ST/ESA/STAT/SER.S/29

**Department of Economic
and Social Affairs**
Statistics Division

**Département des affaires
économiques et sociales**
Division de statistique

Statistical Yearbook

Fifty-third issue

Data available as of October 2009

Annuaire statistique

Cinquante-troisième édition

Données disponibles en octobre 2009

United Nations | Nations Unies

New York, 2009

Department of Economic and Social Affairs

The Department of Economic and Social Affairs of the United Nations Secretariat is a vital interface between global policies in the economic, social and environmental spheres and national action. The Department works in three main inter-linked areas: (i) it compiles, generates and analyses a wide range of economic, social and environmental data and information on which States Members of the United Nations draw to review common problems and to take stock of policy options; (ii) it facilitates the negotiations of Member States in many intergovernmental bodies on joint courses of action to address ongoing or emerging global challenges; and (iii) it advises interested Governments on the ways and means of translating policy frameworks developed in United Nations conferences and summits into programmes at the country level and, through technical assistance, helps build national capacities.

Note

The designations employed and the presentation of the material in this publication do not imply the expression of any opinion whatsoever on the part of the Secretariat of the United Nations concerning the legal status of any country, city or area, or of its authorities, or concerning the delimitation of its frontiers or boundaries.

In general, statistics contained in the present publication are those available to the United Nations Secretariat up to June 2008 and refer to 2007 or earlier. They therefore reflect the country nomenclature currently in use.

The term "country" as used in the text of this publication also refers, as appropriate, to territories or areas.

The designations "developed" and "developing" which appear in some tables are intended for statistical convenience and do not necessarily express a judgement about the stage reached by a particular country or area in the development process.

Symbols of United Nations documents are composed of capital letters combined with figures.

ST/ESA/STAT/SER.S/29

UNITED NATIONS PUBLICATION
Sales No. E/F.09.XVII.1

ISBN 978-92-1-061266-1
ISSN 0082-8459

Département des affaires économiques et sociales

Le Département des affaires économiques et sociales du Secrétariat de l'Organisation des Nations Unies assure le lien essentiel entre les politiques adoptées au plan international dans les domaines économique, social et écologique et les mesures prises au plan national. Il mène ses activités dans trois grands domaines interdépendants : i) il compile, produit et analyse une grande variété de données et d'informations économiques, sociales et écologiques dont les États Membres de l'ONU tirent parti pour examiner les problèmes communs et faire le point sur les possibilités d'action; ii) il facilite les négociations que les États Membres mènent dans un grand nombre d'organes intergouvernementaux sur les moyens d'action à employer conjointement pour faire face aux problèmes mondiaux existants ou naissants; et iii) il aide les gouvernements intéressés à traduire les orientations politiques établies lors des conférences et sommets de l'ONU en programmes nationaux et contribue à renforcer les capacités des pays en leur apportant une assistance technique.

Note

Les appellations employées dans la présente publication et la présentation des données qui y figurent n'impliquent, de la part du Secrétariat de l'Organisation des Nations Unies, aucune prise de position quant au statut juridique des pays, territoires, villes ou zones, ou de leurs autorités, ni quant au tracé de leurs frontières ou limites.

En règle générale, les statistiques contenues dans la présente publication sont celles dont disposait le Secrétariat de l'Organisation des Nations Unies jusqu'à mars 2008 et portent sur la période finissant en 2007. Elles reflètent donc la nomenclature des pays en vigueur à l'époque.

Le terme « pays », tel qu'il est utilisé dans la présente publication, peut également désigner des territoires ou des zones.

Les appellations « développées » et « en développement » qui figurent dans certains tableaux sont employées à des fins exclusivement statistiques et n'expriment pas nécessairement un jugement quant au niveau de développement atteint par tel pays ou telle région.

Les cotes des documents de l'Organisation des Nations Unies se composent de lettres majuscules et de chiffres.

ST/ESA/STAT/SER.S/29

PUBLICATION DES NATIONS UNIES
Numéro de vente : E/F.09.XVII.1

ISBN 978-92-1-061266-1
ISSN 0082-8459

Preface

This is the fifty-third issue of the United Nations *Statistical Yearbook*, prepared by the Statistics Division of the Department of Economic and Social Affairs. Ever since the compilation of data for the *Statistical Yearbook* series was initiated in 1948, it has consistently provided a wide range of internationally available statistics on social and economic conditions and activities at the national, regional and world levels.

The tables include series covering from one to ten years, depending upon data availability (as of 31 October 2009) and space constraints. The ten-year tables generally cover the years 1998 to 2007 or 1999 to 2008.

The *Yearbook* tables are based on data which have been compiled by the Statistics Division mainly from official national and international sources as these are more authoritative and comprehensive, more generally available as time series and more comparable among countries than other sources. These sources include the United Nations Statistics Division in the fields of national accounts, industry, energy and international trade, the United Nations Statistics Division and Population Division in the field of demographic statistics, and over 20 offices of the United Nations system and international organizations in other specialized fields. In some cases, official sources have been supplemented by other sources and estimates, where these have been subjected to professional scrutiny and debate and are consistent with other independent sources.

The United Nations agencies and other international, national and specialized organizations which furnished data are listed under "Statistical sources and references" at the end of the *Yearbook*. Acknowledgement is gratefully made for their generous and valuable cooperation in continually providing data.

The 75 tables of the *Yearbook* are organized in four parts. The first part presents key world and regional aggregates and totals. In the other three parts, the subject matter is generally presented by countries or areas, with world and regional aggregates shown in some cases only. Parts two, three and four cover, respectively, population and social topics, national economic activity and international economic relations. Each chapter ends with brief technical notes on statistical sources and methods for the tables it includes.

The three annexes contain information on country and area nomenclature and the conversion coefficients and factors used in the various tables, and list those tables which were added to or omitted from the last issue of the *Yearbook*.

The *Statistical Yearbook* is prepared by the Statistical Dissemination Section, Statistical Services Branch of the Statistics Division, Department of Economic and Social Affairs of the United Nations

Préface

La présente édition de *l'Annuaire statistique* des Nations Unies est la cinquante-troisième, préparée par la Division de statistique du Département des affaires économiques et sociales. Depuis son instauration en 1948 comme outil de compilation des données statistiques internationales, *l'Annuaire statistique* s'efforce de constamment diffuser un large éventail de statistiques disponibles sur les activités et conditions économiques et sociales, aux niveaux national, régional et mondial.

Les tableaux présentent des séries qui couvrent d'un à dix ans, en fonction de la disponibilité des données (à la date du 31 octobre 2009) et des contraintes d'espace. Les tableaux décennaux couvrent généralement les années 1998 à 2007 ou 1999 à 2008.

Les tableaux de *l'Annuaire* sont construits essentiellement à partir des données compilées par la Division de statistique et provenant de sources officielles, nationales et internationales; c'est en effet la meilleure source si l'on veut des données fiables, complètes et comparables, et si l'on a besoin de séries chronologiques. Ces sources sont: la Division de statistique du Secrétariat de l'Organisation des Nations Unies pour ce qui concerne la comptabilité nationale, l'industrie, l'énergie et le commerce extérieur, la Division de statistique et la Division de la population du Secrétariat de l'Organisation des Nations Unies pour les statistiques démographiques; et plus de 20 bureaux du système des Nations Unies et d'organisations internationales pour les autres domaines spécialisés. Dans quelques cas, les données officielles sont complétées par des informations et des estimations provenant d'autres sources qui ont été examinées par des spécialistes et confirmées par des sources indépendantes.

Les institutions spécialisées des Nations Unies et les autres organisations internationales, nationales et spécialisées qui ont fourni des données sont énumérées dans la section "Sources statistiques et références" figurant à la fin de l'ouvrage. Les auteurs de *l'Annuaire statistique* les remercient de leur précieuse et généreuse collaboration.

Les 75 tableaux de *l'Annuaire* sont regroupés en quatre parties. La première partie présente les principaux agrégats et totaux aux niveaux mondial et régional. Dans les trois parties suivantes, les thèmes sont généralement présentés par pays ou régions. Les agrégats mondiaux ou régionaux ne son indiqués que dans certains cas seulement. Les trois parties autres sont consacrées à la population et aux questions sociales (deuxième partie), à l'activité économique nationale (troisième partie) et aux relations économiques internationales (quatrième partie). Chaque chapitre termine par une brève note technique sur les sources et les méthodes statistiques utilisées pour les tableaux présentés.

Les trois annexes donnent des renseignements sur la nomenclature des pays et des zones, ainsi que sur les coefficients et facteurs de conversion employés dans les différents tableaux. Une liste des tableaux ajoutés et

Secretariat. The programme manager is Mary Jane Holupka and the chief editor is Jacob Assa. They are assisted by David Carter, Anuradha Chimata and Aida Diawara. Bogdan Dragovic developed the software.

Comments on the present *Yearbook* and its future evolution are welcome. They may be sent via e-mail to statistics@un.org or to the United Nations Statistics Division, Statistical Dissemination Section, New York, NY 10017, USA.

supprimés depuis la dernière édition de l'*Annuaire* y est également disponible.

L'*Annuaire statistique* est préparé par la Section de la diffusion des statistiques, Service des statistiques de services de la Division de statistique, Département des affaires économiques et sociales du Secrétariat de l'Organisation des Nations Unies. La responsable du programme est Mary Jane Holupka, et le rédacteur en chef est Jacob Assa. Ils sont secondés par David Carter, Anuradha Chimata et Aida Diawara. Bogdan Dragovic est chargé des logiciels.

Les observations sur la présente édition de l'*Annuaire* et les suggestions de modification pour l'avenir seront reçues avec intérêt. Elles peuvent être envoyées par message électronique à statistics@un.org, ou adressées à la Division de statistique des Nations Unies, Section de la Diffusion Statistique, New York, N.Y. 10017 (États-Unis d'Amérique).

New features in this issue

One objective of the *Statistical Yearbook* is to provide updated information annually for most of the regular tables. In addition, the *Yearbook* team strives to improve the publication and add new and useful features whenever possible. Several such additions have been made to this issue of the *Statistical Yearbook*.

Country and area index

For the first time, the *Statistical Yearbook* now contains a country and area index in addition to the regular subject index. The country index shows the availability of data for each country or area by table and chapter, in order to make the publication more user-friendly and facilitate the use of the *Yearbook* for readers with particular interest in a specific country or area.

New series in existing tables

- Table 60: Gross domestic expenditure on research and development as % of GDP.
- Table 61: Resident filing of patents per million inhabitants.

Les nouveautés de la présente édition

Un objectif de *l'Annuaire statistique* est de fournir, chaque année, les données plus récentes dans la plupart des tableaux régulières. En plus, l'équipe de *l'Annuaire* s'efforce d'améliorer la publication et d'ajouter des nouveautés utiles, chaque fois que possible. Plusieurs de celles améliorations ont été apportés à cette édition de *l'Annuaire statistique*.

Indice de pays et zones

Pour la première fois, *l'Annuaire statistique* comporte un indice de pays et zones outre l'indice conventionnel. L'indice de pays indique la disponibilité des données de chaque pays ou région par tableau et chapitre, pour faire la publication plus facile à utiliser, et pour aider les lecteurs à la recherche d'informations sur un pays ou une région spécifiques.

Nouvelles séries de données dans des tableaux existants

- Tableau 60 : Dépenses intérieures brutes en recherche et développement en % du PIB.
- Tableau 61 : Demandes aux brevets par million d'habitants.

Contents

Preface..iii
New features v
Explanatory notes xi
Introduction...1

Part One: World and region summary

I.   *World and region summary*
   1. World statistics – selected series 9
   2. Population, rate of increase, birth and death
       rates, surface area and density...................... 11
   3. Index numbers of total agricultural and
       food production 13
   4. Index numbers of per capita
       agricultural and food production.................... 13
   5. Index numbers of industrial production 14
   6. Production, trade and consumption
       of commercial energy................................. 20
   7. Total exports and imports: index numbers...... 22
       Technical notes: tables 1-7........................... 24

Part Two: Population and social statistics

II. *Population and human settlements*
   8. Population by sex, rate of population
       increase, surface area and density................. 29
   9. Selected indicators of life expectancy,
       childbearing and mortality 41
   ** Population in urban and rural areas,
       rates of growth and largest urban
       agglomeration population
       Technical notes: tables 8 and 9 49

III. *Gender*
   10. Women in national parliaments.................... 51
   11. Share of women in wage employment in the
       non-agricultural sector................................ 59
   12. Ratio of girls to boys in primary, secondary
       and tertiary education. 67
       Technical notes: tables 10-12 80

IV. *Education*
   13. Education at the primary, secondary and
       tertiary levels.. 83
   14. Public expenditure on education.................... 99
       Technical notes: tables 13 and 14 105

V.   *Culture and communication*
   15. Telephones 107
   16. Cellular mobile telephone subscribers...........119
   17. Internet users...131
   ** Daily newspapers
       Technical notes: tables 15-17.....................143

Table des matières

Préface..iii
Les nouveautés v
Notes explicatives xi
Introduction...1

Première partie: Aperçu mondial et régional

I.   *Aperçu mondial et régional*
   1. Statistiques mondiales - séries principales 9
   2. Population, taux d'accroissement, taux de
       natalité, taux de mortalité, superficie et densité 11
   3. Indices de la production agricole totale
       et de la production alimentaire 13
   4. Indices de la production agricole et de
       la production alimentaire par habitant.................13
   5. Indices de la production industrielle 14
   6. Production, commerce et consommation
       d'énergie commerciale.......................................20
   7. Exportations et importations totales: indices............22
       Notes techniques : tableaux 1 à 7.....................24

Deuxième partie: Population et statistiques sociales

II. *Population et établissements humains*
   8. Population selon le sexe, taux d'accroissement
       de la population, superficie et densité 29
   9. Choix d'indicateurs de l'espérance
       de vie, de la maternité et de la mortalité.................41
   ** Population urbaine, population rurale, taux
       d'accroissement et population de
       l'agglomération urbaine la plus peuplée
       Notes techniques : tableaux 8 et 9........................49

III. *La situation de femmes*
   10. Proportion de sièges occupés par des femmes
       au parlement national 51
   11. Proportion de femmes salariées dans le secteur
       non agricole...59
   12. Rapport filles/garçons dans l'enseignement
       primaire, secondaire et supérieur 67
       Notes techniques : tableaux 10 à 12........................80

IV. *Éducation*
   13. Enseignement primaire, secondaire et supérieur........83
   14. Dépenses publiques afférentes à l'éducation............99
       Notes techniques : tableaux 13 et 14.....................105

V.   *Culture et communication*
   15. Téléphones 107
   16. Abonnés au téléphone mobile..................119
   17. Usagers d'Internet................................131
   ** Journaux quotidiens
       Notes techniques : tableaux 15 à 17......................143

Part Three: Economic activity

VI. *National accounts and industrial production*
  18. Gross domestic product and gross domestic product per capita 147
  19. Gross domestic product by type of expenditure at current prices 165
  20. Value added by industries in current prices ...178
  21. Relationships among the principal national accounting aggregates 193
  22. Government final consumption expenditure by function in current prices 205
  23. Household consumption expenditure by purpose at current prices............................213
  24. Industrial production indices.......................219
  ** Implicit price deflators
     Technical notes: tables 18-24.......................251

VII. *Financial statistics*
  25. Rates of discount of central banks 255
  26. Short-term interest rates............................260
     Technical notes: tables 25 and 26................270

VIII. *Labour force*
  27. Unemployment 271
  ** Employment by economic activity
     Technical notes: table 27 297

IX. *Wages and prices*
  28. Wages in manufacturing 299
  29. Producer price indices 309
  30. Consumer price indices 317
     Technical notes: tables 28-30.......................328

X. *Agriculture, forestry and fishing*
  31. Agricultural production indices 331
  32. Cereals...336
  33. Roundwood 343
  34. Fish production.......................................349
  ** Fertilizers
  ** Livestock
  ** Oil crops
     Technical notes: tables 31-34.......................358

XI. *Manufacturing*
  35. Sugar 361
  36. Beer 371
  37. Cigarettes..376
  38. Fabrics 381
  39. Footwear with uppers of leather 384
  40. Sawnwood 387
  41. Paper and paperboard 394
  42. Cement...399
  43. Pesticides 406

Troisième partie: Activité économique

VI. *Comptabilités nationales et production industrielle*
  18. Produit intérieur brut et produit intérieur brut par habitant................................147
  19. Dépenses imputées au produit intérieur brut aux prix courants..............................165
  20. Valeur ajoutée par branche d'activité aux prix courants.................................178
  21. Relations entre les principaux agrégats de la comptabilité nationale 193
  22. Dépenses de consommation finale des administrations publiques par fonction aux prix courants.......................................205
  23. Dépenses de consommation des ménages par fonction aux prix courants....................213
  24. Indices de la production industrielle 219
  ** Déflateurs implicites des prix
     Notes techniques : tableaux 18 à 24.......................251

VII. *Statistiques financières*
  25. Taux d'escompte des banques centrales 255
  26. Taux d'intérêt à court terme....................260
     Notes techniques : tableaux 25 et 26.......................270

VIII. *Main-d'œuvre*
  27. Chômage 271
  ** Emploi par activité économique
     Notes techniques : tableau 27......................297

IX. *Salaires et prix*
  28. Salaires dans les industries manufacturières 299
  29. Indices des prix à la production 309
  30. Indices des prix à la consommation 317
     Notes techniques : tableaux 28 à 30 328

X. *Agriculture, forêts et pêche*
  31. Indices de la production agricole.......................331
  32. Céréales 336
  33. Bois rond..343
  34. Production halieutique.............................349
  ** Engrais
  ** Cheptel
  ** Cultures oléagineuses
     Notes techniques : tableaux 31 à 34.......................358

XI. *Industries manufacturières*
  35. Sucre...361
  36. Bière 371
  37. Cigarettes...376
  38. Tissus 381
  39. Chaussures à dessus en cuir naturel 384
  40. Sciages 387
  41. Papiers et cartons.......................................394

44. Pig iron and crude steel 408
45. Aluminium 413
46. Radio and television receivers.............416
47. Passenger cars 418
48. Refrigerators for household use............420
49. Household washing and drying machines......423
50. Machine tools 425
51. Trucks..428
** Meat
   Technical notes: tables 35-51......................430

XII. *Energy*
52. Production, trade and consumption of
   commercial energy...............................434
53. Production of selected energy commodities...466
   Technical notes: tables 52 and 53.............484

XIII. *Environment*
54. Land 487
55. CO_2 emissions estimates.....................497
56. Ozone-depleting chlorofluorocarbons
   (CFCs)..505
57. Threatened species.............................513
58. Water and sanitation...........................525
   Technical notes: tables 54-58...................539

XIV. *Science and technology*
59. Personnel in research and development
   (R & D)..543
60. Gross domestic expenditure on R & D by
   source of funds 553
61. Patents 560
   Technical notes: tables 59-61...................564

Part Four: International economic relations

XV. *International merchandise trade*
62. Total imports and exports 569
63. Total imports and exports: index numbers.....586
64. Manufactured goods exports...................593
   Technical notes: tables 62-64...................599

XVI. *International tourism and transport*
65. Tourist/visitor arrivals by region of origin.....603
66. Tourist/visitor arrivals and tourism
   expenditure..633
67. Tourist expenditure in other countries...........646
68. Civil aviation.....................................658
   Technical notes: tables 65-68...................671

42. Ciment 399
43. Pesticides 406
44. Fonte et acier brut 408
45. Aluminium 413
46. Récepteurs de radio et de télévision............416
47. Voitures de tourisme.............................418
48. Réfrigérateurs à usage domestique.............420
49. Machines à laver et à sécher le linge de type
   ménager 423
50. Machines-outils 425
51. Camions..428
** Viande
   Notes techniques : tableaux 35 à 51..............430

XII. *Energie*
52. Production, commerce et consommation
   d'énergie commerciale...........................434
53. Production des principaux biens de l'énergie.........466
   Notes techniques : tableaux 52 et 53.............484

XIII. *Environnement*
54. Terres 487
55. Estimations des émissions de CO_2.............497
56. Chlorofluorocarbones (CFC) qui
   appauvrissent la couche d'ozone...............505
57. Espèces menacées................................513
58. Accès à l'eau et à l'assainissement..............525
   Notes techniques : tableaux 54 à 58..............539

XIV. *Science et technologie*
59. Personnel employé dans la recherche et le
   développement (R – D)............................543
60. Dépenses intérieures brutes de recherche et
   développement par source de financement.............553
61. Brevets 560
   Notes techniques : tableaux 59 à 61..............564

Quatrième partie: Relations économiques internationales

XV. *Commerce international des marchandises*
62. Importations et exportations totales.............569
63. Importations et exportations totales: indices..........586
64. Exportations des produits manufacturés.............593
   Notes techniques : tableaux 62 à 64..............599

XVI. *Tourisme international et transport*
65. Arrivées de touristes/visiteurs par
   régions de provenance...........................603
66. Arrivées de touristes/visiteurs et dépenses
   touristiques.......................................633
67. Dépenses touristiques dans d'autres pays..............646
68. Aviation civile 658
   Notes techniques : tableaux 65 à 68..............671

XVII. *Balance of payments*
 69. Summary of balance of payments.................675
   Technical notes: table 69.................713

XVIII. *International finance*
 70. Exchange rates.................715
 71. International reserves minus gold.................725
 72. Total external and public/publicly guaranteed long-term debt of developing countries.................741
   A. Total external debt.................741
   B. Public and publicly guaranteed long-term debt.................743
   Technical notes: tables 70-72.................748

XIX. *Development assistance*
 73. Disbursements of bilateral and multilateral official development assistance and official aid to individual recipients.................751
 74. Net official development assistance from DAC countries to developing countries and multilateral organizations.................765
 75. Socio-economic development assistance through the United Nations system–Development grants.................766
   Technical notes: tables 73-75.................774

Annexes
I. Country and area nomenclature, regional and other groupings.................775
II. Conversion coefficients and factors.................785
III. Tables added and omitted.................787

Statistical sources and references.................789
Country and area index.................793
Index (English only).................809

XVII. *Balance des paiements*
 69. Résumé des balances des paiements.................675
   Notes techniques : tableau 69.................713

XVIII. *Finances internationales*
 70. Cours des changes.................715
 71. Réserves internationales, or non inclus.................725
 72. Total de la dette extérieure et dette publique extérieure à long terme garantie par l'Etat des pays en développement.................741
   A. Total de la dette extérieure.................741
   B. Dette publique extérieure à long terme.................743
   Notes techniques : tableaux 70 à 72.................748

XIX. *Aide au développement*
 73. Versements d'aide publique au développement et d'aide publique bilatérales et multilatérales aux bénéficiaires.................751
 74. Aide publique au développement nette de pays du CAD aux pays en développement et aux organisations multilatérales.................765
 75. Assistance en matière de développement socioéconomique fournie par le système des Nations Unies – Subventions au développement.................766
   Notes techniques : tableaux 73 à 75.................774

Annexes
I. Nomenclature des pays et des zones, groupements régionaux et autres groupements.................775
II. Coefficients et facteurs de conversion.................785
III. Tableaux ajoutés et supprimés.................787

Sources statistiques et références.................789
Indice de pays et zones.................793

** Asterisks preceding table names identify tables that were presented in previous issues of the *Statistical Yearbook* which are not contained in the present issue. These tables will be updated in future issues of the *Yearbook* when new data become available.

** Ce symbole indique les tableaux publiés dans les éditions précédentes de l'*Annuaire statistique* mais qui n'ont pas été repris dans la présente édition. Ces tableaux seront actualisés dans les futures livraisons de l'*Annuaire* à mesure que des données nouvelles deviendront disponibles.

Explanatory notes

In general, the statistics presented in the present publication are based on information available to the Statistics Division of the United Nations Secretariat up to October 2009.

Units of measurement
The metric system of weights and measures has been employed throughout the *Statistical Yearbook.* For conversion coefficients and factors, see annex II.

Country notes and nomenclature
As a general rule, the data presented in the *Yearbook* relate to a given country or area within its present de facto boundaries. A complete list of countries and territories is presented in Annex I.

It should also be noted that unless otherwise indicated, for statistical purposes, the data for China exclude those for Hong Kong Special Administrative Region of China, Macao Special Administrative Region of China and Taiwan province of China.

Symbols and conventions used in the tables
.   A point is used to indicate decimals.
-   A hyphen between years, for example, 1998-1999, indicates the full period involved, including the beginning and end years.
/   A slash indicates a financial year, school year or crop year, for example 1998/99.
...   Data not available or not applicable.
*   Provisional or estimated figure.
#   Marked break in series.
^0   Not zero but less than half of the unit used.

A space is used as a thousands separator, for example 1 000 is one thousand.

Details and percentages in the tables do not necessarily add to totals because of rounding.

Notes explicatives

En général, les statistiques qui figurent dans la présente publication sont fondées sur les informations dont disposait la Division de statistique du Secrétariat de l'ONU jusqu'à octobre 2009.

Unités de mesure
Le système métrique de poids et mesures a été utilisé dans tout l'*Annuaire statistique*. On trouvera à l'annexe II les coefficients et facteurs de conversion.

Notes sur les pays et nomenclature
En règle générale, les données renvoient au pays ou zone en question dans ses frontières actuelles effectives. Une liste complète des pays et territoires figure à l'annexe I.

Il convient de noter aussi que sauf indication contraire, les données statistiques relatives à la China ne comprennent pas celles qui concernent la région administrative spéciale de Hong Kong, la région administrative spéciale de Macao et la province chinoise de Taiwan.

Signes et conventions employés dans les tableaux
.   Les décimales sont précédées d'un point.
-   Un tiret entre des années, par exemple "1998-1999", indique que la période est embrassée dans sa totalité, y compris la première et la dernière année.
/   Une barre oblique renvoie à un exercice financier, à une année scolaire ou à une campagne agricole, par exemple "1998/99".
...   Données non disponibles ou non applicables.
*   Chiffre provisoire ou estimatif.
#   Discontinuité notable dans la série.
^0   Non nul mais inférieur à la moitié de l'unité employée.

Le séparateur utilisé pour les milliers est l'espace : par exemple, 1 000 correspond à un millier.

Les chiffres étant arrondis, les totaux ne correspondent pas toujours à la somme exacte des éléments ou pourcentages figurant dans les tableaux.

Introduction

This is the fifty-third issue of the United Nations *Statistical Yearbook*, prepared by the Statistics Division, Department of Economic and Social Affairs, of the United Nations Secretariat. The tables include series covering from one to ten years, depending upon data availability and space constraints. The tables generally cover the years 1997 to 2008. For the most part, the statistics presented are those which were available to the Statistics Division as of 31 October 2009.

Objective and content of the Statistical Yearbook

The main purpose of the *Statistical Yearbook* is to provide in a single volume a comprehensive compilation of internationally available statistics on social and economic conditions and activities, at world, regional and national levels, covering a ten-year period to the extent possible.

Most of the statistics presented in the *Yearbook* are extracted from more detailed, specialized databases prepared by the Statistics Division and by many other international statistical services. Thus, while the specialized databases concentrate on monitoring topics and trends in particular social and economic fields, the *Statistical Yearbook* tables aim to provide data for a more comprehensive, overall description of social and economic structures, conditions, changes and activities. The objective has been to collect, systematize, coordinate and present in a consistent way the most essential components of comparable statistical information which can give a broad picture of social and economic processes.

The content of the *Statistical Yearbook* is planned to serve a general readership. The *Yearbook* endeavours to provide information for various bodies of the United Nations system as well as for other international organizations, governments and non-governmental organizations, national statistical, economic and social policy bodies, scientific and educational institutions, libraries and the public. Data published in the *Statistical Yearbook* may also be of interest to companies and enterprises and to agencies engaged in market research. The *Statistical Yearbook* thus provides information on a wide range of social and economic issues which are of concern in the United Nations system and among the governments and peoples of the world. A particular value of the *Yearbook* is that it facilitates meaningful analysis of issues by systematizing and coordinating the data across many fields and shedding light on such interrelated issues as:

- General economic growth and related economic conditions;
- Progress towards the Millennium Development Goals;

Introduction

La présente édition est la cinquante-troisième de *l'Annuaire statistique* des Nations Unies, établi par la Division de statistique du Département des affaires économiques et sociales du Secrétariat de l'Organisation des Nations Unies. Les tableaux présentent des séries qui couvrent d'un à dix ans, en fonction de la disponibilité des données et des contraintes d'espace. Les tableaux couvrent généralement les années 1997 à 2008. La majeure partie des statistiques présentées ici sont celles dont disposait la Division de Statistique à la date du 31 octobre 2009.

Objectif et contenu de l'Annuaire statistique

Le principal objectif de *l'Annuaire statistique* est de fournir en un seul volume un inventaire complet de statistiques internationales concernant la situation et les activités sociales et économiques aux niveaux mondial, régional et national, sur une période s'étalant, dans la mesure du possible, sur dix ans.

La plupart des données qui figurent dans l'*Annuaire statistique* proviennent de bases de données spécialisées davantage détaillées, préparées par la Division de statistique et par bien d'autres services statistiques internationaux. Tandis que les bases de données spécialisées se concentrent sur le suivi de domaines socioéconomiques particuliers, les données de l'*Annuaire* sont présentées de telle sorte qu'elles fournissent une description globale et exhaustive des structures, conditions, transformations et activités socioéconomiques. On a cherché à recueillir, systématiser, coordonner et présenter de manière cohérente les principales informations statistiques comparables, de manière à dresser un tableau général des processus socioéconomiques.

Le contenu de l'*Annuaire statistique* a été élaboré en vue d'un lectorat large. Les renseignements fournis devraient ainsi pouvoir être utilisés par les divers organismes du système des Nations Unies, mais aussi par d'autres organisations internationales, les gouvernements et les organisations non gouvernementales, les organismes nationaux de statistique et de politique économique et sociale, les institutions scientifiques et les établissements d'enseignement, les bibliothèques et les particuliers. Les données publiées dans l'*Annuaire* peuvent également intéresser les sociétés et entreprises, et les organismes spécialisés dans les études de marché. L'*Annuaire* présente des informations sur un large éventail de questions socioéconomiques liées aux préoccupations actuelles du système des Nations Unies, des gouvernements et des peuples du monde entier. Une qualité particulière de l'*Annuaire* est de faciliter une analyse approfondie de ces questions en systématisant et en articulant les données d'un domaine/secteur à l'autre, et en apportant un éclairage sur des sujets interdépendants, tels que :

- La croissance économique générale, et les conditions économiques qui lui sont liées;
- Les progrès accomplis dans la réalisation des Objectifs

- Population, life expectancy, childbearing and mortality;
- Unemployment, inflation and wages;
- Energy production and consumption and the development of new energy sources;
- Expansion of trade;
- The financial situation of countries and external payments and receipts;
- Education, training and eradication of illiteracy;
- Improvement in general living conditions;
- Pollution and protection of the environment;
- Assistance provided to developing countries for social and economic development purposes.

Organization of the Yearbook

The 75 tables of the *Yearbook* are grouped into four broad parts:
- Part One: World and Region Summary (chapter I, tables 1-7);
- Part Two: Population and Social Statistics (chapters II-V: tables 8-17);
- Part Three: Economic Activity (chapters VI-XIV: tables 18-61);
- Part Four: International Economic Relations (chapters XV-XIX: tables 62-75).

The more aggregated information shown in part one provides an overall picture of development at the world and region levels. More specific and detailed information for analysis concerning individual countries or areas is presented in the other three parts. Each of these parts is divided into chapters, by topic, and each chapter ends with a section on "Technical notes", which provides brief descriptions of major statistical concepts, definitions and classifications required for interpretation and analysis of the data. Information on the methodology used for the computation of the figures can be found in the publications on methodology of the United Nations and its agencies, listed in the section "Statistical sources and references" at the end of the *Yearbook*.

Part One, World and Region Summary, comprises seven tables highlighting the principal trends in the world as well as in each of the regions and in the major economic and social sectors. It contains global totals of important aggregate statistics needed for the analysis of economic growth, the structure of the world economy, major changes in world population and expansion of external merchandise trade. The global totals are, as a rule, subdivided into major geographical areas.

Part Two, Population and Social Statistics, comprises ten tables which contain more detailed statistical series on population, gender, education and communication.

Of the 44 tables in Part Three, Economic Activity, 23 provide data on national accounts, index numbers of industrial production, interest rates, labour

du Millénaire pour le Développement;
- La population, l'espérance de vie, la maternité et la mortalité;
- Le chômage, l'inflation et les salaires;
- La production et la consommation d'énergie et le développement de nouvelles sources d'énergie;
- L'expansion des échanges;
- La situation financière, les paiements et recettes extérieurs des pays;
- L'éducation, la formation et l'élimination de l'analphabétisme;
- L'amélioration des conditions de vie;
- La pollution et la protection de l'environnement;
- L'assistance aux pays en développement à des fins socioéconomiques.

Présentation de l'Annuaire

Les 75 tableaux de l'*Annuaire* sont groupés en quatre parties:
- La première partie : Aperçu mondial et régional (chapitre I, tableaux 1 à 7);
- La deuxième partie : Statistiques démographiques et sociales (chapitres II à V, tableaux 8 à 17);
- La troisième partie : Activité économique (chapitres VI à XIV, tableaux 18 à 61);
- La quatrième partie : Relations économiques internationales (chapitres XV à XIX, tableaux 62 à 75).

Les valeurs les plus agrégées qui figurent dans la première partie donnent un tableau global du développement à l'échelon mondial et régional, tandis que les trois autres parties contiennent des renseignements plus précis et détaillés qui se prêtent mieux à une analyse par pays ou par zones. Chacune de ces trois parties est divisée en chapitres portant sur des sujets donnés, et chaque chapitre comprend une section intitulée "Notes techniques" où l'on trouve une brève description des principales notions, définitions et classifications statistiques nécessaires pour interpréter et analyser les données. Les méthodes de calcul utilisées sont décrites dans les publications se référant à la méthodologie des Nations Unies et de leurs organismes, énumérées à la fin de l'*Annuaire* dans la section "Sources et références statistiques".

La première partie, intitulée "Aperçu mondial et régional", comprend sept tableaux présentant les principales tendances dans le monde et dans les régions ainsi que dans les principaux secteurs économiques et sociaux. Elle fournit des chiffres mondiaux pour les principaux agrégats statistiques nécessaires pour analyser la croissance économique, la structure de l'économie mondiale, les principaux changements dans la population mondiale et l'expansion du commerce extérieur de marchandises. En règle générale, les chiffres mondiaux sont répartis par grandes régions géographiques.

La deuxième partie, intitulée "Population et statistiques sociales", comporte dix tableaux où figurent des

force, wages and prices, energy, environment and science and technology; 21 tables provide data on production in the major branches of the economy (using, in general, the *International Standard Industrial Classification*, ISIC), namely agriculture, hunting, forestry and fishing, and manufacturing. Consumption data are combined with the production data in tables on specific commodities, where feasible.

Part Four, International Economic Relations, comprises 14 tables on international merchandise trade, balance of payments, international tourism and transport, international finance and development assistance.

A subject index and a country index (in English only) are provided at the end of the *Yearbook*.

Annexes and regional groupings of countries or areas

The annexes to the *Statistical Yearbook*, and the section "Explanatory notes" preceding the Introduction, provide additional essential information on the *Yearbook*'s contents and presentation of data.

Annex 1 provides information on countries or areas covered in the *Yearbook* tables and on their arrangement in geographical regions and economic or other groupings. The geographical groupings shown in the *Yearbook* are generally based on continental regions unless otherwise indicated. However, strict consistency in this regard is impossible. A wide range of classifications is used for different purposes in the various international agencies and other sources of statistics for the *Yearbook*. These classifications vary in response to administrative and analytical requirements.

Similarly, there is no common agreement in the United Nations system concerning the terms "developed" and "developing" when referring to the stage of development reached by any given country or area, and its corresponding classification in one or the other grouping. The *Yearbook* thus refers more generally to "developed" or "developing" regions on the basis of conventional practice. Following this practice, "developed" regions or areas comprise Canada and the United States in Northern America, Japan in Asia, Australia and New Zealand in Oceania, and Europe, while all of Africa and the remainder of the Americas, Asia and Oceania comprise the "developing regions". These designations are intended for statistical convenience and do not necessarily express a judgement about the stage reached by a particular country or area in the development process.

Annex II provides detailed information on conversion coefficients and factors used in various tables, and annex III provides a list of tables added and omitted in the present edition of the *Yearbook*. Tables for which a sufficient amount of new data is not available are not being published in this *Yearbook*.

séries plus détaillées concernant la population, la situation des femmes, l'éducation et la communication.

La troisième partie, intitulée "Activité économique", comporte 44 tableaux, 23 qui présentent des statistiques concernant les comptes nationaux, les nombres indices relatifs à la production industrielle, les taux d'intérêt, la population active, les prix et les salaires, l'énergie, l'environnement, et la science et technologie; et 21 qui présentent des données sur la production des principales branches d'activité économique (en utilisant en général la *Classification internationale type, par industrie, de toutes les branches d'activité économique*): agriculture, chasse, sylviculture et pêche, et industries manufacturières. Les tableaux traitant de certains produits de base associent autant que possible les données relatives à la consommation aux valeurs concernant la production.

La quatrième partie, intitulée "Relations économiques internationales", comprend 14 tableaux relatifs au commerce international de marchandises, aux balances des paiements, au tourisme et transport internationaux, aux finances internationales, et à l'aide au développement.

Un index de pays figure à la fin de l'*Annuaire*.

Annexes et groupements régionaux des pays et zones

Les annexes à l'*Annuaire statistique,* et la section intitulée "Notes explicatives" qui précède l'introduction, offrent d'importantes informations complémentaires quant à la teneur et à la présentation des données figurant dans le présent ouvrage.

L'annexe I donne des renseignements sur les pays ou zones couverts par les tableaux de l'*Annuaire* et sur leur regroupement en régions géographiques et groupements économiques ou autres. Sauf indication contraire, les groupements géographiques figurant dans l'*Annuaire* sont généralement fondés sur les régions continentales, mais une présentation absolument systématique est impossible à cet égard car les diverses institutions internationales et autres sources de statistiques employées pour la confection de l'*Annuaire* emploient, selon l'objet de l'exercice, des classifications fort différentes en réponse à diverses exigences d'ordre administratif ou analytique.

Il n'existe pas non plus dans le système des Nations Unies de définition commune des termes "développé" et "en développement" pour décrire le niveau atteint en la matière par un pays ou une zone donnés ni pour les classifier dans l'un ou l'autre de ces groupes. Ainsi, dans l'*Annuaire*, on s'en remet à l'usage pour qualifier les régions de "développées" ou "en développement". Selon cet usage, les régions ou zones développées sont le Canada et les Etats-Unis dans l'Amérique septentrionale, le Japon dans l'Asie, l'Australie et la Nouvelle-Zélande dans l'Océanie, et l'Europe, alors que toute l'Afrique et le reste des Amériques, l'Asie et l'Océanie constituent les régions en développement. Ces appellations sont utilisées pour plus de commodité dans la présentation des statistiques et n'impliquent pas nécessairement un jugement quant au

Their titles nevertheless are still listed in the table of contents since it is planned that they will be published in a later issue as new data are compiled by the collecting agency.

Data comparability, quality and relevance

The major challenge continuously facing the *Statistical Yearbook* is to present series which are as nearly comparable across countries as the available statistics permit. Considerable efforts have already been made among the international suppliers of data and by the staff of the *Statistical Yearbook* to ensure the compatibility of various series by coordinating time periods, base years, prices chosen for valuation, and so on. This is indispensable in relating various bodies of data to each other and in facilitating analysis across different sectors. Thus, for example, relating data on short-term interest rates to those on prices makes it possible to arrive at a general understanding about the inflation environment, and relating a country's data on tourism expenditure in other countries to those on its per capita GDP provides a gauge on that country's wealth status. In general, the data presented reflect the methodological recommendations of the United Nations Statistical Commission issued in various United Nations publications, and of other international bodies concerned with statistics. Publications containing these recommendations and guidelines are listed in the section "Statistical sources and references" at the end of the *Yearbook*. The use of international recommendations not only promotes international comparability of the data but also ensures a degree of compatibility regarding the underlying concepts, definitions and classifications relating to different series. However, much work remains to be done in this area and, for this reason, some tables can serve only as a first source of data, which require further adjustment before being used for more in-depth analytical studies. While on the whole, a significant degree of comparability has been achieved in international statistics, there will remain some limitations, for a variety of reasons.

One common cause of non-comparability of economic data is different valuations of statistical aggregates such as national income, wages and salaries, output of industries and so forth. Conversion of these and similar series originally expressed in national prices into a common currency, for example into United States dollars, through the use of exchange rates, is not always satisfactory owing to frequent wide fluctuations in market rates and differences between official rates and rates which would be indicated by unofficial markets or purchasing power parities. The use of different kinds of sources for obtaining data is another cause of incomparability. This is true, for example, in the case of employment and

stade de développement auquel est parvenu tel pays ou telle zone.

L'annexe II fournit des renseignements sur les coefficients et facteurs de conversion employés dans les différents tableaux, et l'annexe III contient la liste de tableaux qui ont été ajoutés ou omis dans la présente édition de l'*Annuaire*. Les tableaux pour lesquels on ne dispose pas d'une quantité suffisante des données nouvelles, n'ont pas été publiés dans cet *Annuaire*. Comme ils seront repris dans une prochaine édition à mesure que des données nouvelles seront dépouillées par l'office statistique d'origine, ses titres figurent toujours dans la table des matières.

Comparabilité, qualité et pertinence des statistiques

Le défi majeur auquel l'*Annuaire Statistique* fait continuellement face est de présenter des séries aussi comparables entre les pays que la disponibilité des statistiques le permettent. Les sources internationales de données et les auteurs de l'*Annuaire* ont réalisé des efforts considérables pour faire en sorte que diverses séries soient compatibles, en harmonisant les périodes de référence, les années de base, les prix utilisés pour les évaluations, etc. Cette démarche est indispensable si l'on veut rapprocher divers ensembles de données, et faciliter l'analyse intersectorielle de l'économie. Ainsi, lier les données concernant les taux d'intérêt à court terme à celles des prix permet d'arriver à une compréhension globale de l'environnement de l'inflation; lier les données de dépenses touristiques d'un pays dans d'autres pays à celles de son PIB par tête fournit un indicateur de la richesse de ce pays. De façon générale, les données sont présentées selon les recommandations méthodologiques formulées par la Commission de statistique des Nations Unies, et par les autres entités internationales impliquées dans les statistiques. Les titres des publications contenant ces recommandations et leurs lignes directrices figurent à la fin de l'*Annuaire*, dans la section "Sources et références statistiques". Le respect des recommandations internationales tend non seulement à promouvoir la comparabilité internationale des données, mais elle assure également une certaine comparabilité entre les concepts, les définitions et classifications utilisés. Mais comme il reste encore beaucoup à faire dans ce domaine, les données présentées dans certains tableaux n'ont qu'une valeur indicative, et nécessiteront des ajustements plus poussés avant de pouvoir servir à des analyses approfondies. Bien que l'on soit parvenu, dans l'ensemble, à un degré de comparabilité appréciable en matière de statistiques internationales, diverses raisons expliquent que subsistent encore de nombreuses limitations.

Une cause commune de non comparabilité des données économiques réside dans la diversité des méthodes d'évaluation employées pour comptabiliser des agrégats tels que le revenu national, les salaires et traitements, la production des différentes branches d'activité industrielle,

uncmployment, where data are obtained from different sources, namely household and labour force sample surveys, establishment censuses or surveys, official estimates, social insurance statistics and employment office statistics, which are not fully comparable in many cases. Non-comparability of data may also result from differences in the institutional patterns of countries. Certain variations in social and economic organization and institutions may have an impact on the comparability of the data even if the underlying concepts and definitions are identical. These and other causes of non-comparability of the data are briefly explained in the technical notes to each chapter.

A further set of challenges relate to timeliness, quality and relevance of the data contained in the *Yearbook*. Users generally demand the most up-to-date statistics. However, due to the different development stages of statistical capacity in different countries, data for the most recent years may only be available for a small number of countries. For a global print publication, therefore, a balance has to be struck between presenting the most updated information and satisfactory country coverage. Of course the UN Statistics Division's website offers greater flexibility in presenting continuously updated information and is therefore a useful complement to the annual print publication. Furthermore, as most of the information presented in this *Yearbook* is collected through specialized United Nations agencies and partners, the timeliness is continuously enhanced by improving the communication and data flow between countries and the specialized agencies on the one hand, and between the UN Statistics Division and the specialized agencies on the other. The development of new XML-based data transfer protocols will address this issue and is expected to make international data flows more efficient in the future.

Data quality at the international level is a function of the data quality at the national level. The UN Statistics Division in close cooperation with its partners in the UN agencies and the international statistical system continues to support countries' efforts to improve both the coverage and the quality of their data. Metadata, as for example reflected in the footnotes and technical notes of this publication, are an important service to the user to allow an informed assessment of the quality of the data. Given the wide variety of sources for the *Yearbook*, there is of course an equally wide variety of data formats and accompanying metadata. An important challenge for the UN Statistics Division and its partners for the future is to work further towards the standardization, or at least harmonization, of metadata.

The final challenge relates to maintaining the relevance of the series included in the *Yearbook*. As new policy concerns enter the developmental debate, the UN Statistics Division will need to introduce new

etc. Il n'est pas toujours satisfaisant de ramener la valeur des séries de ce type—exprimée à l'origine en prix nationaux—à une monnaie commune (par exemple le dollar des États-Unis) car les taux de change du marché connaissent fréquemment de fortes fluctuations, et parce que les taux officiels ne coïncident pas avec ceux des marchés officieux ni avec les parités réelles de pouvoir d'achat. Le recours à des sources diverses pour la collecte des données est un autre facteur qui limite la comparabilité. C'est le cas, par exemple, des données d'emploi et de chômage, obtenues par des moyens aussi peu comparables que les sondages, le dépouillement des registres d'assurances sociales et les enquêtes auprès des entreprises. Dans certains cas, les données ne sont pas comparables en raison de différences entre les structures institutionnelles des pays. Des changements dans l'organisation et les institutions économiques et sociales peuvent affecter la comparabilité des données, même si les concepts et définitions sont fondamentalement identiques. Ces causes, et d'autres, de non comparabilité des données sont brièvement expliquées dans les notes techniques de chaque chapitre.

Un autre ensemble de défis à relever concerne la fraîcheur, la qualité et la pertinence des données présentées dans l'*Annuaire*. Les utilisateurs exigent généralement des données les plus récentes possibles. Toutefois, selon le niveau de développement de la capacité statistique des pays, les données pour les dernières années peuvent n'être disponibles que pour un nombre limité de pays. Dans le cadre d'une publication mondiale, un équilibre doit être trouvé entre la présentation de l'information la plus récente et une couverture géographique satisfaisante. Bien entendu, le site Internet de la Division de statistique des Nations Unies offre une plus grande flexibilité, puisqu'il propose une information actualisée au fil de l'eau, et constitue ainsi un complément utile à la publication papier annuelle. Par ailleurs, étant donné que la plupart des informations présentées dans cet *Annuaire* sont collectées parmi les agences spécialisées des Nations Unies et autres partenaires, la fraîcheur des données est continuellement améliorée, grâce à une meilleure communication et un meilleur échange de données entre les pays et les agences spécialisées d'une part, et entre la Division de statistique des Nations Unies et les agences spécialisées d'autre part. Le développement de nouveaux protocoles de transfert de données basés sur le langage XML devrait contribuer à rendre, à l'avenir, les échanges de données internationales encore plus efficaces.

La qualité des données au niveau international est fonction de la qualité des données au niveau national. La Division de statistique des Nations Unies, en étroite collaboration avec ses partenaires dans les agences de l'ONU et dans le système statistique international, continue de soutenir les efforts des pays pour améliorer à la fois la couverture et la qualité de leurs données. Des métadonnées, comme l'illustrent les notes de bas de page et les notes techniques de cette publication, constituent un important

series that describe concerns that have gained prominence as well as to prune data as they become outdated and continue to update the recurrent *Yearbook* series that still address those issues which are most pertinent. Often choosing the appropriate moment when the statistical information on new topics has matured sufficiently so as to be able to disseminate meaningful global data can be challenging. Furthermore, a balance has to continuously be found between the ever-increasing amount of information available for dissemination and the space limitations of the print version of the *Statistical Yearbook*. International comparability, data availability and data quality will remain the key criteria to guide the UN Statistics Division in its selection.

Needless to say, more can always be done to improve the *Statistical Yearbook*'s scope, coverage, design, metadata and timeliness. The *Yearbook* team continually strives to improve upon each of these aspects and to make its publication as responsive as possible to its users' needs and expectations, while at the same time focusing on a manageable body of data and metadata. Since data disseminated in digital form have clear advantages over those in print, as much of the *Yearbook* information as possible will continue to be included in the Statistics Division's online databases. Still, the *Statistical Yearbook* will continue to claim its rightful place among the products of the Statistics Division as a useful resource for a general understanding of the global social and economic situation.

service fourni à l'utilisateur pour lui permettre d'évaluer de manière avisée la qualité des données. Etant donné la grande variété des sources de *l'Annuaire*, il y a bien entendu une non moins grande variété de formats de données et de métadonnées associées. Un important défi que la Division de statistique des Nations Unies et ses partenaires doivent relever dans le futur est d'aboutir à la standardisation, ou au moins l'harmonisation, des métadonnées.

Le dernier défi concerne la constance de la pertinence des séries présentées dans *l'Annuaire*. Au fur et à mesure que de nouvelles préoccupations politiques pénètrent le débat lié au développement, la Division de statistique des Nations Unies doit introduire dans l'*Annuaire* de nouvelles séries qui leur sont liées, et, ce faisant, effectuer une coupe sombre parmi les données qui lui semblent dépassées, tout en s'assurant de continuer à actualiser les séries récurrentes de qui paraissent encore pertinentes. Souvent, choisir le moment idoine auquel les données statistiques sur de nouveaux thèmes sont suffisamment matures pour qu'elles puissent, au niveau mondial, être diffusées sans hésitation, est un défi en soi. Par ailleurs, un équilibre doit continuellement être trouvé entre le volume toujours croissant d'informations disponibles à la diffusion, et les contraintes d'espace de la version papier de l'*Annuaire statistique*. La comparabilité internationale, la disponibilité des données et leur qualité devront rester le principal critère à considérer par la Division de statistique des Nations Unies dans sa sélection.

Inutile de dire qu'il est toujours possible d'améliorer l'*Annuaire statistique* en ce qui concerne son champ, sa couverture, sa conception générale, ses métadonnées et sa mise à jour. L'équipe en charge de l'*Annuaire* s'évertue en permanence à améliorer chacun de ces aspects, et de faire en sorte que cette publication réponde au plus près aux besoins et aux attentes de ses utilisateurs, sans toutefois oublier de mettre l'accent sur un corpus gérable de données et de métadonnées. Puisqu'il est avéré que les données diffusées de manière digitale ont des avantages comparés à celles diffusées sur papier, autant d'informations de l'*Annuaire* que possible continueront d'être inclues dans les bases de données électroniques de la Division de statistique. L'*Annuaire statistique* garde toujours une place de choix parmi les produits de la Division de statistique comme une ressource utile pour une compréhension général de la situation sociale et économique globale.

Part One
World and region summary

Chapter I   World and region summary (tables 1-7)

This part of the *Statistical Yearbook* presents selected aggregate series on principal economic and social topics for the world as a whole and for the major regions. The topics include population and surface area, agricultural and industrial production, external trade, government financial reserves, and energy production and consumption. More detailed data on individual countries and areas are provided in the subsequent parts of the present *Yearbook*. These comprise Part Two: Population and Social Statistics; Part Three: Economic Activity; and Part Four: International Economic Relations.

Regional totals between series may be incomparable owing to differences in definitions of regions and lack of data for particular regional components. General information on regional groupings is provided in annex I of the *Yearbook*. Supplementary information on regional groupings used in specific series is provided, as necessary, in table footnotes and in the technical notes at the end of chapter I.

Première partie
Aperçu mondial et régional

Chapitre I   Aperçu mondial et régional (tableaux 1 à 7)

Cette partie de l'*Annuaire statistique* présente, pour le monde entier et ses principales subdivisions, un choix d'agrégats ayant trait à des questions économiques et sociales essentielles: population et superficie, production agricole et industrielle, commerce extérieur, réserves financières publiques, et la production et la consommation d'énergie. Des statistiques plus détaillées pour divers pays ou zones figurent dans les parties ultérieures de l'*Annuaire*, c'est-à-dire dans les deuxième, troisième et quatrième parties intitulées respectivement: population et statistiques sociales, activités économiques et relations économiques internationales.

Les totaux régionaux peuvent être incomparables entre les séries en raison de différences dans la définition des régions et de l'absence de données sur tel ou tel élément régional. A l'annexe I de l'*Annuaire*, on trouvera des renseignements généraux sur les groupements régionaux. Des informations complémentaires sur les groupements régionaux pour certaines séries bien précises sont fournies, lorsqu'il y a lieu, dans les notes figurant au bas des tableaux et dans les notes techniques à la fin du chapitre I

1

World statistics: selected series
Population, production, external trade and finance

Statistiques mondiales : séries principales
Population, production, commerce extérieur et finances

Series Séries	Unit or base Unité ou base	1999	2000	2001	2002	2003	2004	2005	2006	2007
Population • Population										
World population [1] Population mondial [1]	Million	6 036	6 115	6 195	6 274	6 354	6 433	6 512	6 592	6 671
Output / production • Production										
Gross domestic product • Produit intérieur brut										
GDP at current prices PIB aux prix courants	billion US $ milliard $ E.-U.	31 075	31 897	31 686	32 997	37 077	41 714	45 103	48 786	54 636
GDP per capita PIB par habitant	US $ $ E.-U.	5 142	5 209	5 109	5 254	5 831	6 481	6 924	7 401	8 191
GDP real rates of growth Taux de l'accroisse. réels	%	3.3%	4.1%	1.7%	2.0%	2.7%	4.0%	3.5%	4.0%	3.8%
Agriculture, forestry and fishing production • Production agricole, forestière et de la pêche										
Index numbers – Indices										
All commodities Tous produits	1999-01 = 100	98	100	101	102	105	110	112	114	116
Food Produits alimentaires	1999-01 = 100	98	100	101	102	105	110	112	113	115
Quantities – Quantités										
Cereals Céréales	million t.	2 086	2 060	2 108	2 028	2 089	2 279	2 267	2 228	2 342
Meat Viande	million t.	230	235	238	245	249	255	263	265	269
Roundwood Bois rond	million m³	3 334	3 405	3 308	3 353	3 388	3 450	3 552	3 511	3 591
Fish production Production halieutique	million t.	122	126	125	128	127	134	136	137	140
Industrial production • Production industrielle										
Index numbers[2] – Indices[2]										
All commodities Tous produits	2000 = 100	95.9	100.0	97.8	98.1	100.4	104.6	108.0	112.7	116.9
Mining Mines	2000 = 100	97.4	100.0	99.0	97.3	101.8	104.4	106.7	108.7	108.5
Manufacturing Manufactures	2000 = 100	95.6	100.0	97.2	97.5	99.5	104.0	107.5	112.8	117.7
Quantities – Quantités										
Coal Houille	million t.	3 249	3 273	3 447	3 498	3 813	4 194	4 510	4 756	4 942
Lignite and brown coal Lignite et charbon brun	million t.	1 287	1 312	1 356	1 356	1 375	1 387	1 401	1 451	1 473
Crude petroleum Pétrole brut	million t.	3 206	3 348	3 353	3 318	3 451	3 539	3 606	3 616	3 604
Natural gas Gaz naturel	petajoules pétajoules	94 706	96 126	97 869	100 445	104 213	106 837	110 082	113 544	116 187
Electricity[3] Electricité[3]	billion kWh milliard kWh	14 825	15 460	15 571	16 187	16 781	17 548	18 345	19 062	19 907
Sugar, raw Sucre, brut	million t.	135	130	131	142	148	147	141	152	166
Woodpulp Pâte de bois	million t.	164	172	166	168	171	176	175	176	177
Sawnwood Sciages	million m³	389	386	380	394	401	425	432	440	431

World statistics: selected series
Population, production, external trade and finance

Statistiques mondiales : séries principales
Population, production, commerce extérieur et finances

Series / Séries	Unit or base / Unité ou base	1999	2000	2001	2002	2003	2004	2005	2006	2007
External trade • Commerce extérieur										
Value – Valeur										
Imports, c.i.f. Importations c.a.f.	billion US $ milliard $ E.-U.	5 462	6 155	5 938	6 156	7 174	8 771	9 958	11 457	13 213
Exports, f.o.b. Exportations f.o.b.	billion US $ milliard $ E.-U.	5 356	5 981	5 755	6 027	7 015	8 543	9 746	11 276	13 082
Volume: index of exports – Volume: indice des exportations										
All commodities Tous produits	2000 = 100	88	100	99	103	109	122	133	147	157
Manufactures Manufacturés	2000 = 100	88	100	100	103	111	128	139	153	...
Unit value: index of exports[4] – Valeur unitaire: indice des exportations[4]										
All commodities Tous produits	2000 = 100	102	100	97	97	107	116	121	126	137
Manufactures Produits manufactures	2000 = 100	103	100	98	98	104	110	111	114	...
Finance • Finances										
International reserves minus gold[5] – Réserves internationales moins l'or[5]										
All countries Tous les pays	billion SDR milliard DTS	1 371.6	1 552.0	1 707.4	1 857.2	2 122.4	2 489.9	2 969.6	3 384.3	4 089.4
Position in IMF Disponibilité au FMI	billion SDR milliard DTS	54.8	47.4	56.9	66.1	66.5	55.8	28.6	17.5	13.7
Foreign exchange Devises	billion SDR milliard DTS	1 298.3	1 486.1	1 630.9	1 771.3	2 035.8	2 413.6	2 920.8	3 348.2	4 057.1
SDR (special drawing rights) DTS (droits de triage sp.)	billion SDR milliard DTS	21.5	21.5	21.5	21.5	21.5	21.5	21.5	21.5	21.5

Source:
Databases of the Food and Agriculture Organization of the United Nations
(FAO), Rome; the International Monetary Fund (IMF), Washington, D.C.; and
the United Nations Statistics Division, New York.

Source:
Les bases de données de l'Organisation des Nations Unies pour
l'alimentation et l'agriculture (FAO), Rome; du Fonds Monétaire
International (FMI), Washington, D.C. ; et de la Division de statistique de
l'Organisation de Nations Unies, New York.

1   Mid-year estimates.
2   Excluding China and the countries of the former USSR (except Russian
     Federation and Ukraine).
3   Electricity generated by establishments for public or private use.

4   Indices computed in US dollars.
5   End of period.

1   Les estimations au milieu de l'année.
2   Non compris la Chine et les pays de l'ancienne URSS (sauf la
     Fédération de Russie et Ukraine).
3   L'électricité produite par des entreprises d'utilisation publique ou
     privée.
4   Indice calculé en dollars des Etats-Unis.
5   Fin de la période.

2

Population, rate of increase, birth and death rates, surface area and density

Population, taux d'accroissement, taux de natalité, taux de mortalité, superficie et densité

Major areas and regions Grandes régions	Mid-year population estimates (millions) Estimations de population au milieu de l'année (millions)							Annual rate of increase Taux d'accrois- sement annuel %	Crude birth rate Taux bruts de natalité (p.1 000)	Crude death rate Taux bruts de mortalité (p.1 000)	Surface area Superficie (000 km²)	Density[1] Densité[1]
	1950	1960	1970	1980	1990	2000	2007	2005 - 2010			2007	2007
World **Monde**	**2 520**	**3 024**	**3 697**	**4 442**	**5 280**	**6 086**	**6 671**	**1.2**	**20**	**9**	**136 127**	**49**
Africa **Afrique**	**224**	**282**	**364**	**479**	**636**	**812**	**965**	**2.2**	**39**	**13**	**30 312**	**32**
Eastern Africa Afrique orientale	65	82	109	146	198	256	303	2.5	39	14	6 361	48
Middle Africa Afrique centrale	26	32	41	54	73	96	119	2.8	45	17	6 613	18
Northern Africa Afrique du Nord	53	67	86	112	144	175	202	1.7	24	6	8 525	24
Southern Africa Afrique australe	16	20	26	33	42	52	56	0.6	23	17	2 675	21
Western Africa Afrique occidentale	64	80	102	134	178	234	284	2.4	40	15	6 138	46
Northern America[2] **Amérique septentrionale[2]**	**172**	**204**	**232**	**256**	**283**	**315**	**342**	**1.0**	**14**	**8**	**21 776**	**16**
Latin America and the Caribbean **Amérique latine et Caraïbes**	**167**	**219**	**285**	**362**	**444**	**523**	**570**	**1.2**	**20**	**6**	**20 546**	**28**
Caribbean Caraïbes	17	20	25	29	34	38	41	0.9	19	8	234	176
Central America Amérique centrale	37	50	68	91	113	136	148	1.3	21	5	2 480	60
South America Amérique du Sud	113	148	192	242	297	349	381	1.2	19	6	17 832	21
Asia[3] **Asie[3]**	**1 396**	**1 699**	**2 140**	**2 630**	**3 169**	**3 676**	**4 029**	**1.1**	**19**	**7**	**31 880**	**126**
Eastern Asia Asie orientale	671	792	987	1 178	1 350	1 479	1 538	0.5	13	7	11 763	131
South-central Asia Asie centrale et du Sud	496	617	780	978	1 226	1 485	1 703	1.5	24	8	10 791	158
South-eastern Asia Asie du Sud-est	178	223	286	358	440	519	568	1.2	20	6	4 495	126
Western Asia Asie occidentale	51	67	88	116	154	193	220	1.8	24	6	4 831	45
Europe[3] **Europe[3]**	**547**	**604**	**656**	**692**	**721**	**728**	**731**	**0.0**	**10**	**12**	**23 049**	**32**
Eastern Europe Europe orientale	220	254	276	295	311	305	294	-0.5	10	15	18 814	16
Northern Europe Europe septentrionale	77	81	86	89	92	94	97	0.4	12	10	1 810	54
Southern Europe Europe méridionale	109	118	127	138	143	146	152	0.3	10	10	1 317	115
Western Europe Europe occidentale	141	152	166	170	176	184	187	0.2	10	10	1 108	169
Oceania[2] **Océanie[2]**	**12.8**	**15.9**	**19.6**	**22.9**	**26.7**	**30.9**	**34.5**	**1.2**	**17**	**7**	**8 564**	**4**
Australia and New Zealand Australie et Nouvelle-Zélande	10.1	12.6	15.5	17.8	20.3	22.9	25.0	1.0	13	7	8 012	3

Major areas and regions Grandes régions	Mid-year population estimates (millions) Estimations de population au milieu de l'année (millions)							Annual rate of increase Taux d'accrois- sement annuel %	Crude birth rate Taux bruts de natalité (p.1 000)	Crude death rate Taux bruts de mortalité (p.1 000)	Surface area Superficie (000 km²)	Density[1] Densité[1]
	1950	1960	1970	1980	1990	2000	2007	2005 - 2010			2007	2007
Melanesia Mélanésie	2.3	2.7	3.4	4.4	5.5	6.9	8.2	1.9	28	9	541	15
Micronesia Micronésie	0.1	0.2	0.2	0.3	0.4	0.5	0.6	1.3	22	5	3	200
Polynesia Polynésie	0.2	0.3	0.4	0.5	0.5	0.6	0.7	1.0	22	5	8	88

Source:
United Nations Statistics Division, New York, *Demographic Yearbook 2007.*

Source:
Organisation des Nations Unies, Division de statistique, New York, *Annuaire démographique 2007.*

1   Population per square kilometre of surface area. Figures are merely the quotients of population divided by surface area and are not to be considered either as reflecting density in the urban sense or as indicating the supporting power of a territory's land and resources.

2   Hawaii, a state of the United States of America, is included in Northern America rather than Oceania.

3   The European portion of Turkey is included in Western Asia rather than Europe.

1   Nombre d'habitants au kilomètre carré. Il s'agit simplement du quotient du chiffre de la population divisé par celui de la superficie, il ne faut pas y voir d'indication de la densité au sens urbain du terme ni de l'effectif de population que les terres et les ressources du territoire sont capables de nourrir.

2   Hawaii, un Etat des Etats-Unis d'Amérique, est comprise en Amérique septentrionale plutôt qu'en Océanie.

3   La partie européenne de la Turquie est comprise en Asie Occidentale plutôt qu'en Europe.

3

Index numbers of total agricultural and food production
1999 – 2001 = 100

Indices de la production agricole totale et de la production alimentaire
1999 – 2001 = 100

Region - Région	1998	1999	2000	2001	2002	2003	2004	2005	2006	2007
World Monde										
Agricultural – agricole	**95.0**	**98.0**	**100.0**	**101.0**	**102.0**	**105.0**	**110.0**	**112.0**	**114.0**	**116.0**
Food – alimentaire	**95.0**	**98.0**	**100.0**	**101.0**	**102.0**	**105.0**	**110.0**	**112.0**	**113.0**	**115.0**
Africa Afrique										
Agricultural – agricole	95.0	98.0	99.0	101.0	105.0	110.0	113.0	117.0	121.0	117.0
Food – alimentaire	94.0	98.0	99.0	101.0	105.0	111.0	114.0	117.0	123.0	118.0
Americas Amériques										
Agricultural – agricole	94.0	98.0	100.0	100.0	101.0	106.0	111.0	113.0	112.0	116.0
Food – alimentaire	94.0	98.0	100.0	100.0	101.0	106.0	111.0	113.0	112.0	116.0
Asia Asie										
Agricultural – agricole	94.0	97.0	100.0	102.0	103.0	107.0	112.0	116.0	120.0	123.0
Food – alimentaire	94.0	97.0	100.0	102.0	104.0	108.0	111.0	116.0	119.0	122.0
Europe Europe										
Agricultural – agricole	98.0	100.0	99.0	99.0	101.0	97.0	105.0	101.0	99.0	99.0
Food – alimentaire	98.0	100.0	100.0	99.0	101.0	97.0	105.0	101.0	99.0	99.0
Oceania Océanie										
Agricultural – agricole	95.0	97.0	99.0	102.0	88.0	99.0	97.0	102.0	88.0	88.0
Food – alimentaire	94.0	97.0	99.0	103.0	88.0	103.0	101.0	104.0	90.0	92.0

4

Index numbers of per capita agricultural and food production
1999 – 2001 – 100

Indices de la production agricole et de la production alimentaire par habitant
1999 – 2001 – 100

Region - Région	1998	1999	2000	2001	2002	2003	2004	2005	2006	2007
World Monde										
Agricultural – agricole	**97.0**	**99.0**	**100.0**	**100.0**	**100.0**	**101.0**	**105.0**	**106.0**	**106.0**	**106.0**
Food – alimentaire	**97.0**	**99.0**	**100.0**	**100.0**	**100.0**	**102.0**	**105.0**	**105.0**	**105.0**	**106.0**
Africa Afrique										
Agricultural – agricole	99.0	100.0	99.0	99.0	100.0	102.0	103.0	104.0	106.0	99.0
Food – alimentaire	99.0	100.0	99.0	99.0	100.0	103.0	104.0	105.0	107.0	101.0
Americas Amériques										
Agricultural – agricole	97.0	99.0	100.0	99.0	99.0	102.0	106.0	106.0	104.0	106.0
Food – alimentaire	97.0	99.0	100.0	99.0	99.0	102.0	105.0	106.0	104.0	107.0
Asia Asie										
Agricultural – agricole	96.0	99.0	100.0	100.0	101.0	103.0	106.0	109.0	111.0	113.0
Food – alimentaire	96.0	99.0	100.0	100.0	101.0	104.0	106.0	109.0	111.0	112.0
Europe Europe										
Agricultural – agricole	98.0	100.0	99.0	99.0	101.0	97.0	104.0	101.0	99.0	98.0
Food – alimentaire	98.0	100.0	100.0	99.0	101.0	97.0	104.0	101.0	99.0	98.0
Oceania Océanie										
Agricultural – agricole	97.0	99.0	99.0	101.0	86.0	95.0	91.0	95.0	81.0	80.0
Food – alimentaire	97.0	99.0	99.0	101.0	86.0	99.0	95.0	97.0	83.0	84.0

Source:
Food and Agriculture Organization of the United Nations (FAO), Rome, FAOSTAT data, last accessed July 2009.

Source:
Organisation des Nations Unies pour l'alimentation et l'agriculture (FAO), Rome, données FAOSTAT, dernier accès juillet 2009.

Region and industry [ISIC Rev. 3] Région et industrie [CITI Rév. 3]	Weight (%) Pondération (%)	2001	2002	2003	2004	2005	2006	2007
World Monde								
Total industry [CDE]								
Total, industrie [CDE]	**100.0**	**97.8**	**98.1**	**100.4**	**104.6**	**108.0**	**112.7**	**116.9**
Total mining [C]								
Total, industries extractives [C]	**10.4**	**99.0**	**97.3**	**101.8**	**104.4**	**106.7**	**108.7**	**108.5**
Coal								
Houille	0.7	103.7	103.4	106.5	111.2	120.7	129.8	131.7
Crude petroleum and natural gas								
Pétrole brut et gaz naturel	8.0	98.7	96.8	101.4	103.6	105.6	107.3	106.7
Metal ores								
Minerais métalliques	1.0	98.1	96.1	101.9	104.6	106.3	107.0	110.7
Total manufacturing [D]								
Total, industries manufacturières [D]	**80.1**	**97.2**	**97.5**	**99.5**	**104.0**	**107.5**	**112.8**	**117.7**
Food, beverages, tobacco								
Industries alimentaires, boissons, tabac	9.4	100.2	101.7	103.8	106.5	110.3	113.4	117.2
Textiles								
Textiles	2.3	94.3	92.4	90.6	91.2	90.0	90.6	91.1
Wearing apparel, leather and footwear								
Articles d'habillement, cuir et chaussures	2.2	93.3	84.5	81.0	79.1	75.1	77.1	77.0
Wood and wood products								
Bois et articles en bois	1.5	95.0	96.0	97.5	100.9	102.4	102.3	98.4
Paper, printing, publishing and recorded media								
Papier, imprimerie, édition et supports enregistré	7.6	96.0	94.4	93.4	95.1	95.7	96.0	96.5
Chemicals and related products								
Produits chimiques et alliés	13.3	99.5	102.4	105.2	109.2	113.0	117.0	120.5
Non-metallic mineral products								
Produits minéraux non métalliques	3.3	98.4	98.9	99.9	103.2	106.5	112.0	115.4
Basic metals								
Métallurgie de base	4.0	96.8	98.6	101.9	108.1	108.5	114.7	118.8
Fabricated metal products								
Fabrications d'ouvrages en métaux	11.2	96.1	94.5	95.1	100.2	103.0	109.3	114.9
Office and related electrical products								
Machines de bureau et autres appareils élect.	12.5	94.2	93.6	100.4	110.0	117.4	132.2	145.4
Transport equipment								
Equipement de transports	8.2	99.8	102.9	104.8	109.9	115.1	118.4	124.3
Electricity, gas, water [E]								
Electricité, gaz et eau [E]	**9.6**	**101.1**	**103.8**	**106.7**	**110.0**	**114.0**	**116.0**	**118.6**
Developed regions[1] Régions développées[1]								
Total industry [CDE]								
Total, industrie [CDE]	**100.0**	**97.3**	**97.0**	**98.1**	**100.8**	**103.0**	**106.6**	**109.8**
Total mining [C]								
Total, industries extractives [C]	**5.9**	**99.2**	**97.6**	**96.7**	**95.7**	**94.1**	**93.9**	**93.7**
Coal								
Houille	0.4	100.8	98.9	97.5	98.4	98.9	99.4	98.5
Crude petroleum and natural gas								
Pétrole brut et gaz naturel	4.2	100.0	98.8	97.9	96.2	92.8	91.9	91.6
Metal ores								
Minerais métalliques	0.8	93.4	88.4	85.3	85.8	90.2	92.1	91.8
Total manufacturing [D]								
Total, industries manufacturières [D]	**84.6**	**96.8**	**96.3**	**97.4**	**100.5**	**102.9**	**107.1**	**110.7**
Food, beverages, tobacco								
Industries alimentaires, boissons, tabac	8.5	100.5	101.3	102.1	103.1	105.1	105.6	107.9
Textiles								
Textiles	1.6	93.4	90.1	86.1	83.2	80.7	76.8	73.9
Wearing apparel, leather and footwear								
Articles d'habillement, cuir et chaussures	1.8	90.7	78.2	72.7	66.3	61.2	59.5	58.8
Wood and wood products								
Bois et articles en bois	1.7	94.7	95.8	96.3	99.3	101.9	102.6	97.3
Paper, printing, publishing and recorded media								
Papier, imprimerie, édition et supports enregistré	9.5	96.0	94.2	92.5	93.7	93.9	93.5	93.5

5

Index numbers of industrial production *(continued)*
2000 = 100
Indices de la production industrielle *(suite)*
2000 = 100

Region and industry [ISIC Rev. 3] Région et industrie [CITI Rév. 3]	Weight (%) Pondération (%)	2001	2002	2003	2004	2005	2006	2007
Chemicals and related products								
Produits chimiques et alliés	13.0	99.2	102.9	104.3	106.8	108.8	111.2	112.5
Non-metallic mineral products								
Produits minéraux non métalliques	3.0	97.5	95.6	95.5	97.7	99.1	101.5	102.0
Basic metals								
Métallurgie de base	3.7	95.5	96.3	97.1	102.3	100.8	104.4	105.8
Fabricated metal products								
Fabrications d'ouvrages en métaux	12.9	95.8	93.2	92.8	96.0	99.0	104.3	108.4
Office and related electrical products								
Machines de bureau et autres appareils élect.	14.3	94.0	91.6	98.6	107.1	113.4	127.9	140.4
Transport equipment								
Equipement de transports	9.5	99.3	101.9	103.0	105.9	109.5	111.9	115.7
Electricity, gas, water [E]								
Electricité, gaz et eau [E]	**9.5**	**100.4**	**102.4**	**104.7**	**106.6**	**109.2**	**109.9**	**111.7**
Developing regions [2] Régions en développement [2]								
Total industry [CDE]								
Total, industrie [CDE]	**100.0**	**99.1**	**100.8**	**106.4**	**114.4**	**120.7**	**128.1**	**134.7**
Total mining [C]								
Total, industries extractives [C]	**21.6**	**98.9**	**97.2**	**105.4**	**110.4**	**115.3**	**118.8**	**118.8**
Coal								
Houille	1.5	105.7	106.5	112.8	120.2	136.1	151.2	155.1
Crude petroleum and natural gas								
Pétrole brut et gaz naturel	17.6	98.0	95.6	103.4	108.2	113.3	116.7	115.8
Metal ores								
Minerais métalliques	1.4	104.9	107.1	125.7	131.4	129.1	128.3	137.6
Total manufacturing [D]								
Total, industries manufacturières [D]	**68.6**	**98.6**	**101.0**	**106.0**	**115.0**	**121.6**	**130.6**	**139.6**
Food, beverages, tobacco								
Industries alimentaires, boissons, tabac	11.8	99.7	102.3	107.0	112.7	119.6	127.5	134.1
Textiles								
Textiles	4.2	95.1	94.7	94.9	98.7	98.9	103.8	107.6
Wearing apparel, leather and footwear								
Articles d'habillement, cuir et chaussures	3.2	97.0	93.8	93.1	97.7	95.2	102.7	103.5
Wood and wood products								
Bois et articles en bois	1.1	96.0	96.6	102.4	107.2	104.3	101.4	102.9
Paper, printing, publishing and recorded media								
Papier, imprimerie, édition et supports enregistré	2.7	95.7	96.2	101.0	107.8	112.3	118.0	122.8
Chemicals and related products								
Produits chimiques et alliés	14.1	100.2	101.2	107.2	114.8	122.7	130.4	139.0
Non-metallic mineral products								
Produits minéraux non métalliques	4.0	100.2	105.0	108.3	113.5	120.7	132.1	140.9
Basic metals								
Métallurgie de base	4.7	99.2	103.2	111.7	119.6	123.9	135.3	144.7
Fabricated metal products								
Fabrications d'ouvrages en métaux	7.1	97.4	100.7	105.7	119.6	121.2	132.0	145.0
Office and related electrical products								
Machines de bureau et autres appareils élect.	8.1	95.2	102.3	108.6	123.2	135.1	151.7	167.6
Transport equipment								
Equipement de transports	4.9	102.5	107.5	113.8	129.3	142.8	150.5	166.4
Electricity, gas, water [E]								
Electricité, gaz et eau [E]	**9.8**	**102.8**	**107.3**	**111.7**	**118.5**	**125.8**	**131.0**	**135.6**
Northern America [3] Amérique septentrionale [3]								
Total industry [CDE]								
Total, industrie [CDE]	**100.0**	**96.2**	**96.6**	**97.9**	**100.3**	**104.4**	**107.5**	**110.5**
Total mining [C]								
Total, industries extractives [C]	**7.5**	**99.1**	**96.2**	**96.6**	**96.8**	**97.2**	**99.8**	**100.2**
Coal								
Houille	0.5	104.7	100.8	98.3	101.6	103.3	106.0	104.5
Crude petroleum and natural gas								
Pétrole brut et gaz naturel	5.4	100.4	98.4	99.7	99.0	97.8	100.7	101.4
Metal ores								
Minerais métalliques	1.4	91.2	84.3	80.8	82.3	87.9	90.6	90.0

Region and industry [ISIC Rev. 3] Région et industrie [CITI Rév. 3]	Weight (%) Pondération (%)	2001	2002	2003	2004	2005	2006	2007
Total manufacturing [D] **Total, industries manufacturières [D]**	**83.5**	**95.6**	**95.9**	**97.3**	**100.0**	**104.5**	**108.1**	**111.2**
Food, beverages, tobacco Industries alimentaires, boissons, tabac	7.7	100.4	100.9	102.5	103.0	106.6	107.4	111.0
Textiles Textiles	1.4	90.2	90.0	85.9	84.6	85.6	77.6	71.1
Wearing apparel, leather and footwear Articles d'habillement, cuir et chaussures	1.4	85.9	68.3	64.0	56.1	54.5	53.3	52.2
Wood and wood products Bois et articles en bois	2.0	93.9	98.3	99.0	102.6	108.2	107.2	96.4
Paper, printing, publishing and recorded media Papier, imprimerie, édition et supports enregistré	11.9	94.4	90.9	88.1	88.8	89.3	87.2	85.9
Chemicals and related products Produits chimiques et alliés	13.1	97.1	103.5	104.5	107.8	111.0	112.6	112.8
Non-metallic mineral products Produits minéraux non métalliques	2.4	96.9	97.3	98.1	101.1	105.3	107.4	105.7
Basic metals Métallurgie de base	2.8	90.5	91.6	90.7	100.0	98.0	102.2	100.4
Fabricated metal products Fabrications d'ouvrages en métaux	12.4	91.2	88.6	87.7	89.5	94.0	98.6	100.3
Office and related electrical products Machines de bureau et autres appareils élect.	12.3	98.5	96.1	106.8	116.0	129.0	147.5	166.8
Transport equipment Equipement de transports	10.2	96.5	99.3	100.2	100.0	104.1	103.9	105.7
Electricity, gas, water [E] **Electricité, gaz et eau [E]**	**9.0**	**99.3**	**102.9**	**104.8**	**106.2**	**108.9**	**108.2**	**111.9**
Latin America and the Caribbean **Amérique latine et Caraïbes**								
Total industry [CDE] **Total, industrie [CDE]**	**100.0**	**98.1**	**97.3**	**99.9**	**107.8**	**112.2**	**117.3**	**123.1**
Total mining [C] **Total, industries extractives [C]**	**11.8**	**100.4**	**97.5**	**96.5**	**100.7**	**103.0**	**105.2**	**105.3**
Coal Houille	0.3	109.9	89.6	86.8	86.9	123.9	130.9	128.6
Crude petroleum and natural gas Pétrole brut et gaz naturel	7.5	98.0	93.8	89.2	92.0	93.8	95.3	92.9
Metal ores Minerais métalliques	2.3	101.7	103.0	112.1	119.2	119.9	122.2	129.3
Total manufacturing [D] **Total, industries manufacturières [D]**	**77.3**	**97.7**	**96.6**	**99.5**	**108.1**	**112.8**	**118.4**	**125.5**
Food, beverages, tobacco Industries alimentaires, boissons, tabac	17.8	99.6	101.4	105.5	112.9	119.0	126.1	131.5
Textiles Textiles	2.9	91.2	83.8	88.2	97.4	98.8	99.6	101.5
Wearing apparel, leather and footwear Articles d'habillement, cuir et chaussures	3.3	91.8	85.2	86.0	91.1	92.4	92.2	97.5
Wood and wood products Bois et articles en bois	1.7	96.0	99.8	106.0	115.3	111.3	109.4	106.8
Paper, printing, publishing and recorded media Papier, imprimerie, édition et supports enregistré	3.6	95.3	94.9	99.1	106.6	112.9	118.0	125.4
Chemicals and related products Produits chimiques et alliés	18.3	97.7	95.6	98.1	105.5	108.8	111.5	116.5
Non-metallic mineral products Produits minéraux non métalliques	3.8	98.1	97.7	98.6	105.8	112.6	121.7	130.1
Basic metals Métallurgie de base	3.6	97.1	99.2	106.2	117.1	121.2	126.7	133.6
Fabricated metal products Fabrications d'ouvrages en métaux	7.6	99.6	96.3	97.9	111.5	114.6	122.3	134.1
Office and related electrical products Machines de bureau et autres appareils élect.	5.4	96.1	89.8	89.2	96.4	103.6	112.4	121.3

Region and industry [ISIC Rev. 3] Région et industrie [CITI Rév. 3]	Weight (%) Pondération (%)	2001	2002	2003	2004	2005	2006	2007
Transport equipment Equipement de transports	6.2	99.1	102.2	103.6	116.0	124.0	133.1	148.6
Electricity, gas, water [E] **Electricité, gaz et eau [E]**	**11.0**	**98.6**	**101.7**	**106.3**	**112.5**	**117.8**	**122.2**	**125.0**
Asia Asie								
Total industry [CDE] **Total, industrie [CDE]**	**100.0**	**96.2**	**97.3**	**101.4**	**107.2**	**111.1**	**117.7**	**122.7**
Total mining [C] **Total, industries extractives [C]**	**11.9**	**98.3**	**96.7**	**103.9**	**106.4**	**110.8**	**113.1**	**111.7**
Coal Houille	1.2	105.8	109.8	117.8	126.5	138.3	155.1	160.2
Crude petroleum and natural gas Pétrole brut et gaz naturel	9.6	97.8	95.4	102.8	105.1	109.6	111.3	109.2
Metal ores Minerais métalliques	0.4	105.1	122.3	116.6	113.3	91.9	94.1	112.4
Total manufacturing [D] **Total, industries manufacturières [D]**	**78.0**	**95.1**	**96.3**	**100.1**	**106.6**	**110.1**	**117.6**	**123.9**
Food, beverages, tobacco Industries alimentaires, boissons, tabac	9.0	99.9	101.4	104.4	106.3	109.8	113.3	117.5
Textiles Textiles	3.1	96.0	96.1	93.1	94.0	93.1	98.1	100.8
Wearing apparel, leather and footwear Articles d'habillement, cuir et chaussures	2.7	93.6	86.7	82.4	80.8	74.3	78.7	75.5
Wood and wood products Bois et articles en bois	0.9	92.3	86.5	87.5	87.5	86.2	84.0	85.4
Paper, printing, publishing and recorded media Papier, imprimerie, édition et supports enregistré	4.8	97.3	96.7	97.1	98.0	99.0	102.4	103.6
Chemicals and related products Produits chimiques et alliés	12.5	100.2	101.7	105.9	110.6	115.5	120.2	124.9
Non-metallic mineral products Produits minéraux non métalliques	3.7	96.5	96.3	96.7	98.4	100.1	104.1	107.1
Basic metals Métallurgie de base	5.6	98.1	100.7	105.4	110.0	110.9	117.2	122.4
Fabricated metal products Fabrications d'ouvrages en métaux	8.2	92.4	90.5	94.4	103.4	105.0	111.0	115.6
Office and related electrical products Machines de bureau et autres appareils élect.	16.5	86.9	90.8	99.9	112.8	117.5	133.8	145.5
Transport equipment Equipement de transports	6.9	101.5	108.2	111.6	121.3	130.4	136.4	146.0
Electricity, gas, water [E] **Electricité, gaz et eau [E]**	**10.1**	**102.3**	**105.3**	**108.2**	**113.5**	**119.0**	**123.1**	**127.1**
Asia excluding Israel and Japan Asie à l'exception de l'Israël et du Japon								
Total industry [CDE] **Total, industrie [CDE]**	**100.0**	**99.6**	**103.6**	**110.4**	**118.9**	**126.4**	**135.1**	**142.6**
Total mining [C] **Total, industries extractives [C]**	**21.4**	**98.3**	**96.7**	**103.9**	**106.4**	**110.8**	**113.1**	**111.6**
Coal Houille	2.2	105.9	110.9	119.0	127.8	140.0	156.9	162.1
Crude petroleum and natural gas Pétrole brut et gaz naturel	17.6	97.8	95.4	102.8	105.0	109.5	111.2	109.1
Metal ores Minerais métalliques	0.7	105.4	122.8	117.0	113.7	91.8	93.8	112.5
Total manufacturing [D] **Total, industries manufacturières [D]**	**69.6**	**99.3**	**104.8**	**111.8**	**122.2**	**130.6**	**141.5**	**151.9**
Food, beverages, tobacco Industries alimentaires, boissons, tabac	9.7	100.8	105.8	112.6	116.5	125.4	135.2	143.9
Textiles Textiles	5.0	96.9	100.1	97.9	100.2	100.3	107.6	112.4
Wearing apparel, leather and footwear Articles d'habillement, cuir et chaussures	3.3	100.9	99.5	98.7	103.9	96.5	111.2	107.7
Wood and wood products Bois et articles en bois	0.8	95.6	92.8	98.4	99.7	99.5	95.3	104.6

5 Index numbers of industrial production *(continued)*
2000 = 100
Indices de la production industrielle *(suite)*
2000 = 100

Region and industry [ISIC Rev. 3] Région et industrie [CITI Rév. 3]	Weight (%) Pondération (%)	2001	2002	2003	2004	2005	2006	2007
Paper, printing, publishing and recorded media Papier, imprimerie, édition et supports enregistré	2.5	95.4	96.8	102.1	107.0	108.3	113.2	113.8
Chemicals and related products Produits chimiques et alliés	13.5	101.4	105.1	112.7	121.8	132.8	141.0	150.6
Non-metallic mineral products Produits minéraux non métalliques	4.2	101.8	109.9	115.2	119.4	124.3	133.3	140.1
Basic metals Métallurgie de base	5.5	101.7	107.2	115.5	123.1	128.2	143.8	155.4
Fabricated metal products Fabrications d'ouvrages en métaux	7.4	95.5	105.2	114.3	129.5	129.5	143.1	157.0
Office and related electrical products Machines de bureau et autres appareils élect.	10.0	94.9	105.8	114.0	130.7	143.9	162.9	180.8
Transport equipment Equipement de transports	4.8	106.5	113.4	125.6	144.8	164.4	170.5	187.7
Electricity, gas, water [E] **Electricité, gaz et eau [E]**	**9.0**	**104.8**	**110.6**	**115.4**	**123.0**	**131.6**	**137.8**	**144.5**
Europe Europe **Total industry [CDE]** **Total, industrie [CDE]**	**100.0**	**100.4**	**99.9**	**100.7**	**103.6**	**104.8**	**108.8**	**112.8**
Total mining [C] **Total, industries extractives [C]**	**6.9**	**99.5**	**100.2**	**99.1**	**98.3**	**94.2**	**91.3**	**90.0**
Coal Houille	0.7	97.2	94.1	93.3	92.5	89.9	89.1	86.9
Crude petroleum and natural gas Pétrole brut et gaz naturel	5.3	100.1	100.8	99.2	98.0	92.7	88.2	86.3
Metal ores Minerais métalliques	0.2	101.1	107.3	112.1	114.7	114.6	116.4	117.6
Total manufacturing [D] **Total, industries manufacturières [D]**	**83.9**	**100.3**	**99.6**	**100.3**	**103.6**	**105.1**	**110.1**	**114.9**
Food, beverages, tobacco Industries alimentaires, boissons, tabac	9.7	101.8	104.4	105.5	107.3	109.6	112.0	114.7
Textiles Textiles	2.2	96.5	92.5	89.7	86.4	82.1	81.4	81.4
Wearing apparel, leather and footwear Articles d'habillement, cuir et chaussures	2.3	96.8	87.6	82.6	77.2	70.2	69.7	69.9
Wood and wood products Bois et articles en bois	1.8	97.0	96.6	98.4	103.2	104.6	108.6	111.1
Paper, printing, publishing and recorded media Papier, imprimerie, édition et supports enregistré	7.6	98.3	98.9	99.1	101.8	101.5	103.0	104.9
Chemicals and related products Produits chimiques et alliés	13.9	101.4	104.2	106.5	109.6	111.6	115.8	119.1
Non-metallic mineral products Produits minéraux non métalliques	3.9	100.0	98.5	99.3	102.6	103.2	108.0	111.8
Basic metals Métallurgie de base	3.8	98.8	98.8	99.6	104.0	102.8	107.8	110.3
Fabricated metal products Fabrications d'ouvrages en métaux	15.4	101.5	100.3	100.5	104.8	107.5	115.1	123.7
Office and related electrical products Machines de bureau et autres appareils élect.	10.7	98.9	93.2	93.6	99.3	103.0	112.7	120.6
Transport equipment Equipement de transports	8.6	101.9	101.7	104.0	109.2	111.4	116.0	122.1
Electricity, gas, water [E] **Electricité, gaz et eau [E]**	**9.2**	**101.7**	**102.6**	**105.5**	**107.2**	**109.5**	**110.8**	**110.7**
Oceania Océanie **Total industry [CDE]** **Total, industrie [CDE]**	**100.0**	**102.8**	**103.9**	**107.4**	**107.6**	**108.3**	**107.7**	**110.2**
Total mining [C] **Total, industries extractives [C]**	**20.3**	**103.2**	**101.6**	**101.8**	**98.0**	**100.6**	**98.2**	**104.9**
Coal Houille	3.2	106.2	112.7	114.4	117.4	124.2	127.3	131.5
Crude petroleum and natural gas Pétrole brut et gaz naturel	9.9	102.6	98.1	93.6	83.2	81.9	78.4	87.7

# Index numbers of industrial production *(continued)*
2000 = 100

Indices de la production industrielle *(suite)*
2000 = 100

Region and industry [ISIC Rev. 3] Région et industrie [CITI Rév. 3]	Weight (%) Pondération (%)	2001	2002	2003	2004	2005	2006	2007
Metal ores Minerais métalliques	6.7	103.9	101.4	107.0	110.1	115.2	112.7	117.3
Total manufacturing [D] **Total, industries manufacturières [D]**	**66.5**	**102.5**	**104.4**	**108.9**	**110.5**	**110.1**	**109.8**	**111.2**
Food, beverages, tobacco Industries alimentaires, boissons, tabac	14.9	104.0	104.1	108.5	110.3	111.4	111.3	111.8
Textiles Textiles	1.5	92.8	82.4	77.2	71.8	60.5	55.7	55.1
Wearing apparel, leather and footwear Articles d'habillement, cuir et chaussures	1.3	92.6	82.7	77.9	72.6	62.0	56.9	56.3
Wood and wood products Bois et articles en bois	2.8	99.2	101.0	104.5	103.8	106.3	102.3	100.1
Paper, printing, publishing and recorded media Papier, imprimerie, édition et supports enregistré	8.9	103.3	105.9	107.6	110.4	109.5	107.4	109.1
Chemicals and related products Produits chimiques et alliés	9.0	102.8	103.4	109.0	103.9	104.6	99.9	99.0
Non-metallic mineral products Produits minéraux non métalliques	3.5	101.8	107.8	116.9	121.5	128.1	141.7	144.4
Basic metals Métallurgie de base	4.8	99.7	107.0	111.1	111.9	108.9	107.7	117.5
Fabricated metal products Fabrications d'ouvrages en métaux	8.1	102.1	106.6	111.8	115.0	113.8	114.5	119.1
Office and related electrical products Machines de bureau et autres appareils élect.	3.5	105.2	105.7	112.5	118.2	119.6	123.7	122.2
Transport equipment Equipement de transports	5.7	104.8	105.2	112.2	118.0	119.0	123.7	122.9
Electricity, gas, water [E] **Electricité, gaz et eau [E]**	**13.2**	**103.4**	**104.8**	**108.1**	**107.6**	**111.0**	**111.9**	**113.6**

Source:
United Nations Statistics Division, New York, the index numbers of industrial production database, last accessed February 2009.

Source:
Organisation des Nations Unies, Division de statistique, New York, la base de données pour les indices de la production industrielle, dernier accès février 2009.

1   Northern America (Canada and the United States), Europe, Australia, Israel, Japan, New Zealand and South Africa.

2   Latin America and the Caribbean, Africa (excluding South Africa), Asia (excluding Israel and Japan), Oceania (excluding Australia and New Zealand).

3   Canada and the United States.

1   Amérique septentrionale (le Canada et les Etats-Unis), Europe, l'Australie, l'Israël, la Nouvelle-Zélande et l'Afrique du Sud.

2   Amérique latine et Caraïbes, Afrique (non compris l'Afrique du Sud), Asie (non compris l'Israël et le Japon), Océanie (non compris l'Australie et la Nouvelle-Zélande).

3   Le Canada et les Etats-Unis.

6

Production, trade and consumption of commercial energy
Thousand metric tons of oil equivalent and kilograms per capita

Production, commerce et consommation d'énergie commerciale
Milliers de tonnes d'équivalent pétrole et kilogrammes par habitant

Region	Year Année	Primary energy production – Production d'énergie primaire					Changes in stocks Variations des stocks	Imports Importations	Exports Exportations
		Total Totale	Solids Solides	Liquids Liquides	Gas Gaz	Electricity Electricité			
World	2000	8 563 245	2 145 185	3 659 492	2 296 403	462 164	-72 032	3 709 615	3 675 212
	2001	8 725 828	2 250 492	3 676 557	2 337 876	460 904	64 344	3 778 790	3 728 435
	2002	8 792 218	2 275 545	3 652 406	2 393 841	470 426	-1 244	3 826 460	3 745 851
	2003	9 200 828	2 446 980	3 797 548	2 485 731	470 568	5 376	4 004 413	3 956 705
	2004	9 635 182	2 650 758	3 941 185	2 547 975	495 265	9 991	4 283 085	4 230 423
	2005	9 960 142	2 825 945	4 005 646	2 618 450	510 100	2 010	4 395 962	4 386 100
	2006	10 247 112	2 977 992	4 037 763	2 706 722	524 636	54 233	4 506 360	4 511 906
Africa	2000	667 862	127 619	412 153	120 259	7 830	-572	77 531	445 595
	2001	663 567	127 120	408 612	119 774	8 061	935	78 012	444 142
	2002	669 769	125 280	406 428	129 381	8 679	427	76 438	440 586
	2003	712 919	129 692	439 097	135 640	8 490	1 521	82 821	477 988
	2004	764 996	131 824	479 831	144 381	8 960	-1 387	87 748	519 849
	2005	820 916	133 136	508 197	170 593	8 990	-649	98 573	559 898
	2006	838 670	132 967	508 317	187 889	9 497	1 012	99 835	586 121
America, North	2000	2 009 724	494 073	659 686	718 717	137 248	-57 151	841 063	428 493
	2001	2 042 507	519 145	664 513	729 890	128 959	66 318	872 388	430 184
	2002	2 026 243	498 017	673 824	716 127	138 275	-19 949	852 548	438 932
	2003	2 032 572	481 383	686 524	727 918	136 748	-6 944	900 042	458 375
	2004	2 048 838	506 542	684 186	717 308	140 801	902	958 051	475 281
	2005	2 032 989	515 239	664 640	709 479	143 631	-3 873	989 545	476 043
	2006	2 069 379	524 172	666 553	731 985	146 668	30 611	989 927	490 944
America, South	2000	511 497	33 755	348 693	82 064	46 985	-25	83 121	248 654
	2001	532 651	36 582	364 123	87 038	44 908	1 933	83 886	260 233
	2002	517 790	36 312	348 688	86 032	46 758	3 427	81 691	244 726
	2003	520 914	39 800	342 758	89 432	48 924	5 105	79 853	238 945
	2004	533 338	42 198	346 772	93 918	50 450	-1 156	90 890	263 532
	2005	558 006	46 620	360 925	97 213	53 248	-151	88 756	269 641
	2006	575 920	50 980	366 472	102 074	56 393	-4 917	91 288	271 750
Asia	2000	3 126 839	975 156	1 542 107	513 779	95 797	-16 450	1 265 088	1 374 911
	2001	3 200 915	1 039 640	1 525 275	536 077	99 922	-7 204	1 266 165	1 387 994
	2002	3 247 648	1 088 403	1 482 248	576 508	100 490	3 379	1 316 079	1 347 720
	2003	3 532 015	1 246 700	1 562 574	621 297	101 444	-2 663	1 384 308	1 457 918
	2004	3 832 682	1 418 934	1 639 561	660 869	113 318	899	1 530 044	1 565 530
	2005	4 094 538	1 568 621	1 695 644	708 497	121 776	-6 328	1 558 445	1 650 338
	2006	4 312 946	1 709 680	1 728 430	745 717	129 119	990	1 626 904	1 728 425
Europe	2000	2 009 697	356 690	658 603	824 135	170 269	7 272	1 408 549	1 021 725
	2001	2 035 912	358 471	675 438	826 688	175 315	-3 239	1 442 742	1 043 413
	2002	2 076 658	352 611	705 523	846 318	172 207	9 762	1 462 819	1 105 144
	2003	2 139 167	362 297	733 598	872 236	171 036	8 013	1 519 522	1 152 601
	2004	2 187 268	356 619	761 129	891 998	177 521	10 469	1 577 797	1 230 560
	2005	2 175 927	358 276	749 647	889 506	178 498	14 063	1 619 414	1 246 811
	2006	2 170 882	355 781	741 994	894 225	178 881	28 077	1 654 720	1 249 834
Oceania	2000	237 626	157 893	38 250	37 448	4 035	-5 105	34 263	155 835
	2001	250 276	169 534	38 595	38 409	3 739	5 600	35 597	162 470
	2002	254 109	174 923	35 694	39 475	4 017	1 711	36 885	168 742
	2003	263 241	187 108	32 998	39 209	3 927	344	37 868	170 879
	2004	268 061	194 640	29 706	39 501	4 214	264	38 556	175 669
	2005	277 765	204 054	26 591	43 163	3 957	-1 053	41 229	183 369
	2006	279 316	204 411	25 997	44 831	4 078	-1 540	43 687	184 831

Source:
United Nations Statistics Division, New York, the energy statistics database, last accessed June 2009.

6 Production, trade and consumption of commercial energy *(continued)*
Thousand metric tons of oil equivalent and kilograms per capita
Production, commerce et consommation d'énergie commerciale *(suite)*
Milliers de tonnes d'équivalent pétrole et kilogrammes par habitant

Bunkers - Soutes		Unallocated	Per capita	Consumption - Consommation						
Air Avion	Sea Maritime	Non distribué	Par habitant	Total Totale	Solids Solides	Liquids Liquides	Gas Gaz	Electricity Electricité	Year Année	Région
105 845	147 929	283 104	1 345	8 125 327	2 250 975	3 096 001	2 316 352	461 999	2000	Monde
102 885	140 574	279 704	1 338	8 180 927	2 261 369	3 135 207	2 322 862	461 489	2001	
105 107	144 784	268 849	1 349	8 346 859	2 317 061	3 158 273	2 400 042	471 483	2002	
108 177	144 504	317 916	1 382	8 661 719	2 505 912	3 196 633	2 488 635	470 540	2003	
113 705	157 657	322 290	1 430	9 073 483	2 715 814	3 324 419	2 537 945	495 305	2004	
121 509	168 444	319 400	1 456	9 346 463	2 850 219	3 370 683	2 615 570	509 991	2005	
123 489	177 722	306 946	1 469	9 568 715	2 988 105	3 398 303	2 657 923	524 383	2006	
5 205	7 208	14 759	347	272 860	95 045	113 610	56 297	7 908	2000	Afrique
4 765	6 895	8 247	344	276 271	95 795	113 772	58 350	8 354	2001	
4 600	5 944	5 188	352	289 158	92 815	120 103	67 365	8 874	2002	
4 514	7 151	8 843	350	295 421	96 479	122 238	68 099	8 604	2003	
4 454	6 122	7 757	363	315 650	103 666	130 529	72 370	9 084	2004	
5 004	6 458	16 190	374	332 303	103 067	134 213	85 925	9 097	2005	
5 060	5 678	7 109	364	333 234	103 367	135 615	84 667	9 585	2006	
23 616	33 601	22 292	4 943	2 400 335	491 580	1 022 400	749 176	137 179	2000	Amérique du Nord
21 657	24 648	29 764	4 770	2 342 701	479 367	1 030 712	703 745	128 877	2001	
21 105	28 096	20 916	4 811	2 390 052	484 785	1 033 341	733 393	138 533	2002	
20 579	23 838	35 805	4 784	2 401 313	488 664	1 049 926	726 080	136 643	2003	
20 963	29 332	33 961	4 825	2 446 827	502 747	1 085 011	718 280	140 790	2004	
21 610	30 409	22 850	4 834	2 475 858	507 655	1 105 879	718 719	143 605	2005	
20 479	32 389	22 428	4 767	2 462 791	500 281	1 097 713	718 250	146 548	2006	
2 012	5 128	25 703	906	312 986	21 055	163 138	81 922	46 871	2000	Amérique du Sud
2 556	6 100	28 270	900	317 288	19 455	166 608	86 396	44 829	2001	
2 588	6 225	28 623	877	313 825	18 843	162 709	85 648	46 625	2002	
2 702	6 072	30 202	877	317 672	20 300	159 253	89 343	48 775	2003	
3 421	6 517	17 043	912	334 721	21 031	169 223	94 007	50 459	2004	
3 402	7 727	17 492	936	348 534	21 776	176 341	97 040	53 376	2005	
3 871	7 310	19 559	979	369 432	21 734	188 820	102 298	56 580	2006	
26 795	55 094	191 187	751	2 753 812	1 132 690	1 013 062	511 604	96 456	2000	Asie
28 270	54 658	188 518	757	2 807 814	1 159 982	1 012 859	534 403	100 571	2001	
31 746	55 309	190 416	780	2 927 441	1 217 650	1 036 224	572 437	101 131	2002	
33 505	58 015	207 820	829	3 151 776	1 373 702	1 059 578	617 033	101 463	2003	
35 195	62 913	226 663	902	3 461 985	1 568 231	1 133 475	646 995	113 284	2004	
38 441	68 715	224 577	944	3 667 397	1 705 334	1 149 538	690 711	121 815	2005	
40 221	74 227	233 959	978	3 852 723	1 835 771	1 150 525	737 180	129 247	2006	
45 091	45 653	35 315	3 109	2 262 397	466 289	736 359	890 199	169 550	2000	Europe
42 252	47 128	32 265	3 189	2 316 199	464 097	765 638	911 344	175 120	2001	
42 232	48 051	26 461	3 180	2 307 077	460 163	763 013	911 598	172 303	2002	
43 497	48 293	37 375	3 256	2 368 032	476 039	761 826	959 040	171 128	2003	
46 242	51 542	39 820	3 277	2 385 316	468 696	762 095	977 052	177 473	2004	
49 221	53 872	40 981	3 275	2 388 092	457 412	758 780	993 760	178 139	2005	
50 307	56 689	24 718	3 308	2 414 966	471 219	779 825	985 576	178 347	2006	
3 127	1 245	-6 132	3 970	122 938	44 317	47 432	27 155	4 035	2000	Océanie
3 385	1 145	-7 361	3 840	120 654	42 672	45 618	28 625	3 739	2001	
2 837	1 159	-2 754	3 740	119 305	42 805	42 883	29 601	4 017	2002	
3 380	1 135	-2 129	3 935	127 506	50 729	43 811	29 040	3 927	2003	
3 429	1 231	-2 954	3 923	128 984	51 443	44 085	29 242	4 214	2004	
3 831	1 264	-2 690	4 025	134 279	54 975	45 933	29 415	3 957	2005	
3 552	1 428	-827	4 002	135 569	55 735	45 805	29 951	4 078	2006	

Source:
Organisation des Nations Unies, Division de statistique, New York, la base de données pour les statistiques de l'énergie, dernier accès juin 2009.

7

Total imports and exports: index numbers
Volume and unit value indices and terms of trade (2000 = 100)

Importations et exportations totales : indices
Indices du volume et de la valeur unitaire et termes de l'échange (2000 = 100)

Region	1999	2001	2002	2003	2004	2005	2006	2007	Région
Total									**Total**
Imports : Volume [1]	90	100	104	111	124	133	143	150	Imp.: Volume [1]
Imports : Unit value indices US $ [2]	99	96	96	104	114	120	128	140	Imp.: Indices de la val. unit. en $ E.-U. [2]
Exports : Volume [1]	88	99	103	109	122	133	147	157	Exp.: Volume [1]
Exports : Unit value indices US $ [2]	102	97	97	107	116	121	126	137	Exp.: Indices de la val. unit. en $ E.-U. [2]
Developed economies [3]									**Economies développées [3]**
Imports : Volume [1]	91	100	103	108	118	125	133	137	Imp.: Volume [1]
Imports : Unit value indices US $ [2]	100	96	96	106	116	122	130	142	Imp.: Indices de la val. unit. en $ E.-U. [2]
Exports : Volume [1]	91	99	102	104	113	118	128	133	Exp.: Volume [1]
Exports : Unit value indices US $ [2]	103	98	99	111	121	126	131	145	Exp.: Indices de la val. unit. en $ E.-U. [2]
Terms of trade [4]	104	102	103	104	104	103	101	102	Termes de l'échange [4]
North America									**Amérique du Nord**
Imports : Volume [1]	91	97	101	106	116	124	130	131	Imp.: Volume [1]
Imports : Unit value indices US $ [2]	94	96	94	97	103	111	116	121	Imp.: Indices de la val. unit. en $ E.-U. [2]
Exports : Volume [1]	91	94	91	92	97	104	113	119	Exp.: Volume [1]
Exports : Unit value indices US $ [2]	98	100	98	101	107	113	117	123	Exp.: Indices de la val. unit. en $ E.-U. [2]
Terms of trade [4]	105	103	104	104	104	102	101	102	Termes de l'échange [4]
Europe									**Europe**
Imports : Volume [1]	91	102	104	108	118	125	135	141	Imp.: Volume [1]
Imports : Unit value indices US $ [2]	104	97	99	114	127	131	139	156	Imp.: Indices de la val. unit. en $ E.-U. [2]
Exports : Volume [1]	90	103	107	109	118	123	134	138	Exp.: Volume [1]
Exports : Unit value indices US $ [2]	107	98	101	117	130	134	140	157	Exp.: Indices de la val. unit. en $ E.-U. [2]
Terms of trade [4]	103	100	102	103	102	102	100	101	Termes de l'échange [4]
Asia and the Pacific									**Asie et le Pacifique**
Imports : Volume [1,5]	91	103	103	111	121	126	133	132	Imp.: Volume [1,5]
Imports : Unit value indices US $ [2]	93	88	88	94	104	113	120	132	Imp.: Indices de la val. unit. en $ E.-U. [2]
Exports : Volume [1]	92	91	97	101	111	113	121	126	Exp.: Volume [1]
Exports : Unit value indices US $ [2]	96	94	91	98	108	115	117	124	Exp.: Indices de la val. unit. en $ E.-U. [2]
Terms of trade [4]	103	107	103	105	104	101	98	94	Termes de l'échange [4]
Africa									**Afrique**
Imports : Volume [1]	100	111	111	113	123	142	...	...	Imp.: Volume [1]
Imports : Unit value indices US $ [2]	100	94	94	113	131	137	...	...	Imp.: Indices de la val. unit. en $ E.-U. [2]
Exports : Volume [1]	84	101	101	109	128	172	190	216	Exp.: Volume [1]
Exports : Unit value indices US $ [2]	95	93	95	109	122	123	124	128	Exp.: Indices de la val. unit. en $ E.-U. [2]
Terms of trade [4]	96	99	101	97	93	90	...	...	Termes de l'échange [4]
Northern Africa									**Afrique du Nord**
Exports : Volume [1]	82	102	98	122	152	207	241	258	Exp.: Volume [1]
Exports : Unit value indices US $ [2]	87	90	93	95	99	100	102	110	Exp.: Indices de la val. unit. en $ E.-U. [2]
Sub-Saharan Africa									**Afrique subsaharienne**
Exports : Volume [1]	85	100	102	101	113	144	154	185	Exp.: Volume [1]
Exports : Unit value indices US $ [2]	101	95	97	119	141	149	148	146	Exp.: Indices de la val. unit. en $ E.-U. [2]
Latin America and the Caribbean									**Amérique latine et Caraïbes**
Imports : Volume [1]	88	99	100	106	114	113	122	132	Imp.: Volume [1]
Imports : Unit value indices US $ [2]	98	99	91	90	101	121	134	148	Imp.: Indices de la val. unit. en $ E.-U. [2]
Exports : Volume [1]	91	102	102	105	120	135	152	162	Exp.: Volume [1]
Exports : Unit value indices US $ [2]	92	94	95	101	109	117	126	133	Exp.: Indices de la val. unit. en $ E.-U. [2]
Terms of trade [4]	94	95	104	113	108	97	94	90	Termes de l'échange [4]
Latin America									**Amérique latine**
Exports : Volume [1]	91	102	102	105	119	134	151	160	Exp.: Volume [1]
Exports : Unit value indices US $ [2]	92	94	95	101	109	118	126	133	Exp.: Indices de la val. unit. en $ E.-U. [2]
Western Asia									**Asie occidentale**
Imports : Volume [1]	89	97	106	113	135	145	160	183	Imp.: Volume [1]
Imports : Unit value indices US $ [2]	96	99	99	109	123	132	144	158	Imp.: Indices de la val. unit. en $ E.-U. [2]
Exports : Volume [1]	76	96	101	115	138	169	191	215	Exp.: Volume [1]
Exports : Unit value indices US $ [2]	102	97	96	105	117	126	131	145	Exp.: Indices de la val. unit. en $ E.-U. [2]
Terms of trade [4]	106	98	97	96	95	95	91	92	Termes de l'échange [4]

7
Total imports and exports: index numbers *(continued)*
Volume and unit value indices and terms of trade (2000 = 100)
Importations et exportations totales : indices *(suite)*
Indices du volume et de la valeur unitaire et termes de l'échange (2000 = 100)

Region	1999	2001	2002	2003	2004	2005	2006	2007	Région
Other Asia									**Autre Asie**
Imports : Volume [1]	84	98	111	128	154	174	193	209	Imp.: Volume [1]
Imports : Unit value indices US $ [2]	94	95	93	96	105	110	116	124	Imp.: Indices de la val. unit. en $ E.-U. [2]
Exports : Volume [1]	83	100	114	131	160	185	215	248	Exp.: Volume [1]
Exports : Unit value indices US $ [2]	99	94	90	93	98	102	106	109	Exp.: Indices de la val. unit. en $ E.-U. [2]
Terms of trade [4]	105	98	97	97	94	93	92	88	Termes de l'échange [4]
Eastern Asia									**Asie orientale**
Imports : Volume [1]	82	99	115	140	169	184	207	233	Imp.: Volume [1]
Imports : Unit value indices US $ [2]	92	94	91	95	104	109	115	120	Imp.: Indices de la val. unit. en $ E.-U. [2]
Exports : Volume [1]	84	101	118	145	179	213	256	302	Exp.: Volume [1]
Exports : Unit value indices US $ [2]	97	93	90	92	98	100	101	103	Exp.: Indices de la val. unit. en $ E.-U. [2]
Terms of trade [4]	105	99	99	97	94	91	87	86	Termes de l'échange [4]
Southern Asia									**Asie australe**
Imports : Volume [1]	94	105	111	123	141	175	213	222	Imp.: Volume [1]
Imports : Unit value indices US $ [2]	96	96	102	113	132	142	137	156	Imp.: Indices de la val. unit. en $ E.-U. [2]
Exports : Volume [1]	80	103	114	121	135	163	181	192	Exp.: Volume [1]
Exports : Unit value indices US $ [2]	103	94	92	105	119	126	141	152	Exp.: Indices de la val. unit. en $ E.-U. [2]
Terms of trade [4]	107	98	90	94	90	88	103	97	Termes de l'échange [4]
South-eastern Asia									**Asie du Sud-est**
Imports : Volume [1]	83	94	101	104	126	141	149	159	Imp.: Volume [1]
Imports : Unit value indices US $ [2]	97	97	95	98	101	110	118	125	Imp.: Indices de la val. unit. en $ E.-U. [2]
Exports : Volume [1]	83	96	106	111	134	145	159	178	Exp.: Volume [1]
Exports : Unit value indices US $ [2]	102	94	90	92	96	102	110	110	Exp.: Indices de la val. unit. en $ E.-U. [2]
Terms of trade [4]	104	96	94	94	95	93	93	88	Termes de l'échange [4]

Source:
United Nations Statistics Division, New York, trade statistics database, last accessed January 2009.

Source:
Organisation des Nations Unies, Division de statistique, New York, la base de données pour les statistiques du commerce extérieur, dernier accès janvier 2009.

1   Volume indices are derived from value data and unit value indices. They are base-period weighted.

2   Regional aggregates are current-period weighted.

3   This classification is intended for statistical convenience and does not, necessarily, express a judgement about the stage reached by a particular country in the development process.

4   Unit value index of exports divided by unit value index of imports.

5   The correction of trade values for Japan (re-exports) in November 2008 led to significant changes in the volume index.

1   Les indices du volume sont calculés à partir des chiffres de la valeur et des indices de valeur unitaire. Ils sont à coefficients de pondération correspondant à la période en base.

2   Les totaux régionaux sont à coefficients de pondération correspondant à la période en cours.

3   Cette classification est utilisée pour plus de commodité dans la présentation des statistiques et n'implique pas nécessairement un jugement quant au stade de développement auquel est parvenu un pays donné.

4   Indice de la valeur unitaire des exportations divisé par l'indice de la valeur unitaire des importations.

5   La correction en Novembre 2008 des valeurs de réexportations du Japon a conduit à des changements significatifs au niveau des indices de volume.

Technical notes: tables 1-7

Table 1: The series of world aggregates on population, output, production, external trade and finance have been compiled from statistical publications and databases of the United Nations and the specialized agencies and other institutions. The sources should be consulted for detailed information on compilation and coverage.

Table 2 presents estimates of population size, rates of population increase, crude birth and death rates, surface area and population density for the world and regions. Unless otherwise specified, all figures are estimates of the order of magnitude and are subject to a substantial margin of error.

The population estimates and rates presented in this table were prepared by the Population Division of the United Nations Secretariat and published in *World Population Prospects: The 2008 Revision.*

The average annual percentage rates of population growth were calculated by the Population Division of the United Nations Secretariat, using an exponential rate of increase formula.

Crude birth and crude death rates are expressed in terms of the average annual number of births and deaths respectively, per 1,000 mid-year population. These rates are estimated.

Surface area totals were obtained by summing the figures for the individual countries or areas.

Density is the number of persons in the 2007 total population per square kilometre of total surface area.

The scheme of regionalization used for the purpose of making these estimates is presented in annex I. Although some continental totals are given, and all can be derived, the basic scheme presents macro regions that are so drawn as to obtain greater homogeneity in sizes of population, types of demographic circumstances and accuracy of demographic statistics.

Tables 3-4: The index numbers in table 3 refer to agricultural production, which is defined to include both crop and livestock products. Seeds and feed are excluded. The index numbers of food refer to commodities which are considered edible and contain nutrients. Coffee, tea and other inedible commodities are excluded.

The index numbers of total agricultural and food production in table 3 are calculated by the Laspeyres formula with the base year period 1999-2001. The latter is provided in order to diminish the impact of annual fluctuations in agricultural output during base years on the indices for the period. Production quantities of each commodity are weighted by 1999-2001 average national producer prices and summed for each year. The index numbers are based on production data for a calendar year.

Index numbers for the world and regions are computed in a similar way to the country index numbers ex-

Notes techniques: tableaux 1 à 7

Tableau 1: Les séries d'agrégats mondiaux sur la population, la production, le commerce extérieur et les finances ont été établies à partir de publications statistiques et bases de données des Nations Unies et les institutions spécialisées et autres organismes. On doit se référer aux sources pour tous renseignements détaillés sur les méthodes de calcul et la portée des statistiques.

Le *Tableau 2* présente les estimations mondiales et régionales de la population, des taux d'accroissement de la population, des taux bruts de natalité et de mortalité, de la superficie et de la densité de population. Sauf indication contraire, tous les chiffres sont des estimations de l'ordre de grandeur et comportent une assez grande marge d'erreur.

Les estimations de la population et tous les taux présentés dans ce tableau ont été établis par la Division de la population du Secrétariat des Nations Unies et publiés dans "*World Population Prospects: The 2008 Revision*".

Les pourcentages annuels moyens de l'accroissement de la population ont été calculés par la Division de la population du Secrétariat des Nations Unies, sur la base d'une formule de taux d'accroissement exponentiel.

Les taux bruts de natalité et de mortalité sont exprimés, respectivement, sur la base du nombre annuel moyen de naissances et de décès par tranche de 1.000 habitants au milieu de l'année. Ces taux sont estimatifs.

On a déterminé les superficies totales en additionnant les chiffres correspondant aux différents pays ou régions.

La densité est le nombre de personnes de la population totale de 2007 par kilomètre carré de la superficie totale.

Le schéma de régionalisation utilisé aux fins de l'établissement de ces estimations est présenté dans l'annexe I. Bien que les totaux de certains continents soient donnés et que tous puissent être déterminés, le schéma de base présente les grandes régions qui sont établies de manière à obtenir une plus grande homogénéité en ce qui concerne l'ampleur des populations, les types de conditions démographiques et la précision des statistiques démographiques.

Tableaux 3-4: Les indices du tableau 3 se rapportent à la production agricole, qui est définie comme comprenant à la fois les produits de l'agriculture et de l'élevage. Les semences et les aliments pour les animaux sont exclus de cette définition. Les indices de la production alimentaire se rapportent aux produits considérés comme comestibles et contenant des éléments nutritifs. Le café, le thé et les produits non comestibles sont exclus.

Les indices de la production agricole et de la production alimentaire présentés au tableau 3 sont calculés selon la formule de Laspeyres avec les années 1999-2001 comme période de référence, cela afin de limiter l'incidence, sur les indices correspondant à la période considérée, des fluctuations annuelles de la production agricole enregistrée pendant les années de référence. Les chiffres de production de chaque produit sont pondérés par les prix nationaux moyens à la production pour la période 1999-2001 et additionnés pour chaque année. Les indices sont fondés sur les

cept that instead of using different commodity prices for each country group, "international commodity prices" derived from the Gheary-Khamis formula are used for all country groupings. This method assigns a single "price" to each commodity.

The indexes in table 4 are calculated as a ratio between the index numbers of total agricultural and food production in table 3 described above and the corresponding index numbers of population.

For further information on the series presented in these tables, see the FAO *Statistical Yearbook* and http://faostat.fao.org.

Table 5: The index numbers of industrial production are classified according to tabulation categories, divisions and combinations of divisions of the International Standard Industrial Classification of All Economic Activities, Revision 3, (ISIC Rev. 3) for mining (category C), manufacturing (category D), and electricity, gas and water (category E)

The indexes indicate trends in value added at constant prices. The measure of value added used is the national accounts concept, which is defined as gross output less intermediate consumption.

Each series is compiled using the Laspeyres formula, that is, the indices are base-weighted arithmetic means. The weight base year is 2000 and value added, generally at factor cost, is used in weighting.

For most countries the estimates of value added used as weights are derived from the results of national industrial censuses or similar inquiries relating to 2000. These data, in national currency, are adjusted to the ISIC where necessary and are subsequently converted into US dollars.

Within each of the ISIC categories (tabulation categories, divisions and combinations of divisions) shown in the tables, the indices for the country aggregations (regions or economic groupings) are calculated directly from the country data. The indices for the World, however, are calculated from the aggregated indices for the groupings of developed and developing countries.

Table 6: For a description of the series in table 6, see the technical notes to chapter XII.

Table 7: For a description of the series in table 7, see the technical notes to chapter XV. The composition of the regions is presented in table 62.

données de production de l'année civile.

Les indices pour le monde et les régions sont calculés de la même façon que les indices par pays, mais au lieu d'appliquer des prix différents aux produits de base pour chaque groupe de pays, on a utilisé des "prix internationaux" établis d'après la formule de Gheary-Khamis pour tous les groupes de pays. Cette méthode attribue un seul "prix" à chaque produit de base.

Les indices du tableau 4 sont calculés comme ratio entre les indices de la production alimentaire et de la production agricole totale du tableau 3 décrits ci-dessus et les indices de population correspondants.

Pour tout renseignement complémentaire sur les séries présentées dans ces tableaux, voir l'*Annuaire Statistique de la FAO* et http://faostat.fao.org.

Tableau 5: Les indices de la production industrielle sont classés selon les catégories de classement, les divisions ou des combinaisons des divisions de la Classification Internationale type, par industrie, de toutes les branches d'activité économique, Révision 3 (CITI Rev. 3) qui concernent les industries extractives (la catégorie C) et les industries manufacturières (la catégorie D), ainsi que l'électricité, le gaz et l'eau (la catégorie E).

Ces indices représentent les tendances de la valeur ajoutée aux prix constants. La mesure utilisée pour la valeur ajoutée correspond à celle qui est appliquée aux fins de la comptabilité nationale, c'est-à-dire égale à la valeur de la production brute diminuée des coûts des matériaux, des fournitures, de la consommation de carburant et d'électricité ainsi que des services reçus.

Chaque série a été établie au moyen de la formule de Laspeyres, ce qui signifie que les indices sont des moyennes arithmétiques affectées de coefficients de pondération. L'année de base de pondération est l'année 2000 et on utilise généralement pour la pondération la valeur ajoutée au coût des facteurs.

Pour la plupart des pays, les estimations de la valeur ajoutée qui sont utilisées comme coefficients de pondération sont tirées des résultats des recensements industriels nationaux ou enquêtes analogues concernant l'année 2000. Ces données, en monnaie nationale, sont ajustées s'il y a lieu aux normes de la CITI et ultérieurement converties en dollars des Etats-Unis.

A l'intérieur de chacune des subdivisions de la CITI (catégories de classement, divisions et combinaisons des divisions) indiquées dans les tableaux, les indices relatifs aux assemblages de pays (régions géographiques ou groupements économiques) sont calculés directement à partir des données des pays. Toutefois, les indices concernant le *Monde* sont calculés à partir des indices agrégés applicables aux groupements de pays développés et de pays en développement.

Tableau 6: On trouvera une description de la série de statistiques du tableau 6 dans les notes techniques du chapitre XII.

Tableau 7: On trouvera une description de la série de statistiques du tableau 7 dans les notes techniques du chapitre XV. La composition des régions est présentée au tableau 62.

Part Two
Population and social statistics

Chapter II Population (tables 8 and 9)

Chapter III Gender (tables 10-12)

Chapter IV Education (tables 13 and 14)

Chapter V Communication (tables 15-17)

Part Two of the *Yearbook* presents statistical series on a wide range of population and social topics for all countries or areas of the world for which data have been made available. The topics include population and population growth, surface area and density; life expectancy, childbearing and mortality; gender; education; telephones; cellular mobile phones and internet users.

Deuxième partie
Population et statistiques sociales

Chapitre II Population (tableaux 8 et 9)

Chapitre III La situation des femmes (tableaux 10 à 12)

Chapitre IV Éducation (tableaux 13 et 14)

Chapitre V Communication (tableaux 15 à 17)

La deuxième partie de l'*Annuaire* présente, pour tous les pays ou zones du monde pour lesquels des données sont disponibles, des séries statistiques concernant une large gamme de questions démographiques et sociales : population et croissance démographique, superficie et densité ; espérance de vie, maternité et mortalité ; éducation ; téléphones ; abonnés au téléphone mobile et usagers d'internet.

Population by sex, rate of population increase, surface area and density

Population selon le sexe, taux d'accroissement de la population, superficie et densité

Country or area+ / Pays ou zone+	Date	Latest census / Dernier recensement Both sexes / Les deux sexes	Men / Hommes	Women / Femmes	Mid-year estimates (thousands) Estimations au milieu de l'année (milliers) 2005	2007	Annual rate of increase Taux d'accroissement annuel % 2005-2007	Surface area Superficie (km²) 2007	Densité 2007&
Africa · Afrique									
Algeria[1] Algérie[1]	16 IV 2008	*34 760 000	...		32 906	34 096	1.8	2 381 741	14
Angola Angola	15 XII 1970	5 646 166	2 943 974	2 702 192	...	...	...	1 246 700	...
Benin Bénin	11 II 2002	6 769 914[1]	3 284 119[1]	3 485 795[1]	*7 395[2]	*8 054[2]	4.3	112 622	72
Botswana Botswana	17 VIII 2001	1 680 863	813 488	867 375	1 708	1 736	0.8	582 000	3
Burkina Faso[1] Burkina Faso[1]	9 XII 2006	14 017 262	6 768 739	7 248 523	12 802	14 252[2]	5.4	274 222	52
Burundi Burundi	16 VIII 1990	5 139 073	2 473 599	2 665 474	...	...	...	27 834	...
Cameroon Cameroun	10 IV 1987	10 493 655	...	...	...	...	...	475 442	...
Cape Verde Cap-Vert	16 VI 2000	436 863	211 479	225 384	475	491	1.7	4 033	122
Central African Rep. Rép. centrafricaine	8 XIII 2003	3 151 072	1 569 446	1 581 626	...	...	...	622 984	...
Chad Tchad	8 IV 1993	6 158 992	2 950 415	3 208 577	...	...	...	1 284 000	...
Comoros Comores	1 IX 2003	575 660[3]	...	...	...	...	...	2 235	...
Congo Congo	6 VI 1996	*2 600 000	...		...	*3 695	...	342 000	11
Côte d'Ivoire Côte d'Ivoire	21 XI 1998	15 366 672	7 844 621	7 522 050	19 097	20 228	2.9	322 463	63
Dem. Rep. of the Congo Rép. dém. du Congo	1 VII 1984	29 916 800	14 543 800	15 373 000	...	...	...	2 344 858	...
Djibouti Djibouti	11 XII 1960	81 200			...	...	...	23 200	...
Egypt Egypte	11 XI 2006	72 798 031[4]	37 219 056[4]	35 578 975[4]	70 653	73 644	2.1	1 002 000	73
Equatorial Guinea Guinée équatoriale	1 II 2002	1 014 999	501 387	513 612	...	...	...	28 051	...
Eritrea Erythrée	9 V 1984	2 748 304	1 374 452	1 373 852	...	...	...	117 600	...
Ethiopia Ethiopie	28 V 2007	73 918 505[5]	37 296 657[5]	36 621 848[5]	73 044	...	...	1 104 300	...
Gabon Gabon	1 XII 2003	*1 269 000	...	...	1 313[6]	...	...	267 668	...
Gambia Gambie	15 IV 2003	*1 364 507	*676 726	*687 781	1 436	...	...	11 295	...
Ghana Ghana	26 III 2000	18 912 079	9 357 382	9 554 697	21 343[2]	...	...	238 539	...
Guinea Guinée	1 XII 1996	7 156 406	3 497 979	3 658 427	...	...	...	245 857	...
Guinea-Bissau Guinée-Bissau	1 XII 1991	983 367	476 210	507 157	1 326[2]	1 389[2]	2.3	36 125	38
Kenya Kenya	24 VIII 1999	28 686 607	14 205 589	14 481 018	35 267	37 184	2.6	580 367	64
Lesotho Lesotho	9 IV 2006	*1 880 661[1]	*916 281[1]	*964 380[1]	...	...	...	30 355	...
Liberia Libéria	21 III 2008	*3 489 072	*1 764 555	*1 724 517	...	...	...	111 369	...

8

Population by sex, rate of population increase, surface area and density *(continued)*
Population selon le sexe, taux d'accroissement de la population, superficie et densité *(suite)*

Country or area[+] Pays ou zone[+]	Date	Latest census Dernier recensement Both sexes Les deux sexes	Men Hommes	Women Femmes	Mid-year estimates (thousands) Estimations au milieu de l'année (milliers) 2005	2007	Annual rate of increase Taux d'accroissement annuel % 2005-2007	Surface area Superficie (km²) 2007	Densité 2007[&]
Libyan Arab Jamah. Jamah. arabe libyenne	11 VIII 1995	4 404 986[7]	2 236 943[7]	2 168 043[7]	...	...	...	1 759 540	...
Madagascar Madagascar	1 VIII 1993	12 238 914	6 088 116	6 150 798	17 730	18 820	3.0	587 041	32
Malawi Malawi	8 VI 2008	*13 066 320	*6 365 771	*6 700 549	12 341[2]	13 188[2]	3.3	118 484	111
Mali Mali	1 IV 1998	9 926 219[8]	4 905 510[8]	5 020 709[8]	11 732[9]	12 378[9]	2.7	1 240 192	10
Mauritania Mauritanie	1 XI 2000	2 548 157	1 240 414	1 307 743	2 906	3 075	2.8	1 025 520	3
Mauritius[1] Maurice[1]	2 VII 2000	1 178 848	583 756	595 092	1 243	1 260	0.7	2 040	618
Mayotte[1] Mayotte[1]	31 VII 2007	186 387	91 405	94 982	...	...	...	...	...
Morocco Maroc	1 IX 2004	29 680 069	14 640 662	15 039 407	30 172	*30 841	1.1	446 550	69
Mozambique Mozambique	1 VIII 2007	*20 530 714	*9 787 135	*10 743 579	19 420[2]	20 367[2]	2.4	801 590	25
Namibia Namibie	27 VIII 2001	1 830 330	887 721[10]	942 572[10]	1 957[2]	2 028[2]	1.8	824 116	2
Niger Niger	20 V 2001	*10 790 352	*5 380 287	*5 410 065	12 628	13 475	3.2	1 267 000	11
Nigeria Nigéria	21 III 2006	*140 003 542	*71 709 859	*68 293 683	133 767[2]	...	...	923 768	...
Réunion[1] Réunion[1]	1 I 2006	781 962	379 176	402 786	777	*798	1.3	2 513	317
Rwanda Rwanda	16 VIII 2002	8 128 553[1]	3 879 448[1]	4 249 105[1]	...	...	...	26 338	...
Saint Helena ex. dep. Sainte-Hélène sans dép.	10 II 2008	*4 255	*2 166	*2 089	...	4	...	122	33
Ascension Ascension	8 III 1998	712[1]	458[1]	254[1]	...	...	...	88	...
Tristan da Cunha Tristan da Cunha	31 XII 1988	296	139	157	...	^0[11]	...	98	3
Sao Tome and Principe Sao Tomé-et-Principe	25 VIII 2001	136 554	67 422	69 132	149	155	1.9	964	161
Senegal Sénégal	8 XII 2002	9 552 442	4 665 730	4 886 712	10 848	...	...	196 722	...
Seychelles Seychelles	26 VIII 2002	81 755[1,12]	40 751[1,12]	41 004[1,12]	83	85	1.3	455	187
Sierra Leone Sierra Leone	4 XII 2004	4 976 871	2 420 218	2 556 653	...	...	...	71 740	...
Somalia Somalie	15 II 1987	7 114 431	3 741 664	3 372 767	...	...	...	637 657	...
South Africa Afrique du Sud	10 X 2001	44 819 778	21 434 041	23 385 737	47 335[13]	48 287[13]	1.0	1 221 037	40
Sudan Soudan	22 IV 2008	*39 154 490	*20 073 977	*19 080 513	35 397	...	...	2 505 813	...
Swaziland Swaziland	11 V 2007	*953 524	*460 498	*493 026	1 126	...	...	17 364	...
Togo Togo	22 XI 1981	2 719 567	1 325 641	1 393 926	5 337	5 465	1.2	56 785	96
Tunisia Tunisie	28 IV 2004	9 910 872	4 965 435	4 945 437	10 029	10 225	1.0	163 610	62
Uganda Ouganda	12 IX 2002	24 442 084	11 929 803	12 512 281	26 495	28 247	3.2	241 038	117
United Rep. of Tanzania Rép.-Unie de Tanzanie	24 VIII 2002	*34 443 603	*16 829 861	*17 613 742	37 379	39 446	2.7	945 087	42

8   Population by sex, rate of population increase, surface area and density *(continued)*
     Population selon le sexe, taux d'accroissement de la population, superficie et densité *(suite)*

Country or area+ Pays ou zone+	Latest census Dernier recensement				Mid-year estimates (thousands) Estimations au milieu de l'année (milliers)		Annual rate of increase Taux d'accroissement annuel %	Surface area Superficie (km²)	Densité
	Date	Both sexes Les deux sexes	Men Hommes	Women Femmes	2005	2007	2005-2007	2007	2007&
Western Sahara [14] Sahara occidental [14]	31 XII 1970	76 425	43 981	32 444	...	...	...	266 000	...
Zambia Zambie	25 X 2000	9 337 425	4 594 290	4 743 135	11 441[2]	*12 161[2]	3.0	752 612	16
Zimbabwe Zimbabwe	17 VIII 2002	11 631 657	5 634 180	5 997 477	...	...	...	390 757	...
America, North · Amérique du Nord									
Anguilla Anguilla	9 V 2001	11 430	5 628	5 802	14	15	4.4	91	164
Antigua and Barbuda Antigua-et-Barbuda	28 V 2001	77 426	37 002	40 424	83	...	...	442	...
Aruba [1] Aruba [1]	14 X 2000	90 508	43 435	47 073	101	104	1.6	180	578
Bahamas Bahamas	1 V 2000	303 611	147 715	155 896	325	334	1.3	13 943	24
Barbados Barbade	1 V 2000	250 010	119 926	130 084	273	274	0.2	430	638
Belize Belize	12 V 2000	240 204	121 278	118 926	292	311	3.3	22 966	14
Bermuda [1] Bermudes [1]	20 V 2000	62 059[15]	29 802[15]	32 257[15]	64	64	0.3	54	1 178
British Virgin Islands Iles Vierges britanniques	21 V 2001	20 647	10 627	10 020	...	...	...	151	...
Canada [1] Canada [1]	16 V 2006	31 612 095[16]	15 475 970[16]	16 136 930[16]	32 312[17]	*32 976[18]	1.0	9 984 670	3
Cayman Islands Iles Caïmanes	10 X 1999	40 786	...	...	48[1]	...	...	264	...
Costa Rica [1] Costa Rica [1]	26 VI 2000	3 810 179	1 902 614	1 907 565	4 266	4 443	2.0	51 100	87
Cuba [1] Cuba [1]	6 IX 2002	11 177 743	5 597 233	5 580 510	11 243	11 238	0.0	109 886	102
Dominica Dominique	12 V 2001	69 625[15]	35 073[15]	34 552[15]	71	...	...	751	...
Dominican Republic Rép. dominicaine	18 X 2002	8 562 541[1]	4 265 215[1]	4 297 326[1]	9 226[2]	9 493[2]	1.4	48 671	195
El Salvador El Salvador	12 V 2007	5 744 113[1]	2 719 371[1]	3 024 742[1]	6 875	7 105	1.6	21 041	338
Greenland [1] Groenland [1]	1 I 2008	56 462[19]	29 885[19]	26 577[19]	57[19]	57[19]	-0.3	2 166 086	^0
Grenada Grenade	25 V 2001	102 632	50 481	52 151	...	107	...	344	312
Guadeloupe [1] Guadeloupe [1]	1 I 2006	400 736	188 720	212 016	*446	*403[9]	-5.0	1 705	236
Guatemala Guatemala	24 XI 2002	11 237 196[1]	5 496 839[1]	5 740 357[1]	12 701[13]	13 345[13]	2.5	108 889	123
Haiti Haïti	11 I 2003	8 373 750[1]	4 039 272[1]	4 334 478[1]	...	...	...	27 750	...
Honduras Honduras	28 VII 2001	6 071 200	3 000 530	3 070 670	7 197	*7 537	2.3	112 492	67
Jamaica [1] Jamaïque [1]	10 IX 2001	2 607 632	1 283 548	1 324 084	2 650	2 676	0.5	10 991	243
Martinique [1] Martinique [1]	1 I 2006	397 732	185 604	212 128	398	*400[9]	0.3	1 128	355
Mexico [1] Mexique [1]	17 X 2005	103 263 388	50 249 955	53 013 433	103 947[2]	105 791[2]	0.9	1 964 375	54
Montserrat Montserrat	12 V 2001	4 491	2 418	2 073	5	5	0.4	102	47

8

Population by sex, rate of population increase, surface area and density *(continued)*
Population selon le sexe, taux d'accroissement de la population, superficie et densité *(suite)*

Country or area[+] Pays ou zone[+]	Date	Latest census Dernier recensement Both sexes Les deux sexes	Men Hommes	Women Femmes	Mid-year estimates (thousands) Estimations au milieu de l'année (milliers) 2005	2007	Annual rate of increase Taux d'accroissement annuel % 2005-2007	Surface area Superficie (km²) 2007	Densité 2007[&]
Netherlands Antilles [1] Antilles néerlandaises [1]	29 I 2001	175 653	82 521	93 132	184[9]	*194[9]	2.7	800	242
Nicaragua [1] Nicaragua [1]	4 VI 2005	5 144 553	2 535 461	2 609 092	5 450	5 596	1.3	130 373	43
Panama Panama	14 V 2000	2 839 177	1 432 566	1 406 611	3 228	3 340	1.7	75 517	44
Puerto Rico [1] Porto Rico [1]	1 IV 2000	3 808 610[20]	1 833 577[20]	1 975 033[20]	3 912[20]	3 942[20]	0.4	8 870	444
Saint Kitts and Nevis Saint-Kitts-et-Nevis	14 V 2001	45 841	22 784	23 057	*39	...	...	261	...
Saint Lucia Sainte-Lucie	22 V 2001	157 164	76 741	80 423	164	168	1.2	539	312
Saint Pierre and Miquelon Saint-Pierre-et-Miquelon	19 I 2006	6 125	...	...	...	...	...	242	...
Saint Vincent-Grenadines Saint Vincent-Grenadines	14 V 2001	109 022[15]	55 456[15]	53 566[15]	104	...	...	389	...
Trinidad and Tobago Trinité-et-Tobago	15 V 2000	1 262 366	633 051	629 315	1 294[21]	1 303[21]	0.3	5 130	254
Turks and Caicos Islands Iles Turques et Caïques	10 IX 2001	19 886	9 897	9 989	31[1]	35[1]	6.5	948[22]	37[1]
United States [1] Etats-Unis [1]	1 IV 2000	281 421 906[23]	138 053 563[23]	143 368 343[23]	295 896[23]	301 621[23]	1.0	9 629 091	31
United States Virgin Is. [1] Iles Vierges américaines [1]	1 IV 2000	108 612[20]	51 864[20]	56 748[20]	110[20]	110[20]	0.1	347	316
America, South · Amérique du Sud									
Argentina Argentine	18 XI 2001	36 260 130	17 659 072	18 601 058	38 592	39 356	1.0	2 780 400	14
Bolivia Bolivie	5 IX 2001	8 274 325	4 123 850	4 150 475	9 427	9 828	2.1	1 098 581	9
Brazil Brésil	1 VIII 2000	169 799 170[1,24]	83 576 015[1,24]	86 223 155[1,24]	183 383[24]	187 642[24]	1.1	8 514 877[25]	22
Chile Chili	24 IV 2002	15 116 435	7 447 695	7 668 740	16 267	16 598	1.0	756 102	22
Colombia Colombie	22 V 2005	41 468 384	20 336 117	21 132 267	42 889[26]	43 926[26]	1.2	1 141 748	38
Ecuador Equateur	25 XI 2001	12 156 608[27]	6 018 353[27]	6 138 255[27]	13 215[2,27]	13 605[2,27]	1.5	256 369	53
Falkland Is. (Malvinas) [28] Iles Falkland (Malvinas) [28]	8 X 2006	2 955	1 569	1 386	...	...	...	12 173	...
French Guiana [1] Guyane française [1]	1 I 2006	205 954	101 930	104 023	*200	214[9]	3.3	83 534	3
Guyana Guyana	15 IX 2002	751 223	376 034	375 189	758	763	0.3	214 969	4
Paraguay Paraguay	28 VIII 2002	5 163 198	2 603 242	2 559 956	5 899	6 120	1.8	406 752	15
Peru Pérou	21 X 2007	27 412 157	13 622 640	13 789 517	27 811[13]	28 482[13]	1.2	1 285 216	22
Suriname [1] Suriname [1]	2 VIII 2004	492 829[29]	247 846[30]	244 618[30]	499	510	1.1	163 820	3
Uruguay Uruguay	1 VI 2004	3 241 003[31]	1 565 533[31]	1 675 470[31]	3 306[13]	3 324[2]	0.3	176 215	19
Venezuela (Bolivarian Rep. of) Venezuela (Rép. bolivarienne du)	30 X 2001	23 054 210[32]	11 402 869[32]	11 651 341[32]	26 577[32]	27 483[32]	1.7	912 050	30

Population by sex, rate of population increase, surface area and density *(continued)*
Population selon le sexe, taux d'accroissement de la population, superficie et densité *(suite)*

| Country or area[+]
Pays ou zone[+] | Date | Latest census
Dernier recensement | | | Mid-year estimates
(thousands)
Estimations au milieu de
l'année (milliers) | | Annual rate of
increase
Taux
d'accroissement
annuel % | Surface
area
Superficie
(km²) | Densité |
		Both sexes Les deux sexes	Men Hommes	Women Femmes	2005	2007	2005-2007	2007	2007[&]
Asia · Asie									
Afghanistan Afghanistan	23 VI 1979	13 051 358[33]	6 712 377[33]	6 338 981[33]	...	...	...	652 090	...
Armenia Arménie	10 X 2001	3 002 594[34]	1 407 220[34]	1 595 374[34]	3 218[1]	3 227[1]	0.1	29 743	108
Azerbaijan Azerbaïdjan	27 I 1999	7 953 438[1]	3 883 155[1]	4 070 283[1]	8 392	8 581	1.1	86 600	99
Bahrain Bahreïn	7 IV 2001	650 604[1]	373 649[1]	276 955[1]	889	1 039	7.8	750	1 386
Bangladesh Bangladesh	22 I 2001	130 522 598[35]	67 731 320[35]	62 791 278[35]	138 600	142 600	1.4	143 998	990
Bhutan Bhoutan	30 V 2005	634 982	333 595	301 387	...	659[36]	...	38 394	17
Brunei Darussalam Brunéi Darussalam	21 VIII 2001	*332 844	*168 974	*163 870	370	390	2.6	5 765	68
Cambodia Cambodge	3 III 2008	*13 388 910	*6 495 512	*6 893 398	*13 661[37]	...	...	181 035	...
China Chine	1 XI 2000	1 242 612 226[1,38,39]	640 275 969[1,38,39]	602 336 257[1,38,39]	1 303 720[40]	1 324 655[41]	0.8	9 596 961	138
China, Hong Kong SAR[1] Chine, Hong Kong RAS[1]	14 VII 2006	6 864 346	3 272 956	3 591 390	6 813	6 926	0.8	1 104	6 273
China, Macao SAR[1] Chine, Macao RAS[1]	19 VIII 2006	502 113[42]	245 167[42]	256 946[42]	473	526	5.2	29	18 131
Cyprus[1] Chypre[1]	1 X 2001	689 565[43]	338 497[43]	351 068[43]	758[44]	784[44]	1.7	9 251	85
Georgia Géorgie	17 I 2002	4 371 535[1]	2 061 753[1]	2 309 782[1]	4 361	4 388	0.3	69 700	63
India Inde	1 III 2001	1 028 610 328[45]	532 156 772[45]	496 453 556[45]	1 101 318[46]	1 134 023[46]	1.5	3 287 263	345
Indonesia Indonésie	30 VI 2000	206 264 595[47]	103 417 180[47]	102 847 415[47]	219 852	225 642	1.3	1 860 360	121
Iran (Islamic Rep. of)[1] Iran (Rép. islamique d')[1]		70 495 782	36 866 362	34 629 420	69 390[48]	71 532[48]	1.5	1 628 750	44
Iraq Iraq	16 X 1997	19 184 543[49]	9 536 570[49]	9 647 973[49]	27 963	29 682	3.0	438 317	68
Israel[1] Israël[1]	4 XI 1995	5 548 523[50]	2 738 175[50]	2 810 348[50]	6 930[50]	7 180[50]	1.8	22 072	325
Japan Japon	1 X 2005	127 767 994[1]	62 348 977[1]	65 419 017[1]	127 773[51]	127 772[51]	0.0	377 930[52]	338
Jordan Jordanie	1 X 2004	5 103 639[53]	2 626 287[53]	2 477 352[53]	5 473[53,54]	5 723[53,54]	2.2	89 342	64
Kazakhstan Kazakhstan	26 II 1999	14 953 126[1]	7 201 785[1]	7 751 341[1]	15 147	15 484	1.1	2 724 900	6
Korea, Dem. P. R. Corée, R. p. dém. de	1 X 2008	*24 051 218	*11 722 403	*12 328 815	...	...	...	120 538	...
Korea, Republic of Corée, République de	1 XI 2005	47 278 951[55]	23 623 954[55]	23 654 997[55]	48 138	48 456	0.3	99 678	486
Kuwait Koweït	20 IV 2005	*2 213 403	*1 310 067	*903 336	2 245	2 411	3.6	17 818	135
Kyrgyzstan Kirghizistan	24 III 1999	4 850 734	2 392 579	2 458 155	5 144	5 235	0.9	199 951	26
Lao People's Dem. Rep. Rép. dém. pop. lao	1 III 2005	5 621 982[1]	2 800 551[1]	2 821 431[1]	5 679[56]	5 874[56]	1.7	236 800	25
Lebanon Liban	3 III 2007	3 759 134[57]	1 857 659[57]	1 901 475[57]	...	...	...	10 452	...
Malaysia Malaisie	5 VII 2000	23 274 690[1,58]	11 853 432[1,58]	11 421 258[1,58]	26 128[59]	27 174[59]	2.0	330 803	82

8 Population by sex, rate of population increase, surface area and density *(continued)*
Population selon le sexe, taux d'accroissement de la population, superficie et densité *(suite)*

Country or area[+] Pays ou zone[+]	Date	Latest census Dernier recensement Both sexes Les deux sexes	Men Hommes	Women Femmes	Mid-year estimates (thousands) Estimations au milieu de l'année (milliers) 2005	2007	Annual rate of increase Taux d'accroissement annuel % 2005-2007	Surface area Superficie (km²) 2007	Densité 2007[&]
Maldives Maldives	21 III 2006	298 968	151 459	147 509	294	305	1.9	300	1 016
Mongolia Mongolie	5 I 2000	2 373 493	1 177 981	1 195 512	2 548	2 615	1.3	1 564 100	2
Myanmar Myanmar	31 III 1983	35 307 913	17 518 255	17 789 658	...	...	...	676 578	...
Nepal[1] Népal[1]	22 VI 2001	23 151 423[60]	11 563 921[60]	11 587 502[60]	25 343	*26 427	2.1	147 181	180
Occupied Palestinian Terr. Terr. palestinien occupé	1 XII 2007	*3 761 646[61]	*1 908 432[61]	*1 853 214[61]	3 508	3 719	2.9	6 020	618
Oman Oman	7 XII 2003	2 340 815	1 313 239	1 027 576	2 514	2 743	4.4	309 500	9
Pakistan Pakistan	2 III 1998	130 579 571[62]	67 840 137[62]	62 739 434[62]	153 960[62]	159 570[62]	1.8	796 095	200
Philippines[1] Philippines[1]	1 VIII 2007	*88 574 614	...	...	84 241	*88 706	2.6	300 000	296
Qatar Qatar	16 III 2004	744 029	496 382	247 647	888	1 226	16.1	11 586	106
Saudi Arabia Arabie saoudite	15 IX 2004	22 678 262	12 557 240	10 121 022	23 119	*24 243	2.4	2 149 690	11
Singapore Singapour	30 VI 2000	4 017 700[63]	2 061 800[63]	1 955 900[63]	4 266	4 589	3.6	705	6 508
Sri Lanka Sri Lanka	17 VII 2001	16 929 689[64]	8 425 607[64]	8 504 082[64]	19 668	20 010	0.9	65 610	305
Syrian Arab Republic Rép. arabe syrienne	3 IX 1994	13 782 315[65]	7 048 906[65]	6 733 409[65]	18 138[65]	19 172[65]	2.8	185 180	104
Tajikistan Tadjikistan	20 I 2000	6 127 493	3 069 100	3 058 393	6 850	7 140	2.1	143 100	50
Thailand[1] Thaïlande[1]	1 IV 2000	60 617 200	29 850 100	30 767 100	64 839[2]	66 042[2]	0.9	513 120	129
Timor-Leste Timor-Leste	11 VII 2004	*924 642	*467 757	*456 885	...	...	...	14 874	...
Turkey Turquie	22 X 2000	67 803 927	34 346 735	33 457 192	72 065	73 875	1.2	783 562	94
Turkmenistan Turkménistan	10 I 1995	4 483 251	2 225 331	2 257 920	...	...	...	488 100	...
United Arab Emirates Emirats arabes unis	5 XII 2005	4 106 427	2 806 141	1 300 286	...	4 488	...	83 600	54
Uzbekistan Ouzbékistan	12 I 1989	19 810 077[1]	9 784 156[1]	10 025 921[1]	...	...	...	447 400	...
Viet Nam Viet Nam	1 IV 1999	76 323 173	37 469 117	38 854 056	83 106	85 172	1.2	331 212	257
Yemen Yémen	16 XII 2004	19 685 161	10 036 953	9 648 208	20 283[54]	21 539[54]	3.0	527 968	41
Europe · Europe									
Åland Islands[1,66] Îles d'Åland[1,66]	31 XII 2000	25 776[19]	12 700[19]	13 076[19]	27[19]	27[19]	0.7	1 552	17
Albania Albanie	1 IV 2001	3 069 300	1 530 500	1 538 800	3 142	3 161	0.3	28 748	110
Andorra Andorre	1 VII 2000	66 089[19]	34 344[19]	31 745[19]	79[19]	82[19]	2.4	468	176
Austria[1] Autriche[1]	15 V 2001	8 032 926	3 889 189	4 143 737	8 233	8 315	0.5	83 871	99
Belarus Bélarus	16 II 1999	10 045 237[1]	4 717 621[1]	5 327 616[1]	9 775	9 702	-0.4	207 600	47
Belgium[1] Belgique[1]	1 X 2001	10 296 350	5 035 446	5 260 904	10 473	10 623	0.7	30 528	348

Country or area[+] Pays ou zone[+]	Date	Latest census Dernier recensement Both sexes Les deux sexes	Men Hommes	Women Femmes	Mid-year estimates (thousands) Estimations au milieu de l'année (milliers) 2005	2007	Annual rate of increase Taux d'accroissement annuel % 2005-2007	Surface area Superficie (km²) 2007	Densité 2007[&]
Bosnia and Herzegovina Bosnie-Herzégovine	31 III 1991	4 377 033[1]	2 183 795[1]	2 193 238[1]	3 843	...	...	51 209	...
Bulgaria Bulgarie	1 III 2001	7 928 901	3 862 465	4 066 436	7 740	7 660	-0.5	110 879	69
Croatia[1] Croatie[1]	31 III 2001	4 437 460	2 135 900	2 301 560	4 442	4 436	-0.1	56 594	78
Czech Republic[1] République tchèque[1]	1 III 2001	10 230 060	4 982 071	5 247 989	10 234	10 334	0.5	78 867	131
Denmark[1,67] Danemark[1,67]	1 I 2001	5 349 212[19]	2 644 319[19]	2 704 893[19]	5 416[19]	5 457[19]	0.4	43 094	127
Estonia Estonie	31 III 2000	1 370 052[1]	631 851[1]	738 201[1]	1 346	1 342	-0.2	45 227	30
Faeroe Islands[1] Iles Féroé[1]	1 I 2008	48 433[19]	25 174[19]	23 259[19]	48	48	0.0	1 393	35
Finland[1] Finlande[1]	31 XII 2000	5 181 115[19]	2 529 341[19]	2 651 774[19]	5 246[19]	5 289[19]	0.4	338 419	16
France[1,68] France[1,68]	1 I 2006	61 399 541[69]	29 714 539[69]	31 685 002[69]	60 996[69]	*61 707[69]	0.6	551 500	112
Germany[1,70] Allemagne[1,70]	28 III 2004	82 491 000[71]	40 330 000[71]	42 161 000[71]	82 464	82 263	-0.1	357 114	230
Gibraltar Gibraltar	12 XI 2001	27 495[72]	13 644[72]	13 851[72]	29[72]	29[73]	0.7	6	4 876
Greece Grèce	18 III 2001	10 964 020[74]	5 427 682[74]	5 536 338[74]	11 104[75]	11 193[75]	0.4	131 957	85
Guernsey Guernesey	29 IV 2001	59 807[1]	29 138[1]	30 669[1]	...	62[76]	...	78	792
Holy See[77] Saint-Siège[77]	1 VII 2000	*798[19]	*529[19]	*269[19]	...	...	...	^0[78]	...
Hungary Hongrie	1 II 2001	10 198 315	4 850 650	5 347 665	10 087	10 056	-0.2	93 028	108
Iceland[1] Islande[1]	1 VII 2000	281 154[19]	140 718[19]	140 436[19]	296[19]	311[19]	2.6	103 000	3
Ireland Irlande	23 IV 2006	4 239 848	2 121 171	2 118 677	4 131[79]	4 339[79]	2.5	70 273	62
Isle of Man[1] Ile de Man[1]	23 IV 2006	80 058	39 523	40 535	79[80]	81[80]	1.3	572	141
Italy Italie	21 X 2001	57 110 144	27 617 335	29 492 809	58 607	59 375	0.7	301 336	197
Jersey Jersey	11 III 2001	87 186[1]	42 484[1]	44 702[1]	88	90	1.1	116	776
Latvia[1] Lettonie[1]	31 III 2000	2 377 383	1 094 964	1 282 419	2 301	2 276	-0.5	64 559	35
Liechtenstein Liechtenstein	5 XII 2000	33 307	16 420	16 887	35	35	0.8	160	221
Lithuania[1] Lituanie[1]	6 IV 2001	3 483 972	1 629 148	1 854 824	3 414	3 376	-0.6	65 300	52
Luxembourg[1] Luxembourg[1]	15 II 2001	439 539	216 541	222 998	465	480	1.6	2 586	186
Malta[1] Malte[1]	27 XI 2005	404 962	200 819	204 143	404	*409	0.7	316	1 295
Monaco Monaco	9 VI 2008	31 109[1]	15 076[1,81]	15 914[1,81]	...	...	...	2	...
Montenegro[1] Monténégro[1]	31 X 2003	620 145	305 225	314 920	623	626	0.2	13 812	45
Netherlands[1] Pays-Bas[1]	1 I 2002	16 105 285[82]	7 971 967[82]	8 133 318[82]	16 320	16 382	0.2	37 354	439
Norway[1,83] Norvège[1,83]	3 XI 2001	4 520 947[8,19]	2 240 281[8,19]	2 280 666[8,19]	4 623[8]	4 709[8]	0.9	323 802	15

Country or area[+] / Pays ou zone[+]	Latest census / Dernier recensement Date	Both sexes / Les deux sexes	Men / Hommes	Women / Femmes	Mid-year estimates (thousands) Estimations au milieu de l'année (milliers) 2005	2007	Annual rate of increase Taux d'accroissement annuel % 2005-2007	Surface area Superficie (km²) 2007	Densité 2007[&]
Poland Pologne	20 V 2002	38 230 080[84]	18 516 403[84]	19 713 677[84]	38 161[84]	38 116[84]	-0.1	312 685[85]	122
Portugal Portugal	12 III 2001	10 356 117	5 000 141	5 355 976	10 549[1]	10 608[1]	0.3	92 090	115
Republic of Moldova République de Moldova	5 X 2004	*3 388 071[86]	*1 632 519[86]	*1 755 549[86]	3 595[1,86]	3 577[1,86]	-0.3	33 846	106
Romania[1] Roumanie[1]	18 III 2002	21 680 974	10 568 741	11 112 233	21 624	21 538	-0.2	238 391	90
Russian Federation[1] Fédération de Russie[1]	9 X 2002	145 166 731[87]	67 605 133[87]	77 561 598[87]	143 114[87]	142 115[87]	-0.4	17 098 242	8
San Marino Saint-Marin	1 VII 2000	26 941[19]	13 185[19]	13 756[19]	31[19]	32[19]	1.5	61	522
Serbia[1] Serbie[1]	31 III 2002	7 498 001[88]	3 645 930[88]	3 852 071[88]	7 441[88]	7 382[88]	-0.4	88 361	84
Slovakia[1] Slovaquie[1]	25 V 2001	5 379 455	2 612 515	2 766 940	5 387	5 398	0.1	49 035	110
Slovenia[1] Slovénie[1]	31 III 2002	1 964 036	958 576	1 005 460	2 001	2 019	0.5	20 273	100
Spain Espagne	1 XI 2001	40 847 371	20 012 882	20 834 489	43 398[1]	44 874[1]	1.7	505 992	89
Svalbard and Jan Mayen Is. Svalbard et îles Jan Mayen	1 XI 1960	3 431[89]	2 545[89]	886[89]	2[90]	...		62 422	...
Sweden[1] Suède[1]	31 XII 2003	8 975 670[19]	4 446 656[19]	4 529 014[19]	9 030[19]	9 148[19]	0.7	441 370	21
Switzerland[1] Suisse[1]	5 XII 2000	7 204 055	3 519 698	3 684 357	7 437	7 551	0.8	41 277[91]	183
TFYR of Macedonia L'ex-R.Y. Macédoine	1 XI 2002	2 022 547[1]	1 015 377[1]	1 007 170[1]	2 037	2 044	0.2	25 713	79
Ukraine Ukraine	5 XII 2001	48 240 902	22 316 317	25 924 585	*47 075	46 646[9]	...	603 500	77
United Kingdom[92] Royaume-Uni[92]	29 IV 2001	58 789 187	28 579 867	30 209 320	60 238	60 975	0.6	242 900	251
Oceania · Océanie									
American Samoa[1] Samoa américaines[1]	1 IV 2000	57 291[20]	29 264[20]	28 027[20]	66[20]	68[20]	2.0	199	343
Australia Australie	8 VIII 2006	20 061 646	9 896 500	10 165 146	20 395[1,13]	21 072[1,13]	1.6	7 692 024	3
Cook Islands[93] Iles Cook[93]	1 XII 2006	*19 569	*9 932	*9 637	20	*21	2.2	236	89
Fiji Fidji	16 IX 2007	837 271	427 176	410 095	825	834	0.5	18 272	46
French Polynesia Polynésie française	20 VIII 2007	*259 596[1]	...	...	253	259	1.2	4 000	65
Guam[1] Guam[1]	1 IV 2000	154 805[20]	79 181[20]	75 624[20]	*169[20]	*173[20]	1.4	541	320
Kiribati Kiribati	7 XII 2005	92 533	45 612	46 921	...	...	...	726	...
Marshall Islands Iles Marshall	1 VI 1999	50 848	26 034	24 814		53	...	181	291
Micronesia (Fed. States of) Micronésie (Etats féd. de)	1 IV 2000	107 008[1]	54 191[1]	52 817[1]	...	...	...	702	...
Nauru Nauru	23 IX 2002	10 065	5 136	4 929	...	...	...	21	...
New Caledonia Nouvelle-Calédonie	31 VIII 2004	*230 789	*116 485	*114 304	234	242	1.7	18 575	13
New Zealand Nouvelle-Zélande	7 III 2006	4 143 282	2 021 277	2 122 005	4 134[1]	4 228[1]	1.1	270 467	16

Country or area[+] / Pays ou zone[+]	Latest census / Dernier recensement				Mid-year estimates (thousands) Estimations au milieu de l'année (milliers)		Annual rate of increase Taux d'accroissement annuel %	Surface area Superficie (km2)	Densité
	Date	Both sexes Les deux sexes	Men Hommes	Women Femmes	2005	2007	2005-2007	2007	2007[&]
Niue Nioué	9 IX 2006	1 625	802	823	2[1]	...	...	260	...
Norfolk Island Ile Norfolk	8 VIII 2006	2 523	1 218	1 305	...	...	...	36	...
Northern Mariana Islands Iles Mariannes du Nord	1 IV 2000	69 221	31 984	37 237	80	85	2.5	464	182
Palau Palaos	1 IV 2005	19 907[1]	10 699[1]	9 208[1]	...	21	...	459	46
Papua New Guinea Papouasie-Nvl-Guinée	9 VII 2000	5 190 786	2 691 744	2 499 042	...	...	...	462 840	
Pitcairn Pitcairn	31 XII 1991	66	...	...	...	0[54]	...	5	13
Samoa Samoa	5 XI 2006	*179 186	*92 961	*86 225	183	187	0.9	2 831	66
Solomon Islands Iles Salomon	21 XI 1999	409 042	211 381	197 661	471	495	2.5	28 896	17
Tokelau Tokélaou	19 X 2006	1 151	583	568	...	...	...	12	...
Tonga Tonga	30 XI 2006	101 991	51 772	50 219	102[2,94]	103[2,94]	0.4	747	138
Tuvalu Tuvalu	1 XI 2002	9 561	4 729	4 832	10	...	...	26	...
Vanuatu Vanuatu	16 XI 1999	186 678[1]	95 682[1]	90 996[1]	...	...	...	12 189	...
Wallis and Futuna Islands Iles Wallis et Futuna	21 VII 2008	*13 484	...	...	...	...	...	142	...

Source:
United Nations Statistics Division, New York, *Demographic Yearbook 2007* and the demographic statistics database.

Source:
Organisation des Nations Unies, Division de statistique, New York, *Annuaire démographique 2007* et la base de données pour les statistiques démographiques.

[+] Unless otherwise indicated, figures refer to de facto (present-in-area) population for the present territory.

[&] Population per square kilometer of surface area in 2007. Figures are merely the quotients of population divided by surface area and are not to be considered either as reflecting density in the urban sense or as indicating the supporting power of a territory's land and resources.

[+] Sauf indication contraire, les chiffres se rapportent à la population effectivement présente sur le territoire (population de fait), tel qu'il est actuellement défini.

[&] Nombre d'habitants au kilomètre carré en 2007. Il s'agit simplement du quotient du chiffre de la population divisé par celui de la superficie: il ne faut pas y voir d'indication de la densité au sens urbain du terme ni de l'effectif de population que les terres et les ressources du territoire sont capables de nourrir.

1	De jure population.	1	Population de droit.
2	Data for estimates refer to national projections.	2	Les données se réfèrent aux projections nationales.
3	Excluding Mayotte.	3	Non compris Mayotte.
4	Excluding border population.	4	À l'exception de la population frontalière.
5	Total includes the estimated population of eight rural kebeles (21,410) in Elidar wereda (Affar Region).	5	Le total comprend l'effectif estimé de la population de huit kebele ruraux (21,410 habitants) du woreda d'Elidar (région Afar).
6	Based on the results of the Gabonese Survey for the Evaluation and Tracking of Poverty.	6	Sur base des résultats de l'enquête gabonaise sur l'évaluation et le suivi de la pauvreté.
7	Data refer to Libyan nationals only.	7	Les données se rapportent aux nationaux libyens seulement.
8	Including residents temporarily outside the country.	8	Y compris les nationaux se trouvant temporairement hors du pays.
9	Data refer to 1 January.	9	Les données se réfèrent au 1er janvier.
10	The number of males and / or females excludes persons whose sex is not stated (18 urban, 19 rural).	10	Il n'est pas tenu compte dans le nombre d'hommes et de femmes des personnes dont le sexe n'est pas indiqué (18 en zone urbaine et 19 en zone rurale).
11	Data refer to 31 December. Based on the results of a population count.	11	Données rapportent au 31 décembre. D'après les résultats d'un comptage de la population.
12	Data have not been adjusted for underenumeration, at estimated at 2.4	12	Les données n'on pas été ajustées pour compenser les lacunes du

	percent.
13	Mid-year estimates have been adjusted for under-enumeration, at latest census.
14	Comprising the Northern Region (former Saguia el Hamra) and Southern Region (former Rio de Oro).
15	Excluding the institutional population.
16	Because of rounding, totals are not in all cases the sum of the parts.
17	Updated postcensal estimates.
18	Preliminary postcensal estimates.
19	Population statistics are compiled from registers.
20	Including armed forces stationed in the area.
21	Based on the results of the population census.
22	Including low water level for all islands (area to shoreline).
23	Excluding armed forces overseas and civilian citizens absent from country for an extended period of time.
24	Data include persons in remote areas, military personnel outside the country, merchant seamen at sea, civilian seasonal workers outside the country, and other civilians outside the country, and exclude nomads, foreign military, civilian aliens temporarily in the country, transients on ships and Indian jungle population.
25	Exact reference date unknown.
26	Data have been adjusted on the basis of the Population Census of 2005.
27	Excluding nomadic Indian tribes.
28	A dispute exists between the governments of Argentina and the United Kingdom of Great Britain and Northern Ireland concerning sovereignty over the Falkland Islands (Malvinas).
29	The previous census was conducted only 16 months earlier (on 31 Mar 2003) but it was repeated because all of its data were destroyed in a fire before they could be fully processed, analyzed, and reported.
30	The previous census was conducted only 16 months earlier (on 31 May 2003) but it was repeated because all of its data were destroyed in a fire before they could be fully processed, analyzed, and reported. Figures for male and female population do not add up to the figure for total population, because they exclude 365 persons of unknown sex.
31	Data refer to resident population in Uruguay according to Census Phase 1, carried out between the months of June and July 2004.
32	Excluding Indian jungle population.
33	Excluding nomad population.
34	The methodology used for calculating the number of the de facto and de jure population in the 2001 census data differs as follows from the methodology used in previous censuses: the duration that defines a person as being ' temporary present ' or ' temporary absent ' is now ' under one year '. The previously applied definition was for 6 months.
35	Census results have been adjusted for underenumeration, estimated at 4.96 per cent.
36	Data refer to projections based on the 2005 population census.
37	Excluding foreign diplomatic personnel and their dependants. Data for estimates based on 1998 census result.
38	For the civilian population of 31 provinces, municipalities and autonomous regions.
39	For statistical purposes, the data for China do not include those for the Hong Kong Special Administrative Region (Hong Kong SAR), Macao Special Administrative Region (Macao SAR) and Taiwan Province of China.
40	For statistical purposes, the data for China do not include those for the Hong Kong Special Administrative Region (Hong Kong SAR), Macao Special Administrative Region (Macao SAR) and Taiwan province of China. Data for 2005 are estimated from the National Sample Survey of 1 per cent population.

	dénombrement, estimées à 2,4 p. 100.
13	Les estimations au milieu de l'année tiennent compte d'une ajustement destiné à compenser les lacunes du dénombrement lors du dernier recensement.
14	Comprend la région septentrionale (ancien Saguia-el-Hamra) et la région méridionale (ancien Rio de Oro).
15	Non compris la population dans les institutions.
16	Les chiffres étant arrondis, les totaux ne correspondent pas toujours rigoureusement à la somme des chiffres partiels.
17	Estimations postcensitaires préliminaires.
18	Estimations postcensitaires préliminaires.
19	Les statistiques de la population sont compilées à partir des registres.
20	Y compris les militaires en garnison sur le territoire.
21	D'après les résultats du recensement de la population.
22	Incluent le niveau de basses eaux pour toutes les iles.
23	Non compris les militaires à l'étranger, et les civils hors du pays pendant une période prolongée.
24	Y compris les personnes dans des régions éloignées, le personnel militaire en dehors du pays, les marins marchands, les ouvriers saisonniers civils de couture en dehors du pays, et autres civils en dehors du pays, et non compris les nomades, les militaires étrangers, les étrangers civils temporairement dans le pays, les transiteurs sur des bateaux et les Indiens de la jungle.
25	La date de référence exacte n'est pas connue.
26	Données ajustées sur la base du recensement de la population de 2005.
27	Non compris les tribus d'Indiens nomades.
28	La souveraineté sur les îles Falkland (Malvinas) fait l'objet d'un différend entre le Gouvernement argentin et le Gouvernement du Royaume-Uni de Grande-Bretagne et d'Irlande du Nord.
29	Le recensement précédent a eu lieu seulement 16 mois auparavant (le 31 mars 2003), mais a dû être refait parce que toutes les données ont été détruites dans un incendie avant que l'on n'ait pu les traiter et les analyser.
30	Le recensement précédent a eu lieu seulement 16 mois auparavant (le 31 mars 2003), mais a du être refait parce que toutes les données ont été détruites dans un incendie avant que l'on n'ait pu les traiter et les analyser. Les chiffres relatifs à la population masculine et féminine ne correspondent pas au chiffre de la population totale, parce que l'on en a exclu 365 personnes de sexe inconnu.
31	Les données se rapportent à la population résidente en Uruguay d'après la phase 1 du recensement, qui a eu lieu entre juin et juillet 2004.
32	Non compris les Indiens de la jungle.
33	Non compris les nomades.
34	La méthode utilisée pour dénombrer la population présente et la population légale dans le contexte du recensement de 2001 diffère de celle qui a été appliquée lors des recensements antérieurs en ce que la durée considérée pour définir la ' présence temporaire ' ou ' l'absence temporaire ' était dorénavant fixée à ' moins d'un an ' alors qu'elle était de 6 mois auparavant.
35	Les données ont été ajustées pour compenser les lacunes du dénombrement, estimées à 4,96 p.100.
36	Les données se réfèrent aux projections basées sur le recensement de la population de 2005.
37	Non compris le personnel diplomatique étranger et les membres de leur famille les accompagnant. Les estimations se réfèrent aux des résultats 1998 de recensement.
38	Pour la population civile seulement de 31 provinces, municipalités et régions autonomes.
39	Pour la présentation des statistiques, les données pour la Chine ne comprennent pas la Région Administrative Spéciale de Hong Kong (Hong Kong RAS), la Région Administrative Spéciale de Macao (Macao RAS) et la province de Taiwan.
40	Pour la présentation des statistiques, les données pour la Chine ne comprennent pas la Région Administrative Spéciale de Hong Kong (Hong Kong RAS), la Région Administrative Spéciale de Macao (Macao RAS) et Taïwan province de Chine. Les données pour 2005 ont été estimées à partir de l'enquête nationale qui a porté sur un échantillon de 1% de la population.

8

Population by sex, rate of population increase, surface area and density *(continued)*
Population selon le sexe, taux d'accroissement de la population, superficie et densité *(suite)*

41	For statistical purposes, the data for China do not include those for the Hong Kong Special Administrative Region (Hong Kong SAR), Macao Special Administrative Region (Macao SAR) and Taiwan province of China. Data have been estimated on the basis of the annual National Sample Surveys on Population Changes.
42	Data derived from the By-Census 2006 held during 19 to 31 of August 2006.
43	Data include all population irrespective of citizenship, who at the time of the census resided in the country or intended to reside for a period of at least one year. It does not distinguish between those present or absent at the time of census.
44	Data refer to government-controlled areas.
45	Including data for the Indian-held part of Jammu and Kashmir, the final status of which has not yet been determined. Excluding Mao-Maram, Paomata and Purul sub-divisions of Senapati district of Manipur. The population of Manipur including the estimated population of the three sub-divisions of Senapati district is 2,291,124 (Males 1,161,173 and females 1,129,952).
46	Including data for the Indian-held part of Jammu and Kashmir, the final status of which has not yet been determined. Data refer to national projections.
47	Census data include an estimated population of 459 557 persons in urban and 1 857 659 persons in rural areas that were not directly enumerated, and a population of 566 403 persons in urban and 1 717 578 persons in rural areas that decline the participation. Also included are 421 399 non permanent residents (the homeless, the crew of ships carrying national flags, boat/floating house people, remote located tribesmen and refugees).
48	Data refer to the Iranian Year which begins on 21 March and ends on 20 March of the following year.
49	For the 1997 population census, data exclude population in three autonomous provinces in the north of the country.
50	Including data for East Jerusalem and Israeli residents in certain other territories under occupation by Israeli military forces since June 1967.
51	Excluding diplomatic personnel outside the country and foreign military and civilian personnel and their dependants stationed in the area.
52	Data refer to 1 October 2007.
53	Excluding data for Jordanian territory under occupation since June 1967 by Israeli military forces. Excluding foreigners, including registered Palestinian refugees.
54	Data refer to 31 December.
55	Excluding usual residents not in country at time of census.
56	Based on the results of the 2005 Population and Housing Census.
57	Based on the results of a household survey.
58	Excluding Malaysian citizens and permanent residents who were away or intended to be away from the country for more than six months Excluding Malaysian military, naval and diplomatic personnel and their families outside the country, and tourists, businessman who intended to be in Malaysia for less than six months.
59	Data refer to projections based on the 2000 population census.
60	Data including estimated population from household listing from Village Development Committees and Wards which could not be enumerated at the time of the census.
61	Data have been adjusted for underenumeration, estimated at 2.70 per cent.
62	Excluding data for the Pakistan-held part of Jammu and Kashmir, the final status of which has not yet been determined.
63	Census results, excluding transients afloat and non-locally domiciled

41	Pour la présentation des statistiques, les données pour la Chine ne comprennent pas la Région Administrative Spéciale de Hong Kong (Hong Kong RAS), la Région Administrative Spéciale de Macao (Macao RAS) et Taïwan province de Chine. Les données on été estimées sur la base de l'enquête annuelle "National Sample Survey on Population Changes".
42	Donnes dérivées du recensement partiel de 2006 organisé entre les 19 et 31 août 2006.
43	Les chiffres comprennent toute la population, quelle que soit la nationalité, qui à l'époque de recensement avait résidé dans le pays, ou avait l'intention de résider, pendant une période d'au moins un an. Il n'y a pas de distinction entre les personnes présentes ou absentes au moment du recensement.
44	Les données se rapportent aux zones contrôlées par le Gouvernement.
45	Y compris les données pour la partie du jammu et du Cachemire occupée par l'Inde dont le statut définitif n'a pas encore été déterminé. Non compris les subdivisions Mao-Maram Paomata et Purul du district de Senapati dans l'État du Manipur. Cet État compte 2 291 125 habitants (1 161 173 hommes et 1 129 952 femmes), y compris la population estimative des trois subdivisions du district de Senapati.
46	Y compris les données pour la partie du Jammu et du Cachemire occupée part l'Inde dont le statut définitif n'a pas encore été déterminé. Les données se réfèrent aux projections nationales.
47	Les données du recensement, y compris l'estimation de 459 557 personnes dans les zones urbaines et de 1 857 659 personnes dans les zones rurales qui n'ont pas été énumérées directement, aussi que 566 403 personnes qui n'ont pas répondu dans les zones urbaines et de 1 717 578 personnes dans les zones rurales. Y compris 421 399 résidants non permanents (les sans abri, l'équipage des bateaux portant le drapeau national, les habitants des embarcations ou des maisons flottantes, les habitants des tribus isolées et les réfugiés).
48	Les données concernent l'année iranienne, qui commence le 21 mars et se termine le 20 mars de l'année suivante.
49	Pour le recensement de 1997, la population des trois provinces autonomes dans le nord du pays est exclue.
50	Y compris les données pour Jérusalem-Est et les résidents israéliens dans certains autres territoires occupés depuis 1967 par les forces armées israéliennes.
51	Non compris le personnel diplomatique hors du pays ni les militaires et agents civils étrangers en poste sur le territoire et les membres de leur famille les accompagnant.
52	Les données se réfèrent au 1er octobre 2007.
53	Non compris les données pour le territoire jordanien occupé depuis juin 1967 par les forces armées israéliennes. Non compris les étrangers, mais y compris les réfugiés de Palestine enregistrés.
54	Les données se réfèrent au 31 décembre.
55	À l'exclusion des résidents habituels qui ne sont pas dans le pays au moment du recensement.
56	Données fondées sur les résultats du recensement de la population et de l'habitat de 2005.
57	D'après les résultats d'une enquête de ménages.
58	Non compris les citoyens Malaisiens et les résidents permanents qui étaient ou qui ont prévu d'être hors du pays pour six mois ou plus. Non compris le personnel militaire Malaisien, le personnel naval ou diplomatique et leurs familles hors du pays, et les touristes et les hommes d'affaires qui avaient l'intention de rester en Malaisie moins de six mois.
59	Les données se réfèrent aux projections basées sur le recensement de la population 2000.
60	Les données incluent la population estimée par les listes des ménages des comités de développement des villages et des circonscriptions qui n'ont pas pu être énumérée au moment du recensement.
61	Les données ont été ajustées pour compenser les lacunes du dénombrement, estimées à 2,70 p. 100.
62	Non compris les données pour le Jammu et Cachemire occupée par le Pakistan dont le statut définitif n'a pas encore été déterminé.
63	Les résultats du recensement, non compris les personnes de passage à bord de

military and civilian services personnel and their dependants and visitors.

64 The Population and Housing Census 2001 did not cover the whole area of the country due to the security problems; the Census was complete in 18 districts only; in three districts it was not possible to conduct it; and in four districts it was partially conducted.

65 Including Palestinian refugees.

66 Also included in Finland

67 Excluding Faeroe Islands and Greenland shown separately, if available.

68 Excluding Overseas Departments, namely French Guiana, Guadeloupe, Martinique and Réunion, shown separately. De jure population but excluding diplomatic personnel outside country and including members of alien armed forces not living in military camps and foreign diplomatic personnel not living in embassies or consulates.

69 Excluding diplomatic personnel outside the country and including members of alien armed forces not living in military camps and foreign diplomatic personnel not living in embassies or consulates.

70 Sample survey, de jure.

71 Data of the microcensus - a 1% household sample survey - refer to a single reference week in spring (usually last week in April).

72 Excluding families of military personnel, visitors and transients.

73 Excluding families of military personnel, visitors and transients. Data refer to 31 December.

74 Census data including armed forces stationed outside the country, but excluding alien armed forces stationed in the area.

75 Mid-year population excludes armed forces stationed outside the country, but includes alien armed forces stationed in the area.

76 Data refer to 1 March.

77 Data refer to the Vatican City State.

78 Surface area is 0.44 Km2.

79 Estimates refer to 15th of April.

80 Data refer to 30 April.

81 Figures for male and female population do not add up to the figure for total population, because they exclude 119 persons of unknown sex.

82 Census results, based on compilation of continuous accounting and sample surveys.

83 Excluding Svalbard and Jan Mayen Island shown separately.

84 Excluding civilian aliens within country, but including civilian nationals temporarily outside country.

85 Surface area includes inland waters as well as part of internal waters.

86 Data do not include information for Transnistria and the municipality of Bender.

87 Data refer to resident population only.

88 Excluding Kosovo and Metohia.

89 Inhabited only during the winter season. Census data are for total population while estimates refer to Norwegian population only. Included also in the de jure population of Norway.

90 Data refer to 1 January. Data refer to Svalbard only.

91 Excluding state forests and communanzas (7.15 km2).

92 Excluding Channel Islands (Guernsey and Jersey) and Isle of Man, shown separately.

93 Excluding Niue, shown separately, which is part of Cook Islands, but because of remoteness is administered separately.

94 Data for estimates based on the results of the 1996 population census not necessarily mid-year estimated.

navires ni les militaires et agents civils non-résidents et les membres de leur famille les accompagnants et visiteurs.

64 Le recensement de la population et de l'habitat en 2001 n' pas couvert la totalité du pays pour des problèmes de sécurité ; le recensement à été complété seulement en 18 districts ; dans 3 districts ça n'a pas été possible de conduire le recensement et dans 4 districts il a été partiallement conduit.

65 Y compris les réfugiés de Palestine.

66 Comprise aussi dans Finlande.

67 Non compris les Illes Féroe et le Gröenland, qui font l'objet de rubriques distinctes, si disponible.

68 Non compris les départements d'outre-mer, c'est-à-dire la Guyane française, la Guadeloupe, la Martinique et la Réunion, qui font l'objet de rubriques distinctes. Population de droit, non compris le personnel diplomatique hors du pays et y compris les militaires étrangers ne vivant pas dans des camps militaires et le personnel diplomatique étranger ne vivant pas dans les ambassades ou les consulats.

69 Non compris le personnel diplomatique hors du pays et y compris les militaires étrangers ne vivant pas dans des camps militaires et le personnel diplomatique étranger ne vivant pas dans les ambassades ou les consulats.

70 Enquête par sondage, Population de droit.

71 Les données du microrecensement (enquête sur les ménages, réalisée sur un échantillon de 1 %) concernent une seule semaine de référence au printemps (habituellement la dernière semaine d'avril).

72 Non compris les familles des militaires, ni les visiteurs et transients.

73 Non compris les familles des militaires, ni les visiteurs et transients. Données se rapportent au 31 décembre.

74 Les données de recensement y compris les militaires hors du pays, mais non compris les militaires étrangers en garnison sur le territoire.

75 Les estimations au milieu de l'année non compris les militaires en garnison hors du pays, mais y compris les militaires étrangers en garnison sur le territoire.

76 Données se rapportent au 1 mars.

77 Les données se réfèrent à la Cité du Vatican.

78 Superficie: 0,44 Km2

79 Les estimations se rapportent au 15 avril.

80 Données se rapportent au 30 avril.

81 Les chiffres relatifs à la population masculine et féminine ne correspondent pas au chiffre de la population totale, parce que l'on en a exclu 119 personnes de sexe inconnu.

82 Les résultats du recensement, d'après les résultats des dénombrements et enquêtes par sondage continue.

83 Non compris Svalbard et Jan Mayen qui font l'objet de rubriques distinctes.

84 Non compris les civils étrangers dans le pays, mais y compris les civils nationaux temporairement hors du pays.

85 Superficie comprends les eaux intérieures et une partie des eaux situées en deçà de la ligne de base de la mer.

86 Les données ne tiennent pas compte de l'information sur la Transnistria et la municipalité de Bender.

87 Pour la population résidante seulement.

88 Non compris Kosovo et Metohia.

89 N'est habitée pendant la saison d'hiver. Les données de recensement se rapportent à la population totale, mais les estimations ne concernent que la population norvégienne, comprise également dans la population de droit de la Norvège.

90 Données se rapportent au 1 janvier. Données ne concernant que le Svalbard.

91 Non comprises les forêts domaniales et communanzas (7,15 km2).

92 Non compris les îles Anglo-Normandes (Guernsey and Jersey) et l'île de Man, qui font l'objet de rubriques distinctes.

93 Non compris Nioué, qui fait l'objet d'une rubrique distincte et qui fait partie des îles Cook, mais qui, en raison de son éloignement, est administrée séparément.

94 Les estimations d'après les résultats du recensement de la population de 1996, pas nécessairement des estimations en milieu d'année.

Selected indicators of life expectancy, childbearing and mortality

Choix d'indicateurs de l'espérance de vie, de la maternité et de la mortalité

| Country or area &
Pays ou zone & | Year
Année | Life expectancy at birth (years)
Espérance de vie à la naissance (en années) | | Total fertility rate
Taux de fécondité | Mortality rates – Taux de mortalité | | | | Maternal –
Maternelle
p. 100 000 |
| | | Males
Hommes | Females
Femmes | | Infant – Infantile
p. 1 000 | | Under 5 years –
Moins de 5 ans
p. 1 000 | | |
					Males Hommes	Females Femmes	Males Hommes	Females Femmes	2005
Afghanistan	2000-2005	42.2	42.1	7.4	171.2	164.8	249.3	254.9	...
Afghanistan	2005-2010	43.9	43.8	6.6	159.9	154.0	232.8	238.3	1 800
Albania	2000-2005	72.6	79.0	2.0	19.3	17.2	21.8	18.5	...
Albanie	2005-2010	73.4	79.7	1.9	16.6	15.6	18.4	16.8	92
Algeria	2000-2005	69.7	72.2	2.5	38.4	36.3	41.5	39.7	...
Algérie	2005-2010	70.9	73.7	2.4	32.7	29.3	35.1	31.3	180
Angola	2000-2005	42.6	46.3	6.6	144.7	120.8	246.1	216.1	...
Angola	2005-2010	44.9	48.8	5.8	129.1	105.5	220.4	189.2	1 400
Argentina	2000-2005	70.6	78.1	2.4	17.0	13.0	19.6	15.1	...
Argentine	2005-2010	71.6	79.1	2.3	15.0	11.8	17.3	13.7	77
Armenia	2000-2005	68.9	75.6	1.7	31.4	26.6	34.9	29.3	...
Arménie	2005-2010	70.2	76.7	1.7	26.8	23.3	29.4	25.4	76
Aruba	2000-2005	71.2	76.6	1.8	21.7	13.0	25.1	14.8	...
Aruba	2005-2010	72.1	77.4	1.7	18.9	12.0	21.6	13.7	...
Australia	2000-2005[1]	78.0	83.0	1.8	5.9	4.8	6.5	5.3	...
Australie	2005-2010	79.1[1]	83.8[1]	1.8[1]	4.8[1]	4.3[1]	5.9[1]	5.2[1]	4
Austria	2000-2005	75.8	81.6	1.4	5.1	3.9	5.9	4.7	...
Autriche	2005-2010	77.2	82.6	1.4	4.7	3.8	5.6	4.7	4
Azerbaijan	2000-2005	65.6	71.2	2.0	52.3	46.8	63.9	57.6	...
Azerbaïdjan	2005-2010	67.7	72.5	2.2	44.2	42.6	53.7	52.1	82
Bahamas	2000-2005	68.4	74.5	2.1	13.8	10.9	21.4	15.7	...
Bahamas	2005-2010	70.6	76.2	2.0	9.2	8.7	14.5	12.3	16
Bahrain	2000-2005	73.5	76.5	2.5	11.2	11.2	14.5	14.5	...
Bahreïn	2005-2010	74.3	77.5	2.3	9.9	9.9	12.6	12.6	32
Bangladesh	2000-2005	62.1	63.9	2.8	59.4	54.9	77.3	75.9	...
Bangladesh	2005-2010	65.0	67.0	2.4	46.4	42.8	57.6	56.5	570
Barbados	2000-2005	72.6	78.9	1.5	13.8	10.2	15.8	11.5	...
Barbade	2005-2010	74.2	79.8	1.5	11.1	9.2	12.4	10.5	16
Belarus	2000-2005	62.5	74.6	1.2	11.2	8.0	13.7	9.8	...
Bélarus	2005-2010	63.2	75.3	1.3	10.9	7.5	14.2	9.4	18
Belgium	2000-2005	75.1	81.2	1.6	5.0	3.7	6.2	4.6	...
Belgique	2005-2010	76.7	82.6	1.8	4.6	3.6	5.8	4.7	8
Belize	2000-2005	72.9	76.6	3.4	20.9	17.6	26.9	22.8	...
Belize	2005-2010	74.4	78.2	2.9	18.2	15.3	22.8	18.7	52
Benin	2000-2005	58.0	60.2	5.8	96.5	90.3	138.8	134.4	...
Bénin	2005-2010	60.1	62.3	5.5	87.7	81.9	122.5	118.4	840
Bhutan	2000-2005	61.8	65.2	3.4	57.2	48.1	82.9	73.5	...
Bhoutan	2005-2010	64.1	67.7	2.7	48.8	40.0	68.8	58.8	440
Bolivia	2000-2005	61.8	66.0	4.0	60.0	51.0	76.8	67.4	...
Bolivie	2005-2010	63.4	67.7	3.5	50.0	41.0	65.1	55.9	290
Bosnia and Herzegovina	2000-2005	71.6	77.2	1.3	15.8	12.2	19.5	14.3	...
Bosnie-Herzégovine	2005-2010	72.4	77.7	1.2	15.1	10.3	17.2	11.8	3
Botswana	2000-2005	47.5	48.7	3.2	66.1	55.6	100.4	87.8	...
Botswana	2005-2010	54.6	54.8	2.9	41.3	31.0	60.0	47.3	380
Brazil	2000-2005	67.2	74.9	2.3	30.9	23.4	38.8	29.4	...
Brésil	2005-2010	68.7	76.0	1.9	26.9	19.9	33.1	24.9	110
Brunei Darussalam	2000-2005	74.2	78.9	2.3	7.2	4.9	8.4	6.4	...
Brunéi Darussalam	2005-2010	75.0	79.7	2.1	6.2	4.8	7.3	6.2	13
Bulgaria	2000-2005	68.7	75.6	1.3	14.5	11.7	17.3	14.2	...
Bulgarie	2005-2010	69.7	76.8	1.4	13.3	10.2	16.6	13.1	11
Burkina Faso	2000-2005	50.1	52.3	6.1	90.4	83.1	174.9	168.6	...
Burkina Faso	2005-2010	51.6	54.2	6.0	83.4	76.7	160.0	154.0	700

Country or area & Pays ou zone &	Year Année	Life expectancy at birth (years) Espérance de vie à la naissance (en années)		Total fertility rate Taux de fécondité	Mortality rates – Taux de mortalité				Maternal – Maternelle p. 100 000
					Infant – Infantile p. 1 000		Under 5 years – Moins de 5 ans p. 1 000		
		Males Hommes	Females Femmes		Males Hommes	Females Femmes	Males Hommes	Females Femmes	2005
Burundi	2000-2005	46.7	49.2	5.4	114.6	96.7	191.4	169.5	...
Burundi	2005-2010	48.8	51.7	4.7	107.0	89.3	176.9	154.7	1 100
Cambodia	2000-2005	55.8	60.0	3.4	76.2	68.4	107.5	101.1	...
Cambodge	2005-2010	59.0	62.6	3.0	66.5	57.9	92.3	84.7	540
Cameroon	2000-2005	50.1	51.5	4.9	95.2	83.4	155.6	142.5	...
Cameroun	2005-2010	50.4	51.5	4.7	93.1	80.5	150.7	136.4	1 000
Canada	2000-2005	77.3	82.3	1.5	5.4	4.7	6.5	5.9	...
Canada	2005-2010	78.3	82.9	1.6	5.1	4.6	6.1	5.6	7
Cape Verde	2000-2005	66.8	72.1	3.4	38.2	24.0	46.5	29.0	...
Cap-Vert	2005-2010	68.3	73.6	2.8	32.1	19.2	38.4	22.8	210
Central African Rep.	2000-2005	44.1	47.8	5.3	124.7	101.2	207.7	175.4	...
Rép. centrafricaine	2005-2010	45.4	48.4	4.9	116.9	93.7	195.7	163.3	980
Chad	2000-2005	47.3	50.1	6.5	139.8	124.0	223.4	204.8	...
Tchad	2005-2010	47.4	50.0	6.2	137.7	121.9	219.9	200.9	1 500
Channel Islands [2]	2000-2005	76.0	80.8	1.4	5.6	5.3	6.7	6.2	...
Iles Anglo-Normandes [2]	2005-2010	76.7	81.5	1.4	5.3	5.0	6.4	5.9	...
Chile	2000-2005	74.8	80.9	2.0	9.0	7.0	10.9	8.5	...
Chili	2005-2010	75.5	81.6	1.9	8.1	6.3	9.8	7.7	16
China [3]	2000-2005	70.5	73.7	1.8	20.4	31.9	26.7	38.1	...
Chine [3]	2005-2010	71.3	74.8	1.8	18.4	28.2	24.6	34.9	45
China, Hong Kong SAR	2000-2005	78.6	84.5	1.0	3.9	3.7	5.1	4.5	...
Chine, Hong Kong RAS	2005-2010	79.4	85.1	1.0	3.7	3.6	4.9	4.4	...
China, Macao SAR	2000-2005	77.0	81.5	0.8	5.2	5.0	6.3	5.9	...
Chine, Macao RAS	2005-2010	78.5	82.8	1.0	4.7	4.6	5.7	5.4	...
Colombia	2000-2005	68.0	75.4	2.6	23.4	17.4	32.0	24.5	...
Colombie	2005-2010	69.2	76.7	2.5	21.9	16.1	29.6	22.3	130
Comoros	2000-2005	60.9	65.1	4.2	64.8	50.2	85.6	68.3	...
Comores	2005-2010	63.0	67.4	4.0	55.2	41.3	71.0	54.0	400
Congo	2000-2005	52.1	54.5	4.8	82.1	71.0	130.3	117.5	...
Congo	2005-2010	52.6	54.5	4.4	84.9	73.5	134.8	121.8	740
Costa Rica	2000-2005	75.9	80.6	2.3	11.8	9.1	13.6	10.7	...
Costa Rica	2005-2010	76.5	81.3	2.0	11.2	8.5	12.8	9.9	30
Côte d'Ivoire	2000-2005	53.8	57.0	5.1	97.4	87.0	139.6	127.1	...
Côte d'Ivoire	2005-2010	56.0	58.6	4.7	92.0	81.5	129.4	116.7	810
Croatia	2000-2005	71.4	78.4	1.4	7.2	6.6	8.5	7.6	...
Croatie	2005-2010	72.8	79.5	1.4	6.3	6.0	7.9	7.1	7
Cuba	2000-2005	75.3	79.1	1.6	6.7	5.5	8.5	6.9	...
Cuba	2005-2010	76.7	80.8	1.5	5.6	4.6	9.5	5.8	45
Cyprus	2000-2005	76.7	81.4	1.6	6.3	5.3	7.5	6.3	...
Chypre	2005-2010	77.3	82.0	1.5	5.9	5.0	7.1	6.0	10
Czech Republic	2000-2005	72.1	78.7	1.2	4.3	3.5	5.3	4.4	...
République tchèque	2005-2010	73.4	79.5	1.4	4.0	3.5	5.0	4.5	4
Dem. Rep. of the Congo	2000-2005	46.0	49.3	6.7	120.7	103.0	208.3	186.9	...
Rép. dém. du Congo	2005-2010	45.9	49.0	6.1	126.1	107.2	208.6	186.6	1 100
Denmark	2000-2005	75.0	79.6	1.8	4.8	4.4	6.2	5.6	...
Danemark	2005-2010	76.0	80.6	1.8	4.4	4.3	5.9	5.6	3
Djibouti	2000-2005	52.4	55.3	4.5	102.7	86.0	148.6	130.6	...
Djibouti	2005-2010	53.9	56.7	4.0	92.7	77.1	133.6	116.4	650
Dominican Republic	2000-2005	69.2	74.2	2.8	39.8	30.1	44.5	34.3	...
Rép. dominicaine	2005-2010	69.8	75.3	2.7	33.7	25.3	37.4	28.6	150
Ecuador	2000-2005	71.3	77.2	2.8	28.8	20.8	34.4	25.1	...
Equateur	2005-2010	72.1	78.1	2.6	24.0	18.0	29.2	22.0	210
Egypt	2000-2005	67.3	70.7	3.2	41.3	37.7	48.1	45.0	...
Egypte	2005-2010	68.3	71.8	2.9	36.5	33.0	42.2	38.9	130

| | | Life expectancy at birth (years) Espérance de vie à la naissance (en années) | | Total fertility rate | Mortality rates – Taux de mortalité | | | | Maternal – Maternelle p. 100 000 |
| | | | | | Infant – Infantile p. 1 000 | | Under 5 years – Moins de 5 ans p. 1 000 | | |
Country or area & Pays ou zone &	Year Année	Males Hommes	Females Femmes	Taux de fécondité	Males Hommes	Females Femmes	Males Hommes	Females Femmes	2005
El Salvador	2000-2005	65.5	75.1	2.6	28.6	24.1	33.6	26.9	...
El Salvador	2005-2010	66.5	76.0	2.4	23.2	19.8	28.9	22.8	170
Equatorial Guinea	2000-2005	47.4	50.2	5.6	113.3	97.7	188.7	170.9	...
Guinée équatoriale	2005-2010	48.9	51.3	5.4	106.9	92.0	176.8	159.7	680
Eritrea	2000-2005	54.7	59.5	5.2	65.1	58.3	92.2	82.6	...
Erythrée	2005-2010	57.0	61.6	4.7	56.8	51.7	78.4	71.2	450
Estonia	2000-2005	65.6	76.9	1.4	8.7	6.3	11.6	8.6	...
Estonie	2005-2010	67.6	78.5	1.6	8.5	6.9	11.2	7.9	25
Ethiopia	2000-2005	51.0	54.0	5.9	94.6	81.3	156.3	140.8	...
Ethiopie	2005-2010	53.6	56.5	5.4	85.2	72.8	138.4	123.6	720
Fiji	2000-2005	65.7	70.1	3.0	22.9	20.2	28.0	26.1	...
Fidji	2005-2010	66.6	71.1	2.8	20.5	18.6	24.6	23.9	210
Finland	2000-2005[4]	74.8	81.6	1.8	3.8	2.8	4.3	3.2	...
Finlande	2005-2010	76.2[4]	83.0[4]	1.8[4]	3.5[4]	2.9[4]	4.5[4]	3.6[4]	7
France	2000-2005	75.8	83.1	1.9	4.7	3.7	5.7	4.5	...
France	2005-2010	77.6	84.7	1.9	4.3	3.5	5.3	4.3	8
French Guiana	2000-2005	71.9	79.1	3.7	19.3	10.0	22.2	11.3	...
Guyane française	2005-2010	72.6	79.9	3.3	17.3	9.2	19.7	10.4	...
French Polynesia	2000-2005	70.6	76.0	2.4	9.3	8.2	11.5	11.3	...
Polynésie française	2005-2010	72.0	76.9	2.2	8.1	7.7	10.4	10.4	...
Gabon	2000-2005	57.3	61.1	3.8	62.5	53.8	94.8	84.7	...
Gabon	2005-2010	59.0	61.7	3.4	54.9	47.2	84.6	75.4	520
Gambia	2000-2005	53.0	56.2	5.5	89.9	80.4	136.4	121.5	...
Gambie	2005-2010	54.2	57.4	5.1	80.9	72.1	122.9	109.4	690
Georgia	2000-2005	68.0	75.0	1.6	37.0	31.7	39.1	33.3	...
Géorgie	2005-2010	68.0	75.0	1.6	37.0	31.7	39.1	33.3	66
Germany	2000-2005	75.8	81.4	1.4	4.5	4.1	5.5	5.2	...
Allemagne	2005-2010	77.1	82.4	1.3	4.2	4.0	5.3	5.0	4
Ghana	2000-2005	56.1	58.1	4.5	72.8	67.9	114.1	112.4	...
Ghana	2005-2010	55.6	57.4	4.3	76.4	70.3	118.7	115.1	560
Greece	2000-2005	75.9	80.4	1.3	4.4	3.6	5.0	4.4	...
Grèce	2005-2010	77.1	81.3	1.4	4.4	3.3	4.6	3.9	3
Grenada	2000-2005	72.8	75.7	2.4	16.6	14.2	18.9	16.4	...
Grenade	2005-2010	73.7	76.8	2.3	14.0	12.7	15.8	14.5	...
Guadeloupe	2000-2005	75.1	81.5	2.1	8.1	6.4	10.5	8.6	...
Guadeloupe	2005-2010	76.0	82.2	2.1	7.5	6.0	9.7	7.9	...
Guam	2000-2005	72.4	77.0	2.7	11.1	8.9	13.0	10.3	...
Guam	2005-2010	73.3	77.9	2.5	9.8	8.3	11.3	9.6	...
Guatemala	2000-2005	65.5	72.5	4.6	44.0	33.0	54.4	42.3	...
Guatemala	2005-2010	66.7	73.8	4.2	35.0	25.0	44.8	33.6	290
Guinea	2000-2005	52.9	56.7	5.8	117.2	102.4	181.8	162.4	...
Guinée	2005-2010	55.6	59.6	5.5	105.0	91.3	156.8	137.8	910
Guinea-Bissau	2000-2005	44.9	48.0	5.8	129.7	111.7	220.8	200.2	...
Guinée-Bissau	2005-2010	46.1	49.2	5.7	123.0	104.9	206.6	185.7	1 100
Guyana	2000-2005	61.1	67.3	2.4	57.3	41.4	78.3	56.7	...
Guyana	2005-2010	64.1	69.9	2.3	49.1	35.3	65.5	47.0	470
Haiti	2000-2005	57.1	62.1	4.0	76.1	62.6	102.0	86.1	...
Haïti	2005-2010	59.5	63.0	3.6	65.6	59.1	89.7	79.9	670
Honduras	2000-2005	68.5	73.4	3.7	35.9	27.1	48.8	38.7	...
Honduras	2005-2010	69.8	74.5	3.3	32.1	23.9	44.1	34.7	280
Hungary	2000-2005	68.3	76.6	1.3	7.3	7.0	8.9	8.3	...
Hongrie	2005-2010	69.2	77.4	1.4	6.9	6.7	8.8	8.1	6
Iceland	2000-2005	79.3	82.7	2.0	3.4	2.8	4.3	3.8	...
Islande	2005-2010	80.2	83.3	2.1	3.1	2.8	4.0	3.9	4

9 Selected indicators of life expectancy, childbearing and mortality *(continued)*
Choix d'indicateurs de l'espérance de vie, de la maternité et de la mortalité *(suite)*

| | | Life expectancy at birth (years) Espérance de vie à la naissance (en années) | | Total fertility rate | Mortality rates – Taux de mortalité | | | | Maternal – Maternelle p. 100 000 |
| | | | | | Infant – Infantile p. 1 000 | | Under 5 years – Moins de 5 ans p. 1 000 | | |
Country or area [&] Pays ou zone [&]	Year Année	Males Hommes	Females Femmes	Taux de fécondité	Males Hommes	Females Femmes	Males Hommes	Females Femmes	2005
India	2000-2005	60.9	63.3	3.1	61.2	62.4	85.9	94.9	...
Inde	2005-2010	62.1	65.0	2.8	54.0	55.2	77.3	86.0	450
Indonesia	2000-2005	66.7	70.5	2.4	38.5	29.7	46.9	36.7	...
Indonésie	2005-2010	68.7	72.7	2.2	30.7	22.3	36.6	26.7	420
Iran (Islamic Rep. of)	2000-2005	68.7	71.2	2.1	34.6	35.5	39.9	42.3	...
Iran (Rép. islamique d')	2005-2010	70.0	72.7	1.8	28.6	29.6	32.6	34.6	140
Iraq	2000-2005	67.5	72.6	4.6	39.2	33.6	47.8	42.4	...
Iraq	2005-2010	63.5	71.7	4.1	35.6	30.6	43.0	38.0	300
Ireland	2000-2005	75.3	80.3	2.0	5.4	5.4	6.7	6.7	...
Irlande	2005-2010	77.5	82.3	2.0	4.5	4.5	5.8	5.8	1
Israel	2000-2005	77.6	81.7	2.9	5.3	4.8	6.3	5.9	...
Israël	2005-2010	78.6	82.8	2.8	5.0	4.5	6.0	5.4	4
Italy	2000-2005	77.2	83.1	1.3	4.5	3.9	5.4	4.6	...
Italie	2005-2010	78.1	84.1	1.4	4.2	3.5	5.0	4.1	3
Jamaica	2000-2005	67.6	74.4	2.5	26.1	25.7	31.2	31.1	...
Jamaïque	2005-2010	68.5	75.2	2.4	23.4	23.3	28.1	28.1	170
Japan	2000-2005	78.3	85.7	1.3	3.2	2.8	4.5	4.0	...
Japon	2005-2010	79.0	86.2	1.3	3.3	3.0	4.6	3.9	6
Jordan	2000-2005	69.7	73.1	3.5	25.3	21.0	28.1	24.4	...
Jordanie	2005-2010	70.8	74.5	3.1	21.7	17.0	23.9	19.5	62
Kazakhstan	2000-2005	59.1	70.4	2.0	36.6	27.2	43.5	33.2	...
Kazakhstan	2005-2010	59.0	71.2	2.3	28.8	22.3	33.6	26.4	140
Kenya	2000-2005	51.0	52.3	5.0	76.3	64.4	121.3	106.0	...
Kenya	2005-2010	53.7	54.5	5.0	69.9	57.6	111.5	95.4	560
Korea, Dem. P. R.	2000-2005	64.2	68.8	1.9	49.9	49.9	65.0	65.0	...
Corée, R. p. dém. de	2005-2010	65.1	69.3	1.9	48.0	48.0	62.5	62.5	370
Korea, Republic of	2000-2005	73.9	80.9	1.2	5.6	4.7	7.2	6.1	...
Corée, République de	2005-2010	75.9	82.5	1.2	4.6	4.3	6.0	5.7	14
Kuwait	2000-2005	75.3	79.2	2.3	10.4	9.1	12.2	9.5	...
Koweït	2005-2010	76.0	79.9	2.2	9.7	8.5	11.3	8.9	4
Kyrgyzstan	2000-2005	62.7	70.6	2.5	43.9	36.6	52.7	44.2	...
Kirghizistan	2005-2010	64.1	71.6	2.6	40.1	34.3	49.0	41.8	150
Lao People's Dem. Rep.	2000-2005	61.1	63.5	3.9	64.0	56.5	84.3	78.6	...
Rép. dém. pop. lao	2005-2010	63.4	66.2	3.5	53.4	45.9	68.2	61.5	660
Latvia	2000-2005	65.3	76.2	1.3	10.7	9.2	13.0	11.0	...
Lettonie	2005-2010	67.3	77.2	1.4	9.5	8.5	12.4	10.4	10
Lebanon	2000-2005	68.9	73.2	2.1	29.7	20.5	35.3	24.4	...
Liban	2005-2010	69.9	74.2	1.9	26.2	17.6	30.9	20.7	150
Lesotho	2000-2005	44.0	47.5	3.8	85.7	72.1	123.3	107.8	...
Lesotho	2005-2010	44.5	45.8	3.4	76.5	62.6	112.0	95.6	960
Liberia	2000-2005	54.4	57.3	5.6	108.0	98.4	164.7	154.2	...
Libéria	2005-2010	56.7	59.4	5.2	99.3	90.8	144.5	135.6	1 200
Libyan Arab Jamah.	2000-2005	70.5	75.7	3.0	22.1	19.5	23.8	22.0	...
Jamah. arabe libyenne	2005-2010	71.7	76.9	2.7	18.9	17.1	20.1	19.2	97
Lithuania	2000-2005	66.3	77.5	1.3	8.4	7.0	10.8	8.6	...
Lituanie	2005-2010	65.8	77.7	1.3	10.8	6.9	14.3	8.6	11
Luxembourg	2000-2005	75.1	81.3	1.7	4.7	4.7	6.9	6.7	...
Luxembourg	2005-2010	76.7	82.1	1.7	4.2	4.2	6.2	6.2	12
Madagascar	2000-2005	56.2	59.2	5.3	80.0	69.4	121.6	112.2	...
Madagascar	2005-2010	58.5	61.8	4.8	70.2	60.2	104.9	95.4	510
Malawi	2000-2005	48.5	51.7	6.0	100.4	92.4	149.3	141.1	...
Malawi	2005-2010	51.8	53.8	5.6	87.7	79.6	125.0	116.7	1 100
Malaysia	2000-2005	70.8	75.5	2.9	11.5	8.5	14.5	11.4	...
Malaisie	2005-2010	72.0	76.7	2.6	9.9	7.9	12.3	10.2	62

Selected indicators of life expectancy, childbearing and mortality *(continued)*
Choix d'indicateurs de l'espérance de vie, de la maternité et de la mortalité *(suite)*

| | | Life expectancy at birth (years) Espérance de vie à la naissance (en années) | | Total fertility rate | Mortality rates – Taux de mortalité | | | | Maternal – Maternelle p. 100 000 |
| | | | | | Infant – Infantile p. 1 000 | | Under 5 years – Moins de 5 ans p. 1 000 | | |
Country or area & Pays ou zone &	Year Année	Males Hommes	Females Femmes	Taux de fécondité	Males Hommes	Females Femmes	Males Hommes	Females Femmes	2005
Maldives	2000-2005	67.2	69.7	2.4	36.5	32.4	44.2	40.5	
Maldives	2005-2010	69.8	72.9	2.1	26.4	21.6	31.0	25.8	...
Mali	2000-2005	45.9	47.1	5.7	117.5	109.3	213.1	206.8	
Mali	2005-2010	47.6	49.0	5.5	110.0	102.7	193.1	187.9	970
Malta	2000-2005	76.4	80.8	1.5	6.9	6.9	8.2	7.9	
Malte	2005-2010	77.8	81.4	1.3	6.3	6.3	7.3	7.3	8
Martinique	2000-2005	75.7	81.6	2.0	7.6	6.4	8.9	8.8	
Martinique	2005-2010	76.5	82.3	1.9	7.1	6.1	8.5	8.2	...
Mauritania	2000-2005	54.6	58.4	4.9	77.8	67.2	127.6	113.4	
Mauritanie	2005-2010	54.7	58.5	4.5	78.0	67.1	127.8	112.3	820
Mauritius	2000-2005[5]	68.3	75.4	1.9	17.8	12.6	21.2	15.4	
Maurice	2005-2010	68.5[5]	75.8[5]	1.8[5]	16.7[5]	12.3[5]	19.6[5]	15.0[5]	15
Mayotte	2000-2005	71.3	79.6	4.0	8.0	6.7	10.9	8.9	
Mayotte	2005-2010	72.1	80.2	3.2	7.3	6.4	10.0	8.4	...
Mexico	2000-2005	72.4	77.4	2.4	22.9	18.0	27.4	21.8	
Mexique	2005-2010	73.8	78.7	2.2	18.7	14.6	22.4	17.8	60
Micronesia (Fed. States of)	2000-2005	66.9	68.2	4.1	37.7	38.2	45.8	49.2	
Micronésie (Etats féd. de)	2005-2010	67.7	69.3	3.6	34.3	33.8	41.3	42.6	...
Mongolia	2000-2005	61.7	67.7	2.1	50.9	43.6	53.6	45.8	
Mongolie	2005-2010	63.2	69.8	2.0	46.0	38.0	48.6	39.9	46
Montenegro	2000-2005	71.9	77.0	1.8	12.7	10.4	14.0	11.3	
Monténégro	2005-2010	71.6	76.5	1.6	8.8	8.6	10.8	9.3	...
Morocco	2000-2005	67.5	71.8	2.5	42.6	32.1	52.8	38.1	
Maroc	2005-2010	69.0	73.4	2.4	35.7	25.3	43.2	29.1	240
Mozambique	2000-2005	46.2	49.1	5.5	110.5	95.2	186.0	167.5	
Mozambique	2005-2010	46.9	48.7	5.1	97.1	83.0	161.9	144.4	520
Myanmar	2000-2005	58.3	62.5	2.5	86.8	69.6	125.2	107.5	
Myanmar	2005-2010	59.0	63.4	2.3	83.8	66.7	120.2	102.0	380
Namibia	2000-2005	55.4	57.8	3.8	54.8	43.9	79.4	65.9	
Namibie	2005-2010	60.3	62.3	3.4	40.0	29.9	57.8	45.3	210
Nepal	2000-2005	63.1	64.0	3.6	54.8	54.6	70.3	75.4	
Népal	2005-2010	65.9	67.2	2.9	42.2	42.1	51.9	55.4	830
Netherlands	2000-2005	76.3	81.0	1.7	5.4	4.3	6.5	5.2	
Pays-Bas	2005-2010	77.8	82.0	1.7	4.8	4.2	5.9	5.2	6
Netherlands Antilles	2000-2005	71.8	79.0	2.1	15.7	12.2	18.5	12.8	
Antilles néerlandaises	2005-2010	72.7	79.4	2.0	13.7	11.7	15.9	12.3	...
New Caledonia	2000-2005	71.9	78.7	2.3	6.9	6.4	9.9	9.1	
Nouvelle-Calédonie	2005-2010	72.8	79.7	2.1	6.3	6.0	8.9	8.4	...
New Zealand	2000-2005	77.0	81.4	2.0	5.7	4.2	7.0	5.6	
Nouvelle-Zélande	2005-2010	78.2	82.2	2.0	5.0	4.1	6.3	5.4	9
Nicaragua	2000-2005	68.0	73.9	3.0	29.9	22.8	36.0	28.0	
Nicaragua	2005-2010	69.9	76.1	2.8	24.3	18.5	28.9	22.4	170
Niger	2000-2005	47.5	48.8	7.4	111.4	104.6	208.0	211.0	
Niger	2005-2010	50.3	52.0	7.2	90.8	85.4	170.9	173.4	1 800
Nigeria	2000-2005	46.2	47.3	5.7	118.3	109.2	201.6	196.9	
Nigéria	2005-2010	47.3	48.3	5.3	114.3	104.4	189.9	184.4	1 100
Norway	2000-2005[6]	76.8	81.8	1.8	4.1	3.4	5.5	4.4	
Norvège	2005-2010	78.3[6]	82.8[6]	1.9[6]	3.5[6]	3.4[6]	4.9[6]	4.4[6]	7
Occupied Palestinian Terr.	2000-2005	70.8	73.9	5.6	23.1	18.5	26.9	21.8	
Terr. palestinien occupé	2005-2010	71.8	75.0	5.1	19.7	15.2	22.6	17.6	...
Oman	2000-2005	72.9	75.9	3.8	16.3	13.9	18.5	16.0	
Oman	2005-2010	74.2	77.5	3.1	12.7	11.9	14.2	13.5	64
Pakistan	2000-2005	64.4	65.1	4.4	68.5	72.7	96.5	104.2	
Pakistan	2005-2010	66.0	66.7	4.0	61.3	66.6	84.9	93.9	320

		Life expectancy at birth (years) Espérance de vie à la naissance (en années)		Total fertility rate	Mortality rates – Taux de mortalité				Maternal – Maternelle p. 100 000
					Infant – Infantile p. 1 000		Under 5 years – Moins de 5 ans p. 1 000		
Country or area & Pays ou zone &	Year Année	Males Hommes	Females Femmes	Taux de fécondité	Males Hommes	Females Femmes	Males Hommes	Females Femmes	2005
Panama	2000-2005	72.3	77.4	2.7	24.1	17.0	30.6	22.9	...
Panama	2005-2010	73.0	78.3	2.6	21.2	15.0	27.1	20.3	130
Papua New Guinea	2000-2005	57.0	61.6	4.4	57.7	55.0	81.3	75.2	...
Papouasie-Nvl-Guinée	2005-2010	58.8	63.2	4.1	51.4	50.1	69.6	68.1	470
Paraguay	2000-2005	68.7	72.9	3.5	40.4	30.4	48.5	36.2	...
Paraguay	2005-2010	69.7	73.9	3.1	36.7	27.2	43.9	32.5	150
Peru	2000-2005	69.0	74.3	2.8	33.8	26.7	45.0	34.5	...
Pérou	2005-2010	70.5	75.9	2.6	23.9	18.3	38.1	27.3	240
Philippines	2000-2005	68.2	72.5	3.3	32.5	22.7	38.9	27.2	...
Philippines	2005-2010	69.5	74.0	3.1	27.5	18.2	32.5	21.4	230
Poland	2000-2005	70.4	78.8	1.3	7.9	6.6	9.2	7.6	...
Pologne	2005-2010	71.3	79.8	1.3	7.3	6.2	8.7	7.3	8
Portugal	2000-2005	74.1	80.8	1.4	4.9	4.1	6.4	5.3	...
Portugal	2005-2010	75.4	81.9	1.4	4.3	4.0	5.6	5.2	11
Puerto Rico	2000-2005	73.7	82.0	1.8	8.5	7.7	10.6	8.8	...
Porto Rico	2005-2010	74.7	82.7	1.8	7.4	7.1	9.2	8.1	...
Qatar	2000-2005	73.4	75.8	2.9	9.8	9.8	11.8	11.8	...
Qatar	2005-2010	74.9	76.9	2.4	8.3	8.3	10.0	10.0	12
Republic of Moldova	2000-2005	63.6	71.2	1.5	21.0	16.6	25.9	20.4	...
République de Moldova	2005-2010	64.7	72.2	1.5	19.9	15.9	25.7	20.6	22
Réunion	2000-2005	71.5	80.0	2.5	7.8	6.5	10.6	8.6	...
Réunion	2005-2010	72.3	80.5	2.4	7.1	6.2	9.7	8.1	...
Romania	2000-2005	67.8	75.1	1.3	18.8	14.4	23.2	16.9	...
Roumanie	2005-2010	69.1	76.2	1.3	16.2	13.0	19.8	15.1	24
Russian Federation	2000-2005	58.5	71.8	1.3	19.6	14.9	24.4	18.5	...
Fédération de Russie	2005-2010	60.3	73.1	1.4	13.2	10.5	17.6	13.8	28
Rwanda	2000-2005	44.4	47.7	5.8	116.6	100.8	182.3	158.8	...
Rwanda	2005-2010	48.1	51.6	5.4	107.5	91.6	166.8	143.0	1 300
Saint Lucia	2000-2005	70.7	74.4	2.1	16.8	12.4	20.9	17.3	...
Sainte-Lucie	2005-2010	71.9	75.6	2.1	14.3	10.7	17.6	14.5	...
Saint Vincent-Grenadines	2000-2005	68.5	72.8	2.2	31.5	21.8	37.6	26.1	...
Saint Vincent-Grenadines	2005-2010	69.5	73.8	2.1	27.7	18.8	32.7	22.1	...
Samoa	2000-2005	67.1	73.5	4.5	27.0	24.4	33.0	29.1	...
Samoa	2005-2010	68.5	74.9	4.0	23.1	21.5	27.9	25.2	...
Sao Tome and Principe	2000-2005	62.5	66.1	4.3	80.7	72.9	106.1	98.3	...
Sao Tomé-et-Principe	2005-2010	63.6	67.4	3.9	76.3	68.1	98.9	90.2	...
Saudi Arabia	2000-2005	69.8	74.0	3.8	26.5	18.2	31.1	21.5	...
Arabie saoudite	2005-2010	70.9	75.3	3.2	22.7	14.8	26.5	17.1	18
Senegal	2000-2005	53.1	56.0	5.4	65.5	58.3	134.7	123.6	...
Sénégal	2005-2010	53.9	57.0	5.0	61.8	55.0	125.0	114.3	980
Serbia	2000-2005	70.9	75.6	1.7	14.3	11.6	16.8	13.8	...
Serbie	2005-2010	71.7	76.3	1.6	12.6	10.8	14.7	12.9	...
Sierra Leone	2000-2005	43.4	46.1	5.3	119.3	100.2	188.0	158.6	...
Sierra Leone	2005-2010	46.1	48.7	5.2	113.3	95.0	159.9	136.0	2 100
Singapore	2000-2005	76.8	80.8	1.4	3.0	2.9	4.0	4.0	...
Singapour	2005-2010	77.9	82.8	1.3	3.0	3.0	4.1	4.1	14
Slovakia	2000-2005	69.8	77.8	1.2	8.0	6.8	9.4	7.8	...
Slovaquie	2005-2010	70.7	78.5	1.3	7.4	6.5	9.2	7.7	6
Slovenia	2000-2005	72.6	80.3	1.2	4.6	3.6	5.4	4.2	...
Slovénie	2005-2010	74.6	81.9	1.4	3.9	3.6	4.8	4.3	6
Solomon Islands	2000-2005	62.9	64.2	4.4	55.8	53.8	71.8	74.1	...
Iles Salomon	2005-2010	65.1	67.0	3.9	45.6	42.9	56.4	56.6	220
Somalia	2000-2005	47.8	51.0	6.5	119.0	102.0	189.8	174.1	...
Somalie	2005-2010	48.2	51.0	6.4	117.1	101.8	186.4	173.8	1 400

Country or area & Pays ou zone &	Year Année	Life expectancy at birth (years) Espérance de vie à la naissance (en années)		Total fertility rate Taux de fécondité	Mortality rates – Taux de mortalité				Maternal – Maternelle p. 100 000
					Infant – Infantile p. 1 000		Under 5 years – Moins de 5 ans p. 1 000		
		Males Hommes	Females Femmes	Taux de fécondité	Males Hommes	Females Femmes	Males Hommes	Females Femmes	2005
South Africa	2000-2005	50.8	55.5	2.8	63.9	54.1	93.4	78.5	
Afrique du Sud	2005-2010	49.9	53.2	2.6	54.7	43.4	79.5	63.8	400
Spain	2000-2005	76.4	83.1	1.3	4.5	3.7	5.6	4.6	...
Espagne	2005-2010	77.6	84.1	1.4	4.2	3.6	5.2	4.5	4
Sri Lanka	2000-2005	69.2	77.2	2.3	19.1	15.6	23.6	19.9	...
Sri Lanka	2005-2010	70.2	77.8	2.3	17.1	14.6	21.2	18.4	58
Sudan	2000-2005	55.1	58.4	4.8	78.9	67.5	126.8	113.3	...
Soudan	2005-2010	56.5	59.5	4.2	74.5	63.4	117.5	104.2	450
Suriname	2000-2005	64.7	71.9	2.6	27.4	19.8	38.0	27.9	...
Suriname	2005-2010	65.4	72.6	2.4	25.4	18.7	35.3	26.1	72
Swaziland	2000-2005	45.4	46.8	4.0	89.7	74.6	135.7	117.0	...
Swaziland	2005-2010	46.3	45.2	3.6	73.2	58.1	110.9	92.1	390
Sweden	2000-2005	77.8	82.3	1.7	3.3	3.1	4.6	4.0	...
Suède	2005-2010	78.7	83.0	1.9	3.1	3.1	4.4	4.0	3
Switzerland	2000-2005	78.0	83.3	1.4	4.7	4.0	5.9	5.0	...
Suisse	2005-2010	79.3	84.1	1.5	4.3	3.8	5.5	4.7	5
Syrian Arab Republic	2000-2005	71.2	74.9	3.6	21.6	15.4	25.0	17.9	...
Rép. arabe syrienne	2005-2010	72.3	76.1	3.3	18.2	13.7	20.8	15.7	130
Tajikistan	2000-2005	60.9	68.6	3.8	66.2	59.8	86.8	77.6	...
Tadjikistan	2005-2010	64.1	69.4	3.5	63.2	57.1	82.5	73.5	170
Thailand	2000-2005	64.0	72.8	1.8	10.7	8.5	16.4	11.3	...
Thaïlande	2005-2010	65.7	72.0	1.8	7.7	6.0	12.9	8.2	110
TFYR of Macedonia	2000-2005	71.1	75.9	1.6	17.5	15.4	20.0	17.7	...
L'ex-R.Y. Macédoine	2005-2010	71.8	76.6	1.4	15.4	14.3	17.4	16.5	10
Timor-Leste	2000-2005	57.5	59.0	7.0	81.6	75.8	111.2	109.8	...
Timor-Leste	2005-2010	60.0	61.7	6.5	69.2	64.0	92.3	90.7	380
Togo	2000-2005	58.3	62.4	4.8	86.8	75.1	121.1	106.3	...
Togo	2005-2010	60.7	64.2	4.3	76.8	66.0	104.6	90.9	510
Tonga	2000-2005	68.8	73.5	4.2	22.4	24.4	26.9	29.0	...
Tonga	2005-2010	69.1	74.7	4.1	21.8	21.8	26.2	25.6	...
Trinidad and Tobago	2000-2005	64.7	72.0	1.6	32.1	25.6	40.9	31.5	...
Trinité-et-Tobago	2005-2010	65.8	73.0	1.6	28.8	23.2	36.9	28.4	45
Tunisia	2000-2005	71.1	75.1	2.0	24.3	20.5	27.4	23.3	...
Tunisie	2005-2010	71.9	76.0	1.9	21.1	18.4	23.5	20.9	100
Turkey	2000-2005	68.5	73.3	2.2	35.5	27.1	41.0	31.5	...
Turquie	2005-2010	69.4	74.3	2.1	31.4	23.5	36.0	27.0	44
Turkmenistan	2000-2005	60.4	68.2	2.8	57.3	45.9	72.7	58.7	...
Turkménistan	2005-2010	60.6	68.9	2.5	56.6	44.1	71.8	56.4	130
Uganda	2000-2005	47.6	48.5	6.7	87.8	76.6	143.8	131.3	...
Ouganda	2005-2010	51.8	53.0	6.4	79.7	68.2	129.2	115.5	550
Ukraine	2000-2005	62.1	73.4	1.2	15.7	11.5	19.5	14.5	...
Ukraine	2005-2010	62.8	73.8	1.3	14.1	10.6	17.7	13.1	18
United Arab Emirates	2000-2005	75.7	78.5	2.5	9.8	10.7	10.8	12.1	...
Emirats arabes unis	2005-2010	76.6	78.8	2.0	8.9	10.4	9.9	11.8	37
United Kingdom	2000-2005	76.1	80.7	1.7	5.5	5.0	6.7	6.1	...
Royaume-Uni	2005-2010	77.2	81.6	1.8	4.9	4.7	6.1	5.8	8
United Rep. of Tanzania	2000-2005	51.1	52.9	5.7	78.7	69.2	130.4	119.1	...
Rép.-Unie de Tanzanie	2005-2010	54.6	56.2	5.6	69.8	59.7	111.7	99.7	950
United States	2000-2005	75.8	80.6	2.0	6.4	6.4	7.7	8.1	...
Etats-Unis	2005-2010	76.9	81.4	2.1	5.9	5.9	7.2	7.6	11
United States Virgin Is.	2000-2005	75.0	81.3	2.2	9.8	10.2	11.0	11.4	...
Iles Vierges américaines	2005-2010	75.9	82.0	2.2	9.0	9.2	10.2	10.3	...
Uruguay	2000-2005	71.6	79.0	2.2	16.0	12.6	19.5	15.5	...
Uruguay	2005-2010	72.8	79.9	2.1	14.4	11.7	17.7	14.6	20

9

Selected indicators of life expectancy, childbearing and mortality *(continued)*
Choix d'indicateurs de l'espérance de vie, de la maternité et de la mortalité *(suite)*

Country or area & Pays ou zone &	Year Année	Life expectancy at birth (years) Espérance de vie à la naissance (en années)		Total fertility rate Taux de fécondité	Mortality rates – Taux de mortalité				Maternal – Maternelle p. 100 000
		Males Hommes	Females Femmes		Infant – Infantile p. 1 000		Under 5 years – Moins de 5 ans p. 1 000		
					Males Hommes	Females Femmes	Males Hommes	Females Femmes	2005
Uzbekistan	2000-2005	64.1	70.4	2.6	54.3	44.6	64.8	54.3	...
Ouzbékistan	2005-2010	64.6	70.9	2.3	52.6	43.2	62.7	52.6	24
Vanuatu	2000-2005	66.8	70.4	4.3	38.4	30.0	46.7	37.1	...
Vanuatu	2005-2010	68.3	72.1	4.0	32.3	24.1	38.7	29.1	...
Venezuela (Bolivarian Rep. of)	2000-2005	69.9	75.8	2.7	21.2	16.4	27.1	21.2	...
Venezuela (Rép. boliv. du)	2005-2010	70.9	76.8	2.6	19.1	14.8	24.4	19.1	57
Viet Nam	2000-2005	71.2	74.9	2.3	25.4	19.2	30.8	23.3	...
Viet Nam	2005-2010	72.3	76.2	2.1	22.2	16.7	26.6	19.9	150
Western Sahara	2000-2005	62.3	65.8	3.0	58.5	47.4	76.0	63.9	...
Sahara occidental	2005-2010	64.3	68.1	2.7	49.5	38.7	62.2	50.0	...
Yemen	2000-2005	58.8	61.8	5.9	74.7	63.5	100.7	89.9	...
Yémen	2005-2010	61.1	64.4	5.3	63.8	53.2	84.1	73.2	430
Zambia	2000-2005	40.9	42.3	6.1	111.1	97.4	185.0	169.3	...
Zambie	2005-2010	44.6	45.6	5.9	101.6	87.5	168.5	151.8	830
Zimbabwe	2000-2005	39.4	42.9	3.7	73.4	64.4	117.4	106.1	...
Zimbabwe	2005-2010	43.4	44.3	3.5	62.0	53.2	99.8	88.5	880

Source:
Life expectancy, total fertility, infant and under 5 years mortality rates: United Nations, *World Population Prospects: The 2008 Revision.*
Maternal mortality: World Health Organization, the United Nations Children's Fund and the United Nations Population Fund, *Maternal Mortality in 2005: Estimates developed by WHO, UNICEF, UNFPA.*

Source :
Espérance de vie à la naissance, taux de fécondité, taux de mortalité infantile, et taux de mortalité des moins de 5 ans : Organisation des Nations Unies, *World Population Prospects: The 2008 Revision.* Taux de mortalité maternelle : Organisation mondiale de la santé, Fonds des Nations Unies pour l'enfance et Fonds des Nations Unies pour la population, *Maternal Mortality in 2005 : Estimates developed by WHO, UNICEF, UNFPA.*

& Countries or areas with a population of 100 000 or more.

& Pays ou zones dont la population est 100 000 ou plus.

1   Including Christmas Island, Cocos (Keeling) Islands and Norfolk Island.
2   Refers to Guernsey and Jersey.
3   For statistical purposes, the data for China do not include those for the Hong Kong Special Administrative Region (Hong Kong SAR) and Macao Special Administrative Region (Macao SAR).

4   Including Aland Islands.
5   Including Agalega, Rodrigues and Saint Brandon.
6   Including Svalbard and Jan Mayen Islands.

1   Y compris les îles Christmas, Cocos (Keeling) et Norfolk.
2   Se rapporte à Guernsey and Jersey.
3   Pour la présentation des statistiques, les données pour la Chine ne comprennent pas la Région Administrative Spéciale de Hong Kong (Hong Kong RAS) et la Région Administrative Spéciale de Macao (Macao RAS).

4   Y compris les Îles d'Åland.
5   Y compris Agalega, Rodrigues et Saint Brandon.
6   Y compris îles Svalbard et Jan Mayen.

Technical notes: tables 8 and 9

Table 8 is based on detailed data on population and its growth and distribution published in the United Nations *Demographic Yearbook*. Only official national population estimates reported to the United Nations Statistics Division are included in this table. For a comprehensive description of methods of evaluation and the limitations of the data, consult the *Demographic Yearbook*.

Unless otherwise indicated, figures refer to de facto (present-in-area) population for the present territory; surface area estimates include inland waters.

Table 9: "Life expectancy at birth", "Infant mortality rate" and "Total fertility rate" are taken from the estimates and projections prepared by the Population Division of the United Nations Secretariat, published in *World Population Prospects: The 2008 Revision*.

"Life expectancy at birth" is an overall estimate of the expected average number of years to be lived by a female or male newborn. Many developing countries lack complete and reliable statistics of births and deaths based on civil registration, so various estimation techniques are used to calculate life expectancy using other sources of data, mainly population censuses and demographic surveys. Life expectancy at birth by sex gives a statistical summary of current differences in male and female mortality across all ages. However, trends and differentials in infant and child mortality rates are the predominant influence on trends and differentials in life expectancy at birth in most developing countries. Thus, life expectancy at birth is of limited usefulness in these countries in assessing levels and differentials in male and female mortality at other ages.

"Total fertility rate" is the average number of children that would be born alive to a hypothetical cohort of women if, throughout their reproductive years, the age specific fertility rates for the specified year remained unchanged.

"Infant mortality rate" is the total number of deaths in a given year of children less than one year old divided by the total number of live births in the same year, multiplied by 1,000. It is an approximation of the number of deaths per 1,000 children born alive who die within one year of birth. In most developing countries where civil registration data are deficient, the most reliable sources are demographic surveys of households. Where these are not available, other sources and general estimates are made which are necessarily of limited reliability. Where countries lack comprehensive and accurate systems of civil registration, infant mortality statistics by sex are difficult to collect or to estimate with any degree of reliability because of reporting biases, and thus are not shown here.

The "under-five mortality rate" is the probability

Notes techniques : tableaux 8 et 9

Le *tableau 8* est fondé sur des données détaillées sur la population, sa croissance et sa distribution, publiées dans l'*Annuaire démographique* des Nations Unies. Le tableau inclut seulement des estimations officielles de la population qui ont été envoyées à la Division de Statistique des Nations Unies. Pour une description complète des méthodes d'évaluation et une indication des limites des données, voir l'*Annuaire démographique*.

Sauf indication contraire, les chiffres se rapportent à la population effectivement présente sur le territoire tel qu'il est actuellement défini; les estimations de superficie comprennent les étendues d'eau intérieures.

Tableau 9 : "L'espérance de vie à la naissance", le "taux de mortalité infantile" et le "taux de fécondité" sont proviennent des estimations et projections de la Division de la population du Secrétariat de l'ONU, qui ont publiées dans "World Population Prospects : The 2008 Revision".

"L'espérance de vie à la naissance" est une estimation globale du nombre d'années qu'un nouveau-né de sexe masculin ou féminin vivant, peut s'attendre à vivre. Comme dans beaucoup de pays en développement, les registres d'état civil ne permettent pas d'établir des statistiques fiables et complètes des naissances et des décès, diverses techniques d'estimation ont été utilisées pour calculer l'espérance de vie à partir d'autres sources et notamment des recensements et enquêtes démographiques. Sur la base des statistiques de l'espérance de vie par sexe, on peut calculer la différence entre la longévité des hommes et celle des femmes à tous les âges. Cependant, ce sont les tendances et les écarts des taux de mortalité infantile et juvénile qui influent de façon prépondérante sur les tendances et les écarts de l'espérance de vie à la naissance dans la plupart des pays en développement. Ainsi, l'espérance de vie à la naissance ne revêt qu'une utilité limitée dans ce pays pour évaluer les niveaux et les écarts de la mortalité des femmes et des hommes à des âges plus avancés.

Le "taux de fécondité" est le nombre moyen d'enfants que mettrait au monde une cohorte hypothétique de femmes si, pendant toutes leurs années d'âge reproductif, les taux de fécondité par âge de l'année en question restaient inchangés.

Le "taux de mortalité infantile" correspond au nombre total de décès au cours d'une année donnée des enfants de moins d'un an divisé par le nombre total de naissances vivantes au cours de la même année, multiplié par 1 000. Il s'agit d'une approximation du nombre de décès pour 1 000 enfants nés vivants qui meurent la première année. Dans la plupart des pays en développement, où les données d'état civil sont déficientes, les sources les plus fiables sont les enquêtes démographiques auprès des ménages. Lorsque de telles enquêtes ne sont pas réalisées, d'autres sources sont

(expressed as a rate per 1,000 live births) of a child born in a specified year dying before reaching the age of five if subject to current age-specific mortality rates.

Data on maternal mortality are estimates developed by the World Health Organization, UNICEF and the United Nations Population Fund and published in *Maternal Mortality in 2005*.

utilisées et des estimations générales sont réalisées qui est nécessairement d'une fiabilité limitée. Lorsqu'il n'a pas dans les pays de systèmes complets et exacts d'enregistrement des faits d'état civil, les statistiques de la mortalité infantile par sexe sont difficiles à rassembler ou à estimer avec quelque fiabilité que ce soit en raison des distorsions de la notification; elles ne sont donc pas indiquées ici.

Le "taux de mortalité des enfants de moins de 5 ans" est la probabilité (exprimée en tant que taux par 1 000 naissances vivantes) qu'un enfant né une année donnée meure avant d'atteindre l'âge de 5 ans compte tenu des taux de mortalité actuels liés à l'âge.

Les données concernant la mortalité maternelle sont des estimations de l'Organisation mondiale de la santé, de l'UNICEF, et du Fonds des Nations Unies pour la Population publiées dans "Maternal Mortality in 2005".

Proportion of seats held by women in national parliament
Percentage, as of 31 January 2009

Proportion de sièges occupés par des femmes au parlement national
Pourcentage, données disponibles en 31 janvier 2009

Country or area Pays ou zone	1990	2001	2002	2003	2004	2005	2006	2007	2008	2009
Afghanistan Afghanistan	3.7	...	...	...	...	...	27.3	27.3	27.7	27.7
Albania Albanie	28.8	5.2	5.7	5.7	5.7	6.4	7.1	7.1	7.1	7.1
Algeria Algérie	2.4	3.4	3.4	6.2	6.2	6.2	6.2	6.2	7.7	7.7
Andorra Andorre	...	7.1	14.3	14.3	14.3	14.3	28.6	28.6	25.0	25.0
Angola Angola	14.5	15.5	15.5	15.5	15.5	15.0	15.0	15.0	15.0	37.3
Antigua and Barbuda Antigua-et-Barbuda	0.0	5.3	5.3	5.3	5.3	10.5	10.5	10.5	10.5	10.5
Argentina Argentine	6.3	26.5	30.7	30.7	30.7	33.7	36.2	35.0	40.0	40.0
Armenia Arménie	35.6	3.1	3.1	3.1	4.6	5.3	5.3	5.3	9.2	8.4
Australia Australie	6.1	23.0	25.3	25.3	25.3	24.7	24.7	24.7	26.7	26.7
Austria Autriche	11.5	26.8	26.8	33.9	33.9	33.9	33.9	32.2	32.8	27.3
Azerbaijan Azerbaïdjan	...	...	10.5	10.5	10.5	10.5	12.0	11.3	11.4	11.4
Bahamas Bahamas	4.1	15.0	15.0	20.0	20.0	20.0	20.0	20.0	12.2	12.2
Bahrain Bahreïn	...	...	...	0.0	0.0	0.0	0.0	2.5	2.5	2.5
Bangladesh Bangladesh	10.3	9.1	...	2.0	2.0	2.0	14.8[1]	...	...	6.3[2]
Barbados Barbade	3.7	10.7	10.7	10.7	13.3	13.3	13.3	13.3	10.0	10.0
Belarus Bélarus	...	...	10.3	10.3	10.3	29.4	29.1	29.1	29.1	31.8
Belgium Belgique	8.5	23.3	23.3	23.3	35.3	34.7	34.7	34.7	35.3	35.3
Belize Belize	0.0	6.9	6.9	6.9	3.3	6.7	6.7	6.7	3.3	0.0
Benin Bénin	2.9	6.0	6.0	6.0	7.2	7.2	7.2	7.2	10.8	10.8
Bhutan Bhoutan	2.0	9.3	9.3	9.3	9.3	9.3	9.3	2.7	2.7	8.5
Bolivia Bolivie	9.2	11.5	11.5	18.5	18.5	19.2	16.9	16.9	16.9	16.9
Bosnia and Herzegovina Bosnie-Herzégovine	...	...	7.1	16.7	16.7	16.7	16.7	14.3	11.9	11.9
Botswana Botswana	5.0	17.0	17.0	17.0	17.0	11.1	11.1	11.1	11.1	11.1
Brazil Brésil	5.3	5.7	6.8	8.6	8.6	8.6	8.6	8.8	9.0	9.0
Bulgaria Bulgarie	21.0	10.8	26.3	26.3	26.3	26.3	22.1	22.1	21.7	21.7
Burkina Faso Burkina Faso	...	8.1	8.1	11.7	11.7	11.7	11.7	11.7	15.3	15.3
Burundi Burundi	...	14.4	19.5	18.4	18.4	18.4	30.5	30.5	30.5	30.5

Proportion of seats held by women in national parliament *(continued)*
Percentage, as of 31 January 2009
Proportion de sièges occupés par des femmes au parlement national *(suite)*
Pourcentage, données disponibles en 31 janvier 2009

Country or area Pays ou zone	1990	2001	2002	2003	2004	2005	2006	2007	2008	2009
Cambodia Cambodge	...	7.4	7.4	7.4	9.8	9.8	9.8	9.8	19.5	16.3
Cameroon Cameroun	14.4	5.6	5.6	8.9	8.9	8.9	8.9	8.9	13.9	13.9
Canada Canada	13.3	20.6	20.6	20.6	20.6	21.1	20.8	20.8	21.3	22.1
Cape Verde Cap-Vert	12.0	11.1	11.1	11.1	11.1	11.1	15.3	15.3	18.1	18.1
Central African Rep. Rép. centrafricaine	3.8	7.3	7.3	7.3	...	...	10.5	10.5	10.5	10.5
Chad Tchad	...	2.4	2.4	5.8	5.8	6.5	6.5	6.5	5.2	5.2
Chile Chili	...	10.8	12.5	12.5	12.5	12.5	15.0	15.0	15.0	15.0
China Chine	21.3	21.8	21.8	21.8	20.2	20.2	20.3	20.3	20.6	21.3
Colombia Colombie	4.5	11.8	11.8	12.0	12.0	12.0	12.1	8.4	8.4	8.4
Comoros Comores	0.0	...	...	...	...	3.0	3.0	3.0	3.0	3.0
Congo Congo	14.3	12.0	12.0	9.3	8.5	8.5	8.5	8.5	7.3	7.3
Costa Rica Costa Rica	10.5	19.3	19.3	35.1	35.1	35.1	35.1	38.6	36.8	36.8
Côte d'Ivoire Côte d'Ivoire	5.7	...	8.5	8.5	8.5	8.5	8.5	8.5	8.9	8.9
Croatia Croatie	...	20.5	20.5	20.5	17.8	21.7	21.7	21.7	20.9	20.9
Cuba Cuba	33.9	27.6	27.6	36.0	36.0	36.0	36.0	36.0	43.2	43.2
Cyprus Chypre	1.8	7.1	10.7	10.7	10.7	16.1	16.1	14.3	14.3	14.3
Czech Republic République tchèque	...	15.0	15.0	17.0	17.0	17.0	17.0	15.5	15.5	15.5
Dem. Rep. of the Congo Rép. dém. du Congo	5.4	...	...	...	12.0	12.0	12.0	8.4	8.4	8.4
Denmark Danemark	30.7	37.4	38.0	38.0	38.0	38.0	36.9	36.9	38.0	38.0
Djibouti Djibouti	0.0	0.0	0.0	10.8	10.8	10.8	10.8	10.8	13.8	13.8
Dominica Dominique	10.0	...	18.8	18.8	18.8	19.4	12.9	12.9	16.1	18.8
Dominican Republic Rép. dominicaine	7.5	16.1	16.1	17.3	17.3	17.3	17.3	19.7	19.7	19.7
Ecuador Equateur	4.5	14.6	14.6	16.0	16.0	16.0	16.0	25.0	25.0	27.6[3]
Egypt Egypte	3.9	...	2.4	2.4	2.4	2.9	2.0	2.0	1.8	1.8
El Salvador El Salvador	11.7	9.5	9.5	9.5	10.7	10.7	10.7	16.7	16.7	19.0
Equatorial Guinea Guinée équatoriale	13.3	5.0	5.0	5.0	5.0	18.0	18.0	18.0	18.0	6.0
Eritrea Erythrée	...	14.7	14.7	22.0	22.0	22.0	22.0	22.0	22.0	22.0
Estonia Estonie	...	17.8	17.8	17.8	18.8	18.8	18.8	18.8	20.8	20.8

Proportion of seats held by women in national parliament *(continued)*
Percentage, as of 31 January 2009
Proportion de sièges occupés par des femmes au parlement national *(suite)*
Pourcentage, données disponibles en 31 janvier 2009

Country or area Pays ou zone	1990	2001	2002	2003	2004	2005	2006	2007	2008	2009
Ethiopia Ethiopie	...	7.7	7.7	7.7	7.7	7.7	21.4	21.9	21.9	21.9
Fiji Fidji	...	...	5.7	5.7	5.7	8.5	8.5[4]	...	...	...
Finland Finlande	31.5	36.5	36.5	36.5	37.5	37.5	37.5	38.0	41.5	41.5
France France	6.9	10.9	10.9	12.2	12.2	12.2	12.2	12.2	18.2	18.2
Gabon Gabon	13.3	9.2	...	9.2	9.2	9.2	9.2	12.5	16.7	16.7
Gambia Gambie	7.8	2.0	...	13.2	13.2	13.2	13.2	9.4	9.4	9.4
Georgia Géorgie	...	7.2	7.2	7.2	7.2	9.4	9.4	9.4	9.4	6.0
Germany Allemagne	...	30.9	31.7	32.2	32.2	32.8	31.8	31.6	31.6	32.2
Ghana Ghana	...	...	9.0	9.0	9.0	10.9	10.9	10.9	10.9	7.9
Greece Grèce	6.7	8.7	8.7	8.7	8.7	14.0	13.0	13.0	14.7	14.7
Grenada Grenade	...	26.7	26.7	26.7	26.7	26.7	26.7	26.7	26.7	13.3
Guatemala Guatemala	7.0	8.8	8.8	8.8	8.2	8.2	8.2	8.2	12.0	12.0
Guinea Guinée	...	8.8	8.8	19.3	19.3	19.3	19.3	19.3	19.3[5]	...
Guinea-Bissau Guinée-Bissau	20.0	7.8	7.8	7.8	...	14.0	14.0	14.0	14.0	10.0
Guyana Guyana	36.9	18.5	20.0	20.0	20.0	30.8	30.8	29.0	29.0	30.0
Haiti Haïti	...	...	3.6	3.6	3.6	3.6	3.6	4.1	4.1	4.1
Honduras Honduras	10.2	9.4	9.4	5.5	5.5	5.5	23.4	23.4	23.4	23.4
Hungary Hongrie	20.7	8.3	8.3	9.8	9.8	9.1	9.1	10.4	11.1	11.1
Iceland Islande	20.6	34.9	34.9	34.9	30.2	30.2	33.3	33.3	33.3	33.3
India Inde	5.0	9.0	8.8	8.8	8.8	8.3	8.3	8.3	9.1	9.1
Indonesia Indonésie	12.4	8.0	8.0	8.0	8.0	11.3	11.3	11.3	11.6	11.6
Iran (Islamic Rep. of) Iran (Rép. islamique d')	1.5	3.4	3.4	4.1	4.1	4.1	4.1	4.1	4.1	2.8
Iraq Iraq	10.8	7.6	7.6	7.6	...	...	25.5	25.5	25.5	25.5
Ireland Irlande	7.8	12.0	12.0	13.3	13.3	13.3	13.3	13.3	13.3	13.3
Israel Israël	6.7	12.5	13.3	15.0	15.0	15.0	15.0	14.2	14.2	14.2
Italy Italie	12.9	11.1	9.8	11.5	11.5	11.5	11.5	17.3	17.3	21.3
Jamaica Jamaïque	5.0	13.3	13.3	11.7	11.7	11.7	11.7	11.7	13.3	13.3
Japan Japon	1.4	7.3	7.3	7.3	7.1	7.1	9.0	9.4	9.4	9.4

10

Proportion of seats held by women in national parliament *(continued)*
Percentage, as of 31 January 2009
Proportion de sièges occupés par des femmes au parlement national *(suite)*
Pourcentage, données disponibles en 31 janvier 2009

Country or area Pays ou zone	1990	2001	2002	2003	2004	2005	2006	2007	2008	2009
Jordan Jordanie	0.0	0.0	1.3	1.3	5.5	5.5	5.5	5.5	6.4	6.4
Kazakhstan Kazakhstan	...	10.4	10.4	10.4	10.4	10.4	10.4	10.4	15.9	15.9
Kenya Kenya	1.1	3.6	3.6	7.1	7.1	7.1	7.1	7.3	7.2[6]	9.8
Kiribati Kiribati	0.0	4.9	4.8	4.8	4.8	4.8	4.8	7.1	4.3	4.3
Korea, Dem. P. R. Corée, R. p. dém. de	21.1	20.1	20.1	20.1	...	20.1	20.1	20.1	20.1	20.1
Korea, Republic of Corée, République de	2.0	5.9	5.9	5.9	5.5	13.0	13.4	13.4	14.4	13.7
Kuwait Koweït	...	0.0	0.0	0.0	0.0	0.0	1.5[7]	1.5[8]	1.5[9]	3.1[10]
Kyrgyzstan Kirghizistan	...	2.3	10.0	10.0	10.0	10.0	0.0	0.0	25.6	25.6
Lao People's Dem. Rep. Rép. dém. pop. lao	6.3	21.2	21.2	22.9	22.9	22.9	22.9	25.2	25.2	25.2
Latvia Lettonie	...	17.0	17.0	21.0	21.0	21.0	21.0	19.0	20.0	20.0
Lebanon Liban	0.0	2.3	2.3	2.3	2.3	2.3	4.7	4.7	4.7	4.7
Lesotho Lesotho	...	3.8	3.8	11.7	11.7	11.7	11.7	11.8	25.0	25.0
Liberia Libéria	...	7.8	7.8	7.8	7.8	5.3	12.5	12.5	12.5	12.5
Libyan Arab Jamah. Jamah. arabe libyenne	...	...	...	...	...	...	4.7	7.7	7.7	7.7
Liechtenstein Liechtenstein	4.0	4.0	12.0	12.0	12.0	12.0	24.0	24.0	24.0	24.0
Lithuania Lituanie	...	10.6	10.6	10.6	10.6	22.0	22.0	24.8	22.7	17.7
Luxembourg Luxembourg	13.3	16.7	16.7	16.7	16.7	23.3	23.3	23.3	23.3	23.3
Madagascar Madagascar	6.5	8.0	8.0	3.8	3.8	6.9	6.9	6.9	7.9	7.9
Malawi Malawi	9.8	9.3	9.3	9.3	9.3	14.0	13.6	13.6	13.0	13.0
Malaysia Malaisie	5.1	10.4	10.4	10.4	10.5	9.1	9.1	9.1	10.0	10.8
Maldives Maldives	6.3	6.0	6.0	6.0	6.0	12.0	12.0	12.0	12.0	12.0
Mali Mali	...	12.2	12.2	10.2	10.2	10.2	10.2	10.2	10.2	10.2
Malta Malte	2.9	9.2	9.2	9.2	9.2	9.2	9.2	9.2	9.2	8.7
Marshall Islands Iles Marshall	...	3.0	3.0	3.0	3.0	3.0	3.0	3.0	3.0	3.0
Mauritania Mauritanie	...	3.8	...	...	3.7	3.7	...	17.9	22.1	22.1
Mauritius Maurice	7.1	5.7	5.7	5.7	5.7	5.7	17.1	17.1	17.1	17.1
Mexico Mexique	12.0	16.0	16.0	16.0	22.6	22.6	24.2	22.6	23.2	23.2
Micronesia (Fed. States of) Micronésie (Etats féd. de)	...	0.0	0.0	0.0	0.0	0.0	0.0	0.0	0.0	0.0

Proportion of seats held by women in national parliament *(continued)*
Percentage, as of 31 January 2009
Proportion de sièges occupés par des femmes au parlement national *(suite)*
Pourcentage, données disponibles en 31 janvier 2009

Country or area Pays ou zone	1990	2001	2002	2003	2004	2005	2006	2007	2008	2009
Monaco Monaco	11.1	22.2	22.2	22.2	20.8	20.8	20.8	20.8	20.8	25.0
Mongolia Mongolie	24.9	10.5	10.5	10.5	10.5	6.8	6.7	6.6	6.6	4.1
Montenegro Monténégro	...	...	...	...	...	...	...	8.6	11.1	11.1
Morocco Maroc	0.0	0.6	0.6	10.8	10.8	10.8	10.8	10.8	10.5	10.5
Mozambique Mozambique	15.7	30.0	30.0	30.0	30.0	34.8	34.8	34.8	34.8	34.8
Namibia Namibie	6.9	25.0	25.0	26.4	26.4	25.0	26.9	26.9	26.9	26.9
Nauru Nauru	5.6	...	0.0	0.0	0.0	0.0	0.0	0.0	0.0	0.0
Nepal Népal	6.1	5.9	5.9[11]	...	...	...	...	17.3[12]	17.3[12]	33.2
Netherlands Pays-Bas	21.3	36.0	36.0	36.7	36.7	36.7	36.7	36.7	39.3	41.3
New Zealand Nouvelle-Zélande	14.4	30.8	30.8	29.2	28.3	28.3	32.2	32.2	33.1	33.6
Nicaragua Nicaragua	14.8	9.7	20.7	20.7	20.7	20.7	20.7	18.5	18.5	18.5
Niger Niger	5.4	1.2	1.2	1.2	1.2	12.4	12.4	12.4	12.4	12.4
Nigeria Nigéria	...	3.4	3.4	3.4	6.7	4.7	6.4	6.1	7.0	7.0
Norway Norvège	35.8	36.4	35.8	36.4	36.4	38.2	37.9	37.9	36.1	36.1
Oman Oman	...	...	...	...	...	2.4	2.4	2.4	0.0	0.0
Pakistan Pakistan	10.1	...	...	21.6	21.6	21.3	21.3	21.3	21.1	22.5
Palau Palaos	...	...	0.0	0.0	0.0	0.0	0.0	0.0	0.0	0.0
Panama Panama	7.5	9.9	9.9	9.9	9.9	16.7	16.7	16.7	16.7	16.7
Papua New Guinea Papouasie-Nvl-Guinée	0.0	1.8	1.8	0.9	0.9	0.9	0.9	0.9	0.9	0.9
Paraguay Paraguay	5.6	2.5	2.5	2.5	10.0	10.0	10.0	10.0	10.0	12.5
Peru Pérou	5.6	20.0	18.3	18.3	18.3	18.3	18.3	29.2	29.2	29.2
Philippines Philippines	9.1	11.3	17.8	17.8	17.8	15.3	15.7	15.3	20.5	20.5
Poland Pologne	13.5	13.0	20.2	20.2	20.2	20.2	20.4	20.4	20.4	20.2
Portugal Portugal	7.6	17.4	18.7	19.1	19.1	19.1	21.3	21.3	28.3	28.3
Qatar Qatar	...	...	...	...	...	...	0.0	0.0	0.0	0.0
Republic of Moldova République de Moldova	...	7.9	12.9	12.9	12.9	15.8	21.8	21.8	21.8	21.8
Romania Roumanie	34.4	10.7	10.7	10.7	10.7	11.4	11.2	11.2	9.4	11.4
Russian Federation Fédération de Russie	...	7.7	7.6	7.6	9.8	9.8	9.8	9.8	14.0	14.0

Proportion of seats held by women in national parliament *(continued)*
Percentage, as of 31 January 2009

Proportion de sièges occupés par des femmes au parlement national *(suite)*
Pourcentage, données disponibles en 31 janvier 2009

Country or area Pays ou zone	1990	2001	2002	2003	2004	2005	2006	2007	2008	2009
Rwanda Rwanda	17.1	25.7	25.7	25.7	48.8	48.8	48.8	48.8	48.8	56.3
Saint Kitts and Nevis Saint-Kitts-et-Nevis	6.7	13.3	13.3	13.3	13.3	0.0	0.0	0.0	6.7	6.7
Saint Lucia Sainte-Lucie	0.0	11.1	...	11.1	11.1	11.1	11.1	5.6[13]	11.1	11.1
Saint Vincent-Grenadines Saint Vincent-Grenadines	9.5	4.8	22.7	22.7	22.7	22.7	18.2	18.2	18.2	18.2
Samoa Samoa	0.0	8.2	6.1	6.1	6.1	6.1	6.1	6.1	8.2	8.2
San Marino Saint-Marin	11.7	13.3	16.7	16.7	16.7	16.7	16.7	11.7	11.7	15.0
Sao Tome and Principe Sao Tomé-et-Principe	11.8	9.1	9.1	9.1	9.1	9.1	9.1	7.3	1.8	7.3
Saudi Arabia Arabie saoudite	...	...	...	0.0	0.0	0.0	0.0	0.0	0.0	0.0
Senegal Sénégal	12.5	12.1	16.7	19.2	19.2	19.2	19.2	19.2	22.0	22.0
Serbia Serbie								20.4	20.4	21.6
Serbia and Montenegro Serbie-et-Monténégro	...	...	7.2	7.2	7.9	7.9	7.9		...	...
Seychelles Seychelles	16.0	23.5	23.5	29.4	29.4	29.4	29.4	29.4	23.5	23.5
Sierra Leone Sierra Leone	...	8.8	8.8	14.5	14.5	14.5	14.5	14.5	13.2	13.2
Singapore Singapour	4.9	6.5	11.8	11.8	16.0	16.0	16.0	24.5	24.5	24.5
Slovakia Slovaquie	...	14.0	14.0	19.3	19.3	16.7	16.7	20.0	19.3	19.3
Slovenia Slovénie	...	12.2	12.2	12.2	12.2	12.2	12.2	12.2	12.2	13.3
Solomon Islands Iles Salomon	0.0	2.0	0.0	0.0	0.0	0.0	0.0	0.0	0.0	0.0
Somalia Somalie	4.0	...	...	...	...	...	8.0	7.8	8.2[14]	...
South Africa Afrique du Sud	2.8	29.8	29.8	29.8	29.8	32.8	32.8	32.8	33.0	33.0
Spain Espagne	14.6	28.3	28.3	28.3	28.3	36.0	36.0	36.0	36.6	36.3
Sri Lanka Sri Lanka	4.9	...	...	4.4	4.4	4.9	4.9	4.9	5.8	5.8
Sudan Soudan	...	...	9.7	9.7	9.7	9.7	14.7	17.8	18.1	18.1
Suriname Suriname	7.8	...	17.6	17.6	17.6	19.6	25.5	25.5	25.5	25.5
Swaziland Swaziland	3.6	3.1	3.1	3.1	10.8	10.8	10.8	10.8	10.8	13.8
Sweden Suède	38.4	42.7	42.7	45.3	45.3	45.3	45.3	47.3	47.0	47.0
Switzerland Suisse	14.0	23.0	23.0	23.0	25.0	25.0	25.0	25.0	28.5	28.5
Syrian Arab Republic Rép. arabe syrienne	9.2	10.4	10.4	10.4	12.0	12.0	12.0	12.0	12.0	12.4
Tajikistan Tadjikistan	...	15.0	12.7	12.7	12.7	12.7	17.5	17.5	17.5	17.5

10

Proportion of seats held by women in national parliament *(continued)*
Percentage, as of 31 January 2009
Proportion de sièges occupés par des femmes au parlement national *(suite)*
Pourcentage, données disponibles en 31 janvier 2009

Country or area Pays ou zone	1990	2001	2002	2003	2004	2005	2006	2007	2008	2009
Thailand Thaïlande	2.8	...	9.2	9.2	9.2	8.8	10.8	8.7	11.7	11.7
TFYR of Macedonia L'ex-R.Y. Macédoine	...	6.7	6.7	18.3	18.3	19.2	19.2	28.3	29.2	31.7
Timor-Leste Timor-Leste	...	...	...	26.1	26.1	25.3	25.3	25.3	29.2	29.2
Togo Togo	5.2	4.9	4.9	7.4	7.4	6.2	7.4	8.6	11.1	11.1
Tonga Tonga	0.0	0.0	0.0	...	0.0	0.0	3.4	3.3	3.3	3.1[15]
Trinidad and Tobago Trinité-et-Tobago	16.7	...	16.7	19.4	19.4	19.4	19.4	19.4	26.8	26.8
Tunisia Tunisie	4.3	11.5	11.5	11.5	11.5	22.8	22.8	22.8	22.8	22.8
Turkey Turquie	1.3	4.2	4.2	4.4	4.4	4.4	4.4	4.4	9.1	9.1
Turkmenistan Turkménistan	26.0	26.0	26.0	26.0	26.0	...	16.0	16.0	16.0	16.8
Tuvalu Tuvalu	7.7	0.0	0.0	0.0	0.0	0.0	0.0	0.0	0.0	0.0
Uganda Ouganda	12.2	17.8	24.7	24.7	24.7	23.9	23.9	29.8	30.7	30.7
Ukraine Ukraine	...	7.8	7.8	5.3	5.3	5.3	5.3	8.7	8.2	8.2
United Arab Emirates Emirats arabes unis	0.0	0.0	0.0	0.0	0.0	0.0	0.0	22.5	22.5	22.5
United Kingdom Royaume-Uni	6.3	18.4	17.9	17.9	17.9	18.1	19.7	19.7	19.5	19.5
United Rep. of Tanzania Rép.-Unie de Tanzanie	...	...	22.3	22.3	21.4	21.4	30.4	30.4	30.4	30.4
United States Etats-Unis	6.6	14.0	14.0	14.3	14.3	14.9	15.2	16.3	16.8	17.0
Uruguay Uruguay	6.1	12.1	12.1	12.1	12.1	12.1	11.1	11.1	12.1	12.1
Uzbekistan Ouzbékistan	...	7.2	7.2	7.2	7.2	17.5	17.5	17.5	17.5	17.5
Vanuatu Vanuatu	4.3	0.0	0.0	1.9	1.9	3.8	3.8	3.8	3.8	3.8
Venezuela (Bolivarian Rep. of) Venezuela (Rép. bolivarienne du)	10.0	9.7	9.7	9.7	9.7	9.7	17.4	18.0	18.6	18.6
Viet Nam Viet Nam	17.7	26.0	26.0	27.3	27.3	27.3	27.3	27.3	25.8	25.8
Yemen Yémen	4.1	0.7	0.7	0.7	0.3	0.3	0.3	0.3	0.3	0.3
Zambia Zambie	6.6	10.1	12.0	12.0	12.0	12.0	12.7	14.6	15.2	15.2
Zimbabwe Zimbabwe	11.0	9.3	10.0	10.0	10.0	10.0	16.0	16.7	16.0	15.2

Source:
International Parliamentary Union (IPU), Geneva, *Women in National Parliaments*, as of 31 January 2009.

Source:
Union interparlementaire, Genève, *Les femmes dans les parlements*, données disponibles en 31 janvier 2009.

10

Proportion of seats held by women in national parliament *(continued)*
Percentage, as of 31 January 2009

Proportion de sièges occupés par des femmes au parlement national *(suite)*
Pourcentage, données disponibles en 31 janvier 2009

1. In 2004, the number of seats in parliament was raised from 300 to 345, with the addition of 45 reserved seats for women. These reserved seats were filled in September and October 2005, being allocated to political parties in proportion to their share of the national vote received in the 2001 election.
2. This figure excludes the 45 reserved seats for women which were not yet filled in January 2009.
3. Data refers to the composition of the Legislative and Oversight Commission which assumed legislative and oversight functions in October 2008. The Commission is to be replaced by a new 124-member National Assembly, as provided for in the new Constitution of 2008, when elections are held in 2009.
4. Parliament has been dissolved or suspended for an indefinite period.
5. The parliament was dissolved following the December 2008 coup.
6. Situation for 1 January 2008 for directly elected members endorsed by the electoral commission. The additional twelve appointed seats and two ex-officio seats had yet to be filled.
7. In June 2005, a woman was appointed Minister for the first time in the country's history. As Cabinet Ministers also sit in Parliament, there was therefore one woman in Parliament.
8. No woman candidate was elected in the 2006 elections. One woman was appointed to the 16-member cabinet. As cabinet ministers also sit in parliament, there is therefore one woman out of a total of 65 members.
9. No woman candidate was elected in the 2006 elections. One woman was appointed to the 16-member cabinet sworn in July 2006. A new cabinet sworn in March 2007 included two women. As cabinet ministers also sit in parliament, there are two women out of a total of 65.
10. No woman candidate was elected in the 2008 elections. Two women were appointed to the 16-member cabinet sworn in June 2008. As cabinet ministers also sit in parliament, there are two women out of a total of 65 members.
11. The parliament (elected in the parliamentary elections in 1999) was dissolved on 22 May 2002. Women held 12 of the 205 (5.9%) seats in the outgoing parliament.
12. After the promulgation of the interim constitution in January 2007, the House of Representatives dissolved itself in favour of a 330-member interim legislature, called the Legislative Parliament. This interim legislature comprises all members of the previous parliament and other appointed members. It was replaced by an elected unicameral Constituent Assembly in April 2008.
13. No woman was elected in the 2006 elections. However one woman was appointed Speaker of the House and therefore became a member of the House.
14. Based on a peace agreement signed in Djibouti in November 2008, the statutory number of the Transitional Federal Parliament (TFP) increased from 275 to 550 members. On 28 January 2009, 200 of the 275 new TFP members were sworn in, bringing the total number of members to 475. However, the final composition, including the number of women members, is not yet available.
15. No women were elected in 2008, however one woman was appointed to the Cabinet. As cabinet ministers also sit in parliament, there is one woman out of a total of 32 members.

1. En 2004, le nombre de sièges parlementaires est passé de 300 à 345, les nouveaux sièges étant réservés aux femmes. Les sièges réservés ont été pourvus en septembre et en octobre 2005, au prorata des voix obtenues par les partis politiques lors des élections nationales de 2001.
2. Ce chiffre exclut les 45 sièges réservés aux femmes toujours vacants en janvier 2009.
3. Les données se réfèrent à la composition de la Commission législative et de contrôle en charge d'assurer les principales fonctions de la branche législative depuis octobre 2008. Après les élections qui seront tenues en 2009, la Commission législative et de contrôle sera remplacée par une nouvelle Assemblée nationale composée de 124 membres comme le prévoyait la nouvelle Constitution de 2008.
4. Le Parlement a été dissous ou suspendu pour une durée indéterminée.
5. L'Assemblée nationale a été dissoute après le coup d'État de décembre 2008.
6. Au 1er janvier 2008, la situation des membres directement élus et approuvés par la commission électorale est la suivante: les sièges des 12 membres nommés et 2 des membres de droits restent vacants.
7. En juin 2005, pour la première fois de son histoire, une femme fut nommée ministre. Comme les ministres du gouvernement siègent de droit au Parlement, il y avait donc une femme au Parlement.
8. Aucune femme n'a été élue en 2006. Une femme a été nommée parmi les 16 membres du gouvernement. Les ministres siégeant également au Parlement, le Parlement compte donc une femme sur un total de 65 membres.
9. Aucune femme n'a été élue en 2006. Une femme a été nommée parmi les 16 membres du gouvernement qui ont prêté serment en juillet 2006. Un nouveau gouvernement dont les membres ont prêté serment en mars 2007 inclut deux femmes. Les ministres siégeant également au Parlement, le Parlement compte donc deux femmes sur un total de 65 membres.
10. Aucune femme n'a été élue en 2008. Deux femmes ont été nommées parmi les 16 membres du gouvernement qui ont prêté serment en juin 2008. Les ministres siégeant également au Parlement, le Parlement compte donc deux femmes sur un total de 65 membres.
11. Le parlement élu aux élections de 1999 a été dissous le 22 mai 2002. Les femmes y occupaient 12 des 205 sièges, soit 5.9%.
12. Après la promulgation de la constitution provisoire en janvier 2007, la Chambre des représentants a prononcé sa dissolution au profit d'une législature provisoire de 330 membres, baptisée Parlement législatif. Cet organe provisoire se compose de tous les membres du parlement précédent, ainsi que de membres nommés. Il a été remplacé en avril 2008 par une Assemblée constituante monocamérale.
13. Aucune femme n'a été élue en 2006. Une femme a cependant été nommée à la présidence de la chambre des députés et est donc devenue membre de cette dernière.
14. Suite à un accord de paix signé à Djibouti en novembre 2008, le nombre réglementaire de membres du Parlement transitoire fédéral (PTF) a été porté de 275 à 550. Le 28 janvier 2009, 200 des 275 nouveaux membres du PTF ont prêté serment, ce qui ramène le nombre total de membres à 475. Cependant, la composition finale ainsi que le nombre de femmes y siégeant n'est pas encore disponible.
15. Aucune femme n'a été élue en 2008. Cependant, une femme a été nommée au Gouvernement. Les ministres siégeant également au Parlement, le Parlement compte donc une femme sur un total de 32 membres.

Share of women in wage employment in the non-agricultural sector
Percentage of total employment

Proportion de femmes salariées dans le secteur non agricole
Pourcentage d'emploi total

Country or area Pays ou zone	Source[&] Source[&]	1990	2000	2001	2002	2003	2004	2005	2006	2007
Afghanistan *[1,2] Afghanistan *[1,2]		17.8	...	...	...	...	...	...	...	...
Albania[3] Albanie[3]	D	...	28.9	26.9	31.6	33.0	...	...	...	...
Algeria[3] Algérie[3]	BA	...	...	13.4	...	14.2	14.5	...	...	...
American Samoa[3] Samoa américaines[3]	A	41.7	...	...	...	...	...	...	...	...
Andorra Andorre	FA	...	...	...	...	45.6	45.7	45.8	46.1	46.6
Anguilla Anguilla	BA	...	...	47.7[3]	*48.8[4]	...	...	...	...	...
Antigua and Barbuda[5] Antigua-et-Barbuda[5]	A	...	...	50.6	...	...	...	...	...	...
Argentina Argentine	BA	37.1	42.6	43.3	45.9	45.5	44.8	45.1	45.0	...
Armenia Arménie	E	...	*47.3[4]	*47.8[4]	49.6[5]	49.7[5]	47.9[5]	45.4[5]	45.7[5]	*45.7[4]
Australia Australie		*44.6[6]	48.1[7]	48.6[7]	48.6[7]	48.9[7]	48.6[7]	48.9[7]	48.9[7]	46.8[7]
Austria Autriche		*41.0[3,8]	*43.7[3,8]	44.2[7]	44.9[7]	45.5[7]	46.2[7]	46.6[7]	46.6[7]	46.3[7]
Azerbaijan[5] Azerbaïdjan[5]	E	...	43.6	45.4	48.4	48.5	48.8	49.1	50.2	50.1
Bahamas[5] Bahamas[5]	BA	...	...	49.8	49.7	50.1	50.4	50.0	49.7	48.0
Bahrain Bahreïn	FA	7.6	12.4	13.2	12.7	12.8	11.5	11.0	10.3	9.8
Bangladesh[3] Bangladesh[3]	BA	...	24.7	...	...	21.6	...	...	20.1	...
Barbados Barbade	BA	*46.8[5]	49.9[3]	50.1[3]	50.0[3]	51.1[3]	51.3[3]	48.7[3]	...	...
Belarus Bélarus	D	*55.4[4]	55.9	56.0	*56.2[4]	*56.3[4]	*56.2[4]	*56.1[4]	*56.0[4]	*56.0[4]
Belgium Belgique		...	43.3[7]	43.4[7]	43.9[7]	44.4[7]	44.8[7]	45.3[7]	45.7[7]	*46.1[9]
Belize *[4] Belize *[4]	BA	...	...	35.0	34.0	...	...	37.6	...	...
Benin[3] Bénin[3]	A	...	...	...	24.3	...	...	...	...	...
Bermuda Bermudes	CA	48.7	49.8	49.3	49.4	48.9	48.7	48.6	48.5	...
Bhutan Bhoutan	A	...	...	...	...	...	...	16.6	...	...
Bolivia *[3] Bolivie *[3]	BA	35.2	38.6	...	...	...	...	...	...	...
Bosnia and Herzegovina[3] Bosnie-Herzégovine[3]	BA	...	...	...	...	...	...	...	35.2	34.7
Botswana Botswana		33.5[6]	*39.4[4,7]	41.1[6]	42.4[6]	40.8[6]	39.5[6]	...	*42.4[4,7]	...
Brazil Brésil		*35.1[7]	40.3[10]	40.7[10]	41.0[10]	*41.4[7]	*41.6[7]	...	...	...

11

Share of women in wage employment in the non-agricultural sector *(continued)*
Percentage of total employment
Proportion de femmes salariées dans le secteur non agricole *(suite)*
Pourcentage d'emploi total

Country or area Pays ou zone	Source[&] Source[&]	1990	2000	2001	2002	2003	2004	2005	2006	2007
British Virgin Islands [4] Iles Vierges britanniques [4]	E	...	49.8	49.9	50.2	50.4	49.3	49.1	...	...
Brunei Darussalam Brunéi Darussalam	CA	...	30.3	28.9	29.0	30.3	...	...	...	...
Bulgaria Bulgarie	D	...	52.8	53.1	53.1	53.1	52.7	52.2	51.4	*51.6[4]
Burkina Faso [4] Burkina Faso [4]	E	12.5	...	...	...	...	...	...	...	...
Burundi [3] Burundi [3]	A	14.3	...	...	...	...	...	...	...	...
Cambodia Cambodge	BA	...	41.1[3]	43.3[3]	...	...	*43.5[4]	...	...	...
Cameroon Cameroun		...	...	22.2	...	...	...	...	...	...
Canada Canada	BA	46.9	48.3	48.8	48.8	49.2	49.4	49.4	49.5	49.8
Cape Verde [3] Cap-Vert [3]	E	38.9	...	...	...	...	...	...	...	...
Cayman Islands Iles Caïmanes	BA	...	...	...	*51.8[4]	*54.2[4]	*52.2[4]	*49.5[4]	49.4[3]	49.3[3]
Central African Rep. [4] Rép. centrafricaine [4]	A	...	...	...	...	46.8	...	...	...	...
Chad Tchad	D	3.8	...	...	...	...	...	...	...	...
Chile Chili	BA	*34.7[5]	35.7[3]	35.4[3]	35.5[3]	36.4[3]	36.8[3]	37.2[3]	36.9[3]	37.4[3]
China Chine	D	37.8	...	...	...	...	...	...	...	...
China, Hong Kong SAR Chine, Hong Kong RAS		41.2	44.8[7]	45.5[7]	45.9[7]	46.8[7]	47.3[7]	47.8[7]	47.9[7]	48.3[7]
China, Macao SAR Chine, Macao RAS	D	42.7	48.9	48.8	50.0	49.0	49.4	49.5	48.1	48.1
Colombia Colombie	BA	41.8	48.8	49.1	*48.7[3]	48.8	48.3	48.5	47.6	48.5
Congo [1,2] Congo [1,2]		26.1	...	...	...	...	...	...	...	...
Cook Islands Iles Cook	D	38.4	...	...	...	...	...	...	...	...
Costa Rica Costa Rica	BA	37.2	39.3	40.1	*39.9[4]	39.5	38.5	39.6	40.7	41.1
Croatia Croatie	D	44.2	47.2	47.1	46.6	46.3	46.2	46.4	46.3	46.3
Cuba Cuba	BA	...	43.3	42.8	42.3	42.8	42.6	42.6	42.7	43.7
Cyprus Chypre	BA	...	44.4	47.4	48.2	49.3	48.2	47.7	48.1	49.1
Czech Republic République tchèque	BA	51.0	46.5	46.6	46.7	46.8	47.1	46.6	46.4	46.3
Denmark Danemark	BA	*48.1[4]	48.5	48.9	49.0	48.3	48.8	48.8	48.8	49.0
Djibouti [4,11] Djibouti [4,11]		...	...	...	26.7	...	...	...	...	...
Dominica [3] Dominique [3]	A	...	...	43.8	...	...	...	...	...	...
Dominican Republic Rép. dominicaine		...	*37.3[3,9]	*36.9[3,9]	*38.2[3,9]	*39.0[3,9]	38.0[7]	37.7[7]	39.3[7]	38.8[7]

Share of women in wage employment in the non-agricultural sector *(continued)*
Percentage of total employment
Proportion de femmes salariées dans le secteur non agricole *(suite)*
Pourcentage d'emploi total

Country or area Pays ou zone	Source& Source&	1990	2000	2001	2002	2003	2004	2005	2006	2007
Ecuador Equateur	BA	*34.1[4]	37.3[3]	36.8[3]	36.2[3]	*37.1[4]	36.6[3]	38.0[3]	36.6[3]	...
Egypt Egypte	BA	20.5	19.0	20.7	22.4	19.9	18.8	17.7	18.1	...
El Salvador El Salvador	BA	*45.6[5]	49.1	48.3	49.5	47.9	47.8	48.5	48.6	...
Equatorial Guinea [1,2] Guinée équatoriale [1,2]		10.5	...							
Estonia Estonie	BA	52.3	51.7	51.7	51.5	51.5	52.2	52.6	52.5	52.3
Ethiopia Ethiopie	BA	...	...			...	40.6	*43.8[4]	*47.3[4]	...
Faeroe Islands [5] Iles Féroé [5]	BA	...						45.8		
Fiji Fidji		29.9[12]	33.2[12]	...	...	*29.6[3,7]	...	...	...	...
Finland Finlande	BA	50.6	50.3	50.2	50.7	50.6	50.7	50.9	51.0	51.0
France France		43.9[9]	46.5[9]	46.6[9]	47.0[9]	47.3[9]	47.5[9]	*47.8[7]	*48.1[7]	*48.5[7]
French Guiana Guyane française	E	36.1	...	...	...	...	...	...	...	...
French Polynesia [3] Polynésie française [3]	FA	...	42.4	41.8	42.5	42.2	42.7	42.5	42.8	42.7
Gambia [1,2] Gambie [1,2]		20.9	...	...		...	...		...	...
Georgia Géorgie	BA	...	...	...	49.6	48.9	50.4	48.6	*49.3[5]	*48.7[5]
Germany Allemagne	BA	...	45.1	45.5	45.9	46.4	46.6	46.6	46.9	46.9
Ghana [3] Ghana [3]	A	...	31.7	...	...	...	...	...	...	...
Gibraltar Gibraltar	BA	34.5	39.7	39.9	40.2	41.6	41.5	41.9	41.5	41.0
Greece Grèce		35.3	39.1[4,9]	39.6[4,9]	39.8[4,9]	40.1[4,9]	40.9[4,9]	41.0[4,9]	41.6	42.0
Greenland Groenland		...	48.8	49.6	49.1	49.4	49.5	49.3	...	...
Guadeloupe Guadeloupe	D	...	...	...	45.7	...	...	...	...	...
Guam Guam		...	45.3[4,7]	47.0	45.7[4,7]	43.6[4,7]	43.0[4,7]	44.6	44.7[4,7]	44.2
Guatemala Guatemala		36.8	*40.0	...	*40.3	*42.0	*39.4	...	*43.0	...
Guinea-Bissau Guinée-Bissau		10.8	...	...	...	...	...	...	...	...
Guyana * Guyana *		...	...	...	34.7	...	...	...	...	...
Haiti [5] Haïti [5]	BA	44.2	...	...	...	...	...	...	...	...
Honduras Honduras	D	*33.3	...	37.6	...	...	34.1	33.4	...	...
Hungary Hongrie	BA	...	48.6	48.6	48.4	49.1	48.9	48.7	48.3	48.0
Iceland Islande		...	52.2[6]	52.3[6]	53.0[6]	52.5[6]	51.8[6]	52.2[6]	50.9	50.0

Share of women in wage employment in the non-agricultural sector *(continued)*
Percentage of total employment

Proportion de femmes salariées dans le secteur non agricole *(suite)*
Pourcentage d'emploi total

Country or area Pays ou zone	Source& Source&	1990	2000	2001	2002	2003	2004	2005	2006	2007
India Inde	BA	12.7	16.6	16.8	17.3	17.6[3]	17.9[3]	18.1[3]	...	...
Indonesia Indonésie		29.2[9]	31.7[9]	30.7[9]	29.7[9]	*29.5[9]	*29.1[9]	*29.9[9]	*30.5	*30.6
Iran (Islamic Rep. of) Iran (Rép. islamique d')		10.5	13.6	11.6	12.0	12.1[4,7]	13.0	16.1	...	...
Iraq Iraq	BA	...	...	...	...	21.3	...	...	...	...
Ireland Irlande		41.7	46.3	46.5[13]	47.6	47.4	47.5	47.7	47.7	48.2
Israel Israël	BA	43.0[5]	48.3	48.4	48.7	48.9	48.7	49.3	49.0	49.0
Italy Italie		*35.9[4,7]	39.8[3,7]	40.6[3,7]	40.9[3,7]	41.2[3,7]	42.7[3,7]	42.6[3,7]	42.8[3,7]	43.0
Jamaica Jamaïque	BA	*46.2	45.0	44.9	46.2	46.3	45.2	45.6	45.8	...
Japan Japon		38.0[7]	40.0[3,7]	40.4[3,7]	40.6[3,7]	40.8[3,7]	41.2[3,7]	41.3[3,7]	41.6	41.6
Jordan Jordanie		23.1	*23.4	*23.4[7]	*24.6[7]	*24.2[7]	*24.3[7]	*25.9	...	...
Kazakhstan Kazakhstan		...	...	48.4	48.1	48.7	49.4	...	...	...
Kenya Kenya		21.4	...	...	...	...	...	...	...	...
Kiribati Kiribati		...	36.8	...	...	...	...	38.5	...	...
Korea, Dem. P. R. Corée, R. p. dém. de	BA	40.7	...	...	...	...	...	...	...	...
Korea, Republic of Corée, République de		38.1	40.1	40.8	41.1	41.2	41.6	41.8	42.0	42.1
Kyrgyzstan Kirghizistan		...	45.8	45.6	44.9	47.3	49.4	51.9[4,13]	52.2	50.8
Lao People's Dem. Rep. Rép. dém. pop. lao	D	...	...	...	...	...	...	50.2	...	...
Latvia Lettonie		...	53.1	52.5	53.1	53.3	53.2	53.4	52.8	52.0
Liberia Libéria		...	...	...	11.4	...	...	...	...	...
Libyan Arab Jamah. [5] Jamah. arabe libyenne [5]	E	...	...	15.8	...	...	...	...	...	...
Liechtenstein Liechtenstein	D	...	38.7	38.7	39.1	38.9	39.1	39.4	...	...
Lithuania Lituanie		*55.4	53.2	52.7	52.6	53.2[7]	53.3[7]	53.0[7]	52.9[7]	52.9[7]
Luxembourg Luxembourg	BA	...	...	...	...	41.2	41.3	41.9	42.8	43.4
Madagascar Madagascar		...	*35.6	*36.2	...	*37.2	...	37.7	...	...
Malawi Malawi		10.5	...	...	...	...	...	...	...	...
Malaysia Malaisie		...	*37.9[3,13]	37.2	37.3	37.9	38.3	38.5	38.7[3,13]	39.0
Maldives Maldives		15.8	40.6	...	...	...	...	...	30.0	...
Mali Mali	BA	...	...	...	...	...	34.6	...	...	...

Share of women in wage employment in the non-agricultural sector *(continued)*
Percentage of total employment
Proportion de femmes salariées dans le secteur non agricole *(suite)*
Pourcentage d'emploi total

Country or area Pays ou zone	Source& Source&	1990	2000	2001	2002	2003	2004	2005	2006	2007
Malta Malte		...	32.7[3,7]	31.2	33.8	33.0	32.9	33.6	34.4	35.5
Marshall Islands Iles Marshall		...	29.3	...	...	...	...	...	...	...
Martinique Martinique		45.4	...	...	48.1	...	...	...	...	...
Mauritania Mauritanie	D	...	35.8							
Mauritius Maurice		36.7	38.6[7]	39.0[7]	38.1[7]	38.4[7]	37.5[7]	36.9[7]	37.2[7]	37.2[7]
Mexico Mexique	BA	...	37.3	37.2	37.5	36.8	37.5	39.1	39.3	39.4
Monaco [5] Monaco [5]	E	...	39.2	...	...	...	...	...	...	...
Mongolia Mongolie		...	50.4	50.7	51.7	51.1	53.1	53.1[3,7]	53.9	53.1
Montenegro Monténégro		...	...	...	...	...	...	43.4	...	...
Morocco Maroc		*28.7[1,2]	26.2	26.5	*26.3	*27.4	*28.3	*28.1	*28.2	28.4
Mozambique [5] Mozambique [5]	BA	11.4	...							...
Myanmar Myanmar		40.6	...	...	...	...	...	...	...	...
Namibia Namibie		...	42.8	*40.7	...	...	41.4	...	...	...
Netherlands Pays-Bas		37.7[4,9]	43.9[3,7]	44.3	45.0	45.7	45.7	46.2	46.7	47.3
Netherlands Antilles Antilles néerlandaises		*42.7	49.9	...	...	...	...	...	...	...
New Zealand Nouvelle-Zélande		43.8	47.3	47.2	47.1[3,7]	47.4[3,7]	47.5[3,7]	47.4[3,7]	51.3	48.5
Nicaragua Nicaragua		...	...	...	39.5	38.6	38.3	38.6	...	...
Niger Niger		11.0	...	...	...	...	...	...	...	...
Nigeria Nigéria		...	18.6	19.3[5,13]	20.1	20.8	21.0	21.1	...	...
Niue Nioué		...	...	43.1	...	...	...	...	...	...
Northern Mariana Islands [5] Iles Mariannes du Nord [5]	BA	44.0	...	...	...	...	...	...	...	...
Norway Norvège		*47.0	48.2[7]	48.3[7]	48.9[7]	49.1[7]	49.2[7]	49.0[7]	49.3[7]	49.2[7]
Occupied Palestinian Terr. Terr. palestinien occupé		...	13.5[6]	15.9[6]	17.0	16.8	17.9	16.1	17.1	17.0
Oman Oman	BA	18.7[5]	24.5[3]	25.3[3]	...	...	...	...	...	...
Pakistan Pakistan		*7.7	13.0[5,13]	13.0	13.6	13.6	13.9	13.9	13.4	13.2
Palau Palaos	BA	...	39.6	...	...	...	...	...	...	...
Panama Panama		...	43.0[13]	43.0	43.5	44.0	43.6	43.4	42.5	43.1
Papua New Guinea Papouasie-Nvl-Guinée	BA	*27.9	32.1[4]	...	...	...	...	...	...	...

Share of women in wage employment in the non-agricultural sector *(continued)*
Percentage of total employment
Proportion de femmes salariées dans le secteur non agricole *(suite)*
Pourcentage d'emploi total

Country or area Pays ou zone	Source[&] Source[&]	1990	2000	2001	2002	2003	2004	2005	2006	2007
Paraguay Paraguay		41.0	*39.3[4,7]	...	*37.7[7]	*38.9[7]	*40.0[7]	*40.1[7]	*38.7[7]	40.2[7]
Peru Pérou	BA	...	*41.3	*42.9	43.4	43.0	41.7	41.8	42.0	42.9
Philippines Philippines		*40.3	41.1[7]	41.9[7]	42.1[7]	41.2[7]	40.4[7]	41.9[7]	41.7[7]	42.3[7]
Poland Pologne	BA	...	46.9	47.0	47.5	47.7	47.2	46.7	46.6	46.7
Portugal Portugal		42.5[6]	45.7[6]	46.2[6]	46.4[6]	46.9[6]	47.4[3,7]	47.3[3,7]	47.3[3,7]	47.6[3,7]
Puerto Rico Porto Rico		46.5	39.6	41.3[7]	40.7	40.1	*39.9[5,13]	*40.5	*40.8	*41.5
Qatar Qatar		...	...	14.5	...	...	*15.5	...	...	...
Republic of Moldova République de Moldova		...	52.8[4,13]	52.6	53.6	54.6	54.6	54.9	53.5	54.6
Romania Roumanie		*41.9	45.5[7]	45.7[7]	45.2[7]	45.3[7]	46.5[7]	46.2[7]	46.6[7]	46.1[7]
Russian Federation Fédération de Russie		...	50.4[11]	50.4	50.6	51.0	50.9	50.9	51.2	51.0
Rwanda[3] Rwanda[3]	BA	...	33.0	...	...	...	...	...	...	...
Saint Helena *[5] Sainte-Hélène *[5]	A	...	24.0	...	...	...	...	...	...	...
Saint Lucia Sainte-Lucie		...	49.4[4,13]	...	*47.8	*45.9	*47.5	...	...	...
Samoa[4] Samoa[4]	E	...	30.2	...	...	...	...	...	...	...
San Marino Saint-Marin		40.4[3,13]	*41.3	41.5	41.7	41.9	42.2	42.1	42.1	38.1
Sao Tome and Principe Sao Tomé-et-Principe		32.1	...	...	...	...	...	...	...	...
Saudi Arabia Arabie saoudite		...	14.0	14.2[9]	14.0	...	...	...	*14.6	*14.8
Senegal Sénégal		...	...	10.6	...	...	...	...	...	...
Serbia Serbie		...	...	...	...	...	43.9	41.6	43.5	43.9
Sierra Leone[3] Sierra Leone[3]	BA	...	...	...	...	...	23.2	...	...	...
Singapore * Singapour *	D	...	...	43.7	43.3	43.6	44.1	...	44.9	45.2
Slovakia Slovaquie		48.6[6]	50.8[7]	51.9[7]	51.9[7]	52.1[7]	52.0[7]	51.4[7]	50.3[7]	50.3[7]
Slovenia Slovénie		*47.8	48.0	47.7	47.9	47.4	47.6	47.4	47.9	46.8
Somalia Somalie		21.7	...	...	...	...	...	...	...	...
South Africa Afrique du Sud	BA	...	43.0	43.9	42.5	43.5	42.6	43.3	43.2	43.9
Spain Espagne		32.3	38.9[3,7]	39.4[3,7]	40.0[3,7]	40.7[3,7]	41.5[3,7]	42.3[3,7]	43.0[3,7]	43.7[3,7]
Sri Lanka Sri Lanka		...	30.5	30.4	30.9	30.0	31.0	30.8	32.2	31.0
Sudan[5] Soudan[5]	BA	22.2	...	...	...	...	...	...	...	...

11

Share of women in wage employment in the non-agricultural sector *(continued)*
Percentage of total employment
Proportion de femmes salariées dans le secteur non agricole *(suite)*
Pourcentage d'emploi total

Country or area Pays ou zone	Source& Source&	1990	2000	2001	2002	2003	2004	2005	2006	2007
Suriname * Suriname *		39.5	...	...	...	...	38.1	...	...	...
Sweden Suède		50.5[5,9]	50.6[7]	50.7[7]	50.9[7]	50.9[7]	50.9[7]	50.5[7]	50.3[7]	50.1[7]
Switzerland Suisse		*43.4	45.7	46.3[3,7]	47.1[5,7]	46.9[5,7]	47.1	47.1	46.9	46.8
Syrian Arab Republic Rép. arabe syrienne	E	...	...	16.1	*15.9	*16.1	...	...	...	...
Tajikistan Tadjikistan		...	40.0	40.9[3,7]	41.6	41.1	39.8	39.4	37.1[7]	...
Thailand Thaïlande		41.9	44.1	44.3[9]	44.2	44.5	44.0	45.4	45.1	45.0
TFYR of Macedonia L'ex-R.Y. Macédoine		38.3	41.6[3,7]	41.9[3,7]	42.2	44.1[3,7]	43.2	42.6[7]	42.6	42.4
Timor-Leste Timor-Leste		...	...	35.0	...	...	...	...	...	...
Togo Togo		41.0	...	...	...	...	...	...	...	...
Tokelau Tokélaou		...	...	37.0	...	...	...	...	...	...
Tonga [3] Tonga [3]	BA	...	...	...	...	38.6	...	...	...	...
Trinidad and Tobago Trinité-et-Tobago		35.6	40.0[4,7]	39.9[4,7]	41.4[4,7]	*41.9[4,7]	*43.5	*43.9	...	...
Tunisia * Tunisie *	BA	...	24.3	24.6	24.9	25.0	...	...	...	...
Turkey Turquie		*16.7	19.1	19.0	20.6[9]	20.6	19.9	20.3	20.9	21.3
Turkmenistan [4] Turkménistan [4]	E	...	...	...	42.1	...	...	...	...	...
Turks and Caicos Islands Iles Turques et Caïques		...	...	43.1	40.4[8]	39.9[8]	40.9[8]	40.7	...	...
Tuvalu Tuvalu		...	...	...	34.3	39.1[5,7]	33.9	...	...	...
Uganda Ouganda	D	...	...	...	...	39.0	...	...	...	...
Ukraine Ukraine		...	52.9	...	54.4	54.4	55.1	54.9[13]	54.6	54.7
United Arab Emirates [3] Emirats arabes unis [3]	BA	...	...	...	...	...	...	13.9	...	...
United Kingdom Royaume-Uni	BA	47.8	*50.5	*50.7	*51.0	*52.4	*52.7	*52.4	*52.4	*52.2
United Rep. of Tanzania [3] Rép.-Unie de Tanzanie [3]	BA	...	...	*29.3	...	...	...	...	30.5	...
United States Etats-Unis		46.6[7]	47.4[7]	47.4[7]	47.5[7]	47.7[3,7]	47.5	47.3[3,7]	47.3[3,7]	47.4[3,7]
Uruguay Uruguay		42.3	46.4	46.5	45.8	*48.1	...	*48.8	*45.1	*45.5
Vanuatu Vanuatu		...	...	...	...	...	37.5[4,7]	37.9	38.3[5,7]	37.8[5,7]
Venezuela (Bolivarian Rep. of) Venezuela (Rép. bolivarienne du)		35.2	39.8[3,7]	41.1[3,7]	41.8[3,7]	42.4[3,7]	*41.8[3,7]	...	40.9	41.4
Viet Nam Viet Nam		...	40.7	40.7	40.8	40.1	40.4	...	...	...
Yemen [3] Yémen [3]	A	...	7.0	...	...	...	...	...	...	...

Share of women in wage employment in the non-agricultural sector *(continued)*
Percentage of total employment
Proportion de femmes salariées dans le secteur non agricole *(suite)*
Pourcentage d'emploi total

Country or area Pays ou zone	Source[&] Source[&]	1990	2000	2001	2002	2003	2004	2005	2006	2007
Zambia Zambie	D	16.6	22.0	...	...	...	...	...	...	...
Zimbabwe Zimbabwe		15.4	20.4	21.5	21.9	...	...	...	...	...

Source:
International Labour Organization (ILO), Geneva, the ILO labour statistics database, last accessed July 2009.

Source:
Bureau international du Travail (BIT), Genève, la base de données du BIT, dernier accès juillet 2009.

[&] Data sources:
  A: Population census.
  B: Household surveys.
  BA: Labour force surveys.
  CA: Labour-related establishment census.
  D: Labour-related establishment survey.
  E: Official estimates.
  FA: Insurance records.
  FD: Administration reports.

[&] Sources de données :
  A: Recensement de la population.
  B: Enquêtes auprès des ménages.
  BA: Enquêtes par sondage sur la main-d'œuvre.
  CA : Recensement concernant les employés mené auprès des entreprises.
  D : Enquête sur les employés menée auprès des entreprises.
  E: Evaluations officielles.
  FA: Fichiers des assurances.
  FD: Rapports administratifs.

1	Economically Active Population in non-agriculture.
2	ILO Economically Active Population Estimates and Projections: 1980-2020.
3	Total paid employment.
4	Total employment.
5	Total employment in non-agriculture.
6	Labour-related establishment survey.
7	Labour Force Survey.
8	Insurance Records.
9	Official Estimates.
10	Administrative reports.
11	MDG report - national estimates.
12	Labour-related establishment census.
13	Population census.

1   Population active dans le secteur non agricole.
2   BIT, estimations et projections de la population active : 1980-2020.
3   Emplois rémunérés (total).
4   Emploi total.
5   Population active totale dans le secteur non agricole.
6   Enquête sur les employés menée auprès des entreprises.
7   Enquête auprès des employés.
8   Données fournies par les assureurs.
9   Estimations officielles.
10 Rapports administratifs.
11 Rapport sur les objectifs du Millénaire pour le développement – estimations nationales.
12 Recensement concernant les employés mené auprès des entreprises.
13 Recensement de population.

Ratio of girls to boys in primary, secondary and tertiary education

Rapport filles/garçons dans l'enseignement primaire, secondaire et supérieur

Country or area	1991	2001	2002	2003	2004	2005	2006	2007	Pays ou zone
Afghanistan									**Afghanistan**
Primary education	0.55	...	0.46	0.57	0.44	0.59	0.64	0.63	Enseignement primaire
Secondary education	0.51	...	...	*0.35	0.21	0.33	0.37	0.38	Enseignement secondaire
Tertiary education	...	...	...	*0.28	0.28	...	...	...	Enseignement supérieur
Albania									**Albanie**
Primary education	1.01	1.00	0.97	0.98	0.99	...	...	...	Enseignement primaire
Secondary education	0.93	1.00	*0.93	0.98	0.96	...	...	...	Enseignement secondaire
Tertiary education	...	1.52	1.57	1.60	1.60	...	...	...	Enseignement supérieur
Algeria									**Algérie**
Primary education	0.85	0.92	0.93	0.93	0.93	0.93	0.93	0.94	Enseignement primaire
Secondary education	0.80	...	*1.05	1.07	1.07	*1.08	...	...	Enseignement secondaire
Tertiary education	...	...	...	...	1.08	1.28	1.26	1.40	Enseignement supérieur
Andorra									**Andorre**
Primary education	...	...	0.99	0.99	*0.98	0.95	1.00	0.98	Enseignement primaire
Secondary education	...	...	1.05	1.05	*1.03	1.12	1.04	1.08	Enseignement secondaire
Tertiary education	...	...	1.05	1.01	*1.00	1.06	1.25	...	Enseignement supérieur
Angola									**Angola**
Primary education	0.92	...	...	...	...	...	...	...	Enseignement primaire
Secondary education	...	0.78	*0.83	...	...	...	...	...	Enseignement secondaire
Tertiary education	...	...	0.66	...	...	...	...	...	Enseignement supérieur
Anguilla									**Anguilla**
Primary education	...	*0.98	0.98	*1.01	*1.03	*1.06	*0.99	...	Enseignement primaire
Secondary education *	...	1.00	1.01	0.99	1.00	0.97	1.02	...	Enseignement secondaire *
Tertiary education *	...	...	...	...	4.23	3.11	4.86	...	Enseignement supérieur *
Antigua and Barbuda									**Antigua-et-Barbuda**
Primary education	...	...	...	...	...	...	...	0.94	Enseignement primaire
Secondary education	...	...	...	...	...	...	...	0.96	Enseignement secondaire
Argentina									**Argentine**
Primary education	...	0.99	0.99	0.99	0.99	0.99	0.98	...	Enseignement primaire
Secondary education	...	1.03	1.03	1.07	1.10	1.11	1.12	...	Enseignement secondaire
Tertiary education	...	1.48	1.49	1.51	1.42	1.45	1.52	...	Enseignement supérieur
Armenia									**Arménie**
Primary education	...	*1.01	1.02	1.02	1.03	1.04	1.04	1.03	Enseignement primaire
Secondary education	...	*1.06	1.06	1.04	1.02	1.03	1.04	1.05	Enseignement secondaire
Tertiary education	...	1.14	1.11	1.12	1.21	1.22	1.18	1.20	Enseignement supérieur
Aruba									**Aruba**
Primary education	...	0.96	0.95	0.94	0.93	0.95	0.98	0.97	Enseignement primaire
Secondary education	...	1.07	1.08	1.09	1.04	1.05	1.04	1.06	Enseignement secondaire
Tertiary education	...	1.56	1.55	1.49	1.55	1.52	1.56	1.45	Enseignement supérieur
Australia									**Australie**
Primary education	0.99	1.00	1.00	1.00	1.00	1.00	1.00	1.00	Enseignement primaire
Secondary education	1.03	0.98	0.97	0.97	0.96	0.96	0.95	0.96	Enseignement secondaire
Tertiary education	1.19	1.23	1.22	1.23	1.24	1.25	1.28	1.29	Enseignement supérieur
Austria									**Autriche**
Primary education	1.00	0.99	0.99	0.99	1.00	1.00	0.99	0.99	Enseignement primaire
Secondary education	0.93	0.96	0.95	0.95	0.95	0.95	0.96	0.96	Enseignement secondaire
Tertiary education	0.88	1.14	1.18	1.19	1.20	1.21	1.21	1.20	Enseignement supérieur
Azerbaijan									**Azerbaïdjan**
Primary education	*0.99	0.98	0.99	0.97	0.98	0.98	0.97	0.99	Enseignement primaire
Secondary education	1.01	0.96	0.97	0.96	0.96	0.96	0.96	0.96	Enseignement secondaire
Tertiary education	0.67	0.71	0.81	0.83	0.88	0.91	0.94	0.88	Enseignement supérieur
Bahamas									**Bahamas**
Primary education	*1.03	*1.00	1.01	*1.01	*1.00	1.00	1.00	1.00	Enseignement primaire
Secondary education	...	*0.95	1.05	*1.02	*1.00	1.00	1.01	1.03	Enseignement secondaire
Bahrain									**Bahreïn**
Primary education	1.00	1.01	1.00	1.01	1.00	0.99	1.00	...	Enseignement primaire
Secondary education	1.04	1.10	1.09	1.07	1.05	1.05	1.04	...	Enseignement secondaire
Tertiary education	1.36	...	...	1.86	*1.95	2.41	2.46	...	Enseignement supérieur

12

Ratio of girls to boys in primary, secondary and tertiary education *(continued)*
Rapport filles/garçons dans l'enseignement primaire, secondaire et supérieur *(suite)*

Country or area	1991	2001	2002	2003	2004	2005	2006	2007	Pays ou zone
Bangladesh									**Bangladesh**
Primary education	...	...	...	...	...	1.05	1.06	1.08	Enseignement primaire
Secondary education	...	1.10	1.11	1.11	1.03	1.07	1.07	1.06	Enseignement secondaire
Tertiary education	...	0.54	0.50	0.50	0.49	0.53	0.57	0.57	Enseignement supérieur
Barbados									**Barbade**
Primary education	*1.00	0.99	1.00	0.99	0.98	1.00	0.98	1.00	Enseignement primaire
Secondary education	...	1.00	1.00	1.02	1.01	1.00	1.04	1.03	Enseignement secondaire
Tertiary education	...	2.46	...	...	...	...	...	2.18	Enseignement supérieur
Belarus									**Bélarus**
Primary education	*0.96	0.99	0.99	0.99	0.97	0.97	0.98	0.99	Enseignement primaire
Secondary education	...	1.04	1.04	1.03	1.02	1.02	1.02	1.02	Enseignement secondaire
Tertiary education	*1.11	1.32	1.36	1.37	1.38	1.36	1.37	1.41	Enseignement supérieur
Belgium									**Belgique**
Primary education	1.01	0.99	0.99	0.99	1.00	1.00	0.99	1.00	Enseignement primaire
Secondary education	1.01	1.11	1.12	1.10	0.97	0.97	0.97	0.97	Enseignement secondaire
Tertiary education	0.97	1.16	1.17	1.18	1.20	1.23	1.25	1.26	Enseignement supérieur
Belize									**Belize**
Primary education	0.96	0.97	*0.96	0.98	0.97	0.96	0.97	0.99	Enseignement primaire
Secondary education	1.09	1.06	*1.04	*1.05	1.04	*1.02	1.06	1.07	Enseignement secondaire
Tertiary education	...	...	...	1.91	2.43	...	...	...	Enseignement supérieur
Benin									**Bénin**
Primary education	0.51	0.71	0.73	0.74	0.77	0.80	0.83	...	Enseignement primaire
Secondary education	*0.42	*0.48	*0.48	0.47	0.48	*0.57	...	...	Enseignement secondaire
Tertiary education	0.15	*0.25	...	...	...	...	...	...	Enseignement supérieur
Bermuda									**Bermudes**
Primary education	...	0.99	1.02	1.00	1.06	1.03	0.85	...	Enseignement primaire
Secondary education	...	1.05	1.06	1.10	1.11	1.09	1.06	...	Enseignement secondaire
Tertiary education	...	1.18	*1.18	...	...	1.80	...	...	Enseignement supérieur
Bhutan									**Bhoutan**
Primary education	...	0.89	*0.92	...	...	0.97	0.98	...	Enseignement primaire
Secondary education	...	0.84	*0.83	...	...	0.88	0.91	...	Enseignement secondaire
Tertiary education	...	*0.53	...	...	...	...	0.59	0.51	Enseignement supérieur
Bolivia									**Bolivie**
Primary education	...	0.99	0.99	0.99	*1.00	...	1.00	1.00	Enseignement primaire
Secondary education	...	0.96	*0.97	0.97	...	...	0.96	0.97	Enseignement secondaire
Bosnia and Herzegovina									**Bosnie-Herzégovine**
Primary education	...	...	...	...	...	...	...	0.93	Enseignement primaire
Secondary education	...	...	...	...	...	...	...	1.03	Enseignement secondaire
Botswana									**Botswana**
Primary education	1.07	1.00	0.99	0.99	0.98	0.99	...	...	Enseignement primaire
Secondary education	1.18	1.05	1.06	1.07	*1.05	1.05	...	...	Enseignement secondaire
Tertiary education	0.73	0.90	0.82	...	0.87	1.00	...	...	Enseignement supérieur
Brazil									**Brésil**
Primary education	...	0.95	0.95	0.95	0.93	0.94	...	0.93	Enseignement primaire
Secondary education	...	1.10	1.10	1.11	1.10	1.10	...	1.11	Enseignement secondaire
Tertiary education	...	1.30	1.32	1.32	1.32	1.30	...	1.29	Enseignement supérieur
British Virgin Islands									**Iles Vierges britanniques**
Primary education	...	*1.00	0.98	0.94	0.96	0.96	0.97	*0.96	Enseignement primaire
Secondary education	...	1.06	1.02	1.16	1.06	1.18	1.13	*1.11	Enseignement secondaire
Tertiary education	...	1.80	2.34	*2.65	2.33	*2.28	...	...	Enseignement supérieur
Brunei Darussalam									**Brunéi Darussalam**
Primary education	0.94	0.99	1.00	1.01	1.00	1.00	0.99	0.99	Enseignement primaire
Secondary education	1.09	1.06	1.05	1.06	1.05	1.04	1.04	1.04	Enseignement secondaire
Tertiary education	...	1.74	1.74	1.85	1.97	2.02	1.99	1.88	Enseignement supérieur
Bulgaria									**Bulgarie**
Primary education	0.98	0.97	0.98	0.98	0.98	0.99	0.99	0.99	Enseignement primaire
Secondary education	1.00	0.98	0.98	0.97	0.96	0.96	0.96	0.96	Enseignement secondaire
Tertiary education	...	1.36	1.24	1.18	1.17	1.15	1.21	1.22	Enseignement supérieur
Burkina Faso									**Burkina Faso**
Primary education	0.64	0.73	0.74	0.75	0.79	0.80	0.82	0.84	Enseignement primaire
Secondary education	*0.54	0.66	*0.66	0.68	*0.69	0.71	0.72	0.73	Enseignement secondaire
Tertiary education	0.30	*0.35	0.35	0.30	*0.30	0.46	0.46	0.46	Enseignement supérieur

Country or area	1991	2001	2002	2003	2004	2005	2006	2007	Pays ou zone
Burundi									**Burundi**
Primary education	0.84	0.80	0.79	0.81	0.83	0.86	0.91	0.93	Enseignement primaire
Secondary education	0.58	...	...	0.77	0.75	*0.74	*0.74	0.72	Enseignement secondaire
Tertiary education	0.36	0.36	0.42	*0.46	0.38	*0.38	0.43	0.46	Enseignement supérieur
Cambodia									**Cambodge**
Primary education	*0.81	0.89	0.90	0.91	0.92	0.93	0.93	0.93	Enseignement primaire
Secondary education	*0.43	0.57	0.60	0.64	*0.69	...	0.79	0.82	Enseignement secondaire
Tertiary education	...	0.38	0.41	*0.41	0.46	0.47	0.50	0.56	Enseignement supérieur
Cameroon									**Cameroun**
Primary education	0.86	0.87	0.86	0.85	0.86	*0.84	0.84	0.86	Enseignement primaire
Secondary education	0.71	0.80	...	*0.84	0.79	0.79	0.79	0.79	Enseignement secondaire
Tertiary education	...	...	*0.64	*0.64	*0.64	0.66	0.72	0.79	Enseignement supérieur
Canada									**Canada**
Primary education	0.98	...	*1.00	...	*0.99	0.99	0.99	...	Enseignement primaire
Secondary education	1.00	...	*1.00	...	*0.97	0.98	0.98	...	Enseignement secondaire
Tertiary education	1.23	...	1.36	...	*1.36	...	...	...	Enseignement supérieur
Cape Verde									**Cap-Vert**
Primary education	*0.94	0.96	0.96	0.95	0.95	0.95	0.95	0.94	Enseignement primaire
Secondary education	...	*1.04	1.05	1.00	1.10	1.07	1.15	1.18	Enseignement secondaire
Tertiary education	...	1.01	1.01	1.10	1.10	1.04	1.09	1.21	Enseignement supérieur
Cayman Islands *									**Iles Caïmanes ***
Primary education	...	0.97	0.98	...	0.95	0.89	...	...	Enseignement primaire
Secondary education	...	1.01	1.09	...	1.10	0.92	...	...	Enseignement secondaire
Tertiary education	...	3.01	...	...	...	...	...	...	Enseignement supérieur
Central African Rep.									**Rép. centrafricaine**
Primary education	0.64	0.68	0.67	0.69	0.66	0.69	0.69	0.70	Enseignement primaire
Secondary education	0.40	...	...	...	...	...	...	...	Enseignement secondaire
Tertiary education	0.15	...	...	...	...	...	0.28	...	Enseignement supérieur
Chad									**Tchad**
Primary education	0.45	0.64	0.65	0.66	0.66	0.68	0.68	0.70	Enseignement primaire
Secondary education	*0.20	*0.28	0.33	*0.32	0.33	*0.33	0.36	0.45	Enseignement secondaire
Tertiary education	...	*0.18	...	0.11	0.14	*0.14	...	...	Enseignement supérieur
Chile									**Chili**
Primary education	0.98	...	0.98	0.97	0.95	0.96	0.95	0.95	Enseignement primaire
Secondary education	1.07	...	1.02	1.01	1.01	1.01	1.02	1.03	Enseignement secondaire
Tertiary education	...	...	0.93	0.94	0.95	0.96	1.00	1.01	Enseignement supérieur
China									**Chine**
Primary education	0.93	1.01	1.00	1.00	...	...	0.99	0.99	Enseignement primaire
Secondary education	0.75	*0.97	...	0.97	...	...	1.01	1.01	Enseignement secondaire
Tertiary education	*0.53	...	...	0.85	0.91	0.93	0.98	1.01	Enseignement supérieur
China, Hong Kong SAR									**Chine, Hong Kong RAS**
Primary education	*1.01	0.95	0.95	0.95	0.95	0.95	...	...	Enseignement primaire
Secondary education	*1.05	0.97	0.97	0.99	1.00	1.01	1.00	1.00	Enseignement secondaire
Tertiary education	...	...	...	0.96	1.02	1.04	1.03	1.03	Enseignement supérieur
China, Macao SAR									**Chine, Macao RAS**
Primary education	0.96	0.95	0.94	0.93	0.92	0.92	0.94	0.92	Enseignement primaire
Secondary education	1.11	1.04	1.04	1.04	1.02	1.01	1.00	1.00	Enseignement secondaire
Tertiary education	...	0.71	0.52	0.52	0.63	0.70	0.81	0.92	Enseignement supérieur
Colombia									**Colombie**
Primary education	1.02	0.99	0.99	*0.99	0.99	0.98	0.99	0.99	Enseignement primaire
Secondary education	1.19	1.10	1.11	*1.10	1.11	1.11	1.11	1.11	Enseignement secondaire
Tertiary education	1.07	1.10	1.08	*1.09	1.08	1.08	1.09	1.09	Enseignement supérieur
Comoros									**Comores**
Primary education	0.73	*0.83	0.82	0.82	0.88	*0.88	...	...	Enseignement primaire
Secondary education	0.65	...	0.84	0.83	0.76	*0.76	...	...	Enseignement secondaire
Tertiary education	...	...	...	0.77	*0.77	...	...	...	Enseignement supérieur
Congo									**Congo**
Primary education	0.90	0.93	0.94	0.93	0.93	0.92	0.90	0.93	Enseignement primaire
Secondary education	*0.72	...	*0.73	0.68	*0.85	...	...	...	Enseignement secondaire
Tertiary education	0.21	0.13	0.19	*0.19	...	...	...	...	Enseignement supérieur

Country or area	1991	2001	2002	2003	2004	2005	2006	2007	Pays ou zone
Cook Islands *									**Îles Cook ***
Primary education	...	0.95	0.97	0.98	0.98	1.01	...	0.97	Enseignement primaire
Secondary education	...	1.09	1.03	1.02	1.02	1.04	...	1.08	Enseignement secondaire
Costa Rica									**Costa Rica**
Primary education	0.99	1.00	0.98	*0.98	0.99	0.99	0.99	0.99	Enseignement primaire
Secondary education	1.06	1.08	1.08	*1.08	1.06	1.06	1.06	1.05	Enseignement secondaire
Tertiary education	...	1.17	1.16	*1.16	1.25	*1.26	...	...	Enseignement supérieur
Côte d'Ivoire									**Côte d'Ivoire**
Primary education	0.71	0.76	0.73	0.79	...	...	0.79	0.79	Enseignement primaire
Secondary education *	0.48	0.55	0.55	...	...	...	...	...	Enseignement secondaire *
Tertiary education	...	...	...	...	...	...	*0.49	0.50	Enseignement supérieur
Croatia									**Croatie**
Primary education	...	0.99	0.99	0.99	...	1.00	1.00	1.00	Enseignement primaire
Secondary education	...	1.02	1.02	1.02	...	1.03	1.03	1.03	Enseignement secondaire
Tertiary education	...	1.15	1.15	1.19	...	1.22	1.23	1.23	Enseignement supérieur
Cuba									**Cuba**
Primary education	0.97	0.96	0.96	0.96	0.96	0.97	0.97	0.98	Enseignement primaire
Secondary education	1.15	1.06	0.99	0.98	1.02	1.01	1.02	1.00	Enseignement secondaire
Tertiary education	1.40	1.16	1.27	1.37	*1.76	1.74	1.65	1.85	Enseignement supérieur
Cyprus									**Chypre**
Primary education	1.00	1.00	1.00	1.00	1.00	1.00	1.00	0.99	Enseignement primaire
Secondary education	1.02	1.01	1.02	1.02	1.03	1.02	1.02	1.02	Enseignement secondaire
Tertiary education	1.11	1.37	1.26	1.03	0.98	1.13	1.05	0.99	Enseignement supérieur
Czech Republic									**République tchèque**
Primary education	1.00	0.99	0.99	0.98	0.99	0.99	0.99	0.99	Enseignement primaire
Secondary education	0.97	1.03	1.03	1.03	1.01	1.02	1.01	1.01	Enseignement secondaire
Tertiary education	0.81	1.05	1.10	1.07	1.10	1.16	1.22	1.26	Enseignement supérieur
Dem. Rep. of the Congo									**Rép. dém. du Congo**
Primary education	0.75	...	0.78	...	...	...	...	0.81	Enseignement primaire
Secondary education	...	...	0.58	...	...	...	...	0.53	Enseignement secondaire
Tertiary education	...	...	...	...	...	...	...	0.35	Enseignement supérieur
Denmark									**Danemark**
Primary education	1.00	1.00	1.00	*1.00	1.00	1.00	1.00	1.00	Enseignement primaire
Secondary education	1.01	1.05	1.05	1.05	1.04	1.03	1.03	1.03	Enseignement secondaire
Tertiary education	1.14	1.34	1.39	1.42	1.41	1.39	1.39	1.41	Enseignement supérieur
Djibouti									**Djibouti**
Primary education	0.72	0.76	0.76	*0.78	0.79	0.82	0.81	0.86	Enseignement primaire
Secondary education	*0.66	0.62	0.62	*0.66	0.69	0.66	0.67	0.69	Enseignement secondaire
Tertiary education	...	0.73	0.81	0.70	0.82	0.73	0.68	0.69	Enseignement supérieur
Dominica									**Dominique**
Primary education	...	0.91	0.97	0.99	0.99	1.02	1.02	...	Enseignement primaire
Secondary education	...	1.06	1.06	1.04	0.99	1.00	0.98	...	Enseignement secondaire
Dominican Republic									**Rép. dominicaine**
Primary education	...	*1.01	1.01	*1.01	0.95	0.95	0.95	0.94	Enseignement primaire
Secondary education	...	*1.21	1.21	*1.21	1.21	1.19	1.20	1.20	Enseignement secondaire
Tertiary education	...	...	...	1.59	*1.59	...	...	...	Enseignement supérieur
Ecuador									**Equateur**
Primary education	*0.99	1.00	1.00	1.00	1.00	1.00	1.00	1.00	Enseignement primaire
Secondary education	...	1.02	1.01	1.02	1.00	1.01	1.02	1.01	Enseignement secondaire
Tertiary education	...	...	...	...	...	...	...	1.22	Enseignement supérieur
Egypt									**Egypte**
Primary education	0.83	*0.93	*0.94	*0.95	*0.96	0.94	0.94	0.95	Enseignement primaire
Secondary education	0.79	*0.93	*0.93	*0.93	*0.94	...	...	...	Enseignement secondaire
Tertiary education *	0.54	...	...	...	...	...	...	...	Enseignement supérieur *
El Salvador									**El Salvador**
Primary education	0.99	0.96	0.95	0.96	0.97	0.96	0.96	1.00	Enseignement primaire
Secondary education	1.13	1.01	1.01	1.02	1.02	1.02	1.04	1.04	Enseignement secondaire
Tertiary education	...	1.20	1.20	1.18	1.27	1.22	1.21	1.22	Enseignement supérieur
Equatorial Guinea									**Guinée équatoriale**
Primary education	*0.96	0.96	0.91	0.97	...	0.95	...	0.95	Enseignement primaire
Secondary education *	...	...	0.57	...	...	...	...	...	Enseignement secondaire *
Tertiary education	0.14	...	...	...	...	...	...	...	Enseignement supérieur

Country or area	1991	2001	2002	2003	2004	2005	2006	2007	Pays ou zone
Eritrea									**Erythrée**
Primary education	0.95	0.82	0.80	0.80	0.80	0.80	0.81	0.83	Enseignement primaire
Secondary education	...	0.70	0.64	0.64	0.56	0.59	0.60	0.70	Enseignement secondaire
Tertiary education	...	0.16	0.15	*0.15	0.15	...	...	...	Enseignement supérieur
Estonia									**Estonie**
Primary education	0.97	0.96	0.96	0.96	0.97	0.97	0.98	0.99	Enseignement primaire
Secondary education	*1.09	1.03	1.02	1.04	1.02	1.01	1.02	1.02	Enseignement secondaire
Tertiary education	*1.04	1.55	1.65	1.66	1.68	1.66	1.67	1.63	Enseignement supérieur
Ethiopia									**Ethiopie**
Primary education	0.66	0.69	0.71	0.73	0.77	0.83	0.86	0.88	Enseignement primaire
Secondary education	0.75	0.66	0.62	0.57	0.57	0.60	0.63	0.67	Enseignement secondaire
Tertiary education	0.22	0.27	0.36	0.34	0.34	0.32	0.32	0.34	Enseignement supérieur
Fiji									**Fidji**
Primary education	1.00	0.99	1.01	0.99	0.98	*0.98	0.98	0.97	Enseignement primaire
Secondary education	0.95	1.08	1.08	1.08	1.07	*1.07	1.10	1.12	Enseignement secondaire
Tertiary education	...	...	...	*1.20	1.20	*1.20	...	...	Enseignement supérieur
Finland									**Finlande**
Primary education	0.99	0.99	0.99	0.99	0.99	0.99	1.00	1.00	Enseignement primaire
Secondary education	1.19	1.11	1.12	1.11	1.05	1.04	1.04	1.05	Enseignement secondaire
Tertiary education	1.13	1.22	1.23	1.20	1.20	1.21	1.22	1.23	Enseignement supérieur
France									**France**
Primary education	0.99	0.99	0.99	0.99	0.99	0.99	0.99	0.99	Enseignement primaire
Secondary education	1.05	1.01	1.01	1.01	1.01	1.01	1.00	1.01	Enseignement secondaire
Tertiary education	1.17	1.23	1.27	1.27	1.27	1.27	1.27	1.27	Enseignement supérieur
Gabon									**Gabon**
Primary education	*0.98	1.00	0.99	0.99	*0.99	...	...	...	Enseignement primaire
Gambia									**Gambie**
Primary education	*0.70	0.92	0.92	0.99	1.04	1.06	1.05	1.05	Enseignement primaire
Secondary education	0.50	0.71	0.72	0.76	0.84	0.84	0.86	0.90	Enseignement secondaire
Tertiary education	...	...	...	...	0.24	...	...	...	Enseignement supérieur
Georgia									**Géorgie**
Primary education	1.00	1.03	1.04	1.02	1.00	1.00	1.03	0.97	Enseignement primaire
Secondary education	0.97	1.00	0.99	0.99	1.00	0.99	*1.04	*1.00	Enseignement secondaire
Tertiary education	*1.18	0.95	0.98	0.95	1.03	1.04	1.13	1.12	Enseignement supérieur
Germany									**Allemagne**
Primary education	*1.01	0.99	0.99	1.00	1.00	1.00	1.00	1.00	Enseignement primaire
Secondary education	*0.97	0.99	0.99	0.98	0.98	0.98	0.97	0.98	Enseignement secondaire
Ghana									**Ghana**
Primary education	0.85	0.94	0.94	0.98	0.94	0.96	0.99	0.99	Enseignement primaire
Secondary education	*0.65	0.84	*0.85	*0.85	0.83	*0.85	0.85	*0.88	Enseignement secondaire
Tertiary education	0.30	0.41	0.40	0.48	0.48	0.56	0.53	0.54	Enseignement supérieur
Greece									**Grèce**
Primary education	0.99	1.00	0.99	0.99	0.99	0.99	1.00	1.00	Enseignement primaire
Secondary education	0.98	1.05	...	1.02	1.01	0.98	0.97	0.95	Enseignement secondaire
Tertiary education	0.99	1.15	1.15	1.14	1.17	1.14	1.13	1.10	Enseignement supérieur
Grenada									**Grenade**
Primary education	*0.85	0.93	*0.89	0.99	0.96	*0.96	...	0.96	Enseignement primaire
Secondary education	1.16	...	*1.05	0.99	1.09	1.03	...	0.99	Enseignement secondaire
Guatemala									**Guatemala**
Primary education	0.87	0.90	0.91	*0.91	0.92	0.92	0.93	0.94	Enseignement primaire
Secondary education	...	0.89	0.89	*0.89	0.90	0.91	0.92	0.92	Enseignement secondaire
Tertiary education	...	...	0.72	*0.72	...	...	0.82	1.00	Enseignement supérieur
Guinea									**Guinée**
Primary education	0.48	0.72	0.75	0.77	0.79	0.82	0.84	0.85	Enseignement primaire
Secondary education	0.34	*0.40	*0.42	*0.46	0.46	*0.51	0.53	*0.57	Enseignement secondaire
Tertiary education	0.07	...	...	*0.19	0.19	0.24	0.28	...	Enseignement supérieur
Guinea-Bissau *									**Guinée-Bissau ***
Primary education	0.55	0.67	...	...	...	...	...	...	Enseignement primaire
Secondary education	...	0.54	...	...	...	...	...	...	Enseignement secondaire
Tertiary education	...	0.18	...	...	...	...	...	...	Enseignement supérieur

Country or area	1991	2001	2002	2003	2004	2005	2006	2007	Pays ou zone
Guyana									**Guyana**
Primary education	0.99	0.98	*0.98	0.98	*0.97	0.99	0.99	0.98	Enseignement primaire
Secondary education	1.06	1.04	*1.03	...	*1.03	0.99	*0.98	0.93	Enseignement secondaire
Tertiary education	...	...	...	...	1.89	2.09	2.17	2.09	Enseignement supérieur
Haiti									**Haïti**
Primary education	0.95	...	...	...	...	...	...	...	Enseignement primaire
Secondary education	0.94	...	...	...	...	...	...	...	Enseignement secondaire
Honduras									**Honduras**
Primary education	1.04	*1.01	...	...	0.99	0.99	0.99	1.00	Enseignement primaire
Secondary education	1.23	...	...	...	...	...	...	1.25	Enseignement secondaire
Tertiary education	0.79	*1.26	*1.39	1.40	*1.41		...	...	Enseignement supérieur
Hungary									**Hongrie**
Primary education	0.99	0.98	0.99	0.99	0.99	0.98	0.98	0.98	Enseignement primaire
Secondary education	1.00	1.01	1.01	1.00	0.99	0.99	0.99	1.00	Enseignement secondaire
Tertiary education	...	1.27	1.29	1.37	1.40	1.46	1.47	1.46	Enseignement supérieur
Iceland									**Islande**
Primary education	*0.99	0.99	0.99	0.98	0.98	0.97	0.99	1.00	Enseignement primaire
Secondary education	0.96	1.06	1.06	1.06	1.03	1.02	1.03	1.06	Enseignement secondaire
Tertiary education	1.39	1.72	1.76	1.80	1.87	1.91	1.87	1.86	Enseignement supérieur
India									**Inde**
Primary education	0.77	0.85	0.87	0.97	*0.97	0.96	0.96	...	Enseignement primaire
Secondary education	*0.60	0.72	0.75	0.81	0.81	0.82	0.83	...	Enseignement secondaire
Tertiary education	0.54	0.69	0.70	0.68	0.72	0.71	0.72	...	Enseignement supérieur
Indonesia									**Indonésie**
Primary education	0.98	0.98	0.98	0.98	0.98	*0.97	0.96	0.96	Enseignement primaire
Secondary education	0.83	0.98	0.99	0.99	0.99	*0.99	1.00	1.01	Enseignement secondaire
Tertiary education	...	0.76	0.87	0.80	0.79	*0.79	...	1.00	Enseignement supérieur
Iran (Islamic Rep. of)									**Iran (Rép. islamique d')**
Primary education	0.90	0.96	0.96	0.97	1.10	1.22	1.27	1.29	Enseignement primaire
Secondary education	0.75	0.94	0.95	0.94	0.94	0.94	...	...	Enseignement secondaire
Tertiary education	*0.48	0.94	1.01	1.08	1.11	1.09	1.11	1.15	Enseignement supérieur
Iraq									**Iraq**
Primary education	0.83	*0.82	*0.83	0.83	0.83	*0.83	...	...	Enseignement primaire
Secondary education	*0.63	0.60	*0.60	0.71	0.66	*0.66	...	...	Enseignement secondaire
Tertiary education	...	...	*0.54	...	0.59	*0.59	...	...	Enseignement supérieur
Ireland									**Irlande**
Primary education	1.00	0.99	1.00	0.99	0.99	1.00	0.99	1.00	Enseignement primaire
Secondary education	1.09	1.08	1.09	1.09	1.08	1.09	1.07	1.07	Enseignement secondaire
Tertiary education	0.90	1.26	1.28	1.31	1.28	1.26	1.27	1.27	Enseignement supérieur
Israel									**Israël**
Primary education	1.04	1.00	1.00	1.00	1.01	1.01	1.02	1.01	Enseignement primaire
Secondary education	1.06	0.99	0.99	0.98	1.00	0.99	0.99	1.00	Enseignement secondaire
Tertiary education	...	1.39	1.38	1.33	1.33	1.34	1.29	1.32	Enseignement supérieur
Italy									**Italie**
Primary education	1.00	0.99	0.98	0.99	1.00	0.99	0.99	0.99	Enseignement primaire
Secondary education	1.00	0.97	0.96	*0.99	0.99	0.99	0.99	0.99	Enseignement secondaire
Tertiary education	0.94	1.32	1.34	1.34	1.34	1.36	1.38	1.40	Enseignement supérieur
Jamaica									**Jamaïque**
Primary education	*0.99	0.99	1.00	1.00	1.00	1.00	...	1.01	Enseignement primaire
Secondary education	*1.06	*1.03	1.03	1.02	1.02	1.03	...	1.05	Enseignement secondaire
Tertiary education	*0.74	*1.97	2.16	*2.29	...	...	...	...	Enseignement supérieur
Japan									**Japon**
Primary education	1.00	1.00	1.00	1.00	1.00	1.00	1.00	1.00	Enseignement primaire
Secondary education	1.02	1.01	1.01	1.00	1.00	1.00	1.00	1.00	Enseignement secondaire
Tertiary education	0.65	0.85	0.86	0.88	0.89	0.89	0.88	0.88	Enseignement supérieur
Jordan									**Jordanie**
Primary education	0.99	...	1.00	1.00	1.00	1.00	1.02	1.02	Enseignement primaire
Secondary education	1.04	...	1.02	1.02	1.01	1.02	1.03	1.03	Enseignement secondaire
Tertiary education	1.12	...	1.00	1.08	1.09	1.05	1.11	1.10	Enseignement supérieur

Country or area	1991	2001	2002	2003	2004	2005	2006	2007	Pays ou zone
Kazakhstan									**Kazakhstan**
Primary education	*0.99	1.00	1.00	1.00	1.00	1.00	1.00	1.00	Enseignement primaire
Secondary education	*1.03	0.98	0.99	1.01	0.99	0.98	0.98	0.99	Enseignement secondaire
Tertiary education	...	1.20	1.25	1.33	1.38	1.43	1.43	1.44	Enseignement supérieur
Kenya									**Kenya**
Primary education	0.97	...	0.95	0.95	0.94	0.96	0.97	0.99	Enseignement primaire
Secondary education	*0.85	...	0.96	1.02	*0.94	*0.95	0.93	0.88	Enseignement secondaire
Tertiary education	...	0.54	*0.54	...	*0.61	*0.61	...	0.57	Enseignement supérieur
Kiribati									**Kiribati**
Primary education	...	*1.01	*0.99	*0.98	*1.03	1.01	...	...	Enseignement primaire
Secondary education	...	*1.39	*1.17	*1.19	*1.18	1.14	...	...	Enseignement secondaire
Korea, Republic of									**Corée, République de**
Primary education	1.01	0.93	0.93	0.94	0.95	0.96	0.97	0.98	Enseignement primaire
Secondary education	0.97	1.00	0.99	0.98	0.96	0.95	0.94	0.93	Enseignement secondaire
Tertiary education	0.49	0.60	0.61	0.62	0.63	0.64	0.65	0.67	Enseignement supérieur
Kuwait									**Koweït**
Primary education	0.95	1.02	1.00	1.01	1.00	0.98	0.99	0.98	Enseignement primaire
Secondary education	*0.98	*1.05	*1.05	1.04	1.06	1.05	1.05	1.02	Enseignement secondaire
Tertiary education	...	*1.90	1.93	2.09	*2.14	2.87	2.32	...	Enseignement supérieur
Kyrgyzstan									**Kirghizistan**
Primary education	...	0.98	0.98	0.99	1.00	0.99	0.99	0.99	Enseignement primaire
Secondary education	1.02	1.00	1.00	1.01	1.01	1.01	1.01	1.01	Enseignement secondaire
Tertiary education	...	1.04	1.14	1.19	1.19	1.25	1.27	1.30	Enseignement supérieur
Lao People's Dem. Rep.									**Rép. dém. pop. lao**
Primary education	0.79	0.86	0.86	0.87	0.88	0.88	0.89	0.90	Enseignement primaire
Secondary education	0.62	0.72	0.73	0.74	0.75	0.76	0.78	0.79	Enseignement secondaire
Tertiary education	...	0.59	0.57	0.57	0.62	0.71	0.68	0.72	Enseignement supérieur
Latvia									**Lettonie**
Primary education	1.00	0.99	0.98	0.97	0.97	0.96	0.96	0.97	Enseignement primaire
Secondary education	1.02	1.02	1.01	1.00	0.99	1.00	1.00	*1.01	Enseignement secondaire
Tertiary education	1.28	1.65	1.64	1.66	1.71	1.79	1.80	1.85	Enseignement supérieur
Lebanon									**Liban**
Primary education	*0.97	0.96	0.96	0.96	0.96	0.97	0.97	0.97	Enseignement primaire
Secondary education	...	1.09	1.09	1.08	1.09	1.10	1.10	1.12	Enseignement secondaire
Tertiary education	...	1.05	1.10	1.16	1.09	1.13	1.16	1.20	Enseignement supérieur
Lesotho									**Lesotho**
Primary education	1.22	1.02	1.02	1.01	1.00	1.00	1.00	...	Enseignement primaire
Secondary education	1.42	1.27	1.28	1.27	1.27	1.26	1.27	...	Enseignement secondaire
Tertiary education	1.30	1.65	1.32	1.52	...	1.27	1.19	...	Enseignement supérieur
Liberia									**Libéria**
Primary education	...	...	...	...	...	...	0.90	...	Enseignement primaire
Libyan Arab Jamah.									**Jamah. arabe libyenne**
Primary education	...	1.01	1.00	0.96	0.96	0.98	0.95	...	Enseignement primaire
Secondary education	...	...	1.06	*1.06	...	*1.19	1.17	...	Enseignement secondaire
Tertiary education	...	*1.04	1.09	*1.10	...	...	...	...	Enseignement supérieur
Liechtenstein									**Liechtenstein**
Primary education	...	...	...	0.98	1.01	...	0.98	0.99	Enseignement primaire
Secondary education	...	...	...	0.88	0.87	...	0.88	0.87	Enseignement secondaire
Tertiary education	...	...	...	0.38	0.37	...	0.44	0.49	Enseignement supérieur
Lithuania									**Lituanie**
Primary education	*0.95	0.99	0.99	0.99	0.99	0.99	0.99	0.99	Enseignement primaire
Secondary education	...	0.99	0.99	0.98	0.99	1.00	1.00	1.00	Enseignement secondaire
Tertiary education	*1.28	1.52	1.57	1.55	1.55	1.56	1.56	1.57	Enseignement supérieur
Luxembourg									**Luxembourg**
Primary education	1.08	1.00	1.00	1.00	1.00	1.01	1.01	1.00	Enseignement primaire
Secondary education	...	1.06	1.06	1.05	1.05	1.06	1.04	1.04	Enseignement secondaire
Tertiary education	...	1.17	*1.16	1.19	*1.17	...	1.12	...	Enseignement supérieur
Madagascar									**Madagascar**
Primary education	0.98	0.96	0.96	0.96	0.96	0.96	0.96	0.97	Enseignement primaire
Secondary education	*0.97	...	...	...	...	*0.96	0.95	*0.95	Enseignement secondaire
Tertiary education	0.82	*0.84	*0.83	*0.83	0.90	0.89	0.87	0.89	Enseignement supérieur

12

Ratio of girls to boys in primary, secondary and tertiary education *(continued)*
Rapport filles/garçons dans l'enseignement primaire, secondaire et supérieur *(suite)*

Country or area	1991	2001	2002	2003	2004	2005	2006	2007	Pays ou zone
Malawi									**Malawi**
Primary education	0.84	0.97	0.97	...	1.03	1.03	1.04	1.04	Enseignement primaire
Secondary education	*0.46	0.77	*0.78	...	0.81	0.82	0.84	0.83	Enseignement secondaire
Tertiary education	0.34	*0.41	*0.41	*0.41	*0.55	*0.55	*0.51	0.51	Enseignement supérieur
Malaysia									**Malaisie**
Primary education	0.99	1.00	1.00	1.00	1.00	1.00	0.99	...	Enseignement primaire
Secondary education	1.05	1.08	1.09	1.12	1.12	1.10	...	...	Enseignement secondaire
Tertiary education	...	1.21	1.25	1.36	1.26	1.29	1.22	...	Enseignement supérieur
Maldives									**Maldives**
Primary education	...	1.00	0.99	0.98	0.97	0.98	0.97	0.97	Enseignement primaire
Secondary education	...	1.07	1.15	1.11	*1.14	...	*1.07	...	Enseignement secondaire
Tertiary education	...	...	...	2.37	*2.37	...	...	...	Enseignement supérieur
Mali									**Mali**
Primary education	0.59	0.72	0.74	0.75	0.76	0.77	0.79	0.80	Enseignement primaire
Secondary education	0.50	...	...	0.53	0.58	*0.60	0.60	0.64	Enseignement secondaire
Tertiary education	0.15	0.49	0.49	*0.51	0.52	*0.52	...	...	Enseignement supérieur
Malta									**Malte**
Primary education	0.96	1.00	0.99	0.99	0.99	0.98	...	...	Enseignement primaire
Secondary education	0.94	0.97	0.99	0.99	0.93	1.00	...	...	Enseignement secondaire
Tertiary education	0.83	1.29	1.40	1.40	1.33	1.35	...	...	Enseignement supérieur
Marshall Islands									**Iles Marshall**
Primary education	...	*0.95	*0.94	*0.94	*0.96	*0.96	...	0.97	Enseignement primaire
Secondary education	...	...	*1.04	*1.04	*1.05	*1.05	...	1.02	Enseignement secondaire
Tertiary education *	...	1.29	1.30	1.30	...	...	...	...	Enseignement supérieur *
Mauritania									**Mauritanie**
Primary education	0.77	0.98	1.01	1.02	1.03	1.06	1.05	1.06	Enseignement primaire
Secondary education	0.49	0.79	0.80	0.84	0.88	0.90	0.86	*0.89	Enseignement secondaire
Tertiary education	0.17	0.21	0.29	0.29	0.33	0.34	0.36	...	Enseignement supérieur
Mauritius									**Maurice**
Primary education	1.00	1.00	1.01	1.01	1.00	1.00	1.00	1.00	Enseignement primaire
Secondary education	*1.04	0.97	1.00	0.99	0.98	*0.99	...	...	Enseignement secondaire
Tertiary education	0.73	1.35	1.29	1.41	1.39	1.26	1.15	...	Enseignement supérieur
Mexico									**Mexique**
Primary education	0.97	0.98	0.98	0.98	0.98	0.97	0.97	0.97	Enseignement primaire
Secondary education	0.99	1.03	1.04	1.05	1.03	1.02	1.02	1.03	Enseignement secondaire
Tertiary education	*0.74	0.94	0.94	0.94	0.94	0.94	0.93	0.93	Enseignement supérieur
Micronesia (Fed. States of)									**Micronésie (Etats féd. de)**
Primary education	...	...	...	...	0.99	0.98	...	1.01	Enseignement primaire
Secondary education	...	...	...	...	1.05	1.07	...	...	Enseignement secondaire
Mongolia									**Mongolie**
Primary education	1.02	1.04	1.03	1.02	1.01	1.02	1.02	1.02	Enseignement primaire
Secondary education	1.14	1.22	1.20	1.16	1.13	1.13	1.12	1.11	Enseignement secondaire
Tertiary education	1.89	1.74	1.75	1.69	1.64	1.62	1.57	1.56	Enseignement supérieur
Montserrat									**Montserrat**
Primary education	...	...	0.96	*0.98	0.97	1.04	*1.00	1.12	Enseignement primaire
Secondary education	...	...	1.13	*1.13	1.10	1.10	*0.98	1.02	Enseignement secondaire
Morocco									**Maroc**
Primary education	0.69	0.87	0.89	0.90	0.90	0.89	0.89	0.90	Enseignement primaire
Secondary education	0.72	*0.80	*0.81	0.82	0.83	*0.84	...	*0.86	Enseignement secondaire
Tertiary education	0.58	0.77	*0.76	0.80	0.83	0.81	0.81	0.89	Enseignement supérieur
Mozambique									**Mozambique**
Primary education	0.74	0.77	0.79	...	0.83	0.84	0.86	0.87	Enseignement primaire
Secondary education	0.57	0.64	0.66	...	0.70	0.69	0.72	0.73	Enseignement secondaire
Tertiary education	...	...	...	0.47	0.46	0.49	...	...	Enseignement supérieur
Myanmar									**Myanmar**
Primary education	0.97	...	...	...	...	...	...	...	Enseignement primaire
Secondary education	0.99	...	...	...	...	...	...	...	Enseignement secondaire
Namibia									**Namibie**
Primary education	1.03	1.00	1.01	1.00	1.00	1.00	1.00	0.99	Enseignement primaire
Secondary education	1.22	1.13	1.12	1.12	1.13	1.13	1.15	1.17	Enseignement secondaire
Tertiary education	...	0.84	1.37	1.14	1.14	0.88	0.88	...	Enseignement supérieur

Country or area	1991	2001	2002	2003	2004	2005	2006	2007	Pays ou zone
Nauru									**Nauru**
Primary education	...	1.07	1.12	*0.99	1.02	1.04	0.97	*1.03	Enseignement primaire
Secondary education	...	1.01	1.21	*1.07	1.16	1.14	1.21	*1.19	Enseignement secondaire
Nepal									**Népal**
Primary education	0.63	0.84	0.86	0.88	0.88	0.91	0.95	0.99	Enseignement primaire
Secondary education	0.46	0.72	0.74	0.77	...	*0.86	*0.89	*0.91	Enseignement secondaire
Tertiary education	0.33	*0.27	0.27	0.34	0.40	...	...	...	Enseignement supérieur
Netherlands									**Pays-Bas**
Primary education	1.03	0.98	0.98	0.98	0.97	0.98	0.98	0.98	Enseignement primaire
Secondary education	0.92	0.97	0.97	0.98	0.98	0.98	0.98	0.98	Enseignement secondaire
Tertiary education	0.83	1.06	1.07	1.08	1.07	1.07	1.08	1.09	Enseignement supérieur
Netherlands Antilles									**Antilles néerlandaises**
Primary education	...	0.87	0.99	*0.99	...	...	...	...	Enseignement primaire
Secondary education	1.19	1.11	1.10	*1.09	...	...	...	...	Enseignement secondaire
Tertiary education	...	1.32	1.43	...	...	...	...	...	Enseignement supérieur
New Zealand									**Nouvelle-Zélande**
Primary education	0.99	0.99	*1.00	1.00	1.00	1.00	1.00	1.01	Enseignement primaire
Secondary education	1.02	...	1.11	1.11	1.07	1.07	1.05	1.03	Enseignement secondaire
Tertiary education	1.14	1.45	1.47	1.46	1.46	1.49	1.51	1.49	Enseignement supérieur
Nicaragua									**Nicaragua**
Primary education	1.06	1.01	0.99	0.99	0.98	0.97	0.98	0.98	Enseignement primaire
Secondary education	*1.20	1.17	1.17	*1.13	1.13	1.13	1.14	1.13	Enseignement secondaire
Tertiary education	0.96	*1.08	1.08	*1.08	...	...	...	...	Enseignement supérieur
Niger									**Niger**
Primary education	0.61	0.70	0.70	0.71	0.72	0.73	0.74	0.75	Enseignement primaire
Secondary education	0.37	*0.61	0.60	0.62	0.61	0.64	0.63	0.61	Enseignement secondaire
Tertiary education	...	...	...	*0.30	0.31	0.34	0.29	0.33	Enseignement supérieur
Nigeria									**Nigéria**
Primary education	0.79	0.82	0.81	*0.82	0.83	0.83	0.85	...	Enseignement primaire
Secondary education	0.72	0.82	0.75	0.77	0.79	0.82	0.81	...	Enseignement secondaire
Tertiary education	...	...	...	*0.53	0.53	0.69	...	...	Enseignement supérieur
Niue									**Nioué**
Primary education	...	0.94	...	...	1.19	0.95	...	...	Enseignement primaire
Secondary education	...	0.98	...	...	0.95	1.07	...	...	Enseignement secondaire
Norway									**Norvège**
Primary education	1.00	1.00	1.00	1.00	1.00	1.00	1.01	1.00	Enseignement primaire
Secondary education	1.03	1.02	1.02	1.02	1.03	1.01	0.99	0.99	Enseignement secondaire
Tertiary education	1.19	1.51	1.54	1.54	1.53	1.53	1.54	1.57	Enseignement supérieur
Occupied Palestinian Terr.									**Terr. palestinien occupé**
Primary education	...	1.01	1.00	1.00	1.00	0.99	1.00	1.00	Enseignement primaire
Secondary education	...	1.08	1.06	1.06	1.05	1.05	1.06	1.06	Enseignement secondaire
Tertiary education	...	0.96	0.98	1.04	1.04	1.03	1.17	1.22	Enseignement supérieur
Oman									**Oman**
Primary education	0.92	0.98	0.98	0.99	1.00	1.00	1.01	1.01	Enseignement primaire
Secondary education	0.81	0.99	0.98	0.96	0.96	0.96	0.96	0.96	Enseignement secondaire
Tertiary education	0.97	...	*0.79	0.79	1.16	1.09	1.04	1.18	Enseignement supérieur
Pakistan									**Pakistan**
Primary education	...	0.68	0.68	0.72	0.73	0.76	0.78	0.82	Enseignement primaire
Secondary education	0.48	...	...	*0.79	*0.78	*0.78	0.78	0.76	Enseignement secondaire
Tertiary education	*0.58	...	*0.81	0.81	0.80	0.88	0.85	0.85	Enseignement supérieur
Palau									**Palaos**
Primary education *	...	...	...	0.78	0.93	0.94	...	1.02	Enseignement primaire *
Secondary education *	...	1.00	...	1.18	1.10	...	...	0.97	Enseignement secondaire *
Tertiary education	...	2.16	*2.15	...	...	...	...	...	Enseignement supérieur
Panama									**Panama**
Primary education	...	0.97	0.97	*0.97	0.97	0.97	0.97	0.97	Enseignement primaire
Secondary education	...	1.07	1.07	*1.07	1.07	1.07	1.09	1.08	Enseignement secondaire
Tertiary education	...	1.71	1.70	1.59	1.66	1.63	1.61	...	Enseignement supérieur
Papua New Guinea									**Papouasie-Nvl-Guinée**
Primary education	0.85	0.85	0.84	0.85	0.86	0.84	0.84	...	Enseignement primaire
Secondary education	0.62	...	...	...	...	...	...	...	Enseignement secondaire

Country or area	1991	2001	2002	2003	2004	2005	2006	2007	Pays ou zone
Paraguay									**Paraguay**
Primary education	0.97	*0.96	0.96	0.97	0.97	0.97	...	...	Enseignement primaire
Secondary education	1.05	1.02	*1.02	1.01	1.02	1.03	...	...	Enseignement secondaire
Tertiary education	...	1.38	*1.40	*1.38	*1.34	*1.13	...	...	Enseignement supérieur
Peru									**Pérou**
Primary education	0.97	1.00	1.00	1.00	1.00	1.01	1.01	1.01	Enseignement primaire
Secondary education	0.94	0.93	0.93	1.00	1.01	1.02	1.03	1.04	Enseignement secondaire
Tertiary education *	...	0.97	1.07	1.07	1.02	1.02	1.06		Enseignement supérieur *
Philippines									**Philippines**
Primary education	0.99	1.00	0.99	0.99	0.99	0.99	0.99	0.98	Enseignement primaire
Secondary education	*1.04	1.10	1.10	1.10	1.11	1.12	1.11	1.10	Enseignement secondaire
Tertiary education	...	...	1.30	1.28	1.28	1.23	1.24	...	Enseignement supérieur
Poland									**Pologne**
Primary education	0.98	0.99	0.99	1.00	1.00	1.00	1.00	1.00	Enseignement primaire
Secondary education	1.02	0.97	0.97	0.96	1.01	0.99	0.99	0.99	Enseignement secondaire
Tertiary education	...	1.43	1.42	1.42	1.40	1.40	1.40	1.40	Enseignement supérieur
Portugal									**Portugal**
Primary education	0.95	0.98	0.96	0.95	0.95	0.95	0.95	0.95	Enseignement primaire
Secondary education	1.16	1.06	...	1.09	1.10	1.09	1.09	1.07	Enseignement secondaire
Tertiary education	1.29	1.37	1.37	1.35	1.32	1.30	1.28	1.22	Enseignement supérieur
Qatar									**Qatar**
Primary education	0.93	0.99	0.96	0.97	0.98	0.99	0.99	0.99	Enseignement primaire
Secondary education	1.06	1.12	1.09	1.05	1.00	1.00	0.97	0.98	Enseignement secondaire
Tertiary education	3.34	3.65	3.60	3.87	3.86	*3.45	*3.41	2.87	Enseignement supérieur
Republic of Moldova									**République de Moldova**
Primary education	1.02	1.00	0.99	0.99	0.99	0.99	0.99	0.98	Enseignement primaire
Secondary education	1.10	1.02	1.03	1.04	1.05	1.04	1.04	1.03	Enseignement secondaire
Tertiary education	...	1.29	1.34	1.32	1.35	1.46	1.38	1.39	Enseignement supérieur
Romania									**Roumanie**
Primary education	1.00	0.98	0.98	0.98	0.98	0.99	0.99	0.99	Enseignement primaire
Secondary education	0.99	1.01	1.02	1.02	1.01	1.01	1.00	0.99	Enseignement secondaire
Tertiary education	0.93	1.20	1.25	1.24	1.27	1.26	1.30	1.33	Enseignement supérieur
Russian Federation									**Fédération de Russie**
Primary education	1.00	0.99	0.99	1.00	...	1.00	1.00	1.00	Enseignement primaire
Secondary education	*1.06	...	...	1.00	0.99	0.99	0.98	0.98	Enseignement secondaire
Tertiary education	1.27	...	...	1.35	1.36	1.36	1.36	1.35	Enseignement supérieur
Rwanda									**Rwanda**
Primary education	0.93	0.98	0.99	1.00	1.02	*1.04	1.04	1.02	Enseignement primaire
Secondary education	0.73	0.96	...	0.89	0.89	*0.90	...	0.89	Enseignement secondaire
Tertiary education	...	0.45	0.47	0.54	0.61	*0.62	...	...	Enseignement supérieur
Saint Kitts and Nevis									**Saint-Kitts-et-Nevis**
Primary education	*1.02	1.09	1.03	1.03	1.07	1.06	...	*1.01	Enseignement primaire
Secondary education	*1.11	*1.02	0.98	1.06	*1.03	*0.98	...	*0.91	Enseignement secondaire
Saint Lucia									**Sainte-Lucie**
Primary education	*0.94	0.97	0.98	0.96	0.96	0.97	0.94	0.97	Enseignement primaire
Secondary education	1.45	1.29	1.32	*1.14	1.12	1.21	1.19	1.13	Enseignement secondaire
Tertiary education	*1.35	...	...	*2.05	3.45	2.79	5.46	2.41	Enseignement supérieur
Saint Vincent-Grenadines									**Saint Vincent-Grenadines**
Primary education	0.98	0.95	0.95	0.96	0.95	0.90	...	0.94	Enseignement primaire
Secondary education	1.24	*1.16	1.11	1.09	*1.07	1.24	...	...	Enseignement secondaire
Samoa									**Samoa**
Primary education	1.02	1.00	0.99	0.99	1.00	*1.00	...	1.00	Enseignement primaire
Secondary education	1.96	1.14	1.12	1.14	1.13	*1.13	...	...	Enseignement secondaire
Tertiary education *	...	0.93	...	...	...	...	...	...	Enseignement supérieur *
Sao Tome and Principe									**Sao Tomé-et-Principe**
Primary education	...	*0.94	*0.96	0.96	0.97	0.97	*0.97	1.00	Enseignement primaire
Secondary education	...	...	*0.85	1.18	1.05	1.07	*1.07	1.08	Enseignement secondaire
Saudi Arabia									**Arabie saoudite**
Primary education	0.85	...	...	...	...	0.97	...	0.96	Enseignement primaire
Secondary education	0.80	...	...	...	...	0.91	...	...	Enseignement secondaire
Tertiary education	0.88	*1.39	*1.62	1.56	1.57	1.50	1.46	...	Enseignement supérieur

Country or area	1991	2001	2002	2003	2004	2005	2006	2007	Pays ou zone
Senegal									**Sénégal**
Primary education	0.73	0.88	0.90	0.92	0.95	0.96	0.98	1.00	Enseignement primaire
Secondary education	*0.53	0.66	0.67	0.69	0.72	0.75	*0.76	*0.76	Enseignement secondaire
Tertiary education	...	...	...	...	...	...	0.46	*0.51	Enseignement supérieur
Serbia									**Serbie**
Primary education	...	*0.99	*0.99	*1.00	*1.00	1.01	1.01	1.00	Enseignement primaire
Secondary education	...	*1.02	*1.03	*1.03	*1.03	1.03	1.03	1.03	Enseignement secondaire
Seychelles									**Seychelles**
Primary education	...	0.99	0.99	1.01	1.01	1.01	...	0.99	Enseignement primaire
Secondary education	...	1.05	1.00	1.04	1.08	0.99	...	1.13	Enseignement secondaire
Sierra Leone									**Sierra Leone**
Primary education	*0.70	0.71	...	...	...	...	...	0.90	Enseignement primaire
Secondary education	0.57	*0.71	...	...	...	...	...	0.69	Enseignement secondaire
Tertiary education	...	0.40	*0.40	...	...	...	...	...	Enseignement supérieur
Slovakia									**Slovaquie**
Primary education	...	0.99	0.99	0.98	0.98	0.98	0.98	0.99	Enseignement primaire
Secondary education	...	1.01	1.01	1.01	1.01	1.01	1.01	1.01	Enseignement secondaire
Tertiary education	...	1.09	1.13	1.18	1.23	1.29	1.42	1.49	Enseignement supérieur
Slovenia									**Slovénie**
Primary education	...	0.99	0.99	1.00	1.00	0.99	0.99	0.99	Enseignement primaire
Secondary education	...	1.02	1.00	0.99	1.00	1.00	1.00	0.99	Enseignement secondaire
Tertiary education	1.32	1.36	1.44	1.36	1.38	1.43	1.46	1.45	Enseignement supérieur
Solomon Islands									**Iles Salomon**
Primary education	0.87	*0.95	0.95	*0.95	*0.96	0.96	...	...	Enseignement primaire
Secondary education	0.61	0.82	0.82	*0.82	*0.84	0.84	...	...	Enseignement secondaire
South Africa									**Afrique du Sud**
Primary education	0.99	0.96	0.97	0.96	0.96	0.96	0.96	0.97	Enseignement primaire
Secondary education	1.18	1.10	1.08	1.07	1.07	1.06	*1.06	*1.05	Enseignement secondaire
Tertiary education	0.83	1.15	1.16	1.17	1.19	1.21	1.24	...	Enseignement supérieur
Spain									**Espagne**
Primary education	0.99	0.99	0.99	0.99	0.99	0.99	0.98	0.99	Enseignement primaire
Secondary education	1.07	1.05	1.06	1.05	1.06	1.06	1.06	1.06	Enseignement secondaire
Tertiary education	1.09	1.16	1.19	1.19	1.22	1.22	1.23	1.24	Enseignement supérieur
Sri Lanka									**Sri Lanka**
Primary education	0.90	0.99	*0.99	*1.00	...	*1.00	1.00	1.00	Enseignement primaire
Secondary education	1.09	...	*1.06	*1.06	*1.02	...	...	...	Enseignement secondaire
Tertiary education *	0.55	...	...	...	...	...	...	...	Enseignement supérieur *
Sudan									**Soudan**
Primary education	0.77	0.85	0.85	0.86	0.87	0.87	0.87	0.86	Enseignement primaire
Secondary education	0.79	0.96	0.94	0.92	0.92	0.94	0.96	0.93	Enseignement secondaire
Tertiary education *	0.88	...	...	...	...	...	...	...	Enseignement supérieur *
Suriname									**Suriname**
Primary education	1.03	1.04	1.03	*1.03	...	1.01	1.00	0.98	Enseignement primaire
Secondary education	1.16	1.16	1.38	*1.34	...	1.33	1.37	1.39	Enseignement secondaire
Tertiary education	...	...	1.62	...	...	...	...	...	Enseignement supérieur
Swaziland									**Swaziland**
Primary education	0.99	0.95	0.93	0.95	0.93	0.93	0.93	0.93	Enseignement primaire
Secondary education	*0.96	1.03	1.02	1.01	0.96	1.00	1.01	0.89	Enseignement secondaire
Tertiary education	0.76	...	1.16	*1.16	1.08	1.06	0.98	...	Enseignement supérieur
Sweden									**Suède**
Primary education	1.00	1.03	1.03	1.03	1.00	1.00	1.00	1.00	Enseignement primaire
Secondary education	1.05	1.26	1.21	1.18	1.03	0.99	0.99	0.99	Enseignement secondaire
Tertiary education	1.22	1.51	1.54	1.55	1.54	1.55	1.55	1.57	Enseignement supérieur
Switzerland									**Suisse**
Primary education	1.01	1.00	1.00	1.00	0.99	0.99	0.99	0.99	Enseignement primaire
Secondary education	0.95	0.94	0.94	0.94	0.94	0.95	0.95	0.96	Enseignement secondaire
Tertiary education	0.57	0.77	0.79	0.82	0.84	0.87	0.90	0.93	Enseignement supérieur
Syrian Arab Republic									**Rép. arabe syrienne**
Primary education	0.90	0.93	0.93	0.94	0.95	0.95	0.96	0.96	Enseignement primaire
Secondary education	0.73	0.90	0.91	0.93	0.93	0.94	0.95	0.97	Enseignement secondaire
Tertiary education	0.65	...	...	...	...	...	...	...	Enseignement supérieur

12

Ratio of girls to boys in primary, secondary and tertiary education *(continued)*
Rapport filles/garçons dans l'enseignement primaire, secondaire et supérieur *(suite)*

Country or area	1991	2001	2002	2003	2004	2005	2006	2007	Pays ou zone
Tajikistan									**Tadjikistan**
Primary education	0.98	0.93	0.96	0.95	0.95	0.96	0.95	0.96	Enseignement primaire
Secondary education	...	0.83	0.82	0.83	0.84	0.83	0.83	0.84	Enseignement secondaire
Tertiary education	...	0.32	0.33	0.34	0.33	0.35	0.37	0.38	Enseignement supérieur
Thailand									**Thaïlande**
Primary education	0.98	1.00	1.00	*1.00	1.00	0.99	1.00	1.00	Enseignement primaire
Secondary education	0.96	*0.98	*1.01	*1.01	1.09	*1.07	1.09	1.10	Enseignement secondaire
Tertiary education	...	1.13	1.11	*1.14	1.18	1.13	1.07	1.23	Enseignement supérieur
TFYR of Macedonia									**L'ex-R.Y. Macédoine**
Primary education	...	1.00	1.01	1.00	1.00	1.00	...	1.00	Enseignement primaire
Secondary education	...	0.97	0.97	0.98	0.98	0.98	...	0.97	Enseignement secondaire
Tertiary education	...	1.32	1.29	1.34	1.39	1.38	...	1.27	Enseignement supérieur
Timor-Leste									**Timor-Leste**
Primary education	...	...	...	...	0.93	0.92	...	0.94	Enseignement primaire
Secondary education	...	...	...	...	0.99	1.00	...	...	Enseignement secondaire
Tertiary education	...	...	1.26	...	...	...	...	...	Enseignement supérieur
Togo									**Togo**
Primary education	0.65	0.79	0.81	0.82	0.84	0.85	0.86	0.86	Enseignement primaire
Secondary education	0.34	0.46	0.48	0.49	0.51	0.53	0.54	*0.53	Enseignement secondaire
Tertiary education	0.16	...	...	...	...	...	...	...	Enseignement supérieur
Tokelau									**Tokélaou**
Primary education	...	1.10	*1.08	*1.29	*1.35	...	...	...	Enseignement primaire
Secondary education	...	1.22	*1.22	*0.87	*0.88	...	...	...	Enseignement secondaire
Tonga									**Tonga**
Primary education	0.98	0.98	0.97	0.96	0.95	0.96	0.95	...	Enseignement primaire
Secondary education	1.04	1.10	1.12	...	*1.09	...	1.04	...	Enseignement secondaire
Tertiary education	...	*1.66	*1.68	1.70	*1.68	...	...	...	Enseignement supérieur
Trinidad and Tobago									**Trinité-et-Tobago**
Primary education	1.00	0.98	0.99	0.98	0.97	0.98	...	0.97	Enseignement primaire
Secondary education	1.04	*1.08	*1.11	*1.09	1.07	1.05	...	*1.07	Enseignement secondaire
Tertiary education	0.78	1.54	1.51	1.61	1.28	*1.28	...	...	Enseignement supérieur
Tunisia									**Tunisie**
Primary education	0.90	0.96	0.97	0.97	0.97	0.97	0.97	0.97	Enseignement primaire
Secondary education	0.79	1.06	1.05	1.09	...	1.10	*1.10	...	Enseignement secondaire
Tertiary education	0.66	*0.98	1.23	1.28	1.36	1.40	1.42	1.51	Enseignement supérieur
Turkey									**Turquie**
Primary education	0.92	*0.92	*0.93	*0.94	*0.94	*0.95	*0.95	*0.95	Enseignement primaire
Secondary education	0.63	*0.75	*0.76	*0.75	*0.75	*0.82	*0.83	*0.82	Enseignement secondaire
Tertiary education	0.53	0.71	0.73	0.75	0.73	0.74	0.75	0.76	Enseignement supérieur
Turks and Caicos Islands									**Iles Turques et Caïques**
Primary education	...	...	0.96	0.95	*1.03	*1.04	...	...	Enseignement primaire
Secondary education *	...	...	1.02	1.00	0.98	0.94	...	...	Enseignement secondaire *
Tuvalu									**Tuvalu**
Primary education	...	1.13	1.13	*1.11	1.07	0.99	0.99	...	Enseignement primaire
Secondary education	...	0.93	...	...	...	...	...	...	Enseignement secondaire
Uganda									**Ouganda**
Primary education	*0.84	0.97	0.99	0.98	0.99	1.00	1.01	1.01	Enseignement primaire
Secondary education	*0.59	*0.77	*0.81	*0.81	0.81	*0.81	*0.83	*0.83	Enseignement secondaire
Tertiary education	0.38	0.53	*0.53	*0.53	0.62	...	...	...	Enseignement supérieur
Ukraine									**Ukraine**
Primary education	1.00	1.00	1.00	1.00	0.99	1.00	1.00	1.00	Enseignement primaire
Secondary education	...	0.99	1.00	1.00	0.99	0.92	0.98	1.00	Enseignement secondaire
Tertiary education	*1.03	1.17	1.19	1.21	1.22	1.23	1.23	1.24	Enseignement supérieur
United Arab Emirates									**Emirats arabes unis**
Primary education	0.97	0.97	0.97	0.98	0.98	0.99	0.99	0.99	Enseignement primaire
Secondary education	1.16	1.04	1.05	1.03	1.02	1.01	1.02	*1.03	Enseignement secondaire
Tertiary education	4.03	*2.84	*2.82	*2.81	...	...	...	...	Enseignement supérieur
United Kingdom									**Royaume-Uni**
Primary education	1.01	1.00	1.00	1.00	1.00	1.00	1.01	1.01	Enseignement primaire
Secondary education	*1.04	1.01	1.01	1.03	1.02	1.03	1.03	1.02	Enseignement secondaire
Tertiary education	0.96	1.22	1.26	1.30	1.37	1.39	1.40	1.40	Enseignement supérieur

Country or area	1991	2001	2002	2003	2004	2005	2006	2007	Pays ou zone
United Rep. of Tanzania									**Rép.-Unie de Tanzanie**
Primary education	0.98	0.98	0.97	0.96	0.96	0.96	0.97	0.98	Enseignement primaire
Secondary education	0.77	...	...	...	...	...	...	...	Enseignement secondaire
Tertiary education	0.19	0.15	*0.31	0.44	0.41	*0.48	...	0.48	Enseignement supérieur
United States									**Etats-Unis**
Primary education	0.98	1.00	1.01	1.00	0.97	0.99	1.01	1.00	Enseignement primaire
Secondary education	1.01	1.01	0.99	1.00	1.02	1.02	0.99	1.01	Enseignement secondaire
Tertiary education	1.25	1.33	1.35	1.37	1.39	1.40	1.41	1.41	Enseignement supérieur
Uruguay									**Uruguay**
Primary education	0.99	0.98	0.98	0.98	0.97	0.98	0.97	0.97	Enseignement primaire
Secondary education	...	1.14	1.13	1.15	1.15	1.15	1.16	0.99	Enseignement secondaire
Tertiary education	...							1.75	Enseignement supérieur
Uzbekistan									**Ouzbékistan**
Primary education	0.98	0.99	0.98	0.99	0.98	0.98	0.98	0.97	Enseignement primaire
Secondary education	*0.91	0.97	0.97	0.96	0.96	0.97	0.97	0.98	Enseignement secondaire
Tertiary education	...	0.81	0.80	0.77	0.79	0.70	0.71	0.71	Enseignement supérieur
Vanuatu									**Vanuatu**
Primary education	0.96	0.99	0.99	0.99	0.98	0.97	0.98	0.97	Enseignement primaire
Secondary education	0.80	0.91	0.94	0.84	0.86	...	...	...	Enseignement secondaire
Tertiary education	...	...	*0.57	0.59	*0.59	...	...	...	Enseignement supérieur
Venezuela (Bolivarian Rep. of)									**Venezuela (Rép. bolivarienne du)**
Primary education	0.99	0.98	0.98	0.98	0.98	0.98	0.98	0.97	Enseignement primaire
Secondary education	1.24	1.17	1.16	1.15	1.14	1.13	1.12	1.12	Enseignement secondaire
Tertiary education *	...	...	1.09	1.08	...	...	...	...	Enseignement supérieur *
Viet Nam									**Viet Nam**
Primary education	*0.93	0.94	...	...	...	...	...	...	Enseignement primaire
Secondary education	...	0.92	...	...	...	...	...	...	Enseignement secondaire
Tertiary education	...	0.74	...	...	...	...	...	...	Enseignement supérieur
Yemen									**Yémen**
Primary education	...	0.63	0.66	0.69	0.71	0.74	...	...	Enseignement primaire
Secondary education	...	*0.42	...	0.45	0.48	0.49	...	...	Enseignement secondaire
Tertiary education	...	...	...	...	0.38	0.37	*0.37	...	Enseignement supérieur
Zambia									**Zambie**
Primary education	...	0.94	0.93	...	0.96	0.95	0.98	0.97	Enseignement primaire
Secondary education	...	0.77	0.83	...	0.79	*0.82	...	0.80	Enseignement secondaire
Zimbabwe									**Zimbabwe**
Primary education	0.97	0.97	0.98	0.98	...	...	0.99	...	Enseignement primaire
Secondary education	0.79	0.89	0.88	0.91	...	...	0.93	...	Enseignement secondaire
Tertiary education *	...	0.58	0.68	0.63	...	...	...	...	Enseignement supérieur *

Source:
United Nations Educational, Scientific and Cultural Organization (UNESCO), Montreal, the UNESCO Institute for Statistics (UIS) database, last accessed July 2009.

Source:
L'Organisation des Nations Unies pour l'éducation, la science et la culture (UNESCO), Montréal, la base de données de l'institut de statistique de l'UNESCO (ISU), dernier accès juillet 2009.

Technical notes: tables 10-12

Tables 10-12: The three tables on gender presented in this chapter are all based on indicators for the Millennium Development Goals (MDGs). For more on MDGs, visit mdgs.un.org

Table 10 shows the percentage of seats held by women members in single or lower chambers of national parliaments. National parliaments can be bicameral or unicameral. This table covers the single chamber in unicameral parliaments and the lower chamber in bicameral parliaments. It does not cover the upper chamber of bicameral parliaments. Seats are usually won by members in general parliamentary elections. Seats may also be filled by nomination, appointment, indirect election, rotation of members and by-election.

The proportion of seats held by women in national parliament is derived by dividing the total number of seats occupied by women by the total number of seats in parliament. There is no weighting or normalizing of statistics.

The source for this table is the Inter-Parliamentary Union (IPU). For more information visit www.ipu.org.

Table 11: The share of women in wage employment in the non-agricultural sector is the share of female workers in wage employment in the non-agricultural sector expressed as a percentage of total wage employment in that same sector.

The non-agricultural sector includes industry and services. "Industry" includes mining and quarrying (including oil production), manufacturing, construction, electricity, gas, and water, corresponding to divisions 2-5 in the International Standard Industrial Classification of All Economic Activities (ISIC-Rev.2) and to tabulation categories C-F in ISIC-Rev. 3. "Services" include wholesale and retail trade and restaurants and hotels; transport, storage, and communications; financing, insurance, real estate, and business services; and community, social, and personal services, corresponding to divisions 6-9 in ISIC-Rev. 2, and to tabulation categories G-Q in ISIC-Rev. 3.

Employment refers to people above a certain age who worked or held a job during a specified reference period (according to the ILO Resolution concerning statistics of the economically active population, employment, unemployment and underemployment, adopted by the Thirteenth International Conference of Labour Statisticians (ICLS), October 1982).

Wage employment refers only to wage earners and salaried employees, or "persons in paid employment jobs". Employees are typically remunerated by wages and salaries, but may be paid by commission from sales, piece-rates, bonuses or payments in kind such as food, housing, training, etc. These persons are in wage employment as opposed to self-employment – that is employers, own-account workers, members of producers'

Notes techniques : tableaux 10 à 12

Tableaux 10-12: ces trois tableaux sur la répartition des sexes figurant dans le présent chapitre reposent tous sur des indicateurs liés aux objectifs du Millénaire pour le développement. Pour plus d'informations sur les objectifs du Millénaire pour le développement, veuillez consulter le site Web suivant : mdgs.un.org.

Tableau 10 : ce tableau indique le pourcentage des sièges des chambres uniques ou basses des parlements nationaux occupés par des femmes. Les parlements nationaux peuvent être bicaméraux ou unicaméraux. Ce tableau porte sur la chambre unique des parlements unicaméraux et sur la chambre basse des parlements bicaméraux. Il ne porte pas sur la chambre haute des parlements bicaméraux. Les sièges sont habituellement attribués aux membres à l'issue d'élections parlementaires générales. Certains sièges peuvent aussi être pourvus à l'issue de nominations, d'élections indirectes, de roulement des membres et d'élections partielles.

La proportion d'élues est obtenue en divisant le nombre total de sièges occupés par des femmes par le nombre total de sièges que compte le parlement. Les statistiques ne sont ni pondérées ni normalisées.

La source de ce tableau est l'Union interparlementaire. Pour plus d'informations, veuillez consulter le site Web suivant : www.ipu.org.

Tableau 11 : la proportion des femmes rémunérées dans le secteur non agricole correspond au pourcentage du nombre total de salariés employés dans le secteur agricole qui sont des femmes.

Le secteur non agricole comprend l'industrie et les services. L'"industrie" comporte les industries extractives (y compris la production pétrolière), le secteur manufacturier, le bâtiment, l'électricité, le gaz et l'eau, correspondant aux divisions 2 à 5 de la Classification internationale type, par industrie, de toutes les branches d'activité économique (CITI) et aux catégories C à F de la CITI-Rev.3. Les "services" comportent le commerce de gros et de détail, la restauration et l'hôtellerie; les transports, l'entreposage et les communications; les finances, les assurances, l'immobilier et les services commerciaux; et les services communautaires, sociaux et personnels, correspondant aux divisions 6 à 9 de la CITI-Rev.2 et aux catégories G à Q de la CITI-Rev.3.

L'emploi se rapporte aux personnes d'un âge minimum donné qui ont travaillé ou occupé un emploi pendant une période donnée de référence (conformément à la résolution de l'OIT sur les statistiques de la population économiquement active, l'emploi, le chômage et le sous-emploi, adoptée par la treizième Conférence internationale des statisticiens du travail (CIST), octobre 1982).

L'emploi salarié se réfère uniquement aux travailleurs salariés ou recevant un traitement et aux personnes dans des emplois rémunérés. Les employés sont généra-

cooperatives and contributing family workers. The different statuses in employment are defined according to the ILO Resolution concerning the International Classification of Status in Employment (ICSE), adopted by the 15th ICLS (1993).

The source for this table is the International Labour Organization (ILO). For more information visit http://laborsta.ilo.org.

Table 12: Ratio of girls to boys (gender parity index) in primary, secondary and tertiary education is the ratio of the number of female students enrolled at primary, secondary and tertiary levels of education to the number of male students in each level. To standardize the effects of the population structure of the appropriate age groups, the Gender Parity Index (GPI) of the Gross Enrolment Ratio (GER) for each level of education is used.

The source for this table is the UNESCO Institute for Statistics (UIS). For more information visit www.uis.unesco.org.

lement rémunérés par des salaires et des traitements, mais leur rémunération peut aussi provenir de commissions, de travaux à la pièce, de primes ou d'avantages en nature tels que repas, logement, formation, etc. Il s'agit de salariés par opposition aux travailleurs indépendants – employeurs, travailleurs à leur compte, membres de coopératives de producteurs et travailleurs familiaux. Les différentes situations d'après la profession sont définies conformément à la résolution de l'OIT concernant la Classification internationale d'après la situation dans la profession (CISP), adoptée par la quinzième Conférence internationale des statisticiens du travail (CIST) (1993).

La source de ce tableau est l'Organisation internationale du Travail (OIT). Pour plus d'informations, veuillez consulter le site Web suivant : http://laborsta.ilo.org.

Tableau 12 : ce tableau indique la proportion de filles par rapport aux garçons (indice de parité des sexes) dans l'enseignement primaire, secondaire et supérieur, à savoir le rapport entre le nombre de filles inscrites dans l'enseignement primaire, secondaire et supérieur et le nombre de garçons à chaque niveau. Pour normaliser les effets de la pyramide des âges, l'indice de parité des sexes du taux brut de scolarisation pour chaque niveau d'enseignement est utilisé.

La source de ce tableau est l'Institut de statistique de l'UNESCO. Pour plus d'informations, veuillez consulter le site Web suivant : www.uis.unesco.org.

Education at the primary, secondary and tertiary levels
Number of students enrolled and percentage female

Enseignement primaire, secondaire et supérieur
Nombre d'élèves inscrits et pourcentage de sexe féminin

Country or area Pays ou zone	Year [t] Année [t]	Primary education Enseignement primaire		Secondary education Enseignement secondaire		Tertiary education Enseignement supérieur	
		Total	% F	Total	% F	Total	% F
Afghanistan	2003	3 781 015	34.8	406 895[1]	24.4[1]	26 211[1]	20.4[1]
Afghanistan	2004	4 430 142	29.1	594 306	16.3	27 648	20.4
	2005	4 318 819	35.7	651 453	23.4	...	...
	2006	4 669 110	37.2	1 006 841	25.4	...	...
	2007	4 718 077	36.9	1 035 782	26.1	...	...
Albania	2003	252 829	48.1	396 139	48.3	43 600	62.3
Albanie	2004	250 487	48.2	397 056	47.9	53 014	62.1
Algeria	2003	4 612 574	47.0	3 548 484	50.5	682 775[1]	...
Algérie	2004	4 507 703	47.0	3 677 107	50.7	716 452	51.0
	2005	4 361 744	47.0	3 755 821[1]	50.7[1]	792 121	55.2
	2006	4 196 580	47.0	...	...	817 968	54.8
	2007	4 078 954	47.2	...	...	901 562	57.4
Andorra	2003	4 142	47.2	3 194	50.2	306	48.7
Andorre	2004	4 264	47.1	3 250	49.9	331	48.6
	2005	4 085	46.9	3 737	50.3	342	50.9
	2006	4 332	47.4	3 843	49.9	401	53.1
	2007	4 427	47.2	3 819	49.4	...	...
Angola	2003	...	...	...	...	48 184	...
Angola	2004	...	...	...	...	37 547	...
	2005	...	...	...	...	48 184	...
	2006	...	...	...	...	48 694	...
Anguilla	2003	1 447	49.7	1 100[1]	50.7[1]	12	100.0
Anguilla	2004	1 433	50.0	1 076	51.1	21	81.0
	2005	1 449	50.8	1 024	50.5	33	75.8
	2006	1 512	48.9	998	51.6	47	83.0
	2007	1 558	48.6	1 001	51.6	54	83.3
	2008	1 610	49.3	1 008	49.9	54	83.3
Antigua and Barbuda Antigua-et-Barbuda	2007	11 569	48.9	7 838	51.1	...	...
Argentina	2003	4 674 869	49.0	3 499 181	50.9	2 101 437	59.7
Argentine	2004	4 701 149	48.9	3 497 541	51.7	2 116 876	58.1
	2005	4 651 255	48.8	3 476 306	51.9	2 082 577	58.7
	2006	4 685 696	48.8	3 481 085	52.1	2 202 032	59.7
Armenia	2003	143 822	48.5	377 727	50.2	73 603	53.7
Arménie	2004	134 664	48.3	369 236	49.6	79 321	55.5
	2005	125 149	48.2	364 234	49.6	86 629	55.5
	2006	121 502	47.8	355 790	49.6	99 293	54.5
	2007	127 546	47.2	336 877	49.7	107 398	54.7
Aruba	2003	9 897	48.0	6 869	51.6	1 672	59.3
Aruba	2004	10 185	47.9	6 973	50.6	1 704	60.2
	2005	10 250	48.3	7 116	50.7	2 106	59.8
	2006	10 390	48.8	7 439	50.4	2 094	60.3
	2007	10 346	48.6	7 853	50.9	2 232	58.4
Australia	2003	1 931 817	48.6	2 568 791	48.1	1 005 977	54.1
Australie	2004	1 934 549	48.6	2 492 235	47.8	1 002 998	54.2
	2005	1 934 941	48.6	2 496 917	47.6	1 024 589	54.5
	2006	1 938 861	48.6	2 536 684	47.4	1 040 153	54.9
	2007	1 973 456	48.6	2 511 214	47.6	1 083 715	55.1
Austria	2003	379 920	48.6	764 426	47.5	229 802	53.0
Autriche	2004	372 963	48.7	770 391	47.4	238 522	53.3
	2005	362 822	48.7	781 292	47.5	244 410	53.7
	2006	355 293	48.5	782 981	47.7	253 139	53.8
	2007	347 249	48.4	777 792	47.8	260 975	53.7
Azerbaijan	2003	635 652	47.7	1 094 387	47.9	121 156	44.7
Azerbaïdjan	2004	607 007	47.8	1 085 632	48.0	122 770	46.0
	2005	568 097	47.7	1 069 980	47.9	128 634	46.7
	2006	538 339	47.1	1 051 591	47.6	131 507	47.5
	2007	512 976	47.2	1 029 853	47.6	135 164	45.7

13

Education at the primary, secondary and tertiary levels *(continued)*
Number of students enrolled and percentage female
Enseignement primaire, secondaire et supérieur *(suite)*
Nombre d'élèves inscrits et pourcentage de sexe féminin

Country or area Pays ou zone	Year [t] Année [t]	Primary education Enseignement primaire		Secondary education Enseignement secondaire		Tertiary education Enseignement supérieur	
		Total	% F	Total	% F	Total	% F
Bahamas Bahamas	2003	34 579	49.4	29 985	50.3	...	...
	2004 [1]	36 070	49.2	30 857	49.6	...	...
	2005	37 050	49.1	32 089	49.7	...	...
	2006	35 921	49.1	32 709	49.8	...	...
	2007	37 122	49.1	34 217	50.4	...	...
Bahrain Bahreïn	2003	81 887	48.9	67 160	50.2	19 079	61.9
	2004	82 708	48.9	69 638	49.9	18 524 [1]	63.1 [1]
	2005	83 299	48.7	71 645	50.0	18 841	67.8
	2006	89 721	48.8	73 767	49.7	18 403	68.3
Bangladesh Bangladesh	2003	...	...	11 051 234	51.3	877 335	32.0
	2004	...	...	10 354 760	49.6	821 364	31.6
	2005	16 219 478	50.1	10 109 395	50.6	911 600	33.5
	2006	16 396 870	50.4	10 250 862	50.4	1 053 566	34.8
	2007	16 312 907	50.7	10 444 714	50.3	1 145 401	34.9
Barbados Barbade	2003	23 074	48.9	20 947	49.7	...	...
	2004	22 327	48.9	21 300	49.7	...	...
	2005	22 249	49.2	21 418	49.4	...	...
	2006	22 461	48.7	20 855	50.2	...	...
	2007	22 584	49.3	20 651	50.0	11 405	68.0
Belarus Bélarus	2003	437 005	48.3	997 760	49.6	488 650	57.1
	2004	403 841	47.8	969 768	49.1	507 360	57.1
	2005	379 577	47.8	928 488	49.1	528 508	56.8
	2006	367 736	48.1	878 943	49.1	544 328	56.8
	2007	361 493	48.2	823 253	49.2	556 526	57.5
Belgium Belgique	2003	761 730	48.7	1 181 327	51.3	374 532	53.3
	2004	747 111	48.8	805 778	48.0	386 110	53.8
	2005	738 580	48.8	814 539	48.0	389 547	54.4
	2006	732 808	48.8	821 996	48.1	394 427	54.7
	2007	732 411	48.9	825 293	48.0	393 687	54.9
Belize Belize	2003	47 187	48.8	27 880 [1]	50.6 [1]	527	64.9 [2]
	2004	48 996	48.7	31 224	50.3	722	70.2
	2005	50 389	48.4	31 377 [1]	49.7 [1]	...	...
	2006	51 497	48.6	30 084	50.7	...	...
	2007	51 898	49.0	30 475	51.0	...	...
	2008	51 994	48.6	31 120	51.4	...	...
Benin Bénin	2003	1 233 214	41.9	312 427 [1]	31.5 [1]	39 406	...
	2004	1 319 648	42.8	344 890	31.7	41 282	...
	2005	1 318 140	43.6	435 449 [1]	35.4 [1]	42 197	...
	2006	1 356 818	44.4	...	...	42 603	...
Bermuda Bermudes	2003	4 879	50.1	4 660	52.4	...	...
	2004	4 810	50.7	4 803	53.1	...	...
	2005	4 760	50.4	4 756	52.4	639	65.1
	2006	4 678	46.2	4 518	51.5	...	...
	2007	...	...	...	...	886	71.1
Bhutan Bhoutan	2005	99 458	48.7	42 144	47.1	...	...
	2006	102 225	48.9	45 035	47.8	4 141	32.7
	2007	...	...	...	...	3 998	30.6
	2008	106 100	49.5	52 098	48.2	...	...
Bolivia Bolivie	2003	1 531 996	48.9	1 048 881	48.4	337 914	...
	2004 [1]	1 541 559	49.0	...	...	346 056	...
	2006	1 508 194	49.0	1 043 127	48.1	...	...
	2007	1 512 002	49.0	1 052 014	48.4	...	...
Bosnia and Herzegovina Bosnie-Herzégovine	2007	191 588	46.9	344 567	49.6	99 414	...
Botswana Botswana	2003	330 376	49.5	166 915	51.4	...	...
	2004	328 692	49.3	169 727 [1]	51.0 [1]	10 197	46.4
	2005	326 500	49.3	168 720	50.9	10 950	49.8
Brazil Brésil	2003	18 919 122	47.7	24 592 569	51.7	3 994 422	56.4
	2004	18 979 209	47.2	25 155 104	51.5	4 275 027	56.3

Education at the primary, secondary and tertiary levels *(continued)*
Number of students enrolled and percentage female
Enseignement primaire, secondaire et supérieur *(suite)*
Nombre d'élèves inscrits et pourcentage de sexe féminin

Country or area Pays ou zone	Year[t] Année[t]	Primary education Enseignement primaire		Secondary education Enseignement secondaire		Tertiary education Enseignement supérieur	
		Total	% F	Total	% F	Total	% F
	2005	18 661 105	47.6	24 863 112	51.6	4 572 297	55.9
	2007	17 996 083	47.2	23 423 870	51.7	5 272 877	55.7
British Virgin Islands Iles Vierges britanniques	2003	2 780	47.9	1 633	53.7	1 025[1]	71.7[1]
	2004	2 824	48.2	1 707	52.1	1 136	69.5
	2005	2 898	48.2	1 882	54.2	1 200[1]	68.8[1]
	2006	2 923	48.3	1 959	53.0	...	...
	2007	3 044	48.8	1 921	53.8	...	...
Brunei Darussalam Brunéi Darussalam	2003	46 242	48.1	40 022	49.3	4 546	64.7
	2004	46 382	47.9	42 167	49.0	4 917	66.0
	2005	46 012	47.9	43 900	48.8	5 023	66.5
	2006	46 086	47.7	45 887	48.9	5 094	66.1
	2007	45 972	47.7	46 173	48.8	5 284	64.5
Bulgaria Bulgarie	2003	333 016	48.2	707 251	48.1	230 513	52.8
	2004	314 221	48.3	704 678	47.7	228 468	52.5
	2005	290 017	48.4	685 640	47.7	237 909	52.1
	2006	273 045	48.3	662 510	47.7	243 464	53.5
	2007	267 584	48.3	633 343	47.7	258 602	53.7
Burkina Faso Burkina Faso	2003	1 012 150	42.1	236 914	39.9	18 200	22.4
	2004	1 139 512	43.2	266 538[1]	40.3[1]	18 868[1]	22.4[1]
	2005	1 270 837	43.7	295 412	40.7	27 942	30.7
	2006	1 390 571	44.2	319 749	41.3	30 472	31.0
	2007	1 561 258	44.8	352 376	41.6	33 459	30.9
	2008	1 742 439	45.6	423 543	41.8	41 779	32.7
Burundi Burundi	2003	894 859	44.6	129 204	43.5	11 915[1]	31.9[1]
	2004	968 488	45.4	152 251	43.0	15 706	27.7
	2005	1 036 859	46.2	171 110[1]	42.5[1]	16 889[1]	27.7[1]
	2006	1 324 937	47.7	192 296[1]	42.6[1]	17 061	30.6
	2007	1 490 844	48.2	209 945	41.9	15 623	31.6
Cambodia Cambodge	2003	2 772 113	46.8	560 197	38.4	43 210	28.8[1]
	2004	2 762 882	47.0	631 508[1]	40.2[1]	45 370	31.3
	2005	2 695 372	47.2	...	...	56 810	31.5
	2006	2 582 250	47.3	811 797	43.3	75 989	32.8
	2007	2 479 644	47.2	875 120	44.2	92 340	35.2
Cameroon Cameroun	2003	2 798 523	45.7	823 068[1]	45.3[1]	81 318	38.8[1]
	2004	2 979 011	45.8	751 580	43.8	83 903[1]	38.8[1]
	2005	2 977 781	45.2[3]	784 203	43.8	99 864[1]	39.5[1]
	2006	2 998 135	45.2	698 444	43.9	120 298	41.8
	2007	3 120 357	45.9	750 777[1]	43.9[1]	132 134	43.9
Canada Canada	2004[1]	2 389 188	48.6	2 572 388	48.0	1 326 711	56.4
	2005	2 320 738	48.6	2 601 926	48.1	...	...
	2006	2 305 211	48.6	2 632 432	48.2	...	...
Cape Verde Cap-Vert	2003	87 841	48.7	49 522	52.0	2 215	52.9
	2004	85 138	48.6	49 790	52.2	3 036	52.6
	2005	82 952	48.5	51 672	51.7	3 910	51.0
	2006	81 434	48.6	61 465	53.5	4 567	52.1
	2007	78 801	48.3	60 783	54.2	5 289	54.6
Cayman Islands Iles Caïmanes	2004	3 361	48.5	2 701	50.8	...	...
	2005	3 240	48.4	2 824	47.8	...	...
	2006	3 461	48.0	2 899	49.0	567	71.6
	2007	3 706	48.2	3 010	49.5	...	...
Central African Rep. Rép. centrafricaine	2003	414 537	41.0	...	...	...	...
	2004	363 158	40.2	...	...	6 384	...
	2005	412 381	41.1	...	...	6 270[1]	...
	2006	418 825	41.0	...	...	4 462	22.5
	2007	494 985	41.4	...	...	...	...
	2008	522 187	41.9	...	...	...	...
Chad Tchad	2003	1 164 093	39.7	212 632[1]	24.3[1]	7 397	10.2
	2004	1 271 985	39.5	227 856	24.8	10 081	12.5
	2005	1 262 393	40.1	236 754[1]	24.8[1]	10 468[1]	12.5[1]

13

Education at the primary, secondary and tertiary levels *(continued)*
Number of students enrolled and percentage female
Enseignement primaire, secondaire et supérieur *(suite)*
Nombre d'élèves inscrits et pourcentage de sexe féminin

Country or area Pays ou zone	Year[t] Année[t]	Primary education Enseignement primaire		Secondary education Enseignement secondaire		Tertiary education Enseignement supérieur	
		Total	% F	Total	% F	Total	% F
	2006	1 296 486	40.2	262 714	26.2	...	...
	2007	1 324 298	40.9	314 470	30.8	...	...
Chile Chili	2003	1 713 538	48.5	1 557 120	49.5	567 114	47.8
	2004	1 755 997	47.9	1 594 966	49.5	580 815	48.0
	2005	1 720 951	48.0	1 630 099	49.5	663 694	48.1
	2006	1 694 765	48.0	1 633 868	49.6	661 142	49.2
	2007	1 679 017	47.8	1 611 631	49.8	753 398	49.4
China[4] Chine[4]	2003	121 662 360	47.2	95 624 760	46.8	15 186 217	43.8
	2004	...	...	...	...	18 090 814	45.5
	2005	...	...	...	...	20 601 219	46.0
	2006	108 925 227	46.8	101 195 119	47.7	23 360 535	47.1
	2007	107 394 752	46.6	101 830 969	47.7	25 346 279	47.9
China, Hong Kong SAR Chine, Hong Kong RAS	2003	487 465	48.1	487 218	48.8	146 039[2]	50.3[2]
	2004	472 863	48.1	492 779	48.9	147 724	51.2
	2005	451 171	48.0	498 354	48.9	152 294	51.0
	2006	429 892	48.0	500 708	48.8	155 324	50.5
	2007	414 501	47.9	504 981	48.8	157 858	50.1
China, Macao SAR Chine, Macao RAS	2003	41 917	46.8	44 425	50.2	26 272	36.5
	2004	39 872	46.7	46 509	49.6	24 815	40.5
	2005	37 401	46.8	46 539	49.4	23 420	42.8
	2006	34 739	47.2	46 393	49.3	23 291	45.9
	2007	32 932	46.9	45 410	49.2	23 868	48.8
Colombia Colombie	2003[1]	5 207 149	48.7	3 788 991	51.6	986 680	51.5
	2004	5 259 033	48.7	4 050 525	51.6	1 112 574	51.3
	2005	5 298 257	48.5	4 297 228	51.6	1 223 594	51.3
	2006	5 296 190	48.6	4 509 406	51.7	1 314 972	51.5
	2007	5 298 567	48.8	4 657 360	51.6	1 372 674	51.5
Comoros Comores	2003	104 274	44.3	38 272	44.9	1 707	43.2
	2004	103 809	46.2	42 919	42.5	1 779[1]	43.2[1]
	2005	106 700[1]	46.2[1]	43 349[1]	42.5	...	...
Congo Congo	2003	509 507	48.2	204 096	40.5	12 456[1]	15.8[1]
	2004	584 370	48.1	232 026[1]	46.0[1]	...	...
	2005	597 304	47.9	...	...	...	...
	2006	617 010	47.2	...	...	...	...
	2007	621 702	48.0	...	...	...	...
Cook Islands Iles Cook	2003	2 254	47.2	1 891	48.7	...	...
	2004[1]	2 265	47.2	1 901	48.6	...	...
	2005	2 201	48.1	1 899	49.2	...	...
	2007	2 031	46.9	1 951	50.1	...	...
Costa Rica Costa Rica	2003	541 494[1]	48.1[1]	305 940	50.5[1]	79 499[1]	52.3[1]
	2004	558 084	48.3	339 763	50.0	108 765	54.3
	2005	542 087	48.3	347 244	50.0	110 717[1]	54.3[1]
	2006	546 542	48.3	374 428	50.1	...	...
	2007	536 436	48.4	377 924	49.8	...	...
Côte d'Ivoire Côte d'Ivoire	2003[2]	2 046 165	44.2	...	...	...	...
	2006	2 111 975	44.1	...	...	149 261[1]	32.7[1]
	2007	2 179 801	44.1	...	...	156 772	33.3
Croatia Croatie	2003	192 004	48.6	399 845	49.3	121 722	53.2
	2005	196 253	48.7	400 123	49.7	134 658	53.8
	2006	194 748	48.6	395 836	49.7	136 646	54.1
	2007	190 693	48.7	392 952	49.7	139 996	54.1
Cuba Cuba	2003	925 335	47.7	938 047	48.3	235 997	56.2
	2004	906 293	47.7	932 338	49.1	396 516	62.3[1]
	2005	895 045	47.8	937 493	49.1	471 858	62.1[1]
	2006	889 834	47.9	928 342	49.1	681 629	60.8
	2007	883 132	47.9	898 833	48.7	864 846	63.6
	2008	871 444	48.0	865 602	48.6	987 250	61.4
Cyprus Chypre	2003	62 868	48.6	64 711	48.9	18 272	49.5
	2004	61 731	48.8	64 534	49.2	20 849	47.9
	2005	61 247	48.7	64 293	49.2	20 078	52.0

Education at the primary, secondary and tertiary levels *(continued)*
Number of students enrolled and percentage female
Enseignement primaire, secondaire et supérieur *(suite)*
Nombre d'élèves inscrits et pourcentage de sexe féminin

Country or area Pays ou zone	Year [‡] Année [‡]	Primary education Enseignement primaire		Secondary education Enseignement secondaire		Tertiary education Enseignement supérieur	
		Total	% F	Total	% F	Total	% F
	2006	59 710	48.8	64 714	49.2	20 587	50.9
	2007	57 785	48.6	64 853	49.3	22 227	50.1
Czech Republic République tchèque	2003	566 581	48.3	1 000 493	49.5	287 001	50.7
	2004	534 366	48.3	982 208	49.1	318 858	51.2
	2005	502 831	48.3	975 284	49.2	336 307	52.6
	2006	473 269	48.4	966 280	49.1	338 009	53.8
	2007	462 820	48.5	937 026	49.1	363 277	54.7
Dem. Rep. of the Congo Rép. dém. du Congo	2007	8 839 888	44.8	2 815 175	34.6	237 836	25.9[2]
Denmark Danemark	2003	417 506[1]	48.7[1]	446 863	50.1	201 746	57.9
	2004	419 806	48.7	449 750	49.8	217 130	57.9
	2005	414 103	48.7	464 952	49.5	232 255	57.4
	2006	415 793	48.7	463 617	49.4	228 893	57.4
	2007	415 793	48.7	475 140	49.4	232 194	57.6
Djibouti Djibouti	2003	46 564[1]	43.3[1]	23 496[1]	39.3[1]	906	40.9
	2004	48 713	43.8	26 549	40.4	1 134	44.8
	2005	50 651	44.6	30 142	39.5	1 606	41.7
	2006	53 745	44.4	30 265	39.8	1 928	40.0
	2007	56 667	45.8	34 667	40.3	2 192	40.4
	2008	56 395	46.5	41 159	40.7	...	...
Dominica Dominique	2003	10 460	48.3	7 724	51.7	...	...
	2004	9 872	48.3	7 477	50.4	...	...
	2005	9 441	48.7	7 476	50.0	...	...
	2006	8 912	48.7	7 475	49.7	...	...
	2007	8 643	48.5	7 481	50.0	...	...
Dominican Republic Rép. dominicaine	2003	1 374 624	49.4[1]	752 096[1]	54.4[1]	286 954	61.3
	2004	1 281 885	47.8	782 690	54.3	293 565[1]	61.3[1]
	2005	1 289 745	47.9	808 352	53.9	...	...
	2006	1 234 450	47.9	794 000	54.1	...	...
	2007	1 355 085	47.5	920 494	54.1	...	...
	2008	1 305 661	47.4	909 331	53.7	...	...
Ecuador Equateur	2003	1 987 465	49.1	972 777	49.6	...	...
	2004	1 989 665	49.0	996 535	49.3	...	...
	2005	1 997 624	49.0	1 053 175	49.4	...	...
	2006	2 006 430	48.9	1 103 258	49.5	...	...
	2007	2 039 168	49.0	1 141 866	49.5	443 509	54.4
Egypt Égypte	2003	7 874 308[1]	47.6[1]	8 384 065[1]	47.3[1]	2 153 865	...
	2004[1]	7 928 380	47.9	8 329 822	47.4	2 512 399	...
	2005	9 563 627	47.3	...	...	2 594 186[1]	...
	2006	9 794 591	47.4	...	...	...	...
	2007	9 988 181	47.6	...	...	...	...
El Salvador El Salvador	2003	1 016 098	48.2	488 515	49.9	116 521	53.9
	2004	1 045 485	48.2	520 332	49.9	120 264	55.7
	2005	1 045 484	48.2	524 202	50.0	122 431	54.7
	2006	1 035 100	48.2	529 057	50.3	124 956	54.7
	2007	1 075 041	49.1	536 017	50.3	132 246	54.8
Equatorial Guinea Guinée équatoriale	2003	73 771	49.2	...	...	...	...
	2005	75 809	48.7	...	...	...	...
	2007	81 099	48.6	...	...	...	...
Eritrea Erythrée	2003	359 299	44.4	161 273	39.2	5 755[1]	13.3[1]
	2004	374 997	44.2	194 124	36.1	4 612	13.1
	2005	377 512	44.4	216 944	37.2	...	...
	2006	364 263	44.4	227 786	37.6	...	...
	2007	331 855	45.1	218 369	41.4	...	...
Estonia Estonie	2003	100 171	47.7	123 074	49.7	63 625	61.5
	2004	92 098	47.9	124 382	49.4	65 659	61.8
	2005	85 539	47.9	124 493	49.1	67 760	61.5
	2006	79 589	48.0	120 286	49.3	68 286	61.6
	2007	76 026	48.3	114 141	49.3	68 767	61.1

13

Education at the primary, secondary and tertiary levels *(continued)*
Number of students enrolled and percentage female
Enseignement primaire, secondaire et supérieur *(suite)*
Nombre d'élèves inscrits et pourcentage de sexe féminin

Country or area Pays ou zone	Year[t] Année[t]	Primary education Enseignement primaire		Secondary education Enseignement secondaire		Tertiary education Enseignement supérieur	
		Total	% F	Total	% F	Total	% F
Ethiopia	2003	7 623 074	41.9	1 857 817	36.4	147 954	25.2
Ethiopie	2004	8 269 663	43.5	2 140 751	36.3	172 111	25.2
	2005	10 019 729	45.1	2 488 465	37.3	191 165	24.4
	2006	10 971 581	46.1	2 992 589	38.5	180 286	24.2
	2007	12 174 719	46.5	3 430 129	40.0	210 456	25.5
Fiji	2003	113 432	48.3	99 210	50.3	12 779[1]	53.2[1]
Fidji	2004	113 449	48.0	102 023	50.1	12 783	53.1
	2005[1]	113 643	48.0	101 741	50.1	12 717	53.1
	2006	109 702	48.0	100 243	50.7	...	...
	2007	103 641	47.8	99 098	51.1	...	...
Finland	2003	392 741	48.8	496 834	51.4	291 664	53.5
Finlande	2004	387 934	48.8	425 966	50.0	299 888	53.4
	2005	381 785	48.9	430 596	50.0	305 996	53.6
	2006	372 128	48.9	432 565	50.0	308 966	53.9
	2007	364 902	48.9	432 607	50.1	309 163	54.0
France	2003	3 791 555	48.6	5 859 127	49.1	2 119 149	55.0
France	2004	3 783 197	48.6	5 826 848	49.0	2 160 300	55.0
	2005	4 015 490	48.5	6 036 192	49.0	2 187 383	55.2
	2006	4 051 861	48.5	5 993 897	48.9	2 201 201	55.3
	2007	4 105 628	48.5	5 940 366	48.9	2 179 505	55.3
Gabon	2003	279 816	49.5	...	...	...	...
Gabon	2004[1]	281 371	49.4	...	...	...	...
Gambia	2003	195 621	49.2	73 060	42.9	...	...
Gambie	2004	180 673	50.4	81 409	45.1	1 530	19.2
	2005	181 289	51.0	94 952	45.2	...	...
	2006	207 635	50.8	126 120	45.9	...	...
	2007	218 341	50.8	101 670	47.0	...	...
	2008	216 516	51.3	104 742	48.4	...	...
Georgia	2003	239 298	48.9	452 685	48.7	155 453	48.8
Géorgie	2004	363 951	48.2	312 333	49.1	155 058	50.5
	2005	338 222	48.3	316 430	48.8	174 255	50.4
	2006	326 597	48.8	314 427	49.8[1]	144 991	52.4
	2007	322 249	47.2	321 171	48.7[1]	141 303	52.0
Germany	2003	3 303 737	48.6	8 446 559	48.3	...	...
Allemagne	2004	3 305 386	48.6	8 381 930	48.2	...	...
	2005	3 306 136	48.7	8 289 699	48.2	...	...
	2006	3 329 349	48.7	8 285 301	48.0	...	...
	2007	3 311 285	48.7	7 981 848	48.2	...	...
Ghana	2003	2 519 272	48.4	1 170 764[1]	45.0[1]	70 293	31.8
Ghana	2004	2 678 912	47.4	1 276 670	44.5	69 968	31.5
	2005	2 929 536	47.9	1 350 410[1]	45.0[1]	119 559	34.9
	2006	3 130 575	48.5	1 454 097	44.9	110 184	33.7
	2007	3 365 762	48.5	1 580 917[1]	45.8[1]	140 017	34.2
	2008	3 616 023	48.6	1 729 141	45.9	...	...
Greece	2003	652 052	48.4	713 850	48.5	561 468	51.0
Grèce	2004	657 492	48.2	695 838	48.3	597 007	51.7
	2005	650 242	48.5	715 537	47.7	646 587	51.1
	2006	645 324	48.6	704 515	47.7	653 003	50.9
	2007	639 083	48.6	682 012	47.1	602 858	50.4
Grenada	2003	16 598	49.6	14 860	48.9	...	...
Grenade	2004	15 819	48.6	13 660	51.4	...	...
	2005	16 072[1]	48.7[1]	13 675[2]	50.1[2]	...	...
	2007	13 733	48.7	13 060	49.0	...	...
Guatemala	2003[1]	2 178 200	47.4	653 492	47.2	114 764	43.0
Guatemala	2004	2 280 706	47.5	698 561	47.4	...	...
	2005	2 345 301	47.6	754 496	47.6	...	...
	2006	2 405 041	47.7	809 131	47.8	112 215[1]	45.9[1]
	2007	2 448 976	47.9	864 154	48.0	233 885	50.8
Guinea	2003	1 073 458	42.7	305 717[1]	30.8[1]	16 858[1]	15.6[1]
Guinée	2004	1 147 388	43.3	344 630	30.7	17 218	15.6

Education at the primary, secondary and tertiary levels *(continued)*
Number of students enrolled and percentage female
Enseignement primaire, secondaire et supérieur *(suite)*
Nombre d'élèves inscrits et pourcentage de sexe féminin

Country or area Pays ou zone	Year[t] Année[t]	Primary education Enseignement primaire		Secondary education Enseignement secondaire		Tertiary education Enseignement supérieur	
		Total	% F	Total	% F	Total	% F
	2005	1 206 743	44.1	420 057[1]	32.9[1]	23 788	18.6
	2006	1 258 038	44.8	482 825	34.0	42 711	21.4
	2007	1 317 791	45.2	530 590[1]	35.3[1]	...	...
Guyana Guyana	2003	110 828	49.0	64 954	...	4 848	...
	2004	114 637[1]	48.7[1]	68 979[1]	50.8[1]	6 933	65.3
	2005	116 756	49.0	70 615	50.0	7 278	67.6
	2006	110 503	49.0	70 848[1]	50.1[1]	7 370	68.7
	2007	109 243	48.7	72 970	48.8	7 532	68.1
Honduras Honduras	2003	...	...	...	...	119 877	58.6
	2004	1 257 358	49.0	...	...	122 874[1]	58.6[1]
	2005	1 231 533	49.1	...	...	...	...
	2006	1 293 333	49.0	...	...	...	...
	2007	1 308 119	49.1	554 297	55.0	...	...
Hungary Hongrie	2003	464 013	48.5	1 029 979	49.0	390 453	56.7
	2004	446 610	48.4	963 242	48.7	422 177	57.3
	2005	430 561	48.3	960 215	48.7	436 012	58.4
	2006	415 858	48.3	948 856	48.7	438 702	58.5
	2007	399 250	48.2	937 323	48.7	431 572	58.3
Iceland Islande	2003	31 470	48.4	34 587	50.4	13 347	63.7
	2004	30 984	48.4	32 700	49.5	14 710	64.5
	2005	30 785	48.3	33 323	49.3	15 169	64.9
	2006	30 421	48.6	33 900	49.5	15 721	64.3
	2007	30 084	49.0	34 434	50.2	15 821	64.1
India Inde	2003	125 568 597	46.8	81 050 129	42.6	11 295 041	38.4
	2004	136 193 772[1]	46.8[1]	84 569 081	42.6	10 009 137	39.7
	2005	138 787 993	46.7	89 461 794	42.9	11 777 296	39.4
	2006	139 169 873	46.6	91 529 430	43.2	12 852 684	39.9
Indonesia Indonésie	2003	29 050 834	48.7	15 872 535	49.0	3 441 429	43.9
	2004	29 142 093	48.7	16 353 933	49.1	3 551 092	43.8
	2005	29 149 746	48.3[1]	15 993 187	49.0[1]	3 660 270[1]	43.7[1]
	2006	28 982 708	48.2	16 797 809	49.3	3 657 429	...
	2007	29 796 705	48.1	18 716 929	49.4	3 755 187	49.5
Iran (Islamic Rep. of) Iran (Rép. islamique d')	2003	7 028 924	47.9	10 024 105	47.2	1 714 433	50.7
	2004	7 306 634	51.1	10 312 561	47.1	1 954 920	51.4
	2005	7 307 056	53.7	9 942 201	47.2	2 126 274	51.0
	2006	7 273 911	54.7	...	...	2 398 811	51.6
	2007	7 152 492	55.1	...	...	2 828 528	52.4
Iraq Iraq	2003	4 280 602	44.5	1 477 616	40.5	...	...
	2004	4 334 609	44.3	1 706 234	38.9	412 545	36.2
	2005[1]	4 430 267	44.3	1 751 164	38.9	424 908	36.2
Ireland Irlande	2003	447 618	48.5	320 620	50.9	181 557	55.7
	2004	450 413	48.5	320 560	50.7	188 315	55.2
	2005	454 060	48.5	317 337	51.0	186 561	54.9
	2006	461 588	48.5	313 479	50.6	186 044	55.1
	2007	475 836	48.5	316 015	50.6	190 349	55.2
Israel Israël	2003	769 856	48.6	603 321	48.3	301 326	55.7
	2004	775 021	48.8	607 224	48.8	301 227	55.8
	2005	784 663	48.9	610 341	48.7	310 937	56.0
	2006	802 555	49.0	613 366	48.6	310 014	55.1
	2007	826 314	48.9	615 973	48.8	327 108	55.8
Italy Italie	2003	2 778 877	48.4	4 528 300	48.5[1]	1 913 352	56.2
	2004	2 768 386	48.4	4 505 699	48.5	1 986 497	56.2
	2005	2 771 247	48.3	4 507 408	48.4	2 014 998	56.6
	2006	2 790 254	48.3	4 531 571	48.4	2 029 023	56.9
	2007	2 820 150	48.3	4 553 163	48.3	2 033 642	57.2
Jamaica Jamaïque	2003	325 302	48.9	229 701	50.1	45 770[1]	69.9[1]
	2004	331 286	48.9	245 533	49.9	...	...
	2005	326 411	48.8	246 332	50.1	...	...
	2007	310 021	49.0	257 186	50.4	...	...

13

Education at the primary, secondary and tertiary levels *(continued)*
Number of students enrolled and percentage female
Enseignement primaire, secondaire et supérieur *(suite)*
Nombre d'élèves inscrits et pourcentage de sexe féminin

Country or area Pays ou zone	Year[t] Année[t]	Primary education Enseignement primaire		Secondary education Enseignement secondaire		Tertiary education Enseignement supérieur	
		Total	% F	Total	% F	Total	% F
Japan	2003	7 268 928	48.8	8 131 217	48.9	3 984 400	45.6
Japon	2004	7 257 223	48.8	7 894 456	48.9	4 031 604	45.8
	2005	7 231 854	48.8	7 710 439	48.8	4 038 302	45.9
	2006	7 229 135	48.8	7 561 241	48.8	4 084 861	45.7
	2007	7 220 111	48.8	7 427 059	48.8	4 032 625	45.6
Jordan	2003	786 154	48.9	613 120	49.3	186 189	51.1
Jordanie	2004	799 888	48.9	615 731	49.2	214 106	51.2
	2005	804 904	48.9	625 682	49.2	217 823	50.3
	2006	805 457	49.3	649 242	49.5	220 103	51.6
	2007	807 702	49.3	670 836	49.5	231 657	51.3
Kazakhstan	2003	1 120 005	48.9	2 067 168	49.2	603 072	56.6
Kazakhstan	2004	1 079 598	48.8	2 090 152	48.6	664 449	57.4
	2005	1 023 974	48.8	2 039 911	48.5	753 181	58.1
	2006	972 931	48.8	1 982 190	48.4	780 783	58.0
	2007	947 807	48.8	1 874 213	48.6	772 600	58.2
	2008	956 019	48.8	1 778 106	48.4	719 802	58.2
Kenya	2003	5 811 381	48.5	2 197 336	50.4	...	...
Kenya	2004	5 926 078	48.3	2 419 856[1]	48.1[1]	104 584[1]	37.7
	2005	6 075 706	48.7	2 464 042[1]	48.6[1]	107 802[1]	37.7[1]
	2006	6 101 390	49.0	2 583 755	48.1	...	...
	2007	6 687 510	49.4	2 729 040	46.5	139 524	36.3
Kiribati	2003	15 798	48.3	11 372	52.9	...	...
Kiribati	2004	15 611	49.6	11 581	52.8	...	...
	2005	16 132	49.4	11 331	51.7	...	...
Korea, Republic of	2003	4 185 330	47.0	3 645 617	47.4	3 223 431	36.6
Corée, République de	2004	4 125 423	47.1	3 692 513	47.2	3 224 875	36.8
	2005	4 031 496	47.2	3 786 224	47.1	3 210 184	37.1
	2006	3 933 186	47.4	3 864 005	46.9	3 204 036	37.5
	2007	3 837 696	47.6	3 917 400	46.8	3 208 591	38.0
Kuwait	2003	154 056	49.0	260 695	49.7	37 153	64.5
Koweït	2004	158 271	49.0	267 114	49.9	36 866[1]	64.3[1]
	2005	202 826	48.5	248 895	49.7	38 630	70.2
	2006	203 423	48.8	236 410	49.8	37 521	65.4
	2007	211 576	48.7	247 233	48.9	...	...
Kyrgyzstan	2003	449 399	48.9	739 259	49.7	201 128	54.1
Kirghizistan	2004	444 417	49.0	732 618	49.6	205 224	54.0
	2005	434 155	48.7	721 205	49.5	220 460	55.3
	2006	423 930	48.8	718 585	49.5	233 463	55.6
	2007	407 669	48.8	713 613	49.5	239 380	56.1
Lao People's Dem. Rep.	2003	875 300	45.6	353 362	41.9	28 117	35.8
Rép. dém. pop. lao	2004	884 629	45.9	379 579	42.2	33 760	38.0
	2005	890 821	46.0	393 856	42.5	47 424	41.2
	2006	891 881	46.1	395 382	43.0	56 716	40.0
	2007	891 807	46.4	403 833	43.4	75 003	41.5
Latvia	2003	103 359	48.2	276 072	48.8	118 944	61.7
Lettonie	2004	92 453	48.1	275 586	48.8	127 656	62.3
	2005	84 369	47.9	271 631	49.0	130 706	63.2
	2006	78 796	47.9	258 432	49.1	131 125	63.3
	2007	75 704	48.1	241 617[1]	49.1[1]	129 497	63.9
Lebanon	2003	449 311	48.2	350 211	51.3	144 050	54.0
Liban	2004	453 578	48.2	359 062	51.4	154 635	52.3
	2005	452 607	48.2	362 366	51.5	165 730	52.8
	2006	447 593	48.4	365 571	51.5	173 123	53.2
	2007	450 566	48.3	368 359	51.9	187 055	54.0
	2008	445 240	48.3	369 691	51.6	196 682	54.7
Lesotho	2003	429 522	50.0	84 318	56.0	6 108	61.3
Lesotho	2004	427 009	49.7	89 468	55.9	...	...
	2005	422 278	49.6	94 460	55.8	7 918	56.9
	2006	424 855	49.6	93 996	56.0	8 500	55.2

Education at the primary, secondary and tertiary levels *(continued)*
Number of students enrolled and percentage female
Enseignement primaire, secondaire et supérieur *(suite)*
Nombre d'élèves inscrits et pourcentage de sexe féminin

Country or area Pays ou zone	Year[t] Année[t]	Primary education Enseignement primaire		Secondary education Enseignement secondaire		Tertiary education Enseignement supérieur	
		Total	% F	Total	% F	Total	% F
Liberia	2006	538 450	47.2	...	...	...	...
Libéria	2008	538 842	46.9	...	...	...	...
Libyan Arab Jamah.	2003	739 028	48.0	797 992[1]	50.5[1]	375 028[1]	51.4[1]
Jamah. arabe libyenne	2004	745 428	48.0	...	...	...	...
	2005	713 902	48.4	701 536	53.3[1]	...	...
	2006	755 338	47.7	732 614	52.9	...	...
Liechtenstein	2003	2 218	49.8	3 255	45.0	440	27.0
Liechtenstein	2004	2 266	49.8	3 273	45.2	532	26.7
	2005	2 242	50.0	3 142	45.6	527	28.8
	2006	2 247	50.7	3 190	45.5	636	30.3
	2007	2 244	50.8	3 169	45.9	673	31.8
Lithuania	2003	183 542	48.5	447 952	48.5	167 606	60.0
Lituanie	2004	170 216	48.6	431 303	48.8	182 656	60.0
	2005	158 105	48.6	423 706	48.8	195 405	60.1
	2006	150 422	48.4	410 507	48.9	198 868	59.9
	2007	143 814	48.3	393 889	48.9	199 855	60.0
Luxembourg	2003	34 081	48.7	34 716	50.2	3 077	53.3
Luxembourg	2004	34 603	48.7	35 208	50.2	3 042[1]	52.9[1]
	2005	35 016	48.8	35 946	50.4	...	...
	2006	35 431	48.9	37 009	50.0	2 692	51.6
	2007	35 668	48.7	38 209	49.8	...	...
Madagascar	2003	2 856 480	48.9	...	...	35 480	45.4[1]
Madagascar	2004	3 366 470	48.9	...	...	42 143	47.3
	2005	3 597 731	48.9	621 173[1]	49.0	44 948	47.0
	2006	3 698 906	49.0	730 406	48.7	49 680	46.5
	2007	3 837 343	49.2	835 539[1]	48.7[1]	58 313	47.0
Malawi	2003	...	...	...	...	4 757[2]	29.2[1]
Malawi	2004	2 841 640	50.3	505 303	44.6	5 782[2]	35.3
	2005	2 867 993	50.2	515 462	44.8	5 810[2]	35.3[1]
	2006	2 933 695	50.5	565 491	45.5	6 298[2]	33.6[1]
	2007	2 943 248	50.4	574 003	45.2	6 458	33.6
Malaysia	2003	3 056 266	48.6	2 518 642	51.9	725 865	57.2
Malaisie	2004	3 159 376	48.6	2 583 993	51.9	731 077	55.4
	2005	3 202 008	48.6	2 489 117	51.3	696 760	56.0
	2006	3 133 399	48.6	...	...	749 165	54.5
Maldives	2003	66 169	47.8	28 612	51.6	73	69.9
Maldives	2004	63 300	47.6	28 878[1]	51.9[1]	73[1]	69.9[1]
	2005	57 873	47.8	...	...	...	...
	2006	54 770	47.7	32 645[1]	50.3[1]	...	...
	2007	50 270	47.8	...	...	...	...
Mali	2003	1 294 672	42.7	349 615	34.6	25 605[1]	33.9[1]
Mali	2004	1 396 791	43.1	388 418	36.7	28 578	34.6
	2005	1 505 903	43.4	429 716	37.5[1]	33 222	34.6[1]
	2006	1 609 979	44.0	474 976	37.5	42 005[1]	...
	2007	1 716 956	44.4	533 849	39.1	50 787	...
Malta	2003	31 710	48.1	37 556	48.4	8 946	57.0
Malte	2004	31 064	48.2	41 723	46.8	7 867	55.9
	2005	29 596	48.0	38 479	48.6	9 441	56.3
Marshall Islands	2003[1]	8 907	47.0	6 460	49.5	919	56.5
Iles Marshall	2004	8 250	47.5	5 846	49.8	...	...
	2005[1]	8 393	47.5	5 901	49.8	...	...
	2007	8 215	47.9	5 369	49.1	...	...
Mauritania	2003	394 401	49.2	84 407	44.4	8 941	21.4[2]
Mauritanie	2004	434 181	49.4	88 926	45.3	9 292	23.7
	2005	443 615	50.0	92 796	45.9	8 758	24.5
	2006	465 970	49.8	98 946[1]	45.0[1]	10 157	25.6
	2007	483 776	50.0	102 130[1]	45.6[1]	11 794	...
Mauritius	2003	129 616	49.4	118 234	49.2	16 764	57.9
Maurice	2004	126 226	49.3	122 556	49.0	17 781	57.6
	2005	123 562	49.2	127 891[1]	49.1[1]	16 852	55.3

13

Education at the primary, secondary and tertiary levels *(continued)*
Number of students enrolled and percentage female
Enseignement primaire, secondaire et supérieur *(suite)*
Nombre d'élèves inscrits et pourcentage de sexe féminin

Country or area Pays ou zone	Year [t] Année [t]	Primary education Enseignement primaire		Secondary education Enseignement secondaire		Tertiary education Enseignement supérieur	
		Total	% F	Total	% F	Total	% F
	2006	121 387	49.2	...	...	16 773	52.9
	2007	119 310	49.2	...	...	...	...
	2008	...	...	...	...	13 509	53.3
Mexico	2003	14 857 191	48.8	10 188 185	51.5	2 236 791	49.6
Mexique	2004	14 781 327	48.8	10 403 853	51.2	2 322 781	50.0
	2005	14 700 005	48.8	10 564 404	51.2	2 384 858	50.3
	2006	14 595 195	48.7	10 883 455	51.3	2 446 726	50.3
	2007	14 631 498	48.8	11 122 276	51.3	2 528 664	50.3
Micronesia (Fed. States of)	2004	19 105	48.3	13 506	48.8	...	...
Micronésie (Etats féd. de)	2005	18 793	48.1	13 634	49.3	...	...
	2007	18 512	49.0	14 742[1]	...	...	...
Monaco	2004	1 831	...	3 078	...	...	...
Monaco	2008	1 852	47.5	3 015	48.0	...	...
Mongolia	2003	238 676	49.6	312 774	53.1	98 031	62.4
Mongolie	2004	235 730	49.4	333 193	52.5	108 738	61.8
	2005	251 205	49.5	339 249	52.4	123 824	61.4
	2006	249 622	49.5	329 269	52.1	138 019	60.7
	2007	239 262	49.4	328 009	51.8	142 411	60.5
Montserrat	2003[1]	465	45.2	285	49.5	...	...
Montserrat	2004	468	44.7	284	48.9	...	...
	2005	509	46.2	298	49.3	...	...
	2006	508	45.9	328	46.3	...	...
	2007	497	49.3	347	46.4	...	...
Morocco	2003	4 101 157	46.4	1 758 057	44.5	335 755	44.9
Maroc	2004	4 070 182	46.5	1 879 483	44.8	343 599	45.7
	2005	4 022 600	46.4	1 952 456[1]	45.1[1]	366 879	45.1
	2006	3 943 831	46.3	2 061 046	...	384 595	45.2
	2007	3 939 177	46.5	2 173 454	45.5[1]	369 142	47.6
Mozambique	2003	...	...	...	...	17 225	32.2
Mozambique	2004	3 569 473	45.3	243 428	41.1	22 256	31.6
	2005	3 942 829	45.7	305 877	40.8	28 298	33.1
	2006	4 172 749	46.2	367 395	41.8	...	...
	2007	4 563 633	46.4	444 926	42.2	...	...
Myanmar	2003	4 889 325	49.7	2 382 608	48.1	...	...
Myanmar	2004	4 932 646	49.7	2 544 437	48.0	...	...
	2005	4 948 198	49.9	2 589 312	49.1	...	...
	2006	4 969 445	49.6	2 696 307	49.3	...	...
	2007	5 013 582	...	2 686 198	49.9	507 660	57.9
Namibia	2003	408 912	49.9	140 976	52.9	11 788	53.2
Namibie	2004	403 412	50.0	144 289	53.0	12 197	53.2
	2005	404 198	49.8	148 104	53.1	13 566	46.7
	2006	402 529	49.8	152 637	53.4	13 185	46.7
	2007	409 508	49.6	158 162	53.9	...	...
Nauru	2003	1 375	46.8	645	50.4	...	...
Nauru	2004	1 529	47.4	508	52.4	...	...
	2005	1 812	48.2	600	50.7	...	...
	2006	1 393	47.1	815	51.7	...	...
	2007	1 235	48.6	689	51.4	...	...
Nepal	2003	3 928 684	45.4	1 822 063	41.9	124 817	24.1
Népal	2004	4 025 692	45.4	...	...	147 123	27.6
	2005	4 030 045	46.3	2 054 165	44.7[1]	...	...
	2006	4 502 697	47.4	1 983 561[1]	45.5[1]	...	...
	2007	4 515 059	48.3	1 998 990[1]	46.2[1]	320 844	...
	2008	4 418 713	48.9	2 305 166	46.7	...	...
Netherlands	2003	1 290 625	48.2	1 415 170	48.6	526 767	51.0
Pays-Bas	2004	1 283 014	48.2	1 396 696	48.5	543 396	50.9
	2005	1 277 990	48.2	1 410 547	48.4	564 983	51.0
	2006	1 277 478	48.2	1 423 262	48.4	579 622	51.1
	2007	1 280 571	48.3	1 444 057	48.4	590 121	51.5

Education at the primary, secondary and tertiary levels *(continued)*
Number of students enrolled and percentage female
Enseignement primaire, secondaire et supérieur *(suite)*
Nombre d'élèves inscrits et pourcentage de sexe féminin

Country or area Pays ou zone	Year[t] Année[t]	Primary education Enseignement primaire		Secondary education Enseignement secondaire		Tertiary education Enseignement supérieur	
		Total	% F	Total	% F	Total	% F
Netherlands Antilles[1] Antilles néerlandaises[1]	2003	22 667	49.2	15 268	52.1	...	...
New Zealand	2003	356 442	48.5	503 706	51.3	195 511	58.6
Nouvelle-Zélande	2004	353 062	48.5	503 241	50.3	243 425	58.4
	2005	352 845	48.5	526 152	50.2	239 983	58.7
	2006	350 810	48.6	522 325	49.8	237 784	59.0
	2007	349 080	48.7	526 974	49.3	242 651	58.7
Nicaragua	2003	927 217	48.7	412 343[1]	52.7[1]	103 577[1]	52.1[1]
Nicaragua	2004	941 957	48.6	416 405	52.7	...	...
	2005	945 089	48.4	437 853	52.7	...	...
	2006	966 206	48.4	448 258	52.6	...	...
	2007	952 964	48.5	470 520	52.4	...	...
Niger	2003	857 592	40.1	126 137	38.9	8 850[1]	27.2[1]
Niger	2004	980 033	40.3	158 343	38.5	8 774	27.4
	2005	1 064 056	40.8	181 641	39.1	10 799	29.6
	2006	1 126 073	41.0	216 961	38.8	11 208	26.6
	2007	1 235 065	41.5	213 991	37.9	10 000	28.6
Nigeria	2003	20 600 798[1]	44.6[1]	5 701 917	43.1	1 234 219[1]	34.6[1]
Nigéria	2004	21 395 510	44.7	6 279 562	43.6	1 289 656	34.6
	2005	22 115 432	44.9	6 397 581	44.6	1 391 527	40.7
	2006	22 861 884	45.4	6 436 449	44.2	...	...
Niue	2004	184	51.1	209	50.7	...	...
Nioué	2005	178	50.6	206	48.1	...	...
Norway	2003	432 618	48.6	385 009	49.3	212 395	59.7
Norvège	2004	432 345	48.7	400 159	49.5	213 845	59.6
	2005	429 652	48.7	403 026	48.9	213 940	59.6
	2006	429 680	48.8	412 311	48.5	214 711	59.7
	2007	430 747	48.7	419 698	48.3	215 237	60.2
Occupied Palestinian Terr.	2003	401 372	49.0	582 736	50.2	104 567	49.5
Terr. palestinien occupé	2004	388 948	48.9	628 495	50.1	121 928	49.5
	2005	387 138	48.8	656 797	50.1	138 139	49.5
	2006	381 904	49.0	685 585	50.3	150 128	52.7
	2007	383 559	49.0	701 715	50.5	169 373	53.7
Oman	2003	314 064	48.5	279 302	48.1	36 826	41.5
Oman	2004	306 210	48.6	286 413	47.9	41 578	51.8
	2005	297 120	48.8	292 783	47.7	48 483	50.8
	2006	287 938	48.9	299 484	47.8	68 154	49.9
	2007	278 461	49.1	306 377	47.0	69 018	53.1
Pakistan	2003	15 093 960	40.6	7 307 218[1]	42.6[1]	401 056	43.2
Pakistan	2004	16 207 286	40.8	8 249 163[1]	42.3[1]	520 666	42.7
	2005	17 257 947	41.8	7 994 299[1]	42.3	782 621	45.1
	2006	16 687 658	42.4	8 421 015	42.3	820 347	44.5
	2007	17 979 190	43.6	9 145 084	41.8	954 698[1]	44.5[1]
Palau	2003[1]	1 809	43.6	2 465	52.2	...	...
Palaos	2004	1 855	48.0	2 273	50.4	...	...
	2005[1]	1 913	48.1	2 282	...	...	...
	2007	1 544	47.8[1]	2 448	49.6[1]	...	...
Panama	2003	424 500[1]	48.2[1]	253 012[1]	50.7[1]	130 026	60.6
Panama	2004	429 837	48.3	253 900	50.8	128 558	61.6
	2005	430 152	48.2	256 224	50.8	126 242	61.2
	2006	436 945	48.3	257 378	51.0	130 838	60.9
	2007	446 176	48.3	260 694	50.8	...	...
Papua New Guinea	2003	496 616	44.6	...	...	...	...
Papouasie-Nvl-Guinée	2004	508 333	44.9	...	...	...	...
	2005	531 759	44.4	...	...	...	...
	2006	532 250	44.3	...	...	...	...
Paraguay	2003	935 722	48.3	510 881	49.6	143 913[1]	57.2[1]
Paraguay	2004	930 918	48.4	526 001	49.7	149 120[1]	56.6[1]
	2005	933 995	48.4	529 309	49.9	156 167[1]	52.3[1]

13

Education at the primary, secondary and tertiary levels *(continued)*
Number of students enrolled and percentage female
Enseignement primaire, secondaire et supérieur *(suite)*
Nombre d'élèves inscrits et pourcentage de sexe féminin

Country or area Pays ou zone	Year[t] Année[t]	Primary education Enseignement primaire		Secondary education Enseignement secondaire		Tertiary education Enseignement supérieur	
		Total	% F	Total	% F	Total	% F
Peru	2003	4 200 489	49.0	2 605 247	49.4	839 584[1]	51.1[1]
Pérou	2004	4 133 386	49.0	2 661 880	49.6	896 501[1]	50.0[1]
	2005	4 077 361	49.1	2 691 311	49.6	909 315[1]	50.0[1]
	2006	4 026 316	49.0	2 760 349	49.8	952 437[1]	50.9[1]
	2007	3 993 965	49.0	2 861 313	50.0	...	...
Philippines	2003	12 970 635	48.6	6 069 063	51.5	2 427 211	55.3
Philippines	2004	13 017 973	48.5	6 308 792	51.6	2 420 997	55.2
	2005	13 083 744	48.6	6 352 482	51.7	2 402 649	54.2
	2006	13 006 648	48.5	6 301 582	51.6	2 483 988	54.5
	2007	13 145 210	48.5	6 365 985	51.4	...	...
Poland	2003	2 983 070	48.6	3 895 167	47.8	1 983 360	57.8
Pologne	2004	2 855 692	48.6	3 480 054	49.1	2 044 298	57.6
	2005	2 723 661	48.6	3 444 903	48.6	2 118 081	57.5
	2006	2 602 020	48.6	3 316 939	48.4	2 145 687	57.4
	2007	2 484 820	48.5	3 205 849	48.5	2 146 926	57.4
Portugal	2003	767 872	47.5	766 172	51.0	400 831	56.6
Portugal	2004	758 476	47.5	665 213	51.4	395 063	56.1
	2005	752 739	47.6	669 529	51.2	380 937	55.7
	2006	750 493	47.6	661 748	51.0	367 312	55.2
	2007	753 646	47.5	680 338	50.7	366 729	54.0
Qatar	2003	66 473	48.3	51 888	49.5	7 826	72.8
Qatar	2004	65 351	48.5	53 953	48.9	9 287	71.4
	2005	69 991	48.7	55 705	49.4	9 760[1]	68.0[1]
	2006	70 927	48.8	58 787	49.2	10 161[1]	67.6[1]
	2007	75 451	48.7	61 226	49.5	8 881	64.3
Republic of Moldova	2003	215 442	48.7	410 590	50.0	114 238	56.4
République de Moldova	2004	201 650	48.6	406 716	50.3	119 981	56.9
	2005	184 159	48.5	394 469	50.1	130 350	58.7
	2006	171 024	48.6	381 543	50.1	143 750	57.4
	2007	160 528	48.5	367 636	49.9	148 449[2]	57.3[2]
Romania	2003	990 807	48.3	2 218 124	49.4	643 911	54.3
Roumanie	2004	1 005 533	48.3	2 154 734	49.3	685 718	54.8
	2005	970 295	48.4	2 089 646	49.2	738 806	54.6
	2006	938 095	48.4	2 013 016	49.0	834 969	55.4
	2007	917 829	48.5	1 954 077	48.7	928 175	56.1
Russian Federation	2003	5 416 925	48.7	14 521 818	48.9	8 099 662	56.8
Fédération de Russie	2004	...	...	13 558 904	48.8	8 605 952	57.0
	2005	5 308 605	48.8	12 433 155	48.7	9 003 208	57.1
	2006	5 164 735	48.9	11 548 337	48.5	9 167 277	56.9
	2007	5 010 284	48.8	10 797 816	48.4	9 370 428	56.8
Rwanda	2003	1 636 563	50.5	189 153	47.5	20 393	36.8
Rwanda	2004	1 752 588	50.8	203 551	47.7	25 233	39.1
	2005[1]	1 851 879	51.3	218 227	47.8	26 378	39.0
	2006	2 019 991	51.3	...	...	...	...
	2007	2 150 430	50.9	266 518	47.6	...	...
Saint Kitts and Nevis	2003	6 401	49.0	4 098	52.6	...	...
Saint-Kitts-et-Nevis	2004	6 394	50.2	3 903[1]	52.0[1]	...	...
	2005	6 350	49.8	3 939[1]	50.7[1]	...	...
	2007	6 172	49.4	4 522	49.6	...	...
Saint Lucia	2003	24 573	48.4	14 110[1]	53.1[1]	2 051[1]	67.7[1]
Sainte-Lucie	2004	23 821	48.3	14 209	52.6	2 285	77.8
	2005	23 573	48.6	13 786	54.3	2 197	73.8
	2006	24 046	47.8	14 377	53.9	1 628	84.6
	2007	22 028	48.6	15 146	52.5	1 438	70.7
Saint Vincent-Grenadines	2003	18 629	48.7	9 624	52.0	...	...
Saint Vincent-Grenadines	2004	17 536	48.4	10 398	51.5[1]	...	...
	2005	17 858	47.0	9 780	55.2	...	...
	2007	15 928	48.3	...	...	...	...
Samoa	2003	31 059	47.8	23 427	50.7	...	...
Samoa	2004	31 175	48.0	23 764	50.6	...	...

Country or area Pays ou zone	Year [t] Année [t]	Primary education Enseignement primaire		Secondary education Enseignement secondaire		Tertiary education Enseignement supérieur	
		Total	% F	Total	% F	Total	% F
	2005 [1]	31 596	47.9	24 242	50.7	...	...
	2007	30 199	48.0	...	...	...	...
San Marino	2004	1 445	...	...	...	...	...
Saint-Marin	2008	1 573	47.6	2 223	48.7	929	57.4
Sao Tome and Principe	2003	29 347	48.5	6 753	53.5	...	...
Sao Tomé-et-Principe	2004	29 784	48.7	7 423	50.5	...	...
	2005	30 468	48.6	8 091	51.1	...	...
	2006 [1]	31 066	48.6	8 142	51.2	...	...
	2007	31 397	49.3	8 997	51.2	...	...
	2008	32 584	49.0	8 518	51.1	...	...
Saudi Arabia	2003	...	...	...	...	525 344	58.2
Arabie saoudite	2004	...	...	...	...	573 732	58.7
	2005	3 097 604 [2]	49.0 [2]	2 609 567	48.0	603 671	58.1
	2006	...	...	...	...	636 445	57.9
	2007	3 173 807	48.8 [2]	2 826 049	...	...	...
Senegal	2003	1 287 093	47.5	309 959	40.6	50 375 [1]	...
Sénégal	2004	1 382 749	48.3	360 016	41.6	52 282	...
	2005	1 444 163	48.6	405 899	42.5	59 127 [1]	...
	2006	1 473 464	49.2	447 425 [1]	42.8 [1]	62 539	31.6
	2007	1 572 178	49.6	505 097 [1]	43.0 [1]	76 949 [1]	33.8 [1]
	2008	...	...	...	...	91 359	35.3
Serbia	2003	334 771 [1]	48.9	655 904 [1]	49.7 [1]	...	...
Serbie	2004 [1]	328 439	48.8	641 743	49.5	...	...
	2005	324 490	48.8	632 761	49.5	...	...
	2006	312 469	48.8	622 854	49.6	...	...
	2007	297 429	48.8	615 522	49.4	...	...
Seychelles	2003	9 477	48.6	7 551	50.2	...	...
Seychelles	2004	8 906	48.8	7 406	50.7	...	...
	2005	9 204	48.3	7 520	48.2	...	...
	2007	8 864	49.3	7 816	50.1	...	...
Sierra Leone							
Sierra Leone	2007	1 322 205	47.5	239 579	41.0		
Singapore							
Singapour	2007	301 101	48.1	232 100	48.2	183 627	48.5
Slovakia	2003	270 004	48.5	669 578	49.1	158 089	53.1
Slovaquie	2004	254 906	48.5	682 780	49.3	164 667	54.1
	2005	242 459	48.5	672 670	49.2	181 419	55.3
	2006	235 378	48.5	650 438	49.2	197 943	57.7
	2007	230 536	48.6	617 109	49.1	217 952	58.9
Slovenia	2003	87 085	48.5	217 587	48.6	101 458	56.2
Slovénie	2004	93 371	48.6	187 817	48.8	104 396	56.9
	2005	93 156	48.4	181 299	48.7	112 228	57.8
	2006	93 274	48.4	174 330	48.7	114 794	58.4
	2007	95 173	48.3	165 467	48.5	115 944	58.3
Solomon Islands	2003 [1]	68 146	46.5	21 885	42.8	...	...
Iles Salomon	2004 [1]	70 906	46.8	22 157	43.5	...	...
	2005	75 082	46.8	22 487	43.5	...	...
South Africa	2003	7 470 476	48.8	4 446 841	51.5	717 793	53.8
Afrique du Sud	2004	7 444 142	48.7	4 593 492	51.5	744 489	54.2
	2005	7 314 449	48.7	4 657 674	51.4	735 073	54.6
	2006	7 256 518	48.7	4 772 456 [1]	51.3 [1]	741 380	55.1
	2007	7 312 258	48.8	4 779 747 [1]	51.0 [1]		
Spain	2003	2 488 319	48.3	3 052 662	50.0	1 840 607	53.1
Espagne	2004	2 497 513	48.4	3 048 188	50.2	1 839 903	53.8
	2005	2 484 903	48.3	3 107 816	50.1	1 809 353	53.7
	2006	2 501 205	48.3	3 091 036	50.1	1 789 254	53.9
	2007	2 555 757	48.3	3 080 161	50.2	1 777 498	54.0
Sri Lanka	2003	1 702 035	49.1 [1]	2 320 093 [1]	50.6 [1]	...	...
Sri Lanka	2004 [1]	1 612 318	...	2 332 326	49.4	...	...
	2005 [1]	1 635 308	49.1	...	...	...	...

13

Education at the primary, secondary and tertiary levels *(continued)*
Number of students enrolled and percentage female
Enseignement primaire, secondaire et supérieur *(suite)*
Nombre d'élèves inscrits et pourcentage de sexe féminin

Country or area Pays ou zone	Year[t] Année[t]	Primary education Enseignement primaire		Secondary education Enseignement secondaire		Tertiary education Enseignement supérieur	
		Total	% F	Total	% F	Total	% F
	2006	1 611 763	49.0	...	...	...	...
	2007	1 621 617	49.0	...	...	...	...
Sudan	2003	3 028 127	45.5	1 278 633	47.1	...	...
Soudan	2004	3 208 186	45.5	1 393 778	47.1	...	...
	2005	3 278 090	45.6	1 369 735	47.5	...	...
	2006	3 880 705	45.6	1 446 539	48.1	...	...
	2007	3 959 310	45.3	1 462 798	47.2	...	...
Suriname	2003[1]	64 659	48.7	41 000	56.3	...	...
Suriname	2005	65 527	48.3	45 818	55.8	...	...
	2006	66 121	48.3	46 725	56.3	...	...
	2007	65 020	47.9	47 235	56.6	...	...
Swaziland	2003	208 444	48.5	62 401	50.2	5 369[1]	54.4[1]
Swaziland	2004	218 352	48.1	67 696	49.1	6 594	52.4
	2005	221 596	48.0	71 124	49.9	5 897	52.0
	2006	229 686	47.9	77 169	50.1	5 692	49.8
	2007	232 572	47.9	83 049	47.1	...	...
Sweden	2003	774 888	49.4	917 978	52.9	414 657	59.6
Suède	2004	690 758	48.6	711 798	49.5	429 623	59.6
	2005	658 461	48.7	735 494	48.6	426 723	59.6
	2006	626 847	48.7	750 567	48.5	422 614	59.6
	2007	601 120	48.6	760 491	48.5	413 710	59.9
Switzerland	2003	535 577	48.6	555 505	47.3	185 965	44.2
Suisse	2004	532 092	48.5	563 701	47.2	195 947	44.9
	2005	524 222	48.6	574 783	47.3	199 696	46.0
	2006	517 056	48.5	584 073	47.3	204 999	46.9
	2007	510 804	48.5	592 454	47.5	213 112	47.6
Syrian Arab Republic	2003	2 149 493	47.5	2 119 690	47.1	...	...
Rép. arabe syrienne	2004	2 192 764	47.6	2 249 116	47.2	...	...
	2005	2 252 145	47.8	2 389 383	47.4	...	...
	2006	2 279 545	47.8	2 464 688	47.7	...	...
	2007	2 310 168	47.8	2 549 444	48.2	...	...
Tajikistan	2003	694 930	48.0	948 341	44.8	97 466	25.0
Tadjikistan	2004	690 270	48.0	973 673	45.1	108 456	24.8
	2005	693 078	48.2	984 410	44.8	119 317	25.9
	2006	687 900	48.0	998 928	44.7	133 385	26.8
	2007	680 308	48.2	1 012 275	45.0	147 294	27.4
Thailand	2003[1]	5 997 390	48.3	4 128 232	49.2	2 205 581	52.9
Thaïlande	2004	6 054 517	48.4	4 253 380	50.9	2 251 453	53.7
	2005	5 974 615	48.1	4 533 173	50.5[1]	2 359 127	52.4
	2006	5 843 512	48.4	4 530 029	50.8	2 338 572	51.0
	2007	5 703 756	48.4	4 789 339	51.1	2 503 572	54.5
	2008	5 564 622	48.4	4 728 761	51.0	2 422 205[1]	54.0[1]
TFYR of Macedonia	2003	116 635	48.4	218 649	48.1	45 624	56.2
L'ex-R.Y. Macédoine	2004	113 362	48.4	215 760	48.0	46 637	57.0
	2005	110 149	48.3	214 005	48.0	49 364	56.7
	2007	100 911	48.2	208 364	47.8	58 199	54.5
Timor-Leste	2003	183 800	...	...	...	...	...
Timor-Leste	2004	183 483	47.1	73 005	48.1	...	...
	2005	177 970	46.9	74 822	48.7	...	...
	2007	173 983	47.5	...	...	...	...
Togo	2003	975 063	45.2	354 965	33.0	...	...
Togo	2004	984 846	45.6	375 385	34.0	...	...
	2005	996 707	45.9	404 470	34.7	...	...
	2006	1 051 872	46.3	430 064	35.3	28 076[1]	...
	2007	1 021 617	46.4	408 964	34.6[1]	32 502	...
Tokelau	2003	227	50.2	191	47.6	...	...
Tokélaou	2004[1]	243	57.2	175	45.1	...	...
Tonga	2003	17 891	46.9	15 743	...	668	60.5
Tonga	2004	17 113	46.9	14 032	49.2[1]	657[1]	59.8[1]

Country or area Pays ou zone	Year[t] Année[t]	Primary education Enseignement primaire		Secondary education Enseignement secondaire		Tertiary education Enseignement supérieur	
		Total	% F	Total	% F	Total	% F
	2005	17 857	47.1	...	...	...	...
	2006	16 941	47.1	13 938	48.4	...	...
Trinidad and Tobago Trinité-et-Tobago	2003	141 036	48.6	107 880[1]	51.4[1]	12 316	61.1
	2004	137 313[2]	48.5[2]	105 381[1]	51.1[1]	16 751	55.4
	2005	129 703[2]	48.6[2]	97 080[1]	50.4[1]	16 920[1]	55.6[1]
	2007	130 242	48.5	98 490[1]	51.0[1]	...	...
Tunisia Tunisie	2003	1 277 124	47.7	1 148 523	50.8	263 414	54.9
	2004	1 228 347	47.7	1 210 012	...	291 842	56.5
	2005	1 184 301	47.7	1 239 468	51.1	311 569	57.2
	2006	1 134 414	47.7	1 247 046	51.0[1]	325 325	57.5
	2007	1 068 822	47.7	1 268 219	...	326 185	59.0
Turkey Turquie	2003	7 904 361[1]	47.5[1]	5 742 070[1]	42.0[1]	1 918 483	42.3
	2004	7 872 546[1]	47.6[1]	5 330 923[1]	42.0[1]	1 972 662	41.4
	2005	7 947 603[1]	47.7[1]	5 075 720[1]	44.2[1]	2 106 351	41.9
	2006	7 949 758[1]	47.9[1]	5 388 119[1]	44.5[1]	2 342 898	42.4
	2007	8 065 193[1]	47.7[1]	5 527 208[1]	44.4[1]	2 453 664	42.6
Turks and Caicos Islands Iles Turques et Caïques	2003	1 810	48.8	1 395[1]	40.2[1]	...	...
	2004	2 117	50.9	1 516	48.9	...	...
	2005	2 220	51.1	1 686[1]	47.8[1]	...	...
Tuvalu Tuvalu	2003	1 344	50.5	...	...	...	...
	2004	1 404	49.9	...	...	...	...
	2005	1 450	48.3	...	...	...	...
	2006	1 460	47.9	...	...	...	...
Uganda Ouganda	2003	7 633 314	49.3	716 736[1]	44.6[1]	74 090[1]	34.5[1]
	2004	7 377 292	49.4	732 792	44.4	88 360	38.4
	2005	7 223 879	49.6	760 337[1]	44.5[1]	...	...
	2006	7 363 721	49.8	849 129[1]	45.0[1]	...	...
	2007	7 537 971	49.9	1 000 580[1]	45.0[1]	...	...
Ukraine Ukraine	2003	1 960 512	48.7	4 824 077	48.7	2 296 221	53.8[2]
	2004	1 850 734	48.6	4 445 974	48.5[2]	2 465 074	53.9[2]
	2005	1 945 715	48.6	4 042 827	46.8[2]	2 604 875	54.1[2]
	2006	1 753 689	48.6	3 896 263	48.4[2]	2 740 342	54.2[2]
	2007	1 647 847	48.7[?]	3 708 736	48.7[2]	2 810 248	54.3[2]
United Arab Emirates Emirats arabes unis	2003	248 370	48.3	273 491	49.4	68 182[1]	66.3[1]
	2004	254 602	48.3	279 496	49.1	...	...
	2005	262 807	48.5	284 978	48.9	...	...
	2006	272 331	48.5	298 447	49.0	...	...
	2007	284 034	48.5	310 999[1]	48.8[1]	...	...
	2008	...	...	...	...	77 428	60.2
United Kingdom Royaume-Uni	2003	4 488 162	48.8	5 530 597	49.6	2 287 833	55.9
	2004	4 685 733	48.8	5 699 526	49.4	2 247 441	57.0
	2005	4 634 991	48.7	5 747 422	49.3	2 287 541	57.2
	2006	4 517 618	48.9	5 357 793	49.3	2 336 111	57.3
	2007	4 409 184	48.9	5 306 368	49.2	2 362 815	57.2
United Rep. of Tanzania Rép.-Unie de Tanzanie	2003	6 562 772	48.7	...	...	31 049	30.7
	2004	7 083 063	48.8	...	...	42 948	29.2
	2005	7 541 208	48.9	...	...	51 080[1]	32.4[1]
	2006	7 959 884	49.1	...	...	...	...
	2007	8 316 925	49.3	...	...	55 134	32.3
	2008	8 624 190	49.8	...	...	...	...
United States Etats-Unis	2003	24 848 518	48.9	23 854 458	48.7	16 611 711	56.6
	2004	24 559 494	48.1	24 185 786	49.2	16 900 471	57.1
	2005	24 454 602	48.5	24 431 934	49.2	17 272 044	57.2
	2006	24 319 033	49.0	24 552 317	48.6	17 487 475	57.4
	2007	24 492 041	48.8	24 731 027	48.9	17 758 870	57.3
Uruguay Uruguay	2003	365 423	48.4	343 617	52.5	...	...
	2004	366 205	48.3	339 057	52.6	...	...
	2005	365 536	48.4	323 087	52.6	...	...
	2006	365 388	48.3	323 027	52.8	...	...
	2007	359 439	48.3	294 852	48.8	158 841	62.9

13

Education at the primary, secondary and tertiary levels *(continued)*
Number of students enrolled and percentage female
Enseignement primaire, secondaire et supérieur *(suite)*
Nombre d'élèves inscrits et pourcentage de sexe féminin

Country or area Pays ou zone	Year [t] Année [t]	Primary education Enseignement primaire		Secondary education Enseignement secondaire		Tertiary education Enseignement supérieur	
		Total	% F	Total	% F	Total	% F
Uzbekistan	2003	2 513 342	49.0	4 258 787	48.3	359 708	43.2
Ouzbékistan	2004	2 451 125	48.7	4 338 358	48.1	376 904	43.6
	2005	2 383 326	48.6	4 515 852	48.4	265 957	40.7
	2006	2 277 191	48.6	4 542 174	48.5	280 837	40.9
	2007	2 164 897	48.5	4 598 037	48.7	288 550	41.0
Vanuatu	2003	39 388	48.1	12 800	44.0	914	36.2
Vanuatu	2004	38 960	47.8	13 837	44.7	955 [1]	36.1 [1]
	2005	38 530	47.7	...	...	...	...
	2006	37 060	47.8	...	...	...	...
	2007	37 518	47.6	...	...	...	...
Venezuela (Bolivarian Rep. of)	2003	3 449 984	48.4	1 866 114	52.5	983 217 [1]	51.0 [1]
Venezuela (Rép. bolivarienne du)	2004	3 453 379	48.4	1 953 506	52.3	1 049 780 [1]	...
	2005	3 449 290	48.4	2 028 388	52.1	...	...
	2006	3 452 062	48.4	2 104 857	51.9	1 381 126 [1]	...
	2007	3 521 139	48.3	2 174 619	51.8	...	...
	2008	3 439 199	48.3	2 224 214	51.4	...	...
Viet Nam	2003	8 841 004	47.5	9 265 801	47.4	829 459	43.0
Viet Nam	2004	8 350 191	47.3	9 588 698	48.0	1 328 485 [1]	40.9 [1]
	2005	7 773 484	47.5	9 939 319	48.6	1 354 543	40.9
	2006	7 317 813	47.9	9 975 113	48.8	...	...
	2007	7 041 312	47.8	9 845 407	49.5	1 587 609	49.3
Yemen	2003	2 950 403	39.8	1 373 362	30.1	...	...
Yémen	2004	3 107 801	40.5	1 446 369	31.2	192 071	26.2
	2005	3 219 564	41.6	1 455 206	32.1	201 043	26.1
	2006 [1]	...	...	...	...	209 386	26.1
Zambia	2004	2 251 357	48.7	363 613	44.1	...	...
Zambie	2005	2 565 419	48.4	408 971 [1]	44.8 [1]	...	...
	2006	2 678 610	49.3	...	...	...	...
	2007	2 790 312	49.1	607 296	46.9	...	...
Zimbabwe	2003	2 361 588	49.5	758 229	47.5	55 689 [1]	38.8 [1]
Zimbabwe	2006	2 445 520	49.6	831 488	48.1	...	...

Source:
United Nations Educational, Scientific and Cultural Organization (UNESCO) Institute for Statistics, Montreal, the UNESCO Institute for Statistics (UIS) database, July 2009.

[t] Data relate to the calendar year in which the academic year ends.

1 UIS estimation.
2 National estimation.
3 Policy change: Introduction of free universal primary education.

4 For statistical purposes, the data for China do not include those for the Hong Kong Special Administrative Region (Hong Kong SAR) and Macao Special Administrative Region (Macao SAR).

Source :
L'Institut de statistique de l'Organisation des Nations Unies pour l'éducation, la science et la culture (UNESCO), Montréal, la base de données de l'institut de statistique de l'UNESCO (ISU), juillet 2009.

[t] Les données se réfèrent à l'année civile durant laquelle l'année scolaire se termine.

1 Estimation de l'ISU.
2 Estimation nationale.
3 Changement de politique: introduction de l'éducation primaire universelle gratuite

4 Pour la présentation des statistiques, les données pour la Chine ne comprennent pas la Région Administrative Spéciale de Hong Kong (Hong Kong RAS) et la Région Administrative Spéciale de Macao (Macao RAS).

Public expenditure on education
Percentage of GNI and of government expenditure

Dépenses publiques afférentes à l'éducation
Pourcentage par rapport au RNB et aux dépenses du gouvernement

Country or area Pays ou zone	As % of Gross National Income (GNI) En % du Revenu National Brut (RNB)				As % of total government expenditure En % des dépenses totales du gouvernement			
	2004	2005	2006	2007	2004	2005	2006	2007
Andorra Andorre	...	1.7	2.3	2.6	...	...	...	...
Angola Angola	...	2.9	3.0	...	...	...	...	...
Anguilla Anguilla	...	4.0	...	...	...	14.0	...	...
Argentina Argentine	4.0	...	4.6	...	13.1	...	14.0	...
Armenia Arménie	2.4	2.6	2.6	...	14.2	14.6	15.0	...
Aruba Aruba	...	5.1	...	...	13.8	15.4	...	...
Australia Australie	5.0	5.0	5.4	...	...	...	...	...
Austria Autriche	5.5	5.5	...	...	10.8	10.9	...	...
Azerbaijan Azerbaïdjan	...	2.7	2.3	2.9	...	19.6	17.4	12.6
Bangladesh Bangladesh	2.1	...	2.3	2.4	14.8	...	14.2	15.8
Barbados Barbade	7.5	7.2	...	6.7	16.7	16.4	...	...
Belarus Bélarus	5.7	5.9	6.1	5.3	13.0	11.3	12.9	9.3
Belgium Belgique	5.9	6.0	6.0	...	12.2	12.1	12.4	...
Belize Belize	5.8	...	...	...	...	...	...	...
Benin Bénin	4.4	...	3.9	...	17.1	...	18.0	...
Bermuda Bermudes	...	2.0	1.2	...	...	...	...	...
Bhutan Bhoutan	...	7.1	...	5.8	...	17.2	...	...
Botswana Botswana	...	10.9	...	8.8	...	21.5	...	21.0
Brazil Brésil	4.1	4.7	5.2	...	12.3	14.5	16.2	...
British Virgin Islands Iles Vierges britanniques	...	3.3	4.0	3.4	17.8	12.4	...	14.6
Bulgaria Bulgarie	2.4	4.5	4.3	...	6.2	...	11.6	...
Burkina Faso Burkina Faso	...	4.5	4.5	...	...	16.4	15.4	...
Burundi Burundi	5.3	5.2	...	...	17.3	17.7	...	...
Cambodia Cambodge	1.8	...	...	1.7	...	...	...	12.4
Cameroon Cameroun	3.4	3.2	3.4	3.9	17.2	15.9	16.8	17.0
Canada Canada	...	5.0	...	...	...	...	...	...

14

Public expenditure on education *(continued)*
Percentage of GNI and of government expenditure
Dépenses publiques afférentes à l'éducation *(suite)*
Pourcentage par rapport au RNB et aux dépenses du gouvernement

Country or area Pays ou zone	As % of Gross National Income (GNI) En % du Revenu National Brut (RNB)				As % of total government expenditure En % des dépenses totales du gouvernement			
	2004	2005	2006	2007	2004	2005	2006	2007
Cape Verde Cap-Vert	7.6	7.0	6.4	5.9	20.7	25.4	15.6	16.4
Cayman Islands Iles Caïmans	...	...	2.9	...	...	...	...	...
Central African Rep. Rép. centrafricaine	...	...	1.3	...	...	...	...	...
Chad Tchad	1.9	2.3	...	...	7.7	10.1	...	...
Chile Chili	3.9	3.7	3.6	3.8	16.8	16.0	16.0	18.2
China, Hong Kong SAR Chine, Hong Kong RAS	4.5	4.1	3.9	3.5	23.3	23.0	23.9	23.2
China, Macao SAR Chine, Macao RAS	...	...	...	...	14.0	14.1	14.9	...
Colombia Colombie	5.1	5.0	4.9	5.1	11.7	11.1	14.2	12.6
Congo Congo	3.3	2.5	...	...	9.0	8.1	...	...
Costa Rica Costa Rica	5.1	...	4.9	4.9	18.5	...	20.6	...
Croatia Croatie	4.6	...	...	...	...	...	...	...
Cuba Cuba	...	...	9.3	13.6	19.4	16.6	14.2	20.6
Cyprus Chypre	6.4	6.6	7.3	...	14.4	14.5	9.5	...
Czech Republic République tchèque	4.6	4.5	4.8	...	10.0	9.5	10.5	...
Denmark Danemark	8.4	8.2	...	...	15.3	15.5	...	...
Djibouti Djibouti	8.4	7.6	7.5	7.8	...	...	22.4	22.8
Dominica Dominique	...	...	...	5.5	...	...	...	...
Dominican Republic Rép. dominicaine	...	...	...	2.6	...	...	...	11.0
Egypt Egypte	4.7	4.8	4.0	3.7	15.5	16.0	12.0	12.6
El Salvador El Salvador	...	2.8	3.1	3.1[1]	...	...	...	13.1[1]
Eritrea Erythrée	3.8	...	2.4	...	...	...	...	...
Estonia Estonie	5.3	5.1	...	...	14.9	14.6	...	...
Ethiopia Ethiopie	...	...	5.5	5.5	...	...	17.5	23.3
Fiji Fidji	6.2	...	...	...	...	...	...	...
Finland Finlande	6.4	6.3	6.1	...	12.8	12.5	12.6	...
France France	5.8	5.6	5.6	...	10.9	10.6	10.6	...
Gambia[1] Gambie[1]	2.1	...	...	...	...	...	...	...

14

Public expenditure on education *(continued)*
Percentage of GNI and of government expenditure
Dépenses publiques afférentes à l'éducation *(suite)*
Pourcentage par rapport au RNB et aux dépenses du gouvernement

Country or area Pays ou zone	As % of Gross National Income (GNI) En % du Revenu National Brut (RNB)				As % of total government expenditure En % des dépenses totales du gouvernement			
	2004	2005	2006	2007	2004	2005	2006	2007
Georgia Géorgie	2.9	2.4	2.9	2.6	13.1	8.8	9.3	7.8
Germany Allemagne	4.6	4.5	4.4	...	9.8	9.7	9.7	...
Ghana Ghana	...	5.5	...	...	...	...	...	...
Greece Grèce	3.4	3.5			8.5	9.2		
Guatemala Guatemala	...	...	3.0	3.1				...
Guinea Guinée	2.0	1.7	...		...	...	...	...
Guyana Guyana	6.1	8.5	8.6	6.5	12.0	14.5	15.5	12.5
Hungary Hongrie	5.8	5.8	5.8	...	11.1	10.9	10.4	...
Iceland Islande	7.8	7.9	8.5	...	16.6	18.0	18.1	...
India Inde	3.4	3.2			...	...	...	...
Indonesia [1] Indonésie [1]	2.9	3.0	3.8	3.6	14.2	14.9	17.2	17.5
Iran (Islamic Rep. of) Iran (Rép. islamique d')	5.0	4.8	5.2	5.6	17.9	22.8	18.6	19.5
Ireland Irlande	5.6	5.6	5.7	...	14.0	13.9	14.4	...
Israel Israël	6.8	6.3	6.3	...	...	...	...	...
Italy Italie	4.6	4.5	4.8	...	9.6	9.2	9.7	
Jamaica Jamaïque	4.7	5.6		7.0	...	8.8		
Japan Japon	3.6	3.5	3.4	...	9.8	9.5	9.5	
Kazakhstan Kazakhstan	2.4	2.5	3.0	3.2	...	...	...	...
Kenya Kenya	6.8	7.3	7.0	...	29.2	17.9		
Korea, Republic of Corée, République de	4.6	4.4		...	16.5	15.3		
Kuwait Koweït	5.2	4.3	3.3 [1]	...	13.6	12.7	12.9 [1]	...
Kyrgyzstan Kirghizistan	4.8	5.0	5.6	5.4	23.1	24.4	25.0	19.2
Lao People's Dem. Rep. Rép. dém. pop. lao	2.4	2.5	3.4	3.6	10.8	11.7	14.0	15.8
Latvia Lettonie	5.2	...	5.2	...	14.2	...	13.4	...
Lebanon Liban	2.7	2.7	2.7	2.7	12.7	11.0	9.8	9.6
Lesotho Lesotho	...	11.3	11.0	...	...	29.8		...
Lithuania Lituanie	5.3	5.1	5.0	...	15.6	14.7	14.4	...

Public expenditure on education *(continued)*
Percentage of GNI and of government expenditure
Dépenses publiques afférentes à l'éducation *(suite)*
Pourcentage par rapport au RNB et aux dépenses du gouvernement

Country or area Pays ou zone	As % of Gross National Income (GNI) En % du Revenu National Brut (RNB)				As % of total government expenditure En % des dépenses totales du gouvernement			
	2004	2005	2006	2007	2004	2005	2006	2007
Madagascar Madagascar	3.4[1]	3.2	3.1	3.4	18.2[1]	25.3	13.9	16.4
Malaysia Malaisie	6.2	7.9	4.7	...	25.2	...	...	...
Maldives Maldives	8.0[1]	8.0	8.3	...	...	15.0	11.0	...
Mali Mali	4.5	4.3	4.9	...	16.9	14.8	16.8	...
Malta Malte	4.9	...	...	...	10.5	...	...	...
Marshall Islands [1] Iles Marshall [1]	9.5	...	...	...	...	...	...	...
Mauritania Mauritanie	3.0[1]	2.3	2.8	...	...	8.3	10.1	...
Mauritius Maurice	4.7	4.5	3.9	...	15.7	14.3	12.7	...
Mexico Mexique	5.5	5.6	5.6	...	25.6	...	...	...
Mongolia Mongolie	4.8	...	...	5.2	...	...	...	...
Morocco Maroc	5.7	6.0	5.6	...	27.8	27.2	26.1	...
Mozambique Mozambique	4.7	5.6	5.8	...	22.6	...	21.0	...
Netherlands Pays-Bas	5.0	5.2	5.4	...	11.2	11.5	12.0	...
New Zealand Nouvelle-Zélande	7.1	7.0	6.7	6.3	...	15.5	19.7	...
Niger Niger	...	...	3.3	...	...	...	17.6	...
Norway Norvège	7.5	7.0	6.6	...	16.6	16.7	16.2	...
Oman Oman	4.2	3.7	4.2	...	24.2	24.2	31.1	...
Pakistan Pakistan	1.9	2.2	2.6	2.8	6.4	10.9	12.2	11.2
Panama [1] Panama [1]	4.1	...	...	...	8.9	...	...	...
Paraguay Paraguay	4.1	...	...	...	10.0	...	...	...
Peru Pérou	3.0	2.9	2.8	2.7	17.0	...	15.4	16.4
Philippines Philippines	2.5	2.3	...	...	16.4	15.2	...	...
Poland Pologne	5.6	5.6	...	...	12.7	...	...	...
Portugal Portugal	5.4	5.6	5.5	...	11.5	11.3	11.3	...
Qatar Qatar	...	...	...	...	...	19.6	...	...
Republic of Moldova République de Moldova	6.0	6.4	6.7	7.3	19.3	19.4	20.2	19.8
Romania Roumanie	3.4	3.6	...	...	8.6	14.3	...	...

14

Public expenditure on education *(continued)*
Percentage of GNI and of government expenditure
Dépenses publiques afférentes à l'éducation *(suite)*
Pourcentage par rapport au RNB et aux dépenses du gouvernement

Country or area Pays ou zone	As % of Gross National Income (GNI) En % du Revenu National Brut (RNB)				As % of total government expenditure En % des dépenses totales du gouvernement			
	2004	2005	2006	2007	2004	2005	2006	2007
Russian Federation Fédération de Russie	3.6	3.9	4.0	...	12.9	...	...	...
Rwanda Rwanda	...	3.4	...	4.9	...	12.2	...	19.0
Saint Kitts and Nevis Saint-Kitts-et-Nevis	4.9[1]	10.9	...	...	...	...	...	...
Saint Lucia Sainte-Lucie	5.1	6.0	6.9	...	15.6	16.9	19.1	...
Saint Vincent-Grenadines Saint Vincent-Grenadines	11.5	8.6	...	7.5	20.5	16.1	...	...
Saudi Arabia Arabie saoudite	6.7	...	...	...	27.6	...	...	...
Senegal Sénégal	3.9	5.2	4.9	...	...	18.9	26.3	...
Seychelles Seychelles	5.7[1]	...	6.6	...	...	...	12.6	...
Sierra Leone [1] Sierra Leone [1]	4.3	3.9	...	...	...	...	...	...
Slovakia Slovaquie	4.3	4.1	3.9	...	10.8	...	10.2	...
Slovenia Slovénie	5.9	5.9	5.9	...	12.6	12.7	12.9	...
South Africa Afrique du Sud	5.5	5.5	5.5	5.5	18.1	17.9	17.6	17.4
Spain Espagne	4.3	4.3	4.4	...	11.0	11.0	11.1	...
Swaziland Swaziland	6.4	7.5	7.9	...	...	...	24.4	...
Sweden Suède	7.4	7.2	7.0	...	12.9	...	12.6	...
Switzerland Suisse	5.5	5.3	5.1	...	...	...	16.3	...
Tajikistan Tadjikistan	2.9	3.6	3.6	3.5	16.9	18.0	19.0	18.2
Thailand Thaïlande	4.4	4.4	4.5	4.0	26.8	25.0	25.0	20.9
Togo Togo	3.5	3.4	3.7	3.8	18.6	18.7	16.6	17.2
Tonga Tonga	4.9	...	...	...	...	...	...	...
Tunisia Tunisie	7.8	7.6	7.5	...	...	20.8	20.5	...
Turkey Turquie	4.1	...	...	...	...	...	...	...
Turks and Caicos Islands Iles Turques et Caïques	...	...	...	...	...	11.8	...	...
Uganda [1] Ouganda [1]	5.3	...	...	...	18.3	...	...	...
Ukraine Ukraine	5.4	6.1	6.3	5.4	18.1	18.9	19.3	20.2
United Arab Emirates [2] Emirats arabes unis [2]	1.6	...	...	...	25.0	28.3	...	...
United Kingdom Royaume-Uni	5.3	5.4	...	...	11.7	12.5	...	...

14

Public expenditure on education *(continued)*
Percentage of GNI and of government expenditure
Dépenses publiques afférentes à l'éducation *(suite)*
Pourcentage par rapport au RNB et aux dépenses du gouvernement

Country or area Pays ou zone	As % of Gross National Income (GNI) En % du Revenu National Brut (RNB)				As % of total government expenditure En % des dépenses totales du gouvernement			
	2004	2005	2006	2007	2004	2005	2006	2007
United States Etats-Unis	5.6	5.4	5.7	...	14.4	13.7	14.8	...
Uruguay Uruguay	2.7	2.9	3.0	...	11.1	12.7	11.6	...
Venezuela (Bolivarian Rep. of) Venezuela (Rép. bolivarienne du)	...	...	3.7	3.7	...	...	...	...
Zambia Zambie	3.0	2.1	...	1.7	14.8	...	...	...

Source:
United Nations Educational, Scientific and Cultural Organization
(UNESCO), Montreal, the UNESCO Institute for Statistics (UIS) database,
last accessed July 2009.

1   UIS estimation.
2   National estimation.

Source:
L'Organisation des Nations Unies pour l'éducation, la science et la culture
(UNESCO), Montréal, la base de données de l'Institut de statistique de
l'UNESCO (ISU), dernier accès juillet 2009.

1   Estimation de l'ISU.
2   Estimation nationale.

Technical notes: tables 13 and 14

Detailed data and explanatory notes on education can be found on the UNESCO Institute for Statistics web site www.uis.unesco.org. Brief notes which pertain to the statistical information shown in tables 13 and 14 are given below.

Table 13: The definitions and classifications applied by UNESCO are those set out in the *Revised Recommendation concerning the International Standardization of Education Statistics* (1978) and the 1976 and 1997 versions of the *International Standard Classification of Education* (ISCED). Data are presented in table 13 according to the terminology of the ISCED-97.

According to the ISCED, these educational levels are defined as follows:

Primary education (ISCED level 1): Programmes normally designed on a unit or project basis to give pupils a sound basic education in reading, writing and mathematics along with an elementary understanding of other subjects such as history, geography, natural science, social science, art and music. Religious instruction may also be featured. It is sometimes called elementary education.

Secondary education (ISCED levels 2 and 3): Lower secondary education (ISCED 2) is generally designed to continue the basic programmes of the primary level but the teaching is typically more subject-focused, requiring more specialized teachers for each subject area. The end of this level often coincides with the end of compulsory education. In upper secondary education (ISCED 3), the final stage of secondary education in most countries, education is often organized even more along subject lines and teachers typically need a higher or more subject-specific qualification than at ISCED level 2.

Tertiary education (ISCED levels 5 and 6): Programmes with an educational content more advanced than what is offered at ISCED levels 3 and 4. The first stage of tertiary education, ISCED level 5, covers level 5A, composed of largely theoretically based programmes intended to provide sufficient qualifications for gaining entry to advanced research programmes and professions with high skill requirements; and level 5B, where programmes are generally more practical, technical and/or occupationally specific. The second stage of tertiary education, ISCED level 6, comprises programmes devoted to advanced study and original research, and leading to the award of an advanced research qualification.

The ISCED-97 also introduced a new category or level between upper secondary and tertiary education called post-secondary non-tertiary education (ISCED level 4). This level includes programmes that lie between the upper-secondary and tertiary levels of education from an international point of view, even though

Notes techniques : tableaux 13 et 14

On trouvera des données détaillées et des notes explicatives sur l'éducation sur le site Web de l'Institut de statistique de l'UNESCO www.uis.unesco.org. Ci-après figurent des notes sommaires, relatives aux principaux éléments d'information statistique figurant dans les tableaux 13 et 14.

Tableau 13: Les définitions et classifications appliquées par l'UNESCO sont tirées de la *Recommandation révisée concernant la normalisation internationale des statistiques de l'éducation* (1978) et des versions de 1976 et de 1997 de la *Classification internationale type de l'éducation* (CITE). La terminologie utilisée dans le tableau 13 est celle de la CITE-1997.

Dans la CITE, les niveaux d'enseignement sont définis comme suit:

Enseignement primaire (niveau 1 de la CITE): Programmes s'articulant normalement autour d'une unité ou d'un projet visant à donner aux élèves un solide enseignement de base en lecture, en écriture et en mathématiques et des connaissances élémentaires dans d'autres matières telles que l'histoire, la géographie, les sciences naturelles, les sciences sociales, le dessin et la musique. Dans certains cas, une instruction religieuse est aussi considérée. Appelé parfois enseignement élémentaire.

Enseignement secondaire (niveaux 2 et 3 de la CITE): Le premier cycle de l'enseignement secondaire (CITE 2) est généralement destiné à compléter les programmes de base de l'enseignement primaire mais dont l'enseignement est généralement plus orienté vers les matières enseignées faisant appel à des enseignants plus spécialisés. La fin de ce niveau coïncide souvent avec celle de la scolarité obligatoire. Dans le deuxième cycle de l'enseignement secondaire (CITE 3), étape finale de l'enseignement secondaire dans plusieurs pays, l'enseignement est souvent organisé en une plus grande spécialisation et les enseignants doivent souvent être plus qualifiés ou spécialisés qu'au niveau 2 de la CITE.

Enseignement supérieur (niveaux 5 et 6 de la CITE): Programmes dont le contenu est plus avancé que celui offert aux niveaux 3 et 4 de la CITE. Le premier cycle de l'enseignement supérieur, niveau 5 de la CITE, couvre le niveau 5A, composé de programmes fondés dans une large mesure sur la théorie et destinés à offrir des qualifications suffisantes pour être admis à suivre des programmes de recherche de pointe ou à exercer une profession exigeant de hautes compétences; et le niveau 5B, dont les programmes sont dans une large mesure d'ordre pratique, technique et/ou spécifiquement professionnel. Le deuxième cycle de l'enseignement supérieur, niveau 6 de la CITE, comprend des programmes consacrés à des études approfondies et à des travaux de recherche originaux, et conduisant à l'obtention d'un titre

they might clearly be considered as upper-secondary or tertiary programmes in a national context. They are often not significantly more advanced than programmes at ISCED 3 (upper secondary) but they serve to broaden the knowledge of participants who have already completed a programme at level 3. The students are usually older than those at level 3. ISCED 4 programmes typically last between six months and two years.

Table 14: Public expenditure on education consists of current and capital expenditures on education by local, regional and national governments, including municipalities. Household contributions are excluded. Current expenditure on education includes expenditure for goods and services consumed within the current year and which would need to be renewed if needed the following year. It includes expenditure on: staff salaries and benefits; contracted or purchased services; other resources including books and teaching materials; welfare services; and other current expenditure such as subsidies to students and households, furniture and equipment, minor repairs, fuel, telecommunications, travel, insurance and rents. Capital expenditure on education includes expenditure for assets that last longer than one year. It includes expenditure for construction, renovation and major repairs of buildings and the purchase of heavy equipment or vehicles.

de chercheur hautement qualifié.

La CITE de 1997 a également introduit une nouvelle catégorie (ou nouveau niveau) entre l'enseignement secondaire et l'enseignement supérieur, appelée enseignement postsecondaire non supérieur (niveau 4 de la CITE). À ce niveau se trouvent des programmes qui, du point de vue des établissements, sont intermédiaires entre le deuxième cycle du secondaire et le premier cycle du supérieur, encore qu'il serait tout à fait possible de les considérer, dans le contexte national, comme appartenant au deuxième cycle du secondaire ou au supérieur. Ils ne sont souvent pas beaucoup plus avancés que des programmes du niveau 3 de la CITE (deuxième cycle du secondaire) mais servent à élargir les connaissances de ceux qui les suivent et qui ont déjà achevé un programme de niveau 3. Les étudiants y sont généralement plus âgés que ceux du niveau 3. Pour la plupart, ces programmes du niveau 4 de la CITE ont une durée comprise entre six mois et deux ans.

Tableau 14: Les données relatives aux dépenses publiques afférentes à l'éducation se rapportent aux dépenses courantes et en capital de l'éducation engagées par l'administration au niveau local, régional, national/central, y inclus les municipalités. Les contributions des ménages sont exclues. Les dépenses ordinaires (ou courantes) en éducation se réfèrent aux dépenses couvrant les biens et les services consommés dans l'année en cours et qui doivent être renouvelées périodiquement. Elles comprennent les dépenses en: salaires et avantages du personnel, services achetés ou assurés sous contrat, l'achat d'autres ressources y compris les manuels scolaires et du matériel pour l'enseignement, les services sociaux et d'autres dépenses de fonctionnement telles que les subventions aux étudiants et aux ménages, les fournitures et l'équipement, les réparations légères, les combustibles, les télécommunications, les voyages, les assurances et les loyers. Dépenses en capital pour l'éducation se réfèrent aux dépenses qui couvrent l'achat de biens d'une durée supérieure à une année. Elles peuvent comprendre les dépenses de construction, de rénovation et de grosses réparations de bâtiments, ainsi que l'achat d'équipements ou véhicules.

Telephones
Main telephone lines in operation (in thousands) and lines per 100 inhabitants

Téléphones
Nombre de lignes téléphoniques en service (en milliers) et lignes pour 100 habitants

Country or area	Fiscal year & Ex. budgét. &	2002	2003	2004	2005	2006	2007	2008	Pays ou zone
Afghanistan									**Afghanistan**
Number (thousands) *		33	37	50	100	90	81	101	Nombre (en milliers) *
Per 100 inhabitants		0.1	0.1	0.2	0.3	0.3	0.3	0.4	Pour 100 habitants
Albania									**Albanie**
Number (thousands)		220	255	275	279	283	300	316	Nombre (en milliers)
Per 100 inhabitants		7.1	8.2	8.8	8.9	9.0	9.4	9.9	Pour 100 habitants
Algeria									**Algérie**
Number (thousands)		1 950	2 147	2 487	2 572	2 841	3 068	...	Nombre (en milliers)
Per 100 inhabitants		6.2	6.7	7.7	7.8	8.5	9.1	...	Pour 100 habitants
American Samoa									**Samoa américaines**
Number (thousands)		14	11	10	...	...	...	...	Nombre (en milliers)
Per 100 inhabitants		23.3	17.3	16.3	...	...	...	...	Pour 100 habitants
Andorra									**Andorre**
Number (thousands)		35[1]	35[1]	35	35	37	37	37	Nombre (en milliers)
Per 100 inhabitants		52.6	52.8	52.3	52.8	51.3	49.8	45.5	Pour 100 habitants
Angola									**Angola**
Number (thousands)		80	85	94	97	98[1]	94	114	Nombre (en milliers)
Per 100 inhabitants		0.5	0.6	0.6	0.6	0.6	0.6	0.7	Pour 100 habitants
Antigua and Barbuda	(01/04)								**Antigua-et-Barbuda**
Number (thousands)		38	38	38	36	38	38	38	Nombre (en milliers)
Per 100 inhabitants		48.4	47.7	47.2	44.8	45.5	45.7	45.9	Pour 100 habitants
Argentina	(30/09)								**Argentine**
Number (thousands) [3]		7 709	8 604	8 761	9 442	9 460	9 500	9 631	Nombre (en milliers) [3]
Per 100 inhabitants		20.5	22.6	22.8	24.4	24.2	24.0	24.1	Pour 100 habitants
Armenia									**Arménie**
Number (thousands)		543	564	579	594	...	...	...	Nombre (en milliers)
Per 100 inhabitants		17.8	18.6	19.1	19.7	...	...	...	Pour 100 habitants
Aruba									**Aruba**
Number (thousands)		37	37[4]	38[4]	38	39	39	38	Nombre (en milliers)
Per 100 inhabitants		39.0	38.7	38.7	38.5	38.4	37.2	37.1	Pour 100 habitants
Australia	(30/06)								**Australie**
Number (thousands) [5]		10 400	10 460	10 370	10 120	9 940	9 760	9 370	Nombre (en milliers) [5]
Per 100 inhabitants		53.3	53.0	52.0	50.2	48.8	47.1	44.7	Pour 100 habitants
Austria									**Autriche**
Number (thousands) [6]		3 883	3 877	3 821	3 739	3 605	3 407	3 342	Nombre (en milliers) [6]
Per 100 inhabitants		47.8	47.6	46.8	45.7	43.9	40.8	39.8	Pour 100 habitants
Azerbaijan									**Azerbaïdjan**
Number (thousands)		924	941	1 013	1 094	1 177	1 253	1 318	Nombre (en milliers)
Per 100 inhabitants		11.2	11.3	12.1	13.0	13.9	14.8	15.4	Pour 100 habitants
Bahamas									**Bahamas**
Number (thousands)		127	132	140	133	132	133	...	Nombre (en milliers)
Per 100 inhabitants		40.8	41.9	43.9	41.2	40.2	40.1	...	Pour 100 habitants
Bahrain									**Bahreïn**
Number (thousands)		175	186	192	194	194	203	220	Nombre (en milliers)
Per 100 inhabitants		25.2	26.3	26.8	26.6	26.3	27.0	28.7	Pour 100 habitants
Bangladesh	(30/06)								**Bangladesh**
Number (thousands)		606	742	831	1 070	1 134	1 187	1 344	Nombre (en milliers)
Per 100 inhabitants		0.5	0.5	0.6	0.8	0.8	0.7	0.8	Pour 100 habitants
Barbados	(01/04)								**Barbade**
Number (thousands)		133	134	136	135	...	...	...	Nombre (en milliers)
Per 100 inhabitants		49.7	50.0	50.5	50.0	...	...	...	Pour 100 habitants
Belarus									**Bélarus**
Number (thousands)		2 967	3 071	3 176	3 284	3 368	3 672	...	Nombre (en milliers)
Per 100 inhabitants		29.9	31.1	32.4	33.7	34.7	37.9	...	Pour 100 habitants
Belgium									**Belgique**
Number (thousands) [6]		4 932	4 875	4 801	4 795	4 728	4 668	4 457	Nombre (en milliers) [6]
Per 100 inhabitants		47.6	47.0	46.2	46.0	45.3	44.6	42.5	Pour 100 habitants
Belize	(01/04)								**Belize**
Number (thousands)		31	33	34	34	34	34	31	Nombre (en milliers)
Per 100 inhabitants		12.4	12.9	12.8	12.5	12.5	11.8	10.6	Pour 100 habitants

15

Telephones *(continued)*
Main telephone lines in operation (in thousands) and lines per 100 inhabitants
Téléphones *(suite)*
Nombre de lignes téléphoniques en service (en milliers) et lignes pour 100 habitants

Country or area	Fiscal year & Ex. budgét. &	2002	2003	2004	2005	2006	2007	2008	Pays ou zone
Benin									**Bénin**
Number (thousands)		63	67	73	76	77	111	...	Nombre (en milliers)
Per 100 inhabitants		0.8	0.8	0.9	0.9	0.9	1.2	...	Pour 100 habitants
Bermuda	(01/04)								**Bermudes**
Number (thousands)		56[4]	54[4]	54	52	58	...	...	Nombre (en milliers)
Per 100 inhabitants		88.3	84.8	84.2	81.8	89.5	...	...	Pour 100 habitants
Bhutan									**Bhoutan**
Number (thousands)		20	24	30	33	32	30	27	Nombre (en milliers)
Per 100 inhabitants		1.0	1.1	1.4	1.5	...	...	...	Pour 100 habitants
Bolivia									**Bolivie**
Number (thousands)		591	610	625	646	667	678	...	Nombre (en milliers)
Per 100 inhabitants		6.8	6.9	6.9	7.0	7.1	7.1	...	Pour 100 habitants
Bosnia and Herzegovina									**Bosnie-Herzégovine**
Number (thousands)[7]		903	938	952	969	989	1 064	1 031	Nombre (en milliers)[7]
Per 100 inhabitants		23.0	23.9	24.3	24.8	25.3	27.1	26.2	Pour 100 habitants
Botswana	(01/04)								**Botswana**
Number (thousands)		148	131	132	136	132	137	142	Nombre (en milliers)
Per 100 inhabitants		8.4	7.4	7.4	7.7	7.5	7.3	7.5	Pour 100 habitants
Brazil									**Brésil**
Number (thousands)[8]		38 811	39 205	39 579	39 853	38 800	39 400	41 141	Nombre (en milliers)[8]
Per 100 inhabitants		21.7	21.6	21.5	21.4	20.5	20.5	21.2	Pour 100 habitants
Brunei Darussalam									**Brunéi Darussalam**
Number (thousands)		81	82	83	84	80	77[4]	...	Nombre (en milliers)
Per 100 inhabitants		23.3	22.9	22.7	22.4	21.0	19.6	...	Pour 100 habitants
Bulgaria									**Bulgarie**
Number (thousands)		2 872	2 818	2 727	2 490	2 399	2 300	2 258	Nombre (en milliers)
Per 100 inhabitants		36.4	36.0	35.0	32.2	31.3	30.1	29.8	Pour 100 habitants
Burkina Faso									**Burkina Faso**
Number (thousands)		62	67	85	91	99	122	...	Nombre (en milliers)
Per 100 inhabitants		0.5	0.5	0.7	0.7	0.7	0.8	...	Pour 100 habitants
Burundi									**Burundi**
Number (thousands)		22	24	28	31[4]	28	29	30	Nombre (en milliers)
Per 100 inhabitants		0.3	0.3	0.4	0.4	0.4	0.3	0.3	Pour 100 habitants
Cambodia									**Cambodge**
Number (thousands)[9]		35	31	32	33	35	38	45	Nombre (en milliers)[9]
Per 100 inhabitants		0.3	0.2	0.2	0.2	0.2	0.3	0.3	Pour 100 habitants
Cameroon									**Cameroun**
Number (thousands)		111	97	99	100	131	189	198	Nombre (en milliers)
Per 100 inhabitants		0.7	0.6	0.6	0.6	0.8	1.0	1.0	Pour 100 habitants
Canada									**Canada**
Number (thousands)		20 622	20 612	20 563	18 148	18 236	18 241[10]	...	Nombre (en milliers)
Per 100 inhabitants		65.9	65.2	64.3	56.2	56.0	55.5	...	Pour 100 habitants
Cape Verde									**Cap-Vert**
Number (thousands)		70	72	72	72	72	72	72	Nombre (en milliers)
Per 100 inhabitants		14.9	14.8	14.5	14.1	13.8	13.5	13.3	Pour 100 habitants
Central African Rep.									**Rép. centrafricaine**
Number (thousands)		9	10	10	10	12	...	...	Nombre (en milliers)
Per 100 inhabitants		0.2	0.2	0.3	0.2	0.3	...	...	Pour 100 habitants
Chad									**Tchad**
Number (thousands)		12	12	13	13	13	...	...	Nombre (en milliers)
Per 100 inhabitants		0.1	0.1	0.1	0.1	0.1	...	...	Pour 100 habitants
Chile									**Chili**
Number (thousands)		3 467	3 252	3 318	3 436	3 384	3 460	3 526	Nombre (en milliers)
Per 100 inhabitants		22.0	20.4	20.6	21.1	20.5	20.7	21.0	Pour 100 habitants
China[11]									**Chine**[11]
Number (thousands)		214 222	262 747	311 756	350 445	367 786	365 637	...	Nombre (en milliers)
Per 100 inhabitants		16.6	20.2	23.8	26.6	27.8	27.5	...	Pour 100 habitants
China, Hong Kong SAR	(01/04)								**Chine, Hong Kong RAS**
Number (thousands)		3 832	3 806	3 763	3 793	3 836	4 125[12]	4 108	Nombre (en milliers)
Per 100 inhabitants		56.3	55.3	54.0	53.9	53.9	57.2	56.4	Pour 100 habitants

15 Telephones *(continued)*
Main telephone lines in operation (in thousands) and lines per 100 inhabitants
Téléphones *(suite)*
Nombre de lignes téléphoniques en service (en milliers) et lignes pour 100 habitants

Country or area	Fiscal year & Ex. budgét. &	2002	2003	2004	2005	2006	2007	2008	Pays ou zone
China, Macao SAR									**Chine, Macao RAS**
Number (thousands)		176	175	174	174	177	178	176	Nombre (en milliers)
Per 100 inhabitants		39.0	38.4	38.0	37.9	38.1	37.0	36.3	Pour 100 habitants
Colombia									**Colombie**
Number (thousands)		7 766	7 848	7 589	7 679	7 860	7 936	6 820	Nombre (en milliers)
Per 100 inhabitants		17.8	17.7	16.9	16.8	17.0	17.2	14.6	Pour 100 habitants
Comoros									**Comores**
Number (thousands)		10	13	15	17	19	...	...	Nombre (en milliers)
Per 100 inhabitants		1.4	1.7	1.9	2.1	2.3	...	...	Pour 100 habitants
Congo									**Congo**
Number (thousands)		22	7	14	16	...	...	...	Nombre (en milliers)
Per 100 inhabitants		0.6	0.2	0.4	0.4	...	...	...	Pour 100 habitants
Costa Rica									**Costa Rica**
Number (thousands)		1 038	1 159	1 343	1 389	1 330	1 437	1 438	Nombre (en milliers)
Per 100 inhabitants		25.3	27.8	31.6	32.1	30.2	32.2	31.7	Pour 100 habitants
Côte d'Ivoire									**Côte d'Ivoire**
Number (thousands)		325	238	258	259	271	...	357	Nombre (en milliers)
Per 100 inhabitants		1.9	1.4	1.4	1.4	1.5	...	1.0	Pour 100 habitants
Croatia									**Croatie**
Number (thousands)		1 825	1 871	1 888	1 883	1 831	1 847	1 851	Nombre (en milliers)
Per 100 inhabitants		40.5	41.4	41.6	41.4	40.2	40.5	40.7	Pour 100 habitants
Cuba									**Cuba**
Number (thousands)		666	724	768	856	962	1 043	1 104	Nombre (en milliers)
Per 100 inhabitants		5.9	6.5	6.8	7.6	8.5	9.3	9.8	Pour 100 habitants
Cyprus									**Chypre**
Number (thousands)		427	424[6]	418	420	408	384	413	Nombre (en milliers)
Per 100 inhabitants		53.0	51.9	50.7	50.3	48.3	44.9	47.9	Pour 100 habitants
Czech Republic									**République tchèque**
Number (thousands)		3 675	3 626	3 428	3 217	2 888	2 403	2 278	Nombre (en milliers)
Per 100 inhabitants		35.9	35.4	33.5	31.5	28.3	23.6	22.4	Pour 100 habitants
Dem. Rep. of the Congo									**Rép. dém. du Congo**
Number (thousands) *		10	10	11	11	10	4	37	Nombre (en milliers) *
Per 100 inhabitants		^0.0	^0.0	^0.0	^0.0	^0.0	^0.0	0.1	Pour 100 habitants
Denmark									**Danemark**
Number (thousands) [6]		3 701	3 614	3 491	3 348	3 099	2 825	2 487	Nombre (en milliers) [6]
Per 100 inhabitants		68.8	67.0	64.5	61.7	56.9	51.9	45.6	Pour 100 habitants
Djibouti									**Djibouti**
Number (thousands)		10	10	11	11	...	...	...	Nombre (en milliers)
Per 100 inhabitants		1.4	1.3	1.4	1.4	...	...	...	Pour 100 habitants
Dominica	(01/04)								**Dominique**
Number (thousands)		24	22	21	...	...	...	...	Nombre (en milliers)
Per 100 inhabitants		30.3	28.7	26.7	...	...	...	...	Pour 100 habitants
Dominican Republic									**Rép. dominicaine**
Number (thousands)		909	909	902	896	897	906	986	Nombre (en milliers)
Per 100 inhabitants		10.7	10.5	10.3	10.1	9.9	9.3	10.0	Pour 100 habitants
Ecuador									**Equateur**
Number (thousands)		1 411	1 531	1 591	1 680	1 775	1 823	1 910	Nombre (en milliers)
Per 100 inhabitants		11.1	11.9	12.2	12.7	13.2	13.7	14.2	Pour 100 habitants
Egypt	(30/06)								**Egypte**
Number (thousands)		7 736	8 736	9 464	10 396	10 967	11 393	12 011	Nombre (en milliers)
Per 100 inhabitants		11.1	12.3	13.0	14.0	14.5	15.1	15.6	Pour 100 habitants
El Salvador									**El Salvador**
Number (thousands)		668	753	888	971	1 037	1 080	1 077	Nombre (en milliers)
Per 100 inhabitants		10.2	11.3	13.1	14.1	14.8	15.8	15.5	Pour 100 habitants
Equatorial Guinea									**Guinée équatoriale**
Number (thousands) *		9	10	11	10	...	...	...	Nombre (en milliers) *
Per 100 inhabitants		1.9	2.0	2.1	2.0	...	...	...	Pour 100 habitants
Eritrea									**Erythrée**
Number (thousands)		36	38	39	38	38	37	40	Nombre (en milliers)
Per 100 inhabitants		0.9	0.9	0.9	0.9	0.8	0.8	0.8	Pour 100 habitants

15

Telephones *(continued)*
Main telephone lines in operation (in thousands) and lines per 100 inhabitants
Téléphones *(suite)*
Nombre de lignes téléphoniques en service (en milliers) et lignes pour 100 habitants

Country or area	Fiscal year & Ex. budgét. &	2002	2003	2004	2005	2006	2007	2008	Pays ou zone
Estonia									**Estonie**
Number (thousands)		475	461	444	442	452	495	498	Nombre (en milliers)
Per 100 inhabitants		35.2	34.4	33.3	33.2	34.1	37.1	37.4	Pour 100 habitants
Ethiopia	(30/06)								**Ethiopie**
Number (thousands)		354	405	484	610	725	880	909	Nombre (en milliers)
Per 100 inhabitants		0.5	0.5	0.6	0.8	0.9	1.1	1.1	Pour 100 habitants
Faeroe Islands									**Iles Féroé**
Number (thousands)		24	24	24	24	23	22	22	Nombre (en milliers)
Per 100 inhabitants		52.8	52.3	51.3	50.7	48.7	45.9	45.2	Pour 100 habitants
Fiji									**Fidji**
Number (thousands)		98	102	105	112	115[4]	122	...	Nombre (en milliers)
Per 100 inhabitants		11.8	12.2	12.5	13.3	13.5	14.5	...	Pour 100 habitants
Finland									**Finlande**
Number (thousands) [13]		2 726	2 568	2 368	2 120	1 910	1 740	1 650[14]	Nombre (en milliers) [13]
Per 100 inhabitants		52.4	49.2	45.2	40.4	36.3	33.0	31.2	Pour 100 habitants
France									**France**
Number (thousands) [6]		34 124	33 913	33 703	33 707	34 125	34 800	35 000	Nombre (en milliers) [6]
Per 100 inhabitants		57.1	56.5	55.9	55.7	56.2	56.5	56.5	Pour 100 habitants
French Polynesia									**Polynésie française**
Number (thousands)		53	54	53	53	54	54[4]	55	Nombre (en milliers)
Per 100 inhabitants		21.7	21.5	21.1	20.8	20.7	20.5	20.5	Pour 100 habitants
Gabon									**Gabon**
Number (thousands)		32	38	39	39	36	27[15]	...	Nombre (en milliers)
Per 100 inhabitants		2.4	2.9	2.8	2.8	2.6	2.0	...	Pour 100 habitants
Gambia	(01/04)								**Gambie**
Number (thousands) [16]		38	42[4]	43[4]	44	46	49	49	Nombre (en milliers) [16]
Per 100 inhabitants		2.7	2.9	2.9	2.9	3.0	2.9	2.8	Pour 100 habitants
Georgia									**Géorgie**
Number (thousands)		640[17]	667	683	570	553	556	...	Nombre (en milliers)
Per 100 inhabitants		13.9	14.6	15.1	12.7	12.5	12.7	...	Pour 100 habitants
Germany									**Allemagne**
Number (thousands) [18]		53 670	54 233	54 526	54 791	54 500	53 400	51 500	Nombre (en milliers) [18]
Per 100 inhabitants		65.0	65.7	66.0	66.3	65.9	64.6	62.4	Pour 100 habitants
Ghana									**Ghana**
Number (thousands)		275	291	313	322	356	377	144	Nombre (en milliers)
Per 100 inhabitants		1.3	1.4	1.4	1.5	1.6	1.6	0.6	Pour 100 habitants
Gibraltar									**Gibraltar**
Number (thousands)		25	...	25	...	24	...	...	Nombre (en milliers)
Per 100 inhabitants		88.4	...	90.9	...	73.1	...	...	Pour 100 habitants
Greece									**Grèce**
Number (thousands) [6]		6 294	6 300	6 352	6 312	6 170	6 010	5 975	Nombre (en milliers) [6]
Per 100 inhabitants		57.0	56.9	57.2	56.8	55.4	53.9	53.5	Pour 100 habitants
Greenland									**Groenland**
Number (thousands)		25	25	25	32	36	23	...	Nombre (en milliers)
Per 100 inhabitants		44.9	44.6	44.3	56.5	62.8	40.4	...	Pour 100 habitants
Grenada									**Grenade**
Number (thousands)		34	33	33	27	28	...	29	Nombre (en milliers)
Per 100 inhabitants		32.9	32.0	32.0	26.6	26.7	...	27.1	Pour 100 habitants
Guam									**Guam**
Number (thousands)		...	66	...	...	...	...	...	Nombre (en milliers)
Per 100 inhabitants		...	40.0	...	...	...	...	...	Pour 100 habitants
Guatemala									**Guatemala**
Number (thousands)		846	944	1 132	1 248	1 355	1 414	1 449	Nombre (en milliers)
Per 100 inhabitants		7.2	7.9	9.2	9.9	10.5	10.6	10.6	Pour 100 habitants
Guernsey									**Guernesey**
Number (thousands) [6]		56	46	45	...	...	...	...	Nombre (en milliers) [6]
Per 100 inhabitants		99.5	81.9	80.9	...	...	...	...	Pour 100 habitants
Guinea									**Guinée**
Number (thousands)		26	26	26	60[4]	...	50	...	Nombre (en milliers)
Per 100 inhabitants		0.3	0.3	0.3	0.6	...	0.5	...	Pour 100 habitants

Telephones *(continued)*
Main telephone lines in operation (in thousands) and lines per 100 inhabitants
Téléphones *(suite)*
Nombre de lignes téléphoniques en service (en milliers) et lignes pour 100 habitants

Country or area	Fiscal year & Ex. budgét. &	2002	2003	2004	2005	2006	2007	2008	Pays ou zone
Guinea-Bissau									**Guinée-Bissau**
Number (thousands)		11	11	10	10	7	5	5	Nombre (en milliers)
Per 100 inhabitants		0.8	0.7	0.6	0.6	0.4	0.3	0.3	Pour 100 habitants
Guyana									**Guyana**
Number (thousands)		80	92	103	110	...	...	...	Nombre (en milliers)
Per 100 inhabitants		10.8	12.3	13.7	14.7	...	...	...	Pour 100 habitants
Haiti									**Haïti**
Number (thousands)[4]		130	140	140	145	150	108	...	Nombre (en milliers)[4]
Per 100 inhabitants		1.6	1.7	1.7	1.7	1.7	1.1	...	Pour 100 habitants
Honduras									**Honduras**
Number (thousands)		323	334	387	494	715	822	826	Nombre (en milliers)
Per 100 inhabitants		4.8	4.9	5.5	6.9	9.7	11.6	11.4	Pour 100 habitants
Hungary									**Hongrie**
Number (thousands)		3 669	3 603	3 564	3 416	3 360	3 251	3 094	Nombre (en milliers)
Per 100 inhabitants		36.1	35.5	35.2	33.8	33.4	32.4	30.9	Pour 100 habitants
Iceland									**Islande**
Number (thousands)[6]		188	193	190	194	189	187	...	Nombre (en milliers)[6]
Per 100 inhabitants		65.6	66.5	65.2	65.0	63.5	62.0		Pour 100 habitants
India	(01/04)								**Inde**
Number (thousands)		41 420[19]	42 000	46 198	50 177	#40 770[20]	39 413	37 900	Nombre (en milliers)
Per 100 inhabitants		3.9	3.9	4.2	4.5	3.6	3.4	3.2	Pour 100 habitants
Indonesia									**Indonésie**
Number (thousands)		7 750[21]	8 058	10 376	13 508	14 821	19 530	30 378	Nombre (en milliers)
Per 100 inhabitants		3.6	3.7	4.7	6.1	6.6	8.4	13.0	Pour 100 habitants
Iran (Islamic Rep. of)	(22/03)								**Iran (Rép. islamique d')**
Number (thousands)		12 888	15 341	16 342	20 339	22 627	23 835	24 800	Nombre (en milliers)
Per 100 inhabitants		19.1	22.5	23.8	29.3	32.1	33.5	34.3	Pour 100 habitants
Iraq	(30/06)								**Iraq**
Number (thousands)		1 128[22]	1 183[22]	*1 034	1 115	1 248	1 365	1 082	Nombre (en milliers)
Per 100 inhabitants		4.2	4.3	3.7	3.9	4.2	4.7	3.7	Pour 100 habitants
Ireland	(01/04)								**Irlande**
Number (thousands)		1 975[6]	1 955[6]	2 015[6]	2 052[6]	2 196[23]	2 237[23]	2 202[23]	Nombre (en milliers)
Per 100 inhabitants		50.2	48.8	49.4	49.5	52.2	52.0	50.3	Pour 100 habitants
Israel									**Israël**
Number (thousands)		3 006	2 913	2 896	2 936	3 005	3 075[4]	2 900	Nombre (en milliers)
Per 100 inhabitants		47.4	45.0	43.9	43.7	43.9	44.4	41.2	Pour 100 habitants
Italy									**Italie**
Number (thousands)[6]		27 142	26 596[24]	25 957[24]	25 049	26 890	25 087	20 031	Nombre (en milliers)[6]
Per 100 inhabitants		46.9	45.9	44.7	43.1	46.3	42.6	34.0	Pour 100 habitants
Jamaica	(01/04)								**Jamaïque**
Number (thousands)		435	459	423	319	343	370	317	Nombre (en milliers)
Per 100 inhabitants		16.6	17.5	16.0	12.0	12.9	13.6	11.6	Pour 100 habitants
Japan	(01/04)								**Japon**
Number (thousands)		60 772	60 219	59 608	58 053[25]	55 165	51 232	...	Nombre (en milliers)
Per 100 inhabitants		47.7	47.1	46.6	45.3	43.0	40.0	...	Pour 100 habitants
Jordan									**Jordanie**
Number (thousands)		675	623	638	628	614	559	519	Nombre (en milliers)
Per 100 inhabitants		12.8	11.5	11.5	11.0	10.5	9.4	8.5	Pour 100 habitants
Kazakhstan									**Kazakhstan**
Number (thousands)		2 082	2 228	2 550	2 708	2 928	3 237	3 410	Nombre (en milliers)
Per 100 inhabitants		14.0	15.0	17.2	18.3	19.8	21.0	22.0	Pour 100 habitants
Kenya	(30/06)								**Kenya**
Number (thousands)		321	328	299	287	293	265	252	Nombre (en milliers)
Per 100 inhabitants		1.0	1.0	0.9	0.8	0.8	0.7	0.7	Pour 100 habitants
Kiribati									**Kiribati**
Number (thousands)		4	4	4	4	4[4]	4[4]	...	Nombre (en milliers)
Per 100 inhabitants		4.8	4.6	4.4	4.2	4.3	...	...	Pour 100 habitants
Korea, Dem. P. R.									**Corée, R. p. dém. de**
Number (thousands) *		916	980	1 000	1 000	1 000	1 180	...	Nombre (en milliers) *
Per 100 inhabitants		4.1	4.4	4.5	4.4	4.4	5.0	...	Pour 100 habitants

Telephones *(continued)*
Main telephone lines in operation (in thousands) and lines per 100 inhabitants
Téléphones *(suite)*
Nombre de lignes téléphoniques en service (en milliers) et lignes pour 100 habitants

Country or area	Fiscal year & Ex. budgét. &	2002	2003	2004	2005	2006	2007	2008	Pays ou zone
Korea, Republic of									**Corée, République de**
Number (thousands) [13]		25 735	25 128	23 568	23 905	22 431	22 397	21 325	Nombre (en milliers) [13]
Per 100 inhabitants		54.4	52.9	49.5	50.0	46.7	46.4	44.1	Pour 100 habitants
Kuwait									**Koweït**
Number (thousands)		482	487	497	505	517	...	...	Nombre (en milliers)
Per 100 inhabitants		19.8	19.3	19.1	18.8	18.7	...	...	Pour 100 habitants
Kyrgyzstan									**Kirghizistan**
Number (thousands)		395	396	416	440	459	482	...	Nombre (en milliers)
Per 100 inhabitants		7.8	7.7	8.0	8.4	8.6	9.1	...	Pour 100 habitants
Lao Peop. Dem. Rep.									**Rép. dém. pop. lao**
Number (thousands)		62	70	75	91	92	95	...	Nombre (en milliers)
Per 100 inhabitants		1.1	1.2	1.3	1.5	1.5	1.6	...	Pour 100 habitants
Latvia									**Lettonie**
Number (thousands)		701	654	650	731	657	644	...	Nombre (en milliers)
Per 100 inhabitants		29.9	28.1	28.1	31.7	28.6	28.3	...	Pour 100 habitants
Lebanon									**Liban**
Number (thousands)		679	700	630	635	681	698[2]	...	Nombre (en milliers)
Per 100 inhabitants		19.6	20.0	17.8	17.7	18.9	17.0	...	Pour 100 habitants
Lesotho	(01/04)								**Lesotho**
Number (thousands) [25]		29	35	37	48	53	...	...	Nombre (en milliers) [25]
Per 100 inhabitants		1.6	2.0	2.1	2.7	3.0	...	...	Pour 100 habitants
Liberia									**Libéria**
Number (thousands)		*7	...	...	...	...	2	...	Nombre (en milliers)
Per 100 inhabitants		0.2	...	...	...	...	0.1	...	Pour 100 habitants
Libyan Arab Jamah.									**Jamah. arabe libyenne**
Number (thousands) [4]		720	750	800	852	...	...	...	Nombre (en milliers) [4]
Per 100 inhabitants		13.0	13.3	13.9	14.6	...	...	...	Pour 100 habitants
Liechtenstein									**Liechtenstein**
Number (thousands)		20	20	20	20	20	20	...	Nombre (en milliers)
Per 100 inhabitants		59.4	58.7	58.4	58.0	56.2	55.6	...	Pour 100 habitants
Lithuania									**Lituanie**
Number (thousands) [5,16]		936	824	820	801	792	799	785	Nombre (en milliers) [5,16]
Per 100 inhabitants		27.0	23.9	23.8	23.3	23.2	23.6	23.3	Pour 100 habitants
Luxembourg									**Luxembourg**
Number (thousands) [5,26]		249	245	245	245	248	248	261	Nombre (en milliers) [5,26]
Per 100 inhabitants		55.6	54.1	53.4	52.6	52.8	53.2	55.2	Pour 100 habitants
Madagascar									**Madagascar**
Number (thousands)		59	60	59	92	130	134	165	Nombre (en milliers)
Per 100 inhabitants		0.3	0.3	0.3	0.5	0.7	0.7	0.8	Pour 100 habitants
Malawi									**Malawi**
Number (thousands)		73	85	93	103	130[4]	175	...	Nombre (en milliers)
Per 100 inhabitants		0.6	0.7	0.7	0.8	1.0	1.3	...	Pour 100 habitants
Malaysia									**Malaisie**
Number (thousands)		4 670	4 572	4 446	4 366	4 342	4 350	4 292	Nombre (en milliers)
Per 100 inhabitants		19.5	18.7	17.9	17.2	16.8	16.4	15.9	Pour 100 habitants
Maldives									**Maldives**
Number (thousands)		29	30	32	32	32	33	47	Nombre (en milliers)
Per 100 inhabitants		9.4	9.6	9.8	9.8	10.8	10.8	15.1	Pour 100 habitants
Mali									**Mali**
Number (thousands)		57	61	66	76	83	80	83	Nombre (en milliers)
Per 100 inhabitants		0.5	0.5	0.5	0.6	0.6	0.6	0.7	Pour 100 habitants
Malta									**Malte**
Number (thousands)		207	208	207	202	208	230	241	Nombre (en milliers)
Per 100 inhabitants		52.3	52.3	51.7	50.3	51.7	56.6	59.1	Pour 100 habitants
Marshall Islands									**Iles Marshall**
Number (thousands)		4	4	...	...	...	4[4]	...	Nombre (en milliers)
Per 100 inhabitants		7.9	7.8	...	...	...	...	...	Pour 100 habitants
Mauritania									**Mauritanie**
Number (thousands)		32	38	39	41	35	40	76	Nombre (en milliers)
Per 100 inhabitants		1.1	1.3	1.3	1.3	1.1	1.3	2.4	Pour 100 habitants

Telephones *(continued)*
Main telephone lines in operation (in thousands) and lines per 100 inhabitants
Téléphones *(suite)*
Nombre de lignes téléphoniques en service (en milliers) et lignes pour 100 habitants

Country or area	Fiscal year & Ex. budgét. &	2002	2003	2004	2005	2006	2007	2008	Pays ou zone
Mauritius									**Maurice**
Number (thousands)		327	348	354	357	357	361	365	Nombre (en milliers)
Per 100 inhabitants		27.1	28.5	28.7	28.7	28.5	28.6	28.7	Pour 100 habitants
Mayotte									**Mayotte**
Number (thousands) *		10	...	...	...	...	...	...	Nombre (en milliers) *
Per 100 inhabitants		6.2	...	...	...	...	...	...	Pour 100 habitants
Mexico									**Mexique**
Number (thousands) [27]		14 975	16 330	18 073[2]	19 512	19 861	19 754	20 539	Nombre (en milliers) [27]
Per 100 inhabitants		14.5	15.7	17.1	18.2	18.3	18.5	19.1	Pour 100 habitants
Micronesia (Fed. States of)									**Micronésie (Et. féd. de)**
Number (thousands)		10	11	12	12	9	9	...	Nombre (en milliers)
Per 100 inhabitants		9.4	10.2	10.9	11.3	8.0	7.8	...	Pour 100 habitants
Mongolia									**Mongolie**
Number (thousands)		128	138	146	156	159	162[4]	...	Nombre (en milliers)
Per 100 inhabitants		5.0	5.3	5.6	5.9	5.9	6.1	...	Pour 100 habitants
Montenegro									**Monténégro**
Number (thousands)		...	...	290	349	353	...	...	Nombre (en milliers)
Per 100 inhabitants		...	...	46.8	57.2	58.9	...	...	Pour 100 habitants
Morocco									**Maroc**
Number (thousands)		1 127	1 219	1 309	1 341	1 266	2 394[28]	2 991[28]	Nombre (en milliers)
Per 100 inhabitants		3.7	4.0	4.2	4.3	4.1	7.7	9.5	Pour 100 habitants
Mozambique									**Mozambique**
Number (thousands)		84	78	70	70	67	78	78	Nombre (en milliers)
Per 100 inhabitants		0.4	0.4	0.4	0.4	0.3	0.4	0.4	Pour 100 habitants
Myanmar									**Myanmar**
Number (thousands)		342	363	425	504	...	709[4]	...	Nombre (en milliers)
Per 100 inhabitants		0.7	0.7	0.8	1.0	...	1.5	...	Pour 100 habitants
Namibia	(30/09)								**Namibie**
Number (thousands)		121	127	128	139	136	138	...	Nombre (en milliers)
Per 100 inhabitants		6.2	6.4	6.4	6.8	6.6	6.7	...	Pour 100 habitants
Nepal	(15/07)								**Népal**
Number (thousands)		328	372	418	485	612	701	805[29]	Nombre (en milliers)
Per 100 inhabitants		1.3	1.4	1.6	1.8	2.2	2.5	2.8	Pour 100 habitants
Netherlands									**Pays-Bas**
Number (thousands) [6]		8 026[4]	7 846	7 861	7 600	7 450[4]	7 404[30]	7 324[30]	Nombre (en milliers) [6]
Per 100 inhabitants		50.0	48.6	48.4	46.6	45.6	45.1	44.5	Pour 100 habitants
New Caledonia									**Nouvelle-Calédonie**
Number (thousands)		52	52	53	55	58	60	63	Nombre (en milliers)
Per 100 inhabitants		23.2	22.7	22.9	23.4	24.0	24.9	25.7	Pour 100 habitants
New Zealand	(01/04)								**Nouvelle-Zélande**
Number (thousands)		1 765	1 798	1 801	1 729	1 762[31]	1 747[31]	1 750[25]	Nombre (en milliers)
Per 100 inhabitants		45.2	45.6	45.1	42.9	43.4	41.8	41.5	Pour 100 habitants
Nicaragua									**Nicaragua**
Number (thousands)		172	205	214	221	248	...	...	Nombre (en milliers)
Per 100 inhabitants		3.3	3.9	4.0	4.0	4.4	...	...	Pour 100 habitants
Niger									**Niger**
Number (thousands)		22	23	24	24	...	...	...	Nombre (en milliers)
Per 100 inhabitants		0.2	0.2	0.2	0.2	...	...	...	Pour 100 habitants
Nigeria									**Nigéria**
Number (thousands)		702	889	1 028	1 223	1 688	1 580[32]	1 308	Nombre (en milliers)
Per 100 inhabitants		0.6	0.7	0.8	0.9	1.3	1.1	0.9	Pour 100 habitants
Norway									**Norvège**
Number (thousands)		2 317	2 236	2 180	2 109	2 055	1 990	...	Nombre (en milliers)
Per 100 inhabitants		50.9	48.9	47.4	45.6	44.3	42.4	...	Pour 100 habitants
Occupied Palest. Terr.									**Terr. palest. occupé**
Number (thousands)		302	252	290	349	341	348	...	Nombre (en milliers)
Per 100 inhabitants		9.0	7.3	8.1	9.4	9.2	9.3	...	Pour 100 habitants
Oman									**Oman**
Number (thousands)		228	236	243	265	270	268	274	Nombre (en milliers)
Per 100 inhabitants		9.1	9.4	9.6	10.3	10.3	10.3	10.3	Pour 100 habitants

15

Telephones *(continued)*
Main telephone lines in operation (in thousands) and lines per 100 inhabitants
Téléphones *(suite)*
Nombre de lignes téléphoniques en service (en milliers) et lignes pour 100 habitants

Country or area	Fiscal year & Ex. budgét. &	2002	2003	2004	2005	2006	2007	2008	Pays ou zone
Pakistan	(30/06)								**Pakistan**
Number (thousands)		3 655	4 047	4 502	5 228	5 240	4 806	4 416	Nombre (en milliers)
Per 100 inhabitants		2.5	2.7	2.9	3.3	3.3	2.9	2.6	Pour 100 habitants
Palau									**Palaos**
Number (thousands)		7	7	8	8	7	7	...	Nombre (en milliers)
Panama									**Panama**
Number (thousands)		387	381	425	470	488	495	496	Nombre (en milliers)
Per 100 inhabitants		12.6	12.2	13.4	14.6	14.9	14.8	14.6	Pour 100 habitants
Papua New Guinea									**Papouasie-Nvl-Guinée**
Number (thousands)		62	63	63	64	62	60	...	Nombre (en milliers)
Per 100 inhabitants		1.1	1.1	1.1	1.1	1.0	0.9	...	Pour 100 habitants
Paraguay									**Paraguay**
Number (thousands)		273	281	303	320	331	394	363	Nombre (en milliers)
Per 100 inhabitants		4.8	4.8	5.0	5.2	5.3	6.4	5.8	Pour 100 habitants
Peru									**Pérou**
Number (thousands)		1 657	1 839	2 050	2 251	2 401	2 673	2 878	Nombre (en milliers)
Per 100 inhabitants		6.2	6.8	7.4	8.0	8.5	9.6	10.2	Pour 100 habitants
Philippines									**Philippines**
Number (thousands)		3 311	3 340	3 437	3 367	3 633	3 940	3 905	Nombre (en milliers)
Per 100 inhabitants		4.2	4.2	4.2	4.1	4.3	4.5	4.4	Pour 100 habitants
Poland									**Pologne**
Number (thousands)[6]		11 860	*12 292	12 553	11 836	11 476	10 336	...	Nombre (en milliers)[6]
Per 100 inhabitants		30.7	31.9	32.6	30.7	29.8	27.1		Pour 100 habitants
Portugal									**Portugal**
Number (thousands)		4 351	4 281	4 238	4 234	4 236	4 195	4 121	Nombre (en milliers)
Per 100 inhabitants		42.1	41.2	40.6	40.3	40.2	39.5	38.7	Pour 100 habitants
Puerto Rico									**Porto Rico**
Number (thousands)[33]		1 276	1 213[2]	1 112[2]	1 038[4]	...	...	...	Nombre (en milliers)[33]
Per 100 inhabitants		32.9	31.0	28.3	26.2	...	...	...	Pour 100 habitants
Qatar									**Qatar**
Number (thousands)		177	185	191	205	228	237	263	Nombre (en milliers)
Per 100 inhabitants		25.7	25.2	24.6	25.3	27.2	28.2	30.8	Pour 100 habitants
Republic of Moldova									**Rép. de Moldova**
Number (thousands)		719	791	863	929	1 018	1 080	...	Nombre (en milliers)
Per 100 inhabitants		16.9	18.7	20.5	22.1	24.3	28.5	...	Pour 100 habitants
Romania									**Roumanie**
Number (thousands)		4 215	4 332	4 388	4 383	4 198	4 257	5 036	Nombre (en milliers)
Per 100 inhabitants		19.2	19.8	20.1	20.2	19.4	19.9	23.6	Pour 100 habitants
Russian Federation									**Fédération de Russie**
Number (thousands)		35 500	36 100	38 500[34]	40 100[34]	43 900	44 200	...	Nombre (en milliers)
Per 100 inhabitants		24.4	25.0	26.8	28.0	30.8	31.0	...	Pour 100 habitants
Rwanda									**Rwanda**
Number (thousands)		25	26	23	24[4]	...	23	17	Nombre (en milliers)
Per 100 inhabitants		0.3	0.3	0.3	0.3	...	0.2	0.2	Pour 100 habitants
Saint Kitts and Nevis	(01/04)								**Saint-Kitts-et-Nevis**
Number (thousands)		24	...	25	...	...	...	...	Nombre (en milliers)
Per 100 inhabitants		57.1	...	59.3	...	...	...	...	Pour 100 habitants
Saint Lucia	(01/04)								**Sainte-Lucie**
Number (thousands)		51	...	...	...	...	...	41	Nombre (en milliers)
Per 100 inhabitants		32.6	...	...	...	...	...	24.5	Pour 100 habitants
Saint Vincent-Grenadines	(01/04)								**Saint Vincent-Grenadines**
Number (thousands)		27	21	19	23	23	23	23	Nombre (en milliers)
Per 100 inhabitants		23.3	18.0	16.1	18.9	19.0	19.0	18.8	Pour 100 habitants
Samoa									**Samoa**
Number (thousands)		12	13	16[4]	20	...	...	...	Nombre (en milliers)
Per 100 inhabitants		6.5	7.3	8.9	10.5	...	...	...	Pour 100 habitants
San Marino									**Saint-Marin**
Number (thousands)		21	21	21	21	21	21	21	Nombre (en milliers)
Per 100 inhabitants		75.1	74.8	74.4	74.2	77.8	68.2	79.1	Pour 100 habitants

15

Telephones *(continued)*
Main telephone lines in operation (in thousands) and lines per 100 inhabitants
Téléphones *(suite)*
Nombre de lignes téléphoniques en service (en milliers) et lignes pour 100 habitants

Country or area	Fiscal year & Ex. budgét. &	2002	2003	2004	2005	2006	2007	2008	Pays ou zone
Sao Tome and Principe									**Sao Tomé-et-Principe**
Number (thousands)		6	7	7	7[4]	8	8	...	Nombre (en milliers)
Per 100 inhabitants		4.4	4.7	4.6	4.5	4.7	4.9	...	Pour 100 habitants
Saudi Arabia									**Arabie saoudite**
Number (thousands)		3 417	3 503	3 695	3 844	3 951	3 996	4 100	Nombre (en milliers)
Per 100 inhabitants		15.1	15.0	15.4	15.6	15.7	16.2	16.2	Pour 100 habitants
Senegal									**Sénégal**
Number (thousands)		225	229	245	267	283	269	238	Nombre (en milliers)
Per 100 inhabitants		2.1	2.1	2.2	2.3	2.4	2.2	1.9	Pour 100 habitants
Serbia									**Serbie**
Number (thousands)		...	...	2 685	2 527	2 719	2 993	3 085	Nombre (en milliers)
Per 100 inhabitants		...	...	...	...	25.9	30.4	31.2	Pour 100 habitants
Serbia and Montenegro									**Serbie-et-Monténégro**
Number (thousands)		2 493	2 612	2 685	2 698[4]	...	...	...	Nombre (en milliers)
Per 100 inhabitants		23.7	24.8	25.6	25.7	...	...	...	Pour 100 habitants
Seychelles	(01/04)								**Seychelles**
Number (thousands)		21	21	21	21	21	23[14,30]	23[2,14]	Nombre (en milliers)
Por 100 inhabitants		27.1	26.8	26.6	26.5	26.1	26.2	27.1	Pour 100 habitants
Sierra Leone									**Sierra Leone**
Number (thousands)		24	...	...	...	...	...	...	Nombre (en milliers)
Per 100 inhabitants		0.5	...	...	...	...	...	...	Pour 100 habitants
Singapore									**Singapour**
Number (thousands)[35]		1 927	1 890	1 857	1 844	1 854[36]	1 862[36]	1 857[36]	Nombre (en milliers)[35]
Per 100 inhabitants		46.3	44.8	43.5	42.6	42.3	42.0	41.4	Pour 100 habitants
Slovakia									**Slovaquie**
Number (thousands)		1 403	1 295	1 250	1 197	1 167	1 151	1 098	Nombre (en milliers)
Per 100 inhabitants		26.0	24.0	23.1	22.2	21.6	21.3	20.4	Pour 100 habitants
Slovenia									**Slovénie**
Number (thousands)[37]		808	812	811	816[14]	837[14]	857[14]	1 010[30]	Nombre (en milliers)[37]
Per 100 inhabitants		41.1	41.3	41.2	41.5	42.6	42.8	50.4	Pour 100 habitants
Solomon Islands	(01/04)								**Iles Salomon**
Number (thousands)[39]		7[40]	6[40]	7	7	8	...	...	Nombre (en milliers)[30]
Per 100 inhabitants		1.5	1.4	1.5	1.6	1.6	...	...	Pour 100 habitants
Somalia									**Somalie**
Number (thousands)[4]		35	100	100	100	100	100	...	Nombre (en milliers)[4]
Per 100 inhabitants		0.5	1.3	1.3	1.2	1.2	1.1	...	Pour 100 habitants
South Africa	(01/04)								**Afrique du Sud**
Number (thousands)		4 844	4 821	4 850	4 729	4 642	4 532	...	Nombre (en milliers)
Per 100 inhabitants		10.4	10.3	10.3	10.0	9.8	9.3	...	Pour 100 habitants
Spain									**Espagne**
Number (thousands)		17 641	17 759	17 934	19 461	19 865	20 192	20 200	Nombre (en milliers)
Per 100 inhabitants		42.4	42.1	42.1	45.2	45.8	45.6	45.3	Pour 100 habitants
Sri Lanka									**Sri Lanka**
Number (thousands)		883	939	991	1 244	1 884	2 742	3 446	Nombre (en milliers)
Per 100 inhabitants		4.4	4.6	4.8	6.0	9.0	14.2	17.8	Pour 100 habitants
Sudan									**Soudan**
Number (thousands)		672	937	1 029	570	499	345	356	Nombre (en milliers)
Per 100 inhabitants		2.0	2.7	2.9	1.6	1.3	0.9	...	Pour 100 habitants
Suriname									**Suriname**
Number (thousands)		79	80	82	81	82	...	...	Nombre (en milliers)
Per 100 inhabitants		17.9	18.0	18.3	18.0	18.0	...	...	Pour 100 habitants
Swaziland	(01/04)								**Swaziland**
Number (thousands)		35	46	45	35	44	...	...	Nombre (en milliers)
Per 100 inhabitants		3.4	4.5	4.3	3.4	4.3	...	...	Pour 100 habitants
Sweden									**Suède**
Number (thousands)[6]		5 585	5 535	5 688	5 635	5 551	5 506	...	Nombre (en milliers)[6]
Per 100 inhabitants		62.5	61.7	63.1	62.3	61.2	60.4	...	Pour 100 habitants
Switzerland									**Suisse**
Number (thousands)[6]		5 388	5 323	5 253	5 150	5 022	4 927	*4 820	Nombre (en milliers)[6]
Per 100 inhabitants		74.7	73.7	72.6	71.0	66.9	65.8	64.2	Pour 100 habitants

15
Telephones *(continued)*
Main telephone lines in operation (in thousands) and lines per 100 inhabitants
Téléphones *(suite)*
Nombre de lignes téléphoniques en service (en milliers) et lignes pour 100 habitants

Country or area	Fiscal year & Ex. budgét. &	2002	2003	2004	2005	2006	2007	2008	Pays ou zone
Syrian Arab Republic									**Rép. arabe syrienne**
Number (thousands)		2 095	2 411	2 658	2 903	3 243	3 452	3 633	Nombre (en milliers)
Per 100 inhabitants		11.8	13.3	14.3	15.2	16.6	17.3	17.8	Pour 100 habitants
Tajikistan									**Tadjikistan**
Number (thousands)		238	245	273	280	320	340	...	Nombre (en milliers)
Per 100 inhabitants		3.8	3.9	4.3	4.3	4.9	5.0	...	Pour 100 habitants
Thailand	(30/09)								**Thaïlande**
Number (thousands)		6 557	6 632	6 812	7 035	7 072	7 024	...	Nombre (en milliers)
Per 100 inhabitants		10.5	10.5	10.7	11.0	10.9	11.0	...	Pour 100 habitants
TFYR of Macedonia									**L'ex-R.Y. Macédoine**
Number (thousands)		560	525	537	534	491	464	457	Nombre (en milliers)
Per 100 inhabitants		27.7	25.9	26.4	26.2	24.1	22.7	22.4	Pour 100 habitants
Timor-Leste									**Timor-Leste**
Number (thousands)[6]		...	2	2	2	2	2	...	Nombre (en milliers)[6]
Per 100 inhabitants		...	0.2	0.2	0.2	0.2	0.2	...	Pour 100 habitants
Togo									**Togo**
Number (thousands)		51	61	66	63[41]	82	99	141	Nombre (en milliers)
Per 100 inhabitants		0.9	1.0	1.1	1.0	1.3	1.5	2.1	Pour 100 habitants
Tonga									**Tonga**
Number (thousands)		11	12[4]	13[4]	14	18	21	26	Nombre (en milliers)
Per 100 inhabitants		11.1	11.8	12.7	13.4	18.0	21.0	25.3	Pour 100 habitants
Trinidad and Tobago	(01/04)								**Trinité-et-Tobago**
Number (thousands)		318	319	322	322	326	307	...	Nombre (en milliers)
Per 100 inhabitants		24.6	24.6	24.8	24.7	24.9	23.0	...	Pour 100 habitants
Tunisia									**Tunisie**
Number (thousands)		1 149	1 164	1 204	1 257	1 268	1 273	1 239	Nombre (en milliers)
Per 100 inhabitants		11.7	11.8	12.0	12.4	12.4	12.3	11.9	Pour 100 habitants
Turkey									**Turquie**
Number (thousands)		18 890	18 917	19 125	18 978	18 832	18 201[12]	17 502	Nombre (en milliers)
Per 100 inhabitants		26.9	26.5	26.5	25.9	25.4	24.3	23.1	Pour 100 habitants
Turkmenistan									**Turkménistan**
Number (thousands)		374	376	388	398	424	458	...	Nombre (en milliers)
Per 100 inhabitants		8.1	8.0	8.1	8.2	8.7	9.2	...	Pour 100 habitants
Tuvalu									**Tuvalu**
Number (thousands)		1	1	1	1	1	1	...	Nombre (en milliers)
Per 100 inhabitants		6.4	6.8	7.2	8.5	10.4	12.1	...	Pour 100 habitants
Uganda	(30/06)								**Ouganda**
Number (thousands)		55	61	72	88	108	162[30]	168	Nombre (en milliers)
Per 100 inhabitants		0.2	0.2	0.3	0.3	0.4	0.5	0.5	Pour 100 habitants
Ukraine									**Ukraine**
Number (thousands)		10 833	11 110	12 142	11 667	12 341	12 859	13 177	Nombre (en milliers)
Per 100 inhabitants		22.6	23.4	25.8	25.1	26.8	27.8	28.7	Pour 100 habitants
United Arab Emirates									**Emirats arabes unis**
Number (thousands)		1 094	1 136	1 188	1 237	1 310	1 386	1 508	Nombre (en milliers)
Per 100 inhabitants		29.1	28.2	27.7	27.5	28.1	31.6	33.5	Pour 100 habitants
United Kingdom	(01/04)								**Royaume-Uni**
Number (thousands)[6]		34 738	34 550	34 576	34 068	33 849	33 815[30]	33 209[30]	Nombre (en milliers)[6]
Per 100 inhabitants		58.8	58.3	58.1	57.1	56.6	55.6	54.4	Pour 100 habitants
United Rep. of Tanzania									**Rép.-Unie de Tanzanie**
Number (thousands)		162	147	148	154	157	163	124	Nombre (en milliers)
Per 100 inhabitants		0.4	0.4	0.4	0.4	0.4	0.4	0.3	Pour 100 habitants
United States									**Royaume-Uni**
Number (thousands)[42]		189 250	182 933	177 691	175 161	167 460	158 437	...	Nombre (en milliers)[42]
Per 100 inhabitants		65.3	62.5	60.2	58.7	55.6	51.8	...	Pour 100 habitants
United States Virgin Is.									**Iles Vierges améric.**
Number (thousands)		69	70	71	72[4]	...	...	...	Nombre (en milliers)
Per 100 inhabitants		62.2	62.4	63.4	64.1	...	...	...	Pour 100 habitants
Uruguay									**Uruguay**
Number (thousands)		947	938	997	1 006	987	965	959	Nombre (en milliers)
Per 100 inhabitants		27.9	27.5	29.0	29.0	28.3	28.9	28.6	Pour 100 habitants

15

Telephones *(continued)*
Main telephone lines in operation (in thousands) and lines per 100 inhabitants
Téléphones *(suite)*
Nombre de lignes téléphoniques en service (en milliers) et lignes pour 100 habitants

Country or area	Fiscal year & Ex. budgét. &	2002	2003	2004	2005	2006	2007	2008	Pays ou zone
Uzbekistan									**Ouzbékistan**
Number (thousands)		1 681	1 717	1 750	1 794	1 842	1 895	1 919	Nombre (en milliers)
Per 100 inhabitants		6.6	6.6	6.7	6.7	6.8	6.9	6.9	Pour 100 habitants
Vanuatu									**Vanuatu**
Number (thousands)		7	7	7	7	8[4]	9[4]	...	Nombre (en milliers)
Per 100 inhabitants		3.3	3.2	3.3	3.3	3.5	3.9	...	Pour 100 habitants
Venezuela (Bol. Rep. of)									**Venezuela (R. bol. du)**
Number (thousands)		2 842	2 956	3 346	3 651	4 217	5 195	6 303	Nombre (en milliers)
Per 100 inhabitants		11.2	11.5	12.7	13.6	15.5	18.8	22.4	Pour 100 habitants
Viet Nam									**Viet Nam**
Number (thousands)		3 929	4 402	10 125	15 845[4]	27 505	28 529	...	Nombre (en milliers)
Per 100 inhabitants		4.9	5.4	12.2	18.8	32.2	32.7	...	Pour 100 habitants
Yemen									**Yémen**
Number (thousands)		542	694	795	901[4]	968	...	...	Nombre (en milliers)
Per 100 inhabitants		2.8	3.5	3.9	4.3	4.5	...	...	Pour 100 habitants
Zambia	(01/04)								**Zambie**
Number (thousands)		88	00	92	95	93	92	91	Nombre (en milliers)
Per 100 inhabitants		0.8	0.8	0.8	0.8	0.8	0.8	0.7	Pour 100 habitants
Zimbabwe	(30/06)								**Zimbabwe**
Number (thousands)		288	301	317	328	336	345	...	Nombre (en milliers)
Per 100 inhabitants		2.3	2.3	2.5	2.5	2.6	2.6	...	Pour 100 habitants

Source:
International Telecommunication Union (ITU), Geneva, the ITU database, last accessed June 2009.

& Fiscal year refers to the fiscal year used in each country or area. Countries or areas whose reference periods coincide with the calendar year ending 31 December are not footnoted. Those that have a fiscal year other than calendar year are denoted as follows:

22/03: Year beginning 22 March
01/04: Year beginning 1 April
30/06: Year ending 30 June
15/07: Year ending 15 July
30/09: Year ending 30 September

Source:
Union internationale des télécommunications (UIT), Genève, la base de données de l'UIT, dernier accès juin 2009.

& Ex. budgét. fait référence à l'exercice budgétaire en vigueur dans chaque pays ou territoire. Les pays ou les territoires dont l'exercice budgétaire terminent le 31 décembre de l'année civile ne sont pas signalés. Dans le cas contraire, ils sont désignés de la manière suivante:

22/03 : Exercice commençant le 22 mars
01/04 : Exercice commençant le 1er avril
30/06 : Exercice se terminant le 30 juin
15/07 : Exercice se terminant le 15 juillet
30/09 : Exercice se terminant le 30 septembre

1	Analogic lines and XDSI lines.	1	Lignes analogiques et "XDSI".
2	June.	2	Juin.
3	1994-2002 only refers to "Telefónica de Argentina S.A. y Telecom Argentina S.A." From 2002 all licensees are included (352 in 2003).	3	Les chiffres de 1994-2002 ne concernent que "Telefónica de Argentina S.A. y Telecom Argentina S.A." À partir de 2002 tous les détenteurs de licence sont compris (352 en 2003).
4	ITU estimate.	4	Estimation de l'UIT.
5	Without ISDN channels.	5	Sans RNIS.
6	Including ISDN channels.	6	RNIS inclus.
7	Including ISDN equivalents.	7	Y compris les équivalents du RNIS.
8	Conventional telephony terminals in service.	8	Terminaux de téléphonie conventionnelle en service.
9	WLL lines included.	9	Y compris les lignes "WLL".
10	Retail lines.	10	Lignes du commerce de détail.
11	For statistical purposes, the data for China do not include those for the Hong Kong Special Administrative Region (Hong Kong SAR), Macao Special Administrative Region (Macao SAR) and Taiwan Province of China.	11	Pour la présentation des statistiques, les données pour la Chine ne comprennent pas la Région Administrative Spéciale de Hong Kong (Hong Kong RAS), la Région Administrative Spéciale de Macao (Macao RAS) et la province de Taiwan.
12	November.	12	Novembre.
13	Telephone subscribers.	13	Abonnés au téléphone.
14	Including fixed VoIP (Voice over internet protocol) lines.	14	Y compris les lignes de téléphonie par Internet (VoIP).
15	Many cancellations of subscribers that had not paid, following privatization (February 2007).	15	Nombreuses résiliations d'abonnements non payés après la privatisation (février 2007).
16	Excluding public call offices.	16	Cabines publiques exclues.
17	Data provided by the Commission based on counts made by technical	17	Données fournies par la Commission fondées sur un dénombrement

	experts.		effectué par des experts techniques.
18	Telephone channels including ISDN and own consumption, excluding public payphones.	18	Voies téléphoniques, y compris RNIS et consommation personnelle, excluant les téléphones publics payants.
19	Subscriber lines.	19	Lignes d'abonnés au téléphone.
20	Excluding WLL-F (Wireless in local loop-fixed) subscribers.	20	À l'exclusion des abonnés ayant un téléphone fixe en boucle locale sans fil.
21	September. Telkom.	21	Septembre. Telkom.
22	Central Organisation for Statistics & IT.	22	"Central Organisation for Statistics & IT".
23	Including PSTN lines, ISDN paths, FWA subscription, public payphones and LLU.	23	Y compris les lignes du RTCP, du RNIS, les abonnements d'accès fixe sans fil, les cabines publiques et l'accès boucle locale dégroupée.
24	Data refer to Telecom Italia Wireline.	24	Les données se réfèrent au "Telecom Italia Wireline".
25	December.	25	Décembre.
26	Including digital lines.	26	Y compris les lignes digitales.
27	Lines in service.	27	Lignes en service.
28	Includes fixed wireless.	28	Y compris les téléphones fixes sans fil.
29	April.	29	Avril.
30	September.	30	Septembre.
31	Includes fibre and satellite fixed telephone connections.	31	Y compris les téléphones fixes sur réseau par fibre et par satellite.
32	Break in comparability: Refers to active Fixed Wired/ Wireless lines.	32	Rupture de comparabilité : concerne les lignes fixes en activité, filaires et sans fil.
33	Switched access lines.	33	Lignes d'accès déviées.
34	October.	34	Octobre.
35	Data refer to fiscal years beginning 1 April.	35	Les données se réfèrent aux exercices budgétaires commençant le 1er avril.
36	This includes direct exchange lines (DEL) and IP telephony subscriptions which function under the Public Switched Telephone Services (PSTS) and the Public Switched Integrated Services Digital Network Services.	36	Les chiffres comprennent les lignes individuelles et les abonnements IP fonctionnant par services RTCP et RNIS.
37	Including ISDN subscribers.	37	Y compris les abonnés au ISDN.
38	Includes ISDN and VoIP connections (network termination points).	38	Y compris les connections ISDN et VoIP.
39	Billable lines.	39	Lignes payables.
40	The number of fixed lines declined due to civil war.	40	Le nombre de lignes fixes a diminué en raison de la guerre civile.
41	Drop results from the termination of contract for clients that had not paid.	41	2005 : la diminution est due à la résiliation des contrats de clients dont le compte était en souffrance.
42	Data up to 1980 refer to main stations reported by FCC. From 1981, data refer to "Local Loops".	42	Les données pour 1980 se réfèrent aux stations principales. Dès 1981, les données se réfèrent aux "Local Loops".

Cellular mobile telephone subscribers
Number (thousands) and per 100 inhabitants

Abonnés au téléphone mobile
Nombre (milliers) et pour 100 habitants

Country or area	Fiscal year & Ex. budgét.&	2002	2003	2004	2005	2006	2007	2008	Pays ou zone
Afghanistan									**Afghanistan**
Number (thousands)		25	200	600	1 200	2 520	4 668	7 899	Nombre (en milliers)
Per 100 inhabitants		^0	1	2	4	8	17	28	Pour 100 habitants
Albania									**Albanie**
Number (thousands)		851	1 100	1 260	1 530	1 900	2 300	3 141	Nombre (en milliers)
Per 100 inhabitants		28	36	40	49	60	72	98	Pour 100 habitants
Algeria									**Algérie**
Number (thousands)		450	1 447	4 882	13 661	20 998	27 563[1]	...	Nombre (en milliers)
Per 100 inhabitants		1	5	15	42	63	81	...	Pour 100 habitants
American Samoa									**Samoa américaines**
Number (thousands)		2	2	2	...	...	...	...	Nombre (en milliers)
Per 100 inhabitants		3	3	4	...	...	...	...	Pour 100 habitants
Andorra									**Andorre**
Number (thousands)		33	52	58	65	69	68	64	Nombre (en milliers)
Per 100 inhabitants		49	78	87	96	97	82	78	Pour 100 habitants
Angola									**Angola**
Number (thousands)		140	350	740	1 611	3 055[2]	4 962	6 773	Nombre (en milliers)
Per 100 inhabitants		1	2	5	10	19	29	39	Pour 100 habitants
Antigua and Barbuda	(01/04)								**Antigua-et-Barbuda**
Number (thousands)		38	46[1]	54	86	110	112	137	Nombre (en milliers)
Per 100 inhabitants		49	58	67	106	134	135	165	Pour 100 habitants
Argentina	(30/09)								**Argentine**
Number (thousands)		6 567	7 842	13 512	22 156	31 510	40 402	46 509	Nombre (en milliers)
Per 100 inhabitants		17	21	35	57	81	102	116	Pour 100 habitants
Armenia									**Arménie**
Number (thousands)		71	114	203	318	1 260	1 876	...	Nombre (en milliers)
Per 100 inhabitants		2	4	7	11	42	62	...	Pour 100 habitants
Aruba									**Aruba**
Number (thousands)		62	70	98	103	135	146	127	Nombre (en milliers)
Per 100 inhabitants		65	72	100	104	135	140	123	Pour 100 habitants
Australia	(30/06)								**Australie**
Number (thousands)		12 670	14 347	16 480	18 420	19 760	21 260	22 120	Nombre (en milliers)
Per 100 inhabitants		65	73	83	91	97	102	106	Pour 100 habitants
Austria									**Autriche**
Number (thousands)		6 736	7 274[3]	7 992	8 665	9 281[4]	9 912[4]	10 816[4]	Nombre (en milliers)
Per 100 inhabitants		83	89	98	106	113	119	129	Pour 100 habitants
Azerbaijan									**Azerbaïdjan**
Number (thousands)		794	1 057	1 457	2 242	3 233	4 519	6 548	Nombre (en milliers)
Per 100 inhabitants		10	13	17	27	38	53	77	Pour 100 habitants
Bahamas									**Bahamas**
Number (thousands)		122	122	186	228	253	374	358	Nombre (en milliers)
Per 100 inhabitants		39	39	58	71	77	113	107	Pour 100 habitants
Bahrain									**Bahreïn**
Number (thousands)		389	443	650	767	907	1 116	1 400	Nombre (en milliers)
Per 100 inhabitants		56	63	91	106	123	148	183	Pour 100 habitants
Bangladesh	(30/06)								**Bangladesh**
Number (thousands)		1 075	1 365	2 782	9 000	19 131	34 370[5]	44 640	Nombre (en milliers)
Per 100 inhabitants		1	1	2	6	13	22	28	Pour 100 habitants
Barbados	(01/04)								**Barbade**
Number (thousands)		97	140	200	206	237	...	...	Nombre (en milliers)
Per 100 inhabitants		36	52	74	76	88	...	...	Pour 100 habitants
Belarus									**Bélarus**
Number (thousands)		463	1 118	2 239	4 100	5 960	6 960	...	Nombre (en milliers)
Per 100 inhabitants		5	11	23	42	61	72	...	Pour 100 habitants
Belgium									**Belgique**
Number (thousands)		8 102[1]	8 606	9 132	9 605	9 847	10 738	11 822	Nombre (en milliers)
Per 100 inhabitants		78	83	88	92	94	103	113	Pour 100 habitants

16

Cellular mobile telephone subscribers *(continued)*
Number (thousands) and per 100 inhabitants
Abonnés au téléphone mobile *(suite)*
Nombre (milliers) et pour 100 habitants

Country or area	Fiscal year & Ex. budgét.&	2002	2003	2004	2005	2006	2007	2008	Pays ou zone
Belize	(01/04)								**Belize**
Number (thousands)		52	60	92	120	121	118	160	Nombre (en milliers)
Per 100 inhabitants		20	23	35	44	44	41	54	Pour 100 habitants
Benin									**Bénin**
Number (thousands)		219	236	459	596	1 056	1 904	3 435¹	Nombre (en milliers)
Per 100 inhabitants		3	3	6	7	12	21	37	Pour 100 habitants
Bermuda	(01/04)								**Bermudes**
Number (thousands)		*30	40	49	53	60	...	...	Nombre (en milliers)
Per 100 inhabitants		47	63	77	82	93	...	...	Pour 100 habitants
Bhutan									**Bhoutan**
Number (thousands)		...	2	19	36	82	149	251	Nombre (en milliers)
Per 100 inhabitants		...	^0	1	2	...	...	...	Pour 100 habitants
Bolivia									**Bolivie**
Number (thousands)		1 023	1 279	1 801	2 421	2 876	3 254	4 830¹	Nombre (en milliers)
Per 100 inhabitants		12	14	20	26	31	34	50	Pour 100 habitants
Bosnia and Herzegovina									**Bosnie-Herzégovine**
Number (thousands)		749	1 075	1 407	1 594	1 888	2 450	3 179	Nombre (en milliers)
Per 100 inhabitants		19	27	36	41	48	62	81	Pour 100 habitants
Botswana	(01/04)								**Botswana**
Number (thousands)		332	445	523	564	823	1 152	1 486	Nombre (en milliers)
Per 100 inhabitants		19	25	30	32	47	61	78	Pour 100 habitants
Brazil									**Brésil**
Number (thousands)		34 881	46 373	65 605	86 210	99 919	120 980	150 641	Nombre (en milliers)
Per 100 inhabitants		19	26	36	46	53	63	78	Pour 100 habitants
Brunei Darussalam									**Brunéi Darussalam**
Number (thousands)		154	177	202	233	301	349¹	...	Nombre (en milliers)
Per 100 inhabitants		44	50	55	62	79	89	...	Pour 100 habitants
Bulgaria									**Bulgarie**
Number (thousands)		2 598	3 501	4 730	6 245	8 253	9 897	10 633	Nombre (en milliers)
Per 100 inhabitants		33	45	61	81	108	130	140	Pour 100 habitants
Burkina Faso									**Burkina Faso**
Number (thousands) [6]		111	238	396	634	1 017	1 611¹	2 553¹	Nombre (en milliers) [6]
Per 100 inhabitants		1	2	3	5	7	11	17	Pour 100 habitants
Burundi									**Burundi**
Number (thousands)		52	64	101	153	200¹	270	481	Nombre (en milliers)
Per 100 inhabitants		1	1	1	2	3	3	5	Pour 100 habitants
Cambodia									**Cambodge**
Number (thousands)		380	498	862	1 062	1 722	2 583	4 237	Nombre (en milliers)
Per 100 inhabitants		3	4	6	8	12	18	29	Pour 100 habitants
Cameroon									**Cameroun**
Number (thousands)		702	1 077	1 531	2 253	3 136	4 536¹	6 161¹	Nombre (en milliers)
Per 100 inhabitants		5	7	10	14	19	24	33	Pour 100 habitants
Canada									**Canada**
Number (thousands)		11 872	13 291	15 020	17 017	18 749	20 277	21 455	Nombre (en milliers)
Per 100 inhabitants		38	42	47	53	58	62	65	Pour 100 habitants
Cape Verde									**Cap-Vert**
Number (thousands)		43	53	66	82	109	152¹	278	Nombre (en milliers)
Per 100 inhabitants		9	11	13	16	21	29	51	Pour 100 habitants
Cayman Islands	(01/04)								**Iles Caïmanes**
Number (thousands)		...	21	34	...	...	...	...	Nombre (en milliers)
Per 100 inhabitants		...	49	77	...	...	...	...	Pour 100 habitants
Central African Rep.									**Rép. centrafricaine**
Number (thousands)		13	40	60	100	110	130	154	Nombre (en milliers)
Per 100 inhabitants		^0	1	2	2	3	3	3	Pour 100 habitants
Chad									**Tchad**
Number (thousands)		34	65	123	210	466	918¹	1 809¹	Nombre (en milliers)
Per 100 inhabitants		^0	1	1	2	5	9	16	Pour 100 habitants
Chile									**Chili**
Number (thousands)		6 244¹	7 268	9 261	10 570	12 451	13 955	14 797	Nombre (en milliers)
Per 100 inhabitants		40	46	57	65	75	84	88	Pour 100 habitants

16

Cellular mobile telephone subscribers *(continued)*
Number (thousands) and per 100 inhabitants
Abonnés au téléphone mobile *(suite)*
Nombre (milliers) et pour 100 habitants

Country or area	Fiscal year & Ex. budgét.&	2002	2003	2004	2005	2006	2007	2008	Pays ou zone
China									**Chine**
Number (thousands)		206 005	269 953	334 824	393 406	461 058	547 306	634 000	Nombre (en milliers)
Per 100 inhabitants		16	21	26	30	35	41	47	Pour 100 habitants
China, Hong Kong SAR	(01/04)								**Chine, Hong Kong RAS**
Number (thousands)		6 396	7 349	8 214	8 544	9 444	10 752[8]	11 374	Nombre (en milliers)
Per 100 inhabitants		94	107	118	121	133	149	156	Pour 100 habitants
China, Macao SAR									**Chine, Macao RAS**
Number (thousands)		276	364	432	533	636	794	933	Nombre (en milliers)
Per 100 inhabitants		61	80	95	116	137	165	193	Pour 100 habitants
Colombia									**Colombie**
Number (thousands)		4 597	6 186	10 401	21 850	29 763	33 941	41 365	Nombre (en milliers)
Per 100 inhabitants		11	14	23	48	64	74	88	Pour 100 habitants
Comoros									**Comores**
Number (thousands)		...	2	8	16	37	40[1]	...	Nombre (en milliers)
Per 100 inhabitants		...	^0	1	2	5	5	...	Pour 100 habitants
Congo									**Congo**
Number (thousands)		222	330	384	558	917	1 288[1]	1 807[1]	Nombre (en milliers)
Per 100 inhabitants		6	9	10	14	22	34	47	Pour 100 habitants
Costa Rica									**Costa Rica**
Number (thousands)		502	778	923	1 101	1 444	1 508	1 887	Nombre (en milliers)
Per 100 inhabitants		12	19	22	25	33	34	42	Pour 100 habitants
Côte d'Ivoire									**Côte d'Ivoire**
Number (thousands)		1 027	1 281	1 674	2 349	4 065	7 468[1]	10 449[1]	Nombre (en milliers)
Per 100 inhabitants		6	7	9	13	22	39	53	Pour 100 habitants
Croatia									**Croatie**
Number (thousands)		2 340	2 537	2 836	3 650	4 395	5 035	5 924[1]	Nombre (en milliers)
Per 100 inhabitants		52	56	62	80	96	111	130	Pour 100 habitants
Cuba									**Cuba**
Number (thousands)		18	35	76	136	153	198	332	Nombre (en milliers)
Per 100 inhabitants		^0	^0	1	1	1	2	3	Pour 100 habitants
Cyprus									**Chypre**
Number (thousands)		418	552	658	783	868	988	1 017	Nombre (en milliers)
Per 100 inhabitants		52	68	80	94	103	116	118	Pour 100 habitants
Czech Republic									**République tchèque**
Number (thousands)		8 610	9 709	10 783	11 776	12 406	13 229	13 780	Nombre (en milliers)
Per 100 inhabitants		84	95	105	115	122	130	135	Pour 100 habitants
Dem. Rep. of the Congo [1]									**Rép. dém. du Congo** [1]
Number (thousands)		560	1 246	1 991	2 746	4 415	6 592	9 263	Nombre (en milliers)
Per 100 inhabitants		1	2	4	5	7	11	14	Pour 100 habitants
Denmark									**Danemark**
Number (thousands)		4 478	4 767	5 167	5 449	5 828	6 310	6 551	Nombre (en milliers)
Per 100 inhabitants		83	88	95	100	107	116	120	Pour 100 habitants
Djibouti									**Djibouti**
Number (thousands)		15	23	34	44	...	...	...	Nombre (en milliers)
Per 100 inhabitants		2	3	4	6	...	...	...	Pour 100 habitants
Dominica	(01/04)								**Dominique**
Number (thousands)		12	24	42	...	...	...	...	Nombre (en milliers)
Per 100 inhabitants		16	30	53	...	...	...	...	Pour 100 habitants
Dominican Republic									**Rép. dominicaine**
Number (thousands)		1 701	2 092	2 534	3 623	4 606	5 513	7 210	Nombre (en milliers)
Per 100 inhabitants		20	24	29	41	51	56	73	Pour 100 habitants
Ecuador									**Equateur**
Number (thousands)		1 561	2 398	3 544	6 246	8 485	9 940	11 595	Nombre (en milliers)
Per 100 inhabitants		12	19	27	47	63	75	86	Pour 100 habitants
Egypt	(30/06)								**Egypte**
Number (thousands)		4 495	5 798	7 643	13 630	18 001	30 065	41 272	Nombre (en milliers)
Per 100 inhabitants		6	8	11	18	24	40	54	Pour 100 habitants
El Salvador									**El Salvador**
Number (thousands)		889	1 150	1 833	2 412	3 852	6 137	6 951	Nombre (en milliers)
Per 100 inhabitants		14	17	27	35	55	90	100	Pour 100 habitants

16

Cellular mobile telephone subscribers *(continued)*
Number (thousands) and per 100 inhabitants
Abonnés au téléphone mobile *(suite)*
Nombre (milliers) et pour 100 habitants

Country or area	Fiscal year & Ex. budgét.&	2002	2003	2004	2005	2006	2007	2008	Pays ou zone
Equatorial Guinea									**Guinée équatoriale**
Number (thousands)		32	42	62	97	140[1]	220[1]	346[1]	Nombre (en milliers)
Per 100 inhabitants		7	9	13	19	27	43	67	Pour 100 habitants
Eritrea									**Erythrée**
Number (thousands)		...	...	20	40	62	84[1]	109	Nombre (en milliers)
Per 100 inhabitants		...	...	^0	1	1	2	2	Pour 100 habitants
Estonia									**Estonie**
Number (thousands)		881	1 050	1 256	1 445	1 659	1 982	2 524	Nombre (en milliers)
Per 100 inhabitants		65	78	94	109	125	148	190	Pour 100 habitants
Ethiopia									**Ethiopie**
Number (thousands)		50	51	156	411	867	1 208	3 168	Nombre (en milliers)
Per 100 inhabitants		^0	^0	^0	1	1	1	4	Pour 100 habitants
Faeroe Islands									**Iles Féroé**
Number (thousands)		35	38	41	42	50	52	55	Nombre (en milliers)
Per 100 inhabitants		75	82	88	89	106	107	114	Pour 100 habitants
Fiji									**Fidji**
Number (thousands)		90	110	142	205	285	530	...	Nombre (en milliers)
Per 100 inhabitants		11	13	17	24	33	63	...	Pour 100 habitants
Finland									**Finlande**
Number (thousands)		4 517	4 747	4 988	5 270	5 670	6 080	6 830	Nombre (en milliers)
Per 100 inhabitants		87	91	95	100	108	115	129	Pour 100 habitants
France									**France**
Number (thousands)		38 585	41 702	44 544	48 088	51 662	55 358	57 972[9]	Nombre (en milliers)
Per 100 inhabitants		65	69	74	79	85	90	94	Pour 100 habitants
French Guiana									**Guyane française**
Number (thousands)		87	92	98	...	...	...	...	Nombre (en milliers)
Per 100 inhabitants		50	52	54	...	...	...	...	Pour 100 habitants
French Polynesia									**Polynésie française**
Number (thousands)		52	60	96	120	152	175	187	Nombre (en milliers)
Per 100 inhabitants		21	24	38	47	59	67	70	Pour 100 habitants
Gabon									**Gabon**
Number (thousands) [10]		279	300	489	737	898	1 169	1 300[1]	Nombre (en milliers) [10]
Per 100 inhabitants		21	22	36	53	64	88	96	Pour 100 habitants
Gambia	(01/04)								**Gambie**
Number (thousands)		100	149	175	247	404	800	1 166	Nombre (en milliers)
Per 100 inhabitants		7	10	12	16	26	47	66	Pour 100 habitants
Georgia									**Géorgie**
Number (thousands)		504	711	841	1 174	1 704	2 600	...	Nombre (en milliers)
Per 100 inhabitants		11	16	19	26	38	59	...	Pour 100 habitants
Germany									**Allemagne**
Number (thousands)		59 128	64 800	71 322	79 271	85 652[11]	97 151[11]	107 245[11]	Nombre (en milliers)
Per 100 inhabitants		72	78	86	96	104	118	130	Pour 100 habitants
Ghana									**Ghana**
Number (thousands)		387	796	1 695	2 875	5 207	7 604	11 570	Nombre (en milliers)
Per 100 inhabitants		2	4	8	13	23	32	48	Pour 100 habitants
Gibraltar									**Gibraltar**
Number (thousands)		12	16[12]	18	...	...	...	...	Nombre (en milliers)
Per 100 inhabitants		44	57	66	...	...	...	...	Pour 100 habitants
Greece									**Grèce**
Number (thousands)		9 314[10]	8 936	9 324	10 260	10 980	12 295[13]	13 799	Nombre (en milliers)
Per 100 inhabitants		84	81	84	92	99	110	124	Pour 100 habitants
Greenland									**Groenland**
Number (thousands)		20	30	39	46	54	66	...	Nombre (en milliers)
Per 100 inhabitants		35	53	69	82	94	116	...	Pour 100 habitants
Grenada									**Grenade**
Number (thousands)		8	42	43	47	46	...	60	Nombre (en milliers)
Per 100 inhabitants		7	41	42	46	45	...	57	Pour 100 habitants
Guadeloupe [9]									**Guadeloupe** [9]
Number (thousands)		299	289	315	...	...	...	...	Nombre (en milliers)
Per 100 inhabitants		68	66	71	...	...	...	...	Pour 100 habitants

Country or area	Fiscal year & Ex. budgét.&	2002	2003	2004	2005	2006	2007	2008	Pays ou zone
Guam									**Guam**
Number (thousands)		71	80	98	...	...	...	...	Nombre (en milliers)
Per 100 inhabitants		44	49	59	...	...	...	...	Pour 100 habitants
Guatemala									**Guatemala**
Number (thousands)		1 577	2 035	3 168	4 510	7 179	11 898	14 949	Nombre (en milliers)
Per 100 inhabitants		13	17	26	36	56	89	109	Pour 100 habitants
Guernsey									**Guernesey**
Number (thousands)		37	42	44	...	...	...	...	Nombre (en milliers)
Per 100 inhabitants		65	74	79	...	...	...	...	Pour 100 habitants
Guinea									**Guinée**
Number (thousands)		91	112	155	189	...	2 000	2 600[1]	Nombre (en milliers)
Per 100 inhabitants		1	1	2	2	...	21	27	Pour 100 habitants
Guinea-Bissau									**Guinée-Bissau**
Number (thousands)		0	1	39	99	157	296	500	Nombre (en milliers)
Per 100 inhabitants		0	^0	3	6	10	17	29	Pour 100 habitants
Guyana[9]									**Guyana**[9]
Number (thousands)		79	138	172	281	...	...	...	Nombre (en milliers)
Per 100 inhabitants		11	18	23	37	...	...	...	Pour 100 habitants
Haiti									**Haïti**
Number (thousands)		140	320	400	500[1]	1 200	2 500	3 200[1]	Nombre (en milliers)
Per 100 inhabitants		2	4	5	6	14	26	33	Pour 100 habitants
Honduras									**Honduras**
Number (thousands)		327	379	707	1 281	2 241	4 185	6 211	Nombre (en milliers)
Per 100 inhabitants		5	6	10	18	30	59	86	Pour 100 habitants
Hungary									**Hongrie**
Number (thousands)		6 886	7 945	8 727[8]	9 320	9 966	11 030	12 224	Nombre (en milliers)
Per 100 inhabitants		68	78	86	92	99	110	122	Pour 100 habitants
Iceland									**Islande**
Number (thousands)		260[1]	280	290	283	302	328	...	Nombre (en milliers)
Per 100 inhabitants		91	97	99	96	102	109	...	Pour 100 habitants
India	(01/04)								**Inde**
Number (thousands)		13 000	33 690	52 220	90 140	166 050	233 620	346 890	Nombre (en milliers)
Per 100 inhabitants		1	3	5	8	15	20	29	Pour 100 habitants
Indonesia									**Indonésie**
Number (thousands)		11 700	18 495	30 337	46 910	63 803	93 387	140 578	Nombre (en milliers)
Per 100 inhabitants		5	9	14	21	28	40	60	Pour 100 habitants
Iran (Islamic Rep. of)	(22/03)								**Iran (Rép. islamique d')**
Number (thousands)		2 279	3 450	5 076	8 511[14]	15 385	29 770	43 000	Nombre (en milliers)
Per 100 inhabitants		3	5	7	12	22	42	60	Pour 100 habitants
Iraq	(30/06)								**Iraq**
Number (thousands)		20	80	574	1 533	9 345	14 021	...	Nombre (en milliers)
Per 100 inhabitants		^0	^0	2	5	32	48	...	Pour 100 habitants
Ireland	(01/04)								**Irlande**
Number (thousands)		3 000	3 500	3 860	4 270	4 741	4 983[15]	5 048[15]	Nombre (en milliers)
Per 100 inhabitants		76	87	95	103	113	116	115	Pour 100 habitants
Israel									**Israël**
Number (thousands)		6 300	6 618	7 222	7 757	8 404	8 902	8 982	Nombre (en milliers)
Per 100 inhabitants		99	102	109	115	123	128	128	Pour 100 habitants
Italy									**Italie**
Number (thousands)		54 200[3]	56 770[16]	62 750	71 500	80 418	89 801	88 580	Nombre (en milliers)
Per 100 inhabitants		94	98	108	123	138	153	150	Pour 100 habitants
Jamaica	(01/04)								**Jamaïque**
Number (thousands)		1 245	1 576	1 838	1 981	2 275	2 684	2 723	Nombre (en milliers)
Per 100 inhabitants		48	60	70	75	85	99	100	Pour 100 habitants
Japan[17]	(01/04)								**Japon**[17]
Number (thousands)		81 118	86 655	91 474	96 484	101 698	107 339	110 395[12]	Nombre (en milliers)
Per 100 inhabitants		64	68	72	75	79	84	86	Pour 100 habitants
Jersey									**Jersey**
Number (thousands)		...	81	84	...	...	...	...	Nombre (en milliers)
Per 100 inhabitants		...	92	95	...	...	...	...	Pour 100 habitants

16

Cellular mobile telephone subscribers *(continued)*
Number (thousands) and per 100 inhabitants
Abonnés au téléphone mobile *(suite)*
Nombre (milliers) et pour 100 habitants

Country or area	Fiscal year & Ex. budgét.&	2002	2003	2004	2005	2006	2007	2008	Pays ou zone
Jordan									**Jordanie**
Number (thousands)		1 220	1 325	1 624	3 138	4 343	4 772	5 314	Nombre (en milliers)
Per 100 inhabitants		23	24	29	55	74	81	87	Pour 100 habitants
Kazakhstan									**Kazakhstan**
Number (thousands)		1 027	1 331	2 447	5 398	7 776	12 323	14 911	Nombre (en milliers)
Per 100 inhabitants		7	9	16	36	52	80	96	Pour 100 habitants
Kenya	(30/06)								**Kenya**
Number (thousands)		1 187[12]	1 591	2 546	4 612	7 340	11 349	16 234	Nombre (en milliers)
Per 100 inhabitants		4	5	8	13	21	30	42	Pour 100 habitants
Kiribati									**Kiribati**
Number (thousands)		^0	1	1	1	1[1]	1[1]	...	Nombre (en milliers)
Per 100 inhabitants		1	1	1	1	1	...	...	Pour 100 habitants
Korea, Republic of									**Corée, République de**
Number (thousands)		32 342	33 592	36 586	38 342	40 197	43 498	45 607	Nombre (en milliers)
Per 100 inhabitants		68	71	77	80	84	90	94	Pour 100 habitants
Kuwait									**Koweït**
Number (thousands)		1 227	1 420	2 000	2 277	2 530	2 774	...	Nombre (en milliers)
Per 100 inhabitants		50	56	77	85	91	97	...	Pour 100 habitants
Kyrgyzstan									**Kirghizistan**
Number (thousands)		53	138	263	542	1 262	2 168	...	Nombre (en milliers)
Per 100 inhabitants		1	3	5	10	24	41	...	Pour 100 habitants
Lao People's Dem. Rep.									**Rép. dém. pop. lao**
Number (thousands)		55	112	204	658	1 010	1 478	...	Nombre (en milliers)
Per 100 inhabitants		1	2	4	11	17	25	...	Pour 100 habitants
Latvia									**Lettonie**
Number (thousands)		917	1 220	1 537	1 872	2 184	2 217	...	Nombre (en milliers)
Per 100 inhabitants		39	52	66	81	95	97	...	Pour 100 habitants
Lebanon [1]									**Liban** [1]
Number (thousands)		775	795	884	994	1 106	1 260	1 430	Nombre (en milliers)
Per 100 inhabitants		22	23	25	28	31	31	35	Pour 100 habitants
Lesotho	(01/04)								**Lesotho**
Number (thousands)		138	126	196	250	358	456[1]	581	Nombre (en milliers)
Per 100 inhabitants		8	7	11	14	20	23	29	Pour 100 habitants
Liberia									**Libéria**
Number (thousands)		...	47[1]	94	160	280[1]	563[1]	732	Nombre (en milliers)
Per 100 inhabitants		...	1	3	5	8	15	19	Pour 100 habitants
Libyan Arab Jamah.									**Jamah. arabe libyenne**
Number (thousands)		70	127	500	2 000	3 928	4 500[1]	...	Nombre (en milliers)
Per 100 inhabitants		1	2	9	34	66	73	...	Pour 100 habitants
Liechtenstein									**Liechtenstein**
Number (thousands)		11	25	26	28	29	32	...	Nombre (en milliers)
Per 100 inhabitants		34	74	75	80	82	91	...	Pour 100 habitants
Lithuania									**Lituanie**
Number (thousands) [9]		1 646	2 102	3 051	4 353	4 718	4 912	5 023	Nombre (en milliers) [9]
Per 100 inhabitants		47	61	89	127	138	145	149	Pour 100 habitants
Luxembourg									**Luxembourg**
Number (thousands)		473[1]	539	470[9]	510[9]	713[9]	685[9]	707[9]	Nombre (en milliers)
Per 100 inhabitants		106	119	102	110	151	147	150	Pour 100 habitants
Madagascar									**Madagascar**
Number (thousands)		163	284	334	510	1 046	2 218	4 835	Nombre (en milliers)
Per 100 inhabitants		1	2	2	3	5	11	24	Pour 100 habitants
Malawi									**Malawi**
Number (thousands)		86	135	222	421	620[1]	1 051	1 781	Nombre (en milliers)
Per 100 inhabitants		1	1	2	3	5	8	12	Pour 100 habitants
Malaysia									**Malaisie**
Number (thousands)		9 053	11 124	14 611	19 545	19 464	23 347	27 125	Nombre (en milliers)
Per 100 inhabitants		38	46	59	77	75	88	100	Pour 100 habitants
Maldives									**Maldives**
Number (thousands)		42	66	113	204	271	314	436	Nombre (en milliers)
Per 100 inhabitants		14	21	35	62	91	103	140	Pour 100 habitants

16

Cellular mobile telephone subscribers *(continued)*
Number (thousands) and per 100 inhabitants
Abonnés au téléphone mobile *(suite)*
Nombre (milliers) et pour 100 habitants

Country or area	Fiscal year & Ex. budgét.&	2002	2003	2004	2005	2006	2007	2008	Pays ou zone
Mali									**Mali**
Number (thousands)		46	247	407	762	1 513	2 531	3 267	Nombre (en milliers)
Per 100 inhabitants		^0	2	3	6	11	21	26	Pour 100 habitants
Malta									**Malte**
Number (thousands)		277	290	306	324	347	372	386	Nombre (en milliers)
Per 100 inhabitants		70	73	77	81	86	91	94	Pour 100 habitants
Marshall Islands									**Iles Marshall**
Number (thousands)		1	1	1	1	1[1]	1[1]	...	Nombre (en milliers)
Per 100 inhabitants		1	1	1	...	...	...	...	Pour 100 habitants
Martinique [9]									**Martinique** [9]
Number (thousands)		298	278	295	...	...	...	...	Nombre (en milliers)
Per 100 inhabitants		76	71	75	...	...	...	...	Pour 100 habitants
Mauritania									**Mauritanie**
Number (thousands)		247	351	522	746	1 060	1 414[1]	2 092	Nombre (en milliers)
Per 100 inhabitants		9	12	18	24	34	45	65	Pour 100 habitants
Mauritius									**Maurice**
Number (thousands)		348	462	548	657	772	929[1]	1 033	Nombre (en milliers)
Per 100 inhabitants		29	38	44	53	62	74	81	Pour 100 habitants
Mayotte [9]									**Mayotte** [9]
Number (thousands)		20	33	48	...	...	...	...	Nombre (en milliers)
Per 100 inhabitants		13	20	29	...	...	...	...	Pour 100 habitants
Mexico									**Mexique**
Number (thousands)		25 928	30 098	38 451	47 129	55 395	66 559	75 303	Nombre (en milliers)
Per 100 inhabitants		25	29	36	44	51	62	70	Pour 100 habitants
Micronesia (Fed. States of)									**Micronésie (Etats féd. de)**
Number (thousands)		^0	6	13	14	19	27	...	Nombre (en milliers)
Per 100 inhabitants		^0	5	12	13	17	25	...	Pour 100 habitants
Mongolia									**Mongolie**
Number (thousands)		216	319	429	557	775	916[1]	...	Nombre (en milliers)
Per 100 inhabitants		8	12	16	21	29	34	...	Pour 100 habitants
Montenegro									**Monténégro**
Number (thousands)		...	...	484	543	644	...	...	Nombre (en milliers)
Per 100 inhabitants		...	...	78	89	107	...	...	Pour 100 habitants
Morocco									**Maroc**
Number (thousands)		6 199	7 360	9 337	12 393	16 005	20 029	22 816	Nombre (en milliers)
Per 100 inhabitants		21	24	30	39	52	64	72	Pour 100 habitants
Mozambique									**Mozambique**
Number (thousands)		255	436	708	1 504	2 339	3 300	4 405	Nombre (en milliers)
Per 100 inhabitants		1	2	4	8	12	15	20	Pour 100 habitants
Myanmar									**Myanmar**
Number (thousands)		48	67	92	129	214	271[1]	376	Nombre (en milliers)
Per 100 inhabitants		^0	^0	^0	^0	^0	1	1	Pour 100 habitants
Namibia	(01/04)								**Namibie**
Number (thousands)		150[12]	224	286	449	609	800	1 052	Nombre (en milliers)
Per 100 inhabitants		8	11	14	22	30	39	50	Pour 100 habitants
Nepal	(15/07)								**Népal**
Number (thousands)		22	82	117	227	1 157	3 269	...	Nombre (en milliers)
Per 100 inhabitants		^0	^0	^0	1	4	12	...	Pour 100 habitants
Netherlands									**Pays-Bas**
Number (thousands)		12 100	13 200	14 800	15 834	17 296	19 285	19 927	Nombre (en milliers)
Per 100 inhabitants		75	82	91	97	106	117	121	Pour 100 habitants
Netherlands Antilles									**Antilles néerlandaises**
Number (thousands)		...	200	200	...	...	...	...	Nombre (en milliers)
Per 100 inhabitants		...	112	111	...	...	...	...	Pour 100 habitants
New Caledonia									**Nouvelle-Calédonie**
Number (thousands)		80	97	116	134	155[1]	176	196	Nombre (en milliers)
Per 100 inhabitants		36	43	50	57	64	73	80	Pour 100 habitants
New Zealand	(01/04)								**Nouvelle-Zélande**
Number (thousands)		2 449	2 599	3 027	3 530	3 802	4 251	4 620[3]	Nombre (en milliers)
Per 100 inhabitants		63	66	76	88	94	102	110	Pour 100 habitants

16

Cellular mobile telephone subscribers *(continued)*
Number (thousands) and per 100 inhabitants
Abonnés au téléphone mobile *(suite)*
Nombre (milliers) et pour 100 habitants

Country or area	Fiscal year & Ex. budgét.&	2002	2003	2004	2005	2006	2007	2008	Pays ou zone
Nicaragua									**Nicaragua**
Number (thousands)		237	467	739	1 119	1 830	2 123	3 039	Nombre (en milliers)
Per 100 inhabitants		5	9	14	20	33	38	54	Pour 100 habitants
Niger									**Niger**
Number (thousands)		58	82	172	324	483	900[1]	1 677[1]	Nombre (en milliers)
Per 100 inhabitants		0	1	1	2	3	6	11	Pour 100 habitants
Nigeria									**Nigéria**
Number (thousands)		1 569	3 149	9 147	18 587	32 322	#40 396	62 988	Nombre (en milliers)
Per 100 inhabitants		1	3	7	14	24	27	42	Pour 100 habitants
Northern Mariana Islands									**Iles Mariannes du Nord**
Number (thousands)		17	19	20	...	...	...	...	Nombre (en milliers)
Per 100 inhabitants		23	24	26	...	...	...	...	Pour 100 habitants
Norway									**Norvège**
Number (thousands)		3 790[1]	4 061	4 525	4 754	5 008	5 192	...	Nombre (en milliers)
Per 100 inhabitants		83	89	98	103	108	111	...	Pour 100 habitants
Occupied Palestinian Terr.[18]									**Terr. palestinien occupé**[18]
Number (thousands)		320	480	974	1 095	822	1 026	...	Nombre (en milliers)
Per 100 inhabitants		10	14	27	30	22	27	...	Pour 100 habitants
Oman									**Oman**
Number (thousands)		463	594	806	1 333	1 818	2 500	3 219	Nombre (en milliers)
Per 100 inhabitants		19	24	32	52	70	96	121	Pour 100 habitants
Pakistan	(30/06)								**Pakistan**
Number (thousands)		1 699	2 404	5 023	12 771	34 507	62 961[12]	88 020	Nombre (en milliers)
Per 100 inhabitants		1	2	3	8	22	38	53	Pour 100 habitants
Palau									**Palaos**
Number (thousands)		2	4	4	6	8	11	...	Nombre (en milliers)
Panama									**Panama**
Number (thousands)		526	692	1 260	1 749	2 174	3 011	3 805	Nombre (en milliers)
Per 100 inhabitants		17	22	40	54	66	90	112	Pour 100 habitants
Papua New Guinea									**Papouasie-Nvl-Guinée**
Number (thousands)		15	18	48	75	100[1]	300[19]	...	Nombre (en milliers)
Per 100 inhabitants		^0	^0	1	1	2	5	...	Pour 100 habitants
Paraguay									**Paraguay**
Number (thousands)		1 667	1 770	1 749	1 887	3 233	4 694	5 791	Nombre (en milliers)
Per 100 inhabitants		29	30	29	31	51	77	93	Pour 100 habitants
Peru									**Pérou**
Number (thousands)		2 307	2 930	4 093	5 583	8 772	15 417	20 952	Nombre (en milliers)
Per 100 inhabitants		9	11	15	20	31	55	74	Pour 100 habitants
Philippines									**Philippines**
Number (thousands)		15 383	22 510	32 936	34 779	42 869	57 345	68 102	Nombre (en milliers)
Per 100 inhabitants		20	28	40	42	51	65	76	Pour 100 habitants
Poland									**Pologne**
Number (thousands)		*13 898	*17 401	23 096	29 166	36 745	41 389	...	Nombre (en milliers)
Per 100 inhabitants		36	45	60	76	95	109	...	Pour 100 habitants
Portugal									**Portugal**
Number (thousands)		8 670	10 003	10 571	11 447	12 226	13 451	14 910	Nombre (en milliers)
Per 100 inhabitants		84	96	101	109	116	127	140	Pour 100 habitants
Puerto Rico									**Porto Rico**
Number (thousands)		1 800	1 860	2 682	3 354[1]	...	...	...	Nombre (en milliers)
Per 100 inhabitants		46	48	68	85	...	...	...	Pour 100 habitants
Qatar									**Qatar**
Number (thousands)		267	377	490	717	920	1 264	1 683	Nombre (en milliers)
Per 100 inhabitants		39	51	63	88	110	150	197	Pour 100 habitants
Republic of Moldova									**République de Moldova**
Number (thousands)		338	476	787	1 090	1 358	1 883	2 420	Nombre (en milliers)
Per 100 inhabitants		8	11	19	26	32	50	64	Pour 100 habitants
Réunion									**Réunion**
Number (thousands)[9]		455	522	579	...	...	...	...	Nombre (en milliers)[9]
Per 100 inhabitants		61	68	75	...	...	...	...	Pour 100 habitants

Cellular mobile telephone subscribers *(continued)*
Number (thousands) and per 100 inhabitants
Abonnés au téléphone mobile *(suite)*
Nombre (milliers) et pour 100 habitants

Country or area	Fiscal year & Ex. budgét.&	2002	2003	2004	2005	2006	2007	2008	Pays ou zone
Romania									**Roumanie**
Number (thousands)		5 111	7 040	10 215	13 354	15 991	20 417	24 467	Nombre (en milliers)
Per 100 inhabitants		23	32	47	62	74	95	115	Pour 100 habitants
Russian Federation									**Fédération de Russie**
Number (thousands)		17 609	36 135	73 722	120 000	150 674[1]	163 300	187 500	Nombre (en milliers)
Per 100 inhabitants		12	25	51	84	106	115	132	Pour 100 habitants
Rwanda									**Rwanda**
Number (thousands)		82	131	137	223	314	635[1]	1 323[1]	Nombre (en milliers)
Per 100 inhabitants		1	1	2	2	3	7	13	Pour 100 habitants
Saint Kitts and Nevis	(01/04)								**Saint-Kitts-et-Nevis**
Number (thousands)		5	...	10	...	...	...	...	Nombre (en milliers)
Per 100 inhabitants		12	...	24	...	...	...	...	Pour 100 habitants
Saint Lucia *	(01/04)								**Sainte-Lucie ***
Number (thousands)		14	...	93	106	...	...	170	Nombre (en milliers)
Per 100 inhabitants		9	...	58	66	...	...	102	Pour 100 habitants
Saint Vincent-Grenadines	(01/04)								**Saint Vincent-Gren.**
Number (thousands)		10	63	72	71	88	110	130	Nombre (en milliers)
Per 100 inhabitants		9	53	61	59	74	92	108	Pour 100 habitants
Samoa									**Samoa**
Number (thousands)		3	11	16	24	46	86[19]	...	Nombre (en milliers)
Per 100 inhabitants		1	6	9	13	25	46	...	Pour 100 habitants
San Marino									**Saint-Marin**
Number (thousands)		17	17	17	17	17	18	18	Nombre (en milliers)
Per 100 inhabitants		61	61	61	61	64	57	66	Pour 100 habitants
Sao Tome and Principe									**Sao Tomé-et-Principe**
Number (thousands)		2	5	8	12	18	30	49	Nombre (en milliers)
Per 100 inhabitants		1	3	5	8	12	19	31	Pour 100 habitants
Saudi Arabia									**Arabie saoudite**
Number (thousands)		5 008	7 238	9 176	14 164	19 663	28 381	36 150	Nombre (en milliers)
Per 100 inhabitants		22	31	38	58	78	115	143	Pour 100 habitants
Senegal									**Sénégal**
Number (thousands)		553	782	1 121	1 730	2 983	3 631	5 389	Nombre (en milliers)
Per 100 inhabitants		5	7	10	15	25	29	42	Pour 100 habitants
Serbia									**Serbie**
Number (thousands)		...	...	4 730	5 511	6 644	8 453	9 619[1]	Nombre (en milliers)
Per 100 inhabitants		...	...	...	...	63	86	97	Pour 100 habitants
Serbia and Montenegro *									**Serbie-et-Monténégro ***
Number (thousands)		2 750	3 635	4 730	5 229	...	...	...	Nombre (en milliers)
Per 100 inhabitants		26	35	45	50	...	...	...	Pour 100 habitants
Seychelles	(01/04)								**Seychelles**
Number (thousands)		45	49	54	59	70	77	85[2]	Nombre (en milliers)
Per 100 inhabitants		57	62	68	73	87	89	101	Pour 100 habitants
Sierra Leone									**Sierra Leone**
Number (thousands)		67	113[1]	...	...	...	776[1]	1 009	Nombre (en milliers)
Per 100 inhabitants		1	2	...	...	...	13	17	Pour 100 habitants
Singapore	(01/04)								**Singapour**
Number (thousands)		3 313	3 577	3 991[12]	4 385	4 789	5 924	6 376	Nombre (en milliers)
Per 100 inhabitants		80	85	93	101	109	134	142	Pour 100 habitants
Slovakia									**Slovaquie**
Number (thousands)		2 923	3 679	4 275	4 540	4 893	6 068	5 520[20]	Nombre (en milliers)
Per 100 inhabitants		54	68	79	84	91	113	102	Pour 100 habitants
Slovenia									**Slovénie**
Number (thousands)		1 667	1 739	1 849	1 759[21]	1 820	1 928	2 055	Nombre (en milliers)
Per 100 inhabitants		85	88	94	89	93	96	103	Pour 100 habitants
Solomon Islands	(01/04)								**Iles Salomon**
Number (thousands)		1	1	3	6	7[1]	11[1]	...	Nombre (en milliers)
Per 100 inhabitants		^0	^0	1	1	1	2	...	Pour 100 habitants
Somalia									**Somalie**
Number (thousands)		100	200[1]	500	500	550[1]	600[1]	...	Nombre (en milliers)
Per 100 inhabitants		1	3	6	6	6	7	...	Pour 100 habitants

16
Cellular mobile telephone subscribers *(continued)*
Number (thousands) and per 100 inhabitants
Abonnés au téléphone mobile *(suite)*
Nombre (milliers) et pour 100 habitants

Country or area	Fiscal year & Ex. budgét. &	2002	2003	2004	2005	2006	2007	2008	Pays ou zone
South Africa	(01/04)								**Afrique du Sud**
Number (thousands)		13 702	16 860	20 839	33 960	39 662	42 300	45 000	Nombre (en milliers)
Per 100 inhabitants		29	36	44	72	83	87	92	Pour 100 habitants
Spain									**Espagne**
Number (thousands)		33 531	37 220	38 623	42 694	45 695	48 422	49 682	Nombre (en milliers)
Per 100 inhabitants		81	88	91	99	105	109	111	Pour 100 habitants
Sri Lanka									**Sri Lanka**
Number (thousands)		931	1 393	2 211	3 362	5 412	7 983	11 082	Nombre (en milliers)
Per 100 inhabitants		5	7	11	16	26	41	57	Pour 100 habitants
Sudan [1]									**Soudan** [1]
Number (thousands)		191	527	1 049	1 828	4 683	8 218	11 187	Nombre (en milliers)
Per 100 inhabitants		1	2	3	5	13	21	...	Pour 100 habitants
Suriname									**Suriname**
Number (thousands)		108	169	213	233	320	...	...	Nombre (en milliers)
Per 100 inhabitants		25	38	48	52	71	...	...	Pour 100 habitants
Swaziland									**Swaziland**
Number (thousands)		68	85[1]	145	200	250	380[1]	457	Nombre (en milliers)
Per 100 inhabitants		7	8	14	19	24	33	40	Pour 100 habitants
Sweden									**Suède**
Number (thousands)		7 949	8 801	8 785[2]	9 104	9 607	10 371	...	Nombre (en milliers)
Per 100 inhabitants		89	98	98	101	106	114	...	Pour 100 habitants
Switzerland	(01/04)								**Suisse**
Number (thousands)		5 736	6 189	6 275	6 834	7 436	8 209	*8 780	Nombre (en milliers)
Per 100 inhabitants		80	86	87	94	99	110	117	Pour 100 habitants
Syrian Arab Republic									**Rép. arabe syrienne**
Number (thousands)		400	1 185	2 346	2 950	4 675	6 235	7 056	Nombre (en milliers)
Per 100 inhabitants		2	7	13	15	24	31	35	Pour 100 habitants
Tajikistan									**Tadjikistan**
Number (thousands)		13	48	135	265	2 150	2 350	...	Nombre (en milliers)
Per 100 inhabitants		^0	1	2	4	33	35	...	Pour 100 habitants
Thailand	(30/09)								**Thaïlande**
Number (thousands)		10 172	21 828	27 379	31 137	40 723	79 066	...	Nombre (en milliers)
Per 100 inhabitants		16	35	43	48	63	124	...	Pour 100 habitants
TFYR of Macedonia									**L'ex-R.Y. Macédoine**
Number (thousands)		365	776	986	1 261	1 417	1 947[2]	2 502[1]	Nombre (en milliers)
Per 100 inhabitants		18	38	49	62	70	95	123	Pour 100 habitants
Timor-Leste									**Timor-Leste**
Number (thousands)		...	20	26	33	49	78[19]	...	Nombre (en milliers)
Per 100 inhabitants		...	2	3	3	5	7	...	Pour 100 habitants
Togo									**Togo**
Number (thousands)		170	244	333	434	708	1 190	1 547[1]	Nombre (en milliers)
Per 100 inhabitants		3	4	6	7	11	18	23	Pour 100 habitants
Tonga [1]									**Tonga** [1]
Number (thousands)		3	11	16	30	30	47	50	Nombre (en milliers)
Per 100 inhabitants		3	11	16	29	29	46	50	Pour 100 habitants
Trinidad and Tobago	(01/04)								**Trinité-et-Tobago**
Number (thousands)		263	336	651	924	1 519	1 510[22]	...	Nombre (en milliers)
Per 100 inhabitants		20	26	50	71	116	113	...	Pour 100 habitants
Tunisia									**Tunisie**
Number (thousands)		574	1 918	3 736	5 681	7 339	7 843	8 569	Nombre (en milliers)
Per 100 inhabitants		6	19	37	56	72	76	82	Pour 100 habitants
Turkey									**Turquie**
Number (thousands)		23 323	27 888	34 708	43 609	52 663	61 976	65 824	Nombre (en milliers)
Per 100 inhabitants		33	39	48	60	71	83	87	Pour 100 habitants
Turkmenistan									**Turkménistan**
Number (thousands)		8	9	50	105[1]	217[1]	348[1]	...	Nombre (en milliers)
Per 100 inhabitants		^0	^0	1	2	4	7	...	Pour 100 habitants
Tuvalu									**Tuvalu**
Number (thousands)		...	...	1	1	2	2	...	Nombre (en milliers)
Per 100 inhabitants		...	...	5	12	15	17	...	Pour 100 habitants

Country or area	Fiscal year & Ex. budgét.&	2002	2003	2004	2005	2006	2007	2008	Pays ou zone
Uganda	(30/06)								**Ouganda**
Number (thousands)		393	776	1 165	1 315	2 009	4 195[1]	8 555	Nombre (en milliers)
Per 100 inhabitants		2	3	4	5	7	14	27	Pour 100 habitants
Ukraine									**Ukraine**
Number (thousands)		3 693	6 498	13 735	30 014	48 987	55 240	55 694	Nombre (en milliers)
Per 100 inhabitants		8	14	29	65	107	120	121	Pour 100 habitants
United Arab Emirates									**Emirats arabes unis**
Number (thousands)		2 428	2 972	3 683	4 534	5 519	7 732	9 358	Nombre (en milliers)
Per 100 inhabitants		65	74	86	101	119	177	208	Pour 100 habitants
United Kingdom	(01/04)								**Royaume-Uni**
Number (thousands)		49 228	54 256	59 688	65 472	69 765	73 224[3]	75 565	Nombre (en milliers)
Per 100 inhabitants		83	92	100	110	117	120	124	Pour 100 habitants
United Rep. of Tanzania									**Rép.-Unie de Tanzanie**
Number (thousands)		607	1 942	1 942	3 390	5 767	8 323	13 007	Nombre (en milliers)
Per 100 inhabitants		2	5	5	9	15	21	31	Pour 100 habitants
United States									**Etats-Unis**
Number (thousands)		141 800	160 637	184 819	213 000	241 800	263 000	270 500	Nombre (en milliers)
Per 100 inhabitants		49	55	63	71	80	86	88	Pour 100 habitants
United States Virgin Is. [1]									**Iles Vierges améric.** [1]
Number (thousands)		45	49	64	80	...	...	...	Nombre (en milliers)
Per 100 inhabitants		40	44	57	72	...	...	...	Pour 100 habitants
Uruguay									**Uruguay**
Number (thousands)		514	498	600	1 155	2 330	3 004	3 508	Nombre (en milliers)
Per 100 inhabitants		15	15	17	33	67	90	105	Pour 100 habitants
Uzbekistan									**Ouzbékistan**
Number (thousands)		187	321	544	720	2 720[1]	5 888	12 650	Nombre (en milliers)
Per 100 inhabitants		1	1	2	3	10	22	46	Pour 100 habitants
Vanuatu									**Vanuatu**
Number (thousands)		5	8	11	13	15[1]	26[19]	...	Nombre (en milliers)
Per 100 inhabitants		2	4	5	6	7	11	...	Pour 100 habitants
Venezuela (Boliv. Rep. of)									**Venezuela (R. bol. du)**
Number (thousands)		6 542	7 015	8 421	12 496	18 789	23 820	27 084	Nombre (en milliers)
Per 100 inhabitants		26	27	32	47	69	86	96	Pour 100 habitants
Viet Nam									**Viet Nam**
Number (thousands)		1 902	2 742	4 960	9 593	15 505	23 730	70 000	Nombre (en milliers)
Per 100 inhabitants		2	3	6	11	18	27	79	Pour 100 habitants
Yemen									**Yémen**
Number (thousands)		487	675	1 483	2 278	2 978	...	...	Nombre (en milliers)
Per 100 inhabitants		3	3	7	11	14	...	...	Pour 100 habitants
Zambia	(01/04)								**Zambie**
Number (thousands)		139	241	464	950	1 663	2 639	3 539	Nombre (en milliers)
Per 100 inhabitants		1	2	4	8	14	22	29	Pour 100 habitants
Zimbabwe	(30/06)								**Zimbabwe**
Number (thousands)		339	364	426	647	849	1 226	1 655	Nombre (en milliers)
Per 100 inhabitants		3	3	3	5	6	9	12	Pour 100 habitants

Source:
International Telecommunication Union (ITU), Geneva, the ITU database, last accessed June 2009.

& Fiscal year refers to the fiscal year used in each country or area. Countries or areas whose reference periods coincide with the calendar year ending 31 December are not footnoted. Those that have a fiscal year other than calendar year are denoted as follows:

22/03: Year beginning 22 March
01/04: Year beginning 1 April
30/06: Year ending 30 June
15/07: Year ending 15 July
30/09: Year ending 30 September

Source:
Union internationale des télécommunications (UIT), Genève, la base de données de l'UIT, dernier accès juin 2009.

& Ex. budgét. fait référence à l'exercice budgétaire en vigueur dans chaque pays ou territoire. Les pays ou les territoires dont l'exercice budgétaire terminent le 31 décembre de l'année civile ne sont pas signalés. Dans le cas contraire, ils sont désignés de la manière suivante:

22/03 : Exercice commençant le 22 mars
01/04 : Exercice commençant le 1er avril
30/06 : Exercice se terminant le 30 juin
15/07 : Exercice se terminant le 15 juillet
30/09 : Exercice se terminant le 30 septembre

16

Cellular mobile telephone subscribers *(continued)*
Number (thousands) and per 100 inhabitants
Abonnés au téléphone mobile *(suite)*
Nombre (milliers) et pour 100 habitants

1	ITU estimate.
2	June.
3	September.
4	Includes subscribers to public mobile data services.
5	December.
6	Including Celtel subscribers.
7	For statistical purposes, the data for China do not include those for the Hong Kong Special Administrative Region (Hong Kong SAR), Macao Special Administrative Region (Macao SAR) and Taiwan Province of China.
8	November.
9	Active mobile subscribers
10	Including inactive subscribers.
11	Including data services.
12	December.
13	Only active subscribers.
14	October.
15	Excluding mobile broadband (HSDPA) subscriptions.
16	30 June.
17	Including Personal Handyphone System.
18	Users use Israel cellular network.
19	Refers to mid-year.
20	New methodology.
21	New methodology of active subscribers.
22	Only one telecom provider.

1	Estimation de l'UIT.
2	Juin.
3	Septembre.
4	Y compris les abonnés aux services mobiles de données sur réseau public.
5	Décembre.
6	Y compris les abonnés au Celtel.
7	Pour la présentation des statistiques, les données pour la Chine ne comprennent pas la Région Administrative Spéciale de Hong Kong (Hong Kong RAS), la Région Administrative Spéciale de Macao (Macao RAS) et la province de Taiwan.
8	Novembre.
9	Nombre d'abonnés actifs de la téléphonie mobile.
10	Y compris d'abonnés inactifs.
11	Services de données compris.
12	Décembre.
13	Abonnements en activité uniquement.
14	Octobre.
15	À l'exclusion des abonnements au très haut débit mobile (HSDPA).
16	30 juin.
17	Y compris "Personal Handyphone System".
18	Les abonnés utilisent le réseau israélien de téléphonie mobile.
19	Données en milieu d'année.
20	Nouvelle méthodologie.
21	Nouvelle méthode de décompte des abonnements en activité.
22	Un seul fournisseur d'accès télécom.

17

Internet users
Estimated number (thousands) and number per 100 inhabitants

Usagers d'Internet
Nombre estimatif (en milliers) et nombre pour 100 habitants

Country or area	Fiscal year & Ex. budgét.&	2002	2003	2004	2005	2006	2007	2008	Pays ou zone
Afghanistan									**Afghanistan**
Number (thousands)		1	20	25	300	535	500	...	Nombre (milliers)
Per 100 inhabitants		^0	^0	^0	1	2	2	...	Pour 100 habitants
Albania									**Albanie**
Number (thousands)		12	30	75	188	471	...	...	Nombre (milliers)
Per 100 inhabitants		^0	1	2	6	15	...	...	Pour 100 habitants
Algeria									**Algérie**
Number (thousands)		500	700	1 500	1 920	2 460	3 500	...	Nombre (milliers)
Per 100 inhabitants		2	2	5	6	7	10	...	Pour 100 habitants
Andorra									**Andorre**
Number (thousands)		...	10	21	30	40	59	59	Nombre (milliers)
Per 100 inhabitants		...	15	31	45	56	79	72	Pour 100 habitants
Angola									**Angola**
Number (thousands)		41	58	75	190	326	498	550	Nombre (milliers)
Per 100 inhabitants		^0	^0	^0	1	2	3	3	Pour 100 habitants
Antigua and Barbuda	(01/04)								**Antigua-et-Barbuda**
Number (thousands)		10	14[1]	20	29	53	60	65	Nombre (milliers)
Per 100 inhabitants		13	18	25	36	64	72	79	Pour 100 habitants
Argentina	(30/09)								**Argentine**
Number (thousands)		4 100	4 530	6 154	6 863	8 184	10 246	11 212	Nombre (milliers)
Per 100 inhabitants		11	12	16	18	21	26	28	Pour 100 habitants
Armenia									**Arménie**
Number (thousands)		60	140	150	161	173	...	...	Nombre (milliers)
Per 100 inhabitants		2	5	5	5	6	...	...	Pour 100 habitants
Aruba									**Aruba**
Number (thousands)		24[1]	24[1]	24[1]	24[1]	24	24	...	Nombre (milliers)
Per 100 inhabitants		25	25	24	24	24	23	...	Pour 100 habitants
Australia	(30/06)								**Australie**
Number (thousands)[1]		11 317	11 837	12 364	12 698	10 600	11 200	11 900	Nombre (milliers)[1]
Per 100 inhabitants		58	60	62	63	52	54	57	Pour 100 habitants
Austria									**Autriche**
Number (thousands)[2]		3 007[3]	3 341[3]	4 249[3]	4 504[3]	5 005[3]	5 602[5]	4 950[3]	Nombre (milliers)[2]
Per 100 inhabitants		37[4]	41[4]	52[4]	55[4]	61[4]	67[4]	59	Pour 100 habitants
Azerbaijan									**Azerbaïdjan**
Number (thousands)		300	350	408	679	829	927	...	Nombre (milliers)
Per 100 inhabitants		4	4	5	8	10	11	...	Pour 100 habitants
Bahamas									**Bahamas**
Number (thousands)		60[1]	84	93	103	110	120	142[1]	Nombre (milliers)
Per 100 inhabitants		19	27	29	32	34	36	42	Pour 100 habitants
Bahrain									**Bahreïn**
Number (thousands)		123	150	153	155	210	250	...	Nombre (milliers)
Per 100 inhabitants		18	21	21	21	28	33	...	Pour 100 habitants
Bangladesh	(30/06)								**Bangladesh**
Number (thousands)		204	243	300	370	450	500	...	Nombre (milliers)
Per 100 inhabitants ^		0	0	0	0	0	0	...	Pour 100 habitants ^
Barbados	(01/04)								**Barbade**
Number (thousands)		30[1]	100	150	160	...	...	...	Nombre (milliers)
Per 100 inhabitants		11	37	56	59	...	...	...	Pour 100 habitants
Belarus									**Bélarus**
Number (thousands)		891	1 607	2 461	...	...	2 810	...	Nombre (milliers)
Per 100 inhabitants		9	16	25	...	...	29	...	Pour 100 habitants
Belgium									**Belgique**
Number (thousands)[2]		4 757	5 153	5 581	6 043	6 471	7 006	...	Nombre (milliers)[2]
Per 100 inhabitants[4]		46	50	54	58	62	67	...	Pour 100 habitants[4]
Belize	(01/04)								**Belize**
Number (thousands)		...	...	16	26	30	32	...	Nombre (milliers)
Per 100 inhabitants		...	...	6	10	11	11	...	Pour 100 habitants

17

Internet users *(continued)*
Estimated number (thousands) and number per 100 inhabitants
Usagers d'Internet *(suite)*
Nombre estimatif (en milliers) et nombre pour 100 habitants

Country or area	Fiscal year & Ex. budgét.&	2002	2003	2004	2005	2006	2007	2008	Pays ou zone
Benin									**Bénin**
Number (thousands)		50	70	90	100	125	150	160	Nombre (milliers)
Per 100 inhabitants		1	1	1	1	1	2	2	Pour 100 habitants
Bermuda	(01/04)								**Bermudes**
Number (thousands)		33	36	39	42	45	48	...	Nombre (milliers)
Per 100 inhabitants		52	57	61	65	70	74	...	Pour 100 habitants
Bhutan									**Bhoutan**
Number (thousands)		10	15	20	25	30	40	40	Nombre (milliers)
Per 100 inhabitants		^0	1	1	1	...	...	...	Pour 100 habitants
Bolivia									**Bolivie**
Number (thousands)		270[1]	310	400	480	580	1 000	...	Nombre (milliers)
Per 100 inhabitants		3	4	4	5	6	10	...	Pour 100 habitants
Bosnia and Herzegovina									**Bosnie-Herzégovine**
Number (thousands)		100	150[1]	585	806	950	1 055	1 308	Nombre (milliers)
Per 100 inhabitants		3	4	15	21	24	27	33	Pour 100 habitants
Botswana	(01/04)								**Botswana**
Number (thousands)		60	60	60	60[1]	80	100	80[1]	Nombre (milliers)
Per 100 inhabitants		3	3	3	3	5	5	4	Pour 100 habitants
Brazil									**Brésil**
Number (thousands)[1,2]		16 389	23 977	35 070	38 418	59 026	67 510	...	Nombre (milliers)[1,2]
Per 100 inhabitants[4]		9	13	19	21	31	35	...	Pour 100 habitants[4]
Brunei Darussalam									**Brunéi Darussalam**
Number (thousands)		53	70	108	135	159	188[1]	...	Nombre (milliers)
Per 100 inhabitants		15	19	29	36	42	48	...	Pour 100 habitants
Bulgaria									**Bulgarie**
Number (thousands)[2]		716	944	1 245	1 545	1 841	2 368	...	Nombre (milliers)[2]
Per 100 inhabitants		9	12	16	20	24	31	...	Pour 100 habitants
Burkina Faso									**Burkina Faso**
Number (thousands)		25	48	53	65	90	110	140	Nombre (milliers)
Per 100 inhabitants		^0	^0	^0	^0	1	1	1	Pour 100 habitants
Burundi									**Burundi**
Number (thousands)		8	14	25	40	50	55	65	Nombre (milliers)
Per 100 inhabitants		^0	^0	^0	1	1	1	1	Pour 100 habitants
Cambodia									**Cambodge**
Number (thousands)		30	35	41	44	66[1]	70[1]	...	Nombre (milliers)
Per 100 inhabitants ^		0	0	0	0	0	0	...	Pour 100 habitants ^
Cameroon									**Cameroun**
Number (thousands)		60	100	170	250	370	548	...	Nombre (milliers)
Per 100 inhabitants		^0	1	1	2	2	3	...	Pour 100 habitants
Canada									**Canada**
Number (thousands)[2]		19 288	20 247	21 092	21 942	22 959	24 000	...	Nombre (milliers)[2]
Per 100 inhabitants[4]		62	64	66	68	71	73	...	Pour 100 habitants[4]
Cape Verde									**Cap-Vert**
Number (thousands)		16[1]	20	25	29	33	41	103	Nombre (milliers)
Per 100 inhabitants		3	4	5	6	6	8	19	Pour 100 habitants
Cayman Islands	(01/04)								**Iles Caïmanes**
Number (thousands)		...	...	...	20[1]	21[1]	22	...	Nombre (milliers)
Per 100 inhabitants		...	...	...	44	46	47	...	Pour 100 habitants
Central African Rep.									**Rép. centrafricaine**
Number (thousands)		5	6	9	11	13	16	19	Nombre (milliers)
Per 100 inhabitants ^		0	0	0	0	0	0	0	Pour 100 habitants ^
Chad									**Tchad**
Number (thousands)		15	30	35	40	60	90	130	Nombre (milliers)
Per 100 inhabitants		^0	^0	^0	^0	1	1	1	Pour 100 habitants
Chile									**Chili**
Number (thousands)		3 007	3 240	3 121	3 511	4 208	5 163	5 457[6]	Nombre (milliers)
Per 100 inhabitants		19	20	19	22	25	31	32	Pour 100 habitants

Internet users *(continued)*
Estimated number (thousands) and number per 100 inhabitants
Usagers d'Internet *(suite)*
Nombre estimatif (en milliers) et nombre pour 100 habitants

Country or area	Fiscal year & Ex. budgét.&	2002	2003	2004	2005	2006	2007	2008	Pays ou zone
China[7]									**Chine**[7]
Number (thousands)		59 100	79 500	94 000	111 847[2]	138 982[2,8,9]	212 581[2]	298 000	Nombre (milliers)
Per 100 inhabitants		5[4]	6[4]	7[4]	9[4]	11[4]	16[4]	22	Pour 100 habitants
China, Hong Kong SAR	(01/04)								**Chine, Hong Kong RAS**
Number (thousands)[10]		2 919	3 213	3 480	3 526	3 770	3 961	4 124	Nombre (milliers)[10]
Per 100 inhabitants		43	47	50	50	53	55	57	Pour 100 habitants
China, Macao SAR									**Chine, Macao RAS**
Number (thousands)		115	120	150	170	217	238	...	Nombre (milliers)
Per 100 inhabitants		25	26	33	37	47	49	...	Pour 100 habitants
Colombia									**Colombie**
Number (thousands)		2 000	3 084[11]	3 866	4 739	6 705	12 100	17 117	Nombre (milliers)
Per 100 inhabitants		5	7	9	10	14	26	37	Pour 100 habitants
Comoros									**Comores**
Number (thousands)		3	5	8	20	21	22	...	Nombre (milliers)
Per 100 inhabitants		^0	1	1	3	3	3	...	Pour 100 habitants
Congo									**Congo**
Number (thousands)		5	15	36	50	70	98	155	Nombre (milliers)
Per 100 inhabitants		^0	^0	1	1	2	3	4	Pour 100 habitants
Costa Rica									**Costa Rica**
Number (thousands)		816	850	885	923	1 214	1 500	...	Nombre (milliers)
Per 100 inhabitants		20	20	21	21	28	34	...	Pour 100 habitants
Côte d'Ivoire									**Côte d'Ivoire**
Number (thousands)		90	140	160	200	300	450	660	Nombre (milliers)
Per 100 inhabitants		1	1	1	1	2	2	3	Pour 100 habitants
Croatia									**Croatie**
Number (thousands)		789	1 014	1 375	1 472	1 685	1 985	2 244	Nombre (milliers)
Per 100 inhabitants		18	22	30	32	37	44	49	Pour 100 habitants
Cuba									**Cuba**
Number (thousands)[12]		#420	585	940	1 090	1 250	1 310	1 450	Nombre (milliers)[12]
Per 100 inhabitants		4	5	8	10	11	12	13	Pour 100 habitants
Cyprus									**Chypre**
Number (thousands)[2]		229	246	264	259	287	325	...	Nombre (milliers)[2]
Per 100 inhabitants		28	30	32	31	34	38	...	Pour 100 habitants
Czech Republic									**République tchèque**
Number (thousands)[2]		2 438	2 867	3 273	3 270	4 492	4 991	...	Nombre (milliers)[2]
Per 100 inhabitants[4]		24	28	32	32	44	49	...	Pour 100 habitants[4]
Dem. Rep. of the Congo									**Rép. dém. du Congo**
Number (thousands)		50	75	113	141	180	230	290	Nombre (milliers)
Per 100 inhabitants ^		0	0	0	0	0	0	0	Pour 100 habitants ^
Denmark									**Danemark**
Number (thousands)[1]		3 443[2]	3 832[2]	4 115[2]	4 182[2]	4 520[2]	4 408[2]	4 630	Nombre (milliers)[1]
Per 100 inhabitants		64[4]	71[4]	76[4]	77[4]	83[4]	81[4]	85	Pour 100 habitants
Djibouti									**Djibouti**
Number (thousands)		5	7	9	10	11	...	...	Nombre (milliers)
Per 100 inhabitants		1	1	1	1	1	...	...	Pour 100 habitants
Dominica	(01/04)								**Dominique**
Number (thousands)		13	16	21	26	27	...	...	Nombre (milliers)
Per 100 inhabitants		16	20	26	33	37	...	...	Pour 100 habitants
Dominican Republic									**Rép. dominicaine**
Number (thousands)		622	731	833	1 095	1 436	1 677	2 563	Nombre (milliers)
Per 100 inhabitants		7	8	9	12	16	17	26	Pour 100 habitants
Ecuador									**Equateur**
Number (thousands)		538	570	625	968	823	1 152	1 310	Nombre (milliers)
Per 100 inhabitants		4	4	5	7	6	9	10	Pour 100 habitants
Egypt	(30/06)								**Egypte**
Number (thousands)		1 900	3 000	3 900	9 027	9 838	10 532	12 569	Nombre (milliers)
Per 100 inhabitants		3	4	5	12	13	14	16	Pour 100 habitants

Country or area	Fiscal year & Ex. budgét.&	2002	2003	2004	2005	2006	2007	2008	Pays ou zone
El Salvador									**El Salvador**
Number (thousands)		300	550	588	637	700[1]	763	...	Nombre (milliers)
Per 100 inhabitants		5	8	9	9	10	11	...	Pour 100 habitants
Equatorial Guinea									**Guinée équatoriale**
Number (thousands)		2	3	5	7	8	10	12	Nombre (milliers)
Per 100 inhabitants		^0	1	1	1	2	2	2	Pour 100 habitants
Eritrea									**Erythrée**
Number (thousands)		9	30	50	80	100	120	150	Nombre (milliers)
Per 100 inhabitants		^0	1	1	2	2	2	3	Pour 100 habitants
Estonia									**Estonie**
Number (thousands)[2]		563	613	668	785	808	855	...	Nombre (milliers)[2]
Per 100 inhabitants[4]		42	46	50	59	61	64	...	Pour 100 habitants[4]
Ethiopia	(30/06)								**Ethiopie**
Number (thousands)		50	75	113	164	238	291	360[1]	Nombre (milliers)
Per 100 inhabitants ^		0	0	0	0	0	0	0	Pour 100 habitants ^
Faeroe Islands									**Iles Féroé**
Number (thousands)		25	28	32	33	34	38	38	Nombre (milliers)
Per 100 inhabitants		54	60	68	70	72	77	78	Pour 100 habitants
Fiji									**Fidji**
Number (thousands)		50	55	61	70	80	91[1]	...	Nombre (milliers)
Per 100 inhabitants		6	7	7	8	9	11	...	Pour 100 habitants
Finland									**Finlande**
Number (thousands)[2,13,14]		3 227	3 446	3 665	3 832	4 052	4 169	...	Nombre (milliers)[2,13,14]
Per 100 inhabitants[4]		62	66	70	73	77	79	...	Pour 100 habitants[4]
France									**France**
Number (thousands)[15]		18 057	21 765	23 732	26 154	30 100	31 571		Nombre (milliers)[15]
Per 100 inhabitants		30	36	39	43	50	51	...	Pour 100 habitants
French Guiana									**Guyane française**
Number (thousands)		25	31	38	42	...	...	...	Nombre (milliers)
Per 100 inhabitants		14	17	21	22	...	...	...	Pour 100 habitants
French Polynesia									**Polynésie française**
Number (thousands)		20	35	45	55	65	75	90	Nombre (milliers)
Per 100 inhabitants		8	14	18	21	25	29	34	Pour 100 habitants
Gabon									**Gabon**
Number (thousands)		25	35	40	67	77	82[1]	90	Nombre (milliers)
Per 100 inhabitants		2	3	3	5	5	6	7	Pour 100 habitants
Gambia	(01/04)								**Gambie**
Number (thousands)		25	35	49	58[1]	82	100	114[1]	Nombre (milliers)
Per 100 inhabitants		2	2	3	4	5	6	7	Pour 100 habitants
Georgia									**Géorgie**
Number (thousands)		74	117	176	271[1]	332	360	...	Nombre (milliers)
Per 100 inhabitants		2	3	4	6	7	8	...	Pour 100 habitants
Germany									**Allemagne**
Number (thousands)		40 429[2]	44 595[2]	50 414[2]	53 748[2]	57 074[2]	59 472[2]	62 500	Nombre (milliers)
Per 100 inhabitants		49[4]	54[4]	61[4]	65[4]	69[4]	72[4]	76	Pour 100 habitants
Ghana									**Ghana**
Number (thousands)		170	250	368	401	610	880	997	Nombre (milliers)
Per 100 inhabitants		1	1	2	2	3	4	4	Pour 100 habitants
Gibraltar									**Gibraltar**
Number (thousands)		6	6	6	6	6	6	...	Nombre (milliers)
Per 100 inhabitants		22	22	23	23	19	18	...	Pour 100 habitants
Greece									**Grèce**
Number (thousands)		1 657[2]	1 772[2]	2 220[2]	2 446[2]	3 231[2]	3 678[2]	3 631	Nombre (milliers)
Per 100 inhabitants		15[4]	16[4]	20[4]	22[4]	29[4]	33[4]	32	Pour 100 habitants
Greenland									**Groenland**
Number (thousands)		25	31	38	45	52	52	...	Nombre (milliers)
Per 100 inhabitants		44	55	67	79	91	91	...	Pour 100 habitants

Internet users *(continued)*
Estimated number (thousands) and number per 100 inhabitants
Usagers d'Internet *(suite)*
Nombre estimatif (en milliers) et nombre pour 100 habitants

Country or area	Fiscal year & Ex. budgét.&	2002	2003	2004	2005	2006	2007	2008	Pays ou zone
Grenada									**Grenade**
Number (thousands)		15	19	20	21	22	23	...	Nombre (milliers)
Per 100 inhabitants		15	19	20	20	21	22	...	Pour 100 habitants
Guadeloupe									**Guadeloupe**
Number (thousands)		50	63	79	85	...	...	...	Nombre (milliers)
Per 100 inhabitants		11	14	18	19	...	...	...	Pour 100 habitants
Guam									**Guam**
Number (thousands)		50	55	60	65	75[1]	80[1]	...	Nombre (milliers)
Per 100 inhabitants		31	34	36	38	44	46	...	Pour 100 habitants
Guatemala									**Guatemala**
Number (thousands)		400	550	760	1 000	1 320	...	...	Nombre (milliers)
Per 100 inhabitants		3	5	6	8	10	...	...	Pour 100 habitants
Guernsey									**Guernesey**
Number (thousands)		30	33	36	39	42	44	...	Nombre (milliers)
Per 100 inhabitants		54	59	65	74	84	...	...	Pour 100 habitants
Guinea									**Guinée**
Number (thousands)		35	40	48	50	60	75	90	Nombre (milliers)
Per 100 inhabitants		^0	^0	0	1	1	1	1	Pour 100 habitants
Guinea-Bissau									**Guinée-Bissau**
Number (thousands)		14	19	26	28	31	34	37	Nombre (milliers)
Per 100 inhabitants		1	1	2	2	2	2	2	Pour 100 habitants
Guyana									**Guyana**
Number (thousands)		125	140	145	160	175	190	...	Nombre (milliers)
Per 100 inhabitants		17	19	19	21	23	26	...	Pour 100 habitants
Haiti									**Haïti**
Number (thousands)		80	150	500	600	650	1 000	...	Nombre (milliers)
Per 100 inhabitants		1	2	6	7	8	10	...	Pour 100 habitants
Honduras									**Honduras**
Number (thousands)		169	186	222	258	344	424	658	Nombre (milliers)
Per 100 inhabitants		3	3	3	4	5	6	9	Pour 100 habitants
Hungary									**Hongrie**
Number (thousands)		1 693[2]	2 191[2]	2 835[2]	3 736[2]	4 532[2]	5 215[2]	5 500	Nombre (milliers)
Per 100 inhabitants		17	22	28	37	45	52	55	Pour 100 habitants
Iceland									**Islande**
Number (thousands)[2]		226	234	239	253	194	202	...	Nombre (milliers)[2]
Per 100 inhabitants[4]		79	81	82	86	65	67	...	Pour 100 habitants[4]
India	(01/04)								**Inde**
Number (thousands)		16 580	18 480[16]	35 000	42 000	76 000	81 000	...	Nombre (milliers)
Per 100 inhabitants		2	2	3	4	7	7	...	Pour 100 habitants
Indonesia									**Indonésie**
Number (thousands)		4 500	5 100	5 628	7 896	20 000	25 000	...	Nombre (milliers)
Per 100 inhabitants		2	2	3	4	9	11	...	Pour 100 habitants
Iran (Islamic Rep. of)	(22/03)								**Iran (Rép. islamique d')**
Number (thousands)		3 168	4 800	10 600	12 300	11 000	13 000	23 000	Nombre (milliers)
Per 100 inhabitants		5	7	15	18	16	18	32	Pour 100 habitants
Iraq	(30/06)								**Iraq**
Number (thousands)		25	30	36	200	275	275	...	Nombre (milliers)
Per 100 inhabitants		^0	^0	^0	1	1	1	...	Pour 100 habitants
Ireland	(01/04)								**Irlande**
Number (thousands)[14]		1 019[2]	1 242[2]	1 387[2]	1 535[2]	2 147[2]	2 452[2]	2 830	Nombre (milliers)[14]
Per 100 inhabitants		26[4]	31[4]	34[4]	37[4]	51[4]	57[4]	65	Pour 100 habitants
Israel									**Israël**
Number (thousands)		1 125	1 265	1 497	1 686	1 899	2 000	...	Nombre (milliers)
Per 100 inhabitants		18	20	23	25	28	29	...	Pour 100 habitants
Italy									**Italie**
Number (thousands)		19 800[2]	22 880[2]	27 170[2]	28 000[2]	30 764[2]	32 000[2]	29 118	Nombre (milliers)
Per 100 inhabitants		34[4]	39[4]	47[4]	48[4]	53[4]	54[4]	49	Pour 100 habitants

17

Internet users *(continued)*
Estimated number (thousands) and number per 100 inhabitants
Usagers d'Internet *(suite)*
Nombre estimatif (en milliers) et nombre pour 100 habitants

Country or area	Fiscal year & Ex. budgét.&	2002	2003	2004	2005	2006	2007	2008	Pays ou zone
Jamaica	(01/04)								**Jamaïque**
Number (thousands)		600	800	1 067	1 232[1]	1 300	1 500	...	Nombre (milliers)
Per 100 inhabitants		23	30	40	46	49	55	...	Pour 100 habitants
Japan	(01/04)								**Japon**
Number (thousands)		59 220[17]	61 640[17]	79 480[18]	85 290[18]	87 540[18]	88 110[18]	...	Nombre (milliers)
Per 100 inhabitants		46	48	62	67	68	69	...	Pour 100 habitants
Jersey									**Jersey**
Number (thousands)		17	20	27	28	28	29	...	Nombre (milliers)
Per 100 inhabitants		19	23	31	31	32	32	...	Pour 100 habitants
Jordan									**Jordanie**
Number (thousands)		307	444	630	720	797	1 127	1 500	Nombre (milliers)
Per 100 inhabitants		6	8	11	13	14	19	25	Pour 100 habitants
Kazakhstan									**Kazakhstan**
Number (thousands)		250	300	400	609	1 291	1 901	...	Nombre (milliers)
Per 100 inhabitants		2	2	3	4	9	12	...	Pour 100 habitants
Kenya	(30/06)								**Kenya**
Number (thousands)		400	1 000	1 055	1 111	2 770	3 000	3 360	Nombre (milliers)
Per 100 inhabitants		1	3	3	3	8	8	9	Pour 100 habitants
Kiribati									**Kiribati**
Number (thousands)		2	2	2	2	2	2	...	Nombre (milliers)
Per 100 inhabitants		2	2	2	2	2	...	...	Pour 100 habitants
Korea, Republic of									**Corée, République de**
Number (thousands)		28 076[2]	31 089[2]	33 446[2]	34 811[2]	35 891[2]	36 795[2]	37 476	Nombre (milliers)
Per 100 inhabitants		59[4]	66[4]	70[4]	73[4]	75[4]	76[4]	77	Pour 100 habitants
Kuwait									**Koweït**
Number (thousands)		250	567	600	700	800	900	...	Nombre (milliers)
Per 100 inhabitants		10	22	23	26	29	32	...	Pour 100 habitants
Kyrgyzstan									**Kirghizistan**
Number (thousands)		152	200	263	550	650	750	...	Nombre (milliers)
Per 100 inhabitants		3	4	5	10	12	14	...	Pour 100 habitants
Lao People's Dem. Rep.									**Rép. dém. pop. lao**
Number (thousands)		15	19	21	50	70	100	...	Nombre (milliers)
Per 100 inhabitants		^0	^0	^0	1	1	2	...	Pour 100 habitants
Latvia									**Lettonie**
Number (thousands)[2]		513	626	765	969	1 148	1 252	...	Nombre (milliers)[2]
Per 100 inhabitants		22	27	33	42	50	55	...	Pour 100 habitants
Lebanon									**Liban**
Number (thousands)		400	500	600	700	950	1 570	...	Nombre (milliers)
Per 100 inhabitants		12	14	17	20	26	38	...	Pour 100 habitants
Lesotho	(01/04)								**Lesotho**
Number (thousands)		21	30	43	51[1]	60	70	73[1]	Nombre (milliers)
Per 100 inhabitants		1	2	2	3	3	3	4	Pour 100 habitants
Liberia									**Libéria**
Number (thousands)		1	1	1	...	...	20	...	Nombre (milliers)
Per 100 inhabitants		^0	^0	^0	...	...	1	...	Pour 100 habitants
Libyan Arab Jamah.									**Jamah. arabe libyenne**
Number (thousands)		125	160	205	232[1]	260[1]	291	...	Nombre (milliers)
Per 100 inhabitants		2	3	4	4	4	5	...	Pour 100 habitants
Liechtenstein									**Liechtenstein**
Number (thousands)		20	20	22	22	23	23	...	Nombre (milliers)
Per 100 inhabitants		60	59	64	64	64	65	...	Pour 100 habitants
Lithuania									**Lituanie**
Number (thousands)		624[2]	829[2]	999[2]	1 167[2]	1 435[2]	1 661[2]	1 777	Nombre (milliers)
Per 100 inhabitants		18	24	29	34	42	49	53	Pour 100 habitants
Luxembourg									**Luxembourg**
Number (thousands)[2]		179	240	298	321	334	364	...	Nombre (milliers)[2]
Per 100 inhabitants		40	53	65	69	71	78	...	Pour 100 habitants

17

Internet users *(continued)*
Estimated number (thousands) and number per 100 inhabitants
Usagers d'Internet *(suite)*
Nombre estimatif (en milliers) et nombre pour 100 habitants

Country or area	Fiscal year & Ex. budgét. &	2002	2003	2004	2005	2006	2007	2008	Pays ou zone
Madagascar									**Madagascar**
Number (thousands)		55	71	90	100	110	121	316	Nombre (milliers)
Per 100 inhabitants		^0	^0	^0	1	1	1	2	Pour 100 habitants
Malawi									**Malawi**
Number (thousands)		27	36	46	53	60	139	316[1]	Nombre (milliers)
Per 100 inhabitants		^0	^0	^0	^0	^0	1	2	Pour 100 habitants
Malaysia									**Malaisie**
Number (thousands)		7 842	8 643	10 637	12 465	13 475	14 793	16 903	Nombre (milliers)
Per 100 inhabitants		33	35	43	49	52	56	63	Pour 100 habitants
Maldives									**Maldives**
Number (thousands) [19]		15	17	19	20	33	50	72	Nombre (milliers) [19]
Per 100 inhabitants		5	5	6	6	11	16	23	Pour 100 habitants
Mali									**Mali**
Number (thousands)		25	35	50	60	88	100	125	Nombre (milliers)
Per 100 inhabitants		^0	^0	^0	^0	1	1	1	Pour 100 habitants
Malta									**Malte**
Number (thousands)		114[9]	126[9]	139[2]	150[2]	167[2]	183[2]	200	Nombre (milliers)
Per 100 inhabitants		29	32	35	38	42	45	49	Pour 100 habitants
Marshall Islands									**Iles Marshall**
Number (thousands)		1	1	2	2	2	2[1]	...	Nombre (milliers)
Per 100 inhabitants		2	2	3	...	...	...	...	Pour 100 habitants
Martinique									**Martinique**
Number (thousands)		60	80	110	130	...	...	...	Nombre (milliers)
Per 100 inhabitants		15	20	28	33	...	...	...	Pour 100 habitants
Mauritania									**Mauritanie**
Number (thousands)		10	12	14	20	30	45	...	Nombre (milliers)
Per 100 inhabitants		^0	^0	^0	1	1	1	...	Pour 100 habitants
Mauritius									**Maurice**
Number (thousands)		125[20]	150	240	300	320	340	380[1]	Nombre (milliers)
Per 100 inhabitants		10	12	19	24	25	27	30	Pour 100 habitants
Mexico									**Mexique**
Number (thousands)		13 661[2]	15 375[2]	17 297[2]	19 450[2]	20 564[2]	22 104[2]	23 260	Nombre (milliers)
Per 100 inhabitants		13	15	16	18	19	21	22	Pour 100 habitants
Micronesia (Fed. States of)									**Micronésie (Etats féd. de)**
Number (thousands)		6	10	12	13	14	15	...	Nombre (milliers)
Per 100 inhabitants		6	9	11	12	13	13	...	Pour 100 habitants
Mongolia									**Mongolie**
Number (thousands)		50	143	200	268	310	320	...	Nombre (milliers)
Per 100 inhabitants		2	6	8	10	12	12	...	Pour 100 habitants
Montenegro									**Monténégro**
Number (thousands)		...	...	160	243	266	280	...	Nombre (milliers)
Per 100 inhabitants		...	...	26	40	44	47	...	Pour 100 habitants
Morocco									**Maroc**
Number (thousands)		700	1 000	3 500[21]	4 600[21]	6 100[21]	6 600[21]	10 300[21]	Nombre (milliers)
Per 100 inhabitants		2	3	11	15	20	21	33	Pour 100 habitants
Mozambique									**Mozambique**
Number (thousands)		50	83	138	178[1]	180	200	350	Nombre (milliers)
Per 100 inhabitants		^0	^0	1	1	1	1	2	Pour 100 habitants
Myanmar									**Myanmar**
Number (thousands)		^0	11	12	32	35	40	...	Nombre (milliers)
Per 100 inhabitants ^		0	0	0	0	0	0	...	Pour 100 habitants ^
Namibia	(30/09)								**Namibie**
Number (thousands)		50	65	75	81[1]	90	101	114[1]	Nombre (milliers)
Per 100 inhabitants		3	3	4	4	4	5	5	Pour 100 habitants
Nepal	(15/07)								**Népal**
Number (thousands)		80	100	120	225	317	398	...	Nombre (milliers)
Per 100 inhabitants		^0	^0	^0	1	1	1	...	Pour 100 habitants
Netherlands									**Pays-Bas**
Number (thousands)		9 800[2]	10 335[2]	11 602[2]	12 876[2]	13 231[2]	13 792[2]	14 273	Nombre (milliers)
Per 100 inhabitants		61[4]	64[4]	72[4]	79[4]	81[4]	84[4]	87	Pour 100 habitants

17

Internet users *(continued)*
Estimated number (thousands) and number per 100 inhabitants
Usagers d'Internet *(suite)*
Nombre estimatif (en milliers) et nombre pour 100 habitants

Country or area	Fiscal year & Ex. budgét.&	2002	2003	2004	2005	2006	2007	2008	Pays ou zone
New Caledonia									**Nouvelle-Calédonie**
Number (thousands)		50	60	70	76	80	85[1]	...	Nombre (milliers)
Per 100 inhabitants		22	26	30	32	33	35	...	Pour 100 habitants
New Zealand	(01/04)								**Nouvelle-Zélande**
Number (thousands) [1]		2 341	2 446	2 513	2 578	2 803	2 925	...	Nombre (milliers) [1]
Per 100 inhabitants		60	62	63	64	69	70	...	Pour 100 habitants
Nicaragua									**Nicaragua**
Number (thousands)		90	100	125	140	155	...	...	Nombre (milliers)
Per 100 inhabitants		2	2	2	3	3	...	...	Pour 100 habitants
Niger									**Niger**
Number (thousands)		15	19	24	29	40	55	80	Nombre (milliers)
Per 100 inhabitants		^0	^0	^0	^0	^0	^0	1	Pour 100 habitants
Nigeria									**Nigéria**
Number (thousands)		420	750	1 769	5 000	8 000	10 000	11 000	Nombre (milliers)
Per 100 inhabitants		^0	1	1	4	6	7	7	Pour 100 habitants
Norway									**Norvège**
Number (thousands) [2,22]		3 306	3 432	3 448	3 696	3 760	3 993	...	Nombre (milliers) [2,22]
Per 100 inhabitants [4]		73	75	75	80	81	85	...	Pour 100 habitants [4]
Occupied Palestinian Terr.									**Terr. palestinien occupé**
Number (thousands)		105	145	160	243	266	355	...	Nombre (milliers)
Per 100 inhabitants		3	4	4	7	7	10	...	Pour 100 habitants
Oman									**Oman**
Number (thousands)		171	183	174	175	222	247	284	Nombre (milliers)
Per 100 inhabitants		7	7	7	7	8	10	11	Pour 100 habitants
Pakistan	(30/06)								**Pakistan**
Number (thousands)		4 000	8 000	10 000	10 500	12 000	17 500	18 500	Nombre (milliers)
Per 100 inhabitants		3	5	6	7	8	11	11	Pour 100 habitants
Palau									**Palaos**
Number (thousands)		4	4	5	...	...	...	...	Nombre (milliers)
Panama									**Panama**
Number (thousands)		261	312	354	371	570	745	779	Nombre (milliers)
Per 100 inhabitants		9	10	11	11	17	22	23	Pour 100 habitants
Papua New Guinea									**Papouasie-Nvl-Guinée**
Number (thousands)		75	80	90	105	110	115[1]	...	Nombre (milliers)
Per 100 inhabitants		1	1	2	2	2	2	...	Pour 100 habitants
Paraguay									**Paraguay**
Number (thousands)		100	120	200	356	367	530[23]	...	Nombre (milliers)
Per 100 inhabitants		2	2	3	6	6	9	...	Pour 100 habitants
Peru									**Pérou**
Number (thousands) [1]		2 400	2 850	3 220	4 600	6 498	7 636	7 128[9]	Nombre (milliers) [1]
Per 100 inhabitants		9	10	12	16	23	27	25	Pour 100 habitants
Philippines									**Philippines**
Number (thousands)		3 500	4 000	4 400	4 615[1]	5 000	5 300	...	Nombre (milliers)
Per 100 inhabitants		4	5	5	6	6	6	...	Pour 100 habitants
Poland									**Pologne**
Number (thousands) [2]		8 108	9 522	11 182	13 485	15 399	16 756	...	Nombre (milliers) [2]
Per 100 inhabitants		21	25	29	35	40	44	...	Pour 100 habitants
Portugal									**Portugal**
Number (thousands)		1 963[2]	2 700[2]	3 028[2]	3 358[2]	3 796[2]	4 249[2]	4 451	Nombre (milliers)
Per 100 inhabitants		19	26	29	32	36	40	42	Pour 100 habitants
Puerto Rico									**Porto Rico**
Number (thousands)		677	764	862	916[1]	1 000	1 000	...	Nombre (milliers)
Per 100 inhabitants		17	20	22	23	25	25	...	Pour 100 habitants
Qatar									**Qatar**
Number (thousands)		70	141	165	219	290	351	436	Nombre (milliers)
Per 100 inhabitants		10	19	21	27	35	42	51	Pour 100 habitants
Republic of Moldova									**République de Moldova**
Number (thousands)		150	288	406	550	728	700	...	Nombre (milliers)
Per 100 inhabitants		4	7	10	13	17	18	...	Pour 100 habitants

17

Internet users *(continued)*
Estimated number (thousands) and number per 100 inhabitants
Usagers d'Internet *(suite)*
Nombre estimatif (en milliers) et nombre pour 100 habitants

Country or area	Fiscal year & Ex. budgét.&	2002	2003	2004	2005	2006	2007	2008	Pays ou zone
Réunion									**Réunion**
Number (thousands) [24]		150	180	200	220	...	...	...	Nombre (milliers) [24]
Per 100 inhabitants		20	24	26	28	...	...	...	Pour 100 habitants
Romania									**Roumanie**
Number (thousands) [2]		1 442	1 942	2 615	3 582	4 542	5 145	...	Nombre (milliers) [2]
Per 100 inhabitants [4]		7	9	12	17	21	24	...	Pour 100 habitants [4]
Russian Federation									**Fédération de Russie**
Number (thousands)		6 000	12 000	18 500	21 800	25 689	30 000	...	Nombre (milliers)
Per 100 inhabitants		4	8	13	15	18	21	...	Pour 100 habitants
Rwanda									**Rwanda**
Number (thousands)		25	31	38	50	100	200	300	Nombre (milliers)
Per 100 inhabitants		^0	^0	^0	1	1	2	3	Pour 100 habitants
Saint Kitts and Nevis	(01/04)								**Saint-Kitts-et-Nevis**
Number (thousands)		10	11	12	13	14	15	...	Nombre (milliers)
Per 100 inhabitants		24	26	28	30	32	35	...	Pour 100 habitants
Saint Lucia	(01/04)								**Sainte-Lucie**
Number (thousands)		24	34	35	36	55	70	100	Nombre (milliers)
Per 100 inhabitants		15	21	22	22	34	42	00	Pour 100 habitants
Saint Vincent-Grenadines	(01/04)								**Saint Vincent-Grenadines**
Number (thousands) [25]		6	7	8	10	35	57	66	Nombre (milliers) [25]
Per 100 inhabitants		5	6	7	8	29	47	55	Pour 100 habitants
Samoa									**Samoa**
Number (thousands)		4	5	6	6	8	9[1]	...	Nombre (milliers)
Per 100 inhabitants		2	3	3	3	4	5	...	Pour 100 habitants
San Marino									**Saint-Marin**
Number (thousands)		14	14	15	15	15	16	16	Nombre (milliers)
Per 100 inhabitants		52	52	54	54	57	50	59	Pour 100 habitants
Sao Tome and Principe									**Sao Tomé-et-Principe**
Number (thousands)		11	15[1]	20[1]	21[1]	22[1]	23[1]	25[1]	Nombre (milliers)
Per 100 inhabitants		8	10	13	13	14	15	15	Pour 100 habitants
Saudi Arabia									**Arabie saoudite**
Number (thousands)		1 400	1 800	2 360	3 000	4 700	6 320	7 200	Nombre (milliers)
Per 100 inhabitants		6	8	10	12	19	26	28	Pour 100 habitants
Senegal									**Sénégal**
Number (thousands)		105	225	482	540	650	820	1 020	Nombre (milliers)
Per 100 inhabitants		1	2	4	5	5	7	8	Pour 100 habitants
Serbia									**Serbie**
Number (thousands)		...	...	1 517	777	1 400	1 500	2 360	Nombre (milliers)
Per 100 inhabitants		...	...	...	...	13	15	24	Pour 100 habitants
Serbia and Montenegro									**Serbie-et-Monténégro**
Number (thousands)		640	847	1 517	...	...	...	...	Nombre (milliers)
Per 100 inhabitants		6	8	14	...	...	...	...	Pour 100 habitants
Seychelles	(01/04)								**Seychelles**
Number (thousands)		12	12	20	21	29	32	32[1]	Nombre (milliers)
Per 100 inhabitants		15	15	25	26	36	37	38	Pour 100 habitants
Sierra Leone									**Sierra Leone**
Number (thousands)		8	9	10	11	12	13	14	Nombre (milliers)
Per 100 inhabitants ^		0	0	0	0	0	0	0	Pour 100 habitants ^
Singapore	(01/04)								**Singapour**
Number (thousands) [1]		2 065	2 236	2 649	2 639	2 611[23]	3 105[26]	...	Nombre (milliers) [1]
Per 100 inhabitants [4]		50	53	62	61	60	70	...	Pour 100 habitants [4]
Slovakia									**Slovaquie**
Number (thousands)		2 160[4]	2 317[2]	2 485[2]	2 700[2]	1 931[2]	2 312[2]	2 771	Nombre (milliers)
Per 100 inhabitants		40	43	46	50	36	43	51	Pour 100 habitants
Slovenia									**Slovénie**
Number (thousands)		554[2]	635[2]	728[2]	924[2]	1 003[2]	1 061[2]	992	Nombre (milliers)
Per 100 inhabitants		28[4]	32[4]	37[4]	47[4]	51[4]	53[4]	50	Pour 100 habitants
Solomon Islands	(01/04)								**Iles Salomon**
Number (thousands)		2	3	3	4	8	9	...	Nombre (milliers)
Per 100 inhabitants		^0	1	1	1	2	2	...	Pour 100 habitants

17

Internet users *(continued)*
Estimated number (thousands) and number per 100 inhabitants
Usagers d'Internet *(suite)*
Nombre estimatif (en milliers) et nombre pour 100 habitants

Country or area	Fiscal year & Ex. budgét.[&]	2002	2003	2004	2005	2006	2007	2008	Pays ou zone
Somalia									**Somalie**
Number (thousands)		9[1]	30[1]	86	90	94	98	...	Nombre (milliers)
Per 100 inhabitants		^0	^0	1	1	1	1	...	Pour 100 habitants
South Africa	(01/04)								**Afrique du Sud**
Number (thousands)		3 100	3 283	4 000	3 600	3 700	3 966	4 187[1]	Nombre (milliers)
Per 100 inhabitants		7	7	8	8	8	8	9	Pour 100 habitants
Spain									**Espagne**
Number (thousands)[27]		8 322[2]	15 593[2]	17 059[2]	18 948[2]	20 822[2]	23 025[2]	26 171[28]	Nombre (milliers)[27]
Per 100 inhabitants		20	37	40	44	48	52	59	Pour 100 habitants
Sri Lanka									**Sri Lanka**
Number (thousands)		200	280	280	350[1]	500	772	1 148	Nombre (milliers)
Per 100 inhabitants		1	1	1	2	2	4	6	Pour 100 habitants
Sudan									**Soudan**
Number (thousands)		160	200	300	500	3 200	3 500	3 800	Nombre (milliers)
Per 100 inhabitants		^0	1	1	1	9	9	...	Pour 100 habitants
Suriname									**Suriname**
Number (thousands)		20	23	30	32	38	44	...	Nombre (milliers)
Per 100 inhabitants		5	5	7	7	8	10	...	Pour 100 habitants
Swaziland	(01/04)								**Swaziland**
Number (thousands)		20	27	36	42[1]	42	47[1]	48[1]	Nombre (milliers)
Per 100 inhabitants		2	3	3	4	4	4	4	Pour 100 habitants
Sweden									**Suède**
Number (thousands)[2]		6 342	6 907	7 386	7 323	7 800	7 295	...	Nombre (milliers)[2]
Per 100 inhabitants[4]		71	77	82	81	86	80	...	Pour 100 habitants[4]
Switzerland									**Suisse**
Number (thousands)		4 470	4 697	4 923	5 077	5 301	5 433	5 739	Nombre (milliers)
Per 100 inhabitants		62	65	68	70	71	73	76	Pour 100 habitants
Syrian Arab Republic									**Rép. arabe syrienne**
Number (thousands)		365	610	800	1 080	1 550	3 470	3 565	Nombre (milliers)
Per 100 inhabitants		2	3	4	6	8	17	17	Pour 100 habitants
Tajikistan									**Tadjikistan**
Number (thousands)		4	4	5	20	...	484	...	Nombre (milliers)
Per 100 inhabitants		^0	^0	^0	^0	...	7	...	Pour 100 habitants
Thailand	(30/09)								**Thaïlande**
Number (thousands)		4 800	6 000	6 970	9 909	11 413	13 416	...	Nombre (milliers)
Per 100 inhabitants		8	10	11	15	18	21	...	Pour 100 habitants
TFYR of Macedonia									**L'ex-R.Y. Macédoine**
Number (thousands)		351[2]	387[2]	426[2]	468[2]	509[2]	556[2]	876	Nombre (milliers)
Per 100 inhabitants		17	19	21	23	25	27	43	Pour 100 habitants
Timor-Leste									**Timor-Leste**
Number (thousands)		0	...	...	1	1	2	...	Nombre (milliers)
Per 100 inhabitants		0	...	...	^0	^0	^0	...	Pour 100 habitants
Togo									**Togo**
Number (thousands)		200	210	221	300	320	341	350	Nombre (milliers)
Per 100 inhabitants		4	4	4	5	5	5	5	Pour 100 habitants
Tonga									**Tonga**
Number (thousands)		3	3	3	3	3	8	8	Nombre (milliers)
Per 100 inhabitants		3	3	3	3	3	8	8	Pour 100 habitants
Trinidad and Tobago	(01/04)								**Trinité-et-Tobago**
Number (thousands)		138[16]	153	160	185[1]	198	213[29]	...	Nombre (milliers)
Per 100 inhabitants		11	12	12	14	15	16	...	Pour 100 habitants
Tunisia									**Tunisie**
Number (thousands)		506	630	835	954	1 295	1 722	2 800	Nombre (milliers)
Per 100 inhabitants		5	6	8	9	13	17	27	Pour 100 habitants
Turkey									**Turquie**
Number (thousands)[30]		7 785[2]	8 550[2]	9 389[2]	10 247[2]	13 150[2]	21 141[2]	24 483	Nombre (milliers)[30]
Per 100 inhabitants		11[4]	12[4]	13[4]	14[4]	18[4]	28[4]	32	Pour 100 habitants
Turkmenistan									**Turkménistan**
Number (thousands)		14[1]	20[1]	36	48[1]	65	70	...	Nombre (milliers)
Per 100 inhabitants		^0	^0	1	1	1	1	...	Pour 100 habitants

17

Internet users *(continued)*
Estimated number (thousands) and number per 100 inhabitants
Usagers d'Internet *(suite)*
Nombre estimatif (en milliers) et nombre pour 100 habitants

Country or area	Fiscal year & Ex. budgét.&	2002	2003	2004	2005	2006	2007	2008	Pays ou zone
Tuvalu									**Tuvalu**
Number (thousands)		1	2	2	1	2	4	...	Nombre (milliers)
Per 100 inhabitants		12	14	19	12	19	37	...	Pour 100 habitants
Uganda	(30/06)								**Ouganda**
Number (thousands)		100	125	200	500	750	1 125	2 500	Nombre (milliers)
Per 100 inhabitants		^0	^0	1	2	3	4	8	Pour 100 habitants
Ukraine									**Ukraine**
Number (thousands)		900	2 500	5 000	8 000[31]	9 000	10 000	10 354	Nombre (milliers)
Per 100 inhabitants		2	5	11	17	20	22	23	Pour 100 habitants
United Arab Emirates									**Emirats arabes unis**
Number (thousands)		1 017	1 110	1 185	1 322	1 708	2 260	3 860	Nombre (milliers)
Per 100 inhabitants		27	28	28	29	37	52	86	Pour 100 habitants
United Kingdom [32]	(01/04)								**Royaume-Uni** [32]
Number (thousands) [32]		33 085[2]	36 162[2]	37 472[2]	39 381[2]	39 499[2]	43 754[2]	48 755	Nombre (milliers) [32]
Per 100 inhabitants		56	61	63	66	66	72	80	Pour 100 habitants
United Rep. of Tanzania									**Rép.-Unie de Tanzanie**
Number (thousands)		80	250	333	384[1]	390	400	520[1]	Nombre (milliers)
Per 100 inhabitants		^0	1	1	1	1	I	1	Pour 100 habitants
United States [1]									**Etats-Unis** [1]
Number (thousands) [1]		172 834[2]	183 196[2]	194 159[2]	205 767[2]	210 720[2]	221 724[2]	220 000	Nombre (milliers) [1]
Per 100 inhabitants		60[4]	63[4]	66[4]	69[4]	70[4]	73[4]	71	Pour 100 habitants
United States Virgin Is.									**Iles Vierges américaines**
Number (thousands)		30	30[1]	30[1]	30[1]	30[1]	30	...	Nombre (milliers)
Per 100 inhabitants		27	27	27	27	27	27	...	Pour 100 habitants
Uruguay									**Uruguay**
Number (thousands)		380	530	567	668	850	968	1 340	Nombre (milliers)
Per 100 inhabitants		11	16	16	19	24	29	40	Pour 100 habitants
Uzbekistan									**Ouzbékistan**
Number (thousands)		275	492	675	880	1 835	2 026	2 416	Nombre (milliers)
Per 100 inhabitants		1	2	3	3	7	7	9	Pour 100 habitants
Vanuatu									**Vanuatu**
Number (thousands)		7	8	10	11	13	17	...	Nombre (milliers)
Per 100 inhabitants		4	4	5	5	6	8	...	Pour 100 habitants
Venezuela (Boliv. Rep. of)									**Venezuela (Rép. bol. du)**
Number (thousands)		1 244	1 935	2 207	3 355	4 140	5 720	7 167	Nombre (milliers)
Per 100 inhabitants		5	7	8	13	15	21	25	Pour 100 habitants
Viet Nam									**Viet Nam**
Number (thousands)		1 500	3 098	6 345	10 711	14 684	17 872	...	Nombre (milliers)
Per 100 inhabitants		2	4	8	13	17	20	...	Pour 100 habitants
Yemen									**Yémen**
Number (thousands)		100	120	180	220[1]	270	320	...	Nombre (milliers)
Per 100 inhabitants		1	1	1	1	1	1	...	Pour 100 habitants
Zambia	(01/04)								**Zambie**
Number (thousands)		52[16]	110	231	335[1]	500	600	700	Nombre (milliers)
Per 100 inhabitants		^0	1	2	3	4	5	6	Pour 100 habitants
Zimbabwe [1]	(30/06)								**Zimbabwe** [1]
Number (thousands) [1]		500	800	820	1 000	1 220	1 351	1 421	Nombre (milliers) [1]
Per 100 inhabitants		4	6	6	8	9	10	11	Pour 100 habitants

Source:
International Telecommunication Union (ITU), Geneva, the ITU database,
last accessed May 2009.

& Fiscal year refers to the fiscal year used in each country or area. Countries
or areas whose reference periods coincide with the calendar year ending 31
December are not footnoted. Those that have a fiscal year other than
calendar year are denoted as follows:

22/03: Year beginning 22 March
01/04: Year beginning 1 April
30/06: Year ending 30 June

Source:
Union internationale des télécommunications (UIT), Genève, la base de données
de l'UIT, dernier accès mai 2009.

& Ex. budgét. fait référence à l'exercice budgétaire en vigueur dans chaque pays
ou territoire. Les pays ou les territoires dont l'exercice budgétaire terminent le
31 décembre de l'année civile ne sont pas signalés. Dans le cas contraire, ils sont
désignés de la manière suivante:

22/03 : Exercice commençant le 22 mars
01/04 : Exercice commençant le 1er avril
30/06 : Exercice se terminant le 30 juin

17

Internet users *(continued)*
Estimated number (thousands) and number per 100 inhabitants
Usagers d'Internet *(suite)*
Nombre estimatif (en milliers) et nombre pour 100 habitants

15/07: Year ending 15 July
30/09: Year ending 30 September

15/07 : Exercice se terminant le 15 juillet
30/09 : Exercice se terminant le 30 septembre

1	ITU estimate.
2	Estimated based on the percentage of Internet users as reported in surveys.
3	Regular users of the Internet, age 14+.
4	Internet users penetration as reported in household surveys.
5	Adult (age 16-74) population using the internet in the last 12 months.
6	Based on subscribers and number of members per household in December 2008.
7	For statistical purposes, the data for China do not include those for the Hong Kong Special Administrative Region (Hong Kong SAR), Macao Special Administrative Region (Macao SAR) and Taiwan Province of China.
8	Online at least one hour per week.
9	Age 6+.
10	Population age 10+ who accessed Internet in previous year.
11	June.
12	Covers all Internet users (both those with full access and those accessing only national networks).
13	Has used at least one other Internet application besides e-mail in last 3 months.
14	Age 15+.
15	Population age 11+ using in the last month.
16	December.
17	PC-based only.
18	Including users accessing internet through cell phones, PHS and game console.
19	Mobile internet users are not included.
20	Age 12+.
21	Persons who have used the Internet at least once during the last month, no matter of location.
22	Norsk Gallup.
23	Refer to users aged 10+
24	France Télécom only.
25	Estimation based on GPRS subscribers, fixed and mobile.
26	Persons aged 7 years and over.
27	At November of year indicated. Age 14+.
28	Adult (age 16-74) population using the internet in the last 3 months.
29	Estimation based on September subscriber data.
30	Persons aged 16 to 74 years.
31	Estimated based on results of user survey applied to resident population aged 15-59 who used internet in the last 4 weeks.
32	Adult (age 16+) population using the internet in the last 3 months.

1	Estimation de l'UIT.
2	Estimations basées sur le pourcentage d'utilisateurs d'Internet d'après les enquêtes.
3	Utilisateurs réguliers de l'Internet âgés de plus de 14 ans.
4	Pénétration des utilisateurs d'Internet basée sur des enquêtes auprès des ménages.
5	Population âgée de 16 à 74 ans qui a utilisé l'internet au cours de l'année écoulée.
6	Basées sur le nombre d'abonnés et le nombre de personnes par ménage en décembre 2008.
7	Pour la présentation des statistiques, les données pour la Chine ne comprennent pas la Région Administrative Spéciale de Hong Kong (Hong Kong RAS), la Région Administrative Spéciale de Macao (Macao RAS) et la province de Taiwan.
8	En ligne au moins une heure par semaine.
9	Population âgée de plus de 6 ans.
10	Population âgée de plus de 10 ans s'étant branchée sur l'Internet au cours de l'année écoulée.
11	Juin.
12	Couvre tous les utilisateurs d'Internet (ceux qui ont un accès libre et ceux qui peuvent uniquement accéder les réseaux nationaux).
13	A utilisé au moins une application Internet autre que le courrier électronique au cours des trois derniers mois. Population âgée de plus de 15 ans.
14	Population âgée de plus de 15 ans.
15	Population âgée de plus de 11 ans utilisant au cours de dernier mois.
16	Décembre.
17	Pour ordinateurs personnels seulement.
18	Comprend les utilisateurs qui naviguent sur Internet au moyen de téléphones mobiles, de téléphones PHS et de consoles de jeux.
19	Les utilisateurs d'Internet mobile ne sont pas inclus.
20	Population âgée de plus de 12 ans.
21	Personnes ayant accédé au moins une fois l'Internet lors du mois précédent quelque soit le lieu.
22	Norsk Gallup.
23	Usagers âgés de plus de 10 ans.
24	France Télécom seulement.
25	Estimation basée sur le nombre d'abonnés aux services GPRS (fixe et mobile).
26	Personnes âgées de 7 ans et plus.
27	En novembre de l'année indiquée. Population âgée de plus de 14 ans.
28	Population âgée de 16 à 74 ans qui a utilisé l'internet au cours des 3 derniers mois.
29	Estimation basée sur le nombre d'abonnés en septembre.
30	Personnes âgées de 16 à 74 ans.
31	Estimation basée sur les résultats d'enquête auprès de la population résidente âgée de 15 à 59 ans qui a utilisé l'internet dans les quatre dernières semaines.
32	Population âgée de plus de 16 ans ayant accédé l'Internet au cours des trois derniers mois.

Technical notes: tables 15-17

The statistics included in *Tables 15-17* were obtained from the statistics database (see www.itu.int) and the *Yearbook of Statistics, Telecommunication Services* of the International Telecommunication Union.

Table 15: This table shows the number of main (fixed) lines in operation and the main lines in operation per 100 inhabitants for the years indicated. Main telephone lines refer to the telephone lines connecting a customer's equipment to the Public Switched Telephone Network (PSTN) and which have a dedicated port on a telephone exchange. Note that in most countries, main lines also include public telephones. The number of main telephone lines per 100 inhabitants is calculated by dividing the number of main lines by the population and multiplying by 100.

Table 16: The number of mobile cellular telephone subscribers (as well as the number of subscribers per 100 inhabitants) refers to users of portable telephones subscribing to an automatic public mobile telephone service using cellular technology, which provides access to the Public Switched Telephone Network (PSTN). Users of both post-paid subscriptions and pre-paid accounts are included. The number of subscribers per 100 inhabitants is calculated by dividing the number of subscribers by the population and multiplying by 100.

Table 17: Many Internet users obtain access without paying directly, either as the member of a household, or from work or school. Therefore the number of Internet users will always be much larger than the number of subscribers, typically by a factor of 2-3 in developed countries or more in developing ones. The estimated number of Internet users is measured in a growing number of countries through regular surveys. In situations where surveys are not available, an estimate can be derived based on the number of subscribers. The number of users per 100 inhabitants is calculated by dividing the number of users by the population and multiplying by 100.

Notes techniques : tableaux 15 à 17

Les données présentées dans les *Tableaux 15 à 17* proviennent de la base de données (voir www.itu.int) et *l'Annuaire statistique, Services de télécommunications* de l'Union internationale des télécommunications.

Tableau 15: Ce tableau indique le nombre de lignes principales (fixes) en service et les lignes principales en service pour 100 habitants pour les années indiquées. Les lignes principales sont des lignes téléphoniques qui relient l'équipement terminal de l'abonné au Réseau de téléphone public connecté (RTPC) et qui possèdent un accès individualisé aux équipements d'un central téléphonique. Pour la plupart des pays, le nombre de lignes principales en service indiqué comprend également les lignes publiques. Le nombre de lignes principales pour 100 habitants se calcule en divisant le nombre de lignes principales par la population et en multipliant par 100.

Tableau 16: Les abonnés mobiles (et les abonnés mobiles pour 100 habitants) désignent les utilisateurs de téléphones portatifs abonnés à un service automatique public de téléphones mobiles ayant accès au Réseau de téléphone public connecté (RTPC). Sont pris en compte aussi bien les abonnements post-payés que les cartes prépayées. Le nombre d'abonnés pour 100 habitants se calcule en divisant le nombre d'abonnés par la population et en multipliant par 100.

Tableau 17: Un certain nombre d'utilisateurs de l'Internet y accèdent sans payer directement, soit en tant que membres d'un ménage, soit parce qu'ils l'utilisent au travail ou à l'école. C'est pourquoi le nombre d'utilisateurs de l'Internet sera toujours bien supérieur au nombre d'abonnés, généralement de deux à trois fois dans les pays développés et plus encore dans les pays en développement. Le nombre d'utilisateurs d'internet est recensé à l'aide d'enquêtes standards dans un nombre croissant de pays. Quand les enquêtes ne sont pas disponibles, il est estimé grâce au nombre d'abonnés. Le nombre d'utilisateurs pour 100 habitants est calculé en divisant le nombre d'utilisateurs par le nombre d'habitants, multiplié par 100.

Part Three
Economic activity

Chapter VI	National accounts and industrial production (tables 18-24)
Chapter VII	Financial statistics (tables 25 and 26)
Chapter VIII	Labour force (table 27)
Chapter IX	Wages and prices (tables 28-30)
Chapter X	Agriculture, forestry and fishing (tables 31-34)
Chapter XI	Manufacturing (tables 35-51)
Chapter XII	Energy (tables 52 and 53)
Chapter XIII	Environment (tables 54-58)
Chapter XIV	Science and technology (tables 59-61)

Part Three of the *Yearbook* presents statistical series on production and consumption for a wide range of economic activities, and other basic series on major economic topics, for all countries or areas of the world for which data are available. Included are basic tables on national accounts, finance, labour force, wages and prices, a wide range of agricultural, mined and manufactured commodities, energy, environment, research and development personnel and expenditure, and patents.

International economic topics such as external trade are covered in Part Four.

Troisième partie
Activité économique

Chapitre VI	Comptabilités nationales et production industrielle (tableaux 18 à 24)
Chapitre VII	Statistiques financières (tableaux 25 et 26)
Chapitre VIII	Main-d'œuvre (tableau 27)
Chapitre IX	Salaires et prix (tableaux 28 à 30)
Chapitre X	Agriculture, forêts et pêche (tableaux 31 à 34)
Chapitre XI	Industries manufacturières (tableaux 35 à 51)
Chapitre XII	Energie (tableaux 52 et 53)
Chapitre XIII	Environnement (tableaux 54 à 58)
Chapitre XIV	Environnement (tableaux 59 à 61)

La troisième partie de l'*Annuaire* présente, pour une large gamme d'activités économiques, des séries statistiques sur la production et la consommation, et, pour tous les pays ou zones du monde pour lesquels des données sont disponibles, d'autres séries fondamentales ayant trait à des questions économiques importantes. Y figurent des tableaux de base consacrés à la comptabilité nationale, aux finances, à la main-d'œuvre, aux salaires et aux prix, à un large éventail de produits agricoles, miniers et manufacturés, à l'énergie, à l'environnement, au personnel employé à des travaux de recherche et développement et dépenses de recherche et développement, et aux brevets.

Les questions économiques internationales comme le commerce extérieur sont traitées dans la quatrième partie.

Gross domestic product and gross domestic product per capita
In millions of US dollars at current and constant 1990 prices; per capita US dollars; real rates of growth

Produit intérieur brut et produit intérieur brut par habitant
En millions de dollars É.-U. aux prix courants et constants de 1990 ; par habitant en dollars É.U. ; taux de croissance réels

Country or area	2001	2002	2003	2004	2005	2006	2007	Pays ou zone
World								**Monde**
GDP at current prices	31 685 709	32 997 458	37 076 887	41 713 704	45 102 992	48 786 093	54 635 982	**PIB aux prix courants**
GDP per capita	5 109	5 254	5 831	6 481	6 924	7 401	8 191	**PIB par habitant**
GDP at constant prices	29 570 558	30 169 255	30 992 198	32 241 209	33 354 836	34 681 649	35 997 411	**PIB aux prix constants**
Growth rates	1.7	2.0	2.7	4.0	3.5	4.0	3.8	**Taux de croissance**
Afghanistan								**Afghanistan**
GDP at current prices	2 618	4 741	4 786	5 700	6 840	7 440	9 358	PIB aux prix courants
GDP per capita	122	213	207	237	273	285	345	PIB par habitant
GDP at constant prices	2 618	4 741	5 420	5 932	6 793	7 295	8 202	PIB aux prix constants
Growth rates	-3.5	81.1	14.3	9.4	14.5	7.4	12.4	Taux de croissance
Albania								**Albanie**
GDP at current prices	4 066	4 443	5 696	7 307	8 184	9 082	10 718	PIB aux prix courants
GDP per capita	1 318	1 434	1 828	2 331	2 595	2 863	3 360	PIB par habitant
GDP at constant prices	2 659	2 771	2 931	3 099	3 279	3 460	3 668	PIB aux prix constants
Growth rates	7.9	4.2	5.8	5.7	5.8	5.5	6.0	Taux de croissance
Algeria								**Algérie**
GDP at current prices	55 181	56 048	68 017	85 032	102 334	116 461	132 462	PIB aux prix courants
GDP per capita	1 783	1 813	2 133	2 627	3 115	3 492	3 912	PIB par habitant
GDP at constant prices	75 036	78 562	83 983	88 350	93 033	94 893	99 259	PIB aux prix constants
Growth rates	2.6	4.7	6.9	5.2	5.3	2.0	4.6	Taux de croissance
Andorra								**Andorre**
GDP at current prices	1 265	1 456	1 918	2 322	2 540	2 824	3 245	PIB aux prix courants
GDP per capita	18 730	21 096	27 116	32 120	34 563	38 042	43 504	PIB par habitant
GDP at constant prices	1 537	1 628	1 738	1 850	1 960	2 093	2 123	PIB aux prix constants
Growth rates	11.8	5.9	6.8	6.5	5.9	6.8	1.4	Taux de croissance
Angola								**Angola**
GDP at current prices	8 936	11 432	13 956	19 775	30 629	49 650	52 237	PIB aux prix courants
GDP per capita	624	776	919	1 265	1 903	2 999	3 068	PIB par habitant
GDP at constant prices	12 044	13 794	14 250	15 844	19 110	22 658	27 445	PIB aux prix constants
Growth rates	3.1	14.5	3.3	11.2	20.6	18.6	21.1	Taux de croissance
Anguilla								**Anguilla**
GDP at current prices	110	113	118	149	170	214	227	PIB aux prix courants
GDP per capita	9 639	9 716	9 934	12 360	13 849	17 216	18 007	PIB par habitant
GDP at constant prices	88	86	89	108	117	142	146	PIB aux prix constants
Growth rates	2.6	-1.4	2.6	21.6	8.3	21.6	3.1	Taux de croissance
Antigua and Barbuda								**Antigua-et-Barbuda**
GDP at current prices	697	715	754	819	873	1 006	1 089	PIB aux prix courants
GDP per capita	8 909	8 977	9 334	9 988	10 518	11 964	12 799	PIB par habitant
GDP at constant prices	546	560	589	632	661	744	790	PIB aux prix constants
Growth rates	2.2	2.5	5.2	7.2	4.7	12.5	6.1	Taux de croissance
Argentina								**Argentine**
GDP at current prices	268 831	102 042	129 596	153 129	183 196	214 267	262 327	PIB aux prix courants
GDP per capita	7 212	2 711	3 410	3 991	4 728	5 475	6 636	PIB par habitant
GDP at constant prices	204 333	182 072	198 162	216 055	235 887	255 857	278 013	PIB aux prix constants
Growth rates	-4.4	-10.9	8.8	9.0	9.2	8.5	8.7	Taux de croissance
Armenia								**Arménie**
GDP at current prices	2 118	2 376	2 807	3 577	4 900	6 387	9 177	PIB aux prix courants
GDP per capita	691	779	924	1 182	1 624	2 122	3 057	PIB par habitant
GDP at constant prices	1 604	1 816	2 070	2 288	2 608	2 957	3 285	PIB aux prix constants
Growth rates	9.6	13.2	14.0	10.5	14.0	13.4	11.1	Taux de croissance
Aruba								**Aruba**
GDP at current prices	1 920	1 941	2 021	2 225	2 323	2 421	2 623	PIB aux prix courants
GDP per capita	20 723	20 322	20 518	22 009	22 579	23 333	25 253	PIB par habitant
GDP at constant prices	1 382	1 352	1 358	1 458	1 473	1 481	1 513	PIB aux prix constants
Growth rates	-0.4	-2.2	0.5	7.4	1.0	0.6	2.1	Taux de croissance
Australia								**Australie**
GDP at current prices	380 520	424 694	545 654	660 151	738 812	787 941	945 674	PIB aux prix courants
GDP per capita	19 648	21 664	27 497	32 875	36 376	38 379	45 590	PIB par habitant
GDP at constant prices	470 980	485 826	505 386	519 782	535 138	552 186	573 823	PIB aux prix constants
Growth rates	3.8	3.2	4.0	2.9	3.0	3.2	3.9	Taux de croissance

18

Gross domestic product and gross domestic product per capita *(continued)*
In millions of US dollars at current and constant 1990 prices; per capita US dollars; real rates of growth

Produit intérieur brut et produit intérieur brut par habitant *(suite)*
En millions de dollars É.-U. aux prix courants et constants de 1990 ; par habitant en dollars É.-U. ; taux de croissance réels

Country or area	2001	2002	2003	2004	2005	2006	2007	Pays ou zone
Austria								**Autriche**
GDP at current prices	193 178	207 840	255 267	293 220	305 091	323 528	373 327	PIB aux prix courants
GDP per capita	23 740	25 434	31 084	35 527	36 794	38 851	44 652	PIB par habitant
GDP at constant prices	214 025	215 859	218 480	223 525	228 092	235 624	243 592	PIB aux prix constants
Growth rates	0.8	0.9	1.2	2.3	2.0	3.3	3.4	Taux de croissance
Azerbaijan								**Azerbaïdjan**
GDP at current prices	5 708	6 236	7 276	8 680	13 245	20 982	31 249	PIB aux prix courants
GDP per capita	697	758	880	1 045	1 586	2 496	3 691	PIB par habitant
GDP at constant prices	4 214	4 660	5 179	5 705	7 214	9 700	12 130	PIB aux prix constants
Growth rates	9.9	10.6	11.2	10.2	26.5	34.5	25.1	Taux de croissance
Bahamas								**Bahamas**
GDP at current prices	5 131	5 389	5 512	5 650	5 986	6 237	6 586	PIB aux prix courants
GDP per capita	16 697	17 307	17 478	17 692	18 516	19 058	19 881	PIB par habitant
GDP at constant prices	3 934	4 023	4 062	4 114	4 215	4 358	4 493	PIB aux prix constants
Growth rates	0.8	2.3	1.0	1.3	2.5	3.4	3.1	Taux de croissance
Bahrain								**Bahreïn**
GDP at current prices	7 971	8 491	9 747	11 235	13 460	15 828	19 664	PIB aux prix courants
GDP per capita	11 988	12 487	14 021	15 820	18 571	21 421	26 127	PIB par habitant
GDP at constant prices	6 974	7 336	7 868	8 312	8 965	9 551	10 185	PIB aux prix constants
Growth rates	4.3	5.2	7.2	5.7	7.9	6.5	6.6	Taux de croissance
Bangladesh								**Bangladesh**
GDP at current prices	45 433	47 195	51 690	55 950	57 628	60 309	67 876	PIB aux prix courants
GDP per capita	320	326	350	372	376	387	428	PIB par habitant
GDP at constant prices	51 366	53 634	56 453	59 993	63 566	67 780	72 193	PIB aux prix constants
Growth rates	5.3	4.4	5.3	6.3	6.0	6.6	6.5	Taux de croissance
Barbados								**Barbade**
GDP at current prices	2 554	2 476	2 695	2 816	3 083	3 422	3 729	PIB aux prix courants
GDP per capita	8 881	8 576	9 298	9 681	10 561	11 681	12 687	PIB par habitant
GDP at constant prices	1 899	1 908	1 946	2 018	2 101	2 182	2 273	PIB aux prix constants
Growth rates	-2.6	0.5	2.0	3.7	4.1	3.9	4.2	Taux de croissance
Belarus								**Bélarus**
GDP at current prices	12 355	14 595	17 825	23 142	30 210	36 962	44 773	PIB aux prix courants
GDP per capita	1 235	1 467	1 801	2 350	3 084	3 794	4 621	PIB par habitant
GDP at constant prices	17 461	18 336	19 618	21 860	23 924	26 316	28 464	PIB aux prix constants
Growth rates	4.7	5.0	7.0	11.4	9.4	10.0	8.2	Taux de croissance
Belgium								**Belgique**
GDP at current prices	231 661	251 896	310 063	359 700	375 524	397 197	454 580	PIB aux prix courants
GDP per capita	22 647	24 525	30 056	34 721	36 115	38 081	43 470	PIB par habitant
GDP at constant prices	252 659	256 471	259 013	266 712	271 175	278 896	286 459	PIB aux prix constants
Growth rates	0.8	1.5	1.0	3.0	1.7	2.9	2.7	Taux de croissance
Belize								**Belize**
GDP at current prices	871	932	988	1 055	1 115	1 214	1 274	PIB aux prix courants
GDP per capita	3 473	3 626	3 752	3 917	4 046	4 309	4 429	PIB par habitant
GDP at constant prices	704	740	809	847	873	922	934	PIB aux prix constants
Growth rates	4.9	5.1	9.3	4.6	3.1	5.6	1.3	Taux de croissance
Benin								**Bénin**
GDP at current prices	2 499	2 808	3 557	4 051	4 358	4 712	5 579	PIB aux prix courants
GDP per capita	335	364	447	493	513	538	618	PIB par habitant
GDP at constant prices	3 051	3 186	3 309	3 413	3 510	3 653	3 872	PIB aux prix constants
Growth rates	6.3	4.4	3.9	3.1	2.9	4.1	6.0	Taux de croissance
Bermuda								**Bermudes**
GDP at current prices	3 622	3 924	4 176	4 450	4 857	5 193	5 581	PIB aux prix courants
GDP per capita	57 360	61 870	65 566	69 592	75 685	80 666	86 450	PIB par habitant
GDP at constant prices	2 617	2 783	2 865	2 966	3 102	3 210	3 343	PIB aux prix constants
Growth rates	0.1	6.4	2.9	3.5	4.6	3.5	4.2	Taux de croissance
Bhutan								**Bhoutan**
GDP at current prices	484	540	628	710	837	922	1 305	PIB aux prix courants
GDP per capita	843	914	1 034	1 140	1 314	1 422	1 982	PIB par habitant
GDP at constant prices	500	550	591	631	672	729	893	PIB aux prix constants
Growth rates	7.2	10.0	7.6	6.8	6.5	8.5	22.4	Taux de croissance

18

Gross domestic product and gross domestic product per capita *(continued)*
In millions of US dollars at current and constant 1990 prices; per capita US dollars; real rates of growth
Produit intérieur brut et produit intérieur brut par habitant *(suite)*
En millions de dollars É.-U. aux prix courants et constants de 1990 ; par habitant en dollars É.-U. ; taux de croissance réels

Country or area	2001	2002	2003	2004	2005	2006	2007	Pays ou zone
Bolivia								**Bolivie**
GDP at current prices	8 142	7 905	8 082	8 773	9 549	11 452	13 120	PIB aux prix courants
GDP per capita	959	913	915	974	1 040	1 224	1 378	PIB par habitant
GDP at constant prices	7 165	7 343	7 542	7 857	8 205	8 598	8 991	PIB aux prix constants
Growth rates	1.7	2.5	2.7	4.2	4.4	4.8	4.6	Taux de croissance
Bosnia and Herzegovina								**Bosnie-Herzégovine**
GDP at current prices	4 795	5 606	7 100	10 022	10 763	12 264	14 771	PIB aux prix courants
GDP per capita	1 247	1 445	1 822	2 566	2 749	3 124	3 754	PIB par habitant
GDP at constant prices	21 697	19 923	18 201	19 345	20 102	21 449	25 465	PIB aux prix constants
Growth rates	-7.8	-8.2	-8.7	6.3	3.9	6.7	18.7	Taux de croissance
Botswana								**Botswana**
GDP at current prices	4 903	5 045	7 341	8 498	9 113	9 275	10 798	PIB aux prix courants
GDP per capita	2 796	2 842	4 089	4 682	4 964	4 992	5 739	PIB par habitant
GDP at constant prices	6 265	6 406	6 834	7 288	7 979	8 030	8 525	PIB aux prix constants
Growth rates	8.5	2.2	6.7	6.6	9.5	0.6	6.2	Taux de croissance
Brazil								**Brésil**
GDP at current prices	554 187	506 041	552 384	663 733	882 044	1 072 453	1 314 199	PIB aux prix courants
GDP per capita	3 136	2 823	3 039	3 601	4 721	5 665	6 852	PIB par habitant
GDP at constant prices	622 973	639 532	040 805	003 010	705 422	731 623	763 710	PIB aux prix constants
Growth rates	1.3	2.7	1.2	5.7	3.2	3.7	4.4	Taux de croissance
British Virgin Islands								**Iles Vierges britanniques**
GDP at current prices	839	813	782	873	972	1 049	1 156	PIB aux prix courants
GDP per capita	40 207	38 385	36 425	40 147	44 150	47 090	51 273	PIB par habitant
GDP at constant prices	850	820	762	842	919	1 000	1 095	PIB aux prix constants
Growth rates	3.8	-3.5	-7.2	10.5	9.2	8.8	9.5	Taux de croissance
Brunei Darussalam								**Brunéi Darussalam**
GDP at current prices	5 601	5 843	6 557	7 872	9 531	11 561	12 388	PIB aux prix courants
GDP per capita	16 404	16 721	18 339	21 527	25 497	30 269	31 759	PIB par habitant
GDP at constant prices	4 357	4 526	4 658	4 681	4 699	4 941	4 960	PIB aux prix constants
Growth rates	2.8	3.9	2.9	0.5	0.4	5.1	0.4	Taux de croissance
Bulgaria								**Bulgarie**
GDP at current prices	13 599	15 600	19 985	24 648	27 188	31 483	39 551	PIB aux prix courants
GDP per capita	1 711	1 976	2 548	3 162	3 511	4 093	5 178	PIB par habitant
GDP at constant prices	18 129	19 143	20 101	21 436	22 775	24 162	25 652	PIB aux prix constants
Growth rates	4.1	5.6	5.0	6.6	6.3	6.1	6.2	Taux de croissance
Burkina Faso								**Burkina Faso**
GDP at current prices	2 792	3 290	4 271	5 108	5 614	6 015	7 136	PIB aux prix courants
GDP per capita	228	260	326	378	403	419	483	PIB par habitant
GDP at constant prices	5 548	5 848	6 318	6 610	7 079	7 512	8 019	PIB aux prix constants
Growth rates	7.1	5.4	8.1	4.6	7.1	6.1	6.7	Taux de croissance
Burundi								**Burundi**
GDP at current prices	662	628	595	680	797	959	1 004	PIB aux prix courants
GDP per capita	97	89	82	90	101	117	118	PIB par habitant
GDP at constant prices	991	1 035	1 023	1 068	1 077	1 132	1 194	PIB aux prix constants
Growth rates	2.1	4.5	-1.2	4.4	0.9	5.1	5.5	Taux de croissance
Cambodia								**Cambodge**
GDP at current prices	3 992	4 289	4 665	5 338	6 293	7 275	8 639	PIB aux prix courants
GDP per capita	307	324	346	389	451	512	598	PIB par habitant
GDP at constant prices	2 932	3 125	3 391	3 741	4 237	4 693	5 172	PIB aux prix constants
Growth rates	8.2	6.6	8.5	10.3	13.3	10.8	10.2	Taux de croissance
Cameroon								**Cameroun**
GDP at current prices	9 633	10 880	13 622	15 775	16 648	17 920	20 606	PIB aux prix courants
GDP per capita	593	654	800	906	936	986	1 111	PIB par habitant
GDP at constant prices	14 475	15 055	15 662	16 242	16 605	17 150	17 716	PIB aux prix constants
Growth rates	4.5	4.0	4.0	3.7	2.2	3.3	3.3	Taux de croissance
Canada								**Canada**
GDP at current prices	715 442	734 653	865 903	992 168	1 134 776	1 274 994	1 425 778	PIB aux prix courants
GDP per capita	23 085	23 465	27 374	31 049	35 164	39 138	43 368	PIB par habitant
GDP at constant prices	790 906	814 036	829 348	854 812	881 025	905 330	929 347	PIB aux prix constants
Growth rates	1.8	2.9	1.9	3.1	3.1	2.8	2.7	Taux de croissance

Gross domestic product and gross domestic product per capita (continued)
In millions of US dollars at current and constant 1990 prices; per capita US dollars; real rates of growth
Produit intérieur brut et produit intérieur brut par habitant (suite)
En millions de dollars É.-U. aux prix courants et constants de 1990 ; par habitant en dollars É.-U. ; taux de croissance réels

Country or area	2001	2002	2003	2004	2005	2006	2007	Pays ou zone
Cape Verde								**Cap-Vert**
GDP at current prices	563	621	814	924	1 006	1 202	1 426	PIB aux prix courants
GDP per capita	1 220	1 315	1 683	1 867	1 986	2 317	2 689	PIB par habitant
GDP at constant prices	630	663	694	724	771	854	913	PIB aux prix constants
Growth rates	6.1	5.3	4.7	4.3	6.5	10.8	6.9	Taux de croissance
Cayman Islands								**Iles Caïmanes**
GDP at current prices	1 779	1 855	1 924	2 027	2 316	2 442	2 701	PIB aux prix courants
GDP per capita	42 868	43 499	44 018	45 355	50 797	52 585	57 222	PIB par habitant
GDP at constant prices	1 267	1 289	1 315	1 327	1 413	1 478	1 534	PIB aux prix constants
Growth rates	0.6	1.7	2.0	0.9	6.5	4.6	3.8	Taux de croissance
Central African Rep.								**Rép. centrafricaine**
GDP at current prices	968	1 042	1 139	1 270	1 350	1 477	1 712	PIB aux prix courants
GDP per capita	246	261	281	308	322	346	394	PIB par habitant
GDP at constant prices	1 778	1 764	1 630	1 651	1 687	1 755	1 829	PIB aux prix constants
Growth rates	1.5	-0.8	-7.6	1.3	2.2	4.0	4.2	Taux de croissance
Chad								**Tchad**
GDP at current prices	1 710	1 987	2 723	4 415	5 885	6 637	7 464	PIB aux prix courants
GDP per capita	195	218	288	450	580	634	692	PIB par habitant
GDP at constant prices	2 422	2 629	3 004	4 016	4 360	4 485	4 514	PIB aux prix constants
Growth rates	11.5	8.5	14.3	33.7	8.6	2.9	0.7	Taux de croissance
Chile								**Chili**
GDP at current prices	68 568	67 266	73 990	95 653	118 250	146 437	163 915	PIB aux prix courants
GDP per capita	4 396	4 264	4 639	5 932	7 257	8 894	9 854	PIB par habitant
GDP at constant prices	64 397	65 803	68 381	72 512	76 543	79 866	83 936	PIB aux prix constants
Growth rates	3.4	2.2	3.9	6.0	5.6	4.3	5.1	Taux de croissance
China[1]								**Chine**[1]
GDP at current prices	1 316 558	1 454 040	1 647 918	1 936 502	2 302 718	2 773 835	3 400 351	PIB aux prix courants
GDP per capita	1 047	1 149	1 293	1 510	1 785	2 137	2 604	PIB par habitant
GDP at constant prices	1 180 869	1 288 328	1 417 161	1 560 294	1 719 444	1 910 302	2 128 077	PIB aux prix constants
Growth rates	8.3	9.1	10.0	10.1	10.2	11.1	11.4	Taux de croissance
China, Hong Kong SAR								**Chine, Hong Kong RAS**
GDP at current prices	166 593	163 781	158 572	165 884	177 831	189 799	206 706	PIB aux prix courants
GDP per capita	24 696	23 992	22 965	23 760	25 198	26 611	28 685	PIB par habitant
GDP at constant prices	113 477	115 566	119 040	129 116	138 307	147 646	157 226	PIB aux prix constants
Growth rates	0.5	1.8	3.0	8.5	7.1	6.8	6.5	Taux de croissance
China, Macao SAR								**Chine, Macao RAS**
GDP at current prices	6 187	6 824	7 925	10 342	11 603	14 408	19 115	PIB aux prix courants
GDP per capita	13 824	15 016	17 179	22 116	24 526	30 171	39 731	PIB par habitant
GDP at constant prices	4 005	4 410	5 035	6 464	6 910	8 088	10 296	PIB aux prix constants
Growth rates	2.9	10.1	14.2	28.4	6.9	17.1	27.3	Taux de croissance
Colombia								**Colombie**
GDP at current prices	81 995	81 243	79 411	98 054	122 935	136 006	168 394	PIB aux prix courants
GDP per capita	1 936	1 889	1 818	2 213	2 735	2 985	3 648	PIB par habitant
GDP at constant prices	62 928	64 145	66 620	69 862	73 161	78 160	83 474	PIB aux prix constants
Growth rates	1.5	1.9	3.9	4.9	4.7	6.8	6.8	Taux de croissance
Comoros								**Comores**
GDP at current prices	220	251	324	362	387	403	467	PIB aux prix courants
GDP per capita	306	340	428	466	485	493	556	PIB par habitant
GDP at constant prices	288	300	308	307	320	322	312	PIB aux prix constants
Growth rates	3.3	4.2	2.5	-0.2	4.2	0.5	-2.9	Taux de croissance
Congo								**Congo**
GDP at current prices	2 794	3 018	3 564	4 342	5 972	7 385	7 304	PIB aux prix courants
GDP per capita	851	896	1 033	1 230	1 654	2 002	1 938	PIB par habitant
GDP at constant prices	3 346	3 507	3 567	3 696	3 980	4 235	4 168	PIB aux prix constants
Growth rates	3.8	4.8	1.7	3.6	7.7	6.4	-1.6	Taux de croissance
Cook Islands								**Iles Cook**
GDP at current prices	86	102	143	171	184	182	211	PIB aux prix courants
GDP per capita	5 565	6 748	9 705	11 940	13 122	13 324	15 813	PIB par habitant
GDP at constant prices	81	83	90	94	94	96	96	PIB aux prix constants
Growth rates	4.9	2.6	8.2	4.3	0.2	1.4	0.4	Taux de croissance

18
Gross domestic product and gross domestic product per capita *(continued)*
In millions of US dollars at current and constant 1990 prices; per capita US dollars; real rates of growth
Produit intérieur brut et produit intérieur brut par habitant *(suite)*
En millions de dollars É.-U. aux prix courants et constants de 1990 ; par habitant en dollars É.-U. ; taux de croissance réels

Country or area	2001	2002	2003	2004	2005	2006	2007	Pays ou zone
Costa Rica								**Costa Rica**
GDP at current prices	16 403	16 844	17 514	18 593	19 973	22 229	25 917	PIB aux prix courants
GDP per capita	4 086	4 111	4 194	4 372	4 616	5 053	5 801	PIB par habitant
GDP at constant prices	12 171	12 523	13 324	13 897	14 718	15 918	16 922	PIB aux prix constants
Growth rates	1.1	2.9	6.4	4.3	5.9	8.2	6.3	Taux de croissance
Côte d'Ivoire								**Côte d'Ivoire**
GDP at current prices	10 735	11 494	13 738	15 701	16 802	18 220	20 650	PIB aux prix courants
GDP per capita	618	650	764	859	904	963	1 072	PIB par habitant
GDP at constant prices	15 156	15 154	15 151	15 153	15 156	15 158	15 406	PIB aux prix constants
Growth rates	^0.0	^0.0	^0.0	^0.0	^0.0	^0.0	1.6	Taux de croissance
Croatia								**Croatie**
GDP at current prices	19 857	23 023	29 593	35 269	38 498	42 925	51 277	PIB aux prix courants
GDP per capita	4 414	5 110	6 544	7 769	8 458	9 422	11 256	PIB par habitant
GDP at constant prices	22 176	23 332	24 329	25 253	26 818	28 095	29 655	PIB aux prix constants
Growth rates	4.4	5.2	4.3	3.8	6.2	4.8	5.6	Taux de croissance
Cuba								**Cuba**
GDP at current prices	33 820	36 089	38 625	41 065	46 162	56 181	52 298	PIB aux prix courants
GDP per capita	3 027	3 221	3 440	3 651	4 100	4 986	4 641	PIB par habitant
GDP at constant prices	27 719	28 218	29 291	30 873	34 525	38 841	41 734	PIB aux prix constants
Growth rates	3.0	1.8	3.8	5.4	11.8	12.5	7.5	Taux de croissance
Cyprus [2]								**Chypre** [2]
GDP at current prices	9 672	10 523	13 303	15 804	16 978	18 357	21 275	PIB aux prix courants
GDP per capita	13 792	14 830	18 461	21 441	22 399	23 951	27 465	PIB par habitant
GDP at constant prices	9 339	9 536	9 717	10 125	10 525	10 951	11 429	PIB aux prix constants
Growth rates	4.0	2.1	1.9	4.2	4.0	4.0	4.4	Taux de croissance
Czech Republic								**République tchèque**
GDP at current prices	61 843	75 276	91 358	109 525	124 710	143 018	171 953	PIB aux prix courants
GDP per capita	6 058	7 379	8 959	10 744	12 236	14 037	16 881	PIB par habitant
GDP at constant prices	38 922	39 660	41 089	42 932	45 668	48 572	51 388	PIB aux prix constants
Growth rates	2.5	1.9	3.6	4.5	6.4	6.4	5.8	Taux de croissance
Dem. Rep. of the Congo								**Rép. dém. du Congo**
GDP at current prices	5 279[3]	5 556	5 682	6 569	7 103	8 544	9 447	PIB aux prix courants
GDP per capita	101[3]	104	103	115	121	141	151	PIB par habitant
GDP at constant prices	5 060[3]	5 234	5 530	5 895	6 278	6 608	7 037	PIB aux prix constants
Growth rates	-2.0	3.4	5.7	6.6	6.5	5.3	6.5	Taux de croissance
Denmark								**Danemark**
GDP at current prices	160 476	173 881	212 623	243 596	258 794	276 152	311 596	PIB aux prix courants
GDP per capita	29 971	32 369	39 463	45 086	47 775	50 856	57 257	PIB par habitant
GDP at constant prices	176 766	177 589	178 270	182 067	187 639	194 245	197 781	PIB aux prix constants
Growth rates	0.7	0.5	0.4	2.1	3.1	3.5	1.8	Taux de croissance
Djibouti								**Djibouti**
GDP at current prices	573	592	628	666	709	770	835	PIB aux prix courants
GDP per capita	767	776	808	843	881	940	1 002	PIB par habitant
GDP at constant prices	526	540	557	574	592	620	650	PIB aux prix constants
Growth rates	1.9	2.6	3.2	3.0	3.2	4.8	4.8	Taux de croissance
Dominica								**Dominique**
GDP at current prices	266	255	263	285	299	316	326	PIB aux prix courants
GDP per capita	3 894	3 734	3 857	4 194	4 415	4 677	4 838	PIB par habitant
GDP at constant prices	192	184	188	200	207	217	219	PIB aux prix constants
Growth rates	-3.8	-4.0	2.1	6.4	3.5	4.9	0.9	Taux de croissance
Dominican Republic								**Rép. dominicaine**
GDP at current prices	24 512	24 913	20 045	21 582	33 542	35 660	41 013	PIB aux prix courants
GDP per capita	2 757	2 757	2 184	2 315	3 542	3 709	4 202	PIB par habitant
GDP at constant prices	17 189	18 184	18 138	18 376	20 078	22 220	24 103	PIB aux prix constants
Growth rates	1.8	5.8	-0.3	1.3	9.3	10.7	8.5	Taux de croissance
Ecuador								**Equateur**
GDP at current prices	21 250	24 899	28 636	32 642	37 187	41 402	44 400	PIB aux prix courants
GDP per capita	1 705	1 973	2 242	2 527	2 847	3 136	3 328	PIB par habitant
GDP at constant prices	14 681	15 304	15 852	17 120	18 148	18 855	19 503	PIB aux prix constants
Growth rates	5.3	4.3	3.6	8.0	6.0	3.9	3.4	Taux de croissance

Gross domestic product and gross domestic product per capita *(continued)*
In millions of US dollars at current and constant 1990 prices; per capita US dollars; real rates of growth
Produit intérieur brut et produit intérieur brut par habitant *(suite)*
En millions de dollars É.-U. aux prix courants et constants de 1990 ; par habitant en dollars É.-U. ; taux de croissance réels

Country or area	2001	2002	2003	2004	2005	2006	2007	Pays ou zone
Egypt								**Egypte**
GDP at current prices	94 438	90 064	77 109	82 429	98 323	112 152	133 599	PIB aux prix courants
GDP per capita	1 394	1 305	1 097	1 152	1 350	1 512	1 770	PIB par habitant
GDP at constant prices	64 801	67 478	70 258	73 436	78 462	84 023	89 890	PIB aux prix constants
Growth rates	3.2	4.1	4.1	4.5	6.8	7.1	7.0	Taux de croissance
El Salvador								**El Salvador**
GDP at current prices	13 813	14 307	15 047	15 798	17 070	18 654	20 373	PIB aux prix courants
GDP per capita	2 194	2 238	2 320	2 402	2 560	2 758	2 971	PIB par habitant
GDP at constant prices	7 660	7 839	8 019	8 168	8 420	8 772	9 180	PIB aux prix constants
Growth rates	1.7	2.3	2.3	1.9	3.1	4.2	4.7	Taux de croissance
Equatorial Guinea								**Guinée équatoriale**
GDP at current prices	1 695	2 084	2 825	4 618	7 295	8 301	10 149	PIB aux prix courants
GDP per capita	3 845	4 617	6 116	9 765	15 069	16 748	19 998	PIB par habitant
GDP at constant prices	1 465	1 761	2 000	2 600	2 842	2 684	3 018	PIB aux prix constants
Growth rates	67.8	20.2	13.6	30.0	9.3	-5.6	12.4	Taux de croissance
Eritrea								**Erythrée**
GDP at current prices	752	729	870	1 109	1 098	1 211	1 316	PIB aux prix courants
GDP per capita	196	182	208	255	243	258	271	PIB par habitant
GDP at constant prices	1 491	1 536	1 495	1 517	1 556	1 541	1 561	PIB aux prix constants
Growth rates	8.8	3.0	-2.7	1.5	2.6	-1.0	1.3	Taux de croissance
Estonia								**Estonie**
GDP at current prices	6 192	7 306	9 816	11 903	13 938	16 611	21 275	PIB aux prix courants
GDP per capita	4 544	5 385	7 258	8 828	10 368	12 396	15 932	PIB par habitant
GDP at constant prices	5 607	6 056	6 495	7 031	7 745	8 611	9 224	PIB aux prix constants
Growth rates	7.7	8.0	7.2	8.3	10.2	11.2	7.1	Taux de croissance
Ethiopia								**Ethiopie**
GDP at current prices	7 767	7 407	8 012	9 467	11 354	13 288	16 712	PIB aux prix courants
GDP per capita	109	101	107	123	144	164	201	PIB par habitant
GDP at constant prices	15 528	15 720	15 168	17 160	18 929	20 943	23 279	PIB aux prix constants
Growth rates	7.7	1.2	-3.5	13.1	10.3	10.6	11.2	Taux de croissance
Fiji								**Fidji**
GDP at current prices	1 662	1 843	2 309	2 728	2 998	3 109	3 366	PIB aux prix courants
GDP per capita	2 059	2 268	2 824	3 315	3 620	3 731	4 014	PIB par habitant
GDP at constant prices	1 699	1 753	1 771	1 865	1 878	1 946	1 870	PIB aux prix constants
Growth rates	2.0	3.2	1.0	5.3	0.7	3.6	-3.9	Taux de croissance
Finland								**Finlande**
GDP at current prices	125 160	135 498	164 709	189 163	195 446	209 577	244 692	PIB aux prix courants
GDP per capita	24 121	26 045	31 574	36 161	37 256	39 834	46 371	PIB par habitant
GDP at constant prices	174 055	176 915	180 053	186 765	192 215	201 837	210 717	PIB aux prix constants
Growth rates	2.6	1.6	1.8	3.7	2.9	5.0	4.4	Taux de croissance
France [4]								**France** [4]
GDP at current prices	1 339 753	1 457 396	1 799 946	2 061 412	2 136 399	2 247 975	2 545 696	PIB aux prix courants
GDP per capita	21 887	23 662	29 030	33 028	34 018	35 590	40 090	PIB par habitant
GDP at constant prices	1 541 628	1 557 453	1 574 389	1 613 280	1 640 882	1 673 525	1 705 370	PIB aux prix constants
Growth rates	1.9	1.0	1.1	2.5	1.7	2.0	1.9	Taux de croissance
French Polynesia								**Polynésie française**
GDP at current prices	3 224	3 564	4 440	5 015	5 226	5 463	6 172	PIB aux prix courants
GDP per capita	13 427	14 599	17 898	19 910	20 444	21 071	23 488	PIB par habitant
GDP at constant prices	3 742	3 904	4 031	4 097	4 217	4 331	4 459	PIB aux prix constants
Growth rates	1.4	4.4	3.2	1.7	2.9	2.7	3.0	Taux de croissance
Gabon								**Gabon**
GDP at current prices	4 656	4 932	6 055	7 178	8 666	9 546	11 285	PIB aux prix courants
GDP per capita	3 863	4 017	4 847	5 651	6 714	7 282	8 481	PIB par habitant
GDP at constant prices	6 252	6 235	6 388	6 457	6 653	6 731	7 105	PIB aux prix constants
Growth rates	1.8	-0.3	2.5	1.1	3.0	1.2	5.6	Taux de croissance
Gambia								**Gambie**
GDP at current prices	418	370	367	401	461	508	644	PIB aux prix courants
GDP per capita	292	250	241	255	285	305	377	PIB par habitant
GDP at constant prices	487	471	504	529	556	581	609	PIB aux prix constants
Growth rates	5.8	-3.3	6.9	5.1	5.0	4.5	4.9	Taux de croissance

18

Gross domestic product and gross domestic product per capita *(continued)*
In millions of US dollars at current and constant 1990 prices; per capita US dollars; real rates of growth
Produit intérieur brut et produit intérieur brut par habitant *(suite)*
En millions de dollars É.-U. aux prix courants et constants de 1990 ; par habitant en dollars É.-U. ; taux de croissance réels

Country or area	2001	2002	2003	2004	2005	2006	2007	Pays ou zone
Georgia								**Géorgie**
GDP at current prices	3 219	3 396	3 991	5 126	6 411	7 745	10 176	PIB aux prix courants
GDP per capita	690	736	875	1 135	1 433	1 747	2 315	PIB par habitant
GDP at constant prices	3 332	3 516	3 904	4 149	4 548	4 974	5 593	PIB aux prix constants
Growth rates	4.8	5.5	11.1	6.3	9.6	9.4	12.4	Taux de croissance
Germany								**Allemagne**
GDP at current prices	1 890 954	2 017 013	2 442 118	2 745 587	2 791 374	2 913 162	3 317 377	PIB aux prix courants
GDP per capita	22 950	24 453	29 577	33 228	33 772	35 251	40 162	PIB par habitant
GDP at constant prices	2 137 266	2 137 266	2 132 621	2 155 210	2 172 099	2 234 376	2 289 897	PIB aux prix constants
Growth rates	1.2	0.0	-0.2	1.1	0.8	2.9	2.5	Taux de croissance
Ghana								**Ghana**
GDP at current prices	5 316	6 161	7 628	8 877	10 726	12 913	15 179	PIB aux prix courants
GDP per capita	258	292	354	402	476	561	647	PIB par habitant
GDP at constant prices	9 882	10 331	10 873	11 502	12 167	12 913	13 738	PIB aux prix constants
Growth rates	4.2	4.6	5.3	5.8	5.8	6.1	6.4	Taux de croissance
Greece								**Grèce**
GDP at current prices	130 881	148 309	193 286	229 988	246 989	268 440	313 355	PIB aux prix courants
GDP per capita	11 886	13 436	17 477	20 759	22 252	24 135	28 111	PIB par habitant
GDP at constant prices	124 075	128 919	135 411	141 609	147 038	153 206	159 339	PIB aux prix constants
Growth rates	4.5	3.9	5.0	4.6	3.8	4.2	4.0	Taux de croissance
Greenland								**Groenland**
GDP at current prices	1 086	1 169	1 426	1 645	1 703	1 919	2 197	PIB aux prix courants
GDP per capita	19 241	20 631	25 064	28 767	29 622	33 203	37 793	PIB par habitant
GDP at constant prices	1 230	1 218	1 214	1 246	1 271	1 304	1 313	PIB aux prix constants
Growth rates	1.3	-1.0	-0.4	2.7	2.0	2.6	0.7	Taux de croissance
Grenada								**Grenade**
GDP at current prices	395	408	444	427	504	508	537	PIB aux prix courants
GDP per capita	3 903	3 980	4 284	4 081	4 788	4 815	5 081	PIB par habitant
GDP at constant prices	333	338	362	342	379	370	382	PIB aux prix constants
Growth rates	-3.0	1.6	7.1	-5.7	11.0	-2.4	3.1	Taux de croissance
Guatemala								**Guatemala**
GDP at current prices	18 703	20 777	21 918	23 965	27 211	30 193	33 432	PIB aux prix courants
GDP per capita	1 626	1 762	1 813	1 933	2 141	2 317	2 504	PIB par habitant
GDP at constant prices	10 446	10 850	11 125	11 475	11 850	12 476	13 185	PIB aux prix constants
Growth rates	2.3	3.9	2.5	3.2	3.3	5.3	5.7	Taux de croissance
Guinea								**Guinée**
GDP at current prices	3 035	3 209	3 621	4 014	3 257	3 285	4 233	PIB aux prix courants
GDP per capita	363	377	418	454	362	358	452	PIB par habitant
GDP at constant prices	4 359	4 540	4 593	4 717	4 874	4 980	5 055	PIB aux prix constants
Growth rates	3.8	4.2	1.2	2.7	3.3	2.2	1.5	Taux de croissance
Guinea-Bissau								**Guinée-Bissau**
GDP at current prices	199	204	239	270	301	304	357	PIB aux prix courants
GDP per capita	141	140	159	174	189	185	211	PIB par habitant
GDP at constant prices	265	246	248	253	262	273	283	PIB aux prix constants
Growth rates	0.2	-7.1	0.6	2.2	3.5	4.2	3.7	Taux de croissance
Guyana								**Guyana**
GDP at current prices	712	726	743	788	826	901	1 059	PIB aux prix courants
GDP per capita	969	986	1 007	1 067	1 117	1 219	1 435	PIB par habitant
GDP at constant prices	653	660	653	675	660	691	728	PIB aux prix constants
Growth rates	2.3	1.1	-1.0	3.3	-2.2	4.8	5.3	Taux de croissance
Haiti								**Haïti**
GDP at current prices	3 365	3 083	2 711	3 511	3 985	4 758	5 869	PIB aux prix courants
GDP per capita	386	348	301	384	429	504	612	PIB par habitant
GDP at constant prices	2 334	2 328	2 336	2 254	2 295	2 348	2 423	PIB aux prix constants
Growth rates	-1.0	-0.3	0.4	-3.5	1.8	2.3	3.2	Taux de croissance
Honduras								**Honduras**
GDP at current prices	7 653	7 860	8 234	8 871	9 757	10 833	12 322	PIB aux prix courants
GDP per capita	1 211	1 219	1 253	1 324	1 428	1 554	1 734	PIB par habitant
GDP at constant prices	5 163	5 356	5 600	5 949	6 309	6 705	7 127	PIB aux prix constants
Growth rates	2.7	3.8	4.6	6.2	6.1	6.3	6.3	Taux de croissance

Gross domestic product and gross domestic product per capita *(continued)*
In millions of US dollars at current and constant 1990 prices; per capita US dollars; real rates of growth
Produit intérieur brut et produit intérieur brut par habitant *(suite)*
En millions de dollars É.-U. aux prix courants et constants de 1990 ; par habitant en dollars É.-U. ; taux de croissance réels

Country or area	2001	2002	2003	2004	2005	2006	2007	Pays ou zone
Hungary								**Hongrie**
GDP at current prices	53 301	66 621	84 441	102 183	110 506	112 920	138 183	PIB aux prix courants
GDP per capita	5 231	6 554	8 328	10 104	10 956	11 226	13 777	PIB par habitant
GDP at constant prices	41 299	43 105	44 905	47 066	49 011	50 911	51 586	PIB aux prix constants
Growth rates	4.1	4.4	4.2	4.8	4.1	3.9	1.3	Taux de croissance
Iceland								**Islande**
GDP at current prices	7 901	8 862	10 947	13 199	16 219	16 265	18 672	PIB aux prix courants
GDP per capita	27 822	30 879	37 751	45 062	54 844	54 503	62 033	PIB par habitant
GDP at constant prices	8 521	8 514	8 748	9 414	10 087	10 351	10 425	PIB aux prix constants
Growth rates	3.9	-0.1	2.7	7.6	7.2	2.6	0.7	Taux de croissance
India								**Inde**
GDP at current prices	483 414	505 671	593 666	689 947	808 884	910 615	1 141 346	PIB aux prix courants
GDP per capita	454	467	540	618	713	791	976	PIB par habitant
GDP at constant prices	585 743	607 572	658 559	713 384	779 245	852 135	926 270	PIB aux prix constants
Growth rates	5.2	3.7	8.4	8.3	9.2	9.4	8.7	Taux de croissance
Indonesia [5]								**Indonésie** [5]
GDP at current prices	160 447	195 661	234 772	256 837	285 869	364 599	432 817	PIB aux prix courants
GDP per capita	748	900	1 065	1 151	1 265	1 593	1 869	PIB par habitant
GDP at constant prices	196 997	205 860	215 701	226 553	239 450	252 644	268 602	PIB aux prix constants
Growth rates	3.6	4.5	4.8	5.0	5.7	5.5	6.3	Taux de croissance
Iran (Islamic Rep. of)								**Iran (Rép. islamique d')**
GDP at current prices	110 411	135 525	136 646	162 747	192 020	222 880	289 933	PIB aux prix courants
GDP per capita	1 654	2 011	2 009	2 370	2 766	3 172	4 072	PIB par habitant
GDP at constant prices	136 821	147 556	157 827	164 765	172 195	181 148	191 733	PIB aux prix constants
Growth rates	3.2	7.9	7.0	4.4	4.5	5.2	5.8	Taux de croissance
Iraq								**Iraq**
GDP at current prices	17 682	17 437	10 621	25 491	33 961	54 831	69 709	PIB aux prix courants
GDP per capita	688	663	395	928	1 213	1 923	2 404	PIB par habitant
GDP at constant prices	15 348	14 289	9 559	11 753	12 136	16 947	17 416	PIB aux prix constants
Growth rates	2.3	-6.9	-33.1	23.0	3.3	39.6	2.8	Taux de croissance
Ireland								**Irlande**
GDP at current prices	104 643	122 549	157 345	184 391	200 838	219 165	256 074	PIB aux prix courants
GDP per capita	27 098	31 218	39 388	45 330	48 473	51 920	59 540	PIB par habitant
GDP at constant prices	100 045	106 628	111 380	116 254	123 255	130 324	136 740	PIB aux prix constants
Growth rates	6.1	6.6	4.5	4.4	6.0	5.7	4.9	Taux de croissance
Israel								**Israël**
GDP at current prices	118 907	109 335	115 715	123 618	131 241	142 075	161 989	PIB aux prix courants
GDP per capita	19 143	17 259	17 926	18 804	19 612	20 863	23 383	PIB par habitant
GDP at constant prices	98 949	98 314	100 528	105 751	111 349	117 151	123 387	PIB aux prix constants
Growth rates	-0.4	-0.6	2.3	5.2	5.3	5.2	5.3	Taux de croissance
Italy								**Italie**
GDP at current prices	1 117 348	1 218 977	1 507 113	1 726 595	1 769 696	1 850 867	2 095 141	PIB aux prix courants
GDP per capita	19 313	20 997	25 864	29 527	30 176	31 489	35 585	PIB par habitant
GDP at constant prices	1 350 718	1 355 337	1 355 841	1 372 160	1 373 368	1 399 074	1 419 454	PIB aux prix constants
Growth rates	1.8	0.3	^0.0	1.2	0.1	1.9	1.5	Taux de croissance
Jamaica								**Jamaïque**
GDP at current prices	8 116	8 471	8 190	8 837	9 715	10 372	11 255	PIB aux prix courants
GDP per capita	3 111	3 223	3 094	3 316	3 622	3 844	4 147	PIB par habitant
GDP at constant prices	5 004	5 060	5 174	5 224	5 299	5 429	5 503	PIB aux prix constants
Growth rates	1.5	1.1	2.3	1.0	1.4	2.5	1.4	Taux de croissance
Japan								**Japon**
GDP at current prices	4 095 483	3 918 334	4 229 098	4 605 939	4 552 191	4 375 994	4 379 624	PIB aux prix courants
GDP per capita	32 179	30 736	33 128	36 041	35 593	34 200	34 225	PIB par habitant
GDP at constant prices	3 423 684	3 432 663	3 481 185	3 576 718	3 645 895	3 733 302	3 812 499	PIB aux prix constants
Growth rates	0.2	0.3	1.4	2.7	1.9	2.4	2.1	Taux de croissance
Jordan								**Jordanie**
GDP at current prices	8 976	9 582	10 196	11 411	12 611	14 101	15 724	PIB aux prix courants
GDP per capita	1 825	1 896	1 958	2 125	2 275	2 461	2 654	PIB par habitant
GDP at constant prices	6 707	7 095	7 391	8 024	8 592	9 133	9 663	PIB aux prix constants
Growth rates	5.3	5.8	4.2	8.6	7.1	6.3	5.8	Taux de croissance

18

Gross domestic product and gross domestic product per capita *(continued)*
In millions of US dollars at current and constant 1990 prices; per capita US dollars; real rates of growth
Produit intérieur brut et produit intérieur brut par habitant *(suite)*
En millions de dollars É.-U. aux prix courants et constants de 1990 ; par habitant en dollars É.-U. ; taux de croissance réels

Country or area	2001	2002	2003	2004	2005	2006	2007	Pays ou zone
Kazakhstan								**Kazakhstan**
GDP at current prices	22 153	24 637	30 834	43 152	57 124	81 004	104 143	PIB aux prix courants
GDP per capita	1 486	1 650	2 055	2 856	3 756	5 289	6 753	PIB par habitant
GDP at constant prices	23 384	25 664	28 058	30 748	33 730	37 298	40 541	PIB aux prix constants
Growth rates	13.6	9.8	9.3	9.6	9.7	10.6	8.7	Taux de croissance
Kenya								**Kenya**
GDP at current prices	12 983	13 151	14 986	16 249	19 132	22 779	29 509	PIB aux prix courants
GDP per capita	405	400	444	469	537	623	786	PIB par habitant
GDP at constant prices	13 815	13 894	14 309	15 025	15 885	16 855	18 035	PIB aux prix constants
Growth rates	4.5	0.6	3.0	5.0	5.7	6.1	7.0	Taux de croissance
Kiribati								**Kiribati**
GDP at current prices	45	48	58	64	61	62	72	PIB aux prix courants
GDP per capita	526	553	658	712	666	659	762	PIB par habitant
GDP at constant prices	46	48	48	47	48	45	46	PIB aux prix constants
Growth rates	1.5	5.3	-1.1	-1.7	1.6	-5.2	2.0	Taux de croissance
Korea, Dem. P. R.								**Corée, R. p. dém. de**
GDP at current prices	11 022	10 910	11 051	11 168	13 031	13 764	14 753	PIB aux prix courants
GDP per capita	476	468	471	473	550	578	618	PIB par habitant
GDP at constant prices	11 960	12 105	12 321	12 597	13 077	12 933	13 144	PIB aux prix constants
Growth rates	3.7	1.2	1.8	2.2	3.8	-1.1	1.6	Taux de croissance
Korea, Republic of								**Corée, République de**
GDP at current prices	481 894	546 935	608 146	680 492	791 429	888 023	956 788	PIB aux prix courants
GDP per capita	10 243	11 568	12 806	14 271	16 533	18 481	19 841	PIB par habitant
GDP at constant prices	494 217	528 666	545 039	570 817	594 778	624 477	655 531	PIB aux prix constants
Growth rates	3.8	7.0	3.1	4.7	4.2	5.0	5.0	Taux de croissance
Kosovo								**Kosovo**
GDP at current prices	2 171	2 438	2 827	3 070	2 988	3 104	3 543	PIB aux prix courants
GDP per capita	844	971	1 146	1 261	1 234	1 283	1 464	PIB par habitant
GDP at constant prices	2 797	2 830	2 664	2 639	2 613	2 694	2 788	PIB aux prix constants
Growth rates	25.7	1.2	-5.9	-1.0	-1.0	3.1	3.5	Taux de croissance
Kuwait								**Koweït**
GDP at current prices	34 890	38 136	47 827	59 267	80 781	98 692	109 981	PIB aux prix courants
GDP per capita	14 918	15 634	18 897	22 647	29 919	35 518	38 574	PIB par habitant
GDP at constant prices	29 727	30 624	35 683	39 426	43 353	46 075	48 183	PIB aux prix constants
Growth rates	0.2	3.0	16.5	10.5	10.0	6.3	4.6	Taux de croissance
Kyrgyzstan								**Kirghizistan**
GDP at current prices	1 527	1 606	1 922	2 212	2 460	2 834	3 745	PIB aux prix courants
GDP per capita	305	317	376	429	473	539	704	PIB par habitant
GDP at constant prices	779	779	834	892	891	918	994	PIB aux prix constants
Growth rates	5.3	^0.0	7.0	7.0	-0.2	3.1	8.2	Taux de croissance
Lao People's Dem. Rep.								**Rép. dém. pop. lao**
GDP at current prices	1 753	1 830	2 130	2 512	2 871	3 485	4 163	PIB aux prix courants
GDP per capita	330	339	388	451	507	605	711	PIB par habitant
GDP at constant prices	1 684	1 784	1 887	2 017	2 164	2 344	2 531	PIB aux prix constants
Growth rates	5.7	5.9	5.8	6.9	7.3	8.3	8.0	Taux de croissance
Latvia								**Lettonie**
GDP at current prices	8 313	9 315	11 186	13 762	16 042	19 935	27 166	PIB aux prix courants
GDP per capita	3 520	3 972	4 802	5 944	6 969	8 709	11 930	PIB par habitant
GDP at constant prices	6 177	6 577	7 050	7 662	8 474	9 511	10 491	PIB aux prix constants
Growth rates	8.0	6.5	7.2	8.7	10.6	12.2	10.3	Taux de croissance
Lebanon								**Liban**
GDP at current prices	17 065	18 712	19 802	21 465	21 558	22 759	24 640	PIB aux prix courants
GDP per capita	4 467	4 836	5 055	5 414	5 375	5 612	6 011	PIB par habitant
GDP at constant prices	5 831	5 754	5 927	6 223	6 285	6 285	6 537	PIB aux prix constants
Growth rates	3.6	-1.3	3.0	5.0	1.0	0.0	4.0	Taux de croissance
Lesotho								**Lesotho**
GDP at current prices	752	687	1 039	1 319	1 426	1 495	1 600	PIB aux prix courants
GDP per capita	394	356	533	671	720	749	797	PIB par habitant
GDP at constant prices	889	915	939	978	1 006	1 078	1 131	PIB aux prix constants
Growth rates	1.8	2.9	2.7	4.2	2.9	7.2	4.9	Taux de croissance

18

Gross domestic product and gross domestic product per capita *(continued)*
In millions of US dollars at current and constant 1990 prices; per capita US dollars; real rates of growth

Produit intérieur brut et produit intérieur brut par habitant *(suite)*
En millions de dollars É.-U. aux prix courants et constants de 1990 ; par habitant en dollars É.-U. ; taux de croissance réels

Country or area	2001	2002	2003	2004	2005	2006	2007	Pays ou zone
Liberia								**Libéria**
GDP at current prices	543	559	435	497	548	612	730	PIB aux prix courants
GDP per capita	171	172	132	148	159	171	195	PIB par habitant
GDP at constant prices	495	513	352	361	380	410	448	PIB aux prix constants
Growth rates	2.9	3.7	-31.3	2.6	5.3	7.8	9.4	Taux de croissance
Libyan Arab Jamah.								**Jamah. arabe libyenne**
GDP at current prices	29 880	20 394	24 542	31 791	42 820	50 321	62 060	PIB aux prix courants
GDP per capita	5 477	3 663	4 319	5 482	7 235	8 333	10 074	PIB par habitant
GDP at constant prices	37 503	37 923	40 601	42 774	45 149	47 677	51 444	PIB aux prix constants
Growth rates	6.1	1.1	7.1	5.4	5.6	5.6	7.9	Taux de croissance
Lithuania								**Lituanie**
GDP at current prices	12 146	14 134	18 558	22 508	25 732	29 760	38 332	PIB aux prix courants
GDP per capita	3 487	4 076	5 373	6 543	7 513	8 732	11 308	PIB par habitant
GDP at constant prices	7 707	8 240	9 090	9 755	10 530	11 336	12 332	PIB aux prix constants
Growth rates	6.7	6.9	10.3	7.3	7.9	7.7	8.8	Taux de croissance
Luxembourg								**Luxembourg**
GDP at current prices	20 199	22 580	29 035	34 070	37 348	42 467	50 489	PIB aux prix courants
GDP per capita	45 780	50 733	64 712	75 307	81 793	92 049	108 217	PIB par habitant
GDP at constant prices	21 231	22 102	22 566	23 666	24 855	26 375	27 756	PIB aux prix constants
Growth rates	2.5	4.1	2.1	4.9	5.0	6.1	5.2	Taux de croissance
Madagascar								**Madagascar**
GDP at current prices	4 530	4 397	5 474	4 364	5 039	5 515	7 417	PIB aux prix courants
GDP per capita	272	256	310	241	270	288	377	PIB par habitant
GDP at constant prices	3 876	3 386	3 717	3 913	4 093	4 298	4 570	PIB aux prix constants
Growth rates	6.0	-12.7	9.8	5.3	4.6	5.0	6.3	Taux de croissance
Malawi								**Malawi**
GDP at current prices	2 365	2 665	2 425	2 625	2 866	3 183	3 574	PIB aux prix courants
GDP per capita	198	217	193	204	217	235	257	PIB par habitant
GDP at constant prices	2 992	3 078	3 265	3 497	3 598	3 876	4 163	PIB aux prix constants
Growth rates	-5.0	2.9	6.1	7.1	2.9	7.7	7.4	Taux de croissance
Malaysia								**Malaisie**
GDP at current prices	92 784	100 846	110 202	124 749	137 954	156 409	186 720	PIB aux prix courants
GDP per capita	3 903	4 157	4 457	4 952	5 378	5 990	7 027	PIB par habitant
GDP at constant prices	91 300	96 221	101 791	108 696	114 492	121 103	128 790	PIB aux prix constants
Growth rates	0.5	5.4	5.8	6.8	5.3	5.8	6.4	Taux de croissance
Maldives								**Maldives**
GDP at current prices	625	641	692	776	751	907	1 055	PIB aux prix courants
GDP per capita	2 253	2 274	2 420	2 672	2 542	3 020	3 454	PIB par habitant
GDP at constant prices	460	488	533	593	563	696	750	PIB aux prix constants
Growth rates	3.3	6.1	9.2	11.3	-5.0	23.5	7.7	Taux de croissance
Mali								**Mali**
GDP at current prices	3 018	3 189	4 222	4 982	5 486	6 123	6 840	PIB aux prix courants
GDP per capita	293	301	386	442	473	512	554	PIB par habitant
GDP at constant prices	4 186	4 367	4 699	4 805	5 100	5 368	5 501	PIB aux prix constants
Growth rates	11.9	4.3	7.6	2.3	6.1	5.3	2.5	Taux de croissance
Malta								**Malte**
GDP at current prices	3 851	4 233	4 994	5 574	5 913	6 373	7 411	PIB aux prix courants
GDP per capita	9 836	10 733	12 569	13 930	14 686	15 744	18 227	PIB par habitant
GDP at constant prices	4 133	4 242	4 229	4 238	4 377	4 525	4 702	PIB aux prix constants
Growth rates	-1.6	2.6	-0.3	0.2	3.3	3.4	3.9	Taux de croissance
Marshall Islands								**Iles Marshall**
GDP at current prices	110	119	124	131	138	144	149	PIB aux prix courants
GDP per capita	2 095	2 229	2 272	2 353	2 426	2 483	2 517	PIB par habitant
GDP at constant prices	59	62	64	67	69	69	71	PIB aux prix constants
Growth rates	2.7	3.8	3.5	5.6	1.7	1.3	2.0	Taux de croissance
Mauritania								**Mauritanie**
GDP at current prices	1 115	1 145	1 281	1 537	1 848	2 661	2 732	PIB aux prix courants
GDP per capita	422	421	457	533	624	874	874	PIB par habitant
GDP at constant prices	1 452	1 467	1 550	1 630	1 738	1 937	1 954	PIB aux prix constants
Growth rates	2.9	1.1	5.6	5.2	6.7	11.5	0.9	Taux de croissance

18

Gross domestic product and gross domestic product per capita *(continued)*
In millions of US dollars at current and constant 1990 prices; per capita US dollars; real rates of growth

Produit intérieur brut et produit intérieur brut par habitant *(suite)*
En millions de dollars É.-U. aux prix courants et constants de 1990 ; par habitant en dollars É.-U. ; taux de croissance réels

Country or area	2001	2002	2003	2004	2005	2006	2007	Pays ou zone
Mauritius								**Maurice**
GDP at current prices	4 537	4 755	5 641	6 386	6 284	6 492	7 376	PIB aux prix courants
GDP per capita	3 789	3 934	4 625	5 189	5 063	5 187	5 846	PIB par habitant
GDP at constant prices	4 462	4 535	4 732	4 994	5 063	5 277	5 553	PIB aux prix constants
Growth rates	2.9	1.6	4.4	5.5	1.4	4.2	5.2	Taux de croissance
Mexico								**Mexique**
GDP at current prices	621 866	648 629	638 797	683 069	767 222	839 500	893 365	PIB aux prix courants
GDP per capita	6 167	6 376	6 231	6 610	7 358	7 969	8 386	PIB par habitant
GDP at constant prices	369 501	372 354	377 530	393 240	404 259	423 546	437 156	PIB aux prix constants
Growth rates	^0.0	0.8	1.4	4.2	2.8	4.8	3.2	Taux de croissance
Micronesia (Fed. States of)								**Micronésie (Etats féd. de)**
GDP at current prices	221	222	222	224	237	245	253	PIB aux prix courants
GDP per capita	2 054	2 058	2 042	2 051	2 153	2 212	2 276	PIB par habitant
GDP at constant prices	166	167	168	166	169	168	168	PIB aux prix constants
Growth rates	0.5	0.9	0.1	-0.7	1.5	-0.7	0.1	Taux de croissance
Monaco								**Monaco**
GDP at current prices	702	761	937	1 070	1 106	1 160	1 311	PIB aux prix courants
GDP per capita	21 887	23 662	29 030	33 028	34 018	35 590	40 090	PIB par habitant
GDP at constant prices	808	814	820	837	849	864	878	PIB aux prix constants
Growth rates	1.6	0.7	0.7	2.1	1.4	1.7	1.7	Taux de croissance
Mongolia								**Mongolie**
GDP at current prices	1 169	1 273	1 448	1 816	2 306	3 188	3 892	PIB aux prix courants
GDP per capita	470	507	572	710	894	1 224	1 481	PIB par habitant
GDP at constant prices	1 491	1 562	1 671	1 849	1 983	2 153	2 366	PIB aux prix constants
Growth rates	3.0	4.7	7.0	10.6	7.3	8.6	9.9	Taux de croissance
Montenegro								**Monténégro**
GDP at current prices	1 159	1 280	1 704	2 073	2 257	2 696	3 118	PIB aux prix courants
GDP per capita	1 745	1 966	2 683	3 346	3 713	4 486	5 214	PIB par habitant
GDP at constant prices	1 466	1 494	1 532	1 599	1 666	1 809	1 936	PIB aux prix constants
Growth rates	1.1	1.9	2.5	4.4	4.2	8.6	7.0	Taux de croissance
Montserrat								**Montserrat**
GDP at current prices	35	38	38	41	43	45	48	PIB aux prix courants
GDP per capita	7 486	8 109	7 590	7 656	7 656	7 839	8 149	PIB par habitant
GDP at constant prices	24	26	25	27	27	25	26	PIB aux prix constants
Growth rates	-6.9	6.6	-3.1	6.8	0.4	-4.9	1.1	Taux de croissance
Morocco[6]								**Maroc**[6]
GDP at current prices	37 766	40 474	49 819	56 392	58 956	65 405	73 429	PIB aux prix courants
GDP per capita	1 280	1 356	1 649	1 845	1 906	2 089	2 316	PIB par habitant
GDP at constant prices	38 294	39 515	41 697	43 467	44 213	47 750	48 801	PIB aux prix constants
Growth rates	6.3	3.2	5.5	4.2	1.7	8.0	2.2	Taux de croissance
Mozambique								**Mozambique**
GDP at current prices	4 075	4 201	4 666	5 698	6 579	6 833	7 756	PIB aux prix courants
GDP per capita	218	220	238	284	320	326	362	PIB par habitant
GDP at constant prices	5 616	6 134	6 532	7 047	7 638	8 247	8 824	PIB aux prix constants
Growth rates	12.3	9.2	6.5	7.9	8.4	8.0	7.0	Taux de croissance
Myanmar								**Myanmar**
GDP at current prices	7 634	10 369	10 000	10 254	11 931	13 739	18 510	PIB aux prix courants
GDP per capita	165	222	212	216	249	284	379	PIB par habitant
GDP at constant prices	11 406	12 778	14 547	16 531	18 779	21 164	22 320	PIB aux prix constants
Growth rates	11.3	12.0	13.8	13.6	13.6	12.7	5.5	Taux de croissance
Namibia								**Namibie**
GDP at current prices	3 216	3 122	4 474	5 650	6 245	6 937	7 410	PIB aux prix courants
GDP per capita	1 681	1 607	2 273	2 834	3 092	3 389	3 573	PIB par habitant
GDP at constant prices	3 625	3 867	4 001	4 267	4 472	4 654	4 859	PIB aux prix constants
Growth rates	2.4	6.7	3.5	6.6	4.8	4.1	4.4	Taux de croissance
Nauru								**Nauru**
GDP at current prices	18	20	24	28	26	28	23	PIB aux prix courants
GDP per capita	1 744	1 974	2 408	2 795	2 569	2 742	2 217	PIB par habitant
GDP at constant prices	17	17	17	17	17	17	17	PIB aux prix constants
Growth rates	0.6	0.8	0.0	0.0	0.0	0.0	0.2	Taux de croissance

18

Gross domestic product and gross domestic product per capita *(continued)*

In millions of US dollars at current and constant 1990 prices; per capita US dollars; real rates of growth

Produit intérieur brut et produit intérieur brut par habitant *(suite)*

En millions de dollars É.-U. aux prix courants et constants de 1990 ; par habitant en dollars É.-U. ; taux de croissance réels

Country or area	2001	2002	2003	2004	2005	2006	2007	Pays ou zone
Nepal								**Népal**
GDP at current prices	6 130	6 321	7 049	8 000	9 058	9 889	11 815	PIB aux prix courants
GDP per capita	246	248	271	301	334	358	419	PIB par habitant
GDP at constant prices	6 684	6 948	7 273	7 500	7 710	7 903	8 100	PIB aux prix constants
Growth rates	0.1	4.0	4.7	3.1	2.8	2.5	2.5	Taux de croissance
Netherlands								**Pays-Bas**
GDP at current prices	400 651	437 827	538 292	609 890	632 945	670 301	766 251	PIB aux prix courants
GDP per capita	25 019	27 189	33 253	37 500	38 765	40 924	46 669	PIB par habitant
GDP at constant prices	410 466	410 779	412 158	421 376	427 740	440 594	455 831	PIB aux prix constants
Growth rates	1.9	0.1	0.3	2.2	1.5	3.0	3.5	Taux de croissance
Netherlands Antilles								**Antilles néerlandaises**
GDP at current prices	2 910	2 935	3 031	3 115	3 204	3 352	3 463	PIB aux prix courants
GDP per capita	16 133	16 213	16 619	16 909	17 188	17 750	18 078	PIB par habitant
GDP at constant prices	2 249	2 256	2 288	2 313	2 334	2 355	2 377	PIB aux prix constants
Growth rates	1.3	0.3	1.4	1.1	0.9	0.9	1.0	Taux de croissance
New Caledonia								**Nouvelle-Calédonie**
GDP at current prices	3 295	3 722	4 904	5 859	6 248	6 802	7 994	PIB aux prix courants
GDP per capita	15 042	16 698	21 633	25 426	26 678	28 584	33 072	PIB par habitant
GDP at constant prices	2 991	3 005	3 009	3 033	3 057	3 073	3 090	PIB aux prix constants
Growth rates	0.5	0.5	0.1	0.8	0.8	0.5	0.5	Taux de croissance
New Zealand								**Nouvelle-Zélande**
GDP at current prices	52 394	60 585	81 153	98 863	110 436	107 246	130 449	PIB aux prix courants
GDP per capita	13 439	15 345	20 289	24 409	26 955	25 907	31 219	PIB par habitant
GDP at constant prices	60 559	63 620	65 854	68 510	70 350	71 453	73 591	PIB aux prix constants
Growth rates	3.8	5.1	3.5	4.0	2.7	1.6	3.0	Taux de croissance
Nicaragua								**Nicaragua**
GDP at current prices	4 125	4 026	4 102	4 465	4 855	5 301	5 675	PIB aux prix courants
GDP per capita	796	766	770	828	889	958	1 013	PIB par habitant
GDP at constant prices	3 950	3 980	4 080	4 297	4 484	4 649	4 843	PIB aux prix constants
Growth rates	3.0	0.8	2.5	5.3	4.4	3.7	4.2	Taux de croissance
Niger								**Niger**
GDP at current prices	1 814	2 065	2 640	2 897	3 327	3 556	4 107	PIB aux prix courants
GDP per capita	157	173	213	226	251	259	289	PIB par habitant
GDP at constant prices	3 219	3 391	3 651	3 621	3 889	4 088	4 216	PIB aux prix constants
Growth rates	7.4	5.4	7.7	-0.8	7.4	5.1	3.1	Taux de croissance
Nigeria								**Nigéria**
GDP at current prices	44 138	59 117	67 656	87 845	112 248	145 430	173 184	PIB aux prix courants
GDP per capita	345	450	502	637	794	1 005	1 169	PIB par habitant
GDP at constant prices	45 562	55 211	60 917	67 365	70 998	75 408	79 178	PIB aux prix constants
Growth rates	8.2	21.2	10.3	10.6	5.4	6.2	5.0	Taux de croissance
Norway								**Norvège**
GDP at current prices	170 924	191 928	225 110	258 579	302 013	336 140	387 427	PIB aux prix courants
GDP per capita	37 835	42 206	49 173	56 109	65 105	71 999	82 465	PIB par habitant
GDP at constant prices	172 601	175 193	176 969	183 807	188 842	192 908	198 514	PIB aux prix constants
Growth rates	2.0	1.5	1.0	3.9	2.7	2.2	2.9	Taux de croissance
Occupied Palestinian Terr.								**Terr. palestinien occupé**
GDP at current prices	3 816	3 484	3 921	4 411	4 844	4 904	5 458	PIB aux prix courants
GDP per capita	1 168	1 029	1 117	1 213	1 288	1 261	1 359	PIB par habitant
GDP at constant prices	3 902	3 756	4 075	4 155	4 405	4 018	4 018	PIB aux prix constants
Growth rates	-6.4	-3.8	8.5	2.0	6.0	-8.8	0.0	Taux de croissance
Oman								**Oman**
GDP at current prices	19 949	20 325	21 784	24 772	30 923	35 729	40 343	PIB aux prix courants
GDP per capita	8 221	8 316	8 858	9 994	12 334	14 031	15 546	PIB par habitant
GDP at constant prices	19 719	20 226	20 632	21 737	23 039	24 706	26 173	PIB aux prix constants
Growth rates	7.5	2.6	2.0	5.4	6.0	7.2	5.9	Taux de croissance
Pakistan								**Pakistan**
GDP at current prices	71 901	81 637	97 669	111 569	127 597	144 462	163 290	PIB aux prix courants
GDP per capita	488	544	640	718	807	898	996	PIB par habitant
GDP at constant prices	83 976	88 046	94 533	101 782	108 825	115 770	122 716	PIB aux prix constants
Growth rates	3.2	4.9	7.4	7.7	6.9	6.4	6.0	Taux de croissance

18 Gross domestic product and gross domestic product per capita *(continued)*
In millions of US dollars at current and constant 1990 prices; per capita US dollars; real rates of growth
Produit intérieur brut et produit intérieur brut par habitant *(suite)*
En millions de dollars É.-U. aux prix courants et constants de 1990 ; par habitant en dollars É.-U. ; taux de croissance réels

Country or area	2001	2002	2003	2004	2005	2006	2007	Pays ou zone
Palau								**Palaos**
GDP at current prices	125	119	123	134	145	158	170	PIB aux prix courants
GDP per capita	6 375	6 046	6 165	6 670	7 188	7 797	8 376	PIB par habitant
GDP at constant prices	80	77	76	80	84	89	94	PIB aux prix constants
Growth rates	1.3	-3.5	-1.3	4.9	5.5	5.7	5.5	Taux de croissance
Panama								**Panama**
GDP at current prices	11 807	12 272	12 933	14 179	15 465	17 134	19 740	PIB aux prix courants
GDP per capita	3 927	4 007	4 146	4 465	4 786	5 212	5 904	PIB par habitant
GDP at constant prices	10 014	10 237	10 580	11 470	12 295	13 359	14 856	PIB aux prix constants
Growth rates	0.6	2.2	3.4	8.4	7.2	8.7	11.2	Taux de croissance
Papua New Guinea								**Papouasie-Nvl-Guinée**
GDP at current prices	3 068	2 993	3 527	3 926	4 589	5 302	6 032	PIB aux prix courants
GDP per capita	556	529	608	662	756	855	953	PIB par habitant
GDP at constant prices	5 143	5 135	5 246	5 388	5 647	5 793	6 153	PIB aux prix constants
Growth rates	-0.1	-0.2	2.2	2.7	4.8	2.6	6.2	Taux de croissance
Paraguay								**Paraguay**
GDP at current prices	6 446	5 092	5 552	6 950	7 473	9 275	12 004	PIB aux prix courants
GDP per capita	1 181	914	977	1 200	1 266	1 542	1 959	PIB par habitant
GDP at constant prices	5 554	5 551	5 765	6 002	6 175	6 442	6 856	PIB aux prix constants
Growth rates	2.1	-0.1	3.9	4.1	2.9	4.3	6.4	Taux de croissance
Peru								**Pérou**
GDP at current prices	53 955	56 775	61 356	69 734	79 466	92 409	108 259	PIB aux prix courants
GDP per capita	2 076	2 157	2 303	2 587	2 914	3 350	3 880	PIB par habitant
GDP at constant prices	43 587	45 775	47 621	50 055	53 431	57 469	62 633	PIB aux prix constants
Growth rates	0.2	5.0	4.0	5.1	6.7	7.6	9.0	Taux de croissance
Philippines								**Philippines**
GDP at current prices	71 216	76 814	79 634	86 930	98 718	117 562	144 129	PIB aux prix courants
GDP per capita	915	966	981	1 049	1 167	1 363	1 639	PIB par habitant
GDP at constant prices	60 873	63 581	66 716	70 972	74 427	78 482	84 235	PIB aux prix constants
Growth rates	1.8	4.5	4.9	6.4	4.9	5.5	7.3	Taux de croissance
Poland								**Pologne**
GDP at current prices	190 421	198 179	216 801	252 769	303 912	340 896	419 205	PIB aux prix courants
GDP per capita	4 961	5 169	5 662	6 609	7 957	8 938	11 008	PIB par habitant
GDP at constant prices	94 680	96 047	99 761	105 093	108 894	115 569	123 102	PIB aux prix constants
Growth rates	1.2	1.4	3.9	5.3	3.6	6.1	6.5	Taux de croissance
Portugal								**Portugal**
GDP at current prices	115 711	127 461	156 407	178 960	185 309	194 655	222 982	PIB aux prix courants
GDP per capita	11 251	12 319	15 025	17 090	17 601	18 401	20 990	PIB par habitant
GDP at constant prices	102 081	102 856	102 027	103 574	104 335	105 584	107 924	PIB aux prix constants
Growth rates	2.0	0.8	-0.8	1.5	0.7	1.2	2.2	Taux de croissance
Puerto Rico								**Porto Rico**
GDP at current prices	71 624	74 827	79 209	82 650	86 464	89 700	93 483	PIB aux prix courants
GDP per capita	18 565	19 280	20 294	21 057	21 907	22 602	23 426	PIB par habitant
GDP at constant prices	50 887	50 910	52 456	52 789	53 114	52 158	52 622	PIB aux prix constants
Growth rates	0.9	0.1	3.0	0.6	0.6	-1.8	0.9	Taux de croissance
Qatar								**Qatar**
GDP at current prices	17 538	19 364	23 534	31 734	42 463	56 770	63 870	PIB aux prix courants
GDP per capita	27 014	28 185	32 378	41 521	53 333	69 121	75 978	PIB par habitant
GDP at constant prices	14 960	16 027	16 586	20 041	21 260	23 459	26 797	PIB aux prix constants
Growth rates	3.3	7.1	3.5	20.8	6.1	10.3	14.2	Taux de croissance
Republic of Moldova								**République de Moldova**
GDP at current prices	1 481	1 662	1 981	2 598	2 988	3 408	4 395	PIB aux prix courants
GDP per capita	362	412	498	662	771	889	1 158	PIB par habitant
GDP at constant prices	1 465	1 579	1 684	1 808	1 944	2 037	2 098	PIB aux prix constants
Growth rates	6.1	7.8	6.6	7.4	7.5	4.8	3.0	Taux de croissance
Romania								**Roumanie**
GDP at current prices	40 181	45 825	59 507	75 519	98 905	122 655	161 279	PIB aux prix courants
GDP per capita	1 824	2 090	2 726	3 476	4 573	5 696	7 523	PIB par habitant
GDP at constant prices	34 327	36 085	37 970	41 181	42 902	46 272	49 033	PIB aux prix constants
Growth rates	5.8	5.1	5.2	8.5	4.2	7.9	6.0	Taux de croissance

18

Gross domestic product and gross domestic product per capita *(continued)*
In millions of US dollars at current and constant 1990 prices; per capita US dollars; real rates of growth
Produit intérieur brut et produit intérieur brut par habitant *(suite)*
En millions de dollars É.-U. aux prix courants et constants de 1990 ; par habitant en dollars É.-U. ; taux de croissance réels

Country or area	2001	2002	2003	2004	2005	2006	2007	Pays ou zone
Russian Federation								**Fédération de Russie**
GDP at current prices	306 618	345 488	431 488	591 666	764 382	984 927	1 289 582	PIB aux prix courants
GDP per capita	2 088	2 364	2 967	4 089	5 310	6 877	9 050	PIB par habitant
GDP at constant prices	402 412	421 501	452 475	484 798	515 825	550 385	594 967	PIB aux prix constants
Growth rates	5.1	4.7	7.4	7.1	6.4	6.7	8.1	Taux de croissance
Rwanda								**Rwanda**
GDP at current prices	1 653	1 672	1 777	1 971	2 387	2 957	3 441	PIB aux prix courants
GDP per capita	194	191	199	218	259	312	354	PIB par habitant
GDP at constant prices	2 822	3 086	3 094	3 257	3 490	3 680	3 902	PIB aux prix constants
Growth rates	6.7	9.3	0.3	5.3	7.2	5.5	6.0	Taux de croissance
Saint Kitts and Nevis								**Saint-Kitts-et-Nevis**
GDP at current prices	342	351	362	399	438	495	527	PIB aux prix courants
GDP per capita	7 338	7 424	7 560	8 230	8 912	9 946	10 447	PIB par habitant
GDP at constant prices	244	246	247	266	279	297	307	PIB aux prix constants
Growth rates	2.0	1.1	0.5	7.6	4.8	6.4	3.3	Taux de croissance
Saint Lucia								**Sainte-Lucie**
GDP at current prices	685	703	746	800	878	925	958	PIB aux prix courants
GDP per capita	4 444	4 512	4 734	5 015	5 442	5 674	5 810	PIB par habitant
GDP at constant prices	506	521	543	572	605	627	648	PIB aux prix constants
Growth rates	-5.4	2.9	4.3	5.3	5.7	3.8	3.2	Taux de croissance
Saint Vincent-Grenadines								**Saint Vincent-Grenadines**
GDP at current prices	346	365	382	414	445	501	561	PIB aux prix courants
GDP per capita	2 964	3 116	3 243	3 495	3 736	4 186	4 660	PIB par habitant
GDP at constant prices	272	282	291	309	321	348	372	PIB aux prix constants
Growth rates	1.0	3.7	3.3	6.1	3.7	8.7	6.7	Taux de croissance
Samoa								**Samoa**
GDP at current prices	241	262	319	377	425	450	514	PIB aux prix courants
GDP per capita	1 345	1 455	1 761	2 068	2 311	2 425	2 750	PIB par habitant
GDP at constant prices	156	159	164	169	178	183	191	PIB aux prix constants
Growth rates	8.1	1.8	3.1	3.4	5.2	2.6	4.7	Taux de croissance
San Marino								**Saint-Marin**
GDP at current prices	815	880	1 123	1 317	1 375	1 469	1 703	PIB aux prix courants
GDP per capita	29 634	31 204	38 796	44 443	45 522	47 952	55 055	PIB par habitant
GDP at constant prices	998	1 001	1 040	1 088	1 113	1 156	1 208	PIB aux prix constants
Growth rates	5.6	0.3	3.9	4.6	2.3	3.9	4.5	Taux de croissance
Sao Tome and Principe								**Sao Tomé-et-Principe**
GDP at current prices	76	92	99	107	114	122	144	PIB aux prix courants
GDP per capita	536	633	671	712	750	788	912	PIB par habitant
GDP at constant prices	144	160	169	180	191	203	216	PIB aux prix constants
Growth rates	3.1	11.6	5.4	6.6	5.7	6.7	6.0	Taux de croissance
Saudi Arabia								**Arabie saoudite**
GDP at current prices	183 012	188 551	214 573	250 339	315 583	352 577	377 318	PIB aux prix courants
GDP per capita	8 569	8 603	9 545	10 862	13 365	14 584	15 255	PIB par habitant
GDP at constant prices	153 314	153 510	165 268	173 973	183 616	189 638	196 287	PIB aux prix constants
Growth rates	0.6	0.1	7.7	5.3	5.5	3.3	3.5	Taux de croissance
Senegal								**Sénégal**
GDP at current prices	4 878	5 334	6 860	8 031	8 687	9 268	11 244	PIB aux prix courants
GDP per capita	460	490	614	700	738	768	908	PIB par habitant
GDP at constant prices	8 776	8 834	9 423	9 977	10 538	10 780	11 324	PIB aux prix constants
Growth rates	4.6	0.7	6.7	5.9	5.6	2.3	5.1	Taux de croissance
Serbia [7]								**Serbie** [7]
GDP at current prices	11 715	15 841	20 345	24 517	26 193	30 412	40 034	PIB aux prix courants
GDP per capita	1 561	2 112	2 720	3 285	3 520	4 092	5 383	PIB par habitant
GDP at constant prices	15 786	16 453	16 864	18 284	19 420	20 527	22 065	PIB aux prix constants
Growth rates	4.8	4.2	2.5	8.4	6.2	5.7	7.5	Taux de croissance
Seychelles								**Seychelles**
GDP at current prices	618	699	706	700	723	775	710	PIB aux prix courants
GDP per capita	7 518	8 407	8 399	8 249	8 449	8 996	8 203	PIB par habitant
GDP at constant prices	552	559	526	511	517	544	573	PIB aux prix constants
Growth rates	-2.2	1.3	-5.9	-2.8	1.2	5.3	5.3	Taux de croissance

Gross domestic product and gross domestic product per capita *(continued)*
In millions of US dollars at current and constant 1990 prices; per capita US dollars; real rates of growth
Produit intérieur brut et produit intérieur brut par habitant *(suite)*
En millions de dollars É.-U. aux prix courants et constants de 1990 ; par habitant en dollars É.-U. ; taux de croissance réels

Country or area	2001	2002	2003	2004	2005	2006	2007	Pays ou zone
Sierra Leone								**Sierra Leone**
GDP at current prices	1 167	1 317	1 432	1 426	1 496	1 655	1 935	PIB aux prix courants
GDP per capita	248	267	277	265	268	288	330	PIB par habitant
GDP at constant prices	505	600	665	729	783	843	898	PIB aux prix constants
Growth rates	18.2	18.8	10.9	9.6	7.5	7.7	6.5	Taux de croissance
Singapore								**Singapour**
GDP at current prices	85 615	88 266	93 152	109 162	119 788	136 566	161 349	PIB aux prix courants
GDP per capita	20 896	21 198	22 069	25 540	27 681	31 166	36 370	PIB par habitant
GDP at constant prices	75 556	78 711	81 469	88 795	95 275	103 059	111 011	PIB aux prix constants
Growth rates	-2.4	4.2	3.5	9.0	7.3	8.2	7.7	Taux de croissance
Slovakia								**Slovaquie**
GDP at current prices	21 106	24 522	32 977	42 015	47 428	55 098	73 852	PIB aux prix courants
GDP per capita	3 917	4 552	6 122	7 800	8 804	10 226	13 702	PIB par habitant
GDP at constant prices	18 530	19 293	20 095	21 184	22 463	24 319	26 434	PIB aux prix constants
Growth rates	3.2	4.1	4.2	5.4	6.0	8.3	8.7	Taux de croissance
Slovenia								**Slovénie**
GDP at current prices	20 135	22 701	28 597	33 231	35 122	38 197	45 908	PIB aux prix courants
GDP per capita	10 132	11 403	14 340	16 639	17 566	19 090	22 936	PIB par habitant
GDP at constant prices	22 080	22 887	23 531	24 577	25 596	27 060	28 701	PIB aux prix constants
Growth rates	3.1	3.7	2.8	4.4	4.2	5.7	6.1	Taux de croissance
Solomon Islands								**Iles Salomon**
GDP at current prices	335	274	289	334	374	424	485	PIB aux prix courants
GDP per capita	784	625	642	725	792	877	978	PIB par habitant
GDP at constant prices	212	207	220	238	249	264	281	PIB aux prix constants
Growth rates	-8.2	-2.7	6.5	8.0	5.0	6.0	6.3	Taux de croissance
Somalia								**Somalie**
GDP at current prices	1 974	2 056	2 100	2 213	2 316	2 532	2 532	PIB aux prix courants
GDP per capita	271	274	272	278	283	300	291	PIB par habitant
GDP at constant prices	786	813	831	854	874	897	921	PIB aux prix constants
Growth rates	3.5	3.5	2.1	2.8	2.4	2.6	2.7	Taux de croissance
South Africa								**Afrique du Sud**
GDP at current prices	118 479	110 874	166 654	216 012	242 332	257 114	283 008	PIB aux prix courants
GDP per capita	2 575	2 380	3 539	4 544	5 055	5 325	5 826	PIB par habitant
GDP at constant prices	137 828	142 883	147 341	154 509	162 235	170 976	179 765	PIB aux prix constants
Growth rates	2.7	3.7	3.1	4.9	5.0	5.4	5.1	Taux de croissance
Spain								**Espagne**
GDP at current prices	609 102	686 278	883 633	1 044 299	1 129 744	1 230 591	1 436 893	PIB aux prix courants
GDP per capita	14 950	16 581	20 987	24 402	26 032	28 040	32 451	PIB par habitant
GDP at constant prices	711 533	730 775	753 402	778 015	806 158	837 277	869 304	PIB aux prix constants
Growth rates	3.7	2.7	3.1	3.3	3.6	3.9	3.8	Taux de croissance
Sri Lanka								**Sri Lanka**
GDP at current prices	16 046	17 091	18 848	20 623	24 272	28 140	32 347	PIB aux prix courants
GDP per capita	853	905	994	1 083	1 269	1 465	1 676	PIB par habitant
GDP at constant prices	13 497	14 035	14 859	15 668	16 647	17 936	19 163	PIB aux prix constants
Growth rates	-1.5	4.0	5.9	5.5	6.2	7.8	6.8	Taux de croissance
Sudan								**Soudan**
GDP at current prices	15 716	18 134	22 197	26 637	33 153	43 888	55 648	PIB aux prix courants
GDP per capita	461	522	626	737	898	1 164	1 443	PIB par habitant
GDP at constant prices	34 194	36 478	38 706	45 608	49 564	54 227	59 931	PIB aux prix constants
Growth rates	6.4	6.7	6.1	17.8	8.7	9.4	10.5	Taux de croissance
Suriname [8]								**Suriname** [8]
GDP at current prices	665	937	1 094	1 283	1 543	1 820	2 044	PIB aux prix courants
GDP per capita	1 510	2 113	2 449	2 853	3 410	3 998	4 463	PIB par habitant
GDP at constant prices	574	589	630	677	716	759	801	PIB aux prix constants
Growth rates	5.9	2.6	6.9	7.5	5.8	5.9	5.5	Taux de croissance
Swaziland								**Swaziland**
GDP at current prices	1 260	1 192	1 904	2 413	2 557	2 724	2 876	PIB aux prix courants
GDP per capita	1 172	1 094	1 727	2 165	2 274	2 403	2 520	PIB par habitant
GDP at constant prices	1 205	1 238	1 268	1 302	1 332	1 360	1 392	PIB aux prix constants
Growth rates	1.7	2.8	2.4	2.7	2.3	2.1	2.4	Taux de croissance

Gross domestic product and gross domestic product per capita *(continued)*
In millions of US dollars at current and constant 1990 prices; per capita US dollars; real rates of growth
Produit intérieur brut et produit intérieur brut par habitant *(suite)*
En millions de dollars É.-U. aux prix courants et constants de 1990 ; par habitant en dollars É.-U. ; taux de croissance réels

Country or area	2001	2002	2003	2004	2005	2006	2007	Pays ou zone
Sweden								**Suède**
GDP at current prices	225 205	248 612	311 038	357 192	366 009	393 000	454 792	PIB aux prix courants
GDP per capita	25 334	27 871	34 724	39 698	40 496	43 291	49 873	PIB par habitant
GDP at constant prices	301 752	309 029	314 939	327 937	338 753	352 604	361 697	PIB aux prix constants
Growth rates	1.1	2.4	1.9	4.1	3.3	4.1	2.6	Taux de croissance
Switzerland								**Suisse**
GDP at current prices	254 987	278 619	325 052	362 992	372 375	387 750	423 434	PIB aux prix courants
GDP per capita	34 969	38 043	44 177	49 106	50 156	52 014	56 579	PIB par habitant
GDP at constant prices	267 921	269 108	268 576	275 378	282 044	291 181	300 197	PIB aux prix constants
Growth rates	1.2	0.4	-0.2	2.5	2.4	3.2	3.1	Taux de croissance
Syrian Arab Republic								**Rép. arabe syrienne**
GDP at current prices	21 174	21 659	20 724	24 473	28 102	32 770	37 525	PIB aux prix courants
GDP per capita	1 249	1 244	1 158	1 331	1 487	1 689	1 883	PIB par habitant
GDP at constant prices	20 702	21 926	22 170	23 659	24 724	25 985	26 994	PIB aux prix constants
Growth rates	5.1	5.9	1.1	6.7	4.5	5.1	3.9	Taux de croissance
Tajikistan								**Tadjikistan**
GDP at current prices	1 081	1 221	1 555	2 076	2 312	2 830	3 738	PIB aux prix courants
GDP per capita	173	193	243	321	353	426	555	PIB par habitant
GDP at constant prices	1 196	1 325	1 472	1 624	1 733	1 828	1 970	PIB aux prix constants
Growth rates	9.6	10.8	11.1	10.3	6.7	5.5	7.8	Taux de croissance
Thailand								**Thaïlande**
GDP at current prices	115 536	126 877	142 640	161 340	176 420	206 703	245 351	PIB aux prix courants
GDP per capita	1 888	2 057	2 296	2 579	2 800	3 258	3 841	PIB par habitant
GDP at constant prices	134 892	142 065	152 209	161 865	169 191	177 832	186 284	PIB aux prix constants
Growth rates	2.2	5.3	7.1	6.3	4.5	5.1	4.8	Taux de croissance
TFYR of Macedonia								**Ex-R.Y. Macédoine**
GDP at current prices	3 437	3 791	4 630	5 369	5 816	6 371	7 549	PIB aux prix courants
GDP per capita	1 705	1 875	2 285	2 644	2 860	3 129	3 703	PIB par habitant
GDP at constant prices	3 974	4 008	4 121	4 290	4 466	4 642	4 874	PIB aux prix constants
Growth rates	-4.5	0.9	2.8	4.1	4.1	4.0	5.0	Taux de croissance
Timor-Leste								**Timor-Leste**
GDP at current prices	368	343	336	339	350	353	453	PIB aux prix courants
GDP per capita	434	383	352	334	328	317	393	PIB par habitant
GDP at constant prices	229	213	200	201	205	198	231	PIB aux prix constants
Growth rates	16.5	-6.7	-6.2	0.4	2.3	-3.4	16.2	Taux de croissance
Togo								**Togo**
GDP at current prices	1 332	1 472	1 674	1 935	2 082	2 197	2 541	PIB aux prix courants
GDP per capita	239	256	283	319	334	343	386	PIB par habitant
GDP at constant prices	1 903	1 899	2 008	2 055	2 080	2 122	2 183	PIB aux prix constants
Growth rates	-2.8	-0.3	5.8	2.3	1.2	2.0	2.9	Taux de croissance
Tonga								**Tonga**
GDP at current prices	136	149	171	197	218	236	248	PIB aux prix courants
GDP per capita	1 383	1 510	1 731	1 995	2 190	2 365	2 470	PIB par habitant
GDP at constant prices	182	184	190	192	188	194	187	PIB aux prix constants
Growth rates	3.0	1.4	3.1	1.1	-2.2	3.2	-3.5	Taux de croissance
Trinidad and Tobago								**Trinité-et-Tobago**
GDP at current prices	8 825	9 008	11 236	12 673	15 089	18 135	20 608	PIB aux prix courants
GDP per capita	6 760	6 876	8 547	9 607	11 399	13 652	15 457	PIB par habitant
GDP at constant prices	8 141	8 786	9 963	10 611	11 455	12 828	13 534	PIB aux prix constants
Growth rates	4.2	7.9	13.4	6.5	8.0	12.0	5.5	Taux de croissance
Tunisia								**Tunisie**
GDP at current prices	19 969	21 048	24 968	28 256	29 029	30 962	35 010	PIB aux prix courants
GDP per capita	2 064	2 152	2 525	2 827	2 873	3 031	3 390	PIB par habitant
GDP at constant prices	20 529	20 900	22 060	23 393	24 321	25 664	27 289	PIB aux prix constants
Growth rates	4.9	1.8	5.6	6.0	4.0	5.5	6.3	Taux de croissance
Turkey								**Turquie**
GDP at current prices	145 573	184 162	239 700	301 999	362 614	403 459	487 552	PIB aux prix courants
GDP per capita	2 105	2 626	3 372	4 193	4 969	5 458	6 511	PIB par habitant
GDP at constant prices	198 103	213 835	226 226	246 431	264 618	280 756	294 984	PIB aux prix constants
Growth rates	-7.5	7.9	5.8	8.9	7.4	6.1	5.1	Taux de croissance

18

Gross domestic product and gross domestic product per capita *(continued)*
In millions of US dollars at current and constant 1990 prices; per capita US dollars; real rates of growth
Produit intérieur brut et produit intérieur brut par habitant *(suite)*
En millions de dollars É.-U. aux prix courants et constants de 1990 ; par habitant en dollars É.-U. ; taux de croissance réels

Country or area	2001	2002	2003	2004	2005	2006	2007	Pays ou zone
Turkmenistan								**Turkménistan**
GDP at current prices [3]	4 442	4 493	4 739	5 119	5 792	6 512	7 253	PIB aux prix courants [3]
GDP per capita [3]	973	970	1 009	1 074	1 198	1 329	1 461	PIB par habitant [3]
GDP at constant prices [3]	2 517	2 503	2 585	2 714	2 974	3 242	3 518	PIB aux prix constants [3]
Growth rates	4.3	-0.6	3.3	5.0	9.6	9.0	8.5	Taux de croissance
Turks and Caicos Islands								**Iles Turques et Caïques**
GDP at current prices	359	367	410	486	579	722	758	PIB aux prix courants
GDP per capita	17 991	17 331	18 283	20 621	23 658	28 758	29 706	PIB par habitant
GDP at constant prices	277	281	307	342	391	461	462	PIB aux prix constants
Growth rates	7.0	1.2	9.3	11.4	14.4	17.9	0.1	Taux de croissance
Tuvalu								**Tuvalu**
GDP at current prices	13	15	19	23	25	25	30	PIB aux prix courants
GDP per capita	1 253	1 421	1 817	2 197	2 395	2 427	2 811	PIB par habitant
GDP at constant prices	14 [9]	15 [9]	15	16	17	17	17	PIB aux prix constants
Growth rates	13.2	5.5	5.5	4.0	4.0	2.0	3.0	Taux de croissance
Uganda								**Ouganda**
GDP at current prices	5 788	6 031	6 498	7 779	9 136	10 160	12 436	PIB aux prix courants
GDP per capita	227	229	239	278	316	340	403	PIB par habitant
GDP at constant prices	7 605	7 966	8 476	8 903	9 390	10 027	10 678	PIB aux prix constants
Growth rates	6.3	4.7	6.4	5.0	5.5	6.8	6.5	Taux de croissance
Ukraine								**Ukraine**
GDP at current prices	38 009	42 393	50 133	64 881	86 142	107 753	141 177	PIB aux prix courants
GDP per capita	785	883	1 052	1 372	1 836	2 314	3 055	PIB par habitant
GDP at constant prices	42 565	44 799	49 097	55 062	56 562	60 719	65 348	PIB aux prix constants
Growth rates	9.2	5.3	9.6	12.2	2.7	7.4	7.6	Taux de croissance
United Arab Emirates								**Emirats arabes unis**
GDP at current prices	69 546	74 959	88 536	106 326	133 583	164 865	191 465	PIB aux prix courants
GDP per capita	20 309	20 805	23 429	26 938	32 547	38 806	43 709	PIB par habitant
GDP at constant prices	56 253	57 743	64 606	70 867	76 673	83 871	90 306	PIB aux prix constants
Growth rates	3.5	2.7	11.9	9.7	8.2	9.4	7.7	Taux de croissance
United Kingdom								**Royaume-Uni**
GDP at current prices	1 444 310	1 582 368	1 825 788	2 168 325	2 243 600	2 395 485	2 767 982	PIB aux prix courants
GDP per capita	24 432	26 644	30 595	36 160	37 241	39 587	45 549	PIB par habitant
GDP at constant prices	1 296 547	1 323 167	1 359 815	1 404 127	1 429 944	1 470 646	1 516 525	PIB aux prix constants
Growth rates	2.4	2.1	2.8	3.3	1.8	2.9	3.1	Taux de croissance
United Rep. of Tanzania [10]								**Rép.-Unie de Tanzanie** [10]
GDP at current prices	9 453	9 772	10 297	11 351	12 586	12 618	14 487	PIB aux prix courants
GDP per capita	280	282	290	311	336	329	368	PIB par habitant
GDP at constant prices	6 914	7 415	7 941	8 476	9 053	9 591	10 288	PIB aux prix constants
Growth rates	6.2	7.2	7.1	6.7	6.8	5.9	7.3	Taux de croissance
United States								**Etats-Unis**
GDP at current prices	10 075 900	10 417 600	10 908 000	11 630 900	12 376 100	13 132 900	13 776 472	PIB aux prix courants
GDP per capita	35 006	35 820	37 123	39 182	41 275	43 366	45 047	PIB par habitant
GDP at constant prices	8 028 989	8 158 495	8 364 302	8 669 584	8 936 186	9 192 914	9 393 837	PIB aux prix constants
Growth rates	0.8	1.6	2.5	3.7	3.1	2.9	2.2	Taux de croissance
Uruguay								**Uruguay**
GDP at current prices	18 561	12 277	11 191	13 216	16 615	19 308	23 087	PIB aux prix courants
GDP per capita	5 582	3 691	3 366	3 976	4 996	5 796	6 913	PIB par habitant
GDP at constant prices	10 961	9 735	9 972	11 159	11 871	12 702	13 652	PIB aux prix constants
Growth rates	-3.4	-11.2	2.4	11.9	6.4	7.0	7.5	Taux de croissance
Uzbekistan								**Ouzbékistan**
GDP at current prices	9 316 [3]	9 877	10 155	12 016	13 751	17 077	19 275	PIB aux prix courants
GDP per capita	371 [3]	388	393	458	517	633	704	PIB par habitant
GDP at constant prices	15 120 [3]	15 755	16 448	17 721	18 983	20 368	21 876	PIB aux prix constants
Growth rates	4.5	4.2	4.4	7.7	7.1	7.3	7.4	Taux de croissance
Vanuatu								**Vanuatu**
GDP at current prices	234	230	280	330	368	389	451	PIB aux prix courants
GDP per capita	1 206	1 153	1 368	1 571	1 708	1 763	1 995	PIB par habitant
GDP at constant prices	216	201	207	219	233	246	258	PIB aux prix constants
Growth rates	-2.7	-7.2	3.2	5.5	6.8	5.5	4.7	Taux de croissance

Gross domestic product and gross domestic product per capita *(continued)*
In millions of US dollars at current and constant 1990 prices; per capita US dollars; real rates of growth
Produit intérieur brut et produit intérieur brut par habitant *(suite)*
En millions de dollars É.-U. aux prix courants et constants de 1990 ; par habitant en dollars É.-U. ; taux de croissance réels

Country or area	2001	2002	2003	2004	2005	2006	2007	Pays ou zone
Venezuela (Boliv. Rep. of)								**Venezuela (Rép. boliv. du)**
GDP at current prices	122 910	92 889	83 529	112 451	145 513	184 509	236 720	PIB aux prix courants
GDP per capita	4 943	3 667	3 238	4 282	5 445	6 786	8 559	PIB par habitant
GDP at constant prices	59 793	54 498	50 272	59 465	65 600	72 388	78 469	PIB aux prix constants
Growth rates	3.4	-8.9	-7.8	18.3	10.3	10.4	8.4	Taux de croissance
Viet Nam								**Viet Nam**
GDP at current prices	32 685	35 064	39 553	45 724	52 832	60 884	71 174	PIB aux prix courants
GDP per capita	407	431	479	545	621	706	815	PIB par habitant
GDP at constant prices	14 359	15 376	16 505	17 791	19 290	20 868	22 595	PIB aux prix constants
Growth rates	6.9	7.1	7.3	7.8	8.4	8.2	8.3	Taux de croissance
Yemen								**Yémen**
GDP at current prices	9 854	10 693	11 778	13 874	16 808	19 082	21 658	PIB aux prix courants
GDP per capita	526	554	593	677	797	878	967	PIB par habitant
GDP at constant prices	7 093	7 372	7 648	7 952	8 397	8 663	8 930	PIB aux prix constants
Growth rates	3.8	3.9	3.8	4.0	5.6	3.2	3.1	Taux de croissance
Zambia								**Zambie**
GDP at current prices	3 637	3 697	4 305	5 440	7 272	10 886	11 613	PIB aux prix courants
GDP per capita	341	340	389	483	634	931	974	PIB par habitant
GDP at constant prices	4 198	4 336	4 523	4 803	5 054	5 367	5 679	PIB aux prix constants
Growth rates	4.9	3.3	4.3	6.2	5.2	6.2	5.8	Taux de croissance
Zanzibar								**Zanzibar**
GDP at current prices	254	265	276	316	350	407	468	PIB aux prix courants
GDP per capita	269	270	273	304	326	374	417	PIB par habitant
GDP at constant prices	192	208	220	235	246	261	280	PIB aux prix constants
Growth rates	9.3	8.6	5.9	6.5	4.9	6.0	7.3	Taux de croissance
Zimbabwe								**Zimbabwe**
GDP at current prices	5 609[3,9]	5 427[3,9]	5 004[3,9]	3 071	2 258	2 203[3]	2 124[3]	PIB aux prix courants
GDP per capita	439[3]	422[3]	387[3]	236	172	167[3]	159[3]	PIB par habitant
GDP at constant prices	9 018[3,9]	8 576[3,9]	7 743[3,9]	7 796	7 488	7 082[3]	6 650[3]	PIB aux prix constants
Growth rates	-2.7	-4.9	-9.7	0.7	-4.0	-5.4	-6.1	Taux de croissance

Source:
United Nations Statistics Division, New York, the national accounts database, last accessed January 2009.

Source:
Organisation des Nations Unies, Division de statistique, New York, la base de données sur les comptes nationaux, dernier accès janvier 2009.

1   For statistical purposes, the data for China do not include those for the Hong Kong Special Administrative Region (Hong Kong SAR), Macao Special Administrative Region (Macao SAR) and Taiwan Province of China.
2   Excludes northern Cyprus.
3   Price-adjusted rates of exchange (PARE) are used for selected years for conversion to US dollars due to large distortions in the dollar levels of per capita GDP with the use of IMF market exchange rates.
4   Includes Guadeloupe, Martinique, Réunion and French Guiana.
5   Beginning 1999, data for Timor-Leste are not included.
6   Including Western Sahara.
7   From 1990, excluding Kosovo and Metohia.
8   Excluding the informal sector.
9   At factor cost.
10   Tanzania mainland only.

1   Pour la présentation des statistiques, les données pour la Chine ne comprennent pas la Région Administrative Spéciale de Hong Kong (Hong Kong RAS), la Région Administrative Spéciale de Macao (Macao RAS) et la province de Taiwan.
2   Exclu Chypre du nord.
3   Pour certaines années, on utilise les Taux de change corrigés des prix (TCCP) pour effectuer la conversion en dollars des États-Unis, en raison des aberrations importantes relevées dans les niveaux du PNB exprimés en dollars après conversion à l'aide des taux de change du marché communiqués par le FMI.
4   Y compris Guadeloupe, Martinique, Réunion et Guyane française.
5   A partir de 1999, les donneés de Timor-Leste ne sont pas inclues.
6   Y compris les données de Sahara occidental.
7   Après 1990, non compris Kosovo et Metohie.
8   Non compris le secteur informel.
9   Au coût des facteurs.
10   Tanzanie continentale seulement.

Gross domestic product by type of expenditure at current prices
Percentage distribution

Dépenses imputées au produit intérieur brut aux prix courants
Répartition en pourcentage

Country or area Pays ou zone	Year Année	GDP in current prices (mil. nat.cur.) PIB aux prix courants (millions monnaie nat.)	% of Gross domestic product – en % du Produit intérieur brut					
			Household final consumption expenditure Consom. finale des ménages	Govt. final consumption expenditure Consom. finale des admin. publiques	Gross fixed capital formation Formation brute de capital fixe	Changes in inventories Variation des stocks	Exports of goods and services Exportations de biens et services	Imports of goods and services Importations de biens et services
Afghanistan[+] Afghanistan[+]	2005	338 541	105.1	9.7	31.3	...	25.2	71.3
	2006	407 673	98.4	9.9	32.8	...	22.9	64.0
	2007	505 630	98.1	10.6	30.6	...	17.3	56.6
Albania Albanie	2003	694 098	75.2[1]	10.9	40.5	-1.8	20.4	45.1
	2004	751 024	78.2[1]	11.0	37.2	-4.0	22.0	44.4
	2005	817 374	76.2[1]	10.8	36.3	1.2	22.8	47.3
Algeria[2] Algérie[2]	2001	4 260 811	43.4	14.7	22.7	4.8	36.4	21.8
	2002	4 537 691	43.8	15.4	24.5	6.4	35.4	25.6
	2003	5 264 187	40.4	14.8	24.0	6.3	38.3	23.8
Angola[2] Angola[2]	1988	239 640	45.5	32.9	14.6	0.0	32.8	25.8
	1989	278 866	48.2	28.9	11.2	0.9	33.8	23.1
	1990	308 062	44.7	28.5	11.1	0.6	38.9	23.8
Anguilla[2] Anguilla[2]	2004	402	86.2	16.4	33.1	...	56.1	91.8
	2005	458	80.7	18.6	34.0	...	67.2	100.6
	2006	578	84.9	20.3	38.4	...	58.9	102.4
Antigua and Barbuda[2] Antigua-et-Barbuda[2]	1984	468	69.8	18.5	23.6	0.0	73.7	85.6
	1985	541	71.5	18.3	28.0	0.0	75.7	93.5
	1986	642	69.7	18.9	36.1	0.0	75.2	99.9
Argentina Argentine	2004	447 643	62.8	11.1	19.2[3]	...	25.7	18.4
	2005	531 939	61.3	11.9	21.5[3]	...	25.1	19.2
	2006	654 439	59.0	12.4	23.4[3]	...	24.8	19.2
Armenia Arménie	2005	2 242 881	75.5[1]	10.6	29.8	0.7[4]	27.3	40.5
	2006	2 657 131	71.8[1]	11.3	33.3	0.3[4]	22.0	36.5
	2007	3 139 354	70.5[1]	11.9	34.2	0.7[4]	18.7	38.1
Aruba Aruba	2004	3 983	51.2	23.2	26.8	1.5	64.6	67.4
	2005	4 159	52.9	22.4	31.3	1.5	68.4	76.5
	2006	4 334	53.6	22.8	33.0	1.5	65.2	76.0
Australia[+] Australie[+]	2004	897 642	58.0[1]	18.1	25.8	0.6	18.7	21.2
	2005	967 454	56.6[1]	17.9	27.0	0.1	20.3	21.8
	2006	1 046 365	55.6[1]	18.3	26.9	0.4	20.6	21.8
Austria Autriche	2005	245 330	56.2[1]	18.1	20.4	0.3[4]	53.4	48.5
	2006	257 897	55.4[1]	18.0	20.6	0.4[4]	56.1	50.5
	2007	272 669	54.2[1]	17.7	20.8	0.1[4]	58.9	51.6
Azerbaijan Azerbaïdjan	2005	12 523	42.1[1]	10.4	41.3	0.2	62.9	52.9
	2006	18 746	37.1[1]	8.5	29.7	0.2	66.5	38.8
	2007[5]	26 815	35.3[1]	6.5	21.2	0.1	72.1	30.2
Bahamas Bahamas	2004	5 650	68.3	14.6	28.7	2.1	46.8	58.8
	2005	5 986	67.5	14.7	33.0	3.2	48.7	66.6
	2006	6 237	68.3	14.7	41.2	3.9	50.4	78.0
Bahrain[2] Bahreïn[2]	2004	4 224	39.1	16.7	24.2	0.6[6]	92.0	72.7
	2005	5 061	36.8	15.7	23.0	1.4[6]	99.5	76.4
	2006[5]	5 951	35.5	14.2	24.8	-0.4[6]	99.0	73.0
Bangladesh[+] Bangladesh[+]	2005	3 707 070	74.5	5.5	24.5	...	16.6	23.1
	2006	4 157 279	74.2	5.5	24.7	...	19.0	25.2
	2007	4 674 973	74.0	5.6	24.3	...	22.0	28.9
Barbados[2] Barbade[2]	2002	4 952	64.1	24.6	16.9	-0.3	50.1	55.3
	2003	5 390	65.7	23.2	16.9	-0.1	50.7	56.3
	2004	5 632	70.7	21.3	19.2	0.2	49.5	60.8
Belarus Bélarus	2005	65 067 100	52.0[1]	20.8	26.5	1.9	59.8	59.1
	2006	79 266 985	51.5[1]	19.2	29.7	2.5	60.1	64.2
	2007	96 087 237	52.3[1]	18.6	30.8	2.4	61.7	67.9

Gross domestic product by type of expenditure at current prices *(continued)*
Percentage distribution
Dépenses imputées au produit intérieur brut aux prix courants *(suite)*
Répartition en pourcentage

Country or area Pays ou zone	Year Année	GDP in current prices (mil. nat.cur.) PIB aux prix courants (millions monnaie nat.)	% of Gross domestic product – en % du Produit intérieur brut					
			Household final consumption expenditure Consom. finale des ménages	Govt. final consumption expenditure Consom. finale des admin. publiques	Gross fixed capital formation Formation brute de capital fixe	Changes in inventories Variation des stocks	Exports of goods and services Exportations de biens et services	Imports of goods and services Importations de biens et services
Belgium Belgique	2005	301 966	52.6[1]	22.8	20.3	0.6	86.6	82.9
	2006	316 622	52.5[1]	22.4	20.8	1.2	87.7	84.5
	2007	330 800	52.4[1]	22.4	21.4	1.0	89.4	86.5
Belize Belize	2004	2 110	75.1	14.0	17.7	1.9	50.7	58.7
	2005	2 230	71.6	14.5	18.5	1.0	54.6	62.7
	2006	2 427	65.2	13.6	19.0	0.4	63.5	61.9
Benin[2] Bénin[2]	2005	2 298 714	76.8	12.0	19.4	-1.2	21.6	28.6
	2006	2 463 700	76.3	12.1	19.5	1.3	18.5	27.7
	2007	2 673 600	74.0	12.0	19.8	1.4	20.3	27.6
Bermuda[+] Bermudes[+]	2004	2 980	76.4[1]	21.2	20.3	1.8	37.5	57.2
	2005	3 265	74.8[1]	20.4	19.4	0.7	37.1	52.5
	2006	3 483	74.3[1]	19.2	18.1	1.0	45.4	57.9
Bhutan[+] Bhoutan[+]	2004	32 320	42.7	20.6	62.1	-0.2	31.1	57.0
	2005	36 581	39.9	21.6	50.8	0.3	38.6	62.0
	2006	41 443	37.5	21.1	45.2	0.3	51.2	59.3
Bolivia[2] Bolivie[2]	2005	77 024[7]	66.3	16.0[8]	13.0	1.3	35.6	32.1
	2006	91 748[7]	62.8	14.4[8]	14.3	-0.4	41.8	32.8
	2007	103 009[7]	63.2	14.1[8]	16.1	-1.0	41.8	34.3
Bosnia and Herzegovina Bosnie-Herzégovine	2004	15 786	95.9[1]	22.4	25.6	3.0	29.4	70.7
	2005	16 927	98.6[1]	21.6	28.9	0.1	33.0	74.7
	2006	19 121	95.4[1]	21.2	24.9	-1.0	36.6	66.4
Botswana[+] Botswana[+]	2005	49 815	27.8[1]	21.7	20.2	17.5	47.1	34.3
	2006	57 851	26.2[1]	20.4	18.4	14.1	49.9	29.0
	2007	70 886	24.1[1]	19.5	18.5	9.4	51.2	27.5
Brazil Brésil	2004	1 941 498	59.8[1]	19.2	16.1	1.0	16.4	12.6
	2005	2 147 239	60.3[1]	19.9	15.9	0.3	15.1	11.5
	2006	2 369 797	60.3[1]	20.0	16.4	0.3	14.4	11.5
British Virgin Islands Iles Vierges britanniques	2005	931	37.2[1]	9.2	24.1	-1.6	108.9	77.7
	2006	1 041	36.7[1]	9.0	24.0	-1.6	109.5	77.5
	2007	1 134	36.2[1]	8.9	24.0	-1.7	110.0	77.4
Brunei Darussalam Brunéi Darussalam	2004	13 306	26.6	22.1	13.4	0.1	68.8	31.8
	2005	15 864	22.5	18.4	11.4	0.0	70.2	27.3
	2006	18 370	19.7	17.9	10.4	0.0	71.2	25.0
Bulgaria Bulgarie	2004	38 823	69.3[1]	18.4	20.5	2.6[4]	57.0	68.5
	2005	42 797	70.2[1]	18.0	24.2	3.8[4]	60.2	76.4
	2006	49 091	69.2[1]	17.4	26.2	5.7[4]	64.0	83.0
Burkina Faso Burkina Faso	2005	2 961 171	72.5	21.5	19.5	1.1	9.7	24.3
	2006	3 144 954	74.9	21.1	19.3	-2.2	11.4	24.5
	2007	3 420 224	74.0	20.5	20.5	-2.2	11.7	24.5
Burundi[2] Burundi[2]	1990	196 656	83.0	19.5	16.4	-0.6	8.0	26.2
	1991	211 898	83.9	17.0	18.1	-0.5	10.0	28.5
	1992	226 384	83.0	15.6	21.1	0.4	9.0	29.0
Cambodia Cambodge	2005	25 754 291	84.3[1]	5.8	18.9	-0.4	64.1	72.8
	2006	29 849 146	81.0[1]	5.3	19.4	1.2	68.6	76.0
	2007	35 039 310	78.2[1]	5.7	19.4	1.4	65.3	73.0
Cameroon[+] Cameroun[+]	2005	8 749 566	72.0[1]	10.0	17.7	1.4	20.5	21.5
	2006	9 387 481	71.5[1]	9.6	16.7	0.2	23.0	21.0
	2007	9 881 963	71.3[1]	...	16.9	-0.1	24.2	22.4
Canada Canada	2004	1 290 829	55.8[1]	19.3	20.3	0.4	38.4	34.1
	2005	1 375 080	55.3[1]	19.1	21.0	0.7	37.8	34.1
	2006	1 446 307	55.6[1]	19.4	22.0	0.5	36.3	33.7
Cape Verde[2] Cap-Vert[2]	2002	72 758	88.5	18.4	35.9	-0.1	20.9	63.7
	2003	79 527	86.5	20.1	31.1	-0.1	14.6	52.1
	2004	82 086	83.7	21.3	38.9	0.5	13.8	58.3

Gross domestic product by type of expenditure at current prices *(continued)*
Percentage distribution

Dépenses imputées au produit intérieur brut aux prix courants *(suite)*
Répartition en pourcentage

				% of Gross domestic product – en % du Produit intérieur brut				
Country or area Pays ou zone	Year Année	GDP in current prices (mil. nat.cur.) PIB aux prix courants (millions monnaie nat.)	Household final consumption expenditure Consom. finale des ménages	Govt. final consumption expenditure Consom. finale des admin. publiques	Gross fixed capital formation Formation brute de capital fixe	Changes in inventories Variation des stocks	Exports of goods and services Exportations de biens et services	Imports of goods and services Importations de biens et services
Cayman Islands [2] Iles Caïmanes [2]	1989	474	65.0	14.1	23.2	...	60.1	68.8
	1990	590	62.5	14.2	21.4	...	64.1	58.5
	1991	616	62.5	15.1	21.8	...	58.9	52.8
Central African Rep. [2] Rép. centrafricaine [2]	1986	388 647	82.1	15.6	12.9	-0.1	18.2	28.6
	1987	360 942	80.6	17.5	12.9	-0.2	17.8	28.6
	1988	376 748	80.7	16.1	9.9	0.7	17.7	25.1
Chad Tchad	2005	3 098 019	24.9	21.0	20.3	4.9	54.5	25.5
	2006	3 294 131	26.2	23.3	16.0	-0.5	57.0	22.1
	2007	3 352 843	28.9	25.4	16.1	0.3	52.0	22.7
Chile Chili	2005	66 192 596	58.2[1]	11.1	21.2	1.0	41.3	32.8
	2006	77 651 822	54.1[1]	10.5	19.5	1.0	45.7	30.8
	2007	85 639 827	54.7	10.5	20.6	0.5	47.1	33.3
China [9] Chine [9]	2004	15 987 830	39.9	14.5	40.7	2.5	34.0	31.4
	2005	18 386 790	38.7	14.5	42.0	1.8	37.3	31.7
	2006	21 087 100	38.0	14.4	42.8	1.9	40.1	32.2
China, Hong Kong SAR Chine, Hong Kong RAS	2004	1 291 902	59.4[1]	9.9	21.3	0.6	190.2	181.3
	2005	1 383 049	58.2[1]	8.8	20.9	-0.3	198.7	186.2
	2006	1 474 329	58.8[1]	8.4	21.5	-0.1	205.4	194.0
China, Macao SAR Chine, Macao RAS	2004	82 966	27.5[1]	8.7	16.2	0.7	105.2	58.2
	2005	92 951	27.1[1]	9.0	26.7	0.7	95.6	59.0
	2006	115 266	24.4[1]	7.8	34.1	0.9	90.9	58.1
Colombia Colombie	2003	228 516 603	64.7[1]	18.6	16.5	0.6[4]	21.2	21.7
	2004	257 746 373	63.9[1]	17.5	18.4	0.7[4]	21.5	22.1
	2005	285 312 900	62.9[1]	17.1	19.9	0.7[4]	21.5	22.3
Comoros [2] Comores [2]	1989	63 397	77.8	27.6	14.4	4.6	14.9	39.3
	1990	66 370	79.7	25.7	12.2	8.0	11.7	37.3
	1991	69 248	80.9	25.3	12.3	4.0	15.5	38.0
Congo [2] Congo [2]	1987	690 523	56.6[1]	20.6	20.9	-1.1	41.7	38.6
	1988	658 964	60.1[1]	21.1	19.6	-1.0	40.6	40.4
	1989	773 524	52.8[1]	18.7	16.4	-0.5	47.6	35.0
Cook Islands [2] Iles Cook [2]	2005	261	...	...	...	...	73.3	61.8
	2006	278	...	...	...	...	80.9	70.5
	2007	287	...	...	...	...	93.8	87.5
Costa Rica Costa Rica	2005	9 538 977	67.3	13.8	18.7	5.6	48.5	54.0
	2006	11 517 822	66.2	13.5	19.9	6.5	49.1	55.3
	2007	13 570 071	66.9	13.3	21.8	2.8	48.8	53.6
Côte d'Ivoire [2] Côte d'Ivoire [2]	1998	7 457 508	65.1[1]	13.7	14.3	0.6	41.3	34.9
	1999	7 734 000	63.2[1]	14.6	14.5	-1.3	39.8	30.8
	2000	7 605 000	67.2[1]	15.5	12.3	-1.0	39.8	33.8
Croatia Croatie	2003	198 422	58.8[1]	21.0	28.6	2.5	47.1	57.9
	2004	214 983	57.9[1]	20.4	28.2	2.5	47.5	56.4
	2005	229 032	57.0	20.4	28.6	2.7	47.1	55.8
Cuba Cuba	2005	42 644	52.9	33.7[1]	9.0	1.8	21.0	18.3
	2006	52 743	55.8	32.2[1]	10.4	1.3	18.7	18.5
	2007	58 604	51.7	35.4[1]	9.7	0.5	20.3	17.6
Cyprus Chypre	2005	7 879	64.6[1]	18.0	19.6	0.4	48.3	50.9
	2006	8 424	64.5[1]	18.6	20.3	0.3	48.2	51.9
	2007	9 066	65.4[1]	17.8	20.8	0.8	47.9	52.7
Czech Republic République tchèque	2004	2 814 762	50.3[1]	22.1	25.8	1.6[4]	70.2	70.1
	2005	2 987 722	49.0[1]	22.0	25.0	0.7[4]	72.2	69.0
	2006	3 231 576	48.8[1]	21.2	24.6	2.2[4]	75.8	72.7
Dem. Rep. of the Congo [2] Rép. dém. du Congo [2]	1987	326 946	77.1	22.4	20.3	5.3	63.2	88.2
	1988	622 822	...	37.3	19.0	3.7	81.0	...
	1989	2 146 811	...	14.4	13.4	3.2	46.5	...

Gross domestic product by type of expenditure at current prices *(continued)*
Percentage distribution

Dépenses imputées au produit intérieur brut aux prix courants *(suite)*
Répartition en pourcentage

			% of Gross domestic product – en % du Produit intérieur brut					
Country or area Pays ou zone	Year Année	GDP in current prices (mil. nat.cur.) PIB aux prix courants (millions monnaie nat.)	Household final consumption expenditure Consom. finale des ménages	Govt. final consumption expenditure Consom. finale des admin. publiques	Gross fixed capital formation Formation brute de capital fixe	Changes in inventories Variation des stocks	Exports of goods and services Exportations de biens et services	Imports of goods and services Importations de biens et services
Denmark	2005	1 548 153	49.1[1]	25.9	19.7	0.3[4]	49.2	44.3
Danemark	2006	1 641 520	49.1[1]	25.7	21.6	0.8[4]	51.9	49.1
	2007	1 696 238	49.6[1]	25.9	22.8	0.4[4]	52.1	51.0
Djibouti[2]	1996	88 233	64.6	33.6	19.3	-0.9	40.3	56.8
Djibouti[2]	1997	87 289	59.3	34.7	21.4	0.2	42.2	57.8
	1998	88 461	67.3	29.0	23.3	0.2	43.4	63.0
Dominica[2]	2004	770	70.0	18.1	27.3	0.0	45.2	67.2
Dominique[2]	2005	809	75.1	18.8	28.6	0.0	42.5	72.1
	2006	854	70.3	18.9	...	...	43.8	69.2
Dominican Republic	2004	909 037	78.1	6.2	14.8	0.2	42.3	41.6
Rép. dominicaine	2005	1 020 002	82.3	6.7	16.4	0.1	30.0	35.5
	2006	1 189 802	82.4	7.2	18.3	0.1	30.0	38.0
Ecuador	2005	37 187	66.0	11.1	22.0	1.8	30.9	31.8
Equateur	2006	41 402	64.9	11.0	21.6	1.5	34.3	33.2
	2007[5]	44 400	66.1	11.4	23.2	1.5	31.9	34.0
Egypt[+]	2004	510 750	72.1[1]	11.1	15.5	0.7	28.8	28.3
Egypte[+]	2005	568 192	72.9[1]	11.1	16.9	0.7	31.3	32.9
	2006	642 986	72.9[1]	10.7	18.7	0.6	32.2	35.1
El Salvador	2004[2]	15 798	91.4	9.7	15.7	0.5	27.8	45.1
El Salvador	2005[2]	17 070	93.4	9.6	15.3	0.4	26.5	45.2
	2006	18 654[2]	94.0[2]	9.6[2]	16.1[2]	0.0	27.2[2]	46.9[2]
Equatorial Guinea[2]	1989	42 256	54.3	22.2	19.6	0.0	40.4	36.6
Guinée équatoriale[2]	1990	44 349	53.2	15.3	34.6	-3.1	59.7	59.7
	1991	46 429	75.9	14.4	18.4	-2.4	28.4	34.7
Estonia	2004	149 923	55.0[1]	18.0	31.4	3.6	74.2	82.2
Estonie	2005	175 392	53.5[1]	17.1	30.6	3.5	79.0	85.3
	2006	207 061	54.1[1]	16.4	34.1	4.2	79.4	90.7
Ethiopia[+]	2005	98 398	79.8	13.8	20.5[3]	...	15.8	34.3
Ethiopie[+]	2006	115 589	80.0	12.4	19.8[3]	...	15.1	32.6
	2007	149 557	80.6	10.8	18.5[3]	...	15.2	30.3
Fiji	2003	4 378	51.2	16.7	21.5	0.6	60.0	68.4
Fidji	2004	4 728	49.1	15.6	18.5	0.7	53.8	70.4
	2005	5 069	47.3	15.2	18.3	0.7	55.0	72.6
Finland	2005	157 335	51.6[1]	22.2	18.9	1.6[4]	41.8	37.4
Finlande	2006	167 041	51.4[1]	21.8	19.3	1.4[4]	45.2	40.2
	2007	178 759	50.6[1]	21.2	20.3	1.9[4]	44.8	40.2
France	2005	1 726 068	56.9[1]	23.7	20.0	0.3[4]	26.1	26.9
France	2006	1 807 462	56.8[1]	23.4	20.8	0.3[4]	26.8	28.1
	2007	1 892 241	56.7[1]	23.2	21.5	0.6[4]	26.5	28.5
French Guiana[2]	1990	6 526	64.4	35.0	47.8	-0.2	67.3	114.3
Guyane française[2]	1991	7 404	60.1	34.4	40.5	1.5	81.1	117.6
	1992	7 976	58.9	34.2	30.8	1.5	65.5	90.8
French Polynesia[2]	2002	324 431	102.5	12.9	26.7[3]	-0.1[4]	19.6	61.6
Polynésie française[2]	2003	338 749	106.5	11.9	25.0[3]	-0.1[4]	17.3	60.6
	2004	345 706	98.7	11.2	25.6[3]	-0.1[4]	17.5	53.0
Gabon[2]	1999	2 855 800	39.3	16.9	25.1	-0.4	...	...
Gabon[2]	2000	3 631 400	32.7	12.8	21.9	0.4	...	...
	2001	3 412 700	35.3	14.1	29.1	-2.3	...	...
Gambia[+][2]	1991	2 920	83.7	13.0	18.2[10]	...	45.3[11]	60.2[12]
Gambie[+][2]	1992	3 078	81.3	13.2	22.4[10]	...	45.2[11]	61.9[12]
	1993	3 243	78.1	15.1	27.1[10]	...	36.6[11]	56.9[12]
Georgia	2005	11 621	67.0[1]	17.3	28.1	0.5[4]	33.8	51.6
Géorgie	2006	13 790	78.7[1]	15.3	25.6	1.1[4]	32.9	57.0
	2007	16 999	70.7[1]	21.9	28.3	0.8[4]	31.5	57.7

Country or area Pays ou zone	Year Année	GDP in current prices (mil. nat.cur.) PIB aux prix courants (millions monnaie nat.)	% of Gross domestic product – en % du Produit intérieur brut					
			Household final consumption expenditure Consom. finale des ménages	Govt. final consumption expenditure Consom. finale des admin. publiques	Gross fixed capital formation Formation brute de capital fixe	Changes in inventories Variation des stocks	Exports of goods and services Exportations de biens et services	Imports of goods and services Importations de biens et services
Germany	2005	2 244 600	59.1[1]	18.8	17.4	-0.4[4]	40.9	35.9
Allemagne	2006	2 322 200	58.5[1]	18.3	18.0	-0.2[4]	45.1	39.6
	2007	2 423 800	56.7[1]	18.0	18.6	-0.3[4]	46.7	39.7
Ghana[2]	2003	66 157 697	75.3[1]	17.7	22.9	^0.0	40.7	56.6
Ghana[2]	2004	79 887 433	77.0[1]	16.5	28.4	^0.0	39.3	60.4
	2005	97 260 628	82.1[1]	15.3	29.0	^0.0	36.1	61.7
Greece	2005	198 609	70.9[1]	16.6	23.4	0.4	21.7	33.0
Grèce	2006	213 985	71.0[1]	15.8	25.8	-0.1	21.9	34.5
	2007	228 949	70.6[1]	16.9	25.7	0.0	22.2	35.4
Greenland[2]	2003	9 397	...	55.7	...	...	24.3[13]	32.3[14]
Groenland[2]	2004	9 855	...	54.0	...	...	23.2[13]	00.0[14]
	2005	10 210	...	51.1	...	...	23.9[13]	35.1[14]
Grenada[2]	2004	1 267	69.1	17.3	40.5	...	40.5	67.4
Grenade[2]	2005	1 495	76.7	16.4	50.7	...	27.8	71.6
	2006	1 516	80.1	16.1	38.0		28.8	62.9
Guadeloupe[2]	1990	15 201	92.8	30.8	33.9	1.1	4.9	63.5
Guadeloupe[2]	1991	16 415	87.3	31.0	33.0	1.0	6.1	58.4
	1992	17 972	84.1	29.3	27.8	1.3	4.5	47.0
Guatemala	2003	174 044	84.5[1]	9.6	18.7	1.6[4]	25.8	40.2
Guatemala	2004	190 440	85.5[1]	8.8	18.3	2.5[4]	27.0	42.1
	2005	207 729	87.7[1]	8.5	18.3	1.4[4]	25.1	41.0
Guinea	2004	8 147 563	66.6	11.8	24.7	1.6	23.0	27.5
Guinée	2005	10 703 666	65.4	8.1	27.6	2.0	32.1	35.2
	2006	15 094 203	64.7	8.2	29.8	2.4	38.0	43.1
Guinea-Bissau[2]	1990	510 094	100.9	11.4	13.8	0.9	12.0	39.0
Guinée-Bissau[2]	1991	854 985	100.6	12.6	10.4	0.9	13.4	38.0
	1992	1 530 010	111.1	10.7	0.0	...	8.2	56.5
Guyana[2]	2004	156 358	54.4	24.1	32.0[3]	...	95.8	109.2
Guyana[2]	2005	165 028	73.3	26.9	32.3[3]	...	84.7	119.9
	2006	180 282	64.7	24.6	45.9[3]	...	-28.5[16]	...
Haiti[+][2]	1997	51 578	...	...	12.5	...	11.5	27.1
Haïti[+][2]	1998	59 055	...	...	12.9	...	13.2	28.6
	1999	66 425	...	...	13.1	...	13.3	28.2
Honduras	2005	183 749	75.3	15.5	24.9	2.7	59.0	77.5
Honduras	2006	204 685	76.0[1]	15.6	27.7	3.6	54.3	77.2
	2007	232 817	77.1[1]	16.4	30.4	3.1	51.5	78.4
Hungary	2005	22 042 476	55.0[1]	22.5	22.8	0.8	66.3	67.4
Hongrie	2006	23 795 306	53.6[1]	22.8	21.7	1.4	77.8	77.3
	2007	25 405 796	53.3[1]	21.4	20.9	2.1	79.9	77.6
Iceland	2005	1 026 251	59.5[1]	24.6	28.4	-0.1	31.6	44.0
Islande	2006	1 167 684	58.7[1]	24.4	33.7	1.2	32.0	50.0
	2007	1 279 379	58.4[1]	24.6	27.5	0.2	35.3	46.0
India[+]	2004	31 494 120	58.4	10.7	28.4	1.9[4]	18.1	19.9
Inde[+]	2005	35 803 440	57.4	10.4	31.0	2.4[4]	19.9	22.7
	2006	41 458 100	55.8	10.3	32.5	2.3[4]	22.1	25.1
Indonesia	2005	2 774 281 100	64.4	8.1	23.6	1.4	34.1	29.9
Indonésie	2006	3 339 479 600	62.7	8.6	24.1	1.3	31.0	25.6
	2007	3 957 403 900	63.5	8.3	24.9	0.0	29.4	25.3
Iran (Islamic Rep. of)[+]	2003	1 119 661 000	45.2[1]	12.6	28.5	6.2	27.0	25.5
Iran (Rép. islamique d')[+]	2004	1 401 899 100	45.7[1]	12.0	28.7	6.0	29.1	26.0
	2005	1 721 260 900	44.5[1]	12.7	27.1	2.5	33.2	24.7
Iraq[2]	2004	37 049 252	48.2	36.7	7.7	17.5	80.0	90.2
Iraq[2]	2005	49 990 680	43.5	29.4	20.4	5.8	79.3	78.3
	2006	80 459 422	44.2	18.6	20.2	2.2	60.6	45.9

19

Gross domestic product by type of expenditure at current prices *(continued)*
Percentage distribution
Dépenses imputées au produit intérieur brut aux prix courants *(suite)*
Répartition en pourcentage

% of Gross domestic product – en % du Produit intérieur brut

Country or area Pays ou zone	Year Année	GDP in current prices (mil. nat.cur.) PIB aux prix courants (millions monnaie nat.)	Household final consumption expenditure Consom. finale des ménages	Govt. final consumption expenditure Consom. finale des admin. publiques	Gross fixed capital formation Formation brute de capital fixe	Changes in inventories Variation des stocks	Exports of goods and services Exportations de biens et services	Imports of goods and services Importations de biens et services
Ireland	2004	148 502	45.6[1]	15.7	23.6	0.2[4]	84.0	69.0
Irlande	2005	161 498	45.6[1]	15.9	26.0	0.1[4]	81.8	69.5
	2006	174 705	45.5[1]	16.0	26.3	0.9[4]	80.0	69.3
Israel	2005	597 773	55.8[1]	25.7	16.4	2.5	42.9	43.2
Israël	2006	640 776	55.1[1]	25.5	17.1	1.9	43.4	43.0
	2007	673 552	56.4[1]	25.2	18.7	1.4	43.2	44.9
Italy	2005	1 428 375	59.0[1]	20.4	20.7	-0.1[4]	26.0	26.0
Italie	2006	1 479 981	59.1[1]	20.2	21.0	0.4[4]	27.8	28.7
	2007	1 535 540	59.0[1]	19.8	21.1	0.3[4]	29.2	29.5
Jamaica[2]	2003	472 918	72.6	15.4	29.7	0.2	40.6	58.5
Jamaïque[2]	2004	540 809	72.4	14.3	30.6	0.1	42.8	60.2
	2005	605 030	72.9	15.2	31.7	0.0	41.1	60.9
Japan	2004	498 328 400	57.1[1]	18.0	22.7	0.3	13.3	11.4
Japon	2005	501 734 400	57.0[1]	18.1	23.3	0.3	14.3	13.0
	2006	508 925 100	57.1[1]	17.7	23.5	0.5	16.1	14.8
Jordan[2]	2004	8 091	81.0[1]	21.3	24.8	2.6	52.2	81.9
Jordanie[2]	2005	8 954	87.2[1]	19.5	30.5	3.5	52.5	93.4
	2006	10 521	80.1[1]	22.3	28.3	2.9	54.7	88.4
Kazakhstan	2005	7 590 594	49.9[1]	11.3	28.0	3.0	53.5	44.7
Kazakhstan	2006	10 213 731	45.7[1]	10.2	30.2	3.7	51.1	40.4
	2007	12 763 212	45.5[1]	11.1	30.3	5.6	49.8	42.9
Kenya	2005	1 418 071	75.2	17.4	18.7	-1.8	28.0	37.0
Kenya	2006	1 620 732	75.1	16.6	19.1	-1.1	27.2	38.0
	2007	1 814 229	76.4	17.2	19.5	0.7	26.6	38.8
Kiribati[2]								
Kiribati[2]	1980	21	92.8	36.4	...	...	22.5	95.7
Korea, Republic of	2005	810 515 869	52.6[1]	14.2	29.3	0.8[4]	42.3	39.9
Corée, République de	2006	848 044 635	53.7[1]	14.8	29.0	0.8[4]	43.0	42.1
	2007	901 188 604	54.1[1]	15.1	28.8	0.6[4]	45.6	44.8
Kuwait[2]	2003	14 253	42.8[1]	23.0	16.0	0.6	52.1	34.5
Koweït[2]	2004	17 466	37.6[1]	19.9	14.9	2.9	57.1	32.5
	2005	23 588	31.4	15.4	17.0	2.8	63.8	30.4
Kyrgyzstan	2005	100 899	84.5[1]	17.5	16.0	0.2[4]	38.3	56.8
Kirghizistan	2006	113 800	95.1[1]	18.0	23.0	0.8[4]	41.7	79.0
	2007	139 749	101.1[1]	17.8	25.2	0.8[4]	44.7	89.9
Latvia	2005	9 059	62.6[1]	17.5	30.6	3.8[4]	47.9	62.2
Lettonie	2006	11 172	65.2[1]	16.6	32.6	7.1[4]	44.9	66.4
	2007	13 957	65.5[1]	18.2	31.6	4.9[4]	44.4	64.7
Lebanon	2003	29 851 000	...	...	19.6	-0.4	16.7	37.8
Liban	2004	32 359 000	...	...	20.6	1.2	19.9	42.2
	2005	32 499 000	...	...	22.0	-0.2	21.1	43.1
Lesotho	2004	8 519	95.2[1]	17.2	35.7	0.1	57.9	106.1
Lesotho	2005	9 065	98.1[1]	18.1	34.4	-0.3	49.7	100.0
	2006	10 120	96.9[1]	18.1	33.3	-0.3	50.5	98.5
Liberia[2]	2005	558	70.3[1]	28.5	1.6	-2.6	1.7	4.2
Libéria[2]	2006	614	76.6[1]	26.4	3.7	-2.7	2.6	5.3
	2007	666	108.9[1]	38.9	3.3[3]	...	41.7	85.6
Libyan Arab Jamah.[2]	1983	8 805	39.2	32.8	25.1	-1.1	42.1	38.0
Jamah. arabe libyenne[2]	1984	8 013	38.6	33.6	25.4	0.5	41.4	39.4
	1985	8 277	37.6	31.7	19.7	0.4	37.4	26.7
Lithuania	2004	62 587	65.2[1]	17.9	22.3	1.6[4]	52.1	59.2
Lituanie	2005	71 380	65.1[1]	17.1	22.8	2.2[4]	58.1	65.4
	2006	81 905	65.3[1]	18.0	24.8	2.2[4]	59.7	70.1

Country or area Pays ou zone	Year Année	GDP in current prices (mil. nat.cur.) PIB aux prix courants (millions monnaie nat.)	Household final consumption expenditure Consom. finale des ménages	Govt. final consumption expenditure Consom. finale des admin. publiques	Gross fixed capital formation Formation brute de capital fixe	Changes in inventories Variation des stocks	Exports of goods and services Exportations de biens et services	Imports of goods and services Importations de biens et services
Luxembourg	2005	30 032	38.6[1]	16.6	20.0	0.2[4]	156.1	133.0
Luxembourg	2006	33 854	36.0[1]	15.3	18.4	0.5[4]	166.1	136.4
	2007	36 137	35.2[1]	15.1	20.2	-0.9[4]	172.5	141.9
Madagascar[2]	2005	10 092 401	86.2	9.0	22.2	...	28.2	45.6
Madagascar[2]	2006	11 815 261	81.9	8.8	25.3	...	29.5	45.5
	2007	13 899 031	79.0	10.1	27.4	...	27.1	43.6
Malawi	2003	236 240	88.1[1]	8.7	14.1	3.0	26.7	40.6
Malawi	2004	285 870	89.6[1]	10.4	16.2	2.0	25.0	43.2
	2005	326 246	94.6[1]	10.8	20.2	2.5	24.1	52.2
Malaysia	2005	522 445	44.8[1]	12.4	20.5	-0.5	117.5	94.6
Malaisie	2006	573 736	44.9[1]	11.9	20.9	0.1	116.7	94.5
	2007	641 864	45.6[1]	12.2	21.7	0.3	110.2	89.9
Maldives	2004	9 939	32.8	23.7	41.8	0.0	86.5	84.8
Maldives	2005	9 607	33.8	38.1	61.3	0.0	67.3	100.5
	2006	11 608	29.8	37.9	55.6	0.0	82.6	105.9
Mali[2]	2006	3 201 472	65.3	17.3	16.5	3.3	30.4	32.9
Mali[2]	2007	3 424 535	64.7	17.4	19.4	4.8	26.5	32.8
	2008	3 850 838	65.5	17.5	18.4	6.8	24.3	32.5
Malta	2005	2 061	64.7[1]	19.7	19.4	1.5[4]	77.1	82.4
Malte	2006	2 187	62.9[1]	20.0	19.8	1.2[4]	93.7	97.5
	2007	2 325	61.1[1]	19.3	19.6	2.9[4]	89.6	92.4
Martinique[2]	1990	19 320	83.6	29.7	26.7	1.9	8.4	50.4
Martinique[2]	1991	20 787	84.0	28.8	25.6	1.4	7.4	47.1
	1992	22 093	84.3	28.8	23.6	-0.9	6.8	42.5
Mauritania	2004	382 285	76.2	19.8	52.0	-6.2	39.9	81.7
Mauritanie	2005	462 779	61.1	31.6	69.2	2.0	40.0	103.8
	2006	692 823	54.6	24.7	25.3	3.6	59.0	67.1
Mauritius	2006	206 328	70.5	14.2	24.3	2.3	61.6	72.9
Maurice	2007	235 530	70.4	13.1	25.1	1.6	58.8	69.0
	2008	264 636	72.4	13.2	25.4	2.2	54.0	67.1
Mexico	2004	7 709 096	68.2[1]	11.9	19.7	2.4	29.6	31.6
Mexique	2005	8 361 107	68.2[1]	11.6	19.3	2.4	30.0	31.6
	2006	9 149 911	67.7[1]	11.7	20.4	1.5	31.9	33.2
Micronesia (Fed. States of)	2004	224	...	...	...	...	15.7	...
Micronésie (Etats féd. de)	2005	232	...	...	...	...	15.9	...
	2006	237	...	...	...	...	15.7	...
Mongolia	2005	2 779 578	55.6[1]	12.4	30.4	6.6[4]	64.3	68.2
Mongolie	2006	3 714 953	48.7[1]	11.5	32.3	2.8[4]	65.3	59.7
	2007	4 599 542	49.8[1]	13.0	37.0	3.4[4]	64.3	65.7
Montserrat[2]	1984	94	96.4	20.6	23.7	2.7	13.6	56.9
Montserrat[2]	1985	100	96.3	20.3	24.7	1.5	11.7	54.5
	1986	114	89.5	18.7	33.0	2.8	10.1	53.9
Morocco	2005	527 679	57.5	19.4	27.5	1.3	32.3	37.9
Maroc	2006	577 344	57.5	18.6	28.1	1.3	34.2	39.7
	2007	616 254	58.4	18.2	31.3	1.2	35.8	44.9
Mozambique	2004	128 668	85.4[1]	13.8	18.7	-0.3	29.8	47.3
Mozambique	2005	151 707	83.3[1]	13.0	18.7	-1.0	30.5	44.4
	2006	173 566	81.7[1]	13.0	19.3	^0.0	29.2	43.1
Myanmar[+][2]	1996	791 980	...	...	14.9	-2.7	0.7	1.5
Myanmar[+][2]	1997	1 109 554	...	...	13.5	-0.9	0.6	1.3
	1998	1 559 996	...	...	11.8	-0.7	0.5	1.0
Namibia	2004	36 496	57.6[1]	24.7	25.2	0.5	45.9	52.0
Namibie	2005	39 711	52.6[1]	24.5	24.5	1.3	47.6	51.0
	2006	46 971	49.4[1]	22.5	26.1	0.7	52.2	52.5

19 Gross domestic product by type of expenditure at current prices *(continued)*
Percentage distribution
Dépenses imputées au produit intérieur brut aux prix courants *(suite)*
Répartition en pourcentage

Country or area Pays ou zone	Year Année	GDP in current prices (mil. nat.cur.) PIB aux prix courants (millions monnaie nat.)	% of Gross domestic product – en % du Produit intérieur brut					
			Household final consumption expenditure Consom. finale des ménages	Govt. final consumption expenditure Consom. finale des admin. publiques	Gross fixed capital formation Formation brute de capital fixe	Changes in inventories Variation des stocks	Exports of goods and services Exportations de biens et services	Imports of goods and services Importations de biens et services
Nepal[+] Népal[+]	2004	589 412	82.6	8.9	19.9	6.5	14.6	29.5
	2005	646 471	86.4	8.8	20.9	5.1	13.6	31.7
	2006	719 477	84.9	8.7	20.3	5.0	12.5	28.5
Netherlands Pays-Bas	2005	508 964	49.1[1]	23.9	19.0	0.1[4]	69.8	61.9
	2006	534 324	47.4[1]	25.4	19.7	^0.0[4]	73.2	65.8
	2007	559 537	47.0[1]	25.3	20.0	-0.2[4]	75.3	67.3
Netherlands Antilles Antilles néerlandaises	2002	5 254	53.2[1]	20.3	29.5	2.4	75.1	81.4
	2003	5 426	53.2[1]	21.2	28.2	0.7	77.6	81.9
	2004	5 576	53.9[1]	20.3	28.2	2.4	82.7	88.5
New Caledonia Nouvelle-Calédonie	2002	471 996	67.1	28.4	24.7	-0.2	18.1	38.1
	2003	518 545	64.0	27.2	28.9	0.6	20.6	41.3
	2004	565 528	62.4	25.6	25.1	1.5	22.0	36.6
New Zealand[+] Nouvelle-Zélande[+]	2004	149 153	58.8[1]	17.6	23.4	1.1[4]	29.1	29.8
	2005	156 849	59.7[1]	18.1	24.1	0.5[4]	27.9	30.3
	2006	165 379	59.6[1]	18.5	23.0	-0.2[4]	29.1	30.6
Nicaragua[+] Nicaragua[+]	2005	81 233	83.4[1]	18.0	28.5	1.1	29.1	58.8
	2006	93 135	81.3[1]	19.1	28.0	1.5	31.1	61.0
	2007	104 702	101.1[16]	19.9	29.9	-1.1	32.5	62.4
Niger Niger	2005	1 755 050	73.8	16.0	21.3	1.5	19.0	31.5
	2006	1 859 458	74.0	15.4	20.9	0.9	18.7	29.9
	2007	1 968 522	74.4	18.3	22.9	0.1	20.3	36.0
Nigeria[+2] Nigéria[+2]	1999	3 320 311	59.3	7.6	5.3	^0.0	49.7	21.9
	2000	4 980 943	49.1	5.2	5.4	^0.0	58.9	18.6
	2001	5 639 863	60.3	4.9	7.0	^0.0	55.4	27.5
Norway Norvège	2005	1 945 716	42.5[1]	19.9	18.8	2.4	44.6	28.2
	2006	2 161 728	40.9[1]	19.2	18.9	2.8	46.5	28.3
	2007	2 276 757	41.6[1]	19.7	20.8	2.3	45.8	30.1
Occupied Palestinian Terr. Terr. palestinien occupé	2001	3 816	94.6[1]	32.8	24.9	0.6	12.1	64.9
	2002	3 484	96.7[1]	34.7	17.9	0.6	11.0	60.8
	2003	3 921	102.1[1]	27.2	23.5	0.2	9.6	62.6
Oman Oman	2004	9 525	44.1	21.3	20.6[3]	...	57.0	42.9
	2005	11 890	35.8	19.3	17.9[3]	...	62.8	35.8
	2006	13 738[5]	38.8	17.9	18.5[3]	...	63.0[5]	38.2
Pakistan[+] Pakistan[+]	2006	7 623 205	75.0	10.8	20.5	1.6	15.2	23.2
	2007	8 723 215	75.1	9.1	21.3	1.6	14.1	21.2
	2008	10 478 194	79.7	8.8	20.0	1.6	12.1	22.1
Panama Panama	2004	14 179	64.0	13.6	16.6	2.1	67.6	63.9
	2005	15 465	62.1	13.2	16.8	1.5	75.5	69.1
	2006	17 134	60.3	12.4	18.3	1.2	77.5	69.6
Papua New Guinea[5] Papouasie-Nvl-Guinée[5]	2004	12 653	51.4	15.3	18.1	1.9	72.2	58.9
	2005	14 236	45.2	16.8	17.5	1.1	79.0	59.5
	2006	16 208	45.6	16.8	14.2	2.2	86.3	65.0
Paraguay Paraguay	2005	46 170 000	73.8	10.9	19.3	0.5	51.2	55.6
	2006	52 270 000	73.7	11.2	19.1	0.6	53.7	58.2
	2007	61 511 651	74.1	10.8	17.4	0.7	50.9	53.9
Peru Pérou	2004	238 015	68.3	10.0	17.9	0.2	21.4	17.8
	2005	261 907	66.1	10.0	18.3	-0.4	25.1	19.2
	2006	302 550	61.8	9.5	19.3	0.7	28.5	19.8
Philippines[2] Philippines[2]	2004	4 871 555	68.7[1]	10.1	16.1	0.7	50.9	54.6
	2005	5 437 905	69.4[1]	9.6	14.4	0.2	47.6	51.8
	2006	6 032 624	70.1[1]	9.7	13.8	0.5	46.4	47.6
Poland Pologne	2005	983 302	63.0[1]	18.1	18.2	1.0[4]	37.1	37.4
	2006	1 060 194	62.0[1]	18.3	19.7	1.4[4]	40.4	41.7
	2007	1 162 903	60.9[1]	17.1	22.3	1.3[4]	41.3	43.0

19

Gross domestic product by type of expenditure at current prices *(continued)*
Percentage distribution
Dépenses imputées au produit intérieur brut aux prix courants *(suite)*
Répartition en pourcentage

| Country or area
Pays ou zone | Year
Année | GDP in
current prices
(mil. nat.cur.)
PIB aux prix
courants
(millions
monnaie nat.) | % of Gross domestic product – en % du Produit intérieur brut | | | | | |
			Household final consumption expenditure Consom. finale des ménages	Govt. final consumption expenditure Consom. finale des admin. publiques	Gross fixed capital formation Formation brute de capital fixe	Changes in inventories Variation des stocks	Exports of goods and services Exportations de biens et services	Imports of goods and services Importations de biens et services
Portugal Portugal	2005	149 124	64.9[1]	21.4	22.2	0.3[4]	28.5	37.4
	2006	155 323	65.0[1]	20.7	21.6	0.5[4]	31.3	39.3
	2007	162 756	64.7[1]	20.3	21.7	0.4[4]	32.9	40.1
Puerto Rico[+2] Porto Rico[+2]	2004	82 809	56.2[1]	12.2	14.4	0.4	79.1	62.2
	2005	86 943	56.9[1]	11.9	13.5	0.4	81.1	63.8
	2006	89 701	57.9[1]	11.7	13.0	0.3	80.5	63.4
Qatar Qatar	2003	85 663	16.5	15.4	30.2	4.6	61.7	28.5
	2004	115 512	17.5	13.1	30.1	3.3	64.2	28.1
	2005	154 564	18.2	11.5	33.6	1.9	68.3	33.5
Republic of Moldova République de Moldova	2005	37 652	93.4[1]	16.4	21.6	6.2	51.2	91.9
	2006	44 754	93.9[1]	20.0	28.4	4.4	45.3	91.9
	2007[5]	53 354	93.1[1]	19.6	33.3	4.9	45.3	96.1
Réunion[2] Réunion[2]	1992	33 787	76.1	28.4	28.6	2.1	3.4	38.6
	1993	33 711	76.4	28.6	25.7	-0.4	3.1	36.2
	1994	35 266	78.0	28.9	28.1	0.1	2.9	38.0
Romania Roumanie	2005	288 955	69.5[1]	17.4	23.7	-0.4	33.1	43.3
	2006	344 651	68.9[1]	16.7	25.6	0.9[4]	32.3	44.3
	2007[17]	412 762	67.3[1]	15.6	30.4	0.7[4]	29.5	43.5
Russian Federation Fédération de Russie	2005	21 625 372	49.6[1]	16.6	17.5	2.3[4]	35.2	21.5
	2006	26 879 762	48.5[1]	17.0	18.2	2.9[4]	33.8	21.0
	2007	32 987 375	48.5[1]	17.6	20.7	3.5[4]	30.5	21.8
Rwanda[2] Rwanda[2]	2000	681 455	90.2	8.9	18.0	...	6.3	23.4
	2001	732 276	90.4	9.5	17.4	...	8.7	26.1
	2002	784 000	91.5	9.5	17.9	...	7.1	24.6
Saint Kitts and Nevis[2] Saint-Kitts-et-Nevis[2]	2004	1 068	53.0	20.4	44.2	...	48.7	66.2
	2005	1 157	51.6	18.6	45.5	...	49.2	64.9
	2006	1 314	57.1	17.7	46.4	...	45.4	66.6
Saint Lucia[2] Sainte-Lucie[2]	2004	2 159	67.6	19.1	20.9	...	50.1	57.7
	2005	2 369	65.5	18.4	23.3	...	47.3	54.5
	2006	2 498	61.4	16.6	29.5	...	46.1	53.5
Saint Vincent-Grenadines[2] Saint Vincent-Grenadines[2]	2004	1 118	69.2	19.8	32.2	...	44.5	65.7
	2005	1 182	68.7	19.8	32.2	...	45.8	66.5
	2006	1 330	69.6	18.8	35.4	...	42.9	66.6
San Marino[2] Saint-Marin[2]	2004	1 061	...	...	53.6	2.2	186.2	190.3
	2005	1 106	...	...	53.0	2.5	184.0	187.7
	2006	1 171	...	...	51.1	2.0	197.0	197.3
Sao Tome and Principe[2] Sao Tomé-et-Principe[2]	1986	2 478	76.1	30.3	13.6	0.9	...	50.8
	1987	3 003	63.1	24.8	15.4	1.1	...	43.1
	1988	4 221	71.8	21.2	15.7	0.0	...	66.8
Saudi Arabia[+2] Arabie saoudite[+2]	2004	938 771	30.4	23.6	16.7	1.5	52.7	24.9
	2005	1 182 514	26.5	22.2	16.5	1.3	59.4	25.9
	2006	1 307 522	25.5	25.2	17.0	0.9	62.2	30.8
Senegal Sénégal	2004	4 242 837	77.8[1]	13.2	22.3	-0.6	27.1	39.8
	2005	4 582 285	77.4[1]	12.9	22.9	2.2	27.1	42.5
	2006	4 846 395	78.1[1]	13.1	26.4	-0.9	25.4	42.1
Serbia Serbie	2004	1 431 313[18]	70.8[1]	19.8	17.7	14.4	23.8[19]	50.8[20]
	2005	1 747 459[18]	70.0[1]	17.9	17.3	9.2	27.7[19]	47.8[20]
	2006	2 042 048[18]	70.4[1]	17.0	19.7	7.4	30.7[19]	50.8[20]
Serbia and Montenegro Serbie-et-Monténégro	1998[2]	148 370	70.7[1]	28.2	11.6	-1.1[4]	23.4	32.8
	1999	191 099	68.0[1]	28.9	12.6	-0.5[4]	11.2	20.3
	2000	381 661	70.5[1]	28.3	15.4	-6.6[4]	9.2	16.8
Seychelles[2] Seychelles[2]	1998	3 201	50.0	31.2	34.0	0.6	-15.8[15]	...
	1999	3 330	45.3	27.8	41.5	1.8	-16.4[15]	...
	2000	3 424	39.4	27.1	35.7	0.5	-2.6[15]	...

			% of Gross domestic product – en % du Produit intérieur brut					
Country or area Pays ou zone	Year Année	GDP in current prices (mil. nat.cur.) PIB aux prix courants (millions monnaie nat.)	Household final consumption expenditure Consom. finale des ménages	Govt. final consumption expenditure Consom. finale des admin. publiques	Gross fixed capital formation Formation brute de capital fixe	Changes in inventories Variation des stocks	Exports of goods and services Exportations de biens et services	Imports of goods and services Importations de biens et services
Sierra Leone[+]	2004	3 853 149	101.9[1]	11.6	6.9	8.1	13.8	42.2
Sierra Leone[+]	2005	4 324 010	92.9[1]	15.1	8.6	7.8	15.3	39.8
	2006	4 902 090	84.9[1]	13.3	5.1	13.4	15.9	32.6
Singapore	2005	199 375	41.1	10.7	21.6	-1.7	238.5	209.8
Singapour	2006	216 995	40.2	11.2	22.7	-2.7	246.2	216.3
	2007	243 169	39.6	10.5	24.9	-2.4	230.9	202.1
Slovakia	2004	1 355 262	56.7[1]	20.0	24.1	1.8[4]	75.2	77.9
Slovaquie	2005	1 471 131	57.4[1]	18.5	26.8	2.3[4]	77.3	82.4
	2006	1 636 263	57.6[1]	18.2	26.4	2.5[4]	85.7	90.3
Slovenia	2005	28 704	54.4[1]	19.0	25.3	1.8[4]	62.2	62.6
Slovénie	2006	31 008	53.0[1]	18.8	26.3	2.4[4]	66.6	67.1
	2007	34 471	52.2[1]	17.7	27.5	3.9[4]	70.2	71.5
Solomon Islands[2]	1986	253	63.1	33.3	25.2	1.0	52.6	75.2[21]
Iles Salomon[2]	1987	293	63.2	36.3	20.4	2.7	55.9	78.4[21]
	1988	367	68.6	31.4	30.0	2.7	52.4	85.0[21]
Somalia[2]	1985	87 290	90.5[22]	10.6[23]	8.9[23]	2.9	4.2[13]	17.0[24]
Somalie[2]	1986	118 781	89.1[22]	9.7[23]	16.8[23]	1.0	5.8[13]	22.4[24]
	1987	169 608	88.8[22]	11.1[23]	16.8[23]	4.8	5.9[13]	27.2[24]
South Africa	2005	1 541 067	62.7	19.5	16.9	1.2	27.5	28.3
Afrique du Sud	2006	1 741 061	62.5	19.5	18.6	1.8	29.6	32.9
	2007	1 993 894	61.9	19.7	20.6	0.8	31.7	34.8
Spain	2005	908 450	57.8[1]	18.0	29.4	0.1	25.7	31.0
Espagne	2006	980 954	57.4[1]	18.1	30.4	0.2	26.0	32.2
	2007	1 049 848	56.9[1]	18.4	31.1	0.2	26.2	32.7
Sri Lanka	2004	2 086 925	71.0	12.7	22.7	2.0	35.4	44.2
Sri Lanka	2005	2 439 328	69.1	13.2	23.5	2.6	32.5	41.5
	2006	2 924 172	67.6	15.4	25.0	2.4	30.3	41.4
Sudan[2]	1994	5 522 838	84.1	4.6	9.4	6.8	4.6	9.5
Soudan[2]	#1996	10 330 678	81.9	7.5	12.3	9.6	8.0	19.2
	1997	16 769 372	85.6	5.4	12.2	5.7	10.2	19.2
Suriname[2]	2004	3 489 032[25]	...	14.7	92.9[3]	...	61.1	68.1
Suriname[2]	2005	4 278 373[25]	...	...	...	...	57.4	73.0
	2006	5 086 746[25]	...	...	...	...	64.1	58.0
Swaziland[+]	2003	14 401	76.2	14.8	18.0	...	77.8	86.9
Swaziland[+]	2004	15 585	63.7	15.2	22.3	...	91.3	92.5
	2005	16 260	65.4	15.4	23.4	...	82.5	86.7
Sweden	2005	2 735 218	48.6[1]	26.4	17.4	-0.2[4]	48.8	41.0
Suède	2006	2 899 653	47.4[1]	26.3	18.1	0.0[4]	51.4	43.2
	2007	3 070 591	46.7[1]	25.9	18.9	0.8[4]	52.4	44.8
Switzerland	2004	451 379	60.3[1]	11.8	20.8	0.1[4]	46.3	39.4
Suisse	2005	463 673	60.3[1]	11.6	21.2	-0.1[4]	48.8	42.3
	2006	486 178	59.2[1]	11.1	21.3	0.0[4]	52.5	44.9
Syrian Arab Republic[2]	2004	1 263 140	64.1	15.7	23.8	-6.4	40.6	37.8
Rép. arabe syrienne[2]	2005	1 490 798	66.6	13.9	24.1	-6.6	41.5	39.5
	2006	1 708 749	66.0	12.8	21.4	-3.9	40.1	36.4
Tajikistan	2004	6 167	74.0[1]	11.8	10.4	1.8	58.8	69.6
Tadjikistan	2005	7 207	81.1[1]	14.6	11.1	0.5	54.3	72.8
	2006	9 335	80.4[1]	13.6	15.5	0.5	58.2	83.0
Thailand[2]	2005	7 092 893	57.3	11.9	28.9	2.5	73.6	74.7
Thaïlande[2]	2006	7 841 297	55.8	11.8	28.0	0.4	73.7	70.2
	2007	8 493 311	53.7	12.2	26.5	0.1	73.2	65.3
TFYR of Macedonia	2004	265 257	78.8[1]	20.0	17.8	4.1[26]	41.1	61.9
L'ex-R.Y. Macédoine	2005	286 619	77.7[1]	18.8	17.1	3.8[26]	45.5	62.8
	2006	310 915	78.2[1]	18.5	18.2	3.7[26]	48.1	66.8

Country or area Pays ou zone	Year Année	GDP in current prices (mil. nat.cur.) PIB aux prix courants (millions monnaie nat.)	% of Gross domestic product – en % du Produit intérieur brut					
			Household final consumption expenditure Consom. finale des ménages	Govt. final consumption expenditure Consom. finale des admin. publiques	Gross fixed capital formation Formation brute de capital fixe	Changes in inventories Variation des stocks	Exports of goods and services Exportations de biens et services	Imports of goods and services Importations de biens et services
Timor-Leste[2] Timor-Leste[2]	2000	393[27]	52.1	43.3	31.7	3.2	21.2	51.6
Togo[2] Togo[2]	1984	304 800	66.0	14.0	21.2	-1.5	51.9	51.6
	1985	332 500	66.0	14.2	23.0	5.2	48.3	56.7
	1986	363 600	69.0	14.4	23.8	5.3	35.6	48.2
Tonga[+2] Tonga[+2]	2004	389	102.5	18.5	17.2	0.8	20.8	59.9
	2005	423	108.3	17.9	17.7	0.7	19.9	64.6
	2006	478	103.9	22.8	16.9	0.6	16.3	60.6
Trinidad and Tobago Trinité-et-Tobago	2003	70 732	54.5	12.8	18.0	0.5	52.1	37.9
	2004	79 826	55.0	12.0	17.0	0.4	57.0	41.4
	2005	95 057	51.0	12.5	15.2	0.3	64.5	43.5
Tunisia Tunisie	2003	32 202	63.1	15.7	23.4	1.7	43.8	47.7
	2004	35 148	63.2	15.4	22.7	1.7	46.8	49.7
	2005	37 311	63.6	15.5	22.5	-0.3	48.8	50.1
Turkey[2] Turquie[2]	2005	648 932	71.7	11.8	21.0	-1.0	21.9	25.4
	2006	758 391	70.5	12.3	22.3	-0.2	22.7	27.6
	2007	856 387	70.7	12.2	21.5	0.7	22.0	27.0
Turkmenistan Turkménistan	2000	25 648 000	70.8[1]	…	…	…	…	…
	2001	35 118 973	70.8[1]	…	…	…	…	…
	2002	45 239 913	70.8[1]	…	…	…	…	…
Turks and Caicos Islands Iles Turques et Caïques	2004	486	31.1	20.5	31.0[3]	…	68.0	50.6
	2005	579	50.3	17.2	38.7[3]	…	56.6	62.7
	2006	722	53.1	19.2	46.7[3]	…	62.8	81.9
Tuvalu[2] Tuvalu[2]	1996	16[28]	…	…	67.6[3]	…	…	…
	1997	18[28]	…	…	51.2[3]	…	…	…
	1998	21[28]	…	…	54.9[3]	…	…	…
Uganda[2] Ouganda[2]	2004	14 081 960	76.6	14.6	22.9	0.1	13.4	27.4
	2005	16 268 320	75.9	14.4	22.7	0.3	14.2	28.3
	2006	18 608 430	78.1	14.3	24.2	0.3	12.8	32.0
Ukraine Ukraine	2005	441 452	58.3[1]	18.2	22.0	0.6[4]	51.5	50.6
	2006	544 153	59.6[1]	18.4	24.6	0.1[4]	46.6	49.5
	2007[5]	712 945	60.1[1]	18.5	27.4	-0.5[4]	45.3	50.9
United Arab Emirates[2] Emirats arabes unis[2]	2005	513 089	47.2	10.1	18.3	1.1	84.0	60.6
	2006[5]	624 623	43.5	9.3	19.4	1.1	85.6	58.8
	2007[5]	729 732	43.8	10.4	20.4	1.0	91.0	66.7
United Kingdom Royaume-Uni	2005	1 233 976	64.2[1]	21.8	17.2	0.3[4]	26.5	30.1
	2006	1 303 915	63.5[1]	22.0	17.8	0.2[4]	28.4	32.0
	2007	1 381 565	63.3[1]	21.6	18.2	0.6[4]	26.1	29.8
United Rep. of Tanzania[+29] Rép.-Unie de Tanzanie[+29]	2005	15 965 296	66.3	17.6	24.7	0.4	20.8	29.7
	2006	17 941 268	68.0	17.5	27.2	0.4	22.6	35.7
	2007	20 948 403	67.9	19.3	29.2	0.4	24.2	41.1
United States Etats-Unis	2004	11 630 900	70.5[1]	15.9	18.5	0.5	10.2	15.5
	2005	12 376 100	70.4[1]	15.9	19.2	0.3	10.6	16.4
	2006	13 132 900	70.2[1]	16.0	19.3	0.4	11.2	17.0
Uruguay[2] Uruguay[2]	2005	406 705	73.8[1]	11.0	12.5	0.0[30]	31.1	28.5
	2006	464 802	74.7[1]	11.0	14.5	0.5[30]	30.0	30.8
	2007	541 869	74.5[1]	11.1	13.9	1.2[30]	29.2	29.9
Uzbekistan Ouzbékistan	1999	2 128 660	62.1[1]	20.6	27.2	-10.1	0.2[15]	…
	2000	3 255 600	61.9[1]	18.7	24.0	-4.4	-0.2[15]	…
	2001	4 868 400	61.6[1]	18.4	25.7	-5.5	-0.3[15]	…
Vanuatu[2] Vanuatu[2]	1993	23 779	49.2	28.5	25.6	2.3	45.3	53.8
	1994	24 961	49.2	27.7	26.5	2.3	47.3	57.2
	1995	27 255	46.9	25.4	29.8	2.1	44.2	53.6

19

Gross domestic product by type of expenditure at current prices *(continued)*
Percentage distribution
Dépenses imputées au produit intérieur brut aux prix courants *(suite)*
Répartition en pourcentage

Country or area Pays ou zone	Year Année	GDP in current prices (mil. nat.cur.) PIB aux prix courants (millions monnaie nat.)	% of Gross domestic product – en % du Produit intérieur brut					
			Household final consumption expenditure Consom. finale des ménages	Govt. final consumption expenditure Consom. finale des admin. publiques	Gross fixed capital formation Formation brute de capital fixe	Changes in inventories Variation des stocks	Exports of goods and services Exportations de biens et services	Imports of goods and services Importations de biens et services
Venezuela (Bolivarian Rep. of)	2003	134 227 833	54.6[1]	12.9	15.5	-0.3[4]	33.9	16.7
Venezuela (Rép. bolivar. du)	2004	212 683 082	48.7[1]	12.0	18.3	3.5[4]	36.2	19.2
	2005	304 086 815	46.3[1]	11.1	20.3	2.7[4]	39.7	20.5
Viet Nam	2005	839 210 857	63.5	6.2	32.9	2.7	-4.2[15]	...
Viet Nam	2006	974 266 206	63.4	6.0	33.4	3.5	-5.1[15]	...
	2007	1 144 014 645	64.9	6.1	37.1	4.5	-13.4[15]	...
Yemen	2004	2 563 490	66.2	12.6	21.0	-0.7	36.4	35.5
Yémen	2005	3 208 501[5]	64.2	12.3	19.0	-0.5	40.9	35.8
	2006	3 760 038[5]	60.9	13.8	17.2	-0.8	41.1	32.2
Zambia[2]	2005	32 456 520	63.3	20.2	27.2	1.1	23.5	35.3
Zambie[2]	2006	39 223 128	58.9	20.0	24.1	1.3	37.7	42.0
	2007	46 483 072	56.3	19.5	26.4	1.3	41.5	44.6
Zimbabwe[2]	2002	1 698 180	107.4[1]	9.5	5.5	-14.3	5.5	9.2
Zimbabwe[2]	2003	5 518 757	112.6[1]	11.0	3.2	-16.2	1.5	3.3
	2004	15 563 920	114.6[1]	32.8	2.7	1.8	61.4	84.1

Source:
United Nations Statistics Division, New York, national accounts database, last accessed February 2009.

Data for most countries have been compiled in accordance with the concepts and definitions of the System of National Accounts 1993 (1993 SNA). Countries that follow the 1968 SNA are footnoted accordingly.

[+] Note: The national accounts data relate to the fiscal year used in each country, unless indicated otherwise. Countries whose reference periods coincide with the calendar year ending 31 December are not listed below.

Year beginning 21 March: Afghanistan, Iran (Islamic Republic).
Year beginning 1 April: Bermuda, India, Myanmar, New Zealand, Nigeria.
Year beginning 1 July: Australia, Bhutan, Cameroon, Gambia, Nicaragua, Pakistan, Puerto Rico, Saudi Arabia, Sierra Leone, Sudan, United Republic of Tanzania.
Year ending 30 June: Bangladesh, Botswana, Egypt, Swaziland, Tonga.
Year ending 7 July: Nepal.
Year ending 30 July: Ethiopia.
Year ending 30 September: Haiti.

1   Including "Non-profit institutions serving households" (NPISHs) final consumption expenditure.
2   Data compiled in accordance with the System of National Accounts 1968 (1968 SNA).
3   Gross capital formation.
4   Including acquisitions less disposals of valuables.
5   Preliminary data.
6   Including net errors and omissions.
7   Refers to Total Individual Consumption.
8   Excludes individual consumption of general government.

Source:
Organisation des Nations Unies, Division de statistique, New York, la base de données sur les comptes nationaux, dernier accès février 2009.

Les données pour la majorité des pays sont compilées selon les concepts et définitions du Système de comptabilité nationale, 1993 (SCN93). Seuls les pays qui suivent toujours le SCN68 seront donc signalés par une note.

[+] Note : Sauf indication contraire, les données sur les comptes nationaux concernent l'exercice budgétaire utilisé dans chaque pays. Les pays ou territoires dont la période de référence coïncide avec l'année civile se terminant le 31 décembre ne sont pas répertoriés ci-dessous.

Exercice commençant le 21 mars: Afghanistan, Iran (République islamique d').
Exercice commençant le 1er avril: Bermudes, Inde, Myanmar, Nigéria, Nouvelle-Zélande.
Exercice commençant le 1er juillet: Arabie saoudite, Australie, Bhoutan, Cameroun, Gambie, Nicaragua, Pakistan, Porto Rico, Sierra Leone, Soudan, Rép.-Unie de Tanzanie.
Exercice se terminant le 30 juin: Bangladesh, Botswana, Égypte, Swaziland, Tonga.
Exercice se terminant le 7 juillet: Népal.
Exercice se terminant le 30 juillet: Éthiopie.
Exercice se terminant le 30 septembre: Haïti.

1   Y compris la consommation finale des institutions sans but lucratif au service des ménages.
2   Données compilées selon le Système de comptabilité nationale de 1968 (SCN 1968).
3   Formation brute de capital.
4   Y compris les acquisitions moins cessions d'objets de valeur.
5   Données préliminaires.
6   Y compris le montant net des erreurs et omissions.
7   Consommation individuelle totale.
8   Non compris la consommation individuelle de l'administration publique.

9	For statistical purposes, the data for China do not include those for the Hong Kong Special Administrative Region (Hong Kong SAR), Macao Special Administrative Region (Macao SAR) and Taiwan Province of China.
10	The estimates refer to central government capital formation only.
11	Including net travel and tourism income.
12	Including net freight and insurance.
13	Exports of goods only.
14	Imports of goods only.
15	Exports less imports.
16	Final consumption expenditure.
17	Semi-final data.
18	As from 1999: excluding Kosovo and Metohia.
19	Includes exports of goods and services to Montenegro.
20	Includes imports of goods and services from Montenegro.
21	Valued f.o.b.
22	Obtained as a residual.
23	Including the value of technical assistance from abroad.
24	Refers to imports of goods and non-factor services.
25	Excluding the informal sector.
26	Includes direct purchases in domestic market by non-residents.
27	Data in US dollars.
28	GDP at market prices.
29	Tanganyika only.
30	Refers to increase in stocks of wool and livestock in the private sector, and to stocks held by the public sector.

9	Pour la présentation des statistiques, les données pour la Chine ne comprennent pas la Région Administrative Spéciale de Hong Kong (Hong Kong RAS), la Région Administrative Spéciale de Macao (Macao RAS) et la province de Taiwan.
10	Les chiffres ne concernent que la formation de capital des administrations centrales.
11	Comprend les recettes nettes des voyages et du tourisme.
12	Comprend les montants nets du fret et de l'assurance.
13	Exportations de biens uniquement.
14	Importations de biens uniquement.
15	Exportations moins importations.
16	Dépenses de consommation finale.
17	Données demi-finales.
18	A partir de 1999: non compris Kosovo et Metohia.
19	Y compris exportations de biens et services à Monténégro.
20	Y compris importations de biens et services de Monténégro.
21	Valeur f.o.b.
22	Obtenu comme valeur résiduelle.
23	Y compris la valeur de l'assistance technique étrangère.
24	Concerne les importations de biens et de services autres que les services des facteurs.
25	Non compris le secteur informel.
26	Y compris les achats directs effectués sur le marché intérieur par les ménages non résidents.
27	Les données sont exprimées en dollars des États-Unis.
28	PIB aux prix du marché.
29	Tanganyika seulement.
30	Concerne les accroissements de stocks de laine et de bétail dans le secteur privé, et les stocks dans le secteur public.

			% of Value added – % de la valeur ajoutée							
Country or area Pays ou zone	Year Année	Value added, gross (mil. nat.cur) Valeur ajoutée, brute (mil. mon. nat.)	Agriculture, hunting, forestry and fishing Agriculture, chasse, sylviculture et pêche	Mining and quarrying Activités extractives	Manu- facturing Activités de fabri- cation	Electricity, gas and water supply Electricité, gaz et eau	Constr- uction Constr- uction	Wholesale, retail trade, restaurants and hotels Commerce, restaurants, hôtels	Transport, storage and commu- nication Transports, entrepôts et communi- cations	Other activities Autres activités
Afghanistan [+][1] Afghanistan [+][1]	2005	327 526	39.5	0.2	15.7	0.1	9.2	8.7	9.6	13.5
	2006	396 094	38.8	0.3	17.2	0.2	9.0	10.3	7.7	13.2
	2007	491 363	37.5	0.4	15.8	0.1	8.7	10.6	9.1	14.5
Albania Albanie	2003	633 247	23.5	0.6	5.2	2.9	13.7	22.1	8.7	23.3
	2004	679 636	22.3	0.8	5.8	3.4	13.9	21.6	9.0	23.2
	2005	740 213	20.7	0.8	5.4	3.5	14.3	22.4	8.9	24.0
Algeria [1] Algérie [1]	2001	4 075 738	10.1	36.5	6.3	1.3	7.9	12.9	8.3	16.8
	2002	4 284 371	9.7	35.5	6.2	1.3	8.6	13.2	8.5	16.9
	2003	4 991 489	10.2	38.5	5.6	1.2	8.0	12.3	8.3	15.9
Andorra [1] Andorre [1]	2005	1 819	0.6	0.0	3.0	0.8	12.2	31.0	3.7	48.6
	2006	1 983	0.6	0.0	3.0	0.8	12.3	29.7	3.6	50.1
	2007	2 094	0.6	0.0	3.0	0.7	11.6	29.0	3.6	51.5
Angola [1] Angola [1]	1988	236 682	16.0	27.1	8.3	0.2	4.1	11.7[2]	3.5	29.1[2]
	1989	276 075	19.3	29.7	6.2	0.2	3.3	11.4[2]	3.0	27.1[2]
	1990	305 831	18.0	32.9	5.0	0.1	2.9	10.7[2]	3.2	27.0[2]
Anguilla [1] Anguilla [1]	2004	340[3]	2.3	1.4	0.9	4.5	12.7	31.3	14.4	32.5
	2005	393[3]	2.0	1.4	2.0	4.9	13.0	31.9	14.7	30.0
	2006	465[3]	1.8	1.8	1.9	4.5	16.7	31.7	12.9	28.7
Antigua and Barbuda [1] Antigua-et-Barbuda [1]	1986	567[3]	4.3	1.7	3.8	3.5	8.9	23.6	15.6	38.5
	1987	649[3]	4.5	2.2	3.5	3.5	11.3	24.1	15.6	35.3
	1988	776[3]	4.1	2.2	3.1	4.0	12.7	23.7	14.3	35.9
Argentina Argentine	2004	414 039[4]	10.4	5.7	24.1	1.7	4.2	14.1	9.0	30.9
	2005	492 825[4]	9.4	5.8	23.2	1.7	4.9	14.3	9.0	31.7
	2006	604 792[4]	8.4	6.0	22.3	1.6	5.8	14.1	8.9	33.0
Armenia Arménie	2005	2 076 259[5]	20.6	3.4	14.6	5.4	21.2	12.7	6.5	15.5
	2006	2 466 689[5]	19.5	2.9	11.6	4.8	26.4	12.3	6.8	15.7
	2007	2 864 580[5]	19.2	2.5	10.2	4.4	28.0	12.1	6.9	16.7
Aruba Aruba	2004	3 850	0.4[6]	...	3.9[7]	8.2[8]	6.5	21.7	8.5	50.8
	2005	4 019	0.4[6]	...	3.9[7]	9.1[8]	6.7	21.5	8.5	49.9
	2006	4 170	0.4[6]	...	3.9[7]	9.5[8]	7.5	19.8	8.3	50.6
Australia [+] Australie [+]	2004	821 859	3.3	5.5	11.8	2.5	7.0	14.1	7.9	48.0[9]
	2005	887 960	3.1	7.3	11.2	2.5	7.0	13.5	7.6	47.8[9]
	2006	961 880	2.3	7.8	11.2	2.3	7.4	13.1	7.7	48.2[9]
Austria Autriche	2004	212 011	1.9	0.5	19.3	2.4	7.6	17.6	7.1	43.8
	2005	220 061	1.6	0.5	19.4	2.4	7.6	17.4	6.8	44.5
	2006	232 494	1.7	0.5	19.9	2.6	7.7	17.1	6.5	44.1
Azerbaijan Azerbaïdjan	2005	11 576[11]	9.9	45.6	7.0	0.8	10.1	7.2	8.1	11.9
	2006	17 722[11]	7.5	53.8	6.1	0.7	8.2	6.2	7.0	11.6
	2007[10]	24 946[11]	6.3	58.8	5.5	0.8	7.6	6.0	6.1	9.6
Bahamas Bahamas	2003	5 718[4]	2.7	1.0	4.4	3.3	7.2	21.6	9.5	50.2
	2004	5 881[4]	2.1	1.0	4.9	3.2	6.7	22.1	9.4	50.6
	2005	6 353[4]	1.9	1.0	4.6	3.3	7.1	22.7	9.4	50.0
Bahrain [1] Bahreïn [1]	2004	4 167[4,11]	0.5	23.5	11.0	1.2	4.2	12.1	7.1	51.0
	2005	5 002[4,11]	0.4	25.7	12.1	1.0	4.6	12.0	6.3	49.1
	2006[10]	5 883[11,12]	0.3	26.8	12.5	0.9	4.8	13.1	6.1	45.9
Bangladesh [+] Bangladesh [+]	2005	3 555 937	20.1	1.1	16.5	1.4	8.2	14.8	10.8	27.0
	2006	4 004 536	19.6	1.2	17.2	1.3	8.2	14.9	10.8	26.7
	2007	4 513 615	18.9	1.2	17.9	1.3	8.1	15.3	10.7	26.6

20

Value added by industries at current prices (continued)
Percentage distribution
Valeur ajoutée par branche d'activité aux prix courants (suite)
Répartition en pourcentage

% of Value added – % de la valeur ajoutée

Country or area Pays ou zone	Year Année	Value added, gross (mil. nat.cur) Valeur ajoutée, brute (mil. mon. nat.)	Agriculture, hunting, forestry and fishing Agriculture, chasse, sylviculture et pêche	Mining and quarrying Activités extractives	Manu- facturing Activités de fabri- cation	Electricity, gas and water supply Electricité, gaz et eau	Constr- uction Constr- uction	Wholesale, retail trade, restaurants and hotels Commerce, restaurants, hôtels	Transport, storage and commu- nication Transports, entrepôts et communi- cations	Other activities Autres activités
Barbados [1] Barbade [1]	2002 2003 2004	4 066[3] 4 335[3] 4 600[3]	3.8 4.5 3.6	0.7 0.7 0.8	6.5 6.8 6.9	3.4 3.3 3.1	5.6 5.4 5.6	28.4 28.9 28.9	7.3 6.7 6.9	44.4 43.9 44.2
Belarus Bélarus	2005 2006 2007	56 678 200 69 637 780 82 727 920	9.6 9.6 9.2	... ...	33.4 32.8 31.8	... ...	7.9 9.1 9.9	11.4 11.9 12.3	10.9 10.7 9.9	26.8 25.9 27.0
Belgium Belgique	2004 2005 2006	257 765 269 027 281 902	1.1 0.9 0.9	0.1 0.1 0.1	17.4 17.2 16.9	2.2 2.0 2.2	4.8 4.8 5.0	14.8 14.7 14.6	8.1 8.4 8.5	51.4 51.9 51.8
Belize Belize	2004 2005 2006	1 822[11] 1 928[11] 2 103[11]	16.5 15.3 14.0	0.5 0.5 0.5	9.1 9.1 12.3	3.6 3.6 4.2	4.5 4.3 4.1	22.1 22.4 21.8	12.4 12.8 12.0	36.6 37.5 36.4
Benin [1] Bénin [1]	2005 2006 2007	2 067 145 2 217 000 2 407 500	35.9 37.1 37.8	0.3 0.3 0.3	8.1 8.3 8.3	1.3 1.3 1.3	4.5 4.5 4.6	18.7 18.3 17.8	8.5 8.4 8.2	22.7 22.0 21.6
Bermuda [+] Bermudes [+]	2004 2005 2006	4 506 4 980 5 591	0.8 0.8 0.8	... ...	1.7 1.6 1.6	1.8 1.6 1.6	6.1[16] 6.5[6] 5.6[6]	13.9 13.1 12.6	6.0 5.8 5.3	69.7 70.6 72.5
Bhutan [+] Bhoutan [+]	2005 2006 2007[13]	34 953 39 662 50 247	23.6 22.3 18.9	1.6 2.4 2.1	7.3 7.4 6.4	10.5 12.9 23.7	17.8 15.2 13.8	6.6 6.7 5.9	11.1 11.3 10.7	21.5 21.7 29.9
Bolivia [1] Bolivie [1]	2005 2006 2007	65 379[5] 74 978[5] 83 242[5]	13.9 13.4 12.4	11.6 14.2 15.2	13.7 13.9 14.1	3.1 2.8 2.7	2.6 2.9 3.0	11.0 11.0 11.3	13.3 12.5 11.6	30.9 29.4 29.7
Bosnia and Herzegovina Bosnie-Herzégovine	2004 2005 2006	13 348 14 344 15 904	10.5 10.3 10.2	2.1 2.3 2.3	11.1 10.9 11.6	6.1 6.1 5.3	4.9 5.0 4.8	17.9 18.3 19.5	9.6 9.2 8.8	37.7[14] 37.9[14] 37.5[14]
Botswana [+] Botswana [+]	2005 2006 2007	47 306[3,5] 55 512[3,5] 68 228[3,5]	1.9 1.9 1.9	40.8 41.0 43.5	3.7 3.4 3.6	2.6 2.5 2.9	4.7 4.4 4.2	10.7 11.0 10.9	3.5 3.9 3.7	32.0 31.9 29.3
Brazil Brésil	2004 2005 2006	1 666 258 1 842 253 2 034 734	6.9 5.7 5.5	1.9 2.5 2.9	19.2 18.1 17.4	3.9 3.8 3.8	5.1 4.9 4.7	18.1 18.4 19.1	8.6 8.9 8.6	36.3 37.7 38.0
British Virgin Islands Iles Vierges brit.	2005 2006 2007	940[5] 1 057[5] 1 150[5]	1.0 0.9 0.8	0.0 0.0 0.0	2.9 2.6 2.3	2.1 2.2 2.2	6.4 4.8 6.9	30.0 30.2 29.6	12.3 12.5 12.2	45.3 47.0 46.1
Brunei Darussalam Brunéi Darussalam	1995 1996 1997	7 583 7 886 8 268	2.5 2.5 3.8[4]	36.5[15] 34.7[15] 33.6[4]	... ... 14.0[4]	1.0 1.0 1.9[4]	5.3 5.8 14.2[4]	11.2 11.9 17.4[4]	4.7 4.8 9.5[4]	38.8 39.3 39.6[4]
Bulgaria Bulgarie	2004 2005 2006	32 437 35 220 39 972	11.0 9.4 8.5	1.6 1.7 2.9	17.6 17.8 18.6	5.2 4.5 4.0	4.9 5.4 5.9	9.6 11.1 11.8	13.7 13.2 12.4	36.4 36.9 35.8
Burkina Faso Burkina Faso	2005 2006 2007	2 771 713[5] 2 902 383[5] 3 143 007[5]	34.1 34.9 34.1	0.5 0.7 0.8	14.6 13.9 14.7	1.2 1.3 1.4	6.5 6.8 7.0	11.7 11.2 11.6	4.4 4.5 4.6	26.9 26.6 25.9
Burundi [1] Burundi [1]	1988 1989 1990	149 067 175 627 192 050	48.9 47.0 52.4	1.0[16] 1.2[16] 0.8[16]	16.5 18.5 16.8	... ...	2.9 3.3 3.4	12.9 10.8 4.9	2.6 3.3 3.1	15.2 16.0 18.5

Value added by industries at current prices *(continued)*
Percentage distribution
Valeur ajoutée par branche d'activité aux prix courants *(suite)*
Répartition en pourcentage

			% of Value added – % de la valeur ajoutée							
Country or area Pays ou zone	Year Année	Value added, gross (mil. nat.cur) Valeur ajoutée, brute (mil. mon. nat.)	Agriculture, hunting, forestry and fishing Agriculture, chasse, sylviculture et pêche	Mining and quarrying Activités extractives	Manu- facturing Activités de fabri- cation	Electricity, gas and water supply Electricité, gaz et eau	Constr- uction Constr- uction	Wholesale, retail trade, restaurants and hotels Commerce, restaurants, hôtels	Transport, storage and commu- nication Transports, entrepôts et communi- cations	Other activities Autres activités
Cambodia	2005	24 409 686	32.4	0.4	18.8	0.5	6.7	14.3	7.8	19.2
Cambodge	2006	28 344 453	31.7	0.4	19.6	0.6	7.0	14.0	7.5	19.3
	2007	32 637 867	31.9	0.4	18.6	0.6	7.2	14.2	7.4	19.7
Cameroon [+]	2005	8 145 956[5]	20.4	9.0	18.7	1.0	3.1	22.9	5.9	19.0
Cameroun [+]	2006	8 700 817[5]	20.9	11.0	17.8	1.1	3.1	22.1	6.2	17.8
	2007	9 157 142	22.6	10.3	15.5	1.1	3.2	22.9	6.5	18.1
Canada	2002	1 068 767	2.2	5.0	17.6	2.9	5.4	13.8	7.2	45.9
Canada	2003	1 128 801	2.1	6.3	16.5	3.0	5.4	13.8	7.0	45.8
	2004	1 200 991	2.2	7.1	16.2	2.8	5.6	13.8	7.0	45.3
Cape Verde [1]	2004	73 094[11]	11.1	2.5	4.2	1.6	8.6	25.0	23.4	27.7
Cap-Vert [1]	2005	79 118[11]	10.2	0.0	0.0	0.0	10.0	2.7[17]	22.0	25.5
	2006	93 656[11]	9.4	0.0	0.0	0.0	10.0	3.3[17]	23.4	25.7
Cayman Islands [1]	1989	473	0.4	0.6	1.9	3.2	11.0	24.5	11.0	47.6
Iles Caïmanes [1]	1990	580	0.3	0.3	1.6	3.1	9.7	24.5	10.9	49.8
	1991	605	0.3	0.3	1.5	3.1	9.1	22.8	10.7	52.1
Central African Rep. [1]	1983	243 350	40.8	2.5	7.8[12]	0.5	2.1	21.2	4.2	20.8[2]
Rép. centrafricaine [1]	1984	268 725	40.7	2.8	8.1[12]	0.9	2.7	21.7	4.3	18.8[2]
	1985	308 549	42.4	2.5	7.5[12]	0.8	2.6	22.0	4.2	17.9[2]
Chad	2005	3 032 473	21.3	46.7	5.8	0.3	1.0	11.1	1.8	12.0
Tchad	2006	3 224 799	21.1	47.0	5.9	0.3	1.0	11.0	1.7	12.0
	2007	3 274 476	21.4	42.5	6.1	0.3	1.1	12.8	1.7	14.1
Chile	2005	62 398 815[4,5]	4.4	16.6	15.8	3.1	6.5	9.5	8.8	35.2
Chili	2006	73 654 092[4,5]	4.0	23.4	14.0	3.0	6.5	8.8	7.8	32.5
	2007	81 049 075[4,5]	4.2	23.1	13.9	2.8	7.3	9.3	7.6	31.8
China [18]	2004	15 987 830[19]	13.4	4.8	32.4	3.6	5.4	9.5	5.8	25.2
Chine [18]	2005	18 386 790[19]	12.5	5.6	32.7	3.7	5.5	7.4	5.9	9.5
	2006	21 087 100[19]	11.7	43.3[20]	...	...	5.6	...	5.7	...
China, Hong Kong SAR	2004	1 244 798[3]	0.1[21]	^0.0	3.6	3.2	3.2	27.7[22]	10.2	52.0
Chine, Hong Kong RAS	2005	1 333 235[3]	0.1[21]	^0.0	3.4	3.0	2.9	29.0[22]	10.1	51.5
	2006	1 424 761[3]	0.1[21]	^0.0	3.1	2.8	2.7	28.0[22]	9.6	53.6
China, Macao SAR	2004	63 979[5]	...	^0.0	5.0	2.0	4.3	12.3	4.9	71.5
Chine, Macao RAS	2005	75 145[5]	...	^0.0	4.2	1.8	8.4	11.5	4.5	69.7
	2006	94 393[5]	...	^0.0	3.7	1.5	12.8	11.0	4.0	66.9
Colombia	2003	217 878 298[5]	12.3	6.2	15.5	4.6	4.6	10.8	7.9	38.2
Colombie	2004	245 368 414[5]	11.7	6.4	15.9	4.5	5.5	10.7	8.1	37.2
	2005	271 138 900[5]	11.8	6.5	15.8	4.4	6.2	10.7	8.1	36.4
Comoros [1]	1989	64 731	40.0	...	3.9	0.8	3.4	25.1	3.9	22.8
Comores [1]	1990	67 992	40.4	...	4.1	0.9	3.1	25.1	4.1	22.3
	1991	71 113	40.8	...	4.2	0.9	2.7	25.1	4.2	22.1
Congo [1]	1987	678 106	12.2	22.9	8.8	1.6	3.2	15.1	10.5	25.8
Congo [1]	1988	643 830	14.2	17.1	8.8	2.0	2.7	16.7	11.3	27.2
	1989	757 088	13.3	28.6	7.2	1.9	1.8	14.7	9.3	23.3
Cook Islands [1]	2005	267[4,5]	12.5	...	3.6	1.8	2.9	39.5	13.4	26.6
Iles Cook [1]	2006	284[4,5]	11.3	...	3.2	2.0	3.4	39.4	12.9	27.9
	2007	293[4,5]	11.9	...	3.6	2.1	3.7	37.9	12.5	28.3
Costa Rica	2005	9 027 072[5]	8.6	0.2	20.7	2.6	4.3	18.8	9.3	35.5
Costa Rica	2006	10 855 048[5]	8.5	0.2	20.7	2.2	4.7	18.7	9.6	35.4
	2007	12 709 110[5]	8.0	0.2	20.5	1.9	5.4	18.9	9.5	35.6

Value added by industries at current prices *(continued)*
Percentage distribution
Valeur ajoutée par branche d'activité aux prix courants *(suite)*
Répartition en pourcentage

% of Value added – % de la valeur ajoutée

Country or area Pays ou zone	Year Année	Value added, gross (mil. nat.cur) Valeur ajoutée, brute (mil. mon. nat.)	Agriculture, hunting, forestry and fishing Agriculture, chasse, sylviculture et pêche	Mining and quarrying Activités extractives	Manu- facturing Activités de fabri- cation	Electricity, gas and water supply Electricité, gaz et eau	Constr- uction Constr- uction	Wholesale, retail trade, restaurants and hotels Commerce, restaurants, hôtels	Transport, storage and commu- nication Transports, entrepôts et communi- cations	Other activities Autres activités
Côte d'Ivoire [1]	1998	6 984 000	25.6	0.6	21.9	1.6	2.3	20.4	6.0	21.3
Côte d'Ivoire [1]	1999	7 449 000	23.2	0.3	22.2	2.0	3.5	21.9	5.7	21.1
	2000	7 323 000	24.8	0.3	22.5	1.6	3.0	19.0	5.5	23.2
Croatia	2002	153 277	8.7	0.7	19.2	3.0	5.3	16.5	9.8	36.8
Croatie	2003	169 338	7.0	0.7	19.2	2.9	6.3	17.5	9.6	36.8
	2004	185 805	7.5	0.8	19.3	3.2	6.6	16.1	10.0	36.4
Cuba	2005	34 906	5.6	1.6	9.5	1.5	6.8	14.1	10.4	50.5
Cuba	2006	43 333	4.5	1.7	9.4	1.6	7.6	18.8	9.2	47.3
	2007	48 072	5.0	2.3	10.1	1.5	6.6	16.9	9.2	48.5
Cyprus	2005	7 086	2.8	0.4	8.8	2.1	8.2	19.8	8.1	49.8
Chypre	2006	7 546	2.6	0.4	8.4	2.0	8.3	19.6	7.8	50.8
	2007	8 051	2.5	0.4	8.1	2.0	8.4	19.7	7.5	51.5
Czech Republic	2004	2 529 678	3.3	1.4	26.8	3.9	6.5	13.7	10.7	33.7
République tchèque	2005	2 679 665	2.9	1.4	26.4	3.7	6.7	14.8	9.9	34.2
	2006	2 910 154	2.6	1.4	26.7	3.7	6.4	15.2	10.3	33.8
Denmark	2003	1 201 067	2.0	2.5	15.0	2.1	5.3	13.6	8.4	51.1
Danemark	2004	1 252 885	1.9	2.9	14.4	2.0	5.4	13.2	8.5	51.2
	2005	1 311 508	1.5	3.9	14.2	1.9	5.6	12.9	9.2	51.1
Djibouti [1]	1996	76 435	3.5[23]	0.2	2.8	6.8[24]	5.7	15.9	21.7	43.4
Djibouti [1]	1997	75 964	3.6[23]	0.2	2.8	6.6[24]	6.0	16.1	23.1	41.6
	1998	78 263	3.6[23]	0.2	2.7	5.3[24]	6.4	16.4	26.0	39.4
Dominica [1]	2004	611[3,11]	18.7	0.8	8.3	6.4	8.3	15.5	13.4	37.0
Dominique [1]	2005	641[3,11]	18.0	0.9	8.1	6.4	8.7	15.9	13.3	37.1
	2006	671[3,11]	17.6	0.9	7.9	5.7	9.2	16.4	13.8	37.0
Dominican Republic	2004	869 150[5]	6.8	0.5	24.3	2.6	4.8	22.1	10.3	28.6
Rép. dominicaine	2005	970 428[5]	7.2	0.4	22.2	2.4	6.1	21.1	10.4	30.2
	2006	1 135 019[5]	6.8	0.5	21.4	2.5	6.8	21.4	10.6	29.9
Ecuador	2004	30 302[5]	7.3	17.6[25]	5.0	1.9	8.8	15.1	12.0	32.2
Equateur	2005	35 067[5]	7.0	21.3[25]	3.5	1.5	8.8	14.3	11.8	31.7
	2006	39 493[5]	7.0	23.8[25]	2.2	1.4	8.8	13.8	11.2	31.7
Egypt +	2004	534 427[5]	14.6	11.9	17.6	1.8	3.6	13.6	8.8	28.2[5]
Egypte +	2005	600 641[5]	14.9	12.5	16.8	1.5	3.8	13.4	10.2	26.9
	2006	675 373[5]	14.6	13.9	16.5	1.9	3.8	13.4	9.2	26.6
El Salvador [1]	2004	15 281[4,5]	9.2	0.4	22.9	1.8	4.3	20.5	9.5	31.5[14]
El Salvador [1]	2005	16 432[4,5]	10.1	0.4	22.0	1.8	4.3	20.8	9.5	31.2[14]
	2006	17 853[4,5]	10.5	0.4	21.5	2.0	4.4	20.7	9.7	30.9[14]
Equatorial Guinea [1]	1989	40 948	56.1	...	1.3	3.1	3.7	8.8	2.0	25.0
Guinée équatoriale [1]	1990	42 765	53.6	...	1.3	3.4	3.8	7.6	2.2	28.0
	1991	43 932	53.1	...	1.4	3.1	3.0	7.6	1.9	30.0
Estonia	2004	133 577	4.0	1.0	17.1	3.4	5.7	17.0	12.7	39.0
Estonie	2005	154 580	3.6	1.0	17.1	3.6	6.7	17.2	12.0	38.7
	2006	181 711	3.1	1.0	16.5	3.5	7.4	17.4	12.2	39.0
Ethiopia +	2005	90 813[5]	46.5	0.6	5.1	2.0	5.4	13.7	5.9	20.7
Ethiopie +	2006	107 202[5]	47.5	0.5	4.6	1.8	5.5	14.0	5.9	20.2
	2007	138 503[5]	47.9	0.5	4.2	1.9	5.7	15.0	5.1	19.6
Fiji	2003	3 684	14.8	...	...	...	4.3	17.0	17.4	...
Fidji	2004	3 991	...	...	...	...	...	19.8	15.7	...
	2005	4 297[11]	14.3	0.8	13.1	2.6	5.3	20.0	17.3	18.8

20

Value added by industries at current prices *(continued)*
Percentage distribution
Valeur ajoutée par branche d'activité aux prix courants *(suite)*
Répartition en pourcentage

% of Value added – % de la valeur ajoutée

Country or area Pays ou zone	Year Année	Value added, gross (mil. nat.cur) Valeur ajoutée, brute (mil. mon. nat.)	Agriculture, hunting, forestry and fishing Agriculture, chasse, sylviculture et pêche	Mining and quarrying Activités extractives	Manu- facturing Activités de fabri- cation	Electricity, gas and water supply Electricité, gaz et eau	Constr- uction Constr- uction	Wholesale, retail trade, restaurants and hotels Commerce, restaurants, hôtels	Transport, storage and commu- nication Transports, entrepôts et communi- cations	Other activities Autres activités
Finland	2004	132 621	3.0	0.3	23.5	2.3	5.4	12.0	10.8	42.6
Finlande	2005	136 595	3.0	0.3	23.0	2.1	5.9	12.2	10.4	43.1
	2006	144 957	2.5	0.4	23.7	2.3	6.0	12.0	10.1	43.0
France	2005	1 547 758	2.3	0.1	13.2	1.6	5.7	12.8	6.5	57.8
France	2006	1 614 703	2.1	0.1	12.7	1.6	6.2	12.7	6.3	58.3
	2007	1 694 998	2.2	0.1	12.2	1.7	6.5	12.3	6.4	58.6
French Guiana [1]	1990	6 454	10.1	7.6	...	0.7	12.8	13.5	7.7	47.5
Guyane française [1]	1991	7 385	7.4	7.6	...	0.5	12.1	13.1	12.3	47.0
	1992	8 052	7.2	9.0	...	0.6	10.8	11.9	11.4	49.1
French Polynesia [1]	1991	305 211	4.1	...	7.5[26]	1.8[26]	5.7	...	...	29.3
Polynésie française [1]	1992	314 265	3.8	...	7.5[26]	2.1[26]	5.9	...	...	29.5
	1993	329 266	3.9	...	6.7[26]	2.1[26]	5.7	...	...	29.0
Gabon [1]	1987	986 000	10.9	28.4	7.1[27]	2.7	7.2	9.2	8.1	26.5
Gabon [1]	1988	965 700	11.2	22.6	7.3[27]	3.0	5.2	14.4	9.1	27.3
	1989	1 128 400	10.4	32.3	5.7[27]	2.5	5.5	12.4	8.2	23.1
Gambia + [1]	1991	2 962	22.3	^0.0	5.5	0.9	4.4	39.1	10.9	17.0
Gambie + [1]	1992	3 100	18.4	^0.0	5.7	1.0	4.7	41.7	11.2	17.4
	1993	3 296	20.2	^0.0	5.1	1.0	4.5	38.3	12.5	18.4
Georgia	2005	10 414[5]	16.5	0.9	13.5	3.1	9.0	16.5	13.9	26.6
Géorgie	2006	12 154[5]	12.7	1.1	12.6	3.1	7.8	18.1	13.1	31.5
	2007	14 779[5]	10.8	1.1	12.2	2.8	7.7	17.6	12.4	35.4
Germany	2004	1 998 740	1.1	0.2	22.6	2.3	4.2	11.8	5.9	52.1
Allemagne	2005	2 026 400	0.9	0.2	22.5	2.4	3.9	12.0	5.7	52.5
	2006	2 094 220	0.9	0.2	22.6	2.5	4.0	12.1	5.8	51.9
Ghana [1]	2006	107 038 630	38.8	5.6	9.2	3.4	10.1	7.7	5.0	20.2
Ghana [1]	2007	129 666 740	36.9	6.3	8.2	2.6	10.7	7.7	5.0	22.5
	2008	155 842 260	36.5	8.3	7.9	2.5	10.9	7.6	4.9	21.4
Greece	2004	165 775	4.7	0.7	11.5	2.1	7.7	22.6	8.9	41.9
Grèce	2005	178 017	4.3	0.6	12.5	2.0	7.2	22.5	8.5	42.5
	2006	190 098	3.7	0.5	13.2	2.0	8.6	22.2	7.9	41.9
Grenada [1]	2005	1 322[4]	4.4	0.5	4.9	4.7	17.1	12.7	19.3	36.5
Grenade [1]	2006	1 331[4]	5.6	0.7	5.1	5.4	12.8	13.4	18.6	38.4
	2007	1 432[4]	5.6	0.6	5.1	5.8	11.8	13.1	19.4	38.7
Guadeloupe [1]	1990	15 036	6.7	5.4[15]	...	1.0	7.4	18.3	5.9	55.2
Guadeloupe [1]	1991	16 278	7.3	6.1[15]	...	1.4	7.0	16.5	6.0	55.5
	1992	17 968	6.7	6.9[15]	...	1.7	6.5	16.2	7.9	54.1
Guatemala	2003	164 065[5]	14.1	1.1	19.6	2.8	5.1	19.1	5.5	32.7
Guatemala	2004	179 718[5]	13.6	1.1	20.0	3.0	5.0	19.2	6.1	32.0
	2005	197 129[5]	13.1	1.2	19.7	2.8	4.9	20.5	6.4	31.4
Guinea	2004	7 445 143[11]	25.5	16.6	6.2	0.5	10.2	18.3	7.9	16.9
Guinée	2005	9 578 049[11]	24.9	19.4	6.5	0.5	9.1	19.1	6.6	16.2
	2006	13 491 019[11]	24.4	19.6	6.3	0.4	8.5	18.6	6.8	18.2
Guinea-Bissau [1]	1989	358 875	44.6	7.9[20]	...	...	9.7	25.7	3.6	8.5
Guinée-Bissau [1]	1990	510 094	44.6	8.2[20]	...	...	10.0	25.7	3.7	7.8
	1991	854 985	44.7	8.5[20]	...	...	8.4	25.8	3.9	8.7
Guyana [1]	2004	130 533[3]	37.8	12.1	3.1[16]	...	5.2[28]	4.1	9.7	27.9
Guyana [1]	2005	137 788[3]	34.7	10.2	3.7[16]	...	6.1[28]	5.1	11.0	29.2
	2006	151 198[3]	34.9	9.3	3.6[16]	...	6.4[28]	5.3	11.4	29.0

Country or area Pays ou zone	Year Année	Value added, gross (mil. nat.cur) Valeur ajoutée, brute (mil. mon. nat.)	% of Value added – % de la valeur ajoutée							
			Agriculture, hunting, forestry and fishing Agriculture, chasse, sylviculture et pêche	Mining and quarrying Activités extractives	Manu- facturing Activités de fabri- cation	Electricity, gas and water supply Electricité, gaz et eau	Constr- uction Constr- uction	Wholesale, retail trade, restaurants and hotels Commerce, restaurants, hôtels	Transport, storage and commu- nication Transports, entrepôts et communi- cations	Other activities Autres activités
Honduras	2005	174 760[5]	13.1	0.7	20.1	1.5	5.4	17.3	7.5	34.5
Honduras	2006	196 516[5]	12.9	0.7	19.4	1.4	5.6	17.3	7.8	34.9[9]
	2007	223 117[5]	12.8	0.7	18.9	1.4	5.8	17.1	7.7	35.6[9]
Hungary	2004	17 655 448	4.8	0.2	22.1	3.1	4.9	12.8	7.9	44.2
Hongrie	2005	18 878 986	4.3	0.2	22.2	2.9	4.9	12.6	7.7	45.2
	2006	20 540 102	4.1	0.2	22.5	2.5	4.8	13.1	7.7	45.0
Iceland	2003	716 948	7.5	0.1	13.3	3.5	7.6	11.4	8.0	49.2
Islande	2004	781 200	6.5	0.1	12.7	3.8	0.5	12.2	7.6	49.3
	2005	852 669	5.8	0.1	10.1	4.0	9.5	12.3	6.2	52.7
India [+]	2003	25 706 444	20.9	2.5	15.4	2.3	6.1	15.4	8.2	29.1
Inde [+]	2004	29 232 421	19.1	2.9	15.9	2.2	7.3	15.8	8.5	28.2
	2005	33 340 889	18.7	2.8	16.1	2.1	8.0	16.2	8.5	27.6
Indonesia	2003	2 013 674 600[29]	15.2	8.3	28.3	1.0	6.2	16.6	5.9	18.5
Indonésie	2004	2 295 826 200[29]	14.3	8.9	28.1	1.0	6.6	16.1	6.2	18.7
	2005	2 774 281 100[29]	13.1	11.1	27.8	1.0	7.1	15.5	6.5	18.2
Iran (Islamic Rep. of) [+]	2003	1 103 857 800	11.7	23.1[30]	11.2	1.5	4.2	11.8	7.5	28.9
Iran (Rép. isl. d') [+]	2004	1 387 903 500	11.0	25.3[30]	11.2	1.4	4.0	11.5	7.0	28.7
	2005	1 718 477 700	9.9	27.7[30]	10.5	1.2	3.6	10.8	6.7	29.5
Iraq [1]	2004	48 206 525[3,5]	7.3	63.4	1.6	0.5	1.0	6.7	7.7	11.9
Iraq [1]	2005	64 227 556[3,5]	6.6	61.3	1.9	0.6	4.6	6.6	7.6	10.7
	2006	96 067 161[3,5]	5.8	55.2	1.5	0.8	3.6	6.6	7.0	19.4
Ireland	2004	132 092	2.4	0.4	26.4	1.2	8.9	12.0	5.5	43.3
Irlande	2005	142 619	2.0	0.4	24.7	1.2	9.5	12.0	5.4	44.9
	2006	153 586	1.7	0.5	23.3	1.3	9.9	11.6	5.2	46.6
Israel	2005	538 180[5]	2.0	...	15.1	2.1	4.7	10.3	7.6	58.2
Israël	2006	578 700[5]	1.9	...	15.9	1.9	4.9	10.4	7.6	57.3
	2007	617 315[5]	1.8	...	15.8	1.9	5.0	10.7	7.6	57.3
Italy	2004	1 252 020	2.5	0.4	18.8	2.0	5.8	15.7	7.7	47.1
Italie	2005	1 283 340	2.2	0.4	18.1	2.0	6.0	15.6	7.6	47.7
	2006	1 319 501	2.1	0.4	18.1	2.0	6.0	15.3	7.6	48.2
Jamaica [1]	2004	523 844[4,31]	5.3	4.3	13.1	3.5	10.2	24.9[32]	11.8	26.8
Jamaïque [1]	2005	586 379[4,31]	5.4	4.1	13.0	4.1	10.4	25.3[32]	11.6	26.1
	2006	656 811[4,31]	5.4	3.8	12.8	4.3	10.0	25.3[32]	11.9	26.5
Japan	2004	516 981 300[33]	1.6	0.1	20.4	2.5	6.4	13.1	6.6	49.4[34,35]
Japon	2005	522 494 500[33]	1.5	0.1	20.6	2.3	6.1	13.2	6.4	49.7[34,35]
	2006	524 570 300[33]	1.4	0.1	20.7	2.2	6.1	13.1	6.4	50.0[34,35]
Jordan [1]	2004	7 415[5]	2.7	3.1	17.0	2.6	4.4	10.8	16.0	43.4
Jordanie [1]	2005	8 304[5]	3.0	3.4	16.9	2.3	4.6	10.7	15.1	44.1
	2006	9 528[5]	2.9	2.8	16.9	2.2	4.5	11.4	15.4	44.0
Kazakhstan	2005	7 288 444[5]	6.6	16.4	12.5	2.0	8.2	13.3	12.3	28.6
Kazakhstan	2006	9 853 931[5]	5.7	16.7	12.1	1.9	10.2	12.7	12.0	28.9
	2007	12 537 674[5]	5.8	15.4	11.5	1.8	10.2	13.4	11.3	30.6
Kenya	2005	1 261 183[11]	27.2	0.5	11.8	2.3	4.5	11.9	11.7	31.0
Kenya	2006	1 440 460[11]	26.8	0.5	11.6	2.0	4.4	12.2	12.7	30.8
	2007	1 603 161[11]	26.1	0.8	11.0	1.8	4.3	12.9	12.9	31.4
Kiribati [1]	2006	79[3,11]	5.4	...	2.8	1.0	3.5	9.4	17.2	66.2[36]
Kiribati [1]	2007	79[3,11]	5.0	...	5.3	0.2	4.7	8.7	16.5	66.7
	2008	83[3,11]	5.4	...	5.6	0.1	5.2	7.9	15.2	68.3

20

Value added by industries at current prices *(continued)*
Percentage distribution
Valeur ajoutée par branche d'activité aux prix courants *(suite)*
Répartition en pourcentage

Country or area Pays ou zone	Year Année	Value added, gross (mil. nat.cur) Valeur ajoutée, brute (mil. mon. nat.)	Agriculture, hunting, forestry and fishing Agriculture, chasse, sylviculture et pêche	Mining and quarrying Activités extractives	Manu- facturing Activités de fabri- cation	Electricity, gas and water supply Electricité, gaz et eau	Constr- uction Constr- uction	Wholesale, retail trade, restaurants and hotels Commerce, restaurants, hôtels	Transport, storage and commu- nication Transports, entrepôts et communi- cations	Other activities Autres activités
Korea, Republic of	2005	721 474 200	3.4	0.4	28.4	2.3	9.2	9.8	7.3	39.3
Corée, République de	2006	754 004 100	3.3	0.3	28.0	2.3	9.0	9.8	7.1	40.2
	2007	800 304 100	3.0	0.4	27.9	2.3	8.9	9.7	7.2	40.8
Kosovo	2002	2 193	8.6	16.4[20]	...	...	9.5	12.1	4.1	49.4
Kosovo	2003	2 067	9.0	15.6[20]	...	...	10.7	12.6	4.2	47.9
	2004	2 076	8.6	15.1[20]	...	...	12.0	13.5	4.8	46.1
Kuwait [1]	2003	14 731[4,5]	0.4	39.5	7.7	2.0	2.4	7.2	5.4	35.4
Koweït [1]	2004	18 028[4,5]	0.4	43.5	8.1	1.7	2.2	6.1	5.8	32.2
	2005	24 251[4,5]	0.3	53.0	7.2	1.3	1.9	4.8	5.3	26.2
Kyrgyzstan	2005	91 698[5]	31.3	0.6	14.1	4.2	3.0	21.1	7.2	18.4
Kirghizistan	2006	101 979[5]	32.0	0.5	12.3	3.9	3.0	22.0	6.8	19.7
	2007	120 800[5]	33.6	0.5	11.3	3.2	3.9	22.6	8.4	16.4
Lao People's Dem. Rep.	2005	30 324 846	44.8	3.1	20.7	2.7	3.0	12.8	6.3	6.9[37]
Rép. dém. pop. lao	2006	31 930 054	32.9	14.2	8.7	3.3	3.3	21.0	5.1	11.6[38]
	2007	37 579 039	32.4	11.7	9.1	2.7	3.8	23.2	5.1	12.1[38]
Latvia	2005	8 029	4.0	0.3	12.6	2.5	6.1	21.6	13.9	39.0
Lettonie	2006	9 836	3.5	0.3	11.8	2.4	7.4	22.7	11.4	40.4
	2007	12 288	3.3	0.4	10.8	2.4	8.4	22.2	10.8	41.7
Lebanon	2003	29 851 000[29]	5.5	...	11.8	0.6	7.4	22.4[39]	7.0	78.7
Liban	2004	32 359 000[29]	5.3	...	11.7	0.2	7.4	24.0[39]	7.4	76.8
	2005	32 499 000[29]	5.2	...	11.7	-0.6	8.2	23.2[39]	7.3	78.7
Lesotho	2004	7 771[3,5]	16.4	2.2	17.8	4.8	14.2	12.5	4.6	27.5
Lesotho	2005	8 293[3,5]	16.4	5.1	16.9	5.2	13.5	9.9	4.9	28.1
	2006	9 371[3,5]	15.6	6.4	17.1	5.1	12.7	10.4	4.8	27.9
Liberia [1]	2005	495	81.6	0.0	6.5	1.0	3.8	13.5	7.9	3.1
Libéria [1]	2006	653	68.1	^0.0	6.7	0.8	3.1	11.8	6.3	2.5
	2007	632	75.0	0.2	7.7	0.8	3.6	14.1	6.8	7.1
Libyan Arab Jamah. [1]	2005	66 921[5]	2.2	65.7	4.7	1.3	4.0	4.0	3.6	14.6
Jamah. arabe libyenne [1]	2006	81 263[5]	2.0	68.5	4.4	1.2	3.9	3.5	3.4	13.1
	2007	89 362[5]	2.1	65.8	4.5	1.1	4.4	3.8	3.7	14.6
Lithuania	2004	56 571	5.8	0.5	20.9	4.4	7.3	19.0	12.7	29.3
Lituanie	2005	64 484	5.7	0.5	20.9	4.0	7.6	19.0	12.8	29.5
	2006	73 816	5.2	0.5	20.5	3.8	8.8	18.4	12.7	30.0
Luxembourg	2004	24 486	0.6	0.1	9.2	1.3	6.2	11.5	10.4	60.6
Luxembourg	2005	26 854	0.4	0.1	8.3	1.2	6.1	11.4	9.9	62.5
	2006	30 611	0.4	0.1	7.9	1.3	5.3	11.0	9.9	64.1
Madagascar [1]	2005	9 228 212	28.1	0.2	14.4	1.1	3.0	11.0	18.9	23.3
Madagascar [1]	2006	10 893 200	27.3	0.2	14.5	1.2	3.7	10.4	19.4	23.4
	2007	12 708 250	26.1	0.2	14.5	1.1	3.9	10.2	19.5	24.5
Malawi	2003	232 520[5]	33.9	1.2	11.1	1.6	4.3	14.3	6.1	27.4
Malawi	2004	273 761[5]	33.5	1.2	9.6	1.8	4.1	16.0	5.7	28.1
	2005	311 933[5]	31.4	1.3	8.7	1.7	4.5	17.4	6.0	29.0
Malaysia	2005	533 387[5]	8.2	14.1	29.0	2.7	2.9	12.5	6.7	23.9[40]
Malaisie	2006	586 143[5]	8.6	14.3	29.0	2.6	2.7	12.4	6.6	23.8[40]
	2007	654 741[5]	10.0	14.2	27.4	2.5	2.7	12.8	6.5	24.0[40]
Mali [1]	2006	2 912 731[5]	36.5	8.3	8.9	2.1	5.0	14.4	5.3	19.5
Mali [1]	2007	3 092 048[5]	36.1	7.4	7.6	2.1	5.5	15.9	6.2	19.3
	2008	3 454 561[5]	37.7	6.8	5.6	2.2	5.8	16.8	6.6	18.5

Value added by industries at current prices *(continued)*
Percentage distribution
Valeur ajoutée par branche d'activité aux prix courants *(suite)*
Répartition en pourcentage

% of Value added – % de la valeur ajoutée

Country or area Pays ou zone	Year Année	Value added, gross (mil. nat.cur) Valeur ajoutée, brute (mil. mon. nat.)	Agriculture, hunting, forestry and fishing Agriculture, chasse, sylviculture et pêche	Mining and quarrying Activités extractives	Manu- facturing Activités de fabri- cation	Electricity, gas and water supply Electricité, gaz et eau	Constr- uction Constr- uction	Wholesale, retail trade, restaurants and hotels Commerce, restaurants, hôtels	Transport, storage and commu- nication Transports, entrepôts et communi- cations	Other activities Autres activités
Malta	2005	1 768	2.7	0.3	17.3	0.9	3.9	19.1	9.9	45.9
Malte	2006	1 876	2.8	0.3	16.4	0.8	4.2	17.8	9.5	48.2
	2007	1 992	2.3	0.3	16.9	0.6	3.8	17.5	9.6	49.2
Marshall Islands +	1995	105	14.9	0.3	2.6	2.0	10.2	17.0	6.2	46.8
Iles Marshall +	1996	95	14.3	0.3	1.6	2.7	7.0	18.7	7.3	48.2
	1997	190	6.8	0.2	0.8	1.5	3.3	8.5	3.8	22.7
Martinique [1]	1990	18 835	5.7	7.9[15]	...	2.5	4.9	18.9	6.2	53.9
Martinique [1]	1991	20 377	5.7	7.8[16]	...	2.4	5.3	18.9	6.3	53.6
	1992	21 869	5.1	8.1[15]	...	2.2	5.2	18.4	6.5	54.5
Mauritania	2004	350 893	24.3	13.5	2.0	0.9	10.1	13.4	6.6	29.1
Mauritanie	2005	430 231	18.0	18.7	6.6	0.9	8.2	12.9	7.4	27.4
	2006	649 007	18.4	30.0	6.2	0.6	7.6	10.8	5.6	20.9
Mauritius	2006	192 126[5]	5.3	0.1	18.9	1.8	5.3	19.8	11.5	37.3
Maurice	2007	218 509[5]	4.5	^0.0	18.8	1.7	6.0	20.6	11.3	37.0
	2008	245 474[5]	4.0	^0.0	17.9	1.8	6.5	20.5	11.0	38.3
Mexico	2002	5 819 424[5]	3.8	1.3[41]	18.4[41]	1.4	5.0	19.7	10.5	39.8
Mexique	2003	6 320 583[5]	3.8	1.3[41]	17.8[41]	1.3	5.2	20.1	10.2	40.4
	2004	7 042 434[5]	3.8	1.4[41]	17.9[41]	1.3	5.4	20.6	10.3	39.3
Mongolia	2005	2 467 840[3,11]	24.7	24.6	4.1	3.2	2.4	10.0	12.5	21.7
Mongolie	2006	3 309 699[3,11]	21.9	33.6	3.9	2.9	1.9	9.0	10.1	20.4
	2007	4 107 675[3,11]	23.0	32.6	4.5	2.5	1.9	8.5	10.7	20.5
Montserrat [1]	1985	90[3]	4.8	1.3	5.7	3.7	7.9	18.0	11.5	47.2
Montserrat [1]	1986	103[3]	4.3	1.4	5.6	3.7	11.3	18.7	11.6	43.4
	1987	118[3]	4.1	1.3	5.7	3.2	11.5	22.1	11.1	41.0
Morocco	2005	473 956[11]	14.7	1.9	16.6	3.1	6.7	14.6	7.3	40.1
Maroc	2006	517 948[11]	16.9	2.0	15.9	2.8	6.4	14.3	7.0	39.6
	2007	545 689[11]	13.7	2.4	15.2	2.9	6.8	14.9	7.9	41.8
Mozambique	2004	119 374	26.7	1.0	17.2	5.3	3.2	11.5	10.4	24.7
Mozambique	2005	140 829	26.4	1.0	15.1	5.4	3.2	14.5	10.3	24.1
	2006	162 262	27.4	1.1	15.0	5.7	3.3	13.7	9.9	23.9
Myanmar + [1]	1996	791 980[29]	60.1	0.6	7.1	0.3[42]	2.4	22.6	3.5	3.4[43,44]
Myanmar + [1]	1997	1 109 554[29]	59.4	0.6	7.1	0.1[42]	2.4	23.2	3.9	3.1[43,44]
	1998	1 559 996[29]	59.1	0.5	7.2	0.1[42]	2.4	23.9	4.0	2.7[43,44]
Namibia	2004	32 930[11]	10.4	10.6	12.2	3.6	3.3	14.1	8.1	38.9
Namibie	2005	35 798[11]	12.1	9.5	11.3	3.8	3.5	13.7	8.4	39.0
	2006	42 698[11]	11.4	12.9	13.2	2.9	4.1	13.9	7.8	35.1
Nepal +	2004	548 485[11]	36.3	0.5	8.2	2.3	6.7	16.2	9.4	23.7
Népal +	2005	603 673[11]	35.0	0.5	7.9	2.2	6.8	16.5	10.7	23.7
	2006	670 589[11]	34.1	0.5	7.7	2.0	6.6	15.8	12.1	24.2
Netherlands	2004	436 874	2.2	2.6	14.3	1.5	5.4	15.1	7.4	51.5
Pays-Bas	2005	451 886	2.1	3.0	14.0	1.5	5.4	14.6	7.2	52.0
	2006	473 610	2.2	3.6	13.3	1.7	5.5	14.8	7.1	51.8
Netherlands Antilles	2004	5 026	0.7	...	6.0	5.1	5.5	16.0	10.5	56.2
Antilles néerlandaises	2005	5 293	0.6	...	6.1	5.1	5.6	17.3	9.7	30.6
	2006	5 560	0.7	...	6.0	5.0	5.9	17.4	9.6	30.9
New Caledonia	2002	435 713[5]	2.0	...	12.1[6]	1.9	9.3	13.4[2]	7.3	54.0[2]
Nouvelle-Calédonie	2003	477 656[5]	1.9	...	14.3[6]	1.7	9.3	13.0[2]	7.4	52.3[2]
	2004	520 059[5]	1.9	...	16.3[6]	1.8	8.9	12.7[2]	7.6	50.7[2]

20

Value added by industries at current prices *(continued)*
Percentage distribution
Valeur ajoutée par branche d'activité aux prix courants *(suite)*
Répartition en pourcentage

			Agriculture, hunting, forestry and fishing	Mining				Wholesale,	Transport, storage and		

% of Value added – % de la valeur ajoutée

Country or area Pays ou zone	Year Année	Value added, gross (mil. nat.cur) Valeur ajoutée, brute (mil. mon. nat.)	Agriculture, hunting, forestry and fishing Agriculture, chasse, sylviculture et pêche	Mining and quarrying Activités extractives	Manu-facturing Activités de fabri-cation	Electricity, gas and water supply Electricité, gaz et eau	Constr-uction Constr-uction	Wholesale, retail trade, restaurants and hotels Commerce, restaurants, hôtels	Transport, storage and commu-nication Transports, entrepôts et communi-cations	Other activities Autres activités
New Zealand [+] Nouvelle-Zélande [+]	2000	111 279[4]	8.6	1.2	16.3	2.5	4.3	14.7	7.4	44.8
	2001	119 882[4]	8.9	1.2	15.8	2.4	4.4	15.5	7.2	44.5
	2002	126 126[4]	7.0	1.2	15.6	2.6	4.6	15.6	7.5	45.9
Nicaragua [+] Nicaragua [+]	2005	75 138[5]	18.1	1.2	17.8	3.0	6.5	14.4	6.2	32.7
	2006	86 087[5]	18.7	1.2	17.5	3.1	6.2	14.1	6.2	33.0
	2007	96 752[5]	17.9	1.1	17.9	3.1	6.8	14.0	6.2	33.1
Niger Niger	2005	1 635 126[5]	45.9	2.2	6.0	1.2	2.5	15.9	7.0	19.2
	2006	1 734 339[5]	47.1	1.7	5.8	1.4	2.5	15.7	7.1	18.6
	2007	1 833 622[5]	45.1	2.8	5.9	1.5	2.5	15.6	7.3	19.2
Nigeria [+][1] Nigéria [+][1]	2003	9 913 518	32.6	41.6	4.7	0.2	1.2	11.3	2.5	5.9
	2004	11 411 067	34.2	37.3	3.1	0.2	1.5	13.3	3.4	7.0
	2005	14 610 881	32.5	38.9	2.8	0.2	1.5	13.5	2.9	7.7
Norway Norvège	2005	1 731 948[5]	1.5	26.1	9.8	2.6	4.4	9.4	7.7	38.5
	2006	1 926 212[5]	1.5	28.1	9.7	2.8	4.6	9.0	7.2	37.3
	2007	2 019 633[5]	1.4	25.5	10.0	2.4	5.2	9.4	7.3	38.8
Occ. Palestinian Terr. Terr. palestinien occupé	2001	3 464[5]	9.8	0.6	13.5	2.0	4.5	10.6	7.4	46.4
	2002	3 192[5]	10.7	0.6	12.8	1.8	3.7	11.8	7.9	46.8
	2003	3 565[5]	10.6	0.3	11.4	2.0	5.5	12.5	6.9	48.8
Oman Oman	2004	9 454[4,11]	1.9	42.7	8.5	1.3	2.9	12.9	7.0	25.2
	2005	11 801[4,11]	1.6	49.2	8.3	1.2	2.5	11.3	7.5	22.3
	2006	13 623[4,10,11]	1.4	48.4	10.4	1.1	2.6	11.6	6.2	20.5
Pakistan [+] Pakistan [+]	2006	7 158 527	20.4	3.1	19.1	2.1	2.5	17.6	12.7	22.5
	2007	8 257 394	20.6	3.0	19.0	2.0	2.6	17.4	12.5	23.0
	2008	9 906 099	20.4	3.1	19.1	1.6	2.8	17.8	11.9	23.4
Palau Palaos	1999	111	4.1	0.2	1.5	3.1	7.4	31.7	8.9	43.3
	2000	115	4.1	0.2	1.5	3.1	7.6	31.3	9.0	43.3
	2001	118	4.0	0.2	1.5	3.2	7.8	31.1	9.2	43.1
Panama Panama	2004	13 680[5]	7.2	1.0	7.5	3.1	5.0	16.3	15.8	44.0
	2005	14 847[5]	6.8	1.0	7.2	3.4	4.7	17.3	16.2	43.4
	2006	16 579[5]	6.8	1.1	7.0	3.0	5.1	17.7	17.8	41.5
Papua New Guinea [10] Papoua.-Nvl-Guinée [10]	2004	12 000[11]	37.9	19.9	7.1	2.2	9.8	7.4	2.5	15.1
	2005	13 578[11]	36.3	23.4	6.9	2.2	8.7	6.9	2.3	15.4
	2006	15 512[11]	33.8	26.8	6.6	2.2	9.0	6.7	2.3	15.1
Paraguay Paraguay	2005	42 086 000	23.2	0.1	15.2	2.2	5.1	22.8	8.4	22.9
	2006	47 584 000	22.2	0.1	15.0	2.2	5.2	24.0	8.3	23.0
	2007	55 843 241	24.2	0.1	14.2	1.9	5.9	22.6	8.7	22.4
Peru Pérou	2004	216 661	7.3	8.4	16.4	2.3	5.9	18.4	8.4	32.9
	2005	238 570	7.1	9.7	16.5	2.3	6.0	17.8	8.4	32.2
	2006	276 553	6.8	12.9	16.3	2.0	6.2	17.4	8.2	30.2
Philippines [1] Philippines [1]	2004	4 871 555[19]	15.1	1.1	23.1	3.2	4.4	15.8	7.5	29.9
	2005	5 437 905[19]	14.3	1.2	23.3	3.6	3.9	16.1	7.6	30.1
	2006	6 032 624[19]	14.2	1.3	22.9	3.6	3.9	16.3	7.4	30.5
Poland Pologne	2004	821 665	5.1	2.5	19.1	3.6	5.5	20.0	7.4	36.7
	2005	866 329	4.5	2.5	18.5	3.6	6.0	20.2	7.2	37.3
	2006	931 343	4.3	2.4	18.9	3.5	6.5	20.3	7.2	37.0
Portugal Portugal	2003	120 465	3.2	0.3	15.7	2.7	7.1	17.4	6.8	46.7
	2004	125 310	3.2	0.3	15.2	2.8	7.1	17.7	6.9	46.9
	2005	128 363	2.8	0.4	14.7	2.6	6.9	17.4	6.9	48.3

20

Value added by industries at current prices *(continued)*
Percentage distribution
Valeur ajoutée par branche d'activité aux prix courants *(suite)*
Répartition en pourcentage

			% of Value added – % de la valeur ajoutée							
Country or area Pays ou zone	Year Année	Value added, gross (mil. nat.cur) Valeur ajoutée, brute (mil. mon. nat.)	Agriculture, hunting, forestry and fishing Agriculture, chasse, sylviculture et pêche	Mining and quarrying Activités extractives	Manu- facturing Activités de fabri- cation	Electricity, gas and water supply Electricité, gaz et eau	Constr- uction Constr- uction	Wholesale, retail trade, restaurants and hotels Commerce, restaurants, hôtels	Transport, storage and commu- nication Transports, entrepôts et communi- cations	Other activities Autres activités
Puerto Rico [+1]	2004	82 665[4]	0.5	0.1	41.8	2.1	2.2[45]	13.3	4.3	35.9
Porto Rico [+1]	2005	86 812[4]	0.4	0.1	42.1	2.2	2.0[45]	13.2	4.3	35.6
	2006	89 515[4]	0.5	0.1	41.0	2.4	2.0[45]	13.2	4.3	36.5
Qatar	2003	87 622[5]	0.2	57.7	7.5	1.4	5.3	5.0	3.3	19.6
Qatar	2004	117 066[5]	0.2	53.7	10.2	1.3	5.5	5.3	3.4	20.4
	2005	157 810[5]	0.1	58.3	8.3	1.4	5.5	4.4	3.2	18.7
Republic of Moldova	2005	32 373[5]	19.1	0.4	15.5	2.4	3.9	13.4	14.2	31.1
République de Moldova	2000	30 455[5]	16.0	0.6	14.6	2.0	4.6	14.6	13.8	33.0
	2007[10]	45 809[6]	11.6	0.6	13.7	2.9	5.6	15.3	14.1	36.1
Réunion [1]	1990	27 417	4.0	9.1[15]	...	4.7	5.9	20.5	4.0	51.7
Réunion [1]	1991	30 371	3.7	9.1[15]	...	4.1	7.1	19.9	4.6	51.5
	1992	32 832	3.5	9.0[15]	...	4.1	6.8	20.0	4.5	50.1
Romania	2005	255 233	9.5	1.5	24.0	2.6	7.4	13.0	11.5	30.5
Roumanie	2006	304 270	8.8	1.6	23.8	2.4	8.4	13.7	11.4	29.9
	2007[46]	365 967	6.4	53.9[20]	...	...	10.1	14.9	11.7	29.9
Russian Federation	2005	18 976 137[5]	5.4	11.0	18.6	3.3	5.3	20.1	10.1	26.1
Fédération de Russie	2006	23 521 033[5]	5.0	10.9	17.8	3.2	5.2	21.1	9.7	27.2
	2007	29 100 911[5]	4.6	10.1	18.5	3.0	5.7	21.0	9.2	27.8
Rwanda [1]	2000	680 822	40.7	0.3	10.0	0.6	8.9	10.4	7.3	22.0
Rwanda [1]	2001	731 919	41.4	0.5	9.9	0.5	8.5	10.2	7.5	21.5
	2002	794 978	43.1	0.5	9.5	0.4	8.1	10.0	7.5	20.9
Saint Kitts and Nevis [1]	2004	981	2.9	0.3	9.1	2.5	13.4	18.4	14.0	39.4
Saint-Kitts-et-Nevis [1]	2005	1 058	2.7	0.3	8.7	2.5	13.3	18.9	14.1	39.5
	2006	1 175	2.2	0.4	8.7	2.4	14.6	19.5	13.5	38.7
Saint Lucia [1]	2004	1 928	4.8	0.3	4.8	5.2	6.2	24.3	18.6	35.9
Sainte-Lucie [1]	2005	2 079	3.6	0.3	5.5	4.7	7.3	24.9	18.5	35.3
	2006	2 206	3.7	0.3	5.7	4.5	8.5	23.9	18.1	35.4
Saint Vincent-Gren. [1]	2004	928[11]	8.2	0.2	5.8	5.9	12.6	21.3	20.4	32.9
Saint Vincent-Gren. [1]	2005	988[11]	8.2	0.2	6.0	5.6	12.1	21.8	19.1	34.9
	2006	1 094[11]	7.7	0.2	5.8	5.1	14.2	21.4	19.6	33.9
Samoa	2004	1 063[4]	13.5	...	15.1	4.4	8.1	21.5	12.1	25.3
Samoa	2005	1 166[4]	12.6	...	14.2	4.5	8.9	22.1	12.4	25.3
	2006	1 264[4]	11.3	...	12.8	4.6	8.9	24.0	12.1	26.3
Sao Tome and Principe [1]	1986	2 259	29.2	...	2.3	0.3	3.4	19.4	5.3	40.1
Sao Tomé-et-Principe [1]	1987	2 797	31.5	...	1.3	1.4	3.8	17.1	5.6	39.2
	1988	3 800	32.1	...	1.7	1.0	4.2	18.8	4.1	38.1
Saudi Arabia [+1]	2004	945 896[4,5]	3.9	40.6	10.1	1.1	5.4	6.1	3.8	28.9
Arabie saoudite [+1]	2005	1 189 138[4,5]	3.2	48.0	9.3	0.9	4.6	5.3	3.2	25.4
	2006	1 314 033[4,5]	3.0	49.9	9.4	0.9	4.5	5.2	3.1	24.0
Senegal	2004	3 715 004	15.7	1.2	16.0	2.6	5.0	21.0	10.6	27.9
Sénégal	2005	3 981 626	16.9	1.1	15.2	2.5	4.9	20.5	11.4	27.6
	2006	4 184 832	15.1	0.9	14.5	2.7	5.7	20.5	12.5	28.1
Serbia	2004	1 201 150	13.7	1.7	17.4	4.4	4.7	10.8	7.9	39.4
Serbie	2005	1 457 375	11.9	1.8	17.3	4.1	4.5	13.4	8.6	38.4
	2006	1 715 647	11.2	1.7	18.1	4.3	4.7	14.0	8.1	37.9
Serbia and Montenegro [47]	2000	358 753	21.1	3.6	22.1	2.5	3.9	11.9	7.1	27.8
Serbie-et-Monténégro [47]	2001	702 402	20.9	4.0	21.8	2.6	3.7	11.1	7.8	28.0
	2002	857 966	16.3	4.3	19.5	4.2	3.8	9.5	9.1	33.3

20

Value added by industries at current prices *(continued)*
Percentage distribution
Valeur ajoutée par branche d'activité aux prix courants *(suite)*
Répartition en pourcentage

Country or area Pays ou zone	Year Année	Value added, gross (mil. nat.cur) Valeur ajoutée, brute (mil. mon. nat.)	% of Value added – % de la valeur ajoutée							
			Agriculture, hunting, forestry and fishing Agriculture, chasse, sylviculture et pêche	Mining and quarrying Activités extractives	Manu- facturing Activités de fabri- cation	Electricity, gas and water supply Electricité, gaz et eau	Constr- uction Constr- uction	Wholesale, retail trade, restaurants and hotels Commerce, restaurants, hôtels	Transport, storage and commu- nication Transports, entrepôts et communi- cations	Other activities Autres activités
Seychelles[1] Seychelles[1]	1999 2000 2001	3 179 3 274 3 278	3.2 3.0 3.1	... ...	15.8[48] 20.6[48] 20.0[48]	2.4 1.5 1.9	10.2 9.1 9.4	8.3 9.9 10.7	32.8 33.8 33.0	21.7 22.6 23.3
Sierra Leone + Sierra Leone +	2004 2005 2006	3 669 740[4,5] 4 175 390[4,5] 4 692 370[4,5]	47.3 51.2 54.0	6.9 5.4 4.3	2.7 2.7 2.7	0.5 0.4 0.3	2.0 1.9 1.9	11.3 9.9 8.6	7.1 7.2 7.4	21.6[9] 21.3[9] 20.7[9]
Singapore Singapour	2005 2006 2007	188 426[11] 205 745[11] 226 657[11]	0.1 0.1 0.1	... ...	27.1 27.5 25.5	1.8 1.7 1.6	3.8 3.7 4.0	19.8 19.9 19.2	14.4 13.9 13.8	37.8 38.4 41.6
Slovakia Slovaquie	2004 2005 2006	1 210 674 1 304 080 1 479 732	4.5 4.3 4.0	0.6 0.6 0.5	23.6 23.4 21.9	4.8 4.9 5.6	6.3 6.8 6.9	15.1 15.7 16.9	10.0 10.4 9.9	35.1 33.9 34.3
Slovenia Slovénie	2005 2006 2007	25 159 27 188 30 231	2.7 2.4 2.4	0.5 0.5 0.4	23.8 23.6 23.4	3.0 3.0 2.6	6.7 7.3 8.0	14.2 14.0 14.6	7.4 7.5 7.7	41.7 41.7 40.9
Solomon Islands[1] Iles Salomon[1]	1984 1985 1986	199 213 224	53.5 50.4 48.3	-0.2 -0.7 -1.2	3.6 3.8 4.5	0.9 1.0 1.2	3.8 4.2 5.1	10.6 10.4 8.4	5.2 5.1 5.8	22.6 25.8 27.9
Somalia[1] Somalie[1]	1985 1986 1987	84 050[3] 112 584[3] 163 175[3]	66.1 62.5 64.9	0.3 0.4 0.3	4.9 5.5 5.1	0.1 0.2 -0.5	2.2 2.7 2.9	10.1 10.3 10.7	6.7 7.3 6.8	9.5 11.1 9.8
South Africa Afrique du Sud	2005 2006 2007	1 372 374 1 543 938 1 768 220	2.7 2.8 3.2	7.5 7.7 7.7	18.5 18.4 18.2	2.3 2.4 2.5	2.5 2.6 2.9	14.1 14.2 13.9	9.8 9.4 9.0	42.6 42.4 42.6
Spain Espagne	2004 2005 2006	756 669 813 434 873 703	3.6 3.2 2.9	0.3 0.3 0.3	16.4 16.2 16.0	1.9 2.0 1.9	10.6 11.6 12.2	18.4 18.2 17.9	7.2 6.9 6.7	41.5 41.8 42.2
Sri Lanka Sri Lanka	2004 2005 2006	1 876 169[3] 2 181 342[3] 2 628 795[3]	14.2 13.6 12.9	1.6 1.6 1.8	19.7 20.6 20.3	2.5 2.6 2.6	6.5 7.4 7.8	19.6 17.3 17.6	12.9 13.3 13.3	23.0 23.5 23.7
Sudan + [1] Soudan + [1]	1994 #1996 1997	4 440 648 9 015 824 15 865 432	40.5 37.1 40.5	6.5[15] 9.6[15] 9.1[15]	... ...	0.7 0.9 0.8	3.8 5.0 6.9	46.6[49] 44.4[49] 39.8[49]	... ...	1.9 3.0 2.8
Suriname[1] Suriname[1]	2004 2005 2006	3 642 655[11] 4 466 449[11] 5 270 164[11]	5.8 5.4 5.4	9.4 9.8 9.7	16.8 20.2 21.0	6.1 5.7 5.2	3.3 3.4 3.8	10.9 11.7 11.3	8.1 7.5 7.2	26.5 25.7 25.5
Swaziland + Swaziland +	2003 2004 2005	8 703[5] 9 340[5] 9 979[5]	12.1 11.3 10.8	0.6 0.6 0.4	37.6 36.9 36.1	1.5 1.4 1.3	6.2 6.3 6.8	9.9 10.1 10.4	5.3 5.4 5.3	26.9 28.0 28.8
Syrian Arab Republic[1] Rép. arabe syrienne[1]	2004 2005 2006	1 263 138[29] 1 490 798[29] 1 708 748[29]	22.5[4] 20.5[4] 20.3[4]	21.5[4] 24.8[4] 25.4[4]	3.9[4] 2.5[4] 1.3[4]	1.2[4] 0.3[4] 0.0[4]	2.9[4] 2.6[4] 2.6[4]	17.7[4] 20.2[4] 20.5[4]	11.3[4] 10.8[4] 11.2[4]	19.0[4] 18.2[4] 18.9[4]
Tajikistan Tadjikistan	2004 2005 2006	5 518[5] 6 428[5] 8 372[5]	21.5 23.8 23.9	... ...	29.8[50] 25.6[50] 23.7[50]	... ...	4.8 5.1 6.8	18.4 18.5 19.0	7.4 8.3 8.0	18.1 18.7 18.5
Thailand[1,19] Thaïlande[1,19]	2005 2006 2007	7 092 893 7 841 297 8 493 311	10.3 10.7 10.8	3.1 3.3 3.3	34.7 35.1 35.6	3.1 3.0 2.9	3.0 3.0 2.9	19.6 19.2 18.9	7.3 7.3 7.3	18.9 18.5 18.3

20

Value added by industries at current prices (*continued*)
Percentage distribution
Valeur ajoutée par branche d'activité aux prix courants (*suite*)
Répartition en pourcentage

Country or area Pays ou zone	Year Année	Value added, gross (mil. nat.cur) Valeur ajoutée, brute (mil. mon. nat.)	% of Value added – % de la valeur ajoutée							
			Agriculture, hunting, forestry and fishing Agriculture, chasse, sylviculture et pêche	Mining and quarrying Activités extractives	Manu- facturing Activités de fabri- cation	Electricity, gas and water supply Electricité, gaz et eau	Constr- uction Constr- uction	Wholesale, retail trade, restaurants and hotels Commerce, restaurants, hôtels	Transport, storage and commu- nication Transports, entrepôts et communi- cations	Other activities Autres activités
TFYR of Macedonia	2004	232 877[5]	12.9	0.4	17.0	4.8	6.3	17.3	8.9	32.4
L'ex-R.Y. Macédoine	2005	248 952[5]	12.5	0.6	17.9	4.1	6.4	17.4	9.5	31.6
	2006	274 484[5]	12.2	0.6	18.5	3.8	6.5	17.7	9.7	31.1
Timor-Leste [1]	1996	368	30.4	1.0[51]	3.0	0.7[24]	19.9	9.7	9.9	25.4
Timor-Leste [1]	1997	342	33.7	1.0[51]	3.1	0.7[24]	18.1	9.1	9.7	24.6
	1998	127	41.1	0.6[51]	2.8	0.8[24]	10.6	7.2	12.0	24.9
Togo [1]	1980	223 479	28.5	9.8	7.4	1.8	6.2	20.6	6.9	5.7
Togo [1]	1981	242 311	28.6	9.3	6.7	1.7	4.6	21.8	7.1	0.2
Tonga +[1]	2004	338[5]	28.1	0.4	4.3	1.8	7.4	16.4	5.9	35.7
Tonga +[1]	2005	362[5]	27.4	0.5	3.8	2.2	7.5	16.4	5.6	36.7
	2006	401[5]	25.1	0.4	3.1	2.4	7.6	14.9	5.4	41.1[52]
Trinidad and Tobago	2002	58 477[4,5]	1.1	15.6	15.2	1.4	6.9	18.2	9.4	28.1
Trinité-et-Tobago	2003	73 225[4,5]	0.8	22.5	17.0	1.2	7.0	15.7	7.5	25.0
	2004	82 715[4,5]	0.6	24.3	16.5	1.1	7.4	15.2	6.7	24.2
Tunisia	2003	28 254[3]	13.8	3.2	20.4	1.6[24]	6.1	17.2	10.0	19.3
Tunisie	2004	30 889[3]	14.4	3.8	20.1	1.7[24]	6.0	17.0	10.4	18.7
	2005	33 180[3]	13.1	...	19.7	1.5[24]	5.9	17.3	11.2	3.3
Turkey	2005	571 714	10.6	1.3	19.6	2.1	5.0	16.6	15.8	29.2
Turquie	2006	668 418	9.4	1.3	19.5	2.0	5.4	16.7	15.6	30.1
	2007	756 728	8.7	1.4	18.7	2.1	5.6	16.2	15.5	31.8
Turkmenistan	1999	20 056 000	24.8	...	31.4[50]	...	12.2	4.1	6.7	20.8
Turkménistan	2000	25 648 000	22.9	...	35.0[50]	...	6.8	3.5	6.6	25.1
	2001	33 863 000	24.7	...	36.6[50]	...	5.7	4.2	5.4	23.5
Turks and Caicos Islands	2004	448[5]	1.4	0.8	2.5	4.5	10.3	34.3	10.5	35.7
Iles Turques et Caïques	2005	535[5]	1.2	1.0	2.2	4.4	12.1	33.4	10.2	35.5
	2006	669[5]	1.0	1.2	1.9	3.8	15.0	33.1	8.6	35.4
Tuvalu [1]	2000	25[53]	17.3	0.8	3.2	4.5	4.6	12.6	10.0	47.0
Tuvalu [1]	2001	27[53]	17.4	0.7	3.3	4.9	4.4	12.3	10.5	46.4
	2002	29[53]	15.9	0.8	3.5	5.0	4.8	12.9	11.9	45.3
Uganda [1]	2004	12 872 976	31.1	0.8	9.3	1.3	10.5	14.1	7.8	25.0
Ouganda [1]	2005	14 097 795	31.3	0.8	9.1	1.2	10.5	14.2	8.6	24.3
	2006	16 975 908	30.3	0.9	8.7	1.0	11.1	14.5	9.8	23.9
Ukraine	2005	396 003[5]	10.3	4.5	21.9	3.8	4.1	14.8	12.0	28.6
Ukraine	2006	487 132[5]	8.4	4.5	22.5	3.8	4.3	15.2	11.5	29.7
	2007[10]	626 945[11]	15.1	4.8	23.4	4.0	5.1	14.6[54]	10.9	46.0[55]
United Arab Emirates [1]	2005	513 089[19]	1.7	36.2	12.1	1.8	7.0	11.9	6.1	25.2
Emirats arabes unis [1]	2006[10]	624 623[19]	1.5	36.1	12.6	1.6	7.4	11.3	6.3	24.9
	2007[10]	729 732[19]	1.3	36.1	12.9	1.5	8.0	10.9	6.0	25.0
United Kingdom	2003	1 030 928[5]	1.0	2.1	14.0	1.6	5.8	14.7	7.4	53.4
Royaume-Uni	2004	1 094 328[5]	0.9	2.0	13.5	1.6	5.9	14.7	7.2	54.2
	2005	1 148 553[5]	0.9	2.2	12.9	2.2	5.7	14.4	7.1	53.8
U. Rep. of Tanzania +[56]	2005	147 390 490	31.5	3.1	8.6	2.3	8.5	14.6	6.7	24.8
Rép.-U. de Tanzanie +[56]	2006	16 447 886	30.1	3.5	8.5	2.1	8.5	15.2	7.0	25.1
	2007	19 198 125	29.6	3.9	8.5	2.2	8.6	15.5	7.2	24.6
United States	2004	10 811 700[3,57]	1.3	1.6	14.4	2.2	5.0	16.4	6.6	60.0[58]
Etats-Unis	2005	11 509 300[3,57]	1.1	2.0	14.1	2.2	5.3	16.2	6.5	60.1[58]
	2006	12 226 000[3,57]	1.0	2.1	13.9	2.2	5.2	16.1	6.5	60.5[58]
Uruguay [1]	2005	412 521[4]	9.1	0.2	22.2	4.9	3.8	12.8	9.5	37.4
Uruguay [1]	2006	470 541[4]	9.1	0.3	22.9	4.6	4.2	13.0	9.6	36.4
	2007	545 451[4]	10.1	0.3	22.6	4.8	4.1	13.4	9.1	35.6

20

Value added by industries at current prices *(continued)*
Percentage distribution
Valeur ajoutée par branche d'activité aux prix courants *(suite)*
Répartition en pourcentage

Country or area Pays ou zone	Year Année	Value added, gross (mil. nat.cur) Valeur ajoutée, brute (mil. mon. nat.)	% of Value added – % de la valeur ajoutée							
			Agriculture, hunting, forestry and fishing Agriculture, chasse, sylviculture et pêche	Mining and quarrying Activités extractives	Manu- facturing Activités de fabri- cation	Electricity, gas and water supply Electricité, gaz et eau	Constr- uction Constr- uction	Wholesale, retail trade, restaurants and hotels Commerce, restaurants, hôtels	Transport, storage and commu- nication Transports, entrepôts et communi- cations	Other activities Autres activités
Uzbekistan	2000	2 788 137	34.9	...	15.8[50]	...	7.0	10.9	9.3	22.2
Ouzbékistan	2002	6 565 515	34.2	...	16.7[50]	...	5.6	11.3	0.0	22.9
	2003	8 369 111	33.3	...	17.6[50]	...	5.2	10.9	0.0	23.3
Vanuatu [1]	1999	34 016[4]	15.5	...	4.4	1.9	2.9	38.3	11.0	26.1
Vanuatu [1]	2000	35 284[4]	14.9	...	4.2	1.7	3.0	38.0	11.6	26.7
	2001	35 712[4]	14.3	...	3.8	1.9	3.0	37.8	12.6	26.5
Venezuela (Bol. Rep. of)	2003	130 552 420[5]	4.4	24.1	17.6	2.1	6.4	10.1	6.4	28.9
Venezuela (Rép. b. du)	2004	200 008 986[5]	4.0	28.3	17.5	1.7	6.9	10.5	6.0	25.1
	2005	283 769 532[5]	4.0	32.4	16.2	1.4	6.9	11.1	5.8	22.2
Viet Nam	2005	839 210 857[19]	21.0	10.6	20.6	3.4	6.3	17.1	4.4	16.6
Viet Nam	2006	974 266 206[19]	20.4	10.2	21.3	3.4	6.6	17.3	4.5	16.2
	2007	1 144 014 645[19]	20.3	9.8	21.4	3.5	7.0	17.6	4.4	16.1
Yemen	2004	2 574 135[5]	11.7	30.9	7.3	0.8	5.9	13.9	11.3	18.1
Yémen	2005	3 239 266[5]	10.4	35.4	7.1	0.7	5.4	12.7	10.9	17.4
	2006	3 815 172[5]	10.0	34.7	7.6	0.7	5.5	12.9	10.7	17.9
Zambia [1]	2005	31 454 842	21.4	3.3	10.9	2.9	11.9	21.5	4.4	23.7
Zambie [1]	2006	36 373 887[11]	21.4	4.4	11.0	3.2	15.0	21.0	4.5	24.5
	2007	43 437 518[11]	21.4	5.1	10.5	3.1	16.6	20.1	4.3	23.8
Zanzibar	2005	345 283	26.8	0.9	5.6	1.9	7.1	20.0	9.1	28.5
Zanzibar	2006	447 968	33.6	0.9	5.2	2.2	8.5	18.8	7.7	23.1
	2007	510 461	31.3	0.9	4.8	2.2	10.1	19.9	8.0	22.8
Zimbabwe [1]	2003	10 247 640	10.9	1.2	18.2	3.3	2.2	18.7	22.4	24.6
Zimbabwe [1]	2004	46 368 560	7.6	10.9	16.8	3.6	1.4	28.4	13.1	18.9
	2005	195 467 770	12.0	17.8	24.0	3.4	0.6	24.1	4.2	14.2

Source:
United Nations Statistics Division, New York, national accounts database, last accessed March 2009.

Data for most countries have been compiled in accordance with the concepts and definitions of the System of National Accounts 1993 (1993 SNA). Countries that follow the 1968 SNA are footnoted accordingly.

[+] Note: The national accounts data generally relate to the fiscal year used in each country, unless indicated otherwise. Countries whose reference periods coincide with the calendar year ending 31 December are not listed below.

Year beginning 21 March: Afghanistan, Iran (Islamic Republic).
Year beginning 1 April: Bermuda, India, Myanmar, New Zealand, Nigeria.
Year beginning 1 July: Australia, Bhutan, Cameroon, Gambia, Nicaragua, Pakistan, Puerto Rico, Saudi Arabia, Sierra Leone, Sudan, United Republic of Tanzania.
Year ending 30 June: Bangladesh, Botswana, Egypt, Swaziland, Tonga.
Year ending 7 July: Nepal.
Year ending 30 July: Ethiopia.
Year ending 30 September: Haiti.

Source:
Organisation des Nations Unies, Division de statistique, New York, la base de données sur les comptes nationaux, dernier accès mars 2009.

Les données pour la majorité des pays sont compilées selon les concepts et définitions du Système de comptabilité nationale, 1993 (SCN93). Seuls les pays qui suivent toujours le SCN68 seront donc signalés par une note.

[+] Note : Sauf indication contraire, les données sur les comptes nationaux concernent généralement l'exercice budgétaire utilisé dans chaque pays. Les pays où territoires dont la période de référence coïncide avec l'année civile se terminant le 31 décembre ne sont pas répertoriés ci-dessous.

Exercice commençant le 21 mars: Afghanistan, Iran (République islamique d').
Exercice commençant le 1er avril: Bermudes, Inde, Myanmar, Nigéria, Nouvelle-Zélande.
Exercice commençant le 1er juillet: Arabie saoudite, Australie, Bhoutan, Cameroun, Gambie, Nicaragua, Pakistan, Porto Rico, Sierra Leone, Soudan, Rép.-Unie de Tanzanie.
Exercice se terminant le 30 juin: Bangladesh, Botswana, Égypte, Swaziland, Tonga.
Exercice se terminant le 7 juillet: Népal.
Exercice se terminant le 30 juillet: Éthiopie.
Exercice se terminant le 30 septembre: Haïti.

1	Data compiled in accordance with the System of National Accounts 1968 (1968 SNA).	1	Données compilées selon le Système de comptabilité nationale de 1968 (SCN 1968).
2	Restaurants and hotels are included in "Other activities".	2	Restaurants et hôtels sont inclus dans "autres activités".
3	At factor cost.	3	Au coût des facteurs.
4	At producers' prices.	4	Aux prix à la production.
5	Including Financial intermediation services indirectly measured (FISIM).	5	Y compris les Services d'intermédiation financière mesurés indirectement (SIFMI).
6	Including mining and quarrying.	6	Y compris les industries extractives.
7	Excludes oil refining.	7	Non compris le raffinage du pétrole.
8	Includes oil refining.	8	Y compris le raffinage du pétrole.
9	Including private households with employed persons.	9	Y compris ménages privés avec les salariés.
10	Preliminary data.	10	Données préliminaires.
11	Excluding Financial intermediation services indirectly measured (FISIM).	11	Non compris les Services d'intermédiation financière mesurés indirectement (SIFMI).
12	Including diamond cutting.	12	Y compris la taille de diamant.
13	Forecast.	13	Prévision.
14	Includes imputed rentals of owner-occupied dwellings.	14	Y compris les loyers fictifs des logements occupés par leur propriétaire.
15	Including "Manufacturing".	15	Y compris "les industries manufacturières".
16	Including "Electricity, gas and water".	16	Y compris "l'électricité, le gaz et l'eau".
17	Hotels and health establishments.	17	Hôtels et établissements de cure.
18	For statistical purposes, the data for China do not include those for the Hong Kong Special Administrative Region (Hong Kong SAR) and Macao Special Administrative Region (Macao SAR).	18	Pour la présentation des statistiques, les données pour la Chine ne comprennent pas la Région Administrative Spéciale de Hong Kong (Hong Kong RAS) et la Région Administrative Spéciale de Macao (Macao RAS).
19	Value added refers to GDP.	19	La valeur ajoutée correspond au Produit Intérieur Brut.
20	Including tabulation categories D - manufacturing and E - electricity, gas and water supply.	20	Y compris les catégories de classement D - activités de fabrication et E - production et distribution d'électricité, de gaz et d'eau.
21	Agriculture and fishing only.	21	Agriculture et la pêche seulement.
22	Refers to Wholesale, retail and import/export trades, restaurants and hotels only. Repair of motor vehicles, motorcycles and personal and households goods are not included.	22	Se réfère à commerce de gros et de détail, commerce des importations/exportations, restaurants et hôtels seulement. Les réparations de véhicules à moteur, de motocycles et d'articles personnels et ménagers ne sont pas inclues.
23	Excluding hunting.	23	Non compris la chasse.
24	Excluding gas.	24	Non compris le gaz.
25	Including petroleum refining.	25	Y compris le raffinage du pétrole.
26	Including manufacturing of energy-generating products.	26	Y compris la fabrication de produits producteurs d'énergie.
27	Including repair services.	27	Y compris les services de réparation.
28	Including engineering and sewage services.	28	Y compris génie civil et services d'égouts.
29	Refers to gross domestic product.	29	Concerné le produit intérieur brut.
30	Including oil production.	30	Y compris la production de pétrole.
31	Derived from available industry breakdown.	31	Donnes dérivées de ventilation industrielle disponible.
32	Excluding repair of motor vehicles, motorcycles and personal and household goods.	32	Non compris les réparations de véhicules à moteur, de motocycles et d'articles personnels et ménagers.
33	Gross value added approximately at market prices.	33	Valeur brute ajoutée à environ aux prix du marché.
34	Including restaurants and hotels.	34	Y compris les restaurants et les hôtels.
35	Including tabulation category K - real estate, renting and business activities.	35	Y compris la catégorie de classement K - immobilier, locations et activités de services aux entreprises.
36	Data refer to non-profit institutions serving households (NPISHs) only.	36	Les données sont la consommation finale des institutions sans but lucratif au service des ménages seulement.
37	Refers to inter-ministerial expenses only.	37	Ne concerne que les dépenses interministérielles.
38	Includes Education, Health, Social Work and other community services from the General Government.	38	Y compris éducation, santé, action sociale et autres services sociaux de gouvernement général.
39	Wholesale and retail trade only.	39	Commerce de gros et de détail seulement.
40	Includes owner occupied dwelling and private non profit services to households.	40	Y compris logements occupés par leur propriétaire et services privées sans but lucratif aux ménages.
41	Basic petroleum manufacturing is included in mining and quarrying.	41	Les industries extractives y compris la fabrication de produits pétroliers de base.
42	Electricity only.	42	Seulement électricité.
43	Including gas.	43	Y compris le gaz.
44	Restaurants and hotels only.	44	Les restaurants et hôtels seulement.
45	Contract construction only.	45	Construction sous contrat seulement.
46	Semi-final data.	46	Données demi-finales.

20

Value added by industries at current prices *(continued)*
Percentage distribution
Valeur ajoutée par branche d'activité aux prix courants *(suite)*
Répartition en pourcentage

47	Excluding Kosovo and Metohia.	47	Non compris Kosovo et Metohia.
48	Includes mining and handicrafts.	48	Y compris l'extraction et l'artisanat.
49	Including Transport, storage and communications; Financial intermediation, real estate, renting and business activities; and Education, health and social work; other community, social and personal services, and Private households with employed persons.	49	Comprend Transports, entreposage et communications ; Intermédiation financière, activités immobilières, de location et commerciales ; Éducation, santé et action sociale ; Autres services communautaires, sociaux et individuels, et Ménages privés comptant des salariés.
50	Including mining and quarrying, electricity, gas and water.	50	Y compris les industries extractives, l'électricité, gaz et l'eau.
51	Refers to non-oil and gas mining only, excluding Quarrying.	51	Activités extractives hormis pétrole et gaz, non compris les carrières.
52	Includes ownership of dwellings.	52	Y compris la propriété des logements.
53	Derived from available data.	53	Calculés à partir des données disponibles.
54	Excluding restaurants and hotels.	54	Non compris les restaurants et hôtels.
55	Includes hotel and restaurants and Fishing.	55	Y compris les restaurants et les hôtels et pêche.
56	Tanganyika only.	56	Tanganyika seulement.
57	Starting 1998 a new classification - NAICS98 - is used to compile data for Value Added.	57	A compter de 1998, une nouvelle classification – NAICS98 – est utilisée pour compiler les donnes sur la valeur ajoutée.
58	From 1998 data, "Repairs and maintenance" is included in "Other communitiy, social and personnal service activities".	58	A compter de 1998, "réparations et entretien" sont inclus dans "Autres activités".

Relationships among the principal national accounting aggregates
As a percentage of Gross Domestic Product (GDP)

Relations entre les principaux agrégats de la comptabilité nationale
En pourcentage du Produit Intérieur Brut (PIB)

As a percentage of GDP - En pourcentage du PIB

Country or area Pays ou zone	Year Année	GDP at current prices (mil.nat.cur.) PIB aux prix courants (millions monnaie nat.)	Plus: Compensation of employees and property income from/to the rest of the world, net Plus: Rémunération des salariés et revenus de la propriété du/au reste du monde, net	Equals: Gross national income Égale: Revenu national brut	Plus: Net current transfers from/to the rest of the world Plus: Transferts courants du/au reste du monde, net	Equals: Gross national disposable income Égale: Revenu national disponible brut	Less: Final consumption expenditure Moins: Dépense de consommation finale	Equals: Gross savings Égale: Épargne brut
Algeria [1]	2001	4 260 811	-2.9[2]	97.1	2.5	99.6	58.0	41.6
Algérie [1]	2002	4 537 691	-3.9[2]	96.2	3.0	99.2	59.2	39.9
	2003	5 264 187	-3.6[2]	96.4	3.5	99.9	55.1	44.8
Angola [1]	1988	239 640	-11.1	88.9	-1.9	87.0	78.4	8.6
Angola [1]	1989	278 866	-10.5	89.5	-1.6	87.9	77.1	10.8
	1990	308 062	-12.4	87.6	-4.2	83.4	73.2	10.2
Anguilla [1]	2004	402	0.5	100.5	3.1	103.6	102.6	1.1
Anguilla [1]	2005	458	1.4	101.4	0.6	102.0	99.3	2.7
	2006	578	2.8	102.8	2.3	105.2	105.1	^0.0
Argentina	2004	447 643	-5.8	94.2	0.4	94.6	73.9	20.6
Argentine	2005	531 939	-3.4	96.6	0.3	96.9	73.2	23.7
	2006	654 439	-2.4	97.6	0.3	97.9	71.4	26.4
Armenia	2003	1 624 643	-1.1	98.9	8.0	106.9	93.5	13.4
Arménie	#2004	1 907 940	-4.0	96.0	11.6	107.6	92.6	15.0
	2005	2 242 881	-3.3	96.7	8.4	105.1	86.0	19.1
Aruba	2000	3 327	-4.7	95.3	-1.7	93.5	72.0	21.5
Aruba	2001	3 399	-6.6	93.4	2.7	96.1	74.1	22.1
	2002	3 421	...	...	...	...	78.9	...
Australia+	2004	897 642	-3.6	96.4	0.0	96.3	76.1	20.2
Australie+	2005	967 454	-4.0	96.0	0.0	95.9	74.5	21.4
	2006	1 046 365	-4.5	95.5	0.0	95.5	73.9	21.6
Austria	2005	245 330	-1.0	99.0	-0.8	98.1	74.3	23.8
Autriche	2006	257 897	-1.3	98.7	-0.9	97.9	73.4	24.4
	2007	272 669	-1.7	98.3	-0.7	97.6	71.9	25.7
Azerbaijan	2004	8 530	-5.9	94.1	8.3	102.4	68.7	33.7
Azerbaïdjan	2005	12 523	-11.4	88.6	8.2	96.8	52.5	44.2
	2006	18 746	-12.0	88.0	5.5	93.6	45.6	47.9
Bahamas	2004	5 650	-2.7	97.3	4.4	101.7	82.9	20.5
Bahamas	2005	5 986	-3.7	96.3	1.4	97.8	82.2	16.0
	2006	6 237	-3.8	96.2	0.8	97.1	83.0	14.6
Bahrain [1]	2004	4 224	-5.1	94.9	-10.0	84.9	55.9	...
Bahreïn [1]	2005	5 061	-3.1	96.9	-9.1	87.8	52.5	...
	2006[3]	5 951	-2.4	97.6	-9.7	87.9	49.7	...
Bangladesh+	2005	3 707 070	5.1	105.1	0.7	105.5	80.0	25.8
Bangladesh+	2006	4 157 279	6.5	106.5	0.9	107.4	79.8	27.7
	2007	4 674 973	...	108.0	...	108.7	79.5	29.1
Barbados [1]	2002	4 952	-4.3	95.7	3.5	99.1	88.7	10.5
Barbade [1]	2003	5 390	-4.0	96.0	3.4	99.5	88.8	10.6
	2004	5 632	-3.8	96.2	3.5	99.7	92.0	7.7
Belarus	2005	65 067 100	0.2	100.2	0.6	100.7	72.8	28.0
Bélarus	2006	79 266 985	-0.3	99.7	0.6	100.2	70.7	29.6
	2007	96 087 237	-0.9	99.1	0.4	99.5	70.9	28.7
Belgium	2005	301 966	0.6	100.6	-1.3	99.3	75.4	23.9
Belgique	2006	316 622	1.2	101.2	-1.1	100.1	74.9	25.2
	2007	330 800	1.1	101.1	-1.2	99.9	74.8	25.1

21

Relationships among the principal national accounting aggregates *(continued)*
As a percentage of Gross Domestic Product (GDP)
Relations entre les principaux agrégats de comptabilité nationale *(suite)*
En pourcentage du Produit Intérieur Brut (PIB)

As a percentage of GDP - En pourcentage du PIB

Country or area Pays ou zone	Year Année	GDP at current prices (mil.nat.cur.) PIB aux prix courants (millions monnaie nat.)	Plus: Compensation of employees and property income from/to the rest of the world, net Plus: Rémunération des salariés et revenus de la propriété du/au reste du monde, net	Equals: Gross national income Égale: Revenu national brut	Plus: Net current transfers from/to the rest of the world Plus: Transferts courants du/au reste du monde, net	Equals: Gross national disposable income Égale: Revenu national disponible brut	Less: Final consumption expenditure Moins: Dépense de consommation finale	Equals: Gross savings Égale: Épargne brut
Belize Belize	2004	2 110	...	...	...	...	89.1	...
	2005	2 230	...	...	...	...	86.1	...
	2006	2 427	...	...	...	...	78.8	...
Benin [1] Bénin [1]	1989	479 200	...	99.2	11.1	110.2	94.4	12.6
	1990	502 300	...	...	...	...	93.6	...
	1991	535 500	...	...	...	...	94.6	...
Bermuda+ Bermudes+	2004	2 980	25.6	127.6	-5.3	122.3	97.6	24.7
	2005	3 265	26.9	128.8	-5.2	123.7	95.2	28.4
	2006	3 483	26.9	129.4	-2.7	126.7	93.4	33.2
Bhutan+ Bhoutan+	2004	32 320	-2.3	97.7	9.3	107.0	63.3	43.1
	2005	36 581	-1.5	98.5	11.7	110.2	61.5	37.9
	2006	41 443	-0.3	99.7	12.3	111.9	58.6	49.3
Bolivia [1] Bolivie [1]	2005	77 024	-3.1	96.9	5.4	102.3	82.3	20.0
	2006	91 748	-4.3	95.7	6.8	102.5	77.1	25.3
	2007	103 009	-1.6	98.4	8.2	106.6	77.3	29.3
Botswana+ Botswana+	2000	28 245	-5.3	83.0	^0.0	83.0	54.4	28.6
	2001	34 787	-4.1	78.2	-0.1	78.1	49.4	28.7
	2002	35 693	-3.8	85.7	-0.1	85.5	55.6	29.9
Brazil Brésil	2004	1 941 498	-3.0	97.0	0.5	97.5	79.0	18.5
	2005	2 147 240	-2.9	97.1	0.4	97.5	80.2	17.3
	2006	2 369 797	-2.5	97.5	0.4	97.9	80.3	17.6
British Virgin Islands Iles Vierges britanniques	2005	931	-7.1	92.9	5.3	98.2	46.4	51.9
	2006	1 041	-6.6	93.5	5.2	98.7	45.7	52.9
	2007	1 134	-6.3	93.7	5.2	98.9	45.2	53.7
Bulgaria Bulgarie	2004	38 823	1.3	101.3	3.7	105.0	87.8	17.3
	2005	42 797	0.9	100.9	3.7	104.7	88.2	16.5
	2006	49 091	-0.1	99.9	2.6	102.5	86.6	15.9
Burkina Faso Burkina Faso	1999	1 836 037	-0.6	99.4	4.8	104.2	96.3	7.9
	2000	1 863 300	-0.8	99.2	4.7	103.9	97.7	6.2
	2001	2 046 308	-0.9	99.1	4.4	103.5	99.8	3.7
Burundi [1] Burundi [1]	1990	196 656	...	98.0	...	...	102.5	...
	1991	211 898	...	99.0	...	...	100.9	...
	1992	226 384	...	98.7	...	...	98.5	...
Cambodia Cambodge	2005	25 754 291	...	85.6	7.0	92.6	90.1	4.3
	2006	29 849 146	...	86.1	6.9	93.0	86.2	9.1
	2007	35 039 310	...	...	...	...	83.9	...
Cameroon+ Cameroun+	2000	6 612 385	-4.4	95.6	1.7	97.3	79.7	17.6
	2001	7 061 440	-3.4	96.6	0.5	97.1	81.0	16.1
	2002	7 583 077	-3.6	96.4	0.3	96.6	81.0	15.6
Canada Canada	2004	1 290 828	-2.0	98.0	^0.0	97.9	75.1	22.8
	2005	1 375 080	-1.8	98.2	-0.1	98.2	74.4	23.7
	2006	1 446 307	-0.7	99.3	^0.0	99.2	74.9	24.3
Cape Verde [1] Cap-Vert [1]	1993	29 078	...	...	...	...	106.8	...
	1994	33 497	...	...	...	...	104.5	...
	1995	37 705	...	...	...	...	109.1	...
Cayman Islands [1] Iles Caïmanes [1]	1989	474	-10.8	89.2	...	92.0	79.3	12.7
	1990	590	-10.3	89.7	...	92.2	76.8	15.4
	1991	616	-9.4	90.6	...	93.0	77.6	15.4

21

Relationships among the principal national accounting aggregates *(continued)*
As a percentage of Gross Domestic Product (GDP)

Relations entre les principaux agrégats de comptabilité nationale *(suite)*
En pourcentage du Produit Intérieur Brut (PIB)

As a percentage of GDP - En pourcentage du PIB

Country or area Pays ou zone	Year Année	GDP at current prices (mil.nat.cur.) PIB aux prix courants (millions monnaie nat.)	Plus: Compensation of employees and property income from/to the rest of the world, net Plus: Rémunération des salariés et revenus de la propriété du/au reste du monde, net	Equals: Gross national income Égale: Revenu national brut	Plus: Net current transfers from/to the rest of the world Plus: Transferts courants du/au reste du monde, net	Equals: Gross national disposable income Égale: Revenu national disponible brut	Less: Final consumption expenditure Moins: Dépense de consommation finale	Equals: Gross savings Égale: Épargne brut
Chad	2004	2 332 367	...	62.9	...	...	...	...
Tchad	2005	3 104 242	...	56.2	...	...	...	...
	2006	3 470 374	...	52.9	...	...	...	...
Chile	2004	58 303 211	-8.2	91.8	1.2	93.0	70.8	22.2
Chili	2005	66 192 596	-8.8	91.2	1.5	92.7	69.3	23.4
	2006	77 661 822	-12.6	87.4	2.3	89.7	64.6	25.2
China	2004	15 987 830	-0.2	99.8	...	...	...	...
Chine	2005	18 386 790	0.5	100.5	...	...	...	...
	2006	21 087 100		100.4	...	...	...	...
China, Hong Kong SAR	2004	1 291 902	1.8	101.8	-1.2	100.6	69.3	31.3
Chine, Hong Kong RAS	2005	1 383 049	0.1	100.1	-1.2	98.9	67.0	31.9
	2006	1 474 329	1.9	101.9	-1.2	100.7	67.1	33.6
Colombia	2003	228 516 603	-4.3	95.7	4.2	99.9	83.3	16.6
Colombie	2004	257 746 373	-4.4	95.6	4.8	100.4	81.4	18.9
	2005	285 312 900	-4.5	95.5	4.2	99.7	80.0	19.7
Comoros [1]	1989	63 397	...	100.7	...	...	...	...
Comores [1]	1990	66 370	...	99.8	12.3	112.1	105.5	6.7
	1991	69 248	...	99.6	...	...	...	...
Congo [1]	1986	640 407	-6.5	93.5	-1.3	92.2	84.4	7.8
Congo [1]	1987	690 523	-11.1	88.9	-1.6	87.3	77.2	10.2
	1988	658 964	-13.7	86.3	-1.8	84.5	81.2	3.3
Costa Rica	2005	9 538 977	-3.9	96.1	1.4	97.4	81.1	16.3
Costa Rica	2006	11 517 822	-3.2	96.8	1.6	98.3	79.7	18.6
	2007	13 570 071	-2.8	97.2	1.8	98.9	80.2	18.7
Côte d'Ivoire [1]	1998	7 457 508	-5.7	94.3	-3.1	91.2	78.7	12.4
Côte d'Ivoire [1]	1999	7 734 000	-6.9	92.1	-2.7	89.1	77.8	11.3
	2000	7 605 000	-5.7	94.3	-3.5	90.8	82.7	8.1
Cuba	2005	42 644	-1.5	98.5	-0.9	97.7	86.6	11.1
Cuba	2006	52 743	-1.2	98.8	0.5	99.4	88.0	11.3
	2007	58 604	-1.6	98.4	-0.3	98.0	87.1	10.9
Cyprus	2005	7 879	...	96.3	...	...	...	...
Chypre	2006	8 424	...	96.8	...	...	...	...
	2007	9 066	...	97.0	...	...	...	...
Czech Republic	2004	2 814 762	-5.5	94.5	-0.1	94.4	72.4	22.0
République tchèque	2005	2 987 722	-5.1	95.1	-0.6	94.5	71.0	23.5
	2006	3 231 576	-5.6	94.6	-0.8	93.8	70.0	23.8
Dem. Rep. of the Congo [1]	1983	59 134	...	95.7	...	...	76.9	...
Rép. dém. du Congo [1]	1984	99 723	...	88.5	...	...	49.5	...
	1985	147 263	...	97.2	...	...	59.4	...
Denmark	2005	1 548 153	1.4[4]	101.4	-1.9	99.5	75.0	24.5
Danemark	2006	1 641 520	1.9[4]	101.9	-2.0	99.9	74.7	25.2
	2007	1 696 238	1.8[4]	101.8	-1.9	100.0	75.5	24.5
Djibouti [1]	1996	88 233	1.0[2]	100.0	9.4	109.4	97.3	12.1
Djibouti [1]	1997	87 289	1.2[2]	99.9	8.3	108.2	94.2	14.0
	1998	88 461	1.2[2]	99.9	8.3	108.3	96.4	11.8
Dominica [1]	1989	423	...	101.0	...	...	92.0	...
Dominique [1]	1990	452	...	101.1	...	...	84.4	...
	1991	479	...	101.0	...	...	91.4	...

21

Relationships among the principal national accounting aggregates *(continued)*
As a percentage of Gross Domestic Product (GDP)
Relations entre les principaux agrégats de comptabilité nationale *(suite)*
En pourcentage du Produit Intérieur Brut (PIB)

As a percentage of GDP - En pourcentage du PIB

Country or area Pays ou zone	Year Année	GDP at current prices (mil.nat.cur.) PIB aux prix courants (millions monnaie nat.)	Plus: Compensation of employees and property income from/to the rest of the world, net Plus: Rémunération des salariés et revenus de la propriété du/au reste du monde, net	Equals: Gross national income Égale: Revenu national brut	Plus: Net current transfers from/to the rest of the world Plus: Transferts courants du/au reste du monde, net	Equals: Gross national disposable income Égale: Revenu national disponible brut	Less: Final consumption expenditure Moins: Dépense de consommation finale	Equals: Gross savings Égale: Épargne brut
Dominican Republic	1994	179 130	-2.2	97.8	6.7	104.5	81.4	23.1
Rép. dominicaine	1995	209 646	-2.3	97.7	6.2	103.9	82.9	21.0
	1996	243 973	-5.4	94.6	6.1	100.7	82.2	18.5
Ecuador	2005	37 187	-5.2	94.8	7.1	101.9	77.1	24.7
Equateur	2006	41 402	-4.8	95.2	7.4	102.6	75.9	26.7
	2007[3]	44 400	...	...	...	...	77.5	...
Egypt[+]	2004	510 751	-0.8	99.2	4.6	103.8	83.2	20.5
Egypte[+]	2005	568 192	-1.1	98.9	5.5	104.4	84.0	20.5
	2006	642 986	-0.4	99.6	4.7	104.3	83.6	20.7
El Salvador[1]	2004	15 798	-2.9	97.1	16.2	113.3	101.0	12.2
El Salvador[1]	2005	17 070	-3.3	96.7	17.8	114.4	103.0	11.5
	2006	18 654	-2.8	97.2	18.7	115.9	103.6	12.4
Estonia	2004	149 923	-5.2	95.1	0.5	95.6	73.0	22.5
Estonie	2005	175 392	-4.1	96.1	^0.0	96.2	70.6	25.6
	2006	207 061	-4.8	95.4	0.3	95.7	70.4	25.2
Ethiopia[+]	2004	81 755	-0.4	99.6	11.5	111.1	92.7	18.4
Ethiopie[+]	2005	98 398	-0.1	99.9	8.9	108.8	93.6	15.2
	2006	115 589	-0.1	99.9	11.7	111.6	92.4	19.3
Fiji	2003	4 378	0.0	100.0	4.2	104.2	67.9	54.7
Fidji	2004	4 728	0.0	100.0	2.9	102.9	64.7	71.0
	2005	5 069	1.4	101.4	4.9	106.3	62.5	79.9
Finland	2005	157 335	0.6	100.6	-1.1	99.5	73.8	25.7
Finlande	2006	167 041	1.0	101.0	-1.0	100.0	73.2	26.8
	2007	178 759	0.7	100.7	-1.0	99.7	71.8	27.9
France	2005	1 726 068	0.6[5]	100.6	-1.6	99.1	80.5	18.5
France	2006	1 807 462	0.7[5]	100.7	-1.5	99.2	80.1	19.1
	2007	1 892 244	0.5[5]	100.5	-1.4	99.1	79.8	19.3
French Guiana[1]	1990	6 526	-1.9[2]	98.1	36.3	134.4	99.4	35.0
Guyane française[1]	1991	7 404	-5.8[2]	94.2	35.9	130.1	94.5	35.6
	1992	7 976	-6.9[2]	93.1	36.4	129.6	93.1	36.4
Gabon[1]	1987	1 020 600	-6.2[2]	93.8	-4.2	89.7	72.4	17.3
Gabon[1]	1988	1 013 600	-7.4[2]	92.6	-7.6	85.0	69.9	15.1
	1989	1 168 066	-8.6[2]	91.4	-6.1	85.3	66.8	18.5
Gambia[+][1]	1991	2 920	...	98.3	...	115.7	96.7	19.0
Gambie[+][1]	1992	3 078	...	98.7	...	114.1	94.4	19.7
	1993	3 243	...	98.5	...	114.4	93.3	21.1
Georgia	2005	11 621	1.4	101.5	5.6	107.1	84.3	22.7
Géorgie	2006	13 790	2.3	102.3	6.7	108.9	94.1	14.9
	2007	16 999	...	102.2	6.1	108.3	92.5	15.7
Germany	2005	2 244 600	0.9[5]	100.9	-1.2	99.7	77.9	21.8
Allemagne	2006	2 322 200	1.0[5]	101.0	-1.2	99.8	76.8	23.0
	2007	2 423 800	1.0[5]	101.0	-1.1	99.9	74.7	25.2
Ghana[1]	1994	5 205 200	...	98.0	...	...	...	...
Ghana[1]	1995	7 752 600	...	98.0	...	...	...	...
	1996	11 339 200	...	98.1	...	...	...	...
Greece	2005	198 609	-2.0[5]	98.0	-0.1	97.9	87.5	10.4
Grèce	2006	213 985	-1.8[5]	98.2	^0.0	98.1	86.8	11.3
	2007	228 949	-2.4[5]	97.6	-0.8	96.8	87.5	9.3

21

Relationships among the principal national accounting aggregates *(continued)*
As a percentage of Gross Domestic Product (GDP)

Relations entre les principaux agrégats de comptabilité nationale *(suite)*
En pourcentage du Produit Intérieur Brut (PIB)

			As a percentage of GDP - En pourcentage du PIB					
Country or area Pays ou zone	Year Année	GDP at current prices (mil.nat.cur.) PIB aux prix courants (millions monnaie nat.)	Plus: Compensation of employees and property income from/to the rest of the world, net Plus: Rémunération des salariés et revenus de la propriété du/au reste du monde, net	Equals: Gross national income Égale: Revenu national brut	Plus: Net current transfers from/to the rest of the world Plus: Transferts courants du/au reste du monde, net	Equals: Gross national disposable income Égale: Revenu national disponible brut	Less: Final consumption expenditure Moins: Dépense de consommation finale	Equals: Gross savings Égale: Épargne brut
Greenland [1] Groenland [1]	2003	9 397	-2.6	97.4	38.7	136.1	...	...
	2004	9 827	-2.5	97.5	36.7	134.2	...	...
	2005	10 210	-2.4	97.6	35.9	133.5	...	...
Grenada [1] Grenade [1]	1984	275	...	98.9	...	...	99.1	...
	1985	311	...	98.9	...	...	99.0	...
	1986	350	...	99.2	...	...	97.7	...
Guadeloupe [1] Guadeloupe [1]	1990	15 201	-2.5[2]	97.5	37.3	134.8	123.6	11.2
	1991	16 415	-3.4[2]	96.6	35.4	132.0	118.3	13.7
	1992	17 972	-3.0[2]	97.0	36.6	133.6	113.4	20.2
Guatemala Guatemala	2003	174 044	-1.5	98.5	10.0	108.5	94.1	14.4
	2004	190 440	-1.4	98.6	11.3	109.9	94.3	15.6
	2005	207 729	-1.2	98.8	11.6	110.4	96.2	14.2
Guinea-Bissau [1] Guinée-Bissau [1]	1986	46 973	-1.7	98.3	2.9	101.3	102.8	-1.5
	1987	92 375	-0.5	99.5	4.1	103.6	100.8	2.8
Guyana [1] Guyana [1]	2004	156 358	...	96.0	...	...	78.6	...
	2005	165 028	...	97.5	...	...	100.2	...
	2006	180 282	...	95.1	...	...	89.3	...
Haiti+ [1] Haïti+ [1]	1995	35 207	...	98.7	22.8	121.5	108.1	13.4
	1996	43 234	...	99.6	17.1	116.7	104.9	11.8
	1997	51 789	...	99.6	14.1	113.7	103.7	10.0
Honduras Honduras	2005	183 749	-4.7	95.3	20.2	115.5	90.9	24.7
	2006	204 685	-5.0	95.0	22.6	117.6	91.6	26.0
	2007	232 817	-4.9	95.1	21.3	116.4	93.4	22.9
Hungary Hongrie	2005	22 042 476	-6.1	93.9	0.4	94.2	77.5	16.7
	2006	23 795 306	-6.6	93.4	0.5	93.9	76.4	17.5
	2007	25 405 796	...	...	...	...	74.7	...
Iceland Islande	2005	1 026 251	-3.6	96.4	-0.2	96.3	84.1	12.2
	2006	1 167 684	-7.2	92.8	-0.2	92.6	83.1	9.5
	2007	1 279 379	-4.7	95.3	-0.3	95.0	82.9	12.1
India+ Inde+	2004	31 494 120	-0.7	99.3	2.9	102.2	69.2	31.8
	2005	35 803 440	-0.7	99.3	3.0	102.3	67.8	34.3
	2006	41 458 100	-0.7	99.3	3.0	102.3	66.1	34.8
Indonesia [1] Indonésie [1]	2001	1 467 660 000	...	95.8	...	...	74.0	...
	2002	1 610 570 000	...	96.6	...	...	77.8	...
	2003	1 786 690 000	...	95.5	...	...	78.5	...
Iran (Islamic Rep. of)+ Iran (Rép. islamique d')+	2003	1 119 661 000	-1.9	98.1	0.0	98.1	57.7	40.3
	2004	1 401 899 100	-1.8	98.2	0.0	98.2	57.7	40.5
	2005	1 721 260 900	-1.8	98.2	0.0	98.2	57.1	41.0
Iraq [1] Iraq [1]	2003	20 562 256	0.2	100.2	9.3	109.5	83.9	25.6
	2004	37 049 252	0.2	100.2	7.5	107.7	85.0	22.8
	2005	49 990 680	2.2	102.2	9.7	111.9	72.9	39.0
Ireland Irlande	2004	148 502	-14.6[5]	85.4	-0.7	84.6	61.3	23.4
	2005	161 498	-14.8[5]	85.2	-1.0	84.2	61.5	22.7
	2006	174 705	-13.9[5]	86.1	-1.0	85.1	61.5	23.6
Israel Israël	2005	597 773	-1.2	98.8	4.5	103.3	81.5	21.8
	2006	640 776	0.1	100.1	5.2	105.2	80.6	24.6
	2007	673 552	^0.0	100.0	4.4	104.4	81.6	22.8

21

Relationships among the principal national accounting aggregates *(continued)*
As a percentage of Gross Domestic Product (GDP)

Relations entre les principaux agrégats de comptabilité nationale *(suite)*
En pourcentage du Produit Intérieur Brut (PIB)

Country or area Pays ou zone	Year Année	GDP at current prices (mil.nat.cur.) PIB aux prix courants (millions monnaie nat.)	Plus: Compensation of employees and property income from/to the rest of the world, net Plus: Rémunération des salariés et revenus de la propriété du/au reste du monde, net	Equals: Gross national income Égale: Revenu national brut	Plus: Net current transfers from/to the rest of the world Plus: Transferts courants du/au reste du monde, net	Equals: Gross national disposable income Égale: Revenu national disponible brut	Less: Final consumption expenditure Moins: Dépense de consommation finale	Equals: Gross savings Égale: Épargne brut
Italy Italie	2005	1 428 375	-0.3	99.7	-0.8	98.9	79.3	19.6
	2006	1 479 981	-0.2	99.8	-1.0	98.9	79.3	19.6
	2007	1 535 540	-0.5	99.5	-0.9	98.6	78.8	19.7
Jamaica [1] Jamaïque [1]	2003	472 918	-6.0	94.0	13.0	107.0	88.0	19.0
	2004	540 809	-4.6	95.4	14.3	109.7	86.8	22.9
	2005	605 030	-8.4	91.6	14.7	106.3	88.0	18.3
Japan Japon	2004	498 328 400	1.9	101.9	-0.1	101.8	75.0	25.8
	2005	501 734 400	2.4	102.4	-0.1	102.3	75.0	26.8
	2006	508 925 100	2.8	102.8	-0.2	102.7	74.8	26.6
Jordan [1] Jordanie [1]	2004	8 091	1.7	101.7	28.5	130.2	102.3	27.9
	2005	8 954	2.4	102.3	21.1	123.3	106.7	16.7
	2006	10 521	3.4	103.4	20.4	123.7	102.5	21.3
Kazakhstan Kazakhstan	2004	5 870 134	-6.6	93.4	-1.1	92.3	65.1	27.1
	2005	7 590 594	-9.4	90.6	-0.7	89.9	61.1	28.8
	2006	10 213 731	-11.5	88.5	-1.5	87.1	55.9	31.2
Kenya Kenya	2005	1 418 071	-0.6[6]	99.4	5.5	106.2	92.6	13.6
	2006	1 620 732	-0.3[6]	99.7	8.0	107.7	91.7	16.0
	2007	1 814 229	-0.7[6]	99.3	7.9	107.2	93.5	13.6
Kiribati [1] Kiribati [1]	2006	84	86.0[5]	186.0	...	...	...	...
	2007	84	86.7[5]	186.7	...	...	...	...
	2008	93	79.4[5]	179.4	...	...	...	...
Korea, Republic of Corée, République de	2005	810 515 900	-0.2	99.9	-0.3	99.5	66.8	32.7
	2006	848 044 600	0.1	100.1	-0.5	99.7	68.5	31.2
	2007	901 188 600	0.2	100.2	-0.4	99.8	69.2	30.6
Kuwait [1] Koweït [1]	1999	9 170	17.0	117.0	-6.7	110.3	78.9	31.4
	2000	11 510	17.9	118.4	-5.2	113.2	63.3	49.8
	2001	10 700	14.0	114.0	-6.0	108.1	69.9	38.2
Kyrgyzstan Kirghizistan	2004	94 351	-4.5	95.5	9.1	104.6	94.2	10.4
	2005	100 899	-3.3	96.7	13.5	110.2	102.1	8.2
	2006	113 800	-1.2	98.8	25.1	123.9	113.1	10.8
Latvia Lettonie	2005	9 059	-1.8	98.7	3.2	101.9	80.0	21.9
	2006	11 172	-3.4	97.0	1.9	99.0	81.8	17.2
	2007	13 957	-4.1	96.3	1.1	97.4	83.7	13.6
Lebanon Liban	2003	29 851 000	-1.2	98.8	17.0	115.8	101.8	14.0
	2004	32 359 000	-3.8	96.2	15.7	111.9	100.4	11.4
	2005	32 499 000	2.1	102.1	12.5	114.6	100.1	14.4
Lesotho Lesotho	2004	8 518	22.9[5]	122.9	21.1	144.0	112.5	31.5
	2005	9 065	21.3[5]	121.3	22.4	143.7	116.2	27.5
	2006	10 120	25.4[5]	125.4	26.8	152.2	115.0	37.2
Liberia [1] Libéria [1]	1987	1 090	...	83.2	...	...	...	...
	1988	1 158	...	84.2	...	...	...	...
	1989	1 194	...	84.9	...	...	...	...
Libyan Arab Jamah. [1] Jamah. arabe libyenne [1]	1983	8 805	-6.9[7]	91.0	-0.2	90.9	72.0	18.9
	1984	8 013	-4.6[7]	92.7	-0.3	92.4	72.2	20.2
	1985	8 277	-2.9[7]	96.7	-0.2	96.5	69.2	27.3
Liechtenstein Liechtenstein	2004	4 296	...	82.7	...	...	...	...
	2005	4 555	...	85.4	...	...	...	...
	2006[3]	5 001	...	87.9	...	...	...	...

21

Relationships among the principal national accounting aggregates *(continued)*
As a percentage of Gross Domestic Product (GDP)
Relations entre les principaux agrégats de comptabilité nationale *(suite)*
En pourcentage du Produit Intérieur Brut (PIB)

As a percentage of GDP - En pourcentage du PIB

Country or area Pays ou zone	Year Année	GDP at current prices (mil.nat.cur.) PIB aux prix courants (millions monnaie nat.)	Plus: Compensation of employees and property income from/to the rest of the world, net Plus: Rémunération des salariés et revenus de la propriété du/au reste du monde, net	Equals: Gross national income Égale: Revenu national brut	Plus: Net current transfers from/to the rest of the world Plus: Transferts courants du/au reste du monde, net	Equals: Gross national disposable income Égale: Revenu national disponible brut	Less: Final consumption expenditure Moins: Dépense de consommation finale	Equals: Gross savings Égale: Épargne brut
Lithuania	2004	62 587	-2.6	97.9	1.7	99.6	83.1	16.4
Lituanie	2005	71 380	-2.4	98.4	1.8	100.2	82.2	17.9
	2006	81 905	-2.8	97.8	2.1	99.9	83.4	16.5
Luxembourg	2004	27 439	-13.1[4]	86.9	...	...	56.5	...
Luxembourg	2005	30 032	-16.7[4]	83.3	...	...	55.2	...
	2006	33 852	-18.2[4]	81.8	...	...	51.3	...
Madagascar [1]								
Madagascar [1]	1980	689 800	...	99.9	...	...		
Malawi [1]	1994	11 209	-3.6	96.4	9.2	105.6	...	...
Malawi [1]	1995	20 246	-3.1	96.9	9.6	105.0	...	...
	1996	23 993	-1.8	98.2	3.4	101.6	...	...
Malaysia	2005	522 445	-4.6	95.4	-3.2	92.2	57.2	35.0
Malaisie	2006	573 736	-3.0	97.0	-2.9	94.0	56.8	37.2
	2007	641 864	-2.1	97.9	-2.5	95.4	57.8	37.6
Maldives	2004	9 939	-5.5[2]	94.5	-7.0	87.5	56.5	31.0
Maldives	2005	9 607	-4.9[2]	95.1	4.9	100.0	71.9	28.1
	2006	11 608	-4.1[2]	95.9	5.7	101.6	67.7	33.9
Mali [1]	1990	683 300	-1.2[2]	98.8	11.5	110.3	94.3	16.1
Mali [1]	1991	691 400	-1.3[2]	98.7	13.0	111.9	100.4	11.5
	1992	737 400	-1.2[2]	98.8	11.4	110.2	96.4	13.8
Malta	2005	2 061	-4.2	95.5	...	...	...	...
Malte	2006	2 187	-4.2	95.6	...	...	...	...
	2007	2 325	-2.4	97.3	...	...	...	...
Martinique [1]	1990	19 320	-4.2[2]	95.8	33.7	...	113.3	...
Martinique [1]	1991	20 787	-4.4[2]	95.6	30.7	...	112.8	...
	1992	22 093	-3.9[2]	96.1	33.4	...	113.1	...
Mauritania	2002	311 087	10.8	110.8	8.8	119.6	96.4	23.2
Mauritanie	2003	336 818	4.6	104.6	10.8	115.4	102.7	12.6
	2004	395 268	4.4	104.4	7.3	111.7	92.9	18.8
Mauritius	2006	206 328	0.8	100.8	1.1	101.9	84.7	17.1
Maurice	2007	235 530	3.2	103.2	1.6	104.7	83.4	21.3
	2008	264 636	...	102.9	...	105.1	85.6	19.6
Mexico	2002	6 263 137	-1.8	98.2	1.6	99.8	81.2	18.6
Mexique	2003	6 891 992	-1.8	98.2	2.2	100.3	81.1	19.2
	2004	7 709 096	-1.5	98.5	2.5	101.0	80.0	21.0
Mongolia	2005	2 779 578	3.6[5]	103.6	...	...	...	...
Mongolie	2006	3 714 953	-0.3[5]	99.7	...	...	...	...
	2007	4 599 541	0.1[5]	100.1	...	...	...	...
Morocco	2005	527 679	-1.1[2]	98.7	9.1	107.8	76.8	31.0
Maroc	2006	577 344	-1.4[2]	98.6	9.6	108.2	76.0	32.2
	2007	616 254	...	98.6			76.6	32.2
Mozambique	2004	128 668	-5.1	94.9	5.4	100.3	99.2	1.1
Mozambique	2005	151 707	-5.3	94.7	4.1	98.8	96.2	2.6
	2006	173 566	-7.1	92.9	7.7	100.6	94.6	5.9
Myanmar+ [1]	1996	791 980	...	100.0	...	100.0	88.5	11.4
Myanmar+ [1]	1997	1 109 554	...	100.0	...	100.0	88.1	11.9
	1998	1 559 996	...	100.0	...	100.0	89.4	10.6

Relationships among the principal national accounting aggregates *(continued)*
As a percentage of Gross Domestic Product (GDP)
Relations entre les principaux agrégats de comptabilité nationale *(suite)*
En pourcentage du Produit Intérieur Brut (PIB)

			As a percentage of GDP - En pourcentage du PIB					
Country or area Pays ou zone	Year Année	GDP at current prices (mil.nat.cur.) PIB aux prix courants (millions monnaie nat.)	Plus: Compensation of employees and property income from/to the rest of the world, net Plus: Rémunération des salariés et revenus de la propriété du/au reste du monde, net	Equals: Gross national income Égale: Revenu national brut	Plus: Net current transfers from/to the rest of the world Plus: Transferts courants du/au reste du monde, net	Equals: Gross national disposable income Égale: Revenu national disponible brut	Less: Final consumption expenditure Moins: Dépense de consommation finale	Equals: Gross savings Égale: Épargne brut
Namibia	2004	36 496	1.5	101.5	11.8	113.3	82.4	30.9
Namibie	2005	39 711	-1.8	98.2	10.7	108.9	77.1	31.8
	2006	46 971	-1.0	99.0	13.8	112.7	71.9	40.9
Nepal[+]	2004	589 412	0.3[8]	100.3	16.6	116.9	88.4	28.4
Népal[+]	2005	646 471	0.8[8]	100.8	19.5	120.3	92.1	28.2
	2006	719 477	...	100.6	18.6	119.2	90.6	28.6
Netherlands	2005	508 964	0.6	100.6	-1.6	99.0	73.0	26.1
Pays-Bas	2006	534 324	1.6	101.6	-1.5	100.1	72.8	27.4
	2007	559 537	2.0	102.0	-1.6	100.4	72.3	28.2
Netherlands Antilles	2002	5 254	0.0	100.0	4.3	104.4	74.5	29.9
Antilles néerlandaises	2003	5 426	-0.2	99.8	4.6	104.4	75.5	28.9
	2004	5 576	-0.3	99.7	2.5	102.2	75.2	26.9
New Zealand[+]	2004	149 153	-6.3	93.7	0.2	93.9	76.4	17.5
Nouvelle-Zélande[+]	2005	156 849	-7.2	92.8	0.2	93.1	77.8	15.3
	2006	165 379	-7.2	92.8	0.4	93.2	78.2	15.1
Nicaragua[+]	2005	81 233	-2.6[2]	97.4	17.0	114.4	100.1	14.3
Nicaragua[+]	2006	93 135	-2.3[2]	97.7	16.1	113.8	100.4	13.4
	2007	104 702	-2.3[2]	97.7	16.1	113.8	101.1	12.7
Niger	2005	1 755 050	-0.3	99.7	5.5	105.2	89.8	15.4
Niger	2006	1 859 458	-0.1	99.9	4.3	104.2	89.4	14.8
	2007	1 968 522	0.9	100.9	5.6	106.5	92.7	13.7
Nigeria[+][1]	1992	549 809	-11.7	88.3	2.3	90.6	77.2	13.4
Nigéria[+][1]	1993	701 473	-10.5	89.5	2.5	92.0	80.6	11.5
	1994	914 334	-7.2	92.8	1.2	94.0	85.5	8.5
Norway	2005	1 945 716	0.7	100.7	-0.9	99.8	62.4	37.4
Norvège	2006	2 161 728	-0.3	99.7	-0.7	99.1	60.1	39.0
	2007	2 276 757	0.4	100.4	-0.7	99.7	61.3	38.5
Occupied Palestinian Terr.	2001	3 816	8.6	108.6	24.6	133.2	127.4	5.8
Terr. palestinien occupé	2002	3 484	6.4	106.4	30.6	137.0	131.4	5.5
	2003	3 921	7.2	107.2	36.2	143.5	129.3	14.1
Oman	2004	9 525	-3.6	96.4	-7.2	89.2	65.4	23.8
Oman	2005	11 890	-6.3	93.7	-7.2	86.5	55.1	31.4
	2006	13 738[3]	-4.9	95.1	-7.7	87.4	56.7	30.8
Pakistan[+]	2006	7 623 205	...	102.0	...	...	85.9	...
Pakistan[+]	2007	8 723 215	...	101.8	...	...	84.2	...
	2008	10 478 194	...	102.2	...	...	88.5	...
Panama	2004	14 179	-8.9	91.1	1.1	92.1	77.6	14.5
Panama	2005	15 465	-9.3	90.7	1.1	91.8	75.2	16.6
	2006	17 134	-9.2	90.8	0.9	91.7	72.7	19.1
Papua New Guinea[3]	2004	12 653	-3.4	90.2	0.7	90.9	66.8	24.2
Papouasie-Nvl-Guinée[3]	2005	14 236	-11.7	82.1	5.7	87.7	61.9	25.8
	2006	16 208	-15.2	78.7	4.5	83.2	62.4	20.8
Paraguay[1]	1993	11 991 719	...	100.4	...	100.4	88.0	12.4
Paraguay[1]	1994	14 960 131	...	100.5	...	100.5	95.2	5.3
	1995	17 699 000	...	100.9	...	100.9	92.5	8.4
Peru[1]	1996	148 278	...	97.3	...	...	80.6	...
Pérou[1]	1997	172 389	...	97.5	...	...	78.7	...
	1998	183 179	...	97.7	...	...	80.9	...

Relationships among the principal national accounting aggregates *(continued)*
As a percentage of Gross Domestic Product (GDP)

Relations entre les principaux agrégats de comptabilité nationale *(suite)*
En pourcentage du Produit Intérieur Brut (PIB)

Country or area Pays ou zone	Year Année	GDP at current prices (mil.nat.cur.) PIB aux prix courants (millions monnaie nat.)	Plus: Compensation of employees and property income from/to the rest of the world, net Plus: Rémunération des salariés et revenus de la propriété du/au reste du monde, net	Equals: Gross national income Égale: Revenu national brut	Plus: Net current transfers from/to the rest of the world Plus: Transferts courants du/au reste du monde, net	Equals: Gross national disposable income Égale: Revenu national disponible brut	Less: Final consumption expenditure Moins: Dépense de consommation finale	Equals: Gross savings Égale: Épargne brut
Philippines [1]	2004	4 871 555	7.7	107.7	0.8	108.5	78.8	29.7
Philippines [1]	2005	5 437 905	8.2	108.2	0.8	109.1	79.0	30.1
	2006	6 032 624	8.9	108.9	0.7	109.6	79.8	29.8
Poland	2004	924 538	-4.1	95.9	1.7	97.6	81.9	15.7
Pologne	2005	983 302	-3.3	96.7	2.1	98.8	81.1	17.7
	2006	1 060 194	-3.9	96.1	2.2	98.3	80.3	18.0
Portugal	2005	149 124	-1.9	98.1	1.0	99.0	86.3	12.8
Portugal	2006	155 323	-3.7	96.3	1.4	97.6	85.8	11.8
	2007	162 756	-4.3	95.7	1.3	97.0	84.9	12.1
Puerto Rico[+][1]	2004	82 809	-35.5	64.5	11.3	75.8	68.4	6.2
Porto Rico[+][1]	2005	86 943	-35.1	64.9	11.6	76.5	68.8	6.4
	2006	89 701	-34.9	65.1	12.1	77.2	69.5	6.5
Qatar	2003	85 663	-1.8[2]	98.2	-7.0	91.2	31.9	59.3
Qatar	2004	115 512	-7.1[2]	92.9	-7.1	85.8	30.5	55.3
	2005	154 564	-3.3[2]	96.7	-6.1	90.6	29.7	60.9
Republic of Moldova	2004	32 032	13.7	113.7	14.0	127.7	104.0	23.8
République de Moldova	2005	37 652	13.5	113.5	19.1	132.6	109.9	22.7
	2006	44 754	11.8	111.8	23.0	134.7	113.9	20.9
Réunion [1]	1990	28 374	-2.5[2]	97.5	44.3	141.7	108.1	33.6
Réunion [1]	1991	31 339	0.1[2]	100.7	42.7	143.4	103.5	39.9
	1992	33 787	-1.5[2]	98.4	43.6	142.1	104.5	37.6
Romania	2005	288 955	-2.9	97.1	4.2	101.3	86.9	14.4
Roumanie	2006	344 651	-3.3	96.7	4.8	101.4	85.6	15.9
	2007[9]	412 762	-3.3	96.7	...	...	...	...
Russian Federation	2004	17 048 122	-2.2	97.8	-0.1	97.7	66.9	30.8
Fédération de Russie	2005	21 620 111	-2.5	97.5	-0.1	97.4	66.4	30.9
	2006	26 781 103	-2.9	97.1	-0.1	97.0	66.3	30.7
Rwanda [1]	1987	171 430	-1.6	98.4	2.5	100.9	93.5	7.4
Rwanda [1]	1988	177 920	-2.0	98.0	2.9	100.9	93.6	7.3
	1989	190 220	-1.2	98.8	2.4	101.3	95.4	5.9
Saint Kitts and Nevis [1]	2004	1 078	-9.7	90.3	4.6	94.8	72.7	22.2
Saint-Kitts-et-Nevis [1]	2005	1 158	-7.8	92.2	4.8	97.0	70.2	26.8
	2006	1 314	-6.9	93.1	4.1	97.3	74.8	22.5
Saint Lucia [1]	2004	2 159	-6.7	93.3	1.7	95.0	86.7	8.3
Sainte-Lucie [1]	2005	2 369	-6.6	93.4	1.6	95.0	84.0	11.0
	2006	2 498	-6.2	93.8	1.5	95.3	78.0	17.3
Saint Vincent-Grenadines [1]	2004	1 118	-6.7	93.3	3.4	96.5	89.0	7.5
Saint Vincent-Grenadines [1]	2005	1 182	-5.9	93.8	4.1	98.0	88.5	9.5
	2006	1 330	-4.2	95.1	4.1	99.2	88.4	11.0
San Marino [1]	2003	995	...	89.5	-12.9	76.7	...	...
Saint-Marin [1]	2004	1 061	...	88.8	-12.8	76.1	...	...
	2005	1 106	...	87.7	-12.7	75.0	...	...
Saudi Arabia[+][1]	2003	804 648	0.3	100.3	-9.3	91.1	58.2	32.9
Arabie saoudite[+][1]	2004	938 771	0.9	100.9	-7.9	92.9	54.1	38.9
	2005	1 182 514	0.9	100.9	-5.8	95.1	48.7	46.4
Senegal	2004	4 242 837	-1.6	99.8[10]	7.9	107.7	91.0	16.7
Sénégal	2005	4 582 285	-1.0	99.3[10]	8.7	108.0	90.3	17.7
	2006	4 846 395	-1.0	97.9[10]	9.6	107.5	91.2	16.3

21 Relationships among the principal national accounting aggregates *(continued)*
As a percentage of Gross Domestic Product (GDP)
Relations entre les principaux agrégats de comptabilité nationale *(suite)*
En pourcentage du Produit Intérieur Brut (PIB)

As a percentage of GDP - En pourcentage du PIB

Country or area Pays ou zone	Year Année	GDP at current prices (mil.nat.cur.) PIB aux prix courants (millions monnaie nat.)	Plus: Compensation of employees and property income from/to the rest of the world, net Plus: Rémunération des salariés et revenus de la propriété du/au reste du monde, net	Equals: Gross national income Égale: Revenu national brut	Plus: Net current transfers from/to the rest of the world Plus: Transferts courants du/au reste du monde, net	Equals: Gross national disposable income Égale: Revenu national disponible brut	Less: Final consumption expenditure Moins: Dépense de consommation finale	Equals: Gross savings Égale: Épargne brut
Seychelles [1]	1998	3 201	...	97.2	...	...	81.2	...
Seychelles [1]	1999	3 330	...	97.3	...	...	73.1	...
	2000	3 424	...	96.3	...	...	66.4	...
Sierra Leone+	2004	3 853 140	-4.7[5]	95.3	9.9	105.2	113.5	-8.2
Sierra Leone+	2005	4 324 020	-3.4[5]	96.6	11.4	108.0	108.0	^0.0
	2006	4 902 090	-2.4[5]	97.6	4.9	102.5	98.2	4.3
Singapore	2005	199 375	-9.1	90.9	-1.1	89.9	51.9	38.5
Singapour	2006	216 995	-7.0	93.0	-1.0	92.0	51.3	41.8
	2007	243 169	-3.5	96.5	-1.0	95.4	50.1	46.8
Slovakia	2004	1 355 262	0.4	100.4	-0.2	100.2	76.7	23.5
Slovaquie	2005	1 471 131	-2.6	97.4	-0.3	97.2	75.9	21.3
	2006	1 636 263	-3.0	97.0	0.0	96.9	75.7	21.2
Slovenia	2005	28 704	-1.1	99.2	-0.5	98.6	73.3	25.3
Slovénie	2006	31 008	-1.4	98.8	-0.7	98.1	71.8	26.3
	2007	34 471	-2.2	98.0	-0.8	97.3	69.9	27.4
Solomon Islands [1]	1984	222	...	94.2	...	100.8	78.2	22.6
Iles Salomon [1]	1985	237	...	95.0	...	101.0	91.6	9.4
	1986	253	...	92.6	...	115.7	94.8	20.9
Somalia [1]	1985	87 290	...	97.8	10.1	107.9	101.1	6.8
Somalie [1]	1986	118 781	...	96.3	14.2	110.5	98.8	11.7
	1987	169 608	...	96.8	21.3	118.0	99.9	18.2
South Africa	2005	1 541 067	-2.0	98.0	-1.2	96.8	82.1	14.0
Afrique du Sud	2006	1 741 061	-2.1	97.9	-1.1	96.9	82.0	14.0
	2007	1 993 894	-3.1	96.9	-1.0	95.8	81.6	14.1
Spain	2005	908 450	-1.4[5]	98.6	-0.8	97.8	75.8	22.0
Espagne	2006	980 954	-1.7[5]	98.3	-1.0	97.3	75.6	21.8
	2007	1 049 848	-2.6[5]	97.4	-0.9	96.5	75.2	21.3
Sri Lanka	2004	2 086 925	-1.0	99.0	6.5	105.6	83.6	21.4
Sri Lanka	2005	2 439 328	-1.2	98.8	7.2	105.9	82.2	23.0
	2006	2 924 172	-1.4	98.6	7.4	106.0	83.1	22.3
Sudan+ [1]	1991	421 819	...	85.5	...	104.0	86.0	18.0
Soudan+ [1]	1992	948 448	...	99.7	...	102.2	88.2	14.0
	1993	1 881 289	...	99.8	...	100.6	88.3	12.3
Suriname [1]	2004	3 489 032	-5.0	95.0	1.1	96.1	...	...
Suriname [1]	2005	4 278 373	-2.6	97.4	1.4	98.8	...	...
	2006	5 086 746	-3.0	97.0	2.0	99.0	...	...
Swaziland+	2003	14 401	3.5[5]	103.5	0.6	104.1	91.0	13.0
Swaziland+	2004	15 585	0.8[5]	100.8	5.2	106.0	78.9	27.1
	2005	16 260	0.8[5]	100.8	5.0	105.8	80.7	25.1
Sweden	2005	2 735 218	-0.2	99.8	-1.5	98.4	75.0	23.4
Suède	2006	2 899 653	1.7	101.7	-1.4	100.3	73.7	26.7
	2007	3 070 591	2.1	102.1	-1.4	100.8	72.6	28.1
Switzerland	2004	451 379	7.1	107.1	-2.6	104.6	72.1	32.9
Suisse	2005	463 673	9.4	109.4	-2.2	107.2	71.9	35.7
	2006	486 178	9.2	109.2	...	...	...	...
Syrian Arab Republic [1]	2004	1 263 138	...	92.4	0.8	93.2	79.8	19.9
Rép. arabe syrienne [1]	2005	1 490 798	...	91.5	0.8	92.3	80.5	18.4
	2006	1 708 747	...	92.2	0.7	92.9	78.8	18.0

21 Relationships among the principal national accounting aggregates *(continued)*
As a percentage of Gross Domestic Product (GDP)
Relations entre les principaux agrégats de comptabilité nationale *(suite)*
En pourcentage du Produit Intérieur Brut (PIB)

As a percentage of GDP - En pourcentage du PIB

Country or area Pays ou zone	Year Année	GDP at current prices (mil.nat.cur.) PIB aux prix courants (millions monnaie nat.)	Plus: Compensation of employees and property income from/to the rest of the world, net Plus: Rémunération des salariés et revenus de la propriété du/au reste du monde, net	Equals: Gross national income Égale: Revenu national brut	Plus: Net current transfers from/to the rest of the world Plus: Transferts courants du/au reste du monde, net	Equals: Gross national disposable income Égale: Revenu national disponible brut	Less: Final consumption expenditure Moins: Dépense de consommation finale	Equals: Gross savings Égale: Épargne brut
Tajikistan	2004	6 167	29.3	129.3	2.3	131.5	85.8	45.7
Tadjikistan	2005	7 207	27.8	127.8	3.1	130.9	95.7	35.2
	2006	9 335	35.1	135.1	4.2	139.3	94.0	45.3
Thailand [1]	2005	7 092 893	-4.9	95.1	1.7	96.9	69.1	27.7
Thaïlande [1]	2006	7 841 297	-4.0	96.0	1.6	97.6	67.6	29.9
	2007	8 493 311	-3.8	96.2	1.6	97.8	65.9	31.8
TFYR of Macedonia	2004	265 257	...	99.3	...	112.3	98.9	13.4
L'ex-R.Y. Macédoine	2005	286 619	...	98.0	...	114.6	96.5	18.1
	2006	310 915	...	99.4	...	117.7	96.7	21.0
Togo [1]	1984	304 800	...	...	...	...	80.0	...
Togo [1]	1985	332 500	...	...	...	...	80.2	...
	1986	363 600	...	...	...	...	83.4	...
Tonga[+][1]	2004	390	1.0	101.0	34.9	135.9	120.8	15.1
Tonga[+][1]	2005	423	-2.1	97.9	35.7	133.6	126.2	7.3
	2006	479	2.7	102.7	34.2	137.0	126.5	10.4
Trinidad and Tobago	2003	70 732	-6.0[2]	94.0	0.5	94.5	67.3	27.2
Trinité-et-Tobago	2004	79 826	-3.1[2]	96.9	0.4	97.3	67.0	30.4
	2005	95 057	-3.7[2]	96.3	0.3	96.7	63.5	33.2
Tunisia	2002	29 924	-4.5	95.5	5.3	100.7	78.6	22.1
Tunisie	2003	32 202	-4.1	95.9	5.1	101.0	78.8	22.2
	2004	35 148	-4.4	95.6	5.3	101.0	78.5	22.4
Turkey [1]	2005	648 932	...	...	...	...	83.5	...
Turquie [1]	2006	758 391	...	...	...	...	82.9	...
	2007	856 387	...	...	...	...	82.9	...
Ukraine	2004	345 113	-1.0	99.0	4.0	103.0	71.2	31.8
Ukraine	2005	441 452	-1.1	98.9	3.4	102.2	76.5	25.7
	2006	544 153	-1.6	98.4	3.0	101.4	78.1	23.3
United Arab Emirates [1]	1988	87 106	0.3	100.3	-1.2	99.1	65.8	33.3
Emirats arabes unis [1]	1989	100 976	0.4	100.4	-0.7	99.7	61.7	38.0
	1990	124 008	-1.0	99.0	-8.9	90.1	54.9	35.1
United Kingdom	2005	1 233 976	2.0	102.0	-0.9	101.1	86.0	15.1
Royaume-Uni	2006	1 303 915	0.5	100.5	-0.8	99.7	85.4	14.2
	2007	1 381 565	0.3	100.3	-0.9	99.4	84.9	14.5
United Rep. of Tanzania[+][11]	2005	15 965 296	-1.3	98.7	3.3	102.0	83.8	18.2
Rép.-Unie de Tanzanie[+][11]	2006	17 941 268	-0.5	99.6	4.2	103.7	85.5	18.2
	2007	20 948 403	-0.3	99.7	4.1	103.7	87.2	16.5
United States	2004	11 630 900	0.7	100.5	-0.7	99.8	86.3	13.4
Etats-Unis	2005	12 376 100	0.6	100.5	-0.7	99.8	86.3	13.5
	2006	13 132 900	0.4	100.6	-0.7	99.9	86.2	13.7
Uruguay [1]	2005	406 705	-3.3[2]	96.7	1.0	97.7	84.9	12.8
Uruguay [1]	2006	464 802	-2.7[2]	97.3	0.8	98.1	85.7	12.4
	2007	541 869	-1.8[2]	98.2	0.6	98.8	85.6	13.2
Vanuatu [1]	1996	28 227	...	91.1	...	...	...	...
Vanuatu [1]	1997	29 477	...	91.7	...	...	...	...
	1998	29 545	...	93.5	...	...	...	...
Venezuela (Bolivarian Rep. of)	2003	134 227 833	-2.6	97.4	0.0	97.4	67.7	29.8
Venezuela (Rép. bol. du)	2004	212 683 082	-3.1	96.9	-0.1	96.8	61.2	35.7
	2005	304 086 815	-1.5	98.5	0.0	98.4	57.8	40.6

21

Relationships among the principal national accounting aggregates *(continued)*
As a percentage of Gross Domestic Product (GDP)

Relations entre les principaux agrégats de comptabilité nationale *(suite)*
En pourcentage du Produit Intérieur Brut (PIB)

As a percentage of GDP - En pourcentage du PIB

Country or area Pays ou zone	Year Année	GDP at current prices (mil.nat.cur.) PIB aux prix courants (millions monnaie nat.)	Plus: Compensation of employees and property income from/to the rest of the world, net Plus: Rémunération des salariés et revenus de la propriété du/au reste du monde, net	Equals: Gross national income Égale: Revenu national brut	Plus: Net current transfers from/to the rest of the world Plus: Transferts courants du/au reste du monde, net	Equals: Gross national disposable income Égale: Revenu national disponible brut	Less: Final consumption expenditure Moins: Dépense de consommation finale	Equals: Gross savings Égale: Épargne brut
Yemen	2004	2 563 490	-9.2	90.8	9.9	100.7	78.8	21.9
Yémen	2005	3 208 501[3]	-9.2	90.8	8.0	98.8	76.4	22.3
	2006	3 760 038[3]	-6.1	93.9	6.8	100.6	74.7	26.0
Zambia [1]	1986	12 963	-18.1[2]	81.9	-1.2	80.7	77.4	3.3
Zambie [1]	1987	19 778	-11.4[2]	88.6	0.5	89.1	82.0	7.1
	1988	27 725	-14.2[2]	85.8	1.0	86.9	79.8	7.1
Zimbabwe [1]	2001	709 214	...	98.3	...	...	...	...
Zimbabwe [1]	2002	1 698 180	...	99.5	...	...	...	...
	2003	5 518 757	...	99.9	...	...	...	...

Source:
United Nations Statistics Division, New York, national accounts database, last accessed February 2009.

Data for most countries have been compiled in accordance with the concepts and definitions of the System of National Accounts 1993 (1993 SNA). Countries that follow the 1968 SNA are footnoted accordingly.

[+] Note: The national accounts data generally relate to the fiscal year used in each country, unless indicated otherwise. Countries whose reference periods coincide with the calendar year ending 31 December are not listed below.

Year beginning 21 March: Afghanistan, Iran (Islamic Republic).
Year beginning 1 April: Bermuda, India, Myanmar, New Zealand, Nigeria.
Year beginning 1 July: Australia, Bhutan, Cameroon, Gambia, Nicaragua, Pakistan, Puerto Rico, Saudi Arabia, Sierra Leone, Sudan, United Republic of Tanzania.
Year ending 30 June: Bangladesh, Botswana, Egypt, Swaziland, Tonga.
Year ending 7 July: Nepal.
Year ending 30 July: Ethiopia.
Year ending 30 September: Haiti.

Source:
Organisation des Nations Unies, Division de statistique, New York, la base de données sur les comptes nationaux, dernier accès février 2009.

Les données pour la majorité des pays sont compilées selon les concepts et définitions du Système de comptabilité nationale, 1993 (SCN93). Seuls les pays qui suivent toujours le SCN68 seront donc signalés par une note.

[+] Note : Sauf indication contraire, les données sur les comptes nationaux concernent généralement l'exercice budgétaire utilisé dans chaque pays. Les pays où territoires dont la période de référence coïncide avec l'année civile se terminant le 31 décembre ne sont pas répertoriés ci-dessous.

Exercice commençant le 21 mars: Afghanistan, Iran (République islamique d').
Exercice commençant le 1er avril: Bermudes, Inde, Myanmar, Nigéria, Nouvelle-Zélande.
Exercice commençant le 1er juillet: Arabie saoudite, Australie, Bhoutan, Cameroun, Gambie, Nicaragua, Pakistan, Porto Rico, Sierra Leone, Soudan, Rép.-Unie de Tanzanie.
Exercice se terminant le 30 juin: Bangladesh, Botswana, Égypte, Swaziland, Tonga.
Exercice se terminant le 7 juillet: Népal.
Exercice se terminant le 30 juillet: Éthiopie.
Exercice se terminant le 30 septembre: Haïti.

1	Data compiled in accordance with the System of National Accounts 1968 (1968 SNA).	
2	Property income - from and to the rest of the world, net.	
3	Preliminary data.	
4	Includes taxes less subsidies, net from-to-the Rest of the world.	
5	Net Primary Income.	
6	Compensation of employee to the rest of the world and property income from and to the rest of the world, net.	
7	Compensation of employees - from and to the rest of the world, net.	
8	Includes taxes less subsidies on production.	
9	Semi-final data.	
10	Includes the adjustment for balance of payments.	
11	Tanzania mainland only.	

1 Données compilées selon le Système de comptabilité nationale de 1968 (SCN 1968).
2 Revenus de la propriété - du et au reste du monde, net.
3 Données préliminaires.
4 Y compris les impôts moins les subventions, net du/au reste du monde.
5 Revenu primaire net.
6 Rémunération des salariés au reste du monde et revenus de la propriété du et au reste du monde, net.
7 Rémunération des salariés - du et au reste du monde, net.
8 Y compris les impôts, moins les subventions à la production.
9 Données demi-finales.
10 Y compris les données ajustées sur la balance des paiements.
11 Tanzanie continentale seulement.

Government final consumption expenditure by function at current prices
Percentage distribution by divisions of Classification of the Functions of Government (COFOG)

Dépenses de consommation finale des administrations publiques par fonction aux prix courants
Répartition en pourcentage par divisions de la Classification des fonctions des administrations publiques (COFOG)

Country or area Pays ou zone	Year Année	Total (m.nat.curr.) Totale (m.monn.nat.)	Div. 01 (%)	Div. 02 (%)	Div. 03 (%)	Div. 04 (%)	Div. 05 (%)	Div. 06 (%)	Div. 07 (%)	Div. 08 (%)	Div. 09 (%)	Div. 10 (%)
Anguilla [1] Anguilla [1]	2004	75	38.4	...	11.6	2.0	...	1.4	^0.0	...	17.9	23.2
	2005	84	36.6	...	12.1	1.9	...	1.4	0.0	...	16.4	25.1
	2006	113	44.3	...	11.4	1.9	...	1.2	0.0	...	14.4	20.6
Antigua and Barbuda [1] Antigua-et-Barbuda [1]	1984	67[2]	22.8	2.2	11.4	22.5	...	6.7	9.7	0.5	15.8	8.4
	1985	81[2]	25.1	2.2	11.4	20.9	...	7.7	11.5	0.6	14.0	6.6
	1986	108[2]	26.1	2.3	11.6	21.2	...	6.4	10.0	0.5	14.7	7.2
Argentina [1] Argentine [1]	1996	43 617	10.8	4.5	3.2	6.0	0.2	2.1	8.4	...	5.9[3]	43.2
	1997	45 156	9.4	4.4	3.1	5.9	0.2	2.1	7.1	...	6.0[3]	42.0
	1998	46 463	9.5	4.2	3.0	5.8	0.2	2.0	6.6	...	6.0[3]	41.0
Armenia Arménie	2003	101 859[4]	85.3[5]	...	...	3.7	...	4.2	...	3.2	...	1.1
	#2004	118 788[4]	84.8[5]	...	...	3.3	...	4.7	...	3.0	...	1.1
	2005	143 786	86.4	...	...	2.3	...	5.4	...	1.2	...	0.8
Australia [+] Australie [+]	2000	110 021	10.3	9.4	7.9	8.1	^0.0	1.3	29.6	3.4	19.8	10.1
	2001	116 297	8.3	9.5	8.0	9.4	0.1	1.4	30.4	3.1	20.0	9.8
	2002	125 330	6.9	9.9	8.3	9.2	0.3	1.5	30.5	2.9	20.2	10.4
Austria Autriche	2005	45 136	12.4	4.8	7.8	9.4	1.1	0.5	28.2	2.6	27.4	5.9
	2006	47 340	11.9	4.9	7.8	9.6	1.0	0.5	28.0	2.6	27.4	6.3
	2007	49 361	11.7	4.9	7.6	9.6	1.0	0.5	28.4	2.6	27.3	6.4
Azerbaijan Azerbaïdjan	2004	1 100	29.7	15.8	1.7	0.5	...	^0.0	17.7	3.4	28.9	2.2
	2005	1 335	24.2	21.6	1.7	0.5	...	0.8	18.6	3.4	27.6	1.7
	2006	1 601	7.2	40.0	1.8	1.3	...	-0.4	19.0	1.9	25.2	4.0
Bahamas Bahamas	1993	408	17.4	4.2	14.5	15.9	...	...	18.6	1.5[6]	24.0	4.2
	1994	511	20.2	3.7	13.3	17.2	...	...	18.0	1.6[6]	23.1	3.5
	1995	484	18.4	3.9	14.5	17.6	...	...	18.0	1.9[6]	22.1	3.9
Bangladesh Bangladesh	2005	148 507	15.1	20.8	12.9	1.4	...	3.6	11.2	0.9	14.3	1.8
	2006	169 764	13.6	19.6	13.8	1.3	...	3.3	11.5	0.8	13.7	1.8
	2007	180 464	14.0	19.2	14.3	1.2	...	3.7	12.2	0.8	15.2	1.9
Belarus Bélarus	2004	4 203 500	69.9	...	...	25.1	...	...	...	...	...	0.5
	2005	5 527 578	67.8	...	...	27.1	...	...	...	...	...	0.6
	2006	6 209 335	67.1	...	...	27.0	...	...	...	...	...	0.6
Belgium Belgique	2004	66 014	13.9	4.8	6.8	9.4	0.9	0.3	29.7	2.6	24.7	6.7
	2005	68 732	14.2	4.5	6.8	9.4	0.7	0.3	29.9	2.5	25.0	6.8
	2006	70 774	14.2	4.4	6.9	9.5	0.7	0.3	29.6	2.5	25.1	6.8
Belize [1] Belize [1]	1989	229	12.7	4.3	5.3	40.3	...	6.3	7.9	1.4	16.5	0.7
	1990	279	12.7	3.4	7.9	37.5	...	6.7	6.8	2.6	15.3	3.3
	1991	321	16.6	3.4	7.0	32.6	...	6.1	6.6	2.4	16.8	4.0
Bermuda [+][1] Bermudes [+][1]	1985	138	36.9	2.0	...	27.1	...	6.0	3.7	2.9	21.3	3.6
	1986	141	34.4	2.1	...	28.3	...	6.4	3.9	2.9	22.2	3.8
	1987	157	34.0	2.3	...	30.1	...	6.2	3.8	2.9	21.5	3.8
Bolivia [1] Bolivie [1]	1991	2 310	74.7	^0.0	...	4.2	...	0.1	^0.0	0.1	7.7	1.9
	1992	2 833	76.2	...	...	3.0	...	0.1	^0.0	0.2	8.1	1.9
	1993	3 270	75.9	...	...	2.5	...	0.2	^0.0	0.2	9.0	2.4
Botswana Botswana	2000	7 525	44.0[7]	...	...	11.2	...	6.2	6.5	2.4	26.4	3.4
	2001	8 742	43.7[7]	...	...	11.0	...	5.2	6.8	2.4	27.4	3.5
	2002	10 553	45.3[7]	...	...	10.8	...	4.3	6.3	2.5	27.4	3.4
Brazil Brésil	2004	373 284	64.4	...	...	...	...	...	14.2	...	18.4	...
	2005	427 553	65.7	...	...	...	...	...	13.2	...	18.4	...
	2006	474 773	63.8	...	...	...	...	...	14.0	...	19.2	...
British Virgin Islands [1] Iles Vierges britanniques [1]	1985	17[2]	23.3	...	10.8	20.7	...	4.1	14.9	0.8	23.6	1.8
	1986	19[2]	21.8	...	11.4	22.1	...	4.4	14.5	0.7	22.7	2.4
	1987	21[2]	23.3	...	11.0	20.2	...	5.5	15.8	0.5	21.1	2.6

Government final consumption expenditure by function at current prices *(continued)*
Percentage distribution by divisions of Classification of the Functions of Government (COFOG)

Dépenses de consommation finale des administrations publiques par fonction aux prix courants *(suite)*
Répartition en pourcentage par divisions de la Classification des fonctions des administrations publiques (COFOG)

Country or area Pays ou zone	Year Année	Total (m.nat.curr.) Totale (m.monn.nat.)	Divisions of the Classification of the Functions of Government (COFOG)[t] Divisions de la Classification des fonctions des administrations publiques (COFOG)[t]									
			Div. 01 (%)	Div. 02 (%)	Div. 03 (%)	Div. 04 (%)	Div. 05 (%)	Div. 06 (%)	Div. 07 (%)	Div. 08 (%)	Div. 09 (%)	Div. 10 (%)
Brunei Darussalam[1]	1982	914	22.9	41.4	5.5	5.0	...	0.7	5.0	4.8	14.2	0.2
Brunéi Darussalam[1]	1983	922	24.6	35.3	6.0	5.5	...	0.7	5.7	5.7	15.2	0.2
	1984	2 512	69.3	12.8	2.7	2.5	...	0.4	2.6	2.3	6.5	0.1
Burkina Faso[1]	1982	38 198[2]	8.2	28.3	8.7	9.9	...	0.3	10.0	2.4	16.6	...
Burkina Faso[1]	1983	38 864[2]	8.1	28.7	9.1	10.5	...	0.4	10.5	2.5	18.3	...
	1984	38 760[2]	7.3	30.4	8.7	10.8	...	0.2	10.3	2.5	19.0	...
Cameroon[+1]	1986	476 700	30.6	12.0	...	10.6	...	6.0	5.7	2.1	19.1	0.7
Cameroun[+1]	1987	391 000	28.3	14.7	...	7.3	...	5.0	6.1	2.3	21.6	0.8
	1988	378 400	35.5	12.4	...	6.2	...	4.9	6.0	2.2	21.5	0.9
Cayman Islands[1]	1989	74[8]	31.1	...	14.9	20.3	...	1.4	13.5	...	13.5	4.1
Iles Caïmanes[1]	1990	94[8]	26.6	...	14.9	19.1	...	1.1	16.0	...	14.9	4.3
	1991	103[8]	27.2	...	14.6	20.4	...	1.9	14.6	...	14.6	5.8
Chad[1]	1997	40 078[9]	1.0[10]	26.6	9.5[11]	6.6[12]	5.2[13]	1.1[14]	6.9[15]	...	23.6	20.7[16]
Tchad[1]	2001	60 157[9]	...	20.2	8.4[11]	5.9[12]	5.2[13]	1.0[14]	6.3[15]	...	25.0	28.0[16]
	2003	74 579[9]	...	24.7	10.0[11]	5.8[12]	...	...	7.2[15]	...	26.9	...
China, Hong Kong SAR	2004	127 327	11.5	29.4[17]	...	9.2	3.3	1.3	29.3	6.0	6.9	3.1
Chine, Hong Kong RAS	2005	121 435	11.4	29.4[17]	...	8.9	3.2	1.1	30.1	6.3	6.7	2.9
	2006	123 436	11.6	29.5[17]	...	8.7	3.2	1.2	30.1	6.3	6.6	2.9
China, Macao SAR	2004	7 200	19.5	...	27.5	11.5	0.2	0.6	15.0	5.2	11.5	9.2
Chine, Macao RAS	2005	8 402	18.1	...	25.9	12.1	0.2	0.6	15.3	8.5	10.5	8.7
	2006	8 991	18.7	...	25.8	12.8	0.2	0.5	15.7	6.6	10.9	8.8
Colombia[1]	1992	3 965 104	29.5	10.8	...	16.6	...	0.6	7.7	0.8	24.8	8.9
Colombie[1]	1993	5 108 076	28.5	10.2	...	16.2	...	0.6	11.0	0.9	24.0	8.2
	1994	7 652 736	36.2	9.8	...	8.5	...	0.4	14.3	0.9	21.0	8.6
Cook Islands[1]	2004	84	17.8	...	4.7	41.2	...	9.7	11.2	0.8	14.6	...
Iles Cook[1]	2005	86	23.3	...	4.8	31.4	...	10.6	13.2	1.0	15.8	...
	2006	95	24.8	...	4.5	33.0	...	9.9	11.5	0.7	15.6	...
Costa Rica	2005	1 316 361	32.3	...	...	...	...	...	34.5	...	33.2	...
Costa Rica	2006	1 559 070	32.1	...	...	...	...	...	35.5	...	32.4	...
	2007	1 810 283	32.0	...	...	...	...	...	36.2	...	31.8	...
Côte d'Ivoire[1]	1996	983 370	73.5	...	...	...	...	...	6.2	...	20.3	...
Côte d'Ivoire[1]	1997	1 029 358	69.3	...	...	...	...	...	19.7	...	11.0	...
	1998	1 018 653	68.3	...	...	...	...	...	19.9	...	11.8	...
Croatia	1996	30 973	6.2	25.1	12.0	15.0	...	8.4	0.5	1.3	11.6	14.2
Croatie	1997	34 395	6.3	20.3	12.1	15.7	...	6.0	0.5	1.6	11.8	18.8
	1998	41 390	8.2	17.8	10.3	15.6	...	6.3	2.0	1.4	11.3	19.4
Cuba	2005	14 192	20.6	...	...	...	...	7.2	24.8	7.9	35.3	4.4
Cuba	2006	16 834	19.5	...	...	...	...	6.6	28.4	8.0	32.9	4.5
	2007	19 772	20.8	...	...	...	...	7.2	29.0	8.2	32.3	2.5
Cyprus	2004	1 320	18.2	10.9	9.0	8.1	0.1	7.8	12.8	2.1	28.5	2.5
Chypre	2005	1 420	17.6	12.9	11.2	7.8	1.1	5.2	11.0	3.7	27.3	2.4
	2006	1 570	18.2	12.4	10.7	7.4	1.0	5.0	12.7	3.1	27.0	2.5
Czech Republic	2004	621 586	11.1	7.1	10.6	12.2	2.8	1.1	27.0	2.8	21.1	4.3
République tchèque	2005	658 188	10.2	8.4	10.4	14.7	2.8	0.8	26.8	2.4	19.7	3.7
	2006	685 350	11.0	6.4	10.5	16.0	2.6	0.9	26.2	2.5	20.2	3.9
Denmark	2005	401 276	6.5	5.6	3.5	7.1	1.4	0.5	25.2	4.5	23.4	22.3
Danemark	2006	421 158	6.5	5.9	3.5	6.8	1.3	0.4	25.3	4.3	23.1	22.8
	2007	438 768	7.0	5.8	3.6	6.5	1.4	0.4	26.3	4.2	22.4	22.3
Dominican Republic	1994	8 265	66.3	...	2.7	...	...	...	12.8	...	18.1	...
Rép. dominicaine	1995	9 115	61.2	...	2.7	...	...	...	12.6	...	23.4	...
	1996	10 843	61.1	...	2.3	...	...	...	12.5	...	24.1	...
Ecuador[1]	1990	777 131[18]	13.0	14.5	7.0	13.9	...	4.4	4.8	0.2	27.5	6.1
Equateur[1]	1991	1 009 000[18]	13.0	15.0	7.1	14.9	...	5.0	4.6	0.3	27.8	6.2
	1992	1 498 000[18]	12.8	15.9	7.3	16.1	...	4.3	3.9	0.2	26.8	7.8

Government final consumption expenditure by function at current prices *(continued)*
Percentage distribution by divisions of Classification of the Functions of Government (COFOG)
Dépenses de consommation finale des administrations publiques par fonction aux prix courants *(suite)*
Répartition en pourcentage par divisions de la Classification des fonctions des administrations publiques (COFOG)

Country or area Pays ou zone	Year Année	Total (m.nat.curr.) Totale (m.monn.nat.)	Div. 01 (%)	Div. 02 (%)	Div. 03 (%)	Div. 04 (%)	Div. 05 (%)	Div. 06 (%)	Div. 07 (%)	Div. 08 (%)	Div. 09 (%)	Div. 10 (%)
Estonia	1996	12 632	11.0	4.6	11.7	11.0	...	4.2	17.3	5.6	27.8	4.1
Estonie	#2003	24 898	11.6	7.3	11.5	8.9	2.7	0.7	18.4	6.0	27.5	5.5
	2004	27 097	11.4	6.7	11.3	9.1	2.8	0.6	19.9	5.7	26.9	5.6
Fiji [1]	2000	561	18.9	12.2	9.3	16.4	...	1.0	14.7	...	27.1	0.4
Fidji [1]	2001	566	20.4	12.0	10.0	19.4	...	1.0	12.8	...	23.9	0.5
	2002	572	16.1	9.8	10.0	18.3	...	1.3	14.3	...	29.4	0.6
Finland	2004	33 314	10.9	6.1	5.1	10.0	0.8	0.8	25.7	3.0	20.4	17.2
Finlande	2005	34 935	10.4	6.4	5.2	9.8	0.8	0.7	26.1	3.0	20.3	17.4
	2006	36 413	10.7	6.2	5.1	9.8	0.8	0.3	26.1	3.0	20.0	18.0
France	2003	378 397	11.5	7.9	5.4	3.6	0.9	4.1	27.8	3.7	21.7	13.3
France	2004	393 629	11.5	8.0	5.4	3.9	0.9	4.1	26.8	3.8	20.7	14.9
	2005	405 600	11.2	7.7	5.6	3.8	0.9	4.2	26.7	3.9	20.6	15.5
Gambia [+][1]	1989	659 [2]	23.3	...	...	25.2	...	3.6	6.3	...	10.3 [19]	0.1
Gambie [+][1]	1990	819 [2]	22.0	...	...	18.6	...	3.0	6.4	...	12.9 [19]	0.1
	1991	804 [2]	22.2	...	...	24.1	...	3.8	5.7	...	12.6 [19]	0.1
Georgia	#1993	1 213	...	1.9	8.2	30.3	...	...	0.6	0.2	5.7	0.5
Géorgie	1994	119 012	...	5.4	10.1	63.6	...	...	3.2	1.2	4.8	9.0
	#1995	295	...	12.9	45.8	5.8	...	...	6.1	6.4	10.2	12.5
Germany	2004	415 590	12.5	6.1	8.6	2.1	0.4	1.4	31.8	2.1	18.7	16.3
Allemagne	2005	421 510	12.8	6.0	8.6	1.5	0.4	1.4	32.4	2.1	18.5	16.2
	2006	425 880	12.8	5.9	8.5	1.5	0.4	1.4	32.9	2.1	18.2	16.3
Ghana [1]	2003	5 976 876	67.2	...	...	...	...	0.2	5.3	...	27.3	...
Ghana [1]	2004	6 703 392	67.2	...	...	...	...	0.2	5.3	...	27.3	...
	2005	7 853 036	67.2	...	...	...	...	0.2	5.3	...	27.3	...
Greece	2004	31 594	25.0	18.3	9.8	3.9	0.0	0.7	15.9	1.6	20.6	4.3
Grèce	2005	32 984	24.7	17.2	8.6	3.9	0.0	0.7	17.0	1.6	21.6	4.6
	2006	33 858	25.8	17.1	8.1	3.4	0.0	0.7	17.6	1.6	22.0	3.7
Greenland [1]	2003	5 238	15.4	5.0	3.9	8.3	...	3.2	16.0	3.1	20.8	17.6
Groenland [1]	2004	5 319	16.0	4.1	4.4	7.7	...	2.8	15.9	3.3	21.1	17.9
	2005	5 221	16.3	4.4	4.3	7.0	...	1.6	16.6	3.2	21.5	18.4
Guinea-Bissau [1]	1986	6 423	44.0	...	...	22.7	...	...	11.8	...	18.4	0.9
Guinée-Bissau [1]	1987	10 776	44.0	...	...	22.7	...	...	11.8	...	18.4	1.2
Honduras [1]	1995	3 495	27.8	9.5	...	...	...	...	20.5	...	39.1	...
Honduras [1]	1996	4 556	26.0	8.2	...	...	...	...	27.6	...	36.7	...
	1997	5 377	31.0	7.3	...	...	...	...	24.9	...	35.2	...
Hungary	2003	4 388 484	21.8	5.7	8.5	5.2	0.7	1.9	22.8	3.9	22.1	7.3
Hongrie	2004	4 636 633	20.3	7.5	8.8	4.2	0.7	2.0	22.8	4.1	21.5	7.9
	2005	4 958 031	21.9	6.3	8.5	4.4	0.4	2.0	22.9	4.1	21.1	8.5
Iceland	2002	196 978	7.6	...	5.5	8.6	...	3.4	31.1	5.4	21.2	8.4
Islande	2003	211 797	7.6	...	5.5	8.6	...	3.4	31.1	5.4	21.2	8.4
	2004	228 244	7.6	...	5.5	8.6	...	3.4	31.1	5.4	21.2	8.4
India [+]	2003	2 305 000	26.6	33.2	...	9.9	0.1	2.5	6.2	0.8	16.3	4.2
Inde [+]	2004	2 503 940	25.6	35.6	...	9.1	0.1	1.4	6.2	0.8	17.0	3.9
	2005	2 773 730	28.2	36.6	...	4.4	0.1	1.9	6.2	0.9	17.0	4.4
Iran (Islamic Rep. of) [+]	2003	140 795 300	13.0	20.7	7.9	12.7	0.1	1.1	7.9	2.9	7.6	16.9
Iran (Rép. islamique d') [+]	2004	168 704 700	12.7	18.6	6.8	16.4	0.1	1.2	7.1	3.1	7.7	18.0
	2005	217 918 500	11.5	19.5	6.4	17.9	0.4	1.9	6.7	2.8	7.0	17.3
Ireland	2004	23 325	9.7	3.4	7.8	10.1	...	3.1	40.3	1.7	17.3	6.5
Irlande	2005	25 595	9.5	3.2	7.5	10.7	...	4.1	39.5	1.5	17.4	6.5
	2006	27 919	9.5	3.2	7.5	10.7	...	4.1	39.5	1.5	17.4	6.5
Israel	2005	153 536	6.8	30.0	6.2	3.6	1.8	1.1	16.8	3.2	24.8	5.7
Israël	2006	163 541	6.9	30.9	6.2	3.5	1.9	1.0	16.1	3.2	24.8	5.6
	2007	169 720	6.8	29.4	6.3	3.7	1.9	1.0	16.4	3.2	25.5	5.8

Government final consumption expenditure by function at current prices *(continued)*
Percentage distribution by divisions of Classification of the Functions of Government (COFOG)
Dépenses de consommation finale des administrations publiques par fonction aux prix courants *(suite)*
Répartition en pourcentage par divisions de la Classification des fonctions des administrations publiques (COFOG)

Country or area Pays ou zone	Year Année	Total (m.nat.curr.) Totale (m.monn.nat.)	Div. 01 (%)	Div. 02 (%)	Div. 03 (%)	Div. 04 (%)	Div. 05 (%)	Div. 06 (%)	Div. 07 (%)	Div. 08 (%)	Div. 09 (%)	Div. 10 (%)
Italy Italie	2004	276 234	15.0	7.0	9.5	6.4	1.3	2.1	32.3	2.0	20.2	4.3
	2005	290 636	14.9	6.9	9.2	6.4	1.3	2.1	32.7	2.0	20.3	4.1
	2006	299 512	14.5	6.9	9.3	6.6	1.3	2.1	33.5	2.0	19.6	4.2
Japan Japon	2004	89 785 100	8.6	4.6	6.3	13.5	6.5	1.4	36.2	0.4	18.8	3.6
	2005	90 576 800	8.3	4.6	6.3	13.8	6.5	1.4	37.0	0.4	18.4	3.4
	2006	89 911 700	8.3	4.6	6.3	13.9	6.0	1.4	37.4	0.4	18.5	3.3
Jordan[1] Jordanie[1]	1993	939	53.6[7]	...	...	...	...	...	10.2	6.4	21.9	1.0
	1994	986	59.3[7]	...	...	...	...	...	8.2	6.0	20.4	1.0
	1995	1 111	60.0[7]	...	...	...	...	...	8.3	5.6	21.3	0.9
Kazakhstan Kazakhstan	2005	853 830	12.1	7.9	18.1	11.5	...	2.3	16.5	4.3	23.9	3.4
	2006	1 039 846	9.9	8.4	17.0	12.8	...	2.8	15.9	5.0	24.8	3.3
	2007	1 420 366	10.0	10.2	16.1	12.6	...	3.0	15.9	4.5	24.6	3.0
Kenya Kenya	2005	246 102	...	...	...	...	...	...	9.1	...	41.7	...
	2006	269 214	...	...	...	...	...	...	9.8	...	40.5	...
	2007	311 211	...	...	...	...	...	...	9.9	...	38.8	...
Korea, Republic of Corée, République de	2004	105 516 900	13.8	17.5	9.1	12.4	1.5	0.6	16.7	1.3	22.5	4.8
	2005	114 838 200	14.7	17.2	8.7	11.5	1.9	0.5	17.2	1.4	22.0	4.9
	2006	125 642 800	14.2	17.0	8.6	11.3	1.9	0.5	18.4	1.5	21.7	5.0
Kuwait[1] Koweït[1]	2003	3 281	...	56.2	...	4.5	...	2.6	9.7	4.4	19.0	3.6
	2004	3 478	...	55.7	...	4.6	...	2.4	9.9	4.5	19.2	3.6
	2005	3 637	...	54.6	...	4.8	...	2.5	10.2	4.4	19.7	3.7
Kyrgyzstan Kirghizistan	2004	17 146	32.2	9.8	4.2	5.2	0.5	1.2	14.5	3.3	23.3	5.1
	2005	17 672	28.3	9.2	4.5	5.4	0.5	1.2	14.7	2.7	21.1	11.5
	2006	20 470	29.6	8.3	4.9	4.9	0.8	1.5	17.5	2.8	22.8	5.9
Latvia Lettonie	2004	1 451	...	3.8	...	...	...	...	16.7	5.4	24.5	3.0
	2005	1 581	...	4.4	...	...	...	...	16.6	4.9	23.6	3.3
	2006	1 855	...	3.9	...	...	...	...	15.9	4.8	24.3	3.7
Lesotho Lesotho	1999	1 188	25.6	...	19.1	4.7	...	10.7	13.1	...	6.1	...
	2000	1 144	27.7	...	20.2	5.5	...	11.6	13.2	...	8.1	...
	2001	1 176	27.4	...	20.6	6.7	...	11.8	14.0	...	7.7	...
Libyan Arab Jamah.[1] Jamah. arabe libyenne[1]	1980	2 351	68.8	...	...	7.7	...	1.2	7.4	0.9	11.5	2.3
Lithuania Lituanie	2004	11 207	10.6	6.7	9.6	9.3	1.7	1.2	21.1	3.3	29.1	7.4
	2005	12 231	8.9	7.1	9.4	9.3	2.0	1.4	22.4	4.0	28.7	6.7
	2006	14 780	9.9	6.8	9.0	10.1	2.3	1.5	22.2	4.5	26.7	7.0
Luxembourg Luxembourg	2005	4 997	16.2	1.3	5.4	10.1	3.4	1.5	24.5	4.1	23.3	10.3
	2006	5 186	15.4	1.3	5.6	10.4	3.2	1.4	24.3	4.3	23.9	10.2
	2007	5 492	15.9	1.4	5.6	9.7	3.0	1.4	24.7	4.4	23.9	10.1
Malaysia Malaisie	2005	64 516	15.9	17.3	8.4	11.5	...	...	12.3	...	29.2	3.7
	2006	68 526	15.0	15.8	8.7	9.0	...	...	13.6	...	31.7	4.4
	2007	78 297	13.8	16.2	9.4	9.2	...	...	13.8	...	31.7	4.2
Maldives[1] Maldives[1]	1984	103	30.4	15.6	...	13.9	...	5.8	7.9	...	14.6	6.8
	1985	121	29.9	15.0	...	11.8	...	8.0	7.9	...	14.5	5.6
	1986	139	32.3	16.3	...	5.6	...	7.8	8.3	...	16.2	5.3
Malta Malte	2005	406	11.5	3.5	6.7	17.0	4.7	1.5	25.0	1.9	22.4	5.9
	2006	437	11.6	3.5	6.5	16.0	5.2	1.4	25.3	1.8	21.8	6.9
	2007	448	11.6	3.5	6.5	16.0	5.2	1.4	25.3	1.8	21.8	7.0
Mauritius Maurice	2003	22 271	22.1	1.3	13.3	11.4	...	5.9	15.6	2.3	25.9	2.3
	2004	25 042	22.8	1.2	13.3	10.5	...	6.0	16.7	1.9	25.3	2.3
	2005	27 171	25.8	1.2	14.0	9.3	...	6.2	15.6	1.9	24.5	1.5
Mexico Mexique	2002	759 866	11.4	...	16.3	7.5	...	...	21.2	5.2	36.8	1.6
	2003	855 747	12.0	...	16.0	7.7	...	...	20.7	5.4	36.6	1.6
	2004	913 971	12.0	...	16.2	7.6	...	...	21.1	5.2	36.4	1.6

22

Government final consumption expenditure by function at current prices *(continued)*
Percentage distribution by divisions of Classification of the Functions of Government (COFOG)

Dépenses de consommation finale des administrations publiques par fonction aux prix courants *(suite)*
Répartition en pourcentage par divisions de la Classification des fonctions des administrations publiques (COFOG)

Country or area Pays ou zone	Year Année	Total (m.nat.curr.) Totale (m.monn.nat.)	Divisions of the Classification of the Functions of Government (COFOG)[t] Divisions de la Classification des fonctions des administrations publiques (COFOG)[t]									
			Div. 01 (%)	Div. 02 (%)	Div. 03 (%)	Div. 04 (%)	Div. 05 (%)	Div. 06 (%)	Div. 07 (%)	Div. 08 (%)	Div. 09 (%)	Div. 10 (%)
Mongolia Mongolie	2005	344 488	14.6	9.3	10.8	6.4	...	0.8	20.4	3.9	31.9	1.9
	2006	425 279	14.5	8.3	10.2	8.3	...	0.8	18.7	4.7	32.6	1.9
	2007	598 566	14.9	8.1	9.9	7.7	...	0.8	18.6	5.0	32.9	2.2
Montserrat[1] Montserrat[1]	1983	18	15.1	0.4	10.9	27.0	...	0.8	17.4	1.4	17.7	9.2
	1984	19	19.6	0.3	10.5	27.2	...	-0.2	15.9	0.6	19.3	6.6
	1985	20	18.7	0.3	11.3	24.5	...	0.9	15.3	1.7	22.4	4.8
Nepal[1] Népal[1]	1986	5 065	14.7	11.7	9.7	23.1	...	2.5	8.0	6.0	23.9	0.7
	1987	5 797	16.9	13.1	8.1	34.6	...	3.2	8.7	0.8	27.5	0.5
	1988	6 895	15.2	7.5	11.0	37.0	...	3.9	3.8	1.6	24.0	1.7
Netherlands Pays-Bas	2004	118 942	9.0	5.5	6.8	12.3	1.6	1.9	17.8	4.0	18.9	22.2
	2005	121 720	9.3	5.3	6.9	12.2	1.6	1.8	18.1	4.0	18.8	22.0
	2006	135 694	8.5	5.2	6.4	11.3	1.5	1.6	22.9	3.6	17.8	21.2
Netherlands Antilles Antilles néerlandaises	2002	1 068	13.6	1.5	14.0	2.1	1.4	...	7.5	1.0	17.4	7.9
	2003	1 150	13.5	1.5	14.1	2.2	1.3	...	7.4	1.0	18.4	7.8
	2004	1 130	14.5	1.6	15.1	2.2	1.6	...	7.7	1.0	19.8	8.4
New Zealand[+] Nouvelle-Zélande[+]	2003	24 386	9.2	6.0	7.4	8.2	3.2	2.0	30.9	2.9	22.2	8.0
	2004	26 238	9.6	5.4	7.2	7.7	3.2	2.0	31.1	2.9	22.5	8.5
	2005	28 659	10.2	4.5	7.6	6.4	3.8	2.3	31.6	2.8	22.2	8.6
Nicaragua[+] Nicaragua[+]	2002	10 078	19.6	4.2	9.9	18.9	1.6	0.4	17.0	0.4	22.3	3.6
	2003	11 354	18.6	4.2	10.1	21.5	1.8	0.5	16.3	0.3	21.7	2.9
	2004	12 887	19.8	3.5	9.6	22.0	1.6	0.4	12.1	0.4	25.8	2.7
Oman Oman	2000	1 580	10.5	29.3[20]	11.6	7.7	...	5.4	10.1	2.8	21.4	1.2
	2001	1 712	10.7	33.2[20]	11.3	6.8	...	4.6	9.4	2.5	20.5	1.1
	2002	1 800	10.8	32.6[20]	12.0	5.9	...	4.7	9.5	2.5	20.8	1.0
Pakistan[+] Pakistan[+]	2006	834 602	35.5	...	5.5	26.0	0.6	0.8	3.9	0.3	14.4	12.1
	2007	811 508	41.8	...	9.5	12.4	0.7	1.2	4.3	0.4	10.3	11.0
	2008	943 751	44.3	...	10.3	14.0	0.8	1.1	5.0	0.4	11.6	9.7
Panama Panama	2004	1 930	22.1	...	14.6	8.0	0.2	0.4	6.4	0.9	24.2	23.1
	2005	2 034	21.4	...	12.0	13.2	0.2	0.5	6.9	0.7	23.3	21.7
	2006	2 116	25.2	...	11.7	9.6	0.5	0.4	6.9	0.8	23.0	21.9
Peru[1] Pérou[1]	1986	43[21]	56.6	...	...	5.7	...	0.2	9.2	1.3	25.0	2.1
	1987	94[21]	55.5	...	...	5.3	...	0.2	7.1	1.8	27.3	2.9
	1988	475[21]	54.1	...	...	6.7	...	0.2	7.6	2.5	26.1	2.7
Poland Pologne	2004	162 656	14.1	4.8	8.6	5.8	1.1	4.5	21.6	2.7	28.2	8.7
	2005	177 785	12.2	4.8	9.1	6.4	1.2	5.0	21.3	2.8	28.1	9.1
	2006	193 707	11.9	5.2	9.4	7.5	1.2	4.1	20.9	3.2	27.2	9.4
Portugal Portugal	2004	29 747	10.0	6.1	8.9	7.8	1.2	1.2	29.1	1.8	29.4	4.6
	2005	31 974	10.4	6.0	8.8	8.3	1.3	1.1	28.6	2.1	28.9	4.5
	2006	32 182	10.0	5.9	8.5	8.1	1.2	1.2	29.8	2.1	28.5	4.7
Republic of Moldova République de Moldova	2005	6 189	34.6[6]	...	...	13.1[23]	...	2.0[24]	4.8	2.4	37.9	2.0
	2006	8 945	29.0[5]	...	...	8.6[23]	...	1.7[24]	20.3	2.8	34.2	1.1
	2007	10 457	26.2[5]	...	...	11.0[23]	...	2.0[24]	20.9	2.8	31.8	2.1
Romania[1] Roumanie[1]	1993	2 473 200	36.5[7]	...	...	11.7	...	...	22.3	4.7	22.6	2.1
	1994	6 851 800	39.0[7]	...	...	8.4	...	...	28.6	4.6	19.4	2.2
	1995	9 877 000	37.3[7]	...	...	14.5	...	...	19.0	5.5	21.4	2.3
Russian Federation Fédération de Russie	2003	2 330 573	53.2[5]	...	...	1.7[25]	...	2.9	22.7	2.9	15.1	...
	2004	2 847 486	52.7[5]	...	...	1.6[25]	...	3.0	23.0	2.9	15.4	...
	2005	3 598 306	8.1	...	29.5	7.9[25]	0.2	2.6	17.1	2.7	19.2	12.6
Saint Vincent-Grenadines[1] Saint Vincent-Grenadines[1]	2004	221	10.9	...	11.8	24.4	...	1.4	17.2	...	24.9	8.1
	2005	234	10.7	...	12.0	24.4	...	1.3	17.1	...	24.8	8.1
	2006	250	10.8	...	12.0	22.4	...	1.6	18.0	...	25.2	8.8
San Marino[1] Saint-Marin[1]	1999	423 728	17.0	0.3	5.0	8.9	...	7.4	20.7	6.5	16.8	17.4
	#2003	271	26.5	4.6	...	...	1.9	3.3	22.7	4.1	14.8	11.5
	2004	314	21.2	4.1	...	...	2.7	4.4	21.0	4.2	12.4	20.3

Government final consumption expenditure by function at current prices *(continued)*
Percentage distribution by divisions of Classification of the Functions of Government (COFOG)

Dépenses de consommation finale des administrations publiques par fonction aux prix courants *(suite)*
Répartition en pourcentage par divisions de la Classification des fonctions des administrations publiques (COFOG)

Country or area Pays ou zone	Year Année	Total (m.nat.curr.) Totale (m.monn.nat.)	Div. 01 (%)	Div. 02 (%)	Div. 03 (%)	Div. 04 (%)	Div. 05 (%)	Div. 06 (%)	Div. 07 (%)	Div. 08 (%)	Div. 09 (%)	Div. 10 (%)
Saudi Arabia[+1]	1999	154 094	19.8	27.4	...	3.4	...	4.7	11.0	2.9[26]	29.4	0.4
Arabie saoudite[+1]	2000	183 804	18.0	27.9	...	4.7	...	5.3	11.7	3.0[26]	27.0	0.5
	2001	188 695	18.4	27.4	...	4.9	...	5.5	11.8	3.0[26]	26.4	0.5
Senegal	2004	559 281	66.8	...	...	...	...	...	5.8	2.0	25.5	...
Sénégal	2005	592 127	63.8	...	...	...	...	...	5.2	2.3	28.7	...
	2006	636 135	64.3	...	...	...	...	...	5.2	2.4	28.1	...
Seychelles[1]	1989	475	9.4	11.5	4.9	17.1	...	2.1	11.8	3.1	29.7	2.6
Seychelles[1]	1990	544	9.5	10.2	5.1	18.3	...	2.6	12.8	5.9	29.2	3.5
	1991	558	10.3	11.0	5.7	17.0	...	2.4	13.7	5.7	26.4	5.2
Sierra Leone[+1]	1988	3 883[2,27]	18.5	7.2	...	28.0	...	0.8	5.9	0.0	13.2	1.0
Sierra Leone[+1]	1989	7 620[2,27]	14.4	7.3	...	45.9	...	1.4	5.0	0.0	10.2	1.4
	1990	32 337[2,27]	11.9	5.6	...	27.9	...	1.0	2.1	^0.0	6.2	0.6
Slovakia Slovaquie	2006	318 497	14.5	3.8	4.6	8.2	1.9	1.9	29.3	2.9	21.4	11.5
Slovenia	2004	5 134	11.2	5.3	9.6	9.0	1.0	1.4	29.8	3.1	25.8	3.7
Slovénie	2005	5 472	11.9	6.3	9.0	9.2	1.0	1.3	29.1	3.0	25.5	3.6
	2006	5 857	12.1	6.4	8.6	9.7	1.0	1.5	28.8	3.0	25.3	3.6
Spain	2004	149 756	8.9	6.1	9.8	8.3	2.5	3.1	29.0	4.2	21.9	6.1
Espagne	2005	163 740	8.8	6.0	9.5	8.1	2.4	3.3	29.7	4.4	21.4	6.4
	2006	177 978	8.9	6.0	9.5	8.2	2.5	3.3	29.2	4.5	21.5	6.5
Sri Lanka	2004	264 069	14.4	21.3	7.2	7.5	...	0.1	12.8	0.3	14.7	21.6
Sri Lanka	2005	321 037	15.9	19.1	5.9	8.4	...	0.2	11.2	0.3	16.0	23.1
	2006	451 429	27.4	17.2	5.3	6.1	...	0.1	10.2	0.4	14.7	18.6
Sudan[+1]	1981	720	25.2[17]	18.6	...	12.4[28]	...	0.1	9.7	3.2	30.9	...
Soudan[+1]	1982	854	27.7[17]	19.0	...	14.4[28]	...	^0.0	8.6	2.6	27.7	...
	1983	1 113	32.4[17]	22.5	...	14.4[28]	...	-0.2	5.1	2.2	23.7	...
Sweden	2004	702 537	9.1	6.2	4.8	5.9	0.2	0.6	24.7	2.7	23.9	21.7
Suède	2005	722 697	9.0	5.8	4.8	6.0	0.4	0.6	24.9	2.8	24.2	21.6
	2006	761 890	8.8	5.5	4.8	6.2	0.4	0.5	24.9	2.8	24.3	21.9
Thailand[1]	2005	843 649	25.0	23.2	...	4.5	...	2.3	11.1	...	33.1	0.8
Thaïlande[1]	2006	927 575	24.3	22.8	...	4.5	...	2.3	10.9	...	33.9	1.1
	2007	1 037 571	23.5	22.9	...	4.4	...	2.1	11.1	...	34.5	1.3
TFYR of Macedonia	1991	199	37.6	...	...	...	...	2.5	21.8	3.8	27.1	6.7
L'ex-R.Y. Macédoine	1992	2 302	38.3	...	...	...	...	1.2	28.9	3.0	23.4	4.7
	1993	12 472	42.6	...	...	...	...	0.4	24.3	3.4	23.5	5.5
Tonga[1]	1985	21	20.7	4.2	7.0	31.9	...	...	12.2	...	13.6	1.9
Tonga[1]	1986	27	22.7	3.7	7.1	29.0	...	...	11.9	...	13.8	1.9
	1987	32	26.9	3.4	6.9	26.3	...	...	10.3	...	13.1	1.9
Trinidad and Tobago	2003	9 042	20.1	...	22.8	16.1	...	6.5	9.8	...	24.2	0.6
Trinité-et-Tobago	2004	9 585	20.1	...	22.2	18.0	...	6.5	9.5	...	23.2	0.6
	2005	11 885	20.9	...	21.8	16.7	...	6.6	8.9	...	24.6	0.6
Ukraine	2005	80 528	13.8	5.8	10.8	5.2	0.5	2.3	19.6	2.8	29.5	9.7
Ukraine	2006	100 350	14.7	4.9	10.6	6.2	0.4	2.2	19.5	2.7	29.0	9.9
	2007	131 938	13.0	5.3	11.6	5.5	0.4	2.2	19.3	2.9	29.1	10.6
United Kingdom	2003	232 699	4.5	12.3	10.3	6.5	2.3	2.2	30.0	3.4	17.4	11.1
Royaume-Uni	2004	250 708	5.4	11.5	10.0	6.4	2.3	2.3	30.7	3.2	17.2	11.1
	2005	267 530	5.7	11.2	10.0	5.4	3.5	2.3	31.2	3.0	16.9	10.7
United Rep. of Tanzania[+29]	2004	2 362 000	3.8	...	...	...	...	...	8.5	...	10.0	...
Rép.-Unie de Tanzanie[+29]	2005	2 805 000	3.3	...	...	...	...	...	8.3	...	8.9	...
	2006	3 144 881	3.0	...	...	...	...	...	8.8	...	8.5	...
United States	2004	1 844 603	9.2	26.2	12.5	11.3	0.0	0.4	4.8	1.4	30.0	4.2
Etats-Unis	2005	1 968 579	9.0	26.3	12.6	11.2	0.0	0.5	5.2	1.4	29.4	4.3
	2006	2 095 462	8.8	26.3	12.8	11.2	0.0	0.5	5.4	1.4	29.1	4.5
Vanuatu[1]	1991	4 693	20.5	8.4	...	22.6	...	18.5[30]	10.3	...	19.8	...
Vanuatu[1]	1992	5 112	22.6	8.7	...	21.2	...	16.1[30]	10.1	...	21.2	...
	1993	5 194	27.1	9.2	...	20.1	...	13.9[30]	9.7	...	20.0	...

22

Government final consumption expenditure by function at current prices *(continued)*
Percentage distribution by divisions of Classification of the Functions of Government (COFOG)

Dépenses de consommation finale des administrations publiques par fonction aux prix courants *(suite)*
Répartition en pourcentage par divisions de la Classification des fonctions des administrations publiques (COFOG)

Country or area Pays ou zone	Year Année	Total (m.nat.curr.) Totale (m.monn.nat.)	Div. 01 (%)	Div. 02 (%)	Div. 03 (%)	Div. 04 (%)	Div. 05 (%)	Div. 06 (%)	Div. 07 (%)	Div. 08 (%)	Div. 09 (%)	Div. 10 (%)
Venezuela (Boliv. Rep. of)	2003	17 276 165	13.7	6.5	5.8	5.2	0.4	3.4	14.6	1.3	41.9	7.2
Venezuela (Rép. bol. du)	2004	25 428 211	14.0	9.2	6.7	4.9	0.9	2.5	17.0	1.3	37.7	5.8
	2005	33 619 547	12.8	8.9	6.4	6.1	0.8	2.5	17.5	1.3	37.9	5.9
Zimbabwe [1]	1989	5 568[31]	6.2	15.7	5.9	14.1	...	1.2	8.1	1.4	28.1	2.6
Zimbabwe [1]	1990	7 425[31]	28.1	13.1	4.9	20.8	...	1.6	6.5	2.0	19.9	3.1
	1991	7 788[31]	16.7	14.3	6.1	23.0	...	1.7	7.4	2.8	26.7	4.1

Source:
United Nations Statistics Division, New York, national accounts database, last accessed February 2009.

Data for most countries have been compiled in accordance with the concepts and definitions of the System of National Accounts 1993 (1993 SNA). Countries that follow the 1968 SNA are footnoted accordingly.

[t] COFOG Divisions:
Div. 01: General public services
Div. 02: Defence
Div. 03: Public order and safety
Div. 04: Economic affairs
Div. 05: Environmental protection
Div. 06: Housing and community amenities
Div. 07: Health
Div. 08: Recreation, culture and religion
Div. 09: Education
Div. 10: Social protection

[+] Note: The national accounts data generally relate to the fiscal year used in each country, unless indicated otherwise. Countries whose reference periods coincide with the calendar year ending 31 December are not listed below.

Year beginning 21 March: Afghanistan, Iran (Islamic Republic).
Year beginning 1 April: Bermuda, India, Myanmar, New Zealand, Nigeria.
Year beginning 1 July: Australia, Bhutan, Cameroon, Gambia, Nicaragua, Pakistan, Puerto Rico, Saudi Arabia, Sierra Leone, Sudan, United Republic of Tanzania.
Year ending 30 June: Bangladesh, Botswana, Egypt, Swaziland, Tonga.
Year ending 7 July: Nepal.
Year ending 30 July: Ethiopia.
Year ending 30 September: Haiti.

1   Data compiled in accordance with the System of National Accounts 1968 (1968 SNA).
2   Central government estimates only.
3   Including expenditure on culture.
4   Data refer only to collective government consumption expenditure (excluding individual consumption).
5   Including "Defence".
6   Including housing and community amenities.
7   Including defence and public order and safety.
8   Total government current expenditure only.
9   Excluding Office of the President, Ministries of Justice, Foreign Affairs, Information, among others.
10   Refers to inter-ministerial expenses only.

Source:
Organisation des Nations Unies, Division de statistique, New York, la base de données sur les comptes nationaux, dernier accès février 2009.

Les données pour la majorité des pays sont compilées selon les concepts et définitions du Système de comptabilité nationale, 1993 (SCN93). Seuls les pays qui suivent toujours le SCN68 seront donc signalés par une note.

[t] Divisions de la COFOG:
Div. 01: Services généraux des administrations publiques
Div. 02: Défense
Div. 03: Ordre et sécurité publics
Div. 04: Affaires économiques
Div. 05: Protection de l'environnement
Div. 06: Logements et équipements collectifs
Div. 07: Santé
Div. 08: Loisirs, culture et culte
Div. 09: Enseignement
Div. 10: Protection sociale

[+] Note : Sauf indication contraire, les données sur les comptes nationaux concernent généralement l'exercice budgétaire utilisé dans chaque pays. Les pays où territoires dont la période de référence coïncide avec l'année civile se terminant le 31 décembre ne sont pas répertoriés ci dessous.

Exercice commençant le 21 mars: Afghanistan, Iran (République islamique d').
Exercice commençant le 1er avril: Bermudes, Inde, Myanmar, Nigéria, Nouvelle-Zélande.
Exercice commençant le 1er juillet: Arabie saoudite, Australie, Bhoutan, Cameroun, Gambie, Nicaragua, Pakistan, Porto Rico, Sierra Leone, Soudan, Rép.-Unie de Tanzanie.
Exercice se terminant le 30 juin: Bangladesh, Botswana, Égypte, Swaziland, Tonga.
Exercice se terminant le 7 juillet: Népal.
Exercice se terminant le 30 juillet: Éthiopie.
Exercice se terminant le 30 septembre: Haïti.

1   Données compilées selon le Système de comptabilité nationale de 1968 (SCN 1968).
2   Administration centrale seulement.
3   Y compris dépenses de culture.
4   Les données ne concernent que les dépenses de consommation collective des administrations publiques (à l'exclusion de la consommation individuelle).
5   Y compris "Défense".
6   Y compris logement et équipements collectifs.
7   Y compris défense et sureté publique.
8   Dépenses publiques courantes seulement.
9   Non compris notamment le Cabinet du Président, et les Ministères de la justice, des affaires étrangères et de l'information.
10   Ne concerne que les dépenses interministérielles.

22 Government final consumption expenditure by function at current prices *(continued)*
Percentage distribution by divisions of Classification of the Functions of Government (COFOG)

Dépenses de consommation finale des administrations publiques par fonction aux prix courants *(suite)*
Répartition en pourcentage par divisions de la Classification des fonctions des administrations publiques (COFOG)

11	Refers to the Ministry of the Interior.	11	Concerne le Ministère de l'intérieur.
12	Refers to the Ministry of Finance and Planning.	12	Concerne le Ministère des finances et de la planification.
13	Refers to the Ministry of Agriculture, Livestock Development and Environmental Protection.	13	Concerne le Ministère de l'agriculture, du développement de l'élevage et de la protection de l'environnement.
14	Refers to the Ministry of Equipment, Transport and Telecommunication.	14	Concerne le Ministère de l'équipement, des transports et des télécommunications.
15	Refers to the Ministry of Health, Public Services and Social Affairs.	15	Concerne le Ministère de la santé, des services publics et des affaires sociales.
16	Twinning projects in the health sector.	16	Projets jumelés dans le secteur de la santé.
17	Including "Public order and safety".	17	Y compris "Ordre et sécurité publics".
18	Including compensation of employees and intermediate consumption of the following departmental enterprises: electricity, gas and steam, water works and supply and medical and other health services.	18	Y compris la rémunération des employés et la consommation intermédiaire des entreprises suivantes : électricité, gaz et vapeur, approvisionnement en eau, services médicaux et autres services sanitaires.
19	Including Recreation, culture and religion.	19	Y compris Loisirs, culture et culte.
20	Data refer to defence affairs and services.	20	Les données se réfèrent aux affaires et services de la défense.
21	Figures in thousands.	21	Données en milliers.
22	Preliminary data.	22	Données préliminaires.
23	Including agriculture, transport, and other branches of the economy.	23	Y compris l'agriculture, les transports, et d'autres branches d'activité.
24	Data refer to real estate transactions.	24	Les données concernent les transactions immobilières.
25	Data refer to agriculture, geology, exploration, hydrometerorology, transport, and communication.	25	Les données concernent l'agriculture, la géologie, l'exploration, l'hydrométéorologie, les transports et les communications.
26	Data refer to other community and social services.	26	Les données concernent les autres services collectifs et sociaux.
27	Including development expenditure.	27	Y compris les dépenses de développement.
28	Including other functions.	28	Y compris les autres fonctions.
29	Tanzania mainland only.	29	Tanzanie continentale seulement.
30	Including "Social protection".	30	Y compris "protection sociale".
31	Central and local government estimates only.	31	Administration centrale et locale seulement.

23
Household consumption expenditure by purpose at current prices
Percentage distribution by divisions of the Classification of Individual Consumption according to Purpose (COICOP)

Dépenses de consommation des ménages par fonction aux prix courants
Répartition en pourcentage par divisions de la Nomenclature des fonctions de la consommation individuelle (COICOP)

Country or area Pays ou zone	Year Année	Total (millions national cur.) Totale (millions monnaie nat.)	Div. 01+02 (%)	Div. 03 (%)	Div. 04 (%)	Div. 05 (%)	Div. 06 (%)	Div. 07+08 (%)	Div. 09 (%)	Div. 10 (%)	Div. 11 (%)	Div. 12 (%)
Andorra [1] Andorre [1]	2001	797	20.2[2]	7.6	14.7	4.0	3.2	19.5[3]	3.9	0.9	7.2	7.8
	2002	870	19.1[2]	7.6	14.9	4.1	3.4	19.6[3]	4.3	0.9	6.3	7.9
	2003	921	18.4[2]	6.3	15.0	4.1	3.6	21.2[3]	4.2	1.0	5.8	8.0
Australia [+] Australie [+]	2004	521 028[4]	14.8	3.8	19.3	5.6	5.1	14.9	12.0	3.3	7.6	13.5
	2005	547 458[4]	14.9	3.7	19.4	5.4	5.2	14.7	12.0	3.4	7.7	13.6
	2006	581 873[4]	15.0	3.6	19.6	5.4	5.2	14.6	11.8	3.4	7.6	13.6
Austria Autriche	2004	128 348	14.4	6.9	20.6	7.9	3.4	16.1	12.3	0.7	12.7	9.8
	2005	133 160	14.4	6.8	21.6	7.8	3.3	16.7	12.2	0.7	12.6	9.1
	2006	138 057	14.4	6.6	21.5	7.7	3.4	16.4	12.2	0.7	12.7	9.5
Azerbaijan Azerbaïdjan	2005	5 211[6]	78.6	5.8	1.3	1.7	1.8	6.2	0.3	3.3	0.4	0.6
	2006	6 873[6]	78.6	5.8	1.3	1.7	1.8	6.2	0.3	3.3	0.4	0.6
	2007[5]	9 439[6]	78.6	5.8	1.3	1.7	1.8	6.2	0.3	3.3	0.4	0.6
Belarus Bélarus	2004	26 130 200	51.5	7.9	12.3	4.4	2.2	11.0	3.4	1.3	2.5	3.5
	2005	32 954 645	49.8	7.6	11.9	4.7	2.1	12.4	3.8	1.5	2.7	3.6
	2006	39 792 291	47.6	7.6	11.9	5.2	2.2	14.2	4.0	1.4	2.5	3.5
Belgium Belgique	2004	149 888	17.0	5.3	22.5	5.3	4.4	16.6	9.1	0.6	5.1	12.1
	2005	156 014	16.6	5.3	22.5	5.4	4.2	16.6	9.1	0.5	5.1	12.6
	2006	163 139	16.3	5.2	22.4	5.4	4.2	16.6	9.2	0.5	5.0	13.2
Bolivia [1] Bolivie [1]	1994	21 444	34.7[7]	6.7	...	...	...	...	...	...	9.2	...
	1995	24 440	34.4[7]	6.5	...	...	...	...	...	...	9.5	...
	1996	28 200	35.7[7]	6.5	...	...	...	...	...	...	9.8	...
Botswana [+] Botswana [+]	1999	6 619	43.3	5.4	12.2	4.1	2.3	7.9	...	6.8	1.1	...
	2000	7 469	42.7	5.1	13.4	3.7	2.4	7.2	...	7.0	1.0	...
	2001	8 001	42.5	3.9	14.5	...	2.7	7.6	...	8.5	1.1	...
British Virgin Islands Iles Vierges brit.	1997	231	16.5	10.4	19.5	6.9	1.7	13.0	2.2	1.3	7.8	21.2
	1998	253	16.2	9.5	20.6	6.7	2.0	12.6	1.6	1.2	7.5	22.1
	1999	280	15.7	10.0	20.7	6.4	2.5	11.8	2.9	1.1	6.1	22.9
Bulgaria Bulgarie	2004	26 732	28.6	3.4	21.9	3.9	4.2	23.3	5.4	0.9	9.4	4.1
	2005	29 842	27.0	3.4	21.2	4.2	4.2	25.5	5.7	0.9	9.5	4.3
	2006	33 762	26.8	3.4	19.8	4.2	4.3	25.8	5.8	0.9	9.8	4.4
Cameroon [+] Cameroun [+]	2002	5 342 410	49.5	12.2	6.9	3.0	0.3	7.6	...	0.9	8.4	11.2
	2003	5 690 774	49.5	12.2	6.9	3.0	0.3	7.6	...	0.0	8.4	11.1
	2004	5 919 214	47.9	13.1	7.0	3.0	0.3	8.2	...	0.9	8.6	10.9
Canada Canada	2004	703 279	13.6	4.9	23.0	6.5	4.1	16.5	10.3	1.3	7.1	12.4
	2005	742 304	13.4	4.8	22.9	6.5	4.2	16.7	10.2	1.3	7.0	12.4
	2006	783 844	13.1	4.7	22.7	6.6	4.3	16.6	10.2	1.3	7.0	12.5
Cape Verde [1] Cap-Vert [1]	1986	13 406	61.2	2.7	14.1	7.2	0.5	...	...	...	...	...
	1987	15 134	60.4	2.9	13.6	7.2	0.6	...	...	...	...	...
	1988	17 848	62.6	2.5	13.5	6.9	0.5	...	...	...	...	...
China, Hong Kong SAR Chine, Hong Kong RAS	2004	710 105	13.8	12.7[8]	20.5[9]	10.8	4.6[10]	10.1	6.6[11]	2.7	...	16.6[12]
	2005	746 842	13.9	12.5[8]	20.4[9]	10.5	4.6[10]	9.7	6.9[11]	2.5	...	18.8[12]
	2006	805 217	13.9	12.6[8]	20.1[9]	10.1	4.5[10]	9.4	7.1[11]	2.4	...	20.5[12]
China, Macao SAR Chine, Macao RAS	2004	21 807	12.5	4.1	16.2	2.6	3.0	14.7	11.8	3.8	14.4	5.2
	2005	24 035	12.7	4.6	16.4	2.6	3.0	14.8	11.4	3.6	14.4	4.9
	2006	26 584	12.4	5.1	16.8	2.8	3.0	14.2	11.6	3.1	14.6	5.9
Colombia Colombie	2003	147 626 161	33.3	4.6	15.9	5.3	4.9	14.4	4.8	4.8	6.3	5.6
	2004	164 474 505	33.0	4.6	15.4	5.4	5.2	15.1	4.6	4.6	6.5	5.7
	2005	179 148 411	32.8	4.8	15.0	5.5	4.9	15.7	4.7	4.5	6.6	5.6
Côte d'Ivoire [1] Côte d'Ivoire [1]	1996	4 046 064	51.1	5.3	7.2	3.8	0.4	9.9	1.8	0.2	2.7	16.8
	1997	4 329 400	49.8	5.3	7.2	4.0	0.5	10.0	1.8	0.2	2.5	17.4
	1998	4 836 550	49.9	5.4	7.2	4.0	0.5	9.3	1.7	0.3	1.9	18.3
Croatia Croatie	2004	123 123	33.3	6.6	21.0	10.6	5.0	18.0	10.3	2.6	10.5	6.6
	2005	131 671	33.6	6.7	21.4	10.8	5.2	17.3	10.4	2.8	10.9	6.7
	2006	140 261	33.9	6.7	21.2	10.6	5.1	17.4	10.3	2.7	10.8	6.7

23

Household consumption expenditure by purpose at current prices *(continued)*
Percentage distribution
Dépenses de consommation des ménages par fonction aux prix courants *(suite)*
Répartition en pourcentage

Country or area Pays ou zone	Year Année	Total (millions national cur.) Totale (millions monnaie nat.)	Div. 01+02 (%)	Div. 03 (%)	Div. 04 (%)	Div. 05 (%)	Div. 06 (%)	Div. 07+08 (%)	Div. 09 (%)	Div. 10 (%)	Div. 11 (%)	Div. 12 (%)
Cyprus	2004	4 702	24.8	7.5	14.3	8.2	4.5	21.1	9.6	3.4	14.1	11.7
Chypre	2005	5 015	25.0	7.4	15.2	8.0	4.6	19.4	9.6	3.5	14.8	11.7
	2006	5 351	25.4	7.4	15.2	8.0	4.5	19.1	9.7	3.5	14.3	11.8
Czech Republic	2004	1 399 200	25.2	5.1	22.8	5.3	1.9	15.2	12.0	0.6	6.7	8.7
République tchèque	2005	1 442 935	25.2	5.1	23.3	5.5	2.0	15.7	12.2	0.7	6.9	8.4
	2006	1 554 404	24.4	4.8	23.7	5.8	2.1	16.1	11.6	0.6	6.5	9.0
Denmark	2003	656 340	16.2	5.0	27.4	5.8	2.6	13.1	11.3	0.8	4.9	12.9
Danemark	2004	696 457	15.4	4.9	26.9	5.7	2.6	14.7	11.4	0.8	4.9	12.7
	2005	748 334	14.8	4.8	26.3	5.7	2.6	15.7	11.1	0.7	4.9	12.8
Dominican Republic	1994	137 616	33.3	4.1	20.6	6.4	5.2	14.2	2.1	2.5	5.6	5.9
Rép. dominicaine	1995	164 689	34.1	4.0	20.3	6.2	5.2	13.5	2.0	2.2	6.9	5.6
	1996	189 675	32.0	3.4	20.1	6.5	5.0	14.1	3.1	2.2	8.8	4.8
Ecuador [1]	1991	8 432 000	38.9	9.9	5.3	7.4	4.2	...	...	...	4.2	17.5
Equateur [1]	1992	13 147 000	38.7	9.5	5.1	7.2	4.5	...	...	...	4.4	18.3
	1993	19 374 000	37.8	9.2	5.2	6.6	4.6	...	...	...	4.4	18.6
Estonia	2004	80 460	28.6	7.5	21.1	5.5	3.4	16.2	9.1	1.2	7.4	8.0
Estonie	2005	91 387	28.5	7.9	19.9	6.0	3.2	17.0	8.9	1.0	7.4	8.0
	2006	109 203	26.1	8.1	18.7	6.4	3.2	17.4	9.1	1.1	7.5	8.0
Fiji [1]	1989	1 197	30.9	8.6	12.4	8.6	2.0	...	...	...	...	...
Fidji [1]	1990	1 277	31.6	8.2	13.1	7.8	2.0	...	...	...	...	...
	1991	1 405	31.2	7.9	13.2	7.9	2.0	...	...	...	...	...
Finland	2004	74 765	17.8	4.8	25.4	5.3	4.1	16.1	11.3	0.5	6.4	8.7
Finlande	2005	77 707	17.5	4.9	25.3	5.5	4.2	15.7	11.4	0.4	6.5	8.7
	2006	82 160	17.4	4.9	24.9	5.5	4.2	15.3	11.8	0.4	6.4	9.4
France	2005	958 656	17.0	4.9	24.6	6.1	3.4	17.7	9.4	0.7	6.3	11.0
France	2006	1 002 014	16.6	4.7	25.1	6.0	3.4	17.4	9.3	0.7	6.2	11.5
	2007	1 047 357	16.3	4.6	25.4	6.0	3.5	17.4	9.3	0.8	6.2	11.7
Germany	2004	1 269 880	14.4	5.2	23.2	6.8	4.6	16.4	9.3	0.7	5.3	11.7
Allemagne	2005	1 290 150	14.4	5.1	23.6	6.7	4.6	16.1	9.2	0.7	5.2	11.9
	2006	1 321 560	14.1	5.1	23.8	6.8	4.7	16.4	9.1	0.7	5.2	11.8
Greece	2005	138 949	21.9	7.1	17.4	6.6	5.3	13.3	8.0	2.6	15.0	9.0
Grèce	2006	150 629	21.4	7.0	17.2	6.5	5.1	13.0	9.3	2.6	14.7	9.1
	2007	160 164	21.6	7.0	17.3	5.1	5.4	12.7	9.0	2.7	14.6	8.8
Guatemala	2003	145 694	38.4	7.6	15.8	7.1	4.8	10.8	3.8	1.5	7.4	4.8
Guatemala	2004	161 241	38.3	7.7	15.6	6.9	4.6	11.8	3.8	1.5	7.3	4.6
	2005	180 485	38.6	7.3	15.1	6.8	4.6	12.6	3.7	1.5	7.1	4.4
Honduras	2003	104 285	39.4	6.7	12.1	4.9	4.6	12.0	4.3	2.7	6.6	7.3
Honduras	2004	118 109	38.9	6.4	12.5	4.8	4.7	12.5	4.3	2.8	6.5	7.2
	2005	136 804	38.8	6.0	12.3	4.8	4.9	13.6	4.3	2.7	6.3	6.9
Hungary	2004	10 965 762	26.7	4.0	18.9	7.4	3.7	19.9	7.9	1.2	5.1	7.9
Hongrie	2005	11 763 968	25.8	3.7	19.0	6.8	3.8	20.9	8.1	1.2	5.1	8.3
	2006	12 384 401	26.7	3.5	19.2	6.6	3.7	21.0	8.1	1.3	5.3	8.1
Iceland	2004	511 178	17.0	4.6	18.6	6.2	3.2	18.4	11.8	1.3	7.8	6.6
Islande	2005	589 654	15.1	4.3	19.3	6.2	2.9	19.5	11.2	1.3	7.5	6.5
	2006	661 811	14.9	4.3	19.6	6.0	2.7	18.6	10.8	1.2	7.7	6.9
India	2004	18 404 060	40.0	5.0	13.0	3.6	4.9	16.9	1.8	2.3	2.3	10.6
Inde	2005	20 553 870	40.1	4.8	12.7	3.7	4.7	17.3	1.8	2.4	2.4	10.5
	2006	23 121 050	40.3	4.5	12.0	3.9	4.4	17.6	1.9	2.4	2.6	10.8
Iran (Islamic Rep. of) [+]	2003	503 164 600	31.0[7]	7.2	30.0	6.3	5.8	11.8[13]	3.3	...	...	4.6
Iran (Rép. islamique d') [+]	2004	636 564 800	30.8[7]	7.5	30.1	6.6	6.1	11.0[13]	3.3	...	...	4.6
	2005	761 075 900	30.8[7]	7.4	30.2	6.5	6.1	11.2[13]	3.3	...	...	4.5
Ireland	2004	64 611	11.5	4.9	20.1	7.1	3.6	15.2	7.6	1.2	16.2	12.3
Irlande	2005	70 570	11.0	5.2	19.7	6.9	3.7	15.9	7.8	1.2	15.6	12.3
	2006	76 048	10.7	5.0	19.8	6.9	3.7	16.0	7.3	1.2	15.3	13.3
Israel	2005	322 854	18.4	3.3	27.8	9.4	4.5	14.5	5.8	3.2	5.3	8.3
Israël	2006	341 613	18.6	3.4	27.0	9.5	4.6	14.7	5.7	3.2	5.6	8.2
	2007	367 683	18.6	3.4	25.6	9.8	4.6	15.3	5.9	3.3	5.7	8.3

Divisions of the Classification of Individual Consumption according to Purpose (COICOP) [‡]
Divisions de la Nomenclature des fonctions de la consommation individuelle (COICOP) [‡]

23 Household consumption expenditure by purpose at current prices *(continued)*
Percentage distribution
Dépenses de consommation des ménages par fonction aux prix courants *(suite)*
Répartition en pourcentage

Country or area / Pays ou zone	Year / Année	Total (millions national cur.) / Totale (millions monnaie nat.)	Div. 01+02 (%)	Div. 03 (%)	Div. 04 (%)	Div. 05 (%)	Div. 06 (%)	Div. 07+08 (%)	Div. 09 (%)	Div. 10 (%)	Div. 11 (%)	Div. 12 (%)
Italy / Italie	2005	836 767	17.7	8.2	20.9	7.8	3.3	16.5	7.0	0.9	9.9	9.6
	2006	868 622	17.7	8.1	21.0	7.7	3.2	16.4	6.9	0.9	10.1	9.9
	2007	900 282	17.6	8.0	21.0	7.7	3.2	16.4	6.8	0.9	10.1	10.1
Jamaica[1] / Jamaïque[1]	1986	8 497	52.6	5.4	15.2	6.8	3.2	...	2.8	0.2	16.1	10.0
	1987	9 849	52.1	6.0	14.5	6.9	3.4	...	2.7	0.2	16.2	10.7
	1988	11 388	49.6	5.8	13.1	6.8	3.5	...	2.5	0.2	13.6	10.6
Japan / Japon	2004	278 310 400	18.5	3.6	24.1	3.7	4.1	13.6	11.1	2.2	7.5	10.7
	2005	279 489 300	17.7	3.5	24.4	3.7	4.3	13.9	10.8	2.2	7.6	11.0
	2006	284 046 700	17.4	3.6	24.5	3.7	4.2	14.1	11.0	2.2	7.6	11.2
Jordan[1] / Jordanie[1]	1984	1 375	#39.6[7]	#6.1	#6.7	#5.1	#4.2[10]	...	#2.9	#3.4	...	...
	1985	1 415	38.5[7]	5.7	6.5	4.8	4.1[10]	...	2.9	3.4	...	...
	1986	1 238	38.8[7]	5.6	6.5	4.9	4.1[10]	...	3.0	3.4	...	...
Kenya	2005	1 066 471[4]	47.5	3.3	8.2	...	2.7	13.1	...	2.6	5.8	
	2006	1 217 635[4]	46.0[7]	3.1	8.4	...	2.6	12.9	...	2.6	6.4	
	2007	1 385 833[4]	44.4[7]	3.1	8.1	...	2.5	13.1	...	2.8	6.8	
Korea, Republic of / Corée, République de	2005	417 425 074	17.6	4.2	16.9	4.0	4.9	16.3	7.2	6.0	7.2	13.6
	2006	444 859 726	16.9	4.4	16.7	4.0	5.1	16.1	7.1	6.1	7.2	13.9
	2007	476 528 591	16.5	4.3	16.4	4.1	5.2	16.1	7.0	6.2	7.0	14.5
Kyrgyzstan / Kirghizistan	2003	63 352	54.0	12.9	11.2	3.1	1.7	9.6	1.7	2.1	1.0	2.6
	2004	69 983	55.3	9.3	7.8	3.3	1.5	13.6	2.4	2.5	3.3	2.4
	2005	83 471	55.9	9.0	8.0	3.4	1.5	13.4	2.2	2.3	3.1	2.2
Latvia / Lettonie	2004	4 606	29.3	7.1	21.1	3.4	4.4	15.0	8.2	2.3	4.1	4.0
	2005	5 578	28.7	6.9	20.6	3.6	4.0	15.1	7.5	2.5	5.3	3.8
	2006	7 184	26.3	7.6	20.2	4.0	4.1	16.6	7.2	2.1	6.1	4.2
Lebanon / Liban	1997	20 158 200	27.1	6.0	15.1	6.4	7.8	13.4[13]	1.2	10.8	2.8	0.7
Lithuania / Lituanie	2004	40 649	35.9	6.6	14.6	5.3	4.2	18.4	6.8	0.7	3.1	6.0
	2005	46 309	33.6	8.3	14.3	5.7	5.0	17.8	6.5	0.8	3.2	6.5
	2006	53 310	32.3	8.2	14.0	5.6	4.2	19.5	6.8	0.8	2.9	6.5
Luxembourg	2004	10 404	24.8	4.7	25.2	9.1	2.1	22.8	9.4	0.4	8.7	11.0
	2005	11 083	23.3	4.5	24.8	8.6	2.4	23.5	9.2	0.4	8.6	11.3
	2006	11 604	21.2	4.4	24.5	8.6	2.4	23.4	9.1	0.5	8.3	12.0
Malaysia / Malaisie	2005	234 112	26.2	3.0	19.4	5.3	2.1	22.0	4.9	1.5	8.9	14.8
	2006	257 284	26.1	3.6	19.6	5.6	2.2	22.2	5.3	1.6	9.1	14.4
	2007	292 594	25.6	3.0	19.1	5.9	2.2	22.3	5.5	1.6	10.1	14.8
Malta / Malte	2005	1 298	22.3	6.9	12.7	10.3	2.8	21.7	12.4	1.4	15.4	10.2
	2006	1 339	22.1	5.6	13.4	9.7	2.9	21.6	12.8	1.5	15.1	10.4
	2007	1 383	23.1	5.2	13.4	9.8	2.6	21.3	13.2	1.6	15.6	10.2
Mexico / Mexique	2002	4 286 979	27.1	3.4	13.4	8.5	4.7	18.8	2.8	3.8	7.8	11.3
	2003	4 690 918	27.3	3.2	13.6	8.2	4.9	18.8	2.7	4.0	7.5	11.5
	2004	5 208 861	27.3	3.1	13.6	8.0	4.7	19.3	2.9	3.9	7.4	11.4
Mongolia / Mongolie	2005	1 523 383	43.9	12.4	18.1	4.2	1.3	9.4	2.8	4.3	0.6	2.8
	2006	1 766 288	44.2	12.3	17.8	4.1	1.5	10.2	2.8	3.6	0.8	2.6
	2007	2 242 734	41.1	13.8	16.1	4.5	2.2	11.5	3.1	2.9	1.6	3.4
Namibia / Namibie	2004	19 916	44.8[7]	6.7	15.3	...	...	...	...	...	...	...
	2005	19 722	46.5[7]	5.0	16.8	...	...	...	...	...	...	...
	2006	21 964	48.0[7]	4.8	16.5	...	...	...	...	...	...	...
Netherlands / Pays-Bas	2004	238 521	13.9	5.4	21.5	6.5	5.1	16.0	10.2	0.6	5.2	15.1
	2005	245 404	13.4	5.2	22.1	6.3	5.3	16.0	10.0	0.5	5.1	15.7
	2006	248 958	13.8	5.5	22.9	6.5	2.2	16.4	10.4	0.5	5.2	16.3
New Zealand[+] / Nouvelle-Zélande[+]	2004	85 750	17.6[2]	4.6	19.4	11.3	3.8	14.9[13]	13.9[14]	...	7.9[15]	11.1[16]
	2005	91 552	17.6[2]	4.7	18.9	11.3	3.7	14.9[13]	13.7[14]	...	8.0[15]	11.0[16]
	2006	96 510	17.8[2]	4.7	18.5	11.4	3.8	14.4[13]	13.8[14]	...	8.0[15]	11.1[16]
Nicaragua[+] / Nicaragua[+]	2002	46 546	41.3	4.4	14.7	6.5	8.3	14.8	2.6	1.8	6.5	1.8
	2003	50 245	40.1	4.2	15.2	6.3	8.5	15.9	2.7	1.8	6.7	1.9
	2004	56 714	40.4	3.9	14.7	6.2	8.5	16.2	2.9	1.8	7.0	2.0

Household consumption expenditure by purpose at current prices *(continued)*
Percentage distribution

Dépenses de consommation des ménages par fonction aux prix courants *(suite)*
Répartition en pourcentage

Country or area Pays ou zone	Year Année	Total (millions national cur.) Totale (millions monnaie nat.)	Div. 01+02 (%)	Div. 03 (%)	Div. 04 (%)	Div. 05 (%)	Div. 06 (%)	Div. 07+08 (%)	Div. 09 (%)	Div. 10 (%)	Div. 11 (%)	Div. 12 (%)
Norway	2003	709 583	17.9	5.4	21.2	6.0	2.9	16.5	12.7	0.5	5.8	9.2
Norvège	2004	754 220	17.4	5.4	20.2	5.9	2.9	17.5	12.6	0.5	5.5	9.5
	2005	792 530	17.2	5.4	19.7	6.0	2.9	17.5	12.5	0.6	5.5	9.8
Panama Panama	1996	5 456	26.3	6.1	25.8	5.2	4.5	15.5	5.4	1.7	4.3	11.9
Peru [1]	1986	255[17]	...	9.3	1.8	12.4	3.9	...	...	...	...	...
Pérou [1]	1987	498[17]	...	10.1	1.4	12.5	4.4	...	...	...	...	...
	1988	3 214[17]	...	11.6	0.8	13.6	4.6	...	...	...	...	...
Philippines [1]	2004	3 346 716	48.6	2.5	4.7[18]	12.7	...	8.3[13]	...	...	...	23.2
Philippines [1]	2005	3 773 038	48.1	2.3	4.9[18]	12.1	...	9.9[13]	...	...	...	22.7
	2006	4 226 120	48.0	2.1	4.9[18]	11.4	...	11.2[13]	...	...	...	22.3
Poland	2004	585 984	27.8	4.8	22.8	4.3	4.2	12.1	7.8	1.4	2.9	11.9
Pologne	2005	610 361	27.7	4.6	23.8	4.4	4.0	12.1	7.6	1.3	2.9	11.8
	2006	647 905	27.5	4.6	23.7	4.4	4.0	11.9	7.3	1.3	2.8	12.5
Portugal	2003	85 075	21.8	7.9	14.5	7.4	5.6	17.2	6.7	1.2	10.8	11.3
Portugal	2004	89 464	21.2	7.6	14.6	7.2	5.7	17.6	6.8	1.3	10.9	11.5
	2005	93 695	20.5	7.4	14.8	7.1	5.8	17.8	6.9	1.3	10.8	11.7
Puerto Rico [+1]	2004	44 676	18.5	6.6	19.0	5.3	13.0	16.4	3.7	3.6	6.4	11.2
Porto Rico [+1]	2005	47 589	18.5	6.5	19.6	5.6	13.1	16.1	3.8	3.5	6.0	11.2
	2006	49 921	18.2	7.0	20.1	5.8	13.0	15.3	3.8	3.4	6.1	10.5
Republic of Moldova	1996	5 243	42.9	6.6	5.0	2.9	9.9	9.3	1.4	12.6	2.2	7.2
République de Moldova	2000	14 031	48.7	7.8	13.0	3.4	3.3	12.9	3.6	1.4	1.3	1.8
	2005	34 694	35.1	4.9	15.6	7.7	4.4	16.0	6.4	1.5	1.8	5.4
Saudi Arabia [+1]	1996	206 336	34.6[7]	7.8	14.7	9.2	0.9	17.9[13]	2.1	...	...	7.2
Arabie saoudite [+1]	1997	206 185	34.7[7]	7.7	14.7	9.1	0.9	17.8[13]	2.1	...	...	7.0
	1998	198 574	37.3[7]	8.2	15.7	9.7	1.0	18.9[13]	2.2	...	...	7.2
Serbia	2004	998 540	37.2	4.7	25.2	4.4	2.5	14.3	3.4	1.3	2.9	4.6
Serbie	2005	1 206 532	35.5	4.5	25.2	5.2	3.1	13.6	4.2	1.5	2.8	5.0
	2006	1 423 177	34.3	4.9	24.3	5.1	3.1	14.4	5.1	1.5	2.7	5.3
Sierra Leone [+]	2003	3 794 745	49.1	7.2	6.0	2.3	13.0	6.2	2.9	1.7	1.1	9.4
Sierra Leone [+]	2004	3 856 375	49.1	7.2	6.0	2.3	13.0	6.2	2.9	1.7	1.1	9.4
	2005	3 983 914	49.1	7.2	6.0	2.3	13.0	6.2	2.9	1.7	1.1	9.4
Singapore	2005	82 006	10.2	3.5	15.3	6.5	6.7	19.7	11.0	2.8	7.9	12.3
Singapour	2006	87 122	9.9	3.5	17.2	6.4	7.0	19.2	10.9	2.8	8.2	12.1
	2007	96 281	9.7	3.5	19.2	6.3	6.9	19.1	10.5	2.8	8.3	12.6
Slovakia	2004	754 351	24.9	3.4	26.1	4.8	2.7	12.9	8.4	1.1	7.1	8.9
Slovaquie	2005	829 771	23.7	3.6	26.2	5.1	2.9	13.0	8.8	1.4	7.3	9.5
	2006	927 159	23.1	3.5	26.8	5.3	2.9	12.6	8.7	1.4	7.9	9.6
Slovenia	2005	15 324	21.1	6.0	20.2	6.3	3.7	20.3	11.4	1.2	6.9	9.6
Slovénie	2006	16 135	20.6	5.7	20.1	6.2	3.6	20.8	11.2	1.2	7.0	9.9
	2007	17 691	20.5	5.9	19.4	6.4	3.7	20.8	11.0	1.4	7.9	10.5
South Africa	2005	965 764	26.2[7]	5.9	12.8	7.8	8.6	17.5[13]	4.1	3.2	2.6	11.3
Afrique du Sud	2006	1 088 852	26.2[7]	5.8	13.0	7.8	8.3	17.5[13]	4.2	3.1	2.7	11.4
	2007	1 234 185	26.6[7]	5.7	13.5	7.6	8.3	16.3[13]	4.2	3.0	2.8	12.0
Spain	2004	479 820	18.4	5.9	17.0	5.6	3.7	15.0	9.6	1.6	19.8	9.4
Espagne	2005	516 818	17.8	5.9	17.2	5.6	3.7	15.2	9.6	1.6	19.6	9.4
	2006	554 495	17.4	5.8	17.5	5.5	3.6	15.3	9.4	1.5	19.5	9.7
Sri Lanka	2004	1 462 192	39.9	10.1	7.8	7.1	1.6	19.7	2.7	0.1	1.1	3.2
Sri Lanka	2005	1 674 210	40.5	9.3	8.2	6.9	1.5	18.4	3.8	0.1	1.8	3.4
	2006	2 015 023	35.9	10.7	10.1	6.9	1.5	22.1	3.6	0.1	1.0	2.5
Sudan [+1]	1981	5 386	62.8	5.6	15.8	4.6	5.2	...	...	...	...	...
Soudan [+1]	1982	7 897	60.4	7.5	15.3	5.6	5.3	...	...	...	...	...
	1983	9 385	64.7	5.3	15.2	5.5	4.1	...	...	...	...	...
Switzerland	2004	263 075	14.3	3.9	23.3	4.5	14.9	10.4	8.5	0.5	8.1	11.5
Suisse	2005	270 092	14.1	4.0	23.5	4.5	14.8	10.7	8.4	0.5	8.0	11.4
	2006	277 965	14.0	4.0	23.5	4.5	14.8	10.7	8.3	0.5	8.1	11.6

Divisions of the Classification of Individual Consumption according to Purpose (COICOP) **‡**
Divisions de la Nomenclature des fonctions de la consommation individuelle (COICOP) **‡**

Country or area Pays ou zone	Year Année	Total (millions national cur.) Totale (millions monnaie nat.)	Divisions of the Classification of Individual Consumption according to Purpose (COICOP) [t] Divisions de la Nomenclature des fonctions de la consommation individuelle (COICOP) [t]									
			Div. 01+02 (%)	Div. 03 (%)	Div. 04 (%)	Div. 05 (%)	Div. 06 (%)	Div. 07+08 (%)	Div. 09 (%)	Div. 10 (%)	Div. 11 (%)	Div. 12 (%)
Thailand [1] Thaïlande [1]	2005	4 060 414	33.5	8.5	8.0	6.7	6.8	18.4	6.9	1.0	9.0	6.6
	2006	4 376 585	35.0	8.1	8.0	6.6	6.8	18.8	6.4	1.0	9.8	6.2
	2007	4 561 528	36.5	7.8	7.9	6.7	6.8	18.3	5.8	1.0	10.1	6.7
TFYR of Macedonia L'ex-R.Y. Macédoine	2004	203 455	36.7	6.0	21.2	3.9	2.1	18.0	2.7	1.4	3.3	5.3
	2005	217 325	38.0	6.2	20.0	4.3	1.7	17.4	2.9	1.6	3.8	4.7
	2006	239 102	36.6	6.4	17.8	5.4	1.9	18.0	3.3	1.6	3.9	5.1
Turkey [1] Turquie [1]	2005	465 402	28.1[7]	7.7	17.6	8.6	4.1	19.5[13]	5.2	1.2	6.3	7.1
	2006	534 849	27.2[7]	7.0	18.7	8.5	4.3	19.8[13]	4.9	1.3	6.4	7.4
	2007	605 236	27.0[7]	6.5	19.8	8.1	4.1	19.2[13]	4.5	1.3	6.4	7.6
Ukraine Ukraine	2005	252 624	45.4	5.2	10.2	3.9	4.4	17.7	5.5	2.1	3.0	2.6
	2006	319 383	44.1	6.1	11.2	3.8	4.1	17.9	5.2	1.9	2.8	2.9
	2007	422 837	42.5	6.4	11.8	3.9	4.0	18.7	5.3	1.7	2.6	3.1
United Kingdom Royaume-Uni	2003	697 160	13.0	5.9	18.5	6.1	1.6	17.2	12.1	1.4	11.3	11.1
	2004	732 531	12.7	5.8	18.8	6.0	1.6	17.2	12.4	1.4	11.4	10.9
	2005	760 869	12.5	5.7	19.4	5.7	1.6	17.0	12.4	1.4	11.7	10.9
United States Etats-Unis	2004	8 195 900[4]	9.0	4.6	17.3	4.8	18.8	13.2	9.1	2.6	6.1	14.4
	2005	8 707 800[4]	9.0	4.6	17.4	4.8	18.8	13.3	9.0	2.6	6.1	14.4
	2006	9 224 500[4]	9.0	4.6	17.4	4.8	19.0	13.0	9.0	2.6	6.2	14.4
Vanuatu [1] Vanuatu [1]	1987	8 198	47.6[7]	5.2	7.5	2.7	...	...	...	...	...	...
	1988	9 562	46.6[7]	5.5	7.4	2.7	...	...	...	...	...	...
	1989	10 545	46.0[7]	4.9	7.9	2.8	...	...	...	...	...	...
Venezuela (Boliv. Rep. of) Venezuela (R. bol. du)	2003	72 324 512	32.4	4.4	12.0	7.4	6.2	15.1	4.3	4.0	9.2	4.2
	2004	103 147 547	31.2	4.9	9.7	8.0	6.1	17.1	4.6	3.3	10.2	4.2
	2005	140 256 814	29.4	4.9	7.9	8.2	6.0	19.1	5.3	2.8	11.7	4.1
Yemen Yémen	2004	1 698 053	55.6	5.9	15.6	3.1	8.0	6.6[13]	0.3	1.8	^0.0	3.1
	2005	2 058 537[5]	55.6	5.9	15.6	3.1	8.0	6.6[13]	0.3	1.8	^0.0	3.1
	2006	2 289 922[5]	55.6	5.9	15.6	3.1	8.0	6.6[13]	0.3	1.8	^0.0	3.1
Zimbabwe [1] Zimbabwe [1]	1985	3 842	25.4[7]	11.6	17.1	7.8	4.2	...	1.4	5.2	9.0	7.1[19]
	1986	4 464	23.3[7]	10.7	15.7	11.8	5.3	...	0.6	5.3	9.0	7.4[19]
	1987	4 324	20.4[7]	10.3	15.4	12.9	7.1	...	0.6	6.0	8.7	7.9[19]

Source:
United Nations Statistics Division, New York, national accounts database, last accessed January 2009.

Data for most countries have been compiled in accordance with the concepts and definitions of the System of National Accounts 1993 (1993 SNA). Countries that follow the 1968 SNA are footnoted accordingly.

[t] COICOP Divisions:

Div. 01+ 02:	Food, beverages, tobacco and narcotics
Div. 03:	Clothing and footwear
Div. 04:	Housing, water, electricity, gas and other fuels
Div. 05:	Furnishings, household equipment and routine household maintenance
Div. 06:	Health
Div. 07 + 08:	Transport and communication
Div. 09:	Recreation and culture
Div. 10:	Education
Div. 11:	Restaurants and hotels
Div. 12:	Miscellaneous goods and services

[+] Data for most countries or areas refers to the western calendar year ending 31 December. The following countries or areas are exceptions, with fiscal years as follows:

Source:
Organisation des Nations Unies, Division de statistique, New York, base de données sur les comptes nationaux, dernier accès janvier 2009.

Les données pour la majorité des pays sont compilées selon les concepts et définitions du Système de comptabilité nationale, 1993 (SCN93). Seuls les pays qui suivent toujours le SCN68 seront donc signalés par une note.

[t] Divisions de la COICOP:

Div. 01 + 02:	Alimentation, boissons, tabac et stupéfiants
Div. 03:	Articles d'habillement et chaussures
Div. 04:	Logement, eau, gaz, électricité et autres combustibles
Div. 05:	Meubles, articles de ménage et entretien courant de l'habitation
Div. 06:	Santé
Div. 07 + 08:	Transports et communication
Div. 09:	Loisirs et culture
Div. 10:	Enseignement
Div. 11:	Restaurants et hôtels
Div. 12:	Biens et services divers

[+] Les données pour la plupart des pays ou territoires concernent l'année civile se terminant le 31 décembre, sauf les pays ou territoires ci-dessous dont les exercices budgétaires sont les suivants:

<u>Year beginning 21 March</u>: Afghanistan, Iran (Islamic Republic).
<u>Year beginning 1 April</u>: Bermuda, India, Myanmar, New Zealand, Nigeria.
<u>Year beginning 1 July</u>: Australia, Bhutan, Cameroon, Gambia, Nicaragua, Pakistan, Puerto Rico, Saudi Arabia, Sierra Leone, Sudan, United Republic of Tanzania.
<u>Year ending 30 June</u>: Bangladesh, Botswana, Egypt, Swaziland, Tonga.
<u>Year ending 7 July</u>: Nepal.
<u>Year ending 30 July</u>: Ethiopia.
<u>Year ending 30 September</u>: Haiti.

<u>Exercice commençant le 21 mars</u>: Afghanistan, Iran (République islamique d').
<u>Exercice commençant le 1er avril</u>: Bermudes, Inde, Myanmar, Nigéria, Nouvelle-Zélande.
<u>Exercice commençant le 1er juillet</u>: Arabie saoudite, Australie, Bhoutan, Cameroun, Gambie, Nicaragua, Pakistan, Porto Rico, Sierra Leone, Soudan, Rép.-Unie de Tanzanie.
<u>Exercice se terminant le 30 juin</u>: Bangladesh, Botswana, Égypte, Swaziland, Tonga.
<u>Exercice se terminant le 7 juillet</u>: Népal.
<u>Exercice se terminant le 30 juillet</u>: Éthiopie.
<u>Exercice se terminant le 30 septembre</u>: Haïti.

1	Data compiled in accordance with the System of National Accounts 1968 (1968 SNA).	1	Données compilées selon le Système de comptabilité nationale de 1968 (SCN 1968).
2	Alcoholic beverages, tobacco and narcotics only.	2	Boissons alcoolisées, tabac et stupéfiants seulement.
3	Communications only.	3	Les communications seulement.
4	Including "Non-profit institutions serving households" (NPISHs) final consumption expenditure.	4	Y compris la consommation finale des institutions sans but lucratif au service des ménages.
5	Preliminary data.	5	Données préliminaires.
6	Excluding direct purchases abroad by resident households and direct purchases in the domestic market by non-resident households.	6	À l'exclusion des achats directs à l'étranger des ménages résidents et des achats directs des ménages non résidents sur le marché intérieur.
7	Food and non-alcoholic beverages only.	7	Alimentation et boissons non alcoolisées seulement.
8	Including personal effects.	8	Y compris les effets personnels.
9	Including housing maintenance charges.	9	Y compris coût d'entretien du logement.
10	Including personal care.	10	Y compris les soins personnels.
11	Including hotel expenditures.	11	Y compris les dépenses d'hôtel.
12	Including restaurant expenditure.	12	Y compris les dépenses de restauration.
13	Transport only.	13	Transports seulement.
14	Including education.	14	Y compris l'enseignement.
15	Including expenditure on alcohol consumed in chartered clubs, taverns and hotels and restaurants.	15	Y compris les dépenses consacrées à l'alcool consommé dans les clubs, les bars, les hôtels et restaurants.
16	Including communication.	16	Y compris communications.
17	Thousands.	17	En milliers.
18	Refers to water, electricity, gas and other fuels only.	18	Données provenant exclusivement l'eau, l'électricité, le gaz et les autres combustibles seulement.
19	Includes personal transport equipment only. Communication is included in Miscellaneous good and services.	19	Ne comprend que le matériel de transport personnel. Les communications sont incluses dans les biens et services divers.

Country or area and industry [ISIC Rev. 3] Pays ou zone et industrie [CITI Rév. 3]	2000	2001	2002	2003	2004	2005	2006	2007
Africa · Afrique								
Algeria Algérie								
Total industry [CDE]								
Total, industrie [CDE]	100.0	99.8	100.8	102.1	102.5	104.1	103.6	102.0
Total mining [C]								
Total, industries extractives [C]	100.0	97.1	104.3	104.9	103.9	114.3	131.7	138.4
Total manufacturing [D]								
Total, industries manufacturières [D]	100.0	99.1	97.5	94.2	91.9	89.8	87.6	82.0
Food, beverages and tobacco								
Aliments, boissons et tabac	100.0	87.5	70.8	56.1	47.4	40.5	37.4	35.2
Textiles, wearing apparel, leather, footwear								
Textiles, habillement, cuir et chaussures	100.0	90.8	94.8	93.2	86.0	83.8	68.4	54.5
Chemicals, petroleum, rubber and plastic products								
Produits chimiques, pétroliers, caoutchouc et plastiques	100.0	104.0	101.4	99.9	89.5	89.8	89.5	88.5
Basic metals								
Métaux de base	100.0	107.9	118.9	145.6	145.4	152.2	171.3	171.1
Metal products								
Produits métalliques	100.0	119.1	115.1	106.8	121.6	115.3	103.6	87.5
Electricity [E]								
Electricité [E]	100.0	105.0	109.6	116.8	123.5	135.3	139.9	148.2
Burkina Faso Burkina Faso								
Total industry [CDE]								
Total, industrie [CDE]	100.0	101.1	106.3	109.5	...	...	...	...
Cameroon [1] Cameroun [1]								
Total industry [DE]								
Total, industrie [DE]	100.0	99.6	102.5	105.3	111.5	110.7	114.3	113.0
Total manufacturing [D]								
Total, industries manufacturières [D]	100.0	116.4	116.3	120.7	127.8	125.6	130.7	126.2
Electricity, gas and water [E]								
Electricité, gaz et eau [E]	100.0	92.0	103.8	109.0	114.7	117.2	120.7	121.5
Côte d'Ivoire Côte d'Ivoire								
Total industry [CDE]								
Total, industrie [CDE]	100.0	96.9	92.6	87.8	90.6	102.9	108.4	104.8
Total mining [C]								
Total, industries extractives [C]	100.0	67.6	121.4	211.3	218.7	362.6	583.8	487.4
Total manufacturing [D]								
Total, industries manufacturières [D]	100.0	97.2	85.6	74.4	76.3	81.8	75.1	76.7
Food, beverages and tobacco								
Aliments, boissons et tabac	100.0	98.3	81.7	75.2	68.4	60.7	55.0	49.6
Textiles and wearing apparel								
Textiles et habillement	100.0	90.2	68.6	48.4	53.4	31.3	22.4	32.1
Chemicals, petroleum, rubber and plastic products								
Produits chimiques, pétroliers, caoutchouc et plastiques	100.0	98.5	103.2	110.9	106.5	112.1	103.1	108.3
Metal products								
Produits métalliques	100.0	80.5	90.1	85.2	82.9	83.9	83.1	83.1
Electricity and water [E]								
Electricité et eau [E]	100.0	102.1	110.2	105.5	110.4	117.1	116.4	115.6
Egypt [2] Egypte [2]								
Total industry [CDE]								
Total, industrie [CDE]	100.0	104.1	112.5	129.7	146.1	161.5	188.4	194.4
Total mining [C]								
Total, industries extractives [C]	100.0	113.1	124.8	201.6	244.2	274.2	333.2	326.0
Total manufacturing [D] [3]								
Total, industries manufacturières [D] [3]	100.0	98.3	104.3	98.6	104.8	115.1	132.8	144.3
Food, beverages and tobacco								
Aliments, boissons et tabac	100.0	75.2	70.0	60.7	61.4	64.3	68.4	73.2
Textiles and wearing apparel								
Textiles et habillement	100.0	91.0	95.5	103.5	90.6	92.4	108.3	111.6
Chemicals, petroleum, rubber and plastic products								
Produits chimiques, pétroliers, caoutchouc et plastiques	100.0	114.9	112.1	146.6	133.7	159.8	247.6	291.4

24 Index numbers of industrial production *(continued)*
2000 = 100
Indices de la production industrielle *(suite)*
2000 = 100

Country or area and industry [ISIC Rev. 3] Pays ou zone et industrie [CITI Rév. 3]	2000	2001	2002	2003	2004	2005	2006	2007
Basic metals Métaux de base	100.0	89.2	92.3	129.2	103.3	93.5	119.1	126.6
Metal products Produits métalliques	100.0	86.9	90.2	79.5	76.3	83.0	97.9	113.3
Electricity, gas and water [E] Electricité, gaz et eau [E]	100.0	110.3	123.4	132.0	145.5	156.1	159.9	165.4
Ethiopia [2] Ethiopie [2]								
Total industry [CDE] Total, industrie [CDE]	100.0	103.6	107.8	109.9	117.2	126.6	137.9	152.7
Total mining [C] Total, industries extractives [C]	100.0	105.2	116.3	121.1	128.8	138.9	150.4	163.8
Total manufacturing [D] Total, industries manufacturières [D]	100.0	103.6	104.9	105.7	112.6	121.7	131.5	147.9
Electricity, gas and water [E] Electricité, gaz et eau [E]	100.0	103.3	113.3	118.2	126.5	136.7	151.5	162.6
Gabon Gabon								
Total industry [DE] Total, industrie [DE]	100.0	111.8	116.7	114.8	117.6	124.2	131.6	...
Total manufacturing [D] Total, industries manufacturières [D]	100.0	113.4	116.9	109.3	111.4	120.3	124.9	...
Food, beverages and tobacco Aliments, boissons et tabac	100.0	113.3	109.9	106.0	105.1	115.9	123.3	...
Chemicals and petroleum products Produits chimiques et pétroliers	100.0	109.3	139.0	124.3	120.2	126.9	128.7	...
Electricity and water [E] Electricité et eau [E]	100.0	110.0	116.7	121.4	125.0	128.9	139.5	...
Ghana Ghana								
Total industry [CDE] [3] Total, industrie [CDE] [3]	100.0	120.2	119.1	126.8	138.6	...	...	...
Total mining [C] Total, industries extractives [C]	100.0	100.8	96.1	100.7	95.4	101.7	111.8	...
Total manufacturing [D] Total, industries manufacturières [D]	100.0	134.3	137.2	154.7	179.0	...	...	...
Food, beverages and tobacco Aliments, boissons et tabac	100.0	148.2	182.4	184.3	222.0	...	...	...
Textiles, wearing apparel, leather, footwear Textiles, habillement, cuir et chaussures	100.0	102.8	106.8	119.9	121.0	...	...	...
Chemicals, petroleum, rubber and plastic products Produits chimiques, pétroliers, caoutchouc et plastiques	100.0	93.8	100.2	128.5	121.9	...	...	...
Basic metals Métaux de base	100.0	70.8	58.8	16.6	12.0	...	...	...
Metal products Produits métalliques	100.0	102.6	83.2	88.4	94.3	...	...	...
Electricity [E] Electricité [E]	100.0	108.8	101.0	81.7	83.6	94.0	116.7	...
Kenya Kenya								
Total industry [CD] [4] Total, industrie [CD] [4]	100.0	101.6	101.9	103.5	111.3	120.2	128.0	136.0
Total mining [C] Total, industries extractives [C]	100.0	124.9	103.3	109.4	137.7	156.0	169.8	172.3
Total manufacturing [D] Total, industries manufacturières [D]	100.0	100.6	101.8	103.3	110.2	118.7	126.3	134.5
Food, beverages and tobacco Aliments, boissons et tabac	100.0	99.2	103.3	105.1	117.1	123.5	130.1	150.1
Textiles, wearing apparel, leather, footwear Textiles, habillement, cuir et chaussures	100.0	103.3	118.5	114.0	104.8	143.7	167.5	170.8
Chemicals, petroleum, rubber and plastic products Produits chimiques, pétroliers, caoutchouc et plastiques	100.0	110.4	104.8	127.8	141.6	139.7	151.1	176.7
Metal products Produits métalliques	100.0	98.4	127.1	128.1	198.9	188.5	222.0	223.1

Country or area and industry [ISIC Rev. 3] Pays ou zone et industrie [CITI Rév. 3]	2000	2001	2002	2003	2004	2005	2006	2007
Madagascar Madagascar								
Total industry [CDE]								
Total, industrie [CDE]	100.0	107.9	105.8	112.3	116.5	130.7	140.1	151.5
Total mining [C]								
Total, industries extractives [C]	100.0	99.4	67.7	80.2	83.6	96.2	104.1	113.0
Total manufacturing [D]								
Total, industries manufacturières [D]	100.0	108.5	84.2	112.4	116.7	129.8	149.2	160.4
Food, beverages and tobacco								
Aliments, boissons et tabac	100.0	108.5	95.1	115.6	118.3	137.6	154.0	162.2
Textiles, wearing apparel, leather, footwear								
Textiles, habillement, cuir et chaussures	100.0	126.4	72.3	93.1	95.4	119.9	131.4	145.9
Chemicals, petroleum, rubber and plastic products								
Produits chimiques, pétroliers, caoutchouc et plastiques	100.0	112.8	70.6	119.3	124.2	108.5	109.3	110.7
Metal products								
Produits métalliques	100.0	110.2	92.1	108.2	106.0	149.2	133.6	143.8
Electricity, gas and water [E]								
Electricité, gaz et eau [E]	100.0	104.3	103.7	116.1	119.8	142.9	151.0	163.2
Malawi Malawi								
Total industry [DE]								
Total, industrie [DE]	100.0	89.8	89.9	87.4	94.3	92.0	94.6	...
Total manufacturing [D]								
Total, industries manufacturières [D]	100.0	85.0	85.1	82.5	89.7	82.6	83.5	...
Food, beverages and tobacco								
Aliments, boissons et tabac	100.0	89.4	85.4	70.7	98.3	89.2	90.2	...
Textiles, wearing apparel, leather, footwear								
Textiles, habillement, cuir et chaussures	100.0	81.4	44.2	44.3	67.1	74.4	61.6	...
Electricity and water [E]								
Electricité et eau [E]	100.0	102.7	107.5	105.1	111.4	121.2	129.4	...
Mali Mali								
Total industry [DE]								
Total, industrie [DE]	100.0	110.0	129.4	130.0	140.2	144.1	160.9	152.6
Food, beverages and tobacco								
Aliments, boissons et tabac	100.0	100.6	103.8	104.3	122.1	129.0	154.1	132.1
Wearing apparel								
Habillement	100.0	88.3	103.3	119.7	151.6	142.2	70.4	55.8
Chemicals and chemical products								
Produits chimiques	100.0	83.8	85.2	81.7	76.1	63.9	68.9	84.4
Mauritius Maurice								
Total industry [CDE]								
Total, industrie [CDE]	100.0	105.2	102.9	103.2	103.4	97.0	100.9	102.1
Total mining [C]								
Total, industries extractives [C]	100.0	94.2	48.0	48.5	48.7	46.9	51.2	46.5
Total manufacturing [D]								
Total, industries manufacturières [D]	100.0	104.7	102.4	101.8	101.3	93.8	97.5	98.4
Food, beverages and tobacco								
Aliments, boissons et tabac	100.0	108.6	109.0	116.2	119.9	121.0	130.2	124.1
Textiles, wearing apparel, leather, footwear								
Textiles, habillement, cuir et chaussures	100.0	103.7	95.9	88.6	80.1	68.8	69.7	75.2
Chemicals, petroleum, rubber and plastic products								
Produits chimiques, pétroliers, caoutchouc et plastiques	100.0	100.5	102.2	120.9	98.2	77.4	75.9	89.6
Basic metals								
Métaux de base	100.0	105.6	124.2	112.6	137.6	101.5	136.6	95.5
Metal products								
Produits métalliques	100.0	101.6	100.3	110.3	181.0	233.9	282.5	306.2
Electricity, gas and water [E]								
Electricité, gaz et eau [E]	100.0	110.7	112.4	121.6	126.6	131.4	136.6	141.1
Morocco Maroc								
Total industry [CDE] [4]								
Total, industrie [CDE] [4]	100.0	106.5	111.4	115.3	121.9	132.3	139.0	145.1
Total mining [C] [5]								
Total, industries extractives [C] [5]	100.0	110.2	115.0	109.5	119.2	127.2	137.9	143.4

Country or area and industry [ISIC Rev. 3] Pays ou zone et industrie [CITI Rév. 3]	2000	2001	2002	2003	2004	2005	2006	2007
Total manufacturing [D] [3] Total, industries manufacturières [D] [3]	100.0	103.3	107.0	110.0	115.2	121.5	127.8	133.6
Food, beverages and tobacco Aliments, boissons et tabac	100.0	101.2	101.2	103.3	109.2	115.1	114.4	117.4
Textiles, wearing apparel, leather, footwear Textiles, habillement, cuir et chaussures	100.0	104.3	105.8	104.0	103.9	108.8	112.4	113.4
Chemicals, petroleum, rubber and plastic products Produits chimiques, pétroliers, caoutchouc et plastiques	100.0	102.3	108.0	104.1	116.4	121.8	126.4	128.8
Basic metals Métaux de base	100.0	103.5	119.3	142.3	140.0	154.7	162.4	174.4
Metal products Produits métalliques	100.0	104.3	106.6	110.0	116.8	122.0	128.9	137.2
Electricity [E] Electricité [E]	100.0	113.9	122.2	132.9	142.1	165.3	171.1	165.6
Namibia Namibie								
Total industry [CDE] Total, industrie [CDE]	100.0	98.1	109.3	111.6	128.6	129.7	131.4	137.5
Total mining [C] Total, industries extractives [C]	100.0	93.9	108.9	103.9	141.8	139.9	160.5	160.8
Total manufacturing [D] Total, industries manufacturières [D]	100.0	105.5	115.7	121.7	125.4	126.7	115.5	130.6
Electricity, gas and water [E] Electricité, gaz et eau [E]	100.0	76.3	76.9	89.0	93.3	105.4	99.3	81.3
Senegal Sénégal								
Total industry [CDE] Total, industrie [CDE]	100.0	100.8	118.4	123.1	137.4	139.9	132.0	144.1
Total mining [C] Total, industries extractives [C]	100.0	87.1	97.0	125.0	113.4	96.6	65.7	65.3
Total manufacturing [D] [4] Total, industries manufacturières [D] [4]	100.0	99.2	121.5	121.5	140.1	141.8	133.6	147.3
Food, beverages and tobacco Aliments, boissons et tabac	100.0	94.9	102.1	109.7	143.1	153.2	180.7	196.6
Textiles Textiles	100.0	125.0	63.5	89.6	71.9	66.6	62.7	68.6
Chemicals, petroleum, rubber and plastic products Produits chimiques, pétroliers, caoutchouc et plastiques	100.0	83.5	122.4	114.3	115.6	104.6	56.2	67.2
Metal products Produits métalliques	100.0	39.0	63.2	64.9	64.1	57.8	56.3	54.5
Electricity and water [E] Electricité et eau [E]	100.0	113.1	110.1	130.1	131.5	144.2	145.0	153.6
South Africa Afrique du Sud								
Total industry [CDE] [4] Total, industrie [CDE] [4]	100.0	102.2	105.8	106.1	111.2	113.5	117.1	120.3
Total mining [C] Total, industries extractives [C]	100.0	101.4	102.2	106.4	112.5	111.7	110.0	109.0
Total manufacturing [D] Total, industries manufacturières [D]	100.0	102.8	107.4	105.4	110.0	113.8	119.3	124.2
Food and beverages Aliments et boissons	100.0	105.0	102.0	103.9	111.8	118.7	119.7	124.5
Textiles, wearing apparel, leather, footwear Textiles, habillement, cuir et chaussures	100.0	96.4	102.7	95.4	99.5	97.2	99.3	102.5
Chemicals, petroleum, rubber and plastic products Produits chimiques, pétroliers, caoutchouc et plastiques	100.0	103.9	112.6	107.0	111.5	115.0	119.6	129.3
Basic metals Métaux de base	100.0	99.3	104.4	106.8	110.7	105.7	114.1	114.0
Metal products Produits métalliques	100.0	106.4	113.6	110.3	113.4	117.9	127.7	133.7
Electricity [E] Electricité [E]	100.0	99.7	104.7	111.1	116.1	116.2	120.4	125.0

24

Index numbers of industrial production *(continued)*
2000 = 100
Indices de la production industrielle *(suite)*
2000 = 100

Country or area and industry [ISIC Rev. 3] Pays ou zone et industrie [CITI Rév. 3]	2000	2001	2002	2003	2004	2005	2006	2007
Swaziland Swaziland								
Total industry [CDE] [4]								
Total, industrie [CDE] [4]	100.0	100.8	111.3	120.7	126.6	127.6	130.6	...
Total mining [C]								
Total, industries extractives [C]	100.0	80.1	89.5	71.0	78.0	60.8	70.9	...
Total manufacturing [D]								
Total, industries manufacturières [D]	100.0	100.9	111.1	121.7	128.2	129.4	132.0	...
Electricity, gas and water [E]								
Electricité, gaz et eau [E]	100.0	105.4	120.4	123.3	120.3	124.9	131.2	...
Tunisia Tunisie								
Total industry [CDE]								
Total, industrie [CDE]	100.0	105.4	106.0	105.7	110.0	110.9	114.3	125.0
Total mining [C]								
Total, industries extractives [C]	100.0	98.1	97.5	94.1	98.4	99.7	94.1	112.5
Total manufacturing [D]								
Total, industries manufacturières [D]	100.0	106.7	107.3	107.1	111.3	111.8	116.8	126.4
Food, beverages and tobacco								
Aliments, boissons et tabac	100.0	99.6	102.9	104.7	112.7	111.5	117.0	121.2
Textiles, wearing apparel, leather, footwear								
Textiles, habillement, cuir et chaussures	100.0	111.0	108.5	102.4	101.5	95.9	94.4	100.1
Chemicals, petroleum, rubber and plastic products								
Produits chimiques, pétroliers, caoutchouc et plastiques	100.0	100.2	102.1	102.9	100.4	98.1	95.5	96.2
Basic metals								
Métaux de base	100.0	96.4	86.0	71.3	69.5	84.7	94.7	111.6
Metal products								
Produits métalliques	100.0	111.2	115.0	120.3	125.6	136.7	163.1	206.7
Electricity and water [E]								
Electricité et eau [E]	100.0	107.3	110.5	117.1	121.7	127.2	132.1	138.1
Uganda Ouganda								
Total manufacturing [D]								
Total, industries manufacturières [D]	100.0	118.6	122.1	126.8	141.4	146.1	150.3	...
Food, beverages and tobacco								
Aliments, boissons et tabac	100.0	98.8	106.5	115.0	123.1	121.7	130.8	...
Textiles, wearing apparel, leather, footwear								
Textiles, habillement, cuir et chaussures	100.0	74.0	93.1	98.9	102.7	82.9	72.5	...
Chemicals, rubber and plastic products								
Produits chimiques, caoutchouc et plastiques	100.0	128.5	120.1	130.0	142.6	158.3	150.6	...
Basic metals								
Métaux de base	100.0	107.1	182.6	159.3	200.2	246.6	272.5	...
Metal products								
Produits métalliques	100.0	103.2	116.7	95.9	116.1	87.4	80.8	...
United Rep. of Tanzania Rép.-Unie de Tanzanie								
Total manufacturing [D]								
Total, industries manufacturières [D]	100.0	104.1	119.6	135.4	146.0	156.7	158.4	254.3
Food, beverages and tobacco								
Aliments, boissons et tabac	100.0	106.3	119.3	151.5	146.2	172.9	177.8	233.2
Textiles, leather and footwear								
Textiles, cuir et chaussures	100.0	116.4	144.1	174.8	181.1	170.3	186.7	407.6
Chemicals, rubber and plastic products								
Produits chimiques, caoutchouc et plastiques	100.0	101.2	90.7	138.0	94.8	156.8	115.5	513.0
Basic metals								
Métaux de base	100.0	106.2	140.9	165.1	162.9	166.0	175.3	178.9
Metal products								
Produits métalliques	100.0	106.2	83.4	92.6	84.3	87.9	72.9	31.7
Zambia Zambie								
Total industry [CDE]								
Total, industrie [CDE]	100.0	105.1	103.6	113.1	122.9	133.3	142.0	153.0
Total mining [C]								
Total, industries extractives [C]	100.0	113.9	111.4	126.7	147.6	168.3	183.6	201.4
Total manufacturing [D]								
Total, industries manufacturières [D]	100.0	96.3	97.4	105.5	111.3	115.8	118.6	127.6

Country or area and industry [ISIC Rev. 3] Pays ou zone et industrie [CITI Rév. 3]	2000	2001	2002	2003	2004	2005	2006	2007
Food, beverages and tobacco Aliments, boissons et tabac	100.0	112.6	122.1	129.4	137.0	141.9	148.2	166.6
Textiles and wearing apparel Textiles et habillement	100.0	68.0	72.2	74.5	73.1	71.0	65.1	53.1
Chemicals, petroleum, rubber and plastic products Produits chimiques, pétroliers, caoutchouc et plastiques	100.0	67.9	73.8	79.6	85.0	87.7	91.2	95.1
Basic metals Métaux de base	100.0	56.6	59.0	67.9	70.0	68.6	68.4	65.2
Metal products Produits métalliques	100.0	95.4	71.0	84.2	88.2	94.8	96.8	103.0
Electricity and water [E] Electricité et eau [E]	100.0	115.4	106.9	106.8	103.5	109.9	124.4	125.1
Zimbabwe Zimbabwe								
Total industry [CDE] [4] Total, industrie [CDE] [4]	100.0	92.8	83.7	77.5	74.6	...	...	...
Total mining [C] Total, industries extractives [C]	100.0	86.0	87.9	76.8	106.7	...	...	...
Total manufacturing [D] Total, industries manufacturières [D]	100.0	90.9	78.1	71.2	62.6	64.1	68.3	...
Food, beverages and tobacco Aliments, boissons et tabac	100.0	85.6	69.6	59.5	54.6	54.0	52.5	...
Textiles, wearing apparel, leather, footwear Textiles, habillement, cuir et chaussures	100.0	98.1	77.4	53.6	63.3	69.6	93.1	...
Chemicals, petroleum, rubber and plastic products Produits chimiques, pétroliers, caoutchouc et plastiques	100.0	99.9	104.2	89.5	88.0	86.6	69.7	...
Basic metals and metal products Métaux de base et produits métalliques	100.0	88.9	77.6	81.0	63.5	68.5	61.7	...
Electricity [E] Electricité [E]	100.0	112.2	120.9	124.0	136.4	147.0	...	...
America, North · Amérique du Nord								
Barbados Barbade								
Total industry [CDE] Total, industrie [CDE]	100.0	93.9	94.3	93.6	95.4	97.1	98.4	98.1
Total mining [C] Total, industries extractives [C]	100.0	83.8	70.8	66.7	64.1	69.3	67.1	63.1
Total manufacturing [D] Total, industries manufacturières [D]	100.0	92.3	92.8	91.8	93.2	95.0	94.2	92.8
Food, beverages and tobacco Aliments, boissons et tabac	100.0	97.2	99.2	99.0	99.3	99.1	93.9	97.0
Wearing apparel Habillement	100.0	63.0	47.0	44.0	46.0	45.1	39.7	36.7
Chemicals and petroleum products Produits chimiques et pétroliers	100.0	93.9	90.0	86.8	109.6	115.6	112.1	108.8
Metal products Produits métalliques	100.0	69.6	68.1	59.6	65.8	51.3	55.4	47.6
Electricity and gas [E] Electricité et gaz [E]	100.0	103.6	105.4	108.2	110.8	110.1	119.2	122.1
Belize Belize								
Total industry [DE] Total, industrie [DE]	100.0	99.6	101.5	107.9	109.3	108.8	136.7	...
Total manufacturing [D] Total, industries manufacturières [D]	100.0	97.4	97.2	97.1	107.3	106.9	96.8	...
Food, beverages and tobacco Aliments, boissons et tabac	100.0	96.4	96.0	95.8	105.1	105.5	94.6	...
Wearing apparel Habillement	100.0	112.6	115.4	117.5	144.0	128.0	131.9	...
Chemicals and chemical products Produits chimiques	100.0	123.9	126.4	128.9	131.5	134.1	136.8	...
Electricity and water [E] Electricité et eau [E]	100.0	100.4	103.1	111.8	110.1	109.5	151.2	...

Country or area and industry [ISIC Rev. 3] Pays ou zone et industrie [CITI Rév. 3]	2000	2001	2002	2003	2004	2005	2006	2007
Canada Canada								
Total industry [CDE]								
Total, industrie [CDE]	100.0	96.2	97.9	97.9	99.7	101.5	101.3	101.3
Total mining [C]								
Total, industries extractives [C]	100.0	100.1	102.5	105.4	107.1	107.8	109.3	110.0
Total manufacturing [D]								
Total, industries manufacturières [D]	100.0	95.3	96.1	95.1	97.1	98.4	97.9	97.1
Food, beverages and tobacco								
Aliments, boissons et tabac	100.0	104.9	104.5	102.6	103.7	106.7	107.7	108.8
Textiles, wearing apparel, leather, footwear								
Textiles, habillement, cuir et chaussures	100.0	95.5	91.9	85.5	77.2	68.4	60.9	56.2
Chemicals, petroleum, rubber and plastic products								
Produits chimiques, pétroliers, caoutchouc et plastiques	100.0	102.1	107.0	108.5	109.4	109.4	109.6	107.9
Basic metals								
Métaux de base	100.0	98.0	102.5	100.9	107.1	109.3	109.9	108.9
Metal products								
Produits métalliques	100.0	89.1	86.4	85.4	88.2	91.2	92.4	93.5
Electricity, gas and water [E]								
Electricité, gaz et eau [E]	100.0	97.7	104.3	106.0	106.9	112.6	111.6	116.2
Costa Rica Costa Rica								
Total industry [DE] [4]								
Total, industrie [DE] [4]	100.0	93.8	97.4	105.0	109.1	119.6	130.9	137.8
Total manufacturing [D]								
Total, industries manufacturières [D]	100.0	90.9	94.0	101.9	106.0	117.4	129.6	138.0
Food, beverages and tobacco								
Aliments, boissons et tabac	100.0	94.1	92.1	94.0	93.6	98.7	108.2	111.7
Textiles, wearing apparel, leather, footwear								
Textiles, habillement, cuir et chaussures	100.0	90.3	88.4	85.7	88.8	90.7	86.2	86.5
Chemicals, petroleum, rubber and plastic products								
Produits chimiques, pétroliers, caoutchouc et plastiques	100.0	108.8	127.8	132.8	134.0	136.9	147.9	153.7
Metal products								
Produits métalliques	100.0	92.1	99.0	99.3	102.0	108.2	113.7	119.2
Electricity and water [E]								
Electricité et eau [E]	100.0	104.1	109.6	116.1	120.7	127.8	135.6	137.3
Cuba Cuba								
Total industry [CDE]								
Total, industrie [CDE]	100.0	100.6	82.7	76.7	78.3	74.6	75.1	78.1
Total mining [C]								
Total, industries extractives [C]	100.0	101.5	118.8	122.8	113.7	107.3	120.3	...
Total manufacturing [D]								
Total, industries manufacturières [D]	100.0	102.2	93.3	92.9	93.5	95.5	97.3	101.6
Food, beverages and tobacco								
Aliments, boissons et tabac	100.0	110.9	105.7	105.3	109.1	120.0	123.1	119.5
Textiles, wearing apparel, leather, footwear								
Textiles, habillement, cuir et chaussures	100.0	100.9	74.0	68.0	64.0	57.7	55.0	53.0
Chemicals, petroleum, rubber and plastic products								
Produits chimiques, pétroliers, caoutchouc et plastiques	100.0	98.5	67.9	70.4	67.2	63.3	66.7	71.2
Basic metals								
Métaux de base	100.0	102.9	99.8	93.5	98.4	100.1	95.9	98.3
Metal products								
Produits métalliques	100.0	104.9	92.4	94.6	80.4	34.5	37.8	40.4
Electricity and water [E]								
Electricité et eau [E]	100.0	101.8	104.5	105.2	104.1	102.1	109.6	...
Dominican Republic Rép. dominicaine								
Total industry [CDE]								
Total, Industrie [CDE]	100.0	98.8	104.0	104.6	105.4	111.8	115.8	118.9
Total mining [C]								
Total, industries extractives [C]	100.0	86.5	93.2	101.4	107.2	107.1	118.9	117.2
Total manufacturing [D]								
Total, industries manufacturières [D]	100.0	98.1	102.9	103.9	106.4	113.1	116.8	119.6
Electricity and water [E]								
Electricité et eau [E]	100.0	115.1	126.3	117.6	92.0	103.9	113.9	119.1

Country or area and industry [ISIC Rev. 3] Pays ou zone et industrie [CITI Rév. 3]	2000	2001	2002	2003	2004	2005	2006	2007
El Salvador El Salvador								
Total industry [CDE] Total, industrie [CDE]	100.0	104.2	107.3	109.8	110.5	112.3	115.9	120.3
Total mining [C] Total, industries extractives [C]	100.0	111.4	117.8	121.9	102.4	105.1	110.1	116.8
Total manufacturing [D] Total, industries manufacturières [D]	100.0	104.0	107.1	109.5	110.5	112.2	115.7	120.0
Food and beverages Aliments et boissons	100.0	105.1	106.7	108.9	112.1	115.1	119.3	125.3
Textiles, wearing apparel, leather, footwear Textiles, habillement, cuir et chaussures	100.0	93.2	93.1	92.4	95.0	99.6	103.1	104.7
Chemicals, petroleum, rubber and plastic products Produits chimiques, pétroliers, caoutchouc et plastiques	100.0	104.5	107.2	108.6	107.3	111.0	116.3	122.9
Basic metals and metal products Métaux de base et produits métalliques	100.0	102.6	106.1	108.7	110.9	114.2	117.8	117.7
Electricity [E] Electricité [E]	100.0	106.6	114.2	119.8	121.2	130.7	141.0	144.8
Guatemala Guatemala								
Total industry [CDE] Total, industrie [CDE]	100.0	100.1	102.1	104.7	109.1	111.8	116.3	120.6
Total mining [C] Total, industries extractives [C]	100.0	100.8	116.9	109.9	96.8	93.6	110.1	125.4
Total manufacturing [D] Total, industries manufacturières [D]	100.0	101.1	102.3	104.8	109.9	112.8	117.0	120.6
Electricity and water [E] Electricité et eau [E]	100.0	97.0	102.0	107.0	110.9	113.8	117.2	124.6
Haïti [6] Haïti [6]								
Total industry [DE] [4] Total, industrie [DE] [4]	100.0	99.4	101.0	105.7	107.3	115.4	119.8	121.9
Total manufacturing [D] Total, industries manufacturières [D]	100.0	102.4	104.0	108.4	110.1	116.6	124.3	126.7
Food, beverages and tobacco Aliments, boissons et tabac	100.0	103.7	105.2	105.7	107.9	118.5	...	
Chemicals and chemical products Produits chimiques	100.0	103.4	105.8	121.1	119.7	126.1	130.2	142.2
Electricity [E] Electricité [E]	100.0	69.5	70.4	77.4	78.6	103.1	74.0	72.6
Honduras Honduras								
Total industry [CDE] Total, industrie [CDE]	100.0	102.5	108.2	113.0	117.4	128.5	135.5	140.4
Total mining [C] Total, industries extractives [C]	100.0	99.2	134.4	126.6	129.7	128.8	132.9	137.6
Total manufacturing [D] Total, industries manufacturières [D]	100.0	103.8	111.9	119.1	123.9	132.6	139.7	144.6
Food, beverages and tobacco Aliments, boissons et tabac	100.0	101.7	111.4	115.4	119.6	121.3	129.8	135.3
Textiles, wearing apparel, leather, footwear Textiles, habillement, cuir et chaussures	100.0	109.7	117.3	133.0	145.4	162.1	164.8	167.6
Chemicals, petroleum, rubber and plastic products Produits chimiques, pétroliers, caoutchouc et plastiques	100.0	103.4	103.1	109.8	107.1	118.5	125.0	131.4
Basic metals Métaux de base	100.0	111.1	120.2	86.9	92.4	69.5	75.1	75.7
Metal products Produits métalliques	100.0	104.6	108.8	116.5	116.7	133.3	142.9	152.6
Electricity, gas and water [E] Electricité, gaz et eau [E]	100.0	86.0	74.3	59.0	62.7	95.6	101.6	106.8
Mexico Mexique								
Total industry [CDE] [7] Total, industrie [CDE] [7]	100.0	96.6	96.4	96.3	99.8	102.4	107.9	110.0
Total mining [C] Total, industries extractives [C]	100.0	101.4	101.9	105.6	107.0	106.7	108.1	104.4

Country or area and industry [ISIC Rev. 3] Pays ou zone et industrie [CITI Rév. 3]	2000	2001	2002	2003	2004	2005	2006	2007
Total manufacturing [D] Total, industries manufacturières [D]	100.0	96.2	95.6	94.3	98.0	101.5	106.8	109.7
Food, beverages and tobacco Aliments, boissons et tabac	100.0	102.6	104.3	106.1	110.4	114.3	116.9	119.1
Textiles and wearing apparel Textiles et habillement	100.0	91.9	86.1	80.2	81.4	79.3	78.7	74.8
Chemicals, petroleum, rubber and plastic products Produits chimiques, pétroliers, caoutchouc et plastiques	100.0	96.2	95.9	97.4	102.1	104.0	106.5	107.2
Basic metals Métaux de base	100.0	92.9	94.1	98.0	101.7	107.9	113.6	112.1
Metal products Produits métalliques	100.0	93.1	91.2	86.8	90.1	94.5	104.0	111.4
Electricity [E] Electricité [E]	100.0	102.2	103.3	104.9	109.1	111.3	124.8	133.7
Panama Panama								
Total industry [CDE] [4] Total, industrie [CDE] [4]	100.0	94.0	97.2	100.0	102.8	106.2	112.6	121.3
Total mining [C] Total, industries extractives [C]	100.0	96.9	113.3	141.5	158.8	159.7	186.8	229.2
Total manufacturing [D] Total, industries manufacturières [D]	100.0	93.4	94.7	96.0	96.6	99.4	105.1	110.7
Food, beverages and tobacco Aliments, boissons et tabac	100.0	98.7	98.7	100.1	101.2	104.5	109.4	113.7
Textiles, wearing apparel, leather, footwear Textiles, habillement, cuir et chaussures	100.0	87.3	74.3	55.2	44.8	38.7	38.3	37.7
Chemicals, petroleum, rubber and plastic products Produits chimiques, pétroliers, caoutchouc et plastiques	100.0	87.3	89.2	89.0	81.7	84.3	87.5	88.9
Basic metals Métaux de base	100.0	40.6	51.6	52.1	56.8	54.1	53.8	54.8
Metal products Produits métalliques	100.0	90.6	60.9	56.0	64.0	69.3	68.8	71.4
Electricity and water [E] Electricité et eau [E]	100.0	95.3	101.7	103.3	109.7	116.0	119.8	130.4
Trinidad and Tobago Trinité-et-Tobago								
Total industry [DE] Total, industrie [DE]	100.0	107.7	128.2	140.4	148.9	164.0	178.9	...
Total manufacturing [D] [4] Total, industries manufacturières [D] [4]	100.0	109.3	130.3	144.2	153.1	169.1	185.1	...
Food, beverages and tobacco Aliments, boissons et tabac	100.0	119.1	87.5	85.9	103.1	123.2	147.7	...
Textiles, leather and footwear Textiles, cuir et chaussures	100.0	90.3	85.2	133.4	154.8	181.6	193.3	...
Chemicals and petroleum products Produits chimiques et pétroliers	100.0	100.4	122.1	150.7	172.7	235.4	209.8	...
Metal products Produits métalliques	100.0	116.3	130.6	171.5	313.6	398.4	610.8	...
Electricity [E] Electricité [E]	100.0	87.6	103.6	94.2	98.4	103.1	104.7	...
United States Etats-Unis								
Total industry [CDE] Total, industrie [CDE]	100.0	96.5	96.4	97.7	100.1	103.4	105.7	107.4
Total mining [C] Total, industries extractives [C]	100.0	100.6	96.0	96.2	95.6	94.3	97.3	97.4
Total manufacturing [D] Total, industries manufacturières [D]	100.0	95.9	95.8	97.0	99.8	103.9	106.4	108.1
Food, beverages and tobacco Aliments, boissons et tabac	100.0	99.9	100.5	102.4	103.0	106.6	107.4	111.3
Textiles, wearing apparel, leather, footwear Textiles, habillement, cuir et chaussures	100.0	87.3	78.0	74.0	69.9	70.4	66.0	62.3
Chemicals, petroleum, rubber and plastic products Produits chimiques, pétroliers, caoutchouc et plastiques	100.0	96.8	103.2	104.2	107.7	111.1	112.8	113.1

24
Index numbers of industrial production *(continued)*
2000 = 100
Indices de la production industrielle *(suite)*
2000 = 100

Country or area and industry [ISIC Rev. 3] Pays ou zone et industrie [CITI Rév. 3]	2000	2001	2002	2003	2004	2005	2006	2007
Basic metals Métaux de base	100.0	89.2	89.8	89.0	98.7	96.1	100.9	99.0
Metal products Produits métalliques	100.0	95.8	95.0	99.1	103.0	110.8	119.4	127.9
Electricity and gas [E] Electricité et gaz [E]	100.0	99.6	102.7	104.6	106.1	108.2	107.6	111.2
America, South · Amérique du Sud								
Argentina Argentine								
Total manufacturing [D] Total, industries manufacturières [D]	100.0	88.8	80.2	94.2	107.4	117.3	128.1	140.0
Food, beverages and tobacco Aliments, boissons et tabac	100.0	91.4	87.0	98.0	108.7	116.9	123.8	136.0
Textiles, wearing apparel, leather, footwear Textiles, habillement, cuir et chaussures	100.0	85.7	67.8	94.6	104.9	116.6	122.2	135.3
Chemicals, petroleum, rubber and plastic products Produits chimiques, pétroliers, caoutchouc et plastiques	100.0	91.6	87.5	97.6	104.6	111.2	121.2	128.2
Basic metals Métaux de base	100.0	94.2	99.8	111.0	122.1	130.9	143.3	146.8
Metal products Produits métalliques	100.0	83.7	68.3	88.2	111.4	124.7	142.8	162.7
Bolivia Bolivie								
Total industry [CDE] [4] Total, industrie [CDE] [4]	100.0	98.5	99.1	101.5	101.6	108.1	116.5	...
Total mining [C] Total, industries extractives [C]	100.0	96.7	96.9	97.6	91.3	102.7	109.1	...
Total manufacturing [D] Total, industries manufacturières [D]	100.0	99.2	99.9	103.4	106.9	110.4	120.2	...
Food, beverages and tobacco Aliments, boissons et tabac	100.0	102.4	105.4	108.4	108.2	108.5	119.9	...
Textiles, wearing apparel, leather, footwear Textiles, habillement, cuir et chaussures	100.0	84.1	79.9	95.6	95.3	107.9	114.5	...
Chemicals, petroleum, rubber and plastic products Produits chimiques, pétroliers, caoutchouc et plastiques	100.0	97.3	98.5	104.5	123.3	122.5	127.1	...
Basic metals Métaux de base	100.0	87.4	91.1	98.5	99.4	98.4	99.1	...
Metal products Produits métalliques	100.0	92.3	79.9	64.7	67.9	53.7	64.4	...
Electricity, gas and water [E] Electricité, gaz et eau [E]	100.0	100.7	104.5	106.0	109.2	115.6	123.0	...
Brazil Brésil								
Total industry [CD] Total, industrie [CD]	100.0	101.6	104.4	104.4	113.2	116.6	119.9	127.1
Total mining [C] Total, industries extractives [C]	100.0	103.4	123.0	128.8	134.3	148.0	158.9	168.5
Total manufacturing [D] Total, industries manufacturières [D]	100.0	101.3	101.8	101.6	110.3	113.3	116.2	123.2
Food, beverages and tobacco Aliments, boissons et tabac	100.0	103.8	101.7	99.4	104.5	106.4	109.8	113.0
Textiles, wearing apparel, leather, footwear Textiles, habillement, cuir et chaussures	100.0	93.5	95.0	87.4	92.6	89.6	88.5	91.3
Chemicals, petroleum, rubber and plastic products Produits chimiques, pétroliers, caoutchouc et plastiques	100.0	98.6	97.2	95.9	100.5	101.9	103.2	107.5
Basic metals and metal products Métaux de base et produits métalliques	100.0	100.2	103.8	110.1	113.7	111.5	114.6	122.4
Metal products Produits métalliques	100.0	107.0	112.0	115.4	132.1	136.1	139.0	156.8
Chile Chili								
Total industry [CDE] [4] Total, industrie [CDE] [4]	100.0	101.6	102.5	108.3	117.6	122.2	125.6	131.4
Total mining [C] Total, industries extractives [C]	100.0	101.6	98.0	104.4	114.9	114.0	114.8	119.3

Country or area and industry [ISIC Rev. 3] Pays ou zone et industrie [CITI Rév. 3]	2000	2001	2002	2003	2004	2005	2006	2007
Total manufacturing [D]								
Total, industries manufacturières [D]	100.0	101.2	103.7	109.1	117.8	124.4	128.5	134.5
Food, beverages and tobacco								
Aliments, boissons et tabac	100.0	103.9	107.0	110.5	118.7	125.1	138.5	141.7
Textiles, wearing apparel, leather, footwear								
Textiles, habillement, cuir et chaussures	100.0	87.3	82.9	90.1	100.1	97.9	85.6	85.7
Chemicals, petroleum, rubber and plastic products								
Produits chimiques, pétroliers, caoutchouc et plastiques	100.0	106.1	110.7	114.4	119.3	135.9	130.7	137.9
Basic metals								
Métaux de base	100.0	104.7	103.6	120.7	153.4	164.1	153.7	169.9
Metal products								
Produits métalliques	100.0	101.7	95.6	96.5	102.8	112.6	111.0	113.0
Electricity [E]								
Electricité [E]	100.0	104.3	107.0	114.3	123.5	130.3	137.4	145.8
Colombia Colombie								
Total industry [CDE] [4]								
Total, industrie [CDE] [4]	100.0	104.3	100.5	114.5	123.4	130.2	143.1	153.5
Total mining [C]								
Total, industries extractives [C]	100.0	113.3	06.0	145.2	163.6	177.8	196.8	203.3
Total manufacturing [D]								
Total, industries manufacturières [D]	100.0	100.7	100.8	103.5	110.1	114.3	126.8	140.3
Food, beverages and tobacco								
Aliments, boissons et tabac	100.0	101.6	102.8	102.3	102.5	101.2	109.8	116.2
Textiles, wearing apparel, leather, footwear								
Textiles, habillement, cuir et chaussures	100.0	99.3	88.7	92.4	99.7	98.5	105.6	116.5
Chemicals, petroleum, rubber and plastic products								
Produits chimiques, pétroliers, caoutchouc et plastiques	100.0	95.8	97.3	102.5	110.2	113.2	119.5	127.9
Basic metals								
Métaux de base	100.0	96.1	103.8	135.1	156.2	174.5	211.6	251.7
Metal products								
Produits métalliques	100.0	112.1	112.8	112.1	134.9	153.9	183.0	216.9
Electricity [E]								
Electricité [E]	100.0	105.3	107.6	113.1	116.8	122.8	127.5	130.6
Ecuador Equateur								
Total industry [CDE]								
Total, industrie [CDE]	100.0	102.5	102.2	107.6	124.5	129.4	133.6	132.8
Total mining [C]								
Total, industries extractives [C]	100.0	101.1	98.5	104.5	130.9	132.4	133.8	127.4
Total manufacturing [D] [3]								
Total, industries manufacturières [D] [3]	100.0	104.9	107.5	112.5	114.0	124.3	135.0	149.0
Food, beverages and tobacco								
Aliments, boissons et tabac	100.0	107.1	109.4	118.5	116.9	128.4	143.2	158.6
Textiles, wearing apparel, leather, footwear								
Textiles, habillement, cuir et chaussures	100.0	100.7	101.4	101.0	108.4	112.4	114.0	115.1
Chemicals and chemical products								
Produits chimiques	100.0	102.8	100.7	100.5	101.7	106.8	103.7	122.3
Basic metals and metal products								
Métaux de base et produits métalliques	100.0	116.8	119.8	128.3	129.5	154.2	178.5	222.7
Electricity and water [E]								
Electricité et eau [E]	100.0	100.6	108.9	110.2	100.6	101.9	102.4	118.2
Paraguay Paraguay								
Total manufacturing [D]								
Total, industries manufacturières [D]	100.0	101.4	100.5	100.7	105.0	109.6	114.3	112.9
Food, beverages and tobacco								
Aliments, boissons et tabac	100.0	102.9	98.7	100.9	102.9	108.0	115.1	113.6
Textiles, wearing apparel, leather, footwear								
Textiles, habillement, cuir et chaussures	100.0	101.0	102.0	115.5	121.3	111.7	114.3	112.9
Chemicals, petroleum, rubber and plastic products								
Produits chimiques, pétroliers, caoutchouc et plastiques	100.0	105.0	97.6	93.5	83.1	70.9	63.8	61.5

Country or area and industry [ISIC Rev. 3] Pays ou zone et industrie [CITI Rév. 3]	2000	2001	2002	2003	2004	2005	2006	2007
Basic metals								
Métaux de base	100.0	97.4	87.2	94.0	101.6	105.8	104.6	106.6
All machinery and transport equipment								
Fabrication de machines et de matériel de transport	100.0	107.4	107.2	95.0	90.9	109.0	133.0	156.9
Peru Pérou								
Total industry [CDE]								
Total, industrie [CDE]	100.0	100.3	105.5	109.6	115.1	122.5	132.0	143.9
Total mining [C]								
Total, industries extractives [C]	100.0	109.9	123.1	129.8	136.7	148.1	150.2	154.2
Total manufacturing [D]								
Total, industries manufacturières [D]	100.0	100.6	106.4	110.1	118.6	127.2	136.7	151.4
Food, beverages and tobacco								
Aliments, boissons et tabac	100.0	97.4	100.8	101.4	107.7	114.0	124.0	136.3
Textiles, wearing apparel, leather, footwear								
Textiles, habillement, cuir et chaussures	100.0	95.9	108.0	117.8	132.4	136.9	133.7	142.7
Chemicals, petroleum, rubber and plastic products								
Produits chimiques, pétroliers, caoutchouc et plastiques	100.0	103.3	107.3	108.7	115.0	127.8	138.9	156.0
Basic metals								
Métaux de base	100.0	103.6	100.8	103.8	105.6	105.6	109.9	104.3
Metal products								
Produits métalliques	100.0	98.6	94.8	96.4	97.4	107.2	128.4	161.5
Electricity [E]								
Electricité [E]	100.0	101.7	107.2	111.1	116.1	122.6	131.1	142.1
Uruguay Uruguay								
Total manufacturing [D]								
Total, industries manufacturières [D]	100.0	101.7	107.2	118.9	146.2	164.3	179.6	190.2
Food, beverages and tobacco								
Aliments, boissons et tabac	100.0	93.2	93.3	92.2	111.9	135.8	150.4	160.7
Textiles, wearing apparel, leather, footwear								
Textiles, habillement, cuir et chaussures	100.0	81.0	61.9	74.9	89.4	90.5	84.2	87.5
Chemicals, petroleum, rubber and plastic products								
Produits chimiques, pétroliers, caoutchouc et plastiques	100.0	91.8	86.7	98.5	119.1	120.1	119.7	119.1
Basic metals								
Métaux de base	100.0	98.7	98.7	120.9	155.2	173.3	203.9	219.4
Metal products								
Produits métalliques	100.0	81.5	47.7	76.9	103.2	128.4	142.7	152.3
Venezuela (Bolivarian Rep. of) Venezuela (Rép. bolivarienne du)								
Total industry [CDE]								
Total, industrie [CDE]	100.0	103.8	92.5	87.1	104.0	115.2	125.6	133.7
Total mining [C]								
Total, industries extractives [C]	100.0	102.8	107.2	102.4	117.0	120.6	126.0	128.6
Total manufacturing [D]								
Total, industries manufacturières [D]	100.0	103.9	86.4	78.8	101.5	113.0	124.4	132.9
Food, beverages and tobacco								
Aliments, boissons et tabac	100.0	105.7	98.6	86.7	93.9	100.8	112.9	123.3
Textiles, wearing apparel, leather, footwear								
Textiles, habillement, cuir et chaussures	100.0	98.5	59.1	57.9	90.4	102.5	106.1	112.1
Chemicals, petroleum, rubber and plastic products								
Produits chimiques, pétroliers, caoutchouc et plastiques	100.0	101.0	88.4	91.5	116.0	114.4	112.9	125.8
Basic metals								
Métaux de base	100.0	95.1	94.9	93.1	113.7	114.1	120.4	128.3
Metal products								
Produits métalliques	100.0	102.0	68.3	56.5	83.4	101.4	124.1	111.7
Electricity [E]								
Electricité [E]	100.0	105.2	107.8	108.6	116.7	125.9	134.3	137.2
Asia · Asie								
Armenia Arménie								
Total industry [CDE]								
Total, industrie [CDE]	100.0	105.3	120.7	143.0	140.1	152.2	147.0	151.1
Total mining [C]								
Total, industries extractives [C]	100.0	119.7	143.2	160.2	177.0	168.9	179.4	185.3

Country or area and industry [ISIC Rev. 3] Pays ou zone et industrie [CITI Rév. 3]	2000	2001	2002	2003	2004	2005	2006	2007
Total manufacturing [D]								
Total, industries manufacturières [D]	100.0	109.6	137.3	163.6	162.7	178.8	175.2	177.7
Food, beverages and tobacco								
Aliments, boissons et tabac	100.0	106.8	118.6	136.5	141.9	150.8	154.9	164.4
Textiles, wearing apparel, leather, footwear								
Textiles, habillement, cuir et chaussures	100.0	114.8	115.2	141.2	176.3	132.4	136.9	125.7
Chemicals, petroleum, rubber and plastic products								
Produits chimiques, pétroliers, caoutchouc et plastiques	100.0	86.6	80.2	94.8	136.9	199.6	205.4	275.4
Basic metals								
Métaux de base	100.0	144.7	178.3	192.3	188.5	250.9	262.7	299.2
Metal products								
Produits métalliques	100.0	137.6	159.7	205.4	261.9	226.1	243.7	274.0
Electricity and gas [E]								
Electricité et gaz [E]	100.0	92.7	79.3	81.3	92.7	105.5	104.9	114.0
Azerbaijan Azerbaïdjan								
Total industry [CDE]								
Total, industrie [CDE]	100.0	105.1	108.9	115.5	122.1	163.1	222.7	276.1
Total mining [C]								
Total, industries extractives [C]	100.0	105.9	108.5	110.0	112.5	159.2	230.4	297.4
Total manufacturing [D]								
Total, industries manufacturières [D]	100.0	102.8	108.5	127.7	140.7	163.2	174.5	187.2
Food, beverages and tobacco								
Aliments, boissons et tabac	100.0	113.6	112.8	118.7	118.8	126.2	131.8	142.3
Textiles, wearing apparel, leather, footwear								
Textiles, habillement, cuir et chaussures	100.0	86.2	95.8	104.9	109.2	160.3	140.1	109.4
Chemicals, petroleum, rubber and plastic products								
Produits chimiques, pétroliers, caoutchouc et plastiques	100.0	76.9	83.2	87.6	99.1	109.8	115.5	111.7
Basic metals and metal products								
Métaux de base et produits métalliques	100.0	121.4	133.5	286.3	457.1	595.2	665.7	656.1
Electricity, gas and water [E]								
Electricité, gaz et eau [E]	100.0	100.6	105.3	122.6	125.4	131.4	143.0	132.2
Bangladesh [2] Bangladesh [2]								
Total industry [CDE]								
Total, Industrie [CDE]	100.0	107.1	112.2	119.5	128.0	138.3	152.9	165.4
Total mining [C]								
Total, industries extractives [C]	100.0	112.2	117.8	126.5	136.0	144.2	157.8	169.0
Total manufacturing [D]								
Total, industries manufacturières [D]	100.0	105.4	110.1	117.3	127.2	135.9	150.9	166.0
Food, beverages and tobacco								
Aliments, boissons et tabac	100.0	102.8	119.2	121.1	124.3	134.7	144.4	151.7
Textiles, wearing apparel, leather, footwear								
Textiles, habillement, cuir et chaussures	100.0	107.5	115.8	121.5	128.7	150.0	176.0	196.8
Chemicals, petroleum, rubber and plastic products								
Produits chimiques, pétroliers, caoutchouc et plastiques	100.0	108.8	106.4	127.4	127.7	133.1	133.3	142.5
Basic metals								
Métaux de base	100.0	110.8	116.0	120.1	122.8	139.0	148.4	166.0
Metal products								
Produits métalliques	100.0	95.0	100.3	94.0	97.9	118.3	128.3	135.8
Electricity [E]								
Electricité [E]	100.0	110.3	118.2	125.3	136.2	143.7	153.1	152.1
Brunei Darussalam Brunéi Darussalam								
Total industry [CDE]								
Total, industrie [CDE]	100.0	100.0	104.2	107.9	107.0	104.4	109.2	...
Total mining [C]								
Total, industries extractives [C]	100.0	99.9	103.2	107.0	106.2	103.3	109.6	...
Total manufacturing [D]								
Total, industries manufacturières [D]	100.0	100.1	107.0	110.2	108.9	106.8	107.7	...
Electricity, gas and water [E]								
Electricité, gaz et eau [E]	100.0	102.9	108.5	112.6	113.0	117.7	117.8	...

24

Index numbers of industrial production *(continued)*
2000 = 100
Indices de la production industrielle *(suite)*
2000 = 100

Country or area and industry [ISIC Rev. 3] Pays ou zone et industrie [CITI Rév. 3]	2000	2001	2002	2003	2004	2005	2006	2007
China, Hong Kong SAR Chine, Hong Kong RAS								
Total industry [DE] [4]								
Total, industrie [DE] [4]	100.0	98.3	94.0	90.1	93.1	95.7	96.9	96.4
Total manufacturing [D]								
Total, industries manufacturières [D]	100.0	95.6	86.2	78.3	80.6	82.6	84.4	83.1
Food, beverages and tobacco								
Aliments, boissons et tabac	100.0	98.3	106.4	94.1	99.4	100.6	110.3	125.6
Textiles and wearing apparel								
Textiles et habillement	100.0	99.8	92.9	89.4	87.6	83.4	82.2	70.1
Chemicals and other non-metallic mineral products								
Produits chimiques et minéraux non-métalliques	100.0	92.2	76.3	77.3	76.0	77.3	82.9	91.2
Basic metals and metal products								
Métaux de base et produits métalliques	100.0	91.3	70.3	56.0	62.1	68.4	66.4	58.9
Electricity and gas [E]								
Electricité et gaz [E]	100.0	103.2	108.2	111.5	115.8	119.4	119.6	120.5
China, Macao SAR Chine, Macao RAS								
Total industry [CDE]								
Total, industrie [CDE]	100.0	106.2	119.0	132.6	131.6	116.8	108.5	102.1
Total manufacturing [D]								
Total, industries manufacturières [D]	100.0	105.6	122.6	143.9	135.4	105.9	104.9	99.3
Textiles and wearing apparel								
Textiles et habillement	100.0	105.2	123.7	144.1	138.0	102.9	98.7	94.1
Basic metals and other non-metallic products								
Métaux de base et autre produits non-métalliques	100.0	99.8	69.6	153.4	163.3	381.3	532.1	520.4
Electricity and gas [E]								
Electricité et gaz [E]	100.0	108.6	115.1	116.3	128.1	137.1	112.9	102.8
Cyprus Chypre								
Total industry [CDE]								
Total, industrie [CDE]	100.0	99.7	99.8	107.8	109.8	110.8	111.8	115.3
Total mining [C]								
Total, industries extractives [C]	100.0	95.3	106.1	110.1	115.3	119.8	118.4	123.3
Total manufacturing [D]								
Total, industries manufacturières [D]	100.0	98.1	95.7	103.7	105.4	104.8	104.5	107.7
Food, beverages and tobacco								
Aliments, boissons et tabac	100.0	100.4	98.1	99.7	97.4	97.8	90.9	92.8
Textiles, wearing apparel, leather, footwear								
Textiles, habillement, cuir et chaussures	100.0	95.7	79.1	56.3	48.1	41.6	35.1	35.5
Chemicals, petroleum, rubber and plastic products								
Produits chimiques, pétroliers, caoutchouc et plastiques	100.0	105.1	106.4	101.3	99.7	95.8	100.8	112.3
Metal products								
Produits métalliques	100.0	102.5	112.0	102.9	107.9	107.7	119.0	120.8
Electricity, gas and water [E]								
Electricité, gaz et eau [E]	100.0	107.5	116.6	125.7	129.7	136.8	143.6	148.5
Georgia Géorgie								
Total industry [CDE]								
Total, industrie [CDE]	100.0	95.0	115.2	137.9	144.6	194.5	263.2	287.3
Total mining [C]								
Total, industries extractives [C]	100.0	106.9	135.8	172.7	139.7	139.8	146.4	177.8
Total manufacturing [D]								
Total, industries manufacturières [D]	100.0	97.8	131.6	162.8	177.7	249.8	349.3	382.7
Electricity, gas and water [E]								
Electricité, gaz et eau [E]	100.0	89.4	76.9	78.5	71.4	77.0	83.3	84.8
India [8] Inde [8]								
Total industry [CDE]								
Total, industrie [CDE]	100.0	102.7	108.7	116.2	126.0	136.2	151.7	164.8
Total mining [C]								
Total, industries extractives [C]	100.0	101.2	107.1	112.8	117.7	118.9	124.9	131.7
Total manufacturing [D]								
Total, industries manufacturières [D]	100.0	102.9	109.1	117.2	127.8	139.5	156.7	171.1
Food, beverages and tobacco								
Aliments, boissons et tabac	100.0	98.4	110.6	111.7	116.1	127.8	140.6	151.7

24

Index numbers of industrial production *(continued)*
2000 = 100
Indices de la production industrielle *(suite)*
2000 = 100

Country or area and industry [ISIC Rev. 3] Pays ou zone et industrie [CITI Rév. 3]	2000	2001	2002	2003	2004	2005	2006	2007
Textiles, wearing apparel, leather, footwear								
Textiles, habillement, cuir et chaussures	100.0	99.2	100.3	102.2	110.8	114.5	126.6	134.9
Chemicals, petroleum, rubber and plastic products								
Produits chimiques, pétroliers, caoutchouc et plastiques	100.0	105.9	110.4	118.6	132.2	141.7	156.2	172.0
Basic metals								
Métaux de base	100.0	104.3	113.9	124.3	131.1	151.7	186.4	209.0
Metal products								
Produits métalliques	100.0	99.2	109.1	125.5	141.4	155.4	177.4	192.2
Electricity [E]								
Electricité [E]	100.0	103.0	106.3	111.7	117.5	123.6	132.6	140.9
Indonesia Indonésie								
Total industry [CDE][4]								
Total, industrie [CDE][4]	100.0	110.5	106.7	111.2	99.2	116.9	99.0	94.1
Total mining [C]								
Total, industries extractives [C]	100.0	120.3	118.9	109.6	84.0	115.4	83.6	68.6
Total manufacturing [D]								
Total, industries manufacturières [D]	100.0	99.0	92.0	113.6	117.4	118.9	116.9	123.4
Food, beverages and tobacco								
Aliments, boissons et tabac	100.0	99.6	97.4	110.6	118.8	142.5	157.1	167.2
Textiles, wearing apparel, leather, footwear								
Textiles, habillement, cuir et chaussures	100.0	93.2	92.5	94.1	104.3	91.9	127.5	111.3
Chemicals, petroleum, rubber and plastic products								
Produits chimiques, pétroliers, caoutchouc et plastiques	100.0	102.5	102.2	111.6	126.7	166.6	188.0	213.0
Basic metals								
Métaux de base	100.0	102.1	89.8	70.6	75.2	73.2	89.4	100.2
Metal products								
Produits métalliques	100.0	123.1	141.8	175.6	210.7	220.7	238.1	321.4
Electricity [E]								
Electricité [E]	100.0	101.1	99.2	103.6	110.2	101.6	120.2	131.1
Iran (Islamic Rep. of) Iran (Rép. islamique d')								
Total manufacturing [D]								
Total, industries manufacturières [D]	100.0	103.8	107.7	111.5	115.4	...	...	...
Food and beverages								
Aliments et boissons	100.0	96.4	114.5	126.1	130.8	...	...	...
Textiles, wearing apparel, leather, footwear								
Textiles, habillement, cuir et chaussures	100.0	119.3	119.2	97.4	93.9	...	...	...
Chemicals, rubber and plastic products								
Produits chimiques, caoutchouc et plastiques	100.0	106.2	113.8	127.7	140.8	...	...	...
Metal products								
Produits métalliques	100.0	114.2	179.4	257.7	311.6	...	...	...
Israel Israël								
Total industry [CD]								
Total, industrie [CD]	100.0	95.1	93.2	93.0	99.4	103.1	113.2	118.3
Total mining [C]								
Total, industries extractives [C]	100.0	102.0	110.0	106.7	103.7	105.9	105.6	104.6
Total manufacturing [D]								
Total, industries manufacturières [D]	100.0	94.9	92.9	92.7	99.3	103.0	113.4	118.6
Food, beverages and tobacco								
Aliments, boissons et tabac	100.0	98.9	97.5	95.3	96.9	97.4	99.4	102.2
Textiles								
Textiles	100.0	91.4	87.5	84.3	84.7	85.0	88.4	83.1
Chemicals, petroleum, rubber and plastic products								
Produits chimiques, pétroliers, caoutchouc et plastiques	100.0	104.9	119.0	125.8	138.8	147.2	173.4	175.8
Basic metals								
Métaux de base	100.0	92.9	84.5	75.1	80.9	82.7	82.9	88.1
Metal products								
Produits métalliques	100.0	94.7	91.9	90.2	92.8	96.0	106.4	110.6
Japan Japon								
Total industry [CDE]								
Total, industrie [CDE]	100.0	93.6	92.5	95.4	100.5	101.7	106.3	109.2
Total mining [C]								
Total, industries extractives [C]	100.0	99.6	93.6	95.5	95.5	98.5	101.0	105.0

24

Index numbers of industrial production *(continued)*
2000 = 100
Indices de la production industrielle *(suite)*
2000 = 100

Country or area and industry [ISIC Rev. 3] Pays ou zone et industrie [CITI Rév. 3]	2000	2001	2002	2003	2004	2005	2006	2007
Total manufacturing [D] Total, industries manufacturières [D]	100.0	93.2	92.0	95.0	99.5	100.8	105.4	108.3
Food, beverages and tobacco Aliments, boissons et tabac	100.0	99.2	98.1	98.3	98.6	97.9	96.6	97.3
Textiles, wearing apparel, leather, footwear Textiles, habillement, cuir et chaussures	100.0	89.8	79.6	73.0	67.6	62.2	59.4	56.4
Chemicals, petroleum, rubber and plastic products Produits chimiques, pétroliers, caoutchouc et plastiques	100.0	99.1	98.6	100.1	101.0	101.0	102.5	103.2
Basic metals Métaux de base	100.0	96.9	98.4	101.9	105.4	104.8	107.8	110.6
Metal products Produits métalliques	100.0	89.8	90.5	96.0	105.2	108.1	118.1	124.9
Electricity and gas [E] Electricité et gaz [E]	100.0	100.2	101.0	102.4	105.8	108.8	111.0	113.1
Jordan Jordanie								
Total industry [CDE] Total, industrie [CDE]	100.0	111.8	118.5	108.4	121.4	133.9	141.6	146.1
Total mining [C] Total, industries extractives [C]	100.0	102.3	109.7	107.5	103.3	102.1	93.6	92.3
Total manufacturing [D] Total, industries manufacturières [D]	100.0	113.6	120.3	108.6	123.7	138.0	146.8	150.2
Food, beverages and tobacco Aliments, boissons et tabac	100.0	105.7	120.1	105.2	120.4	142.2	151.7	149.7
Textiles, wearing apparel, leather, footwear Textiles, habillement, cuir et chaussures	100.0	77.9	78.3	72.9	86.2	82.1	88.6	80.4
Chemicals, petroleum, rubber and plastic products Produits chimiques, pétroliers, caoutchouc et plastiques	100.0	112.3	111.9	104.9	117.5	127.6	131.4	131.4
Basic metals Métaux de base	100.0	124.6	119.0	130.1	143.0	166.3	138.6	147.4
Electricity [E] Electricité [E]	100.0	102.9	108.7	107.7	121.8	131.0	153.2	180.8
Kazakhstan Kazakhstan								
Total industry [CDE] Total, industrie [CDE]	100.0	113.8	125.7	137.2	151.5	158.7	170.2	177.8
Total mining [C] Total, industries extractives [C]	100.0	114.0	132.1	145.6	165.1	169.6	181.4	186.2
Total manufacturing [D] Total, industries manufacturières [D]	100.0	115.0	124.3	134.1	146.5	157.6	170.4	181.8
Food, beverages and tobacco Aliments, boissons et tabac	100.0	108.4	117.9	130.3	142.4	165.2	177.1	188.8
Textiles and wearing apparel Textiles et habillement	100.0	125.6	145.6	138.6	143.3	163.4	167.8	142.2
Chemicals and chemical products Produits chimiques	100.0	126.2	138.3	157.9	167.3	186.3	194.7	218.6
Metal and Metal Products, except machinery and equip. Metallurgie et travail des métaux à l'exclusion de la fabrication de machines et d'équipements	100.0	107.2	113.8	115.0	120.3	113.2	120.9	124.3
All machinery and transport equipment Fabrication de machines et de matériel de transport	100.0	141.2	154.8	188.2	247.8	309.1	369.0	403.7
Electricity, gas and water [E] Electricité, gaz et eau [E]	100.0	108.6	110.7	122.1	124.5	130.0	133.6	143.4
Korea, Republic of Corée, République de								
Total industry [CDE] Total, industrie [CDE]	100.0	100.5	108.6	114.7	126.5	134.6	145.9	155.9
Total mining [C] Total, industries extractives [C]	100.0	99.8	104.2	103.1	99.5	91.7	87.9	83.3
Total manufacturing [D] Total, industries manufacturières [D]	100.0	100.1	108.2	114.3	126.5	134.6	146.3	156.5
Food, beverages and tobacco Aliments, boissons et tabac	100.0	105.2	108.0	108.3	111.1	108.6	110.8	111.5
Textiles, wearing apparel, leather, footwear Textiles, habillement, cuir et chaussures	100.0	90.8	86.8	76.6	70.7	64.6	66.3	66.4

Country or area and industry [ISIC Rev. 3] Pays ou zone et industrie [CITI Rév. 3]	2000	2001	2002	2003	2004	2005	2006	2007
Chemicals, petroleum, rubber and plastic products								
Produits chimiques, pétroliers, caoutchouc et plastiques	100.0	101.1	104.2	107.8	112.6	115.9	120.9	127.5
Basic metals								
Métaux de base	100.0	101.3	106.4	111.8	117.6	117.9	122.3	127.5
Metal products								
Produits métalliques	100.0	99.9	110.1	116.2	130.0	138.9	151.5	163.6
Electricity and gas [E]								
Electricité et gaz [E]	100.0	106.9	115.0	121.3	128.5	137.6	143.2	149.7
Kyrgyzstan Kirghizistan								
Total industry [CDE]								
Total, industrie [CDE]	100.0	105.4	93.9	122.4	136.8	124.8	109.8	108.6
Total mining [C]								
Total, industries extractives [C]	100.0	100.2	101.8	100.2	147.9	143.6	139.3	138.4
Total manufacturing [D]								
Total, industries manufacturières [D]	100.0	109.3	97.1	130.8	145.6	129.3	106.9	101.9
Food, beverages and tobacco								
Aliments, boissons et tabac	100.0	94.0	102.0	110.0	115.0	114.3	123.7	129.0
Textiles and wearing apparel								
Textiles et habillement	100.0	116.0	135.0	132.0	184.0	208.6	248.4	315.9
Chemicals and chemical products								
Produits chimiques	100.0	107.0	179.0	191.0	272.9	236.9	211.7	299.1
Metal and Metal Products, except machinery and equip.								
Metallurgie et travail des métaux à l'exclusion de la fabrication de machines et d'équipements	100.0	114.0	79.0	99.0	94.3	71.8	46.1	45.9
All machinery and transport equipment								
Fabrication de machines et de matériel de transport	100.0	120.6	126.9	141.8	139.6	110.7	103.9	88.4
Electricity, gas and water [E]								
Electricité, gaz et eau [E]	100.0	92.2	81.6	98.6	108.1	109.3	114.7	127.2
Malaysia Malaisie								
Total industry [CDE]								
Total, industrie [CDE]	100.0	95.9	100.2	109.6	122.5	127.5	133.3	136.1
Total mining [C]								
Total, industries extractives [C]	100.0	102.8	104.6	110.2	117.0	117.6	111.2	113.6
Total manufacturing [D]								
Total, industries manufacturières [D]	100.0	93.4	97.6	107.8	123.0	129.3	139.0	141.6
Food, beverages and tobacco								
Aliments, boissons et tabac	100.0	106.4	112.6	125.4	130.0	139.5	146.8	153.0
Textiles, wearing apparel, leather, footwear								
Textiles, habillement, cuir et chaussures	100.0	93.6	88.5	84.9	78.3	82.0	86.2	78.8
Chemicals, petroleum, rubber and plastic products								
Produits chimiques, pétroliers, caoutchouc et plastiques	100.0	105.0	104.2	116.5	126.2	138.2	148.5	153.7
Basic metals								
Métaux de base	100.0	99.4	101.7	112.8	111.7	105.8	109.0	124.8
Metal products								
Produits métalliques	100.0	87.8	91.7	98.2	113.6	116.4	125.2	127.5
Electricity [E]								
Electricité [E]	100.0	108.6	118.7	126.7	137.2	145.1	152.5	158.4
Mongolia Mongolie								
Total industry [CDE]								
Total, industrie [CDE]	100.0	112.0	130.5	135.9	152.6	145.2	157.3	173.9
Total mining [C]								
Total, industries extractives [C]	100.0	106.8	103.1	102.5	119.5	134.5	139.3	141.1
Total manufacturing [D]								
Total, industries manufacturières [D]	100.0	128.0	209.9	232.0	252.2	189.6	246.7	340.9
Food and beverages								
Aliments et boissons	100.0	120.0	123.2	139.9	143.3	140.1	159.0	211.8
Textiles, wearing apparel, leather, footwear								
Textiles, habillement, cuir et chaussures	100.0	157.3	402.0	542.7	525.8	214.6	319.7	319.4
Chemicals and chemical products								
Produits chimiques	100.0	132.3	127.5	113.9	129.8	80.1	93.7	138.1

Country or area and industry [ISIC Rev. 3] Pays ou zone et industrie [CITI Rév. 3]	2000	2001	2002	2003	2004	2005	2006	2007
Basic metals 　Métaux de base	100.0	78.0	151.6	197.4	316.8	434.7	673.4	1 504.0
Electricity, gas and water [E] 　Electricité, gaz et eau [E]	100.0	103.1	107.1	108.5	115.9	120.4	122.0	126.3
Oman　Oman								
Total industry [CDE] 　Total, industrie [CDE]	100.0	104.0	103.6	98.9	99.2	102.9	106.9	...
Total mining [C] 　Total, industries extractives [C]	100.0	99.7	96.2	88.3	87.0	88.6	89.0	...
Total manufacturing [D] 　Total, industries manufacturières [D]	100.0	130.1	146.0	155.6	161.7	178.1	204.4	...
Electricity, gas and water [E] 　Electricité, gaz et eau [E]	100.0	106.8	115.2	128.6	143.9	148.8	154.1	...
Pakistan [1]　Pakistan [1]								
Total industry [CDE] [4] 　Total, industrie [CDE] [4]	100.0	107.5	117.6	132.7	152.4	167.0	177.4	182.1
Total mining [C] 　Total, industries extractives [C]	100.0	99.2	109.8	114.1	118.1	133.0	136.3	131.2
Total manufacturing [D] 　Total, industries manufacturières [D]	100.0	103.8	111.5	132.4	156.8	171.4	184.3	191.6
Electricity [E] 　Electricité [E]	100.0	119.6	135.5	139.6	153.5	167.7	174.7	176.1
Philippines　Philippines								
Total industry [CDE] [4] 　Total, industrie [CDE] [4]	100.0	99.4	94.6	95.3	97.1	99.3	91.2	79.1
Total mining [C] 　Total, industries extractives [C]	100.0	95.8	141.1	167.2	175.5	189.4	184.2	228.6
Total manufacturing [D] 　Total, industries manufacturières [D]	100.0	98.2	92.3	92.2	93.2	95.2	85.8	70.5
Food, beverages and tobacco 　Aliments, boissons et tabac	100.0	96.5	94.9	87.4	85.9	92.3	92.6	105.9
Textiles and wearing apparel 　Textiles et habillement	100.0	92.4	110.9	130.4	127.2	144.5	129.3	92.7
Chemicals, petroleum, rubber and plastic products 　Produits chimiques, pétroliers, caoutchouc et plastiques	100.0	85.7	75.2	70.7	77.3	82.8	78.4	58.1
Basic metals 　Métaux de base	100.0	91.3	82.5	106.8	135.4	106.8	145.7	144.2
Metal products 　Produits métalliques	100.0	102.2	103.0	98.9	104.3	99.7	79.3	76.7
Electricity and water [E] 　Electricité et eau [E]	100.0	107.9	105.7	109.0	116.7	118.7	119.5	123.5
Saudi Arabia　Arabie saoudite								
Total industry [CDE] 　Total, industrie [CDE]	100.0	98.3	93.7	107.3	114.4	123.4	125.7	...
Total mining [C] 　Total, industries extractives [C]	100.0	95.6	87.6	103.6	110.4	119.6	119.4	...
Total manufacturing [D] 　Total, industries manufacturières [D]	100.0	104.4	108.0	115.7	123.6	132.1	140.8	...
Electricity, gas and water [E] 　Electricité, gaz et eau [E]	100.0	111.1	116.3	123.5	131.5	138.6	147.5	...
Singapore　Singapour								
Total industry [DE] [4] 　Total, industrie [DE] [4]	100.0	91.0	98.0	100.8	112.9	123.0	135.7	143.5
Total manufacturing [D] 　Total, industries manufacturières [D]	100.0	88.4	95.9	98.8	112.6	123.1	137.8	146.0
Food, beverages and tobacco 　Aliments, boissons et tabac	100.0	104.2	101.3	101.0	102.8	110.1	114.4	127.2
Textiles, wearing apparel, leather, footwear 　Textiles, habillement, cuir et chaussures	100.0	85.5	71.5	70.0	68.1	58.1	53.0	47.4
Chemicals, petroleum, rubber and plastic products 　Produits chimiques, pétroliers, caoutchouc et plastiques	100.0	102.2	130.4	122.8	129.5	132.4	136.3	142.8

Country or area and industry [ISIC Rev. 3] Pays ou zone et industrie [CITI Rév. 3]	2000	2001	2002	2003	2004	2005	2006	2007
Basic metals								
Métaux de base	100.0	100.6	103.2	88.7	105.4	123.0	145.1	131.9
Metal products								
Produits métalliques	100.0	84.6	88.4	90.2	103.1	114.7	126.4	136.9
Electricity [E]								
Electricité [E]	100.0	104.5	109.5	111.6	115.0	122.7	124.3	129.9
Sri Lanka Sri Lanka								
Total manufacturing [D]								
Total, industries manufacturières [D]	100.0	103.6	108.1	108.9	112.2	116.2	120.4	126.8
Food, beverages and tobacco								
Aliments, boissons et tabac	100.0	102.8	107.1	113.0	117.1	123.0	130.2	138.4
Textiles, wearing apparel, leather, footwear								
Textiles, habillement, cuir et chaussures	100.0	98.0	95.7	93.3	100.9	105.4	109.3	116.2
Chemicals, petroleum, rubber and plastic products								
Produits chimiques, pétroliers, caoutchouc et plastiques	100.0	103.1	104.8	109.1	114.6	130.5	140.6	150.7
Basic metals								
Métaux de base	100.0	101.6	105.8	109.7	119.0	126.4	134.1	143.0
Metal products								
Produits métalliques	100.0	102.5	105.8	108.3	111.2	114.3	118.6	124.3
Syrian Arab Republic Rép. arabe syrienne								
Total industry [CDE]								
Total, industrie [CDE]	100.0	106.0	112.0	105.0	95.0	91.0	91.0	88.0
Total mining [C]								
Total, industries extractives [C]	100.0	106.0	113.0	109.0	85.0	78.0	75.0	69.0
Total manufacturing [D]								
Total, industries manufacturières [D]	100.0	106.0	110.0	98.0	109.0	107.0	111.0	111.0
Food, beverages and tobacco								
Aliments, boissons et tabac	100.0	104.3	115.0	110.4	118.3	111.0	119.5	121.3
Textiles, wearing apparel, leather, footwear								
Textiles, habillement, cuir et chaussures	100.0	106.4	111.6	103.9	114.2	114.6	112.2	104.8
Chemicals, petroleum, rubber and plastic products								
Produits chimiques, pétroliers, caoutchouc et plastiques	100.0	122.1	114.7	102.9	119.4	104.0	97.4	94.3
Basic metals								
Métaux de base	100.0	109.0	95.0	92.0	84.0	94.0	90.0	79.0
Metal products								
Produits métalliques	100.0	182.4	148.0	118.0	150.9	143.1	146.9	119.5
Electricity and water [E]								
Electricité et eau [E]	100.0	107.1	113.1	119.4	127.6	145.8	148.0	152.0
Tajikistan Tadjikistan								
Total industry [CDE]								
Total, industrie [CDE]	100.0	114.6	124.4	139.0	156.1	173.2	182.9	...
Total mining [C]								
Total, industries extractives [C]	100.0	103.8	110.0	123.7	122.5	123.7	132.1	...
Total manufacturing [D]								
Total, industries manufacturières [D]	100.0	116.7	127.8	138.9	163.9	183.3	191.7	...
Electricity, gas and water [E]								
Electricité, gaz et eau [E]	100.0	103.7	112.1	119.6	116.8	122.4	129.0	...
Thailand Thaïlande								
Total manufacturing [D]								
Total, industries manufacturières [D]	100.0	102.7	112.0	127.8	142.7	155.6	167.1	180.7
Turkey Turquie								
Total industry [CDE]								
Total, industrie [CDE]	100.0	91.3	99.9	108.7	119.2	125.7	133.1	140.2
Total mining [C]								
Total, industries extractives [C]	100.0	91.9	84.4	81.5	84.8	96.5	100.7	110.4
Total manufacturing [D]								
Total, industries manufacturières [D]	100.0	90.5	100.4	109.7	121.1	126.9	134.0	140.4
Food, beverages and tobacco								
Aliments, boissons et tabac	100.0	98.6	101.9	107.3	103.3	110.3	119.6	120.0
Textiles, wearing apparel, leather, footwear								
Textiles, habillement, cuir et chaussures	100.0	94.9	104.3	106.2	106.7	93.5	92.0	94.0

Country or area and industry [ISIC Rev. 3] Pays ou zone et industrie [CITI Rév. 3]	2000	2001	2002	2003	2004	2005	2006	2007
Chemicals, petroleum, rubber and plastic products								
Produits chimiques, pétroliers, caoutchouc et plastiques	100.0	97.5	108.6	116.1	122.5	129.2	131.2	140.0
Basic metals								
Métaux de base	100.0	95.0	104.6	117.0	130.6	135.0	149.3	166.8
Metal products								
Produits métalliques	100.0	76.7	92.4	109.3	142.7	156.5	175.8	184.9
Electricity, gas and water [E]								
Electricité, gaz et eau [E]	100.0	98.3	103.6	112.3	120.0	129.1	140.8	153.0
Turkmenistan Turkménistan								
Total industry [CDE]								
Total, industrie [CDE]	100.0	130.0	157.0	187.0	...	...	...	...
Uzbekistan Ouzbékistan								
Total industry [CDE]								
Total, industrie [CDE]	100.0	107.6	116.5	123.5	135.1	144.9	160.5	...
Viet Nam Viet Nam								
Total industry [CDE]								
Total, industrie [CDE]	100.0	116.3	131.6	153.8	179.3	210.1	245.7	288.0
Total mining [C]								
Total, industries extractives [C]	100.0	105.5	110.9	119.9	137.1	140.3	138.3	140.5
Total manufacturing [D]								
Total, industries manufacturières [D]	100.0	117.6	135.2	160.0	187.4	223.4	266.3	316.3
Food, beverages and tobacco								
Aliments, boissons et tabac	100.0	114.4	128.9	149.0	171.7	198.0	232.7	276.3
Textiles, wearing apparel, leather, footwear								
Textiles, habillement, cuir et chaussures	100.0	113.6	127.2	154.3	183.7	215.8	265.0	323.8
Chemicals, petroleum, rubber and plastic products								
Produits chimiques, pétroliers, caoutchouc et plastiques	100.0	119.6	139.2	156.8	195.3	240.9	283.7	332.5
Basic metals								
Métaux de base	100.0	122.0	144.0	176.4	189.8	235.9	265.6	311.6
Metal products								
Produits métalliques	100.0	123.5	147.0	179.5	211.5	266.2	323.6	391.9
Electricity, gas and water [E]								
Electricité, gaz et eau [E]	100.0	123.2	132.4	150.7	169.6	194.3	221.1	252.6
Europe · Europe								
Albania Albanie								
Total industry [CDE]								
Total, industrie [CDE]	100.0	75.3	88.9	101.1	103.6	119.6	...	...
Total mining [C]								
Total, industries extractives [C]	100.0	88.3	91.8	164.8	143.3	159.2	...	...
Total manufacturing [D]								
Total, industries manufacturières [D]	100.0	66.9	75.9	82.1	92.3	126.0	...	...
Electricity, gas and water [E]								
Electricité, gaz et eau [E]	100.0	77.9	102.8	116.4	102.3	86.8	...	...
Austria Autriche								
Total industry [CDE]								
Total, industrie [CDE]	100.0	103.0	103.8	106.0	112.6	117.3	125.9	132.1
Total mining [C]								
Total, industries extractives [C]	100.0	97.6	100.7	100.2	94.6	93.0	102.3	101.7
Total manufacturing [D]								
Total, industries manufacturières [D]	100.0	102.0	101.9	104.3	111.9	116.5	125.1	132.0
Food, beverages and tobacco								
Aliments, boissons et tabac	100.0	101.5	104.8	104.9	106.1	108.6	113.7	115.8
Textiles, wearing apparel, leather, footwear								
Textiles, habillement, cuir et chaussures	100.0	97.4	96.4	94.7	86.8	82.5	80.0	78.2
Chemicals, petroleum, rubber and plastic products								
Produits chimiques, pétroliers, caoutchouc et plastiques	100.0	104.0	97.9	101.0	107.1	114.4	123.9	133.1
Basic metals								
Métaux de base	100.0	106.2	107.2	107.8	117.3	122.2	130.6	137.6

24

Index numbers of industrial production *(continued)*
2000 = 100
Indices de la production industrielle *(suite)*
2000 = 100

Country or area and industry [ISIC Rev. 3] Pays ou zone et industrie [CITI Rév. 3]	2000	2001	2002	2003	2004	2005	2006	2007
Metal products								
Produits métalliques	100.0	102.1	102.9	105.6	118.4	125.5	137.2	146.8
Electricity, gas and water [E]								
Electricité, gaz et eau [E]	100.0	112.5	119.7	120.5	120.9	127.1	134.9	136.4
Belarus Bélarus								
Total industry [CDE]								
Total, industrie [CDE]	100.0	106.1	111.0	118.9	137.9	152.5	169.4	184.3
Total mining [C]								
Total, industries extractives [C]	100.0	111.2	114.7	125.5	136.9	147.7	151.6	161.1
Total manufacturing [D]								
Total, industries manufacturières [D]	100.0	105.6	110.4	118.1	137.3	151.7	169.3	184.1
Electricity [E]								
Electricité [E]	100.0	98.9	101.9	102.8	115.8	115.0	118.5	117.0
Belgium Belgique								
Total industry [CDE]								
Total, industrie [CDE]	100.0	99.6	101.0	101.7	105.2	104.8	110.0	113.0
Total mining [C]								
Total, industries extractives [C]	100.0	101.0	131.9	125.9	127.4	135.2	141.6	144.3
Total manufacturing [D]								
Total, industries manufacturières [D]	100.0	99.9	100.8	101.3	105.6	103.5	108.5	111.7
Food, beverages and tobacco								
Aliments, boissons et tabac	100.0	103.6	108.6	112.2	117.8	119.8	124.5	130.7
Textiles, wearing apparel, leather, footwear								
Textiles, habillement, cuir et chaussures	100.0	94.7	89.8	85.5	87.1	82.5	88.5	90.0
Chemicals, petroleum, rubber and plastic products								
Produits chimiques, pétroliers, caoutchouc et plastiques	100.0	97.9	104.9	110.7	116.7	111.7	114.9	114.3
Basic metals								
Métaux de base	100.0	88.6	89.3	91.6	83.8	69.6	72.1	72.9
Metal products								
Produits métalliques	100.0	104.0	100.5	97.3	104.9	106.5	114.1	121.0
Electricity, gas and water [E]								
Electricité, gaz et eau [E]	100.0	97.4	99.8	102.4	100.3	110.9	118.0	119.2
Bulgaria Bulgarie								
Total industry [CDE]								
Total, industrie [CDE]	100.0	98.9	106.9	122.0	142.8	152.3	161.3	176.2
Total mining [C]								
Total, industries extractives [C]	100.0	91.3	90.8	97.1	117.4	117.8	119.8	110.7
Total manufacturing [D]								
Total, industries manufacturières [D]	100.0	101.4	108.9	129.3	156.7	169.4	181.8	196.8
Food, beverages and tobacco								
Aliments, boissons et tabac	100.0	96.6	97.2	115.1	133.3	139.8	139.6	155.6
Textiles, wearing apparel, leather, footwear								
Textiles, habillement, cuir et chaussures	100.0	110.5	135.6	174.5	199.7	196.6	217.5	227.0
Chemicals, petroleum, rubber and plastic products								
Produits chimiques, pétroliers, caoutchouc et plastiques	100.0	101.2	96.7	112.6	117.2	129.0	129.1	138.6
Basic metals								
Métaux de base	100.0	83.7	90.1	112.8	191.5	205.9	219.7	216.1
Metal products								
Produits métalliques	100.0	107.6	126.4	141.3	170.9	198.7	217.7	247.0
Electricity, gas and water [E]								
Electricité, gaz et eau [E]	100.0	108.4	106.9	109.9	113.1	117.2	118.8	141.3
Croatia Croatie								
Total industry [CDE]								
Total, industrie [CDE]	100.0	106.0	111.8	116.3	120.6	126.7	138.9	139.8
Total mining [C]								
Total, industries extractives [C]	100.0	102.0	119.4	122.1	118.1	114.6	125.5	129.9
Total manufacturing [D]								
Total, industries manufacturières [D]	100.0	106.4	111.1	116.8	121.5	129.5	139.2	144.2
Food, beverages and tobacco								
Aliments, boissons et tabac	100.0	106.6	112.5	118.2	121.6	128.3	132.8	139.6
Textiles, wearing apparel, leather, footwear								
Textiles, habillement, cuir et chaussures	100.0	104.4	93.9	89.1	75.3	70.2	69.1	72.2

24

Index numbers of industrial production *(continued)*
2000 = 100
Indices de la production industrielle *(suite)*
2000 = 100

Country or area and industry [ISIC Rev. 3] Pays ou zone et industrie [CITI Rév. 3]	2000	2001	2002	2003	2004	2005	2006	2007
Chemicals, petroleum, rubber and plastic products								
Produits chimiques, pétroliers, caoutchouc et plastiques	100.0	95.3	99.3	98.8	102.0	100.0	91.1	95.1
Basic metals								
Métaux de base	100.0	104.2	93.9	98.7	123.9	129.7	134.4	133.9
Metal products								
Produits métalliques	100.0	115.3	120.0	125.4	134.2	150.0	157.8	171.4
Electricity, gas and water [E]								
Electricité, gaz et eau [E]	100.0	104.8	106.6	110.1	114.7	113.5	154.9	116.7
Czech Republic République tchèque								
Total industry [CDE]								
Total, industrie [CDE]	100.0	106.7	108.7	114.7	125.7	134.0	149.0	162.4
Total mining [C]								
Total, industries extractives [C]	100.0	100.8	101.7	102.0	101.4	101.9	104.5	102.7
Total manufacturing [D]								
Total, industries manufacturières [D]	100.0	107.4	109.6	115.5	127.9	137.6	154.2	169.3
Food, beverages and tobacco								
Aliments, boissons et tabac	100.0	102.0	103.6	103.8	102.4	98.7	99.3	101.5
Textiles, wearing apparel, leather, footwear								
Textiles, habillement, cuir et chaussures	100.0	101.2	93.6	91.6	90.6	90.4	84.6	84.2
Chemicals, petroleum, rubber and plastic products								
Produits chimiques, pétroliers, caoutchouc et plastiques	100.0	107.5	110.9	118.6	131.3	143.6	155.4	169.7
Basic metals								
Métaux de base	100.0	101.7	98.3	110.7	120.6	112.6	123.6	109.6
Metal products								
Produits métalliques	100.0	110.6	117.0	124.4	145.8	164.4	196.0	231.9
Electricity, gas and water [E]								
Electricité, gaz et eau [E]	100.0	101.7	101.8	110.8	111.9	110.5	113.4	115.3
Denmark Danemark								
Total industry [CDE]								
Total, industrie [CDE]	100.0	101.6	103.0	103.2	103.2	104.9	108.6	109.0
Total mining [C]								
Total, industries extractives [C]	100.0	98.4	104.0	102.1	107.3	111.9	105.8	95.2
Total manufacturing [D]								
Total, industries manufacturières [D]	100.0	102.0	103.0	102.3	102.0	103.8	108.1	112.3
Food, beverages and tobacco								
Aliments, boissons et tabac	100.0	100.0	107.5	114.2	110.8	109.7	111.0	118.8
Textiles, wearing apparel, leather, footwear								
Textiles, habillement, cuir et chaussures	100.0	90.3	85.3	81.3	67.5	65.5	67.0	59.6
Chemicals, petroleum, rubber and plastic products								
Produits chimiques, pétroliers, caoutchouc et plastiques	100.0	106.9	108.7	105.9	98.6	108.9	107.6	103.8
Basic metals								
Métaux de base	100.0	90.7	68.6	73.4	67.8	66.4	65.6	70.5
Metal products								
Produits métalliques	100.0	104.7	105.9	104.2	106.7	106.9	115.8	125.2
Electricity, gas and water [E]								
Electricité, gaz et eau [E]	100.0	103.7	101.9	120.5	112.3	105.6	123.2	90.7
Estonia Estonie								
Total industry [CDE]								
Total, industrie [CDE]	100.0	108.9	117.8	130.7	144.4	160.3	176.2	188.0
Total mining [C]								
Total, industries extractives [C]	100.0	103.6	119.6	125.8	114.7	127.7	139.1	154.1
Total manufacturing [D]								
Total, industries manufacturières [D]	100.0	110.2	119.8	132.7	148.8	166.4	184.5	193.9
Food, beverages and tobacco								
Aliments, boissons et tabac	100.0	109.8	112.0	114.8	120.7	127.2	135.3	139.3
Textiles, wearing apparel, leather, footwear								
Textiles, habillement, cuir et chaussures	100.0	110.8	117.9	124.0	119.7	111.0	114.6	107.5
Chemicals, rubber and plastic products								
Produits chimiques, caoutchouc et plastiques	100.0	112.3	123.8	148.9	173.3	199.1	231.3	239.7
Basic metals								
Métaux de base	100.0	153.3	199.1	343.1	268.3	243.4	247.5	380.7

Country or area and industry [ISIC Rev. 3] Pays ou zone et industrie [CITI Rév. 3]	2000	2001	2002	2003	2004	2005	2006	2007
Metal products Produits métalliques	100.0	116.2	136.2	156.3	191.9	224.2	253.4	287.2
Electricity and gas [E] Electricité et gaz [E]	100.0	101.2	101.8	116.3	118.7	117.5	113.2	131.3
Finland Finlande								
Total industry [CDE] Total, industrie [CDE]	100.0	100.1	102.2	103.4	109.0	109.1	119.4	124.7
Total mining [C] Total, industries extractives [C]	100.0	120.7	131.9	132.5	116.2	152.0	191.9	150.7
Total manufacturing [D] Total, industries manufacturières [D]	100.0	99.5	101.5	101.9	108.1	109.3	118.8	125.2
Food, beverages and tobacco Aliments, boissons et tabac	100.0	103.8	106.5	108.6	109.7	107.6	107.6	110.0
Textiles, wearing apparel, leather, footwear Textiles, habillement, cuir et chaussures	100.0	101.9	99.8	91.5	89.6	89.3	90.5	89.0
Chemicals, petroleum, rubber and plastic products Produits chimiques, pétroliers, caoutchouc et plastiques	100.0	99.0	98.7	98.6	102.6	102.1	109.4	111.0
Basic metals Métaux de base	100.0	99.7	100.5	103.1	107.5	99.6	103.8	94.5
Metal products Produits métalliques	100.0	99.9	103.8	104.2	116.3	120.5	134.0	149.2
Electricity, gas and water [E] Electricité, gaz et eau [E]	100.0	105.6	107.0	118.8	120.3	101.0	116.1	114.4
France France								
Total industry [CDE] Total, industrie [CDE]	100.0	101.3	100.0	99.7	102.0	102.3	102.8	104.1
Total mining [C] Total, industries extractives [C]	100.0	98.9	93.9	92.7	91.9	89.5	91.9	92.9
Total manufacturing [D] Total, industries manufacturières [D]	100.0	101.1	99.7	98.9	101.4	102.3	102.4	104.0
Food, beverages and tobacco Aliments, beverages et tabac	100.0	100.8	103.3	102.2	102.6	102.6	103.6	105.9
Textiles, wearing apparel, leather, footwear Textiles, habillement, cuir et chaussures	100.0	93.2	81.4	71.8	65.7	57.4	52.8	50.8
Chemicals, petroleum, rubber and plastic products Produits chimiques, pétroliers, caoutchouc et plastiques	100.0	102.2	102.3	105.2	108.5	110.5	111.9	115.2
Basic metals Métaux de base	100.0	97.8	95.7	92.7	95.0	91.1	93.0	91.1
Metal products Produits métalliques	100.0	102.5	101.0	100.0	103.4	104.5	105.6	107.7
Electricity, gas and water [E] Electricité, gaz et eau [E]	100.0	103.2	103.2	106.1	108.1	108.3	107.2	106.5
Germany Allemagne								
Total industry [CDE] Total, industrie [CDE]	100.0	100.1	99.1	99.5	102.5	106.0	112.2	119.1
Total mining [C] Total, industries extractives [C]	100.0	93.4	92.0	91.2	88.3	86.9	84.2	83.7
Total manufacturing [D] Total, industries manufacturières [D]	100.0	100.4	99.3	99.5	102.6	106.4	113.3	121.1
Food, beverages and tobacco Aliments, boissons et tabac	100.0	99.4	99.9	99.6	100.5	104.7	106.6	109.0
Textiles, wearing apparel, leather, footwear Textiles, habillement, cuir et chaussures	100.0	95.7	87.9	81.7	79.1	75.0	71.7	71.3
Chemicals, petroleum, rubber and plastic products Produits chimiques, pétroliers, caoutchouc et plastiques	100.0	98.4	100.9	101.4	104.6	108.6	112.8	118.5
Basic metals Métaux de base	100.0	101.2	101.9	99.9	103.6	104.5	111.7	118.0
Metal products Produits métalliques	100.0	102.6	101.2	102.3	106.7	111.9	121.7	132.8
Electricity and gas [E] Electricité et gaz [E]	100.0	98.1	98.4	102.1	104.7	104.8	105.9	102.2

Country or area and industry [ISIC Rev. 3] Pays ou zone et industrie [CITI Rév. 3]	2000	2001	2002	2003	2004	2005	2006	2007
Greece Grèce								
Total industry [CDE]								
Total, industrie [CDE]	100.0	98.2	99.0	99.3	100.5	99.4	100.1	102.3
Total mining [C]								
Total, industries extractives [C]	100.0	102.4	112.3	106.5	106.6	100.9	98.0	97.1
Total manufacturing [D]								
Total, industries manufacturières [D]	100.0	97.5	97.4	97.0	98.1	97.4	98.2	99.9
Food, beverages and tobacco								
Aliments, boissons et tabac	100.0	101.7	102.9	100.8	106.8	105.2	106.7	109.8
Textiles, wearing apparel, leather, footwear								
Textiles, habillement, cuir et chaussures	100.0	93.3	88.8	86.5	80.0	67.7	59.6	64.0
Chemicals, petroleum, rubber and plastic products								
Produits chimiques, pétroliers, caoutchouc et plastiques	100.0	101.0	104.2	105.2	107.1	108.2	106.9	112.2
Basic metals								
Métaux de base	100.0	103.8	110.9	109.2	114.8	116.8	120.2	120.8
Metal products								
Produits métalliques	100.0	91.0	87.2	88.9	89.7	90.1	94.4	92.6
Electricity and gas [E]								
Electricité et gaz [E]	100.0	99.2	100.8	108.1	109.6	110.6	109.9	115.1
Hungary Hongrie								
Total industry [CDE]								
Total, industrie [CDE]	100.0	103.9	107.3	114.4	122.9	131.6	145.1	157.0
Total mining [C]								
Total, industries extractives [C]	100.0	116.4	105.4	101.8	111.9	108.2	125.6	104.2
Total manufacturing [D]								
Total, industries manufacturières [D]	100.0	104.2	107.9	115.5	125.3	134.8	149.5	162.6
Food, beverages and tobacco								
Aliments, boissons et tabac	100.0	99.7	101.1	99.9	95.9	90.9	92.0	88.5
Textiles, wearing apparel, leather, footwear								
Textiles, habillement, cuir et chaussures	100.0	102.9	97.8	88.8	83.5	75.4	76.9	76.3
Chemicals, petroleum, rubber and plastic products								
Produits chimiques, pétroliers, caoutchouc et plastiques	100.0	101.0	104.7	107.0	114.1	122.1	127.3	134.4
Basic metals								
Métaux de base	100.0	96.6	100.7	108.9	116.6	111.3	127.7	119.8
Metal products								
Produits métalliques	100.0	114.7	121.6	129.1	145.8	160.7	185.9	211.7
Electricity and gas [E]								
Electricité et gaz [E]	100.0	100.4	104.3	108.6	107.7	108.3	109.3	113.2
Ireland Irlande								
Total industry [CDE]								
Total, industrie [CDE]	100.0	110.1	118.0	123.5	123.9	127.6	134.1	143.8
Total mining [C]								
Total, industries extractives [C]	100.0	99.9	95.0	115.7	113.2	112.8	123.0	128.2
Total manufacturing [D]								
Total, industries manufacturières [D]	100.0	110.4	118.7	124.1	124.3	128.2	135.0	144.9
Food, beverages and tobacco								
Aliments, boissons et tabac	100.0	106.5	110.7	114.8	120.6	122.1	127.8	129.9
Textiles, wearing apparel, leather, footwear								
Textiles, habillement, cuir et chaussures	100.0	104.9	73.4	65.1	63.6	54.0	44.5	39.3
Chemicals, rubber and plastic products								
Produits chimiques, caoutchouc et plastiques	100.0	121.4	149.7	156.0	141.9	142.5	147.7	158.8
Basic metals								
Métaux de base	100.0	89.5	88.1	84.3	80.0	91.2	95.3	106.2
Metal products								
Produits métalliques	100.0	106.3	100.7	106.2	111.9	118.4	127.0	132.9
Electricity, gas and water [E]								
Electricité, gaz et eau [E]	100.0	106.5	110.0	113.2	117.8	119.8	120.6	124.4
Italy Italie								
Total industry [CDE]								
Total, industrie [CDE]	100.0	99.2	97.9	96.9	97.8	96.0	97.9	98.4
Total mining [C]								
Total, industries extractives [C]	100.0	92.3	107.9	110.0	107.7	116.0	112.5	113.4

Country or area and industry [ISIC Rev. 3] Pays ou zone et industrie [CITI Rév. 3]	2000	2001	2002	2003	2004	2005	2006	2007
Total manufacturing [D] Total, industries manufacturières [D]	100.0	99.2	97.3	95.6	96.3	93.9	95.8	96.4
Food, beverages and tobacco Aliments, boissons et tabac	100.0	103.7	104.9	107.0	106.6	107.5	108.0	107.7
Textiles, wearing apparel, leather, footwear Textiles, habillement, cuir et chaussures	100.0	99.6	92.3	88.9	85.3	78.3	77.7	79.4
Chemicals, petroleum, rubber and plastic products Produits chimiques, pétroliers, caoutchouc et plastiques	100.0	98.1	98.9	97.9	99.3	97.6	99.9	100.8
Basic metals Métaux de base	100.0	96.0	94.9	96.2	100.6	101.1	107.5	107.5
Metal products Produits métalliques	100.0	98.4	95.6	92.8	93.6	91.0	95.0	95.6
Electricity and gas [E] Electricité et gaz [E]	100.0	100.6	102.0	107.2	111.2	113.8	115.7	115.5
Latvia Lettonie								
Total industry [CDE] Total, industrie [CDE]	100.0	106.9	113.1	120.5	127.7	134.9	141.4	142.1
Total mining [C] Total, industries extractives [C]	100.0	104.8	114.3	120.4	133.6	167.7	183.3	208.3
Total manufacturing [D] Total, industries manufacturières [D]	100.0	107.5	114.2	123.2	130.8	139.3	146.0	144.5
Food, beverages and tobacco Aliments, boissons et tabac	100.0	105.2	111.3	118.1	125.7	132.0	138.3	136.7
Textiles, wearing apparel, leather, footwear Textiles, habillement, cuir et chaussures	100.0	103.8	103.5	99.9	99.0	107.4	117.9	117.9
Chemicals, rubber and plastic products Produits chimiques, caoutchouc et plastiques	100.0	112.2	*129.6	123.2	145.8	168.6	203.0	210.3
Basic metals Métaux de base	100.0	116.6	114.6	140.1	151.5	143.9	148.0	149.2
Metal products Produits métalliques	100.0	108.2	116.5	136.7	147.1	157.4	165.5	171.4
Electricity, gas and water [E] Electricité, gaz et eau [E]	100.0	105.4	110.0	113.1	118.8	122.3	127.1	132.4
Lithuania Lituanie								
Total industry [CDE] Total, industrie [CDE]	100.0	116.0	119.5	138.8	153.9	164.8	176.9	183.9
Total mining [C] Total, industries extractives [C]	100.0	132.8	126.6	137.2	126.8	116.8	115.5	116.7
Total manufacturing [D] Total, industries manufacturières [D]	100.0	115.8	119.1	135.9	152.0	165.1	179.4	187.1
Food, beverages and tobacco Aliments, boissons et tabac	100.0	102.3	100.4	109.8	114.2	124.9	140.9	161.4
Textiles, wearing apparel, leather, footwear Textiles, habillement, cuir et chaussures	100.0	109.6	109.0	105.7	104.6	100.2	107.7	108.8
Chemicals, petroleum, rubber and plastic products Produits chimiques, pétroliers, caoutchouc et plastiques	100.0	126.9	132.3	152.0	175.0	194.7	209.7	214.1
Basic metals Métaux de base	100.0	103.7	82.5	60.8	47.3	58.9	50.1	62.7
Metal products Produits métalliques	100.0	115.2	123.2	145.5	179.1	207.1	256.8	327.4
Electricity, gas and water [E] Electricité, gaz et eau [E]	100.0	115.1	121.3	157.3	168.8	168.7	168.7	172.6
Luxembourg Luxembourg								
Total industry [CDE] Total, industrie [CDE]	100.0	103.5	106.0	109.8	114.1	114.8	117.2	117.5
Total mining [C] Total, industries extractives [C]	100.0	101.0	91.9	81.5	80.0	78.7	61.7	62.7
Total manufacturing [D] Total, industries manufacturières [D]	100.0	102.5	104.3	108.6	113.5	115.5	117.7	118.8
Food and beverages Aliments et boissons	100.0	113.4	115.7	113.7	117.3	126.2	117.4	117.8

24 Index numbers of industrial production *(continued)*
2000 = 100
Indices de la production industrielle *(suite)*
2000 = 100

Country or area and industry [ISIC Rev. 3] Pays ou zone et industrie [CITI Rév. 3]	2000	2001	2002	2003	2004	2005	2006	2007
Textiles, wearing apparel, leather, footwear								
Textiles, habillement, cuir et chaussures	100.0	102.0	104.1	108.4	108.6	113.2	115.5	114.7
Chemicals, rubber and plastic products								
Produits chimiques, caoutchouc et plastiques	100.0	107.5	116.5	124.1	129.8	134.0	134.6	133.5
Basic metals								
Métaux de base	100.0	98.6	95.6	98.1	101.7	91.9	107.0	107.0
Metal products								
Produits métalliques	100.0	95.3	95.2	97.7	97.9	108.7	111.7	119.6
Electricity and gas [E]								
Electricité et gaz [E]	100.0	108.8	115.8	119.9	121.4	120.4	117.3	112.3
Malta Malte								
Total industry [CDE]								
Total, industrie [CDE]	100.0	91.9	...	...	...	...	...	...
Total mining [C]								
Total, industries extractives [C]	100.0	101.9	...	...	...	...	...	...
Total manufacturing [D]								
Total, industries manufacturières [D]	100.0	90.8	...	...	...	...	...	...
Food, beverages and tobacco								
Aliments, boissons et tabac	100.0	98.5	...	...	...	...	...	...
Textiles, wearing apparel, leather, footwear								
Textiles, habillement, cuir et chaussures	100.0	103.7	...	...	...	...	...	...
Chemicals, petroleum, rubber and plastic products								
Produits chimiques, pétroliers, caoutchouc et plastiques	100.0	89.5	...	...	...	...	...	...
Metal products								
Produits métalliques	100.0	94.9	...	...	...	...	...	...
Electricity and water [E]								
Electricité et eau [E]	100.0	103.2	...	...	...	...	...	...
Netherlands Pays-Bas								
Total industry [CDE]								
Total, industrie [CDE]	100.0	101.0	101.9	100.5	104.6	105.0	106.5	109.0
Total mining [C]								
Total, industries extractives [C]	100.0	107.1	107.5	104.2	115.5	95.1	91.0	92.0
Total manufacturing [D]								
Total, industries manufacturières [D]	100.0	99.8	99.9	98.8	102.2	104.2	107.1	110.5
Food, beverages and tobacco								
Aliments, boissons et tabac	100.0	100.1	102.0	101.6	102.9	107.1	109.7	111.2
Textiles, wearing apparel, leather, footwear								
Textiles, habillement, cuir et chaussures	100.0	98.3	94.0	91.9	80.2	81.0	84.9	87.6
Chemicals, petroleum, rubber and plastic products								
Produits chimiques, pétroliers, caoutchouc et plastiques	100.0	104.1	114.8	114.8	121.1	123.2	127.4	132.0
Basic metals								
Métaux de base	100.0	98.8	101.4	105.0	118.7	115.0	113.2	118.7
Metal products								
Produits métalliques	100.0	96.3	90.0	88.8	93.2	95.9	99.4	104.8
Electricity, gas and water [E]								
Electricité, gaz et eau [E]	100.0	104.0	115.7	113.9	114.4	131.7	130.1	129.2
Norway Norvège								
Total industry [CDE]								
Total, industrie [CDE]	100.0	98.6	99.4	95.4	97.5	96.8	94.5	93.7
Total mining [C] [9]								
Total, industries extractives [C] [9]	100.0	103.0	101.3	99.7	98.4	95.3	90.6	86.6
Total manufacturing [D]								
Total, industries manufacturières [D]	100.0	98.9	98.1	93.9	95.2	98.2	102.5	106.7
Food, beverages and tobacco								
Aliments, boissons et tabac	100.0	99.1	97.5	93.6	93.6	91.0	92.0	93.0
Textiles, wearing apparel, leather, footwear								
Textiles, habillement, cuir et chaussures	100.0	95.2	87.0	75.0	72.0	72.5	79.8	77.2
Chemicals, petroleum, rubber and plastic products								
Produits chimiques, pétroliers, caoutchouc et plastiques	100.0	99.9	98.8	98.4	100.7	104.1	105.3	107.7
Basic metals								
Métaux de base	100.0	95.7	93.8	94.2	103.7	102.8	104.5	105.6

24
Index numbers of industrial production *(continued)*
2000 = 100
Indices de la production industrielle *(suite)*
2000 = 100

Country or area and industry [ISIC Rev. 3] Pays ou zone et industrie [CITI Rév. 3]	2000	2001	2002	2003	2004	2005	2006	2007
Metal products								
Produits métalliques	100.0	100.3	102.1	95.3	95.4	101.1	112.0	121.8
Electricity and gas [E]								
Electricité et gaz [E]	100.0	85.1	90.7	75.0	76.2	95.0	83.9	94.5
Poland Pologne								
Total industry [CDE]								
Total, industrie [CDE]	100.0	100.4	101.8	110.7	124.8	129.9	145.5	159.4
Total mining [C]								
Total, industries extractives [C]	100.0	94.9	92.0	90.3	93.0	90.4	91.7	89.2
Total manufacturing [D]								
Total, industries manufacturières [D]	100.0	99.9	101.7	112.4	128.8	134.7	153.1	169.6
Food, beverages and tobacco								
Aliments, boissons et tabac	100.0	102.5	106.1	111.6	118.3	123.7	132.1	141.5
Textiles, wearing apparel, leather, footwear								
Textiles, habillement, cuir et chaussures	100.0	96.3	95.6	95.0	95.4	88.1	92.3	97.8
Chemicals, petroleum, rubber and plastic products								
Produits chimiques, pétroliers, caoutchouc et plastiques	100.0	103.8	108.1	122.2	135.4	140.4	157.8	168.7
Basic metals								
Métaux de base	100.0	84.1	80.5	83.8	100.7	94.0	107.8	114.6
Metal products								
Produits métalliques	100.0	101.0	103.7	119.1	144.9	161.2	190.6	225.9
Electricity, gas and water [E]								
Electricité, gaz et eau [E]	100.0	108.1	107.9	108.4	109.6	112.9	113.1	116.1
Portugal Portugal								
Total industry [CDE]								
Total, industrie [CDE]	100.0	103.1	102.6	102.7	100.0	100.3	103.1	104.9
Total mining [C]								
Total, industries extractives [C]	100.0	101.9	96.5	87.4	91.1	89.1	80.3	88.6
Total manufacturing [D]								
Total, industries manufacturières [D]	100.0	102.3	102.7	102.2	101.4	99.8	102.1	105.4
Food, beverages and tobacco								
Aliments, boissons et tabac	100.0	102.0	104.9	104.4	107.0	106.8	110.7	116.0
Textiles, wearing apparel, leather, footwear								
Textiles, habillement, cuir et chaussures	100.0	100.8	95.6	88.1	81.8	74.2	70.1	68.1
Chemicals, petroleum, rubber and plastic products								
Produits chimiques, pétroliers, caoutchouc et plastiques	100.0	98.6	103.9	106.9	106.9	110.2	111.6	114.7
Basic metals								
Métaux de base	100.0	92.4	93.1	91.9	94.5	90.7	99.0	103.2
Metal products								
Produits métalliques	100.0	105.2	104.3	101.6	99.8	98.7	104.8	111.9
Electricity and gas [E]								
Electricité et gaz [E]	100.0	109.0	103.3	108.9	91.2	104.1	113.8	103.2
Republic of Moldova République de Moldova								
Total industry [CDE]								
Total, industrie [CDE]	100.0	113.7	126.0	145.7	157.6	168.7	160.6	158.5
Total mining [C]								
Total, industries extractives [C]	100.0	109.0	135.3	170.7	211.0	220.0	281.4	291.5
Total manufacturing [D]								
Total, industries manufacturières [D]	100.0	115.1	130.4	153.9	168.2	179.3	167.7	164.6
Food, beverages and tobacco								
Aliments, boissons et tabac	100.0	108.6	105.1	119.3	122.9	126.5	102.3	94.4
Textiles, wearing apparel, leather, footwear								
Textiles, habillement, cuir et chaussures	100.0	119.6	136.8	150.1	174.5	178.8	204.0	216.2
Chemicals, rubber and plastic products								
Produits chimiques, caoutchouc et plastiques	100.0	119.6	164.5	196.5	222.1	268.0	323.3	342.4
Basic metals								
Métaux de base	100.0	131.2	102.1	119.0	132.0	196.4	239.2	245.6
Metal products								
Produits métalliques	100.0	103.6	128.9	166.4	192.7	155.5	183.1	199.7
Electricity, gas and water [E]								
Electricité, gaz et eau [E]	100.0	109.0	107.0	109.8	109.9	121.8	127.9	127.4

Country or area and industry [ISIC Rev. 3] Pays ou zone et industrie [CITI Rév. 3]	2000	2001	2002	2003	2004	2005	2006	2007
Romania Roumanie								
Total industry [CDE]								
Total, industrie [CDE]	100.0	108.5	113.4	117.2	122.5	125.4	135.0	141.7
Total mining [C]								
Total, industries extractives [C]	100.0	105.8	100.2	99.5	101.7	101.0	103.7	103.4
Total manufacturing [D]								
Total, industries manufacturières [D]	100.0	110.1	117.1	121.8	128.5	132.3	143.7	152.1
Food, beverages and tobacco								
Aliments, boissons et tabac	100.0	120.8	134.6	141.5	134.4	139.6	161.8	176.5
Textiles, wearing apparel, leather, footwear								
Textiles, habillement, cuir et chaussures	100.0	110.8	115.6	130.3	127.0	110.7	101.7	92.3
Chemicals, petroleum, rubber and plastic products								
Produits chimiques, pétroliers, caoutchouc et plastiques	100.0	102.8	111.8	116.5	136.6	142.3	149.6	158.2
Basic metals								
Métaux de base	100.0	113.0	137.5	111.2	126.6	128.9	130.1	134.7
Metal products								
Produits métalliques	100.0	107.0	108.4	114.1	121.8	127.1	141.0	151.5
Electricity, gas and water [E]								
Electricité, gaz et eau [E]	100.0	96.9	94.2	95.7	92.5	91.4	94.9	93.9
Russian Federation Fédération de Russie								
Total industry [CDE]								
Total, industrie [CDE]	100.0	102.9	106.2	116.2	125.6	130.6	136.7	149.5
Total mining [C]								
Total, industries extractives [C]	100.0	106.0	113.1	122.9	131.3	133.1	136.3	138.7
Total manufacturing [D]								
Total, industries manufacturières [D]	100.0	102.0	103.1	114.4	125.3	133.0	140.5	160.7
Food, beverages and tobacco								
Aliments, boissons et tabac	100.0	108.3	116.3	125.5	131.9	140.6	151.2	161.9
Textiles, wearing apparel, leather, footwear								
Textiles, habillement, cuir et chaussures	100.0	108.9	109.2	112.8	109.7	113.3	129.7	128.5
Chemicals, petroleum, rubber and plastic products								
Produits chimiques, pétroliers, caoutchouc et plastiques	100.0	101.3	103.1	107.5	113.8	120.2	129.6	139.0
Basic metals								
Métaux de base	100.0	101.8	106.8	114.5	118.5	121.7	132.3	134.6
Metal products								
Produits métalliques	100.0	101.3	96.5	113.8	132.7	147.9	166.3	186.8
Electricity and gas [E]								
Electricité et gaz [E]	100.0	101.4	106.3	109.8	111.1	112.6	117.6	116.8
Serbia Serbie								
Total industry [CDE]								
Total, industrie [CDE]	100.0	100.1	102.0	99.2	106.8	107.3	112.4	116.5
Total mining [C]								
Total, industries extractives [C]	100.0	87.3	89.1	90.2	89.1	90.9	94.1	93.5
Total manufacturing [D]								
Total, industries manufacturières [D]	100.0	100.8	103.8	99.2	109.1	108.2	114.0	118.9
Food, beverages and tobacco								
Aliments, boissons et tabac	100.0	97.3	105.2	103.0	106.7	112.8	120.3	127.1
Textiles, wearing apparel, leather, footwear								
Textiles, habillement, cuir et chaussures	100.0	101.5	81.3	57.8	54.7	50.3	48.7	45.8
Chemicals, petroleum, rubber and plastic products								
Produits chimiques, pétroliers, caoutchouc et plastiques	100.0	117.0	122.0	132.2	153.0	159.5	167.9	176.1
Basic metals								
Métaux de base	100.0	97.3	103.3	105.3	137.8	168.8	208.5	205.8
Metal products								
Produits métalliques	100.0	89.0	94.6	84.3	95.8	88.1	83.9	91.8
Electricity, gas and water [E]								
Electricité, gaz et eau [E]	100.0	100.7	98.6	101.8	103.5	108.7	111.1	114.2
Slovakia Slovaquie								
Total industry [CDE]								
Total, industrie [CDE]	100.0	106.9	113.6	119.3	124.2	128.2	141.1	159.1
Total mining [C]								
Total, industries extractives [C]	100.0	87.0	111.9	105.7	94.1	90.8	82.1	83.4

Country or area and industry [ISIC Rev. 3] Pays ou zone et industrie [CITI Rév. 3]	2000	2001	2002	2003	2004	2005	2006	2007
Total manufacturing [D]								
Total, industries manufacturières [D]	100.0	109.9	119.0	127.8	133.9	139.9	157.5	181.5
Food, beverages and tobacco								
Aliments, boissons et tabac	100.0	101.6	106.4	103.7	103.3	102.7	103.1	103.1
Textiles, wearing apparel, leather, footwear								
Textiles, habillement, cuir et chaussures	100.0	109.0	116.6	112.4	106.7	104.5	118.8	114.6
Chemicals, petroleum, rubber and plastic products								
Produits chimiques, pétroliers, caoutchouc et plastiques	100.0	104.1	113.3	114.7	119.0	120.9	126.9	135.9
Basic metals								
Métaux de base	100.0	103.9	114.5	120.9	117.4	115.3	120.8	127.1
Metal products								
Produits métalliques	100.0	117.1	131.4	153.0	167.5	182.1	222.6	279.9
Electricity, gas and water [E]								
Electricité, gaz et eau [E]	100.0	98.1	92.3	87.8	91.0	88.4	86.3	79.8
Slovenia Slovénie								
Total industry [CDE]								
Total, industrie [CDE]	100.0	102.9	105.4	106.9	112.8	116.5	123.7	131.3
Total mining [C]								
Total, industries extractives [C]	100.0	92.1	99.2	104.9	97.6	104.2	115.0	119.2
Total manufacturing [D]								
Total, industries manufacturières [D]	100.0	102.8	104.8	106.5	111.6	115.7	123.2	132.4
Food, beverages and tobacco								
Aliments, boissons et tabac	100.0	102.4	100.9	102.0	91.1	89.7	89.6	88.5
Textiles, wearing apparel, leather, footwear								
Textiles, habillement, cuir et chaussures	100.0	94.1	79.7	70.3	61.9	56.9	56.4	51.6
Chemicals, petroleum, rubber and plastic products								
Produits chimiques, pétroliers, caoutchouc et plastiques	100.0	105.8	109.7	119.9	137.3	146.7	163.1	193.1
Basic metals								
Métaux de base	100.0	104.5	107.5	114.8	105.9	109.2	130.5	139.3
Metal products								
Produits métalliques	100.0	107.6	114.0	117.2	134.9	143.9	155.6	169.7
Electricity and gas [E]								
Electricité et gaz [E]	100.0	109.3	115.3	111.3	132.9	130.9	129.6	115.2
Spain Espagne								
Total industry [CDE]								
Total, industrie [CDE]	100.0	98.8	98.9	100.5	102.3	102.4	106.2	108.6
Total mining [C]								
Total, industries extractives [C]	100.0	96.8	96.3	96.3	91.7	88.0	90.2	89.0
Total manufacturing [D]								
Total, industries manufacturières [D]	100.0	98.0	98.4	99.9	101.1	100.8	104.9	107.4
Food, beverages and tobacco								
Aliments, boissons et tabac	100.0	101.1	105.0	107.4	109.0	110.7	110.5	110.2
Textiles, wearing apparel, leather, footwear								
Textiles, habillement, cuir et chaussures	100.0	96.6	86.8	80.7	75.4	66.8	64.9	62.5
Chemicals, petroleum, rubber and plastic products								
Produits chimiques, pétroliers, caoutchouc et plastiques	100.0	99.8	104.1	108.8	108.6	108.5	111.6	112.9
Basic metals								
Métaux de base	100.0	96.4	102.6	103.8	110.2	107.8	113.7	113.6
Metal products								
Produits métalliques	100.0	96.0	92.6	93.7	95.7	95.0	102.5	108.2
Electricity and gas [E]								
Electricité et gaz [E]	100.0	104.3	104.3	107.3	114.8	119.5	120.8	122.5
Sweden Suède								
Total industry [CDE]								
Total, industrie [CDE]	100.0	99.0	99.0	100.4	106.0	108.7	111.9	115.6
Total mining [C]								
Total, industries extractives [C]	100.0	97.6	99.1	98.1	106.7	113.0	114.1	121.0
Total manufacturing [D]								
Total, industries manufacturières [D]	100.0	99.0	100.0	102.6	107.4	109.9	115.0	118.7
Food, beverages and tobacco								
Aliments, boissons et tabac	100.0	102.9	100.1	95.5	96.2	96.5	96.9	96.7

Country or area and industry [ISIC Rev. 3] Pays ou zone et industrie [CITI Rév. 3]	2000	2001	2002	2003	2004	2005	2006	2007
Chemicals, petroleum, rubber and plastic products Produits chimiques, pétroliers, caoutchouc et plastiques	100.0	105.5	110.3	118.2	125.0	125.2	135.2	109.9
Basic metals Métaux de base	100.0	108.0	112.8	111.3	117.9	113.7	109.1	109.8
Metal products Produits métalliques	100.0	96.5	94.7	98.5	106.0	110.9	117.4	128.1
Electricity, gas and water [E] Electricité, gaz et eau [E]	100.0	98.5	89.4	82.7	92.2	96.0	87.4	90.3
Switzerland Suisse								
Total industry [CDE] Total, industrie [CDE]	100.0	99.3	94.2	94.2	98.4	101.0	108.9	119.2
Total mining [C] Total, industries extractives [C]	100.0	100.5	99.0	98.3	102.4	97.1	106.6	113.1
Total manufacturing [D] Total, industries manufacturières [D]	100.0	98.9	93.7	93.6	98.1	101.2	109.7	120.6
Food, beverages and tobacco Aliments, boissons et tabac	100.0	95.8	95.8	95.0	96.3	97.2	101.0	106.0
Textiles and wearing apparel Textiles et habillement	100.0	87.2	80.3	76.6	81.9	83.1	87.1	105.1
Chemicals and chemical products Produits chimiques	100.0	105.5	111.5	121.0	126.6	137.4	151.0	173.8
Basic metals and metal products Métaux de base et produits métalliques	100.0	98.0	87.8	84.5	88.0	89.3	96.8	106.6
Electricity, gas and water [E] Electricité, gaz et eau [E]	100.0	104.3	100.0	102.0	101.6	99.2	101.1	103.4
TFYR of Macedonia Ex-R.Y. Macédoine								
Total industry [CDE] Total, industrie [CDE]	100.0	89.9	85.1	89.1	87.2	93.3	96.7	100.2
Total mining [C] Total, industries extractives [C]	100.0	98.2	74.1	45.2	42.9	56.5	63.0	69.2
Total manufacturing [D] Total, industries manufacturières [D]	100.0	96.6	92.1	97.5	95.4	102.5	106.2	111.7
Food, beverages and tobacco Aliments, boissons et tabac	100.0	97.6	90.9	108.1	101.0	104.6	105.4	112.0
Textiles, wearing apparel, leather, footwear Textiles, habillement, cuir et chaussures	100.0	96.3	85.5	66.4	65.9	67.7	70.9	61.7
Chemicals, petroleum, rubber and plastic products Produits chimiques, pétroliers, caoutchouc et plastiques	100.0	98.4	97.6	88.9	89.9	94.6	96.4	95.7
Basic metals Métaux de base	100.0	94.8	77.2	91.7	104.6	139.5	152.0	204.0
Metal products Produits métalliques	100.0	98.3	106.1	72.6	61.0	63.3	64.1	73.7
Electricity, gas and water [E] Electricité, gaz et eau [E]	100.0	100.1	96.2	105.7	102.9	105.6	106.4	96.4
Ukraine Ukraine								
Total industry [CDE] Total, industrie [CDE]	100.0	112.9	120.4	139.6	156.1	160.5	169.7	187.1
Total mining [C] Total, industries extractives [C]	100.0	103.0	105.7	111.4	116.0	120.0	127.1	130.4
Total manufacturing [D] Total, industries manufacturières [D]	100.0	115.7	124.9	148.0	168.1	172.6	182.5	203.8
Food, beverages and tobacco Aliments, boissons et tabac	100.0	118.6	128.3	154.5	174.1	197.8	216.8	240.0
Textiles, wearing apparel, leather, footwear Textiles, habillement, cuir et chaussures	100.0	115.4	116.2	120.1	137.3	139.5	135.2	135.3
Chemicals, petroleum, rubber and plastic products Produits chimiques, pétroliers, caoutchouc et plastiques	100.0	114.3	124.8	144.6	163.4	175.0	178.1	188.6
Metal and Metal Products, except machinery and equip. Metallurgie et travail des métaux à l'exclusion de la fabrication de machines et d'équipements	100.0	105.9	110.1	125.9	141.4	139.4	151.9	165.2

24

Index numbers of industrial production *(continued)*
2000 = 100
Indices de la production industrielle *(suite)*
2000 = 100

Country or area and industry [ISIC Rev. 3] Pays ou zone et industrie [CITI Rév. 3]	2000	2001	2002	2003	2004	2005	2006	2007
All machinery and transport equipment								
Fabrication de machines et de matériel de transport	100.0	120.3	132.8	178.1	225.0	250.7	275.3	350.6
Electricity, gas and water [E]								
Electricité, gaz et eau [E]	100.0	102.2	103.7	106.4	105.3	107.7	114.7	118.4
United Kingdom Royaume-Uni								
Total industry [CDE]								
Total, industrie [CDE]	100.0	98.7	96.9	96.3	97.5	96.0	96.7	97.3
Total mining [C]								
Total, industries extractives [C]	100.0	94.5	94.9	90.0	83.1	76.1	70.4	69.2
Total manufacturing [D]								
Total, industries manufacturières [D]	100.0	98.7	96.5	96.3	98.7	98.0	99.9	100.6
Food, beverages and tobacco								
Aliments, boissons et tabac	100.0	100.9	103.5	101.8	104.2	105.4	104.7	104.1
Textiles, wearing apparel, leather, footwear								
Textiles, habillement, cuir et chaussures	100.0	87.6	81.8	80.6	72.0	70.3	70.7	69.8
Chemicals, petroleum, rubber and plastic products								
Produits chimiques, pétroliers, caoutchouc et plastiques	100.0	102.1	101.4	101.5	104.3	105.5	108.5	108.3
Basic metals								
Métaux de base	100.0	96.1	87.2	86.1	88.6	88.5	86.8	86.9
Metal products								
Produits métalliques	100.0	98.1	93.0	93.1	96.5	95.3	98.1	99.6
Electricity, gas and water [E]								
Electricité, gaz et eau [E]	100.0	103.2	103.5	105.3	106.4	106.1	105.8	107.3
Oceania · Océanie								
Australia [2] Australie [2]								
Total industry [CDE]								
Total, industrie [CDE]	100.0	103.7	104.7	106.9	106.6	107.2	107.8	111.6
Total mining [C]								
Total, industries extractives [C]	100.0	106.7	106.5	105.4	102.2	106.4	107.6	115.7
Total manufacturing [D]								
Total, industries manufacturières [D]	100.0	102.3	104.4	108.2	109.2	107.8	107.3	109.4
Food, beverages and tobacco								
Aliments, boissons et tabac	100.0	104.4	103.9	104.9	104.7	105.7	104.9	105.9
Textiles, wearing apparel, leather, footwear								
Textiles, habillement, cuir et chaussures	100.0	93.0	81.6	75.1	69.4	56.5	52.6	51.8
Chemicals, petroleum, rubber and plastic products								
Produits chimiques, pétroliers, caoutchouc et plastiques	100.0	102.3	103.3	109.2	104.4	104.4	100.1	98.8
Basic metals and metal products								
Métaux de base et produits métalliques	100.0	102.3	105.7	111.5	114.8	113.7	116.2	121.1
Electricity, gas and water [E]								
Electricité, gaz et eau [E]	100.0	101.5	100.7	101.7	102.3	103.1	104.5	103.2
Fiji Fidji								
Total industry [CDE]								
Total, industrie [CDE]	100.0	105.9	107.7	108.1	120.6	105.5	106.3	104.6
Total mining [C]								
Total, industries extractives [C]	100.0	101.9	98.8	93.0	106.7	77.6	43.4	7.5
Total manufacturing [D]								
Total, industries manufacturières [D]	100.0	106.9	106.6	104.7	117.6	98.3	100.2	101.1
Food, beverages and tobacco								
Aliments, boissons et tabac	100.0	110.1	118.9	126.3	136.3	151.6	164.8	166.9
Textiles and wearing apparel								
Textiles et habillement	100.0	130.9	115.0	103.2	127.7	57.6	41.7	43.8
Chemicals and chemical products								
Produits chimiques	100.0	96.0	111.0	95.2	111.0	129.8	144.4	135.3
Electricity and water [E]								
Electricité et eau [E]	100.0	106.2	114.2	126.0	136.7	138.8	147.7	148.3
New Zealand [10] Nouvelle-Zélande [10]								
Total industry [CDE] [11]								
Total, industrie [CDE] [11]	100.0	102.3	102.4	110.6	112.9	116.4	114.2	112.6
Total mining [C]								
Total, industries extractives [C]	100.0	102.6	103.3	104.9	95.1	91.3	90.1	89.0

Country or area and industry [ISIC Rev. 3] Pays ou zone et industrie [CITI Rév. 3]	2000	2001	2002	2003	2004	2005	2006	2007
Total manufacturing [D] Total, industries manufacturières [D]	100.0	102.5	103.5	112.4	116.4	120.0	118.2	115.9
Food, beverages and tobacco Aliments, boissons et tabac	100.0	102.3	104.2	122.2	131.8	132.8	135.2	133.7
Textiles, wearing apparel, leather, footwear Textiles, habillement, cuir et chaussures	100.0	88.5	84.3	86.5	80.6	82.9	73.9	74.0
Chemicals, petroleum, rubber and plastic products Produits chimiques, pétroliers, caoutchouc et plastiques	100.0	105.8	104.1	107.9	100.9	105.7	98.6	100.3
Basic metals and metal products Métaux de base et produits métalliques	100.0	106.3	109.7	115.0	121.5	124.0	121.3	114.1
Electricity, gas and water [E] Electricité, gaz et eau [E]	100.0	101.1	97.3	104.6	105.0	110.7	105.9	109.0

Source:
United Nations Statistics Division, New York, the index numbers of industrial production database, last accessed March 2009.

Source:
Organisation des Nations Unies, Division de statistique, New York, la base de données pour les indices de la production industrielle, dernier accès mars 2009.

1	Twelve months beginning 1 July of the year stated.	Période de 12 mois commençant le 1er juillet de l'année indiquée.
2	Twelve months ending 30 June of the year stated.	Période de 12 mois finissant le 30 juin de l'année indiquée.
3	Excluding petroleum refineries.	Non compris les raffineries de pétrole.
4	Calculated by the Statistics Division of the United Nations from component national indices.	Calculé par la Division de Statistiques de l'Organisation des Nations Unies à partir d'indices nationaux plus détaillés.
5	Excluding coal mining and crude petroleum.	Non compris l'extraction du charbon et de pétrole brut.
6	Twelve months ending 30 September of the year stated.	Période de 12 mois finissant le 30 septembre de l'année indiquée.
7	Including construction.	Y compris la construction.
8	Twelve months beginning 1 April of the year stated.	Période de 12 mois commençant le 1er avril de l'année indiquée.
9	Excluding gas and oil extraction.	Non compris l'extraction de gaz et de pétrole brut.
10	Twelve months ending 31 March of the year stated.	Période de 12 mois finissant le 31 mars de l'année indiquée.
11	Including forestry and fishing.	Y compris l'exploitation forestière et la pêche.

Technical notes: tables 18-24

Detailed internationally comparable data on national accounts are compiled and published annually by the Statistics Division, Department of Economic and Social Affairs of the United Nations Secretariat. Data for national accounts aggregates for countries or areas are based on the concepts and definitions contained in *A System of National Accounts* (1968 SNA) and in *System of National Accounts 1993* (1993 SNA). A summary of the conceptual framework, classifications and definitions of transactions is found in the annual United Nations publication, *National Accounts Statistics: Main Aggregates and Detailed Tables*, which presents, in the form of analytical tables, a summary of selected principal national accounts aggregates based on official detailed national accounts data of over 200 countries and areas. Every effort has been made to present the estimates of the various countries or areas in a form designed to facilitate international comparability. The data for some countries or areas has been compiled according to the 1993 SNA. Data for those countries or areas which still follow the concepts and definitions of the 1968 SNA is indicated with a footnote. To the extent possible, any other differences in concept, scope, coverage and classification are footnoted as well. Detailed footnotes identifying these differences are also available in the annual national accounts publication mentioned above. Such differences should be taken into account in order to avoid misleading comparisons among countries or areas.

Table 18 shows gross domestic product (GDP) and GDP per capita in US dollars at current prices, GDP at constant 1990 prices and the corresponding real rates of growth. The table is designed to facilitate international comparisons of levels of income generated in production. In order to present comparable coverage for as many countries as possible, the official GDP national currency data are supplemented by estimates prepared by the Statistics Division, based on a variety of data derived from national and international sources. The conversion rates used to translate national currency data into US dollars are the period averages of market exchange rates (MERs) for members of the International Monetary Fund (IMF). These rates, which are published in the *International Financial Statistics*, are communicated to the IMF by national central banks and consist of three types: (a) market rates, determined largely by market forces; (b) official rates, determined by government authorities; and (c) principal rates for countries maintaining multiple exchange rate arrangements. Market rates always take priority and official rates are used only when a free market rate is not available.

For non-members of the IMF, averages of the United Nations operational rates, used for accounting pur-

Notes techniques: tableaux 18 à 24

La Division de statistique du Département des affaires économiques et sociales du Secrétariat de l'Organisation des Nations Unies établit et publie chaque année des données détaillées, comparables au plan international, sur les comptes nationaux. Les données relatives aux agrégats des différents pays et territoires sont établies en fonction des concepts et des définitions du *Système de comptabilité nationale* (SCN de 1968) et du *Système de comptabilité nationale 1993* (SCN de 1993). On trouvera un résumé de l'appareil conceptuel, des classifications et des définitions des opérations dans "*National Accounts Statistics: Main Aggregates and Detailed Tables*", publication annuelle des Nations Unies, qui présente, sous forme de tableaux analytiques, un choix d'agrégats essentiels de comptabilité nationale, issus des comptes nationaux détaillés de plus que 200 pays et territoires. On n'a rien négligé pour présenter les chiffres des différents pays et territoires sous une forme facilitant les comparaisons internationales. Pour plusieurs pays, les chiffres ont été établis selon le SCN de 1993. Les données des pays et territoires qui encore appliquent les concepts et les définitions du SCN de 1968 sont signalés par une note. Dans la mesure du possible, on signale également au moyen de notes les cas où les concepts, la portée, la couverture et la classification ne seraient pas les mêmes. Il y a en outre des notes détaillées explicitant ces différences dans la publication annuelle mentionnée plus haut. Il y a lieu de tenir compte de ces différences pour éviter de tenter des comparaisons qui donneraient matière à confusion.

Le *tableau 18* fait apparaître le produit intérieur brut (PIB) total et par habitant, exprimé en dollars des États-Unis aux prix courants et à prix constants (base 1990), ainsi que les taux de croissance correspondants. Le tableau est conçu pour faciliter les comparaisons internationales du revenu issu de la production. Afin que la couverture soit comparable pour le plus grand nombre possible de pays, la Division de statistique s'appuie non seulement sur les chiffres officiels du PIB exprimé dans la monnaie nationale, mais aussi sur diverses données provenant de sources nationales et internationales. Les taux de conversion utilisés pour exprimer les données nationales en dollars des États-Unis sont, pour les membres du Fonds monétaire international (FMI), les moyennes pour la période considérée des taux de change du marché. Ces derniers, publiés dans *Statistiques financières internationales*, sont communiqués au FMI par les banques centrales des pays et reposent sur trois types de taux : a) taux du marché, déterminés dans une large mesure par les facteurs du marché; b) taux officiels, déterminés par les pouvoirs publics; c) taux principaux, pour les pays pratiquant différents arrangements en matière de taux de change. On donne toujours la priorité aux taux du marché, n'utilisant

poses in United Nations transactions with member countries, are applied. These are based on official, commercial and/or tourist rates of exchange.

It should be noted that there are practical constraints in the use of MERs for conversion purposes. Their use may result in excessive fluctuations or distortions in the dollar income levels of a number of countries, particularly in those with multiple exchange rates, those coping with inordinate levels of inflation or countries experiencing misalignments caused by market fluctuations. Caution is therefore urged when making inter-country comparisons of incomes as expressed in US dollars.

Alternative methods of making international comparisons have been developed in recent years. One is the Purchasing Power Parities (PPPs) which have been developed as part of the International Comparison Programme; another is the World Bank Atlas method of conversion based on the average of the exchange rates of the current year and the two immediately preceding years that have been adjusted for differences in inflation rates between individual countries and the average of G-5 countries (Germany, France, Japan, the United Kingdom, and the United States). The Statistics Division of the United Nations has developed the Price-Adjusted Rates of Exchange method (PARE) which, like the Atlas method, is designed to adjust exchange rates that do not adequately reflect relative movements of domestic and international inflation. PARE is mainly applied to countries with fixed exchange rate regimes and countries going through a period of high inflation (e.g. transition countries from 1990-1995).

The GDP at constant price series, based primarily on data officially provided by countries or areas and partly on estimates made by the Statistics Division, is transformed into index numbers and rebased to 1990=100. The resulting data are then converted into US dollars at the rate prevailing in the base year 1990. The growth rates are based on the estimates of GDP at constant 1990 prices. The growth rate of the year in question is obtained by dividing the GDP of that year by the GDP of the preceding year.

Table 19 features the percentage distribution of GDP at current prices by expenditure breakdown. It shows the portions of GDP spent on consumption by the household sector (including the non-profit institutions serving households) and the government, the portions spent on gross fixed capital formation, on changes in inventories, and on exports of goods and services, deducting imports of goods and services. The percentages are derived from official data reported to the United Nations by the countries and published in the annual national accounts publication.

Table 20 shows the percentage distribution of va-

les taux officiels que lorsqu'on n'a pas de taux du marché libre.

Pour les pays qui ne sont pas membres du FMI, on utilise les moyennes des taux de change opérationnels de l'ONU (qui servent à des fins comptables pour les opérations de l'ONU avec les pays qui en sont membres). Ces taux reposent sur les taux de change officiels, les taux du commerce et/ou les taux touristiques.

Il faut noter que l'utilisation des taux de change du marché pour la conversion des données se heurte à des obstacles pratiques. On risque, ce faisant, d'aboutir à des fluctuations excessives ou à des distorsions du revenu en dollars de certains pays, surtout dans le cas des pays qui pratiquent plusieurs taux de change et de ceux qui connaissent des taux d'inflation exceptionnels ou des décalages provenant des fluctuations du marché. Les comparaisons de revenu entre pays sont donc sujettes à caution lorsqu'on se fonde sur le revenu exprimé en dollars des États-Unis.

D'autres méthodes ont été élaborées ces dernières années pour les comparaisons internationales. L'une, celle de la parité de pouvoir d'achat (PPA), procède du Programme de comparaison internationale ; une autre méthode de conversion, celle de l'Atlas de la Banque mondiale, est basée sur la moyenne des taux de change de l'année en cours et des deux années immédiatement précédentes, ajustés en fonction des différences d'inflation entre les pays considérés et la moyenne des pays du G-5 (Allemagne, États-Unis, France, Japon, et Royaume-Uni). La Division de statistique de l'ONU a mis au point la méthode des Taux de Change Corrigés des Prix (TCCP) qui, comme celle de l'Atlas, est conçue pour corriger les taux de change qui ne rendent pas convenablement compte de l'évolution relative de l'inflation dans un pays par rapport à l'inflation à l'échelon international. Le TCCP sert surtout pour les pays à taux de change fixe et ceux qui connaissent une période de forte inflation (par ex. les pays en transition entre 1990 et 1995).

La série de statistiques du PIB à prix constants est fondée principalement sur des données officiellement communiquées par les pays, et en partie sur des estimations de la Division de statistique; les données permettent de calculer des indices, la base 100 correspondant à 1990. Les chiffres ainsi obtenus sont alors convertis en dollars des États-Unis au taux de change de l'année de base (1990). Les taux de croissance sont calculés à partir des estimations du PIB aux prix constants de 1990. Le taux de croissance de l'année considérée est obtenu en divisant le PIB de l'année par celui de l'année précédente.

Le *tableau 19* montre la répartition (en pourcentage) du PIB aux prix courants par catégorie de dépense. Il indique la part du PIB consacrée aux dépenses de consommation du secteur des ménages (y compris les institutions sans but lucratif au service des ménages) et des

lue added originating from the various industry components of the *International Standard Industrial Classification of All Economic Activities, Revision 3* (ISIC Rev. 3). This table reflects the economic structure of production in the different countries or areas. The percentages are based on official gross value added at basic current prices broken down by the kind of economic activity: agriculture, hunting, forestry and fishing (categories A+B); mining and quarrying (C); manufacturing (D); electricity, gas and water supply (E); construction (F); wholesale and retail trade, repair of motor vehicles, motorcycles and personal and household goods, restaurants and hotels (G+H); transport, storage and communication (I) and "other activities", comprised of financial intermediation (J), real estate, renting and business activities (K), public administration and defence, compulsory social security (L), education (M), health and social work (N), other community, social and personal service activities (O) and private households with employed persons (P).

Table 21 presents the relationships among the principal national accounting aggregates, namely: gross domestic product (GDP), gross national income (GNI), gross national disposable income (GNDI) and gross savings. GNI is the term used in the 1993 SNA instead of the term Gross National Product (GNP) which was used in the 1968 SNA. The ratio of each aggregate to GDP is derived cumulatively by adding net primary income (or net factor income) from the rest of the world (GNI), adding net current transfers from the rest of the world (GNDI), and deducting final consumption to arrive at gross saving.

Table 22 presents the distribution of government final consumption expenditure by function at current prices. The breakdown by function includes: general public services; defence; public order and safety; economic affairs; environmental protection; housing and community amenities; health; recreation, culture and religion; education; and social protection. The government expenditure is equal to the service produced by general government for its own use. These services are not sold; they are valued in the GDP at their cost to the government.

Table 23 shows the distribution of household final consumption expenditure in the domestic market by purpose at current prices. The percentage shares include: food, beverages, tobacco and narcotics; clothing and footwear; housing, water, electricity, gas and other fuels; furnishings, household equipment and routine maintenance of the house; health; transport and communication; recreation and culture; education; restaurants and hotels; and miscellaneous goods and services.

Table 24: The national indices in this table are shown for the categories "Mining and Quarrying", "Manu-

administrations publiques et celle qui est consacrée à l'investissement fixe brut, celle qui correspond aux variations de stocks et celle qui correspond aux exportations de biens et services, déduction faite des importations de biens et services. Ces pourcentages sont calculés à partir des chiffres officiels communiqués à l'ONU par les pays, publiés dans l'ouvrage annuel.

Le *tableau 20* montre la répartition (en pourcentage) de la valeur ajoutée par branche d'activité, selon le classement retenu dans la *Classification internationale type, par industrie, de toutes les branches d'activité économique, Révision 3* (CITI Révision 3). Il rend donc compte de la structure économique de la production dans chaque pays. Les pourcentages sont établis à partir des chiffres officiels de valeur ajoutée brute aux prix de base courants, répartis selon les différentes catégories d'activité économique: agriculture, chasse, sylviculture et pêche (catégories A + B); activités extractives (C); activités de fabrication (D); production et distribution d'électricité, de gaz et d'eau (E); construction (F); commerce de gros et de détail, réparation de véhicules automobiles, de motocycles et de biens personnels et domestiques, hôtels et restaurants (G + H); transports, entreposage et communications (I) et "autres activités", y compris intermédiation financière (J), immobilier, locations et activités de services aux entreprises (K), administration publique et défense, sécurité sociale obligatoire (L), éducation (M), santé et action sociale (N), autres activités de services collectifs, sociaux et personnels (O), et ménages privés employant du personnel domestique (P).

Le *tableau 21* montre les rapports entre les principaux agrégats de la comptabilité nationale, à savoir le produit intérieur brut (PIB), le revenu national brut (RNB), le revenu national brut disponible et l'épargne brute. Le revenu national brut est l'agrégat qui remplace dans le SCN de 1993 le produit national brut, utilisé dans le SCN de 1968. Chacun d'entre eux est obtenu par rapport au PIB, en ajoutant les revenus primaires nets (ou revenus nets de facteurs) engendrés dans le reste du monde, pour obtenir le revenu national brut; en ajoutant les transferts courants nets reçus de non-résidents, pour obtenir le revenu national disponible; en soustrayant la consommation finale pour obtenir l'épargne brute.

Le *tableau 22* donne la répartition des dépenses de consommation finale des administrations publiques, par fonction, aux prix courants. La répartition par fonction est la suivante: services généraux des administrations publiques; défense; ordre et sécurité publiques; affaires économiques; protection de l'environnement; logements et équipements collectifs; santé; loisirs, culture et culte; enseignement ; protection sociale. Les dépenses des administrations sont considérées comme égales aux services produits par l'administration pour son propre usage. Ces services ne sont pas vendus et ils sont évalués, dans le

facturing" and "Electricity, gas and water". These categories are classified according to Tabulation Categories C, D and E of the ISIC Revision 3 at the 2-digit level. Major deviations from ISIC in the scope of the indices for the above categories are indicated by footnotes to the table.

The category "Total industry" covers Mining, Manufacturing and Electricity, gas and water. The indices for "Total industry", however, are the combination of the components shown and share all deviations from ISIC as footnoted for the component series.

The weights used in the calculation of the indices for a particular country are the value added contribution to the gross domestic product (GDP) of the given industry during the base year (value added = output - intermediate consumption). These value added contributions are measured at factor cost. Ideally, every five years the base year is changed, the corresponding base weights are updated and the indices of subsequent years are rebased. Currently, the national indices have been rebased to 2000=100.

PIB, à leur coût pour l'administration.

Le *tableau 23* donne la répartition des dépenses de consommation finale des ménages sur le marché intérieur par fonction aux prix courants. La répartition en pourcentage distingue les rubriques suivantes: alimentation, boissons, tabac et stupéfiants; articles d'habillement et chaussures; logement, eau, gaz, électricité et autres combustibles; meubles, articles de ménage et entretien courant de l'habitation; santé; transports et communication; loisirs et culture; enseignement; restaurants et hôtels; et autres fonctions, y compris les biens et services divers.

Tableau 24: Les indices nationaux de ce tableau sont donnés pour les catégories "Industries extractives et carrières", "Industries manufacturières" et "Électricité, gaz et eau". Les catégories correspondent à celles des catégories C, D et E de la Classification internationale type, par industrie, de toutes les branches d'activité économique (CITI Révision 3) au niveau des classes à deux chiffres. Tous les indices pour lesquels les catégories s'écartent sensiblement de celles de la CITI sont signalés en note au tableau.

La catégorie "Ensemble de l'industrie" comprend les Industries extractives et carrières, les Industries manufacturières et l'Électricité, gaz et eau. Les indices pour "Ensemble de l'industrie", toutefois, combinent les composantes indiquées et présentent tous les écarts par rapport à la CITI que signalent les notes concernant les séries des composantes.

Les coefficients de pondération utilisés pour le calcul des indices d'un pays donné correspondent à la part de la valeur ajoutée de la branche considérée dans le produit intérieur brut (PIB) pendant l'année de référence (valeur ajoutée = production - consommation intermédiaire). Cette part de la valeur ajoutée est mesurée au coût des facteurs. En principe, l'année de référence change tous les cinq ans, les coefficients de pondération correspondants sont actualisés et les indices des années suivantes sont calculés sur une nouvelle base. À l'heure actuelle, la nouvelle base des indices est 2000=100.

25

Rates of discount of central banks
Per cent per annum, end of period

Taux d'escompte des banques centrales
Pour cent par année, fin de la période

Country or area Pays ou zone	1999	2000	2001	2002	2003	2004	2005	2006	2007	2008
Albania [1] Albanie [1]	18.00	10.82	7.00	8.50	6.50	5.25	5.00	5.50	6.25	6.25
Algeria Algérie	8.50	6.00	6.00	5.50	4.50	4.00	4.00	4.00	4.00	4.00
Angola Angola	120.00	150.00	150.00	150.00	150.00	95.00	95.00	14.00	19.57	19.57
Anguilla Anguilla	8.00	8.00	7.00	7.00	6.50	6.50	6.50	6.50	6.50	6.50
Antigua and Barbuda Antigua-et-Barbuda	8.00	8.00	7.00	7.00	6.50	6.50	6.50	6.50	6.50	6.50
Aruba [1] Aruba [1]	6.50	6.50	6.50	6.50	5.00	5.00	5.00	5.00	5.00	5.00
Azerbaijan [2] Azerbaïdjan [2]	10.00	10.00	10.00	7.00	7.00	7.00	9.00	9.50	13.00	8.00
Bahamas Bahamas	5.75	5.75	5.75	5.75	5.75	5.75	5.25	5.25	5.25	5.25
Bangladesh Bangladesh	7.00	7.00	6.00	6.00	5.00	5.00	5.00	5.00	5.00	5.00
Barbados [1] Barbade [1]	10.00	10.00	7.50	7.50	7.50	7.50	10.00	12.00	12.00	...
Belarus [2] Bélarus [2]	23.40	#80.00	48.00	38.00	28.00	17.00	11.00	10.00	10.00	12.00
Belize [3] Belize [3]	12.00	12.00	12.00	12.00	12.00	12.00	12.00	12.00	12.00	12.00
Benin Bénin	6.00	6.00	6.00	6.00	4.50	4.00	4.00	4.25	4.25	4.75
Bolivia Bolivie	12.50	10.00	8.50	12.50	7.50	6.00	5.25	5.25	6.50	13.00
Botswana [3] Botswana [3]	13.75	14.25	14.25	15.25	14.25	14.25	14.50	15.00	14.50	15.50
Brazil Brésil	21.37	#18.52	21.43	30.42	23.92	24.55	25.34	19.98	17.85	20.48
Bulgaria [1] Bulgarie [1]	4.46	4.63	4.65	3.31	2.83	2.37	#2.05	3.26	4.58	5.77
Burkina Faso Burkina Faso	6.00	6.00	6.00	6.00	4.50	4.00	4.00	4.25	4.25	4.75
Burundi [4] Burundi [4]	12.00	14.00	14.00	15.50	14.50	14.50	14.50	11.07	10.12	10.08
Cameroon Cameroun	7.30	7.00	6.50	6.30	6.00	6.00	5.50	5.25	5.25	4.75
Canada [1] Canada [1]	5.00	6.00	2.50	3.00	3.00	2.75	3.50	4.50	4.50	1.75
Cape Verde Cap-Vert	...	...	11.50	10.00	8.50	8.50	8.50	8.50	8.50	7.50
Central African Rep. Rép. centrafricaine	7.60	7.00	6.50	6.30	6.00	6.00	5.50	5.25	5.25	4.75
Chad Tchad	7.60	7.00	6.50	6.30	6.00	6.00	5.50	5.25	5.25	4.75
Chile Chili	7.44	8.73	6.50	3.00	2.45	2.25	4.50	5.25	6.00	8.25
China [1] Chine [1]	3.24	3.24	3.24	2.70	2.70	3.33	3.33	3.33	3.33	2.79

25

Rates of discount of central banks *(continued)*
Per cent per annum, end of period
Taux d'escompte des banques centrales *(suite)*
Pour cent par année, fin de la période

Country or area Pays ou zone	1999	2000	2001	2002	2003	2004	2005	2006	2007	2008
China, Hong Kong SAR Chine, Hong Kong RAS	7.00	8.00	3.25	2.75	2.50	3.75	5.75	6.75	5.75	0.50
Colombia Colombie	23.05	18.28	13.25	10.00	12.00	11.25	10.75	9.50	11.50	11.50
Comoros Comores	#6.36	5.63	5.89	4.79	3.82	3.55	3.59	4.34	5.36	5.36
Congo Congo	7.60	7.00	6.50	6.30	6.00	6.00	5.50	5.25	5.25	4.75
Costa Rica[5] Costa Rica[5]	34.00	31.50	28.75	31.25	26.00	26.00	27.00	24.75	17.00	25.00
Côte d'Ivoire Côte d'Ivoire	6.00	6.00	6.00	6.00	4.50	4.00	4.00	4.25	4.25	4.75
Croatia Croatie	7.90	5.90	5.90	4.50	4.50	4.50	4.50	4.50	9.00	9.00
Cyprus Chypre	7.00	7.00	5.50	5.00	4.50	5.50	4.25	4.50	5.00	...
Czech Republic[1] République tchèque[1]	5.25	5.25	4.50	2.75	2.00	2.50	2.00	2.50	3.50	2.25
Dem. Rep. of the Congo Rép. dém. du Congo	120.00	120.00	140.00	24.00	8.00	...	...	...	...	...
Denmark Danemark	3.00	4.75	3.25	2.86	2.00	2.00	2.25	3.50	4.00	3.50
Dominica Dominique	8.00	8.00	7.00	7.00	6.50	6.50	6.50	6.50	6.50	6.50
Ecuador Equateur	64.40	#13.82	17.48	15.36	11.67	10.23	9.96	9.54	10.72	9.14
Egypt Egypte	12.00	12.00	11.00	10.00	10.00	10.00	10.00	9.00	9.00	11.50
Equatorial Guinea Guinée équatoriale	7.60	7.00	6.50	6.30	6.00	6.00	5.50	5.25	5.25	4.75
Euro Area[6,7] Zone euro[6,7]	4.00	5.75	4.25	3.75	3.00	3.00	3.25	4.50	5.00	3.00
Fiji[1] Fidji[1]	2.50	8.00	1.75	1.75	1.75	2.25	2.75	5.25	9.25	6.32
Gabon Gabon	7.60	7.00	6.50	6.30	6.00	6.00	5.50	5.25	5.25	4.75
Gambia Gambie	10.50	10.00	13.00	18.00	29.00	28.00	14.00	9.00	10.00	...
Ghana Ghana	27.00	27.00	27.00	24.50	21.50	18.50	15.50	12.50	13.50	17.00
Grenada Grenade	8.00	8.00	7.00	7.00	6.50	6.50	6.50	6.50	6.50	6.50
Guinea[2] Guinée[2]	...	11.50	16.25	16.25	16.25	16.25	22.25	...	...	...
Guinea-Bissau Guinée-Bissau	6.00	6.00	6.00	6.00	4.50	4.00	4.00	4.25	4.25	4.75
Guyana Guyana	13.25	11.75	8.75	6.25	5.50	6.00	6.00	6.75	6.50	6.75
Hungary Hongrie	14.50	11.00	9.75	8.50	12.50	9.50	6.00	8.00	7.50	10.00
Iceland Islande	10.00	12.40	12.00	8.20	7.70	10.25	12.00	15.25	15.25	22.00
India[1] Inde[1]	8.00	8.00	6.50	6.25	6.00	6.00	6.00	6.00	6.00	6.00
Indonesia Indonésie	12.51	14.53	17.62	12.93	8.31	7.43	12.75	9.75	8.00	10.83

25

Rates of discount of central banks *(continued)*
Per cent per annum, end of period
Taux d'escompte des banques centrales *(suite)*
Pour cent par année, fin de la période

Country or area Pays ou zone	1999	2000	2001	2002	2003	2004	2005	2006	2007	2008
Iraq Iraq	...	...	...	...	...	6.00	6.33	10.42	20.00	...
Israel Israël	11.20	8.21	5.67	9.18	5.20	3.90	4.44	5.00	4.00	2.50
Japan Japon	0.50	0.50	0.10	0.10	0.10	0.10	0.10	0.40	0.75	0.30
Jordan Jordanie	8.00	6.50	5.00	4.50	2.50	3.75	6.50	7.50	7.00	6.25
Kazakhstan [2] Kazakhstan [2]	18.00	14.00	9.00	7.50	7.00	7.00	8.00	9.00	11.00	10.50
Kenya Kenya	26.46	...	...	...	...	...	...	...	...	...
Korea, Republic of Corée, République de	3.00	3.00	2.50	2.50	2.50	2.00	2.00	2.75	3.25	1.75
Kuwait Koweït	6.75	7.25	4.25	3.25	3.25	4.75	6.00	6.25	6.25	3.75
Lao People's Dem. Rep. [1] Rép. dém. pop. lao [1]	34.89	35.17	35.00	20.00	20.00	20.00	20.00	20.00	12.67	7.67
Latvia Lettonie	4.00	3.50	3.50	3.00	3.00	4.00	4.00	5.00	6.00	6.00
Lebanon Liban	25.00	20.00	20.00	20.00	20.00	20.00	12.00	12.00	12.00	12.00
Lesotho Lesotho	19.00	15.00	13.00	16.19	15.00	13.00	13.00	10.76	12.82	14.05
Libyan Arab Jamah. Jamah. arabe libyenne	5.00	5.00	5.00	5.00	5.00	4.00	4.00	4.00	4.00	5.00
Lithuania [1] Lituanie [1]	...	...	...	...	...	...	3.02	3.79	4.85	4.73
Madagascar Madagascar	15.00	...	...	...	...	...	...	...	...	...
Malawi Malawi	47.00	50.23	46.80	40.00	35.00	25.00	25.00	20.00	15.00	...
Maldives Maldives	...	...	18.00	18.54	19.00	18.25	18.00	#12.00	12.50	13.00
Mali [1] Mali [1]	6.00	6.00	6.00	6.00	4.50	4.00	4.00	4.25	4.25	4.75
Malta Malte	4.75	4.75	4.25	3.75	#3.00	3.00	3.25	3.75	...	...
Mauritania Mauritanie	18.00	13.00	11.00	11.00	11.00	11.00	14.00	14.00	12.00	...
Mongolia [1] Mongolie [1]	11.40	8.65	8.60	9.90	11.50	15.75	4.40	6.42	9.87	14.78
Montserrat Montserrat	8.00	8.00	7.00	7.00	6.50	6.50	6.50	6.50	6.50	6.50
Morocco Maroc	5.42	5.00	4.71	3.79	3.25	3.25	3.25	3.25	3.25	3.32
Mozambique Mozambique	9.95	9.95	9.95	9.95	9.95	9.95	9.95	9.95	9.95	9.95
Myanmar [1] Myanmar [1]	12.00	10.00	10.00	10.00	10.00	10.00	10.00	12.00	12.00	12.00
Namibia [8] Namibie [8]	11.50	11.25	9.25	12.75	7.75	7.50	7.00	9.00	10.50	10.00
Nepal [1] Népal [1]	9.00	7.50	6.50	5.50	5.50	5.50	6.00	6.25	6.25	...
Netherlands Antilles Antilles néerlandaises	6.00	6.00	6.00	6.00	...	...	...	...	...	...

25

Rates of discount of central banks *(continued)*
Per cent per annum, end of period
Taux d'escompte des banques centrales *(suite)*
Pour cent par année, fin de la période

Country or area Pays ou zone	1999	2000	2001	2002	2003	2004	2005	2006	2007	2008
New Zealand Nouvelle-Zélande	5.00	6.50	4.75	5.75	5.00	6.50	7.25	7.25	8.25	5.00
Niger Niger	6.00	6.00	6.00	6.00	4.50	4.00	4.00	4.25	4.25	4.75
Nigeria Nigéria	18.00	14.00	20.50	16.50	15.00	15.00	13.00	10.00	9.50	9.75
Norway Norvège	7.50	9.00	8.50	8.50	4.25	3.75	4.25	5.50	6.25	4.00
Oman Oman	7.30	7.30	7.50	7.50	7.50	#0.69	3.12	3.63	1.98	0.91
Pakistan Pakistan	13.00	13.00	10.00	7.50	7.50	7.50	9.00	9.50	10.00	15.00
Papua New Guinea Papouasie-Nvl-Guinée	16.66	9.79	11.73	11.71	#15.50	12.67	9.67	8.13	7.38	7.00
Paraguay Paraguay	20.00	20.00	20.00	20.00	20.00	20.00	20.00	20.00	20.00	20.00
Peru Pérou	17.80	14.00	5.00	4.50	3.25	3.75	4.00	5.25	5.75	7.25
Philippines Philippines	7.89	13.81	8.30	4.19	5.53	8.36	5.70	5.04	4.28	6.00
Poland Pologne	16.50	19.00	11.50	6.75	5.25	6.50	4.50	4.00	5.00	5.00
Qatar Qatar	...	...	...	1.70	1.33	2.60	4.50	5.50	5.50	5.50
Russian Federation[2] Fédération de Russie[2]	55.00	25.00	25.00	21.00	16.00	13.00	12.00	11.00	10.00	13.00
Rwanda Rwanda	11.19	11.69	13.00	13.00	14.50	14.50	12.50	12.50	12.50	11.25
Saint Kitts and Nevis Saint-Kitts-et-Nevis	8.00	8.00	7.00	7.00	6.50	6.50	6.50	6.50	6.50	6.50
Saint Lucia Sainte-Lucie	8.00	8.00	7.00	7.00	6.50	6.50	6.50	6.50	6.50	6.50
Saint Vincent-Grenadines Saint Vincent-Grenadines	8.00	8.00	7.00	7.00	6.50	6.50	6.50	6.50	6.50	6.50
Sao Tome and Principe Sao Tomé-et-Principe	17.00	17.00	15.50	15.50	14.50	14.50	18.20	28.00	28.00	28.00
Senegal Sénégal	6.00	6.00	6.00	6.00	4.50	4.00	4.00	4.25	4.25	4.75
Serbia[1] Serbie[1]	...	...	18.67	9.72	10.63	#17.21	19.16	15.35	9.57	17.75
Seychelles Seychelles	5.50	5.50	5.50	5.50	4.67	3.51	3.87	4.44	5.13	...
Slovakia Slovaquie	8.80	8.80	#7.75	6.50	6.00	4.00	3.00	4.75	4.25	...
Slovenia[1] Slovénie[1]	9.00	11.00	12.00	10.50	7.25	5.00	5.00	4.50	...	...
South Africa Afrique du Sud	12.00	12.00	9.50	13.50	8.00	7.50	7.00	9.00	11.00	11.50
Sri Lanka[4] Sri Lanka[4]	16.00	25.00	...	18.00	15.00	15.00	15.00	15.00	15.00	15.00
Swaziland Swaziland	12.00	11.00	9.50	13.50	8.00	7.50	7.00	9.00	11.00	11.00
Sweden[1] Suède[1]	1.50	2.00	2.00	#4.50	3.00	2.00	1.50	2.50	3.50	2.00
Switzerland Suisse	0.50	#3.20	1.59	0.50	0.11	0.54	0.73	1.90	2.05	0.05

25
Rates of discount of central banks *(continued)*
Per cent per annum, end of period
Taux d'escompte des banques centrales *(suite)*
Pour cent par année, fin de la période

Country or area Pays ou zone	1999	2000	2001	2002	2003	2004	2005	2006	2007	2008
Syrian Arab Republic Rép. arabe syrienne	5.00	5.00	5.00	5.00	...	...	...	...	5.00	...
Tajikistan [2] Tadjikistan [2]	20.10	20.60	20.00	#24.75	#15.00	10.00	9.00	12.00	15.00	...
Thailand Thaïlande	4.00	3.00	3.75	3.25	2.75	3.50	5.50	6.50	3.75	3.25
TFYR of Macedonia [1] L'ex-R.Y. Macédoine [1]	8.90	7.90	10.70	10.70	6.50	6.50	6.50	6.50	6.50	6.50
Togo Togo	6.00	6.00	6.00	6.00	4.50	4.00	4.00	4.25	4.25	4.75
Trinidad and Tobago [1] Trinité-et-Tobago [1]	13.00	13.00	13.00	7.25	7.00	7.00	8.00	10.00	10.00	10.75
Turkey Turquie	60.00	60.00	60.00	55.00	43.00	38.00	23.00	27.00	25.00	25.00
Uganda [1] Ouganda [1]	15.75	18.86	8.88	13.08	25.62	16.15	14.36	16.30	14.68	...
Ukraine [2] Ukraine [2]	45.00	27.00	12.50	7.00	7.00	9.00	9.50	8.50	8.00	12.00
United Rep. of Tanzania Rép.-Unie de Tanzanie	20.20	10.70	8.70	9.18	12.34	14.42	19.33	20.07	16.40	15.99
United States Etats-Unis	5.00	6.00	1.33	0.75	#2.00	3.15	5.16	6.25	4.83	0.86
Uruguay [9] Uruguay [9]	66.39	57.26	71.66	316.01	46.27	10.00	10.00	10.00	10.00	10.00
Vanuatu Vanuatu	7.00	7.00	6.50	6.50	6.50	6.50	6.25	6.00	6.00	6.00
Venezuela (Bolivarian Rep. of) Venezuela (Rép. boliv. du)	38.00	38.00	37.00	40.00	28.50	28.50	28.50	28.50	28.50	33.50
Viet Nam [2] Viet Nam [2]	6.00	6.00	4.80	4.80	5.00	5.00	5.00	6.50	6.50	10.25
Zambia Zambie	32.93	25.67	40.10	27.87	14.35	16.68	14.81	8.79	11.73	14.49
Zimbabwe [1] Zimbabwe [1]	74.41	57.84	57.20	29.65	300.00	110.00	540.00	500.00	975.00	...

Source:
International Monetary Fund (IMF), Washington, D.C., the International Financial Statistics database, last accessed June 2009.

Source:
Fonds monétaire international (FMI), Washington, D.C., la base de données de Statistiques Financières Internationales, dernier accès juin 2009.

1   Central Bank rate.
2   Refinance rate.
3   Lending rate.
4   Advance rate.
5   Discount rate: commercial.
6   "Euro Area" is an official descriptor for the European Economic and Monetary Union (EMU). The participating member states of the EMU are Austria, Belgium, Cyprus (beginning 2008), Finland, France, Germany, Greece (beginning 2001), Ireland, Italy, Luxembourg, Malta (beginning 2008), Netherlands, Portugal, Slovenia (beginning 2007), and Spain.
7   Marginal lending facility rate.
8   Bank of Namibia overdraft rate.
9   Domestic currency.

1   Taux de la Banque centrale.
2   Taux de refinancement.
3   Taux prêteur.
4   Avances ordinaires à l'état.
5   Taux de l'escompte : effet de commerce.
6   L'expression "zone euro" est un intitulé officiel pour l'Union économique et monétaire (UEM) européenne. L'UEM est composée des pays membres suivants : Allemagne, Autriche, Belgique, Chypre (à partir de 2008), Espagne, Finlande, France, Grèce (à partir de 2001), Irlande, Italie, Luxembourg, Malte (à partir de 2008), Pays-Bas, Portugal et Slovénie (à partir de 2007).
7   Taux de facilité de prêt marginal.
8   Taux de découvert à la "Bank of Namibia".
9   Monnaie locale.

Short-term interest rates
Treasury bill and money market rates: per cent per annum

Taux d'intérêt à court terme
Taux des bons du trésor et du marché monétaire : pour cent par année

Country or area Pays ou zone	1999	2000	2001	2002	2003	2004	2005	2006	2007	2008
Afghanistan Afghanistan										
Money market										
Marché monétaire	...	...	...	...	...	...	...	2.50	5.65	...
Money market B [1]										
Marché monétaire B [1]	...	...	...	...	...	...	...	5.23	4.53	2.23
Albania Albanie										
Treasury bill										
Bons du trésor	17.54	10.80	7.72	9.49	8.81	6.79	5.52	5.49	5.93	6.24
Algeria Algérie										
Money market										
Marché monétaire	9.99	9.49	5.37	2.80	2.74	1.64	1.43	2.05	3.13	3.27
Treasury bill										
Bons du trésor	10.04	9.54	5.85	2.86	1.67	0.87	0.75	2.14	0.96	0.33
Anguilla Anguilla										
Money market										
Marché monétaire	5.25	5.25	#5.64	6.32	6.07	4.67	4.01	4.76	5.24	4.92
Antigua and Barbuda Antigua-et-Barbuda										
Money market										
Marché monétaire	5.25	5.25	#5.64	6.32	6.07	4.67	4.01	4.76	5.24	4.92
Treasury bill										
Bons du trésor	7.00	7.00	7.00	7.00	7.00	7.00	7.00	6.52	6.33	6.02
Argentina Argentine										
Money market										
Marché monétaire	6.99	8.15	24.90	41.35	3.74	1.96	4.11	7.20	8.67	10.07
Money market B [1]										
Marché monétaire B [1]	6.07	7.53	12.76	13.01	1.64	2.03	2.86	3.32	4.55	3.37
Armenia Arménie										
Money market										
Marché monétaire	23.65	18.63	19.40	12.29	7.51	4.18	3.17	4.34	4.47	6.75
Treasury bill										
Bons du trésor	55.10	24.40	#20.59	14.75	11.91	5.27	4.05	4.87	6.09	7.69
Aruba Aruba										
Money market										
Marché monétaire	2.62	3.37	2.19	0.45	0.18	0.11	0.51	2.27	2.53	0.45
Australia Australie										
Money market										
Marché monétaire	#4.78	5.90	5.06	4.55	4.81	5.25	5.46	5.81	6.39	6.67
Treasury bill A [2]										
Bons du trésor A [2]	4.76	5.98	4.80	...	...	...	...	...	...	...
Azerbaijan Azerbaïdjan										
Treasury bill										
Bons du trésor	18.31	16.73	16.51	14.12	8.00	4.62	7.52	10.04	10.64	...
Bahamas Bahamas										
Treasury bill										
Bons du trésor	1.97	1.03	1.94	2.50	1.78	0.56	0.14	0.87	2.66	2.73
Bahrain Bahreïn										
Money market B [3]										
Marché monétaire B [3]	5.58	6.89	3.85	2.02	1.24	1.74	3.64	5.33	...	...
Treasury bill										
Bons du trésor	5.46	6.56	3.78	1.75	1.13	1.56	3.57	5.04	4.86	...
Barbados Barbade										
Treasury bill										
Bons du trésor	5.83	5.29	3.14	2.10	1.41	1.20	4.62	5.96	5.65	...
Belgium Belgique										
Treasury bill										
Bons du trésor	2.72	4.02	4.16	3.17	2.23	1.97	2.02	2.73	3.80	3.63
Belize [4] Belize [4]										
Treasury bill B										
Bons du trésor B	5.91	5.91	5.91	4.59	3.22	3.22	3.22	3.22	3.22	3.22

26
Short-term interest rates *(continued)*
Treasury bill and money market rates: per cent per annum
Taux d'intérêt à court terme *(suite)*
Taux des bons du trésor et du marché monétaire : pour cent par année

Country or area Pays ou zone	1999	2000	2001	2002	2003	2004	2005	2006	2007	2008
Benin [5] Bénin [5]										
Money market A										
Marché monétaire A	4.95	4.95	4.95	4.95	4.95	4.95	4.95	4.95	3.93	3.94
Bolivia Bolivie										
Money market										
Marché monétaire	13.49	7.40	6.99	8.41	4.07	4.05	3.53	3.80	4.27	7.68
Money market B [1]										
Marché monétaire B [1]	8.29	5.68	3.57	2.96	2.12	3.02	3.37	4.62	4.59	6.36
Treasury bill										
Bons du trésor	14.07	10.99	11.48	12.41	9.93	7.41	4.96	4.56	6.04	8.31
Treasury bill B [1]										
Bons du trésor B [1]	7.84	7.02	4.19	3.56	2.53	3.34	2.85	3.68	4.31	4.87
Brazil Brésil										
Money market										
Marché monétaire	26.26	17.59	17.47	19.11	23.37	16.24	19.12	15.28	11.98	12.36
Treasury bill										
Bons du trésor	26.39	18.51	20.06	19.43	22.11	17.14	18.76	14.38	11.50	13.68
Treasury bill B [1]										
Bons du trésor B [1]	...	...	11.46	...	...	...	...	...	...	...
Bulgaria Bulgarie										
Money market B [3]										
Marché monétaire B [3]	2.93	3.02	3.74	2.47	1.95	1.95	#2.02	2.79	4.03	5.16
Treasury bill										
Bons du trésor	5.43	4.21	4.57	4.29	2.81	2.64	2.23	#2.58	3.79	...
Burkina Faso [5] Burkina Faso [5]										
Money market A										
Marché monétaire A	4.95	4.95	4.95	4.95	4.95	4.95	4.95	4.95	3.93	3.94
Burundi Burundi										
Treasury bill										
Bons du trésor	11.04	11.74	16.59	19.19	16.55	14.95	7.92	8.84	...	...
Canada Canada										
Money market A [6]										
Marché monétaire A [6]	4.74	5.52	4.11	2.45	2.93	2.25	2.66	4.02	4.35	2.96
Treasury bill										
Bons du trésor	4.72	5.49	3.77	2.59	2.87	2.22	2.73	4.03	4.15	2.39
Cape Verde Cap-Vert										
Treasury bill										
Bons du trésor	7.19	8.53	10.33	8.04	5.81	6.42	4.07	2.70	3.41	3.41
Chile Chili										
Money market										
Marché monétaire	...	10.09	6.81	4.08	2.72	1.88	3.48	5.02	5.36	7.11
China, Hong Kong SAR Chine, Hong Kong RAS										
Money market										
Marché monétaire	5.75	7.13	2.69	1.50	0.07	0.13	4.25	3.94	1.88	0.23
Treasury bill										
Bons du trésor	4.94	5.69	1.69	1.35	-0.08	0.07	3.65	3.29	1.96	0.05
China, Macao SAR [3] Chine, Macao RAS [3]										
Money market B										
Marché monétaire B	5.70	6.29	2.11	1.48	0.11	0.27	4.09	3.91	3.27	0.30
Colombia [3] Colombie [3]										
Money market B										
Marché monétaire B	18.81	10.87	10.43	6.06	6.95	7.01	6.19	6.49	8.66	9.73
Côte d'Ivoire [5] Côte d'Ivoire [5]										
Money market A										
Marché monétaire A	4.95	4.95	4.95	4.95	4.95	4.95	4.95	4.95	3.93	3.94
Croatia Croatie										
Money market										
Marché monétaire	10.43	6.88	3.42	1.75	3.31	5.11	3.10	2.06	4.27	5.99

26

Short-term interest rates *(continued)*
Treasury bill and money market rates: per cent per annum
Taux d'intérêt à court terme *(suite)*
Taux des bons du trésor et du marché monétaire : pour cent par année

Country or area Pays ou zone	1999	2000	2001	2002	2003	2004	2005	2006	2007	2008
Cyprus Chypre										
Money market										
Marché monétaire	5.15	5.96	4.93	3.42	3.35	4.01	3.27	2.90	4.01	...
Treasury bill										
Bons du trésor	5.54	6.02	5.80	4.04	3.51	4.44	4.34	2.56	3.59	...
Czech Republic République tchèque										
Money market										
Marché monétaire	5.58	5.42	4.69	2.63	2.08	2.56	2.17	2.55	4.11	3.63
Treasury bill										
Bons du trésor	5.71	5.37	5.06	2.72	2.04	2.57	1.96	2.51	3.55	3.62
Denmark[7] Danemark[7]										
Money market B										
Marché monétaire B	3.37	4.98	...	3.56	2.38	2.16	2.20	3.18	#4.33	4.88
Dominica Dominique										
Money market										
Marché monétaire	5.25	5.25	#5.64	6.32	6.07	4.67	4.01	4.76	5.24	4.92
Treasury bill										
Bons du trésor	6.40	6.40	6.40	6.40	6.40	6.40	6.40	6.40	6.40	6.40
Dominican Republic Rép. dominicaine										
Money market										
Marché monétaire	15.30	18.28	13.47	14.50	24.24	36.76	12.57	10.60	8.24	12.24
Egypt Egypte										
Treasury bill										
Bons du trésor	9.00	9.10	7.20	5.50	6.90	9.90	8.57	9.53	6.85	11.37
El Salvador El Salvador										
Money market										
Marché monétaire	10.68	6.93	5.28	4.40	3.86	4.36	5.18	6.00	5.25	...
Estonia Estonie										
Money market										
Marché monétaire	5.39	#5.68	5.31	3.88	2.92	2.50	2.38	3.16	4.87	6.66
Ethiopia Ethiopie										
Treasury bill										
Bons du trésor	3.65	2.74	3.06	1.30	#1.31	0.57	0.25	0.09	...	...
Euro Area[8] Zone euro[8]										
Money market A										
Marché monétaire A	2.96	4.39	4.26	3.26	2.26	2.05	2.12	3.01	3.98	3.78
Fiji Fidji										
Money market A[9]										
Marché monétaire A[9]	1.27	2.58	0.79	0.92	0.86	0.90	1.28	4.78	4.74	0.96
Treasury bill										
Bons du trésor	2.00	3.63	1.51	1.66	1.06	1.56	1.94	7.45	4.48	...
Finland[10] Finlande[10]										
Money market B										
Marché monétaire B	2.96	4.39	4.26	3.32	2.33	2.11	2.19	3.08	4.28	4.63
France[11] France[11]										
Treasury bill A										
Bons du trésor A	2.73	4.24	4.26	3.30	2.28	2.02	2.07	2.89	3.86	3.62
Georgia Géorgie										
Money market										
Marché monétaire	31.26	16.77	17.54	27.69	16.88	11.87	7.71	9.46	7.42	...
Treasury bill										
Bons du trésor	...	...	29.93	43.42	44.26	19.16	...	...	...	...
Germany Allemagne										
Money market B[7]										
Marché monétaire B[7]	2.73	4.11	4.37	3.28	2.32	2.05	2.09	2.84	3.86	3.82
Treasury bill										
Bons du trésor	2.88	4.32	3.66	2.97	1.98	2.00	2.03	3.08	...	...

26

Short-term interest rates *(continued)*
Treasury bill and money market rates: per cent per annum
Taux d'intérêt à court terme *(suite)*
Taux des bons du trésor et du marché monétaire : pour cent par année

Country or area Pays ou zone	1999	2000	2001	2002	2003	2004	2005	2006	2007	2008
Ghana Ghana										
Money market										
Marché monétaire	...	...	...	...	24.71	15.73	14.70	10.57	12.00	15.64
Treasury bill B [12]										
Bons du trésor B [12]	26.37	36.28	40.96	25.11	27.25	16.57	14.89	9.95	9.66	16.96
Greece [13] Grèce [13]										
Treasury bill A										
Bons du trésor A	8.30	#6.22	4.08	3.50	2.34	2.27	2.33	3.44	4.45	4.81
Grenada Grenade										
Money market										
Marché monétaire	5.25	5.25	#5.64	6.32	6.07	4.67	4.01	4.76	5.24	4.94
Treasury bill										
Bons du trésor	6.50	6.50	#7.00	7.00	6.50	5.50	5.50	6.25	6.38	6.25
Guatemala Guatemala										
Money market										
Marché monétaire	9.23	9.33	10.58	9.11	6.65	6.16	6.54	6.56	...	...
Guinea-Bissau Guinée-Bissau										
Money market										
Marché monétaire	4.95	4.95	4.95	4.95	4.95	4.95	4.95	4.95	3.93	3.94
Guyana Guyana										
Treasury bill										
Bons du trésor	11.31	9.88	7.78	4.94	3.04	3.62	3.79	3.95	3.94	3.99
Hungary Hongrie										
Treasury bill										
Bons du trésor	14.68	11.03	10.79	8.91	8.22	11.33	6.95	6.87	7.67	8.90
Iceland Islande										
Money market										
Marché monétaire	9.24	11.61	14.51	11.21	5.14	6.22	9.05	12.41	13.96	16.05
Treasury bill B [14]										
Bons du trésor B [14]	8.61	11.12	11.03	8.01	4.93	6.04	8.80	13.41	15.13	...
India [7] Inde [7]										
Money market B										
Marché monétaire B	...	...	...	...	...	...	...	...	15.29	11.55
Indonesia [7] Indonésie [7]										
Money market B										
Marché monétaire B	23.58	10.32	15.03	13.54	7.76	5.38	6.78	9.18	6.02	8.48
Iraq [15] Iraq [15]										
Money market B										
Marché monétaire B	...	...	...	...	...	...	8.90	9.49	21.00	...
Ireland [16] Irlande [16]										
Money market A										
Marché monétaire A	3.14	4.84	3.31	2.88	2.08	2.13	2.40	3.64	4.71	2.99
Israel Israël										
Treasury bill										
Bons du trésor	11.41	8.81	6.50	7.38	7.00	4.78	4.34	5.54	4.33	3.90
Italy Italie										
Money market										
Marché monétaire	2.95	4.39	4.26	3.32	2.33	2.10	2.18	3.09	4.29	4.67
Treasury bill										
Bons du trésor	3.01	4.53	4.05	3.26	2.19	2.08	2.17	3.18	4.04	3.76
Jamaica Jamaïque										
Money market										
Marché monétaire	21.50	19.90	19.10	15.09	25.53	12.79	10.96	9.37	9.04	10.78
Treasury bill										
Bons du trésor	20.75	18.24	16.71	15.54	25.94	15.47	13.39	12.79	12.56	15.89
Japan [7] Japon [7]										
Money market B										
Marché monétaire B	0.06	0.11	0.06	0.01	^0.00	^0.00	^0.00	0.13	0.47	0.46
Jordan Jordanie										
Money market										
Marché monétaire	5.19	5.28	4.63	3.49	2.58	2.18	3.59	5.55	5.70	4.94

26

Short-term interest rates *(continued)*
Treasury bill and money market rates: per cent per annum
Taux d'intérêt à court terme *(suite)*
Taux des bons du trésor et du marché monétaire : pour cent par année

Country or area Pays ou zone	1999	2000	2001	2002	2003	2004	2005	2006	2007	2008
Kazakhstan Kazakhstan										
Treasury bill										
Bons du trésor	15.63	6.59	5.28	5.20	5.86	3.28	3.28	3.28	7.01	7.00
Kenya Kenya										
Treasury bill										
Bons du trésor	13.87	12.05	12.60	8.95	3.51	3.17	8.43	6.73	6.49	...
Korea, Republic of Corée, République de										
Money market										
Marché monétaire	5.01	5.16	4.69	4.21	4.00	3.65	3.33	4.19	4.77	4.78
Money market B [17]										
Marché monétaire B [17]	8.86	9.35	7.05	6.56	5.43	4.73	4.68	5.17	5.70	7.02
Kuwait Koweït										
Money market A [18]										
Marché monétaire A [18]	6.32	6.82	4.62	2.99	2.47	2.14	2.83	5.62	4.88	2.78
Treasury bill A [11,19]										
Bons du trésor A [11,19]	6.08	6.83	4.23	2.83	2.33	1.75	1.99	...	...	...
Kyrgyzstan Kirghizistan										
Money market										
Marché monétaire	43.71	24.26	11.92	6.30	4.65	4.78	3.24	2.83	3.18	7.62
Treasury bill										
Bons du trésor	47.19	32.26	19.08	10.15	7.21	4.94	4.40	4.75	4.90	13.16
Lao People's Dem. Rep. Rép. dém. pop. lao										
Treasury bill										
Bons du trésor	30.00	29.94	22.70	21.41	24.87	20.37	18.61	18.34	18.36	12.48
Latvia Lettonie										
Money market										
Marché monétaire	4.72	2.97	5.23	3.01	2.86	3.25	2.49	3.24	5.07	4.09
Treasury bill										
Bons du trésor	6.23	#4.85	5.63	3.52	3.24	3.43	2.56	4.13	4.23	6.99
Lebanon Liban										
Treasury bill										
Bons du trésor	11.57	11.18	11.18	10.90	6.46	5.25	5.22	5.22	5.22	5.21
Lesotho Lesotho										
Treasury bill										
Bons du trésor	12.45	9.06	9.49	11.34	11.96	8.52	7.23	6.87	7.81	9.75
Libyan Arab Jamah. [20] Jamah. arabe libyenne [20]										
Money market B										
Marché monétaire B	4.00	4.00	4.00	4.00	4.00	4.00	...	...	...	...
Lithuania Lituanie										
Money market										
Marché monétaire	6.26	3.60	3.37	2.21	1.79	1.53	1.97	2.76	4.18	3.95
Money market B [1]										
Marché monétaire B [1]	5.05	6.10	4.03	1.92	1.72	1.73	2.59	3.06	4.25	2.92
Treasury bill										
Bons du trésor	11.14	#9.27	5.68	3.72	2.61	2.25	2.36	2.95	4.23	...
Madagascar Madagascar										
Money market										
Marché monétaire	17.25	16.00	9.00	9.00	10.50	16.50	16.50	14.50	11.00	11.50
Treasury bill										
Bons du trésor	...	...	10.28	...	11.94	12.95	18.84	21.16	11.84	8.81
Malawi Malawi										
Treasury bill										
Bons du trésor	42.85	39.52	42.41	41.75	39.27	28.58	24.40	19.27	13.95	...
Malaysia Malaisie										
Money market A [9]										
Marché monétaire A [9]	3.38	2.66	2.79	2.73	2.74	2.70	2.72	3.38	3.50	3.47
Treasury bill A [11]										
Bons du trésor A [11]	3.53	2.86	2.79	2.73	2.79	2.40	2.48	3.23	3.43	3.39

26

Short-term interest rates *(continued)*
Treasury bill and money market rates: per cent per annum
Taux d'intérêt à court terme *(suite)*
Taux des bons du trésor et du marché monétaire : pour cent par année

Country or area Pays ou zone	1999	2000	2001	2002	2003	2004	2005	2006	2007	2008
Maldives Maldives										
Money market B [7]										
Marché monétaire B [7]	6.80	6.80	...	...	...	...	...	...	...	...
Treasury bill										
Bons du trésor	...	...	...	...	...	...	...	5.00	5.50	6.00
Mali [5] Mali [5]										
Money market A										
Marché monétaire A	4.95	4.95	4.95	4.95	4.95	4.95	4.95	4.95	3.93	3.94
Malta [11] Malte [11]										
Treasury bill A										
Bons du trésor A	5.15	4.89	4.93	4.03	3.29	2.94	3.18	3.49	4.25	4.54
Mauritania Mauritanie										
Treasury bill										
Bons du trésor	14.16	10.93	3.14	6.01	7.65	7.22	11.84	11.50	10.43	...
Mauritius Maurice										
Money market										
Marché monétaire	10.01	7.66	7.25	6.20	3.22	1.33	2.45	5.59	8.52	7.52
Mexico Mexique										
Money market B [21]										
Marché monétaire B [21]	24.10	16.96	12.89	8.17	6.83	7.15	9.59	7.51	7.66	8.28
Treasury bill										
Bons du trésor	21.41	15.24	11.31	7.09	6.23	6.82	9.20	7.19	7.19	7.68
Montenegro Monténégro										
Treasury bill										
Bons du trésor	...	...	...	...	...	...	6.03	1.15	0.49	0.49
Montserrat Montserrat										
Money market										
Marché monétaire	5.25	5.25	#5.64	6.32	6.07	4.67	4.01	4.76	5.24	4.92
Morocco Maroc										
Money market										
Marché monétaire	5.64	5.41	4.44	2.99	3.22	2.39	2.78	2.58	3.31	3.37
Mozambique Mozambique										
Money market										
Marché monétaire	9.92	16.12	#25.00	20.40	13.34	9.87	6.35	15.25	15.15	12.84
Treasury bill										
Bons du trésor	...	16.97	24.77	29.55	15.31	12.37	9.10	15.05	15.16	13.76
Namibia Namibie										
Money market										
Marché monétaire	13.17	9.19	9.53	10.46	10.03	6.93	6.93	7.12	8.61	9.37
Treasury bill										
Bons du trésor	13.28	10.26	9.29	11.00	10.51	7.78	7.09	7.26	8.59	9.64
Nepal Népal										
Treasury bill										
Bons du trésor	4.30	5.30	5.00	3.80	3.85	2.40	2.20	1.98	3.59	...
Netherlands Antilles [11] Antilles néerlandaises [11]										
Treasury bill A										
Bons du trésor A	6.15	6.15	6.15	5.15	2.80	3.86	3.52	5.39	6.04	4.40
New Zealand Nouvelle-Zélande										
Money market										
Marché monétaire	4.33	6.12	5.76	5.40	5.33	5.77	6.76	7.30	7.93	7.55
Treasury bill A [22]										
Bons du trésor A [22]	4.58	6.39	5.56	5.52	5.21	5.85	6.52	7.05	7.55	7.01
Niger [5] Niger [5]										
Money market A										
Marché monétaire A	4.95	4.95	4.95	4.95	4.95	4.95	4.95	4.95	3.93	3.94
Nigeria Nigéria										
Treasury bill										
Bons du trésor	17.82	15.50	17.50	19.03	14.79	14.34	7.63	9.99	6.85	8.20
Norway [7] Norvège [7]										
Money market B										
Marché monétaire B	6.87	6.72	7.38	7.05	4.45	2.17	2.26	3.12	...	6.06

26

Short-term interest rates *(continued)*
Treasury bill and money market rates: per cent per annum
Taux d'intérêt à court terme *(suite)*
Taux des bons du trésor et du marché monétaire : pour cent par année

Country or area Pays ou zone	1999	2000	2001	2002	2003	2004	2005	2006	2007	2008
Oman[9] Oman[9]										
Money market A										
Marché monétaire A	...	...	...	...	...	0.66	2.25	3.40	1.47	0.29
Pakistan Pakistan										
Money market B[7]										
Marché monétaire B[7]	9.04	8.57	8.49	5.53	2.14	2.70	6.83	8.89	9.30	11.93
Treasury bill A[23]										
Bons du trésor A[23]	...	8.38	10.71	6.08	1.87	2.49	7.18	8.54	8.99	11.37
Panama Panama										
Money market										
Marché monétaire	...	...	...	2.22	1.50	1.90	3.13	5.06	5.05	...
Papua New Guinea Papouasie-Nvl-Guinée										
Money market B[3]										
Marché monétaire B[3]	...	9.54	11.05	9.11	13.58	7.79	4.36	3.29	3.00	5.50
Treasury bill A[24]										
Bons du trésor A[24]	22.70	17.00	12.36	10.93	18.69	8.85	3.81	4.01	4.67	6.19
Paraguay Paraguay										
Money market										
Marché monétaire	17.26	10.70	13.45	13.19	13.02	1.33	2.29	8.33	3.93	4.25
Peru[3] Pérou[3]										
Money market										
Marché monétaire	16.91	11.41	3.15	3.80	2.51	3.00	3.34	4.51	4.99	6.54
Money market B[1]										
Marché monétaire B[1]	6.60	8.40	2.07	2.22	1.09	2.19	4.19	5.37	5.92	1.02
Philippines Philippines										
Money market										
Marché monétaire	10.16	10.84	9.75	7.15	6.97	7.05	7.31	7.84	7.02	5.48
Treasury bill A[15]										
Bons du trésor A[15]	10.00	9.91	9.73	5.49	5.87	7.32	6.13	5.29	3.38	...
Poland Pologne										
Money market										
Marché monétaire	13.89	17.55	17.14	9.49	5.69	5.67	5.34	4.10	4.42	5.75
Treasury bill										
Bons du trésor	12.99	17.42	14.73	8.22	5.38	6.60	4.90	4.19	4.70	6.27
Portugal[25] Portugal[25]										
Money market A										
Marché monétaire A	2.71	...	...	...	...	...	...	...	...	...
Qatar Qatar										
Money market										
Marché monétaire	...	...	...	...	...	2.09	3.13	4.77	4.38	1.06
Republic of Moldova République de Moldova										
Money market										
Marché monétaire	32.60	20.77	11.04	5.13	11.51	13.19	5.87	9.50	12.19	15.58
Money market B[1]										
Marché monétaire B[1]	11.88	6.86	9.06	4.80	2.51	0.78	2.49	4.13	3.96	2.57
Treasury bill										
Bons du trésor	28.49	22.20	14.24	5.89	15.08	11.89	3.70	7.30	13.10	18.07
Romania Roumanie										
Money market										
Marché monétaire	80.76	44.78	40.97	29.05	18.95	20.01	8.99	8.34	7.55	11.37
Treasury bill A[15]										
Bons du trésor A[15]	74.21	51.86	42.18	27.03	15.07	...	...	...	7.11	10.42
Russian Federation Fédération de Russie										
Money market										
Marché monétaire	14.79	7.14	10.10	8.19	3.77	3.33	2.68	3.43	4.43	5.48
Treasury bill										
Bons du trésor	...	12.12	12.45	12.72	5.35	...	...	...	...	...
Rwanda Rwanda										
Money market B[3]										
Marché monétaire B[3]	...	...	10.29	10.09	10.13	11.02	8.28	8.26	7.21	7.13
Treasury bill										
Bons du trésor	...	...	8.89	9.32	11.18	12.52	8.35	9.86	#7.24	...

26
Short-term interest rates *(continued)*
Treasury bill and money market rates: per cent per annum
Taux d'intérêt à court terme *(suite)*
Taux des bons du trésor et du marché monétaire : pour cent par année

Country or area Pays ou zone	1999	2000	2001	2002	2003	2004	2005	2006	2007	2008
Saint Kitts and Nevis **Saint-Kitts-et-Nevis**										
Money market										
Marché monétaire	5.25	5.25	#5.64	6.32	6.07	4.67	4.01	4.76	5.24	4.92
Treasury bill										
Bons du trésor	6.50	6.50	7.50	7.50	7.17	7.00	7.00	7.00	7.00	7.00
Saint Lucia **Sainte-Lucie**										
Money market										
Marché monétaire	5.25	5.25	#5.64	6.32	6.07	4.67	4.01	4.76	5.24	4.92
Treasury bill										
Bons du trésor	6.02	6.02	5.84	5.84	5.44	5.50	4.64	5.17	#5.65	5.60
Saint Vincent-Grenadines **Saint Vincent-Grenadines**										
Money market										
Marché monétaire	5.25	5.25	#5.64	6.32	6.07	4.67	4.01	4.76	5.24	4.92
Treasury bill										
Bons du trésor	6.50	6.50	7.00	7.00	5.73	4.61	4.85	5.62	5.75	5.56
Senegal **Sénégal**										
Money market										
Marché monétaire	4.95	4.95	4.95	4.95	4.95	4.95	4.95	4.95	3.93	3.94
Serbia **Serbie**										
Money market										
Marché monétaire	...	...	31.91	15.48	12.69	12.86	20.51	16.51	10.31	18.52
Treasury bill										
Bons du trésor	...	...	...	...	20.02	21.17	14.58	10.24	4.42	9.61
Seychelles **Seychelles**										
Treasury bill										
Bons du trésor	5.00	5.00	5.00	5.00	4.61	3.17	3.34	3.70	3.92	7.07
Sierra Leone **Sierra Leone**										
Treasury bill										
Bons du trésor	32.42	26.22	13.74	15.15	15.68	26.14	22.98	17.71	18.41	15.48
Singapore **Singapour**										
Money market A [8]										
Marché monétaire A [8]	2.04	2.57	1.99	0.96	0.74	1.04	2.28	3.46	2.72	1.31
Treasury bill										
Bons du trésor	1.12	2.18	1.69	0.81	0.64	0.96	2.04	2.95	2.34	0.87
Slovakia **Slovaquie**										
Money market										
Marché monétaire	...	8.08	7.76	6.33	6.08	3.82	3.02	4.83	4.25	...
Slovenia **Slovénie**										
Money market										
Marché monétaire	6.87	6.95	6.90	4.93	5.59	4.40	3.73	3.38	4.08	4.27
Treasury bill										
Bons du trésor	8.63	10.94	10.88	8.73	6.53	4.17	3.66	3.30	3.90	3.88
Solomon Islands [11] **Iles Salomon** [11]										
Treasury bill A										
Bons du trésor A	6.00	7.05	8.23	7.52	5.85	6.00	4.53	#3.41	3.17	3.20
South Africa **Afrique du Sud**										
Money market										
Marché monétaire	13.06	9.54	#8.49	11.11	10.93	7.15	6.62	7.19	#9.22	11.32
Treasury bill										
Bons du trésor	12.85	10.11	9.68	11.16	10.67	7.53	6.91	7.34	9.12	10.81
Spain **Espagne**										
Money market B [7]										
Marché monétaire B [7]	2.72	4.11	4.36	3.28	2.31	2.04	2.09	2.83	3.85	3.85
Treasury bill										
Bons du trésor	3.01	4.61	3.92	3.34	2.21	2.17	2.19	3.26	4.07	3.71
Sri Lanka **Sri Lanka**										
Money market B [26]										
Marché monétaire B [26]	16.69	17.30	21.24	12.33	9.68	8.87	10.15	12.89	30.88	21.22
Treasury bill										
Bons du trésor	12.51	14.02	17.57	12.47	8.09	7.71	9.03	10.98	16.60	18.91

26
Short-term interest rates *(continued)*
Treasury bill and money market rates: per cent per annum
Taux d'intérêt à court terme *(suite)*
Taux des bons du trésor et du marché monétaire : pour cent par année

Country or area Pays ou zone	1999	2000	2001	2002	2003	2004	2005	2006	2007	2008
Swaziland Swaziland										
Money market										
Marché monétaire	8.86	5.54	5.06	7.31	6.98	4.12	3.47	4.40	6.67	8.17
Treasury bill										
Bons du trésor	11.19	8.30	7.16	8.59	10.61	7.94	7.08	7.54	9.03	10.77
Sweden Suède										
Money market B[7]										
Marché monétaire B[7]	3.14	3.81	4.09	4.19	3.29	...	...	...	...	...
Treasury bill A[27]										
Bons du trésor A[27]	3.12	3.95	4.00	4.07	3.03	2.11	1.72	2.33	3.55	3.91
Switzerland Suisse										
Money market										
Marché monétaire	1.09	3.50	1.65	0.44	0.09	0.55	0.63	1.94	2.00	0.01
Treasury bill										
Bons du trésor	1.17	2.93	2.68	0.94	0.16	0.37	0.71	1.36	2.16	1.33
Thailand Thaïlande										
Money market										
Marché monétaire	1.77	1.95	2.00	1.76	1.31	1.23	2.62	4.64	3.75	3.28
Togo[5] Togo[5]										
Money market A										
Marché monétaire A	4.95	4.95	4.95	4.95	4.95	4.95	4.95	4.95	3.93	3.94
Trinidad and Tobago Trinité-et-Tobago										
Treasury bill										
Bons du trésor	10.40	10.56	8.55	4.83	4.71	4.77	4.86	6.07	6.91	7.01
Tunisia Tunisie										
Money market										
Marché monétaire	5.99	5.88	6.04	5.94	5.14	5.00	5.00	5.07	5.24	5.21
Turkey Turquie										
Money market B[3]										
Marché monétaire B[3]	73.53	56.72	91.95	49.51	36.16	21.42	14.73	15.59	17.24	16.00
Treasury bill										
Bons du trésor	...	37.77	93.24	59.50	34.90	22.08	15.49	18.37	17.65	...
Uganda[15] Ouganda[15]										
Treasury bill A										
Bons du trésor A	7.43	13.19	11.00	5.85	16.87	9.02	8.50	8.12	9.05	8.74
Ukraine Ukraine										
Money market										
Marché monétaire	44.98	18.34	16.57	5.50	7.90	6.34	4.16	3.59	2.27	13.71
Money market B[1]										
Marché monétaire B[1]	5.44	6.27	5.87	3.14	3.61	2.15	2.85	4.13	4.82	4.30
United Kingdom Royaume-Uni										
Money market A[28]										
Marché monétaire A[28]	5.20	5.77	5.08	3.89	3.59	4.29	4.70	4.77	5.67	4.65
Treasury bill										
Bons du trésor	5.04	5.80	4.77	3.86	3.55	4.43	4.55	4.65	5.52	4.30
Treasury bill B[29]										
Bons du trésor B[29]	5.14	5.83	4.79	3.96	3.55	4.44	4.59	4.67	5.60	4.35
United Rep. of Tanzania Rép.-Unie de Tanzanie										
Treasury bill										
Bons du trésor	10.05	9.78	4.21	3.53	6.26	8.35	10.67	11.64	13.38	8.11
United States Etats-Unis										
Money market A[30]										
Marché monétaire A[30]	5.18	6.31	3.61	1.69	1.11	1.49	3.38	5.03	4.99	2.12
Money market B[31]										
Marché monétaire B[31]	4.97	6.24	3.89	1.67	1.13	1.35	3.21	4.96	5.02	1.93
Treasury bill										
Bons du trésor	4.66	5.84	3.45	1.61	1.01	1.37	3.15	4.72	4.41	1.46
Treasury bill A[11]										
Bons du trésor A[11]	4.77	6.00	3.48	1.63	1.02	1.39	3.21	4.85	4.45	1.37

Short-term interest rates *(continued)*
Treasury bill and money market rates: per cent per annum

Taux d'intérêt à court terme *(suite)*
Taux des bons du trésor et du marché monétaire : pour cent par année

Country or area Pays ou zone	1999	2000	2001	2002	2003	2004	2005	2006	2007	2008
Uruguay Uruguay										
Money market										
Marché monétaire	13.96	14.82	22.10	86.10	20.76	3.57	1.25	1.60	4.10	9.80
Treasury bill										
Bons du trésor	...	...	...	...	32.53	14.75	4.14	4.54	7.11	...
Vanuatu[32] Vanuatu[32]										
Money market B										
Marché monétaire B	6.99	5.58	5.50	5.50	5.50	5.50	5.50	5.50	5.50	5.78
Venezuela (Bolivarian Rep. of) Venezuela (Rép. bolivarienne du)										
Money market										
Marché monétaire	7.48	8.14	13.33	28.87	13.23	4.38	2.62	5.26	8.72	11.09
Viet Nam Viet Nam										
Treasury bill										
Bons du trésor	...	5.42	5.49	5.92	5.83	5.69	6.13	4.73	4.15	...
Yemen Yémen										
Treasury bill										
Bons du trésor	20.57	14.16	13.25	11.55	12.92	13.84	14.89	15.65	15.86	15.20
Zambia Zambie										
Treasury bill										
Bons du trésor	36.19	31.37	44.28	34.54	29.98	12.60	16.32	10.37	11.95	13.47
Zimbabwe Zimbabwe										
Money market A[8]										
Marché monétaire A[8]	53.13	64.98	21.52	32.35	110.05	129.58	...	...	...	...
Treasury bill										
Bons du trésor	50.48	64.78	17.60	28.51	52.72	125.68	185.11	322.36	248.77	...

Source:
International Monetary Fund (IMF), Washington, D.C., the database on International Financial Statistics, last accessed July 2009.

1	Foreign currency.
2	13 weeks.
3	Interbank.
4	Discount rate.
5	Overnight advances.
6	Overnight rate.
7	Call money rate.
8	3-month interbank rate.
9	Overnight interbank.
10	Average cost of Central Bank debt.
11	3 months.
12	Discounted.
13	12 months.
14	Yield.
15	91 days.
16	1-month fixed rate.
17	Corporate bond rate.
18	Interbank deposit rate (3 months).
19	Central Bank bill rate.
20	Interbank call loans (maximum rate).
21	Bankers' acceptances.
22	New issue rate: 3-month treasury bills.
23	6 months.
24	182 days.
25	Up-to-5-days interbank deposit.
26	Interbank call loans.
27	3-month discount notes.
28	Overnight interbank minimum.
29	Bond equivalent.
30	Commercial paper (3 months).
31	Federal funds rate.
32	Interbank borrowing rate.

Source:
Fonds monétaire international (FMI), Washington, D.C., la base de données de Statistiques Financières Internationales, dernier accès juillet 2009.

1	Devises.
2	Treize semaines.
3	Interbancaire.
4	Taux de l'escompte.
5	Taux des avances à un jour.
6	Taux à un jour.
7	Taux de l'argent au jour le jour.
8	Taux interbancaire à trois mois.
9	Taux interbancaire à un jour.
10	Coût moyen de la dette à la Banque centrale.
11	Trois mois.
12	Taux actualisé.
13	Douze mois.
14	Rendement.
15	Quatre-vingt-onze jours.
16	Taux forfaitaire à un mois.
17	Taux des obligations de société.
18	Taux des dépôts interbancaires (à trois mois).
19	Taux d'escompte de la Banque Centrale (a trois mois).
20	Prêts interbancaires remboursables sur demande (taux maximum).
21	Traite bancaire.
22	Taux des émissions nouvelles : bons du Trésor à trois mois.
23	Six mois.
24	182 jours.
25	Dépôts interbancaires jusqu'à cinq jours.
26	Prêts interbancaires remboursables sur demande.
27	Billets à escompte à trois mois.
28	Taux minimum des prêts interbancaires à un jour.
29	Équivalant à obligation.
30	Effet de commerce (à trois mois).
31	Taux des fonds fédéraux.
32	Taux des prêts interbancaires.

Technical notes: tables 25 and 26

Detailed information and current figures relating to tables 25 and 26 are contained in *International Financial Statistics*, published by the International Monetary Fund (see also www.imf.org) and in the United Nations *Monthly Bulletin of Statistics*.

Table 25: The discount rates shown represent the rates at which the central bank lends or discounts eligible paper for deposit money banks, typically shown on an end-of-period basis.

Table 26: The rates shown represent short-term treasury bill rates and money market rates. The treasury bill rate is the rate at which short-term securities are issued or traded in the market. The money market rate is the rate on short-term lending between financial institutions. The naming conventions for money market rates and treasury bill yields sometimes vary among countries. In table 26, three money market and treasury bill descriptions are used: (i) "Money market"/"Treasury bill", (ii) "Money market A"/"Treasury bill A" and (iii) "Money market B"/"Treasury bill B". These distinctions are shown for those countries for which more than one type of money market rate or treasury bill yield is differentiated by the International Monetary Fund in *International Financial Statistics*. In this table, "Money market A" and "Treasury bill A" generally refer to those interest rates or yields whose durations have been specified (e.g. overnight, one month, 91 days, etc.) and "Money market B" and "Treasury bill B" refer to all others containing specific descriptors such as "call money rate", "foreign currency", "interbank", "discounted rate", etc.

Notes techniques : tableaux 25 et 26

Les informations détaillées et les chiffres courants concernant les tableaux 25 et 26 figurent dans les *Statistiques financières internationales* publiées par le Fonds monétaire international (voir aussi www.imf.org) et dans le *Bulletin mensuel de statistique* des Nations Unies.

Tableau 25: Les taux d'escomptes indiqués représentent les taux que la banque centrale applique à ses prêts ou auquel elle réescompte les effets escomptables des banques créatrices de monnaie (généralement, taux de fin de période).

Tableau 26: Les taux indiqués représentent le taux des bons du Trésor et le taux du marché monétaire à court terme. Le taux des bons du Trésor est le taux auquel les effets à court terme sont émis ou négociés sur le marché. Le taux du marché monétaire est le taux prêteur à court terme entre institutions financières. La manière dont par convention on dénomme les taux du marché monétaire et le rendement des bons du Trésor peut varier selon les pays. Dans le tableau 26, on utilise trois termes pour le marché monétaire et les bons du Trésor : i) "Marché monétaire"/ "Bons du Trésor", ii) "Marché monétaire A"/ "Bons du Trésor A", iii) "Marché monétaire B"/ "Bons du Trésor B". Ces distinctions apparaissent pour les pays où le Fonds monétaire international distingue dans *Statistiques financières internationales* plus d'un type de taux du marché monétaire ou de rendement de bons du Trésor. En général, dans ce tableau, "Marché monétaire A" et "Bons du Trésor A" désignent les taux d'intérêt ou les rendements dont la durée a été précisée (au jour le jour, à un mois, à 91 jours, etc.), "Marché monétaire B" et "Bons du Trésor B" désignant tous les autres assortis de descripteurs précis tels que taux de l'argent au jour le jour, en devises, interbancaire, taux escompté, etc.

Country or area, source [§] Pays ou zone, source [§]	2001	2002	2003	2004	2005	2006	2007	2008
Afghanistan [1] Afghanistan [1]								
MF [BA]	...	...	...	...	363.8	...	...	...
M [BA]	...	...	...	...	172.7	...	...	...
F [BA]	...	...	...	...	191.1	...	...	...
%MF [BA]	...	...	...	...	8.5	...	...	...
%M [BA]	...	...	...	...	7.6	...	...	...
%F [BA]	...	...	...	...	9.5	...	...	...
Albania [1] Albanie [1]								
MF [A] [2]	305.5	...	...	...	...	...		
M [A] [2]	150.1	...	...	...	...	...		
F [A] [2]	155.4	...	...	...	...	...		
MF [FB] [3]	180.5	172.4	163.0	157.0	153.3	149.8		
M [FB] [3]	96.0	91.0	86.0	82.0	79.0	77.0		
F [FB] [3]	85.0	81.4	77.0	75.0	74.0	73.0		
%MF [FB] [3]	16.4	15.8	15.0	14.4	14.1	13.8		
%M [FB] [3]	14.2	13.6	12.9	12.4	12.1	11.8		
%F [FB] [3]	19.9	19.1	18.2	17.5	17.2	16.8		
Algeria [1] Algérie [1]								
MF [BA]	2 339.4	2 247.3	2 078.0	1 671.5	1 474.5	1 240.8	1 374.6	...
M [BA]	1 934.9	...	1 759.9	1 370.4	1 221.0	988.3	1 072.0	...
F [BA]	404.5	...	318.3	301.1	253.5	252.6	302.7	...
%MF [BA]	27.3	25.9	23.7	17.7	15.3	12.3	13.8	...
%M [BA]	26.6	...	23.4	17.5	14.9	11.8	12.9	...
%F [BA]	31.4	...	25.4	18.1	17.5	14.4	18.4	...
Anguilla [1] Anguilla [1]								
MF [A] [4]	0.4	...	...	...	...	...	...	...
M [A] [4]	0.2	...	...	...	...	...	...	...
F [A] [4]	0.2	...	...	...	...	...	...	...
%MF [A] [4]	6.7	...	...	...	...	...	...	...
%M [A] [4]	6.5	...	...	...	...	...	...	...
%F [A] [4]	7.0	...	...	...	...	...	...	...
MF [BA] [5]	...	0.5	...	...	...	...	...	...
M [BA] [5]	...	0.2	...	...	...	...	...	...
F [BA] [5]	...	0.3	...	...	...	...	...	...
%MF [BA] [5]	...	7.8	...	...	...	...	...	...
%M [BA] [5]	...	6.3	...	...	...	...	...	...
%F [BA] [5]	...	9.5	...	...	...	...	...	...
Antigua and Barbuda [1,4] Antigua-et-Barbuda [1,4]								
MF [A]	3.3	...	...	...	...	...	...	...
M [A]	1.6	...	...	...	...	...	...	...
F [A]	1.7	...	...	...	...	...	...	...
Argentina Argentine								
MF [A] [6,7]	4 351.6	...	...	...	...	...	...	...
M [A] [6,7]	2 212.8	...	...	...	...	...	...	...
F [A] [6,7]	2 138.8	...	...	...	...	...	...	...
MF [BA] [9]	#1 709.8 [10,11]	1 955.8 [10,11]	#1 633.0 [8,10]	1 361.6 [8,10]	1 141.5 [8,10]	1 049.2 [8,12]	936.0 [12,13]	898.0 [12,13]
M [BA] [9]	#1 021.9 [10,11]	1 175.2 [10,11]	#824.8 [8,10]	687.6 [8,10]	561.7 [8,10]	488.9 [8,12]	...	...
F [BA] [9]	#688.4 [10,11]	780.6 [10,11]	#808.2 [8,10]	673.9 [8,10]	579.8 [8,10]	560.3 [8,12]	...	...
%MF [BA] [9]	#17.4 [10,11]	19.6 [10,11]	#15.4 [8,10]	12.6 [8,10]	10.6 [8,10]	9.5 [8,12]	...	...
%M [BA] [9]	#17.4 [10,11]	20.2 [10,11]	#13.8 [8,10]	11.2 [8,10]	9.2 [8,10]	7.8 [8,12]	...	...
%F [BA] [9]	#17.2 [10,11]	18.8 [10,11]	#17.5 [8,10]	14.5 [8,10]	12.4 [8,10]	11.7 [8,12]	...	...
Armenia Arménie								
MF [A] [1,14]	570.5	...	...	...	...	...	...	...
M [A] [1,14]	268.8	...	...	...	...	...	...	...
F [A] [1,14]	301.7	...	...	...	...	...	...	...
MF [BA] [15]	...	...	...	...	...	...	470.9	...
M [BA] [15]	...	...	...	...	...	...	183.7	...
F [BA] [16]	...	...	...	...	...	...	287.2	...
%MF [BA] [15]	...	...	...	...	...	...	28.4	...

27

Unemployment *(continued)*
Number (thousands) and percentage unemployed, by sex
Chômage *(suite)*
Nombre (milliers) et pourcentage des chômeurs, par sexe

Country or area, source [§] Pays ou zone, source [§]	2001	2002	2003	2004	2005	2006	2007	2008
%M [BA] [15]	...	...	...	...	...	...	21.9	...
%F [BA] [15]	...	...	...	...	...	...	35.0	...
MF [E] [16]	146.8	133.7	124.8	114.8	98.0	88.9	82.8	...
M [E] [16]	50.9	44.9	40.1	35.0	29.0	25.5	22.9	...
F [E] [16]	95.9	88.8	84.7	79.8	69.0	63.4	59.9	...
%MF [E] [16]	10.4	10.8	10.1	9.6	8.2	7.5	7.1	...
%M [E] [16]	6.9	7.2	5.9	5.2	4.6	4.1	3.8	...
%F [E] [16]	14.1	14.5	14.4	14.3	12.1	11.3	10.8	...
MF [FB] [3,16]	138.4	127.3	118.6	108.6	89.0	84.6	75.1	74.7
M [FB] [3,16]	47.1	85.7	37.0	32.3	26.0	23.9	19.9	18.3
F [FB] [3,16]	91.3	41.6	81.6	76.3	63.0	60.7	55.2	56.4
Aruba [1,14] Aruba [1,14]								
MF [BA]	...	...	...	...	...	...	3.1	...
M [BA]	...	...	...	...	...	...	1.4	...
F [BA]	...	...	...	...	...	...	1.7	...
%MF [BA]	...	...	...	...	...	...	5.7	...
%M [BA]	...	...	...	...	...	...	5.0	...
%F [BA]	...	...	...	...	...	...	6.5	...
Australia [1,17] Australie [1,17]								
MF [BA]	663.5	631.2	596.0	554.7	529.0	517.7	487.5	470.9
M [BA]	381.8	360.9	324.9	299.4	283.1	277.5	245.7	236.9
F [BA]	281.7	270.3	271.1	255.4	245.9	240.1	241.7	234.0
%MF [BA]	6.8	6.4	5.9	5.5	5.0	4.8	4.4	4.2
%M [BA]	7.1	6.6	5.9	5.3	4.9	4.7	4.1	3.9
%F [BA]	6.5	6.2	6.0	5.6	5.2	4.9	4.8	4.6
Austria [1] Autriche [1]								
MF [A] [4]	255.2	...	...	...	...	...	...	...
M [A] [4]	138.9	...	...	...	...	...	...	...
F [A] [4]	115.3	...	...	...	...	...	...	...
MF [BA]	142.5[18]	161.0[18]	168.8	#194.6	207.7	195.6	185.6	162.3
M [BA]	77.0[18]	91.7[18]	94.7	#98.0	107.8	97.1	89.7	81.8
F [BA]	65.5[18]	69.3[18]	74.3	#96.6	100.0	98.5	95.8	80.5
%MF [BA]	3.6[18]	4.0[18]	4.3	#4.9	5.2	4.7	4.4	3.8
%M [BA]	3.5[18]	4.1[18]	4.3	#4.5	4.9	4.3	3.9	3.6
%F [BA]	3.8[18]	3.9[18]	4.2	#5.4	5.5	5.2	5.0	4.1
MF [FB]	203.9	232.4	240.1	243.9	252.7	239.2	222.2	212.3
M [FB]	115.3	134.4	139.7	140.2	144.2	135.8	124.3	118.8
F [FB]	88.6	98.0	100.4	103.6	108.4	103.4	97.9	93.4
%MF [FB]	6.1	6.9	7.0	7.1	7.3	6.8	6.2	5.8
%M [FB]	6.2	7.2	7.5	7.5	7.7	7.1	6.5	6.1
%F [FB]	5.9	6.4	6.5	6.6	6.8	6.4	6.0	5.6
Azerbaijan [19] Azerbaïdjan [19]								
MF [BA]	...	...	404.7	...	...	291.2	281.1	261.4
M [BA]	...	...	210.5	...	...	157.0	169.9	156.9
F [BA]	...	...	194.2	...	...	134.2	111.2	104.5
%MF [BA]	...	...	10.7	...	...	6.8	6.5	6.1
%M [BA]	...	...	9.6	...	...	6.9	7.8	7.1
%F [BA]	...	...	12.2	...	...	6.7	5.3	4.9
MF [E]	...	...	400.9	348.7	317.8	...	...	...
M [E]	...	...	206.2	179.8	164.1	...	...	...
F [E]	...	...	194.7	168.9	153.7	...	...	...
%MF [E]	...	...	9.7	8.4	7.6	...	...	...
%M [E]	...	...	9.5	8.3	7.5	...	...	...
%F [E]	...	...	9.8	8.5	7.7	...	...	...
MF [FB] [3]	48.4	51.0	54.4	55.9	56.3	53.9	50.7	44.5
M [FB] [3]	21.8	23.1	25.3	26.7	27.3	26.3	25.3	23.6
F [FB] [3]	26.6	27.9	29.1	29.3	29.1	27.5	25.3	20.9
%MF [FB] [3]	1.3	1.3	1.3	1.3	1.4	1.3	1.2	1.0
%M [FB] [3]	1.1	1.2	1.2	1.2	1.2	1.2	1.2	1.1
%F [FB] [3]	1.5	1.5	1.5	1.5	1.5	1.3	1.2	1.0

27

Unemployment *(continued)*
Number (thousands) and percentage unemployed, by sex
Chômage *(suite)*
Nombre (milliers) et pourcentage des chômeurs, par sexe

Country or area, source [§] Pays ou zone, source [§]	2001	2002	2003	2004	2005	2006	2007	2008
Bahamas[1] Bahamas[1]								
MF [BA]	11.3[20]	15.3[20]	18.8[20]	18.0[20]	18.2[20]	13.8[4]	14.6[20]	...
M [BA]	5.7[20]	7.6[20]	8.8[20]	8.5[20]	8.4[20]	6.4[4]	6.4[20]	...
F [BA]	5.6[20]	7.7[20]	10.1[20]	9.5[20]	9.8[20]	7.5[4]	8.2[20]	...
%MF [BA]	6.9[20]	9.1[20]	10.8[20]	10.2[20]	10.2[20]	7.6[4]	7.9[20]	...
%M [BA]	6.7[20]	8.8[20]	10.0[20]	9.4[20]	9.2[20]	6.9[4]	6.7[20]	...
%F [BA]	7.0[20]	9.4[20]	11.7[20]	11.0[20]	11.2[20]	8.4[4]	9.1[20]	...
Bahrain Bahreïn								
MF [A][1,2]	17.0	...	...	...	...	...	...	...
M [A][1,2]	10.0	...	...	...	...	...	...	...
F [A][1,2]	7.0	...	...	...	...	...	...	...
MF [FB][21]	...	8.7[1]	11.8[1]	6.3[1]	6.4[1]	6.8[1]	9.5[1]	5.3[22]
M [FB][21]	...	4.4[1]	6.0[1]	3.1[1]	2.9[1]	1.5[1]	1.2[1]	0.8[22]
F [FB][21]	...	4.4[1]	5.7[1]	3.2[1]	3.5[1]	5.3[1]	8.3[1]	4.5[22]
Bangladesh[1,23] Bangladesh[1,23]								
MF [BA]	...		2 002.0	...	2 104.0	...	...	...
M [BA]	...	...	1 500.0	...	1 256.0	...	...	...
F [BA]	...	...	502.0	...	854.0	...	...	...
%MF [BA]	...	...	4.3	...	4.3	...	...	...
%M [BA]	...	...	4.2	...	3.4	...	...	...
%F [BA]	...	...	4.9	...	7.0	...	...	...
Barbados[1] Barbade[1]								
MF [BA]	14.3	14.8	16.0	14.3	13.3	12.5	10.7	11.6
M [BA]	6.0	6.4	7.1	6.7	5.5	5.6	4.8	5.0
F [BA]	8.3	8.4	8.9	7.5	7.8	6.8	5.9	6.6
%MF [BA]	9.9	10.3	11.0	9.8	9.1	8.7	7.4	8.1
%M [BA]	8.0	8.2	9.6	9.0	7.3	7.6	6.4	6.8
%F [BA]	11.9	12.4	12.6	10.6	10.9	9.7	8.5	9.4
Belarus[3,24] Bélarus[3,24]								
MF [FB]	102.9	130.5	136.1	83.0	67.9	52.0	44.1	37.3
M [FB]	40.9	47.8	46.1	25.5	21.1	17.7	15.2	14.7
F [FB]	62.0	82.7	90.0	57.5	46.8	34.3	28.9	22.6
%MF [FB]	2.3	3.0	3.1	1.9	1.5	1.2	1.0	0.8
%M [FB]	1.9	2.3	1.2	1.2	1.0	0.8	0.7	0.7
%F [FB]	2.6	3.5	3.9	2.4	2.0	1.5	1.2	0.9
Belgium Belgique								
MF [BA][1]	286.4	332.1	364.3	380.3	390.3	383.2	353.0	333.7
M [BA][1]	147.9	168.1	193.0	191.4	196.0	191.0	174.4	170.4
F [BA][1]	138.4	164.0	171.3	188.9	194.3	192.2	178.6	163.2
%MF [BA][1]	6.6	7.5	8.2	8.5	8.5	8.3	7.5	7.0
%M [BA][1]	6.0	6.7	7.7	7.6	7.7	7.5	6.7	6.5
%F [BA][1]	7.5	8.7	8.9	9.6	9.6	9.4	8.5	7.6
MF [FB]	469.7	491.5	538.1	...	...	...	...	...
M [FB]	210.8	228.1	253.1	...	...	...	...	...
F [FB]	258.9	263.4	285.1	...	...	...	...	...
%MF [FB]	10.8	11.2	12.3	...	...	...	...	...
%M [FB]	8.7	9.4	10.4	...	...	...	...	...
%F [FB]	13.4	13.6	14.7	...	...	...	...	...
Belize[6] Belize[6]								
MF [BA]	8.6[20]	9.5[20]	...	...	12.2[20]	10.6[20]	10.4[20]	10.2[4]
M [BA][20]	3.6	4.7	...	...	5.2	4.5	4.5	...
F [BA][20]	5.0	4.7	...	...	7.0	6.1	5.9	...
%MF [BA]	9.1[20]	10.0[20]	...	...	11.0[20]	9.4[20]	8.5[20]	8.2[4]
%M [BA][20]	5.8	7.5	...	...	7.4	6.2	5.8	...
%F [BA][20]	15.4	15.3	...	...	17.2	15.0	13.1	...
Benin[21] Bénin[21]								
MF [A]	...	20.5	...	...	...	...	...	...
M [A]	...	13.6	...	...	...	...	...	...
F [A]	...	6.8	...	...	...	...	...	...

Country or area, source [§] Pays ou zone, source [§]	2001	2002	2003	2004	2005	2006	2007	2008
Bhutan [1,4] **Bhoutan** [1,4]								
MF [A]	...	...	...	...	7.9	...	...	...
M [A]	...	...	...	...	4.8	...	...	...
F [A]	...	...	...	...	3.1	...	...	...
Bolivia [7,9] **Bolivie** [7,9]								
MF [BA]	214.9	221.6	...	182.4	245.2	243.5	255.0	...
M [BA]	99.4	97.4	...	84.2	112.1	119.1	122.4	...
F [BA]	115.2	124.2	...	98.2	133.1	124.5	132.6	...
%MF [BA]	5.2	5.5	...	4.2	5.4	5.1	5.2	...
%M [BA]	4.5	4.3	...	3.6	4.5	4.5	4.5	...
%F [BA]	6.2	6.9	...	4.9	6.5	5.7	6.0	...
Bosnia and Herzegovina [1] **Bosnie-Herzégovine** [1]								
MF [BA]	...	...	...	...	...	366.0	347.0	272.0
M [BA]	...	...	...	...	...	215.0	203.0	156.0
F [BA]	...	...	...	...	...	151.0	144.0	116.0
%MF [BA]	...	...	...	...	...	31.1	29.0	23.4
%M [BA]	...	...	...	...	...	28.9	26.7	21.4
%F [BA]	...	...	...	...	...	34.9	32.9	26.8
Botswana [25] **Botswana** [25]								
MF [A] [26]	109.5	...	...	...	...	...	...	...
M [A] [26]	51.9	...	...	...	...	...	...	...
F [A] [26]	57.6	...	...	...	...	...	...	...
%MF [A] [26]	19.6	...	...	...	...	...	...	...
%M [A] [26]	16.4	...	...	...	...	...	...	...
%F [A] [26]	23.9	...	...	...	...	...	...	...
MF [BA]	...	...	144.5	...	...	114.4	...	...
M [BA]	...	...	66.9	...	...	50.9	...	...
F [BA]	...	...	77.6	...	...	63.5	...	...
%MF [BA]	...	...	23.8	...	...	17.6	...	...
%M [BA]	...	...	21.4	...	...	15.3	...	...
%F [BA]	...	...	26.3	...	...	19.9	...	...
Brazil [9,27] **Brésil** [9,27]								
MF [BA]	7 853.4 [28]	7 958.5 [28]	8 640.0	8 263.8	8 953.0	8 210.0	8 059.6	...
M [BA]	3 674.9 [28]	3 685.1 [28]	3 972.8	3 590.7	3 859.0	3 510.0	3 390.9	...
F [BA]	4 178.5 [28]	4 273.3 [28]	4 667.1	4 673.1	5 094.0	4 700.0	4 668.7	...
%MF [BA]	9.4 [28]	9.2 [28]	9.7	8.9	9.3	8.4	8.2	...
%M [BA]	7.5 [28]	7.4 [28]	7.8	6.8	7.1	6.4	6.1	...
%F [BA]	11.9 [28]	11.6 [28]	12.3	11.7	12.2	11.0	10.8	...
Brunei Darussalam **Brunéi Darussalam**								
MF [FB]	8.6	5.6	7.1	...	...	...	...	...
M [FB]	3.3	2.1	3.1	...	...	...	...	...
F [FB]	5.3	3.4	4.0	...	...	...	...	...
Bulgaria **Bulgarie**								
MF [A] [1,29]	1 257.0	...	...	...	...	...	...	...
M [A] [1,29]	682.5	...	...	...	...	...	...	...
F [A] [1,29]	574.5	...	...	...	...	...	...	...
MF [BA] [1]	661.1 [32]	599.2 [32]	449.1	399.8	334.2	305.7	240.2	199.7
M [BA] [1]	363.2 [32]	328.7 [32]	246.1	221.6	182.5	156.4	120.7	103.9
F [BA] [1]	297.8 [32]	270.4 [32]	203.0	178.2	151.6	149.3	119.5	95.8
%MF [BA] [1]	19.4 [32]	17.6 [32]	13.7	12.0	10.1	9.0	6.9	5.6
%M [BA] [1]	20.2 [32]	18.3 [32]	14.1	12.5	10.3	8.6	6.5	5.5
%F [BA] [1]	18.4 [32]	16.9 [32]	13.2	11.5	9.8	9.3	7.3	5.8
MF [FB] [3,30,31]	662.3	602.5	500.7	450.6	397.3	337.8	255.9	232.3
M [FB] [3,30,31]	321.1	281.1	227.1	201.6	171.8	140.0	100.0	86.7
F [FB] [3,30,31]	341.2	321.5	273.6	249.0	225.5	197.8	156.0	145.6
%MF [FB] [3,30,31]	17.3	16.3	13.5	12.2	10.7	9.1	6.9	6.3
Cambodia [33] **Cambodge** [33]								
MF [BA]	115.8 [9]	...	...	503.4 [34]	...	...	...	...
M [BA]	44.9 [9]	...	...	259.5 [34]	...	...	...	...
F [BA]	71.0 [9]	...	...	243.9 [34]	...	...	...	...
%MF [BA] [9]	1.8	...	...	7.1	...	...	...	...

27

Unemployment *(continued)*
Number (thousands) and percentage unemployed, by sex
Chômage *(suite)*
Nombre (milliers) et pourcentage des chômeurs, par sexe

Country or area, source [§] Pays ou zone, source [§]	2001	2002	2003	2004	2005	2006	2007	2008
%M [BA][9]	1.5	...	...	7.6	...	...	...	...
%F [BA][9]	2.2	...	...	6.7	...	...	...	...
Cameroon[1] Cameroun[1]								
MF [B]	468.0	...	...	...	...	...	...	...
M [B]	263.0	...	...	...	...	...	...	...
F [B]	205.0	...	...	...	...	...	...	...
%MF [B]	7.5	...	...	...	...	...	...	...
%M [B]	8.2	...	...	...	...	...	...	...
%F [B]	6.7	...	...	...	...	...	...	...
Canada[1] Canada[1]								
MF [A][4]	1 176.9	...	...	...	...	...	...	...
M [A][4]	641.7	...	...	...	...	...	...	...
F [A][4]	535.2	...	...	...	...	...	...	...
MF [BA][35]	1 163.6	1 268.9	1 286.2	1 235.3	1 172.8	1 108.4	1 079.4	1 119.3
M [BA][35]	655.1	721.7	719.6	685.4	649.0	608.3	603.9	632.6
F [BA][35]	508.5	547.2	566.6	549.9	523.8	500.1	475.5	486.6
%MF [BA][35]	7.2	7.7	7.6	7.2	6.8	6.3	6.0	6.1
%M [BA][35]	7.5	8.1	7.9	7.5	7.0	6.5	6.4	6.6
%F [BA][35]	6.9	7.1	7.2	6.9	6.5	6.1	5.6	5.7
Cayman Islands[1] Iles Caïmanes[1]								
MF [BA]	2.1[14]	1.6[14]	1.1[14]	1.3[2]	1.3[14]	0.9[2]	1.4[14]	1.5[14]
M [BA]	...	...	...	...	...	0.5[2]	0.7	0.8
F [BA]	...	...	...	...	...	0.5[2]	0.7	0.8
%MF [BA]	7.5[14]	5.4[14]	3.6[14]	4.3[2]	3.5[14]	2.6[2]	3.8[14]	4.0[14]
%M [BA][14]	...	...	...	...	...	...	3.5	3.8
%F [BA][14]	...	...	...	...	...	...	4.2	4.1
Chile[1,36] Chili[1,36]								
MF [BA]	469.4	468.7	453.1	494.7	440.4	#409.9	510.7	544.7
M [BA]	302.6	298.5	279.2	280.8	248.2	#239.3	280.1	306.7
F [BA]	166.9	170.2	173.9	213.9	192.2	#170.6	230.6	238.0
%MF [BA]	7.9	7.8	7.4	7.8	6.9	#6.0	7.2	7.5
%M [BA]	7.6	7.5	6.9	6.9	6.1	#5.5	6.3	6.7
%F [BA]	8.4	8.5	8.3	9.5	8.5	#7.0	8.8	8.7
China[1,3,37,38] Chine[1,3,37,38]								
MF [E]	6 810.0	7 700.0	8 000.0	8 270.0	8 390.0	8 470.0	8 300.0	8 860.0
%MF [E]	3.6	4.0	4.3	4.2	4.2	4.1	4.0	4.2
China, Hong Kong SAR[1,39] Chine, Hong Kong RAS[1,39]								
MF [BA]	174.3	254.2	275.2	239.2	197.6	171.1	145.7	130.1
M [BA]	117.8	164.0	180.0	151.8	127.5	110.2	89.2	79.4
F [BA]	56.5	90.1	95.3	87.4	70.1	60.8	56.5	50.7
%MF [BA]	5.1	7.3	7.9	6.8	5.6	4.8	4.0	3.6
%M [BA]	6.0	8.4	9.3	7.8	6.5	5.7	4.6	4.1
%F [BA]	3.9	6.0	6.3	5.6	4.4	3.8	3.4	3.0
China, Macao SAR[6] Chine, Macao RAS[6]								
MF [BA]	14.0	13.7	13.1	11.2	10.3	10.4	9.5	10.1
M [BA]	9.5	9.1	8.3	6.8	5.8	5.6	5.6	5.7
F [BA]	4.5	4.6	4.8	4.4	4.5	4.8	3.9	4.3
%MF [BA]	6.4	6.3	6.0	4.9	4.1	3.8	3.1	3.0
%M [BA]	8.1	7.9	7.1	5.6	4.4	3.8	3.4	3.2
%F [BA]	4.4	4.5	4.7	4.0	3.8	3.8	2.7	2.8
Colombia[9,40,41] Colombie[9,40,41]								
MF [BA]	2 708.8	2 848.6	2 797.3	2 462.0	2 260.6	2 424.8	2 097.1	2 245.7
M [BA]	1 257.6	1 341.3	1 264.8	1 132.1	1 019.4	1 093.9	996.4	1 033.0
F [BA]	1 451.2	1 507.3	1 532.5	1 329.9	1 241.2	1 330.9	1 092.8	1 212.7
%MF [BA]	14.6	15.2	14.4	12.8	11.6	12.7	10.9	11.4
%M [BA]	11.5	12.2	11.1	9.9	8.8	9.7	8.7	8.9
%F [BA]	19.1	19.7	18.9	16.9	15.7	17.0	14.1	15.1
Cook Islands[1,42] Iles Cook[1,42]								
MF [A]	0.9	...	...	...	...	...	...	...
M [A]	0.4	...	...	...	...	...	...	...
F [A]	0.4	...	...	...	...	...	...	...

27

Unemployment *(continued)*
Number (thousands) and percentage unemployed, by sex
Chômage *(suite)*
Nombre (milliers) et pourcentage des chômeurs, par sexe

Country or area, source [§] Pays ou zone, source [§]	2001	2002	2003	2004	2005	2006	2007	2008
Costa Rica [25,43] **Costa Rica** [25,43]								
MF [BA]	100.4	108.5	117.2	114.9	126.2	116.0	92.8	101.9
M [BA]	55.8	61.6	66.0	62.5	60.2	53.8	41.3	53.5
F [BA]	44.6	46.9	51.2	52.4	66.0	62.3	51.5	48.4
%MF [BA]	6.1	6.4	6.7	6.5	6.6	6.0	4.6	4.9
%M [BA]	5.2	5.6	5.8	5.4	5.0	4.4	3.3	4.2
%F [BA]	7.6	7.9	8.2	8.5	9.6	8.7	6.8	6.2
Croatia **Croatie**								
MF [A] [1,29]	399.0	...	...	...	...	...	...	...
M [A] [1,29]	214.1	...	...	...	...	...	...	...
F [A] [1,29]	184.9	...	...	...	...	...	...	...
MF [BA] [1]	276.2	265.8	255.7	249.7	229.1	198.7	171.0	149.2
M [BA] [1]	134.8	129.7	127.7	120.0	114.4	94.4	81.6	67.9
F [BA] [1]	141.4	136.0	128.1	129.7	114.7	104.2	89.4	81.3
%MF [BA] [1]	15.8	14.8	14.3	13.8	12.7	11.1	9.6	8.4
%M [BA] [1]	14.2	13.4	13.1	12.0	11.7	9.8	8.3	7.0
%F [BA] [1]	17.9	16.6	15.7	15.7	14.0	12.7	11.1	10.0
MF [FB] [44]	380.0	390.0	330.0	310.0	309.0	292.0	264.0	237.0
M [FB] [44]	177.0	177.0	140.0	129.0	128.0	117.0	102.0	90.0
F [FB] [44]	203.0	213.0	190.0	181.0	181.0	175.0	162.0	147.0
%MF [FB] [44]	22.0	22.3	19.2	18.0	17.9	16.6	14.8	...
%M [FB] [44]	19.5	19.3	15.5	14.3	14.1	12.6	11.0	...
%F [FB] [44]	24.7	25.6	23.2	22.2	22.0	20.9	19.1	...
Cuba [42,45] **Cuba** [42,45]								
MF [BA]	191.6	156.1	109.7	87.7	93.9	92.7	88.6	79.7
M [BA]	93.8	76.9	51.3	49.7	55.0	52.6	53.3	42.0
F [BA]	97.8	79.2	58.4	38.0	38.9	40.1	35.3	37.7
%MF [BA]	4.1	3.3	2.3	1.9	1.9	1.9	1.8	1.6
%M [BA]	3.1	2.6	1.7	1.7	1.8	1.7	1.7	1.3
%F [BA]	5.8	4.6	3.4	2.2	2.2	2.2	1.9	2.0
Cyprus [1] **Chypre** [1]								
MF [A] [14]	10.5	...	...	...	...	...	...	...
M [A] [14]	5.7	...	...	...	...	...	...	...
F [A] [14]	4.7	...	...	...	...	...	...	...
MF [BA] [46]	12.8	10.8	14.1	16.7	19.5	17.0	15.4	14.5
M [BA] [46]	4.8	4.7	7.1	7.0	9.0	8.0	7.3	7.0
F [BA] [46]	8.1	6.0	7.0	9.7	10.4	9.0	8.1	7.6
%MF [BA] [46]	4.0	3.3	4.1	4.7	5.3	4.5	3.9	3.7
%M [BA] [46]	2.6	2.6	3.8	3.5	4.4	3.9	3.4	3.2
%F [BA] [46]	5.7	4.2	4.6	6.2	6.5	5.4	4.6	4.2
MF [FB] [46]	9.5	10.6	12.0	12.7	13.2	12.8	12.0	11.5
M [FB] [46]	4.5	4.7	5.1	5.4	5.8	5.7	5.2	4.9
F [FB] [46]	5.0	5.9	6.8	7.2	7.3	7.1	6.8	6.6
%MF [FB] [46]	2.9	3.2	3.5	3.6	3.7	...	...	...
%M [FB] [46]	2.3	2.3	2.5	2.6	2.9	...	...	...
%F [FB] [46]	3.8	4.3	5.0	5.1	4.7	...	...	...
Czech Republic **République tchèque**								
MF [BA] [1]	418.0	374.0	399.0	426.0	410.0	371.0	276.0	229.8
M [BA] [1]	193.0	169.0	175.0	201.0	187.0	169.0	124.0	102.6
F [BA] [1]	225.0	205.0	224.0	225.0	223.0	202.0	153.0	127.2
%MF [BA] [1]	8.1	7.3	7.8	8.3	7.9	7.1	5.3	4.4
%M [BA] [1]	6.8	5.9	6.1	7.0	6.5	5.8	4.2	3.5
%F [BA] [1]	9.9	9.0	9.9	9.9	9.8	8.8	6.7	5.6
MF [FB] [3]	462.0	514.0	542.0	542.0	510.0	449.0	355.0	352.0
M [FB] [3]	230.0	257.0	270.0	266.0	244.0	210.0	164.0	168.0
F [FB] [3]	232.0	257.0	272.0	276.0	266.0	239.0	191.0	184.0
%MF [FB] [3]	8.9	9.8	10.3	9.5	8.9	7.7	6.0	6.0
%M [FB] [3]	7.9	8.7	9.2	8.3	7.6	6.4	4.9	5.0
%F [FB] [3]	10.1	11.2	11.8	10.9	10.5	9.3	7.4	7.2

27 Unemployment *(continued)*
Number (thousands) and percentage unemployed, by sex
Chômage *(suite)*
Nombre (milliers) et pourcentage des chômeurs, par sexe

Country or area, source [§] Pays ou zone, source [§]	2001	2002	2003	2004	2005	2006	2007	2008
Denmark Danemark								
MF [A] [1,21]	...	...	119.3					
M [A] [1,21]	...	...	60.3	...	...	...	...	...
F [A] [1,21]	...	...	58.9	...	...	...	...	...
MF [BA] [47]	137.0	134.0	157.6	162.6	143.3	117.9	114.5	98.4
M [BA] [47]	66.0	66.0	75.7	79.9	69.4	53.4	55.1	47.1
F [BA] [47]	71.0	68.0	81.8	82.7	73.9	64.5	59.5	51.3
%MF [BA] [47]	4.8	4.7	5.5	5.6	5.0	4.1	4.0	3.4
%M [BA] [47]	4.4	4.4	5.0	5.2	4.6	3.5	3.6	3.0
%F [BA] [47]	5.3	5.1	6.2	6.1	5.5	4.7	4.4	3.7
MF [FB]	#130.6[48]	133.0[48]	159.1[48]	160.4[48]	140.2[48]	108.4[49]	77.2[49]	51.7[49]
M [FB]	#61.1[48]	64.4[48]	78.6[48]	77.6[48]	65.6[48]	48.3[49]	33.8[49]	25.8[49]
F [FB]	#69.5[48]	68.6[48]	80.5[48]	82.8[48]	74.6[48]	60.1[49]	43.4[49]	25.9[49]
%MF [FB]	#4.7[48]	4.8[48]	5.8[48]	5.8[48]	5.1[48]	3.9[49]	2.8[49]	1.8[49]
%M [FB]	#4.1[48]	4.4[48]	5.4[48]	5.4[48]	4.5[48]	3.3[49]	2.3[49]	1.8[49]
%F [FB]	#5.2[48]	5.2[48]	6.1[48]	6.3[48]	5.7[48]	4.5[49]	3.2[49]	1.9[49]
Dominica [1,4] Dominique [1,4]								
MF [A]	3.1	...	...	...	...	...	...	...
M [A]	2.0	...	...	...	...	...	...	...
F [A]	1.0	...	...	...	...	...	...	...
%MF [A]	11.0	...	...	...	...	...	...	...
%M [A]	11.9	...	...	...	...	...	...	...
%F [A]	9.5	...	...	...	...	...	...	...
Dominican Republic [9] Rép. dominicaine [9]								
MF [A] [29]	...	509.6	...	...	...	...	...	...
M [A] [29]	...	264.8	...	...	...	...	...	...
F [A] [29]	...	244.8	...	...	...	...	...	...
MF [BA]	556.3	596.3	619.7	723.7	715.8	661.4	654.0	602.5
M [BA]	208.0	215.5	243.0	252.5	269.6	233.5	240.7	218.3
F [BA]	348.2	380.8	376.8	471.2	446.3	428.0	413.3	384.2
%MF [BA]	15.6	16.1	16.7	18.4	17.9	16.0	15.6	14.2
%M [BA]	9.4	9.5	10.6	10.5	11.0	9.3	9.3	8.5
%F [BA]	26.0	26.6	26.6	30.7	28.8	26.3	25.4	22.8
Ecuador [9,50] Equateur [9,50]								
MF [BA]	450.9[5]	352.9[33]	461.1[33]	362.1[33]	333.6[33]	341.8[33]	260.4[42]	320.4[42]
M [BA]	169.0[5]	136.2[33]	215.0[33]	160.7[33]	143.3[33]	143.4[33]	123.2[42]	142.1[42]
F [BA]	282.0[5]	216.7[33]	246.1[33]	201.4[33]	190.3[33]	198.4[33]	137.2[42]	178.3[42]
%MF [BA]	11.0[5]	9.3[33]	11.5[33]	8.6[33]	7.9[33]	7.8[33]	6.1[42]	7.3[42]
%M [BA]	7.1[5]	6.0[33]	9.1[33]	6.6[33]	5.8[33]	5.6[33]	4.9[42]	5.6[42]
%F [BA]	16.2[5]	14.0[33]	15.0[33]	11.4[33]	10.8[33]	10.9[33]	7.6[42]	9.6[42]
Egypt [51,52] Egypte [51,52]								
MF [BA]	1 783.0	2 020.6	2 240.7	2 153.9	2 450.0	2 434.5	2 135.1	...
M [BA]	851.8	983.2	1 186.7	942.6	1 194.5	1 207.7	1 077.6	...
F [BA]	931.2	1 037.4	1 054.0	1 211.3	1 255.5	1 226.8	1 057.5	...
%MF [BA]	9.2	10.2	11.0	10.3	11.2	10.6	8.9	...
%M [BA]	5.6	6.3	7.5	5.9	7.1	6.8	5.9	...
%F [BA]	22.6	23.9	23.3	25.1	24.3	24.0	18.6	...
El Salvador [9,42] El Salvador [9,42]								
MF [BA]	170.3	147.4	169.4	164.0	177.6	164.2	166.6	...
M [BA]	119.6	113.7	134.5	127.3	129.6	123.9	126.6	...
F [BA]	50.7	33.7	34.9	36.7	48.1	40.4	40.0	...
%MF [BA]	7.0	6.2	6.9	6.8	7.2	6.6	6.4	...
%M [BA]	8.1	8.1	9.2	8.7	8.9	8.5	8.3	...
%F [BA]	5.2	3.5	3.5	3.8	4.8	3.9	3.8	...
Estonia Estonie								
MF [BA] [53]	83.1	67.2	66.2	63.6	52.2	40.5	32.0	38.4
M [BA] [53]	43.7	36.1	34.2	34.7	28.9	21.3	18.9	20.2
F [BA] [53]	39.3	31.0	32.0	28.9	23.3	19.2	13.1	18.1
%MF [BA] [53]	12.6	10.3	10.0	9.7	7.9	5.9	4.7	5.5
%M [BA] [53]	12.9	10.8	10.2	10.4	8.8	6.2	5.4	5.8
%F [BA] [53]	12.2	9.7	9.9	8.9	7.1	5.6	3.9	5.3

Unemployment *(continued)*
Number (thousands) and percentage unemployed, by sex
Chômage *(suite)*
Nombre (milliers) et pourcentage des chômeurs, par sexe

Country or area, source [§] Pays ou zone, source [§]	2001	2002	2003	2004	2005	2006	2007	2008
MF [FB][53]	54.1	...	...	...	...	...	...	...
%MF [FB]	#7.1	6.4	5.8	4.9	3.9	2.2	...	...
Ethiopia[9,50] Ethiopie[9,50]								
MF [BA]	...	...	...	845.9[2]	894.2[29]	767.1[5]	...	...
M [BA]	...	...	...	304.5[2]	292.7[29]	273.1[5]	...	...
F [BA]	...	...	...	541.4[2]	601.5[29]	493.9[5]	...	...
%MF [BA]	...	...	...	22.9[2]	...	16.7[5]	...	...
%M [BA]	...	...	...	15.8[2]	...	11.5[5]	...	...
%F [BA]	...	...	...	30.6[2]	...	22.1[5]	...	...
Faeroe Islands[15,54] Iles Féroé[15,54]								
MF [BA]	1.0	...	1.0	1.0	0.9	...	...	...
M [BA]	...	...	...	...	0.4	...	...	...
F [BA]	...	...	...	...	0.5	...	...	...
Fiji[55] Fidji[55]								
MF [BA]	...	...	...	...	15.5	...	...	...
M [BA]	...	...	...	...	9.4	...	...	...
F [BA]	...	...	...	...	6.1	...	...	...
%MF [BA]	...	...	...	...	4.6	...	...	...
%M [BA]	...	...	...	...	4.1	...	...	...
%F [BA]	...	...	...	...	5.9	...	...	...
Finland Finlande								
MF [BA][53]	238.0	237.0	235.0	229.0	220.0	204.0	183.0	#172.0
M [BA][53]	117.0	123.0	124.0	118.0	111.0	101.0	90.0	#85.0
F [BA][53]	121.0	114.0	111.0	111.0	109.0	103.0	93.0	#87.0
%MF [BA][53]	9.1	9.1	9.0	8.8	8.3	7.7	6.8	#6.4
%M [BA][53]	8.6	9.1	9.2	8.7	8.1	7.4	6.4	#6.1
%F [BA][53]	9.7	9.1	8.9	8.9	8.6	8.1	7.2	#6.7
MF [FB][1,56,57]	302.0	294.0	288.0	288.0	275.0	250.0	217.0	204.0
M [FB][1,56,57]	153.0	154.0	153.0	152.0	144.0	129.0	111.0	108.0
F [FB][1,56,57]	149.0	140.0	135.0	136.0	131.0	120.0	106.0	96.0
France France								
MF [BA][1]	2 075.0[58]	2 137.0[58]	2 295.0	2 408.0	2 429.0	2 435.0	2 222.0	2 070.0
M [BA][1]	938.0[58]	1 024.0[58]	1 097.0	1 153.0	1 163.0	1 175.0	1 092.0	1 018.0
F [BA][1]	1 137.0[58]	1 113.0[58]	1 198.0	1 255.0	1 266.0	1 260.0	1 130.0	1 053.0
%MF [BA][1]	7.8[58]	7.9[58]	8.5	8.9	8.9	8.8	8.0	7.4
%M [BA][1]	6.5[58]	7.1[58]	7.6	8.0	8.0	8.1	7.5	6.9
%F [BA][1]	9.2[58]	8.9[58]	9.5	9.8	9.8	9.7	8.6	7.9
MF [E][1]	2 088.1	2 150.6	2 320.9	2 434.1	2 451.7	2 455.2	2 236.0	...
M [E][1]	948.0	1 037.7	1 119.1	1 176.6	1 187.8	1 200.9	1 110.0	...
F [E][1]	1 140.0	1 112.9	1 201.8	1 257.5	1 264.0	1 254.3	1 126.0	...
%MF [E][1]	7.9	8.0	8.6	9.0	9.0	8.9	8.2	...
%M [E][1]	6.6	7.2	7.7	8.1	8.1	8.2	7.6	...
%F [E][1]	9.4	9.0	9.6	10.0	9.9	9.7	8.7	...
MF [FB][15]	2 479.8	2 589.3	2 718.2	2 702.8	2 563.5	2 260.5	2 015.0	...
M [FB][15]	1 150.6	1 246.0	1 324.9	1 314.6	1 239.6	1 099.2	979.0	...
F [FB][15]	1 329.2	1 343.3	1 393.3	1 388.2	1 323.9	1 161.3	1 037.0	...
French Guiana[1,59] Guyane française[1,59]								
MF [BA]	15.0	13.5	14.1	15.2	15.9	18.4	12.8	...
M [BA]	7.4	6.4	6.6	7.3	7.9	8.2	5.9	...
F [BA]	7.6	7.1	7.5	8.0	8.0	10.3	6.9	...
%MF [BA]	26.3	23.4	24.5	26.3	26.5	29.1	...	...
%M [BA]	23.0	19.8	20.5	22.6	23.8	23.9	...	...
%F [BA]	30.5	27.8	29.6	30.8	29.7	35.3	...	...
French Polynesia[1] Polynésie française[1]								
MF [A]	...	11.7	...	...	...	...	...	...
M [A]	...	6.3	...	...	...	...	...	...
F [A]	...	5.3	...	...	...	...	...	...
Georgia[1] Géorgie[1]								
MF [BA]	235.6	265.0	235.9	257.6	279.3	274.5	261.0	...
M [BA]	126.9	155.5	124.2	143.2	159.2	165.4	143.7	...
F [BA]	108.7	109.5	111.7	114.4	120.1	109.1	117.3	...
%MF [BA]	11.0	12.3	11.5	12.6	13.8	13.6	13.3	...

27

Unemployment *(continued)*
Number (thousands) and percentage unemployed, by sex
Chômage *(suite)*
Nombre (milliers) et pourcentage des chômeurs, par sexe

Country or area, source [§] Pays ou zone, source [§]	2001	2002	2003	2004	2005	2006	2007	2008
%M [BA]	11.6	13.7	11.5	13.4	14.8	15.2	13.9	...
%F [BA]	10.7	10.7	11.5	11.8	12.6	11.7	12.6	...
MF [FB][3]	97.8	#21.9	42.9	46.6	34.2	...	...	...
M [FB][3]	40.1	#12.1	23.2	24.1	17.1	...	...	...
F [FB][3]	57.7	#9.8	19.7	22.5	17.1	...	...	...
%MF [FB][3]	5.5	#1.2	...	...	...	...	...	...
Germany Allemagne								
MF [A][1,2]	3 138.7	...	...	...	...	...	...	...
M [A][1,2]	1 730.2	...	...	...	...	...	...	...
F [A][1,2]	1 408.5	...	...	...	...	...	...	...
MF [BA][1]	3 150.0[60]	3 486.0	4 023.0[4]	4 388.0[29]	#4 583.0	4 279.0	3 608.0	3 141.0
M [BA][1]	1 754.0[60]	1 982.0	2 316.0[4]	2 551.0[29]	#2 574.0	2 358.0	1 944.0	1 690.0
F [BA][1]	1 396.0[60]	1 504.0	1 707.0[4]	1 836.0[29]	#2 009.0	1 921.0	1 664.0	1 451.0
%MF [BA][1]	7.9[60]	8.7	10.0[4]	11.0[29]	#11.1	10.3	8.6	7.5
%M [BA][1]	7.8[60]	8.9	10.4[4]	11.5[29]	#11.3	10.3	8.5	7.4
%F [BA][1]	7.9[60]	8.5	9.5[4]	10.3[29]	#10.9	10.2	8.8	7.6
MF [FB][51]	3 852.6[61]	4 061.3[61]	4 376.8[61]	#4 381.0[61]	4 861.0[61]	4 487.0[61]	3 776.0[61]	3 268.0
M [FB][51]	2 063.9[61]	2 239.9[61]	2 446.2[61]	#2 449.0[61]	2 606.0[61]	2 338.0[61]	1 900.0[61]	1 668.0
F [FB][51]	1 788.7[61]	1 821.4[61]	1 930.6[61]	#1 932.0[61]	2 255.0[61]	2 149.0[61]	1 873.0[61]	1 600.0
%MF [FB][51]	10.4[61]	10.8[61]	11.6[61]	#11.7[61]	13.0[61]	12.0[61]	10.1[61]	8.7
%M [FB][51]	10.4[61]	11.3[61]	12.4[61]	#12.5[61]	13.4[61]	12.0[61]	9.8[61]	8.6
%F [FB][51]	10.2[61]	10.3[61]	10.8[61]	#10.8[61]	12.7[61]	12.0[61]	10.4[61]	8.9
Gibraltar[62] Gibraltar[62]								
MF [FB]	0.4	0.5	0.5	0.4	0.5	0.5	0.5	0.5
M [FB]	0.2	0.3	0.3	0.3	0.3	0.3	0.3	0.3
F [FB]	0.2	0.2	0.2	0.2	0.2	0.2	0.2	0.2
Greece[1] Grèce[1]								
MF [A][29]	508.2	...	...	...	...	...	...	...
M [A][29]	277.1	...	...	...	...	...	...	...
F [A][29]	231.1	...	...	...	...	...	...	...
MF [BA][13]	478.4	462.1	441.8	492.7	466.7	427.4	398.0	357.1
M [BA][13]	191.4	180.5	170.8	181.7	166.8	160.9	144.0	136.6
F [BA][13]	287.0	281.6	271.0	311.0	299.9	266.5	254.0	220.5
%MF [BA][13]	10.4	9.9	9.3	10.2	9.6	8.8	8.1	7.2
%M [BA][13]	6.9	6.4	6.0	6.3	5.8	5.6	5.0	4.6
%F [BA][13]	15.9	15.2	14.3	15.9	15.2	13.4	12.6	10.9
Greenland[1,63] Groenland[1,63]								
MF [E]	2.5	2.3	2.7	2.8	2.5	2.3	...	...
M [E]	1.5	1.3	1.6	1.7	1.5	1.4	...	...
F [E]	1.0	1.0	1.1	1.2	1.1	0.9	...	...
%MF [E]	9.5	8.8	10.3	10.4	9.3	...	...	...
%M [E]	11.3	9.8	11.9	12.0	10.4	...	...	...
%F [E]	7.7	7.8	8.6	8.8	8.0	...	...	...
Guadeloupe[1,59] Guadeloupe[1,59]								
MF [BA]	43.7	41.5	44.0	40.3	42.0	46.2	38.0	...
M [BA]	19.1	19.0	20.9	17.5	18.1	20.8	15.9	...
F [BA]	24.6	22.5	23.1	22.8	23.9	25.4	22.1	...
%MF [BA]	27.6	25.7	26.9	24.7	26.0	27.3	22.7	...
%M [BA]	23.4	22.6	24.6	21.0	22.0	24.2	19.2	...
%F [BA]	32.0	29.1	29.4	28.5	30.1	30.5	26.1	...
Guatemala[9] Guatemala[9]								
MF [BA]	62.2	154.3	172.2	156.2	...	#100.1	...	...
M [BA]	34.4	77.1	79.4	91.7	...	#50.6	...	...
F [BA]	27.8	77.2	92.8	64.5	...	#49.5	...	...
%MF [BA]	1.3	3.1	3.4	3.1	...	#1.8	...	...
%M [BA]	1.3	2.5	2.5	2.8	...	#1.5	...	...
%F [BA]	1.4	4.3	4.9	3.7	...	#2.4	...	...
Guyana[1] Guyana[1]								
MF [A]	...	32.1	...	...	...	...	...	...
M [A]	...	19.5	...	...	...	...	...	...
F [A]	...	12.6	...	...	...	...	...	...

27

Unemployment *(continued)*
Number (thousands) and percentage unemployed, by sex
Chômage *(suite)*
Nombre (milliers) et pourcentage des chômeurs, par sexe

Country or area, source [§] Pays ou zone, source [§]	2001	2002	2003	2004	2005	2006	2007	2008
Honduras[9] Honduras[9]								
MF [BA]	93.0	93.7	130.3	153.2	107.8	87.4	85.3	...
M [BA]	58.9	56.8	74.9	81.1	55.2	46.8	55.9	...
F [BA]	34.1	37.0	55.5	72.2	52.6	40.7	29.5	...
%MF [BA]	3.9	3.8	5.1	5.9	4.1	3.1	2.9	...
%M [BA]	3.7	3.4	4.4	4.7	3.1	2.5	2.9	...
%F [BA]	4.3	4.7	6.4	8.3	6.1	4.2	2.9	...
Hungary Hongrie								
MF [BA][53]	232.9	238.8[64]	244.5	252.9	303.9	316.8	311.9	329.2
M [BA][53]	142.7	138.0[64]	138.5	136.8	159.1	164.6	164.2	174.3
F [BA][53]	90.2	100.8[64]	106.0	116.1	144.8	152.2	147.7	154.9
%MF [BA][53]	5.7	5.8[64]	5.7	6.1	7.2	7.5	7.4	7.8
%M [BA][53]	6.3	6.1[64]	6.1	6.1	7.0	7.2	7.1	7.6
%F [BA][53]	5.0	5.4[64]	5.3	6.1	7.5	7.8	7.6	8.1
MF [FB][3]	342.8	344.9	359.9	400.6	410.6	403.4	445.0	477.4
M [FB][3]	188.7	186.8	189.4	209.6	213.7	210.1	232.7	250.9
F [FB][3]	154.1	158.1	170.5	191.0	197.0	193.3	212.3	226.5
%MF [FB][3]	...	...	8.4	...	...	...	...	...
%M [FB][3]	...	...	7.9	...	...	...	...	...
%F [FB][3]	...	...	8.9	...	...	...	...	...
Iceland Islande								
MF [BA][65,66]	3.7	5.3	5.4	4.9	4.3	5.0	4.2	5.5
M [BA][65,66]	1.8	3.1	3.1	2.7	2.3	2.6	2.3	3.3
F [BA][65,66]	1.9	2.2	2.4	2.2	2.0	2.4	1.9	2.2
%MF [BA][65]	2.3	3.3	3.4	3.1	2.6	2.9	2.3	3.0
%M [BA][65]	2.0	3.6	3.6	2.9	2.6	2.7	2.3	3.3
%F [BA][65]	2.5	2.9	3.1	2.9	2.6	3.1	2.3	2.6
MF [FB][15]	2.0	3.6	4.9	...	...	...	...	...
M [FB][15]	0.8	1.8	2.5	...	...	...	...	...
F [FB][15]	1.2	1.8	2.4	...	...	...	...	...
%MF [FB][15]	1.4	2.5	3.4	...	...	...	...	...
%M [FB][15]	1.0	2.1	3.0	...	...	...	...	...
%F [FB][15]	1.9	3.0	3.9	...	...	...	...	...
India[3,6] Inde[3,6]								
MF [FB]	41 996.0	41 171.0	41 389.0	40 458.0	39 348.0	41 466.0	39 974.0	39 112.0
M [FB]	31 111.0	30 521.0	30 636.0	29 746.0	28 742.0	29 685.0	27 972.0	26 785.0
F [FB]	10 885.0	10 650.0	10 752.0	10 712.0	10 606.0	11 781.0	12 002.0	12 327.0
Indonesia[1] Indonésie[1]								
MF [BA]	8 005.0[67]	9 132.1[67]	9 939.3[67]	10 251.4[67]	11 899.3[7]	10 932.0[67]	10 011.1[67]	9 394.5[67]
M [BA]	4 032.4[67]	4 727.8[67]	5 100.1[67]	5 345.7[67]	6 292.4[7]	5 772.6[67]	5 571.9[67]	5 245.1[67]
F [BA]	3 972.6[67]	4 404.3[67]	4 839.2[67]	4 905.7[67]	5 606.8[7]	5 159.4[67]	4 439.2[67]	4 149.5[67]
%MF [BA]	8.1[67]	9.1[67]	9.7[67]	9.9[67]	11.2[7]	10.3[67]	9.1[67]	8.4[67]
%M [BA]	6.6[67]	7.5[67]	7.9[67]	8.1[67]	9.3[7]	8.5[67]	8.1[67]	7.6[67]
%F [BA]	10.6[67]	11.8[67]	12.7[67]	12.9[67]	14.7[7]	13.4[67]	10.8[67]	9.7[67]
Iran (Islamic Rep. of)[9] Iran (Rép. islamique d')[9]								
MF [BA]	...	...	...	...	2 675.0	2 643.0	2 486.0	2 392.0
M [BA]	...	...	...	...	1 856.0	1 878.0	1 764.0	1 715.0
F [BA]	...	...	...	...	819.0	765.0	722.0	677.0
%MF [BA]	...	...	...	...	11.5	11.3	10.5	10.4
%M [BA]	...	...	...	...	10.0	10.0	9.3	9.1
%F [BA]	...	...	...	...	17.0	16.2	15.8	16.7
Iraq[1] Iraq[1]								
%MF [BA]	...	...	28.1	26.8	...	...	...	...
%M [BA]	...	...	30.2	29.4	...	...	...	...
%F [BA]	...	...	16.0	15.0	...	...	...	...
Ireland Irlande								
MF [BA][1,13]	65.4	77.1	82.6	84.6	86.5	92.6	100.3	115.5
M [BA][1,13]	39.8	48.8	51.9	54.6	53.7	55.9	60.0	78.0
F [BA][1,13]	25.6	28.4	30.6	30.0	32.9	36.7	40.3	37.5
%MF [BA][1,13]	3.7	4.2	4.4	4.4	4.2	4.6	4.6	5.2
%M [BA][1,13]	3.8	4.5	4.8	4.9	4.6	4.5	4.8	6.2
%F [BA][1,13]	3.5	3.7	3.9	3.8	3.8	4.0	4.3	3.9

27

Unemployment *(continued)*
Number (thousands) and percentage unemployed, by sex
Chômage *(suite)*
Nombre (milliers) et pourcentage des chômeurs, par sexe

Country or area, source [§] Pays ou zone, source [§]	2001	2002	2003	2004	2005	2006	2007	2008
MF [FB] [15]	142.3	162.5	172.4	166.0	153.3	...	...	...
M [FB] [15]	83.0	96.3	100.2	96.1	91.0	...	...	...
F [FB] [15]	59.3	66.2	72.2	70.0	62.3	...	...	...
%MF [FB] [15]	3.9	4.4	4.6	4.4	4.2	...		
Isle of Man Ile de Man								
MF [A] [1]	0.6	...	...	...	...	1.0[2]	...	...
M [A] [1]	0.4	...	...	...	...	0.6[2]	...	...
F [A] [1]	0.3	...	...	...	...	0.4[2]	...	...
%MF [A] [1]	1.6	...	...	...	...	2.4[2]	...	...
%M [A] [1]	1.7	...	...	...	...	2.8[2]	...	...
%F [A] [1]	1.5	...	...	...	...	2.0[2]	...	
MF [FB]	0.2	0.2	0.3	0.4	0.6	0.6	0.6	0.6
M [FB]	0.1	0.1	0.2	0.3	0.4	0.4	0.4	0.4
F [FB]	0.1	0.1	0.1	0.1	0.2	0.2	0.2	0.2
%MF [FB]	0.5	0.5	0.8	1.0	1.4	1.4	1.4	1.4
%M [FB]	0.6	0.7	1.0	1.3	1.8	1.7	1.7	1.8
%F [FB]	0.3	0.4	0.5	0.6	0.9	1.0	1.1	1.0
Israel [1] Israël [1]								
MF [BA]	233.9	262.4	279.9	277.7	246.4	236.1	211.8	180.4
M [BA]	120.9	138.4	142.8	136.5	124.9	118.5	104.8	90.8
F [BA]	113.0	124.0	137.1	141.2	121.5	117.6	107.0	89.6
%MF [BA]	9.4	10.3	10.7	10.4	9.0	8.4	7.3	6.1
%M [BA]	8.9	10.1	10.2	9.5	8.5	7.9	6.8	5.7
%F [BA]	9.9	10.6	11.3	11.4	9.5	9.0	7.9	6.5
Italy [1] Italie [1]								
MF [BA]	2 267.0	2 163.0	2 096.0	#1 960.0	1 889.0	1 673.0	1 506.0	1 691.9
M [BA]	1 066.0	1 016.0	996.0	#925.0	902.0	801.0	722.4	820.4
F [BA]	1 201.0	1 147.0	1 100.0	#1 036.0	986.0	873.0	783.6	871.5
%MF [BA]	9.5	9.0	8.7	#8.0	7.7	6.8	6.1	6.7
%M [BA]	7.3	6.9	6.7	#6.4	6.2	5.4	4.9	5.5
%F [BA]	13.0	12.2	11.6	#10.5	10.1	8.8	7.9	8.5
Jamaica [6] Jamaïque [6]								
MF [BA]	165.4[68]	171.8	128.9	136.8	133.3	119.6	119.4	134.6
M [BA]	63.4[68]	65.7	47.6	54.0	50.0	48.0	37.8	52.8
F [BA]	102.1[68]	106.1	81.3	82.8	83.3	71.6	81.6	81.8
%MF [BA]	15.0[68]	14.3	10.9	11.4	10.9	9.6	9.3	10.3
%M [BA]	10.3[68]	9.9	7.2	8.1	7.4	6.9	5.3	7.4
%F [BA]	21.0[68]	19.8	15.6	15.7	15.3	13.0	14.0	13.8
Japan [1] Japon [1]								
MF [BA]	3 400.0[69,70]	3 590.0	3 500.0	3 130.0	2 940.0	2 750.0	2 570.0	2 650.0
M [BA]	2 090.0[69,70]	2 190.0	2 150.0	1 920.0	1 780.0	1 680.0	1 540.0	1 590.0
F [BA]	1 310.0[69,70]	1 400.0	1 350.0	1 210.0	1 160.0	1 070.0	1 030.0	1 060.0
%MF [BA]	5.0[69,70]	5.4	5.3	4.7	4.4	4.1	3.9	4.0
%M [BA]	5.2[69,70]	5.5	5.5	4.9	4.6	4.3	3.9	4.1
%F [BA]	4.7[69,70]	5.1	4.9	4.4	4.2	3.9	3.7	3.8
Jersey Jersey								
MF [A] [15]	1.0	...	...	...	...	...	...	...
M [A] [15]	0.6	...	...	...	...	...	...	...
F [A] [15]	0.4	...	...	...	...	...	...	...
MF [FB] [42]	0.2	0.2	0.7	0.5	0.4	0.4	0.3	0.7
%MF [FB] [42]	...	...	...	...	...	...	0.6	2.3
Kazakhstan Kazakhstan								
MF [BA] [1]	780.3	690.7	672.1	658.8	640.7	625.4	597.2	557.8
M [BA] [1]	338.0	283.8	281.4	281.1	270.6	262.5	244.5	226.5
F [BA] [1]	442.3	406.9	390.7	377.7	370.2	362.8	352.6	331.4
%MF [BA] [1]	10.4	9.3	8.8	8.4	8.1	7.8	7.3	6.6
%M [BA] [1]	8.9	7.5	7.2	7.0	6.7	6.4	5.9	5.3
%F [BA] [1]	12.0	11.2	10.4	9.8	9.6	9.2	8.7	7.9
MF [FB] [44]	216.1	193.7	142.8	117.7	94.0	75.2	54.7	48.4
M [FB] [44]	97.9	79.8	55.7	43.7	33.4	20.7	16.2	15.6
F [FB] [44]	118.3	113.9	87.2	74.0	60.6	51.4	38.5	32.8
%MF [FB] [44]	2.8	2.6	1.8	1.5	1.2	0.9	0.7	0.6

27

Unemployment *(continued)*
Number (thousands) and percentage unemployed, by sex
Chômage *(suite)*
Nombre (milliers) et pourcentage des chômeurs, par sexe

Country or area, source [§] Pays ou zone, source [§]	2001	2002	2003	2004	2005	2006	2007	2008
%M [FB][44]	2.6	2.1	1.4	1.1	0.8	0.5	0.4	0.4
%F [FB][44]	3.2	3.1	2.3	1.9	1.6	1.3	0.9	0.8
Korea, Republic of[1] Corée, République de[1]								
MF [BA]	899.0	752.0	818.0	860.0	887.0	827.0	783.0	769.0
M [BA]	591.0	491.0	508.0	534.0	553.0	533.0	517.0	505.0
F [BA]	308.0	261.0	309.7	325.9	334.0	294.0	266.0	265.0
%MF [BA]	4.0	3.3	3.6	3.7	3.7	3.5	3.2	3.2
%M [BA]	4.5	3.7	3.8	3.9	4.0	3.8	3.7	3.6
%F [BA]	3.3	2.8	3.3	3.4	3.4	2.9	2.8	2.6
Kosovo[51] Kosovo[51]								
%MF [BA]	57.0	55.0	49.7	39.7	41.4	44.9	46.3	...
%M [BA]	52.0	45.2	40.3	31.5	32.9	34.6	38.5	...
%F [BA]	70.0	74.5	71.9	60.7	60.5	61.6	55.2	...
Kuwait Koweït								
MF [A][1]	...	...	...	...	22.4	...	...	...
M [A][1]	...	...	...	...	17.1	...	...	...
F [A][1]	...	...	...	...	5.2	...	...	...
MF [FD][59]	9.5	15.1	18.1	23.2	25.7	24.9	...	...
M [FD][59]	7.6	9.4	10.1	11.6	12.8	11.9	...	...
F [FD][59]	1.9	5.6	7.9	11.6	12.9	13.0	...	...
%MF [FD][59]	0.8	1.1	1.3	1.4	1.5	1.3	...	...
%M [FD][59]	0.8	1.0	1.0	0.9	1.0	0.8	...	...
%F [FD][59]	0.6	1.7	2.2	2.9	3.1	2.9	...	...
Kyrgyzstan Kirghizistan								
MF [BA][1,33]	...	265.5	212.3	185.7	183.5	188.9	191.1	...
M [BA][1,33]	...	132.6	113.1	98.8	95.7	101.5	102.5	...
F [BA][1,33]	...	132.9	99.2	86.9	87.8	87.5	88.6	...
%MF [BA][1,33]	...	12.5	9.9	8.5	8.1	8.3	8.2	...
%M [BA][1,33]	...	11.2	9.4	8.0	7.4	7.7	7.6	...
%F [BA][1,33]	...	14.3	10.5	9.3	9.1	9.0	9.0	...
MF [FB]	60.5	60.2	57.4	58.2	68.0	73.4	71.3	...
M [FB]	28.0	27.6	26.5	26.8	32.2	37.9	35.8	...
F [FB]	32.5	32.6	30.9	31.4	35.8	35.5	35.5	...
Lao People's Dem. Rep.[1,21] Rép. dém. pop. lao[1,21]								
MF [A]	...	...	...	...	37.5	...	...	...
M [A]	...	...	...	...	18.6	...	...	...
F [A]	...	...	...	...	18.9	...	...	...
Latvia Lettonie								
MF [BA]	144.7[1]	134.5[53]	119.2[53]	118.6[53]	99.1[53]	79.9[53]	72.1[53]	91.6[53]
M [BA]	81.9[1]	74.9[53]	61.7[53]	61.7[53]	52.8[53]	43.7[53]	39.4[53]	50.3[53]
F [BA]	62.7[1]	59.6[53]	57.5[53]	56.9[53]	46.2[53]	36.2[53]	32.7[53]	41.4[53]
%MF [BA]	13.1[1]	12.0[53]	10.6[53]	10.4[53]	8.7[53]	6.8[53]	6.0[53]	7.5[53]
%M [BA]	14.4[1]	12.9[53]	10.7[53]	10.6[53]	9.0[53]	7.2[53]	6.4[53]	8.1[53]
%F [BA]	11.7[1]	11.0[53]	10.5[53]	10.3[53]	8.4[53]	6.4[53]	5.7[53]	7.0[53]
MF [FB][44,71]	91.6	89.7	90.6	90.8	78.5	68.9	52.3	...
M [FB][44,71]	39.1	37.0	37.6	37.3	31.5	27.0	20.1	...
F [FB][44,71]	52.6	52.7	53.0	53.5	47.0	42.0	32.2	...
%MF [FB][44,71]	7.7	8.5	8.6	8.5	7.4	6.5	4.9	...
%M [FB][44,71]	6.4	6.7	6.8	...	...	...	...	...
%F [FB][44,71]	9.0	10.5	10.6	...	...	...	...	...
Lebanon[1] Liban[1]								
MF [B]	...	...	...	94.4	...	...	110.4	...
M [B]	...	...	...	67.3	...	...	79.3	...
F [B]	...	...	...	27.1	...	...	31.1	...
%MF [B]	...	...	...	7.9	...	...	9.0	...
%M [B]	...	...	...	7.3	...	...	8.6	...
%F [B]	...	...	...	9.5	...	...	10.1	...
Liechtenstein Liechtenstein								
MF [E]	0.4	0.4	0.7	0.7	...	...	...	...
Lithuania Lituanie								
MF [BA][1,72]	284.0	224.4	203.9	184.4	132.9	89.3	69.0	94.3
M [BA][1,72]	165.6	121.1	105.4	90.6	67.1	46.7	34.6	49.5

27

Unemployment *(continued)*
Number (thousands) and percentage unemployed, by sex
Chômage *(suite)*
Nombre (milliers) et pourcentage des chômeurs, par sexe

Country or area, source [§] Pays ou zone, source [§]	2001	2002	2003	2004	2005	2006	2007	2008
F [BA] [1,72]	118.4	103.3	98.4	93.8	65.8	42.6	34.3	44.8
%MF [BA] [1,72]	17.4	13.8	12.4	11.4	8.3	5.6	4.3	5.8
%M [BA] [1,72]	19.9	14.6	12.7	11.0	8.2	5.8	4.3	6.0
%F [BA] [1,72]	14.7	12.9	12.2	11.8	8.3	5.4	4.3	5.6
MF [FB] [44,49]	224.0	191.2	158.8	126.4	87.2	79.3	69.7	95.0
M [FB] [44,49]	117.7	95.1	73.7	53.8	33.9	29.9	27.4	49.0
F [FB] [44,49]	106.3	96.1	85.1	72.6	53.3	49.4	42.3	46.0
%MF [FB] [44,49]	12.9	10.9	9.8	7.8	5.4	5.0	4.3	5.9
%M [FB] [44,49]	13.5	10.8	9.0	6.5	4.1	3.7	3.4	6.0
%F [FB] [44,49]	12.2	11.0	10.5	9.1	6.8	6.3	5.3	5.8
Luxembourg Luxembourg								
MF [BA] [1]	...	...	...	...	...	9.7	8.9	10.4
M [BA] [1]	...	...	...	...	...	4.0	4.3	4.9
F [BA] [1]	...	...	...	...	...	5.7	4.6	5.5
%MF [BA] [1]	...	...	...	...	...	...	...	4.8
%M [BA] [1]	...	...	...	...	...	...	...	4.0
%F [BA] [1]	...	...	...	...	...	...	...	5.8
MF [FB] [49]	4.9	5.8	7.6	8.7	9.8	9.5	0.6	9.9
M [FB] [49]	2.6	3.2	4.1	4.7	5.4	5.0	4.9	5.2
F [FB] [49]	2.3	2.7	3.5	4.0	4.4	4.5	4.7	4.7
%MF [FB] [49]	2.7	3.0	3.8	4.2	4.7	4.6	4.5	...
%M [FB] [49]	...	...	...	...	...	4.3	...	...
%F [FB] [49]	...	...	...	...	...	5.0	...	...
Madagascar Madagascar								
MF [B] [73]	...	...	383.0 [76]	...	274.3	...	...	...
M [B] [73]	...	...	149.8 [76]	...	100.4	...	...	...
F [B] [73]	...	...	233.2 [76]	...	173.8	...	...	...
%MF [B] [73]	...	...	4.5	...	2.8	...	...	...
%M [B] [73]	...	...	3.5	...	2.0	...	...	...
%F [B] [73]	...	...	5.6	...	3.6	...	...	...
MF [BA] [9,74,75]	47.4	...	...	...	...	...	...	...
M [BA] [9,74,75]	24.7	...	...	...	...	...	...	...
F [BA] [9,74,75]	22.7	...	...	...	...	...	...	...
%MF [BA] [9,74,75]	5.3	...	...	...	...	...	...	...
%M [BA] [9,74,75]	5.3	...	...	...	...	...	...	...
%F [BA] [9,74,75]	5.4	...	...	...	...	...	...	...
Malaysia Malaisie								
MF [BA] [51]	342.4	343.5	369.8	366.6	368.1	353.6	351.4	368.5
M [BA] [51]	212.3	210.5	235.8	224.7	230.4	224.9	216.4	223.5
F [BA] [51]	130.1	133.1	134.0	142.0	137.7	128.7	135.0	145.0
%MF [BA] [51]	3.5	3.5	3.6	3.5	3.5	3.3	3.2	3.3
%M [BA] [51]	3.4	3.3	3.6	3.4	3.4	3.3	3.1	3.2
%F [BA] [51]	3.8	3.8	3.6	3.8	3.7	3.4	3.4	3.7
MF [FB] [1]	33.5	37.2	34.8	...	...	...	...	...
Maldives [1] Maldives [1]								
MF [A]	...	...	...	...	...	18.6	...	...
M [A]	...	...	...	...	...	6.0	...	...
F [A]	...	...	...	...	...	12.6	...	...
Mali [1] Mali [1]								
MF [BA]	...	...	...	227.5	...	...	...	...
M [BA]	...	...	...	107.0	...	...	...	...
F [BA]	...	...	...	120.5	...	...	...	...
%MF [BA]	...	...	...	8.8	...	...	...	...
%M [BA]	...	...	...	7.2	...	...	...	...
%F [BA]	...	...	...	10.9	...	...	...	...
Malta Malte								
MF [BA] [1]	10.1	11.0	12.1	11.5	11.7	11.9	10.7	10.4
M [BA] [1]	6.8	7.2	7.8	7.1	7.3	7.2	6.5	6.4
F [BA] [1]	3.2	3.8	4.3	4.4	4.5	4.7	4.3	3.9
%MF [BA] [1]	6.4	7.0	7.6	7.2	7.3	7.3	6.5	6.1
%M [BA] [1]	6.2	6.6	7.1	6.4	6.6	6.5	5.8	5.7
%F [BA] [1]	7.0	7.7	8.7	9.0	8.9	8.9	7.7	6.9

27

Unemployment *(continued)*
Number (thousands) and percentage unemployed, by sex
Chômage *(suite)*
Nombre (milliers) et pourcentage des chômeurs, par sexe

Country or area, source [§] Pays ou zone, source [§]	2001	2002	2003	2004	2005	2006	2007	2008
MF [FB] [3,77]	6.8	6.8	#8.2	8.1	7.4	7.2	6.2	...
M [FB] [3,77]	5.6	5.6	#6.6	6.5	5.7	5.5	4.7	...
F [FB] [3,77]	1.1	1.2	#1.6	1.6	1.7	1.6	1.5	...
%MF [FB] [3,77]	4.7	4.7	#5.7	5.4	5.1	5.0	4.1	...
%M [FB] [3,77]	5.4	5.4	#6.4	6.1	5.6	5.5	4.5	...
%F [FB] [3,77]	2.7	2.9	#3.8	3.8	3.9	3.9	3.2	...
Martinique [1,59] Martinique [1,59]								
MF [BA]	39.8	#35.8	36.1	35.9	34.8	42.2	34.5	...
M [BA]	16.3	#15.4	16.1	15.9	16.2	19.1	16.3	...
F [BA]	23.6	#20.4	20.1	20.0	18.6	23.1	18.2	...
%MF [BA]	24.7	#22.3	22.3	22.4	21.7	25.2	21.2	...
%M [BA]	20.1	#19.2	19.9	19.9	20.1	23.1	20.7	...
%F [BA]	29.3	#25.4	24.6	24.7	20.1	27.3	21.7	...
Mauritius Maurice								
MF [BA]	...	...	...	45.1[1]	52.1[1]	50.1[1]	46.8[15]	40.4[15]
M [BA]	...	...	...	20.3[1]	20.2[1]	19.5[1]	18.6[15]	14.6[15]
F [BA]	...	...	...	24.8[1]	31.8[1]	30.6[1]	28.2[15]	25.8[15]
%MF [BA]	...	...	...	8.5[1]	9.6[1]	9.1[1]	8.5[15]	7.2[15]
%M [BA]	...	...	...	5.8[1]	5.8[1]	5.5[1]	5.3[15]	4.1[15]
%F [BA]	...	...	...	13.5[1]	16.5[1]	15.5[1]	14.4[15]	12.7[15]
MF [E]	47.7	50.8	54.4	...	...	...	...	...
M [E]	30.5	29.6	31.7	...	...	...	...	...
F [E]	17.2	21.2	22.7	...	...	...	...	...
%MF [E]	9.1	9.7	10.2	...	...	...	...	...
%M [E]	8.8	8.5	9.0	...	...	...	...	...
%F [E]	9.8	12.0	12.6	...	...	...	...	...
MF [FB] [1,78]	21.6	22.0	23.4	22.0	33.6	...	36.1	20.6
M [FB] [1,78]	10.5	10.1	10.1	10.5	15.4	...	17.9	7.1
F [FB] [1,78]	11.1	11.9	13.3	11.4	18.2	...	18.2	13.4
%MF [FB] [1,78]	...	...	...	...	...	...	...	7.1
%M [FB] [1,78]	...	...	...	...	...	...	...	4.1
%F [FB] [1,78]	...	...	...	...	...	...	...	12.7
Mexico [6,13] Mexique [6,13]								
MF [BA]	996.1	1 145.6	1 195.6	1 539.8	1 482.5	1 377.7	1 505.2	1 593.3
M [BA]	550.6	656.5	687.0	828.7	917.8	811.5	885.6	927.4
F [BA]	445.5	489.0	508.7	711.0	564.7	566.2	619.6	665.9
%MF [BA]	2.6	2.9	3.0	3.7	3.5	3.2	3.4	3.5
%M [BA]	2.2	2.5	2.6	3.1	3.4	3.0	3.2	3.3
%F [BA]	3.3	3.5	3.6	4.7	3.6	3.5	3.7	3.9
Mongolia [3,15] Mongolie [3,15]								
MF [E]	40.3	30.9	33.3	35.6	32.9	32.9	29.9	29.8
M [E]	18.5	14.1	15.3	15.9	14.6	14.2	12.9	17.6
F [E]	21.9	16.8	18.1	19.6	18.3	18.7	17.0	12.2
%MF [E]	4.6	3.5	3.5	3.6	3.3	3.2	2.8	2.8
%M [E]	4.2	3.4	3.2	3.3	3.0	2.8	2.5	2.3
%F [E]	5.1	3.8	3.8	3.9	3.6	3.5	3.2	3.2
Montenegro [51,79] Monténégro [51,79]								
MF [BA]	...	...	...	...	77.8	...	...	...
M [BA]	...	...	...	...	37.4	...	...	...
F [BA]	...	...	...	...	40.3	...	...	...
%MF [BA]	...	...	...	...	30.3	...	...	...
%M [BA]	...	...	...	...	26.2	...	...	...
%F [BA]	...	...	...	...	35.5	...	...	...
Morocco [1] Maroc [1]								
MF [BA]	1 275.0	1 202.7	1 299.0	1 192.5	1 226.4	1 062.5	1 092.1	1 077.8
M [BA]	952.0	878.4	922.4	851.2	877.6	774.1	794.5	781.2
F [BA]	323.0	324.3	376.6	341.4	348.8	288.4	297.6	296.7
%MF [BA]	12.5	11.6	11.9	10.8	11.0	9.7	9.6	9.4
%M [BA]	12.5	11.6	11.5	10.6	10.8	9.7	9.6	9.4
%F [BA]	12.5	12.5	13.0	11.4	11.5	9.7	9.5	9.5
Myanmar [22] Myanmar [22]								
MF [FB]	398.4	435.7	326.5	291.3	189.7	183.4	118.7	137.8

Country or area, source [§] Pays ou zone, source [§]	2001	2002	2003	2004	2005	2006	2007	2008
Namibia[80] Namibie[80]								
MF [BA]	...	...	...	108.1	...	...	...	...
M [BA]	...	...	...	52.0	...	...	...	...
F [BA]	...	...	...	56.1	...	...	...	...
%MF [BA]	...	...	...	21.9	...	...	...	...
%M [BA]	...	...	...	19.4	...	...	...	...
%F [BA]	...	...	...	25.0	...	...	...	...
Netherlands Pays-Bas								
MF [BA][51]	204.0	252.0	332.0	411.0	425.0	354.0	300.0	257.0
M [BA][51]	93.0	126.0	178.0	219.0	220.0	174.0	143.0	128.0
F [BA][51]	111.0	125.0	153.0	192.0	205.0	180.0	157.0	128.0
%MF [BA][51]	2.5	3.1	4.0	5.0	5.1	4.2	3.5	3.0
%M [BA][51]	2.0	2.7	3.9	4.8	4.8	3.8	3.1	2.8
%F [BA][51]	3.1	3.5	4.2	5.2	5.5	4.7	4.0	3.2
MF [FB][49]	146.0	170.0	255.0	319.0	311.0	260.0	182.0	145.0
M [FB][49]	77.0	91.0	144.0	179.0	164.0	133.0	93.0	77.0
F [FB][49]	69.0	79.0	111.0	141.0	146.0	127.0	89.0	68.0
%MF [FB][49]	2.0	2.3	3.5	4.3	4.2	3.5	2.4	1.9
%M [FB][49]	1.8	2.1	3.3	4.1	3.8	3.1	2.2	1.8
%F [FB][49]	2.3	2.6	3.6	4.6	4.7	4.0	2.7	2.0
Netherlands Antilles[1,79,81] Antilles néerlandaises[1,79,81]								
MF [BA]	...	9.1	9.3	9.9	11.4	8.9	7.7	6.5
M [BA]	...	4.1	4.0	4.5	5.2	3.3	3.0	2.5
F [BA]	...	4.9	5.3	5.4	6.2	5.6	4.6	4.0
%MF [BA]	...	15.6	15.1	16.1	18.2	14.6	12.4	10.3
%M [BA]	...	14.0	13.1	15.1	17.1	11.3	10.2	8.1
%F [BA]	...	17.1	17.1	17.0	19.2	17.7	14.4	12.4
New Caledonia[15] Nouvelle-Calédonie[15]								
MF [FB]	9.9	10.5	10.2	9.6	8.7	7.0	6.6	...
M [FB]	4.4	4.8	4.6	...	...	...	...	...
F [FB]	5.4	5.7	5.6	...	...	...	...	...
New Zealand Nouvelle-Zélande								
MF [BA][1]	106.3	106.4	97.0	84.0	82.5	85.4	82.8	95.0
M [BA][1]	58.1	56.2	49.3	40.7	40.9	42.3	41.0	49.8
F [BA][1]	48.2	50.2	48.5	44.2	41.6	43.1	41.7	45.2
%MF [BA][1]	5.4	5.3	4.8	4.0	3.8	3.8	3.7	4.2
%M [BA][1]	5.5	5.1	4.5	3.6	3.5	3.6	3.4	4.1
%F [BA][1]	5.4	5.5	5.1	4.5	4.1	4.2	4.0	4.2
MF [FB][82,83]	192.2	168.3	...	...	...	...	...	...
M [FB][82,83]	103.5	89.1	...	...	...	...	...	...
F [FB][82,83]	88.7	79.2	...	...	...	...	...	...
Nicaragua[9] Nicaragua[9]								
MF [BA]	...	...	160.5	138.0	122.5	114.5	106.9	...
M [BA]	...	...	97.1	74.2	73.4	74.1	65.9	...
F [BA]	...	...	63.4	63.8	49.1	40.3	41.0	...
%MF [BA]	...	...	7.7	6.5	5.6	5.2	4.9	...
%M [BA]	...	...	7.6	5.7	5.4	5.4	4.8	...
%F [BA]	...	...	7.9	8.0	5.9	4.9	5.0	...
MF [E]	122.5	135.3	...	...	...	...	...	...
M [E]	77.3	84.0	...	...	...	...	...	...
F [E]	45.2	51.3	...	...	...	...	...	...
%MF [E]	11.3	12.2	...	...	...	...	...	...
Niger[9] Niger[9]								
MF [A]	57.6	...	...	...	...	...	...	...
M [A]	44.9	...	...	...	...	...	...	...
F [A]	12.7	...	...	...	...	...	...	...
Niue[1] Nioué[1]								
MF [A]	^0.0	...	...	...	...	...	...	...
M [A]	^0.0	...	...	...	...	...	...	...
F [A]	^0.0	...	...	...	...	...	...	...

27

Unemployment *(continued)*
Number (thousands) and percentage unemployed, by sex
Chômage *(suite)*
Nombre (milliers) et pourcentage des chômeurs, par sexe

Country or area, source [§] Pays ou zone, source [§]	2001	2002	2003	2004	2005	2006	2007	2008
Northern Mariana Islands [15] **Îles Mariannes du Nord** [15]								
MF [BA]	...	...	1.8	...	...	...	...	...
M [BA]	...	...	0.8	...	...	...	...	...
F [BA]	...	...	1.0	...	...	...	...	...
%MF [BA]	...	...	4.6	...	...	...	...	...
%M [BA]	...	...	5.0	...	...	...	...	...
%F [BA]	...	...	4.3	...	...	...	...	...
Norway **Norvège**								
MF [BA]	84.0[65]	92.0[65]	107.0[65]	106.0[65]	111.0[65]	84.0[53]	63.0[53]	67.0[53]
M [BA]	46.0[65]	52.0[65]	62.0[65]	62.0[65]	61.0[65]	45.0[53]	34.0[53]	38.0[53]
F [BA]	38.0[65]	40.0[65]	45.0[65]	45.0[65]	49.0[65]	39.0[53]	29.0[53]	30.0[53]
%MF [BA]	3.6[65]	3.9[65]	4.5[65]	4.5[65]	4.6[65]	3.4[53]	2.5[53]	2.6[53]
%M [BA]	3.7[65]	4.1[65]	4.9[65]	4.9[65]	4.8[65]	3.5[53]	2.6[53]	2.8[53]
%F [BA]	3.4[65]	3.6[65]	4.0[65]	4.0[65]	4.4[65]	3.4[53]	2.5[53]	2.4[53]
MF [FB]	62.7[65]	75.2[65]	92.6[65]	91.6[65]	83.5[65]	63.0[53]	46.0[53]	43.0[53]
M [FB]	35.7[65]	42.6[65]	54.0[65]	52.2[65]	45.7[65]	33.0[53]	24.0[53]	24.0[53]
F [FB]	27.0[65]	32.6[65]	38.6[65]	39.4[65]	37.8[65]	30.0[53]	22.0[53]	19.0[53]
%MF [FB]	2.7[65]	3.2[65]	3.9[65]	3.9[65]	3.5[65]	2.6[53]	1.9[53]	1.7[53]
%M [FB]	...	...	4.3[65]	4.1[65]	3.6[65]	2.6[53]	1.9[53]	1.8[53]
%F [FB]	...	...	3.5[65]	3.5[65]	3.4[65]	2.7[53]	1.9[53]	1.6[53]
Occupied Palestinian Terr. [9,84] **Terr. palestinien occupé** [9,84]								
MF [BA]	170.5	217.5	194.3	212.2	194.5	206.2	183.7	228.0
M [BA]	158.0	201.5	172.2	185.8	164.6	175.2	153.7	190.1
F [BA]	12.5	16.0	22.1	26.4	30.1	31.0	30.0	37.9
%MF [BA]	25.2	31.2	25.4	26.7	23.3	23.2	21.3	25.7
%M [BA]	26.9	33.5	26.7	28.0	23.6	23.9	21.8	26.2
%F [BA]	14.0	17.0	18.4	20.0	22.1	20.1	18.7	23.5
Pakistan **Pakistan**								
MF [BA] [9,21]	3 181.0	3 506.0	3 594.0	3 499.0	3 566.0	3 103.0	2 680.0	...
M [BA] [9,21]	2 082.0	2 381.0	2 441.0	2 461.0	2 508.0	2 166.0	1 807.0	...
F [BA] [9,21]	1 099.0	1 125.0	1 153.0	1 038.0	1 058.0	937.0	873.0	...
%MF [BA] [9,21]	7.8	8.3	8.3	7.7	7.7	6.2	5.3	...
%M [BA] [9,21]	6.1	6.7	6.7	6.6	6.6	5.4	4.5	...
%F [BA] [9,21]	17.3	16.5	16.5	12.8	12.8	6.2	8.4	...
MF [FB] [85]	477.0	493.0	505.0	576.0	587.0	420.0	...	...
M [FB] [85]	428.0	442.0	453.0	477.0	486.0	360.0	...	...
F [FB] [85]	49.0	51.0	52.0	99.0	101.0	60.0	...	...
Panama [1,67] **Panama** [1,67]								
MF [BA]	169.7	172.4	170.4	159.9	136.8	121.4	92.0	82.9
M [BA]	92.0	86.5	82.9	76.3	66.7	60.2	44.5	40.2
F [BA]	77.8	85.9	87.3	83.6	70.2	61.1	47.5	42.7
%MF [BA]	14.7	14.1	13.6	12.4	10.3	9.1	6.8	5.8
%M [BA]	12.2	11.2	10.5	9.4	8.1	7.2	5.3	4.6
%F [BA]	19.3	19.2	18.8	17.3	14.0	12.4	9.3	7.8
Paraguay [9] **Paraguay** [9]								
MF [A] [26]	...	109.0	...	...	...	...	...	...
M [A] [26]	...	61.9	...	...	...	...	...	...
F [A] [26]	...	47.1	...	...	...	...	...	...
MF [BA] [26]	...	272.6	206.0	...	...	...	161.2	170.6
M [BA] [86]	...	141.9	105.6	...	...	...	74.6	83.9
F [BA] [86]	...	130.9	100.4	...	...	...	86.6	86.7
%MF [BA] [86]	...	10.8	8.1	...	...	...	5.6	5.7
%M [BA] [86]	...	9.0	6.7	...	...	...	4.3	4.6
%F [BA] [86]	...	13.6	10.1	...	...	...	7.5	7.4
Peru [6,87] **Pérou** [6,87]								
MF [BA]	...	359.4[86]	316.0[88]	339.5	333.4	297.6	300.1	308.0
M [BA]	...	194.0[86]	182.5[88]	159.4	155.4	136.3	139.1	131.3
F [BA]	...	165.4[86]	133.6[88]	180.1	178.0	161.3	161.0	176.6
%MF [BA]	...	7.7[86]	7.2[88]	7.4	7.5	7.2	6.7	6.8
%M [BA]	...	7.5[86]	7.3[88]	6.6	7.1	6.0	5.8	5.4
%F [BA]	...	7.8[86]	7.0[88]	8.3	8.1	8.6	7.8	8.3

Unemployment *(continued)*
Number (thousands) and percentage unemployed, by sex
Chômage *(suite)*
Nombre (milliers) et pourcentage des chômeurs, par sexe

Country or area, source [§] Pays ou zone, source [§]	2001	2002	2003	2004	2005	2006	2007	2008
Philippines[1] Philippines[1]								
MF [BA]	3 653.0	3 874.0	3 936.0	4 249.0	#2 748.0	2 829.0	2 653.0	2 716.0
M [BA]	2 174.0	2 295.0	2 343.0	2 558.0	#1 685.0	1 798.0	1 675.0	1 714.0
F [BA]	1 478.0	1 579.0	1 592.0	1 692.0	#1 062.0	1 031.0	978.0	1 002.0
%MF [BA]	11.1	11.4	11.4	11.8	#7.8	8.0	7.3	7.4
%M [BA]	10.8	11.1	11.0	11.5	#7.8	8.2	7.5	7.6
%F [BA]	11.6	11.8	11.9	12.4	#7.8	7.6	7.0	7.1
Poland Pologne								
MF [A][1,4]	...	3 558.2	...	...	...	...	...	...
M [A][1,4]	...	1 851.5	...	...	...	...	...	...
F [A][1,4]	...	1 706.7	...	...	...	...	...	...
MF [BA][53]	3 170.0	3 431.0	3 329.0	3 230.0	3 045.0	2 344.0	1 619.0	1 211.0
M [BA][53]	1 583.0	1 779.0	1 741.0	1 681.0	1 553.0	1 202.0	831.0	599.0
F [BA][53]	1 587.0	1 652.0	1 588.0	1 550.0	1 493.0	1 140.0	788.0	612.0
%MF [BA][53]	18.2	19.9	19.6	19.0	17.7	13.8	9.6	7.1
%M [BA][53]	16.9	19.1	19.0	18.2	16.6	13.0	9.0	6.4
%F [BA][53]	19.8	20.9	20.4	19.9	19.1	14.9	10.3	8.0
MF [FB][3,89]	3 115.1	#3 217.0	3 175.7	2 999.6	2 773.0	2 309.4	1 746.6	1 473.8
M [FB][3,89]	1 473.0	#1 571.2	1 541.0	1 431.1	1 286.6	1 003.7	729.3	640.4
F [FB][3,89]	1 642.1	#1 645.8	1 634.7	1 568.5	1 486.4	1 305.7	1 017.3	833.4
%MF [FB][3,89]	17.5	#20.0	20.0	19.1	17.6	14.9	11.4	9.5
Portugal[1] Portugal[1]								
MF [A][29]	339.3	...	...	...	...	...	...	...
M [A][29]	142.9	...	...	...	...	...	...	...
F [A][29]	196.3	...	...	...	...	...	...	...
MF [BA]	213.5	270.5	342.3	365.0	422.3	427.8	448.6	427.1
M [BA]	91.6	121.4	160.9	172.9	198.1	194.8	196.8	194.3
F [BA]	122.0	149.1	181.4	192.2	224.1	233.1	251.1	232.7
%MF [BA]	4.0	5.0	6.3	6.7	7.6	7.7	8.0	7.6
%M [BA]	3.2	4.1	5.5	5.8	6.7	6.5	6.6	6.5
%F [BA]	5.0	6.0	7.2	7.6	8.7	9.0	9.6	8.8
MF [FB]	324.7	344.6	427.3	461.0	477.2	456.1	410.3	...
M [FB]	127.0	139.6	182.3	199.5	206.0	194.4	167.1	...
F [FB]	197.7	205.3	245.0	261.5	271.6	264.1	243.1	...
Puerto Rico[15,56] Porto Rico[15,56]								
MF [BA]	145.0	163.0	164.0	145.0	160.0	156.0	152.0	158.0
M [BA]	97.0	101.0	99.0	92.0	97.0	90.0	93.0	97.0
F [BA]	48.0	62.0	65.0	53.0	63.0	66.0	59.0	60.0
%MF [BA]	11.4	12.3	12.0	10.6	11.3	11.1	10.9	11.5
%M [BA]	13.0	13.2	12.8	11.8	12.2	11.5	12.1	12.9
%F [BA]	9.1	10.9	10.9	9.0	10.2	10.5	9.5	9.9
Qatar[1,29] Qatar[1,29]								
MF [A]	...	...	...	6.6	...	...	...	...
M [A]	...	...	...	4.0	...	...	...	...
F [A]	...	...	...	2.6	...	...	...	...
MF [BA]	12.6	...	...	...	...	...	4.3	...
M [BA]	6.1	...	...	...	...	...	1.6	...
F [BA]	6.5	...	...	...	...	...	2.7	...
%MF [BA]	3.9	...	...	...	...	...	...	...
%M [BA]	2.3	...	...	...	...	...	...	...
%F [BA]	12.6	...	...	...	...	...	...	...
Republic of Moldova République de Moldova								
MF [BA][1]	117.7	110.0	117.1	116.5	103.7	99.9	66.7	51.7
M [BA][1]	70.1	64.4	69.9	70.1	59.8	61.7	41.5	30.0
F [BA][1]	47.6	45.4	47.2	46.4	43.9	38.2	25.2	21.8
%MF [BA][1]	7.3	6.8	7.9	8.1	7.3	7.4	5.1	4.0
%M [BA][1]	8.7	8.1	9.6	10.0	8.7	8.9	6.3	4.6
%F [BA][1]	5.9	5.5	6.4	6.3	6.0	5.7	3.9	3.4
MF [FB][3]	27.6	24.0	19.7	21.0	21.7	20.4	18.9	17.8
M [FB][3]	13.6	11.7	10.3	11.7	11.3	9.6	8.3	7.3
F [FB][3]	14.0	12.3	9.4	9.3	10.4	10.8	10.6	10.5
%MF [FB][3]	2.2	2.1	2.0	2.0	2.0	1.9	1.9	1.6

Country or area, source [§] Pays ou zone, source [§]	2001	2002	2003	2004	2005	2006	2007	2008
Réunion[1,13] Réunion[1,13]								
MF [BA]	83.3	80.9	90.1	96.2	88.9	86.7	75.9	78.0
M [BA]	44.5	41.9	48.9	52.3	45.7	46.8	39.9	39.4
F [BA]	38.8	39.0	41.3	43.9	43.2	39.9	36.0	38.7
%MF [BA]	29.7	28.3	30.8	32.2	29.5	27.5	24.2	24.5
%M [BA]	28.0	26.0	29.5	30.7	26.6	26.5	22.9	22.8
%F [BA]	32.1	31.1	32.5	34.1	33.3	28.8	25.9	26.5
Romania[1] Roumanie[1]								
MF [A][29]	...	1 040.1	...	...	...	...	...	...
M [A][29]	...	682.4	...	...	...	...	...	...
F [A][29]	...	357.7	...	...	...	...	...	...
MF [BA]	749.9	845.2[90]	691.7	799.5	704.5	728.4	641.0	575.5
M [BA]	436.0	494.0[90]	408.0	490.7	420.3	452.4	398.7	369.2
F [BA]	313.9	351.1[90]	283.7	308.7	284.1	276.0	242.3	206.3
%MF [BA]	6.6	8.4[90]	7.0	8.0	7.2	7.3	6.4	5.8
%M [BA]	7.1	8.9[90]	7.5	9.0	7.7	8.2	7.3	6.7
%F [BA]	5.9	7.7[90]	6.4	6.9	6.4	6.1	5.4	4.7
MF [FB][3]	826.9	760.6	658.9	557.9	523.0	460.5	367.8	403.4
M [FB][3]	445.8	421.1	372.6	323.3	303.8	269.0	201.2	216.2
F [FB][3]	381.1	339.5	286.3	234.6	219.2	191.5	166.6	187.2
%MF [FB][3]	8.8	8.4	7.4	6.3	5.9	5.2	4.0	4.4
%M [FB][3]	9.2	8.9	7.8	7.0	6.4	5.7	4.2	4.5
%F [FB][3]	8.4	7.8	6.8	5.6	5.2	4.6	3.9	4.4
Russian Federation Fédération de Russie								
MF [BA][91]	6 424.0	5 698.0	5 959.0	5 675.0	5 263.0	5 312.0	4 588.0	4 791.0
M [BA][91]	3 450.0	3 014.0	3 121.0	2 975.0	2 725.0	2 811.0	2 453.0	2 542.0
F [BA][91]	2 974.0	2 685.0	2 838.0	2 699.0	2 538.0	2 501.0	2 136.0	2 250.0
%MF [BA][91]	8.9	7.9	8.0	7.8	7.2	7.2	6.1	6.3
%M [BA][91]	9.3	7.9	8.3	7.6	7.3	7.5	6.4	6.6
%F [BA][91]	8.5	7.9	7.8	8.0	7.0	6.8	5.8	6.1
MF [FB][3]	1 123.0	1 500.0	1 639.0	1 920.0	1 830.0	1 742.0	1 553.0	1 522.0
M [FB][3]	360.0	487.0	533.0	647.0	630.0	610.0	570.0	604.0
F [FB][3]	763.0	1 013.0	1 106.0	1 273.0	1 200.0	1 132.0	983.0	918.0
%MF [FB][3]	1.6	2.1	2.3	2.6	2.5	2.3	2.1	2.0
Rwanda[26] Rwanda[26]								
MF [A]	...	30.6	...	...	...	...	...	...
M [A]	...	17.7	...	...	...	...	...	...
F [A]	...	12.9	...	...	...	...	...	...
Saint Helena[1] Sainte-Hélène[1]								
MF [FB]	0.3	...	0.2	0.2	0.1	0.1	0.1	...
M [FB]	0.2	...	0.2	0.1	0.1	0.1	0.0	...
F [FB]	0.1	...	0.1	0.1	0.0	0.0	0.0	...
Saint Lucia[1] Sainte-Lucie[1]								
MF [A][4]	8.7	...	...	...	...	...	...	...
M [A][4]	5.0	...	...	...	...	...	...	...
F [A][4]	3.6	...	...	...	...	...	...	...
MF [BA]	...	15.0	18.2	16.5	...	...	...	...
M [BA]	...	6.7	7.6	7.4	...	...	...	...
F [BA]	...	8.3	10.6	9.1	...	...	...	...
%MF [BA]	...	20.4	22.3	21.0	...	...	...	...
%M [BA]	...	17.3	17.3	17.5	...	...	...	...
%F [BA]	...	23.8	28.0	25.0	...	...	...	...
Samoa[1] Samoa[1]								
MF [A]	2.6	...	...	...	...	...	...	...
M [A]	1.6	...	...	...	...	...	...	...
F [A]	1.0	...	...	...	...	...	...	...
San Marino[1,42] Saint-Marin[1,42]								
MF [E]	0.5	0.7	0.6	0.6	0.7	0.6	0.6	0.7
M [E]	0.2	0.2	0.2	0.1	0.2	0.1	0.2	0.2
F [E]	0.4	0.5	0.5	0.4	0.5	0.5	0.4	0.5
%MF [E]	2.6	3.6	3.1	2.8	2.1	1.6	...	...

Country or area, source [§] Pays ou zone, source [§]	2001	2002	2003	2004	2005	2006	2007	2008
%M [E]	1.4	1.6	1.5	1.1	1.7	1.2	...	...
%F [E]	4.3	6.3	5.5	5.2	2.6	2.0	...	...
Sao Tome and Principe [1] Sao Tomé-et-Principe [1]								
MF [E]	8.2	9.5	9.0	8.3	8.7	8.9	...	...
M [E]	3.1	3.7	3.3	3.4	3.4	3.4	...	...
F [E]	5.2	5.8	5.7	4.9	5.4	5.4	...	...
Saudi Arabia [1] Arabie saoudite [1]								
MF [BA]	281.2	326.6	...	...	...	501.9[2]	463.3	418.1
M [BA]	202.6	225.0	...	...	...	319.1[2]	295.5	250.4
F [BA]	78.6	103.7	...	...	...	182.8[2]	167.8	167.7
%MF [BA]	4.6	5.2	...	...	...	6.3[2]	5.6	5.0
%M [BA]	3.9	4.2	...	...	...	4.7[2]	4.2	3.5
%F [BA]	9.1	11.5	...	...	...	14.7[2]	13.2	13.0
Senegal [1] Sénégal [1]								
MF [B]	...	...	...	...	...	351.4	...	...
M [B]	...	...	...	...	...	176.8	...	...
F [B]	...	...	...	...	...	174.6	...	...
%MF [B]	...	...	...	...	...	11.1	...	...
%M [B]	...	...	...	...	...	7.9	...	...
%F [B]	...	...	...	...	...	13.6	...	...
Serbia [1,14] Serbie [1,14]								
MF [BA]	...	...	...	665.4	719.9	693.0	585.5	445.4
M [BA]	...	...	...	303.2	329.8	339.8	289.8	217.5
F [BA]	...	...	...	362.2	390.1	353.2	295.7	227.9
%MF [BA]	...	...	...	18.5	20.8	20.9	18.1	13.6
%M [BA]	...	...	...	15.1	16.8	17.9	15.1	11.9
%F [BA]	...	...	...	22.9	26.2	24.7	21.0	15.8
Serbia and Montenegro Serbie-et-Monténégro								
MF [BA][1,79]	490.2	517.3	562.4	...	...	...	...	...
M [BA][1,79]	242.5	261.5	306.4	...	...	...	...	...
F [BA][1,79]	247.7	255.8	256.0	...	...	...	...	...
%MF [BA][1,79]	12.8	13.8	15.2	...	...	...	...	...
%M [BA][1,79]	11.1	12.4	14.4	...	...	...	...	...
%F [BA][1,79]	15.0	15.8	16.4	...	...	...	...	...
MF [FB][92]	850.0	923.2	1 019.0	...	...	...	...	...
M [FB][92]	369.6	408.7	461.2	...	...	...	...	...
F [FB][92]	480.4	514.5	557.8	...	...	...	...	...
%MF [FB][92]	22.3	24.7	27.6	...	...	...	...	...
%M [FB][92]	22.6	...	...	...	...	...	...	...
%F [FB][92]	22.1	...	...	...	...	...	...	...
Seychelles [1,26] Seychelles [1,26]								
MF [A]	...	4.3	...	...	...	...	...	...
Sierra Leone [9,42,93] Sierra Leone [9,42,93]								
MF [A]	...	...	...	68.3	...	...	...	...
M [A]	...	...	...	45.9	...	...	...	...
F [A]	...	...	...	22.3	...	...	...	...
%MF [A]	...	...	...	2.8	...	...	...	...
%M [A]	...	...	...	3.1	...	...	...	...
%F [A]	...	...	...	2.5	...	...	...	...
Singapore Singapour								
MF [BA][32,94]	61.9	94.2	101.0	101.3	...	84.2	74.8	76.2
M [BA][32,94]	35.7	55.3	57.6	56.8	...	44.7	40.0	39.6
F [BA][32,94]	26.2	39.0	43.4	44.5	...	39.5	34.8	36.6
%MF [BA][32,94]	3.8	5.6	5.9	5.8	...	4.5	4.0	4.0
%M [BA][32,94]	3.7	5.6	5.7	5.6	...	4.1	3.7	3.6
%F [BA][32,94]	3.9	5.8	6.2	6.2	...	4.9	4.3	4.4
MF [FB][6]	6.4	11.6	13.9	#49.6	43.8	#22.2	16.7	13.4
M [FB][6]	3.2	5.6	6.8	#25.3	22.0	#11.2	8.3	6.5
F [FB][6]	3.2	6.0	7.1	#24.3	21.8	#11.0	8.4	6.9
Slovakia [1] Slovaquie [1]								
MF [A][4]	561.2	...	...	...	...	...	...	...
M [A][4]	313.2	...	...	...	...	...	...	...

27

Unemployment *(continued)*
Number (thousands) and percentage unemployed, by sex
Chômage *(suite)*
Nombre (milliers) et pourcentage des chômeurs, par sexe

Country or area, source [§] Pays ou zone, source [§]	2001	2002	2003	2004	2005	2006	2007	2008
F [A][4]	248.0	...	...	...	...	...	...	...
MF [BA][95]	508.0	486.9	459.2	481.0	427.5	353.4	291.9	257.5
M [BA][95]	282.5	263.9	246.5	250.0	223.6	179.5	143.5	124.6
F [BA][95]	225.5	223.0	212.7	231.0	203.8	173.9	148.4	132.8
%MF [BA][95]	19.2	18.5	17.4	18.1	16.2	13.3	11.0	9.6
%M [BA][95]	19.5	18.4	17.2	17.3	15.3	12.0	9.8	8.4
%F [BA][95]	18.8	18.7	17.7	19.1	17.2	14.7	12.5	11.1
MF [FB]	520.6	513.2	443.4	409.0	340.4	299.2	250.9	230.4
M [FB]	284.7	280.8	240.0	211.0	167.9	143.6	118.3	107.0
F [FB]	235.9	232.4	203.4	198.0	172.5	155.6	132.6	123.4
%MF [FB]	18.3	17.8	15.2	14.3	11.6	10.4	8.4	7.7
%M [FB]	18.9	19.0	15.3	13.7	10.8	9.2	7.3	6.5
%F [FB]	17.5	16.5	15.0	14.9	12.7	11.8	9.9	9.1
Slovenia[1] Slovénie[1]								
MF [A][29]	...	130.8	...	...	...	...	...	...
M [A][29]	...	66.8	...	...	...	...	...	...
F [A][29]	...	63.9	...	...	...	...	...	...
MF [BA][13]	57.0	58.0	63.0	61.0	58.0	61.0	48.0	43.0
M [BA][13]	29.0	30.0	32.0	31.0	30.0	28.0	20.0	20.0
F [BA][13]	28.0	28.0	31.0	30.0	28.0	33.0	28.0	23.0
%MF [BA][13]	5.9	5.9	6.6	6.1	5.8	5.9	4.6	4.2
%M [BA][13]	5.6	5.7	6.1	5.7	5.5	5.1	3.6	3.5
%F [BA][13]	6.3	6.3	7.1	6.4	6.1	6.8	5.8	4.9
MF [FB][44]	101.9	102.6	97.7	93.1	91.9	80.0	71.3	...
M [FB][44]	50.2	50.1	46.1	43.8	42.4	38.8	32.2	...
F [FB][44]	51.7	52.1	51.6	49.3	49.4	47.0	39.1	...
%MF [FB][44]	11.6	11.6	11.2	10.6	10.1	9.4	7.7	...
%M [FB][44]	10.4	10.4	9.7	9.1	...	7.7	6.3	...
%F [FB][44]	12.9	13.1	13.0	12.4	...	11.5	9.6	...
South Africa Afrique du Sud								
MF [BA]	4 655.0[1,27]	4 936.0[1,27]	4 434.0[1,27]	4 135.0[1,27]	4 487.0[1,27]	4 391.0[1,27]	3 945.0[1,27]	4 075.0[51]
M [BA]	2 236.0[1,27]	2 316.0[1,27]	2 166.0[1,27]	2 029.0[1,27]	2 057.0[1,27]	1 967.0[1,27]	1 883.0[1,27]	1 917.0[51]
F [BA]	2 420.0[1,27]	2 619.0[1,27]	2 268.0[1,27]	2 103.0[1,27]	2 428.0[1,27]	2 424.0[1,27]	2 059.0[1,27]	2 158.0[51]
%MF [BA]	29.4[1,27]	30.4[1,27]	28.0[1,27]	26.2[1,27]	26.7[1,27]	25.5[1,27]	23.0[1,27]	22.9[51]
%M [BA]	25.8[1,27]	25.9[1,27]	24.7[1,27]	23.1[1,27]	22.6[1,27]	21.2[1,27]	20.0[1,27]	20.0[51]
%F [BA]	33.8[1,27]	35.9[1,27]	32.0[1,27]	30.2[1,27]	31.7[1,27]	30.7[1,27]	26.7[1,27]	26.3[51]
Spain[49] Espagne[49]								
MF [BA]	1 904.4	2 155.3	2 242.2	2 213.6	#1 912.5	1 837.1	1 833.9	2 590.6
M [BA]	828.1	929.3	976.4	970.8	#862.9	791.5	815.2	1 311.0
F [BA]	1 076.3	1 226.0	1 265.8	1 242.8	#1 049.6	1 045.6	1 018.7	1 279.6
%MF [BA]	10.6	11.5	11.5	11.0	#9.2	8.5	8.3	11.3
%M [BA]	7.5	8.2	8.4	8.2	#7.0	6.3	6.4	10.1
%F [BA]	15.2	16.4	16.0	15.0	#12.2	11.6	10.9	13.0
MF [FB]	1 930.2	2 049.6	2 096.9	2 113.7	#2 069.9	2 039.4	2 039.0	2 539.9
M [FB]	771.5	836.7	851.1	854.3	#818.0	788.2	791.8	1 146.9
F [FB]	1 158.7	1 212.9	1 245.8	1 259.4	#1 251.8	1 251.2	1 247.2	1 393.0
%MF [FB]	10.7	10.9	10.7	10.5	#9.9	9.4	9.2	11.1
%M [FB]	7.0	7.4	7.3	7.2	#6.7	6.3	6.2	8.8
%F [FB]	16.4	16.2	15.8	15.2	#14.5	13.8	13.3	14.2
Sri Lanka[9] Sri Lanka[9]								
MF [BA]	537.2[105]	626.0[105]	641.0[96]	667.3[97]	623.4[98]	493.4[105]	447.0[105]	394.0[105]
M [BA]	280.1[105]	310.4[105]	310.7[96]	323.5[97]	301.6[98]	226.7[105]	209.7[105]	175.2[105]
F [BA]	257.1[105]	315.5[105]	330.2[96]	343.9[97]	321.7[98]	266.8[105]	237.3[105]	218.8[105]
%MF [BA]	7.9[105]	8.8[105]	8.4[96]	8.3[97]	7.7[98]	6.5[105]	6.0[105]	5.2[105]
%M [BA]	6.2[105]	6.6[105]	6.0[96]	6.0[97]	5.5[98]	4.7[105]	4.3[105]	3.6[105]
%F [BA]	11.5[105]	12.9[105]	13.2[96]	12.8[97]	11.9[98]	9.7[105]	9.0[105]	8.0[105]
Sudan[9] Soudan[9]								
MF [E]	...	...	...	...	...	...	2 300.0	...
Suriname[1,26] Suriname[1,26]								
MF [A]	...	...	...	16.4	...	...	...	...
M [A]	...	...	...	7.7	...	...	...	...
F [A]	...	...	...	8.7	...	...	...	...

27

Unemployment *(continued)*
Number (thousands) and percentage unemployed, by sex
Chômage *(suite)*
Nombre (milliers) et pourcentage des chômeurs, par sexe

Country or area, source [§] Pays ou zone, source [§]	2001	2002	2003	2004	2005	2006	2007	2008
Sweden Suède								
MF [BA]	175.0[49]	176.0[49]	217.0[49]	246.0[49]	#270.0[49]	246.0[49]	298.0[53]	305.0[53]
M [BA]	99.0[49]	101.0[49]	123.0[49]	137.0[49]	#148.0[49]	131.0[49]	149.0[53]	152.0[53]
F [BA]	76.0[49]	76.0[49]	94.0[49]	109.0[49]	#123.0[49]	114.0[49]	148.0[53]	152.0[53]
%MF [BA]	4.0[49]	4.0[49]	4.9[49]	5.5[49]	#6.0[49]	5.4[49]	6.1[53]	6.2[53]
%M [BA]	4.3[49]	4.4[49]	5.3[49]	5.9[49]	#6.2[49]	5.5[49]	5.9[53]	5.9[53]
%F [BA]	3.6[49]	3.6[49]	4.4[49]	5.1[49]	#5.7[49]	5.2[49]	6.5[53]	6.6[53]
MF [FB] [1]	193.0	185.8	223.0	239.2	241.4	210.9	169.5	150.4
M [FB] [1]	107.2	105.4	127.4	135.1	132.0	114.2	90.3	80.9
F [FB] [1]	85.8	80.4	95.6	104.1	109.4	96.7	79.2	69.5
%MF [FB] [1]	4.4	4.2	4.9	5.5	5.3	4.6	3.5	2.5
%M [FB] [1]	4.7	4.6	5.3	5.9	...	4.7	3.6	2.7
%F [FB] [1]	4.1	3.8	4.4	5.1	...	4.4	3.5	2.4
Switzerland [1] Suisse [1]								
MF [BA] [99]	101.0	119.0	170.0	179.0	185.0	169.0	156.0	147.0
M [BA] [99]	38.0	62.0	86.0	89.0	88.0	78.0	68.0	66.0
F [BA] [99]	63.0	57.0	84.0	89.0	97.0	91.0	88.0	80.0
%MF [BA] [99]	2.5	2.9	4.1	4.3	4.4	4.0	3.6	3.4
%M [BA] [99]	1.7	2.8	3.8	3.9	3.9	3.4	2.9	2.8
%F [BA] [99]	3.5	3.1	4.5	4.8	5.1	4.7	4.5	4.0
MF [FB]	67.2	100.5	145.7	153.1	148.5	131.5	109.2	101.7
M [FB]	35.4	55.9	81.7	83.6	78.8	68.1	56.3	53.5
F [FB]	31.8	44.6	64.0	69.5	69.7	63.4	52.9	48.3
%MF [FB]	1.7	2.5	3.7	3.9	3.8	3.3	2.8	2.6
%M [FB]	1.6	2.5	3.7	3.8	3.6	3.1	2.6	2.4
%F [FB]	1.8	2.6	3.7	4.0	4.0	3.6	3.0	2.8
Syrian Arab Republic [1,27] Rép. arabe syrienne [1,27]								
MF [BA]	613.4	637.8	#512.9	...	...	...	454.8	...
M [BA]	348.4	355.8	#311.6	...	...	...	237.3	...
F [BA]	265.0	282.0	#201.3	...	...	...	217.5	...
%MF [BA]	11.2	11.7	#10.3	...	...	...	8.4	...
%M [BA]	8.0	8.3	#7.6	...	...	...	5.2	...
%F [BA]	23.9	24.1	#20.9	...	...	...	25.7	...
Tajikistan [1] Tadjikistan [1]								
MF [FB]	42.9	46.7	42.9	38.8	43.8	46.5	51.7	...
M [FB]	20.2	21.0	19.7	16.9	19.8	21.2	23.4	...
F [FB]	22.7	25.7	23.2	21.9	23.8	25.3	28.3	...
%MF [FB]	2.3	2.5	2.4	2.0	2.0	2.2	2.5	...
United Republic of Tanzania [9,29,106] République Unie de Tanzanie [9,29,106]								
MF [BA]	912.8	...	...	...	...	...	...	...
M [BA]	388.4	...	...	...	...	...	...	...
F [BA]	524.4	...	...	...	...	...	...	...
%MF [BA]	5.1	...	...	...	...	...	...	...
%M [BA]	4.4	...	...	...	...	...	...	...
%F [BA]	5.8	...	...	...	...	...	...	...
Thailand [1,41] Thaïlande [1,41]								
MF [BA]	896.3	616.3	543.7	548.9	495.8	449.9	442.2	450.9
M [BA]	511.2	372.1	314.7	324.2	289.9	259.7	258.1	268.1
F [BA]	385.1	244.2	229.0	224.7	206.0	190.2	184.1	182.8
%MF [BA]	2.6	1.8	1.5	1.5	1.4	1.2	1.2	1.2
%M [BA]	2.7	2.0	1.6	1.6	1.5	1.3	1.3	1.3
%F [BA]	2.5	1.6	1.4	1.4	1.2	1.1	1.1	1.0
TFYR of Macedonia L'ex-R.Y. Macédoine								
MF [BA] [1]	263.2[20]	263.5[20]	315.9[20]	309.3	323.9	321.3	316.9	310.4
M [BA] [1]	149.4[20]	159.1[20]	191.9[20]	186.2	191.1	191.9	189.3	188.2
F [BA] [1]	113.8[20]	104.3[20]	124.0[20]	123.1	132.8	129.4	127.6	122.2
%MF [BA] [1]	30.5[20]	31.9[20]	36.7[20]	37.2	37.3	36.0	34.9	33.8
%M [BA] [1]	29.5[20]	31.7[20]	37.0[20]	36.7	36.5	35.3	34.5	33.5
%F [BA] [1]	32.0[20]	32.3[20]	36.3[20]	37.8	38.4	37.2	35.5	34.2
MF [FB] [1]	360.3	374.1	390.4	391.1	360.0	366.6	357.0	...
M [FB] [1]	...	...	222.4	224.6	208.4	213.9	209.0	...
F [FB] [1]	...	...	167.9	166.5	151.6	152.6	148.0	...

27

Unemployment *(continued)*
Number (thousands) and percentage unemployed, by sex
Chômage *(suite)*
Nombre (milliers) et pourcentage des chômeurs, par sexe

Country or area, source [§] Pays ou zone, source [§]	2001	2002	2003	2004	2005	2006	2007	2008
Tonga[1] Tonga[1]								
MF [BA]	...	...	1.9	...	...	...	...	...
M [BA]	...	...	0.8	...	...	...	...	...
F [BA]	...	...	1.1	...	...	...	...	...
%MF [BA]	...	...	5.2	...	...	...	...	...
%M [BA]	...	...	3.6	...	...	...	...	...
%F [BA]	...	...	7.4	...	...	...	...	...
Trinidad and Tobago[1] Trinité-et-Tobago[1]								
MF [BA]	62.4	61.1	62.4	51.1	49.7	39.0	34.5	29.0
M [BA]	30.7	27.9	29.8	23.4	21.3	16.4	14.4	12.9
F [BA]	31.7	33.2	32.6	27.7	28.4	22.6	20.1	16.1
%MF [BA]	10.8	10.4	10.5	8.3	8.0	6.2	5.5	4.6
%M [BA]	8.6	7.8	8.3	6.4	5.8	4.5	3.9	3.5
%F [BA]	14.4	14.5	13.8	11.2	11.0	8.7	7.9	6.2
Tunisia Tunisie								
MF [BA][1]	469.2[101]	485.5[101]	473.4[101]	473.9	486.4	...	...	...
M [BA][1]	341.4[101]	351.6[101]	334.7[101]	322.7	328.8	...	...	...
F [BA][1]	127.8[101]	133.9[101]	138.6[101]	151.2	157.6	...	...	...
%MF [BA][1]	15.1[101]	15.3[101]	14.5[101]	14.2	14.2	...	...	...
%M [BA][1]	14.5[101]	14.9[101]	13.9[101]	13.2	13.1	...	...	...
%F [BA][1]	16.2[101]	16.3[101]	16.2[101]	17.1	17.3	...	...	...
MF [FB][22,101,107]	71.9	73.5	77.9	...	...	...	...	...
M [FB][22,101,107]	40.5	40.5	41.6	...	...	...	...	...
F [FB][22,101,107]	31.5	33.1	36.2	...	...	...	...	...
Turkey Turquie								
MF [BA][1]	1 967.0	2 464.0	2 493.0	2 498.0	2 519.0	2 446.0	2 376.0	2 611.0
M [BA][1]	1 485.0	1 826.0	1 830.0	1 878.0	1 867.0	1 777.0	1 716.0	1 877.0
F [BA][1]	482.0	638.0	663.0	620.0	652.0	670.0	660.0	734.0
%MF [BA][1]	8.4	10.3	10.5	10.3	10.3	9.9	10.3	11.0
%M [BA][1]	8.7	10.7	10.7	10.5	10.3	9.7	10.0	10.7
%F [BA][1]	7.5	9.4	10.1	9.7	10.3	10.3	11.0	11.6
MF [FB][3,6]	718.7	464.3	587.4	811.9	881.3	1 061.9	696.5	987.8
M [FB][3,6]	582.9	379.8	469.4	611.3	656.2	782.7	520.1	724.3
F [FB][3,6]	135.8	84.5	118.0	200.6	225.0	279.2	176.4	263.5
Turks and Caicos Islands[1] Iles Turques et Caïques[1]								
MF [BA]	...	...	3.7	4.2	4.9	6.4	6.8	...
%F [BA]	...	...	7.8	9.9	8.0	7.4	5.4	...
MF [E]	1.1	0.8	1.2	1.7	1.5	...	...	...
Tuvalu[1] Tuvalu[1]								
MF [A]	...	0.2	...	...	...	...	...	...
M [A]	...	0.1	...	...	...	...	...	...
F [A]	...	0.1	...	...	...	...	...	...
%MF [A]	...	6.5	...	...	...	...	...	...
%M [A]	...	4.9	...	...	...	...	...	...
%F [A]	...	8.6	...	...	...	...	...	...
Uganda[9] Ouganda[9]								
MF [BA]	...	...	346.0	...	...	...	...	...
M [BA]	...	...	128.0	...	...	...	...	...
F [BA]	...	...	218.0	...	...	...	...	...
%MF [BA]	...	...	3.2	...	...	...	...	...
%M [BA]	...	...	2.5	...	...	...	...	...
%F [BA]	...	...	3.9	...	...	...	...	...
Ukraine Ukraine								
MF [BA][102]	2 455.0	2 140.7	2 008.0	1 906.7	1 600.8	1 515.0	1 417.6	1 425.1
M [BA][102]	1 263.0	1 106.5	1 055.7	1 001.6	862.5	804.1	770.7	768.9
F [BA][102]	1 192.0	1 034.2	952.3	905.1	738.3	710.9	646.9	656.2
%MF [BA][102]	10.9	9.6	9.1	8.6	7.2	6.8	6.4	6.4
%M [BA][102]	11.0	9.8	9.4	8.9	7.5	7.0	6.7	6.6
%F [BA][102]	10.8	9.5	8.7	8.3	6.8	6.6	6.0	6.1
MF [FB][24,44]	1 008.1	1 034.2	988.9	981.8	881.5	759.5	642.3	844.9
M [FB][24,44]	362.5	369.2	361.3	361.9	345.9	300.4	256.5	379.7
F [FB][24,44]	645.6	665.0	627.6	619.9	535.6	459.1	385.8	465.2

Unemployment *(continued)*
Number (thousands) and percentage unemployed, by sex
Chômage *(suite)*
Nombre (milliers) et pourcentage des chômeurs, par sexe

Country or area, source § Pays ou zone, source §	2001	2002	2003	2004	2005	2006	2007	2008
%MF [FB][24,44]	4.8	5.0	4.8	4.8	4.3	3.7	3.1	4.1
%M [FB][24,44]	3.3	3.4	3.4	3.4	3.2	2.7	2.3	3.4
%F [FB][24,44]	6.4	6.7	6.3	6.3	5.6	4.8	4.0	4.9
United Arab Emirates[1] **Emirats arabes unis**[1]								
MF [A]	...	...	...	...	79.8[42]	...	...	...
M [A]	...	...	...	...	55.4[42]	...	...	...
F [A]	...	...	...	...	24.4[42]	...	...	...
MF [BA][103]	...	...	...	...	...	...	...	77.1
M [BA][103]	...	...	...	...	...	...	...	30.3
F [BA][103]	...	...	...	...	...	...	...	46.9
%MF [BA][103]	...	...	...	...	...	...	...	4.0
%M [BA][103]	...	...	...	...	...	...	...	2.0
%F [BA][103]	...	...	...	...	...	...	...	12.0
United Kingdom Royaume-Uni								
MF [BA][13,15]	1 423.0	1 472.0	1 420.0	1 394.0	1 397.0	1 649.0	1 621.0	1 643.0
M [BA][13,15]	861.0	892.0	867.0	824.0	817.0	959.0	930.0	969.0
F [BA][13,15]	562.0	580.0	553.0	570.0	580.0	690.0	691.0	674.0
%MF [BA][13,15]	4.9	5.0	4.8	4.7	4.6	5.4	5.3	5.3
%M [BA][13,15]	5.4	5.6	5.4	5.1	5.0	5.8	5.6	5.7
%F [BA][13,15]	4.2	4.3	4.1	4.2	4.2	4.9	4.9	4.7
MF [FA][56,104]	983.0	958.8	945.9	866.1	874.4	956.7	873.0	...
M [FA][56,104]	746.8	723.8	707.6	643.0	...	...	...	...
F [FA][56,104]	236.2	235.0	238.5	223.2	...	...	...	...
%MF [FA][56,104]	3.3	3.2	3.1	2.8	2.8	3.0	2.7	...
%M [FA][56,104]	4.6	4.4	4.3	3.8	...	...	...	...
%F [FA][56,104]	1.7	1.7	1.7	1.6	...	...	...	...
United Rep. of Tanzania[9] **Rép.-Unie de Tanzanie**[9]								
MF [BA]	...	...	...	...	...	892.2	...	...
M [BA]	...	...	...	...	...	281.7	...	...
F [BA]	...	...	...	...	...	610.5	...	...
%MF [BA]	...	...	...	...	...	4.3	...	...
%M [BA]	...	...	...	...	...	2.8	...	...
%F [BA]	...	...	...	...	...	5.8	...	...
United States[15] **Etats-Unis**[15]								
MF [BA]	6 742.0	8 378.0	8 774.0	8 149.0	7 591.0	7 001.0	7 078.0	8 924.0
M [BA]	3 663.0	4 597.0	4 906.0	4 456.0	4 059.0	3 753.0	3 882.0	5 033.0
F [BA]	3 079.0	3 781.0	3 868.0	3 694.0	3 531.0	3 247.0	3 196.0	3 891.0
%MF [BA]	4.8	5.8	6.0	5.5	5.1	4.6	4.6	5.8
%M [BA]	4.8	5.9	6.3	5.6	5.1	4.6	4.7	6.1
%F [BA]	4.7	5.6	5.7	5.4	5.1	4.6	4.5	5.4
Uruguay[6] **Uruguay**[6]								
MF [BA]	193.2[50]	211.3[50]	208.5[50]	...	154.9[50]	167.0	149.3	...
M [BA]	80.4[50]	93.3[50]	92.2[50]	...	65.4[50]	70.0	60.0	...
F [BA]	112.8[50]	118.0[50]	116.2[50]	...	89.5[50]	96.9	89.3	...
%MF [BA]	15.3[50]	17.0[50]	16.9[50]	...	12.2[50]	10.6	9.2	...
%M [BA]	11.5[50]	13.5[50]	13.5[50]	...	9.5[50]	7.8	6.6	...
%F [BA]	19.7[50]	21.2[50]	20.8[50]	...	15.3[50]	14.1	12.4	...
Uzbekistan[1] **Ouzbékistan**[1]								
MF [FB]	37.5	35.0	32.0	34.9	27.7	...	...	...
%MF [FB]	0.4	...	...	0.4	0.3	...	...	...
Venezuela (Bolivarian Rep. of) Venezuela (Rép. bolivarienne du)								
MF [A][9,14]	755.7	...	...	...	...	...	...	...
M [A][9,14]	565.3	...	...	...	...	...	...	...
F [A][9,14]	190.5	...	...	...	...	...	...	...
MF [BA][1,8]	1 419.2	1 887.7	2 014.9	1 687.7	1 374.3	1 143.7	928.2	872.9
M [BA][1,8]	788.1	1 017.1	1 034.2	900.9	762.4	618.9	536.7	506.3
F [BA][1,8]	631.1	870.6	980.7	786.8	611.9	524.8	391.5	366.6
%MF [BA][1,8]	12.8	16.2	16.8	13.9	11.4	9.3	7.5	6.9
%M [BA][1,8]	11.6	14.4	14.4	12.3	10.3	8.2	7.1	6.5
%F [BA][1,8]	14.6	18.8	20.3	16.4	13.0	11.1	8.1	7.4

27
Unemployment *(continued)*
Number (thousands) and percentage unemployed, by sex
Chômage *(suite)*
Nombre (milliers) et pourcentage des chômeurs, par sexe

Country or area, source [§] Pays ou zone, source [§]	2001	2002	2003	2004	2005	2006	2007	2008
Viet Nam [1,43] Viet Nam [1,43]								
MF [BA]	1 107.4	871.0	949.0	926.4	...	...	...	...
M [BA]	457.9	398.0	402.4	409.8	...	...	...	...
F [BA]	649.6	473.0	546.6	516.6	...	...	...	...
%MF [BA]	2.8	2.1	2.3	2.1	...	...	...	...
%M [BA]	2.3	1.9	1.9	1.9	...	...	...	...
%F [BA]	3.3	2.3	2.6	2.4	...	...	...	...

Source:
International Labour Office (ILO), Geneva, the ILO labour statistics database. Last accessed November 2009.

Source:
Bureau international du Travail (BIT), Genève, la base de données du BIT, dernier accès novembre 2009.

[§] Data sources:

    A: Population census.
    B: Household surveys.
    BA: Labour force sample surveys.
    E: Official estimates.
    FA: Insurance records.
    FB: Employment office records.
    FD: Administration reports.

[§] Sources de données :

    A: Recensement de la population.
    B: Enquêtes auprès des ménages.
    BA: Enquêtes par sondage sur la main-d'œuvre.
    E: Evaluations officielles.
    FA: Fichiers des assurances.
    FB: Fichiers des bureaux de placement.
    FD: Rapports administratifs.

1	Persons aged 15 years and over.	1	Personnes âgées de 15 ans et plus.
2	April.	2	Avril.
3	December of each year.	3	Décembre de chaque année.
4	May.	4	Mai.
5	July.	5	Juillet.
6	Persons aged 14 years and over.	6	Personnes âgées de 14 ans et plus.
7	November.	7	Novembre.
8	Second semester.	8	Second semestre.
9	Persons aged 10 years and over.	9	Personnes âgées de 10 ans et plus.
10	28 urban agglomerations.	10	28 agglomérations urbaines.
11	May and October.	11	Mai et octobre.
12	31 urban agglomerations.	12	31 agglomérations urbaines.
13	Second quarter.	13	Deuxième trimestre.
14	October.	14	Octobre.
15	Persons aged 16 years and over.	15	Personnes âgées de 16 ans et plus.
16	Persons aged 16 to 63 years.	16	Personnes âgées de 16 à 63 ans.
17	Excluding armed forces.	17	Non compris les militaires.
18	May and November of each year.	18	Mai et novembre de chaque année.
19	Men aged 15 to 61 years; women aged 15 to 56 years.	19	Hommes âgés de 15 à 61 ans; femmes âgées de 15 à 56 ans.
20	April of each year.	20	Avril de chaque année.
21	January.	21	Janvier.
22	Persons aged 18 years and over.	22	Personnes âgées de 18 ans et plus.
23	Year ending in June of the year indicated.	23	Année se terminant en juin de l'année indiquée.
24	Men aged 16 to 59 years; women aged 16 to 54 years.	24	Hommes âgés de 16 à 59 ans; femmes âgées de 16 à 54 ans.
25	Persons aged 12 years and over.	25	Personnes âgées de 12 ans et plus.
26	August.	26	Août.
27	September of each year.	27	Septembre de chaque année.
28	Excluding rural population of Rondônia, Acre, Amazonas, Roraima, Pará and Amapá.	28	Non compris la population rurale de Rondônia, Acre, Amazonas, Roraima, Pará et Amapá.
29	March.	29	Mars.
30	After 1999, age limits vary according to the year.	30	Après 1999, les limites d'âge varient selon l'année.
31	Men aged 16 to 60, women aged 16 to 55	31	Hommes âgés de 16 à 60 ans; femmes âgées de 16 à 55 ans.
32	June.	32	Juin.
33	November of each year.	33	Novembre de chaque année.
34	Persons aged 7 years and over.	34	Personnes âgées de 7 ans et plus.
35	Excluding residents of the Territories and indigenous persons living on reserves.	35	Non compris les habitants des Territoires et les populations indigènes vivant dans les réserves.
36	Fourth quarter of each year.	36	Quatrième trimestre de chaque année.
37	For statistical purposes, the data for China do not include those for the Hong Kong Special Administrative Region (Hong Kong SAR)	37	Pour la présentation des statistiques, les données pour la Chine ne comprennent pas la Région Administrative Spéciale de Hong Kong

27

Unemployment *(continued)*
Number (thousands) and percentage unemployed, by sex
Chômage *(suite)*
Nombre (milliers) et pourcentage des chômeurs, par sexe

	and Macao Special Administrative Region (Macao SAR).		(Hong Kong RAS) et la Région Administrative Spéciale de Macao (Macao RAS).
38	Unemployed in urban areas.	38	Chômeurs dans les régions urbaines.
39	Excluding marine, military and institutional populations.	39	A l'exclusion des populations marines, militaires et institutionnelles.
40	Figures revised on the basis of the 2005 census results.	40	Données révisées sur la base des résultats du Recensement de 2005.
41	Third quarter.	41	Troisième trimestre.
42	December.	42	Décembre.
43	July of each year.	43	Juillet de chaque année.
44	31 December of each year.	44	31 décembre de chaque année.
45	Men aged 17 to 60 years; women aged 17 to 55 years.	45	Hommes âgés de 17 à 60 ans; femmes âgées de 17 à 55 ans.
46	Government-controlled area.	46	Région sous contrôle gouvernemental.
47	Persons aged 15 to 66 years.	47	Personnes âgées de 15 à 66 ans.
48	Persons aged 16 to 66 years.	48	Personnes âgées de 16 à 66 ans.
49	Persons aged 16 to 64 years.	49	Personnes âgées de 16 à 64 ans.
50	Urban areas.	50	Régions urbaines.
51	Persons aged 15 to 64 years.	51	Personnes âgées de 15 à 64 ans.
52	May and November.	52	Mai et novembre.
53	Persons aged 15 to 74 years.	53	Personnes âgées de 15 à 74 ans.
54	September.	54	Septembre.
55	Persons aged 15 to 55 years.	55	Personnes âgées de 15 à 55 ans.
56	Excluding persons temporarily laid off.	56	Non compris les personnes temporairement mises à pied.
57	Excluding elderly unemployment pensioners no longer seeking work.	57	Non compris chômeurs âgés devenus non demandeurs d'emploi.
58	March of each year.	58	Mars de chaque année.
59	June of each year.	59	Juin de chaque année.
60	April of each year.	60	Avril de chaque année.
61	Due to methodology revised, total may not equal sum of components.	61	En raison des changements méthodologiques, le total peut différer de la somme des composantes.
62	Persons aged 15 to 65 years.	62	Personnes âgées de 15 à 65 ans.
63	January of each year.	63	Janvier de chaque année.
64	Estimates based on the 2001 Population Census results.	64	Estimations basées sur les résultats du Recensement de la population de 2001.
65	Persons aged 16 to 74 years.	65	Personnes âgées de 16 à 74 ans.
66	April and November of each year.	66	Avril et novembre de chaque année.
67	August of each year.	67	Août de chaque année.
68	First and second quarters.	68	Premier et deuxième trimestres.
69	February of each year.	69	Février de chaque année.
70	Special Labour Force Survey.	70	Enquête spéciale sur la population active.
71	Age limits vary according to the year.	71	Les limites d'âge varient selon l'année.
72	Including the unemployed whose last job was 8 years ago or over.	72	Y compris les personnes sans emploi dont le dernier emploi remonte à 8 ans ou plus.
73	Persons aged 6 years and over.	73	Personnes âgées de 6 ans et plus.
74	7 main cities.	74	7 villes principales.
75	May of each year.	75	Mai de chaque année.
76	Totals include persons still attending school (incl. full-time tertiary students).	76	Les totaux incluent les personnes encore en cours d'études (y compris les étudiants à plein temps de l'enseignement supérieur).
77	Persons aged 16 to 61 years.	77	Personnes âgées de 16 à 61 ans.
78	Excluding Rodrigues.	78	Non compris Rodrigues.
79	October of each year.	79	Octobre de chaque année.
80	Persons aged 15 to 69 years.	80	Personnes âgées de 15 à 69 ans.
81	Curaçao.	81	Curaçao.
82	Including students seeking vacation work.	82	Y compris les étudiants qui cherchent un emploi pendant les vacances.
83	Persons aged 15 to 60 years.	83	Personnes âgées de 15 à 60 ans.
84	West Bank and Gaza.	84	Cisjordanie et Gaza.
85	Persons aged 18 to 60 years.	85	Personnes âgées de 18 à 60 ans.
86	Fourth quarter.	86	Quatrième trimestre.
87	Metropolitan Lima.	87	Lima métropolitaine.
88	May-December.	88	Mai - décembre.
89	Men aged 18 to 64 years; women aged 18 to 59 years (with the exception of juvenile graduates).	89	Hommes âgés de 18 à 64 ans; femmes âgées de 18 à 59 ans (à l'exception des jeunes diplômés).
90	Estimates based on the 2002 Population Census results.	90	Estimations basées sur les résultats du Recensement de la population de 2002
91	Persons aged 15 to 72 years.	91	Personnes âgées de 15 à 72 ans.
92	Excluding Kosovo and Metohia.	92	Non compris Kosovo et Metohia.

27

Unemployment *(continued)*
Number (thousands) and percentage unemployed, by sex
Chômage *(suite)*
Nombre (milliers) et pourcentage des chômeurs, par sexe

93	The data refer to the usually active population.	93	Les données se réfèrent à la population habituellement active.
94	The data refer to the residents (Singapore citizens and permanent residents) aged 15 years and over.	94	Les données font référence aux résidents (citoyens Singapouriens et résidents permanents) âgés de 15 ans ou plus.
95	Excluding persons on child-care leave.	95	Non compris les personnes en congé parental.
96	Excluding Northern province.	96	Non compris la province du Nord.
97	Excluding Mullativu and Killinochchi districts.	97	Ne comprend pas les districts de Mullativu et Killinochchi.
98	Whole country.	98	Ensemble du pays.
99	Second quarter of each year.	99	Deuxième trimestre de chaque année.
100	Prior to 2001: persons aged 10 years and over.	100	Avant 2001: personnes âgées de 10 ans et plus.
101	Figures revised on the basis of the 2004 census results.	101	Chiffres révisés sur la base des chiffres du recensement de 2004.
102	Persons aged 15-70 years.	102	Personnes âgées de 15 à 70 ans.
103	February.	103	Février.
104	Claimants at unemployment benefits offices.	104	Demandeurs auprès des bureaux de prestations de chômage.
105	Excluding the Northern and Eastern provinces	105	Non compris les provinces du Nord et de l'Est.
106	Tanganyika only.	106	Tanganyika seulement.
107	Work applicants.	107	Demandeurs d'emploi.

Technical notes: table 27

Detailed data on labour force and related topics are published in the ILO *Yearbook of Labour Statistics* and on the ILO web site http://laborsta.ilo.org. The series shown in the *Statistical Yearbook* give an overall picture of the availability and disposition of labour resources and, in conjunction with other macroeconomic indicators, can be useful for an overall assessment of economic performance. The ILO *Yearbook of Labour Statistics* provides a comprehensive description of the methodology underlying the labour series. Brief definitions of the major categories of labour statistics are given below.

"Unemployment" is defined to include persons above a certain age who, during a specified period of time were:

(a) "Without work", i.e. were not in paid employment or self-employment;

(b) "Currently available for work", i.e. were available for paid employment or self-employment during the reference period; and

(c) "Seeking work", i.e. had taken specific steps in a specified period to find paid employment or self-employment.

Persons not considered to be unemployed include:

(a) Persons intending to establish their own business or farm, but who had not yet arranged to do so and who were not seeking work for pay or profit;

(b) Former unpaid family workers not at work and not seeking work for pay or profit.

For various reasons, national definitions of employment and unemployment often differ from the recommended international standard definitions and thereby limit international comparability. Inter-country comparisons are also complicated by a variety of types of data collection systems used to obtain information on employed and unemployed persons.

Table 27: Figures are presented in absolute numbers and in percentages. Data are normally annual averages of monthly, quarterly or semi-annual data.

The series generally represent the total number of persons wholly unemployed or temporarily laid-off. Percentage figures, where given, are calculated by comparing the number of unemployed to the total members of that group of the labour force on which the unemployment data are based.

Notes techniques : tableau 27

Des données détaillées sur la main-d'œuvre et des sujets connexes sont publiées dans l'*Annuaire des Statistiques du Travail* du BIT et sur le site Web du BIT http://laborsta.ilo.org. Les séries indiquées dans l'*Annuaire des Statistiques* donnent un tableau d'ensemble des disponibilités de main-d'œuvre et de l'emploi de ces ressources et, combinées à d'autres indicateurs économiques, elles peuvent être utiles pour une évaluation générale de la performance économique. L'*Annuaire des statistiques du Travail* du BIT donne une description complète de la méthodologie employée pour établir les séries sur la main-d'œuvre. On trouvera ci-dessous quelques brèves définitions des grandes catégories de statistiques du travail.

Par "chômeurs", on entend les personnes dépassant un âge déterminé qui, pendant une période donnée, étaient:

(a) "sans emploi", c'est-à-dire sans emploi rémunéré ou indépendant;

(b) "disponibles", c'est-à-dire qui pouvaient être engagées pour un emploi rémunéré ou pouvaient s'adonner à un emploi indépendant au cours de la période de référence; et

(c) "à la recherche d'un emploi", c'est-à-dire qui avaient pris des mesures précises à un certain moment pour trouver un emploi rémunéré ou un emploi indépendant.

Ne sont pas considérés comme chômeurs:

(a) Les personnes qui, pendant la période de référence, avaient l'intention de créer leur propre entreprise ou exploitation agricole, mais n'avaient pas encore pris les dispositions nécessaires à cet effet et qui n'étaient pas à la recherche d'un emploi en vue d'une rémunération ou d'un profit;

(b) Les anciens travailleurs familiaux non rémunérés qui n'avaient pas d'emploi et n'étaient pas à la recherche d'un emploi en vue d'une rémunération ou d'un profit.

Pour diverses raisons, les définitions nationales de l'emploi et du chômage diffèrent souvent des définitions internationales types recommandées, limitant ainsi les possibilités de comparaison entre pays. Ces comparaisons se trouvent en outre compliquées par la diversité des systèmes de collecte de données utilisés pour recueillir des informations sur les personnes employées et les chômeurs.

Tableau 27: Les chiffres sont présentés en valeur absolue et en pourcentage. Les données sont normalement des moyennes annuelles des données mensuelles, trimestrielles ou semestrielles.

Les séries représentent généralement le nombre total des chômeurs complets ou des personnes temporairement mises à pied. Les données en pourcentage, lorsqu'elles figurent dans le tableau, sont calculées en comparant le nombre de chômeurs au nombre total des personnes du groupe de main-d'œuvre sur lequel sont basées les données relatives au chômage.

28

Wages in manufacturing
By hour, day, week or month, and by gender

Salaires dans les industries manufacturières
Par heure, jour, semaine ou mois, et par sexe

Country or area § Pays ou zone §	2001	2002	2003	2004	2005	2006	2007	2008
Albania (lek) Albanie (lek)								
MF(I) - month mois	14 056.0	14 334.0	16 572.0	17 559.0	18 333.0	19 750.0	...	...
Andorra (euro) Andorre (euro)								
MF(I) - month mois	1 334.2	1 424.3	1 508.9	1 585.9	1 680.3	1 801.6	1 902.5	...
M(I) - month mois	...	...	1 680.0	1 778.2	1 894.8	2 024.5	2 108.9	...
F(I) - month mois	...	...	1 165.3	1 215.5	1 263.0	1 367.4	1 503.1	...
Argentina [1,2] (Argentine peso) Argentine [1,2] (peso argentin)								
MF(II) - hour heure	4.3	4.5	5.1	6.3	7.6	9.7	...	...
Armenia (dram) Arménie (dram)								
MF(I) - month mois	35 848.0	30 061.0	41 881.0	48 191.0	54 536.0	61 490.0	71 834.0	92 559.0
M(I) - month mois			...	...	...	78 214.0	88 692.0	...
F(I) - month mois	...	...				46 410.0	54 844.0	...
Australia [3,4] (Australian dollar) Australie [3,4] (dollar australien)								
MF(I) - hour heure	...	20.5	...	22.8	...	25.4	...	...
M(I) - hour heure	...	20.8	...	23.4	...	26.1	...	...
F(I)- hour heure	...	18.5	...	19.9	...	23.6	...	...
Austria (euro) Autriche (euro)								
MF(I) - hour heure [5,6]	13.0	13.4	13.8	14.0	14.4	14.9	15.3	...
MF(I) - month mois	2 501.0	2 549.0	2 618.0	...	...	...	...	...
M(I) - month mois	2 837.0	2 871.0	2 941.0	...	...	...	...	...
F(I) - month mois	1 716.0	1 758.0	1 809.0	...	...	...	...	...
MF(II) - month mois	2 046.0	2 047.0	2 093.0	...	...	...	...	...
M(II) - month mois	2 271.0	2 257.0	2 303.0	...	...	...	...	...
F(II) - month mois	1 394.0	1 412.0	1 444.0	...	...	...	...	...
MF(V) - month mois	3 273.0	3 358.0	3 436.0	...	...	...	...	...
M(V) - month mois	3 979.0	4 054.0	4 132.0	...	...	...	...	...
F(V) - month mois	2 090.0	2 141.0	2 198.0	...	...	...	...	...
Azerbaijan (manat) Azerbaïdjan (manat)								
MF(I) - month mois	303 163.6	348 815.6	445 436.5	491 330.2	115.0[7]	141.0	192.3	251.8
M(I) - month mois	...	...	...	...	...	...	...	283.2
F(I) - month mois	...	...	...	...	...	...	...	159.0
Bahrain [8,9] (Bahrain dinar) Bahreïn [8,9] (dinar de Bahreïn)								
MF(I) - month mois	215.0	228.0	230.0	234.0	228.0	219.0	225.0	...
M(I) - month mois	241.0	252.0	250.0	249.0	239.0	226.0	230.0	...
F(I) - month mois	100.0	111.0	125.0	138.0	145.0	155.0	177.0	...
Belarus [10,11] (Belarussian rouble) Bélarus [10,11] (rouble bélarussien)								
MF(I) - month mois	187.0	255.0	337.0	467.0	616.0	728.0	881.0	1 091.0
M(I) - month mois	214.0	290.0	338.0	539.0	711.0	828.0	1 010.0	1 284.0
F(I) - month mois	157.0	216.0	280.0	384.0	502.0	608.0	723.0	859.0
Belgium [12] (euro) Belgique [12] (euro)								
MF(I) - hour heure	14.0	14.3	14.9	15.6	16.1	16.4	16.6	...
M(I) - hour heure	14.5	14.9	15.5	16.1	16.6	16.9	17.2	...
F(I)- hour heure	12.2	12.3	12.7	13.6	14.0	14.5	14.7	...
MF(I) - month mois	2 350.0	2 391.0	2 520.0	2 609.0	2 660.0	2 695.0	2 740.0	...
M(I) - month mois	2 464.0	2 513.0	2 653.0	2 737.0	2 784.0	2 815.0	2 869.0	...
F(I) - month mois	1 945.0	1 992.0	2 051.0	2 160.0	2 218.0	2 251.0	2 279.0	...
MF(II) - hour heure [13]	12.3	12.6	13.1	13.5	...	...	...	...
M(II) - hour heure [13]	12.7	13.0	13.6	14.0	...	...	...	...
F(II) - hour heure [13]	10.4	10.4	10.8	11.3	...	...	...	...
MF(II) - month mois [13]	2 096.0	2 136.0	2 256.0	2 316.0	2 328.0	2 405.0	...	...
M(II) - month mois [13]	2 160.0	2 198.0	2 275.0	2 333.0	2 396.0	2 465.0	...	...
F(II) - month mois [13]	1 727.0	1 762.0	1 831.0	1 893.0	1 901.0	1 999.0	...	...
MF(V) - hour heure [13]	17.5	17.9	18.5	19.4	...	...	...	...
M(V) - hour heure [13]	19.1	19.5	20.2	21.1	...	...	...	...
F(V) - hour heure [13]	14.3	14.3	14.9	15.8	...	...	...	...
MF(V) - month mois [13]	3 065.0	3 108.0	3 292.0	3 395.0	3 479.0	3 541.0	...	...

28

Wages in manufacturing *(continued)*
By hour, day, week or month, and by gender
Salaires dans les industries manufacturières *(suite)*
Par heure, jour, semaine ou mois, et par sexe

Country or area § Pays ou zone §	2001	2002	2003	2004	2005	2006	2007	2008
M(V) - month mois [13]	3 275.0	3 316.0	3 496.0	3 590.0	...	...	...	...
F(V) - month mois [13]	2 292.0	2 266.0	2 422.0	2 541.0	...	...	...	...
Bermuda [14] (Bermuda dollar) Bermudes [14] (dollar des Bermudes)								
MF(I) - month mois	...	...	...	4 167.0	3 561.0	3 692.0	3 950.0	...
M(I) - month mois	...	...	...	4 333.0	3 691.0	3 792.0	4 101.0	...
F(I) - month mois	...	...	...	2 375.0	3 347.0	3 490.0	3 740.0	...
Bosnia and Herzegovina [15] (convertible marka) Bosnie-Herzégovine [15] (marka convertible)								
MF(I) - month mois	...	...	...	...	...	672.8	...	...
Botswana [16] (pula) Botswana [16] (pula)								
MF(I) - month mois	891.0[17]	889.0[17]	944.0[18]	1 173.0[17]	1 219.0[18]	1 314.0[17]	...	...
M(I) - month mois	...	1 200.0[17]	1 296.0[18]	1 490.0[17]	1 608.0[18]	1 597.0[17]	...	...
F(I) - month mois	681.0[17]	651.0[17]	671.0[18]	876.0[17]	720.0[18]	1 059.0[17]	...	...
Brazil [11] (real) Brésil [11] (real)								
MF(I) - month mois	844.6	901.9	...	...	...	...	...	...
M(I) - month mois	946.9	1 009.8	...	...	...	...	...	...
F(I) - month mois	576.5	618.6	...	...	...	...	...	...
Bulgaria [19] (lev) Bulgarie [19] (lev)								
MF(I) - month mois	227.0	236.0	246.0	262.0	289.0	320.0	383.0	474.0
M(I) - month mois	271.0	284.0	293.0	311.0	343.0	378.0	452.0	...
F(I) - month mois	185.0	192.0	203.0	216.0	237.0	264.0	315.0	...
Canada [20] (Canadian dollar) Canada [20] (dollar canadien)								
MF(I) - week semaine	796.7	818.6	837.4	860.6	895.4	904.7	939.6	947.4
MF(II) - hour heure [21]	18.4	18.6	19.4	20.0	20.5	20.5	21.6	22.0
Chile [22,23] (Chilean peso) Chili [22,23] (peso chilien)								
MF(I) - month mois	213 394.0[9]	218 740.0[9]	221 860.0[9]	229 575.0[9]	242 160.0[9]	300 948.0	315 408.0	351 684.0
China [24] (yuan) Chine [24] (yuan)								
MF(I) - month mois	814.5	916.8	1 041.3	1 169.4	1 313.1	1 497.2	1 740.3	2 016.0
China, Hong Kong SAR [9] (Hong Kong dollar) Chine, Hong Kong RAS [9] (dollar de Hong Kong)								
MF(I) - month mois [25,26]	...	...	10 000.0	9 500.0	9 800.0	...	10 300.0	...
M(I) - month mois [25,26]	...	...	...	...	11 000.0	...	12 000.0	...
F(I) - month mois [25,26]	...	...	...	...	7 000.0	...	7 500.0	...
MF(II) - day jour	342.6	326.1	322.2	324.3	279.0	321.7	342.8	341.2
M(II) - day jour	428.5	419.2	406.1	380.4	282.4	420.8	436.4	430.3
F(II) - day jour	280.6	268.2	262.7	280.0	273.8	256.9	259.6	259.9
MF(V) - month mois	12 133.1	11 951.0	11 508.8	11 498.1	11 622.0	11 972.0	11 878.0	11 881.0
M(V) - month mois	12 929.7	12 810.0	12 082.7	11 880.7	12 249.0	12 483.0	12 596.7	12 470.0
F(V) - month mois	11 395.0	11 123.0	11 021.1	11 139.3	11 015.0	11 552.0	11 282.4	11 336.0
China, Macao SAR (Macao pataca) Chine, Macao RAS (pataca de Macao)								
MF(I) - month mois [27]	4 102.0	3 970.0	4 010.0	4 178.0	4 390.0	4 652.0	4 990.0	5 447.0
M(I) - month mois [27]	5 382.0	5 250.0	5 335.0	5 750.0	5 961.0	6 193.0	6 716.0	7 072.0
F(I) - month mois [27]	3 683.0	3 575.0	3 584.0	3 689.0	3 860.0	4 074.0	4 272.0	4 689.0
MF(VI) - month mois [25]	2 758.0	2 758.0	2 834.0	2 983.0	3 101.0	3 140.0	4 000.0	4 000.0
M(VI) - month mois [25]	4 527.0	4 469.0	4 363.0	4 829.0	4 765.0	5 462.0	6 500.0	5 300.0
F(VI) - month mois [25]	2 429.0	2 430.0	2 542.0	2 652.0	2 795.0	2 698.0	3 100.0	3 500.0
Colombia [28,29,30] (Colombian peso) Colombie [28,29,30] (peso colombien)								
MF(I) - month mois	...	353 590.0	442 510.0	468 406.0	506 020.0	608 137.0	694 244.0	...
M(I) - month mois	...	457 189.0	531 791.0	557 571.0	605 537.0	707 408.0	847 898.0	...
F(I) - month mois	...	258 415.0	347 588.0	365 782.0	394 964.0	473 334.0	505 713.0	...
Costa Rica [31] (Costa Rican colón) Costa Rica [31] (colón costa-ricien)								
MF(I) - hour heure	...	...	...	...	953.0	993.3	1 210.2	1 195.1
M(I) - hour heure	...	...	...	...	1 006.1	1 028.5	1 325.5	1 209.1
F(I)- hour heure	...	...	...	...	793.6	890.3	923.4	1 144.0
MF(VI) - month mois	128 207.0	...	...	...	393 518.0	...	...	549 285.0
M(VI) - month mois	135 707.0	...	...	...	410 986.0	...	...	580 373.0
F(VI) - month mois	112 596.0	...	...	...	335 824.0	...	...	472 590.0
Croatia [32] (kuna) Croatie [32] (kuna)								
MF(I) - month mois	4 465.0	4 794.0	4 952.0	5 189.0	5 452.0	5 833.0	6 161.0	...
M(I) - month mois	...	...	5 412.0	5 680.0	5 969.0	6 377.0	6 734.0	...
F(I) - month mois	...	...	4 196.0	4 359.0	4 560.0	4 874.0	5 148.0	...
Cuba [9,33] (Cuban peso) Cuba [9,33] (peso cubain)								
MF(I) - month mois	255.0	263.0	275.0	290.0	338.0	404.0	433.0	430.0

28

Wages in manufacturing *(continued)*
By hour, day, week or month, and by gender
Salaires dans les industries manufacturières *(suite)*
Par heure, jour, semaine ou mois, et par sexe

Country or area § Pays ou zone §	2001	2002	2003	2004	2005	2006	2007	2008
Cyprus [12,23,34] (Cyprus pound)	**Chypre [12,23,34] (livre chypriote)**							
MF(I) - hour heure	4.3	4.5	4.6	4.8	4.9	5.0	...	...
M(I) - hour heure	4.9	5.2	5.4	5.7	5.8	5.7	...	...
F(I)- hour heure	3.2	3.2	3.4	3.5	3.6	3.7	...	...
MF(II) - hour heure	3.7	3.9	4.1	4.2	4.3	4.9	...	...
M(II) - hour heure	4.3	4.6	4.8	5.0	5.1	5.3	...	...
F(II) - hour heure	2.8	2.7	2.9	2.9	3.0	3.2	...	...
MF(II) - week semaine	152.4	157.3	165.7	169.4	171.8	200.6	...	...
M(II) - week semaine	176.6	186.3	194.9	203.3	202.9	223.1	...	...
F(II) - week semaine	109.0	105.5	113.5	108.8	115.6	125.1	...	...
MF(V) - month mois	814.5	842.0	876.6	928.4	936.8	887.2	...	...
M(V) - month mois	967.2	1 005.7	1 038.9	1 108.2	1 105.0	1 035.1	...	...
F(V) - month mois	593.2	604.3	641.1	667.5	692.9	654.8		
Czech Republic (Czech koruna)	**République tchèque (couronne tchèque)**							
MF(I) - month mois	...	14 589.0	15 329.0	16 560.0	17 337.0	18 482.0	...	...
MF(II) - month mois [35]	11 769.0	12 324.0	13 049.0	14 095.0	14 662.0	...	...	...
M(II) - month mois [35]	13 629.0	14 272.0	15 112.0	16 323.0	16 980.0	...	...	...
F(II) - month mois [35]	8 912.0	9 332.0	9 881.0	10 674.0	11 103.0		...	
Denmark [8,36] (Danish krone)	**Danemark [8,36] (couronne danoise)**							
MF(I) - hour heure	199.1	207.0	215.3	217.2	226.6	235.6	248.8	
M(I) - hour heure	207.7	215.3	223.8	226.1	235.5	244.6	258.5	
F(I)- hour heure	178.8	186.8	194.5	196.8	204.7	213.4	223.7	
Dominican Republic (Dominican peso)	**Rép. dominicaine (peso dominicain)**							
MF(I) - hour heure	28.2	29.4	32.7	50.8	...	...	...	...
Ecuador (U.S. dollar)	**Equateur (dollar des Etats-Unis)**							
MF(I) - month mois	257.2	294.3	338.2	370.6	...	...	...	...
MF(II) - hour heure	1.3	...			...		...	...
Egypt [12,37] (Egyptian pound)	**Egypte [12,37] (livre égyptienne)**							
MF(II) - week semaine	136.0	147.0	150.0	162.0	179.0	203.0	220.0	...
M(II) - week semaine	142.0	154.0	157.0	168.0	187.0	210.0	231.0	...
F(II) week semaine	97.0	104.0	104.0	126.0	134.0	159.0	153.0	...
El Salvador (El Salvadoran colón, U.S. dollar)	**El Salvador (cólon salvadorien, dollar des Etats-Unis)**							
MF(I) - month mois	1 750.4[39]	#208.7	209.6	211.3	229.0	235.1	...	...
M(I) - month mois	2 117.4[39]	#253.8	249.6	261.8	280.6	284.8	...	...
F(I) - month mois	1 370.5[39]	#167.7	171.2	162.5	178.1	181.3	...	...
MF(II) - hour heure [38]	...	1.2	1.3	1.4	1.5	1.2	...	...
M(II) - hour heure [38]	10.3[39]	#1.3	1.5	1.7	1.5	1.4	1.3	1.6
F(II) - hour heure [38]	9.5[39]	...	#1.2	1.2	1.2	1.1	1.1	1.7
Estonia (Estonian kroon)	**Estonie (couronne estonienne)**							
MF(I) - month mois	5 337.0	5 884.0	6 403.0	7 012.0	7 760.0	9 158.0	11 047.7	12 366.4
Finland [40] (euro)	**Finlande [40] (euro)**							
MF(I) - month mois [41]	2 275.0	2 357.0	2 463.0[42]	2 564.0[42]	2 641.0[42]	2 788.0[42]	2 915.0[42]	...
M(I) - month mois [41]	2 402.0	2 475.0	2 581.0[42]	2 685.0[42]	2 772.0[42]	2 921.0[42]	3 048.0[42]	...
F(I) - month mois [41]	1 969.0	2 063.0	2 160.0[42]	2 252.0[42]	2 315.0[42]	2 447.0[42]	2 568.0[42]	...
MF(II) - hour heure [8]	...	...	...	...	13.9	14.5	15.1	...
M(II) - hour heure [8]	...	...	...	...	14.4	15.1	15.7	...
F(II) - hour heure [8]	...	...	...	...	12.2	12.6	13.1	...
France (euro)	**France (euro)**							
MF(I) - hour heure [43]	14.7	15.3	15.9	16.4	16.8	17.3	17.9	...
M(I) - hour heure [43]	15.6	16.2	16.8	17.3	17.7	18.2	18.8	...
F(I)- hour heure [43]	12.4	13.0	13.5	14.0	14.5	15.0	15.6	...
MF(I) - month mois [44]	1 506.9	1 562.7[45]	...	...	...	...	...	...
M(I) - month mois [44]	1 618.5	1 668.8[45]	...	...	...	...	...	...
F(I) - month mois [44]	1 241.7	1 307.9[45]	...	...	...	...	...	...
MF(II) - hour heure	10.6	11.5	12.0	12.3	12.6	12.9	13.3	...
M(II) - hour heure	11.1	12.0	12.4	12.8	13.0	13.4	13.8	...
F(II) - hour heure	9.1	10.0	10.3	10.7	11.0	11.3	11.7	...
French Polynesia (CFP franc)	**Polynésie française (franc CFP)**							
M(I) - month mois	202 046.0	205 866.0	213 876.0	...	...	...	...	...
F(I) - month mois	176 580.0	177 719.0	186 653.0	...	...	...	...	...

Country or area § Pays ou zone §	2001	2002	2003	2004	2005	2006	2007	2008
Georgia (lari) Géorgie (lari)								
MF(I) - month mois	120.8	143.4	152.5	183.9	212.1	260.5	368.1	...
M(I) - month mois	141.5	165.1	174.9	210.2	243.5	293.7	475.6	...
F(I) - month mois	82.7	101.6	108.4	132.2	147.7	...	240.2	...
Germany (euro) Allemagne (euro)								
MF(I) - hour heure	...	...	...	...	...	...	19.1	19.5
M(I) - hour heure	...	...	...	...	...	...	20.0	20.5
F(I)- hour heure	...	...	...	...	...	...	15.3	15.6
MF(II) - hour heure	14.4	14.7	15.1	15.4	15.6	15.7[45]	...	...
M(II) - hour heure	15.1	15.4	15.7	16.0	16.2	16.4[45]	...	...
F(II) - hour heure	11.1	11.4	11.6	11.9	12.0	12.1[45]	...	...
Gibraltar [12,46] (Gibraltar pound) Gibraltar [12,46] (livre de Gibraltar)								
MF(II) - hour heure	6.6	7.0	7.2	8.0	8.4	8.9	8.8	...
M(II) - hour heure	6.7	7.2	7.2	8.1	8.6	9.1	8.9	...
F(II) - hour heure	5.7	5.7	5.9	6.0	6.9	6.9	7.2	...
MF(II) - week semaine [9]	299.5	311.3	323.8	400.6	419.1	...	...	
M(II) - week semaine	...	...	...	...	...	447.4	437.2	
F(II) - week semaine	...	...	...	...	...	253.7	267.9	
Greece (euro) Grèce (euro)								
MF(I) - month mois			...	...	...	1 800.7		
MF(II) - month mois [37]	...	1 140.0	...	...	...	...		
Guam [8,9,11] (US dollar) Guam [8,9,11] (dollar des Etats-Unis)								
MF(II) - hour heure	11.6	13.1	12.2	12.5	12.3	14.9	14.4	...
Guatemala [9] (quetzal) Guatemala [9] (quetzal)								
MF(I) - month mois	1 732.3	1 837.3	1 911.4	2 100.1	2 199.7	2 482.1	2 579.4	2 737.2
Guyana [47] (Guyana dollar) Guyana [47] (dollar guyanais)								
MF(I) - month mois	...	...	29 678.0	47 800.0	...	55 615.0	47 150.0	
Hungary [41,48] (forint) Hongrie [41,48] (forint)								
MF(I) - month mois	101 700.0	114 297.0	124 770.0	136 992.0	147 234.0	156 812.7	171 564.5	184 184.8
M(I) - month mois	115 830.0	127 916.0	140 244.0	153 396.0	164 230.0	175 199.4	191 594.8	
F(I) - month mois	82 761.0	94 882.0	102 585.0	112 946.0	121 082.0	128 302.2	139 856.3	
Iceland (Icelandic króna) Islande (couronne islandaise)								
MF(I) - hour heure	1 219.0	1 336.0	1 404.0	1 494.0	1 622.0	1 762.0	1 946.0	2 033.0
M(I) - hour heure	1 383.0	1 496.0	1 568.0	1 670.0	1 812.0	1 961.0	2 131.0	2 216.0
F(I)- hour heure	941.0	1 074.0	1 122.0	1 200.0	1 312.0	1 425.0	1 597.0	1 675.0
MF(I) - month mois	253 000.0	269 000.0	283 000.0	304 000.0	331 000.0	361 000.0	390 000.0	407 000.0
M(I) - month mois [49]	282 000.0	297 000.0	312 000.0	335 000.0	365 000.0	398 000.0	426 000.0	443 000.0
F(I) - month mois [49]	180 000.0	200 000.0	212 000.0	231 000.0	254 000.0	272 000.0	303 000.0	318 000.0
India [9,50] (Indian rupee) Inde [9,50] (roupie indienne)								
MF(II) - month mois	1 893.2	1 158.6	1 078.9	1 731.8	1 234.4	3 525.9	...	...
Iran (Islamic Rep. of) (Iranian rial) Iran (Rép. islamique d') (rial iranien)								
MF(I) - month mois	1 014 285.0	1 189 654.0	...	...	...	...	...	...
M(I) - month mois	1 029 232.0	1 198 461.0	...	...	...	...	...	...
F(I) - month mois	828 265.0	1 078 610.0	...	...	...	...	...	...
Ireland [37] (euro) Irlande [37] (euro)								
MF(I) - week semaine [51]	543.9	569.8	603.5	632.8	659.4	678.3	...	...
MF(II) - hour heure	11.5	12.3	12.9	13.5	13.9	...	...	...
M(II) - hour heure	12.4	13.3	13.8	14.4	14.8	15.3	...	...
F(II) - hour heure	9.4	10.1	10.7	11.1	11.6	12.3	...	...
MF(II) - week semaine [52]	457.0	483.0	511.8	534.2	557.6	575.2	...	...
M(II) - week semaine [52]	512.4	538.4	564.9	588.9	609.9	624.5	...	...
F(II) - week semaine [52]	347.3	365.2	393.8	406.8	430.2	451.1	...	...
Isle of Man [53] (pound sterling) Île de Man [53] (livre sterling)								
MF(I) - hour heure	9.0	10.3	9.7	10.4	10.6	11.0	12.0	12.9
M(I) - hour heure	9.2	10.9	11.0	10.3	10.9	11.1	12.7	12.6
F(I)- hour heure	8.5	7.7	7.5	10.7	9.2	10.7	9.0	14.2
MF(I) - week semaine	361.4	392.0	409.6	412.4	441.0	445.8	482.4	540.0
M(I) - week semaine	381.5	417.3	504.5	455.4	468.0	463.2	518.2	545.4
F(I) - week semaine	278.3	292.8	253.9	265.2	325.0	401.1	323.0	...

Wages in manufacturing *(continued)*
By hour, day, week or month, and by gender
Salaires dans les industries manufacturières *(suite)*
Par heure, jour, semaine ou mois, et par sexe

Country or area § Pays ou zone §	2001	2002	2003	2004	2005	2006	2007	2008
Israel (new sheqel) Israël (nouveau sheqel)								
MF(I) - month mois [54,55]	9 051.0	...	...	...			...	...
MF(II) - month mois [56]	...	...	...	...	9 915.0	10 377.0	10 694.0	10 982.0
Jamaica [9] (Jamaican dollar) Jamaïque [9] (dollar jamaïcain)								
MF(I) - week semaine	5 725.2	6 092.9	...				...	...
Japan [57,58] (yen) Japon [57,58] (yen)								
MF(I) - month mois	297 500.0	296 400.0	296 500.0	293 100.0	292 100.0	299 600.0	296 800.0	293 400.0
M(I) - month mois	331 400.0	328 300.0	327 800.0	323 100.0	323 800.0	332 300.0	328 500.0	322 600.0
F(I) - month mois	195 000.0	195 600.0	195 800.0	194 100.0	190 900.0	194 600.0	197 700.0	198 000.0
Jersey [53,59,60] (pound) Jersey [53,59,60] (livre)								
MF(I) - week semaine	450.0	460.0	480.0	500.0	530.0	530.0	550.0	...
Jordan [12] (Jordan dinar) Jordanie [12] (dinar jordanien)								
MF(I) - month mois	185.0	186.7	198.0	186.0	203.0	211.0	237.0	...
M(I) - month mois	195.0	196.0	208.0	201.0	222.0	234.0	254.0	...
F(I) - month mois	126.0	129.3	136.0	130.0	136.0	142.0	174.0	...
Korea, Republic of [10,61] (Korean won) Corée, République de [10,61] (won coréen)								
MF(I) - month mois	1 702.4	1 907.0	2 074.0	2 279.7	2 458.0	2 594.8	2 772.0	2 757.8
M(I) - month mois	1 936.0	2 177.0	2 369.7	2 599.8	2 798.6	2 931.9	3 123.6	...
F(I) - month mois	1 121.3	1 211.0	1 320.0	1 419.7	1 556.1	1 675.6	1 785.3	...
Kyrgyzstan (Kyrgyz som) Kirghizistan (som kirghize)								
MF(I) - month mois	2 390.6	2 834.0	3 182.6	3 758.6	4 229.6	6 211.0	6 254.0	...
Latvia [62] (lats) Lettonie [62] (lats)								
MF(I) - month mois	140.3	145.5	159.3	176.4	200.3	239.6	315.0	394.0
M(I) - month mois	150.9	157.3	172.8	192.1	217.9	263.1	350.3	430.2
F(I) - month mois	127.1	131.1	142.0	155.9	177.3	209.0	269.7	346.7
Lithuania [63] (litas) Lituanie [63] (litas)								
MF(I) - hour heure [64]	6.3	6.5	6.6	6.9	7.6	8.9	11.0	12.8
M(I) - hour heure [64]	7.1	7.2	7.5	7.7	8.6	10.2	12.7	14.9
F(I)- hour heure [64]	5.5	5.7	5.8	5.9	6.5	7.5	9.0	10.4
MF(I) - month mois	963.0	982.0	1 016.0	1 085.0	1 184.0	1 387.0	1 727.0	2 035.0
Luxembourg [12] (euro) Luxembourg [12] (euro)								
MF(II) - hour heure	12.6	13.1	13.5	14.2	14.7	14.7	14.8	15.1
M(II) - hour heure	13.1	13.6	14.0	14.7	15.2	15.2	15.3	15.6
F(II) - hour heure	9.5	9.8	10.2	10.6	11.1	11.0	11.1	11.4
MF(V) - month mois	3 816.0	3 941.0	4 090.0	4 189.0	4 334.0	4 374.0	4 506.0	4 650.0
M(V) - month mois	4 104.0	4 251.0	4 412.0	4 510.0	4 663.0	4 710.0	4 876.0	5 007.0
F(V) - month mois	2 710.0	2 782.0	2 911.0	3 030.0	3 185.0	3 229.0	3 280.0	3 489.0
Madagascar (Malagasy ariary) Madagascar (ariary malgache)								
MF(I) - hour heure	...	...	...	...	2 033.0	...	...	...
M(I) - hour heure	...	...	...	...	2 106.0	...	...	...
F(I)- hour heure	...	...	...	...	1 794.0	...	...	...
Malaysia [9] (ringgit) Malaisie [9] (ringgit)								
MF(I) - month mois	1 530.7				...	...	...	...
Malta [11,65] (Maltese lira, euro) Malte [11,65] (lire maltaise, euro)								
MF(VI) - hour heure	2.2	2.3	2.3	2.3	2.4	2.6	2.6	6.4[66]
M(VI)- hour heure	2.3	2.4	2.4	2.4	2.5	2.6	2.7	6.6[66]
F(VI) - hour heure	1.9	2.1	2.2	2.2	2.2	2.3	2.3	5.8[66]
Mauritius [37,67] (Mauritian rupee) Maurice [37,67] (roupie mauricienne)								
MF(I) - month mois	5 856.0	6 155.0	6 668.0	7 299.0	7 798.0	8 214.0	8 622.0	8 979.0
Mexico (Mexican peso) Mexique (peso mexicain)								
MF(I) - day jour [9]	143.6	...	...	...	...	...	...	...
MF(I) - hour heure	17.8	18.0	19.4	...	...	...	...	...
M(I) - hour heure	19.3	19.8	21.2	...	...	...	...	...
F(I)- hour heure	14.7	14.4	15.7	...	...	...	...	...
MF(I) - month mois [68,69]	3 399.8	3 554.8	3 757.3	3 887.9	4 140.3	4 422.6	4 689.2	4 679.3
M(I) - month mois [68,69]	3 789.6	3 988.9	4 176.6	4 273.8	4 625.6	4 839.5	5 242.5	5 172.2
F(I) - month mois [68,69]	2 646.1	2 714.7	2 911.7	3 114.6	3 217.5	3 628.3	3 651.1	3 715.3
MF(II) - hour heure	23.5	25.2	26.9	...	...	...	...	...

Country or area § Pays ou zone §	2001	2002	2003	2004	2005	2006	2007	2008
Mongolia [10] (togrog) Mongolie [10] (togrog)								
MF(I) - month mois	...	68.7	82.7	92.8	100.5	124.1	160.2	268.0
M(I) - month mois	65.9	69.3	86.9	98.1	114.9	142.7	189.4	315.9
F(I) - month mois	64.8	68.2	75.6	89.1	88.9	105.2	135.6	225.2
Montenegro (euro) Monténégro (euro)								
MF(I) - month mois	...	...	...	...	...	...	530.0	615.0
Myanmar [9,70,71] (kyat) Myanmar [9,70,71] (kyat)								
M(I) - hour heure	19.0	20.8	22.8	29.9	31.9	94.0	132.7	180.6
F(I)- hour heure	17.5	19.6	20.3	27.2	28.4	90.6	116.3	158.6
Netherlands [11,72] (euro) Pays-Bas [11,72] (euro)								
MF(I) - hour heure	16.5	17.1	17.8	18.2	18.5	...	...	...
M(I) - hour heure	17.2	17.8	18.5	18.9	19.1	...	...	...
F(I)- hour heure	13.5	14.1	14.7	15.4	15.6	...	...	...
MF(I) - month mois [13]	2 392.0	2 487.0	2 572.0	2 637.0	2 689.0	...	...	...
M(I) - month mois [13]	2 458.0	2 549.0	2 634.0	2 692.0	2 740.0	...	...	...
F(I) - month mois [13]	1 944.0	2 039.0	2 123.0	2 221.0	2 282.0	...	...	...
New Zealand [59,73,74] (New Zealand dollar) Nouvelle-Zélande [59,73,74] (dollar néo-zélandais)								
MF(I) - hour heure	17.5	18.1	18.5	19.3	19.6	20.5	21.5	22.4
M(I) - hour heure	18.3	19.1	19.5	20.2	20.5	21.5	22.5	23.6
F(I)- hour heure	14.9	15.3	15.5	16.6	16.8	17.6	18.5	19.2
Nicaragua [9] (córdoba) Nicaragua [9] (córdoba)								
MF(I) - hour heure	...	...	13.5	13.5	13.7	13.9	...	...
MF(I) - month mois	...	...	3 279.0	3 283.0	3 331.0	3 393.0	...	...
Norway [12,41,75] (Norwegian krone) Norvège [12,41,75] (couronne norvégienne)								
MF(I) - month mois	24 426.0	25 991.0	26 944.0	27 920.0	28 908.0	30 162.0	31 983.0	33 977.0
M(I) - month mois	...	...	27 625.0	28 588.0	29 513.0	30 767.0	32 710.0	34 638.0
F(I) - month mois	...	...	24 260.0	25 290.0	26 432.0	27 649.0	29 124.0	31 301.0
Occupied Palestinian Terr. [44,65,76] (new shekel) Terr. palestinien occupé [44,65,76] (nouveau shekel)								
MF(I) - day jour	68.0	70.1	68.5	66.8	74.0	77.7	71.1	81.4
M(I) - day jour	73.5	74.7	71.7	70.9	77.8	81.8	76.4	86.6
F(I) - day jour	35.2	36.8	41.6	30.8	40.8	44.5	40.4	43.4
Pakistan [9] (Pakistan rupee) Pakistan [9] (roupie pakistanaise)								
MF(I) - month mois	3 002.2	4 113.7	...	...	...	...	...	...
Panama [25,65,77] (balboa) Panama [25,65,77] (balboa)								
MF(VI) - hour heure	...	1.8	1.7	1.9	2.2	2.2	2.2	2.0
M(VI)- hour heure	...	1.8	1.7	1.9	2.1	2.1	2.2	2.1
F(VI) - hour heure	...	1.9	1.8	2.1	2.7	2.7	2.1	2.0
Paraguay [10,40] (guaraní) Paraguay [10,40] (guaraní)								
MF(I) - month mois	...	...	...	...	...	...	5 399.1	5 907.1
M(I) - month mois	...	...	...	...	...	...	5 550.4	5 827.6
F(I) - month mois	...	...	...	...	...	...	4 745.9	6 303.2
Philippines (Philippine peso) Philippines (peso philippin)								
MF(I) - day jour	226.2	229.0	237.4	239.4	246.6	265.0	277.2	289.6
M(I) - day jour	237.2	238.9	246.3	247.7	254.0	270.5	290.9	299.1
F(I) - day jour	210.6	215.3	225.0	227.4	236.5	257.4	257.9	275.8
MF(I) - month mois [78,79]	9 936.0	...	11 166.0	...	...	...	...	...
Poland [80,81] (zloty) Pologne [80,81] (zloty)								
MF(I) - month mois	1 938.9	2 000.0	2 058.7	2 140.7	2 202.0	2 337.0	2 562.0	2 805.0
Portugal (Portugese escudo, euro) Portugal (escudo portugais, euro)								
MF(I) - month mois	133 939.0 [82]	#705.0	775.0	806.0	837.0	868.0	893.0	932.0
M(I) - month mois	159 822.0 [82]	#840.0	905.0	934.0	968.2	1 008.0	1 026.0	1 065.0
F(I) - month mois	103 835.0 [82]	#547.0	596.0	622.0	648.4	675.0	696.0	729.0
MF(II) - hour heure	673.0	375.0 [83]	#3.7	3.8	3.9	4.0	4.1	4.3
M(II) - hour heure	784.0	430.0 [83]	#4.2	4.4	4.5	4.6	4.7	4.8
F(II) - hour heure	536.0	294.0 [83]	#2.9	3.0	3.0	3.1	3.2	3.3
Puerto Rico [9] (US dollar) Porto Rico [9] (dollar des Etats-Unis)								
MF(II) - hour heure	9.8	10.3	10.5	10.8	11.1	11.5	11.9	12.1

28 Wages in manufacturing *(continued)*
By hour, day, week or month, and by gender
Salaires dans les industries manufacturières *(suite)*
Par heure, jour, semaine ou mois, et par sexe

Country or area § / Pays ou zone §	2001	2002	2003	2004	2005	2006	2007	2008
Qatar (Qatar riyal) Qatar (riyal qatarien)								
MF(I) - month mois [84]	...	...	...	...	...	3 677.0	5 060.0	...
M(I) - month mois [84]	...	...	...	...	...	3 668.0	5 027.0	...
F(I) - month mois [84]	...	...	...	...	...	4 092.0	7 118.0	...
MF(VI) - month mois [22,65]	1 546.0	...	...	...	...	...	...	...
M(VI) - month mois [22,65]	1 543.0	...	...	...	...	...	...	...
F(VI) - month mois [22,65]	2 987.0	...	...	...	...	...	...	...
Republic of Moldova [35] (Moldovan leu) République de Moldova [35] (leu moldove)								
MF(I) - month mois	813.1	971.8	1 216.1	1 417.8	1 651.6	1 914.5	2 314.1	2 762.8
Romania (Romanian leu) Roumanie (leu roumain)								
MF(I) - month mois	3 734 701.0	4 632 583.0	5 804 147.0	7 196 971.0	829.0[85]	950.0	1 146.0	...
M(I) - month mois	...	...	6 662 800.0	8 167 249.0	945.0[85]	1 087.0	1 302.0	...
F(I) - month mois	...	...	4 915 058.0	6 203 325.0	710.0[85]	807.0	976.0	...
Russian Federation (ruble) Fédération de Russie (ruble)								
MF(I) - month mois		...	...	...	8 421.0	10 199.0	12 879.0	16 050.0
Saint Helena [86] (pound sterling) Sainte-Hélène [86] (livre sterling)								
MF(I) - month mois	263.4	296.8	...	...	...	...	...	...
M(I) - month mois	272.9	317.1	...	...	...	...	...	...
F(I) - month mois	229.0	229.5	...	...	...	...	...	...
Saint Lucia [87] (EC dollar) Sainte-Lucie [87] (dollar des Caraïbes orientales)								
M(II) - hour heure [88]	6.3	5.3	7.0	...	...	...	...	...
F(II) - hour heure [88]	4.1	4.5	5.0	...	...	...	...	...
M(V) - hour heure	10.0	...	14.5	...	...	...	...	...
F(V) - hour heure	10.2	14.9	11.7	...	...	...	...	...
M(V) - month mois	1 656.3	2 901.7	...	...	...	...	...	...
F(V) - month mois	1 588.0	2 435.1	...	...	...	...	...	...
Saint Vincent-Grenadines (EC dollar) Saint Vincent-Grenadines (dollar des Caraïbes orientales)								
MF(I) - day jour	26.5	26.5	...	...	...	...	...	...
San Marino (lira, euro) Saint-Marin (lira, euro)								
MF(I) - month mois	3 289 004.2[89]	#1 868.2	1 922.1	1 900.0	1 933.6	2 021.1	...	...
Serbia [90] (dinar) Serbie [90] (dinar)								
MF(I) - month mois	...	...	12 996.0	16 065.0	20 366.0	25 830.0	30 620.0	...
Serbia and Montenegro [90] (new dinar) Serbie-et-Monténégro [90] (nouveau dinar)								
MF(I) - month mois	4 786.0[44,91]	#11 065.0	...	...	...	...	...	...
Seychelles (Seychelles rupee) Seychelles (roupie seychelloises)								
MF(I) - month mois	3 235.0	3 300.0	2 986.0	3 042.0	3 314.0	3 350.0	3 306.0	...
Singapore (Singapore dollar) Singapour (dollar singapourien)								
MF(I) - month mois	3 117.0	3 154.0	3 265.0	3 350.0	3 495.0[92]	3 618.0	3 764.0	3 955.0
M(I) - month mois	3 752.0	3 762.0	3 881.0	3 969.0	4 111.0[92]	4 218.0	4 359.0	4 559.0
F(I) - month mois	2 226.0	2 283.0	2 374.0	2 442.0	2 563.0[92]	2 682.0	2 815.0	2 974.0
Slovakia [93] (Slovak koruna) Slovaquie [93] (couronne slovaque)								
MF(I) - month mois	12 908.0	13 837.0	14 873.0	16 378.0	17 604.0	18 817.0	20 024.0	21 449.0
Slovenia (tolar, euro) Slovénie (tolar, euro)								
MF(I) - month mois	178 596.0[94]	196 220.0[94]	211 060.0[94]	226 029.0[94]	238 985.0[94,95]	252 162.0[94]	1 123.6	1 208.2
South Africa [9] (rand) Afrique du Sud [9] (rand)								
MF(I) - month mois	4 701.0	5 197.0[45]	...	...	6 546.5	6 911.8	7 430.0	8 240.0
Spain [96] (euro) Espagne [96] (euro)								
MF(I) - hour heure	10.5	11.0	11.5	12.0	12.4	12.9	13.4	14.1
Sri Lanka [9,71] (Sri Lanka rupee) Sri Lanka [9,71] (roupie sri-lankaise)								
MF(II) - day jour	230.7	273.1	306.3	309.0	336.5	356.1	412.2	432.6
M(II) - day jour	233.1	278.1	311.2	312.1	338.1	357.5	419.0	489.2
F(II) - day jour	201.3	235.1	253.0	270.0	327.9	346.2	394.4	376.0
MF(II) - hour heure	27.1	31.9	33.2	35.5	36.9	39.9	45.4	49.9
M(II) - hour heure	27.5	32.1	33.6	35.8	37.1	40.0	46.1	55.2
F(II) - hour heure	22.6	28.0	28.9	31.2	35.1	39.1	43.0	44.6
Sweden [8,17,34,97] (Swedish krona) Suède [8,17,34,97] (couronne suédoise)								
MF(II) - hour heure	114.9	118.2	122.0	126.1	129.9	133.8	139.5	...
M(II) - hour heure	116.9	120.2	124.1	128.4	132.2	136.1	142.1	...
F(II) - hour heure	106.6	109.4	112.9	116.8	119.9	124.1	128.6	...

28

Wages in manufacturing *(continued)*
By hour, day, week or month, and by gender
Salaires dans les industries manufacturières *(suite)*
Par heure, jour, semaine ou mois, et par sexe

Country or area § Pays ou zone §	2001	2002	2003	2004	2005	2006	2007	2008
Switzerland [98] (Swiss franc) Suisse [98] (franc suisse)								
MF(I) - month mois	...	6 155.0	...	6 349.0	...	6 527.0	...	...
M(I) - month mois	...	6 552.0	...	6 726.0	...	6 915.0	...	...
F(I) - month mois	...	4 926.0	...	5 162.0	...	5 353.0	...	...
Thailand (baht) Thaïlande (baht)								
MF(I) - month mois	6 064.6	6 795.3	6 432.2	...	...	...	...	...
M(I) - month mois	7 112.7	7 449.2	7 344.8	...	...	...	...	...
F(I) - month mois	5 122.4	6 143.7	5 538.8	...	...	...	...	...
TFYR of Macedonia [44] (TFYR Macedonian denar) L'ex-R.Y. Macédoine [44] (denar de l'ex-R.Y. Macédoine)								
MF(I) - month mois	...	9 944.0	10 028.0	10 486.0	10 298.0	10 624.0	11 653.0	12 613.0
Trinidad and Tobago (Trinidad and Tobago dollar) Trinité-et-Tobago (dollar de la Trinité-et-Tobago)								
MF(I) - week semaine	1 161.2	1 161.6	...	...	...	...	...	...
Turkey (new Turkish Lira) Turquie (nouveau livre turque)								
MF(I) - day jour	...	28 340.5	36 069.1	42 629.9	46 184.1	...	...	...
MF(I) - hour heure	...	3 778.7	4 809.2	5 684.0	6 157.9	...	...	...
MF(I) - month mois	...	680 172.4	865 658.0	1 023 118.2	1 108 419.2	...	...	...
Ukraine (hryvnia) Ukraine (hryvnia)								
MF(I) - month mois	368.3	441.3	552.9	700.0	905.1	1 137.3	1 456.4	1 849.0
M(I) - month mois		509.0	640.8	809.0	1 042.3	1 302.1	1 667.0	2 103.2
F(I) - month mois		358.9	443.5	562.9	727.0	920.0	1 175.3	1 503.5
United Kingdom [41] (pound sterling) Royaume-Uni [41] (livre sterling)								
MF(I) - hour heure	9.3	9.9	10.3	10.5	11.2	11.4	11.7	12.3
M(I) - hour heure	9.9	10.4	10.8	11.0	11.6	11.8	12.3	12.9
F(I)- hour heure	7.6	8.4	8.6	9.2	10.0	10.1	10.1	10.7
MF(I) - week semaine	395.0	414.0	431.0	437.0	467.0	477.0	491.0	513.0
M(I) - week semaine	421.0	438.0	456.0	462.0	486.0	495.0	517.0	521.0
F(I) - week semaine	301.0	326.0	340.0	348.0	393.0	406.0	401.0	425.0
United States (US dollar) Etats-Unis (dollar des Etats-Unis)								
MF(I) - hour heure [8,99,100]	14.8	15.3	15.7	16.1	16.6	16.8	17.3	17.7
MF(II) - week semaine [9,101]	603.6	625.8[45]	...	...	...	...	...	...
United States Virgin Is. (US dollar) Iles Vierges américaines (dollar des Etats-Unis)								
MF(II) - hour heure	22.6	23.0	23.4	23.4	23.5	26.5	26.4	28.1
Uruguay [102] (Uruguayan peso) Uruguay [102] (peso uruguayen)								
MF(I) - month mois	6 856.0	...	...	...	...	...	...	...
Zimbabwe [9] (Zimbabwe dollar) Zimbabwe [9] (dollar zimbabwéen)								
MF(I) - hour heure	80.2	144.0	...	...	...	...	...	...
MF(I) - month mois	12 823.7							

Source:
International Labour Office (ILO), Geneva, the ILO labour statistics database, last accessed October 2009.

§ I.   Employees.
   II. Wage earners.
  III. Skilled wage earners.
  IV. Unskilled wage earners.
  V. Salaried employees.
  VI. Total employment.

Data are classified according to ISIC Rev. 3 unless indicated otherwise.

1   Production and related workers.
2   Local units with 10 or more workers.
3   May of each year.
4   Full-time adult non-managerial employees.
5   Including mining and quarrying.
6   Per hour paid.
7   New denomination of AZM; 1 AZN=5000 AZM.
8   Private sector.
9   Data classified according to ISIC Rev. 2.
10 Figures in thousands.

Source:
Bureau international du Travail (BIT), Genève, la base de données du BIT, dernier accès Octobre 2009.

§ I.   Salariés.
   II. Ouvriers.
  III. Ouvriers qualifiés.
  IV. Ouvriers non qualifiés.
  V. Employés.
  VI. Emploi total.

Sauf indication contraire, les données sont classifiées selon la CITI, Rév. 3.

1   Ouvriers à la production et assimilés.
2   Unités locales occupant 10 ouvriers et plus.
3   Mai de chaque année.
4   Salariés adultes à plein temps, non compris les cadres dirigeants.
5   Y compris les industries extractives.
6   Salaire horaire.
7   Nouvelle dénomination de l'AZM; 1 AZN = 5000 AZM.
8   Secteur privé.
9   Données classifiées selon la CITI, Rév. 2.
10 Données en milliers.

11	December of each year.	11	Décembre de chaque année.
12	October of each year.	12	Octobre de chaque année.
13	Full-time employees only.	13	Salariés à plein temps seulement.
14	Last week of Aug. of each year.	14	Dernière semaine d'août de chaque année.
15	Data refer to the Federation of Bosnia and Herzegovina.	15	Les données se réfèrent à la Fédération de Bosnie et Herzégovine.
16	Citizens only.	16	Nationaux seulement.
17	September of each year.	17	Septembre de chaque année.
18	March.	18	Mars.
19	Employees under labour contract.	19	Salariés sous contrat de travail.
20	Including overtime.	20	Y compris les heures supplémentaires.
21	Employees paid by the hour.	21	Salariés rémunérés à l'heure.
22	April of each year.	22	Avril de chaque année.
23	Including family allowances and the value of payments in kind.	23	Y compris les allocations familiales et la valeur des paiements en nature.
24	State-owned units, urban collective-owned units and other ownership units.	24	Unités d'Etat, unités collectives urbaines et autres.
25	Median.	25	Médiane.
26	Including outworkers.	26	Y compris les travailleurs externes.
27	Third quarter of each year.	27	Troisième trimestre de chaque année.
28	Excluding armed forces.	28	Non compris les militaires.
29	Persons aged 10 years and over.	29	Personnes âgées de 10 ans et plus.
30	Fourth quarter.	30	Quatrième trimestre.
31	Main occupation; July of each year.	31	Occupation principale; juillet de chaque année.
32	Excluding employees in craft and trade.	32	Non compris les salariés dans l'artisanat et dans le commerce.
33	State sector (civilian).	33	Secteur d'Etat (civils).
34	Adults.	34	Adultes.
35	Enterprises with 20 or more employees.	35	Entreprises occupant 20 salariés et plus.
36	Excluding young people aged less than 18 years and trainees.	36	Non compris les jeunes gens âgés de moins de 18 ans et les apprentis.
37	Establishments with 10 or more persons employed.	37	Etablissements occupant 10 personnes et plus.
38	Urban areas.	38	Régions urbaines.
39	Prior to 2002: colones; 8.75 colones=1 US dollar.	39	Avant 2002: colones; 8.75 colones=1 dollar EU.
40	Fourth quarter of each year.	40	Quatrième trimestre de chaque année.
41	Full-time employees.	41	Salariés à plein temps.
42	From 2003: excl. seasonal and end-of-year bonuses.	42	A partir de 2003: non compris les primes saisonnières et de fin d'année.
43	Including managerial staff and intermediary occupations.	43	Y compris les cadres et les professions intermédiaires.
44	Net earnings.	44	Gains nets.
45	Series discontinued.	45	Série arrêtée.
46	Excluding part-time workers and juveniles.	46	Non compris les travailleurs à temps partiel et les jeunes.
47	July.	47	Juillet.
48	Enterprises with 5 or more employees.	48	Entreprises occupant 5 salariés et plus.
49	Full-time adult employees.	49	Salariés adultes à plein temps.
50	Fluctuations due to various changes in workers' coverage.	50	Fluctuations dues à divers changements dans la couverture des travailleurs.
51	Adult and non-adult rates of pay.	51	Taux de rémunération des adultes et des mineurs.
52	Wage-earners on adult rates of pay.	52	Salariés rémunérés sur la base du taux de rémunération des adultes.
53	June of each year.	53	Juin de chaque année.
54	Incl. payments subject to income tax.	54	Y compris les versements soumis à l'impôt sur le revenu.
55	Including workers from the Judea, Samaria and Gaza areas.	55	Y compris les travailleurs des régions de Judée, Samarie et Gaza.
56	Israeli workers only.	56	Travailleurs israéliens seulement.
57	Regular scheduled cash earnings.	57	Gains en espèce tarifés réguliers.
58	Private sector; establishments with 10 or more regular employees; June of each year.	58	Secteur privé; établissements occupant 10 salariés stables ou plus; juin de chaque années.
59	Full-time equivalent employees.	59	Salariés en équivalents à plein temps.
60	Approximate levels since survey aims at measuring changes; excl. bonuses.	60	Niveaux approximatifs étant donné que l'enquête vise à mesurer l'évolution; non compris les primes.
61	Establishments with 10 or more regular employees.	61	Etablissements occupant 10 salariés stables ou plus.
62	First quarter of each year.	62	Le premier trimestre de chaque année.
63	All employees converted into full-time units.	63	Ensemble des salariés convertis en unités à plein temps.
64	Excluding individual unincorporated enterprises.	64	Non compris les entreprises individuelles non constituées en société.
65	Persons aged 15 years and over.	65	Personnes âgées de 15 ans et plus.
66	Euros; 1 Euro=0.429300 MTL.	66	Euros; 1 Euro=0.429300 MTL.
67	March of each year.	67	Mars de chaque année.
68	Second quarter of each year.	68	Deuxième trimestre de chaque année.
69	Persons aged 14 years and over.	69	Personnes âgées de 14 ans et plus.
70	Temporary workers.	70	Personnel temporairement.
71	March and Sep. of each year	71	Mars et sept. de chaque année.

72	Excluding overtime payments.	72	Non compris la rémunération des heures supplémentaires.
73	February of each year.	73	Février de chaque année.
74	Establishments with the equivalent of more than 0.5 full-time paid employees.	74	Etablissements occupant plus de l'équivalent de 0.5 salarié à plein temps.
75	Only remuneration in cash; excl. overtime payments.	75	Seulement rémunération en espèces; non compris les paiements pour heures supplémentaires.
76	West Bank and Gaza.	76	Cisjordanie et Gaza.
77	August of each year.	77	Août de chaque année.
78	Computed on the basis of annual wages.	78	Calculés sur la base de salaires annuels.
79	Establishments with 20 or more persons employed.	79	Entreprises occupant 20 salariés et plus.
80	Including the value of payments in kind.	80	Y compris la valeur des paiements en nature.
81	Economic units with 10 or more persons employed.	81	Unités économiques composées 10 travailleurs et plus.
82	Prior to 2002: PTE; 1 Euro= 200.482 PTE.	82	Avant 2002: PTE; 1 Euro= 200,482 PTE.
83	Prior to 2003: PTE; 1 Euro= 200.482 PTE.	83	Avant 2003: PTE; 1 Euro= 200.482 PTE.
84	October.	84	Octobre.
85	New denomination: 1 leu = 10 000 old lei.	85	Nouvelle dénomination: 1 leu = 1,000 anciens lei.
86	Year ending in March of the year indicated.	86	Année se terminant en mars de l'année indiquée.
87	Unweighted survey results.	87	Résultats d'enquête non pondérés.
88	Minimum rates.	88	Taux minima.
89	Prior to 2002: ITL; 1 Euro=1936.27 ITL.	89	Avant 2002: ITL; 1 Euro=1936,27 ITL.
90	Excluding Kosovo and Metohia.	90	Non compris Kosovo et Metohia.
91	Excluding private sector.	91	Non compris le secteur privé.
92	Methodology revised; data not strictly comparable.	92	Méthodologie révisée; les données ne sont pas strictement comparables.
93	Excluding enterprises with less than 20 employees.	93	Non compris les entreprises occupant moins de 20 salariés.
94	Prior to 2007: SIT; 1 Euro = 239.64 SIT.	94	Avant 2007: SIT; 1 Euro=239.64 SIT.
95	Beginning 2005, methodology revised: excl. family allowances and the value of payments in kind.	95	A partir de 2005, méthodologie révisée: non compris les allocations familiales et la valeur des paiements en nature.
96	Including overtime payments and irregular gratuities.	96	Y compris la rémunération des heures supplémentaires et les prestations versées irrégulièrement.
97	Excl. holidays, sick-leave and overtime payments.	97	Non compris les versements pour les vacances, congés maladie ainsi que la rémunération des heures supplémentaires.
98	Standardised monthly earnings (40 hours x 4 1/3 weeks).	98	Gains mensuels standardisés (40 heures x 4 1/3 semaines).
99	National classification not strictly compatible with ISIC.	99	Classification nationale non strictement compatible avec la CITI.
100	Not all employees covered; only production and non-supervisory workers.	100	Salariés inclus: seuls les travailleurs de production à l'exception du personnel d'encadrement.
101	Private sector: production and construction workers and non-supervisory employees.	101	Secteur privé: travailleurs de production ou d'entreprise de construction et salariés sans fonction d'encadrement.
102	Establishments with 5 or more persons employed.	102	Entreprises occupant 5 salariés et plus.

Producer price indices
Index base: 2000 = 100

Indices des prix à la production
Base de l'indice: 2000= 100

Country or area	2002	2003	2004	2005	2006	2007	2008	Pays ou zone
Argentina								**Argentine**
Domestic supply [1,2]	173	204	219	234	260	...	...	Offre intérieure [1,2]
Domestic production	168	200	216	232	258	...	...	Production intérieure
Agricultural products [2]	242	251	267	239	281	...	...	Produits agricoles [2]
Industrial products [2,3]	160	190	205	217	237	...	...	Produits industriels [2,3]
Imported goods [3]	253	258	266	268	289	...	...	Produits importés [3]
Armenia [4]								**Arménie** [4]
Industrial products	100	...	...	...	...	144	156	Produits industriels
Australia [5,6]								**Australie** [5,6]
Domestic supply	102	103	105	109	113	116	120	Offre intérieure
Domestic production	102	105	109	115	120	125	132	Production intérieure
Agricultural products	126	124	121	...	131	132	155	Produits agricoles
Industrial products [2,3,7]	103	...	104	111	119	125	131	Produits industriels [2,3,7]
Imported goods	104	98	88	88	91	90	90	Produits importés
Raw materials	95	97	96	101	109	115	116	Matières premières
Intermediate goods	102	103	101	107	113	119	131	Produits intermédiaires
Consumer goods	102	103	103	105	109	112	116	Biens de consommation
Capital goods	102	104	108	112	116	119	124	Biens d'équipement
Austria								**Autriche**
Domestic supply [2,8]	101	103	108	110	113	118	126	Offre intérieure [2,8]
Agricultural products	102	108	109	102	106	136	159	Produits agricoles
Intermediate goods	100	102	113	116	123	133	147	Produits intermédiaires
Consumer goods [2]	103	105	106	109	110	113	118	Biens de consommation [2]
Capital goods [2]	100	100	100	99	98	95	92	Biens d'équipement [2]
Bangladesh [6]								**Bangladesh** [6]
Domestic supply [2,8]	102	108	112				...	Offre intérieure [2,8]
Agricultural products [2,9]	102	108	112	...	...	...	...	Produits agricoles [2,9]
Industrial products [2,3,9]	105	107	110	...	...	...	...	Produits industriels [2,3,9]
Raw materials	103	113	107	...	...	...	...	Matières premières
Belarus								**Bélarus**
Domestic production	241	332	412	461	500	582	...	Production intérieure
Intermediate goods	259	389	489	551	601	732	...	Produits intermédiaires
Consumer goods	223	273	332	366	390	422	...	Biens de consommation
Capital goods	224	272	337	384		447	...	Biens d'équipement
Belgium								**Belgique**
Domestic production [10]	102	103	107	110	...	...	...	Production intérieure [10]
Industrial products	101	100	107	107	...	...	...	Produits industriels
Intermediate goods	101	102	108	112	...	...	...	Produits intermédiaires
Consumer goods	98	95	94	96	...	...	...	Biens de consommation
Capital goods	100	100	102	104	...	...	...	Biens d'équipement
Bolivia								**Bolivie**
Industrial products	104	107	...	...	...	...	...	Produits industriels
Raw materials	108	117	...	...	...	...	...	Matières premières
Consumer goods	103	106	...	...	...	...	...	Biens de consommation
Capital goods	109	111	...	...	...	...	...	Biens d'équipement
Botswana								**Botswana**
Domestic supply	112	123	133	...	...	...	...	Offre intérieure
Brazil								**Brésil**
Domestic supply [11]	130	164	185	195	197	#311	...	Offre intérieure [11]
Agricultural products [11]	142	186	197	192	185	#363	...	Produits agricoles [11]
Industrial products [11]	127	161	180	196	200	#289	...	Produits industriels [11]
Raw materials [11]	133	169	191	192	187	...	...	Matières premières [11]
Consumer goods [11]	130	165	176	184	186	#295	...	Biens de consommation [11]
Capital goods	121	147	...	190	194	...	...	Biens d'équipement
Bulgaria								**Bulgarie**
Domestic supply	106	109	115	123	134	144	163	Offre intérieure

Country or area	2002	2003	2004	2005	2006	2007	2008	Pays ou zone
Canada								**Canada**
Agricultural products [2]	111	107	104	102	101	110	120	Produits agricoles [2]
Industrial products [2,3]	101	100	103	104	107	109	113	Produits industriels [2,3]
Raw materials	98	100	112	127	141	152	171	Matières premières
Intermediate goods	99	99	104	107	112	114	120	Produits intermédiaires
Chile								**Chili**
Domestic supply	115	123	126	133	142	151	...	Offre intérieure
Domestic production	112	120	126	135	146	156	183	Production intérieure
Agricultural products	113	113	120	129	141	169	175	Produits agricoles
Industrial products	112	121	125	133	141	149	175	Produits industriels
Imported goods	90	95	91	92	96	100	115	Produits importés
China, Hong Kong SAR								**Chine, Hong Kong RAS**
Industrial products	96	95	98	98	101	104	109	Produits industriels
Colombia								**Colombie**
Domestic supply [2]	115	125	132	136	142	143	153	Offre intérieure [2]
Domestic production	118	127	136	142	149	156	170	Production intérieure
Agricultural products	112	119	125	133	139	144	154	Produits agricoles
Industrial products	115	126	132	134	140	139	147	Produits industriels
Imported goods	115	130	129	125	128	115	116	Produits importés
Raw materials	118	130	143	145	150	150	158	Matières premières
Intermediate goods	115	127	134	139	147	148	161	Produits intermédiaires
Consumer goods	115	122	128	133	138	142	153	Biens de consommation
Capital goods	115	128	127	123	126	116	114	Biens d'équipement
Croatia								**Croatie**
Agricultural products [12]	92	91	95	...	94	98	112	Produits agricoles [12]
Industrial products	95	95	98	101	103	107	116	Produits industriels
Consumer goods	102	104	102	106	107	110	115	Biens de consommation
Capital goods	96	92	91	92	94	94	94	Biens d'équipement
Cyprus [13]								**Chypre [13]**
Industrial products	105	108	117	121	125	131	141	Produits industriels
Czech Republic								**République tchèque**
Agricultural products	98	96	103	94	95	121	...	Produits agricoles
Denmark								**Danemark**
Domestic supply [2,11]	102	102	105	109	113	118	126	Offre intérieure [2,11]
Domestic production [2,11]	104	105	109	113	119	127	139	Production intérieure [2,11]
Imported goods [11]	100	99	100	104	107	110	114	Produits importés [11]
Raw materials	94	94	106	128	...	...	...	Matières premières
Consumer goods	104	105	107	109	...	...	...	Biens de consommation
Ecuador								**Equateur**
Domestic supply	...	...	125	143	160	...	199	Offre intérieure
Domestic production	110	...	...	140	146	...	...	Production intérieure
Agricultural products	...	...	...	121	123	...	171	Produits agricoles
Egypt [6]								**Egypte [6]**
Domestic supply [8]	103	119	139	154	180	193	217	Offre intérieure [8]
Agricultural products	...	...	...	148	210	236	267	Produits agricoles
Raw materials	...	...	162	169	176	199	316	Matières premières
Intermediate goods	103	118	143	148	190	205	199	Produits intermédiaires
Consumer goods	...	...	132	126	126	...	138	Biens de consommation
Capital goods	103	110	146	169	208	191	197	Biens d'équipement
Finland								**Finlande**
Domestic supply	99	96	100	104	110	114	120	Offre intérieure
Domestic production	101	101	101	104	109	114	121	Production intérieure
Industrial products	95	93	93	95	100	103	106	Produits industriels
Imported goods	94	94	97	103	111	114	118	Produits importés
Intermediate goods [14]	99	96	99	102	111	117	117	Produits intermédiaires [14]
Consumer goods [15]	99	98	96	94	94	94	94	Biens de consommation [15]
Capital goods	94	90	89	89	90	92	93	Biens d'équipement
France								**France**
Domestic supply [16]	...	...	...	100	104	107	112	Offre intérieure [16]
Intermediate goods	102	101	104	107	111	...	...	Produits intermédiaires
Consumer goods	...	101	101	101	101	...	...	Biens de consommation
Capital goods	...	101	101	102	103	...	...	Biens d'équipement

Country or area	2002	2003	2004	2005	2006	2007	2008	Pays ou zone
Georgia								**Géorgie**
Industrial products	110	114	119	128	142	158	174	Produits industriels
Germany								**Allemagne**
Domestic supply	104	103	104	108	112	114	119	Offre intérieure
Domestic production [16]	...	...	...	100	105	107	113	Production intérieure [16]
Agricultural products	98	98	99	102	110	120	124	Produits agricoles
Industrial products	107	104	106	111	117	119	118	Produits industriels
Imported goods	98	96	97	101	106	106	111	Produits importés
Intermediate goods	111	100	102	105	109	113	115	Produits intermédiaires
Consumer goods	106	104	104	106	107	110	113	Biens de consommation
Capital goods	93	102	102	102	103	104	103	Biens d'équipement
Greece								**Grèce**
Domestic supply [17,18]	105	107	111	116	124	...	...	Offre intérieure [17,18]
Domestic production [17,18]	106	109	112	119	127	...	...	Production intérieure [17,18]
Agricultural products [17,19]	122	133	130	...	...	...	...	Produits agricoles [17,19]
Industrial products [17,18]	105	108	111	116	124	...	...	Produits industriels [17,18]
Imported goods [17,18]	102	102	107	111	115	...	...	Produits importés [17,18]
Intermediate goods	105	106	109	112	120	...	...	Produits intermédiaires
Consumer goods	108	111	116	118	123	...	...	Biens de consommation
Capital goods	102	103	107	109	111	...	...	Biens d'équipement
Guatemala								**Guatemala**
Domestic supply	109	114	120	125	...	...	...	Offre intérieure
Domestic production	112	115	121	125	...	...	...	Production intérieure
Agricultural products	...	112	112	113	...	...	...	Produits agricoles
Industrial products	...	117	127	136	...	...	...	Produits industriels
Imported goods	...	112	118	124	...	...	...	Produits importés
India [20]								**Inde [20]**
Domestic supply	107	109	115	122	...	134	140	Offre intérieure
Agricultural products	102	104	109	110	...	121	130	Produits agricoles
Industrial products [3]	104	105	111	118	...	127	133	Produits Industriels [3]
Raw materials [21]	97	100	112	119	...	127	142	Matières premières [21]
Indonesia								**Indonésie**
Domestic supply [18]	117	120	130	151	172	229	288	Offre intérieure [18]
Domestic production	126	130	135	151	186	272	342	Production intérieure
Agricultural products	134	134	138	148	172	286	368	Produits agricoles
Industrial products [3]	122	127	133	152	195	266	333	Produits industriels [3]
Imported goods [18]	111	110	120	137	162	208	262	Produits importés [18]
Raw materials	110	116	137	176	179	241	307	Matières premières
Intermediate goods	119	119	130	151	176	240	305	Produits intermédiaires
Consumer goods	126	126	129	140	162	235	290	Biens de consommation
Capital goods	107	107	112	121	128	147	170	Biens d'équipement
Iran (Islamic Rep. of)								**Iran (Rép. islamique d')**
Domestic supply [2]	119	...	...	166	182	209	296	Offre intérieure [2]
Agricultural products [9]	122	...	158	176	191	229	290	Produits agricoles [9]
Industrial products [9]	97	100	119	127	136	157	217	Produits industriels [9]
Raw materials [9]	118	...	...	183	206	241	...	Matières premières [9]
Ireland								**Irlande**
Domestic supply [2,22]	103	98	101	...	...	...	...	Offre intérieure [2,22]
Agricultural products [2,22]	100	99	...	103	107	116	124	Produits agricoles [2,22]
Industrial products [2,3,22]	101	92	...	...	...	...	...	Produits industriels [2,3,22]
Capital goods [9]	92	80	...	...	...	...	...	Biens d'équipement [9]
Israel [18]								**Israël [18]**
Industrial products	105	108	113	118	123	128	137	Produits industriels
Italy								**Italie**
Domestic supply [2,18]	102	105	107	111	117	121	125	Offre intérieure [2,18]
Intermediate goods	100	103	108	111	117	122	125	Produits intermédiaires
Consumer goods	104	107	108	108	110	113	117	Biens de consommation
Capital goods	102	103	105	107	109	111	116	Biens d'équipement

Country or area	2002	2003	2004	2005	2006	2007	2008	Pays ou zone
Japan								**Japon**
Domestic supply[2]	99	96	97	100	105	108	114	Offre intérieure[2]
Domestic production	96	95	96	98	100	102	106	Production intérieure
Agricultural products[9]	97	98	103	100	98	97	99	Produits agricoles[9]
Industrial products[9]	96	95	96	98	100	102	106	Produits industriels[9]
Imported goods	90	93	102	114	129	139	152	Produits importés
Raw materials	104	108	119	144	174	191	240	Matières premières
Intermediate goods	97	97	99	103	109	113	120	Produits intermédiaires
Consumer goods	97	95	95	95	94	95	96	Biens de consommation
Capital goods	92	89	87	85	85	84	83	Biens d'équipement
Jordan								**Jordanie**
Domestic supply[2]	97	98	106	114	121	154	240	Offre intérieure[2]
Agricultural products	98	99	112	124	133	106	123	Produits agricoles
Intermediate goods	92	92	98	103	112	...	...	Produits intermédiaires
Consumer goods	97	98	98	100	...	...	...	Biens de consommation
Korea, Republic of								**Corée, République de**
Domestic supply	99	101	108	110	111	113	122	Offre intérieure
Agricultural products[9,23]	106	113	127	122	118	122	123	Produits agricoles[9,23]
Industrial products	96	98	106	109	112	109	113	Produits industriels
Raw materials	104	110	132	156	176	187	280	Matières premières
Intermediate goods	96	98	107	108	108	111	131	Produits intermédiaires
Consumer goods	100	102	105	106	106	106	112	Biens de consommation
Capital goods	95	94	96	94	92	91	100	Biens d'équipement
Kuwait								**Koweït**
Domestic supply	105	107	108	...	...	119	...	Offre intérieure
Domestic production	102	102	102	...	...	112	...	Production intérieure
Agricultural products	102	106	116	...	...	178	...	Produits agricoles
Industrial products	105	107	107	...	...	...	...	Produits industriels
Imported goods	106	109	109	...	...	121	...	Produits importés
Latvia								**Lettonie**
Domestic supply	103	106	115	124	137	159	...	Offre intérieure
Intermediate goods[16]	...	...	...	100	111	132	138	Produits intermédiaires[16]
Capital goods[16]	...	...	...	100	112	125	136	Biens d'équipement[16]
Lithuania								**Lituanie**
Domestic supply	93	93	100	113	121	128	151	Offre intérieure
Luxembourg								**Luxembourg**
Industrial products	100	100	109	118	127	139	151	Produits industriels
Imported goods	104	107	116	121	...	146	...	Produits importés
Intermediate goods	97	98	111	122	133	143	154	Produits intermédiaires
Consumer goods[15]	111	105	105	106	105	105	107	Biens de consommation[15]
Capital goods	104	105	109	109	111	115	120	Biens d'équipement
Malaysia								**Malaisie**
Domestic supply	99	105	114	122	127	133	...	Offre intérieure
Domestic production	99	106	117	126	131	136	...	Production intérieure
Imported goods	117	118	120	122	123	128	...	Produits importés
Mexico[24]								**Mexique**[24]
Domestic supply[8,25]	94	100	109	113	121	...	...	Offre intérieure[8,25]
Agricultural products	95	100	112	123	130	...	...	Produits agricoles
Industrial products	92	100	103	107	111	...	...	Produits industriels
Consumer goods[9,25]	94	100	109	113	117	...	...	Biens de consommation[9,25]
Capital goods[8,9,25]	92	100	110	113	123	...	...	Biens d'équipement[8,9,25]
Morocco								**Maroc**
Agricultural products	102	97	97	98	103	109	...	Produits agricoles
Industrial products	97	98	103	113	119	121	...	Produits industriels

29

Producer price indices *(continued)*
Index base: 2000= 100
Indices des prix à la production *(suite)*
Base de l'indice: 2000= 100

Country or area	2002	2003	2004	2005	2006	2007	2008	Pays ou zone
Netherlands								**Pays-Bas**
Agricultural products [26,27]	103	105	...	...	...	...	...	Produits agricoles [26,27]
Industrial products	102	101	105	104	105	108	...	Produits industriels
Raw materials	97	98	105	...	...	...	...	Matières premières
Intermediate goods	101	102	106	...	...	...	...	Produits intermédiaires
Consumer goods	104	105	108	...	...	...	...	Biens de consommation
Capital goods	105	106	108	...	...	...	...	Biens d'équipement
New Zealand								**Nouvelle-Zélande**
Agricultural products [2]	123	112	113	113	116	122	138	Produits agricoles [2]
Industrial products [2,28]	105	104	106	110	114	118	129	Produits industriels [2,28]
Intermediate goods [29]	107	106	108	114	121	124	136	Produits intermédiaires [29]
Norway								**Norvège**
Domestic supply	105	106	107	107	111	120	130	Offre intérieure
Domestic production	106	106	107	107	110	113	117	Production intérieure
Industrial products	101	103	106	110	113	118	127	Produits industriels
Imported goods	...	...	...	...	100	105	109	Produits importés
Raw materials	88	89	98	99	106	127	121	Matières premières
Intermediate goods	99	99	104	106	110	116	123	Produits intermédiaires
Consumer goods	104	104	106	108	112	113	117	Biens de consommation
Capital goods	105	97	108	110	111	115	118	Biens d'équipement
Occupied Palestinian Terr. [30]								**Terr. palestinien occupé** [30]
Domestic supply	...	...	94	96	98	100	108	Offre intérieure
Domestic production	...	...	94	96	98	100	109	Production intérieure
Agricultural products	...	...	93	96	98	100	102	Produits agricoles
Imported goods	...	...	96	97	99	100	105	Produits importés
Oman [31]								**Oman** [31]
Domestic supply	103	104	107	...	...	...	...	Offre intérieure
Pakistan [6]								**Pakistan** [6]
Domestic supply [2,8]	108	113	120	131	142	154	...	Offre intérieure [2,8]
Agricultural products	105	108	119	130	139	156	...	Produits agricoles
Industrial products	103	109	113	115	119	122	...	Produits industriels
Raw materials	116	125	122	115	130	147	...	Matières premières
Panama								**Panama**
Domestic supply	94	95	100	105	...	...	...	Offre intérieure
Peru								**Pérou**
Domestic supply	100	...	109	110	113	...	...	Offre intérieure
Domestic production	100	...	107	110	113	...	...	Production intérieure
Agricultural products [32]	97	...	107	109	114	...	...	Produits agricoles [32]
Industrial products [3,9]	101	...	108	111	114	...	...	Produits industriels [3,9]
Imported goods	100	...	108	109	113	...	...	Produits importés
Philippines [33]								**Philippines** [33]
Domestic supply	106	...	...	149	161	...	...	Offre intérieure
Poland [16]								**Pologne** [16]
Domestic production	...	...	...	100	99	108	113	Production intérieure
Industrial products	...	...	...	100	102	104	106	Produits industriels
Raw materials	...	...	...	100	106	111	126	Matières premières
Intermediate goods	...	...	...	100	105	112	116	Produits intermédiaires
Consumer goods	...	...	...	100	99	101	101	Biens de consommation
Capital goods	...	...	...	100	99	99	98	Biens d'équipement
Portugal								**Portugal**
Domestic supply	...	104	107	111	116	120	126	Offre intérieure
Intermediate goods	...	100	103	104	108	112	117	Produits intermédiaires
Consumer goods	...	106	107	108	110	112	114	Biens de consommation
Capital goods	102	103	105	106	109	112	114	Biens d'équipement
Romania								**Roumanie**
Industrial products	176	213	242	267	298	322	373	Produits industriels
Russian Federation [34]								**Fédération de Russie** [34]
Agricultural products	54	57	68	69	72	83	...	Produits agricoles
Industrial products	47	50	64	70	79	90	...	Produits industriels

Country or area	2002	2003	2004	2005	2006	2007	2008	Pays ou zone
Serbia[35]								**Serbie**[35]
Agricultural products	...	...	...	...	100	113	133	Produits agricoles
Industrial products	...	...	...	...	100	106	106	Produits industriels
Singapore								**Singapour**
Domestic supply[8]	97	99	102	112	118	118	127	Offre intérieure[8]
Domestic production[2,3]	101	97	96	101	103	102	105	Production intérieure[2,3]
Imported goods	100	100	99	104	107	105	108	Produits importés
Slovakia[36]								**Slovaquie**[36]
Agricultural products	...	101	103	102	101	106	111	Produits agricoles
Industrial products	...	...	110	115	121	116	120	Produits industriels
Slovenia								**Slovénie**
Agricultural products	111	114	111	112	118	127	147	Produits agricoles
Industrial products	115	118	123	126	129	136	144	Produits industriels
Intermediate goods	114	116	123	127	132	140	148	Produits intermédiaires
Consumer goods	118	123	126	129	131	135	142	Biens de consommation
Capital goods	107	106	108	112	113	114	118	Biens d'équipement
South Africa								**Afrique du Sud**
Domestic production[37]	122	125	128	132	143	158	181	Production intérieure[37]
Agricultural products	139	131	129	120	143	176	188	Produits agricoles
Imported goods	127	122	117	121	131	143	167	Produits importés
Spain								**Espagne**
Domestic supply[18]	102	104	107	113	119	123	131	Offre intérieure[18]
Intermediate goods	102	103	107	111	118	125	132	Produits intermédiaires
Consumer goods	106	108	111	114	118	121	126	Biens de consommation
Capital goods	103	104	106	108	111	115	118	Biens d'équipement
Sweden[18,38]								**Suède**[18,38]
Domestic supply[2]	104	103	105	111	117	121	128	Offre intérieure[2]
Domestic production[2]	103	103	106	109	114	120	126	Production intérieure[2]
Imported goods	105	102	105	113	119	122	128	Produits importés
Switzerland								**Suisse**
Domestic supply[2,8]	99	102	104	...	...	111	...	Offre intérieure[2,8]
Domestic production[2,8]	100	104	107	...	...	113	...	Production intérieure[2,8]
Agricultural products[2]	92	122	119	...	...	121	...	Produits agricoles[2]
Industrial products	100	103	105	...	...	109	...	Produits industriels
Imported goods[8]	96	98	100	...	...	107	...	Produits importés[8]
Intermediate goods	99	105	109	...	...	116	...	Produits intermédiaires
Capital goods	102	102	102	...	...	109	...	Biens d'équipement
Syrian Arab Republic								**Rép. arabe syrienne**
Raw materials	100	...	...	104	104	...	...	Matières premières
Intermediate goods	...	...	...	85	87	...	...	Produits intermédiaires
Consumer goods[39]	...	...	...	102	109	...	...	Biens de consommation[39]
Thailand								**Thaïlande**
Domestic supply[2,11]	...	108	116	126	135	...	...	Offre intérieure[2,11]
Agricultural products	...	128	147	176	211	...	...	Produits agricoles
Industrial products[3]	...	106	111	119	125	...	...	Produits industriels[3]
Raw materials	...	120	133	154	174	...	...	Matières premières
Intermediate goods	...	108	119	128	138	...	...	Produits intermédiaires
Consumer goods	110	116	125	143	158	...	...	Biens de consommation
Capital goods	...	106	108	117	117	...	...	Biens d'équipement
TFYR of Macedonia[16]								**L'ex-R.Y. Macédoine**[16]
Domestic supply	...	...	...	100	107	110	121	Offre intérieure
Intermediate goods	...	...	...	100	103	111	126	Produits intermédiaires
Capital goods	...	...	...	100	102	102	105	Biens d'équipement
Trinidad and Tobago								**Trinité-et-Tobago**
Domestic supply[39]	129	130	135	...	...	...	...	Offre intérieure[39]
Industrial products	102	103	...	...	...	...	...	Produits industriels
Tunisia								**Tunisie**
Agricultural products	107	111	116	...	...	...	...	Produits agricoles
Industrial products	106	109	112	117	125	130	145	Produits industriels

Country or area	2002	2003	2004	2005	2006	2007	2008	Pays ou zone
Turkey								**Turquie**
Domestic supply [2,18,40]	243	305	349	370	403	430	484	Offre intérieure [2,18,40]
Agricultural products	223	298	369	375	403	431	484	Produits agricoles
Industrial products	247	306	340	368	405	429	481	Produits industriels
Ukraine								**Ukraine**
Agricultural products	...	...	...	127	130	179	192	Produits agricoles
Industrial products	...	...	...	169	186	222	301	Produits industriels
United Kingdom								**Royaume-Uni**
Domestic supply [41]	105	101	104	107	109	113	...	Offre intérieure [41]
Agricultural products	...	...	...	110	115	128	...	Produits agricoles
Industrial products [42]	101	102	103	105	107	110	...	Produits industriels [42]
Imported goods	95	96	95	102	108	112	...	Produits importés
Raw materials	97	96	99	111	122	126	...	Matières premières
Intermediate goods	97	100	107	124	142	143	...	Produits intermédiaires
Consumer goods	103	104	106	108	109	112	...	Biens de consommation
Capital goods	99	98	97	100	101	104	...	Biens d'équipement
United States								**Etats-Unis**
Domestic supply [2]	99	104	111	119	124	130	143	Offre intérieure [2]
Agricultural products [2]	100	112	125	119	118	144	162	Produits agricoles [2]
Industrial products [2,43]	98	103	110	119	125	130	143	Produits industriels [2,43]
Raw materials	90	113	132	152	154	173	210	Matières premières
Intermediate goods	99	104	110	119	127	132	146	Produits intermédiaires
Consumer goods	101	105	110	116	120	125	135	Biens de consommation
Capital goods	100	101	102	104	106	108	111	Biens d'équipement
Uruguay [44,45]								**Uruguay** [44,45]
Domestic production	141	195	224	218	231	259	302	Production intérieure
Agricultural products	166	250	285	240	243	304	373	Produits agricoles
Industrial products [8]	132	177	204	211	227	243	279	Produits industriels [8]
Venezuela (Bol. Rep. of) [8]								**Venezuela (Rép. bol. du)** [8]
Domestic supply	...	253	...	...	435	507	...	Offre intérieure
Domestic production	...	237	...	...	421	497	...	Production intérieure
Agricultural products	...	184	...	...	380	493	...	Produits agricoles
Industrial products	...	191	...	...	322	373	...	Produits industriels
Imported goods	...	294	...	...	450	500	...	Produits importés
Viet Nam								**Viet Nam**
Agricultural products [46]	...	...	...	123	127	145	203	Produits agricoles [46]
Industrial products	...	...	...	120	125	133	162	Produits industriels
Imported goods	...	...	...	120	125	131	155	Produits importés

Source:
United Nations Statistics Division, New York, price statistics database, last accessed October 2009.

Source:
Organisation des Nations Unies, Division de statistique, New York, la base de données pour les statistiques des prix, dernier accès octobre 2009.

1	Domestic agricultural products only.
2	Including exported products.
3	Manufacturing industry only.
4	Index base: 2002=100.
5	Including service industries.
6	Annual average refers to average of 12 months ending June.
7	Prices relate only to products for sale or transfer to other sectors or for use as capital equipment.
8	Excluding mining and quarrying.
9	Including imported products.
10	Excluding construction.
11	Agricultural products and products of manufacturing industry.
12	Forestry and fishing.
13	Data refer to government-controlled areas.
14	Including raw materials.
15	Durable goods only.
16	Index base: 2005=100.

1	Produits agricoles intérieurs seulement.
2	Y compris les produits exportés.
3	Industries manufacturières seulement.
4	Base de l'indice: 2002=100.
5	Y compris industries de service.
6	La moyenne annuelle est la moyenne de douze mois finissant en juin.
7	Uniquement les prix des produits destinés à être vendus ou transférés à d'autres secteurs ou à être utilisés comme biens d'équipement.
8	Non compris les industries extractives.
9	Y compris les produits importés.
10	Non compris construction.
11	Produits agricoles et produits des industries manufacturières.
12	Exploitation forestière et pêche.
13	Les données se rapportent aux zones contrôlées par le Gouvernement.
14	Y compris les matières premières.
15	Biens durables seulement.
16	Base de l'indice: 2005=100.

17	Finished products only.	17	Produits finis uniquement.
18	Excluding electricity, gas and water.	18	Non compris l'électricité, le gaz et l'eau.
19	Including mining and quarrying.	19	Y compris les industries extractives.
20	Annual average refers to average of 12 months ending March.	20	La moyenne annuelle est la moyenne de douze mois finissant en mars.
21	Primary articles include food, non-food articles and minerals.	21	Les articles primaires comprennent des articles des produits alimentaires, non- alimentaires et des minéraux.
22	Excluding Value Added Tax.	22	Non compris taxe sur la valeur ajoutée.
23	Including marine foods.	23	Y compris l'alimentation marine.
24	Index base: 2003=100.	24	Base de l'indice: 2003=100.
25	Mexico City.	25	Mexico.
26	Excluding forestry, fishing and hunting.	26	Non compris sylviculture, pêche et chasse.
27	Crop growing production only, excluding livestock production.	27	Cultures uniquement, non compris les produits de l'élevage.
28	Including all outputs of manufacturing.	28	Y compris toute la production du secteur manufacturière.
29	Including all industrial inputs.	29	Tous les intrants industriels.
30	Index base: 2007=100	30	Base de l'indice: 2007=100.
31	Muscat.	31	Muscat.
32	Excluding fishing.	32	Non compris la pêche.
33	Metro Manila.	33	L'agglomération de Manille.
34	Index base: 2007 December=100.	34	Base de l'indice : 2007 décembre=100.
35	Index base: 2006=100.	35	Base de l'indice: 2006=100.
36	Prices of producers are surveyed without value added tax and without excise taxes.	36	Les enquêtes sur le prix à la production ne prennent pas en considération les taxes à la valeur ajoutée et excise.
37	Excluding gold mining.	37	Non compris l'extraction de l'or.
38	Excluding agriculture.	38	Non compris l'agriculture.
39	Index base: 1990=100.	39	Base de l'indice: 1990=100.
40	Excluding industrial finished goods.	40	Non compris les produits finis industriels.
41	Data refers to the output of manufactured products.	41	Les données se réfèrent à production brute des industries manufacturières.
42	Excluding food, beverages, petroleum and tobacco.	42	Non compris les produits alimentaires, les boissons, le pétrole et le tabac.
43	Excluding foods and feeds production.	43	Non compris les produits alimentaires et d'affouragement.
44	Montevideo.	44	Montevideo.
45	Index base: 2001 August = 100	45	Base de l'indice: 2001 August = 100
46	Excluding forestry and fishing.	46	Non compris l'exploitation forestière et la pêche.

Country or area	2001	2002	2003	2004	2005	2006	2007	2008	Pays ou zone
Albania									**Albanie**
General	103.1	108.4	110.8	114.0	116.7	119.5	123.0	127.1[1]	Généraux
Food	103.7	110.2	115.0	114.9	114.3	115.6	119.0	125.5[1]	Alimentation
Algeria									**Algérie**
General	103.5	105.8	109.5	114.5	116.7	118.8	123.5	128.9	Généraux
Food	104.4	106.2	111.0	116.4	116.6	119.3	126.7	134.6	Alimentation
American Samoa									**Samoa américaines**
General [2]	101.2	103.4	108.4	116.1	122.1	125.7	...	...	Généraux [2]
Food	101.6	103.1	109.7	123.5	130.4	132.2	...	...	Alimentation
Andorra [3]									**Andorre [3]**
General (2001 = 100)	100.0	104.5	107.5	111.1	114.6	118.2	122.8	125.3	Généraux (2001 = 100)
Food (2001 = 100) [4]	100.0	106.2	109.9	111.9	113.1	116.2	119.8	123.2	Alimentation (2001 = 100) [4]
Angola (Luanda)									**Angola**
General	252.6	527.6[1]	1 045.8	1 501.2	1 846.0	2 091.6	2 347.7[1]	2 640.5	Généraux
Food	251.1[1]	508.6	1 062.4[1]	1 587.5	1 957.0	2 292.4	2 617.7	3 103.8	Alimentation
Anguilla									**Anguilla**
General (2001 = 100)	100.0[5]	100.5	103.8	108.3	113.5	122.7	129.1	137.9	Généraux (2001 = 100)
Food (2001 = 100)	100.0[5]	100.5	98.0	102.1	105.4	112.4	119.4	137.5	Alimentation (2001 = 100)
Antigua and Barbuda									**Antigua-et-Barbuda**
General	101.5	...	...	...	...	...	...	...	Généraux
Food	103.6	...	...	...	...	...	...	...	Alimentation
Argentina [6] (Buenos Aires)									**Argentine [6]**
General	98.9	124.5	141.3	147.5	161.7	179.4	195.2[1]	211.9	Généraux
Food	98.1	132.0	157.3	165.1	183.3	205.5	228.5[1]	243.9	Alimentation
Armenia									**Arménie**
General	103.1	104.2[1]	109.2	116.3	117.0[1]	121.1	126.5	137.8	Généraux
Food	104.7	107.0[1]	114.4	125.8	126.8[1]	132.0	140.9	156.5	Alimentation
Aruba									**Aruba**
General	102.9[1]	106.3	110.2	113.0	116.8	121.0	128.3	139.0[1]	Généraux
Food	103.3[1]	106.7	110.1	114.4	118.7	124.1	137.6	156.8[1]	Alimentation
Australia									**Australie**
General	104.4	107.6	110.5	113.1	116.1	120.2	123.1	128.3	Généraux
Food	106.5	110.4	114.4	117.1	120.0	129.2	132.3	138.5	Alimentation
Austria									**Autriche**
General	102.7	104.5	105.9	108.1	110.6	112.3[1]	114.7	118.3	Généraux
Food	103.3[7]	105.2[7]	107.3[7]	109.5[7]	111.0[7]	112.5[1]	117.1	124.5	Alimentation
Azerbaijan									**Azerbaïdjan**
General	101.5	104.4	106.7	113.9	124.8	135.2	157.7	190.6	Généraux
Food [8]	102.7	106.5	109.9	120.9	134.1	150.2	174.6	224.4	Alimentation [8]
Bahamas (New Providence)									**Bahamas**
General	102.1	104.2	107.4	108.6	110.8	112.8	115.6	120.8	Généraux
Food	102.1	104.1	104.7	107.8	111.2	116.4	120.6	128.6	Alimentation
Bahrain									**Bahreïn**
General	98.8	98.3	100.0	102.3	104.9	107.1[1]	110.6	114.4	Généraux
Food [8]	98.6	97.6	96.2	98.3	101.3	103.3[1]	108.0	119.8	Alimentation [8]
Bangladesh [9]									**Bangladesh [9]**
General	101.5	105.4	111.5[1]	118.4	126.7	135.3	147.6	160.7	Généraux
Food	100.8	103.4	110.1[1]	118.3	127.8	137.5	151.9	168.7	Alimentation
Barbados									**Barbade**
General	102.6[1]	103.0	104.6	106.1	112.5	120.8	125.7	135.8	Généraux
Food	105.2[1]	107.1	110.1	115.0	123.1	132.8	142.2	161.4	Alimentation
Belarus									**Bélarus**
General	161.1	229.8	295.0	348.3	384.3	411.2	445.9	512.0	Généraux
Food	156.8	217.9	267.6	320.1	358.2	380.1	417.4	491.1	Alimentation
Belgium									**Belgique**
General	102.5	104.2	105.8	108.0[1]	111.0	113.0	115.1	120.3	Généraux
Food	104.2	106.5	108.7	110.4[1]	112.5	115.0	119.1	126.1	Alimentation
Belize									**Belize**
General	101.2	103.4	106.1	109.3	113.1	118.2	120.9	128.6	Généraux
Food [8]	100.5	101.6	104.2	106.9	111.8	116.6	122.7	139.0	Alimentation [8]

30 Consumer price indices *(continued)*
General and food (Index base: 2000 = 100)
Indices des prix à la consommation *(suite)*
Généraux et alimentation (Indices base : 2000 = 100)

Country or area	2001	2002	2003	2004	2005	2006	2007	2008	Pays ou zone
Benin (Cotonou)									**Bénin**
General	103.9	106.5	108.1	109.0	114.9	119.2	120.8	130.3	Généraux
Food [10]	102.3	108.0	105.5	104.7	114.4	113.8	112.6	132.9	Alimentation [10]
Bermuda									**Bermudes**
General	102.9	105.3	108.6	112.5	116.0	119.5[1]	124.1	130.0	Généraux
Food	102.0	103.5	105.6	108.2	111.4	113.6[1]	117.6	124.1	Alimentation
Bhutan									**Bhoutan**
General	103.4	106.0	107.6	110.9[1]	116.8	122.6	129.0	139.8	Généraux
Food	101.5	103.6	104.5	102.9[1]	108.8	114.2	123.5	138.2	Alimentation
Bolivia [11]									**Bolivie** [11]
General	101.6	102.5	105.9	110.6	116.6	121.6	132.2	150.7[1]	Généraux
Food	100.6	99.7	103.2	109.3	115.7	122.2	138.9	174.5	Alimentation
Bosnia and Herzegovina									**Bosnie-Herzégovine**
General (2005 = 100)	...	...	...	...	100.0	106.1	107.7	115.7	Généraux (2005 = 100)
Food (2005 = 100)	...	...	...	...	100.0	108.3	111.4	124.8	Alimentation (2005 = 100)
Botswana									**Botswana**
General	106.6	115.1	125.8	134.4	146.1	163.0[1]	174.5	196.6	Généraux
Food	102.6	112.2	125.0	130.9	137.9	155.2[1]	172.7	207.7	Alimentation
Brazil									**Brésil**
General	106.8	115.9	132.9	141.7	151.4	157.8	163.5	172.8	Généraux
Food [7]	106.7	117.0	140.8	146.5	151.0	151.0	161.2	182.3	Alimentation [7]
British Virgin Islands									**Iles Vierges britanniques**
General	103.1	103.5	107.2	108.3	110.4	...	...	...	Généraux
Food	104.3	105.3	107.1	108.4	112.1	...	...	...	Alimentation
Brunei Darussalam									**Brunéi Darussalam**
General	100.6	98.3[1]	98.6	99.5	100.5	100.7	101.0	103.8	Généraux
Food	100.5	100.8[1]	100.0	101.7	102.2	102.5	104.7	109.9	Alimentation
Bulgaria									**Bulgarie**
General	107.4	113.6	116.3	123.4	129.6	139.0	150.7	169.3	Généraux
Food	106.5	106.5	105.4	112.5	117.0	123.4	140.0	163.4	Alimentation
Burkina Faso (Ouagadougou)									**Burkina Faso**
General	104.9	107.3	109.5	109.0	116.0	118.8	118.5	131.1	Généraux
Food	108.8	112.2	110.3	104.9	120.2	120.0	117.9	145.4	Alimentation
Burundi (Bujumbura)									**Burundi**
General	108.1	106.7	118.1	127.9	144.8	148.6	161.0	...	Généraux
Food	100.6	95.5	107.5	119.0	139.4	139.5	151.6	...	Alimentation
Cambodia (Phnom Penh)									**Cambodge**
General	99.4[1]	102.7	103.9	107.9	114.1	119.5	126.5	151.4	Généraux
Food [8]	98.0[1]	99.7	101.2	107.6	116.6	124.2	136.6	181.7	Alimentation [8]
Cameroon									**Cameroun**
General	104.4	107.4	108.1[12]	108.4	110.5	116.2	117.2	123.5	Généraux
Food	107.0	112.1	111.4[12]	109.2	110.3	117.9	119.1	130.0	Alimentation
Canada									**Canada**
General	102.6	104.8	107.8	109.8	112.2	114.4	116.9[1]	119.6	Généraux
Food	104.5	107.2	109.1	111.3	114.1	116.8	119.9[1]	124.1	Alimentation
Cape Verde									**Cap-Vert**
General	99.6	105.4	106.5	104.5	104.9	110.6	115.5[1]	123.4	Généraux
Food (2003 = 100)	105.3	...	100.0[13]	96.5	96.4	102.7	107.9	117.7	Alimentation (2003 = 100)
Cayman Islands									**Iles Caïmanes**
General	101.1	103.6	104.2	108.8	116.8	117.7	121.1	126.1	Généraux
	103.5	105.7	109.1	113.9	117.0	120.1	126.3	133.4	Alimentation
Central African Rep. (Bangui)									**Rép. centrafricaine**
General [2]	103.7	105.2	110.9	108.6	111.7	119.1	120.3	131.5	Généraux [2]
Food	104.7	106.8	112.4	107.2	110.9	118.9	121.1	134.9	Alimentation
Chad (N'Djamena)									**Tchad**
General	112.4	117.5[1]	115.4	109.3	117.8	127.5	115.9	127.7[1]	Généraux
Food	119.3	125.8[1]	122.6	116.0	129.2	144.0	129.9[1]	151.2	Alimentation
Chile (Santiago)									**Chili**
General	103.6	106.1	109.1	110.3	113.6	117.5	122.7	133.4	Généraux
Food	100.8	102.9	105.8	104.4	107.4	110.6	120.5	139.8	Alimentation

Country or area	2001	2002	2003	2004	2005	2006	2007	2008	Pays ou zone
China									**Chine**
General	100.7	99.9	101.1	105.0	106.9	108.5	113.7	...	Généraux
Food	100.0	99.4	102.8	113.0	116.2	118.9	133.5	...	Alimentation
China, Hong Kong SAR									**Chine, Hong Kong RAS**
General	98.4	95.4	93.0	92.6	93.6[1]	95.5	97.4	101.6	Généraux
Food	99.2	97.1	95.7	96.7	98.4[1]	100.1	104.4	115.0	Alimentation
China, Macao SAR									**Chine, Macao RAS**
General	98.0	95.4	93.9	94.9	99.0[1]	104.1	109.9	119.4	Généraux
Food	98.6	96.5	95.2	97.4	101.3[1]	105.0	113.6	133.2	Alimentation
Colombia [14]									**Colombie** [14]
General	108.7	116.5	125.0	132.5	139.6	145.2	153.4	166.0	Généraux
Food	108.7	118.4	127.2	134.6	143.1	150.5	162.5	182.6	Alimentation
Congo [38] (Brazzaville)									**Congo**
General	100.1	104.4	103.8	106.4	109.6	116.8	119.9	128.7	Généraux
Food	98.3	102.9	96.9	90.8	95.6	105.3	...	...	Alimentation
Cook Islands (Rarotonga)									**Iles Cook**
General	108.7	112.4	114.6	115.6	118.5	122.4	125.5[1]	135.4	Généraux
Food [15]	109.4	116.9	119.9	120.9	122.3	125.2	125.5[1]	132.9	Alimentation [15]
Costa Rica [16]									**Costa Rica** [16]
General	111.3	121.5	132.9	149.3	169.9	189.4[1]	207.1	234.9	Généraux
Food	110.8[10]	121.8[10]	133.3[10]	151.6[10]	176.5[10]	...	100.0[17]	123.9	Alimentation
Côte d'Ivoire [38] (Abidjan)									**Côte d'Ivoire**
General	104.4	107.6	111.1	112.7	117.1	119.9	122.2	130.0	Généraux
Food [10]	105.7	111.6	116.1	111.6	114.3	117.5	123.8	137.8	Alimentation [10]
Croatia									**Croatie**
General	104.5[1]	106.3	108.2	110.4	114.0[1]	117.7	121.1	128.4	Généraux
Food	102.1[1]	102.3	104.0	105.5	110.4[1]	113.1	116.9	128.6	Alimentation
Cuba									**Cuba**
General	111.9	106.1	108.2	105.9	108.9	114.5	122.5	124.5	Généraux
Food [10]	114.3	113.5	110.2	107.0	110.3	117.8	124.7	126.3	Alimentation [10]
Cyprus									**Chypre**
General	102.0	104.8	109.2	111.7	114.5	117.4[1]	120.2	125.8	Généraux
Food	104.1	108.9	114.4	119.0	120.9	126.7[1]	133.7	143.8	Alimentation
Czech Republic									**République tchèque**
General	104.7	106.6	106.6	109.7	111.7	114.6	117.9	125.4	Généraux
Food [18]	104.3	104.3	104.0	109.0	110.3	111.5	118.0	127.9	Alimentation [18]
Denmark									**Danemark**
General	102.4	104.8	107.0	108.3	110.2	112.3	114.2	118.1	Généraux
Food	103.9	106.1	107.7	106.6	107.3	110.2	115.1	123.8	Alimentation
Dominica									**Dominique**
General (2001 = 100)	100.0[5]	100.2	101.6	104.1	105.8	108.6	112.1	119.2	Généraux (2001 = 100)
Food (2001 = 100)	100.0[5]	101.5	101.9	104.8	107.4	111.8	117.7	131.5	Alimentation (2001 = 100)
Dominican Republic									**Rép. dominicaine**
General	108.9	114.6	146.1	221.2	230.5	247.9	263.1	291.1	Généraux
Food [10]	106.1	110.7	140.1	237.0	233.2	242.8	258.8	295.7	Alimentation [10]
Ecuador									**Equateur**
General	137.7	154.9	167.1	171.7	175.5[1]	181.2	185.4	200.9	Généraux
Food (2005 = 100)	132.0[10]	142.5[10]	146.0[10]	147.7[10]	100.0[19]	106.0	109.5	128.4	Alimentation (2005 = 100)
Egypt									**Egypte**
General	102.2	105.0	109.5	127.4[1]	133.7	143.9	157.6[1]	186.4	Généraux
Food (2004 = 100)	101.1[8]	105.3[8]	112.3[8]	100.0[20]	105.0	115.7	130.6[1]	162.0	Alimentation (2004 = 100)
El Salvador [11]									**El Salvador** [11]
General	103.7	105.7	107.9	112.7	118.0	122.8	128.4	137.7	Généraux
Food	104.6	106.6	108.6	115.5	122.6	126.3	134.2	150.5	Alimentation
Equatorial Guinea (Malabo)									**Guinée équatoriale**
General	108.8	117.0	125.5	130.9	...	144.5	...	...	Généraux
Food	111.5	122.2	130.0	135.7	...	153.6	...	...	Alimentation
Estonia									**Estonie**
General	105.8	109.5	111.0	114.4	119.0	124.4	132.5	146.3	Généraux
Food	108.3	111.6	109.6	114.2	118.3	124.2	135.8	155.1	Alimentation

Country or area	2001	2002	2003	2004	2005	2006	2007	2008	Pays ou zone
Ethiopia									**Ethiopie**
General (2001 = 100)	100.0	101.6	119.6	123.6	138.0	156.6	184.8[1]	266.8	Généraux (2001 = 100)
Food (2001 = 100)	100.0	102.6	102.6	134.8	153.3	175.2	214.3[1]	343.0	Alimentation (2001 = 100)
Faeroe Islands									**Iles Féroé**
General	104.9	105.2[1]	106.5	107.2	109.3	111.0	114.9	122.2	Généraux
Food	106.2	108.9[1]	109.4	109.9	111.1	114.1	118.9	127.1	Alimentation
Falk. Is. (Malvinas) (Stanley)									**Iles Falkland (Malvinas)**
General	101.3	102.0	103.2	...	...	...	...	...	Généraux
Fiji									**Fidji**
General	104.3	105.0	109.4	112.5	115.1	118.1	123.7[1]	133.3	Généraux
Food	104.1	104.6	111.0	115.2	117.1	119.2	130.8[1]	145.8	Alimentation
Finland									**Finlande**
General	102.6	104.2	105.1	105.3	106.2	107.9[1]	110.6	115.0	Généraux
Food	104.4	107.4	108.1	108.9	109.2	110.7[1]	113.0	122.7	Alimentation
France									**France**
General	101.7	103.6	105.8	108.0	109.9	111.8	113.4	116.6	Généraux
Food	105.1	107.8	110.2	110.9	111.0	112.7	114.3	119.9	Alimentation
French Guiana									**Guyane française**
General	101.6	103.1	105.2	106.4	108.2	110.4	114.2	118.2	Généraux
Food	102.7	105.3	109.3	109.8	110.5	111.4	113.6	119.0	Alimentation
French Polynesia									**Polynésie française**
General	101.0	103.9	104.3[1]	104.8	105.8	108.7	110.9	114.4[1]	Généraux
Food	102.2	107.4	108.2[1]	110.6	113.2	117.5	121.0	126.6[1]	Alimentation
Gabon [38] **(Libreville)**									**Gabon**
General	102.1	102.3	104.4	104.9	104.9	109.1	112.7[1]	118.5	Généraux
Food	105.0[10]	105.2[10]	107.1[10]	105.1[10]	105.5[10]	112.2[10]	100.0[21]	107.8	Alimentation
Gambia (Banjul, Kombo St.Mary)									**Gambie**
General	104.5	113.5	132.8	151.7	156.5	159.7[1]	168.3	175.8	Généraux
Food	99.3	117.2	141.2	164.0	169.2	172.2[1]	185.8	197.1	Alimentation
Georgia [22]									**Géorgie** [22]
General	104.7	110.5	115.8	122.4	132.5	144.6	158.0	173.8[1]	Généraux
Food [8]	106.6	114.6	122.7	132.2	149.6	167.1	183.4	204.0[1]	Alimentation [8]
Germany									**Allemagne**
General	102.0	103.4	104.5	106.2	108.3	110.1	112.5[1]	115.4	Généraux
Food	104.5	105.3	105.2	104.8	105.3	107.3	111.5[1]	118.3	Alimentation
Ghana									**Ghana**
General	132.9	151.8	193.3	217.7	250.7	278.0	331.9[1]	386.8	Généraux
Food	123.2	145.6	181.6	211.8	244.7	267.2	300.6[1]	346.2	Alimentation
Gibraltar									**Gibraltar**
General	101.8	102.5	105.2	107.6	110.9	113.8	116.9	121.2	Généraux
Food	103.5	107.1	111.3	115.1	117.4	120.4	124.4	132.1	Alimentation
Greece									**Grèce**
General	103.4	107.1	110.9	114.1	118.2[1]	122.0	125.5	130.7	Généraux
Food	105.1	110.7	116.2	116.8	117.5[1]	121.9	125.9	132.6	Alimentation
Greenland									**Groenland**
General	103.0	107.2	109.0	112.0	113.3	116.2	118.5	126.3	Généraux
Food	103.4	107.6	109.8	111.4	114.5	117.4	120.9	130.5	Alimentation
Grenada									**Grenade**
General	103.2[21]	104.3	106.6	109.0	...	...	...	...	Généraux
Food	101.8[21]	101.4	102.1	105.3	...	...	...	...	Alimentation
Guadeloupe									**Guadeloupe**
General	102.6	105.0	107.1	108.6	112.1	114.3	115.8	118.4	Généraux
Food	105.3	108.0	111.7	113.1	116.1	115.7	118.1	122.9	Alimentation
Guam									**Guam**
General	98.7	99.4	102.0	108.1	116.3	129.8	138.6	147.1[1]	Généraux
Food	106.0	112.6	118.9	130.1	140.8	150.0	154.6	168.6[1]	Alimentation
Guatemala (Guatemala)									**Guatemala**
General	107.3[1]	116.0	122.5	131.8	143.8	153.2	163.7	182.3	Généraux
Food	110.0[1]	121.5	128.5	141.7	160.5	171.9	188.9	217.5	Alimentation
Guinea (Conakry)									**Guinée**
General	105.4	108.4	122.4	141.1[1]	185.3	249.6	306.6	362.9	Généraux
Food	...	114.4[1,23]	138.8	168.3	230.6	328.6	422.2	509.2	Alimentation

30

Consumer price indices *(continued)*
General and food (Index base: 2000 = 100)
Indices des prix à la consommation *(suite)*
Généraux et alimentation (Indices base : 2000 = 100)

Country or area	2001	2002	2003	2004	2005	2006	2007	2008	Pays ou zone
Guinea-Bissau (Bissau)									**Guinée-Bissau**
General (2003 = 100)	...	...	100.0	100.9	104.3	106.4	111.2	122.9	Généraux (2003 = 100)
Food (2003 = 100) [10]	...	...	100.0[13]	101.1	104.7	105.2	111.3	129.1	Alimentation (2003 = 100) [10]
Guyana (Georgetown)									**Guyana**
General	102.7	108.2	114.6	120.0	128.3	136.9	153.6	166.0	Généraux
Food [8]	100.6	104.4	108.5	113.3	121.7	130.0	150.3	172.3	Alimentation [8]
Haïti [6]									**Haïti** [6]
General	114.0	125.3	174.5	214.3	255.4[1]	286.9	311.3	359.6	Généraux
Food [10]	115.5	127.4	174.2	223.2	263.2[1]	300.2	324.5	388.6	Alimentation [10]
Honduras									**Honduras**
General	109.6	118.0	127.1	137.5	149.5	157.9	168.9	188.1	Généraux
Food	108.7	112.8	117.0	124.9	137.5	143.7	159.2	189.3	Alimentation
Hungary									**Hongrie**
General	109.2	115.0	120.3	128.5	133.1	138.3	149.3	158.4	Généraux
Food	113.8	119.9	123.2	131.2	134.5	144.8	161.5	177.9	Alimentation
Iceland [24]									**Islande** [24]
General	106.7	111.8	114.2	117.8	122.6	130.9	137.5	154.5	Généraux
Food	107.4	111.1	108.4	100.7	106.7	115.7	113.8	132.3	Alimentation
India [39]									**Inde**
General	103.9	108.2	112.5	116.6	121.5	127.7[1]	136.0	147.5	Généraux
Food	102.2	104.9	108.4	111.5	115.0	124.7[1]	137.0	152.3	Alimentation
Indonesia									**Indonésie**
General	111.5	124.7	133.0	141.3[1]	156.0	176.5	187.8[1]	207.2	Généraux
Food	108.5	120.2	121.2	128.3[1]	140.3	161.9	180.4[1]	210.9	Alimentation
Iran (Islamic Rep. of)									**Iran (Rép. islamique d')**
General	111.3	127.3	148.2	170.1	192.9	215.9	240.1[1]	309.1	Généraux
Food	106.6[7]	124.0[7]	145.9[7]	164.8[7]	186.3[7]	205.5[7]	100.0[21]	131.0	Alimentation
Iraq									**Iraq**
General (1990 = 100)	116.4	138.9	185.5	235.6	322.6	491.3	646.8	664.0	Généraux (1990 = 100)
Food (1990 = 100)	108.2	118.0	137.5	149.5	182.9	237.4	270.4	300.0	Alimentation (1990 = 100)
Ireland									**Irlande**
General	104.8[1]	109.7	113.5	116.0	118.8	123.5	129.5[1]	134.8	Généraux
Food	107.0[1]	110.7	112.3	111.9	111.2	112.7	116.0[1]	123.5	Alimentation
Isle of Man									**Ile de Man**
General	101.7	104.1	107.3	112.8	117.5	121.0	125.9	132.4	Généraux
Food	104.9	113.0	119.6	126.3	131.0	135.1	141.2	152.3	Alimentation
Israel									**Israël**
General	101.1	106.9[1]	107.6	107.2	108.6	111.0[1]	111.5	116.6	Généraux
Food	102.5	105.4[1]	108.4	108.0	109.9	115.1[1]	119.5	133.2	Alimentation
Italy									**Italie**
General [25]	102.8	105.4	108.2	110.5	112.4	114.7	116.9	120.7	Généraux [25]
Food	104.1	107.9	111.3	113.7	113.7	115.6	119.0	125.4	Alimentation
Jamaica									**Jamaïque**
General	107.0	114.6	126.4	143.6	165.5	179.8	196.8[1]	240.1	Généraux
Food	103.4[7]	109.7[7]	120.2[7]	136.5[7]	161.4[7]	172.0[7]	194.8[1]	254.6	Alimentation
Japan									**Japon**
General	99.3	98.4	98.1	98.1	97.8	98.1	98.1	99.5	Généraux
Food	99.4	98.6	98.4	99.3	98.4	98.9	99.2	101.7	Alimentation
Jersey [26]									**Jersey** [26]
General	103.9	108.3	112.9	118.3	122.6	126.2	131.6	139.0	Généraux
Food	105.1	107.3	109.6	114.0	114.4	117.0	122.1	137.9	Alimentation
Jordan									**Jordanie**
General	101.8	103.6[1]	105.3	108.9	112.7	119.7	126.2	145.0	Généraux
Food [8]	100.3	100.5[1]	103.1	107.8	113.4	121.8	133.1	158.2	Alimentation [8]
Kazakhstan									**Kazakhstan**
General	108.4	114.7	122.1	130.5	140.3	152.4	168.8	197.5	Généraux
Food [10]	111.5	119.0	127.3	137.1	148.2	161.0	180.7	223.1	Alimentation [10]
Kenya [14]	Nairobi								**Kenya** [14]
General	103.6	105.3	116.7	133.5	149.1	178.3	195.1	249.6	Généraux
Food	102.4	103.9	120.9	143.8	164.8	210.8	233.8	315.9	Alimentation

Country or area	2001	2002	2003	2004	2005	2006	2007	2008	Pays ou zone
Kiribati (Tarawa)									**Kiribati**
General	106.0	109.4	111.4	110.3	110.0	108.3	112.9	125.3	Généraux
Food	106.1	109.7	112.8	112.8	112.7	108.3	114.4	133.4	Alimentation
Korea, Republic of									**Corée, République de**
General	104.1	106.9	110.7	114.7	117.8[1]	120.4	123.5	129.2	Généraux
Food	103.5[7]	107.7[7]	112.4[7]	119.5[7]	128.6[21]	129.2	132.4	139.1	Alimentation
Kosovo									**Kosovo**
General (2003 = 100)	...	98.8[27]	100.0	98.9	97.6	98.2	102.6	112.1	Généraux (2003 = 100)
Food (2003 = 100)	...	97.6[27]	100.0	98.9	96.5	99.7	100.7	116.8	Alimentation (2003 = 100)
Kuwait									**Koweït**
General	101.8	102.3	103.2	104.5	108.8	112.1	118.3	130.8	Généraux
Food	100.4	101.1	106.6	110.0	119.4	124.0	129.9	145.0	Alimentation
Kyrgyzstan									**Kirghizistan**
General	106.9	109.1	112.5	117.1	122.2	129.0	...	...	Généraux
Food	105.7	105.9	108.9	112.4	118.3	128.7	...	...	Alimentation
Lao People's Dem. Rep.									**Rép. dém. pop. lao**
General	107.7	119.3	137.7	152.1	163.0	174.1	182.0	...	Généraux
Food	106.6	117.0	134.8	148.8	160.2	...	...	...	Alimentation
Latvia									**Lettonie**
General	102.5	104.5	107.5	114.2	121.9	129.9	143.0	165.0	Généraux
Food	104.8[10]	108.4[10]	111.2[10]	119.5[10]	130.5[21]	141.1	160.1	189.4	Alimentation
Lebanon (Beirut)									**Liban**
General	97.0	95.3	...	...	...	...	...	...	Généraux
Lesotho									**Lesotho**
General [2]	106.9	120.1	129.0	135.5	140.1	148.4	160.6	177.8	Généraux [2]
Food [28]	106.5	134.8	142.4	148.1	152.0	165.9	189.9	220.0	Alimentation [28]
Lithuania									**Lituanie**
General	101.3	101.6	100.4	101.6	104.3[1]	108.2	114.4	126.9	Généraux
Food	103.5	102.8	99.0	101.2	105.3[1]	111.7	124.3	144.1	Alimentation
Luxembourg									**Luxembourg**
General	102.7	104.8	106.9	109.3	112.0[1]	115.0	117.7	121.7	Généraux
Food	104.8	108.9	111.0	113.0	114.8[1]	117.6	121.5	128.1	Alimentation
Madagascar (Cinq regions)									**Madagascar**
General	107.4	125.1	123.0	139.9	165.9	183.7	202.6	221.4	Généraux
Food [4]	101.9	117.2	112.9	134.7	170.2	180.8	202.1	223.2	Alimentation [4]
Malawi									**Malawi**
General	122.7	140.8	154.3	172.0	198.5	226.1	244.1	265.4	Généraux
Food	117.6	136.4	143.6	154.4	181.0	209.1	224.7	240.3	Alimentation
Malaysia									**Malaisie**
General	101.4	103.2	104.4	105.9	109.1[1]	113.0	115.3	121.5	Généraux
Food	100.7	101.4	102.7	105.0	108.8[1]	112.5	115.9	126.1	Alimentation
Maldives (Male)									**Maldives**
General	100.7	101.6	98.7	105.0	108.5	110.0[1]	117.5	131.6	Généraux
Food (2005 = 100)	102.1[10]	105.7[10]	99.3[10]	115.2[10]	117.6[10]	104.0[19]	120.8	143.9	Alimentation (2005 = 100)
Mali (Bamako)									**Mali**
General	105.1	110.4	109.1	105.6	112.3	114.1	115.7	126.3	Généraux
Food [29]	108.0	115.8	111.1	103.3	115.1	114.6	117.3	132.6	Alimentation [29]
Malta									**Malte**
General	102.9	105.1	105.8[1]	108.7	112.0	115.0	116.5	121.4	Généraux
Food	106.0	107.4	109.2[1]	109.5	111.4	113.6	118.5	128.1	Alimentation
Marshall Islands (Majuro)									**Iles Marshall**
General	101.8	103.0	100.1	102.3	106.9	111.5	115.0	135.2	Généraux
Food	100.3	102.7	102.5	106.0	106.3	109.4	110.8	129.4	Alimentation
Martinique									**Martinique**
General	102.1	104.2	106.4	108.6	111.2	113.9	116.7	119.9	Généraux
Food	103.8	108.8	112.5	114.6	118.3	120.5	124.5	131.2	Alimentation
Mauritania									**Mauritanie**
General	104.7	108.9	114.4	124.2[1]	139.3	147.9	158.7	170.4	Généraux
Food	106.5	111.3	117.9[30]	131.2[1]	149.3	157.3	173.9	190.6	Alimentation
Mauritius									**Maurice**
General	105.4	112.2[1]	116.5	122.1	128.1	139.5	154.9[1,31]	166.5	Généraux
Food	104.0	112.2[1]	115.4	122.3	129.5	142.4	168.9[1,31]	190.7	Alimentation

Country or area	2001	2002	2003	2004	2005	2006	2007	2008	Pays ou zone
Mexico									**Mexique**
General	106.4	111.7[1]	116.8	122.3	127.2	131.8	137.0	144.0	Généraux
Food [10]	105.4	109.6[1]	115.1	122.9	129.4	134.1	142.6	154.1	Alimentation [10]
Mongolia (Ulan Bator)									**Mongolie**
General	106.3[1]	107.3	112.8	122.1	137.6	...	157.7[1]	...	Généraux
Food [10]	101.5	98.5	105.5	118.5	139.4	...	...	...	Alimentation [10]
Morocco									**Maroc**
General	100.6	103.4	104.6	106.2	107.2	110.8	113.0	117.4	Généraux
Food [8]	99.0	103.2	104.6	106.2	106.5	110.7	114.3	122.1	Alimentation [8]
Mozambique									**Mozambique**
General	111.2	130.4	145.4	162.0	173.3[1]	196.9	214.9	...	Généraux
Food	110.6	132.3	148.8	164.9[1]	173.9	203.6	224.6	...	Alimentation
Myanmar (Yangon)									**Myanmar**
General	121.1	190.2	259.8	271.6	297.1	356.5	481.3	610.3	Généraux
Food	119.5	201.2	274.3	277.5	303.2	365.7	493.9	638.3	Alimentation
Namibia									**Namibie**
General (2002 = 100)	...	100.0	107.1	111.6	114.1	119.9	127.9	141.1	Généraux (2002 = 100)
Food (2002 = 100)	...	100.0	109.5	110.4	112.0	119.3	133.8	156.6	Alimentation (2002 = 100)
Nepal									**Népal**
General	102.7	105.9	112.0	115.2	123.2	132.6	140.5	156.9	Généraux
Food	101.3	104.4	110.1	112.9	120.3	129.1	139.6	158.8	Alimentation
Netherlands									**Pays-Bas**
General	104.2	107.6	109.9	111.2	113.1	114.4	116.2[1]	119.1	Généraux
Food	107.0	110.5	111.7	107.8	106.5	108.3	109.4	115.6	Alimentation
Netherlands Antilles (Curaçao)									**Antilles néerlandaises**
General	101.8	102.1	103.8	105.2	109.4	113.0	116.4[1]	124.4	Généraux
Food	103.4	107.3	109.5	114.7	123.3	133.0	145.0[1]	171.6	Alimentation
New Caledonia (Nouméa)									**Nouvelle-Calédonie**
General	102.3	104.1	105.4	106.2	107.6	110.7	111.8	115.1	Généraux
Food	102.6	105.0	107.0	108.2	109.7	113.0	114.5	119.1	Alimentation
New Zealand									**Nouvelle-Zélande**
General	102.6	105.4	107.2	109.7	113.0	116.8[1]	119.6	124.4	Généraux
Food	106.0	109.4	109.4	110.3	113.1	116.2[1]	120.6	130.2	Alimentation
Nicaragua (Managua)									**Nicaragua**
General (1999 = 100)	113.5	117.7	124.0	134.5	147.4	160.9	178.8	214.2	Généraux (1999 = 100)
Food (1999 = 100)	112.1	115.7	120.7	133.6	149.0	162.5	188.9	242.8	Alimentation (1999 = 100)
Niger [38] (Niamey)									**Niger**
General [2]	104.0	106.7	105.1	105.2	113.5	113.6	113.6	126.5	Généraux [2]
Food [8]	107.1	111.9	106.7	105.1	120.7	118.4	117.6	141.8	Alimentation [8]
Nigeria									**Nigéria**
General	118.9	134.2	153.1[1]	176.0	207.4	224.5	236.6	263.9	Généraux
Food	128.0	144.8	153.8[1]	175.8	216.3	228.3	232.6	270.0	Alimentation
Niue									**Nioué**
General	106.8	109.7	112.3[1]	116.6[32]	117.0	119.7	127.8	139.3	Généraux
Food	111.2	115.1	118.3[1]	121.2[32]	122.0	127.2	134.9	150.0	Alimentation
Norfolk Island									**Ile Norfolk**
General	103.1	105.9	109.1	118.6	125.2	134.4	...	...	Généraux
Food	104.5	112.4	118.4	123.4	129.9	137.3	...	...	Alimentation
Northern Mariana Is. (Saipan)									**Iles Mariannes du Nord**
General	99.2	99.4	98.4[1]	99.3	99.8	104.7	111.9	117.2	Généraux
Food	96.6	93.0	90.7[1]	94.9	93.9	91.4	96.0	103.7	Alimentation
Norway									**Norvège**
General	103.0	104.4	106.9	107.4	109.1	111.6	112.4	116.7	Généraux
Food	98.1	96.5	99.7	101.5	103.1	104.6	107.3	111.9	Alimentation
Occ. Palestinian Terr.									**Terr. palestinien occupé**
General	101.2	107.0	111.7	115.1	119.1	123.5	126.9	139.2[1]	Généraux
Food	99.5	102.1	106.8	109.1	113.3	118.8	124.3	147.4[1]	Alimentation
Oman (Muscat)									**Oman**
General	99.0	98.3	97.9	98.3	100.2[1]	103.3	108.5	122.5	Généraux
Food [8]	99.4	98.3	98.2	98.5	102.7[1]	108.3	118.9	144.9	Alimentation [8]

Country or area	2001	2002	2003	2004	2005	2006	2007	2008	Pays ou zone
Pakistan									**Pakistan**
General	103.2	107.4[1]	110.5	118.7	129.5	139.7	150.3	180.8	Généraux
Food	101.8	105.9[1]	108.6	120.2	132.1	143.3	158.8	202.6	Alimentation
Panama[11]									**Panama[11]**
General (2003 = 100)	...	...	100.0	100.4	103.3	105.9	110.3	119.9	Généraux (2003 = 100)
Food (2003 = 100)	...	...	100.0	101.3	105.6	107.0	114.2	131.3	Alimentation (2003 = 100)
Papua New Guinea									**Papouasie-Nvl-Guinée**
General	109.3	122.2	140.2	143.2	145.7	149.2	150.6	166.8	Généraux
Food	109.6	128.3	145.3	146.1	151.2	159.3	160.3	187.0	Alimentation
Paraguay (Asunción)									**Paraguay**
General	107.3	118.5	135.4	141.3	149.5	165.4	178.8	196.9[1]	Généraux
Food	103.8	114.4	139.3	149.7	156.2	182.5	213.2	246.1[1]	Alimentation
Peru[6] (Lima)									**Pérou[6]**
General	102.0	102.2[1]	104.5	108.3	110.1	112.3	114.3	120.9	Généraux
Food	100.5	100.2[1]	101.0	106.6	107.6	110.2	113.0	123.3	Alimentation
Philippines									**Philippines**
General	106.8	110.1	113.9	120.6	129.8	137.9	141.8	155.0	Généraux
Food[10]	104.7	107.1	109.4	116.3	123.8	130.6	134.9	152.3	Alimentation[10]
Poland									**Pologne**
General	105.5	107.5	108.4	112.2	114.6	115.7	118.6	123.6	Généraux
Food[7]	105.1	104.6	103.0	108.6	110.6	111.2	115.9	122.5	Alimentation[7]
Portugal									**Portugal**
General[2]	104.3	108.0[1]	111.6	114.2	116.7	120.4	123.3	126.4	Généraux[2]
Food	106.5	108.1[1]	110.9	112.1	111.3	114.2	117.0	121.1	Alimentation
Puerto Rico									**Porto Rico**
General	107.0	113.6	122.5	137.1	156.1	178.9	191.1[1]	209.4	Généraux
Food	114.1	127.8	145.8	176.3	212.1	257.1	281.0[1]	331.5	Alimentation
Qatar									**Qatar**
General	101.5	101.6	104.0	111.0	120.9	135.2	153.6	176.9	Généraux
Food[8]	99.8	101.1	100.7	104.4	107.7	115.1	123.6	148.2	Alimentation[8]
Republic of Moldova									**République de Moldova**
General	109.8	115.6	129.2	145.3	162.7	183.5	206.2	232.5	Généraux
Food	110.7	115.5	131.2	147.9	168.0	183.4	203.4	234.8	Alimentation
Réunion									**Réunion**
General	102.3	105.1	106.3	108.1	110.4	113.2	114.8	118.2	Généraux
Food	101.5	108.3	107.5	107.5	108.8	111.2	114.0	121.5	Alimentation
Romania									**Roumanie**
General	134.5	164.8	189.9	212.5	231.7	246.9	258.8	279.1	Généraux
Food	135.7	160.5	184.1	201.5	213.8	222.0	230.6	251.9	Alimentation
Russian Federation									**Fédération de Russie**
General	121.5[1]	140.6	159.9	177.3	199.7	219.1	238.8	272.5	Généraux
Food	121.7[1]	136.5	151.8	167.4	190.3	208.4	227.2	274.6	Alimentation
Rwanda (Kigali)									**Rwanda**
General	103.4	105.4	113.2[1]	126.7	138.3	150.6	164.2	189.5	Généraux
Food	106.0	104.7	119.2[1]	141.7	156.1	171.5	185.0	215.2	Alimentation
Saint Helena									**Sainte-Hélène**
General	103.5	104.2	108.1	112.5	115.8	120.8	126.4	136.5	Généraux
Food	102.5	99.0	102.7	108.8	112.7	117.1	117.2	131.2	Alimentation
Saint Lucia									**Sainte-Lucie**
General	101.8	105.0	106.0	107.6	111.8	114.4	...	...	Généraux
Food	103.2	101.9	104.1	104.9	112.3	116.0	...	...	Alimentation
Saint Pierre and Miquelon									**Saint-Pierre-et-Miquelon**
General	102.3	102.5	104.8	106.9	114.0	...	...	...	Généraux
Food	103.5	106.1	106.7	104.9	109.7	...	...	...	Alimentation
Saint Vincent-Gren. (St. Vincent)									**Saint Vincent-Grenadines**
General	100.8[1]	101.5	101.8	104.8	108.7	112.0	119.8	131.8	Généraux
Food	101.0[1]	101.6	100.9	105.6	111.3	115.3	123.9	142.1	Alimentation
Samoa									**Samoa**
General[2]	103.7	112.2	112.3	130.5[1]	133.0	138.1	145.7	162.4	Généraux[2]
	105.1	117.3	115.1	146.2[1]	146.7	152.5	164.3	187.5	Alimentation

Country or area	2001	2002	2003	2004	2005	2006	2007	2008	Pays ou zone
San Marino									**Saint-Marin**
General (2003 = 100)	...	...	100.0[13]	101.4	103.1	105.3	107.9	112.6	Généraux (2003 = 100)
Food (2003 = 100)	...	...	100.0[13]	103.3	108.9	115.0	120.7	130.4	Alimentation (2003 = 100)
Saudi Arabia[33]									**Arabie saoudite**[33]
General	99.2	98.6	97.2	99.5[1]	100.2	102.4	106.7	117.2	Généraux
Food[8]	100.6	100.0	96.9	104.4[1]	107.5	113.3	121.2	138.3	Alimentation[8]
Senegal (Dakar)									**Sénégal**
General	103.0	105.4	105.3	105.9	107.7	110.0	116.4	123.1	Généraux
Food[8]	104.9	110.1	109.4	110.3	114.5	116.0	124.4	136.4	Alimentation[8]
Serbia									**Serbie**
General	195.0	233.0	256.1	284.2	330.0	368.6	392.4	442.8	Généraux
Food	191.9	209.8	211.5	235.1	280.9	310.1	328.7	397.4	Alimentation
Seychelles									**Seychelles**
General	106.0[1]	106.2	109.7	114.0	115.0	114.6	122.1[1]	167.3	Généraux
Food	104.9[1]	105.6	108.2	109.2	110.3	114.3	125.6[1]	173.8	Alimentation
Sierra Leone									**Sierra Leone**
General (2003 = 100)	...	...	100.0	114.9	131.8	142.5	160.8	182.6	Généraux (2003 = 100)
Food (2003 = 100)	...	...	100.0	120.1	137.6	141.0	159.3	186.4	Alimentation (2003 = 100)
Singapore									**Singapour**
General	101.0	100.6	101.1	102.8[1]	103.2	104.2	106.4	113.4	Généraux
Food	100.5	100.5	101.1	103.2[1]	104.6	106.2	109.4	117.8	Alimentation
Slovakia									**Slovaquie**
General	107.1[1]	110.7	120.2	129.2	132.8	138.7	142.5	149.0	Généraux
Food	105.8[1]	107.3	111.0	116.4	114.7	116.4	121.0	130.3	Alimentation
Slovenia[11]									**Slovénie**[11]
General	108.4	116.5	123.0	127.4	130.6[1]	133.8	138.6	146.5	Généraux
Food	109.0	117.5	123.1	124.2	124.3[1]	127.1	137.0	150.8	Alimentation
Solomon Islands (Honiara)									**Iles Salomon**
General	107.8	119.5	129.4	138.7	149.3	161.2	178.1[1]	208.9	Généraux
Food	108.9	122.1	125.0	136.8	145.1	156.7	168.1[1]	208.7	Alimentation
South Africa									**Afrique du Sud**
General	105.7	115.4	122.1	123.8	128.0	134.0	143.5	160.0	Généraux
Food[20]	105.4	122.0	131.9	134.9	137.9	147.8	163.1	190.0	Alimentation[28]
Spain									**Espagne**
General (2001 = 100)	100.0[5]	103.5	106.7	109.9	113.6	117.6[1]	120.9	125.8	Généraux (2001 = 100)
Food (2001 = 100)	100.0[5]	104.7	109.0	113.2	116.3	121.5[1]	126.0	133.4	Alimentation (2001 = 100)
Sri Lanka (Colombo)									**Sri Lanka**
General	114.2	125.1	133.0	143.0	159.7	181.5	163.1[40]	199.9	Généraux
Food	115.2	127.5	134.9	145.5	163.0	184.6	163.4[40]	213.3	Alimentation
Suriname (Paramaribo)									**Suriname**
General (2001 = 100)	100.0[1]	115.9	...	156.9[34]	171.4	190.7	203.0	232.8	Généraux (2001 = 100)
Food (2001 = 100)	100.0[1]	118.1	...	157.8[34]	174.2	182.7	198.0	246.8	Alimentation (2001 = 100)
Swaziland									**Swaziland**
General	107.7	120.2	129.0	133.5	139.9	147.3	159.2[1]	179.8	Généraux
Food	106.5	129.8	145.7	155.7	169.2	194.1[1]	228.3	271.5	Alimentation
Sweden									**Suède**
General	102.4	104.6	106.6	107.0	107.5	109.0	111.4	115.2	Généraux
Food	102.9	106.2	106.6	106.1	105.4	106.2	108.3	115.8	Alimentation
Switzerland									**Suisse**
General	101.0	101.7	102.3	103.1	104.4	105.4[1]	106.1	108.8	Généraux
Food	102.1	104.4	105.7	106.3	105.5	105.4	106.0	109.3	Alimentation
Syrian Arab Republic									**Rép. arabe syrienne**
General	100.4	101.4	108.8[1]	113.5	121.9	134.1[1]	140.1	161.4	Généraux
Food	100.2	99.6	107.2[1]	112.8	122.5	138.1[1]	150.6	181.8	Alimentation
Thailand									**Thaïlande**
General	101.6	102.3	104.1	107.0[1]	111.8	117.0	119.6	126.1	Généraux
Food	100.7	101.0	104.7	109.4[1]	114.9	120.1	125.0	139.4	Alimentation
TFYR of Macedonia									**L'ex-R.Y. Macédoine**
General	105.5	107.4	108.7	108.2	108.8	112.3	114.8	124.4	Généraux
Food	106.9	108.8	107.3	104.0	102.7	105.0	109.1	125.8	Alimentation

Country or area	2001	2002	2003	2004	2005	2006	2007	2008	Pays ou zone
Togo (Lomé)									**Togo**
General	103.9	107.1	106.0	106.5	113.7	116.3	117.3	127.5	Généraux
Food [10]	105.2	109.3	103.1	101.9	113.0	111.7	114.9	138.3	Alimentation [10]
Tonga									**Tonga**
General [2]	108.3	119.5[1]	133.5	148.1	160.4	172.0	180.8	198.9	Généraux [2]
Food	111.8	130.6[1]	143.1	156.1	165.5	170.4	182.9	197.7	Alimentation
Trinidad and Tobago									**Trinité-et-Tobago**
General	105.6	109.9	114.2[1]	118.3	126.5	137.0	147.9	165.7	Généraux
Food	114.0	125.6	142.9[1]	161.1	198.1	244.1	286.6	360.9	Alimentation
Tunisia									**Tunisie**
General	102.0	104.8	107.6	111.5	113.8	118.9	122.6	128.8	Généraux
Food	102.0	106.1	109.7	115.1	115.2	121.4	124.8	132.6	Alimentation
Turkey									**Turquie**
General	154.4	223.8	280.4	310.1	329.5[1]	361.1	392.7	433.7	Généraux
Food	150.3[10]	225.3[10]	290.0[10]	316.1[10]	112.1	123.0	138.2	155.9	Alimentation
Tuvalu (Funafuti)									**Tuvalu**
General	101.5	106.7[1]	110.2	113.3	117.0	119.0	121.6[1]	...	Généraux
Food	105.3	109.4[1]	117.4	120.8	127.4	129.2	128.6[1]	...	Alimentation
Uganda									**Ouganda**
General	101.9	101.6	110.5	114.5	124.1	133.3	141.4[1]	158.5	Généraux
Food	96.6	92.5	106.7	111.4	126.1	139.1	142.8[1]	171.1	Alimentation
Ukraine									**Ukraine**
General	112.0	112.8	118.7	129.4	146.9	160.2	180.8	226.4	Généraux
Food [10]	114.4	114.4	121.5	135.1	157.5	166.5	182.4	247.0	Alimentation [10]
United Arab Emirates									**Emirats arabes unis**
General	102.8	105.8	109.1	114.6	121.7	133.0	147.8	166.0[1]	Généraux
Food	101.0[10]	102.4[10]	104.7[10]	112.0[10]	117.0[10]	123.5[10]	130.4[1]	116.3	Alimentation
United Kingdom									**Royaume-Uni**
General	101.8	103.5	106.5	109.6	112.7	116.3	121.3	126.1	Généraux
Food	103.3	104.0	105.4	106.0	107.3	109.6	114.6	125.2	Alimentation
U. Rep. of Tanzania [35]									**Rép.-Unie de Tanzanie** [35]
General	105.1	109.9[1]	115.8	121.3	127.4	136.6	146.2	161.2	Généraux
Food	106.1	110.5[1]	117.8	127.5	133.5	142.9	152.9	172.2	Alimentation
United States [36]									**Etats-Unis** [36]
General	102.8	104.5	106.9	109.7	113.4	117.1	120.4	125.0	Généraux
Food	103.2	105.0	107.3	111.0	113.6	116.3	120.9	127.6	Alimentation
Uruguay (Montevideo)									**Uruguay**
General	104.4	118.9	142.0	155.0	162.3	172.7	186.7	201.4	Généraux
Food	103.1	117.2	142.5	159.2	165.7	176.0	202.5	230.3	Alimentation
Vanuatu									**Vanuatu**
General	103.6	105.7	108.8	110.4	111.7	114.0	118.5	124.2	Généraux
Food	102.2	102.7	105.0	108.5	108.1	111.8	116.1	125.4	Alimentation
Venezuela (Bol. R. of) (Caracas)									**Venezuela (Rép. bol. du)**
General	112.5	137.8	180.6	219.9	255.0	289.8	343.9	452.1[1]	Généraux
Food	116.1	149.0	205.2	274.6	332.5	399.3	506.3	738.0[1]	Alimentation
Viet Nam									**Viet Nam**
General	99.7	103.7	107.0	115.0	125.5[1]	133.4[1]	143.8	177.0	Généraux
Food	98.6[10]	106.1[10]	108.7[10]	119.8[10]	136.2[21]	144.8[1]	156.0	192.1	Alimentation
Yemen									**Yémen**
General	111.9	125.6	139.2	156.6	174.5	211.6	232.8	249.1[1]	Généraux
Food	115.7	121.2	141.4	168.3	199.9	269.5	317.9	323.2[1]	Alimentation
Zambia									**Zambie**
General	121.4	148.4	180.1	212.5	251.4	274.1	303.3	341.1	Généraux
Food [10]	118.9	151.1	184.5	214.7	254.5	267.1	281.1	319.9	Alimentation [10]
Zimbabwe [37]									**Zimbabwe** [37]
General	0.2[1]	0.4	1.9	8.4	28.3	316.6	21 602.0	...	Généraux
Food	0.2[1]	0.4	1.8	8.6	27.9	316.0	23 620.2	...	Alimentation

Source:
International Labour Organization (ILO), Geneva, the ILO labour statistics database, last accessed October 2009.

Source:
Bureau international du Travail (BIT), Genève, la base de données du BIT, dernier accès octobre 2009.

1	Series linked to former series.	1	Série enchaînée à la précédente.
2	Excluding rent.	2	Non compris le groupe "Loyer".
3	December.	3	Décembre.
4	Including beverages and tobacco.	4	Y compris les boissons et le tabac.
5	Series (base 2001 = 100) replacing former series.	5	Série (base 2001 = 100) remplaçant la précédente.
6	Metropolitan area.	6	Région métropolitaine.
7	Including alcoholic beverages.	7	Y compris les boissons alcoolisées.
8	Including tobacco.	8	Y compris le tabac.
9	Government officials.	9	Fonctionnaires.
10	Including alcoholic beverages and tobacco.	10	Y compris les boissons alcoolisées et le tabac.
11	Urban areas.	11	Régions urbaines.
12	Prior to December 2003: Douala and Yaoundé only.	12	Avant déc. 2003: Douala et Yaoundé seulement.
13	Series (base 2003=100) replacing former series.	13	Série (base 2003=100) remplaçant la précédente.
14	Low-income group.	14	Familles à revenu modique.
15	Excluding beverages.	15	Non compris les boissons.
16	Central area.	16	Région centrale.
17	Index base: 2007=100	17	Base de l'indice: 2007=100.
18	Including tobacco, beverages and public catering.	18	Y compris le tabac, les boissons et la restauration.
19	Series (base 2005=100) replacing former series.	19	Série (base 2005=100) remplaçant la précédente.
20	Series (base 2004=100) replacing former series.	20	Série (base 2004=100) remplaçant la précédente.
21	Series replacing former series.	21	Série remplaçant la précédente.
22	Five cities.	22	Cinq villes.
23	Average July to December.	23	Moyenne de juillet à décembre.
24	Annual averages are based on the months Feb.-Dec. and the mean of January both years.	24	Les moyennes annuelles sont basées sur les mois de fév.-déc. et la moyenne de janvier des deux années.
25	Excluding tobacco.	25	Non compris le tabac.
26	June of each year.	26	Juin de chaque année.
27	May-December.	27	Mai-décembre.
28	Food only.	28	Alimentation seulement.
29	Beginning January 1998, including alcoholic beverages and tobacco.	29	A partir de janvier, y compris les boissons alcoolisées et le tabac.
30	January-November.	30	Janvier-novembre.
31	July-December.	31	Juillet-décembre.
32	Average of the last three quarters.	32	Moyenne des trois derniers trimestres.
33	All cities.	33	Ensemble des villes.
34	March-December.	34	Mars-décembre.
35	Tanganyika only.	35	Tanganyika seulement.
36	All urban consumers.	36	Tous les consommateurs urbains.
37	Due to lack of space, multiply each figure by 1000.	37	En raison du manque de place, multiplier chaque chiffre par 1000.
38	African population.	38	Population Africaine.
39	Industrial workers.	39	Ouvriers industriels.
40	Series (base 2002=100) replacing former series.	40	Série (base 2002=100) remplaçant la précédente.

Technical notes: tables 28-30

Table 28: The series generally relate to the average earnings per worker in manufacturing industries, according to the *International Standard Industrial Classification of All Economic Activities* (ISIC) Revision 2 or Revision 3. The data are published in the ILO *Yearbook of Labour Statistics* and on the ILO web site http://laborsta.ilo.org and generally cover all employees (i.e. wage earners and salaried employees) of both sexes, irrespective of age. Data which refer exclusively to wage earners (i.e. manual or production workers), salaried employees (i.e. non-manual workers), or to total employment are also shown when available. Earnings generally include bonuses, cost of living allowances, taxes, social insurance contributions payable by the employed person and, in some cases, payments in kind, and normally exclude social insurance contributions payable by the employers, family allowances and other social security benefits. The time of year to which the figures refer is not the same for all countries. In some cases, the series may show wage rates instead of earnings; this is indicated in footnotes.

Table 29: The producer price index (PPI) can be generally described as an index for measuring the average change in the prices of goods and services either as they leave the place of production or as they enter the production process. As such, producer price indices can represent input prices (at purchasers' prices) and output prices (at basic or producer prices) with different levels of aggregation.

The industrial coverage of the PPI can vary across countries. Normally, the PPIs refer to indices related to the agricultural, mining, manufacturing, transport and telecommunications, and public utilities sectors. Many countries are progressively developing service industry PPIs for incorporation within their larger PPI frameworks. PPI prices should be actual transaction prices recorded at the time the transaction occurs (i.e. when ownership changes).

PPIs can be calculated in a number of different combinations. In this publication, the PPIs are classified according to the following scheme:

    (a)   Components of supply
           Domestic supply
           Domestic production for domestic market
           Agricultural products
           Industrial products
           Imported goods
    (b)   Stage of processing
           Raw materials
           Intermediate goods
    (c)   End-use

Notes techniques : tableaux 28 à 30

Tableau 28: Les séries se rapportent généralement aux gains moyens des salariés des industries manufacturières (activités de fabrication), suivant la *Classification internationale type, par industrie, de toutes les branches d'activité économique* (CITI, Rev. 2 ou Rev.3). Les données sont publiées dans *l'Annuaire des statistiques du travail* du BIT et sur le site Web du BIT http://laborsta.ilo.org et généralement portent sur l'ensemble des salariés (qu'ils perçoivent un salaire ou un traitement au mois) des deux sexes, indépendamment de leur âge. Les données qui portent exclusivement sur les salariés horaires (ouvriers, travailleurs manuels), sur les employés percevant un traitement (travailleurs autres que manuels, cadres), ou sur l'emploi total sont aussi présentées si elles sont disponibles. Les gains comprennent en général les primes, les indemnités pour coût de la vie, les impôts, les cotisations de sécurité sociale à la charge de l'employé, et dans certains cas des paiements en nature, mais ne comprennent pas en règle générale la part patronale des cotisations d'assurance sociale, les allocations familiales et les autres prestations de sécurité sociale. La période de l'année visée par les données n'est pas la même pour tous les pays. Dans certains cas, les séries présentent les taux horaires et non pas les gains, ce présente qui est alors signalé en note.

Tableau 29: L'indice des prix à la production peut être caractérisé de manière générale comme un indice permettant de mesurer le changement moyen des prix des biens et des services soit au moment où ils quittent le lieu de production soit au moment où ils arrivent au processus de production. Les indices des prix à la production peuvent donc représenter les prix des intrants (aux prix d'acquisition) et les prix à la sortie de fabrique (aux prix de base, ou prix à la production), les agrégats étant de différents niveaux.

Les branches d'activité couvertes par l'indice des prix à la production peuvent n'être pas les mêmes d'un pays à l'autre. Normalement, l'indice concerne l'agriculture, les industries extractives, les industries manufacturières, les transports et télécommunications et les services publics de distribution. Nombre de pays mettent peu à peu au point des indices des prix à la production pour les services, de manière à pouvoir les intégrer à leurs indices des prix à la production plus généraux. Les prix servant pour ces indices doivent être des prix effectifs de transaction enregistrés au moment où s'effectue la transaction (au moment où le propriétaire change).

Les indices des prix à la production peuvent se calculer selon plusieurs combinaisons différentes. Dans la présente publication, on les classe de la manière ci-après:

Consumer goods
Capital goods

Though a few countries are still compiling the wholesale price index (WPI), which is the precedent of the PPI, the WPI has been replaced in most countries by the PPI because of the broader coverage provided by the PPI in terms of products and industries and the conceptual concordance between the PPI and the System of National Accounts. The WPI would normally cover the price of products as they flow from the wholesaler to the retailer and is an index for measuring the price level changes in markets other than retail.

For a more detailed explanation about the PPI, please refer to the *Producer Price Index Manual: Theory and Practice* published by the International Monetary Fund in 2004.

Table 30: A consumer price index is usually estimated as a series of summary measures of the period-to-period proportional change in the prices of a fixed set of consumer goods and services of constant quantity and characteristics, acquired, used or paid for by the reference population. Each summary measure is constructed as a weighted average of a large number of elementary aggregate indices. Each of the elementary aggregate indices is estimated using a sample of prices for a defined set of goods and services obtained in, or by residents of, a specific region from a given set of outlets or other sources of consumption goods and services.

The table presents the general consumer price index for all groups of consumption items combined, and the food index including nonalcoholic beverages only. Where alcoholic beverages and/or tobacco are included, this is indicated in footnotes.

(a) Eléments de l'offre
  Offre intérieure
  Production nationale pour le marché intérieur
  Produits agricoles
  Produits industriels
  Produits importés
(b) Stade de la transformation
  Matières premières
  Produits intermédiaires
(c) Utilisation finale
  Biens de consommation
  Biens d'équipement

Même s'il y a encore quelques pays qui compilent l'indice des prix de gros, qui est l'ancêtre de l'indice des prix à la production, la plupart l'ont remplacé par ce dernier, qui offre une couverture plus large de produits et de branches d'activité, et coïncide dans ses concepts avec le Système de comptabilité nationale. L'indice des prix de gros suivait normalement le prix des produits à mesure qu'ils passaient du grossiste au détaillant il permet de mesurer les changements du niveau des prix sur les marchés autres que le marché de détail.

Pour un complément de détails sur l'indice des prix à la production, on se reportera au "Producer Price Index Manual, Theory and Practice" publié par le Fonds monétaire international en 2004.

Tableau 30: Un indice est généralement estimé à partir d'une suite de mesures synthétiques des variations relatives, d'une période à l'autre, des prix d'un ensemble fixe de biens et de services de consommation constants en quantité et par leurs caractéristiques, acquis, utilisés ou payés par la population de référence. Chaque mesure synthétique est obtenue comme une moyenne pondérée d'un grand nombre d'indices de prix d'agrégats élémentaires. L'indice de chaque agrégat élémentaire est estimé au moyen d'un échantillon de prix pour un ensemble fixe de biens et de services que se procurent les individus de la population de référence dans une région donnée, ou qui habitent cette région, auprès d'un ensemble spécifié de points de vente ou auprès d'autres fournisseurs de biens et de services de consommation.

Le tableau présente les indices généraux des prix à la consommation pour tous les groupes d'articles de consommation combinés, et un indice "Alimentation", y compris les boissons non alcoolisées seulement. Dans le cas où les boissons alcoolisées et/ou le tabac sont compris dans le groupe "alimentation", l'utilisateur sera informé par un appel de note.

Region, country or area Région, pays ou zone	Agriculture - Agriculture					Food - Produits alimentaires				
	2003	2004	2005	2006	2007	2003	2004	2005	2006	2007
World – Monde	**105**	**110**	**112**	**114**	**116**	**105**	**110**	**112**	**113**	**115**
Africa – Afrique	**110**	**113**	**117**	**121**	**117**	**111**	**114**	**117**	**123**	**118**
Algeria – Algérie	125	136	137	142	135	125	136	137	143	136
Angola – Angola	129	137	146	148	149	129	138	147	150	151
Benin – Bénin	114	120	114	106	102	116	123	120	114	107
Botswana – Botswana	102	109	112	111	111	103	109	113	111	111
Burkina Faso – Burkina Faso	126	119	137	142	123	124	110	126	127	123
Burundi – Burundi	107	109	112	102	100	107	107	114	100	101
Cameroon – Cameroun	108	108	113	110	109	108	112	115	112	113
Cape Verde – Cap-Vert	88	99	102	109	118	88	99	102	109	118
Central African Rep. – Rép. centrafricaine	103	106	106	107	100	107	110	111	111	104
Chad – Tchad	110	109	119	115	104	114	108	120	121	110
Comoros – Comores	104	104	99	102	106	104	104	99	102	106
Congo – Congo	106	113	117	120	122	106	113	116	120	122
Côte d'Ivoire – Côte d'Ivoire	99	100	105	107	106	103	108	109	113	114
Dem. Rep. of the Congo – Rép. dém. du Congo	96	97	97	103	97	97	97	97	103	97
Djibouti – Djibouti	114	113	115	154	153	114	113	115	154	153
Egypt – Egypte	110	114	114	119	114	111	114	116	121	115
Equatorial Guinea – Guinée équatoriale	95	94	94	95	95	93	95	95	95	95
Eritrea – Erythrée	88	87	103	104	102	87	87	104	104	102
Ethiopia – Ethiopie	113	121	132	135	135	114	123	134	136	135
Gabon – Gabon	100	100	100	101	103	100	100	100	101	103
Gambia – Gambie	83	105	89	95	66	83	105	89	95	66
Ghana – Ghana	117	121	126	127	124	117	122	127	128	124
Guinea – Guinée	106	110	114	119	123	108	112	116	121	125
Guinea-Bissau – Guinée-Bissau	105	108	114	114	115	105	108	113	114	114
Kenya – Kenya	112	113	115	129	134	113	113	115	131	136
Lesotho – Lesotho	90	88	92	68	88	89	88	92	70	88
Liberia – Libéria	97	103	107	106	117	96	100	107	109	122
Libyan Arab Jamah. – Jamah. arabe libyenne	105	102	104	100	101	105	102	104	100	101
Madagascar – Madagascar	97	102	116	118	119	98	103	118	119	121
Malawi – Malawi	100	105	90	123	140	99	102	87	121	142
Mali – Mali	124	115	123	122	127	120	111	127	133	146
Mauritania – Mauritanie	107	109	114	113	114	107	109	114	113	114
Mauritius – Maurice	108	112	106	104	100	109	113	107	104	101
Morocco – Maroc	129	132	124	146	119	130	132	124	147	119
Mozambique – Mozambique	110	117	123	127	114	104	109	111	109	99
Namibia – Namibie	103	99	103	102	101	102	99	102	101	101
Niger – Niger	133	112	130	139	145	133	113	130	140	146
Nigeria – Nigéria	109	115	121	130	119	109	115	121	130	119
Réunion – Réunion	100	103	99	100	95	100	103	99	100	95
Rwanda – Rwanda	113	113	120	121	120	114	113	120	121	120
Sao Tome and Principe – Sao Tomé-et-Principe	108	105	110	111	114	108	105	110	111	114
Senegal – Sénégal	86	85	100	83	73	83	85	100	82	73
Seychelles – Seychelles	90	88	87	88	90	89	88	87	89	89
Sierra Leone – Sierra Leone	132	146	165	200	180	133	147	168	204	183
Somalia – Somalie	104	105	107	103	103	104	105	107	103	103

31

Agricultural production *(continued)*
Index base: 1999-01=100
Production agricole *(suite)*
Indices base : 1999-01 = 100

Region, country or area Région, pays ou zone	Agriculture - Agriculture					Food - Produits alimentaires				
	2003	2004	2005	2006	2007	2003	2004	2005	2006	2007
South Africa – Afrique du Sud	104	107	112	108	108	104	108	113	110	109
Sudan – Soudan	116	113	116	125	123	116	112	116	125	123
Swaziland – Swaziland	105	107	115	111	109	109	110	118	113	111
Togo – Togo	106	109	100	103	107	103	106	110	118	121
Tunisia – Tunisie	129	111	117	116	117	130	111	118	116	118
Uganda – Ouganda	108	108	106	104	106	109	108	107	105	106
United Rep. of Tanzania – Rép.-Unie de Tanzanie	102	131	125	132	132	102	130	122	130	132
Western Sahara – Sahara occidental	100	100	100	97	97	100	100	100	97	97
Zambia – Zambie	113	119	128	119	117	112	112	113	120	115
Zimbabwe – Zimbabwe	79	81	70	70	72	89	96	82	88	84
Americas – Amériques	**106**	**111**	**113**	**112**	**116**	**106**	**111**	**113**	**112**	**116**
Antigua and Barbuda – Antigua-et-Barbuda	107	108	103	102	105	107	108	103	102	104
Argentina – Argentine	104	106	117	117	125	104	106	117	117	125
Bahamas – Bahamas	100	104	107	99	100	100	104	107	99	100
Barbados – Barbade	93	100	108	109	116	93	100	108	109	116
Belize – Belize	99	115	115	113	112	99	115	115	113	112
Bermuda – Bermudes	98	94	92	93	96	98	94	92	93	96
Bolivia – Bolivie	114	112	118	112	113	114	112	118	112	113
Brazil – Brésil	121	127	130	126	132	121	125	129	125	131
British Virgin Islands – Iles Vierges britanniques	100	100	100	100	100	100	100	100	100	100
Canada – Canada	96	106	111	110	106	97	107	111	110	106
Cayman Islands – Iles Caïmanes	100	100	100	101	102	100	100	100	101	102
Chile – Chili	108	112	118	118	115	108	112	119	118	115
Colombia – Colombie	105	111	114	100	99	105	111	114	100	98
Costa Rica – Costa Rica	101	99	108	112	118	102	102	111	116	122
Cuba – Cuba	108	112	92	80	83	109	113	93	80	83
Dominica – Dominique	85	87	85	97	99	85	87	85	97	99
Dominican Republic – Rép. dominicaine	117	119	125	137	135	119	121	127	139	137
Ecuador – Equateur	104	112	111	106	109	106	114	112	109	112
El Salvador – El Salvador	87	94	98	102	109	92	99	103	109	115
Falkland Is. (Malvinas) – Iles Falkland (Malvinas)	99	99	99	99	103	96	96	96	96	103
French Guiana – Guyane française	97	99	90	87	79	97	99	90	87	79
Greenland – Groenland	99	99	99	99	99	100	99	99	99	99
Grenada – Grenade	95	102	70	84	89	95	102	70	84	89
Guadeloupe – Guadeloupe	97	96	89	81	80	97	96	89	81	80
Guatemala – Guatemala	105	106	119	121	130	108	110	125	128	137
Guyana – Guyana	106	104	90	101	100	106	104	90	101	100
Haiti – Haïti	102	101	103	100	100	103	102	104	101	101
Honduras – Honduras	121	127	132	136	139	126	132	138	142	144
Jamaica – Jamaïque	100	97	94	99	98	100	97	93	99	98
Martinique – Martinique	97	98	100	99	99	97	98	100	99	99
Mexico – Mexique	107	110	110	117	120	108	110	110	118	121
Montserrat – Montserrat	100	99	99	99	101	100	99	99	99	101
Nicaragua – Nicaragua	120	116	129	126	128	121	120	130	129	129
Panama – Panama	101	102	106	108	111	101	102	106	108	110
Paraguay – Paraguay	115	115	115	122	146	117	114	117	125	150
Peru – Pérou	111	113	123	131	134	112	113	124	131	136
Puerto Rico – Porto Rico	96	101	91	93	94	95	100	91	93	93
Saint Kitts and Nevis – Saint-Kitts-et-Nevis	98	124	63	57	61	98	124	63	57	61

31

Agricultural production *(continued)*
Index base: 1999-01=100
Production agricole *(suite)*
Indices base : 1999-01 = 100

Region, country or area Région, pays ou zone	Agriculture - Agriculture					Food - Produits alimentaires				
	2003	2004	2005	2006	2007	2003	2004	2005	2006	2007
Saint Lucia – Sainte-Lucie	88	91	81	85	89	88	91	81	85	89
Saint Pierre and Miq. – Saint-Pierre-et-Miquelon	101	106	99	106	94	101	106	99	106	94
Saint Vincent-Gren. – Saint Vincent-Grenadines	97	99	96	98	100	96	99	96	98	100
Suriname – Suriname	95	96	96	106	106	95	96	96	106	106
Trinidad and Tobago – Trinité-et-Tobago	117	111	109	108	109	117	111	109	107	109
United States – Etats-Unis	101	107	106	104	108	101	106	105	104	109
United States Virgin Is. – Iles Vierges américaines	99	99	99	99	101	99	99	99	99	101
Uruguay – Uruguay	96	118	116	128	124	97	120	118	131	126
Venezuela (Bol. R. of) – Venezuela (Rép. bol. du)	98	94	106	104	108	98	95	106	105	108
Asia – Asie	**107**	**112**	**116**	**120**	**123**	**108**	**111**	**116**	**119**	**122**
Afghanistan – Afghanistan	111	107	122	110	120	112	108	124	111	122
Armenia – Arménie	111	128	148	158	169	112	129	150	160	172
Azerbaijan – Azerbaïdjan	118	120	135	134	136	121	120	133	136	140
Bahrain – Bahreïn	121	117	122	119	117	121	117	122	119	117
Bangladesh – Bangladesh	106	104	116	118	116	106	104	117	118	117
Bhutan – Bhoutan	106	117	152	157	154	106	117	152	158	154
Brunei Darussalam – Brunéi Darussalam	107	124	105	127	140	107	124	104	127	140
Cambodia – Cambodge	116	111	143	154	164	117	112	143	155	165
China [1] – Chine [1]	109	116	120	123	125	109	116	120	123	125
Cyprus – Chypre	103	107	97	94	91	103	107	97	94	91
Georgia – Géorgie	104	97	109	69	81	106	98	111	72	85
India – Inde	104	103	108	113	121	104	102	107	112	119
Indonesia – Indonésie	115	122	126	132	137	115	122	126	131	136
Iran (Islamic Rep. of) – Iran (Rép. islamique d')	115	117	124	127	123	116	117	125	129	125
Iraq – Iraq	95	97	108	112	94	96	97	109	113	95
Israel – Israël	108	114	111	110	93	108	114	111	110	93
Japan – Japon	94	97	98	95	98	94	96	98	96	99
Jordan – Jordanie	120	134	143	144	135	120	134	144	144	135
Kazakhstan – Kazakhstan	108	105	114	124	136	106	103	112	123	137
Korea, Dem . P. R. – Corée, R. p. dém. de	112	111	114	113	111	112	112	115	114	111
Korea, Republic of – Corée, République de	90	94	94	94	95	91	94	94	94	96
Kuwait – Koweït	123	133	121	128	129	123	133	121	129	130
Kyrgyzstan – Kirghizistan	101	103	101	102	100	103	105	103	103	103
Lao People's Dem. Rep. – Rép. dém. pop. lao	110	116	119	124	132	113	118	122	128	132
Lebanon – Liban	99	107	102	103	104	100	107	103	104	104
Malaysia – Malaisie	113	119	126	132	131	113	118	126	131	131
Maldives – Maldives	103	113	78	109	50	103	113	78	109	50
Mongolia – Mongolie	67	78	74	78	78	66	79	74	78	78
Myanmar – Myanmar	121	129	133	147	157	122	130	134	148	158
Nepal – Népal	110	114	115	118	117	110	114	115	118	117
Occ. Palestinian Terr. – Terr. palestinien occupé	110	101	112	113	117	110	101	112	113	117
Oman – Oman	86	104	119	105	107	85	104	119	105	107
Pakistan – Pakistan	103	111	115	117	122	105	109	114	117	124
Philippines – Philippines	109	117	119	123	128	110	116	118	122	127
Qatar – Qatar	89	100	67	63	77	89	100	67	63	77
Saudi Arabia – Arabie saoudite	117	134	116	113	115	117	134	116	113	115
Singapore – Singapour	113	132	100	123	181	113	132	100	123	181
Sri Lanka – Sri Lanka	103	99	107	109	108	103	98	108	110	109
Syrian Arab Republic – Rép. arabe syrienne	114	120	119	132	118	118	123	121	137	120

31

Agricultural production *(continued)*
Index base: 1999-01=100
Production agricole *(suite)*
Indices base : 1999-01 = 100

Region, country or area Région, pays ou zone	Agriculture - Agriculture					Food - Produits alimentaires				
	2003	2004	2005	2006	2007	2003	2004	2005	2006	2007
Tajikistan – Tadjikistan	133	145	146	147	152	128	145	153	158	166
Thailand – Thaïlande	110	111	110	114	121	110	110	109	113	121
Timor-Leste – Timor-Leste	110	116	120	118	108	111	117	122	120	108
Turkey – Turquie	103	104	110	110	101	103	104	111	111	101
Turkmenistan – Turkménistan	112	125	126	118	125	126	128	131	136	132
United Arab Emirates – Emirats arabes unis	51	58	58	54	55	51	58	58	54	55
Uzbekistan – Ouzbékistan	107	116	124	130	131	112	117	124	136	139
Viet Nam – Viet Nam	114	120	122	126	128	114	120	122	124	127
Yemen – Yémen	113	115	117	124	129	114	115	117	123	128
Europe – Europe	97	105	101	99	99	97	105	101	99	99
Albania – Albanie	108	112	111	117	113	109	113	112	119	115
Austria – Autriche	93	96	94	92	95	93	96	94	92	95
Belarus – Bélarus	106	121	127	135	139	106	121	126	135	139
Bosnia and Herzegovina – Bosnie-Herzégovine	96	120	119	127	126	96	120	119	127	126
Bulgaria – Bulgarie	79	95	77	90	73	76	93	75	89	72
Croatia – Croatie	86	91	88	94	99	85	91	88	94	98
Czech Republic – République tchèque	87	106	96	95	96	87	106	96	95	96
Denmark – Danemark	100	101	102	102	102	100	101	102	102	102
Estonia – Estonie	109	107	116	115	127	109	107	116	115	127
Faeroe Islands – Iles Féroé	30	59	78	68	67	30	59	78	68	67
Finland – Finlande	101	101	106	103	102	101	101	106	103	102
France – France	94	101	97	94	93	94	101	97	94	93
Germany – Allemagne	92	100	96	93	95	92	100	96	93	96
Greece – Grèce	87	94	96	85	82	87	94	96	89	87
Hungary – Hongrie	86	119	103	101	97	86	119	103	101	98
Iceland – Islande	104	105	104	104	104	105	106	105	106	106
Ireland – Irlande	96	97	95	94	92	96	97	95	94	92
Italy – Italie	91	101	99	95	94	91	101	99	95	94
Latvia – Lettonie	109	111	126	116	128	109	111	126	117	128
Liechtenstein – Liechtenstein	100	100	100	100	96	100	100	100	100	96
Lithuania – Lituanie	117	120	124	113	128	117	120	124	113	129
Luxembourg – Luxembourg	94	94	89	53	56	94	94	89	53	56
Malta – Malte	97	97	90	98	95	97	97	90	98	95
Netherlands – Pays-Bas	90	95	92	91	92	90	95	92	91	92
Norway – Norvège	97	101	98	97	98	97	101	98	97	98
Poland – Pologne	101	110	104	102	103	101	110	104	102	103
Portugal – Portugal	94	103	96	100	96	94	103	96	100	96
Republic of Moldova – République de Moldova	107	113	115	112	87	110	116	119	115	89
Romania – Roumanie	105	126	105	107	91	105	127	106	108	91
Russian Federation – Fédération de Russie	104	112	115	118	123	103	112	115	118	123
Serbia and Montenegro – Serbie-et-Monténégro	100	113	105	...	...	100	113	106	...	...
Slovakia – Slovaquie	95	110	109	89	82	95	111	110	89	82
Slovenia – Slovénie	103	106	102	100	103	103	106	102	100	103
Spain – Espagne	111	107	94	101	99	112	107	94	102	99
Sweden – Suède	99	102	100	98	99	99	102	100	98	100
Switzerland – Suisse	97	101	100	99	102	97	101	100	99	103
TFYR of Macedonia – L'ex-R.Y. Macédoine	93	104	105	104	109	93	105	105	105	111
Ukraine – Ukraine	99	111	118	116	108	99	111	118	116	108
United Kingdom – Royaume-Uni	97	98	98	96	92	97	98	98	96	93

31

Agricultural production *(continued)*
Index base: 1999-01=100
Production agricole *(suite)*
Indices base : 1999-01 = 100

Region, country or area Région, pays ou zone	Agriculture - Agriculture					Food - Produits alimentaires				
	2003	2004	2005	2006	2007	2003	2004	2005	2006	2007
Oceania – Océanie	99	97	102	88	88	103	101	104	90	92
American Samoa – Samoa américaines	127	121	121	127	128	127	121	121	127	128
Australia – Australie	94	87	96	74	73	98	92	98	74	76
Cook Islands – Iles Cook	60	51	51	51	63	60	51	51	51	63
Fiji – Fidji	92	96	99	101	92	92	96	99	101	92
French Polynesia – Polynésie française	109	109	119	112	112	109	109	119	112	112
Guam – Guam	103	107	107	108	108	103	107	107	108	108
Kiribati – Kiribati	100	124	124	123	126	100	124	124	123	126
Micronesia (Fed. St. of) – Micronésie (Et. féd. de)	100	100	100	100	103	100	100	100	100	103
Nauru – Nauru	100	100	100	99	108	100	100	100	99	108
New Caledonia – Nouvelle-Calédonie	97	103	97	95	98	97	102	97	95	99
New Zealand – Nouvelle-Zélande	111	116	114	117	119	112	118	116	119	121
Niue – Nioué	100	100	101	101	105	100	100	101	101	105
Papua New Guinea – Papouasie-Nvl-Guinée	104	106	109	108	110	105	108	100	111	111
Samoa – Samoa	104	104	106	106	106	104	104	106	106	106
Solomon Islands – Iles Salomon	101	110	117	116	117	101	110	117	116	117
Tokelau – Tokélaou	100	100	100	100	100	100	100	100	100	100
Tonga – Tonga	103	103	103	104	104	103	103	103	104	104
Tuvalu – Tuvalu	108	111	111	111	114	108	111	111	111	114
Vanuatu – Vanuatu	94	108	107	107	109	94	108	107	107	109
Wallis and Futuna Islands – Iles Wallis et Futuna	100	99	99	101	103	100	99	99	101	103

Source:
Food and Agriculture Organization of the United Nations (FAO), Rome,
FAOSTAT database, last accessed October 2009.

Source:
Organisation des Nations Unies pour l'alimentation et l'agriculture (FAO), Rome, la
base de données FAOSTAT, dernier accès octobre 2009.

1   For statistical purposes, the data for China do not include those for the
     Hong Kong Special Administrative Region (Hong Kong SAR) and
     Macau Special Administrative Region (Macao SAR).

1   Pour la présentation des statistiques, les données pour la Chine ne
     comprennent pas la Région Administrative Spéciale de Hong Kong (Hong
     Kong RAS) et la Région Administrative Spéciale de Macao (Macao
     RAS).

Region, country or area Région, pays ou zone	1998	1999	2000	2001	2002	2003	2004	2005	2006	2007
World **Monde**	**2 083 560**	**2 085 858**	**2 060 370**	**2 108 250**	**2 028 395**	**2 088 796**	**2 279 241**	**2 266 604**	**2 228 041**	**2 342 427**
Africa **Afrique**	**115 028**	**114 179**	**111 879**	**116 432**	**117 693**	**132 983**	**132 454**	**142 094**	**150 312**	**146 475**
Algeria Algérie	3 026	2 021	935	2 659	1 953	4 266	4 033	3 528	4 018	4 133
Angola Angola	610	541	510	586	717	717	668	871	724	731
Benin Bénin	867	974	993	943	926	1 043	1 109	1 152	934	1 221
Botswana Botswana	15	21	25	23	35	36	36	36	45	48
Burkina Faso Burkina Faso	2 657	2 700	2 286	3 109	3 119	3 564	2 902	3 650	3 681	3 736
Burundi Burundi	261	265	245	273	282	279	280	288	269	279
Cameroon Cameroun	1 412	1 185	1 275	1 356	1 499	1 584	1 684	1 660	1 407	1 567
Cape Verde Cap-Vert	5	36	24	20	5	12	10	4	12	12
Central African Rep. Rép. centrafricaine	148	161	166	183	193	202	210	230	172	201
Chad Tchad	1 312	1 231	930	1 321	1 212	1 618	1 213	1 853	1 913	3 083
Comoros Comores	21	21	21	21	21	21	21	21	21	21
Congo Congo	13	9	10	18	18	20	21	21	9	10
Côte d'Ivoire Côte d'Ivoire	1 243	1 264	1 286	1 308	1 330	1 334	1 378	1 423	1 400	1 396
Dem. Rep. of the Congo Rép. dém. du Congo	1 621	1 593	1 572	1 546	1 520	1 521	1 522	1 523	1 524	1 522
Egypt Egypte	17 964	19 401	20 106	18 561	20 194	20 682	20 823	22 996	22 991	22 059
Eritrea Erythrée	458	319	121	183	52	99	80	152	199	177
Ethiopia Ethiopie	7 210	8 393	8 020	9 586	9 002	9 533	10 697	13 365	13 393	13 666
Gabon Gabon	27	28	27	26	25	32	32	32	32	34
Gambia Gambie	107	151	176	200	139	205	224	206	215	281
Ghana Ghana	1 788	1 686	1 711	1 627	2 155	2 041	1 830	1 948	1 919	1 852
Guinea Guinée	1 572	1 656	1 801	1 721	1 846	1 984	2 136	2 290	2 445	2 601
Guinea-Bissau Guinée-Bissau	139	145	178	162	151	143	171	213	225	203
Kenya Kenya	2 927	2 802	2 591	3 369	3 046	3 351	3 199	3 585	3 955	3 755
Lesotho Lesotho	169	174	179	242	195	127	105	102	89	73
Liberia Libéria	209	196	183	145	110	100	110	155	107	155

32

Cereals *(continued)*
Production: thousand metric tons
Céréales *(suite)*
Production: milliers de tonnes

Region, country or area Région, pays ou zone	1998	1999	2000	2001	2002	2003	2004	2005	2006	2007
Libyan Arab Jamah. Jamah. arabe libyenne	213	213	222	218	217	217	218	234	210	209
Madagascar Madagascar	2 610	2 756	2 660	2 853	2 787	3 129	3 391	3 795	3 991	4 109
Malawi Malawi	1 904	2 636	2 631	1 866	1 711	2 143	1 718	1 302	2 752	3 637
Mali Mali	2 548	2 894	2 310	2 584	2 532	3 402	2 845	3 399	3 693	3 510
Mauritania Mauritanie	189	194	180	124	113	117	120	175	175	155
Mauritius Maurice	^0	^0	1	^0	^0	^0	^0	^0	^0	^0
Morocco Maroc	6 632	3 846	2 002	4 607	5 293	7 973	8 603	4 283	9 239	2 541
Mozambique Mozambique	1 688	1 912	1 587	1 585	1 662	1 813	2 007	1 922	2 107	2 173
Namibia Namibie	70	74	121	107	100	97	117	106	139	114
Niger Niger	2 973	2 853	2 127	3 162	3 243	3 568	2 730	3 669	4 030	3 840
Nigeria Nigéria	22 040	22 405	21 370	20 090	21 373	22 736	24 321	26 031	28 884	30 850
Réunion Réunion	12	12	12	12	12	12	12	12	12	14
Rwanda Rwanda	194	179	240	285	308	298	319	413	366	341
Sao Tome and Principe Sao Tomé-et-Principe	1	1	2	3	3	3	3	3	3	3
Senegal Sénégal	717	1 131	1 026	1 023	785	1 452	1 054	1 433	988	885
Sierra Leone Sierra Leone	373	280	222	334	466	496	614	824	1 157	739
Somalia Somalie	201	299	392	429	442	403	366	359	261	196
South Africa Afrique du Sud	10 221	10 065	14 528	10 706	13 046	11 821	12 028	14 177	9 454	9 547
Sudan Soudan	5 583	3 066	3 259	5 339	3 714	6 373	3 498	5 500	6 742	6 572
Swaziland Swaziland	119	125	114	84	69	70	69	76	68	69
Togo Togo	624	759	741	715	801	815	799	833	889	820
Tunisia Tunisie	1 697	1 837	1 118	1 391	550	2 318	2 164	2 136	1 646	2 020
Uganda Ouganda	2 085	2 178	2 112	2 309	2 368	2 508	2 274	2 459	2 557	2 631
United Rep. of Tanzania Rép.-Unie de Tanzanie	3 854	4 485	3 785	4 497	4 826	4 141	5 262	5 422	5 793	5 895
Western Sahara Sahara occidental	3	3	2	2	2	2	2	2	2	2
Zambia Zambie	798	1 003	1 208	950	755	1 366	1 381	1 067	1 604	1 537
Zimbabwe Zimbabwe	1 899	2 001	2 539	1 973	767	1 197	2 044	1 162	1 849	1 251

32

Cereals *(continued)*
Production: thousand metric tons
Céréales *(suite)*
Production: milliers de tonnes

Region, country or area Région, pays ou zone	1998	1999	2000	2001	2002	2003	2004	2005	2006	2007
Northern America **Amérique septentrionale**	**400 437**	**389 630**	**393 899**	**368 473**	**333 168**	**397 493**	**439 879**	**417 507**	**387 090**	**462 839**
Canada Canada	50 993	54 078	51 090	43 391	36 047	49 189	50 778	50 962	48 577	48 773
United States Etats-Unis	349 445	335 553	342 809	325 082	297 121	348 304	389 101	366 544	338 513	414 066
Latin America and the Caribbean **Amérique latine et Caraïbes**	**130 432**	**133 815**	**138 003**	**150 713**	**138 022**	**162 430**	**163 200**	**153 473**	**156 360**	**173 464**
Argentina Argentine	37 808	35 036	38 751	35 936	31 730	33 984	35 752	38 168	34 107	41 961
Barbados Barbade	1	^0	^0	^0	^0	^0	^0	^0	^0	^0
Belize Belize	52	62	48	57	57	56	49	61	55	56
Bolivia Bolivie	1 146	1 128	1 256	1 280	1 257	1 460	1 296	1 705	1 872	1 332
Brazil Brésil	40 743	47 431	45 897	57 117	50 879	67 453	63 951	55 390	59 149	68 832
Chile Chili	3 098	2 168	2 590	3 116	3 380	3 693	3 999	3 989	3 566	3 694
Colombia Colombie	2 893	3 411	3 765	3 827	3 794	4 729	5 085	4 687	3 786	3 851
Costa Rica Costa Rica	263	292	285	229	201	198	210	196	173	167
Cuba Cuba	619	797	826	900	1 001	1 076	889	732	744	895
Dominican Republic Rép. dominicaine	530	605	610	771	766	656	620	634	734	750
Ecuador Equateur	1 485	1 847	1 909	1 644	1 940	2 113	2 704	2 410	2 379	2 226
El Salvador El Salvador	783	857	779	760	814	791	822	895	937	1 050
French Guiana Guyane française	25	20	20	32	22	23	26	18	24	23
Guatemala Guatemala	1 164	1 134	1 161	1 199	1 155	1 147	1 170	1 158	1 275	1 195
Guyana Guyana	526	565	453	498	446	550	505	424	472	479
Haiti Haïti	403	475	431	363	389	401	436	455	383	380
Honduras Honduras	590	562	607	603	579	594	502	531	529	615
Jamaica Jamaïque	2	2	2	2	2	2	2	2	2	2
Mexico Mexique	29 123	27 419	27 991	31 057	28 770	31 387	32 312	29 060	32 155	32 362
Nicaragua Nicaragua	642	572	783	755	911	1 002	799	964	891	963
Panama Panama	233	265	303	342	371	409	341	334	360	364
Paraguay Paraguay	1 156	1 156	1 003	1 455	1 371	1 643	1 979	1 579	1 871	1 845
Peru Pérou	2 845	3 395	3 554	3 737	3 844	3 920	3 438	4 132	4 163	4 252

32

Cereals *(continued)*
Production: thousand metric tons
Céréales *(suite)*
Production: milliers de tonnes

Region, country or area Région, pays ou zone	1998	1999	2000	2001	2002	2003	2004	2005	2006	2007
Puerto Rico Porto Rico	1	1	^0	^0	^0	^0	^0	^0	1	1
Saint Vincent-Grenadines Saint Vincent-Grenadines	2	1	1	1	1	1	1	1	1	1
Suriname Suriname	189	180	164	191	157	194	175	164	195	195
Trinidad and Tobago Trinité-et-Tobago	12	4	7	5	7	5	5	5	5	5
Uruguay Uruguay	1 961	2 194	1 860	1 718	1 606	1 827	2 523	2 192	2 485	2 565
Venezuela (Bolivarian Rep. of) Venezuela (Rép. boliv. du)	2 134	2 234	2 948	3 117	2 569	3 116	3 606	3 584	4 044	3 402
Asia **Asie**	**1 016 747**	**1 035 979**	**996 270**	**1 001 382**	**982 924**	**997 600**	**1 037 900**	**1 084 679**	**1 109 755**	**1 141 044**
Afghanistan Afghanistan	3 876	3 257	1 940	2 108	3 737	4 382	3 447	5 265	4 459	4 840
Armenia Arménie	323	297	221	364	412	310	460	399	216	267
Azerbaijan Azerbaïdjan	918	1 069	1 496	1 956	2 133	1 993	2 087	2 056	2 012	1 978
Bangladesh Bangladesh	31 577	36 403	39 503	38 029	39 341	40 018	37 759	41 152	44 790	44 669
Bhutan Bhoutan	173	157	107	115	93	108	158	193	194	196
Brunei Darussalam Brunéi Darussalam	^0	^0	^0	^0	^0	1	1	1	1	1
Cambodia Cambodge	3 558	4 136	4 183	4 285	3 971	5 026	4 427	6 234	6 641	6 375
China Chine	458 396	455 193	407 336	398 395	399 998	376 123	413 165	429 371	444 065	460 353
Cyprus Chypre	66	127	48	127	142	165	111	70	66	70
Georgia Géorgie	589	771	418	704	662	742	663	680	428	226
India Inde	226 877	236 206	234 866	242 964	206 635	236 593	229 845	239 997	242 887	252 121
Indonesia Indonésie	59 406	60 070	61 575	59 808	61 075	63 024	65 314	66 675	66 066	69 430
Iran (Islamic Rep. of) Iran (Rép. islamique d')	18 979	14 186	12 874	14 945	19 861	20 942	21 986	21 906	22 409	23 097
Iraq Iraq	2 432	1 605	904	1 819	4 125	3 516	3 308	3 697	3 335	2 710
Israel Israël	249	123	183	242	271	306	273	308	237	273
Japan Japon	11 934	12 283	12 796	12 255	12 184	10 824	11 994	12 434	11 742	12 029
Jordan Jordanie	76	27	57	48	115	80	53	102	62	81
Kazakhstan Kazakhstan	6 380	14 248	11 539	15 866	15 929	14 739	12 334	13 728	16 462	20 495
Korea, Dem. P. R. Corée, R. p. dém. de	4 420	3 837	2 945	3 880	4 211	4 393	4 485	5 156	4 733	4 244
Korea, Republic of Corée, République de	7 132	7 458	7 501	7 860	7 083	6 355	7 115	6 816	6 647	6 269
Kuwait Koweït	3	3	3	3	5	3	3	3	4	4

32
Cereals *(continued)*
Production: thousand metric tons
Céréales *(suite)*
Production: milliers de tonnes

Region, country or area Région, pays ou zone	1998	1999	2000	2001	2002	2003	2004	2005	2006	2007
Kyrgyzstan Kirghizistan	1 608	1 618	1 550	1 795	1 712	1 634	1 709	1 622	1 505	1 419
Lao People's Dem. Rep. Rép. dém. pop. lao	1 784	2 199	2 319	2 447	2 541	2 518	2 733	2 941	3 114	3 320
Lebanon Liban	103	93	123	153	140	146	165	177	174	168
Malaysia Malaisie	1 994	2 094	2 206	2 162	2 267	2 329	2 336	2 315	2 234	2 314
Mongolia Mongolie	195	170	142	142	126	165	139	76	139	115
Myanmar Myanmar	17 636	20 774	21 964	22 717	22 695	24 165	25 842	26 644	31 874	33 720
Nepal Népal	6 390	6 930	7 116	7 120	7 215	7 360	7 747	7 767	7 657	7 329
Occupied Palestinian Terr. Terr. palestinien occupé	53	14	68	40	77	68	62	68	55	63
Oman Oman	10	11	12	13	14	14	19	15	14	14
Pakistan Pakistan	27 985	27 756	30 461	27 048	27 173	28 964	30 311	33 508	32 864	35 553
Philippines Philippines	12 377	16 371	16 901	17 480	17 590	18 116	19 910	19 856	21 409	22 730
Qatar Qatar	6	7	7	7	7	7	5	7	7	7
Saudi Arabia Arabie saoudite	2 202	2 454	2 167	2 592	2 853	2 949	3 189	2 999	2 790	3 089
Sri Lanka Sri Lanka	2 731	2 894	2 896	2 728	2 890	3 106	2 668	3 295	3 396	3 193
Syrian Arab Republic Rép. arabe syrienne	5 270	3 301	3 513	6 921	5 932	6 227	5 281	5 631	5 823	5 453
Tajikistan Tadjikistan	491	465	545	478	688	866	860	903	880	896
Thailand Thaïlande	28 265	28 661	30 523	31 215	30 526	31 485	33 021	34 508	33 201	31 702
Timor-Leste Timor-Leste	96	104	139	123	147	136	152	140	155	105
Turkey Turquie	33 187	28 886	32 249	29 571	30 831	30 807	34 045	36 354	34 637	30 212
Turkmenistan Turkménistan	1 278	1 567	1 751	1 832	2 461	2 667	2 785	3 035	3 489	2 886
Uzbekistan Ouzbékistan	4 132	4 311	3 914	4 056	5 535	6 106	5 860	6 531	6 511	6 372
Viet Nam Viet Nam	30 758	33 149	34 537	34 272	36 960	37 707	39 581	39 549	39 648	39 881
Yemen Yémen	833	694	672	700	560	418	490	496	727	774
Europe **Europe**	**386 687**	**375 978**	**384 981**	**431 396**	**436 586**	**355 683**	**470 378**	**428 078**	**404 451**	**395 473**
Albania Albanie	606	498	566	503	519	489	499	511	508	494
Austria Autriche	4 776	4 809	4 494	4 830	4 461	4 519	5 606	5 195	4 460	4 595
Belarus Bélarus	4 497	3 413	4 565	4 871	5 710	5 117	6 590	6 089	5 686	7 016
Belgium Belgique	...	...	2 513	2 359	2 639	2 561	2 932	2 787	2 606	2 519

32

Cereals *(continued)*
Production: thousand metric tons
Céréales *(suite)*
Production: milliers de tonnes

Region, country or area Région, pays ou zone	1998	1999	2000	2001	2002	2003	2004	2005	2006	2007
Belgium-Luxembourg Belgique-Luxembourg	2 601	2 449	...	...	...	...	...	...	...	...
Bosnia and Herzegovina Bosnie-Herzégovine	1 327	1 369	930	1 138	1 308	793	1 439	1 350	1 341	1 001
Bulgaria Bulgarie	5 378	5 221	4 389	6 076	6 770	3 814	7 463	5 839	5 532	3 180
Croatia Croatie	3 210	2 883	2 770	3 396	3 722	2 355	3 248	3 041	3 048	2 607
Czech Republic République tchèque	6 676	6 935	6 460	7 347	6 784	5 773	8 792	7 668	6 386	7 066
Denmark Danemark	9 334	8 774	9 413	9 423	8 804	9 051	8 963	9 283	8 632	8 220
Estonia Estonie	576	402	697	558	525	506	608	760	619	860
Finland Finlande	2 780	2 882	4 103	3 671	3 938	3 791	3 619	4 059	3 790	4 181
France France	60 064	64 342	65 698	60 237	69 657	54 940	70 517	64 104	61 813	58 707
Germany Allemagne	44 575	44 461	45 271	49 686	43 391	39 320	51 110	45 888	43 475	42 295
Greece Grèce	4 611	4 576	4 968	4 939	4 827	4 710	5 088	5 084	4 702	3 808
Hungary Hongrie	13 038	11 392	10 036	15 046	11 703	8 770	16 779	16 212	14 467	14 047
Ireland Irlande	1 866	2 011	2 174	2 166	1 964	2 147	2 501	1 940	2 090	1 969
Italy Italie	20 731	21 068	20 661	19 933	21 248	17 864	23 283	21 423	20 207	20 499
Latvia Lettonie	959	784	924	928	1 029	932	1 060	1 314	1 159	1 535
Lithuania Lituanie	2 717	2 048	2 657	2 344	2 531	2 632	2 859	2 811	1 858	3 017
Luxembourg Luxembourg	...	...	153	144	169	164	179	161	161	151
Malta Malte	11	11	12	12	12	12	12	12	11	11
Montenegro Monténégro	...	...	...	...	...	...	...	...	14	14
Netherlands Pays-Bas	1 497	1 368	1 732	1 672	1 740	1 820	1 823	1 775	1 730	1 506
Norway Norvège	1 358	1 218	1 300	1 220	1 143	1 287	1 445	1 298	1 229	1 250
Poland Pologne	27 159	25 750	22 341	26 960	26 877	23 391	29 635	26 928	21 776	27 365
Portugal Portugal	1 622	1 678	1 608	1 298	1 497	1 186	1 363	790	1 167	1 103
Republic of Moldova République de Moldova	2 428	2 142	1 905	2 550	2 539	1 583	2 943	2 772	2 222	885
Romania Roumanie	15 453	17 037	10 499	18 900	14 357	12 966	24 402	19 350	15 760	7 461
Russian Federation Fédération de Russie	46 937	53 845	64 326	83 398	84 859	65 562	76 231	76 564	76 866	80 495
Serbia Serbie	...	...	...	...	...	...	...	...	8 277	6 125
Serbia and Montenegro Serbie-et-Monténégro	8 667	8 615	5 391	9 040	8 327	5 541	9 893	9 534	...	...

Region, country or area Région, pays ou zone	1998	1999	2000	2001	2002	2003	2004	2005	2006	2007
Slovakia Slovaquie	3 486	2 830	2 204	3 414	3 196	2 491	3 798	3 585	2 929	2 950
Slovenia Slovénie	559	480	497	500	614	402	586	580	494	532
Spain Espagne	22 557	17 988	24 556	18 050	21 710	21 412	24 809	14 364	19 353	24 135
Sweden Suède	5 618	4 931	5 604	5 382	5 398	5 290	5 508	5 051	4 128	5 059
Switzerland Suisse	1 263	1 055	1 206	1 094	1 101	847	1 089	1 057	1 008	1 049
TFYR of Macedonia Ex-R.Y. Macédoine	660	638	563	475	556	472	682	645	602	364
Ukraine Ukraine	25 724	23 950	23 807	38 879	37 995	19 662	40 997	37 258	33 511	28 035
United Kingdom Royaume-Uni	22 768	22 125	23 989	18 959	22 966	21 511	22 028	20 998	20 832	19 369
Oceania **Océanie**	**34 229**	**36 278**	**35 337**	**39 853**	**20 001**	**42 606**	**35 430**	**40 774**	**20 072**	**23 132**
Australia Australie	33 339	35 369	34 447	38 877	19 029	41 631	34 564	39 870	19 229	22 145
Fiji Fidji	6	18	14	15	14	17	15	16	14	16
New Caledonia Nouvelle-Calédonie	2	2	5	5	4	6	5	4	7	7
New Zealand Nouvelle-Zélande	869	873	854	938	936	936	829	866	805	945
Papua New Guinea Papouasie-Nvl-Guinée	10	11	11	13	13	10	10	11	11	12
Solomon Islands Iles Salomon	1	5	5	5	5	5	6	6	6	6
Vanuatu Vanuatu	1	1	1	1	1	1	1	1	1	1

Source:
Food and Agriculture Organization of the United Nations (FAO), Rome,
FAOSTAT data, last accessed March 2009.

Source:
Organisation des Nations Unies pour l'alimentation et l'agriculture (FAO),
Rome, données FAOSTAT, dernier accès mars 2009.

Roundwood
Production (solid volume of roundwood without bark): million cubic metres

Bois rond
Production (volume solide de bois rond sans écorce) : millions de mètres cubes

Region, country or area Région, pays ou zone	1998	1999	2000	2001	2002	2003	2004	2005	2006	2007
World **Monde**	**3 225.4**	**3 334.4**	**3 405.3**	**3 307.9**	**3 335.3**	**3 388.2**	**3 450.4**	**3 551.6**	**3 510.6**	**3 591.4**
Africa **Afrique**	**585.0**	**588.8**	**594.9**	**591.1**	**599.8**	**611.3**	**619.6**	**636.1**	**664.9**	**672.1**
Algeria Algérie	7.3	7.4	7.2	7.4	7.5	7.5	7.7	7.7	7.8	8.0
Angola Angola	4.0	4.2	4.3	4.3	4.4	4.5	4.6	4.7	4.8	4.8
Benin Bénin	6.2	6.2	6.2	0.5	0.5	0.5	0.5	6.4	6.6	6.6
Botswana Botswana	0.7	0.7	0.7	0.7	0.7	0.8	0.8	0.8	0.8	0.8
Burkina Faso Burkina Faso	11.3	7.8	8.0	8.0	7.2	7.3	9.2	11.7	13.2	13.4
Burundi Burundi	7.7	5.6	5.8	8.3	8.4	8.6	8.7	8.9	9.0	9.2
Cameroon Cameroun	11.1	10.9	11.0	10.5	10.6	11.0	11.2	11.3	11.4	11.4
Central African Rep. Rép. centrafricaine	3.5	2.9	3.0	3.0	2.9	2.8	2.8	2.8	2.8	2.8
Chad Tchad	6.3	6.5	6.6	6.8	6.9	7.0	7.1	7.2	7.4	7.5
Congo Congo	2.7	2.4	2.5	2.8	3.1	3.3	3.5	3.6	3.6	3.7
Côte d'Ivoire Côte d'Ivoire	11.8	11.7	11.9	11.2	10.7	10.2	10.3	10.0	10.1	10.3
Dem. Rep. of the Congo Rép. dém. du Congo	66.0	67.3	68.6	69.8	71.1	72.5	73.9	75.3	76.4	77.7
Egypt Egypte	16.1	16.3	16.4	16.6	16.8	16.9	17.1	17.2	17.3	17.4
Equatorial Guinea Guinée equatoriale	0.9	1.2	1.1	1.1	1.0	0.9	0.9	0.9	0.9	0.6
Eritrea Erythrée	2.1	2.2	2.2	2.3	1.3	1.3	2.4	2.4	2.5	2.5
Ethiopia Ethiopie	86.5	88.2	89.9	91.3	92.7	94.5	96.0	97.4	98.6	100.1
Gabon Gabon	3.3	2.8	3.1	3.1	2.2	4.6	4.6	3.7	4.0	3.9
Gambia Gambie	0.6	0.6	0.7	0.7	0.7	0.7	0.8	0.8	0.8	0.8
Ghana Ghana	21.9	21.8	21.7	21.9	21.8	22.1	22.0	21.9	34.3	35.5
Guinea Guinée	8.7	12.2	12.1	12.1	12.2	12.2	12.3	12.3	12.4	12.4
Guinea-Bissau Guinée-Bissau	0.6	0.6	0.6	0.6	0.6	0.6	0.6	0.6	0.6	0.6
Kenya Kenya	21.3	21.5	21.6	21.7	21.8	21.9	22.2	26.7	27.6	27.6
Lesotho Lesotho	1.6	2.0	2.0	2.0	2.0	2.0	2.0	2.1	2.1	2.1
Liberia Libéria	4.1	4.5	5.8	6.1	6.7	6.3	5.9	6.1	6.4	6.6
Libyan Arab Jamah. Jamah. arabe libyenne	0.7	0.7	0.7	0.7	0.7	0.7	0.7	0.7	1.0	1.0
Madagascar Madagascar	9.2	9.5	9.8	10.0	10.3	10.7	11.0	11.2	13.3	13.3

33

Roundwood *(continued)*
Production (solid volume of roundwood without bark): million cubic metres
Bois rond *(suite)*
Production (volume solide de bois rond sans écorce) : millions de mètres cubes

Region, country or area Région, pays ou zone	1998	1999	2000	2001	2002	2003	2004	2005	2006	2007
Malawi Malawi	5.4	5.4	5.5	5.5	5.5	5.6	5.6	5.7	5.7	5.8
Mali Mali	5.0	5.1	5.1	5.2	5.3	5.3	5.4	5.4	5.5	5.6
Mauritania Mauritanie	1.4	1.4	1.4	1.5	1.5	1.5	1.6	1.6	1.7	1.7
Morocco Maroc	1.7	1.1	1.1	1.0	0.9	0.9	0.9	1.0	0.9	1.0
Mozambique Mozambique	18.0	18.0	18.0	18.0	18.0	18.0	18.0	18.0	18.0	18.0
Niger Niger	7.8	8.0	8.2	3.3	8.6	8.8	9.0	9.2	9.4	9.6
Nigeria Nigéria	67.8	68.3	68.8	69.1	69.5	69.9	70.3	70.7	71.0	71.4
Rwanda Rwanda	7.5	7.8	5.4	5.5	5.5	5.5	5.5	5.5	9.9	10.0
Senegal Sénégal	5.8	5.9	5.9	5.9	6.0	6.0	6.0	6.1	6.1	6.1
Sierra Leone Sierra Leone	5.2	5.3	5.5	5.5	5.5	5.5	5.5	5.5	5.6	5.6
Somalia Somalie	8.6	9.0	9.3	9.6	9.9	10.3	10.6	10.9	11.2	11.6
South Africa Afrique du Sud	30.6	30.6	30.6	30.6	30.6	33.2	33.3	30.2	30.1	30.1
Sudan Soudan	18.6	18.7	18.9	19.0	19.2	19.4	19.7	19.9	20.1	20.3
Swaziland Swaziland	0.9	0.9	0.9	0.9	0.9	0.9	0.9	0.9	1.3	1.3
Togo Togo	5.7	5.7	5.8	5.8	5.8	5.9	4.7	5.9	6.0	6.0
Tunisia Tunisie	2.3	2.3	2.3	2.3	2.3	2.3	2.3	2.4	2.4	2.4
Uganda Ouganda	36.4	36.9	37.3	37.8	38.3	38.9	39.4	40.0	40.5	41.1
United Rep. of Tanzania Rép.-Unie de Tanzanie	23.0	23.1	23.1	23.3	23.4	23.6	23.8	24.0	24.2	24.4
Zambia Zambie	8.0	8.1	8.9	8.7	8.9	9.2	9.5	9.8	10.1	10.0
Zimbabwe Zimbabwe	9.0	9.3	9.1	9.1	9.1	9.1	9.1	8.9	9.2	9.2
Northern America Amérique septentrionale	**671.0**	**663.2**	**668.4**	**635.0**	**646.1**	**628.2**	**669.8**	**670.5**	**645.2**	**639.9**
Canada Canada	176.9	193.9	201.8	185.9	198.1	179.6	208.1	203.1	188.2	195.9
United States Etats-Unis	494.0	469.3	466.5	449.1	448.0	448.5	461.7	467.3	457.0	444.0
Latin America and the Caribbean Amérique latine et Caraïbes	**399.2**	**418.4**	**425.0**	**412.7**	**421.0**	**450.0**	**446.3**	**463.8**	**447.6**	**462.1**
Argentina Argentine	5.7	10.6	10.0	9.3	9.3	13.7	14.9	14.2	13.9	13.9
Belize Belize	0.2	0.2	0.2	0.2	0.2	0.2	0.2	0.2	0.2	0.7
Bolivia Bolivie	2.9	2.6	2.6	2.7	2.7	2.9	3.0	3.1	3.1	3.1
Brazil Brésil	213.7	231.6	235.4	223.6	231.0	256.1	243.4	255.9	239.5	245.0

Roundwood *(continued)*
Production (solid volume of roundwood without bark): million cubic metres
Bois rond *(suite)*
Production (volume solide de bois rond sans écorce) : millions de mètres cubes

Region, country or area Région, pays ou zone	1998	1999	2000	2001	2002	2003	2004	2005	2006	2007
Chile Chili	31.7	34.0	36.6	37.8	37.8	37.0	42.6	45.6	46.7	52.9
Colombia Colombie	10.1	10.6	13.1	12.5	11.6	12.0	10.5	11.9	10.5	10.4
Costa Rica Costa Rica	5.2	5.2	5.2	5.2	5.2	5.1	4.5	4.6	4.6	4.6
Cuba Cuba	3.5	1.6	1.8	1.7	2.8	2.6	2.5	2.6	2.3	2.3
Dominican Republic Rép. dominicaine	0.6	0.6	0.6	0.6	0.6	0.6	0.6	0.6	0.9	0.9
Ecuador Equateur	11.5	5.5	5.7	6.1	6.2	6.3	6.6	6.7	5.8	6.1
El Salvador El Salvador	5.1	5.2	5.2	5.2	5.2	4.8	4.9	4.9	4.9	4.9
French Guiana Guyane française	0.1	0.1	0.1	0.1	0.2	0.2	0.2	0.2	0.2	0.2
Guatemala Guatemala	14.1	14.7	15.0	15.3	15.7	15.9	16.3	16.7	17.1	17.4
Guyana Guyana	1.3	1.3	1.2	1.2	1.2	1.2	1.3	1.4	1.4	1.4
Haiti Haïti	2.2	2.2	2.2	2.2	2.2	2.2	2.2	2.2	2.2	2.3
Honduras Honduras	9.5	9.6	9.5	9.6	9.7	9.5	9.6	9.6	9.5	9.5
Jamaica Jamaïque	0.8	0.9	0.9	0.9	0.9	0.9	0.9	0.8	0.8	0.8
Mexico Mexique	45.0	45.4	45.7	45.2	44.0	44.4	45.2	44.6	44.7	44.9
Nicaragua Nicaragua	5.9	5.9	6.0	5.9	6.0	6.0	6.0	6.0	6.1	6.1
Panama Panama	1.3	1.3	1.3	1.3	1.3	1.3	1.3	1.4	1.3	1.3
Paraguay Paraguay	9.5	9.6	9.6	9.7	9.8	9.9	10.0	10.1	10.2	10.3
Peru Pérou	9.2	9.2	9.3	8.6	8.8	8.4	8.9	9.1	9.3	9.4
Suriname Suriname	0.2	0.1	0.2	0.2	0.2	0.2	0.2	0.2	0.2	0.2
Trinidad and Tobago Trinité-et-Tobago	0.1	0.1	0.1	0.1	0.1	0.1	0.1	0.1	0.1	0.1
Uruguay Uruguay	5.2	5.1	2.9	3.0	3.4	3.7	5.1	5.7	6.4	7.2
Venezuela (Bolivarian Rep. of) Venezuela (Rép. bolivarienne du)	4.6	5.3	4.7	4.6	5.1	4.8	5.3	5.3	5.6	6.1
Asia **Asie**	**1 044.3**	**1 076.8**	**1 065.1**	**1 044.0**	**1 029.2**	**1 028.9**	**1 031.6**	**1 031.4**	**1 022.6**	**1 026.6**
Afghanistan Afghanistan	2.9	3.0	3.0	3.1	3.1	3.1	3.2	3.2	3.3	3.3
Armenia Arménie	0.0	0.0	0.1	^0.0	0.1	0.1	0.1	^0.0	0.1	0.0
Azerbaijan Azerbaïdjan	^0.0	^0.0	^0.0	^0.0	0.1	^0.0	^0.0	^0.0	^0.0	^0.0
Bangladesh Bangladesh	28.5	28.5	28.5	28.4	28.0	28.0	28.0	27.9	27.9	27.8
Bhutan Bhoutan	4.1	4.3	4.4	4.4	4.5	4.5	4.6	4.7	4.7	4.8

33

Roundwood *(continued)*
Production (solid volume of roundwood without bark): million cubic metres
Bois rond *(suite)*
Production (volume solide de bois rond sans écorce) : millions de mètres cubes

Region, country or area Région, pays ou zone	1998	1999	2000	2001	2002	2003	2004	2005	2006	2007
Brunei Darussalam Brunéi Darussalam	0.2	0.1	0.1	0.1	0.1	0.1	0.1	0.1	0.1	0.1
Cambodia Cambodge	11.6	11.2	10.3	10.0	9.9	9.7	9.5	9.3	9.3	9.0
China Chine	298.0	331.8	323.6	316.9	312.0	309.9	305.9	302.0	298.2	294.4
Georgia Géorgie	0.0	0.0	0.0	0.3	0.4	0.4	0.5	0.6	0.6	0.6
India Inde	296.3	296.6	296.1	296.7	319.4	321.0	326.6	328.7	329.4	330.2
Indonesia Indonésie	135.6	130.2	122.5	112.2	115.6	112.0	109.1	104.4	98.8	103.4
Iran (Islamic Rep. of) Iran (Rép. islamique d')	1.3	1.1	1.1	1.3	0.7	0.9	0.8	0.8	0.8	0.9
Iraq Iraq	0.2	0.1	0.1	0.1	0.1	0.1	0.1	0.1	0.1	0.1
Israel Israël	0.1	0.1	0.1	^0.0	^0.0	^0.0	^0.0	^0.0	^0.0	^0.0
Japan Japon	19.6	19.0	18.1	15.9	15.2	15.3	15.7	16.3	16.7	17.8
Jordan Jordanie	0.2	0.2	0.2	0.2	0.2	0.2	0.3	0.3	0.3	0.3
Kazakhstan Kazakhstan	0.0	0.5	0.6	0.7	0.5	0.3	0.5	0.9	0.9	0.9
Korea, Dem. P. R. Corée, R. p. dém. de	6.9	6.9	7.0	7.1	7.1	7.2	7.2	7.3	7.3	7.4
Korea, Republic of Corée, République de	3.9	4.1	4.0	4.0	4.1	4.1	4.7	4.8	4.9	5.2
Lao People's Dem. Rep. Rép. dém. pop. lao	6.4	6.7	6.4	6.5	6.3	6.3	6.2	6.1	6.1	6.1
Lebanon Liban	0.1	^0.0	^0.0	0.1	0.1	0.1	0.1	0.1	0.1	0.1
Malaysia Malaisie	26.8	26.8	27.7	23.5	22.7	26.5	28.5	28.3	26.2	25.1
Mongolia Mongolie	0.6	0.6	0.6	0.7	0.7	0.7	0.7	0.7	0.7	0.8
Myanmar Myanmar	34.3	37.6	38.1	39.4	38.9	42.2	41.8	42.5	42.5	42.5
Nepal Népal	13.9	13.9	14.0	14.0	14.0	14.0	14.0	14.0	13.9	13.9
Pakistan Pakistan	31.8	33.1	33.6	33.2	27.7	28.0	28.7	29.3	29.0	29.2
Philippines Philippines	42.0	43.0	44.0	44.4	16.0	16.0	16.1	16.1	16.1	15.8
Sri Lanka Sri Lanka	6.6	6.6	6.6	6.5	6.5	6.4	6.3	6.3	6.3	6.1
Syrian Arab Republic Rép. arabe syrienne	0.1	0.1	0.1	0.1	0.1	0.1	0.1	0.1	0.1	0.1
Tajikistan Tadjikistan	0.0	0.0	0.0	0.0	0.0	0.0	0.1	0.1	0.1	0.1
Thailand Thaïlande	23.4	23.4	26.8	27.5	28.1	28.8	28.7	28.6	28.4	28.3
Turkey Turquie	17.7	16.6	15.9	15.3	16.1	15.8	16.5	16.2	18.1	17.7
Viet Nam Viet Nam	31.0	30.2	30.9	30.8	30.7	26.4	26.5	31.1	31.0	34.2

33

Roundwood *(continued)*
Production (solid volume of roundwood without bark): million cubic metres
Bois rond *(suite)*
Production (volume solide de bois rond sans écorce) : millions de mètres cubes

Region, country or area Région, pays ou zone	1998	1999	2000	2001	2002	2003	2004	2005	2006	2007
Yemen Yémen	0.3	0.3	0.3	0.3	0.3	0.3	0.4	0.4	0.4	0.4
Europe **Europe**	**472.4**	**531.7**	**592.2**	**564.6**	**578.8**	**608.3**	**622.2**	**689.7**	**670.0**	**728.9**
Albania Albanie	^0.0	0.2	0.4	0.3	0.3	0.3	0.3	0.3	0.3	0.3
Austria Autriche	14.0	14.1	13.3	13.5	14.8	17.1	16.5	16.5	19.1	21.3
Belarus Bélarus	5.9	6.6	6.1	6.5	6.9	7.5	8.6	8.7	8.8	8.8
Belgium Belgique	...	...	4.5	4.2	4.5	4.8	4.9	5.0	5.1	4.9
Belgium-Luxembourg Belgique-Luxembourg	4.8	5.1	...	...	...	...	...	...	...	...
Bosnia and Herzegovina Bosnie-Herzégovine	4.1	4.1	4.3	3.8	4.2	4.1	4.0	3.8	4.1	3.8
Bulgaria Bulgarie	3.2	4.4	4.8	4.0	4.8	4.8	6.0	5.9	6.0	5.7
Croatia Croatie	3.4	3.5	3.7	3.5	3.6	3.8	3.8	4.0	4.5	4.2
Czech Republic République tchèque	14.0	14.2	14.4	14.4	14.5	15.1	15.6	15.5	17.7	18.5
Denmark Danemark	1.6	1.6	3.0	1.6	1.4	1.6	1.5	3.0	2.4	2.6
Estonia Estonie	6.1	6.7	8.9	10.2	10.5	10.5	6.8	5.5	5.4	5.9
Finland Finlande	53.7	53.6	54.3	52.2	53.4	54.2	54.4	52.3	50.8	56.9
France France	35.5	36.0	45.8	39.8	35.4	32.8	33.6	63.2	61.8	62.8
Germany Allemagne	39.1	37.6	53.7	39.5	42.4	51.2	54.5	56.9	62.3	76.7
Greece Grèce	1.7	2.2	2.2	1.9	1.6	1.7	1.7	1.5	1.6	1.7
Hungary Hongrie	4.2	5.2	5.9	5.8	5.8	5.8	5.7	5.9	5.9	5.6
Ireland Irlande	2.3	2.6	2.7	2.5	2.6	2.7	2.6	2.6	2.7	2.7
Italy Italie	9.6	11.1	9.3	8.1	7.5	8.2	8.7	8.7	8.6	8.1
Latvia Lettonie	10.0	14.0	14.3	12.8	13.5	12.9	12.8	12.8	12.8	12.2
Lithuania Lituanie	4.9	4.9	5.5	5.7	6.1	6.3	6.1	6.1	5.6	5.9
Luxembourg Luxembourg	...	...	0.3	0.3	0.3	0.3	0.3	0.2	0.3	0.3
Montenegro Monténégro	...	...	...	...	...	...	...	...	0.5	0.5
Netherlands Pays-Bas	1.0	1.0	1.0	0.9	0.8	1.0	1.0	1.1	1.1	1.0
Norway Norvège	8.2	8.4	8.2	9.0	8.7	8.3	8.8	9.7	9.8	10.5
Poland Pologne	23.1	24.3	26.0	25.0	27.1	30.8	32.7	31.9	32.4	35.9
Portugal Portugal	8.5	9.0	10.8	8.9	8.7	9.7	10.9	10.7	10.8	10.8
Republic of Moldova République de Moldova	0.4	^0.0	0.1	0.1	0.1	0.2	0.2	0.2	0.2	0.2

Roundwood *(continued)*
Production (solid volume of roundwood without bark): million cubic metres
Bois rond *(suite)*
Production (volume solide de bois rond sans écorce) : millions de mètres cubes

Region, country or area Région, pays ou zone	1998	1999	2000	2001	2002	2003	2004	2005	2006	2007
Romania Roumanie	11.6	12.7	13.1	12.4	15.2	15.4	15.8	14.5	14.0	15.3
Russian Federation Fédération de Russie	95.0	143.6	158.1	164.7	165.0	174.0	178.4	185.0	190.6	207.0
Serbia Serbie	...	...	...	...	...	...	...	...	2.9	3.0
Serbia and Montenegro Serbie-et-Monténégro	2.7	2.5	3.4	2.5	2.9	3.2	3.5	3.2	...	...
Slovakia Slovaquie	5.5	5.8	6.2	5.8	5.8	6.4	7.2	9.3	7.9	8.9
Slovenia Slovénie	2.1	2.1	2.3	2.3	2.3	2.6	2.6	2.7	3.2	2.9
Spain Espagne	14.9	14.8	14.3	15.1	15.8	16.1	16.3	15.5	15.7	14.5
Sweden Suède	60.6	58.7	63.3	63.2	66.6	67.1	67.3	98.2	64.6	77.2
Switzerland Suisse	4.3	4.7	9.2	5.7	4.6	5.1	5.1	5.3	5.7	5.7
TFYR of Macedonia Ex-R.Y. Macédoine	0.7	0.8	1.1	0.7	0.7	0.8	0.8	0.8	0.8	0.8
Ukraine Ukraine	8.5	7.9	9.9	9.9	12.3	13.8	14.9	14.6	15.8	16.9
United Kingdom Royaume-Uni	7.3	7.5	7.8	7.9	7.8	8.0	8.3	8.5	8.4	9.0
Oceania **Océanie**	**53.5**	**55.6**	**59.8**	**60.5**	**60.4**	**61.6**	**60.9**	**60.2**	**60.4**	**61.8**
Australia Australie	28.1	27.7	31.2	31.1	29.7	31.6	31.9	31.9	31.8	32.3
Fiji Fidji	0.5	0.5	0.5	0.5	0.4	0.4	0.5	0.5	0.5	0.5
New Zealand Nouvelle-Zélande	15.3	17.7	19.3	20.7	22.1	21.2	19.8	19.0	19.3	20.3
Papua New Guinea Papouasie-Nvl-Guinée	8.6	8.6	7.7	7.2	7.2	7.2	7.2	7.2	7.2	7.2
Samoa Samoa	0.1	0.1	0.1	0.1	0.1	0.1	0.1	0.1	0.1	0.1
Solomon Islands Iles Salomon	0.9	0.9	0.9	0.7	0.7	0.9	1.2	1.3	1.3	1.3
Vanuatu Vanuatu	0.1	0.1	0.1	0.1	0.1	0.1	0.1	0.1	0.1	0.1

Source:
Food and Agriculture Organization of the United Nations (FAO), Rome, FAOSTAT database, last accessed March 2009.

Source:
Organisation des Nations Unies pour l'alimentation et l'agriculture (FAO), Rome, la base de données de la FAOSTAT, dernier accès mars 2009.

Fish production
Capture and aquaculture: metric tons

Production halieutique
Pêche de capture et aquaculture: tonnes

Country or area Pays ou zone	Capture production Captures					Aquaculture production Production de l'aquaculture				
	2003	2004	2005	2006	2007	2003	2004	2005	2006	2007
Afghanistan [1] Afghanistan [1]	900	1 000	1 000	1 000	1 000	...	...	...	...	...
Albania Albanie	2 800[1]	4 549	5 000	5 729	5 497	1 473	1 569	1 473	1 970	2 008
Algeria Algérie	141 528	113 462	126 839	145 762	148 436	417[1]	586[1]	368	288	405
American Samoa Samoa américaines	4 984	4 039	3 985	5 433	6 587	...	...	...	...	...
Angola Angola	211 539	240 002	202 616	225 449	312 440	...	...	...	...	...
Anguilla Anguilla	250[1]	250	250	250	250	...	...	...	...	...
Antigua and Barbuda Antigua-et-Barbuda	2 587	2 527	2 999	3 092	3 092	...	...	...	...	...
Argentina Argentine	915 994	945 943	931 333	1 181 980	989 380	1 647	1 848	2 430	2 528	2 957
Armenia Arménie	569	218	250[1]	350[1]	3 000[1]	1 064	813	739[1]	1 056[1]	1 566[1]
Aruba Aruba	160[1]	162	162[1]	145	159	...	...	...	...	...
Australia Australie	215 259	230 679	236 484	197 108	184 996	38 793	44 142	42 787	49 376	54 316
Austria Autriche	372	400	370	360	350	2 233	2 267	2 420	2 503	2 525
Azerbaijan Azerbaïdjan	6 435	9 258	9 001	3 983	2 943	122	184	114	110	113
Bahamas Bahamas	12 611	11 347	11 064	10 598	3 749	42	10	10	22	0
Bahrain Bahreïn	13 638	14 334	11 854	15 594	15 012	4	8	3	2	1
Bangladesh Bangladesh	1 141 241	1 187 274	1 333 866	1 436 496	1 494 199	856 956	914 752	882 091	892 049	945 812
Barbados Barbade	2 838	2 148	2 182	1 974	1 800[1]	...	...	...	...	...
Belarus Bélarus	6 925	890	900[1]	900[1]	900[1]	5 393	4 150	4 150[1]	4 150[1]	4 150[1]
Belgium Belgique	26 831	26 735	24 567	23 019	24 541	1 261	739	414	128	128
Belize Belize	6 618	4 148	4 165	4 217	6 682	10 160	11 428	10 858	7 624	7 700[1]
Benin Bénin	41 648	39 988	38 035	38 021	30 261	7[1]	7	350	415	178
Bermuda Bermudes	352	379	406	380	420	...	...	...	...	...
Bhutan [1] Bhoutan [1]	300	300	300	300	300	...	...	...	...	...
Bolivia Bolivie	6 599	6 746	6 660	6 350[1]	6 000	375	450	430	455[1]	585
Bosnia and Herzegovina Bosnie-Herzégovine	2 005[1]	2 005[1]	2 005[1]	2 005[1]	2 005[1]	6 635	6 394	7 070	7 621	7 620[1]
Botswana Botswana	122	161	132	81	123	...	...	...	...	...

34

Fish production *(continued)*
Capture and aquaculture: metric tons
Production halieutique *(suite)*
Pêche de capture et aquaculture: tonnes

Country or area Pays ou zone	Capture production Captures					Aquaculture production Production de l'aquaculture				
	2003	2004	2005	2006	2007	2003	2004	2005	2006	2007
Brazil Brésil	712 144	746 217	750 261	779 113	783 177	273 268	269 699	257 783	271 696	289 648
British Indian Ocean Terr Terr. brit. de l'océan Indien	28	28	28	21	24	...	...	...	...	...
British Virgin Islands Iles Vierges britanniques	2 771	1 262	1 300[1]	1 308[1]	1 300[1]	...	...	...	...	...
Brunei Darussalam Brunéi Darussalam	2 226	2 428	2 407	1 992	2 241	160	709	454	475	622
Bulgaria Bulgarie	12 035	8 252	5 434	7 544	8 897	4 465	2 489	3 145	3 257	4 032
Burkina Faso Burkina Faso	9 000	9 000[1]	9 000	9 500	10 200	5	5[1]	55[1]	200	298
Burundi Burundi	14 697	13 855	14 000[1]	14 000[1]	14 000[1]	200	200	200[1]	200[1]	200[1]
Cambodia Cambodge	364 357	305 817	384 000	482 500	480 000[1]	18 500	20 675	26 000	34 200	34 200[1]
Cameroon Cameroun	117 801	129 000[1]	142 345	137 232	138 612	320	330[1]	337	340[1]	340[1]
Canada Canada	1 107 991	1 172 578	1 103 853	1 068 977	1 005 966	167 798	145 018	154 587	170 990	168 769[1]
Cape Verde Cap-Vert	8 169	10 397	21 617	24 589	18 328	...	...	...	...	...
Cayman Islands Iles Caïmanes	125	125	125	125	125	...	...	...	...	...
Central African Rep. [1] Rép. centrafricaine [1]	15 000	15 000	15 000	15 000	15 000	...	...	...	...	...
Chad [1] Tchad [1]	70 000	70 000	70 000	70 000	70 000	...	...	...	...	...
Channel Islands Iles Anglo-Normandes	3 526	3 201	3 505	3 468	3 566	684	775	650	660[1]	791
Chile Chili	3 612 644	4 926 741	4 328 732	4 160 848	3 806 085	563 435	665 421	698 214	802 410	829 842
China [2] Chine [2]	14 347 274[1]	14 464 803[1]	14 588 940[1]	14 631 018[1]	14 659 036	25 083 253[1]	26 567 201[1]	28 120 690[1]	29 856 841[1]	31 420 275
China, Hong Kong SAR Chine, Hong Kong RAS	157 444	167 544	161 964	154 536	154 147	4 857	4 615	4 130	4 125	4 514
China, Macao SAR [1] Chine, Macao RAS [1]	1 500	1 500	1 500	1 500	1 500	...	...	...	...	...
Colombia Colombie	129 792	124 951	94 806	95 000[1]	96 000[1]	60 895	60 072	60 072[1]	60 100[1]	60 100[1]
Comoros Comores	14 115	14 935	15 070	15 070[1]	16 000	...	...	...	...	...
Congo Congo	54 659	54 234	58 368	59 485	59 941	69	72	80	21	25
Cook Islands Iles Cook	3 250	4 194	3 994	3 700	3 200	0	0	0	0	^0
Costa Rica Costa Rica	29 397	20 850	22 340	22 000[1]	21 735	20 546	24 708	24 038	19 962	25 765
Côte d'Ivoire Côte d'Ivoire	69 539	54 401	31 521	32 644	32 599[1]	866	866	866[1]	817	817[1]
Croatia Croatie	19 946	30 164	34 665	37 853	40 199	8 387	10 367	11 104	13 556	12 884
Cuba Cuba	40 350	36 089	28 664	27 567	36 690	26 897	27 562	22 635	27 186	25 416

34

Fish production *(continued)*
Capture and aquaculture: metric tons
Production halieutique *(suite)*
Pêche de capture et aquaculture: tonnes

Country or area Pays ou zone	Capture production Captures					Aquaculture production Production de l'aquaculture				
	2003	2004	2005	2006	2007	2003	2004	2005	2006	2007
Cyprus Chypre	1 791	1 567	1 916	2 155	2 446	1 821	2 175	2 387	2 633	2 504
Czech Republic République tchèque	5 127	4 528	4 242	4 646	4 276	19 670	19 384	20 455	20 431	20 447
Dem. Rep. of the Congo Rép. dém. du Congo	235 765	237 372	236 640	236 588	236 000	2 965[1]	2 965[1]	2 965[1]	2 970[1]	2 970[1]
Denmark Danemark	1 031 221	1 090 596	910 667	867 855	653 023	37 772	42 814	39 012	37 188	31 168
Djibouti Djibouti	260[1]	260[1]	260[1]	260[1]	265	...	...	...	...	...
Dominica Dominique	950	700	579	694	776	3[1]	3[1]	...	...	...
Dominican Republic Rép. dominicaine	18 097	14 223	11 193	12 956	13 709	1 944[1]	2 000[1]	980	980[1]	980[1]
Ecuador Equateur	397 764	338 910	407 376	448 828	383 725	95 278	108 673	138 562	169 588	171 020[1]
Egypt Egypte	430 809	393 494	349 553	375 894	372 491	445 181	471 535	539 748	595 030	635 516
El Salvador El Salvador	35 410	42 415	41 114	43 218	48 639	1 131	2 219	2 203	3 078	3 729
Equatorial Guinea Guinée équatoriale	3 550[1]	3 500[1]	3 500[1]	3 450[1]	3 583	...	...	...	0	^0
Eritrea Erythrée	6 689	7 404	4 027	8 813	1 932	...	...	...	...	...
Estonia Estonie	79 082	87 906	98 772	86 490	97 836	372	252	555	703	778
Ethiopia Ethiopie	9 213	10 005	9 450	9 890	13 253	0	0	0	0	0
Faeroe Islands Iles Féroé	620 991	599 386	565 260	623 122	582 134	62 746	46 077	23 455	18 574	29 954[1]
Falkland Is. (Malvinas) Iles Falkland (Malvinas)	74 898	55 369	84 546	75 288	72 147	0	21	2	2	2
Fiji Fidji	34 689	46 656	42 500[1]	46 080	48 677	144	99	99[1]	428	180
Finland Finlande	121 954	135 427	131 741	149 444	164 381	12 558	12 821	14 355	12 891	13 031
France France	638 338	599 460	573 614	574 433	512 276	239 583	242 634	245 115	238 119	237 618
French Guiana Guyane française	5 565[1]	5 514[1]	5 285[1]	4 458	4 874	37	37	37	37	...
French Polynesia Polynésie française	14 099[1]	12 198[1]	12 152	13 409	13 080	60	65	75	64	46
Gabon Gabon	45 479	45 998	43 863	41 521	39 000[1]	80	80	78	126	124
Gambia Gambie	37 364	32 423	34 586	36 912	43 574	...	...	...	...	...
Georgia Géorgie	3 306	11 988	9 974[1]	9 709[1]	18 197	56	72	72[1]	75[1]	180
Germany Allemagne	260 867	262 103	285 668	297 837	248 763	74 280	57 233	44 685	35 379	44 994
Ghana Ghana	390 770	399 389	391 867	366 919	320 725	938	950	1 154	1 150[1]	1 150[1]
Greece Grèce	93 383	93 886	92 423	98 238	96 094	101 434	97 143	106 268	113 307	113 258

34

Fish production *(continued)*
Capture and aquaculture: metric tons
Production halieutique *(suite)*
Pêche de capture et aquaculture: tonnes

Country or area Pays ou zone	Capture production Captures					Aquaculture production Production de l'aquaculture				
	2003	2004	2005	2006	2007	2003	2004	2005	2006	2007
Greenland Groenland	175 321	228 400	247 011	247 011[1]	247 011[1]	...	...	...	...	...
Grenada Grenade	2 544	2 039	2 053	2 169	2 407	...	...	...	...	...
Guadeloupe Guadeloupe	10 100	10 100	10 100	10 100	10 100	31	31	31	31	37[1]
Guam Guam	458	596	320	609	642	...	...	...	162	162
Guatemala Guatemala	23 696[1]	10 012[1]	18 366	18 667	17 587	6 346[1]	4 908[1]	9 008[1]	16 293	16 400[1]
Guinea Guinée	120 242	93 947	105 137	100 000[1]	100 000[1]	...	...	...	...	...
Guinea-Bissau [1] Guinée-Bissau [1]	6 153	6 200	6 200	6 200	6 200	...	...	...	...	...
Guyana Guyana	59 695	56 719	53 370	53 000[1]	47 440	608[1]	608[1]	608	660[1]	660
Haiti [1] Haïti [1]	8 000	8 300	9 000	10 000	10 000	...	...	...	...	...
Honduras Honduras	7 667[1]	12 105[1]	16 558[1]	16 894[1]	12 878[1]	23 547	27 036	49 249	55 356[1]	54 689
Hungary Hongrie	6 536	7 242	7 609	7 543	7 024	11 870	12 744	13 661	14 686	15 864
Iceland Islande	1 986 539	1 733 702	1 664 657	1 327 097	1 399 167	6 214	9 003	8 325[1]	8 345[1]	4 899[1]
India Inde	3 712 149	3 391 009	3 691 362	3 844 837	3 953 476	2 312 971	2 794 636	2 961 978	3 169 303	3 354 754
Indonesia Indonésie	4 644 715	4 653 888	4 709 074	4 823 587	4 936 629	996 659	1 045 051	1 197 109	1 292 899	1 392 904
Iran (Islamic Rep. of) Iran (Rép. islamique d')	350 122	369 990	410 558	445 852	403 635	91 714	104 330	112 001	129 708	158 789
Iraq Iraq	17 200	12 936	29 929	59 259	57 779	2 000[1]	13 947	17 941	14 867	15 810[1]
Ireland Irlande	266 218	280 229	262 548	211 110	227 145	62 516	58 359	60 050	53 122	57 101
Isle of Man Ile de Man	2 984	2 627	2 764	1 209	3 760	...	...	...	...	...
Israel Israël	4 055	3 340	4 151	3 820	3 820[1]	20 776	22 303	22 404	22 216	22 416[1]
Italy Italie	295 694	287 084	296 889	315 436	286 645	191 884	118 217	181 101	172 833	178 992
Jamaica Jamaïque	8 702	13 471	13 096	17 830[1]	16 548	2 969	4 495	5 670	8 019	5 616
Japan Japon	4 670 393	4 315 734	4 389 206	4 344 513	4 211 201	823 873	776 421	746 221	733 891	765 846
Jordan Jordanie	481	494	510	485	506	650	487	561	560	509
Kazakhstan Kazakhstan	25 938	33 856	36 785	34 620	41 242	820	589	1 102	528	386
Kenya Kenya	120 051	126 867	147 304	158 684	131 765	1 012	1 035	1 047	1 012	4 240
Kiribati Kiribati	31 650	29 000[1]	28 500[1]	23 600[1]	21 598[1]	9	9[1]	12	12	5
Korea, Dem. P. R. [1] Corée, R. p. dém. de [1]	205 000	205 000	205 000	205 000	205 000	63 700	63 700	63 700	63 700	63 700

Fish production *(continued)*
Capture and aquaculture: metric tons
Production halieutique *(suite)*
Pêche de capture et aquaculture: tonnes

Country or area Pays ou zone	Capture production Captures					Aquaculture production Production de l'aquaculture				
	2003	2004	2005	2006	2007	2003	2004	2005	2006	2007
Korea, Republic of Corée, République de	1 643 148	1 575 475	1 641 026	1 775 437	1 858 206	387 791	405 748	436 571	513 568	606 122
Kuwait Koweït	4 059	4 833	4 895	5 635	4 373	366	375	327	568	348
Kyrgyzstan Kirghizistan	14	7	7[1]	7[1]	34	12	20	20[1]	20[1]	107
Lao People's Dem. Rep. Rép. dém. pop. lao	29 800	29 800	26 560	26 925	26 925[1]	64 900	64 900	78 000	78 000[1]	78 000[1]
Latvia Lettonie	114 543	125 391	150 618	140 389	155 276	637	545	542	565	729
Lebanon Liban	3 898	3 866	3 798	3 811	3 811	790	790	803	803	803
Lesotho Lesotho	42	45	45	45	48	4	2	1	2	131
Liberia Libéria	10 004	14 525	13 347	10 494	16 245	14[1]	...	...	...	...
Libyan Arab Jamah. Jamah. arabe libyenne	41 828[1]	39 898	37 391[1]	34 647[1]	31 921	...	288	388[1]	388[1]	240[1]
Lithuania Lituanie	157 205	161 988	139 785	154 548	187 513	2 356	2 697	2 013	2 224	3 377
Madagascar Madagascar	129 525	134 916	133 252	133 842	147 778	9 457	8 793	9 376	11 213	11 257[1]
Malawi Malawi	53 543	56 463	58 783	71 287	66 500	666	733	812	1 500	1 500
Malaysia Malaisie	1 287 084	1 335 764	1 214 183	1 296 335	1 385 703	167 160	171 270	175 834	168 317	178 239
Maldives Maldives	155 415	158 164	185 923	184 158	143 597	...	...	...	...	...
Mali Mali	100 000[1]	100 000[1]	100 000[1]	100 000[1]	100 000	1 008[1]	1 008[1]	1 008[1]	1 000[1]	640
Malta Malte	1 138	1 138	1 406	1 330	1 235	887	868	736	1 115	2 548
Marshall Islands Iles Marshall	38 775	47 576	57 164	43 349	60 409	...	...	...	...	...
Martinique Martinique	6 200	6 200	5 500	6 300	6 300	100	92	92	92	0
Mauritania Mauritanie	199 650[1]	270 733	304 877	165 312	201 588[1]	...	...	...	...	...
Mauritius Maurice	10 968	9 971	9 855	8 681	7 906	33	350	400	443	570
Mayotte Mayotte	3 464	2 306	2 194	5 772	11 661	213	170	164	140	128[1]
Mexico Mexique	1 357 251	1 258 973	1 320 049	1 357 366	1 340 000[1]	84 475	104 354	133 131	154 451	156 002[1]
Micronesia (Fed. States of) Micronésie (Etats féd. de)	32 379[1]	30 021	29 852	12 324	16 990	0	0	0	0	^0
Monaco [1] Monaco [1]	3	3	2	1	1	...	...	...	...	...
Mongolia Mongolie	382	305	366	326	185	...	...	...	...	...
Montenegro [1] Monténégro [1]	...	...	...	900	900	...	...	...	11	11
Montserrat [1] Montserrat [1]	50	50	50	50	50	...	...	...	...	...

34

Fish production *(continued)*
Capture and aquaculture: metric tons
Production halieutique *(suite)*
Pêche de capture et aquaculture: tonnes

Country or area Pays ou zone	Capture production Captures					Aquaculture production Production de l'aquaculture				
	2003	2004	2005	2006	2007	2003	2004	2005	2006	2007
Morocco Maroc	939 964	944 882	1 026 509	867 877	880 443	1 538	1 718	2 257	1 161	1 636
Mozambique Mozambique	99 282[1]	99 589[1]	93 995[1]	101 899[1]	92 270	409	446	1 222	1 048	838
Myanmar Myanmar	1 343 860	1 586 600	1 732 250	2 006 790	2 235 580	252 010	400 360	485 220	574 990	604 660
Namibia Namibie	637 227	571 708	553 995	509 395	415 518	50[1]	50[1]	50[1]	50[1]	25
Nauru Nauru	44	18	39	39[1]	39[1]	...	...	...	...	...
Nepal Népal	18 888	19 947	19 983	20 016	20 100	17 680	20 000	22 480	25 409	26 679
Netherlands Pays-Bas	526 281	521 636	549 208	435 335	413 602	66 540	78 598	71 370	45 553	56 761[1]
Netherlands Antilles Antilles néerlandaises	20 149	17 286	650	6 247	3 662	...	...	...	...	...
New Caledonia Nouvelle-Calédonie	3 657	3 767	3 315	3 151	3 510	1 784	2 290	2 533	2 365	1 931
New Zealand Nouvelle-Zélande	550 943	545 950	545 118	476 884	488 960	84 641	92 220	105 302	107 524	111 908[1]
Nicaragua Nicaragua	15 326	19 554	31 054	35 633	26 426	7 005	7 880	9 983	11 220	11 533
Niger Niger	55 860	51 466	50 018	29 835	29 728	40	40	40	40	40
Nigeria Nigéria	475 162	465 251	523 182	552 323	530 420	30 677	43 950	56 355	84 578	85 087
Niue [1] Nioué [1]	200	200	203	200	200	...	...	...	...	...
Northern Mariana Islands Iles Mariannes du Nord	173	170	196	187	231	...	...	...	...	...
Norway Norvège	2 548 975	2 524 464	2 392 970	2 256 413	2 378 950	584 423	636 802	661 811	712 281	830 190
Occupied Palestinian Terr. Terr. palestinien occupé	1 507	2 951	1 814	2 323	2 702	...	...	...	...	...
Oman Oman	138 481	165 082	157 326	147 669	151 744	352	503	173	89[1]	90[1]
Pakistan Pakistan	491 834	480 340	434 850	489 421	440 190	73 047	76 653	80 622	121 825	130 092
Palau Palaos	1 047	1 079	932	967	985	4	5	5	5[1]	18[1]
Panama Panama	219 299	208 840	220 333	226 825	206 732	6 228	7 048	7 778	8 744	8 837[1]
Papua New Guinea Papouasie-Nvl-Guinée	222 124	256 384	290 115	280 137	263 960	15[1]	...	...	...	0
Paraguay [1] Paraguay [1]	23 000	22 000	21 000	20 000	20 000	1 300	2 100	2 100	2 100	2 100
Peru Pérou	6 086 060	9 604 527	9 388 488	7 017 491	7 210 544	13 621	22 114	25 964	28 393	39 531
Philippines Philippines	2 165 812	2 211 245	2 269 668	2 318 981	2 499 634	459 615	512 220	557 251	623 369	709 715
Pitcairn [1] Pitcairn [1]	5	3	3	3	3	...	...	...	...	...
Poland Pologne	180 399	192 108	155 247	145 479	151 820	35 436	35 131	37 920	35 867	35 628

34

Fish production *(continued)*
Capture and aquaculture: metric tons
Production halieutique *(suite)*
Pêche de capture et aquaculture: tonnes

Country or area Pays ou zone	Capture production Captures					Aquaculture production Production de l'aquaculture				
	2003	2004	2005	2006	2007	2003	2004	2005	2006	2007
Portugal Portugal	212 073	221 316	211 756	229 078	252 802	8 033	6 700	6 696	7 893	7 473
Puerto Rico Porto Rico	2 919	2 428	2 551	2 042	1 675	269	417	311	266	44
Qatar Qatar	11 295	11 134	13 935	16 376	15 190	0	0	11	36	36
Republic of Moldova République de Moldova	343	487	531	612	1 160	2 638	4 470	4 470	5 000	4 700
Réunion Réunion	2 904	3 373	4 282	3 548	3 925	121	107	161	161	0
Romania Roumanie	9 890	5 095	6 068	6 664	6 184	9 042	8 137	7 284	8 088	10 312
Russian Federation Fédération de Russie	3 281 448	2 941 533	3 197 564	3 284 285	3 454 214	108 684	109 802	114 752	105 525	105 503
Rwanda Rwanda	7 400	7 826	7 800[1]	8 400[1]	9 050	1 027	386	386[1]	400[1]	4 038
Saint Helena Sainte-Hélène	985	1 061	1 130	1 120	837	...	...	...	...	...
Saint Kitts and Nevis Saint-Kitts-et-Nevis	400[1]	484	450[1]	450[1]	450[1]	...	...	...	...	...
Saint Lucia Sainte-Lucie	1 462	1 508	1 409	1 496	1 555	2[1]	1	1	0	^0
Saint Pierre and Miquelon Saint-Pierre-et-Miquelon	3 894	4 399	4 694	2 855	5 113	...	...	...	...	...
Saint Vincent-Grenadines Saint Vincent-Grenadines	4 784	8 634	1 740	4 739	5 250	...	...	...	...	...
Samoa Samoa	4 494[1]	4 795	3 200[1]	3 750	4 606	0	...	...	...	3
Sao Tome and Principe Sao Tomé-et-Principe	4 038	4 141	4 197[1]	4 150[1]	4 150[1]	...	...	...	...	...
Saudi Arabia Arabie saoudite	55 440	55 418	60 407	65 471	70 000[1]	11 824	11 172	14 375	15 586	18 410
Senegal Sénégal	478 284	445 338	412 131	378 927	421 317	98	204	193[1]	200[1]	200[1]
Serbia Serbie	...	...	...	2 628	2 631	...	...	...	4 904	6 528
Serbia and Montenegro Serbie-et-Monténégro	1 798	2 388	2 468[1]	...	...	3 194	4 616	4 554	...	...
Seychelles Seychelles	85 990	100 671	108 688	93 121	65 871	1 084	1 175	772	704	368
Sierra Leone Sierra Leone	96 926	134 440	145 993	148 146	144 535	...	...	...	...	...
Singapore Singapour	2 085	2 173	1 920	3 103	3 522	5 024	5 406	5 917	8 573	4 503
Slovakia Slovaquie	1 646	1 603	1 693	1 718	2 872	881	1 180	955	1 263	1 199
Slovenia Slovénie	1 281	1 022	1 223	1 131	1 111	1 353	1 571	1 346	1 369	1 352
Solomon Islands[1] Iles Salomon[1]	35 813	32 766	30 094	39 336	31 272	...	...	...	...	...
Somalia[1] Somalie[1]	30 000	30 000	30 000	30 000	30 000	...	...	...	...	...
South Africa Afrique du Sud	822 936	888 106	817 666	618 616	670 571	3 778	3 109	2 895	3 037[1]	2 789[1]

34

Fish production *(continued)*
Capture and aquaculture: metric tons
Production halieutique *(suite)*
Pêche de capture et aquaculture: tonnes

Country or area Pays ou zone	Capture production Captures					Aquaculture production Production de l'aquaculture				
	2003	2004	2005	2006	2007	2003	2004	2005	2006	2007
Spain Espagne	894 827	808 109	848 844	950 714	808 682	268 201	293 319	219 367	292 918	281 240
Sri Lanka Sri Lanka	328 319	333 360	190 856	274 025	309 755	3 462	4 003	4 304	5 652	8 233
Sudan Soudan	59 000	63 000	59 000	57 000	65 509	1 600[1]	1 600[1]	1 600[1]	1 600[1]	1 950[1]
Suriname Suriname	32 482	30 402	27 410	30 621	29 627	260	288	242	180	52
Swaziland [1] Swaziland [1]	70	70	70	70	70	...	...	...	...	...
Sweden Suède	286 875	269 922	256 359	269 251	238 253	6 334	5 989	5 880	7 549	5 365
Switzerland Suisse	1 815	1 602	1 475	1 422	1 377	1 100	1 205	1 214	1 214	1 217
Syrian Arab Republic Rép. arabe syrienne	8 911	8 528	8 447	8 264	9 456	7 217	8 682	8 533	8 902	8 425
Tajikistan Tadjikistan	158	184	146	146[1]	146[1]	167	26	26	26	26
Thailand Thaïlande	2 849 724	2 839 612	2 814 295	2 698 803	2 468 784	1 064 409	1 259 983	1 304 213	1 406 981	1 390 031[1]
TFYR of Macedonia L'ex-R.Y. Macédoine	162	213	246	89	122	910	959	868	646	1 096
Timor-Leste [1] Timor-Leste [1]	350	350	350	350	350	...	...	...	...	...
Togo Togo	27 485	28 013	27 744	24 879	19 905	1 221	1 525[1]	1 535	3 020	5 000
Tokelau [1] Tokélaou [1]	200	200	200	200	200	...	...	...	...	...
Tonga Tonga	4 435	1 645	2 000[1]	2 500[1]	2 545[1]	22	3	1	5	4
Trinidad and Tobago Trinité-et-Tobago	9 915	10 034	13 414	8 445	8 406	7[1]	...	...	...	...
Tunisia Tunisie	90 226	111 531	109 117	111 288	103 163	2 086	2 308	2 603	2 634	3 367
Turkey Turquie	507 772	550 482	426 496	533 048	632 450	79 943	94 450	119 567	129 025	140 021
Turkmenistan Turkménistan	14 543	14 992	15 000[1]	15 000[1]	15 000[1]	24	16	16[1]	16[1]	16[1]
Turks and Caicos Islands Iles Turques et Caïques	5 100	5 677	5 491	6 018	4 830	25	4	4	4	1
Tuvalu Tuvalu	1 500	2 400	2 560	2 200[1]	2 200[1]	5	1	1	1[1]	1[1]
Uganda Ouganda	241 810	371 789	416 758	367 099	500 000	5 500	5 539	10 817	32 392	51 110
Ukraine Ukraine	222 349	202 676	244 945	238 734	213 508	25 616	26 223	28 745	4 030	27 841
United Arab Emirates Emirats arabes unis	95 150	90 000[1]	86 735	87 000[1]	87 000[1]	2 300	570[1]	570[1]	570[1]	570[1]
United Kingdom Royaume-Uni	635 486	653 408	669 905	623 823	619 691	181 838[1]	207 203	172 813	171 848	174 203
United Rep. of Tanzania Rép.-Unie de Tanzanie	371 984	385 998	399 538	358 607	352 397	2	11	10[1]	10	10[1]
United States Etats-Unis	4 938 956	4 959 826	4 892 967	4 852 283	4 767 596	544 329	606 549	513 107	518 693	526 281

Fish production *(continued)*
Capture and aquaculture: metric tons
Production halieutique *(suite)*
Pêche de capture et aquaculture: tonnes

Country or area Pays ou zone	Capture production Captures					Aquaculture production Production de l'aquaculture				
	2003	2004	2005	2006	2007	2003	2004	2005	2006	2007
United States Virgin Is. Iles Vierges américaines	1 492	1 522	1 269	1 615	1 127	0	0	0	10	10[1]
Uruguay Uruguay	117 273	122 989	125 818	133 955	108 720	24	21	47	37	30
Uzbekistan Ouzbékistan	1 349	1 230	2 000[1]	3 400	2 802	3 118	3 093	3 800	3 800	3 424
Vanuatu Vanuatu	57 758	111 477	146 991	88 085	85 356	0	1	1	114	31
Venezuela (Bolivarian Rep. of) Venezuela (Rép. bolivarienne du)	520 773	487 000[1]	470 000[1]	460 000[1]	455 000[1]	19 821	22 210	22 210[1]	22 210[1]	22 210[1]
Viet Nam Viet Nam	1 856 105	1 879 488	1 929 900	1 970 600	2 121 400	937 502	1 198 617	1 437 300	1 657 727	2 156 500
Wallis and Futuna Islands Iles Wallis et Futuna	300	300[1]	300[1]	600	600[1]	...	...	...	...	...
Yemen Yémen	228 116	256 300	238 400	229 660	179 916	...	...	...	...	...
Zambia Zambie	65 000[1]	65 000[1]	65 000[1]	65 000[1]	65 000[1]	4 501	5 125	5 125[1]	5 125[1]	5 125[1]
Zimbabwe Zimbabwe	10 600[1]	10 500[1]	10 420[1]	10 500[1]	10 500[1]	2 600	2 955	2 452	2 450[1]	2 450[1]

Source:
Food and Agriculture Organization of the United Nations (FAO), Rome, FISHSTAT database, last accessed May 2009

Source:
Organisation des Nations Unies pour l'alimentation et l'agriculture (FAO), Rome, les données des pêches de FISHSTAT, dernier accès mai 2009.

1   FAO estimate.
2   For statistical purposes, the data for China do not include those for the Hong Kong Special Administrative Region (Hong Kong SAR), Macao Special Administrative Region (Macao SAR) and Taiwan Province of China.

1   Estimation de la FAO.
2   Pour la présentation des statistiques, les données pour la Chine ne comprennent pas la Région Administrative Spéciale de Hong Kong (Hong Kong RAS), la Région Administrative Spéciale de Macao (Macao RAS) et la province de Taiwan.

Technical notes: tables 31-34

The series shown on agriculture and fishing have been furnished by the Food and Agriculture Organization of the United Nations (FAO). They refer mainly to the long-term trends in the growth of agricultural output and the food supply, the output of principal agricultural commodities and fish production.

Agricultural production is defined to include all crops and livestock products except those used for seed and fodder and other intermediate uses in agriculture; for example deductions are made for eggs used for hatching. Intermediate input of seeds and fodder and similar items refer to both domestically produced and imported commodities. For further details, reference may be made to *FAO Statistical Yearbook*. FAO data are also available through the Internet at http://faostat.fao.org.

Table 31: "Agriculture" relates to the production of all crops and livestock products. The "Food Index" includes those commodities which are considered edible and contain nutrients.

The index numbers of agricultural output and food production are calculated by the Laspeyres formula with the base year period 1999-2001. The latter is provided in order to diminish the impact of annual fluctuations in agricultural output during base years on the indices for the period. Production quantities of each commodity are weighted by 1999-2001 average national producer prices and summed for each year. The index numbers are based on production data for a calendar year. These may differ in some instances from those actually produced and published by the individual countries themselves due to variations in concepts, coverage, weights and methods of calculation. Efforts have been made to estimate these methodological differences to achieve a better international comparability of data.

Detailed data on agricultural production are published by FAO in its *Statistical Yearbook*.

Table 32: The data on the production of cereals relate to crops harvested for dry grain only. Cereals harvested for hay, green feed or used for grazing are excluded.

Table 33: The data on roundwood refer to wood in the rough, wood in its natural state as felled or otherwise harvested, with or without bark, round, split, roughly squared or in other form (i.e. roots, stumps, burls, etc.). It may also be impregnated (e.g. telegraph poles) or roughly shaped or pointed. It comprises all wood obtained from removals, i.e. the quantities removed from forests and from trees outside the forest, including wood recovered from natural, felling and logging losses during the period—calendar year or forest year.

Table 34: The data cover (i) capture production from marine and inland fisheries and (ii) aquaculture,

Notes techniques : tableaux 31 à 34

Les séries présentées sur l'agriculture et la pêche ont été fournies par l'Organisation des Nations Unies pour l'alimentation et l'agriculture (FAO) et portent principalement sur les tendances à long terme de la croissance de la production agricole et des approvisionnements alimentaires, et sur la production des principales denrées agricoles et la production halieutique.

La production agricole se définit comme comprenant l'ensemble des produits agricoles et des produits de l'élevage à l'exception de ceux utilisés comme semences et comme aliments pour les animaux, et pour les autres utilisations intermédiaires en agriculture; par exemple, on déduit les œufs utilisés pour la reproduction. L'apport intermédiaire de semences et d'aliments pour les animaux et d'autres éléments similaires se rapportent à la fois à des produits locaux et importés. Pour tous détails complémentaires, on se reportera à *l'annuaire statistique de la FAO*. Des statistiques peuvent également être consultées sur le site Web de la FAO http://faostat.fao.org.

Tableau 31: "L'agriculture" se rapporte à la production de tous les produits de l'agriculture et de l'élevage. "L'indice des produits alimentaires" comprend les produits considérés comme comestibles et qui contiennent des éléments nutritifs.

Les indices de la production agricole et de la production alimentaire sont calculés selon la formule de Laspeyres avec les années 1999-2001 pour période de base. Le choix d'une période de plusieurs années permet de diminuer l'incidence des fluctuations annuelles de la production agricole pendant les années de base sur les indices pour cette période. Les quantités produites de chaque denrée sont pondérées par les prix nationaux moyens à la production de 1999-2001, et additionnées pour chaque année. Les indices sont fondés sur les données de production d'une année civile. Ils peuvent différer dans certains cas des indices effectivement établis et publiés par les pays eux-mêmes par suite de différences dans les concepts, la couverture, les pondérations et les méthodes de calcul. On s'est efforcé d'estimer ces différences méthodologiques afin de rendre les données plus facilement comparables à l'échelle internationale.

Des chiffres détaillés de production sont publiés dans l'*Annuaire statistique de la FAO*.

Tableau 32: Les données sur la production de céréales se rapportent uniquement aux céréales récoltées pour le grain sec; celles cultivées pour le foin, le fourrage vert ou le pâturage en sont exclues.

Tableau 33: Les données sur le bois rond se réfèrent au bois brut, bois à l'état naturel, tel qu'il a été abattu ou récolté autrement, avec ou sans écorce, fendu, grossièrement équarri ou sous une autre forme (par

and are expressed in terms of live weight. They include fish, crustaceans and molluscs but exclude sponges, corals, pearls, seaweed, crocodiles, and aquatic mammals (such as whales and dolphins).

The flag of the vessel is considered as the paramount indication of the nationality of the catch. Marine fisheries data include landings by domestic craft in foreign ports and exclude landings by foreign craft in domestic ports.

To separate aquaculture from capture fisheries production, at least two criteria must apply i.e., the human intervention in one or more of the phases of the growth cycle, and individual, corporate or state ownership of the organism reared and harvested.

Data on aquaculture production are published in the *FAO Yearbook of Fishery Statistics, Aquaculture Production*; capture production statistics are published in the *FAO Yearbook of Fishery Statistics, Capture Production.*

exemple, racines, souches, loupes, etc.). Il peut être également imprégné (par exemple, dans le cas des poteaux télégraphiques) et dégrossi ou taillé en pointe. Cette catégorie comprend tous les bois provenant des quantités enlevées en forêt ou provenant des arbres poussant hors forêt, y compris le volume récupéré sur les déchets naturels et les déchets d'abattage et de transport pendant la période envisagée (année civile ou forestière).

Tableau 34: Les données ont trait (i) à la pêche maritime et intérieure et (ii) à l'aquaculture, et sont exprimées en poids vif. Elles comprennent poissons, crustacés et mollusques, mais excluent éponges, coraux, perles, algues, crocodiles et les mammifères aquatiques (baleines, dauphins, etc.).

Le pavillon du navire est considéré comme la principale indication de la nationalité de la prise. Les données de pêche maritime comprennent les quantités débarquées par des bateaux nationaux dans des ports étrangers et excluent les quantités débarquées par des bateaux étrangers dans des ports nationaux.

Pour séparer la production d'aquaculture de la pêche de capture, au moins deux critères doivent se vérifier, c'est-à-dire l'intervention humaine dans une ou plusieurs des phases du cycle de croissance, et l'appartenance de l'organisme élevé et récolté à une personne physique, à une personne morale ou à l'état.

Les données sur la production de l'aquaculture sont publiées dans *l'Annuaire statistique des pêches, production de l'aquaculture*; celles sur les captures sont publiées dans *l'Annuaire statistique des pêches, captures*.

Sugar
Production and consumption: thousand metric tons; consumption per capita: kilograms

Sucre
Production et consommation : milliers de tonnes ; consommation per habitant : kilogrammes

Country or area	2001	2002	2003	2004	2005	2006	2007	Pays ou zone
World								**Monde**
Production	**130 650**	**142 088**	**148 122**	**147 261**	**141 354**	**152 087**	**166 319**	**Production**
Consumption	**127 740**	**134 072**	**137 477**	**142 572**	**143 468**	**148 266**	**152 828**	**Consommation**
Consumption per capita	**22**	**22**	**23**	**23**	**23**	**24**	**24**	**Consommation par habitant**
Afghanistan								**Afghanistan**
Consumption *	60	70	90	120	140	150	160	Consommation *
Consumption per capita	3	3	4	5	6	7	7	Consommation par habitant
Albania								**Albanie**
Production *	3	3	3	3	3	5	4	Production *
Consumption *	68	75	85	88	90	90	95	Consommation *
Consumption per capita	22	24	27	28	29	29	30	Consommation par habitant
Algeria								**Algérie**
Consumption *	965	1 040	1 100	1 135	1 185	1 215	1 245	Consommation *
Consumption per capita	31	33	35	35	36	36	37	Consommation par habitant
Angola								**Angola**
Consumption *	155	185	195	205	225	245	255	Consommation *
Consumption per capita	11	13	13	13	14	15	15	Consommation par habitant
Argentina								**Argentine**
Production	*1 630	*1 680	1 952	1 857	2 165	2 470	2 198	Production
Consumption	*1 520	*1 515	1 515	1 574	1 654	1 866	1 874	Consommation
Consumption per capita	41	40	39	41	42	47	47	Consommation par habitant
Armenia								**Arménie**
Production	0	0	0	0	2	2	3	Production
Consumption	*73	*74	87	*87	*87	*87	*88	Consommation
Consumption per capita	19	23	27	27	27	27	27	Consommation par habitant
Australia								**Australie**
Production	4 768	5 614	5 315	5 530	5 393	4 729	4 627	Production
Consumption	1 068	1 100	1 089	1 043	1 034	*1 035	*1 040	Consommation
Consumption per capita	55	56	55	52	51	50	50	Consommation par habitant
Azerbaijan								**Azerbaïdjan**
Production	...	...	...	...	2	*60	138	Production
Consumption *	160	165	175	180	185	185	190	Consommation *
Consumption per capita	20	20	21	21	22	22	22	Consommation par habitant
Bahamas								**Bahamas**
Consumption	8	9	11	12	13	14	14	Consommation
Consumption per capita	27	32	35	38	41	44	44	Consommation par habitant
Bangladesh								**Bangladesh**
Production	109	229	*166	*125	*120	*145	*170	Production
Consumption *	550	635	695	790	880	995	1 055	Consommation *
Consumption per capita	4	5	5	6	6	6	7	Consommation par habitant
Barbados								**Barbade**
Production	*50	*45	*36	*35	*40	32	*34	Production
Consumption *	15	15	15	15	15	15	15	Consommation *
Consumption per capita	56	56	56	56	56	56	55	Consommation par habitant
Belarus								**Bélarus**
Production	196	162	*255	*340	*435	*480	*495	Production
Consumption	422	410	*410	*415	*420	*425	*425	Consommation
Consumption per capita	42	41	42	42	43	43	44	Consommation par habitant
Belize								**Belize**
Production	114	119	111	125	102	120	100	Production
Consumption	12[1]	12	12	12	12	13	14	Consommation
Consumption per capita	46	44	44	42	42	44	45	Consommation par habitant
Benin								**Bénin**
Production *	5	5	4	4	5	10	10	Production *
Consumption	22	*28	*35	*36	*37	*38	*39	Consommation
Consumption per capita	3	4	5	5	5	5	4	Consommation par habitant
Bermuda								**Bermudes**
Consumption	2	2	2	2	2	2	2	Consommation
Consumption per capita	25	25	25	25	25	25	25	Consommation par habitant

35

Sugar *(continued)*
Production and consumption: thousand metric tons; consumption per capita: kilograms
Sucre *(suite)*
Production et consommation : milliers de tonnes ; consommation par habitant : kilogrammes

Country or area	2001	2002	2003	2004	2005	2006	2007	Pays ou zone
Bolivia								**Bolivie**
Production	390	426	387	464	*400	*370	*375	Production
Consumption *	295	300	305	310	320	325	335	Consommation *
Consumption per capita	34	34	34	34	34	34	34	Consommation par habitant
Bosnia and Herzegovina								**Bosnie-Herzégovine**
Consumption *	110	120	130	130	135	135	140	Consommation *
Consumption per capita	29	31	34	34	35	35	36	Consommation par habitant
Botswana								**Botswana**
Consumption	46	47	48	48	50	51	51	Consommation
Consumption per capita	28	28	28	28	29	29	29	Consommation par habitant
Brazil								**Brésil**
Production	20 336	23 567	25 730	27 290	28 135	31 622	33 199	Production
Consumption	*9 800	10 520	10 217	10 857	10 950	12 513	12 474	Consommation
Consumption per capita	57	60	58	59	59	66	68	Consommation par habitant
Brunei Darussalam								**Brunéi Darussalam**
Consumption	10	10	11	11	11	11	11	Consommation
Consumption per capita	30	29	31	31	30	29	29	Consommation par habitant
Bulgaria [2]								**Bulgarie** [2]
Production *	3	3	3	3	5	4	...	Production *
Consumption *	240	255	265	270	275	280	...	Consommation *
Consumption per capita	30	33	34	35	36	37	...	Consommation par habitant
Burkina Faso								**Burkina Faso**
Production *	35	40	40	40	40	40	40	Production *
Consumption *	55	60	65	65	75	80	85	Consommation *
Consumption per capita	5	5	5	5	6	6	6	Consommation par habitant
Burundi								**Burundi**
Production	20	20	22	22	23	25	24	Production
Consumption	23	25	26	27	29	29	30	Consommation
Consumption per capita	4	3	3	4	4	4	4	Consommation par habitant
Cameroon								**Cameroun**
Production	94	104	*120	*125	119	126	100	Production
Consumption	112	145	*150	*145	92	112	129	Consommation
Consumption per capita	7	10	10	8	5	6	7	Consommation par habitant
Canada								**Canada**
Production *	95	64	85	115	105	135	130	Production *
Consumption *	1 240	1 255	1 400	1 425	1 425	1 430	1 435	Consommation *
Consumption per capita	40	40	44	45	44	43	43	Consommation par habitant
Cape Verde								**Cap-Vert**
Consumption *	15	16	17	17	17	17	18	Consommation *
Consumption per capita	34	36	37	36	35	35	37	Consommation par habitant
Central African Rep.								**Rép. centrafricaine**
Consumption *	4	5	6	9	11	11	11	Consommation *
Consumption per capita	1	1	2	3	4	4	4	Consommation par habitant
Chad								**Tchad**
Production	*32	*32	*33	*30	*35	*35	35	Production
Consumption	*57	*65	*75	*80	*85	*90	90	Consommation
Consumption per capita	7	8	9	9	10	10	10	Consommation par habitant
Chile								**Chili**
Production	*430	576	374	401	386	372	*370	Production
Consumption	*685	*685	*685	673	682	*695	*700	Consommation
Consumption per capita	44	46	43	41	41	42	42	Consommation par habitant
China [3]								**Chine** [3]
Production	7 161	9 805	11 433	10 912	*9 785	*10 682	*13 895	Production
Consumption	*8 900	*9 975	11 065	11 613	*11 785	*11 975	*13 825	Consommation
Consumption per capita	7	8	9	9	9	9	10	Consommation par habitant
China, Hong Kong SAR								**Chine, Hong Kong RAS**
Consumption *	181	181	185	185	185	185	190	Consommation *
Consumption per capita	27	27	27	27	27	27	27	Consommation par habitant
China, Macao SAR								**Chine, Macao RAS**
Consumption	7	8	8	8	8	8	7	Consommation
Consumption per capita	17	17	18	21	17	15	12	Consommation par habitant

Sugar *(continued)*
Production and consumption. thousand metric tons; consumption per capita: kilograms
Sucre *(suite)*
Production et consommation : milliers de tonnes ; consommation par habitant : kilogrammes

Country or area	2001	2002	2003	2004	2005	2006	2007	Pays ou zone
Colombia								**Colombie**
Production	2 260	2 523	2 646	2 740	2 683	2 415	2 277	Production
Consumption	1 309[4]	1 356[4]	1 348	1 521	1 512	1 460	1 547[4]	Consommation
Consumption per capita	30	31	30	34	33	34	35	Consommation par habitant
Comoros								**Comores**
Consumption	8	9	9	9	9	9	10	Consommation
Consumption per capita	11	11	11	11	12	12	13	Consommation par habitant
Congo								**Congo**
Production	*45	33	*45	*55	63	*65	56	Production
Consumption	*45	32	*50	*55	76	*80	*80	Consommation
Consumption per capita	15	10	17	18	24	25	27	Consommation par habitant
Costa Rica								**Costa Rica**
Production	358	*360	*358	*405	398	348	373	Production
Consumption	*210	*225	*230	*230	225	*230	235	Consommation
Consumption per capita	54	56	56	54	53	56	55	Consommation par habitant
Côte d'Ivoire								**Côte d'Ivoire**
Production *	155	170	145	120	145	145	145	Production *
Consumption *	190	200	205	210	215	220	230	Consommation *
Consumption per capita	11	11	11	11	11	11	11	Consommation par habitant
Croatia								**Croatie**
Production	131	160	116	173	204	*230	*225	Production
Consumption *	175	180	185	190	200	200	200	Consommation *
Consumption per capita	40	41	42	43	45	45	45	Consommation par habitant
Cuba								**Cuba**
Production	3 748	3 522	2 278	*2 600	*1 300	1 239	1 193	Production
Consumption	698	698	682	*700	*700	741	690	Consommation
Consumption per capita	63	62	61	62	62	66	61	Consommation par habitant
Cyprus [2]								**Chypre** [2]
Consumption	32	33	36	...	...	...	...	Consommation
Consumption per capita	42	46	47	...	...	...	...	Consommation par habitant
Czech Republic [2]								**République tchèque** [2]
Production	484	523	522	...	...	...	...	Production
Consumption	450	475	399	...	...	...	...	Consommation
Consumption per capita	44	47	39	...	...	...	...	Consommation par habitant
Dem. Rep. of the Congo								**Rép. dém. du Congo**
Production *	60	65	65	60	60	65	65	Production *
Consumption *	75	85	85	90	95	105	120	Consommation *
Consumption per capita	1	2	2	2	2	2	2	Consommation par habitant
Djibouti								**Djibouti**
Consumption	13	13	14	15	16	16	16	Consommation
Consumption per capita	15	15	16	17	18	18	18	Consommation par habitant
Dominican Republic								**Rép. dominicaine**
Production	491	516	525	*530	*475	487	488	Production
Consumption	352	366	322	*360	*370	338	325	Consommation
Consumption per capita	41	44	36	39	38	36	34	Consommation par habitant
Ecuador								**Equateur**
Production	*495	*475	*505	*490	*470	520	*495	Production
Consumption *	465	480	485	485	488	490	495	Consommation *
Consumption per capita	37	38	38	37	37	37	36	Consommation par habitant
Egypt								**Egypte**
Production	*1 585	*1 490	*1 425	1 489	*1 625	*1 725	1 851	Production
Consumption	*2 325	*2 400	*2 500	*2 600	*2 675	*2 700	2 700	Consommation
Consumption per capita	36	36	35	35	37	36	36	Consommation par habitant
El Salvador								**El Salvador**
Production	527	476	530	555	633	542	560	Production
Consumption	244	217	209	212	225	240	237	Consommation
Consumption per capita	38	33	33	33	35	35	37	Consommation par habitant
Eritrea								**Erythrée**
Consumption	8	9	15	16	20	20	25	Consommation
Consumption per capita	2	2	3	4	4	4	5	Consommation par habitant

35

Sugar *(continued)*
Production and consumption: thousand metric tons; consumption per capita: kilograms
Sucre *(suite)*
Production et consommation : milliers de tonnes ; consommation par habitant : kilogrammes

Country or area	2001	2002	2003	2004	2005	2006	2007	Pays ou zone
Estonia[2]								**Estonie**[2]
Consumption	73	73	80	...	...	...	...	Consommation
Consumption per capita	53	49	60	...	...	...	...	Consommation par habitant
Ethiopia								**Ethiopie**
Production	*305	287	*295	*325	*345	*360	*340	Production
Consumption	*240	211	*260	*295	*320	*350	*370	Consommation
Consumption per capita	4	3	4	4	4	5	5	Consommation par habitant
European Union[2]								**Union européenne**[2]
Production	15 500	18 268	16 578	21 843	21 698	18 098	18 445	Production
Consumption	13 588	14 370	14 137	17 691	16 765	17 527	19 315	Consommation
Consumption per capita	36	38	37	39	36	38	39	Consommation par habitant
Fiji								**Fidji**
Production	327	334	330	330	306	324	254	Production
Consumption	45[5]	53[5]	55	58[5]	55	61[5]	70[5]	Consommation
Consumption per capita	55	64	66	69	66	71	85	Consommation par habitant
Gabon								**Gabon**
Production	*18	*18	25	*19	*21	21	*21	Production
Consumption	*19	*20	*21	*21	*21	21	*22	Consommation
Consumption per capita	15	16	16	16	15	15	15	Consommation par habitant
Gambia								**Gambie**
Consumption *	60	65	70	70	70	75	75	Consommation *
Consumption per capita	42	45	48	47	47	50	49	Consommation par habitant
Georgia								**Géorgie**
Consumption *	110	120	125	135	135	135	137	Consommation *
Consumption per capita	25	28	29	31	31	31	31	Consommation par habitant
Ghana								**Ghana**
Consumption *	155	170	185	200	205	215	220	Consommation *
Consumption per capita	8	9	9	10	10	10	10	Consommation par habitant
Gibraltar								**Gibraltar**
Consumption	2	2	2	2	2	1	1	Consommation
Consumption per capita	73	55	60	67	53	37	...	Consommation par habitant
Guatemala								**Guatemala**
Production	1 661	1 910	1 801	2 092	2 015	1 961	2 364	Production
Consumption	496	534	585	585	657	637	716	Consommation
Consumption per capita	42	45	48	47	52	49	54	Consommation par habitant
Guinea								**Guinée**
Production *	25	25	26	26	25	25	25	Production *
Consumption *	95	100	110	110	120	125	130	Consommation *
Consumption per capita	11	12	13	12	13	13	13	Consommation par habitant
Guinea-Bissau								**Guinée-Bissau**
Consumption	7	7	8	9	14	14	15	Consommation
Consumption per capita	6	6	6	7	11	10	11	Consommation par habitant
Guyana								**Guyana**
Production	284	331	*302	*320	246	*255	*265	Production
Consumption	24	24	*25	*26	22	*25	*26	Consommation
Consumption per capita	35	31	33	35	29	33	34	Consommation par habitant
Haiti								**Haïti**
Production *	5	5	...	...	...	...	...	Production *
Consumption *	165	170	175	175	185	185	190	Consommation *
Consumption per capita	20	21	22	22	23	23	23	Consommation par habitant
Honduras								**Honduras**
Production	316	*320	300	357	*360	*385	*390	Production
Consumption	237	*240	249	250	*250	*250	*260	Consommation
Consumption per capita	39	33	36	35	36	36	37	Consommation par habitant
Hungary[2]								**Hongrie**[2]
Production	434	347	257	...	...	...	...	Production
Consumption	317	313	282	...	...	...	...	Consommation
Consumption per capita	31	31	28	...	...	...	...	Consommation par habitant
Iceland								**Islande**
Consumption *	12	12	12	12	11	11	11	Consommation *
Consumption per capita	41	41	41	41	37	36	35	Consommation par habitant

Sugar *(continued)*
Production and consumption: thousand metric tons; consumption per capita: kilograms
Sucre *(suite)*
Production et consommation : milliers de tonnes ; consommation par habitant : kilogrammes

Country or area	2001	2002	2003	2004	2005	2006	2007	Pays ou zone
India								**Inde**
Production	19 906	19 525	21 702	14 432	15 216	22 347	29 090	Production
Consumption	17 274	17 857	18 625	19 858	20 110	20 110	20 878	Consommation
Consumption per capita	17	17	18	19	20	18	17	Consommation par habitant
Indonesia								**Indonésie**
Production	*1 850	*2 150	*1 780	*2 225	*2 435	2 510	2 814	Production
Consumption *	3 500	3 675	3 800	3 915	4 052	4 195	4 400	Consommation *
Consumption per capita	17	17	18	18	18	19	20	Consommation par habitant
Iran (Islamic Rep. of)								**Iran (Rép. islamique d')**
Production *	900	995	1 270	1 310	1 300	1 425	1 250	Production *
Consumption *	1 965	1 975	2 025	2 060	2 110	2 160	2 225	Consommation *
Consumption per capita	30	30	30	31	31	31	31	Consommation par habitant
Iraq								**Iraq**
Consumption *	425	500	650	675	675	685	700	Consommation *
Consumption per capita	17	20	25	25	24	24	24	Consommation par habitant
Israel								**Israël**
Consumption *	400	410	425	440	455	460	470	Consommation *
Consumption per capita	62	62	64	65	66	65	66	Consommation par habitant
Jamaica								**Jamaïque**
Production	205	175	154	181	126	144	163	Production
Consumption	136	126	129	111	123	98	109	Consommation
Consumption per capita	52	48	49	42	46	36	40	Consommation par habitant
Japan								**Japon**
Production	823	901	934	976	965	909	859	Production
Consumption	2 339	2 433	2 415	2 403	2 397	2 229	2 452	Consommation
Consumption per capita	18	19	19	19	19	17	19	Consommation par habitant
Jordan								**Jordanie**
Consumption	*190	*200	216	*235	*255	*270	*280	Consommation
Consumption per capita	38	39	41	44	47	48	49	Consommation par habitant
Kazakhstan								**Kazakhstan**
Production	*25	46	62	40	*22	*26	*30	Production
Consumption *	365	438	442	450	455	460	465	Consommation *
Consumption per capita	25	29	30	30	30	30	30	Consommation par habitant
Kenya								**Kenya**
Production	377	537	448	562	532	517	520	Production
Consumption	*625	652	692	728	756	781	741	Consommation
Consumption per capita	20	21	21	22	23	23	20	Consommation par habitant
Korea, Dem. P. R.								**Corée, R. p. dém. de**
Consumption *	70	70	75	85	90	90	90	Consommation *
Consumption per capita	3	3	3	4	4	4	4	Consommation par habitant
Korea, Republic of [6]								**Corée, République de** [6]
Consumption	1 086	1 129	1 134	1 171	1 198	1 156	1 107	Consommation
Consumption per capita	23	24	24	24	25	24	23	Consommation par habitant
Kuwait								**Koweït**
Consumption *	75	80	80	85	90	90	95	Consommation *
Consumption per capita	34	35	34	36	37	36	36	Consommation par habitant
Kyrgyzstan								**Kirghizistan**
Production	29	41	75	88	45	*40	*15	Production
Consumption *	110	115	120	120	120	125	130	Consommation *
Consumption per capita	22	23	24	24	23	24	25	Consommation par habitant
Lao People's Dem. Rep.								**Rép. dém. pop. lao**
Consumption *	25	30	30	35	45	45	50	Consommation *
Consumption per capita	5	5	5	6	8	8	9	Consommation par habitant
Latvia [2]								**Lettonie** [2]
Production	56	77	75	...	...	...	...	Production
Consumption	78	78	73	...	...	...	...	Consommation
Consumption per capita	33	33	31	...	...	...	...	Consommation par habitant
Lebanon								**Liban**
Production	0	0	0	0	4	*5	*5	Production
Consumption	*135	*140	*145	*150	151	*145	*150	Consommation
Consumption per capita	38	36	39	43	42	40	41	Consommation par habitant

Country or area	2001	2002	2003	2004	2005	2006	2007	Pays ou zone
Liberia								**Libéria**
Consumption	9	10	10	10	15	15	16	Consommation
Consumption per capita	3	3	3	3	4	4	4	Consommation par habitant
Libyan Arab Jamah.								**Jamah. arabe libyenne**
Consumption *	230	240	250	255	265	270	275	Consommation *
Consumption per capita	43	45	46	46	47	47	47	Consommation par habitant
Lithuania [2]								**Lituanie** [2]
Production	118	150	143	...	...	...	...	Production
Consumption	111	89	89	...	...	...	...	Consommation
Consumption per capita	32	26	26	...	...	...	...	Consommation par habitant
Madagascar								**Madagascar**
Production	*50	32	27	26	27	*20	*20	Production
Consumption	*98	104	117	129	132	*135	*140	Consommation
Consumption per capita	6	7	7	7	7	7	7	Consommation par habitant
Malawi								**Malawi**
Production	*205	261	*257	*255	*265	*230	*280	Production
Consumption *	140	145	150	155	160	165	170	Consommation *
Consumption per capita	13	13	13	13	13	13	13	Consommation par habitant
Malaysia								**Malaisie**
Production *	105	110	80	80	80	55	60	Production *
Consumption *	1 050	1 090	1 175	1 215	1 225	1 250	1 275	Consommation *
Consumption per capita	44	44	47	47	47	47	47	Consommation par habitant
Maldives								**Maldives**
Consumption	5	5	5	5	6	6	...	Consommation
Consumption per capita	16	18	17	17	19	21	...	Consommation par habitant
Mali								**Mali**
Production *	32	32	34	35	35	34	34	Production *
Consumption *	80	90	95	95	100	105	110	Consommation *
Consumption per capita	8	8	9	8	9	9	9	Consommation par habitant
Malta [2]								**Malte** [2]
Consumption	23	23	25	...	...	...	...	Consommation
Consumption per capita	59	59	63	...	...	...	...	Consommation par habitant
Mauritania								**Mauritanie**
Consumption *	135	135	140	140	145	155	165	Consommation *
Consumption per capita	50	48	48	45	44	45	45	Consommation par habitant
Mauritius								**Maurice**
Production	685	553	538	606	524	505	462	Production
Consumption	44	43	41	42	39	39	42	Consommation
Consumption per capita	36	35	34	34	32	31	33	Consommation par habitant
Mexico								**Mexique**
Production	5 614	5 073	5 442	5 672	5 619	5 412	5 420	Production
Consumption	4 857	5 069	5 328	5 300	4 877	4 979	4 944	Consommation
Consumption per capita	48	49	52	50	47	47	47	Consommation par habitant
Mongolia								**Mongolie**
Consumption	20	21	22	23	25	25	26	Consommation
Consumption per capita	8	9	9	9	10	10	10	Consommation par habitant
Morocco								**Maroc**
Production	*530	*505	*505	*540	513	*450	*505	Production
Consumption	*1 050	*1 100	1 057	*1 150	1 163	*1 170	*1 190	Consommation
Consumption per capita	36	37	35	38	39	38	39	Consommation par habitant
Mozambique								**Mozambique**
Production	*60	*170	*225	205	265	243	244	Production
Consumption	*95	*110	*120	134	135	144	169	Consommation
Consumption per capita	5	5	7	7	7	7	8	Consommation par habitant
Myanmar								**Myanmar**
Production *	125	125	135	150	150	155	160	Production *
Consumption *	90	120	135	150	155	165	175	Consommation *
Consumption per capita	2	2	3	3	3	3	3	Consommation par habitant
Namibia								**Namibie**
Consumption *	47	48	50	55	55	60	60	Consommation *
Consumption per capita	26	26	27	30	30	33	33	Consommation par habitant

35

Sugar *(continued)*
Production and consumption: thousand metric tons; consumption per capita: kilograms
Sucre *(suite)*
Production et consommation : milliers de tonnes ; consommation par habitant : kilogrammes

Country or area	2001	2002	2003	2004	2005	2006	2007	Pays ou zone
Nepal								**Népal**
Production *	65	110	125	140	130	135	140	Production *
Consumption *	120	125	125	130	135	135	140	Consommation *
Consumption per capita	5	5	5	5	5	5	5	Consommation par habitant
Netherlands Antilles								**Antilles néerlandaises**
Consumption *	14	14	15	15	16	16	16	Consommation *
Consumption per capita	82	82	83	82	87	87	88	Consommation par habitant
New Zealand								**Nouvelle-Zélande**
Consumption *	215	220	225	230	230	230	230	Consommation *
Consumption per capita	55	56	56	57	56	55	54	Consommation par habitant
Nicaragua								**Nicaragua**
Production	*390	*370	333	*440	*470	*435	*505	Production
Consumption *	160	175	190	200	205	210	215	Consommation *
Consumption per capita	31	33	36	37	38	38	38	Consommation par habitant
Niger								**Niger**
Production *	10	10	15	10	10	10	10	Production *
Consumption *	55	65	70	70	75	75	80	Consommation *
Consumption per capita	5	6	6	6	6	6	6	Consommation par habitant
Nigeria								**Nigeria**
Production	7	7	0	0	0	*30	55	Production
Consumption	975	1 317	1 046	1 222	1 236	*1 265	*1 295	Consommation
Consumption per capita	8	11	8	9	9	8	9	Consommation par habitant
Norway								**Norvège**
Consumption *	180	175	175	170	170	165	165	Consommation *
Consumption per capita	40	39	38	37	37	35	35	Consommation par habitant
Pakistan								**Pakistan**
Production	2 720	3 334	4 063	4 481	2 839	3 263	*4 355	Production
Consumption	*3 390	*3 490	3 875	4 004	4 075	3 951	*4 250	Consommation
Consumption per capita	24	24	26	29	27	25	27	Consommation par habitant
Panama								**Panama**
Production	146	152	147	157	157	168	164	Production
Consumption *	105	110	113	115	117	120	123	Consommation *
Consumption per capita	36	36	38	36	37	36	36	Consommation par habitant
Papua New Guinea								**Papouasie-Nvl-Guinée**
Production	45	50	50	46	44	*35	*35	Production
Consumption	35	37	35	35	35	*35	*37	Consommation
Consumption per capita	7	8	7	6	6	6	7	Consommation par habitant
Paraguay								**Paraguay**
Production *	95	115	116	115	117	120	120	Production *
Consumption *	110	110	115	115	120	120	125	Consommation *
Consumption per capita	20	20	20	20	20	20	20	Consommation par habitant
Peru								**Pérou**
Production	*755	*850	*970	813	695	805	*905	Production
Consumption	*950	*975	*995	967	896	*960	*1 025	Consommation
Consumption per capita	36	36	37	35	32	34	36	Consommation par habitant
Philippines								**Philippines**
Production	1 895	1 988	2 245	2 423	2 184	2 413	2 147	Production
Consumption	1 974	2 059	2 117	2 102	2 037	2 021	1 939	Consommation
Consumption per capita	26	26	26	25	24	23	22	Consommation par habitant
Poland [2]								**Pologne** [2]
Production	1 626	2 038	1 912	...	...	...	...	Production
Consumption	1 740	1 745	1 760	...	...	...	...	Consommation
Consumption per capita	45	45	46	...	...	...	...	Consommation par habitant
Republic of Moldova								**République de Moldova**
Production	130	*125	107	111	133	161	75	Production
Consumption	*105	*110	*115	106	*125	*130	*105	Consommation
Consumption per capita	29	26	32	29	35	36	29	Consommation par habitant
Romania [2]								**Roumanie** [2]
Production	71	75	57	*55	67	*125	...	Production
Consumption	*565	*570	*590	584	*595	*600	...	Consommation
Consumption per capita	25	26	27	27	28	28	...	Consommation par habitant

35

Sugar *(continued)*
Production and consumption: thousand metric tons; consumption per capita: kilograms
Sucre *(suite)*
Production et consommation : milliers de tonnes ; consommation par habitant : kilogrammes

Country or area	2001	2002	2003	2004	2005	2006	2007	Pays ou zone
Russian Federation								**Fédération de Russie**
Production	1 757	1 757	1 892	2 496	2 719	3 459	*3 405	Production
Consumption	5 848	6 673	*6 850	*6 700	*6 600	*6 500	*6 500	Consommation
Consumption per capita	41	47	47	46	46	46	46	Consommation par habitant
Rwanda								**Rwanda**
Consumption *	10	11	11	11	14	15	15	Consommation *
Consumption per capita	1	1	1	1	2	2	2	Consommation par habitant
Saint Kitts-Nevis								**Saint-Kitts-et-Nevis**
Production *	20	20	15	15	10	0	0	Production *
Consumption *	3	3	3	3	3	3	3	Consommation *
Consumption per capita	50	42	42	42	42	42	36	Consommation par habitant
Samoa								**Samoa**
Production	2	2	2	2	2	3	3	Production
Consumption	2	3	4	4	4	4	5	Consommation
Consumption per capita	8	12	15	15	15	15	...	Consommation par habitant
Saudi Arabia								**Arabie saoudite**
Consumption *	620	650	690	720	760	780	800	Consommation *
Consumption per capita	30	30	31	32	33	33	33	Consommation par habitant
Senegal								**Sénégal**
Production *	95	95	90	90	90	95	95	Production *
Consumption *	170	175	175	180	185	190	200	Consommation *
Consumption per capita	18	18	17	17	17	17	18	Consommation par habitant
Serbia								**Serbie**
Production	209	*230	*270	*335	*415	*505	*490	Production
Consumption *	300	300	310	315	320	325	325	Consommation *
Consumption per capita	40	40	41	42	43	44	44	Consommation par habitant
Sierra Leone								**Sierra Leone**
Production *	7	7	5	6	6	6	6	Production *
Consumption *	20	21	22	25	26	27	28	Consommation *
Consumption per capita	4	4	4	5	5	5	5	Consommation par habitant
Singapore								**Singapour**
Consumption *	300	305	310	310	315	315	320	Consommation *
Consumption per capita	73	73	74	73	72	70	69	Consommation par habitant
Slovakia [2]								**Slovaquie** [2]
Production	173	197	171	...	...	...	...	Production
Consumption	235	240	206	...	...	...	...	Consommation
Consumption per capita	44	45	38	...	...	...	...	Consommation par habitant
Slovenia [2]								**Slovénie** [2]
Production	50	44	55	...	...	...	...	Production
Consumption	90	90	100	...	...	...	...	Consommation
Consumption per capita	45	45	50	...	...	...	...	Consommation par habitant
Somalia								**Somalie**
Production *	20	20	20	20	15	20	20	Production *
Consumption *	185	190	200	200	205	205	220	Consommation *
Consumption per capita	20	19	25	23	22	21	21	Consommation par habitant
South Africa								**Afrique du Sud**
Production	2 311	2 767	2 418	2 234	2 507	2 234	2 286	Production
Consumption	1 341	1 478	1 436	1 484	1 565	2 387	2 255	Consommation
Consumption per capita	30	33	31	32	33	50	47	Consommation par habitant
Sri Lanka								**Sri Lanka**
Production *	20	20	21	60	60	70	75	Production *
Consumption *	575	535	610	630	640	660	685	Consommation *
Consumption per capita	31	28	32	32	32	33	34	Consommation par habitant
Sudan								**Soudan**
Production	719	744	686	789	728	767	743	Production
Consumption	523	568	568	624	877	910	916	Consommation
Consumption per capita	17	17	16	18	25	26	26	Consommation par habitant
Suriname								**Suriname**
Production *	10	10	5	5	5	7	7	Production *
Consumption *	19	20	20	20	21	21	22	Consommation *
Consumption per capita	40	42	42	42	42	42	44	Consommation par habitant

Sugar *(continued)*
Production and consumption: thousand metric tons; consumption per capita: kilograms
Sucre *(suite)*
Production et consommation : milliers de tonnes ; consommation par habitant : kilogrammes

Country or area	2001	2002	2003	2004	2005	2006	2007	Pays ou zone
Swaziland								**Swaziland**
Production	567	675	616	594	653	623	631	Production
Consumption	107	107	109	112	*114	*115	*116	Consommation
Consumption per capita	107	112	99	98	97	100	122	Consommation par habitant
Switzerland								**Suisse**
Production	*187	222	185	*225	221	198	*260	Production
Consumption	*385	393	463	*475	526	558	*560	Consommation
Consumption per capita	53	54	63	64	70	75	75	Consommation par habitant
Syrian Arab Republic								**Rép. arabe syrienne**
Production	121	*120	*120	*105	*110	148	*160	Production
Consumption *	745	760	775	790	800	825	835	Consommation *
Consumption per capita	45	44	44	44	44	45	45	Consommation par habitant
Tajikistan								**Tadjikistan**
Consumption *	60	70	80	85	105	110	115	Consommation *
Consumption per capita	10	11	12	13	15	16	16	Consommation par habitant
Thailand								**Thaïlande**
Production	5 370	6 438	7 737	7 462	4 589	5 646	7 147	Production
Consumption	1 955	1 978	2 073	2 303	2 352	2 464	2 476	Consommation
Consumption per capita	31	31	33	36	36	38	38	Consommation par habitant
TFYR of Macedonia								**Ex-R.Y. Macédoine**
Production	6	*10	16	16	16	19	36	Production
Consumption *	60	65	65	70	70	75	75	Consommation *
Consumption per capita	30	32	32	34	34	37	37	Consommation par habitant
Togo								**Togo**
Consumption *	45	45	48	50	60	65	68	Consommation *
Consumption per capita	9	9	10	10	11	12	12	Consommation par habitant
Trinidad and Tobago								**Trinité-et-Tobago**
Production	89	104	67	43	33	*25	*30	Production
Consumption	79	70	70	*75	*75	*75	*75	Consommation
Consumption per capita	62	54	55	59	59	59	59	Consommation par habitant
Tunisia								**Tunisie**
Consumption	309	319	*330	335	332	362	375	Consommation
Consumption per capita	32	33	33	34	33	36	37	Consommation par habitant
Turkey								**Turquie**
Production	2 360	2 128	2 136	2 053	2 171	2 091	1 919	Production
Consumption	1 973	1 782	1 725	1 894	1 978	2 208	1 999	Consommation
Consumption per capita	29	26	24	27	27	30	28	Consommation par habitant
Turkmenistan								**Turkménistan**
Production	0	0	1	*2	*3	*3	*4	Production
Consumption *	70	70	75	75	80	85	90	Consommation *
Consumption per capita	14	15	15	14	14	13	13	Consommation par habitant
Uganda								**Ouganda**
Production	146	180	192	213	211	208	197	Production
Consumption	*160	*180	225	257	263	260	250	Consommation
Consumption per capita	7	8	9	10	10	10	9	Consommation par habitant
Ukraine								**Ukraine**
Production	1 802	*1 545	1 690	*1 945	*2 060	*2 800	*2 025	Production
Consumption *	2 005	2 100	2 300	2 300	2 350	2 350	2 350	Consommation *
Consumption per capita	41	44	48	48	49	49	49	Consommation par habitant
United Arab Emirates								**Emirats arabes unis**
Consumption *	105	113	119	127	140	151	163	Consommation *
Consumption per capita	32	30	30	31	34	36	39	Consommation par habitant
United Rep. of Tanzania								**Rép.-Unie de Tanzanie**
Production	*115	187	218	211	278	257	267	Production
Consumption	*200	165	218	221	268	300	307	Consommation
Consumption per capita	6	5	6	6	7	8	8	Consommation par habitant
United States								**Etats-Unis**
Production	7 774	6 805	7 964	7 647	6 784	7 034	7 678	Production
Consumption	9 139[7]	9 079	8 844	8 994	9 248	9 228	9 107	Consommation
Consumption per capita	32	32	30	31	31	31	30	Consommation par habitant

35

Sugar *(continued)*
Production and consumption: thousand metric tons; consumption per capita: kilograms
Sucre *(suite)*
Production et consommation : milliers de tonnes ; consommation par habitant : kilogrammes

Country or area	2001	2002	2003	2004	2005	2006	2007	Pays ou zone
Uruguay								**Uruguay**
Production *	7	7	6	7	6	6	6	Production *
Consumption *	105	110	115	120	125	130	130	Consommation *
Consumption per capita	32	33	35	36	38	39	39	Consommation par habitant
Uzbekistan								**Ouzbékistan**
Production	*7	*7	0	0	0	0	0	Production
Consumption *	475	490	495	495	505	510	510	Consommation *
Consumption per capita	19	19	19	19	20	20	20	Consommation par habitant
Venezuela (Boliv. Rep. of)								**Venezuela (Rép. boliv. du)**
Production	*585	*550	*510	694	*690	*700	*700	Production
Consumption	*910	*925	*930	1 020	*1 050	*1 070	*1 080	Consommation
Consumption per capita	37	37	36	39	40	40	39	Consommation par habitant
Viet Nam								**Viet Nam**
Production	*850	*890	*975	*1 070	875	*995	*1 251	Production
Consumption	*875	*950	*1 005	*1 035	906	*1 170	*1 299	Consommation
Consumption per capita	11	12	12	13	11	13	15	Consommation par habitant
Yemen								**Yémen**
Consumption *	425	445	470	480	495	510	525	Consommation *
Consumption per capita	23	23	23	23	23	24	24	Consommation par habitant
Zambia								**Zambie**
Production	199	233	230	245	248	*250	237	Production
Consumption	102	116	104	115	95	*115	118	Consommation
Consumption per capita	11	11	9	10	8	10	10	Consommation par habitant
Zimbabwe								**Zimbabwe**
Production	548	565	482	456	430	446	349	Production
Consumption	305	335	315	311	295	263	234	Consommation
Consumption per capita	24	27	25	27	25	23	22	Consommation par habitant

Source:
International Sugar Organization (ISO), London, the ISO database and the *Sugar Yearbook 2008*.

Source:
Organisation internationale du sucre (OIS), Londres, la base de données de l'OIS et l'*Annuaire du sucre 2008*.

1	Including store losses of 1 159 tons and accidental losses of 129 tons.
2	Beginning 2004, data for Cyprus, Czech Republic, Estonia, Hungary, Latvia, Lithuania, Malta, Poland, Slovakia, and Slovenia are incorporated in the European Union data. From 2007 including figures of Bulgaria and Romania.
3	For statistical purposes, the data for China do not include those for the Hong Kong Special Administrative Region (Hong Kong SAR), Macao Special Administrative Region (Macao SAR) and Taiwan Province of China.
4	Including non-human consumption: 2001 - 13 534 tons; 2002 – 16 750 tons; 2007 - 22 335 tons.
5	Including 6 444 tons sold to other Pacific Island nations in tons in 2001; 7 546 tons in 2002; 10 686 tons in 2004; 15 515 tons in 2006 and 13 398 tons in 2007.
6	Including sugar used for the production of mono-sodium glutamate and llysin: 2001 - 210 498 tons; 2002 - 197 939 tons; 2003 - 226 191 tons; 2004 - 235 773 tons; 2005 - 241 101 tons; 2006 - 232 665 tons; 2007 - 223 344 tons.
7	Including 19 780 tons used for livestock feed.

1 Y compris des pertes de 1 159 tonnes au cours du stockage et des pertes accidentelles de 129 tonnes.

2 À partir de 2004, les données pour Chypre, République tchèque, Estonie, Hongrie, Lettonie, Lituanie, Malta, Pologne, Slovaquie, Slovénie sont inclues dans les données de l'Union européenne. À partir de 2007, les données incluent également la Bulgarie et la Roumaine.

3 Pour la présentation des statistiques, les données pour la Chine ne comprennent pas la Région Administrative Spéciale de Hong Kong (Hong Kong RAS), la Région Administrative Spéciale de Macao (Macao RAS) et la province de Taiwan.

4 Dont consommation non humaine : 2001 - 13 534 tonnes; 2002 – 16 750 tonnes.

5 Y compris 6 444 tonnes vendues aux autres îles pacifiques en 2001; 7 546 tonnes en 2002; 10 686 tonnes en 2004, 15 515 tonnes en 2006 et 13 398 tonnes en 2007.

6 Y compris la sucre utilisée pour la production du glutamate monosodium et lysine: 2001 - 210 498 tonnes; 2002 - 197 939 tonnes; 2003 - 226 191 tonnes; 2004 - 235 773 tonnes; 2005 – 241 101 tonnes; 2006 - 232 665 tonnes; 2007 - 223 344 tonnes.

7 Y compris 19 780 tonnes utilisées pour les aliments du bétail.

Beer
Production: thousand hectoliters

Bière
Production: milliers d'hectolitres

Country or area Pays ou zone	1997	1998	1999	2000	2001	2002	2003	2004	2005	2006
Albania Albanie	151	93	87	86	117	150	144	296	285	348
Algeria Algérie	370	382	383	453	435	283	166	124	...	...
Angola [1] Angola [1]	1 150	1 288	1 609	...	...	...	...	...	...	...
Argentina Argentine	12 687	12 395	12 448	12 685	12 390	11 990	12 950	13 410	13 960	14 825
Armenia Arménie	50	133	84	79	100	71	73	88	108	126
Australia [2,3] Australie [2,3]	17 350	17 570	17 380	17 680	17 450	17 440	17 270	17 360	16 850	17 141
Austria Autriche	9 303	8 837	8 884	8 725	8 528	8 745	8 980	...	...	...
Azerbaijan Azerbaïdjan	16	12	69	71	117	125	133	184	249	309
Barbados Barbade	75	87	76	69	67	68	69	80	87	89
Belarus Bélarus	2 413	2 604	2 728	2 371	2 174	2 026	2 056	2 272	2 715	3 322
Belgium Belgique	14 758	14 763	15 094[4]	15 509[4]	15 068[4]	15 063[4]	15 924[4]			
Belize Belize	37	42	66	92	...	...	...	...	...	...
Benin [5] Bénin [5]	364	329	347	...	...	...	...	...	...	...
Bolivia Bolivie	187	186	166	...	...	...	...	...	...	...
Bosnia and Herzegovina Bosnie-Herzégovine	745	844	975	676[6]	480[6]	652[6]	#1 316			
Botswana Botswana	1 005	1 019	1 591	1 976	1 692	1 396	1 198	...	...	...
Brazil Brésil	66 582	66 453	62 491	87 882	91 372	79 883	76 921	86 633	92 164	100 176
Bulgaria Bulgarie	3 031	3 765	3 890	3 977	4 097	3 888	4 355	3 997	4 287	4 827
Burkina Faso [5] Burkina Faso [5]	460	501	516	...	...	...	...	...	...	...
Burundi Burundi	1 161	1 036	1 084	892	702	752	876	973	1 013	1 220
Cameroon Cameroun	3 124	3 370	3 373	3 340	3 740	4 196	4 597	4 287	4 439	
Canada Canada	21 816	24 352	24 605	24 515	25 551	25 368	19 299	...	...	...
Central African Rep. [5] Rép. centrafricaine [5]	209	219	243	...	...	...	...	...	...	...
Chad [5] Tchad [5]	123	...	...	...	...	...	...	...	...	...
Chile Chili	3 640	3 666	3 343	3 221	3 374	3 401	3 490	...	4 627	5 562
China [7,8] Chine [7,8]	154 610	162 693	...	...	...	...	...	...	...	...
China, Hong Kong SAR Chine, Hong Kong RAS	894	...	...	...	...	...	...	...	...	...

36

Beer *(continued)*
Production: thousand hectoliters
Bière *(suite)*
Production: milliers d'hectolitres

Country or area Pays ou zone	1997	1998	1999	2000	2001	2002	2003	2004	2005	2006
Colombia Colombie	18 290	16 461	14 213	...	...	...	...	...	...	...
Congo Congo	342	494	480	526	623	661	658	674	...	...
Croatia Croatie	3 607	3 759	3 663	3 847	3 799	3 624	3 679	3 606	3 496	3 689
Cuba Cuba	1 639	1 759	2 009	2 136	2 197	2 331	2 313	2 221	2 255	2 298
Cyprus Chypre	333	365	405	409	404	383	367	371	377	374
Czech Republic République tchèque	18 558	18 290	17 945	17 796	17 734	17 987	18 216	18 596	18 885	20 134
Denmark Danemark	9 181	8 044	8 205	7 455	7 233	8 202	8 352	8 550	8 493	7 915
Dominica Dominique	11	11	8	11	9	10	...	...	...	...
Dominican Republic Rép. dominicaine	2 593	2 993	3 484	3 666	3 176	3 554	3 553	3 547	4 408	2 134
Ecuador Equateur	238	633	555	353	...	...	...	...	...	...
Egypt Egypte	...	...	352	261	122	...	...	...	...	...
Estonia Estonie	543	744	957	950	1 015	1 044	1 040	1 189	1 346	1 411
Ethiopia Ethiopie	843[9]	831[9]	921[9]	1 111[9]	1 605[9]	1 812	2 123	...	...	...
Fiji Fidji	170	170	185	179	180	200	150	200	220	220
Finland Finlande	4 840	4 341	4 733	4 574	4 650	4 777	4 606	4 948	4 527	4 557
France France	17 010	16 551	16 623	18 353	18 539	17 899	17 989	17 477	17 199	...
Gabon Gabon	801	847	778	812	867	792	754	...	...	...
Georgia Géorgie	79	97	126	234	257	273	284	476	...	...
Germany Allemagne	108 729	106 993	107 479	106 877	106 372	102 133	98 933	97 748	94 806	96 937
Greece Grèce	3 797	4 139	4 342	4 423	4 494	4 548	4 090	3 890	...	...
Guatemala Guatemala	1 303	1 363	1 443	1 406	...	...	...	...	...	...
Guyana Guyana	136	137	136	130	120	131	105	110	119	...
Hungary Hongrie	6 973	7 163	6 996	7 194	7 142	7 237	7 255	6 467	6 770	7 157
Iceland Islande	64	71	77	88	123	103	108	...	...	...
India Inde	4 331[10]	4 332[10]	3 632[10]	3 025	2 352	2 696	7 101	7 365	8 996	...
Indonesia Indonésie	531	502	401	...	437	237	...	...	...	...
Iran (Islamic Rep. of) Iran (Rép. islamique d')	130[11]	155[11]	127[11]	145[11]	...	...	...	352	518	663
Ireland Irlande	12 095	12 584	...	...	...	...	...	...	...	...

36

Beer *(continued)*
Production: thousand hectoliters
Bière *(suite)*
Production: milliers d'hectolitres

Country or area Pays ou zone	1997	1998	1999	2000	2001	2002	2003	2004	2005	2006
Italy Italie	10 379	11 073	11 123	11 173	11 375	11 208	13 994	13 692	...	...
Jamaica Jamaïque	674	670	656	697	784	774	585	590	633	669
Japan [12] Japon [12]	66 971	63 297	58 573	55 081	51 855	46 215	41 323	37 833	36 169	34 079
Kazakhstan Kazakhstan	693	850	824	1 357	1 732	2 020	2 348	2 780	3 235	3 638
Kenya Kenya	2 704	2 630	1 885	2 029	1 843	1 919	2 223	2 447	2 663	3 116
Korea, Republic of Corée, République de	16 907	14 080	14 866	16 544	17 765	18 224	17 863	18 033	17 489	17 400
Kyrgyzstan Kirghizistan	145	128	122	124	87	71	77	116	123	110
Lao People's Dem. Rep. Rép. dém. pop. lao	...	...	...	480	576	652	702	827	927	1 059
Latvia Lettonie	715	721	946	931	989	1 199	1 364	1 313	1 285	1 408
Lesotho Lesotho	...	...	...	349	288	333	358	325	285	295
Lithuania Lituanie	1 406	1 557	1 852	2 065	2 174	2 683	2 520	2 782	2 916	2 958
Luxembourg Luxembourg	481	469	450	438	397	386	391	...	...	...
Madagascar Madagascar	234	297	446	467	502	439	...	92	93	103
Malawi Malawi	780	678	684	739	1 033	...	...	...	...	...
Mali Mali	65	66	62	74	71	75	78	78	149	101
Mauritius Maurice	340	376	358	375	328	348	378	364	389	360
Mexico Mexique	51 315	54 569	57 905	59 851	61 632	63 530	65 462	67 575	72 030	78 040
Montenegro Monténégro	...	...	...	...	...	301	553	491	52	517
Mozambique Mozambique	631	75	95	989	982	779	1 044	1 025	1 412	...
Nepal [13] Népal [13]	215	139	188	217	233	228	242	250	260	...
Netherlands Pays-Bas	23 780[14,15]	23 040[14,15]	23 799[14,15]	24 956[14,15]	24 605[15]	24 774[15]	25 699	24 546[14,15]	23 851[14,15]	...
New Zealand Nouvelle-Zélande	3 214	3 206	3 146	2 980	3 070	3 093	3 127	3 060	3 036	...
Niger Niger	72	70	69	72	68	65	...	...	...	...
Nigeria Nigéria	...	...	...	...	4 049	4 142	4 011	4 067	4 073	...
Norway Norvège	2 396	1 833	2 651	...	2 462	2 377	...	2 352	2 442	2 410
Panama Panama	1 335	1 448	1 461	1 399	...	...	...	...	...	...
Peru Pérou	7 650	6 557	6 168	5 706	5 296	6 170	6 483	6 733	7 970	...
Poland Pologne	19 281	21 017	23 360	#24 739	15 069	26 715	28 412	29 794	31 343	33 661

36

Beer *(continued)*
Production: thousand hectoliters
Bière *(suite)*
Production: milliers d'hectolitres

Country or area Pays ou zone	1997	1998	1999	2000	2001	2002	2003	2004	2005	2006
Portugal Portugal	6 494	6 617	6 641	6 718	6 509	6 689	7 110	7 712	7 702	8 337
Puerto Rico Porto Rico	317	263	259	...	...	...	...	...	...	...
Republic of Moldova[16] République de Moldova[16]	238	278	202	249	318	438	566	653	724	
Romania Roumanie	7 651	9 989	11 133	12 664	12 087	11 513	13 087	14 159	14 713	17 554
Russian Federation Fédération de Russie	26 103	33 631	44 484	51 563	63 780	70 266	75 540	83 787	90 986	100 051
Saint Kitts and Nevis Saint-Kitts-et-Nevis	19	20	20	20	20	20		...	...	...
Serbia Serbie	...	...	...	...	...	...	...	...	6 569	6 451
Serbia and Montenegro Serbie-et-Monténégro	6 106	6 630	#6 786	6 734	6 063	5 764	6 049	...	...	...
Seychelles Seychelles	71	72	68	70	72	76	65	63	63	67
Sierra Leone Sierra Leone	187	489	...	382	983	1 116	924	942	1 012	1 101
Slovakia Slovaquie	5 577	4 478	4 473	4 491	4 216	4 747	4 684	3 877	3 810	3 987
Slovenia Slovénie	...	1 976	2 084	2 463	2 449	...	...	...	...	...
Spain Espagne	24 786	22 428	26 007	26 388	26 802	28 631	31 028	31 467	31 156	34 032
Sweden Suède	5 129	4 763	4 718	4 686	4 522	4 527	4 255	3 870	3 952	4 381
Syrian Arab Republic Rép. arabe syrienne	97	97	121	91	100	104	100	109	111	...
Tajikistan Tadjikistan	6	9	7	4	8	9	9	11	13	16
Thailand Thaïlande	8 740	9 770	10 420	11 650	12 380	12 750	16 020	16 320	16 950	20 110
TFYR of Macedonia L'ex-R.Y. Macédoine	600	578	652	661	618	657	680	716	695	670
Togo Togo	...	...	...	...	...	...	...	313	325	345
Trinidad and Tobago Trinité-et-Tobago	407	517	522	625	...	...	...	...	...	...
Tunisia Tunisie	780	813	912	1 066	1 087	1 100	997	...	...	...
Turkey Turquie	7 656	7 130	7 188	7 649	7 441	7 845	8 363	8 812	8 936	9 059
Turkmenistan Turkménistan	44	29	37	52	79	84	...	...	...	...
Uganda Ouganda	896	1 105	1 178	1 261	1 079	989	826	1 149	1 359	1 616
Ukraine Ukraine	6 125	6 842	8 407	10 765	13 059	15 000	17 012	19 373	23 805	26 750
United Kingdom Royaume-Uni	64 816	60 915	62 510	54 206	57 032	60 646	64 253	73 622	...	...
United Rep. of Tanzania Rép.-Unie de Tanzanie	1 483	1 707	1 674	1 830	1 756	1 759	1 941	2 026	2 166	2 990[17]
Uruguay Uruguay	939	860	741	706	629	507	415	...	...	...

Beer *(continued)*
Production: thousand hectoliters
Bière *(suite)*
Production: milliers d'hectolitres

Country or area Pays ou zone	1997	1998	1999	2000	2001	2002	2003	2004	2005	2006
Uzbekistan Ouzbékistan	619	569[18]	422[18]	609[18]	...	...	...	...	...	...
Viet Nam Viet Nam	5 811	6 700	6 898	7 791	8 712	9 398	11 189	13 428	14 606	15 472
Zimbabwe Zimbabwe	...	...	...	...	4 747	2 957	...	...	...	...

Source:
United Nations Statistics Division, New York, the *Industrial Commodity Statistics Yearbook 2006* and the industrial statistics database, last accessed April 2009.

Source:
Organisation des Nations Unies, Division de statistique, New York, *l'Annuaire de statistiques industrielles par produit 2006* et la base de données pour les statistiques industrielles, dernier accès avril 2009.

1	Source: *Economist Intelligence Unit* (London).
2	Twelve months ending 30 June of the year stated.
3	Excluding light beer containing less than 1.15% by volume of alcohol.
4	Incomplete coverage.
5	Source: Afristat: Sub-Saharan African Observatory of Economics and Statistics (Bamako, Mali).
6	Excluding the Federation of Bosnia and Herzegovina.
7	For statistical purposes, the data for China do not include those for the Hong Kong Special Administrative Region (Hong Kong SAR), Macao Special Administrative Region (Macao SAR) and Taiwan Province of China.
8	Original data in metric tons.
9	Twelve months ending 7 July of the year stated.
10	Production by large- and medium-scale establishments only.
11	Production by establishments employing 10 or more persons.
12	Twelve months beginning 1 April of the year stated.
13	Twelve months beginning 16 July of the year stated.
14	Production by establishments employing 20 or more persons.
15	Sales.
16	Excluding the Transnistria region.
17	Tanganyika only.
18	Source: *Statistical Yearbook for Asia and the Pacific*, United Nations Economic and Social Commission for Asia and the Pacific (Bangkok).

1	Source: *Economist Intelligence Unit* (London).
2	Période de 12 mois finissant le 30 juin de l'année indiquée.
3	Non compris la bière légère contenant moins de 1.15 p. 100 en volume d'alcool.
4	Couverture incomplète.
5	Source : Afristat : Observatoire Economique et Statistique d'Afrique Subsaharienne (Bamako, Mali).
6	Non compris la Fédération de Bosnie et Herzégovine.
7	Pour la présentation des statistiques, les données pour la Chine ne comprennent pas la Région Administrative Spéciale de Hong Kong (Hong Kong RAS), la Région Administrative Spéciale de Macao (Macao RAS) et la province de Taiwan.
8	Données d'origine exprimées en tonnes.
9	Période de 12 mois finissant le 7 juillet de l'année indiquée.
10	Production des grandes et moyennes entreprises seulement.
11	Production des établissements employant 10 personnes ou plus.
12	Période de 12 mois commençant le 1er avril de l'année indiquée.
13	Période de 12 mois commençant le 16 juillet de l'année indiquée.
14	Production des établissements employant 20 personnes ou plus.
15	Ventes.
16	Non compris la région de Transnistria.
17	Tanganyika seulement.
18	Source : *Annuaire des Statistiques de l'Asie et Pacifique*, Commission économique et sociale des Nations Unies pour l'Asie et le Pacifique (Bangkok).

Cigarettes
Production: millions

Country or area Pays ou zone	1997	1998	1999	2000	2001	2002	2003	2004	2005	2006
Albania Albanie	414[1]	764[1]	647[1]	372[1]	126[1]	50	15	...	...	...
Andorra Andorre	...	1	1	1	1	1	2	2	3	1
Argentina Argentine	1 940	1 967	1 996	1 843	1 740	1 812	1 990	1 890	1 862	1 993
Armenia Arménie	815	2 489	3 132	2 109	1 623	2 815	3 222	2 720	3 020	2 825
Azerbaijan Azerbaïdjan	827	241	416	2 363	6 808	6 296	6 611	3 671	5 008	6 224
Bangladesh[2] Bangladesh[2]	18 601	19 889	19 558	19 732	20 120	20 384	22 499	...	...	...
Belarus Bélarus	6 787	7 296	9 259	10 356	11 182	10 524	10 442	12 627	12 008	15 650
Belgium Belgique	18 061	17 519	14 713[3]	...	...	...	...	...	...	...
Belize Belize	88	94	91	84	...	...	...	...	...	...
Bolivia Bolivie	1 484	1 538	1 404	...	...	...	...	...	...	...
Bosnia and Herzegovina Bosnie-Herzégovine	3 886	4 830	5 974	...	...	...	5 062	...	...	...
Brazil Brésil	...	...	...	17 860	15 820	100 193	21 099	96 828	120 167	120 228
Bulgaria Bulgarie	43 315	33 181	25 715	26 681	26 659	23 227	25 914	24 462	23 318	17 353
Burundi Burundi	377	317	353	286	293	312	354	376	419	410
Cameroon Cameroun	2 704	3 084	3 249	2 984	2 814	2 785	1 903	1 966	1 755	...
Canada Canada	47 263	48 854	47 224	46 068	44 403	37 127	...	...	...	...
Chad[4] Tchad[4]	786	...	...	...	...	...	...	...	...	...
Chile Chili	12 522	12 904	13 271	13 796	13 305	13 839	13 776	...	16 635	18 096
China[5] Chine[5]	34	34	33	34	34	35	36	...	...	...
China, Hong Kong SAR Chine, Hong Kong RAS	20 929	13 470	...	...	...	...	...	...	...	...
China, Macao SAR Chine, Macao RAS	...	0	...	...	...	...	...	...	...	...
Colombia Colombie	11 662	12 472	15 182	...	...	...	...	...	...	...
Congo Congo	380	...	...	...	102	662	748	750	...	...
Croatia Croatie	11 416	11 987	12 785	13 692	14 738	15 047	15 613	14 256	14 578	14 457
Cuba Cuba	10 700	11 655	13 432	12 086	11 769	12 519	14 300	12 766	14 022	13 151
Cyprus Chypre	3 662	4 362	4 783	4 980	3 803	2 534	2 661	3 845	...	...

Country or area Pays ou zone	1997	1998	1999	2000	2001	2002	2003	2004	2005	2006
Denmark Danemark	12 262	12 392	11 749	11 413	11 089	12 039	12 898	13 458	14 867	14 553
Dominican Republic Rép. dominicaine	3 972	4 098	4 005	3 898	3 338	3 509	3 469	3 446	3 300	...
Ecuador Equateur	1 678	1 997	2 178	2 773	...	...	2 975	...	...	...
Egypt Egypte	50 000	52 000	52 336	56 614	61 000	62 018	63 396	63 395	55 468	55 123
Ethiopia Ethiopie	2 024[6]	2 029[6]	1 829[6]	1 931[6]	1 904[6]	1 511	1 511	...	...	...
Fiji Fidji	450	410	446	396	389	422	416	454	420	457
Finland Finlande	6 790	4 062	4 877	3 981	3 999	4 130	3 946	868	...	...
France France	44 646	43 304	42 405	42 058	42 980	42 500	42 700	48 163	46 500	...
Gabon Gabon	331	463	670	859	880	860	...	...	...	...
Georgia Géorgie	917	601	132	296	1 615	1 894	2 972	2 808	...	...
Germany Allemagne	181 747	181 904	204 631	206 770	213 793	212 500	205 237	208 347	212 428	216 042
Ghana Ghana	1 747	1 399	1 158	1 166	1 481	1 800	...	...	...	...
Greece Grèce	29 529	31 705	31 535	34 256	25 516	28 091	26 249	28 048	...	...
Guatemala Guatemala	2 198	4 184	4 376	4 262	...	...	...	...	...	...
Guyana Guyana	221	...	...	...	...	...	...	...	...	...
Honduras Honduras	...	3 814	4 586	5 655	5 984	6 010	...	...	...	...
Hungary Hongrie	26 057	26 849	22 985	21 608	20 787	21 748	20 181	12 119	...	...
India Inde	83 162[7]	79 313[7]	82 504[7]	82 504[7]	60 577[8]	54 991[8]	75 675	...	81 598	...
Iran (Islamic Rep. of) Iran (Rép. islamique d')	10 304[9]	14 335	20 081	13 800	13 363	12 700	12 200	13 930	14 270	14 200
Iraq Iraq	...	...	...	...	...	...	...	812	...	68
Ireland Irlande	4 605	6 452	6 176	6 461	6 807	6 599	...	...	...	...
Italy Italie	51 894[1]	50 785	45 159	43 694[1]	45 368[1]	37 342	40 350	...	...	...
Jamaica Jamaïque	1 175	1 160	1 073	995	1 027	1 049	889	979	889	...
Japan[10] Japon[10]	328 000	336 600	332 200	324 500	313 900	...	...	...	...	...
Jordan[11] Jordanie[11]	1 853	1 144	*1 602	*1 300	...	...	...	...	...	...
Kazakhstan Kazakhstan	24 109	21 747	18 773	19 293	21 395	23 453	25 715	28 038	30 008	30 834
Kenya Kenya	8 898	7 599	7 231	6 009	5 850	4 631	4 753	5 351	7 324	10 262
Korea, Republic of Corée, République de	96 725	101 011	95 995	94 531	94 116	94 433	123 166	133 206	107 247	119 966

Country or area Pays ou zone	1997	1998	1999	2000	2001	2002	2003	2004	2005	2006
Kyrgyzstan Kirghizistan	716	843	2 103	3 169	3 013	2 927	3 102	3 170	3 179	3 086
Lao People's Dem. Rep. Rép. dém. pop. lao	856[10]	1 104[10]	...	41	41	55	68	84	105	...
Latvia Lettonie	1 775	2 018	1 909	...	...	...	...	...	...	...
Lebanon[1] Liban[1]	793	672	945	1 009	...	...	...	...	...	...
Lithuania Lituanie	5 755	7 427	8 217	7 207	...	...	...	...	...	...
Madagascar Madagascar	2 826	3 303	...	...	...	...	...	8	8	8
Malawi Malawi	731	501	...	...	...	...	...	...	...	...
Mali Mali	655	473	350	231	106	90	198	328	330	626
Mauritius Maurice	1 144	1 034	979	1 049	928	928	938	918	764	726
Mexico Mexique	38 786	44 917	45 373	44 400	44 904	43 834	41 856	40 752	41 439	44 295
Montenegro Monténégro	...	...	...	...		1 141	793	2 000	1 282	433
Mozambique Mozambique	250	950	1 084	1 417	1 359	1 255	1 390	...	...	...
Myanmar[12] Myanmar[12]	1 991	2 040	2 270	2 559	2 650	2 657	2 806	3 183		
Nepal[13] Népal[13]	7 944	8 127	7 315	6 584	6 979	6 900	6 812	7 268		
New Zealand Nouvelle-Zélande	3 234	3 086	2 949	2 916	2 396	2 509	2 176	2 122	2 211	1 253
Nicaragua Nicaragua	1 580	1 789	780[14]	...	...	...	...	...	...	...
Nigeria Nigéria	...	...	...	...	1 798	1 854	1 776	1 809	1 813	...
Pakistan[2] Pakistan[2]	46	48	52	47	58	55	49	55	61	64
Panama Panama	752	...	...	...	...	...	...	...	...	...
Peru Pérou	3 029	3 115	3 581	3 605	3 310	3 766	2 707	2 168	1 460	...
Poland Pologne	95 798	96 741	95 056	#78 792	82 421	78 746	78 792	83 376	95 531	106 641
Portugal Portugal	14 606	15 889	18 189	20 561	23 376	25 581	24 950	26 415	27 013	26 608
Republic of Moldova[15] République de Moldova[15]	9 539	7 512	8 731	9 262	9 421	6 310	7 126	7 050	6 195	5 031
Romania Roumanie	25 943	...	...	...	...	38 033	37 808	28 677	34 541	31 881
Russian Federation Fédération de Russie	140 000	196 000	266 000	334 000	356 000	383 000	376 000	377 000	402 000	409 697
Serbia Serbie	...	...	...	...	...	...	...	...	18 127	18 267
Serbia and Montenegro Serbie-et-Monténégro	10 988	14 597	#13 126	14 451	13 968	15 388	...	...	...	...
Seychelles Seychelles	70	61	60	40	36	24	50	22	30	19

Country or area Pays ou zone	1997	1998	1999	2000	2001	2002	2003	2004	2005	2006
Spain Espagne	77 315	81 940	74 873	74 799	...	...	...	48 651	47 506	39 798
Sri Lanka Sri Lanka	5 712	5 797	5 333	4 889	*4 973	5 015[16]	4 765[16]	5 003[16]	...	...
Sweden Suède	6 291	5 692	6 060	5 958	5 959	...	...	...	...	...
Switzerland Suisse	37 638	34 453	32 139	34 299	33 565	37 160	38 140	39 059	42 190	48 937
Syrian Arab Republic[1] Rép. arabe syrienne[1]	10 137	10 398	10 991	11 097	12 007	12 863	13 412	...	...	...
Tajikistan Tadjikistan	153	191	209	667	1 155	585	468	508	714	497
Thailand Thaïlande	43 387	34 585	31 146	30 732	29 807	30 772	31 908	34 761	32 978	28 588
TFYR of Macedonia L'ex-R.Y. Macédoine	...	...	...	...	7 766	6 567	5 120	5 654	5 763	5 123
Trinidad and Tobago Trinité-et-Tobago	1 386	1 680	1 945	2 050	...	...	...	...	...	...
Tunisia Tunisie	7 735	9 813	11 066	12 231	12 354	13 230	13 227	...	...	...
Turkey Turquie	74 984[1]	81 616[1]	75 135[1]	76 613[1]	77 160	131 561	111 881	103 371	104 170	128 278
Uganda Ouganda	1 846	1 866	1 602	1 344	1 220	1 092	...	...	...	...
Ukraine Ukraine	54 488	59 275	54 052	58 774	69 731	81 088	96 776	108 946	120 218	120 333
United Kingdom Royaume-Uni	167 670	152 998	143 794	139 125	109 025	124 896	89 639	85 691	...	...
United Rep. of Tanzania[17] Rép.-Unie de Tanzanie[17]	4 710	4 012	3 371	3 745	3 491	3 778	3 920	4 308	4 445	5 095
United States Etats-Unis	719 600	679 700	611 929	...	...	...	...	...	...	...
Uruguay Uruguay	6 872	10 187	11 161	10 894	9 616	8 449	5 718	...	...	...
Uzbekistan Ouzbékistan	8 521	7 582[10]	10 668[10]	7 766[10]	...	...	...	...	...	...
Viet Nam Viet Nam	2 123	2 196	2 147	2 836	3 075	3 375	3 871	4 192	4 485	3 941
Yemen Yémen	6 800	5 980	5 760	4 780	6 020	5 780	5 960	...	...	...

Source:
United Nations Statistics Division, New York, the industrial statistics database, last accessed April 2009.

Source:
Organisation des Nations Unies, Division de statistique, New York, et la base de données sur les statistiques industrielles, dernier accès avril 2009.

1	Original data in units of weight. Computed on the basis of one million cigarettes per ton.
2	Twelve months ending 30 June of the year stated.
3	Incomplete coverage.
4	Source: Afristat: Sub-Saharan African Observatory of Economics and Statistics (Bamako, Mali).
5	For statistical purposes, the data for China do not include those for the Hong Kong Special Administrative Region (Hong Kong SAR), Macao Special Administrative Region (Macao SAR) and Taiwan Province of China.
6	Twelve months ending 7 July of the year stated.
7	Production by large- and medium-scale establishments only.

1	Données d'origine exprimées en poids. Calcul sur la base d'un million de cigarettes par tonne.
2	Période de 12 mois finissant le 30 juin de l'année indiquée.
3	Couverture incomplète.
4	Source : Afristat : Observatoire Economique et Statistique d'Afrique Subsaharienne (Bamako, Mali).
5	Pour la présentation des statistiques, les données pour la Chine ne comprennent pas la Région Administrative Spéciale de Hong Kong (Hong Kong RAS), la Région Administrative Spéciale de Macao (Macao RAS) et la province de Taiwan.
6	Période de 12 mois finissant le 7 juillet de l'année indiquée.
7	Production des grandes et moyennes entreprises seulement.

8	Production by establishments employing 50 or more persons.
9	Production by establishments employing 10 or more persons.
10	Source: *Statistical Yearbook for Asia and the Pacific*, United Nations Economic and Social Commission for Asia and the Pacific (Bangkok).
11	Source: *Bulletin of Industrial Statistics for the Arab Countries*, United Nations Economic and Social Commission for Western Asia (Beirut).
12	Government production only.
13	Twelve months beginning 16 July of the year stated.
14	Beginning August 1999, national production discontinued.
15	Excluding the Transnistria region.
16	Source: *Country Economic Review*, Asian Development Bank (Manila).
17	Tanganyika only.

8	Production des établissements occupant 50 personnes ou plus.
9	Production des établissements occupant 10 personnes ou plus.
10	Source : *Annuaire des Statistiques de l'Asie et Pacifique*, Commission économique et sociale des Nations Unies pour l'Asie et le Pacifique (Bangkok).
11	Source: *Bulletin of Industrial Statistics for the Arab Countries*, Commission économique et sociale pour l'Asie occidentale (Beyrouth).
12	Production de l'état seulement.
13	Période de 12 mois commençant le 16 juillet de l'année indiquée.
14	A partir d'août 1999, la production nationale a été discontinuée.
15	Non compris la région de Transnistrie.
16	Source: *La Revue Economique du Pays*, La Banque de Développement Asiatique (Manille).
17	Tanganyika seulement.

38

Fabrics
Woven cotton and wool: thousand square metres

Tissus
Tissus de coton et tissages de laine : milliers de mètres carrés

Country or area Pays ou zone		2000	2001	2002	2003	2004	2005	2006	2007
Algeria[1]	**Algérie[1]**								
Cotton	Coton	...	...	...	...	14 802	...	...	...
Wool	Laines	...	...	...	...	1 161	...	...	...
Australia	**Australie**								
Cotton	Coton	47 230[2]	39 305[2]	33 780[2]	26 439[2]	19 565[2]	12 350[2]	8 046	...
Wool	Laines	5 427[2]	4 013[2]	3 641[2]	3 082[2]	2 105[2]	1 894[2]	1 362	...
Azerbaijan	**Azerbaïdjan**								
Cotton	Coton	621	3 263	2 709	2 783	3 723	2 758	2 113	1 690
Wool	Laines	32	0	0	0	0	18	0	0
Belarus	**Bélarus**								
Cotton	Coton	66 598	60 011	64 202	64 347	71 502	63 763	76 597	78 283
Wool	Laines	9 322	6 479	5 176	4 675	5 001	5 475	5 610	6 714
Bulgaria	**Bulgarie**								
Cotton	Coton	25 698[1]	31 766	28 040	27 106	32 717	25 696	25 037	26 997
Wool	Laines	4 000[1]	7 298	8 530	6 080	7 959	9 701	14 922	6 407
Cameroon	**Cameroun**								
Cotton	Coton	27	29	28	22	21	21	...	...
Chile[1]	**Chili[1]**								
Cotton	Coton	...	...	...	...	...	37 041	35 376	34 767
Wool	Laines	...	...	...	...	...	4 876	5 263	1 586
China, Hong Kong SAR	**Chine, Hong Kong RAS**								
Cotton	Coton	305 634	378 467	333 379	221 089	157 419	199 779	...	...
China, Macao SAR	**Chine, Macao RAS**								
Cotton	Coton	7 247	39	0	0	...	...	...	...
Croatia	**Croatie**								
Cotton	Coton	...	...	...	...	29 326	23 055	26 578	17 203
Wool	Laines	...	...	...	...	1 145	701	0	688
Cuba	**Cuba**								
Cotton	Coton	18 177	13 880	12 001	8 100	6 700	6 400	7 500	6 100
Czech Republic	**République tchèque**								
Cotton	Coton	226 088	231 917	210 333	182 286	167 141	128 331	131 373	120 968
Wool	Laines	14 297	13 517	13 268	16 073	16 107	16 913	20 853	16 851
Denmark	**Danemark**								
Cotton	Coton	10 131	9 949	6 236	4 257	3 424	4 807	5 332	2 832
Wool	Laines	516	1 807	1 565	1 372	1 352	1 711	1 656	1 698
Egypt[3]	**Egypte[3]**								
Cotton	Coton	1 559 000	...	...	...	...	...	...	...
Wool	Laines	6 000	...	...	...	...	...	...	...
Estonia	**Estonie**								
Cotton	Coton	...	...	...	...	72 665	62 032	9 668	8 973
Finland	**Finlande**								
Cotton	Coton	7 327	7 295	7 229	9 865	5 766	6 652	881	1 178
Wool	Laines	18	17	22	19	18	0	11	13
Germany	**Allemagne**								
Cotton	Coton	423 968	414 320	361 647	362 292	316 277	283 900	268 112	245 508
Wool	Laines	57 179	55 549	44 909	35 321	35 435	28 591	22 746	21 665
Hungary	**Hongrie**								
Cotton	Coton	...	...	12 788	8 141	14 943	10 721	8 435	6 219
Iran (Islamic Rep. of)	**Iran (Rép. islamique d')**								
Cotton	Coton	...	...	...	...	50 910	54 141	38 463	46 221
Wool	Laines	...	...	...	...	17 706	23 889	18 819	25 000
Iraq	**Iraq**								
Cotton	Coton	...	...	...	...	10 262	...	...	...
Wool	Laines	...	...	...	...	245	...	...	...
Japan	**Japon**								
Cotton	Coton	762 000	695 000	...	...	...	...	...	...
Wool	Laines	168 000	164 000	...	...	...	...	...	...

38

Fabrics *(continued)*
Woven cotton and wool: thousand square metres
Tissus *(suite)*
Tissus de coton et tissages de laine : milliers de mètres carrés

Country or area Pays ou zone	2000	2001	2002	2003	2004	2005	2006	2007
Kazakhstan Kazakhstan								
Cotton Coton	5 289	7 616	14 204	19 979	16 401	30 441	47 639	42 423
Wool Laines	259	416	575	...	...	...	...	...
Kenya Kenya								
Cotton Coton	16 327	15 483	8 953	10 246	10 252	9 582	8 498[1]	9 088[1]
Korea, Republic of Corée, République de								
Wool Laines	8 837	9 319	8 788	7 040	5 449	4 732	...	...
Kyrgyzstan Kirghizistan								
Cotton Coton	6 119	5 398	3 630	553	49	442	954	202
Wool Laines	750	477	374	302	591	634	284	201
Latvia Lettonie								
Cotton Coton	12 980	15 486	18 215	24 630	25 082	...	...	...
Wool Laines	...	11	21	24	17	...	...	...
Lithuania Lituanie								
Cotton Coton	42 507	33 841	23 891	15 079	11 688	9 455	8 252	1 827
Wool Laines	15 161	19 588	22 095	23 261	23 028	20 961	22 631	19 035
Mali Mali								
Cotton Coton	7 725	9 587	10 175	9 193	6 889	5 908	5 522	7 290
Montenegro Monténégro								
Cotton Coton	...	...	538	536	211	7	...	...
Wool Laines	...	...	194	104	67	55	60	...
Niger[1] Niger[1]								
Cotton Coton	6 749	7 361	7 675	...	...	...	...	...
Nigeria Nigéria								
Cotton Coton	...	24 912	25 119	24 830	24 953	24 967	...	...
Pakistan[2] Pakistan[2]								
Cotton Coton	437 190	490 164	568 436	582 145	683 390	924 670	903 810	964 800
Peru Pérou								
Cotton Coton	52 002	51 002	46 264	42 784	43 735	41 505		
Poland Pologne								
Cotton Coton	292 020	226 667	213 847	189 439	170 962	155 662	145 651	...
Wool Laines	6 059	5 182	3 370	3 602	3 500	2 988	2 570	...
Portugal Portugal								
Cotton Coton	146 579	152 396	132 377	126 729	140 442	93 027	88 569	...
Wool Laines	9 978	10 534	8 488	4 813	2 976	2 515	2 754	...
Romania Roumanie								
Cotton Coton	...	...	73 647	81 499	75 416	74 892	78 182	77 004
Wool Laines	...	...	6 086	4 401	4 308	3 732	2 828	1 865
Russian Federation Fédération de Russie								
Cotton Coton	1 822 000	2 094 000	2 264 000	2 329 000	2 149 000	2 225 000	2 222 000	2 108 000
Wool Laines	54 600	56 500	47 900	44 600	36 000	30 300	29 000	28 700
Serbia Serbie								
Cotton Coton	...	...	...	...	...	...	9 885	...
Wool Laines	...	...	...	...	...	83	41	...
Slovenia Slovénie								
Cotton Coton	...	...	...	...	...	42 282	33 375	31 819
South Africa[3] Afrique du Sud[3]								
Cotton Coton	219	216	215	198	...	...	...	...
Wool Laines	7 391	8 313	9 107	7 726	...	...	...	...
Spain Espagne								
Cotton Coton	...	...	...	...	290 293	251 111	...	...
Wool Laines	...	...	...	...	15 636	14 052	11 661	11 060
Sweden Suède								
Cotton Coton	...	...	...	...	...	...	...	2 521
Wool Laines	...	...	...	...	...	...	0	570
Tajikistan Tadjikistan								
Cotton Coton	11 485	13 617	19 521	21 450	19 377	24 156	21 176	30 514
TFYR of Macedonia L'ex-R.Y. Macédoine								
Cotton Coton	...	3 272	4 090	3 312	2 579	2 254	2 022	1 540
Wool Laines	...	967	335	182	270	149	119	95

38

Fabrics (continued)
Woven cotton and wool: thousand square metres

Tissus (suite)
Tissus de coton et tissages de laine : milliers de mètres carrés

Country or area Pays ou zone		2000	2001	2002	2003	2004	2005	2006	2007
Turkmenistan[4]	**Turkménistan[4]**								
Cotton	Coton	34 000	61 000	78 000	...	...	...	...	...
Uganda[3]	**Ouganda[3]**								
Cotton	Coton	8 000	6 000	8 000	...	...	...	...	...
Ukraine	**Ukraine**								
Cotton	Coton	...	...	...	34 428	45 105	52 989	42 719	52 106
Wool	Laines	...	...	...	5 180	8 341	8 287	8 110	7 043
United Rep. of Tanzania[5]	**Rép.-Unie de Tanzanie[5]**								
Cotton	Coton	65 473	74 978	100 021	108 997	111 637	99 134	107 884	109 843
United States	**Etats-Unis**								
Cotton	Coton	3 717 511[7]	3 100 592[7]	2 946 508[7]	2 422 538[7]	2 106 257[7]	2 416 580	2 329 714	...
Wool	Laines	56 742[7,8]	44 450[7,8]	23 224[7,8]	19 205[7,8]	15 910[7,8]	21 844[8]	22 360[8]	18 008

Source:
United Nations Statistics Division, New York, the *Industrial Commodity Statistics Yearbook 2006* and the industrial statistics database, last accessed April 2009.

1 In thousand metres.
2 Twelve months ending 30 June of the year stated.
3 Source: *African Statistical Yearbook*, Economic Commission for Africa (Addis Ababa).
4 Source: *Statistical Yearbook for Asia and the Pacific*, United Nations Economic and Social Commission for Asia and the Pacific (Bangkok).
5 Tanganyika only.
6 Production of gray broadwoven fabrics; fabric blends are based upon chief weight of fibre.
7 Shipments.
8 Production of gray broadwoven fabrics; fabric blends are based upon chief weight of fibre.

Source:
Organisation des Nations Unies, Division de statistique, New York, *l'Annuaire de statistiques industrielles par produit 2006* et la base de données pour les statistiques industrielles, dernier accès avril 2009.

1 En milliers de mètres.
2 Période de 12 mois finissant le 30 juin de l'année indiquée.
3 Source : *Annuaire des Statistiques de l'Afrique*, Conseil Economique pour l'Afrique (Addis-Abeba).
4 Source : *Annuaire des Statistiques de l'Asie et Pacifique*, Commission économique et sociale des Nations Unies pour l'Asie et le Pacifique (Bangkok).
5 Tanganyika seulement.
6 Production de tissus à armure large; les tissus mélangés sont basées sur le poids principal des fibres.
7 Expéditions.
8 Production de tissus à armure large; les tissus mélanges sont basés sur le poids principal des fibres.

Country or area Pays ou zone	1997	1998	1999	2000	2001	2002	2003	2004	2005	2006
Armenia Arménie	...	...	31	63	51	36	23	23	22	23
Azerbaijan Azerbaïdjan	...	...	...	114	218	339	456	288	261	311
Belarus Bélarus	12 495	12 533	12 449	12 455	11 275	9 346	8 635	9 020	8 821	9 487
Bolivia Bolivie	615	175	251	...	...	...	...	...	...	...
Botswana Botswana	...	...	...	...	367 552	...	...	...	...	...
Brazil Brésil	...	...	...	205 040	212 569	197 153	190 027	210 046	216 116	208 863
Bulgaria Bulgarie	...	3 713	2 562	2 492	2 507	3 542	4 556	2 985	3 003	2 889
Chile Chili	...	...	...	...	...	...	...	...	5 730	4 049
China [1] Chine [1]	2 473 427	1 205 617	1 013 751	1 468 379	1 335 864	1 522 824	1 816 469	2 743 931	2 525 475	3 003 002
China, Hong Kong SAR Chine, Hong Kong RAS	752	178	200	381	542	523	572	504	...	...
China, Macao SAR Chine, Macao RAS	962	881	...	...	4 254	4 640	6 679	...	...	...
Croatia Croatie	...	...	...	...	...	...	...	4 312	3 914	3 805
Cuba Cuba	3 281	2 666	2 918	2 526	2 765	1 665	971	1 300	1 051	457
Cyprus Chypre	...	...	...	...	...	548	313	194	193	205
Czech Republic République tchèque	9 776	6 455	4 922	3 398	2 937	1 776	1 202	1 074	963	1 154
Denmark Danemark	9 576	9 784	9 673	9 590	1 584	1 811	1 738	1 781	1 897	1 887
El Salvador El Salvador	3 399	1 152	...	...	...	...	...	...	...	...
Estonia Estonie	...	...	...	...	...	...	...	1 124	778	879
Finland Finlande	...	2 569	2 294	1 895	1 866	1 877	1 698	1 651	1 584	1 171
Georgia Géorgie	...	...	...	17	7	^0	3	12	...	...
Germany Allemagne	20 267	22 203	20 675	17 501	16 129	21 183	17 418	19 294	18 648	14 733
Greece [2] Grèce [2]	5 300	4 836	...	...	...	...	...	...	...	...
Hungary Hongrie	...	...	...	...	...	3 347	3 739	2 999	2 098	1 555
Iran (Islamic Rep. of) Iran (Rép. islamique d')	...	...	...	...	...	...	...	5 004	7 076	12 615
Iraq Iraq	...	...	...	...	...	...	...	164	...	118
Ireland Irlande	508	359	370	286	270	239	32	41	...	...
Italy Italie	...	...	...	...	...	...	205 316	218 417	...	...

Footwear with uppers of leather *(continued)*
Production: thousand pairs

Chaussures à dessus en cuir naturel *(suite)*
Production : milliers de paires

Country or area Pays ou zone	1997	1998	1999	2000	2001	2002	2003	2004	2005	2006
Japan Japon	...	58 656	54 768	50 806	45 841	40 860	37 024	37 516	36 632	32 472
Kazakhstan Kazakhstan	...	116	59	127	264	218	206	210	367	314
Kenya Kenya	899	828	3 783	4 342	3 842	4 416	7 949	7 915	12 455	15 869
Kuwait Koweït	0	0	0	0	0	51	91	94	100	205
Kyrgyzstan Kirghizistan	173	59	63	56	30	24	6	8	6	7
Latvia Lettonie	...	...	382	305	285	...	...	...	...	...
Lesotho Lesotho	...	...	...	6 477	7 158	6 476	6 032	5 395	2 165	2 176
Lithuania Lituanie	1 106	785	1 056	609	848	781	566	680	402	300
Mexico Mexique	24 104	23 591	23 909	24 292	22 094	21 846	21 535	22 442	22 856	24 791
Montenegro Monténégro	...	...	...	...	...	327	241	12	...	...
Mozambique Mozambique	...	...	...	...	...	...	12	22	34	...
Nigeria Nigéria	...	...	...	...	1 779	1 798	1 770	1 782	1 783	...
Norway Norvège	...	...	...	...	...	...	33	...	...	...
Poland Pologne	...	...	...	...	...	12 933	12 439	10 898	10 877	11 993
Portugal Portugal	65 791	61 912	70 153	69 303	71 431	68 366	62 121	58 167	53 157	51 234
Republic of Moldova[3] République de Moldova[3]	...	...	...	...	...	...	...	1 557	1 814	1 801
Romania Roumanie	...	...	...	...	...	53 981	62 100	56 447	55 315	55 191
Russian Federation Fédération de Russie	21 952	16 986	18 918	21 048	22 095	21 443	22 512	21 330	21 162	22 984
Serbia Serbie	...	...	...	...	...	...	...	...	...	3 508
Slovakia Slovaquie	...	...	...	...	5 975	6 486	9 871	11 813	12 388	12 770
Slovenia Slovénie	4 679	4 279	3 480	3 359	3 258	2 942	2 462	2 485	2 083	1 862
Spain Espagne	...	...	...	...	...	...	...	87 210	72 668	70 844
Sweden Suède	681	582	691	540	498	544	351	379	360	334
Tajikistan Tadjikistan	107	123	72	110	100	84	46	49	33	30
TFYR of Macedonia L'ex-R.Y. Macédoine	...	...	...	...	1 376	1 530	1 484	1 767	1 515	1 124
Ukraine Ukraine	...	...	...	...	...	...	10 476	9 742	8 899	9 465
United Kingdom Royaume-Uni	33 294	29 904	26 230[4]	22 369	20 331[5]	...	...	...	...	...
United Rep. of Tanzania[6] Rép.-Unie de Tanzanie[6]	152	...	71	...	0	0	0	0	0	...

Country or area Pays ou zone	1997	1998	1999	2000	2001	2002	2003	2004	2005	2006
Viet Nam Viet Nam	79 289	77 037	89 928	107 944	102 259	113 070	133 570	155 118	218 039	234 181

Source:
United Nations Statistics Division, New York, the *Industrial Commodity Statistics Yearbook 2006* and the industrial statistics database, last accessed April 2009.

1   For statistical purposes, the data for China do not include those for the Hong Kong Special Administrative Region (Hong Kong SAR), Macao Special Administrative Region (Macao SAR) and Taiwan Province of China.

2   Excluding children's sandals with leather uppers (incl. thong type sandals, flip flops).

3   Excluding the Transnistria region.

4   Excluding women's sandals with leather uppers (including thong type sandals and flip flops).

5   Excluding footwear with wood; cork or other outer soles and leather uppers (except outer soles of rubber, plastics or leather).

6   Tanganyika only.

Source:
Organisation des Nations Unies, Division de statistique, New York, *l'Annuaire de statistiques industrielles par produit 2006* et la base de données sur les statistiques industrielles, dernier accès avril 2009.

1   Pour la présentation des statistiques, les données pour la Chine ne comprennent pas la Région Administrative Spéciale de Hong Kong (Hong Kong RAS), la Région Administrative Spéciale de Macao (Macao RAS) et la province de Taiwan.

2   Sandales pour enfants avec dessus en cuir naturel non comprises.

3   Non compris la région de Transnistria.

4   Sandales pour femmes avec dessus en cuir naturel non comprises.

5   Chaussures à dessus en cuir avec des semelles en bois ou en liège non comprises.

6   Tanganyika seulement.

Sawnwood
Production (sawn): thousand cubic metres

Sciages
Production (sciés): milliers de mètres cubes

Region, country or area Région, pays ou zone	1998	1999	2000	2001	2002	2003	2004	2005	2006	2007
World **Monde**	**378 716**	**389 088**	**386 090**	**379 906**	**394 274**	**400 942**	**424 973**	**432 399**	**439 603**	**431 042**
Africa **Afrique**	**7 423**	**7 415**	**8 320**	**7 921**	**7 490**	**8 474**	**9 516**	**9 044**	**9 146**	**9 100**
Algeria Algérie	13	13	13	13	13	13	13	13	13	13
Angola Angola	5	5	5	5	5	5	5	5	5	5
Benin Bénin	13	13	13	32	46	31	31	31	146	84
Burkina Faso Burkina Faso	1	1	1	1	2	2	1	1	1	1
Burundi Burundi	33	80	83	83	83	83	83	83	83	83
Cameroon Cameroun	588	600	1 154	800	652	658	702	702	702	702
Central African Rep. Rép. centrafricaine	91	79	102	150	97	69	69	69	69	69
Chad Tchad	2	2	2	2	2	2	2	2	2	2
Congo Congo	73	74	93	126	170	168	200	209	268	268
Côte d'Ivoire Côte d'Ivoire	623	611	603	630	620	503	503	363	442	456
Dem. Rep. of the Congo Rép. dém. du Congo	80	70	40	10	35	15	15	15	15	15
Egypt Egypte	3	4	4	2	3	3	2	2	2	2
Equatorial Guinea Guinée équatoriale	4	4	4	4	4	4	4	4	4	4
Ethiopia Ethiopie	60	60	60	60	14	18	18	18	18	18
Gabon Gabon	60	98	88	112	176	231	133	230	235	230
Gambia Gambie	1	1	1	1	1	1	1	1	1	1
Ghana Ghana	590	454	475	480	461	496	480	520	527	520
Guinea Guinée	26	26	26	26	26	26	26	3	2	2
Guinea-Bissau Guinée-Bissau	16	16	16	16	16	16	16	16	16	16
Kenya Kenya	185	185	185	84	78	78	78	136	142	142
Liberia Libéria	6	4	10	20	30	25	50	50	60	60
Libyan Arab Jamah. Jamah. arabe libyenne	31	31	31	31	31	31	31	31	31	31
Madagascar Madagascar	84	102	485	400	95	493	893	893	887	888
Malawi Malawi	45	45	45	45	45	45	45	45	45	45

40

Sawnwood *(continued)*
Production (sawn): thousand cubic metres
Sciages *(suite)*
Production (sciés): milliers de mètres cubes

Region, country or area Région, pays ou zone	1998	1999	2000	2001	2002	2003	2004	2005	2006	2007
Mali Mali	13	13	13	13	13	13	13	13	13	13
Mauritania Mauritanie	...	...	...	...	...	...	...	7	14	14
Mauritius Maurice	5	5	3	3	3	3	3	3	4	3
Morocco Maroc	83	83	83	83	83	83	83	83	83	83
Mozambique Mozambique	28	28	28	28	28	28	32	38	43	57
Niger Niger	4	4	4	4	4	4	4	4	4	4
Nigeria Nigéria	2 000	2 000	2 000	2 000	2 000	2 000	2 000	2 000	2 000	2 000
Réunion Réunion	2	2	2	2	2	2	2	2	2	2
Rwanda Rwanda	76	79	79	79	79	79	79	79	79	79
Sao Tome and Principe Sao Tomé-et-Principe	5	5	5	5	5	5	5	5	5	5
Senegal Sénégal	23	23	23	23	23	23	23	23	23	23
Sierra Leone Sierra Leone	5	5	5	5	5	5	5	5	5	5
Somalia Somalie	14	14	14	14	14	14	14	14	14	14
South Africa Afrique du Sud	1 498	1 498	1 498	1 498	1 498	2 171	2 824	2 217	2 091	2 091
Sudan Soudan	51	51	51	51	51	51	51	51	51	51
Swaziland Swaziland	102	102	102	102	102	102	102	102	102	102
Togo Togo	18	21	19	15	13	13	13	14	14	14
Tunisia Tunisie	20	20	20	20	20	20	20	20	20	20
Uganda Ouganda	245	264	264	264	264	264	264	125	117	117
United Rep. of Tanzania Rép.-Unie de Tanzanie	24	24	24	24	24	24	24	24	24	24
Zambia Zambie	157	157	157	157	157	157	157	157	157	157
Zimbabwe Zimbabwe	416	438	386	397	397	397	397	617	565	565
Northern America **Amérique septentrionale**	**136 176**	**143 026**	**141 541**	**139 723**	**147 124**	**143 051**	**154 019**	**157 206**	**151 613**	**136 648**
Canada Canada	47 185	50 412	50 465	53 708	58 481	56 892	60 952	60 187	58 709	52 284
United States Etats-Unis	88 991	92 615	91 076	86 015	88 643	86 159	93 067	97 020	92 903	84 363
Latin America and the Caribbean **Amérique latine et Caraïbes**	**35 935**	**36 621**	**36 653**	**38 169**	**39 249**	**39 961**	**41 623**	**41 914**	**44 673**	**45 116**
Argentina Argentine	1 377	1 408	821	2 130	2 130	1 388	1 562	1 739	2 103	2 103

40

Sawnwood *(continued)*
Production (sawn): thousand cubic metres
Sciages *(suite)*
Production (sciés): milliers de mètres cubes

Region, country or area Région, pays ou zone	1998	1999	2000	2001	2002	2003	2004	2005	2006	2007
Bahamas Bahamas	1	1	1	1	1	1	1	1	1	1
Belize Belize	35	35	35	35	35	35	35	35	35	35
Bolivia Bolivie	515	244	239	308	299	347	402	408	408	408
Brazil Brésil	19 520	20 530	21 600	21 950	22 488	23 090	23 480	23 557	23 797	24 414
Chile Chili	4 551	5 254	5 698	5 872	6 439	7 004	8 015	8 298	8 718	8 340
Colombia Colombie	910	730	587	539	527	599	622	407	389	382
Costa Rica Costa Rica	780	780	812	812	812	812	426	488	1 132	1 132
Cuba Cuba	130	146	179	190	147	181	189	220	243	243
Dominica Dominique	...	...	...	...	...	47	66	66	66	66
Dominican Republic Rép. dominicaine	0	0	0	0	0	0	0	15	58	56
Ecuador Equateur	2 079	1 455	715	794	750	750	755	755	1 382	1 480
El Salvador El Salvador	58	58	58	58	68	68	16	16	16	16
French Guiana Guyane française	15	15	15	15	15	15	15	15	15	15
Guadeloupe Guadeloupe	1	1	1	1	1	1	1	1	1	1
Guatemala Guatemala	308	235	340	340	340	366	366	366	366	366
Guyana Guyana	50	50	29	30	31	38	36	58	68	74
Haiti Haïti	14	14	14	14	14	14	14	14	14	14
Honduras Honduras	369	419	442	419	470	421	454	400	412	379
Jamaica Jamaïque	66	66	66	66	66	66	66	66	66	66
Martinique Martinique	1	1	1	1	1	1	1	1	1	1
Mexico Mexique	3 260	3 110	3 110	2 829	2 691	2 740	2 962	2 674	2 650	2 687
Nicaragua Nicaragua	148	148	148	65	45	45	67	54	54	54
Panama Panama	8	46	48	42	24	27	30	30	30	30
Paraguay Paraguay	550	550	550	550	550	550	550	550	550	550
Peru Pérou	590	835	646	506	626	528	671	743	856	948
Suriname Suriname	41	28	60	56	47	56	58	65	69	57
Trinidad and Tobago Trinité-et-Tobago	27	18	32	41	43	39	32	41	41	41
Uruguay Uruguay	269	269	203	203	224	230	252	268	293	308

Sawnwood *(continued)*
Production (sawn): thousand cubic metres
Sciages *(suite)*
Production (sciés): milliers de mètres cubes

Region, country or area Région, pays ou zone	1998	1999	2000	2001	2002	2003	2004	2005	2006	2007
Venezuela (Bolivarian Rep. of) Venezuela (Rép. boliv. du)	261	174	202	301	364	501	479	562	838	348
Asia **Asie**	**72 096**	**71 648**	**61 905**	**59 616**	**63 742**	**68 334**	**71 815**	**73 291**	**79 035**	**81 547**
Afghanistan Afghanistan	400	400	400	400	400	400	400	400	400	400
Armenia Arménie	...	...	4	4	4	3	2	2	2	1
Azerbaijan Azerbaïdjan	...	...	1	^0	^0	^0	^0	^0	^0	2
Bangladesh Bangladesh	70	70	70	70	255	388	388	388	388	388
Bhutan Bhoutan	18	22	31	31	31	31	31	31	31	31
Brunei Darussalam Brunéi Darussalam	90	67	56	51	54	51	51	51	51	51
Cambodia Cambodge	40	26	20	5	10	4	6	4	2	4
China Chine	18 716	16 700	7 345	8 549	9 431	12 211	16 236	18 814	25 776	29 202
Cyprus Chypre	11	12	9	9	7	6	5	4	4	9
Georgia Géorgie	5	10	10	44	59	71	69	222	162	115
India Inde	8 400	8 400	7 900	7 900	10 990	11 880	13 661	14 789	14 789	14 789
Indonesia Indonésie	7 125	6 625	6 500	6 750	6 230	7 620	4 330	1 472	679	525
Iran (Islamic Rep. of) Iran (Rép. islamique d')	129	96	106	106	170	79	68	62	50	52
Iraq Iraq	12	12	12	12	12	12	12	12	12	12
Japan Japon	18 625	17 952	17 094	15 485	14 402	13 929	13 603	12 825	12 554	11 632
Kazakhstan Kazakhstan	182	183	244	224	232	265	134	139	139	139
Korea, Dem. P. R. Corée, R. p. dém. de	280	280	280	280	280	280	280	280	280	280
Korea, Republic of Corée, République de	2 240	4 300	4 544	4 420	4 410	4 380	4 366	4 366	4 366	4 366
Kyrgyzstan Kirghizistan	23	23	6	6	6	15	22	22	22	22
Lao People's Dem. Rep. Rép. dém. pop. lao	389	439	200	185	192	125	125	130	130	130
Lebanon Liban	9	9	9	9	9	9	9	9	9	9
Malaysia Malaisie	5 091	5 237	5 590	4 696	4 643	4 769	4 934	5 173	5 129	5 122
Mongolia Mongolie	300	300	300	300	300	300	300	300	300	300
Myanmar Myanmar	299	298	545	671	1 012	1 001	1 056	1 530	1 530	1 530
Nepal Népal	630	630	630	630	630	630	630	630	630	630
Pakistan Pakistan	1 051	1 075	1 087	1 180	1 180	1 180	1 260	1 288	1 313	1 313

40

Sawnwood *(continued)*
Production (sawn): thousand cubic metres
Sciages *(suite)*
Production (sciés): milliers de mètres cubes

Region, country or area Région, pays ou zone	1998	1999	2000	2001	2002	2003	2004	2005	2006	2007
Philippines Philippines	222	288	151	199	163	246	339	288	432	362
Singapore Singapour	25	25	25	25	25	25	25	25	25	25
Sri Lanka Sri Lanka	5	5	29	61	61	61	61	61	61	61
Syrian Arab Republic Rép. arabe syrienne	9	9	9	9	9	9	9	9	9	9
Thailand Thaïlande	103	178	220	233	288	288	288	288	288	288
Turkey Turquie	4 891	5 039	5 528	5 036	5 579	5 615	6 215	6 445	6 471	6 599
Viet Nam Viet Nam	2 705	2 937	2 950	2 036	2 667	2 450	2 900	3 232	3 000	3 150
Europe **Europe**	**119 718**	**122 822**	**129 501**	**126 558**	**127 933**	**132 212**	**138 674**	**141 757**	**145 869**	**149 036**
Albania Albanie	28	35	90	197	97	97	97	97	97	97
Austria Autriche	8 737	9 628	10 390	10 227	10 415	10 473	11 133	11 074	10 507	11 262
Belarus Bélarus	2 131	2 175	1 808	2 058	2 182	2 304	2 727	2 737	2 458	2 458
Belgium Belgique	...	...	1 150	1 275	1 175	1 215	1 235	1 285	1 520	1 555
Belgium-Luxembourg Belgique-Luxembourg	1 267	1 189	...	...	...	...	...	...	...	...
Bosnia and Herzegovina Bosnie-Herzégovine	330	330	320	310	738	888	1 319	1 319	1 358	1 358
Bulgaria Bulgarie	253	325	312	332	332	332	569	569	683	690
Croatia Croatie	676	685	642	574	640	585	582	624	669	702
Czech Republic République tchèque	3 427	3 584	4 106	3 889	3 800	3 805	3 940	4 003	5 080	5 454
Denmark Danemark	238	344	364	283	244	248	196	196	300	300
Estonia Estonie	850	1 200	1 436	1 623	1 825	1 954	2 029	2 063	1 958	1 750
Finland Finlande	12 300	12 768	13 420	12 770	13 390	13 745	13 544	12 269	12 227	12 477
France France	10 220	10 236	10 536	10 518	9 815	9 539	9 774	9 715	9 992	10 190
Germany Allemagne	14 972	16 096	16 340	16 131	17 119	17 596	19 538	21 931	24 420	25 170
Greece Grèce	137	140	123	123	196	191	191	191	108	108
Hungary Hongrie	298	308	291	264	293	299	205	215	186	235
Ireland Irlande	675	811	888	925	818	1 005	939	1 015	1 094	985
Italy Italie	1 600	1 630	1 630	1 600	1 605	1 590	1 580	1 590	1 748	1 700
Latvia Lettonie	3 200	3 640	3 900	3 840	3 947	3 951	3 988	4 227	4 320	3 459
Lithuania Lituanie	1 150	1 150	1 300	1 200	1 300	1 400	1 450	1 445	1 466	1 380

40

Sawnwood *(continued)*
Production (sawn): thousand cubic metres
Sciages *(suite)*
Production (sciés): milliers de mètres cubes

Region, country or area Région, pays ou zone	1998	1999	2000	2001	2002	2003	2004	2005	2006	2007
Luxembourg Luxembourg	...	...	133	133	133	133	133	133	133	133
Montenegro Monténégro	...	...	...	...	...	...	...	...	42	42
Netherlands Pays-Bas	349	362	390	268	258	269	273	279	265	271
Norway Norvège	2 525	2 336	2 280	2 253	2 225	2 186	2 230	2 326	2 389	2 402
Poland Pologne	4 320	4 137	4 262	3 083	3 180	3 360	3 743	3 360	3 607	3 304
Portugal Portugal	1 490	1 430	1 427	1 492	1 298	1 383	1 060	1 010	1 010	1 010
Republic of Moldova République de Moldova	30	6	5	5	5	31	31	31	31	31
Romania Roumanie	2 200	2 818	3 396	3 059	3 696	4 246	4 588	4 321	3 476	4 143
Russian Federation Fédération de Russie	19 580	19 100	20 000	19 600	19 240	20 155	21 380	22 033	22 127	23 200
Serbia Serbie	...	...	...	...	...	...	...	...	493	602
Serbia and Montenegro Serbie-et-Monténégro	438	364	504	391	432	514	575	497	...	...
Slovakia Slovaquie	1 265	1 265	1 265	1 265	1 265	1 651	1 837	2 621	2 440	2 781
Slovenia Slovénie	664	455	439	460	506	511	461	527	580	628
Spain Espagne	3 178	3 178	3 760	4 275	3 524	3 630	3 730	3 660	3 806	3 332
Sweden Suède	15 124	14 858	16 176	15 988	16 172	16 800	16 900	17 600	18 300	18 600
Switzerland Suisse	1 400	1 525	1 625	1 400	1 392	1 345	1 505	1 591	1 668	1 541
TFYR of Macedonia L'ex-R.Y. Macédoine	27	37	36	23	20	21	28	18	17	14
Ukraine Ukraine	2 258	2 141	2 127	1 995	1 950	2 019	2 392	2 416	2 385	2 525
United Kingdom Royaume-Uni	2 382	2 537	2 630	2 728	2 705	2 742	2 772	2 770	2 907	3 146
Oceania **Océanie**	**7 369**	**7 556**	**8 171**	**7 920**	**8 736**	**8 910**	**9 325**	**9 187**	**9 269**	**9 595**
Australia Australie	3 789	3 743	4 093	3 921	4 215	4 411	4 668	4 687	4 784	5 064
Fiji Fidji	131	64	72	72	84	84	112	125	125	125
New Caledonia Nouvelle-Calédonie	3	3	3	3	3	3	3	3	3	3
New Zealand Nouvelle-Zélande	3 178	3 653	3 910	3 821	4 301	4 289	4 419	4 249	4 234	4 280
Papua New Guinea Papouasie-Nvl-Guinée	218	40	40	40	70	60	60	60	60	60
Samoa Samoa	21	21	21	21	21	21	21	21	21	21
Solomon Islands Iles Salomon	12	12	12	12	12	12	12	12	12	12
Tonga Tonga	2	2	2	2	2	2	2	2	2	2

Sawnwood *(continued)*
Production (sawn): thousand cubic metres
Sciages *(suite)*
Production (sciés): milliers de mètres cubes

Region, country or area Région, pays ou zone	1998	1999	2000	2001	2002	2003	2004	2005	2006	2007
Vanuatu Vanuatu	15	18	18	28	28	28	28	28	28	28

Source:
Food and Agriculture Organization of the United Nations (FAO), Rome,
FAOSTAT database, last accessed March 2009.

Source:
Organisation des Nations Unies pour l'alimentation et l'agriculture (FAO),
Rome, la base de données de la FAOSTAT, dernier accès mars 2009.

Paper and paperboard
Production: thousand metric tons

Papiers et cartons
Production: milliers de tonnes

Region, country or area Région, pays ou zone	1998	1999	2000	2001	2002	2003	2004	2005	2006	2007
World **Monde**	**301 671**	**315 848**	**324 048**	**320 425**	**331 361**	**340 745**	**355 447**	**364 381**	**376 037**	**383 603**
Africa **Afrique**	**3 027**	**3 782**	**3 965**	**4 486**	**4 526**	**4 674**	**4 890**	**4 998**	**4 167**	**4 285**
Algeria Algérie	94	47	46	48	38	42	46	45	45	45
Dem. Rep. of the Congo Rép. dém. du Congo	3	3	3	3	3	3	3	3	3	3
Egypt Egypte	343	343	440	460	460	460	460	460	460	460
Ethiopia Ethiopie	6	10	12	12	11	14	16	16	16	16
Kenya Kenya	129	129	129	67	80	100	165	273	279	279
Libyan Arab Jamah. Jamah. arabe libyenne	6	6	6	6	6	6	6	6	6	6
Madagascar Madagascar	13	7	11	10	9	10	10	10	10	10
Mauritania Mauritanie	...	...	...	...	...	...	...	1	1	1
Morocco Maroc	110	109	109	129	129	129	129	129	129	129
Nigeria Nigéria	19	19	19	19	19	19	19	19	19	19
South Africa Afrique du Sud	2 105	2 900	2 982	3 523	3 579	3 645	3 774	3 774	2 915	3 033
Sudan Soudan	3	3	3	3	3	3	3	3	3	3
Tunisia Tunisie	88	94	94	94	77	95	106	106	106	106
Uganda Ouganda	3	3	3	3	3	3	3	3	3	3
United Rep. of Tanzania Rép.-Unie de Tanzanie	25	25	25	25	25	25	25	25	25	25
Zambia Zambie	4	4	4	4	4	4	4	4	4	4
Zimbabwe Zimbabwe	76	80	80	80	80	117	121	121	144	144
Northern America **Amérique septentrionale**	**105 326**	**108 950**	**107 211**	**101 083**	**101 952**	**100 676**	**102 546**	**103 195**	**102 506**	**101 939**
Canada Canada	18 875	20 280	20 959	19 834	20 073	19 964	20 462	19 498	18 189	18 113
United States Etats-Unis	86 451	88 670	86 252	81 249	81 879	80 712	82 084	83 697	84 317	83 826
Latin America and the Caribbean **Amérique latine et Caraïbes**	**13 624**	**13 837**	**14 498**	**15 507**	**15 772**	**16 601**	**17 949**	**18 812**	**16 514**	**16 636**
Argentina Argentine	978	1 012	1 270	1 141	1 417	1 444	1 586	2 080	1 545	1 545
Barbados Barbade	...	...	...	...	...	...	...	2	2	2
Bolivia Bolivie	2	0	0	0	0	0	0	0	0	0

Paper and paperboard *(continued)*
Production: thousand metric tons

Papiers et cartons *(suite)*
Production: milliers de tonnes

Region, country or area Région, pays ou zone	1998	1999	2000	2001	2002	2003	2004	2005	2006	2007
Brazil Brésil	6 524	6 255	6 473	7 354	7 354	7 811	8 221	8 411	5 834	5 836
Chile Chili	598	824	861	877	1 016	1 098	1 168	1 215	1 231	1 344
Colombia Colombie	712	733	771	771	847	864	899	919	990	1 013
Costa Rica Costa Rica	20	20	20	20	20	20	20	20	20	20
Cuba Cuba	57	57	57	57	25	33	27	30	27	25
Dominican Republic Rép. dominicaine	130	130	130	130	130	130	130	130	130	130
Ecuador Equateur	91	91	91	91	94	101	100	100	99	100
El Salvador El Salvador	56	56	56	56	56	56	56	56	56	56
Guatemala Guatemala	31	31	31	31	31	31	31	31	31	31
Honduras Honduras	95	95	95	95	95	95	95	95	95	95
Mexico Mexique	3 673	3 784	3 865	4 056	3 987	4 149	4 689	4 841	5 566	5 594
Paraguay Paraguay	13	13	13	13	13	13	13	13	13	13
Peru Pérou	63	63	83	86	88	91	91	91	124	132
Uruguay Uruguay	88	92	88	88	89	89	100	98	98	90
Venezuela (Boliv. Rep. of) Venezuela (Rép. boliv. du)	493	581	594	641	510	576	723	680	653	610
Asia **Asie**	**85 484**	**91 224**	**94 516**	**96 593**	**103 426**	**110 036**	**116 222**	**122 317**	**134 307**	**141 702**
Armenia Arménie	...	...	20	1	2	2	2	4	20	18
Azerbaijan Azerbaïdjan	...	...	28	146	144	8	8	5	3	^0
Bahrain Bahreïn	...	...	...	...	...	15	15	15	15	15
Bangladesh Bangladesh	46	46	46	46	46	83	58	58	58	58
China Chine	32 203	33 627	34 894	36 529	42 329	47 529	54 029	60 526	69 526	78 026
India Inde	3 320	3 845	3 794	4 094	4 105	4 075	4 434	4 183	4 183	4 183
Indonesia Indonésie	5 487	6 978	6 977	6 995	6 995	7 040	7 223	7 223	7 223	7 223
Iran (Islamic Rep. of) Iran (Rép. islamique d')	20	25	46	46	415	411	411	411	411	411
Iraq Iraq	20	20	30	33	33	27	33	33	33	33
Israel Israël	242	275	275	275	275	275	275	275	275	275
Japan Japon	29 886	30 631	31 828	30 717	30 686	30 457	29 253	29 295	29 459	28 930
Jordan Jordanie	32	32	19	27	25	54	54	54	54	54

41

Paper and paperboard *(continued)*
Production: thousand metric tons
Papiers et cartons *(suite)*
Production: milliers de tonnes

Region, country or area Région, pays ou zone	1998	1999	2000	2001	2002	2003	2004	2005	2006	2007
Kazakhstan Kazakhstan	...	3	24	47	64	58	69	81	81	81
Korea, Dem. P. R. Corée, R. p. dém. de	80	80	80	80	80	80	80	80	80	80
Korea, Republic of Corée, République de	7 750	8 875	9 308	9 332	9 812	10 148	10 511	10 254	10 703	10 932
Kuwait Koweït	...	...	42	42	42	56	56	56	56	56
Kyrgyzstan Kirghizistan	...	...	2	7	16	3	2	2	2	2
Lebanon Liban	42	42	64	66	66	100	103	103	103	103
Malaysia Malaisie	761	859	791	851	851	983	946	954	1 069	1 062
Myanmar Myanmar	41	37	39	42	49	45	43	45	45	45
Nepal Népal	13	13	13	13	13	13	13	13	13	13
Pakistan Pakistan	527	574	592	1 165	1 165	1 165	986	1 010	1 010	1 010
Philippines Philippines	987	1 010	1 107	1 056	1 056	1 091	1 097	1 097	1 097	1 097
Saudi Arabia Arabie saoudite	...	...	50	70	70	214	279	279	279	279
Singapore Singapour	87	87	87	87	87	87	87	87	87	87
Sri Lanka Sri Lanka	25	25	24	25	25	25	25	25	25	25
Syrian Arab Republic Rép. arabe syrienne	1	1	11	15	15	62	75	75	75	75
Thailand Thaïlande	2 367	2 434	2 312	2 445	2 444	3 420	3 433	3 452	5 305	4 484
Turkey Turquie	1 357	1 349	1 567	1 513	1 643	1 643	1 643	1 643	1 643	1 643
United Arab Emirates Emirats arabes unis	...	...	55	58	58	78	81	81	81	81
Uzbekistan Ouzbékistan	...	...	8	8	9	11	11	11	11	11
Viet Nam Viet Nam	190	356	384	762	807	779	888	888	1 282	1 309
Europe **Europe**	**90 825**	**94 675**	**100 144**	**99 245**	**102 166**	**104 857**	**109 825**	**110 863**	**114 380**	**114 977**
Albania Albanie	44	1	3	3	3	3	3	3	3	3
Austria Autriche	4 009	4 142	4 386	4 250	4 419	4 565	4 852	4 950	5 213	5 199
Belarus Bélarus	195	208	236	224	216	279	257	284	285	285
Belgium Belgique	...	...	1 727	1 662	1 704	1 919	1 957	1 897	1 897	1 897
Belgium-Luxembourg Belgique-Luxembourg	1 831	1 727	...	...	...	...	...	...	...	...
Bosnia and Herzegovina Bosnie-Herzégovine	...	...	...	...	...	60	81	81	118	118
Bulgaria Bulgarie	153	126	136	171	171	171	326	326	313	442

41

Paper and paperboard *(continued)*
Production: thousand metric tons
Papiers et cartons *(suite)*
Production: milliers de tonnes

Region, country or area Région, pays ou zone	1998	1999	2000	2001	2002	2003	2004	2005	2006	2007
Croatia Croatie	403	417	406	451	467	463	464	592	564	545
Czech Republic République tchèque	768	770	804	864	870	950	934	969	1 042	1 023
Denmark Danemark	393	397	263	389	384	388	402	423	423	423
Estonia Estonie	43	48	54	70	75	64	66	64	78	72
Finland Finlande	12 703	12 947	13 509	12 502	12 789	13 058	14 036	12 391	14 140	14 334
France France	9 161	9 603	10 006	9 625	9 809	9 939	10 255	10 332	10 006	9 871
Germany Allemagne	16 311	16 742	18 182	17 879	18 526	19 310	20 391	21 679	22 656	23 172
Greece Grèce	622	545	496	495	493	493	510	510	412	409
Hungary Hongrie	434	473	506	495	517	546	579	571	553	552
Ireland Irlande	42	42	43	43	44	45	45	45	0	0
Italy Italie	8 254	8 568	9 129	8 926	9 317	9 491	9 667	9 999	10 011	10 112
Latvia Lettonie	18	19	16	24	33	38	38	39	57	60
Lithuania Lituanie	37	37	53	68	78	92	99	113	119	124
Netherlands Pays-Bas	3 180	3 256	3 332	3 174	3 346	3 339	3 459	3 471	3 367	3 224
Norway Norvège	2 260	2 241	2 300	2 220	2 114	2 186	2 294	2 223	2 109	2 010
Poland Pologne	1 718	1 839	1 934	2 086	2 342	2 461	2 635	2 732	2 857	2 992
Portugal Portugal	1 136	1 163	1 290	1 419	1 537	1 530	1 664	1 570	1 644	1 644
Romania Roumanie	301	289	340	395	370	443	454	371	432	558
Russian Federation Fédération de Russie	3 595	4 535	5 310	5 625	5 978	6 377	6 830	7 126	7 434	7 559
Serbia Serbie	...	...	...	...	...	...	...	...	231	245
Serbia and Montenegro Serbie-et-Monténégro	326	230	180	241	254	148	159	229	...	...
Slovakia Slovaquie	597	738	925	988	710	674	798	858	888	915
Slovenia Slovénie	491	417	411	633	704	417	497	763	760	794
Spain Espagne	3 545	4 435	4 765	5 131	5 365	5 437	5 526	5 697	6 898	6 714
Sweden Suède	9 879	10 071	10 782	10 534	10 724	11 062	11 589	11 775	12 066	11 902
Switzerland Suisse	1 592	1 748	1 589	1 729	1 805	1 818	1 777	1 751	1 526	1 536
TFYR of Macedonia Ex-R.Y. Macédoine	15	14	17	15	19	18	16	20	20	23
Ukraine Ukraine	293	311	411	480	532	618	723	768	804	937

Region, country or area Région, pays ou zone	1998	1999	2000	2001	2002	2003	2004	2005	2006	2007
United Kingdom Royaume-Uni	6 477	6 576	6 605	6 434	6 452	6 455	6 442	6 241	5 454	5 284
Oceania **Océanie**	**3 385**	**3 381**	**3 713**	**3 511**	**3 519**	**3 900**	**4 014**	**4 195**	**4 162**	**4 064**
Australia Australie	2 541	2 564	2 836	2 672	2 645	3 090	3 097	3 244	3 221	3 192
New Zealand Nouvelle-Zélande	844	817	877	839	874	810	917	951	941	872

Source:
Food and Agriculture Organization of the United Nations (FAO), Rome,
FAOSTAT database, last accessed March 2009.

Source:
Organisation des Nations Unies pour l'alimentation et l'agriculture (FAO),
Rome, la base de données de la FAOSTAT, dernier accès mars 2009.

42

Cement
Production: thousand metric tons

Ciment
Production: milliers de tonnes

Country or area Pays ou zone	1997	1998	1999	2000	2001	2002	2003	2004	2005	2006
Afghanistan Afghanistan	116[1]	116[1]	116[1]	25[1]	16[1]	27[1]	24	70[2]	30[3]	...
Albania Albanie	100[1]	84[1]	107[1]	180[1]	30[1]	50[1]	578	530	473	356
Algeria Algérie	7 146[1]	7 836[1]	7 685	8 703	8 710	8 941	8 192	9 543	...	...
Angola [2] Angola [2]	301	*350	207	201	*200	*250	250	250	...	...
Argentina Argentine	6 769	7 092	7 187	6 121	5 545	3 911	5 217	6 254	7 595	8 929
Armenia Arménie	293	314	287	219	275	355	384	501	605	625
Australia [4] Australie [4]	6 701	7 236	7 704	7 937	6 821	7 236	7 731	8 460	8 925	8 910
Austria Autriche	3 852	...	...	3 776[2]	3 863[2]	3 800[2]	3 800[2]	3 800[2]	...	...
Azerbaijan Azerbaïdjan	303[1]	201[1]	171[1]	251[1]	523[1]	848[1]	1 012[1]	1 428[1]	1 538	1 639
Bahrain Bahreïn	172[1]	230[1]	156[1]	89[1]	89[1]	67[1]	70[2]	75[2]	...	...
Bangladesh Bangladesh	610[1]	468[1]	1 514[1]	1 868[1]	2 340[4]	2 514[4]	2 565[4]	2 695[4]	2 943[4]	3 211[4]
Barbados Barbade	176	257	257	268	250	298	325	322	342	338
Belarus Bélarus	1 876	2 035	1 998	1 847	1 803	2 171	2 472	2 731	3 131	3 495
Belgium Belgique	6 996	6 852	7 463	7 150[2]	*7 500[2]	*8 000[2]	8 000[2]	8 000[2]	...	...
Benin Bénin	442[1]	520[1]	520[1]	250[1]	250[1]	250[1]	*250[2]	250[2]	...	...
Bhutan *[2] Bhoutan *[2]	160	150	150	150	160	160	160	170	...	...
Bolivia Bolivie	762	938	1 234	1 072	983	1 011[5]	1 138[5]	1 276[5]	1 440	...
Bosnia and Herzegovina Bosnie-Herzégovine	414	563	683	164[6]	145[6]	213[6]	#891	1 045[2]	...	...
Brazil Brésil	37 995	39 942	40 248	37 562	38 302	37 462	34 653	34 159	38 864	41 555
Brunei Darussalam Brunéi Darussalam	...	...	222	241[1]	234[1]	220[1]	235[2]	240[2]	234	184
Bulgaria Bulgarie	1 654	1 723	2 047	2 207	2 061	2 141	2 398	2 943	3 600	4 064
Burkina Faso Burkina Faso	50[2]	50[2]	50[2]	50[1]	50[1]	50[1]	*30[2]	30[2]	...	...
Cambodia [2] Cambodge [2]	...	150	...	...	...	...	...	...	...	...
Cameroon Cameroun	633[1]	740[1]	852[1]	1 570[1]	980[1]	950[1]	949	930[2]	1 026	...
Canada Canada	11 736[7]	12 168	12 643	12 753	12 793	13 081	13 424[2]	14 017[2]	...	...
Chile Chili	3 718	3 890	2 508	2 686	3 145	3 462[2]	3 622[2]	3 798[2]	4 016	4 127
China [8] Chine [8]	511 738	536 000	573 000	597 000	661 040	725 000	862 081	966 820	1 068 848	1 236 765

42

Cement *(continued)*
Production: thousand metric tons
Ciment *(suite)*
Production: milliers de tonnes

Country or area Pays ou zone	1997	1998	1999	2000	2001	2002	2003	2004	2005	2006
China, Hong Kong SAR Chine, Hong Kong RAS	1 925	1 539	1 387	1 284	1 279	1 206	1 189	1 039	1 005	1 255
Colombia Colombie	10 878	8 673	6 677	7 131	6 776	6 633	7 337[5]	7 822[5]	9 959[5]	...
Congo Congo	20	0	0	0	...	...	...	...	...	...
Costa Rica[2] Costa Rica[2]	940	1 085	1 100	1 050	1 200	1 200	1 320	1 300	...	...
Côte d'Ivoire Côte d'Ivoire	1 100[1]	650[1]	650[1]	650[1]	650[1]	650[1]	650[2]	650[2]	...	...
Croatia Croatie	2 134	3 873	2 712	2 852	3 246	3 378	3 571	3 514	3 481	3 622
Cuba Cuba	1 701	1 724	1 797	1 643	1 335	1 336	1 357	1 409	1 576	1 714
Cyprus Chypre	910	1 207	1 157	1 398	1 367	1 445	1 638	1 688	1 800	1 786
Czech Republic République tchèque	4 874	4 599	4 241	4 093	3 591	3 249	3 502	3 829	3 978	4 239
Dem. Rep. of the Congo[2] Rép. dém. du Congo[2]	125	134	159	161	192	*190	190	...	...	...
Denmark Danemark	2 544	2 548	2 422	2 536	2 576	2 545	2 580	2 892	2 881	2 937
Dominican Republic Rép. dominicaine	1 822	1 872	2 295	2 505	2 746	3 050	2 783	2 654	2 779	1 888
Ecuador Equateur	2 900[2]	2 539	2 262	2 800[2]	2 947	3 113	3 100[2]	3 100[2]	...	...
Egypt Egypte	15 569[1]	15 569[1]	11 933[1]	25 101[1]	26 811[1]	23 000[1]	16 281	...	...	...
El Salvador El Salvador	1 667	1 073	1 031[2]	1 064[2]	1 174[2]	1 318[2]	1 390[2]	1 400[2]	...	...
Eritrea[2] Erythrée[2]	60	50	*45	*45	*45	*45	*45	45	...	...
Estonia Estonie	422	321	358	329	405	466	506	614	733	856
Ethiopia Ethiopie	775[9]	783[9]	767[9]	816[9]	819	919	890	1 300[2]	...	...
Fiji Fidji	96	89	99	87	98	102	100	111	143	143
Finland Finlande	1 152	1 232	1 310	1 422	1 325	1 198	1 493	1 691	1 321	1 513
France France	18 309	19 434	20 302	20 000[2]	20 652	20 244	20 544	...	...	...
French Guiana[2] Guyane française[2]	51	88	*88	*88	*58	*62	*62	62	...	...
Gabon Gabon	200[1]	198[1]	162[1]	166[1]	240[1]	257[1]	261	350[2]	...	...
Georgia Géorgie	94	199	341	348	335	347	345	442	...	...
Germany Allemagne	37 210	38 464	39 970	38 088	33 689	32 012	32 349[2]	31 954[2]	...	...
Ghana Ghana	1 446	1 573	1 851	1 673	1 490	1 414	1 900[2]	2 000[2]	...	...
Greece Grèce	13 660	14 207	13 624	14 147	15 563	15 500[2]	18 742[10]	15 000[2]	...	...
Guadeloupe *[2] Guadeloupe *[2]	230	230	230	230	230	230	230	230	...	...

Cement (continued)
Production: thousand metric tons
Ciment (suite)
Production: milliers de tonnes

Country or area Pays ou zone	1997	1998	1999	2000	2001	2002	2003	2004	2005	2006
Guatemala Guatemala	1 480	1 496	2 120	2 039	1 976	2 068	1 900[2]	1 900[2]	...	...
Guinea Guinée	260[1]	277[1]	297[1]	300[1]	300[1]	300[1]	360[2]	360[2]	...	...
Haiti[2] Haïti[2]	...	...	...	...	204	290	200	300		...
Honduras Honduras	*1 041[2]	896[2]	980[2]	1 284[2]	*1 321[2]	*1 360[2]	1 400[2]	1 400[2]	1 384[5]	...
Hungary Hongrie	2 811	2 999	2 980	3 326	3 452	3 510	3 575	3 363	3 235	3 571
Iceland Islande	110	118	131	144	125	83	85	...	...	...
India Inde	82 873	87 646	100 230	99 227	106 491	111 778	117 035	125 000[2]	140 512[3]	...
Indonesia[1] Indonésie[1]	20 702	22 344	22 808	27 789	18 629	33 000	40 476	32 448	...	...
Iran (Islamic Rep. of) Iran (Rép. islamique d')	18 349[1]	20 049[1]	22 219[1]	23 276[1]	24 755[1]	30 000[1]	30 000[2]	30 000[2]	33 049	21 536
Iraq Iraq	2 500[1]	2 000[1]	2 000[1]	2 000[1]	2 000[1]	2 000[1]	*1 000[2]	*3 000[2]	...	2 887
Ireland Irlande	2 247	2 395	2 616	2 784	2 779	2 693	3 065	3 348	...	...
Israel Israël	5 916	6 476[2]	6 354[2]	*5 703[2]	*4 700[2]	*4 584[2]	*4 632[2]	*4 494[2]	...	...
Italy Italie	33 718	35 512	36 827	39 588	40 494	42 050	37 021[11]	37 843[11]	...	...
Jamaica Jamaïque	588	558	504[5]	521[5]	596	622	608	808	848[5]	763
Japan Japon	91 938	81 328	80 120	81 097	76 550	...	...	...	...	...
Jordan Jordanie	3 250[1]	2 650[1]	2 688[1]	2 640[1]	3 149[1]	3 558	3 515	3 908	4 046	3 967
Kazakhstan Kazakhstan	657[1]	622	838	1 175	2 029	2 128[1]	2 580[1]	3 660[1]	...	...
Kenya Kenya	1 580	1 453	1 389	1 348	1 319	1 537	1 659	1 886	2 182	2 406
Korea, Dem. P. R.[2] Corée, R. p. dém. de[2]	7 000	7 000	*4 000	*4 600	*5 160	*5 320	*5 540	5 500	...	...
Korea, Republic of Corée, République de	60 317	46 791	48 579	51 417	53 062	56 823	60 725	56 955	52 224	55 021
Kuwait Koweït	1 370[1]	2 310[1]	947[1]	1 187[1]	921[1]	1 584[1]	1 863[1]	2 635	2 690	2 837
Kyrgyzstan Kirghizistan	386	546	658	453	469	533	757	870	973	1 051
Lao People's Dem. Rep. Rép. dém. pop. lao	84[2]	80[2]	*80[2]	*92[2]	*92[2]	263	280	282	400	...
Latvia Lettonie	246	366	...	...	...	...	...	...	...	...
Lebanon Liban	3 126[1]	3 316[1]	2 714[1]	2 808[1]	2 890[1]	2 852[1]	2 900[2]	2 900[2]	...	2 297
Liberia *[2] Libéria *[2]	7	10	15	71	63	54	30	30	...	...
Libyan Arab Jamah.[2] Jamah. arabe libyenne[2]	3 000	3 000	3 000	3 000	3 000	3 300	3 500	3 600	...	...
Lithuania Lituanie	710	781	668	559	541	601	599	753	840	1 054

Cement (*continued*)
Production: thousand metric tons
Ciment (*suite*)
Production: milliers de tonnes

Country or area Pays ou zone	1997	1998	1999	2000	2001	2002	2003	2004	2005	2006
Luxembourg Luxembourg	683	699	742	749	725	729	709	750[2]	...	...
Madagascar Madagascar	36	44	46[2]	48[2]	51	34	33[2]	23	29	33
Malawi Malawi	70	83	104	156[2]	111	174[2]	190[2]	190[2]	...	...
Malaysia Malaisie	12 668[1]	10 379[1]	10 104[1]	11 445[1]	13 820[1]	14 336[1]	17 244[1]	17 328[1]	16 659	19 456
Mali Mali	10[1]	10[1]	10[1]	10[1]	18[12]	...	...	...	...	...
Martinique *[2] Martinique *[2]	220	220	220	255	255	221	225	225		
Mauritania Mauritanie	125[1]	50[1]	50[1]	156[1]	181[1]	174[1]	*200[2]	*200[2]		
Mexico Mexique	29 526	30 728	31 802	33 228	32 134	33 372	33 594	34 992	37 452	40 362
Mongolia Mongolie	*112[2]	109	104	92	68	148	162	62	112[3]	141
Morocco Maroc	7 236[1]	7 155[1]	7 194[1]	7 497[1]	8 058[1]	8 486	9 277	9 796	10 289	11 357
Mozambique Mozambique	217[1]	264[1]	266[1]	348[1]	421[1]	274[1]	582	552	564	...
Myanmar Myanmar	524[13]	371[13]	343[13]	400[13]	384[13]	462[13]	581[13]	527[13]	552[3]	552[3]
Nepal [14] Népal [14]	227	139	191	206	215	233	255	279	278	...
Netherlands Pays-Bas	3 230	3 200	3 200	3 200	*3 450[2]	*3 400[2]	*3 400[2]	*3 400[2]		
New Caledonia Nouvelle-Calédonie	84	89	93	91	100	100	100[2]	115[2]	119	133
New Zealand [2] Nouvelle-Zélande [2]	976	950	*1 030	1 070	1 080	1 090	1 100	1 110	...	...
Nicaragua Nicaragua	361	412	536	568	588	507[5]	533[5]	521[5]	530[5]	...
Niger Niger	30[1]	30[1]	30[1]	40[1]	40[1]	55[1]	40[2]	40[2]	...	...
Nigeria Nigéria	2 520[1]	2 700[1]	2 500[1]	2 500[1]	1 756	1 760	1 747	1 754	1 754	...
Norway [2] Norvège [2]	1 724	1 676	1 827	1 851	*1 870	...	...	...	...	...
Occupied Palestinian Terr. [1] Terr. palestinien occupé [1]	...	...	...	...	40	29	...	...	...	...
Oman Oman	1 233[1]	1 217[1]	1 990[1]	1 815[1]	1 370[1]	1 523[15]	1 593[15]	1 648[15]	...	...
Pakistan Pakistan	9 536	9 364	9 635	9 314	9 672	9 935	11 316[1]	12 862[4]	16 353[4]	18 564[4]
Panama Panama	752	814	976	849[5]	698[5]	748[5]	889[5]	1 042[5]	...	...
Paraguay Paraguay	603	586	556	516	505	447	505	660[2]	...	...
Peru Pérou	4 092	4 069	3 327	3 658	3 589	4 115	4 203	4 602	5 108	...
Philippines Philippines	14 681	12 888	12 557	11 959	11 378	11 396	10 000[2]	13 057[3]	12 368[3]	12 033[3]
Poland Pologne	15 003	14 970	15 555	#14 943	12 090	11 213	11 624	12 148	12 190	14 695

Cement *(continued)*
Production: thousand metric tons
Ciment *(suite)*
Production: milliers de tonnes

Country or area Pays ou zone	1997	1998	1999	2000	2001	2002	2003	2004	2005	2006
Portugal Portugal	9 445	9 845	10 057	10 293	10 168	9 728	8 598	8 839	8 427	8 327
Puerto Rico Porto Rico	1 586	1 646	1 757	...	...	...	...	...	...	...
Qatar Qatar	584[1]	857[1]	959[1]	1 029[1]	1 209[1]	1 346[15]	1 340[15]	1 200[15]	...	...
Republic of Moldova [16] République de Moldova [16]	122	74	50	222	158	279	255	440	641	...
Réunion Réunion	200	342	263	258	*380[2]	*380[2]	*380[2]	*380[2]	...	...
Romania Roumanie	6 553	7 300	6 252	8 411	5 668	5 767	5 879	6 211	7 023	8 263
Russian Federation Fédération de Russie	26 688	25 974	28 529	32 389	35 271	37 705	40 998	45 615	48 534	54 731
Rwanda Rwanda	61	60	68	71[2]	91[2]	101[2]	105[2]	104[2]	...	...
Saudi Arabia Arabie saoudite	15 448[1]	15 776[1]	16 381[1]	18 296[1]	20 976	23 452	24 200	25 470	26 064	...
Senegal Sénégal	854[1]	847[1]	1 014	1 341	1 539	1 653	1 694	2 391	2 623	2 884
Serbia Serbie	...	...	...	...	...	...	...	...	2 276	2 565
Serbia and Montenegro Serbie-et-Monténégro	2 011	2 253	#1 575	2 117	2 418	2 396	2 075	2 240[2]	...	...
Sierra Leone Sierra Leone	40	41	45	73	113	144	170	181	172	163
Singapore [2] Singapour [2]	*3 300	2 340	1 660	1 150	*600	*200	150	150	...	...
Slovakia Slovaquie	5 856	3 066	3 084	3 045	3 011	3 121	3 115	3 031	3 282	3 389
Slovenia Slovénie	...	...	...	...	1 186	...	...	...	...	...
South Africa Afrique du Sud	7 891	7 676	8 211	8 715	8 036[2]	8 525[2]	8 883[2]	12 348[2]	...	...
Spain Espagne	27 860	27 943[2]	...	...	...	...	...	...	...	...
Sri Lanka Sri Lanka	966	2 151	2 354	2 432	2 123	973	1 163	1 400[2]	3 928[3]	4 579[3]
Sudan Soudan	276[17]	198[17]	231[17]	146[17]	190[17]	220[17]	320[17]	244	244	227
Suriname Suriname	65[1]	65[1]	65[1]	60[1]	65[1]	65[1]	*65[2]	*65[2]	...	...
Sweden Suède	2 320	2 373	2 293	2 613	2 644	2 765	2 841	2 731	2 791	3 074
Switzerland Suisse	3 568[2]	*3 600[2]	3 548[2]	3 771[2]	3 950[2]	*4 000[2]	3 800[2]	3 955	...	...
Syrian Arab Republic Rép. arabe syrienne	4 838	5 016	5 134	4 631	5 428	5 399	5 224	5 098	5 218	...
Tajikistan Tadjikistan	36[1]	18[1]	33[1]	55[1]	69[1]	89[1]	168[1]	192[1]	253	282
Thailand Thaïlande	37 115	22 722	25 354	25 499	27 913	31 679	32 530	35 626	37 872	39 408
TFYR of Macedonia Ex-R.Y. Macédoine	610	461	563	801	630	778	832	812	887	924
Togo Togo	421[1]	500[1]	600[1]	1 393	1 381	1 270	1 196	1 164	1 018	1 102

42
Cement *(continued)*
Production: thousand metric tons
Ciment *(suite)*
Production: milliers de tonnes

Country or area Pays ou zone	1997	1998	1999	2000	2001	2002	2003	2004	2005	2006
Trinidad and Tobago Trinité-et-Tobago	677	700	740	743	697	744	766	768	686	883
Tunisia[1] Tunisie[1]	4 378	4 588	4 860	5 647	5 721	6 020	6 480	6 192	...	...
Turkey Turquie	36 035	38 175	34 215	36 238	30 111	32 546	35 264	38 594	41 100	47 906
Turkmenistan Turkménistan	601[1]	750[1]	780[1]	420[1]	448[1]	486[1]	200	450[2]	...	...
Ukraine Ukraine	5 101	5 591	5 828	5 311	5 786	7 157	8 923	10 648	12 165	13 739
United Arab Emirates Emirats arabes unis	6 330[1]	7 066[1]	7 069[1]	6 100[1]	6 100[1]	6 500[1]	*8 000[2]	*8 000[2]		
United Kingdom Royaume-Uni	14 307[11]	14 764[11]	14 544[11]	12 452[2]	11 854[2]	*11 089[2]	11 215[2]	11 250[2]	...	...
United Rep. of Tanzania Rép.-Unie de Tanzanie	621	778[2]	833	833	901[18]	1 026	1 187[18]	1 281[18]	1 367[18]	1 369[18]
United States[19] Etats-Unis[19]	82 582	83 931	85 952	87 546	88 900	89 732	92 843	97 434	99 319	98 167
Uruguay Uruguay	818	940	839	688	1 015[2]	442[20]	489[20]	658[20]	691[20]	...
Uzbekistan Ouzbékistan	3 286[1]	3 400[1]	3 300[1]	3 284[1]	3 722[3]	3 927[3]	4 062[3]	4 805[3]	5 068[3]	5 583[3]
Venezuela (Boliv. Rep. of)[5] Venezuela (R. bol. du)[5]	7 867	7 870	7 875	7 527	7 329	6 126	7 398	9 000	10 000	...
Viet Nam Viet Nam	8 019	9 738	10 489	13 298	16 073	21 121	24 127	26 153	30 808	32 690
Yemen Yémen	1 038[1]	1 195[1]	1 454[1]	1 406[1]	1 449[1]	1 582[1]	1 541	1 546[2]	...	...
Zambia Zambie	384[2]	351[2]	300[2]	335	309	343	424	480[2]	...	...
Zimbabwe Zimbabwe	954	1 066	1 105	1 000	549	*600[2]	*400[2]	*400[2]	...	...

Source:
United Nations Statistics Division, New York, the *Industrial Commodity Statistics Yearbook 2006* and the industrial statistics database, last accessed April 2009.

Source:
Organisation des Nations Unies, Division de statistique, New York, *l'Annuaire de statistiques industrielles par produit 2006* et la base de données sur les statistiques industrielles, dernier accès avril 2009.

1	Source: Organization of the Islamic Conference (Jeddah, Saudi Arabia).	1	Source: Organisation de la Conférence islamique (Djeddah, Arabie saoudite).
2	Source: U. S. Geological Survey (Washington, D. C.).	2	Source: "U. S. Geological Survey" (Washington, D. C.).
3	Source: "Country Economic Review", Asian Development Bank (Manila).	3	Source: "La Revue Economique du Pays", La Banque de Développement Asiatique (Manille).
4	Twelve months ending 30 June of the year stated.	4	Période de 12 mois finissant le 30 juin de l'année indiquée.
5	Source: United Nations Economic Commission for Latin America and the Caribbean (Santiago).	5	Source: Commission économique des Nations Unies pour l'Amérique Latine et des Caraïbes (Santiago).
6	Excluding the Federation of Bosnia and Herzegovina.	6	Non compris la Fédération de Bosnie et Herzégovine.
7	Shipments.	7	Expéditions.
8	For statistical purposes, the data for China do not include those for the Hong Kong Special Administrative Region (Hong Kong SAR), Macao Special Administrative Region (Macao SAR) and Taiwan Province of China.	8	Pour la présentation des statistiques, les données pour la Chine ne comprennent pas la Région Administrative Spéciale de Hong Kong (Hong Kong RAS), la Région Administrative Spéciale de Macao (Macao RAS) et la province de Taiwan.
9	Twelve months ending 7 July of the year stated.	9	Période de 12 mois finissant le 7 juillet de l'année indiquée.
10	Incomplete coverage.	10	Couverture incomplète.
11	Excluding Prodcom code 26.51.12.50.	11	Code Prodcom 26.51.12.50 non compris.
12	Source: Afristat: Sub-Saharan African Observatory of Economics and Statistics (Bamako, Mali).	12	Source : Afristat : Observatoire Economique et Statistique d'Afrique Subsaharienne (Bamako, Mali).
13	Government production only.	13	Production de l'état seulement.

42

Cement *(continued)*
Production: thousand metric tons
Ciment *(suite)*
Production: milliers de tonnes

14	Twelve months beginning 16 July of the year stated.
15	Source: Arab Gulf Cooperation Council (Riyadh).
16	Excluding the Transnistria region.
17	Source: "African Statistical Yearbook", Economic Commission for Africa (Addis Ababa).
18	Tanganyika only.
19	Excluding Puerto Rico.
20	Portland cement only.

14	Période de 12 mois commençant le 16 juillet de l'année indiquée.
15	Source: "Arab Gulf Cooperation Council (Riyad)".
16	Non compris la région de Transnistria.
17	Source : "Annuaire des Statistiques de l'Afrique", Conseil Economique pour l'Afrique (Addis-Abeba).
18	Tanganyika seulement.
19	Non compris Porto Rico.
20	Ciment Portland uniquement.

Pesticides
Production: metric tons

Pesticides
Production : tonnes

Country or area Pays ou zone	1997	1998	1999	2000	2001	2002	2003	2004	2005	2006
Austria Autriche	20 485	16 744	12 429	15 578	20 163	17 913	20 851	...	...	...
Bangladesh [1] Bangladesh [1]	6 354	7 701	9 086	9 063	8 880	8 577	3 773	...	...	...
Belgium [2] Belgique [2]	...	...	153 757	182 351	188 988	179 187	179 720			
Bulgaria Bulgarie	5 292	...	...	...	...	...	...	...	3 576	3 282
Chile Chili	...	...	...	...	...	...	...	...	7 758	10 921
China [3] Chine [3]	380 600	382 100	386 500	397 200	411 800	481 400	420 000	485 300	434 300	505 300
Croatia Croatie	10 167	8 676	7 039	7 070	8 120	7 370	5 861	6 034	3 442	3 167
Cuba Cuba	4 147	5 965	6 944	6 896	9 099	3 840	3 469	2 304	2 757	1 616
Czech Republic République tchèque	20 904	21 432	19 128	19 064	18 037	18 687	18 759	16 727	17 264	18 457
Denmark Danemark	16 693	17 228	18 765	20 537	21 860	21 064	21 560	23 094	24 024	23 218
Ecuador Equateur	3 360	537	575	1 881	...	...	6 342	...	...	...
Egypt Egypte	42 648	42 537	...	...	...	...	...	...	...	...
Estonia Estonie	...	...	...	...	...	...	...	...	82	...
Finland Finlande	...	2 039	1 835	1 842	...	...	...	...	...	...
Germany Allemagne	109 086[4]	110 481[4]	97 261[4]	84 137[4]	85 849[4]	87 667[4]	93 616[4]	94 840[4]	129 313	122 699
Greece Grèce	22 192	11 368	11 249	11 366	8 960	...	8 797[2]	...	...	...
Hungary Hongrie	21 712	18 105	14 526	14 688	15 087	11 848	14 559	11 425	9 318	5 825
India Inde	...	...	...	...	...	...	1 569	462	138	...
Indonesia Indonésie	...	10 700	22 109	...	...	...	...	...	...	...
Iran (Islamic Rep. of) Iran (Rép. islamique d')	18 976[5]	16 618[5]	28 634[5]	15 958[5]	26 340[5]	...	...	25 342	22 039	12 907
Ireland Irlande	17 708	5 362	6 614	3 198	4 771	1 459	7 664	10 356	...	...
Kazakhstan Kazakhstan	...	...	1 702	1 765	1 682	1 258	2 091	1 888	2 373	3 004
Kenya Kenya	885	1 180	1 188	679	370	530	1 331	2 234	1 616	1 628
Korea, Republic of Corée, République de	97 690	85 266	92 681	77 903	83 675	75 858	74 917	66 924	73 369	65 858
Latvia Lettonie	26	30	...	...	...	...	...	...	...	...
Lithuania Lituanie	348	354	295	372	613	0	469[4]	499[4]	461[4]	417[4]
Mexico Mexique	58 367	58 637	61 206	62 062	54 938	58 340	58 359	51 449	62 297	65 197

Pesticides *(continued)*
Production: metric tons
Pesticides *(suite)*
Production : tonnes

Country or area Pays ou zone	1997	1998	1999	2000	2001	2002	2003	2004	2005	2006
Mozambique Mozambique	...	...	...	...	...	...	...	62	54	...
Peru Pérou	1 628	1 975	1 405	1 185	1 191	1 139	1 192	1 216	1 446	...
Poland Pologne	27 881	29 930	30 219	#0	22 547	22 251	27 013	28 403	35 102	34 973
Portugal[4] Portugal[4]	19 963	20 167	21 586	15 583	18 206	20 694	20 849	20 727	21 376	19 932
Romania Roumanie	8 277	5 197	4 154	3 611	3 669	2 921[4]	2 901[4]	2 786[4]	...	...
Russian Federation Fédération de Russie	11 296	5 830	9 756	10 641	12 864	10 916	8 275	8 369	10 115	12 815
Serbia Serbie	...	...	...	...	...	...	...	...	5 805	6 157
Serbia and Montenegro Serbie-et-Monténégro	8 788	8 630	#5 643	6 937	6 406	6 396	...	...	...	...
Slovakia Slovaquie	2 637	3 371	2 795	3 384	3 402[4]	4 115[4]	3 624[4]	3 684[4]	3 154[4]	2 764
Slovenia Slovénie	1 362	1 508	1 166	1 358	1 575	1 617	1 441	...	...	...
South Africa Afrique du Sud	35 024[6]	...	...	...	67 062	39 545	...	...	...	...
Spain Espagne	89 448	92 770	98 925	104 510	118 363	...	...	163 817	...	137 731
Sweden Suède	3 429	2 262	2 004	2 021	2 126	5 822	4 958	3 828	3 680	5 472
TFYR of Macedonia L'ex-R.Y. Macédoine	119	172	127	177	39	46	55	59	75	170
Turkey Turquie	24 153	25 580	26 039	29 682	25 674	30 417	24 010	34 282	19 300	...
Ukraine Ukraine	2 736	1 852	1 840	1 070	2 669	1 894	1 825	1 541	1 862	1 960
United Kingdom Royaume-Uni	330 490	259 097	49 224	41 098	...	40 253	40 185	...	...	...
United Rep. of Tanzania[7] Rép.-Unie de Tanzanie[7]	258	40	30	16	24	65	31	688	523	880
Uzbekistan Ouzbékistan	1 184	...	...	...	...	...	...	...	...	...
Viet Nam Viet Nam	19 078[1]	20 223[1]	*18 849[1]	25 291	28 354	38 325	48 101	64 561	66 997	64 314

Source:
United Nations Statistics Division, New York, the *Industrial Commodity Statistics Yearbook 2006* and the industrial statistics database, last accessed April 2009.

1   Insecticides only.
2   Incomplete coverage.
3   For statistical purposes, the data for China do not include those for the Hong Kong Special Administrative Region (Hong Kong SAR), Macao Special Administrative Region (Macao SAR) and Taiwan Province of China.
4   On the basis of 100 per cent active substances.
5   Production by establishments employing 10 or more persons.
6   Excluding products usually measured in units of volume.
7   Tanganyika only.

Source:
Organisation des Nations Unies, Division de statistique, New York, l'*Annuaire de statistiques industrielles par produit 2006*, et la base de données sur les statistiques industrielles, dernier accès avril 2009.

1   Insecticides seulement.
2   Couverture incomplète.
3   Pour la présentation des statistiques, les données pour la Chine ne comprennent pas la Région Administrative Spéciale de Hong Kong (Hong Kong RAS), la Région Administrative Spéciale de Macao (Macao RAS) et la province de Taiwan.
4   Sur la base de 100 pour cent de substances actives.
5   Production des établissements employant 10 personnes ou plus.
6   Non compris les produits habituellement mesurés en unités de volume.
7   Tanganyika seulement.

Pig iron and crude steel
Production: thousand metric tons

Fonte et acier brut
Production : milliers de tonnes

Country or area	1999	2000	2001	2002	2003	2004	2005	2006	Pays ou zone
Albania									**Albanie**
Crude steel and semi-finished prod.	16[1]	5[1]	80[1]	140[1]	140[1]	143[1]	145[1]	123	Acier brut et demi-produits
Algeria									**Algérie**
Pig iron and spiegeleisen [1,2]	807	762	895	959	1 026	977	952	1 093	Fontes brutes et fontes spiegel [1,2]
Crude steel and semi-finished prod.	675	689	861	991	964	978	1 007[1]	1 158[1]	Acier brut et demi-produits
Angola [1]									**Angola** [1]
Crude steel and semi-finished prod.	9	9	...	...	...	...	...	...	Acier brut et demi-produits
Argentina									**Argentine**
Pig iron and spiegeleisen	2 973	3 602	3 193	3 650	4 140	4 148	4 467	4 428	Fontes brutes et fontes spiegel
Crude steel and semi-finished prod.	3 799	4 472	4 107	4 354	5 033	5 133	5 386	5 533	Acier brut et demi-produits
Australia [1]									**Australie** [1]
Pig iron and spiegeleisen [2]	7 047	7 049	6 017	6 106	6 116	5 735	6 203	6 433	Fontes brutes et fontes spiegel [2]
Crude steel and semi-finished prod.	8 172	7 129	7 033	7 527	7 544	7 414	7 757	7 881	Acier brut et demi-produits
Austria [1]									**Autriche** [1]
Pig iron and spiegeleisen [2]	3 913	4 318	4 375	4 669	4 677	4 847	5 444	5 547	Fontes brutes et fontes spiegel [2]
Crude steel and semi-finished prod.	5 202	5 707	5 869	6 189	6 261	6 530	7 031	7 129	Acier brut et demi-produits
Azerbaijan									**Azerbaïdjan**
Pig iron and spiegeleisen	...	0	1	1	1	1	2	1	Fontes brutes et fontes spiegel
Crude steel and semi-finished prod.	...	...	5	33	55	88	284	55	Acier brut et demi-produits
Belarus									**Bélarus**
Crude steel and semi-finished prod.	1 449	1 623	1 611	1 607	1 694	1 920[1]	2 076	2 297	Acier brut et demi-produits
Belgium [1]									**Belgique** [1]
Pig iron and spiegeleisen [2]	8 430	8 471	7 732	7 988	7 813	8 224	7 254	7 516	Fontes brutes et fontes spiegel [2]
Crude steel and semi-finished prod.	10 931	11 636	10 762	11 343	11 114	11 698	10 422	11 631	Acier brut et demi-produits
Bosnia and Herzegovina [1]									**Bosnie-Herzégovine** [1]
Crude steel and semi-finished prod.	60	77	84	74	75	75	269	490	Acier brut et demi-produits
Brazil									**Brésil**
Pig iron and spiegeleisen	24 549[1,2]	27 723[1,2]	27 391[1,2]	29 644[1,2]	32 038[1,2]	8 455[2]	10 326	10 110	Fontes brutes et fontes spiegel
Crude steel and semi-finished prod.	24 996[1]	27 865[1]	26 717[1]	29 604[1]	31 147[1]	18 814	18 620	19 039	Acier brut et demi-produits
Bulgaria									**Bulgarie**
Pig iron and spiegeleisen	1 152[1,2]	0	0	0	0	1 158[1,2]	...	...	Fontes brutes et fontes spiegel
Crude steel and semi-finished prod.	1 889[1]	98	300	0	0	282	104	160	Acier brut et demi-produits
Canada [1]									**Canada** [1]
Pig iron and spiegeleisen [2]	8 857	8 904	8 302	8 670	8 554	8 828	8 274	8 305	Fontes brutes et fontes spiegel [2]
Crude steel and semi-finished prod.	16 235	16 595	15 276	16 002	15 929	16 305	15 327	15 493	Acier brut et demi-produits
Chile [1]									**Chili** [1]
Pig iron and spiegeleisen [2]	1 030	1 024	897	964	988	1 137	1 074	1 115	Fontes brutes et fontes spiegel [2]
Crude steel and semi-finished prod.	1 290	1 352	1 247	1 279	1 377	1 579	1 537	1 627	Acier brut et demi-produits
China [1,3]									**Chine** [1,3]
Pig iron and spiegeleisen [2]	125 330	131 034	147 067	170 745	213 785	256 738	344 732	413 635	Fontes brutes et fontes spiegel [2]
Crude steel and semi-finished prod.	123 954	127 236	150 906	182 249	222 413	280 486	355 790	422 660	Acier brut et demi-produits
Colombia [1]									**Colombie** [1]
Pig iron and spiegeleisen [2]	264	285	319	311	283	312	325	360	Fontes brutes et fontes spiegel [2]
Crude steel and semi-finished prod.	534	660	638	664	668	730	842	1 220	Acier brut et demi-produits
Croatia									**Croatie**
Crude steel and semi-finished prod.	74[1]	71[1]	58[1]	34[1]	41[1]	86[1]	73[1]	93	Acier brut et demi-produits
Cuba									**Cuba**
Pig iron and spiegeleisen	303	327	270	264	210	193	245	257	Fontes brutes et fontes spiegel
Crude steel and semi-finished prod.	278	304	250	247	193	178	245[1]	237	Acier brut et demi-produits
Czech Republic									**République tchèque**
Pig iron and spiegeleisen [1,2]	4 023	4 621	4 671	4 840	5 207	5 384	...	...	Fontes brutes et fontes spiegel [1,2]
Crude steel and semi-finished prod.	5 616[1]	6 216[1]	6 316[1]	6 512[1]	6 783[1]	7 033[1]	5 363	5 955	Acier brut et demi-produits
Dem. Rep. of the Congo [1]									**Rép. dém. du Congo** [1]
Crude steel and semi-finished prod.	30	30	30	30	30	30	30	30	Acier brut et demi-produits
Denmark									**Danemark**
Crude steel and semi-finished prod.	729[1]	801[1]	751[1]	392[1]	...	...	43	0	Acier brut et demi-produits
Dominican Republic [1]									**Rép. dominicaine** [1]
Crude steel and semi-finished prod.	43	39	...	...	...	...	...	...	Acier brut et demi-produits
Ecuador [1]									**Equateur** [1]
Crude steel and semi-finished prod.	53	58	60	69	80	72	84	85	Acier brut et demi-produits

Pig iron and crude steel *(continued)*
Production: thousand metric tons
Fonte et acier brut *(suite)*
Production : milliers de tonnes

Country or area	1999	2000	2001	2002	2003	2004	2005	2006	Pays ou zone
Egypt									**Egypte**
Pig iron and spiegeleisen [1,2]	1 020	990	1 160	1 100	1 080	1 000	1 100	1 100	Fontes brutes et fontes spiegel [1,2]
Crude steel and semi-finished prod.	0	0	0	4 316[1]	4 398[1]	4 810[1]	5 603[1]	6 054[1]	Acier brut et demi-produits
El Salvador [1]									**El Salvador** [1]
Crude steel and semi-finished prod.	34	41	39	49	57	59	48	72	Acier brut et demi-produits
Estonia [1]									**Estonie** [1]
Crude steel and semi-finished prod.	1	1	1	1	1	1	1	...	Acier brut et demi-produits
Finland									**Finlande**
Pig iron and spiegeleisen	2 954[1,2]	2 983[1,2]	2 852[1,2]	2 828[1,2]	3 092[1,2]	3 037[1,2]	4 000	3 158[1,2]	Fontes brutes et fontes spiegel
Crude steel and semi-finished prod.	3 956[1]	4 096[1]	3 938[1]	4 003[1]	4 766[1]	4 832[1]	4 738[1]	274	Acier brut et demi-produits
France [1]									**France** [1]
Pig iron and spiegeleisen [2]	13 852	13 916	12 298	13 510	12 972	13 198	12 705	13 013	Fontes brutes et fontes spiegel [2]
Crude steel and semi-finished prod.	20 200	20 954	19 343	20 258	19 758	20 770	19 481	19 852	Acier brut et demi-produits
Georgia [1]									**Géorgie** [1]
Crude steel and semi-finished prod.	7	...	...	...	...	...	...	...	Acier brut et demi-produits
Germany									**Allemagne**
Pig iron and spiegeleisen	27 934[1,2]	1 304	1 393	1 661	1 694	1 595	1 523	1 702	Fontes brutes et fontes spiegel
Crude steel and semi-finished prod.	42 062[1]	20 261	21 534	12 404	12 631	12 469	11 655	11 828	Acier brut et demi-produits
Ghana [1]									**Ghana** [1]
Crude steel and semi-finished prod.	26	26	26	26	25	25	25	25	Acier brut et demi-produits
Greece [1]									**Grèce** [1]
Crude steel and semi-finished prod.	951	1 088	1 281	1 835	1 701	1 967	2 266	2 416	Acier brut et demi-produits
Guatemala [1]									**Guatemala** [1]
Crude steel and semi-finished prod.	...	167	202	216	226	232	207	292	Acier brut et demi-produits
Hungary									**Hongrie**
Pig iron and spiegeleisen	1 310[1,2]	1 340[1,2]	1 226[1,2]	1 335[1,2]	1 333[1,2]	1	...	...	Fontes brutes et fontes spiegel
Crude steel and semi-finished prod.	1 813[1]	1 871[1]	1 956[1]	2 053[1]	1 989[1]	118	164	138	Acier brut et demi-produits
India [1]									**Inde** [1]
Pig iron and spiegeleisen [2]	20 139	21 321	21 875	24 315	26 550	25 117	27 125	28 256	Fontes brutes et fontes spiegel [2]
Crude steel and semi-finished prod.	24 296	26 924	27 291	28 814	31 779	32 626	45 780	49 450	Acier brut et demi-produits
Indonesia [1]									**Indonésie** [1]
Crude steel and semi-finished prod.	2 891	2 848	2 781	2 462	2 042	3 682	3 675	3 759	Acier brut et demi-produits
Iran (Islamic Rep. of)									**Iran (Rép. islamique d')**
Pig iron and spiegeleisen	2 112[1,2]	2 202[1,2]	2 100[1,2]	2 102[1,2]	2 201[1,2]	2 000[1,2]	2 005[1,2]	222	Fontes brutes et fontes spiegel
Crude steel and semi-finished prod.	6 070[1]	6 600[1]	6 916[1]	7 321[1]	7 869[1]	8 682[1]	9 404[1]	28 449	Acier brut et demi-produits
Ireland [1]									**Irlande** [1]
Crude steel and semi-finished prod.	335	360	150	...	...	...	...	...	Acier brut et demi-produits
Israel [1]									**Israël** [1]
Crude steel and semi-finished prod.	280	280	280	280	280	280	300	300	Acier brut et demi-produits
Italy [1]									**Italie** [1]
Pig iron and spiegeleisen [2]	10 621	11 220	11 220	9 775	10 148	10 604	11 423	11 497	Fontes brutes et fontes spiegel [2]
Crude steel and semi-finished prod.	24 878	26 759	26 545	26 066	27 058	28 604	29 350	31 624	Acier brut et demi-produits
Japan									**Japon**
Pig iron and spiegeleisen	6 928	5 244	5 325	5 153	4 904	4 759	4 457	84 270[1,2]	Fontes brutes et fontes spiegel
Crude steel and semi-finished prod.	10 800	11 884	11 350	11 965	12 476	14 340	13 452	14 044	Acier brut et demi-produits
Jordan [1]									**Jordanie** [1]
Crude steel and semi-finished prod.	30	30	30	134	135	140	150	150	Acier brut et demi-produits
Kazakhstan									**Kazakhstan**
Pig iron and spiegeleisen	3 438	4 010	3 906	4 009	4 138	4 283	3 582	3 369	Fontes brutes et fontes spiegel
Crude steel and semi-finished prod.	4 105	4 799	4 691	9 081	9 360	9 903	7 196	5 007	Acier brut et demi-produits
Kenya [1]									**Kenya** [1]
Crude steel and semi-finished prod.	20	20	20	20	20	20	20	20	Acier brut et demi-produits
Korea, Dem. P. R. [1]									**Corée, R. p. dém. de** [1]
Pig iron and spiegeleisen [2]	250	250	250	250	250	250	250	250	Fontes brutes et fontes spiegel [2]
Crude steel and semi-finished prod.	300	300	300	300	300	300	300	300	Acier brut et demi-produits
Korea, Republic of									**Corée, République de**
Pig iron and spiegeleisen [1,2]	23 329	24 937	25 898	26 570	27 314	27 556	27 309	27 559	Fontes brutes et fontes spiegel [1,2]
Crude steel and semi-finished prod.	41 502	43 423	44 199	45 482	46 561	46 466	46 123	48 259	Acier brut et demi-produits
Latvia [1]									**Lettonie** [1]
Crude steel and semi-finished prod.	482	498	515	520	520	520	550	550	Acier brut et demi-produits
Lesotho									**Lesotho**
Crude steel and semi-finished prod.	...	12 025	11 980	22 790	19 942	27 928	22 635	53 038	Acier brut et demi-produits

44

Pig iron and crude steel *(continued)*
Production: thousand metric tons
Fonte et acier brut *(suite)*
Production : milliers de tonnes

Country or area	1999	2000	2001	2002	2003	2004	2005	2006	Pays ou zone
Libyan Arab Jamah. [1]									**Jamah. arabe libyenne** [1]
Crude steel and semi-finished prod.	966	1 055	846	886	1 007	1 026	1 255	1 151	Acier brut et demi-produits
Luxembourg [1]									**Luxembourg** [1]
Crude steel and semi-finished prod.	2 600	2 571	2 725	2 719	2 675	2 684	2 194	2 802	Acier brut et demi-produits
Malaysia [1]									**Malaisie** [1]
Crude steel and semi-finished prod.	2 770	3 650	4 100	4 722	3 960	5 698	5 296	5 834	Acier brut et demi-produits
Mauritania [1]									**Mauritanie** [1]
Crude steel and semi-finished prod.	5	5	5	5	5	5	5	5	Acier brut et demi-produits
Mexico									**Mexique**
Pig iron and spiegeleisen [1,2]	4 822	4 856	4 373	3 996	4 183	4 278	4 047	3 790	Fontes brutes et fontes spiegel [1,2]
Crude steel and semi-finished prod.	13 517	13 881	12 706	12 831	14 080	15 238	14 619	14 738	Acier brut et demi-produits
Mongolia [1]									**Mongolie** [1]
Crude steel and semi-finished prod.	...	35	35	35	35	35	35	35	Acier brut et demi-produits
Montenegro									**Monténégro**
Crude steel and semi-finished prod.	...	...	...	17	6	30	28	20	Acier brut et demi-produits
Morocco [1]									**Maroc** [1]
Pig iron and spiegeleisen [2]	15	15	15	15	15	15	15	15	Fontes brutes et fontes spiegel [2]
Crude steel and semi-finished prod.	5	5	5	5	5	5	205	314	Acier brut et demi-produits
Myanmar [1]									**Myanmar** [1]
Crude steel and semi-finished prod.	25	25	25	25	25	25	25	25	Acier brut et demi-produits
Netherlands [1]									**Pays-Bas** [1]
Pig iron and spiegeleisen [2]	5 307	4 970	5 305	5 367	5 846	6 011	6 031	5 417	Fontes brutes et fontes spiegel [2]
Crude steel and semi-finished prod.	6 075	5 666	6 037	6 117	6 571	6 848	6 919	6 372	Acier brut et demi-produits
New Zealand [1]									**Nouvelle-Zélande** [1]
Pig iron and spiegeleisen [2]	620	603	646	617	700	719	652	664	Fontes brutes et fontes spiegel [2]
Crude steel and semi-finished prod.	775	702	826	765	853	885	889	810	Acier brut et demi-produits
Nigeria [1]									**Nigéria** [1]
Crude steel and semi-finished prod.	...	...	...	...	...	40	100	100	Acier brut et demi-produits
Norway									**Norvège**
Pig iron and spiegeleisen	70 [1,2]	70 [1,2]	70 [1,2]	0	0	0	100 [1,2]	100 [1,2]	Fontes brutes et fontes spiegel
Crude steel and semi-finished prod.	610 [1]	679 [1]	640 [1]	0	0	0	705 [1]	684 [1]	Acier brut et demi-produits
Pakistan									**Pakistan**
Pig iron and spiegeleisen [2]	1 000 [1]	1 000 [1]	1 067 [1]	1 000 [1]	1 000 [1]	1 180 [4]	1 137 [4]	768 [4]	Fontes brutes et fontes spiegel [2]
Crude steel and semi-finished prod. [1]	900	950	953	970	1 000	1 145	825	1 040	Acier brut et demi-produits [1]
Paraguay [1]									**Paraguay** [1]
Pig iron and spiegeleisen [2]	61	82	72	87	98	119	123	128	Fontes brutes et fontes spiegel [2]
Crude steel and semi-finished prod.	56	77	71	80	91	107	101	115	Acier brut et demi-produits
Peru [1]									**Pérou** [1]
Pig iron and spiegeleisen [2]	197	327	316	240	226	272	263	306	Fontes brutes et fontes spiegel [2]
Crude steel and semi-finished prod.	559	751	690	611	669	726	790	896	Acier brut et demi-produits
Philippines [1]									**Philippines** [1]
Crude steel and semi-finished prod.	530	426	500	550	500	400	470	558	Acier brut et demi-produits
Poland [1]									**Pologne** [1]
Pig iron and spiegeleisen [2]	5 233	6 492	5 440	5 294	5 632	6 400	4 477	5 333	Fontes brutes et fontes spiegel [2]
Crude steel and semi-finished prod.	8 848	10 498	8 809	8 368	9 107	10 593	8 336	10 008	Acier brut et demi-produits
Portugal									**Portugal**
Pig iron and spiegeleisen	389 [1,2]	379 [1,2]	82 [1,2]	0	0	0	0	0	Fontes brutes et fontes spiegel
Crude steel and semi-finished prod.	1 044 [1]	1 088 [1]	728 [1]	920	1 000	...	...	1 400 [1]	Acier brut et demi-produits
Qatar [1]									**Qatar** [1]
Crude steel and semi-finished prod.	629	729	891	1 027	1 055	1 089	1 057	1 003	Acier brut et demi-produits
Republic of Moldova [5]									**République de Moldova** [5]
Crude steel and semi-finished prod.	796 [1]	908 [1]	967 [1]	514 [1]	850 [1]	1 012	0	785 [1]	Acier brut et demi-produits
Romania [1]									**Roumanie** [1]
Pig iron and spiegeleisen [2]	3 006	2 985	3 085	3 976	4 101	4 244	4 098	3 975	Fontes brutes et fontes spiegel [2]
Crude steel and semi-finished prod.	4 354	4 672	4 935	5 491	5 691	6 042	6 280	6 263	Acier brut et demi-produits
Russian Federation									**Fédération de Russie**
Pig iron and spiegeleisen	40 856	44 584	45 016	46 691	48 812	50 427	49 175	52 362	Fontes brutes et fontes spiegel
Crude steel and semi-finished prod.	51 518	59 150	59 030	59 883	62 839	65 646	66 262	70 816	Acier brut et demi-produits
Saudi Arabia [1]									**Arabie saoudite** [1]
Crude steel and semi-finished prod.	2 610	2 981	3 413	3 570	3 944	3 902	4 186	3 974	Acier brut et demi-produits

Pig iron and crude steel *(continued)*
Production: thousand metric tons
Fonte et acier brut *(suite)*
Production : milliers de tonnes

Country or area	1999	2000	2001	2002	2003	2004	2005	2006	Pays ou zone
Serbia									**Serbie**
Pig iron and spiegeleisen	...	...	...	...	...	...	1 115	1 529	Fontes brutes et fontes spiegel
Crude steel and semi-finished prod.	...	...	...	...	...	...	...	1	Acier brut et demi-produits
Serbia and Montenegro [1]									**Serbie-et-Monténégro** [1]
Pig iron and spiegeleisen [2]	139	598	456	485	635	1 003	1 208	1 762	Fontes brutes et fontes spiegel [2]
Crude steel and semi-finished prod.	230	696	595	591	711	1 175	1 292	1 823	Acier brut et demi-produits
Singapore [1]									**Singapour** [1]
Crude steel and semi-finished prod.	590	603	456	460	561	610	572	607	Acier brut et demi-produits
Slovakia									**Slovaquie**
Pig iron and spiegeleisen [1,2]	2 987	3 166	3 255	3 533	3 892	3 765	3 681	4 145	Fontes brutes et fontes spiegel [1,2]
Crude steel and semi-finished prod.	3 569	3 733	181	119	95	515	280	663	Acier brut et demi-produits
Slovenia									**Slovénie**
Crude steel and semi-finished prod.	5	6	...	481[1]	...	...	583[1]	...	Acier brut et demi-produits
South Africa [1]									**Afrique du Sud** [1]
Pig iron and spiegeleisen [2]	6 005	6 292	5 820	5 823	6 234	6 011	6 130	6 159	Fontes brutes et fontes spiegel [2]
Crude steel and semi-finished prod.	7 857	8 481	8 821	9 095	9 481	9 500	9 494	9 718	Acier brut et demi-produits
Spain									**Espagne**
Pig iron and spiegeleisen	4 058[1,2]	4 059[1,2]	4 219[1,2]	4 021[1,2]	3 645[1,2]	4 036[1,2]	4 160[1,2]	0	Fontes brutes et fontes spiegel
Crude steel and semi-finished prod.	14 882[1]	15 874[1]	16 504[1]	16 408[1]	16 286[1]	17 621[1]	502	600	Acier brut et demi-produits
Sri Lanka [1]									**Sri Lanka** [1]
Crude steel and semi-finished prod.	30	30	30	30	30	30	30	30	Acier brut et demi-produits
Sweden									**Suède**
Pig iron and spiegeleisen	3 212[1,2]	3 145[1,2]	3 614[1,2]	3 703[1,2]	3 710[1,2]	3 871[1,2]	0	0	Fontes brutes et fontes spiegel
Crude steel and semi-finished prod.	5 066[1]	5 227[1]	5 518[1]	5 754[1]	5 707[1]	5 978[1]	3 154	3 192	Acier brut et demi-produits
Switzerland [1]									**Suisse** [1]
Pig iron and spiegeleisen [2]	80	80	80	80	80	80	80	80	Fontes brutes et fontes spiegel [2]
Crude steel and semi-finished prod.	800	1 000	1 000	1 000	1 000	1 000	1 158	1 252	Acier brut et demi-produits
Syrian Arab Republic [1]									**Rép. arabe syrienne** [1]
Crude steel and semi-finished prod.	70	70	70	70	70	70	70	70	Acier brut et demi-produits
Thailand [1]									**Thaïlande** [1]
Crude steel and semi-finished prod.	1 532	2 100	2 127	2 538	3 551	4 533	5 161	5 210	Acier brut et demi-produits
TFYR of Macedonia									**L'ex-R.Y. Macédoine**
Crude steel and semi-finished prod.	45[1]	161[1]	260[1]	260[1]	291[1]	309[1]	313	354	Acier brut et demi-produits
Trinidad and Tobago									**Trinité-et-Tobago**
Crude steel and semi-finished prod.	729[1]	741[1]	668[1]	817	896	790	712	673	Acier brut et demi-produits
Tunisia [1]									**Tunisie** [1]
Pig iron and spiegeleisen [2]	180	195	191	152	45	...	...	...	Fontes brutes et fontes spiegel [2]
Crude steel and semi-finished prod.	231	229	239	200	86	66	115	160	Acier brut et demi-produits
Turkey									**Turquie**
Pig iron and spiegeleisen [1,2]	5 181	5 333	5 289	5 003	5 706	5 836	5 970	5 952	Fontes brutes et fontes spiegel [1,2]
Crude steel and semi-finished prod.	14 313[1]	14 325[1]	14 981[1]	16 467[1]	18 298[1]	20 478[1]	20 965[1]	23 308	Acier brut et demi-produits
Uganda [1]									**Ouganda** [1]
Crude steel and semi-finished prod.	30	30	30	30	30	30	30	30	Acier brut et demi-produits
Ukraine									**Ukraine**
Pig iron and spiegeleisen	23 010	25 699	26 379	27 633	29 459	30 978	30 746	32 929	Fontes brutes et fontes spiegel
Crude steel and semi-finished prod.	27 453[1]	31 767[1]	33 108[1]	34 050[1]	46 911	47 429	46 615	50 181	Acier brut et demi-produits
United Arab Emirates [1]									**Emirats arabes unis** [1]
Crude steel and semi-finished prod.	90	90	90	90	90	90	90	90	Acier brut et demi-produits
United Kingdom [1]									**Royaume-Uni** [1]
Pig iron and spiegeleisen [2]	12 139	10 890	9 870	8 561	10 228	10 180	10 189	10 696	Fontes brutes et fontes spiegel [2]
Crude steel and semi-finished prod.	16 298	15 155	13 543	11 667	13 268	13 766	13 239	13 871	Acier brut et demi-produits
United States									**Etats-Unis**
Pig iron and spiegeleisen [2]	46 300	47 900	42 100	40 200	40 600	42 300	37 200	37 900	Fontes brutes et fontes spiegel [2]
Crude steel and semi-finished prod.	97 400	102 000	90 100	91 600	93 700	99 700	94 900	98 200	Acier brut et demi-produits
Uruguay [1]									**Uruguay** [1]
Crude steel and semi-finished prod.	45	38	31	34	40	58	64	57	Acier brut et demi-produits
Uzbekistan [1]									**Ouzbékistan** [1]
Crude steel and semi-finished prod.	344	407	433	450	499	602	595	730	Acier brut et demi-produits
Venezuela (Bolivarian Rep. of) [1]									**Venezuela (Rép. bolivarienne du)** [1]
Crude steel and semi-finished prod.	3 261	3 835	3 813	4 164	3 930	4 561	4 910	4 864	Acier brut et demi-produits

Country or area	1999	2000	2001	2002	2003	2004	2005	2006	Pays ou zone
Viet Nam									**Viet Nam**
Pig iron and spiegeleisen	66[1,2]	41	31	172	380	294	91	80	Fontes brutes et fontes spiegel
Crude steel and semi-finished prod.	308[1]	36	231	412	591	670	474	827	Acier brut et demi-produits
Zimbabwe [1]									**Zimbabwe** [1]
Pig iron and spiegeleisen [2]	270	277	156	122	182	125	129	38	Fontes brutes et fontes spiegel [2]
Crude steel and semi-finished prod.	255	258	149	105	152	135	107	24	Acier brut et demi-produits

Source:
United Nations Statistics Division, New York, the *Industrial Commodity Statistics Yearbook 2006* and the industrial statistics database, last accessed April 2009.

Source:
Organisation des Nations Unies, Division de statistique, New York, l'*Annuaire de statistiques industrielles par produit 2006* et la base de données sur les statistiques industrielles, dernier accès avril 2009.

1   Source: International Iron and Steel Institute (Brussels).
2   Excluding spiegeleisen.
3   For statistical purposes, the data for China do not include those for the Hong Kong Special Administrative Region (Hong Kong SAR), Macao Special Administrative Region (Macao SAR) and Taiwan Province of China.
4   Twelve months ending 30 June of the year stated.
5   Excluding the Transnistria region.

1   Source: Institut international de sidérurgie (Bruxelles).
2   Non compris la fonte spiegel.
3   Pour la présentation des statistiques, les données pour la Chine ne comprennent pas la Région Administrative Spéciale de Hong Kong (Hong Kong RAS), la Région Administrative Spéciale de Macao (Macao RAS) et la province de Taiwan.
4   Période de 12 mois finissant le 30 juin de l'année indiquée.
5   Non compris la région de Transnistria.

Country or area Pays ou zone	1997	1998	1999	2000	2001	2002	2003	2004	2005	2006
Argentina Argentine	187	187	206	261	248	269	272	272	271	273
Australia[1] Australie[1]	1 395	1 589	1 686	...	...	...	...	...	...	...
Austria Autriche	119[2]	126	143[2]	158[2]	158[2]	...	...	...	...	...
Azerbaijan Azerbaïdjan	...	...	...	...	...	...	19[3]	30[3]	0	0
Bahrain Bahreïn	490[3]	501[3]	502	512	523[3]	519[3]	532[3]	530[3]	...	...
Bosnia and Herzegovina Bosnie-Herzégovine	...	32	57	95[3]	96[3]	103[3]	113	115[3]	...	...
Brazil Brésil	1 369[2]	1 388[2]	1 440[3]	1 035	951	1 449	1 195	1 275	1 307	1 267
Bulgaria Bulgarie	...	...	...	1	...	...	0	0	0	0
Cameroon Cameroun	98	89	94	100	85	72	79	86	86	...
Canada Canada	2 433[2]	2 485[2]	2 502	2 373[3]	2 583[3]	2 709[3]	808	2 592[3]	...	...
China[4] Chine[4]	2 180	2 362	2 809	2 989	3 576	4 511	5 866	6 690	7 787	9 266
Croatia Croatie	18	16	14	14	15	15	...	...	...	...
Czech Republic République tchèque	45[3]	45[3]	40[3]	40[3]	...	...	...	...	0	0
Denmark Danemark	0	0	0	0	0	0	0	0	3	1
Egypt Egypte	119[5]	187[5]	193[3]	189[3]	191[3]	195[3]	195[3]	215[3]	...	...
Finland Finlande	2	2	...	...	...	...	...	...	0	0
France * France *	635	663	694	701	713	713	685	...	...	...
Germany Allemagne	349	375	395	404	404	410	438	...	329	225
Ghana Ghana	152	56	114	156	162	133	...	...	...	...
Greece Grèce	132	161	161	168[3]	166[3]	165[3]	166[6]	165[3]	...	...
Hungary Hongrie	98	92	89	89[3]	110[3]	...	...	2	...	...
Iceland Islande	123	160	161	167	169	194	286	192	180	...
India Inde	539	542[3]	614[3]	644[3]	624[3]	671[3]	...	124	209	...
Indonesia Indonésie	219[2]	133[2]	112[2,7]	160[3]	180[3]	*160[3]	200[3]	230[3]	...	...
Iran (Islamic Rep. of) Iran (Rép. islamique d')	125[2]	137[2]	164[2]	146[3]	160[3]	169[3]	170[0]	170[3]	336	218
Italy Italie	631	690	689	757	766	782	#74	76	...	...
Japan[8] Japon[8]	1 330	...	...	...	...	...	...	...	...	...

Country or area Pays ou zone	1997	1998	1999	2000	2001	2002	2003	2004	2005	2006
Korea, Republic of Corée, République de	...	...	...	312	325	357	356	454	463	...
Kuwait Koweït	6	4	7	7	7	6	6	6	7	10
Mozambique Mozambique	...	...	...	54^3	266^3	273^3	409	548	539	...
Netherlands Pays-Bas	382	366	391	405	294^3	284^3	278^3	326^3	...	...
New Zealand Nouvelle-Zélande	318^2	389^2	348^3	328^3	322^3	335^3	340^3	350^3	...	...
Norway Norvège	977^2	$1\ 058^2$	$1\ 199^3$	$1\ 280^3$	$1\ 291^3$	...	...	...	...	...
Poland Pologne	54	54	51	#12	12	14	15	14	11	18
Romania [8,9] Roumanie [8,9]	164	175	174	181	183	190	205	...	...	...
Russian Federation [3] Fédération de Russie [3]	2 906	3 005	3 146	3 245	3 300	3 347	3 478	3 593	...	...
Serbia Serbie	...	...	...	...	...	...	...	...	^0	1
Serbia and Montenegro Serbie-et-Monténégro	67	61	#73	88	100	112	117	115^3	...	...
Slovakia Slovaquie	110^2	121	109	110	...	...	...	...	...	...
South Africa [3] Afrique du Sud [3]	673	677	689	673	662	707	738	863	...	...
Spain Espagne	533^2	570^2	588^2	366^3	376^3	380^3	389^3	...	...	...
Suriname Suriname	29	28	7	...	...	2	...	...	...	...
Sweden Suède	34	31	36	35	35	29	28	0	0	^0
Switzerland Suisse	35^2	47^2	41^2	36^3	36^3	40^3	44^3	45^3	...	...
Tajikistan Tadjikistan	189	196	229	269^3	289^3	306^3	319^3	358^3	...	...
TFYR of Macedonia L'ex-R.Y. Macédoine	5	7	6	4	3	5	5	...	...	...
Turkey Turquie	62	62	62	62	62	63	63	60^3	27	...
Ukraine [3] Ukraine [3]	101	178	226	104	106	112	...	...	...	...
United Arab Emirates [3] Emirats arabes unis [3]	...	...	...	^0	1	1	1	1	...	...
United Kingdom Royaume-Uni	114	494^3	547^3	305^3	341^3	344^3	343^3	360^3	...	...
United States Etats-Unis	3 603	3 713	3 779	3 668	2 637	2 707	2 703	2 516	2 481	2 284
Venezuela (Bolivarian Rep. of) Venezuela (Rép. bolivarienne du)	668^2	617^2	595^2	571^3	571^3	605^3	601^3	624^3	...	...

Source:
United Nations Statistics Division, New York, the *Industrial Commodity Statistics Yearbook 2006* and the industrial statistics database, last accessed April 2009.

Source:
Organisation des Nations Unies, Division de statistique, *l'Annuaire de statistiques industrielles par produit 2006* et la base de données sur les statistiques industrielles, dernier accès avril 2009.

1	Twelve months ending 30 June of the year stated.
2	Source: *World Metal Statistics* (London).
3	Source: *U. S. Geological Survey* (Washington, D. C.).
4	For statistical purposes, the data for China do not include those for the Hong Kong Special Administrative Region (Hong Kong SAR), Macao Special Administrative Region (Macao SAR) and Taiwan Province of China.
5	Including aluminium plates, shapes and bars.
6	Incomplete coverage.
7	Primary metal production only.
8	Including alloys.
9	Including pure content of virgin alloys.

1	Période de 12 mois finissant le 30 juin de l'année indiquée.
2	Source: *World Metal Statistics* (Londres).
3	Source: *U. S. Geological Survey* (Washington, D. C.).
4	Pour la présentation des statistiques, les données pour la Chine ne comprennent pas la Région Administrative Spéciale de Hong Kong (Hong Kong RAS), la Région Administrative Spéciale de Macao (Macao RAS) et la province de Taiwan.
5	Y compris les tôles, les profilés et les barres d'aluminium.
6	Couverture incomplète.
7	Production du métal de première fusion seulement.
8	Y compris les alliages.
9	Y compris la teneur pure des alliages de première fusion.

46

Radio and television receivers
Production: thousands

Récepteurs de radio et de télévision
Production : milliers

Country or area Pays ou zone	Radio receivers Récepteurs de radio					Television receivers Récepteurs de télévision				
	2003	2004	2005	2006	2007	2003	2004	2005	2006	2007
Algeria Algérie	...	...	...	...	...	292	206	...	...	...
Argentina Argentine	203	340	301	517	...	332	941	1 627	2 042	2 219
Azerbaijan Azerbaïdjan	...	...	...	...	...	...	...	7	5	0
Bangladesh [1] Bangladesh [1]	13	15	20	24	...	131	141	172	192	...
Belarus Bélarus	31	22	13	8	5	690	1 262	1 308	1 067	702
Brazil Brésil	3 905	6 335	5 813	5 913	...	6 952	10 872	13 236	15 346	...
Bulgaria Bulgarie	...	...	...	...	...	...	...	159	249	...
Cuba Cuba	6	66	214	522	26	325	100	128	150	118
Czech Republic République tchèque	...	...	...	...	8 795	...	...	...	...	...
Denmark Danemark	68	64	49	125	107	...	...	273	84	0
Finland Finlande	...	...	...	...	...	...	...	3	0	0
France France	3 498	...	...	...	...	...	...	...	...	...
Germany Allemagne	...	...	...	...	...	1 565	2 564	2 209	2 207	2 009
Hungary Hongrie	2 991	2 840	2 248	2 258	2 341	...	4 892	5 832	8 350	9 891
India Inde	0	...	...	...	...	3 572	5 044	6 060	5 853	...
Iran (Islamic Rep. of) Iran (Rép. islamique d')	^0	^0	562	821	301	...	...	...	...	...
Iraq Iraq	...	...	...	29	...	...	...	...	4	...
Ireland Irlande	174	1 490	...	...	...	...	...	...	...	...
Japan Japon	2 892	1 605	1 769	1 456	1 941	10 404	10 521	11 072	15 740	13 798
Kazakhstan Kazakhstan	...	...	^0	0	0	...	...	346	410	323
Korea, Republic of Corée, République de	318	31	1	...	...	7 336	6 425	5 843	...	...
Kyrgyzstan Kirghizistan	...	...	...	...	...	8	3	2	0	22
Malaysia Malaisie	27 634	28 587	19 245	28 433	46 253	9 915	9 895	10 409	7 594	6 028
Mexico Mexique	1 580	1 310	903	781	1 068	...	...	...	...	...
Nigeria Nigéria	26	26	26	...	...	3	3	3	...	...
Poland Pologne	...	...	15	18	...	...	...	6 525	8 920	...

46

Radio and television receivers *(continued)*
Production: thousands
Récepteurs de radio et de télévision *(suite)*
Production : milliers

Country or area Pays ou zone	Radio receivers Récepteurs de radio					Television receivers Récepteurs de télévision				
	2003	2004	2005	2006	2007	2003	2004	2005	2006	2007
Portugal Portugal	7 310	7 805	9 487	10 592	...	...	...	...	...	...
Republic of Moldova République de Moldova	3	6	3	^0	...	...	...	...	...	...
Romania Roumanie	0	...	0	0	0	...	...	...	...	...
Russian Federation Fédération de Russie	278	194	313	184	152	2 383	4 691	6 278	4 601	6 823
South Africa[2] Afrique du Sud[2]	...	...	...	...	...	359	...	...	...	...
Spain Espagne	47	71	110	151	150	...	...	3 084	2 991	3 010
Sweden Suède	...	...	275	145	367	...	...	344	0	0
Thailand Thaïlande	...	...	...	...	...	6 538	6 942	6 916	6 255	6 074
Tunisia ^[2] Tunisie ^[2]	...	...	...	...	...	0	...	...	...	...
Ukraine Ukraine	21	106	18	2	1	415	443	651	434	514
Viet Nam Viet Nam	24	24	25	23	...	...	...	...	...	...

Source:
United Nations Statistics Division, New York, the *Industrial Commodity Statistics Yearbook 2006* and the industrial statistics database, last accessed April 2009.

1   Twelve months ending 30 June of the year stated.
2   Source: *African Statistical Yearbook*, Economic Commission for Africa (Addis Abaha).

Source:
Organisation des Nations Unies, Division de statistique, New York, *l'Annuaire de statistiques industrielles par produit 2006* et la base de données sur les statistiques industrielles, dernier accès avril 2009.

1   Période de 12 mois finissant le 30 juin de l'année indiquée.
2   Source : *Annuaire des Statistiques de l'Afrique*, Conseil Economique pour l'Afrique (Addis-Abeba).

Country or area Pays ou zone	1997	1998	1999	2000	2001	2002	2003	2004	2005	2006
Argentina Argentine	425	435	291	325	227	153	161	244	299	409
Australia Australie	304[1]	313[1]	340[1]	314[1]	340[1]	319[1]	358[1]	414[1]	399[1]	352
Azerbaijan Azerbaïdjan	...	...	...	...	...	...	...	^0	^0	1
Bangladesh[1] Bangladesh[1]	...	...	...	...	1	1	1	1	^0	^0
Belarus Bélarus	1	1	^0	^0	0	0	0	0	0	^0
Brazil Brésil	...	...	...	1 320	1 467	1 444	1 472	1 876	2 182	3 706
Denmark Danemark	2	1	1	1	1	1	1	1	1	^0
Finland Finlande	34	31	34	38	42	41	19	10	22	33
Germany Allemagne	4 757	5 459	...	...	...	5 561	5 624	...	5 945	5 965
Hungary Hongrie	...	...	...	...	...	...	...	116	...	182
India Inde	...	...	...	506	573	575	538	732	1 031	...
Japan Japon	...	...	...	...	...	#9 244	9 409	9 605	9 588	10 684
Kazakhstan Kazakhstan	...	...	...	...	...	...	3	3	2	3
Kenya Kenya	...	...	...	...	...	^0	1	^0	^0	^0
Korea, Republic of Corée, République de	2 137	1 437	1 924	2 626	2 477	2 653	2 767	3 133	3 356	3 489
Malaysia Malaisie	362	149	258	301	384	419	348	385	423	366
Mexico Mexique	858	947	988	1 294	1 273	1 247	1 028	993	1 128	1 430
Nigeria Nigéria	...	...	...	...	2	2	2	2	2	...
Poland Pologne	...	...	...	534	365	292	333	522	540	631
Portugal Portugal	190	189	184	187	195	190	168	157	142	148
Romania Roumanie	...	...	...	...	...	66	74	104	173	200
Russian Federation Fédération de Russie	986	840	954	969	1 022	981	1 012	1 110	1 069	1 178
Serbia Serbie	...	...	...	...	...	...	...	...	16	11
Slovakia Slovaquie	...	...	...	...	182	226	242	186	177	263
Slovenia Slovénie	...	126	...	...	...	...	...	...	...	...
Spain Espagne	...	...	...	...	...	...	...	2 482	2 375	2 220

Passenger cars *(continued)*
Production: thousands
Voitures de tourisme *(suite)*
Production: milliers

Country or area Pays ou zone	1997	1998	1999	2000	2001	2002	2003	2004	2005	2006
Sudan Soudan	...	...	...	...	...	...	...	1	2	2
Sweden Suède	221	214	235	278	272	260	297	318	309	310
Thailand Thaïlande	112	32	73	97	156	169	252	299	278	299
Ukraine Ukraine	2	26	10	17	26	44	98	174	192	267
United Kingdom [4] Royaume-Uni [4]	...	...	2 208	...	...	...	...	...	...	...
Viet Nam Viet Nam	7	5	6	14	21	30	48	51	59	48

Source:
United Nations Statistics Division, New York, the *Industrial Commodity Statistics Yearbook 2006* and the industrial statistics database, last accessed April 2009.

Source:
Organisation des Nations Unies, Division de statistique, New York, *l'Annuaire de statistiques industrielles par produit 2006* et la base de données sur les statistiques industrielles, dernier accès avril 2009.

1   Twelve months ending 30 June of the year stated.
2   Government production only.
3   Including lorries (trucks), including articulated vehicles, produced.
4   Excluding motor vehicles with a petrol engine less than or equal to 1000 cm³ (excl. vehicles for transporting 10 or more persons, snowmobiles, golf cars and similar vehicles).

1   Période de 12 mois finissant le 30 juin de l'année indiquée.
2   Production de l'état seulement.
3   Y compris les camions et les véhicules articulés produits.
4   Non compris les voitures particulières à moteurs à étincelles, d'une cylindrée inférieur ou égal à 1000 cm³ (sauf les véhicules pour le transport de 10 personnes ou plus, les scooters des neiges, les voiturettes de golf et véhicules similaires).

Country or area Pays ou zone	1997	1998	1999	2000	2001	2002	2003	2004	2005	2006
Algeria Algérie	175	215	181	117	64	153	150	215	...	...
Argentina [1] Argentine [1]	492	512	456	405	311	197	200	321	458	532
Australia Australie	398	441	427	...	...	...	...	...	...	...
Azerbaijan Azerbaïdjan	0	3	1	1	2	4	5	10	13	14
Belarus Bélarus	795	802	802	812	830	856	886	953	995	1 050
Brazil Brésil	3 592	3 034	2 796	...	...	...	...	...	...	...
Bulgaria Bulgarie	21	...	...	...	...	...	...	...	...	...
Chile Chili	268	229	242	271	280	230	232	...	0	
China [2] Chine [2]	10 444	10 600	12 100	12 790	13 513	15 989	22 426	30 076	29 871	35 309
Cuba Cuba	...	6	10	9	9	10	8	7	0	0
Denmark Danemark	1 091	1 046	1 061	1 008	863	805	798	667	511	515
Ecuador Equateur	133	88	38	55	...	...	142	...	...	...
Egypt Egypte	...		527	191	451	640	808	663	685	698
Finland Finlande	102	107	...	...	...	0	...	...	...	13
France France	490	640	509	555	542	528	544	...	...	...
Germany Allemagne	...	...	...	...	...	2 354	2 107	2 061	2 152	2 460
Greece [3,4] Grèce [3,4]	...	...	...	...	...	...	381	...	...	...
Hungary Hongrie	835	708	849	995	1 058	1 866	1 883	1 625	1 535	1 683
India Inde	1 600	1 902	2 012	2 009	2 469	2 735	3 715	...	...	...
Indonesia Indonésie	573	417	240	774	...	...	...	...	...	...
Iran (Islamic Rep. of) Iran (Rép. islamique d')	786 [5]	1 200	1 236	973	917	978	946	799	775	854
Ireland Irlande	160	...	15	...	10	10	11	12	...	...
Italy Italie	5 562	6 280	6 582	6 987	6 936	7 088	7 197	7 201	...	...
Japan Japon	5 369	4 851	4 543	4 224	3 875	3 317	2 859	...	...	...
Kazakhstan Kazakhstan	...	...	...	2	...	...	...	...	0	0
Korea, Republic of Corée, République de	4 257	3 790	4 735	6 304	6 448	8 254	7 267	7 122	6 960	6 579

Refrigerators for household use *(continued)*
Production: thousands
Réfrigérateurs à usage domestique *(suite)*
Production : milliers

Country or area Pays ou zone	1997	1998	1999	2000	2001	2002	2003	2004	2005	2006
Lithuania Lituanie	88	116	118	101	94	111	98	107	89	84
Malaysia Malaisie	249	206	194	215	186	172	187	...	...	...
Mexico Mexique	1 943	1 986	2 083	2 049	2 071	2 222	2 162	2 291	2 844	3 043
Peru Pérou	101	118	42	51	*68	64	*46	69	76	...
Poland Pologne	705	714	726	#172	152	101	215	273	329	251
Portugal Portugal	333	403	430	424	417	440	452	399	166	208
Republic of Moldova[6] République de Moldova[6]	2	0	...	...	...	...	...	...	...	...
Romania Roumanie	429[4]	366[4]	323[4]	341[1]	313[4]	212	319	260	261	424
Russian Federation Fédération de Russie	1 186	1 043	1 173	1 327	1 719	1 938	2 218	2 589	2 778	2 995
Serbia and Montenegro Serbie-et-Monténégro	81	48	#5	20	0	10	...	...	...	...
Slovakia Slovaquie	258	228	206	177	53	...	...	...	...	...
South Africa Afrique du Sud	388	399	440	508	662	702	711	...	...	...
Spain Espagne	1 960	2 415	2 107	2 153	...	...	...	...	...	...
Sudan Soudan	...	...	...	...	...	...	...	47	47	48
Sweden Suède	428	668	649	575	593	627	655	639	625	632
Syrian Arab Republic Rép. arabe syrienne	138	137	120	96	110	113	97	112	142	...
Tajikistan Tadjikistan	2	1	2	2	2	1	1	2	1	1
Thailand Thaïlande	2 384	1 631[7]	...	...	...	...	...	...	...	...
TFYR of Macedonia L'ex-R.Y. Macédoine	12	4	0	0	9	1	0	0	0	0
Turkey Turquie	1 945	1 993	2 083	2 405	2 245	3 017	4 011	4 867	5 099	6 223
Ukraine Ukraine	404	407	427	474	548	635	340	313	313	437
United Kingdom[8] Royaume-Uni[8]	746	662	620	581	565	476	745	317	...	...
United States[9,10] Etats-Unis[9,10]	12 092	11 279	11 716	12 355	11 776	11 145	11 639	...	...	...
Uzbekistan Ouzbékistan	13	16[11]	2[11]	1[11]	...	...	...	...	...	...
Viet Nam Viet Nam	...	...	...	174	223	342	479	621	693	793

Source:
United Nations Statistics Division, New York, the *Industrial Commodity Statistics Yearbook 2006* and the industrial statistics database, last accessed April 2009.

Source:
Organisation des Nations Unies, Division de statistique, New York, *l'Annuaire de statistiques industrielles par produit 2006* et la base de données sur les statistiques industrielles, dernier accès avril 2009.

1	All refrigerators, freezers and combined refrigerator-freezers.	1	Tous réfrigérateurs, congélateurs et combinaisons réfrigérateurs-congélateurs.
2	For statistical purposes, the data for China do not include those for the Hong Kong Special Administrative Region (Hong Kong SAR), Macao Special Administrative Region (Macao SAR) and Taiwan Province of China.	2	Pour la présentation des statistiques, les données pour la Chine ne comprennent pas la Région Administrative Spéciale de Hong Kong (Hong Kong RAS), la Région Administrative Spéciale de Macao (Macao RAS) et la province de Taiwan.
3	Incomplete coverage.	3	Couverture incomplète.
4	Including freezers.	4	Y compris les congélateurs.
5	Production by establishments employing 10 or more persons.	5	Production des établissements occupant 10 personnes ou plus.
6	Excluding the Transnistria region.	6	Non compris la région de Transnistrie.
7	Beginning 1999, series discontinued.	7	A partir de 1999, les séries ont été discontinuées.
8	Excluding chest freezers of a capacity less than or equal to 800 litres.	8	Non compris congélateurs-conservateurs de type coffre, à capacité inférieur ou égal à 800 litres.
9	Shipments.	9	Expéditions.
10	Electric domestic refrigerators only.	10	Réfrigérateurs électriques de ménage seulement.
11	Source: *Statistical Yearbook for Asia and the Pacific*, United Nations Economic and Social Commission for Asia and the Pacific (Bangkok).	11	Source : *Annuaire des Statistiques de l'Asie et Pacifique*, Commission économique et sociale des Nations Unies pour l'Asie et le Pacifique (Bangkok).

Household washing and drying machines
Production: thousands

Machines à laver et à sécher le linge, de type ménager
Production: en milliers

Country or area Pays ou zone	1998	1999	2000	2001	2002	2003	2004	2005	2006	2007
Argentina Argentine	624	635	694	558	263	608	919	1 102	1 243	1 546
Australia Australie	321	354	...	...	...	...	...	...	...	...
Azerbaijan Azerbaïdjan	...	...	...	...	...	...	...	...	36	...
Belarus Bélarus	91	92	88	81	66	63	50	37	13	163
Brazil Brésil	1 851	1 940	3 216	2 495	2 875	4 428	3 708	3 794	4 402	...
Chile Chili	...	...	...	...	...	...	...	117	440	449
China[1] Chine[1]	12 073	13 422	14 430	13 416	15 958	19 645	25 334	30 355	35 605	40 051
Cuba Cuba	...	...	35	49	45	15	5	...	...	...
Egypt Egypte	201	159	7	7	27	86	...	...	...	...
Finland Finlande	...	...	...	...	...	...	...	...	6	4
France France	1 941[2]	2 229[2]	2 751	3 259	3 404	3 618	...	...	...	...
Germany Allemagne	...	5 857	5 770	5 789	5 988	5 836	5 319	4 233	3 299	...
Greece[3] Grèce[3]	...	...	...	...	...	5	...	...	...	...
Hungary Hongrie	...	...	...	...	...	...	26	...	...	...
India Inde	...	...	715	779	1 165	1 539	1 748	1 625	...	...
Indonesia Indonésie	33	48	110	92	96	...	...	...	...	...
Iran (Islamic Rep. of) Iran (Rép. islamique d')	175	193	288	296	411	363	335	430	418	780
Italy Italie	8 119	7 367	8 186	8 507	8 884	9 905	9 829	...	...	...
Japan Japon	5 076	4 833	4 662	4 546	3 982	3 882	3 930	3 839	3 848	3 159
Kazakhstan Kazakhstan	3	2	5	11	17	20	50	73	102	127
Korea, Republic of Corée, République de	2 643	2 822	3 271	3 529	4 183	4 977	5 226	5 665	...	...
Latvia Lettonie	2	...	...	...	...	...	...	...	...	...
Mexico Mexique	1 037	1 250	1 337	1 240	1 220	1 091	1 074	988	1 042	962
Poland Pologne	416	448	...	...	...	...	...	2 338	3 287	...
Republic of Moldova République de Moldova	43	18	25	25	40	48	55	36	22	...
Romania Roumanie	36	28	25	24	28	37	43	25	23	23

49 Household washing and drying machines *(continued)*
Production: thousands
Machines à laver et à sécher le linge, de type ménager *(suite)*
Production: en milliers

Country or area Pays ou zone	1998	1999	2000	2001	2002	2003	2004	2005	2006	2007
Russian Federation Fédération de Russie	862	999	954	1 039	1 369	1 330	1 452	1 582	2 016	2 713
Serbia and Montenegro Serbie-et-Monténégro	30	#12	10	5	4	...	...	...	...	...
South Africa Afrique du Sud	44	45	35	...	...	...	...	...	...	...
Spain Espagne	2 281	...	...	...	2 702	...	2 809	...	2 716	2 478
Sweden Suède	170	182	176	206	189	182	182	187	179	151
Syrian Arab Republic Rép. arabe syrienne	68	65	66	62	85	85	87	77	...	...
Thailand [5] Thaïlande [5]	800	...	...	...	...	...	...	...	...	...
Turkey Turquie	1 408	1 249	1 346	1 034	1 687	2 471	4 058	4 433	5 410	...
Ukraine Ukraine	138[6]	127[6]	125[6]	166[6]	232[6]	255	345	322	208	173
United Kingdom Royaume-Uni	1 111	1 321[7]	1 350[7]	1 549[7]	1 592[7]	1 450[7]	1 670[7]	...	...	...
United States Etats-Unis	7 504[2]	7 991[2]	8 043	7 992[2]	8 959[2]	9 531[2]	...	...	...	...
Uzbekistan [8] Ouzbékistan [8]	5	0	0	...	...	...	...	...	...	...
Viet Nam Viet Nam	...	...	159	168	211	283	514	337	340	...

Source:
United Nations Statistics Division, New York, the *Industrial Commodity Statistics Yearbook 2006* and the industrial statistics database, last accessed April 2009.

Source:
Organisation des Nations Unies, Division de statistique, New York, *l'Annuaire de statistiques industrielles par produit 2006* et la base de données pour les statistiques industrielles, dernier accès avril 2009.

1   For statistical purposes, the data for China do not include those for the Hong Kong Special Administrative Region (Hong Kong SAR) and Macao Special Administrative Region (Macao SAR).

2   Shipments.

3   Incomplete coverage.

4   Break in series; data prior to the sign not comparable to following years.

5   Beginning 1999, series discontinued.

6   Excluding household drying machines.

7   Excluding fully-automatic washing machines of a dry linen capacity less than or equal to 10 kg (including machines which both wash and dry).

8   Source: *Statistical Yearbook*, Commonwealth of Independent States (Moscow).

1   Pour la présentation des statistiques, les données pour la Chine ne comprennent pas la Région Administrative Spéciale de Hong Kong (Hong Kong RAS) et la Région Administrative Spéciale de Macao (Macao RAS).

2   Expéditions.

3   Couverture incomplète.

4   Marque une interruption dans la série et la non-comparabilité des données précédant le symbole.

5   A partir de 1999, les séries ont été discontinuées.

6   Non compris les machines à sécher le linge, de type ménager.

7   Non compris machines entièrement automatiques à laver le linge, d'une capacité inférieur ou égal à 10 kg de linge sec.

8   Source: *Annuaire des Statistiques*, Communauté des États indépendants (Moscou).

Machine tools
Production: number

Machines-outils
Production : nombre

Country or area Pays ou zone	1998	1999	2000	2001	2002	2003	2004	2005	2006	2007
Algeria Algérie										
Lathes										
Tours	14	...	38	27	30	47	...	...	...	...
Armenia Arménie										
Lathes										
Tours	71	33	40	47	115	95	44	10	28	7
Austria Autriche										
Lathes										
Tours	1 914	...	...	1 091	1 031	...	...	...	...	...
Azerbaijan[1] Azerbaïdjan[1]										
Lathes										
Tours	40	6	4	...	...	...	...	...	...	...
Belarus Bélarus										
Drilling, boring and milling machines										
Perceuses et fraiseuses	1 715	1 663	1 939	1 686	1 970	1 885	1 528	680	1 172	981
Lathes										
Tours	131	96	122	146	150	141	124	209	176	246
Brazil Brésil										
Drilling, boring and milling machines										
Perceuses et fraiseuses	...	...	9 328	11 800	10 940	11 311	*14 012	10 950	5 495	...
Lathes										
Tours	...	...	3 044	3 106	3 359	7 381	18 767	5 498	67 999	...
Bulgaria Bulgarie										
Drilling, boring and milling machines										
Perceuses et fraiseuses	930	973	1 470	1 233	1 154	958	866	934	618	521
Lathes										
Tours	1 794	1 726	1 555	1 937	1 813	2 068	2 324	2 134	2 008	2 075
Croatia Croatie										
Lathes										
Tours	144	186	122	74	152	0	...	...	...	...
Czech Republic République tchèque										
Drilling, boring and milling machines										
Perceuses et fraiseuses	2 469	1 807	1 812	1 746	1 280	1 044	1 032	1 061	1 017	1 087
Lathes										
Tours	994	989	1 046	1 254	1 044	861	653	575	906	1 172
Denmark Danemark										
Drilling, boring and milling machines										
Perceuses et fraiseuses	57	35	36	39	32	24	49	34	55	53
Lathes										
Tours	35	98	0	0	74	59	0	0	0	0
Egypt Egypte										
Drilling, boring and milling machines										
Perceuses et fraiseuses	...	...	...	...	...	4	...	...	...	...
Finland Finlande										
Drilling, boring and milling machines										
Perceuses et fraiseuses	67	50	89	58	56	60	36	46	64	61
Lathes										
Tours	...	...	...	...	...	152	...	0	0	0
Georgia Géorgie										
Drilling, boring and milling machines										
Perceuses et fraiseuses	21	2	3	2	25	30	...	...	...	...
Lathes										
Tours	...	...	...	...	9	23	...	...	...	...
Germany Allemagne										
Drilling, boring and milling machines										
Perceuses et fraiseuses	16 744	20 195	23 924	...	...	...	17 330	...	19 576	15 721
Lathes										
Tours	6 607	6 307	6 684	...	5 775	4 824	5 207	5 035	5 783	6 574

50

Machine tools *(continued)*
Production: number
Machines-outils *(suite)*
Production : nombre

Country or area Pays ou zone	1998	1999	2000	2001	2002	2003	2004	2005	2006	2007
Hungary Hongrie										
Drilling, boring and milling machines										
Perceuses et fraiseuses	...	...	...	...	68	68	234	29	22	13
Lathes										
Tours	...	51	100	...	220	...	35	...	...	...
India Inde										
Lathes										
Tours	6 902[2]	12 436[2]	21 579[2]	20 469[2]	14 623[2]	13 522	...	...	...	...
Indonesia Indonésie										
Lathes										
Tours	4	4	...	...	...	...	...	...	...	...
Iran (Islamic Rep. of)[3] Iran (Rép. islamique d')[3]										
Lathes										
Tours	2 836	1 529	1 474	1 691	...	...	...	...	...	...
Japan Japon										
Drilling, boring and milling machines										
Perceuses et fraiseuses	24 901	19 304	16 178	9 520	6 593	7 796	9 031	13 040	9 885	16 544
Lathes										
Tours	22 652	16 924	22 027	19 813	...	...	...	...	...	...
Kazakhstan Kazakhstan										
Drilling, boring and milling machines										
Perceuses et fraiseuses	...	...	...	...	4	8	...	0	0	0
Lathes										
Tours	...	...	...	...	11	...	...	0	0	0
Korea, Republic of Corée, République de										
Drilling, boring and milling machines										
Perceuses et fraiseuses	825	2 242	3 731	2 496	2 634	2 341	2 716	2 729	2 234	2 082
Lathes										
Tours	1 140	1 962	2 497	1 703	1 747	1 366	1 577	1 624	...	...
Kyrgyzstan Kirghizistan										
Lathes										
Tours	10[4]	...	3[4]	...	3[4]	10[4]	0	3	...	...
Latvia Lettonie										
Lathes										
Tours	29	...	...	...	...	...	...	...	...	...
Lithuania Lituanie										
Drilling, boring and milling machines										
Perceuses et fraiseuses	290	216	183	137	122	131	104	45	29	15
Lathes										
Tours	6	6	6	5	0	0	0	0	0	0
Poland Pologne										
Drilling, boring and milling machines										
Perceuses et fraiseuses	...	...	...	...	1 207	1 205	1 183	1 035	1 283	...
Lathes										
Tours	963	732	#748	1 055	399	408	357	470	571	...
Portugal Portugal										
Drilling, boring and milling machines										
Perceuses et fraiseuses	923	1 009	1 012	25	10	14	13	4	7	...
Lathes										
Tours	...	...	...	...	...	...	0	0	1	...
Romania Roumanie										
Drilling, boring and milling machines										
Perceuses et fraiseuses	...	...	...	...	1 202	809	697	525	291	189
Lathes										
Tours	573	330	307	388	299	65	48	61	123	54
Russian Federation Fédération de Russie										
Drilling, boring and milling machines										
Perceuses et fraiseuses	1 846	1 849	1 589	1 205	1 098	1 228	1 425	1 572	2 066	2 225
Lathes										
Tours	1 798	1 681	2 067	2 444	1 959	1 597	1 699	1 325	1 334	1 315

50

Machine tools *(continued)*
Production: number
Machines-outils *(suite)*
Production : nombre

Country or area Pays ou zone	1998	1999	2000	2001	2002	2003	2004	2005	2006	2007
Serbia and Montenegro Serbie-et-Monténégro										
Lathes										
Tours	213	#231	181	...	...	...	...	...	...	...
Slovakia Slovaquie										
Drilling, boring and milling machines										
Perceuses et fraiseuses	...	...	...	1 011	1 019	923	519	...	...	...
Lathes										
Tours	1 660	1 786	1 769	1 683	1 215	1 247	2 598	1 100	1 085	...
Spain Espagne										
Drilling, boring and milling machines										
Perceuses et fraiseuses	...	...	...	...	...	...	5 858	6 062	4 659	6 012
Lathes										
Tours	3 509	3 559	3 492	4 240	3 143	2 785	2 404	2 573	1 955	2 004
Sweden Suède										
Drilling, boring and milling machines										
Perceuses et fraiseuses	3 789	3 394	3 727	1 933	1 956	1 422	1 400	1 881	1 974	1 979
Lathes										
Tours	22	25	17	18	23	0	3	6	151	6
Ukraine Ukraine										
Drilling, boring and milling machines										
Perceuses et fraiseuses	...	...	...	...	...	194	172	120	156	160
Lathes										
Tours	234	213	260	293	195	121	136	158	114	148
United Kingdom Royaume-Uni										
Lathes										
Tours	3 478	2 047	3 317[5]	2 937[5]	...	...	...	...	...	...
United States [6,7] Etats-Unis [6,7]										
Drilling, boring and milling machines										
Perceuses et fraiseuses	9 228	7 845	7 822	4 793	2 327	3 343	3 930	8 807	10 097	9 246
Lathes										
Tours	5 089	3 807	3 278	2 949	1 793	1 816	4 038	4 852	5 769	6 210

Source:
United Nations Statistics Division, New York, the *Industrial Commodity Statistics Yearbook 2006* and the industrial statistics database, last accessed April 2009.

Source:
Organisation des Nations Unies, Division de statistique, New York, *l'Annuaire de statistiques industrielles par produit 2006* et la base de données pour les statistiques industrielles, dernier accès avril 2009.

1	Source: *Statistical Yearbook*, Commonwealth of Independent States (Moscow).
2	All metal-cutting machines.
3	Production by establishments employing 10 or more persons.
4	Source: *Statistical Yearbook*, Commonwealth of Independent States (Moscow).
5	Excluding numerically controlled horizontal lathes, automatic lathes (excl. turning centres).
6	Excluding machines valued under $3025 each.
7	Shipments.

1   Source: *Annuaire des Statistiques*, Communauté d'Etats indépendants (Moscou).
2   Machines-outils tous types pour le travail des métaux.
3   Production des établissements occupant 10 personnes ou plus.
4   Source: *Annuaire des Statistiques*, Communauté des États indépendants (Moscou).
5   Non compris tours automatiques, horizontaux, à commande numérique.
6   Non compris les machines evaluées au-dessous de $3025 par pièce.
7   Expéditions.

Country or area Pays ou zone	1998	1999	2000	2001	2002	2003	2004	2005	2006	2007
Algeria Algérie	...	...	...	...	...	...	2 698	...	...	...
Argentina Argentine	81 929	66 544	85 945	57 509	41 778	50 799	72 493	116 444	145 754	162 497
Azerbaijan Azerbaïdjan	...	...	0	0	0	0	...	...	7	64
Belarus Bélarus	12 799	13 370	14 656	16 524	16 544	18 138	21 506	22 251	23 175	25 540
Brazil Brésil	...	...	222 877	147 054	152 321	155 516	225 615	105 874	95 572	...
Czech Republic République tchèque	39 098	23 113	23 641	4 701	1 095	666	306	229	222	...
Denmark Danemark	160	151	123	90	103	0	0	0	0	0
Finland Finlande	716	721	655	616	596	702	784	910	1 003	1 006
Georgia Géorgie	39	38	45	4	5	...	...	...	...	...
Germany Allemagne	292 489	291 688	298 950	282 610	...	...	...	299 498	314 331	392 678
Iran (Islamic Rep. of) Iran (Rép. islamique d')	41 094	42 338	38 642	49 810	57 638	79 131	99 838	155 941	174 668	193 425
Ireland Irlande	718	1 008	474	406	433	568	461	...	...	...
Kazakhstan Kazakhstan	...	...	225	97	338	84	18	144	1 523	2 043
Kenya Kenya	...	...	...	...	2 439	3 254	4 667	1 873	3 779	2 845
Korea, Republic of Corée, République de	178 401	256 467	254 039	242 030	274 698	233 720	210 008	218 902	...	...
Lithuania Lituanie	0	0	0	41	126	182	778	803	1 133	1 457
Mexico Mexique	455 864	476 894	582 004	552 797	519 101	514 417	526 585	496 806	556 961	552 663
Nigeria Nigéria	...	...	...	1 319	1 340	1 309	1 322	1 324	...	...
Poland Pologne	...	...	59 219	25 718	21 851	17 502	59 541	67 967	75 216	...
Portugal Portugal	15 661	12 750	5 235	...	...	...	...	3 528	3 443	...
Romania Roumanie	...	...	...	...	13 829	19 421	23 060	20 449	12 272	7 706
Russian Federation Fédération de Russie	141 000	176 000	184 000	173 000	173 000	193 000	200 000	205 085	245 291	285 030
Serbia Serbie	...	...	...	...	...	...	...	501	441	...
South Africa Afrique du Sud	117 092	113 310	15 440	12 736	7 479	6 061	...	...	...	...
Spain Espagne	...	...	...	...	...	...	456 542	472 014	493 529	494 442
Sweden Suède	...	...	...	...	...	...	...	37 042	32 764	37 872
Thailand Thaïlande	124 112	248 614	308 632	298 460	394 683	489 608	655 809	847 301	894 794	971 348

Trucks *(continued)*
Production: number of units
Camions *(suite)*
Production : nombre

Country or area Pays ou zone	1998	1999	2000	2001	2002	2003	2004	2005	2006	2007
Turkey Turquie	...	...	...	...	...	18 707	31 125	39 324	35 142	...
Ukraine Ukraine	...	...	...	...	...	4 348	10 651	13 731	11 760	10 844
United Kingdom[1] Royaume-Uni[1]	...	150 397	...	...	...	...	...	...	...	...

Source:
United Nations Statistics Division, New York, the *Industrial Commodity Statistics Yearbook 2006* and the industrial statistics database, last accessed April 2009.

Source:
Organisation des Nations Unies, Division de statistique, New York, *l'Annuaire de statistiques industrielles par produit 2006* et la base de données pour les statistiques industrielles, dernier accès avril 2009.

1   Excluding goods vehicles with a spark-ignition internal combustion piston engine, of a gross vehicle weight less than or equal to 5 tonnes (excl. dumpers designed for off-highway use).

1   Non compris véhicules utilitaires à moteurs à étincelles, d'un poids en charge maximal inférieur ou égal à 5 tonnes (sauf Tombereaux automoteurs utilisés en dehors du réseau routier)

Technical notes: tables 35-51

Industrial activity includes mining and quarrying, manufacturing and the production of electricity, gas and water. These activities correspond to the major divisions 2, 3 and 4 respectively of the *International Standard Industrial Classification of All Economic Activities*.

Many of the tables are based primarily on data compiled for the United Nations *Industrial Commodity Statistics Yearbook*. Data taken from alternate sources are footnoted.

The methods used by countries for the computation of industrial output are, as a rule, consistent with those described in the United Nations *International Recommendations for Industrial Statistics* and provide a satisfactory basis for comparative analysis. In some cases, however, the definitions and procedures underlying computations of output differ from approved guidelines. The differences, where known, are indicated in the footnotes to each table.

Table 35: The statistics on sugar were obtained from the database and the *Sugar Yearbook* of the International Sugar Organization. The data shown cover the production and consumption of centrifugal sugar from both beet and cane, and refer to calendar years.

The consumption data relate to the apparent consumption of centrifugal sugar in the country concerned, including sugar used for the manufacture of sugar-containing products whether exported or not and sugar used for purposes other than human consumption as food. Unless otherwise specified, the statistics are expressed in terms of raw value (i.e. sugar polarizing at 96 degrees). The world total also includes data for countries not shown separately whose sugar consumption was less than 10,000 metric tons.

Table 36: The data refer to beer made from malt, including ale, stout, and porter.

Table 37 presents data on cigarettes only, unless otherwise indicated.

Table 38: the data refer to two types of fabrics: (i) woven fabrics of cotton, containing 85 % or more by weight of cotton, unbleached, bleached, dyed, of yarns of different colours and printed; woven fabrics of cotton, containing less than 85 % by weight of cotton, mixed mainly or solely with man-made fibres, unbleached, bleached, dyed, of yarns of different colours and printed and other woven fabrics of cotton; (ii) woven fabrics of carded or combed wool or of carded or combed fine animal hair for clothing, home furnishing textiles, household linens or for technical or industrial uses.

Table 39 presents data on footwear with uppers of leather, other than sports footwear, footwear incorporating a protective metal toe-cap and miscellaneous special footwear.

Notes techniques : tableaux 35 à 51

L'activité industrielle comprend les industries extractives (mines et carrières), les industries manufacturières et la production d'électricité, de gaz et d'eau. Ces activités correspondent aux grandes divisions 2, 3 et 4, respectivement, de la *Classification internationale type par industrie de toutes les branches d'activité économique*.

Un grand nombre de ces tableaux sont établis principalement sur la base de données compilée pour l'*Annuaire de statistiques industrielles par produit* des Nations Unies. Les données tirées d'autres sources sont signalées par une note.

En règle générale, les méthodes employées par les pays pour le calcul de leur production industrielle sont conformes à celles dans *Recommandations internationales concernant les statistiques industrielles* des Nations Unies et offrent une base satisfaisante pour une analyse comparative. Toutefois, dans certains cas, les définitions des méthodes sur lesquelles reposent les calculs de la production diffèrent des directives approuvées. Lorsqu'elles sont connues, les différences sont indiquées par une note.

Tableau 35: Les données sur le sucre proviennent de la base de données et de l'*Annuaire du sucre* de l'Organisation internationale du sucre. Les données présentées portent sur la production et la consommation de sucre centrifugé à partir de la betterave et de la canne à sucre, et se rapportent à des années civiles.

Les données de la consommation se rapportent à la consommation apparente de sucre centrifugé dans le pays en question, y compris le sucre utilisé pour la fabrication de produits à base de sucre, exportés ou non, et le sucre utilisé à d'autres fins que pour la consommation alimentaire humaine. Sauf indication contraire, les statistiques sont exprimées en valeur brute (sucre polarisant à 96 degrés). Le total mondial compris également les données relatives aux pays où la consommation de sucre est inférieure à 10.000 tonnes.

Tableau 36: Les données se rapportent à la bière produite à partir du malte, y compris ale, stout et porter (bière anglaise, blonde et brune).

Le *tableau 37* se rapporte seulement aux cigarettes, sauf indication contraire.

Le *tableau 38 :* Les données se rapportent aux deux types de tissus : (i) tissus de coton, contenant au moins 85 % en poids de coton, écrus, blanchis, teints, en fils de diverses couleurs et imprimés; tissus de coton, contenant moins de 85 % en poids de coton, mélangés principalement ou uniquement avec des fibres synthétiques ou artificielles, écrus, blanchis, teints, en fils de diverses couleurs et imprimés et autres tissus de coton; (ii) tissages de laine cardée ou peignée, ou de poils fins cardés ou peignés, destinés à l'habillement, aux textiles d'ameublement, au linge de maison ou à des usages tech-

Table 40: The data refer to the aggregate of sawnwood and sleepers, coniferous or non-coniferous. The data cover wood planed, unplaned, grooved, tongued and the like, sawn lengthwise or produced by a pro-file-chipping process, and planed wood which may also be finger-jointed, tongued or grooved, chamfered, rabbeted, V-jointed, beaded and so on. Wood flooring is excluded. Sleepers may be sawn or hewn.

Table 41 presents statistics on the production of all paper and paper board. The data cover newsprint, printing and writing paper, construction paper and paperboard, household and sanitary paper, special thin paper, wrapping and packaging paper and paperboard.

Table 42: Statistics on all hydraulic cements used for construction (Portland, aluminous, slag, and so on) are shown, except in the form of clinkers.

Table 43 presents statistics on pesticides, including insecticides, rodenticides, fungicides, herbicides, anti-sprouting products and plant-growth regulators, disinfectants and similar products, put up in forms or packings for retail sale or as preparations or articles (for example, sulphur-treated bands, wicks and candles, and fly-papers).

Table 44: The data on crude steel and steel semi-finished products refer to ingots, other primary forms, and semi-finished products of iron, non-alloy steel, stainless steel or other alloy steel.

The data on pig iron and spiegeleisen refer to non-alloy pig iron, alloy pig iron and spiegeleisen, in pigs, blocks or other primary forms.

Table 45: The data refer to unwrought aluminium obtained by electrolytic reduction of alumina (primary) and re-melting metal waste or scrap (secondary).

Table 46: The data on radio receivers include radio-broadcast receivers capable of operating without an external source of power, including apparatus capable of receiving also radio-telephony or radio-telegraphy, whether combined with sound recording or reproducing apparatus or not; radio-broadcast receivers not capable of operating without an external source of power, of a kind used in motor vehicles, including apparatus capable of receiving also radio-telephony or radio-telegraphy, whether combined with sound recording or reproducing apparatus or not; other radio-broadcast receivers, including apparatus capable of receiving also radio-telephony or radio-telegraphy, whether combined with sound recording or reproducing apparatus or not.

The data on television receivers include colour, black and white and other monochrome. Also includes television receivers with a video recorder or player, flat panel colour TV receivers, tuner blocks for CTV/VCR and cable TV receiver units and satellite TV receivers/decoders.

niques ou industriels.

Le *tableau 39* se rapporte aux chaussures à dessus en cuir naturel, autres que les chaussures de sport, les chaussures comportant à l'avant une coquille de protection en métal et les chaussures spéciales diverses.

Tableau 40: Les données font référence à un agrégat des sciages de bois de conifères et de non-conifères et de traverses de chemins de fer. Elles comprennent les bois rabotés, non rabotés, rainés, languetés, etc. sciés en long ou obtenus à l'aide d'un procédé de profilage par enlèvement de copeaux et les bois rabotés qui peuvent être également à joints digitiformes languetés ou rainés, chanfreinés, à feuillures, à joints en V, à rebords, etc. Cette rubrique ne comprend pas les éléments de parquet en bois. Les traverses de chemin de fer comprennent les traverses sciées ou équarries à la hache.

Le *tableau 41* présente les statistiques sur la production de tout papier et carton. Les données comprennent le papier journal, les papiers d'impression et d'écriture, les papiers et cartons de construction, les papiers de ménage et les papiers hygiéniques, les papiers minces spéciaux, les papiers d'empaquetage et d'emballage et carton.

Tableau 42: Les données sur tous les ciments hydrauliques utilisés dans la construction (portland, alumineux, de laitier, etc.) sont présentées, autres que sous forme de "clinkers".

Le *tableau 43* présente les statistiques sur la production des pesticides, y compris des insecticides, antirongeurs, fongicides, herbicides, inhibiteurs de germination et régulateurs de croissance pour plantes, désinfectants et produits similaires, présentés dans des formes ou emballages de vente au détail ou à l'état de préparations ou sous forme d'articles (rubans, mèches et bougies soufrés et papier tue mouches, par exemple).

Tableau 44: Les données sur l'acier brut et demi-produits se rapportent aux lingots, autres formes primaires, et demi produits en fer, en aciers non alliés, aciers inoxydables ou autres aciers alliés.

Les données sur les fontes brutes et fontes spiegel se rapportent aux fontes brutes non alliées, fontes brutes alliées et fontes spiegel, en gueuses, saumons ou autres formes primaires.

Tableau 45: Les données se rapportent à la production d'aluminium non travaillé obtenue par réduction électrolytique de l'alumine (formes primaires) et par refonte de déchets et débris de métal (formes secondaires).

Tableau 46: Les données sur les récepteurs de radio comprennent les appareils récepteurs de radiodiffusion pouvant fonctionner sans source d'énergie extérieure, y compris les appareils pouvant recevoir également la radiotéléphonie ou la radiotélégraphie, même combinés à un appareil d'enregistrement ou de reproduction du son; appareils récepteurs de radiodiffusion ne pouvant fonctionner qu'avec une source d'énergie extérieure, du type utilisé

Table 47 presents statistics on passenger cars, including motor cars and other motor vehicles principally designed for the transport of persons (except public-transport type vehicles, vehicles specially designed for travelling on snow, and golf cars and similar vehicles).

Table 48: The data refer to refrigerators of household type such as compression-type, absorption-type, electrical, and other household type refrigerators; freezers of the chest type, not exceeding 800 l capacity; freezers of the upright type, not exceeding 900 l capacity.

Table 49 presents statistics on household washing machines and drying machines, including machines that both wash and dry.

Table 50: The data on machine tools presented in this table include two types: (i) machine-tools (including way-type unit head machines) for drilling, boring, milling, threading or tapping by removing metal, other than lathes and turning centres; (ii) lathes including turning centres for removing metal, horizontal, numerically controlled or otherwise.

Table 51 presents statistics on trucks - motor vehicles not elsewhere classified for the transport of goods except for dumpers designed for off-highway use.

dans les véhicules automobiles, y compris les appareils pouvant recevoir également la radiotéléphonie ou la radiotélégraphie, même combinés à un appareil d'enregistrement ou de reproduction du son; autres appareils récepteurs de radiodiffusion, y compris les appareils pouvant recevoir également la radiotéléphonie ou la radiotélégraphie, même combinés à un appareil d'enregistrement ou de reproduction du son.

Les données sur les appareils récepteurs de télévision y compris couleur, en noir et blanc ou en autres monochromes. Y compris les appareils incorporant un appareil d'enregistrement ou de reproduction vidéo phonique, les récepteurs de télévision avec écran plat (écran à cristaux liquides ou écran à plasma), récepteurs de signaux vidéo phoniques (tuner) et autres appareils récepteur téléviseur sans écran.

Le *tableau 47* présente les statistiques sur les voitures de tourisme et autres véhicules automobiles principalement conçus pour le transport des personnes (autres que les véhicules automobiles pour le transport en commun des personnes, les véhicules spécialement conçus pour se déplacer sur la neige et les véhicules spéciaux pour le transport des personnes sur les terrains de golf et véhicules similaires).

Tableau 48: Les données se rapportent à la production des réfrigérateurs de type ménager comme les réfrigérateurs à compression, à absorption, électriques, et autres réfrigérateurs de type ménager; meubles congélateurs conservateurs du type coffre, d'une capacité n'excédant pas 800 litres; meubles congélateurs conservateurs du type armoire, d'une capacité n'excédant pas 900 litres.

Le *tableau 49* présente les statistiques sur les machines à laver le linge, même avec dispositif de séchage, et machines à sécher le linge.

Tableau 50: Les données se rapportent sur les machines-outils présentés dans ce tableau comprennent deux types : (i) machines (y compris les unités d'usinage à glissières) à percer, aléser, fraiser, fileter ou tarauder les métaux par enlèvement de matière, autres que les tours et centres de tournage ; (ii) tours y compris les centres de tournage travaillant par enlèvement de métal, horizontaux, à commande numérique ou autres.

Le *tableau 51* présente les statistiques sur les camions - véhicules automobiles n.c.a. pour le transport de marchandises à l'exception des tombereaux automoteurs conçus pour être utilisés en dehors du réseau routier.

Production, trade and consumption of commercial energy
Thousand metric tons of oil equivalent and kilograms per capita

Production, commerce et consommation d'énergie commerciale
Milliers de tonnes d'équivalent pétrole et kilogrammes par habitant

Region, country or area	Year Année	Primary energy production – Production d'énergie primaire Total Totale	Solids Solides	Liquids Liquides	Gas Gaz	Electricity Electricité	Changes in stocks Variations des stocks	Imports Importations	Exports Exportations
World	2003	9 200 828	2 446 980	3 797 548	2 485 731	470 568	5 376	4 004 413	3 956 705
	2004	9 635 182	2 650 758	3 941 185	2 547 975	495 265	9 991	4 283 085	4 230 423
	2005	9 960 142	2 825 945	4 005 646	2 618 450	510 100	2 010	4 395 962	4 386 100
	2006	10 247 112	2 977 992	4 037 763	2 706 722	524 636	54 233	4 506 360	4 511 906
Africa	2003	712 919	129 692	439 097	135 640	8 490	1 521	82 821	477 988
	2004	764 996	131 824	479 831	144 381	8 960	-1 387	87 748	519 849
	2005	820 916	133 136	508 197	170 593	8 990	-649	98 573	559 898
	2006	838 670	132 967	508 317	187 889	9 497	1 012	99 835	586 121
Algeria	2003	183 893	...	106 283	77 587	23	-42	972	136 335
	2004	187 780	...	110 940	76 819	22	*153	1 235	141 768
	2005	199 780	...	114 076	85 657	48	65	1 118	144 513
	2006	203 933	...	112 081	91 833	19	717	1 355	151 819
Angola	2003	43 780	...	43 083	590	107	217	733	41 293
	2004	50 274	...	49 443	681	150	780	800	47 110
	2005	63 186	...	62 314	681	191	129	904	60 642
	2006	71 197	...	70 242	726	229	612	1 206	68 043
Benin	2003	0	...	...	...	0	11	1 133	324
	2004	0	...	...	...	0	21	1 296	436
	2005	0	...	...	...	0	-15	1 195	311
	2006	0	...	...	...	0	-14	1 595	531
Burkina Faso	2003	*8	...	...	...	*8	...	*237	0
	2004	*9	...	...	...	*9	...	*237	0
	2005	*9	...	...	...	*9	...	*243	0
	2006	*9	...	...	...	*9	...	*243	0
Burundi	2003	10	2	...	...	9	-4	56	...
	2004	10	2	...	...	8	*12	72	...
	2005	10	2	...	...	9	*-4	62	...
	2006	10	*2	...	...	8	2	74	...
Cameroon	2003	4 414	...	4 111	...	303	-156	2 713	5 517
	2004	4 693	...	4 356	...	337	3	2 314	5 479
	2005	4 417	...	4 081	...	336	-110	1 963	5 012
	2006	4 646	...	4 326	...	320	-10	2 276	5 273
Cape Verde	2003	0	...	...	...	0	...	*90	...
	2004	1	...	...	...	1	...	*96	...
	2005	1	...	...	...	1	...	*109	...
	2006	1	...	...	...	1	...	*111	...
Central African Rep. *	2003	7	...	...	...	7	...	105	...
	2004	7	...	...	...	7	...	105	...
	2005	7	...	...	...	7	...	105	...
	2006	7	...	...	...	7	...	112	...
Chad	2003	1 798	...	1 798	...	...	...	*74	1 728
	2004	8 505	...	8 505	...	...	...	*77	8 440
	2005	8 808	...	8 808	...	...	...	*82	8 741
	2006	7 874	...	7 874	...	...	...	*82	7 806
Comoros *	2003	0	...	...	...	0	...	30	...
	2004	0	...	...	...	0	...	30	...
	2005	0	...	...	...	0	...	30	...
	2006	0	...	...	...	0	...	30	...
Congo	2003	11 222	...	11 177	16	29	...	31	10 875
	2004	11 679	...	11 626	18	34	...	81	11 124
	2005	12 717	...	12 665	21	31	...	116	12 314
	2006	14 382	...	14 328	22	32	...	133	14 035
Côte d'Ivoire	2003	2 326	...	1 028	1 141	158	*166	2 989	2 680
	2004	2 726	...	1 126	1 450	150	-238	3 617	3 340
	2005	3 737	...	1 994	1 619	123	*-31	4 265	4 516
	2006	4 786	...	3 135	1 521	130	-204	3 724	5 711

52

Production, trade and consumption of commercial energy *(continued)*
Thousand metric tons of oil equivalent and kilograms per capita
Production, commerce et consommation d'énergie commerciale *(suite)*
Milliers de tonnes d'équivalent pétrole et kilogrammes par habitant

Bunkers - Soutes			Consumption - Consommation							
Air Avion	Sea Maritime	Unallocated Non distribué	Per capita Par habitant	Total Totale	Solids Solides	Liquids Liquides	Gas Gaz	Electricity Electricité	Year Année	Région, pays ou zone
108 177	**144 504**	**317 916**	**1 382**	**8 661 719**	**2 505 912**	**3 196 633**	**2 488 635**	**470 540**	**2003**	**Monde**
113 705	**157 657**	**322 290**	**1 430**	**9 073 483**	**2 715 814**	**3 324 419**	**2 537 945**	**495 305**	**2004**	
121 509	**168 444**	**319 400**	**1 456**	**9 346 463**	**2 850 219**	**3 370 683**	**2 615 570**	**509 991**	**2005**	
123 489	**177 722**	**306 946**	**1 469**	**9 568 715**	**2 988 105**	**3 398 303**	**2 657 923**	**524 383**	**2006**	
4 514	7 151	8 843	350	295 421	96 479	122 238	68 099	8 604	2003	**Afrique**
4 454	6 122	7 757	363	315 650	103 666	130 529	72 370	9 084	2004	
5 004	6 458	16 190	374	332 303	103 067	134 213	85 925	9 097	2005	
5 060	5 678	7 109	364	333 234	103 367	135 615	84 667	9 585	2006	
273	217	5 140	1 341	42 705	761	20 543	21 377	24	2003	Algérie
219	332	2 727	1 346	43 575	524	23 020	20 008	23	2004	
318	331	3 025	1 593	52 417	644	22 008	29 720	45	2005	
371	317	4 486	1 414	47 343	734	19 900	26 604	26	2006	
301	0	213	222	2 489	...	1 792	590	107	2003	Angola
343	0	258	227	2 583	...	1 751	681	150	2004	
286	1	252	237	2 780	...	1 908	681	191	2005	
340	1	323	257	3 084	...	2 129	726	229	2006	
26	...	...	97	772	...	728	...	44	2003	Bénin
25	...	...	99	814	...	764	...	50	2004	
24	...	...	103	875	...	824	...	51	2005	
25	...	...	120	1 055	...	1 004	...	51	2006	
...	...	...	*19	*245	0	*237	...	*8	2003	Burkina Faso
...	...	...	*19	*246	0	*237	...	*9	2004	
...	...	...	*20	*252	0	*243	...	*9	2005	
...	...	...	*18	*252	0	*243	...	*9	2006	
4	...	...	9	67	2	52	...	13	2003	Burundi
7	...	...	8	63	2	48	...	13	2004	
7	...	...	9	69	2	53	...	15	2005	
7	...	...	9	75	*2	60	...	13	2006	
71	14	433	73	1 249	...	945	...	303	2003	Cameroun
71	15	158	74	1 281	...	944	...	337	2004	
64	12	107	73	1 295	...	959	...	336	2005	
73	42	228	72	1 315	...	995	...	320	2006	
...	*6	...	*183	*84	...	*84	...	0	2003	Cap-Vert
...	*7	...	*190	*89	...	*89	...	1	2004	
...	*10	...	*208	*99	...	*99	...	1	2005	
...	*10	...	*209	*102	...	*101	...	1	2006	
27	...	...	21	85	...	78	...	7	2003	Rép. centrafricaine *
27	...	...	21	85	...	78	...	7	2004	
27	...	...	20	85	...	78	...	7	2005	
29	...	...	21	91	...	83	...	7	2006	
*19	...	0	*13	*125	...	*125	...	...	2003	Tchad
*19	...	0	*13	*124	...	*124	...	...	2004	
*20	...	-1	*13	*131	...	*131	...	...	2005	
*20	...	-1	*13	*131	...	*131	...	...	2006	
...	...	...	47	30	...	30	...	0	2003	Comores *
...	...	...	46	30	...	30	...	0	2004	
...	...	...	45	30	...	30	...	0	2005	
...	...	...	43	30	...	30	...	0	2006	
...	...	46	96	331	...	256	16	60	2003	Congo
...	...	253	108	383	...	295	18	69	2004	
...	...	118	111	401	...	314	21	66	2005	
...	...	25	123	454	...	365	22	67	2006	
*108	91	159	120	2 111	...	927	1 141	44	2003	Côte d'Ivoire
92	91	435	141	2 623	...	1 143	1 450	29	2004	
92	75	658	141	2 692	...	1 069	1 619	3	2005	
92	65	168	136	2 679	...	1 120	1 521	38	2006	

52

Production, trade and consumption of commercial energy *(continued)*
Thousand metric tons of oil equivalent and kilograms per capita
Production, commerce et consommation d'énergie commerciale *(suite)*
Milliers de tonnes d'équivalent pétrole et kilogrammes par habitant

Region, country or area	Year Année	Primary energy production – Production d'énergie primaire					Changes in stocks Variations des stocks	Imports Importations	Exports Exportations
		Total Totale	Solids Solides	Liquids Liquides	Gas Gaz	Electricity Electricité			
Dem. Rep. of the Congo	2003	1 693	73	1 083	...	536	...	513	1 202
	2004	1 696	76	1 033	...	587	...	689	1 163
	2005	1 704	84	984	...	636	...	689	1 144
	2006	1 649	87	886	...	676	...	701	1 046
Djibouti	2003	...	...	...	...	...	...	287	...
	2004	...	...	...	...	...	...	307	...
	2005	...	...	...	...	...	...	318	...
	2006	...	...	...	...	...	...	331	...
Egypt	2003	70 118	26	40 013	28 996	1 082	*454	2 623	11 684
	2004	70 426	23	37 948	31 323	1 132	*-398	3 901	10 848
	2005	83 332	20	37 269	44 908	1 135	0	6 959	18 484
	2006	80 836	15	33 419	46 238	1 164	-89	7 075	19 963
Equatorial Guinea	2003	13 795	...	13 346	448	*0	...	*55	13 346
	2004	18 110	...	17 662	447	*0	...	*48	17 662
	2005	18 421	...	17 973	447	*0	...	*48	17 973
	2006	17 592	...	17 144	447	*0	...	*52	17 144
Eritrea	2003	0	...	...	...	0	11	257	0
	2004	0	...	...	...	0	-25	233	3
	2005	0	...	...	...	0	-40	211	0
	2006	0	...	...	...	0	-30	153	0
Ethiopia	2003	196	...	...	...	196	-272	1 274	...
	2004	217	...	...	...	217	-397	1 349	...
	2005	245	...	...	...	245	-209	1 504	...
	2006	280	...	...	...	280	-218	1 676	...
Gabon	2003	11 239	...	11 056	106	77	-224	116	10 703
	2004	10 930	...	10 736	117	77	-190	88	10 351
	2005	10 877	...	10 690	117	70	-190	149	10 270
	2006	10 935	...	10 736	117	81	-265	183	10 363
Gambia	2003	...	...	...	...	...	...	*108	2
	2004	...	...	...	...	...	...	*109	2
	2005	...	...	...	...	...	...	*109	2
	2006	...	...	...	...	...	...	*114	2
Ghana	2003	334	...	...	...	334	-6	2 653	333
	2004	454	...	...	...	454	0	2 469	454
	2005	484	...	...	...	484	-6	2 726	458
	2006	483	...	...	...	483	-6	3 170	293
Guinea *	2003	36	...	...	...	36	...	405	...
	2004	37	...	...	...	37	...	405	...
	2005	37	...	...	...	37	...	412	...
	2006	37	...	...	...	37	...	413	...
Guinea-Bissau *	2003	...	...	...	...	...	...	100	...
	2004	...	...	...	...	...	...	100	...
	2005	...	...	...	...	...	...	100	...
	2006	...	...	...	...	...	...	103	...
Kenya	2003	348	...	...	...	348	0	2 992	322
	2004	336	...	...	...	336	0	3 667	424
	2005	336	...	...	...	336	48	3 599	241
	2006	359	...	...	...	359	-201	3 723	223
Liberia	2003	...	...	...	...	...	...	*180	1
	2004	...	...	...	...	...	...	205	1
	2005	...	...	...	...	...	...	236	1
	2006	...	...	...	...	...	...	*252	1
Libyan Arab Jamah.	2003	76 752	...	70 943	5 809	...	...	0	57 845
	2004	84 912	...	77 597	7 315	...	...	0	64 978
	2005	93 497	...	83 241	10 256	...	...	13	74 316
	2006	101 124	...	87 691	13 433	...	...	11	81 924

52

Production, trade and consumption of commercial energy *(continued)*
Thousand metric tons of oil equivalent and kilograms per capita
Production, commerce et consommation d'énergie commerciale *(suite)*
Milliers de tonnes d'équivalent pétrole et kilogrammes par habitant

Bunkers - Soutes		Unallocated	Consumption - Consommation							
Air Avion	Sea Maritime	Non distribué	Per capita Par habitant	Total Totale	Solids Solides	Liquids Liquides	Gas Gaz	Electricity Electricité	Year Année	Région, pays ou zone
*97	2	0	17	904	232	249	...	422	2003	Rép. dém. du Congo
121	2	0	20	1 099	251	385	...	463	2004	
120	2	0	20	1 128	264	382	...	482	2005	
120	2	0	19	1 182	278	382	...	522	2006	
99	*72	...	149	116	...	116	...	...	2003	Djibouti
99	*75	...	169	133	...	133	...	...	2004	
104	*74	...	173	139	...	139	...	...	2005	
104	*84	...	174	143	...	143	...	...	2006	
490	2 737	3 347	802	53 963	395	24 296	28 264	1 007	2003	Egypte
712	1 843	2 900	819	58 366	893	28 423	27 978	1 072	2004	
761	1 973	5 834	883	63 182	893	30 363	30 859	1 068	2005	
801	1 082	1 980	881	64 119	780	31 335	30 869	1 134	2006	
...	...	0	1 091	504	...	*55	448	*0	2003	Guinée équatoriale
...	...	0	*1 040	*406	...	*48	*447	*0	2004	
...	...	0	*1 024	*496	...	*48	*447	*0	2005	
...	...	0	*1 008	*500	...	*52	*447	*0	2006	
11	...	...	56	234	...	234	...	0	2003	Erythrée
11	...	...	56	244	...	244	...	0	2004	
9	...	...	53	241	...	241	...	0	2005	
7	...	...	37	175	...	175	...	0	2006	
88	...	...	24	1 654	...	1 458	...	196	2003	Ethiopie
99	...	...	27	1 864	...	1 647	...	217	2004	
151	...	...	25	1 808	...	1 563	...	245	2005	
183	...	...	27	1 992	...	1 711	...	280	2006	
81	145	49	462	601	...	418	106	77	2003	Gabon
67	149	35	444	606	...	412	117	77	2004	
68	153	25	501	700	...	512	117	70	2005	
64	155	97	493	704	...	505	117	81	2006	
...	...	...	*71	*106	...	*106	...	...	2003	Gambie
...	...	...	*69	*107	...	*107	...	...	2004	
...	...	...	*67	*107	...	*107	...	...	2005	
...	...	...	*68	*112	...	*112	...	...	2006	
141	...	-42	122	2 560	...	2 219	...	341	2003	Ghana
116	...	-79	112	2 433	...	1 960	...	472	2004	
128	...	-70	122	2 700	...	2 201	...	499	2005	
162	...	18	138	3 186	...	2 714	...	472	2006	
22	...	...	48	419	...	383	...	36	2003	Guinée *
22	...	...	48	420	...	383	...	37	2004	
23	...	...	47	426	...	389	...	37	2005	
23	...	...	47	428	...	390	...	37	2006	
10	...	...	71	90	...	90	...	...	2003	Guinée-Bissau *
10	...	...	69	90	...	90	...	...	2004	
10	...	...	68	90	...	90	...	...	2005	
10	...	...	68	93	...	93	...	...	2006	
...	13	45	91	2 960	65	2 532	...	363	2003	Kenya
...	37	331	94	3 211	76	2 792	...	343	2004	
...	42	114	99	3 490	76	3 079	...	336	2005	
...	47	135	106	3 878	84	3 440	...	354	2006	
*3	*13	...	*47	*163	...	*163	...	...	2003	Libéria
*3	*13	...	54	188	...	188	...	...	2004	
*3	*13	...	61	219	...	219	...	...	2005	
*3	*13	...	*64	*235	...	*235	...	...	2006	
213	89	2 439	2 599	16 166	...	11 038	5 128	0	2003	Jamah. arabe libyenne
215	89	2 467	2 673	17 164	...	10 937	6 226	0	2004	
191	89	2 486	2 478	16 428	...	11 069	5 355	4	2005	
179	89	2 384	2 471	16 559	...	10 756	5 800	3	2006	

52
Production, trade and consumption of commercial energy *(continued)*
Thousand metric tons of oil equivalent and kilograms per capita
Production, commerce et consommation d'énergie commerciale *(suite)*
Milliers de tonnes d'équivalent pétrole et kilogrammes par habitant

Region, country or area Région, country or area	Year Année	Primary energy production – Production d'énergie primaire					Changes in stocks Variations des stocks	Imports Importations	Exports Exportations
		Total Totale	Solids Solides	Liquids Liquides	Gas Gaz	Electricity Electricité			
Madagascar	2003	52	...	...	...	52	...	*860	20
	2004	55	...	...	...	55	...	*924	20
	2005	*57	...	...	...	*57	...	*943	20
	2006	*58	...	...	...	*58	...	*955	20
Malawi	2003	*145	46	...	...	*99	...	271	11
	2004	*158	*49	...	...	*109	...	*284	11
	2005	*146	31	...	...	*114	...	*289	11
	2006	*154	*38	...	...	*115	...	*274	8
Mali	2003	*20	...	...	...	*20	...	201	...
	2004	*21	...	...	...	*21	...	*210	...
	2005	*22	...	...	...	*22	...	*211	...
	*2006	23	...	...	...	23	...	211	...
Mauritania	2003	*4	...	...	...	*4	...	452	...
	2004	*4	...	...	...	*4	...	485	...
	2005	*4	...	...	...	*4	...	501	...
	2006	*5	...	...	...	*5	...	493	...
Mauritius	2003	10	...	...	...	10	-30	1 185	...
	2004	10	...	...	...	10	14	1 260	...
	2005	10	...	...	...	10	-15	1 343	...
	2006	7	...	...	...	7	-68	1 406	...
Morocco	2003	192	...	10	39	143	93	11 208	296
	2004	214	...	11	47	156	-194	12 488	778
	2005	190	...	7	43	140	38	14 745	576
	2006	226	...	11	62	153	-31	13 901	324
Mozambique	2003	963	26	...	3	935	42	1 276	840
	2004	2 265	12	...	1 249	1 003	-8	1 422	2 162
	2005	3 245	2	...	2 103	1 140	-15	1 337	3 073
	2006	3 811	29	...	2 516	1 265	19	1 412	3 555
Niger	2003	132	132	...	...	...	...	190	...
	2004	140	140	...	...	...	...	187	...
	2005	127	127	...	...	...	...	186	...
	2006	*128	*128	...	...	...	...	186	...
Nigeria	2003	136 383	16	117 964	17 729	674	-396	7 501	124 399
	2004	150 196	2	128 734	20 866	594	224	7 680	136 250
	2005	154 656	6	133 807	20 318	526	-133	7 959	135 690
	2006	152 250	6	125 027	26 554	663	-42	7 749	137 266
Réunion	2003	*50	...	...	...	*50	...	*774	...
	2004	*50	...	...	...	*50	...	*783	...
	2005	*50	...	...	...	*50	...	*783	...
	2006	*50	...	...	...	*50	...	*783	...
Rwanda	2003	10	...	...	0	10	...	*196	1
	2004	*11	...	...	0	*11	...	199	1
	2005	*12	...	...	1	*11	...	*207	1
	2006	10	...	...	1	10	...	*216	1
Saint Helena	*2003	...	...	...	...	...	...	4	...
	2004	...	...	...	...	...	...	3	...
	*2005	...	...	...	...	...	...	3	...
	*2006	...	...	...	...	...	...	3	...
Sao Tome and Principe *	2003	1	...	...	...	1	...	31	...
	2004	1	...	...	...	1	...	31	...
	2005	1	...	...	...	1	...	34	...
	2006	1	...	...	...	1	...	35	...
Senegal	2003	39	...	...	10	29	40	1 779	190
	2004	38	...	...	12	25	-84	1 673	187
	2005	36	...	...	13	23	89	1 982	273
	2006	32	...	...	12	21	-132	1 158	145

52

Production, trade and consumption of commercial energy *(continued)*
Thousand metric tons of oil equivalent and kilograms per capita
Production, commerce et consommation d'énergie commerciale *(suite)*
Milliers de tonnes d'équivalent pétrole et kilogrammes par habitant

| Bunkers - Soutes | | Unallocated | Consumption - Consommation | | | | | | | |
Air Avion	Sea Maritime	Non distribué	Per capita Par habitant	Total Totale	Solids Solides	Liquids Liquides	Gas Gaz	Electricity Electricité	Year Année	Région, pays ou zone
*2	*17	*142	*44	*731	*7	*672	...	52	2003	Madagascar
*2	*17	*145	*46	*795	*7	*733	...	55	2004	
*2	*17	*144	*46	*817	*7	*753	...	*57	2005	
*2	*17	*146	*45	*828	*7	*763	...	*58	2006	
...	...	...	35	405	37	270	...	*98	2003	Malawi
...	...	...	*36	*431	*40	*283	...	*109	2004	
...	...	...	*34	*424	*42	*268	...	*113	2005	
...	...	...	*33	*420	*35	*271	...	*114	2006	
20	...	...	18	201	...	181	...	*20	2003	Mali
21	...	...	*19	*211	...	*189	...	*21	2004	
21	...	...	*18	*212	...	*190	...	*22	2005	
21	...	...	18	213	...	190	...	23	*2006	
0	*5	...	157	450	0	443	...	*7	2003	Mauritanie
0	*5	...	167	484	0	478	...	*6	2004	
0	*5	...	172	500	0	492	...	*8	2005	
0	*5	...	165	493	0	484	...	*9	2006	
92	135	...	825	998	221	766	...	10	2003	Maurice
91	146	...	835	1 019	202	806	...	10	2004	
100	192	...	866	1 077	255	812	...	10	2005	
103	182	...	955	1 196	339	850	...	7	2006	
301	13	669	348	10 027	3 227	6 496	39	264	2003	Maroc
331	*13	987	362	10 787	3 612	6 842	47	286	2004	
380	13	1 152	423	12 775	4 455	7 690	421	209	2005	
430	13	995	406	12 395	3 879	7 659	532	325	2006	
39	45	...	68	1 273	0	532	3	739	2003	Mozambique
41	43	...	75	1 449	0	541	3	906	2004	
45	3	...	76	1 476	0	475	68	933	2005	
56	3	...	80	1 589	0	501	79	1 009	2006	
10	...	...	26	311	132	154	...	25	2003	Niger
12	...	...	26	315	140	148	...	27	2004	
13	...	...	24	300	127	142	...	31	2005	
11	...	...	23	303	*128	142	...	33	2006	
400	628	700	144	18 152	18	10 713	6 747	674	2003	Nigéria
197	523	719	155	19 963	4	10 354	9 011	594	2004	
497	476	6 075	150	20 011	7	10 497	8 980	526	2005	
235	609	524	153	21 406	7	10 736	10 000	663	2006	
...	81	...	*985	*743	...	*694	...	*50	2003	Réunion
...	83	...	*980	*751	...	*701	...	*50	2004	
...	83	...	*966	*751	...	*701	...	*50	2005	
...	83	...	*943	*751	...	*701	...	*50	2006	
*12	...	...	*22	*193	...	*171	0	22	2003	Rwanda
*12	...	...	22	197	...	176	*0	20	2004	
*12	...	...	*22	*206	...	*185	*1	*21	2005	
*12	...	...	*23	*213	...	*194	*1	18	2006	
...	...	...	558	4	...	4	...	...	*2003	Sainte-Hélène
...	...	...	415	3	...	3	...	...	2004	
...	...	...	454	3	...	3	...	...	*2005	
...	...	...	451	3	...	3	...	...	*2006	
...	...	...	221	32	...	31	...	1	2003	Sao Tomé-et-Principe *
...	...	...	216	32	...	31	...	1	2004	
...	...	...	233	35	...	34	...	1	2005	
...	...	...	236	36	...	35	...	1	2006	
*233	11	5	132	1 340	*84	1 217	10	29	2003	Sénégal
253	0	26	126	1 329	89	1 203	12	25	2004	
252	0	9	129	1 395	106	1 252	13	23	2005	
250	0	-12	85	939	117	790	12	21	2006	

52

Production, trade and consumption of commercial energy *(continued)*
Thousand metric tons of oil equivalent and kilograms per capita
Production, commerce et consommation d'énergie commerciale *(suite)*
Milliers de tonnes d'équivalent pétrole et kilogrammes par habitant

Region, country or area	Year Année	Primary energy production – Production d'énergie primaire					Changes in stocks Variations des stocks	Imports Importations	Exports Exportations
		Total Totale	Solids Solides	Liquids Liquides	Gas Gaz	Electricity Electricité			
Seychelles	2003	...	...	...	...	...	...	281	2
	2004	...	...	...	...	...	...	392	2
	2005	...	...	...	...	...	...	357	2
	2006	...	...	...	...	...	...	381	2
Sierra Leone	2003	1	...	...	...	1	...	*368	17
	2004	1	...	...	...	1	...	*454	20
	2005	2	...	...	...	2	...	*459	22
	2006	*2	...	...	...	*2	...	*444	23
Somalia	2003	...	...	...	...	...	...	*178	36
	2004	...	...	...	...	...	...	*184	36
	2005	...	...	...	...	...	...	*187	31
	2006	...	...	...	...	...	...	*186	59
South Africa[1]	2003	130 145	126 717	693	1 199	1 536	1 183	25 557	43 781
	2004	134 142	128 947	1 680	1 843	1 672	-1 282	25 787	40 904
	2005	135 154	130 133	1 555	1 982	1 485	*-13	29 652	45 115
	2006	135 000	130 050	1 506	1 804	1 641	*3	30 632	44 165
Sudan	2003	13 350	...	13 250	...	100	135	350	10 460
	2004	15 091	...	15 000	...	91	116	385	11 820
	2005	15 357	...	15 250	...	107	-171	314	12 013
	2006	16 668	...	16 550	...	118	907	538	12 482
Togo	2003	10	...	...	...	10	2	430	...
	2004	7	...	...	...	7	-1	420	...
	2005	6	...	...	...	6	-18	394	...
	2006	8	...	...	...	8	-46	311	...
Tunisia	2003	5 242	...	3 259	1 966	17	222	5 583	3 532
	2004	5 526	...	3 436	2 074	17	39	5 677	3 884
	2005	5 598	...	3 484	2 098	16	-113	5 720	3 953
	2006	5 628	...	3 363	2 254	11	60	5 776	3 719
Uganda	2003	154	...	...	...	154	...	*488	14
	2004	167	...	...	...	167	...	518	15
	2005	158	...	...	...	158	...	663	14
	2006	107	...	...	...	107	...	785	4
Un. Rep. of Tanzania	2003	258	38	...	0	219	...	1 126	...
	2004	367	45	...	119	203	...	1 209	...
	2005	534	52	...	329	153	...	1 293	...
	2006	528	56	...	349	123	...	1 366	...
Western Sahara *	2003	...	...	...	...	...	...	85	...
	2004	...	...	...	...	...	...	85	...
	2005	...	...	...	...	...	...	85	...
	2006	...	...	...	...	...	...	85	...
Zambia	2003	840	130	...	...	710	56	627	54
	2004	865	137	...	...	727	56	657	35
	2005	908	144	...	...	764	60	691	37
	2006	946	144	...	...	802	51	720	42
Zimbabwe	2003	2 946	2 485	...	...	461	18	1 097	144
	2004	2 865	2 390	...	...	475	12	822	144
	2005	3 036	2 535	...	...	502	4	967	128
	2006	2 890	2 413	...	...	477	-4	929	129
America, North	**2003**	**2 032 572**	**481 383**	**686 524**	**727 918**	**136 748**	**-6 944**	**900 042**	**458 375**
	2004	**2 048 838**	**506 542**	**684 186**	**717 308**	**140 801**	**902**	**958 051**	**475 281**
	2005	**2 032 989**	**515 239**	**664 640**	**709 479**	**143 631**	**-3 873**	**989 545**	**476 043**
	2006	**2 069 379**	**524 172**	**666 553**	**731 985**	**146 668**	**30 611**	**989 927**	**490 944**
Anguilla	2003	...	...	...	...	...	...	13	...
	2004	...	...	...	...	...	...	14	...
	2005	...	...	...	...	...	...	17	...
	2006	...	...	...	...	...	...	18	...

52

Production, trade and consumption of commercial energy *(continued)*
Thousand metric tons of oil equivalent and kilograms per capita
Production, commerce et consommation d'énergie commerciale *(suite)*
Milliers de tonnes d'équivalent pétrole et kilogrammes par habitant

Bunkers - Soutes		Unallocated	Consumption - Consommation							
Air Avion	Sea Maritime	Non distribué	Per capita Par habitant	Total Totale	Solids Solides	Liquids Liquides	Gas Gaz	Electricity Electricité	Year Année	Région, pays ou zone
*27	*71	...	2 191	181	...	184	...	-2	2003	Seychelles
*31	*103	...	3 100	256	...	258	...	-2	2004	
*27	*100	...	2 753	228	...	230	...	-2	2005	
*30	*106	...	2 877	243	...	246	...	-2	2006	
*27	*88	*69	*30	*169	...	*168	...	1	2003	Sierra Leone
27	*91	*94	*39	*223	...	*222	...	1	2004	
*27	*92	*107	*36	*214	...	*212	...	2	2005	
*29	*87	*101	*34	*207	...	*205	...	*2	2006	
*52	*20	*-102	*22	*172	...	*172	...	...	2003	Somalie
*52	*20	*-96	*22	*172	...	*172	...	...	2004	
*52	*21	*-96	*22	*179	...	*179	...	...	2005	
*52	*21	*-124	*21	*179	...	*179	...	...	2006	
886	2 601	-4 709	2 193	111 961	88 808	20 330	1 199	1 624	2003	Afrique du Sud [1]
781	2 390	-3 922	2 275	121 057	95 430	20 811	3 090	1 727	2004	
766	2 647	-4 117	2 249	120 408	93 600	21 124	4 037	1 648	2005	
794	2 604	-4 237	2 257	122 303	94 495	21 876	4 242	1 690	2006	
136	8	93	86	2 868	...	2 768	...	100	2003	Soudan
142	8	212	92	3 178	...	3 087	...	91	2004	
201	8	188	97	3 431	...	3 324	...	107	2005	
226	8	-337	108	3 921	...	3 803	...	118	2006	
27	7	...	81	405	...	355	...	50	2003	Togo
40	5	...	75	383	...	333	...	49	2004	
50	3	...	68	365	...	315	...	50	2005	
35	2	...	61	327	...	276	...	51	2006	
...	0	106	708	6 965	16	3 902	3 032	15	2003	Tunisie
...	0	63	727	7 217	0	4 040	3 162	15	2004	
...	0	135	732	7 344	0	4 074	3 257	13	2005	
...	9	165	736	7 451	0	4 092	3 348	12	2006	
...	...	...	*25	*628	...	*488	...	140	2003	Ouganda
...	...	...	25	670	...	518	...	152	2004	
...	...	...	29	807	...	663	...	144	2005	
...	...	...	30	887	...	785	...	102	2006	
74	23	...	36	1 287	38	1 021	0	227	2003	Rép.Un. de Tanzanie
79	23	...	41	1 473	45	1 097	119	212	2004	
86	23	...	46	1 719	52	1 173	329	165	2005	
91	23	...	47	1 781	56	1 242	349	134	2006	
6	...	...	301	79	...	79	...	...	2003	Sahara occidental [4]
6	...	...	294	79	...	79	...	...	2004	
6	...	...	290	79	...	79	...	...	2005	
6	...	...	286	79	...	79	...	...	2006	
49	...	41	118	1 267	85	516	...	667	2003	Zambie
51	...	43	121	1 338	90	540	...	708	2004	
53	...	46	122	1 404	95	566	...	743	2005	
56	...	46	125	1 471	101	590	...	780	2006	
36	...	...	297	3 844	2 350	760	...	735	2003	Zimbabwe
8	...	...	270	3 522	2 261	611	...	650	2004	
8	...	...	294	3 863	2 442	664	...	758	2005	
8	...	...	279	3 686	2 325	640	...	721	2006	
20 579	**23 838**	**35 805**	**4 784**	**2 401 313**	**488 664**	**1 049 926**	**726 080**	**136 643**	**2003**	**Amérique du Nord**
20 963	**29 332**	**33 961**	**4 825**	**2 446 827**	**502 747**	**1 085 011**	**718 280**	**140 790**	**2004**	
21 610	**30 409**	**22 850**	**4 834**	**2 475 858**	**507 655**	**1 105 879**	**718 719**	**143 605**	**2005**	
20 479	**32 389**	**22 428**	**4 767**	**2 462 791**	**500 281**	**1 097 713**	**718 250**	**146 548**	**2006**	
...	...	...	1 052	13	...	13	...	...	2003	Anguilla
...	...	...	1 092	14	...	14	...	...	2004	
...	...	...	1 250	17	...	17	...	...	2005	
...	...	...	1 242	18	...	18	...	...	2006	

52

Production, trade and consumption of commercial energy *(continued)*
Thousand metric tons of oil equivalent and kilograms per capita
Production, commerce et consommation d'énergie commerciale *(suite)*
Milliers de tonnes d'équivalent pétrole et kilogrammes par habitant

Region, country or area	Year Année	Primary energy production – Production d'énergie primaire					Changes in stocks Variations des stocks	Imports Importations	Exports Exportations
		Total Totale	Solids Solides	Liquids Liquides	Gas Gaz	Electricity Electricité			
Antigua and Barbuda *	2003	...	...	...	...	...	...	190	8
	2004	...	...	...	...	...	...	196	8
	2005	...	...	...	...	...	...	199	9
	2006	...	...	...	...	...	...	205	10
Aruba	2003	*120	...	*120	...	...	...	*10 706	10 495
	2004	*120	...	*120	...	...	...	*10 706	10 495
	2005	*120	...	*120	...	...	...	10 713	10 495
	*2006	120	...	120	...	...	...	10 713	10 495
Bahamas	*2003	...	...	...	...	...	50	3 163	2 206
	2004	...	...	...	...	...	0	*3 209	*2 247
	2005	...	...	...	...	...	0	*3 265	*2 257
	2006	...	...	...	...	...	0	*3 273	*2 256
Barbados	2003	99	...	75	24	...	...	324	74
	2004	89	...	65	23	...	...	351	64
	2005	90	...	66	25	...	...	364	64
	2006	77	...	52	25	...	...	372	51
Belize *	2003	9	...	...	...	9	...	300	...
	2004	9	...	...	...	9	...	305	...
	2005	9	...	...	...	9	...	316	...
	2006	9	...	...	...	9	...	316	...
Bermuda *	2003	...	...	...	...	...	...	196	...
	2004	...	...	...	...	...	...	203	...
	2005	...	...	...	...	...	...	209	...
	2006	...	...	...	...	...	...	211	...
British Virgin Islands *	2003	...	...	...	...	...	...	26	...
	2004	...	...	...	...	...	...	29	...
	2005	...	...	...	...	...	...	30	...
	2006	...	...	...	...	...	...	33	...
Canada	2003	376 493	30 390	142 603	167 960	35 540	-4 339	76 138	214 676
	2004	385 115	32 622	147 681	167 591	37 221	-7 315	78 304	223 268
	2005	388 279	31 907	145 830	171 231	39 311	-5 933	78 231	223 133
	2006	397 145	32 724	153 089	172 121	39 211	-1 541	74 225	227 192
Cayman Islands *	2003	...	...	...	...	...	...	180	...
	2004	...	...	...	...	...	...	186	...
	2005	...	...	...	...	...	...	189	...
	2006	...	...	...	...	...	...	195	...
Costa Rica	2003	636	...	...	...	636	-98	2 010	48
	2004	684	...	...	...	684	15	2 161	88
	2005	695	...	...	...	695	-16	2 106	9
	2006	696	...	...	...	696	17	2 356	34
Cuba	2003	4 335	...	3 711	613	11	30	4 411	...
	2004	3 948	...	3 284	656	8	*23	4 424	...
	2005	3 614	...	2 916	692	6	402	5 314	...
	2006	3 958	...	2 938	1 011	8	-17	6 172	...
Dominica	2003	2	...	...	...	2	...	38	...
	2004	3	...	...	...	3	...	36	...
	2005	2	...	...	...	2	...	*38	...
	*2006	3	...	...	...	3	...	39	...
Dominican Republic	2003	103	...	...	...	103	0	6 577	...
	2004	136	...	...	...	136	36	6 217	...
	2005	163	...	...	...	163	-5	6 224	...
	2006	121	...	...	...	121	-19	6 325	...
El Salvador	2003	209	...	...	...	209	44	2 240	188
	2004	206	...	...	...	206	38	2 284	274
	2005	234	...	...	...	234	65	2 215	122
	2006	267	...	...	...	267	53	2 157	78

Production, trade and consumption of commercial energy *(continued)*
Thousand metric tons of oil equivalent and kilograms per capita
Production, commerce et consommation d'énergie commerciale *(suite)*
Milliers de tonnes d'équivalent pétrole et kilogrammes par habitant

Bunkers - Soutes		Unallocated	Consumption - Consommation							
Air Avion	Sea Maritime	Non distribué	Per capita Par habitant	Total Totale	Solids Solides	Liquids Liquides	Gas Gaz	Electricity Electricité	Year Année	Région, pays ou zone
48	3	...	1 628	130	...	130	...	...	2003	Antigua-et-Barbuda *
50	3	...	1 671	135	...	135	...	...	2004	
50	3	...	1 659	137	...	137	...	...	2005	
50	3	...	1 695	143	...	143	...	...	2006	
*75	...	*5	2 636	251	...	251	...	...	2003	Aruba
*75	...	*5	2 566	251	...	251	...	...	2004	
*77	...	5	2 541	256	...	256	...	...	2005	
77	...	5	2 487	256	...	256	...	...	*2006	
43	244	...	1 941	619	2	617	...	...	*2003	Bahamas
*44	*254	...	*2 217	*664	*2	*662	...	...	2004	
*46	*266	...	*2 156	*696	*2	*694	...	...	2005	
*47	*264	...	*2 160	*706	*3	*703	...	...	2006	
...	...	0	1 285	349	...	325	24	...	2003	Barbade
...	...	0	1 376	375	...	352	23	...	2004	
...	...	0	1 429	390	...	366	25	...	2005	
...	...	0	1 451	398	...	373	25	...	2006	
22	12	...	1 006	275	...	264	...	11	2003	Belize *
23	12	...	989	279	...	268	...	11	2004	
24	13	...	988	288	...	277	...	12	2005	
24	13	...	946	288	...	277	...	12	2006	
17	3	...	2 795	176	...	176	...	...	2003	Bermudes *
18	3	...	2 883	183	...	183	...	...	2004	
18	3	...	2 964	188	...	188	...	...	2005	
20	3	...	2 954	188	...	188	...	...	2006	
...	...	...	1 208	26	...	26	...	...	2003	Iles Vierges brit. *
...	...	...	1 330	29	...	29	...	...	2004	
...	...	...	1 357	30	...	30	...	...	2005	
...	...	...	1 464	33	...	33	...	...	2006	
699	507	2 456	7 534	238 633	26 284	88 806	88 587	34 956	2003	Canada
885	617	5 419	7 518	240 545	25 689	91 840	86 695	36 321	2004	
835	604	5 308	7 507	242 562	25 141	90 544	89 617	37 260	2005	
825	549	4 007	7 361	240 337	24 673	89 775	88 322	37 568	2006	
22	...	...	3 639	159	...	159	...	...	2003	Iles Caïmanes *
23	...	...	3 699	164	...	164	...	...	2004	
23	...	...	3 447	167	...	167	...	...	2005	
24	...	...	3 285	171	...	171	...	...	2006	
...	...	136	626	2 559	100	1 830	...	629	2003	Costa Rica
...	...	89	635	2 653	83	1 906	...	664	2004	
...	...	56	645	2 751	60	1 995	...	696	2005	
...	...	26	683	2 974	82	2 189	...	703	2006	
221	67	820	673	7 608	18	6 966	613	11	2003	Cuba
223	72	351	679	7 702	18	7 020	656	8	2004	
225	73	58	727	8 170	23	7 449	692	6	2005	
*212	*55	1 130	778	8 750	*20	7 710	1 011	8	2006	
...	...	...	582	41	...	38	...	2	2003	Dominique
...	...	...	558	39	...	36	...	3	2004	
...	...	...	*589	*41	...	*38	...	2	2005	
...	...	...	614	42	...	39	...	3	*2006	
92	...	630	666	5 958	740	5 012	103	103	2003	Rép. dominicaine
101	...	192	663	6 023	544	5 218	125	136	2004	
100	...	156	665	6 135	333	5 386	253	163	2005	
99	...	54	675	6 311	560	5 322	309	121	2006	
70	...	32	319	2 115	1	1 878	...	236	2003	El Salvador
75	...	-28	315	2 131	1	1 891	...	239	2004	
78	...	149	296	2 035	1	1 775	...	258	2005	
75	...	48	310	2 170	1	1 903	...	267	2006	

52

Production, trade and consumption of commercial energy *(continued)*
Thousand metric tons of oil equivalent and kilograms per capita
Production, commerce et consommation d'énergie commerciale *(suite)*
Milliers de tonnes d'équivalent pétrole et kilogrammes par habitant

Region, country or area	Year Année	Primary energy production – Production d'énergie primaire					Changes in stocks Variations des stocks	Imports Importations	Exports Exportations
		Total Totale	Solids Solides	Liquids Liquides	Gas Gaz	Electricity Electricité			
Greenland *	2003	...	...	...	...	...	...	196	7
	2004	...	...	...	...	...	...	197	7
	2005	...	...	...	...	...	...	200	7
	2006	...	...	...	...	...	...	204	7
Grenada	2003	...	...	...	...	...	...	83	...
	2004	...	...	...	...	...	...	82	...
	2005	...	...	...	...	...	...	86	...
	2006	...	...	...	...	...	...	88	...
Guadeloupe *	2003	...	...	...	...	...	...	742	...
	2004	...	...	...	...	...	...	748	...
	2005	...	...	...	...	...	...	772	...
	2006	...	...	...	...	...	...	781	...
Guatemala	2003	1 434	...	1 221	...	213	0	3 352	1 152
	2004	1 208	...	999	...	209	25	3 519	955
	2005	1 225	...	910	...	315	169	3 718	846
	2006	1 167	...	818	...	349	-210	3 477	920
Haiti	2003	22	...	...	...	22	...	538	...
	2004	22	...	...	...	22	...	561	...
	2005	23	...	...	...	23	...	565	...
	2006	23	...	...	...	23	...	580	...
Honduras	2003	187	...	...	...	187	243	2 204	18
	2004	202	...	...	...	202	5	2 278	27
	2005	148	...	...	...	148	17	2 374	25
	2006	167	...	...	...	167	277	2 460	38
Jamaica	2003	13	...	...	...	13	35	3 802	129
	2004	14	...	...	...	14	12	3 717	124
	2005	13	...	...	...	13	26	3 431	0
	2006	14	...	...	...	14	-11	4 121	0
Martinique	2003	...	...	...	...	...	...	765	*225
	2004	...	...	...	...	...	...	793	*225
	2005	...	...	...	...	...	...	814	*225
	2006	...	...	...	...	...	...	840	*225
Mexico	2003	233 827	2 944	190 001	37 726	3 157	-1 055	22 525	109 390
	2004	237 911	3 044	191 899	39 440	3 528	1 643	24 544	109 241
	2005	236 409	3 292	188 168	41 004	3 945	445	26 902	104 304
	2006	236 443	3 516	183 762	45 037	4 128	621	30 544	104 114
Montserrat *	2003	...	...	...	...	...	...	24	...
	2004	...	...	...	...	...	...	24	...
	2005	...	...	...	...	...	...	24	...
	2006	...	...	...	...	...	...	25	...
Netherlands Antilles	2003	...	...	...	...	...	...	12 784	7 683
	2004	...	...	...	...	...	...	13 751	8 151
	2005	...	...	...	...	...	...	14 734	9 355
	2006	...	...	...	...	...	...	14 169	8 680
Nicaragua	2003	49	...	...	...	49	41	1 321	5
	2004	50	...	...	...	50	-42	1 286	5
	2005	61	...	...	...	61	31	1 317	6
	2006	59	...	...	...	59	14	1 382	18
Panama	2003	248	...	...	...	248	-20	2 054	209
	2004	335	...	...	...	335	-186	1 770	220
	2005	333	...	...	...	333	0	2 038	226
	2006	336	...	...	...	336	0	2 188	229
Puerto Rico	2003	22	...	...	...	22	...	686	...
	2004	12	...	...	...	12	...	633	...
	2005	12	...	...	...	12	...	633	...
	2006	*13	...	...	...	*13	...	633	...

52

Production, trade and consumption of commercial energy *(continued)*
Thousand metric tons of oil equivalent and kilograms per capita
Production, commerce et consommation d'énergie commerciale *(suite)*
Milliers de tonnes d'équivalent pétrole et kilogrammes par habitant

Bunkers - Soutes		Unallocated	Consumption - Consommation							
Air Avion	Sea Maritime	Non distribué	Per capita Par habitant	Total Totale	Solids Solides	Liquids Liquides	Gas Gaz	Electricity Electricité	Year Année	Région, pays ou zone
8	...	...	3 196	180	...	180	...	...	2003	Groenland *
8	...	...	3 214	181	...	181	...	...	2004	
8	...	...	3 268	184	...	184	...	...	2005	
9	...	...	3 324	187	...	187	...	...	2006	
*8	...	...	715	75	...	75	...	...	2003	Grenade
*8	...	...	707	74	...	74	...	...	2004	
*7	...	...	749	79	...	79	...	...	2005	
*7	...	...	765	81	...	81	...	...	2006	
103	...	...	1 455	639	...	639	...	...	2003	Guadeloupe *
103	...	...	1 449	644	...	644	...	...	2004	
108	...	...	1 491	664	...	664	...	...	2005	
110	...	...	1 467	672	...	672	...	...	2006	
41	122	106	278	3 365	258	2 928	...	179	2003	Guatemala
44	122	83	282	3 497	291	3 033	...	173	2004	
38	122	76	291	3 693	285	3 119	...	288	2005	
38	122	106	282	3 668	300	3 027	...	342	2006	
27	...	...	64	533	...	511	...	22	2003	Haïti
24	...	...	66	559	...	537	...	22	2004	
24	...	...	66	564	...	541	...	23	2005	
25	...	...	67	579	...	555	...	23	2006	
26	...	...	307	2 104	118	1 770	...	215	2003	Honduras
29	...	...	344	2 419	122	2 064	...	233	2004	
28	...	...	340	2 450	128	2 170	...	153	2005	
30	...	...	310	2 281	133	1 980	...	168	2006	
195	30	24	1 279	3 400	59	3 328	...	13	2003	Jamaïque
*186	25	59	1 243	3 327	46	3 267	...	14	2004	
183	30	7	1 207	3 199	42	3 144	...	13	2005	
236	30	12	1 452	3 868	22	3 831	...	14	2006	
*3	*44	*-106	*1 533	*599	...	*599	...	...	2003	Martinique
*4	*45	*-97	*1 564	*616	...	*616	...	...	2004	
*4	*45	*-80	*1 560	*620	...	*620	...	...	2005	
*4	*45	*-62	*1 568	*627	...	*627	...	...	2006	
2 593	815	7 001	1 349	137 609	5 638	82 246	46 643	3 082	2003	Mexique
2 491	774	5 314	1 388	142 992	5 070	85 907	48 570	3 445	2004	
2 581	877	7 033	1 424	148 071	6 068	89 044	49 117	3 842	2005	
2 763	880	5 392	1 461	153 217	6 125	89 062	53 968	4 062	2006	
...	1	...	2 580	23	...	23	...	...	2003	Montserrat *
...	1	...	2 510	23	...	23	...	...	2004	
...	1	...	2 484	23	...	23	...	...	2005	
...	1	...	2 512	24	...	24	...	...	2006	
72	1 707	1 735	8 877	1 586	...	1 586	...	...	2003	Antilles néerland.
73	1 709	1 521	12 538	2 296	...	2 296	...	...	2004	
74	1 712	2 300	6 972	1 293	...	1 293	...	...	2005	
75	1 716	2 493	6 354	1 204	...	1 204	...	...	2006	
...	...	35	243	1 289	...	1 241	...	48	2003	Nicaragua
...	...	30	249	1 342	...	1 293	...	50	2004	
...	...	35	239	1 306	...	1 244	...	62	2005	
...	...	48	246	1 361	...	1 298	...	63	2006	
2	...	0	677	2 111	0	1 878	...	233	2003	Panama
0	...	0	653	2 071	1	1 746	...	324	2004	
0	...	0	665	2 146	1	1 816	...	329	2005	
0	...	0	699	2 295	1	1 962	...	331	2006	
...	...	...	183	709	...	...	686	22	2003	Porto Rico
...	...	...	166	645	...	...	633	12	2004	
...	...	...	165	646	...	...	633	12	2005	
...	...	...	165	646	...	...	633	*13	2006	

Production, trade and consumption of commercial energy *(continued)*
Thousand metric tons of oil equivalent and kilograms per capita
Production, commerce et consommation d'énergie commerciale *(suite)*
Milliers de tonnes d'équivalent pétrole et kilogrammes par habitant

Region, country or area	Year Année	Primary energy production – Production d'énergie primaire					Changes in stocks Variations des stocks	Imports Importations	Exports Exportations
		Total Totale	Solids Solides	Liquids Liquides	Gas Gaz	Electricity Electricité			
Saint Kitts and Nevis *	2003	...	...	...	...	...	...	42	...
	2004	...	...	...	...	...	...	42	...
	2005	...	...	...	...	...	...	45	...
	2006	...	...	...	...	...	...	45	...
Saint Lucia *	2003	...	...	...	...	...	...	121	...
	2004	...	...	...	...	...	...	127	...
	2005	...	...	...	...	...	...	132	...
	2006	...	...	...	...	...	...	135	...
Saint Pierre and Miq. *	2003	...	...	...	...	...	...	28	...
	2004	...	...	...	...	...	...	27	...
	2005	...	...	...	...	...	...	28	...
	2006	...	...	...	...	...	...	28	...
Saint Vincent-Gren	2003	2	...	...	...	2	...	*64	...
	2004	2	...	...	...	2	...	*64	...
	*2005	2	...	...	...	2	...	64	...
	*2006	2	...	...	...	2	...	66	...
Trinidad and Tobago	2003	31 184	...	7 974	23 210	...	324	4 702	22 437
	2004	31 847	...	7 385	24 462	...	313	3 449	21 483
	2005	33 934	...	8 444	25 490	...	78	4 577	24 016
	2006	39 884	...	8 226	31 658	...	-427	4 737	29 306
United States	2003	1 383 577	448 050	340 819	498 383	96 325	-2 200	737 498	89 422
	2004	1 386 925	470 876	332 753	485 136	98 160	6 335	791 813	98 400
	2005	1 367 623	480 041	318 187	471 037	98 358	847	817 660	100 944
	2006	1 388 875	487 932	317 547	482 133	101 263	31 853	816 815	107 292
America, South	**2003**	**520 914**	**39 800**	**342 758**	**89 432**	**48 924**	**5 105**	**79 853**	**238 945**
	2004	**533 338**	**42 198**	**346 772**	**93 918**	**50 450**	**-1 156**	**90 890**	**263 532**
	2005	**558 006**	**46 620**	**360 925**	**97 213**	**53 248**	**-151**	**88 756**	**269 641**
	2006	**575 920**	**50 980**	**366 472**	**102 074**	**56 393**	**-4 917**	**91 288**	**271 750**
Argentina	2003	88 284	53	44 918	39 747	3 567	57	1 804	25 272
	2004	87 597	30	43 338	40 921	3 307	-115	3 093	22 204
	2005	85 423	15	41 612	40 253	3 544	147	4 587	20 082
	2006	88 438	252	42 083	42 155	3 948	-155	3 544	16 418
Bolivia	2003	8 279	...	1 978	6 108	193	*-64	329	4 297
	2004	10 946	...	2 267	8 494	185	-510	193	7 903
	2005	13 220	...	2 441	10 568	211	-472	255	10 291
	2006	14 151	...	2 654	11 312	186	-925	376	10 762
Brazil	2003	125 927	2 064	86 941	9 495	27 427	654	44 579	20 787
	2004	127 868	2 402	86 852	10 032	28 582	-775	51 604	22 419
	2005	139 024	2 779	96 133	10 249	29 863	-226	46 181	23 303
	2006	146 068	2 613	101 894	10 386	31 174	-424	47 919	29 438
Chile	2003	4 464	391	369	1 760	1 944	150	19 923	1 597
	2004	3 939	128	368	1 615	1 829	100	21 913	1 475
	2005	4 925	369	343	1 965	2 248	406	22 596	1 619
	2006	5 425	269	330	1 882	2 945	734	23 592	1 942
Colombia	2003	69 814	32 517	28 027	6 157	3 114	616	334	45 393
	2004	71 600	34 900	26 770	6 481	3 449	8	319	48 347
	2005	74 924	38 391	26 301	6 800	3 430	357	947	50 662
	2006	80 907	42 637	26 901	7 684	3 685	-1 324	688	55 668
Ecuador	2003	22 504	...	21 499	388	617	1 133	2 117	15 229
	2004	28 703	...	27 466	600	637	305	2 108	20 335
	2005	27 834	...	26 606	488	740	98	2 783	19 596
	2006	28 373	...	26 812	795	766	-253	3 240	20 709

52

Production, trade and consumption of commercial energy *(continued)*
Thousand metric tons of oil equivalent and kilograms per capita
Production, commerce et consommation d'énergie commerciale *(suite)*
Milliers de tonnes d'équivalent pétrole et kilogrammes par habitant

Bunkers - Soutes		Unallocated	Consumption - Consommation							
Air Avion	Sea Maritime	Non distribué	Per capita Par habitant	Total Totale	Solids Solides	Liquids Liquides	Gas Gaz	Electricity Electricité	Year Année	Région, pays ou zone
...	...	...	946	42	...	42	...	...	2003	Saint-Kitts-et-Nevis *
...	...	...	957	42	...	42	...	...	2004	
...	...	...	1 051	45	...	45	...	...	2005	
...	...	...	1 051	45	...	45	...	...	2006	
...	5	...	720	116	...	116	...	...	2003	Sainte-Lucie *
...	5	...	753	122	...	122		...	2004	
...	6	...	762	126	...	126		...	2005	
...	6	...	771	129	...	129	...	...	2006	
...	6	...	3 065	21	...	21	...	...	2003	Saint-Pierre-et-Miq. *
...	6	...	2 920	20	...	20	...	...	2004	
...	6	...	3 060	21	...	21	...	...	2005	
...	6	...	3 054	21	...	21	...	...	2006	
...	...	...	*626	*66	...	*64	...	2	2003	Saint Vincent-Gren.
...	...	...	*634	*66	...	*64	...	2	2004	
...	...	...	639	66	...	64	...	2	*2005	
...	...	...	662	69	...	66	...	2	*2006	
8	744	548	8 996	11 830	...	734	11 096	...	2003	Trinité-et-Tobago
6	898	286	9 338	12 317	...	666	11 651	...	2004	
60	264	942	9 937	13 157	...	987	12 170	...	2005	
75	*250	451	11 274	14 972	...	1 312	13 660	...	2006	
16 183	19 528	22 383	6 794	1 976 104	455 445	845 455	578 327	96 877	2003	Etats-Unis
16 469	24 786	20 737	6 854	2 012 384	470 879	872 447	569 926	99 132	2004	
17 020	26 383	6 805	6 861	2 033 642	475 570	891 377	566 211	100 484	2005	
15 653	28 445	8 718	6 749	2 014 060	468 361	882 531	560 321	102 847	2006	
2 702	**6 072**	**30 202**	**877**	**317 672**	**20 300**	**159 253**	**89 343**	**48 775**	**2003**	**Amérique du Sud**
3 421	**6 517**	**17 043**	**912**	**334 721**	**21 031**	**169 223**	**94 007**	**50 459**	**2004**	
3 402	**7 727**	**17 492**	**936**	**348 534**	**21 776**	**176 341**	**97 040**	**53 376**	**2005**	
3 871	**7 310**	**19 559**	**979**	**369 432**	**21 734**	**188 820**	**102 298**	**56 580**	**2006**	
...	588	4 875	1 566	59 320	525	21 259	33 536	4 000	2003	Argentine
...	542	5 047	1 649	63 040	580	23 972	34 882	3 606	2004	
...	695	3 968	1 688	65 145	897	24 688	35 683	3 877	2005	
...	741	5 049	1 795	69 960	753	27 175	37 882	4 151	2006	
...	...	354	446	4 021	...	1 727	2 101	194	2003	Bolivie
...	...	402	363	3 346	...	1 619	1 541	185	2004	
...	...	562	328	3 096	...	1 997	887	212	2005	
...	...	1 025	381	3 668	...	2 195	1 287	186	2006	
1 100	3 219	6 886	770	137 786	13 809	79 185	14 171	30 621	2003	Brésil
1 090	3 348	6 479	808	146 750	14 363	83 079	17 512	31 796	2004	
1 100	3 497	6 442	820	150 968	13 923	85 252	18 572	33 220	2005	
1 271	3 393	6 106	824	153 992	13 779	86 057	19 441	34 714	2006	
544	881	824	1 280	20 392	2 445	8 677	7 159	2 111	2003	Chili
602	961	961	1 351	21 753	3 287	9 350	7 124	1 992	2004	
640	1 246	812	1 399	22 799	3 313	9 423	7 630	2 433	2005	
683	1 404	-28	1 478	24 285	3 948	9 948	7 247	3 141	2006	
589	249	1 847	481	21 454	2 746	9 533	6 157	3 018	2003	Colombie
587	395	989	477	21 593	1 941	9 863	6 481	3 308	2004	
616	415	1 355	488	22 466	2 700	9 685	6 800	3 281	2005	
663	468	2 558	504	23 564	2 467	9 882	7 684	3 531	2006	
...	258	650	572	7 351	...	6 250	388	714	2003	Equateur
...	226	2 557	567	7 389	...	6 010	600	779	2004	
...	672	707	722	9 543	...	8 169	488	887	2005	
...	*297	657	761	10 203	...	8 507	795	901	2006	

52

Production, trade and consumption of commercial energy *(continued)*
Thousand metric tons of oil equivalent and kilograms per capita
Production, commerce et consommation d'énergie commerciale *(suite)*
Milliers de tonnes d'équivalent pétrole et kilogrammes par habitant

Region, country or area	Year Année	Primary energy production – Production d'énergie primaire					Changes in stocks	Imports	Exports
		Total Totale	Solids Solides	Liquids Liquides	Gas Gaz	Electricity Electricité	Variations des stocks	Imports Importations	Exports Exportations
Falkland Is. (Malvinas) *	2003	3	3	...	...	...	...	12	...
	2004	3	3	...	...	...	...	12	...
	2005	3	3	...	...	...	...	13	...
	2006	3	3	...	...	...	...	13	...
French Guiana *	2003	...	...	...	...	...	...	287	...
	2004	...	...	...	...	...	...	287	...
	2005	...	...	...	...	...	...	287	...
	2006	...	...	...	...	...	...	298	...
Guyana	2003	...	...	...	...	...	...	508	...
	2004	...	...	...	...	...	...	492	...
	2005	...	...	...	...	...	...	508	...
	2006	...	...	...	...	...	...	513	...
Paraguay	2003	4 451	...	0	...	4 451	-71	1 226	3 884
	2004	4 464	...	0	...	4 464	-12	1 292	3 869
	2005	4 403	...	5	...	4 399	-26	1 179	3 765
	2006	4 628	...	5	...	4 624	-13	1 241	3 929
Peru	2003	7 307	11	5 086	616	1 594	883	6 438	3 393
	2004	7 588	15	5 103	963	1 507	36	6 542	2 924
	2005	8 746	29	5 376	1 624	1 717	-94	6 550	3 452
	2006	10 680	73	6 900	1 859	1 847	1 180	6 631	3 339
Suriname	2003	653	...	588	...	65	...	268	129
	2004	678	...	612	...	66	...	272	142
	2005	708	...	637	...	71	...	284	148
	2006	731	...	656	...	75	...	290	152
Uruguay	2003	733	...	...	...	733	132	2 030	258
	2004	411	...	...	...	411	78	2 763	353
	2005	575	...	...	...	575	-129	2 586	444
	2006	309	...	...	...	309	39	2 942	239
Venezuela (Bol. R. of)	2003	188 495	4 762	153 351	25 163	5 219	1 614	...	118 706
	2004	189 543	4 721	153 997	24 812	6 013	-271	...	133 560
	2005	198 223	5 034	161 473	25 266	6 451	-211	...	136 278
	2006	196 206	5 134	158 237	26 002	6 834	-3 776	...	129 154
Asia	**2003**	**3 532 015**	**1 246 700**	**1 562 574**	**621 297**	**101 444**	**-2 663**	**1 384 308**	**1 457 918**
	2004	**3 832 682**	**1 418 934**	**1 639 561**	**660 869**	**113 318**	**899**	**1 530 044**	**1 565 530**
	2005	**4 094 538**	**1 568 621**	**1 695 644**	**708 497**	**121 776**	**-6 328**	**1 558 445**	**1 650 338**
	2006	**4 312 946**	**1 709 680**	**1 728 430**	**745 717**	**129 119**	**990**	**1 626 904**	**1 728 425**
Afghanistan	2003	86	24	...	6	56	...	*164	...
	2004	76	24	...	3	50	...	197	...
	*2005	77	23	...	2	51	...	210	...
	*2006	77	23	...	2	51	...	210	...
Armenia	2003	342	...	...	...	342	...	1 470	50
	2004	380	...	...	...	380	...	1 586	99
	2005	386	...	...	...	386	...	1 924	129
	2006	393	...	...	...	393	...	1 928	85
Azerbaijan	2003	20 221	...	15 391	4 618	212	-3	3 886	10 973
	2004	20 457	...	15 565	4 655	237	42	4 861	11 405
	2005	27 652	...	22 232	5 161	259	904	4 734	16 771
	2006	38 598	...	32 289	6 092	217	-133	4 412	27 985
Bahrain	2003	16 488	...	10 187	6 300	...	-603	3 283	10 344
	2004	16 720	...	10 168	6 552	...	-315	3 326	9 927
	2005	17 083	...	10 143	6 941	...	-250	3 980	10 082
	2006	17 324	...	9 970	7 354	...	-513	3 760	9 746
Bangladesh	2003	10 591	...	108	10 386	97	-133	4 227	...
	2004	11 374	...	97	11 171	105	-56	4 269	...
	2005	12 225	...	104	12 010	111	-326	4 495	...
	2006	13 191	...	100	12 972	119	-117	4 537	...

52

Production, trade and consumption of commercial energy *(continued)*
Thousand metric tons of oil equivalent and kilograms per capita

Production, commerce et consommation d'énergie commerciale *(suite)*
Milliers de tonnes d'équivalent pétrole et kilogrammes par habitant

Bunkers - Soutes		Unallocated	Consumption - Consommation							
Air Avion	Sea Maritime	Non distribué	Per capita Par habitant	Total Totale	Solids Solides	Liquids Liquides	Gas Gaz	Electricity Electricité	Year Année	Région, pays ou zone
...	...	...	5 112	15	3	12	...	...	2003	Iles Falkland (Malvinas) *
...	...	...	5 095	15	3	12	...	...	2004	
...	...	...	5 350	16	3	13	...	...	2005	
...	...	...	5 341	16	3	13	...	...	2006	
18	...	...	1 488	269	...	269	...	...	2003	Guyane française *
18	...	...	1 408	269	...	269	...	...	2004	
18	...	...	1 378	269	...	269	...	...	2005	
20	...	...	1 413	278	...	278	...	...	2006	
12		...	659	496	...	496	...	...	2003	Guyana
12		...	635	479	...	479	...	...	2004	
13		...	653	495	...	495		...	2005	
13		...	658	500	...	500		...	2006	
26	...	1	323	1 836	...	1 270	...	567	2003	Paraguay
19	...	2	324	1 878	...	1 282	...	595	2004	
19	...	1	309	1 823	...	1 189	...	634	2005	
24	...	0	321	1 929	...	1 235	...	694	2006	
139	44	-566	366	9 837	730	6 897	616	1 594	2003	Pérou
443	57	-586	415	11 233	857	7 906	963	1 507	2004	
313	228	258	409	11 107	902	6 864	1 624	1 717	2005	
466	100	-266	455	12 457	745	8 006	1 859	1 847	2006	
...	...	137	1 362	655	...	590	...	65	2003	Suriname
...	...	144	1 348	664	...	598	...	66	2004	
...	...	149	1 394	696	...	624	...	71	2005	
...	...	155	1 416	714	...	639	...	75	2006	
33	317	17	589	2 007	1	1 279	54	673	2003	Uruguay
45	340	25	706	2 332	1	1 626	94	611	2004	
43	356	91	712	2 355	1	1 626	89	639	2005	
57	248	104	774	2 565	2	1 909	102	552	2006	
241	517	15 177	2 034	52 232	41	21 809	25 163	5 219	2003	Venezuela (Rép. bol. du)
606	649	1 023	2 066	53 980	0	23 156	24 812	6 013	2004	
640	618	3 147	2 173	57 756	36	26 047	25 266	6 406	2005	
674	658	4 201	2 416	65 301	36	32 476	26 002	6 787	2006	
33 505	**58 015**	**207 820**	**829**	**3 151 776**	**1 373 702**	**1 059 578**	**617 033**	**101 463**	**2003**	**Asie**
35 195	**62 913**	**226 663**	**902**	**3 461 985**	**1 568 231**	**1 133 475**	**646 995**	**113 284**	**2004**	
38 441	**68 715**	**224 577**	**944**	**3 667 397**	**1 705 334**	**1 149 538**	**690 711**	**121 815**	**2005**	
40 221	**74 227**	**233 959**	**978**	**3 852 723**	**1 835 771**	**1 150 525**	**737 180**	**129 247**	**2006**	
*8	...	...	*11	*241	24	*147	6	64	2003	Afghanistan
0	...	...	12	273	24	188	3	58	2004	
10	...	...	12	276	23	191	2	60	*2005	
10	...	...	12	276	23	191	2	60	*2006	
27	...	0	457	1 735	19	316	1 081	318	2003	Arménie
39	...	0	569	1 828	0	311	1 201	315	2004	
45	...	0	664	2 136	0	333	1 488	316	2005	
40	...	0	682	2 196	1	312	1 525	358	2006	
201	...	490	1 511	12 445	...	3 819	8 280	347	2003	Azerbaïdjan
228	...	38	1 638	13 605	...	4 209	9 042	354	2004	
428	...	198	1 678	14 085	...	4 678	9 045	362	2005	
500	...	156	1 709	14 501	...	4 271	9 938	293	2006	
477	...	1 683	11 114	7 662	...	1 362	6 300	...	2003	Bahreïn
521	...	1 719	11 297	7 989	...	1 437	6 552	...	2004	
563	...	1 854	11 852	8 589	...	1 648	6 941	...	2005	
577	...	1 801	12 458	9 251	...	1 897	7 354	...	2006	
234	36	474	105	14 207	350	3 374	10 386	97	2003	Bangladesh
242	36	430	110	14 991	350	3 364	11 171	105	2004	
279	36	479	117	16 253	350	3 782	12 010	111	2005	
274	36	469	120	17 067	350	3 626	12 972	119	2006	

52

Production, trade and consumption of commercial energy *(continued)*
Thousand metric tons of oil equivalent and kilograms per capita
Production, commerce et consommation d'énergie commerciale *(suite)*
Milliers de tonnes d'équivalent pétrole et kilogrammes par habitant

Region, country or area	Year Année	Primary energy production – Production d'énergie primaire					Changes in stocks Variations des stocks	Imports Importations	Exports Exportations
		Total Totale	Solids Solides	Liquids Liquides	Gas Gaz	Electricity Electricité			
Bhutan	2003	235	46	...	...	189	...	*69	159
	2004	238	21	...	...	217	...	*82	173
	2005	262	59	...	...	202	...	*68	173
	2006	296	69	...	...	228	...	*69	213
Brunei Darussalam	2003	22 016	...	10 492	11 524		*-96	0	19 924
	2004	21 739	...	10 338	11 401		55	0	19 378
	2005	21 309	...	10 116	11 193		*-83	26	19 143
	2006	22 598	...	10 833	11 765		*-212	0	20 537
Cambodia	2003	3	...	...	...	3	...	1 079	...
	2004	2	...	...	...	2	...	1 202	...
	2005	4	...	...	...	4	...	1 278	...
	2006	5	...	...	...	5	...	1 404	...
China[2]	2003	1 098 103	860 139	169 600	40 246	28 119	-278	128 182	80 862
	2004	1 242 421	995 163	175 873	36 897	34 488	-124	179 041	72 578
	2005	1 366 651	1 101 259	181 353	45 337	38 702	-4 162	182 116	68 796
	2006	1 460 396	1 185 310	184 766	47 662	42 659	-3 286	203 060	63 566
China, Hong Kong SAR	2003	...	...	...	...	...	-114	22 620	1 481
	2004	...	...	...	...	...	-2	24 563	1 635
	2005	...	...	...	...	...	-542	24 146	2 697
	2006	...	...	...	...	...	630	25 378	1 597
China, Macao SAR	2003	...	...	...	...	...	-4	625	...
	2004	...	...	...	...	...	18	763	...
	2005	...	...	...	...	...	-2	787	...
	2006	...	...	...	...	...	8	827	...
Cyprus	2003	0	...	...	...	0	-67	2 652	...
	2004	0	...	...	...	0	-62	2 398	...
	2005	0	...	...	...	0	71	2 799	...
	2006	0	...	...	...	0	120	2 959	...
Georgia	2003	723	5	140	17	561	-23	1 514	124
	2004	634	5	98	11	520	0	1 699	106
	2005	618	3	67	12	536	0	2 067	90
	2006	549	6	64	16	463	0	2 343	77
India	2003	285 806	215 981	37 557	24 270	7 998	978	110 674	12 850
	2004	299 690	228 921	37 958	24 075	8 738	1 532	120 102	15 877
	2005	314 387	243 028	36 651	24 490	10 217	5 996	130 539	16 996
	2006	330 904	257 084	38 468	24 006	11 347	6 494	146 423	24 196
Indonesia	2003	200 166	73 898	57 095	67 850	1 324	6	32 844	132 882
	2004	214 165	89 579	52 909	70 273	1 404	578	40 533	141 777
	2005	229 071	108 674	50 122	68 782	1 493	570	37 727	150 854
	2006	261 321	142 862	48 091	68 968	1 400	524	32 935	177 604
Iran (Islamic Rep. of)	2003	267 945	862	192 585	73 544	954	-132	10 575	131 710
	2004	283 629	872	200 067	81 776	914	0	12 821	137 022
	2005	308 277	931	217 351	88 610	1 384	0	12 807	153 293
	2006	315 942	1 064	215 973	97 334	1 571	0	16 036	151 762
Iraq	2003	67 456	...	66 003	1 416	37	0	393	41 737
	2004	101 419	...	99 016	2 360	42	459	4 473	76 100
	2005	94 215	...	91 766	2 405	45	448	5 133	68 533
	2006	99 276	...	96 058	3 177	42	-1 749	5 312	74 679
Israel	2003	111	96	3	8	4	-103	23 863	3 092
	2004	1 143	97	2	1 041	3	-201	23 248	3 590
	2005	1 529	91	2	1 433	3	548	22 888	3 926
	2006	2 105	99	2	2 002	1	-186	23 318	3 290
Japan	2003	33 517	...	670	2 884	29 963	-446	430 934	4 845
	2004	37 244	...	692	2 994	33 558	-1 135	437 983	5 087
	2005	38 006	...	734	3 215	34 057	2 445	442 087	9 000
	2006	38 996	...	726	3 547	34 723	-1 174	437 804	10 365

52

Production, trade and consumption of commercial energy *(continued)*
Thousand metric tons of oil equivalent and kilograms per capita

Production, commerce et consommation d'énergie commerciale *(suite)*
Milliers de tonnes d'équivalent pétrole et kilogrammes par habitant

Bunkers - Soutes		Unallocated	Consumption - Consommation							
Air Avion	Sea Maritime	Non distribué	Per capita Par habitant	Total Totale	Solids Solides	Liquids Liquides	Gas Gaz	Electricity Electricité	Year Année	Région, pays ou zone
...	...	...	238	146	39	*49	...	57	2003	Bhoutan
...	...	...	237	148	35	*53	...	60	2004	
...	...	...	247	157	40	*53	...	64	2005	
...	...	...	236	152	36	*53	...	63	2006	
...	...	-358	7 264	2 539	...	1 131	1 409	...	2003	Brunéi Darussalam
...	...	-519	7 831	2 817	...	1 243	1 574	...	2004	
...	...	-511	7 512	2 780	...	1 186	1 594	...	2005	
...	...	-560	7 380	2 826	...	1 253	1 573	...	2006	
23	...	...	81	1 060	...	1 052	...	8	2003	Cambodge
21	...	...	88	1 184	...	1 176	...	7	2004	
21	...	...	92	1 261	...	1 250	...	11	2005	
26	...	...	97	1 383	...	1 369	...	14	2006	
339	2 503	64 698	837	1 078 160	810 955	200 849	38 871	27 486	2003	Chine[2]
129	289	80 617	978	1 267 972	957 800	241 481	34 725	33 966	2004	
321	927	78 315	1 077	1 404 569	1 078 356	245 348	42 695	38 170	2005	
439	1 440	86 892	1 153	1 514 405	1 173 291	253 880	45 167	42 067	2006	
3 547	5 411	...	1 805	12 295	5 743	4 498	1 418	635	2003	Chine, Hong Kong RAS
3 243	7 722	...	1 764	11 965	5 244	4 091	2 049	580	2004	
3 763	5 717	...	1 836	12 512	5 840	4 065	2 048	559	2005	
3 835	7 329	...	1 747	11 986	5 733	3 542	2 164	548	2006	
...	...	...	1 402	629	...	613	...	15	2003	Chine, Macao RAS
...	...	...	1 601	745	...	732	...	13	2004	
...	...	...	1 616	789	...	760	...	29	2005	
...	...	...	1 631	819	...	736	...	83	2006	
330	124	36	3 092	2 228	37	2 191	...	0	2003	Chypre
304	55	6	2 842	2 095	40	2 055	...	0	2004	
300	291	0	2 819	2 137	37	2 100	...	0	2005	
310	296	0	2 898	2 234	38	2 196	...	0	2006	
27	...	54	475	2 055	30	528	857	640	2003	Géorgie
38	...	21	502	2 168	7	527	1 004	630	2004	
38	...	15	583	2 542	19	676	1 195	652	2005	
38	...	15	628	2 762	18	682	1 533	530	2006	
2 470	31	33 221	325	346 950	230 306	84 230	24 270	8 144	2003	Inde
2 900	7	31 354	341	368 142	246 275	88 909	24 075	8 884	2004	
3 400	5	33 907	351	384 640	259 810	89 990	24 490	10 351	2005	
4 101	2	34 694	365	407 858	277 908	94 364	24 006	11 580	2006	
811	490	1 592	454	97 231	10 870	54 384	30 652	1 324	2003	Indonésie
794	358	1 364	506	109 829	15 513	59 516	33 396	1 404	2004	
729	374	2 398	509	111 880	17 781	59 492	33 115	1 493	2005	
717	360	2 155	508	112 904	22 375	54 240	34 889	1 400	2006	
800	585	496	2 182	145 057	1 287	67 044	75 723	1 003	2003	Iran (Rép. islamique d')
812	619	88	2 340	157 905	1 117	71 864	83 982	942	2004	
880	556	-4 389	2 494	170 739	1 267	79 122	89 025	1 325	2005	
1 032	459	-5 052	2 607	183 771	1 351	83 032	97 838	1 550	2006	
418	...	3 648	837	22 052	...	20 599	1 416	37	2003	Iraq
1 200	...	1 382	986	26 757	...	24 242	2 360	156	2004	
774	...	1 637	1 017	27 963	...	25 394	2 405	164	2005	
812	...	2 040	1 000	28 814	...	25 484	3 177	154	2006	
*4	272	400	3 036	20 309	8 963	11 461	8	-123	2003	Israël
*4	229	-240	3 085	21 009	9 110	10 980	1 041	-122	2004	
*4	259	-1 272	3 023	20 952	8 578	11 080	1 433	-140	2005	
4	261	-412	3 188	22 465	9 194	11 427	2 002	-157	2006	
6 720	5 120	19 575	3 395	428 636	115 430	203 996	79 247	29 963	2003	Japon
6 952	5 360	18 757	3 487	440 206	126 224	201 990	78 435	33 558	2004	
7 000	6 024	19 089	3 459	436 536	123 219	200 831	78 429	34 057	2005	
6 498	5 666	20 847	3 445	434 598	124 717	189 085	86 073	34 723	2006	

52
Production, trade and consumption of commercial energy *(continued)*
Thousand metric tons of oil equivalent and kilograms per capita
Production, commerce et consommation d'énergie commerciale *(suite)*
Milliers de tonnes d'équivalent pétrole et kilogrammes par habitant

Region, country or area	Year Année	Primary energy production – Production d'énergie primaire					Changes in stocks	Imports Importations	Exports Exportations
		Total Totale	Solids Solides	Liquids Liquides	Gas Gaz	Electricity Electricité	Variations des stocks		
Jordan	2003	243	...	2	237	*5	-46	5 241	0
	2004	247	...	1	241	5	113	6 393	0
	2005	205	...	1	199	5	143	7 117	0
	2006	191	...	1	185	5	-7	6 942	3
Kazakhstan	2003	105 442	37 297	51 933	15 470	742	407	12 575	69 026
	2004	119 676	38 198	60 185	20 601	693	400	17 216	81 703
	2005	124 352	38 071	62 329	23 277	675	359	16 889	83 103
	2006	133 974	42 271	66 444	24 591	668	267	19 103	89 742
Korea, Dem. P. R.	2003	20 154	19 147	...	...	1 008	...	1 354	528
	2004	21 217	20 142	...	...	1 075	...	1 368	1 100
	2005	23 187	22 058	...	...	1 129	...	1 202	1 963
	2006	23 435	22 350	...	...	1 085	...	989	1 737
Korea, Republic of	2003	13 232	1 484	2	0	11 746	2 482	191 647	22 427
	2004	13 190	1 436	4	0	11 750	959	201 224	25 402
	2005	14 908	1 274	65	490	13 079	-4 504	199 350	29 636
	2006	15 137	1 271	87	517	13 262	2 943	211 149	32 370
Kuwait	2003	124 723	...	114 453	10 269	...	...	589	85 707
	2004	135 274	...	124 221	11 053	...	...	113	93 408
	2005	150 065	...	137 670	12 394	...	...	0	105 226
	2006	155 098	...	141 990	13 108	...	...	0	111 831
Kyrgyzstan	2003	1 380	123	69	25	1 162	-23	1 646	303
	2004	1 448	135	74	27	1 212	-10	1 791	464
	2005	1 422	99	74	23	1 226	0	1 715	357
	2006	1 463	95	71	18	1 280	0	1 668	320
Lao People's Dem. Rep.	2003	*529	*267	...	...	263	...	*144	318
	*2004	561	284	...	...	277	...	149	313
	*2005	585	296	...	...	289	...	155	319
	*2006	598	299	...	...	298	...	151	318
Lebanon	2003	59	...	...	...	59	-566	5 191	...
	2004	97	...	...	...	97	1	5 002	...
	2005	90	...	...	...	90	-417	4 812	...
	2006	60	...	...	...	60	0	4 443	...
Malaysia	2003	89 382	107	39 102	49 679	494	-587	23 747	45 829
	2004	90 133	268	37 275	52 089	501	397	29 557	49 128
	2005	95 925	477	37 627	57 375	446	500	27 722	52 132
	2006	100 550	631	37 003	62 308	608	114	26 597	52 605
Maldives	2003	...	...	...	...	...	...	199	...
	2004	...	...	...	...	...	...	250	...
	2005	...	...	...	...	...	...	225	...
	2006	...	...	...	...	...	...	288	...
Mongolia	2003	1 742	1 742	...	...	...	...	542	101
	2004	2 111	2 111	...	...	...	...	595	361
	2005	2 311	2 311	...	...	...	...	582	490
	2006	2 482	2 482	...	...	...	...	669	569
Myanmar	2003	9 109	609	977	7 330	193	-88	976	6 389
	2004	11 906	645	1 026	10 028	207	0	1 154	9 128
	2005	12 646	794	1 114	10 480	258	0	1 269	9 654
	2006	12 998	807	1 059	10 847	286	57	907	9 669
Nepal	2003	202	8	...	...	195	...	932	18
	2004	213	6	...	...	207	...	883	10
	2005	231	6	...	...	225	...	1 011	11
	2006	236	6	...	...	230	...	1 033	12
Occ. Palestinian Terr.	2003	...	...	...	...	...	-1	629	0
	2004	...	...	...	...	...	*0	862	15
	2005	...	...	...	...	...	0	1 185	18
	2006	...	...	...	...	...	0	*1 264	*26

Production, trade and consumption of commercial energy *(continued)*
Thousand metric tons of oil equivalent and kilograms per capita

Production, commerce et consommation d'énergie commerciale *(suite)*
Milliers de tonnes d'équivalent pétrole et kilogrammes par habitant

Bunkers - Soutes		Unallocated	Consumption - Consommation							
Air Avion	Sea Maritime	Non distribué	Per capita Par habitant	Total Totale	Solids Solides	Liquids Liquides	Gas Gaz	Electricity Electricité	Year Année	Région, pays ou zone
62	8	65	1 032	5 395	...	5 126	237	32	2003	Jordanie
79	48	188	1 217	6 212	...	4 807	1 329	76	2004	
*77	79	342	1 220	6 680	...	5 073	1 538	69	2005	
76	41	162	1 225	6 857	...	4 808	2 004	46	2006	
171	...	544	3 211	47 868	26 683	7 255	13 314	615	2003	Kazakhstan
223	...	2 145	3 492	52 422	27 583	8 982	15 351	506	2004	
241	...	290	3 780	57 248	28 217	8 942	19 364	725	2005	
256	...	775	4 053	62 038	30 318	10 122	20 858	740	2006	
...	...	15	894	20 966	18 865	1 093	...	1 008	2003	Corée, R. p. dém. de
...	...	13	909	21 473	19 296	1 102	...	1 075	2004	
...	...	10	949	22 417	20 362	925	...	1 129	2005	
...	...	7	957	22 681	20 887	708	...	1 085	2006	
1 176	6 480	16 462	3 257	155 852	49 832	69 821	24 453	11 746	2003	Corée, République de
1 286	7 135	23 234	3 253	156 398	51 909	64 502	26 097	11 750	2004	
2 374	10 169	19 516	3 252	157 066	52 231	61 326	30 429	13 079	2005	
2 891	10 182	22 002	3 228	155 899	53 603	57 039	31 995	13 262	2006	
739	556	9 894	11 684	27 171	...	16 902	10 269	...	2003	Koweït
552	567	9 993	12 412	29 673	...	18 620	11 053	...	2004	
594	528	9 880	13 309	32 704	...	20 310	12 394	...	2005	
572	634	8 845	12 681	32 031	...	18 923	13 108	...	2006	
...	...	5	544	2 741	588	448	681	1 024	2003	Kirghizistan
...	...	2	546	2 783	555	559	744	926	2004	
...	...	-8	542	2 788	516	591	686	995	2005	
...	...	-13	544	2 824	480	564	717	1 063	2006	
...	...	...	*63	*355	*221	*125	...	9	2003	Rép. dém. pop. lao
...	...	...	68	397	229	131	...	38	*2004	
...	...	...	75	421	236	131	...	55	*2005	
...	...	...	75	430	239	132	...	59	*2006	
129	16	...	1 447	5 671	140	5 472	...	59	2003	Liban
131	17	...	1 248	4 950	140	4 695	...	115	2004	
152	17	...	1 284	5 151	140	4 882	...	129	2005	
106	17	...	1 080	4 379	140	4 100	...	140	2006	
1 853	71	10 501	2 214	55 467	5 336	19 592	30 045	494	2003	Malaisie
2 074	85	8 689	2 319	59 320	9 293	20 819	28 753	456	2004	
1 954	59	8 626	2 300	60 084	7 575	21 143	31 113	254	2005	
2 010	50	7 471	2 424	64 587	7 800	21 062	35 334	391	2006	
...	...	...	697	199	...	199	...	...	2003	Maldives
...	...	...	863	250	...	250	...	...	2004	
...	...	...	767	225	...	225	...	...	2005	
...	...	...	965	288	...	288	...	...	2006	
...	...	...	877	2 183	1 642	527	...	14	2003	Mongolie
...	...	...	931	2 345	1 751	580	...	14	2004	
...	...	...	943	2 403	1 822	567	...	13	2005	
...	...	...	1 001	2 582	1 915	655	...	13	2006	
69	3	216	66	3 496	97	1 722	1 484	193	2003	Myanmar
66	3	60	70	3 802	102	1 797	1 696	207	2004	
51	3	56	75	4 150	106	1 878	1 909	258	2005	
77	3	50	72	4 047	120	1 667	1 975	286	2006	
40	...	...	44	1 077	204	683	...	190	2003	Népal
54	...	...	42	1 032	180	635	...	218	2004	
60	...	...	46	1 170	287	653	...	231	2005	
61	...	...	46	1 197	294	667	...	236	2006	
...	...	...	179	630	0	431	...	199	2003	Terr. palestinien occ.
...	...	...	233	847	*1	623	...	223	2004	
...	...	...	310	1 166	0	920	...	*246	2005	
...	...	...	*318	*1 238	0	*997	...	*241	2006	

52

Production, trade and consumption of commercial energy *(continued)*
Thousand metric tons of oil equivalent and kilograms per capita
Production, commerce et consommation d'énergie commerciale *(suite)*
Milliers de tonnes d'équivalent pétrole et kilogrammes par habitant

Region, country or area	Year Année	Total Totale	Solids Solides	Liquids Liquides	Gas Gaz	Electricity Electricité	Variations des stocks	Imports Importations	Exports Exportations
		Primary energy production – Production d'énergie primaire					Changes in stocks		
Oman	2003	57 595	...	41 078	16 517	...	-1 562	299	47 510
	2004	56 115	...	39 249	16 866	...	-1 016	422	46 370
	2005	56 557	...	38 879	17 678	...	-1 485	701	46 644
	2006	59 443	...	37 019	22 424	...	2	735	44 346
Pakistan	2003	31 806	1 566	3 314	24 457	2 468	-225	13 106	503
	2004	34 686	2 169	3 415	26 653	2 448	-68	16 347	301
	2005	36 632	2 304	3 490	27 971	2 867	*-17	16 664	411
	2006	36 438	1 723	3 540	28 231	2 944	5	19 560	440
Philippines	2003	6 107	2 149	20	2 416	1 523	116	19 242	881
	2004	5 227	1 273	19	2 311	1 624	-253	20 370	613
	2005	6 126	1 477	29	3 047	1 573	-900	19 068	1 164
	2006	6 072	*1 518	26	2 768	1 761	82	18 752	1 564
Qatar	2003	67 754	...	38 489	29 265	...	2 598	...	51 311
	2004	77 326	...	40 820	36 506	...	-768	...	60 852
	2005	84 149	...	41 463	42 686	...	-1 307	...	63 588
	2006	99 767	...	53 633	46 134	...	-41	...	77 998
Saudi Arabia	2003	528 555	...	481 008	47 547	...	40	1 275	388 105
	2004	547 073	...	495 418	51 655	...	-46	1 524	396 053
	2005	575 237	...	518 469	56 768	...	25	1 875	415 194
	2006	569 645	...	510 048	59 598	...	-119	3 561	405 752
Singapore	2003	...	...	...	...	...	-3 342	85 999	42 078
	2004	...	...	...	...	...	-2 310	97 980	47 157
	2005	...	...	...	...	...	-4 405	105 496	50 712
	2006	...	...	...	...	...	-4 509	112 321	55 656
Sri Lanka	2003	285	...	...	...	285	-114	3 496	0
	2004	255	...	...	...	255	-2	4 086	38
	2005	297	...	...	...	297	41	4 013	0
	2006	399	...	...	...	399	120	4 174	0
Syrian Arab Republic	2003	34 409	...	28 000	6 168	241	11	1 100	17 010
	2004	30 113	...	23 355	6 393	365	-20	1 410	12 610
	2005	28 030	...	22 241	5 493	296	18	1 718	10 202
	2006	26 839	...	20 823	5 673	343	18	1 305	8 085
Tajikistan	2003	1 479	26	18	30	1 405	...	2 111	400
	2004	1 498	41	19	33	1 405	...	2 236	387
	2005	1 565	57	22	27	1 459	...	2 316	372
	2006	1 541	65	22	18	1 436	...	2 539	371
Thailand	2003	35 923	8 289	10 113	16 893	628	-936	52 192	7 870
	2004	36 439	8 824	10 348	16 747	520	-981	58 712	8 564
	2005	39 556	9 184	11 871	18 002	499	-1 285	57 150	8 938
	2006	40 128	8 359	12 880	18 191	699	-1 969	58 056	10 311
Timor-Leste	2003	*7 317	...	*7 317	...	...	...	*53	7 242
	2004	*7 367	...	*7 367	...	...	...	*58	7 291
	2005	*7 394	...	*7 394	...	...	...	*58	7 318
	2006	*7 407	...	*7 407	...	...	...	*58	7 330
Turkey	2003	16 544	10 630	2 351	512	3 051	437	62 760	3 729
	2004	17 000	10 144	2 251	629	3 975	-453	65 413	4 515
	2005	19 151	12 657	2 258	821	3 415	-644	70 292	4 939
	2006	20 727	13 914	2 162	828	3 823	203	78 121	5 998
Turkmenistan	2003	63 928	...	10 390	53 538	0	...	87	45 415
	2004	63 541	...	10 148	53 393	0	...	87	46 693
	2005	66 862	...	9 849	57 013	0	...	87	49 066
	2006	67 359	...	10 120	57 239	0	...	87	48 820
United Arab Emirates	2003	169 311	...	127 590	41 722	...	...	12 458	108 690
	2004	176 233	...	133 114	43 119	...	...	13 420	113 577
	2005	178 003	...	134 642	43 361	...	...	15 078	114 860
	2006	188 485	...	144 378	44 106	...	...	15 792	123 385

52

Production, trade and consumption of commercial energy (continued)
Thousand metric tons of oil equivalent and kilograms per capita
Production, commerce et consommation d'énergie commerciale (suite)
Milliers de tonnes d'équivalent pétrole et kilogrammes par habitant

Bunkers - Soutes		Unallocated		Consumption - Consommation							
Air Avion	Sea Maritime	Non distribué	Per capita Par habitant	Total Totale	Solids Solides	Liquids Liquides	Gas Gaz	Electricity Electricité	Year Année	Région, pays ou zone
369	1	223	4 851	11 354	...	3 310	8 044	...	2003	Oman
*200	1	153	4 483	10 830	...	3 356	7 474	...	2004	
281	1	415	4 545	11 404	...	3 605	7 799	...	2005	
*322	0	777	5 717	14 732	...	4 331	10 402	...	2006	
142	15	1 165	297	43 313	2 659	13 716	24 463	2 474	2003	Pakistan
168	63	1 292	331	49 277	4 460	15 700	26 660	2 457	2004	
214	80	1 727	332	50 884	4 272	15 758	27 974	2 880	2005	
176	103	1 528	343	53 748	4 667	17 887	28 235	2 959	2006	
588	185	984	279	22 595	4 304	14 353	2 416	1 523	2003	Philippines
*619	139	867	286	23 612	4 947	14 730	2 311	1 624	2004	
*722	120	785	273	23 302	4 767	13 915	3 047	1 573	2005	
828	129	690	248	21 532	*4 862	12 141	2 768	1 761	2006	
615	...	-127	18 216	13 357	...	1 769	11 587	...	2003	Qatar
366	...	1 139	20 255	15 737	...	1 862	13 875	...	2004	
468	...	1 173	24 884	20 227	...	2 244	17 983	...	2005	
596	...	798	21 805	20 416	...	2 622	17 794	...	2006	
1 774	2 211	9 333	5 445	119 897	...	72 350	47 547	...	2003	Arabie saoudite
1 695	2 249	7 265	5 907	133 284	...	81 629	51 655	...	2004	
1 707	2 282	8 207	6 122	141 530	...	84 762	56 768	...	2005	
1 774	2 661	6 862	6 281	148 719	...	89 121	59 598	...	2006	
2 420	20 662	10 803	3 196	13 378	8	8 387	4 983	...	2003	Singapour
2 980	23 395	13 254	3 186	13 504	6	7 623	5 875	...	2004	
3 184	25 292	15 944	3 402	14 769	2	8 171	6 595	...	2005	
3 440	27 788	15 420	3 240	14 526	4	7 829	6 692	...	2006	
115	114	131	184	3 536	68	3 183	...	285	2003	Sri Lanka
132	119	118	202	3 937	67	3 615	...	255	2004	
134	169	139	195	3 828	67	3 464	...	297	2005	
123	137	253	198	3 940	67	3 474	...	399	2006	
100	...	1 666	953	16 721	3	10 309	6 168	241	2003	Rép. arabe syrienne
120	...	1 151	990	17 662	3	10 901	6 393	365	2004	
108	...	1 894	959	17 526	3	11 735	5 493	296	2005	
105	...	1 798	969	18 139	3	12 121	5 673	343	2006	
4	...	13	483	3 173	31	1 226	511	1 405	2003	Tadjikistan
4	...	15	496	3 327	45	1 319	528	1 436	2004	
4	...	17	509	3 488	60	1 411	537	1 480	2005	
4	...	16	517	3 690	68	1 590	543	1 488	2006	
...	...	8 040	1 142	73 099	13 281	35 103	23 899	815	2003	Thaïlande
...	...	7 612	1 245	79 904	14 859	39 977	24 289	779	2004	
...	...	8 480	1 242	80 530	14 367	39 101	26 238	823	2005	
...	...	8 993	1 237	80 802	14 539	38 509	26 675	1 078	2006	
...	...	*0	*54	*53	...	*53	...	...	2003	Timor-Leste
...	...	*0	*57	*58	...	*58	...	...	2004	
...	...	*0	*56	*58	...	*58	...	...	2005	
...	...	*0	*55	*58	...	*58	...	...	2006	
904	626	3 063	1 004	70 545	22 127	25 629	19 690	3 100	2003	Turquie
974	1 008	3 462	1 025	72 907	22 646	25 556	20 788	3 917	2004	
1 090	1 072	3 720	1 100	79 266	25 530	25 097	25 324	3 315	2005	
986	991	4 559	1 180	86 111	28 587	24 985	28 859	3 680	2006	
...	...	26	3 954	18 575	...	4 404	14 262	-91	2003	Turkménistan
...	...	26	3 548	16 909	...	4 249	12 760	-101	2004	
...	...	25	3 695	17 858	...	4 341	13 625	-108	2005	
...	...	30	3 796	18 595	...	5 031	13 679	-115	2006	
3 419	9 332	3 788	15 938	56 597	...	21 536	35 062	...	2003	Emirats arabes unis
3 276	10 832	3 845	15 470	58 182	...	22 031	36 151	...	2004	
3 609	12 050	3 571	14 380	59 052	...	22 342	36 710	...	2005	
3 704	13 143	3 519	14 327	60 589	...	23 078	37 511	...	2006	

Production, trade and consumption of commercial energy *(continued)*
Thousand metric tons of oil equivalent and kilograms per capita
Production, commerce et consommation d'énergie commerciale *(suite)*
Milliers de tonnes d'équivalent pétrole et kilogrammes par habitant

Region, country or area	Year Année	Primary energy production – Production d'énergie primaire					Changes in stocks Variations des stocks	Imports Importations	Exports Exportations
		Total Totale	Solids Solides	Liquids Liquides	Gas Gaz	Electricity Electricité			
Uzbekistan	2003	61 512	516	8 046	52 405	546	12	2 296	8 059
	2004	62 239	727	7 533	53 415	564	17	2 174	10 300
	2005	61 935	809	6 173	54 425	527	19	1 952	12 404
	2006	63 778	842	5 763	56 628	545	20	1 984	12 645
Viet Nam	2003	33 463	11 690	17 131	3 009	1 633	0	10 437	21 571
	2004	45 340	17 850	20 844	5 127	1 519	700	11 526	27 018
	2005	50 874	22 677	19 462	6 890	1 845	633	12 347	32 271
	2006	53 941	26 529	18 382	7 000	2 029	800	12 258	34 045
Yemen	2003	21 300	...	21 300		...	567	2 425	17 065
	2004	20 050	...	20 050		...	908	2 738	15 348
	2005	19 852	...	19 852		...	920	2 829	14 911
	2006	18 212	...	18 212		...	1 527	3 553	12 996
Europe	**2003**	**2 139 167**	**362 297**	**733 598**	**872 236**	**171 036**	**8 013**	**1 519 522**	**1 152 601**
	2004	**2 187 268**	**356 619**	**761 129**	**891 998**	**177 521**	**10 469**	**1 577 797**	**1 230 560**
	2005	**2 175 927**	**358 276**	**749 647**	**889 506**	**178 498**	**14 063**	**1 619 414**	**1 246 811**
	2006	**2 170 882**	**355 781**	**741 994**	**894 225**	**178 881**	**28 077**	**1 654 720**	**1 249 834**
Albania	2003	853	19	375	15	444	...	935	64
	2004	933	26	420	17	470	...	1 029	28
	2005	949	22	447	18	462	...	955	0
	2006	975	22	505	18	430	...	920	0
Austria	2003	6 386	300	1 033	1 985	3 067	-68	26 858	3 265
	2004	6 456	61	1 099	1 865	3 431	235	27 688	3 766
	2005	5 951	0	1 018	1 498	3 436	185	29 688	4 329
	2006	6 206	0	1 067	1 751	3 388	727	30 369	5 106
Belarus	2003	2 467	410	1 820	234	2	-190	33 858	9 878
	2004	2 498	453	1 804	237	3	203	37 874	12 693
	2005	2 524	525	1 785	210	3	-102	39 380	14 746
	2006	2 469	483	1 780	202	3	16	42 362	15 894
Belgium	2003	4 229	35	0	...	4 195	51	77 231	23 216
	2004	4 267	49	0	...	4 219	114	79 205	25 014
	2005	4 292	29	13	...	4 250	389	78 144	25 702
	2006	4 212	8	22	...	4 182	107	77 003	24 193
Bosnia-Herzegovina	2003	5 479	5 092	...	...	387	0	1 353	448
	2004	5 657	5 143	...	...	514	3	1 776	578
	2005	5 938	5 423	...	...	516	-15	2 012	681
	2006	6 300	5 796	...	...	504	-15	2 184	825
Bulgaria	2003	6 343	4 513	30	31	1 770	-332	11 508	2 089
	2004	6 421	4 345	30	311	1 735	461	12 340	2 899
	2005	6 523	4 040	30	442	2 011	-7	13 092	3 306
	2006	6 745	4 210	34	429	2 072	-178	14 276	4 394
Croatia	2003	3 729	...	1 317	1 987	424	-142	7 171	1 842
	2004	3 876	...	1 274	1 995	606	-6	7 676	2 216
	2005	3 833	...	1 206	2 072	554	4	7 859	2 326
	2006	4 156	...	1 165	2 463	528	69	7 835	2 605
Czech Republic	2003	24 448	21 365	558	146	2 379	127	19 716	7 240
	2004	24 590	21 259	640	206	2 485	-44	19 394	6 690
	2005	23 861	20 594	681	197	2 388	395	20 900	6 858
	2006	24 053	20 897	443	189	2 524	407	21 626	7 573
Denmark	2003	26 669	...	18 183	8 006	480	-130	14 442	21 755
	2004	29 326	...	19 319	9 438	569	129	13 772	24 395
	2005	29 580	...	18 580	10 429	571	323	13 163	24 561
	2006	27 820	...	16 926	10 367	527	-521	13 743	22 768
Estonia	2003	3 441	3 439	...	...	2	40	1 975	253
	2004	3 220	3 217	...	...	3	-112	2 238	250
	2005	3 381	3 375	...	...	7	1	2 030	210
	2006	3 300	3 292	...	...	8	130	2 161	153

Production, trade and consumption of commercial energy *(continued)*
Thousand metric tons of oil equivalent and kilograms per capita

Production, commerce et consommation d'énergie commerciale *(suite)*
Milliers de tonnes d'équivalent pétrole et kilogrammes par habitant

Bunkers - Soutes		Unallocated	Consumption - Consommation							
Air Avion	Sea Maritime	Non distribué	Per capita Par habitant	Total Totale	Solids Solides	Liquids Liquides	Gas Gaz	Electricity Electricité	Year Année	Région, pays ou zone
...	...	-2 064	2 238	57 801	503	9 793	46 967	538	2003	Ouzbékistan
...	...	-1 924	2 137	56 021	710	9 159	45 597	556	2004	
...	...	-1 469	1 991	52 934	790	7 398	44 226	520	2005	
...	...	-1 432	2 021	54 529	822	6 967	46 203	537	2006	
159	...	0	274	22 173	7 280	10 251	3 009	1 633	2003	Viet Nam
266	...	0	352	28 884	10 430	11 808	5 127	1 519	2004	
265	...	0	362	30 055	10 157	12 592	5 461	1 845	2005	
246	...	0	370	31 112	11 009	12 526	5 548	2 029	2006	
94	126	678	276	5 194	...	5 194	...	...	2003	Yémen
105	126	869	280	5 431	...	5 431	...	...	2004	
105	126	865	288	5 754	...	5 754	...	...	2005	
116	126	783	302	6 217	...	6 217	...	...	2006	
43 497	**48 293**	**37 375**	**3 256**	**2 368 032**	**476 039**	**761 826**	**959 040**	**171 128**	**2003**	**Europe**
46 242	**51 542**	**39 820**	**3 277**	**2 385 316**	**468 696**	**762 095**	**977 052**	**177 473**	**2004**	
49 221	**53 872**	**40 981**	**3 275**	**2 388 092**	**457 412**	**758 780**	**993 760**	**178 139**	**2005**	
50 307	**56 689**	**24 718**	**3 308**	**2 414 966**	**471 219**	**779 825**	**985 576**	**178 347**	**2006**	
48	...	157	431	1 519	21	961	13	523	2003	Albanie
59	...	157	551	1 718	28	1 187	15	487	2004	
71	...	232	509	1 601	25	1 066	16	494	2005	
86	...	241	497	1 567	25	1 044	16	483	2006	
428	...	1 093	3 536	28 526	4 170	12 412	8 394	3 550	2003	Autriche
502	...	1 110	3 505	28 530	3 984	12 383	8 467	3 696	2004	
566	...	853	3 620	29 705	4 095	12 836	9 109	3 665	2005	
593	...	1 109	3 507	29 041	4 044	12 728	8 292	3 977	2006	
...	...	3 444	2 349	23 193	647	4 938	17 018	590	2003	Bélarus
...	...	3 040	2 487	24 436	553	5 130	18 469	283	2004	
...	...	2 442	2 539	24 817	547	5 095	18 825	350	2005	
...	...	3 131	2 650	25 790	522	5 722	19 168	378	2006	
1 478	7 098	4 369	4 369	45 249	6 216	18 285	16 002	4 746	2003	Belgique
1 360	7 978	3 846	4 344	45 161	6 122	17 963	16 189	4 887	2004	
1 287	7 895	3 689	4 162	43 473	5 501	17 430	15 750	4 792	2005	
1 182	8 545	2 820	4 221	44 368	4 774	17 811	16 728	5 056	2006	
...	...	4	1 665	6 380	4 930	964	179	307	2003	Bosnie-Herzégovine
...	...	21	1 778	6 830	5 070	1 131	283	347	2004	
...	...	9	1 893	7 275	5 482	1 060	336	397	2005	
...	...	9	1 994	7 663	5 864	1 122	355	322	2006	
160	139	1 065	1 883	14 730	7 209	3 445	2 778	1 298	2003	Bulgarie
154	117	517	1 878	14 613	6 976	3 638	2 770	1 230	2004	
189	112	810	1 965	15 206	6 840	3 891	3 116	1 359	2005	
181	108	916	2 026	15 601	6 979	3 993	3 223	1 406	2006	
24	22	-144	2 086	9 264	764	5 123	2 618	759	2003	Croatie
29	24	239	2 030	9 013	816	4 545	2 731	922	2004	
40	25	121	2 058	9 140	783	4 721	2 641	994	2005	
40	20	147	2 044	9 076	733	4 719	2 612	1 012	2006	
203	...	1 764	3 414	34 829	18 694	6 436	8 714	985	2003	République tchèque
291	...	2 057	3 428	34 990	18 419	6 784	8 653	1 133	2004	
318	...	2 315	3 408	34 875	18 020	6 988	8 565	1 302	2005	
335	...	2 235	3 415	35 128	18 322	6 954	8 415	1 438	2006	
720	991	-107	3 384	17 883	5 702	7 257	5 179	-255	2003	Danemark
821	806	-88	3 154	17 037	4 398	7 169	5 149	322	2004	
864	833	71	2 971	16 091	3 738	6 776	4 888	689	2005	
869	1 081	-11	3 198	17 377	5 490	6 915	5 041	-69	2006	
19	114	...	3 687	4 990	3 537	859	756	-161	2003	Estonie
28	153	...	3 809	5 139	3 545	885	861	-152	2004	
42	122	...	3 741	5 035	3 388	891	889	-132	2005	
29	216	...	3 672	4 933	3 209	883	898	-57	2006	

52

Production, trade and consumption of commercial energy *(continued)*
Thousand metric tons of oil equivalent and kilograms per capita

Production, commerce et consommation d'énergie commerciale *(suite)*
Milliers de tonnes d'équivalent pétrole et kilogrammes par habitant

Region, country or area	Year Année	Primary energy production – Production d'énergie primaire					Changes in stocks Variations des stocks	Imports Importations	Exports Exportations
		Total Totale	Solids Solides	Liquids Liquides	Gas Gaz	Electricity Electricité			
Faeroe Islands	2003	8	...	...	...	8	...	*219	...
	2004	8	...	...	...	8	...	*219	...
	*2005	8	...	...	...	8	...	220	...
	*2006	8	...	...	...	8	...	220	...
Finland	2003	4 637	1 850	...	...	2 787	498	28 305	5 682
	2004	4 179	920	...	...	3 260	-1 403	26 656	5 745
	2005	5 462	2 261	...	...	3 201	701	23 675	4 685
	2006	6 322	3 351	...	...	2 972	562	26 088	5 262
France [3]	2003	48 383	1 454	1 968	1 424	43 538	-705	167 386	26 362
	2004	48 025	566	1 995	1 231	44 234	-1 036	171 722	27 881
	2005	47 066	415	1 833	1 010	43 809	1 158	178 207	30 488
	2006	47 435	293	1 770	1 176	44 196	1 844	174 552	30 412
Germany	2003	96 089	56 034	4 412	17 699	17 944	-1 512	240 938	28 754
	2004	96 712	56 882	4 448	16 379	19 003	1 329	249 098	34 693
	2005	95 507	55 309	5 613	15 816	18 769	1 596	251 332	38 721
	2006	94 542	52 216	7 137	15 627	19 562	1 279	255 599	41 600
Gibraltar	2003	...	...	...	...	...	...	1 239	...
	2004	...	...	...	...	...	...	1 278	...
	2005	...	...	...	...	...	...	1 308	...
	2006	...	...	...	...	...	...	1 341	...
Greece	2003	8 895	8 176	138	34	546	-863	28 920	5 299
	2004	9 255	8 545	134	32	544	1 017	30 704	5 044
	2005	9 249	8 536	101	20	591	-498	29 730	5 664
	2006	8 806	7 936	137	29	703	382	32 301	6 815
Hungary	2003	8 225	2 743	1 959	2 561	962	466	20 298	2 797
	2004	7 817	2 182	1 942	2 650	1 043	13	19 897	2 620
	2005	7 357	1 748	1 790	2 611	1 208	124	22 364	3 256
	2006	7 366	1 818	1 709	2 661	1 177	155	22 420	3 777
Iceland	2003	946	...	...	215	730	-52	921	...
	2004	963	...	...	222	741	31	1 047	...
	2005	953	...	...	207	746	20	1 032	...
	2006	1 083	...	...	230	853	-28	1 050	...
Ireland	2003	1 945	1 220	0	604	121	271	15 346	1 599
	2004	1 880	974	0	765	141	446	15 225	1 241
	2005	1 569	877	1	512	179	53	15 256	1 394
	2006	1 511	819	3	456	233	146	15 666	1 283
Italy [4]	2003	22 757	157	5 570	12 635	4 394	-1 699	184 480	21 546
	2004	22 474	62	5 698	11 795	4 920	-191	188 826	22 767
	2005	21 685	60	6 288	10 985	4 353	-1 621	194 455	26 805
	2006	20 438	13	5 966	9 991	4 468	3 159	198 832	25 400
Latvia	2003	201	2	0	...	199	63	3 226	9
	2004	274	3	0	...	272	455	3 862	392
	2005	294	3	2	...	290	125	3 756	557
	2006	249	3	9	...	236	204	3 855	290
Lithuania	2003	1 862	10	382	53	1 416	129	10 566	6 248
	2004	1 745	11	305	49	1 380	156	12 277	7 749
	2005	1 250	16	227	48	960	85	12 828	7 598
	2006	1 071	13	196	48	814	138	12 472	6 892
Luxembourg	2003	81	...	0	...	81	6	4 509	253
	2004	79	...	1	...	78	-13	4 936	284
	2005	83	...	1	...	82	-19	5 013	284
	2006	87	...	1	...	86	29	5 064	289
Malta	2003	...	...	...	...	...	...	909	...
	2004	...	...	...	...	...	...	957	...
	2005	...	...	...	...	...	...	945	...
	2006	...	...	...	...	...	...	918	...

52

Production, trade and consumption of commercial energy *(continued)*
Thousand metric tons of oil equivalent and kilograms per capita
Production, commerce et consommation d'énergie commerciale *(suite)*
Milliers de tonnes d'équivalent pétrole et kilogrammes par habitant

Bunkers - Soutes		Unallocated	Consumption - Consommation							
Air Avion	Sea Maritime	Non distribué	Per capita Par habitant	Total Totale	Solids Solides	Liquids Liquides	Gas Gaz	Electricity Electricité	Year Année	Région, pays ou zone
*2	...	...	*4 683	*224	...	*217	...	8	2003	Iles Féroé
*2	...	...	*4 650	*224	...	*217	...	8	2004	
2	...	...	4 671	225	...	218	...	8	*2005	
2	...	...	4 671	225	...	218	...	8	*2006	
362	650	-1 358	5 200	27 107	8 398	10 966	4 538	3 205	2003	Finlande
418	524	-2 000	5 270	27 551	7 680	11 761	4 432	3 678	2004	
420	515	-2 393	4 805	25 208	4 971	11 536	4 037	4 664	2005	
467	566	-2 740	5 372	28 292	7 604	12 381	4 355	3 952	2006	
5 079	2 693	9 855	2 866	172 486	14 805	76 167	43 687	37 827	2003	France[3]
5 427	3 051	9 666	2 886	174 758	14 267	76 971	44 609	38 911	2004	
5 490	2 781	10 855	2 865	174 500	14 784	75 454	45 641	38 622	2005	
5 714	2 889	6 530	2 859	174 597	13 634	78 187	44 027	38 750	2006	
5 737	2 641	6 453	3 574	294 954	83 442	105 926	87 923	17 663	2003	Allemagne
6 201	2 704	6 292	3 571	294 592	84 125	104 211	87 479	18 778	2004	
6 674	2 532	6 410	3 528	290 905	80 236	102 453	89 840	18 376	2005	
7 014	2 624	4 952	3 553	292 672	80 593	105 649	88 328	18 102	2006	
4	1 115	...	4 277	120	...	120	...	...	2003	Gibraltar
4	1 150	...	4 422	124	...	124	...	...	2004	
4	1 176	...	4 568	128	...	128	...	...	2005	
4	1 209	...	4 427	128	...	128	...	...	2006	
785	3 237	1 263	2 778	30 621	8 909	18 734	2 251	726	2003	Grèce
809	3 263	-699	2 760	30 525	9 124	18 138	2 476	787	2004	
781	2 909	-1 317	2 831	31 439	8 970	18 937	2 615	916	2005	
937	3 141	-1 982	2 854	31 814	8 208	19 490	3 052	1 064	2006	
204	...	587	2 416	24 471	3 652	6 054	13 207	1 559	2003	Hongrie
233	...	740	2 386	24 111	3 342	6 070	13 014	1 685	2004	
270	...	1 127	2 473	24 946	2 952	6 813	13 438	1 743	2005	
273	...	955	2 445	24 628	2 967	7 138	12 726	1 797	2006	
103	68	335	4 882	1 412	91	591	...	730	2003	Islande
119	71	348	4 925	1 441	103	597	...	741	2004	
134	65	335	4 838	1 431	99	586	...	746	2005	
179	35	392	5 108	1 555	78	624	...	853	2006	
731	172	62	3 633	14 456	2 802	7 375	4 058	221	2003	Irlande
691	151	6	3 603	14 569	2 501	7 741	4 050	276	2004	
798	105	136	3 472	14 340	2 917	7 213	3 855	355	2005	
814	125	-141	3 530	14 950	2 607	7 497	4 459	386	2006	
2 700	3 234	-1 070	3 169	182 524	15 272	87 786	70 690	8 776	2003	Italie[4]
2 704	3 381	1 611	3 112	181 027	17 190	81 638	73 354	8 844	2004	
2 864	3 411	1 110	3 132	183 571	16 978	79 512	78 501	8 580	2005	
3 052	3 515	2 865	3 076	181 278	17 154	78 909	76 880	8 336	2006	
40	190	8	1 340	3 117	63	1 131	1 497	425	2003	Lettonie
48	205	3	1 311	3 033	51	1 050	1 480	452	2004	
59	264	4	1 323	3 043	61	999	1 509	475	2005	
66	200	20	1 453	3 324	55	1 254	1 563	452	2006	
22	111	140	1 673	5 779	211	2 138	2 661	769	2003	Lituanie
11	115	151	1 699	5 839	206	2 221	2 651	761	2004	
46	146	120	1 782	6 083	226	2 355	2 797	704	2005	
53	141	-105	1 893	6 424	311	2 563	2 773	777	2006	
392	...	...	8 722	3 939	78	2 279	1 182	400	2003	Luxembourg
427	...	...	9 424	4 317	94	2 522	1 333	368	2004	
433	...	...	9 453	4 397	82	2 644	1 310	362	2005	
407	...	...	9 364	4 426	110	2 553	1 371	391	2006	
79	23	...	2 017	806	...	806	...	...	2003	Malte
101	23	...	2 069	833	...	833	...	...	2004	
91	23	...	2 052	831	...	831	...	...	2005	
77	23	...	2 012	818	...	818	...	...	2006	

52

Production, trade and consumption of commercial energy *(continued)*
Thousand metric tons of oil equivalent and kilograms per capita
Production, commerce et consommation d'énergie commerciale *(suite)*
Milliers de tonnes d'équivalent pétrole et kilogrammes par habitant

| Region, country or area | Year Année | Primary energy production – Production d'énergie primaire | | | | | Changes in stocks Variations des stocks | Imports Importations | Exports Exportations |
		Total Totale	Solids Solides	Liquids Liquides	Gas Gaz	Electricity Electricité			
Netherlands	2003	61 676	...	3 195	58 013	468	-235	129 157	98 288
	2004	71 903	...	2 975	68 428	500	432	130 747	107 467
	2005	65 701	...	2 652	62 517	532	1 178	144 202	112 600
	2006	64 302	...	2 161	61 595	545	95	152 384	121 450
Norway[5]	2003	238 901	1 976	154 140	73 633	9 152	1 071	5 871	214 946
	2004	242 795	1 949	153 183	78 243	9 419	-396	6 087	218 699
	2005	239 221	987	141 691	84 756	11 787	346	5 166	208 827
	2006	230 036	1 608	130 942	87 127	10 359	516	5 548	207 304
Poland	2003	76 233	71 132	794	4 013	294	260	32 287	18 156
	2004	75 846	70 253	900	4 364	330	341	34 192	18 265
	2005	74 058	68 448	958	4 316	336	1 954	36 595	18 307
	2006	72 304	66 758	953	4 312	282	-288	40 542	18 048
Portugal	2003	1 431	...	0	...	1 431	449	23 415	1 575
	2004	950	...	0	...	950	-413	23 948	1 703
	2005	599	...	0	...	599	415	25 992	2 148
	2006	1 315	...	70	...	1 245	55	24 633	3 186
Republic of Moldova	2003	6	...	0	...	6	52	3 540	12
	2004	13	...	8	...	5	-7	3 560	43
	2005	10	...	5	...	5	0	3 747	21
	2006	11	...	4	...	7	-20	3 546	22
Romania	2003	24 783	5 724	5 909	11 587	1 562	-249	14 001	3 833
	2004	24 654	5 502	5 724	11 531	1 897	1 010	16 383	4 633
	2005	24 129	5 383	5 751	10 780	2 215	-340	16 852	6 259
	2006	24 408	6 044	5 676	10 625	2 063	-837	17 360	5 737
Russian Federation	2003	1 108 766	106 842	419 673	555 733	26 517	12 165	25 533	493 928
	2004	1 160 339	108 768	457 537	566 269	27 764	6 775	22 063	544 716
	2005	1 188 192	119 007	467 819	573 466	27 899	6 859	20 337	565 719
	2006	1 210 122	119 645	477 262	584 652	28 563	13 924	20 843	563 023
Serbia and Montenegro	2003	10 522	8 574	773	328	847	0	5 433	400
	2004	10 661	8 767	652	285	956	0	6 888	755
	2005	9 457	7 519	649	254	1 035	0	6 682	943
	2006	9 663	7 812	646	262	943	-21	7 260	917
Slovakia	2003	3 047	907	52	236	1 852	-55	16 483	4 185
	2004	2 959	864	53	215	1 826	581	17 426	4 697
	2005	2 930	735	65	197	1 932	93	17 366	4 860
	2006	2 910	645	69	255	1 942	-176	17 168	5 091
Slovenia	2003	1 774	1 050	0	5	719	40	4 255	588
	2004	1 872	1 045	0	5	821	40	4 402	737
	2005	1 794	987	0	4	804	9	4 660	862
	2006	1 778	983	5	4	786	-93	4 787	1 011
Spain	2003	17 680	6 811	515	219	10 137	-82	116 795	5 569
	2004	17 235	6 632	474	344	9 785	-782	125 425	7 026
	2005	15 669	6 331	426	160	8 752	1 777	134 433	7 229
	2006	16 154	6 082	313	61	9 699	2 795	136 366	9 214
Sweden	2003	10 765	233	68	...	10 464	1 037	32 929	10 490
	2004	12 312	258	144	...	11 910	-435	31 998	12 102
	2005	12 982	205	208	...	12 570	765	31 728	11 786
	2006	11 605	179	273	...	11 152	-731	31 320	11 652
Switzerland[6]	2003	5 562	...	0	27	5 535	-160	18 126	3 463
	2004	5 400	...	3	28	5 370	15	17 976	2 963
	2005	4 887	...	7	26	4 854	138	19 241	3 230
	2006	5 261	...	8	31	5 223	73	19 011	3 215
TFYR of Macedonia	2003	2 108	1 989	...	...	118	-37	1 376	336
	2004	2 080	1 953	...	...	127	4	1 314	210
	2005	1 983	1 854	...	...	128	-60	1 517	330
	2006	1 931	1 789	...	...	142	16	1 627	360

52

Production, trade and consumption of commercial energy *(continued)*
Thousand metric tons of oil equivalent and kilograms per capita
Production, commerce et consommation d'énergie commerciale *(suite)*
Milliers de tonnes d'équivalent pétrole et kilogrammes par habitant

Bunkers - Soutes		Unallocated	Consumption - Consommation							
Air Avion	Sea Maritime	Non distribué	Per capita Par habitant	Total Totale	Solids Solides	Liquids Liquides	Gas Gaz	Electricity Electricité	Year Année	Région, pays ou zone
3 288	13 774	-16 387	5 684	92 047	8 535	41 585	39 998	1 929	2003	Pays-Bas
3 518	14 965	-14 635	5 590	90 881	8 333	39 826	40 828	1 895	2004	
3 616	17 178	-13 689	5 451	88 965	7 992	39 338	39 531	2 105	2005	
3 666	17 830	-14 303	5 384	87 948	7 506	39 678	38 374	2 391	2006	
210	567	391	5 848	26 782	789	10 220	5 944	9 829	2003	Norvège[5]
242	520	1 798	5 844	26 936	921	9 929	5 684	10 402	2004	
272	701	4 375	5 951	27 628	776	10 319	5 782	10 751	2005	
378	507	-2 484	6 086	28 364	713	11 905	5 313	10 432	2006	
292	290	1 742	2 298	87 779	57 998	17 849	12 512	-580	2003	Pologne
286	258	1 921	2 330	88 967	57 023	19 213	13 201	-469	2004	
324	328	2 123	2 296	87 617	55 376	19 273	13 594	-625	2005	
431	300	2 371	2 412	91 983	58 252	20 645	13 748	-663	2006	
635	589	1 247	1 949	20 351	3 381	12 370	2 929	1 671	2003	Portugal
695	670	1 102	2 013	21 140	3 420	12 542	3 670	1 507	2004	
721	589	1 227	2 037	21 490	3 408	12 729	4 167	1 186	2005	
772	647	961	1 921	20 328	3 516	11 055	4 044	1 713	2006	
12	...	0	960	3 468	89	597	2 480	302	2003	Rép. de Moldova
11	...	0	978	3 526	84	639	2 545	258	2004	
12	...	0	1 036	3 723	76	646	2 726	275	2005	
12	...	0	988	3 542	91	630	2 513	309	2006	
118	...	401	1 596	34 681	8 111	8 821	16 366	1 383	2003	Roumanie
137	...	1 535	1 556	33 722	8 125	8 316	15 486	1 795	2004	
111	...	1 089	1 566	33 862	7 915	8 491	15 491	1 966	2005	
137	...	1 597	1 628	35 134	8 554	8 654	16 231	1 695	2006	
4 876	...	10 042	4 242	613 288	90 429	116 825	380 667	25 367	2003	Féd. de Russie
4 789	...	7 686	4 300	618 435	87 514	118 633	385 179	27 109	2004	
5 178	...	9 604	4 340	621 169	86 988	118 825	388 521	26 835	2005	
5 470	...	9 231	4 487	639 317	89 809	123 741	398 564	27 203	2006	
64	...	593	1 408	14 897	8 921	2 867	2 022	1 087	2003	Serbie-et-Monténégro
47	...	752	1 521	15 994	9 265	3 227	2 569	933	2004	
50	...	706	1 379	14 440	8 031	3 391	2 151	867	2005	
54	...	594	1 472	15 380	8 621	3 673	2 213	873	2006	
34	...	468	2 770	14 898	4 228	2 714	6 299	1 658	2003	Slovaquie
27	...	129	2 778	14 951	4 113	3 063	6 109	1 666	2004	
39	...	162	2 810	15 141	3 826	3 126	6 537	1 652	2005	
40	...	313	2 747	14 810	4 112	2 981	5 975	1 741	2006	
26	0	4	2 692	5 370	1 324	2 306	1 007	733	2003	Slovénie
20	0	52	2 717	5 425	1 340	2 331	999	754	2004	
23	22	56	2 740	5 483	1 293	2 382	1 032	776	2005	
25	30	54	2 758	5 539	1 300	2 449	999	790	2006	
2 798	7 150	7 699	2 651	111 341	20 379	56 991	23 726	10 245	2003	Espagne
3 103	7 376	7 884	2 765	118 055	21 887	58 674	27 969	9 525	2004	
3 113	8 094	5 893	2 857	123 996	21 296	60 904	33 160	8 636	2005	
3 245	8 451	5 257	2 804	123 557	18 904	60 770	34 466	9 417	2006	
513	1 645	2 291	3 094	27 718	2 633	12 530	987	11 567	2003	Suède
628	1 937	2 027	3 119	28 052	2 908	12 432	983	11 729	2004	
634	1 978	2 099	3 040	27 449	2 580	11 998	936	11 934	2005	
663	2 126	1 914	3 006	27 300	2 624	12 025	980	11 672	2006	
1 210	10	27	2 607	19 137	142	10 808	2 920	5 268	2003	Suisse[6]
1 155	9	7	2 580	19 227	133	10 772	3 012	5 309	2004	
1 180	12	6	2 623	19 562	149	10 920	3 092	5 400	2005	
1 247	9	-17	2 638	19 744	138	11 144	3 007	5 455	2006	
7	...	6	1 565	3 172	2 088	809	74	200	2003	L'ex-R.Y. Macédoine
6	...	12	1 558	3 162	2 046	823	65	229	2004	
6	...	11	1 577	3 212	2 026	849	71	266	2005	
5	...	24	1 545	3 153	1 888	894	75	296	2006	

52

Production, trade and consumption of commercial energy *(continued)*
Thousand metric tons of oil equivalent and kilograms per capita

Production, commerce et consommation d'énergie commerciale *(suite)*
Milliers de tonnes d'équivalent pétrole et kilogrammes par habitant

Region, country or area	Year Année	Primary energy production – Production d'énergie primaire					Changes in stocks Variations des stocks	Imports Importations	Exports Exportations
		Total Totale	Solids Solides	Liquids Liquides	Gas Gaz	Electricity Electricité			
Ukraine	2003	62 903	33 201	4 008	17 885	7 809	0	87 422	17 094
	2004	62 772	30 809	4 370	19 087	8 507	308	87 354	18 159
	2005	63 791	31 236	4 471	19 374	8 710	-2 690	77 322	12 797
	2006	65 053	31 902	4 615	19 655	8 882	1 720	68 533	7 832
United Kingdom	2003	234 940	17 038	106 727	102 926	8 249	-2 203	100 592	111 137
	2004	214 822	15 121	95 998	96 006	7 697	1 209	118 337	101 443
	2005	193 210	12 350	85 332	87 581	7 947	720	126 231	88 720
	2006	178 878	11 163	80 127	80 009	7 579	2 436	140 934	86 241
Oceania	**2003**	**263 241**	**187 108**	**32 998**	**39 209**	**3 927**	**344**	**37 868**	**170 879**
	2004	**268 061**	**194 640**	**29 706**	**39 501**	**4 214**	**264**	**38 556**	**175 669**
	2005	**277 765**	**204 054**	**26 591**	**43 163**	**3 957**	**-1 053**	**41 229**	**183 369**
	2006	**279 316**	**204 411**	**25 997**	**44 831**	**4 078**	**-1 540**	**43 687**	**184 831**
Australia	2003	250 455	184 899	29 308	34 790	1 458	493	27 344	166 100
	2004	255 823	192 389	26 451	35 557	1 426	146	27 428	171 451
	2005	265 665	201 765	23 085	39 372	1 443	-1 020	29 931	178 585
	2006	266 467	201 883	22 130	40 928	1 526	-1 755	32 190	179 566
Cook Islands	2003	...	...	...	...	...	...	13	...
	2004	...	...	...	...	...	...	18	...
	2005	...	...	...	...	...	...	20	...
	2006	...	...	...	...	...	...	*21	...
Fiji	2003	*57	...	...	...	*57	...	1 023	*118
	2004	*58	...	...	...	*58	...	1 066	*134
	2005	*58	...	...	...	*58	...	950	*124
	2006	*59	...	...	...	*59	...	984	*119
French Polynesia	2003	10	...	...	...	10	...	312	...
	2004	13	...	...	...	13	...	311	...
	2005	11	...	...	...	11	...	333	...
	2006	14	...	...	...	14	...	326	...
Kiribati *	2003	...	...	...	...	...	...	10	...
	2004	...	...	...	...	...	...	10	...
	2005	...	...	...	...	...	...	10	...
	2006	...	...	...	...	...	...	12	...
Marshall Islands *	2003	...	...	...	...	...	...	28	...
	2004	...	...	...	...	...	...	29	...
	2005	...	...	...	...	...	...	29	...
	2006	...	...	...	...	...	...	30	...
Nauru *	2003	...	...	...	...	...	...	53	...
	2004	...	...	...	...	...	...	53	...
	2005	...	...	...	...	...	...	53	...
	2006	...	...	...	...	...	...	53	...
New Caledonia	2003	28	...	...	...	28	...	868	30
	2004	29	...	...	...	29	...	808	30
	2005	31	...	...	...	31	...	892	*31
	2006	37	...	...	...	37	...	939	*32
New Zealand	2003	10 046	2 209	1 262	4 287	2 289	-224	6 686	2 267
	2004	9 815	2 250	1 121	3 837	2 606	322	7 168	1 908
	2005	9 215	2 289	1 044	3 549	2 333	-33	7 089	2 142
	2006	9 534	2 528	1 000	3 643	2 363	-78	7 161	2 389
Niue *	2003	...	...	...	...	...	...	1	...
	2004	...	...	...	...	...	...	1	...
	2005	...	...	...	...	...	...	1	...
	2006	...	...	...	...	...	...	1	...
Palau *	2003	2	...	...	...	2	...	54	...
	2004	2	...	...	...	2	...	54	...
	2005	2	...	...	...	2	...	54	...
	2006	2	...	...	...	2	...	54	...

52

Production, trade and consumption of commercial energy *(continued)*
Thousand metric tons of oil equivalent and kilograms per capita
Production, commerce et consommation d'énergie commerciale *(suite)*
Milliers de tonnes d'équivalent pétrole et kilogrammes par habitant

Air Avion	Sea Maritime	Non distribué	Per capita Par habitant	Total Totale	Solids Solides	Liquids Liquides	Gas Gaz	Electricity Electricité	Year Année	Région, pays ou zone
372	...	3 002	2 716	129 856	37 115	13 016	72 340	7 385	2003	Ukraine
378	...	3 358	2 706	127 924	33 042	13 641	73 192	8 049	2004	
376	...	-153	2 778	130 783	33 823	14 008	74 960	7 992	2005	
335	...	-494	2 656	124 192	36 671	14 813	64 724	7 984	2006	
9 720	1 770	454	3 618	214 669	40 264	70 547	95 424	8 435	2003	Royaume-Uni
10 759	2 092	-827	3 660	218 507	39 947	73 122	97 097	8 341	2004	
12 122	2 056	543	3 576	215 304	41 160	71 150	94 332	8 663	2005	
11 451	2 352	-1 644	3 615	218 997	45 235	75 467	90 069	8 225	2006	
3 380	**1 135**	**-2 129**	**3 935**	**127 506**	**50 729**	**43 811**	**29 040**	**3 927**	**2003**	**Océanie**
3 429	**1 231**	**-2 954**	**3 923**	**128 984**	**51 443**	**44 085**	**29 242**	**4 214**	**2004**	
3 831	**1 264**	**-2 690**	**4 025**	**134 279**	**54 975**	**45 933**	**29 415**	**3 957**	**2005**	
3 552	**1 428**	**-827**	**4 002**	**135 569**	**55 735**	**45 805**	**29 951**	**4 078**	**2006**	
2 246	733	-1 960	5 537	110 192	49 338	34 775	24 621	1 458	2003	Australie
2 266	842	-2 803	5 529	111 356	50 072	34 583	25 274	1 426	2004	
2 654	857	-2 633	5 741	117 160	53 500	36 605	25 612	1 443	2005	
2 387	988	-934	5 720	118 415	54 250	36 602	26 037	1 526	2006	
*2	...	...	616	11	...	11	...	...	2003	Iles Cook
0	...	...	909	18	...	18	...	...	2004	
0	...	...	1 014	20	...	20	...	...	2005	
0	...	...	*1 009	*21	...	*21	...	...	2006	
*300	*71	...	713	591	*9	524	...	*57	2003	Fidji
*232	*81	...	809	676	*9	609	...	*58	2004	
*227	*71	...	696	586	*8	520	...	*58	2005	
*290	*66	...	666	569	*8	501	...	*59	2006	
*6	*36	...	1 131	280	...	269	...	10	2003	Polynésie française
*6	*46	...	1 085	272	...	259	...	13	2004	
*6	*47	...	1 145	291	...	280	...	11	2005	
*6	*50	...	1 108	284	...	270	...	14	2006	
2	...	...	88	8	...	8	...	...	2003	Kiribati *
2	...	...	82	8	...	8	...	...	2004	
2	...	...	80	8	...	8	...	...	2005	
2	...	...	98	10	...	10	...	...	2006	
...	...	...	502	28	...	28	...	...	2003	Iles Marshall *
...	...	...	503	29	...	29	...	...	2004	
...	...	...	488	29	...	29	...	...	2005	
...	...	...	503	30	...	30	...	...	2006	
7	...	...	3 658	46	...	46	...	...	2003	Nauru *
7	...	...	3 590	46	...	46	...	...	2004	
7	...	...	3 524	46	...	46	...	...	2005	
7	...	...	3 457	46	...	46	...	...	2006	
9	...	...	3 759	857	219	610	...	28	2003	Nouvelle-Calédonie
11	...	...	3 451	796	197	571	...	29	2004	
10	...	...	3 768	882	182	669	...	31	2005	
14	...	...	3 905	929	198	695	...	37	2006	
753	262	-162	3 451	13 837	1 162	6 099	4 287	2 289	2003	Nouvelle-Zélande
846	231	-287	3 439	13 966	1 165	6 333	3 860	2 606	2004	
867	258	-370	3 279	13 442	1 284	6 263	3 562	2 333	2005	
786	292	-119	3 241	13 427	1 278	6 131	3 656	2 363	2006	
...	...	...	574	1	...	1	...	...	2003	Nioué *
...	...	...	576	1	...	1	...	...	2004	
...	...	...	602	1	...	1	...	...	2005	
...	...	...	625	1	...	1	...	...	2006	
15	...	...	1 969	40	...	38	...	2	2003	Palaos *
15	...	...	1 940	40	...	38	...	2	2004	
15	...	...	1 912	40	...	38	...	2	2005	
15	...	...	1 845	40	...	38	...	2	2006	

Production, trade and consumption of commercial energy *(continued)*
Thousand metric tons of oil equivalent and kilograms per capita
Production, commerce et consommation d'énergie commerciale *(suite)*
Milliers de tonnes d'équivalent pétrole et kilogrammes par habitant

| Region, country or area | Year Année | Primary energy production – Production d'énergie primaire | | | | | Changes in stocks | Imports Importations | Exports Exportations |
		Total Totale	Solids Solides	Liquids Liquides	Gas Gaz	Electricity Electricité	Variations des stocks		
Papua New Guinea	2003	2 639	...	2 427	132	80	*75	1 279	2 364
	2004	2 318	...	2 134	107	77	*-204	1 410	2 147
	2005	2 780	...	2 462	241	77	0	1 666	2 487
	2006	3 200	...	2 867	259	74	294	1 713	2 726
Samoa *	2003	3	...	...	...	3	...	50	...
	2004	3	...	...	...	3	...	52	...
	2005	3	...	...	...	3	...	53	...
	2006	3	...	...	...	3	...	53	...
Solomon Islands *	2003	...	...	...	...	...	...	61	...
	2004	...	...	...	...	...	...	61	...
	2005	...	...	...	...	...	...	61	...
	2006	...	...	...	...	...	...	63	...
Tonga	2003	...	...	...	...	...	...	47	...
	2004	...	...	...	...	...	...	46	...
	*2005	...	...	...	...	...	...	45	...
	*2006	...	...	...	...	...	...	45	...
Vanuatu *	2003	...	...	...	...	...	...	30	...
	2004	...	...	...	...	...	...	30	...
	2005	...	...	...	...	...	...	30	...
	2006	...	...	...	...	...	...	31	...
Wallis and Futuna Is.	*2003	...	...	...	...	...	...	9	...
	2004	...	...	...	...	...	...	9	...
	2005	...	...	...	...	...	...	9	...
	2006	...	...	...	...	...	...	9	...

Source:
United Nations Statistics Division, New York, the energy statistics database, last accessed June 2009.

1   Refers to the Southern African Customs Union.
2   For statistical purposes, the data for China do not include those for the Hong Kong Special Administrative Region (Hong Kong SAR), Macao Special
     Administrative Region (Macao SAR) and Taiwan Province of China.
3   Including Monaco.
4   Including San Marino.
5   Including Svalbard and Jan Mayen Islands.
6   Including Liechtenstein.

52

Production, trade and consumption of commercial energy *(continued)*
Thousand metric tons of oil equivalent and kilograms per capita
Production, commerce et consommation d'énergie commerciale *(suite)*
Milliers de tonnes d'équivalent pétrole et kilogrammes par habitant

Bunkers - Soutes		Unallocated	Consumption - Consommation							
Air Avion	Sea Maritime	Non distribué	Per capita Par habitant	Total Totale	Solids Solides	Liquids Liquides	Gas Gaz	Electricity Electricité	Year Année	Région, pays ou zone
										Papouasie-Nvl-Guinée
*33	*32	-7	245	1 420	...	1 208	132	80	2003	
*38	*32	136	266	1 579	...	1 395	107	77	2004	
*38	*32	312	260	1 577	...	1 259	241	77	2005	
*39	*32	226	257	1 596	...	1 263	259	74	2006	
...	...	...	297	54	...	50	...	3	2003	Samoa *
...	...	...	303	55	...	52	...	3	2004	
...	...	...	306	56	...	53	...	3	2005	
...	...	...	303	56	...	53	...	3	2006	
3	...	...	130	58	...	58	...	...	2003	Iles Salomon *
3	...	...	127	58	...	58	...	...	2004	
3	...	...	124	58	...	58	...	...	2005	
3	...	...	123	59	...	59	...	...	2006	
*1	...	...	458	46	...	46	...	...	2003	Tonga
*1	...	...	443	45	...	45	...	...	2004	
1	...	...	432	44	...	44	...	...	*2005	
1	...	...	437	44	...	44	...	...	*2006	
...	...	...	140	30	...	30	...	...	2003	Vanuatu *
...	...	...	139	30	...	30	...	...	2004	
...	...	...	138	30	...	30	...	...	2005	
...	...	...	139	31	...	31	...	...	2006	
1	...	...	558	8	...	8	...	...	*2003	Iles Wallis et Futuna
1	...	...	564	9	...	9	...	...	2004	
1	...	...	555	9	...	9	...	...	2005	
1	...	...	537	9	...	9	...	...	2006	

Source:
Organisation des Nations Unies, Division de statistique, New York, la base de données pour les statistiques de l'énergie, dernier accès juin 2009.

1   Se réfèrent à l'Union douanière d'Afrique australe.
2   Pour la présentation des statistiques, les données pour la Chine ne comprennent pas la Région Administrative Spéciale de Hong Kong (Hong Kong RAS), la Région Administrative Spéciale de Macao (Macao RAS) et la province de Taiwan.
3   Y compris Monaco.
4   Y compris Saint-Marin.
5   Y compris îles Svalbard et Jan Mayen.
6   Y compris Liechtenstein.

Region, country or area Région, pays ou zone	Year Année	Hard coal, lignite and peat Houille, lignite et tourbe	Crude petroleum and NGL Pétrole brut et LGN	Motor gasoline Essence auto	Jet fuel Carbu-réacteurs	Gas-diesel oil Gazole/ carburant diesel	Residual fuel oil Mazout résiduel	Liquefied petroleum gas Gaz de pétrole liquéfiés	Natural gas Gaz naturel Terajoules Térajoules	Electricity Electricité Million kWh Millions de kWh
		Thousand metric tons						Milliers de tonnes		
World **Monde**	2003	5 205 138	3 758 384	872 360	205 889	1 078 043	594 417	220 197	104 039 984	16 784 964
	2004	5 590 725	3 898 109	893 725	218 075	1 123 160	601 312	231 966	106 644 763	17 549 588
	2005	5 926 425	3 957 962	895 220	225 774	1 162 425	598 400	233 905	109 598 318	18 340 700
	2006	6 224 491	3 983 445	895 350	229 540	1 180 533	595 209	236 492	113 290 917	19 048 038
Africa **Afrique**	2003	244 273[1]	434 435	22 575	7 977	35 441	33 990	12 827	5 678 973	509 131
	2004	248 325[1]	475 045	21 343	8 034	36 087	34 162	12 369	6 044 955	539 446
	2005	250 740[1]	503 192	18 611	8 429	37 797	35 051	12 600	7 142 386	563 972
	2006	250 448[1]	503 567	20 361	7 941	38 959	34 147	12 191	7 866 551	592 544
Algeria Algérie	2003	...	102 501	1 893	1 315	6 186	6 093	9 756	3 248 416	29 571
	2004	...	107 144	1 925	986	6 340	5 560	9 223	3 216 262	31 250
	2005	...	110 285	2 059	1 069	5 946	5 055	9 337	3 586 296	32 875
	2006	...	108 534	2 320	965	6 385	5 337	8 750	3 844 884	35 226
Angola Angola	2003	...	43 083[2]	108	352	683	609	40	24 700	1 995
	2004	...	49 443[2]	96	302	669	604	28	28 500	2 240
	2005	...	62 314[2]	134	290	675	609	24	28 500	2 632
	2006	...	70 242[2]	98	323	681	644	24	30 400	2 959
Benin Bénin	2003	...	...	...	...	...	...	...	...	80
	2004	...	...	...	...	...	...	...	...	81
	2005	...	...	...	...	...	...	...	...	107
	2006	...	...	...	...	...	...	...	...	128
Burkina Faso Burkina Faso	2003	...	...	...	...	...	...	...	...	445
	2004	...	...	...	...	...	...	...	...	473
	2005	...	...	...	...	...	...	...	...	516
	2006	...	...	...	...	...	...	...	...	548
Burundi Burundi	2003	5[3]	...	...	...	...	...	...	...	104
	2004	5[3]	...	...	...	...	...	...	...	94
	2005	5[3]	...	...	...	...	...	...	...	102
	2006	*5[3]	...	...	...	...	...	...	...	95
Cameroon Cameroun	2003	...	4 111[2]	290	69	446	327	21	...	3 684
	2004	...	4 356[2]	402	69	607	388	28	...	4 110
	2005	...	4 081[2]	393	62	610	341	26	...	4 145
	2006	...	4 326[2]	354	71	577	354	22	...	3 954
Cape Verde Cap-Vert	2003	...	...	...	...	...	...	...	...	200
	2004	...	...	...	...	...	...	...	...	220
	2005		...							237
	2006	...	...	...	...	...	...	...	...	252
Central African Rep. * Rép. centrafricaine *	2003	...	...	...	...	...	...	...	...	110
	2004	...	...	...	...	...	...	...	...	111
	2005	...	...	...	...	...	...	...	...	113
	2006	...	...	...	...	...	...	...	...	114
Chad Tchad	2003	...	1 798[2]	...	...	...	...	...	...	*94
	2004	...	8 505[2]	...	...	...	...	...	...	*97
	2005	...	8 808[2]	...	...	...	...	...	...	*100
	2006	...	7 874[2]	...	...	...	...	...	...	*104
Comoros * Comores *	2003	...	...	...	...	...	...	...	...	20
	2004	...	...	...	...	...	...	...	...	21
	2005	...	...	...	...	...	...	...	...	21
	2006	...	...	...	...	...	...	...	...	22
Congo Congo	2003	...	11 142	53	38	119	287	4	650	408
	2004	...	11 595	49	47	120	295	5	769	465
	2005	...	12 636	47	45	110	210	5	890	434
	2006	...	14 296	53	53	123	377	7	923	453

Region, country or area Région, pays ou zone	Year Année	Hard coal, lignite and peat Houille, lignite et tourbe	Crude petroleum and NGL Pétrole brut et LGN	Motor gasoline Essence auto	Jet fuel Carbu-réacteurs	Gas-diesel oil Gazole/ carburant diesel	Residual fuel oil Mazout résiduel	Liquefied petroleum gas Gaz de pétrole liquéfiés	Natural gas Gaz naturel Terajoules Térajoules	Electricity Electricité Million kWh Millions de kWh
				Thousand metric tons Milliers de tonnes						
Côte d'Ivoire Côte d'Ivoire	2003	...	1 028[2]	359	104	788	318	72	47 770	5 093
	2004	...	1 126[2]	436	88	1 180	431	96	60 709	5 403
	2005	...	1 994[2]	494	88	1 205	687	87	67 803	5 566
	2006	...	3 135[2]	605	88	1 269	521	101	63 681	5 535
Dem. Rep. of the Congo Rép. dém. du Congo	2003	105[4]	1 083[2]	...	...	...	...	...	...	6 258
	2004	108[4]	1 033[2]	...	...	...	...	...	...	6 852
	2005	120[4]	984[2]	...	...	...	...	...	...	7 419
	2006	124[4]	886[2]	...	...	...	...	...	...	7 886
Djibouti Djibouti	2003	...	...	...	...	...	...	...	...	200
	2004	...	...	...	...	...	...	...	...	215
	2005	...	...	...	...	...	...	...	...	255
	2006	...	...	...	...	...	...	...	...	280
Egypt Egypte	2003	37[4]	39 644	6 306	1 469	8 235	10 532	1 739	1 214 024	91 932
	2004	33[4]	37 605	*5 000	2 080	7 922	11 273	1 724	1 311 413	101 299
	2005	33[4]	36 931	2 972	2 146	8 179	11 643	1 713	1 880 223	111 690
	2006	25[4]	33 076	3 659	2 033	8 440	10 653	1 711	1 935 875	118 407
Equatorial Guinea Guinée équatoriale	2003	...	13 346[2]	...	...	...	...	...	18 773	*26
	2004	...	17 662[2]	...	...	...	...	...	*18 730	*27
	2005	...	17 973[2]	...	...	...	...	...	*18 730	*28
	2006	...	17 144[2]	...	...	...	...	...	*18 730	*29
Eritrea Erythrée	2003	...	...	...	...	...	...	...	...	276
	2004	...	...	...	...	...	...	...	...	283
	2005	...	...	...	...	...	...	...	...	289
	2006	...	...	...	...	...	...	...	...	269
Ethiopia Ethiopie	2003	...	...	...	...	...	...	...	...	2 302
	2004	...	...	...	...	...	...	...	...	2 540
	2005	...	...	...	...	...	...	...	...	2 872
	2006	...	...	...	...	...	...	...	...	3 270
Gabon Gabon	2003	...	11 056[2]	69	54	210	302	9	4 421	1 504
	2004	...	10 736[2]	68	45	228	324	9	4 912	1 537
	2005	...	10 690[2]	79	59	225	305	10	4 912	1 611
	2006	...	10 736[2]	44	55	213	324	7	4 912	1 726
Gambia * Gambie *	2003	...	...	...	...	...	...	...	...	151
	2004	...	...	...	...	...	...	...	...	156
	2005	...	...	...	...	...	...	...	...	161
	2006	...	...	...	...	...	...	...	...	166
Ghana Ghana	2003	...	...	434	91	493	216	53	...	5 905
	2004	...	...	580	107	625	239	66	...	6 044
	2005	...	...	567	113	520	242	78	...	6 793
	2006	...	...	294	46	294	156	36	...	8 435
Guinea * Guinée *	2003	...	...	...	...	...	...	...	...	782
	2004	...	...	...	...	...	...	...	...	801
	2005	...	...	...	...	...	...	...	...	816
	2006	...	...	...	...	...	...	...	...	836
Guinea-Bissau * Guinée-Bissau *	2003	...	...	...	...	...	...	...	...	61
	2004	...	...	...	...	...	...	...	...	63
	2005	...	...	...	...	...	...	...	...	64
	2006	...	...	...	...	...	...	...	...	66
Kenya Kenya	2003	...	...	263	204	411	524	24	...	5 506
	2004	...	...	275	212	387	620	27	...	5 889
	2005	...	...	266	205	374	549	26	...	6 003
	2006	...	...	179	226	368	596	30	...	6 477

Region, country or area Région, pays ou zone	Year Année	Hard coal, lignite and peat Houille, lignite et tourbe	Crude petroleum and NGL Pétrole brut et LGN	Motor gasoline Essence auto	Jet fuel Carbu-réacteurs	Gas-diesel oil Gazole/ carburant diesel	Residual fuel oil Mazout résiduel	Liquefied petroleum gas Gaz de pétrole liquéfiés	Natural gas Gaz naturel Terajoules Térajoules	Electricity Electricité Million kWh Millions de kWh
					Thousand metric tons Milliers de tonnes					
Liberia Libéria	2003	...	...	...	...	...	...	...	...	320
	2004	...	...	...	...	...	...	...	...	330
	*2005	...	...	...	...	...	...	...	...	338
	*2006	...	...	...	...	...	...	...	...	351
Libyan Arab Jamah. Jamah. arabe libyenne	2003	...	70 781	1 517	1 491	4 737	4 556	310	243 200	18 943
	2004	...	77 427	1 507	1 504	4 782	4 597	310	306 280	20 202
	2005	...	83 021	1 237	1 339	4 849	4 443	350	429 400	22 317
	2006	...	87 369	1 237	1 255	4 503	4 419	395	562 400	23 992
Madagascar Madagascar	2003	...	...	*113	*1	*57	*77	*6	...	900
	2004	...	...	*113	*1	*57	*77	*6	...	990
	*2005	...	...	114	1	58	78	6	...	1 035
	*2006	...	...	114	1	58	78	6	...	1 065
Malawi Malawi	2003	66[4]	...	...	...	...	...	...	...	1 337
	2004	*70[4]	...	...	...	...	...	...	...	1 477
	2005	45[4]	...	...	...	...	...	...	...	1 544
	2006	*55[4]	...	...	...	...	...	...	...	1 556
Mali * Mali *	2003	...	...	...	...	...	...	...	...	449
	2004	...	...	...	...	...	...	...	...	465
	2005	...	...	...	...	...	...	...	...	475
	2006	...	...	...	...	...	...	...	...	489
Mauritania Mauritanie	2003	...	...	...	...	...	...	...	...	242
	2004	...	...	...	...	...	...	...	...	263
	2005	...	...	...	...	...	...	...	...	250
	2006	...	...	...	...	...	...	...	...	277
Mauritius Maurice	2003	...	...	...	...	...	...	...	...	2 082
	2004	...	...	...	...	...	...	...	...	2 165
	2005	...	...	...	...	...	...	...	...	2 271
	2006	...	...	...	...	...	...	...	...	2 350
Morocco Maroc	2003	...	10[2]	132	108	1 535	1 747	67	1 633	18 107
	2004	...	11[2]	257	174	2 254	2 264	104	1 977	19 336
	2005	...	7[2]	372	264	2 295	2 545	204	1 782	22 456
	2006	...	11[2]	373	236	2 033	2 265	192	2 600	23 192
Mozambique Mozambique	2003	37[4]	...	...	...	...	...	...	106	10 907
	2004	17[4]	...	...	...	...	...	...	52 312	11 714
	2005	3[4]	...	...	...	...	...	...	88 029	13 285
	2006	41[4]	...	...	...	...	...	...	105 358	14 737
Niger Niger	2003	189[4]	...	...	...	...	...	...	...	*192
	2004	200[4]	...	...	...	...	...	...	...	*212
	2005	182[4]	...	...	...	...	...	...	...	*195
	*2006	183[4]	...	...	...	...	...	...	...	179
Nigeria Nigéria	2003	23[4]	117 666	1 036	386	1 418	1 838	17	742 296	20 183
	2004	3[4]	128 308	534	189	1 179	1 866	17	873 602	20 224
	2005	8[4]	133 199	275	480	980	1 894	17	850 658	20 468
	2006	8[4]	124 541	993	226	1 260	2 159	20	1 111 761	23 110
Réunion * Réunion *	2003	...	...	...	...	...	...	...	...	1 618
	2004	...	...	...	...	...	...	...	...	1 652
	2005	...	...	...	...	...	...	...	...	1 680
	2006	...	...	...	...	...	...	...	...	1 710
Rwanda Rwanda	2003	...	...	...	...	...	...	...	12	123
	*2004	...	...	...	...	...	...	...	20	130
	*2005	...	...	...	...	...	...	...	23	135
	2006	...	...	...	...	...	...	...	*24	118

Region, country or area Région, pays ou zone	Year Année	Hard coal, lignite and peat Houille, lignite et tourbe	Crude petroleum and NGL Pétrole brut et LGN	Motor gasoline Essence auto	Jet fuel Carbu- réacteurs	Gas- diesel oil Gazole/ carburant diesel	Residual fuel oil Mazout résiduel	Liquefied petroleum gas Gaz de pétrole liquéfiés	Natural gas Gaz naturel Terajoules Térajoules	Electricity Electricité Million kWh Millions de kWh
		Thousand metric tons — Milliers de tonnes								
Saint Helena	*2003	...	...	...	...	...	...	...	...	7
Sainte-Hélène	2004	...	...	...	...	...	...	...	...	8
	*2005	...	...	...	...	...	...	...	...	8
	*2006	...	...	...	...	...	...	...	...	8
Sao Tome and Principe *	2003	...	...	...	...	...	...	...	...	18
Sao Tomé-et-Principe *	2004	...	...	...	...	...	...	...	...	18
	2005	...	...	...	...	...	...	...	...	19
	2006	...	...	...	...	...	...	...	...	19
Senegal	2003	...	...	151	126	463	316	12	423	2 157
Sénégal	2004	...	...	148	132	471	327	10	506	2 354
	2005	...	...	118	89	356	279	3	533	2 595
	2006	...	...	46	31	115	100	0	483	2 433
Seychelles	2003	...	...	...	...	...	...	...	...	224
Seychelles	2004	...	...	...	...	...	...	...	...	226
	2005	...	...	...	...	...	...	...	...	231
	2006	...	...	...	...	...	...	...	...	252
Sierra Leone	2003	...	...	*31	*20	*74	*55	...	...	144
Sierra Leone	2004	...	...	*32	*21	*60	*45	...	...	120
	2005	...	...	*32	*21	*60	*35	...	...	84
	*2006	...	...	33	22	60	40	...	...	99
Somalia	2003	...	...	5	*80	10	20	0	...	280
Somalie	2004	...	...	5	*80	10	25	0	...	280
	2005	...	...	5	*75	10	25	0	...	290
	2006	...	...	5	*75	10	25	31	...	295
South Africa [5]	2003	239 985 [4]	684	8 360	1 874	7 593	5 162	307	50 218	237 177
Afrique du Sud [5]	2004	244 175 [4]	1 665	8 343	1 778	7 141	4 192	305	77 172	247 331
	2005	246 404 [4]	1 541	7 858	1 840	9 201	5 040	297	82 976	247 959
	2006	246 236 [4]	1 492	7 938	1 908	9 873	4 906	327	75 529	256 882
Sudan	2003	...	13 250 [2]	1 111	170	1 273	328	284	...	3 354
Soudan	2004	...	15 000 [2]	1 228	192	1 400	361	300	...	3 883
	2005	...	15 250 [2]	1 247	214	1 423	377	305	...	4 124
	2006	...	16 550 [2]	1 712	294	1 952	504	419	...	4 209
Togo	2003	...	...	...	...	...	...	...	...	176
Togo	2004	...	...	...	...	...	...	...	...	186
	2005	...	...	...	...	...	...	...	...	189
	2006	...	...	...	...	...	...	...	...	221
Tunisia	2003	...	3 252	234	0	502	609	103	82 331	11 829
Tunisie	2004	...	3 429	226	0	432	595	108	86 816	12 455
	2005	...	3 478	216	0	482	609	109	87 857	13 007
	2006	...	3 355	178	4	506	604	110	94 391	14 122
Uganda	2003	...	...	...	...	...	...	...	...	1 802
Ouganda	2004	...	...	...	...	...	...	...	...	1 942
	2005	...	...	...	...	...	...	...	...	1 836
	2006	...	...	...	...	...	...	...	...	1 615
United Rep. of Tanzania	2003	55 [4]	...	...	...	...	...	...	0	2 658
Rép.-Unie de Tanzanie	2004	65 [4]	...	...	...	...	...	...	4 975	2 893
	2005	75 [4]	...	...	...	...	...	...	13 774	3 035
	2006	80 [4]	...	...	...	...	...	...	14 600	2 776
Western Sahara	2003	...	...	...	...	...	...	...	...	90
Sahara occidental	2004	...	...	...	...	...	...	...	...	90
	2005	...	...	...	...	...	...	...	...	90
	*2006	...	...	...	...	...	...	...	...	90

Region, country or area / Région, pays ou zone	Year / Année	Hard coal, lignite and peat / Houille, lignite et tourbe	Crude petroleum and NGL / Pétrole brut et LGN	Motor gasoline / Essence auto	Jet fuel / Carbu-réacteurs	Gas-diesel oil / Gazole/ carburant diesel	Residual fuel oil / Mazout résiduel	Liquefied petroleum gas / Gaz de pétrole liquéfiés	Natural gas / Gaz naturel	Electricity / Electricité
		Thousand metric tons / Milliers de tonnes							Terajoules / Térajoules	Million kWh / Millions de kWh
Zambia	2003	221[4]	...	110	25	208	74	3	...	8 308
Zambie	2004	233[4]	...	118	27	223	79	3	...	8 512
	2005	244[4]	...	126	29	239	85	3	...	8 938
	2006	244[4]	...	126	29	239	85	3	...	9 385
Zimbabwe	2003	3 550[4]	...	...	...	...	...	...	...	8 799
Zimbabwe	2004	3 415[4]	...	...	...	...	...	...	...	9 718
	2005	3 621[4]	...	...	...	...	...	...	...	10 269
	2006	3 447[4]	...	...	...	...	...	...	...	9 776
America, North	**2003**	**1 044 040**[6]	**674 005**	**406 361**	**78 650**	**239 843**	**80 680**	**64 804**	**30 476 452**	**4 997 761**
Amérique du Nord	**2004**	**1 095 008**[6]	**670 077**	**409 008**	**82 407**	**247 074**	**79 551**	**67 431**	**30 032 263**	**5 108 687**
	2005	**1 114 691**[6]	**649 538**	**407 872**	**82 969**	**254 143**	**76 647**	**64 382**	**29 704 467**	**5 271 402**
	2006	**1 145 829**[6]	**649 011**	**404 041**	**79 673**	**259 052**	**73 497**	**62 159**	**30 646 765**	**5 281 822**
Anguilla	2003	...	...	...	...	...	...	...	...	58
Anguilla	2004	...	...	...	...	...	...	...	...	62
	2005	...	...	...	...	...	...	...	...	72
	2006	...	...	...	...	...	...	...	...	80
Antigua and Barbuda *	2003	...	...	...	...	...	...	...	...	109
Antigua-et-Barbuda *	2004	...	...	...	...	...	...	...	...	111
	2005	...	...	...	...	...	...	...	...	114
	2006	...	...	...	...	...	...	...	...	116
Aruba	2003	...	*120[2]	...	...	...	...	...	...	842
Aruba	2004	...	*120[2]	...	...	...	...	...	...	866
	2005	...	*120[2]	...	...	...	...	...	...	911
	2006	...	*120[2]	...	...	...	...	...	...	910
Bahamas	2003	...	...	...	...	...	...	...	...	1 990
Bahamas	*2004	...	...	...	...	...	...	...	...	2 087
	*2005	...	...	...	...	...	...	...	...	2 090
	*2006	...	...	...	...	...	...	...	...	2 090
Barbados	2003	...	75	...	...	...	...	1	1 020	871
Barbade	2004	...	65	...	...	...	...	1	973	895
	2005	...	65	...	...	...	...	1	1 028	930
	2006	...	52	...	...	...	...	1	1 048	948
Belize *	2003	...	...	...	...	...	...	...	...	169
Belize *	2004	...	...	...	...	...	...	...	...	177
	2005	...	...	...	...	...	...	...	...	183
	2006	...	...	...	...	...	...	...	...	191
Bermuda	2003	...	...	...	...	...	...	...	...	664
Bermudes	*2004	...	...	...	...	...	...	...	...	661
	*2005	...	...	...	...	...	...	...	...	685
	*2006	...	...	...	...	...	...	...	...	696
British Virgin Islands *	2003	...	...	...	...	...	...	...	...	45
Iles Vierges britanniques *	2004	...	...	...	...	...	...	...	...	45
	2005	...	...	...	...	...	...	...	...	45
	2006	...	...	...	...	...	...	...	...	48
Canada	2003	62 163[6]	140 928	33 689	4 200	31 136	7 989	1 991	7 032 164	589 967
Canada	2004	65 997[6]	145 983	33 024	4 597	31 590	8 724	1 955	7 016 682	598 514
	2005	65 345[6]	144 080	32 270	4 363	30 745	8 263	1 779	7 169 112	628 194
	2006	66 440[6]	151 265	30 889	3 869	30 704	7 763	1 730	7 206 362	612 594
Cayman Islands	2003	...	...	...	...	...	...	...	...	490
Iles Caïmanes	2004	...	...	...	...	...	...	...	...	433
	2005	...	...	...	...	...	...	...	...	454
	2006	...	...	...	...	...	...	...	...	536

Region, country or area / Région, pays ou zone	Year / Année	Hard coal, lignite and peat Houille, lignite et tourbe	Crude petroleum and NGL Pétrole brut et LGN	Motor gasoline Essence auto	Jet fuel Carbu-réacteurs	Gas-diesel oil Gazole/ carburant diesel	Residual fuel oil Mazout résiduel	Liquefied petroleum gas Gaz de pétrole liquéfiés	Natural gas Gaz naturel Terajoules Térajoules	Electricity Electricité Million kWh Millions de kWh
				Thousand metric tons / Milliers de tonnes						
Costa Rica	2003	...	...	0	...	168	222	2	...	7 565
Costa Rica	2004	...	...	14	...	163	247	2	...	8 040
	2005	...	...	85	...	153	227	2	...	8 252
	2006	...	...	105	...	230	295	4	...	8 697
Cuba	2003	...	3 680[2]	412	...	444	1 024	93	25 675	15 811
Cuba	2004	...	3 253[2]	331	...	385	858	63	27 470	15 652
	2005	...	2 876[2]	407	...	395	879	82	28 992	15 341
	2006	...	2 900[2]	317	...	420	892	62	42 337	16 469
Dominica	2003	...	...	...	...	...	...	...	...	79
Dominique	2004	...	...	...	...	...	...	...	...	79
	2005	...	...	...	...	...	...	...	...	84
	*2006	...	...	...	...	...	...	...	...	85
Dominican Republic	2003	...	...	284	54	411	449	42	...	13 489
Rép. dominicaine	2004	...	...	445	54	417	839	33	...	13 759
	2005	...	...	447	56	423	812	35	...	12 899
	2006	...	...	440	59	424	762	33	...	14 150
El Salvador	2003	...	...	135	45	195	485	12	...	4 128
El Salvador	2004	...	...	143	49	199	543	14	...	4 468
	2005	...	...	112	51	198	419	16	...	4 788
	2006	...	...	112	39	176	437	17	...	5 597
Greenland *	2003	...	...	...	...	...	...	...	...	305
Groenland *	2004	...	...	...	...	...	...	...	...	305
	2005	...	...	...	...	...	...	...	...	305
	2006	...	...	...	...	...	...	...	...	305
Grenada	2003	...	...	...	...	...	...	...	...	153
Grenade	2004	...	...	...	...	...	...	...	...	157
	2005	...	...	...	...	...	...	...	...	166
	2006	...	...	...	...	...	...	...	...	171
Guadeloupe	2003	...	...	...	...	...	...	...	...	1 165
Guadeloupe	*2004	...	...	...	...	...	...	...	...	1 180
	*2005	...	...	...	...	...	...	...	...	1 190
	*2006	...	...	...	...	...	...	...	...	1 225
Guatemala	2003	...	1 221[2]	0	...	0	...	...	...	6 561
Guatemala	2004	...	999[2]	0	...	0	...	...	...	7 009
	2005	...	910[2]	1	...	25	...	...	...	7 550
	2006	...	818[2]	1	...	22	...	...	...	7 911
Haiti	2003	...	...	...	...	...	...	...	...	535
Haïti	2004	...	...	...	...	...	...	...	...	547
	2005	...	...	...	...	...	...	...	...	556
	2006	...	...	...	...	...	...	...	...	570
Honduras	2003	...	...	...	...	...	...	...	...	4 530
Honduras	2004	...	...	...	...	...	...	...	...	4 877
	2005	...	...	...	...	...	...	...	...	5 545
	2006	...	...	...	...	...	...	...	...	5 356
Jamaica	2003	...	...	111	62	158	495	7	...	7 146
Jamaïque	2004	...	...	95	63	129	370	7	...	7 217
	2005	...	...	52	41	87	268	0	...	7 526
	2006	...	...	124	63	226	561	9	...	7 473
Martinique *	2003	...	...	161	...	177	300	26	...	1 185
Martinique *	2004	...	...	163	...	178	310	27	...	1 195
	2005	...	...	164	...	179	310	27	...	1 205
	2006	...	...	164	...	179	312	27	...	1 215

Region, country or area Région, pays ou zone	Year Année	Hard coal, lignite and peat Houille, lignite et tourbe	Crude petroleum and NGL Pétrole brut et LGN	Motor gasoline Essence auto	Jet fuel Carbu- réacteurs	Gas- diesel oil Gazole/ carburant diesel	Residual fuel oil Mazout résiduel	Liquefied petroleum gas Gaz de pétrole liquéfiés	Natural gas Gaz naturel Terajoules Térajoules	Electricity Electricité Million kWh Millions de kWh
		Thousand metric tons Milliers de tonnes								
Mexico	2003	9 599[6]	189 016	18 587	2 717	15 182	22 581	1 059	1 579 524	217 867
Mexique	2004	9 882[6]	190 897	19 855	2 770	16 057	21 089	1 056	1 651 290	224 077
	2005	10 755[6]	187 205	20 399	3 125	17 157	20 019	1 039	1 716 773	234 895
	2006	11 487[6]	182 794	20 658	3 172	17 692	16 914	1 014	1 885 615	249 648
Montserrat	2003	...	...	...	...	...	...	...	...	21
Montserrat	2004	...	...	...	...	...	...	...	...	21
	*2005	...	...	...	...	...	...	...	...	22
	*2006	...	...	...	...	...	...	...	...	22
Netherlands Antilles	2003	...	...	1 412	768	2 102	4 269	85	...	1 181
Antilles néerlandaises	2004	...	...	1 788	786	2 182	4 257	78	...	1 210
	2005	...	...	1 925	872	2 631	4 712	119	...	1 248
	2006	...	...	1 524	825	2 652	4 540	90	...	1 271
Nicaragua	2003	...	...	96	...	211	400	21	...	2 708
Nicaragua	2004	...	...	99	...	210	427	17	...	2 822
	2005	...	...	87	...	183	378	15	...	2 866
	2006	...	...	91	...	199	404	15	...	2 958
Panama	2003	...	...	...	...	...	...	...	...	5 308
Panama	2004	...	...	...	...	...	...	...	...	5 504
	2005	...	...	...	...	...	...	...	...	5 702
	2006	...	...	...	...	...	...	...	...	5 962
Puerto Rico	2003	...	...	...	...	...	...	...	...	23 280
Porto Rico	2004	...	...	...	...	...	...	...	...	24 130
	2005	...	...	...	...	...	...	...	...	24 960
	*2006	...	...	...	...	...	...	...	...	25 800
Saint Kitts and Nevis	2003	...	...	...	...	...	...	...	...	127
Saint-Kitts-et-Nevis	*2004	...	...	...	...	...	...	...	...	130
	*2005	...	...	...	...	...	...	...	...	133
	*2006	...	...	...	...	...	...	...	...	135
Saint Lucia	2003	...	...	...	...	...	...	...	...	299
Sainte-Lucie	2004	...	...	...	...	...	...	...	...	309
	2005	...	...	...	...	...	...	...	...	324
	2006	...	...	...	...	...	...	...	...	331
Saint Pierre and Miquelon *	2003	...	...	...	...	...	...	...	...	52
Saint-Pierre-et-Miquelon *	2004	...	...	...	...	...	...	...	...	52
	2005	...	...	...	...	...	...	...	...	54
	2006	...	...	...	...	...	...	...	...	54
Saint Vincent-Grenadines	2003	...	...	...	...	...	...	...	...	108
Saint Vincent-Grenadines	2004	...	...	...	...	...	...	...	...	121
	*2005	...	...	...	...	...	...	...	...	124
	*2006	...	...	...	...	...	...	...	...	127
Trinidad and Tobago	2003	...	7 898	1 216	685	1 522	3 247	726	971 764	6 437
Trinité-et-Tobago	2004	...	7 308	1 096	615	1 421	2 971	710	1 024 185	6 430
	2005	...	8 373	1 350	827	1 764	3 180	686	1 067 201	7 058
	2006	...	8 145	1 388	773	1 861	2 951	771	1 325 454	6 901
Turks and Caicos Islands *	2003	...	...	...	...	...	...	...	...	10
Iles Turques et Caïques *	2004	...	...	...	...	...	...	...	...	11
	2005	...	...	...	...	...	...	...	...	12
	2006	...	...	...	...	...	...	...	...	14
United States	2003	972 278[6]	331 067	350 258	70 119	188 137	39 219	60 739	20 866 305	4 081 466
Etats-Unis	2004	1 019 129[6]	321 452	351 954	73 473	194 143	38 916	63 468	20 311 663	4 174 484
	2005	1 038 591[6]	305 908	350 574	73 634	200 203	37 180	60 581	19 721 361	4 293 860
	2006	1 067 902[6]	302 917	348 229	70 873	204 267	37 666	58 386	20 185 949	4 300 103

Region, country or area Région, pays ou zone	Year Année	Hard coal, lignite and peat Houille, lignite et tourbe	Crude petroleum and NGL Pétrole brut et LGN	Motor gasoline Essence auto	Jet fuel Carbu- réacteurs	Gas- diesel oil Gazole/ carburant diesel	Residual fuel oil Mazout résiduel	Liquefied petroleum gas Gaz de pétrole liquéfiés	Natural gas Gaz naturel Terajoules Térajoules	Electricity Electricité Million kWh Millions de kWh
		Thousand metric tons Milliers de tonnes								
United States Virgin Is. *	2003	...	...	...	...	...	...	...	...	1 040
Iles Vierges américaines *	2004	...	...	...	...	...	...	...	...	1 050
	2005	...	...	...	...	...	...	...	...	1 060
	2006	...	...	...	...	...	...	...	...	1 065
America, South	**2003**	**62 171**[4]	**333 973**	**41 760**	**10 007**	**66 813**	**42 985**	**14 979**	**3 744 351**	**745 700**
Amérique du Sud	**2004**	**66 120**[4]	**337 672**	**45 264**	**10 659**	**71 887**	**46 406**	**16 477**	**3 932 148**	**790 558**
	2005	**73 137**[4]	**350 896**	**48 020**	**10 844**	**71 026**	**44 668**	**18 234**	**4 070 096**	**822 595**
	2006	**79 756**[4]	**354 735**	**46 702**	**10 448**	**71 939**	**46 554**	**18 287**	**4 273 621**	**866 989**
Argentina	2003	89[4]	44 418	4 830	1 135	9 957	1 946	4 143	1 664 109	92 609
Argentine	2004	51[4]	42 765	4 018	1 209	10 590	2 368	4 431	1 713 297	100 260
	2005	25[4]	41 047	4 348	1 264	10 143	2 795	4 290	1 685 308	107 053
	2006	427[4]	41 478	4 305	1 191	10 733	3 422	4 643	1 764 945	115 197
Bolivia	2003	...	1 956	406	121	482	0	301	255 726	4 269
Bolivie	2004	...	2 243	455	122	622	0	322	355 620	4 542
	2005	...	2 416	430	125	601	0	333	442 468	5 230
	2006	...	2 628	500	131	620	1	353	473 592	5 293
Brazil	2003	4 646[4]	79 081	13 477	3 073	30 608	15 779	4 934	397 527	364 339
Brésil	2004	5 406[4]	78 846	13 738	3 357	34 079	16 074	5 144	420 030	387 451
	2005	6 255[4]	87 325	14 337	3 337	33 368	15 461	5 780	429 095	402 938
	2006	5 881[4]	92 144	14 981	3 037	33 597	15 661	5 405	434 855	419 336
Chile	2003	576[4]	355	2 265	574	3 865	1 814	533	73 681	48 780
Chili	2004	188[4]	353	2 384	650	3 693	2 294	681	67 617	51 984
	2005	544[4]	329	2 257	574	3 534	2 306	621	82 254	54 383
	2006	396[4]	316	2 482	660	3 717	2 646	530	78 786	57 555
Colombia	2003	50 025[4]	28 018	4 756	1 254	3 308	2 932	868	257 762	47 682
Colombie	2004	53 693[4]	26 766	4 963	861	3 689	3 330	688	271 346	50 228
	2005	59 064[4]	26 283	4 252	858	3 660	3 056	689	284 720	50 665
	2006	65 596[4]	26 768	3 618	718	4 457	2 792	694	321 698	54 755
Ecuador	2003	...	21 493	1 516	239	1 600	3 646	231	16 234	11 546
Equateur	2004	...	27 460	895	279	1 621	3 657	215	25 108	12 585
	2005	...	26 599	1 615	297	1 787	3 492	228	20 411	13 404
	2006	...	26 807	1 226	348	1 715	3 922	242	33 281	14 814
Falkland Is. (Malvinas) *	2003	12[3]	...	...	...	...	...	...	...	16
Iles Falkland (Malvinas) *	2004	12[3]	...	...	...	...	...	...	...	16
	2005	11[3]	...	...	...	...	...	...	...	16
	2006	11[3]	...	...	...	...	...	...	...	16
French Guiana	2003	...	...	...	...	...	...	...	...	440
Guyane française	2004	...	...	...	...	...	...	...	...	430
	2005	...	...	...	...	...	...	...	...	430
	2006	...	...	...	...	...	...	...	...	430
Guyana	2003	...	...	...	...	...	...	...	...	820
Guyana	2004	...	...	...	...	...	...	...	...	835
	2005	...	...	...	...	...	...	...	...	862
	2006	...	...	...	...	...	...	...	...	867
Paraguay	2003	...	...	10	...	42	30	...	...	51 762
Paraguay	2004	...	...	8	...	33	20	...	...	51 921
	2005	...	...	4	...	16	11	...	...	51 156
	2006	...	...	0	...	0	0	...	...	53 774
Peru	2003	16[4]	5 058	1 470	382	1 883	3 245	319	25 802	23 128
Pérou	2004	22[4]	5 031	1 744	418	1 999	3 324	355	40 321	24 415
	2005	43[4]	5 267	2 220	270	2 415	2 958	738	68 008	25 660
	2006	107[4]	6 687	2 208	504	2 638	2 878	777	77 826	27 358

Region, country or area Région, pays ou zone	Year Année	Hard coal, lignite and peat Houille, lignite et tourbe	Crude petroleum and NGL Pétrole brut et LGN	Motor gasoline Essence auto	Jet fuel Carbu-réacteurs	Gas-diesel oil Gazole/carburant diesel	Residual fuel oil Mazout résiduel	Liquefied petroleum gas Gaz de pétrole liquéfiés	Natural gas Gaz naturel Terajoules Térajoules	Electricity Electricité Million kWh Millions de kWh
		Thousand metric tons — Milliers de tonnes								
Suriname Suriname	2003	...	588[2]	...	...	39	333	...	...	1 496
	2004	...	612[2]	...	...	39	335	...	...	1 509
	2005	...	637[2]	...	...	41	349	...	...	1 571
	2006	...	656[2]	...	...	41	360	...	...	1 618
Uruguay Uruguay	2003	...	...	321	24	618	448	66	...	8 578
	2004	...	...	503	44	807	518	86	...	5 899
	2005	...	...	447	41	810	505	91	...	7 683
	2006	...	...	396	53	760	381	77	...	5 618
Venezuela (Boliv. Rep. of) Venezuela (Rép. bol. du)	2003	6 807[4]	153 006	12 903	3 205	14 411	12 812	3 585	1 053 511	90 235
	2004	6 748[4]	153 596	16 555	3 719	14 715	14 486	4 555	1 038 809	98 482
	2005	7 195[4]	160 993	18 110	4 078	14 651	13 735	5 464	1 057 831	101 544
	2006	7 338[4]	157 251	16 986	3 806	13 661	14 491	5 566	1 088 638	110 357
Asia **Asie**	**2003**	**2 452 876**[6]	**1 553 705**	**193 697**	**56 842**	**386 074**	**249 050**	**85 938**	**26 012 452**	**5 656 352**
	2004	**2 782 240**[6]	**1 629 718**	**203 143**	**63 406**	**413 993**	**247 470**	**92 658**	**27 669 272**	**6 130 540**
	2005	**3 072 046**[6]	**1 684 951**	**206 205**	**70 031**	**434 225**	**246 917**	**94 930**	**29 663 356**	**6 622 834**
	2006	**3 335 032**[6]	**1 717 559**	**209 617**	**75 899**	**444 683**	**246 599**	**98 022**	**31 221 693**	**7 155 055**
Afghanistan Afghanistan	2003	35[4]	...	...	...	...	...	...	242	976
	2004	34[4]	...	...	...	...	...	...	119	929
	*2005	33[4]	...	...	...	...	...	...	100	960
	*2006	33[4]	...	...	...	...	...	...	100	960
Armenia Arménie	2003	...	...	...	...	...	...	...	...	5 501
	2004	...	...	...	...	...	...	...	...	6 030
	2005	...	...	...	...	...	...	...	...	6 317
	2006	...	...	...	...	...	...	...	...	6 041
Azerbaijan Azerbaïdjan	2003	...	15 381	720	521	1 641	2 470	148	193 326	21 286
	2004	...	15 549	852	536	1 789	2 521	182	194 905	21 743
	2005	...	22 214	906	630	2 101	3 061	185	216 096	22 872
	2006	...	32 267	1 043	693	2 095	2 899	195	255 073	24 542
Bahrain Bahreïn	2003	...	10 130	810	1 866	4 295	3 008	201	263 779	7 768
	2004	...	10 111	755	2 178	4 500	2 734	204	274 330	8 448
	2005	...	10 081	789	2 276	4 702	2 857	218	290 590	8 698
	2006	...	9 909	766	2 210	4 566	2 775	215	307 881	9 822
Bangladesh Bangladesh	2003	...	100[7]	150	2	303	58	20	434 849	19 170
	2004	...	90[7]	136	2	274	53	16	467 723	20 820
	2005	...	96[7]	145	1	293	57	12	502 829	22 006
	2006	...	93[7]	140	1	284	55	8	543 096	23 703
Bhutan Bhoutan	2003	66[4]	...	...	...	...	...	...	...	2 200
	2004	30[4]	...	...	...	...	...	...	...	2 529
	2005	85[4]	...	...	...	...	...	...	...	2 355
	2006	98[4]	...	...	...	...	...	...	...	2 648
Brunei Darussalam Brunéi Darussalam	2003	...	10 452	202	82	165	77	14	482 490	3 169
	2004	...	10 291	201	80	173	89	15	477 318	3 236
	2005	...	10 075	196	78	178	92	15	468 618	3 264
	2006	...	10 788	209	79	190	103	15	492 586	3 298
Cambodia Cambodge	2003	...	...	...	...	...	...	...	...	637
	2004	...	...	...	...	...	...	...	...	743
	2005	...	...	...	...	...	...	...	...	880
	2006	...	...	...	...	...	...	...	...	1 235
China[8] Chine[8]	2003	1 722 000[4]	169 600[2]	47 909	...	85 328	20 048	12 117	1 685 000	1 907 380
	2004	1 992 324[4]	175 873[2]	52 236	...	98 436	20 293	14 170	1 544 800	2 193 736
	2005	2 204 729[4]	181 353[2]	53 884	...	110 902	17 674	14 327	1 898 173	2 497 441
	2006	2 373 000[4]	184 766[2]	55 473	...	117 624	17 847	17 453	1 995 497	2 865 726

Region, country or area Région, pays ou zone	Year Année	Hard coal, lignite and peat Houille, lignite et tourbe	Crude petroleum and NGL Pétrole brut et LGN	Motor gasoline Essence auto	Jet fuel Carbu-réacteurs	Gas-diesel oil Gazole/ carburant diesel	Residual fuel oil Mazout résiduel	Liquefied petroleum gas Gaz de pétrole liquéfiés	Natural gas Gaz naturel Terajoules Térajoules	Electricity Electricité Million kWh Millions de kWh
		Thousand metric tons — Milliers de tonnes								
China, Hong Kong SAR	2003	...	...	...	...	...	...	...	...	35 506
Chine, Hong Kong RAS	2004	...	...	...	...	...	...	...	...	37 129
	2005	...	...	...	...	...	...	...	...	38 448
	2006	...	...	...	...	...	...	...	...	38 613
China, Macao SAR	2003	...	...	...	...	...	...	...	...	1 779
Chine, Macao RAS	2004	...	...	...	...	...	...	...	...	1 956
	2005	...	...	...	...	...	...	...	...	2 027
	2006	...	...	...	...	...	...	...	...	1 668
Cyprus	2003	...	...	146	...	327	362	28		4 053
Chypre	2004	...	...	40	...	88	112	9		4 200
	2005	...	...	0	...	0	0	0		4 377
	2006	...	...	0	...	0	0	0		4 652
Georgia	2003	8[4]	140[2]	...	...	2	13	...	712	7 160
Géorgie	2004	8[4]	98[2]	...	...	2	14	...	461	6 924
	2005	5[4]	67[2]	...	...	1	4	...	516	7 267
	2006	11[4]	64[2]	...	...	0	4	...	649	7 599
India	2003	389 204[6]	37 249	10 999	4 180	41 966	13 372	7 551	1 016 146	633 275
Inde	2004	412 952[6]	37 665	11 057	5 201	47 426	14 970	7 825	1 007 951	665 873
	2005	437 105[6]	36 323	10 502	6 196	48 495	14 305	7 710	1 025 355	697 234
	2006	461 980[6]	38 138	12 539	7 805	54 268	15 697	8 408	1 005 064	744 119
Indonesia	2003	119 726[6]	56 851	8 584	1 349	13 786	11 755	2 007	2 840 729	112 944
Indonésie	2004	142 054[6]	52 658	8 825	1 414	14 661	10 995	2 514	2 942 183	120 160
	2005	171 052[6]	49 835	8 325	1 418	13 889	10 105	1 819	2 879 750	127 369
	2006	221 182[6]	47 793	8 411	1 256	13 216	9 686	1 279	2 887 554	133 108
Iran (Islamic Rep. of)	2003	1 232[4]	192 067	10 730	868	22 958	26 566	3 750	3 079 135	152 599
Iran (Rép. Islamique d')	2004	1 246[4]	199 433	10 836	795	23 771	25 840	4 146	3 423 814	166 016
	2005	1 330[4]	216 309	11 394	848	24 375	26 241	3 689	3 709 933	180 390
	2006	1 520[4]	214 886	12 047	1.042	24 762	26 351	4 086	4 075 188	201 029
Iraq	2003	...	65 949	3 097	573	6 610	7 404	848	59 280	28 340
Iraq	2004	...	98 951	3 278	607	4 906	8 257	938	98 799	32 295
	2005	...	91 669	3 185	590	4 766	8 022	951	100 700	34 000
	2006	...	95 985	3 233	599	4 838	8 392	1 032	132 998	31 869
Israel	2003	437[9]	3[2]	2 231	...	2 977	3 440	474	321	47 041
Israël	2004	439[9]	2[2]	2 467	...	2 750	3 168	532	43 585	48 481
	2005	413[9]	2[2]	2 729	...	3 042	3 504	566	59 988	49 843
	2006	452[9]	2[2]	2 592	...	3 231	3 223	471	83 815	51 811
Japan	2003	...	642	43 140	7 671	57 402	34 028	4 527	120 758	1 047 041
Japon	2004	...	663	42 715	7 902	57 059	30 985	4 448	125 356	1 076 244
	2005	...	703	43 259	8 896	57 700	31 419	4 895	134 612	1 098 315
	2006	...	693	42 437	10 433	54 711	28 315	4 647	148 485	1 100 364
Jordan	2003	...	2[2]	667	268	1 160	1 251	134	9 902	8 044
Jordanie	2004	...	1[2]	579	291	1 223	1 516	116	10 098	8 970
	2005	...	1[2]	613	300	1 395	1 466	118	8 315	9 651
	2006	...	1[2]	675	312	1 412	1 345	139	7 754	11 120
Kazakhstan	2003	84 906[6]	51 451	1 841	257	2 128	2 584	1 179	647 698	63 866
Kazakhstan	2004	86 875[6]	59 485	1 928	244	2 888	2 708	1 507	862 531	66 942
	2005	86 586[6]	61 486	2 359	207	3 705	3 874	1 478	974 571	67 916
	2006	96 231[6]	65 554	2 345	260	4 065	3 333	1 106	1 029 558	71 653
Korea, Dem. P. R.	2003	30 224[6]	...	185	...	201	116	...	...	20 999
Corée, R. p. dém. de	2004	31 711[6]	...	188	...	203	117	...	...	21 974
	2005	34 610[6]	...	159	...	171	98	...	...	22 913
	2006	35 107[6]	...	122	...	131	75	...	...	22 436

Region, country or area / Région, pays ou zone	Year / Année	Hard coal, lignite and peat / Houille, lignite et tourbe	Crude petroleum and NGL / Pétrole brut et LGN	Motor gasoline / Essence auto	Jet fuel / Carbu-réacteurs	Gas-diesel oil / Gazole/ carburant diesel	Residual fuel oil / Mazout résiduel	Liquefied petroleum gas / Gaz de pétrole liquéfiés	Natural gas / Gaz naturel Terajoules / Térajoules	Electricity / Electricité Million kWh / Millions de kWh
		Thousand metric tons / Milliers de tonnes								
Korea, Republic of	2003	3 298[4]	0[2]	8 564	6 944	27 801	30 095	3 613	0	345 192
Corée, République de	2004	3 191[4]	0[2]	8 850	9 665	29 048	29 912	3 326	0	368 162
	2005	2 832[4]	54[2]	8 654	10 755	31 508	31 305	3 213	20 495	389 390
	2006	2 824[4]	45[2]	8 707	12 021	32 392	30 793	3 098	21 631	404 021
Kuwait	2003	...	113 765	1 355	2 227	12 426	9 800	3 250	429 950	39 802
Koweït	2004	...	123 501	1 931	2 258	12 204	9 760	3 515	462 773	41 256
	2005	...	136 982	2 812	1 586	12 397	9 166	3 368	518 914	43 734
	2006	...	141 245	3 023	2 619	11 079	11 951	3 671	548 804	47 607
Kyrgyzstan	2003	416[6]	69[2]	27	...	22	39	...	1 054	15 576
Kirghizistan	2004	461[6]	74[2]	19	...	27	42	...	1 132	16 312
	2005	335[6]	74[2]	13	...	31	42	...	975	16 415
	2006	322[6]	71[2]	10	...	31	42	...	741	17 082
Lao People's Dem. Rep.	2003	*535[6]	...	...	...	...	...	...	...	3 372
Rép. dém. pop. lao	*2004	590[6]	...	...	...	...	...	...	...	3 541
	*2005	620[6]	...	...	...	...	...	...	...	3 685
	*2006	624[6]	...	...	...	...	...	...	...	3 799
Lebanon	2003	...	...	...	...	...	...	...	...	11 787
Liban	2004	...	...	...	...	...	...	...	...	11 054
	2005	...	...	...	...	...	...	...	...	11 125
	2006	...	...	...	...	...	...	...	...	10 654
Malaysia	2003	153[4]	39 044	4 363	2 293	8 922	1 777	1 582	2 079 956	78 427
Malaisie	2004	382[4]	37 237	4 496	2 608	9 463	1 828	1 303	2 180 862	82 282
	2005	682[4]	37 468	4 040	2 472	9 020	1 792	2 470	2 402 160	87 300
	2006	902[4]	36 844	4 270	2 523	8 734	1 992	2 503	2 608 702	91 563
Maldives	2003	...	...	...	...	...	...	...	...	141
Maldives	2004	...	...	...	...	...	...	...	...	160
	*2005	...	...	...	...	...	...	...	...	185
	2006	...	...	...	...	...	...	...	...	212
Mongolia	2003	5 666[6]	...	...	...	...	...	...	...	3 138
Mongolie	2004	6 865[6]	...	...	...	...	...	...	...	3 303
	2005	7 517[6]	...	...	...	...	...	...	...	3 419
	2006	8 074[6]	...	...	...	...	...	...	...	3 544
Myanmar	2003	978[6]	976	307	65	249	67	16	306 893	5 426
Myanmar	2004	1 052[6]	1 025	309	61	196	49	20	419 860	5 608
	2005	1 360[6]	1 113	302	46	173	48	19	438 767	6 015
	2006	1 386[6]	1 058	357	52	274	41	10	454 124	6 164
Nepal	2003	11[4]	...	...	...	...	...	...	...	2 267
Népal	2004	9[4]	...	...	...	...	...	...	...	2 416
	2005	9[4]	...	...	...	...	...	...	...	2 622
	2006	9[4]	...	...	...	...	...	...	...	2 684
Occupied Palestinian Terr.	2003	...	...	...	...	...	...	...	...	342
Terr. palestinien occupé	2004	...	...	...	...	...	...	...	...	396
	2005	...	...	...	...	...	...	...	...	501
	*2006	...	...	...	...	...	...	...	...	520
Oman	2003	...	41 058	642	217	878	2 259	117	691 553	10 714
Oman	2004	...	39 226	593	178	864	2 121	116	706 149	11 499
	2005	...	38 859	618	183	894	2 167	*95	740 145	12 648
	2006	...	36 998	597	292	905	2 244	*118	938 861	13 585
Pakistan	2003	3 312[4]	3 302	1 075	997	2 937	3 058	380	1 023 969	80 830
Pakistan	2004	4 587[4]	3 402	1 326	1 185	3 603	3 132	412	1 115 913	85 698
	2005	4 871[4]	3 474	1 195	1 258	3 419	3 358	557	1 171 106	93 832
	2006	3 643[4]	3 522	1 218	1 165	3 383	3 193	436	1 181 984	98 350

Region, country or area / Région, pays ou zone	Year / Année	Hard coal, lignite and peat Houille, lignite et tourbe	Crude petroleum and NGL Pétrole brut et LGN	Motor gasoline Essence auto	Jet fuel Carbu-réacteurs	Gas-diesel oil Gazole/ carburant diesel	Residual fuel oil Mazout résiduel	Liquefied petroleum gas Gaz de pétrole liquéfiés	Natural gas Gaz naturel Terajoules Térajoules	Electricity Electricité Million kWh Millions de kWh
		Thousand metric tons / Milliers de tonnes								
Philippines Philippines	2003	4 603[6]	20[2]	1 844	634	3 851	3 899	397	101 146	52 897
	2004	2 726[6]	19[2]	1 501	590	3 004	3 537	263	96 743	55 957
	2005	3 164[6]	29[2]	1 629	665	3 399	3 463	322	127 566	56 549
	2006	*3 252[6]	25[2]	1 582	740	3 612	3 150	333	115 873	56 818
Qatar Qatar	2003	...	38 129	1 815	921	965	429	122	1 225 260	12 012
	2004	...	40 458	1 709	956	979	618	128	1 528 453	13 233
	2005	...	41 078	1 722	916	924	356	131	1 787 162	14 396
	2006	...	53 269	1 729	1 035	994	724	151	1 931 540	15 325
Saudi Arabia Arabie saoudite	2003	...	477 702	12 600	4 519	28 899	25 432	27 093	1 990 700	153 000
	2004	...	491 685	13 605	4 923	31 486	25 944	29 719	2 162 680	159 875
	2005	...	514 624	13 400	6 627	31 685	26 722	30 979	2 376 770	176 124
	2006	...	506 289	12 025	6 193	32 412	27 177	30 641	2 495 244	179 782
Singapore Singapour	2003	...	...	3 350	6 322	9 938	6 084	870	...	35 331
	2004	...	...	3 948	6 481	11 711	7 170	872	...	36 810
	2005	...	...	4 879	7 610	14 474	8 862	848	...	38 213
	2006	...	...	4 699	7 458	13 939	8 534	634	...	39 442
Sri Lanka Sri Lanka	2003	...	...	196	96	622	745	15	...	7 711
	2004	...	...	203	126	693	855	15	...	8 158
	2005	...	...	161	114	591	762	13	...	8 769
	2006	...	...	194	131	628	716	15	...	9 389
Syrian Arab Republic Rép. arabe syrienne	2003	...	28 000[2]	1 262	204	3 906	4 921	286	258 245	29 534
	2004	...	23 355[2]	1 338	245	4 123	5 015	286	267 670	32 077
	2005	...	22 241[2]	1 257	221	3 934	4 938	328	229 970	34 935
	2006	...	20 823[2]	1 345	215	3 934	5 288	321	237 510	37 283
Tajikistan Tadjikistan	2003	47[6]	18[2]	...	...	...	...	...	1 254	16 509
	2004	68[6]	19[2]	...	...	...	...	...	1 368	16 491
	2005	91[6]	22[2]	...	...	...	...	...	1 113	17 090
	2006	102[6]	22[2]	...	...	...	...	...	760	16 935
Thailand Thaïlande	2003	18 843[9]	9 721	6 012	3 253	15 608	5 947	3 446	707 276	116 983
	2004	20 060[9]	9 903	6 674	3 774	17 511	6 335	3 917	701 157	125 727
	2005	20 878[9]	11 418	6 428	3 711	16 378	6 409	4 011	753 708	132 197
	2006	19 001[9]	12 406	6 331	4 299	16 737	6 578	4 032	761 621	138 742
Timor-Leste * Timor-Leste *	2003	...	6 789	...	...	...	...	2 193	...	300
	2004	...	6 835	...	...	...	...	2 200	...	307
	2005	...	6 860	...	...	...	...	2 210	...	314
	2006	...	6 872	...	...	...	...	2 215	...	320
Turkey Turquie	2003	48 563[6]	2 351[2]	3 837	1 682	8 087	8 038	758	21 448	140 581
	2004	46 377[6]	2 251[2]	3 479	1 767	7 665	7 845	762	26 350	150 698
	2005	58 340[6]	2 258[2]	3 609	1 997	7 601	7 208	766	34 355	161 956
	2006	64 255[6]	2 160[2]	3 659	1 644	7 549	7 271	808	34 662	176 299
Turkmenistan Turkménistan	2003	...	10 332	1 321	309	2 622	1 822	...	2 241 513	10 800
	2004	...	10 091	1 270	297	2 522	1 752	...	2 235 451	11 920
	2005	...	9 794	1 313	307	2 607	1 811	...	2 387 007	12 820
	2006	...	10 063	1 564	366	3 105	2 157	...	2 396 479	13 650
United Arab Emirates Emirats arabes unis	2003	...	126 150	1 498	5 454	4 609	1 173	6 985	1 746 810	49 450
	2004	...	131 629	1 746	5 400	4 754	1 291	7 252	1 805 310	52 417
	2005	...	133 143	1 866	5 404	4 262	1 299	7 526	1 815 450	60 698
	2006	...	142 835	2 626	5 385	4 428	1 173	7 807	1 846 650	66 768
Uzbekistan Ouzbékistan	2003	1 913[9]	7 788	1 842	314	1 993	1 925	44	2 194 105	49 400
	2004	2 699[9]	7 295	1 736	296	1 879	1 814	40	2 236 391	51 030
	2005	3 003[9]	5 985	1 418	242	1 535	1 482	32	2 278 677	47 706
	2006	3 126[9]	5 583	1 323	226	1 433	1 383	30	2 370 882	49 299

Region, country or area Région, pays ou zone	Year Année	Hard coal, lignite and peat Houille, lignite et tourbe	Crude petroleum and NGL Pétrole brut et LGN	Motor gasoline Essence auto	Jet fuel Carbu-réacteurs	Gas-diesel oil Gazole/ carburant diesel	Residual fuel oil Mazout résiduel	Liquefied petroleum gas Gaz de pétrole liquéfiés	Natural gas Gaz naturel Terajoules Térajoules	Electricity Electricité Million kWh Millions de kWh
		Thousand metric tons — Milliers de tonnes								
Viet Nam	2003	16 700[4]	17 092	...	...	...	...	307	125 993	40 925
Viet Nam	2004	25 500[4]	20 804	...	...	...	...	335	214 663	46 029
	2005	32 396[4]	19 399	...	...	...	...	343	288 471	53 463
	2006	37 899[4]	18 310	...	...	...	...	483	293 076	56 494
Yemen	2003	...	21 251	1 059	388	819	586	87	...	4 094
Yémen	2004	...	19 999	1 138	317	883	268	89	...	4 337
	2005	...	19 802	1 195	369	959	399	84	...	4 741
	2006	...	18 159	1 188	413	801	378	69	...	5 337
Europe	**2003**	**1 054 935**	**729 481**	**193 339**	**47 501**	**336 425**	**186 043**	**39 799**	**36 486 165**	**4 597 760**
Europe	**2004**	**1 041 680**	**756 139**	**199 860**	**48 702**	**340 617**	**192 201**	**41 552**	**37 312 306**	**4 693 652**
	2005	**1 043 202**	**742 999**	**199 595**	**48 304**	**352 249**	**193 453**	**42 314**	**37 210 883**	**4 762 228**
	2006	**1 040 207**	**732 833**	**200 915**	**50 436**	**354 085**	**192 875**	**43 996**	**37 405 317**	**4 847 282**
Albania	2003	81[9]	375[2]	6	1	95	45	0	544	5 230
Albanie	2004	109[9]	420[2]	35	16	73	67	1	636	5 559
	2005	92[9]	447[2]	14	0	72	68	0	670	5 443
	2006	92[9]	505[2]	35	0	99	48	0	670	5 094
Austria	2003	1 153[10]	1 011	1 811	446	3 849	1 062	50	82 603	60 100
Autriche	2004	236[10]	1 061	1 738	455	3 529	1 032	57	77 550	64 125
	2005	1[3]	965	1 798	592	3 894	1 009	107	62 081	65 681
	2006	1[3]	983	1 615	526	3 685	915	50	72 756	63 445
Belarus	2003	1 802[3]	1 820[2]	1 895	...	4 913	4 790	216	9 810	26 627
Bélarus	2004	1 993[3]	1 804[2]	2 842	...	5 845	5 501	418	9 942	31 210
	2005	2 308[3]	1 785[2]	3 330	...	6 426	6 313	459	8 806	30 961
	2006	2 125[3]	1 780[2]	3 498	...	6 616	6 329	483	8 458	31 811
Belgium	2003	129[9]	...	5 865	2 048	13 013	8 689	627	...	84 630
Belgique	2004	181[9]	...	5 789	2 143	12 327	8 380	511	...	85 643
	2005	109[9]	...	5 056	1 678	11 938	8 042	462	...	86 944
	2006	29[9]	...	5 357	1 744	12 660	7 128	403	...	85 391
Bosnia and Herzegovina	2003	12 230[6]	...	9	...	19	36	1	...	11 266
Bosnie-Herzégovine	2004	12 275[6]	...	26	...	42	78	3	...	12 734
	2005	12 665[6]	...	18	...	31	74	2	...	12 637
	2006	13 741[6]	...	18	...	31	74	2	...	13 346
Bulgaria	2003	27 335[6]	30[2]	967	144	1 878	718	85	597	42 600
Bulgarie	2004	26 485[6]	30[2]	1 401	142	1 915	965	103	12 432	41 621
	2005	24 695[6]	30[2]	1 381	144	2 270	1 230	105	17 884	44 365
	2006	25 678[6]	28[2]	1 560	151	2 521	1 512	127	17 391	45 843
Croatia	2003	...	1 291	1 261	75	1 873	1 036	437	83 205	12 620
Croatie	2004	...	1 246	1 226	91	1 741	1 012	443	83 528	13 295
	2005	...	1 178	1 168	99	1 603	1 160	431	86 769	12 462
	2006	...	1 139	1 083	67	1 565	1 097	399	103 113	12 430
Czech Republic	2003	63 906[6]	457[2]	1 344	140	2 590	445	168	6 098	83 227
République tchèque	2004	64 076[6]	565[2]	1 289	147	2 673	394	181	7 555	84 333
	2005	62 026[6]	569[2]	1 467	132	3 067	581	184	7 170	82 578
	2006	62 453[6]	344[2]	1 594	121	3 128	381	204	6 853	84 361
Denmark	2003	...	18 143[2]	2 082	611	3 451	1 519	168	335 062	46 181
Danemark	2004	...	19 262[2]	1 986	606	3 329	1 557	164	395 033	40 433
	2005	...	18 517[2]	1 919	507	3 224	1 405	145	436 520	36 355
	2006	...	16 839[2]	1 987	608	3 298	1 471	166	433 718	45 716
Estonia	2003	15 254[10]	...	...	...	...	...	...	...	10 159
Estonie	2004	14 272[10]	...	...	...	...	...	...	...	10 128
	2005	14 969[10]	...	...	...	...	...	...	...	10 002
	2006	14 602[10]	...	...	...	...	...	...	...	9 508

Region, country or area Région, pays ou zone	Year Année	Hard coal, lignite and peat Houille, lignite et tourbe	Crude petroleum and NGL Pétrole brut et LGN	Motor gasoline Essence auto	Jet fuel Carbu-réacteurs	Gas-diesel oil Gazole/ carburant diesel	Residual fuel oil Mazout résiduel	Liquefied petroleum gas Gaz de pétrole liquéfiés	Natural gas Gaz naturel Terajoules Térajoules	Electricity Electricité Million kWh Millions de kWh
		Thousand metric tons Milliers de tonnes								
Faeroe Islands Iles Féroé	2003 2004 *2005 *2006	... ...	... ...	... ...	... ...	... ...	... ...	... ...	... ...	270 290 290 295
Finland Finlande	2003 2004 2005 2006	7 305[3] 3 633[3] 8 928[3] 13 235[3]	... ...	4 304 4 321 4 061 4 298	614 714 592 715	5 038 5 078 4 964 5 502	1 267 1 445 1 318 1 272	273 267 315 402	... ...	84 230 85 847 70 550 82 304
France[11] France[11]	2003 2004 2005 2006	2 243[6] 872[4] 617[4] 452[4]	1 559 1 561 1 354 1 119	16 804 16 926 16 305 17 214	5 169 5 616 5 478 5 633	34 979 34 421 33 590 33 733	10 919 11 887 11 823 11 955	3 071 2 979 2 868 2 774	59 621 51 530 42 275 49 242	566 948 574 278 576 170 574 473
Germany Allemagne	2003 2004 2005 2006	207 983 211 210 206 054 200 184	3 690[2] 3 463[2] 3 471[2] 3 383[2]	26 449 26 467 27 240 26 576	4 194 4 424 4 252 4 412	48 638 49 551 52 137 50 854	12 232 14 013 13 340 13 684	3 056 2 918 2 951 2 925	740 615 685 342 661 721 653 696	606 719 615 287 620 574 636 761
Gibraltar Gibraltar	2003 2004 2005 2006	... ...	... ...	... ...	... ...	... ...	... ...	... ...	... ...	134 136 145 151
Greece Grèce	2003 2004 2005 2006	68 299[9] 70 041[9] 69 398[9] 64 521[9]	137 133 100 94	3 653 3 629 4 058 4 327	1 630 1 720 1 737 1 423	6 053 5 369 5 653 6 452	7 456 7 095 6 956 6 953	672 598 655 653	1 442 1 337 851 1 209	58 471 59 346 60 020 60 789
Hungary Hongrie	2003 2004 2005 2006	13 301[9] 11 242[9] 9 570[9] 9 952[9]	1 898 1 878 1 723 1 637	1 477 1 465 1 321 1 302	202 239 266 280	3 124 2 989 3 515 3 498	367 313 218 232	392 408 393 373	106 329 110 100 108 422 110 660	34 145 33 708 35 756 35 859
Iceland Islande	2003 2004 2005 2006	... ...	... ...	... ...	... ...	... ...	... ...	... ...	... ...	8 500 8 623 8 683 9 930
Ireland Irlande	2003 2004 2005 2006	5 504[3] 4 395[3] 3 956[3] 3 694[3]	... ...	639 552 683 634	... ...	988 964 1 097 1 121	1 005 966 948 1 101	59 53 57 51	25 293 32 025 21 437 19 107	25 317 25 569 25 970 28 046
Italy[12] Italie[12]	2003 2004 2005 2006	250[4] 98[4] 95[4] 21[4]	5 570[2] 5 445[2] 6 111[2] 5 769[2]	20 699 20 662 21 189 20 967	4 187 3 787 3 910 4 081	38 389 39 536 39 844 39 805	18 018 17 543 19 032 17 621	2 610 2 613 2 517 2 275	529 017 493 813 459 905 418 301	293 884 303 347 303 699 314 121
Latvia Lettonie	2003 2004 2005 2006	8[3] 13[3] 12[3] 14[3]	... ...	... ...	... ...	... ...	... ...	... ...	... ...	3 975 4 689 4 905 4 891
Lithuania Lituanie	2003 2004 2005 2006	46[3] 50[3] 70[3] 55[3]	382[2] 302[2] 216[2] 181[2]	1 882 2 331 2 462 2 163	695 850 832 764	2 064 2 523 2 781 2 246	1 381 1 673 1 799 1 938	435 526 555 474	... ...	19 488 19 274 14 784 12 482
Luxembourg Luxembourg	2003 2004 2005 2006	... ...	... ...	... ...	... ...	... ...	... ...	... ...	... ...	3 620 4 121 4 135 4 333

Region, country or area Région, pays ou zone	Year Année	Hard coal, lignite and peat Houille, lignite et tourbe	Crude petroleum and NGL Pétrole brut et LGN	Motor gasoline Essence auto	Jet fuel Carbu-réacteurs	Gas-diesel oil Gazole/ carburant diesel	Residual fuel oil Mazout résiduel	Liquefied petroleum gas Gaz de pétrole liquéfiés	Natural gas Gaz naturel Terajoules Térajoules	Electricity Electricité Million kWh Millions de kWh
		Thousand metric tons Milliers de tonnes								
Malta	2003	...	...	...	...	...	...	...	...	2 236
Malte	2004	...	...	...	...	...	...	...	...	2 216
	2005	...	...	...	...	...	...	...	...	2 240
	2006	...	...	...	...	...	...	...	...	2 296
Netherlands	2003	...	3 129	15 730	6 669	20 787	12 333	4 780	2 428 905	96 763
Pays-Bas	2004	...	2 910	15 539	6 935	20 234	13 073	5 070	2 864 924	100 770
	2005	...	2 530	14 234	6 990	21 346	12 394	4 579	2 617 469	100 219
	2006	...	2 022	13 794	6 914	19 685	12 151	4 069	2 578 865	96 733
Norway [13]	2003	2 944[4]	153 616	3 546	415	6 635	1 702	6 167	3 082 859	107 405
Norvège [13]	2004	2 904[4]	152 615	3 261	423	6 241	1 845	6 423	3 275 892	110 598
	2005	1 471[4]	141 024	3 829	644	6 835	1 610	6 628	3 548 571	138 108
	2006	2 395[4]	130 239	4 134	644	7 101	1 957	8 255	3 647 849	121 663
Poland	2003	163 794[6]	765[2]	3 871	647	6 722	3 253	269	167 997	151 631
Pologne	2004	162 428[6]	886[2]	3 978	679	7 371	2 754	259	182 698	154 159
	2005	159 540[6]	848[2]	4 117	644	7 459	2 537	284	180 700	156 936
	2006	156 067[6]	796[2]	4 155	853	8 336	2 824	282	180 514	161 742
Portugal	2003	...	...	2 732	703	4 955	2 388	379	...	46 852
Portugal	2004	...	...	2 551	779	4 703	2 969	365	...	45 105
	2005	...	...	2 466	854	4 906	3 062	391	...	46 575
	2006	...	...	2 750	856	5 102	2 920	406	...	49 041
Republic of Moldova	2003	...	...	...	...	...	...	...	...	3 453
République de Moldova	2004	...	8[2]	...	...	...	...	...	...	3 613
	2005	...	5[2]	...	...	...	...	...	...	3 864
	2006	...	4[2]	...	...	...	...	...	...	3 829
Romania	2003	*33 073	*5 890	3 295	158	3 988	1 562	327	485 135	55 140
Roumanie	2004	31 800	*5 705	3 419	177	4 170	1 559	366	482 759	56 499
	2005	*31 114	*5 733	4 237	191	4 709	1 707	658	451 305	59 413
	2006	34 932	*5 659	4 145	238	4 593	1 303	677	444 656	62 697
Russian Federation	2003	258 106	418 582	29 315	9 453	53 930	56 377	8 571	23 252 111	916 286
Fédération de Russie	2004	260 431	456 253	30 505	9 283	55 389	58 330	8 760	23 693 333	931 865
	2005	284 530	466 448	32 011	10 036	60 000	62 365	9 428	23 996 973	953 074
	2006	285 928	475 827	34 368	10 602	64 166	65 189	10 368	24 463 654	995 785
Serbia	2003	40 279[6]	773[2]	617	85	1 254	919	79	13 723	35 366
Serbie	2004	41 157[6]	652[2]	821	56	1 315	853	95	11 951	37 686
	2005	35 244[6]	649[2]	770	53	1 234	801	89	10 631	36 474
	2006	36 780[9]	646[2]	648	45	1 038	674	75	10 970	36 481
Slovakia	2003	3 097[9]	48	1 597	63	2 349	635	152	7 745	31 178
Slovaquie	2004	2 952[9]	42	1 670	61	2 598	585	206	6 603	30 567
	2005	2 511[9]	34	1 584	36	2 455	543	181	5 876	31 455
	2006	2 201[9]	31	1 449	46	2 587	654	137	8 187	31 418
Slovenia	2003	4 830[9]	...	...	...	...	...	...	199	14 019
Slovénie	2004	4 809[9]	...	...	...	...	...	...	201	15 271
	2005	4 540[9]	...	...	...	...	...	...	160	15 117
	2006	4 522[9]	...	...	...	...	...	...	160	15 115
Spain	2003	20 562[6]	322[2]	9 047	3 061	21 631	10 130	1 211	9 149	260 727
Espagne	2004	20 487[6]	255[2]	10 434	2 713	21 563	9 125	1 058	14 398	280 007
	2005	19 481[6]	166[2]	10 152	2 653	23 457	9 019	1 050	6 694	294 077
	2006	18 447[6]	139[2]	10 038	2 612	23 844	9 245	1 522	2 545	303 051
Sweden	2003	806[3]	...	4 309	109	6 942	5 170	360	...	135 435
Suède	2004	893[3]	...	4 506	208	7 238	5 450	423	...	151 726
	2005	708[3]	...	4 045	70	6 951	5 576	433	...	158 434
	2006	621[3]	...	4 182	179	7 204	5 226	302	...	143 299

Region, country or area Région, pays ou zone	Year Année	Hard coal, lignite and peat Houille, lignite et tourbe	Crude petroleum and NGL Pétrole brut et LGN	Motor gasoline Essence auto	Jet fuel Carbu-réacteurs	Gas-diesel oil Gazole/ carburant diesel	Residual fuel oil Mazout résiduel	Liquefied petroleum gas Gaz de pétrole liquéfiés	Natural gas Gaz naturel	Electricity Electricité
				Thousand metric tons — Milliers de tonnes					Terajoules Térajoules	Million kWh Millions de kWh
Switzerland [14]	2003	...	...	1 072	344	1 893	759	178	...	67 166
Suisse [14]	2004	...	...	1 362	350	2 148	701	196	...	65 299
	2005	...	...	1 268	212	2 170	611	197	...	59 612
	2006	...	...	1 465	228	2 573	583	223	...	64 038
TFYR of Macedonia	2003	7 382[9]	...	126	0	322	343	21	...	6 737
L'ex-R.Y. Macédoine	2004	7 245[9]	...	146	0	359	282	20	...	6 665
	2005	6 881[9]	...	183	23	394	295	24	...	6 942
	2006	6 639[9]	...	190	33	443	327	29	...	7 006
Ukraine	2003	64 954	3 920	4 308	361	6 484	7 970	978	748 794	180 354
Ukraine	2004	60 296	4 269	4 394	473	6 544	7 766	988	799 130	182 157
	2005	61 119	4 374	4 609	512	5 533	5 889	948	811 148	186 055
	2006	62 298	4 521	3 926	400	4 519	3 834	938	822 932	193 381
United Kingdom	2003	28 279[4]	106 073	22 627	5 277	27 579	11 517	4 007	4 309 312	398 671
Royaume-Uni	2004	25 097[4]	95 374	24 589	5 615	28 839	12 988	5 080	4 019 594	395 853
	2005	20 498[4]	84 722	22 620	5 167	28 691	11 728	5 218	3 666 845	400 524
	2006	18 528[4]	79 148	21 443	6 261	26 080	12 277	4 952	3 349 811	398 327
Oceania	**2003**	**346 843[6]**	**32 785**	**14 628**	**4 912**	**13 448**	**1 669**	**1 850**	**1 641 590**	**278 260**
Océanie	**2004**	**357 352[6]**	**29 458**	**15 107**	**4 867**	**13 503**	**1 521**	**1 479**	**1 653 819**	**286 705**
	2005	**372 609[6]**	**26 387**	**14 917**	**5 198**	**12 985**	**1 664**	**1 445**	**1 807 130**	**297 669**
	2006	**373 219[6]**	**25 740**	**13 714**	**5 143**	**11 815**	**1 537**	**1 836**	**1 876 971**	**304 345**
American Samoa	2003	...	...	...	...	...	...	...	...	188
Samoa américaines	2004	...	...	...	...	...	...	...	...	188
	2005	...	...	...	...	...	...	...	...	189
	*2006	...	...	...	...	...	...	...	...	193
Australia	2003	341 663[6]	29 111	13 108	4 080	11 430	1 310	1 694	1 456 588	228 118
Australie	2004	352 197[6]	26 218	13 453	3 937	11 590	1 071	1 312	1 488 699	234 542
	2005	367 342[6]	22 895	13 218	4 221	10 790	1 085	1 271	1 648 435	245 495
	2006	367 452[6]	21 886	12 153	4 128	9 466	1 051	1 679	1 713 590	251 659
Cook Islands	2003	...	...	...	...	...	...	...	...	29
Iles Cook	2004	...	...	...	...	...	...	...	...	30
	2005	...	...	...	...	...	...	...	...	30
	2006	...	...	...	...	...	...	...	...	32
Fiji *	2003	...	...	...	...	...	...	...	...	812
Fidji *	2004	...	...	...	...	...	...	...	...	816
	2005	...	...	...	...	...	...	...	...	823
	2006	...	...	...	...	...	...	...	...	840
French Polynesia	2003	...	...	...	...	...	...	...	...	602
Polynésie française	2004	...	...	...	...	...	...	...	...	643
	2005	...	...	...	...	...	...	...	...	631
	2006	...	...	...	...	...	...	...	...	667
Guam	2003	...	...	...	...	...	...	...	...	1 777
Guam	2004	...	...	...	...	...	...	...	...	1 878
	2005	...	...	...	...	...	...	...	...	1 897
	2006	...	...	...	...	...	...	...	...	1 891
Kiribati *	2003	...	...	...	...	...	...	...	...	14
Kiribati *	2004	...	...	...	...	...	...	...	...	14
	2005	...	...	...	...	...	...	...	...	15
	2006	...	...	...	...	...	...	...	...	15
Marshall Islands	2003	...	...	...	...	...	...	...	...	96
Iles Marshall	2004	...	...	...	...	...	...	...	...	101
	2005	...	...	...	...	...	...	...	...	101
	*2006	...	...	...	...	...	...	...	...	104

Region, country or area Région, pays ou zone	Year Année	Hard coal, lignite and peat Houille, lignite et tourbe	Crude petroleum and NGL Pétrole brut et LGN	Motor gasoline Essence auto	Jet fuel Carbu-réacteurs	Gas-diesel oil Gazole/ carburant diesel	Residual fuel oil Mazout résiduel	Liquefied petroleum gas Gaz de pétrole liquéfiés	Natural gas Gaz naturel Terajoules Térajoules	Electricity Electricité Million kWh Millions de kWh
					Thousand metric tons Milliers de tonnes					
Nauru * Nauru *	2003	...	...	...	...	...	...	...	...	31
	2004	...	...	...	...	...	...	...	...	32
	2005	...	...	...	...	...	...	...	...	33
	2006	...	...	...	...	...	...	...	...	33
New Caledonia Nouvelle-Calédonie	2003	...	...	...	...	...	...	...	...	1 758
	2004	...	...	...	...	...	...	...	...	1 678
	2005	...	...	...	...	...	...	...	...	1 883
	2006	...	...	...	...	...	...	...	...	1 926
New Zealand Nouvelle-Zélande	2003	5 180[6]	1 247	1 520	832	2 018	359	156	179 476	41 249
	2004	5 155[6]	1 106	1 627	930	1 763	350	167	160 640	42 901
	2005	5 267[6]	1 030	1 645	887	1 785	439	156	148 597	43 136
	2006	5 767[6]	987	1 482	909	1 819	381	135	152 529	43 519
Niue * Nioué *	2003	...	...	...	...	...	...	...	...	3
	2004	...	...	...	...	...	...	...	...	3
	2005	...	...	...	...	...	...	...	...	3
	2006	...	...	...	...	...	...	...	...	3
Palau Palaos	2003	...	...	...	...	...	...	...	...	128
	*2004	...	...	...	...	...	...	...	...	128
	*2005	...	...	...	...	...	...	...	...	134
	*2006	...	...	...	...	...	...	...	...	151
Papua New Guinea Papouasie-Nvl-Guinée	2003	...	2 427[2]	0	0	0	0	0	5 526	3 178
	2004	...	2 134[2]	27	0	150	100	0	4 480	3 468
	2005	...	2 462[2]	54	90	410	140	18	10 098	3 002
	2006	...	2 867[2]	79	106	530	105	22	10 852	3 012
Samoa * Samoa *	2003	...	...	...	...	...	...	...	...	106
	2004	...	...	...	...	...	...	...	...	110
	2005	...	...	...	...	...	...	...	...	111
	2006	...	...	...	...	...	...	...	...	112
Solomon Islands Iles Salomon	*2003	...	...	...	...	...	...	...	...	63
	2004	...	...	...	...	...	...	...	...	63
	2005	...	...	...	...	...	...	...	...	74
	2006	...	...	...	...	...	...	...	...	75
Tonga Tonga	2003	...	...	...	...	...	...	...	...	45
	2004	...	...	...	...	...	...	...	...	47
	*2005	...	...	...	...	...	...	...	...	48
	*2006	...	...	...	...	...	...	...	...	48
Vanuatu * Vanuatu *	2003	...	...	...	...	...	...	...	...	44
	2004	...	...	...	...	...	...	...	...	44
	2005	...	...	...	...	...	...	...	...	45
	2006	...	...	...	...	...	...	...	...	45
Wallis and Futuna Islands Iles Wallis et Futuna	2003	...	...	...	...	...	...	...	...	19
	2004	...	...	...	...	...	...	...	...	19
	2005	...	...	...	...	...	...	...	...	20
	2006	...	...	...	...	...	...	...	...	20

Source:
United Nations Statistics Division, New York, the energy statistics database, last accessed June 2009.

Source:
Organisation des Nations Unies, Division de statistique, New York, la base de données pour les statistiques de l'énergie, dernier accès juin 2009.

1 Hard coal and peat only.
2 Crude petroleum only.
3 Peat only.
4 Hard coal only.
5 Refers to the Southern African Customs Union.

1 Houille et tourbe seulement.
2 Pétrole brut seulement.
3 Tourbe seulement.
4 Houille seulement.
5 Se réfèrent à l'Union douanière d'Afrique australe.

6	Hard coal and lignite only.	6	Houille et lignite seulement.
7	Natural gas liquids only.	7	Liquides de gaz naturel seulement.
8	For statistical purposes, the data for China do not include those for the Hong Kong Special Administrative Region (Hong Kong SAR), Macao Special Administrative Region (Macao SAR) and Taiwan Province of China.	8	Pour la présentation des statistiques, les données pour la Chine ne comprennent pas la Région Administrative Spéciale de Hong Kong (Hong Kong RAS), la Région Administrative Spéciale de Macao (Macao RAS) et la province de Taiwan.
9	Lignite only.	9	Lignite seulement.
10	Lignite and peat only.	10	Lignite et tourbe seulement.
11	Including Monaco.	11	Y compris Monaco.
12	Including San Marino.	12	Y compris Saint-Marin.
13	Including Svalbard and Jan Mayen Islands.	13	Y compris îles Svalbard et Jan Mayen.
14	Including Liechtenstein.	14	Y compris Liechtenstein.

Technical notes: tables 52 and 53

Table 52: Data are presented in metric tons of oil equivalent (TOE), to which the individual energy commodities are converted in the interests of international uniformity and comparability.

To convert from original units to TOE, the data in original units (metric tons, terajoules, kilowatt hours, cubic metres) are multiplied by conversion factors. For a list of the relevant conversion factors and a detailed description of methods, see the United Nations Energy Statistics Yearbook and related methodological publications.

Included in the production of commercial primary energy for solids are hard coal, lignite, peat and oil shale; liquids are comprised of crude petroleum and natural gas liquids; gas comprises natural gas; and electricity is comprised of primary electricity generation from hydro, nuclear, geothermal, wind, tide, wave and solar sources.

International trade of energy commodities is based on the "general trade" system, that is, all goods entering and leaving the national boundary of a country are recorded as imports and exports.

Sea/air bunkers refer to the amounts of fuels delivered to ocean-going ships or aircraft of all flags engaged in international traffic. Consumption by ships engaged in transport in inland and coastal waters, or by aircraft engaged in domestic flights, is not included.

Data on consumption refer to "apparent consumption" and are derived from the formula "production + imports – exports – bunkers +/- stock changes". Accordingly, the series on apparent consumption may in some cases represent only an indication of the magnitude of actual gross inland availability.

Included in the consumption of commercial energy for solids are consumption of primary forms of solid fuels, net imports and changes in stocks of secondary fuels; liquids are comprised of consumption of energy petroleum products including feedstocks, natural gasoline, condensate, refinery gas and input of crude petroleum to thermal power plants; gases include the consumption of natural gas, net imports and changes in stocks of gasworks and coke oven gas; and electricity is comprised of production of primary electricity and net imports of electricity.

Table 53: The definitions of the energy commodities are as follows:

– Hard coal: Coal that has a high degree of coalification with a gross calorific value above 23,865 KJ/kg (5,700 kcal/kg) on an ash free but moist basis, and a mean random reflectance of vitrinite of at least 0.6. Slurries, middlings and other low-grade coal products, which cannot be classified according to the type of coal

Notes techniques : tableaux 52 et 53

Tableau 52 : Les données relatives aux divers produits énergétiques ont été converties en tonnes d'équivalent pétrole (TEP), dans un souci d'uniformité et pour permettre les comparaisons entre la production de différents pays.

Pour passer des unités de mesure d'origine à l'unité commune, les données en unités d'origine (tonnes, terajoules, kilowattheures, mètres cubes) sont multipliées par des facteurs de conversion. Pour une liste des facteurs de conversion appropriée et pour des descriptions détaillées des méthodes appliquées, se reporter à l'Annuaire des statistiques de l'énergie des Nations Unies et aux publications méthodologiques apparentées.

Sont compris dans la production d'énergie primaire commerciale: pour les solides, la houille, le lignite, la tourbe et le schiste bitumineux; pour les liquides, le pétrole brut et les liquides de gaz naturel; pour les gaz, le gaz naturel; pour l'électricité, l'électricité primaire de source hydraulique, nucléaire, géothermique, éolienne, marémotrice, des vagues et solaire.

En général, les variations des stocks se rapportent aux différences entre les stocks des producteurs, des importateurs ou des consommateurs industriels au début et à la fin de chaque année.

Le commerce international des produits énergétiques est fondé sur le système du "commerce général", c'est-à-dire que tous les biens entrant sur le territoire national d'un pays ou en sortant sont respectivement enregistrés comme importations et exportations.

Les soutes maritimes/aériens se rapportent aux quantités de combustibles livrées aux navires de mer et aéronefs assurant des liaisons commerciales internationales, quel que soit leur pavillon. La consommation des navires effectuant des opérations de transport sur les voies navigables intérieures ou dans les eaux côtières n'est pas incluse, tout comme celle des aéronefs effectuant des vols intérieurs.

Les données sur la consommation se rapportent à la "consommation apparente" et sont obtenues par la formule "production + importations – exportations – soutes +/- variations des stocks". En conséquence, les séries relatives à la consommation apparente peuvent occasionnellement ne donner qu'une indication de l'ordre de grandeur des disponibilités intérieures brutes réelles.

Sont compris dans la consommation d'énergie commerciale: pour les solides, la consommation de combustibles solides primaires, les importations nettes et les variations de stocks de combustibles solides secondaires; pour les liquides, la consommation de produits pétroliers énergétiques y compris les charges d'alimentation des usines de traitement, l'essence naturelle, le condensat et le gaz de raffinerie ainsi que le pétrole brut consommé dans les centrales thermiques pour la production d'électricité; pour les gaz, la consommation de gaz naturel, les importations nettes et les variations de stocks de gaz d'usines à gaz et de gaz de cokerie; pour l'électricité, la production d'électricité primaire et les importations nettes d'électricité.

from which they are obtained, are included under hard coal.

– Lignite: Non-agglomerating coal with a low degree of coalification which retained the anatomical structure of the vegetable matter from which it was formed. Its gross calorific value is less than 17,435 KJ/kg (4,165 kcal/kg), and it contains greater than 31 per cent volatile matter on a dry mineral matter free basis.

– Peat: a solid fuel formed from the partial decomposition of dead vegetation under conditions of high humidity and limited air access (initial stage of coalification). Only peat used as fuel is included. Its principal use is as a household fuel.

– Crude petroleum: A mineral oil consisting of a mixture of hydrocarbons of natural origin, yellow to black in colour, of variable density and viscosity. Data in this category also includes lease or field condensate (separator liquids) which is recovered from gaseous hydrocarbons in lease separation facilities, as well as synthetic crude oil, mineral oils extracted from bituminous minerals such as shales and bituminous sand, and oils from coal liquefaction.

– Natural gas liquids (NGL): Liquid or liquefied hydrocarbons produced in the manufacture, purification and stabilization of natural gas. NGLs include, but are not limited to, ethane, propane, butane, pentane, natural gasoline, and plant condensate.

– Motor gasoline: Light hydrocarbon oil for use in internal combustion engines such as motor vehicles, excluding aircraft. It distills between 35°C and 200°C, and is treated to reach a sufficiently high octane number of generally between 80 and 100 RON. Treatment may be by re-forming, blending with an aromatic fraction, or the addition of benzole or other additives (such as tetra-ethyl lead).

– Jet fuel: Consists of gasoline-type jet fuel and kerosene-type jet fuel. Gasoline-type jet fuel: All light hydro-carbon oils for use in aviation gas-turbine engines. It distills between 100°C and 250°C with at least 20% of volume distilling at 143°C. It is obtained by blending kerosene and gasoline or naphtha in such a way that the aromatic content does not exceed 25% in volume. Additives are included to reduce the freezing point to -58°C or lower, and to keep the Reid vapour pressure between 0.14 and 0.21 kg/cm2. Kerosene-type jet fuel: Medium oil for use in aviation gas-turbine engines with the same distillation characteristics and flash point as kerosene, with a maxi-mum aromatic content of 20% in volume. It is treated to give a kinematic viscosity of less than 15 cSt at -34°C and a freezing point below -50°C.

– Gas-diesel oil (distillate fuel oil): Heavy oils distilling between 200°C and 380°C, but distilling less

Tableau 53: Les définitions des produits énergétiques sont données ci-après :

– Houille: Charbon à haut degré de houillification et à pouvoir calorifique brut supérieur à 23 865 kJ/kg (5 700 kcal/kg), valeur mesurée pour un combustible exempt de cendres, mais humide et ayant un indice moyen de réflectance de la vitrinite au moins égal à 0,6. Les schlamms, les mixtes et autres produits du charbon de faible qualité qui ne peuvent être classés en fonction du type de charbon dont ils sont dérivés, sont inclus dans cette rubrique.

– Lignite: Le charbon non agglutinant d'un faible degré de houillification qui a gardé la structure anatomique des végétaux dont il est issu. Son pouvoir calorifique supérieur est inférieur à 17 435 kJ/kg (4 165 kcal/kg) et il contient plus de 31% de matières volatiles sur produit sec exempt de matières minérales.

–Tourbe : Combustible solide issu de la décomposition particlle de végétaux morts dans des conditions de forte humidité et de faible circulation d'air (phase initiale de la houillification). N'est prise en considération ici que la tourbe utilisée comme combustible. La tourbe est utilisée principalement comme combustible domestique.

– Pétrole brut: Huile minérale constituée d'un mélange d'hydrocarbures d'origine naturelle, de couleur variant du jaune au noir, d'une densité et d'une viscosité variable. Figurent également dans cette rubrique les condensats directement récupérés sur les sites d'exploitation des hydrocarbures gazeux (dans les installations prévues pour la séparation des phases liquide et gazeuse), le pétrole brut synthétique, les huiles minérales brutes extraites des roches bitumineuses telles que schistes, sables asphaltiques et les huiles issues de la liquéfaction du charbon.

– Liquides de gaz naturel (LGN): Hydrocarbures liquides ou liquéfiés produits lors de la fabrication, de la purification et de la stabilisation du gaz naturel. Les liquides de gaz naturel comprennent l'éthane, le propane, le butane, le pentane, l'essence naturelle et les condensats d'usine, sans que la liste soit limitative.

– Essence auto : Hydrocarbure léger utilisé dans les moteurs à combustion interne, tels que ceux des véhicules à moteur, à l'exception des aéronefs. Sa température de distillation se situe entre 35°C et 200°C et il est traité de façon à atteindre un indice d'octane suffisamment élevé, généralement entre 80 et 100 IOR. Le traitement peut consister en reformage, mélange avec une fraction aromatique, ou adjonction de benzol ou d'autres additifs (tels que du plomb tétraéthyle).

– Carburéacteurs: Comprennent les carburéacteurs du type essence et les carburéacteurs du type kérosène. Carburéacteurs du type essence: Comprennent tous les hydrocarbures légers utilisés dans les turboréacteurs d'aviation. Leur température de distillation se situe entre 100°C et 250°C et donne au moins 20% en volume de distillat à 143°C. Ils sont obtenus par mélange de pétrole lampant et d'essence ou de naphta de façon que la teneur en composés aromatiques ne dépasse pas 25% en volume. Des additifs y sont ajoutés afin d'abaisser le point de congélation à -58°C ou au-dessous, et de maintenir la tension de vapeur Reid

than 65% in volume at 250°C, including losses, and 85% or more at 350°C. Its flash point is always above 50°C and its specific gravity is higher than 0.82. Heavy oils obtained by blending are grouped together with gas oils on the condition that their kinematic viscosity does not exceed 27.5 cSt at 38°C. Also included are middle distillates intended for the petrochemical industry. Gas-diesel oils are used as a fuel for internal combustion in diesel engines, as a burner fuel in heating installations, such as furnaces, and for enriching water gas to increase its luminosity. Other names for this product are diesel fuel, diesel oil and gas oil.

– Residual fuel oil: heavy oil that makes up the distillation residue. It comprises all fuels (including those obtained by blending) with a kinematic viscosity above 27.5 cSt at 38°C. Its flash point is always above 50°C and its specific gravity is higher than 0.90. It is commonly used by ships and industrial large-scale heating installations as a fuel in furnaces or boilers.

– Liquefied petroleum gas (LPG): Hydrocarbons which are gaseous under conditions of normal temperature and pressure but are liquefied by compression or cooling to facilitate storage, handling and transportation. It comprises propane, butane, or a combination of the two. Also included is ethane from petroleum refineries or natural gas producers' separation and stabilization plants.

– Natural gas: Gases consisting mainly of methane occurring naturally in underground deposits. It includes both non associated gas (originating from fields producing only hydrocarbons in gaseous form) and associated gas (originating from fields producing both liquid and gaseous hydrocarbons), as well as methane recovered from coal mines and sewage gas. Production of natural gas refers to dry marketable production, measured after purification and extraction of natural gas liquids and sulphur. Extraction losses and the amounts that have been re-injected, flared, and vented are excluded from the data on production.

– Electricity production refers to gross production, which includes the consumption by station auxiliaries and any losses in the transformers that are considered integral parts of the station. Included also is total electric energy produced by pumping installations without deduction of electric energy absorbed by pumping.

entre 0,14 et 0,21 kg/cm2. Carburéacteurs du type kerosene: Huiles moyennement visqueuses utilisées dans les turboréacteurs d'aviation, ayant les mêmes caractéristiques de distillation et le même point d'éclair que le pétrole lampant et une teneur en composés aromatiques ne dépassant pas 20% en volume. Elles sont traitées de façon à atteindre une viscosité cinématique de moins de 15 cSt à -34°C et un point de congélation inférieur à -50°C.

– Gazole/carburant diesel (mazout distillé):Huiles lourdes dont la température de distillation se situe entre 200°C et 380°C, mais qui donnent moins de 65% en volume de distillat à 250°C (y compris les pertes) et 85% ou davantage à 350°C. Leur point d'éclair est toujours supérieur à 50°C et leur densité supérieure à 0,82. Les huiles lourdes obtenues par mélange sont classées dans la même catégorie que les gazoles à condition que leur viscosité cinématique ne dépasse pas 27,5 cSt à 38°C. Sont compris dans cette rubrique les distillats moyens destinés à l'industrie pétrochimique. Les gazoles servent de carburant pour la combustion interne dans les moteurs diesel, de combustible dans les installations de chauffage telles que les chaudières, et d'additifs destinés à augmenter la luminosité de la flamme du gaz à l'eau. Ce produit est aussi connu sous les appellations de gazole ou gasoil et carburant ou combustible diesel.

– Gaz de pétrole liquéfiés (GPL): Hydrocarbures qui sont à l'état gazeux dans des conditions de température et de pression normales mais sont liquéfiés par compression ou refroidissement pour en faciliter l'entreposage, la manipulation et le transport. Dans cette rubrique figurent le propane et le butane ou un mélange de ces deux hydrocarbures. Est également inclus l'éthane produit dans les raffineries ou dans les installations de séparation et de stabilisation des producteurs de gaz naturel.

– Gaz naturel: gaz constitué essentiellement de méthane, extraits de gisements naturels souterrains. Il peut s'agir aussi bien de gaz non associé (provenant de gisements qui produisent uniquement des hydrocarbures gazeux) que de gaz associé (provenant de gisements qui produisent à la fois des hydrocarbures liquides et gazeux) ou de méthane récupéré dans les mines de charbon et le gaz de gadoues. La production de gaz naturel se rapporte à la production de gaz commercialisable sec, mesurée après purification et extraction des condensats de gaz naturel et du soufre. Les quantités réinjectées, brûlées à la torchère ou éventées et les pertes d'extraction sont exclues des données sur la production.

– La production d'électricité se rapporte à la production brute, qui comprend la consommation des équipements auxiliaires des centrales et les pertes au niveau des transformateurs considérés comme faisant partie intégrante de ces centrales, ainsi que la quantité totale d'énergie électrique produite par les installations de pompage sans déductions de l'énergie électrique absorbée par ces dernières.

Land
As of 2007, thousand hectares

Terres
En 2007, milliers d'hectares

Country or area Pays ou zone	Area – Superficie				Net change from 2000 to 2007 Variation nette de 2000 à 2007		
	Total land Superficie totale	Arable land Terres arables	Permanent crops Cultures permanentes	Forest cover Superficie forestière	Arable land Terres arables	Permanent crops Cultures permanentes	Forest cover Superficie forestière
World [1] **Monde [1]**	**13 009 115**	**1 411 117**	**142 571**	**3 937 326**	**13 158**	**10 175**	**-51 284**
Africa [1] **Afrique [1]**	**2 964 396**	**219 183**	**27 342**	**627 336**	**19 403**	**2 155**	**-28 277**
Americas [1] **Amériques [1]**	**3 894 456**	**364 368**	**29 075**	**1 528 151**	**652**	**543**	**-32 159**
Asia [1] **Asie [1]**	**3 093 949**	**504 537**	**68 747**	**573 583**	**7 056**	**8 228**	**7 020**
Europe [1] **Europe [1]**	**2 207 219**	**277 456**	**15 979**	**1 002 715**	**-10 244**	**-809**	**4 624**
Oceania [1] **Océanie [1]**	**849 095**	**45 573**	**1 428**	**205 542**	**-3 709**	**57**	**-2 492**
Afghanistan [2] Afghanistan [2]	65 223	8 531	130	808	828	-5	-207
Albania Albanie	2 740[2]	578	120	804[2]	0	-1	35[2]
Algeria Algérie	238 174	7 469	921	2 330[2]	-193	391	186[2]
American Samoa Samoa américaines	20	2[2]	3[2]	18[2]	0[2]	0[2]	0[2]
Andorra Andorre	47	1[2]	...	16[2]	0[2]	...	0[2]
Angola Angola	124 670	3 300[2]	290[2]	58 854[2]	300[2]	-10[2]	-874[2]
Anguilla Anguilla	9	...	...	6[2]	...	...	0[2]
Antigua and Barbuda Antigua-et-Barbuda	44	8[2]	1[2]	9[2]	0[2]	0[2]	0[2]
Argentina [2] Argentine [2]	273 669	32 500	1 000	32 721	4 600	0	-1 049
Armenia Arménie	2 820[2]	406[2]	54	274[2]	-36[2]	16	-31[2]
Aruba Aruba	18	2[2]	...	0[2]	0[2]	...	0[2]
Australia Australie	768 230	44 180[2]	350[2]	163 291[2]	-3 124[2]	54[2]	-1 354[2]
Austria Autriche	8 245	1 382	68	3 872[2]	-17	-3	34[2]
Azerbaijan Azerbaïdjan	8 263	1 854	225	936[2]	28	-12	0[2]
Bahamas [2] Bahamas [2]	1 001	8	4	515	1	0	0
Bahrain [2] Bahreïn [2]	71	2	4	1	0	0	0
Bangladesh [2] Bangladesh [2]	13 017	7 970	480	866	-114	80	-17
Barbados Barbade	43	16[2]	1[2]	2[2]	0[2]	0[2]	0[2]
Belarus [2] Bélarus [2]	20 290	5 535	120	7 912	-598	-4	64

54

Land *(continued)*
As of 2007, thousand hectares
Terres *(suite)*
En 2007, milliers d'hectares

Country or area Pays ou zone	Total land Superficie totale	Area – Superficie Arable land Terres arables	Permanent crops Cultures permanentes	Forest cover Superficie forestière	Net change from 2000 to 2007 Variation nette de 2000 à 2007 Arable land Terres arables	Permanent crops Cultures permanentes	Forest cover Superficie forestière
Belgium Belgique	3 028	840	23	667[2]	-22	2	0[2]
Belize[2] Belize[2]	2 281	70	32	1 653	6	-3	0
Benin[2] Bénin[2]	11 062	2 700	270	2 221	320	5	-454
Bermuda Bermudes	5	1	...	1[2]	0	...	0[2]
Bhutan Bhoutan	3 839	128[2]	27[2]	3 217[2]	-2[2]	3[2]	76[2]
Bolivia Bolivie	108 330	3 609[2]	219	58 200[2]	609[2]	51	-1 891[2]
Bosnia and Herzegovina Bosnie-Herzégovine	5 120[2]	1 022	95	2 185[2]	22	-5	0[2]
Botswana[2] Botswana[2]	56 673	250	2	11 706	-100	1	-829
Brazil[2] Brésil[2]	845 942	59 500	7 000	471 492	1 800	-500	-21 721
British Indian Ocean Terr[2] Terr. brit. de l'océan Indien[2]	8	...	...	3	...	...	0
British Virgin Islands Iles Vierges britanniques	15	2[2]	1[2]	4[2]	-1[2]	0[2]	0[2]
Brunei Darussalam[2] Brunéi Darussalam[2]	527	3	5	274	1	1	-14
Bulgaria Bulgarie	10 861	3 086	195	3 725[2]	-440	-57	350[2]
Burkina Faso[2] Burkina Faso[2]	27 360	5 200	60	6 746	1 160	0	-168
Burundi[2] Burundi[2]	2 568	995	350	134	35	-10	-64
Cambodia[2] Cambodge[2]	17 652	3 800	155	10 009	100	15	-1 532
Cameroon Cameroun	47 271	5 960[2]	1 200[2]	20 805[2]	0[2]	0[2]	-1 540[2]
Canada Canada	909 351	45 100[2]	7 050[2,3]	310 134[2]	-710[2]	682[2,3]	0[2]
Cape Verde Cap-Vert	403	50[2]	3[2]	85[2]	6[2]	1[2]	2[2]
Cayman Islands Iles Caïmanes	26	1	...	12[2]	0[2]	...	0[2]
Central African Rep.[2] Rép. centrafricaine[2]	62 300	1 925	80	22 696	-5	-14	-207
Chad[2] Tchad[2]	125 920	4 300	30	11 763	780	0	-554
Channel Islands Iles Anglo-Normandes	19[4]	3[2]	...	1[2]	-1[2]	...	0[2]
Chile Chili	74 380[2]	1 294	459	16 236[2]	-456	99	402[2]
China[2] Chine[2]	932 749	140 630	12 201	205 406	7 459	1 015	28 405
Colombia Colombie	110 950	1 998[2]	1 572[2]	60 634[2]	-820[2]	-155[2]	-329[2]

54

Land *(continued)*
As of 2007, thousand hectares
Terres *(suite)*
En 2007, milliers d'hectares

Country or area Pays ou zone	Area – Superficie				Net change from 2000 to 2007 Variation nette de 2000 à 2007		
	Total land Superficie totale	Arable land Terres arables	Permanent crops Cultures permanentes	Forest cover Superficie forestière	Arable land Terres arables	Permanent crops Cultures permanentes	Forest cover Superficie forestière
Comoros Comores	186	80[2]	55[2]	4[2]	0[2]	5[2]	-4[2]
Congo[2] Congo[2]	34 150	495	50	22 437	5	0	-119
Cook Islands Iles Cook	24	3[2]	1[2]	16[2]	-1[2]	-1[2]	0[2]
Costa Rica[2] Costa Rica[2]	5 106	200	300	2 397	-10	20	21
Côte d'Ivoire[2] Côte d'Ivoire[2]	31 800	2 800	4 200	10 436	0	400	108
Croatia Croatie	5 391	852[5]	80	2 137[2]	-249	-49	8[2]
Cuba Cuba	10 982[2]	3 573[2]	418	2 824[2]	69[2]	-132	389[2]
Cyprus[6] Chypre[6]	924	115	41	175[2]	17	-1	2[2]
Czech Republic République tchèque	7 725	3 032	239	2 652[2]	-50	3	15[2]
Dem. Rep. of the Congo[2] Rép. dém. du Congo[2]	226 705	6 700	950	132 971	0	-150	-2 236
Denmark Danemark	4 243	2 306	7	506[2]	25	-1	20[2]
Djibouti Djibouti	2 318[2]	1	...	6[2]	0	...	0[2]
Dominica Dominique	75	5[2]	16[2]	46[2]	0[2]	2[2]	-2[2]
Dominican Republic[2] Rép. dominicaine[2]	4 832	820	500	1 376	2	0	0
Ecuador Equateur	27 684[2]	1 195	1 220	10 458[2]	-421	-143	-1 383[2]
Egypt[2] Egypte[2]	99 545	3 018	520	70	217	30	11
El Salvador El Salvador	2 072[2]	682[2]	237	288[2]	32[2]	-13	-36[2]
Equatorial Guinea Guinée équatoriale	2 805	130[2]	90[2]	1 602[2]	0[2]	-10[2]	-107[2]
Eritrea[2] Erythrée[2]	10 100	640	2	1 550	80	-1	-26
Estonia Estonie	4 239	598	9	2 300[2]	-245	-3	57[2]
Ethiopia Ethiopie	100 000[2]	14 038	1 039	12 718[2]	4 038	377	-987[2]
Faeroe Islands Iles Féroé	140	3[2]	...	0[2]	0[2]	...	0[2]
Falkland Is. (Malvinas) Iles Falkland (Malvinas)	1 217	...	...	0[2]	...	...	0[2]
Fiji Fidji	1 827	170[2]	83[2]	1 000[2]	0[2]	0[2]	0[2]
Finland Finlande	30 409	2 253	8	22 510[2]	70	-1	35[2]
France France	54 766	18 433	1 086	15 635[2]	-7	-56	284[2]

54

Land *(continued)*
As of 2007, thousand hectares
Terres *(suite)*
En 2007, milliers d'hectares

Country or area Pays ou zone	Area – Superficie				Net change from 2000 to 2007 Variation nette de 2000 à 2007		
	Total land Superficie totale	Arable land Terres arables	Permanent crops Cultures permanentes	Forest cover Superficie forestière	Arable land Terres arables	Permanent crops Cultures permanentes	Forest cover Superficie forestière
French Guiana[2] Guyane française[2]	8 815	12	4	8 063	0	0	0
French Polynesia[2] Polynésie française[2]	366	3	22	105	0	2	0
Gabon[2] Gabon[2]	25 767	325	170	21 755	0	0	-71
Gambia[2] Gambie[2]	1 000	348	6	475	63	1	14
Georgia Géorgie	6 949[2]	463	114	2 760[2]	-330	-155	0[2]
Germany Allemagne	34 877[2]	11 877	198	11 076[2]	73	-18	0[2]
Ghana[2] Ghana[2]	22 754	4 100	2 400	5 286	150	250	-808
Gibraltar Gibraltar	1	...	...	0[2]	...	...	0[2]
Greece[2] Grèce[2]	12 890	2 548	1 132	3 812	-193	19	211
Greenland Groenland	41 045	...	...	0[2]	...	...	0[2]
Grenada Grenade	34	2[2]	10[2]	4[2]	1[2]	0[2]	0[2]
Guadeloupe Guadeloupe	169	21[2]	3[2]	79[2]	2[2]	-3[2]	-2[2]
Guam[2] Guam[2]	54	1	10	26	-1	0	0
Guatemala Guatemala	10 716	1 576	938	3 830[2]	181	368	-378[2]
Guinea[2] Guinée[2]	24 572	2 200	670	6 652	830	45	-252
Guinea-Bissau[2] Guinée-Bissau[2]	2 812	300	250	2 052	0	2	-68
Guyana[2] Guyana[2]	19 685	420	30	15 104	-30	2	0
Haiti[2] Haïti[2]	2 756	900	300	103	0	-20	-6
Honduras[2] Honduras[2]	11 189	1 068	360	4 335	0	1	-1 095
Hungary Hongrie	8 961	4 592	198	2 004[2]	-10	-3	97[2]
Iceland[2] Islande[2]	10 025	7	...	49	0	...	11
India[2] Inde[2]	297 319	158 650	10 850	67 760	-4 067	1 650	206
Indonesia Indonésie	181 157	22 000[2]	15 500[2]	84 752[2]	1 500[2]	2 400[2]	-13 100[2]
Iran (Islamic Rep. of) Iran (Rép. islamique d')	162 855	16 869	1 680	11 075[2]	1 945	320	0[2]
Iraq[2] Iraq[2]	43 737	5 200	250	824	200	-50	6
Ireland Irlande	6 889	1 060	3	693[2]	-17	1	84[2]

54
Land *(continued)*
As of 2007, thousand hectares
Terres *(suite)*
En 2007, milliers d'hectares

Country or area Pays ou zone	Total land Superficie totale	Area – Superficie		Net change from 2000 to 2007 Variation nette de 2000 à 2007		
		Arable land Terres arables	Permanent crops Cultures permanentes	Forest cover Superficie forestière	Arable land Terres arables	Permanent crops Cultures permanentes	Forest cover Superficie forestière
Isle of Man Ile de Man	57	7^2	...	4^2	-3^2	...	0^2
Israel Israël	$2\ 164^7$	307^2	69^2	174^2	-31^2	-17^2	10^2
Italy Italie	29 414	7 171	2 531	$10\ 192^2$	-1 308	-274	745^2
Jamaica[2] Jamaïque[2]	1 083	174	110	338	0	0	-3
Japan Japon	$36\ 450^2$	4 326	324	$24\ 865^2$	-148	-32	-11^2
Jordan Jordanie	8 824	140	81	83^2	-50	-7	0^2
Kazakhstan[2] Kazakhstan[2]	269 970	22 700	100	3 326	1 165	-36	-39
Kenya[2] Kenya[2]	56 914	5 200	500	3 498	309	20	-84
Kiribati[2] Kiribati[2]	81	2	35	2	0	0	0
Korea, Dem. P. R.[2] Corée, R. p. dém. dc[2]	12 041	2 800	200	5 933	200	0	-888
Korea, Republic of Corée, République de	$9\ 692^2$	1 597	185	$6\ 251^2$	-121	-15	-49^2
Kuwait[2] Koweït[2]	1 782	15	3	6	5	1	1
Kyrgyzstan Kirghizistan	$19\ 180^2$	1 280	73	874^2	-76	6	15^2
Lao People's Dem. Rep. Rép. dém. pop. lao	23 080	$1\ 170^2$	81^2	$15\ 986^2$	293^2	0^2	-546^2
Latvia Lettonie	6 225	1 188	10	$2\ 963^2$	218	-2	78^2
Lebanon Liban	$1\ 023^2$	144^2	143	139^2	15^2	2	8^2
Lesotho[2] Lesotho[2]	3 035	300	4	8	-30	0	1
Liberia[2] Libéria[2]	9 632	385	215	3 034	5	5	-421
Libyan Arab Jamah. Jamah. arabe libyenne	175 954	$1\ 750^2$	300^2	217^2	-65^2	-35^2	0^2
Liechtenstein Liechtenstein	16	4^2	...	7^2	0^2	...	0^2
Lithuania Lituanie	6 268	1 835	30	$2\ 131^2$	-1 043	-13	111^2
Luxembourg Luxembourg	259	61	2	87^2	-1	1	0^2
Madagascar[2] Madagascar[2]	58 154	2 950	600	12 764	50	0	-259
Malawi[2] Malawi[2]	9 408	3 000	120	3 336	250	0	-231
Malaysia[2] Malaisie[2]	32 855	1 800	5 785	20 610	-20	0	-981
Maldives Maldives	30	4^2	8^2	1^2	0^2	3^2	0^2

54

Land *(continued)*
As of 2007, thousand hectares
Terres *(suite)*
En 2007, milliers d'hectares

Country or area Pays ou zone	Area – Superficie				Net change from 2000 to 2007 Variation nette de 2000 à 2007		
	Total land Superficie totale	Arable land Terres arables	Permanent crops Cultures permanentes	Forest cover Superficie forestière	Arable land Terres arables	Permanent crops Cultures permanentes	Forest cover Superficie forestière
Mali [2] Mali [2]	122 019	4 850	130	12 372	261	45	-700
Malta Malte	32	8	1	0[2]	0	0	0[2]
Marshall Islands Iles Marshall	18	2[2]	8[2]	...	1[2]	0[2]	...
Martinique Martinique	106[2]	11	7	47[2]	0	-3	0[2]
Mauritania Mauritanie	103 070	450[2]	12[2]	247[2]	-38[2]	0[2]	-70[2]
Mauritius Maurice	203	90[2]	4[2]	37[2]	-10[2]	0[2]	-1[2]
Mayotte Mayotte	37	7[2]	13[2]	5[2]	0[2]	0[2]	0[2]
Mexico [2] Mexique [2]	194 395	24 500	2 400	63 717	-600	100	-1 823
Micronesia (Fed. States of) Micronésie (Etats féd. de)	70	3[2]	18[2]	63[2]	0[2]	0[2]	0[2]
Mongolia Mongolie	155 356[2]	851	2[2]	10 087[2]	-323	0[2]	-578[2]
Montenegro Monténégro	1 345[2]	174	16	625[2]	0[8]	0[8]	2[2,8]
Montserrat Montserrat	10	2[2]	...	4[2]	0[2]	...	0[2]
Morocco Maroc	44 630[2]	8 065	895	4 378[2]	-702	10	50[2]
Mozambique Mozambique	78 638	4 450[2]	350[2]	19 162[2]	550[2]	100[2]	-350[2]
Myanmar Myanmar	65 352	10 577	1 101	31 289[2]	668	512	-3 265[2]
Namibia [2] Namibie [2]	82 329	800	5	7 512	-16	1	-521
Nauru Nauru	2	...	...	0[2]	...	...	0[2]
Nepal Népal	14 335	2 357	118	3 530[2]	3	13	-370[2]
Netherlands Pays-Bas	3 376	1 059	34	367[2]	149	0	7[2]
Netherlands Antilles Antilles néerlandaises	80	8[2]	...	1[2]	0[2]	...	0[2]
New Caledonia [2] Nouvelle-Calédonie [2]	1 828	9	4	717	3	0	0
New Zealand Nouvelle-Zélande	26 771[2,9]	866[9]	66[9]	8 342[2]	-634[9]	16[9]	116[2]
Nicaragua Nicaragua	11 999	1 950[2]	234[2]	4 979[2]	33[2]	0[2]	-560[2]
Niger [2] Niger [2]	126 670	14 720	15	1 241	735	0	-87
Nigeria [2] Nigéria [2]	91 077	36 500	3 000	10 270	6 500	350	-2 867
Niue Nioué	26	3[2]	3[2]	14[2]	0[2]	0[2]	-1[2]

54

Land *(continued)*
As of 2007, thousand hectares
Terres *(suite)*
En 2007, milliers d'hectares

Country or area Pays ou zone	Total land Superficie totale	Arable land Terres arables	Permanent crops Cultures permanentes	Forest cover Superficie forestière	Arable land Terres arables	Permanent crops Cultures permanentes	Forest cover Superficie forestière
		Area – Superficie			Net change from 2000 to 2007 Variation nette de 2000 à 2007		
Norfolk Island Ile Norfolk	4	...	...	...	...	...	...
Northern Mariana Islands Iles Mariannes du Nord	46	1[2]	1[2]	33[2]	0[2]	0[2]	-1[2]
Norway Norvège	30 428	854	5	9 421[2]	-25	0	120[2]
Occupied Palestinian Terr. Terr. palestinien occupé	602	109[2]	114[2]	9[2]	3[2]	-6[2]	0[2]
Oman Oman	30 950	60[2]	39	2[2]	22[2]	-3	0[2]
Pakistan Pakistan	77 088	21 500[2]	800[2]	1 816[2]	208[2]	142[2]	-300[2]
Palau[2] Palaos[2]	46	1	2	41	0	0	1
Panama Panama	7 434	548[2]	147[2]	4 289[2]	0[2]	0[2]	-18[2]
Papua New Guinea[2] Papouasie-Nvl-Guinée[2]	45 286	250	600	29 159	45	-20	-974
Paraguay[2] Paraguay[2]	39 730	4 300	100	18 118	1 280	10	-1 250
Peru[2] Pérou[2]	128 000	3 700	860	68 554	0	275	-659
Philippines[2] Philippines[2]	29 817	5 100	4 900	6 847	66	250	-1 102
Pitcairn Pitcairn	5	...	...	4[2]	...	...	0[2]
Poland Pologne	30 425	12 502	404	9 245[2]	-1 491	67	186[2]
Portugal Portugal	9 150[2]	1 083	589	3 863[2]	-557	-111	280[2]
Puerto Rico Porto Rico	887	62[2]	37[2]	408[2]	2[2]	-5[2]	1[2]
Qatar Qatar	1 159	18[2]	3[2]	0[2]	0[2]	0[2]	0[2]
Republic of Moldova République de Moldova	3 289	1 820	303	330[2]	-7	-32	4[2]
Réunion Réunion	250[2]	33	3	83[2]	-4	-1	-4[2]
Romania Roumanie	22 989	8 553	460	6 372[2]	-828	-67	6[2]
Russian Federation Fédération de Russie	1 637 774	121 574	1 794	808 599[2]	-2 800	-70	-670[2]
Rwanda[2] Rwanda[2]	2 467	1 200	275	534	300	25	190
Saint Helena[2,10] Sainte-Hélène[2,10]	39	4	...	2	0	...	0
Saint Kitts and Nevis[2] Saint-Kitts-et-Nevis[2]	26	4	0	5	-3	-1	0
Saint Lucia Sainte-Lucie	61[2]	3[2]	7	17[2]	1[2]	-6	0[2]
Saint Pierre and Miquelon[2] Saint-Pierre-et-Miquelon[2]	23	3	...	3	0	...	0

54

Land (continued)
As of 2007, thousand hectares
Terres (suite)
En 2007, milliers d'hectares

Country or area Pays ou zone	Area – Superficie				Net change from 2000 to 2007 Variation nette de 2000 à 2007		
	Total land Superficie totale	Arable land Terres arables	Permanent crops Cultures permanentes	Forest cover Superficie forestière	Arable land Terres arables	Permanent crops Cultures permanentes	Forest cover Superficie forestière
Saint Vincent-Grenadines Saint Vincent-Grenadines	39	7[2]	5[2]	11[2]	2[2]	2[2]	1[2]
Samoa[2] Samoa[2]	283	25	58	171	0	0	0
San Marino Saint-Marin	6	1[2]	...	0[2]	0[2]	...	0[2]
Sao Tome and Principe[2] Sao Tomé-et-Principe[2]	96	9	47	27	3	2	0
Saudi Arabia[2] Arabie saoudite[2]	214 969	3 400	225	2 728	-192	32	0
Senegal[2] Sénégal[2]	19 253	2 985	52	8 583	-65	-3	-315
Serbia Serbie	8 836[2]	3 299	299	2 087[2]	-19[8]	-1[8]	7[2,8]
Seychelles[2] Seychelles[2]	46	1	5	40	0	0	0
Sierra Leone[2] Sierra Leone[2]	7 162	900	80	2 716	410	20	-135
Singapore[2] Singapour[2]	70	1	^0	2	0	0	0
Slovakia Slovaquie	4 810	1 377	25	1 932[2]	-151	-22	11[2]
Slovenia Slovénie	2 014	177	26	1 275[2]	4	-5	35[2]
Solomon Islands[2] Iles Salomon[2]	2 799	16	60	2 092	2	5	-279
Somalia[2] Somalie[2]	62 734	1 000	27	6 977	-43	3	-538
South Africa[2] Afrique du Sud[2]	121 447	14 500	950	9 203	-253	-9	0
Spain[2] Espagne[2]	49 898	12 700	4 860	18 507	-700	-44	2 071
Sri Lanka[2] Sri Lanka[2]	6 463	970	950	1 873	55	-45	-209
Sudan Soudan	237 600	19 321	225[2]	66 368[2]	3 088	108[2]	-4 123[2]
Suriname Suriname	15 600	58[2]	7[2]	14 776[2]	1[2]	-3[2]	0[2]
Swaziland[2] Swaziland[2]	1 720	178	14	550	0	1	33
Sweden Suède	41 033	2 643[2]	5[2]	27 550[2]	-60[2]	2[2]	76[2]
Switzerland Suisse	4 000[2]	408	23	1 230[2]	-5	-1	31[2]
Syrian Arab Republic Rép. arabe syrienne	18 363	4 736	947	473[2]	194	137	41[2]
Tajikistan[2] Tadjikistan[2]	13 996	710	101	410	-74	-1	0
Thailand[2] Thaïlande[2]	51 089	15 200	3 750	14 402	-454	370	-412
TFYR of Macedonia L'ex-R.Y. Macédoine	2 543[2]	431	36	906[2]	-124	-8	0[2]

54

Land *(continued)*
As of 2007, thousand hectares
Terres *(suite)*
En 2007, milliers d'hectares

Country or area Pays ou zone	Area – Superficie				Net change from 2000 to 2007 Variation nette de 2000 à 2007		
	Total land Superficie totale	Arable land Terres arables	Permanent crops Cultures permanentes	Forest cover Superficie forestière	Arable land Terres arables	Permanent crops Cultures permanentes	Forest cover Superficie forestière
Timor-Leste Timor-Leste	1 487	170[2]	68[2]	776[2]	50[2]	1[2]	-78[2]
Togo[2] Togo[2]	5 439	2 460	170	346	-50	50	-140
Tokelau Tokélaou	1	...	...	0[2]	...	...	0[2]
Tonga[2] Tonga[2]	72	15	12	4	0	1	0
Trinidad and Tobago Trinité-et-Tobago	513	25[2]	22[2]	225[2]	-10[2]	-3[2]	-3[2]
Tunisia[2] Tunisie[2]	15 536	2 757	2 174	1 095	-107	48	136
Turkey Turquie	76 963	21 929	2 908	10 224[2]	-1 897	355	172[2]
Turkmenistan[2] Turkménistan[2]	46 993	1 850	63	4 127	150	-2	0
Turks and Caicos Islands Iles Turques et Caïques	95	1[2]	...	34[2]	0[2]	...	0[2]
Tuvalu Tuvalu	3	...	2[2]	1[2]	...	0[2]	0[2]
Uganda[2] Ouganda[2]	19 710	5 500	2 200	3 454	440	100	-605
Ukraine Ukraine	57 933	32 434	899	9 601[2]	-130	-33	91[2]
United Arab Emirates Emirats arabes unis	8 360	70[2]	220[2]	313[2]	10[2]	33[2]	3[2]
United Kingdom Royaume-Uni	24 193	6 085	46	2 866[2]	209	-6	73[2]
United Rep. of Tanzania Rép.-Unie de Tanzanie	88 580	9 000[2]	1 200[2]	34 433[2]	200[2]	0[2]	-2 885[2]
United States Etats-Unis	916 192	170 428[2]	2 730[2]	303 407[2]	-4 940[2]	30[2]	1 113[2]
United States Virgin Is. Iles Vierges américaines	35	1[2]	1[2]	9[2]	-1[2]	0[2]	-1[2]
Uruguay Uruguay	17 502	1 350[2]	33[2]	1 545[2]	-23[2]	-9[2]	136[2]
Uzbekistan Ouzbékistan	42 540	4 300[2]	340[2]	3 328[2]	-175[2]	-10[2]	116[2]
Vanuatu[2] Vanuatu[2]	1 219	20	85	440	0	0	0
Venezuela (Boliv. Rep. of)[2] Venezuela (Rép. boliv. du)[2]	88 205	2 650	700	47 138	55	-100	-2 013
Viet Nam[2] Viet Nam[2]	31 007	6 350	3 080	13 413	150	1 142	1 688
Wallis and Futuna Islands Iles Wallis et Futuna	14	1[2]	5[2]	5[2]	0[2]	0[2]	-1[2]
Western Sahara Sahara occidental	26 600	4[2]	...	1 011[2]	-1[2]	...	0[2]
Yemen[2] Yémen[2]	52 797	1 375	250	549	-170	126	0
Zambia[2] Zambie[2]	74 339	5 260	29	41 562	0	2	-3 114

Country or area Pays ou zone	Area – Superficie				Net change from 2000 to 2007 Variation nette de 2000 à 2007		
	Total land Superficie totale	Arable land Terres arables	Permanent crops Cultures permanentes	Forest cover Superficie forestière	Arable land Terres arables	Permanent crops Cultures permanentes	Forest cover Superficie forestière
Zimbabwe [2] Zimbabwe [2]	38 685	3 230	120	16 914	0	0	-2 191

Source:
Food and Agriculture Organization of the United Nations (FAO), Rome, FAOSTAT data, last accessed July 2009.

1   May include official, semi-official or estimated data.
2   FAO estimate.
3   Data relating to "Permanent Crops" is largely the area on farms that is covered by "Forest and Woodland": whereas, the area used to cultivate fruit and fibre crops, which is less than one percent of the land in crops is included in the "Arable Land" category.

4   Country data reported by international organizations where the country is a member.
5   The "Arable land" figures exclude non-cultivated arable land.

6   Data refer to government-controlled areas.
7   Data relating to "Land area" include the Golan Heights.

8   Net change from 2006 to 2007.
9   "Land area" category actually refers to the total area of the country, as the area of "Inland waters" is not available; "Arable land" category includes other land in farms; "Permanent crops" category includes area of planted production forest.

10   Including Ascension and Tristan da Cunha.

Source :
Organisation des Nations Unies pour l'alimentation et l'agriculture (FAO), Rome, données FAOSTAT, dernier accès juillet 2009.

1   Les données peuvent être officielles, semi-officielles ou estimatives.
2   Estimation de la FAO.
3   Les données relatives aux "Cultures permanentes" représentent la superficie des terres des exploitations agricoles couvertes par "Superficie forestière", tandis que la superficie des terres utilisées pour la culture des fruits et des plantes textiles, qui représente moins de un pour cent des terres cultivées est comprise dans "Terres arables".

4   Statistiques nationales fournies par les organisations internationales dont le pays est membre.
5   Les chiffres relatifs aux terres arables excluent les terres arables non cultivées.

6   Les données se rapportent aux zones contrôlées par le Gouvernement.
7   Les données relatives aux terres émergées englobent le plateau du Golan.

8   Variation nette de 2006 à 2007.
9   La catégorie portant sur les terres émergées correspond à la superficie totale du pays, puisque les données sur les eaux intérieures ne sont pas disponibles; les "terres arables" comprennent d'autres terres faisant partie des exploitations agricoles; les "récoltes permanentes" comprennent les zones boisées a des fins d'exploitations.

10   Y compris Ascension et Tristan da Cunha.

55

CO$_2$ emission estimates
From fossil fuel combustion, cement production and gas flared (thousand metric tons of carbon dioxide)

Estimation des émissions de CO$_2$
Dues à la combustion de combustibles fossiles, à la production de ciment et au gaz brûlés à la torchère (milliers de tonnes de dioxyde de carbone)

Country or area Pays ou zone	1997	1998	1999	2000	2001	2002	2003	2004	2005	2006
Afghanistan Afghanistan	1 115	1 056	832	781	645	359	583	704	700	697
Albania Albanie	1 544	1 753	2 992	3 029	3 230	3 773	4 191	5 075	4 536	4 301
Algeria Algérie	88 187	107 070	117 242	116 853	113 751	120 468	121 436	120 857	138 178	132 715
Angola Angola	7 381	7 308	9 156	9 541	9 731	12 236	8 070	9 097	9 856	10 582
Anguilla Anguilla	18	26	26	33	37	37	40	44	51	51
Antigua and Barbuda Antigua et Barbuda	337	334	340	345	345	363	389	407	411	425
Argentina Argentine	134 666	137 661	145 475	141 064	140 459	132 836	144 540	156 031	158 939	173 536
Armenia Arménie	3 278	3 406	3 058	3 465	3 542	3 003	3 428	3 645	4 349	4 371
Aruba Aruba	1 877	1 694	1 709	2 259	2 266	2 288	2 292	2 292	2 310	2 310
Australia Australie	334 070	350 002	328 005	329 061	322 450	336 138	339 596	340 630	365 790	372 013
Austria Autriche	61 299	62 836	61 758	61 721	63 602	65 149	70 371	69 472	72 820	71 834
Azerbaijan Azerbaïdjan	29 964	31 592	29 297	30 543	29 436	29 909	31 676	33 381	35 284	35 050
Bahamas Bahamas	1 742	1 793	1 797	1 797	1 797	2 083	1 870	2 009	2 108	2 138
Bahrain Bahreïn	17 318	18 403	18 018	19 756	15 081	16 823	17 578	18 055	19 683	21 292
Bangladesh Bangladesh	25 062	24 039	25 230	27 859	32 446	33 697	35 486	37 088	40 110	41 609
Barbados Barbade	902	1 140	1 210	1 188	1 221	1 228	1 192	1 272	1 316	1 338
Belarus Bélarus	62 487	59 708	58 454	59 195	58 612	59 888	62 601	65 142	64 335	68 849
Belgium Belgique	118 393	121 308	117 579	117 414	117 740	109 417	116 442	113 311	109 391	107 199
Belize Belize	389	370	601	689	711	744	781	792	818	818
Benin Bénin	1 217	1 214	1 562	1 617	1 738	2 053	2 281	2 387	2 567	3 109
Bermuda Bermudes	477	462	495	495	495	528	528	550	565	565
Bhutan Bhoutan	392	385	385	392	403	436	378	374	392	381
Bolivia Bolivie	9 841	10 325	9 768	8 554	7 722	7 245	10 560	9 071	9 566	11 403
Bosnia and Herzegovina Bosnie-Herzégovine	12 804	16 691	19 397	22 700	20 288	22 132	22 810	24 182	25 612	27 438
Botswana Botswana	3 205	3 824	3 535	4 272	4 334	4 484	4 264	4 385	4 525	4 770
Brazil Brésil	321 178	313 991	322 047	330 103	339 874	335 163	324 735	341 150	349 950	352 524

CO$_2$ emission estimates *(continued)*
From fossil fuel combustion, cement production and gas flared (thousand metric tons of carbon dioxide)

Estimation des émissions de CO$_2$ *(suite)*
Dues à la combustion de combustibles fossiles, à la production de ciment et au gaz brûlés à la torchère (milliers de tonnes de dioxyde de carbone)

Country or area Pays ou zone	1997	1998	1999	2000	2001	2002	2003	2004	2005	2006
British Virgin Islands Iles Vierges britanniques	59	59	59	59	59	66	77	84	88	99
Brunei Darussalam Brunéi Darussalam	5 812	5 984	4 598	6 527	6 197	6 153	6 021	6 076	5 907	5 911
Bulgaria Bulgarie	52 448	50 270	43 120	43 054	45 518	43 494	46 878	45 287	46 992	48 085
Burkina Faso Burkina Faso	682	697	770	748	733	752	766	766	788	788
Burundi Burundi	315	301	293	301	216	220	172	161	169	198
Cambodia Cambodge	1 907	2 233	2 196	2 255	2 644	2 860	3 128	3 498	3 722	4 074
Cameroon Cameroun	3 216	3 208	3 080	3 432	3 421	3 417	4 616	3 839	3 718	3 645
Canada Canada	483 223	478 859	477 862	537 372	527 113	521 811	554 635	553 898	559 783	544 680
Cape Verde Cap-Vert	143	154	172	187	209	246	253	268	297	308
Cayman Islands Iles Caïmanes	286	286	282	455	455	469	480	495	502	517
Central African Rep. Rép. centrafricaine	246	249	264	268	246	246	235	235	235	249
Chad Tchad	114	114	121	176	172	169	381	374	392	396
Chile Chili	58 289	57 508	62 693	59 704	49 815	52 184	52 419	58 403	59 440	60 100
China Chine	3 354 516	3 175 850	3 318 396	3 405 849	3 488 613	3 701 782	4 353 228	5 099 142	5 625 561	6 103 493
China, Hong Kong SAR Chine, Hong Kong RAS	30 855	39 230	42 753	40 583	38 867	37 613	40 806	38 889	41 092	39 039
China, Macao SAR Chine, Macao RAS	1 500	1 566	1 533	1 635	1 687	1 848	1 863	2 226	2 310	2 237
Colombia Colombie	64 904	65 974	56 507	57 919	56 272	55 656	57 416	53 871	59 173	63 422
Comoros Comores	81	70	81	84	81	81	88	88	88	88
Congo Congo	2 343	777	821	1 049	862	708	1 085	1 903	1 606	1 463
Cook Islands Iles Cook	22	22	29	29	33	29	33	55	62	66
Costa Rica Costa Rica	4 987	5 317	5 522	5 474	5 760	6 325	6 860	7 106	7 278	7 854
Côte d'Ivoire Côte d'Ivoire	8 173	6 912	6 266	6 791	7 726	7 286	5 460	7 663	8 166	6 882
Croatia Croatie	19 778	21 109	21 124	20 247	21 241	22 389	24 042	23 584	23 617	23 683
Cuba Cuba	24 603	24 442	25 274	26 037	25 450	26 074	25 436	24 240	24 871	29 627
Cyprus Chypre	6 109	6 640	6 754	6 849	6 846	7 025	7 759	7 322	7 502	7 788
Czech Republic République tchèque	123 827	118 917	105 567	117 201	116 373	113 689	116 336	115 841	114 719	114 858
Dem. Rep. of the Congo Rép. dém. du Congo	2 541	2 534	2 248	1 646	1 566	1 591	1 624	2 105	2 145	2 200
Denmark Danemark	57 563	55 114	50 351	46 937	48 730	48 609	55 858	50 714	46 827	53 944

CO$_2$ emission estimates *(continued)*
From fossil fuel combustion, cement production and gas flared (thousand metric tons of carbon dioxide)
Estimation des émissions de CO$_2$ *(suite)*
Dues à la combustion de combustibles fossiles, à la production de ciment et au gaz brûlés à la torchère (milliers de tonnes de dioxyde de carbone)

Country or area Pays ou zone	1997	1998	1999	2000	2001	2002	2003	2004	2005	2006
Djibouti Djibouti	440	411	444	403	385	400	407	458	473	488
Dominica Dominique	81	77	81	103	114	103	114	106	114	117
Dominican Republic Rép. dominicaine	18 238	18 682	18 869	20 115	20 233	21 498	21 531	19 969	19 892	20 357
Ecuador Equateur	18 542	22 645	21 622	21 347	23 980	24 596	23 984	29 729	30 668	31 328
Egypt Egypte	108 207	122 254	125 184	141 317	125 814	140 092	140 004	153 399	173 481	166 800
El Salvador El Salvador	5 760	5 812	5 698	5 742	5 947	6 039	6 380	6 178	6 292	6 461
Equatorial Guinea Guinée équatoriale	147	150	249	268	700	4 371	4 363	4 341	4 341	4 356
Eritrea Erythrée	528	590	620	609	634	638	730	763	752	554
Estonia Estonie	19 177	17 684	15 994	15 990	16 397	15 972	18 370	18 744	18 216	17 523
Ethiopia Ethiopie	4 275	5 027	5 075	5 830	4 308	4 481	4 946	5 606	5 489	6 006
Faeroe Islands Iles Féroé	656	664	671	656	660	667	675	675	678	678
Falkland Is. (Malvinas) Iles Falkland (Malvinas)	48	37	37	37	44	44	48	48	51	51
Fiji Fidji	759	730	832	862	1 126	920	1 665	1 921	1 665	1 610
Finland Finlande	59 935	57 031	55 543	52 272	56 899	61 281	69 612	67 672	54 795	66 693
France [1] France [1]	379 911	410 711	372 662	367 129	386 503	380 772	389 994	392 410	394 647	383 148
French Guiana Guyane française	898	968	939	843	836	851	851	851	851	876
French Polynesia Polynésie française	576	572	576	649	737	748	821	788	854	821
Gabon Gabon	3 828	1 753	1 562	1 214	1 371	1 492	1 514	1 591	1 870	2 057
Gambia Gambie	216	235	257	275	286	315	315	319	319	334
Georgia Géorgie	4 437	4 961	4 345	4 536	3 769	3 388	3 773	3 927	4 800	5 518
Germany Allemagne	895 822	890 509	819 856	827 218	849 999	824 960	828 894	821 817	803 649	805 090
Ghana Ghana	6 395	6 409	6 560	6 299	6 919	7 414	7 594	6 703	7 473	9 240
Gibraltar Gibraltar	121	312	323	334	345	348	363	374	385	385
Greece Grèce	84 564	87 204	86 992	92 195	94 992	93 089	95 729	97 251	98 919	96 382
Greenland Groenland	524	532	543	532	539	539	543	546	557	565
Grenada Grenade	205	191	205	205	220	216	220	216	235	242
Guadeloupe Guadeloupe	1 544	1 525	1 588	2 075	2 090	2 028	2 042	2 061	2 119	2 141
Guatemala Guatemala	7 597	8 752	8 928	9 915	10 285	10 982	11 004	11 557	11 869	11 766

55

CO₂ emission estimates *(continued)*
From fossil fuel combustion, cement production and gas flared (thousand metric tons of carbon dioxide)

Estimation des émissions de CO₂ *(suite)*
Dues à la combustion de combustibles fossiles, à la production de ciment et au gaz brûlés à la torchère (milliers de tonnes de dioxyde de carbone)

Country or area Pays ou zone	1997	1998	1999	2000	2001	2002	2003	2004	2005	2006
Guinea Guinée	1 280	1 243	1 272	1 280	1 298	1 324	1 338	1 338	1 360	1 360
Guinea-Bissau Guinée-Bissau	290	231	249	253	260	271	271	271	271	279
Guyana Guyana	1 602	1 654	1 650	1 580	1 518	1 547	1 500	1 445	1 492	1 507
Haiti Haïti	1 423	1 232	1 331	1 368	1 591	1 683	1 668	1 756	1 767	1 811
Honduras Honduras	4 158	4 649	4 741	5 031	5 713	5 969	6 428	7 410	7 784	7 194
Hungary Hongrie	61 277	59 440	59 099	56 005	56 782	56 239	59 580	57 889	58 821	57 644
Iceland Islande	2 105	2 101	2 068	2 163	2 101	2 171	2 167	2 226	2 185	2 215
India Inde	1 043 966	1 071 935	1 144 414	1 186 706	1 203 796	1 246 161	1 302 165	1 363 028	1 423 844	1 510 351
Indonesia Indonésie	269 456	200 666	224 781	245 916	270 670	284 269	282 069	320 841	330 777	333 483
Iran (Islamic Rep. of) Iran (Rép. islamique d')	290 591	316 147	316 642	339 211	357 053	365 372	394 951	420 101	436 036	466 976
Iraq Iraq	68 303	72 365	72 321	74 532	86 761	92 484	77 832	83 178	88 631	92 572
Ireland Irlande	37 209	38 878	41 140	42 266	45 107	44 583	43 699	43 941	44 033	43 806
Israel Israël	63 397	62 773	62 150	62 685	65 743	67 085	69 113	67 430	63 664	70 440
Italy [2] Italie [2]	431 882	441 485	437 151	447 623	448 206	451 290	467 221	469 678	470 140	474 148
Jamaica Jamaïque	10 630	9 728	9 772	10 318	10 626	10 307	10 729	10 534	10 164	12 151
Japan Japon	1 293 340	1 253 432	1 227 849	1 260 215	1 249 585	1 265 095	1 287 719	1 312 003	1 300 189	1 293 409
Jordan Jordanie	14 417	14 542	14 568	15 506	16 001	16 885	17 490	19 235	21 333	20 724
Kazakhstan Kazakhstan	129 587	125 070	116 501	127 776	147 921	151 954	153 828	172 168	177 239	193 508
Kenya Kenya	8 265	10 036	10 171	10 417	9 368	7 968	8 840	10 586	10 952	12 151
Kiribati Kiribati	29	33	29	33	26	26	26	26	26	29
Korea, Dem. P. R. Corée, R. p. dém. de	234 678	64 926	71 394	76 963	79 915	76 527	78 203	79 919	83 472	84 799
Korea, Republic of Corée, République de	435 413	372 878	410 791	447 594	455 371	478 584	479 479	494 098	474 181	475 248
Kuwait Koweït	62 245	63 415	65 996	71 100	67 459	63 976	73 256	81 330	89 870	86 599
Kyrgyzstan Kirghizistan	5 621	5 988	4 679	4 646	3 850	4 950	5 379	5 760	5 570	5 566
Lao People's Dem. Rep. Rép. dém. pop. lao	719	895	902	1 060	1 177	1 294	1 338	1 382	1 408	1 426
Latvia Lettonie	8 243	7 880	6 633	6 098	6 776	6 560	7 003	7 066	7 062	7 462
Lebanon Liban	15 646	15 998	16 599	15 352	16 207	16 038	18 729	16 889	17 494	15 330
Liberia Libéria	356	389	407	436	466	466	506	627	737	785

55

CO$_2$ emission estimates *(continued)*
From fossil fuel combustion, cement production and gas flared (thousand metric tons of carbon dioxide)
Estimation des émissions de CO$_2$ *(suite)*
Dues à la combustion de combustibles fossiles, à la production de ciment et au gaz brûlés à la torchère (milliers de tonnes de dioxyde de carbone)

Country or area Pays ou zone	1997	1998	1999	2000	2001	2002	2003	2004	2005	2006
Libyan Arab Jamah. Jamah. arabe libyenne	51 242	48 129	47 227	49 749	51 069	50 420	51 902	53 082	54 894	55 495
Lithuania Lituanie	15 338	16 196	13 691	12 192	12 698	12 782	12 910	13 325	13 999	14 190
Luxembourg Luxembourg	7 916	7 355	7 685	8 235	8 580	9 423	9 918	11 066	11 326	11 312
Madagascar Madagascar	1 701	1 738	1 925	2 270	2 314	2 314	2 574	2 750	2 798	2 834
Malawi Malawi	759	792	1 100	1 030	1 030	1 008	1 038	1 067	1 049	1 049
Malaysia Malaisie	124 810	114 176	107 925	126 592	136 704	140 767	167 900	174 416	183 304	187 865
Maldives Maldives	367	334	466	499	576	689	598	752	678	869
Mali Mali	524	517	539	543	546	554	539	565	568	568
Malta Malte	3 366	2 145	2 347	2 152	2 475	2 156	2 512	2 596	2 589	2 548
Marshall Islands Iles Marshall	66	70	66	77	81	84	84	88	84	92
Martinique Martinique	2 042	2 057	2 006	2 042	1 602	1 555	1 646	1 727	1 793	1 870
Mauritania Mauritanie	2 999	1 111	1 199	1 195	1 283	1 412	1 452	1 613	1 650	1 665
Mauritius Maurice	1 998	2 196	2 468	2 768	2 966	2 981	3 146	3 197	3 410	3 850
Mexico Mexique	397 866	400 481	384 091	383 915	395 292	389 107	403 949	408 104	429 378	436 150
Mongolia Mongolie	7 715	7 707	7 557	7 506	7 883	8 287	8 034	8 554	8 811	9 442
Montserrat Montserrat	48	51	48	55	59	66	70	70	70	70
Morocco Maroc	31 860	32 036	33 150	33 906	37 715	38 232	37 484	40 363	47 531	45 316
Mozambique Mozambique	1 126	1 133	1 188	1 349	1 580	1 588	1 918	1 932	1 855	2 039
Myanmar Myanmar	7 498	8 078	8 829	8 888	7 348	8 173	9 599	9 775	10 472	10 025
Namibia Namibie	1 903	1 995	1 771	1 764	2 086	2 339	2 464	2 600	2 724	2 831
Nauru Nauru	139	139	136	136	139	139	143	143	143	143
Nepal Népal	2 783	2 251	3 219	3 234	3 454	2 710	2 952	2 710	3 168	3 241
Netherlands Pays-Bas	180 928	178 746	165 154	168 997	172 234	175 164	177 650	179 344	175 017	168 513
Netherlands Antilles Antilles néerlandaises	8 558	3 392	3 230	3 293	3 333	3 538	3 843	3 751	3 755	4 312
New Caledonia Nouvelle-Calédonie	1 826	1 804	2 035	2 299	2 119	2 427	2 750	2 552	2 801	2 941
New Zealand Nouvelle-Zélande	29 432	28 483	30 096	31 148	32 340	31 849	31 181	30 723	30 103	30 488
Nicaragua Nicaragua	3 135	3 421	3 626	3 843	4 015	4 019	4 327	4 290	4 154	4 334
Niger Niger	1 140	1 137	1 144	858	858	931	986	997	928	935

55

CO$_2$ emission estimates *(continued)*
From fossil fuel combustion, cement production and gas flared (thousand metric tons of carbon dioxide)
Estimation des émissions de CO$_2$ *(suite)*
Dues à la combustion de combustibles fossiles, à la production de ciment et au gaz brûlés à la torchère (milliers de tonnes de dioxyde de carbone)

Country or area Pays ou zone	1997	1998	1999	2000	2001	2002	2003	2004	2005	2006
Nigeria Nigéria	40 187	40 179	44 785	79 174	83 343	98 116	93 130	97 585	113 868	97 262
Niue Nioué	4	4	4	4	4	4	4	4	4	4
Norway Norvège	34 137	34 591	40 957	38 786	41 103	37 440	42 559	49 687	60 856	40 220
Occupied Palestinian Terr. Terr. palestinien occupé	414	609	660	799	1 357	1 170	1 283	2 211	2 754	2 985
Oman Oman	15 594	16 665	20 816	22 055	24 127	30 426	31 548	31 064	31 467	41 378
Pakistan Pakistan	94 706	97 658	100 379	106 443	108 277	111 485	110 873	129 914	134 057	142 659
Palau Palaos	117	117	117	117	110	110	117	117	117	117
Panama Panama	5 958	5 947	5 669	5 790	7 007	5 834	6 153	5 757	5 980	6 428
Papua New Guinea Papouasie-Nvl-Guinée	2 556	2 838	2 464	2 688	3 230	3 513	3 945	4 481	4 613	4 620
Paraguay Paraguay	4 195	4 503	4 503	3 689	3 821	3 898	4 070	4 088	3 832	3 986
Peru Pérou	27 386	27 830	29 799	30 485	27 705	27 735	26 921	33 092	37 162	38 643
Philippines Philippines	77 396	75 643	73 014	78 885	76 945	78 364	72 904	76 908	76 424	68 328
Poland Pologne	349 532	324 727	314 706	301 176	303 296	296 912	306 486	308 565	303 567	318 219
Portugal Portugal	53 357	58 175	64 790	63 364	62 718	67 228	61 644	63 257	65 461	60 001
Qatar Qatar	36 285	32 399	31 405	34 727	27 999	28 959	28 288	36 989	46 710	46 193
Republic of Moldova République de Moldova	10 795	9 629	6 538	6 600	7 139	6 802	7 352	7 685	8 144	7 821
Réunion Réunion	2 347	2 512	2 369	2 475	2 490	2 475	2 493	2 515	2 515	2 523
Romania Roumanie	115 977	103 671	86 236	87 699	93 284	89 826	93 419	92 660	91 857	98 490
Russian Federation Fédération de Russie	1 482 510	1 422 311	1 424 027	1 443 673	1 442 514	1 433 043	1 481 869	1 500 019	1 515 514	1 564 669
Rwanda Rwanda	693	678	704	708	719	722	730	741	766	796
Saint Helena Sainte-Hélène	15	18	22	11	11	11	11	11	11	11
Saint Kitts and Nevis Saint-Kitts-et-Nevis	103	103	103	103	103	114	125	125	136	136
Saint Lucia Sainte-Lucie	312	308	319	330	363	326	348	363	374	381
Saint Pierre and Miquelon Saint-Pierre-et-Miquelon	48	55	55	55	55	59	66	62	66	66
Saint Vincent-Grenadines Saint Vincent-Grenadines	136	165	169	158	180	187	194	194	194	198
Samoa Samoa	132	132	139	139	143	143	150	154	158	158
Sao Tome and Principe Sao Tomé-et-Principe	77	81	88	88	92	92	92	92	103	103
Saudi Arabia Arabie saoudite	216 806	207 269	227 209	297 722	295 816	323 429	323 668	346 016	367 033	381 564

CO₂ emission estimates *(continued)*
From fossil fuel combustion, cement production and gas flared (thousand metric tons of carbon dioxide)

Estimation des émissions de CO₂ *(suite)*
Dues à la combustion de combustibles fossiles, à la production de ciment et au gaz brûlés à la torchère (milliers de tonnes de dioxyde de carbone)

Country or area Pays ou zone	1997	1998	1999	2000	2001	2002	2003	2004	2005	2006
Senegal Sénégal	3 263	3 428	3 700	3 938	4 253	4 616	4 913	5 309	5 577	4 261
Serbia and Montenegro Serbie-et-Monténégro	51 029	53 658	36 993	41 092	44 128	47 197	50 472	55 194	49 933	53 266
Seychelles Seychelles	414	440	513	565	642	543	557	774	697	744
Sierra Leone Sierra Leone	634	594	583	631	752	788	766	1 005	1 005	994
Singapore Singapour	69 234	61 890	52 342	52 342	52 543	51 143	49 133	50 919	59 558	56 217
Slovakia Slovaquie	40 506	42 317	38 592	35 354	37 888	37 855	38 078	37 209	37 693	37 459
Slovenia Slovénie	15 899	15 173	15 026	14 443	14 502	14 641	14 872	14 920	14 927	15 173
Solomon Islands Iles Salomon	161	161	165	165	172	172	180	180	180	180
Somalia Somalie	...	...	...	517	502	209	216	235	253	172
South Africa Afrique du Sud	371 353	372 244	371 059	368 636	362 769	347 714	380 908	415 334	409 090	414 649
Spain Espagne	263 963	275 359	285 490	295 981	298 584	316 540	322 425	343 530	356 455	352 235
Sri Lanka Sri Lanka	7 506	7 762	8 536	10 160	10 245	10 960	10 611	11 913	11 590	11 876
Sudan Soudan	5 419	4 697	5 093	5 533	6 369	8 118	8 998	10 373	11 000	10 813
Suriname Suriname	2 141	2 163	2 152	2 127	2 266	2 251	2 240	2 284	2 380	2 438
Swaziland Swaziland	1 203	1 214	1 239	1 188	1 144	1 126	1 041	1 030	1 019	1 016
Sweden Suède	54 516	54 897	51 025	49 669	50 926	57 233	54 655	54 336	51 491	50 875
Switzerland Suisse	41 576	42 002	40 696	39 090	42 992	40 751	40 234	40 436	41 353	41 826
Syrian Arab Republic Rép. arabe syrienne	52 290	62 704	64 907	63 338	60 654	66 495	65 212	66 198	66 598	68 460
Tajikistan Tadjikistan	5 078	5 445	5 522	4 268	4 976	4 646	5 049	5 427	5 804	6 391
Thailand Thaïlande	210 052	186 498	196 940	201 538	217 078	230 626	246 158	268 132	271 091	272 521
TFYR of Macedonia L'ex-R.Y. Macédoine	10 633	12 624	11 722	12 063	11 997	11 026	11 312	11 227	11 238	10 875
Timor-Leste Timor-Leste	...	...	...	...	...	161	161	176	176	176
Togo Togo	986	1 166	1 481	1 313	1 162	1 232	1 463	1 397	1 338	1 221
Tonga Tonga	114	110	128	121	106	114	139	136	132	132
Trinidad and Tobago Trinité-et-Tobago	19 228	19 316	22 814	24 512	25 021	26 888	27 694	27 837	30 954	33 601
Tunisia Tunisie	16 944	18 000	18 330	19 921	20 816	21 014	21 395	22 444	22 799	23 126
Turkey Turquie	202 840	207 471	200 794	223 021	200 831	209 161	221 613	226 908	248 475	269 452
Turkmenistan Turkménistan	29 927	26 044	35 112	35 644	39 677	41 070	43 157	39 637	41 756	44 103

CO₂ emission estimates *(continued)*
From fossil fuel combustion, cement production and gas flared (thousand metric tons of carbon dioxide)
Estimation des émissions de CO₂ *(suite)*
Dues à la combustion de combustibles fossiles, à la production de ciment et au gaz brûlés à la torchère (milliers de tonnes de dioxyde de carbone)

Country or area Pays ou zone	1997	1998	1999	2000	2001	2002	2003	2004	2005	2006
Uganda Ouganda	1 133	1 338	1 393	1 533	1 632	1 705	1 720	1 833	2 339	2 706
Ukraine Ukraine	328 321	314 692	317 775	304 986	305 844	312 092	337 447	328 794	327 235	319 158
United Arab Emirates Emirats arabes unis	44 711	98 883	89 030	126 742	113 773	95 847	127 409	132 070	135 692	139 553
United Kingdom Royaume-Uni	553 916	556 699	537 218	548 453	559 119	539 293	550 711	554 917	553 641	568 520
United Rep. of Tanzania Rép.-Unie de Tanzanie	2 882	2 556	2 537	2 651	3 128	3 590	3 806	4 352	5 086	5 372
United States [3] Etats-Unis [3]	5 472 834	5 483 533	5 556 445	5 741 725	5 628 777	5 694 198	5 688 236	5 798 012	5 841 315	5 752 289
Uruguay Uruguay	5 555	5 687	6 725	5 306	5 093	4 620	4 594	5 826	5 991	6 864
Uzbekistan Ouzbékistan	101 772	118 041	117 410	118 840	120 952	125 862	121 275	118 371	112 563	115 672
Vanuatu Vanuatu	88	84	84	81	84	84	88	88	88	92
Venezuela (Bolivarian Rep. of) Venezuela (Rép. boliv. du)	131 883	159 192	165 249	145 112	169 561	166 544	172 517	135 945	152 530	171 593
Viet Nam Viet Nam	45 657	47 802	48 059	53 592	59 972	71 144	76 094	98 039	101 838	106 132
Wallis and Futuna Islands Iles Wallis et Futuna	...	...	...	...	...	...	26	26	29	29
Western Sahara Sahara occidental	220	224	235	238	238	238	238	238	238	238
Yemen Yémen	15 473	12 199	13 900	14 626	16 258	16 284	17 138	19 140	20 174	21 201
Zambia Zambie	2 391	2 314	1 808	1 819	1 907	1 969	2 127	2 288	2 365	2 471
Zimbabwe Zimbabwe	15 220	15 088	16 808	14 813	13 438	12 767	11 378	10 648	11 550	11 081

Source:
Carbon Dioxide Information Analysis Center (CDIAC) of the Oak Ridge National Laboratory, Oak Ridge, Tennessee, U.S.A., database on national CO₂ emission estimates, last updated July 2009.

Source:
"Carbon Dioxide Information Analysis Center (CDIAC) of the Oak Ridge National Laboratory, Oak Ridge, Tennessee, U.S.A.", la base de données des estimations nationales des émissions de CO₂, dernier accès juillet 2009.

1   Including Monaco.
2   Including San Marino.
3   Including territories.

1   Y compris Monaco.
2   Y compris Saint-Marin.
3   Y compris les territoires.

Ozone-depleting chlorofluorocarbons (CFCs)
Consumption: ozone-depleting potential (ODP) metric tons

Chlorofluorocarbones (CFC) qui appauvrissent la couche d'ozone
Consommation : tonnes de potentiel de destruction de l'ozone (PDO)

Country or area Pays ou zone	1998	1999	2000	2001	2002	2003	2004	2005	2006	2007
Afghanistan Afghanistan	...	...	...	...	...	...	177.9	141.2	94.5	55.2
Albania Albanie	46.5	53.1	61.9	68.8	49.9	35.0	36.6	14.3	15.2	4.1
Algeria Algérie	1 549.2	1 502.2	1 474.6	1 021.8	1 761.8	1 761.8	1 045.0	859.0	302.6	200.0
Angola Angola	115.9	...	107.0	114.8	105.0	104.2	75.6	52.0	42.1	17.0
Antigua and Barbuda Antigua-et-Barbuda	26.5	-2.0[1]	5.0	3.1	3.7	1.5	1.9	1.1	1.1	0.0
Argentina Argentine	3 546.3	4 316.3	2 396.7	3 293.1	2 139.2	2 255.2	2 211.6	1 675.5	1 654.2	529.0
Armenia Arménie	185.9	9.0	25.0	162.7	172.7	172.7	110.7	84.0	59.0	25.0
Australia Australie	195.1	274.1	6.5	6.0	9.8	1.1	-61.8[1]	-51.4[1]	-80.0[1]	-55.0[1]
Azerbaijan Azerbaïdjan	152.2	99.9	87.8	52.0	12.0	10.2	15.1	21.9	0.0	0.0
Bahamas Bahamas	54.6	53.8	65.9	63.0	55.4	29.6	18.8	13.0	4.0	0.0
Bahrain Bahreïn	149.5	129.0	113.1	106.0	94.6	85.8	64.8	58.7	32.4	14.7
Bangladesh Bangladesh	830.4	800.6	805.0	807.9	328.0	333.0	294.9	263.0	196.2	154.9
Barbados Barbade	22.5	16.5	8.1	12.5	9.5	8.6	14.1	6.7	7.9	1.9
Belarus Bélarus	256.2	193.7	0.0	0.0	0.0	0.0	0.0	0.0	0.0	0.0
Belize Belize	25.0	25.1	15.5	28.0	21.7	15.1	12.2	9.6	3.9	2.2
Benin Bénin	54.2	56.6	54.6	54.0	35.5	17.3	11.5	10.0	14.2	7.9
Bhutan Bhoutan	0.0	0.0	0.0	...	...	...	0.1	0.1	0.1	0.0
Bolivia Bolivie	74.1	72.2	78.8	76.7	65.5	32.1	42.4	26.7	33.1	2.4
Bosnia and Herzegovina Bosnie-Herzégovine	45.1	151.0	175.9	199.7	243.6	230.0	187.9	50.8	32.6	22.1
Botswana Botswana	2.6	2.6	2.5	4.0	3.6	5.1	2.7	1.9	0.7	0.6
Brazil Brésil	9 542.9	11 612.0	9 275.1	6 230.9	3 000.6	3 224.3	1 870.5	967.2	477.8	318.1
Brunei Darussalam Brunéi Darussalam	63.5	36.7	46.6	31.4	43.4	32.3	60.2	39.0	27.8	9.9
Bulgaria Bulgarie	0.0	0.0	0.0	0.0	0.0	0.0	0.0	0.0	0.0	...
Burkina Faso Burkina Faso	37.0	30.6	25.4	19.6	16.3	13.2	10.5	7.4	5.2	4.2
Burundi Burundi	64.5	59.6	53.8	46.5	19.1	9.2	3.9	3.5	3.5	3.1
Cambodia Cambodge	94.2	94.2	94.2	94.2	94.2	86.7	70.4	44.5	28.3	11.6

56

Ozone-depleting chlorofluorocarbons (CFCs) *(continued)*
Consumption: ozone-depleting potential (ODP) metric tons
Chlorofluorocarbones (CFC) qui appauvrissent la couche d'ozone *(suite)*
Consommation : tonnes de potentiel de destruction de l'ozone (PDO)

Country or area Pays ou zone	1998	1999	2000	2001	2002	2003	2004	2005	2006	2007
Cameroon Cameroun	311.8	361.5	368.7	364.1	226.0	220.5	148.5	120.0	103.0	25.0
Canada Canada	42.2	-4.8[1]	10.1	0.1	-12.6[1]	-0.2[1]	0.0	0.0	0.0	0.0
Cape Verde Cap-Vert	2.1	2.0	1.9	1.9	1.8	1.8	1.5	0.9	0.0	0.0
Central African Rep. Rép. centrafricaine	7.0	1.4	4.3	4.0	4.4	4.1	3.9	2.6	2.0	1.3
Chad Tchad	38.1	37.5	36.5	31.6	27.1	22.8	14.2	11.3	9.2	5.1
Chile Chili	737.9	657.5	576.0	470.2	370.2	424.5	230.8	221.5	181.8	19.2
China[2] Chine[2]	55 414.2	42 983.4	39 123.6	33 922.6	30 621.2	22 808.8	17 902.5	13 123.8	12 414.9	5 832.1
Colombia Colombie	1 224.0	985.5	1 149.3	1 164.8	907.0	1 058.1	898.5	556.9	660.4	263.1
Comoros Comores	3.6	2.5	2.7	1.9	1.8	1.2	1.1	0.9	0.8	0.3
Congo Congo	6.6	9.3	11.4	2.5	5.5	7.0	4.7	3.7	3.3	1.5
Cook Islands Iles Cook	0.5	0.0	0.0	...	...	0.0	0.0	0.0	0.0	0.0
Costa Rica Costa Rica	-204.2[1]	152.3	105.9	144.6	137.4	142.5	111.5	96.1	55.7	27.9
Côte d'Ivoire Côte d'Ivoire	267.8	166.2	206.4	148.0	106.5	93.4	79.4	70.1	85.5	35.5
Croatia Croatie	85.7	141.5	171.2	113.8	140.1	88.7	78.2	43.5	-31.4[1]	-5.0[1]
Cuba Cuba	531.4	571.4	533.7	504.0	488.8	481.0	445.1	208.6	239.5	83.5
Cyprus Chypre	81.0	114.9	165.0	137.6	131.8	62.5	...	...	...	...
Czech Republic République tchèque	7.9	11.2	5.1	2.9	3.7	-4.4[1]	...	...	...	...
Dem. Rep. of the Congo Rép. dém. du Congo	688.5	368.1	386.6	639.4	569.4	566.9	329.1	268.7	170.7	48.9
Djibouti Djibouti	20.6	20.6	20.7	18.0	15.8	12.1	8.8	7.1	3.1	2.2
Dominica Dominique	2.1	1.1	2.1	1.6	3.0	1.4	1.0	1.4	0.5	0.0
Dominican Republic Rép. dominicaine	311.4	752.1	401.9	485.8	329.8	266.5	310.4	204.3	156.2	46.6
Ecuador Equateur	271.7	153.0	230.5	207.0	229.6	256.3	147.4	132.5	63.0	28.3
Egypt Egypte	1 540.0	1 373.6	1 267.0	1 334.8	1 294.0	1 102.2	1 047.6	821.2	593.6	241.6
El Salvador El Salvador	194.6	109.5	99.1	116.9	101.6	97.5	75.6	119.2	64.4	34.7
Equatorial Guinea Guinée équatoriale	31.4	21.4	23.2	23.8	17.5	13.6	10.0	8.1	4.6	4.6
Eritrea Erythrée	25.5	25.2	48.8	...	...	...	...	30.2	4.2	3.1
Estonia Estonie	69.8	56.3	15.7	-0.4[1]	0.0	0.0	...	...	...	...

Ozone-depleting chlorofluorocarbons (CFCs) *(continued)*
Consumption: ozone-depleting potential (ODP) metric tons
Chlorofluorocarbones (CFC) qui appauvrissent la couche d'ozone *(suite)*
Consommation : tonnes de potentiel de destruction de l'ozone (PDO)

Country or area Pays ou zone	1998	1999	2000	2001	2002	2003	2004	2005	2006	2007
Ethiopia Ethiopie	38.2	39.2	39.2	34.6	30.0	28.0	16.0	15.0	12.9	4.9
European Union (EU) Union européenne (UE)	4 341.8[3]	4 746.4[3]	2 168.8[3]	2 136.4[3]	-265.8[1,3]	294.6[3]	195.8[4]	-1 151.6[1,4]	-2.5[1,4]	-106.7[1,5]
Fiji Fidji	13.1	9.4	0.0	0.0	0.0	0.0	0.0	0.0	0.0	0.0
Gabon Gabon	12.0	7.8	13.7	6.4	5.0	5.0	4.5	2.1	1.2	0.0
Gambia Gambie	10.9	6.9	6.1	5.8	4.7	5.1	0.2	0.7	1.0	0.6
Georgia Géorgie	26.0	21.5	21.5	18.8	15.5	12.6	8.6	8.2	5.8	2.7
Ghana Ghana	50.3	46.8	47.0	35.6	21.2	32.0	35.8	17.5	13.1	4.2
Grenada Grenade	3.8	2.9	2.9	1.3	2.1	2.1	1.9	0.6	0.0	0.0
Guatemala Guatemala	188.7	191.1	187.9	265.0	239.6	147.1	65.4	57.5	12.7	5.9
Guinea Guinée	41.8	39.9	37.5	35.4	31.3	25.9	16.7	9.3	4.9	2.9
Guinea-Bissau Guinée-Bissau	27.1	26.0	26.0	26.9	27.2	29.4	25.2	12.5	13.1	2.9
Guyana Guyana	29.2	39.9	24.4	19.8	14.3	10.4	11.9	23.5	8.8	0.1
Haiti Haïti	...	...	169.0	169.0	181.2	115.9	132.5	81.4	50.4	9.0
Honduras Honduras	157.4	334.8	172.3	121.6	131.2	219.1	167.8	122.6	94.7	39.7
Hungary Hongrie	1.3	0.6	0.5	0.0	0.3	-1.3[1]	...	...	...	
Iceland Islande	0.0	0.0	0.0	0.0	0.0	0.0	0.0	0.0	0.0	0.0
India Inde	5 264.7	4 142.9	5 614.3	4 514.3	3 917.7	2 631.5	2 241.6	1 957.8	3 560.3	998.2
Indonesia Indonésie	6 182.8	5 865.8	5 411.1	5 003.3	5 506.3	4 829.3	3 925.5	2 385.3	231.0	202.6
Iran (Islamic Rep. of) Iran (Rép. islamique d')	5 571.0	4 399.0	4 156.5	4 204.8	4 437.8	4 088.8	3 471.9	2 221.0	953.3	549.5
Iraq Iraq	...	...	...	...	...	...	...	...	1 414.1	1 686.1
Israel Israël	0.0	0.0	0.0	0.0	0.0	0.0	0.0	0.0	0.0	0.0
Jamaica Jamaïque	199.0	210.4	59.8	48.6	31.7	16.2	16.0	5.0	0.0	0.0
Japan Japon	-208.0[1]	23.2	-24.2[1]	-5.5[1]	19.5	4.0	0.0	0.0	0.0	-5.0[1]
Jordan Jordanie	647.2	398.0	354.0	321.0	90.0	74.4	58.4	59.6	21.8	24.0
Kazakhstan Kazakhstan	1 025.5	730.0	523.9	290.0	112.0	30.4	11.2	0.0	0.0	0.0
Kenya Kenya	245.3	241.1	203.3	168.6	152.3	168.6	131.7	160.6	57.7	22.7
Kiribati Kiribati	0.5	0.0	0.0	0.0	0.0	0.0	0.0	0.0	0.0	0.0

56

Ozone-depleting chlorofluorocarbons (CFCs) *(continued)*
Consumption: ozone-depleting potential (ODP) metric tons
Chlorofluorocarbones (CFC) qui appauvrissent la couche d'ozone *(suite)*
Consommation : tonnes de potentiel de destruction de l'ozone (PDO)

Country or area Pays ou zone	1998	1999	2000	2001	2002	2003	2004	2005	2006	2007
Korea, Dem. P. R. Corée, R. p. dém. de	112.0	106.0	77.0	320.8	299.0	587.4	7.3	91.8	24.5	40.7
Korea, Republic of Corée, République de	5 298.8	7 402.6	7 395.4	6 802.2	6 646.6	5 171.6	5 012.2	2 730.0	3 026.2	1 209.6
Kuwait Koweït	399.2	450.0	419.9	354.2	349.0	247.4	233.0	152.7	106.8	68.0
Kyrgyzstan Kirghizistan	56.8	52.4	53.5	53.0	38.0	33.0	22.9	8.1	5.3	4.2
Lao People's Dem. Rep. Rép. dém. pop. lao	43.3	44.1	44.6	41.2	42.3	35.3	23.1	19.5	17.8	6.4
Latvia Lettonie	25.3	21.6	35.2	0.0	0.0	0.0	...	...	...	...
Lebanon Liban	475.3	463.4	527.9	533.4	491.7	480.2	347.0	287.3	224.4	74.5
Lesotho Lesotho	3.4	2.8	2.4	1.8	1.6	1.4	1.2	0.0	0.0	0.0
Liberia Libéria	31.1	18.2	41.4	25.1	32.8	26.3	14.2	5.0	5.0	1.8
Libyan Arab Jamah. Jamah. arabe libyenne	659.8	894.0	985.4	985.4	985.4	704.1	459.0	252.0	115.7	57.5
Liechtenstein Liechtenstein	-0.1[1]	0.0	0.0	0.0	0.0	0.0	-0.1[1]	0.0	0.0	0.0
Lithuania Lituanie	103.8	85.3	36.5	0.0	0.0	0.0	...	...	...	...
Madagascar Madagascar	23.9	26.3	12.4	9.9	7.8	7.2	7.1	7.0	2.3	2.1
Malawi Malawi	56.9	50.4	21.5	19.0	19.0	18.7	11.4	5.6	3.6	2.3
Malaysia Malaisie	2 333.7	2 010.1	1 979.8	1 946.9	1 605.5	1 174.4	1 128.5	668.3	564.2	234.2
Maldives Maldives	0.9	1.5	4.6	14.0	2.8	0.0	0.0	0.0	2.1	0.0
Mali Mali	113.1	37.1	29.2	27.0	26.0	26.0	25.0	25.0	16.2	11.0
Malta Malte	106.6	97.2	67.6	63.1	10.3	14.0	...	...	...	...
Marshall Islands Iles Marshall	0.6	1.1	0.5	0.2	0.2	0.2	0.0	0.0	0.0	0.0
Mauritania Mauritanie	14.7	13.4	14.2	15.0	14.7	14.3	7.1	6.1	3.0	1.3
Mauritius Maurice	39.0	18.6	19.1	14.5	7.3	4.0	3.4	-0.1[1]	1.0	0.0
Mexico Mexique	3 482.9	2 837.9	3 059.5	2 223.9	1 946.7	1 983.2	3 208.4	1 604.0	-441.3[1]	-480.6[1]
Micronesia (Fed. States of) Micronésie (Etats féd. de)	1.2	1.2	1.0	1.1	1.9	1.7	1.5	0.4	0.0	0.5
Monaco Monaco	0.0	0.0	0.0	0.0	0.0	0.0	0.0	0.0	0.0	0.0
Mongolia Mongolie	13.2	12.4	11.2	9.3	6.9	5.7	4.1	3.7	2.2	1.0
Montenegro Monténégro	...	...	...	...	...	...	...	...	14.0	3.5
Morocco Maroc	923.6	870.6	564.0	435.2	668.6	474.8	329.0	38.7	40.0	24.1

56

Ozone-depleting chlorofluorocarbons (CFCs) *(continued)*
Consumption: ozone-depleting potential (ODP) metric tons

Chlorofluorocarbones (CFC) qui appauvrissent la couche d'ozone *(suite)*
Consommation : tonnes de potentiel de destruction de l'ozone (PDO)

Country or area Pays ou zone	1998	1999	2000	2001	2002	2003	2004	2005	2006	2007
Mozambique Mozambique	3.2	13.8	9.9	8.4	9.9	1.7	1.6	1.2	2.7	2.3
Myanmar Myanmar	52.3	30.7	26.3	39.4	43.5	51.6	29.6	14.8	0.0	0.0
Namibia Namibie	16.4	16.8	22.1	24.0	20.0	17.2	7.7	0.0	0.0	0.0
Nauru Nauru	0.5	0.4	0.4	0.4	0.0	0.0	0.0	0.0	0.0	0.0
Nepal Népal	32.9	25.0	94.0	0.0	0.0	0.0	0.0	0.0	0.0	0.0
New Zealand Nouvelle-Zélande	0.0	0.0	-2.6[1]	0.0	-4.7[1]	0.0	-1.1[1]	0.0	0.0	0.0
Nicaragua Nicaragua	37.3	52.6	44.4	35.2	54.9	29.9	48.4	36.0	27.6	3.7
Niger Niger	60.7	58.3	39.9	29.1	26.6	24.5	23.0	15.1	15.9	4.3
Nigeria Nigéria	4 761.5	4 286.2	4 094.8	3 665.5	3 286.7	2 662.4	2 116.1	466.1	454.0	17.5
Niue Nioué	0.0	0.0	0.0	...	...	0.0	0.0	0.0	0.0	0.0
Norway [1] Norvège [1]	-16.4	-60.2	-39.8	-48.1	-73.5	-65.5	-54.6	-21.8	-26.7	-64.2
Oman Oman	261.1	259.6	282.1	207.3	179.5	134.5	98.7	54.3	25.8	10.1
Pakistan Pakistan	1 196.0	1 421.8	1 945.3	1 666.3	1 647.0	1 124.0	805.0	453.0	626.0	170.3
Palau Palaos	2.1	0.4	0.6	0.6	0.1	1.0	0.9	0.2	0.1	0.1
Panama Panama	346.0	301.1	249.9	180.4	195.3	168.5	134.7	92.8	43.7	28.4
Papua New Guinea Papouasie-Nvl-Guinée	45.2	35.5	47.9	15.0	34.6	22.7	17.2	15.1	3.1	4.5
Paraguay Paraguay	113.4	345.3	153.5	116.0	96.9	91.8	141.0	250.7	102.9	12.3
Peru Pérou	326.7	295.6	347.0	189.0	196.5	178.4	145.7	127.7	87.2	0.0
Philippines Philippines	2 130.2	2 087.6	2 905.2	2 049.4	1 644.5	1 422.4	1 389.8	1 014.2	603.4	143.1
Poland Pologne	314.1	187.0	174.8	179.0	201.5	126.3	...	...	...	...
Qatar Qatar	120.8	89.0	85.8	85.4	86.7	95.1	63.7	37.0	31.4	13.0
Republic of Moldova République de Moldova	40.5	11.1	31.7	23.5	29.6	18.9	20.0	14.4	12.0	9.2
Romania Roumanie	582.0	338.1	360.6	185.7	359.4	362.1	116.7	180.2	0.0	...
Russian Federation Fédération de Russie	11 821.1	14 824.4	23 820.8	0.0	0.0	258.0	373.6	349.0	394.7	363.0
Rwanda Rwanda	37.7	30.1	30.1	30.1	30.1	30.1	27.1	12.3	12.0	4.1
Saint Kitts and Nevis Saint-Kitts-et-Nevis	1.6	2.6	7.0	6.6	5.3	2.8	3.3	1.5	0.6	0.1
Saint Lucia Sainte-Lucie	6.3	3.2	4.2	4.1	7.6	2.5	0.8	1.5	0.8	0.0

56

Ozone-depleting chlorofluorocarbons (CFCs) *(continued)*
Consumption: ozone-depleting potential (ODP) metric tons

Chlorofluorocarbones (CFC) qui appauvrissent la couche d'ozone *(suite)*
Consommation : tonnes de potentiel de destruction de l'ozone (PDO)

Country or area Pays ou zone	1998	1999	2000	2001	2002	2003	2004	2005	2006	2007
Saint Vincent-Grenadines Saint Vincent-Grenadines	2.3	10.0	6.0	6.9	6.0	3.1	2.1	1.0	0.5	0.2
Samoa Samoa	2.6	6.1	0.6	2.0	2.2	0.0	0.0	0.0	0.0	0.0
Sao Tome and Principe Sao Tomé-et-Principe	3.8	3.4	3.9	4.1	4.3	4.6	4.0	2.3	1.7	0.4
Saudi Arabia Arabie saoudite	1 921.8	1 710.4	1 593.6	1 593.0	1 531.0	1 300.0	1 150.0	878.5	850.0	657.8
Senegal Sénégal	128.5	121.1	116.5	98.0	71.9	51.0	40.0	30.0	25.0	15.0
Serbia Serbie	519.4	548.6	309.7	263.3	371.7	412.0	282.8	52.1	233.8	53.5
Seychelles Seychelles	2.0	1.1	0.8	0.7	1.5	0.6	0.0	0.0	0.0	0.0
Sierra Leone Sierra Leone	81.0	75.9	75.9	92.9	80.8	66.3	64.5	26.2	18.2	10.4
Singapore Singapour	16.7	24.1	21.7	21.6	0.9	11.1	6.6	-0.7[1]	0.0	0.0
Slovakia Slovaquie	1.4	1.4	1.7	3.3	0.8	0.6	...	...	...	...
Slovenia Slovénie	0.1	0.1	0.3	2.6	0.4	0.6	...	...	...	...
Solomon Islands Iles Salomon	0.8	6.2	0.3	0.6	0.5	0.8	1.1	0.9	1.4	0.0
Somalia Somalie	246.9	48.6	65.6	86.9	98.5	108.2	97.2	88.2	84.6	79.5
South Africa Afrique du Sud	155.1	117.3	80.5	16.0	86.6	60.8	61.8	30.0	0.0	0.0
Sri Lanka Sri Lanka	250.4	216.4	220.3	190.4	185.0	179.9	155.7	149.2	105.3	62.2
Sudan Soudan	294.5	294.5	291.5	266.0	253.0	216.0	203.0	185.0	120.0	61.0
Suriname Suriname	42.0	43.0	44.0	46.0	46.0	12.3	9.2	7.5	0.1	0.1
Swaziland Swaziland	2.2	2.1	0.1	1.3	1.2	1.9	3.1	1.5	0.2	0.0
Switzerland Suisse	-28.1[1]	-4.5[1]	-5.8[1]	-1.6[1]	-3.4[1]	-9.1[1]	-19.0[1]	-30.0[1]	0.0	0.0
Syrian Arab Republic Rép. arabe syrienne	1 245.6	1 280.7	1 174.7	1 392.2	1 201.6	1 124.6	928.3	869.7	541.2	282.0
Tajikistan Tadjikistan	56.3	50.7	28.0	28.3	11.8	4.7	0.0	0.0	0.0	0.0
Thailand Thaïlande	3 783.0	3 610.6	3 568.3	3 375.1	2 177.3	1 857.0	1 358.3	1 259.9	453.7	321.6
TFYR of Macedonia L'ex-R.Y. Macédoine	62.8	191.9	49.5	46.7	34.1	49.3	8.8	11.8	7.0	0.0
Togo Togo	36.7	41.7	37.5	34.7	35.3	33.7	26.4	18.6	10.1	5.0
Tonga Tonga	0.0	83.4	0.5	0.7	0.8	0.3	0.0	0.0	0.0	0.0
Trinidad and Tobago Trinité-et-Tobago	155.6	81.7	101.3	79.2	63.6	62.5	35.0	18.3	2.9	0.0
Tunisia Tunisie	790.6	566.0	555.0	570.0	465.8	362.5	271.0	205.0	59.0	17.7

56

Ozone-depleting chlorofluorocarbons (CFCs) *(continued)*
Consumption: ozone-depleting potential (ODP) metric tons
Chlorofluorocarbones (CFC) qui appauvrissent la couche d'ozone *(suite)*
Consommation : tonnes de potentiel de destruction de l'ozone (PDO)

Country or area Pays ou zone	1998	1999	2000	2001	2002	2003	2004	2005	2006	2007
Turkey Turquie	3 985.0	1 791.1	820.2	731.2	698.9	440.9	257.6	132.8	0.2	0.0
Turkmenistan Turkménistan	25.3	18.6	21.0	57.7	10.5	43.4	58.4	17.9	16.8	5.6
Tuvalu Tuvalu	0.3	0.2	0.0	0.0	0.0	0.0	0.0	0.0	0.0	0.0
Uganda Ouganda	11.4	12.2	12.7	13.4	12.7	4.1	0.2	0.2	0.0	0.0
Ukraine Ukraine	1 100.7	951.2	838.7	1 076.5	119.7	77.8	80.0	53.1	0.0	0.0
United Arab Emirates Emirats arabes unis	737.4	529.2	476.2	423.4	370.4	317.5	291.0	264.6	132.3	79.4
United Rep. of Tanzania Rép.-Unie de Tanzanie	131.5	88.9	215.5	131.2	71.5	148.2	98.8	98.9	54.0	26.5
United States Etats-Unis	2 706.0	2 903.8	2 613.0	2 805.2	1 357.2	1 605.2	1 153.6	1 496.6	752.7	-68.6[1]
Uruguay Uruguay	194.0	111.4	106.8	102.3	75.2	111.4	90.9	97.6	81.9	29.3
Uzbekistan Ouzbékistan	119.8	52.8	41.7	15.3	0.0	0.0	0.0	0.0	0.0	0.0
Vanuatu Vanuatu	0.0	0.0	0.0	0.0	0.0	0.0	0.0	0.0	2.3	0.3
Venezuela (Boliv. Rep. of) Venezuela (Rép. boliv. du)	3 213.9	1 922.1	2 705.9	2 546.2	1 552.8	1 313.5	2 944.6	1 841.8	2 641.8	-114.4[1]
Viet Nam Viet Nam	392.0	293.9	220.0	243.0	235.5	243.7	241.0	234.8	148.7	37.8
Yemen Yémen	1 060.8	1 040.7	1 045.0	1 023.4	959.9	758.6	746.4	710.5	394.7	268.7
Zambia Zambie	26.7	24.3	23.3	11.8	10.6	10.4	10.0	9.5	6.6	4.1
Zimbabwe Zimbabwe	390.2	229.1	145.0	259.4	129.1	117.5	112.9	49.0	63.0	54.3

Source:
United Nations Environment Programme (UNEP), Ozone Secretariat
(Nairobi), data access centre, last accessed July 2009.

Source:
Secrétariat de l'ozone du programme des Nations Unies pour l'environnement
(PNUE) (Nairobi), centre de communication de données, dernier accès juillet 2009.

1 Negative numbers can occur when destruction and/or exports exceed
production plus imports, implying that the destruction and/or exports
are from stockpiles.

2 Data include those for Hong Kong Special Administrative Region
(Hong Kong SAR) and Taiwan Province of China.

3 European Community (EC) consumption figures for the years between
1995 and 2003 cover 15 members of the community at the time, namely
, namely Austria, Belgium, Denmark, Finland, France, Germany,
Greece, Ireland, Italy, Luxembourg, Netherlands, Portugal, Spain,
Sweden and United Kingdom of Great Britain and Northern Ireland.

4 European Community (EC) consumption figures for the years between
2004 and 2006 cover 25 members of the community at the time, namely
, namely Austria, Belgium, Cyprus, Czech Republic, Denmark, Estonia,
Finland, France, Germany, Greece, Hungary, Ireland, Italy, Latvia,
Lithuania, Luxembourg, Malta, Netherlands, Poland, Portugal,
Slovakia, Slovenia, Spain, Sweden and United Kingdom of Great
Britain and Northern Ireland.

1 Il peut y avoir des chiffres négatifs, lorsque les quantités exportées, ajoutées
aux quantités détruites, sont supérieures aux quantités effectivement produites
ajoutées aux quantités importées, ce qui est le cas par exemple lorsque les
exportations proviennent des stocks reportés d'un exercice précédent.

2 Les données comprennent les chiffres pour la Région Administrative Spéciale
de Hong Kong (Hong Kong RAS), et la province de Taiwan.

3 Les chiffres sur la consommation dans la Communauté européenne pour les
années comprises entre 1995 et 2003 englobent des données communiquées
par les 15 pays qui étaient alors membres de la Communauté, à savoir
l'Allemagne, l'Autriche, la Belgique, le Danemark, l'Espagne, la Finlande, la
France, la Grèce, l'Irlande, l'Italie, le Luxembourg, les Pays-Bas, le Portugal,
le Royaume-Uni de Grande-Bretagne et d'Irlande du Nord et la Suède.

4 Les chiffres sur la consommation dans la Communauté européenne pour les
années comprises entre 2004 et 2006 englobent des données communiquées
par les 25 pays qui étaient alors membres de la Communauté, à savoir
l'Allemagne, l'Autriche, la Belgique, Chypre, le Danemark, l'Espagne,
l'Estonie, la Finlande, la France, la Grèce, la Hongrie, l'Irlande, l'Italie, la
Lettonie, la Lituanie, le Luxembourg, Malte, les Pays-Bas, la Pologne, le
Portugal, la République tchèque, le Royaume-Uni de Grande-Bretagne et
d'Irlande du Nord, la Slovaquie, la Slovénie et la Suède.

56

Ozone-depleting chlorofluorocarbons (CFCs) *(continued)*
Consumption: ozone-depleting potential (ODP) metric tons

Chlorofluorocarbones (CFC) qui appauvrissent la couche d'ozone *(suite)*
Consommation : tonnes de potentiel de destruction de l'ozone (PDO)

5   European Community (EC) consumption figures for the years starting 2007 onwards covers 27 members of the community at the time, namely , namely Austria, Belgium, Bulgaria, Cyprus, Czech Republic, Denmark, Estonia, Finland, France, Germany, Greece, Hungary, Ireland, Italy, Latvia, Lithuania, Luxembourg, Malta, Netherlands, Poland, Portugal, Romania, Slovakia, Slovenia, Spain,. Sweden and United Kingdom of Great Britain and Northern Ireland.

5   Les chiffres sur la consommation dans la Communauté européenne depuis 2007 englobent des données communiquées par les 27 pays qui étaient alors membres de la Communauté, à savoir l'Allemagne, l'Autriche, la Belgique, la Bulgarie, Chypre, le Danemark, l'Espagne, l'Estonie, la Finlande, la France, la Grèce, la Hongrie, l'Irlande, l'Italie, la Lettonie, la Lituanie, le Luxembourg, Malte, les Pays-Bas, la Pologne, le Portugal, la République tchèque, la Roumanie, le Royaume-Uni de Grande-Bretagne et d'Irlande du Nord, la Slovaquie, la Slovénie et la Suède.

Threatened species
Number by taxonomic group

Espèces menacées
Nombre par groupe taxonomique

Country or area Pays ou zone	Year Année	Mammals Mammifères	Birds Oiseaux	Reptiles Reptiles	Amphibians Amphibiens	Fishes Poissons	Molluscs Mollusques	Invertebrates Invertébrés	Plants Plantes	Total
Afghanistan	2004	12	17	1	1	0	0	1	1	33
Afghanistan	2006	16	18	1	1	0	0	1	1	38
	2008	11	13	1	1	3	0	1	2	32
Albania	2004	1	9	4	2	17	0	4	0	37
Albanie	2006	2	9	4	2	22	0	4	0	43
	2008	3	6	4	2	33	0	4	0	52
Algeria	2004	12	11	2	1	10	0	12	2	50
Algérie	2006	15	13	7	3	18	0	14	3	73
	2008	14	11	7	3	23	0	14	3	75
American Samoa	2004	3	9	2	0	4	5	0	1	24
Samoa américaines	2006	3	11	2	0	5	5	0	1	27
	2008	1	8	2	0	8	5	52	1	77
Andorra	2004	1	0	0	0	0	1	3	0	5
Andorre	2006	2	0	1	0	1	1	3	0	8
	2008	2	0	1	0	2	1	3	0	9
Angola	2004	11	20	4	0	9	5	1	26	76
Angola	2006	14	21	5	0	16	5	1	26	88
	2008	14	18	4	0	22	4	1	26	89
Anguilla	2004	0	0	4	0	11	0	0	3	18
Anguilla	2006	1	0	4	0	12	0	0	3	20
	2008	1	0	3	0	14	0	10	3	31
Antigua and Barbuda	2004	0	2	5	0	11	0	0	4	22
Antigua-et-Barbuda	2006	1	1	5	0	12	0	0	4	23
	2008	2	1	6	0	14	0	11	4	38
Argentina	2004	32	55	5	30	12	0	10	42	186
Argentine	2006	32	57	5	33	22	0	10	44	203
	2008	35	49	5	29	31	0	10	44	203
Armenia	2004	9	12	5	0	1	0	7	1	35
Arménie	2006	11	12	5	0	1	0	6	1	36
	2008	9	12	5	0	4	0	6	1	37
Aruba	2004	1	1	3	0	12	0	1	0	18
Aruba	2006	2	2	3	0	13	0	1	0	21
	2008	3	1	2	0	15	0	1	0	22
Australia	2004	63	60	38	47	74	176	107	56	621
Australie	2006	64	65	39	47	85	176	107	56	639
	2008	57	49	38	48	84	175	282	55	788
Austria	2004	5	8	0	0	7	22	22	3	67
Autriche	2006	6	12	1	0	7	22	21	4	73
	2008	4	9	1	0	9	22	21	4	70
Azerbaijan	2004	11	11	5	0	5	0	6	0	38
Azerbaïdjan	2006	11	13	5	0	5	0	5	0	39
	2008	7	15	5	0	9	0	4	0	40
Bahamas	2004	5	10	6	0	15	0	1	5	42
Bahamas	2006	5	10	7	0	17	0	1	5	45
	2008	7	5	6	0	20	0	11	5	54
Bahrain	2004	1	7	4	0	6	0	0	0	18
Bahreïn	2006	2	7	4	0	6	0	0	0	19
	2008	3	4	4	0	6	0	13	0	30
Bangladesh	2004	22	23	20	0	8	0	0	12	85
Bangladesh	2006	31	32	21	2	13	0	0	12	111
	2008	34	28	20	1	12	0	2	12	109
Barbados	2004	0	3	4	0	11	0	0	2	20
Barbade	2006	1	3	4	0	12	0	0	2	22
	2008	3	1	4	0	15	0	10	2	35
Belarus	2004	6	4	0	0	0	0	8	0	18
Bélarus	2006	6	5	0	0	0	0	8	0	19
	2008	4	4	0	0	1	0	8	0	17

57

Threatened species *(continued)*
Number by taxonomic group
Espèces menacées *(suite)*
Nombre par groupe taxonomique

Country or area Pays ou zone	Year Année	Mammals Mammifères	Birds Oiseaux	Reptiles Reptiles	Amphibians Amphibiens	Fishes Poissons	Molluscs Mollusques	Invertebrates Invertébrés	Plants Plantes	Total
Belgium	2004	9	10	0	0	6	4	7	0	36
Belgique	2006	9	12	0	0	8	4	8	0	41
	2008	3	2	0	0	9	4	8	1	27
Belize	2004	5	3	4	6	18	0	1	30	67
Belize	2006	5	3	5	6	19	0	1	30	69
	2008	7	3	5	6	22	0	12	30	85
Benin	2004	6	2	1	0	8	0	0	14	31
Bénin	2006	12	2	5	0	12	0	0	14	45
	2008	10	4	4	0	15	0	0	14	47
Bermuda	2004	2	3	2	0	11	0	25	4	47
Bermudes	2006	2	3	2	0	13	0	25	4	49
	2008	4	1	2	0	12	0	28	4	51
Bhutan	2004	21	18	0	1	0	0	1	7	48
Bhoutan	2006	25	18	1	2	0	0	1	7	54
	2008	28	17	1	1	0	0	1	7	55
Bolivia	2004	26	30	2	21	0	0	1	70	150
Bolivie	2006	24	32	3	23	0	0	1	71	154
	2008	19	29	2	39	0	0	1	71	161
Bosnia and Herzegovina	2004	8	8	1	1	11	0	10	1	40
Bosnie-Herzégovine	2006	8	9	2	1	25	0	10	1	56
	2008	4	6	2	1	27	0	10	1	51
Botswana	2004	6	9	0	0	0	0	0	0	15
Botswana	2006	8	9	0	0	0	0	0	0	17
	2008	6	7	0	0	2	0	0	0	15
Brazil	2004	74	120	22	24	42	21	13	381	697
Brésil	2006	73	124	22	28	58	21	13	382	721
	2008	82	122	22	30	64	21	15	382	738
British Indian Ocean Terr	2004	0	0	2	0	4	0	0	1	7
Terr. brit. de l'océan Indien	2006	0	0	2	0	5	0	0	1	8
	2008	0	0	2	0	9	0	65	1	77
British Virgin Islands	2004	0	2	6	2	10	0	0	10	30
Iles Vierges britanniques	2006	1	1	6	2	11	0	0	10	31
	2008	1	1	6	2	12	0	10	10	42
Brunei Darussalam	2004	11	25	4	3	6	0	0	99	148
Brunéi Darussalam	2006	15	25	5	15	7	0	0	101	168
	2008	35	21	5	3	8	0	0	99	171
Bulgaria	2004	12	11	2	0	10	0	9	0	44
Bulgarie	2006	13	12	2	0	12	0	8	0	47
	2008	7	12	2	0	17	0	7	0	45
Burkina Faso	2004	6	2	1	0	0	0	0	2	11
Burkina Faso	2006	9	3	1	0	0	0	0	2	15
	2008	8	5	1	0	0	0	0	2	16
Burundi	2004	7	9	0	6	0	1	3	2	28
Burundi	2006	12	11	0	6	18	1	4	2	54
	2008	9	8	0	6	18	1	4	2	48
Cambodia	2004	23	24	10	3	12	0	0	31	103
Cambodge	2006	29	25	15	6	15	0	0	32	122
	2008	37	25	12	3	18	0	67	31	193
Cameroon	2004	42	18	1	50	35	1	3	334	484
Cameroun	2006	43	18	4	53	39	1	1	355	514
	2008	41	15	3	53	43	1	3	355	514
Canada	2004	16	19	2	1	24	1	10	1	74
Canada	2006	18	21	3	1	26	2	10	1	82
	2008	12	16	3	1	26	2	10	2	72
Cape Verde	2004	3	4	0	0	14	0	0	2	23
Cap-Vert	2006	3	5	3	0	15	0	0	2	28
	2008	3	4	1	0	18	0	0	2	28
Cayman Islands	2004	0	3	3	0	10	1	0	2	19
Iles Caïmanes	2006	0	3	6	0	11	1	0	2	23
	2008	1	1	4	0	14	1	10	2	33

Threatened species *(continued)*
Number by taxonomic group
Espèces menacées *(suite)*
Nombre par groupe taxonomique

Country or area Pays ou zone	Year Année	Mammals Mammifères	Birds Oiseaux	Reptiles Reptiles	Amphibians Amphibiens	Fishes Poissons	Molluscs Mollusques	Invertebrates Invertébrés	Plants Plantes	Total
Central African Rep.	2004	11	3	1	0	0	0	0	15	30
Rép. centrafricaine	2006	12	3	1	0	0	0	0	15	31
	2008	7	5	1	0	0	0	0	15	28
Chad	2004	12	5	1	0	0	1	0	2	21
Tchad	2006	14	5	1	0	0	1	0	2	23
	2008	12	7	1	0	0	1	0	2	23
Chile	2004	22	32	0	20	9	0	0	40	123
Chili	2006	22	35	1	21	12	0	2	39	132
	2008	21	32	1	21	18	0	8	40	141
China[1]	2004	80	82	31	86	47	1	3	443	773
Chine[1]	2006	84	88	34	91	59	1	5	442	804
	2008	74	85	30	90	70	1	20	446	816
China, Hong Kong SAR	2004	1	20	1	3	7	1	0	6	39
Chine, Hong Kong RAS	2006	1	20	1	3	9	1	2	6	43
	2008	2	16	1	5	13	1	4	6	48
China, Macao SAR	2004	0	2	0	0	3	0	0	0	5
Chine, Macao RAS	2008	0	4	0	0	6	0	0	0	10
Christmas Is.	2004	0	5	3	0	4	0	0	1	13
Ile Christmas	2006	0	5	3	0	5	0	0	1	14
	2008	1	5	3	0	5	0	16	1	31
Cocos (Keeling) Islands	2004	0	1	1	0	3	0	0	0	5
Iles des Cocos (Keeling)	2006	0	1	1	0	4	1	0	0	7
	2008	2	0	1	0	7	0	17	0	27
Colombia	2004	39	86	15	208	23	0	0	222	593
Colombie	2006	38	88	16	217	28	0	2	225	614
	2008	52	86	15	214	31	0	31	223	652
Comoros	2004	2	10	2	0	4	0	4	5	27
Comores	2006	3	10	2	0	5	0	4	5	29
	2008	5	8	2	0	7	0	62	5	89
Congo	2004	14	4	1	0	10	1	0	35	65
Congo	2006	14	4	2	0	12	1	4	36	73
	2008	11	3	2	0	15	1	3	35	70
Cook Islands	2004	1	15	2	0	4	0	0	1	23
Iles Cook	2006	1	15	2	0	6	0	0	1	25
	2008	1	15	1	0	7	0	25	1	50
Costa Rica	2004	13	18	8	60	13	0	9	110	231
Costa Rica	2006	11	19	8	64	15	0	12	111	240
	2008	8	17	8	59	19	0	28	111	250
Côte d'Ivoire	2004	23	11	2	14	11	1	0	105	167
Côte d'Ivoire	2006	25	11	5	15	15	1	0	109	181
	2008	24	14	4	13	19	1	0	105	180
Croatia	2004	7	9	1	2	27	0	11	0	57
Croatie	2006	7	11	2	2	40	0	13	0	75
	2008	7	11	2	2	46	0	15	1	84
Cuba	2004	11	18	7	47	23	0	3	163	272
Cuba	2006	11	18	7	47	26	0	5	163	277
	2008	14	17	8	49	28	0	15	163	294
Cyprus	2004	3	11	3	0	7	0	0	1	25
Chypre	2006	4	12	4	0	9	0	0	7	36
	2008	5	5	4	0	12	0	0	7	33
Czech Republic	2004	6	9	0	0	7	2	17	4	45
République tchèque	2006	7	11	0	0	10	2	16	4	50
	2008	2	6	0	0	5	2	16	4	35
Dem. Rep. of the Congo	2004	29	30	2	13	10	14	8	65	171
Rép. dém. du Congo	2006	29	30	4	13	24	14	13	66	193
	2008	29	31	3	13	25	13	11	65	190
Denmark	2004	4	10	0	0	7	1	10	3	35
Danemark	2006	4	12	0	0	10	1	10	3	40
	2008	2	2	0	0	13	1	10	3	31

57

Threatened species *(continued)*
Number by taxonomic group
Espèces menacées *(suite)*
Nombre par groupe taxonomique

Country or area Pays ou zone	Year Année	Mammals Mammifères	Birds Oiseaux	Reptiles Reptiles	Amphibians Amphibiens	Fishes Poissons	Molluscs Mollusques	Invertebrates Invertébrés	Plants Plantes	Total
Djibouti	2004	4	6	0	0	9	0	0	2	21
Djibouti	2006	7	6	2	0	12	0	0	2	29
	2008	8	7	0	0	14	0	50	2	81
Dominica	2004	1	4	4	2	11	0	0	11	33
Dominique	2006	2	5	4	2	13	0	0	11	37
	2008	3	3	3	2	15	0	11	11	48
Dominican Republic	2004	5	16	10	31	10	0	2	30	104
Rép. dominicaine	2006	5	14	10	31	12	0	6	30	108
	2008	6	14	11	30	15	0	18	30	124
Ecuador	2004	34	69	10	163	12	48	0	1 815	2 151
Equateur	2006	34	76	11	165	14	48	0	1 832	2 180
	2008	43	69	11	171	15	48	12	1 839	2 208
Egypt	2004	6	17	6	0	14	0	1	2	46
Egypte	2006	14	18	11	0	17	0	1	2	63
	2008	17	10	11	0	24	0	46	2	110
El Salvador	2004	2	3	5	8	5	0	1	25	49
El Salvador	2006	4	4	7	11	7	0	0	26	59
	2008	5	3	7	10	7	0	6	26	64
Equatorial Guinea	2004	17	6	2	5	8	0	2	61	101
Guinée équatoriale	2006	18	5	3	5	10	0	0	63	104
	2008	18	5	4	4	13	0	0	63	107
Eritrea	2004	9	7	6	0	9	0	0	3	34
Erythrée	2006	13	8	6	0	12	0	0	3	42
	2008	9	9	6	0	14	0	50	3	91
Estonia	2004	4	3	0	0	1	0	4	0	12
Estonie	2006	5	4	0	0	2	0	4	0	15
	2008	1	3	0	0	4	0	4	0	12
Ethiopia	2004	35	20	1	9	0	3	3	22	93
Ethiopie	2006	40	21	1	9	3	3	12	22	111
	2008	31	22	1	9	2	3	11	22	101
Faeroe Islands	2004	4	0	0	0	7	0	0	0	11
Iles Féroé	2006	4	0	0	0	8	0	0	0	12
	2008	5	0	0	0	9	0	0	0	14
Falkland Is. (Malvinas)	2004	4	16	0	0	1	0	0	5	26
Iles Falkland (Malvinas)	2006	4	18	0	0	2	0	0	5	29
	2008	4	10	0	0	5	0	0	5	24
Fiji	2004	5	13	6	1	8	2	0	66	101
Fidji	2006	5	12	6	1	9	3	0	66	102
	2008	6	10	6	1	11	3	87	66	190
Finland	2004	3	10	0	0	1	1	9	1	25
Finlande	2006	4	11	0	0	3	1	9	1	29
	2008	1	4	0	0	5	1	9	1	21
France	2004	16	15	3	3	16	34	31	2	120
France	2006	16	17	5	2	23	34	29	7	133
	2008	9	6	5	2	31	34	40	8	135
French Guiana	2004	10	0	7	3	13	0	0	16	49
Guyane française	2006	9	0	7	3	18	0	0	16	53
	2008	6	0	6	3	21	0	0	16	52
French Polynesia	2004	3	33	1	0	9	29	0	47	122
Polynésie française	2006	3	35	2	0	10	30	0	47	127
	2008	1	32	1	0	13	29	26	47	149
Gabon	2004	11	5	1	2	12	0	1	107	139
Gabon	2006	13	5	4	4	16	0	0	108	150
	2008	13	5	3	3	21	0	0	108	153
Gambia	2004	3	2	1	0	11	0	0	4	21
Gambie	2006	10	2	2	0	14	0	0	4	32
	2008	9	5	2	0	16	0	0	4	36
Georgia	2004	11	8	7	1	6	0	10	0	43
Géorgie	2006	13	10	7	1	9	0	9	0	49
	2008	10	10	7	1	12	0	9	0	49

Threatened species *(continued)*
Number by taxonomic group

Espèces menacées *(suite)*
Nombre par groupe taxonomique

Country or area Pays ou zone	Year Année	Mammals Mammifères	Birds Oiseaux	Reptiles Reptiles	Amphibians Amphibiens	Fishes Poissons	Molluscs Mollusques	Invertebrates Invertébrés	Plants Plantes	Total
Germany	2004	9	14	0	0	12	9	22	12	78
Allemagne	2006	10	16	0	0	15	9	21	12	83
	2008	6	6	0	0	20	9	21	12	74
Ghana	2004	15	8	2	10	8	0	0	117	160
Ghana	2006	18	9	5	10	13	0	0	117	172
	2008	17	8	4	10	17	0	1	117	174
Gibraltar	2004	1	5	0	0	10	2	0	0	18
Gibraltar	2006	1	5	0	0	10	2	0	0	18
	2008	5	3	0	0	10	2	0	0	20
Greece	2004	11	14	6	4	27	1	10	2	75
Grèce	2006	12	15	5	5	49	1	13	11	111
	2008	10	11	5	5	62	1	13	11	118
Greenland	2004	7	0	0	0	4	0	0	1	12
Groenland	2006	8	3	0	0	6	0	0	1	18
	2008	6	0	0	0	6	0	0	1	13
Grenada	2004	1	2	4	1	12	0	0	3	23
Grenade	2006	1	3	4	1	13	0	0	3	25
	2008	3	1	4	1	15	0	10	3	37
Guadeloupe	2004	5	2	5	2	11	1	0	7	33
Guadeloupe	2006	6	4	6	3	12	1	0	7	39
	2008	5	1	5	3	14	1	15	7	51
Guam	2004	2	6	2	0	6	5	0	3	24
Guam	2006	2	11	2	0	7	6	0	4	32
	2008	2	12	2	0	9	6	0	4	35
Guatemala	2004	7	10	10	74	14	2	6	85	208
Guatemala	2006	9	11	11	79	16	2	5	86	219
	2008	16	11	13	80	16	2	7	83	228
Guinea	2004	18	10	1	5	8	0	3	22	67
Guinée	2006	22	10	3	8	15	0	3	22	83
	2008	22	12	2	5	19	0	4	22	86
Guinea-Bissau	2004	5	1	1	0	10	0	1	4	22
Guinée-Bissau	2006	9	1	3	0	15	0	0	4	32
	2008	11	2	2	0	18	0	0	4	37
Guyana	2004	13	3	6	6	13	0	1	23	65
Guyana	2006	11	3	6	9	18	0	1	23	71
	2008	8	3	5	7	22	0	1	22	68
Haltl	2004	4	15	9	46	12	0	2	28	116
Haïti	2006	4	13	9	47	13	0	4	29	119
	2008	5	13	8	46	15	0	14	29	130
Honduras	2004	10	6	10	53	14	0	2	111	206
Honduras	2006	9	6	11	59	16	0	1	110	212
	2008	6	7	11	59	19	0	18	110	230
Hungary	2004	7	9	1	0	8	1	24	1	51
Hongrie	2006	9	12	1	0	10	1	26	1	60
	2008	2	9	1	0	9	1	25	1	48
Iceland	2004	7	0	0	0	8	0	0	0	15
Islande	2006	8	2	0	0	10	0	0	0	20
	2008	5	0	0	0	12	0	0	0	17
India	2004	85	79	25	66	28	2	21	246	552
Inde	2006	89	82	26	68	35	2	20	247	569
	2008	96	76	25	65	40	2	109	246	659
Indonesia	2004	146	121	28	33	91	3	28	383	833
Indonésie	2006	146	121	28	39	105	3	28	387	857
	2008	183	115	27	33	111	3	229	386	1 087
Iran (Islamic Rep. of)	2004	21	18	8	4	14	0	3	1	69
Iran (Rép. islamique d')	2006	25	19	9	4	15	0	5	1	78
	2008	16	20	9	4	21	0	19	1	90
Iraq	2004	9	18	2	1	3	0	2	0	35
Iraq	2006	12	18	2	2	5	0	2	0	41
	2008	13	18	2	1	6	0	15	0	55

57

Threatened species *(continued)*
Number by taxonomic group
Espèces menacées *(suite)*
Nombre par groupe taxonomique

Country or area Pays ou zone	Year Année	Mammals Mammifères	Birds Oiseaux	Reptiles Reptiles	Amphibians Amphibiens	Fishes Poissons	Molluscs Mollusques	Invertebrates Invertébrés	Plants Plantes	Total
Ireland	2004	4	8	0	0	6	1	2	1	22
Irlande	2006	4	9	0	0	7	1	2	1	24
	2008	5	1	0	0	16	1	2	1	26
Israel	2004	13	18	4	0	12	5	5	0	57
Israël	2006	16	21	10	0	24	5	6	0	82
	2008	15	13	10	1	31	5	52	0	127
Italy	2004	12	15	4	5	17	16	42	3	114
Italie	2006	12	16	5	6	30	16	42	20	147
	2008	7	8	5	8	33	16	42	19	138
Jamaica	2004	5	12	8	17	12	0	5	208	267
Jamaïque	2006	5	12	9	17	13	0	5	208	269
	2008	5	10	9	17	15	0	15	209	280
Japan	2004	37	53	11	20	27	25	20	12	205
Japon	2006	38	56	11	20	35	25	18	12	215
	2008	27	40	12	20	40	25	133	12	309
Jordan	2004	7	14	1	0	5	0	3	0	30
Jordanie	2006	12	15	5	0	12	0	3	0	47
	2008	13	8	5	0	14	0	49	0	89
Kazakhstan	2004	15	23	2	1	7	0	4	1	53
Kazakhstan	2008	16	21	2	1	13	0	4	16	73
Kenya	2004	33	28	5	4	29	16	11	103	229
Kenya	2006	32	27	5	6	68	16	16	104	274
	2008	27	27	5	7	71	16	55	103	311
Kiribati	2004	0	5	1	0	4	1	0	0	11
Kiribati	2006	0	6	2	0	4	1	0	0	13
	2008	1	5	1	0	7	1	72	0	87
Korea, Dem. P. R.	2004	12	22	0	1	5	0	1	3	44
Corée, R. p. dém. de	2006	13	23	0	1	8	0	2	3	50
	2008	9	20	0	1	8	0	2	3	43
Korea, Republic of	2004	12	34	0	1	7	0	1	0	55
Corée, République de	2006	12	35	0	1	10	0	2	0	60
	2008	9	30	0	2	14	0	3	0	58
Kuwait	2004	1	12	1	0	6	0	0	0	20
Koweït	2006	5	12	2	0	9	0	0	0	28
	2008	6	8	2	0	10	0	13	0	39
Kyrgyzstan	2004	6	4	2	0	0	0	3	1	16
Kirghizistan	2006	9	6	2	0	0	0	3	1	21
	2008	6	12	2	0	3	0	3	14	40
Lao People's Dem. Rep.	2004	30	21	11	4	6	0	0	19	91
Rép. dém. pop. lao	2006	35	24	12	9	6	0	0	20	106
	2008	46	23	11	5	6	0	3	21	115
Latvia	2004	4	8	0	0	3	0	8	0	23
Lettonie	2006	5	9	0	0	4	0	9	0	27
	2008	1	4	0	0	6	1	9	0	21
Lebanon	2004	5	10	1	0	9	0	1	0	26
Liban	2006	9	10	7	0	10	0	3	0	39
	2008	10	6	6	0	15	0	3	0	40
Lesotho	2004	3	7	0	0	1	0	1	1	13
Lesotho	2006	3	7	0	2	1	0	1	1	15
	2008	2	5	0	0	1	0	2	1	11
Liberia	2004	20	11	2	4	8	1	2	46	94
Libéria	2006	21	11	4	11	14	1	1	46	109
	2008	20	11	4	4	19	1	6	46	111
Libyan Arab Jamah.	2004	5	7	3	0	9	0	0	1	25
Jamah. arabe libyenne	2006	9	8	5	0	8	0	0	1	31
	2008	12	0	5	0	14	0	0	1	36
Liechtenstein	2004	2	1	0	0	0	0	5	0	8
Liechtenstein	2006	2	1	0	0	0	0	4	0	7
	2008	0	0	0	0	0	0	4	0	4

57

Threatened species *(continued)*
Number by taxonomic group
Espèces menacées *(suite)*
Nombre par groupe taxonomique

Country or area Pays ou zone	Year Année	Mammals Mammifères	Birds Oiseaux	Reptiles Reptiles	Amphibians Amphibiens	Fishes Poissons	Molluscs Mollusques	Invertebrates Invertébrés	Plants Plantes	Total
Lithuania	2004	5	4	0	0	3	0	5	0	17
Lituanie	2006	6	5	0	0	4	0	6	0	21
	2008	3	4	0	0	6	0	6	0	19
Luxembourg	2004	3	3	0	0	0	2	2	0	10
Luxembourg	2006	3	3	0	0	0	2	2	0	10
	2008	0	0	0	0	1	2	2	0	5
Madagascar	2004	49	34	18	55	66	24	8	276	530
Madagascar	2006	48	36	18	55	72	24	8	277	538
	2008	62	35	19	64	75	24	76	281	636
Malawi	2004	7	13	0	5	0	9	2	14	50
Malawi	2006	7	13	0	5	102	9	7	14	157
	2008	6	12	0	5	101	9	7	14	154
Malaysia	2004	50	40	21	45	34	17	2	683	892
Malaisie	2006	51	43	22	47	45	19	2	688	917
	2008	70	42	21	47	49	19	207	686	1 141
Maldives	2004	0	2	2	0	8	0	0	0	12
Maldives	2006	1	2	2	0	10	0	0	0	15
	2008	2	0	3	0	12	0	38	0	55
Mali	2004	12	5	1	0	1	0	0	6	25
Mali	2006	15	7	1	0	1	0	0	6	30
	2008	11	6	1	0	1	0	0	6	25
Malta	2004	1	10	0	0	11	3	0	0	25
Malte	2006	1	10	0	0	11	3	0	3	28
	2008	3	3	0	0	13	3	0	3	25
Marshall Islands	2004	1	2	2	0	7	1	0	0	13
Iles Marshall	2006	1	2	2	0	8	1	0	0	14
	2008	2	5	1	0	10	1	66	0	85
Martinique	2004	0	3	5	1	11	1	0	8	29
Martinique	2006	1	4	5	2	12	1	0	8	33
	2008	2	2	6	2	10	1	0	8	31
Mauritania	2004	7	5	2	0	11	0	1	0	26
Mauritanie	2006	12	6	3	0	17	0	1	0	39
	2008	14	8	3	0	23	0	1	0	49
Mauritius	2004	3	13	5	0	7	27	5	87	147
Maurice	2006	4	17	7	0	9	27	5	88	157
	2008	6	11	7	0	11	27	69	88	219
Mayotte	2004	0	3	2	0	1	0	1	0	7
Mayotte	2006	1	4	2	0	1	0	1	0	9
	2008	1	3	2	0	3	0	59	0	68
Mexico	2004	72	57	21	190	106	5	36	261	748
Mexique	2006	74	62	21	204	109	5	35	261	771
	2008	100	54	95	211	114	5	57	261	897
Micronesia (Fed. States of)	2004	6	8	2	0	6	4	0	4	30
Micronésie (Etats féd. de)	2006	5	8	2	0	8	4	0	6	33
	2008	6	9	3	0	13	4	104	5	144
Monaco	2004	0	0	0	0	9	0	0	0	9
Monaco	2006	0	0	0	0	6	0	0	0	6
	2008	2	0	0	0	12	0	0	0	14
Mongolia	2004	13	22	0	0	1	0	3	0	39
Mongolie	2006	14	22	0	0	1	0	3	0	40
	2008	11	21	0	0	1	0	3	0	36
Montserrat	2004	1	2	3	1	11	0	0	3	21
Montserrat	2006	2	2	5	1	12	0	0	3	25
	2008	3	2	2	1	14	0	11	3	36
Morocco	2004	12	13	2	2	11	0	8	2	50
Maroc	2006	17	14	10	2	25	0	9	2	79
	2008	18	10	10	2	31	0	9	2	82
Mozambique	2004	12	23	5	3	21	4	1	46	115
Mozambique	2006	15	24	5	7	39	4	2	47	143
	2008	11	21	5	3	45	4	54	46	189

57

Threatened species *(continued)*
Number by taxonomic group
Espèces menacées *(suite)*
Nombre par groupe taxonomique

Country or area Pays ou zone	Year Année	Mammals Mammifères	Birds Oiseaux	Reptiles Reptiles	Amphibians Amphibiens	Fishes Poissons	Molluscs Mollusques	Invertebrates Invertébrés	Plants Plantes	Total
Myanmar	2004	39	41	20	0	7	1	1	38	147
Myanmar	2006	40	49	26	7	15	1	1	38	177
	2008	45	41	22	0	17	1	63	38	227
Namibia	2004	10	18	4	1	11	1	0	24	69
Namibie	2006	10	22	5	2	16	1	1	24	81
	2008	11	21	4	1	21	0	0	24	82
Nauru	2004	0	2	0	0	3	0	0	0	5
Nauru	2006	0	2	0	0	5	0	0	0	7
	2008	1	2	0	0	8	0	62	0	73
Nepal	2004	29	31	6	3	0	0	1	7	77
Népal	2006	32	34	9	3	0	0	0	7	85
	2008	32	32	7	3	0	0	0	7	81
Netherlands	2004	9	11	0	0	7	1	6	0	34
Pays-Bas	2006	10	13	0	0	9	1	6	0	39
	2008	4	2	0	0	11	1	5	0	23
Netherlands Antilles	2004	3	4	6	0	13	0	0	2	28
Antilles néerlandaises	2006	2	4	6	0	13	0	0	2	27
	2008	4	1	6	0	15	0	11	2	39
New Caledonia	2004	6	16	2	0	10	10	1	217	262
Nouvelle-Calédonie	2006	6	16	3	0	12	11	1	217	266
	2008	9	14	2	0	17	11	84	218	355
New Zealand	2004	8	74	12	4	16	5	9	21	149
Nouvelle-Zélande	2006	8	80	12	4	16	5	9	21	155
	2008	8	69	12	4	14	5	10	21	143
Nicaragua	2004	6	8	8	10	17	2	0	39	90
Nicaragua	2006	6	8	8	10	19	2	3	39	95
	2008	5	9	8	10	21	2	17	39	111
Niger	2004	10	2	0	0	0	0	1	2	15
Niger	2006	13	2	1	0	2	0	1	2	21
	2008	11	5	0	0	2	0	1	2	21
Nigeria	2004	25	9	2	13	12	0	1	170	232
Nigéria	2006	30	10	5	19	16	0	1	172	253
	2008	27	12	4	13	21	0	3	171	251
Niue	2004	0	8	1	0	3	0	0	0	12
Nioué	2006	0	8	1	0	4	0	0	0	13
	2008	2	8	1	0	7	0	23	0	41
Norfolk Island	2004	0	17	2	0	2	12	0	1	34
Ile Norfolk	2006	0	19	2	0	2	12	0	1	36
	2008	0	15	2	0	2	12	9	1	41
Northern Mariana Islands	2004	2	13	2	0	5	2	0	4	28
Iles Mariannes du Nord	2006	2	13	2	0	6	4	0	5	32
	2008	5	14	1	0	9	4	47	5	85
Norway	2004	9	6	0	0	7	1	8	2	33
Norvège	2006	10	7	0	0	9	1	8	2	37
	2008	7	2	0	0	14	1	8	2	34
Occupied Palestinian Terr.	2004	0	4	0	0	0	0	0	0	4
Terr. palestinien occupé	2006	0	4	4	0	0	0	1	0	9
	2008	3	7	4	1	1	0	1	0	17
Oman	2004	12	14	4	0	18	0	1	6	55
Oman	2006	13	14	4	0	21	0	4	6	62
	2008	9	9	4	0	20	0	26	6	74
Pakistan	2004	17	30	9	0	14	0	0	2	72
Pakistan	2006	23	32	9	0	20	0	0	2	86
	2008	23	27	10	0	22	0	15	2	99
Palau	2004	3	2	2	0	6	5	0	3	21
Palaos	2006	3	2	2	0	7	5	0	4	23
	2008	4	2	2	0	12	5	97	4	126
Panama	2004	17	20	7	52	17	0	2	195	310
Panama	2006	18	20	7	60	19	0	2	196	322
	2008	14	17	7	49	19	0	20	194	320

57

Threatened species *(continued)*
Number by taxonomic group
Espèces menacées *(suite)*
Nombre par groupe taxonomique

Country or area Pays ou zone	Year Année	Mammals Mammifères	Birds Oiseaux	Reptiles Reptiles	Amphibians Amphibiens	Fishes Poissons	Molluscs Mollusques	Invertebrates Invertébrés	Plants Plantes	Total
Papua New Guinea	2004	58	33	9	10	31	2	10	142	295
Papouasie-Nvl-Guinée	2006	58	32	10	10	37	2	10	142	301
	2008	41	36	9	11	38	2	167	142	446
Paraguay	2004	11	27	2	0	0	0	0	10	50
Paraguay	2006	9	29	2	2	0	0	0	12	54
	2008	8	27	2	0	0	0	0	10	47
Peru	2004	46	94	6	78	8	0	2	274	508
Pérou	2006	46	98	8	86	8	0	2	276	524
	2008	53	93	6	96	10	0	3	275	536
Philippines	2004	50	70	8	48	49	3	16	212	456
Philippines	2006	51	74	9	48	58	3	17	215	475
	2008	39	67	9	48	60	3	199	216	641
Pitcairn	2004	0	11	1	0	3	5	0	7	27
Pitcairn	2006	0	11	1	0	4	5	0	7	28
	2008	2	10	0	0	6	5	10	7	40
Poland	2004	12	12	0	0	3	1	14	4	46
Pologne	2006	13	14	0	0	4	1	15	4	51
	2008	5	6	0	0	6	1	15	4	37
Portugal	2004	15	15	1	0	20	67	15	15	148
Portugal	2006	15	16	3	0	36	67	15	15	167
	2008	11	8	2	1	38	67	16	16	159
Puerto Rico	2004	2	12	8	13	9	0	1	52	97
Porto Rico	2006	2	13	8	13	11	0	1	54	102
	2008	3	8	9	14	13	0	1	53	101
Qatar	2004	0	7	1	0	4	0	0	0	12
Qatar	2006	1	7	2	0	6	0	0	0	16
	2008	2	4	1	0	7	0	13	0	27
Republic of Moldova	2004	4	8	1	0	9	0	5	0	27
République de Moldova	2006	5	8	1	0	9	0	4	0	27
	2008	4	9	1	0	9	0	4	0	27
Réunion	2004	3	8	2	0	5	14	2	14	48
Réunion	2006	4	10	2	0	5	14	2	16	53
	2008	5	6	0	0	6	14	58	15	104
Romania	2004	15	13	2	0	10	0	22	1	63
Roumanie	2006	15	14	2	0	13	0	22	1	67
	2008	7	12	2	0	16	0	22	1	60
Russian Federation	2004	43	47	6	0	18	1	29	7	151
Fédération de Russie	2006	44	53	6	0	22	1	28	7	161
	2008	33	51	6	0	32	1	28	7	158
Rwanda	2004	13	9	0	8	0	0	4	3	37
Rwanda	2006	17	12	0	8	9	0	5	3	54
	2008	19	10	0	8	9	0	3	3	52
Saint Helena	2004	1	20	1	0	10	0	2	26	60
Sainte-Hélène	2006	1	20	1	0	11	0	2	26	61
	2008	2	18	1	0	11	0	2	26	60
Saint Kitts and Nevis	2004	1	2	3	0	11	0	0	2	19
Saint-Kitts-et-Nevis	2006	1	1	5	1	12	0	0	2	22
	2008	2	1	5	1	14	0	10	2	35
Saint Lucia	2004	2	5	6	0	10	0	0	6	29
Sainte-Lucie	2006	2	5	6	0	11	0	0	6	30
	2008	2	5	5	0	15	0	11	6	44
Saint Pierre and Miquelon	2004	0	1	0	0	1	0	0	0	2
Saint-Pierre-et-Miquelon	2006	0	0	0	0	1	0	0	0	1
	2008	3	1	0	0	1	0	0	0	5
Saint Vincent-Grenadines	2004	2	2	4	1	11	0	0	4	24
Saint Vincent-Grenadines	2006	3	3	4	1	12	0	0	4	27
	2008	2	2	3	1	16	0	10	4	38
Samoa	2004	3	7	1	0	4	1	0	2	18
Samoa	2006	3	8	2	0	5	1	0	2	21
	2008	2	7	1	0	8	1	52	2	73

57

Threatened species *(continued)*
Number by taxonomic group
Espèces menacées *(suite)*
Nombre par groupe taxonomique

Country or area Pays ou zone	Year Année	Mammals Mammifères	Birds Oiseaux	Reptiles Reptiles	Amphibians Amphibiens	Fishes Poissons	Molluscs Mollusques	Invertebrates Invertébrés	Plants Plantes	Total
San Marino										
Saint-Marin	2008	0	0	0	0	1	0	0	0	1
Sao Tome and Principe	2004	3	10	1	3	7	1	1	35	61
Sao Tomé-et-Principe	2008	5	10	3	3	8	1	1	35	66
Saudi Arabia	2004	9	17	2	0	9	0	1	3	41
Arabie saoudite	2006	12	18	2	0	13	0	2	3	50
	2008	9	14	2	0	16	0	53	3	97
Senegal	2004	11	5	6	0	18	0	0	7	47
Sénégal	2006	15	6	7	0	23	0	0	7	58
	2008	15	8	6	0	28	0	0	7	64
Seychelles	2004	3	13	3	6	10	2	2	45	84
Seychelles	2006	4	13	10	6	12	2	3	45	95
	2008	5	10	10	6	14	2	63	45	155
Sierra Leone	2004	12	10	3	2	8	0	4	47	86
Sierra Leone	2006	15	10	3	2	12	0	2	47	91
	2008	16	10	3	2	16	0	0	47	94
Singapore	2004	3	10	4	0	13	0	1	54	85
Singapour	2006	5	14	5	0	20	0	1	55	100
	2008	12	14	4	0	22	0	161	54	267
Slovakia	2004	7	11	1	0	8	6	13	2	48
Slovaquie	2006	8	13	1	0	9	6	13	2	52
	2008	3	7	1	0	7	6	13	2	39
Slovenia	2004	7	7	0	2	16	0	42	0	74
Slovénie	2006	7	8	1	2	21	0	42	0	81
	2008	4	4	1	2	24	0	42	0	77
Solomon Islands	2004	20	21	4	2	5	2	4	16	74
Iles Salomon	2006	20	20	4	2	7	2	4	16	75
	2008	17	20	4	2	12	2	138	16	211
Somalia	2004	15	13	2	0	16	1	0	17	64
Somalie	2006	15	13	3	0	21	1	1	17	71
	2008	14	12	3	0	26	1	50	17	123
South Africa	2004	29	36	20	21	49	18	109	75	357
Afrique du Sud	2006	28	38	20	21	58	18	123	73	379
	2008	23	35	19	21	65	24	137	74	398
Spain	2004	20	20	8	4	24	27	36	14	153
Espagne	2006	20	21	18	6	44	27	35	48	219
	2008	16	15	18	6	52	27	35	49	218
Sri Lanka	2004	21	16	8	44	23	0	2	280	394
Sri Lanka	2006	21	17	8	52	29	0	52	280	459
	2008	30	13	8	53	31	0	119	280	534
Sudan	2004	16	10	2	0	8	0	2	17	55
Soudan	2006	19	11	3	0	11	0	2	17	63
	2008	14	13	3	0	13	0	45	17	105
Suriname	2004	12	0	6	2	12	0	0	27	59
Suriname	2006	11	0	6	2	19	0	0	27	65
	2008	7	0	5	1	20	0	0	26	59
Svalbard and Jan Mayen Is.	2004	5	2	0	0	2	0	0	0	9
Svalbard et îles Jan Mayen	2006	6	3	0	0	2	0	0	0	11
	2008	1	0	0	0	2	0	0	0	3
Swaziland	2004	6	6	0	0	0	0	0	11	23
Swaziland	2006	8	8	0	1	0	0	0	11	28
	2008	4	7	0	0	3	0	0	11	25
Sweden	2004	5	9	0	0	6	1	12	3	36
Suède	2006	5	11	0	0	9	1	12	3	41
	2008	1	3	0	0	12	1	12	3	32
Switzerland	2004	4	8	0	1	4	0	30	2	49
Suisse	2006	4	9	0	1	8	0	29	3	54
	2008	2	2	0	1	11	0	29	3	48

57 Threatened species *(continued)*
Number by taxonomic group
Espèces menacées *(suite)*
Nombre par groupe taxonomique

Country or area Pays ou zone	Year Année	Mammals Mammifères	Birds Oiseaux	Reptiles Reptiles	Amphibians Amphibiens	Fishes Poissons	Molluscs Mollusques	Invertebrates Invertébrés	Plants Plantes	Total
Syrian Arab Republic	2004	3	11	3	0	9	0	3	0	29
Rép. arabe syrienne	2006	10	14	7	0	22	0	5	0	58
	2008	16	13	6	0	27	0	6	0	68
Tajikistan	2004	7	9	1	0	3	0	2	2	24
Tadjikistan	2006	10	10	1	0	5	0	2	2	30
	2008	8	9	1	0	8	0	2	14	42
Thailand	2004	36	42	19	3	36	1	0	84	221
Thaïlande	2006	38	49	22	3	49	1	0	88	250
	2008	57	44	22	4	50	1	179	86	443
TFYR of Macedonia	2004	9	9	2	0	4	0	5	0	29
L'ex-R.Y. Macédoine	2006	9	11	2	0	8	0	5	0	35
	2008	5	10	2	0	14	0	5	0	36
Timor-Leste	2004	0	7	1	0	3	0	0	0	11
Timor-Leste	2008	4	5	1	0	5	0	0	0	15
Togo	2004	7	2	2	3	8	0	0	10	32
Togo	2006	12	2	4	3	12	0	0	10	43
	2008	10	2	3	3	16	0	0	10	44
Tokelau	2004	0	1	2	0	3	0	0	0	6
Tokélaou	2006	0	1	2	0	4	0	0	0	7
	2008	0	1	1	0	7	0	31	0	40
Tonga	2004	2	3	2	0	4	2	0	3	16
Tonga	2006	2	4	3	0	5	2	0	3	19
	2008	2	4	2	0	9	2	33	4	56
Trinidad and Tobago	2004	1	2	5	9	15	0	0	1	33
Trinité-et-Tobago	2006	1	4	5	9	18	0	0	1	38
	2008	2	2	5	9	19	0	10	1	48
Tunisia	2004	10	9	3	0	9	0	5	0	36
Tunisie	2006	15	9	4	2	14	0	7	0	51
	2008	14	8	4	1	20	0	7	0	54
Turkey	2004	15	14	12	5	30	0	13	3	92
Turquie	2006	18	16	13	10	52	0	11	3	123
	2008	17	15	13	10	60	0	13	3	131
Turkmenistan	2004	12	13	2	0	8	0	5	0	40
Turkménistan	2006	16	14	1	0	9	0	5	0	45
	2008	9	15	1	0	12	0	5	3	45
Turks and Caicos Islands	2004	0	3	5	0	10	0	0	2	20
Iles Turques et Caïques	2006	1	2	5	0	11	0	0	2	21
	2008	2	2	4	0	14	0	10	2	34
Tuvalu	2004	0	1	1	0	5	1	0	0	8
Tuvalu	2006	0	1	2	0	6	2	0	0	11
	2008	2	1	1	0	8	1	70	0	83
Uganda	2004	29	15	0	6	27	10	9	38	134
Ouganda	2006	28	15	1	10	49	10	17	40	170
	2008	21	18	0	6	54	10	12	38	159
Ukraine	2004	14	13	2	0	11	0	14	1	55
Ukraine	2006	17	13	2	0	14	0	14	1	61
	2008	11	12	2	0	20	0	14	1	60
United Arab Emirates	2004	5	11	1	0	6	0	0	0	23
Emirats arabes unis	2006	7	12	2	0	8	0	2	0	31
	2008	7	8	2	0	9	0	16	0	42
United Kingdom	2004	10	10	0	0	12	2	8	13	55
Royaume-Uni	2006	10	13	0	0	14	2	8	13	60
	2008	5	2	0	0	34	2	8	14	65
United Rep. of Tanzania	2004	34	37	5	40	28	17	16	239	416
Rép.-Unie de Tanzanie	2006	35	39	5	41	130	17	25	241	533
	2008	34	40	5	49	138	17	66	240	589
United States	2004	40	71	27	50	154	261	300	240	1 143
Etats-Unis	2006	41	79	27	53	159	273	303	243	1 178
	2008	37	74	32	56	164	273	312	244	1 192

57

Threatened species *(continued)*
Number by taxonomic group
Espèces menacées *(suite)*
Nombre par groupe taxonomique

Country or area Pays ou zone	Year Année	Mammals Mammifères	Birds Oiseaux	Reptiles Reptiles	Amphibians Amphibiens	Fishes Poissons	Molluscs Mollusques	Invertebrates Invertébrés	Plants Plantes	Total
United States Virgin Is.	2004	1	5	5	1	10	0	0	9	31
Iles Vierges américaines	2006	2	5	5	2	10	0	0	11	35
	2008	1	1	6	2	12	0	10	10	42
Uruguay	2004	6	24	3	4	11	0	1	1	50
Uruguay	2006	7	26	3	4	22	0	1	1	64
	2008	10	24	4	4	28	0	1	1	72
Uzbekistan	2004	7	16	2	0	4	0	1	1	31
Ouzbékistan	2006	10	16	2	0	5	0	1	1	35
	2008	11	15	2	0	8	0	1	15	52
Vanuatu	2004	5	7	2	0	5	0	0	10	29
Vanuatu	2006	5	8	2	0	7	2	0	10	34
	2008	8	8	2	0	11	1	78	10	118
Venezuela (Bolivarian Rep. of)	2004	26	25	13	68	19	0	1	67	219
Venezuela (Rép. boliv. du)	2006	26	25	13	71	26	0	3	69	233
	2008	32	26	13	71	29	0	19	69	259
Viet Nam	2004	41	41	24	15	23	0	0	145	289
Viet Nam	2006	45	42	27	18	30	0	0	148	310
	2008	54	39	27	17	33	0	91	147	408
Wallis and Futuna Islands	2004	0	9	0	0	3	0	0	1	13
Iles Wallis et Futuna	2006	0	9	1	0	3	0	0	1	14
	2008	0	9	0	0	6	0	57	1	73
Western Sahara	2004	4	3	0	0	11	0	1	0	19
Sahara occidental	2006	9	4	2	0	14	0	1	0	30
	2008	11	1	0	0	19	0	1	0	32
Yemen	2004	6	14	2	1	11	2	0	159	195
Yémen	2006	9	14	2	1	13	2	4	159	204
	2008	9	13	3	1	18	2	61	159	266
Zambia	2004	11	12	0	1	0	4	3	8	39
Zambie	2006	12	12	0	1	6	4	3	8	46
	2008	8	12	0	1	10	3	1	8	43
Zimbabwe	2004	8	10	0	6	0	0	2	17	43
Zimbabwe	2006	10	11	0	6	0	0	5	18	50
	2008	8	11	0	6	3	0	4	17	49

Source:
The World Conservation Union (IUCN) / Species Survival Commission (SSC), Gland, Switzerland and Cambridge, United Kingdom, IUCN Red List of Threatened Species, 2004, 2006 and 2008.

1   For statistical purposes, the data for China do not include those for the Hong Kong Special Administrative Region (Hong Kong SAR), Macao Special Administrative Region (Macao SAR) and Taiwan Province of China.

Source:
Union mondiale pour la nature (UICN) / Commission de la sauvergarde des espèces, Gland, Suisse, et Cambridge, Royaume-Uni, La liste rouge des espèces menacées de l'UICN, 2004, 2006 et 2008.

1   Pour la présentation des statistiques, les données pour la Chine ne comprennent pas la Région Administrative Spéciale de Hong Kong (Hong Kong RAS), la Région Administrative Spéciale de Macao (Macao RAS) et la province de Taiwan.

Country or area Pays ou zone	Year Année	Proportion of population with access to: - Pourcentage de la population ayant accès à :					
		Improved drinking water sources Un système amélioré de distribution d'eau potable			Improved sanitation facilities Un système amélioré d'assainissement		
		Urban (%) Urbaine (%)	Rural (%) Rurale (%)	Total (%) Totale (%)	Urban (%) Urbaine (%)	Rural (%) Rurale (%)	Total (%) Totale (%)
Afghanistan	1995	37	17	21	42	29	32
Afghanistan	2000	37	17	21	43	27	30
	2006	37	17	22	45	25	30
Albania	1990	100	...	...	97	...	...
Albanie	1995	100	93	96	97	79	86
	2000	100	94	97	97	83	89
	2006	97	97	97	98	97	97
Algeria	1990	99	88	94	99	77	88
Algérie	1995	98	87	93	99	78	90
	2000	93	84	89	99	82	92
	2006	87	81	85	98	87	94
Andorra	1990	100	100	100	100	100	100
Andorre	1995	100	100	100	100	100	...
	2000	100	100	100	100	100	...
	2006	100	100	100	100	100	100
Angola	1990	37	40	39	55	9	26
Angola	1995	39	40	40	57	9	30
	2000	49	39	44	67	13	40
	2006	62	39	51	79	16	50
Anguilla	1990	...	...	...	99	...	...
Anguilla	1995	60	...	...	99	...	...
	2000	60	...	...	99	...	...
	2006	...	...	...	99	...	...
Antigua and Barbuda	1990	95	...	...	98	...	...
Antigua-et-Barbuda	1995	95	89	91	98	94	95
	2000	95	89	91	98	94	95
	2006	95	...	...	98	...	...
Argentina	1990	97	72	94	86	45	81
Argentine	1995	98	75	95	89	59	85
	2000	98	78	96	91	74	89
	2006	98	80	96	92	83	91
Armenia	1990	99	...	...	94	...	...
Arménie	1995	99	75	91	94	78	89
	2000	99	83	93	95	79	89
	2006	99	96	98	96	81	91
Aruba	1990	100	100	100	...	...	...
Aruba	1995	100	100	100	...	...	...
	2000	100	100	100	...	...	...
	2006	100	100	100	...	...	...
Australia	1990	100	100	100	100	100	100
Australie	1995	100	100	100	100	100	100
	2000	100	100	100	100	100	100
	2006	100	100	100	100	100	100
Austria	1990	100	100	100	100	100	100
Autriche	1995	100	100	100	100	100	100
	2000	100	100	100	100	100	100
	2006	100	100	100	100	100	100
Azerbaijan	1990	82	51	68	...	...	...
Azerbaïdjan	1995	85	53	70	90	70	80
	2000	93	58	76	90	70	80
	2006	95	59	78	90	70	80
Bahamas	1990	98	...	...	100	100	100
Bahamas	1995	98	86	96	100	100	100
	2000	98	86	97	100	100	100
	2006	98	...	...	100	100	100

Country or area Pays ou zone	Year Année	Improved drinking water sources Un système amélioré de distribution d'eau potable			Improved sanitation facilities Un système amélioré d'assainissement		
		Urban (%) Urbaine (%)	Rural (%) Rurale (%)	Total (%) Totale (%)	Urban (%) Urbaine (%)	Rural (%) Rurale (%)	Total (%) Totale (%)
Bahrain Bahreïn	1990	100	...	...	100	...	...
	1995	100	...	...	100	...	...
	2000	100	...	...	100	...	...
	2006	100	...	...	100	...	...
Bangladesh [1] Bangladesh [1]	1990	88	76	78	56	18	26
	1995	87	76	78	54	21	28
	2000	86	77	79	51	26	32
	2006	85	78	80	48	32	36
Barbados Barbade	1990	100	100	100	99	100	100
	1995	100	100	100	99	100	100
	2000	100	100	100	99	100	100
	2006	100	100	100	99	100	99
Belarus Bélarus	1990	100	100	100	...	...	...
	1995	100	100	100	91	96	93
	2000	100	100	100	91	96	92
	2006	100	99	100	91	97	93
Belgium Belgique	1990	100	...	...	...	...	...
	1995	100	...	...	...	...	...
	2000	100	...	...	...	...	...
	2006	100	...	...	...	...	...
Belize Belize	1990	100	...	...	...	...	...
	1995	100	-82	91	71	25	47
	2000	100	82	91	71	25	47
	2006	100	...	...	...	...	...
Benin Bénin	1990	73	57	63	32	2	12
	1995	74	57	63	42	5	19
	2000	76	57	64	51	8	24
	2006	78	57	65	59	11	30
Bhutan Bhoutan	2000	98	79	81	71	50	52
	2006	98	79	81	71	50	52
Bolivia Bolivie	1990	91	49	72	47	15	33
	1995	93	56	78	49	17	36
	2000	94	62	82	52	19	39
	2006	96	69	86	54	22	43
Bosnia and Herzegovina Bosnie-Herzégovine	1990	99	96	97	99	...	...
	1995	99	96	97	99	94	96
	2000	99	96	97	99	93	96
	2006	100	98	99	99	92	95
Botswana Botswana	1990	100	88	93	60	22	38
	1995	100	89	94	60	25	42
	2000	100	90	95	60	28	45
	2006	100	90	96	60	30	47
Brazil Brésil	1990	93	54	83	82	37	71
	1995	95	55	86	83	37	73
	2000	96	57	89	83	37	74
	2006	97	58	91	84	37	77
British Virgin Islands Iles Vierges britanniques	1990	98	98	98	100	100	100
	1995	98	98	98	100	100	100
	2000	98	98	98	100	100	100
	2006	98	98	98	100	100	100
Bulgaria Bulgarie	1990	100	97	99	100	96	99
	1995	100	97	99	100	96	99
	2000	100	97	99	100	96	99
	2006	100	97	99	100	96	99
Burkina Faso Burkina Faso	1990	62	29	34	23	2	5
	1995	71	39	44	27	3	7
	2000	83	51	56	33	4	9
	2006	97	66	72	41	6	13

Country or area Pays ou zone	Year Année	Proportion of population with access to: - Pourcentage de la population ayant accès à :					
		Improved drinking water sources Un système amélioré de distribution d'eau potable			Improved sanitation facilities Un système amélioré d'assainissement		
		Urban (%) Urbaine (%)	Rural (%) Rurale (%)	Total (%) Totale (%)	Urban (%) Urbaine (%)	Rural (%) Rurale (%)	Total (%) Totale (%)
Burundi	1990	97	68	70	41	44	44
Burundi	1995	93	68	70	42	43	43
	2000	89	69	71	43	42	42
	2006	84	70	71	44	41	41
Cambodia	1995	47	14	19	43	2	8
Cambodge	2000	60	33	38	51	9	16
	2006	80	61	65	62	19	28
Cameroon	1990	76	31	49	47	34	39
Cameroun	1995	80	36	56	50	37	43
	2000	84	41	63	54	39	47
	2006	88	47	70	58	42	51
Canada	1990	100	99	100	100	99	100
Canada	1995	100	99	100	100	99	100
	2000	100	99	100	100	99	100
	2006	100	99	100	100	99	100
Cape Verde	1995	86	73	79	61	19	40
Cap-Vert	2000	86	73	80	61	19	41
Central African Rep.	1990	78	47	58	21	5	11
Rép. centrafricaine	1995	80	47	59	25	9	15
	2000	85	49	63	32	16	22
	2006	90	51	66	40	25	31
Chad	1990	...	16	...	19	1	5
Tchad	1995	26	23	24	20	2	6
	2000	46	30	34	21	3	7
	2006	71	40	48	23	4	9
Chile	1990	99	49	91	91	48	84
Chili	1995	99	57	92	93	58	88
	2000	98	65	93	95	67	91
	2006	98	72	95	97	74	94
China	1990	97	55	67	61	43	48
Chine	1995	97	63	74	65	48	53
	2000	97	71	80	69	53	59
	2006	98	81	88	74	59	65
Colombia	1990	98	68	89	81	39	68
Colombie	1995	98	71	90	82	45	71
	2000	98	73	91	83	51	74
	2006	99	77	93	85	58	78
Comoros	1990	98	91	93	34	12	18
Comores	1995	96	88	90	36	17	23
	2000	93	85	88	42	22	29
	2006	91	81	85	49	26	35
Congo	2000	95	35	70	19	21	20
Congo	2006	95	35	71	19	21	20
Cook Islands	1990	99	87	94	100	91	96
Iles Cook	1995	99	87	94	100	92	97
	2000	99	87	95	100	99	100
	2006	98	88	95	100	100	100
Costa Rica	1990	...	88	...	96	92	94
Costa Rica	1995	99	92	96	96	93	95
	2000	99	95	97	96	95	96
	2006	99	96	98	96	95	96
Côte d'Ivoire	1990	71	65	67	39	8	20
Côte d'Ivoire	1995	79	66	71	38	9	21
	2000	87	66	75	38	10	22
	2006	98	66	81	38	12	24

Country or area Pays ou zone	Year Année	Proportion of population with access to: - Pourcentage de la population ayant accès à :					
		Improved drinking water sources Un système amélioré de distribution d'eau potable			Improved sanitation facilities Un système amélioré d'assainissement		
		Urban (%) Urbaine (%)	Rural (%) Rurale (%)	Total (%) Totale (%)	Urban (%) Urbaine (%)	Rural (%) Rurale (%)	Total (%) Totale (%)
Croatia Croatie	1990	100	98	99	99	98	99
	1995	100	98	99	99	98	99
	2000	100	98	99	99	98	99
	2006	100	98	99	99	98	99
Cuba Cuba	1990	95	...	...	99	95	98
	1995	95	78	91	99	95	98
	2000	95	78	91	99	95	98
	2006	95	78	91	99	95	98
Cyprus Chypre	1990	100	100	100	100	100	100
	1995	100	100	100	100	100	100
	2000	100	100	100	100	100	100
	2006	100	100	100	100	100	100
Czech Republic République tchèque	1990	100	100	100	100	98	100
	1995	100	100	100	100	98	99
	2000	100	100	100	100	98	99
	2006	100	100	100	100	98	99
Dem. Rep. of the Congo Rép. dém. du Congo	1990	90	25	43	53	1	15
	1995	89	26	44	51	3	17
	2000	85	28	45	45	17	25
	2006	82	29	46	42	25	31
Denmark Danemark	1990	100	100	100	100	100	100
	1995	100	100	100	100	100	100
	2000	100	100	100	100	100	100
	2006	100	100	100	100	100	100
Djibouti Djibouti	1990	79	68	76	...	...	...
	1995	81	66	78	...	...	...
	2000	88	61	83	76	11	65
	2006	98	54	92	76	11	67
Dominica Dominique	1990	100	...	...	...	...	...
	1995	100	90	97	86	75	83
	2000	100	90	97	86	75	83
	2006	100	...	...	...	...	...
Dominican Republic Rép. dominicaine	1990	98	66	84	77	57	68
	1995	97	75	88	78	62	71
	2000	97	84	92	79	67	74
	2006	97	91	95	81	74	79
Ecuador Equateur	1990	82	61	73	88	50	71
	1995	87	71	80	89	57	75
	2000	92	81	88	90	65	80
	2006	98	91	95	91	72	84
Egypt Egypte	1990	97	92	94	68	37	50
	1995	98	94	96	73	42	55
	2000	99	95	97	79	47	61
	2006	99	98	98	85	52	66
El Salvador El Salvador	1990	90	48	69	88	59	73
	1995	91	54	74	88	65	77
	2000	92	60	79	89	72	82
	2006	94	68	84	90	80	86
Equatorial Guinea Guinée équatoriale	1990	45	42	43	60	46	51
	1995	45	42	43	60	46	51
	2000	45	42	43	60	46	51
	2006	45	42	43	60	46	51
Eritrea Erythrée	1990	62	39	43	20	0	3
	1995	64	42	46	19	0	3
	2000	70	50	54	16	2	4
	2006	74	57	60	14	3	5

Country or area Pays ou zone	Year Année	Proportion of population with access to: - Pourcentage de la population ayant accès à :					
		Improved drinking water sources Un système amélioré de distribution d'eau potable			Improved sanitation facilities Un système amélioré d'assainissement		
		Urban (%) Urbaine (%)	Rural (%) Rurale (%)	Total (%) Totale (%)	Urban (%) Urbaine (%)	Rural (%) Rurale (%)	Total (%) Totale (%)
Estonia Estonie	1990	100	99	100	96	94	95
	1995	100	99	100	96	94	95
	2000	100	99	100	96	94	95
	2006	100	99	100	96	94	95
Ethiopia Ethiopie	1990	74	4	13	19	2	4
	1995	79	10	20	21	2	5
	2000	87	19	29	24	4	7
	2006	96	31	42	27	8	11
Fiji Fidji	1990	43	51	48	87	55	68
	1995	43	51	47	87	55	70
	2000	43	51	47	87	55	70
	2006	43	51	47	87	55	71
Finland Finlande	1990	100	100	100	100	100	100
	1995	100	100	100	100	100	100
	2000	100	100	100	100	100	100
	2006	100	100	100	100	100	100
France France	1990	100	...	...	...	...	...
	1995	100	100	100	...	...	...
	2000	100	100	100	...	...	...
	2006	100	100	100	...	...	...
French Guiana Guyane française	1995	88	71	84	85	57	78
	2000	88	71	84	85	57	78
French Polynesia Polynésie française	1990	100	100	100	99	97	98
	1995	100	100	100	99	97	98
	2000	100	100	100	99	97	98
	2006	100	100	100	99	97	98
Gabon Gabon	1990	95	...	...	...	...	...
	1995	95	47	83	37	30	35
	2000	95	47	85	37	30	36
	2006	95	47	87	37	30	36
Gambia Gambie	1995	96	76	85	48	47	47
	2000	95	77	86	49	49	49
	2006	91	81	86	50	55	52
Georgia Géorgie	1990	91	58	76	96	91	94
	1995	92	61	78	96	91	94
	2000	95	78	87	95	91	93
	2006	100	97	99	94	92	93
Germany Allemagne	1990	100	100	100	100	100	100
	1995	100	100	100	100	100	100
	2000	100	100	100	100	100	100
	2006	100	100	100	100	100	100
Ghana Ghana	1990	86	39	56	11	3	6
	1995	87	49	64	12	4	7
	2000	88	59	72	14	5	9
	2006	90	71	80	15	6	10
Greece Grèce	1990	99	91	96	100	93	97
	1995	100	94	98	99	94	97
	2000	100	97	99	99	96	98
	2006	100	99	100	99	97	98
Grenada Grenade	1990	97	...	...	96	97	97
	1995	97	93	94	96	97	97
	2000	97	93	94	96	97	97
	2006	97	...	...	96	97	97
Guadeloupe Guadeloupe	1990	98	...	...	...	...	...
	1995	98	93	98	64	61	64
	2000	98	93	98	64	61	64
	2006	98	...	...	...	...	...

Country or area Pays ou zone	Year Année	Proportion of population with access to: - Pourcentage de la population ayant accès à :					
		Improved drinking water sources Un système amélioré de distribution d'eau potable			Improved sanitation facilities Un système amélioré d'assainissement		
		Urban (%) Urbaine (%)	Rural (%) Rurale (%)	Total (%) Totale (%)	Urban (%) Urbaine (%)	Rural (%) Rurale (%)	Total (%) Totale (%)
Guam Guam	1990	100	100	100	99	98	99
	1995	100	100	100	99	98	99
	2000	100	100	100	99	98	99
	2006	100	100	100	99	98	99
Guatemala Guatemala	1990	89	72	79	87	58	70
	1995	93	79	85	88	65	75
	2000	96	86	91	89	72	80
	2006	99	94	96	90	79	84
Guinea Guinée	1990	72	35	45	19	10	13
	1995	78	42	53	23	10	14
	2000	84	50	61	28	11	16
	2006	91	59	70	33	12	19
Guinea-Bissau Guinée-Bissau	1995	78	50	58	48	21	29
	2000	79	49	58	48	22	30
	2006	82	47	57	48	26	33
Guyana Guyana	1995	97	85	88	86	80	82
	2000	97	86	89	86	80	82
	2006	98	91	93	85	80	81
Haiti Haïti	1990	62	48	52	49	20	29
	1995	65	49	54	45	19	27
	2000	67	50	56	38	16	24
	2006	70	51	58	29	12	19
Honduras Honduras	1990	91	60	72	68	29	45
	1995	93	65	77	71	37	51
	2000	94	69	80	74	45	58
	2006	95	74	84	78	55	66
Hungary Hongrie	1990	98	91	96	100	100	100
	1995	99	94	97	100	100	100
	2000	100	98	99	100	100	100
	2006	100	100	100	100	100	100
Iceland Islande	1990	100	100	100	100	100	100
	1995	100	100	100	100	100	100
	2000	100	100	100	100	100	100
	2006	100	100	100	100	100	100
India Inde	1990	90	65	71	44	4	14
	1995	92	71	77	46	8	18
	2000	94	77	82	49	13	23
	2006	96	86	89	52	18	28
Indonesia Indonésie	1990	92	63	72	73	42	51
	1995	91	65	74	71	40	51
	2000	90	68	77	69	39	52
	2006	89	71	80	67	37	52
Iran (Islamic Rep. of) Iran (Rép. islamique d')	1990	99	84	92	86	78	83
	1995	99	84	93	86	78	83
	2000	99	84	94	86	78	83
	2006	99	...	...	...	...	...
Iraq Iraq	1990	99	46	83	75	...	...
	1995	98	47	82	76	59	71
	2000	94	51	80	77	63	72
	2006	88	56	77	80	69	76
Ireland Irlande	1990	100	...	...	...	...	...
	1995	100	...	...	...	...	...
	2000	100	...	...	...	...	...
	2006	100	...	...	...	...	...
Israel Israël	1990	100	100	100	100	...	...
	1995	100	100	100	100	...	...
	2000	100	100	100	100	...	...
	2006	100	100	100	100	...	...

Country or area Pays ou zone	Year Année	Improved drinking water sources Un système amélioré de distribution d'eau potable			Improved sanitation facilities Un système amélioré d'assainissement		
		Urban (%) Urbaine (%)	Rural (%) Rurale (%)	Total (%) Totale (%)	Urban (%) Urbaine (%)	Rural (%) Rurale (%)	Total (%) Totale (%)
Italy Italie	1990	100	...	...	...	...	...
	1995	100	...	...	...	...	...
	2000	100	...	...	...	...	...
	2006	100	...	...	...	...	...
Jamaica Jamaïque	1990	98	86	92	82	83	83
	1995	98	87	93	82	83	82
	2000	98	87	93	82	84	83
	2006	97	88	93	82	84	83
Japan Japon	1990	100	100	100	100	100	100
	1995	100	100	100	100	100	100
	2000	100	100	100	100	100	100
	2006	100	100	100	100	100	100
Jordan Jordanie	1990	99	91	97	...	...	...
	1995	99	91	97	98	86	95
	2000	99	91	97	93	78	90
	2006	99	91	98	88	71	85
Kazakhstan Kazakhstan	1990	99	91	96	97	96	97
	1995	99	91	95	97	96	97
	2000	99	91	96	97	97	97
	2006	99	91	96	97	98	97
Kenya Kenya	1990	90	30	41	18	44	39
	1995	88	36	46	18	45	40
	2000	87	42	51	19	46	41
	2006	85	49	57	19	48	42
Kiribati Kiribati	1990	76	33	48	26	20	22
	1995	77	41	54	34	20	25
	2000	77	50	62	43	20	30
	2006	77	53	65	46	20	33
Korea, Dem. P. R. Corée, R. p. dém. de	1990	100	...	...	...	...	...
	1995	100	100	100	58	60	59
	2000	100	100	100	58	60	59
	2006	100	100	100	...	...	...
Korea, Republic of Corée, République de	1990	97	...	...	...	...	...
	1995	97	71	91	...	...	...
	2000	97	71	92	...	...	...
	2006	97	...	...	...	...	...
Kyrgyzstan Kirghizistan	1990	97	...	...	...	...	...
	1995	97	65	77	93	92	92
	2000	98	73	82	93	93	93
	2006	99	83	89	94	93	93
Lao People's Dem. Rep. Rép. dém. pop. lao	1995	73	34	41	48	6	13
	2000	76	39	46	57	14	22
	2006	86	53	60	87	38	48
Latvia Lettonie	1990	100	96	99	...	...	...
	1995	100	96	99	...	...	...
	2000	100	96	99	82	71	78
	2006	100	96	99	82	71	78
Lebanon Liban	1990	100	100	100	100	...	...
	1995	100	100	100	100	87	98
	2000	100	100	100	100	87	98
	2006	100	100	100	100	...	...
Lesotho Lesotho	1990	...	...	...	...	30	...
	1995	93	74	77	43	31	33
	2000	93	74	77	43	32	34
	2006	93	74	78	43	34	36

Country or area Pays ou zone	Year Année	Proportion of population with access to: - Pourcentage de la population ayant accès à :					
		Improved drinking water sources Un système amélioré de distribution d'eau potable			Improved sanitation facilities Un système amélioré d'assainissement		
		Urban (%) Urbaine (%)	Rural (%) Rurale (%)	Total (%) Totale (%)	Urban (%) Urbaine (%)	Rural (%) Rurale (%)	Total (%) Totale (%)
Liberia	1990	85	34	57	59	24	40
Libéria	1995	80	42	61	55	17	36
	2000	75	49	63	51	10	32
	2006	72	52	64	49	7	32
Libyan Arab Jamah.	1990	72	68	71	97	96	97
Jamah. arabe libyenne	1995	72	68	71	97	96	97
	2000	72	68	71	97	96	97
	2006	...	...	...	97	96	97
Luxembourg	1990	100	100	100	100	100	100
Luxembourg	1995	100	100	100	100	100	100
	2000	100	100	100	100	100	100
	2006	100	100	100	100	100	100
Madagascar	1990	80	27	39	15	6	8
Madagascar	1995	79	30	42	16	8	10
	2000	78	33	45	17	9	11
	2006	76	36	47	18	10	12
Malawi	1990	92	34	41	50	46	46
Malawi	1995	93	46	52	51	51	51
	2000	94	58	63	51	56	55
	2006	96	72	76	51	62	60
Malaysia	1990	100	96	98	95	...	...
Malaisie	1995	100	96	98	95	...	...
	2000	100	96	98	95	93	94
	2006	100	96	99	95	93	94
Maldives	1990	100	95	96	100	...	...
Maldives	1995	100	93	95	100	42	57
	2000	99	82	87	100	42	58
	2006	98	76	83	100	42	59
Mali	1990	50	28	33	53	30	35
Mali	1995	62	35	42	55	33	39
	2000	74	42	51	57	36	42
	2006	86	48	60	59	39	45
Malta	1990	100	100	100	100	...	...
Malte	1995	100	100	100	100	...	...
	2000	100	100	100	100	...	...
	2006	100	100	100	100	...	...
Marshall Islands	1990	95	97	96	88	51	75
Iles Marshall	1995	89	97	92	90	54	77
	2000	83	96	88	93	57	81
Mauritania	1990	30	41	37	33	11	20
Mauritanie	1995	36	43	40	34	11	20
	2000	52	48	50	39	11	22
	2006	70	54	60	44	10	24
Mauritius	1990	100	100	100	95	94	94
Maurice	1995	100	100	100	95	94	94
	2000	100	100	100	95	94	94
	2006	100	100	100	95	94	94
Mexico	1990	94	72	88	74	8	56
Mexique	1995	95	76	90	81	25	66
	2000	97	81	93	88	42	76
	2006	98	85	95	91	48	81
Micronesia (Fed. States of)	1990	93	86	88	54	20	29
Micronésie (Etats féd. de)	1995	94	89	90	56	18	28
	2000	94	92	92	59	16	26
	2006	95	94	94	61	14	25

| | | Proportion of population with access to: - Pourcentage de la population ayant accès à : | | | | | |
| | | Improved drinking water sources Un système amélioré de distribution d'eau potable | | | Improved sanitation facilities Un système amélioré d'assainissement | | |
Country or area Pays ou zone	Year Année	Urban (%) Urbaine (%)	Rural (%) Rurale (%)	Total (%) Totale (%)	Urban (%) Urbaine (%)	Rural (%) Rurale (%)	Total (%) Totale (%)
Monaco Monaco	1990	100	...	...	100	...	...
	1995	100	...	...	100	...	...
	2000	100	...	...	100	...	...
	2006	100	...	...	100	...	...
Mongolia Mongolie	1990	97	21	64	...	...	...
	1995	96	24	65	66	23	47
	2000	93	35	68	65	26	48
	2006	90	48	72	64	31	50
Montenegro Monténégro	2006	100	96	98	96	86	91
Montserrat Montserrat	1990	100	100	100	96	96	96
	1995	100	100	100	96	96	96
	2000	100	100	100	96	96	96
	2006	100	100	100	96	96	96
Morocco Maroc	1990	94	58	75	80	25	52
	1995	96	58	78	82	34	59
	2000	98	58	80	83	43	65
	2006	100	58	83	85	54	72
Mozambique Mozambique	1995	83	24	39	49	12	22
	2000	77	25	41	51	16	27
	2006	71	26	42	53	19	31
Myanmar Myanmar	1990	86	47	57	47	15	23
	1995	85	53	61	55	26	34
	2000	83	66	71	74	53	59
	2006	80	80	80	85	81	82
Namibia Namibie	1990	98	42	57	73	8	26
	1995	99	57	70	71	11	29
	2000	99	72	81	68	15	32
	2006	99	90	93	66	18	35
Nepal Népal	1990	97	70	72	36	6	9
	1995	96	76	78	39	12	15
	2000	95	81	83	42	17	20
	2006	94	88	89	45	24	27
Netherlands Pays-Bas	1990	100	100	100	100	100	100
	1995	100	100	100	100	100	100
	2000	100	100	100	100	100	100
	2006	100	100	100	100	100	100
New Zealand Nouvelle-Zélande	1990	100	82	97	...	88	...
	1995	100	82	97	...	88	...
	2000	100	...	...	...	...	...
	2006	100	...	...	...	...	...
Nicaragua Nicaragua	1990	91	46	70	59	23	42
	1995	91	53	74	58	28	44
	2000	90	59	77	57	32	46
	2006	90	63	79	57	34	48
Niger Niger	1990	59	38	41	16	1	3
	1995	69	36	41	19	2	5
	2000	79	34	41	23	2	5
	2006	91	32	42	27	3	7
Nigeria Nigéria	1990	80	34	50	33	22	26
	1995	76	33	50	34	23	27
	2000	71	32	49	34	24	28
	2006	65	30	47	35	25	30
Niue Nioué	1990	100	100	100	100	100	100
	1995	100	100	100	100	100	100
	2000	100	100	100	100	100	100
	2006	100	100	100	100	100	100

Country or area Pays ou zone	Year Année	Proportion of population with access to: - Pourcentage de la population ayant accès à :					
		Improved drinking water sources Un système amélioré de distribution d'eau potable			Improved sanitation facilities Un système amélioré d'assainissement		
		Urban (%) Urbaine (%)	Rural (%) Rurale (%)	Total (%) Totale (%)	Urban (%) Urbaine (%)	Rural (%) Rurale (%)	Total (%) Totale (%)
Northern Mariana Islands Iles Mariannes du Nord	1990	98	100	98	85	78	84
	1995	98	99	98	89	86	89
	2000	98	97	98	92	93	92
	2006	98	97	98	94	96	94
Norway Norvège	1990	100	100	100	...	...	...
	1995	100	100	100	...	...	...
	2000	100	100	100	...	...	...
	2006	100	100	100	...	...	...
Occupied Palestinian Terr. Terr. palestinien occupé	1995	99	90	96	84	69	80
	2000	95	89	93	84	69	80
	2006	90	88	89	84	69	80
Oman Oman	1990	85	73	81	97	61	85
	1995	85	73	82	97	61	87
	2000	85	73	82	97	61	87
	2006	...	...	...	97	...	...
Pakistan Pakistan	1990	96	81	86	76	14	33
	1995	96	83	87	80	22	40
	2000	95	85	88	85	30	48
	2006	95	87	90	90	40	58
Palau Palaos	1990	73	98	90	76	54	61
	1995	74	97	90	81	53	61
	2000	78	95	90	92	52	65
	2006	79	94	89	96	52	67
Panama Panama	1990	100	...	...	...	...	...
	1995	100	79	92	77	43	63
	2000	98	80	92	77	53	69
	2006	96	81	92	78	63	74
Papua New Guinea Papouasie-Nvl-Guinée	1990	88	32	39	67	41	44
	1995	88	32	39	67	41	44
	2000	88	32	39	67	41	44
	2006	88	32	40	67	41	45
Paraguay Paraguay	1990	78	28	52	88	34	60
	1995	84	36	61	88	37	64
	2000	89	44	69	88	40	67
	2006	94	52	77	89	42	70
Peru Pérou	1990	88	46	75	73	15	55
	1995	90	51	79	76	22	60
	2000	91	56	81	80	28	65
	2006	92	63	84	85	36	72
Philippines Philippines	1990	92	75	83	71	46	58
	1995	93	79	87	75	55	66
	2000	94	84	90	78	64	72
	2006	96	88	93	81	72	78
Poland Pologne	1990	100	...	...	...	...	...
	1995	100	...	...	...	...	...
	2000	100	...	...	...	...	...
	2006	100	...	...	...	...	...
Portugal Portugal	1990	98	94	96	97	88	92
	1995	98	96	97	98	92	95
	2000	99	98	99	99	95	97
	2006	99	100	99	99	98	99
Qatar Qatar	1990	100	100	100	100	100	100
	1995	100	100	100	100	100	100
	2000	100	100	100	100	100	100
	2006	100	100	100	100	100	100

| Country or area
Pays ou zone | Year
Année | Proportion of population with access to: - Pourcentage de la population ayant accès à : | | | | | |
| | | Improved drinking water sources
Un système amélioré de distribution d'eau potable | | | Improved sanitation facilities
Un système amélioré d'assainissement | | |
		Urban (%) Urbaine (%)	Rural (%) Rurale (%)	Total (%) Totale (%)	Urban (%) Urbaine (%)	Rural (%) Rurale (%)	Total (%) Totale (%)
Republic of Moldova	1990	98	...	...	...	...	...
République de Moldova	1995	98	89	93	86	72	78
	2000	97	88	92	86	72	78
	2006	96	85	90	85	73	79
Romania	1990	93	55	76	88	52	72
Roumanie	1995	95	62	80	88	53	72
	2000	97	70	85	88	54	73
	2006	99	76	88	88	54	72
Russian Federation	1990	97	86	94	93	70	87
Fédération de Russie	1995	98	87	95	93	70	87
	2000	99	88	96	93	70	87
	2006	100	88	97	93	70	87
Rwanda	1990	94	63	65	31	25	25
Rwanda	1995	90	62	64	37	32	32
	2000	86	62	65	44	39	40
	2006	82	61	65	51	47	48
Saint Kitts and Nevis	1990	99	99	99	96	96	96
Saint-Kitts-et-Nevis	1995	99	99	99	96	96	96
	2000	99	99	99	96	96	96
	2006	99	99	99	96	96	96
Saint Lucia	1990	98	98	98	...	...	...
Sainte-Lucie	1995	98	98	98	89	89	89
	2000	98	98	98	89	89	89
	2006	98	98	98	...	...	...
Saint Vincent-Grenadines	1990	...	...	...	...	96	...
Saint Vincent-Grenadines	1995	...	93	...	...	96	...
	2000	...	93	...	...	96	...
	2006	...	...	...	...	96	...
Samoa	1990	99	89	91	100	98	98
Samoa	1995	96	88	90	100	99	99
	2000	92	88	89	100	100	100
	2006	90	87	88	100	100	100
Sao Tome and Principe	1995	89	69	79	28	15	21
Sao Tomé-et-Principe	2000	89	73	82	28	15	22
	2006	88	83	86	29	18	24
Saudi Arabia	1990	97	63	89	100	...	...
Arabie saoudite	1995	97	63	90	100	...	...
	2000	97	...	...	100	...	...
	2006	97	...	...	100	...	...
Senegal	1990	91	51	67	52	9	26
Sénégal	1995	91	55	69	53	9	27
	2000	92	59	72	53	9	27
	2006	93	65	77	54	9	28
Serbia Serbie	2006	99	98	99	96	88	92
Seychelles	1990	100	...	...	...	100	...
Seychelles	1995	100	75	88	...	100	...
	2000	100	75	87	...	100	...
	2006	100	...	...	...	100	...
Sierra Leone	1995	72	50	57	21	7	12
Sierra Leone	2000	75	46	57	21	6	12
	2006	83	32	53	20	5	11
Singapore	1990	100	...	...	100	...	...
Singapour	1995	100	...	...	100	...	...
	2000	100	...	...	100	...	...
	2006	100	...	...	100	...	...

Country or area Pays ou zone	Year Année	Proportion of population with access to: - Pourcentage de la population ayant accès à :					
		Improved drinking water sources Un système amélioré de distribution d'eau potable			Improved sanitation facilities Un système amélioré d'assainissement		
		Urban (%) Urbaine (%)	Rural (%) Rurale (%)	Total (%) Totale (%)	Urban (%) Urbaine (%)	Rural (%) Rurale (%)	Total (%) Totale (%)
Slovakia Slovaquie	1990	100	100	100	100	99	100
	1995	100	100	100	100	99	100
	2000	100	100	100	100	99	100
	2006	100	100	100	100	99	100
Solomon Islands Iles Salomon	1990	94	65	69	98	18	29
	1995	94	65	69	98	18	30
	2000	94	65	70	98	18	31
	2006	94	65	70	98	18	32
Somalia Somalie	1995	22	20	21	41	12	21
	2000	36	17	23	44	10	21
	2006	63	10	29	51	7	23
South Africa Afrique du Sud	1990	98	62	81	64	45	55
	1995	98	65	83	64	46	56
	2000	99	75	89	65	47	57
	2006	100	82	93	66	49	59
Spain Espagne	1990	100	100	100	100	100	100
	1995	100	100	100	100	100	100
	2000	100	100	100	100	100	100
	2006	100	100	100	100	100	100
Sri Lanka Sri Lanka	1990	91	62	67	85	68	71
	1995	93	67	71	86	74	76
	2000	96	73	77	88	80	81
	2006	98	79	82	89	86	86
Sudan Soudan	1990	85	57	64	53	26	33
	1995	82	60	67	52	25	33
	2000	79	63	69	51	24	34
	2006	78	64	70	50	24	35
Suriname Suriname	1990	99	...	...	90	...	...
	1995	99	71	91	90	66	83
	2000	98	73	91	90	65	83
	2006	97	79	92	89	60	82
Swaziland Swaziland	1995	87	51	59	64	46	50
	2000	87	51	59	64	46	50
	2006	87	51	60	64	46	50
Sweden Suède	1990	100	100	100	100	100	100
	1995	100	100	100	100	100	100
	2000	100	100	100	100	100	100
	2006	100	100	100	100	100	100
Switzerland Suisse	1990	100	100	100	100	100	100
	1995	100	100	100	100	100	100
	2000	100	100	100	100	100	100
	2006	100	100	100	100	100	100
Syrian Arab Republic Rép. arabe syrienne	1990	96	70	83	94	69	81
	1995	96	71	83	95	71	83
	2000	95	77	86	95	79	87
	2006	95	83	89	96	88	92
Tajikistan Tadjikistan	1995	91	42	56	88	81	83
	2000	92	47	59	91	84	86
	2006	93	58	67	95	91	92
Thailand Thaïlande	1990	98	94	95	92	72	78
	1995	98	95	96	93	82	85
	2000	98	96	97	94	92	93
	2006	99	97	98	95	96	96
TFYR of Macedonia L'ex-R.Y. Macédoine	2000	100	99	100	92	81	88
	2006	100	99	100	92	81	89
Timor-Leste Timor-Leste	2000	77	56	61	64	32	40
	2006	77	56	62	64	32	41

Country or area Pays ou zone	Year Année	Proportion of population with access to: - Pourcentage de la population ayant accès à :					
		Improved drinking water sources Un système amélioré de distribution d'eau potable			Improved sanitation facilities Un système amélioré d'assainissement		
		Urban (%) Urbaine (%)	Rural (%) Rurale (%)	Total (%) Totale (%)	Urban (%) Urbaine (%)	Rural (%) Rurale (%)	Total (%) Totale (%)
Togo Togo	1990	79	36	49	25	8	13
	1995	81	37	52	25	6	12
	2000	83	39	55	24	5	12
	2006	86	40	59	24	3	12
Tokelau Tokélaou	1990	...	94	...	...	39	...
	1995	...	94	...	...	43	...
	2000	...	90	...	...	65	...
	2006	...	88	...	...	78	...
Tonga Tonga	1990	100	100	100	98	96	96
	1995	100	100	100	98	96	96
	2000	100	100	100	98	96	96
	2006	100	100	100	98	96	96
Trinidad and Tobago Trinité-et-Tobago	1990	92	88	88	93	93	93
	1995	94	90	90	93	93	93
	2000	95	91	91	92	92	92
	2006	97	93	94	92	92	92
Tunisia Tunisie	1990	95	62	82	95	44	74
	1995	96	69	86	95	51	78
	2000	98	76	90	95	57	81
	2006	99	84	94	96	64	85
Turkey Turquie	1990	92	74	85	96	69	85
	1995	94	80	89	96	70	86
	2000	96	87	93	96	71	87
	2006	98	95	97	96	72	88
Turks and Caicos Islands Îles Turques et Caïques	1990	100	100	100	98	...	...
	1995	100	100	100	98	94	96
	2000	100	100	100	98	94	96
	2006	100	100	100	98	...	...
Tuvalu Tuvalu	1990	92	89	90	83	74	78
	1995	93	90	92	87	78	83
	2000	94	91	93	90	81	86
	2006	94	92	93	93	84	89
Uganda Ouganda	1990	78	39	43	27	29	29
	1995	81	45	49	27	31	31
	2000	85	52	56	28	32	32
	2006	90	60	64	29	34	33
Ukraine Ukraine	1990	100	...	...	98	93	96
	1995	100	90	97	98	93	96
	2000	100	92	97	98	91	96
	2006	97	97	97	97	83	93
United Arab Emirates Emirats arabes unis	1990	100	100	100	98	95	97
	1995	100	100	100	98	95	97
	2000	100	100	100	98	95	97
	2006	100	100	100	98	95	97
United Kingdom Royaume-Uni	1990	100	100	100	...	...	...
	1995	100	100	100	...	...	...
	2000	100	100	100	...	...	...
	2006	100	100	100	...	...	...
United Rep. of Tanzania Rép.-Unie de Tanzanie	1990	90	39	49	29	36	35
	1995	87	41	50	30	36	35
	2000	84	44	53	31	35	34
	2006	81	46	55	31	34	33
United States Etats-Unis	1990	100	94	99	100	99	100
	1995	100	94	99	100	99	100
	2000	100	94	99	100	99	100
	2006	100	94	99	100	99	100

Country or area Pays ou zone	Year Année	Proportion of population with access to: - Pourcentage de la population ayant accès à :					
		Improved drinking water sources Un système amélioré de distribution d'eau potable			Improved sanitation facilities Un système amélioré d'assainissement		
		Urban (%) Urbaine (%)	Rural (%) Rurale (%)	Total (%) Totale (%)	Urban (%) Urbaine (%)	Rural (%) Rurale (%)	Total (%) Totale (%)
Uruguay	1990	100	100	100	100	99	100
Uruguay	1995	100	100	100	100	99	100
	2000	100	100	100	100	99	100
	2006	100	100	100	100	99	100
Uzbekistan	1990	97	85	90	97	91	93
Ouzbékistan	1995	97	85	90	97	92	94
	2000	98	83	89	97	93	94
	2006	98	82	88	97	95	96
Vanuatu	1990	93	53	61	...	...	...
Vanuatu	1995	90	53	61	78	42	49
	2000	86	52	59	78	42	50
Venezuela (Bolivarian Rep. of)	1990	93	70	89	90	47	83
Venezuela (Rép. boliv. du)	1995	93	72	90	91	51	86
Viet Nam	1990	87	43	52	62	21	29
Viet Nam	1995	90	57	64	70	32	40
	2000	94	72	77	78	43	51
	2006	98	90	92	88	56	65
Wallis and Futuna Islands	1990	...	100		...	...	...
Iles Wallis et Futuna	1995	...	100		...	80	...
	2000	...	100		...	80	...
	2006	...	100		...	...	...
Yemen	1990	...	...	...	79	14	28
Yémen	1995	84	68	72	82	19	34
	2000	77	67	70	84	24	39
	2006	68	65	66	88	30	46
Zambia	1990	86	27	50	49	38	42
Zambie	1995	88	32	53	51	42	45
	2000	89	36	54	53	47	49
	2006	90	41	58	55	51	52
Zimbabwe	1990	99	70	78	65	35	44
Zimbabwe	1995	99	70	79	65	35	45
	2000	99	71	80	64	36	45
	2006	98	72	81	63	37	46

Source:
World Health Organization (WHO) and United Nations Children's Fund (UNICEF), Geneva and New York, the WHO/UNICEF Joint Monitoring Programme for the Water and Sanitation database, last accessed July 2008.

Source :
Organisation mondial de la santé (OMS) et Fonds des Nations Unies pour l'enfance (UNICEF), Genève et New York, la base de données de la Programme commun OMS/UNICEF de surveillance de l'eau et de l'assainissement, dernier accès juillet 2008.

1   The drinking water estimates for Bangladesh have been adjusted for arsenic contamination levels based on the national surveys conducted and approved by the Government of Bangladesh.

1   Les estimations concernant l'eau potable pour le Bangladesh ont été ajustées afin de tenir compte des taux de pollution à l'arsenic constatés lors d'enquêtes nationales effectuées et approuvées par le Gouvernement bangladais.

Technical notes: tables 54-58

Table 54: The data on land are compiled by the Food and Agriculture Organization of the United Nations (FAO). FAO's definitions of the land categories are as follows:

Land area: Total area excluding area under inland water bodies. The definition of inland water bodies generally includes major rivers and lakes.

Arable land: Land under temporary crops (double-cropped areas are counted only once); temporary meadows for mowing or pasture; land under market and kitchen gardens; and land temporarily fallow (less than five years). Abandoned land resulting from shifting cultivation is not included in this category. Data for "arable land" are not meant to indicate the amount of land that is potentially cultivable.

Permanent crops: Land cultivated with crops that occupy the land for long periods and need not be replanted after each harvest, such as cocoa, coffee and rubber. This category includes land under flowering shrubs, fruit trees, nut trees and vines, but excludes land under trees grown for wood or timber.

Forest: In the *Global Forest Resources Assessment 2005* the following definition is used for forest: forest includes natural forests and forest plantations and is used to refer to land with a tree crown cover (or equivalent stocking level) of more than 10 per cent and area of more than 0.5 hectares. The trees should be able to reach a minimum height of 5 metres at maturity *in situ*. Forest may consist either of closed forest formations where trees of various storeys and undergrowth cover a high proportion of the ground; or open forest formations with a continuous vegetation cover in which the tree crown cover exceeds 10 per cent. Young natural stands and all plantations established for forestry purposes that have yet to reach a crown density of 10 per cent or tree height of 5 metres are included under forest, as are areas normally forming part of the forest area that are temporarily unstocked as a result of human intervention or natural causes but that are expected to revert to forest.

Table 55: The source of the data presented on the emissions of carbon dioxide (CO_2) is the Carbon Dioxide Information Analysis Centre (CDIAC) of the Oak Ridge National Laboratory in the USA.

The CDIAC estimates of CO_2 emissions are derived primarily from United Nations energy statistics on the consumption of liquid and solid fuels and gas consumption and flaring, and from cement production estimates from the Bureau of Mines of the U.S. Department of Interior. The emissions presented in the table are in units of 1,000 metric tons of CO_2; to convert CO_2 into carbon, divide the data by 3.66406. Full details of the

Notes techniques : tableaux 54 à 58

Tableau 54: Les données relatives aux terres sont compilées par l'Organisation des Nations Unies pour l'alimentation et l'agriculture (FAO). Les définitions de la FAO en ce qui concerne les terres sont les suivantes:

Superficie totale des terres: Superficie totale, à l'exception des eaux intérieures. Les eaux intérieures désignent généralement les principaux fleuves et lacs.

Terres arables: Terres affectées aux cultures temporaires (les terres sur lesquelles est pratiquée la double culture ne sont comptabilisées qu'une fois), prairies temporaires à faucher ou à pâturer, jardins maraîchers ou potagers et terres en jachère temporaire (moins de cinq ans). Cette définition ne comprend pas les terres abandonnées du fait de la culture itinérante. Les données relatives aux terres arables ne peuvent être utilisées pour calculer la superficie des terres aptes à l'agriculture.

Cultures permanentes: Superficie des terres avec des cultures qui occupent la terre pour de longues périodes et qui ne nécessitent pas d'être replantées après chaque récolte, comme le cacao, le café et le caoutchouc. Cette catégorie comprend les terres plantées d'arbustes à fleurs, d'arbres fruitiers, d'arbres à noix et de vignes, mais ne comprend pas les terres plantées d'arbres destinés à la coupe.

Superficie forestière: Dans *l'Évaluation des ressources forestières mondiales 2005*, la FAO a défini les forêts comme suit : les forêts, qui comprennent les forêts naturelles et les plantations forestières, sont des terres où le couvert arboré (ou la densité de peuplement équivalente) est supérieur à 10 % et représente une superficie de plus de 0,5 hectares. Les arbres doivent être susceptibles d'atteindre sur place, à leur maturité, une hauteur de 5 mètres minimum. Il peut s'agir de forêts denses, où les arbres de différente hauteur et le sous-bois couvrent une proportion importante du sol, ou de forêts claires, avec un couvert végétal continu, où le couvert arboré est supérieur à 10 %. Les jeunes peuplements naturels et toutes les plantations d'exploitation forestière n'ayant pas encore atteint une densité de couvert arboré de 10 % ou une hauteur de 5 mètres sont inclus dans les forêts, de même que les aires formant naturellement partie de la superficie forestière mais temporairement déboisées du fait d'une intervention de l'homme ou de causes naturelles, mais devant redevenir boisées.

Tableau 55: Les données sur les émissions de dioxyde de carbone (CO_2) proviennent du "Carbon Dioxide Information Analysis Center" (CDIAC) du "Oak Ridge National Laboratory" (États-Unis).

Les estimations du "Carbon Dioxide Information Analysis Center" sont obtenues essentiellement à partir des statistiques de l'énergie des Nations Unies relatives à la consommation de combustibles liquides et solides, à la production et à la consommation de gaz de torche, et des chiffres de production de ciment du "Bureau of Mines" du "Depart-

procedures for calculating emissions are given in Global, Regional, and National Annual C0$_2$ Emissions Estimates from Fossil Fuel Burning, Hydraulic Cement Production, and Gas Flaring and in the CDIAC web site (see http://cdiac.esd.ornl.gov). Relative to other industrial sources for which CO$_2$ emissions are estimated, statistics on gas flaring activities are sparse and sporadic. In countries where gas flaring activities account for a considerable proportion of the total CO$_2$ emissions, the sporadic nature of gas flaring statistics may produce spurious or misleading trends in national CO$_2$ emissions over the period covered by the table.

Table 56: Chlorofluorocarbons (CFCs) are synthetic compounds formerly used as refrigerants and aerosol propellants and known to be harmful to the ozone layer of the atmosphere. In the Montreal Protocol on Substances that Deplete the Ozone Layer, CFCs to be measured are found in vehicle air conditioning units, domestic and commercial refrigeration and air conditioning/heat pump equipment, aerosol products, portable fire extinguishers, insulation boards, panels and pipe covers, and pre-polymers.

The Parties to the Montreal Protocol on Substances that Deplete the Ozone Layer report data on CFCs to the Ozone Secretariat of the United Nations Environment Programme. The data on CFCs are shown in ozone depleting potential (ODP) tons that are calculated by multiplying the quantities in metric tons reported by the Parties, by the ODP of that substance, and added together.

Consumption is defined as production plus imports, minus exports of controlled substances. Feedstocks are exempt and are therefore subtracted from the imports and/or production. Similarly, the destroyed amounts are also subtracted. Negative numbers can occur when destruction and/or exports exceed production plus imports, implying that the destruction and/or exports are from stockpiles.

Table 57: Data on the number of threatened species in each group of animals and plants are compiled by the World Conservation Union (IUCN)/Species Survival Commission (SSC) and published in the IUCN Red List of Threatened Species.

The list provides a catalogue of those species that are considered globally threatened. The categories used in the Red List are as follows: Extinct, Extinct in the Wild, Critically Endangered, Endangered, Vulnerable, Near Threatened and Data Deficient.

Table 58: The proportion of the population with sustainable access to an improved water source, urban and rural, is the percentage of the population who use any of the following types of water supply for drinking: piped water, public tap, borehole or pump, protected well, protected spring or rainwater. Improved water sources do not include vendor-provided water, bottled water, tanker trucks or unprotected wells and springs.

ment of Interior" des États-Unis. Les émissions sont indiquées en milliers de tonnes de dioxyde de carbone (à diviser par 3.66406 pour avoir les chiffres de carbone). On peut voir dans le détail les méthodes utilisées pour calculer les émissions dans "Global, Regional, and National Annual C0$_2$ Emissions Estimates from Fossil Fuel Burning, Hydraulic Cement Production, and Gas Flaring" et sur le site Web du Carbon Dioxide Information Analysis Center (voir http://cdiac.esd.ornl.gov). Par rapport à d'autres sources industrielles pour lesquelles on calcule les émissions de CO$_2$, les statistiques sur la production de gaz de torche sont rares et sporadiques. Dans les pays où cette production représente une proportion considérable de l'ensemble des émissions de dioxyde de carbone, on peut voir apparaître de ce fait des chiffres parasites ou trompeurs pour ce qui est des tendances des émissions nationales de dioxyde de carbone durant la période visée par le tableau.

Tableau 56: Les chlorofluorocarbones (CFC) sont des substances de synthèse utilisées comme réfrigérants et propulseurs d'aérosols, dont on sait qu'elles appauvrissent la couche d'ozone. Aux termes du Protocole de Montréal relatif à des substances qui appauvrissent la couche d'ozone, la production de certains CFC doit être mesurée : ils sont utilisés dans les climatiseurs de véhicules, le matériel domestique et commercial de réfrigération et de climatisation (pompes à chaleur), les produits sous forme d'aérosols, les extincteurs d'incendie portables, les planches, panneaux et gaines isolants, et les prépolymères.

Les Parties au Protocole de Montréal communiquent leurs données concernant les CFC au secrétariat de l'ozone du Programme des Nations Unies pour l'environnement. Les données sur les CFC, indiquées en tonnes de potentiel de destruction de l'ozone (PDO), sont calculées en multipliant le nombre de tonnes signalé par les Parties par le potentiel de destruction coefficient de la substance considérée, et en faisant la somme de ces PDO.

La consommation est définie comme production de substances contrôlées, plus les importations, moins les exportations. Les produits intermédiaires de l'industrie sont exemptés, et on les soustrait donc des importations et/ou de la production. De même, on soustrait aussi les quantités détruites. On peut obtenir des quantités négatives, lorsque les quantités détruites et/ou exportées sont supérieures à la somme production + importations, ce qui signifie que les quantités détruites ou exportées ont été prélevées sur les stocks accumulés.

Tableau 57: Les données relatives aux espèces menacées pour chaque groupe d'animaux et de plantes, réunies par la Commission de la sauvegarde des espèces de l'Union mondiale pour la nature (UICN), sont publiées dans la Liste rouge des espèces menacées de l'UICN.

Cette liste répertorie les espèces animales considérées comme menacées à l'échelle mondiale, réparties entre les catégories ci-après : éteintes, éteintes à l'état sauvage, gravement menacées d'extinction, menacées d'extinction, vulnérables, quasi menacées, et catégorie à données insuffisantes.

Tableau 58: La proportion de la population ayant accès de

Proportion of the urban and rural population with access to improved sanitation refers to the percentage of the population with access to facilities that hygienically separate human excreta from human, animal and insect contact. Facilities such as sewers or septic tanks, poor-flush latrines and simple pit or ventilated improved pit latrines are assumed to be adequate, provided that they are not public, according to the World Health Organization and United Nations Children's Fund's Global Water Supply and Sanitation Assessment 2000 Report. To be effective, facilities must be correctly constructed and properly maintained.

façon durable à une source d'eau améliorée (zones urbaines et rurales) est le pourcentage de la population qui utilise l'un quelconque des types suivants d'approvisionnement en eau de boisson : eau courante, fontaine publique, forage ou pompe, puits protégé, source protégée ou eau de pluie. Les sources d'eau améliorées ne comprennent pas l'eau fournie par un vendeur, l'eau en bouteille, l'eau fournie par un camion-citerne ou les puits et sources non protégés.

La proportion de la population ayant accès à un système d'assainissement amélioré (zones urbaines et rurales) se réfère au pourcentage de la population ayant accès aux installations qui dans des conditions hygiéniques empêchent l'homme, l'animal ou l'insecte d'entrer en contact avec des excréta humains. Les dispositifs tels que les égouts ou les fosses septiques, les latrines à siphon hydraulique et les latrines simples ou les latrines améliorées à fosse ventilée sont considérés comme appropriés, à condition de ne pas être publics, aux termes du Rapport sur l'évaluation de la situation mondiale de l'approvisionnement en eau et de l'assainissement en 2000 de l'Organisation mondiale de la santé et du Fonds des Nations Unies pour l'enfance. Pour être efficaces, ces installations doivent être bien construites et correctement entretenues.

Country or area Pays ou zone	Year Année	Total R & D personnel Total du personnel de R - D	Researchers Chercheurs Total M & W Total H & F	Women Femmes	Technicians and equivalent staff Techniciens et personnel assimilé Total M & W Total H & F	Women Femmes	Other supporting staff Autre personnel de soutien Total M & W Total H & F	Women Femmes
Algeria Algérie	2005	7 331[1]	5 593[1]	2 043	1 134[1]	...	604[1]	...
American Samoa[1] Samoa américaines[1]	2002	5	5	...	...	...	...	...
	2003	24	24	...	...	...	...	...
	2004	9	9	...	...	...	...	...
	2005	6	6	...	...	...	...	...
Argentina Argentine	2001	37 444	25 656	12 071	6 211	...	5 577	...
	2002	37 413	26 083	12 593	6 072	...	5 258	...
	2003	39 393	27 367	13 271	6 428	...	5 598	...
	2004	42 454	29 471	14 370	6 967	...	6 016	...
	2005	45 361	31 868	15 416	7 788	...	5 705	...
	2006	49 359	35 040	17 081	8 151	...	6 168	...
	2007	53 187	38 681	...	7 732	...	6 774	...
Armenia[2] Arménie[2]	2001	6 965[1,3]	5 087[1,3]	2 175	415[1,3]	...	1 463[1,3]	...
	2002	6 737[1,3]	4 927[1,3]	2 314	451[1,3]	...	1 359[1,3]	...
	2003	6 277[1,3]	4 667[1,3]	2 138	313[1,3]	...	1 297[1,3]	...
	2004	6 685[1,3]	4 788[1,3]	2 235	423[1,3]	...	1 474[1,3]	...
	2005	6 892[1,3]	5 056[1,3]	2 329	345[1,3]	...	1 491[1,3]	...
	2006	6 723[1,3]	4 838[1,3]	2 217	296[1,3]	...	782[1,3]	...
	2007[1]	5 669[3]	4 114[3]	1 840	331[3]	...	811[3]	...
Australia Australie	2002	107 209	73 173	...	18 651	...	15 383	...
	2004	116 194	81 192	...	17 601	...	17 402	...
	2006	125 770	87 270	...	20 479	...	18 021	...
Austria Autriche	2002	38 893	24 124	3 811	10 194	2 683	4 575	2 068
	2004	42 891	25 955	4 740	12 067	2 901	4 869	2 471
	2005[4]	47 275	28 148	...	...	...	...	...
	2006	49 377	29 199	5 669	14 822	3 486	5 357	2 452
	2007	53 019	31 352	...	...	...	...	...
Azerbaijan[2] Azerbaïdjan[2]	2001	15 929[3]	10 139	5 069	1 552	...	4 238[3]	...
	2002	16 019[3]	10 195	5 236	1 609	...	4 215[3]	...
	2003	17 190[3]	10 830	5 541	1 825	...	2 814[3]	...
	2004	17 712[3]	11 531	6 110	1 749	...	2 849	...
	2005	18 164[3]	11 603	6 056	1 825	...	3 086	...
	2006	17 973[3]	11 698	6 029	2 013	...	2 905	...
	2007	18 079[3]	11 280	5 866	2 073	...	3 194	...
Belarus[2] Bélarus[2]	2001	28 186	19 133	8 648	2 332	...	6 721	...
	2002	26 871	18 557	8 361	2 050	...	6 264	...
	2003	#29 981[3]	17 702	7 785	2 337	...	5 999	...
	2004	#28 750	17 034	7 556	2 068	...	5 844	...
	2005	#30 222	18 267	7 897	2 112	...	5 763	...
	2006	#30 544	18 494	8 078	2 263	...	5 715	...
	2007	#31 294	18 995	8 228	2 312	...	5 880	...
Belgium Belgique	2001	55 949	32 237	8 254	15 038	4 497	8 675	2 804
	2002	52 054	30 668	8 316	15 358	4 498	6 028	2 640
	2003	52 257	30 917	8 585	15 293	4 572	6 046	2 669
	2004	52 253	32 400	9 287	14 722	4 425	5 130	2 606
	2005	53 517	33 146	9 769	15 047	4 585	5 324	2 702
	2006[5]	55 204	34 921	...	...	...	...	...
	2007[5]	56 244	35 937	...	...	...	...	...
Benin[1,2,4] Bénin[1,2,4]	2007	...	1 000	...	...	...	...	...
Bolivia[2] Bolivie[2]	2001	1 500	1 250	495	...	...	250	150
Bosnia and Herzegovina[1] Bosnie-Herzégovine[1]	2003	614	232	...	170	...	213	...
	2004	688	239	...	197	...	250	...
	2005	731	253	...	198	...	280	...
	2006	1 284	671	...	245	...	368	...
	2007	1 554	745	...	270	...	536	...
Botswana[2] Botswana[2]	2005	2 140[1]	1 728[1]	529	412[1]	...	...	...
Brazil[2] Brésil[2]	2001	212 667	116 570	51 290	...	...	96 097	...
	2002	216 405	122 716	56 450	...	...	93 689	...
	2003	246 782	135 080	62 137	...	...	111 702	...
	2004	283 146	149 247	74 145	...	...	133 899	...

Country or area Pays ou zone	Year Année	Total R & D personnel Total du personnel de R - D	Researchers Chercheurs		Technicians and equivalent staff Techniciens et personnel assimilé		Other supporting staff Autre personnel de soutien	
			Total M & W Total H & F	Women Femmes	Total M & W Total H & F	Women Femmes	Total M & W Total H & F	Women Femmes
	2005	328 932	177 941	83 633	...	...	150 991	...
	2006	354 100	190 937	95 084	...	...	163 163	...
Brunei Darussalam [1,6]	2002	140	99	...	...	...	...	...
Brunéi Darussalam [1,6]	2003	140	98	...	...	...	...	...
	2004	...	102	...	...	...	...	...
Bulgaria	2001	14 949	9 217	4 247	3 786	2 355	1 946	1 305
Bulgarie	2002	15 029	9 223	4 353	3 713	2 374	2 093	1 379
	2003	15 453	9 589	4 535	3 735	2 294	2 129	1 396
	2004	15 647	9 827	4 642	3 721	2 236	2 099	1 371
	2005	15 853	10 053	4 673	3 778	2 256	2 022	1 349
	2006	16 321	10 336	4 690	3 843	2 263	2 142	1 362
	2007	16 940	11 203	...	...	...	...	...
Burkina Faso [2]	2001	828 [1]	236 [1]	34	244 [1]	...	348 [1]	...
Burkina Faso [2]	2002	828 [1]	236 [1]	34	244 [1]	...	348 [1]	...
	2003	888 [1]	251 [1]	32	260 [1]	...	377 [1]	...
	2004	890 [1]	293 [1]	34	227 [1]	...	370 [1]	...
	2005	942 [1]	301 [1]	37	225 [1]	...	416 [1]	...
	2007	1 054 [1]	187 [1]	#25	391 [1]	...	476 [1]	...
Cambodia [4]								
Cambodge [4]	2002	494 [1]	223 [1]	50	170 [1]		102 [1]	
Cameroon [2]								
Cameroun [2]	2005	...	462 [1]	88	...	...	...	...
Canada	2001	179 450	114 640	...	40 590	...	24 220	...
Canada	2002	183 360	115 960	...	42 680	...	24 720	...
	2003	195 730	122 550	...	46 060	...	27 120	...
	2004 [4,5]	206 180	127 840	...	50 240	...	28 100	...
	2005 [4,5]	213 930	134 300	...	51 540	...	28 090	...
Cape Verde [1]	2001	130	45	...	14	...	71	...
Cap-Vert [1]	2002	151	60	...	15	...	76	...
Central African Rep. [2]	2005 [1]	...	11	...	...	...	...	...
Rép. centrafricaine [2]	2006 [1]	...	20	...	...	...	...	...
	2007	...	41 [1]	17	...	...	...	...
Chile [2]	2001	13 838	7 778	...	...	...	6 060	...
Chili [2]	2002	...	8 507	2 785	...	...	...	...
	#2003	28 220	17 212	5 168	7 273	...	3 735	...
	2004	30 583	18 365	5 503	7 912	...	4 306	...
China [7,8]	2001	956 482	742 726	...	...	...	...	...
Chine [7,8]	2002	1 035 200	810 525	...	...	...	...	...
	2003	1 094 830	862 108	...	...	...	...	...
	2004	1 152 620	926 252	...	...	...	...	...
	2005	1 364 800	1 118 700	...	...	...	...	...
	2006	1 502 470	1 223 760	...	...	...	...	...
	2007	1 736 160	1 423 380	...	...	...	...	...
China, Hong Kong SAR	2001	11 041	9 149	...	1 162	...	730	...
Chine, Hong Kong RAS	2002	12 890	10 639	...	1 532	...	719	...
	2003	16 864	13 497	...	2 138	...	1 228	...
	2004	18 846	14 594	...	2 904	...	1 348	...
	2005	22 053	18 024	...	2 346	...	1 683	...
	2006	22 977	18 326	...	3 176	...	1 475	...
China, Macao SAR [4]	2001	196 [1]	114 [1]	20	74 [1]	...	8 [1]	...
Chine, Macao RAS [4]	2002	196 [1]	105 [1]	16	81 [1]	...	10 [1]	...
	2003	249 [1]	147 [1]	27	94 [1]	...	8 [1]	...
	2004	349 [1]	244 [1]	48	97 [1]	...	8 [1]	...
	2005	409 [1]	298 [1]	62	102 [1]	...	9 [1]	...
Colombia [2]	2001	...	6 414	2 160	...	...	...	...
Colombie [2]	2002	...	8 598	2 942	...	...	...	...
	2003	...	9 578	3 327	...	...	...	...
	2004	...	10 580	3 767	...	...	...	...
	2005	...	10 962	3 974	...	...	...	...
	2006	...	10 634	3 816	...	...	...	...
Costa Rica [2]	2002	...	1 193	453	...	...	...	...
Costa Rica [2]	2003	...	1 171	480	...	...	...	...
	2004	...	1 076	447	...	...	...	...
	2005	...	1 444	569	...	...	...	...

Country or area Pays ou zone	Year Année	Total R & D personnel Total du personnel de R - D	Researchers Chercheurs		Technicians and equivalent staff Techniciens et personnel assimilé		Other supporting staff Autre personnel de soutien	
			Total M & W Total H & F	Women Femmes	Total M & W Total H & F	Women Femmes	Total M & W Total H & F	Women Femmes
Côte d'Ivoire Côte d'Ivoire	2005	...	1 269[1]	210	...	...	...	...
Croatia Croatie	2001	10 043	6 656	2 964	1 676	...	1 711	...
	2002	12 960	8 572	3 651	1 981	1 086	2 407	1 744
	2003	9 148	5 861	2 799	2 056	1 046	1 231	934
	2004	11 162	7 140	3 256	2 573	1 226	1 449	1 051
	2005	9 270	5 727	2 710	2 633	1 196	910	584
	2006	9 516	5 778	2 680	2 843	1 359	895	597
	2007	10 124	6 129	2 893	2 846	1 433	1 149	795
Cuba[2] Cuba[2]	2001	32 721	5 849	...	...	...	26 872[9]	...
	2002	34 326	6 057	...	...	...	28 269[9]	...
	2003	33 855	5 075	...	...	...	28 780[9]	...
	2004	34 094	5 115	...	...	...	28 979[9]	...
	2005	33 988	5 526	2 703	...	...	28 462[9]	...
	2006	29 810	5 401	2 724	...	...	24 319	...
	2007	#17 915	5 236	2 408	...	...	12 679[9]	...
Cyprus Chypre	2001	690	333	105	187	66	170	87
	2002	822	435	137	206	80	181	95
	2003	922	490	157	239	87	194	107
	2004	1 017	583	197	243	95	191	105
	2005	1 157	682	239	273	98	201	105
	2006	1 226	748	254	270	103	207	108
	2007[5]	1 285	795	...	...	...	...	...
Czech Republic République tchèque	2001	26 107	14 987	3 853	8 109	3 447	3 011	1 399
	2002	26 032	14 974	3 917	8 090	3 216	2 968	1 351
	2003	27 957	15 809	4 121	9 001	3 347	3 147	1 403
	2004	28 765	16 300	4 052	9 445	3 407	3 020	1 349
	#2005	43 370	24 169	6 349	13 773	5 153	5 429	2 633
	2006	47 729	26 267	6 652	15 840	5 672	5 622	2 731
	2007	49 192	27 878	7 093	15 431	5 641	5 883	2 916
Dem. Rep. of the Congo[2] Rép. dém. du Congo[2]	2004	31 923	9 072	...	1 444	...	21 407	...
	2005	33 478	10 411	...	1 510	...	21 557	
Denmark Danemark	2001	39 892	19 453[4]	6 660[10]	...	...	...	...
	2002	42 406	25 547[4]	6 802[10]	...	...	...	...
	2003	41 607	24 882	6 926	...	...	...	...
	2004	42 687	26 167	...	...	...	...	...
	2005	43 499	28 179	8 113	10 782	5 364	4 538	2 534
	2006	44 878	28 846	...	10 894	...	5 138	...
	2007	46 029[4]	29 572	...	...	...	...	...
Ecuador[2] Equateur[2]	2001	1 164	648	157	...	...	516	...
	2002	1 271	696	160	...	...	575	...
	2003	1 555	845	241	...	...	710	...
	#2006	2 301	1 555	645	414	171	332	332
	2007	2 853	1 615	725	471	211	767	...
Egypt[1] Egypte[1]	2007	...	49 363	...	30 295	...	...	...
El Salvador[2] El Salvador[2]	2003	...	252	78	...	...	...	...
	2004	...	258	80	...	...	...	...
	2005	...	260	81	...	...	...	...
	2006	...	263	82	...	...	...	...
	2007	...	274	85	...	...	...	...
Estonia Estonie	2001	3 745	2 681	1 125	472	296	592	390
	2002	4 129	3 059	1 262	524	317	546	394
	2003	4 144	3 017	1 273	573	362	554	393
	2004	4 735	3 369	1 390	654	370	712	488
	2005	4 362	3 331	1 317	567	274	464	305
	2006	4 741	3 513	1 418	776	339	452	237
	2007	5 002	3 690	1 531	805	368	507	266
Ethiopia Ethiopie	2005	5 112	1 608	111	779	...	2 725	...
	2007	6 051	1 615	125	978	...	3 458	...
Faeroe Islands Iles Féroé	2003	131	86	21	41	...	4	...
Finland[2] Finlande[2]	2001	69 788	47 534	13 813	...	...	...	...
	2002	73 121	50 215	15 025	...	...	...	...
	2003	74 773	#53 430	#15 931	...	...	...	...
	2004	76 687	51 219	14 834	...	...	...	...

Country or area Pays ou zone	Year Année	Total R & D personnel Total du personnel de R - D	Researchers Chercheurs		Technicians and equivalent staff Techniciens et personnel assimilé		Other supporting staff Autre personnel de soutien	
			Total M & W Total H & F	Women Femmes	Total M & W Total H & F	Women Femmes	Total M & W Total H & F	Women Femmes
	2005	77 275	50 773	15 349	...	...	...	...
	2006	79 911	53 273	16 808	...	...	...	...
	2007	79 507	53 420	16 824	...	...	...	...
France France	2001	333 518	177 372	...	...	...	...	...
	2002	339 847	186 420	...	...	...	...	...
	2003	342 307	192 790	...	...	...	...	...
	2004	352 003	202 377	...	106 415	...	43 211	...
	2005	349 681	202 507	...	105 171	...	42 003	...
	2006	363 867	211 129	...	108 501	...	44 237	...
Gabon[2] Gabon[2]	2004	188[1]	80[1]	25	68[1]	...	40[1]	...
	2006	322[1]	150[1]	37	42[1]	13	130[1]	40
Gambia[2] Gambie[2]	2001	77[1]	40[1]	0	25[1]	...	12[1]	...
	2002	77[1]	40[1]	0	25[1]	...	12[1]	...
	2003	81[1]	44[1]	0	25[1]	...	12[1]	...
	2004	82[1]	44[1]	3	28[1]	...	10[1]	...
	2005	84[1]	46[1]	4	28[1]	...	10[1]	...
Georgia[2] Géorgie[2]	2001	15 100	12 400	6 400	1 180	...	1 520	...
	2002	16 031	11 997	6 165	1 246	...	2 788	...
	2003	17 819	11 572	5 809	1 895	...	4 352	...
	2004	16 698	10 910	5 664	2 262	...	3 526	...
	2005	13 415	8 112	4 275	1 810	...	3 493	...
Germany Allemagne	2001	480 606	264 385	42 588	...	...	...	...
	2002[4]	480 004	265 812	...	...	...	...	...
	2003	472 533	268 942	43 855	89 956	...	113 634	...
	2004	470 729	270 215	...	87 873	...	112 640	...
	2005	475 278	272 148	48 205	94 578	...	108 553	...
	2006	487 260	279 452	...	98 900	...	108 908	...
	2007	493 858	284 305	...	...	...	...	...
Greece Grèce	2001	30 226	14 371	4 710	9 636	...	6 219	...
	2003	31 849	15 631	5 198	9 207	2 661	7 011	3 223
	2005	33 603	19 593	6 213	8 450	3 070	5 559	3 007
	2006[4]	35 140	19 907	...	...	...	...	...
	2007[4]	35 629	20 817	...	...	...	...	...
Greenland Groenland	2001[4]	35	30	10	5[11]	...	...	...
	2002	34	30	9	3[4]	...	...	...
	2003[4]	41	37	12	5[11]	...	...	...
	2004	48	40	11	8[4]	...	...	...
Guam Guam	2003	48	45	...	...	...	...	...
	2004	53	50	...	...	...	...	...
	2005	51	48	...	...	...	...	...
Guatemala[1,2] Guatemala[1,2]	2005	1 177	615	262	192	52	370	90
	2006	1 122	547	135	189	50	386	69
Honduras[2] Honduras[2]	2001	2 262	525	164	...	...	1 737	677
	2002	2 321	516	149	...	...	1 805	830
	2003	2 280	539	143	...	...	1 741	731
Hungary Hongrie	2001[12]	22 942	14 666	...	4 752	...	3 524	...
	2002[12]	23 703	14 965	...	4 936	...	3 802	...
	2003[12]	23 311	15 180	...	4 641	...	3 490	...
	2004[12]	22 826	14 904	...	4 713	...	3 209	...
	2005	23 239	15 878	...	4 591	...	2 770	...
	2006	25 971	17 547	5 505	4 943	3 176	3 481	2 116
	2007	25 954	17 391	5 505	5 141	3 014	3 422	1 985
Iceland Islande	2001	2 901	1 859	647	...	...	...	...
	2002[4]	2 797	...	...	...	...	...	...
	2003	2 940	1 917	690	594	...	429	...
	2005	3 226	2 155	784	669	299	402	181
	2006	3 415	2 400	874	652	282	363	156
	2007	2 982	2 208	805	517	213	257	102
India Inde	2005	...	154 827[4,13]	19 663[14]	...	...	...	...
Indonesia[2] Indonésie[2]	2001[6]	...	92 817	...	...	...	...	...
	2005	#55 118[1]	35 564[6]	#10 874	#9 253[1]	...	#10 301[1]	...
Iran (Islamic Rep. of)[2] Iran (Rép. islamique d')[2]	2004	91 584	51 899	10 300	22 186	...	17 499	...
	2006	101 457	67 795	15 587	18 429	...	15 233	...

Country or area Pays ou zone	Year Année	Total R & D personnel Total du personnel de R - D	Researchers Chercheurs		Technicians and equivalent staff Techniciens et personnel assimilé		Other supporting staff Autre personnel de soutien	
			Total M & W Total H & F	Women Femmes	Total M & W Total H & F	Women Femmes	Total M & W Total H & F	Women Femmes
Ireland	2001	13 317	8 949	...	2 347		2 021	
Irlande	2002	13 582	9 376	2 602	2 369	586	1 837	672
	2003	14 450	10 039	2 883	2 511	633	1 900	702
	2004	15 713	11 010	3 069	2 717	729	1 986	834
	2005	16 690	11 587	3 241	3 043	797	2 060	881
	2006[4]	17 660	12 169	...	3 133	...	2 358	
	2007[4]	18 556	...	...	...	...	...	...
Italy	2001	153 905	66 702	...	...	...	...	...
Italie	2002	164 023	71 242	...	...	...	...	...
	2003	161 828	70 332	20 105	...	...	...	...
	2004	164 026	72 012	20 938	...	...	...	...
	2005	175 248	82 489	26 797	...	...	...	...
	2006	192 002	88 430	29 107	...	...	...	...
Japan[2]	2001	1 050 410	792 699	85 207	85 257	22 433	172 458	61 731
Japon[2]	2002	1 032 830	791 224	88 674	76 190	22 964	165 112	61 044
	2003	1 081 100	830 545	96 133	82 007	24 650	168 546	62 433
	2004	1 096 080	830 474	98 690	87 886	25 696	177 719	65 308
	2005	1 122 680	861 901	102 948	85 509	27 562	175 269	65 753
	2006	1 148 840	874 690	108 547	87 721	27 774	186 425	67 387
	2007	1 157 570	883 386	114 942	93 841	30 051	180 343	65 469
Jordan[2]								
Jordanie[2]	2003	42 153	15 891	3 385	19 322	2 073	6 940	2 101
Kazakhstan[2]	2001	15 339[3]	9 223	4 624	1 140	...	2 793	...
Kazakhstan[2]	2002	15 998[3]	9 366	4 558	1 364	...	2 990	...
	2003	16 578[3]	9 899	4 809	1 300	...	3 018	...
	2004	16 715[3]	10 382	5 017	1 102	...	3 112	...
	2005	18 912[3]	11 910	6 013	1 270	...	3 133	...
	2006	19 563[3]	12 404	6 140	1 281	...	3 214	...
	2007	17 774[3]	11 524	5 987	1 290	...	2 824	...
Korea, Republic of[2]	2001[15]	261 802	178 937	19 930	62 738	15 243	20 127	7 167
Corée, République de[2]	2002[15]	279 806	189 888	22 057	69 021	17 460	20 897	7 792
	2003[15]	297 060	198 171	22 613	75 283	18 158	23 606	8 845
	2004[15]	312 314	209 979	25 198	76 730	18 908	25 605	9 401
	2005[15]	335 428	234 702	30 174	75 179	19 123	25 547	9 732
	2006[16]	365 794	256 598	33 682	80 079	21 223	29 117	10 478
	2007	421 549[16]	289 098[15]	42 977[17]	94 319[17]	28 734[17]	38 132[17]	14 713[16]
Kuwait	2001[1]	730	336	...	84	...	310	...
Koweït	2002[1]	744	346	...	86	...	312	...
	2003[1]	771	358	...	90	...	323	...
	2004[1]	786	373	...	93	...	320	...
	2005[1]	800	384	...	96	...	320	...
	2006[1]	812	392	...	98	...	322	...
	2007	869[1]	472[1]	166	94	...	303	...
Kyrgyzstan[2]	2001	2 958	2 099	1 001	248	...	611	...
Kirghizistan[2]	2002	2 922	2 065	1 019	257	...	600	...
	2003	#3 207[3]	1 979	990	229	...	491	...
	2004	#3 369	2 019	971	307	...	518	...
	2005	#3 419	2 187	977	226	...	498	...
	2006	#3 287	2 154	967	205	...	457	...
	2007	#3 140	2 034	888	204	...	480	...
Lao People's Dem. Rep.[1,6]								
Rép. dém. pop. lao[1,6]	2002	268	87	...	...	...	...	...
Latvia	2001	5 476	3 497	1 927	809	536	1 170	639
Lettonie	2002	5 294	3 451	1 835	660	367	1 183	726
	2003	4 858	3 203	1 707	742	416	913	598
	2004	5 103	3 324	1 806	802	456	977	619
	2005	5 483	3 282	1 636	1 062	554	1 139	594
	2006	6 520	4 024	1 868	1 483	711	1 013	623
	2007	6 378	4 223	2 063	1 126	596	1 029	661
Lesotho	2002	26[1]	12[1]	5[14]	5[1]	...	9[1]	...
Lesotho	2003	26[1]	15[1]	8[14]	5[1]	...	6[1]	...
	2004	51[1]	20[1]	10[14]	21[1]	...	10[1]	...
Lithuania	2001	11 949	8 075	3 766	1 725	1 215	2 149	1 405
Lituanie	2002	9 531	6 326	2 989	1 490	1 058	1 715	1 054
	2003	9 648	6 606	3 196	1 476	1 029	1 566	970
	2004	10 557	7 356	3 481	1 531	992	1 670	1 054

59

Personnel in research and development (R & D) *(continued)*
Full-time equivalent (FTE)
Personnel employé dans la recherche et le développement (R - D) *(suite)*
Equivalent temps plein (ETP)

Country or area Pays ou zone	Year Année	Total R & D personnel Total du personnel de R - D	Researchers Chercheurs		Technicians and equivalent staff Techniciens et personnel assimilé		Other supporting staff Autre personnel de soutien	
			Total M & W Total H & F	Women Femmes	Total M & W Total H & F	Women Femmes	Total M & W Total H & F	Women Femmes
	2005	11 002	7 637	3 706	1 436	939	1 929	1 280
	2006	11 443	8 036	3 907	1 402	899	2 005	1 323
	2007	12 656	8 489	4 116	1 778	1 017	2 389	1 612
Luxembourg	2003	4 010	1 949	...	1 685[4]	...	376[4]	...
Luxembourg	2004	4 318	2 031	...	...	...	...	...
	2005	4 392	2 227	392	1 558	258	607	250
	2006	4 377	2 054	...	1 284	...	1 038	...
	2007	4 585[5]	2 174[5]	...	1 342[4]	...	1 069[4]	...
Madagascar	2001	1 741[1]	822[1]	253	243[1]	...	676[1]	...
Madagascar	2002	1 712[1]	788[1]	241	245[1]	...	679[1]	...
	2003	1 696[1]	814[1]	259	188[1]	...	694[1]	...
	2004	1 706[1]	848[1]	279	175[1]	...	683[1]	...
	2005	1 686[1]	879[1]	298	195[1]	...	612[1]	...
	2006	1 715[1]	899[1]	303	278[1]	...	538[1]	...
	2007	1 778[1]	937[1]	320	280[1]	...	561[1]	...
Malaysia	2002	10 731	7 157	2 451	1 379	...	2 195	...
Malaisie	2004	17 887	12 670	4 701	1 598	...	3 619	...
	2006	13 416	9 694	3 757	1 142	...	2 579	...
Mali								
Mali	2006	672[1]	513[1]	68	159[1,11]	...	...	...
Malta	2002	475	272	...	45	...	158	...
Malte	2003	413	276	...	...	...	...	...
	#2004	717	436	109	147	17	134	64
	2005	825	479	121	222	20	124	65
	2006	862	521	132	221	23	120	63
	#2007	845	515	...	221	...	109	...
Mexico	2001	43 455	...	...	...	...	...	...
Mexique	2003	59 875	33 558	...	15 304	...	11 013	...
	2004	80 685[4]	44 614[4]	...	#22 597	...	#13 474	...
	2005	89 398	48 401	...	27 109	...	13 888	...
Monaco	2004	18[1]	9[1]	4	6[1]	...	3[1]	...
Monaco	2005	18[1]	10[1]	5	5[1]	...	3[1]	...
Mongolia[2]	2001	2 752[1]	2 087[1]	901	215[1]	...	450[1]	...
Mongolie[2]	2002	2 879[1]	1 973[1]	923	177[1]	...	729[1]	...
	2003	2 638[1]	1 995[1]	909	154[1]	...	489[1]	...
	2004	2 642[1]	1 991[1]	907	146[1]	...	505[1]	...
	2005	2 283[1]	1 731[1]	819	81[1]	...	471[1]	...
	2006	2 316[1]	1 707[1]	822	114[1]	...	495[1]	...
	2007	2 379[1]	1 740[1]	837	120[1]	...	519[1]	...
Montenegro[2]	2003	1 227	602	235	312	...	313	...
Monténégro[2]	2004	1 200	597	236	259	...	344	...
	2005	1 246	633	252	290	...	323	...
	2006	1 233	602	231	282	...	349	...
	2007	1 344	671	277	276	...	397	...
Morocco[2]	2001	...	24 719[1]	5 061[14]	...	...	...	...
Maroc[2]	2002	...	25 790[1]	5 133[14]	...	...	...	...
	2003	26 571[1]	23 559[1]	6 049[14]	1 420[1]	...	1 592[1]	...
	2004	27 495[1]	24 483[1]	6 872	1 420[1]	...	1 592[1]	...
	2005	27 549[1]	24 835[1]	6 580	1 042[1]	...	1 672[1]	...
	2006	31 326[1]	28 089[1]	7 322[14]	1 467[1]	...	1 770[1]	...
Mozambique[2]	2002[13]	2 467[14]	468[14]	...	1 999[11]	...	...	...
Mozambique[2]	2006	1 532[13,14]	337[13,14]	113	753[11,13]	...	#442[1]	...
Myanmar[1]	2001	4 373	574	...	3 754	...	46	...
Myanmar[1]	2002	7 418	837	...	6 499	...	82	...
Nauru[2]								
Nauru[2]	2003	77[1]	19[1]	3	18[1]	...	36[1]	...
Nepal[2,4]								
Népal[2,4]	2002	13 500	3 000	450	6 000	...	4 500	...
Netherlands[2]	2002	109 224	46 730	...	34 840	...	27 654	...
Pays-Bas[2]	2003	106 980	45 554	7 852	34 893	7 767	26 533	9 593
	2004[4,5]	118 104	52 505	...	35 999	...	29 600	...
	2005	113 773[4]	49 979[4]	8 980[5]	36 725[4]	8 475[5]	27 067[4]	10 070[5]

Country or area Pays ou zone	Year Année	Total R & D personnel Total du personnel de R - D	Researchers Chercheurs Total M & W Total H & F	Women Femmes	Technicians and equivalent staff Techniciens et personnel assimilé Total M & W Total H & F	Women Femmes	Other supporting staff Autre personnel de soutien Total M & W Total H & F	Women Femmes
New Zealand[2] Nouvelle-Zélande[2]	2001	30 183	22 045	8 657	4 200	1 617	3 938	2 789
	2003	36 875	25 486	...	5 554	...	5 835	...
	2005	37 310	27 570	...	5 303	...	4 437	...
	2007	43 600	29 700	...	7 700	...	6 250	...
Nicaragua[2] Nicaragua[2]	2002	456	256	96[14]	...	...	200	...
	2004	371	326	...	45	15	...	...
Niger[1] Niger[1]	2001	611	109	...	122	...	380	...
	2002	594	104	...	118	...	372	...
	2003	569	100	...	115	...	354	...
	2004	599	106	...	133	...	360	...
	2005	595	101	...	137	...	357	...
Nigeria[2] Nigéria[2]	2001	50 229[1]	19 447[1]	3 691	9 261[1]	...	21 521[1]	...
	2002	50 271[1]	18 973[1]	3 475	8 986[1]	...	22 312[1]	...
	2003	55 556[1]	22 690[1]	4 246	9 107[1]	...	23 759[1]	...
	2004	...	24 727[1]	4 286	9 047[1]	...	...	...
	2005	66 574[1]	28 533[1]	4 839	10 854[1]	...	27 187[1]	...
Norway[2] Norvège[2]	2001	48 691	34 864	9 883	...	...	...	...
	2002	51 086	...	...	...	...	...	...
	2003	51 175	35 700	10 505	...	...	...	...
	2005	54 341	36 998	11 740	...	...	...	...
	2007	59 590	41 752	13 924	...	...	...	...
Occupied Palestinian Terr.[1,2] Terr. palestinien occupé[1,2]	2001	75	...	...	...	...	...	...
	2002	81	...	...	...	...	...	...
	2003	141	...	...	...	...	...	...
	2004	209	...	...	...	...	...	...
	2005	195	...	...	...	...	...	...
Pakistan Pakistan	2005	53 159	12 689	2 053	6 471	...	33 999	...
	2007	#69 619	#26 338	6 153	11 113	...	32 168	...
Panama[2] Panama[2]	2001	1 530	841	297	...	...	689	231
	2002	1 688	#416	154	...	...	#1 272	442
	2003	1 795	432	158	...	...	1 363	477
	2004	#1 446	484	199	332	130	#630	245[18]
	2005	#1 802	507	...	...	...	#1 295	...
Paraguay[2] Paraguay[2]	2001	1 358	587	294	...	...	771	471
	2002	1 721	794	398	...	...	927	515
	2003	1 734	800	406	...	...	934	504
	2004	1 873	864	444	...	...	1 009	525
	2005	#1 142	787	368	...	...	#355	#179
Peru[2] Pérou[2]	2004	8 434	4 965	...	1 757	...	1 712	...
Philippines Philippines	2003	9 390[3]	5 860	3 089[18]	938	...	2 502	...
	2005	9 407[3]	6 896	3 500	897	...	1 440	...
Poland[2] Pologne[2]	2001	123 840	89 596	...	18 279	...	15 965	...
	2002	122 987	90 842	...	17 458	...	14 687	...
	2003	126 241	94 432	37 065	16 876	8 430	14 933	9 799
	2004	127 356	96 531	37 594	15 686	7 844	15 139	9 865
	2005	123 431	97 875	38 426	13 989	6 613	11 567	7 606
	2006	121 283	96 374	38 065	13 533	6 358	11 376	7 167
	2007	121 623	97 289	38 802	13 500	6 167	10 834	6 854
Portugal Portugal	2001	22 970	17 725	7 940	2 874	1 056	2 371	1 048
	2002[4]	24 250	18 984	8 538	3 031	1 164	2 235	1 131
	2003	25 529	20 242	9 136	3 189	1 272	2 098	1 214
	2004[4]	25 629	20 684	9 333	3 054	1 224	1 891	1 084
	2005	25 728	21 126	9 530	2 918	1 177	1 683	954
	2006[4]	30 160	24 556	...	3 529	...	2 075	...
	2007[4]	34 593	27 986	...	4 140	...	2 466	...
Republic of Moldova République de Moldova	2003	5 005[14]	2 737[14]	1 242	403[14]	...	1 865[14]	...
	2004	4 797[14]	2 725[14]	1 220	354[14]	...	1 718[14]	...
	2005	4 672[14]	2 583[14]	1 120	334[14]	...	1 755[14]	...
	2006	4 505[14]	2 507[14]	1 045	362[14]	...	1 636[14]	...
	2007	4 587[14]	2 592[14]	1 170	417[14]	...	1 578[14]	...
Romania Roumanie	2001	32 639	19 726	8 551	5 952	3 447	6 961	3 499
	2002	32 799	20 286	9 181	6 436	3 540	6 077	2 763
	2003	33 077	20 965	9 340	5 434	3 174	6 678	3 147
	2004	33 361	21 257	9 480	5 525	3 199	6 579	2 916
	2005	33 222	22 958	10 617	4 998	2 859	5 266	2 414

Country or area Pays ou zone	Year Année	Total R & D personnel Total du personnel de R - D	Researchers Chercheurs		Technicians and equivalent staff Techniciens et personnel assimilé		Other supporting staff Autre personnel de soutien	
			Total M & W Total H & F	Women Femmes	Total M & W Total H & F	Women Femmes	Total M & W Total H & F	Women Femmes
	2006	30 802	20 506	8 956	4 496	2 625	5 800	2 734
	2007	28 977	18 808	8 242	4 361	2 392	5 808	2 631
Russian Federation [2,14]	2001	885 568	422 176	185 609	75 416	...	387 976	...
Fédération de Russie [2,14]	2002	870 878	414 676	179 120	74 599	...	381 603	...
	2003	858 470	409 775	177 538	71 729	...	376 966	...
	2004	839 338	401 425	172 177	69 963	...	367 950	...
	2005	813 207	391 121	165 993	65 982	...	356 104	...
	2006	807 066	388 939	163 972	66 031	...	352 096	...
	2007	801 135	392 849	164 385	64 569	...	343 717	...
Saint Vincent-Grenadines [2]	2001	129	20	...	109	...	...	...
Saint Vincent-Grenadines [2]	2002	131	21	...	110	...	...	...
Saudi Arabia [2]	2001	3 708[1]	1 239[1]	225[14]	1 498[1]	...	971[1]	...
Arabie saoudite [2]	2002	4 182[1]	1 513[1]	263	1 674[1]	...	995[1]	...
	2007[1]	1 612	1 024	...	419	...	169	...
Senegal [4]	2006	3 299[1]	3 011[1]	301	...	...	288[1]	...
Sénégal [4]	2007	3 565[1]	3 277[1]	327	...	...	288[1]	...
Serbia								
Serbie	2007	15 921	8 806	4 155	2 204		4 911	
Seychelles								
Seychelles	2005	180[1]	13[1]	4	53[1]	...	114[1]	...
Singapore [2]	2001	25 162	20 645	...	2 371	...	2 146	...
Singapour [2]	2002	26 824	21 531	5 517	2 398	953	2 895	1 701
	2003	28 825	23 513	5 938	2 549	1 009	2 763	1 823
	2004	31 006	25 251	6 506	2 823	1 121	2 932	1 901
	2005	34 522	27 969	7 346	3 265	1 326	3 288	2 095
	2006	36 191	29 478	7 986	3 291	1 311	3 422	2 290
	2007	38 255	31 657	8 665	3 224	1 279	3 374	2 278
Slovakia	2001	14 422	9 585	3 816	3 323	1 798	1 514	920
Slovaquie	2002	13 631	9 181	3 749	3 032	1 586	1 418	828
	2003	13 354	9 627	3 946	2 483	1 433	1 244	735
	2004	14 329	10 718	4 427	2 403	1 331	1 209	664
	2005	14 404	10 921	4 484	2 245	1 218	1 238	670
	2006	15 028	11 776	4 959	2 284	1 220	969	603
	2007	15 421	12 354	5 116	2 238	1 238	829	533
Slovenia	2001	8 608	4 498	1 547	3 146	1 256	964	543
Slovénie	2002	8 615	4 642	1 606	3 140	1 199	833	450
	2003	6 805	3 775	1 202	2 281	838	749	415
	2004	7 132	4 030	1 288	2 323	882	779	427
	2005	8 994	5 253	1 777	2 820	1 067	921	501
	2006	9 793	5 857	1 941	2 954	1 148	982	535
	2007	10 369	6 250	...	3 089	...	1 030	...
South Africa	2001	21 196	14 182	4 923	3 374	996	3 640	1 360
Afrique du Sud	2003	25 189	14 131	5 059	5 142	1 992	5 916	2 300
	2004	29 697	17 915	6 623	5 176	1 631	6 606	2 913
	2005	28 798	17 303	6 272	5 248	1 749	6 247	2 928
	2006	30 985	18 574	...	6 332	...	6 080	...
Spain	2001	125 750	80 081	28 208	28 460	7 437	17 209	6 779
Espagne	2002	134 258	83 318	29 767	30 376	9 561	20 564	9 068
	2003	151 487	92 523	33 985	36 278	11 381	22 687	9 891
	2004	161 933	100 994	37 580	37 871	12 578	23 068	10 353
	2005	174 773	109 720	41 371	39 904	13 259	25 149	11 390
	2006	188 978	115 798	43 431	44 842	15 809	28 337	12 932
	2007	201 108	122 624	...	...	...	...	...
Sri Lanka	2004	5 475	2 679[4]	861	1 474	...	1 322	...
Sri Lanka	2006	4 513	1 833	754	1 272	...	1 408	...
Sudan [2,4]	2001	16 050	7 850	1 664	3 170	...	5 030	...
Soudan [2,4]	2002	18 604	9 100	2 754	3 674	...	5 830	...
	2003	18 808	9 200	2 784	3 714	...	5 894	...
	2004	19 772	9 340	2 830	4 641	...	5 791	...
	2005	23 726	11 208	4 483	5 569	...	6 949	...
Sweden	2001	72 190	45 995	...	...	...	...	...
Suède	2003	72 978	48 186	...	...	...	...	...
	2004	72 459	48 784	...	...	...	...	...
	2005	#77 704	#55 090	16 002[10]	...	...	...	...

Country or area Pays ou zone	Year Année	Total R & D personnel Total du personnel de R - D	Researchers Chercheurs Total M & W Total H & F	Women Femmes	Technicians and equivalent staff Techniciens et personnel assimilé Total M & W Total H & F	Women Femmes	Other supporting staff Autre personnel de soutien Total M & W Total H & F	Women Femmes
	2006	78 715	55 729	...	...	...	...	...
	#2007[5]	76 815	47 762	13 714[10]	...	...	...	...
Switzerland[2] Suisse[2]	2004	84 090	43 220	11 555	19 775	3 590	21 095	10 960
Tajikistan[2] Tadjikistan[2]	2001	2 799[3]	1 845	908	391	...	563[3]	...
	2002	2 628[3]	1 752	701	312	...	564[3]	...
	2003	2 425[3]	1 544	438	270	...	611[3]	...
	2004	2 487[3]	1 548	407	247	...	692[3]	...
	2005	3 220[3]	1 993	...	324	...	903[3]	...
	2006	3 110[3]	1 895	735	202	...	1 013[3]	...
	2007	2 075[3]	1 286		253	...	536[3]	...
Thailand Thaïlande	2001	32 011	17 710	...	7 110	...	7 191	...
	2003	42 379	18 114	...	13 139	...	11 126	...
	2005	36 967	20 506	10 241	10 520	...	5 941	...
TFYR of Macedonia L'ex-R.Y. Macédoine	2001	1 630	1 240	596	199	...	191	...
	2002	1 518	1 164	571	140	...	214	...
	2003	1 464	1 118	557	137	...	209	...
	2004	1 447	1 069	538	195	...	183	...
	2005	1 434	1 113	576	168	...	153	...
	2006	1 357	1 062	547	152	...	143	...
Togo Togo	2003	235	142	...	93	...	...	...
	2004	228	137	...	91[18]	...	...	...
	2005	#312	#186	...	126[18]	...	...	...
	2006	230	136	...	94	...	...	...
	2007	#320	#216	#21	104[18]	...	...	...
Trinidad and Tobago[2] Trinité-et-Tobago[2]	2001	...	509	192	...	...	...	...
	2003	...	518	208	...	...	...	...
	2004	#908	550	213	#358	132	...	...
	2005	1 103	603	203	500	229	...	...
	2006	1 243	690	267	553	261	...	...
Tunisia Tunisie	2001	10 090	8 515[3]	...	294[1]	...	1 281[1]	...
	2002	11 510	9 910[3]		329[1]	...	1 271[1]	...
	2003	12 857	11 265[3]	5 471	357[1]	...	1 235[1]	...
	2004	14 556	12 950[3]	6 145	379[1]	...	1 227[1]	...
	2005	16 289	14 650[3]	6 995	413[1]	...	1 226[1]	...
	2006	17 466	15 833[3]	...	428[1]	...	1 205[1]	...
Turkey Turquie	2001	27 698[14]	22 702	8 527	2 560[14]	434[14]	2 436[14]	510[14]
	2002	28 964[14]	23 995	8 211	2 567[14]	415[14]	2 402[14]	511[14]
	2003	38 308[14]	32 660	11 229	3 092[14]	565[14]	2 556[14]	650[14]
	2004	39 960[14]	33 876	11 815	3 341[14]	637[14]	2 743[14]	677[14]
	2005	49 251[14]	39 139	13 381	4 753[14]	988[14]	5 360[14]	978[14]
	2006	54 444[14]	42 664	14 567	5 724[14]	1 074[14]	6 056[14]	1 131[14]
	2007	63 377[14]	49 668	16 942	7 420[14]	1 291[14]	6 289[14]	1 258[14]
Uganda[2] Ouganda[2]	2001	1 278	568	213	366	...	344	...
	2002	1 370	630	236	384	...	356	...
	2003	1 468	675	253	411	...	382	...
	2004	1 573	724	272	440	...	409	...
	2005	1 686	776	291	472	...	438	...
	2006	1 807	831	312	506	...	470	...
	2007	1 937	891	365	542	...	504	...
Ukraine[2] Ukraine[2]	2001	147 116	86 366	36 164	26 975	...	33 775	...
	2002	142 763	85 211	36 557	22 236	...	35 316	...
	2003	139 470	83 890	36 174	20 951	...	34 629	...
	2004	140 284	85 742	37 634	20 861	...	33 681	...
	2005	#170 579[3]	85 246	37 586	20 266	...	32 052	...
	2006	#160 788	80 497	35 542	19 748	...	30 204	...
	2007	#155 549	78 832	34 596	17 988	...	28 896	...
United Kingdom Royaume-Uni	2001[19]	311 982	167 019	...	...	...	...	...
	2002[19]	321 543	174 433	...	...	...	...	...
	2003[19]	319 239	178 035	...	...	...	...	...
	2004[19]	315 963	176 040	...	...	...	...	...
	2005	311 054[19]	174 557[19]	...	41 494[4]	...	...	...
	2006	318 356[19]	176 213[19]	...	44 465[4]	...	...	...
	2007	333 671[19]	175 476[19]	...	53 502[4]	...	...	...
United States[19] Etats-Unis[19]	2001	...	1 319 710	...	...	...	...	...
	2002	...	1 342 450	...	...	...	...	...

Country or area Pays ou zone	Year Année	Total R & D personnel Total du personnel de R - D	Researchers Chercheurs Total M & W Total H & F	Women Femmes	Technicians and equivalent staff Techniciens et personnel assimilé Total M & W Total H & F	Women Femmes	Other supporting staff Autre personnel de soutien Total M & W Total H & F	Women Femmes
	2003	...	1 430 550	...	...	...	...	...
	2004	...	1 393 520	...	...	...	...	...
	2005	...	1 387 880	...	...	...	...	...
	2006	...	1 425 550	...	...	...	...	...
United States Virgin Is. [2] Iles Vierges américaines [2]	2001	36[1]	6[1]	0	15[1]	...	15[1]	...
	2002	36[1]	6[1]	0	15[1]	...	15[1]	...
	2003	27[1]	3[1]	0	7[1]	...	10[1]	...
	2004	27[1]	3[1]	0	7[1]	...	10[1]	...
	2005	37[1]	6[1]	0	12[1]	...	11[1]	...
	2006	40[1]	6[1]	0	13[1]	...	12[1]	...
	2007	42[1]	6[1]	0	13[1]	...	14[1]	...
Uruguay [2] Uruguay [2]	2002	4 323	3 839	1 813	...	...	484	114
	2006	3 436	3 182	1 349	172	84	82	69
Venezuela (Boliv. Rep. of) [2] Venezuela (R. bol. du) [2]	2001	...	2 077[1]	923	...	...	...	...
	2002	...	2 077[1]	923	...	...	...	...
	2003	...	2 827[1]	1 345	...	...	...	...
	2004	...	3 148[1]	1 529	...	...	...	...
	2005	...	3 710[1]	1 843	...	...	...	...
	2006	...	4 626[1]	2 330	...	...	...	...
	2007	...	5 222[1]	2 710	...	...	...	...
Viet Nam Viet Nam	2002	11 356	9 328	...	...	...	...	
Zambia [2] Zambie [2]	#2002	1 084[1]	268[1]	31[14]	276[1]	...	540[1]	...
	2003	1 141[1]	288[1]	#36	295[1]	...	558[1]	...
	2004	1 307[1]	356[1]	#79	376[1]	...	575[1]	...
	2005	3 285[1]	792[1]	#116	1 240[1]	...	1 253[1]	...

Source:
United Nations Educational, Scientific and Cultural Organization (UNESCO) Institute for Statistics, Montreal, the UNESCO Institute of Statistics database, last accessed October 2009.

Source:
L'Institut de statistique de l'Organisation des Nations Unies pour l'éducation, la science et la culture (UNESCO), Montréal, la base de données de l'Institut de statistique de l'UNESCO, dernier accès octobre 2009.

1	Partial data.
2	Head count instead of full-time equivalent.
3	Overestimated or based on overestimated data.
4	National estimation.
5	Provisional data.
6	Source: Regional publication.
7	Do not correspond exactly to Frascati Manual recommendations.
8	For statistical purposes, the data for China do not include those for the Hong Kong Special Administrative Region (Hong Kong SAR) and Macao Special Administrative Region (Macao SAR).
9	Including technicians and equivalent staff.
10	University graduates instead of researchers.
11	Including other supporting staff.
12	Defence excluded (all or mostly).
13	Source: National publication.
14	Underestimated or based on underestimated data.
15	Excluding R&D in the Social sciences and Humanities.
16	Excluding R&D in the Social sciences.
17	Excluding R&D in the Humanities.
18	UIS estimation.
19	OECD estimation.

1	Données partielles.
2	Personnes physiques au lieu d'Equivalents temps plein.
3	Surestimé ou fondé sur des données surestimées.
4	Estimation nationale.
5	Données provisoires.
6	Source: Publication régionale.
7	Ne corresponds pas exactement aux recommandations du Manuel de Frascati.
8	Pour la présentation des statistiques, les données pour la Chine ne comprennent pas la Région Administrative Spéciale de Hong Kong (Hong Kong RAS) et la Région Administrative Spéciale de Macao (Macao RAS).
9	Y compris les techniciens y le personnel assimilé.
10	Diplômes universitaires au lieu de chercheurs.
11	Y compris autre personnel de soutien.
12	A l'exclusion de la défense (en totalité ou en grande partie).
13	Source : Publication statistique nationale.
14	Sous-estimé ou basé sur des données sous-estimées.
15	À l'exclusion de la recherche-développement en sciences sociales et sciences humaines.
16	À l'exclusion de la recherche-développement en sciences sociales.
17	À l'exclusion de la recherche-développement en sciences humaines.
18	Estimation de l'ISU.
19	Estimation de l'OCDE.

Gross domestic expenditure on R & D
As a percentage of GDP and by source of funds

Dépenses intérieures brutes de recherche et développement
En pourcentage du PIB et répartition par source de financement

			Source of funds (%) / Source de financement (%)					
Country or area Pays ou zone	Year Année	Expenditure on R&D as a % of GDP Dépenses en R - D en % du PIB	Business enterprises Entreprises	Government Etat	Higher education Enseignement supérieur	Private non-profit Institut. privées sans but lucratif	Funds from abroad Fonds de l'étranger	Not distributed Non répartis
Algeria [1] Algérie [1]	2003	0.2	...	...	...	...	...	...
	2004	0.2	...	...	...	...	...	...
	2005	0.1	...	...	...	...	...	...
Argentina Argentine	2005	0.5	31.0	65.3	1.4	1.5	0.8	0.0
	2006	0.5	29.4	66.7	1.6	1.6	0.8	0.0
	2007	0.5	29.3	67.5	1.4	1.1	0.6	0.0
Armenia Arménie	2005	0.2[1]	...	53.8	...	...	5.7	40.5
	2006	0.2[1]	...	64.2	...	...	10.1	25.0
	2007	0.2[1]	...	50.3	...	...	11.3	38.5
Australia Australie	2002	1.8	50.7	41.2	0.2	#1.7	3.6	2.7[2]
	2004	1.9	...	...	0.4	1.7	2.9	...
	2006	2.2	57.2	38.4	0.2	1.7	2.6	0.0
Austria Autriche	2005[3]	2.4	45.7	36.2	...	0.4	17.7	...
	2006	2.5	48.4	32.3	0.5	0.4	18.4	0.0
	2007[3]	2.5	47.7	35.6	...	0.4	16.3	...
Azerbaijan Azerbaïdjan	2005	0.2[4]	18.7	77.5	0.0	1.3	2.4	0.0
	2006	0.2	18.3	79.7	...	2.0	0.0	0.0
	2007	0.2	20.8	76.5	...	2.6	0.1	0.0
Belarus Bélarus	2005	0.7	21.2	71.9	0.7	0.0	6.3	0.0
	2006	0.7	20.7	71.8	0.7	0.0	6.8	0.0
	2007	1.0	#45.1	#49.2	0.3	0.1	5.3	0.0
Belgium Belgique	2003	1.9	60.3	23.5	2.7	0.5	12.9	0.0
	2004	1.9	60.2	24.4	2.6	0.5	12.3	0.0
	2005	1.9	59.7	24.7	2.6	0.6	12.4	0.0
Bermuda Bermudes	1997	0.1	...	...	...	...	...	...
Bolivia Bolivie	2000	0.3	22.0	22.0	32.0	15.0	9.0	0.0
	2001	0.3	18.0	21.0	33.0	17.0	11.0	0.0
	2002	0.3	16.0	20.0	31.0	19.0	14.0	0.0
Botswana Botswana	2005	0.4	...	...	...	...	...	...
Brazil Brésil	2004	0.8	39.9	57.9	2.2	...	...	0.0
	2005	1.0	48.4	49.6	2.0	...	...	0.0
	2006	1.0	47.9	50.1	2.0	...	...	0.0
Brunei Darussalam Brunéi Darussalam	2002	0.0[1,5]	8.8	91.2	0.0	0.0	...	0.0
	2003	0.0[1,5]	6.7	86.8	0.0	0.0	6.6	0.0
	2004	0.0[1,5]	#1.6	#91.0	#7.4	0.0	0.0	0.0
Bulgaria Bulgarie	2004	0.5	28.2	65.8	0.3	0.2	5.5	0.0
	2005	0.5	27.8	63.9	0.4	0.3	7.6	0.0
	2006	0.5	30.6	61.9	0.7	0.4	6.5	0.0
Burkina Faso Burkina Faso	2004	0.2[1]	...	100.0	...	...	...	...
	2005	0.2[1]	...	100.0	...	...	...	...
	2007	0.1[1]	...	#72.3	...	...	#24.5	#3.2
Cambodia Cambodge	2002	0.0[1,3]	0.0	17.9[3]	0.0	43.0[3]	28.4[3]	10.6[3]
Canada Canada	2005	2.1	48.9	31.6[3]	7.3[3]	2.8	9.5	0.0
	2006	2.0	49.6	31.3[3]	7.3[3]	2.9	9.0	0.0
	2007	*2.0	*49.4	31.4[3]	7.3[3]	*2.9	*9.0	...
Chile Chili	2002	0.7	33.2	54.6	0.4	0.3	11.3	0.0
	2003	0.7	43.7	43.3	0.8	0.4	12.0	0.0
	2004	0.7	45.9	44.5	0.8	0.3	8.7	0.0

60

Gross domestic expenditure on R & D *(continued)*
As a percentage of GDP and by source of funds

Dépenses intérieures brutes de recherche et développement *(suite)*
En pourcentage du PIB et répartition par source de financement

Country or area Pays ou zone	Year Année	Expenditure on R&D as a % of GDP Dépenses en R - D en % du PIB	Source of funds (%) / Source de financement (%)					
			Business enterprises Entreprises	Government Etat	Higher education Enseignement supérieur	Private non-profit Institut. privées sans but lucratif	Funds from abroad Fonds de l'étranger	Not distributed Non répartis
China	2005	1.3	67.0	26.3	...	...	0.9	5.7[2]
Chine	2006	1.4	69.1	24.7	...	...	1.6	4.6[2]
	2007	1.5	70.4	24.6	...	...	1.3	3.7[2]
China, Hong Kong SAR	2004	0.7	47.8[6]	47.0	0.1	...	5.1	0.0
Chine, Hong Kong RAS	2005	0.8	53.0[6]	44.1	0.4	...	2.5	0.0
	2006	0.8	52.8[6]	43.1	0.2	...	3.9	0.0
China, Macao SAR [1,3]	2003	0.1	...	...	...	...	...	...
Chine, Macao RAS [1,3]	2004	0.1	...	...	...	...	...	...
	2005	0.1	...	...	...	...	...	...
Colombia	2004	0.2	26.7	31.0	37.3	2.3	4.2	0.0
Colombie	2005	0.2	27.2	37.4	27.8	2.7	5.4	0.0
	2006	0.2	27.0	39.6	25.8	4.0	4.4	0.0
Costa Rica	2000	0.4	...	...	...	...	...	...
Costa Rica	2003	0.4	...	...	...	...	...	...
	2004	0.4	...	...	...	...	...	...
Croatia	2005	1.0	34.3	58.1	4.9	0.0	2.6	0.0
Croatie	2006	0.9	34.6	55.8	2.5	0.2	6.8	0.0
	2007	0.9	35.5	50.4	3.0	0.2	10.9	0.0
Cuba	2005	0.5	35.0	60.0	...	...	5.0	0.0
Cuba	2006	0.4	35.0	60.0	...	...	5.0	0.0
	2007	0.4	35.0	60.0	...	...	5.0	0.0
Cyprus	2004	0.4[4]	18.9	64.1	3.9	1.6	11.5	0.0
Chypre	2005	0.4[4]	16.8	67.0	4.2	1.2	10.9	0.0
	2006	0.4[4]	15.9	66.5	4.1	1.3	12.1	0.0
Czech Republic	2005	1.4	54.1	40.9	1.1	0.0	4.0	0.0
République tchèque	2006	1.5	56.9	39.0	1.0	0.0	3.1	0.0
	2007	1.6	54.0	41.2	0.8	0.0	4.1	0.0
Dem. Rep. of the Congo	2004	0.4[7,8]	...	100.0	...	...	...	...
Rép. dém. du Congo	2005	0.5[7,8]	...	100.0	...	...	...	...
Denmark	2001	2.4	61.4	28.2	...	2.6	7.8	...
Danemark	2003	2.6	59.9	27.1	...	2.7	10.3	...
	2005	2.4	59.5	27.6	...	2.8	10.1	...
Ecuador	2003	0.1	...	...	...	...	...	...
Equateur	#2006	0.1	17.4	69.3	4.0	1.2	4.2	4.0
	2007	0.2	21.5	58.1	3.9	3.3	7.0	6.2
Egypt [1]	2005	0.2	...	...	...	...	...	...
Egypte [1]	2006	0.3	...	...	...	...	...	...
	2007	0.2	...	...	...	...	...	...
El Salvador								
El Salvador	1998	0.1	1.2	51.9	13.2	10.4	23.4	0.0
Estonia	2005	0.9	38.5	43.5	0.8	0.2	17.1	0.0
Estonie	2006	1.1	38.1	44.6	0.9	0.1	16.3	0.0
	2007	1.1	41.6	45.6	0.9	0.2	11.7	0.0
Ethiopia	2005	0.2[1]	...	69.2	...	0.1	30.8	0.0
Ethiopie	2007	0.2[1]	...	71.7	...	0.7	27.0	0.5
Finland	2005	3.5	66.9	25.7	0.2	1.0	#6.3	0.0
Finlande	2006	3.4	66.6	25.1	0.3	1.0	7.1	0.0
	2007	3.5	68.2	24.1	0.3	1.0	6.5	0.0
France	2004	2.1[4]	#50.7	#38.7	#0.9	#0.9	#8.8	0.0
France	2005	2.1	51.9	38.6	1.0	0.9	7.5	0.0
	2006	2.1[4]	52.4	38.4	1.3	0.8	7.0	0.0
Georgia	2003	0.2	...	...	...	...	...	...
Géorgie	2004	0.2	...	...	...	...	...	...
	2005	0.2	...	...	...	...	...	...

60

Gross domestic expenditure on R & D *(continued)*
As a percentage of GDP and by source of funds
Dépenses intérieures brutes de recherche et développement *(suite)*
En pourcentage du PIB et répartition par source de financement

Country or area Pays ou zone	Year Année	Expenditure on R&D as a % of GDP Dépenses en R - D en % du PIB	Source of funds (%) / Source de financement (%)					
			Business enterprises Entreprises	Government Etat	Higher education Enseignement supérieur	Private non-profit Institut. privées sans but lucratif	Funds from abroad Fonds de l'étranger	Not distributed Non répartis
Germany	2004	2.5	66.6	30.5	...	0.4	2.5	...
Allemagne	2005	2.5	67.6	28.4	...	0.3	3.7	...
	2006	2.5	68.1	27.8	...	0.4	3.8	...
Greece	2001	0.5	33.0	46.6	1.6	0.4	18.4	0.0
Grèce	2003	0.5	28.2	46.4	2.6	1.2	21.6	0.0
	2005	0.5	31.1	46.8	1.7	1.5	19.0	0.0
Guatemala	2005	^0.0[1]	...	42.1	57.9	...	...	0.0
Guatemala	2006	^0.0[1]	...	36.5	23.7	...	39.8	0.0
Hungary	2005	0.9	39.4	49.4[9]	...	0.3	10.7	0.1[2]
Hongrie	2006	1.0	43.3	44.8	...	0.6	11.3	...
	2007	1.0	43.9	44.4	...	0.6	11.1	...
Iceland	2005	2.8	48.0	40.5	0.0	0.3	11.2	0.0
Islande	2006	3.1	49.3	39.6	0.0	0.6	10.6	0.0
	2007	2.8	50.3	38.8	0.0	0.8	10.0	0.0
India	2002	0.7	20.3[7,10]	75.6	4.2[7,10]	...	...	0.0
Inde	2003	0.7[3]	20.0[6,7,10]	75.4[3]	4.5[7,10]	...	...	0.0
	2004	0.7[3]	19.8[6,7,10]	75.3[3]	4.9[7,10]	...	...	0.0
Indonesia	2000	0.1[1,5]	25.7[1,6]	72.7	1.1	...	...	0.5
Indonésie	2001	^0.0[1,5]	14.7[1,6]	84.5	0.2	...	...	0.7
	2005[1]	^0.0	...	...	...	...	...	...
Iran (Islamic Rep. of)	2004	0.6	19.6	69.0	11.4	...	...	0.0
Iran (Rép. islamique d')	2005	0.7	12.2	76.2	11.6	...	...	0.0
	2006	0.7	14.2	74.6	11.2	...	...	0.0
Ireland	2004	1.2	58.6	31.1	1.7	0.0	8.6	0.0
Irlande	2005	1.3	57.4	32.0	1.7	0.2	8.6	0.0
	2006	1.3	59.3	30.1	0.2	1.5	8.9	0.0
Israel [9]	2003	4.5	68.9	23.4	3.0	1.4	3.4	0.0
Israël [9]	2004	4.4	72.9	20.1	2.5	1.2	3.3	0.0
	2005	4.5	75.4	17.8	2.1	1.4	3.3	0.0
Italy	2004	1.1	...	...	...	...	...	...
Italie	2005	1.1	39.7	50.7	0.1	1.6	8.0	0.0
	2006	1.1	40.4	48.3	0.1	2.9	8.3	0.0
Jamaica	2001	0.1	...	...	...	...	...	...
Jamaïque	2002	0.1	...	...	...	...	...	...
Japan	2005	3.3	76.1	16.8[11]	6.1[11]	0.7	0.3	0.0
Japon	2006	3.4	77.1	16.2[11]	5.7[11]	0.7	0.4	0.0
	2007	3.4	77.7	15.6[11]	5.6[11]	0.7	0.3	0.0
Jordan								
Jordanie	2002	0.3	...	...	...	...	...	...
Kazakhstan	2005	0.3	39.1	44.5	13.4	1.3	1.5	0.0
Kazakhstan	2006	0.2	35.2	50.7	12.0	1.1	1.0	0.0
	2007	0.2	44.5	37.4	15.3	1.1	1.7	0.0
Korea, Republic of	2005[12]	3.0	75.0	23.0	0.9	0.4	0.7	0.0
Corée, République de	2006[12]	3.2	75.4	23.1	0.8	0.3	0.3	0.0
	2007[13]	3.5	73.7	24.8	1.0	0.3	0.2	0.0
Kuwait	2005	0.1[1]	7.3	92.3	...	0.4	...	...
Koweït	2006	0.1[1]	6.6	93.4	...	...	...	...
	2007	0.1[1]	2.4	97.6	...	...	...	...
Kyrgyzstan	2003	0.2	53.7	45.1	0.1	0.0	1.1	0.0
Kirghizistan	2004	0.2	45.9	53.4	0.0	0.0	0.7	0.0
	2005	0.2	36.4	63.6	0.0	0.0	0.0	0.0
Lao People's Dem. Rep. Rép. dém. pop. lao	2002	^0.0[1,5]	36.0	8.0	2.0	0.0	54.0	0.0
Latvia	2005	0.6	34.3	46.0	1.2	...	18.5	0.0
Lettonie	2006	0.7	52.7	38.2	1.5	...	7.5	0.0
	2007	0.6	36.4	55.2	0.9	...	7.5	0.0

60

Gross domestic expenditure on R & D *(continued)*
As a percentage of GDP and by source of funds
Dépenses intérieures brutes de recherche et développement *(suite)*
En pourcentage du PIB et répartition par source de financement

Country or area Pays ou zone	Year Année	Expenditure on R&D as a % of GDP Dépenses en R - D en % du PIB	Source of funds (%) / Source de financement (%)					
			Business enterprises Entreprises	Government Etat	Higher education Enseignement supérieur	Private non-profit Institut. privées sans but lucratif	Funds from abroad Fonds de l'étranger	Not distributed Non répartis
Lesotho [1]	2002	^0.0	...	...	...	...	...	...
Lesotho [1]	2003	^0.0	...	...	...	...	...	...
	2004	0.1	...	...	...	...	...	...
Lithuania	2005	0.8	20.8	62.7	5.7	0.2	10.5	0.0
Lituanie	2006	0.8	26.2	53.6	5.3	0.6	14.3	0.0
	2007	0.8	24.5	47.9	7.5	0.5	19.6	0.0
Luxembourg	2000	1.7	90.7	7.7	...	...	1.6	
Luxembourg	2003	1.7	80.4	11.2	0.0	0.1	8.3	0.0
	2005	1.6	79.7	16.6	0.0	0.1	3.6	0.0
Madagascar	2005	0.2[1]	...	38.6	51.2	...	10.2	...
Madagascar	2006	0.2[1]	...	28.4	52.4	...	19.2	...
	2007	0.1[1]	...	32.0	59.6	...	8.4	...
Malaysia	2002	0.7	51.5	32.1	4.9	0.0	11.5	0.0
Malaisie	2004	0.6	71.2	21.5	6.9	0.0	0.4	0.0
	2006	0.6	84.7	5.0	9.7	0.0	0.2	0.4
Malta	2005	0.6[4]	46.8	25.9	0.4	0.1	26.9	0.0
Malte	2006	0.6[4]	45.7	#3.8	#23.1	...	27.5	0.0
	2007	0.6[4]	45.4	3.3	22.9	...	28.4	0.0
Mauritius	2003	0.4[7,8]	...	100.0	...	...	...	...
Maurice	2004	0.4[7,8]	...	100.0	...	...	...	...
	2005	0.4[7,8]	...	100.0	...	...	...	...
Mexico	2003	0.4	34.7	56.1	7.7	0.8	0.8	0.0
Mexique	#2004	0.5	44.0	47.4	7.0	0.7	0.8	0.0
	2005	0.5	46.5	45.3	6.6	0.8	0.7	0.0
Monaco	2004	...	...	97.0	...	...	...	3.0
Monaco	2005	...	...	98.8	...	...	...	1.2
Mongolia	2005	0.3[1]	10.4	77.8	0.8	0.0	4.4	6.5
Mongolie	2006	0.2[1]	8.2	79.5	0.8	0.0	1.7	9.8
	2007	0.2[1]	3.1	82.4	0.5	0.0	1.6	12.4
Montenegro	2005	0.9	...	...	...	...	...	...
Monténégro	2006	1.2	...	...	...	...	...	...
	2007	1.2	...	...	...	...	...	...
Morocco	2002	0.5	21.6	37.1	41.2	0.0	...	0.0
Maroc	2003	0.7	12.3	40.3	47.4	0.0	...	0.0
	2006	0.6	22.7	74.7	...	0.0	2.6	0.0
Mozambique Mozambique	2002	0.5[7,8,14]	...	34.7	...	...	65.3	...
Myanmar [1]	2000	0.1	...	...	...	...	...	...
Myanmar [1]	2001	0.1	...	...	...	...	...	...
	2002	0.2	...	...	...	...	...	...
Netherlands	2001	1.8	51.9	35.8	0.1	1.2	11.0	0.0
Pays-Bas	2002	1.7	50.0	37.1	0.1	1.1	11.6	0.0
	2003	1.8	51.1	36.2	0.1	1.3	11.3	0.0
New Zealand	2003	1.2	38.2	43.8	8.8	2.1	7.1	0.0
Nouvelle-Zélande	2005	1.2	41.1	43.2	8.9	1.7	5.2	0.0
	2007	1.3	40.1	42.7	8.7	3.7	4.8	0.0
Nicaragua	1997	0.1	...	...	...	...	...	...
Nicaragua	2002	0.0	...	...	...	...	...	...
Norway	2003	1.7	49.2	41.9	0.6	0.8	7.4	0.0
Norvège	2005	1.5	46.4	44.0	0.7	0.9	8.0	0.0
	2007	1.7	45.3	44.9	0.6	0.9	8.3	0.0
Pakistan	2002	0.2[1]	...	100.0[3]	...	...	...	...
Pakistan	2005	0.4	...	87.0	11.9	...	0.3	0.8
	2007	0.7	...	82.9	12.9	1.8	1.0	1.5

60

Gross domestic expenditure on R & D *(continued)*
As a percentage of GDP and by source of funds

Dépenses intérieures brutes de recherche et développement *(suite)*
En pourcentage du PIB et répartition par source de financement

Country or area Pays ou zone	Year Année	Expenditure on R&D as a % of GDP Dépenses en R - D en % du PIB	Source of funds (%) / Source de financement (%)					
			Business enterprises Entreprises	Government Etat	Higher education Enseignement supérieur	Private non-profit Institut. privées sans but lucratif	Funds from abroad Fonds de l'étranger	Not distributed Non répartis
Panama	2003	0.3	0.6	25.5	1.8	1.0	71.0	0.1
Panama	2004	0.2	0.1	35.0	2.6	2.5	59.8	0.0
	2005	0.2	0.4	38.5	1.4	0.7	58.9	0.0
Paraguay	2003	0.1	0.0	63.2	12.7	2.3	21.8	0.0
Paraguay	2004	0.1	0.0	63.1	12.7	2.3	21.9	0.0
	2005	0.1	0.3	74.9	8.6	2.0	14.2	0.0
Peru	2002	0.1	...	...	...	...	...	...
Pérou	2003	0.1	...	...	...	...	...	...
	2004	0.1	...	...	...	...	...	...
Philippines	2002	0.1	68.6	19.1	5.9	0.2	5.5	0.7
Philippines	2003	0.1	69.1	21.9	4.8	0.4	3.8	0.1
	2005	0.1	62.6	25.6	0.0	0.7	4.8	0.3
Poland	2005	0.6	33.4	57.7	2.9	0.3	5.7	0.0
Pologne	2006	0.6	33.1	57.5	2.2	0.3	7.0	0.0
	2007	0.6	34.3	58.6	0.2	0.2	6.7	0.0
Portugal	2003	0.7	31.7	60.1	1.3	1.9	5.0	0.0
Portugal	2004[3]	0.8	34.2	57.5	1.1	2.4	4.8	0.0
	2005	0.8	36.3	55.2	1.0	2.8	4.7	0.0
Republic of Moldova	2005	0.4	...	...	...	...	3.8	96.2
République de Moldova	2006	0.4	...	...	...	...	2.6	97.4
	2007	0.5	...	...	...	...	2.7	97.3
Romania	2005	0.4[4]	37.2	53.5	4.0	0.0	5.3	0.0
Roumanie	2006	0.5	30.4	64.1	1.2	0.2	4.1	0.0
	2007	0.5	26.9	67.1	1.4	0.0	4.5	0.0
Russian Federation	2005	1.1	30.0	61.9	0.4	0.0	7.6	0.0
Fédération de Russie	2006	1.1	28.8	61.1	0.6	0.1	9.4	0.0
	2007	1.1	29.4	62.6	0.6	0.1	7.2	0.0
Saint Lucia[7]	1998	0.7	...	...	...	...	...	...
Sainte-Lucie[7]	1999	0.4	...	...	...	...	...	...
Saint Vincent-Grenadines	2001	0.1	...	...	...	...	...	...
Saint Vincent-Grenadines	2002	0.2	...	...	...	...	...	...
Senegal[3]								
Sénégal[3]	2005	0.1[1]	...	100.0	...	...	...	...
Serbia[15]	2005	0.4	...	...	...	...	...	...
Serbie[15]	2006	0.5	...	...	...	...	...	...
	2007	0.3	...	...	...	...	...	...
Seychelles	2003	0.4	...	...	...	...	...	...
Seychelles	2004	0.4	...	...	...	...	...	...
	2005	0.4	...	...	...	...	...	...
Singapore	2005	2.3	58.8	36.4	0.5	...	4.4	...
Singapour	2006	2.3	58.3	36.4	0.9	...	4.4	...
	2007	2.6	59.8	34.9	0.9	...	4.3	...
Slovakia	2005	0.5	36.6	57.0[9]	0.3	0.0	6.0	0.0
Slovaquie	2006	0.5	35.0	55.6[9]	0.3	0.1	9.1	0.0
	2007	0.5	35.6	53.9[9]	0.2	0.1	10.2	0.0
Slovenia	2005	1.5[4]	54.8	37.2	0.7	0.0	7.3	0.0
Slovénie	2006	1.6[4]	59.3	34.4	0.3	0.2	5.8	0.0
	2007	1.5	58.3	35.6	0.4	0.0	5.8	0.0
South Africa	2003	0.8	52.1	27.9	3.5	5.5	10.9	0.0
Afrique du Sud	2004	0.9	44.5	23.7	9.2	6.8	15.8	0.0
	2005	0.9	43.9	29.7	11.5	1.4	13.6	0.0
Spain	2004	1.1	48.0	41.0	4.1	0.7	6.2	0.0
Espagne	2005	1.1	46.3	43.0	4.1	0.9	5.7	0.0
	2006	1.2	47.1	42.5	3.9	0.6	5.9	0.0

60

Gross domestic expenditure on R & D *(continued)*
As a percentage of GDP and by source of funds
Dépenses intérieures brutes de recherche et développement *(suite)*
En pourcentage du PIB et répartition par source de financement

Country or area Pays ou zone	Year Année	Expenditure on R&D as a % of GDP Dépenses en R - D en % du PIB	Source of funds (%) / Source de financement (%)					
			Business enterprises Entreprises	Government Etat	Higher education Enseignement supérieur	Private non-profit Institut. privées sans but lucratif	Funds from abroad Fonds de l'étranger	Not distributed Non répartis
Sri Lanka	2000[3]	0.1[1]	7.7	51.7	18.5	0.0	4.5	17.5
Sri Lanka	2004[3]	0.2	#0.6	#67.5	...	...	22.6	9.3
	2006	0.2	19.0[3]	65.2[3]	...	...	4.8	10.9
Sudan [3]	2003	0.3	...	...	...	...	...	...
Soudan [3]	2004	0.3	...	...	...	...	...	...
	2005	0.3	...	...	...	...	...	...
Sweden [16]	2001	4.2	71.7	22.3	0.2	2.5	3.4	0.0
Suède [16]	2003	3.9	65.1	24.3	0.1	3.1	7.3	0.0
	2005	3.7	63.9	24.4	0.7	2.9	8.1	0.0
Switzerland	1996	2.7	67.5	26.9	1.3	1.2	3.1	0.0
Suisse	2000	2.6	69.1	23.2	2.1	1.4	4.3	0.0
	2004	2.9	69.7	22.7	1.5	0.8	5.2	0.0
Tajikistan	2003	0.1	7.9	65.1	...	...	...	27.0
Tadjikistan	2004	0.1	4.8	64.7	0.1	...	...	30.4
	2005	0.1	2.2	91.9	0.3	...	...	5.5
Thailand	2003	0.3	41.8	38.6	15.1	0.6	2.6	1.3
Thaïlande	2004	0.3[3]	35.5	...	...	...	...	64.5
	2005	0.2	48.7	31.5	14.9	0.7	1.8	2.4
TFYR of Macedonia	2000	0.4	7.7[3]	79.8[3]	3.6[3]	2.0[3]	7.0[3]	0.0
L'ex-R.Y. Macédoine	2001	0.3	10.0[3]	70.3[3]	6.9[3]	3.3[3]	9.4[3]	0.0
	2002	0.3	7.8[3]	76.3[3]	7.3[3]	...	8.6[3]	0.0
Trinidad and Tobago	2004	0.1	...	...	...	...	...	...
Trinité-et-Tobago	2005	0.1	...	...	...	...	...	...
	2006	0.1	...	...	...	...	...	...
Tunisia	2003	0.7	9.6	47.0	34.2	0.0	7.5	1.7
Tunisie	2004	1.0	12.6	35.4	28.0	0.0	9.4	14.6
	2005[3]	1.0	14.1	45.1	30.5	0.0	10.4	0.0
Turkey	2005	0.6[4]	43.3	50.1	0.0	5.8[18,19]	0.8	0.0
Turquie	2006	0.6	46.0	48.6	0.0[17]	4.8[19]	0.5	0.0
	2007	0.7	48.4	47.1	0.0[17]	4.0[19]	0.5	0.0
Uganda	2005	0.2	1.7	41.5	0.0	0.0	56.9	0.0
Ouganda	2006	0.3	0.0	50.1	0.0	0.0	49.9	0.0
	2007	0.4	7.5	41.7	0.0	0.0	50.7	0.0
Ukraine	2005	1.0	32.3[2]	40.1[2]	0.1[2]	0.4[2]	24.4[2]	2.8[2]
Ukraine	2006	0.9	32.5[2]	46.3[2]	0.1[2]	0.1[2]	19.4[2]	1.5[2]
	2007	0.9	30.2	52.2	0.2	0.1	15.9	1.3
United Kingdom	2005	1.8	42.1	32.7	1.2	4.7	19.3	0.0
Royaume-Uni	2006	1.8	45.2	31.9	1.3	4.6	17.0	0.0
	*2007	1.8	47.2	29.3	1.2	4.6	17.7	0.0
United States	2005	2.6[20]	64.2[19,20]	30.1[20]	2.6[20]	3.1[20]	0.0	0.0
Etats-Unis	2006	2.6[20]	65.2[19,20]	29.1[20]	2.7[20]	3.0[20]	0.0	0.0
	2007	2.7[20]	66.4[19,20]	27.7[20]	2.7[20]	3.2[20]	0.0	0.0
Uruguay	2000	0.2	39.3	20.3	35.7	...	4.8	0.0
Uruguay	2002	0.3	46.7	17.1	31.4	0.1	4.7	0.0
	2006	0.4	32.8	40.0	26.9	...	0.3	0.0
Viet Nam Viet Nam	2002	0.2	18.1	74.1	0.7[6]	...	6.3	0.8

Source:
United Nations Educational, Scientific and Cultural Organization
(UNESCO) Institute for Statistics, Montreal, the UNESCO Institute of
Statistics database, last accessed September 2009.

Source:
L'Institut de statistique de l'Organisation des Nations Unies pour
l'éducation, la science et la culture (UNESCO), Montréal, la base
de données de l'Institut de statistique de l'UNESCO, dernier accès septembre
2009.

60

Gross domestic expenditure on R & D *(continued)*
As a percentage of GDP and by source of funds

Dépenses intérieures brutes de recherche et développement *(suite)*
En pourcentage du PIB et répartition par source de financement

1	Partial data.
2	UIS estimation.
3	National estimation.
4	Data have been converted from the former national currency using the appropriate conversion rate.
5	Source: Regional publication.
6	Including private non-profit funds.
7	Overestimated or based on overestimated data.
8	Based on R&D budget instead of R&D expenditure.
9	Defence excluded (all or mostly).
10	Do not correspond exactly to Frascati Manual recommendations.
11	OECD estimation.
12	Excluding R&D in the Social sciences and Humanities.
13	Excluding R&D in the Social sciences.
14	Source: National publication.
15	Excluding data from some regions, provinces or states.
16	Underestimated or based on underestimated data.
17	Included elsewhere.
18	Including higher education.
19	Including other classes.
20	Excluding most or all capital expenditure.

1	Données partielles.
2	Estimation de l'ISU.
3	Estimation nationale.
4	Les données ont été converties à partir de l'ancienne monnaie nationale et du taux de conversion approprié.
5	Source: Publication régionale.
6	Y compris les fonds privés à but non lucratif.
7	Surestimé ou fondé sur des données surestimées.
8	Basé sur le budget de la recherche-développement au lieu des dépenses.
9	A l'exclusion de la défense (en totalité ou en grande partie).
10	Ne corresponds pas exactement aux recommandations du Manuel de Frascati.
11	Estimation de l'OCDE.
12	À l'exclusion de la recherche-développement en sciences sociales et sciences humaines.
13	À l'exclusion de la recherche-développement en sciences sociales.
14	Source : Publication statistique nationale.
15	Non compris les données de certaines régions, provinces ou états.
16	Sous-estimé ou basé sur des données sous-estimées.
17	Inclus ailleurs.
18	Y compris l'enseignement supérieur.
19	Comprend d'autres catégories.
20	A l'exclusion des dépenses d'équipement (en totalité ou en grande partie).

Patents
Filings, grants and patents in force

Brevets
Demandes, délivrances et brevets en vigueur

Country or area Pays ou zone	Resident filings (per million pop.) Demandes émanant de résidents (par million d'hab.)			Grants of patents Brevets délivrés			Patents in force Brevets en vigueur		
	2005	2006	2007	2005	2006	2007	2005	2006	2007
Algeria Algérie	1.8	1.7	2.5	550	479	214	2 074	2 334	...
Antigua and Barbuda Antigua-et-Barbuda	...	...	...	...	...	9	...	...	...
Armenia Arménie	68.3	63.8	...	126	213	...	110	404	...
Australia Australie	125.3	137.1	129.3	10 979	9 426	11 236	96 403	95 912	106 756
Austria Autriche	275.7	274.2	...	938	1 564	...	10 126	10 326	...
Azerbaijan Azerbaïdjan	33.5	...	...	...	...	...	...	...	...
Bangladesh Bangladesh	0.3	0.1	...	182	162	...	...	...	...
Belarus Bélarus	119.3	122.1	...	955	1 130	...	...	...	...
Belgium Belgique	49.3	46.5	42.7	708	548	519	...	...	...
Belize Belize	...	3.4	...	...	7	...	...	...	...
Bosnia and Herzegovina Bosnie-Herzégovine	17.5	14.6	...	46	272	...	120	178	...
Brazil Brésil	20.9	20.1	...	2 439	2 465	...	32 571	31 223	...
Bulgaria Bulgarie	33.7	31.6	27.6	313	317	264	2 203	3 441	2 046
Canada Canada	160.4	169.1	151.6	15 516	14 972	18 550	125 110	115 639	121 889
Chile Chili	22.2	17.7	...	311	406	...	...	...	...
China Chine	71.7	93.3	116.1	53 305	57 786	67 948	182 396	...	...
China, Hong Kong SAR Chine, Hong Kong RAS	22.9	25.1	23.1	6 518	5 146	4 839	...	141 766	197 822
China, Macao SAR Chine, Macao RAS	6.3	...	2.1	5	17	63	12	28	81
Colombia Colombie	...	...	2.8	...	...	227	...	...	5 522
Croatia Croatie	81.7	71.4	77.6	140	183	147	1 094	1 163	1 326
Cuba Cuba	9.3	8.3	6.6	64	73	70	653	...	1 423
Cyprus Chypre	23.9	...	3.5	68	...	...	...	...	452
Czech Republic République tchèque	57.3	62.4	69.3	1 551	1 324	1 203	10 165	10 298	10 310
Denmark Danemark	306.1	276.4	304.0	389	162	221	4 518	3 688	2 661
Ecuador Equateur	0.8	...	...	...	...	33	38	...	33

61

Patents *(continued)*
Filings, grants and patents in force
Brevets *(suite)*
Demandes, délivrances et brevets en vigueur

Country or area Pays ou zone	Resident filings (per million pop.) Demandes émanant de résidents (par million d'hab.)			Grants of patents Brevets délivrés			Patents in force Brevets en vigueur		
	2005	2006	2007	2005	2006	2007	2005	2006	2007
Egypt Egypte	5.9	...	6.8	147	...	300	...	...	300
Estonia Estonie	17.1	26.8	32.8	...	...	1 056	...	2 033	2 909
Eurasian Patent Organization [1] Organisation eurasienne de brevets [1]	...	...	...	1 201	1 251	1 704	...	...	2 909
European Patent Office [2] Office européen de brevets [2]	...	...	...	53 258	62 780	54 699	244 361	268 384	...
Finland Finlande	348.8	344.8	341.1	1 757	1 059	921	39 450	43 345	44 363
France France	235.4	236.8	238.6	11 473	13 788	12 112	343 512	377 755	390 341
Georgia Géorgie	50.3	53.2	10.9	315	287	71	1 040	2 606	1 733
Germany Allemagne	586.5	582.8	581.7	17 063	21 034	17 739	434 663	460 657	492 604
Greece Grèce	54.9	62.1	69.0	323	4 994	4 245	...	33 870	33 709
Guatemala Guatemala	...	2.2	0.7	71	...	110	1 030	...	433
Hungary Hongrie	69.9	71.3	68.5	1 126	1 089	637	9 125	8 408	11 850
Iceland Islande	158.4	148.1	196.1	101	112	138	375	505	654
India Inde	4.1	4.8	...	4 320	7 539	...	...	...	...
Indonesia Indonésie	1.1	1.3	...	...	...	...	...	...	...
Ireland Irlande	189.7	196.7	194.0	349	357	314	...	...	140 296
Israel Israël	45.6	36.4	224.9	...	2 584	2 489	...	6 941	21 217
Italy Italie	...	...	155.9	...	...	6 508	...	...	...
Jamaica Jamaïque	3.8	7.9	...	...	43	...	527	...	...
Japan Japon	2 879.8	2 716.6	2 610.1	122 944	141 399	164 954	...	...	...
Kazakhstan Kazakhstan	100.6	93.6	...	...	...	...	...	...	...
Kenya Kenya	...	1.0	...	...	24	...	...	120	...
Korea, Dem. P. R. Corée, R. p. dém. de	248.2	267.9	287.9	3 583	4 150	4 301	...	...	...
Korea, Republic of Corée, République de	2 538.3	2 598.0	2 656.0	73 512	120 790	123 705	420 906	465 988	566 965
Kyrgyzstan Kirghizistan	...	...	29.6	...	...	84	...	...	297
Latvia Lettonie	48.7	49.8	...	122	120	...	4 012	4 167	...
Lithuania Lituanie	19.9	19.2	18.4	116	89	69	768	739	729

61

Patents *(continued)*
Filings, grants and patents in force
Brevets *(suite)*
Demandes, délivrances et brevets en vigueur

Country or area Pays ou zone	Resident filings (per million pop.) Demandes émanant de résidents (par million d'hab.)			Grants of patents Brevets délivrés			Patents in force Brevets en vigueur		
	2005	2006	2007	2005	2006	2007	2005	2006	2007
Luxembourg Luxembourg	52.6	55.0	31.3	29	55	46	25 500	25 728	...
Madagascar Madagascar	...	0.2	...	32	28	...	249	255	...
Malaysia Malaisie	20.4	20.3	25.2	2 508	6 749	6 983	...	...	...
Malta Malte	...	...	24.4	...	653	317	...	1 746	2 101
Mexico Mexique	5.7	5.5	6.0	8 098	9 632	9 957	48 374	54 722	66 865
Monaco Monaco	61.5	184.1	336.4	9	5	16	37 483	45 507	45 068
Mongolia Mongolie	39.2	39.9	...	197	174	...	13 663	13 621	...
Morocco Maroc	4.6	5.8	...	556	699	...	9 872	...	...
Netherlands Pays-Bas	135.9	132.6	126.9	2 373	2 361	2 319	14 091	14 084	16 532
New Zealand Nouvelle-Zélande	457.9	514.5	447.5	4 189	3 412	3 592	34 182	34 291	34 468
Norway Norvège	247.2	246.5	259.7	...	...	1 774	...	...	17 801
Pakistan Pakistan	...	...	...	258	299	...	...	...	...
Peru Pérou	1.0	1.4	1.0	388	306	327	2 252	2 167	2 239
Philippines Philippines	2.5	2.7	...	1 653	1 053	...	...	...	...
Poland Pologne	53.1	56.6	62.8	2 522	2 686	3 534	14 578	...	17 251
Portugal Portugal	15.0	17.4	23.6	231	125	187	4 502	37 848	38 894
Republic of Moldova République de Moldova	97.3	79.1	87.6	269	288	268	1 108	1 196	1 033
Romania Roumanie	42.3	37.7	38.4	759	787	684	8 627	8 458	9 263
Russian Federation Fédération de Russie	165.2	195.7	193.6	23 390	23 299	23 028	123 089	123 817	129 910
Saint Lucia Sainte-Lucie	...	...	...	...	34	...	...	...	...
Samoa Samoa	...	...	...	...	...	11	...	...	...
Saudi Arabia Arabie saoudite	5.2	5.0	5.3	225	1 044	274	...	...	...
Serbia Serbie	...	...	53.5	...	...	278	...	...	1 274
Singapore Singapour	133.4	142.2	151.7	7 530	7 393	7 478	42 700	46 823	...
Slovakia Slovaquie	28.8	35.8	44.3	560	543	574	4 033	4 830	7 122
Slovenia Slovénie	172.0	143.0	164.0	285	228	...	6 229	7 063	...
Spain Espagne	70.1	70.5	72.8	2 769	2 165	2 667	242 292	155 621	160 368

61

Patents *(continued)*
Filings, grants and patents in force
Brevets *(suite)*
Demandes, délivrances et brevets en vigueur

Country or area Pays ou zone	Resident filings (per million pop.) Demandes émanant de résidents (par million d'hab.)			Grants of patents Brevets délivrés			Patents in force Brevets en vigueur		
	2005	2006	2007	2005	2006	2007	2005	2006	2007
Sri Lanka Sri Lanka	7.6	7.7	7.6	180	137	91	...	...	...
Sweden Suède	279.5	269.4	276.2	1 911	1 490	1 287	102 741	104 710	105 571
Switzerland Suisse	220.9	232.5	224.1	...	948	737	...	6 573	8 064
Syrian Arab Republic Rép. arabe syrienne	5.6	6.4	...	...	...	...	...	...	...
Tajikistan Tadjikistan	4.6	3.9	...		437		...	257	...
Thailand Thaïlande	14.1	14.4	13.7	553	1 121	232	...	8 026	6 742
Trinidad and Tobago Trinité-et-Tobago	...	...	...		81		...	...	...
Tunisia Tunisie	5.6	...	...						
Turkey Turquie	12.9	14.7	24.5	823	659	628	...	...	9 015
Uganda Ouganda	0.1	0.4	0.2	...	...	...	...	...	...
Ukraine Ukraine	75.1	74.3	...	3 719	3 705	...	37 336	32 399	...
United Kingdom Royaume-Uni	296.1	288.5	284.8	10 159	7 907	5 930	383 501	...	...
United States Etats-Unis	702.5	742.4	800.2	143 806	173 770	157 283	1 683 968	1 774 742	1 814 939
Uzbekistan Ouzbékistan	10.1	12.2	12.1	407	272	312	1 263	1 370	1 568
Viet Nam Viet Nam	2.2	...	...	...	...	...	...	...	...
Yemen Yémen	1.0	0.6	0.5	...	...	...	...	...	...

Source:
World Intellectual Property Organization (WIPO), Geneva, *World Intellectual Property Indicators 2009*.

Source :
Organisation mondiale de la propriété intellectuelle (OMPI), Genève, *Indicateurs mondiaux relatifs à la propriété intellectuelle pour l'année 2009*.

1   Members of the Eurasian Patent Organization (EAPO), which includes Armenia, Azerbaijan, Belarus, Georgia, Kazakhstan, Kyrgyzstan, Republic of Moldova, the Russian Federation, Tajikistan, Ukraine, Turkmenistan.

2   The following states are currently members of the European Patent Organization (EPO): Austria, Belgium, Bulgaria, Switzerland, Cyprus, Czech Republic, Germany, Denmark, Estonia, Spain, Finland, France, United Kingdom, Greece, Croatia, Hungary, Ireland, Iceland, Italy, Liechtenstein, Lithuania, Luxembourg, Latvia, Monaco, Former Yugoslav Republic of Macedonia, Malta, Netherlands, Norway, Poland, Portugal, Romania, Sweden, Slovenia, Slovakia, San Marino, and Turkey.

1   Les membres de l'Organisation eurasienne de la propriété intellectuelle (EAPO) incluent: Arménie, Azerbaïdjan, Bélarus, Fédération de Russie, Géorgie, Kazakhstan, Kirghizistan, République de Moldova, Tadjikistan, Turkménistan, Ukraine.

2   Les États suivants sont membres de l'Organisation européenne des brevets (OEB): Autriche, Belgique, Bulgarie, Suisse, Chypre, République tchèque, Allemagne, Danemark, Estonie, Espagne, Finlande, France, Royaume-Uni, Grèce, Hongrie, Croatie, Irlande, Islande, Italie, Liechtenstein, Lituanie, Luxembourg, Lettonie, Monaco, L'ex-République yougoslave de Macédoine, Malte, Pays-Bas, Norvège, Pologne, Portugal, Roumanie, Suède, Slovénie, Slovaquie, Saint-Marin, and Turquie.

Technical notes: tables 59-61

Research and experimental development (R&D) is defined as any creative work undertaken on a systematic basis in order to increase the stock of knowledge, including knowledge of man, culture and society, and the use of this stock of knowledge to devise new applications.

Table 59: The data presented on human resources in research and development (R&D) are compiled by the UNESCO Institute for Statistics. Data for certain countries are provided to UNESCO by OECD, EUROSTAT and the Network on Science and Technology Indicators (RICYT).

The definitions and classifications applied by UNESCO in the table are based on those set out in the *Recommendation concerning the International Standardization of Statistics on Science and Technology* (UNESCO, 1978) and in the *Frascati Manual* (OECD, 2002).

The three categories of personnel shown are defined as follows:

Researchers are professionals engaged in the conception or creation of new knowledge, products, processes, methods and systems, and in the planning and management of R&D projects. Postgraduate students engaged in R&D are considered as researchers.

Technicians and equivalent staff comprise persons whose main tasks require technical knowledge and experience in one or more fields of engineering, physical and life sciences, or social sciences and humanities. They participate in R&D by performing scientific and technical tasks involving the application of concepts and operational methods, normally under the supervision of researchers. As distinguished from technicians participating in the R&D under the supervision of researchers in engineering, physical and life sciences, equivalent staff perform the corresponding R&D tasks in the social sciences and humanities.

Other supporting staff includes skilled and unskilled craftsmen, secretarial and clerical staff participating in or directly associated with R&D projects. Included in this category are all managers and administrators dealing mainly with financial and personnel matters and general administration, insofar as their activities are a direct service to R&D.

Headcount data reflect the total number of persons employed in R&D, independently from their dedication. Full-time equivalent may be thought of as one person-year. Thus, a person who normally spends 30% of his/her time on R&D and the rest on other activities (such as teaching, university administration and student counselling) should be considered as 0.3 FTE. Similarly, if a full-time R&D worker is employed at an R&D unit for only six months, this results in an FTE of 0.5.

Notes techniques : tableaux 59 à 61

La recherche et le développement expérimental (R-D) englobe tous les travaux de création entrepris de façon systématique en vue d'accroître la somme des connaissances, y compris la connaissance de l'homme, de la culture et de la société, ainsi que l'utilisation de cette somme de connaissances pour de nouvelles applications.

Tableau 59: Les données présentées sur le personnel employé dans la recherche et le développement (R-D) sont compilées par l'Institut de statistique de l'UNESCO. Les données de certains pays ont été fournies à l'UNESCO par l'OCDE, EUROSTAT et "la Red de Indicadores de Ciencia y Technología (RICYT)".

Les définitions et classifications appliquées par l'UNESCO sont basées sur la *Recommandation concernant la normalisation internationale des statistiques relatives à la science et à la technologie* (UNESCO, 1978) et sur le *Manuel de Frascati* (OCDE, 2002).

Les trois catégories du personnel présentées sont définies comme suivant:

Les chercheurs sont des spécialistes travaillant à la conception ou à la création de connaissances, de produits, de procédés, de méthodes et de systèmes, et dans la planification et la gestion de projets de R-D. Les étudiants diplômés ayant des activités de R-D sont considérés comme des chercheurs.

Techniciens et personnel assimilé comprend des personnes dont les tâches principales requièrent des connaissances et une expérience technique dans un ou plusieurs domaines de l'ingénierie, des sciences physiques et de la vie ou des sciences sociales et humaines. Ils participent à la R-D en exécutant des tâches scientifiques et techniques faisant intervenir l'application de principes et de méthodes opérationnelles, généralement sous le contrôle de chercheurs. Pour se distinguer des techniciens qui participent à la R-D sous le contrôle de chercheurs dans les domaines de l'ingénierie, des sciences physiques et de la vie, le personnel assimilé effectue des travaux correspondants dans les sciences sociales et humaines.

Autre personnel de soutien comprend les travailleurs, qualifiés ou non, et le personnel de secrétariat et de bureau qui participent à l'exécution des projets de R-D ou qui sont directement associés à l'exécution de tels projets. Sont inclus dans cette catégorie les gérants et administrateurs qui s'occupent principalement de problèmes financiers, le personnel et l'administration en général, dans la mesure où leurs activités ont une relation directe avec la R-D.

Personnes physiques est le nombre total de personnes qui sont principalement ou partiellement affectées à la R-D. Ce dénombrement inclut les employés à 'temps plein' et les employés à 'temps partiel'. Équivalent temps plein (ETP) peut être considéré comme une année-personne. Ainsi, une personne qui consacre 30% de son temps en R&D et le reste à d'autres activités (enseignement, administration universitaire ou direction d'étudiants) compte pour 0.3 ETP en R&D. De

More information can be found on the UNESCO Institute for Statistics web site www.uis.unesco.org.

Table 60: The data presented on gross domestic expenditure on research and development are compiled by the UNESCO Institute for Statistics. Data for certain countries are provided to UNESCO by OECD, EUROSTAT and the Network on Science and Technology Indicators (RICYT).

Gross domestic expenditure on R&D (GERD) is total intramural expenditure on R&D performed on the national territory during a given period. It includes R&D performed within a country and funded from abroad but excludes payments made abroad for R&D.

The sources of funds for GERD are classified according to the following five categories:

Business enterprise funds include funds allocated to R&D by all firms, organizations and institutions whose primary activity is the market production of goods and services (other than the higher education sector) for sale to the general public at an economically significant price, and those private non-profit institutes mainly serving these firms, organizations and institutions.

Government funds refer to funds allocated to R&D by the central (federal), state or local government authorities. These include all departments, offices and other bodies which furnish, but normally do not sell to the community, those common services, other than higher education, which cannot be conveniently and economically provided, as well as those that administer the state and the economic and social policy of the community. Public enterprises funds are included in the business enterprise funds sector. Government funds also include private non-profit institutes controlled and mainly financed by government.

Higher education funds include funds allocated to R&D by institutions of higher education comprising all universities, colleges of technology, other institutes of post-secondary education, and all research institutes, experimental stations and clinics operating under the direct control of or administered by or associated with higher educational establishments.

Private non-profit funds are funds allocated to R&D by non-market, private non-profit institutions serving the general public, as well as by private individuals and households.

Funds from abroad refer to funds allocated to R&D by institutions and individuals located outside the political frontiers of a country except for vehicles, ships, aircraft and space satellites operated by domestic organizations and testing grounds acquired by such organizations, and by all international organizations (except business enterprises) including their facilities and operations within the country's borders.

façon analogue, si un employé travaille à temps plein dans un centre de R&D pendant six mois seulement, il compte pour 0.5 ETP.

Pour tout renseignement complémentaire, voir le site Web de l'Institut de statistique de l'UNESCO www.uis.unesco.org.

Tableau 60: Les données présentées sur les dépenses intérieures brutes de recherche et développement sont compilées par l'Institut de statistique de l'UNESCO. Les données de certains pays ont été fournies à l'UNESCO par l'OCDE, EUROSTAT et "la Red de Indicadores de Ciencia y Tecnología (RICYT)".

La dépense intérieure brute de R-D (DIRD) est la dépense totale intra-muros afférente aux travaux de R-D exécutés sur le territoire national pendant une période donnée. Elle comprend la R-D exécutée sur le territoire national et financée par l'étranger mais ne tient pas compte des paiements effectués à l'étranger pour des travaux de R-D.

Les sources de financement pour la DIRD sont classées selon les cinq catégories suivantes:

Les fonds des entreprises incluent les fonds alloués à la R-D par toutes les firmes, organismes et institutions dont l'activité première est la production marchande de biens ou de services (autres que dans le secteur d'enseignement supérieur) en vue de leur vente au public, à un prix qui correspond à la réalité économique, et les institutions privées sans but lucratif principalement au service de ces entreprises, organismes et institutions.

Les fonds de l'Etat sont les fonds fournis à la R-D par le gouvernement central (fédéral), d'état ou par les autorités locales. Ceci inclut tous les ministères, bureaux et autres organismes qui fournissent, sans normalement les vendre, des services collectifs autres que d'enseignement supérieur, qu'il n'est pas possible d'assurer de façon pratique et économique par d'autres moyens et qui, de surcroît, administrent les affaires publiques et appliquent la politique économique et sociale de la collectivité. Les fonds des entreprises publiques sont compris dans ceux du secteur des entreprises. Les fonds de l'Etat incluent également les institutions privées sans but lucratif contrôlées et principalement financées par l'Etat.

Les fonds de l'enseignement supérieur inclut les fonds fournis à la R-D par les établissements d'enseignement supérieur tels que toutes les universités, grandes écoles, instituts de technologie et autres établissements postsecondaires, ainsi que tous les instituts de recherche, les stations d'essais et les cliniques qui travaillent sous le contrôle direct des établissements d'enseignement supérieur ou qui sont administrés par ces derniers ou leur sont associés.

Les fonds d'institutions privées sans but lucratif sont les fonds destinés à la R-D par les institutions privées sans but lucratif non marchandes au service du public, ainsi que par les simples particuliers ou les ménages.

Les fonds étrangers concernent les fonds destinés à la R-D par les institutions et les individus se trouvant en dehors

The absolute figures for R&D expenditure should not be compared country by country. Such comparisons would require the conversion of national currencies into a common currency by means of special R&D exchange rates. Official exchange rates do not always reflect the real costs of R&D activities and comparisons are based on such rates can result in misleading conclusions, although they can be used to indicate a gross order of magnitude.

More information can be found on the UNESCO Institute for Statistics web site www.uis.unesco.org.

Table 61: A patent is granted by a national patent office or by a regional office that does the work for a number of countries, such as the European Patent Office and the African Regional Intellectual Property Organization. Under such regional systems, an applicant requests protection for the invention in one or more countries, and each country decides as to whether to offer patent protection within its borders. The World Intellectual Property Organization (WIPO)-administered Patent Cooperation Treaty (PCT) provides for the filing of a single international patent application which has the same effect as national applications filed in the designated countries.

Data include patent intensity, patents granted and patents in force. Patent intensity is presented as the resident patent filings per million population, where a resident Intellectual Property (IP) filing refers to an application filed by an applicant at its national IP office. IP grant (registration) data are based on the same concept. In Force refers to a patent or other form of IP protection that is currently valid.

Country of origin is used to categorize IP data by resident (domestic) and non-resident (foreign). The residence of the first-named applicant (or inventor) recorded in the IP document (e.g. patent or trademark application) is used to classify IP data by country of origin.

The data are compiled and published by the WIPO.

des frontières politiques d'un pays, à l'exception des véhicules, navires, avions et satellites utilisés par des institutions nationales, ainsi que des terrains d'essai acquis par ces institutions, et par toutes les organisations internationales (à l'exception des entreprises), y compris leurs installations et leurs activités à l'intérieur des frontières d'un pays.

Il faut éviter de comparer les chiffres absolus concernant les dépenses de R-D d'un pays à l'autre. On ne pourrait procéder à des comparaisons détaillées qu'en convertissant en une même monnaie les sommes libellées en monnaie nationale au moyen de taux de change spécialement applicables aux activités de R-D. Les taux de change officiels ne reflètent pas toujours le coût réel des activités de R-D, et les comparaisons établies sur la base de ces taux peuvent conduire à des conclusions trompeuses; toutefois, elles peuvent être utilisées pour donner une idée de l'ordre de grandeur.

Pour tout renseignement complémentaire, voir le site Web de l'Institut de statistique de l'UNESCO www.uis.unesco.org.

Tableau 61: Les brevets sont délivrés par les offices nationaux des brevets, ou par des offices régionaux qui desservent plusieurs pays, par exemple l'Office européen des brevets et l'Organisation régionale africaine de la propriété intellectuelle. Dans le cadre de ces systèmes régionaux, le déposant demande la protection de son invention dans un ou plusieurs pays, et chaque pays décide d'accorder ou non cette protection dans les limites de ses frontières. Le Traité de coopération en matière de brevets (PCT) administré par l'Organisation mondiale de la propriété intellectuelle (OMPI) prévoit le dépôt d'une demande internationale unique, qui a le même effet que des demandes nationales qui auraient été déposées dans les pays désignés.

Les données relatives aux brevets comprennent l'intensité de l'activité brevets, les brevets délivrés et les brevets en vigueur. L'intensité de l'activité est présente sous la forme du nombre de demandes de brevet émanant de résidents par million d'habitants. Un dépôt émanant d'un résident renvoie à une demande déposée auprès de l'office d'un État ou agissant pour le compte d'un État dans lequel est domicilié le déposant de la demande concernée nommé en premier. La délivrance de brevet obéit au même principe. En vigueur se dit d'un brevet ou tout autre titre de propriété industrielle qui est encore valable.

Les demandes de brevet contiennent des renseignements relatifs au pays dans lequel sont domiciliés l'inventeur et le déposant (ou cessionnaire). Les statistiques fondées sur le pays dans lequel est domicilié l'inventeur peuvent indiquer l'endroit où se situe l'invention, alors que les données relatives au pays dans lequel est domicilié le déposant (ou cessionnaire) fournissent des informations sur le titulaire du brevet au moment du dépôt de la demande.

Les données sont compilées et publiées par l'OMPI.

Part Four
International economic relations

Chapter XV   International merchandise trade (tables 62-64)

Chapter XVI   International tourism and transport (tables 65-68)

Chapter XVII   Balance of payments (table 69)

Chapter XVIII International finance (tables 70-72)

Chapter XIX   Development assistance (tables 73-75)

Part Four of the *Yearbook* presents statistics on international economic relations in areas of international merchandise trade, international tourism and transport balance of payments and assistance to developing countries. The series cover all countries or areas of the world for which data have been made available.

Quatrième partie
Relations économiques internationales

Chapitre XV   Commerce international des marchandises (tableaux 62 à 64)

Chapitre XVI   Tourisme international et transport (tableaux 65 à 68)

Chapitre XVII Balance des paiements (tableau 69)

Chapitre XVIII Finances internationales (tableaux 70 à 72)

Chapitre XIX Aide au développement (tableaux 73 à 75)

La quatrième partie de l'*Annuaire* présente des statistiques sur les relations économiques internationales dans les domaines du commerce international des marchandises, du tourisme international et transport, de la balance des paiements et l'assistance aux pays en développement. Les séries couvrent tous les pays ou les zones du monde pour lesquels de données sont disponibles.

Total imports and exports
Imports c.i.f., exports f.o.b. and balance, value in million US dollars

Importations et exportations totales
Importations c.a.f., exportations f.o.b. et balance, valeur en millions de dollars E.-U.

Region, country or area [&]	Sys.[t]	2001	2002	2003	2004	2005	2006	2007	Région, pays ou zone [&]
World [1,2,3]									**Monde** [1,2,3]
Imports		5 937 624	6 156 456	7 174 499	8 771 067	9 958 064	11 456 676	13 212 623	**Importations**
Exports		5 755 336	6 026 752	7 015 148	8 543 107	9 746 388	11 276 159	13 081 665	**Exportations**
Balance		-182 288	-129 703	-159 351	-227 960	-211 676	-180 517	-130 959	**Balance**
Developed economies [2,4,5]									**Economies développées** [2,4,5]
Imports		4 215 839	4 341 556	5 044 293	6 014 449	6 681 920	7 570 436	8 537 448	**Importations**
Exports		3 897 390	4 037 130	4 652 050	5 483 984	5 957 818	6 723 904	7 703 199	**Exportations**
Balance		-318 449	-304 426	-392 243	-530 465	-724 102	-846 532	-834 249	**Balance**
Asia and the Pacific - Developed economies									**Asie et Pacifique - Economies développées**
Imports		406 243	402 927	465 383	557 900	634 374	707 909	773 795	**Importations**
Exports		460 591	474 126	534 726	643 237	690 417	758 290	835 441	**Exportations**
Balance		54 348	71 199	69 343	85 337	56 043	50 381	61 646	**Balance**
Australia	G								**Australie**
Imports		63 890	72 693	89 089	109 383	125 283	139 279	165 364	Importations
Exports		63 389	65 036	71 551	86 420	105 833	123 316	141 122	Exportations
Balance		-501	-7 657	-17 539	-22 962	-19 449	-15 963	-24 241	Balance
Japan	G								**Japon**
Imports		349 189	337 209	383 085	454 592	514 988	579 609	619 845	Importations
Exports		403 616	416 730	471 999	565 743	594 986	649 948	709 668	Exportations
Balance		54 427	79 520	88 914	111 150	79 998	70 340	89 823	Balance
New Zealand	G								**Nouvelle-Zélande**
Imports		13 308	15 046	18 559	23 195	26 234	26 430	30 885	Importations
Exports		13 730	14 382	16 527	20 344	21 729	22 434	26 949	Exportations
Balance		422	-664	-2 033	-2 850	-4 505	-3 996	-3 936	Balance
Europe - Developed economies									**Europe - Economies dév.**
Imports		2 487 216	2 594 139	3 123 471	3 763 930	4 112 531	4 726 959	5 512 861	**Importations**
Exports		2 527 201	2 696 046	3 207 549	3 824 971	4 122 848	4 672 186	5 436 374	**Exportations**
Balance		39 986	101 907	84 078	61 041	10 317	-54 773	-76 487	**Balance**
Andorra	S								**Andorre**
Imports		1 042	1 200	1 510	1 702	1 790	1 780	1 917	Importations
Exports		52	63	89	123	142	150	127	Exportations
Balance		-990	-1 136	-1 424	-1 639	-1 654	-1 630	-1 790	Balance
Austria	S								**Autriche**
Imports		70 492	72 796	91 595	113 344	119 950	130 937	156 107	Importations
Exports		66 492	73 113	89 257	111 720	117 722	130 361	156 661	Exportations
Balance		-3 999	316	-2 339	-1 623	-2 228	-576	554	Balance
Belgium	S								**Belgique**
Imports		178 715	198 125	234 947	285 596	318 768	351 908	413 960	Importations
Exports		190 361	215 877	255 598	306 816	335 868	366 938	432 316	Exportations
Balance		11 646	17 752	20 650	21 220	17 100	15 030	18 356	Balance
Croatia	G								**Croatie**
Imports		9 147	10 722	14 209	16 589	18 560	21 488	25 830	Importations
Exports		4 666	4 904	6 187	8 024	8 773	10 376	12 364	Exportations
Balance		-4 481	-5 818	-8 022	-8 565	-9 788	-11 112	-13 465	Balance
Czech Republic	S								**République tchèque**
Imports		38 308	42 773	53 807	71 635	76 343	93 453	118 508	Importations
Exports		33 399	38 488	48 715	67 198	77 988	95 165	122 790	Exportations
Balance		-4 909	-4 285	-5 092	-4 438	1 645	1 712	4 282	Balance
Denmark	S								**Danemark**
Imports		44 132	48 890	56 227	66 845	74 265	85 102	98 860	Importations
Exports		51 077	56 308	65 280	75 568	83 569	91 705	102 863	Exportations
Balance		6 945	7 418	9 052	8 723	9 303	6 603	4 003	Balance
Estonia [6]	S								**Estonie** [6]
Imports		4 280	4 810	6 480	8 334	10 189	13 154	15 105	Importations
Exports		3 298	3 448	4 539	5 934	7 676	9 586	10 952	Exportations
Balance		-982	-1 363	-1 942	-2 400	-2 513	-3 568	-4 153	Balance
Faeroe Islands	G								**Iles Féroé**
Imports		498	...	...	...	...	...	...	Importations

62

Total imports and exports *(continued)*
Imports c.i.f., exports f.o.b., and balance, value in million US dollars
Importations et exportations totales *(suite)*
Importations c.a.f., exportations f.o.b. et balance, valeur en millions de dollars E.-U.

Region, country or area [&]	Sys.[t]	2001	2002	2003	2004	2005	2006	2007	Région, pays ou zone [&]
Exports		514	...	...	...	...	...	...	Exportations
Balance		16	...	...	...	...	...	...	Balance
Finland	G								**Finlande**
Imports		32 114	33 642	41 601	50 677	58 474	69 447	81 756	Importations
Exports		42 802	44 671	52 514	60 916	65 240	77 287	90 091	Exportations
Balance		10 688	11 029	10 913	10 239	6 765	7 840	8 335	Balance
France[7]	S								**France**[7]
Imports		302 016	312 164	370 574	443 056	484 721	536 996	617 784	Importations
Exports		297 278	312 105	365 761	425 110	439 131	483 157	542 009	Exportations
Balance		-4 739	-59	-4 813	-17 947	-45 590	-53 838	-75 775	Balance
Germany	S								**Allemagne**
Imports		486 055	490 157	604 729	718 269	780 514	922 376	1 059 644	Importations
Exports		571 459	615 705	751 824	911 858	977 970	1 122 112	1 329 053	Exportations
Balance		85 404	125 548	147 095	193 589	197 456	199 736	269 410	Balance
Gibraltar									**Gibraltar**
Imports		435	385	468	535	550	...	...	Importations
Exports		120	148	147	199	199	...	...	Exportations
Balance		-315	-236	-320	-336	-351	...	...	Balance
Greece	S								**Grèce**
Imports		29 928	31 164	44 375	51 559	49 817	59 121	75 100	Importations
Exports		9 483	10 315	13 195	14 996	15 511	20 180	23 472	Exportations
Balance		-20 444	-20 849	-31 180	-36 564	-34 306	-38 940	-51 628	Balance
Greenland	G								**Groenland**
Imports		324	388	461	547	598	615	670	Importations
Exports		268	305	348	380	403	397	430	Exportations
Balance		-56	-82	-113	-166	-196	-219	-240	Balance
Hungary[6]	S								**Hongrie**[6]
Imports		33 724	37 787	47 602	59 636	65 783	77 206	94 373	Importations
Exports		30 530	34 512	42 532	54 893	62 179	74 217	93 379	Exportations
Balance		-3 195	-3 276	-5 070	-4 744	-3 604	-2 989	-994	Balance
Iceland	G								**Islande**
Imports		2 253	2 274	2 788	3 551	4 554	5 077	6 391	Importations
Exports		2 021	2 227	2 385	2 896	2 944	3 241	4 509	Exportations
Balance		-231	-47	-403	-654	-1 610	-1 835	-1 882	Balance
Ireland	G								**Irlande**
Imports		51 305	51 508	53 315	61 413	69 177	83 889	85 626	Importations
Exports		83 020	87 497	92 431	104 204	109 605	104 639	122 624	Exportations
Balance		31 715	35 990	39 117	42 791	40 428	20 750	36 998	Balance
Italy	S								**Italie**
Imports		236 128	246 613	297 405	355 269	384 837	440 770	509 900	Importations
Exports		244 253	254 219	299 468	353 544	372 962	416 145	499 910	Exportations
Balance		8 125	7 606	2 063	-1 726	-11 875	-24 626	-9 990	Balance
Latvia	S								**Lettonie**
Imports		3 504	4 053	5 242	7 048	8 592	11 430	15 185	Importations
Exports		2 001	2 284	2 893	3 983	5 108	5 896	7 892	Exportations
Balance		-1 504	-1 769	-2 350	-3 066	-3 483	-5 535	-7 293	Balance
Lithuania	G								**Lituanie**
Imports		6 060	7 524	9 668	12 386	15 510	19 413	24 445	Importations
Exports		4 279	5 231	6 970	9 307	11 782	14 153	17 162	Exportations
Balance		-1 781	-2 294	-2 698	-3 079	-3 729	-5 259	-7 283	Balance
Luxembourg	S								**Luxembourg**
Imports		11 153	11 602	13 694	16 829	17 565	19 434	22 157	Importations
Exports		8 239	8 499	9 980	12 181	12 699	14 172	16 099	Exportations
Balance		-2 914	-3 103	-3 714	-4 648	-4 866	-5 262	-6 057	Balance
Malta	G								**Malte**
Imports		2 726	2 840	3 399	3 824	3 807	4 073	4 508	Importations
Exports		1 958	2 223	2 468	2 628	2 376	2 705	2 985	Exportations
Balance		-768	-616	-931	-1 196	-1 432	-1 368	-1 523	Balance
Netherlands	S								**Pays-Bas**
Imports		195 569	194 130	234 014	284 020	310 600	358 510	421 381	Importations
Exports		216 180	219 857	264 849	318 066	349 844	399 635	476 804	Exportations
Balance		20 611	25 727	30 835	34 046	39 244	41 125	55 423	Balance

Total imports and exports *(continued)*
Imports c.i.f., exports f.o.b., and balance, value in million US dollars
Importations et exportations totales *(suite)*
Importations c.a.f., exportations f.o.b. et balance, valeur en millions de dollars E.-U.

Region, country or area [&]	Sys.[t]	2001	2002	2003	2004	2005	2006	2007	Région, pays ou zone [&]
Norway	G								**Norvège**
Imports		32 954	34 889	39 284	48 062	54 786	63 349	79 778	Importations
Exports		59 193	59 576	67 103	81 709	101 917	120 550	137 975	Exportations
Balance		26 239	24 687	27 818	33 646	47 131	57 200	58 197	Balance
Poland	S								**Pologne**
Imports		50 378	55 141	68 153	89 094	100 759	127 260	162 437	Importations
Exports		36 159	41 032	53 699	74 831	89 214	110 941	138 756	Exportations
Balance		-14 219	-14 108	-14 454	-14 264	-11 545	-16 319	-23 680	Balance
Portugal	S								**Portugal**
Imports		39 422	38 326	40 843	49 225	53 407	65 605	76 367	Importations
Exports		24 449	25 536	30 714	33 023	32 137	42 890	50 240	Exportations
Balance		-14 973	-12 791	-10 129	-16 201	-21 270	-22 716	-26 127	Balance
Slovakia	S								**Slovaquie**
Imports		15 501	17 460	23 760	30 469	36 168	47 250	62 102	Importations
Exports		12 641	14 478	21 966	27 605	31 997	41 939	57 766	Exportations
Balance		-2 860	-2 983	-1 794	-2 864	-4 171	-5 311	-4 336	Balance
Slovenia	S								**Slovénie**
Imports		10 148	10 933	13 853	17 571	19 626	23 014	29 481	Importations
Exports		9 252	10 357	12 767	15 879	17 896	20 985	26 553	Exportations
Balance		-895	-576	-1 086	-1 692	-1 730	-2 029	-2 928	Balance
Spain	S								**Espagne**
Imports		153 634	163 575	208 553	257 672	287 610	326 046	382 651	Importations
Exports		115 175	123 563	156 024	182 156	191 021	213 350	246 752	Exportations
Balance		-38 459	-40 012	-52 529	-75 516	-96 589	-112 697	-135 899	Balance
Sweden	G								**Suède**
Imports		64 316	67 667	84 197	100 792	111 324	126 609	148 744	Importations
Exports		78 173	82 965	102 405	123 306	130 205	147 235	166 898	Exportations
Balance		13 857	15 298	18 208	22 514	18 881	20 626	18 153	Balance
Switzerland	S								**Suisse**
Imports		77 086	82 387	95 600	110 324	119 784	132 030	153 181	Importations
Exports		78 082	87 370	100 744	117 820	126 099	141 679	164 809	Exportations
Balance		996	4 983	5 144	7 496	6 314	9 649	11 627	Balance
United Kingdom	G								**Royaume-Uni**
Imports		320 956	335 458	380 821	451 715	483 064	547 508	622 743	Importations
Exports		267 357	276 317	304 268	341 621	371 406	428 357	435 963	Exportations
Balance		-53 599	-59 142	-76 553	-110 094	-111 658	-119 151	-186 780	Balance
North America - Developed economies									**Amerique du Nord - Economies développées**
Imports		**1 322 381**	**1 344 490**	**1 455 439**	**1 692 619**	**1 935 015**	**2 135 567**	**2 250 793**	**Importations**
Exports		**909 599**	**866 959**	**909 775**	**1 015 776**	**1 144 552**	**1 293 428**	**1 431 384**	**Exportations**
Balance		**-412 782**	**-477 532**	**-545 664**	**-676 843**	**-790 463**	**-842 140**	**-819 409**	**Balance**
Bermuda	G								**Bermudes**
Imports		720	747	833	988	985	1 094	1 150	Importations
Exports		36	56	52	73	49	25	23	Exportations
Balance		-684	-691	-781	-915	-936	-1 069	-1 127	Balance
Canada[8]	G								**Canada**[8]
Imports		221 757	221 962	239 085	273 084	323 365	348 958	379 794	Importations
Exports		259 858	252 407	272 699	304 623	359 411	389 513	416 432	Exportations
Balance		38 101	30 445	33 614	31 538	36 046	40 555	36 637	Balance
United States[9]	G								**Etats-Unis**[9]
Imports		1 179 180	1 200 230	1 303 050	1 525 680	1 732 350	1 919 430	2 017 330	Importations
Exports		729 100	693 103	724 771	818 520	907 158	1 038 270	1 162 980	Exportations
Balance		-450 080	-507 127	-578 279	-707 160	-825 192	-881 160	-854 350	Balance
South-eastern Europe									**Europe du Sud-est**
Imports		**33 810**	**39 318**	**51 445**	**69 210**	**82 504**	**103 035**	**139 123**	**Importations**
Exports		**20 680**	**24 112**	**30 658**	**40 847**	**48 524**	**60 653**	**75 738**	**Exportations**
Balance		**-13 129**	**-15 206**	**-20 787**	**-28 363**	**-33 980**	**-42 382**	**-63 385**	**Balance**
Albania	G								**Albanie**
Imports		1 327	1 503	1 864	2 309	2 618	3 058	4 196	Importations
Exports		307	340	448	605	658	798	1 073	Exportations
Balance		-1 020	-1 164	-1 416	-1 703	-1 960	-2 261	-3 124	Balance

62

Total imports and exports *(continued)*
Imports c.i.f., exports f.o.b., and balance, value in million US dollars
Importations et exportations totales *(suite)*
Importations c.a.f., exportations f.o.b. et balance, valeur en millions de dollars E.-U.

Region, country or area [&]	Sys.[t]	2001	2002	2003	2004	2005	2006	2007	Région, pays ou zone [&]
Bosnia and Herzegovina	S								**Bosnie-Herzégovine**
Imports		3 354	3 909	4 769	5 918	7 073	7 344	9 772	Importations
Exports		1 032	1 015	1 369	1 794	2 401	3 324	4 166	Exportations
Balance		-2 322	-2 894	-3 399	-4 124	-4 673	-4 020	-5 606	Balance
Bulgaria	S								**Bulgarie**
Imports		7 263	7 987	10 887	14 467	18 162	23 270	30 086	Importations
Exports		5 115	5 749	7 540	9 931	11 739	15 101	18 575	Exportations
Balance		-2 148	-2 238	-3 346	-4 536	-6 423	-8 168	-11 511	Balance
Montenegro	S								**Monténégro**
Imports		...	...	...	...	...	1 848	2 953	Importations
Exports		...	...	...	...	...	791	828	Exportations
Balance		...	...	...	...	...	-1 057	-2 125	Balance
Romania	S								**Roumanie**
Imports		15 561	17 862	24 003	32 664	40 463	51 106	69 602	Importations
Exports		11 391	13 876	17 619	23 485	27 730	32 336	40 042	Exportations
Balance		-4 170	-3 986	-6 384	-9 179	-12 733	-18 770	-29 560	Balance
Serbia	S								**Serbie**
Imports		...	...	...	...	...	13 188	18 400	Importations
Exports		...	...	...	...	...	6 437	8 817	Exportations
Balance		...	...	...	...	...	-6 752	-9 584	Balance
Serbia and Montenegro	S								**Serbie-et-Monténégro**
Imports		4 837	6 320	7 952	11 366	...	...	...	Importations
Exports		1 903	2 275	2 650	3 801	...	...	...	Exportations
Balance		-2 934	-4 045	-5 302	-7 565	...	...	...	Balance
TFYR of Macedonia	S								**Ex-R.Y. Macédoine**
Imports		1 694	1 995	2 306	2 932	3 228	3 752	5 177	Importations
Exports		1 158	1 116	1 367	1 676	2 041	2 398	3 302	Exportations
Balance		-536	-880	-939	-1 256	-1 187	-1 355	-1 875	Balance
CIS [§]									**CEI [§]**
Imports		**82 436**	**88 907**	**113 258**	**149 627**	**187 533**	**253 604**	**349 826**	**Importations**
Exports		**142 099**	**152 352**	**191 024**	**262 649**	**338 753**	**426 183**	**508 668**	**Exportations**
Balance		**59 663**	**63 445**	**77 766**	**113 022**	**151 220**	**172 579**	**158 842**	**Balance**
Asia									**Asie**
Imports		**15 737**	**15 771**	**20 115**	**27 055**	**33 985**	**46 054**	**58 772**	**Importations**
Exports		**17 985**	**19 167**	**23 752**	**33 824**	**46 278**	**66 134**	**83 577**	**Exportations**
Balance		**2 248**	**3 396**	**3 637**	**6 769**	**12 293**	**20 080**	**24 804**	**Balance**
Armenia	S								**Arménie**
Imports		874	987	1 280	1 351	1 768	2 194	3 282	Importations
Exports		343	505	686	715	950	1 004	1 219	Exportations
Balance		-532	-482	-594	-636	-818	-1 190	-2 063	Balance
Azerbaijan	G								**Azerbaïdjan**
Imports		1 431	1 666	2 626	3 516	4 211	5 269	5 709	Importations
Exports		2 314	2 167	2 590	3 615	7 449	13 015	21 269	Exportations
Balance		883	502	-36	99	3 238	7 745	15 561	Balance
Georgia	G								**Géorgie**
Imports		753	796	1 141	1 846	2 490	3 678	5 217	Importations
Exports		318	346	461	647	865	993	1 240	Exportations
Balance		-436	-450	-680	-1 199	-1 624	-2 685	-3 977	Balance
Kazakhstan	G								**Kazakhstan**
Imports		6 446	6 584	8 409	12 781	17 353	24 956	32 940	Importations
Exports		8 639	9 670	12 927	20 093	27 849	40 470	46 540	Exportations
Balance		2 193	3 086	4 518	7 312	10 497	15 515	13 600	Balance
Kyrgyzstan	S								**Kirghizistan**
Imports		467	587	717	941	1 102	1 848	2 475	Importations
Exports		476	486	582	733	672	796	1 105	Exportations
Balance		9	-101	-135	-208	-431	-1 052	-1 370	Balance
Tajikistan	G								**Tadjikistan**
Imports		688	721	881	1 191	1 354	1 723	2 455	Importations
Exports		652	737	797	915	891	1 399	1 468	Exportations
Balance		-36	16	-84	-276	-464	-324	-987	Balance
Turkmenistan	G								**Turkménistan**
Imports		...	2 119	2 512	...	...	...	...	Importations

62

Total imports and exports *(continued)*
Imports c.i.f., exports f.o.b., and balance, value in million US dollars

Importations et exportations totales *(suite)*
Importations c.a.f., exportations f.o.b. et balance, valeur en millions de dollars E.-U.

Region, country or area [&]	Sys.[t]	2001	2002	2003	2004	2005	2006	2007	Région, pays ou zone [&]
Exports		...	2 856	2 632	...	...	...	...	Exportations
Balance		...	736	120	...	...	...	...	Balance
Europe									**Europe**
Imports		**66 699**	**73 136**	**93 143**	**122 572**	**153 548**	**207 550**	**291 053**	**Importations**
Exports		**124 114**	**133 185**	**167 273**	**228 825**	**292 475**	**360 048**	**425 091**	**Exportations**
Balance		**57 415**	**60 049**	**74 130**	**106 253**	**138 927**	**152 499**	**134 038**	**Balance**
Belarus	G								**Bélarus**
Imports		8 286	9 092	11 558	16 491	16 708	22 351	28 693	Importations
Exports		7 451	8 021	9 946	13 774	15 979	19 734	24 275	Exportations
Balance		-836	-1 071	-1 612	-2 717	-729	-2 618	-4 418	Balance
Republic of Moldova	G								**République de Moldova**
Imports		893	1 039	1 403	1 773	2 293	2 710	3 690	Importations
Exports		568	644	789	980	1 091	1 060	1 342	Exportations
Balance		-325	-395	-614	-793	-1 202	-1 650	-2 348	Balance
Russian Federation	G								**Fédération de Russie**
Imports		41 883	46 177	57 347	75 569	98 708	137 807	199 793	Importations
Exports		99 969	106 712	133 656	181 663	241 473	301 244	351 919	Exportations
Balance		58 086	60 535	76 309	106 093	142 766	163 437	152 126	Balance
Ukraine	G								**Ukraine**
Imports		15 775	16 977	23 020	28 997	36 136	45 039	60 618	Importations
Exports		16 265	17 957	23 067	32 666	34 228	38 368	49 296	Exportations
Balance		490	980	47	3 669	-1 908	-6 671	-11 322	Balance
Northern Africa									**Afrique du Nord**
Imports		**47 433**	**50 108**	**52 778**	**67 663**	**79 835**	**87 050**	**111 014**	**Importations**
Exports		**47 760**	**47 842**	**60 632**	**78 504**	**108 798**	**129 489**	**149 013**	**Exportations**
Balance		**327**	**-2 266**	**7 854**	**10 841**	**28 963**	**42 439**	**37 998**	**Balance**
Algeria	S								**Algérie**
Imports		9 941	11 969	12 392	18 166	20 356	20 985	...	Importations
Exports		19 139	18 801	23 206	31 300	46 000	52 760	...	Exportations
Balance		9 198	6 832	10 814	13 133	25 644	31 775	...	Balance
Egypt [10]	S								**Egypte** [10]
Imports		12 756	12 552	11 170	12 859	19 851	20 784	27 092	Importations
Exports		4 128	4 708	6 327	7 530	10 672	13 736	16 218	Exportations
Balance		-8 628	-7 844	-4 842	-5 329	-9 179	-7 048	-10 874	Balance
Libyan Arab Jamah.	G								**Jamah. arabe libyenne**
Imports		4 363	4 412	4 311	6 333	6 058	6 965	8 626	Importations
Exports		10 931	9 837	14 557	20 403	30 869	39 271	45 075	Exportations
Balance		6 567	5 425	10 246	14 069	24 811	32 306	36 449	Balance
Morocco	S								**Maroc**
Imports		11 038	11 864	14 250	17 807	20 805	23 977	31 715	Importations
Exports		7 144	7 849	8 778	9 917	11 185	12 744	14 665	Exportations
Balance		-3 893	-4 014	-5 472	-7 890	-9 621	-11 233	-17 050	Balance
Tunisia	G								**Tunisie**
Imports		9 529	9 526	10 910	12 818	13 177	14 865	18 980	Importations
Exports		6 621	6 871	8 027	9 685	10 494	11 513	15 029	Exportations
Balance		-2 908	-2 655	-2 883	-3 133	-2 683	-3 352	-3 951	Balance
Sub-Saharan Africa									**Afrique subsaharienne**
Imports		**84 871**	**83 042**	**108 724**	**136 621**	**166 490**	**192 369**	**236 829**	**Importations**
Exports		**87 637**	**90 333**	**110 083**	**146 681**	**196 924**	**209 640**	**248 475**	**Exportations**
Balance		**2 766**	**7 291**	**1 359**	**10 060**	**30 435**	**17 271**	**11 646**	**Balance**
Angola [8]	S								**Angola** [8]
Imports		3 179	3 760	5 480	5 832	8 353	11 600	...	Importations
Exports		6 380	7 516	9 508	13 475	24 109	31 084	...	Exportations
Balance		3 201	3 756	4 028	7 643	15 756	19 484	...	Balance
Benin	S								**Bénin**
Imports		623	725	892	894	895	990	1 110	Importations
Exports		372	450	555	564	564	574	593	Exportations
Balance		-251	-275	-337	-330	-330	-416	-517	Balance
Botswana	G								**Botswana**
Imports		1 817	1 865	2 472	3 236	3 177	3 045	4 050	Importations

62

Total imports and exports *(continued)*
Imports c.i.f., exports f.o.b., and balance, value in million US dollars

Importations et exportations totales *(suite)*
Importations c.a.f., exportations f.o.b. et balance, valeur en millions de dollars E.-U.

Region, country or area [&]	Sys.[t]	2001	2002	2003	2004	2005	2006	2007	Région, pays ou zone [&]
Exports		2 544	2 445	2 809	3 516	4 464	4 487	5 053	Exportations
Balance		726	580	337	280	1 287	1 442	1 003	Balance
Burkina Faso	G								**Burkina Faso**
Imports		655	746	932	1 273	1 374	1 504	1 707	Importations
Exports		226	248	320	480	467	588	660	Exportations
Balance		-429	-498	-612	-793	-907	-916	-1 047	Balance
Burundi	S								**Burundi**
Imports		139	129	157	176	267	431	319	Importations
Exports		39	30	38	47	56	58	62	Exportations
Balance		-101	-99	-119	-129	-211	-372	-257	Balance
Cameroon	S								**Cameroun**
Imports		1 849	1 876	2 176	2 411	2 725	3 161	3 776	Importations
Exports		1 746	1 814	2 297	2 481	2 785	3 590	3 769	Exportations
Balance		-104	-62	122	70	60	430	-7	Balance
Cape Verde	G								**Cap-Vert**
Imports		234	276	352	432	438	543	755	Importations
Exports		10	11	13	15	18	21	19	Exportations
Balance		-224	-266	-339	-417	-420	-522	-736	Balance
Central African Rep.	S								**Rép. centrafricaine**
Imports		108	122	119	152	175	203	231	Importations
Exports		142	150	128	126	127	159	196	Exportations
Balance		35	27	9	-26	-48	-44	-34	Balance
Chad	S								**Tchad**
Imports		680	1 638	788	953	954	1 304	1 495	Importations
Exports		189	184	599	2 192	3 164	3 398	3 438	Exportations
Balance		-491	-1 454	-189	1 239	2 210	2 093	1 943	Balance
Comoros	S								**Comores**
Imports		51	53	70	86	98	116	120	Importations
Exports		17	19	27	19	12	10	9	Exportations
Balance		-34	-34	-43	-67	-86	-106	-112	Balance
Congo	S								**Congo**
Imports		703	695	856	905	1 503	1 909	2 985	Importations
Exports		2 053	2 290	2 686	3 435	4 733	6 315	6 116	Exportations
Balance		1 350	1 596	1 830	2 530	3 230	4 406	3 130	Balance
Côte d'Ivoire	S								**Côte d'Ivoire**
Imports		2 420	2 462	3 237	4 299	5 246	5 222	6 110	Importations
Exports		3 955	5 279	5 803	6 955	7 693	8 368	8 423	Exportations
Balance		1 535	2 817	2 566	2 655	2 447	3 146	2 313	Balance
Dem. Rep. of the Congo	S								**Rép. dém. du Congo**
Imports		807	1 081	1 594	1 986	2 270	2 740	2 950	Importations
Exports		901	1 132	1 374	1 850	2 190	2 320	2 600	Exportations
Balance		94	51	-220	-137	-80	-420	-350	Balance
Djibouti	G								**Djibouti**
Imports		196	197	238	261	277	336	410	Importations
Exports		32	36	37	38	40	55	60	Exportations
Balance		-164	-161	-201	-223	-238	-281	-350	Balance
Equatorial Guinea	G								**Guinée équatoriale**
Imports		812	508	1 237	1 563	2 108	2 624	3 098	Importations
Exports		1 732	2 121	2 803	4 588	6 989	8 227	10 095	Exportations
Balance		921	1 613	1 566	3 024	4 880	5 602	6 996	Balance
Ethiopia	G								**Ethiopie**
Imports		1 807	1 622	2 119	3 087	4 127	4 805	5 317	Importations
Exports		456	480	496	678	903	1 036	1 293	Exportations
Balance		-1 351	-1 142	-1 623	-2 409	-3 224	-3 768	-4 024	Balance
Gabon	S								**Gabon**
Imports		858	943	1 043	1 213	1 473	1 726	2 198	Importations
Exports		2 519	2 413	2 827	3 612	4 863	5 254	5 943	Exportations
Balance		1 661	1 470	1 784	2 398	3 390	3 528	3 746	Balance
Gambia	G								**Gambie**
Imports		134	159	156	229	237	259	306	Importations
Exports		10	12	8	10	8	11	13	Exportations
Balance		-124	-147	-148	-219	-229	-248	-294	Balance

62

Total imports and exports *(continued)*
Imports c.i.f., exports f.o.b., and balance, value in million US dollars
Importations et exportations totales *(suite)*
Importations c.a.f., exportations f.o.b. et balance, valeur en millions de dollars E.-U.

Region, country or area [&]	Sys.[t]	2001	2002	2003	2004	2005	2006	2007	Région, pays ou zone [&]
Ghana	G								**Ghana**
Imports		3 156	2 712	3 210	4 074	5 754	6 497	7 976	Importations
Exports		...	...	...	...	2 802	3 735	4 321	Exportations
Balance		...	...	...	...	-2 952	-2 762	-3 655	Balance
Guinea-Bissau	G								**Guinée-Bissau**
Imports		62	59	66	83	105	99	111	Importations
Exports		62	54	65	75	90	64	70	Exportations
Balance		1	-5	-1	-8	-15	-35	-42	Balance
Kenya	G								**Kenya**
Imports		3 189	3 245	3 725	4 553	6 149	7 311	8 989	Importations
Exports		1 943	2 116	2 411	2 684	3 293	3 437	4 080	Exportations
Balance		-1 246	-1 129	-1 314	-1 869	-2 856	-3 874	-4 910	Balance
Lesotho	G								**Lesotho**
Imports		748	815	1 121	1 440	1 410	1 466	1 733	Importations
Exports		278	376	485	713	675	690	810	Exportations
Balance		-470	-438	-636	-727	-735	-776	-922	Balance
Madagascar	S								**Madagascar**
Imports		1 119	629	1 311	1 616	1 685	1 796	2 625	Importations
Exports		932	490	863	946	837	983	1 214	Exportations
Balance		-187	-139	-449	-670	-848	-814	-1 411	Balance
Malawi	G								**Malawi**
Imports		579	691	785	932	1 163	1 206	1 380	Importations
Exports		458	405	520	483	501	541	670	Exportations
Balance		-121	-286	-265	-449	-662	-665	-710	Balance
Mali	S								**Mali**
Imports		989	927	1 270	1 365	1 623	1 843	1 999	Importations
Exports		724	873	926	979	1 092	1 553	1 631	Exportations
Balance		-265	-54	-345	-386	-531	-290	-367	Balance
Mauritius	G								**Maurice**
Imports		1 987	2 159	2 364	2 771	3 157	3 627	3 896	Importations
Exports		1 628	1 801	1 899	1 993	2 138	2 329	2 231	Exportations
Balance		-359	-358	-465	-778	-1 018	-1 298	-1 665	Balance
Mozambique	S								**Mozambique**
Imports		1 063	1 543	1 753	2 035	2 408	2 869	3 210	Importations
Exports		703	810	1 045	1 504	1 783	2 381	2 650	Exportations
Balance		-360	-733	-708	-531	-625	-488	-560	Balance
Namibia	G								**Namibie**
Imports		1 542	1 484	1 999	2 432	2 659	2 904	3 348	Importations
Exports		1 180	1 077	1 269	1 833	2 067	2 638	2 992	Exportations
Balance		-362	-407	-730	-600	-592	-266	-355	Balance
Niger	S								**Niger**
Imports		412	474	630	757	797	956	982	Importations
Exports		273	278	353	439	479	520	651	Exportations
Balance		-139	-196	-277	-318	-319	-436	-331	Balance
Nigeria	G								**Nigéria**
Imports		11 586	7 547	10 853	14 164	21 314	22 222	37 576	Importations
Exports		17 261	15 107	19 887	31 148	55 145	45 403	65 133	Exportations
Balance		5 675	7 560	9 034	16 984	33 831	23 181	27 557	Balance
Rwanda	G								**Rwanda**
Imports		250	203	245	284	432	484	736	Importations
Exports		85	56	58	98	125	135	176	Exportations
Balance		-165	-147	-187	-186	-306	-349	-559	Balance
Sao Tome and Principe	S								**Sao Tomé-et-Principe**
Imports		29	31	41	41	50	71	79	Importations
Exports		3	5	7	4	3	4	4	Exportations
Balance		-26	-26	-34	-38	-46	-67	-75	Balance
Senegal	G								**Sénégal**
Imports		1 727	2 038	2 395	2 844	3 193	3 442	4 261	Importations
Exports		1 002	1 070	1 259	1 506	1 576	1 559	1 663	Exportations
Balance		-726	-968	-1 136	-1 337	-1 617	-1 884	-2 597	Balance
Seychelles	G								**Seychelles**
Imports		478	421	412	497	676	758	777	Importations

62

Total imports and exports *(continued)*
Imports c.i.f., exports f.o.b., and balance, value in million US dollars
Importations et exportations totales *(suite)*
Importations c.a.f., exportations f.o.b. et balance, valeur en millions de dollars E.-U.

Region, country or area [&]	Sys.[t]	2001	2002	2003	2004	2005	2006	2007	Région, pays ou zone [&]
Exports		217	227	274	291	340	380	356	Exportations
Balance		-262	-194	-138	-206	-336	-378	-421	Balance
Sierra Leone	S								**Sierra Leone**
Imports		182	264	303	286	345	389	445	Importations
Exports		29	49	92	139	159	216	244	Exportations
Balance		-153	-216	-211	-148	-186	-173	-200	Balance
South Africa[11,12]	G								**Afrique du Sud**[11,12]
Imports		28 264	29 281	41 120	53 518	62 325	...	...	Importations
Exports		29 283	29 733	36 503	46 148	51 640	58 197	69 788	Exportations
Balance		1 019	452	-4 617	-7 370	-10 685	...	...	Balance
Sudan[13]	G								**Soudan**[13]
Imports		2 301	2 446	2 882	4 075	6 757	8 074	8 450	Importations
Exports		1 699	1 949	2 542	3 778	4 824	5 657	...	Exportations
Balance		-602	-497	-340	-297	-1 933	-2 417	...	Balance
Swaziland	G								**Swaziland**
Imports		1 042	1 037	1 654	1 961	2 138	2 379	2 460	Importations
Exports		1 122	964	1 536	1 938	2 226	2 479	2 657	Exportations
Balance		80	-73	-118	-23	88	100	197	Balance
Togo	S								**Togo**
Imports		553	595	775	883	1 194	1 346	1 483	Importations
Exports		357	430	600	601	659	619	705	Exportations
Balance		-196	-165	-176	-281	-535	-726	-778	Balance
Uganda	G								**Ouganda**
Imports		1 594	1 112	1 251	2 020	1 895	2 503	3 466	Importations
Exports		457	442	563	885	821	970	1 557	Exportations
Balance		-1 137	-670	-688	-1 136	-1 075	-1 533	-1 909	Balance
United Rep. of Tanzania	G								**Rép.-Unie de Tanzanie**
Imports		1 715	1 661	2 125	2 515	2 661	4 254	5 337	Importations
Exports		777	902	1 129	1 336	1 479	1 655	2 022	Exportations
Balance		-937	-758	-996	-1 179	-1 182	-2 598	-3 315	Balance
Zambia	S								**Zambie**
Imports		1 309	1 284	1 576	2 018	2 567	2 931	...	Importations
Exports		993	961	981	1 576	1 780	3 828	4 915	Exportations
Balance		-316	-323	-595	-442	-786	896	...	Balance
Zimbabwe	G								**Zimbabwe**
Imports		1 715	1 751	1 710	2 204	2 330	2 250	2 420	Importations
Exports		1 207	2 012	1 670	1 887	1 840	2 020	2 050	Exportations
Balance		-508	261	-40	-317	-490	-230	-370	Balance
Latin America and the Caribbean									**Amérique latine et Caraïbes**
Imports		367 321	343 463	355 639	434 427	514 124	612 810	732 387	**Importations**
Exports		339 673	343 895	374 904	461 485	558 366	674 410	758 969	**Exportations**
Balance		-27 647	432	19 265	27 058	44 242	61 600	26 582	**Balance**
Caribbean									**Caraïbes**
Imports		25 408	26 051	26 712	29 711	36 998	42 942	48 775	**Importations**
Exports		10 286	9 894	11 734	13 938	17 605	23 930	26 422	**Exportations**
Balance		-15 122	-16 157	-14 978	-15 773	-19 393	-19 012	-22 353	**Balance**
Anguilla	S								**Anguilla**
Imports		82	74	80	105	133	143	...	Importations
Exports		4	4	4	6	7	13	...	Exportations
Balance		-79	-69	-76	-100	-126	-130	...	Balance
Antigua and Barbuda	G								**Antigua-et-Barbuda**
Imports		386	400	422	454	497	615	750	Importations
Exports		41	39	45	57	82	72	77	Exportations
Balance		-345	-360	-377	-397	-415	-543	-673	Balance
Aruba	S								**Aruba**
Imports		841	841	848	875	1 028	1 041	1 114	Importations
Exports		149	128	83	80	102	109	98	Exportations
Balance		-693	-713	-764	-796	-927	-932	-1 016	Balance
Bahamas[14]	G								**Bahamas**[14]
Imports		1 912	1 728	1 762	1 905	2 230	2 401	2 449	Importations
Exports		423	446	425	477	562	674	485	Exportations
Balance		-1 489	-1 282	-1 337	-1 428	-1 668	-1 726	-1 965	Balance

62
Total imports and exports *(continued)*
Imports c.i.f., exports f.o.b., and balance, value in million US dollars
Importations et exportations totales *(suite)*
Importations c.a.f., exportations f.o.b. et balance, valeur en millions de dollars E.-U.

Region, country or area [&]	Sys.[t]	2001	2002	2003	2004	2005	2006	2007	Région, pays ou zone [&]
Barbados	G								**Barbade**
Imports		1 069	1 071	1 195	1 413	1 604	1 586	1 709	Importations
Exports		259	242	250	278	359	385	419	Exportations
Balance		-809	-829	-946	-1 135	-1 245	-1 201	-1 291	Balance
Cayman Islands	G								**Iles Caïmanes**
Imports		621	605	678	884	1 214	1 066	1 058	Importations
Exports		4	3	24	24	59	25	26	Exportations
Balance		-616	-602	-654	-860	-1 155	-1 041	-1 032	Balance
Cuba	S								**Cuba**
Imports		3 736	4 151	4 613	5 562	8 130	10 174	10 889	Importations
Exports		1 354	1 504	1 672	2 188	2 159	2 980	3 998	Exportations
Balance		-2 382	-2 647	-2 941	-3 374	-5 972	-7 194	-6 892	Balance
Dominica	S								**Dominique**
Imports		131	116	128	144	165	167	190	Importations
Exports		46	46	41	44	46	...	...	Exportations
Balance		-85	-70	-87	-101	-119	...	...	Balance
Dominican Republic [8,15]	G								**Rép. dominicaine** [8,15]
Imports		5 937	6 037	5 266	5 368	7 207	8 745	11 289	Importations
Exports		805	834	1 041	1 251	1 398	1 933	2 674	Exportations
Balance		-5 132	-5 204	-4 225	-4 117	-5 809	-6 812	-8 615	Balance
Grenada	S								**Grenade**
Imports		219	202	254	233	319	280	...	Importations
Exports		60	58	42	30	39	20	...	Exportations
Balance		-160	-144	-213	-203	-279	-260	...	Balance
Haïti	G								**Haïti**
Imports		1 017	1 122	1 187	1 317	1 449	1 880	1 681	Importations
Exports		275	279	346	394	470	480	522	Exportations
Balance		-742	-842	-841	-923	-979	-1 401	-1 159	Balance
Jamaica	G								**Jamaïque**
Imports		3 361	3 533	3 633	3 772	4 458	5 314	6 415	Importations
Exports		1 220	1 114	1 177	1 390	1 499	1 874	2 074	Exportations
Balance		-2 140	-2 419	-2 457	-2 382	-2 959	-3 440	-4 341	Balance
Saint Kitts and Nevis	S								**Saint-Kitts-et-Nevis**
Imports		189	201	205	182	210	250	275	Importations
Exports		31	27	48	42	34	40	40	Exportations
Balance		-158	-174	-157	-140	-176	-210	-235	Balance
Saint Lucia	S								**Sainte-Lucie**
Imports		355	309	403	437	479	592	635	Importations
Exports		51	49	85	63	64	65	...	Exportations
Balance		-304	260	-318	-374	-415	-527	...	Balance
Saint Vincent-Grenadines	S								**Saint Vincent-Grenadines**
Imports		186	174	201	226	240	271	310	Importations
Exports		41	38	38	37	40	38	50	Exportations
Balance		144	-136	-163	-189	-201	-233	-260	Balance
Trinidad and Tobago	S								**Trinité-et-Tobago**
Imports		3 576	3 644	3 892	4 858	5 725	6 484	7 482	Importations
Exports		4 275	3 883	5 178	6 374	9 611	14 154	14 744	Exportations
Balance		698	239	1 286	1 516	3 887	7 670	7 262	Balance
Latin America									**Amérique latine**
Imports		**341 912**	**317 412**	**328 927**	**404 716**	**477 126**	**569 869**	**683 612**	**Importations**
Exports		**329 387**	**334 001**	**363 170**	**447 547**	**540 761**	**650 480**	**732 547**	**Exportations**
Balance		**-12 525**	**16 589**	**34 243**	**42 831**	**63 635**	**80 611**	**48 935**	**Balance**
Argentina	S								**Argentine**
Imports		20 320	8 990	13 834	22 445	28 688	34 158	44 707	Importations
Exports		26 543	25 650	29 566	34 576	40 351	46 569	55 779	Exportations
Balance		6 223	16 660	15 732	12 131	11 664	12 411	11 072	Balance
Belize	G								**Belize**
Imports		517	525	552	514	593	676	684	Importations
Exports		169	169	205	213	208	266	254	Exportations
Balance		-348	-356	-347	-301	-385	-410	-430	Balance
Bolivia	G								**Bolivie**
Imports		1 708	1 770	1 616	1 844	2 341	2 814	3 457	Importations

62

Total imports and exports *(continued)*
Imports c.i.f., exports f.o.b., and balance, value in million US dollars
Importations et exportations totales *(suite)*
Importations c.a.f., exportations f.o.b. et balance, valeur en millions de dollars E.-U.

Region, country or area [&]	Sys.[t]	2001	2002	2003	2004	2005	2006	2007	Région, pays ou zone [&]
Exports		1 285	1 299	1 598	2 146	2 791	3 875	4 458	Exportations
Balance		-423	-471	-18	302	450	1 060	1 001	Balance
Brazil	G								**Brésil**
Imports		58 672	49 723	50 881	66 433	77 628	95 845	126 566	Importations
Exports		58 287	60 439	73 203	96 678	118 529	137 807	160 649	Exportations
Balance		-385	10 716	22 322	30 244	40 901	41 962	34 083	Balance
Chile	S								**Chili**
Imports		17 429	17 092	19 322	24 794	32 735	38 405	47 125	Importations
Exports		18 272	18 180	21 664	32 520	41 267	58 486	67 644	Exportations
Balance		843	1 088	2 342	7 727	8 532	20 081	20 519	Balance
Colombia	G								**Colombie**
Imports		12 834	12 711	13 889	16 746	21 204	26 046	33 164	Importations
Exports		12 290	11 911	13 080	16 224	21 146	24 388	29 786	Exportations
Balance		-544	-800	-809	-522	-59	-1 658	-3 378	Balance
Costa Rica	S								**Costa Rica**
Imports		6 569	7 188	7 663	8 268	9 812	11 520	12 955	Importations
Exports		5 021	5 264	6 102	6 301	7 026	8 216	9 360	Exportations
Balance		-1 547	-1 924	-1 561	-1 967	-2 786	-3 305	-3 596	Balance
Ecuador	G								**Equateur**
Imports		5 363	6 431	6 703	8 226	10 287	12 114	13 565	Importations
Exports		4 678	5 042	6 223	7 753	10 100	12 728	13 852	Exportations
Balance		-684	-1 390	-480	-473	-187	615	287	Balance
El Salvador	S								**El Salvador**
Imports		5 027	5 184	5 754	6 329	6 834	7 628	8 677	Importations
Exports		2 864	2 995	3 128	3 305	3 387	3 513	3 977	Exportations
Balance		-2 163	-2 189	-2 626	-3 024	-3 448	-4 115	-4 700	Balance
Guatemala	S								**Guatemala**
Imports		5 606	6 304	6 722	7 812	8 810	10 157	11 861	Importations
Exports		2 464	2 473	2 632	2 939	3 477	3 665	4 468	Exportations
Balance		-3 143	-3 831	-4 090	-4 873	-5 333	-6 492	-7 393	Balance
Guyana	S								**Guyana**
Imports		583	576	576	652	788	889	1 059	Importations
Exports		490	496	513	593	553	588	679	Exportations
Balance		-93	-81	-63	-59	-235	-301	-381	Balance
Honduras	S								**Honduras**
Imports		3 069	3 082	3 448	4 212	4 853	5 695	6 762	Importations
Exports		1 264	1 240	1 359	1 640	1 892	2 054	2 120	Exportations
Balance		-1 805	-1 842	-2 089	-2 572	-2 960	-3 641	-4 642	Balance
Mexico[8,16]	G								**Mexique**[8,16]
Imports		168 276	168 679	170 490	197 347	221 414	256 130	283 264	Importations
Exports		158 547	160 682	165 396	189 084	213 891	250 441	272 055	Exportations
Balance		-9 729	-7 997	-5 094	-8 263	-7 523	-5 689	-11 209	Balance
Nicaragua	G								**Nicaragua**
Imports		1 775	1 754	1 879	2 212	2 595	3 000	3 579	Importations
Exports		589	561	605	756	858	1 027	1 194	Exportations
Balance		-1 186	-1 193	-1 275	-1 457	-1 737	-1 973	-2 385	Balance
Panama[17]	S								**Panama**[17]
Imports		2 964	2 982	3 086	3 594	4 180	4 831	6 872	Importations
Exports		911	846	864	944	1 018	1 093	1 164	Exportations
Balance		-2 053	-2 136	-2 222	-2 651	-3 162	-3 738	-5 709	Balance
Paraguay	S								**Paraguay**
Imports		2 182	1 672	2 228	3 097	3 790	6 090	...	Importations
Exports		990	951	1 242	1 627	1 688	1 906	2 785	Exportations
Balance		-1 192	-721	-986	-1 470	-2 102	-4 184	...	Balance
Peru[8]	S								**Pérou**[8]
Imports		7 273	7 440	8 244	9 812	12 084	14 897	19 580	Importations
Exports		7 026	7 714	9 091	12 617	16 587	23 749	27 680	Exportations
Balance		-248	274	846	2 805	4 503	8 852	8 099	Balance
Suriname	G								**Suriname**
Imports		461	492	704	742	770	820	940	Importations
Exports		403	469	638	895	950	1 200	1 310	Exportations
Balance		-58	-23	-66	152	180	380	370	Balance

Total imports and exports *(continued)*
Imports c.i.f., exports f.o.b., and balance, value in million US dollars
Importations et exportations totales *(suite)*
Importations c.a.f., exportations f.o.b. et balance, valeur en millions de dollars E.-U.

Region, country or area [&]	Sys.[t]	2001	2002	2003	2004	2005	2006	2007	Région, pays ou zone [&]
Uruguay	G								**Uruguay**
Imports		3 061	1 964	2 190	3 114	3 879	4 757	5 667	Importations
Exports		2 060	1 861	2 206	2 931	3 405	3 953	4 485	Exportations
Balance		-1 000	-103	16	-183	-474	-804	-1 182	Balance
Venezuela (Boliv. Rep. of) [8]	G								**Venezuela (Rép. boliv. du)** [8]
Imports		18 323	12 963	9 256	16 679	24 027	33 607	46 097	Importations
Exports		25 353	25 890	23 990	33 994	51 859	65 210	69 165	Exportations
Balance		7 030	12 927	14 734	17 315	27 832	31 603	23 068	Balance
Eastern Asia									**Asie orientale**
Imports		**522 820**	**583 412**	**740 940**	**978 656**	**1 128 323**	**1 334 891**	**1 566 229**	**Importations**
Exports		**558 102**	**633 488**	**788 880**	**1 032 705**	**1 256 278**	**1 529 464**	**1 842 965**	**Exportations**
Balance		**35 282**	**50 076**	**47 941**	**54 049**	**127 954**	**194 573**	**276 735**	**Balance**
China [18]	S								**Chine** [18]
Imports		243 553	295 170	412 760	561 229	659 953	791 605	956 284	Importations
Exports		266 098	325 596	438 228	593 326	761 953	969 380	1 217 815	Exportations
Balance		22 545	30 426	25 468	32 097	102 000	177 775	261 531	Balance
China, Hong Kong SAR	G								**Chine, Hong Kong RAS**
Imports		201 076	207 644	231 896	271 074	299 533	334 681	367 864	Importations
Exports		189 894	200 092	223 762	259 260	289 337	316 816	344 629	Exportations
Balance		-11 182	-7 552	-8 134	-11 814	-10 196	-17 865	-23 235	Balance
China, Macao SAR	G								**Chine, Macao RAS**
Imports		2 386	2 530	2 755	3 478	3 913	4 565	5 366	Importations
Exports		2 300	2 356	2 581	2 812	2 476	2 557	2 543	Exportations
Balance		-87	-174	-174	-666	-1 438	-2 008	-2 823	Balance
Korea, Republic of	G								**Corée, République de**
Imports		141 098	152 126	178 827	224 463	261 238	309 383	356 648	Importations
Exports		150 439	162 471	193 817	253 845	284 419	325 465	371 554	Exportations
Balance		9 341	10 345	14 990	29 382	23 181	16 082	14 906	Balance
Mongolia	G								**Mongolie**
Imports		638	691	801	1 021	1 184	1 486	2 117	Importations
Exports		521	524	616	870	1 065	1 543	1 889	Exportations
Balance		-116	-167	-185	-151	-119	57	-228	Balance
Southern Asia									**Asie australe**
Imports		**95 234**	**106 677**	**131 001**	**175 365**	**235 506**	**277 116**	**328 030**	**Importations**
Exports		**88 774**	**94 697**	**115 926**	**145 417**	**186 938**	**232 475**	**265 798**	**Exportations**
Balance		**-6 460**	**-11 980**	**-15 075**	**-29 948**	**-48 568**	**-44 641**	**-62 231**	**Balance**
Afghanistan	G								**Afghanistan**
Imports		1 696	2 452	2 101	2 177	...	...	...	Importations
Exports		68	100	144	314	...	...	...	Exportations
Balance		-1 628	-2 352	-1 957	-1 863	...	...	...	Balance
Bangladesh	G								**Bangladesh**
Imports		8 349	7 913	9 516	12 611	12 881	14 964	17 263	Importations
Exports		4 826	4 566	5 263	6 615	7 233	9 103	10 233	Exportations
Balance		-3 523	-3 348	-4 253	-5 996	-5 648	-5 861	-7 030	Balance
Bhutan	G								**Bhoutan**
Imports		191	196	249	411	387	419	480	Importations
Exports		106	113	133	183	258	414	601	Exportations
Balance		-85	-84	-116	-228	-129	-5	120	Balance
India [19]	G								**Inde** [19]
Imports		50 391	56 496	72 559	99 757	142 865	175 243	215 510	Importations
Exports		43 352	50 353	58 964	76 647	99 618	120 862	145 429	Exportations
Balance		-7 038	-6 143	-13 595	-23 110	-43 247	-54 381	-70 080	Balance
Iran (Islamic Rep. of) [20,21]	S								**Iran (Rép. islamique d')** [20,21]
Imports		16 709	20 617	24 798	31 976	40 041	40 772	45 000	Importations
Exports		25 689	24 440	33 750	41 697	56 252	77 012	83 000	Exportations
Balance		8 980	3 823	8 952	9 721	16 211	36 240	38 000	Balance
Maldives	G								**Maldives**
Imports		393	392	471	642	745	927	1 096	Importations
Exports		76	90	113	122	103	135	108	Exportations
Balance		-317	-301	-358	-519	-641	-791	-989	Balance
Nepal	G								**Népal**
Imports		1 475	1 418	1 755	1 939	2 284	2 490	2 911	Importations

Total imports and exports *(continued)*
Imports c.i.f., exports f.o.b., and balance, value in million US dollars
Importations et exportations totales *(suite)*
Importations c.a.f., exportations f.o.b. et balance, valeur en millions de dollars E.-U.

Region, country or area [&]	Sys.[t]	2001	2002	2003	2004	2005	2006	2007	Région, pays ou zone [&]
Exports		738	568	662	772	863	838	889	Exportations
Balance		-737	-850	-1 093	-1 167	-1 421	-1 652	-2 022	Balance
Pakistan	G								**Pakistan**
Imports		10 192	11 227	13 038	17 949	25 356	29 828	32 590	Importations
Exports		9 238	9 908	11 930	13 379	16 050	16 932	17 838	Exportations
Balance		-953	-1 319	-1 107	-4 570	-9 306	-12 896	-14 752	Balance
Sri Lanka	G								**Sri Lanka**
Imports		5 973	6 105	6 672	7 973	8 833	10 259	11 301	Importations
Exports		4 815	4 699	5 125	5 757	6 347	6 886	7 740	Exportations
Balance		-1 158	-1 406	-1 547	-2 216	-2 487	-3 373	-3 560	Balance
South-eastern Asia[3]									**Asie du Sud-est**[3]
Imports		**287 556**	**301 858**	**319 859**	**400 697**	**485 700**	**552 285**	**619 703**	**Importations**
Exports		**327 981**	**346 840**	**374 241**	**468 351**	**538 906**	**636 400**	**714 511**	**Exportations**
Balance		**40 425**	**44 982**	**54 382**	**67 654**	**53 206**	**84 115**	**94 808**	**Balance**
Brunei Darussalam	S								**Brunéi Darussalam**
Imports		1 142	1 556	1 327	1 427	...	...	...	Importations
Exports		3 642	3 701	4 424	5 069	...	...	...	Exportations
Balance		2 499	2 145	3 097	3 642	...	...	...	Balance
Cambodia	S								**Cambodge**
Imports		2 094	2 318	2 560	3 193	3 927	4 749	5 300	Importations
Exports		1 500	1 923	2 118	2 798	3 200	3 800	4 400	Exportations
Balance		-594	-395	-442	-395	-727	-949	-900	Balance
Indonesia	S								**Indonésie**
Imports		37 534	38 340	42 244	54 877	75 533	80 333	93 088	Importations
Exports		57 360	59 164	64 107	70 767	86 996	103 486	118 728	Exportations
Balance		19 826	20 824	21 863	15 890	11 463	23 153	25 640	Balance
Lao People's Dem. Rep.	S								**Rép. dém. pop. lao**
Imports		510	447	462	713	882	1 060	1 067	Importations
Exports		320	301	335	363	553	882	842	Exportations
Balance		-191	-146	-127	-349	-329	-177	-225	Balance
Malaysia	G								**Malaisie**
Imports		73 866	79 869	81 948	105 298	114 410	131 079	146 772	Importations
Exports		88 005	93 265	99 369	125 745	140 870	160 574	176 026	Exportations
Balance		14 139	13 396	17 421	20 446	26 460	29 495	29 254	Balance
Myanmar	G								**Myanmar**
Imports		2 877	2 348	2 092	2 196	1 910	2 564	3 277	Importations
Exports		2 382	3 046	2 485	2 380	3 778	4 585	6 313	Exportations
Balance		-496	698	392	184	1 869	2 021	3 036	Balance
Philippines	G								**Philippines**
Imports		34 944	37 202	39 502	42 345	46 963	54 077	57 708	Importations
Exports		32 664	36 510	36 231	39 680	39 879	47 413	50 270	Exportations
Balance		-2 280	-692	-3 271	-2 664	-7 084	-6 665	-7 438	Balance
Singapore	G								**Singapour**
Imports		116 004	116 448	127 935	163 851	200 050	238 711	263 155	Importations
Exports		121 755	125 177	144 183	198 633	229 652	271 809	299 270	Exportations
Balance		5 752	8 729	16 248	34 782	29 602	33 098	36 115	Balance
Thailand	S								**Thaïlande**
Imports		61 961	64 645	75 824	94 410	118 158	128 654	140 812	Importations
Exports		64 919	68 108	80 324	96 248	110 178	130 795	153 092	Exportations
Balance		2 959	3 463	4 499	1 838	-7 980	2 142	12 280	Balance
Viet Nam	G								**Viet Nam**
Imports		16 218	19 746	25 256	31 969	36 978	44 410	60 869	Importations
Exports		15 029	16 706	20 149	26 485	32 442	39 605	48 302	Exportations
Balance		-1 189	-3 040	-5 107	-5 484	-4 536	-4 805	-12 567	Balance
Western Asia									**Asie occidentale**
Imports		**193 273**	**210 450**	**247 297**	**334 239**	**385 182**	**460 677**	**577 710**	**Importations**
Exports		**240 722**	**251 640**	**311 190**	**416 188**	**548 028**	**645 401**	**804 809**	**Exportations**
Balance		**47 450**	**41 189**	**63 893**	**81 949**	**162 846**	**184 724**	**227 100**	**Balance**
Bahrain	G								**Bahreïn**
Imports		4 306	4 988	5 657	7 385	8 790	9 022	11 293	Importations
Exports		5 578	5 786	6 624	7 556	10 160	11 625	13 394	Exportations
Balance		1 272	798	966	171	1 370	2 603	2 101	Balance

62

Total imports and exports *(continued)*
Imports c.i.f., exports f.o.b., and balance, value in million US dollars
Importations et exportations totales *(suite)*
Importations c.a.f., exportations f.o.b. et balance, valeur en millions de dollars E.-U.

Region, country or area [&]	Sys.[t]	2001	2002	2003	2004	2005	2006	2007	Région, pays ou zone [&]
Cyprus	G								**Chypre**
Imports		3 922	3 863	4 288	5 659	6 282	6 951	8 687	Importations
Exports		976	770	834	1 081	1 303	1 153	1 254	Exportations
Balance		-2 946	-3 094	-3 455	-4 577	-4 979	-5 798	-7 433	Balance
Israel[22]	S								**Israël**[22]
Imports		35 449	35 517	36 303	42 864	47 142	50 334	59 039	Importations
Exports		29 081	29 347	31 784	38 618	42 770	46 789	54 065	Exportations
Balance		-6 368	-6 170	-4 519	-4 245	-4 371	-3 544	-4 973	Balance
Jordan	G								**Jordanie**
Imports		4 871	5 076	5 743	8 128	10 506	11 447	13 511	Importations
Exports		2 294	2 770	3 082	3 922	4 302	5 175	5 725	Exportations
Balance		-2 577	-2 306	-2 662	-4 206	-6 204	-6 272	-7 786	Balance
Kuwait	S								**Koweït**
Imports		7 869	9 007	10 992	12 630	15 534	15 960	19 417	Importations
Exports		16 203	15 363	20 677	28 599	45 189	55 719	62 163	Exportations
Balance		8 334	6 356	9 685	15 968	29 655	39 759	42 747	Balance
Lebanon	G								**Liban**
Imports		7 380	6 560	7 315	9 609	9 633	9 647	12 251	Importations
Exports		1 093	1 238	1 813	2 199	2 337	2 814	3 574	Exportations
Balance		-6 287	-5 322	-5 502	-7 410	-7 296	-6 833	-8 677	Balance
Occupied Palestinian Terr.	S								**Terr. palestinien occupé**
Imports		...	1 516	...	2 373	2 667	2 835	...	Importations
Exports		273	241	...	322	335	339	...	Exportations
Balance		...	-1 275	...	-2 052	-2 331	-2 496	...	Balance
Oman	G								**Oman**
Imports		5 798	6 005	6 572	8 865	8 827	10 915	15 978	Importations
Exports		11 074	11 172	11 669	13 341	18 692	21 585	24 136	Exportations
Balance		5 276	5 166	5 096	4 476	9 865	10 670	8 158	Balance
Qatar	S								**Qatar**
Imports		3 758	4 052	4 897	6 005	10 061	16 441	22 045	Importations
Exports		10 871	10 978	13 383	18 684	25 762	34 052	36 970	Exportations
Balance		7 114	6 926	8 485	12 680	15 702	17 610	14 925	Balance
Saudi Arabia	S								**Arabie saoudite**
Imports		31 181	32 293	36 915	44 744	59 458	69 800	90 218	Importations
Exports		67 973	72 453	93 245	125 997	180 736	211 306	...	Exportations
Balance		36 792	40 160	56 331	81 253	121 278	141 506	...	Balance
Syrian Arab Republic	S								**Rép. arabe syrienne**
Imports		4 773	5 097	5 119	8 411	10 862	...	...	Importations
Exports		5 257	6 520	5 731	7 485	9 174	...	...	Exportations
Balance		484	1 423	611	-926	-1 688	...	...	Balance
Turkey	S								**Turquie**
Imports		41 399	49 663	65 637	96 368	98 998	133 584	168 527	Importations
Exports		31 334	34 561	46 576	61 683	71 928	81 912	106 851	Exportations
Balance		-10 065	-15 101	-19 061	-34 685	-27 070	-51 672	-61 676	Balance
United Arab Emirates	G								**Emirats arabes unis**
Imports		37 293	42 652	52 074	72 082	84 654	97 864	121 100	Importations
Exports		48 414	52 163	67 135	90 997	117 287	142 505	154 000	Exportations
Balance		11 121	9 511	15 061	18 915	32 633	44 641	32 900	Balance
Yemen	S								**Yémen**
Imports		2 473	2 927	3 680	3 988	4 885	5 300	5 892	Importations
Exports		3 373	3 683	3 923	4 676	6 376	7 315	7 160	Exportations
Balance		900	755	243	688	1 491	2 015	1 268	Balance
Oceania									**Océanie**
Imports		**7 031**	**7 665**	**9 265**	**10 113**	**10 947**	**12 404**	**14 324**	**Importations**
Exports		**4 515**	**4 423**	**5 559**	**6 296**	**7 055**	**8 141**	**9 520**	**Exportations**
Balance		**-2 516**	**-3 241**	**-3 706**	**-3 818**	**-3 892**	**-4 263**	**-4 804**	**Balance**
American Samoa[23]	S								**Samoa américaines**[23]
Imports		516	499	624	604	521	579	...	Importations
Exports		318	388	460	446	374	439	...	Exportations
Balance		-198	-111	-164	-158	-147	-141	...	Balance
Cook Islands	G								**Iles Cook**
Imports		47	47	71	76	81	100	175	Importations

62

Total imports and exports *(continued)*
Imports c.i.f., exports f.o.b., and balance, value in million US dollars

Importations et exportations totales *(suite)*
Importations c.a.f., exportations f.o.b. et balance, valeur en millions de dollars E.-U.

Region, country or area [&]	Sys.[t]	2001	2002	2003	2004	2005	2006	2007	Région, pays ou zone [&]
Exports		7	5	9	7	5	3	5	Exportations
Balance		-40	-42	-62	-69	-76	-96	-170	Balance
Fiji	G								**Fidji**
Imports		886	906	1 208	1 444	1 607	1 802	1 801	Importations
Exports		534	519	674	693	701	679	755	Exportations
Balance		-352	-386	-533	-751	-906	-1 123	-1 046	Balance
French Polynesia	S								**Polynésie française**
Imports		1 017	1 268	1 560	1 478	1 702	1 650	1 859	Importations
Exports		174	168	151	185	210	198	194	Exportations
Balance		-842	-1 100	-1 410	-1 293	-1 492	-1 451	-1 665	Balance
Guam	G								**Guam**
Imports		...	...	...	...	...	501	...	Importations
Exports		...	...	...	53	52	53	...	Exportations
Balance		...	...	...	...	...	-448	...	Balance
Kiribati [8]	G								**Kiribati** [8]
Imports		41	...	...	...	...	...	...	Importations
Exports		5	...	...	...	...	...	...	Exportations
Balance		-36	...	...	...	...	...	...	Balance
New Caledonia	S								**Nouvelle-Calédonie**
Imports		932	1 008	1 541	1 637	1 774	2 132	2 825	Importations
Exports		453	476	785	1 034	1 086	1 208	1 906	Exportations
Balance		-479	-532	-756	-603	-688	-924	-919	Balance
Niue	G								**Nioué**
Imports		2	2	2	8	...	...	...	Importations
Exports [^]		0	0	0	0	0	...	...	Exportations [^]
Balance		-2	-2	-2	-8	...	...	...	Balance
Papua New Guinea	G								**Papouasie-Nvl-Guinée**
Imports		1 071	1 235	1 368	1 681	1 728	2 287	2 945	Importations
Exports		1 805	1 641	2 206	2 552	3 273	4 166	4 683	Exportations
Balance		734	406	838	871	1 546	1 879	1 737	Balance
Samoa	S								**Samoa**
Imports		120	127	128	155	187	219	227	Importations
Exports		16	14	15	11	12	11	15	Exportations
Balance		-104	-114	-113	-145	-175	-208	-212	Balance
Solomon Islands	S								**Iles Salomon**
Imports		88	67	83	85	185	210	250	Importations
Exports		46	58	74	97	105	120	166	Exportations
Balance		-42	-9	-9	12	-80	-90	-84	Balance
Tonga	G								**Tonga**
Imports		72	89	94	105	120	130	143	Importations
Exports		7	14	18	15	10	11	9	Exportations
Balance		-66	-75	-76	-90	-110	-119	-134	Balance
Vanuatu	G								**Vanuatu**
Imports		86	90	106	128	149	160	202	Importations
Exports		19	20	27	38	38	37	30	Exportations
Balance		-67	-70	-79	-90	-111	-123	-172	Balance
Non Petroleum Exports of Asia Middle East [24]									**Exp. non pétrolières de Moyen-Orient d'Asie** [24]
Exports		**100 182**	**92 853**	**86 061**	**79 766**	**73 931**	**68 523**	**63 510**	**Exportations**

Additional country groupings · Groupements supplémentaires de pays

		2001	2002	2003	2004	2005	2006	2007	
ANCOM [§]									**ANCOM** [§]
Imports		45 442	41 255	39 652	53 231	69 837	89 330	115 658	Importations
Exports		50 573	51 795	53 926	72 656	102 376	129 801	144 736	Exportations
Balance		5 131	10 540	14 273	19 426	32 539	40 471	29 078	Balance
APEC [§]									**CEAP** [§]
Imports		2 765 551	2 863 833	3 227 877	3 926 257	4 536 110	5 163 466	5 743 698	Importations
Exports		2 535 246	2 608 400	2 931 404	3 569 139	4 135 705	4 842 647	5 532 839	Exportations
Balance		-230 304	-255 433	-296 473	-357 118	-400 405	-320 819	-210 858	Balance
ASEAN [§]									**ANASE** [§]
Imports		287 556	301 858	319 638	400 430	485 378	551 897	619 235	Importations
Exports		327 981	346 840	374 212	468 319	538 872	636 363	714 471	Exportations
Balance		40 425	44 982	54 574	67 889	53 494	84 466	95 236	Balance

Total imports and exports *(continued)*
Imports c.i.f., exports f.o.b., and balance, value in million US dollars
Importations et exportations totales *(suite)*
Importations c.a.f., exportations f.o.b. et balance, valeur en millions de dollars E.-U.

Region, country or area [&]	Sys.[t]	2001	2002	2003	2004	2005	2006	2007	Région, pays ou zone [&]
CACM[§]									**MCAC**[§]
Imports		22 046	23 512	25 466	28 833	32 904	37 999	43 833	Importations
Exports		12 202	12 532	13 825	14 941	16 640	18 475	21 118	Exportations
Balance		-9 844	-10 980	-11 641	-13 892	-16 264	-19 524	-22 715	Balance
CARICOM[§]									**CARICOM**[§]
Imports		13 371	13 453	14 485	16 165	18 673	21 335	24 041	Importations
Exports		7 175	6 694	8 378	10 180	13 641	18 981	19 925	Exportations
Balance		-6 196	-6 759	-6 107	-5 985	-5 032	-2 353	-4 116	Balance
COMESA[§]									**COMESA**[§]
Imports		35 678	34 749	37 238	47 392	61 178	68 615	82 719	Importations
Exports		26 880	27 057	35 450	46 334	62 256	77 777	90 859	Exportations
Balance		-8 798	-7 693	-1 788	-1 058	1 078	9 162	8 139	Balance
ECOWAS[§]									**CEDEAO**[§]
Imports		22 959	19 190	25 222	31 619	42 343	44 999	64 431	Importations
Exports		26 509	26 340	32 189	44 922	70 562	62 857	83 659	Exportations
Balance		3 550	7 151	6 967	13 303	28 219	17 858	19 228	Balance
EMCCA[§]									**CEMAC**[0]
Imports		5 010	5 782	6 218	7 198	8 939	10 927	13 783	Importations
Exports		8 382	8 972	11 340	16 434	22 661	26 942	29 556	Exportations
Balance		3 372	3 190	5 122	9 236	13 723	16 015	15 773	Balance
LAIA[§]									**ALAI**[§]
Imports		319 117	293 525	303 210	376 023	446 101	534 889	641 168	Importations
Exports		316 626	321 062	348 874	432 260	523 666	631 943	712 129	Exportations
Balance		-2 491	27 537	45 664	56 237	77 564	97 055	70 961	Balance
LDC[§ 3]									**PMA**[§ 3]
Imports		46 107	48 374	58 248	70 959	82 933	99 328	113 183	Importations
Exports		33 166	36 525	43 436	58 244	78 727	96 609	109 648	Exportations
Balance		-12 941	-11 849	-14 812	-12 715	-4 206	-2 719	-3 534	Balance
MERCOSUR[§]									**MERCOSUR**[§]
Imports		84 234	62 348	69 133	95 089	113 985	140 850	184 233	Importations
Exports		87 880	88 900	106 217	135 811	163 973	190 236	223 697	Exportations
Balance		3 646	26 552	37 084	40 722	49 988	49 385	39 465	Balance
NAFTA[§]									**ALENA**[§]
Imports		1 489 591	1 511 991	1 624 559	1 888 295	2 154 652	2 389 717	2 531 862	Importations
Exports		1 067 883	1 027 312	1 074 800	1 204 411	1 357 983	1 543 422	1 702 941	Exportations
Balance		-421 708	-484 679	-549 759	-683 885	-796 669	-846 294	-828 922	Balance
OECD[§]									**OCDE**[§]
Imports		4 526 952	4 666 997	5 401 189	6 460 465	7 180 266	8 168 857	9 221 879	Importations
Exports		4 210 553	4 364 460	5 019 530	5 939 598	6 470 708	7 313 365	8 370 025	Exportations
Balance		-316 399	-302 537	-381 659	-520 867	-709 557	-855 492	-851 854	Balance
OPEC[§]									**OPEP**[§]
Imports		192 683	199 833	225 860	301 834	388 530	444 994	555 455	Importations
Exports		321 240	325 906	398 743	530 831	747 950	889 970	1 072 323	Exportations
Balance		128 557	126 073	172 883	228 998	359 420	444 977	516 868	Balance
EU-25									**UE-25**
Imports		2 367 132	2 465 164	2 972 759	3 587 360	3 916 861	4 507 593	5 251 619	Importations
Exports		2 382 937	2 541 529	3 030 567	3 613 845	3 882 117	4 395 034	5 115 255	Exportations
Balance		15 805	76 365	57 808	26 485	-34 744	-112 559	-136 364	Balance
Extra-EU-25[25]									**Extra-UE-25**[25]
Imports		880 948	889 542	1 063 891	1 283 863	1 470 417	1 702 321	1 955 505	Importations
Exports		801 722	854 112	999 614	1 205 484	1 331 083	1 489 696	1 740 937	Exportations
Balance		-79 227	-35 430	-64 277	-78 379	-139 334	-212 625	-214 568	Balance
EU-27									**UE-27**
Imports		2 389 956	2 491 013	3 007 649	3 634 491	3 975 487	4 581 969	5 351 307	Importations
Exports		2 399 443	2 561 153	3 055 726	3 647 262	3 921 586	4 442 472	5 173 872	Exportations
Balance		9 487	70 141	48 077	12 771	-53 901	-139 497	-177 435	Balance
Extra-EU-27[25]									**Extra-UE-27**[25]
Imports		876 828	884 628	1 057 654	1 277 883	1 465 464	1 698 154	1 956 917	Importations
Exports		791 773	843 095	984 114	1 185 129	1 307 916	1 457 176	1 703 336	Exportations
Balance		-85 055	-41 534	-73 540	-92 753	-157 548	-240 978	-253 581	Balance
World exc. intra-EU27									**Monde excl. intra-UE27**
Imports		4 424 496	4 550 072	5 224 504	6 414 458	7 448 041	8 572 861	9 818 233	Importations

62

Total imports and exports *(continued)*
Imports c.i.f., exports f.o.b., and balance, value in million US dollars

Importations et exportations totales *(suite)*
Importations c.a.f., exportations f.o.b. et balance, valeur en millions de dollars E.-U.

Region, country or area [&]	Sys.[t]	2001	2002	2003	2004	2005	2006	2007	Région, pays ou zone [&]
Exports		4 147 665	4 308 694	4 943 536	6 080 974	7 132 718	8 290 863	9 611 129	Exportations
Balance		-276 830	-241 378	-280 968	-333 484	-315 323	-281 998	-207 104	Balance

Source:
United Nations Statistics Division, New York, trade statistics database, last accessed January 2009.

Source:
Organisation des Nations Unies, Division de statistique, New York, la base de données pour les statistiques du commerce extérieur, dernier accès janvier 2009.

[&] The regional totals for imports and exports have been adjusted to exclude the re-exports of countries or areas comprising each region.

[&] Les totaux régionaux pour importations et exportations ont été ajustés pour exclure les réexportations des pays ou zones qui comprennent la région.

[§] For member states of this grouping, see Annex I – Other groupings. The totals have been calculated for all periods shown according to the current composition.

[§] Pour les Etats membres de ce groupements, voir annexe I – Autres groupements. Les totales ont été calculés pour toutes les périodes données suivant la composition présente.

[t] Systems of trade: Two systems of recording trade, the General trade system (G) and the Special trade system (S), are in common use. They differ mainly in the way warehoused and re-exported goods are recorded. See the Technical notes for an explanation of the trade systems.

[t] Systèmes de commerce : Deux systèmes d'enregistrement du commerce sont couramment utilisés, le Commerce général (G) et le Commerce spécial (S). Ils ne diffèrent que par la façon dont sont enregistrées les marchandises entreposées et les marchandises réexportées. Voir les Notes techniques pour une explication des Systèmes de commerce.

1 In April 2006, regional totals have been revised downwards due to the additional identification of re-exports, in particular for Singapore and Italy.
2 In November 2008, extrapolated figures for re-exports of Japan were replaced with actual data for the years 1999-2007 which lead to an increase of exports and imports on world level by 17 billion in 2004, 35 billion in 2005, 62 billion in 2006 and 103 billion in 2007.

3 In February 2008, the regional total for South-eastern Asia and the World total have been revised upwards very significantly for 2006 and the first three quarters of 2007 due to a correction of estimated data (re-exports) used in the calculation of these totals.

4 Developed economies of the Asia-Pacific region, Europe, and North America.
5 This classification is intended for statistical convenience and does not, necessarily, express a judgement about the stage reached by a particular country in the development process.

6 Data exclude re-exports.
7 Trade data for France include the import and export values of French Guiana, Guadeloupe, Martinique, and Réunion.

8 Imports FOB.
9 Including the trade of the U.S. Virgin Islands and Puerto Rico but excluding shipments of merchandise between the United States and its other possessions (Guam, American Samoa, etc.). Data include imports and exports of non-monetary gold.

10 Imports exclude petroleum imported without stated value. Exports cover domestic exports.
11 Exports include gold.
12 Beginning in January 1998, foreign trade data refer to South Africa only, excluding intra-trade of the Southern African Common Customs Area. Prior to January 1998, trade data refer to the Southern African Common Customs Area, which includes Botswana, Lesotho, Namibia, South Africa and Swaziland.

1 En avril 2006, les totaux régionaux ont été diminués à cause d'une identification additionnelle des réexportations, en particulier celles du Singapour et de l'Italie.
2 En novembre 2008, les statistiques de réexportations du Japon, jusque la estimées ont été mises à jour avec des données actuelles pour 1999-2007. Ceci a conduit à une augmentation des exportations et importations mondiales de 17 milliards en 2004, 35 milliards en 2005, 62 milliards en 2006 and 103 milliards en 2007.

3 En février 2008, le total régional de l'Asie du sud-est et le total du monde ont été révisés vers le haut très significativement pour l'année 2006 et les premiers trois trimestres de l'année 2007 à cause d'une correction des données estimées (des réexportations) qui sont utilisées dans ces totaux.

4 Économies développées de la région Asie-Pacifique, de l'Europe, et de l'Amérique de Nord.
5 Cette classification est utilisée pour plus de commodité dans la présentation des statistiques et n'implique pas nécessairement un jugement quant au stage de développement auquel est parvenu un pays donné.

6 Les données non compris les réexportations.
7 Les valeurs de commerce pour la France comprennent les valeurs des importations et des exportations de la Guyane française, la Guadeloupe, la Martinique, et la Réunion.

8 Importations FOB.
9 Y compris le commerce des Iles Vierges américaines et de Porto Rico mais non compris les échanges de marchandises, entre les Etats-Unis et leurs autres possessions (Guam, Samoa américaines, etc.). Les données comprennent les importations et exportations d'or non-monétaire.

10 Non compris le pétrole brute dont la valeur des importations ne sont pas stipulée. Les exportations sont les exportations d'intérieur.
11 Les exportations comprennent l'or.
12 A compter de janvier 1998, les données sur le commerce extérieur ne se rapportent qu'à l'Afrique du Sud. et ne tiennent pas compte des échanges commerciaux entre les pays de l'Union douanière de l'Afrique du Sud, qui incluait l'Afrique du Sud, Botswana, Lesotho, Namibie, et Swaziland.

62

Total imports and exports *(continued)*
Imports c.i.f., exports f.o.b., and balance, value in million US dollars

Importations et exportations totales *(suite)*
Importations c.a.f., exportations f.o.b. et balance, valeur en millions de dollars E.-U.

13	Year ending June 30 through 1994. Year ending December 31 thereafter.	13	Année finissant juin 30 à 1994. Année finissant décembre 31 ensuite.
14	Trade statistics exclude certain oil and chemical products.	14	Les statistiques commerciales font exclusion de certains produits pétroliers et chimiques.
15	Export and import values exclude trade in the processing zone.	15	Les valeurs à l'exportation et à l'importation excluent le commerce de la zone de transformation.
16	Trade data include maquiladoras and exclude goods from customs-bonded warehouses. Total exports include revaluation and exports of silver.	16	Les statistiques du commerce extérieur comprennent maquiladoras et ne comprennent pas les marchandises provenant des entrepôts en douane. Les exportations comprennent la réévaluation et les données sur les exportations d'argent.
17	Exports include re-exports and petroleum products.	17	Exportations comprennent réexportations et produits pétroliers.
18	For statistical purposes, the data for China do not include those for the Hong Kong Special Administrative Region (Hong Kong SAR), Macao Special Administrative Region (Macao SAR) and Taiwan Province of China.	18	Pour la présentation des statistiques, les données pour la Chine ne comprennent pas la Région Administrative Spéciale de Hong Kong (Hong Kong RAS), la Région Administrative Spéciale de Macao (Macao RAS) et la province de Taiwan.
19	Excluding military goods, fissionable materials, bunkers, ships, and aircraft.	19	A l'exclusion des marchandises militaires, des matières fissibles, des soutes, des bateaux, et de l'avion.
20	Data include oil and gas. Data on the value and volume of oil exports and on the value of total exports are rough estimates based on information published in various petroleum industry journals.	20	Les données comprennent le petrole et le gaz. La valeur des exportations de pétrole et des exportations totales sont des évaluations grossières basées sur l'information publiée à divers journaux d'industrie de pétrole.
21	Year ending 20 March of the years stated.	21	Année finissant le 20 mars de l'année indiquée.
22	Imports and exports net of returned goods. The figures also exclude Judea and Samaria and the Gaza area.	22	Importations et exportations nets, ne comprenant pas les marchandises retournées. Sont également exclues les données de la Judée et de Samara et ainsi que la zone de Gaza.
23	Year ending 30 September.	23	Année finissant le 30 septembre.
24	Data refer to total exports less petroleum exports of Asia Middle East countries where petroleum, in this case, is the sum of SITC groups 333, 334 and 335.	24	Les données se rapportent aux exportations totales moins les exportations pétrolières de Moyen-Orient d'Asie. Dans ce cas, le pétrole est la somme des groupes CTCI 333, 334 et 335.
25	Excluding intra-EU trade.	25	Non compris le commerce de l'intra-UE.

Country or area	1998	1999	2001	2002	2003	2004	2005	2006	2007	Pays ou zone
Argentina										**Argentine**
Imports: volume	117	101	83	38	58	87	108	125	150	Importations : volume
Imports: unit value	106	100	97	94	94	102	105	108	115	Importations : valeur unitaire
Exports: volume	98	97	104	105	110	118	135	143	154	Exportations : volume
Exports: unit value	102	91	97	93	102	111	113	122	137	Exportations : valeur unitaire
Terms of trade	97	91	99	99	108	110	107	114	119	Termes de l'échange
Purchasing power of exports	94	89	104	104	120	129	145	163	183	Pouvoir d'achat des exportations
Australia										**Australie**
Imports: volume	84	92	96	108	120	137	129	145	155	Importations : volume
Imports: unit value [1]	102	102	94	95	104	111	117	120	128	Importations : valeur unitaire [1]
Exports: volume	87	91	103	104	102	106	119	141	144	Exportations : volume
Exports: unit value [1]	101	96	98	100	111	129	153	175	196	Exportations : valeur unitaire [1]
Terms of trade	100	94	104	106	106	116	131	146	153	Termes de l'échange
Purchasing power of exports	86	86	107	110	108	123	156	205	220	Pouvoir d'achat des exportations
Austria										**Autriche**
Imports: volume	86	87	103	107	111	118	125	133	196	Importations : volume
Imports: unit value	124	115	97	100	114	125	123	130	142	Importations : valeur unitaire
Exports: volume	91	94	106	112	117	127	132	139	195	Exportations : volume
Exports: unit value	126	105	95	101	114	126	126	132	145	Exportations : valeur unitaire
Terms of trade	102	91	98	101	100	101	102	102	102	Termes de l'échange
Purchasing power of exports	93	86	104	114	117	128	135	142	200	Pouvoir d'achat des exportations
Belgium										**Belgique**
Imports: volume	91	91	101	109	111	118	126	132	140	Importations : volume
Imports: unit value	106	102	100	103	120	136	143	151	168	Importations : valeur unitaire
Exports: volume	88	91	102	111	113	121	126	131	135	Exportations : volume
Exports: unit value	111	105	99	104	121	135	142	149	170	Exportations : valeur unitaire
Terms of trade	104	102	100	101	100	99	99	99	101	Termes de l'échange
Purchasing power of exports	92	93	102	112	113	120	125	130	137	Pouvoir d'achat des exportations
Bolivia										**Bolivie**
Exports: volume	96	88	107	129	145	173	195	215	228	Exportations : volume
Exports: unit value	79	78	92	81	90	122	146	244	296	Exportations : valeur unitaire
Brazil										**Brésil**
Imports: volume	98	92	101	99	136	111	101	110	128	Importations : volume
Imports: unit value	105	96	99	86	64	102	131	148	167	Importations : valeur unitaire
Exports: volume	94	93	111	121	131	154	162	173	189	Exportations : volume
Exports: unit value	100	94	95	91	101	114	133	144	155	Exportations : valeur unitaire
Terms of trade	95	98	96	106	158	112	101	97	92	Termes de l'échange
Purchasing power of exports	89	91	107	128	208	173	165	168	174	Pouvoir d'achat des exportations
Bulgaria										**Bulgarie**
Imports: unit value	...	...	96	98	112	130	140	156	182	Importations : valeur unitaire
Exports: unit value	...	...	95	95	114	133	142	162	194	Exportations : valeur unitaire
Terms of trade	...	...	99	98	102	102	102	104	107	Termes de l'échange
Canada										**Canada**
Imports: volume	86	96	94	96	100	108	116	123	130	Importations : volume
Imports: unit value	92	93	96	95	100	106	114	122	128	Importations : valeur unitaire
Exports: volume	82	91	96	97	95	100	102	103	105	Exportations : volume
Exports: unit value	98	98	101	96	106	117	130	140	150	Exportations : valeur unitaire
Terms of trade	107	105	105	101	106	110	114	114	117	Termes de l'échange
Purchasing power of exports	88	96	101	97	101	111	117	118	123	Pouvoir d'achat des exportations
China, Hong Kong SAR										**Chine, Hong Kong RAS**
Imports: volume	85	85	98	106	119	136	148	163	179	Importations : volume
Imports: unit value	102	100	97	93	93	96	98	101	102	Importations : valeur unitaire
Exports: volume	82	85	97	105	120	138	154	169	183	Exportations : volume
Exports: unit value	104	101	98	95	94	95	96	97	99	Exportations : valeur unitaire
Terms of trade	102	101	101	102	101	99	98	97	97	Termes de l'échange
Purchasing power of exports	84	86	97	107	121	137	151	164	178	Pouvoir d'achat des exportations
Colombia										**Colombie**
Imports: unit value	110	103	98	95	95	103	114	114	117	Importations : valeur unitaire
Exports: unit value	103	96	89	84	87	96	111	119	130	Exportations : valeur unitaire
Terms of trade	93	93	91	89	92	93	97	104	111	Termes de l'échange

Country or area	1998	1999	2001	2002	2003	2004	2005	2006	2007	Pays ou zone
Czech Republic										**République tchèque**
Imports: unit value	105	99	101	107	123	137	148	158	175	Importations : valeur unitaire
Exports: unit value	114	105	102	111	130	147	155	164	185	Exportations : valeur unitaire
Terms of trade	108	105	101	104	105	107	105	104	106	Termes de l'échange
Denmark										**Danemark**
Imports: volume	93	93	102	108	106	113	122	136	145	Importations : volume
Imports: unit value	113	108	98	102	119	133	138	142	156	Importations : valeur unitaire
Exports: volume	86	92	103	109	107	110	116	122	128	Exportations : volume
Exports: unit value	112	108	99	103	122	136	143	150	160	Exportations : valeur unitaire
Terms of trade	99	100	101	101	102	102	104	105	103	Termes de l'échange
Purchasing power of exports	85	92	104	110	109	113	121	129	132	Pouvoir d'achat des exportations
Dominica										**Dominique**
Imports: volume	94	97	98	82	...	...	...	...	...	Importations : volume
Imports: unit value	116	95	95	91	...	...	...	...	...	Importations : valeur unitaire
Exports: volume	94	92	78	72	...	...	...	...	...	Exportations : volume
Exports: unit value	113	113	101	101	...	...	...	...	...	Exportations : valeur unitaire
Terms of trade	90	119	100	111	...	...	...	...	...	Termes de l'échange
Purchasing power of exports	91	110	82	80	...	...	...	...	...	Pouvoir d'achat des exportations
Ecuador										**Equateur**
Imports: volume	166	96	119	148	161	168	204	229	262	Importations : volume
Exports: volume	96	93	101	99	107	133	117	143	139	Exportations : volume
Exports: unit value	64	77	88	94	107	118	150	182	208	Exportations : valeur unitaire
Estonia										**Estonie**
Imports: unit value	113	109	98	103	121	135	140	147	166	Importations : valeur unitaire
Exports: unit value	113	107	129	136	173	194	199	210	247	Exportations : valeur unitaire
Terms of trade	99	98	132	132	143	144	143	143	148	Termes de l'échange
Finland										**Finlande**
Imports: volume	95	96	97	104	103	108	114	127	128	Importations : volume
Imports: unit value	102	101	98	97	115	131	146	152	170	Importations : valeur unitaire
Exports: volume	89	92	99	104	106	112	111	124	120	Exportations : volume
Exports: unit value	105	102	96	94	107	117	127	126	141	Exportations : valeur unitaire
Terms of trade	103	101	97	97	93	89	87	83	83	Termes de l'échange
Purchasing power of exports	92	93	97	101	98	99	96	103	100	Pouvoir d'achat des exportations
France										**France**
Imports: volume	79	87	116	112	112	125	136	148	150	Importations : volume
Imports: unit value	129	108	96	95	114	123	122	124	137	Importations : valeur unitaire
Exports: volume	83	89	119	112	110	118	125	138	137	Exportations : volume
Exports: unit value	137	114	97	97	118	127	127	127	139	Exportations : valeur unitaire
Terms of trade	106	105	102	103	104	104	104	102	101	Termes de l'échange
Purchasing power of exports	87	93	121	115	114	123	130	141	139	Pouvoir d'achat des exportations
Germany										**Allemagne**
Imports: volume	85	89	101	100	110	121	126	133	147	Importations : volume
Imports: unit value	111	104	97	98	111	121	123	140	158	Importations : valeur unitaire
Exports: volume	83	87	103	104	115	129	136	151	163	Exportations : volume
Exports: unit value	118	111	99	102	119	129	130	135	153	Exportations : valeur unitaire
Terms of trade	107	107	102	104	107	107	105	97	97	Termes de l'échange
Purchasing power of exports	89	93	105	109	123	139	143	146	158	Pouvoir d'achat des exportations
Greece										**Grèce**
Imports: volume	85	90	...	...	...	...	...	...	...	Importations : volume
Imports: unit value [1]	119	115	100	106	127	144	158	166	186	Importations : valeur unitaire [1]
Exports: volume	90	96	...	...	...	...	...	...	...	Exportations : volume
Exports: unit value [1]	111	107	98	104	124	143	149	157	174	Exportations : valeur unitaire [1]
Terms of trade	93	93	98	98	98	99	95	94	93	Termes de l'échange
Purchasing power of exports	84	90	...	...	...	...	...	...	...	Pouvoir d'achat des exportations
Honduras										**Honduras**
Exports: volume	77	70	102	100	93	112	103	110	118	Exportations : volume
Exports: unit value	134	101	101	96	83	102	136	142	149	Exportations : valeur unitaire
Hungary										**Hongrie**
Imports: volume	72	83	104	109	120	139	147	166	189	Importations : volume
Imports: unit value	111	106	101	107	123	135	138	142	156	Importations : valeur unitaire
Exports: volume	71	82	108	114	125	147	164	194	224	Exportations : volume
Exports: unit value	116	108	101	107	122	134	134	136	149	Exportations : valeur unitaire

63 Total imports and exports: index numbers *(continued)*
Index base : 2000 = 100
Importations et exportations totales : indices *(suite)*
Indices base : 2000 = 100

Country or area	1998	1999	2001	2002	2003	2004	2005	2006	2007	Pays ou zone
Terms of trade	104	103	100	100	100	99	97	95	95	Termes de l'échange
Purchasing power of exports	74	84	107	114	124	146	159	185	214	Pouvoir d'achat des exportations
Iceland										**Islande**
Imports: volume	92	96	90	...	...	...	...	...	...	Importations : volume
Imports: unit value	104	101	97	...	...	...	...	...	...	Importations : valeur unitaire
Exports: volume	93	100	107	...	...	...	...	...	...	Exportations : volume
Exports: unit value	110	106	99	...	...	...	...	...	...	Exportations : valeur unitaire
Terms of trade	105	104	102	...	...	...	...	...	...	Termes de l'échange
Purchasing power of exports	97	104	109	...	...	...	...	...	...	Pouvoir d'achat des exportations
India										**Inde**
Imports: volume	92	101	105	115	139	155	151	...	...	Importations : volume
Imports: unit value	91	96	96	104	113	134	143	135	...	Importations : valeur unitaire
Exports: volume	70	81	104	126	134	152	184	...	...	Exportations : volume
Exports: unit value	107	101	94	92	107	122	130	148	...	Exportations : valeur unitaire
Terms of trade	117	105	98	89	95	91	91	109	...	Termes de l'échange
Purchasing power of exports	82	85	102	112	127	138	168	...	...	Pouvoir d'achat des exportations
Indonesia										**Indonésie**
Exports: volume	102	84	121	100	97	101	64	...	...	Exportations : volume
Exports: unit value	81	65	90	96	103	120	81	...	...	Exportations : valeur unitaire
Ireland										**Irlande**
Imports: volume	79	86	99	97	90	98	112	117	119	Importations : volume
Imports: unit value	109	107	100	101	112	120	121	126	137	Importations : valeur unitaire
Exports: volume	72	84	105	104	99	110	113	117	120	Exportations : volume
Exports: unit value	110	110	99	104	115	116	119	118	125	Exportations : valeur unitaire
Terms of trade	101	103	98	102	103	97	99	94	91	Termes de l'échange
Purchasing power of exports	73	86	103	107	103	107	111	110	110	Pouvoir d'achat des exportations
Israel										**Israël**
Imports: volume	77	88	93	93	92	103	105	106	114	Importations : volume
Imports: unit value	100	97	99	99	104	112	120	127	138	Importations : valeur unitaire
Exports: volume	74	80	96	97	101	116	119	124	136	Exportations : volume
Exports: unit value	99	100	96	96	100	106	114	119	127	Exportations : valeur unitaire
Terms of trade	99	103	98	98	96	95	95	94	92	Termes de l'échange
Purchasing power of exports	73	82	94	95	97	110	113	117	125	Pouvoir d'achat des exportations
Italy										**Italie**
Imports: volume	90	93	101	101	102	108	108	113	115	Importations : volume
Imports: unit value	103	99	98	102	122	138	149	165	185	Importations : valeur unitaire
Exports: volume	94	92	103	101	99	104	104	110	113	Exportations : volume
Exports: unit value	109	107	99	106	126	142	149	158	181	Exportations : valeur unitaire
Terms of trade	107	108	101	103	104	103	100	96	98	Termes de l'échange
Purchasing power of exports	100	99	104	104	103	106	104	105	111	Pouvoir d'achat des exportations
Japan										**Japon**
Imports: volume	82	90	99	100	107	115	118	123	119	Importations : volume
Imports: unit value	90	91	87	86	91	101	112	120	133	Importations : valeur unitaire
Exports: volume	90	91	90	97	102	113	114	123	130	Exportations : volume
Exports: unit value	91	95	94	89	96	104	109	110	115	Exportations : valeur unitaire
Terms of trade	101	105	107	104	105	103	98	92	86	Termes de l'échange
Purchasing power of exports	90	96	97	101	108	116	111	113	112	Pouvoir d'achat des exportations
Jordan										**Jordanie**
Imports: volume	85	84	103	104	109	136	155	154	162	Importations : volume
Imports: unit value	100	97	102	105	115	130	148	162	184	Importations : valeur unitaire
Exports: volume	90	93	123	142	152	190	182	188	173	Exportations : volume
Exports: unit value	107	105	101	102	102	114	131	143	170	Exportations : valeur unitaire
Terms of trade	107	107	99	97	88	87	88	88	92	Termes de l'échange
Purchasing power of exports	97	100	122	137	135	166	161	166	160	Pouvoir d'achat des exportations
Kenya										**Kenya**
Imports: volume	96	87	...	...	...	...	...	...	...	Importations : volume
Imports: unit value	105	98	...	...	...	...	...	...	...	Importations : valeur unitaire
Exports: unit value	125	101	...	...	...	...	...	...	...	Exportations : valeur unitaire
Terms of trade	119	103	...	...	...	...	...	...	...	Termes de l'échange
Korea, Republic of										**Corée, République de**
Imports: volume	65	84	98	110	118	132	140	155	169	Importations : volume
Imports: unit value	88	87	91	88	96	107	117	126	134	Importations : valeur unitaire

Country or area	1998	1999	2001	2002	2003	2004	2005	2006	2007	Pays ou zone
Exports: volume	74	83	101	114	134	163	178	202	223	Exportations : volume
Exports: unit value	103	100	87	83	85	92	93	93	96	Exportations : valeur unitaire
Terms of trade	117	114	96	95	89	85	79	74	72	Termes de l'échange
Purchasing power of exports	86	95	96	108	119	140	141	149	160	Pouvoir d'achat des exportations
Latvia										**Lettonie**
Imports: unit value	102	97	98	106	122	140	150	166	191	Importations : valeur unitaire
Exports: unit value	108	105	99	104	121	145	153	169	209	Exportations : valeur unitaire
Terms of trade	106	108	101	98	99	104	102	102	109	Termes de l'échange
Libyan Arab Jamah.										**Jamah. arabe libyenne**
Imports: volume	156	147	173	214	...	...	...	...	...	Importations : volume
Imports: unit value	96	115	83	48	...	...	...	...	...	Importations : valeur unitaire
Exports: volume	94	108	110	95	...	...	...	...	...	Exportations : volume
Exports: unit value	53	72	87	88	...	...	...	...	...	Exportations : valeur unitaire
Terms of trade	55	63	104	185	...	...	...	...	...	Termes de l'échange
Purchasing power of exports	52	68	115	175	...	...	...	...	...	Pouvoir d'achat des exportations
Lithuania										**Lituanie**
Imports: volume	...	...	120	143	155	182	209	233	229	Importations : volume
Imports: unit value	99	95	97	101	117	127	138	151	174	Importations : valeur unitaire
Exports: volume	...	...	125	145	161	185	214	234	227	Exportations : volume
Exports: unit value	97	94	97	101	120	137	151	160	185	Exportations : valeur unitaire
Terms of trade	98	99	101	100	102	108	109	106	106	Termes de l'échange
Purchasing power of exports	...	...	126	146	164	199	233	247	241	Pouvoir d'achat des exportations
Malaysia										**Malaisie**
Imports: volume	...	...	92	97	...	...	...	...	...	Importations : volume
Imports: unit value	...	...	98	99	...	...	...	...	...	Importations : valeur unitaire
Exports: volume	...	...	96	102	...	...	...	...	...	Exportations : volume
Exports: unit value	...	...	94	93	...	...	...	...	...	Exportations : valeur unitaire
Terms of trade	...	...	96	94	...	...	...	...	...	Termes de l'échange
Purchasing power of exports	...	...	92	96	...	...	...	...	...	Pouvoir d'achat des exportations
Mauritius										**Maurice**
Imports: volume	99	107	98	103	96	100	106	110	115	Importations : volume
Imports: unit value	99	100	97	99	80	90	98	102	111	Importations : valeur unitaire
Exports: volume	95	98	116	121	92	89	96	107	96	Exportations : volume
Exports: unit value	111	106	92	98	84	92	90	89	96	Exportations : valeur unitaire
Terms of trade	112	106	95	98	105	101	92	87	86	Termes de l'échange
Purchasing power of exports	107	103	110	119	96	90	89	93	82	Pouvoir d'achat des exportations
Mexico										**Mexique**
Imports: unit value	98	97	101	100	103	108	114	119	125	Importations : valeur unitaire
Exports: unit value	90	93	98	100	105	117	127	137	144	Exportations : valeur unitaire
Terms of trade	91	96	97	100	102	108	112	115	114	Termes de l'échange
Morocco										**Maroc**
Imports: volume	...	89	98	105	113	127	140	154	176	Importations : volume
Imports: unit value	109	107	97	98	110	121	129	134	152	Importations : valeur unitaire
Exports: volume	...	92	102	107	104	103	107	111	131	Exportations : volume
Exports: unit value	115	110	94	99	116	127	128	135	150	Exportations : valeur unitaire
Terms of trade	105	103	97	101	105	105	99	100	98	Termes de l'échange
Purchasing power of exports	...	95	99	107	110	108	106	112	129	Pouvoir d'achat des exportations
Netherlands										**Pays-Bas**
Imports: volume	89	96	97	95	98	106	115	126	132	Importations : volume
Imports: unit value	108	103	101	101	118	131	133	139	159	Importations : valeur unitaire
Exports: volume	88	92	102	103	106	116	122	132	133	Exportations : volume
Exports: unit value	109	101	100	100	116	127	133	141	169	Exportations : valeur unitaire
Terms of trade	101	98	99	98	99	96	100	102	106	Termes de l'échange
Purchasing power of exports	88	90	100	101	104	112	122	134	141	Pouvoir d'achat des exportations
New Zealand										**Nouvelle-Zélande**
Imports: volume	91	103	102	111	124	142	151	152	165	Importations : volume
Imports: unit value	99	100	94	98	109	118	125	126	136	Importations : valeur unitaire
Exports: volume	92	95	103	109	112	119	118	120	127	Exportations : volume
Exports: unit value	99	99	101	99	111	129	138	138	159	Exportations : valeur unitaire
Terms of trade	99	99	107	102	102	109	111	110	117	Termes de l'échange
Purchasing power of exports	92	93	110	111	115	130	130	131	150	Pouvoir d'achat des exportations

Country or area	1998	1999	2001	2002	2003	2004	2005	2006	2007	Pays ou zone
Norway										**Norvège**
Imports: volume[2]	94	94	101	103	106	118	129	142	155	Importations : volume[2]
Imports: unit value[2]	118	109	98	104	116	127	133	139	159	Importations : valeur unitaire[2]
Exports: volume[2]	93	95	105	107	107	108	108	105	107	Exportations : volume[2]
Exports: unit value[2]	71	78	93	94	104	127	161	194	213	Exportations : valeur unitaire[2]
Terms of trade	61	71	95	91	90	100	122	139	134	Termes de l'échange
Purchasing power of exports	56	68	99	97	97	109	131	147	143	Pouvoir d'achat des exportations
Pakistan										**Pakistan**
Imports: volume	90	101	112	123	123	142	165	153	169	Importations : volume
Imports: unit value	86	93	94	95	109	122	138	151	167	Importations : valeur unitaire
Exports: volume	79	89	102	109	110	103	126	127	124	Exportations : volume
Exports: unit value	118	109	94	90	96	103	103	106	110	Exportations : valeur unitaire
Terms of trade	137	118	100	95	89	85	75	70	66	Termes de l'échange
Purchasing power of exports	109	105	102	104	98	87	95	89	81	Pouvoir d'achat des exportations
Panama										**Panama**
Exports: volume	143	105	...	81	84	83	98	...	...	Exportations : volume
Papua New Guinea										**Papouasie-Nvl-Guinée**
Exports: volume	...	...	94	88	105	99	106	92	94	Exportations : volume
Exports: unit value	80	79	90	85	101	126	156	247	271	Exportations : valeur unitaire
Peru										**Pérou**
Exports: volume	78	88	114	126	122	136	150	144	161	Exportations : volume
Exports: unit value	70	75	84	87	97	100	170	264	231	Exportations : valeur unitaire
Philippines										**Philippines**
Imports: volume	85	95	98	116	118	137	127	...	...	Importations : volume
Imports: unit value[1]	121	118	84	83	82	81	94	...	...	Importations : valeur unitaire[1]
Exports: volume	80	87	89	104	98	110	104	...	...	Exportations : volume
Exports: unit value[1]	105	121	84	77	79	75	84	...	...	Exportations : valeur unitaire[1]
Terms of trade	87	103	100	93	96	93	89	...	...	Termes de l'échange
Purchasing power of exports	70	89	88	97	94	102	93	...	...	Pouvoir d'achat des exportations
Poland										**Pologne**
Imports: volume	87	90	104	111	119	140	148	173	200	Importations : volume
Imports: unit value[1]	111	103	100	101	116	131	141	151	171	Importations : valeur unitaire[1]
Exports: volume	79	80	114	122	143	170	189	220	242	Exportations : volume
Exports: unit value[1]	115	108	102	107	118	139	150	160	186	Exportations : valeur unitaire[1]
Terms of trade	103	105	102	105	102	107	107	107	109	Termes de l'échange
Purchasing power of exports	82	83	116	129	146	182	201	235	263	Pouvoir d'achat des exportations
Portugal										**Portugal**
Imports: volume	...	...	97	94	94	...	...	...	...	Importations : volume
Imports: unit value[1]	110	106	89	91	110	...	...	...	...	Importations : valeur unitaire[1]
Exports: volume	...	...	95	95	97	...	...	...	...	Exportations : volume
Exports: unit value[1]	116	109	93	96	112	...	...	...	...	Exportations : valeur unitaire[1]
Terms of trade	106	103	105	106	102	...	...	...	...	Termes de l'échange
Purchasing power of exports	...	...	99	101	99	...	...	...	...	Pouvoir d'achat des exportations
Republic of Moldova										**République de Moldova**
Imports: volume	...	...	118	139	180	205	248	...	...	Importations : volume
Imports: unit value	...	...	97	92	95	119	124	...	...	Importations : valeur unitaire
Exports: volume	...	...	122	142	170	199	215	...	...	Exportations : volume
Exports: unit value	...	...	93	87	88	107	107	...	...	Exportations : valeur unitaire
Terms of trade	...	...	96	95	93	90	86	...	...	Termes de l'échange
Purchasing power of exports	...	...	117	134	158	178	186	...	...	Pouvoir d'achat des exportations
Romania										**Roumanie**
Imports: volume	...	...	124	143	169	207	244	293	...	Importations : volume
Imports: unit value	117	105	96	96	106	106	112	116	...	Importations : valeur unitaire
Exports: volume	...	...	112	132	144	166	179	191	...	Exportations : volume
Exports: unit value	109	102	98	102	119	125	137	148	...	Exportations : valeur unitaire
Terms of trade	93	97	102	106	112	118	122	127	...	Termes de l'échange
Purchasing power of exports	...	...	114	139	161	195	218	244	...	Pouvoir d'achat des exportations
Russian Federation										**Fédération de Russie**
Imports: volume	...	...	123	136	168	222	288	398	...	Importations : volume
Exports: volume	...	...	99	105	133	180	240	303	...	Exportations : volume

Country or area	1998	1999	2001	2002	2003	2004	2005	2006	2007	Pays ou zone
Serbia										**Serbie**
Imports: volume	...	...	...	...	...	...	...	...	129	Importations : volume
Imports: unit value	...	...	...	...	...	...	...	...	106	Importations : valeur unitaire
Exports: volume	...	...	...	...	...	...	...	...	126	Exportations : volume
Exports: unit value	...	...	...	...	...	...	...	...	110	Exportations : valeur unitaire
Terms of trade	...	...	...	...	...	...	...	...	104	Termes de l'échange
Purchasing power of exports	...	...	...	...	...	...	...	...	131	Pouvoir d'achat des exportations
Seychelles										**Seychelles**
Imports: volume	83	105	...	...	...	...	...	...	...	Importations : volume
Imports: unit value	136	120	...	...	...	...	...	...	...	Importations : valeur unitaire
Exports: volume	51	78	...	...	...	...	...	...	...	Exportations : volume
Exports: unit value	143	114	...	...	...	...	...	...	...	Exportations : valeur unitaire
Terms of trade	105	94	...	...	...	...	...	...	...	Termes de l'échange
Purchasing power of exports	54	73	...	...	...	...	...	...	...	Pouvoir d'achat des exportations
Singapore										**Singapour**
Imports: volume	83	88	89	90	96	117	134	149	158	Importations : volume
Imports: unit value [1]	93	93	97	96	99	104	111	120	124	Importations : valeur unitaire [1]
Exports: volume	82	86	95	100	110	155	173	192	208	Exportations : volume
Exports: unit value [1]	97	96	93	91	90	93	96	103	104	Exportations : valeur unitaire [1]
Terms of trade	104	103	96	94	91	89	87	86	84	Termes de l'échange
Purchasing power of exports	86	89	91	95	106	139	151	165	176	Pouvoir d'achat des exportations
Slovakia										**Slovaquie**
Imports: unit value	...	...	...	106	129	147	157	177	196	Importations : valeur unitaire
Exports: unit value	...	...	...	105	139	174	191	204	221	Exportations : valeur unitaire
Terms of trade	...	...	...	99	108	118	121	116	112	Termes de l'échange
Slovenia										**Slovénie**
Imports: volume	88	96	101	105	111	...	...	...	...	Importations : volume
Imports: unit value	113	104	100	104	124	141	152	164	175	Importations : valeur unitaire
Exports: volume	86	89	105	110	115	...	...	...	...	Exportations : volume
Exports: unit value	119	109	100	106	126	142	149	159	169	Exportations : valeur unitaire
Terms of trade	105	105	100	102	102	101	98	97	96	Termes de l'échange
Purchasing power of exports	90	94	105	112	117	...	...	...	...	Pouvoir d'achat des exportations
South Africa										**Afrique du Sud**
Imports: volume	101	93	100	105	115	131	144	...	...	Importations : volume
Imports: unit value	99	98	94	93	116	136	144	...	...	Importations : valeur unitaire
Exports: volume	90	91	102	102	103	105	112	...	...	Exportations : volume
Exports: unit value	104	100	96	96	123	148	156	...	...	Exportations : valeur unitaire
Terms of trade	105	102	101	104	107	109	109	...	...	Termes de l'échange
Purchasing power of exports	94	92	103	106	109	114	122	...	...	Pouvoir d'achat des exportations
Spain										**Espagne**
Imports: volume	...	92	104	109	117	129	...	...	...	Importations : volume
Imports: unit value [1]	108	102	96	99	116	131	138	143	158	Importations : valeur unitaire [1]
Exports: volume	...	89	104	107	114	120	...	...	...	Exportations : volume
Exports: unit value [1]	115	109	98	102	121	134	140	148	166	Exportations : valeur unitaire [1]
Terms of trade	107	106	101	103	104	102	102	103	105	Termes de l'échange
Purchasing power of exports	...	94	106	111	118	123	...	...	...	Pouvoir d'achat des exportations
Sri Lanka										**Sri Lanka**
Imports: volume	89	90	91	101	111	122	126	135	140	Importations : volume
Imports: unit value	...	...	98	90	...	...	...	...	...	Importations : valeur unitaire
Exports: volume	81	84	92	93	98	106	113	97	126	Exportations : volume
Exports: unit value	110	101	97	91	97	101	104	109	114	Exportations : valeur unitaire
Terms of trade	...	...	98	101	...	...	...	...	...	Termes de l'échange
Purchasing power of exports	...	...	90	94	...	...	...	...	...	Pouvoir d'achat des exportations
Sweden										**Suède**
Imports: volume	86	89	95	94	100	108	116	126	138	Importations : volume
Imports: unit value [1]	104	103	93	99	117	132	139	149	167	Importations : valeur unitaire [1]
Exports: volume	85	90	98	101	106	117	122	133	136	Exportations : volume
Exports: unit value [1]	112	106	90	94	111	121	124	131	149	Exportations : valeur unitaire [1]
Terms of trade	107	104	97	95	95	92	90	88	89	Termes de l'échange
Purchasing power of exports	91	93	96	96	101	108	109	117	121	Pouvoir d'achat des exportations

Country or area	1998	1999	2001	2002	2003	2004	2005	2006	2007	Pays ou zone
Switzerland										**Suisse**
Imports: volume	87	93	101	99	100	104	106	117	125	Importations : volume
Imports: unit value	112	107	100	105	121	135	143	149	161	Importations : valeur unitaire
Exports: volume	91	93	103	105	105	111	115	132	139	Exportations : volume
Exports: unit value	110	109	101	107	124	137	141	143	158	Exportations : valeur unitaire
Terms of trade	99	103	101	102	102	102	99	96	98	Termes de l'échange
Purchasing power of exports	90	95	104	106	107	113	114	127	136	Pouvoir d'achat des exportations
Thailand										**Thaïlande**
Imports: volume	67	82	89	100	112	137	162	164	171	Importations : volume
Imports: unit value	98	95	109	102	107	110	117	124	131	Importations : valeur unitaire
Exports: volume	73	82	92	101	109	119	124	135	133	Exportations : volume
Exports: unit value	107	102	102	97	105	118	130	140	126	Exportations : valeur unitaire
Terms of trade	109	107	93	95	99	108	111	112	96	Termes de l'échange
Purchasing power of exports	80	88	85	96	108	128	138	152	128	Pouvoir d'achat des exportations
Turkey										**Turquie**
Imports: volume	76	75	75	91	113	137	153	166	187	Importations : volume
Imports: unit value	101	96	100	98	111	129	138	150	164	Importations : valeur unitaire
Exports: volume	87	90	122	142	169	192	212	238	265	Exportations : volume
Exports: unit value	112	104	97	96	108	126	133	138	155	Exportations : valeur unitaire
Terms of trade	111	109	98	97	97	98	97	92	95	Termes de l'échange
Purchasing power of exports	96	98	119	137	164	188	205	220	251	Pouvoir d'achat des exportations
United Kingdom										**Royaume-Uni**
Imports: volume	86	91	105	110	112	120	128	143	138	Importations : volume
Imports: unit value [1]	106	104	94	96	104	116	120	126	138	Importations : valeur unitaire [1]
Exports: volume	86	89	102	101	101	102	111	123	113	Exportations : volume
Exports: unit value [1]	111	106	94	98	108	121	126	131	145	Exportations : valeur unitaire [1]
Terms of trade	104	102	99	102	104	105	105	105	105	Termes de l'échange
Purchasing power of exports	90	91	101	103	105	107	117	129	118	Pouvoir d'achat des exportations
United States										**Etats-Unis**
Imports: volume	81	90	97	101	107	118	125	132	133	Importations : volume
Imports: unit value [1]	93	94	96	94	97	102	110	115	120	Importations : valeur unitaire [1]
Exports: volume [3]	88	90	94	90	93	101	109	120	128	Exportations : volume [3]
Exports: unit value [1,3]	100	98	99	98	100	104	107	111	116	Exportations : valeur unitaire [1,3]
Terms of trade	107	105	103	104	103	101	97	96	97	Termes de l'échange
Purchasing power of exports	94	95	97	94	96	102	105	115	124	Pouvoir d'achat des exportations
Uruguay										**Uruguay**
Imports: unit value	101	96	94	87	...	...	...	...	...	Importations : valeur unitaire
Exports: unit value	118	101	98	93	...	...	...	...	...	Exportations : valeur unitaire
Terms of trade	117	106	104	106	...	...	...	...	...	Termes de l'échange
Venezuela (Bolivarian Rep. of) [1]										**Venezuela (Rép. boliv. du) [1]**
Imports: unit value	102	102	105	105	112	123	126	132	151	Importations : valeur unitaire

Source:
United Nations Statistics Division, New York, trade statistics database, last accessed January 2009.

Source:
Organisation des Nations Unies, Division de statistique, New York, la base de données pour les statistiques du commerce extérieur, dernier accès janvier 2009.

1	Price indices.	1	Les indices des prix.
2	Index numbers exclude ships.	2	Les indices excluent les navires.
3	Excluding military goods.	3	Non compris les biens militaires.

64

Manufactured goods exports
Unit value and volume indices: 2000 = 100; value: thousand million US dollars

Exportations des produits manufacturés
Indices de valeur unitaire et de volume: 2000 = 100; valeur: milliards de dollars des E.-U.

Region, country or area Région, pays ou zone	1998	1999	2000	2001	2002	2003	2004	2005	2006	2007
Total Total										
Unit value indices, US $ [1]										
Indices de valeur unitaire, $ des E.-U. [1]	108	103	100	98	98	104	110	111	114	...
Unit value indices, SDRs										
Indices de valeur unitaire, DTS	106	99	100	102	99	99	97	99	102	...
Volume indices										
Indices de volume	82	88	100	100	103	111	128	139	153	...
Value, thousand million US $										
Valeur, milliards de $ des E.-U.	4 094.8	4 194.4	4 620.8	4 548.3	4 648.6	5 356.1	6 495.7	7 135.9	8 104.2	...
Developed economies Economies développées										
Unit value indices, US $										
Indices de valeur unitaire, $ des E.-U.	110	105	100	98	99	108	117	120	123	133
Unit value indices, SDRs										
Indices de valeur unitaire, DTS	107	101	100	102	100	102	103	107	110	114
Volume indices										
Indices de volume	84	89	100	102	101	105	115	120	130	136
Value, thousand million US $										
Valeur, milliards de $ des E.-U.	2 983.8	3 021.0	3 209.4	3 215.6	3 196.4	3 653.2	4 312.7	4 590.7	5 128.2	5 795.9
Americas Amériques										
Unit value indices, US $										
Indices de valeur unitaire, $ des E.-U.	100	99	100	99	100	103	106	108	111	115
Volume indices										
Indices de volume	87	91	100	101	88	88	97	104	113	119
Value, thousand million US $										
Valeur, milliards de $ des E.-U.	675.6	703.7	780.3	781.7	685.3	704.0	803.2	872.2	983.2	1 070.3
Canada Canada										
Unit value indices, US $										
Indices de valeur unitaire, $ des E.-U.	101	99	100	98	96	103	112	119	128	135
Unit value indices, national currency Indices de val. unitaire, monnaie nationale	101	99	100	102	102	98	98	97	98	97
Volume indices Indices de volume	80	90	100	94	94	92	97	100	99	100
Value, thousand million US $ Valeur, milliards de $ des E.-U.	148.7	165.6	184.0	169.1	166.6	173.6	200.2	219.2	234.6	247.8
United States Etats-Unis										
Unit value indices, US $ [2] Indices de valeur unitaire, $ des E.-U. [2]	100	99	100	100	102	103	104	104	107	110
Unit value indices, national currency [2] Indices de val. unitaire, monnaie nationale [2]	100	99	100	100	102	103	104	104	107	110
Volume indices Indices de volume	89	91	100	103	86	87	97	105	118	126
Value, thousand million US $ Valeur, milliards de $ des E.-U.	527.0	538.1	596.3	612.6	518.8	530.4	603.0	653.1	748.6	822.5
Europe Europe										
Unit value indices, US $										
Indices de valeur unitaire, $ des E.-U.	118	110	100	99	100	112	122	125	130	142
Volume indices										
Indices de volume	84	89	100	106	108	113	124	128	139	145
Value, thousand million US $										
Valeur, milliards de $ des E.-U.	1 884.5	1 856.3	1 903.5	1 986.4	2 051.3	2 426.2	2 877.4	3 055.3	3 426.3	3 930.0
Austria Autriche										
Unit value indices, US $										
Indices de valeur unitaire, $ des E.-U.	141	118	100	94	100	...	...	...	...	...
Unit value indices, national currency Indices de val. unitaire, monnaie nationale	117	102	100	98	98	...	...	...	...	...
Volume indices Indices de volume	74	86	100	124	118	...	...	...	...	...

64

Manufactured goods exports *(continued)*
Unit value and volume indices: 2000 = 100; value: thousand million US dollars

Exportations des produits manufacturés *(suite)*
Indices de valeur unitaire et de volume: 2000 = 100; valeur: milliards de dollars des E.-U.

Region, country or area Région, pays ou zone	1998	1999	2000	2001	2002	2003	2004	2005	2006	2007
Value, thousand million US $ Valeur, milliards de $ des E.-U.	51.7	50.4	49.8	58.3	59.0	76.8	96.7	100.2	114.0	133.6
Belgium Belgique										
Unit value indices, US $ Indices de valeur unitaire, $ des E.-U.	114	108	100	99	106	125	141	148	156	178
Unit value indices, national currency Indices de val. unitaire, monnaie nationale	95	94	100	102	103	103	105	110	115	120
Volume indices Indices de volume	87	92	100	100	100	100	106	107	107	109
Value, thousand million US $ Valeur, milliards de $ des E.-U.	132.2	131.8	132.5	131.6	139.5	166.3	198.7	209.9	222.3	258.2
Denmark Danemark										
Unit value indices, US $ Indices de valeur unitaire, $ des E.-U.	116	112	100	100	103	122	136	138	141	145
Unit value indices, national currency Indices de val. unitaire, monnaie nationale	96	97	100	102	100	101	101	102	103	97
Volume indices Indices de volume	84	95	100	105	114	119	119	129	137	149
Value, thousand million US $ Valeur, milliards de $ des E.-U.	31.2	33.8	31.8	33.5	37.2	46.4	51.4	56.6	61.1	68.8
Finland Finlande										
Unit value indices, US $ Indices de valeur unitaire, $ des E.-U.	107	104	100	95	100	117	120	131	141	166
Unit value indices, national currency Indices de val. unitaire, monnaie nationale	89	90	100	98	98	96	89	97	104	112
Volume indices Indices de volume	89	89	100	103	98	98	109	108	116	116
Value, thousand million US $ Valeur, milliards de $ des E.-U.	38.0	36.7	39.7	38.9	38.9	45.4	51.8	56.1	65.1	76.8
France France										
Unit value indices, US $ Indices de valeur unitaire, $ des E.-U.	120	113	100	98	84	101	111	111	109	118
Unit value indices, national currency Indices de val. unitaire, monnaie nationale	100	98	100	101	83	83	82	82	81	80
Volume indices Indices de volume	82	86	100	119	120	118	127	132	148	152
Value, thousand million US $ Valeur, milliards de $ des E.-U.	244.3	242.5	249.2	290.2	251.9	298.5	351.8	365.3	404.9	449.2
Germany Allemagne										
Unit value indices, US $ Indices de valeur unitaire, $ des E.-U.	124	111	100	99	104	118	128	128	132	143
Unit value indices, national currency Indices de val. unitaire, monnaie nationale	103	97	100	102	102	96	95	95	97	97
Volume indices Indices de volume	80	86	100	105	107	114	128	138	152	166
Value, thousand million US $ Valeur, milliards de $ des E.-U.	477.9	461.1	481.0	499.2	534.8	644.3	790.3	849.0	970.0	1 143.7
Greece Grèce										
Unit value indices, US $ Indices de valeur unitaire, $ des E.-U.	113	107	100	...	...	...	...	...	...	...
Unit value indices, national currency Indices de val. unitaire, monnaie nationale	91	90	100	...	...	...	...	...	...	...
Volume indices Indices de volume	93	86	100	...	...	...	...	...	...	...
Value, thousand million US $ Valeur, milliards de $ des E.-U.	6.3	5.6	6.1	6.0	5.7	8.7	8.5	10.7	12.0	14.0

64

Manufactured goods exports *(continued)*
Unit value and volume indices: 2000 = 100; value: thousand million US dollars

Exportations des produits manufacturés *(suite)*
Indices de valeur unitaire et de volume: 2000 = 100; valeur: milliards de dollars des E.-U.

Region, country or area Région, pays ou zone	1998	1999	2000	2001	2002	2003	2004	2005	2006	2007
Iceland Islande										
Unit value indices, US $ [3]										
Indices de valeur unitaire, $ des E.-U. [3]	100	...	100	...	...	...	...	...	...	...
Volume indices										
Indices de volume	72	...	100	...	...	...	...	...	...	...
Value, thousand million US $										
Valeur, milliards de $ des E.-U.	0.4	0.6	0.6	0.7	0.7	0.8	1.0	1.1	1.3	1.9
Ireland Irlande										
Unit value indices, US $ [3]										
Indices de valeur unitaire, $ des E.-U. [3]	96	...	100	...	...	...	...	...	...	...
Volume indices										
Indices de volume	86	...	100	...	...	...	...	...	...	...
Value, thousand million US $										
Valeur, milliards de $ des E.-U.	53.6	59.6	65.6	75.1	77.7	79.4	88.7	94.0	96.5	101.9
Italy Italie										
Unit value indices, US $ [3]										
Indices de valeur unitaire, $ des E.-U. [3]	119	113	100	100	...	104	...	118	125	136
Volume indices										
Indices de volume	87	86	100	105	...	119	...	128	135	148
Value, thousand million US $										
Valeur, milliards de $ des E.-U.	219.7	206.7	212.6	223.2	226.1	262.5	309.7	320.2	357.9	426.3
Netherlands Pays-Bas										
Unit value indices, US $ [3]										
Indices de valeur unitaire, $ des E.-U. [3]	115	109	100	104	104	120	130	139	144	175
Unit value indices, national currency										
Indices de val. unitaire, monnaie nationale	95	95	100	107	102	98	97	103	106	118
Volume indices										
Indices de volume	83	88	100	115	117	122	135	136	147	148
Value, thousand million US $										
Valeur, milliards de $ des E.-U.	121.7	122.2	127.5	152.8	154.6	186.1	224.7	240.4	271.0	331.4
Norway Norvège										
Unit value indices, US $										
Indices de valeur unitaire, $ des E.-U.	112	106	100	97	100	110	126	131	145	169
Unit value indices, national currency										
Indices de val. unitaire, monnaie nationale	96	94	100	99	91	89	96	96	106	112
Volume indices										
Indices de volume	95	96	100	92	110	110	112	119	129	141
Value, thousand million US $										
Valeur, milliards de $ des E.-U.	17.7	16.8	16.6	14.8	18.3	20.3	23.5	25.9	31.1	39.5
Portugal Portugal										
Unit value indices, US $ [3]										
Indices de valeur unitaire, $ des E.-U. [3]	115	110	100	99	...	...	...	...	...	...
Volume indices										
Indices de volume	88	93	100	103	...	...	...	...	...	...
Value, thousand million US $										
Valeur, milliards de $ des E.-U.	21.1	21.3	21.0	21.4	22.4	27.5	30.5	28.8	32.1	32.9
Spain Espagne										
Unit value indices, US $ [3]										
Indices de valeur unitaire, $ des E.-U. [3]	115	...	100	...	...	...	...	...	...	...
Volume indices										
Indices de volume	84	...	100	...	...	...	...	...	...	...
Value, thousand million US $										
Valeur, milliards de $ des E.-U.	86.3	88.7	89.4	91.4	99.0	124.0	142.8	150.1	166.8	196.8
Sweden Suède										
Unit value indices, US $										
Indices de valeur unitaire, $ des E.-U.	112	106	100	...	...	...	...	...	...	...
Unit value indices, national currency										
Indices de val. unitaire, monnaie nationale	97	96	100	...	...	...	...	...	...	...

64

Manufactured goods exports *(continued)*
Unit value and volume indices: 2000 = 100; value: thousand million US dollars

Exportations des produits manufacturés *(suite)*
Indices de valeur unitaire et de volume: 2000 = 100; valeur: milliards de dollars des E.-U.

Region, country or area Région, pays ou zone	1998	1999	2000	2001	2002	2003	2004	2005	2006	2007
Volume indices Indices de volume	91	100	100	...	...	...	...	...	...	...
Value, thousand million US $ Valeur, milliards de $ des E.-U.	68.7	71.1	67.2	58.7	66.9	82.4	101.0	111.0	124.1	143.1
Switzerland Suisse										
Unit value indices, US $ Indices de valeur unitaire, $ des E.-U.	111	109	100	104	109	...	...	...	...	...
Volume indices Indices de volume	87	94	100	97	99	...	...	...	...	...
Value, thousand million US $ Valeur, milliards de $ des E.-U.	75.7	80.0	78.2	78.8	84.5	96.8	113.7	123.3	138.2	160.6
United Kingdom Royaume-Uni										
Unit value indices, US $ Indices de valeur unitaire, $ des E.-U.	114	108	100	95	98	108	120	120	123	133
Unit value indices, national currency Indices de val. unitaire, monnaie nationale	104	101	100	99	99	100	99	100	101	101
Volume indices Indices de volume	89	90	100	96	102	103	104	111	124	113
Value, thousand million US $ Valeur, milliards de $ des E.-U.	236.4	225.6	232.5	210.2	232.6	258.1	290.2	310.5	355.4	348.4
Other developed economies Autres économies développées										
Unit value indices, US $ Indices de valeur unitaire, $ des E.-U.	**99**	**98**	**100**	**93**	**91**	**97**	**107**	**113**	**114**	**119**
Volume indices Indices de volume	**82**	**90**	**100**	**91**	**96**	**103**	**112**	**112**	**120**	**127**
Value, thousand million US $ Valeur, milliards de $ des E.-U.	**423.7**	**461.0**	**525.6**	**447.5**	**459.8**	**523.1**	**632.1**	**663.2**	**718.6**	**795.7**
Australia Australie										
Unit value indices, US $ Indices de valeur unitaire, $ des E.-U.	98	97	100	93	92	101	133	151	203	245
Unit value indices, national currency Indices de val. unitaire, monnaie nationale	90	87	100	104	97	89	104	114	156	169
Volume indices Indices de volume	83	91	100	99	104	103	88	88	73	73
Value, thousand million US $ Valeur, milliards de $ des E.-U.	17.3	18.7	21.2	19.5	20.2	22.0	25.0	28.2	31.6	38.1
Israel Israël										
Unit value indices, US $ Indices de valeur unitair , $ des E.-U.	77	83	100	98	95	95	99	109	118	124
Volume indices Indices de volume	95	98	100	95	98	105	124	125	123	134
Value, thousand million US $ Valeur, milliards de $ des E.-U.	21.7	24.2	29.7	27.6	27.5	29.5	36.5	40.5	43.3	49.4
Japan Japon										
Unit value indices, US $ Indices de valeur unitaire, $ des E.-U.	100	98	100	94	92	97	107	112	112	117
Unit value indices, national currency Indices de val. unitaire, monnaie nationale	121	104	100	110	106	105	107	114	121	127
Volume indices Indices de volume	81	89	100	89	94	100	110	109	117	123
Value, thousand million US $ Valeur, milliards de $ des E.-U.	369.6	397.5	454.8	378.0	391.8	443.3	534.1	553.7	597.3	654.1
New Zealand Nouvelle-Zélande										
Unit value indices, US $ Indices de valeur unitaire, $ des E.-U.	101	96	100	98	99	112	125	136	140	155
Unit value indices, national currency Indices de val. unitaire, monnaie nationale	85	83	100	105	97	88	86	88	98	96

Manufactured goods exports *(continued)*
Unit value and volume indices: 2000 = 100; value: thousand million US dollars

Exportations des produits manufacturés *(suite)*
Indices de valeur unitaire et de volume: 2000 = 100; valeur: milliards de dollars des E.-U.

Region, country or area Région, pays ou zone	1998	1999	2000	2001	2002	2003	2004	2005	2006	2007
Volume indices Indices de volume	92	99	100	108	105	109	116	115	117	119
Value, thousand million US $ Valeur, milliards de $ des E.-U.	4.3	4.5	4.7	5.0	4.9	5.7	6.8	7.3	7.7	8.6
South Africa Afrique du Sud										
Value, thousand million US $ Valeur, milliards de $ des E.-U.	10.8	16.1	15.2	17.5	15.3	22.5	29.7	33.5	38.7	45.5
Developing regions Régions en développement										
Unit value indices, US $										
Indices de valeur unitaire, $ des E.-U.	**104**	**97**	**100**	**98**	**96**	**97**	**99**	**98**	**102**	...
Unit value indices, SDRs										
Indices de valeur unitaire, DTS	**101**	**93**	**100**	**102**	**98**	**92**	**87**	**87**	**91**	...
Volume indices										
Indices de volume	**76**	**86**	**100**	**96**	**107**	**124**	**157**	**184**	**208**	...
Value, thousand million US $										
Valeur, milliards de $ des E.-U.	**1 111.0**	**1 173.3**	**1 411.4**	**1 332.7**	**1 452.2**	**1 702.8**	**2 183.0**	**2 545.1**	**2 976.0**	...
China, Hong Kong SAR Chine, Hong Kong RAS										
Unit value indices, US $ Indices de valeur unitaire, $ des E.-U.	104	102	100	95	93	93	94	96	93	94
Unit value indices, national currency Indices de val. unitaire, monnaie nationale	103	101	100	96	93	93	94	96	93	94
Volume indices Indices de volume	100	93	100	88	93	70	71	75	77	60
Value, thousand million US $ Valeur, milliards de $ des E.-U.	23.3	21.2	22.4	18.9	19.4	14.7	15.1	16.3	16.0	12.5
India Inde										
Unit value indices, US $ Indices de valeur unitaire, $ des E.-U.	107	121	100	92	99	...	...	...	...	...
Unit value indices, national currency Indices de val. unitaire, monnaie nationale	98	116	100	95	107	...	...	...	...	...
Volume indices Indices de volume	67	69	100	105	115	...	...	...	...	...
Value, thousand million US $ Valeur, milliards de $ des E.-U.	25.3	29.3	35.0	33.5	39.9	48.8	59.1	74.1	86.1	96.9
Korea, Republic of Corée, République de										
Unit value indices, US $ Indices de valeur unitaire, $ des E.-U.	101	96	100	92	82	83	92	96	101	106
Unit value indices, national currency Indices de val. unitaire, monnaie nationale	125	101	100	105	91	87	93	87	85	87
Volume indices Indices de volume	73	87	100	95	97	118	145	175	188	203
Value, thousand million US $ Valeur, milliards de $ des E.-U.	116.3	130.6	156.9	137.3	125.4	153.0	207.9	262.8	297.5	338.6
Pakistan Pakistan										
Unit value indices, US $ Indices de valeur unitaire, $ des E.-U.	115	106	100	100	96	101	108	106	108	108
Unit value indices, national currency Indices de val. unitaire, monnaie nationale	99	100	100	117	108	111	119	119	123	124
Volume indices Indices de volume	79	90	100	101	114	140	137	155	160	163
Value, thousand million US $ Valeur, milliards de $ des E.-U.	7.1	7.4	7.7	7.8	8.4	10.9	11.4	12.7	13.4	13.6
Singapore Singapour										
Unit value indices, US $ Indices de valeur unitaire, $ des E.-U.	105	101	100	98	100	99	98	78	81	109
Unit value indices, national currency Indices de val. unitaire, monnaie nationale	...	...	...	...	...	...	...	76	75	95

Manufactured goods exports *(continued)*
Unit value and volume indices: 2000 = 100; value: thousand million US dollars

64

Exportations des produits manufacturés *(suite)*
Indices de valeur unitaire et de volume: 2000 = 100; valeur: milliards de dollars des E.-U.

Region, country or area Région, pays ou zone	1998	1999	2000	2001	2002	2003	2004	2005	2006	2007
Volume indices Indices de volume	75	82	100	89	90	104	129	188	225	180
Value, thousand million US $ Valeur, milliards de $ des E.-U.	94.2	99.7	119.3	103.7	106.7	122.8	151.7	175.7	217.4	233.8
Turkey Turquie										
Unit value indices, US $[4] Indices de valeur unitaire, $ des E.-U. [4]	109	105	100	99	96	108	124	130	127	137
Volume indices Indices de volume	83	88	100	114	138	162	189	204	240	279
Value, thousand million US $ Valeur, milliards de $ des E.-U.	21.0	21.2	23.1	26.1	30.8	40.3	54.2	61.1	70.9	88.7

Source:
United Nations Statistics Division, New York, trade statistics database, last accessed January 2009.

Source:
Organisation des Nations Unies, Division de statistique, New York, la base de données pour les statistiques du commerce extérieur, dernier accès janvier 2009.

1   Excluding trade of the countries of Eastern Europe and the former USSR.
2   Derived from price indices; national unit value index is discontinued.
3   Calculated by the United Nations Statistics Division.
4   Industrial products.

1   Non compris le commerce des pays de l'Europe de l'Est et l'ex-URSS.
2   Calculés à partir des indices des prix; l'indice de la valeur unitaire nationale est discontinué.
3   Calculés par la Division de statistique des Nations Unies.
4   Produits industriels.

Technical notes: tables 62-64

Current data (annual, monthly and/or quarterly) for most of the series are published regularly by the Statistics Division in the United Nations *Monthly Bulletin of Statistics*. More detailed descriptions of the tables and notes on methodology appear in the *International Trade Statistics Yearbook*.

Data are obtained from data supplied by the governments for dissemination in United Nations publications, from national published sources and from data published by other international organisations.

Statistical Territory

The statistics reported by each country refer to its statistical territory which may coincide with its economic territory or with some part of it.

Systems of trade

There are two trade systems in common use by which international merchandise trade statistics are compiled - the general trade system and the special trade system:

(a) The general trade system is in use when the statistical territory of a country coincides with its economic territory.

(b) The special trade system (strict definition) is in use when the statistical territory comprises only the free circulation area, that is, the part within which goods may be disposed of without customs restriction. A "relaxed" definition of the special trade system is in use when (i) goods that enter a country for or leave it after inward processing and (ii) goods that enter or leave an industrial free zone are also recorded and included in international merchandise trade statistics.

Valuation

Goods are, in general, valued based on the transaction value. It is recommended that the statistical value of imported goods be a CIF-type value and the statistical value of exported goods an FOB-type value. FOB-type values include the transaction value of the goods and the value of services performed to deliver goods to the border of the exporting country. CIF-type values include the transaction value of the goods, the value of services performed to deliver goods to the border of the exporting country and the value of the services performed to deliver the goods from the border of the exporting country to the border of the importing country.

Currency conversion

Conversion of values from national currencies into United States dollars is done by means of external trade conversion factors which are generally weighted averages of exchange rates, the weight being the corresponding monthly value of imports or exports.

Notes techniques : tableaux 62 à 64

La Division de statistique des Nations Unies publie régulièrement dans le *Bulletin mensuel de statistique* des données courantes (annuelles, mensuelles et/ou trimestrielles) pour la plupart des séries de ces tableaux. Des descriptions plus détaillées des tableaux et des notes méthodologiques figurent dans l'*Annuaire statistique du Commerce international*.

Les données proviennent de publications nationales, des informations fournies par les gouvernements pour les publications des Nations Unies ainsi que des publications d'autres organisations internationales.

Territoire statistique

Les statistiques fournies par chaque pays se rapportent au territoire statistique. Celui-ci peut coïncider avec le territoire économique en totalité ou en partie.

Systèmes de commerce

Il existe deux systèmes de commerce qui servent couramment pour les statistiques du commerce international de marchandises - le système de commerce général et le système de commerce spécial:

(a) Le système de commerce général est utilisé lorsque le territoire statistique d'un pays coïncide avec son territoire économique.

(b) Le système de commerce spécial (définition stricte) est appliqué lorsque le territoire statistique ne comprend que la zone de libre circulation, c'est-à-dire la zone à l'intérieur de laquelle les biens peuvent être écoulés librement sans restriction douanière. Une définition "assouplie" du système de commerce spécial est utilisée lorsque (i) les biens qui entrent dans un pays en vue de ou le quittent après un perfectionnement actif et (ii) les biens qui entrent ou quittent une zone franche industrielle sont également enregistrés et inclus dans les statistiques du commerce international de marchandises.

Evaluation

En général, les marchandises sont évaluées à la valeur de la transaction. Il est recommandé d'adopter une valeur de type CIF pour la valeur statistique des biens importés et une valeur de type FOB pour la valeur statistique des biens exportés. Les valeurs FOB comprennent la valeur transactionnelle des biens et la valeur des services fournis pour acheminer les biens jusqu'à la frontière du pays exportateur. Les valeurs CIF comprennent la valeur transactionnelle des biens, la valeur des services fournis pour acheminer les biens jusqu'à la frontière du pays exportateur et la valeur des services fournis pour acheminer les biens de la frontière du pays exportateur jusqu'à la frontière du pays importateur.

Coverage

The statistics relate to merchandise trade. It is recommended that international merchandise trade statistics record all goods which add to or subtract from the stock of material resources of a country by entering (imports) or leaving (exports) its economic territory. Goods simply being transported through a country (goods in transit) or temporarily admitted or withdrawn (except for goods for inward or outward processing) do not add to or subtract from the stock of material resources of a country and are not included in the international merchandise trade statistics. For details and a list of inclusions and exclusions see *International Merchandise Trade Statistics, Concepts and Definitions, Revision 2*.

Commodity classification

The commodity classification of trade is in accordance with the United Nations *Standard International Trade Classification* (SITC).

World and regional totals

The regional, economic and world totals have been adjusted: (a) to include estimates for countries or areas for which full data are not available; (b) to include countries or areas not listed separately; and (c) where possible, to eliminate incomparabilities owing to geographical changes, by adjusting the figures for periods before the change to be comparable to those for periods after the change.

Volume and unit value index numbers

These index numbers show the changes in the volume of imports or exports (volume index) and the average price of imports or exports (unit value or price index).

Description of tables

Table 62: The regional totals for imports and exports have been adjusted to exclude the re-exports of countries or areas comprising each region. Estimates for certain countries or areas not shown separately as well as for those shown separately but for which no data are yet available are included in the regional and world totals.

Export and import values in terms of U.S. dollars are obtained from data published by the International Monetary Fund (IMF) in the publication *International Financial Statistics*, from the replies to the *Monthly Bulletin of Statistics* questionnaires and from national sources.

Table 63: These index numbers show the changes in the volume (quantum index) and the average price (unit value or price index) of total imports and exports.

The indices are obtained from data published by the International Monetary Fund (IMF) in the publication *International Financial Statistics*, from the replies

Conversion des monnaies

La conversion en dollars des Etats-Unis de valeurs exprimées en monnaie nationale se fait par application de coefficients de conversion du commerce extérieur, qui sont généralement les moyennes pondérées des taux de change, le poids étant la valeur mensuelle correspondante des importations ou des exportations.

Couverture

Les statistiques se rapportent au commerce des marchandises. Il est recommandé d'enregistrer dans les statistiques du commerce international de marchandises tous les biens dont l'entrée (importations) ou la sortie (exportations) du territoire économique fait augmenter ou diminuer le stock des ressources matérielles du territoire économique du pays considéré. Les biens simplement transportés à travers le pays (biens en transit) ou admis ou expédiés temporairement (à l'exception des biens destinés au perfectionnement actif ou passif) ne font ni augmenter ni diminuer le stock de ressources matérielles d'un pays et ne sont donc pas à inclure dans les statistiques du commerce international de marchandises. Pour plus de détails et une liste des inclusions et exclusions, voir *Statistiques du commerce international des marchandises : concepts et définitions, révision 2*.

Classification par marchandise

La classification par marchandise du commerce extérieur est celle adoptée dans la *Classification Type pour le Commerce International* des Nations Unies (CTCI).

Totaux mondiaux et régionaux

Les totaux économiques, régionaux et mondiaux ont été ajustés de manière: (a) à inclure les estimations pour les pays ou régions pour lesquels on ne disposait pas de données complètes; (b) à inclure les pays ou régions non indiqués séparément ; et (c) à éliminer, dans la mesure du possible, les données non comparables par suite de changements géographiques, en ajustant les chiffres correspondant aux périodes avant le changement de manière à les rendre comparables à ceux des périodes après le changement.

Indices de volume et de valeur unitaire

Ces indices indiquent les variations du volume des importations ou des exportations (indice de volume) et du prix moyen des importations ou des exportations (indice de valeur unitaire ou de prix).

Description des tableaux

Tableau 62: Les totaux régionaux des importations et des exportations ont été ajustés afin d'exclure les réexportations des pays ou zones que comprend une région donnée. Les totaux régionaux et mondiaux comprennent des estimations pour certains pays ou zones ne figurant

to the *Monthly Bulletin of Statistics* questionnaires and from national sources.

Unit value indices obtained from national indices are rebased, where necessary, so that 2000=100. Indices in national currency are converted into US dollars using conversion factors obtained by dividing the weighted average exchange rate of a given currency in the current period by the weighted average exchange rate in the base period. The terms of trade figures are calculated by dividing export unit value indices by the corresponding import unit value indices. The product of the terms of trade and the volume index of exports is called the index of the purchasing power of exports. The footnotes to countries appearing in table 62 also apply to the index numbers in this table.

Table 64: Manufactured goods are defined here to comprise sections 5 through 8 of the Standard International Trade Classification (SITC). These sections are: chemicals and related products, manufactured goods classified chiefly by material, machinery and transport equipment and miscellaneous manufactured articles.

The unit value indices are obtained from national sources including replies to the *Monthly Bulletin of Statistics* questionnaires, except those of a few countries which the United Nations Statistics Division compiles using their quantity and value figures. For countries that do not compile indices for manufactured goods exports conforming to the above definition, sub-indices are aggregated to approximate an index of SITC sections 5-8.

Unit value indices obtained from national indices are rebased, where necessary, so that 2000=100. Indices in national currency are converted into US dollars using conversion factors obtained by dividing the weighted average exchange rate of a given currency in the current period by the weighted average exchange rate in the base period. All aggregate unit value indices are current period weighted.

The indices in Special Drawing Rights (SDRs) are calculated by multiplying the equivalent aggregate indices in United States dollars by conversion factors obtained by dividing the SDR/US$ exchange rate in the current period by the rate in the base period.

The volume indices are derived from the value data and the unit value indices. All aggregate volume indices are base period weighted.

pas séparément mais pour lesquels les données ne sont pas encore disponibles.

Les valeurs en dollars des E.-U. des exportations et des importations ont été obtenues à partir des données publiées par le Fonds Monétaire International dans *Statistiques Financières Internationales,* des réponses aux questionnaires du *Bulletin Mensuel de Statistique* et des sources nationales.

Tableau 63: Ces indices indiquent les variations du volume (indice de quantum) et du prix moyen (indice de valeur unitaire ou de prix) des importations et des exportations totales.

Les indices sont obtenus à partir des données publiées par le Fonds Monétaire International dans *Statistiques Financières Internationales,* des réponses aux questionnaires du *Bulletin Mensuel de Statistique* et des sources nationales.

Les indices de valeur unitaire obtenus à partir des indices nationaux sont ajustés sur la base 2000=100. On convertit les indices en monnaie nationale en indices en dollars des Etats-Unis en utilisant des facteurs de conversion obtenus en divisant la moyenne pondérée des taux de change d'une monnaie donnée pendant la période courante par la moyenne pondérée des taux de change de la période de base. Les chiffres relatifs aux termes de l'échange se calculent en divisant les indices de valeur unitaire des exportations par les indices correspondants de valeur unitaire des importations. Le produit de la valeur des termes de l'échange et de l'indice du volume des exportations est appelé indice du pouvoir d'achat des exportations. Les notes figurant au bas du tableau 62 concernant certains pays s'appliquent également aux indices du présent tableau.

Tableau 64: Les produits manufacturés se définissent comme correspondant aux sections 5 à 8 de la Classification Type pour le Commerce International (CTCI). Ces sections sont: produits chimiques et produits liés connexes, biens manufacturés classés principalement par matière première, machines et équipements de transport et articles divers manufacturés.

Les indices de valeur unitaire sont obtenus de sources nationales y compris les réponses aux questionnaires du *Bulletin Mensuel de Statistique*, à l'exception de ceux de certains pays que la Division de statistique des Nations Unies compile en utilisant les chiffres de ces pays relatifs aux quantités et aux valeurs. Pour les pays qui n'établissent pas d'indices conformes à la définition ci-dessus pour leurs exportations de produits manufacturés, on fait la synthèse de sous-indices de manière à établir un indice proche de celui des sections 5 à 8 de la CTCI.

Le cas échéant, les indices de valeur unitaire obtenus à partir des indices nationaux sont ajustés sur la base

2000=100. On convertit les indices en monnaie nationale en indices en dollars des Etats-Unis en utilisant des facteurs de conversion obtenus en divisant la moyenne pondérée des taux de change d'une monnaie donnée pendant la période courante par la moyenne pondérée des taux de change de la période de base. Tous les indices globaux de valeur unitaire sont pondérés pour la période courante.

On calcule les indices en Droits de Tirages Spéciaux (DTS) en multipliant les indices globaux équivalents en dollars des Etats-Unis par les facteurs de conversion obtenus en divisant le taux de change DTS/dollars E.-U. de la période courante par le taux correspondant de la période de base.

On détermine les indices de volume à partir des données de valeur et des indices de valeur unitaire. Tous les indices globaux de volume sont pondérés par rapport à la période de base.

Country or area of destination and region of origin[+]	Series[&] Série[&]	2003	2004	2005	2006	2007	Pays ou zone de destination et région de provenance[+]
Albania	VFN						**Albanie**
Total		557 210	645 409	747 837	937 038	1 126 514	Total
Africa		233	174	174	220	319	Afrique
Americas		18 895	25 519	34 816	42 241	51 881	Amériques
East Asia/Pacific		3 805	4 288	5 444	7 592	9 674	Asie de l'Est/Pacifique
Europe		531 927	609 821	703 205	857 358	1 060 975	Europe
Middle East		896	775	837	1 068	1 262	Moyen-Orient
South Asia		424	410	354	376	376	Asie du Sud
Region not specified		1 030	4 422	3 007	28 183	2 027	Région non spécifiée
Algeria	VFN						**Algérie**
Total[1]		1 166 287	1 233 719	1 443 090	1 637 582	1 743 084	Total[1]
Africa		111 941	131 066	161 182	159 869	157 554	Afrique
Americas		4 949	6 830	8 117	9 724	10 271	Amériques
East Asia/Pacific		8 260	9 401	15 157	19 207	27 590	Asie de l'Est/Pacifique
Europe		157 093	198 230	227 618	252 553	270 881	Europe
Middle East		22 671	23 035	29 132	37 005	44 892	Moyen-Orient
Region not specified		861 373	865 157	1 001 884	1 159 224	1 231 896	Région non spécifiée
American Samoa	TFN						**Samoa américaines**
Total		...	...	24 496	25 347	...	Total
Africa		...	...	11	7	...	Afrique
Americas		...	...	6 899	7 205	...	Amériques
East Asia/Pacific		...	...	16 933	17 640	...	Asie de l'Est/Pacifique
Europe		...	...	382	358	...	Europe
Middle East		...	...	8	5	...	Moyen-Orient
South Asia		...	...	37	49	...	Asie du Sud
Region not specified		...	...	226	83	...	Région non spécifiée
Andorra	TFR						**Andorre**
Total		3 137 738	2 791 116	2 418 409	2 226 922	2 189 421	Total
Europe		3 137 738	2 791 116	2 418 409	2 226 922	2 189 421	Europe
Angola	TFR						**Angola**
Total		106 625	194 329	209 956	121 426	194 730	Total
Africa		30 915	41 873	43 138	18 921	33 098	Afrique
Americas		14 770	34 045	36 140	20 847	38 067	Amériques
East Asia/Pacific		5 396	16 061	15 358	15 248	28 299	Asie de l'Est/Pacifique
Europe		55 190	101 180	110 025	63 459	89 344	Europe
Middle East		354	1 170	3 151	896	1 639	Moyen-Orient
South Asia		...	...	2 144	2 055	4 283	Asie du Sud
Anguilla	TFR						**Anguilla**
Total[2]		46 915	53 987	62 084	72 962	77 652	Total[2]
Americas		39 295	44 799	52 054	61 746	63 792	Amériques
Europe		6 308	7 667	8 113	9 218	10 795	Europe
Region not specified		1 312	1 521	1 917	1 998	3 065	Région non spécifiée
Antigua and Barbuda	TFR						**Antigua-et-Barbuda**
Total[2,3]		224 032	245 797	238 804	253 669	261 802	Total[2,3]
Americas		121 563	129 316	126 096	138 547	145 506	Amériques
Europe		98 665	113 033	105 735	106 538	115 454	Europe
Region not specified		3 804	3 448	6 973	8 584	842	Région non spécifiée
Argentina	TFN						**Argentine**
Total[2]		2 995 271	3 456 526	3 822 666	*4 172 533	*4 561 510	Total[2]
Americas		2 424 735	2 721 888	2 983 895	3 282 925	3 608 887	Amériques
Europe		455 998	546 184	630 888	661 694	737 502	Europe
Region not specified		114 538	188 454	207 883	227 914	215 121	Région non spécifiée
Armenia	TFR						**Arménie**
Total		206 094	262 959	318 563	381 136	...	Total
Africa		133	184	335	396	...	Afrique
Americas		58 258	75 496	85 994	96 525	...	Amériques
East Asia/Pacific		5 669	9 355	13 592	15 557	...	Asie de l'Est/Pacifique
Europe		98 884	127 242	160 479	203 539	...	Europe
Middle East		19 155	23 131	28 182	32 621	...	Moyen-Orient
South Asia		23 995	27 551	29 981	32 498	...	Asie du Sud

Country or area of destination and region of origin[+]	Series[&] Série[&]	2003	2004	2005	2006	2007	Pays ou zone de destination et région de provenance[+]
Aruba	TFR						**Aruba**
Total		641 906	728 157	732 514	694 372	771 822	Total
Americas		584 651	665 489	666 454	629 925	703 367	Amériques
East Asia/Pacific		162	211	191	199	148	Asie de l'Est/Pacifique
Europe		54 711	60 428	63 181	61 993	67 446	Europe
Region not specified		2 382	2 029	2 688	2 255	861	Région non spécifiée
Australia	VFR						**Australie**
Total[4]		4 745 855	5 214 981	5 499 050	5 532 435	5 644 077	Total[4]
Africa		69 535	67 711	70 877	77 615	85 570	Afrique
Americas		537 494	561 454	584 395	611 140	628 777	Amériques
East Asia/Pacific		2 811 834	3 205 477	3 374 765	3 314 747	3 386 617	Asie de l'Est/Pacifique
Europe		1 228 033	1 261 477	1 330 233	1 367 738	1 355 280	Europe
Middle East		34 432	43 484	49 195	52 401	62 743	Moyen-Orient
South Asia		63 264	75 233	89 356	108 324	124 690	Asie du Sud
Region not specified		1 263	145	229	470	400	Région non spécifiée
Austria	TCER						**Autriche**
Total[5]		19 077 630	19 372 816	19 952 350	20 261 292	20 766 189	Total[5]
Africa		27 206	32 114	42 259	42 501	40 471	Afrique
Americas		599 474	673 695	691 644	780 218	755 874	Amériques
East Asia/Pacific		618 852	755 406	792 197	797 479	747 284	Asie de l'Est/Pacifique
Europe		17 386 722	17 445 939	18 030 663	18 257 289	18 788 063	Europe
Middle East		37 667	43 202	67 833	75 217	91 353	Moyen-Orient
South Asia		29 619	39 882	39 204	49 684	46 206	Asie du Sud
Region not specified		378 090	382 578	288 550	258 904	296 938	Région non spécifiée
Azerbaijan	VFR						**Azerbaïdjan**
Total		1 013 811	1 348 655	1 177 277	1 193 742	1 332 701	Total
Africa		320	661	544	807	829	Afrique
Americas		7 951	12 358	11 272	10 133	11 021	Amériques
East Asia/Pacific		4 271	6 051	6 825	7 205	8 391	Asie de l'Est/Pacifique
Europe		746 916	1 050 943	945 662	1 007 670	1 104 267	Europe
Middle East		1 684	2 143	1 942	1 888	1 854	Moyen-Orient
South Asia		252 669	275 147	211 032	165 144	205 242	Asie du Sud
Region not specified		...	1 352	...	895	1 097	Région non spécifiée
Bahamas	TFR						**Bahamas**
Total		1 510 169	1 561 312	1 608 153	1 600 862	1 527 726	Total
Africa		1 409	1 427	1 302	1 397	1 477	Afrique
Americas		1 392 578	1 455 375	1 484 921	1 485 158	1 403 999	Amériques
East Asia/Pacific		6 285	6 890	7 145	6 910	6 720	Asie de l'Est/Pacifique
Europe		93 714	84 121	85 857	82 791	87 874	Europe
Middle East		346	616	361	452	465	Moyen-Orient
South Asia		381	347	285	443	506	Asie du Sud
Region not specified		15 456	12 536	28 282	23 711	26 685	Région non spécifiée
Bahrain	VFN						**Bahreïn**
Total[2]		4 844 497	5 667 331	6 313 232	7 288 716	7 833 609	Total[2]
Africa		59 989	76 325	82 121	98 749	109 114	Afrique
Americas		192 206	200 481	189 778	234 467	267 496	Amériques
East Asia/Pacific		211 749	267 978	287 257	374 335	390 262	Asie de l'Est/Pacifique
Europe		260 698	333 920	357 623	429 750	506 891	Europe
Middle East		3 558 805	4 140 624	4 676 446	5 209 825	5 451 041	Moyen-Orient
South Asia		561 050	648 003	720 007	941 590	1 108 805	Asie du Sud
Bangladesh	TFN						**Bangladesh**
Total		244 509	271 270	207 662	200 311	289 110	Total
Africa		2 012	2 147	1 730	1 953	2 001	Afrique
Americas		30 795	37 404	18 673	25 129	45 706	Amériques
East Asia/Pacific		42 824	51 230	35 887	37 032	57 135	Asie de l'Est/Pacifique
Europe		63 749	77 307	48 961	56 709	77 345	Europe
Middle East		2 626	3 243	2 861	4 021	4 530	Moyen-Orient
South Asia		102 503	99 939	99 458	75 467	102 393	Asie du Sud
Region not specified		...	...	92	...	...	Région non spécifiée

Tourist/visitor arrivals by region of origin *(continued)*
Number
Arrivées de touristes/visiteurs par région de provenance *(suite)*
Nombre

Country or area of destination and region of origin[+]	Series[&] Série[&]	2003	2004	2005	2006	2007	Pays ou zone de destination et région de provenance[+]
Barbados	TFR						**Barbade**
Total		531 211	551 502	547 534	562 558	574 533	Total
Africa		668	753	1 117	988	3 331	Afrique
Americas		291 623	301 268	311 222	312 317	303 404	Amériques
East Asia/Pacific		4 027	2 679	2 710	2 758	10 450	Asie de l'Est/Pacifique
Europe		233 791	245 919	230 167	241 141	250 924	Europe
Middle East		160	145	154	230	481	Moyen-Orient
South Asia		466	627	756	784	3 538	Asie du Sud
Region not specified		476	111	1 408	4 340	2 405	Région non spécifiée
Belarus	TFN						**Bélarus**
Total[6]		64 190	67 297	90 588	89 101	104 890	Total[6]
Africa		65	47	399	148	499	Afrique
Americas		3 522	5 892	4 663	4 292	5 587	Amériques
East Asia/Pacific		1 833	2 150	1 860	1 815	2 386	Asie de l'Est/Pacifique
Europe		57 916	58 524	82 247	80 956	95 003	Europe
Middle East		382	415	825	1 318	818	Moyen-Orient
South Asia		472	269	594	572	597	Asie du Sud
Belgium	TCER						**Belgique**
Total[7]		6 689 998	6 709 740	6 747 123	6 994 819	7 044 719	Total[7]
Africa		62 755	60 872	62 455	65 438	62 449	Afrique
Americas		368 814	382 249	390 160	407 403	420 845	Amériques
East Asia/Pacific		294 364	318 231	298 360	304 773	301 959	Asie de l'Est/Pacifique
Europe		5 846 966	5 800 440	5 835 628	6 035 866	6 061 187	Europe
Middle East		17 502	17 664	19 793	20 978	20 284	Moyen-Orient
South Asia		32 362	33 152	34 844	32 673	43 785	Asie du Sud
Region not specified		67 235	97 132	105 883	127 688	134 210	Région non spécifiée
Belize	TFN						**Belize**
Total[1]		220 574	230 835	236 573	247 309	255 890	Total[1]
Africa		337	349	348	359	490	Afrique
Americas		174 784	185 254	190 301	199 315	205 384	Amériques
East Asia/Pacific		3 754	4 285	4 384	4 516	5 672	Asie de l'Est/Pacifique
Europe		33 530	32 768	33 466	34 373	34 505	Europe
Middle East		370	481	369	381	445	Moyen-Orient
Region not specified		7 799	7 698	7 705	8 365	9 394	Région non spécifiée
Benin	TFR						**Bénin**
Total *		175 000	173 500	176 000	180 006	186 394	Total *
Africa		148 646	147 536	140 185	152 000	153 016	Afrique
Americas		471	360	500	972	2 299	Amériques
East Asia/Pacific		225	261	321	633	780	Asie de l'Est/Pacifique
Europe		25 403	25 157	31 500	22 257	26 283	Europe
Middle East		112	61	518	644	1 762	Moyen-Orient
South Asia		137	125	2 956	3 500	2 254	Asie du Sud
Region not specified		6	...	20	...	...	Région non spécifiée
Bermuda	TFR						**Bermudes**
Total[3]		256 579	271 620	269 591	298 973	305 548	Total[3]
Americas		222 396	235 546	232 661	255 400	257 342	Amériques
East Asia/Pacific		503	834	639	647	...	Asie de l'Est/Pacifique
Europe		25 938	25 873	26 678	32 347	35 938	Europe
Region not specified		7 742	9 367	9 613	10 579	12 268	Région non spécifiée
Bhutan	TFN						**Bhoutan**
Total		6 261	9 249	13 626	17 348	21 094	Total
Africa		14	14	45	88	65	Afrique
Americas		2 034	3 607	5 168	5 627	6 653	Amériques
East Asia/Pacific		1 415	1 680	2 759	4 317	5 393	Asie de l'Est/Pacifique
Europe		2 774	3 905	5 619	7 267	8 929	Europe
Middle East		...	...	7	12	15	Moyen-Orient
South Asia		12	19	17	30	39	Asie du Sud
Region not specified		12	24	11	7	...	Région non spécifiée

Country or area of destination and region of origin[+]	Series[&] Série[&]	2003	2004	2005	2006	2007	Pays ou zone de destination et région de provenance[+]
Bolivia	THSN						**Bolivie**
Total[8]		367 036	390 888	413 267	496 489	...	Total[8]
Africa		1 117	1 278	1 661	1 484	...	Afrique
Americas		209 715	227 280	250 107	300 893	...	Amériques
East Asia/Pacific		15 291	18 917	19 878	26 999	...	Asie de l'Est/Pacifique
Europe		140 913	143 413	141 621	167 113	...	Europe
Bonaire	TFR						**Bonaire**
Total		62 179	63 156	62 550	63 552	74 309	Total
Americas		32 771	34 576	32 244	35 093	42 191	Amériques
Europe		29 079	27 973	30 066	28 202	31 427	Europe
Region not specified		329	607	240	257	691	Région non spécifiée
Bosnia and Herzegovina	TCER						**Bosnie-Herzégovine**
Total		165 465	190 300	217 273	255 764	306 452	Total
Americas		7 339	8 442	8 030	10 195	10 341	Amériques
East Asia/Pacific		1 870	2 177	2 355	2 869	4 399	Asie de l'Est/Pacifique
Europe		152 246	176 588	203 564	238 976	286 280	Europe
Middle East		94	132	46	175	134	Moyen-Orient
South Asia		189	116	265	51	233	Asie du Sud
Region not specified		3 727	2 845	3 013	3 498	5 065	Région non spécifiée
Botswana	TFR						**Botswana**
Total		1 405 535	1 522 807	...	...	...	Total
Africa		1 235 404	1 353 125	...	...	...	Afrique
Americas		18 025	21 023	...	...	...	Amériques
East Asia/Pacific		12 442	11 848	...	...	...	Asie de l'Est/Pacifique
Europe		55 054	58 432	...	...	...	Europe
South Asia		1 889	2 223	...	...	...	Asie du Sud
Region not specified		82 721	76 156	...	...	...	Région non spécifiée
Brazil	TFR						**Brésil**
Total		4 132 847	4 793 703	5 358 170	5 017 251	5 025 834	Total
Africa		52 489	64 678	75 676	83 721	75 923	Afrique
Americas		2 396 832	2 703 442	2 998 060	2 717 273	2 774 867	Amériques
East Asia/Pacific		128 640	155 605	177 381	216 976	205 572	Asie de l'Est/Pacifique
Europe		1 543 559	1 860 259	2 097 357	1 979 817	1 942 132	Europe
Middle East		5 595	6 064	7 002	18 172	25 967	Moyen-Orient
Region not specified		5 732	3 655	2 694	1 292	1 373	Région non spécifiée
British Virgin Islands	TFR						**Iles Vierges britanniques**
Total		317 758	...	...	...	...	Total
Americas		261 201	...	...	...	...	Amériques
Europe		49 952	...	...	...	...	Europe
Region not specified		6 605	...	...	...	...	Région non spécifiée
Brunei Darussalam	TFN						**Brunéi Darussalam**
Total[3]		...	...	126 217	158 095	178 540	Total[3]
Americas		...	...	3 313	3 943	5 116	Amériques
East Asia/Pacific		...	...	75 781	100 160	144 488	Asie de l'Est/Pacifique
Europe		...	...	14 428	20 847	20 796	Europe
Middle East		...	...	210	654	574	Moyen-Orient
South Asia		...	...	...	...	5 195	Asie du Sud
Region not specified		...	...	32 485	32 491	2 371	Région non spécifiée
Bulgaria	VFR						**Bulgarie**
Total		6 240 932	6 981 597	7 282 455	7 499 117	7 725 747	Total
Africa		3 848	2 937	2 774	2 668	1 734	Afrique
Americas		54 701	67 605	76 514	85 158	89 790	Amériques
East Asia/Pacific		26 521	32 067	35 127	38 186	43 563	Asie de l'Est/Pacifique
Europe		6 088 039	6 806 650	7 087 954	7 286 509	7 371 761	Europe
Middle East		15 132	16 124	17 569	14 284	18 823	Moyen-Orient
South Asia		11 613	12 199	11 396	13 267	15 000	Asie du Sud
Region not specified		41 078	44 015	51 121	59 045	185 076	Région non spécifiée
Burkina Faso	THSN						**Burkina Faso**
Total[1]		163 123	222 201	244 728	263 978	288 965	Total[1]
Africa		65 459	96 385	100 674	108 019	121 174	Afrique
Americas		10 025	12 991	14 724	15 814	20 473	Amériques

65

Tourist/visitor arrivals by region of origin *(continued)*
Number
Arrivées de touristes/visiteurs par région de provenance *(suite)*
Nombre

Country or area of destination and region of origin+	Series& Série&	2003	2004	2005	2006	2007	Pays ou zone de destination et région de provenance+
East Asia/Pacific		3 271	4 550	6 582	6 387	11 563	Asie de l'Est/Pacifique
Europe		76 743	99 742	113 496	123 426	126 544	Europe
Middle East		1 447	1 982	2 220	2 022	2 066	Moyen-Orient
Region not specified		6 178	6 551	7 032	8 310	7 145	Région non spécifiée
Burundi	TFN						**Burundi**
Total [9]		74 116	133 228	148 418	201 241	...	Total [9]
Africa		24 706	1 333	49 473	140 868	...	Afrique
Americas		2 308	5 908	9 956	4 025	...	Amériques
East Asia/Pacific		1 162	4 528	4 023	10 062	...	Asie de l'Est/Pacifique
Europe		7 620	29 409	29 486	32 199	...	Europe
Region not specified		38 320	92 050	55 480	14 087	...	Région non spécifiéc
Cambodia	VFR						**Cambodge**
Total		701 014	1 055 202 [10]	1 421 615 [11]	1 700 041 [12]	2 015 128 [13]	Total
Africa		...	...	...	...	3 270	Afrique
Americas		88 662	122 169	152 328	159 429	194 706	Amériques
East Asia/Pacific		412 245	589 230	786 506	1 022 181	1 241 002	Asie de l'Est/Pacifique
Europe		183 353	242 811	310 006	314 194	417 096	Europe
Middle East		...	...	...	...	1 059	Moyen-Orient
South Asia		5 286	7 132	7 516	9 245	14 554	Asie du Sud
Region not specified		11 468	93 860	165 259	194 992	142 561	Région non spécifiée
Cameroon	THSN						**Cameroun**
Total		...	189 856	176 372	184 549	...	Total
Africa		...	80 013	88 739	97 596	...	Afrique
Americas		...	11 593	10 002	8 999	...	Amériques
East Asia/Pacific		...	4 248	4 580	5 042	...	Asie de l'Est/Pacifique
Europe		...	83 272	68 058	62 668	...	Europe
Middle East		...	4 583	2 007	3 501	...	Moyen-Orient
Region not specified		...	6 147	2 986	6 743	...	Région non spécifiée
Canada	TFR						**Canada**
Total		17 534 329	19 144 810	18 770 552	18 265 406	17 931 061	Total
Africa		52 437	58 210	61 842	72 388	75 525	Afrique
Americas		14 588 822	15 518 243	14 867 460	14 372 551	13 942 626	Amériques
East Asia/Pacific		900 328	1 221 981	1 282 007	1 282 472	1 266 536	Asie de l'Est/Pacifique
Europe		1 872 693	2 202 397	2 397 419	2 359 997	2 443 093	Europe
Middle East		40 257	47 637	52 131	59 270	67 512	Moyen-Orient
South Asia		79 792	96 342	109 693	118 728	135 769	Asie du Sud
Cape Verde	THSR						**Cap-Vert**
Total		150 048	157 052	197 844	241 742	267 188	Total
Africa		5 225	10 034	9 432	4 659	307	Afrique
Americas		1 740	1 472	2 102	5 949	4 932	Amériques
Europe		134 749	136 304	173 318	207 964	228 165	Europe
Region not specified		8 334	9 242	12 992	23 170	33 784	Région non spécifiée
Cayman Islands	TFR						**Iles Caïmanes**
Total [3]		293 513	259 929	167 802	267 257	291 503	Total [3]
Africa		373	321	325	435	530	Afrique
Americas		272 381	242 012	152 735	247 420	268 141	Amériques
East Asia/Pacific		1 201	1 216	1 129	1 370	1 720	Asie de l'Est/Pacifique
Europe		19 001	15 938	13 221	17 516	20 432	Europe
Middle East		65	72	24	53	116	Moyen-Orient
South Asia		274	176	97	158	158	Asie du Sud
Region not specified		218	194	271	305	406	Région non spécifiée
Central African Rep.	TFN						**Rép. centrafricaine**
Total [3]		5 687	8 156	11 969	*13 764	...	Total [3]
Africa		3 111	3 501	6 156	7 079	...	Afrique
Americas		374	449	639	735	...	Amériques
East Asia/Pacific		288	317	373	429	...	Asie de l'Est/Pacifique
Europe		1 881	3 674	4 349	5 001	...	Europe
Middle East		18	192	397	457	...	Moyen-Orient
Region not specified		15	23	55	63	...	Région non spécifiée

65

Tourist/visitor arrivals by region of origin *(continued)*
Number
Arrivées de touristes/visiteurs par région de provenance *(suite)*
Nombre

Country or area of destination and region of origin[+]	Series[&] Série[&]	2003	2004	2005	2006	2007	Pays ou zone de destination et région de provenance[+]
Chad	THSN						**Tchad**
Total		20 974	25 899	29 356	15 863	24 794	Total
Africa		5 141	5 855	6 695	4 226	6 365	Afrique
Americas		4 368	5 609	5 976	2 316	5 002	Amériques
East Asia/Pacific		297	398	550	490	1 427	Asie de l'Est/Pacifique
Europe		10 029	12 690	14 805	8 723	11 250	Europe
Middle East		1 139	1 347	1 330	108	750	Moyen-Orient
Chile	TFN						**Chili**
Total		1 613 523	1 785 024	2 027 082	2 252 952	2 506 756	Total
Africa		2 872	3 653	3 544	4 150	4 286	Afrique
Americas		1 242 956	1 360 342	1 553 381	1 754 599	1 967 792	Amériques
East Asia/Pacific		54 476	69 883	74 927	83 683	90 673	Asie de l'Est/Pacifique
Europe		309 008	344 774	384 886	401 775	436 770	Europe
Middle East		637	812	682	2 015	1 297	Moyen-Orient
South Asia		2 039	3 605	4 257	4 100	4 410	Asie du Sud
Region not specified		1 535	1 955	5 405	2 630	1 528	Région non spécifiée
China[14]	VFN						**Chine**[14]
Total		91 662 082	109 038 218	120 292 255	124 942 096	131 873 287	Total
Africa		91 949	154 223	210 533	255 288	327 142	Afrique
Americas		1 132 937	1 789 500	2 145 758	2 405 829	2 721 034	Amériques
East Asia/Pacific		87 214 341	102 393 763	112 053 459	115 700 406	120 956 213	Asie de l'Est/Pacifique
Europe		2 789 888	4 096 999	5 165 588	5 769 346	6 936 600	Europe
Middle East		46 856	84 376	110 966	136 429	179 771	Moyen-Orient
South Asia		383 121	514 163	599 435	670 505	749 103	Asie du Sud
Region not specified		2 990	5 194	6 516	4 293	3 424	Région non spécifiée
China, Hong Kong SAR	TFR						**Chine, Hong Kong RAS**
Total		9 676 300	13 655 100	14 773 200	15 821 400	17 153 900	Total
Africa		68 100	91 100	116 600	123 400	126 500	Afrique
Americas		713 400	1 091 600	1 196 700	1 229 500	1 330 100	Amériques
East Asia/Pacific		8 154 000	11 368 600	12 124 500	12 989 900	14 022 400	Asie de l'Est/Pacifique
Europe		588 000	888 700	1 083 900	1 198 700	1 368 600	Europe
Middle East		39 100	55 600	71 000	88 100	101 600	Moyen-Orient
South Asia		113 700	159 500	180 500	191 800	204 700	Asie du Sud
China, Macao SAR	VFN						**Chine, Macao RAS**
Total[15,16]		11 887 876	16 672 556	18 711 187	21 998 580	26 992 995	Total[15,16]
Africa		4 668	6 042	8 082	13 693	30 049	Afrique
Americas		95 502	147 953	182 830	218 728	306 510	Amériques
East Asia/Pacific		11 673 256	16 361 807	18 321 056	21 525 911	26 325 474	Asie de l'Est/Pacifique
Europe		94 078	128 887	161 204	188 196	252 322	Europe
Middle East		1 171	1 905	2 679	3 747	7 276	Moyen-Orient
South Asia		17 324	23 771	32 335	42 604	64 532	Asie du Sud
Region not specified		1 877	2 191	3 001	5 701	6 832	Région non spécifiée
Colombia	VFN						**Colombie**
Total[17]		624 910	790 940	933 243	1 053 348	*1 195 443	Total[17]
Africa		897	935	1 380	1 703	3 929	Afrique
Americas		484 379	617 896	730 495	826 746	943 562	Amériques
East Asia/Pacific		11 272	13 294	15 395	17 118	24 427	Asie de l'Est/Pacifique
Europe		125 073	155 657	182 822	204 533	219 810	Europe
Middle East		1 004	1 399	1 167	1 349	1 339	Moyen-Orient
South Asia		1 119	1 404	1 618	1 819	2 292	Asie du Sud
Region not specified		1 166	355	366	80	84	Région non spécifiée
Comoros	TFN						**Comores**
Total[3]		14 229	17 603	19 551	17 060	14 582	Total[3]
Africa		5 590	6 344	8 793	6 123	4 241	Afrique
Americas		26	162	83	358	420	Amériques
East Asia/Pacific		610	165	543	582	382	Asie de l'Est/Pacifique
Europe		8 003	10 562	9 625	9 470	9 450	Europe
Region not specified		...	370	507	527	89	Région non spécifiée

65

Tourist/visitor arrivals by region of origin *(continued)*
Number
Arrivées de touristes/visiteurs par région de provenance *(suite)*
Nombre

Country or area of destination and region of origin[+]	Series[&] Série[&]	2003	2004	2005	2006	2007	Pays ou zone de destination et région de provenance[+]
Cook Islands	TFR						**Iles Cook**
Total[18]		78 328	83 333	88 405	92 251	*97 019	Total[18]
Americas		11 390	8 445	6 463	7 677	7 074	Amériques
East Asia/Pacific		45 008	53 962	63 319	65 972	73 247	Asie de l'Est/Pacifique
Europe		21 559	20 410	18 162	18 112	15 162	Europe
Region not specified		371	516	461	490	1 536	Région non spécifiée
Costa Rica	TFN						**Costa Rica**
Total		1 238 692	1 452 926	1 679 051	1 725 261	1 979 789	Total
Africa		1 048	1 194	1 164	1 204	1 621	Afrique
Americas		1 017 831	1 213 784	1 411 640	1 456 947	1 670 551	Amériques
East Asia/Pacific		16 403	16 043	23 687	23 425	25 730	Asie de l'Est/Pacifique
Europe		198 242	215 072	241 751	243 100	281 515	Europe
Region not specified		5 168	6 833	809	585	372	Région non spécifiée
Croatia	TCER						**Croatie**
Total[19]		7 408 590	7 911 874	8 466 886	8 658 876	9 306 691	Total[19]
Americas		84 470	119 485	140 031	182 016	217 055	Amériques
East Asia/Pacific		43 173	58 370	83 273	132 824	170 336	Asie de l'Est/Pacifique
Europe		7 244 346	7 692 506	8 192 055	8 281 634	8 839 689	Europe
Region not specified		36 601	41 513	51 527	61 502	78 811	Région non spécifiée
Cuba	VFR						**Cuba**
Total		1 905 682	2 048 572	2 319 334	2 220 567	2 152 221	Total
Africa		6 679	5 868	6 619	6 636	6 611	Afrique
Americas		916 818	1 025 756	1 215 857	1 149 135	1 172 933	Amériques
East Asia/Pacific		32 463	33 861	41 858	43 819	42 311	Asie de l'Est/Pacifique
Europe		942 052	976 727	1 047 669	1 013 273	924 025	Europe
Middle East		1 514	1 517	1 622	1 643	1 734	Moyen-Orient
South Asia		5 559	4 176	5 149	5 248	4 021	Asie du Sud
Region not specified		597	667	560	813	586	Région non spécifiée
Curaçao	TFR						**Curaçao**
Total[3]		221 395	223 439	222 061	234 400	299 779	Total[3]
Americas		125 794	128 873	123 353	126 522	174 321	Amériques
Europe		91 384	89 752	94 957	104 248	121 424	Europe
Region not specified		4 217	4 814	3 751	3 630	4 034	Région non spécifiée
Cyprus	TFR						**Chypre**
Total		2 303 246	2 349 012	2 470 063	2 400 924	2 416 081	Total
Africa		6 752	4 936	7 097	6 641	7 139	Afrique
Americas		23 246	22 924	28 984	26 353	30 352	Amériques
East Asia/Pacific		12 266	13 042	15 043	16 262	16 548	Asie de l'Est/Pacifique
Europe		2 207 434	2 263 145	2 375 402	2 307 885	2 304 366	Europe
Middle East		49 413	41 379	40 233	39 291	50 896	Moyen-Orient
South Asia		3 130	1 992	2 777	3 808	6 432	Asie du Sud
Region not specified		1 005	1 594	527	684	348	Région non spécifiée
Czech Republic	TCEN						**République tchèque**
Total		5 075 756	6 061 225	6 336 128	6 435 474	6 679 704	Total
Africa		14 097	15 394	18 539	19 411	19 520	Afrique
Americas		282 239	380 056	400 840	435 280	441 493	Amériques
East Asia/Pacific		251 411	351 652	420 989	492 842	503 899	Asie de l'Est/Pacifique
Europe		4 528 009	5 314 123	5 495 760	5 487 941	5 714 792	Europe
Dem. Rep. of the Congo	TFN						**Rép. dém. du Congo**
Total		35 141[3]	36 238[3]	61 007	55 148	*47 492[3]	Total
Africa		20 380	14 531	36 489	33 089	27 767	Afrique
Americas		2 568	4 592	3 824	3 309	2 933	Amériques
East Asia/Pacific		3 156	3 998	5 943	5 515	5 478	Asie de l'Est/Pacifique
Europe		9 037	13 117	14 751	13 235	11 314	Europe
Denmark	TCER						**Danemark**
Total		3 473 808	4 421 442	4 698 668	4 652 780	4 680 947	Total
Americas		78 382	126 276	147 289	159 593	140 200	Amériques
East Asia/Pacific		46 850	82 957	110 098	109 878	102 544	Asie de l'Est/Pacifique
Europe		3 253 489	4 065 043	4 357 752	4 272 987	4 325 458	Europe
Region not specified		95 087	147 166	83 529	110 322	112 745	Région non spécifiée

Country or area of destination and region of origin[+]	Series[&] Série[&]	2003	2004	2005	2006	2007	Pays ou zone de destination et région de provenance[+]
Dominica	TFR						**Dominique**
Total		73 190	80 087	79 257	84 041	81 086	Total
Americas		61 536	69 115	68 164	71 832	69 429	Amériques
East Asia/Pacific		486	387	529	495	514	Asie de l'Est/Pacifique
Europe		10 772	10 208	10 258	11 303	10 784	Europe
Region not specified		396	377	306	411	359	Région non spécifiée
Dominican Republic	TFR						**Rép. dominicaine**
Total[1,3]		3 282 138	3 450 180	3 690 692	*3 965 055	*3 979 582	Total[1,3]
Americas		1 503 896	1 597 342	1 711 341	1 947 796	2 046 288	Amériques
East Asia/Pacific		3 417	3 511	4 280	4 631	7 672	Asie de l'Est/Pacifique
Europe		1 250 608	1 271 299	1 371 663	1 388 757	1 343 209	Europe
South Asia		236	249	337	279	663	Asie du Sud
Region not specified		523 981	577 779	603 071	623 592	581 750	Région non spécifiée
Ecuador	VFN						**Equateur**
Total[2]		760 776	818 927	859 888	840 555	937 487	Total[2]
Africa		1 720	2 191	1 919	1 240	1 360	Afrique
Americas		617 088	662 019	690 743	642 075	729 610	Amériques
East Asia/Pacific		17 831	21 195	20 222	19 488	25 223	Asie de l'Est/Pacifique
Europe		124 137	133 495	146 537	144 682	179 700	Europe
Region not specified		...	27	467	33 070	1 594	Région non spécifiée
Egypt	VFN						**Egypte**
Total[2]		6 044 160	8 103 609	8 607 807	9 082 777	11 090 863	Total[2]
Africa		183 035	244 662	263 847	301 866	387 221	Afrique
Americas		187 828	257 418	297 675	340 530	429 863	Amériques
East Asia/Pacific		226 756	296 189	411 048	389 304	526 196	Asie de l'Est/Pacifique
Europe		4 203 687	5 919 575	6 047 194	6 259 732	7 936 508	Europe
Middle East		1 188 994	1 317 883	1 511 285	1 706 423	1 686 953	Moyen-Orient
South Asia		51 042	63 310	73 000	80 501	105 874	Asie du Sud
Region not specified		2 818	4 572	3 758	4 421	18 248	Région non spécifiée
El Salvador	TFN						**El Salvador**
Total		719 963	950 745	1 127 141	1 278 927	1 338 543	Total
Africa		368	580	624	753	569	Afrique
Americas		681 953	908 148	1 086 016	1 239 978	1 285 051	Amériques
East Asia/Pacific		7 474	9 408	9 716	9 677	11 699	Asie de l'Est/Pacifique
Europe		30 144	32 597	30 759	28 503	41 190	Europe
Middle East		24	12	26	16	34	Moyen-Orient
Eritrea	VFN						**Erythrée**
Total[1]		80 029	87 298	83 307	78 451	80 503	Total[1]
Africa		3 147	4 503	3 182	3 645	5 051	Afrique
Americas		2 321	2 559	2 263	1 474	983	Amériques
East Asia/Pacific		1 953	2 484	2 267	2 275	1 935	Asie de l'Est/Pacifique
Europe		8 367	10 142	8 364	5 983	5 408	Europe
Middle East		2 857	4 196	3 862	3 241	2 249	Moyen-Orient
South Asia		2 580	2 420	2 985	2 895	2 973	Asie du Sud
Region not specified		58 804	60 994	60 384	58 938	61 904	Région non spécifiée
Estonia	TCER						**Estonie**
Total		1 112 746	1 374 414	1 453 418	1 427 583	1 380 323	Total
Africa		542	641	1 033	723	1 013	Afrique
Americas		14 823	23 448	24 037	24 359	27 787	Amériques
East Asia/Pacific		10 663	13 456	15 130	17 663	17 101	Asie de l'Est/Pacifique
Europe		1 080 977	1 333 979	1 411 062	1 382 143	1 332 798	Europe
Region not specified		5 741	2 890	2 156	2 695	1 624	Région non spécifiée
Ethiopia	TFR						**Ethiopie**
Total[9,20]		179 910	184 079	227 398	290 458	303 241	Total[9,20]
Africa		82 152	65 744	85 501	89 923	87 181	Afrique
Americas		27 456	33 895	41 380	61 353	67 641	Amériques
East Asia/Pacific		7 645	9 825	12 188	20 058	25 725	Asie de l'Est/Pacifique
Europe		43 647	47 955	57 103	76 466	86 891	Europe
Middle East		14 366	20 618	22 162	30 556	27 219	Moyen-Orient
South Asia		3 602	4 641	7 125	7 975	8 584	Asie du Sud
Region not specified		1 042	1 401	1 939	4 127	...	Région non spécifiée

Country or area of destination and region of origin[+]	Series[&] Série[&]	2003	2004	2005	2006	2007	Pays ou zone de destination et région de provenance[+]
Fiji	TFR						**Fidji**
Total[2]		430 800	504 075	549 911	545 168	539 881	Total[2]
Americas		69 313	77 646	85 536	81 955	81 679	Amériques
East Asia/Pacific		288 321	352 743	383 691	377 697	387 941	Asie de l'Est/Pacifique
Europe		71 641	70 388	78 507	80 586	61 096	Europe
Region not specified		1 525	3 298	2 177	4 930	9 165	Région non spécifiée
Finland	TCER						**Finlande**
Total		2 047 444	2 083 487[21]	2 080 194	2 316 967	2 472 449	Total
Africa		3 370	3 185	4 123	5 147	5 340	Afrique
Americas		102 034	111 245	105 992	110 530	117 098	Amériques
East Asia/Pacific		146 652	167 808	158 128	188 447	193 835	Asie de l'Est/Pacifique
Europe		1 683 624	1 698 936	1 712 228	1 884 448	2 017 072	Europe
Middle East		3 463	3 168	3 613	3 824	3 316	Moyen-Orient
South Asia		5 361	5 965	7 445	10 707	15 651	Asie du Sud
Region not specified		102 940	93 180	88 665	110 004	120 137	Région non spécifiée
France	TFR						**France**
Total		75 048 000[22]	75 121 000[23]	75 908 000[23]	78 853 000[23]	*81 940 200[23]	Total
Africa		889 000	895 000	1 252 000	1 222 000	1 384 000	Afrique
Americas		3 954 000	4 206 000	5 086 000	5 399 000	5 829 200	Amériques
East Asia/Pacific		1 890 000	2 058 000	3 192 000	3 116 000	3 004 100	Asie de l'Est/Pacifique
Europe		68 072 000	67 711 000	66 029 000	68 592 000	71 154 600	Europe
Middle East		210 000	237 000	349 000	524 000	568 300	Moyen-Orient
Region not specified		33 000	14 000	...	...	...	Région non spécifiée
French Guiana	TFR						**Guyane française**
Total		...	...	94 920	...	108 801	Total
Americas		...	...	25 439	...	37 101	Amériques
East Asia/Pacific		...	...	63 501	...	67 130	Asie de l'Est/Pacifique
Region not specified		...	...	5 980	...	4 570	Région non spécifiée
French Polynesia	TFR						**Polynésie française**
Total[2,3]		212 692	211 828	208 045	221 549	218 241	Total[2,3]
Africa		294	257	235	255	764	Afrique
Americas		89 454	86 032	80 067	88 991	81 445	Amériques
East Asia/Pacific		42 235	45 083	45 655	48 344	50 260	Asie de l'Est/Pacifique
Europe		80 182	79 944	81 643	82 580	85 205	Europe
Middle East		163	172	165	226	343	Moyen-Orient
South Asia		62	75	69	116	224	Asie du Sud
Region not specified		302	265	211	1 037	...	Région non spécifiée
Gambia	TFN						**Gambie**
Total[24]		73 485	90 095	107 904	124 800	142 626	Total[24]
Africa		4 542	1 330	11 497	18 135	17 541	Afrique
Americas		643	3 248	1 387	2 189	1 639	Amériques
East Asia/Pacific		...	...	...	...	147	Asie de l'Est/Pacifique
Europe		63 625	81 955	86 181	91 194	121 038	Europe
Region not specified		4 675	3 562	8 839	13 282	2 261	Région non spécifiée
Georgia	VFR						**Géorgie**
Total		313 442	368 312	560 021	983 114	1 051 769	Total
Africa		306	788	431	777	883	Afrique
Americas		8 731	11 209	14 842	19 417	16 861	Amériques
East Asia/Pacific		6 756	4 952	3 244	13 732	9 415	Asie de l'Est/Pacifique
Europe		288 648	342 596	533 129	935 747	1 009 669	Europe
Middle East		1 835	1 563	973	2 105	2 481	Moyen-Orient
South Asia		6 683	6 635	6 641	9 977	10 869	Asie du Sud
Region not specified		483	569	761	1 359	1 591	Région non spécifiée
Germany	TCER						**Allemagne**
Total		18 399 093	20 136 979	21 500 067	23 569 145	24 420 672	Total
Africa		143 156	146 454	144 391	167 005	163 564	Afrique
Americas		2 048 770	2 337 209	2 397 527	2 782 911	2 705 989	Amériques
East Asia/Pacific		1 605 064	1 931 265	2 000 752	2 176 143	2 104 663	Asie de l'Est/Pacifique
Europe		13 877 895	14 918 028	16 099 891	17 504 005	18 423 468	Europe
Middle East		142 732	160 110	185 497	202 369	222 556	Moyen-Orient
Region not specified		581 476	643 913	672 009	736 712	800 432	Région non spécifiée

65

Tourist/visitor arrivals by region of origin *(continued)*
Number
Arrivées de touristes/visiteurs par région de provenance *(suite)*
Nombre

Country or area of destination and region of origin[+]	Series[&] Série[&]	2003	2004	2005	2006	2007	Pays ou zone de destination et région de provenance[+]
Ghana	TFN						**Ghana**
Total[1]		530 827	583 819	428 533	497 129	...	Total[1]
Africa		180 609	198 638	172 913	140 066	...	Afrique
Americas		44 581	49 031	62 572	73 858	...	Amériques
East Asia/Pacific		25 532	28 081	11 186	7 917	...	Asie de l'Est/Pacifique
Europe		131 587	144 724	100 509	95 728	...	Europe
Middle East		4 026	4 428	10 632	9 602	...	Moyen-Orient
South Asia		...	...	10 900	14 132	...	Asie du Sud
Region not specified		144 492	158 917	59 821	155 826	...	Région non spécifiée
Greece	TFN						**Grèce**
Total[25]		13 969 393	13 312 629	14 765 463	16 039 216	17 517 791	Total[25]
Africa		19 184	23 073	22 961	30 296	27 894	Afrique
Americas		219 391	236 274	416 746	513 402	579 607	Amériques
East Asia/Pacific		212 791	226 973	253 686	315 691	318 990	Asie de l'Est/Pacifique
Europe		13 459 272	12 766 224	13 996 356	15 104 338	16 518 090	Europe
Middle East		54 836	55 257	72 057	70 616	68 559	Moyen-Orient
South Asia		3 919	4 828	3 657	4 873	4 651	Asie du Sud
Grenada	TFN						**Grenade**
Total[1]		142 355	133 865	98 548	118 654	130 096	Total[1]
Africa		522	562	325	461	965	Afrique
Americas		80 126	77 126	58 629	65 292	63 796	Amériques
East Asia/Pacific		1 062	722	1 054	1 515	3 382	Asie de l'Est/Pacifique
Europe		43 167	36 222	22 423	32 556	42 111	Europe
Middle East		109	132	121	110	87	Moyen-Orient
Region not specified		17 369	19 101	15 996	18 720	19 755	Région non spécifiée
Guadeloupe	THSR						**Guadeloupe**
Total		438 819[26]	455 981[26]	371 985[27]	...	...	Total
Europe		386 737	406 204	369 800	...	...	Europe
Region not specified		52 082	49 777	2 185	...	...	Région non spécifiée
Guam	TFR						**Guam**
Total[18]		909 506	1 159 881	1 227 587	1 211 674	1 225 323	Total[18]
Americas		41 160	46 754	46 362	44 813	49 578	Amériques
East Asia/Pacific		808 623	1 068 997	1 133 807	1 134 264	1 125 858	Asie de l'Est/Pacifique
Europe		...	1 511	1 750	1 380	1 564	Europe
Region not specified		59 723	42 619	45 668	31 217	48 323	Région non spécifiée
Guatemala	VFN						**Guatemala**
Total		880 223	1 181 526	1 315 646	1 502 069	1 627 552	Total
Americas		703 841	1 006 614	1 148 318	1 325 209	1 443 662	Amériques
East Asia/Pacific		21 999	23 167	24 921	27 914	30 246	Asie de l'Est/Pacifique
Europe		150 920	149 871	139 996	147 227	151 807	Europe
Middle East		603	365	1 182	485	454	Moyen-Orient
Region not specified		2 860	1 509	1 229	1 234	1 383	Région non spécifiée
Guinea	TFR						**Guinée**
Total[28]		43 966	42 041	45 334	46 096	...	Total[28]
Africa		19 227	17 915	17 008	6 562	...	Afrique
Americas		4 064	4 377	5 336	2 260	...	Amériques
East Asia/Pacific		1 833	2 160	2 545	2 002	...	Asie de l'Est/Pacifique
Europe		17 114	15 564	18 007	13 717	...	Europe
Middle East		938	1 040	628	755	...	Moyen-Orient
South Asia		641	985	1 251	20 800	...	Asie du Sud
Region not specified		149	...	559	...	...	Région non spécifiée
Guinea-Bissau	TFN						**Guinée-Bissau**
Total[29]		...	...	4 978	11 617	30 092	Total[29]
Africa		...	...	1 224	2 705	13 354	Afrique
Americas		...	...	451	1 992	2 409	Amériques
East Asia/Pacific		...	...	102	1 601	2 884	Asie de l'Est/Pacifique
Europe		...	...	3 123	5 063	10 289	Europe
Middle East		...	...	12	94	356	Moyen-Orient
South Asia		...	...	66	162	800	Asie du Sud

65

Tourist/visitor arrivals by region of origin *(continued)*
Number
Arrivées de touristes/visiteurs par région de provenance *(suite)*
Nombre

Country or area of destination and region of origin[+]	Series[&] Série[&]	2003	2004	2005	2006	2007	Pays ou zone de destination et région de provenance[+]
Guyana	TFR						**Guyana**
Total[30]		100 911	121 989	116 596	113 474	131 487	Total[30]
Americas		91 022	111 078	105 468	102 627	88 369	Amériques
Europe		8 136	9 056	8 704	8 390	9 686	Europe
Region not specified		1 753	1 855	2 424	2 457	33 432	Région non spécifiée
Haiti	TFR						**Haïti**
Total[3]		136 031	96 439	112 267	107 783	386 060[9]	Total[3]
Americas		125 214	90 615	103 595	98 898	331 986	Amériques
Europe		7 659	4 246	6 720	6 782	23 372	Europe
Region not specified		3 158	1 578	1 952	2 103	30 702	Région non spécifiée
Honduras	TFN						**Honduras**
Total		610 535	640 981	673 035	738 667	831 433	Total
Africa		206	251	231	330	209	Afrique
Americas		557 262	584 831	610 179	666 017	785 225	Amériques
East Asia/Pacific		7 115	7 542	8 437	11 009	7 001	Asie de l'Est/Pacifique
Europe		45 152	47 504	53 482	60 324	38 226	Europe
Middle East		102	109	90	135	100	Moyen-Orient
South Asia		260	278	321	396	250	Asie du Sud
Region not specified		438	466	295	396	422	Région non spécifiée
Hungary	TCEN						**Hongrie**
Total[31]		2 948 224	3 269 868	3 446 362	3 309 753	3 451 186	Total[31]
Africa		5 756	12 379	10 310	7 557	9 540	Afrique
Americas		173 862	202 180	218 304	244 890	252 473	Amériques
East Asia/Pacific		77 189	104 805	132 564	122 687	116 151	Asie de l'Est/Pacifique
Europe		2 626 677	2 860 588	2 985 842	2 827 586	3 073 022	Europe
Region not specified		64 740	89 916	99 342	107 033	...	Région non spécifiée
Hungary	VFN						**Hongrie**
Total[32]		36 168 616	36 104 954	38 554 561	40 962 830	42 466 159	Total[32]
Africa		18 093	14 050	13 502	16 675	18 382	Atrique
Americas		454 083	478 255	490 440	521 151	532 683	Amériques
East Asia/Pacific		201 527	236 915	272 207	290 992	312 426	Asie de l'Est/Pacifique
Europe		35 448 201	35 318 166	37 744 758	40 100 380	41 558 891	Europe
Middle East		23 181	9 593	9 538	9 477	13 527	Moyen-Orient
South Asia		14 966	14 630	15 179	15 500	17 533	Asie du Sud
Region not specified		8 565	33 345	8 937	8 655	12 717	Région non spécifiée
Iceland	TCEN						**Islande**
Total		771 323	836 230	871 401	970 821	1 054 016	Total
Africa		...	...	1 104	1 508	1 356	Afrique
Americas		72 174	74 857	84 839	86 650	85 847	Amériques
East Asia/Pacific		9 013	10 520	29 723	32 943	29 481	Asie de l'Est/Pacifique
Europe		642 762	706 580	714 982	785 148	850 326	Europe
Region not specified		47 374	44 273	40 753	64 572	87 006	Région non spécifiée
India	TFN						**Inde**
Total[2]		2 726 214	3 457 477	3 918 610	4 447 167	5 081 504	Total[2]
Africa		89 201	111 711	130 753	137 285	151 355	Afrique
Americas		540 128	690 169	804 394	912 051	1 049 595	Amériques
East Asia/Pacific		393 281	511 681	584 753	702 147	822 575	Asie de l'Est/Pacifique
Europe		942 061	1 257 239	1 434 983	1 662 362	1 900 413	Europe
Middle East		68 917	80 073	86 450	98 439	118 469	Moyen-Orient
South Asia		666 889	790 698	841 969	908 916	982 468	Asie du Sud
Region not specified		25 737	15 906	35 308	25 967	56 629	Région non spécifiée
Indonesia	TFR						**Indonésie**
Total		4 467 021	5 321 165	5 002 101	4 871 351	5 505 759	Total
Africa		30 244	35 507	27 450	22 655	27 777	Afrique
Americas		175 546	209 779	209 511	184 525	220 202	Amériques
East Asia/Pacific		3 575 842	4 265 551	3 837 107	3 795 481	4 315 873	Asie de l'Est/Pacifique
Europe		605 904	720 706	798 408	730 398	796 730	Europe
Middle East		31 371	35 783	60 601	55 033	55 348	Moyen-Orient
South Asia		48 114	53 839	69 024	83 259	89 829	Asie du Sud

Country or area of destination and region of origin[+]	Series[&] Série[&]	2003	2004	2005	2006	2007	Pays ou zone de destination et région de provenance[+]
Ireland	TFR						**Irlande**
Total		6 764 000	6 953 000	7 334 000	8 001 000	8 333 000	Total
Africa		32 000	42 000	39 000	48 000	39 000	Afrique
Americas		913 000	975 000	956 000	1 058 000	1 099 000	Amériques
East Asia/Pacific		196 000	259 000	226 000	237 000	249 000	Asie de l'Est/Pacifique
Europe		5 623 000	5 677 000	6 113 000	6 658 000	6 946 000	Europe
Israel	TFR						**Israël**
Total[2]		1 063 381	1 505 606	1 902 787	1 825 207	2 066 852	Total[2]
Africa		29 547	40 122	41 450	54 337	66 023	Afrique
Americas		347 622	486 508	602 578	606 771	672 870	Amériques
East Asia/Pacific		42 384	65 953	87 572	94 407	109 134	Asie de l'Est/Pacifique
Europe		598 231	857 133	1 107 142	1 015 624	1 167 525	Europe
Middle East		23 159	28 561	29 946	20 613	13 433	Moyen-Orient
South Asia		10 172	15 155	22 911	23 219	27 631	Asie du Sud
Region not specified		12 266	12 174	11 188	10 236	10 236	Région non spécifiée
Italy	TFN						**Italie**
Total[33]		39 604 118	37 070 775	36 512 500	41 057 834	43 654 122	Total[33]
Africa		122 472	205 617	250 705	253 863	264 662	Afrique
Americas		1 680 228	2 988 244	3 250 284	3 579 393	3 440 062	Amériques
East Asia/Pacific		1 074 563	1 088 281	1 111 603	1 188 781	1 326 583	Asie de l'Est/Pacifique
Europe		36 583 819	32 521 819	31 571 338	35 594 161	38 136 255	Europe
Middle East		76 035	129 760	212 716	246 956	242 048	Moyen-Orient
South Asia		67 001	135 290	115 193	189 745	173 235	Asie du Sud
Region not specified		...	1 764	661	4 935	71 277	Région non spécifiée
Jamaica	TFR						**Jamaïque**
Total[3,9]		1 350 285	1 414 786	1 478 663	1 678 905	1 700 785	Total[3,9]
Africa		1 084	1 139	889	1 032	1 449	Afrique
Americas		1 119 679	1 161 840	1 233 846	1 411 339	1 398 318	Amériques
East Asia/Pacific		9 051	7 971	8 129	8 240	8 620	Asie de l'Est/Pacifique
Europe		219 406	242 904	234 952	257 224	290 269	Europe
Middle East		363	350	347	394	477	Moyen-Orient
South Asia		643	554	464	600	1 604	Asie du Sud
Region not specified		59	28	36	76	48	Région non spécifiée
Japan	VFN						**Japon**
Total[2]		5 211 725	6 137 905	6 727 926	7 334 077	8 346 969	Total[2]
Africa		16 434	16 946	20 583	18 678	20 114	Afrique
Americas		824 345	951 074	1 032 140	1 035 300	1 054 019	Amériques
East Asia/Pacific		3 625 013	4 337 788	4 761 395	5 362 608	6 267 798	Asie de l'Est/Pacifique
Europe		665 187	744 142	817 092	817 670	897 944	Europe
Middle East		3 166	3 285	3 072	3 218	3 294	Moyen-Orient
South Asia		76 217	83 856	92 676	95 555	102 860	Asie du Sud
Region not specified		1 363	814	968	1 048	940	Région non spécifiée
Jordan	TFN						**Jordanie**
Total[1]		2 353 087	2 852 803	2 986 589	3 225 409	3 430 954	Total[1]
Africa		17 537	19 938	30 234	50 670	54 708	Afrique
Americas		64 545	93 477	111 975	163 918	177 782	Amériques
East Asia/Pacific		43 883	60 121	64 191	82 943	126 069	Asie de l'Est/Pacifique
Europe		314 858	374 428	391 846	424 583	570 859	Europe
Middle East		1 464 910	1 780 755	1 828 735	1 879 541	1 689 532	Moyen-Orient
South Asia		27 034	37 885	42 947	41 884	64 895	Asie du Sud
Region not specified		420 320	486 199	516 661	581 870	747 109	Région non spécifiée
Kazakhstan	VFR						**Kazakhstan**
Total		3 236 788	4 291 040	4 364 949	4 706 742	5 310 582	Total
Africa		1 064	1 506	1 703	5 023	2 272	Afrique
Americas		23 203	32 345	30 768	31 978	33 222	Amériques
East Asia/Pacific		72 359	96 660	113 842	152 929	219 908	Asie de l'Est/Pacifique
Europe		3 114 377	4 125 909	4 194 081	4 486 983	5 018 562	Europe
Middle East		2 917	1 984	2 276	3 212	4 551	Moyen-Orient
South Asia		17 733	20 849	19 036	21 811	26 372	Asie du Sud
Region not specified		5 135	11 787	3 243	4 806	5 695	Région non spécifiée

65

Tourist/visitor arrivals by region of origin *(continued)*
Number
Arrivées de touristes/visiteurs par région de provenance *(suite)*
Nombre

Country or area of destination and region of origin[+]	Series[&] Série[&]	2003	2004	2005	2006	2007	Pays ou zone de destination et région de provenance[+]
Kenya	VFR						**Kenya**
Total[2,34]		1 146 099	...	...	...	...	Total[2,34]
Africa		311 819	...	...	...	...	Afrique
Americas		97 389	...	...	...	...	Amériques
East Asia/Pacific		50 681	...	...	...	...	Asie de l'Est/Pacifique
Europe		658 384	...	...	...	...	Europe
South Asia		27 479	...	...	...	...	Asie du Sud
Region not specified		347	...	...	...	...	Région non spécifiée
Kiribati	TFN						**Kiribati**
Total[3]		4 905[35]	3 616[36]	3 037[36]	4 406[35]	4 709[35]	Total[3]
Americas		786	123	300	760	1 072	Amériques
East Asia/Pacific		2 875	2 463	2 185	2 744	2 573	Asie de l'Est/Pacifique
Europe		388	387	133	232	190	Europe
Region not specified		856	643	419	670	874	Région non spécifiée
Korea, Republic of	VFN						**Corée, République de**
Total[37]		4 753 604	5 818 138	6 022 752	6 155 046	6 448 240	Total[37]
Africa		14 834	14 649	14 464	16 071	19 210	Afrique
Americas		505 067	610 562	640 050	673 118	716 336	Amériques
East Asia/Pacific		3 334 633	4 252 976	4 441 757	4 554 010	4 696 553	Asie de l'Est/Pacifique
Europe		514 403	531 257	540 694	571 648	605 440	Europe
Middle East		8 045	11 155	13 050	14 964	15 859	Moyen-Orient
South Asia		86 000	95 398	92 189	95 430	100 662	Asie du Sud
Region not specified		290 622	302 141	280 548	229 805	294 180	Région non spécifiée
Kuwait	VFN						**Koweït**
Total		2 602 302	3 056 093	3 474 267	3 899 105	4 481 616	Total
Africa		26 169	29 144	35 339	43 420	54 708	Afrique
Americas		103 447	115 260	131 644	155 203	189 775	Amériques
East Asia/Pacific		124 868	158 006	184 548	226 747	235 562	Asie de l'Est/Pacifique
Europe		94 168	125 509	136 877	154 765	177 528	Europe
Middle East		1 505 733	1 769 220	2 004 725	2 222 558	2 618 506	Moyen-Orient
South Asia		745 679	855 730	977 946	1 092 846	1 191 690	Asie du Sud
Region not specified		2 238	3 224	3 188	3 566	13 847	Région non spécifiée
Kyrgyzstan	TFR						**Kirghizistan**
Total[38]		341 990	398 078	319 303	765 850	1 654 089	Total[38]
Americas		12 744	12 266	13 023	14 140	15 407	Amériques
East Asia/Pacific		14 005	16 766	21 993	26 288	29 611	Asie de l'Est/Pacifique
Europe		269 575	356 982	273 696	715 435	1 594 672	Europe
Middle East		...	...	108	134	168	Moyen-Orient
South Asia		5 395	5 864	6 364	5 142	7 262	Asie du Sud
Region not specified		40 271	6 200	4 119	4 711	6 969	Région non spécifiée
Lao People's Dem. Rep.	VFN						**Rép. dém. pop. lao**
Total		636 361	894 806	1 095 315	1 215 107	1 623 943	Total
Americas		39 453	47 153	60 061	60 883	61 463	Amériques
East Asia/Pacific		495 253	728 262	897 177	1 006 564	1 404 095	Asie de l'Est/Pacifique
Europe		97 314	116 180	134 472	143 716	152 023	Europe
South Asia		2 932	1 845	2 096	2 100	2 361	Asie du Sud
Region not specified		1 409	1 366	1 509	1 844	4 001	Région non spécifiée
Latvia	TCER						**Lettonie**
Total		414 924	545 366	730 146	816 297	844 828	Total
Africa		151	83	71	137	132	Afrique
Americas		14 128	21 091	20 423	22 517	20 849	Amériques
East Asia/Pacific		7 603	9 511	9 941	10 131	11 387	Asie de l'Est/Pacifique
Europe		386 070	500 979	680 362	757 385	794 241	Europe
Middle East		131	196	524	233	390	Moyen-Orient
South Asia		294	308	570	620	626	Asie du Sud
Region not specified		6 547	13 198	18 255	25 274	17 203	Région non spécifiée
Lebanon	TFN						**Liban**
Total[39]		1 015 793	1 278 469	1 139 524	1 062 625	1 017 072	Total[39]
Africa		39 453	45 095	31 073	39 021	59 861	Afrique
Americas		120 239	152 175	136 904	130 117	121 596	Amériques
East Asia/Pacific		65 581	92 285	87 813	74 461	63 579	Asie de l'Est/Pacifique

65

Tourist/visitor arrivals by region of origin *(continued)*
Number
Arrivées de touristes/visiteurs par région de provenance *(suite)*
Nombre

Country or area of destination and region of origin[+]	Series[&] Série[&]	2003	2004	2005	2006	2007	Pays ou zone de destination et région de provenance[+]
Europe		267 077	337 337	316 561	269 263	277 873	Europe
Middle East		421 148	520 230	436 549	433 323	388 292	Moyen-Orient
South Asia		102 035	128 120	129 315	115 243	104 729	Asie du Sud
Region not specified		260	3 227	1 309	1 197	1 142	Région non spécifiée
Lesotho	VFR						**Lesotho**
Total		329 301	303 530	303 578	356 913	300 350	Total
Africa		302 924	290 295	289 342	329 838	271 475	Afrique
Americas		2 842	1 375	1 490	3 412	3 385	Amériques
East Asia/Pacific		4 009	2 551	2 657	3 456	4 816	Asie de l'Est/Pacifique
Europe		12 569	7 568	7 930	19 641	19 772	Europe
Middle East		...	...	...	117	400	Moyen-Orient
South Asia		...	...	...	318	304	Asie du Sud
Region not specified		6 957	1 741	2 159	131	198	Région non spécifiée
Libyan Arab Jamah.	VFN						**Jamah. arabe libyenne**
Total * [40]		957 896	999 343	...	...	...	Total * [40]
Africa		457 721	482 704	...	...	...	Afrique
Americas		1 926	2 201	...	...	...	Amériques
East Asia/Pacific		6 601	6 942	...	...	...	Asie de l'Est/Pacifique
Europe		42 056	45 657	...	...	...	Europe
Middle East		445 561	458 124	...	...	...	Moyen-Orient
South Asia		4 031	3 704	...	...	...	Asie du Sud
Region not specified		...	11	...	...	...	Région non spécifiée
Liechtenstein	THSR						**Liechtenstein**
Total		49 002	48 501	49 767	54 856	58 258	Total
Africa		214	198	170	189	216	Afrique
Americas		2 414	2 739	2 888	2 999	3 156	Amériques
East Asia/Pacific		1 634	1 728	1 635	1 740	1 724	Asie de l'Est/Pacifique
Europe		44 740	43 836	44 944	49 818	53 053	Europe
South Asia		...	...	47	59	62	Asie du Sud
Region not specified		...	...	83	51	47	Région non spécifiée
Lithuania	TCER						**Lituanie**
Total		438 299	590 043	681 487	759 041	849 006	Total
Africa		400	525	1 159	1 360	961	Afrique
Americas		16 324	22 385	23 626	25 955	27 188	Amériques
East Asia/Pacific		11 003	15 472	15 032	16 260	15 953	Asie de l'Est/Pacifique
Europe		400 338	538 078	623 045	694 241	791 281	Europe
Region not specified		10 234	13 583	18 625	21 225	13 623	Région non spécifiée
Luxembourg	TCER						**Luxembourg**
Total		867 048	877 712	912 798	908 171	917 334	Total
Americas		28 562	29 777	32 249	34 516	33 255	Amériques
Europe		801 138	806 575	840 259	831 114	841 388	Europe
Region not specified		37 348	41 360	40 290	42 541	42 691	Région non spécifiée
Madagascar	TFN						**Madagascar**
Total [3]		139 230	228 785	277 422	311 730	344 348	Total [3]
Africa		21 725	39 302	52 277	58 520	64 013	Afrique
Americas		4 177	9 180	13 853	15 587	13 671	Amériques
East Asia/Pacific		4 872	3 432	6 404	7 206	14 084	Asie de l'Est/Pacifique
Europe		99 271	175 727	202 530	228 452	246 837	Europe
Region not specified		9 185	1 144	2 358	1 965	5 743	Région non spécifiée
Malawi	TFR						**Malawi**
Total [32]		424 000	427 360	437 718	637 780	714 315	Total [32]
Africa		320 360	335 651	336 856	483 615	541 649	Afrique
Americas		18 070	20 828	18 725	36 162	40 502	Amériques
East Asia/Pacific		9 940	11 313	8 698	10 030	11 234	Asie de l'Est/Pacifique
Europe		67 500	48 929	60 437	94 266	105 578	Europe
Middle East		...	...	...	5 730	6 418	Moyen-Orient
South Asia		3 620	6 815	9 549	...	...	Asie du Sud
Region not specified		4 510	3 824	3 453	7 977	8 934	Région non spécifiée
Malaysia	TFR						**Malaisie**
Total [41]		10 576 915	15 703 406	16 431 055	17 546 863	20 972 822	Total [41]
Africa		133 762	136 587	128 208	157 342	307 797	Afrique

Country or area of destination and region of origin[+]	Series[&] Série[&]	2003	2004	2005	2006	2007	Pays ou zone de destination et région de provenance[+]
Americas		270 157	271 901	274 915	312 478	472 164	Amériques
East Asia/Pacific		9 073 882	13 983 381	14 685 975	15 478 386	17 656 571	Asie de l'Est/Pacifique
Europe		456 351	540 306	618 188	673 118	829 653	Europe
Middle East		78 324	124 331	145 448	173 750	225 153	Moyen-Orient
South Asia		209 120	248 673	321 246	390 189	686 614	Asie du Sud
Region not specified		355 319	398 227	257 075	361 600	794 870	Région non spécifiée
Maldives	TFN						**Maldives**
Total[3]		563 593	616 716	395 320	601 923	675 889	Total[3]
Africa		3 984	5 325	3 460	4 169	4 846	Afrique
Americas		7 660	9 385	7 238	10 813	14 198	Amériques
East Asia/Pacific		83 640	99 735	55 985	102 277	124 674	Asie de l'Est/Pacifique
Europe		443 093	475 707	306 856	457 535	495 371	Europe
Middle East		3 636	4 517	2 404	4 372	6 450	Moyen-Orient
South Asia		21 580	22 047	19 377	22 757	30 350	Asie du Sud
Mali	THSN						**Mali**
Total		110 005	112 654	142 814	152 660	164 124	Total
Africa		27 816	29 256	35 985	38 892	29 378	Afrique
Americas		9 393	12 494	13 287	18 507	17 564	Amériques
East Asia/Pacific		1 200	3 117	2 090	1 636	1 416	Asie de l'Est/Pacifique
Europe		62 744	64 252	80 968	86 443	104 308	Europe
Middle East		2 712	1 524	1 064	1 128	1 190	Moyen-Orient
Region not specified		6 500	2 011	9 420	6 054	10 268	Région non spécifiée
Malta	TFN						**Malte**
Total		1 126 601	1 156 028[42]	1 230 610[42]	1 124 233[42]	1 243 508[42]	Total
Americas		20 657	18 720	18 136	16 970	20 423	Amériques
Europe		939 793	982 623	1 066 530	955 176	1 030 784	Europe
Middle East		20 218	12 831	10 662	9 198	9 259	Moyen-Orient
Region not specified		145 933	141 854	135 282	142 889	183 042	Région non spécifiée
Marshall Islands	TFR						**Iles Marshall**
Total		7 195[3]	9 007[18]	9 173[18]	5 780[3]	7 200[3]	Total
Americas		2 189	2 099	1 721	1 472	1 703	Amériques
East Asia/Pacific		4 422	4 466	5 577	3 850	4 382	Asie de l'Est/Pacifique
Europe		196	160	160	180	278	Europe
Region not specified		388	2 282	1 715	278	837	Région non spécifiée
Martinique	TFR						**Martinique**
Total		453 159	470 890	484 127	503 475	501 491	Total
Americas		71 559	73 011	81 247	79 335	92 980	Amériques
Europe		379 922	396 138	399 083	422 453	405 231	Europe
Region not specified		1 678	1 741	3 797	1 687	3 280	Région non spécifiée
Mauritius	TFR						**Maurice**
Total		702 018	718 861	761 063	788 276	906 971	Total
Africa		173 996	175 295	184 821	189 026	210 553	Afrique
Americas		8 106	8 380	8 791	9 759	10 462	Amériques
East Asia/Pacific		21 934	27 026	28 924	34 103	39 681	Asie de l'Est/Pacifique
Europe		465 620	477 347	503 037	510 872	596 132	Europe
Middle East		4 800	3 883	3 737	4 715	4 591	Moyen-Orient
South Asia		27 277	26 558	31 087	39 070	44 762	Asie du Sud
Region not specified		285	372	666	731	790	Région non spécifiée
Mexico	TFN						**Mexique**
Total[9]		...	...	21 914 917	21 352 605	21 423 545	Total[9]
Americas		...	...	19 012 275	18 713 395	18 867 770	Amériques
East Asia/Pacific		...	...	92 007	99 723	109 488	Asie de l'Est/Pacifique
Europe		...	...	1 134 228	1 295 430	1 423 432	Europe
Region not specified		...	...	1 676 407	1 244 057	1 022 855	Région non spécifiée
Mexico	TFR						**Mexique**
Total[9]		18 665 384	20 617 746	21 914 917	21 352 605	21 423 545	Total[9]
Americas		18 155 315	19 705 636	20 691 415	20 094 345	20 045 546	Amériques
Europe		443 366	...	...	...	...	Europe
Region not specified		66 703	912 110	1 223 502	1 258 260	1 377 999	Région non spécifiée

Tourist/visitor arrivals by region of origin *(continued)*
Number
Arrivées de touristes/visiteurs par région de provenance *(suite)*
Nombre

65

Country or area of destination and region of origin[+]	Series[&] Série[&]	2003	2004	2005	2006	2007	Pays ou zone de destination et région de provenance[+]
Micronesia (Fed. States of)	TFR						**Micronésie (Etats féd. de)**
Total[43]		18 211	19 260	18 958	19 136	21 146	Total[43]
Americas		7 671	7 744	7 955	8 256	8 471	Amériques
East Asia/Pacific		8 884	9 982	8 895	8 361	10 082	Asie de l'Est/Pacifique
Europe		1 568	1 408	2 019	2 398	2 452	Europe
Region not specified		88	126	89	121	141	Région non spécifiée
Monaco	THSN						**Monaco**
Total		234 638	250 159	285 675	313 070	327 985	Total
Africa		2 228	2 230	2 601	2 826	3 293	Afrique
Americas		23 660	25 132	28 626	34 071	40 910	Amériques
East Asia/Pacific		9 781	12 653	11 746	10 632	12 382	Asie de l'Est/Pacifique
Europe		186 972	190 326	214 131	239 872	244 497	Europe
Middle East		3 320	3 367	3 190	3 694	4 318	Moyen-Orient
Region not specified		8 677	16 451	25 381	21 975	22 585	Région non spécifiée
Mongolia	TFN						**Mongolie**
Total		201 153	300 537	337 790	385 989	...	Total
Africa		209	263	297	502	...	Afrique
Americas		6 863	12 198	12 913	14 433	...	Amériques
East Asia/Pacific		120 691	188 250	223 411	245 760	...	Asie de l'Est/Pacifique
Europe		72 345	98 592	100 123	124 002	...	Europe
Middle East		229	249	232	159	...	Moyen-Orient
South Asia		803	966	792	1 129	...	Asie du Sud
Region not specified		13	19	22	4	...	Région non spécifiée
Montenegro	TCEN						**Monténégro**
Total		141 787	188 060	272 005	377 798	984 138	Total
Americas		2 657	3 354	4 302	7 324	8 894	Amériques
East Asia/Pacific		427	682	973	1 488	2 075	Asie de l'Est/Pacifique
Europe		135 329	180 286	259 596	359 937	963 214	Europe
Region not specified		3 374	3 738	7 134	9 049	9 955	Région non spécifiée
Montserrat	TFR						**Montserrat**
Total		8 390	10 138	9 690	7 991	7 746	Total
Americas		5 932	6 822	6 448	5 427	5 311	Amériques
East Asia/Pacific		...	...	...	...	5	Asie de l'Est/Pacifique
Europe		2 414	3 197	3 196	2 501	2 366	Europe
Region not specified		44	119	46	63	64	Région non spécifiée
Morocco	TFN						**Maroc**
Total[1]		4 761 271	5 476 712	5 843 360	6 558 269	7 407 617	Total[1]
Africa		103 194	123 070	143 855	165 307	192 668	Afrique
Americas		107 877	127 974	140 194	173 258	196 154	Amériques
East Asia/Pacific		41 651	48 874	51 745	65 234	73 910	Asie de l'Est/Pacifique
Europe		1 880 177	2 309 477	2 607 239	3 024 876	3 405 703	Europe
Middle East		78 639	84 298	91 029	105 632	115 832	Moyen-Orient
South Asia		5 383	6 486	7 723	8 795	11 592	Asie du Sud
Region not specified		2 544 350	2 776 533	2 801 575	3 015 167	3 411 758	Région non spécifiée
Mozambique	VFR						**Mozambique**
Total		726 099	711 060	954 433	1 095 000	1 259 000	Total
Africa		591 647	623 240	851 999	977 468	1 043 310	Afrique
Americas		5 035	5 647	12 399	14 226	18 799	Amériques
East Asia/Pacific		...	...	8 036	9 220	12 680	Asie de l'Est/Pacifique
Europe		42 698	56 508	47 999	55 074	66 233	Europe
Region not specified		86 719	25 665	34 000	39 012	117 978	Région non spécifiée
Myanmar	TFN						**Myanmar**
Total[44]		205 610	241 938	232 218	263 514	248 076	Total[44]
Africa		390	395	488	502	432	Afrique
Americas		16 426	20 451	20 701	22 880	19 331	Amériques
East Asia/Pacific		115 614	141 683	129 922	148 282	144 484	Asie de l'Est/Pacifique
Europe		60 364	65 411	67 933	80 791	72 827	Europe
Middle East		1 148	1 831	1 920	2 177	2 281	Moyen-Orient
South Asia		11 668	12 167	11 254	8 882	8 721	Asie du Sud

65

Tourist/visitor arrivals by region of origin *(continued)*
Number
Arrivées de touristes/visiteurs par région de provenance *(suite)*
Nombre

Country or area of destination and region of origin[+]	Series[&] Série[&]	2003	2004	2005	2006	2007	Pays ou zone de destination et région de provenance[+]
Namibia	TFN						**Namibie**
Total		695 221	...	777 888	833 344	928 914	Total
Africa		525 885	...	601 737	628 588	690 148	Afrique
Americas		11 775	...	11 979	16 325	19 342	Amériques
East Asia/Pacific		4 280	...	4 274	4 645	5 783	Asie de l'Est/Pacifique
Europe		141 834	...	146 361	166 972	194 605	Europe
Region not specified		11 447	...	13 537	16 814	19 036	Région non spécifiée
Nepal	TFR						**Népal**
Total		338 132	385 297	375 398	383 926	526 705	Total
Africa		1 501	1 346	1 285	1 571	1 309	Afrique
Americas		25 156	29 791	26 385	27 991	41 348	Amériques
East Asia/Pacific		91 582	96 565	92 733	95 407	139 615	Asie de l'Est/Pacifique
Europe		111 822	131 999	112 341	108 166	157 505	Europe
South Asia		108 071	124 804	139 288	137 059	168 041	Asie du Sud
Region not specified		...	792	3 366	13 732	18 887	Région non spécifiée
Netherlands	TCER						**Pays-Bas**
Total		9 180 600	9 646 500	10 011 900	10 738 700	11 008 000	Total
Africa		130 600	117 300	101 100	92 700	91 900	Afrique
Americas		996 100	1 131 500	1 222 200	1 325 000	1 273 600	Amériques
East Asia/Pacific		622 100	753 700	748 700	722 600	738 500	Asie de l'Est/Pacifique
Europe		7 431 800	7 644 000	7 939 900	8 598 400	8 904 000	Europe
New Caledonia	TFR						**Nouvelle-Calédonie**
Total[9]		101 983	99 515	100 651	100 491	103 363	Total[9]
Africa		489	615	637	705	628	Afrique
Americas		1 753	1 676	1 785	1 854	1 918	Amériques
East Asia/Pacific		65 382	65 892	67 753	66 074	68 449	Asie de l'Est/Pacifique
Europe		32 492	29 992	30 268	31 850	32 252	Europe
Region not specified		1 867	1 340	208	8	116	Région non spécifiée
New Zealand	VFR						**Nouvelle-Zélande**
Total[9,45]		2 104 420	2 334 153	2 365 529	2 400 888	2 455 204	Total[9,45]
Africa		19 395	18 673	19 709	20 643	24 251	Afrique
Americas		266 245	275 699	275 616	294 450	289 860	Amériques
East Asia/Pacific		1 271 657	1 468 307	1 484 424	1 512 292	1 550 926	Asie de l'Est/Pacifique
Europe		460 938	488 674	521 267	515 716	517 080	Europe
Middle East		7 048	8 122	8 871	9 607	10 758	Moyen-Orient
South Asia		17 028	17 830	19 833	22 507	24 216	Asie du Sud
Region not specified		62 109	56 848	35 809	33 673	38 193	Région non spécifiée
Nicaragua	TFN						**Nicaragua**
Total		525 775[2]	614 782[2]	712 444[1]	749 184[1]	799 996[1]	Total
Africa		378	515	621	643	471	Afrique
Americas		464 176	552 846	619 305	623 470	671 603	Amériques
East Asia/Pacific		10 674	8 326	11 235	12 792	9 096	Asie de l'Est/Pacifique
Europe		49 147	52 564	58 964	58 319	52 525	Europe
Middle East		89	76	82	129	157	Moyen-Orient
South Asia		1 254	437	1 522	861	444	Asie du Sud
Region not specified		57	18	20 715	52 970	65 700	Région non spécifiée
Niger	TFN						**Niger**
Total		55 344	57 004	59 920	60 332	47 539	Total
Africa		37 344	38 000	35 952	36 199	23 770	Afrique
Americas		2 000	2 500	4 194	4 223	3 898	Amériques
East Asia/Pacific		1 400	1 500	2 996	3 017	1 778	Asie de l'Est/Pacifique
Europe		14 344	14 500	16 778	16 893	17 589	Europe
Middle East		...	...	...	...	504	Moyen-Orient
Region not specified		256	504	...	...	...	Région non spécifiée
Nigeria	VFN						**Nigéria**
Total		2 253 115	2 646 411	2 778 365	3 055 800	...	Total
Africa		1 554 308	1 825 312	1 916 246	2 107 870	...	Afrique
Americas		94 486	111 020	116 563	129 219	...	Amériques
East Asia/Pacific		130 228	153 020	160 666	177 001	...	Asie de l'Est/Pacifique
Europe		372 846	438 093	459 985	506 000	...	Europe

65

Tourist/visitor arrivals by region of origin *(continued)*
Number
Arrivées de touristes/visiteurs par région de provenance *(suite)*
Nombre

Country or area of destination and region of origin[+]	Series[&] Série[&]	2003	2004	2005	2006	2007	Pays ou zone de destination et région de provenance[+]
Middle East		40 608	47 714	50 095	55 104	...	Moyen-Orient
South Asia		52 523	61 714	64 796	72 000	...	Asie du Sud
Region not specified		8 116	9 538	10 014	8 606	...	Région non spécifiée
Niue	TFR						**Nioué**
Total[46]		2 706[3]	2 550[3]	2 793[3]	3 008[3]	3 463[18]	Total[46]
Americas		178	138	181	161	208	Amériques
East Asia/Pacific		2 247	2 217	2 272	2 588	3 026	Asie de l'Est/Pacifique
Europe		235	168	295	237	206	Europe
Region not specified		46	27	45	22	23	Région non spécifiée
Northern Mariana Islands	VFN						**Iles Mariannes du Nord**
Total		459 458	535 873	506 846	435 494	389 345	Total
Americas		34 670	37 334	37 989	32 582	28 082	Amériques
East Asia/Pacific		422 811	494 826	465 360	398 952	355 921	Asie de l'Est/Pacifique
Europe		439	666	1 300	2 324	4 676	Europe
Region not specified		1 538	3 047	2 197	1 636	666	Région non spécifiée
Norway	TFN						**Norvège**
Total[47]		3 269 000	3 628 000	3 824 000	4 070 000	4 290 000	Total[47]
Americas		144 000	176 000	146 000	163 000	170 000	Amériques
East Asia/Pacific		35 000	35 000	41 000	37 000	34 000	Asie de l'Est/Pacifique
Europe		3 009 000	3 307 000	3 508 000	3 698 000	3 860 000	Europe
Region not specified		81 000	110 000	129 000	172 000	226 000	Région non spécifiée
Occupied Palestinian Terr.	THSN						**Terr. palestinien occupé**
Total		36 722	56 011	88 360	122 616	264 168	Total
Africa		604	641	971	1 643	4 951	Afrique
Americas		6 407	10 649	13 735	18 728	32 440	Amériques
East Asia/Pacific		4 872	8 399	16 490	16 595	20 424	Asie de l'Est/Pacifique
Europe		23 701	35 210	55 324	83 178	203 468	Europe
Middle East		1 138	1 112	1 840	2 472	2 885	Moyen-Orient
Oman	THSN						**Oman**
Total		629 525	908 466	989 390	1 306 128	1 130 735	Total
Africa		19 035	28 266	14 598	15 161	15 310	Afrique
Americas		36 356	40 154	17 938	47 639	43 872	Amériques
East Asia/Pacific		51 026	54 971	56 245	82 616	78 338	Asie de l'Est/Pacifique
Europe		163 855	280 727	403 962	577 546	362 242	Europe
Middle East		204 586	249 285	240 506	230 777	189 844	Moyen-Orient
South Asia		101 971	130 565	140 832	133 180	174 657	Asie du Sud
Region not specified		52 696	124 498	115 309	219 209	266 472	Région non spécifiée
Pakistan	TFN						**Pakistan**
Total		500 918	647 993	798 260	898 389	839 500	Total
Africa		11 721	12 521	14 691	18 970	15 797	Afrique
Americas		85 910	103 104	146 548	160 713	160 615	Amériques
East Asia/Pacific		43 521	59 503	83 607	99 063	87 092	Asie de l'Est/Pacifique
Europe		192 854	280 877	356 804	393 919	386 672	Europe
Middle East		19 593	28 365	31 920	37 661	35 887	Moyen-Orient
South Asia		146 655	160 345	158 549	182 144	148 856	Asie du Sud
Region not specified		664	3 278	6 141	5 919	4 581	Région non spécifiée
Palau	TFR						**Palaos**
Total[48]		68 296	94 895	86 124	87 206	93 031	Total[48]
Americas		4 511	6 507	5 910	8 932	6 250	Amériques
East Asia/Pacific		61 400	84 381	75 501	73 714	82 297	Asie de l'Est/Pacifique
Europe		818	1 837	2 390	2 203	2 298	Europe
Region not specified		1 567	2 170	2 323	2 357	2 186	Région non spécifiée
Panama	VFR						**Panama**
Total[49]		468 686	498 415	576 050	703 745	948 946	Total[49]
Africa		354	335	390	477	646	Afrique
Americas		410 957	438 872	507 185	619 526	835 948	Amériques
East Asia/Pacific		13 968	13 919	16 095	20 241	27 001	Asie de l'Est/Pacifique
Europe		43 355	45 254	52 339	63 451	85 283	Europe
Middle East		52	35	41	50	68	Moyen-Orient

65 Tourist/visitor arrivals by region of origin *(continued)*
Number
Arrivées de touristes/visiteurs par région de provenance *(suite)*
Nombre

Country or area of destination and region of origin[+]	Series[&] Série[&]	2003	2004	2005	2006	2007	Pays ou zone de destination et région de provenance[+]
Papua New Guinea	TFR						**Papouasie-Nvl-Guinée**
Total		56 282	59 013	69 251	77 730	104 122	Total
Africa		193	241	353	500	725	Afrique
Americas		5 215	5 440	6 491	7 355	7 868	Amériques
East Asia/Pacific		45 999	47 963	57 516	63 325	85 026	Asie de l'Est/Pacifique
Europe		4 218	4 739	4 155	5 548	8 563	Europe
South Asia		657	630	736	1 002	1 940	Asie du Sud
Paraguay	TFN						**Paraguay**
Total[4,50]		268 175	309 287	340 845	388 465	415 702	Total[4,50]
Africa		185	211	253	358	484	Afrique
Americas		248 364	284 325	311 628	349 105	369 993	Amériques
East Asia/Pacific		4 251	4 718	5 466	8 058	9 174	Asie de l'Est/Pacifique
Europe		15 375	19 788	23 201	30 531	35 133	Europe
Middle East		...	96	97	184	377	Moyen-Orient
South Asia		...	148	200	229	427	Asie du Sud
Region not specified		...	1	...	...	114	Région non spécifiée
Peru	TFR						**Pérou**
Total		1 135 769[1]	1 349 959	1 570 566[9,51]	1 720 746[9,51]	1 916 400[9,51]	Total
Africa		2 127	2 760	3 435	3 130	3 819	Afrique
Americas		762 290	983 592	1 126 506	1 247 653	1 399 083	Amériques
East Asia/Pacific		49 918	64 572	76 852	84 847	94 271	Asie de l'Est/Pacifique
Europe		252 435	296 684	360 297	378 296	414 588	Europe
Middle East		117	155	229	185	249	Moyen-Orient
South Asia		1 294	1 245	1 831	1 965	2 755	Asie du Sud
Region not specified		67 588	951	1 416	4 670	1 635	Région non spécifiée
Philippines	TFR						**Philippines**
Total[1]		1 907 226	2 291 352	2 623 084	2 843 345	3 091 993	Total[1]
Africa		1 442	1 700	2 294	2 246	3 090	Afrique
Americas		444 264	545 867	604 793	651 705	674 921	Amériques
East Asia/Pacific		1 128 540	1 359 256	1 565 359	1 690 939	1 829 095	Asie de l'Est/Pacifique
Europe		177 338	212 305	246 449	264 353	300 372	Europe
Middle East		16 736	20 683	24 532	27 544	31 759	Moyen-Orient
South Asia		21 543	24 997	28 485	31 975	37 596	Asie du Sud
Region not specified		117 363	126 544	151 172	174 583	215 160	Région non spécifiée
Poland	VFN						**Pologne**
Total		52 129 778	61 917 759	64 606 085	65 114 865	66 207 767	Total
Africa		9 538	11 114	13 217	14 914	16 861	Afrique
Americas		294 313	345 181	439 417	466 299	452 903	Amériques
East Asia/Pacific		88 693	123 114	163 414	193 899	228 844	Asie de l'Est/Pacifique
Europe		51 691 151	61 385 787	63 926 773	64 366 590	65 373 132	Europe
Middle East		6 065	6 471	7 636	8 265	9 507	Moyen-Orient
South Asia		9 483	11 710	13 219	15 246	19 721	Asie du Sud
Region not specified		30 535	34 382	42 409	49 652	106 799	Région non spécifiée
Poland	TCER						**Pologne**
Total		3 331 870	3 934 064	4 310 401	4 313 578	4 387 404	Total
Africa		6 009	5 483	5 637	6 969	6 657	Afrique
Americas		182 309	232 723	242 264	250 413	234 350	Amériques
East Asia/Pacific		66 951	98 239	110 944	117 857	121 185	Asie de l'Est/Pacifique
Europe		3 022 645	3 521 865	3 882 651	3 870 392	3 964 327	Europe
Middle East		3 780	4 403	3 648	5 742	5 288	Moyen-Orient
South Asia		4 843	8 659	8 293	7 093	10 504	Asie du Sud
Region not specified		45 333	62 692	56 964	55 112	45 093	Région non spécifiée
Portugal	TFR						**Portugal**
Total		11 707 228[2]	10 639 000[9,52]	10 612 000[9]	11 282 000[9]	12 321 000[9]	Total
Americas		480 544	367 000	413 000	499 000	600 000	Amériques
East Asia/Pacific		40 055	43 000	37 000	32 000	40 000	Asie de l'Est/Pacifique
Europe		10 887 861	9 343 000	9 271 000	9 831 000	10 693 000	Europe
Region not specified		298 768	886 000	891 000	920 000	988 000	Région non spécifiée

65 Tourist/visitor arrivals by region of origin *(continued)*
Number
Arrivées de touristes/visiteurs par région de provenance *(suite)*
Nombre

Country or area of destination and region of origin[+]	Series[&] Série[&]	2003	2004	2005	2006	2007	Pays ou zone de destination et région de provenance[+]
Puerto Rico	TFR						**Porto Rico**
Total[3,53]		3 238 300	3 541 000	3 685 900	3 722 000	3 687 000	Total[3,53]
Americas		2 470 500	2 754 400	2 847 400	2 929 900	2 886 700	Amériques
Region not specified		767 800	786 600	838 500	792 100	800 300	Région non spécifiée
Qatar	THSR						**Qatar**
Total[54]		556 965	732 454	912 997	945 970	963 573	Total[54]
East Asia/Pacific		127 348	145 974	159 279	180 543	203 465	Asie de l'Est/Pacifique
Europe		88 620	195 732	233 315	201 187	265 965	Europe
Middle East		282 538	295 335	364 977	413 523	361 139	Moyen-Orient
Region not specified		58 459	95 413	155 426	150 717	133 004	Région non spécifiée
Republic of Moldova	VFN						**République de Moldova**
Total[55]		23 598	26 045	25 073	14 239	14 722	Total[55]
Africa		45	71	15	9	7	Afrique
Americas		2 556	2 564	3 161	1 123	580	Amériques
East Asia/Pacific		295	307	277	243	293	Asie de l'Est/Pacifique
Europe		20 152	22 686	21 223	12 741	13 794	Europe
Middle East		525	392	362	114	27	Moyen-Orient
South Asia		25	25	35	9	21	Asie du Sud
Réunion	TFR						**Réunion**
Total		432 000	430 000	409 000	278 800	380 547	Total
Africa		27 367	26 222	24 815	20 109	33 245	Afrique
Americas		...	...	...	...	1 721	Amériques
East Asia/Pacific		...	...	...	...	2 491	Asie de l'Est/Pacifique
Europe		366 725	370 474	349 113	224 065	303 307	Europe
South Asia		...	...	...	...	418	Asie du Sud
Region not specified		37 908	33 304	35 072	34 626	39 365	Région non spécifiée
Romania	VFR						**Roumanie**
Total		5 594 828	6 600 115	5 839 374	6 036 999	7 721 741	Total
Africa		5 461	6 585	6 992	9 274	10 701	Afrique
Americas		115 373	139 463	154 244	171 930	188 807	Amériques
East Asia/Pacific		41 610	49 309	57 028	61 921	79 998	Asie de l'Est/Pacifique
Europe		5 391 609	6 360 587	5 580 091	5 751 503	7 394 449	Europe
Middle East		26 867	27 760	24 090	25 049	29 195	Moyen-Orient
South Asia		12 856	15 344	15 566	15 774	17 106	Asie du Sud
Region not specified		1 052	1 067	1 363	1 548	1 485	Région non spécifiée
Russian Federation	VFN						**Fédération de Russie**
Total		22 521 059	22 064 213	22 200 649	22 486 043	22 908 625	Total
Africa		28 985	29 217	26 909	28 288	29 964	Afrique
Americas		420 857	477 338	457 301	532 991	466 404	Amériques
East Asia/Pacific		1 106 605	1 313 669	1 315 480	1 345 870	1 381 412	Asie de l'Est/Pacifique
Europe		20 236 821	19 607 077	19 690 628	19 872 873	20 395 436	Europe
Middle East		31 792	31 765	33 405	33 029	23 998	Moyen-Orient
South Asia		58 804	62 927	68 421	71 917	100 150	Asie du Sud
Region not specified		637 195	542 220	608 505	601 075	511 261	Région non spécifiée
Saba	TFR						**Saba**
Total		10 261	11 012	11 462	11 012	11 673	Total
Americas		4 106	4 764	4 933	4 712	5 210	Amériques
Europe		4 387	4 628	5 097	4 776	5 287	Europe
Region not specified		1 768	1 620	1 432	1 524	1 176	Région non spécifiée
Saint Eustatius	TFR						**Saint-Eustache**
Total[56]		10 451	11 056	10 355	9 584	11 568	Total[56]
Americas		3 483	3 732	3 457	3 177	3 928	Amériques
Europe		5 272	5 505	5 400	4 851	5 893	Europe
Region not specified		1 696	1 819	1 498	1 556	1 747	Région non spécifiée
Saint Kitts and Nevis	TFR						**Saint-Kitts-et-Nevis**
Total[3]		90 562	117 638	140 504	139 268	117 347	Total[3]
Americas		75 783	103 093	125 031	123 530	101 580	Amériques
Europe		11 467	11 004	11 149	11 148	10 770	Europe
Region not specified		3 312	3 541	4 324	4 590	4 997	Région non spécifiée

Country or area of destination and region of origin[+]	Series[&] Série[&]	2003	2004	2005	2006	2007	Pays ou zone de destination et région de provenance[+]
Saint Lucia	TFR						**Sainte-Lucie**
Total[2]		276 948	298 431	317 939	302 510	287 407	Total[2]
Americas		183 349	197 433	214 621	214 463	192 018	Amériques
East Asia/Pacific		373	282	260	329	212	Asie de l'Est/Pacifique
Europe		90 193	96 793	101 790	85 565	89 647	Europe
Region not specified		3 033	3 923	1 268	2 153	5 530	Région non spécifiée
Saint Maarten	TFN						**Saint-Martin**
Total[57,58]		427 587	475 032	467 861	467 804	469 407	Total[57,58]
Americas		301 018	338 242	331 841	328 450	335 410	Amériques
Europe		88 259	96 403	93 821	97 058	96 365	Europe
Region not specified		38 310	40 387	42 199	42 296	37 632	Région non spécifiée
Saint Vincent-Grenadines	TFR						**Saint Vincent-Grenadines**
Total[3]		78 535	86 722	95 506	97 432	89 637	Total[3]
Americas		60 315	66 871	74 173	74 193	64 518	Amériques
Europe		17 201	18 652	10 028	21 901	23 454	Europe
Region not specified		1 019	1 199	1 405	1 278	1 665	Région non spécifiée
Samoa	TFR						**Samoa**
Total		92 486	98 155	101 807	115 882	122 352	Total
Americas		8 959	8 311	9 682	9 067	8 493	Amériques
East Asia/Pacific		78 155	84 882	87 217	101 915	109 130	Asie de l'Est/Pacifique
Europe		5 136	4 756	4 632	4 581	4 417	Europe
Region not specified		236	206	276	319	312	Région non spécifiée
San Marino	VFN						**Saint-Marin**
Total[59]		2 882 207	2 812 488	2 107 092[60]	2 135 589	2 164 419	Total[59]
Africa		...	...	111	140	193	Afrique
Americas		...	...	17 479	22 131	36 690	Amériques
East Asia/Pacific		...	...	53 328	36 340	26 475	Asie de l'Est/Pacifique
Europe		...	...	2 035 386	2 075 681	2 099 431	Europe
Middle East		...	...	270	88	696	Moyen-Orient
South Asia		...	...	436	...	693	Asie du Sud
Region not specified		2 882 207	2 812 488	82	1 209	241	Région non spécifiée
Sao Tome and Principe	TFN						**Sao Tomé-et-Principe**
Total		10 039	10 576	15 746	12 266	...	Total
Africa		2 550	2 076	4 361	2 751	...	Afrique
Americas		638	710	580	525	...	Amériques
East Asia/Pacific		...	...	156	...	...	Asie de l'Est/Pacifique
Europe		6 742	6 803	10 299	7 568	...	Europe
Middle East		...	...	35	...	...	Moyen-Orient
South Asia		...	...	23	...	...	Asie du Sud
Region not specified		109	987	292	1 422	...	Région non spécifiée
Saudi Arabia	TFN						**Arabie saoudite**
Total		7 332 233	8 599 430	8 036 613	8 620 465	11 530 834	Total
Africa		525 045	675 441	436 292	488 751	601 614	Afrique
Americas		46 496	53 190	70 196	66 464	235 900	Amériques
East Asia/Pacific		612 340	752 905	439 021	595 438	578 805	Asie de l'Est/Pacifique
Europe		334 159	424 297	340 310	484 575	656 937	Europe
Middle East		3 923 873	4 752 257	5 607 356	5 515 980	7 443 786	Moyen-Orient
South Asia		1 868 897	1 932 990	1 142 202	1 469 257	2 013 792	Asie du Sud
Region not specified		21 423	8 350	1 236	...	...	Région non spécifiée
Senegal	TFN						**Sénégal**
Total		...	666 616	769 489	866 154	874 623	Total
Africa		...	209 226	265 113	429 955	437 970	Afrique
Americas		...	24 686	26 274	25 921	26 004	Amériques
Europe		...	348 852	392 767	323 721	324 080	Europe
Region not specified		...	83 852	85 335	86 557	86 569	Région non spécifiée
Senegal	THSN						**Sénégal**
Total		353 539	363 490	386 565	405 827	386 793	Total
Africa		85 664	89 660	87 565	106 396	97 398	Afrique
Americas		10 025	12 431	13 989	14 684	22 976	Amériques
East Asia/Pacific		2 273	3 705	3 837	3 846	3 620	Asie de l'Est/Pacifique
Europe		252 568	242 944	274 439	271 231	253 506	Europe

65

Tourist/visitor arrivals by region of origin *(continued)*
Number
Arrivées de touristes/visiteurs par région de provenance *(suite)*
Nombre

Country or area of destination and region of origin[+]	Series[&] Série[&]	2003	2004	2005	2006	2007	Pays ou zone de destination et région de provenance[+]
Middle East		1 253	1 672	1 467	1 882	2 313	Moyen-Orient
Region not specified		1 756	13 078	5 268	7 788	6 980	Région non spécifiée
Serbia	TCEN						**Serbie**
Total		339 283	391 826	452 679	468 842	696 045	Total
Americas		14 155	13 483	15 789	17 038	19 083	Amériques
East Asia/Pacific		3 680	4 879	5 675	6 402	7 433	Asie de l'Est/Pacifique
Europe		312 666	363 345	419 058	435 400	655 782	Europe
Region not specified		8 782	10 119	12 157	10 002	13 747	Région non spécifiée
Seychelles	TFR						**Seychelles**
Total		122 038	120 765	128 654	140 627	161 273	Total
Africa		13 578	12 598	12 478	13 408	16 847	Afrique
Americas		3 477	4 030	3 867	3 398	3 915	Amériques
East Asia/Pacific		1 977	2 135	2 647	2 996	3 793	Asie de l'Est/Pacifique
Europe		99 961	98 654	103 581	114 211	130 046	Europe
Middle East		1 770	1 911	4 458	4 731	4 930	Moyen-Orient
South Asia		1 275	1 437	1 623	1 883	1 742	Asie du Sud
Sierra Leone	TFR						**Sierra Leone**
Total[3]		38 107	43 560	40 023	33 704	32 223	Total[3]
Africa		23 341	24 446	21 798	10 122	10 846	Afrique
Americas		4 699	4 790	4 713	6 669	6 169	Amériques
East Asia/Pacific		1 995	2 257	2 343	4 898	2 916	Asie de l'Est/Pacifique
Europe		6 460	9 476	9 879	10 470	11 327	Europe
Middle East		1 612	2 591	1 290	1 545	965	Moyen-Orient
Singapore	VFR						**Singapour**
Total[61]		6 127 291	8 328 720	8 943 029	9 751 141	10 284 545	Total[61]
Africa		55 997	70 626	78 803	87 132	93 600	Afrique
Americas		314 728	422 167	470 493	509 774	524 178	Amériques
East Asia/Pacific		4 426 237	6 072 703	6 445 012	7 012 238	7 322 529	Asie de l'Est/Pacifique
Europe		885 146	1 081 336	1 136 024	1 220 172	1 276 669	Europe
Middle East		29 844	55 450	56 165	65 923	78 353	Moyen-Orient
South Asia		415 151	626 165	751 437	849 808	968 389	Asie du Sud
Region not specified		188	273	5 095	6 094	20 827	Région non spécifiée
Slovakia	TCEN						**Slovaquie**
Total		1 386 791	1 401 189	1 514 980	1 611 808	1 684 526	Total
Africa		2 581	2 482	2 252	2 726	2 276	Afrique
Americas		33 981	38 712	42 100	39 118	43 697	Amériques
East Asia/Pacific		32 258	42 249	55 992	69 102	73 658	Asie de l'Est/Pacifique
Europe		1 316 120	1 316 705	1 412 628	1 499 394	1 558 688	Europe
Middle East		241	314	328	272	3 592	Moyen-Orient
South Asia		1 305	384	603	443	1 229	Asie du Sud
Region not specified		305	343	1 077	753	1 386	Région non spécifiée
Slovenia	TCEN						**Slovénie**
Total		1 373 137	1 498 852	1 554 969	1 616 650	1 751 332	Total
Africa		...	...	1 546	1 409	2 100	Afrique
Americas		35 945	45 880	59 303	67 159	66 900	Amériques
East Asia/Pacific		17 141	24 237	39 626	52 371	65 277	Asie de l'Est/Pacifique
Europe		1 307 775	1 410 671	1 454 494	1 495 711	1 617 055	Europe
Region not specified		12 276	18 064	...	...	...	Région non spécifiée
Solomon Islands	TFR						**Iles Salomon**
Total		6 595	...	9 400[62]	11 482	13 748	Total
Americas		600	...	642	879	1 048	Amériques
East Asia/Pacific		5 406	...	8 128	9 755	11 628	Asie de l'Est/Pacifique
Europe		464	...	545	708	925	Europe
Region not specified		125	...	85	140	147	Région non spécifiée
South Africa	TFR						**Afrique du Sud**
Total[63]		6 504 890	6 677 844	7 368 742	8 395 833	9 090 880	Total[63]
Africa		4 450 212	4 638 371	5 370 137	6 280 500	6 861 295	Afrique
Americas		262 496	290 625	322 099	358 096	387 379	Amériques
East Asia/Pacific		224 610	238 829	238 885	257 666	281 567	Asie de l'Est/Pacifique
Europe		1 338 976	1 306 389	1 328 521	1 402 643	1 474 879	Europe
Middle East		15 048	16 037	17 194	19 806	17 836	Moyen-Orient

65

Tourist/visitor arrivals by region of origin *(continued)*
Number
Arrivées de touristes/visiteurs par région de provenance *(suite)*
Nombre

Country or area of destination and region of origin[+]	Series[&] Série[&]	2003	2004	2005	2006	2007	Pays ou zone de destination et région de provenance[+]
South Asia		41 018	36 172	36 045	44 337	51 823	Asie du Sud
Region not specified		172 530	151 421	55 861	32 785	16 101	Région non spécifiée
Spain	TFR						**Espagne**
Total		50 853 816	52 429 833	55 913 776	58 004 459	58 665 505	Total
Americas		1 893 951	2 079 063	2 232 850	2 377 815	2 312 521	Amériques
East Asia/Pacific		237 391	150 584	181 052	255 309	346 047	Asie de l'Est/Pacifique
Europe		47 835 339	49 238 603	52 189 868	54 312 738	54 926 634	Europe
Region not specified		887 135	961 583	1 310 006	1 058 597	1 080 303	Région non spécifiée
Sri Lanka	TFR						**Sri Lanka**
Total[2]		500 642	566 202	549 308	559 603	494 008	Total[2]
Africa		1 991	1 855	2 340	3 235	2 712	Afrique
Americas		25 744	30 500	47 162	36 098	32 317	Amériques
East Asia/Pacific		84 145	91 076	99 736	98 476	75 778	Asie de l'Est/Pacifique
Europe		265 802	298 776	236 481	242 666	220 021	Europe
Middle East		6 789	10 463	10 236	10 315	10 554	Moyen-Orient
South Asia		116 171	133 532	153 353	168 783	149 626	Asie du Sud
Sudan	TFN						**Soudan**
Total		52 291	60 577	245 798[9]	328 148[9]	436 295[9]	Total
Africa		7 000	9 000	58 991	50 665	65 444	Afrique
Americas		...	...	20 751	11 607	15 526	Amériques
East Asia/Pacific		14 000	17 000	109 380	222 157	296 680	Asie de l'Est/Pacifique
Europe		14 000	17 000	55 796	43 719	56 718	Europe
Region not specified		17 291	17 577	880		1 927	Région non spécifiée
Suriname	TFN						**Suriname**
Total[64]		82 298	74 887	...	...	...	Total[64]
Africa		187	177	...	...	...	Afrique
Americas		6 903	7 986	...	...	...	Amériques
East Asia/Pacific		998	2 522	...	...	...	Asie de l'Est/Pacifique
Europe		74 153	64 011	...	...	...	Europe
South Asia		55	165	...	...	...	Asie du Sud
Region not specified		2	26	...	...	...	Région non spécifiée
Suriname	TFR						**Suriname**
Total		...	137 808	160 022	152 895	162 509	Total
Africa		...	...	279	...	223	Afrique
Americas		...	44 802	56 338	48 627	50 857	Amériques
East Asia/Pacific		...	...	3 247	...	2 327	Asie de l'Est/Pacifique
Europe		...	86 913	99 265	98 292	108 134	Europe
Middle East		...	...	...	...	25	Moyen-Orient
South Asia		...	...	498	...	506	Asie du Sud
Region not specified		...	6 093	395	5 976	437	Région non spécifiée
Swaziland	THSR						**Swaziland**
Total[54]		218 813	352 040	311 656	316 082	299 226	Total[54]
Africa		110 054	151 879	134 456	167 347	176 417	Afrique
Americas		11 092	4 968	4 398	3 576	9 832	Amériques
East Asia/Pacific		2 343	3 485	3 085	5 423	8 044	Asie de l'Est/Pacifique
Europe		87 999	110 709	98 009	114 249	92 332	Europe
Region not specified		7 325	80 999	71 708	25 487	12 601	Région non spécifiée
Sweden	TFR						**Suède**
Total[65]		7 627 000	...	...	...	...	Total[65]
Africa		46 000	...	...	...	...	Afrique
Americas		467 000	...	...	...	...	Amériques
East Asia/Pacific		380 000	...	...	...	...	Asie de l'Est/Pacifique
Europe		6 696 000	...	...	...	...	Europe
Region not specified		38 000	...	...	...	...	Région non spécifiée
Switzerland	THSR						**Suisse**
Total		6 530 108[66]	...	7 228 851[67]	7 862 957[67]	8 447 718[67]	Total
Africa		72 786	...	78 143	85 460	85 463	Afrique
Americas		757 015	...	829 551	933 715	954 115	Amériques
East Asia/Pacific		727 005	...	846 703	896 031	941 200	Asie de l'Est/Pacifique
Europe		4 821 157	...	5 304 949	5 747 455	6 225 587	Europe

65

Tourist/visitor arrivals by region of origin *(continued)*
Number
Arrivées de touristes/visiteurs par région de provenance *(suite)*
Nombre

Country or area of destination and region of origin[+]	Series[&] Série[&]	2003	2004	2005	2006	2007	Pays ou zone de destination et région de provenance[+]
Middle East		67 460	...	76 033	85 241	108 957	Moyen-Orient
South Asia		84 685	...	93 472	115 055	132 396	Asie du Sud
Syrian Arab Republic	VFN						**Rép. arabe syrienne**
Total[2,68]		4 388 119	6 153 653	5 837 980	6 009 483	6 004 061	Total[2,68]
Africa		73 487	89 664	92 585	81 136	77 526	Afrique
Americas		43 901	58 032	57 795	59 408	59 584	Amériques
East Asia/Pacific		25 897	36 852	35 088	35 155	34 998	Asie de l'Est/Pacifique
Europe		651 800	933 239	946 853	709 697	731 744	Europe
Middle East		3 325 490	4 760 773	4 369 669	4 734 283	4 654 385	Moyen-Orient
South Asia		228 357	217 947	268 952	289 658	355 530	Asie du Sud
Region not specified		39 187	57 146	67 038	100 146	90 294	Région non spécifiée
Syrian Arab Republic	TCEN						**Rép. arabe syrienne**
Total[68,69]		2 084 956	3 029 964	3 367 935	4 422 482	4 565 813	Total[68,69]
Africa		73 487	89 664	92 585	71 796	69 117	Afrique
Americas		43 901	57 032	57 795	54 583	54 738	Amériques
East Asia/Pacific		25 897	36 852	35 088	32 378	32 879	Asie de l'Est/Pacifique
Europe		204 445	313 956	430 120	467 151	486 063	Europe
Middle East		1 470 289	2 259 703	2 416 358	3 458 290	3 531 298	Moyen-Orient
South Asia		228 357	217 947	268 952	264 998	325 135	Asie du Sud
Region not specified		38 580	54 810	67 037	73 286	66 583	Région non spécifiée
Thailand	TFR						**Thaïlande**
Total		10 082 109[1]	11 737 413[1]	11 567 341[1]	13 821 802[2]	14 464 228[2]	Total
Africa		67 121	82 711	72 875	96 117	104 941	Afrique
Americas		576 587	692 792	739 703	825 079	817 564	Amériques
East Asia/Pacific		6 510 375	7 500 966	7 194 866	8 568 558	8 712 488	Asie de l'Est/Pacifique
Europe		2 320 807	2 706 062	2 778 693	3 439 010	3 812 782	Europe
Middle East		118 339	172 699	178 718	239 171	330 879	Moyen-Orient
South Asia		411 224	495 473	552 081	653 867	685 574	Asie du Sud
Region not specified		77 656	86 710	50 405	...	...	Région non spécifiée
TFYR of Macedonia	TCEN						**L'ex-R.Y. Macédoine**
Total		157 692	165 306	197 216	202 357	230 080	Total
Americas		8 373	8 362	8 439	9 181	8 947	Amériques
East Asia/Pacific		2 362	2 143	2 747	3 490	4 799	Asie de l'Est/Pacifique
Europe		143 387	151 215	182 534	186 519	212 365	Europe
Region not specified		3 570	3 586	3 496	3 167	3 969	Région non spécifiée
Togo	THSR						**Togo**
Total		60 592	82 686	80 763	94 096	86 175	Total
Africa		31 334	43 842	45 967	52 549	48 526	Afrique
Americas		1 785	2 738	2 633	3 314	2 928	Amériques
East Asia/Pacific		1 452	3 492	2 627	3 205	2 649	Asie de l'Est/Pacifique
Europe		24 484	30 018	27 092	33 266	31 181	Europe
Middle East		1 495	2 500	2 371	1 635	772	Moyen-Orient
Region not specified		42	96	73	127	119	Région non spécifiée
Tonga	TFR						**Tonga**
Total[3]		40 110	41 208	41 862	39 451	46 040	Total[3]
Americas		7 930	8 202	8 147	6 345	6 298	Amériques
East Asia/Pacific		27 932	28 972	30 424	29 634	36 524	Asie de l'Est/Pacifique
Europe		4 131	3 408	2 908	2 875	2 868	Europe
Region not specified		117	626	383	597	350	Région non spécifiée
Trinidad and Tobago	TFR						**Trinité-et-Tobago**
Total[3]		409 069	442 596	463 191	457 434	449 453	Total[3]
Africa		935	1 017	1 299	1 389	1 508	Afrique
Americas		324 175	347 181	365 311	364 888	356 177	Amériques
East Asia/Pacific		3 313	2 925	3 046	4 082	5 762	Asie de l'Est/Pacifique
Europe		79 236	89 512	91 424	84 243	82 495	Europe
Middle East		239	221	338	363	367	Moyen-Orient
South Asia		1 136	1 411	1 632	2 365	3 005	Asie du Sud
Region not specified		35	329	141	104	139	Région non spécifiée
Tunisia	TFN						**Tunisie**
Total[2]		5 114 304	5 997 918	6 378 430	6 549 549	6 761 906	Total[2]
Africa		872 251	984 538	993 378	1 010 195	1 045 637	Afrique

Country or area of destination and region of origin[+]	Series[&] Série[&]	2003	2004	2005	2006	2007	Pays ou zone de destination et région de provenance[+]
Americas		23 217	30 347	35 202	33 947	36 450	Amériques
East Asia/Pacific		9 389	10 784	13 710	15 442	16 702	Asie de l'Est/Pacifique
Europe		2 840 307	3 482 041	3 869 030	3 956 274	4 048 429	Europe
Middle East		1 355 878	1 471 752	1 440 387	1 507 155	1 581 512	Moyen-Orient
Region not specified		13 262	18 456	26 723	26 536	33 176	Région non spécifiée
Turkey	TFN						**Turquie**
Total		13 340 956	16 826 062	20 272 877	18 916 436	22 248 328	Total
Africa		119 122	131 148	154 489	152 983	166 883	Afrique
Americas		213 136	282 586	390 884	458 898	523 496	Amériques
East Asia/Pacific		241 996	288 326	421 643	471 280	585 706	Asie de l'Est/Pacifique
Europe		11 871 694	14 946 162	17 663 077	16 268 842	19 039 593	Europe
Middle East		359 281	498 095	625 686	630 140	787 561	Moyen-Orient
South Asia		522 054	660 787	994 620	917 360	1 124 724	Asie du Sud
Region not specified		13 673	18 958	22 478	16 933	20 365	Région non spécifiée
Turkmenistan	TFN						**Turkménistan**
Total		8 214	14 799	11 611	5 620	8 177	Total
Africa		...	...	1	...	13	Afrique
Americas		207	374	384	548	775	Amériques
East Asia/Pacific		466	1 053	753	872	943	Asie de l'Est/Pacifique
Europe		1 855	3 915	3 284	2 721	4 296	Europe
Middle East		37	32	4	...	7	Moyen-Orient
South Asia		5 649	9 425	7 185	1 479	2 143	Asie du Sud
Turks and Caicos Islands	TFR						**Îles Turques et Caïques**
Total		164 100	173 081	176 130	248 343	...	Total
Americas		149 072	148 711	156 674	221 372	...	Amériques
Europe		12 626	13 807	17 613	24 834	...	Europe
Region not specified		2 402	10 563	1 843	2 137	...	Région non spécifiée
Tuvalu	TFN						**Tuvalu**
Total		1 377	1 290	1 085	1 135	1 130	Total
Americas		130	79	101	63	65	Amériques
East Asia/Pacific		1 101	1 043	828	852	851	Asie de l'Est/Pacifique
Europe		97	108	104	120	87	Europe
Region not specified		49	60	52	100	127	Région non spécifiée
Uganda	TFR						**Ouganda**
Total		304 656	512 379	467 728	538 586	641 743	Total
Africa		233 043	405 706	337 188	397 031	479 802	Afrique
Americas		16 409	23 438	28 557	35 749	42 388	Amériques
East Asia/Pacific		4 845	8 150	10 046	12 003	14 466	Asie de l'Est/Pacifique
Europe		39 207	48 847	62 312	71 131	77 283	Europe
Middle East		1 976	3 133	3 766	4 111	4 971	Moyen-Orient
South Asia		7 647	12 139	13 879	14 339	14 803	Asie du Sud
Region not specified		1 529	10 966	11 980	4 222	8 030	Région non spécifiée
Ukraine	TFR						**Ukraine**
Total		12 513 883	15 629 213	17 630 760	18 935 775	23 122 157	Total
Africa		12 367	6 586	7 259	8 611	10 216	Afrique
Americas		83 451	99 135	95 540	142 519	167 103	Amériques
East Asia/Pacific		26 362	32 494	34 946	45 241	48 651	Asie de l'Est/Pacifique
Europe		12 345 396	15 450 129	17 442 407	18 679 863	22 825 500	Europe
Middle East		18 720	20 130	25 501	23 474	26 308	Moyen-Orient
South Asia		13 978	13 434	14 544	16 019	17 572	Asie du Sud
Region not specified		13 609	7 305	10 563	20 048	26 807	Région non spécifiée
United Arab Emirates	THSN						**Emirats arabes unis**
Total[70]		5 871 023	6 195 006	...	...	...	Total[70]
Africa		306 872	315 418	...	...	...	Afrique
Americas		254 362	285 627	...	...	...	Amériques
East Asia/Pacific		427 506	444 575	...	...	...	Asie de l'Est/Pacifique
Europe		1 584 792	2 007 600	...	...	...	Europe
Middle East		1 583 258	1 544 557	...	...	...	Moyen-Orient
South Asia		921 698	909 339	...	...	...	Asie du Sud
Region not specified		792 535	687 890	...	...	...	Région non spécifiée

Country or area of destination and region of origin[+]	Series[&] Série[&]	2003	2004	2005	2006	2007	Pays ou zone de destination et région de provenance[+]
United Kingdom	VFR						**Royaume-Uni**
Total		24 715 000	27 755 000	29 970 000	32 712 920	32 778 102	Total
Africa		569 000	639 000	659 000	701 468	653 917	Afrique
Americas		4 326 000	4 692 000	4 596 000	5 166 674	4 826 687	Amériques
East Asia/Pacific		1 809 000	2 086 000	2 231 000	2 310 449	2 315 607	Asie de l'Est/Pacifique
Europe		17 370 000	19 581 000	21 706 000	23 541 245	24 020 354	Europe
Middle East		347 000	386 000	384 000	471 856	489 559	Moyen-Orient
South Asia		294 000	371 000	394 000	521 228	471 978	Asie du Sud
United Rep. of Tanzania	VFR						**Rép.-Unie de Tanzanie**
Total		576 198	582 807	612 754	644 124	719 031	Total
Africa		267 940	256 455	275 718	293 440	305 748	Afrique
Americas		49 781	53 437	61 604	71 278	80 699	Amériques
East Asia/Pacific		27 208	22 928	24 714	28 222	29 760	Asie de l'Est/Pacifique
Europe		191 025	221 865	220 255	229 048	274 410	Europe
Middle East		13 742	11 594	10 528	6 815	11 444	Moyen-Orient
South Asia		26 502	16 528	19 935	15 321	16 970	Asie du Sud
United States	TFR						**Etats-Unis**
Total		41 217 876	46 085 774	49 205 624	50 977 532	55 986 236	Total
Africa		236 067	240 488	251 654	251 841	276 300	Afrique
Americas		26 367 961	29 195 347	31 178 504	33 128 737	36 470 970	Amériques
East Asia/Pacific		5 192 366	6 086 708	6 518 211	6 427 817	6 562 889	Asie de l'Est/Pacifique
Europe		8 981 711	10 055 657	10 701 847	10 530 566	11 839 074	Europe
Middle East		110 111	137 259	144 131	164 283	195 960	Moyen-Orient
South Asia		329 660	370 315	411 277	474 288	641 043	Asie du Sud
United States Virgin Is.	THSN						**Iles Vierges américaines**
Total		623 394	603 944	617 603	700 985	679 459	Total
Africa		134	289	162	59	115	Afrique
Americas		531 270	560 581	568 908	648 842	651 074	Amériques
East Asia/Pacific		363	379	501	350	351	Asie de l'Est/Pacifique
Europe		7 747	15 819	18 821	15 020	14 834	Europe
Region not specified		83 880	26 876	29 211	36 714	13 085	Région non spécifiée
Uruguay	VFN						**Uruguay**
Total[1]		1 508 055	1 870 858	1 917 049	1 824 340	1 815 281	Total[1]
Americas		1 159 580	1 457 944	1 497 756	1 402 957	1 406 790	Amériques
East Asia/Pacific		6 230	7 221	11 686	12 877	12 855	Asie de l'Est/Pacifique
Europe		73 230	97 223	119 553	124 215	132 636	Europe
Middle East		131	489	182	172	234	Moyen-Orient
Region not specified		268 884	307 981	287 872	284 119	262 766	Région non spécifiée
Uzbekistan	TFR						**Ouzbékistan**
Total		231 000	261 600	...	559 500	903 100	Total
Africa		1 000	1 000	...	2 000	2 000	Afrique
Americas		2 000	12 000	...	6 000	8 000	Amériques
East Asia/Pacific		145 000	140 000	...	295 900	442 700	Asie de l'Est/Pacifique
Europe		51 000	68 600	...	215 600	370 400	Europe
Middle East		24 000	30 000	...	30 000	50 000	Moyen-Orient
South Asia		8 000	10 000	...	10 000	30 000	Asie du Sud
Vanuatu	TFR						**Vanuatu**
Total		50 400	61 453	62 123	68 179[71]	81 344	Total
Americas		1 625	1 954	1 625	1 896	2 578	Amériques
East Asia/Pacific		44 876	55 027	55 894	61 023	73 214	Asie de l'Est/Pacifique
Europe		3 003	3 388	3 504	4 021	3 785	Europe
Region not specified		896	1 084	1 100	1 239	1 767	Région non spécifiée
Venezuela (Boliv. Rep. of)	TFN						**Venezuela (Rép. bol. du)**
Total		336 974	486 401	706 103	747 930	770 567	Total
Africa		438	640	787	914	738	Afrique
Americas		154 334	217 699	374 460	411 772	440 560	Amériques
East Asia/Pacific		3 201	4 475	16 360	17 106	15 548	Asie de l'Est/Pacifique
Europe		175 159	258 178	296 310	297 601	295 205	Europe
Middle East		371	492	9 957	10 324	9 098	Moyen-Orient
South Asia		270	344	1 801	1 931	1 727	Asie du Sud
Region not specified		3 201	4 573	6 428	8 282	7 691	Région non spécifiée

Country or area of destination and region of origin[+]	Series[&] Série[&]	2003	2004	2005	2006	2007	Pays ou zone de destination et région de provenance[+]
Viet Nam	VFR						**Viet Nam**
Total[9]		2 428 735	2 927 873	3 467 757	3 583 488	4 243 626	Total[9]
Americas		258 991	326 286	396 997	459 398	508 202	Amériques
East Asia/Pacific		1 669 541	2 008 366	2 365 222	2 361 258	2 715 593	Asie de l'Est/Pacifique
Europe		293 636	354 735	425 774	480 585	634 461	Europe
Region not specified		206 567	238 486	279 764	282 247	385 370	Région non spécifiée
Yemen	THSN						**Yémen**
Total		154 667	273 732	336 070	382 332	379 390	Total
Africa		8 627	10 853	12 628	13 025	10 485	Afrique
Americas		12 932	17 099	18 253	18 771	17 613	Amériques
East Asia/Pacific		15 966	22 512	24 437	18 839	21 668	Asie de l'Est/Pacifique
Europe		13 733	28 608	26 456	32 788	33 079	Europe
Middle East		103 409	175 679	238 524	278 385	278 238	Moyen-Orient
South Asia		...	18 981	15 772	20 524	18 307	Asie du Sud
Zambia	TFR						**Zambie**
Total		412 675	515 000	668 862	756 860	897 413	Total
Africa		298 485	366 918	461 000	510 270	660 551	Afrique
Americas		22 667	29 053	37 580	52 457	50 606	Amériques
East Asia/Pacific		17 297	23 107	39 912	38 171	28 095	Asie de l'Est/Pacifique
Europe		71 363	91 863	121 712	143 304	145 729	Europe
South Asia		2 863	4 059	8 658	12 658	12 432	Asie du Sud
Zimbabwe	VFR						**Zimbabwe**
Total		2 256 205	1 854 488	1 558 501	2 286 572	2 508 255	Total
Africa		1 942 052	1 523 090	1 356 384	2 082 724	2 289 308	Afrique
Americas		61 181	75 161	43 976	44 746	40 388	Amériques
East Asia/Pacific		68 414	90 405	38 767	53 908	56 720	Asie de l'Est/Pacifique
Europe		169 938	155 767	112 608	96 849	109 119	Europe
Middle East		2 209	3 749	1 989	4 145	4 502	Moyen-Orient
South Asia		12 411	6 316	4 777	4 200	5 023	Asie du Sud
Region not specified		...	...	...	...	3 195	Région non spécifiée

Source:
World Tourism Organization (UNWTO), Madrid, UNWTO statistics database and the *Yearbook of Tourism Statistics*, 2009 edition.

[+] For a listing of the Member States of the regions of origin, see Annex I, with the following exceptions:

Africa includes the countries and territories listed under Africa in Annex I but excludes Egypt and Libyan Arab Jamahiriya.
Americas is as shown in Annex I
Europe is as shown in Annex I, but also includes Armenia, Azerbaijan, Cyprus, Georgia, Israel, Kazakhstan, Kyrgyzstan, Tajikistan, Turkey, Turkmenistan and Uzbekistan.
East Asia and the Pacific includes the countries and territories listed under Eastern Asia, South-eastern Asia, and Oceania in Annex I except for Canton and Enderbury Islands, Christmas Island, Cocos Island, Johnston Island, Midway Islands, and Wake Island.
South Asia is as shown in Annex I under South-central Asia, but excludes Kazakhstan, Kyrgyzstan, Tajikistan, Turkmenistan and Uzbekistan.
Middle east is as shown in Annex I under Western Asia, but excludes Armenia, Azerbaijan, Cyprus, Georgia, Israel, and Turkey. The Western Asia group also includes Egypt and the Libyan Arab Jamahiriya.

Source:
Organisation mondiale du tourisme (OMT), Madrid, la base de données de l'OMT, et l'*Annuaire des statistiques du tourisme*, édition 2009.

[+] On se reportera à l'Annexe I pour les États Membres classés dans les différentes régions de provenance, avec les exceptions ci-après :

Afrique – Comprend les États et territoires énumérés dans l'Annexe I, sauf l'Égypte et la Jamahiriya arabe libyenne.
Amériques – Comprend les États et territoires énumérés dans l'Annexe I.
Europe – Comprend les États et territoires énumérés dans l'Annexe I, mais comprend en revanche l'Arménie, l'Azerbaïdjan, Chypre, la Géorgie, l'Israël, le Kazakhstan, le Kirghizistan, le Tadjikistan, la Turquie, le Turkménistan, et l'Ouzbékistan.
L'Asie de l'Est et le Pacifique– Comprend les États et territoires énumérés dans l'Annexe I dans les Groupes Asie de l'Est, Asie du Sud-est et Océanie sauf les îles Canton et Enderbury, l'île Christmas, les îles Cocos, l'île Johnston, les îles Midway, Nauru, et l'île Wake.
Asie du Sud – Comprend les États et territoires énumérés dans l'Annexe I dans le groupe Asie centrale et du sud, sauf le Kazakhstan, le Kirghizistan, l'Ouzbékistan, le Tadjikistan et le Turkménistan.
Le Moyen-Orient – Comprend les États et territoires énumérés dans l'Annexe I dans le groupe Asie occidentale, sauf l'Arménie, l'Azerbaïdjan, Chypre, la Géorgie, Israël, la Turquie. Le Groupe comprend en revanche l'Égypte et la Jamahiriya arabe libyenne.

65 Tourist/visitor arrivals by region of origin *(continued)*
Number
Arrivées de touristes/visiteurs par région de provenance *(suite)*
Nombre

& Series:

TFN: Arrivals of non-resident tourists at national borders (excluding same-day visitors), by nationality.

TFR: Arrivals of non-resident tourists at national borders (excluding same- day visitors), by country of residence.

TCEN: Arrivals of non-resident tourists in all types of accommodation establishments, by nationality.

TCER: Arrivals of non-resident tourists in all types of accommodation establishments, by country of residence.

THSN: Arrivals of non-resident tourists in hotels and similar establishments, by nationality.

THSR: Arrivals of non-resident tourists in hotels and similar establishments, by country of residence.

VFN: Arrivals of non-resident visitors at national borders (including tourists and same-day visitors), by nationality.

VFR: Arrivals of non-resident visitors at national borders (including tourists and same-day visitors), by country of residence.

& Série :

TFN : Arrivées de touristes non résidents aux frontières nationales (à l'exclusion de visiteurs de la journée), par nationalité.

TFR : Arrivées de touristes non résidents aux frontières nationales (à l'exclusion de visiteurs de la journée), par pays de résidence.

TCEN : Arrivées de touristes non résidents dans tous les types d'établissements d'hébergement, par nationalité.

TCER : Arrivées de touristes non résidents dans tous les types d'établissements d'hébergement, par pays de résidence.

THSN : Arrivées de touristes non résidents dans les hôtels et établissements assimilés, par nationalité.

THSR : Arrivées de touristes non résidents dans les hôtels et établissements assimilés, par pays de résidence.

VFN : Arrivées de visiteurs non résidents aux frontières nationales (y compris touristes et visiteurs de la journée), par nationalité.

VFR : Arrivées de visiteurs non résidents aux frontières nationales (y compris touristes et visiteurs de la journée), par pays de résidence.

Footnotes on the totals also apply to the other regions.

Les notes sur les totaux s'appliquent aussi aux autres régions.

1 Arrivals of nationals residing abroad are included in the total and are all accounted for in "region not specified" only.

2 Excluding nationals of the country residing abroad.

3 Air arrivals.

4 Excluding nationals residing abroad and crew members.

5 Including private accommodation.

6 Organized tourism.

7 Hotels establishments, campings, holiday centres, holiday villages and specific categories of accommodation.

8 International tourist arrivals in hotels of regional capitals.

9 Arrivals of nationals residing abroad are included in the total and are also accounted for in the individual regions.

10 Arrivals in the Phreah Vihear temple are included in the total and are all accounted for in "Region not specified": 67 843.

11 Arrivals in the Phreah Vihear temple are included in the total and are all accounted for in "region not specified": 88 615.

12 Arrivals in the Phreah Vihear temple are included in the total and are all accounted for in "region not specified": 108 691.

13 Arrivals in the Phreah Vihear temple are included in the total and are all accounted for in "region not specified": 142,561.

14 For statistical purposes, the data for China do not include those for the Hong Kong Special Administrative Region (Hong Kong SAR), Macao Special Administrative Region (Macao SAR) and Taiwan Province of China.

15 Including arrivals by sea, land and by air.

16 Including stateless and Chinese people who do not have permanent residency in Hong Kong SAR, China.

17 Source:"Dirección de Extranjería, Departamento Administrativo de Seguridad (DAS)".

18 Air and sea arrivals.

19 Including arrivals in ports of nautical tourism.

20 Arrivals through all ports of entry.

21 Due to a change in the methodology, data are not comparable to previous years.

22 Estimated based on surveys at national borders (1996-2000).

23 Non-resident visitor survey (EVE).

1 Les arrivées de nationaux résidant à l'étranger sont comprises dans le total, et sont toutes comptabilisées uniquement dans la catégorie Région non spécifiée.

2 A l'exclusion des nationaux du pays résidant à l'étranger.

3 Arrivées par voie aérienne.

4 A l'exclusion des nationaux du pays résidant à l'étranger et des membres des équipages.

5 Y compris l'hébergement privé.

6 Tourisme organisé.

7 Établissements hôteliers, terrains de camping, centres de vacances, villages de vacances et catégories spécifiques d'hébergement.

8 Arrivées de touristes internationaux dans les hôtels des capitales de département.

9 Les arrivées de nationaux résidant à l'étranger sont comprises dans le total, et comptabilisées aussi dans chacune des régions.

10 Les arrivées dans le temple de Phreah Vihear sont comprises dans le total, et sont toutes prises en compte dans "Région non spécifiée" : 67 843.

11 Les arrivées dans le temple de Phreah Vihear sont comprises dans le total, et sont toutes prises en compte dans "Région non spécifiée": 88 615.

12 Les arrivées dans le temple de Phreah Vihear sont comprises dans le total, et sont toutes prises en compte dans "Région non spécifiée": 108 691.

13 Les arrivées dans le temple "Phreah Vihear" sont comprises dans le total, et sont toutes prises en compte dans "Région non spécifiée": 142.561.

14 Pour la présentation des statistiques, les données pour la Chine ne comprennent pas la Région Administrative Spéciale de Hong Kong (Hong Kong RAS), la Région Administrative Spéciale de Macao (Macao RAS) et la province de Taiwan.

15 Y compris les arrivées par mer, terre et air.

16 Y compris les chinois qui ne résident pas de manière permanente à Hong Kong SAR, Chine.

17 Source:"Dirección de Extranjería, Departamento Administrativo de Seguridad (DAS)".

18 Arrivées par voie aérienne et maritime.

19 Y compris les arrivées dans des ports à tourisme nautique.

20 Arrivées à travers tous les ports d'entrée.

21 Dû à un changement dans la méthodologie, l'information n'est pas comparable à celle des années précédentes.

22 Estimations à partir d'enquêtes aux frontières (1996-2000).

23 Enquête auprès des visiteurs venant de l'étranger (EVE).

24	Charter tourists only.	24	Arrivées en vols à la demande seulement.
25	Information based on administrative data.	25	Information tirée de données administratives.
26	Estimates for continental Guadeloupe (without Saint-Martin and Saint-Barthélemy).	26	Estimations pour la Guadeloupe continentale (sans Saint-Martin et Saint-Barthélemy).
27	Data based on a survey conducted at Guadeloupe airport.	27	Données tirées d'une enquête réalisée à l'aéroport de Guadeloupe.
28	Air arrivals at Conakry airport.	28	Arrivées par voie aérienne à l'aéroport de Conakry.
29	Arrivals at "Osvaldo Vieira" Airport.	29	Arrivées à l'aéroport "Osvaldo Vieira".
30	Arrivals to Timehri airport only.	30	Arrivées à l'aéroport de Timehri seulement.
31	Collective accommodation establishments.	31	Etablissements d'hébergement collectif.
32	Departures.	32	Départs.
33	Excluding seasonal and border workers.	33	A l'exclusion des travailleurs saisoniers et frontaliers.
34	All data are estimates, projected using 1989 market shares. Source: Economic survey various years.	34	Toutes les données représentent des estimations, dont la projection a été faite sur la base des taux de marché de l'année 1989. Source: Enquête économique de diverses années.
35	Tarawa and Christmas Island.	35	Tarawa et Ile Christmas.
36	Tarawa only.	36	Tarawa uniquement.
37	Including nationals residing abroad and crew members.	37	Y compris les nationaux résidant à l'étranger et membres des équipages.
38	New data source: Department of Customs Control.	38	Nouvelle source d'information: Département du Contrôle douanier.
39	Excluding Syrian nationals, Palestinians and students.	39	A l'exclusion des ressortissants syriens, palestiniens et sous-études.
40	Travellers.	40	Voyageurs.
41	Including Singapore residents crossing the frontier by road through Johore Causeway.	41	Y compris les résidents de Singapour traversant la frontière par voie terrestre à travers le Johore Causeway.
42	Departures by air and by sea.	42	Départs par voies aérienne et maritime.
43	Data refer to the states of Pohnpei, Truk and Yap.	43	Les données se réfèrent aux états de Pohnpei, Truk et Yap.
44	Including tourist arrivals through border entry points to Yangon.	44	Comprenant les arrivées de touristes aux postes-frontières de Yangon.
45	Data regarding to short term movements are compiled from a random sample of passenger declarations. Source: Statistics New Zealand, External Migration.	45	Les données relatives aux mouvements de courte durée sont obtenues à partir d'un échantillon aléatoire de déclarations des passagers. Source : Statistiques de la Nouvelle Zélande, Immigration.
46	Including Niuans residing usually in New Zealand.	46	Y compris les nationaux de Niue résidant habituellement en Nouvelle-Zélande.
47	Figures are based on "The Guest survey" carried out by "Institute of Transport Economics".	47	Les chiffres se fondent sur "l'enquête auprès de la clientèle" de l'Institut d'économie des transports.
48	Air arrivals (Palau International Airport).	48	Arrivées par voie aérienne (Aéroport international de Palau).
49	Total number of visitors broken down by permanent residence who arrived in Panama at Tocumen International Airport.	49	Nombre total de visiteurs arrivées au Panama par l'aéroport international de Tocúmen.
50	E/D cards in the "Silvio Petirossi" airport and passenger counts at the national border crossings - National Police and SENATUR.	50	Cartes d'embarquement et de débarquement à l'aéroport Silvio Petirossi et comptages des passagers lors du franchissement des frontières nationales – Police Nationale et SENATUR.
51	Preliminary estimates.	51	Estimations préliminaires.
52	Due to a change in the methodology, from 2004 the data are not comparable with those of previous years.	52	La méthodologie a été modifiée et pour cela, à partir de 2004 les données ne sont pas comparables avec celles des années précédentes.
53	Fiscal year July to June.	53	Année fiscale de juillet à juin.
54	Arrivals in hotels only.	54	Arrivées dans les hôtels uniquement.
55	Visitors who have benefited from tourism services provided by the tourism agencies and tour operators (titulars of tourism licences). Excluding the left side of the river Nistru and the municipality of Bender.	55	Visiteurs qui ont bénéficié des services touristiques des agences de tourisme et des voyagistes (titulaires d'une licence touristique). À l'exception de la rive gauche de la rivière Nistru et de la municipalité de Bender.
56	Excluding Netherlands Antillean residents.	56	A l'exclusion des résidents des Antilles Néerlandaises.
57	Arrivals at Princess Juliana International airport.	57	Arrivées à l'aéroport international "Princess Juliana".
58	Including visitors to Saint Martin (the French side of the island).	58	Y compris les visiteurs à Saint Martin (partie française de l'île).
59	Including Italian visitors.	59	Y compris les visiteurs italiens.
60	New methodology.	60	Nouvelle méthodologie.
61	Excluding Malaysian citizens arriving by land.	61	Non compris les arrivées de malaysiens par voie terrestre.
62	Without 1st quarter.	62	À l'exclusion du 1er trimestre.
63	Excluding arrivals by work and contract workers.	63	À l'exclusion des arrivées par travail et les travailleurs contractuels.
64	Arrivals at Zanderij Airport.	64	Arrivées à l'aéroport de Zanderij.
65	Data according to IBIS-Survey (Incoming Visitors to Sweden) during the years 2001 to 2003, (no data collected before 2001 or after 2003). Source: Swedish Tourist Authority and Statistics Sweden.	65	Données reposant sur l'enquête IBIS (auprès des visiteurs du tourisme récepteur) portant sur les années 2001 à 2003 (aucune donnée n'a été collectée avant 2001 ni après 2003). Source: "Swedish Tourist Authority" et "Statistics Sweden".
66	Hotels, motels and inns.	66	Hôtels, motels et auberges.
67	Hotels and health establishments.	67	Hôtels et établissements de cure.
68	Survey of the incoming tourism in 2004, 2006 and 2007.	68	Enquête du tourisme récepteur en 2004, 2006 et 2007.
69	Excluding private accommodation.	69	À l'exclusion de l'hébergement chez des particuliers.

70   Domestic tourism and arrivals of nationals residing abroad are included in the total and are all accounted for in "Region not specified" only.

71   From November 2006, including arrivals to Luganville.

70   Les touristes nationaux et les arrivées de nationaux résidant à l'étranger sont compris dans le total, et sont tous pris en compte uniquement dans "Région non spécifiée" seulement.

71   À partir de novembre 2006, les arrivées à Luganville sont inclues.

Tourist/visitor arrivals and tourism expenditure
Thousands arrivals and millions of US dollars

Arrivées de touristes/visiteurs et dépenses touristiques
Milliers d'arrivées et millions de dollars E.-U.

Country or area of destination	Series[&] Série[&]	2002	2003	2004	2005	2006	2007	Pays ou zone de destination
Albania								**Albanie**
Tourist/visitor arrivals[1]	THS	36	41	32	48	60	57	Arrivées de touristes/visiteurs[1]
Tourism expenditure		492	537	756	880	1 057	1 055	Dépenses touristiques
Algeria								**Algérie**
Tourist/visitor arrivals[2]	VF	988	1 166	1 234	1 443	1 638	1 743	Arrivées de touristes/visiteurs[2]
Tourism expenditure[3]		111	112	178	184	215	219	Dépenses touristiques[3]
American Samoa								**Samoa américaines**
Tourist/visitor arrivals	TF	...	...	...	24	25	...	Arrivées de touristes/visiteurs
Andorra								**Andorre**
Tourist/visitor arrivals	TF	3 387	3 138	2 791	2 418	2 227	2 189	Arrivées de touristes/visiteurs
Angola								**Angola**
Tourist/visitor arrivals	TF	91	107	194	210	121	195	Arrivées de touristes/visiteurs
Tourism expenditure		51	63	82	103	91	236	Dépenses touristiques
Anguilla								**Anguilla**
Tourist/visitor arrivals[4]	TF	44	47	54	62	73	78	Arrivées de touristes/visiteurs[4]
Tourism expenditure[5]		57	64	69	86	107	119	Dépenses touristiques[5]
Antigua and Barbuda								**Antigua-et-Barbuda**
Tourist/visitor arrivals[4]	TF	218	239	268	267	273	262	Arrivées de touristes/visiteurs[4]
Tourism expenditure[5]		274	300	337	309	327	338	Dépenses touristiques[5]
Argentina[6]								**Argentine[6]**
Tourist/visitor arrivals	TF	2 820	2 995	3 457	3 823	4 173	4 562	Arrivées de touristes/visiteurs
Tourism expenditure		1 716	2 306	2 660	3 209	3 899	4 984	Dépenses touristiques
Armenia								**Arménie**
Tourist/visitor arrivals	TF	162	206	263	319	381	...	Arrivées de touristes/visiteurs
Tourism expenditure		81	90	188	240	307	343	Dépenses touristiques
Aruba								**Aruba**
Tourist/visitor arrivals	TF	643	642	728	733	694	772	Arrivées de touristes/visiteurs
Tourism expenditure		835	859	1 056[5]	1 094[5]	1 081	1 257	Dépenses touristiques
Australia								**Australie**
Tourist/visitor arrivals[7]	VF	4 841	4 746	5 215	5 499	5 532	5 644	Arrivées de touristes/visiteurs[7]
Tourism expenditure		13 624	16 647	20 453	22 566	23 729	26 619	Dépenses touristiques
Austria								**Autriche**
Tourist/visitor arrivals	TCE	18 611	19 078	19 373	19 952	20 261	20 766	Arrivées de touristes/visiteurs
Tourism expenditure		13 046	16 342	18 385	19 310	18 886	21 292	Dépenses touristiques
Azerbaijan								**Azerbaïdjan**
Tourist/visitor arrivals	TF	576	767	988	861	903	1 010	Arrivées de touristes/visiteurs
Tourism expenditure		63	70	79	100	201	317	Dépenses touristiques
Bahamas								**Bahamas**
Tourist/visitor arrivals	TF	1 513	1 510	1 561	1 608	1 601	1 528	Arrivées de touristes/visiteurs
Tourism expenditure		1 773	1 770	1 897	2 081	2 066	2 198	Dépenses touristiques
Bahrain								**Bahreïn**
Tourist/visitor arrivals	TF	3 167	2 955	3 514	3 914	4 519	4 935	Arrivées de touristes/visiteurs
Tourism expenditure		985	1 206	1 504	1 603	1 786	1 854	Dépenses touristiques
Bangladesh								**Bangladesh**
Tourist/visitor arrivals	TF	207	245	271	208	200	289	Arrivées de touristes/visiteurs
Tourism expenditure		59	59	76	79	80	76[5]	Dépenses touristiques
Barbados								**Barbade**
Tourist/visitor arrivals	TF	498	531	552	548	563	575	Arrivées de touristes/visiteurs
Tourism expenditure		666	767	785	905	974	...	Dépenses touristiques
Belarus								**Bélarus**
Tourist/visitor arrivals[8]	TF	63	64	67	91	89	105	Arrivées de touristes/visiteurs[8]
Tourism expenditure		295	339	362	346	401	479	Dépenses touristiques
Belgium								**Belgique**
Tourist/visitor arrivals	TCE	6 720	6 690	6 710	6 747	6 995	7 045	Arrivées de touristes/visiteurs
Tourism expenditure		7 598	8 848	10 089	10 881	11 625	12 176	Dépenses touristiques
Belize								**Belize**
Tourist/visitor arrivals	TF	200	221	231	237	247	256	Arrivées de touristes/visiteurs
Tourism expenditure[5]		121	150	168	214	271	289	Dépenses touristiques[5]

66

Tourist/visitor arrivals and tourism expenditure *(continued)*
Thousands arrivals and millions of US dollars
Arrivées de touristes/visiteurs et dépenses touristiques *(suite)*
Milliers d'arrivées et millions de dollars E.-U.

Country or area of destination	Series[&] Série[&]	2002	2003	2004	2005	2006	2007	Pays ou zone de destination
Benin								**Bénin**
Tourist/visitor arrivals [9]	TF	72	175	174	176	180	186	Arrivées de touristes/visiteurs [9]
Tourism expenditure		95	108	121	108	122	124	Dépenses touristiques
Bermuda								**Bermudes**
Tourist/visitor arrivals [10]	TF	284	257	272	270	299	306	Arrivées de touristes/visiteurs [10]
Tourism expenditure [3]		378	348	426	429	494	569	Dépenses touristiques [3]
Bhutan								**Bhoutan**
Tourist/visitor arrivals	TF	6	6	9	14	17	21	Arrivées de touristes/visiteurs
Tourism expenditure [3]		8	8	13	19	24	30	Dépenses touristiques [3]
Bolivia								**Bolivie**
Tourist/visitor arrivals	TF	334	427	480	524	521	556	Arrivées de touristes/visiteurs
Tourism expenditure		143	243	283	345	330	294	Dépenses touristiques
Bonaire								**Bonaire**
Tourist/visitor arrivals	TF	52	62	63	63	64	74	Arrivées de touristes/visiteurs
Tourism expenditure [5,11]		65	84	87	87	91	110	Dépenses touristiques [5,11]
Bosnia and Herzegovina								**Bosnie-Herzégovine**
Tourist/visitor arrivals	TCE	160	165	190	217	256	306	Arrivées de touristes/visiteurs
Tourism expenditure		307	404	507	557	658	798	Dépenses touristiques
Botswana								**Botswana**
Tourist/visitor arrivals	TF	1 274	1 406	1 523	1 675	...	...	Arrivées de touristes/visiteurs
Tourism expenditure		324	459	582	561	539	549	Dépenses touristiques
Brazil								**Brésil**
Tourist/visitor arrivals	TF	3 785	4 133	4 794	5 358	5 017	5 026	Arrivées de touristes/visiteurs
Tourism expenditure		2 142	2 673	3 389	4 168	4 577	5 284	Dépenses touristiques
British Virgin Islands								**Iles Vierges britanniques**
Tourist/visitor arrivals	TF	282	318	304	337	356	358	Arrivées de touristes/visiteurs
Tourism expenditure [3]		345	342	393	437	...	...	Dépenses touristiques [3]
Brunei Darussalam								**Brunéi Darussalam**
Tourist/visitor arrivals [10]	VF	...	...	...	815	836	877	Arrivées de touristes/visiteurs [10]
Tourism expenditure [5]		114	124	181	191	224	...	Dépenses touristiques [5]
Bulgaria								**Bulgarie**
Tourist/visitor arrivals	TF	3 433	4 048	4 630	4 837	5 158	5 151	Arrivées de touristes/visiteurs
Tourism expenditure		1 392	2 051	2 796	3 063	3 317	3 975	Dépenses touristiques
Burkina Faso								**Burkina Faso**
Tourist/visitor arrivals	THS	150	163	222	245	264	289	Arrivées de touristes/visiteurs
Tourism expenditure [12]		...	...	40[5]	45	55	...	Dépenses touristiques [12]
Burundi								**Burundi**
Tourist/visitor arrivals [2]	TF	74	74	133	148	201	...	Arrivées de touristes/visiteurs [2]
Tourism expenditure		2	1	2	2	2	2	Dépenses touristiques
Cambodia								**Cambodge**
Tourist/visitor arrivals [13]	VF	787	701	1 055	1 422	1 700	2 015	Arrivées de touristes/visiteurs [13]
Tourism expenditure		509	441	673	929	1 080	1 284	Dépenses touristiques
Cameroon								**Cameroun**
Tourist/visitor arrivals	THS	226	...	190	176	185	...	Arrivées de touristes/visiteurs
Tourism expenditure		124	266	212	229	231	221	Dépenses touristiques
Canada								**Canada**
Tourist/visitor arrivals [14]	TF	20 057	17 534	19 145	18 771	18 265	17 931	Arrivées de touristes/visiteurs [14]
Tourism expenditure		12 744	12 236	15 135	16 006	16 978	17 985	Dépenses touristiques
Cape Verde								**Cap-Vert**
Tourist/visitor arrivals	TF	126	150	157	198	242	267	Arrivées de touristes/visiteurs
Tourism expenditure		100	135	153	177	286	426	Dépenses touristiques
Cayman Islands								**Iles Caïmanes**
Tourist/visitor arrivals [10]	TF	303	294	260	168	267	292	Arrivées de touristes/visiteurs [10]
Tourism expenditure [3]		607	518	523	356	513	479	Dépenses touristiques [3]
Central African Rep.								**Rép. centrafricaine**
Tourist/visitor arrivals [15]	TF	3	6	8	12	14	...	Arrivées de touristes/visiteurs [15]
Tourism expenditure [16]		3	4	4	...	...	...	Dépenses touristiques [16]
Chad								**Tchad**
Tourist/visitor arrivals	THS	32	21	26	29	16	25	Arrivées de touristes/visiteurs
Tourism expenditure [16]		25	...	...	...	...	...	Dépenses touristiques [16]

Tourist/visitor arrivals and tourism expenditure *(continued)*
Thousands arrivals and millions of US dollars
Arrivées de touristes/visiteurs et dépenses touristiques *(suite)*
Milliers d'arrivées et millions de dollars E.-U.

Country or area of destination	Series[&] Série[&]	2002	2003	2004	2005	2006	2007	Pays ou zone de destination
Chile								**Chili**
Tourist/visitor arrivals	TF	1 412	1 614	1 785	2 027	2 253	2 507	Arrivées de touristes/visiteurs
Tourism expenditure		1 221	1 309	1 571	1 682	1 893	2 172	Dépenses touristiques
China[17]								**Chine**[17]
Tourist/visitor arrivals	TF	36 803	32 970	41 761	46 809	49 913	54 720	Arrivées de touristes/visiteurs
Tourism expenditure		21 742	18 707	27 755	31 842	37 132	41 126	Dépenses touristiques
China, Hong Kong SAR								**Chine, Hong Kong RAS**
Tourist/visitor arrivals	TF	10 689	9 676	13 655	14 773	15 821	17 154	Arrivées de touristes/visiteurs
Tourism expenditure[18]		9 849	9 004	11 874	13 588	15 476	18 015	Dépenses touristiques[18]
China, Macao SAR[9]								**Chine, Macao RAS**[9]
Tourist/visitor arrivals	TF	6 565	6 309	8 324	9 014	10 683	12 942	Arrivées de touristes/visiteurs[9]
Tourism expenditure		4 519	5 319	7 704	8 236	10 135	13 939	Dépenses touristiques
Colombia								**Colombie**
Tourist/visitor arrivals	VF	567	625	791	933	1 053	1 195	Arrivées de touristes/visiteurs
Tourism expenditure		1 237	1 191	1 369	1 574	2 009	2 262	Dépenses touristiques
Comoros								**Comores**
Tourist/visitor arrivals	TF	19	21	23	26	29	15	Arrivées de touristes/visiteurs
Tourism expenditure[19]		11	16	21	24	27	...	Dépenses touristiques[19]
Congo								**Congo**
Tourist/visitor arrivals	THS	22	...	...	...	...	...	Arrivées de touristes/visiteurs
Tourism expenditure		26	30	23	40[5]	45[5]	54[5]	Dépenses touristiques
Cook Islands								**Iles Cook**
Tourist/visitor arrivals	TF	73	78	83	88	92	97	Arrivées de touristes/visiteurs
Tourism expenditure[3]		46	69	72	91	90	...	Dépenses touristiques[3]
Costa Rica								**Costa Rica**
Tourist/visitor arrivals	TF	1 113	1 239	1 453	1 679	1 725	1 980	Arrivées de touristes/visiteurs
Tourism expenditure		1 292	1 424	1 586	1 810	1 890	2 224	Dépenses touristiques
Côte d'Ivoire								**Côte d'Ivoire**
Tourism expenditure		56	76	91	93	104	104[5]	Dépenses touristiques
Croatia								**Croatie**
Tourist/visitor arrivals	TCE	6 944	7 409	7 912	8 467	8 659	9 307	Arrivées de touristes/visiteurs
Tourism expenditure		3 952	6 513	6 945	7 625	8 296	9 576	Dépenses touristiques
Cuba								**Cuba**
Tourist/visitor arrivals[10]	TF	1 656	1 847	2 017	2 261	2 150	2 119	Arrivées de touristes/visiteurs[10]
Tourism expenditure[3]		1 769	1 999	2 114	2 399	2 414	2 415	Dépenses touristiques[3]
Curaçao								**Curaçao**
Tourist/visitor arrivals[10]	TF	218	221	223	222	234	300	Arrivées de touristes/visiteurs[10]
Tourism expenditure[3]		290	286	296	284	...	...	Dépenses touristiques[3]
Cyprus								**Chypre**
Tourist/visitor arrivals	TF	2 418	2 303	2 349	2 470	2 401	2 416	Arrivées de touristes/visiteurs
Tourism expenditure		2 178	2 325	2 552	2 644	2 691	3 109	Dépenses touristiques
Czech Republic								**République tchèque**
Tourist/visitor arrivals	TCE	4 743	5 076	6 061	6 336	6 435	6 680	Arrivées de touristes/visiteurs
Tourism expenditure		3 376	4 069	4 931	5 635	6 359	7 496	Dépenses touristiques
Dem. Rep. of the Congo								**Rép. dém. du Congo**
Tourist/visitor arrivals	TF	28[10]	35[10]	36[10]	61	55	47[10]	Arrivées de touristes/visiteurs
Denmark								**Danemark**
Tourist/visitor arrivals[20]	TCE	3 436	3 474	4 421[21]	4 699	4 653[21]	4 681	Arrivées de touristes/visiteurs[20]
Tourism expenditure[5]		4 791	5 271	5 652	5 293	5 587	6 218	Dépenses touristiques[5]
Djibouti								**Djibouti**
Tourist/visitor arrivals	THS	23	23	26	30	40	40	Arrivées de touristes/visiteurs
Tourism expenditure[5]		9	7	7	7	9	...	Dépenses touristiques[5]
Dominica								**Dominique**
Tourist/visitor arrivals	TF	69	73	80	79	84	81	Arrivées de touristes/visiteurs
Tourism expenditure[5]		46	52	61	57	72	71	Dépenses touristiques[5]
Dominican Republic								**Rép. dominicaine**
Tourist/visitor arrivals[2,10]	TF	2 811	3 282	3 450	3 691	3 965	3 980	Arrivées de touristes/visiteurs[2,10]
Tourism expenditure[5]		2 730	3 128	3 152	3 518	3 917	4 082	Dépenses touristiques[5]
Ecuador								**Equateur**
Tourist/visitor arrivals[4]	VF	683	761	819	860	841	937	Arrivées de touristes/visiteurs[4]
Tourism expenditure		449	408	464	488	492	626	Dépenses touristiques

66
Tourist/visitor arrivals and tourism expenditure *(continued)*
Thousands arrivals and millions of US dollars
Arrivées de touristes/visiteurs et dépenses touristiques *(suite)*
Milliers d'arrivées et millions de dollars E.-U.

Country or area of destination	Series[&] Série[&]	2002	2003	2004	2005	2006	2007	Pays ou zone de destination
Egypt								**Egypte**
Tourist/visitor arrivals	TF	4 906	5 746	7 795	8 244	8 646	10 610	Arrivées de touristes/visiteurs
Tourism expenditure		4 133	4 704	6 328	7 206	8 133	10 327	Dépenses touristiques
El Salvador								**El Salvador**
Tourist/visitor arrivals	TF	798	720	951	1 127	1 279	1 339	Arrivées de touristes/visiteurs
Tourism expenditure		521	665	748	838	1 097	1 158	Dépenses touristiques
Eritrea								**Erythrée**
Tourist/visitor arrivals[2]	VF	101	80	87	83	78	81	Arrivées de touristes/visiteurs[2]
Tourism expenditure[18]		73	74	73	66	60	60	Dépenses touristiques[18]
Estonia								**Estonie**
Tourist/visitor arrivals	TF	1 362	1 462	1 750[22,23]	1 917[22,23]	1 940[22,23]	1 900[22,23]	Arrivées de touristes/visiteurs
Tourism expenditure		737	883	1 111	1 229	1 362	1 415	Dépenses touristiques
Ethiopia								**Ethiopie**
Tourist/visitor arrivals[24]	TF	156	180	184	227	290	303	Arrivées de touristes/visiteurs[24]
Tourism expenditure		261	336	458	533	639	792	Dépenses touristiques
Fiji								**Fidji**
Tourist/visitor arrivals[4]	TF	398	431	504	550	545	540	Arrivées de touristes/visiteurs[4]
Tourism expenditure		379	490	585	676	636	...	Dépenses touristiques
Finland								**Finlande**
Tourist/visitor arrivals	TF	2 875	2 601	2 840[25]	3 140	3 375	3 519	Arrivées de touristes/visiteurs
Tourism expenditure		2 236	2 678	2 975	3 070	3 509	3 890	Dépenses touristiques
France								**France**
Tourist/visitor arrivals	TF	77 012[26]	75 048[26]	75 121[27]	75 908[27]	78 853[27]	*81 940[27]	Arrivées de touristes/visiteurs
Tourism expenditure		38 110	43 406	52 607	52 150	54 415	63 609	Dépenses touristiques
French Guiana								**Guyane française**
Tourist/visitor arrivals	TF	65	...	...	95[28]	...	109	Arrivées de touristes/visiteurs
Tourism expenditure[3]		45	...	...	44	...	49	Dépenses touristiques[3]
French Polynesia								**Polynésie française**
Tourist/visitor arrivals[4]	TF	189	213	212	208	222	218	Arrivées de touristes/visiteurs[4]
Tourism expenditure		471	651	737	759	781	876	Dépenses touristiques
Gabon								**Gabon**
Tourist/visitor arrivals[29]	TF	208	222	...	...	...	...	Arrivées de touristes/visiteurs[29]
Tourism expenditure		77	84	74	13	...	...	Dépenses touristiques
Gambia								**Gambie**
Tourist/visitor arrivals[30]	TF	81	73	90	108	125	143	Arrivées de touristes/visiteurs[30]
Tourism expenditure		...	58	51	57	69	77	Dépenses touristiques
Georgia								**Géorgie**
Tourist/visitor arrivals	VF	298	313	368	560	983	1 052	Arrivées de touristes/visiteurs
Tourism expenditure		144	172	209	287	361	441	Dépenses touristiques
Germany								**Allemagne**
Tourist/visitor arrivals	TCE	17 969	18 399	20 137	21 500	23 569	24 421	Arrivées de touristes/visiteurs
Tourism expenditure		26 690	30 104	35 569	38 220	42 921	46 860	Dépenses touristiques
Ghana								**Ghana**
Tourist/visitor arrivals[2]	TF	483	531	584	429	497	...	Arrivées de touristes/visiteurs[2]
Tourism expenditure		383	441	495	867	910	990	Dépenses touristiques
Greece								**Grèce**
Tourist/visitor arrivals[31]	TF	14 180	13 969	13 313	14 765	16 039	17 518	Arrivées de touristes/visiteurs[31]
Tourism expenditure		10 005	10 842	12 809	13 453	14 495	15 687	Dépenses touristiques
Grenada								**Grenade**
Tourist/visitor arrivals	TF	132	142	134	99	119	130	Arrivées de touristes/visiteurs
Tourism expenditure[5]		91	104	84	71	93	110	Dépenses touristiques[5]
Guadeloupe								**Guadeloupe**
Tourist/visitor arrivals[10,32,33]	TCE	...	439[34]	456[34]	372[35]	393	408	Arrivées de touristes/visiteurs[10,32,33]
Tourism expenditure[3]		...	...	...	306	299	344	Dépenses touristiques[3]
Guam								**Guam**
Tourist/visitor arrivals	TF	1 059	910	1 160	1 228	1 212	1 225	Arrivées de touristes/visiteurs
Guatemala								**Guatemala**
Tourist/visitor arrivals	VF	884	880	1 182	1 316	1 502	1 628	Arrivées de touristes/visiteurs
Tourism expenditure		647	646	630[5]	791[5]	919[5]	1 055[5]	Dépenses touristiques

66

Tourist/visitor arrivals and tourism expenditure *(continued)*
Thousands arrivals and millions of US dollars
Arrivées de touristes/visiteurs et dépenses touristiques *(suite)*
Milliers d'arrivées et millions de dollars E.-U.

Country or area of destination	Series[&] Série[&]	2002	2003	2004	2005	2006	2007	Pays ou zone de destination
Guinea								**Guinée**
Tourist/visitor arrivals	TF	43	44[36]	45	45[36]	46[36]	...	Arrivées de touristes/visiteurs
Tourism expenditure		...	...	...	...	...	1	Dépenses touristiques
Guinea-Bissau								**Guinée-Bissau**
Tourist/visitor arrivals [10]	TF	...	...	...	5	12	30	Arrivées de touristes/visiteurs [10]
Tourism expenditure		2[5]	2	2	2[5]	3[5]	...	Dépenses touristiques
Guyana								**Guyana**
Tourist/visitor arrivals [37]	TF	104	101	122	117	113	131	Arrivées de touristes/visiteurs [37]
Tourism expenditure		53	28	27[5]	35[5]	37[5]	50[5]	Dépenses touristiques
Haiti								**Haïti**
Tourist/visitor arrivals [10]	TF	140	136	96	112	108	386[2]	Arrivées de touristes/visiteurs [10]
Tourism expenditure [5]		108	96	87	80	135	140	Dépenses touristiques [5]
Honduras								**Honduras**
Tourist/visitor arrivals	TF	550	611	641	673	739	831	Arrivées de touristes/visiteurs
Tourism expenditure		305	364	420	466	490	559	Dépenses touristiques
Hungary								**Hongrie**
Tourist/visitor arrivals	TCE	3 013	2 948	3 270	3 446	3 310	3 451	Arrivées de touristes/visiteurs
Tourism expenditure		3 774	4 119	4 129	4 717	4 943	5 693	Dépenses touristiques
Iceland								**Islande**
Tourist/visitor arrivals	TCE	705	771	836	871	971	1 054	Arrivées de touristes/visiteurs
Tourism expenditure		415	486	558	630	663	887	Dépenses touristiques
India								**Inde**
Tourist/visitor arrivals [4]	TF	2 384	2 726	3 457	3 919	4 447	5 082	Arrivées de touristes/visiteurs [4]
Tourism expenditure		3 300	4 560	6 307	7 652	8 927	10 729[5]	Dépenses touristiques
Indonesia								**Indonésie**
Tourist/visitor arrivals	TF	5 033	4 467	5 321	5 002	4 871	5 506	Arrivées de touristes/visiteurs
Tourism expenditure		5 797	4 461	5 226	5 094	4 890	5 833	Dépenses touristiques
Iran (Islamic Rep. of)								**Iran (Rép. islamique d')**
Tourist/visitor arrivals	TF	1 585	1 546	1 659	1 889	2 735	...	Arrivées de touristes/visiteurs
Tourism expenditure [38]		1 607	1 266	1 305	1 364	1 760	1 834	Dépenses touristiques [38]
Iraq								**Iraq**
Tourism expenditure		45[5,39]			186	170	...	Dépenses touristiques
Ireland								**Irlande**
Tourist/visitor arrivals [40]	TF	6 476	6 764	6 953	7 333	8 001	8 332	Arrivées de touristes/visiteurs [40]
Tourism expenditure		4 228	5 206	6 075	6 780	7 664	8 863	Dépenses touristiques
Israel								**Israël**
Tourist/visitor arrivals [4]	TF	862	1 063	1 506	1 903	1 825	2 067	Arrivées de touristes/visiteurs [4]
Tourism expenditure		2 426	2 473	2 862	3 358	3 317	3 712	Dépenses touristiques
Italy								**Italie**
Tourist/visitor arrivals [41]	TF	39 799	39 604	37 071	36 513	41 058	43 654	Arrivées de touristes/visiteurs [41]
Tourism expenditure		28 192	32 591	37 870	38 374	41 644	46 144	Dépenses touristiques
Jamaica								**Jamaïque**
Tourist/visitor arrivals [2,42]	TF	1 266	1 350	1 415	1 479	1 679	1 701	Arrivées de touristes/visiteurs [2,42]
Tourism expenditure		1 482	1 621	1 733	1 783	2 094	2 137	Dépenses touristiques
Japan								**Japon**
Tourist/visitor arrivals [4]	VF	5 239	5 212	6 138	6 728	7 334	8 347	Arrivées de touristes/visiteurs [4]
Tourism expenditure		6 069	11 475	14 343	15 555	11 490	12 422	Dépenses touristiques
Jordan								**Jordanie**
Tourist/visitor arrivals [2]	TF	2 384	2 353	2 853	2 987	3 225	3 431	Arrivées de touristes/visiteurs [2]
Tourism expenditure		1 254	1 266	1 621	1 759	2 426	2 755	Dépenses touristiques
Kazakhstan								**Kazakhstan**
Tourist/visitor arrivals	TF	2 832	2 410	3 073	3 143	3 468	3 876	Arrivées de touristes/visiteurs
Tourism expenditure		680	638	803	801	973	1 213	Dépenses touristiques
Kenya								**Kenya**
Tourist/visitor arrivals	TF	825	927	1 193	1 536	1 644	...	Arrivées de touristes/visiteurs
Tourism expenditure		513	619	799	969	1 181	1 507	Dépenses touristiques
Kiribati [10]								**Kiribati** [10]
Tourist/visitor arrivals	TF	5	5[43]	4[44]	3[44]	4[43]	5[43]	Arrivées de touristes/visiteurs
Korea, Republic of								**Corée, République de**
Tourist/visitor arrivals [45]	VF	5 347	4 753	5 818	6 023	6 155	6 448	Arrivées de touristes/visiteurs [45]
Tourism expenditure		7 621	7 005	8 226	8 290	8 508	8 947	Dépenses touristiques

66

Tourist/visitor arrivals and tourism expenditure *(continued)*
Thousands arrivals and millions of US dollars
Arrivées de touristes/visiteurs et dépenses touristiques *(suite)*
Milliers d'arrivées et millions de dollars E.-U.

Country or area of destination	Series[&] Série[&]	2002	2003	2004	2005	2006	2007	Pays ou zone de destination
Kuwait								**Koweït**
Tourist/visitor arrivals	VF	2 316	2 602	3 056	3 474	3 899	4 482	Arrivées de touristes/visiteurs
Tourism expenditure		320	328	412	410	469	512	Dépenses touristiques
Kyrgyzstan								**Kirghizistan**
Tourist/visitor arrivals	TF	140	342[46]	398[46]	319[46]	766[46]	1 654[46]	Arrivées de touristes/visiteurs
Tourism expenditure		48	62	92	94	189	392	Dépenses touristiques
Lao People's Dem. Rep.								**Rép. dém. pop. lao**
Tourist/visitor arrivals	TF	215	196	407	672	842	1 142	Arrivées de touristes/visiteurs
Tourism expenditure[5,47]		113	87	119	147	173	233	Dépenses touristiques [5,47]
Latvia								**Lettonie**
Tourist/visitor arrivals[48]	TF	848	971	1 079	1 116	1 535	1 653	Arrivées de touristes/visiteurs [48]
Tourism expenditure		201	271	343	446	622	880	Dépenses touristiques
Lebanon								**Liban**
Tourist/visitor arrivals[49]	TF	956	1 016	1 278	1 140	1 063	1 017	Arrivées de touristes/visiteurs [49]
Tourism expenditure		4 284[5]	6 782	5 931	5 969	5 441	5 573	Dépenses touristiques
Lesotho								**Lesotho**
Tourist/visitor arrivals	VF	287	329	304	304	357	300	Arrivées de touristes/visiteurs
Tourism expenditure		20	28	42	26	27	43	Dépenses touristiques
Liberia[5]								**Libéria**[5]
Tourism expenditure		...	...	59	67	124	131	Dépenses touristiques
Libyan Arab Jamah.								**Jamah. arabe libyenne**
Tourist/visitor arrivals	TF	135	142	149	...	...	...	Arrivées de touristes/visiteurs
Tourism expenditure		202	243	261	301	244	99	Dépenses touristiques
Liechtenstein								**Liechtenstein**
Tourist/visitor arrivals	THS	49	49	49	50	55	58	Arrivées de touristes/visiteurs
Lithuania								**Lituanie**
Tourist/visitor arrivals	TF	1 428	1 491	1 800	2 000	2 180	1 486	Arrivées de touristes/visiteurs
Tourism expenditure		556	700	834	975	1 077	1 192	Dépenses touristiques
Luxembourg								**Luxembourg**
Tourist/visitor arrivals	TCE	885	867	878	913	908	917	Arrivées de touristes/visiteurs
Tourism expenditure		2 547	3 149	3 880	3 612[5]	3 620[5]	4 009[5]	Dépenses touristiques
Madagascar								**Madagascar**
Tourist/visitor arrivals[50]	TF	62	139	229	277	312	344	Arrivées de touristes/visiteurs [50]
Tourism expenditure		109	119	239	290	386	506	Dépenses touristiques
Malawi								**Malawi**
Tourist/visitor arrivals[51]	TF	383	424	427	438	638	714	Arrivées de touristes/visiteurs [51]
Tourism expenditure[52]		45	35	36	43	43	48	Dépenses touristiques [52]
Malaysia								**Malaisie**
Tourist/visitor arrivals[53]	TF	13 292	10 577	15 703	16 431	17 547	20 973	Arrivées de touristes/visiteurs [53]
Tourism expenditure		8 084	6 799	9 183	10 389	12 355	16 798	Dépenses touristiques
Maldives								**Maldives**
Tourist/visitor arrivals[10]	TF	485	564	617	395	602	676	Arrivées de touristes/visiteurs [10]
Tourism expenditure[5]		337	402	471	287	512	586	Dépenses touristiques [5]
Mali								**Mali**
Tourist/visitor arrivals[10]	THS	96	110	113	143	153	164	Arrivées de touristes/visiteurs [10]
Tourism expenditure		105	136	142	149	175	...	Dépenses touristiques
Malta								**Malte**
Tourist/visitor arrivals	TF	1 134	1 127	1 156[54]	1 171[54]	1 124[54]	1 244[54]	Arrivées de touristes/visiteurs
Tourism expenditure		757	869	949	924	966	1 143	Dépenses touristiques
Marshall Islands								**Iles Marshall**
Tourist/visitor arrivals	TF	6[10]	7[10]	9[56]	9[56]	6[10]	7[10]	Arrivées de touristes/visiteurs
Tourism expenditure[3,55]		3	4	5	6	7	5	Dépenses touristiques [3,55]
Martinique								**Martinique**
Tourist/visitor arrivals	TF	447	453	471	484	503	501	Arrivées de touristes/visiteurs
Tourism expenditure[3]		237	247	291	280	306	299	Dépenses touristiques [3]
Mauritius								**Maurice**
Tourist/visitor arrivals	TF	682	702	719	761	788	907	Arrivées de touristes/visiteurs
Tourism expenditure		829	960	1 156	1 189	1 302	1 663	Dépenses touristiques
Mexico								**Mexique**
Tourist/visitor arrivals[2]	TF	19 667	18 665	20 618	21 915	21 353	21 424	Arrivées de touristes/visiteurs [2]
Tourism expenditure		9 547	10 058	11 609	12 801	13 329	14 072	Dépenses touristiques

66

Tourist/visitor arrivals and tourism expenditure *(continued)*
Thousands arrivals and millions of US dollars
Arrivées de touristes/visiteurs et dépenses touristiques *(suite)*
Milliers d'arrivées et millions de dollars E.-U.

Country or area of destination	Series[&] Série[&]	2002	2003	2004	2005	2006	2007	Pays ou zone de destination
Micronesia (Fed. States of)								**Micronésie (Etats féd. de)**
Tourist/visitor arrivals[57]	TF	19	18	19	19	19	21	Arrivées de touristes/visiteurs[57]
Tourism expenditure[3,55]		17	17	17	17	18	...	Dépenses touristiques[3,55]
Monaco								**Monaco**
Tourist/visitor arrivals	THS	263	235	250	286	313	328	Arrivées de touristes/visiteurs
Mongolia								**Mongolie**
Tourist/visitor arrivals[58]	TF	229	201	301	338	386	452	Arrivées de touristes/visiteurs[58]
Tourism expenditure		143	154	205	203	261	...	Dépenses touristiques
Montenegro								**Monténégro**
Tourist/visitor arrivals	TCE	136	142	188	272	378	984	Arrivées de touristes/visiteurs
Tourism expenditure[3]		...	...	...	222	271	457	Dépenses touristiques[3]
Montserrat								**Montserrat**
Tourist/visitor arrivals	TF	10	8	10	10	8	8	Arrivées de touristes/visiteurs
Tourism expenditure[5]		9	7	9	9	8	7	Dépenses touristiques[5]
Morocco								**Maroc**
Tourist/visitor arrivals[2]	TF	4 453	4 761	5 477	5 843	6 558	7 408	Arrivées de touristes/visiteurs[2]
Tourism expenditure		3 157	3 802	4 540	5 426	6 900	8 307	Dépenses touristiques
Mozambique								**Mozambique**
Tourist/visitor arrivals	TF	541	441	470	578	664	771	Arrivées de touristes/visiteurs
Tourism expenditure		65	106	96	138	145	182	Dépenses touristiques
Myanmar								**Myanmar**
Tourist/visitor arrivals[59]	TF	217	206	242	232	264	248	Arrivées de touristes/visiteurs[59]
Tourism expenditure		136	70	97	85	59	...	Dépenses touristiques
Namibia								**Namibie**
Tourist/visitor arrivals	TF	757	695	...	778	833	929	Arrivées de touristes/visiteurs
Tourism expenditure		251	383	426	363	473	542	Dépenses touristiques
Nepal								**Népal**
Tourist/visitor arrivals[60]	TF	275	338	385	375	384	527	Arrivées de touristes/visiteurs[60]
Tourism expenditure		134	232	260	160	157	234	Dépenses touristiques
Netherlands								**Pays-Bas**
Tourist/visitor arrivals	TCE	9 595	9 181	9 646	10 012	10 739	11 008	Arrivées de touristes/visiteurs
Tourism expenditure		11 720	14 603	16 495	16 528	17 529	19 922	Dépenses touristiques
New Caledonia								**Nouvelle-Calédonie**
Tourist/visitor arrivals[2]	TF	104	102	100	101	100	103	Arrivées de touristes/visiteurs[2]
Tourism expenditure[5]		156	196	241	149	169	197	Dépenses touristiques[5]
New Zealand								**Nouvelle-Zélande**
Tourist/visitor arrivals	VF	2 045	2 104	2 334	2 365	2 409	2 455	Arrivées de touristes/visiteurs
Tourism expenditure[5]		3 158	4 201	5 031	5 162	4 777	5 406	Dépenses touristiques[5]
Nicaragua								**Nicaragua**
Tourist/visitor arrivals	TF	472	526	615	712[2]	749[2]	800[2]	Arrivées de touristes/visiteurs
Tourism expenditure[5]		135	160	192	206	231	255	Dépenses touristiques[5]
Niger								**Niger**
Tourist/visitor arrivals	TF	39	55	57	60	60	48	Arrivées de touristes/visiteurs
Tourism expenditure		20	28	32	44	39	41	Dépenses touristiques
Nigeria								**Nigéria**
Tourist/visitor arrivals	TF	887	924	962	1 010	1 111	...	Arrivées de touristes/visiteurs
Tourism expenditure		256	58	49	46	51	340	Dépenses touristiques
Niue								**Nioué**
Tourist/visitor arrivals[61]	TF	2[10]	3[10]	3[10]	3[10]	3[10]	4[56]	Arrivées de touristes/visiteurs[61]
Tourism expenditure[3]		...	1	1	1	1	2	Dépenses touristiques[3]
Northern Mariana Islands[10]								**Iles Mariannes du Nord**[10]
Tourist/visitor arrivals	TF	466	452	525	498	429	385	Arrivées de touristes/visiteurs
Norway								**Norvège**
Tourist/visitor arrivals[62]	TF	3 111	3 269	3 628	3 824	4 070	4 290	Arrivées de touristes/visiteurs[62]
Tourism expenditure		2 581	2 989	3 531	4 030	4 251	5 021	Dépenses touristiques
Occupied Palestinian Terr.								**Terr. palestinien occupé**
Tourist/visitor arrivals	THS	33	37	56	88	123	264	Arrivées de touristes/visiteurs
Tourism expenditure[5,63]		33	107	56	121	...	...	Dépenses touristiques[5,63]
Oman								**Oman**
Tourist/visitor arrivals	THS	643	630	908	989	1 306	1 144	Arrivées de touristes/visiteurs
Tourism expenditure		539	546	604	599	743	902	Dépenses touristiques

66

Tourist/visitor arrivals and tourism expenditure *(continued)*
Thousands arrivals and millions of US dollars
Arrivées de touristes/visiteurs et dépenses touristiques *(suite)*
Milliers d'arrivées et millions de dollars E.-U.

Country or area of destination	Series[&] Série[&]	2002	2003	2004	2005	2006	2007	Pays ou zone de destination
Pakistan								**Pakistan**
Tourist/visitor arrivals	TF	498	501	648	798	898	840	Arrivées de touristes/visiteurs
Tourism expenditure		562	620	765	828	919	900	Dépenses touristiques
Palau								**Palaos**
Tourist/visitor arrivals[64]	TF	59	68	95	86	87	93	Arrivées de touristes/visiteurs[64]
Tourism expenditure[3]		57	76	97	97	90	...	Dépenses touristiques[3]
Panama								**Panama**
Tourist/visitor arrivals	TF	534	566	621	702	843	1 103	Arrivées de touristes/visiteurs
Tourism expenditure		710	804	903	1 108	1 450	1 796	Dépenses touristiques
Papua New Guinea								**Papouasie-Nvl-Guinée**
Tourist/visitor arrivals	TF	54	56	59	69	78	104	Arrivées de touristes/visiteurs
Tourism expenditure		3[5]	4[5]	6	4	...	...	Dépenses touristiques
Paraguay								**Paraguay**
Tourist/visitor arrivals[7,65]	TF	250	268	309	341	388	416	Arrivées de touristes/visiteurs[7,65]
Tourism expenditure		76	81	87	96	112	121	Dépenses touristiques
Peru								**Pérou**
Tourist/visitor arrivals[2,66]	TF	1 064	1 136	1 350	1 571	1 721	1 916	Arrivées de touristes/visiteurs[2,66]
Tourism expenditure		836	1 023	1 232	1 438	1 782	2 222	Dépenses touristiques
Philippines								**Philippines**
Tourist/visitor arrivals[2]	TF	1 933	1 907	2 291	2 623	2 843	3 092	Arrivées de touristes/visiteurs[2]
Tourism expenditure		2 018	1 821	2 390	2 755	4 019	5 518	Dépenses touristiques
Poland								**Pologne**
Tourist/visitor arrivals	TF	13 980	13 720	14 290	15 200	15 670	14 975	Arrivées de touristes/visiteurs
Tourism expenditure		4 971	4 733	6 499	7 128	8 122	11 686	Dépenses touristiques
Portugal								**Portugal**
Tourist/visitor arrivals	TF	11 644[4]	11 707[4]	10 639[2,25]	10 612[2]	11 282[2]	12 321[2]	Arrivées de touristes/visiteurs
Tourism expenditure		6 595	7 634	8 858	9 009	10 061	12 917	Dépenses touristiques
Puerto Rico								**Porto Rico**
Tourist/visitor arrivals[67]	TF	3 087	3 238	3 541	3 686	3 722	3 687	Arrivées de touristes/visiteurs[67]
Tourism expenditure[3]		2 486	2 677	3 024	3 239	3 369	3 414	Dépenses touristiques[3]
Qatar								**Qatar**
Tourist/visitor arrivals[1]	THS	587	557	732	913	946	964	Arrivées de touristes/visiteurs[1]
Tourism expenditure[5,68]		285	369	498	760	874	...	Dépenses touristiques[5,68]
Republic of Moldova								**République de Moldova**
Tourist/visitor arrivals[69]	TF	18	21	24	23	13	13	Arrivées de touristes/visiteurs[69]
Tourism expenditure		72	79	112	138	145	221	Dépenses touristiques
Réunion								**Réunion**
Tourist/visitor arrivals	TF	426	432	430	409	279	381	Arrivées de touristes/visiteurs
Tourism expenditure[3]		329	413	448	442	308	446	Dépenses touristiques[3]
Romania								**Roumanie**
Tourist/visitor arrivals	VF	4 794	5 595	6 600	5 839	6 037	7 722	Arrivées de touristes/visiteurs
Tourism expenditure		400	523	607	1 325	1 676	1 922	Dépenses touristiques
Russian Federation								**Fédération de Russie**
Tourist/visitor arrivals	VF	23 309	22 521	22 064	22 201	22 486	22 909	Arrivées de touristes/visiteurs
Tourism expenditure		5 428	5 879	7 262	7 806	9 720	12 587	Dépenses touristiques
Rwanda								**Rwanda**
Tourist/visitor arrivals	VF	...	...	...	...	...	826	Arrivées de touristes/visiteurs
Tourism expenditure		31[5]	30[5]	44[5]	49[5]	31[5]	66	Dépenses touristiques
Saba								**Saba**
Tourist/visitor arrivals	TF	11	10	11	11	11	12	Arrivées de touristes/visiteurs
Saint Eustatius[70]								**Saint-Eustache**[70]
Tourist/visitor arrivals	TF	10	10	11	10	10	12	Arrivées de touristes/visiteurs
Saint Kitts and Nevis								**Saint-Kitts-et-Nevis**
Tourist/visitor arrivals[42]	TF	69	91	118	141	139	117	Arrivées de touristes/visiteurs[42]
Tourism expenditure[5]		57	75	103	121	122	106	Dépenses touristiques[5]
Saint Lucia								**Sainte-Lucie**
Tourist/visitor arrivals[4]	TF	253	277	298	318	303	287	Arrivées de touristes/visiteurs[4]
Tourism expenditure[5]		210	282	326	356	285	296	Dépenses touristiques[5]
Saint Maarten								**Saint-Martin**
Tourist/visitor arrivals[71]	TF	381	428	475	468	468	469	Arrivées de touristes/visiteurs[71]
Tourism expenditure[5,72]		489	538	626	659	651	662	Dépenses touristiques[5,72]

66

Tourist/visitor arrivals and tourism expenditure *(continued)*
Thousands arrivals and millions of US dollars
Arrivées de touristes/visiteurs et dépenses touristiques *(suite)*
Milliers d'arrivées et millions de dollars E.-U.

Country or area of destination	Series& Série&	2002	2003	2004	2005	2006	2007	Pays ou zone de destination
Saint Vincent-Grenadines								**Saint Vincent-Grenadines**
Tourist/visitor arrivals[42]	TF	78	79	87	96	97	90	Arrivées de touristes/visiteurs[42]
Tourism expenditure[5]		91	91	96	104	113	119	Dépenses touristiques[5]
Samoa								**Samoa**
Tourist/visitor arrivals	TF	89	92	98	102	116	122	Arrivées de touristes/visiteurs
Tourism expenditure		45[5,47]	54[5,47]	70	80	91	107	Dépenses touristiques
San Marino[73]								**Saint-Marin[73]**
Tourist/visitor arrivals	THS	46	41	42	50	50	69	Arrivées de touristes/visiteurs
Sao Tome and Principe								**Sao Tomé-et-Principe**
Tourist/visitor arrivals	TF	9	10	11	16	12	...	Arrivées de touristes/visiteurs
Tourism expenditure[5]		7	7	8	7	7	3	Dépenses touristiques[5]
Saudi Arabia								**Arabie saoudite**
Tourist/visitor arrivals[3]	TF	7 511	7 332	8 599	8 037	8 620	11 531	Arrivées de touristes/visiteurs
Tourism expenditure[3]		...	3 418	6 916	5 626	5 391	6 020	Dépenses touristiques[3]
Senegal								**Sénégal**
Tourist/visitor arrivals	TF	...	495	667	769	866	875	Arrivées de touristes/visiteurs
Tourism expenditure		210	260	207	334	329	...	Dépenses touristiques
Serbia								**Serbie**
Tourist/visitor arrivals	TCE	312[74]	339[74]	392[74]	453[74]	469[74]	696	Arrivées de touristes/visiteurs
Tourism expenditure[3]		77	159	220	308	398	1 011	Dépenses touristiques[3]
Seychelles								**Seychelles**
Tourist/visitor arrivals	TF	132	122	121	129	141	161	Arrivées de touristes/visiteurs
Tourism expenditure		247	258	256	269	323	366	Dépenses touristiques
Sierra Leone								**Sierra Leone**
Tourist/visitor arrivals[10]	TF	28	38	44	40	34	32	Arrivées de touristes/visiteurs[10]
Tourism expenditure[5]		38	60	58	64	23	22	Dépenses touristiques[5]
Singapore								**Singapour**
Tourist/visitor arrivals	TF	5 855	4 703	6 553	7 079	7 588	7 957	Arrivées de touristes/visiteurs
Tourism expenditure		4 428	3 783	5 229	5 909	7 204	8 680	Dépenses touristiques
Slovakia								**Slovaquie**
Tourist/visitor arrivals	TCE	1 399	1 387	1 401	1 515	1 612	1 685	Arrivées de touristes/visiteurs
Tourism expenditure		742	876	931	1 282	1 655	2 352	Dépenses touristiques
Slovenia								**Slovénie**
Tourist/visitor arrivals	TCE	1 302	1 373	1 499	1 555	1 617	1 751	Arrivées de touristes/visiteurs
Tourism expenditure		1 152	1 427	1 725	1 894	1 911	2 400	Dépenses touristiques
Solomon Islands								**Iles Salomon**
Tourist/visitor arrivals	TF	...	7	...	9[75]	11	14	Arrivées de touristes/visiteurs
Tourism expenditure		1	2	4	8	10	4[5]	Dépenses touristiques
South Africa								**Afrique du Sud**
Tourist/visitor arrivals[76]	TF	6 430	6 505	6 678	7 369	8 396	9 091	Arrivées de touristes/visiteurs[76]
Tourism expenditure		3 695	6 533	7 380	8 448	8 967	9 890	Dépenses touristiques
Spain								**Espagne**
Tourist/visitor arrivals	TF	50 331	50 854	52 430	55 914	58 004	58 666	Arrivées de touristes/visiteurs
Tourism expenditure		35 468	43 863	49 996	53 066	57 543	65 136	Dépenses touristiques
Sri Lanka								**Sri Lanka**
Tourist/visitor arrivals[4]	TF	393	501	566	549	560	494	Arrivées de touristes/visiteurs[4]
Tourism expenditure		594	709	808	729	733	750	Dépenses touristiques
Sudan								**Soudan**
Tourist/visitor arrivals	TF	52	52	61	246[2]	328[2]	436[2]	Arrivées de touristes/visiteurs
Tourism expenditure[5]		108	17	21	89	167	262	Dépenses touristiques[5]
Suriname								**Suriname**
Tourist/visitor arrivals	TF	60[77]	82[77]	138	160	153	163	Arrivées de touristes/visiteurs
Tourism expenditure		17	18	52	96	109	73	Dépenses touristiques
Swaziland								**Swaziland**
Tourist/visitor arrivals	THS	256[1]	461	459	839	873	870	Arrivées de touristes/visiteurs
Tourism expenditure		45	70	75	77	75	32	Dépenses touristiques
Sweden								**Suède**
Tourist/visitor arrivals[78]	TCE	2 989	2 952	3 003	3 133	3 270	3 434	Arrivées de touristes/visiteurs[78]
Tourism expenditure		5 671	6 548	7 686	8 589	10 485	13 706	Dépenses touristiques

66

Tourist/visitor arrivals and tourism expenditure *(continued)*
Thousands arrivals and millions of US dollars

Arrivées de touristes/visiteurs et dépenses touristiques *(suite)*
Milliers d'arrivées et millions de dollars E.-U.

Country or area of destination	Series[&] Série[&]	2002	2003	2004	2005	2006	2007	Pays ou zone de destination
Switzerland								**Suisse**
Tourist/visitor arrivals	THS	6 868	6 530	...	7 229	7 863	8 448	Arrivées de touristes/visiteurs
Tourism expenditure		9 117	10 493	11 404	11 937	12 923	14 777	Dépenses touristiques
Syrian Arab Republic								**Rép. arabe syrienne**
Tourist/visitor arrivals	TF	2 186	2 085	3 030	3 368	4 422	4 566	Arrivées de touristes/visiteurs
Tourism expenditure		970[5]	877	1 883	2 035	2 113	3 297	Dépenses touristiques
Tajikistan								**Tadjikistan**
Tourism expenditure		5	7	9	10	11	16	Dépenses touristiques
Thailand								**Thaïlande**
Tourist/visitor arrivals	TF	10 873[2]	10 082[2]	11 737[2]	11 567[2]	13 822	14 464	Arrivées de touristes/visiteurs
Tourism expenditure		10 388	10 456	13 054	12 102	16 614	20 623	Dépenses touristiques
TFYR of Macedonia								**L'ex-R.Y. Macédoine**
Tourist/visitor arrivals	TCE	123	158	165	197	202	230	Arrivées de touristes/visiteurs
Tourism expenditure		55	86	103	116	156	219	Dépenses touristiques
Togo								**Togo**
Tourist/visitor arrivals	THS	58	61	83	81	94	86	Arrivées de touristes/visiteurs
Tourism expenditure		16	26	25	27	23	...	Dépenses touristiques
Tonga								**Tonga**
Tourist/visitor arrivals [10]	TF	37	40	41	42	39	46	Arrivées de touristes/visiteurs [10]
Tourism expenditure [5]		6	10	13	15	16	16	Dépenses touristiques [5]
Trinidad and Tobago								**Trinité-et-Tobago**
Tourist/visitor arrivals [10]	TF	384	409	443	463	457	449	Arrivées de touristes/visiteurs [10]
Tourism expenditure		402	437	568	593	517	621	Dépenses touristiques
Tunisia								**Tunisie**
Tourist/visitor arrivals [4]	TF	5 064	5 114	5 998	6 378	6 550	6 762	Arrivées de touristes/visiteurs [4]
Tourism expenditure		1 831	1 935	2 432	2 800	2 999	3 373	Dépenses touristiques
Turkey								**Turquie**
Tourist/visitor arrivals	TF	12 790	13 341	16 826	20 273	18 916	22 248	Arrivées de touristes/visiteurs
Tourism expenditure [79]		11 901[47]	13 203	15 888	19 720	18 520	20 649	Dépenses touristiques [79]
Turkmenistan								**Turkménistan**
Tourist/visitor arrivals	TF	11	8	15	12	6	8	Arrivées de touristes/visiteurs
Turks and Caicos Islands								**Iles Turques et Caïques**
Tourist/visitor arrivals	TF	155	164	173	176	248	265	Arrivées de touristes/visiteurs
Tourism expenditure [3]		292	...	...	...	...	...	Dépenses touristiques [3]
Tuvalu								**Tuvalu**
Tourist/visitor arrivals	TF	1	1	1	1	1	1	Arrivées de touristes/visiteurs
Uganda								**Ouganda**
Tourist/visitor arrivals	TF	254	305	512	468	539	642	Arrivées de touristes/visiteurs
Tourism expenditure		194	185	268	382	310	359	Dépenses touristiques
Ukraine								**Ukraine**
Tourist/visitor arrivals	TF	10 517	12 514	15 629	17 631	18 936	23 122	Arrivées de touristes/visiteurs
Tourism expenditure		1 001	1 204	2 931	3 542	4 018	5 317	Dépenses touristiques
United Arab Emirates								**Emirats arabes unis**
Tourist/visitor arrivals [1,80]	THS	5 445	5 871	6 195	7 126	...	...	Arrivées de touristes/visiteurs [1,80]
Tourism expenditure [3]		1 332	1 438	1 593	3 218	4 972	6 059	Dépenses touristiques [3]
United Kingdom								**Royaume-Uni**
Tourist/visitor arrivals	TF	22 307	22 787	25 678	28 039	30 654	30 870	Arrivées de touristes/visiteurs
Tourism expenditure		27 819	30 736	37 166	39 569	42 888	47 109	Dépenses touristiques
United Rep. of Tanzania								**Rép.-Unie de Tanzanie**
Tourist/visitor arrivals	TF	550	552	566	590	622	692	Arrivées de touristes/visiteurs
Tourism expenditure		639	654	762	835	986	1 053	Dépenses touristiques
United States								**Etats-Unis**
Tourist/visitor arrivals [81]	TF	43 581	41 218	46 086	49 206	50 978	55 986	Arrivées de touristes/visiteurs [81]
Tourism expenditure		101 798	99 207	112 957	123 039	128 871	144 808	Dépenses touristiques
United States Virgin Is.								**Iles Vierges américaines**
Tourist/visitor arrivals	TF	520	538	544	582	570	510	Arrivées de touristes/visiteurs
Tourism expenditure [3]		1 195	1 257	1 356	1 490	1 466	1 433	Dépenses touristiques [3]
Uruguay								**Uruguay**
Tourist/visitor arrivals	TF	1 258	1 420	1 756	1 808	1 749	1 752	Arrivées de touristes/visiteurs
Tourism expenditure		409	419	591	699	710	927	Dépenses touristiques

Tourist/visitor arrivals and tourism expenditure *(continued)*
Thousands arrivals and millions of US dollars
Arrivées de touristes/visiteurs et dépenses touristiques *(suite)*
Milliers d'arrivées et millions de dollars E.-U.

Country or area of destination	Series[&] Série[&]	2002	2003	2004	2005	2006	2007	Pays ou zone de destination
Uzbekistan								**Ouzbékistan**
Tourist/visitor arrivals	TF	332	231	262	242	560	903	Arrivées de touristes/visiteurs
Tourism expenditure [3]		68	48	57	28[5]	43[5]	51[5]	Dépenses touristiques [3]
Vanuatu								**Vanuatu**
Tourist/visitor arrivals	TF	49	50	61	62	68	...	Arrivées de touristes/visiteurs
Tourism expenditure		72	83	93	104	109	142	Dépenses touristiques
Venezuela (Boliv. Rep. of)								**Venezuela (Rép. boliv. du)**
Tourist/visitor arrivals	TF	432	337	486	706	748	771	Arrivées de touristes/visiteurs
Tourism expenditure		484	378	554	722	843	894	Dépenses touristiques
Viet Nam								**Viet Nam**
Tourist/visitor arrivals	VF	2 628	2 429	2 928	3 468	3 583	4 244	Arrivées de touristes/visiteurs
Tourism expenditure [3]		...	1 400	1 700	1 880	3 200	...	Dépenses touristiques [3]
Yemen								**Yémen**
Tourist/visitor arrivals	THS	98	155	274	336	382	379	Arrivées de touristes/visiteurs
Tourism expenditure [5]		38	139	139	181	181	425	Dépenses touristiques [5]
Zambia								**Zambie**
Tourist/visitor arrivals	TF	565	413	515	669	757	897	Arrivées de touristes/visiteurs
Tourism expenditure		64	88	92	98	110	138	Dépenses touristiques
Zimbabwe								**Zimbabwe**
Tourist/visitor arrivals	VF	2 041	2 256	1 854	1 559	2 287	2 508	Arrivées de touristes/visiteurs
Tourism expenditure [3]		76	61	194	99	338	365	Dépenses touristiques [3]

Source:
World Tourism Organization (UNWTO), Madrid, UNWTO statistics database and the *Yearbook of Tourism Statistics*, 2009 edition.

The majority of the expenditure data have been provided to the WTO by the International Monetary Fund (IMF). Exceptions are footnoted.

[&]Series:
TF: Arrivals of non-resident tourists at national borders.
VF: Arrivals of non-resident visitors at national borders.
THS: Arrivals of non-resident tourists in hotels and similar establishments.
TCE: Arrivals of non-resident tourists in all types of accommodation establishments.

1 Arrivals in hotels only.
2 Including nationals of the country residing abroad.
3 The expenditure figures are those provided by the country to UNWTO, which do not appear in the International Monetary Fund data.
4 Excluding nationals of the country residing abroad.
5 Excluding passenger transport.
6 Starting 2004, as a result of the importance of the "Survey on International Tourism", the estimates of the series of the "Travel" item of the Balance of Payments were modified. For this reason, the data are not rigorously comparable with those of previous years.

7 Excluding nationals residing abroad and crew members.

8 Organized tourism.
9 Country estimates.
10 Air arrivals.
11 Source: Central Bank of the Netherlands Antilles.
12 Source: "Banque Centrale des Etats de l'Afrique de l'Ouest".
13 International tourist arrivals by all means of transport.
14 Different types of methodological changes that affect the estimates for 2000 and 2001 for expenditures and characteristics of international tourists to Canada have been introduced in 2002.

Source:
Organisation mondiale du tourisme (OMT), Madrid, la base de données de l'OMT, et l'*Annuaire des statistiques du tourisme*, édition 2009.

La majorité des données sur les dépenses touristiques sont celles que le Fonds monétaire international (FMI) a fournies à l'Organisation mondiale du tourisme (OMT). Les exceptions sont signalées par une note.

[&]Série:
TF : Arrivées de touristes non résidents aux frontières nationales.
VF: Arrivées de visiteurs non résidents aux frontières nationales.
THS: Arrivées de touristes non résidents dans les hôtels et établissements assimilés.
TCE: Arrivées de touristes non résidents dans tous les types d'établissements d'hébergement touristique.

1 Arrivées dans les hôtels uniquement.
2 Y compris les nationaux du pays résidant à l'étranger.
3 Les chiffres de dépense sont ceux que le pays a fournis à l'OMT mais ils ne figurent pas dans les données du Fonds monétaire international.
4 A l'exclusion des nationaux du pays résidant à l'étranger.
5 Non compris le transport de passagers.
6 À partir de 2004, vu l'importance de l'"Enquête sur le tourisme international", des modifications ont été apportées aux estimations de la série du poste "Voyages" de la balance des paiements. C'est la raison pour laquelle les données ne sont pas rigoureusement comparables avec celles des années précédentes.

7 A l'exclusion des nationaux du pays résidant à l'étranger et des membres des équipages.

8 Tourisme organisé.
9 Estimations du pays.
10 Arrivées par voie aérienne.
11 Source: "Central Bank of the Netherlands Antilles".
12 Source: Banque Centrale des Etats de l'Afrique de l'Ouest.
13 Touristes étrangers, tous moyens de transport confondus.
14 En 2002, il a été adopté différents types de changements méthodologiques qui ont eu des effets sur les estimations des dépenses et des caractéristiques des touristes internationaux ayant

66

Tourist/visitor arrivals and tourism expenditure *(continued)*
Thousands arrivals and millions of US dollars
Arrivées de touristes/visiteurs et dépenses touristiques *(suite)*
Milliers d'arrivées et millions de dollars E.-U.

Therefore, Statistics Canada advises not to compare the estimates for 2000 and 2001 with the years prior because of these methodological changes for the non-count estimates (one of the reasons ALS numbers are not provided).

15	Arrivals by air to Bangui only.
16	Source: "Banque des Etats de l'Afrique Centrale (B.E.A.C.)".
17	For statistical purposes, the data for China do not include those for the Hong Kong Special Administrative Region (Hong Kong SAR), Macao Special Administrative Region (Macao SAR) and Taiwan Province of China.
18	The expenditure figures used were the ones provided by the country to UNWTO, as this data series is more complete than that provided by the International Monetary Fund (IMF).
19	Source: "Banque centrale des Comores".
20	New accommodation coverage from 2000.
21	New methodology.
22	Calculated on the basis of accommodation statistics and "Foreign Visitor Survey" carried out by the Statistical Office of Estonia.
23	Starting from 2004, border statistics are not collected any more.
24	Arrivals through all ports of entry. Including nationals residing abroad.
25	Due to a change in the methodology, data are not comparable to previous years.
26	Estimated based on surveys at national borders.
27	Non-resident visitor survey (EVE).
28	2005 survey at Cayenne-Rochambeau airport on departure.
29	Arrivals of non-resident tourists at Libreville airport.
30	Charter tourists only.
31	Information based on administrative data.
32	Excluding the north islands (Saint Maarten and Saint Bartholemy).
33	Non-resident tourists staying in all types of accommodation establishments.
34	Arrivals of non-resident tourists in hotels only.
35	Data based on a survey conducted at Guadeloupe airport.
36	Air arrivals at Conakry airport.
37	Arrivals to Timehri airport only.
38	Source: Central Bank of Islamic Republic of Iran.
39	Source: Central Bank of Iraq.
40	Including tourists from Northern Ireland.
41	Excluding seasonal and border workers.
42	Arrivals of non-resident tourists by air. E/D cards.
43	Tarawa and Christmas Island.
44	Tarawa only.
45	Including nationals residing abroad and crew members.
46	New data source: Department of Customs Control.
47	Country data.
48	Non-resident departures. Survey of persons crossing the state border.
49	Excluding Syrian nationals.
50	Arrivals of non-resident tourists by air.
51	Departures.
52	Source: Reserve Bank of Malawi.
53	Including Singapore residents crossing the frontier by road through Johore Causeway.
54	Departures by air and by sea.
55	Fiscal years (October 1 to September 30).
56	Air and sea arrivals.
57	Arrivals in the States of Kosrae, Chuuk, Pohnpei and Yap. Excluding FSM citizens.
58	Excluding diplomats and foreign residents in Mongolia.
59	Including tourist arrivals through border entry points to Yangon.

visité le Canada en 2000 et 2001. Pour 2000 et 2001, Statistique Canada conseille par conséquent de ne pas comparer les estimations ne reposant pas sur des comptages aux données des années précédentes (c'est une des raisons pour lesquelles les données DMS ne sont pas fournies).

15	Arrivées par voie aérienne à Bangui uniquement.
16	Source: Banque des Etats de l'Afrique Centrale (B.E.A.C.).
17	Pour la présentation des statistiques, les données pour la Chine ne comprennent pas la Région Administrative Spéciale de Hong Kong (Hong Kong RAS), la Région Administrative Spéciale de Macao (Macao RAS) et la province de Taiwan.
18	Les données de dépense sont celles que le pays a fournies à l'OMT car il s'agit d'une série plus complète que celle obtenue du Fonds monétaire international (FMI).
19	Source: Banque centrale des Comores.
20	Porte sur les nouveaux logements depuis 2000.
21	Nouvelle méthodologie.
22	Calculé sur la base des statistiques d'hébergement et de la "Foreign Visitor Survey" menée par la "Statistical Office of Estonia".
23	À partir de 2004, les statistiques de frontière ne sont plus collectées.
24	Arrivées à travers tous les ports d'entrée. Y compris les nationaux résidant à l'étranger.
25	Dû à un changement dans la méthodologie, l'information n'est pas comparable à celle des années précédentes.
26	Estimations à partir d'enquêtes aux frontières.
27	Enquête auprès des visiteurs venant de l'étranger (EVE).
28	Enquête 2005 au départ de l'aéroport de Cayenne-Rochambeau.
29	Arrivées de touristes non résidents à l'aéroport de Libreville.
30	Arrivées en vols à la demande seulement.
31	Information tirée de données administratives.
32	Excluant les îles du Nord (Saint Martin et Saint Barthélemy).
33	Arrivées de touristes non résidents dans tous les types d'établissements d'hébergement touristique.
34	Arrivées de touristes non résidents dans les hôtels seulement.
35	Données tirées d'une enquête réalisée à l'aéroport de Guadeloupe.
36	Arrivées par voie aérienne à l'aéroport de Conakry.
37	Arrivées à l'aéroport de Timehri seulement.
38	Source: "Central Bank of Islamic Republic of Iran".
39	Source: "Central Bank of Iraq".
40	Y compris touristes à Irlande du Nord.
41	A l'exclusion des travailleurs saisonniers et frontaliers.
42	Arrivées de touristes non résidents par voie aérienne. Cartes d'embarquement
43	Tarawa et Ile Christmas.
44	Tarawa uniquement.
45	Y compris les nationaux résidant à l'étranger et membres des équipages.
46	Nouvelle source d'information: Département du Contrôle douanier.
47	Données du pays.
48	Départs de non-résidents. Enquête menée auprès de personnes franchissant la frontière de l'État.
49	A l'exclusion des ressortissants syriens.
50	Arrivées de touristes non résidents par voie aérienne.
51	Départs.
52	Source: "Reserve Bank of Malawi".
53	Y compris les résidents de Singapour traversant la frontière par voie terrestre à travers le Johore Causeway.
54	Départs par voies aérienne et maritime.
55	Années fiscales (du 1er octobre au 30 septembre).
56	Arrivées par voie aérienne et maritime.
57	Arrivées dans les États de Kosrae, Chuuk, Pohnpei et Yap. Excluant les citoyens de EFM.
58	Sont exclus les diplomates et les étrangers qui résident en Mongolie.
59	Comprenant les arrivées de touristes aux postes-frontières de

66

Tourist/visitor arrivals and tourism expenditure *(continued)*
Thousands arrivals and millions of US dollars
Arrivées de touristes/visiteurs et dépenses touristiques *(suite)*
Milliers d'arrivées et millions de dollars E.-U.

			Yangon.
60	Including arrivals from India.	60	Y compris les arrivées à Inde.
61	Arrivals by air, including Niueans residing usually in New Zealand.	61	Arrivées par voie aérienne et y compris les nationaux de Niue résidant habituellement en Nouvelle-Zélande.
62	Non-resident tourists staying in registered hotels.	62	Non résidents touristes dans les hôtels enregistrés.
63	West Bank and Gaza.	63	Cisjordanie et Gaza.
64	Air arrivals (Palau International Airport).	64	Arrivées par voie aérienne (Aéroport international de Palau).
65	E/D cards in the "Silvio Petirossi" airport and passenger counts at the national border crossings - National Police and SENATUR.	65	Cartes d'embarquement et de débarquement à l'aéroport Silvio Petirossi et comptages des passagers lors du franchissement des frontières nationales – Police Nationale et SENATUR.
66	From 2002, new estimated series including tourists with identity document other than a passport.	66	À partir de 2002, nouvelle série estimée comprenant les touristes avec une pièce d'identité autre qu'un passeport.
67	Arrivals by air. Source: "Junta de Planificación de Puerto Rico".	67	Arrivées par voie aérienne. Source: "Junta de Planificación de Puerto Rico".
68	Source: Qatar Central Bank.	68	Source: "Qatar Central Bank".
69	Visitors who enjoyed the services of the economic agents officially registered under tourism activity and accommodation (excluding the regions of the left bank of the Dniestr and the municipality of Bender).	69	Visiteurs qui ont bénéficié des services des agents économiques officiellement enregistrés avec le type d'activité tourisme et des unités d'hébergement qui leur appartiennent (à l'exception des régions de la partie gauche du Dniestr et de la municipalité de Bender).
70	Excluding Netherlands Antillean residents.	70	A l'exclusion des résidents des Antilles Néerlandaises.
71	Including air arrivals to Saint Martin (the French side of the island).	71	Y compris les arrivées par voie aérienne à Saint-Martin (côté français de l'île).
72	Source: Central Bank of the Netherlands Antilles - Including the estimates for Saba and Saint Eustatius.	72	Source : Banque centrale des Antilles néerlandaises. Comprend des estimations concernant Saint-Eustache et Saba.
73	Including Italian visitors.	73	Y compris les visiteurs italiens.
74	Figures provided by the country to the World Tourism Organisation (UNWTO).	74	Les chiffres de dépense sont ceux que le pays a fournis à l'Organisation mondiale du tourisme (OMT).
75	Without 1st quarter.	75	À l'exclusion du 1er trimestre.
76	Excluding arrivals by work and contract workers.	76	À l'exclusion des arrivées par travail et les travailleurs contractuels.
77	Arrivals at Zanderij Airport.	77	Arrivées à l'aéroport de Zanderij.
78	Excluding camping.	78	Camping exclu.
79	Including expenditure of the nationals residing abroad.	79	Y compris dépenses des nationaux résidant à l'étranger.
80	Including domestic tourism and nationals of the country residing abroad.	80	Y compris le tourisme interne et les nationaux résidant à l'étranger.
81	Including Mexicans staying one or more nights in the United States.	81	Incluant Mexicains passant 1 nuit ou plus aux EU.

67

Tourism expenditure in other countries
Total, travel and passenger transport: million US dollars

Dépenses touristiques dans d'autres pays
Totale, voyage et transport de passagers : millions de dollars E.-U.

Country or area	2003	2004	2005	2006	2007	Pays ou zone
Albania						**Albanie**
Total	507	669	808	989	940	Total
Travel	489	642	786	965	923	Voyage
Passenger transport	18	27	22	24	17	Transport de passagers
Algeria[1]						**Algérie**[1]
Total	255	341	370	381	377	Total
Angola						**Angola**
Total	49	86	135	393	473	Total
Travel	12	39	74	148	212	Voyage
Passenger transport	37	47	61	245	261	Transport de passagers
Anguilla						**Anguilla**
Travel	9	9	10	13	15	Voyage
Antigua and Barbuda						**Antigua-et-Barbuda**
Travel	35	38	40	45	51	Voyage
Argentina						**Argentine**
Total	2 997	3 208	3 564	*4 046	*5 071	Total
Travel	2 511	2 604[2]	2 790[2]	*3 099[2]	*3 921[2]	Voyage
Passenger transport	486	604	774	*947	*1 150	Transport de passagers
Armenia						**Arménie**
Total	97	216	284	321	345	Total
Travel	67	179	236	286	294	Voyage
Passenger transport	30	37	48	35	51	Transport de passagers
Aruba						**Aruba**
Total	214	248	242	257	301	Total
Travel	189	218	218	234	282	Voyage
Passenger transport	25	30	24	23	19	Transport de passagers
Australia						**Australie**
Total	10 135	14 224	15 593	16 393	20 003	Total
Travel	7 270	10 242	11 253	11 690	14 244	Voyage
Passenger transport	2 865	3 982	4 340	4 703	5 759	Transport de passagers
Austria						**Autriche**
Total	12 894	13 411	12 755	11 719	12 839	Total
Travel	11 757	11 834	10 994	9 626	10 566	Voyage
Passenger transport	1 137	1 577	1 761	2 093	2 273	Transport de passagers
Azerbaijan						**Azerbaïdjan**
Total	120	140	188	256	381	Total
Travel	111	126	164	201	264	Voyage
Passenger transport	9	14	24	55	117	Transport de passagers
Bahamas						**Bahamas**
Total	404	469	528	541	538	Total
Travel	305	316	344	385	377	Voyage
Passenger transport	99	153	184	156	161	Transport de passagers
Bahrain						**Bahreïn**
Total	492	528	574	639	671	Total
Travel	372	387	414	455	479	Voyage
Passenger transport	120	141	160	184	192	Transport de passagers
Bangladesh						**Bangladesh**
Total	389	442	375	444	514	Total
Travel	165	161	136	140	156	Voyage
Passenger transport	224	281	239	304	358	Transport de passagers
Barbados						**Barbade**
Total	153	163	153	167	...	Total
Travel	104	108	96	105	...	Voyage
Passenger transport	49	55	57	62	...	Transport de passagers
Belarus						**Bélarus**
Total	436	500	516	675	724	Total
Travel	399	450	448	586	606	Voyage
Passenger transport	37	50	68	89	118	Transport de passagers

Tourism expenditure in other countries *(continued)*
Total, travel and passenger transport: million US dollars
Dépenses touristiques dans d'autres pays *(suite)*
Totale, voyage et transport de passagers : millions de dollars E.-U.

Country or area	2003	2004	2005	2006	2007	Pays ou zone
Belgium						**Belgique**
Total	13 402	15 456	16 771	17 891	19 095	Total
Travel	12 210	13 956	14 948	15 574	17 268	Voyage
Passenger transport	1 192	1 500	1 823	2 317	1 827	Transport de passagers
Belize						**Belize**
Total	50	47	45	43	46	Total
Travel	46	43	42	41	43	Voyage
Passenger transport	4	4	3	2	3	Transport de passagers
Benin						**Bénin**
Total	53	59	58	71	75	Total
Travel	21	29	27	34	35	Voyage
Passenger transport	32	30	31	37	40	Transport de passagers
Bermuda [1]						**Bermudes** [1]
Total	248	217	239	278	287	Total
Bolivia						**Bolivie**
Total	197	232	257	360	325	Total
Travel	138	164	186	273	249	Voyage
Passenger transport	59	68	71	87	76	Transport de passagers
Bonaire [3]						**Bonaire** [3]
Travel	3	6	5	5	6	Voyage
Bosnia and Herzegovina						**Bosnie-Herzégovine**
Total	145	162	158	195	232	Total
Travel	106	117	122	156	186	Voyage
Passenger transport	39	45	36	39	46	Transport de passagers
Botswana						**Botswana**
Total	235	280	301	285	281	Total
Travel	230	276	282	277	278	Voyage
Passenger transport	5	4	19	8	3	Transport de passagers
Brazil						**Brésil**
Total	2 874	3 752	5 905	7 501	10 434	Total
Travel	2 261	2 871	4 720	5 764	8 211	Voyage
Passenger transport	613	881	1 185	1 737	2 223	Transport de passagers
Brunei Darussalam						**Brunéi Darussalam**
Travel	468	382	374	408	...	Voyage
Bulgaria						**Bulgarie**
Total	1 467	1 935	1 858	2 093	2 597	Total
Travel	1 033	1 363	1 309	1 474	1 829	Voyage
Passenger transport	434	572	549	619	768	Transport de passagers
Burkina Faso [4]						**Burkina Faso** [4]
Total	...	...	53	84	...	Total
Travel	...	39	46	55	...	Voyage
Passenger transport	...	...	7	29	...	Transport de passagers
Burundi						**Burundi**
Total	...	29	62	126	106	Total
Travel	15	23	60	125	104	Voyage
Passenger transport	...	6	2	1	2	Transport de passagers
Cambodia						**Cambodge**
Total	60	80	138	176	194	Total
Travel	36	48	97	122	123	Voyage
Passenger transport	24	32	41	54	71	Transport de passagers
Cameroon						**Cameroun**
Total	272	394	480	521	476	Total
Travel	171	323	355	412	318	Voyage
Passenger transport	101	71	125	109	158	Transport de passagers
Canada						**Canada**
Total	16 309	19 267	22 734	26 075	31 365	Total
Travel	13 337	15 524	18 017	20 620	24 882	Voyage
Passenger transport	2 972	3 743	4 717	5 455	6 483	Transport de passagers
Cape Verde						**Cap-Vert**
Total	89	93	82	104	132	Total
Travel	73	78	67	82	107	Voyage
Passenger transport	16	15	15	22	25	Transport de passagers

Tourism expenditure in other countries *(continued)*
Total, travel and passenger transport: million US dollars

Dépenses touristiques dans d'autres pays *(suite)*
Totale, voyage et transport de passagers : millions de dollars E.-U.

Country or area	2003	2004	2005	2006	2007	Pays ou zone
Central African Rep. [5]						**Rép. centrafricaine** [5]
Total	31	32	...	...	...	Total
Chile						**Chili**
Total	1 109	1 251	1 355	1 573	2 140	Total
Travel	850	977	1 051	1 239	1 762	Voyage
Passenger transport	259	274	304	334	378	Transport de passagers
China [6]						**Chine** [6]
Total	16 716	21 360	24 715	28 242	33 264	Total
Travel	15 187	19 149	21 759	24 322	29 786	Voyage
Passenger transport	1 529	2 211	2 956	3 920	3 478	Transport de passagers
China, Hong Kong SAR [7]						**Chine, Hong Kong RAS** [7]
Travel	11 447	13 270	13 305	14 044	15 086	Voyage
China, Macao SAR						**Chine, Macao RAS**
Total	312	357	428	452	530	Total
Travel	291	332	358	378	456	Voyage
Passenger transport	21	25	70	74	74	Transport de passagers
Colombia						**Colombie**
Total	1 349	1 469	1 565	1 799	2 093	Total
Travel	1 062	1 111	1 130	1 332	1 537	Voyage
Passenger transport	287	358	435	467	556	Transport de passagers
Comoros [8]						**Comores** [8]
Total	8	9	10	11	...	Total
Congo						**Congo**
Total	118	176	...	...	...	Total
Travel	78	103	112	132	168	Voyage
Passenger transport	40	73	...	...	...	Transport de passagers
Costa Rica						**Costa Rica**
Total	434	481	556	577	731	Total
Travel	353	406	470	485	628	Voyage
Passenger transport	81	75	86	92	103	Transport de passagers
Côte d'Ivoire						**Côte d'Ivoire**
Total	551	571	549	583	...	Total
Travel	387	381	354	373	396	Voyage
Passenger transport	164	190	195	210	...	Transport de passagers
Croatia						**Croatie**
Total	709	881	786	770	1 025	Total
Travel	672	848	754	737	985	Voyage
Passenger transport	37	33	32	33	40	Transport de passagers
Cyprus						**Chypre**
Total	700	907	1 001	1 031	1 554	Total
Travel	611	811	932	967	1 479	Voyage
Passenger transport	89	96	69	64	75	Transport de passagers
Czech Republic						**République tchèque**
Total	2 177	2 682	2 603	2 874	3 771	Total
Travel	1 934	2 280	2 405	2 765	3 647	Voyage
Passenger transport	243	402	198	109	124	Transport de passagers
Denmark						**Danemark**
Travel	6 659	7 279	6 850	7 428	8 791	Voyage
Djibouti						**Djibouti**
Total	10	14	14	15	...	Total
Travel	3	3	3	4	...	Voyage
Passenger transport	7	11	12	12	...	Transport de passagers
Dominica						**Dominique**
Travel	9	9	10	10	10	Voyage
Dominican Republic						**Rép. dominicaine**
Total	408	448	511	495	531	Total
Travel	272	310	352	333	326	Voyage
Passenger transport	136	138	159	162	205	Transport de passagers
Ecuador						**Equateur**
Total	500	577	644	706	733	Total
Travel	354	391	429	466	504	Voyage
Passenger transport	146	186	215	240	229	Transport de passagers

67

Country or area	2003	2004	2005	2006	2007	Pays ou zone
Egypt						**Egypte**
Total	1 465	1 543	1 932	2 156	2 886	Total
Travel	1 321	1 257	1 629	1 784	2 446	Voyage
Passenger transport	144	286	303	372	440	Transport de passagers
El Salvador						**El Salvador**
Total	312	373	430	606	690	Total
Travel	230	292	347	523	605	Voyage
Passenger transport	82	81	83	83	85	Transport de passagers
Estonia						**Estonie**
Total	404	486	528	706	804	Total
Travel	319	399	437	586	670	Voyage
Passenger transport	85	87	91	120	134	Transport de passagers
Ethiopia						**Ethiopie**
Total	63	59	...	...	...	Total
Travel	50	58	77	97	107	Voyage
Passenger transport	13	1	...	...	...	Transport de passagers
Fiji						**Fidji**
Total	87	118	132	123	...	Total
Travel	69	94	106	101	...	Voyage
Passenger transport	18	24	26	22	...	Transport de passagers
Finland						**Finlande**
Total	2 954	3 383	3 622	4 094	4 632	Total
Travel	2 433	2 821	3 057	3 424	3 986	Voyage
Passenger transport	521	562	565	670	646	Transport de passagers
France						**France**
Total	28 143	34 674	37 546	37 913	44 544	Total
Travel	23 392	28 703	30 458	31 264	36 743	Voyage
Passenger transport	4 751	5 971	7 088	6 649	7 801	Transport de passagers
French Polynesia						**Polynésie française**
Total	335	425	430	560	600	Total
Travel	236	311	312	314	343	Voyage
Passenger transport	99	114	118	246	257	Transport de passagers
Gabon						**Gabon**
Total	239	275	346	...	...	Total
Travel	194	214	274	...	...	Voyage
Passenger transport	45	61	72	...	...	Transport de passagers
Gambia						**Gambie**
Total	8	6	7	8	...	Total
Travel	4	4	5	6	7	Voyage
Passenger transport	4	2	2	2	...	Transport de passagers
Georgia						**Géorgie**
Total	170	196	237	257	277	Total
Travel	130	147	169	167	176	Voyage
Passenger transport	40	49	68	90	101	Transport de passagers
Germany						**Allemagne**
Total	72 777	79 438	82 228	83 066	93 515	Total
Travel	65 234	71 187	74 189	74 123	82 966	Voyage
Passenger transport	7 543	8 251	8 039	8 943	10 549	Transport de passagers
Ghana						**Ghana**
Total	216	270	472	575	816	Total
Travel	138	186	303	345	558	Voyage
Passenger transport	78	84	169	230	258	Transport de passagers
Greece						**Grèce**
Total	2 439	2 880	3 045	3 004	3 430	Total
Travel	2 431	2 872	3 039	2 997	3 423	Voyage
Passenger transport	8	8	6	7	7	Transport de passagers
Grenada						**Grenade**
Travel	8	9	10	16	10	Voyage
Guatemala						**Guatemala**
Total	373	488	531	654	736	Total
Travel	312	385	420	528	597	Voyage
Passenger transport	61	103	111	126	139	Transport de passagers

67

Tourism expenditure in other countries *(continued)*
Total, travel and passenger transport: million US dollars
Dépenses touristiques dans d'autres pays *(suite)*
Totale, voyage et transport de passagers : millions de dollars E.-U.

Country or area	2003	2004	2005	2006	2007	Pays ou zone
Guinea						**Guinée**
Total	36	29	...	...	96	Total
Travel	26	25	...	...	29	Voyage
Passenger transport	10	4	...	...	67	Transport de passagers
Guinea-Bissau						**Guinée-Bissau**
Total	21	22	18	...	...	Total
Travel	13	13	10	16	...	Voyage
Passenger transport	8	9	8	...	...	Transport de passagers
Guyana						**Guyana**
Total	30	...	...	...	...	Total
Travel	26	30	40	49	58	Voyage
Passenger transport	4	...	...	...	...	Transport de passagers
Haiti						**Haïti**
Total	202	206	172	233	332	Total
Travel	42	72	55	56	55	Voyage
Passenger transport	160	134	117	177	277	Transport de passagers
Honduras						**Honduras**
Total	271	307	327	353	385	Total
Travel	211	245	262	283	306	Voyage
Passenger transport	60	62	65	70	79	Transport de passagers
Hungary						**Hongrie**
Total	2 700	2 909	2 826	2 568	3 468	Total
Travel	2 594	2 848	2 382	2 126	2 949	Voyage
Passenger transport	106	61	444	442	519	Transport de passagers
Iceland						**Islande**
Total	524	699	991	1 084	1 351	Total
Travel	523	697	980	1 076	1 341	Voyage
Passenger transport	1	2	11	8	10	Transport de passagers
India						**Inde**
Total	4 385	5 783	7 798	9 296	...	Total
Travel	3 585	4 816	6 013	7 352	...	Voyage
Passenger transport	800	967	1 785	1 944	...	Transport de passagers
Indonesia						**Indonésie**
Total	4 427	4 569	4 740	5 458	6 120	Total
Travel	3 082	3 507	3 584	4 030	4 446	Voyage
Passenger transport	1 345	1 062	1 156	1 428	1 674	Transport de passagers
Iran (Islamic Rep. of) [9]						**Iran (Rép. islamique d')** [9]
Total	4 120	4 402	4 560	5 767	6 526	Total
Travel	3 842	4 093	4 202	5 315	6 002	Voyage
Passenger transport	278	309	358	452	524	Transport de passagers
Iraq						**Iraq**
Total	...	...	627	526	...	Total
Travel	...	...	439	395	...	Voyage
Passenger transport	...	...	188	131	...	Transport de passagers
Ireland						**Irlande**
Total	4 832	5 291	6 186	6 978	8 811	Total
Travel	4 736	5 177	6 074	6 862	8 682	Voyage
Passenger transport	96	114	112	116	129	Transport de passagers
Israel						**Israël**
Total	3 341	3 663	3 780	3 870	4 250	Total
Travel	2 550	2 796	2 895	2 983	3 260	Voyage
Passenger transport	791	867	885	887	990	Transport de passagers
Italy						**Italie**
Total	23 731	24 064	26 774	27 437	32 754	Total
Travel	20 589	20 460	22 370	23 152	27 329	Voyage
Passenger transport	3 142	3 604	4 404	4 285	5 425	Transport de passagers
Jamaica						**Jamaïque**
Total	269	318	290	315	340	Total
Travel	252	286	249	273	298	Voyage
Passenger transport	17	32	41	42	42	Transport de passagers

Tourism expenditure in other countries *(continued)*
Total, travel and passenger transport: million US dollars
Dépenses touristiques dans d'autres pays *(suite)*
Totale, voyage et transport de passagers : millions de dollars E.-U.

Country or area	2003	2004	2005	2006	2007	Pays ou zone
Japan						**Japon**
Total	36 505	48 175	48 102	37 659	37 261	Total
Travel	#28 958	38 252	37 565	#26 876	26 511	Voyage
Passenger transport	7 547	9 923	10 537	10 783	10 750	Transport de passagers
Jordan						**Jordanie**
Total	503	585	653	956	1 024	Total
Travel	452	524	585	837	883	Voyage
Passenger transport	51	61	68	119	141	Transport de passagers
Kazakhstan						**Kazakhstan**
Total	783	997	940	1 060	1 355	Total
Travel	669	844	753	821	1 041	Voyage
Passenger transport	114	153	187	239	314	Transport de passagers
Kenya						**Kenya**
Travel	127	108	124	178	262	Voyage
Korea, Republic of						**Corée, République de**
Total	11 063	13 507	16 924	20 989	23 359	Total
Travel	10 103	12 350	15 406	18 851	20 090	Voyage
Passenger transport	960	1 157	1 518	2 138	2 469	Transport de passagers
Kuwait						**Koweït**
Total	3 750	4 148	4 741	5 754	6 678	Total
Travel	3 348	3 701	4 277	5 253	6 128	Voyage
Passenger transport	402	447	464	501	550	Transport de passagers
Kyrgyzstan						**Kirghizistan**
Total	35	73	94	142	193	Total
Travel	17	50	58	92	90	Voyage
Passenger transport	18	23	36	50	103	Transport de passagers
Latvia						**Lettonie**
Total	365	428	655	788	1 021	Total
Travel	328	377	584	704	927	Voyage
Passenger transport	37	51	71	84	94	Transport de passagers
Lebanon						**Liban**
Total	3 319	3 719	3 565	3 783	3 914	Total
Travel	2 943	3 170	2 908	3 006	3 114	Voyage
Passenger transport	376	549	657	777	800	Transport de passagers
Lesotho						**Lesotho**
Total	30	37	36	22	24	Total
Travel	26	30	27	19	16	Voyage
Passenger transport	4	7	9	3	8	Transport de passagers
Liberia						**Libéria**
Total	...	27	31	41	48	Total
Travel	...	13	15	17	21	Voyage
Passenger transport	...	14	16	24	27	Transport de passagers
Libyan Arab Jamah.						**Jamah. arabe libyenne**
Total	689	789	920	915	1 009	Total
Travel	557	603	680	668	888	Voyage
Passenger transport	132	186	240	247	121	Transport de passagers
Lithuania						**Lituanie**
Total	476	643	757	931	1 167	Total
Travel	471	636	744	909	1 143	Voyage
Passenger transport	5	7	13	22	24	Transport de passagers
Luxembourg						**Luxembourg**
Total	2 445	2 950	...	...	...	Total
Travel	2 423	2 911	2 976	3 136	3 552	Voyage
Passenger transport	22	39	...	...	...	Transport de passagers
Madagascar						**Madagascar**
Total	67	108	80	...	...	Total
Travel	64	93	74	86	94	Voyage
Passenger transport	3	15	6	...	...	Transport de passagers
Malawi[10]						**Malawi**[10]
Total	61	59	75	75	84	Total
Travel	48	50	65	65	73	Voyage
Passenger transport	13	9	10	10	11	Transport de passagers

67

Tourism expenditure in other countries *(continued)*
Total, travel and passenger transport: million US dollars
Dépenses touristiques dans d'autres pays *(suite)*
Totale, voyage et transport de passagers : millions de dollars E.-U.

Country or area	2003	2004	2005	2006	2007	Pays ou zone
Malaysia						**Malaisie**
Total	3 401	3 822	4 339	4 847	6 245	Total
Travel	2 846	3 178	3 711	4 020	5 252	Voyage
Passenger transport	555	644	628	827	993	Transport de passagers
Maldives						**Maldives**
Total	60	75	92	105	126	Total
Travel	46	56	68	77	92	Voyage
Passenger transport	14	19	24	28	34	Transport de passagers
Mali						**Mali**
Total	94	125	133	196	...	Total
Travel	48	66	77	120	...	Voyage
Passenger transport	46	59	56	76	...	Transport de passagers
Malta						**Malte**
Total	238	291	311	362	420	Total
Travel	215	255	268	320	376	Voyage
Passenger transport	23	36	43	42	44	Transport de passagers
Mauritius						**Maurice**
Total	236	277	295	347	388	Total
Travel	216	255	275	327	361	Voyage
Passenger transport	20	22	20	20	27	Transport de passagers
Mexico						**Mexique**
Total	7 252	8 034	8 951	9 387	9 843	Total
Travel	6 253	6 959	7 600	8 108	8 378	Voyage
Passenger transport	999	1 075	1 351	1 279	1 465	Transport de passagers
Micronesia (Fed. States of) [1,11]						**Micronésie (Etats féd. de)** [1,11]
Total	6	5	6	6	...	Total
Mongolia						**Mongolie**
Total	144	207	173	212	...	Total
Travel	138	193	157	188	...	Voyage
Passenger transport	6	14	16	24	...	Transport de passagers
Montserrat						**Montserrat**
Travel	2	2	3	3	3	Voyage
Morocco						**Maroc**
Total	845	912	999	1 113	1 418	Total
Travel	548	574	612	693	880	Voyage
Passenger transport	297	338	387	420	538	Transport de passagers
Mozambique						**Mozambique**
Total	141	140	187	205	209	Total
Travel	140	134	176	179	180	Voyage
Passenger transport	1	6	11	26	29	Transport de passagers
Myanmar						**Myanmar**
Total	36	32	34	40	...	Total
Travel	32	29	31	37	...	Voyage
Passenger transport	4	3	3	3	...	Transport de passagers
Namibia						**Namibie**
Travel	101	123	108	118	132	Voyage
Nepal						**Népal**
Total	119	205	221	261	402	Total
Travel	81	154	163	185	274	Voyage
Passenger transport	38	51	58	76	128	Transport de passagers
Netherlands						**Pays-Bas**
Total	15 887	16 937	16 621	17 453	19 477	Total
Travel	15 265	16 348	16 140	17 087	19 110	Voyage
Passenger transport	622	589	481	366	367	Transport de passagers
New Caledonia						**Nouvelle-Calédonie**
Travel	128	167	122	129	149	Voyage
New Zealand						**Nouvelle-Zélande**
Travel	1 649	2 217	2 657	2 526	3 066	Voyage
Nicaragua						**Nicaragua**
Total	139	154	162	171	195	Total
Travel	75	89	91	97	121	Voyage
Passenger transport	64	65	71	74	74	Transport de passagers

Tourism expenditure in other countries *(continued)*
Total, travel and passenger transport: million US dollars
Dépenses touristiques dans d'autres pays *(suite)*
Totale, voyage et transport de passagers : millions de dollars E.-U.

Country or area	2003	2004	2005	2006	2007	Pays ou zone
Niger						**Niger**
Total	39	42	42	42	45	Total
Travel	22	22	30	28	30	Voyage
Passenger transport	17	20	12	14	15	Transport de passagers
Nigeria						**Nigéria**
Total	2 076	1 469	1 385	2 078	3 494	Total
Travel	1 795	1 161	1 109	1 664	2 444	Voyage
Passenger transport	281	308	276	414	1 050	Transport de passagers
Norway						**Norvège**
Total	7 089	8 894	10 591	12 072	14 109	Total
Travel	6 716	8 489	10 111	11 586	14 032	Voyage
Passenger transport	373	405	480	486	77	Transport de passagers
Occupied Palestinian Terr. [12]						**Terr. palestinien occupé** [12]
Travel	317	286	265	...	...	Voyage
Oman						**Oman**
Total	804	848	887	919	944	Total
Travel	630	669	692	711	744	Voyage
Passenger transport	174	179	195	208	200	Transport de passagers
Pakistan						**Pakistan**
Total	1 163	1 612	1 753	2 029	2 043	Total
Travel	925	1 268	1 280	1 545	1 593	Voyage
Passenger transport	238	344	473	484	450	Transport de passagers
Palau [1]						**Palaos** [1]
Total	1	2	2	1	...	Total
Panama						**Panama**
Total	267	294	388	403	457	Total
Travel	208	239	271	271	307	Voyage
Passenger transport	59	55	117	132	150	Transport de passagers
Papua New Guinea						**Papouasle-Nvl-Guinée**
Total	...	72	56	...	...	Total
Travel	52	71	56	...	...	Voyage
Passenger transport	...	1	1	...	...	Transport de passagers
Paraguay						**Paraguay**
Total	115	121	130	144	184	Total
Travel	67	71	79	92	109	Voyage
Passenger transport	48	50	51	52	75	Transport de passagers
Peru						**Pérou**
Total	847	852	970[13]	1 034[13]	1 274[13]	Total
Travel	641	643	752[13]	789[13]	1 007[13]	Voyage
Passenger transport	206	209	218[13]	245[13]	267[13]	Transport de passagers
Philippines						**Philippines**
Total	1 649	1 526	1 547	1 558	2 007	Total
Travel	1 413	1 275	1 279	1 232	1 615	Voyage
Passenger transport	236	251	268	326	392	Transport de passagers
Poland						**Pologne**
Total	3 286	5 092	5 894	7 654	8 341	Total
Travel	3 085	4 776	5 548	7 224	7 753	Voyage
Passenger transport	201	316	346	430	588	Transport de passagers
Portugal						**Portugal**
Total	2 982	3 369	3 744	4 098	4 836	Total
Travel	2 409	2 763	3 050	3 340	3 922	Voyage
Passenger transport	573	606	694	758	914	Transport de passagers
Puerto Rico [1,14]						**Porto Rico** [1,14]
Total	1 420	1 584	1 663	1 752	1 743	Total
Travel	985	1 085	1 143	1 205	1 192	Voyage
Passenger transport	435	499	520	547	551	Transport de passagers
Qatar [15]						**Qatar** [15]
Travel	471	691	1 759	3 751	...	Voyage
Republic of Moldova						**République de Moldova**
Total	118	135	170	220	270	Total
Travel	99	113	141	187	213	Voyage
Passenger transport	19	22	29	33	57	Transport de passagers

67

Tourism expenditure in other countries *(continued)*
Total, travel and passenger transport: million US dollars

Dépenses touristiques dans d'autres pays *(suite)*
Totale, voyage et transport de passagers : millions de dollars E.-U.

Country or area	2003	2004	2005	2006	2007	Pays ou zone
Romania						**Roumanie**
Total	572	672	1 073	1 459	1 719	Total
Travel	479	539	925	1 310	1 535	Voyage
Passenger transport	93	133	148	149	184	Transport de passagers
Russian Federation						**Fédération de Russie**
Total	13 427	16 082	18 425	19 601	24 289	Total
Travel	12 880	15 285	17 434	18 235	22 258	Voyage
Passenger transport	547	797	991	1 366	2 031	Transport de passagers
Rwanda						**Rwanda**
Travel	26	31	37	35	69	Voyage
Saint Kitts and Nevis						**Saint-Kitts-et-Nevis**
Travel	8	10	11	14	15	Voyage
Saint Lucia						**Sainte-Lucie**
Travel	36	37	39	39	41	Voyage
Saint Maarten [16]						**Saint-Martin** [16]
Travel	144	80	94	86	86	Voyage
Saint Vincent-Grenadines						**Saint Vincent-Grenadines**
Travel	13	14	15	16	17	Voyage
Samoa						**Samoa**
Total	...	12	17	16	14	Total
Travel	...	5	9	6	5	Voyage
Passenger transport	...	7	8	10	9	Transport de passagers
Sao Tome and Principe						**Sao Tomé-et-Principe**
Total	2	2	1	1	1	Total
Travel	1	1	^0	^0	^0	Voyage
Passenger transport	1	2	^0	1	1	Transport de passagers
Saudi Arabia [1]						**Arabie saoudite** [1]
Total	4 165	4 600	4 178	2 316	6 279	Total
Travel	...	4 428	3 975	1 804	4 880	Voyage
Passenger transport	...	172	203	512	1 399	Transport de passagers
Senegal						**Sénégal**
Total	129	138	144	139	...	Total
Travel	55	57	65	54	...	Voyage
Passenger transport	74	81	79	85	...	Transport de passagers
Serbia						**Serbie**
Total	144[17]	208[17]	260[17]	322[17]	1 194	Total
Travel	...	...	...	...	1 042	Voyage
Passenger transport	...	...	...	...	152	Transport de passagers
Seychelles						**Seychelles**
Total	54	53	59	56	70	Total
Travel	36	34	39	36	40	Voyage
Passenger transport	18	19	20	20	30	Transport de passagers
Sierra Leone						**Sierra Leone**
Total	38	30	34	15	17	Total
Travel	37	30	32	12	14	Voyage
Passenger transport	1	^0	2	3	3	Transport de passagers
Singapore						**Singapour**
Travel	8 260	9 197	10 011	10 989	11 844	Voyage
Slovakia						**Slovaquie**
Total	662	900	1 122	1 230	1 825	Total
Travel	573	745	844	1 060	1 533	Voyage
Passenger transport	89	155	278	170	292	Transport de passagers
Slovenia						**Slovénie**
Total	805	937	1 019	1 058	1 219	Total
Travel	753	868	950	974	1 103	Voyage
Passenger transport	52	69	69	84	116	Transport de passagers
Solomon Islands						**Iles Salomon**
Total	6	8	11	11	...	Total
Travel	4	4	5	4	8	Voyage
Passenger transport	2	3	7	7	...	Transport de passagers

67

Tourism expenditure in other countries *(continued)*
Total, travel and passenger transport: million US dollars

Dépenses touristiques dans d'autres pays *(suite)*
Totale, voyage et transport de passagers : millions de dollars E.-U.

Country or area	2003	2004	2005	2006	2007	Pays ou zone
South Africa						**Afrique du Sud**
Total	3 654	4 237	4 811	5 229	6 103	Total
Travel	2 889	3 157	3 373	3 384	3 927	Voyage
Passenger transport	765	1 080	1 438	1 845	2 176	Transport de passagers
Spain						**Espagne**
Total	11 330	14 864	18 441	20 348	24 179	Total
Travel	9 071	12 153	15 046	16 697	19 724	Voyage
Passenger transport	2 259	2 711	3 395	3 651	4 455	Transport de passagers
Sri Lanka						**Sri Lanka**
Total	462	499	552	666	709	Total
Travel	279	296	314	373	393	Voyage
Passenger transport	183	203	238	293	316	Transport de passagers
Sudan						**Soudan**
Travel	119	176	667	1 413	1 477	Voyage
Suriname						**Suriname**
Total	68	85	94	33	28	Total
Travel	6	14	17	10	22	Voyage
Passenger transport	62	71	77	15	6	Transport de passagers
Swaziland						**Swaziland**
Total	23	54	60	54	63	Total
Travel	22	48	49	49	51	Voyage
Passenger transport	1	6	11	5	12	Transport de passagers
Sweden						**Suède**
Total	9 375	11 088	11 844	12 837	15 696	Total
Travel	8 296	10 165	10 771	11 529	13 972	Voyage
Passenger transport	1 079	923	1 073	1 308	1 724	Transport de passagers
Switzerland						**Suisse**
Total	8 614	9 924	10 579	11 199	12 449	Total
Travel	6 883	8 104	8 782	9 252	10 265	Voyage
Passenger transport	1 731	1 820	1 797	1 947	2 184	Transport de passagers
Syrian Arab Republic						**Rép. arabe syrienne**
Total	734	688	584	585	791	Total
Travel	700	650	550	540	719	Voyage
Passenger transport	34	38	34	45	72	Transport de passagers
Tajikistan						**Tadjikistan**
Travel	2	3	4	6	7	Voyage
Thailand						**Thaïlande**
Total	3 538	5 343	4 917	6 173	6 887	Total
Travel	2 921	4 514	3 800	4 598	5 143	Voyage
Passenger transport	617	829	1 117	1 575	1 744	Transport de passagers
TFYR of Macedonia						**L'ex-R.Y. Macédoine**
Total	71	85	97	110	147	Total
Travel	48	55	62	71	102	Voyage
Passenger transport	23	30	35	39	45	Transport de passagers
Togo						**Togo**
Total	37	38	42	42	...	Total
Travel	7	8	8	5	...	Voyage
Passenger transport	30	30	34	37	...	Transport de passagers
Tonga						**Tonga**
Travel	3	6	4	8	10	Voyage
Trinidad and Tobago						**Trinité-et-Tobago**
Total	143	141	234	146	155	Total
Travel	107	96	180	93	94	Voyage
Passenger transport	36	45	54	53	61	Transport de passagers
Tunisia						**Tunisie**
Total	355	427	452	498	530	Total
Travel	300	340	374	410	437	Voyage
Passenger transport	55	87	78	88	93	Transport de passagers
Turkey						**Turquie**
Total	...	...	3 210	3 155	3 720	Total
Travel	2 113	2 524	2 872	2 743	3 260	Voyage
Passenger transport	...	...	338	412	460	Transport de passagers

67

Tourism expenditure in other countries *(continued)*
Total, travel and passenger transport: million US dollars

Dépenses touristiques dans d'autres pays *(suite)*
Totale, voyage et transport de passagers : millions de dollars E.-U.

Country or area	2003	2004	2005	2006	2007	Pays ou zone
Uganda						**Ouganda**
Total	...	111	128	168	200	Total
Travel	...	108	124	95	112	Voyage
Passenger transport	2	3	4	73	88	Transport de passagers
Ukraine						**Ukraine**
Total	953	2 660	3 078	3 202	3 743	Total
Travel	789	2 463	2 805	2 834	3 293	Voyage
Passenger transport	164	197	273	368	450	Transport de passagers
United Arab Emirates [1]						**Emirats arabes unis** [1]
Total	3 956	4 472	6 186	8 827	11 263	Total
United Kingdom						**Royaume-Uni**
Total	58 627	69 463	73 672	78 351	88 478	Total
Travel	47 853	56 444	59 532	63 319	72 436	Voyage
Passenger transport	10 774	13 019	14 140	15 032	16 042	Transport de passagers
United Rep. of Tanzania						**Rép.-Unie de Tanzanie**
Total	375	470	577	571	666	Total
Travel	353	445	554	534	645	Voyage
Passenger transport	22	25	23	37	21	Transport de passagers
United States						**Etats-Unis**
Total	81 924	94 344	99 469	104 447	109 578	Total
Travel	60 935	69 626	73 320	76 946	81 092	Voyage
Passenger transport	20 989	24 718	26 149	27 501	28 486	Transport de passagers
Uruguay						**Uruguay**
Total	236	267	331	305	349	Total
Travel	169	194	252	213	239	Voyage
Passenger transport	67	73	79	92	110	Transport de passagers
Vanuatu						**Vanuatu**
Total	14	15	13	11	13	Total
Travel	12	13	11	9	11	Voyage
Passenger transport	2	2	2	2	2	Transport de passagers
Venezuela (Bolivarian Rep. of)						**Venezuela (Rép. bolivarienne du)**
Total	1 311	1 604	1 843	1 807	2 101	Total
Travel	859	1 077	1 276	1 229	1 394	Voyage
Passenger transport	452	527	567	578	707	Transport de passagers
Yemen						**Yémen**
Total	134	183	224	225	247	Total
Travel	77	126	167	162	184	Voyage
Passenger transport	57	57	57	63	63	Transport de passagers
Zambia						**Zambie**
Total	115	86	88	97	98	Total
Travel	49	55	58	68	56	Voyage
Passenger transport	66	31	30	29	42	Transport de passagers

Source:
World Tourism Organization (UNWTO), Madrid, UNWTO statistics
database and the *Yearbook of Tourism Statistics*, 2009 edition. The
majority of the data have been provided to the UNWTO by the
International Monetary Fund (IMF). Exceptions are footnoted.

Source:
Organisation mondiale du tourisme (OMT), Madrid, la base de données de
l'OMT, et *l'Annuaire des statistiques du tourisme*, édition 2009. La
majorité des données sont celles que le Fonds monétaire international (FMI)
a fournies à l'Organisation mondiale du tourisme (OMT). Les exceptions
sont signalées par une note.

1 The expenditure figures are those provided by the country to
UNWTO, which do not appear in the International Monetary Fund
data.

2 Starting 2004, as a result of the importance of the "Survey on
International Tourism", the estimates of the series of the "Travel"
item of the Balance of Payments were modified. For this reason,
the data are not rigorously comparable with those of this previous
years.

3 Source: Central Bank of the Netherlands Antilles.

4 Source: "Banque Centrale des Etats de l'Afrique de l'Ouest".

5 Source: "Banque des Etats de l'Afrique Centrale (B.E.A.C.)".

6 For statistical purposes, the data for China do not include those for

1 Les chiffres de dépense sont ceux que le pays a fournis à l'OMT mais ils
ne figurent pas dans les données du Fonds monétaire international.

2 À partir de 2004, vu l'importance de l'"Enquête sur le tourisme
international", des modifications ont été apportées aux estimations de la
série du poste "Voyages" de la balance des paiements. C'est la raison
pour laquelle les données ne sont pas rigoureusement comparables avec
celles des années précédentes.

3 Source: "Central Bank of the Netherlands Antilles".

4 Source: Banque Centrale des Etats de l'Afrique de l'Ouest.

5 Source: Banque des Etats de l'Afrique Centrale (B.E.A.C.).

6 Pour la présentation des statistiques, les données pour la Chine ne

67

Tourism expenditure in other countries *(continued)*
Total, travel and passenger transport: million US dollars

Dépenses touristiques dans d'autres pays *(suite)*
Totale, voyage et transport de passagers : millions de dollars E.-U.

the Hong Kong Special Administrative Region (Hong Kong SAR), Macao Special Administrative Region (Macao SAR) and Taiwan Province of China.	comprennent pas la Région Administrative Spéciale de Hong Kong (Hong Kong RAS), la Région Administrative Spéciale de Macao (Macao RAS) et la province de Taiwan.

7	Source: Census and Statistics Department.		7	Source: "Census and Statistics Department".
8	The Central Bank of Comoros		8	Banque centrale des Comores.
9	Source: Central Bank of Islamic Republic of Iran.		9	Source: "Central Bank of Islamic Republic of Iran".
10	Source: Reserve Bank of Malawi.		10	Source: "Reserve Bank of Malawi".
11	Fiscal years (October 1 to September 30).		11	Années fiscales (du 1er octobre au 30 septembre).
12	West Bank and Gaza.		12	Cisjordanie et Gaza.
13	Preliminary data.		13	Données préliminaires.
14	Fiscal years (July-June).		14	Années fiscales (juillet-juin).
15	Source: Qatar Central Bank.		15	Source: "Qatar Central Bank".
16	Source: Central Bank of the Netherlands Antilles - Including the estimates for Saba and Saint Eustatius.		16	Source : Banque centrale des Antilles néerlandaises. Comprend des estimations concernant Saint-Eustache et Saba.
17	Figures provided by the country to the World Tourism Organisation (UNWTO).		17	Les chiffres de dépense sont ceux que le pays a fournis à l'Organisation mondiale du tourisme (OMT).

Country or area and traffic	Total traffic (domestic and international) Trafic total (intérieur et international)				International traffic Trafic international				Pays ou zone et trafic
	2003	2004	2005	2006	2003	2004	2005	2006	
Albania				.					**Albanie**
Kilometres flown	2	3	3	3	2	3	3	3	Kilomètres parcourus
Passengers carried	159	180	196	213	159	180	196	213	Passagers transportés
Passenger-kilometres	121	136	149	161	121	136	149	161	Passagers-kilomètres
Total tonne-kilometres	11	12	13	14	11	12	13	14	Tonnes-kilomètres totales
Algeria									**Algérie**
Kilometres flown	41	44	40	38	27	30	27	24	Kilomètres parcourus
Passengers carried	3 293	3 236	3 037	2 900	2 019	1 913	1 842	1 702	Passagers transportés
Passenger-kilometres	3 415	3 353	3 101	2 964	2 672	2 652	2 505	2 378	Passagers-kilomètres
Total tonne-kilometres	328	323	311	293	258	258	255	237	Tonnes-kilomètres totales
Angola									**Angola**
Kilometres flown	5	6	6	7	4	4	5	5	Kilomètres parcourus
Passengers carried	198	222	240	263	99	113	122	136	Passagers transportés
Passenger-kilometres	479	548	605	655	417	479	532	575	Passagers-kilomètres
Total tonne-kilometres	98	111	121	136	92	105	115	128	Tonnes-kilomètres totales
Antigua and Barbuda									**Antigua-et-Barbuda**
Kilometres flown	12	5	5	5	12	5	5	5	Kilomètres parcourus
Passengers carried	1 428	714	778	755	1 428	714	778	755	Passagers transportés
Passenger-kilometres	325	114	123	118	325	114	123	118	Passagers-kilomètres
Total tonne-kilometres	32	10	11	11	32	10	11	11	Tonnes-kilomètres totales
Argentina									**Argentine**
Kilometres flown	104	111	110	101	48	50	51	46	Kilomètres parcourus
Passengers carried	5 946	6 795	6 938	6 636	1 709	1 872	1 860	1 818	Passagers transportés
Passenger-kilometres	12 381	14 450	15 025	14 489	7 764	9 036	9 224	8 882	Passagers-kilomètres
Total tonne-kilometres	1 218	1 413	1 481	1 441	787	918	948	926	Tonnes-kilomètres totales
Armenia									**Arménie**
Kilometres flown	8	12	12	13	8	12	12	13	Kilomètres parcourus
Passengers carried	370	510	556	606	370	510	556	606	Passagers transportés
Passenger-kilometres	716	974	1 071	1 157	716	974	1 071	1 157	Passagers-kilomètres
Total tonne-kilometres	70	97	106	113	70	97	106	113	Tonnes-kilomètres totales
Australia									**Australie**
Kilometres flown	482	547	579	599	204	235	249	249	Kilomètres parcourus
Passengers carried	36 400	41 597	44 657	46 620	7 452	8 464	8 762	8 392	Passagers transportés
Passenger-kilometres	83 886	94 811	99 614	104 687	49 244	54 712	56 275	58 010	Passagers-kilomètres
Total tonne-kilometres	9 524	11 075	12 081	12 641	6 212	7 273	7 984	8 231	Tonnes-kilomètres totales
Austria									**Autriche**
Kilometres flown	130	149	159	170	126	145	155	166	Kilomètres parcourus
Passengers carried	6 903	7 619	8 038	8 785	6 461	7 166	7 583	8 289	Passagers transportés
Passenger-kilometres	14 558	17 530	18 835	19 921	14 440	17 407	18 713	19 790	Passagers-kilomètres
Total tonne-kilometres	1 983	2 366	2 542	2 696	1 971	2 353	2 529	2 682	Tonnes-kilomètres totales
Azerbaijan									**Azerbaïdjan**
Kilometres flown	12	14	15	15	9	11	12	12	Kilomètres parcourus
Passengers carried	684	1 007	1 134	1 253	245	501	570	607	Passagers transportés
Passenger-kilometres	751	1 276	1 431	1 519	497	983	1 107	1 146	Passagers-kilomètres
Total tonne-kilometres	135	149	141	153	111	121	109	114	Tonnes-kilomètres totales
Bahamas									**Bahamas**
Kilometres flown	6	7	8	8	4	3	4	4	Kilomètres parcourus
Passengers carried	1 601	900	1 020	1 033	984	398	470	456	Passagers transportés
Passenger-kilometres	388	219	277	276	287	129	184	176	Passagers-kilomètres
Total tonne-kilometres	48	20	26	25	35	12	17	16	Tonnes-kilomètres totales
Bahrain									**Bahreïn**
Kilometres flown	40	50	48	47	40	50	48	46	Kilomètres parcourus
Passengers carried	1 850	2 285	2 234	2 355	1 850	2 285	2 234	2 126	Passagers transportés
Passenger-kilometres	4 494	5 954	5 822	5 801	4 494	5 954	5 822	5 633	Passagers-kilomètres
Total tonne-kilometres	769	981	933	902	769	981	933	881	Tonnes-kilomètres totales
Bangladesh									**Bangladesh**
Kilometres flown	29	30	31	33	27	29	30	31	Kilomètres parcourus
Passengers carried	1 579	1 650	1 634	1 729	1 205	1 324	1 338	1 392	Passagers transportés

68

Civil aviation: scheduled airline traffic *(continued)*
Passengers carried (thousands); kilometres (millions)
Aviation civile : trafic régulier des lignes aériennes *(suite)*
Passagers transportés (milliers) ; kilomètres (millions)

Country or area and traffic	Total traffic (domestic and international) Trafic total (intérieur et international)				International traffic Trafic international				Pays ou zone et trafic
	2003	2004	2005	2006	2003	2004	2005	2006	
Passenger-kilometres	4 662	5 042	5 381	5 607	4 583	4 972	5 317	5 530	Passagers-kilomètres
Total tonne-kilometres	704	747	796	828	697	740	789	821	Tonnes-kilomètres totales
Belarus									**Bélarus**
Kilometres flown	7	7	6	7	7	7	6	7	Kilomètres parcourus
Passengers carried	234	274	282	307	232	274	282	307	Passagers transportés
Passenger-kilometres	338	399	383	414	337	399	383	414	Passagers-kilomètres
Total tonne-kilometres	32	38	36	39	32	38	36	39	Tonnes-kilomètres totales
Belgium									**Belgique**
Kilometres flown	103	125	124	132	103	125	124	132	Kilomètres parcourus
Passengers carried	2 904	3 265	3 341	3 641	2 904	3 265	3 341	3 641	Passagers transportés
Passenger-kilometres	3 958	4 738	4 918	5 312	3 958	4 738	4 918	5 312	Passagers-kilomètres
Total tonne-kilometres	961	1 130	1 126	1 205	961	1 130	1 126	1 205	Tonnes-kilomètres totales
Bhutan									**Bhoutan**
Kilometres flown	2	2	2	2	2	2	2	2	Kilomètres parcourus
Passengers carried	36	45	49	51	36	45	40	51	Passagers transportés
Passenger-kilometres	56	69	74	77	56	69	74	77	Passagers-kilomètres
Total tonne-kilometres	5	6	7	7	5	6	7	7	Tonnes-kilomètres totales
Bolivia									**Bolivie**
Kilometres flown	22	22	22	17	14	15	15	11	Kilomètres parcourus
Passengers carried	1 771	1 844	1 892	1 443	568	586	614	424	Passagers transportés
Passenger-kilometres	1 744	1 787	1 903	1 413	1 311	1 341	1 434	1 034	Passagers-kilomètres
Total tonne-kilometres	187	186	196	136	145	145	151	100	Tonnes-kilomètres totales
Bosnia and Herzegovina									**Bosnie-Herzégovine**
Kilometres flown	1	...	...	...	1	...	...	...	Kilomètres parcourus
Passengers carried	73	...	...	...	73	...	...	...	Passagers transportés
Passenger-kilometres	47	...	...	...	47	...	...	...	Passagers-kilomètres
Total tonne-kilometres	6	...	...	...	6	...	...	...	Tonnes-kilomètres totales
Botswana									**Botswana**
Kilometres flown	3	3	4	3	2	2	2	2	Kilomètres parcourus
Passengers carried	189	213	230	214	131	149	161	153	Passagers transportés
Passenger-kilometres	83	95	104	110	55	60	70	79	Passagers-kilomètres
Total tonne-kilometres	8	9	10	10	5	6	7	7	Tonnes-kilomètres totales
Brazil									**Brésil**
Kilometres flown	443	441	467	478	123	129	136	111	Kilomètres parcourus
Passengers carried	32 293	35 264	37 662	40 945	3 448	3 727	3 980	3 121	Passagers transportés
Passenger-kilometres	44 192	47 462	50 689	49 218	20 252	21 286	22 733	17 824	Passagers-kilomètres
Total tonne-kilometres	5 447	5 844	6 173	5 879	2 875	3 013	3 174	2 523	Tonnes-kilomètres totales
Brunei Darussalam									**Brunéi Darussalam**
Kilometres flown	28	30	29	30	28	30	29	30	Kilomètres parcourus
Passengers carried	956	1 080	978	1 041	956	1 080	978	1 041	Passagers transportés
Passenger-kilometres	3 591	3 852	3 762	4 058	3 591	3 852	3 762	4 058	Passagers-kilomètres
Total tonne-kilometres	473	478	473	497	473	478	473	497	Tonnes-kilomètres totales
Bulgaria									**Bulgarie**
Kilometres flown	7	11	14	19	7	10	14	19	Kilomètres parcourus
Passengers carried	311	476	654	808	270	431	603	753	Passagers transportés
Passenger-kilometres	457	747	1 123	1 359	442	731	1 104	1 339	Passagers-kilomètres
Total tonne-kilometres	42	71	105	141	41	69	104	139	Tonnes-kilomètres totales
Burkina Faso									**Burkina Faso**
Kilometres flown	1	1	1	1	1	1	1	1	Kilomètres parcourus
Passengers carried	54	61	66	73	36	41	44	50	Passagers transportés
Passenger-kilometres	29	33	37	40	24	28	31	34	Passagers-kilomètres
Total tonne-kilometres	3	3	3	4	2	3	3	3	Tonnes-kilomètres totales
Cambodia									**Cambodge**
Kilometres flown	2	2	2	4	1	1	2	3	Kilomètres parcourus
Passengers carried	165	162	169	252	70	74	101	171	Passagers transportés
Passenger-kilometres	106	98	165	317	82	77	148	297	Passagers-kilomètres
Total tonne-kilometres	12	12	16	29	11	10	14	28	Tonnes-kilomètres totales

68

Civil aviation: scheduled airline traffic *(continued)*
Passengers carried (thousands); kilometres (millions)

Aviation civile : trafic régulier des lignes aériennes *(suite)*
Passagers transportés (milliers) ; kilomètres (millions)

Country or area and traffic	Total traffic (domestic and international) Trafic total (intérieur et international) 2003	2004	2005	2006	International traffic Trafic international 2003	2004	2005	2006	Pays ou zone et trafic
Cameroon									**Cameroun**
Kilometres flown	9	11	12	12	8	9	10	11	Kilomètres parcourus
Passengers carried	315	356	384	425	225	257	277	310	Passagers transportés
Passenger-kilometres	629	720	797	861	562	646	717	775	Passagers-kilomètres
Total tonne-kilometres	77	88	97	108	70	81	89	100	Tonnes-kilomètres totales
Canada									**Canada**
Kilometres flown	870	936	974	1 004	338	373	388	405	Kilomètres parcourus
Passengers carried	36 264	40 701	45 230	46 727	12 191	12 936	14 376	14 543	Passagers transportés
Passenger-kilometres	76 328	87 025	94 680	98 241	45 875	51 151	55 650	59 581	Passagers-kilomètres
Total tonne-kilometres	8 816	9 886	10 590	10 916	5 406	5 978	6 335	6 683	Tonnes-kilomètres totales
Cape Verde									**Cap-Vert**
Kilometres flown	5	9	11	11	3	7	8	8	Kilomètres parcourus
Passengers carried	253	560	690	754	86	224	304	341	Passagers transportés
Passenger-kilometres	285	804	1 078	1 165	242	725	986	1 065	Passagers-kilomètres
Total tonne-kilometres	27	74	99	110	23	66	90	101	Tonnes-kilomètres totales
Chile									**Chili**
Kilometres flown	107	110	119	120	71	72	76	75	Kilomètres parcourus
Passengers carried	5 247	5 464	5 939	6 017	2 387	2 479	2 742	2 659	Passagers transportés
Passenger-kilometres	12 187	12 874	14 067	13 858	9 140	9 648	10 529	10 108	Passagers-kilomètres
Total tonne-kilometres	2 237	2 260	2 336	2 272	1 913	1 922	1 961	1 882	Tonnes-kilomètres totales
China [1]									**Chine** [1]
Kilometres flown	1 195	1 542	1 731	2 009	209	287	315	370	Kilomètres parcourus
Passengers carried	86 041	119 789	136 722	158 013	6 641	10 553	11 991	13 659	Passagers transportés
Passenger-kilometres	124 591	176 268	201 961	234 505	24 346	39 179	44 603	51 329	Passagers-kilomètres
Total tonne-kilometres	17 641	22 912	25 765	30 090	6 246	7 679	8 387	9 976	Tonnes-kilomètres totales
China, Hong Kong SAR									**Chine, Hong Kong RAS**
Kilometres flown	272	338	383	414	272	338	383	414	Kilomètres parcourus
Passengers carried	13 025	17 893	20 230	21 799	13 025	17 893	20 230	21 799	Passagers transportés
Passenger-kilometres	46 402	62 094	70 603	77 539	46 402	62 094	70 603	77 539	Passagers-kilomètres
Total tonne-kilometres	10 278	12 939	14 606	16 197	10 278	12 939	14 606	16 197	Tonnes-kilomètres totales
China, Macao SAR									**Chine, Macao RAS**
Kilometres flown	15	23	27	24	15	23	27	24	Kilomètres parcourus
Passengers carried	1 212	1 800	2 041	2 430	1 212	1 800	2 041	2 430	Passagers transportés
Passenger-kilometres	1 566	2 127	2 406	2 949	1 566	2 127	2 406	2 949	Passagers-kilomètres
Total tonne-kilometres	198	320	410	487	198	320	410	487	Tonnes-kilomètres totales
Colombia									**Colombie**
Kilometres flown	110	118	127	142	54	69	75	85	Kilomètres parcourus
Passengers carried	8 665	8 829	9 984	10 616	1 714	1 781	2 120	2 275	Passagers transportés
Passenger-kilometres	8 299	9 045	9 688	10 478	4 210	4 382	4 782	5 131	Passagers-kilomètres
Total tonne-kilometres	1 390	1 926	1 982	2 022	953	1 442	1 455	1 457	Tonnes-kilomètres totales
Congo									**Congo**
Kilometres flown	1	...	...	...	^0	...	...	...	Kilomètres parcourus
Passengers carried	52	...	...	...	2	...	...	...	Passagers transportés
Passenger-kilometres	31	...	...	...	4	...	...	...	Passagers-kilomètres
Total tonne-kilometres	3	...	...	...	^0	...	...	...	Tonnes-kilomètres totales
Costa Rica									**Costa Rica**
Kilometres flown	20	24	27	26	16	19	21	21	Kilomètres parcourus
Passengers carried	750	901	953	943	584	706	748	726	Passagers transportés
Passenger-kilometres	1 671	2 173	2 306	2 216	1 654	2 152	2 284	2 193	Passagers-kilomètres
Total tonne-kilometres	122	157	156	150	120	155	154	148	Tonnes-kilomètres totales
Croatia									**Croatie**
Kilometres flown	12	12	14	13	10	10	11	11	Kilomètres parcourus
Passengers carried	1 267	1 336	1 361	1 389	795	866	897	942	Passagers transportés
Passenger-kilometres	869	941	974	1 005	726	796	827	861	Passagers-kilomètres
Total tonne-kilometres	81	88	91	93	68	74	77	80	Tonnes-kilomètres totales
Cuba									**Cuba**
Kilometres flown	19	21	22	22	16	18	19	19	Kilomètres parcourus
Passengers carried	664	743	813	812	429	480	523	508	Passagers transportés
Passenger-kilometres	2 036	2 241	2 422	2 337	1 945	2 140	2 311	2 219	Passagers-kilomètres
Total tonne-kilometres	224	246	263	254	211	232	247	237	Tonnes-kilomètres totales

68

Civil aviation: scheduled airline traffic *(continued)*
Passengers carried (thousands); kilometres (millions)
Aviation civile : trafic régulier des lignes aériennes *(suite)*
Passagers transportés (milliers) ; kilomètres (millions)

Country or area and traffic	Total traffic (domestic and international) Trafic total (intérieur et international)				International traffic Trafic international				Pays ou zone et trafic
	2003	2004	2005	2006	2003	2004	2005	2006	
Cyprus									**Chypre**
Kilometres flown	30	32	32	32	30	32	32	32	Kilomètres parcourus
Passengers carried	1 883	2 013	1 921	1 944	1 883	2 013	1 921	1 944	Passagers transportés
Passenger-kilometres	3 935	4 230	4 184	4 293	3 935	4 230	4 184	4 293	Passagers-kilomètres
Total tonne-kilometres	408	442	428	437	408	442	428	437	Tonnes-kilomètres totales
Czech Republic									**République tchèque**
Kilometres flown	53	67	75	74	52	66	74	73	Kilomètres parcourus
Passengers carried	3 391	4 219	4 706	4 922	3 339	4 157	4 626	4 814	Passagers transportés
Passenger-kilometres	4 938	5 988	6 605	6 652	4 923	5 970	6 583	6 624	Passagers-kilomètres
Total tonne-kilometres	485	584	638	643	483	582	636	641	Tonnes-kilomètres totales
Denmark									**Danemark**
Kilometres flown	78	82	102	108	73	78	76	82	Kilomètres parcourus
Passengers carried	5 886	5 923	9 721	10 373	4 855	5 088	5 389	5 902	Passagers transportés
Passenger-kilometres	7 202	7 857	9 904	10 581	6 968	7 685	7 955	8 636	Passagers-kilomètres
Total tonne-kilometres	885	952	1 175	1 259	863	935	980	1 005	Tonnes-kilomètres totales
Ecuador									**Equateur**
Kilometres flown	9	11	11	16	^0	^0	^0	^0	Kilomètres parcourus
Passengers carried	1 521	1 828	2 011	2 505	16	13	14	14	Passagers transportés
Passenger-kilometres	674	788	867	1 083	9	3	3	6	Passagers-kilomètres
Total tonne-kilometres	64	75	83	102	1	^0	^0	1	Tonnes-kilomètres totales
Egypt									**Egypte**
Kilometres flown	63	69	76	84	58	63	70	78	Kilomètres parcourus
Passengers carried	4 181	4 621	4 888	4 954	2 916	3 260	3 402	3 525	Passagers transportés
Passenger-kilometres	8 103	8 918	9 401	10 336	7 517	8 298	8 720	9 683	Passagers-kilomètres
Total tonne-kilometres	975	1 053	1 194	1 360	921	997	1 129	1 294	Tonnes-kilomètres totales
El Salvador									**El Salvador**
Kilometres flown	34	40	40	35	34	40	40	35	Kilomètres parcourus
Passengers carried	2 271	2 391	2 541	2 289	2 182	2 391	2 541	2 241	Passagers transportés
Passenger-kilometres	3 644	4 236	4 419	3 808	3 616	4 236	4 419	3 799	Passagers-kilomètres
Total tonne-kilometres	339	407	417	365	336	407	417	364	Tonnes-kilomètres totales
Estonia									**Estonie**
Kilometres flown	7	8	9	9	7	8	9	9	Kilomètres parcourus
Passengers carried	395	510	578	598	389	510	578	598	Passagers transportés
Passenger-kilometres	415	547	660	682	413	547	660	682	Passagers-kilomètres
Total tonne-kilometres	39	51	61	63	39	51	61	63	Tonnes-kilomètres totales
Ethiopia									**Ethiopie**
Kilometres flown	35	42	49	61	32	38	46	57	Kilomètres parcourus
Passengers carried	1 147	1 403	1 667	1 954	881	1 110	1 358	1 642	Passagers transportés
Passenger-kilometres	3 573	4 394	5 418	6 640	3 460	4 270	5 286	6 504	Passagers-kilomètres
Total tonne-kilometres	484	595	725	888	474	584	713	876	Tonnes-kilomètres totales
Fiji									**Fidji**
Kilometres flown	21	22	23	25	17	18	18	19	Kilomètres parcourus
Passengers carried	766	837	871	932	516	587	601	625	Passagers transportés
Passenger-kilometres	2 233	2 430	2 403	2 506	2 190	2 389	2 360	2 455	Passagers-kilomètres
Total tonne-kilometres	298	318	332	346	294	314	329	342	Tonnes-kilomètres totales
Finland									**Finlande**
Kilometres flown	97	108	109	119	80	92	95	104	Kilomètres parcourus
Passengers carried	6 184	7 049	7 075	7 597	3 971	4 796	5 019	5 581	Passagers transportés
Passenger-kilometres	9 056	11 142	11 900	13 418	7 981	10 009	10 870	12 419	Passagers-kilomètres
Total tonne-kilometres	1 086	1 342	1 439	1 628	991	1 242	1 348	1 541	Tonnes-kilomètres totales
France [2]									**France** [2]
Kilometres flown	860	867	886	960	620	663	677	731	Kilomètres parcourus
Passengers carried	47 641	46 507	50 246	59 538	23 904	24 863	28 732	34 832	Passagers transportés
Passenger-kilometres	112 260	116 850	126 702	144 096	79 027	86 476	99 670	123 395	Passagers-kilomètres
Total tonne-kilometres	15 293	16 147	17 347	19 917	12 029	13 158	14 675	17 437	Tonnes-kilomètres totales
Gabon									**Gabon**
Kilometres flown	8	9	9	...	5	6	7	...	Kilomètres parcourus
Passengers carried	386	431	465	...	170	194	209	...	Passagers transportés
Passenger-kilometres	655	750	829	...	571	656	728	...	Passagers-kilomètres
Total tonne-kilometres	112	128	140	...	104	119	130	...	Tonnes-kilomètres totales

68

Civil aviation: scheduled airline traffic *(continued)*
Passengers carried (thousands); kilometres (millions)
Aviation civile : trafic régulier des lignes aériennes *(suite)*
Passagers transportés (milliers) ; kilomètres (millions)

Country or area and traffic	Total traffic (domestic and international) Trafic total (intérieur et international)				International traffic Trafic international				Pays ou zone et trafic
	2003	2004	2005	2006	2003	2004	2005	2006	
Georgia									**Géorgie**
Kilometres flown	6	7	8	7	6	7	8	7	Kilomètres parcourus
Passengers carried	180	229	249	231	180	229	249	231	Passagers transportés
Passenger-kilometres	384	473	520	505	384	473	520	505	Passagers-kilomètres
Total tonne-kilometres	37	46	50	48	37	46	50	48	Tonnes-kilomètres totales
Germany									**Allemagne**
Kilometres flown	1 070	1 198	1 285	1 397	952	1 082	1 149	1 267	Kilomètres parcourus
Passengers carried	72 693	82 100	90 789	98 717	53 645	63 493	69 144	77 969	Passagers transportés
Passenger-kilometres	149 672	170 628	182 508	204 118	141 313	162 427	172 799	194 717	Passagers-kilomètres
Total tonne-kilometres	21 937	24 736	25 457	28 091	21 097	23 911	24 509	27 176	Tonnes-kilomètres totales
Ghana									**Ghana**
Kilometres flown	12	5	...	...	12	5	...	...	Kilomètres parcourus
Passengers carried	241	96	...	...	241	96	...	...	Passagers transportés
Passenger-kilometres	906	363	...	...	906	363	...	...	Passagers-kilomètres
Total tonne-kilometres	101	41	...	...	101	41	...	...	Tonnes-kilomètres totales
Greece									**Grèce**
Kilometres flown	80	96	88	89	55	67	61	61	Kilomètres parcourus
Passengers carried	7 657	9 277	9 452	9 481	2 855	3 587	3 722	3 614	Passagers transportés
Passenger-kilometres	7 650	9 166	9 410	9 225	6 177	7 421	7 656	7 439	Passagers-kilomètres
Total tonne-kilometres	785	927	956	945	640	759	787	774	Tonnes-kilomètres totales
Hungary									**Hongrie**
Kilometres flown	46	52	54	57	46	52	54	57	Kilomètres parcourus
Passengers carried	2 362	2 546	2 735	3 073	2 362	2 546	2 735	3 073	Passagers transportés
Passenger-kilometres	3 130	3 510	3 806	4 140	3 130	3 510	3 806	4 140	Passagers-kilomètres
Total tonne-kilometres	314	344	368	401	314	344	368	401	Tonnes-kilomètres totales
Iceland									**Islande**
Kilometres flown	25	29	32	34	25	29	32	34	Kilomètres parcourus
Passengers carried	1 134	1 333	1 529	1 536	1 134	1 333	1 529	1 536	Passagers transportés
Passenger-kilometres	2 998	3 635	4 308	4 253	2 998	3 635	4 308	4 253	Passagers-kilomètres
Total tonne-kilometres	378	481	551	565	378	481	551	565	Tonnes-kilomètres totales
India									**Inde**
Kilometres flown	277	327	372	503	94	115	147	179	Kilomètres parcourus
Passengers carried	19 455	23 934	27 879	40 311	4 348	5 250	6 103	7 193	Passagers transportés
Passenger-kilometres	31 196	38 888	47 023	60 754	17 221	21 617	26 495	29 728	Passagers-kilomètres
Total tonne-kilometres	3 410	4 238	5 046	6 310	2 011	2 497	2 997	3 343	Tonnes-kilomètres totales
Indonesia									**Indonésie**
Kilometres flown	211	263	266	287	40	55	49	50	Kilomètres parcourus
Passengers carried	20 358	26 781	26 836	27 831	1 984	2 823	2 713	2 775	Passagers transportés
Passenger-kilometres	21 274	28 447	28 243	29 919	6 487	8 800	7 589	7 736	Passagers-kilomètres
Total tonne-kilometres	2 164	2 963	2 924	3 104	776	1 080	928	964	Tonnes-kilomètres totales
Iran (Islamic Rep. of)									**Iran (Rép. islamique d')**
Kilometres flown	89	91	99	107	34	37	39	40	Kilomètres parcourus
Passengers carried	11 664	11 878	12 708	13 507	2 282	2 554	2 887	2 944	Passagers transportés
Passenger-kilometres	10 231	11 657	12 194	12 620	3 761	4 925	5 250	5 204	Passagers-kilomètres
Total tonne-kilometres	1 002	1 136	1 169	1 190	401	509	539	522	Tonnes-kilomètres totales
Ireland									**Irlande**
Kilometres flown	197	236	292	350	197	236	292	350	Kilomètres parcourus
Passengers carried	28 923	34 749	42 873	50 738	28 890	34 749	42 873	50 738	Passagers transportés
Passenger-kilometres	27 441	34 597	44 792	54 272	27 433	34 597	44 792	54 272	Passagers-kilomètres
Total tonne-kilometres	2 573	3 216	4 156	5 026	2 572	3 216	4 156	5 026	Tonnes-kilomètres totales
Israel									**Israël**
Kilometres flown	89	99	101	108	83	93	96	103	Kilomètres parcourus
Passengers carried	3 678	4 969	4 392	4 384	2 581	3 970	3 352	3 408	Passagers transportés
Passenger-kilometres	12 465	14 674	16 362	17 098	12 157	14 381	16 057	16 800	Passagers-kilomètres
Total tonne-kilometres	2 535	2 695	2 710	2 696	2 507	2 669	2 683	2 668	Tonnes-kilomètres totales
Italy									**Italie**
Kilometres flown	398	407	448	428	265	284	313	294	Kilomètres parcourus
Passengers carried	36 077	35 922	36 116	35 894	13 613	14 729	15 129	14 922	Passagers transportés
Passenger-kilometres	40 823	43 237	51 127	50 039	28 559	32 136	39 141	37 909	Passagers-kilomètres
Total tonne-kilometres	5 343	5 626	6 426	6 343	4 171	4 572	5 278	5 192	Tonnes-kilomètres totales

68

Civil aviation: scheduled airline traffic *(continued)*
Passengers carried (thousands); kilometres (millions)

Aviation civile : trafic régulier des lignes aériennes *(suite)*
Passagers transportés (milliers) ; kilomètres (millions)

Country or area and traffic	Total traffic (domestic and international) Trafic total (intérieur et international)				International traffic Trafic international				Pays ou zone et trafic
	2003	2004	2005	2006	2003	2004	2005	2006	
Jamaica									**Jamaïque**
Kilometres flown	48	53	53	52	48	53	53	52	Kilomètres parcourus
Passengers carried	1 838	2 008	1 574	1 527	1 838	2 008	1 574	1 527	Passagers transportés
Passenger-kilometres	5 005	5 060	3 855	3 700	5 005	5 060	3 855	3 700	Passagers-kilomètres
Total tonne-kilometres	484	499	369	355	484	499	369	355	Tonnes-kilomètres totales
Japan									**Japon**
Kilometres flown	834	838	863	852	420	432	449	431	Kilomètres parcourus
Passengers carried	103 650	101 741	102 279	101 741	14 411	16 259	16 484	15 890	Passagers transportés
Passenger-kilometres	146 856	151 810	153 289	150 495	73 610	81 674	82 227	78 842	Passagers-kilomètres
Total tonne-kilometres	21 071	22 027	21 992	21 635	14 643	15 803	15 691	15 271	Tonnes-kilomètres totales
Jordan									**Jordanie**
Kilometres flown	36	42	44	50	36	42	44	50	Kilomètres parcourus
Passengers carried	1 353	1 660	1 737	2 046	1 353	1 660	1 732	1 998	Passagers transportés
Passenger-kilometres	4 498	5 327	5 390	5 589	4 498	5 327	5 389	5 576	Passagers-kilomètres
Total tonne-kilometres	602	740	716	769	602	740	716	768	Tonnes-kilomètres totales
Kazakhstan									**Kazakhstan**
Kilometres flown	31	22	35	39	17	13	18	19	Kilomètres parcourus
Passengers carried	1 010	835	1 160	1 283	405	308	395	411	Passagers transportés
Passenger-kilometres	2 149	1 898	2 470	2 722	1 404	1 197	1 515	1 575	Passagers-kilomètres
Total tonne-kilometres	222	185	241	264	151	118	151	157	Tonnes-kilomètres totales
Kenya									**Kenya**
Kilometres flown	41	43	48	51	35	40	43	48	Kilomètres parcourus
Passengers carried	1 732	2 005	2 424	2 548	1 250	1 513	1 821	2 006	Passagers transportés
Passenger-kilometres	4 245	5 310	6 540	7 268	4 050	5 105	6 292	7 045	Passagers-kilomètres
Total tonne-kilometres	527	674	850	953	509	655	826	933	Tonnes-kilomètres totales
Korea, Dem. P. R.									**Corée, R. p. dém. de**
Kilometres flown	1	1	1	1	1	1	1	1	Kilomètres parcourus
Passengers carried	75	94	101	105	75	94	101	105	Passagers transportés
Passenger-kilometres	32	39	42	43	32	39	42	43	Passagers-kilomètres
Total tonne-kilometres	5	6	6	6	5	6	6	6	Tonnes-kilomètres totales
Korea, Republic of									**Corée, République de**
Kilometres flown	370	407	398	425	311	355	351	381	Kilomètres parcourus
Passengers carried	33 373	34 511	33 888	35 298	13 051	15 917	17 198	18 861	Passagers transportés
Passenger-kilometres	57 624	67 131	69 292	74 187	50 104	60 103	62 896	67 849	Passagers-kilomètres
Total tonne-kilometres	12 134	14 140	13 687	14 592	11 402	13 443	13 053	13 970	Tonnes-kilomètres totales
Kuwait									**Koweït**
Kilometres flown	39	44	43	42	39	44	43	42	Kilomètres parcourus
Passengers carried	2 186	2 496	2 433	2 435	2 186	2 496	2 433	2 435	Passagers transportés
Passenger-kilometres	6 311	7 285	7 282	6 946	6 311	7 285	7 282	6 946	Passagers-kilomètres
Total tonne-kilometres	795	892	905	891	795	892	905	891	Tonnes-kilomètres totales
Kyrgyzstan									**Kirghizistan**
Kilometres flown	6	6	6	5	5	5	4	4	Kilomètres parcourus
Passengers carried	206	246	226	245	103	125	116	138	Passagers transportés
Passenger-kilometres	372	418	368	402	332	370	324	359	Passagers-kilomètres
Total tonne-kilometres	39	40	35	38	35	36	31	34	Tonnes-kilomètres totales
Lao People's Dem. Rep.									**Rép. dém. pop. lao**
Kilometres flown	3	3	3	4	1	1	1	1	Kilomètres parcourus
Passengers carried	219	272	293	327	58	72	78	81	Passagers transportés
Passenger-kilometres	90	113	124	141	37	45	48	50	Passagers-kilomètres
Total tonne-kilometres	9	12	13	14	4	5	6	6	Tonnes-kilomètres totales
Latvia									**Lettonie**
Kilometres flown	7	13	21	26	7	13	21	26	Kilomètres parcourus
Passengers carried	340	594	1 032	1 410	340	594	1 032	1 409	Passagers transportés
Passenger-kilometres	245	581	1 161	1 510	245	581	1 161	1 510	Passagers-kilomètres
Total tonne-kilometres	23	53	106	149	23	53	106	149	Tonnes-kilomètres totales
Lebanon									**Liban**
Kilometres flown	20	22	22	24	20	22	22	24	Kilomètres parcourus
Passengers carried	935	1 087	1 076	969	935	1 087	1 076	969	Passagers transportés
Passenger-kilometres	1 905	2 197	2 168	1 940	1 905	2 197	2 168	1 940	Passagers-kilomètres
Total tonne-kilometres	253	292	291	257	253	292	291	257	Tonnes-kilomètres totales

Civil aviation: scheduled airline traffic *(continued)*
Passengers carried (thousands); kilometres (millions)
Aviation civile : trafic régulier des lignes aériennes *(suite)*
Passagers transportés (milliers) ; kilomètres (millions)

Country or area and traffic	Total traffic (domestic and international) Trafic total (intérieur et international)				International traffic Trafic international				Pays ou zone et trafic
	2003	2004	2005	2006	2003	2004	2005	2006	
Libyan Arab Jamah.									**Jamah. arabe libyenne**
Kilometres flown	8	9	18	17	4	5	13	13	Kilomètres parcourus
Passengers carried	742	850	...	1 152	115	161	...	355	Passagers transportés
Passenger-kilometres	825	985	1 572	1 507	346	454	918	888	Passagers-kilomètres
Total tonne-kilometres	69	82	142	137	31	41	92	89	Tonnes-kilomètres totales
Lithuania									**Lituanie**
Kilometres flown	10	12	14	14	10	12	14	14	Kilomètres parcourus
Passengers carried	329	448	505	460	329	447	505	459	Passagers transportés
Passenger-kilometres	395	557	700	623	395	557	700	622	Passagers-kilomètres
Total tonne-kilometres	37	52	65	58	37	52	65	58	Tonnes-kilomètres totales
Luxembourg									**Luxembourg**
Kilometres flown	74	78	91	93	74	78	91	93	Kilomètres parcourus
Passengers carried	854	856	851	928	854	856	851	928	Passagers transportés
Passenger-kilometres	548	573	566	611	548	573	566	611	Passagers-kilomètres
Total tonne-kilometres	4 397	4 722	5 201	5 325	4 397	4 722	5 201	5 325	Tonnes-kilomètres totales
Madagascar									**Madagascar**
Kilometres flown	9	11	13	13	4	6	8	9	Kilomètres parcourus
Passengers carried	452	514	575	573	140	167	207	215	Passagers transportés
Passenger-kilometres	715	911	1 174	1 172	562	736	982	987	Passagers-kilomètres
Total tonne-kilometres	74	95	121	124	60	78	103	107	Tonnes-kilomètres totales
Malawi									**Malawi**
Kilometres flown	4	5	5	5	2	3	3	3	Kilomètres parcourus
Passengers carried	109	122	132	146	68	78	84	94	Passagers transportés
Passenger-kilometres	147	167	182	197	86	99	110	119	Passagers-kilomètres
Total tonne-kilometres	16	18	20	23	11	12	14	15	Tonnes-kilomètres totales
Malaysia									**Malaisie**
Kilometres flown	247	278	291	291	179	207	218	225	Kilomètres parcourus
Passengers carried	16 710	19 227	20 369	21 009	6 949	8 369	9 353	10 113	Passagers transportés
Passenger-kilometres	38 415	44 642	49 578	47 442	32 309	37 823	42 416	39 390	Passagers-kilomètres
Total tonne-kilometres	5 689	6 672	7 103	6 971	5 126	6 047	6 445	6 187	Tonnes-kilomètres totales
Maldives									**Maldives**
Kilometres flown	2	2	2	3	...	...	...	...	Kilomètres parcourus
Passengers carried	60	76	82	93	...	...	...	...	Passagers transportés
Passenger-kilometres	28	35	39	47	...	...	...	...	Passagers-kilomètres
Total tonne-kilometres	3	3	4	4	...	...	...	...	Tonnes-kilomètres totales
Malta									**Malte**
Kilometres flown	22	22	24	25	22	22	24	25	Kilomètres parcourus
Passengers carried	1 309	1 365	1 372	1 495	1 309	1 365	1 372	1 495	Passagers transportés
Passenger-kilometres	2 174	2 282	2 292	2 476	2 174	2 282	2 292	2 476	Passagers-kilomètres
Total tonne-kilometres	209	212	218	233	209	212	218	233	Tonnes-kilomètres totales
Marshall Islands									**Iles Marshall**
Kilometres flown	1	1	1	1	^0	^0	...	^0	Kilomètres parcourus
Passengers carried	27	29	26	30	1	1	...	1	Passagers transportés
Passenger-kilometres	36	38	34	42	1	1	...	1	Passagers-kilomètres
Total tonne-kilometres	4	4	4	4	^0	^0	...	^0	Tonnes-kilomètres totales
Mauritania									**Mauritanie**
Kilometres flown	1	1	1	1	^0	^0	^0	1	Kilomètres parcourus
Passengers carried	116	128	139	149	14	17	18	20	Passagers transportés
Passenger-kilometres	49	56	60	65	17	19	22	23	Passagers-kilomètres
Total tonne-kilometres	5	5	6	6	2	2	2	2	Tonnes-kilomètres totales
Mauritius									**Maurice**
Kilometres flown	33	44	47	47	32	43	46	46	Kilomètres parcourus
Passengers carried	1 043	1 089	1 146	1 150	929	991	1 064	1 067	Passagers transportés
Passenger-kilometres	5 243	5 739	6 266	6 293	5 175	5 680	6 217	6 245	Passagers-kilomètres
Total tonne-kilometres	687	739	778	770	680	733	774	766	Tonnes-kilomètres totales
Mexico									**Mexique**
Kilometres flown	344	366	386	392	149	163	185	191	Kilomètres parcourus
Passengers carried	19 642	21 168	21 858	21 243	5 383	6 071	6 905	6 755	Passagers transportés
Passenger-kilometres	28 927	31 924	34 123	34 991	13 517	15 499	17 713	18 354	Passagers-kilomètres
Total tonne-kilometres	3 300	3 645	3 869	3 811	1 739	1 979	2 206	2 262	Tonnes-kilomètres totales

68

Civil aviation: scheduled airline traffic *(continued)*
Passengers carried (thousands); kilometres (millions)
Aviation civile : trafic régulier des lignes aériennes *(suite)*
Passagers transportés (milliers) ; kilomètres (millions)

Country or area and traffic	Total traffic (domestic and international) Trafic total (intérieur et international)				International traffic Trafic international				Pays ou zone et trafic
	2003	2004	2005	2006	2003	2004	2005	2006	
Monaco									**Monaco**
Kilometres flown	1	1	1	1	1	1	1	1	Kilomètres parcourus
Passengers carried	95	84	88	96	95	84	88	96	Passagers transportés
Passenger-kilometres	6	4	5	5	6	4	5	5	Passagers-kilomètres
Total tonne-kilometres	1	^0	^0	^0	1	^0	^0	^0	Tonnes-kilomètres totales
Mongolia									**Mongolie**
Kilometres flown	9	9	9	9	5	5	6	6	Kilomètres parcourus
Passengers carried	289	310	295	332	139	162	178	223	Passagers transportés
Passenger-kilometres	691	735	753	843	552	611	657	756	Passagers-kilomètres
Total tonne-kilometres	71	74	76	84	58	63	66	76	Tonnes-kilomètres totales
Montenegro									**Monténégro**
Kilometres flown	...	...	...	6	...	...	...	6	Kilomètres parcourus
Passengers carried	...	...	...	375	...	...	...	295	Passagers transportés
Passenger-kilometres	...	...	...	373	...	...	...	350	Passagers-kilomètres
Total tonne-kilometres	...	...	...	35	...	...	...	33	Tonnes-kilomètres totales
Morocco									**Maroc**
Kilometres flown	59	70	76	96	56	67	71	91	Kilomètres parcourus
Passengers carried	2 638	3 004	3 493	4 150	2 049	2 363	2 738	3 425	Passagers transportés
Passenger-kilometres	4 905	5 551	6 434	8 086	4 710	5 341	6 181	7 832	Passagers-kilomètres
Total tonne-kilometres	528	642	714	768	507	617	687	744	Tonnes-kilomètres totales
Mozambique									**Mozambique**
Kilometres flown	6	7	8	9	3	3	3	4	Kilomètres parcourus
Passengers carried	281	294	347	350	103	100	126	114	Passagers transportés
Passenger-kilometres	405	372	445	356	214	133	211	100	Passagers-kilomètres
Total tonne-kilometres	43	37	45	38	23	14	21	10	Tonnes-kilomètres totales
Myanmar									**Myanmar**
Kilometres flown	16	19	20	22	11	13	14	15	Kilomètres parcourus
Passengers carried	1 117	1 392	1 504	1 621	691	863	932	970	Passagers transportés
Passenger-kilometres	1 083	1 339	1 448	1 559	848	1 043	1 116	1 161	Passagers-kilomètres
Total tonne-kilometres	100	122	132	142	78	94	100	104	Tonnes-kilomètres totales
Namibia									**Namibie**
Kilometres flown	11	11	11	11	8	8	10	10	Kilomètres parcourus
Passengers carried	266	283	399	401	222	235	354	355	Passagers transportés
Passenger-kilometres	930	913	1 569	1 588	904	885	1 540	1 559	Passagers-kilomètres
Total tonne-kilometres	139	147	157	159	136	144	154	156	Tonnes-kilomètres totales
Nauru									**Nauru**
Kilometres flown	3	3	3	4	3	3	3	4	Kilomètres parcourus
Passengers carried	156	195	211	219	156	195	211	219	Passagers transportés
Passenger-kilometres	275	338	361	376	275	338	361	376	Passagers-kilomètres
Total tonne-kilometres	28	34	36	37	28	34	36	37	Tonnes-kilomètres totales
Nepal									**Népal**
Kilometres flown	8	9	10	10	6	8	8	8	Kilomètres parcourus
Passengers carried	356	445	480	510	279	349	377	392	Passagers transportés
Passenger-kilometres	663	816	873	911	652	802	858	892	Passagers-kilomètres
Total tonne-kilometres	64	77	82	86	63	76	81	84	Tonnes-kilomètres totales
Netherlands[3]									**Pays-Bas[3]**
Kilometres flown	429	460	481	503	428	459	481	502	Kilomètres parcourus
Passengers carried	22 590	24 627	26 133	27 454	22 482	24 526	26 057	27 411	Passagers transportés
Passenger-kilometres	68 688	75 706	82 269	86 833	68 673	75 692	82 258	86 826	Passagers-kilomètres
Total tonne-kilometres	11 331	12 487	13 235	13 710	11 329	12 486	13 234	13 709	Tonnes-kilomètres totales
New Zealand									**Nouvelle-Zélande**
Kilometres flown	164	176	185	195	109	116	122	128	Kilomètres parcourus
Passengers carried	10 334	11 305	11 952	12 382	4 042	4 338	4 623	4 790	Passagers transportés
Passenger-kilometres	23 280	24 710	26 093	27 032	20 440	21 536	22 766	23 586	Passagers-kilomètres
Total tonne-kilometres	3 203	3 307	3 486	3 621	2 902	2 970	3 133	3 255	Tonnes-kilomètres totales
Nigeria									**Nigéria**
Kilometres flown	12	12	14	21	4	5	6	11	Kilomètres parcourus
Passengers carried	520	540	748	1 308	51	51	100	296	Passagers transportés
Passenger-kilometres	638	683	935	1 767	15	10	153	754	Passagers-kilomètres
Total tonne-kilometres	61	64	89	161	2	2	16	69	Tonnes-kilomètres totales

68

Civil aviation: scheduled airline traffic *(continued)*
Passengers carried (thousands); kilometres (millions)

Aviation civile : trafic régulier des lignes aériennes *(suite)*
Passagers transportés (milliers) ; kilomètres (millions)

Country or area and traffic	Total traffic (domestic and international) Trafic total (intérieur et international)				International traffic Trafic international				Pays ou zone et trafic
	2003	2004	2005	2006	2003	2004	2005	2006	
Norway									**Norvège**
Kilometres flown	127	128	110	107	66	68	68	67	Kilomètres parcourus
Passengers carried	12 806	12 277	10 398	10 344	4 407	4 410	4 849	5 040	Passagers transportés
Passenger-kilometres	10 506	10 321	9 408	9 779	6 726	6 958	7 152	7 596	Passagers-kilomètres
Total tonne-kilometres	1 211	1 199	1 125	1 183	834	864	904	969	Tonnes-kilomètres totales
Oman									**Oman**
Kilometres flown	45	52	52	53	43	50	51	50	Kilomètres parcourus
Passengers carried	2 777	3 267	3 369	3 580	2 617	3 094	3 167	3 114	Passagers transportés
Passenger-kilometres	5 899	7 455	7 538	7 551	5 765	7 313	7 369	7 183	Passagers-kilomètres
Total tonne-kilometres	746	945	951	944	731	931	934	903	Tonnes-kilomètres totales
Pakistan									**Pakistan**
Kilometres flown	68	79	79	88	52	63	64	72	Kilomètres parcourus
Passengers carried	4 522	5 097	5 364	5 715	2 433	2 985	3 171	3 400	Passagers transportés
Passenger-kilometres	11 880	13 459	14 304	15 110	10 154	11 713	12 496	13 163	Passagers-kilomètres
Total tonne-kilometres	1 432	1 629	1 708	1 800	1 239	1 433	1 504	1 587	Tonnes-kilomètres totales
Panama									**Panama**
Kilometres flown	43	46	55	67	43	46	55	67	Kilomètres parcourus
Passengers carried	1 313	1 501	1 796	2 174	1 313	1 501	1 796	2 174	Passagers transportés
Passenger-kilometres	3 529	4 100	5 206	6 557	3 529	4 100	5 206	6 557	Passagers-kilomètres
Total tonne-kilometres	375	442	553	693	375	442	553	693	Tonnes-kilomètres totales
Papua New Guinea									**Papouasie-Nvl-Guinée**
Kilometres flown	11	12	12	14	5	5	5	5	Kilomètres parcourus
Passengers carried	691	763	819	919	127	146	148	154	Passagers transportés
Passenger-kilometres	576	667	695	771	334	389	394	410	Passagers-kilomètres
Total tonne-kilometres	76	84	92	100	50	57	59	61	Tonnes-kilomètres totales
Paraguay									**Paraguay**
Kilometres flown	6	7	7	7	5	7	7	7	Kilomètres parcourus
Passengers carried	299	373	446	433	288	366	442	429	Passagers transportés
Passenger-kilometres	320	433	501	481	318	431	500	480	Passagers-kilomètres
Total tonne-kilometres	29	39	45	43	29	39	45	43	Tonnes-kilomètres totales
Peru									**Pérou**
Kilometres flown	44	50	66	66	29	31	39	40	Kilomètres parcourus
Passengers carried	2 226	3 225	4 332	4 218	547	741	922	1 068	Passagers transportés
Passenger-kilometres	2 796	3 901	5 298	5 752	1 727	2 296	2 959	3 469	Passagers-kilomètres
Total tonne-kilometres	382	594	602	631	265	417	386	416	Tonnes-kilomètres totales
Philippines									**Philippines**
Kilometres flown	75	82	87	87	53	57	61	59	Kilomètres parcourus
Passengers carried	6 435	7 388	8 057	8 305	2 416	2 765	3 110	3 109	Passagers transportés
Passenger-kilometres	13 904	15 739	17 123	16 800	11 387	12 845	14 022	13 512	Passagers-kilomètres
Total tonne-kilometres	1 729	1 929	2 085	2 040	1 468	1 630	1 773	1 714	Tonnes-kilomètres totales
Poland									**Pologne**
Kilometres flown	68	73	77	81	61	66	70	74	Kilomètres parcourus
Passengers carried	3 252	3 493	3 554	3 701	2 495	2 678	2 749	2 844	Passagers transportés
Passenger-kilometres	5 434	5 861	6 223	6 720	5 213	5 622	5 988	6 469	Passagers-kilomètres
Total tonne-kilometres	608	654	687	735	589	634	667	714	Tonnes-kilomètres totales
Portugal									**Portugal**
Kilometres flown	128	149	158	171	110	124	133	147	Kilomètres parcourus
Passengers carried	7 590	9 052	10 140	9 449	4 994	5 756	5 900	6 449	Passagers transportés
Passenger-kilometres	13 562	16 093	16 834	19 010	11 904	13 634	14 519	16 603	Passagers-kilomètres
Total tonne-kilometres	1 455	1 723	1 789	2 050	1 289	1 467	1 547	1 800	Tonnes-kilomètres totales
Qatar									**Qatar**
Kilometres flown	59	87	118	145	59	87	118	145	Kilomètres parcourus
Passengers carried	3 184	4 453	6 041	7 071	3 184	4 453	6 041	7 071	Passagers transportés
Passenger-kilometres	8 003	12 172	17 890	24 032	8 003	12 172	17 890	24 032	Passagers-kilomètres
Total tonne-kilometres	1 003	1 579	2 494	3 068	1 003	1 579	2 494	3 068	Tonnes-kilomètres totales
Republic of Moldova									**République de Moldova**
Kilometres flown	5	6	6	5	5	6	6	5	Kilomètres parcourus
Passengers carried	179	201	232	270	179	201	232	270	Passagers transportés
Passenger-kilometres	223	257	325	363	223	257	325	363	Passagers-kilomètres
Total tonne-kilometres	22	26	35	40	22	26	35	40	Tonnes-kilomètres totales

Civil aviation: scheduled airline traffic *(continued)*
Passengers carried (thousands); kilometres (millions)
Aviation civile : trafic régulier des lignes aériennes *(suite)*
Passagers transportés (milliers) ; kilomètres (millions)

Country or area and traffic	Total traffic (domestic and international) Trafic total (intérieur et international)				International traffic Trafic international				Pays ou zone et trafic
	2003	2004	2005	2006	2003	2004	2005	2006	
Romania									**Roumanie**
Kilometres flown	26	28	36	40	24	26	33	38	Kilomètres parcourus
Passengers carried	1 255	1 338	1 708	2 047	1 034	1 150	1 484	1 804	Passagers transportés
Passenger-kilometres	1 696	1 532	1 967	2 430	1 634	1 463	1 886	2 343	Passagers-kilomètres
Total tonne-kilometres	160	144	188	234	155	137	181	226	Tonnes-kilomètres totales
Russian Federation									**Fédération de Russie**
Kilometres flown	602	694	680	749	199	250	245	279	Kilomètres parcourus
Passengers carried	22 723	25 949	26 522	28 837	6 972	8 404	8 560	9 634	Passagers transportés
Passenger-kilometres	53 894	62 010	63 192	69 499	20 478	25 151	25 413	29 332	Passagers-kilomètres
Total tonne-kilometres	6 018	7 064	7 285	8 242	2 513	3 224	3 339	4 061	Tonnes-kilomètres totales
Samoa									**Samoa**
Kilometres flown	4	5	5	6	3	4	4	4	Kilomètres parcourus
Passengers carried	198	247	267	288	121	151	164	170	Passagers transportés
Passenger-kilometres	279	343	368	384	270	332	355	370	Passagers-kilomètres
Total tonne-kilometres	27	32	35	36	26	31	33	35	Tonnes-kilomètres totales
Sao Tome and Principe									**Sao Tomé-et-Principe**
Kilometres flown	^0	1	1	...	^0	^0	^0	...	Kilomètres parcourus
Passengers carried	36	40	43	...	21	24	25	...	Passagers transportés
Passenger-kilometres	15	17	18	...	7	8	9	...	Passagers-kilomètres
Total tonne-kilometres	1	2	2	...	1	1	1	...	Tonnes-kilomètres totales
Saudi Arabia									**Arabie saoudite**
Kilometres flown	125	135	141	154	72	81	85	88	Kilomètres parcourus
Passengers carried	13 822	14 943	15 933	16 831	4 801	5 251	5 538	5 914	Passagers transportés
Passenger-kilometres	20 801	22 557	23 793	25 314	13 693	14 897	15 534	16 545	Passagers-kilomètres
Total tonne-kilometres	2 739	3 000	3 174	3 353	2 014	2 229	2 351	2 487	Tonnes-kilomètres totales
Senegal									**Sénégal**
Kilometres flown	6	8	9	10	6	8	9	0	Kilomètres parcourus
Passengers carried	130	416	450	501	96	379	409	463	Passagers transportés
Passenger-kilometres	388	767	851	937	378	756	839	927	Passagers-kilomètres
Total tonne-kilometres	35	69	77	94	34	68	76	93	Tonnes-kilomètres totales
Serbia									**Serbie**
Kilometres flown	...	...	...	10	...	...	...	10	Kilomètres parcourus
Passengers carried	...	...	...	716	...	...	...	560	Passagers transportés
Passenger-kilometres	...	...	...	715	...	...	...	668	Passagers-kilomètres
Total tonne-kilometres	...	...	...	67	...	...	...	62	Tonnes-kilomètres totales
Serbia and Montenegro									**Serbie-et-Monténégro**
Kilometres flown	18	20	18	...	16	17	16	...	Kilomètres parcourus
Passengers carried	1 298	1 414	1 302	...	871	943	877	...	Passagers transportés
Passenger-kilometres	1 199	1 286	1 169	...	1 061	1 137	1 032	...	Passagers-kilomètres
Total tonne-kilometres	156	122	109	...	137	108	97	...	Tonnes-kilomètres totales
Seychelles									**Seychelles**
Kilometres flown	12	14	15	16	11	13	14	15	Kilomètres parcourus
Passengers carried	413	462	499	545	187	213	230	258	Passagers transportés
Passenger-kilometres	986	1 134	1 258	1 359	976	1 123	1 246	1 346	Passagers-kilomètres
Total tonne-kilometres	114	131	145	163	113	130	144	162	Tonnes-kilomètres totales
Sierra Leone									**Sierra Leone**
Kilometres flown	1	1	2	2	1	1	2	2	Kilomètres parcourus
Passengers carried	14	16	17	19	14	16	17	19	Passagers transportés
Passenger-kilometres	74	85	94	101	74	85	94	101	Passagers-kilomètres
Total tonne-kilometres	13	15	17	19	13	15	17	19	Tonnes-kilomètres totales
Singapore									**Singapour**
Kilometres flown	341	397	425	444	341	397	425	444	Kilomètres parcourus
Passengers carried	14 737	16 996	17 744	19 566	14 737	16 996	17 744	19 566	Passagers transportés
Passenger-kilometres	65 387	79 085	82 904	90 126	65 387	79 085	82 904	90 126	Passagers-kilomètres
Total tonne-kilometres	13 062	14 206	14 913	15 902	13 062	14 206	14 913	15 902	Tonnes-kilomètres totales
Slovakia									**Slovaquie**
Kilometres flown	5	12	13	14	4	11	12	13	Kilomètres parcourus
Passengers carried	190	636	712	780	159	601	674	741	Passagers transportés
Passenger-kilometres	220	848	949	1 029	211	837	938	1 018	Passagers-kilomètres
Total tonne-kilometres	20	65	73	78	19	64	72	77	Tonnes-kilomètres totales

Civil aviation: scheduled airline traffic *(continued)*
Passengers carried (thousands); kilometres (millions)

Aviation civile : trafic régulier des lignes aériennes *(suite)*
Passagers transportés (milliers) ; kilomètres (millions)

Country or area and traffic	Total traffic (domestic and international) Trafic total (intérieur et international)				International traffic Trafic international				Pays ou zone et trafic
	2003	2004	2005	2006	2003	2004	2005	2006	
Slovenia									**Slovénie**
Kilometres flown	13	14	15	15	13	14	15	15	Kilomètres parcourus
Passengers carried	758	765	758	850	758	765	758	850	Passagers transportés
Passenger-kilometres	700	711	707	773	700	711	707	773	Passagers-kilomètres
Total tonne-kilometres	67	67	66	72	67	67	66	72	Tonnes-kilomètres totales
Solomon Islands									**Iles Salomon**
Kilometres flown	2	3	3	3	1	1	1	1	Kilomètres parcourus
Passengers carried	68	85	91	101	23	28	31	32	Passagers transportés
Passenger-kilometres	59	73	79	85	47	58	62	65	Passagers-kilomètres
Total tonne-kilometres	6	7	8	8	5	6	6	7	Tonnes-kilomètres totales
South Africa									**Afrique du Sud**
Kilometres flown	188	194	218	217	104	109	122	124	Kilomètres parcourus
Passengers carried	9 160	9 879	11 845	12 921	2 996	3 156	3 397	3 688	Passagers transportés
Passenger-kilometres	24 666	26 048	29 191	30 797	18 852	19 684	21 289	22 097	Passagers-kilomètres
Total tonne-kilometres	3 125	3 270	3 580	3 845	2 505	2 618	2 760	2 968	Tonnes-kilomètres totales
Spain									**Espagne**
Kilometres flown	473	520	561	575	279	308	323	330	Kilomètres parcourus
Passengers carried	42 507	45 540	49 855	53 114	13 515	14 704	15 911	17 417	Passagers transportés
Passenger-kilometres	57 594	64 141	70 975	77 100	38 723	43 509	48 008	53 057	Passagers-kilomètres
Total tonne-kilometres	6 096	6 859	7 459	8 093	4 268	4 858	5 265	5 811	Tonnes-kilomètres totales
Sri Lanka									**Sri Lanka**
Kilometres flown	34	43	42	45	34	43	42	45	Kilomètres parcourus
Passengers carried	1 958	2 413	2 818	3 101	1 958	2 413	2 818	3 101	Passagers transportés
Passenger-kilometres	6 910	8 310	8 599	9 271	6 910	8 310	8 599	9 271	Passagers-kilomètres
Total tonne-kilometres	864	1 068	1 089	1 164	864	1 068	1 089	1 164	Tonnes-kilomètres totales
Sudan									**Soudan**
Kilometres flown	7	8	8	9	5	6	7	7	Kilomètres parcourus
Passengers carried	420	473	511	563	264	301	326	365	Passagers transportés
Passenger-kilometres	786	898	992	1 072	659	758	841	908	Passagers-kilomètres
Total tonne-kilometres	103	116	128	142	88	100	110	124	Tonnes-kilomètres totales
Suriname									**Suriname**
Kilometres flown	5	5	6	6	4	5	5	5	Kilomètres parcourus
Passengers carried	258	289	315	307	253	283	308	299	Passagers transportés
Passenger-kilometres	1 470	1 616	1 746	1 676	1 469	1 616	1 745	1 675	Passagers-kilomètres
Total tonne-kilometres	183	201	214	205	183	201	214	205	Tonnes-kilomètres totales
Sweden									**Suède**
Kilometres flown	129	133	119	110	86	89	76	68	Kilomètres parcourus
Passengers carried	11 873	11 624	10 808	10 561	5 900	5 976	5 030	5 022	Passagers transportés
Passenger-kilometres	11 638	11 976	11 389	10 237	8 846	9 304	8 774	7 687	Passagers-kilomètres
Total tonne-kilometres	1 410	1 452	1 410	1 224	1 142	1 197	1 157	978	Tonnes-kilomètres totales
Switzerland									**Suisse**
Kilometres flown	218	172	166	165	216	170	164	162	Kilomètres parcourus
Passengers carried	10 118	9 287	9 663	10 849	9 642	8 624	9 013	10 096	Passagers transportés
Passenger-kilometres	23 295	20 602	20 476	22 140	23 186	20 456	20 334	21 987	Passagers-kilomètres
Total tonne-kilometres	3 617	2 986	2 994	3 282	3 605	2 971	2 979	3 267	Tonnes-kilomètres totales
Syrian Arab Republic									**Rép. arabe syrienne**
Kilometres flown	9	11	12	24	9	11	12	23	Kilomètres parcourus
Passengers carried	940	1 170	1 240	1 252	908	1 135	1 203	1 193	Passagers transportés
Passenger-kilometres	1 744	2 212	2 520	2 340	1 727	2 193	2 500	2 311	Passagers-kilomètres
Total tonne-kilometres	173	219	249	228	171	217	247	225	Tonnes-kilomètres totales
Tajikistan									**Tadjikistan**
Kilometres flown	10	11	9	8	8	9	8	7	Kilomètres parcourus
Passengers carried	413	498	479	394	291	342	313	239	Passagers transportés
Passenger-kilometres	854	1 000	942	708	803	937	877	645	Passagers-kilomètres
Total tonne-kilometres	84	96	91	69	79	90	85	63	Tonnes-kilomètres totales
Thailand									**Thaïlande**
Kilometres flown	204	223	229	246	175	193	200	215	Kilomètres parcourus
Passengers carried	17 892	20 343	18 903	20 102	11 774	13 671	12 946	14 154	Passagers transportés
Passenger-kilometres	45 449	51 564	50 809	56 378	41 910	47 699	47 385	52 863	Passagers-kilomètres
Total tonne-kilometres	5 920	6 579	6 646	7 258	5 579	6 209	6 317	6 928	Tonnes-kilomètres totales

68

Civil aviation: scheduled airline traffic *(continued)*
Passengers carried (thousands); kilometres (millions)
Aviation civile : trafic régulier des lignes aériennes *(suite)*
Passagers transportés (milliers) ; kilomètres (millions)

Country or area and traffic	Total traffic (domestic and international) Trafic total (intérieur et international)				International traffic Trafic international				Pays ou zone et trafic
	2003	2004	2005	2006	2003	2004	2005	2006	
TFYR of Macedonia									**L'ex-R.Y. Macédoine**
Kilometres flown	3	3	3	3	3	3	3	3	Kilomètres parcourus
Passengers carried	201	211	192	209	201	211	192	209	Passagers transportés
Passenger-kilometres	280	276	249	269	280	276	249	269	Passagers-kilomètres
Total tonne-kilometres	25	25	22	24	25	25	22	24	Tonnes-kilomètres totales
Tonga									**Tonga**
Kilometres flown	1	1	...	...	...	...	...	...	Kilomètres parcourus
Passengers carried	61	75	...	...	...	...	...	...	Passagers transportés
Passenger-kilometres	15	19	...	...	...	...	...	...	Passagers-kilomètres
Total tonne-kilometres	1	2	...	...	...	...	...	...	Tonnes-kilomètres totales
Trinidad and Tobago									**Trinité-et-Tobago**
Kilometres flown	31	28	27	27	31	28	27	26	Kilomètres parcourus
Passengers carried	1 084	1 132	1 055	1 024	972	1 088	1 044	1 013	Passagers transportés
Passenger-kilometres	2 671	3 013	3 100	2 976	2 662	3 009	3 100	2 976	Passagers-kilomètres
Total tonne-kilometres	276	314	328	315	275	314	328	315	Tonnes-kilomètres totales
Tunisia									**Tunisie**
Kilometres flown	25	28	30	31	25	28	30	31	Kilomètres parcourus
Passengers carried	1 720	1 940	1 997	2 014	1 720	1 940	1 997	2 014	Passagers transportés
Passenger-kilometres	2 459	2 853	2 995	2 976	2 459	2 853	2 995	2 976	Passagers-kilomètres
Total tonne-kilometres	261	299	312	308	261	299	312	308	Tonnes-kilomètres totales
Turkey									**Turquie**
Kilometres flown	142	161	186	227	111	119	136	168	Kilomètres parcourus
Passengers carried	10 745	14 276	16 944	19 361	5 239	6 094	7 194	8 341	Passagers transportés
Passenger-kilometres	16 451	20 500	24 297	27 890	13 343	15 422	18 259	21 145	Passagers-kilomètres
Total tonne-kilometres	2 071	2 448	2 814	3 256	1 756	1 959	2 247	2 619	Tonnes-kilomètres totales
Turkmenistan									**Turkménistan**
Kilometres flown	22	17	16	17	12	11	11	12	Kilomètres parcourus
Passengers carried	1 412	1 612	1 654	1 843	307	436	420	437	Passagers transportés
Passenger-kilometres	1 538	1 916	1 905	2 072	1 005	1 363	1 337	1 391	Passagers-kilomètres
Total tonne-kilometres	150	182	182	197	102	131	129	135	Tonnes-kilomètres totales
Uganda									**Ouganda**
Kilometres flown	2	3	3	3	2	3	3	3	Kilomètres parcourus
Passengers carried	40	46	49	55	40	46	49	55	Passagers transportés
Passenger-kilometres	237	272	302	327	237	272	302	327	Passagers-kilomètres
Total tonne-kilometres	44	50	55	61	44	50	55	61	Tonnes-kilomètres totales
Ukraine									**Ukraine**
Kilometres flown	38	54	56	62	30	44	44	50	Kilomètres parcourus
Passengers carried	1 476	2 200	2 513	2 770	1 054	1 610	1 802	1 951	Passagers transportés
Passenger-kilometres	2 351	3 826	4 087	4 929	2 115	3 282	3 549	4 472	Passagers-kilomètres
Total tonne-kilometres	231	372	405	491	211	325	352	450	Tonnes-kilomètres totales
United Arab Emirates									**Emirats arabes unis**
Kilometres flown	207	277	321	382	207	277	321	381	Kilomètres parcourus
Passengers carried	11 610	14 314	16 210	19 102	11 610	14 314	16 210	18 873	Passagers transportés
Passenger-kilometres	41 504	54 703	65 121	79 704	41 504	54 703	65 121	79 536	Passagers-kilomètres
Total tonne-kilometres	6 760	8 979	10 669	12 903	6 760	8 979	10 669	12 882	Tonnes-kilomètres totales
United Kingdom [4]									**Royaume-Uni** [4]
Kilometres flown	1 087	1 205	1 324	1 400	965	1 066	1 177	1 251	Kilomètres parcourus
Passengers carried	76 389	86 055	93 603	97 545	55 604	63 515	70 475	74 692	Passagers transportés
Passenger-kilometres	166 518	182 736	200 333	213 335	157 503	173 205	190 543	203 537	Passagers-kilomètres
Total tonne-kilometres	20 689	22 260	24 008	25 385	19 942	21 474	23 173	24 551	Tonnes-kilomètres totales
United Rep. of Tanzania									**Rép.-Unie de Tanzanie**
Kilometres flown	4	5	8	5	3	3	5	3	Kilomètres parcourus
Passengers carried	150	243	257	221	61	82	74	67	Passagers transportés
Passenger-kilometres	151	216	246	225	102	135	148	130	Passagers-kilomètres
Total tonne-kilometres	16	22	24	22	10	14	14	13	Tonnes-kilomètres totales
United States [5]									**Etats-Unis** [5]
Kilometres flown	10 526	11 634	12 197	12 228	1 937	2 161	2 352	2 518	Kilomètres parcourus
Passengers carried	615 944	676 655	719 023	724 054	61 639	70 458	79 064	84 822	Passagers transportés
Passenger-kilometres	1 035 277	1 160 236	1 239 844	1 270 646	261 070	303 202	333 554	357 431	Passagers-kilomètres
Total tonne-kilometres	130 979	144 508	151 465	156 679	42 991	48 560	51 386	55 086	Tonnes-kilomètres totales

68

Civil aviation: scheduled airline traffic *(continued)*
Passengers carried (thousands); kilometres (millions)

Aviation civile : trafic régulier des lignes aériennes *(suite)*
Passagers transportés (milliers) ; kilomètres (millions)

Country or area and traffic	Total traffic (domestic and international) Trafic total (intérieur et international)				International traffic Trafic international				Pays ou zone et trafic
	2003	2004	2005	2006	2003	2004	2005	2006	
Uruguay									**Uruguay**
Kilometres flown	8	9	8	8	8	9	8	8	Kilomètres parcourus
Passengers carried	464	564	586	569	464	564	586	569	Passagers transportés
Passenger-kilometres	1 029	1 076	980	940	1 029	1 076	980	940	Passagers-kilomètres
Total tonne-kilometres	118	101	92	89	118	101	92	89	Tonnes-kilomètres totales
Uzbekistan									**Ouzbékistan**
Kilometres flown	40	44	42	42	33	37	36	36	Kilomètres parcourus
Passengers carried	1 466	1 588	1 639	1 665	1 048	1 183	1 220	1 297	Passagers transportés
Passenger-kilometres	3 889	4 454	4 409	4 599	3 646	4 215	4 171	4 377	Passagers-kilomètres
Total tonne-kilometres	424	486	479	483	401	464	457	462	Tonnes-kilomètres totales
Vanuatu									**Vanuatu**
Kilometres flown	3	3	3	3	3	3	3	3	Kilomètres parcourus
Passengers carried	83	104	112	117	83	104	112	117	Passagers transportés
Passenger-kilometres	176	217	232	241	176	217	232	241	Passagers-kilomètres
Total tonne-kilometres	18	21	23	23	18	21	23	23	Tonnes-kilomètres totales
Venezuela (Bol. Rep. of)									**Venezuela (Rép. bol. du)**
Kilometres flown	50	57	59	61	17	21	20	19	Kilomètres parcourus
Passengers carried	3 887	4 944	5 043	5 226	726	1 018	870	844	Passagers transportés
Passenger-kilometres	2 048	2 469	2 579	2 635	841	991	985	945	Passagers-kilomètres
Total tonne-kilometres	187	218	234	236	78	88	91	87	Tonnes-kilomètres totales
Viet Nam									**Viet Nam**
Kilometres flown	48	60	65	68	32	43	46	48	Kilomètres parcourus
Passengers carried	3 969	5 050	5 454	6 631	1 644	2 298	2 482	2 989	Passagers transportés
Passenger-kilometres	6 246	8 518	9 219	11 717	4 459	6 428	6 878	8 923	Passagers-kilomètres
Total tonne-kilometres	726	983	1 060	1 297	523	745	790	980	Tonnes-kilomètres totales
Yemen									**Yémen**
Kilometres flown	18	22	24	22	17	21	23	22	Kilomètres parcourus
Passengers carried	844	1 022	1 083	978	622	778	825	952	Passagers transportés
Passenger-kilometres	1 956	2 473	2 812	2 815	1 876	2 382	2 716	2 771	Passagers-kilomètres
Total tonne-kilometres	225	282	320	291	217	274	311	287	Tonnes-kilomètres totales
Zambia									**Zambie**
Kilometres flown	2	2	2	2	1	1	1	1	Kilomètres parcourus
Passengers carried	45	50	54	59	17	19	21	23	Passagers transportés
Passenger-kilometres	14	16	17	19	6	7	8	8	Passagers-kilomètres
Total tonne-kilometres	1	1	2	2	1	1	1	1	Tonnes-kilomètres totales
Zimbabwe									**Zimbabwe**
Kilometres flown	6	6	7	10	5	6	6	9	Kilomètres parcourus
Passengers carried	201	225	243	239	102	116	126	171	Passagers transportés
Passenger-kilometres	437	500	553	671	391	450	499	642	Passagers-kilomètres
Total tonne-kilometres	58	67	74	76	54	62	68	73	Tonnes-kilomètres totales

Source:
International Civil Aviation Organization (ICAO), Montreal, the ICAO Integrated Statistical Database (ISDB), last accessed September 2009.

1   For statistical purposes, the data for China do not include those for the Hong Kong Special Administrative Region (Hong Kong SAR), Macao Special Administrative Region (Macao SAR) and Taiwan Province of China.

2   Including data for airlines based in the territories and dependencies of France.

3   Including data for airlines based in the territories and dependencies of the Netherlands.

4   Including data for airlines based in the territories and dependencies of the United Kingdom (2001 and 2002).

5   Including data for airlines based in the territories and dependencies of the United States.

Source:
Organisation de l'aviation civile internationale (OACI), Montréal, la base de données statistique intégrée (ISDB), dernier accès septembre 2009.

1   Pour la présentation des statistiques, les données pour la Chine ne comprennent pas la Région Administrative Spéciale de Hong Kong (Hong Kong RAS), la Région Administrative Spéciale de Macao (Macao RAS) et la province de Taiwan.

2   Y compris les données relatives aux compagnies aériennes ayant des bases d'opérations dans les territoires et dépendances de France.

3   Y compris les données relatives aux compagnies aériennes ayant des bases d'opérations dans les territoires et dépendances des Pays-Bas.

4   Y compris les données relatives aux compagnies aériennes ayant des bases d'opération dans les territoires et dépendances du Royaume-Uni (2001 et 2002).

5   Y compris les données relatives aux compagnies aériennes ayant des bases d'opérations dans les territoires et dépendances des Etats-Unis.

Technical notes: tables 65-68

The data on international tourism have been supplied by the United Nations World Tourism Organization (UNWTO) from detailed tourism information published in the *Compendium of Tourism Statistics* and in the *Tourism Factbook* online available from http://www.unwto.org/statistics/index.htm.

For statistical purposes, the term "international visitor" describes "any person who travels to a country other than that in which he/she has his/her usual residence but outside his/her usual environment for a period not exceeding 12 months and whose main purpose of visit is other than the exercise of an activity remunerated from within the country visited".

International visitors include: (a) *tourists* (overnight visitors): "visitors who stay at least one night in a collective or private accommodation in the country visited"; and (b) *same-day visitors*: "visitors who do not spend the night in a collective or private accommodation in the country visited". The figures do not include immigrants, residents in a frontier zone, persons domiciled in one country or area and working in an adjoining country or area, members of the armed forces and diplomats and consular representatives when they travel from their country of origin to the country in which they are stationed and vice-versa. The figures also exclude persons in transit who do not formally enter the country through passport control, such as air transit passengers who remain for a short period in a designated area of the air terminal or ship passengers who are not permitted to disembark. This category includes passengers transferred directly between airports or other terminals. Other passengers in transit through a country are classified as visitors.

Tables 65 and 66: Data on arrivals of non-resident (or international) visitors may be obtained from different sources. In some cases data are obtained from border statistics derived from administrative records (police, immigration, traffic counts and other types of controls), border surveys and registrations at accommodation establishments.

Unless otherwise stated, table 65 shows the number of non-resident tourist/visitor arrivals at national borders classified by their region of origin. Totals correspond to the total number of arrivals from the regions indicated in the table. However, these totals may not correspond to the number of tourist arrivals shown in table 66. The latter excludes same day visitors except when indicated whereas they may be included in table 65.

When a person visits the same country several times a year, an equal number of arrivals is recorded. Likewise, if a person visits several countries during the course of a single trip, his/her arrival in each country is recorded separately. Consequently, arrivals cannot be assumed to be equal to the number of persons travelling.

Expenditure associated with tourism activity of visitors has been traditionally identified with the travel item of the Balance of Payments (BOP): in the case of inbound tourism, those expenditures in the country of reference associated with non-resident visitors are registered as "credits" in the BOP and refer to "travel receipts".

Notes techniques : tableaux 65 à 68

Les données sur le tourisme international ont été fournies par l'Organisation mondiale du tourisme (l'OMT) qui publie des renseignements détaillés sur le tourisme dans *le Compendium de statistiques du tourisme* et dans le *"Tourism Factbook"* en ligne au http://www.unwto.org/statistics/index.htm.

A des fins statistiques, l'expression "visiteur international" désigne "toute personne qui se rend dans un pays autre que celui où elle a son lieu de résidence habituelle, mais différent de son environnement habituel, pour une période de 12 mois au maximum, dans un but principal autre que celui d'y exercer une profession rémunérée".

Entrent dans cette catégorie: (a) *les touristes* (visiteurs passant la nuit), c'est à dire "les visiteurs qui passent une nuit au moins en logement collectif ou privé dans le pays visité"; et (b) *les visiteurs ne restant que la journée*, c'est à dire "les visiteurs qui ne passent pas la nuit en logement collectif ou privé dans le pays visité". Ces chiffres ne comprennent pas les immigrants, les résidents frontaliers, les personnes domiciliées dans une zone ou un pays donné et travaillant dans une zone ou pays limitrophe, les membres des forces armées et les membres des corps diplomatique et consulaire lorsqu'ils se rendent de leur pays d'origine au pays où ils sont en poste, et vice versa. Ne sont pas non plus inclus les voyageurs en transit, qui ne pénètrent pas officiellement dans le pays en faisant contrôler leurs passeports, tels que les passagers d'un vol en escale, qui demeurent pendant un court laps de temps dans une aire distincte de l'aérogare, ou les passagers d'un navire qui ne sont pas autorisés à débarquer. Cette catégorie comprend également les passagers transportés directement d'une aérogare à l'autre ou à un autre terminal. Les autres passagers en transit dans un pays sont classés parmi les visiteurs.

Tableaux 65 et 66: Les données relatives aux arrivées des visiteurs non résidents (ou internationaux) peuvent être obtenues de différentes sources. Dans certains cas, elles proviennent des statistiques des frontières tirées des registres administratifs (contrôles de police, de l'immigration, de la circulation et autres effectués aux frontières nationales), des enquêtes statistiques aux frontières et des enregistrements d'établissements d'hébergement touristique.

Sauf indication contraire, le tableau 65 indique le nombre d'arrivées de touristes/visiteurs non résidents aux frontières nationales par région de provenance. Les totaux correspondent au nombre total d'arrivées de touristes des régions indiquées sur le tableau. Les chiffres totaux peuvent, néanmoins, ne pas coïncider avec le nombre des arrivées de touristes indiqué dans le tableau 66, qui sauf indication contraire ne comprend pas les visiteurs ne restant que la journée, lesquels peuvent au contraire être inclus dans les chiffres du tableau 65.

Lorsqu'une personne visite le même pays plusieurs fois dans l'année, il est enregistré un nombre égal d'arrivées. En outre, si une personne visite plusieurs pays au cours d'un seul et même voyage, son arrivée dans chaque pays est enregistrée séparément. Par conséquent, on ne peut pas partir du postulat que les arrivées

The new conceptual framework approved by the United Nations Statistical Commission in relation to the measurement of tourism macroeconomic activity (the so-called Tourism Satellite Account) considers that "tourism industries and products" includes transport of passengers. Consequently, a better estimate of tourism-related expenditures by resident and non-resident visitors in an international scenario would be, in terms of the BOP, the value of the travel item plus that of the passenger transport item.

Nevertheless, users should be aware that BOP estimates include, in addition to expenditures associated with visitors, those related to other types of individuals.

The data published should allow international comparability and therefore correspond to those published by the International Monetary Fund (and provided by the Central Banks). Exceptions are footnoted.

Table 67: Indicators on expenditure (in other countries) are equivalent to those for inbound tourism but are registered as "debits" in the BOP's *travel* and *passenger transport* items. The data published are also provided by the International Monetary Fund and the same previous warning is applicable.

More detailed tourism information from the United Nations World Tourism Organization is available in the *Compendium of Tourism Statistics* and from http://www.unwto.org/statistics/index.htm; information on the balance of payments is published by the International Monetary Fund in the *Balance of Payments Statistics Yearbook*.

Table 68: Data for total traffic cover both domestic and international scheduled services operated by airlines registered in each country. Scheduled services include supplementary services occasioned by overflow traffic on regularly scheduled trips and preparatory flights for newly scheduled services. The data are prepared by the International Civil Aviation Organization (see also www.icao.int).

The following terms have been used in the table:
- Kilometres flown - aircraft kilometres performed, which is the sum of the products obtained by multiplying the number of revenue flight stages flown by the corresponding stage distance.
- Passengers carried - the number of passengers carried is obtained by counting each passenger on a particular flight (with one flight number) once only and not repeatedly on each individual stage of that flight, with a single exception that a passenger flying on both the international and domestic stages of the same flight should be counted as both a domestic and an international passenger.
- Passenger-kilometres performed - a passenger-kilometre is performed when a passenger is carried one kilometre. Calculation of passenger-kilometres equals the sum of the products obtained by multiplying the number of revenue passengers carried on each flight stage by the stage distance. The resultant figure is equal to the number of kilometres travelled by all passengers.
- Tonne-kilometres performed - a metric tonne of revenue load carried one kilometre. Tonne-kilometres

sont égales au nombre de personnes qui voyagent.

Les dépenses associées à l'activité touristique des visiteurs sont traditionnellement identifiées au poste "Voyages" de la balance des paiements. Dans le cas du tourisme récepteur, ces dépenses associées aux visiteurs non résidents sont enregistrées dans la balance des paiements comme des "crédits" et il s'agit de "recettes au titre des voyages".

Le cadre conceptuel approuvé par la Commission de statistique de l'Organisation des Nations Unies concernant l'évaluation de l'activité touristique à l'échelle macroéconomique (cadre qu'il est convenu d'appeler compte satellite du tourisme) considère que la notion "industries et produits touristiques " englobe le transport de passagers. Par conséquent, une meilleure estimation des dépenses liées au tourisme international que font les visiteurs résidents et non résidents serait, sous l'angle de la balance des paiements, la somme des valeurs des postes "Voyages" et "Transport de passagers".

Néanmoins, les utilisateurs doivent être conscients que les estimations de la balance des paiements comprennent, outre les dépenses associées aux visiteurs, celles liées à d'autres types d'individus.

Les données publiées doivent permettre la comparabilité internationale et donc correspondre à celles publiées par le Fonds monétaire international (FMI) qui viennent des banques centrales. Les exceptions sont signalées par une note de pied.

Tableau 67: Les indicateurs relatifs aux dépenses touristiques dans d'autres pays sont équivalents à ceux du tourisme récepteur mais ils sont enregistrés comme "débits" aux postes "Voyages" et "Transport de passagers" de la balance des paiements.

Les données publiées sont également fournies par le FMI. Il y a lieu de faire la même mise en garde que plus haut. On trouvera plus de renseignements publiés par l'Organisation mondiale du tourisme dans le *Compendium des statistiques du tourisme* et au http://www.unwto.org/statistics/index.htm; des renseignements sur la balance des paiements sont publiés par le Fonds monétaire international dans "*Balance of Payments Statistics Yearbook*".

Tableau 68: Les données relatives au trafic total se rapportent aux services réguliers, intérieurs ou internationaux des compagnies de transport aérien enregistrées dans chaque pays. Les services réguliers comprennent aussi les vols supplémentaires nécessités par un surcroît d'activité des services réguliers et les vols préparatoires en vue de nouveaux services réguliers. Les données sont préparées par l'Organisation de l'aviation civile internationale (voir aussi www.icao.int).

Les termes ci-après ont été utilisés dans le tableau:
- Kilomètres parcourus – le nombre de kilomètres parcourus équivaut à la somme des produits du nombre de vols payants effectués sur chaque étape par la longueur de l'étape.
- Passagers transportés – pour calculer le nombre de passagers transportés, on compte chaque passager d'un vol donné (correspondant à un numéro de vol) une seule fois et non pour chacune des étapes de ce vol; toutefois,

performed equals the sum of the product obtained by multiplying the number of total tonnes of revenue load (passengers, freight and mail) carried on each flight stage by the stage distance. See http://www.icaodata.com/Terms.aspx for more information.

les passagers qui voyagent sur une étape internationale et sur une étape intérieure d'un même vol doivent être comptés à la fois comme passagers d'un vol intérieur et comme passagers d'un vol international.

- Passager-kilomètre réalisé – un passager-kilomètre est réalisé lorsqu'un passager est transporté sur une distance d'un kilomètre. Le nombre de passagers-kilomètres réalisés équivaut à la somme des produits du nombre de passagers payants transportés sur chaque étape par la longueur de l'étape. Le total obtenu est égal au nombre de kilomètres parcourus par l'ensemble des passagers.
- Tonnes-kilomètres réalisées – la tonne-kilomètre est une unité de mesure qui correspond au déplacement d'une tonne métrique de charge payante sur un kilomètre. Les tonnes-kilomètres réalisées sont la somme des produits du nombre de tonnes de charge payante (passagers, fret, envois postaux) transportées sur chaque étape par la longueur de l'étape. Pour plus de détails, voir http://www.icaodata.com/Terms.aspx.

Balance of payments summary
Millions of US dollars

Résumé de la balance des paiements
Millions de dollars des E.-U.

Country or area	2001	2002	2003	2004	2005	2006	2007	Pays ou zone
Albania								**Albanie**
Current account	-217	-408	-407	-358	-571	-671	-831	Compte des transac. courantes
Goods: exports f.o.b.	305	330	447	603	656	793	786	Biens : exportations f.à.b.
Goods: imports f.o.b.	-1 332	-1 485	-1 783	-2 195	-2 478	-2 916	-2 890	Biens : importations f.à.b.
Services: credit	534	585	720	1 003	1 165	1 504	1 415	Services : crédit
Services: debit	-444	-590	-803	-1 055	-1 383	-1 585	-1 402	Services : débit
Income: credit	163	148	195	204	227	332	279	Revenus : crédit
Income: debit	-14	-21	-24	-28	-53	-69	-62	Revenus : débit
Current transfers: credit	648	684	924	1 200	1 519	1 426	1 220	Transferts courants : crédit
Current transfers: debit	-77	-59	-82	-91	-225	-157	-177	Transferts courants : débit
Capital account, n.i.e.	118	121	157	132	123	180	90	Compte de capital, n.i.a.
Financial account, n.i.e.	110	213	201	396	393	523	744	Compte financier, n.i.a.
Net errors and omissions	136	108	147	115	204	237	151	Erreurs et omissions nettes
Reserves and related items	-147	-36	-98	-286	-148	-269	-153	Réserves et postes apparentés
Angola								**Angola**
Current account	-1 431	-150	-720	686	5 138	10 690	9 402	Compte des transac. courantes
Goods: exports f.o.b.	6 534	8 328	9 508	13 475	24 109	31 862	44 396	Biens : exportations f.à.b.
Goods: imports f.o.b.	-3 179	-3 760	-5 480	-5 832	-8 353	-8 778	-13 662	Biens : importations f.à.b.
Services: credit	203	207	201	323	177	1 484	311	Services : crédit
Services: debit	-3 518	-3 322	-3 321	-4 803	-6 791	-7 511	-12 643	Services : débit
Income: credit	23	18	12	33	26	145	33	Revenus : crédit
Income: debit	-1 584	-1 652	-1 739	-2 517	-4 057	-6 323	-8 811	Revenus : débit
Current transfers: credit	208	142	186	124	173	60	46	Transferts courants : crédit
Current transfers: debit	-118	-110	-87	-118	-146	-250	-268	Transferts courants : débit
Capital account, n.i.e.	4	0	0	0	0	0	7	Compte de capital, n.i.a.
Financial account, n.i.e.	950	-357	1 371	-623	-3 115	-5 601	-11 910	Compte financier, n.i.a.
Net errors and omissions	-309	150	-388	277	-378	290	-462	Erreurs et omissions nettes
Reserves and related items	786	356	-263	-340	-1 645	-5 378	2 963	Réserves et postes apparentés
Anguilla								**Anguilla**
Current account	-40	-36	-40	-47	-52	-172	-255	Compte des transac. courantes
Goods: exports f.o.b.	4	4	4	6	15	12	14	Biens : exportations f.à.b.
Goods: imports f.o.b.	-68	-62	-08	-90	-114	-216	-280	Biens : importations f.à.b.
Services: credit	70	66	73	78	99	124	138	Services : crédit
Services: debit	-39	-39	-44	-47	-56	-101	-131	Services : débit
Income: credit	2	2	2	8	12	15	17	Revenus : crédit
Income: debit	-9	-8	-8	-7	8	-7	-8	Revenus : débit
Current transfers: credit	10	9	10	14	11	14	11	Transferts courants : crédit
Current transfers: debit	-9	-8	-10	-10	-10	-14	-16	Transferts courants : débit
Capital account, n.i.e.	9	8	8	8	13	18	13	Compte de capital, n.i.a.
Financial account, n.i.e.	20	18	46	42	47	155	246	Compte financier, n.i.a.
Net errors and omissions	15	12	-7	-2	-3	2	-1	Erreurs et omissions nettes
Reserves and related items	-4	-2	-7	-1	-5	-2	-3	Réserves et postes apparentés
Antigua and Barbuda								**Antigua-et-Barbuda**
Current account	-57	-82	-98	-96	-171	-309	-402	Compte des transac. courantes
Goods: exports f.o.b.	45	34	45	57	83	74	83	Biens : exportations f.à.b.
Goods: imports f.o.b.	-317	-303	-352	-402	-455	-560	-653	Biens : importations f.à.b.
Services: credit	401	394	418	477	463	477	498	Services : crédit
Services: debit	-169	-171	-182	-190	-227	-259	-294	Services : débit
Income: credit	19	8	9	12	18	27	31	Revenus : crédit
Income: debit	-43	-50	-47	-57	-60	-91	-87	Revenus : débit
Current transfers: credit	23	23	29	25	26	41	42	Transferts courants : crédit
Current transfers: debit	-13	-17	-16	-17	-18	-19	-22	Transferts courants : débit
Capital account, n.i.e.	12	14	10	21	214	32	11	Compte de capital, n.i.a.
Financial account, n.i.e.	60	102	100	99	-32	296	395	Compte financier, n.i.a.
Net errors and omissions	1	-25	13	-19	-4	-3	-4	Erreurs et omissions nettes
Reserves and related items	-16	-8	-26	-6	-7	-15	-1	Réserves et postes apparentés
Argentina								**Argentine**
Current account	-3 780	8 767	8 140	3 212	5 281	7 706	7 122	Compte des transac. courantes
Goods: exports f.o.b.	26 543	25 651	29 939	34 576	40 387	46 546	55 780	Biens : exportations f.à.b.
Goods: imports f.o.b.	-19 158	-8 473	-13 134	-21 311	-27 300	-32 588	-42 525	Biens : importations f.à.b.

69
Summary of balance of payments *(continued)*
Millions of US dollars
Résumé de la balance des paiements *(suite)*
Millions de dollars des E.-U.

Country or area	2001	2002	2003	2004	2005	2006	2007	Pays ou zone
Services: credit	4 627	3 495	4 500	5 288	6 635	7 987	10 306	Services : crédit
Services: debit	-8 490	-4 956	-5 693	-6 619	-7 620	-8 529	-10 828	Services : débit
Income: credit	5 358	3 039	3 104	3 721	4 313	5 674	6 639	Revenus : crédit
Income: debit	-13 085	-10 530	-11 080	-13 004	-11 617	-11 834	-12 568	Revenus : débit
Current transfers: credit	856	818	942	1 110	1 226	1 412	1 583	Transferts courants : crédit
Current transfers: debit	-431	-278	-438	-549	-742	-962	-1 265	Transferts courants : débit
Capital account, n.i.e.	157	406	70	196	89	97	112	Compte de capital, n.i.a.
Financial account, n.i.e.	-14 971	-20 685	-15 860	-10 949	1 898	4 888	3 771	Compte financier, n.i.a.
Net errors and omissions	-2 810	-1 890	-1 428	548	377	1 556	571	Erreurs et omissions nettes
Reserves and related items	21 405	13 402	9 077	6 993	-7 644	-14 247	-11 576	Réserves et postes apparentés
Armenia								**Arménie**
Current account	-200	-148	-189	-20	-52	-117	-590	Compte des transac. courantes
Goods: exports f.o.b.	353	514	696	738	1 005	1 025	1 197	Biens : exportations f.à.b.
Goods: imports f.o.b.	-773	-883	-1 130	-1 196	-1 593	-1 921	-2 797	Biens : importations f.à.b.
Services: credit	187	184	207	333	411	485	580	Services : crédit
Services: debit	-204	-225	-276	-432	-531	-615	-793	Services : débit
Income: credit	104	137	166	397	458	624	811	Revenus : crédit
Income: debit	-39	-48	-71	-290	-325	-409	-532	Revenus : débit
Current transfers: credit	201	200	245	515	604	792	1 025	Transferts courants : crédit
Current transfers: debit	-27	-26	-27	-85	-80	-98	-80	Transferts courants : débit
Capital account, n.i.e.	30	68	90	41	73	86	143	Compte de capital, n.i.a.
Financial account, n.i.e.	175	147	174	17	163	434	1 008	Compte financier, n.i.a.
Net errors and omissions	11	-4	-2	6	2	-16	-2	Erreurs et omissions nettes
Reserves and related items	-17	-63	-73	-33	-187	-387	-560	Réserves et postes apparentés
Aruba								**Aruba**
Current account	314	-338	-163	-7	-198	-43	215	Compte des transac. courantes
Goods: exports f.o.b.	2 423	1 488	2 052	2 724	3 483	3 669	2 691	Biens : exportations f.à.b.
Goods: imports f.o.b.	-2 372	-2 024	-2 400	-3 004	-3 460	-3 790	-2 850	Biens : importations f.à.b.
Services: credit	988	1 001	1 047	1 248	1 304	1 323	1 492	Services : crédit
Services: debit	-613	-606	-727	-794	-917	-1 002	-941	Services : débit
Income: credit	50	32	32	35	42	61	79	Revenus : crédit
Income: debit	-105	-165	-82	-111	-526	-183	-157	Revenus : débit
Current transfers: credit	42	41	41	45	53	55	58	Transferts courants : crédit
Current transfers: debit	-100	-105	-127	-149	-177	-177	-157	Transferts courants : débit
Capital account, n.i.e.	-1	21	100	19	19	-14	18	Compte de capital, n.i.a.
Financial account, n.i.e.	-224	348	3	-16	155	111	-197	Compte financier, n.i.a.
Net errors and omissions	-6	9	23	5	2	1	7	Erreurs et omissions nettes
Reserves and related items	-83	-40	36	-2	22	-55	-43	Réserves et postes apparentés
Australia								**Australie**
Current account	-7 411	-15 809	-28 684	-38 854	-41 032	-41 504	-57 682	Compte des transac. courantes
Goods: exports f.o.b.	63 626	65 014	70 523	87 166	107 011	124 913	142 435	Biens : exportations f.à.b.
Goods: imports f.o.b.	-61 890	-70 528	-85 862	-105 230	-120 383	-134 509	-160 205	Biens : importations f.à.b.
Services: credit	18 092	19 594	23 747	28 485	31 047	33 088	40 437	Services : crédit
Services: debit	-17 351	-18 388	-21 941	-27 943	-30 505	-32 219	-39 252	Services : débit
Income: credit	8 200	8 522	10 487	14 311	16 445	21 748	32 501	Revenus : crédit
Income: debit	-18 132	-19 974	-25 456	-35 327	-44 166	-54 131	-73 318	Revenus : débit
Current transfers: credit	2 296	2 373	2 743	3 114	3 333	3 698	4 405	Transferts courants : crédit
Current transfers: debit	-2 254	-2 422	-2 926	-3 431	-3 813	-4 092	-4 686	Transferts courants : débit
Capital account, n.i.e.	645	583	889	1 076	1 252	1 737	1 632	Compte de capital, n.i.a.
Financial account, n.i.e.	8 155	16 249	34 694	39 374	47 617	49 901	20 777	Compte financier, n.i.a.
Net errors and omissions	-293	-900	-22	-429	-581	-412	125	Erreurs et omissions nettes
Reserves and related items	-1 096	-122	-6 877	-1 166	-7 256	-9 722	35 148	Réserves et postes apparentés
Austria								**Autriche**
Current account	-1 512	5 464	4 186	6 074	6 245	7 807	12 031	Compte des transac. courantes
Goods: exports f.o.b.	66 900	73 668	88 105	109 875	119 228	133 844	162 147	Biens : exportations f.à.b.
Goods: imports f.o.b.	-70 140	-72 375	-89 799	-110 905	-120 977	-133 419	-160 302	Biens : importations f.à.b.
Services: credit	23 978	25 861	32 455	37 945	42 589	46 112	55 736	Services : crédit
Services: debit	-17 555	-18 727	-23 738	-27 986	-30 730	-33 514	-39 033	Services : débit
Income: credit	12 343	14 168	16 514	20 193	25 914	28 027	37 858	Revenus : crédit
Income: debit	-15 324	-15 630	-17 611	-21 403	-27 957	-31 701	-43 024	Revenus : débit
Current transfers: credit	2 065	2 356	2 954	3 449	3 949	4 290	5 050	Transferts courants : crédit
Current transfers: debit	-3 779	-3 857	-4 693	-5 096	-5 770	-5 833	-6 402	Transferts courants : débit
Capital account, n.i.e.	-528	-379	8	-342	-237	-1 009	-90	Compte de capital, n.i.a.
Financial account, n.i.e.	1 772	-4 021	-2 515	-2 823	-917	-6 862	-6 045	Compte financier, n.i.a.

69 Summary of balance of payments *(continued)*
Millions of US dollars
Résumé de la balance des paiements *(suite)*
Millions de dollars des É.-U.

Country or area	2001	2002	2003	2004	2005	2006	2007	Pays ou zone
Net errors and omissions	-1 620	-2 787	-3 703	-4 758	-5 841	-797	-3 371	Erreurs et omissions nettes
Reserves and related items	1 888	1 723	2 023	1 849	750	861	-2 525	Réserves et postes apparentés
Azerbaijan								**Azerbaïdjan**
Current account	-52	-768	-2 021	-2 589	167	3 708	9 019	Compte des transac. courantes
Goods: exports f.o.b.	2 079	2 305	2 625	3 743	7 649	13 015	21 269	Biens : exportations f.à.b.
Goods: imports f.o.b.	-1 465	-1 823	-2 723	-3 582	-4 350	-5 269	-6 045	Biens : importations f.à.b.
Services: credit	290	362	432	492	683	940	1 248	Services : crédit
Services: debit	-665	-1 298	-2 047	-2 730	-2 653	-2 863	-3 379	Services : débit
Income: credit	41	37	53	65	202	280	328	Revenus : crédit
Income: debit	-409	-422	-495	-766	-1 847	-2 961	-5 407	Revenus : débit
Current transfers: credit	176	228	225	263	626	748	1 313	Transferts courants : crédit
Current transfers: debit	-100	-158	-91	-74	-142	-182	-308	Transferts courants : débit
Capital account, n.i.e.	...	-29	-23	-4	41	-4	-3	Compte de capital, n.i.a.
Financial account, n.i.e.	126	918	2 280	2 960	78	-2 105	-6 874	Compte financier, n.i.a.
Net errors and omissions	-1	-87	-112	-50	-126	-256	-361	Erreurs et omissions nettes
Reserves and related items	-73	-34	-124	-317	-161	-1 343	-1 781	Réserves et postes apparentés
Bahamas								**Bahamas**
Current account	-645	-423	-474	-307	-701	-1 406	-1 316	Compte des transac. courantes
Goods: exports f.o.b.	417	422	427	477	549	704	802	Biens : exportations f.à.b.
Goods: imports f.o.b.	-1 804	-1 749	-1 759	-1 907	-2 377	-2 768	-2 958	Biens : importations f.à.b.
Services: credit	1 804	2 062	2 055	2 244	2 511	2 436	2 599	Services : crédit
Services: debit	-973	-1 016	-1 092	-1 231	-1 286	-1 611	-1 580	Services : débit
Income: credit	185	108	79	80	97	119	121	Revenus : crédit
Income: debit	-383	-292	-232	-221	-279	-337	-353	Revenus : débit
Current transfers: credit	121	55	60	265	103	66	71	Transferts courants : crédit
Current transfers: debit	-11	-13	-11	-14	-18	-14	-19	Transferts courants : débit
Capital account, n.i.e.	-21	-25	-37	-48	-60	-64	-76	Compte de capital, n.i.a.
Financial account, n.i.e.	265	405	535	358	822	1 280	1 031	Compte financier, n.i.a.
Net errors and omissions	371	103	85	180	-149	109	315	Erreurs et omissions nettes
Reserves and related items	31	-60	-110	-183	88	80	46	Réserves et postes apparentés
Bahrain								**Bahreïn**
Current account	226	-50	200	472	1 474	2 188	2 907	Compte des transac. courantes
Goods: exports f.o.b.	5 656	5 888	6 721	7 660	10 349	12 340	13 790	Biens : exportations f.à.b.
Goods: imports f.o.b.	-4 029	-4 678	-5 298	-6 923	-8 871	-9 954	-10 925	Biens : importations f.à.b.
Services: credit	950	1 068	1 260	2 070	3 048	3 322	3 524	Services : crédit
Services: debit	-766	-945	-907	-1 248	-1 416	-1 605	-1 701	Services : débit
Income: credit	3 794	1 679	1 267	2 544	5 016	7 634	10 374	Revenus : crédit
Income: debit	-4 116	-2 204	-1 760	-3 119	-5 428	-8 019	-10 672	Revenus : débit
Current transfers: credit	23	15	0	0	0	0	0	Transferts courants : crédit
Current transfers: debit	-1 287	-872	-1 082	-1 120	-1 223	-1 531	-1 483	Transferts courants : débit
Capital account, n.i.e.	100	102	50	50	50	75	50	Compte de capital, n.i.a.
Financial account, n.i.e.	-417	-1 234	493	-391	-1 380	-1 452	-1 552	Compte financier, n.i.a.
Net errors and omissions	215	1 217	-700	27	150	11	10	Erreurs et omissions nettes
Reserves and related items	-123	-35	-44	-158	-294	-822	-1 415	Réserves et postes apparentés
Bangladesh								**Bangladesh**
Current account	-535	739	132	-279	-176	1 196	857	Compte des transac. courantes
Goods: exports f.o.b.	6 085	6 102	7 050	8 151	9 302	11 554	12 474	Biens : exportations f.à.b.
Goods: imports f.o.b.	-8 133	-7 780	-9 492	-11 157	-12 502	-14 443	-16 669	Biens : importations f.à.b.
Services: credit	752	849	1 012	1 083	1 249	1 334	1 617	Services : crédit
Services: debit	-1 522	-1 406	-1 711	-1 931	-2 207	-2 340	-2 884	Services : débit
Income: credit	77	57	57	103	117	177	244	Revenus : crédit
Income: debit	-362	-322	-361	-474	-910	-1 018	-1 212	Revenus : débit
Current transfers: credit	2 573	3 245	3 586	3 960	4 785	5 941	7 297	Transferts courants : crédit
Current transfers: debit	-5	-6	-8	-13	-11	-8	-10	Transferts courants : débit
Capital account, n.i.e.	235	364	387	142	262	153	701	Compte de capital, n.i.a.
Financial account, n.i.e.	262	-256	289	665	142	120	735	Compte financier, n.i.a.
Net errors and omissions	-106	-349	81	-25	-644	-604	-920	Erreurs et omissions nettes
Reserves and related items	144	-497	-889	-503	416	-865	-1 373	Réserves et postes apparentés
Barbados								**Barbade**
Current account	-111	-168	-170	-337	-387	...	...	Compte des transac. courantes
Goods: exports f.o.b.	271	253	264	293	379	...	...	Biens : exportations f.à.b.
Goods: imports f.o.b.	-952	-955	-1 066	-1 264	-1 464	...	...	Biens : importations f.à.b.
Services: credit	1 069	1 041	1 165	1 224	1 457	...	...	Services : crédit
Services: debit	-499	-491	-519	-556	-680	...	...	Services : débit

69
Summary of balance of payments *(continued)*
Millions of US dollars
Résumé de la balance des paiements *(suite)*
Millions de dollars des E.-U.

Country or area	2001	2002	2003	2004	2005	2006	2007	Pays ou zone
Income: credit	73	72	75	75	85	...	...	Revenus : crédit
Income: debit	-166	-174	-182	-197	-257	...	...	Revenus : débit
Current transfers: credit	126	120	127	126	160	...	...	Transferts courants : crédit
Current transfers: debit	-32	-34	-34	-38	-67	...	...	Transferts courants : débit
Capital account, n.i.e.	1	0	0	0	0	...	...	Compte de capital, n.i.a.
Financial account, n.i.e.	285	119	203	135	391	...	...	Compte financier, n.i.a.
Net errors and omissions	47	25	34	45	18	...	...	Erreurs et omissions nettes
Reserves and related items	-222	24	-67	157	-22	...	...	Réserves et postes apparentés
Belarus								**Bélarus**
Current account	-401	-334	-426	-1 193	436	-1 447	-3 060	Compte des transac. courantes
Goods: exports f.o.b.	7 334	7 965	10 076	13 942	16 109	19 835	24 329	Biens : exportations f.à.b.
Goods: imports f.o.b.	-8 188	-8 945	-11 397	-16 214	-16 746	-22 104	-28 400	Biens : importations f.à.b.
Services: credit	1 142	1 341	1 500	1 747	2 073	2 397	3 254	Services : crédit
Services: debit	-794	-842	-841	-970	-1 093	-1 658	-2 021	Services : débit
Income: credit	27	45	126	158	168	247	276	Revenus : crédit
Income: debit	-76	-97	-112	-159	-239	-367	-687	Revenus : débit
Current transfers: credit	202	260	292	391	267	317	348	Transferts courants : crédit
Current transfers: debit	-49	-62	-70	-88	-102	-113	-160	Transferts courants : débit
Capital account, n.i.e.	56	53	69	49	41	74	92	Compte de capital, n.i.a.
Financial account, n.i.e.	332	753	429	1 152	-65	1 691	5 200	Compte financier, n.i.a.
Net errors and omissions	-1	-289	-13	270	109	-302	505	Erreurs et omissions nettes
Reserves and related items	13	-183	-58	-278	-520	-16	-2 737	Réserves et postes apparentés
Belgium								**Belgique**
Current account	...	11 611	12 906	12 537	9 945	8 035	7 216	Compte des transac. courantes
Goods: exports f.o.b.	...	169 166	204 962	245 426	263 056	281 135	323 708	Biens : exportations f.à.b.
Goods: imports f.o.b.	...	-159 648	-194 003	-235 718	-257 137	-277 778	-322 023	Biens : importations f.à.b.
Services: credit	...	37 822	44 708	52 708	56 144	59 516	79 113	Services : crédit
Services: debit	...	-35 863	-42 862	-49 023	-51 172	-53 250	-72 578	Services : débit
Income: credit	...	36 372	40 213	48 891	59 028	74 277	98 581	Revenus : crédit
Income: debit	...	-31 897	-33 732	-43 269	-53 604	-69 324	-92 765	Revenus : débit
Current transfers: credit	...	5 275	6 515	7 949	9 355	8 812	8 681	Transferts courants : crédit
Current transfers: debit	...	-9 616	-12 894	-14 427	-15 724	-15 353	-15 500	Transferts courants : débit
Capital account, n.i.e.	...	-585	-1 021	-497	-894	-405	-1 499	Compte de capital, n.i.a.
Financial account, n.i.e.	...	-6 483	-12 518	-10 660	-8 929	-9 116	-6 634	Compte financier, n.i.a.
Net errors and omissions	...	-4 579	-1 093	-2 103	-2 298	1 641	2 142	Erreurs et omissions nettes
Reserves and related items	...	35	1 725	723	2 176	-156	-1 226	Réserves et postes apparentés
Belgium-Luxembourg [1]								**Belgique-Luxembourg** [1]
Current account	9 392	...	...	...	...	...	...	Compte des transac. courantes
Goods: exports f.o.b.	163 498	...	...	...	...	...	...	Biens : exportations f.à.b.
Goods: imports f.o.b.	-159 790	...	...	...	...	...	...	Biens : importations f.à.b.
Services: credit	50 314	...	...	...	...	...	...	Services : crédit
Services: debit	-43 316	...	...	...	...	...	...	Services : débit
Income: credit	78 906	...	...	...	...	...	...	Revenus : crédit
Income: debit	-75 999	...	...	...	...	...	...	Revenus : débit
Current transfers: credit	7 316	...	...	...	...	...	...	Transferts courants : crédit
Current transfers: debit	-11 535	...	...	...	...	...	...	Transferts courants : débit
Capital account, n.i.e.	26	...	...	...	...	...	...	Compte de capital, n.i.a.
Financial account, n.i.e.	-7 978	...	...	...	...	...	...	Compte financier, n.i.a.
Net errors and omissions	3	...	...	...	...	...	...	Erreurs et omissions nettes
Reserves and related items	-1 442	...	...	...	...	...	...	Réserves et postes apparentés
Belize								**Belize**
Current account	-190	-165	-184	-155	-151	-16	-51	Compte des transac. courantes
Goods: exports f.o.b.	269	310	316	308	325	427	426	Biens : exportations f.à.b.
Goods: imports f.o.b.	-478	-497	-522	-481	-556	-612	-642	Biens : importations f.à.b.
Services: credit	166	176	212	235	302	374	398	Services : crédit
Services: debit	-120	-130	-141	-147	-159	-150	-168	Services : débit
Income: credit	9	4	5	4	7	10	7	Revenus : crédit
Income: debit	-76	-72	-95	-121	-121	-139	-165	Revenus : débit
Current transfers: credit	54	59	59	61	68	92	137	Transferts courants : crédit
Current transfers: debit	-14	-16	-18	-15	-17	-18	-43	Transferts courants : débit
Capital account, n.i.e.	6	14	4	10	3	9	4	Compte de capital, n.i.a.
Financial account, n.i.e.	165	151	204	117	144	69	98	Compte financier, n.i.a.
Net errors and omissions	9	-9	-35	-4	-8	-13	-28	Erreurs et omissions nettes
Reserves and related items	11	8	11	31	11	-49	-22	Réserves et postes apparentés

69

Summary of balance of payments *(continued)*
Millions of US dollars

Résumé de la balance des paiements *(suite)*
Millions de dollars des E.-U.

Country or area	2001	2002	2003	2004	2005	2006	2007	Pays ou zone
Benin								**Bénin**
Current account	-160	-239	-349	-317	-270	-327	...	Compte des transac. courantes
Goods: exports f.o.b.	373	448	541	569	578	735	...	Biens : exportations f.à.b.
Goods: imports f.o.b.	-553	-679	-819	-842	-866	-1 046	...	Biens : importations f.à.b.
Services: credit	147	152	172	216	194	217	...	Services : crédit
Services: debit	-192	-209	-254	-287	-279	-352	...	Services : débit
Income: credit	22	21	23	23	25	24	...	Revenus : crédit
Income: debit	-36	-47	-61	-60	-43	-54	...	Revenus : débit
Current transfers: credit	87	93	57	73	153	206	...	Transferts courants : crédit
Current transfers: debit	-10	-19	-8	-8	-33	-57	...	Transferts courants : débit
Capital account, n.i.e.	49	38	34	52	99	83	...	Compte de capital, n.i.a.
Financial account, n.i.e.	40	-61	32	-28	105	-901	...	Compte financier, n.i.a.
Net errors and omissions	4	2	182	-10	9	28	...	Erreurs et omissions nettes
Reserves and related items	69	261	100	303	57	1 117	...	Réserves et postes apparentés
Bolivia								**Bolivie**
Current account	-274	-352	76	337	622	1 317	1 800	Compte des transac. courantes
Goods: exports f.o.b.	1 285	1 299	1 598	2 146	2 791	3 875	4 490	Biens : exportations f.à.b.
Goods: imports f.o.b.	-1 580	-1 639	-1 497	-1 725	-2 183	-2 632	-3 249	Biens : importations f.à.b.
Services: credit	236	257	364	416	489	477	468	Services : crédit
Services: debit	-399	-433	-551	-607	-683	-827	-828	Services : débit
Income: credit	121	103	71	76	121	235	370	Revenus : crédit
Income: debit	-333	-308	-374	-461	-498	-633	-543	Revenus : débit
Current transfers: credit	432	408	511	543	649	895	1 163	Transferts courants : crédit
Current transfers: debit	-35	-38	-46	-52	-65	-73	-72	Transferts courants : débit
Capital account, n.i.e.	0	0	0	0	9	1 813	1 180	Compte de capital, n.i.a.
Financial account, n.i.e.	441	649	36	361	181	-1 589	-1 034	Compte financier, n.i.a.
Net errors and omissions	-203	-640	-174	-625	-374	-103	-80	Erreurs et omissions nettes
Reserves and related items	36	343	62	-73	-437	-1 439	-1 865	Réserves et postes apparentés
Bosnia and Herzegovina								**Bosnie-Herzégovine**
Current account	-743	-1 191	-1 631	-1 639	-1 844	-973	-1 931	Compte des transac. courantes
Goods: exports f.o.b.	1 134	1 110	1 477	2 087	2 555	3 381	4 243	Biens : exportations f.à.b.
Goods: imports f.o.b.	-4 092	-4 449	-5 637	-6 656	-7 454	-7 680	-9 947	Biens : importations f.à.b.
Services: credit	497	524	721	864	989	1 161	1 365	Services : crédit
Services: debit	-269	-305	-384	-432	-436	-488	-567	Services : débit
Income: credit	625	605	654	675	682	733	894	Revenus : crédit
Income: debit	-93	-97	-121	-170	-213	-316	-495	Revenus : débit
Current transfers: credit	1 528	1 524	1 781	2 204	2 172	2 399	2 775	Transferts courants : crédit
Current transfers: debit	-73	-102	-123	-210	-140	-165	-200	Transferts courants : débit
Capital account, n.i.e.	400	412	466	301	281	294	309	Compte de capital, n.i.a.
Financial account, n.i.e.	995	552	1 056	1 389	1 828	1 243	2 180	Compte financier, n.i.a.
Net errors and omissions	100	98	323	409	227	197	249	Erreurs et omissions nettes
Reserves and related items	-752	129	-214	-459	-491	-761	-806	Réserves et postes apparentés
Botswana								**Botswana**
Current account	598	157	462	309	1 597	1 940	2 434	Compte des transac. courantes
Goods: exports f.o.b.	2 315	2 319	3 024	3 696	4 444	4 521	5 158	Biens : exportations f.à.b.
Goods: imports f.o.b.	-1 604	-1 642	-2 127	-2 864	-2 686	-2 617	-3 447	Biens : importations f.à.b.
Services: credit	340	490	643	780	854	771	935	Services : crédit
Services: debit	-513	-510	-652	-793	-857	-835	-970	Services : débit
Income: credit	358	268	383	217	456	529	473	Revenus : crédit
Income: debit	-495	-980	-1 098	-1 254	-1 292	-1 301	-819	Revenus : débit
Current transfers: credit	383	400	538	743	896	1 073	1 368	Transferts courants : crédit
Current transfers: debit	-185	-188	-248	-217	-218	-202	-263	Transferts courants : débit
Capital account, n.i.e.	6	16	22	32	31	24	89	Compte de capital, n.i.a.
Financial account, n.i.e.	-509	-217	-379	-276	54	-67	-665	Compte financier, n.i.a.
Net errors and omissions	76	106	66	-122	-319	-142	-124	Erreurs et omissions nettes
Reserves and related items	-170	-61	-171	57	-1 364	-1 756	-1 734	Réserves et postes apparentés
Brazil								**Brésil**
Current account	-23 215	-7 637	4 177	11 738	13 984	13 620	1 550	Compte des transac. courantes
Goods: exports f.o.b.	58 223	60 362	73 084	96 475	118 308	137 807	160 649	Biens : exportations f.à.b.
Goods: imports f.o.b.	-55 572	-47 241	-48 290	-62 809	-73 606	-91 350	-120 618	Biens : importations f.à.b.
Services: credit	9 322	9 551	10 447	12 584	16 048	19 462	23 954	Services : crédit
Services: debit	-17 081	-14 509	-15 378	-17 260	-24 356	-29 116	-37 173	Services : débit
Income: credit	3 280	3 295	3 339	3 199	3 194	6 438	11 493	Revenus : crédit
Income: debit	-23 023	-21 486	-21 891	-23 719	-29 162	-33 927	-40 784	Revenus : débit

69 Summary of balance of payments *(continued)*
Millions of US dollars

Résumé de la balance des paiements *(suite)*
Millions de dollars des E.-U.

Country or area	2001	2002	2003	2004	2005	2006	2007	Pays ou zone
Current transfers: credit	1 934	2 627	3 132	3 582	4 050	4 846	4 972	Transferts courants : crédit
Current transfers: debit	-296	-237	-265	-314	-493	-541	-943	Transferts courants : débit
Capital account, n.i.e.	-36	433	498	339	663	869	756	Compte de capital, n.i.a.
Financial account, n.i.e.	20 331	-3 909	-157	-3 333	13 144	15 113	88 330	Compte financier, n.i.a.
Net errors and omissions	-498	-154	-933	-2 145	-225	967	-3 152	Erreurs et omissions nettes
Reserves and related items	3 418	11 266	-3 586	-6 599	-27 566	-30 569	-87 484	Réserves et postes apparentés
Brunei Darussalam								**Brunéi Darussalam**
Current account	1 775	1 531	2 279	2 896	4 038	5 232	...	Compte des transac. courantes
Goods: exports f.o.b.	3 640	3 702	4 422	5 066	6 247	7 627	...	Biens : exportations f.à.b.
Goods: imports f.o.b.	-1 082	-1 475	-1 258	-1 338	-1 413	-1 586	...	Biens : importations f.à.b.
Services: credit	482	427	437	544	617	744	...	Services : crédit
Services: debit	-1 053	-876	-1 032	-1 075	-1 110	-1 213	...	Services : débit
Income: credit	244	235	214	236	263	248	...	Revenus : crédit
Income: debit	-186	-172	-214	-228	-190	-183	...	Revenus : débit
Current transfers: debit	-269	-310	-290	-309	-376	-405	...	Transferts courants : débit
Capital account, n.i.e.	-1	-1	-1	-11	-11	-7	...	Compte de capital, n.i.a.
Financial account, n.i.e.	234	612	-627	-1 152	-85	575	...	Compte financier, n.i.a.
Net errors and omissions	-2 016	-2 102	-1 628	-1 705	-3 950	-5 770	...	Erreurs et omissions nettes
Reserves and related items	8	-40	-23	-28	9	-30	...	Réserves et postes apparentés
Bulgaria								**Bulgarie**
Current account	-805	-319	-1 022	-1 671	-3 347	-5 659	-8 716	Compte des transac. courantes
Goods: exports f.o.b.	5 113	5 354	7 081	9 931	11 754	15 101	18 575	Biens : exportations f.à.b.
Goods: imports f.o.b.	-6 693	-7 013	-9 657	-13 619	-17 204	-22 130	-28 646	Biens : importations f.à.b.
Services: credit	2 163	2 203	2 961	4 029	4 404	5 289	6 336	Services : crédit
Services: debit	-1 910	-1 755	-2 447	-3 238	-3 404	-4 100	-4 821	Services : débit
Income: credit	706	924	1 298	1 539	1 516	1 607	2 103	Revenus : crédit
Income: debit	-681	-581	-954	-1 236	-1 426	-2 271	-2 727	Revenus : débit
Current transfers: credit	599	654	865	1 121	1 238	1 066	1 253	Transferts courants : crédit
Current transfers: debit	-100	-106	-170	-199	-225	-222	-789	Transferts courants : débit
Capital account, n.i.e.	^0	^0	^0	204	290	228	505	Compte de capital, n.i.a.
Financial account, n.i.e.	663	3 513	2 738	3 428	6 903	8 625	15 008	Compte financier, n.i.a.
Net errors and omissions	515	-716	-889	371	-1 219	-907	-2 074	Erreurs et omissions nettes
Reserves and related items	-373	-2 478	-827	-2 332	-2 626	-2 287	-4 724	Réserves et postes apparentés
Burkina Faso								**Burkina Faso**
Current account	-381	...	...	...	...	...	...	Compte des transac. courantes
Goods: exports f.o.b.	223	...	...	...	...	...	...	Biens : exportations f.à.b.
Goods: imports f.o.b.	-509	...	...	...	...	...	...	Biens : importations f.à.b.
Services: credit	37	...	...	...	...	...	...	Services : crédit
Services: debit	-141	...	...	...	...	...	...	Services : débit
Income: credit	15	...	...	...	...	...	...	Revenus : crédit
Income: debit	-40	...	...	...	...	...	...	Revenus : débit
Current transfers: credit	72	...	...	...	...	...	...	Transferts courants : crédit
Current transfers: debit	-38	...	...	...	...	...	...	Transferts courants : débit
Capital account, n.i.e.	165	...	...	...	...	...	...	Compte de capital, n.i.a.
Financial account, n.i.e.	25	...	...	...	...	...	...	Compte financier, n.i.a.
Net errors and omissions	3	...	...	...	...	...	...	Erreurs et omissions nettes
Reserves and related items	187	...	...	...	...	...	...	Réserves et postes apparentés
Burundi								**Burundi**
Current account	-109	-111	-131	-166	-226	-324	-276	Compte des transac. courantes
Goods: exports f.o.b.	39	31	38	48	57	59	53	Biens : exportations f.à.b.
Goods: imports f.o.b.	-108	-105	-130	-145	-189	-245	-258	Biens : importations f.à.b.
Services: credit	5	8	7	16	35	34	31	Services : crédit
Services: debit	-38	-43	-45	-87	-134	-202	-177	Services : débit
Income: credit	2	1	1	1	3	5	9	Revenus : crédit
Income: debit	-16	-13	-19	-20	-21	-13	-15	Revenus : débit
Current transfers: credit	10	13	20	24	27	41	82	Transferts courants : crédit
Current transfers: debit	-3	-3	-3	-3	-3	-3	^0	Transferts courants : débit
Capital account, n.i.e.	^0	^0	-1	18	24	46	79	Compte de capital, n.i.a.
Financial account, n.i.e.	-4	-41	-50	-23	-11	-16	-42	Compte financier, n.i.a.
Net errors and omissions	-31	2	-14	-19	-80	4	-35	Erreurs et omissions nettes
Reserves and related items	144	150	196	190	293	289	273	Réserves et postes apparentés
Cambodia								**Cambodge**
Current account	-88	-107	-233	-183	-360	-339	-506	Compte des transac. courantes
Goods: exports f.o.b.	1 571	1 770	2 087	2 589	2 910	3 694	4 089	Biens : exportations f.à.b.

69

Summary of balance of payments *(continued)*
Millions of US dollars

Résumé de la balance des paiements *(suite)*
Millions de dollars des E.-U.

Country or area	2001	2002	2003	2004	2005	2006	2007	Pays ou zone
Goods: imports f.o.b.	-2 094	-2 361	-2 668	-3 269	-3 928	-4 749	-5 424	Biens : importations f.à.b.
Services: credit	525	604	548	805	1 118	1 296	1 548	Services : crédit
Services: debit	-347	-376	-434	-514	-647	-792	-903	Services : débit
Income: credit	58	51	44	49	68	90	112	Revenus : crédit
Income: debit	-195	-234	-223	-270	-322	-380	-472	Revenus : débit
Current transfers: credit	404	448	425	444	461	527	570	Transferts courants : crédit
Current transfers: debit	-8	-9	-12	-15	-21	-25	-26	Transferts courants : débit
Capital account, n.i.e.	45	8	66	68	95	268	253	Compte de capital, n.i.a.
Financial account, n.i.e.	59	165	244	219	335	324	672	Compte financier, n.i.a.
Net errors and omissions	26	2	-40	-46	5	-44	-4	Erreurs et omissions nettes
Reserves and related items	-42	-67	-36	-58	-74	-208	-414	Réserves et postes apparentés
Cameroon								**Cameroun**
Current account	-376	-445	-628	-626	-777	-151	547	Compte des transac. courantes
Goods: exports f.o.b.	1 891	1 964	2 483	2 904	3 265	3 849	4 345	Biens : exportations f.à.b.
Goods: imports f.o.b.	-1 797	-1 812	-2 214	-2 695	-2 890	-3 179	-4 050	Biens : importations f.à.b.
Services: credit	858	939	645	940	687	672	607	Services : crédit
Services: debit	-1 082	-1 212	-1 222	-1 485	-1 455	-1 475	-1 481	Services : débit
Income: credit	47	43	108	98	45	46	58	Revenus : crédit
Income: debit	-380	-420	-549	-545	-665	-377	-443	Revenus : débit
Current transfers: credit	147	127	205	206	332	527	593	Transferts courants : crédit
Current transfers: debit	-61	-75	-83	-49	-95	-214	-177	Transferts courants : débit
Capital account, n.i.e.	56	61	112	-105	204	1 586	356	Compte de capital, n.i.a.
Financial account, n.i.e.	326	593	-603	210	67	69	936	Compte financier, n.i.a.
Net errors and omissions	-124	-130	93	113	-32	113	93	Erreurs et omissions nettes
Reserves and related items	119	-79	1 026	408	538	-1 617	-839	Réserves et postes apparentés
Canada								**Canada**
Current account	16 281	12 604	10 696	22 946	22 179	17 859	12 639	Compte des transac. courantes
Goods: exports f.o.b.	271 849	263 908	285 186	330 011	371 899	400 056	432 028	Biens : exportations f.à.b.
Goods: imports f.o.b.	-226 132	-227 410	-244 904	-279 508	-320 181	-356 514	-387 665	Biens : importations f.à.b.
Services: credit	38 804	40 481	44 242	50 286	55 444	59 330	62 988	Services : crédit
Services: debit	-43 843	-45 070	-52 454	-58 776	-65 434	-72 295	-80 837	Services : débit
Income: credit	16 823	19 444	21 050	29 374	39 944	56 912	66 958	Revenus : crédit
Income: debit	-42 238	-38 745	-42 295	-47 926	-58 401	-68 662	-79 946	Revenus : débit
Current transfers: credit	4 500	4 387	4 814	5 518	6 754	8 532	8 938	Transferts courants : crédit
Current transfers: debit	-3 480	-4 391	-4 943	-6 033	-7 845	-9 498	-9 826	Transferts courants : débit
Capital account, n.i.e.	3 721	3 145	3 020	3 416	4 828	3 642	3 899	Compte de capital, n.i.a.
Financial account, n.i.e.	-11 609	-14 360	-18 070	-31 510	-25 568	17 986	-15 803	Compte financier, n.i.a.
Net errors and omissions	-6 220	-1 574	1 098	2 313	-104	-2 689	3 171	Erreurs et omissions nettes
Reserves and related items	-2 172	185	3 255	2 836	-1 335	-826	-3 906	Réserves et postes apparentés
Cape Verde								**Cap-Vert**
Current account	-56	-72	-91	-130	-41	-83	-197	Compte des transac. courantes
Goods: exports f.o.b.	37	42	53	57	89	96	82	Biens : exportations f.à.b.
Goods: imports f.o.b.	-232	-278	-361	-435	-438	-560	-746	Biens : importations f.à.b.
Services: credit	130	153	202	239	269	382	491	Services : crédit
Services: debit	-119	-142	-189	-207	-209	-250	-294	Services : débit
Income: credit	8	6	16	18	19	19	27	Revenus : crédit
Income: debit	-13	-18	-29	-36	-53	-59	-58	Revenus : débit
Current transfers: credit	156	182	235	278	312	334	406	Transferts courants : crédit
Current transfers: debit	-22	-16	-18	-43	-31	-45	-104	Transferts courants : débit
Capital account, n.i.e.	24	9	25	24	21	17	27	Compte de capital, n.i.a.
Financial account, n.i.e.	39	81	82	124	82	203	282	Compte financier, n.i.a.
Net errors and omissions	-24	-8	-12	10	2	-10	-1	Erreurs et omissions nettes
Reserves and related items	17	-10	-4	-28	-63	-127	-111	Réserves et postes apparentés
Chile								**Chili**
Current account	-1 100	-580	-779	2 074	1 449	6 838	7 200	Compte des transac. courantes
Goods: exports f.o.b.	18 272	18 180	21 664	32 520	41 267	58 486	67 644	Biens : exportations f.à.b.
Goods: imports f.o.b.	-16 428	-15 794	-17 941	-22 935	-30 492	-35 899	-43 991	Biens : importations f.à.b.
Services: credit	4 138	4 386	5 070	6 034	7 134	7 824	8 786	Services : crédit
Services: debit	-4 983	-5 087	-5 688	-6 780	-7 756	-8 452	-9 947	Services : débit
Income: credit	1 458	1 114	1 552	1 983	2 452	3 457	5 587	Revenus : crédit
Income: debit	-3 985	-3 960	-6 041	-9 820	-12 939	-21 876	-23 853	Revenus : débit
Current transfers: credit	713	954	901	1 411	2 199	3 801	3 574	Transferts courants : crédit
Current transfers: debit	-286	-372	-296	-339	-416	-504	-600	Transferts courants : débit
Capital account, n.i.e.	0	83	0	5	41	13	16	Compte de capital, n.i.a.

69

Summary of balance of payments *(continued)*
Millions of US dollars

Résumé de la balance des paiements *(suite)*
Millions de dollars des E.-U.

Country or area	2001	2002	2003	2004	2005	2006	2007	Pays ou zone
Financial account, n.i.e.	1 362	1 634	1 145	-2 001	1 550	-5 057	-9 436	Compte financier, n.i.a.
Net errors and omissions	-861	-952	-724	-270	-1 329	204	-993	Erreurs et omissions nettes
Reserves and related items	599	-185	357	191	-1 711	-1 998	3 214	Réserves et postes apparentés
China [2]								**Chine** [2]
Current account	17 401	35 422	45 875	68 659	160 818	253 268	371 833	Compte des transac. courantes
Goods: exports f.o.b.	266 075	325 651	438 270	593 393	762 484	969 682	1 220 000	Biens : exportations f.à.b.
Goods: imports f.o.b.	-232 058	-281 484	-393 618	-534 410	-628 295	-751 936	-904 618	Biens : importations f.à.b.
Services: credit	33 334	39 745	46 734	62 434	74 404	91 999	122 206	Services : crédit
Services: debit	-39 267	-46 528	-55 306	-72 133	-83 796	-100 833	-130 111	Services : débit
Income: credit	9 388	8 344	16 095	20 544	38 959	54 642	83 030	Revenus : crédit
Income: debit	-28 563	-23 290	-23 933	-24 067	-28 324	-39 485	-57 342	Revenus : débit
Current transfers: credit	9 125	13 795	18 483	24 326	27 735	31 578	42 646	Transferts courants : crédit
Current transfers: debit	-633	-811	-848	-1 428	-2 349	-2 378	-3 978	Transferts courants : débit
Capital account, n.i.e.	-54	-50	-48	-69	4 102	4 020	3 099	Compte de capital, n.i.a.
Financial account, n.i.e.	34 832	32 341	52 774	110 729	58 862	2 642	70 410	Compte financier, n.i.a.
Net errors and omissions	-4 732	7 504	17 985	26 834	-16 441	-13 075	16 349	Erreurs et omissions nettes
Reserves and related items	-47 447	-75 217	-116 586	-206 153	-207 342	-246 855	-461 691	Réserves et postes apparentés
China, Hong Kong SAR								**Chine, Hong Kong RAS**
Current account	9 786	12 412	16 470	15 731	20 181	22 928	25 746	Compte des transac. courantes
Goods: exports f.o.b.	190 926	200 300	224 656	260 263	289 579	317 600	345 979	Biens : exportations f.à.b.
Goods: imports f.o.b.	-199 257	-205 353	-230 435	-269 575	-297 206	-331 634	-365 679	Biens : importations f.à.b.
Services: credit	41 135	44 601	46 555	55 160	63 709	72 735	83 563	Services : crédit
Services: debit	-24 899	-25 964	-26 126	-31 138	-33 933	-37 060	-41 234	Services : débit
Income: credit	48 058	41 511	43 181	52 003	64 806	83 865	114 720	Revenus : crédit
Income: debit	-44 398	-40 787	-39 525	-48 997	-64 604	-80 346	-109 027	Revenus : débit
Current transfers: credit	605	777	529	626	943	960	938	Transferts courants : crédit
Current transfers: debit	-2 385	-2 673	-2 366	-2 611	-3 067	-3 194	-3 513	Transferts courants : débit
Capital account, n.i.e.	-1 174	-2 011	-1 065	-329	-634	-373	1 324	Compte de capital, n.i.a.
Financial account, n.i.e.	-6 626	-19 751	-20 953	-20 094	-21 448	-20 621	-19 855	Compte financier, n.i.a.
Net errors and omissions	2 699	6 973	6 542	7 977	3 279	4 082	7 490	Erreurs et omissions nettes
Reserves and related items	-4 684	2 377	-994	-3 286	-1 378	-6 016	-14 704	Réserves et postes apparentés
China, Macao SAR								**Chine, Macao RAS**
Current account	...	2 719	3 160	4 240	3 367	2 927	5 863	Compte des transac. courantes
Goods: exports f.o.b.	...	2 358	2 585	2 816	2 478	2 559	2 545	Biens : exportations f.à.b.
Goods: imports f.o.b.	...	-3 277	-3 678	-4 658	-5 271	-6 495	-7 639	Biens : importations f.à.b.
Services: credit	...	4 758	5 605	8 063	8 612	10 538	14 411	Services : crédit
Services: debit	...	-1 071	-1 175	-1 364	-1 576	-1 883	-2 732	Services : débit
Income: credit	...	450	395	387	806	1 426	1 945	Revenus : crédit
Income: debit	...	-468	-547	-959	-1 582	-2 983	-2 099	Revenus : débit
Current transfers: credit	...	69	83	79	83	108	101	Transferts courants : crédit
Current transfers: debit	...	-99	-108	-124	-184	-343	-668	Transferts courants : débit
Capital account, n.i.e.	...	139	88	274	515	438	319	Compte de capital, n.i.a.
Financial account, n.i.e.	...	-1 084	-1 680	-1 558	-264	-814	4 893	Compte financier, n.i.a.
Net errors and omissions	...	-1 572	-1 077	-1 932	-2 492	-494	-7 568	Erreurs et omissions nettes
Reserves and related items	...	-202	-491	-1 024	-1 126	-2 058	-3 507	Réserves et postes apparentés
Colombia								**Colombie**
Current account	-1 091	-1 304	-982	-913	-1 884	-2 992	-5 866	Compte des transac. courantes
Goods: exports f.o.b.	12 869	12 384	13 813	17 224	21 730	25 181	30 577	Biens : exportations f.à.b.
Goods: imports f.o.b.	-12 269	-12 078	-13 258	-15 878	-20 134	-24 859	-31 173	Biens : importations f.à.b.
Services: credit	2 190	1 867	1 921	2 258	2 668	3 377	3 636	Services : crédit
Services: debit	-3 602	-3 302	-3 360	-3 938	-4 770	-5 496	-6 243	Services : débit
Income: credit	895	703	543	664	1 072	1 516	1 843	Revenus : crédit
Income: debit	-3 528	-3 584	-3 951	-4 967	-6 531	-7 454	-9 737	Revenus : débit
Current transfers: credit	2 656	3 010	3 565	3 994	4 342	5 037	5 642	Transferts courants : crédit
Current transfers: debit	-302	-304	-256	-270	-260	-293	-410	Transferts courants : débit
Capital account, n.i.e.	0	0	0	0	0	0	0	Compte de capital, n.i.a.
Financial account, n.i.e.	2 453	1 304	652	3 134	3 234	2 901	10 338	Compte financier, n.i.a.
Net errors and omissions	-161	124	133	241	373	114	232	Erreurs et omissions nettes
Reserves and related items	-1 202	-124	197	-2 463	-1 724	-23	-4 704	Réserves et postes apparentés
Congo								**Congo**
Current account	-28	-34	520	674	696	124	-2 181	Compte des transac. courantes
Goods: exports f.o.b.	2 055	2 289	2 637	3 433	4 745	6 066	5 808	Biens : exportations f.à.b.
Goods: imports f.o.b.	-681	-691	-831	-969	-1 305	-2 003	-2 858	Biens : importations f.à.b.
Services: credit	144	165	194	197	220	266	319	Services : crédit

69
Summary of balance of payments *(continued)*
Millions of US dollars
Résumé de la balance des paiements *(suite)*
Millions de dollars des E.-U.

Country or area	2001	2002	2003	2004	2005	2006	2007	Pays ou zone
Services: debit	-852	-927	-875	-1 016	-1 417	-2 426	-3 528	Services : débit
Income: credit	15	6	10	13	18	20	23	Revenus : crédit
Income: debit	-694	-866	-596	-962	-1 596	-1 773	-1 908	Revenus : débit
Current transfers: credit	18	13	26	34	87	38	43	Transferts courants : crédit
Current transfers: debit	-34	-23	-44	-56	-57	-63	-81	Transferts courants : débit
Capital account, n.i.e.	13	5	17	13	11	10		Compte de capital, n.i.a.
Financial account, n.i.e.	-653	-464	-701	-775	-227	426	2 547	Compte financier, n.i.a.
Net errors and omissions	-12	-220	-116	-93	30	143	-201	Erreurs et omissions nettes
Reserves and related items	681	713	280	181	-510	-702	-196	Réserves et postes apparentés
Costa Rica								**Costa Rica**
Current account	-603	-857	-880	-796	-981	-1 053	-1 578	Compte des transac. courantes
Goods: exports f.o.b.	4 923	5 270	6 163	6 370	7 099	8 068	9 266	Biens : exportations f.à.b.
Goods: imports f.o.b.	-5 743	-6 548	-7 252	-7 791	-9 258	-10 838	-12 290	Biens : importations f.à.b.
Services: credit	1 926	1 868	2 021	2 242	2 622	2 979	3 630	Services : crédit
Services: debit	-1 180	-1 183	-1 245	-1 384	-1 506	-1 616	-1 803	Services : débit
Income: credit	193	158	146	144	807	1 135	722	Revenus : crédit
Income: debit	-872	-598	-922	-589	-1 015	-1 131	-1 572	Revenus : débit
Current transfers: credit	266	297	369	371	471	586	734	Transferts courants : crédit
Current transfers: debit	-118	-121	-160	-159	-200	-237	-265	Transferts courants : débit
Capital account, n.i.e.	18	12	24	11	16	1	21	Compte de capital, n.i.a.
Financial account, n.i.e.	271	857	595	472	878	1 885	2 389	Compte financier, n.i.a.
Net errors and omissions	168	-51	35	64	144	182	145	Erreurs et omissions nettes
Reserves and related items	146	38	226	249	-57	-1 015	-978	Réserves et postes apparentés
Côte d'Ivoire								**Côte d'Ivoire**
Current account	-61	768	294	241	40	479	-146	Compte des transac. courantes
Goods: exports f.o.b.	3 946	5 275	5 788	6 919	7 697	8 477	8 476	Biens : exportations f.à.b.
Goods: imports f.o.b.	-2 418	-2 456	-3 231	-4 291	-5 251	-5 368	-5 932	Biens : importations f.à.b.
Services: credit	578	585	664	763	832	845	943	Services : crédit
Services: debit	-1 271	-1 545	-1 780	-2 033	-2 124	-2 233	-2 444	Services : débit
Income: credit	137	141	171	190	194	196	215	Revenus : crédit
Income: debit	-723	-771	-830	-841	-847	-906	-1 025	Revenus : débit
Current transfers: credit	89	132	196	187	195	218	459	Transferts courants : crédit
Current transfers: debit	-399	-594	-683	-653	-657	-749	-838	Transferts courants : débit
Capital account, n.i.e.	10	8	14	146	185	33	90	Compte de capital, n.i.a.
Financial account, n.i.e.	-66	-1 029	-1 035	-263	-482	-279	332	Compte financier, n.i.a.
Net errors and omissions	31	-26	-888	27	-58	-10	45	Erreurs et omissions nettes
Reserves and related items	86	278	1 615	-150	315	-223	-321	Réserves et postes apparentés
Croatia								**Croatie**
Current account	-729	-1 925	-2 162	-1 875	-2 555	-3 295	-4 447	Compte des transac. courantes
Goods: exports f.o.b.	4 767	5 006	6 311	8 214	8 960	10 644	12 623	Biens : exportations f.à.b.
Goods: imports f.o.b.	-8 860	-10 652	-14 216	-16 560	-18 301	-21 131	-25 556	Biens : importations f.à.b.
Services: credit	4 884	5 582	8 569	9 373	9 921	10 802	12 525	Services : crédit
Services: debit	-1 949	-2 414	-2 982	-3 565	-3 400	-3 548	-3 925	Services : débit
Income: credit	434	437	508	879	889	1 126	1 760	Revenus : crédit
Income: debit	-988	-975	-1 760	-1 701	-2 099	-2 578	-3 305	Revenus : débit
Current transfers: credit	1 193	1 375	1 741	1 974	2 027	2 061	2 164	Transferts courants : crédit
Current transfers: debit	-209	-285	-334	-488	-552	-670	-734	Transferts courants : débit
Capital account, n.i.e.	137	463	119	39	64	-157	47	Compte de capital, n.i.a.
Financial account, n.i.e.	2 431	2 725	4 363	3 128	4 826	6 448	6 568	Compte financier, n.i.a.
Net errors and omissions	-441	-448	-918	-1 224	-1 313	-1 269	-1 186	Erreurs et omissions nettes
Reserves and related items	-1 398	-815	-1 401	-68	-1 022	-1 727	-982	Réserves et postes apparentés
Cyprus								**Chypre**
Current account	-322	-379	-292	-827	-971	-1 279	-2 595	Compte des transac. courantes
Goods: exports f.o.b.	975	852	925	1 173	1 545	1 393	1 483	Biens : exportations f.à.b.
Goods: imports f.o.b.	-3 553	-3 735	-4 108	-5 222	-5 792	-6 335	-7 957	Biens : importations f.à.b.
Services: credit	4 340	4 531	5 372	6 235	6 502	7 160	8 802	Services : crédit
Services: debit	-1 615	-1 742	-2 237	-2 644	-2 706	-2 939	-3 764	Services : débit
Income: credit	559	757	905	1 160	1 635	2 139	3 349	Revenus : crédit
Income: debit	-1 083	-1 158	-1 295	-1 697	-2 247	-2 904	-4 494	Revenus : débit
Current transfers: credit	147	270	386	585	631	822	822	Transferts courants : crédit
Current transfers: debit	-93	-153	-242	-417	-539	-616	-836	Transferts courants : débit
Capital account, n.i.e.	6	20	38	134	87	33	8	Compte de capital, n.i.a.
Financial account, n.i.e.	965	826	46	912	1 421	2 270	2 624	Compte financier, n.i.a.

69

Summary of balance of payments *(continued)*
Millions of US dollars

Résumé de la balance des paiements *(suite)*
Millions de dollars des E.-U.

Country or area	2001	2002	2003	2004	2005	2006	2007	Pays ou zone
Net errors and omissions	-38	-77	21	152	165	-12	-287	Erreurs et omissions nettes
Reserves and related items	-611	-389	188	-371	-703	-1 012	250	Réserves et postes apparentés
Czech Republic								**République tchèque**
Current account	-3 273	-4 265	-5 785	-5 749	-1 577	-3 783	-3 232	Compte des transac. courantes
Goods: exports f.o.b.	33 404	38 480	48 705	67 220	77 951	95 151	122 791	Biens : exportations f.à.b.
Goods: imports f.o.b.	-36 482	-40 720	-51 224	-67 749	-75 430	-92 308	-116 878	Biens : importations f.à.b.
Services: credit	7 092	7 083	7 789	9 643	11 765	13 941	17 180	Services : crédit
Services: debit	-5 567	-6 439	-7 320	-9 008	-10 217	-11 883	-14 397	Services : débit
Income: credit	2 233	2 052	2 681	3 405	4 390	5 674	6 977	Revenus : crédit
Income: debit	-4 422	-5 632	-6 966	-9 497	-10 364	-13 778	-18 017	Revenus : débit
Current transfers: credit	959	1 465	1 663	2 081	3 219	2 482	3 466	Transferts courants : crédit
Current transfers: debit	-489	-553	-1 114	-1 845	-2 892	-3 061	-4 353	Transferts courants : débit
Capital account, n.i.e.	-9	-4	-3	-602	196	380	1 026	Compte de capital, n.i.a.
Financial account, n.i.e.	4 569	10 621	5 620	7 036	6 379	4 205	4 921	Compte financier, n.i.a.
Net errors and omissions	499	266	611	-422	-1 118	-710	-1 844	Erreurs et omissions nettes
Reserves and related items	-1 787	-6 618	-442	-263	-3 879	-92	-872	Réserves et postes apparentés
Denmark								**Danemark**
Current account	4 848	3 460	6 963	5 941	11 104	7 963	2 379	Compte des transac. courantes
Goods: exports f.o.b.	50 466	55 473	64 537	75 050	82 486	90 570	100 449	Biens : exportations f.à.b.
Goods: imports f.o.b.	-43 048	-47 810	-54 840	-65 524	-75 153	-87 671	-100 836	Biens : importations f.à.b.
Services: credit	25 134	26 667	31 672	36 304	43 372	51 961	61 608	Services : crédit
Services: debit	-22 121	-24 305	-28 254	-33 401	-37 002	-45 123	-53 889	Services : débit
Income: credit	10 737	9 265	11 180	12 784	24 929	27 726	34 660	Revenus : crédit
Income: debit	-13 748	-12 805	-13 796	-15 114	-23 331	-24 899	-34 484	Revenus : débit
Current transfers: credit	3 719	3 466	4 615	5 120	3 562	3 535	4 133	Transferts courants : crédit
Current transfers: debit	-6 291	-6 489	-8 151	-9 279	-7 758	-8 136	-9 263	Transferts courants : débit
Capital account, n.i.e.	14	152	-7	13	518	5	55	Compte de capital, n.i.a.
Financial account, n.i.e.	-5 712	3 819	-5 129	-19 023	-10 578	-8 609	-4 817	Compte financier, n.i.a.
Net errors and omissions	4 167	-1 887	2 846	11 644	-2 550	-5 347	2 172	Erreurs et omissions nettes
Reserves and related items	-3 317	-5 546	-4 674	1 426	1 506	5 988	211	Réserves et postes apparentés
Djibouti								**Djibouti**
Current account	-38	-17	-34	-68	-55	-98	-254	Compte des transac. courantes
Goods: exports f.o.b.	32	36	37	38	40	55	58	Biens : exportations f.à.b.
Goods: imports f.o.b.	-196	-197	-238	-261	-277	-336	-473	Biens : importations f.à.b.
Services: credit	182	192	216	213	248	251	248	Services : crédit
Services: debit	-66	-62	-67	-77	-84	-89	-108	Services : débit
Income: credit	21	24	31	33	32	35	35	Revenus : crédit
Income: debit	-9	-9	-10	-11	-11	-12	-11	Revenus : débit
Current transfers: credit	1	1	3	3	3	4	4	Transferts courants : crédit
Current transfers: debit	-2	-2	-6	-6	-6	-7	-7	Transferts courants : débit
Capital account, n.i.e.	5	10	-7	20	27	9	35	Compte de capital, n.i.a.
Financial account, n.i.e.	-65	-58	-37	-36	-33	64	190	Compte financier, n.i.a.
Net errors and omissions	34	9	1	-16	-45	-52	-81	Erreurs et omissions nettes
Reserves and related items	64	56	77	100	107	77	109	Réserves et postes apparentés
Dominica								**Dominique**
Current account	-61	-51	-56	-62	-81	-54	-93	Compte des transac. courantes
Goods: exports f.o.b.	44	44	41	43	43	44	40	Biens : exportations f.à.b.
Goods: imports f.o.b.	-116	-102	-113	-128	-146	-147	-174	Biens : importations f.à.b.
Services: credit	77	80	77	88	86	100	100	Services : crédit
Services: debit	-50	-54	-45	-46	-50	-52	-59	Services : débit
Income: credit	4	3	2	4	6	6	6	Revenus : crédit
Income: debit	-29	-31	-29	-37	-35	-23	-23	Revenus : débit
Current transfers: credit	16	17	17	22	24	23	23	Transferts courants : crédit
Current transfers: debit	-7	-7	-8	-6	-9	-6	-6	Transferts courants : débit
Capital account, n.i.e.	18	20	19	27	18	28	31	Compte de capital, n.i.a.
Financial account, n.i.e.	30	21	22	12	59	29	45	Compte financier, n.i.a.
Net errors and omissions	7	16	10	15	9	6	15	Erreurs et omissions nettes
Reserves and related items	5	-6	5	8	-6	-9	2	Réserves et postes apparentés
Dominican Republic								**Rép. dominicaine**
Current account	-741	-798	1 036	1 041	-473	-1 288	-2 068	Compte des transac. courantes
Goods: exports f.o.b.	5 276	5 165	5 471	5 936	6 145	6 610	7 160	Biens : exportations f.à.b.
Goods: imports f.o.b.	-8 779	-8 838	-7 627	-7 888	-9 869	-12 174	-13 597	Biens : importations f.à.b.
Services: credit	3 110	3 071	3 469	3 504	3 935	4 567	4 812	Services : crédit
Services: debit	-1 284	-1 314	-1 219	-1 213	-1 478	-1 582	-1 773	Services : débit

69

Summary of balance of payments *(continued)*
Millions of US dollars
Résumé de la balance des paiements *(suite)*
Millions de dollars des E.-U.

Country or area	2001	2002	2003	2004	2005	2006	2007	Pays ou zone
Income: credit	271	300	341	322	418	700	812	Revenus : crédit
Income: debit	-1 363	-1 452	-1 734	-2 146	-2 320	-2 553	-2 891	Revenus : débit
Current transfers: credit	2 232	2 452	2 512	2 701	2 908	3 366	3 663	Transferts courants : crédit
Current transfers: debit	-205	-183	-176	-174	-211	-222	-254	Transferts courants : débit
Capital account, n.i.e.	0	0	0	0	0	254	249	Compte de capital, n.i.a.
Financial account, n.i.e.	1 707	383	-16	118	1 636	1 344	2 065	Compte financier, n.i.a.
Net errors and omissions	-452	-139	-1 568	-981	-456	-147	374	Erreurs et omissions nettes
Reserves and related items	-515	554	548	-178	-707	-164	-620	Réserves et postes apparentés
Ecuador								**Equateur**
Current account	-654	-1 272	-422	-542	347	1 615	1 598	Compte des transac. courantes
Goods: exports f.o.b.	4 821	5 258	6 446	7 968	10 468	13 188	14 864	Biens : exportations f.à.b.
Goods: imports f.o.b.	-5 178	-6 160	-6 366	-7 684	-9 709	-11 423	-13 067	Biens : importations f.à.b.
Services: credit	862	884	881	1 014	1 012	1 037	1 175	Services : crédit
Services: debit	-1 434	-1 600	-1 624	-1 968	-2 142	-2 341	-2 572	Services : débit
Income: credit	48	30	27	37	86	165	259	Revenus : crédit
Income: debit	-1 412	-1 335	-1 555	-1 940	-2 029	-2 114	-2 306	Revenus : débit
Current transfers: credit	1 686	1 710	1 791	2 049	2 781	3 234	3 395	Transferts courants : crédit
Current transfers: debit	-47	-58	-22	-18	-120	-130	-149	Transferts courants : débit
Capital account, n.i.e.	15	16	8	8	13	19	22	Compte de capital, n.i.a.
Financial account, n.i.e.	626	1 193	322	244	-515	-2 050	-257	Compte financier, n.i.a.
Net errors and omissions	-301	-157	163	681	424	342	45	Erreurs et omissions nettes
Reserves and related items	313	221	-70	-391	-269	74	-1 407	Réserves et postes apparentés
Egypt								**Egypte**
Current account	-388	622	3 743	3 922	2 103	2 635	412	Compte des transac. courantes
Goods: exports f.o.b.	7 025	7 118	8 987	12 320	16 073	20 546	24 455	Biens : exportations f.à.b.
Goods: imports f.o.b.	-13 960	-12 879	-13 189	-18 895	-23 818	-28 984	-39 354	Biens : importations f.à.b.
Services: credit	9 042	9 320	11 073	14 197	14 643	16 135	19 943	Services : crédit
Services: debit	-7 037	-6 629	-6 474	-8 020	-10 508	-11 569	-14 342	Services : débit
Income: credit	1 468	698	578	572	1 425	2 560	3 309	Revenus : crédit
Income: debit	-885	-965	-832	-818	-1 460	-1 822	-1 921	Revenus : débit
Current transfers: credit	4 056	4 002	3 708	4 615	5 831	5 933	8 562	Transferts courants : crédit
Current transfers: debit	-98	-42	-109	-48	-82	-163	-240	Transferts courants : débit
Capital account, n.i.e.	...	0	...	...	-40	-36	2	Compte de capital, n.i.a.
Financial account, n.i.e.	190	-3 333	-5 725	-4 461	5 591	-297	3 023	Compte financier, n.i.a.
Net errors and omissions	-1 146	1 906	1 575	-45	-2 427	634	251	Erreurs et omissions nettes
Reserves and related items	1 345	804	407	584	-5 226	-2 937	-3 687	Réserves et postes apparentés
El Salvador								**El Salvador**
Current account	-150	-405	-702	-628	-569	-677	-1 119	Compte des transac. courantes
Goods: exports f.o.b.	2 892	3 020	3 153	3 339	3 447	3 758	4 035	Biens : exportations f.à.b.
Goods: imports f.o.b.	-4 824	-4 885	-5 439	-6 000	-6 385	-7 300	-8 108	Biens : importations f.à.b.
Services: credit	704	783	949	1 090	1 128	1 426	1 492	Services : crédit
Services: debit	-954	-1 023	-1 056	-1 154	-1 214	-1 505	-1 734	Services : débit
Income: credit	169	159	140	144	175	234	286	Revenus : crédit
Income: debit	-435	-483	-563	-602	-754	-762	-865	Revenus : débit
Current transfers: credit	2 374	2 111	2 200	2 615	3 106	3 549	3 835	Transferts courants : crédit
Current transfers: debit	-75	-88	-86	-60	-71	-77	-60	Transferts courants : débit
Capital account, n.i.e.	199	209	113	100	94	106	150	Compte de capital, n.i.a.
Financial account, n.i.e.	230	688	1 050	123	777	1 032	600	Compte financier, n.i.a.
Net errors and omissions	-457	-615	-144	352	-361	-389	649	Erreurs et omissions nettes
Reserves and related items	178	124	-316	53	59	-72	-280	Réserves et postes apparentés
Estonia								**Estonie**
Current account	-325	-779	-1 115	-1 413	-1 382	-2 759	-3 772	Compte des transac. courantes
Goods: exports f.o.b.	3 367	3 508	4 597	5 887	7 792	9 755	11 078	Biens : exportations f.à.b.
Goods: imports f.o.b.	-4 142	-4 626	-6 164	-7 877	-9 704	-12 777	-14 756	Biens : importations f.à.b.
Services: credit	1 607	1 706	2 224	2 848	3 187	3 512	4 394	Services : crédit
Services: debit	-963	-1 106	-1 393	-1 747	-2 150	-2 440	-3 072	Services : débit
Income: credit	173	205	249	436	731	1 091	1 518	Revenus : crédit
Income: debit	-454	-530	-785	-1 074	-1 300	-1 956	-3 092	Revenus : débit
Current transfers: credit	115	126	266	417	466	524	707	Transferts courants : crédit
Current transfers: debit	-29	-61	-110	-303	-404	-466	-548	Transferts courants : débit
Capital account, n.i.e.	14	38	50	86	103	352	240	Compte de capital, n.i.a.
Financial account, n.i.e.	269	752	1 275	1 616	1 574	2 982	3 490	Compte financier, n.i.a.
Net errors and omissions	-1	59	-39	-18	90	45	150	Erreurs et omissions nettes
Reserves and related items	42	-69	-169	-271	-386	-620	-109	Réserves et postes apparentés

69

Summary of balance of payments *(continued)*
Millions of US dollars
Résumé de la balance des paiements *(suite)*
Millions de dollars des E.-U.

Country or area	2001	2002	2003	2004	2005	2006	2007	Pays ou zone
Ethiopia								**Ethiopie**
Current account	-373	-137	-136	-668	-1 568	-1 786	-828	Compte des transac. courantes
Goods: exports f.o.b.	456	480	496	678	917	1 025	1 285	Biens : exportations f.à.b.
Goods: imports f.o.b.	-1 626	-1 455	-1 895	-2 768	-3 701	-4 106	-5 155	Biens : importations f.à.b.
Services: credit	523	585	762	1 005	1 012	1 174	1 368	Services : crédit
Services: debit	-524	-580	-709	-958	-1 194	-1 171	-1 752	Services : débit
Income: credit	16	14	19	32	43	56	76	Revenus : crédit
Income: debit	-48	-37	-43	-60	-48	-38	-37	Revenus : débit
Current transfers: credit	854	876	1 267	1 421	1 426	1 297	3 415	Transferts courants : crédit
Current transfers: debit	-24	-21	-33	-17	-24	-23	-28	Transferts courants : débit
Capital account, n.i.e.	...	...	0	0	0	0	0	Compte de capital, n.i.a.
Financial account, n.i.e.	-178	-83	247	73	759	976	448	Compte financier, n.i.a.
Net errors and omissions	-229	-915	-390	-354	486	1 161	-157	Erreurs et omissions nettes
Reserves and related items	781	1 134	280	949	323	-352	537	Réserves et postes apparentés
Euro Area								**Zone euro**
Current account	-19 744	54 783	38 776	79 763	22 534	1 548	38 556	Compte des transac. courantes
Goods: exports f.o.b.	920 862	998 201	1 172 750	1 406 250	1 527 090	1 759 890	2 073 030	Biens : exportations f.à.b.
Goods: imports f.o.b.	-855 641	-876 731	-1 053 440	-1 276 970	-1 460 100	-1 726 950	-1 989 900	Biens : importations f.à.b.
Services: credit	287 120	316 488	378 515	452 270	500 040	545 193	670 470	Services : crédit
Services: debit	-290 550	-299 880	-353 270	-416 897	-460 035	-497 780	-606 538	Services : débit
Income: credit	244 241	232 381	275 923	362 745	470 108	607 850	763 685	Revenus : crédit
Income: debit	-279 959	-269 598	-317 875	-373 615	-463 320	-589 072	-757 141	Revenus : débit
Current transfers: credit	71 185	81 081	93 237	101 777	104 836	108 626	120 358	Transferts courants : crédit
Current transfers: debit	-117 001	-127 158	-157 059	-175 801	-196 083	-206 203	-235 416	Transferts courants : débit
Capital account, n.i.e.	5 619	9 697	14 315	20 558	13 864	11 714	19 076	Compte de capital, n.i.a.
Financial account, n.i.e.	-41 164	-16 938	-49 002	-38 967	-14 408	129 852	118 430	Compte financier, n.i.a.
Net errors and omissions	38 840	-44 566	-36 891	-76 913	-44 902	-140 553	-170 106	Erreurs et omissions nettes
Reserves and related items	16 449	-2 977	32 802	15 560	22 912	-2 562	-5 956	Réserves et postes apparentés
Faeroe Islands								**Iles Féroé**
Current account	146	126	-7	...	...	...	...	Compte des transac. courantes
Goods: exports f.o.b.	516	537	594	...	...	...	...	Biens : exportations f.à.b.
Goods: imports f.o.b.	-479	-472	-684	...	...	...	...	Biens : importations f.à.b.
Services: credit	57	71	78	...	...	...	...	Services : crédit
Services: debit	-105	-132	-147	...	...	...	...	Services : débit
Income: credit	91	92	106	...	...	...	...	Revenus : crédit
Income: debit	-76	-73	-76	...	...	...	...	Revenus : débit
Current transfers: credit	147	109	128	...	...	...	...	Transferts courants : crédit
Current transfers: debit	-4	-7	-6	...	...	...	...	Transferts courants : débit
Fiji								**Fidji**
Current account	-113	-21	-96	-372	-399	-719	...	Compte des transac. courantes
Goods: exports f.o.b.	507	484	679	653	698	711	...	Biens : exportations f.à.b.
Goods: imports f.o.b.	-777	-800	-1 064	-1 286	-1 462	-1 640	...	Biens : importations f.à.b.
Services: credit	404	502	614	688	810	774	...	Services : crédit
Services: debit	-297	-290	-397	-486	-525	-542	...	Services : débit
Income: credit	67	72	92	145	80	65	...	Revenus : crédit
Income: debit	-84	-68	-103	-156	-126	-186	...	Revenus : débit
Current transfers: credit	122	133	164	165	229	211	...	Transferts courants : crédit
Current transfers: debit	-55	-55	-81	-96	-102	-111	...	Transferts courants : débit
Capital account, n.i.e.	-10	-10	-6	-12	-18	-17	...	Compte de capital, n.i.a.
Financial account, n.i.e.	44	98	36	236	107	417	...	Compte financier, n.i.a.
Net errors and omissions	94	-96	2	230	159	171	...	Erreurs et omissions nettes
Reserves and related items	-15	29	64	-82	150	148	...	Réserves et postes apparentés
Finland								**Finlande**
Current account	12 077	12 078	8 534	12 542	6 993	9 436	10 121	Compte des transac. courantes
Goods: exports f.o.b.	42 980	44 863	52 740	61 139	65 451	77 552	90 196	Biens : exportations f.à.b.
Goods: imports f.o.b.	-30 321	-32 022	-39 790	-48 369	-55 887	-66 046	-78 216	Biens : importations f.à.b.
Services: credit	9 205	10 441	11 470	15 168	17 010	17 520	23 189	Services : crédit
Services: debit	-8 105	-9 870	-12 149	-14 563	-17 732	-18 641	-22 118	Services : débit
Income: credit	8 568	8 607	9 349	13 129	14 406	18 304	23 082	Revenus : crédit
Income: debit	-9 573	-9 210	-11 980	-12 884	-14 754	-17 576	-24 116	Revenus : débit
Current transfers: credit	1 562	1 621	1 911	2 040	1 953	1 951	2 225	Transferts courants : crédit
Current transfers: debit	-2 239	-2 353	-3 016	-3 118	-3 453	-3 628	-4 119	Transferts courants : débit
Capital account, n.i.e.	83	125	149	188	336	223	236	Compte de capital, n.i.a.

Summary of balance of payments *(continued)*
Millions of US dollars
Résumé de la balance des paiements *(suite)*
Millions de dollars des E.-U.

Country or area	2001	2002	2003	2004	2005	2006	2007	Pays ou zone
Financial account, n.i.e.	-10 942	-7 312	-9 217	-9 475	-3 610	-15 480	-7 158	Compte financier, n.i.a.
Net errors and omissions	-808	-5 005	26	-2 441	-3 898	1 500	-2 879	Erreurs et omissions nettes
Reserves and related items	-410	115	508	-814	180	4 321	-320	Réserves et postes apparentés
France								**France**
Current account	26 191	19 703	14 757	12 361	-13 565	-15 452	-31 249	Compte des transac. courantes
Goods: exports f.o.b.	294 181	307 201	361 930	421 106	439 452	484 768	546 039	Biens : exportations f.à.b.
Goods: imports f.o.b.	-290 666	-299 576	-358 499	-425 953	-467 293	-521 698	-600 923	Biens : importations f.à.b.
Services: credit	80 125	86 160	98 814	114 629	122 209	126 287	145 736	Services : crédit
Services: debit	-62 372	-68 960	-82 898	-98 371	-105 692	-113 734	-130 749	Services : débit
Income: credit	75 927	66 875	89 357	119 722	149 023	195 417	252 730	Revenus : crédit
Income: debit	-56 357	-57 507	-74 489	-97 080	-124 180	-159 139	-213 425	Revenus : débit
Current transfers: credit	17 180	19 767	24 050	25 443	25 406	26 894	28 076	Transferts courants : crédit
Current transfers: debit	-31 826	-34 257	-43 508	-47 135	-52 490	-54 248	-58 734	Transferts courants : débit
Capital account, n.i.e.	-333	-215	-8 260	1 810	662	-272	2 470	Compte de capital, n.i.a.
Financial account, n.i.e.	-33 089	-20 294	13 531	-6 273	-9 444	96 371	27 405	Compte financier, n.i.a.
Net errors and omissions	1 660	-3 164	-18 737	-3 790	13 299	-68 863	1 047	Erreurs et omissions nettes
Reserves and related items	5 570	3 970	-1 291	-4 108	9 047	-11 783	327	Réserves et postes apparentés
Gabon								**Gabon**
Current account	517	000	766	924	1 983	...	...	Compte des transac. courantes
Goods: exports f.o.b.	2 614	2 556	3 178	4 072	5 464	...	...	Biens : exportations f.à.b.
Goods: imports f.o.b.	-847	-935	-1 043	-1 216	-1 359	...	...	Biens : importations f.à.b.
Services: credit	168	86	172	156	146	...	...	Services : crédit
Services: debit	-710	-759	-840	-939	-1 042	...	...	Services : débit
Income: credit	30	18	48	13	36	...	...	Revenus : crédit
Income: debit	-659	-496	-570	-978	-994	...	...	Revenus : débit
Current transfers: credit	34	5	7	10	18	...	...	Transferts courants : crédit
Current transfers: debit	-113	-136	-188	-194	-287	...	...	Transferts courants : débit
Capital account, n.i.e.	3	3	43	0	0	...	...	Compte de capital, n.i.a.
Financial account, n.i.e.	-674	-437	-650	-499	-1 342	...	...	Compte financier, n.i.a.
Net errors and omissions	-104	-125	-260	-357	-415	...	...	Erreurs et omissions nettes
Reserves and related items	258	222	101	-68	-226	...	...	Réserves et postes apparentés
Gambia								**Gambie**
Current account	...	...	-2	-44	-50	-72	-59	Compte des transac. courantes
Goods: exports f.o.b.	...	...	78	109	101	109	118	Biens : exportations f.à.b.
Goods: imports f.o.b.	...	...	-156	-207	-215	-222	-245	Biens : importations f.à.b.
Services: credit	...	...	84	73	80	92	114	Services : crédit
Services: debit	...	...	-36	-46	-45	-94	-77	Services : débit
Income: credit	...	...	5	2	3	4	8	Revenus : crédit
Income: debit	...	...	-32	-30	-35	-42	-48	Revenus : débit
Current transfers: credit	...	...	89	78	88	107	90	Transferts courants : crédit
Current transfers: debit	...	...	-33	-24	-26	-27	-19	Transferts courants : débit
Capital account, n.i.e.	...	...	5	5	1	0	^0	Compte de capital, n.i.a.
Financial account, n.i.e.	...	...	-10	47	68	78	78	Compte financier, n.i.a.
Net errors and omissions	...	...	3	-9	-54	-6	-29	Erreurs et omissions nettes
Reserves and related items	...	...	5	1	36	^0	9	Réserves et postes apparentés
Georgia								**Géorgie**
Current account	-212	-239	-391	-430	-772	-1 255	-2 118	Compte des transac. courantes
Goods: exports f.o.b.	496	603	831	1 092	1 472	1 667	2 088	Biens : exportations f.à.b.
Goods: imports f.o.b.	-1 046	-1 092	-1 469	-2 008	-2 687	-3 686	-4 984	Biens : importations f.à.b.
Services: credit	314	408	458	555	715	885	1 094	Services : crédit
Services: debit	-237	-363	-397	-485	-632	-727	-933	Services : débit
Income: credit	98	161	177	252	263	341	482	Revenus : crédit
Income: debit	-65	-149	-164	-173	-201	-178	-442	Revenus : débit
Current transfers: credit	246	222	208	389	351	506	656	Transferts courants : crédit
Current transfers: debit	-18	-29	-36	-51	-54	-63	-80	Transferts courants : débit
Capital account, n.i.e.	-5	18	20	41	59	169	128	Compte de capital, n.i.a.
Financial account, n.i.e.	210	14	313	446	666	1 348	2 197	Compte financier, n.i.a.
Net errors and omissions	35	16	-6	11	28	68	-11	Erreurs et omissions nettes
Reserves and related items	-28	191	64	-68	19	-330	-195	Réserves et postes apparentés
Germany								**Allemagne**
Current account	2 998	42 967	47 449	128 073	145 202	178 332	252 929	Compte des transac. courantes
Goods: exports f.o.b.	565 870	611 843	747 369	907 794	983 068	1 135 730	1 354 120	Biens : exportations f.à.b.
Goods: imports f.o.b.	-478 455	-486 088	-602 624	-721 727	-788 727	-934 861	-1 075 430	Biens : importations f.à.b.
Services: credit	87 775	102 217	123 661	146 321	163 515	188 218	217 133	Services : crédit

69

Summary of balance of payments *(continued)*
Millions of US dollars
Résumé de la balance des paiements *(suite)*
Millions de dollars des E.-U.

Country or area	2001	2002	2003	2004	2005	2006	2007	Pays ou zone
Services: debit	-138 462	-141 973	-172 836	-195 534	-208 335	-224 589	-259 012	Services : débit
Income: credit	91 209	97 983	118 531	170 228	199 652	245 550	318 012	Revenus : crédit
Income: debit	-100 956	-115 005	-135 518	-144 627	-167 882	-198 210	-260 118	Revenus : débit
Current transfers: credit	14 306	14 696	18 004	19 036	20 613	24 466	25 435	Transferts courants : crédit
Current transfers: debit	-38 288	-40 707	-49 139	-53 418	-56 701	-57 967	-67 206	Transferts courants : débit
Capital account, n.i.e.	-327	-225	353	521	-1 665	-238	237	Compte de capital, n.i.a.
Financial account, n.i.e.	-16 122	-40 749	-71 612	-152 990	-165 904	-192 585	-323 022	Compte financier, n.i.a.
Net errors and omissions	7 985	-3 971	23 127	22 588	19 767	10 839	71 090	Erreurs et omissions nettes
Reserves and related items	5 466	1 979	684	1 807	2 601	3 652	-1 234	Réserves et postes apparentés
Ghana								**Ghana**
Current account	-325	-32	278	-567	-1 105	-1 043	-2 151	Compte des transac. courantes
Goods: exports f.o.b.	1 867	2 015	2 562	2 704	2 802	3 727	4 172	Biens : exportations f.à.b.
Goods: imports f.o.b.	-2 969	-2 707	-3 233	-4 297	-5 347	-6 754	-8 066	Biens : importations f.à.b.
Services: credit	532	555	630	702	1 106	1 396	1 832	Services : crédit
Services: debit	-606	-621	-900	-1 058	-1 273	-1 533	-1 994	Services : débit
Income: credit	16	15	21	45	43	73	84	Revenus : crédit
Income: debit	-124	-189	-202	-242	-230	-201	-223	Revenus : débit
Current transfers: credit	978	912	1 408	1 580	1 794	2 248	2 043	Transferts courants : crédit
Current transfers: debit	-19	-12	-9	0	0	0	0	Transferts courants : débit
Capital account, n.i.e.	0	0	0	251	331	230	188	Compte de capital, n.i.a.
Financial account, n.i.e.	392	-21	340	202	834	1 255	2 430	Compte financier, n.i.a.
Net errors and omissions	-189	39	-115	115	65	78	-52	Erreurs et omissions nettes
Reserves and related items	121	14	-504	-1	-126	-520	-414	Réserves et postes apparentés
Greece								**Grèce**
Current account	-9 400	-9 582	-12 804	-13 476	-18 233	-29 565	-44 587	Compte des transac. courantes
Goods: exports f.o.b.	10 615	9 865	12 578	15 739	17 631	20 300	23 991	Biens : exportations f.à.b.
Goods: imports f.o.b.	-29 702	-31 321	-38 184	-47 360	-51 900	-64 585	-81 041	Biens : importations f.à.b.
Services: credit	19 456	20 142	24 283	33 085	33 914	35 762	43 080	Services : crédit
Services: debit	-11 589	-9 819	-11 250	-14 020	-14 742	-16 367	-20 270	Services : débit
Income: credit	1 885	1 532	2 911	3 495	4 072	4 566	6 345	Revenus : crédit
Income: debit	-3 652	-3 488	-7 414	-8 920	-11 102	-13 524	-18 814	Revenus : débit
Current transfers: credit	4 592	5 536	7 202	7 901	8 615	8 587	9 053	Transferts courants : crédit
Current transfers: debit	-1 005	-2 029	-2 930	-3 396	-4 722	-4 305	-6 931	Transferts courants : débit
Capital account, n.i.e.	2 153	1 530	1 411	2 990	2 563	3 822	5 957	Compte de capital, n.i.a.
Financial account, n.i.e.	537	11 578	6 417	6 836	15 633	25 661	38 027	Compte financier, n.i.a.
Net errors and omissions	1 011	-1 663	253	373	-67	361	1 060	Erreurs et omissions nettes
Reserves and related items	5 699	-1 863	4 723	3 277	104	-279	-457	Réserves et postes apparentés
Grenada								**Grenade**
Current account	-103	-126	-146	-55	-186	-193	-222	Compte des transac. courantes
Goods: exports f.o.b.	64	41	46	38	33	31	48	Biens : exportations f.à.b.
Goods: imports f.o.b.	-197	-181	-228	-222	-294	-263	-316	Biens : importations f.à.b.
Services: credit	134	131	134	157	116	130	147	Services : crédit
Services: debit	-83	-91	-83	-92	-95	-99	-108	Services : débit
Income: credit	4	4	4	6	11	13	13	Revenus : crédit
Income: debit	-45	-52	-54	-62	-40	-42	-44	Revenus : débit
Current transfers: credit	31	32	48	126	88	49	50	Transferts courants : crédit
Current transfers: debit	-9	-10	-12	-5	-5	-13	-13	Transferts courants : débit
Capital account, n.i.e.	43	32	43	40	47	62	31	Compte de capital, n.i.a.
Financial account, n.i.e.	47	100	96	27	132	132	194	Compte financier, n.i.a.
Net errors and omissions	19	24	-10	30	-20	4	10	Erreurs et omissions nettes
Reserves and related items	-6	-31	17	-42	27	-5	-13	Réserves et postes apparentés
Guatemala								**Guatemala**
Current account	-1 253	-1 235	-1 039	-1 236	-1 300	-1 573	-1 754	Compte des transac. courantes
Goods: exports f.o.b.	2 860	2 819	3 060	5 105	5 459	6 082	7 012	Biens : exportations f.à.b.
Goods: imports f.o.b.	-5 142	-5 791	-6 176	-8 737	-9 650	-10 934	-12 482	Biens : importations f.à.b.
Services: credit	1 045	1 145	1 059	1 100	1 308	1 519	1 709	Services : crédit
Services: debit	-928	-1 066	-1 126	-1 344	-1 450	-1 785	-2 029	Services : débit
Income: credit	317	161	179	220	302	453	551	Revenus : crédit
Income: debit	-402	-479	-497	-630	-786	-1 115	-1 321	Revenus : débit
Current transfers: credit	1 024	2 078	2 559	3 086	3 555	4 244	4 817	Transferts courants : crédit
Current transfers: debit	-28	-101	-97	-35	-38	-37	-11	Transferts courants : débit
Capital account, n.i.e.	93	124	134	0	0	142	0	Compte de capital, n.i.a.
Financial account, n.i.e.	1 547	1 197	1 516	878	748	1 190	1 629	Compte financier, n.i.a.

69

Summary of balance of payments *(continued)*
Millions of US dollars
Résumé de la balance des paiements *(suite)*
Millions de dollars des E.-U.

Country or area	2001	2002	2003	2004	2005	2006	2007	Pays ou zone
Net errors and omissions	87	-65	-61	891	731	431	283	Erreurs et omissions nettes
Reserves and related items	-474	-21	-550	-533	-178	-190	-157	Réserves et postes apparentés
Guinea								**Guinée**
Current account	-102	-200	-188	-175	...	...	-463	Compte des transac. courantes
Goods: exports f.o.b.	731	709	609	726	...	...	1 203	Biens : exportations f.à.b.
Goods: imports f.o.b.	-562	-669	-644	-688	...	...	-1 218	Biens : importations f.à.b.
Services: credit	103	90	134	85	...	...	49	Services : crédit
Services: debit	-319	-331	-307	-275	...	...	-296	Services : débit
Income: credit	11	6	13	10	...	...	61	Revenus : crédit
Income: debit	-114	-52	-124	-37	...	...	-124	Revenus : débit
Current transfers: credit	92	71	195	55	...	...	35	Transferts courants : crédit
Current transfers: debit	-44	-25	-62	-50	...	...	-174	Transferts courants : débit
Capital account, n.i.e.	0	92	58	-30	...	...	90	Compte de capital, n.i.a.
Financial account, n.i.e.	-12	-115	59	78	...	...	444	Compte financier, n.i.a.
Net errors and omissions	-2	143	-157	69	...	...	117	Erreurs et omissions nettes
Reserves and related items	117	80	229	59	...	...	-188	Réserves et postes apparentés
Guinea-Bissau								**Guinée-Bissau**
Current account	-27	-9	-7	-13	...	...	...	Compte des transac. courantes
Goods: exports f.o.b.	63	54	65	76	...	...	...	Biens : exportations f.à.b.
Goods: imports f.o.b.	-62	-59	-65	-83	...	...	...	Biens : importations f.à.b.
Services: credit	4	6	6	8	...	...	...	Services : crédit
Services: debit	-30	-27	-36	-44	...	...	...	Services : débit
Income: credit	1	1	2	1	...	...	...	Revenus : crédit
Income: debit	-13	-10	-11	-11	...	...	...	Revenus : débit
Current transfers: credit	10	30	40	47	...	...	...	Transferts courants : crédit
Current transfers: debit	^0	-5	-7	-7	...	...	...	Transferts courants : débit
Capital account, n.i.e.	25	39	43	27	...	...	...	Compte de capital, n.i.a.
Financial account, n.i.e.	-17	-21	-13	1	...	...	...	Compte financier, n.i.a.
Net errors and omissions	6	-3	6	-4	...	...	...	Erreurs et omissions nettes
Reserves and related items	13	-6	-29	-11	...	...	...	Réserves et postes apparentés
Guyana								**Guyana**
Current account	-91	-62	-45	-20	-96	-181	-166	Compte des transac. courantes
Goods: exports f.o.b.	485	490	508	584	546	580	675	Biens : exportations f.à.b.
Goods: imports f.o.b.	-541	-514	-525	-592	-717	-810	-983	Biens : importations f.à.b.
Services: credit	172	172	157	161	148	148	173	Services : crédit
Services: debit	-192	-196	-172	-208	-201	-245	-273	Services : débit
Income: credit	10	8	5	4	3	3	3	Revenus : crédit
Income: debit	-69	-63	-60	-43	-42	-72	-48	Revenus : débit
Current transfers: credit	98	129	127	194	262	311	424	Transferts courants : crédit
Current transfers: debit	-54	-89	-84	-120	-95	-95	-137	Transferts courants : débit
Capital account, n.i.e.	32	31	44	46	52	351	427	Compte de capital, n.i.a.
Financial account, n.i.e.	84	54	35	39	127	-52	-227	Compte financier, n.i.a.
Net errors and omissions	-45	-1	-20	-43	-68	-84	-37	Erreurs et omissions nettes
Reserves and related items	19	-22	-14	-21	-14	-33	3	Réserves et postes apparentés
Haiti								**Haïti**
Current account	-132	-189	-182	-156	-358	-447	-460	Compte des transac. courantes
Goods: exports f.o.b.	305	274	334	377	455	492	522	Biens : exportations f.à.b.
Goods: imports f.o.b.	-1 055	-980	-1 116	-1 210	-1 309	-1 548	-1 618	Biens : importations f.à.b.
Services: credit	139	147	136	142	145	203	207	Services : crédit
Services: debit	-260	-270	-301	-345	-542	-588	-703	Services : débit
Income: credit	0	0	0	0	2	19	25	Revenus : crédit
Income: debit	-9	-14	-14	-12	-37	-12	-18	Revenus : débit
Current transfers: credit	769	676	811	932	986	1 063	1 222	Transferts courants : crédit
Current transfers: debit	-19	-22	-31	-39	-60	-76	-96	Transferts courants : débit
Capital account, n.i.e.	0	0	0	0	0	0	0	Compte de capital, n.i.a.
Financial account, n.i.e.	82	-33	-60	22	-22	140	112	Compte financier, n.i.a.
Net errors and omissions	44	41	102	73	49	26	182	Erreurs et omissions nettes
Reserves and related items	5	181	140	60	331	280	166	Réserves et postes apparentés
Honduras								**Honduras**
Current account	-479	-282	-553	-683	-304	-510	-1 225	Compte des transac. courantes
Goods: exports f.o.b.	3 423	3 745	3 754	4 534	5 048	5 195	5 594	Biens : exportations f.à.b.
Goods: imports f.o.b.	-4 152	-4 382	-4 774	-5 827	-6 545	-7 317	-8 556	Biens : importations f.à.b.
Services: credit	505	542	591	645	700	686	750	Services : crédit
Services: debit	-711	-732	-753	-849	-929	-984	-1 037	Services : débit

69

Summary of balance of payments *(continued)*
Millions of US dollars

Résumé de la balance des paiements *(suite)*
Millions de dollars des E.-U.

Country or area	2001	2002	2003	2004	2005	2006	2007	Pays ou zone
Income: credit	123	85	68	87	145	198	224	Revenus : crédit
Income: debit	-381	-386	-430	-539	-619	-739	-822	Revenus : débit
Current transfers: credit	840	983	1 092	1 374	2 042	2 589	2 774	Transferts courants : crédit
Current transfers: debit	-125	-137	-101	-109	-147	-138	-152	Transferts courants : débit
Capital account, n.i.e.	160	85	49	51	594	1 485	1 158	Compte de capital, n.i.a.
Financial account, n.i.e.	288	170	304	991	55	-408	-4	Compte financier, n.i.a.
Net errors and omissions	-43	22	5	47	-188	-186	-53	Erreurs et omissions nettes
Reserves and related items	73	5	194	-405	-156	-380	124	Réserves et postes apparentés
Hungary								**Hongrie**
Current account	-3 205	-4 693	-6 721	-8 716	-8 261	-8 610	-8 635	Compte des transac. courantes
Goods: exports f.o.b.	31 081	34 792	42 943	55 431	61 688	73 457	93 855	Biens : exportations f.à.b.
Goods: imports f.o.b.	-33 318	-36 911	-46 221	-58 898	-64 416	-76 029	-93 403	Biens : importations f.à.b.
Services: credit	7 029	7 417	9 211	10 769	12 857	13 390	17 099	Services : crédit
Services: debit	-5 550	-6 849	-9 150	-10 178	-11 448	-11 798	-15 662	Services : débit
Income: credit	1 302	1 236	1 371	3 267	3 521	7 957	11 531	Revenus : crédit
Income: debit	-4 152	-4 870	-5 541	-8 633	-9 767	-15 043	-21 387	Revenus : débit
Current transfers: credit	781	1 070	1 283	1 689	2 608	3 169	4 102	Transferts courants : crédit
Current transfers: debit	-377	-579	-616	-2 164	-3 305	-3 712	-4 770	Transferts courants : débit
Capital account, n.i.e.	317	191	-27	328	885	604	1 586	Compte de capital, n.i.a.
Financial account, n.i.e.	2 775	2 565	6 858	11 905	14 301	12 095	9 791	Compte financier, n.i.a.
Net errors and omissions	29	145	226	-1 535	-2 021	-2 986	-2 589	Erreurs et omissions nettes
Reserves and related items	84	1 792	-336	-1 981	-4 904	-1 102	-154	Réserves et postes apparentés
Iceland								**Islande**
Current account	-336	145	-534	-1 317	-2 645	-4 234	-3 179	Compte des transac. courantes
Goods: exports f.o.b.	2 016	2 240	2 386	2 896	3 107	3 477	4 792	Biens : exportations f.à.b.
Goods: imports f.o.b.	-2 091	-2 090	-2 596	-3 415	-4 590	-5 716	-6 181	Biens : importations f.à.b.
Services: credit	1 086	1 118	1 378	1 623	2 041	1 834	2 251	Services : crédit
Services: debit	-1 074	-1 123	-1 503	-1 838	-2 560	-2 553	-2 949	Services : débit
Income: credit	171	305	376	470	1 456	2 587	5 006	Revenus : crédit
Income: debit	-435	-318	-559	-1 035	-2 072	-3 827	-6 050	Revenus : débit
Current transfers: credit	8	36	12	10	11	8	16	Transferts courants : crédit
Current transfers: debit	-17	-22	-28	-27	-38	-42	-66	Transferts courants : débit
Capital account, n.i.e.	4	-1	-5	-3	-27	-26	-30	Compte de capital, n.i.a.
Financial account, n.i.e.	172	-64	444	1 925	2 354	7 417	3 087	Compte financier, n.i.a.
Net errors and omissions	111	-19	401	-404	389	-1 906	230	Erreurs et omissions nettes
Reserves and related items	48	-61	-307	-202	-71	-1 252	-108	Réserves et postes apparentés
India								**Inde**
Current account	1 410	7 060	8 773	780	-7 835	-9 415	...	Compte des transac. courantes
Goods: exports f.o.b.	44 793	51 141	60 893	77 939	102 176	123 617	...	Biens : exportations f.à.b.
Goods: imports f.o.b.	-51 212	-54 702	-68 081	-95 539	-134 702	-166 695	...	Biens : importations f.à.b.
Services: credit	17 337	19 478	23 902	38 281	55 831	75 354	...	Services : crédit
Services: debit	-20 099	-21 039	-24 878	-35 641	-47 989	-63 537	...	Services : débit
Income: credit	3 524	3 188	3 491	4 690	5 082	7 795	...	Revenus : crédit
Income: debit	-7 666	-7 097	-8 386	-8 742	-11 475	-12 059	...	Revenus : débit
Current transfers: credit	15 140	16 789	22 401	20 615	24 120	27 449	...	Transferts courants : crédit
Current transfers: debit	-407	-698	-570	-822	-877	-1 340	...	Transferts courants : débit
Capital account, n.i.e.	0	0	0	0	0	0	...	Compte de capital, n.i.a.
Financial account, n.i.e.	7 995	11 985	16 421	22 229	21 622	37 776	...	Compte financier, n.i.a.
Net errors and omissions	-715	-190	471	637	769	-4 623	...	Erreurs et omissions nettes
Reserves and related items	-8 690	-18 854	-25 665	-23 646	-14 555	-23 737	...	Réserves et postes apparentés
Indonesia								**Indonésie**
Current account	6 901	7 824	8 107	1 563	278	10 859	10 492	Compte des transac. courantes
Goods: exports f.o.b.	57 365	59 165	64 109	70 767	86 995	103 528	118 014	Biens : exportations f.à.b.
Goods: imports f.o.b.	-34 669	-35 652	-39 546	-50 615	-69 462	-73 868	-85 260	Biens : importations f.à.b.
Services: credit	5 500	6 663	5 293	12 045	12 927	11 520	12 487	Services : crédit
Services: debit	-15 880	-17 045	-17 400	-20 856	-22 049	-21 392	-24 328	Services : débit
Income: credit	2 004	1 318	1 054	1 995	2 338	2 585	3 469	Revenus : crédit
Income: debit	-8 940	-8 365	-7 272	-12 912	-15 264	-16 377	-18 994	Revenus : débit
Current transfers: credit	1 520	2 210	2 053	2 433	5 993	6 079	6 801	Transferts courants : crédit
Current transfers: debit	0	-470	-184	-1 294	-1 200	-1 216	-1 697	Transferts courants : débit
Capital account, n.i.e.	0	0	0	0	334	350	546	Compte de capital, n.i.a.
Financial account, n.i.e.	-7 617	-1 103	-949	-667	-2 587	2 738	3 045	Compte financier, n.i.a.
Net errors and omissions	701	-1 763	-3 510	-3 094	-136	1 010	-1 377	Erreurs et omissions nettes
Reserves and related items	15	-4 958	-3 647	2 198	2 111	-14 958	-12 706	Réserves et postes apparentés

69

Summary of balance of payments *(continued)*
Millions of US dollars
Résumé de la balance des paiements *(suite)*
Millions de dollars des E.-U.

Country or area	2001	2002	2003	2004	2005	2006	2007	Pays ou zone
Iraq								**Iraq**
Current account	...	...	...	...	-7 513	1 252	...	Compte des transac. courantes
Goods: exports f.o.b.	...	...	...	...	23 697	30 529	...	Biens : exportations f.à.b.
Goods: imports f.o.b.	...	...	...	...	-20 002	-18 708	...	Biens : importations f.à.b.
Services: credit	...	...	...	...	355	357	...	Services : crédit
Services: debit	...	...	...	...	-6 095	-5 490	...	Services : débit
Income: credit	...	...	...	...	680	1 206	...	Revenus : crédit
Income: debit	...	...	...	...	-5 207	-4 751	...	Revenus : débit
Current transfers: credit	...	...	...	...	552	261	...	Transferts courants : crédit
Current transfers: debit	...	...	...	...	-1 493	-2 153	...	Transferts courants : débit
Capital account, n.i.e.	...	...	...	...	3 889	2 769	...	Compte de capital, n.i.a.
Financial account, n.i.e.	...	...	...	...	-1 350	-2 600	...	Compte financier, n.i.a.
Net errors and omissions	...	...	...	...	451	112	...	Erreurs et omissions nettes
Reserves and related items	...	...	...	...	4 523	-1 533	...	Réserves et postes apparentés
Ireland								**Irlande**
Current account	-690	-1 101	89	-1 081	-7 150	-9 095	-12 695	Compte des transac. courantes
Goods: exports f.o.b.	77 623	84 216	88 590	100 116	102 825	104 667	115 517	Biens : exportations f.à.b.
Goods: imports f.o.b.	-50 360	-50 769	-51 709	-61 102	-67 730	-72 779	-84 226	Biens : importations f.à.b.
Services: credit	23 465	29 901	42 061	52 718	59 920	69 191	88 994	Services : crédit
Services: debit	-35 339	-42 829	-54 597	-65 384	-71 437	-78 528	-94 472	Services : débit
Income: credit	28 850	27 200	34 095	43 457	53 862	75 321	103 989	Revenus : crédit
Income: debit	-45 202	-49 515	-58 879	-71 388	-84 876	-106 422	-140 840	Revenus : débit
Current transfers: credit	7 400	7 538	7 027	6 626	6 963	6 648	6 459	Transferts courants : crédit
Current transfers: debit	-7 128	-6 842	-6 500	-6 123	-6 679	-7 192	-8 117	Transferts courants : débit
Capital account, n.i.e.	635	512	126	368	323	283	54	Compte de capital, n.i.a.
Financial account, n.i.e.	16	468	-3 481	3 301	-2 501	10 732	14 115	Compte financier, n.i.a.
Net errors and omissions	434	-171	1 375	-4 023	7 552	-2 032	-1 457	Erreurs et omissions nettes
Reserves and related items	-395	292	1 890	1 435	1 776	112	-16	Réserves et postes apparentés
Israel								**Israël**
Current account	-1 287	-928	1 323	2 659	3 980	8 078	4 523	Compte des transac. courantes
Goods: exports f.o.b.	27 663	27 244	29 918	36 329	39 722	43 278	49 779	Biens : exportations f.à.b.
Goods: imports f.o.b.	-31 713	-31 971	-33 294	-39 488	-43 868	-47 125	-55 789	Biens : importations f.à.b.
Services: credit	12 852	12 186	13 661	16 035	17 447	19 248	21 122	Services : crédit
Services: debit	-11 846	-10 902	-11 201	-12 822	-13 715	-14 866	-17 842	Services : débit
Income: credit	2 730	2 458	2 814	3 004	5 800	8 419	10 486	Revenus : crédit
Income: debit	-7 632	-6 727	-6 986	-6 675	-7 177	-8 334	-10 511	Revenus : débit
Current transfers: credit	7 790	8 165	7 556	7 358	7 010	8 575	8 549	Transferts courants : crédit
Current transfers: debit	-1 132	-1 380	-1 145	-1 081	-1 038	-1 117	-1 270	Transferts courants : débit
Capital account, n.i.e.	720	207	534	667	727	786	782	Compte de capital, n.i.a.
Financial account, n.i.e.	391	-139	-3 758	-7 399	-6 856	-12 825	-1 928	Compte financier, n.i.a.
Net errors and omissions	385	-166	1 858	1 111	3 769	-172	-2 942	Erreurs et omissions nettes
Reserves and related items	-209	1 026	43	2 962	-1 619	4 132	-436	Réserves et postes apparentés
Italy								**Italie**
Current account	-652	-9 369	-19 407	-16 456	-29 714	-48 045	-51 032	Compte des transac. courantes
Goods: exports f.o.b.	244 931	252 618	298 118	352 171	372 378	418 074	502 384	Biens : exportations f.à.b.
Goods: imports f.o.b.	-229 392	-239 206	-286 641	-341 278	-371 814	-430 585	-498 142	Biens : importations f.à.b.
Services: credit	57 676	60 439	71 767	84 524	89 216	98 984	111 999	Services : crédit
Services: debit	-57 753	-63 166	-74 332	-83 246	-90 081	-100 511	-121 450	Services : débit
Income: credit	38 574	43 303	48 780	53 118	61 324	72 350	88 075	Revenus : crédit
Income: debit	-48 911	-57 854	-69 003	-71 457	-78 434	-89 426	-114 993	Revenus : débit
Current transfers: credit	16 137	20 871	20 650	21 833	23 574	22 006	27 459	Transferts courants : crédit
Current transfers: debit	-21 915	-26 375	-28 745	-32 120	-35 876	-38 937	46 364	Transferts courants : débit
Capital account, n.i.e.	846	-80	2 667	2 172	1 240	2 390	3 679	Compte de capital, n.i.a.
Financial account, n.i.e.	-3 570	11 224	20 437	8 426	25 283	30 933	37 615	Compte financier, n.i.a.
Net errors and omissions	2 787	1 395	-2 583	3 014	2 160	14 156	11 632	Erreurs et omissions nettes
Reserves and related items	588	-3 169	-1 115	2 844	1 030	566	-1 893	Réserves et postes apparentés
Jamaica								**Jamaïque**
Current account	-759	-1 074	-773	-509	-1 072	-1 183	-1 744	Compte des transac. courantes
Goods: exports f.o.b.	1 454	1 309	1 386	1 602	1 664	2 134	2 226	Biens : exportations f.à.b.
Goods: imports f.o.b.	-3 073	-3 180	-3 328	-3 546	-4 246	-5 077	-5 789	Biens : importations f.à.b.
Services: credit	1 897	1 912	2 138	2 297	2 330	2 649	2 702	Services : crédit
Services: debit	-1 514	-1 597	-1 586	-1 725	-1 722	-2 021	-2 261	Services : débit
Income: credit	218	221	218	270	328	378	521	Revenus : crédit
Income: debit	-656	-826	-789	-852	-1 004	-994	-1 182	Revenus : débit

69

Summary of balance of payments *(continued)*
Millions of US dollars

Résumé de la balance des paiements *(suite)*
Millions de dollars des E.-U.

Country or area	2001	2002	2003	2004	2005	2006	2007	Pays ou zone
Current transfers: credit	1 091	1 338	1 524	1 892	1 935	2 088	2 386	Transferts courants : crédit
Current transfers: debit	-177	-251	-334	-446	-357	-340	-346	Transferts courants : débit
Capital account, n.i.e.	-22	-17	^0	2	-18	-28	-36	Compte de capital, n.i.a.
Financial account, n.i.e.	1 661	911	314	1 216	1 297	1 312	1 289	Compte financier, n.i.a.
Net errors and omissions	-14	-61	28	-14	22	129	50	Erreurs et omissions nettes
Reserves and related items	-865	241	431	-695	-230	-230	440	Réserves et postes apparentés
Japan								**Japon**
Current account	87 798	112 447	136 216	172 059	165 783	170 517	210 490	Compte des transac. courantes
Goods: exports f.o.b.	383 592	395 581	449 119	538 999	567 572	615 813	678 090	Biens : exportations f.à.b.
Goods: imports f.o.b.	-313 378	-301 751	-342 723	-406 866	-473 614	-534 509	-573 337	Biens : importations f.à.b.
Services: credit	64 516	65 712	77 621	97 611	110 210	117 298	129 117	Services : crédit
Services: debit	-108 249	-107 940	-111 528	-135 514	-134 256	-135 556	-150 367	Services : débit
Income: credit	103 095	91 478	95 211	113 331	141 062	165 802	199 460	Revenus : crédit
Income: debit	-33 874	-25 709	-23 971	-27 628	-37 618	-47 647	-60 959	Revenus : débit
Current transfers: credit	6 152	10 038	6 508	6 907	9 738	6 184	6 771	Transferts courants : crédit
Current transfers: debit	-14 056	-14 960	-14 020	-14 782	-17 311	-16 868	-18 285	Transferts courants : débit
Capital account, n.i.e.	-2 869	-3 321	-3 998	-4 787	-4 878	-4 757	-4 029	Compte de capital, n.i.a.
Financial account, n.i.e.	-48 160	-63 381	71 924	22 500	-122 682	-102 343	-187 240	Compte financier, n.i.a.
Net errors and omissions	3 718	388	-16 990	-28 918	-15 898	-31 437	17 303	Erreurs et omissions nettes
Reserves and related items	-40 487	-46 134	-187 153	-160 854	-22 325	-31 982	-36 524	Réserves et postes apparentés
Jordan								**Jordanie**
Current account	5	544	1 245	89	-2 200	-1 598	-2 776	Compte des transac. courantes
Goods: exports f.o.b.	2 294	2 770	3 082	3 883	4 301	5 204	5 700	Biens : exportations f.à.b.
Goods: imports f.o.b.	-4 301	-4 501	-5 078	-7 261	-9 317	-10 260	-12 022	Biens : importations f.à.b.
Services: credit	1 487	1 774	1 748	2 073	2 334	2 907	3 410	Services : crédit
Services: debit	-1 726	-1 883	-1 889	-2 146	-2 542	-2 971	-3 479	Services : débit
Income: credit	652	492	550	649	791	1 032	1 395	Revenus : crédit
Income: debit	-461	-372	-374	-326	-383	-451	-560	Revenus : débit
Current transfers: credit	2 366	2 524	3 501	3 562	3 030	3 379	3 511	Transferts courants : crédit
Current transfers: debit	-307	-260	-295	-346	-414	-439	-732	Transferts courants : débit
Capital account, n.i.e.	22	69	94	2	8	63	13	Compte de capital, n.i.a.
Financial account, n.i.e.	-191	337	-211	-103	1 638	2 994	2 400	Compte financier, n.i.a.
Net errors and omissions	-90	-56	149	192	814	-17	1 254	Erreurs et omissions nettes
Reserves and related items	255	-894	-1 277	-180	-261	-1 442	-890	Réserves et postes apparentés
Kazakhstan								**Kazakhstan**
Current account	-1 390	-1 024	-273	335	-1 056	-1 999	-7 333	Compte des transac. courantes
Goods: exports f.o.b.	8 928	10 027	13 233	20 603	28 301	38 762	48 351	Biens : exportations f.à.b.
Goods: imports f.o.b.	-7 944	-8 040	-9 554	-13 818	-17 979	-24 120	-33 260	Biens : importations f.à.b.
Services: credit	1 260	1 540	1 712	2 009	2 228	2 819	3 555	Services : crédit
Services: debit	-2 635	-3 538	-3 753	-5 108	-7 496	-8 760	-11 627	Services : débit
Income: credit	225	234	255	423	680	1 431	3 463	Revenus : crédit
Income: debit	-1 462	-1 361	-2 002	-3 286	-6 377	-10 922	-15 656	Revenus : débit
Current transfers: credit	394	426	279	353	810	904	904	Transferts courants : crédit
Current transfers: debit	-156	-312	-443	-841	-1 223	-2 111	-3 063	Transferts courants : débit
Capital account, n.i.e.	-185	-120	-28	-21	14	32	-38	Compte de capital, n.i.a.
Financial account, n.i.e.	2 614	1 359	2 766	4 701	898	16 169	7 312	Compte financier, n.i.a.
Net errors and omissions	-654	320	-932	-1 016	-1 800	-3 128	-2 970	Erreurs et omissions nettes
Reserves and related items	-385	-535	-1 534	-3 999	1 944	-11 075	3 029	Réserves et postes apparentés
Kenya								**Kenya**
Current account	-320	-118	132	-132	-260	-479	-1 102	Compte des transac. courantes
Goods: exports f.o.b.	1 891	2 162	2 412	2 726	3 455	3 516	4 123	Biens : exportations f.à.b.
Goods: imports f.o.b.	-3 238	-3 159	-3 569	-4 351	-5 602	-6 769	-8 381	Biens : importations f.à.b.
Services: credit	1 120	1 054	1 198	1 557	1 880	2 461	2 699	Services : crédit
Services: debit	-810	-708	-691	-939	-1 137	-1 402	-1 459	Services : débit
Income: credit	46	35	60	45	73	99	113	Revenus : crédit
Income: debit	-168	-179	-148	-172	-182	-170	-304	Revenus : débit
Current transfers: credit	854	689	884	1 045	1 319	1 833	2 149	Transferts courants : crédit
Current transfers: debit	-16	-12	-14	-43	-67	-48	-40	Transferts courants : débit
Capital account, n.i.e.	51	81	163	145	103	168	157	Compte de capital, n.i.a.
Financial account, n.i.e.	148	-174	406	40	511	674	2 071	Compte financier, n.i.a.
Net errors and omissions	131	194	-277	-67	-238	218	-315	Erreurs et omissions nettes
Reserves and related items	-10	16	-425	13	-117	-581	-811	Réserves et postes apparentés

69

Summary of balance of payments (*continued*)
Millions of US dollars

Résumé de la balance des paiements (*suite*)
Millions de dollars des E.-U.

Country or area	2001	2002	2003	2004	2005	2006	2007	Pays ou zone
Korea, Republic of								**Corée, République de**
Current account	8 033	5 394	11 950	28 174	14 981	5 385	5 954	Compte des transac. courantes
Goods: exports f.o.b.	151 478	163 414	197 289	257 710	288 971	331 842	378 982	Biens : exportations f.à.b.
Goods: imports f.o.b.	-137 990	-148 637	-175 337	-220 141	-256 288	-303 937	-349 573	Biens : importations f.à.b.
Services: credit	29 055	28 388	32 957	41 882	45 129	49 891	63 034	Services : crédit
Services: debit	-32 927	-36 585	-40 381	-49 928	-58 788	-68 851	-83 609	Services : débit
Income: credit	6 650	6 900	7 176	9 410	10 432	14 547	19 327	Revenus : crédit
Income: debit	-7 848	-6 467	-6 850	-8 328	-11 994	-14 014	-18 558	Revenus : débit
Current transfers: credit	6 687	7 314	7 859	9 151	10 004	9 588	10 934	Transferts courants : crédit
Current transfers: debit	-7 072	-8 932	-10 764	-11 583	-12 486	-13 680	-14 583	Transferts courants : débit
Capital account, n.i.e.	-731	-1 087	-1 398	-1 753	-2 340	-3 126	-2 390	Compte de capital, n.i.a.
Financial account, n.i.e.	3 025	7 338	15 308	9 359	7 104	21 098	8 622	Compte financier, n.i.a.
Net errors and omissions	2 951	124	-68	2 895	119	-1 267	2 922	Erreurs et omissions nettes
Reserves and related items	-13 278	-11 769	-25 791	-38 675	-19 864	-22 090	-15 109	Réserves et postes apparentés
Kuwait								**Koweït**
Current account	8 324	4 265	9 424	18 162	34 308	51 571	47 471	Compte des transac. courantes
Goods: exports f.o.b.	16 237	15 367	21 795	30 089	46 971	58 638	63 681	Biens : exportations f.à.b.
Goods: imports f.o.b.	-7 047	-8 117	-9 880	-11 663	-14 238	-14 331	-20 625	Biens : importations f.à.b.
Services: credit	1 664	1 648	3 144	3 743	4 723	7 931	9 636	Services : crédit
Services: debit	-5 355	-5 838	-6 615	-7 586	-8 604	-10 215	-13 082	Services : débit
Income: credit	5 427	3 716	3 733	6 584	9 413	14 667	15 688	Revenus : crédit
Income: debit	-524	-369	-372	-456	-556	-1 499	-2 751	Revenus : débit
Current transfers: credit	53	50	66	88	86	113	127	Transferts courants : crédit
Current transfers: debit	-2 132	-2 192	-2 446	-2 638	-3 487	-3 733	-5 203	Transferts courants : débit
Capital account, n.i.e.	2 931	1 672	1 431	433	797	882	1 573	Compte de capital, n.i.a.
Financial account, n.i.e.	-5 478	-5 038	-12 106	-16 836	-31 087	-47 962	-37 285	Compte financier, n.i.a.
Net errors and omissions	-2 869	-1 869	-574	-1 130	-3 398	-907	-8 541	Erreurs et omissions nettes
Reserves and related items	-2 908	970	1 824	-629	-619	-3 583	-3 218	Réserves et postes apparentés
Kyrgyzstan								**Kirghizistan**
Current account	-52	-61	-61	3	-60	-299	-263	Compte des transac. courantes
Goods: exports f.o.b.	480	498	590	733	687	906	1 337	Biens : exportations f.à.b.
Goods: imports f.o.b.	-449	-571	-723	-904	-1 106	-1 792	-2 635	Biens : importations f.à.b.
Services: credit	83	142	158	210	259	379	684	Services : crédit
Services: debit	-125	-148	-160	-223	-291	-461	-582	Services : débit
Income: credit	12	6	5	8	17	42	43	Revenus : crédit
Income: debit	-71	-64	-67	-109	-102	-85	-95	Revenus : débit
Current transfers: credit	23	79	143	307	514	762	1 065	Transferts courants : crédit
Current transfers: debit	-4	-3	-7	-18	-38	-50	-79	Transferts courants : débit
Capital account, n.i.e.	-32	-8	-1	-20	-21	-44	-75	Compte de capital, n.i.a.
Financial account, n.i.e.	46	110	28	180	85	337	354	Compte financier, n.i.a.
Net errors and omissions	24	-21	81	-19	64	182	276	Erreurs et omissions nettes
Reserves and related items	13	-20	-47	-145	-68	-177	293	Réserves et postes apparentés
Lao People's Dem. Rep.								**Rép. dém. pop. lao**
Current account	-82	3	-62	-189	-193	50	107	Compte des transac. courantes
Goods: exports f.o.b.	311	301	335	363	553	882	923	Biens : exportations f.à.b.
Goods: imports f.o.b.	-528	-447	-462	-713	-882	-1 060	-1 065	Biens : importations f.à.b.
Services: credit	166	176	127	179	204	224	278	Services : crédit
Services: debit	-32	-32	-37	-41	-56	-62	-76	Services : débit
Income: credit	6	5	4	4	5	16	44	Revenus : crédit
Income: debit	-40	-47	-51	-60	-84	-76	-94	Revenus : débit
Current transfers: credit	34	48	21	79	67	127	98	Transferts courants : crédit
Current transfers: debit	...	0	0	0	0	0	0	Transferts courants : débit
Capital account, n.i.e.	...	0	0	0	0	0	0	Compte de capital, n.i.a.
Financial account, n.i.e.	136	69	119	94	155	230	397	Compte financier, n.i.a.
Net errors and omissions	-57	-13	-35	115	56	-180	-307	Erreurs et omissions nettes
Reserves and related items	4	-59	-22	-19	-18	-100	-198	Réserves et postes apparentés
Latvia								**Lettonie**
Current account	-626	-625	-921	-1 762	-1 992	-4 522	-6 485	Compte des transac. courantes
Goods: exports f.o.b.	2 243	2 545	3 171	4 221	5 361	6 140	8 227	Biens : exportations f.à.b.
Goods: imports f.o.b.	-3 578	-4 024	-5 173	-7 002	-8 379	-11 271	-15 125	Biens : importations f.à.b.
Services: credit	1 179	1 238	1 506	1 779	2 163	2 642	3 671	Services : crédit
Services: debit	-671	-701	-929	-1 178	-1 557	-1 980	-2 702	Services : débit
Income: credit	278	289	368	500	772	1 078	1 488	Revenus : crédit
Income: debit	-221	-235	-393	-775	-948	-1 610	-2 425	Revenus : débit

69

Summary of balance of payments *(continued)*
Millions of US dollars

Résumé de la balance des paiements *(suite)*
Millions de dollars des E.-U.

Country or area	2001	2002	2003	2004	2005	2006	2007	Pays ou zone
Current transfers: credit	373	538	924	1 289	1 373	1 789	2 035	Transferts courants : crédit
Current transfers: debit	-229	-275	-394	-595	-776	-1 310	-1 654	Transferts courants : débit
Capital account, n.i.e.	41	21	76	144	212	239	578	Compte de capital, n.i.a.
Financial account, n.i.e.	900	687	937	2 013	2 600	6 141	7 063	Compte financier, n.i.a.
Net errors and omissions	^0	-71	-13	8	-296	120	-173	Erreurs et omissions nettes
Reserves and related items	-314	-12	-79	-403	-524	-1 979	-982	Réserves et postes apparentés
Lebanon								**Liban**
Current account	...	-4 541	-5 139	-4 406	-2 748	-1 312	-1 395	Compte des transac. courantes
Goods: exports f.o.b.	...	1 420	1 998	2 397	2 652	3 207	4 077	Biens : exportations f.à.b.
Goods: imports f.o.b.	...	-6 245	-7 001	-9 175	-9 239	-9 345	-11 926	Biens : importations f.à.b.
Services: credit	...	4 429	9 462	9 704	10 858	11 565	12 993	Services : crédit
Services: debit	...	-3 354	-6 488	-8 230	-7 895	-8 734	-9 988	Services : débit
Income: credit	...	395	1 399	1 060	1 733	2 440	3 113	Revenus : crédit
Income: debit	...	-1 263	-4 836	-1 878	-1 919	-2 256	-2 371	Revenus : débit
Current transfers: credit	...	2 591	4 079	5 325	4 399	5 053	5 219	Transferts courants : crédit
Current transfers: debit	...	-2 513	-3 751	-3 609	-3 337	-3 242	-2 510	Transferts courants : débit
Capital account, n.i.e.	...	13	29	50	27	1 940	590	Compte de capital, n.i.a.
Financial account, n.i.e.	...	348	6 344	4 309	3 786	1 524	5 831	Compte financier, n.i.a.
Net errors and omissions	...	4 845	3 802	-733	-608	-2 007	-5 691	Erreurs et omissions nettes
Reserves and related items	...	-664	-5 037	780	-458	-146	665	Réserves et postes apparentés
Lesotho								**Lesotho**
Current account	-95	-143	-135	-68	-102	66	212	Compte des transac. courantes
Goods: exports f.o.b.	279	357	475	707	650	694	805	Biens : exportations f.à.b.
Goods: imports f.o.b.	-679	-763	-994	-1 302	-1 306	-1 361	-1 604	Biens : importations f.à.b.
Services: credit	40	35	50	72	52	59	76	Services : crédit
Services: debit	-49	-55	-85	-96	-103	-95	-110	Services : débit
Income: credit	235	207	304	379	370	413	517	Revenus : crédit
Income: debit	-57	-45	-54	-76	-65	-32	-97	Revenus : débit
Current transfers: credit	137	123	172	251	304	392	629	Transferts courants : crédit
Current transfers: debit	-3	-2	-2	-3	-3	-3	-4	Transferts courants : débit
Capital account, n.i.e.	17	24	27	33	21	11	32	Compte de capital, n.i.a.
Financial account, n.i.e.	89	89	98	63	127	4	85	Compte financier, n.i.a.
Net errors and omissions	155	-98	-56	-25	-3	110	-59	Erreurs et omissions nettes
Reserves and related items	-166	128	65	-4	-44	-191	-270	Réserves et postes apparentés
Liberia								**Libéria**
Current account	...	...	...	-165	-199	-369	-383	Compte des transac. courantes
Goods: exports f.o.b.	...	...	...	105	132	155	196	Biens : exportations f.à.b.
Goods: imports f.o.b.	...	...	...	-279	-306	-441	-498	Biens : importations f.à.b.
Services: credit	...	...	...	211	211	336	346	Services : crédit
Services: debit	...	...	...	-770	-844	-1 275	-1 244	Services : débit
Income: credit	...	...	...	5	9	18	20	Revenus : crédit
Income: debit	...	...	...	-168	-156	-167	-170	Revenus : débit
Current transfers: credit	...	...	...	731	755	1 004	967	Transferts courants : crédit
Current transfers: debit	...	...	...	0	0	0	0	Transferts courants : débit
Capital account, n.i.e.	...	...	...	0	0	0	0	Compte de capital, n.i.a.
Financial account, n.i.e.	...	...	...	46	54	87	113	Compte financier, n.i.a.
Net errors and omissions	...	...	...	-49	-36	-21	-9	Erreurs et omissions nettes
Reserves and related items	...	...	...	167	181	303	279	Réserves et postes apparentés
Libyan Arab Jamah.								**Jamah. arabe libyenne**
Current account	3 332	694	3 402	4 616	14 945	22 170	28 454	Compte des transac. courantes
Goods: exports f.o.b.	10 634	9 851	12 878	17 425	28 849	37 473	46 970	Biens : exportations f.à.b.
Goods: imports f.o.b.	-4 825	-7 408	-7 200	-8 768	-11 174	-13 219	-17 701	Biens : importations f.à.b.
Services: credit	184	401	442	437	534	489	99	Services : crédit
Services: debit	-1 034	-1 544	-1 597	-1 914	-2 349	-2 564	-2 666	Services : débit
Income: credit	684	1 773	1 689	1 339	1 837	2 180	4 471	Revenus : crédit
Income: debit	-1 583	-1 508	-1 149	-1 394	-2 118	-2 775	-2 500	Revenus : débit
Current transfers: credit	20	13	255	254	418	1 646	598	Transferts courants : crédit
Current transfers: debit	-748	-884	-1 916	-2 763	-1 052	-1 060	-817	Transferts courants : débit
Capital account, n.i.e.	0	0	0	0	0	0	0	Compte de capital, n.i.a.
Financial account, n.i.e.	-977	89	-166	-238	392	-4 731	-6 409	Compte financier, n.i.a.
Net errors and omissions	-1 206	362	1 890	1 733	-1 497	2 008	-1 183	Erreurs et omissions nettes
Reserves and related items	-1 149	-1 145	-5 126	-6 111	-13 840	-19 447	-20 862	Réserves et postes apparentés

69

Summary of balance of payments *(continued)*
Millions of US dollars
Résumé de la balance des paiements *(suite)*
Millions de dollars des E.-U.

Country or area	2001	2002	2003	2004	2005	2006	2007	Pays ou zone
Lithuania								**Lituanie**
Current account	-574	-721	-1 278	-1 725	-1 831	-3 218	-5 692	Compte des transac. courantes
Goods: exports f.o.b.	4 889	6 028	7 658	9 306	11 774	14 151	17 162	Biens : exportations f.à.b.
Goods: imports f.o.b.	-5 997	-7 343	-9 362	-11 689	-14 690	-18 360	-23 036	Biens : importations f.à.b.
Services: credit	1 157	1 464	1 878	2 444	3 104	3 623	4 025	Services : crédit
Services: debit	-700	-915	-1 264	-1 632	-2 055	-2 540	-3 393	Services : débit
Income: credit	206	192	235	355	448	590	793	Revenus : crédit
Income: debit	-385	-375	-717	-967	-1 075	-1 407	-2 407	Revenus : débit
Current transfers: credit	262	232	302	612	951	1 425	2 071	Transferts courants : crédit
Current transfers: debit	-4	-3	-8	-154	-289	-700	-908	Transferts courants : débit
Capital account, n.i.e.	1	56	68	287	331	351	690	Compte de capital, n.i.a.
Financial account, n.i.e.	778	1 048	1 642	1 141	2 262	4 663	6 272	Compte financier, n.i.a.
Net errors and omissions	154	79	181	192	-49	-289	-54	Erreurs et omissions nettes
Reserves and related items	-359	-463	-613	104	-712	-1 507	-1 216	Réserves et postes apparentés
Luxembourg								**Luxembourg**
Current account	1 674	2 306	2 409	4 088	4 148	4 435	4 928	Compte des transac. courantes
Goods: exports f.o.b.	8 996	9 467	10 942	13 526	14 602	16 383	18 257	Biens : exportations f.à.b.
Goods: imports f.o.b.	-11 395	-11 612	-13 937	-17 078	-18 802	-20 795	-23 066	Biens : importations f.à.b.
Services: credit	19 945	20 504	25 499	30 957	40 842	50 906	64 524	Services : crédit
Services: debit	-13 708	-12 413	-15 531	-20 940	-24 594	-30 218	-37 453	Services : débit
Income: credit	52 302	60 400	69 291	76 855	90 229	117 521	162 971	Revenus : crédit
Income: debit	-53 941	-63 759	-73 247	-81 166	-96 950	-128 091	-177 946	Revenus : débit
Current transfers: credit	2 269	3 579	3 889	4 025	4 716	5 612	6 134	Transferts courants : crédit
Current transfers: debit	-2 794	-3 860	-4 497	-5 090	-5 895	-6 882	-8 492	Transferts courants : débit
Capital account, n.i.e.	...	-89	-140	-772	1 183	-299	-166	Compte de capital, n.i.a.
Financial account, n.i.e.	...	-2 456	-2 084	-3 528	-5 883	-4 631	-5 097	Compte financier, n.i.a.
Net errors and omissions	...	275	-76	220	504	467	247	Erreurs et omissions nettes
Reserves and related items	...	-35	-108	-8	48	28	89	Réserves et postes apparentés
Madagascar								**Madagascar**
Current account	-170	-528	-458	-541	-626	...	...	Compte des transac. courantes
Goods: exports f.o.b.	928	859	854	990	834	...	...	Biens : exportations f.à.b.
Goods: imports f.o.b.	-955	-1 066	-1 111	-1 427	-1 427	...	...	Biens : importations f.à.b.
Services: credit	351	397	322	425	498	...	...	Services : crédit
Services: debit	-511	-704	-619	-637	-615	...	...	Services : débit
Income: credit	24	46	16	15	24	...	...	Revenus : crédit
Income: debit	-106	-178	-94	-89	-104	...	...	Revenus : débit
Current transfers: credit	114	156	357	245	208	...	...	Transferts courants : crédit
Current transfers: debit	-15	-36	-183	-62	-45	...	...	Transferts courants : débit
Capital account, n.i.e.	113	102	143	182	192	...	...	Compte de capital, n.i.a.
Financial account, n.i.e.	-139	-96	-126	251	-6	...	...	Compte financier, n.i.a.
Net errors and omissions	-57	29	67	-35	91	...	...	Erreurs et omissions nettes
Reserves and related items	253	493	374	143	349	...	...	Réserves et postes apparentés
Malawi								**Malawi**
Current account	-60	-201	...	...	...	...	...	Compte des transac. courantes
Goods: exports f.o.b.	428	422	...	...	...	...	...	Biens : exportations f.à.b.
Goods: imports f.o.b.	-472	-573	...	...	...	...	...	Biens : importations f.à.b.
Services: credit	44	49	...	...	...	...	...	Services : crédit
Services: debit	-171	-222	...	...	...	...	...	Services : débit
Income: credit	12	6	...	...	...	...	...	Revenus : crédit
Income: debit	-43	-45	...	...	...	...	...	Revenus : débit
Current transfers: credit	149	170	...	...	...	...	...	Transferts courants : crédit
Current transfers: debit	-6	-9	...	...	...	...	...	Transferts courants : débit
Capital account, n.i.e.	0	0	...	...	...	...	...	Compte de capital, n.i.a.
Financial account, n.i.e.	213	134	...	...	...	...	...	Compte financier, n.i.a.
Net errors and omissions	-221	157	...	...	...	...	...	Erreurs et omissions nettes
Reserves and related items	68	-90	...	...	...	...	...	Réserves et postes apparentés
Malaysia								**Malaisie**
Current account	7 287	7 190	13 381	15 079	19 980	25 488	28 931	Compte des transac. courantes
Goods: exports f.o.b.	87 981	93 383	104 999	126 817	141 808	160 842	176 403	Biens : exportations f.à.b.
Goods: imports f.o.b.	-69 597	-75 248	-79 289	-99 244	-108 653	-124 144	-139 075	Biens : importations f.à.b.
Services: credit	14 455	14 878	13 578	17 111	19 576	21 831	28 272	Services : crédit
Services: debit	-16 657	-16 448	-17 532	-19 269	-21 956	-23 720	-27 986	Services : débit
Income: credit	1 847	2 139	3 448	4 329	5 373	8 463	11 302	Revenus : crédit
Income: debit	-8 590	-8 734	-9 376	-10 751	-11 691	-13 192	-15 297	Revenus : débit

69

Summary of balance of payments *(continued)*
Millions of US dollars
Résumé de la balance des paiements *(suite)*
Millions de dollars des E.-U.

Country or area	2001	2002	2003	2004	2005	2006	2007	Pays ou zone
Current transfers: credit	537	661	508	422	299	313	342	Transferts courants : crédit
Current transfers: debit	-2 689	-3 442	-2 955	-4 335	-4 776	-4 904	-5 029	Transferts courants : débit
Capital account, n.i.e.	...	0	0	0	0	...	-28	Compte de capital, n.i.a.
Financial account, n.i.e.	-3 892	-3 142	-3 196	5 091	-9 806	-11 894	-10 850	Compte financier, n.i.a.
Net errors and omissions	-2 394	-391	-4	1 880	-6 555	-6 731	-4 910	Erreurs et omissions nettes
Reserves and related items	-1 000	-3 657	-10 181	-22 050	-3 620	-6 864	-13 144	Réserves et postes apparentés
Maldives								**Maldives**
Current account	-65	-45	-31	-122	-271	-300	-423	Compte des transac. courantes
Goods: exports f.o.b.	104	123	152	181	162	225	228	Biens : exportations f.à.b.
Goods: imports f.o.b.	-346	-345	-414	-565	-655	-815	-965	Biens : importations f.à.b.
Services: credit	354	363	432	508	323	552	628	Services : crédit
Services: debit	-110	-111	-120	-158	-212	-230	-269	Services : débit
Income: credit	8	6	6	10	11	16	22	Revenus : crédit
Income: debit	-45	-41	-45	-45	-42	-56	-63	Revenus : débit
Current transfers: credit	20	11	13	8	211	91	99	Transferts courants : crédit
Current transfers: debit	-50	-50	-55	-61	-70	-83	-103	Transferts courants : débit
Capital account, n.i.e.	0	0	0	0	0	0	0	Compte de capital, n.i.a.
Financial account, n.i.e.	34	74	51	153	264	294	445	Compte financier, n.i.a.
Net errors and omissions	1	11	7	13	-16	51	54	Erreurs et omissions nettes
Reserves and related items	30	-40	-26	-44	23	-45	-76	Réserves et postes apparentés
Mali								**Mali**
Current account	-310	-149	-271	-409	-438	-231	...	Compte des transac. courantes
Goods: exports f.o.b.	725	875	928	976	1 101	1 550	...	Biens : exportations f.à.b.
Goods: imports f.o.b.	-735	-712	-988	-1 093	-1 245	-1 475	...	Biens : importations f.à.b.
Services: credit	151	169	224	241	274	313	...	Services : crédit
Services: debit	-421	-387	-482	-532	-588	-675	...	Services : débit
Income: credit	22	36	21	24	32	33	...	Revenus : crédit
Income: debit	-188	-276	-181	-219	-239	-303	...	Revenus : débit
Current transfers: credit	161	182	266	251	286	381	...	Transferts courants : crédit
Current transfers: debit	-25	-36	-58	-58	-58	-56	...	Transferts courants : débit
Capital account, n.i.e.	107	104	114	151	149	141	...	Compte de capital, n.i.a.
Financial account, n.i.e.	146	189	289	100	333	-1 910	...	Compte financier, n.i.a.
Net errors and omissions	9	-6	45	-26	-29	-35	...	Erreurs et omissions nettes
Reserves and related items	47	-138	-177	184	-16	2 035	...	Réserves et postes apparentés
Malta								**Malte**
Current account	-150	106	-156	-353	-524	-585	-462	Compte des transac. courantes
Goods: exports f.o.b.	2 023	2 342	2 592	2 720	2 587	2 937	3 304	Biens : exportations f.à.b.
Goods: imports f.o.b.	-2 575	-2 681	-3 232	-3 583	-3 709	-4 143	-4 661	Biens : importations f.à.b.
Services: credit	1 099	1 201	1 379	1 676	2 007	2 666	3 411	Services : crédit
Services: debit	-759	-798	-894	-1 052	-1 204	-1 770	-2 250	Services : débit
Income: credit	839	857	905	973	1 208	1 841	2 682	Revenus : crédit
Income: debit	-800	-833	-934	-1 026	-1 455	-2 103	-2 854	Revenus : débit
Current transfers: credit	201	281	276	230	343	528	725	Transferts courants : crédit
Current transfers: debit	-178	-263	-248	-291	-300	-540	-819	Transferts courants : débit
Capital account, n.i.e.	1	7	17	83	193	194	72	Compte de capital, n.i.a.
Financial account, n.i.e.	143	231	259	-40	611	495	680	Compte financier, n.i.a.
Net errors and omissions	261	-56	24	102	-64	7	205	Erreurs et omissions nettes
Reserves and related items	-255	-288	-144	207	-217	-111	-495	Réserves et postes apparentés
Mauritius								**Maurice**
Current account	276	249	93	-112	-324	-604	-408	Compte des transac. courantes
Goods: exports f.o.b.	1 628	1 801	1 898	1 993	2 138	2 329	2 231	Biens : exportations f.à.b.
Goods: imports f.o.b.	-1 846	-2 013	-2 201	-2 573	-2 935	-3 409	-3 656	Biens : importations f.à.b.
Services: credit	1 222	1 149	1 280	1 456	1 618	1 671	2 205	Services : crédit
Services: debit	-810	-793	-906	-1 023	-1 198	-1 317	-1 545	Services : débit
Income: credit	75	80	47	52	143	374	817	Revenus : crédit
Income: debit	-61	-67	-77	-66	-151	-324	-578	Revenus : débit
Current transfers: credit	193	195	163	168	162	179	254	Transferts courants : crédit
Current transfers: debit	-125	-104	-111	-119	-101	-108	-135	Transferts courants : débit
Capital account, n.i.e.	-1	-2	-1	-2	-2	-3	-2	Compte de capital, n.i.a.
Financial account, n.i.e.	-240	84	90	8	142	173	519	Compte financier, n.i.a.
Net errors and omissions	-86	9	40	78	19	294	327	Erreurs et omissions nettes
Reserves and related items	52	-341	-222	27	165	140	-436	Réserves et postes apparentés

69

Summary of balance of payments *(continued)*
Millions of US dollars
Résumé de la balance des paiements *(suite)*
Millions de dollars des E.-U.

Country or area	2001	2002	2003	2004	2005	2006	2007	Pays ou zone
Mexico								**Mexique**
Current account	-17 725	-14 155	-7 204	-5 176	-4 213	-4 226	-8 115	Compte des transac. courantes
Goods: exports f.o.b.	158 780	161 046	164 766	187 999	214 233	249 925	271 875	Biens : exportations f.à.b.
Goods: imports f.o.b.	-168 397	-168 679	-170 546	-196 810	-221 820	-256 059	-281 949	Biens : importations f.à.b.
Services: credit	12 701	12 740	12 617	14 047	16 137	16 392	17 658	Services : crédit
Services: debit	-17 194	-17 660	-18 141	-19 779	-21 440	-22 833	-24 068	Services : débit
Income: credit	5 326	4 051	3 858	5 617	5 359	6 406	7 876	Revenus : crédit
Income: debit	-18 256	-15 905	-15 244	-14 997	-18 805	-23 993	-25 916	Revenus : débit
Current transfers: credit	9 336	10 287	15 524	18 827	22 180	26 022	26 516	Transferts courants : crédit
Current transfers: debit	-22	-35	-37	-80	-57	-88	-108	Transferts courants : débit
Capital account, n.i.e.	0	0	0	0	0	0	0	Compte de capital, n.i.a.
Financial account, n.i.e.	28 263	23 355	19 154	13 108	15 800	-1 644	20 660	Compte financier, n.i.a.
Net errors and omissions	-3 223	-1 841	-2 133	-3 827	-4 623	4 567	-2 294	Erreurs et omissions nettes
Reserves and related items	-7 314	-7 359	-9 817	-4 104	-6 965	1 303	-10 250	Réserves et postes apparentés
Mongolia								**Mongolie**
Current account	-154	-158	-148	-25	-5	109	...	Compte des transac. courantes
Goods: exports f.o.b.	523	524	627	872	1 069	1 545	...	Biens : exportations f.à.b.
Goods: imports f.o.b.	-624	-680	-827	-901	-1 097	-1 357	...	Biens : importations f.à.b.
Services: credit	114	184	208	338	414	486	...	Services : crédit
Services: debit	-205	-266	-257	-504	-476	-523	...	Services : débit
Income: credit	15	14	14	17	11	17	...	Revenus : crédit
Income: debit	-17	-19	-25	-28	-61	-162	...	Revenus : débit
Current transfers: credit	40	127	167	231	178	180	...	Transferts courants : crédit
Current transfers: debit	0	-42	-55	-50	-41	-77	...	Transferts courants : débit
Capital account, n.i.e.	0	0	0	0	...	...	...	Compte de capital, n.i.a.
Financial account, n.i.e.	107	157	5	-23	46	181	...	Compte financier, n.i.a.
Net errors and omissions	-32	14	-6	1	-75	-8	...	Erreurs et omissions nettes
Reserves and related items	79	-13	149	46	34	-283	...	Réserves et postes apparentés
Montserrat								**Montserrat**
Current account	-6	-10	-8	-9	-16	-8	-9	Compte des transac. courantes
Goods: exports f.o.b.	1	2	2	5	2	2	3	Biens : exportations f.à.b.
Goods: imports f.o.b.	-17	-22	-25	-25	-26	-27	-26	Biens : importations f.à.b.
Services: credit	15	14	12	15	15	15	15	Services : crédit
Services: debit	-22	-16	-19	-23	-26	-17	-19	Services : débit
Income: credit	1	1	1	1	2	3	2	Revenus : crédit
Income: debit	-2	-4	-2	-5	-5	-5	-6	Revenus : débit
Current transfers: credit	22	21	27	28	28	25	28	Transferts courants : crédit
Current transfers: debit	-4	-5	-5	-5	-6	-4	-6	Transferts courants : débit
Capital account, n.i.e.	8	13	14	12	11	9	12	Compte de capital, n.i.a.
Financial account, n.i.e.	-4	-3	-8	-2	6	3	-2	Compte financier, n.i.a.
Net errors and omissions	4	1	3	^0	^0	-3	^0	Erreurs et omissions nettes
Reserves and related items	-2	-1	-1	-1	-1	-1	^0	Réserves et postes apparentés
Morocco								**Maroc**
Current account	1 606	1 472	1 552	922	949	1 315	-224	Compte des transac. courantes
Goods: exports f.o.b.	7 142	7 839	8 771	9 922	10 690	11 926	15 146	Biens : exportations f.à.b.
Goods: imports f.o.b.	-10 164	-10 900	-13 117	-16 408	-18 894	-21 683	-29 316	Biens : importations f.à.b.
Services: credit	4 029	4 360	5 478	6 710	8 098	9 789	12 165	Services : crédit
Services: debit	-2 118	-2 413	-2 861	-3 451	-3 845	-4 473	-5 416	Services : débit
Income: credit	326	377	370	505	689	750	961	Revenus : crédit
Income: debit	-1 159	-1 115	-1 162	-1 176	-1 072	-1 227	-1 365	Revenus : débit
Current transfers: credit	3 670	3 441	4 214	4 974	5 441	6 410	7 786	Transferts courants : crédit
Current transfers: debit	-120	-115	-141	-154	-158	-177	-185	Transferts courants : débit
Capital account, n.i.e.	-9	-6	-10	-8	-5	-3	-3	Compte de capital, n.i.a.
Financial account, n.i.e.	-966	-1 336	-1 091	102	-88	-185	-718	Compte financier, n.i.a.
Net errors and omissions	230	-182	-297	-282	-407	-499	105	Erreurs et omissions nettes
Reserves and related items	-861	52	-154	-733	-449	-628	840	Réserves et postes apparentés
Mozambique								**Mozambique**
Current account	-657	-869	-816	-607	-761	-773	-795	Compte des transac. courantes
Goods: exports f.o.b.	726	810	1 044	1 504	1 745	2 381	2 412	Biens : exportations f.à.b.
Goods: imports f.o.b.	-997	-1 476	-1 648	-1 850	-2 242	-2 649	-2 811	Biens : importations f.à.b.
Services: credit	250	339	304	256	342	386	459	Services : crédit
Services: debit	618	-577	-574	-531	-649	-758	-856	Services : débit
Income: credit	56	52	56	75	99	160	194	Revenus : crédit
Income: debit	-291	-655	-221	-374	-459	-794	-785	Revenus : débit

69

Summary of balance of payments *(continued)*
Millions of US dollars

Résumé de la balance des paiements *(suite)*
Millions de dollars des E.-U.

Country or area	2001	2002	2003	2004	2005	2006	2007	Pays ou zone
Current transfers: credit	255	827	293	371	479	574	658	Transferts courants : crédit
Current transfers: debit	-37	-189	-70	-57	-76	-74	-65	Transferts courants : débit
Capital account, n.i.e.	257	222	271	578	188	489	415	Compte de capital, n.i.a.
Financial account, n.i.e.	-25	-732	373	-47	95	-1 502	353	Compte financier, n.i.a.
Net errors and omissions	-60	-60	208	216	281	144	84	Erreurs et omissions nettes
Reserves and related items	485	1 439	-35	-141	197	1 643	-57	Réserves et postes apparentés
Myanmar								**Myanmar**
Current account	-154	97	-19	112	588	802	...	Compte des transac. courantes
Goods: exports f.o.b.	2 522	2 421	2 710	2 927	3 788	4 555	...	Biens : exportations f.à.b.
Goods: imports f.o.b.	-2 444	-2 022	-1 912	-1 999	-1 759	-2 343	...	Biens : importations f.à.b.
Services: credit	408	426	249	255	259	280	...	Services : crédit
Services: debit	-361	-309	-420	-460	-502	-563	...	Services : débit
Income: credit	37	37	29	40	56	98	...	Revenus : crédit
Income: debit	-549	-620	-771	-786	-1 427	-1 346	...	Revenus : débit
Current transfers: credit	249	188	118	161	198	161	...	Transferts courants : crédit
Current transfers: debit	-14	-23	-23	-27	-24	-39	...	Transferts courants : débit
Capital account, n.i.e.	0	0	0	0	0	0	...	Compte de capital, n.i.a.
Financial account, n.i.e.	348	-32	137	125	166	253	...	Compte financier, n.i.a.
Net errors and omissions	-14	-19	-79	-143	-610	-632	...	Erreurs et omissions nettes
Reserves and related items	-180	-45	-39	-94	-144	-423	...	Réserves et postes apparentés
Namibia								**Namibie**
Current account	-20	57	204	384	267	1 016	693	Compte des transac. courantes
Goods: exports f.o.b.	1 147	1 072	1 262	1 827	2 070	2 647	2 922	Biens : exportations f.à.b.
Goods: imports f.o.b.	-1 349	-1 283	-1 726	-2 110	-2 326	-2 544	-3 102	Biens : importations f.à.b.
Services: credit	294	272	414	475	413	526	599	Services : crédit
Services: debit	-276	-234	-276	-420	-369	-430	-514	Services : débit
Income: credit	121	110	185	217	225	256	273	Revenus : crédit
Income: debit	-269	-122	-54	-212	-353	-319	-432	Revenus : débit
Current transfers: credit	347	270	426	642	651	926	998	Transferts courants : crédit
Current transfers: debit	-36	-30	-27	-35	-45	-45	-52	Transferts courants : débit
Capital account, n.i.e.	96	41	68	77	80	83	83	Compte de capital, n.i.a.
Financial account, n.i.e.	-435	-366	-582	-779	-875	-1 525	-1 467	Compte financier, n.i.a.
Net errors and omissions	-28	16	-89	115	128	122	490	Erreurs et omissions nettes
Reserves and related items	388	252	398	202	401	305	201	Réserves et postes apparentés
Nepal								**Népal**
Current account	-339	56	120	-45	1	-10	-130	Compte des transac. courantes
Goods: exports f.o.b.	721	632	703	773	903	849	925	Biens : exportations f.à.b.
Goods: imports f.o.b.	-1 486	-1 425	-1 666	-1 908	-2 276	-2 441	-2 933	Biens : importations f.à.b.
Services: credit	413	305	372	461	380	386	511	Services : crédit
Services: debit	-215	-237	-266	-385	-435	-493	-723	Services : débit
Income: credit	70	57	49	63	140	158	224	Revenus : crédit
Income: debit	-59	-71	-69	-78	-92	-96	-88	Revenus : débit
Current transfers: credit	240	828	1 022	1 092	1 441	1 696	1 994	Transferts courants : crédit
Current transfers: debit	-24	-33	-25	-63	-61	-69	-42	Transferts courants : débit
Capital account, n.i.e.	0	102	25	16	40	46	75	Compte de capital, n.i.a.
Financial account, n.i.e.	-217	-405	-354	-488	-277	3	-132	Compte financier, n.i.a.
Net errors and omissions	257	-67	310	416	139	109	19	Erreurs et omissions nettes
Reserves and related items	300	313	-101	102	96	-147	168	Réserves et postes apparentés
Netherlands								**Pays-Bas**
Current account	9 810	11 018	29 867	46 100	46 618	63 043	59 586	Compte des transac. courantes
Goods: exports f.o.b.	203 201	209 516	264 966	313 429	344 734	390 785	462 226	Biens : exportations f.à.b.
Goods: imports f.o.b.	-184 015	-190 950	-228 447	-272 590	-297 088	-342 317	-407 317	Biens : importations f.à.b.
Services: credit	51 248	56 138	63 227	73 772	80 086	84 809	96 727	Services : crédit
Services: debit	-53 713	-57 204	-63 897	-69 444	-73 307	-75 481	-84 536	Services : débit
Income: credit	43 458	40 304	59 006	80 671	98 776	131 137	159 667	Revenus : crédit
Income: debit	-43 631	-40 245	-57 773	-69 306	-94 839	-112 858	-154 853	Revenus : débit
Current transfers: credit	4 475	4 961	8 444	9 764	11 177	12 521	13 983	Transferts courants : crédit
Current transfers: debit	-11 214	-11 501	-15 660	-20 197	-22 921	-25 555	-26 309	Transferts courants : débit
Capital account, n.i.e.	-3 200	-545	-3 069	-1 614	-1 764	-2 617	-3 450	Compte de capital, n.i.a.
Financial account, n.i.e.	-3 852	-4 527	-23 964	-46 181	-39 415	-60 397	-28 812	Compte financier, n.i.a.
Net errors and omissions	-3 110	-6 077	-3 272	785	-7 229	752	-28 733	Erreurs et omissions nettes
Reserves and related items	351	132	437	911	1 790	-780	1 409	Réserves et postes apparentés

Summary of balance of payments *(continued)*
Millions of US dollars

Résumé de la balance des paiements *(suite)*
Millions de dollars des E.-U.

Country or area	2001	2002	2003	2004	2005	2006	2007	Pays ou zone
Netherlands Antilles								**Antilles néerlandaises**
Current account	-210	-59	5	-113	-148	-260	-590	Compte des transac. courantes
Goods: exports f.o.b.	637	577	654	776	971	695	676	Biens : exportations f.à.b.
Goods: imports f.o.b.	-1 747	-1 598	-1 672	-1 956	-2 285	-2 209	-2 543	Biens : importations f.à.b.
Services: credit	1 651	1 626	1 701	1 799	1 847	1 991	2 100	Services : crédit
Services: debit	-790	-793	-812	-801	-813	-758	-803	Services : débit
Income: credit	104	91	90	95	103	137	176	Revenus : crédit
Income: debit	-84	-90	-97	-105	-108	-138	-166	Revenus : débit
Current transfers: credit	212	361	395	311	401	329	296	Transferts courants : crédit
Current transfers: debit	-193	-233	-254	-233	-265	-306	-327	Transferts courants : débit
Capital account, n.i.e.	37	28	26	79	96	100	122	Compte de capital, n.i.a.
Financial account, n.i.e.	298	90	-36	^0	21	140	515	Compte financier, n.i.a.
Net errors and omissions	92	-6	32	42	80	36	82	Erreurs et omissions nettes
Reserves and related items	-218	-52	-27	-8	-49	-16	-129	Réserves et postes apparentés
New Zealand								**Nouvelle-Zélande**
Current account	-1 428	-2 376	-3 479	-6 264	-9 281	-9 265	-10 635	Compte des transac. courantes
Goods: exports f.o.b.	13 871	14 495	16 804	20 466	22 006	22 576	27 291	Biens : exportations f.à.b.
Goods: imports f.o.b.	-12 449	-14 351	-17 315	-21 888	-24 583	-24 573	-29 052	Biens : importations f.à.b.
Services: credit	4 443	5 405	6 860	8 140	8 602	8 108	9 282	Services : crédit
Services: debit	-4 326	-4 788	-5 760	-7 225	-8 253	-7 887	-9 114	Services : débit
Income: credit	611	1 133	1 430	1 596	1 554	1 554	2 765	Revenus : crédit
Income: debit	-3 730	-4 343	-5 651	-7 438	-8 844	-9 456	-12 224	Revenus : débit
Current transfers: credit	585	642	855	900	1 242	1 292	1 425	Transferts courants : crédit
Current transfers: debit	-433	-568	-703	-814	-1 006	-880	-1 009	Transferts courants : débit
Capital account, n.i.e.	480	813	-1 917	-2 589	-195	-214	-559	Compte de capital, n.i.a.
Financial account, n.i.e.	866	2 157	2 875	8 089	11 004	12 765	14 497	Compte financier, n.i.a.
Net errors and omissions	-106	487	3 346	1 394	914	969	-216	Erreurs et omissions nettes
Reserves and related items	188	-1 082	-825	-630	-2 441	-4 255	-3 087	Réserves et postes apparentés
Nicaragua								**Nicaragua**
Current account	-805	-744	-663	-649	-734	-679	-1 048	Compte des transac. courantes
Goods: exports f.o.b.	895	914	1 056	1 369	1 654	2 034	2 313	Biens : exportations f.à.b.
Goods: imports f.o.b.	-1 805	-1 853	-2 027	-2 457	-2 956	-3 451	-4 117	Biens : importations f.à.b.
Services: credit	223	226	258	286	309	341	372	Services : crédit
Services: debit	-364	-355	-377	-409	-448	-478	-556	Services : débit
Income: credit	15	9	7	9	23	41	48	Revenus : crédit
Income: debit	-255	-215	-205	-202	-173	-170	-183	Revenus : débit
Current transfers: credit	486	530	625	755	857	1 003	1 075	Transferts courants : crédit
Current transfers: debit	0	0	0	0	0	0	0	Transferts courants : débit
Capital account, n.i.e.	298	312	284	307	300	348	418	Compte de capital, n.i.a.
Financial account, n.i.e.	-171	359	37	361	183	515	490	Compte financier, n.i.a.
Net errors and omissions	235	-319	-119	-415	-57	-152	43	Erreurs et omissions nettes
Reserves and related items	443	391	462	396	309	-33	97	Réserves et postes apparentés
Niger								**Niger**
Current account	-92	-165	-219	-231	-312	-314	...	Compte des transac. courantes
Goods: exports f.o.b.	272	279	352	437	478	508	...	Biens : exportations f.à.b.
Goods: imports f.o.b.	-331	-371	-488	-590	-769	-748	...	Biens : importations f.à.b.
Services: credit	57	51	63	93	88	91	...	Services : crédit
Services: debit	-147	-152	-193	-262	-279	-329	...	Services : débit
Income: credit	12	13	17	26	37	42	...	Revenus : crédit
Income: debit	-27	-37	-43	-39	-47	-41	...	Revenus : débit
Current transfers: credit	88	65	83	129	217	199	...	Transferts courants : crédit
Current transfers: debit	-16	-12	-10	-25	-35	-36	...	Transferts courants : débit
Capital account, n.i.e.	40	92	92	249	49	220	...	Compte de capital, n.i.a.
Financial account, n.i.e.	61	69	97	-173	174	35	...	Compte financier, n.i.a.
Net errors and omissions	14	-9	-15	116	121	-18	...	Erreurs et omissions nettes
Reserves and related items	-22	12	44	39	-33	77	...	Réserves et postes apparentés
Nigeria								**Nigéria**
Current account	2 478	1 083	3 391	16 840	24 202	...	21 972	Compte des transac. courantes
Goods: exports f.o.b.	17 992	15 613	23 976	34 766	48 069	...	65 086	Biens : exportations f.à.b.
Goods: imports f.o.b.	-11 097	-10 876	-16 152	-15 009	-17 288	...	-31 948	Biens : importations f.à.b.
Services: credit	1 653	2 524	3 473	3 336	4 164	...	1 682	Services : crédit
Services: debit	-4 640	-4 922	-5 715	-5 973	-7 321	...	-14 118	Services : débit
Income: credit	199	184	82	157	705	...	2 581	Revenus : crédit
Income: debit	-2 997	-2 854	-3 325	-2 689	-7 437	...	-19 327	Revenus : débit

69

Summary of balance of payments *(continued)*
Millions of US dollars

Résumé de la balance des paiements *(suite)*
Millions de dollars des E.-U.

Country or area	2001	2002	2003	2004	2005	2006	2007	Pays ou zone
Current transfers: credit	1 373	1 422	1 063	2 273	3 329	...	18 168	Transferts courants : crédit
Current transfers: debit	-6	-9	-12	-21	-18	...	-151	Transferts courants : débit
Capital account, n.i.e.	0	55	20	36	23	...	0	Compte de capital, n.i.a.
Financial account, n.i.e.	-3 035	-6 609	-10 285	-13 061	-23 586	...	5 159	Compte financier, n.i.a.
Net errors and omissions	779	782	5 614	4 676	9 758	...	-18 095	Erreurs et omissions nettes
Reserves and related items	-223	4 689	1 260	-8 491	-10 397	...	-9 035	Réserves et postes apparentés
Norway								**Norvège**
Current account	27 546	24 269	27 698	33 000	49 003	58 323	60 459	Compte des transac. courantes
Goods: exports f.o.b.	59 448	59 555	68 666	83 164	104 011	122 789	137 297	Biens : exportations f.à.b.
Goods: imports f.o.b.	-33 046	-35 263	-40 504	-49 035	-55 094	-62 933	-77 026	Biens : importations f.à.b.
Services: credit	18 355	19 488	21 663	25 263	29 928	33 328	40 592	Services : crédit
Services: debit	-15 798	-17 972	-20 569	-24 304	-29 182	-31 957	-39 758	Services : débit
Income: credit	9 671	10 351	14 077	17 117	24 557	30 988	39 273	Revenus : crédit
Income: debit	-9 502	-9 654	-12 712	-16 570	-22 586	-31 610	-37 272	Revenus : débit
Current transfers: credit	1 815	1 877	2 049	2 553	3 458	3 304	3 554	Transferts courants : crédit
Current transfers: debit	-3 398	-4 112	-4 972	-5 188	-6 090	-5 587	-6 201	Transferts courants : débit
Capital account, n.i.e.	-90	-191	678	-154	-290	-146	-163	Compte de capital, n.i.a.
Financial account, n.i.e.	-28 720	-10 534	-21 745	-22 300	-38 694	-38 690	-30 665	Compte financier, n.i.a.
Net errors and omissions	-1 216	-6 814	-6 303	-5 319	-5 508	-14 012	-28 586	Erreurs et omissions nettes
Reserves and related items	2 481	-6 730	-328	-5 227	-4 511	-5 475	-1 045	Réserves et postes apparentés
Occupied Palestinian Terr.[3]								**Terr. palestinien occupé**[3]
Current account	-741	-458	-979	-1 417	-1 107	...	...	Compte des transac. courantes
Goods: exports f.o.b.	448	365	384	410	412	...	...	Biens : exportations f.à.b.
Goods: imports f.o.b.	-2 117	-1 836	-2 280	-2 710	-3 050	...	...	Biens : importations f.à.b,
Services: credit	178	192	214	181	265	...	...	Services : crédit
Services: debit	-702	-651	-516	-489	-487	...	...	Services : débit
Income: credit	504	392	458	459	610	...	...	Revenus : crédit
Income: debit	-19	-11	-2	-33	-36	...	...	Revenus : débit
Current transfers: credit	1 068	1 187	917	904	1 309	...	...	Transferts courants : crédit
Current transfers: debit	-101	-97	-153	-139	-129	...	...	Transferts courants : débit
Capital account, n.i.e.	226	301	305	670	422	...	...	Compte de capital, n.i.a.
Financial account, n.i.e.	367	11	888	728	657	...	...	Compte financier, n.i.a.
Net errors and omissions	133	161	-113	46	3	...	...	Erreurs et omissions nettes
Reserves and related items	16	-15	-100	-27	26	...	...	Réserves et postes apparentés
Oman								**Oman**
Current account	2 082	1 941	1 454	908	4 935	5 087	1 918	Compte des transac. courantes
Goods: exports f.o.b.	11 074	11 170	11 670	13 381	18 692	21 587	24 723	Biens : exportations f.à.b.
Goods: imports f.o.b.	-5 308	-5 633	-6 086	-7 873	-8 029	-9 880	-14 343	Biens : importations f.à.b.
Services: credit	606	606	655	739	754	931	1 163	Services : crédit
Services: debit	-1 899	-1 880	-2 573	-3 123	-3 255	-3 847	-4 996	Services : débit
Income: credit	307	242	317	761	830	1 549	2 026	Revenus : crédit
Income: debit	-1 165	-962	-857	-1 152	-1 801	-2 464	-2 985	Revenus : débit
Current transfers: credit	0	0	0	0	0	0	0	Transferts courants : crédit
Current transfers: debit	-1 532	-1 602	-1 672	-1 826	-2 257	-2 788	-3 670	Transferts courants : débit
Capital account, n.i.e.	-10	5	10	21	-16	-96	827	Compte de capital, n.i.a.
Financial account, n.i.e.	-502	-798	-261	360	-1 437	-2 826	2 384	Compte financier, n.i.a.
Net errors and omissions	-555	-842	-547	-427	-673	41	1 159	Erreurs et omissions nettes
Reserves and related items	-1 015	-307	-656	-861	-2 809	-2 206	-6 287	Réserves et postes apparentés
Pakistan								**Pakistan**
Current account	1 878	3 854	3 573	-817	-3 606	-6 750	-8 295	Compte des transac. courantes
Goods: exports f.o.b.	9 131	9 832	11 869	13 297	15 432	17 049	18 121	Biens : exportations f.à.b.
Goods: imports f.o.b.	-9 741	-10 428	-11 978	-16 693	-21 773	-26 696	-28 761	Biens : importations f.à.b.
Services: credit	1 459	2 429	2 968	2 749	3 678	3 506	3 758	Services : crédit
Services: debit	-2 330	-2 241	-3 294	-5 333	-7 508	-8 418	-8 764	Services : débit
Income: credit	113	128	180	221	658	864	1 357	Revenus : crédit
Income: debit	-2 189	-2 414	-2 404	-2 584	-3 172	-3 995	-5 092	Revenus : débit
Current transfers: credit	5 496	6 593	6 300	7 666	9 169	11 030	11 215	Transferts courants : crédit
Current transfers: debit	-61	-45	-68	-140	-90	-89	-129	Transferts courants : débit
Capital account, n.i.e.	...	40	1 138	591	202	345	176	Compte de capital, n.i.a.
Financial account, n.i.e.	-389	-784	-1 751	-1 810	4 079	7 436	10 008	Compte financier, n.i.a.
Net errors and omissions	708	974	-52	685	-200	520	238	Erreurs et omissions nettes
Reserves and related items	-2 197	-4 084	-2 908	1 351	-475	-1 551	-2 127	Réserves et postes apparentés

69 Summary of balance of payments *(continued)*
Millions of US dollars

Résumé de la balance des paiements *(suite)*
Millions de dollars des E.-U.

Country or area	2001	2002	2003	2004	2005	2006	2007	Pays ou zone
Panama								**Panama**
Current account	-170	-96	-537	-1 003	-1 022	-527	-1 422	Compte des transac. courantes
Goods: exports f.o.b.	5 992	5 315	5 072	6 080	7 375	8 478	9 338	Biens : exportations f.à.b.
Goods: imports f.o.b.	-6 689	-6 350	-6 274	-7 617	-8 933	-10 190	-12 521	Biens : importations f.à.b.
Services: credit	1 993	2 278	2 540	2 794	3 231	3 938	4 924	Services : crédit
Services: debit	-1 103	-1 310	-1 300	-1 457	-1 811	-1 728	-2 107	Services : débit
Income: credit	1 384	953	805	791	1 055	1 403	1 876	Revenus : crédit
Income: debit	-1 974	-1 226	-1 614	-1 811	-2 180	-2 681	-3 187	Revenus : débit
Current transfers: credit	278	299	299	298	338	388	416	Transferts courants : crédit
Current transfers: debit	-52	-55	-64	-81	-97	-136	-163	Transferts courants : débit
Capital account, n.i.e.	2	0	0	0	16	15	44	Compte de capital, n.i.a.
Financial account, n.i.e.	1 301	194	178	497	2 040	375	2 774	Compte financier, n.i.a.
Net errors and omissions	-499	45	90	110	-358	308	-775	Erreurs et omissions nettes
Reserves and related items	-634	-144	269	396	-676	-172	-620	Réserves et postes apparentés
Papua New Guinea								**Papouasie-Nvl-Guinée**
Current account	282	-129	-35	-82	423	...	...	Compte des transac. courantes
Goods: exports f.o.b.	1 813	1 640	2 201	2 555	3 278	...	...	Biens : exportations f.à.b.
Goods: imports f.o.b.	-932	1 077	-1 187	-1 459	-1 525	...	...	Biens : importations f.à.b.
Services: credit	285	162	233	203	302	...	...	Services : crédit
Services: debit	-662	-678	-868	-998	-1 167	...	...	Services : débit
Income: credit	20	27	16	20	26	...	...	Revenus : crédit
Income: debit	-250	-229	-493	-456	-565	...	...	Revenus : débit
Current transfers: credit	76	86	144	130	167	...	...	Transferts courants : crédit
Current transfers: debit	-67	-59	-81	-77	-94	...	...	Transferts courants : débit
Capital account, n.i.e.	0	0	0	0	0	...	...	Compte de capital, n.i.a.
Financial account, n.i.e.	-152	56	-282	-42	-752	...	...	Compte financier, n.i.a.
Net errors and omissions	-2	91	40	26	47	...	...	Erreurs et omissions nettes
Reserves and related items	-129	19	277	98	282	...	...	Réserves et postes apparentés
Paraguay								**Paraguay**
Current account	-266	93	129	143	53	219	126	Compte des transac. courantes
Goods: exports f.o.b.	1 890	1 858	2 170	2 861	3 352	4 409	5 463	Biens : exportations f.à.b.
Goods: imports f.o.b.	-2 504	-2 138	-2 446	-3 105	-3 814	-5 022	-6 008	Biens : importations f.à.b.
Services: credit	555	568	574	628	693	809	853	Services : crédit
Services: debit	-390	-355	-329	-301	-343	-384	-463	Services : débit
Income: credit	256	196	166	165	206	301	319	Revenus : crédit
Income: debit	-240	-153	-171	-299	-264	-320	-411	Revenus : débit
Current transfers: credit	168	118	166	196	225	430	375	Transferts courants : crédit
Current transfers: debit	-2	-2	-2	-2	-2	-4	-2	Transferts courants : débit
Capital account, n.i.e.	15	4	15	16	20	30	28	Compte de capital, n.i.a.
Financial account, n.i.e.	151	44	132	19	301	177	639	Compte financier, n.i.a.
Net errors and omissions	53	-263	-41	96	-211	-43	-168	Erreurs et omissions nettes
Reserves and related items	47	123	-236	-273	-163	-383	-625	Réserves et postes apparentés
Peru								**Pérou**
Current account	-1 203	-1 110	-949	19	1 148	2 755	1 505	Compte des transac. courantes
Goods: exports f.o.b.	7 026	7 714	9 091	12 809	17 368	23 800	27 956	Biens : exportations f.à.b.
Goods: imports f.o.b.	-7 204	-7 393	-8 205	-9 805	-12 082	-14 866	-19 599	Biens : importations f.à.b.
Services: credit	1 437	1 455	1 716	1 993	2 289	2 647	3 343	Services : crédit
Services: debit	-2 400	-2 449	-2 616	-2 725	-3 123	-3 429	-4 270	Services : débit
Income: credit	670	370	322	332	625	1 033	1 567	Revenus : crédit
Income: debit	-1 771	-1 827	-2 466	-4 017	-5 701	-8 616	-9 985	Revenus : débit
Current transfers: credit	1 048	1 028	1 215	1 439	1 781	2 194	2 504	Transferts courants : crédit
Current transfers: debit	-8	-8	-6	-6	-10	-10	-10	Transferts courants : débit
Capital account, n.i.e.	-155	-112	-112	-86	-123	-127	-134	Compte de capital, n.i.a.
Financial account, n.i.e.	1 534	1 983	820	2 286	24	1 096	9 294	Compte financier, n.i.a.
Net errors and omissions	255	249	801	236	362	-503	-322	Erreurs et omissions nettes
Reserves and related items	-432	-1 010	-561	-2 456	-1 411	-3 221	-10 344	Réserves et postes apparentés
Philippines								**Philippines**
Current account	-1 744	-279	288	1 633	1 984	5 347	6 301	Compte des transac. courantes
Goods: exports f.o.b.	31 313	34 403	35 339	38 794	40 263	46 526	49 512	Biens : exportations f.à.b.
Goods: imports f.o.b.	-37 578	-39 933	-41 190	-44 478	-48 036	-53 258	-57 723	Biens : importations f.à.b.
Services: credit	3 072	3 428	3 389	4 043	4 525	6 444	8 448	Services : crédit
Services: debit	-5 360	-5 430	-5 352	-5 815	-5 865	-6 307	-7 371	Services : débit
Income: credit	3 553	3 306	3 330	3 725	3 937	4 388	5 488	Revenus : crédit
Income: debit	-3 604	-3 733	-3 614	-3 796	-4 231	-5 643	-6 030	Revenus : débit

69

Summary of balance of payments *(continued)*
Millions of US dollars
Résumé de la balance des paiements *(suite)*
Millions de dollars des E.-U.

Country or area	2001	2002	2003	2004	2005	2006	2007	Pays ou zone
Current transfers: credit	7 119	7 948	8 626	9 420	11 711	13 511	14 397	Transferts courants : crédit
Current transfers: debit	-259	-268	-240	-260	-320	-314	-420	Transferts courants : débit
Capital account, n.i.e.	62	27	54	17	40	138	24	Compte de capital, n.i.a.
Financial account, n.i.e.	366	394	481	-1 671	1 441	1 351	3 015	Compte financier, n.i.a.
Net errors and omissions	629	33	-902	-282	-1 803	-1 594	-633	Erreurs et omissions nettes
Reserves and related items	687	-175	79	303	-1 662	-5 242	-8 707	Réserves et postes apparentés
Poland								**Pologne**
Current account	-5 945	-5 544	-5 473	-10 067	-3 716	-9 394	-18 595	Compte des transac. courantes
Goods: exports f.o.b.	41 663	46 742	61 007	81 862	96 395	117 468	144 609	Biens : exportations f.à.b.
Goods: imports f.o.b.	-49 324	-53 991	-66 732	-87 484	-99 161	-124 474	-160 162	Biens : importations f.à.b.
Services: credit	9 753	10 037	11 174	13 471	16 258	20 592	28 790	Services : crédit
Services: debit	-8 967	-9 262	-10 931	-13 392	-15 520	-19 856	-24 072	Services : débit
Income: credit	3 401	2 776	3 284	5 305	6 998	9 040	10 039	Revenus : crédit
Income: debit	-4 015	-3 837	-5 745	-13 549	-13 695	-18 768	-26 292	Revenus : débit
Current transfers: credit	2 529	3 049	3 769	6 878	9 766	11 955	15 241	Transferts courants : crédit
Current transfers: debit	-985	-1 058	-1 299	-3 158	-4 757	-5 351	-6 748	Transferts courants : débit
Capital account, n.i.e.	76	-7	-46	1 180	995	2 105	4 771	Compte de capital, n.i.a.
Financial account, n.i.e.	3 173	7 180	8 686	8 038	15 228	13 101	39 832	Compte financier, n.i.a.
Net errors and omissions	2 269	-981	-1 961	1 650	-4 361	-3 323	-12 965	Erreurs et omissions nettes
Reserves and related items	427	-648	-1 206	-801	-8 146	-2 489	-13 044	Réserves et postes apparentés
Portugal								**Portugal**
Current account	-11 445	-10 264	-9 593	-13 616	-17 619	-19 640	-21 418	Compte des transac. courantes
Goods: exports f.o.b.	24 456	25 975	32 055	36 986	38 577	43 592	51 746	Biens : exportations f.à.b.
Goods: imports f.o.b.	-38 362	-39 286	-46 337	-55 386	-58 916	-64 510	-75 853	Biens : importations f.à.b.
Services: credit	9 379	10 357	12 354	14 701	15 193	17 839	23 156	Services : crédit
Services: debit	-6 826	-7 146	-8 293	-9 746	-10 456	-11 758	-13 950	Services : débit
Income: credit	5 669	4 900	6 622	8 040	9 307	13 518	17 332	Revenus : crédit
Income: debit	-9 127	-7 891	-9 260	-11 747	-14 151	-21 492	-27 467	Revenus : débit
Current transfers: credit	5 677	5 544	6 544	7 297	7 226	8 054	8 709	Transferts courants : crédit
Current transfers: debit	-2 312	-2 717	-3 278	-3 761	-4 398	-4 884	-5 090	Transferts courants : débit
Capital account, n.i.e.	1 069	1 906	2 977	2 773	2 115	1 527	2 837	Compte de capital, n.i.a.
Financial account, n.i.e.	10 606	8 796	-830	9 728	14 629	14 326	19 171	Compte financier, n.i.a.
Net errors and omissions	623	580	991	-749	-866	1 430	-1 552	Erreurs et omissions nettes
Reserves and related items	-852	-1 017	6 455	1 863	1 741	2 357	962	Réserves et postes apparentés
Republic of Moldova								**République de Moldova**
Current account	-37	-25	-130	-47	-248	-384	-748	Compte des transac. courantes
Goods: exports f.o.b.	565	660	805	994	1 105	1 059	1 368	Biens : exportations f.à.b.
Goods: imports f.o.b.	-880	-1 038	-1 428	-1 748	-2 296	-2 644	-3 676	Biens : importations f.à.b.
Services: credit	171	217	250	332	399	489	650	Services : crédit
Services: debit	-209	-257	-294	-353	-420	-484	-630	Services : débit
Income: credit	174	229	341	490	539	606	710	Revenus : crédit
Income: debit	-78	-73	-110	-133	-128	-204	-296	Revenus : débit
Current transfers: credit	236	256	334	407	597	855	1 207	Transferts courants : crédit
Current transfers: debit	-16	-19	-28	-36	-43	-60	-80	Transferts courants : débit
Capital account, n.i.e.	-21	-19	-19	-18	-17	-23	-8	Compte de capital, n.i.a.
Financial account, n.i.e.	19	21	84	113	200	359	989	Compte financier, n.i.a.
Net errors and omissions	16	-24	47	101	178	64	139	Erreurs et omissions nettes
Reserves and related items	23	48	18	-148	-114	-16	-372	Réserves et postes apparentés
Romania								**Roumanie**
Current account	-2 229	-1 525	-3 311	-6 382	-8 621	-12 785	-23 032	Compte des transac. courantes
Goods: exports f.o.b.	11 385	13 876	17 618	23 485	27 730	32 336	40 555	Biens : exportations f.à.b.
Goods: imports f.o.b.	-14 354	-16 487	-22 155	-30 150	-37 348	-47 172	-65 121	Biens : importations f.à.b.
Services: credit	2 032	2 347	3 028	3 614	5 083	7 032	9 502	Services : crédit
Services: debit	-2 153	-2 338	-2 958	-3 879	-5 518	-7 027	-8 879	Services : débit
Income: credit	455	413	372	433	1 533	2 176	3 287	Revenus : crédit
Income: debit	-737	-872	-1 077	-3 582	-4 432	-6 255	-8 987	Revenus : débit
Current transfers: credit	1 417	1 808	2 200	4 188	4 939	6 995	9 871	Transferts courants : crédit
Current transfers: debit	-274	-272	-339	-491	-607	-870	-3 260	Transferts courants : débit
Capital account, n.i.e.	95	93	213	643	731	-34	1 142	Compte de capital, n.i.a.
Financial account, n.i.e.	2 938	4 079	4 400	10 835	14 089	18 899	29 267	Compte financier, n.i.a.
Net errors and omissions	731	-856	-289	1 093	612	521	-1 098	Erreurs et omissions nettes
Reserves and related items	-1 535	-1 791	-1 013	-6 189	-6 811	-6 602	-6 279	Réserves et postes apparentés

Summary of balance of payments *(continued)*
Millions of US dollars
Résumé de la balance des paiements *(suite)*
Millions de dollars des E.-U.

Country or area	2001	2002	2003	2004	2005	2006	2007	Pays ou zone
Russian Federation								**Fédération de Russie**
Current account	33 935	29 280	35 410	59 512	84 409	94 340	76 241	Compte des transac. courantes
Goods: exports f.o.b.	101 884	111 204	135 929	183 207	243 798	303 550	354 401	Biens : exportations f.à.b.
Goods: imports f.o.b.	-53 764	-64 323	-76 070	-97 382	-125 434	-164 281	-223 486	Biens : importations f.à.b.
Services: credit	11 442	13 987	16 229	20 595	24 970	31 102	39 416	Services : crédit
Services: debit	-20 572	-23 937	-27 122	-33 287	-38 865	-44 839	-59 188	Services : débit
Income: credit	6 800	5 795	11 057	11 998	17 382	29 505	46 784	Revenus : crédit
Income: debit	-11 038	-12 773	-24 228	-24 769	-36 405	-59 160	-78 180	Revenus : débit
Current transfers: credit	744	1 490	2 537	3 467	4 490	6 403	8 423	Transferts courants : crédit
Current transfers: debit	-1 561	-2 164	-2 922	-4 317	-5 528	-7 940	-11 929	Transferts courants : débit
Capital account, n.i.e.	-9 378	-16 579	-993	-1 624	-12 764	191	-10 224	Compte de capital, n.i.a.
Financial account, n.i.e.	-3 732	2 101	3 024	-5 128	1 145	3 194	96 119	Compte financier, n.i.a.
Net errors and omissions	-9 558	-7 594	-9 179	-5 870	-7 821	9 741	-13 208	Erreurs et omissions nettes
Reserves and related items	-11 266	-7 208	28 262	-46 890	-64 968	-107 466	-148 928	Réserves et postes apparentés
Rwanda								**Rwanda**
Current account	-102	-126	-121	-198	-84	-180	-147	Compte des transac. courantes
Goods: exports f.o.b.	93	67	63	98	128	145	184	Biens : exportations f.à.b.
Goods: imports f.o.b.	-245	-233	-229	-276	-355	-488	-637	Biens : importations f.à.b.
Services: credit	66	65	76	103	129	131	179	Services : crédit
Services: debit	-189	-202	-204	-240	-304	-243	-272	Services : débit
Income: credit	14	8	6	6	27	27	48	Revenus : crédit
Income: debit	-34	-27	-37	-39	-44	-48	-63	Revenus : débit
Current transfers: credit	210	215	223	169	352	319	435	Transferts courants : crédit
Current transfers: debit	-18	-20	-20	-18	-18	-23	-22	Transferts courants : débit
Capital account, n.i.e.	50	66	41	61	93	1 323	161	Compte de capital, n.i.a.
Financial account, n.i.e.	-44	81	-21	-21	59	-1 204	35	Compte financier, n.i.a.
Net errors and omissions	71	-8	23	-9	26	87	4	Erreurs et omissions nettes
Reserves and related items	26	-13	78	168	23	-26	-53	Réserves et postes apparentés
Saint Kitts and Nevis								**Saint-Kitts-et-Nevis**
Current account	-107	-125	-116	-68	-65	-90	-135	Compte des transac. courantes
Goods: exports f.o.b.	55	63	57	59	64	58	57	Biens : exportations f.à.b.
Goods: imports f.o.b.	-167	-178	-176	-161	-185	-220	-240	Biens : Importations f.à.b.
Services: credit	98	90	108	135	163	173	161	Services : crédit
Services: debit	-75	-79	-80	-81	-95	-102	-114	Services : débit
Income: credit	5	6	6	8	11	13	14	Revenus : crédit
Income: debit	-39	-44	-49	-46	-46	-46	-45	Revenus : débit
Current transfers: credit	27	28	30	31	37	45	46	Transferts courants : crédit
Current transfers: debit	-11	-12	-11	-13	-13	-13	-14	Transferts courants : débit
Capital account, n.i.e.	11	15	5	5	15	13	10	Compte de capital, n.i.a.
Financial account, n.i.e.	114	116	105	75	29	90	136	Compte financier, n.i.a.
Net errors and omissions	-6	2	4	1	14	4	-4	Erreurs et omissions nettes
Reserves and related items	-12	-9	1	-14	7	-17	-7	Réserves et postes apparentés
Saint Lucia								**Sainte-Lucie**
Current account	-108	-106	-147	-87	-150	-303	-320	Compte des transac. courantes
Goods: exports f.o.b.	54	69	72	96	89	97	100	Biens : exportations f.à.b.
Goods: imports f.o.b.	-272	-272	-355	-348	-418	-521	-541	Biens : importations f.à.b.
Services: credit	274	250	318	367	410	334	347	Services : crédit
Services: debit	-131	-129	-145	-148	-172	-169	-176	Services : débit
Income: credit	3	4	5	6	8	10	6	Revenus : crédit
Income: debit	-50	-40	-56	-75	-81	-66	-68	Revenus : débit
Current transfers: credit	29	28	29	30	30	31	32	Transferts courants : crédit
Current transfers: debit	-15	-16	-16	-16	-17	-19	-20	Transferts courants : débit
Capital account, n.i.e.	25	20	17	3	5	11	6	Compte de capital, n.i.a.
Financial account, n.i.e.	87	94	136	106	123	309	327	Compte financier, n.i.a.
Net errors and omissions	8	-2	13	4	7	-4	6	Erreurs et omissions nettes
Reserves and related items	-13	-6	-18	-27	15	-14	-19	Réserves et postes apparentés
Saint Vincent-Grenadines								**Saint Vincent-Grenadines**
Current account	-37	-42	-79	-102	-99	-120	-149	Compte des transac. courantes
Goods: exports f.o.b.	43	41	40	39	43	41	51	Biens : exportations f.à.b.
Goods: imports f.o.b.	-152	-158	-177	-199	-212	-240	-276	Biens : importations f.à.b.
Services: credit	133	137	133	145	158	171	181	Services : crédit
Services: debit	-57	-57	-65	-73	-79	-88	-98	Services : débit
Income: credit	2	3	4	5	8	14	15	Revenus : crédit
Income: debit	-19	-21	-28	-33	-35	-38	-41	Revenus : débit

69

Summary of balance of payments *(continued)*
Millions of US dollars
Résumé de la balance des paiements *(suite)*
Millions de dollars des E.-U.

Country or area	2001	2002	2003	2004	2005	2006	2007	Pays ou zone
Current transfers: credit	23	24	24	25	26	32	33	Transferts courants : crédit
Current transfers: debit	-11	-12	-11	-11	-8	-12	-13	Transferts courants : débit
Capital account, n.i.e.	9	11	14	19	14	8	162	Compte de capital, n.i.a.
Financial account, n.i.e.	49	15	49	83	63	113	-24	Compte financier, n.i.a.
Net errors and omissions	-11	9	16	25	19	11	9	Erreurs et omissions nettes
Reserves and related items	-9	7	1	-25	3	-12	2	Réserves et postes apparentés
Samoa								**Samoa**
Current account	...	...	...	-26	-25	-49	-38	Compte des transac. courantes
Goods: exports f.o.b.	...	...	...	12	12	10	14	Biens : exportations f.à.b.
Goods: imports f.o.b.	...	...	...	-155	-187	-219	-227	Biens : importations f.à.b.
Services: credit	...	...	...	95	113	133	139	Services : crédit
Services: debit	...	...	...	-42	-56	-57	-55	Services : débit
Income: credit	...	...	...	4	6	6	7	Revenus : crédit
Income: debit	...	...	...	-22	-20	-18	-24	Revenus : débit
Current transfers: credit	...	...	...	96	115	107	119	Transferts courants : crédit
Current transfers: debit	...	...	...	-14	-8	-13	-10	Transferts courants : débit
Capital account, n.i.e.	...	...	...	39	39	52	29	Compte de capital, n.i.a.
Financial account, n.i.e.	...	...	...	-2	-8	-3	6	Compte financier, n.i.a.
Net errors and omissions	...	...	...	-3	-7	-5	12	Erreurs et omissions nettes
Reserves and related items	...	...	...	-8	1	5	-9	Réserves et postes apparentés
Sao Tome and Principe								**Sao Tomé-et-Principe**
Current account	-27	-27	-28	-38	-36	-58	-67	Compte des transac. courantes
Goods: exports f.o.b.	3	6	7	5	7	8	7	Biens : exportations f.à.b.
Goods: imports f.o.b.	-27	-28	-34	-38	-42	-59	-65	Biens : importations f.à.b.
Services: credit	8	9	9	10	9	8	4	Services : crédit
Services: debit	-12	-12	-14	-16	-11	-18	-19	Services : débit
Income: credit	1	1	1	1	2	6	7	Revenus : crédit
Income: debit	-4	-4	-4	-4	-5	-3	-2	Revenus : débit
Current transfers: credit	5	4	7	8	7	5	6	Transferts courants : crédit
Current transfers: debit	-1	-1	-1	-4	-4	-5	-5	Transferts courants : débit
Capital account, n.i.e.	17	15	19	18	66	24	62	Compte de capital, n.i.a.
Financial account, n.i.e.	10	6	9	16	12	36	-144	Compte financier, n.i.a.
Net errors and omissions	1	2	3	-4	2	4	2	Erreurs et omissions nettes
Reserves and related items	-2	3	-2	7	-43	-6	146	Réserves et postes apparentés
Saudi Arabia								**Arabie saoudite**
Current account	9 353	11 873	28 048	51 926	90 060	99 066	95 080	Compte des transac. courantes
Goods: exports f.o.b.	67 973	72 464	93 244	125 998	180 712	211 305	234 145	Biens : exportations f.à.b.
Goods: imports f.o.b.	-28 607	-29 624	-33 868	-41 050	-54 595	-63 914	-82 598	Biens : importations f.à.b.
Services: credit	5 008	5 177	5 713	5 852	6 677	7 297	7 901	Services : crédit
Services: debit	-7 155	-7 152	-7 936	-11 057	-14 520	-19 390	-30 798	Services : débit
Income: credit	4 125	3 714	2 977	4 278	4 964	10 376	15 014	Revenus : crédit
Income: debit	-4 644	-3 925	-4 277	-3 800	-4 963	-9 734	-14 776	Revenus : débit
Current transfers: credit	0	0	0	0	0	0	0	Transferts courants : crédit
Current transfers: debit	-27 346	-28 782	-27 804	-28 293	-28 215	-36 874	-33 808	Transferts courants : débit
Capital account, n.i.e.	0	0	0	0	0	0	0	Compte de capital, n.i.a.
Financial account, n.i.e.	-11 262	-9 137	-26 440	-47 428	-90 525	-98 172	-88 912	Compte financier, n.i.a.
Net errors and omissions	0	0	0	0	^0	0	^0	Erreurs et omissions nettes
Reserves and related items	1 909	-2 736	-1 608	-4 498	465	-894	-6 168	Réserves et postes apparentés
Senegal								**Sénégal**
Current account	-245	-317	-436	-513	-677	-861	...	Compte des transac. courantes
Goods: exports f.o.b.	1 003	1 067	1 257	1 509	1 578	1 594	...	Biens : exportations f.à.b.
Goods: imports f.o.b.	-1 428	-1 604	-2 066	-2 496	-2 889	-3 194	...	Biens : importations f.à.b.
Services: credit	398	456	569	670	774	804	...	Services : crédit
Services: debit	-414	-474	-591	-698	-805	-839	...	Services : débit
Income: credit	62	65	86	95	95	121	...	Revenus : crédit
Income: debit	-166	-195	-223	-226	-185	-185	...	Revenus : débit
Current transfers: credit	354	414	596	715	859	974	...	Transferts courants : crédit
Current transfers: debit	-53	-46	-65	-83	-105	-137	...	Transferts courants : débit
Capital account, n.i.e.	146	127	150	750	199	2 291	...	Compte de capital, n.i.a.
Financial account, n.i.e.	-103	-88	3	-54	118	-1 581	...	Compte financier, n.i.a.
Net errors and omissions	8	31	11	16	-2	28	...	Erreurs et omissions nettes
Reserves and related items	194	247	273	-199	362	122	...	Réserves et postes apparentés

69
Summary of balance of payments *(continued)*
Millions of US dollars
Résumé de la balance des paiements *(suite)*
Millions de dollars des E.-U.

Country or area	2001	2002	2003	2004	2005	2006	2007	Pays ou zone
Serbia								**Serbie**
Current account	...	...	...	...	...	...	-6 346	Compte des transac. courantes
Goods: exports f.o.b.	...	...	...	...	...	...	8 776	Biens : exportations f.à.b.
Goods: imports f.o.b.	...	...	...	...	...	...	-17 916	Biens : importations f.à.b.
Services: credit	...	...	...	...	...	...	3 168	Services : crédit
Services: debit	...	...	...	...	...	...	-3 516	Services : débit
Income: credit	...	...	...	...	...	...	710	Revenus : crédit
Income: debit	...	...	...	...	...	...	-1 539	Revenus : débit
Current transfers: credit	...	...	...	...	...	...	4 285	Transferts courants : crédit
Current transfers: debit	...	...	...	...	...	...	-315	Transferts courants : débit
Capital account, n.i.e.	...	...	...	...	...	...	-408	Compte de capital, n.i.a.
Financial account, n.i.e.	...	...	...	...	...	...	7 693	Compte financier, n.i.a.
Net errors and omissions	...	...	...	...	...	...	323	Erreurs et omissions nettes
Reserves and related items	...	...	...	...	...	...	-1 263	Réserves et postes apparentés
Seychelles								**Seychelles**
Current account	-158	-108	-12	-64	-188	-145	-275	Compte des transac. courantes
Goods: exports f.o.b.	216	237	286	301	351	420	392	Biens : exportations f.à.b.
Goods: imports f.o.b.	-429	-380	-376	-456	-650	-710	-804	Biens : importations f.à.b.
Services: credit	294	313	330	327	369	430	472	Services : crédit
Services: debit	-216	-217	-220	-216	-235	-274	-303	Services : débit
Income: credit	8	7	12	9	10	10	10	Revenus : crédit
Income: debit	-37	-75	-55	-43	-50	-54	-81	Revenus : débit
Current transfers: credit	8	8	13	17	21	43	49	Transferts courants : crédit
Current transfers: debit	-4	-2	-3	-3	-4	-10	-11	Transferts courants : débit
Capital account, n.i.e.	9	5	7	1	30	13	5	Compte de capital, n.i.a.
Financial account, n.i.e.	94	131	-31	-30	129	224	295	Compte financier, n.i.a.
Net errors and omissions	1	-10	-5	1	-1	2	2	Erreurs et omissions nettes
Reserves and related items	54	-17	41	93	29	-94	-27	Réserves et postes apparentés
Sierra Leone								**Sierra Leone**
Current account	-98	-125	-99	-141	-171	-135	-238	Compte des transac. courantes
Goods: exports f.o.b.	29	60	111	154	184	262	293	Biens : exportations f.à.b.
Goods: imports f.o.b.	-165	-255	-311	-274	-362	-351	-395	Biens : importations f.à.b.
Services: credit	52	38	66	61	78	43	42	Services : crédit
Services: debit	-111	-81	-94	-92	-91	-86	-94	Services : débit
Income: credit	4	18	2	4	5	12	43	Revenus : crédit
Income: debit	-15	-21	-17	-71	-56	-52	-148	Revenus : débit
Current transfers: credit	121	119	149	80	74	73	156	Transferts courants : crédit
Current transfers: debit	-13	-4	-5	-3	-2	-36	-135	Transferts courants : débit
Capital account, n.i.e.	^0	8	16	18	37	224	240	Compte de capital, n.i.a.
Financial account, n.i.e.	30	19	34	76	63	36	108	Compte financier, n.i.a.
Net errors and omissions	97	-16	-50	-54	-58	-64	-140	Erreurs et omissions nettes
Reserves and related items	-30	114	100	100	130	-60	30	Réserves et postes apparentés
Singapore								**Singapour**
Current account	10 715	11 170	21 593	18 256	22 223	29 800	39 106	Compte des transac. courantes
Goods: exports f.o.b.	136 609	140 776	161 702	199 393	232 512	275 288	303 136	Biens : exportations f.à.b.
Goods: imports f.o.b.	-119 358	-121 972	-132 266	-168 330	-195 477	-231 855	-254 036	Biens : importations f.à.b.
Services: credit	27 405	29 525	36 288	46 804	52 940	61 100	69 829	Services : crédit
Services: debit	-31 762	-33 436	-40 081	-50 143	-55 630	-63 744	-72 419	Services : débit
Income: credit	14 382	14 175	17 421	21 535	27 239	32 200	42 982	Revenus : crédit
Income: debit	-14 960	-16 445	-20 065	-29 663	-38 097	-41 780	-48 690	Revenus : débit
Current transfers: credit	124	127	131	136	138	145	152	Transferts courants : crédit
Current transfers: debit	-1 727	-1 581	-1 538	-1 477	-1 402	-1 553	-1 847	Transferts courants : débit
Capital account, n.i.e.	-161	-160	-168	-184	-202	-231	-259	Compte de capital, n.i.a.
Financial account, n.i.e.	-11 772	-10 304	-17 815	-8 516	-12 673	-14 105	-18 388	Compte financier, n.i.a.
Net errors and omissions	301	551	3 093	2 636	2 966	1 543	-818	Erreurs et omissions nettes
Reserves and related items	917	-1 256	-6 703	-12 193	-12 315	-17 008	-19 640	Réserves et postes apparentés
Slovakia								**Slovaquie**
Current account	...	-1 955	-282	-3 296	-4 005	-3 937	-4 103	Compte des transac. courantes
Goods: exports f.o.b.	...	14 460	21 944	27 663	31 851	41 735	57 806	Biens : exportations f.à.b.
Goods: imports f.o.b.	...	-16 626	-22 593	-29 220	-34 214	-44 283	-58 715	Biens : importations f.à.b.
Services: credit	...	2 812	3 297	3 735	4 405	5 436	7 063	Services : crédit
Services: debit	...	-2 351	-3 056	-3 466	-4 078	-4 675	-6 531	Services : débit
Income: credit	...	342	907	1 002	1 585	1 959	2 340	Revenus : crédit
Income: debit	...	-791	-1 026	-3 184	-3 570	-4 051	-5 628	Revenus : débit

69

Summary of balance of payments *(continued)*
Millions of US dollars

Résumé de la balance des paiements *(suite)*
Millions de dollars des E.-U.

Country or area	2001	2002	2003	2004	2005	2006	2007	Pays ou zone
Current transfers: credit	...	480	537	890	1 403	1 623	2 070	Transferts courants : crédit
Current transfers: debit	...	-282	-292	-717	-1 386	-1 681	-2 508	Transferts courants : débit
Capital account, n.i.e.	...	110	102	135	-18	-42	465	Compte de capital, n.i.a.
Financial account, n.i.e.	...	5 230	1 661	4 838	6 219	1 155	7 023	Compte financier, n.i.a.
Net errors and omissions	...	298	27	56	324	167	302	Erreurs et omissions nettes
Reserves and related items	...	-3 684	-1 508	-1 732	-2 521	2 656	-3 688	Réserves et postes apparentés
Slovenia								**Slovénie**
Current account	31	244	-216	-893	-681	-1 088	-2 293	Compte des transac. courantes
Goods: exports f.o.b.	9 343	10 471	12 916	16 065	18 146	21 397	27 123	Biens : exportations f.à.b.
Goods: imports f.o.b.	-9 962	-10 719	-13 539	-17 322	-19 404	-22 856	-29 432	Biens : importations f.à.b.
Services: credit	1 961	2 316	2 791	3 455	3 976	4 344	5 650	Services : crédit
Services: debit	-1 458	-1 732	-2 183	-2 603	-2 915	-3 254	-4 231	Services : débit
Income: credit	463	468	589	667	781	1 135	1 400	Revenus : crédit
Income: debit	-444	-617	-821	-1 060	-1 143	-1 642	-2 400	Revenus : débit
Current transfers: credit	390	473	538	698	878	988	1 251	Transferts courants : crédit
Current transfers: debit	-261	-416	-508	-792	-998	-1 202	-1 654	Transferts courants : débit
Capital account, n.i.e.	-3	-159	-191	-123	-138	-169	-72	Compte de capital, n.i.a.
Financial account, n.i.e.	1 204	1 987	567	702	844	-129	2 707	Compte financier, n.i.a.
Net errors and omissions	53	-255	150	17	181	-270	-541	Erreurs et omissions nettes
Reserves and related items	-1 285	-1 817	-310	296	-206	1 656	199	Réserves et postes apparentés
Solomon Islands								**Iles Salomon**
Current account	-65	-68	-40	-19	-90	-97	...	Compte des transac. courantes
Goods: exports f.o.b.	40	33	67	86	105	122	...	Biens : exportations f.à.b.
Goods: imports f.o.b.	-85	-69	-94	-121	-185	-217	...	Biens : importations f.à.b.
Services: credit	52	16	25	31	41	60	...	Services : crédit
Services: debit	-81	-49	-62	-41	-58	-95	...	Services : débit
Income: credit	7	3	4	11	9	19	...	Revenus : crédit
Income: debit	-7	-10	-7	-8	-7	-13	...	Revenus : débit
Current transfers: credit	31	29	46	50	41	69	...	Transferts courants : crédit
Current transfers: debit	-21	-20	-19	-25	-36	-42	...	Transferts courants : débit
Capital account, n.i.e.	4	8	12	1	28	29	...	Compte de capital, n.i.a.
Financial account, n.i.e.	15	-4	-29	-19	-9	-32	...	Compte financier, n.i.a.
Net errors and omissions	49	55	35	-6	54	74	...	Erreurs et omissions nettes
Reserves and related items	-3	9	22	43	18	25	...	Réserves et postes apparentés
South Africa								**Afrique du Sud**
Current account	343	884	-1 902	-7 003	-9 723	-16 121	-20 780	Compte des transac. courantes
Goods: exports f.o.b.	31 064	31 772	38 700	48 237	55 284	64 163	75 920	Biens : exportations f.à.b.
Goods: imports f.o.b.	-25 809	-27 016	-35 270	-48 518	-56 279	-70 031	-81 661	Biens : importations f.à.b.
Services: credit	4 845	4 985	8 298	9 682	11 157	12 014	13 562	Services : crédit
Services: debit	-5 232	-5 504	-8 045	-10 328	-12 155	-14 290	-16 563	Services : débit
Income: credit	2 480	2 179	2 857	3 259	4 640	6 078	6 882	Revenus : crédit
Income: debit	-6 267	-4 975	-7 447	-7 576	-9 569	-11 238	-15 967	Revenus : débit
Current transfers: credit	126	139	252	257	240	261	265	Transferts courants : crédit
Current transfers: debit	-865	-695	-1 248	-2 015	-3 041	-3 078	-3 218	Transferts courants : débit
Capital account, n.i.e.	-31	-15	44	52	30	30	28	Compte de capital, n.i.a.
Financial account, n.i.e.	-1 188	-707	-1 961	7 651	12 583	15 291	22 038	Compte financier, n.i.a.
Net errors and omissions	855	-485	3 466	5 623	2 875	4 510	4 451	Erreurs et omissions nettes
Reserves and related items	22	322	354	-6 324	-5 766	-3 711	-5 737	Réserves et postes apparentés
Spain								**Espagne**
Current account	-24 065	-22 239	-30 886	-54 865	-83 388	-110 124	-145 355	Compte des transac. courantes
Goods: exports f.o.b.	117 522	127 162	158 049	185 209	196 580	220 774	256 681	Biens : exportations f.à.b.
Goods: imports f.o.b.	-152 039	-161 794	-203 205	-251 939	-281 784	-325 444	-380 197	Biens : importations f.à.b.
Services: credit	55 651	60 247	74 308	86 078	94 663	106 628	129 303	Services : crédit
Services: debit	-35 182	-38 712	-47 951	-59 188	-67 129	-78 423	-98 900	Services : débit
Income: credit	20 243	21 536	27 209	33 948	39 445	55 855	72 688	Revenus : crédit
Income: debit	-31 509	-33 194	-38 910	-48 986	-60 701	-81 814	-115 931	Revenus : débit
Current transfers: credit	12 143	14 575	17 048	20 366	20 194	21 563	26 058	Transferts courants : crédit
Current transfers: debit	-10 893	-12 059	-17 434	-20 353	-24 656	-29 263	-35 058	Transferts courants : débit
Capital account, n.i.e.	4 811	7 236	9 274	10 450	10 107	7 857	6 291	Compte de capital, n.i.a.
Financial account, n.i.e.	18 169	17 782	4 353	36 964	73 885	104 951	134 004	Compte financier, n.i.a.
Net errors and omissions	-257	912	1 769	1 039	-2 524	-2 106	5 275	Erreurs et omissions nettes
Reserves and related items	1 341	-3 690	15 490	6 412	1 920	-578	-215	Réserves et postes apparentés

69

Summary of balance of payments *(continued)*
Millions of US dollars
Résumé de la balance des paiements *(suite)*
Millions de dollars des E.-U.

Country or area	2001	2002	2003	2004	2005	2006	2007	Pays ou zone
Sri Lanka								**Sri Lanka**
Current account	-237	-268	-106	-677	-743	-1 599	-1 465	Compte des transac. courantes
Goods: exports f.o.b.	4 817	4 699	5 133	5 757	6 347	6 883	7 741	Biens : exportations f.à.b.
Goods: imports f.o.b.	-5 377	-5 495	-6 005	-7 200	-7 977	-9 228	-10 170	Biens : importations f.à.b.
Services: credit	1 355	1 268	1 411	1 527	1 540	1 625	1 712	Services : crédit
Services: debit	-1 749	-1 584	-1 679	-1 908	-2 089	-2 394	-2 603	Services : débit
Income: credit	108	75	170	157	76	312	449	Revenus : crédit
Income: debit	-375	-328	-341	-360	-375	-700	-807	Revenus : débit
Current transfers: credit	1 155	1 287	1 414	1 564	1 968	2 161	2 502	Transferts courants : crédit
Current transfers: debit	-172	-190	-209	-214	-233	-258	-288	Transferts courants : débit
Capital account, n.i.e.	50	65	74	64	250	291	269	Compte do capital, n.i.a.
Financial account, n.i.e.	-136	-196	-219	-133	67	687	14	Compte financier, n.i.a.
Net errors and omissions	15	136	-114	-189	-73	-96	-192	Erreurs et omissions nettes
Reserves and related items	308	262	365	935	498	717	1 374	Réserves et postes apparentés
Sudan								**Soudan**
Current account	-618	-1 008	-955	-871	-3 013	-5 199	-3 447	Compte des transac. courantes
Goods: exports f.o.b.	1 699	1 949	2 542	3 778	4 824	5 657	8 879	Biens : exportations f.à.b.
Goods: imports f.o.b.	-1 395	-2 294	-2 536	-3 586	-5 946	-7 105	-7 722	Biens : importations f.à.b.
Services: credit	15	132	36	44	114	247	384	Services : crédit
Services: debit	-660	-818	-830	-1 065	-1 844	-2 800	-2 939	Services : débit
Income: credit	18	29	10	22	44	89	184	Revenus : crédit
Income: debit	-572	-638	-879	-1 135	-1 406	-2 103	-2 437	Revenus : débit
Current transfers: credit	730	1 086	1 218	1 580	1 681	1 900	2 321	Transferts courants : crédit
Current transfers: debit	-453	-454	-517	-510	-480	-1 084	-2 118	Transferts courants : débit
Capital account, n.i.e.	-93	0	0	0	0	0	0	Compte de capital, n.i.a.
Financial account, n.i.e.	561	761	1 284	1 428	2 885	4 739	2 996	Compte financier, n.i.a.
Net errors and omissions	-24	479	-14	212	727	-131	27	Erreurs et omissions nettes
Reserves and related items	175	-232	-315	769	-598	591	424	Réserves et postes apparentés
Suriname								**Suriname**
Current account	-84	-131	-159	-138	-144	110	185	Compte des transac. courantes
Goods: exports f.o.b.	437	369	488	782	1 212	1 174	1 359	Biens : exportations f.à.b.
Goods: imports f.o.b.	-297	-322	-458	-740	-1 189	-1 013	-1 185	Biens : importations f.à.b.
Services: credit	59	39	59	141	204	234	245	Services : crédit
Services: debit	-174	-166	-195	-271	-352	-269	-317	Services : débit
Income: credit	5	8	12	16	24	28	44	Revenus : crédit
Income: debit	-113	-51	-60	-79	-64	-80	-35	Revenus : débit
Current transfers: credit	2	13	25	76	52	74	138	Transferts courants : crédit
Current transfers: debit	-3	-21	-30	-63	-30	-38	-62	Transferts courants : débit
Capital account, n.i.e.	2	6	9	19	15	19	8	Compte de capital, n.i.a.
Financial account, n.i.e.	104	-38	-37	-24	-21	-181	-177	Compte financier, n.i.a.
Net errors and omissions	56	144	194	218	169	145	161	Erreurs et omissions nettes
Reserves and related items	-78	19	-7	-76	-20	-94	-177	Réserves et postes apparentés
Swaziland								**Swaziland**
Current account	9	33	89	71	-103	-197	-66	Compte des transac. courantes
Goods: exports f.o.b.	1 039	1 079	1 667	1 806	1 637	1 663	1 745	Biens : exportations f.à.b.
Goods: imports f.o.b.	-1 120	-1 027	-1 540	-1 715	-1 895	-1 915	-2 016	Biens : importations f.à.b.
Services: credit	114	93	205	250	283	283	455	Services : crédit
Services: debit	-208	-210	-349	-378	-403	-373	-507	Services : débit
Income: credit	136	127	61	128	271	242	281	Revenus : crédit
Income: debit	-43	-124	-105	-125	-93	-228	-217	Revenus : débit
Current transfers: credit	230	216	337	371	340	366	403	Transferts courants : crédit
Current transfers: debit	-138	-120	-186	-265	-242	-235	-209	Transferts courants : débit
Capital account, n.i.e.	^0	^0	0	-1	-3	25	-30	Compte de capital, n.i.a.
Financial account, n.i.e.	-144	-166	-89	-204	148	261	431	Compte financier, n.i.a.
Net errors and omissions	210	62	-92	168	-41	-238	-701	Erreurs et omissions nettes
Reserves and related items	-75	70	92	-35	-1	149	365	Réserves et postes apparentés
Sweden								**Suède**
Current account	6 696	12 784	22 844	24 127	25 526	33 159	38 416	Compte des transac. courantes
Goods: exports f.o.b.	76 200	84 172	102 080	123 187	131 976	148 789	170 462	Biens : exportations f.à.b.
Goods: imports f.o.b.	-62 368	-67 541	-83 147	-100 217	-112 274	-128 290	-152 230	Biens : importations f.à.b.
Services: credit	21 997	24 009	30 654	39 023	42 887	49 797	63 587	Services : crédit
Services: debit	-23 020	-23 958	-28 771	-33 138	-35 273	-39 571	-47 954	Services : débit
Income: credit	17 934	18 018	22 934	31 332	38 196	50 620	62 457	Revenus : crédit
Income: debit	-20 786	-19 044	-22 638	-31 310	-35 412	-43 241	-52 923	Revenus : débit

69

Summary of balance of payments *(continued)*
Millions of US dollars
Résumé de la balance des paiements *(suite)*
Millions de dollars des E.-U.

Country or area	2001	2002	2003	2004	2005	2006	2007	Pays ou zone
Current transfers: credit	2 578	3 345	3 577	4 067	5 027	5 107	4 741	Transferts courants : crédit
Current transfers: debit	-5 839	-6 218	-1 845	-8 817	-9 601	-10 051	-9 724	Transferts courants : débit
Capital account, n.i.e.	509	-79	-46	34	308	-2 556	-441	Compte de capital, n.i.a.
Financial account, n.i.e.	1 824	-10 704	-20 163	-26 010	-28 483	-32 016	-22 075	Compte financier, n.i.a.
Net errors and omissions	-10 078	-1 336	-558	750	2 899	2 702	-16 348	Erreurs et omissions nettes
Reserves and related items	1 048	-665	-2 076	1 100	-250	-1 289	447	Réserves et postes apparentés
Switzerland								**Suisse**
Current account	22 223	24 914	43 398	54 695	51 284	56 060	43 946	Compte des transac. courantes
Goods: exports f.o.b.	95 897	104 281	118 837	141 874	151 309	167 221	200 490	Biens : exportations f.à.b.
Goods: imports f.o.b.	-94 264	-97 584	-111 831	-126 089	-145 442	-162 213	-187 740	Biens : importations f.à.b.
Services: credit	29 568	30 991	36 269	43 941	49 766	55 274	66 374	Services : crédit
Services: debit	-15 366	-16 150	-18 533	-23 760	-27 411	-28 317	-33 373	Services : débit
Income: credit	51 896	41 331	62 761	71 334	101 978	108 873	126 193	Revenus : crédit
Income: debit	-40 004	-32 024	-38 489	-46 093	-67 956	-75 429	-118 592	Revenus : débit
Current transfers: credit	9 721	10 635	13 198	14 300	15 504	17 639	22 883	Transferts courants : crédit
Current transfers: debit	-15 225	-16 567	-18 815	-20 811	-26 464	-26 989	-32 288	Transferts courants : débit
Capital account, n.i.e.	1 523	-1 159	-667	-1 409	-665	-2 770	-2 299	Compte de capital, n.i.a.
Financial account, n.i.e.	-36 679	-22 789	-24 311	-64 032	-86 182	-70 691	-29 764	Compte financier, n.i.a.
Net errors and omissions	13 555	1 584	-15 016	12 363	17 348	17 771	-8 423	Erreurs et omissions nettes
Reserves and related items	-622	-2 549	-3 405	-1 618	18 215	-370	-3 461	Réserves et postes apparentés
Syrian Arab Republic								**Rép. arabe syrienne**
Current account	1 221	1 440	728	587	295	890	...	Compte des transac. courantes
Goods: exports f.o.b.	5 706	6 668	5 762	7 220	8 602	10 245	...	Biens : exportations f.à.b.
Goods: imports f.o.b.	-4 282	-4 458	-4 430	-6 957	-8 742	-9 359	...	Biens : importations f.à.b.
Services: credit	1 781	1 559	1 331	2 613	2 910	2 924	...	Services : crédit
Services: debit	-1 694	-1 883	-1 806	-2 235	-2 359	-2 520	...	Services : débit
Income: credit	379	250	282	385	395	428	...	Revenus : crédit
Income: debit	-1 162	-1 175	-1 139	-1 114	-1 258	-1 363	...	Revenus : débit
Current transfers: credit	512	499	743	690	763	770	...	Transferts courants : crédit
Current transfers: debit	-19	-20	-15	-16	-16	-235	...	Transferts courants : débit
Capital account, n.i.e.	17	20	20	18	18	18	...	Compte de capital, n.i.a.
Financial account, n.i.e.	-244	-250	-436	-97	-162	-1 052	...	Compte financier, n.i.a.
Net errors and omissions	26	-160	383	-256	-137	-588	...	Erreurs et omissions nettes
Reserves and related items	-1 020	-1 050	-695	-251	-14	732	...	Réserves et postes apparentés
Tajikistan								**Tadjikistan**
Current account	...	-15	-5	-57	-19	-21	-495	Compte des transac. courantes
Goods: exports f.o.b.	...	699	906	1 097	1 108	1 512	1 557	Biens : exportations f.à.b.
Goods: imports f.o.b.	...	-823	-1 026	-1 232	-1 431	-1 955	-3 115	Biens : importations f.à.b.
Services: credit	...	69	89	123	146	134	149	Services : crédit
Services: debit	...	-105	-122	-213	-252	-394	-592	Services : débit
Income: credit	...	1	1	2	10	12	22	Revenus : crédit
Income: debit	...	-42	-71	-59	-50	-76	-73	Revenus : débit
Current transfers: credit	...	202	285	348	600	1 146	1 794	Transferts courants : crédit
Current transfers: debit	...	-16	-67	-123	-150	-400	-237	Transferts courants : débit
Capital account, n.i.e.	...	0	0	0	0	^0	33	Compte de capital, n.i.a.
Financial account, n.i.e.	...	72	63	93	101	276	811	Compte financier, n.i.a.
Net errors and omissions	...	-56	-30	-32	-76	-265	-363	Erreurs et omissions nettes
Reserves and related items	...	-2	-28	-4	-6	10	14	Réserves et postes apparentés
Thailand								**Thaïlande**
Current account	5 101	4 654	4 772	2 759	-7 647	2 175	15 755	Compte des transac. courantes
Goods: exports f.o.b.	63 082	66 052	78 083	94 979	109 369	127 929	150 026	Biens : exportations f.à.b.
Goods: imports f.o.b.	-54 539	-57 008	-66 909	-84 194	-105 981	-114 085	-124 479	Biens : importations f.à.b.
Services: credit	13 024	15 391	15 798	19 040	20 163	24 822	30 357	Services : crédit
Services: debit	-14 610	-16 720	-18 169	-23 077	-27 027	-33 015	-38 425	Services : débit
Income: credit	3 917	3 421	3 150	3 244	3 640	4 659	6 772	Revenus : crédit
Income: debit	-6 375	-7 084	-8 123	-9 364	-10 813	-11 502	-12 433	Revenus : débit
Current transfers: credit	990	979	1 326	2 479	3 351	3 764	4 395	Transferts courants : crédit
Current transfers: debit	-389	-375	-385	-348	-348	-396	-457	Transferts courants : débit
Capital account, n.i.e.	0	0	0	0	...	...	...	Compte de capital, n.i.a.
Financial account, n.i.e.	-2 498	-540	-4 385	3 664	11 082	5 649	-3 015	Compte financier, n.i.a.
Net errors and omissions	-327	1 423	132	-710	1 981	4 845	4 337	Erreurs et omissions nettes
Reserves and related items	-2 276	-5 537	-518	-5 713	-5 417	-12 669	-17 077	Réserves et postes apparentés

69

Summary of balance of payments *(continued)*
Millions of US dollars
Résumé de la balance des paiements *(suite)*
Millions de dollars des E.-U.

Country or area	2001	2002	2003	2004	2005	2006	2007	Pays ou zone
TFYR of Macedonia								**Ex-R.Y. Macédoine**
Current account	-236	-377	-184	-453	-158	-56	-247	Compte des transac. courantes
Goods: exports f.o.b.	1 155	1 112	1 363	1 675	2 041	2 396	3 349	Biens : exportations f.à.b.
Goods: imports f.o.b.	-1 682	-1 918	-2 214	-2 814	-3 104	-3 681	-4 976	Biens : importations f.à.b.
Services: credit	245	253	380	452	515	601	818	Services : crédit
Services: debit	-264	-275	-387	-507	-549	-573	-783	Services : débit
Income: credit	53	51	60	85	98	135	213	Revenus : crédit
Income: debit	-81	-95	-123	-124	-211	-172	-248	Revenus : débit
Current transfers: credit	372	535	774	825	1 095	1 279	1 480	Transferts courants : crédit
Current transfers: debit	-35	-41	-38	-45	-43	-42	-100	Transferts courants : débit
Capital account, n.i.e.	1	8	-7	-5	-2	-1	-2	Compte de capital, n.i.a.
Financial account, n.i.e.	321	249	281	467	578	435	474	Compte financier, n.i.a.
Net errors and omissions	-1	-11	-34	19	-7	8	-27	Erreurs et omissions nettes
Reserves and related items	-86	131	-55	-28	-411	-385	-199	Réserves et postes apparentés
Togo								**Togo**
Current account	-169	-140	-162	-206	-461	-340	...	Compte des transac. courantes
Goods: exports f.o.b.	357	424	598	601	660	754	...	Biens : exportations f.à.b.
Goods: imports f.o.b.	-516	-576	-755	-853	-1 172	-1 219	...	Biens : importations f.à.b.
Services: credit	72	90	95	150	177	216	...	Services : crédit
Services: debit	-130	-148	-204	-239	-279	-298	...	Services : débit
Income: credit	26	26	27	39	44	48	...	Revenus : crédit
Income: debit	-55	-48	-50	-73	-79	-86	...	Revenus : débit
Current transfers: credit	88	113	161	207	229	285	...	Transferts courants : crédit
Current transfers: debit	-11	-22	-34	-37	-42	-41	...	Transferts courants : débit
Capital account, n.i.e.	21	14	21	40	51	64	...	Compte de capital, n.i.a.
Financial account, n.i.e.	151	151	143	292	287	414	...	Compte financier, n.i.a.
Net errors and omissions	-5	5	-10	14	9	20	...	Erreurs et omissions nettes
Reserves and related items	2	-30	9	-141	113	-158	...	Réserves et postes apparentés
Tonga								**Tonga**
Current account	-11	-3	-10	-15	-14	-15	-24	Compte des transac. courantes
Goods: exports f.o.b.	7	18	21	19	18	10	9	Biens : exportations f.à.b.
Goods: imports f.o.b.	-64	-73	-75	-86	-100	-86	-127	Biens : importations f.à.b.
Services: credit	20	23	26	27	37	31	33	Services : crédit
Services: debit	-28	-32	-44	-52	-50	-58	-52	Services : débit
Income: credit	6	7	8	5	8	11	11	Revenus : crédit
Income: debit	-2	-4	-4	-7	-2	-3	-4	Revenus : débit
Current transfers: credit	63	75	67	92	87	93	119	Transferts courants : crédit
Current transfers: debit	-12	-16	-8	-13	-12	-13	-13	Transferts courants : débit
Capital account, n.i.e.	10	13	10	11	13	7	18	Compte de capital, n.i.a.
Financial account, n.i.e.	1	-3	8	28	3	12	22	Compte financier, n.i.a.
Net errors and omissions	2	^0	-2	-6	-6	-4	^0	Erreurs et omissions nettes
Reserves and related items	-2	-7	-6	-19	4	1	-16	Réserves et postes apparentés
Trinidad and Tobago								**Trinité-et-Tobago**
Current account	416	76	985	1 647	3 594	7 271	5 364	Compte des transac. courantes
Goods: exports f.o.b.	4 304	3 920	5 205	6 403	9 672	14 217	13 391	Biens : exportations f.à.b.
Goods: imports f.o.b.	-3 586	-3 682	-3 912	-4 894	-5 725	-6 517	-7 670	Biens : importations f.à.b.
Services: credit	574	637	685	851	897	814	924	Services : crédit
Services: debit	-370	-373	-371	-371	-541	-363	-377	Services : débit
Income: credit	109	64	78	66	84	262	267	Revenus : crédit
Income: debit	-648	-544	-759	-464	-844	-1 198	-1 231	Revenus : débit
Current transfers: credit	64	96	101	99	102	105	121	Transferts courants : crédit
Current transfers: debit	-31	-42	-42	-42	-52	-49	-61	Transferts courants : débit
Capital account, n.i.e.	0	0	0	0	0	0	0	Compte de capital, n.i.a.
Financial account, n.i.e.	322	397	-446	-673	-1 553	-5 367	-3 250	Compte financier, n.i.a.
Net errors and omissions	-235	-357	-218	-469	-653	-808	-593	Erreurs et omissions nettes
Reserves and related items	-502	-116	-321	-506	-1 388	-1 096	-1 521	Réserves et postes apparentés
Tunisia								**Tunisie**
Current account	-840	-746	-730	-551	-299	-619	-904	Compte des transac. courantes
Goods: exports f.o.b.	6 628	6 857	8 027	9 679	10 632	11 689	15 148	Biens : exportations f.à.b.
Goods: imports f.o.b.	-8 997	-8 981	-10 297	-12 110	-12 595	-14 202	-18 024	Biens : importations f.à.b.
Services: credit	2 912	2 681	2 937	3 629	4 021	4 295	4 909	Services : crédit
Services: debit	-1 425	-1 450	-1 612	-1 986	-2 191	-2 455	-2 803	Services : débit
Income: credit	195	177	224	277	316	367	563	Revenus : crédit
Income: debit	-1 045	-1 061	-1 180	-1 418	-1 794	-1 756	-2 316	Revenus : débit

69

Summary of balance of payments *(continued)*
Millions of US dollars
Résumé de la balance des paiements *(suite)*
Millions de dollars des E.-U.

Country or area	2001	2002	2003	2004	2005	2006	2007	Pays ou zone
Current transfers: credit	916	1 050	1 200	1 401	1 340	1 470	1 650	Transferts courants : crédit
Current transfers: debit	-24	-19	-29	-24	-28	-27	-32	Transferts courants : débit
Capital account, n.i.e.	53	76	59	107	127	145	152	Compte de capital, n.i.a.
Financial account, n.i.e.	1 058	845	1 101	1 439	1 136	2 595	1 477	Compte financier, n.i.a.
Net errors and omissions	19	-35	-47	-18	-28	-38	-36	Erreurs et omissions nettes
Reserves and related items	-288	-140	-383	-977	-936	-2 082	-689	Réserves et postes apparentés
Turkey								**Turquie**
Current account	3 760	-626	-7 515	-14 431	-22 137	-31 893	-37 697	Compte des transac. courantes
Goods: exports f.o.b.	34 729	40 719	52 394	68 535	78 365	93 611	115 356	Biens : exportations f.à.b.
Goods: imports f.o.b.	-38 092	-47 109	-65 883	-91 271	-111 353	-134 552	-162 025	Biens : importations f.à.b.
Services: credit	15 234	14 046	18 013	22 960	26 648	25 312	28 853	Services : crédit
Services: debit	-6 098	-6 161	-7 502	-10 163	-11 376	-11 481	-14 974	Services : débit
Income: credit	2 753	2 486	2 246	2 651	3 608	4 383	6 384	Revenus : crédit
Income: debit	-7 753	-7 040	-7 803	-8 260	-9 483	-11 074	-13 527	Revenus : débit
Current transfers: credit	3 045	2 477	1 081	1 155	1 475	2 244	2 778	Transferts courants : crédit
Current transfers: debit	-58	-44	-61	-38	-21	-336	-542	Transferts courants : débit
Capital account, n.i.e.	0	0	0	0	0	0	0	Compte de capital, n.i.a.
Financial account, n.i.e.	-14 558	1 190	7 192	17 730	43 502	42 691	48 567	Compte financier, n.i.a.
Net errors and omissions	-2 090	-778	4 410	961	1 811	-177	1 182	Erreurs et omissions nettes
Reserves and related items	12 888	214	-4 087	-4 260	-23 176	-10 621	-12 052	Réserves et postes apparentés
Uganda								**Ouganda**
Current account	-370	-362	-354	-316	-414	-323	-745	Compte des transac. courantes
Goods: exports f.o.b.	476	481	563	759	1 017	1 188	1 686	Biens : exportations f.à.b.
Goods: imports f.o.b.	-975	-1 052	-1 246	-1 427	-1 746	-2 216	-2 983	Biens : importations f.à.b.
Services: credit	217	225	266	370	507	452	499	Services : crédit
Services: debit	-506	-558	-502	-627	-777	-950	-1 178	Services : débit
Income: credit	37	24	28	36	50	72	98	Revenus : crédit
Income: debit	-203	-148	-171	-329	-299	-298	-377	Revenus : débit
Current transfers: credit	889	1 023	923	1 144	1 184	1 763	1 816	Transferts courants : crédit
Current transfers: debit	-304	-357	-214	-242	-351	-334	-307	Transferts courants : débit
Capital account, n.i.e.	0	0	0	0	0	3 428	0	Compte de capital, n.i.a.
Financial account, n.i.e.	441	178	359	443	494	628	1 329	Compte financier, n.i.a.
Net errors and omissions	19	9	-8	-4	2	41	62	Erreurs et omissions nettes
Reserves and related items	-91	175	3	-123	-82	-3 774	-646	Réserves et postes apparentés
Ukraine								**Ukraine**
Current account	1 402	3 174	2 891	6 909	2 531	-1 617	-5 272	Compte des transac. courantes
Goods: exports f.o.b.	17 091	18 669	23 739	33 432	35 024	38 949	49 840	Biens : exportations f.à.b.
Goods: imports f.o.b.	-16 893	-17 959	-23 221	-29 691	-36 159	-44 143	-60 412	Biens : importations f.à.b.
Services: credit	3 995	4 682	5 214	7 859	9 354	11 290	14 161	Services : crédit
Services: debit	-3 580	-3 535	-4 444	-6 622	-7 548	-9 164	-11 741	Services : débit
Income: credit	167	165	254	389	758	1 332	3 656	Revenus : crédit
Income: debit	-834	-769	-835	-1 034	-1 743	-3 054	-4 315	Revenus : débit
Current transfers: credit	1 516	1 967	2 270	2 671	3 111	3 533	4 147	Transferts courants : crédit
Current transfers: debit	-60	-46	-86	-95	-266	-360	-608	Transferts courants : débit
Capital account, n.i.e.	3	17	-17	7	-65	3	3	Compte de capital, n.i.a.
Financial account, n.i.e.	-260	-1 071	133	-4 521	8 126	3 929	15 127	Compte financier, n.i.a.
Net errors and omissions	-152	-889	-834	128	133	94	-452	Erreurs et omissions nettes
Reserves and related items	-993	-1 231	-2 173	-2 523	-10 725	-2 409	-9 406	Réserves et postes apparentés
United Kingdom								**Royaume-Uni**
Current account	-30 281	-27 858	-30 002	-45 936	-59 132	-83 078	-78 765	Compte des transac. courantes
Goods: exports f.o.b.	272 279	279 866	307 799	349 652	384 318	447 592	441 968	Biens : exportations f.à.b.
Goods: imports f.o.b.	-331 567	-351 636	-387 254	-461 140	-509 044	-588 251	-620 705	Biens : importations f.à.b.
Services: credit	120 978	135 308	158 615	196 989	208 104	234 633	281 813	Services : crédit
Services: debit	-100 193	-110 023	-127 250	-149 652	-163 016	-175 625	-203 398	Services : débit
Income: credit	200 927	184 547	203 108	254 376	338 701	439 589	584 816	Revenus : crédit
Income: debit	-183 327	-152 662	-169 020	-217 339	-296 562	-419 115	-536 149	Revenus : débit
Current transfers: credit	20 037	18 410	19 700	25 217	31 660	33 545	29 891	Transferts courants : crédit
Current transfers: debit	-29 415	-31 669	-35 701	-44 040	-53 294	-55 446	-57 002	Transferts courants : débit
Capital account, n.i.e.	1 890	1 420	2 425	3 779	2 825	1 806	5 262	Compte de capital, n.i.a.
Financial account, n.i.e.	34 316	36 263	34 809	35 881	55 484	76 194	65 111	Compte financier, n.i.a.
Net errors and omissions	-10 382	-10 460	-9 824	6 683	2 555	3 776	10 964	Erreurs et omissions nettes
Reserves and related items	4 456	635	2 592	-407	-1 732	1 301	-2 572	Réserves et postes apparentés

69
Summary of balance of payments *(continued)*
Millions of US dollars
Résumé de la balance des paiements *(suite)*
Millions de dollars des E.-U.

Country or area	2001	2002	2003	2004	2005	2006	2007	Pays ou zone
United Rep. of Tanzania								**Rép.-Unie de Tanzanie**
Current account	-395	-37	-118	-362	-864	-1 172	-1 856	Compte des transac. courantes
Goods: exports f.o.b.	851	980	1 221	1 482	1 679	1 918	2 227	Biens : exportations f.à.b.
Goods: imports f.o.b.	-1 560	-1 511	-1 933	-2 483	-2 998	-3 864	-4 861	Biens : importations f.à.b.
Services: credit	915	920	948	1 139	1 269	1 528	1 714	Services : crédit
Services: debit	-649	-633	-726	-975	-1 207	-1 249	-1 474	Services : débit
Income: credit	55	68	87	82	81	54	81	Revenus : crédit
Income: debit	-208	-157	-226	-195	-185	-147	-160	Revenus : débit
Current transfers: credit	280	357	574	654	564	655	689	Transferts courants : crédit
Current transfers: debit	-80	-61	-63	-65	-68	-66	-72	Transferts courants : débit
Capital account, n.i.e.	1 004	786	693	460	393	5 218	958	Compte de capital, n.i.a.
Financial account, n.i.e.	-353	277	247	279	665	-3 952	1 031	Compte financier, n.i.a.
Net errors and omissions	-304	-702	-350	-173	-418	367	283	Erreurs et omissions nettes
Reserves and related items	49	-323	-472	-204	224	-461	-416	Réserves et postes apparentés
United States								**Etats-Unis**
Current account	-384 698	-461 276	-523 403	-624 995	-728 994	-788 115	-731 209	Compte des transac. courantes
Goods: exports f.o.b.	721 842	685 933	716 704	811 010	898 458	1 026 850	1 152 570	Biens : exportations f.à.b.
Goods: imports f.o.b.	-1 148 260	-1 167 400	-1 264 340	-1 477 130	-1 681 810	-1 861 410	-1 967 870	Biens : importations f.à.b.
Services: credit	283 054	288 788	301 053	349 576	385 295	430 159	493 157	Services : crédit
Services: debit	-221 764	-231 049	-250 328	-291 191	-313 511	-348 889	-378 114	Services : débit
Income: credit	290 799	280 942	320 457	413 739	535 262	685 151	817 782	Revenus : crédit
Income: debit	-259 076	-253 545	-275 150	-346 519	-462 906	-627 954	-736 031	Revenus : débit
Current transfers: credit	9 011	12 296	14 991	20 281	18 965	25 173	22 327	Transferts courants : crédit
Current transfers: debit	-60 306	-77 244	-86 786	-104 763	-108 749	-117 200	-135 032	Transferts courants : débit
Capital account, n.i.e.	-1 271	-1 470	-3 481	-2 368	-4 036	-3 880	-1 843	Compte de capital, n.i.a.
Financial account, n.i.e.	405 163	504 197	531 356	529 526	686 622	836 690	774 467	Compte financier, n.i.a.
Net errors and omissions	-14 268	-37 759	-6 002	95 033	32 309	-47 097	-41 290	Erreurs et omissions nettes
Reserves and related items	-4 927	-3 693	1 529	2 804	14 100	2 392	-125	Réserves et postes apparentés
Uruguay								**Uruguay**
Current account	-498	382	-87	3	24	-369	-186	Compte des transac. courantes
Goods: exports f.o.b.	2 140	1 922	2 281	3 145	3 774	4 407	5 063	Biens : exportations f.à.b.
Goods: imports f.o.b.	-2 915	-1 874	-2 098	-2 992	-3 753	-4 867	-5 554	Biens : importations f.à.b.
Services: credit	1 123	771	771	1 112	1 311	1 392	1 762	Services : crédit
Services: debit	-807	-618	-636	-786	939	-987	-1 249	Services : débit
Income: credit	833	453	242	372	563	734	878	Revenus : crédit
Income: debit	-901	-344	-730	-960	-1 057	-1 175	-1 220	Revenus : débit
Current transfers: credit	48	84	95	127	143	150	159	Transferts courants : crédit
Current transfers: debit	-18	-12	-12	-14	-17	-24	-25	Transferts courants : débit
Capital account, n.i.e.	0	0	4	5	4	7	4	Compte de capital, n.i.a.
Financial account, n.i.e.	490	-1 885	7	-82	924	2 840	1 226	Compte financier, n.i.a.
Net errors and omissions	287	-2 394	1 034	378	-173	-110	-39	Erreurs et omissions nettes
Reserves and related items	-279	3 897	-958	-304	-778	-2 367	-1 005	Réserves et postes apparentés
Vanuatu								**Vanuatu**
Current account	-15	-31	-34	-42	-53	-50	-54	Compte des transac. courantes
Goods: exports f.o.b.	20	20	27	38	38	38	34	Biens : exportations f.à.b.
Goods: imports f.o.b.	-78	-78	-92	-113	-131	-148	-176	Biens : importations f.à.b.
Services: credit	119	94	111	122	139	146	186	Services : crédit
Services: debit	-73	-52	-61	-66	-74	-71	-76	Services : débit
Income: credit	17	22	24	27	28	32	36	Revenus : crédit
Income: debit	-21	-34	-39	-46	-54	-52	-61	Revenus : débit
Current transfers: credit	40	6	5	5	7	10	7	Transferts courants : crédit
Current transfers: debit	-38	-9	-10	-10	6	-5	-3	Transferts courants : débit
Capital account, n.i.e.	-16	8	7	13	20	34	30	Compte de capital, n.i.a.
Financial account, n.i.e.	13	26	38	48	38	33	15	Compte financier, n.i.a.
Net errors and omissions	8	-21	-22	-25	-17	-4	-4	Erreurs et omissions nettes
Reserves and related items	10	18	11	5	11	-13	13	Réserves et postes apparentés
Venezuela (Bolivarian Rep. of)								**Venezuela (Rép. bolivarienne du)**
Current account	1 983	7 599	11 796	15 519	25 110	27 149	20 001	Compte des transac. courantes
Goods: exports f.o.b.	26 667	26 781	27 230	39 668	55 647	65 210	69 165	Biens : exportations f.à.b.
Goods: imports f.o.b.	-19 211	-13 360	-10 483	-17 021	-24 195	-32 498	-45 463	Biens : importations f.à.b.
Services: credit	1 376	1 013	878	1 114	1 341	1 572	1 673	Services : crédit
Services: debit	-4 681	-3 922	-3 512	-4 497	-5 349	-6 005	-7 524	Services : débit
Income: credit	2 603	1 474	1 729	2 050	4 146	7 934	10 114	Revenus : crédit
Income: debit	-4 623	-4 230	-4 066	-5 723	-6 411	-9 026	-7 549	Revenus : débit

69

Summary of balance of payments *(continued)*
Millions of US dollars

Résumé de la balance des paiements *(suite)*
Millions de dollars des E.-U.

Country or area	2001	2002	2003	2004	2005	2006	2007	Pays ou zone
Current transfers: credit	356	288	257	227	249	296	285	Transferts courants : crédit
Current transfers: debit	-504	-445	-237	-299	-318	-334	-700	Transferts courants : débit
Capital account, n.i.e.	0	0	0	0	0	0	0	Compte de capital, n.i.a.
Financial account, n.i.e.	-211	-9 246	-5 547	-10 861	-16 480	-19 244	-22 919	Compte financier, n.i.a.
Net errors and omissions	-3 601	-2 781	-795	-2 503	-3 205	-2 828	-2 439	Erreurs et omissions nettes
Reserves and related items	1 829	4 428	-5 454	-2 155	-5 425	-5 077	5 357	Réserves et postes apparentés
Viet Nam								**Viet Nam**
Current account	682	-604	-1 931	-957	-560	-164	-6 992	Compte des transac. courantes
Goods: exports f.o.b.	15 027	16 706	20 149	26 485	32 447	39 826	48 561	Biens : exportations f.à.b.
Goods: imports f.o.b.	-14 546	-17 760	-22 730	-28 772	-34 886	-42 602	-58 921	Biens : importations f.à.b.
Services: credit	2 810	2 948	3 272	3 867	4 176	5 100	6 030	Services : crédit
Services: debit	-3 382	-3 698	-4 050	-4 739	-4 472	-5 108	-6 924	Services : débit
Income: credit	318	167	125	188	364	668	1 093	Revenus : crédit
Income: debit	-795	-888	-936	-1 079	-1 569	-2 097	-3 261	Revenus : débit
Current transfers: credit	1 250	1 921	2 239	3 093	3 380	4 049	6 430	Transferts courants : crédit
Current transfers: debit	0	0	...	...	...	...	...	Transferts courants : débit
Capital account, n.i.e.	0	0	...	...	...	...	...	Compte de capital, n.i.a.
Financial account, n.i.e.	371	2 090	3 279	2 807	3 087	3 088	17 540	Compte financier, n.i.a.
Net errors and omissions	-847	-1 038	798	-915	-397	1 400	-342	Erreurs et omissions nettes
Reserves and related items	-206	-448	-2 146	-935	-2 130	-4 324	-10 206	Réserves et postes apparentés
Yemen								**Yémen**
Current account	667	538	149	225	624	206	-1 328	Compte des transac. courantes
Goods: exports f.o.b.	3 367	3 621	3 934	4 676	6 413	7 316	7 131	Biens : exportations f.à.b.
Goods: imports f.o.b.	-2 600	-2 932	-3 557	-3 859	-4 713	-5 926	-7 212	Biens : importations f.à.b.
Services: credit	166	166	318	370	372	549	643	Services : crédit
Services: debit	-848	-935	-1 004	-1 059	-1 241	-1 855	-2 125	Services : débit
Income: credit	179	135	99	104	178	316	385	Revenus : crédit
Income: debit	-869	-901	-1 008	-1 450	-1 791	-1 551	-1 537	Revenus : débit
Current transfers: credit	1 344	1 457	1 442	1 493	1 458	1 402	1 436	Transferts courants : crédit
Current transfers: debit	-71	-73	-75	-49	-53	-46	-49	Transferts courants : débit
Capital account, n.i.e.	50	0	5	163	202	94	94	Compte de capital, n.i.a.
Financial account, n.i.e.	-53	-157	20	-69	-606	632	747	Compte financier, n.i.a.
Net errors and omissions	-110	43	156	53	213	180	132	Erreurs et omissions nettes
Reserves and related items	-553	-425	-330	-373	-434	-1 112	354	Réserves et postes apparentés
Zambia								**Zambie**
Current account	-724	-643	-707	-463	-731	-78	-780	Compte des transac. courantes
Goods: exports f.o.b.	911	989	1 087	1 845	2 247	3 929	4 594	Biens : exportations f.à.b.
Goods: imports f.o.b.	-1 253	-1 204	-1 393	-1 727	-2 161	-2 636	-3 611	Biens : importations f.à.b.
Services: credit	144	115	165	232	273	228	279	Services : crédit
Services: debit	-367	-375	-403	-447	-471	-587	-914	Services : débit
Income: credit	21	42	32	32	13	18	35	Revenus : crédit
Income: debit	-161	-190	-177	-382	-608	-1 187	-1 419	Revenus : débit
Current transfers: credit	0	0	36	48	53	248	351	Transferts courants : crédit
Current transfers: debit	-20	-20	-55	-64	-77	-93	-96	Transferts courants : débit
Capital account, n.i.e.	222	236	240	239	287	197	223	Compte de capital, n.i.a.
Financial account, n.i.e.	287	204	407	78	-1 567	-1 606	729	Compte financier, n.i.a.
Net errors and omissions	-470	-418	-399	-90	-75	-303	-140	Erreurs et omissions nettes
Reserves and related items	685	620	459	237	2 086	1 791	-32	Réserves et postes apparentés

Source:
International Monetary Fund (IMF), Washington, D.C., *International Financial Statistics*, April 2009 and the IMF database.

1   Balance of payments data for the Belgium-Luxembourg Economic Union (BLEU) were available until December 31, 2001. From January 1, 2002, Belgium and Luxembourg have separate balance of payments data.

2   For statistical purposes, the data for China do not include those for the Hong Kong Special Administrative Region (Hong Kong SAR), Macao Special Administrative Region (Macao SAR) and Taiwan Province of China.

3   West Bank and Gaza.

Source:
Fonds monétaire international (FMI), Washington, D.C., *Statistiques Financières Internationales*, avril 2009 et la base de données du FMI.

1   Les données sur la balance des paiements pour l'Union économique belgo-luxembourgeoise (UEBL) sont disponibles jusqu'au 31 décembre 2001. À partir du 1er janvier 2002, les données sur la balance des paiements de la Belgique et du Luxembourg sont séparées.

2   Pour la présentation des statistiques, les données pour la Chine ne comprennent pas la Région Administrative Spéciale de Hong Kong (Hong Kong RAS), la Région Administrative Spéciale de Macao (Macao RAS) et la province de Taiwan.

3   Cisjordanie et Gaza.

Technical notes: table 69

A balance of payments can be broadly described as the record of an economy's international economic transactions. It shows (a) transactions in goods, services and income between an economy and the rest of the world, (b) changes of ownership and other changes in that economy's monetary gold, special drawing rights (SDRs) and claims on and liabilities to the rest of the world, and (c) unrequited transfers and counterpart entries needed to balance in the accounting sense any entries for the foregoing transactions and changes which are not mutually offsetting.

The balance of payments data are presented on the basis of the methodology and presentation of the fifth edition of the *Balance of Payments Manual* (BPM5), published by the International Monetary Fund in September 1993. The BPM5 incorporates several major changes to take account of developments in international trade and finance over the years, and to better harmonize the Fund's balance of payments methodology with the methodology of the 1993 *System of National Accounts* (SNA). The Fund's balance of payments has been converted for all periods from the BPM4 basis to the BPM5 basis; thus the time series conform to the BPM5 methodology with no methodological breaks.

The detailed definitions concerning the content of the basic categories of the balance of payments are given in the *Balance of Payments Manual (fifth edition)*. Brief explanatory notes are given below to clarify the scope of the major items.

Goods: exports f.o.b. and *Goods: imports f.o.b.* are both measured on the "free-on-board" (f.o.b.) basis — that is, by the value of the goods at the border of the exporting country; in the case of imports, this excludes the cost of freight and insurance incurred beyond the border of the exporting country.

Services and *income* cover transactions in real resources between residents and non-residents other than those classified as merchandise, including (a) shipment and other transportation services, including freight, insurance and other distributive services in connection with the movement of commodities, (b) travel, i.e. goods and services acquired by non-resident travellers in a given country and similar acquisitions by resident travellers abroad, and (c) investment income which covers income of non-residents from their financial assets invested in the compiling economy (debit) and similar income of residents from their financial assets invested abroad (credit).

Current transfers, n.i.e.: *credit* comprises all current transfers received by the reporting country, except those made to the country to finance its "overall balance", hence, the label "n.i.e." (not included elsewhere).

Notes techniques: tableau 69

La balance des paiements peut se définir d'une façon générale comme le relevé des transactions économiques internationales d'une économie. Elle indique (a) les transactions sur biens, services et revenus entre une économie et le reste du monde, (b) les transferts de propriété et autres variations intervenues au niveau des avoirs en or monétaire de cette économie, de ses avoirs en droits de tirages spéciaux (DTS) ainsi que de ses créances financières sur le reste du monde ou de ses engagements financiers envers lui et (c) les "inscriptions de transferts sans contrepartie" et de "contrepartie" destinées à équilibrer, d'un point de vue comptable, les transactions et changements précités qui ne se compensent pas réciproquement.

Les données de la balance des paiements sont présentées conformément à la méthodologie et à la classification recommandées dans la cinquième édition du *Manuel de la balance des paiements*, publiée en septembre 1993 par le Fonds monétaire international. La cinquième édition fait état de plusieurs changements importants qui ont été opérés de manière à rendre compte de l'évolution des finances et des changes internationaux pendant les années et à harmoniser davantage la méthodologie de la balance des paiements du FMI avec celle du *Système de comptabilité nationale* (SCN) de 1993. Les statistiques incluses dans la balance des paiements du FMI ont été converties et sont désormais établies, pour toutes les périodes, sur la base de la cinquième et non plus de la quatrième édition; en conséquence, les séries chronologiques sont conformes aux principes de la cinquième édition, sans rupture due à des différences d'ordre méthodologique.

Les définitions détaillées relatives au contenu des postes fondamentaux de la balance des paiements figurent dans le *Manuel de la balance des paiements (cinquième édition)*. De brèves notes explicatives sont présentées ci-après pour clarifier la portée de ces principales rubriques.

Les Biens: exportations, f.à.b. et *Biens: importations, f.à.b.* sont évalués sur la base f.à.b. (franco à bord) - c'est-à-dire à la frontière du pays exportateur; dans le cas des importations, cette valeur exclut le coût du fret et de l'assurance au-delà de la frontière du pays exportateur.

Services et *revenus*: transactions en ressources effectuées entre résidents et non résidents, autres que celles qui sont considérées comme des marchandises, notamment: (a) expéditions et autres services de transport, y compris le fret, l'assurance et les autres services de distribution liés aux mouvements de marchandises; (b) voyages, à savoir les biens et services acquis par des voyageurs non résidents dans un pays donné et achats

(Note: some of the capital and financial accounts labelled "n.i.e." denote that *Exceptional financing items* and *Liabilities constituting foreign authorities' reserves* (LCFARs) have been excluded.)

Capital account, n.i.e. refers mainly to capital transfers linked to the acquisition of a fixed asset other than transactions relating to debt forgiveness plus the disposal of nonproduced, nonfinancial assets, and to capital transfers linked to the disposal of fixed assets by the donor or to the financing of capital formation by the recipient, plus the acquisition of nonproduced, nonfinancial assets.

Financial account, n.i.e. is the net sum of the balance of direct investment, portfolio investment, and other investment transactions.

Net errors and omissions is a residual category needed to ensure that all debit and credit entries in the balance of payments statement sum to zero and reflects statistical inconsistencies in the recording of the credit and debit entries.

Reserves and related items is the sum of transactions in reserve assets, LCFARs, exceptional financing, and use of Fund credit and loans.

For further information see *International Financial Statistics* and www.imf.org.

similaires faits par des résidents voyageant à l'étranger; et (c) revenus des investissements, qui correspondent aux revenus que les non résidents tirent de leurs avoirs financiers placés dans l'économie déclarante (débit) et les revenus similaires que les résidents tirent de leurs avoirs financiers placés à l'étranger (crédit).

Les transferts courants, n.i.a: crédit englobent tous les transferts courants reçus par l'économie qui établit sa balance des paiements, à l'exception de ceux qui sont destinés à financer sa "balance globale"—c'est ce qui explique la mention "n.i.a." (non inclus ailleurs). (Note: comptes de capital et d'opérations financières portent la mention "n.i.a.", ce qui signifie que les postes de *Financement exceptionnel* et les *Engagements constituant des réserves pour les autorités étrangères* ont été exclus de ces composantes du compte de capital et d'opérations financières.)

Le Compte de capital, n.i.a retrace principalement les transferts de capital liés à l'acquisition d'un actif fixe autres que les transactions ayant trait à des remises de dettes plus les cessions d'actifs non financiers non produits, et les transferts de capital liés à la cession d'actifs fixes par le donateur ou au financement de la formation de capital par le bénéficiaire, plus les acquisitions d'actifs non financiers non produits.

Le Compte financier, n.i.a est la somme des soldes des investissements directs, des investissements de portefeuille et des autres investissements.

Le poste des *Erreurs et omissions nettes* est une catégorie résiduelle qui est nécessaire pour assurer que la somme de toutes les inscriptions effectuées au débit et au crédit est égal à zéro et qui laisse apparaître les écarts entre les montants portés au débit et ceux qui sont inscrits au crédit.

Le montant de *Réserves et postes apparentés* est égal à la somme de transactions afférentes aux avoirs de réserve, aux engagements constituant des réserves pour les autorités étrangères, au financement exceptionnel et à l'utilisation des crédits et des prêts du FMI.

Pour plus de renseignements, voir *Statistiques financières internationales* et www.imf.org.

Country or area Pays ou zone		2000	2001	2002	2003	2004	2005	2006	2007	2008
Afghanistan [1,2] (afghani)	**Afghanistan [1,2] (afghani)**									
End of period	Fin de période	...	47.259	47.263	#48.865	48.220	50.410	49.850	49.720	52.140
Period average	Moyenne sur période	61.629	65.690	41.459	48.762	47.845	49.495	49.925	49.962	50.250
Albania (lek)	**Albanie (lek)**									
End of period	Fin de période	142.640	136.550	133.740	106.580	92.640	103.580	94.140	82.890	87.910
Period average	Moyenne sur période	143.709	143.485	140.155	121.863	102.780	99.870	98.103	90.428	83.895
Algeria (Algerian dinar)	**Algérie (dinar algérien)**									
End of period	Fin de période	75.343	77.820	79.723	72.613	72.614	73.380	71.158	66.830	71.183
Period average	Moyenne sur période	75.260	77.215	79.682	77.395	72.061	73.276	72.647	69.292	64.583
Angola (readjusted kwanza)	**Angola (réajusté kwanza)**									
End of period	Fin de période	16.818	31.949	58.666	79.082	85.988	80.780	80.264	75.023	75.169
Period average	Moyenne sur période	10.041	22.058	43.530	74.606	83.541	87.159	80.368	76.706	75.033
Anguilla (EC dollar)	**Anguilla (dollar des Caraïbes orientales)**									
End of period	Fin de période	2.700	2.700	2.700	2.700	2.700	2.700	2.700	2.700	2.700
Period average	Moyenne sur période	2.700	2.700	2.700	2.700	2.700	2.700	2.700	2.700	2.700
Antigua and Barbuda (EC dollar)	**Antigua-et-Barbuda (dollar des Caraïbes orientales)**									
End of period	Fin de période	2.700	2.700	2.700	2.700	2.700	2.700	2.700	2.700	2.700
Period average	Moyenne sur période	2.700	2.700	2.700	2.700	2.700	2.700	2.700	2.700	2.700
Argentina [3] (Argentine peso)	**Argentine [3] (peso argentin)**									
End of period	Fin de période	1.000	1.000	3.320	2.905	2.959	3.012	3.042	3.129	3.433
Period average	Moyenne sur période	1.000	1.000	3.063	2.901	2.923	2.904	3.054	3.096	3.144
Armenia (dram)	**Arménie (dram)**									
End of period	Fin de période	552.180	561.810	584.890	566.000	485.840	450.190	363.500	304.220	306.730
Period average	Moyenne sur période	539.526	555.078	573.353	578.763	533.451	457.687	416.040	342.079	305.969
Aruba (Aruban florin)	**Aruba (florin de Aruba)**									
End of period	Fin de période	1.790	1.790	1.790	1.790	1.790	1.790	1.790	1.790	1.790
Period average	Moyenne sur période	1.790	1.790	1.790	1.790	1.790	1.790	1.790	1.790	1.790
Australia (Australian dollar)	**Australie (dollar australien)**									
End of period	Fin de période	1.805	1.958	1.766	1.333	1.284	1.363	1.264	1.134	1.443
Period average	Moyenne sur période	1.725	1.933	1.841	1.542	1.360	1.309	1.328	1.195	1.192
Azerbaijan (manat)	**Azerbaïdjan (manat)**									
End of period	Fin de période	0.913	0.955	0.979	0.985	0.981	0.919	#0.871	0.845	0.801
Period average	Moyenne sur période	0.895	0.931	0.972	0.982	0.983	0.945	#0.893	0.858	0.822
Bahamas [1] (Bahamian dollar)	**Bahamas [1] (dollar des Bahamas)**									
End of period	Fin de période	1.000	1.000	1.000	1.000	1.000	1.000	1.000	1.000	1.000
Period average	Moyenne sur période	1.000	1.000	1.000	1.000	1.000	1.000	1.000	1.000	1.000
Bahrain (Bahrain dinar)	**Bahreïn (dinar de Bahreïn)**									
End of period	Fin de période	0.376	0.376	0.376	0.376	0.376	0.376	0.376	0.376	0.376
Period average	Moyenne sur période	0.376	0.376	0.376	0.376	0.376	0.376	0.376	0.376	0.376
Bangladesh [1] (taka)	**Bangladesh [1] (taka)**									
End of period	Fin de période	54.000	57.000	57.900	58.782	60.742	66.210	69.065	68.576	68.920
Period average	Moyenne sur période	52.142	55.807	57.888	58.150	59.513	64.328	68.933	68.875	68.598
Barbados (Barbados dollar)	**Barbade (dollar de la Barbade)**									
End of period	Fin de période	2.000	2.000	2.000	2.000	2.000	2.000	2.000	2.000	2.000
Period average	Moyenne sur période	2.000	2.000	2.000	2.000	2.000	2.000	2.000	2.000	2.000
Belarus (Belarussian rouble)	**Bélarus (rouble bélarussien)**									
End of period	Fin de période	1 180.000	1 580.000	1 920.000	2 156.000	2 170.000	2 152.000	2 140.000	2 150.000	2 200.000
Period average	Moyenne sur période	876.750	1 390.000	1 790.920	2 051.270	2 160.260	2 153.820	2 144.560	2 146.080	2 136.400
Belize (Belize dollar)	**Belize (dollar du Belize)**									
End of period	Fin de période	2.000	2.000	2.000	2.000	2.000	2.000	2.000	2.000	2.000
Period average	Moyenne sur période	2.000	2.000	2.000	2.000	2.000	2.000	2.000	2.000	2.000
Benin (CFA franc)	**Bénin (franc CFA)**									
End of period	Fin de période	704.951	744.306	625.495	519.364	481.578	556.037	498.069	445.593	471.335
Period average	Moyenne sur période	711.976	733.039	696.988	581.200	528.285	527.468	522.890	479.267	447.805
Bhutan (ngultrum)	**Bhoutan (ngultrum)**									
End of period	Fin de période	46.750	48.180	48.030	45.605	43.585	45.065	44.245	39.415	48.455
Period average	Moyenne sur période	44.942	47.186	48.610	46.583	45.317	44.100	45.307	41.349	43.505
Bolivia (boliviano)	**Bolivie (boliviano)**									
End of period	Fin de période	6.390	6.820	7.490	7.830	8.050	8.040	7.980	7.620	7.020
Period average	Moyenne sur période	6.184	6.607	7.170	7.659	7.936	8.066	8.012	7.851	7.238

70

Exchange rates *(continued)*
National currency per US dollar
Cours des changes *(suite)*
Valeur du dollar E.-U. en monnaie nationale

Country or area Pays ou zone		2000	2001	2002	2003	2004	2005	2006	2007	2008
Bosnia and Herzegovina (convertible marka)	**Bosnie-Herzégovine (marka convertible)**									
End of period	Fin de période	2.102	2.219	1.865	1.549	1.436	1.658	1.485	1.329	1.405
Period average	Moyenne sur période	2.123	2.186	2.078	1.733	1.575	1.573	1.559	1.429	1.335
Botswana (pula)	**Botswana (pula)**									
End of period	Fin de période	5.362	6.983	5.467	4.442	4.281	5.513	6.031	6.006	7.519
Period average	Moyenne sur période	5.102	5.841	6.328	4.950	4.693	5.110	5.837	6.139	6.827
Brazil (real)	**Brésil (real)**									
End of period	Fin de période	1.955	2.320	3.533	2.888	2.654	2.340	2.137	1.771	2.336
Period average	Moyenne sur période	1.829	2.350	2.920	3.077	2.925	2.434	2.175	1.947	1.834
Brunei Darussalam (Brunei dollar)	**Brunéi Darussalam (dollar du Brunéi)**									
End of period	Fin de période	1.732	1.851	1.737	1.701	1.634	1.664	1.534	1.441	1.439
Period average	Moyenne sur période	1.724	1.792	1.791	1.742	1.690	1.664	1.589	1.507	1.417
Bulgaria (lev)	**Bulgarie (lev)**									
End of period	Fin de période	2.102	2.219	1.885	1.549	1.436	1.658	1.485	1.331	1.387
Period average	Moyenne sur période	2.123	2.185	2.077	1.733	1.575	1.574	1.559	1.429	1.337
Burkina Faso (CFA franc)	**Burkina Faso (franc CFA)**									
End of period	Fin de période	704.951	744.306	625.495	519.364	481.578	556.037	498.069	445.593	471.335
Period average	Moyenne sur période	711.976	733.039	696.988	581.200	528.285	527.468	522.890	479.267	447.805
Burundi (Burundi franc)	**Burundi (franc burundais)**									
End of period	Fin de période	778.200	864.200	1 071.230	1 093.000	1 109.510	997.780	1 002.470	1 119.540	1 234.980
Period average	Moyenne sur période	720.673	830.353	930.749	1 082.620	1 100.900	1 081.580	1 028.680	1 081.870	1 185.730
Cambodia (riel)	**Cambodge (riel)**									
End of period	Fin de période	3 905.000	3 895.000	3 930.000	3 984.000	4 027.000	4 112.000	4 057.000	3 999.000	4 077.000
Period average	Moyenne sur période	3 840.750	3 916.330	3 912.080	3 973.330	4 016.250	4 092.500	4 103.250	4 056.170	4 054.170
Cameroon (CFA franc)	**Cameroun (franc CFA)**									
End of period	Fin de période	704.951	744.306	625.495	519.364	481.578	556.037	498.069	445.593	471.335
Period average	Moyenne sur période	711.976	733.039	696.988	581.200	528.285	527.468	522.890	479.267	447.805
Canada (Canadian dollar)	**Canada (dollar canadien)**									
End of period	Fin de période	1.500	1.593	1.580	1.292	1.204	1.165	1.165	0.988	1.225
Period average	Moyenne sur période	1.485	1.549	1.569	1.401	1.301	1.212	1.134	1.074	1.067
Cape Verde (Cape Verde escudo)	**Cap-Vert (escudo du Cap-Vert)**									
End of period	Fin de période	118.506	125.122	105.149	87.308	80.956	93.473	83.728	74.907	79.234
Period average	Moyenne sur période	119.687	123.228	117.168	97.703	88.808	88.670	87.901	80.567	75.279
Central African Rep. (CFA franc)	**Rép. centrafricaine (franc CFA)**									
End of period	Fin de période	704.951	744.306	625.495	519.364	481.578	556.037	498.069	445.593	471.335
Period average	Moyenne sur période	711.976	733.039	696.988	581.200	528.285	527.468	522.890	479.267	447.805
Chad (CFA franc)	**Tchad (franc CFA)**									
End of period	Fin de période	704.951	744.306	625.495	519.364	481.578	556.037	498.069	445.593	471.335
Period average	Moyenne sur période	711.976	733.039	696.988	581.200	528.285	527.468	522.890	479.267	447.805
Chile[1] (Chilean peso)	**Chili[1] (peso chilien)**									
End of period	Fin de période	572.680	656.200	712.380	599.420	559.830	514.210	534.430	495.820	629.110
Period average	Moyenne sur période	539.588	634.938	688.937	691.398	609.529	559.768	530.275	522.464	522.461
China[1] (yuan)	**Chine[1] (yuan)**									
End of period	Fin de période	8.277	8.277	8.277	8.277	8.277	8.070	7.809	7.305	6.835
Period average	Moyenne sur période	8.279	8.277	8.277	8.277	8.277	8.194	7.973	7.608	6.949
China, Hong Kong SAR (Hong Kong dollar)	**Chine, Hong Kong RAS (dollar de Hong Kong)**									
End of period	Fin de période	7.796	7.797	7.798	7.763	7.774	7.753	7.775	7.802	7.751
Period average	Moyenne sur période	7.791	7.799	7.799	7.787	7.788	7.777	7.768	7.801	7.787
China, Macao SAR (Macao pataca)	**Chine, Macao RAS (pataca de Macao)**									
End of period	Fin de période	8.034	8.031	8.033	7.997	8.010	7.987	8.006	8.034	7.982
Period average	Moyenne sur période	8.026	8.034	8.033	8.021	8.022	8.011	8.001	8.036	8.020
Colombia (Colombian peso)	**Colombie (peso colombien)**									
End of period	Fin de période	2 187.020	2 301.330	2 864.790	2 780.820	2 412.100	2 284.220	2 225.440	1 987.810	2 198.090
Period average	Moyenne sur période	2 087.900	2 299.630	2 504.240	2 877.650	2 628.610	2 320.830	2 361.140	2 078.290	1 967.710
Comoros (Comorian franc)	**Comores (franc comorien)**									
End of period	Fin de période	528.714	558.230	469.122	389.523	361.183	417.028	373.552	334.195	353.501
Period average	Moyenne sur période	533.982	549.779	522.741	435.900	396.214	395.601	392.168	359.450	335.854
Congo (CFA franc)	**Congo (franc CFA)**									
End of period	Fin de période	704.951	744.306	625.495	519.364	481.578	556.037	498.069	445.593	471.335
Period average	Moyenne sur période	711.976	733.039	696.988	581.200	528.285	527.468	522.890	479.267	447.805

70

Exchange rates *(continued)*
National currency per US dollar
Cours des changes *(suite)*
Valeur du dollar E.-U. en monnaie nationale

Country or area Pays ou zone		2000	2001	2002	2003	2004	2005	2006	2007	2008
Costa Rica (Costa Rican colón)	**Costa Rica (colón costa-ricien)**									
End of period	Fin de période	318.020	341.670	378.720	418.530	458.610	496.680	517.895	498.100	555.470
Period average	Moyenne sur période	308.187	328.871	359.818	398.662	437.935	477.787	511.302	516.617	526.236
Côte d'Ivoire (CFA franc)	**Côte d'Ivoire (franc CFA)**									
End of period	Fin de période	704.951	744.306	625.495	519.364	481.578	556.037	498.069	445.593	471.335
Period average	Moyenne sur période	711.976	733.039	696.988	581.200	528.285	527.468	522.890	479.267	447.805
Croatia (kuna)	**Croatie (kuna)**									
End of period	Fin de période	8.155	8.356	7.146	6.119	5.637	6.234	5.578	4.985	5.156
Period average	Moyenne sur période	8.278	8.342	7.872	6.705	6.034	5.949	5.838	5.365	4.935
Cyprus (Cyprus pound, euro)	**Chypre (livre chypriote, euro)**									
End of period	Fin de période	0.617	0.650	0.547	0.465	0.425	0.484	0.439	0.398	#0.719
Period average	Moyenne sur période	0.622	0.643	0.611	0.517	0.469	0.464	0.459	0.426	#0.683
Czech Republic (Czech koruna)	**République tchèque (couronne tchèque)**									
End of period	Fin de période	37.813	36.259	30.141	25.654	22.365	24.588	20.876	18.078	19.346
Period average	Moyenne sur période	38.598	38.035	32.739	28.209	25.700	23.957	22.596	20.294	17.072
Dem. Rep. of the Congo (Congo franc)	**Rép. dém. du Congo (franc congolais)**									
End of period	Fin de période	50.000	313.600	382.140	#372.520	444.088	431.279	503.430	502.986	639.320
Period average	Moyenne sur période	21.831	206.739	346.688	#405.397	399.476	473.908	468.279	516.750	559.293
Denmark (Danish krone)	**Danemark (couronne danoise)**									
End of period	Fin de période	8.021	8.410	7.082	5.958	5.468	6.324	5.661	5.075	5.285
Period average	Moyenne sur période	8.083	8.323	7.895	6.588	5.991	5.997	5.947	5.444	5.098
Djibouti (Djibouti franc)	**Djibouti (franc djiboutien)**									
End of period	Fin de période	177.721	177.721	177.721	177.721	177.721	177.721	177.721	177.721	177.721
Period average	Moyenne sur période	177.721	177.721	177.721	177.721	177.721	177.721	177.721	177.721	177.721
Dominica (EC dollar)	**Dominique (dollar des Caraïbes orientales)**									
End of period	Fin de période	2.700	2.700	2.700	2.700	2.700	2.700	2.700	2.700	2.700
Period average	Moyenne sur période	2.700	2.700	2.700	2.700	2.700	2.700	2.700	2.700	2.700
Dominican Republic [1] (Dominican peso)	**Rép. dominicaine [1] (peso dominicain)**									
End of period	Fin de période	16.674	17.149	21.194	37.250	31.109	34.879	33.797	34.342	35.458
Period average	Moyenne sur période	16.415	16.952	18.610	30.831	42.120	30.409	33.365	33.263	34.624
Egypt [1] (Egyptian pound)	**Egypte [1] (livre égyptienne)**									
End of period	Fin de période	3.690	4.490	4.500	6.153	6.131	5.732	5.704	5.504	5.504
Period average	Moyenne sur période	3.472	3.973	4.500	5.851	6.196	5.779	5.733	5.635	5.433
El Salvador [1] (El Salvadoran colón)	**El Salvador [1] (cólon salvadorien)**									
End of period	Fin de période	8.755	8.750	8.750	8.750	8.750	8.750	8.750	8.750	8.750
Period average	Moyenne sur période	8.755	8.750	8.750	8.750	8.750	8.750	8.750	8.750	8.750
Equatorial Guinea (CFA franc)	**Guinée équatoriale (franc CFA)**									
End of period	Fin de période	704.951	744.306	625.495	519.364	481.578	556.037	498.069	445.593	471.335
Period average	Moyenne sur période	711.976	733.039	696.988	581.200	528.285	527.468	522.890	479.267	447.805
Eritrea (nakfa)	**Erythrée (nakfa)**									
End of period	Fin de période	10.200	13.798	14.309	13.788	13.788	15.375	15.375	15.375	15.375
Period average	Moyenne sur période	9.625	11.310	13.958	13.878	13.788	15.368	15.375	15.375	15.375
Estonia (Estonian kroon)	**Estonie (couronne estonienne)**									
End of period	Fin de période	16.820	17.692	14.936	12.410	11.471	13.221	11.882	10.638	11.105
Period average	Moyenne sur période	16.969	17.478	16.612	13.856	12.596	12.584	12.466	11.434	10.694
Ethiopia (Ethiopian birr)	**Ethiopie (birr éthiopien)**									
End of period	Fin de période	8.314	8.558	8.581	8.621	8.652	8.681	8.776	9.201	9.957
Period average	Moyenne sur période	8.217	8.457	8.568	8.600	8.636	8.666	8.699	8.966	9.600
Euro Area [4] (euro)	**Zone euro [4] (euro)**									
End of period	Fin de période	1.075	1.135	0.954	0.792	0.734	0.848	0.759	0.679	0.719
Period average	Moyenne sur période	1.085	1.118	1.063	0.886	0.805	0.804	0.797	0.731	0.683
Fiji (Fiji dollar)	**Fidji (dollar des Fidji)**									
End of period	Fin de période	2.186	2.309	2.065	1.722	1.645	1.745	1.664	1.551	1.764
Period average	Moyenne sur période	2.129	2.277	2.187	1.896	1.733	1.691	1.731	1.610	1.594
Gabon (CFA franc)	**Gabon (franc CFA)**									
End of period	Fin de période	704.951	744.306	625.495	519.364	481.578	556.037	498.069	445.593	471.335
Period average	Moyenne sur période	711.976	733.039	696.988	581.200	528.285	527.468	522.890	479.267	447.805
Gambia (dalasi)	**Gambie (dalasi)**									
End of period	Fin de période	14.888	16.932	23.392	30.960	29.674	28.135	28.047	22.539	...
Period average	Moyenne sur période	12.788	15.687	19.918	27.306	30.030	28.575	28.066	24.875	...

70

Exchange rates *(continued)*
National currency per US dollar
Cours des changes *(suite)*
Valeur du dollar E.-U. en monnaie nationale

Country or area Pays ou zone		2000	2001	2002	2003	2004	2005	2006	2007	2008
Georgia (lari)	**Géorgie (lari)**									
End of period	Fin de période	1.975	2.060	2.090	2.075	1.825	1.793	1.714	1.592	1.667
Period average	Moyenne sur période	1.976	2.073	2.196	2.146	1.917	1.813	1.780	1.670	1.491
Ghana [1] (cedi)	**Ghana [1] (cedi)**									
End of period	Fin de période	0.705	0.732	0.844	0.885	0.905	0.913	0.924	...	...
Period average	Moyenne sur période	0.545	0.717	0.793	0.867	0.900	0.907	0.917	0.935	...
Greece (drachmas, euro)	**Grèce (drachmas, euro)**									
End of period	Fin de période	365.620	#1.135	0.954	0.792	0.734	0.848	0.759	0.679	0.719
Period average	Moyenne sur période	365.399	#1.118	1.063	0.886	0.805	0.804	0.797	0.731	0.683
Grenada (EC dollar)	**Grenade (dollar des Caraïbes orientales)**									
End of period	Fin de période	2.700	2.700	2.700	2.700	2.700	2.700	2.700	2.700	2.700
Period average	Moyenne sur période	2.700	2.700	2.700	2.700	2.700	2.700	2.700	2.700	2.700
Guatemala (quetzal)	**Guatemala (quetzal)**									
End of period	Fin de période	7.731	8.000	7.807	8.041	7.748	7.610	7.624	7.631	7.774
Period average	Moyenne sur période	7.763	7.859	7.822	7.941	7.947	7.634	7.603	7.673	7.560
Guinea (Guinean franc)	**Guinée (franc guinéen)**									
End of period	Fin de période	1 882.270	1 988.330	1 976.000	2 000.000	2 550.000	4 500.000	...	...	...
Period average	Moyenne sur période	1 746.870	1 950.560	1 975.840	1 984.930	2 225.030	3 644.330	...	...	...
Guinea-Bissau (CFA franc)	**Guinée-Bissau (franc CFA)**									
End of period	Fin de période	704.951	744.306	625.495	519.364	481.578	556.037	498.069	445.593	471.335
Period average	Moyenne sur période	711.976	733.039	696.988	581.200	528.285	527.468	522.890	479.267	447.805
Guyana [1] (Guyana dollar)	**Guyana [1] (dollar guyanais)**									
End of period	Fin de période	184.750	189.500	191.750	194.250	199.750	200.250	201.000	203.500	205.250
Period average	Moyenne sur période	182.430	187.321	190.665	193.878	198.307	199.875	200.188	202.347	203.633
Haïti [1] (gourde)	**Haïti [1] (gourde)**									
End of period	Fin de période	22.524	26.339	37.609	42.085	37.232	43.000	37.591	36.784	39.818
Period average	Moyenne sur période	21.171	24.429	29.251	42.367	38.352	40.449	40.409	36.861	39.108
Honduras [1] (lempira)	**Honduras [1] (lempira)**									
End of period	Fin de période	15.141	15.920	16.923	17.748	18.633	18.895	18.895	18.895	18.895
Period average	Moyenne sur période	14.839	15.474	16.433	17.345	18.206	18.832	18.895	18.895	18.904
Hungary (forint)	**Hongrie (forint)**									
End of period	Fin de période	284.730	279.030	225.160	207.920	180.290	213.580	191.620	172.610	187.910
Period average	Moyenne sur période	282.179	286.490	257.887	224.307	202.746	199.582	210.390	183.626	172.113
Iceland (Icelandic króna)	**Islande (couronne islandaise)**									
End of period	Fin de période	84.700	102.950	80.580	70.990	61.040	62.980	71.660	61.850	120.580
Period average	Moyenne sur période	78.616	97.425	91.662	76.709	70.192	62.982	70.180	64.055	87.948
India (Indian rupee)	**Inde (roupie indienne)**									
End of period	Fin de période	46.750	48.180	48.030	45.605	43.585	45.065	44.245	39.415	48.455
Period average	Moyenne sur période	44.942	47.186	48.610	46.583	45.317	44.100	45.307	41.349	43.505
Indonesia (Indonesian rupiah)	**Indonésie (roupie indonésien)**									
End of period	Fin de période	9 595.000	10 400.000	8 940.000	8 465.000	9 290.000	9 830.000	9 020.000	9 419.000	10 950.000
Period average	Moyenne sur période	8 421.780	10 260.900	9 311.190	8 577.130	8 938.850	9 704.740	9 159.320	9 141.000	9 698.960
Iran (Islamic Rep. of) (Iranian rial)	**Iran (Rép. islamique d') (rial iranien)**									
End of period	Fin de période	2 262.930	1 750.950	#7 951.980	8 272.110	8 793.000	9 091.000	9 223.000	9 282.000	9 825.000
Period average	Moyenne sur période	1 767.390	1 756.500	#6 907.450	8 193.890	8 613.990	8 963.960	9 170.940	9 281.150	9 428.530
Iraq [1] (Iraqi dinar)	**Iraq [1] (dinar iraquien)**									
End of period	Fin de période	0.310	0.310	0.310	...	#1 469.000	1 487.000	1 325.000	1 215.000	1 172.000
Period average	Moyenne sur période	0.311	0.311	0.311	...	1 453.420	1 472.000	1 467.420	1 254.570	1 193.080
Israel (new sheqel)	**Israël (nouveau sheqel)**									
End of period	Fin de période	4.041	4.416	4.737	4.379	4.308	4.603	4.225	3.846	3.802
Period average	Moyenne sur période	4.077	4.206	4.738	4.554	4.482	4.488	4.456	4.108	3.588
Jamaica (Jamaican dollar)	**Jamaïque (dollar jamaïcain)**									
End of period	Fin de période	45.415	47.286	50.762	60.517	61.450	64.381	67.032	70.618	80.217
Period average	Moyenne sur période	42.986	45.996	48.416	57.741	61.197	62.281	65.744	68.950	72.797
Japan (yen)	**Japon (yen)**									
End of period	Fin de période	114.900	131.800	119.900	107.100	104.120	117.970	118.950	114.000	90.750
Period average	Moyenne sur période	107.765	121.529	125.388	115.933	108.193	110.218	116.299	117.754	103.359
Jordan (Jordan dinar)	**Jordanie (dinar jordanien)**									
End of period	Fin de période	0.709	0.709	0.709	0.709	0.709	0.709	0.709	0.709	0.709
Period average	Moyenne sur période	0.709	0.709	0.709	0.709	0.709	0.709	0.709	0.709	0.710

70

Exchange rates *(continued)*
National currency per US dollar
Cours des changes *(suite)*
Valeur du dollar E.-U. en monnaie nationale

Country or area Pays ou zone		2000	2001	2002	2003	2004	2005	2006	2007	2008
Kazakhstan (tenge)	**Kazakhstan (tenge)**									
End of period	Fin de période	144.500	150.200	154.600	144.220	130.000	133.980	127.000	120.300	120.790
Period average	Moyenne sur période	142.133	146.736	153.279	149.576	136.035	132.880	126.089	122.554	120.299
Kenya (Kenya shilling)	**Kenya (shilling kényen)**									
End of period	Fin de période	78.036	78.600	77.072	76.139	77.344	72.367	69.397	62.675	77.711
Period average	Moyenne sur période	76.176	78.563	78.749	75.936	79.174	75.554	72.101	67.318	69.175
Kiribati (Australian dollar)	**Kiribati (dollar australien)**									
End of period	Fin de période	1.805	1.958	1.766	1.333	1.284	1.363	1.264	1.134	1.443
Period average	Moyenne sur période	1.725	1.933	1.841	1.542	1.360	1.309	1.328	1.195	1.192
Korea, Republic of (Korean won)	**Corée, République de (won coréen)**									
End of period	Fin de période	1 264.500	1 313.500	1 186.200	1 192.600	1 035.100	1 011.600	929.800	936.100	1 259.500
Period average	Moyenne sur période	1 130.960	1 290.990	1 251.090	1 191.610	1 145.320	1 024.120	954.791	929.257	1 102.050
Kuwait (Kuwaiti dinar)	**Koweït (dinar koweïtien)**									
End of period	Fin de période	0.305	0.308	0.300	0.295	0.295	0.292	0.289	0.273	0.276
Period average	Moyenne sur période	0.307	0.307	0.304	0.298	0.295	0.292	0.290	0.284	0.269
Kyrgyzstan (Kyrgyz som)	**Kirghizistan (som kirghize)**									
End of period	Fin de période	48.304	47.719	46.095	44.190	41.625	41.301	38.124	35.499	39.418
Period average	Moyenne sur période	47.704	48.378	46.937	43.648	42.650	41.012	40.153	37.316	36.575
Lao People's Dem. Rep. (kip)	**Rép. dém. pop. lao (kip)**									
End of period	Fin de période	8 218.000	9 490.000	10 680.000	10 467.000	10 376.500	10 743.000	9 696.480	9 346.000	8 478.940
Period average	Moyenne sur période	7 887.640	8 954.580	10 056.300	10 569.000	10 585.400	10 655.200	10 159.900	9 603.160	8 744.060
Latvia (lats)	**Lettonie (lats)**									
End of period	Fin de période	0.613	0.638	0.594	0.541	0.516	0.593	0.536	0.484	0.495
Period average	Moyenne sur période	0.607	0.628	0.618	0.571	0.540	0.565	0.580	0.514	0.481
Lebanon (Lebanese pound)	**Liban (livre libanaise)**									
End of period	Fin de période	1 507.500	1 507.500	1 507.500	1 507.500	1 507.500	1 507.500	1 507.500	1 507.500	1 507.500
Period average	Moyenne sur période	1 507.500	1 507.500	1 507.500	1 507.500	1 507.500	1 507.500	1 507.500	1 507.500	1 507.500
Lesotho [1] (loti)	**Lesotho [1] (loti)**									
End of period	Fin de période	7.569	12.127	8.640	6.640	5.630	6.325	6.970	6.810	9.305
Period average	Moyenne sur période	6.940	8.609	10.541	7.565	6.460	6.359	6.772	7.045	8.261
Liberia [1] (Liberian dollar)	**Libéria [1] (dollar libérien)**									
End of period	Fin de période	42.750	49.500	65.000	50.500	54.500	56.500	59.500	62.500	64.000
Period average	Moyenne sur période	40.953	48.583	61.754	59.379	54.906	57.096	58.013	61.272	63.208
Libyan Arab Jamah. (Libyan dinar)	**Jamah. arabe libyenne (dinar libyen)**									
End of period	Fin de période	0.540	0.650	1.210	1.300	1.244	1.352	1.284	1.223	1.255
Period average	Moyenne sur période	0.512	0.605	1.271	1.293	1.305	1.308	1.314	1.263	1.224
Lithuania (litas)	**Lituanie (litas)**									
End of period	Fin de période	4.000	4.000	3.311	2.762	2.535	2.910	2.630	2.357	2.451
Period average	Moyenne sur période	4.000	4.000	3.677	3.061	2.781	2.774	2.752	2.524	2.357
Madagascar [5] (Malagasy ariary)	**Madagascar [5] (ariary malgache)**									
End of period	Fin de période	1 310.090	1 326.240	1 286.950	1 219.620	1 869.400	#2 159.820	2 013.950	1 786.690	1 860.360
Period average	Moyenne sur période	1 353.500	1 317.700	1 366.390	1 238.330	1 868.860	2 003.030	2 142.300	1 873.880	1 708.370
Malawi (Malawi kwacha)	**Malawi (kwacha malawien)**									
End of period	Fin de période	80.076	67.294	87.139	108.566	108.943	123.781	139.343	140.316	...
Period average	Moyenne sur période	59.544	72.197	76.687	97.433	108.898	118.420	136.014	139.957	...
Malaysia (ringgit)	**Malaisie (ringgit)**									
End of period	Fin de période	3.800	3.800	3.800	3.800	3.800	3.780	3.532	3.307	3.464
Period average	Moyenne sur période	3.800	3.800	3.800	3.800	3.800	3.787	3.668	3.438	3.336
Maldives [6] (rufiyaa)	**Maldives [6] (rufiyaa)**									
End of period	Fin de période	11.770	12.800	12.800	12.800	12.800	12.800	12.800	12.800	12.800
Period average	Moyenne sur période	11.770	12.242	12.800	12.800	12.800	12.800	12.800	12.800	12.800
Mali (CFA franc)	**Mali (franc CFA)**									
End of period	Fin de période	704.951	744.306	625.495	519.364	481.578	556.037	498.069	445.593	471.335
Period average	Moyenne sur période	711.976	733.039	696.988	581.200	528.285	527.468	522.890	479.267	447.805
Malta (Maltese lira, euro)	**Malte (lire maltaise, euro)**									
End of period	Fin de période	0.438	0.452	0.399	0.343	0.319	0.363	0.326	0.292	#0.719
Period average	Moyenne sur période	0.438	0.450	0.434	0.377	0.345	0.346	0.341	0.312	#0.683
Mauritania (ouguiya)	**Mauritanie (ouguiya)**									
End of period	Fin de période	252.300	264.120	268.710	265.600	257.190	270.610	270.610	252.880	...
Period average	Moyenne sur période	238.923	255.629	271.739	263.030	...	265.528	268.600	258.587	...

70

Exchange rates *(continued)*
National currency per US dollar
Cours des changes *(suite)*
Valeur du dollar E.-U. en monnaie nationale

Country or area Pays ou zone		2000	2001	2002	2003	2004	2005	2006	2007	2008
Mauritius (Mauritian rupee) Maurice (roupie mauricienne)										
End of period	Fin de période	27.882	30.394	29.197	26.088	28.204	30.667	34.337	28.216	31.756
Period average	Moyenne sur période	26.250	29.129	29.962	27.902	27.499	29.496	31.708	31.314	28.453
Mexico[1] (Mexican peso) Mexique[1] (peso mexicain)										
End of period	Fin de période	9.572	9.142	10.313	11.236	11.265	10.778	10.881	10.866	13.538
Period average	Moyenne sur période	9.456	9.342	9.656	10.789	11.286	10.898	10.899	10.928	11.130
Micronesia (Fed. States of) (US dollar) Micronésie (Etats féd. de) (dollar des Etats-Unis)										
End of period	Fin de période	1.000	1.000	1.000	1.000	1.000	1.000	1.000	1.000	1.000
Period average	Moyenne sur période	1.000	1.000	1.000	1.000	1.000	1.000	1.000	1.000	1.000
Mongolia (togrog) Mongolie (togrog)										
End of period	Fin de période	1 097.000	1 102.000	1 125.000	1 168.000	1 209.000	1 221.000	1 165.000	1 170.000	1 267.510
Period average	Moyenne sur période	1 076.670	1 097.700	1 110.310	1 146.540	1 185.280	1 205.220	1 165.370	1 170.960	1 165.740
Montenegro (euro) Monténégro (euro)										
End of period	Fin de période	...	...	...	...	...	...	0.759	0.679	0.719
Period average	Moyenne sur période	...	...	...	...	...	...	0.797	0.731	0.683
Montserrat (EC dollar) Montserrat (dollar des Caraïbes orientales)										
End of period	Fin de période	2.700	2.700	2.700	2.700	2.700	2.700	2.700	2.700	2.700
Period average	Moyenne sur période	2.700	2.700	2.700	2.700	2.700	2.700	2.700	2.700	2.700
Morocco (Moroccan dirham) Maroc (dirham marocain)										
End of period	Fin de période	10.619	11.560	10.167	8.750	8.218	9.249	8.457	7.713	8.098
Period average	Moyenne sur période	10.626	11.303	11.021	9.574	8.868	8.865	8.796	8.192	7.750
Mozambique[1,7] (new metical) Mozambique[1,7] (nouveau metical)										
End of period	Fin de période	17.141	23.320	23.854	23.857	18.899	24.183	#25.970	23.820	25.500
Period average	Moyenne sur période	15.227	20.704	23.678	23.782	22.581	23.061	25.401	25.840	24.301
Myanmar (kyat) Myanmar (kyat)										
End of period	Fin de période	6.530	6.770	6.258	5.726	5.479	5.953	5.656	5.384	5.524
Period average	Moyenne sur période	6.426	6.684	6.573	6.076	5.746	5.761	5.784	5.560	5.388
Namibia (Namibia dollar) Namibie (dollar namibien)										
End of period	Fin de période	7.569	12.127	8.640	6.640	5.630	6.325	6.970	6.810	9.305
Period average	Moyenne sur période	6.940	8.609	10.541	7.565	6.460	6.359	6.772	7.045	8.261
Nepal (Nepalese rupee) Népal (roupie népalaise)										
End of period	Fin de période	74.300	76.475	78.300	74.040	71.800	74.050	71.100	63.550	77.650
Period average	Moyenne sur période	71.094	74.949	77.877	76.141	73.674	71.368	72.756	66.415	69.762
Netherlands Antilles (Netherlands Antillean guilder) Antilles néerlandaises (florin des Antilles néerlandaises)										
End of period	Fin de période	1.790	1.790	1.790	1.790	1.790	1.790	1.790	1.790	1.790
Period average	Moyenne sur période	1.790	1.790	1.790	1.790	1.790	1.790	1.790	1.790	1.790
New Zealand (New Zealand dollar) Nouvelle-Zélande (dollar néo-zélandais)										
End of period	Fin de période	2.272	2.407	1.899	1.538	1.392	1.468	1.417	1.292	1.729
Period average	Moyenne sur période	2.201	2.379	2.162	1.722	1.509	1.420	1.542	1.361	1.423
Nicaragua[1] (córdoba) Nicaragua[1] (córdoba)										
End of period	Fin de période	13.057	13.841	14.671	15.552	16.329	17.146	18.003	18.903	19.848
Period average	Moyenne sur période	12.684	13.372	14.251	15.105	15.937	16.733	17.570	18.449	19.372
Niger (CFA franc) Niger (franc CFA)										
End of period	Fin de période	704.951	744.306	625.495	519.364	481.578	556.037	498.069	445.593	471.335
Period average	Moyenne sur période	711.976	733.039	696.988	581.200	528.285	527.468	522.890	479.267	447.805
Nigeria[1] (naira) Nigéria[1] (naira)										
End of period	Fin de période	109.550	112.950	126.400	136.500	132.350	129.000	128.270	117.968	132.563
Period average	Moyenne sur période	101.697	111.231	120.578	129.222	132.888	131.274	128.652	125.808	118.546
Norway (Norwegian krone) Norvège (couronne norvégienne)										
End of period	Fin de période	8.849	9.012	6.966	6.680	6.040	6.770	6.260	5.410	7.000
Period average	Moyenne sur période	8.802	8.992	7.984	7.080	6.741	6.443	6.413	5.862	5.640
Oman (rial Omani) Oman (rial omani)										
End of period	Fin de période	0.385	0.385	0.385	0.385	0.385	0.385	0.385	0.385	0.385
Period average	Moyenne sur période	0.385	0.385	0.385	0.385	0.385	0.385	0.385	0.385	0.385
Pakistan (Pakistan rupee) Pakistan (roupie pakistanaise)										
End of period	Fin de période	58.029	60.864	58.534	57.215	59.124	59.830	60.918	61.221	79.098
Period average	Moyenne sur période	53.648	61.927	59.724	57.752	58.258	59.515	60.271	60.739	70.408
Panama (balboa) Panama (balboa)										
End of period	Fin de période	1.000	1.000	1.000	1.000	1.000	1.000	1.000	1.000	1.000
Period average	Moyenne sur période	1.000	1.000	1.000	1.000	1.000	1.000	1.000	1.000	1.000

70
Exchange rates *(continued)*
National currency per US dollar
Cours des changes *(suite)*
Valeur du dollar E.-U. en monnaie nationale

Country or area Pays ou zone		2000	2001	2002	2003	2004	2005	2006	2007	2008
Papua New Guinea (kina)	**Papouasie-Nvl-Guinée (kina)**									
End of period	Fin de période	3.072	3.762	4.019	3.333	3.125	3.096	3.030	2.837	2.677
Period average	Moyenne sur période	2.782	3.389	3.895	3.563	3.223	3.102	3.057	2.965	2.700
Paraguay (guaraní)	**Paraguay (guaraní)**									
End of period	Fin de période	3 526.900	4 682.000	7 103.590	6 114.960	6 250.000	6 120.000	5 190.000	4 875.000	4 945.000
Period average	Moyenne sur période	3 486.350	4 105.930	5 716.260	6 424.340	5 974.580	6 177.960	5 635.460	5 032.720	4 363.240
Peru (new sol)	**Pérou (nouveau sol)**									
End of period	Fin de période	3.527	3.444	3.514	3.463	3.282	3.430	3.196	2.996	3.140
Period average	Moyenne sur période	3.490	3.507	3.517	3.478	3.413	3.296	3.274	3.128	2.924
Philippines (Philippine peso)	**Philippines (peso philippin)**									
End of period	Fin de période	49.998	51.404	53.096	55.569	56.267	53.067	49.132	41.401	47.485
Period average	Moyenne sur période	44.192	50.993	51.604	54.203	56.040	55.086	51.314	46.148	44.475
Poland (zloty)	**Pologne (zloty)**									
End of period	Fin de période	4.143	3.986	3.839	3.741	2.990	3.261	2.911	2.435	2.962
Period average	Moyenne sur période	4.346	4.094	4.080	3.889	3.658	3.235	3.103	2.768	2.409
Qatar (Qatar riyal)	**Qatar (riyal qatarien)**									
End of period	Fin de période	3.640	3.640	3.640	3.640	3.640	3.640	3.640	3.640	3.640
Period average	Moyenne sur période	3.640	3.640	3.640	3.640	3.640	3.640	3.640	3.640	3.640
Republic of Moldova (Moldovan leu)	**République de Moldova (leu moldove)**									
End of period	Fin de période	12.383	13.091	13.822	13.220	12.461	12.832	12.905	11.319	10.400
Period average	Moyenne sur période	12.434	12.865	13.571	13.945	12.330	12.600	13.131	12.140	10.392
Romania [1,8] (Romanian leu)	**Roumanie [1,8] (leu roumain)**									
End of period	Fin de période	2.593	3.160	3.350	3.260	2.907	#3.108	2.568	2.456	2.834
Period average	Moyenne sur période	2.171	2.906	3.306	3.320	3.264	2.914	2.809	2.438	2.519
Russian Federation [9] (ruble)	**Fédération de Russie [9] (ruble)**									
End of period	Fin de période	28.160	30.140	31.784	29.455	27.749	28.783	26.331	24.546	29.380
Period average	Moyenne sur période	28.129	29.169	31.349	30.692	28.814	28.284	27.191	25.581	24.853
Rwanda (Rwanda franc)	**Rwanda (franc rwandais)**									
End of period	Fin de période	430.486	457.900	511.854	580.280	566.860	553.719	548.650	544.220	558.898
Period average	Moyenne sur période	389.696	442.992	475.365	537.655	577.449	557.823	551.710	546.955	546.848
Saint Kitts and Nevis (EC dollar)	**Saint-Kitts-et-Nevis (dollar des Caraïbes orientales)**									
End of period	Fin de période	2.700	2.700	2.700	2.700	2.700	2.700	2.700	2.700	2.700
Period average	Moyenne sur période	2.700	2.700	2.700	2.700	2.700	2.700	2.700	2.700	2.700
Saint Lucia (EC dollar)	**Sainte-Lucie (dollar des Caraïbes orientales)**									
End of period	Fin de période	2.700	2.700	2.700	2.700	2.700	2.700	2.700	2.700	2.700
Period average	Moyenne sur période	2.700	2.700	2.700	2.700	2.700	2.700	2.700	2.700	2.700
Saint Vincent-Grenadines (EC dollar)	**Saint Vincent-Grenadines (dollar des Caraïbes orientales)**									
End of period	Fin de période	2.700	2.700	2.700	2.700	2.700	2.700	2.700	2.700	2.700
Period average	Moyenne sur période	2.700	2.700	2.700	2.700	2.700	2.700	2.700	2.700	2.700
Samoa (tala)	**Samoa (tala)**									
End of period	Fin de période	3.341	3.551	3.216	2.778	2.673	2.764	2.685	2.558	2.904
Period average	Moyenne sur période	3.286	3.478	3.376	2.973	2.781	2.710	2.779	2.617	2.644
San Marino (euro)	**Saint-Marin (euro)**									
End of period	Fin de période	1.075	1.135	0.954	0.792	0.734	0.848	0.759	0.679	0.719
Period average	Moyenne sur période	1.085	1.118	1.063	0.886	0.805	0.804	0.797	0.731	0.683
Sao Tome and Principe (dobra)	**Sao Tomé-et-Principe (dobra)**									
End of period	Fin de période	8 610.650	9 019.710	9 191.840	9 455.900	10 104.000	11 929.700	13 073.900	14 362.300	15 228.100
Period average	Moyenne sur période	7 978.170	8 842.110	9 088.330	9 347.580	9 902.320	10 558.000	12 448.600	13 536.800	14 695.200
Saudi Arabia (Saudi Arabian riyal)	**Arabie saoudite (riyal saoudien)**									
End of period	Fin de période	3.750	3.750	3.750	3.750	3.750	3.745	3.745	3.750	3.750
Period average	Moyenne sur période	3.750	3.750	3.750	3.750	3.750	3.747	3.745	3.748	3.750
Senegal (CFA franc)	**Sénégal (franc CFA)**									
End of period	Fin de période	704.951	744.306	625.495	519.364	481.578	556.037	498.069	445.593	471.335
Period average	Moyenne sur période	711.976	733.039	696.988	581.200	528.285	527.468	522.890	479.267	447.805
Serbia (dinar)	**Serbie (dinar)**									
End of period	Fin de période	63.166	67.670	58.985	54.637	57.936	72.219	59.976	53.727	62.900
Period average	Moyenne sur période	63.166	66.914	64.398	57.585	58.381	66.714	67.146	58.454	55.724
Seychelles (Seychelles rupee)	**Seychelles (roupie seychelloises)**									
End of period	Fin de période	6.269	5.752	5.055	5.500	5.500	5.500	5.796	7.998	#16.573
Period average	Moyenne sur période	5.714	5.858	5.480	5.401	5.500	5.500	5.520	6.701	9.457

70

Exchange rates *(continued)*
National currency per US dollar
Cours des changes *(suite)*
Valeur du dollar E.-U. en monnaie nationale

Country or area Pays ou zone		2000	2001	2002	2003	2004	2005	2006	2007	2008
Sierra Leone (leone)	**Sierra Leone (leone)**									
End of period	Fin de période	1 666.670	2 161.270	2 191.730	2 562.180	2 860.490	2 932.520	2 973.940	2 977.600	3 044.250
Period average	Moyenne sur période	2 092.120	1 986.150	2 099.030	2 347.940	2 701.300	2 889.590	2 961.910	2 985.190	2 980.650
Singapore (Singapore dollar)	**Singapour (dollar singapourien)**									
End of period	Fin de période	1.732	1.851	1.737	1.701	1.634	1.664	1.534	1.441	1.439
Period average	Moyenne sur période	1.724	1.792	1.791	1.742	1.690	1.664	1.589	1.507	1.415
Slovakia (Slovak koruna)	**Slovaquie (couronne slovaque)**									
End of period	Fin de période	47.389	48.467	40.036	32.920	28.496	31.948	26.246	22.870	21.385
Period average	Moyenne sur période	46.035	48.355	45.327	36.773	32.257	31.018	29.697	24.694	21.361
Slovenia (tolar, euro)	**Slovénie (tolar, euro)**									
End of period	Fin de période	227.377	250.946	221.071	189.367	176.243	202.430	181.931	#0.679	0.719
Period average	Moyenne sur période	222.656	242.749	240.248	207.114	192.381	192.705	191.028	#0.731	0.683
Solomon Islands (Solomon Islands dollar)	**Iles Salomon (dollar des Iles Salomon)**									
End of period	Fin de période	5.099	5.565	7.457	7.491	7.508	7.576	7.616	7.663	8.000
Period average	Moyenne sur période	5.089	5.278	6.749	7.506	7.485	7.530	7.609	7.652	7.748
South Africa[1] (rand)	**Afrique du Sud[1] (rand)**									
End of period	Fin de période	7.569	12.127	8.640	6.640	5.630	6.325	6.970	6.810	9.305
Period average	Moyenne sur période	6.940	8.609	10.541	7.565	6.460	6.359	6.772	7.045	8.261
Sri Lanka (Sri Lanka rupee)	**Sri Lanka (roupie sri-lankaise)**									
End of period	Fin de période	82.580	93.159	96.725	96.738	104.605	102.117	107.706	108.719	113.140
Period average	Moyenne sur période	77.005	89.383	95.662	96.521	101.194	100.498	103.914	110.623	108.334
Sudan[1] (Sudanese pound)	**Soudan[1] (livre soudanaise)**									
End of period	Fin de période	2.574	2.614	2.617	2.602	2.506	2.305	2.013	#2.053	2.184
Period average	Moyenne sur période	2.571	2.587	2.633	2.610	2.579	2.436	2.172	2.016	2.090
Suriname[10] (Surinamese dollar)	**Suriname[10] (dollar surinamais)**									
End of period	Fin de période	2.179	2.179	2.515	#2.625	#2.715	2.740	2.745	2.745	2.745
Period average	Moyenne sur période	1.322	2.178	2.347	#2.601	2.734	2.732	2.744	2.745	2.745
Swaziland (lilangeni)	**Swaziland (lilangeni)**									
End of period	Fin de période	7.569	12.127	8.640	6.640	5.630	6.325	6.970	6.810	9.305
Period average	Moyenne sur période	6.940	8.609	10.541	7.565	6.460	6.359	6.772	7.045	8.261
Sweden (Swedish krona)	**Suède (couronne suédoise)**									
End of period	Fin de période	9.535	10.668	8.825	7.189	6.615	7.958	6.864	6.414	7.811
Period average	Moyenne sur période	9.162	10.329	9.737	8.086	7.349	7.473	7.378	6.759	6.591
Switzerland (Swiss franc)	**Suisse (franc suisse)**									
End of period	Fin de période	1.637	1.677	1.387	1.237	1.132	1.314	1.220	1.126	1.064
Period average	Moyenne sur période	1.689	1.688	1.559	1.347	1.244	1.245	1.254	1.200	1.083
Syrian Arab Republic[1] (Syrian pound)	**Rép. arabe syrienne[1] (livre syrienne)**									
End of period	Fin de période	11.225	11.225	11.225	11.225	11.225	11.225	11.225	11.225	11.225
Period average	Moyenne sur période	11.225	11.225	11.225	11.225	11.225	11.225	11.225	...	...
Tajikistan (somoni)	**Tadjikistan (somoni)**									
End of period	Fin de période	#2.200	2.550	3.000	2.957	3.037	3.199	3.427	3.465	3.452
Period average	Moyenne sur période	#2.076	2.372	2.764	3.061	2.971	3.117	3.298	3.442	3.431
Thailand (baht)	**Thaïlande (baht)**									
End of period	Fin de période	43.268	44.222	43.152	39.591	39.061	41.030	36.046	33.718	34.898
Period average	Moyenne sur période	40.112	44.432	42.960	41.485	40.222	40.220	37.882	34.518	33.313
TFYR of Macedonia (TFYR Macedonian denar)	**L'ex-R.Y. Macédoine (denar de l'ex-R.Y. Macédoine)**									
End of period	Fin de période	66.328	69.172	58.598	49.050	45.068	51.859	46.450	41.656	43.561
Period average	Moyenne sur période	65.904	68.037	64.350	54.322	49.410	49.284	48.802	44.730	41.868
Togo (CFA franc)	**Togo (franc CFA)**									
End of period	Fin de période	704.951	744.306	625.495	519.364	481.578	556.037	498.069	445.593	471.335
Period average	Moyenne sur période	711.976	733.039	696.988	581.200	528.285	527.468	522.890	479.267	447.805
Tonga (pa'anga)	**Tonga (pa'anga)**									
End of period	Fin de période	1.977	2.207	2.229	2.020	1.912	2.060	2.000	1.887	2.134
Period average	Moyenne sur période	1.759	2.124	2.195	2.146	1.972	1.943	2.026	1.971	1.942
Trinidad and Tobago (Trinidad and Tobago dollar)	**Trinité-et-Tobago (dollar de la Trinité-et-Tobago)**									
End of period	Fin de période	6.300	6.290	6.300	6.300	6.300	6.310	6.312	6.341	6.299
Period average	Moyenne sur période	6.300	6.233	6.249	6.295	6.299	6.300	6.312	6.328	6.289
Tunisia (Tunisian dinar)	**Tunisie (dinar tunisien)**									
End of period	Fin de période	1.385	1.468	1.334	1.208	1.199	1.363	1.297	1.221	1.310
Period average	Moyenne sur période	1.371	1.439	1.422	1.288	1.245	1.297	1.331	1.281	1.232

70

Exchange rates *(continued)*
National currency per US dollar
Cours des changes *(suite)*
Valeur du dollar E.-U. en monnaie nationale

Country or area Pays ou zone		2000	2001	2002	2003	2004	2005	2006	2007	2008
Turkey [11] (new Turkish Lira)	**Turquie [11] (nouveau livre turque)**									
End of period	Fin de période	0.673	1.450	1.644	1.397	1.340	#1.345	1.409	1.171	1.525
Period average	Moyenne sur période	0.625	1.226	1.507	1.501	1.426	1.344	1.428	1.303	1.302
Turkmenistan (Turkmen manat)	**Turkménistan (manat turkmène)**									
End of period	Fin de période	5 200.000	5 200.000	...	...	...	...	...	...	...
Period average	Moyenne sur période	5 200.000	5 200.000	...	...	...	...	...	...	...
Uganda [1] (Uganda shilling)	**Ouganda [1] (shilling ougandais)**									
End of period	Fin de période	1 766.680	1 727.400	1 852.570	1 935.320	1 738.590	1 816.860	1 741.440	1 697.340	1 949.180
Period average	Moyenne sur période	1 644.480	1 755.660	1 797.550	1 963.720	1 810.300	1 780.670	1 831.450	1 723.490	1 720.440
Ukraine (hryvnia)	**Ukraine (hryvnia)**									
End of period	Fin de période	5.435	5.299	5.332	5.332	5.305	5.050	5.050	5.050	7.700
Period average	Moyenne sur période	5.440	5.372	5.327	5.333	5.319	5.125	5.050	5.050	5.267
United Arab Emirates (UAE dirham)	**Emirats arabes unis (dirham des EAU)**									
End of period	Fin de période	3.673	3.673	3.673	3.673	3.673	3.673	3.673	3.673	3.673
Period average	Moyenne sur période	3.673	3.673	3.673	3.673	3.673	3.673	3.673	3.673	3.673
United Kingdom (pound sterling)	**Royaume-Uni (livre sterling)**									
End of period	Fin de période	0.670	0.689	0.620	0.560	0.518	0.581	0.509	0.499	0.686
Period average	Moyenne sur période	0.661	0.695	0.667	0.612	0.546	0.550	0.543	0.500	0.544
United Rep. of Tanzania (Tanzania shilling)	**Rép.-Unie de Tanzanie (shilling tanzanien)**									
End of period	Fin de période	803.260	916.300	976.300	1 063.620	1 042.960	1 165.510	1 261.640	1 132.090	1 280.300
Period average	Moyenne sur période	800.409	876.412	966.583	1 038.420	1 089.330	1 128.930	1 251.900	1 245.040	1 196.310
United States (US dollar)	**Etats-Unis (dollar des Etats-Unis)**									
End of period	Fin de période	1.000	1.000	1.000	1.000	1.000	1.000	1.000	1.000	1.000
Period average	Moyenne sur période	1.000	1.000	1.000	1.000	1.000	1.000	1.000	1.000	1.000
Uruguay (Uruguayan peso)	**Uruguay (peso uruguayen)**									
End of period	Fin de période	12.515	14.768	27.200	29.300	26.350	24.100	24.400	21.500	24.350
Period average	Moyenne sur période	12.100	13.319	21.257	28.209	28.704	24.479	24.073	23.471	20.949
Uzbekistan (Uzbek sum)	**Ouzbékistan (sum ouzbek)**									
Period average	Moyenne sur période	236.608	...	...	...	...	...	...	...	...
Vanuatu (vatu)	**Vanuatu (vatu)**									
End of period	Fin de période	142.810	146.740	133.170	111.810	106.530	112.330	106.480	99.860	112.620
Period average	Moyenne sur période	137.643	145.313	139.198	122.189	111.790	109.246	110.641	102.438	101.334
Venezuela (Bolivarian Rep. of) (bolívar)	**Venezuela (Rép. bolivarienne du) (bolívar)**									
End of period	Fin de période	0.699	0.762	1.400	1.596	1.916	2.145	2.145	2.145	2.145
Period average	Moyenne sur période	0.679	0.723	1.160	1.605	1.889	2.087	2.145	2.145	2.145
Viet Nam (dong)	**Viet Nam (dong)**									
End of period	Fin de période	14 514.000	15 084.000	15 403.000	15 646.000	15 777.000	15 916.000	16 054.000	16 114.000	16 977.000
Period average	Moyenne sur période	14 167.700	14 725.200	15 279.500	15 509.600	15 746.000	15 858.900	15 994.300	16 105.100	16 302.300
Yemen (Yemeni rial)	**Yémen (rial yéménite)**									
End of period	Fin de période	165.590	173.270	179.010	184.310	185.870	195.080	198.500	199.540	200.080
Period average	Moyenne sur période	161.718	168.672	175.625	183.448	184.776	191.509	197.049	198.953	199.764
Zambia (Zambia kwacha)	**Zambie (kwacha zambie)**									
End of period	Fin de période	4 157.830	3 830.400	4 334.400	4 645.480	4 771.310	3 508.980	4 406.670	3 844.810	4 832.260
Period average	Moyenne sur période	3 110.840	3 610.940	4 398.590	4 733.270	4 778.880	4 463.500	3 603.070	4 002.520	3 745.660
Zimbabwe (Zimbabwe dollar)	**Zimbabwe (dollar zimbabwéen)**									
End of period	Fin de période	0.057	0.057	0.057	0.853	5.936	80.774	#258.920	30 000.000	...
Period average	Moyenne sur période	0.044	0.055	0.055	0.697	5.069	22.364	164.361	9 675.780	...

Source:
International Monetary Fund (IMF), Washington, D.C., database on International Financial Statistics, last accessed August 2009.

Source:
Fonds monétaire international (FMI), Washington, D.C., la base de données de Statistiques Financières Internationales, dernier accès août 2009.

1   Principal rate.
2   In October 2002, Afghanistan redenominated its currency. One afghani is equal to 1,000 old afghanis.
3   A unified floating exchange rate regime was introduced on 11 Feb. 2002, with the exchange rate determined by market conditions.

1   Taux principal.
2   L'Afghanistan a changé en octobre 2002 la valeur de sa monnaie : un afghani vaut 1 000 afghanis anciens.
3   Un régime de taux de change flottant unifié a été introduit le 11 février 2002, le taux de change étant déterminé par le marché.

70

Exchange rates *(continued)*
National currency per US dollar
Cours des changes *(suite)*
Valeur du dollar E.-U. en monnaie nationale

4	"Euro Area" is an official descriptor for the European Economic and Monetary Union (EMU). The participating member states of the EMU are Austria, Belgium, Cyprus (beginning 2008), Finland, France, Germany, Greece (beginning 2001), Ireland, Italy, Luxembourg, Malta (beginning 2008), Netherlands, Portugal, Slovenia (beginning 2007), and Spain.	4	L'expression "zone euro" est un intitulé officiel pour l'Union économique et monétaire (UEM) européenne. L'UEM est composée des pays membres suivants : Allemagne, Autriche, Belgique, Chypre (à partir de 2008), Espagne, Finlande, France, Grèce (à partir de 2001), Irlande, Italie, Luxembourg, Malte (à partir de 2008), Pays-Bas, Portugal et Slovénie (à partir de 2007).
5	Effective 1 January 2005, Madagascar announced a new currency, the ariary. One ariary is equal to 5 Malagasy francs.	5	À compter du 1er janvier 2005, Madagascar a adopté une nouvelle monnaie, l'ariary, qui vaut 5 francs malgaches.
6	Effective 19 October 1994, the official rate of the rufiyaa was pegged to the US dollar at a rate of Rf 11.77 per US dollar. Effective 25 July 2001, the rufiyaa was devalued and fixed at Rf 12.80 per US dollar.	6	À compter du 19 octobre 1994, le taux de change officiel du rufiyaa est indexé sur le dollar des États-Unis, et établi à 11.77 Rf pour 1 dollar. À compter du 25 juillet 2001, le rufiyaa a été dévalué et le taux de change fixe est de 12.80 Rf pour 1 dollar.
7	On July 1, 2006, the new metical (MTn), equivalent to 1,000 of the old metical (MT) was introduced.	7	En 1er juillet 2006, le nouveau metical (MTn), valant 1 000 metical anciens, a été introduit.
8	Effective 1 July 2005, Romania redenominated its currency. One new leu is equal to 10,000 old lei.	8	À compter du 1er juillet 2005, la Roumanie a changé la valeur de sa monnaie : un nouveau leu vaut 10 000 lei anciens.
9	The post-1 January 1998 ruble is equal to 1,000 pre-January 1998 rubles.	9	Le rouble ayant cours après le 1er janvier 1998 vaut 1 000 roubles de la période antérieure à cette date.
10	On 1 January 2004, the Surinamese dollar, equal to 1 000 Surinamese guilders, replaced the guilder as the currency unit.	10	Le 1er janvier 2004, le dollar de Suriname, égal à 1 000 florins de Suriname, a remplacé le florin comme unité monétaire.
11	Effective 1 January 2005, Turkey adopted a new currency, the new Turkish lira. One new Turkish lira (yeni Türk lirasi) is equal to 1,000,000 Turkish lira (Türk lirasi).	11	À compter du 1er janvier 2005, la Turquie a adopté une nouvelle monnaie, la nouvelle livre turque (yeni Türk lirasi), qui vaut 1 000 000 de livres turques (Türk lirasi).

International reserves minus gold
Millions of US dollars, end of period

Réserves internationales, moins l'or
Millions de dollars E.-U., fin de période

Country or area Pays ou zone	1999	2000	2001	2002	2003	2004	2005	2006	2007	2008
Albania Albanie										
Total reserves minus gold										
Rés. totale, moins l'or	488.3	615.6	739.9	838.8	1 009.4	1 357.6	1 404.1	1 768.8	2 104.2	2 319.8
Foreign exchange										
Devises étrangères	406.7	535.3	654.2	752.6	913.8	1 251.6	1 386.8	1 754.8	2 097.0	2 307.4
Algeria Algérie										
Total reserves minus gold										
Rés. totale, moins l'or	4 525.7	12 023.9	18 081.4	23 237.5	33 125.2	43 246.4	56 303.1	77 913.7	110 318.0	143 243.0
Foreign exchange										
Devises étrangères	4 407.0	11 910.0	17 963.0	23 108.0	32 942.0	43 113.0	56 178.0	77 781.0	110 180.0	143 102.0
Angola Angola										
Total reserves minus gold										
Rés. totale, moins l'or	496.1	1 198.2	731.9	375.5	634.2	1 374.1	3 196.9	8 598.6	11 196.8	18 359.4
Foreign exchange										
Devises étrangères	495.9	1 198.0	731.7	375.4	634.0	1 373.8	3 196.6	8 598.4	11 196.5	18 359.2
Anguilla Anguilla										
Total reserves minus gold										
Rés. totale, moins l'or	19.9	20.3	24.2	26.2	33.3	34.3	39.7	41.8	44.9	41.0
Foreign exchange										
Devises étrangères	19.9	20.3	24.2	26.2	33.3	34.3	39.7	41.8	44.9	41.0
Antigua and Barbuda Antigua-et-Barbuda										
Total reserves minus gold										
Rés. totale, moins l'or	69.7	63.6	79.7	87.6	113.8	120.1	127.3	142.6	143.8	138.0
Foreign exchange										
Devises étrangères	69.7	63.6	79.7	87.6	113.7	120.1	127.3	142.6	143.8	138.0
Argentina Argentine										
Total reserves minus gold										
Rés. totale, moins l'or	26 252.1	25 146.9	14 553.1	10 489.3	14 153.4	18 884.3	27 178.9	30 903.5	44 682.1	44 854.6
Foreign exchange										
Devises étrangères	26 114.3	24 414.4	14 542.4	10 395.1	13 144.8	18 007.5	22 742.0	30 420.9	44 175.1	44 360.4
Armenia Arménie										
Total reserves minus gold										
Rés. totale, moins l'or	290.9	302.0	317.2	415.6	502.0	547.8	669.5	1 071.9	1 659.1	1 406.8
Foreign exchange										
Devises étrangères	250.2	280.4	307.0	385.5	483.1	535.8	659.3	1 058.0	1 649.5	1 403.9
Aruba Aruba										
Total reserves minus gold										
Rés. totale, moins l'or	219.9	208.0	293.7	339.7	295.2	295.4	273.5	337.8	372.1	604.9
Foreign exchange										
Devises étrangères	219.9	208.0	293.7	339.7	295.2	295.4	273.5	337.8	372.1	604.9
Australia Australie										
Total reserves minus gold										
Rés. totale, moins l'or	21 212.2	18 118.1	17 955.3	20 688.5	32 188.7	35 802.5	41 941.2	53 448.1	24 768.5	30 690.9
Foreign exchange										
Devises étrangères	19 507.4	16 781.8	16 434.2	18 617.8	29 966.2	33 901.3	40 972.0	52 820.9	24 236.9	29 867.3
Austria Autriche										
Total reserves minus gold										
Rés. totale, moins l'or	#15 120.5	14 318.6	12 509.1	9 683.2	8 470.0	7 858.4	6 839.1	7 010.0	10 688.5	8 912.0
Foreign exchange										
Devises étrangères	14 016.2	13 492.2	11 443.7	8 539.6	7 143.5	6 762.8	6 298.4	6 573.2	10 260.5	8 244.4
Azerbaijan Azerbaïdjan										
Total reserves minus gold										
Rés. totale, moins l'or	672.6	679.6	725.0	720.5	802.8	1 075.1	1 177.7	2 500.4	4 273.1	6 467.2
Foreign exchange										
Devises étrangères	665.5	673.0	722.5	719.8	784.8	1 060.5	1 163.8	2 484.9	4 262.9	6 465.5
Bahamas Bahamas										
Total reserves minus gold										
Rés. totale, moins l'or	410.5	349.6	319.3	380.6	491.1	674.4	586.3	461.3	464.5	567.9
Foreign exchange										
Devises étrangères	401.9	341.4	311.3	372.1	481.8	664.7	577.3	451.9	454.5	558.2

International reserves minus gold *(continued)*
Millions of US dollars, end of period
Réserves internationales, moins l'or *(suite)*
Millions de dollars des E.-U., fin de période

Country or area Pays ou zone	1999	2000	2001	2002	2003	2004	2005	2006	2007	2008
Bahrain Bahreïn										
Total reserves minus gold										
Rés. totale, moins l'or	1 369.0	1 564.1	1 684.0	1 725.8	1 778.4	1 940.5	...	...	...	...
Foreign exchange										
Devises étrangères	1 283.4	1 478.3	1 598.5	1 631.4	1 673.8	1 829.6	...	...	...	...
Bangladesh Bangladesh										
Total reserves minus gold										
Rés. totale, moins l'or	1 603.6	1 486.0	1 275.0	1 683.2	2 577.9	3 172.4	2 767.2	3 805.6	5 183.4	5 689.3
Foreign exchange										
Devises étrangères	1 602.5	1 485.3	1 273.6	1 680.7	2 574.4	3 170.9	2 766.0	3 803.9	5 182.2	5 686.7
Barbados Barbade										
Total reserves minus gold										
Rés. totale, moins l'or	301.9	472.7	690.4	668.5	737.9	579.9	603.5	636.1	839.4	...
Foreign exchange										
Devises étrangères	295.5	466.6	684.4	661.9	730.5	571.8	595.9	627.9	830.5	...
Belarus Bélarus										
Total reserves minus gold										
Rés. totale, moins l'or	294.3	350.5	390.7	618.8	594.8	749.4	1 136.6	1 068.6	3 952.1	2 687.0
Foreign exchange										
Devises étrangères	293.8	350.3	390.3	618.5	594.8	749.3	1 136.6	1 068.5	3 952.1	2 686.0
Belgium Belgique										
Total reserves minus gold										
Rés. totale, moins l'or	#10 937.7	9 994.4	11 266.2	11 855.1	10 989.4	10 361.1	8 241.2	8 783.4	10 383.9	9 318.4
Foreign exchange										
Devises étrangères	#8 377.4	7 988.3	8 743.4	8 908.7	7 651.3	7 714.9	6 815.1	7 618.9	9 297.8	7 767.1
Belize Belize										
Total reserves minus gold										
Rés. totale, moins l'or	71.3	122.9	112.0	114.5	84.7	48.3	71.4	113.7	108.5	166.2
Foreign exchange										
Devises étrangères	64.1	115.8	105.0	106.7	76.1	39.1	62.8	104.4	98.4	156.1
Benin Bénin										
Total reserves minus gold										
Rés. totale, moins l'or	400.1	458.1	578.1	615.7	717.9	640.0	656.8	912.2	1 209.2	1 260.5
Foreign exchange										
Devises étrangères	396.9	455.2	574.9	612.6	714.4	636.5	653.5	908.9	1 205.6	1 257.1
Bhutan Bhoutan										
Total reserves minus gold										
Rés. totale, moins l'or	292.3	317.6	323.4	354.9	366.6	398.6	467.4	545.3	699.0	764.8
Foreign exchange										
Devises étrangères	290.7	316.1	321.8	353.2	364.7	396.6	465.5	543.3	696.8	762.6
Bolivia Bolivie										
Total reserves minus gold										
Rés. totale, moins l'or	974.9	926.4	886.4	580.5	716.8	872.4	1 327.6	2 614.8	4 554.0	6 927.4
Foreign exchange										
Devises étrangères	925.3	879.3	840.9	531.2	663.3	817.3	1 276.7	2 561.2	4 497.7	6 871.4
Bosnia and Herzegovina Bosnie-Herzégovine										
Total reserves minus gold										
Rés. totale, moins l'or	452.3	496.6	1 221.2	1 321.4	1 795.6	2 407.9	2 530.9	3 371.6	4 524.8	3 515.5
Foreign exchange										
Devises étrangères	444.7	485.9	1 215.1	1 318.2	1 792.2	2 407.4	2 530.5	3 371.3	4 524.5	3 515.3
Botswana Botswana										
Total reserves minus gold										
Rés. totale, moins l'or	6 228.8	6 318.2	5 897.3	5 473.9	5 339.8	5 661.4	6 309.1	7 992.4	9 789.7	9 118.6
Foreign exchange										
Devises étrangères	6 159.3	6 256.2	5 829.6	5 397.2	5 244.9	5 576.1	6 247.6	7 927.5	9 722.0	9 044.7
Brazil Brésil										
Total reserves minus gold										
Rés. totale, moins l'or	35 279.3	32 434.0	35 563.0	37 462.0	48 846.6	52 461.8	53 245.2	85 156.2	179 433.0	192 844.0
Foreign exchange										
Devises étrangères	35 269.3	32 433.6	35 552.5	37 187.3	48 844.3	52 457.6	53 216.4	85 147.8	179 431.0	192 843.0

International reserves minus gold *(continued)*
Millions of US dollars, end of period
Réserves internationales, moins l'or *(suite)*
Millions de dollars des E.-U., fin de période

Country or area Pays ou zone	1999	2000	2001	2002	2003	2004	2005	2006	2007	2008
Brunei Darussalam Brunéi Darussalam										
Total reserves minus gold										
Rés. totale, moins l'or	516.8	408.3	381.8	449.0	474.7	488.9	491.9	513.6	667.5	748.7
Foreign exchange										
Devises étrangères	463.3	355.8	329.6	369.1	376.5	384.7	431.2	459.8	625.5	708.1
Bulgaria Bulgarie										
Total reserves minus gold										
Rés. totale, moins l'or	2 892.1	3 154.9	3 290.8	4 407.1	6 291.0	8 776.3	8 040.5	10 943.0	16 477.9	16 815.5
Foreign exchange										
Devises étrangères	2 765.5	3 027.6	3 247.3	4 361.8	6 174.6	8 712.1	7 992.4	10 892.1	16 424.2	16 757.4
Burkina Faso Burkina Faso										
Total reserves minus gold										
Rés. totale, moins l'or	295.0	243.6	260.5	313.4	752.2	669.1	438.4	554.9	1 029.2	926.3
Foreign exchange										
Devises étrangères	284.4	233.8	250.9	303.1	741.1	657.6	427.7	543.7	1 017.4	914.8
Burundi Burundi										
Total reserves minus gold										
Rés. totale, moins l'or	48.0	32.9	17.7	58.8	67.0	65.8	100.1	130.5	176.3	265.7
Foreign exchange										
Devises étrangères	39.8	25.2	17.2	58.1	66.3	64.8	99.3	129.7	175.4	265.0
Cambodia Cambodge										
Total reserves minus gold										
Rés. totale, moins l'or	393.2	501.7	586.8	776.1	815.5	943.2	953.0	1 157.3	1 806.9	2 291.6
Foreign exchange										
Devises étrangères	388.0	501.5	586.3	775.6	815.3	943.1	952.7	1 157.1	1 806.7	2 291.4
Cameroon Cameroun										
Total reserves minus gold										
Rés. totale, moins l'or	4.4	212.0	331.8	629.7	639.6	829.3	949.4	1 716.2	2 906.8	3 086.4
Foreign exchange										
Devises étrangères	1.1	203.6	331.1	627.7	637.2	827.6	946.2	1 710.5	2 900.7	3 080.6
Canada Canada										
Total reserves minus gold										
Rés. totale, moins l'or	28 126.4	32 102.3	33 961.8	36 984.1	36 222.1	34 428.7	32 962.1	34 993.8	40 991.2	43 777.5
Foreign exchange										
Devises étrangères	24 432.0	29 019.0	30 484.0	32 685.0	31 537.0	30 166.0	30 664.0	33 198.0	39 314.0	41 537.0
Cape Verde Cap-Vert										
Total reserves minus gold										
Rés. totale, moins l'or	42.6	28.3	45.4	79.8	93.6	139.5	174.0	254.5	281.2	258.5
Foreign exchange										
Devises étrangères	42.6	28.2	45.4	79.8	93.6	139.5	173.9	254.4	281.1	258.2
Central African Rep. Rép. centrafricaine										
Total reserves minus gold										
Rés. totale, moins l'or	136.3	133.3	118.8	123.2	132.4	148.3	139.2	125.3	82.6	121.8
Foreign exchange										
Devises étrangères	136.1	133.1	118.6	123.1	132.2	145.6	138.9	124.4	81.6	121.5
Chad Tchad										
Total reserves minus gold										
Rés. totale, moins l'or	95.0	110.7	122.4	218.7	187.1	221.7	225.6	625.1	955.1	1 345.5
Foreign exchange										
Devises étrangères	94.6	110.3	122.0	218.3	186.7	221.2	225.1	624.6	954.5	1 344.9
Chile Chili										
Total reserves minus gold										
Rés. totale, moins l'or	14 616.6	15 034.9	14 379.0	15 341.1	15 839.6	15 993.8	16 929.2	19 392.0	16 836.8	23 072.4
Foreign exchange										
Devises étrangères	14 187.1	14 686.1	14 041.3	14 813.9	15 211.0	15 495.4	16 689.1	19 224.9	16 695.3	22 848.6
China [1] Chine [1]										
Total reserves minus gold										
Rés. totale, moins l'or	157 728.0	168 278.0	215 605.0	291 128.0	408 151.0	614 500.0	821 514.0	1 068 490.0	1 530 280.0	...
Foreign exchange										
Devises étrangères	154 675.0	165 574.0	212 165.0	286 407.0	403 251.0	609 932.0	818 872.0	1 066 340.0	1 528 250.0	...

71

International reserves minus gold *(continued)*
Millions of US dollars, end of period
Réserves internationales, moins l'or *(suite)*
Millions de dollars des E.-U., fin de période

Country or area Pays ou zone	1999	2000	2001	2002	2003	2004	2005	2006	2007	2008
China, Hong Kong SAR　Chine, Hong Kong RAS										
Total reserves minus gold										
Rés. totale, moins l'or	96 236.0	107 542.0	111 155.0	111 896.0	118 360.0	123 540.0	124 244.0	133 168.0	152 637.0	182 469.0
Foreign exchange										
Devises étrangères	96 236.0	107 542.0	111 155.0	111 896.0	118 360.0	123 540.0	124 244.0	133 168.0	152 637.0	182 469.0
China, Macao SAR　Chine, Macao RAS										
Total reserves minus gold										
Rés. totale, moins l'or	2 857.4	3 323.0	3 508.4	3 800.3	4 343.4	5 436.1	6 689.4	9 132.1	13 229.9	15 930.1
Foreign exchange										
Devises étrangères	2 857.4	3 323.0	3 508.4	3 800.3	4 343.4	5 436.1	6 689.4	9 132.1	13 229.9	15 930.1
Colombia　Colombie										
Total reserves minus gold										
Rés. totale, moins l'or	8 007.9	8 916.0	10 153.7	10 732.4	10 783.9	13 393.8	14 787.0	15 296.2	20 767.3	23 478.8
Foreign exchange										
Devises étrangères	7 485.0	8 409.0	9 659.0	10 190.0	10 188.0	12 769.0	14 206.0	14 673.0	20 096.0	22 810.0
Comoros　Comores										
Total reserves minus gold										
Rés. totale, moins l'or	37.1	43.2	62.3	79.9	94.3	103.7	85.8	93.5	117.2	112.2
Foreign exchange										
Devises étrangères	36.2	42.3	61.6	79.2	93.5	102.9	85.0	92.7	116.3	111.3
Congo　Congo										
Total reserves minus gold										
Rés. totale, moins l'or	39.4	222.0	68.9	31.6	34.8	119.6	731.8	1 840.9	2 174.3	3 871.8
Foreign exchange										
Devises étrangères	38.5	221.3	68.0	27.7	33.4	111.5	728.6	1 839.9	2 173.2	3 870.7
Costa Rica　Costa Rica										
Total reserves minus gold										
Rés. totale, moins l'or	1 460.4	1 317.8	1 329.8	1 501.7	1 839.2	1 921.8	2 312.7	3 114.6	4 113.6	3 798.7
Foreign exchange										
Devises étrangères	1 432.1	1 291.3	1 304.6	1 474.4	1 809.4	1 890.6	2 284.0	3 084.5	4 081.9	3 767.5
Côte d'Ivoire　Côte d'Ivoire										
Total reserves minus gold										
Rés. totale, moins l'or	630.4	667.9	1 019.0	1 863.3	1 303.9	1 693.6	1 321.6	1 797.7	2 519.0	2 252.1
Foreign exchange										
Devises étrangères	626.6	666.2	1 017.9	1 861.5	1 302.7	1 692.5	1 320.0	1 795.7	2 517.3	2 249.7
Croatia　Croatie										
Total reserves minus gold										
Rés. totale, moins l'or	3 025.0	3 524.4	4 703.2	5 884.9	8 190.5	8 758.2	8 800.3	11 487.8	13 674.5	12 957.3
Foreign exchange										
Devises étrangères	2 835.3	3 376.9	4 595.6	5 883.2	8 190.2	8 757.9	8 799.8	11 487.4	13 674.0	12 956.8
Cyprus　Chypre										
Total reserves minus gold										
Rés. totale, moins l'or	1 832.9	1 741.1	2 267.8	3 022.1	3 256.7	3 910.0	4 191.1	5 646.8	6 118.6	#616.8
Foreign exchange										
Devises étrangères	1 783.8	1 694.0	2 221.9	2 953.2	3 154.5	3 832.7	4 155.9	5 621.5	6 100.1	#585.5
Czech Republic　République tchèque										
Total reserves minus gold										
Rés. totale, moins l'or	12 806.1	13 019.2	14 341.2	23 555.6	26 770.6	28 259.3	29 330.4	31 181.7	34 549.6	36 642.1
Foreign exchange										
Devises étrangères	12 806.1	13 015.9	14 189.0	23 315.2	26 293.8	27 844.1	29 137.7	31 053.7	34 445.2	36 459.2
Dem. Rep. of the Congo　Rép. dém. du Congo										
Total reserves minus gold										
Rés. totale, moins l'or	...	...	...	73.9	97.8	236.2	131.2	154.5	180.7	77.7
Foreign exchange										
Devises étrangères	...	...	...	65.5	89.8	230.7	129.8	154.2	177.4	71.8
Denmark　Danemark										
Total reserves minus gold										
Rés. totale, moins l'or	22 286.9	15 108.2	17 110.2	26 985.7	37 105.0	39 083.7	#32 930.4	29 723.7	32 534.4	40 465.8
Foreign exchange										
Devises étrangères	21 145.0	14 469.0	16 117.0	25 901.0	36 004.0	38 196.0	#32 510.0	29 160.0	32 029.0	39 823.0

International reserves minus gold *(continued)*
Millions of US dollars, end of period
Réserves internationales, moins l'or *(suite)*
Millions de dollars des E.-U., fin de période

Country or area Pays ou zone	1999	2000	2001	2002	2003	2004	2005	2006	2007	2008
Djibouti Djibouti										
Total reserves minus gold										
Rés. totale, moins l'or	70.6	67.8	70.3	73.7	100.1	93.9	89.3	120.3	132.1	175.5
Foreign exchange										
Devises étrangères	69.0	66.0	68.8	71.2	98.4	91.2	87.7	117.8	130.3	173.7
Dominica Dominique										
Total reserves minus gold										
Rés. totale, moins l'or	31.6	29.4	31.2	45.5	47.7	42.3	49.2	63.0	60.5	55.2
Foreign exchange										
Devises étrangères	31.6	29.4	31.2	45.5	47.7	42.3	49.1	63.0	60.5	55.1
Dominican Republic Rép. dominicaine										
Total reserves minus gold										
Rés. totale, moins l'or	694.0	627.2	1 099.5	468.4	253.1	798.3	1 843.2	2 115.6	2 546.4	2 271.6
Foreign exchange										
Devises étrangères	693.7	626.8	1 099.0	468.1	253.0	796.7	1 842.6	2 091.2	2 447.8	2 235.6
Ecuador Equateur										
Total reserves minus gold										
Rés. totale, moins l'or	1 642.4	946.9	839.8	714.6	812.6	1 069.6	1 714.2	1 489.5	2 816.4	3 738.2
Foreign exchange										
Devises étrangères	1 616.5	924.3	815.9	689.4	786.1	986.9	1 667.9	1 456.1	2 764.9	3 685.5
Egypt Egypte										
Total reserves minus gold										
Rés. totale, moins l'or	14 484.1	13 117.6	12 925.8	13 242.4	13 588.7	14 273.2	20 609.1	24 461.6	30 187.7	32 216.1
Foreign exchange										
Devises étrangères	14 278.0	12 913.0	12 891.0	13 151.0	13 400.0	14 108.0	20 508.0	24 341.0	30 054.0	32 108.0
El Salvador El Salvador										
Total reserves minus gold										
Rés. totale, moins l'or	1 819.8	1 772.6	1 593.7	1 472.8	1 792.3	1 754.0	1 722.8	1 814.9	2 110.0	2 443.1
Foreign exchange										
Devises étrangères	1 785.5	1 740.0	1 562.3	1 438.9	1 755.2	1 715.2	1 687.1	1 777.3	2 070.5	2 404.6
Equatorial Guinea Guinée équatoriale										
Total reserves minus gold										
Rés. totale, moins l'or	3.4	23.0	70.9	88.5	237.7	945.0	2 102.5	3 066.7	3 845.9	4 431.2
Foreign exchange										
Devises étrangères	3.4	22.9	69.9	87.9	237.7	944.3	2 101.9	3 066.1	3 845.2	4 430.5
Eritrea Erythrée										
Total reserves minus gold										
Rés. totale, moins l'or	34.2	25.5	39.8	30.3	24.7	34.7	27.9	25.4	34.3	57.9
Foreign exchange										
Devises étrangères	34.2	25.5	39.7	30.3	24.7	34.7	27.9	25.3	34.3	57.9
Estonia Estonie										
Total reserves minus gold										
Rés. totale, moins l'or	853.5	920.6	820.2	1 000.4	1 373.4	1 788.2	1 943.2	2 781.2	3 262.7	3 964.9
Foreign exchange										
Devises étrangères	852.1	920.6	820.2	1 000.3	1 373.3	1 788.1	1 943.1	2 781.1	3 262.6	3 964.8
Ethiopia Ethiopie										
Total reserves minus gold										
Rés. totale, moins l'or	458.5	306.3	433.2	881.7	955.6	1 496.8	1 121.5	832.7	1 289.9	870.5
Foreign exchange										
Devises étrangères	448.7	297.1	424.1	871.9	944.8	1 485.1	1 111.0	821.6	1 278.1	859.0
Euro Area Zone euro										
Total reserves minus gold										
Rés. totale, moins l'or	256 780.0	242 327.0	234 931.0	247 168.0	223 145.0	211 971.0	184 714.0	197 006.0	215 296.0	218 717.0
Foreign exchange										
Devises étrangères	227 989.0	218 633.0	207 817.0	215 812.0	188 173.0	181 196.0	167 150.0	184 034.0	203 189.0	201 875.0
Fiji Fidji										
Total reserves minus gold										
Rés. totale, moins l'or	428.7	411.8	366.4	358.8	423.6	478.1	314.7	...	...	...
Foreign exchange										
Devises étrangères	402.6	386.5	341.5	331.5	393.3	446.1	284.9	...	...	...

71

International reserves minus gold *(continued)*
Millions of US dollars, end of period
Réserves internationales, moins l'or *(suite)*
Millions de dollars des E.-U., fin de période

Country or area Pays ou zone	1999	2000	2001	2002	2003	2004	2005	2006	2007	2008
Finland Finlande										
Total reserves minus gold										
Rés. totale, moins l'or	8 219.7	7 976.9	7 983.4	9 285.0	10 514.9	12 221.5	10 521.1	6 494.2	7 063.2	6 979.4
Foreign exchange										
Devises étrangères	7 292.4	7 340.7	7 197.6	8 436.8	9 544.5	11 425.3	10 075.8	6 134.6	6 689.2	6 397.6
France France										
Total reserves minus gold										
Rés. totale, moins l'or	#39 701.5	37 039.2	31 749.1	28 365.3	30 186.5	35 314.0	27 752.9	42 651.6	45 709.7	33 617.5
Foreign exchange										
Devises étrangères	33 933.4	32 114.3	26 363.2	21 965.0	23 121.7	29 076.7	23 996.3	40 287.0	43 587.4	30 382.2
Gabon Gabon										
Total reserves minus gold										
Rés. totale, moins l'or	17.9	190.1	9.9	139.7	196.6	443.4	668.6	1 113.4	1 227.2	1 923.5
Foreign exchange										
Devises étrangères	17.8	189.8	9.6	139.4	196.3	436.9	668.1	1 112.2	1 226.0	1 922.3
Gambia Gambie										
Total reserves minus gold										
Rés. totale, moins l'or	111.2	109.4	106.0	106.9	59.3	83.8	98.3	120.6	142.8	...
Foreign exchange										
Devises étrangères	108.5	107.3	104.1	104.8	57.1	80.7	96.0	116.9	140.2	...
Georgia Géorgie										
Total reserves minus gold										
Rés. totale, moins l'or	144.4	116.0	161.9	202.2	196.2	386.7	478.6	930.8	1 361.2	1 480.2
Foreign exchange										
Devises étrangères	135.9	112.7	158.0	199.3	191.3	375.4	477.6	929.9	1 346.3	1 467.8
Germany Allemagne										
Total reserves minus gold										
Rés. totale, moins l'or	#61 038.8	56 890.5	51 403.9	51 170.6	50 694.0	48 822.7	45 139.7	41 686.5	44 326.5	43 137.2
Foreign exchange										
Devises étrangères	#52 661.1	49 667.3	43 709.8	42 495.4	41 095.5	39 898.6	39 765.3	37 718.9	40 768.3	38 557.0
Ghana Ghana										
Total reserves minus gold										
Rés. totale, moins l'or	453.8	232.1	298.2	539.7	1 352.8	1 626.7	1 752.9	2 090.3	...	...
Foreign exchange										
Devises étrangères	379.1	231.5	294.2	536.1	1 306.0	1 605.9	1 751.8	2 089.1	...	...
Greece Grèce										
Total reserves minus gold										
Rés. totale, moins l'or	18 122.3	13 424.3	#5 154.2	8 082.8	4 361.5	1 191.0	506.4	565.9	631.1	343.8
Foreign exchange										
Devises étrangères	17 726.0	13 115.5	#4 787.2	7 629.3	3 843.3	743.7	309.1	408.3	518.2	158.7
Grenada Grenade										
Total reserves minus gold										
Rés. totale, moins l'or	50.8	57.7	63.9	87.8	83.2	121.7	94.3	100.0	110.6	105.3
Foreign exchange										
Devises étrangères	50.8	57.7	63.9	87.8	83.2	121.7	94.2	99.8	110.4	104.1
Guatemala Guatemala										
Total reserves minus gold										
Rés. totale, moins l'or	1 189.2	1 746.4	2 292.2	2 299.1	2 833.2	3 426.3	3 663.8	3 915.0	4 129.9	4 461.9
Foreign exchange										
Devises étrangères	1 177.7	1 736.6	2 283.7	2 290.9	2 825.0	3 418.3	3 657.3	3 909.3	4 125.6	4 458.4
Guinea Guinée										
Total reserves minus gold										
Rés. totale, moins l'or	199.7	147.9	200.2	171.4	...	110.5	95.1	...	...	...
Foreign exchange										
Devises étrangères	198.3	147.6	199.3	169.6	...	110.4	94.9	...	...	...
Guinea-Bissau Guinée-Bissau										
Total reserves minus gold										
Rés. totale, moins l'or	35.3	66.7	69.5	102.7	32.9	73.1	79.8	82.0	112.9	124.5
Foreign exchange										
Devises étrangères	35.2	66.7	69.3	102.3	31.7	72.4	79.2	81.5	112.8	124.4

International reserves minus gold *(continued)*
Millions of US dollars, end of period
Réserves internationales, moins l'or *(suite)*
Millions de dollars des E.-U., fin de période

Country or area Pays ou zone	1999	2000	2001	2002	2003	2004	2005	2006	2007	2008
Guyana Guyana										
Total reserves minus gold										
Rés. totale, moins l'or	268.3	305.0	287.3	284.5	276.4	231.8	251.9	279.6	313.0	355.9
Foreign exchange										
Devises étrangères	267.0	295.8	284.8	279.8	271.5	224.7	251.4	278.0	312.5	355.9
Haiti Haïti										
Total reserves minus gold										
Rés. totale, moins l'or	264.0	182.1	141.4	81.7	62.0	114.4	133.1	253.1	452.0	541.4
Foreign exchange										
Devises étrangères	263.1	182.0	140.8	81.1	61.6	114.1	120.7	245.1	444.4	534.3
Honduras Honduras										
Total reserves minus gold										
Rés. totale, moins l'or	1 257.6	1 313.0	1 415.6	1 524.1	1 430.0	1 970.4	2 327.2	2 628.5	2 528.0	2 473.4
Foreign exchange										
Devises étrangères	1 244.8	1 301.7	1 404.4	1 511.9	1 417.1	1 956.9	2 314.6	2 615.5	2 514.3	2 460.0
Hungary Hongrie										
Total reserves minus gold										
Rés. totale, moins l'or	10 954.0	11 189.6	10 727.2	10 348.5	12 751.4	15 922.1	18 552.1	21 527.0	23 969.8	33 787.9
Foreign exchange										
Devises étrangères	10 707.0	10 915.0	10 302.0	9 721.0	12 029.0	15 326.0	18 296.0	21 316.0	23 773.0	33 620.0
Iceland Islande										
Total reserves minus gold										
Rés. totale, moins l'or	478.4	388.9	338.2	440.1	792.3	1 046.2	1 035.7	2 301.3	2 578.7	3 515.2
Foreign exchange										
Devises étrangères	452.9	364.6	314.8	414.7	764.6	1 017.3	1 009.1	2 273.2	2 549.1	3 486.2
India Inde										
Total reserves minus gold										
Rés. totale, moins l'or	32 666.7	37 902.2	45 870.5	67 665.5	98 937.9	126 593.0	131 924.0	170 738.0	266 988.0	247 419.0
Foreign exchange										
Devises étrangères	31 992.0	37 264.0	45 251.0	66 994.0	97 617.0	125 164.0	131 018.0	170 187.0	266 553.0	246 603.0
Indonesia Indonésie										
Total reserves minus gold										
Rés. totale, moins l'or	26 445.0	29 501.9	27 246.2	30 970.7	34 962.3	34 952.5	33 140.5	41 103.1	54 976.4	49 596.7
Foreign exchange										
Devises étrangères	26 245.0	28 280.4	27 047.5	30 754.3	34 742.4	34 724.1	32 925.5	40 866.0	54 737.3	49 338.9
Iraq Iraq										
Total reserves minus gold										
Rés. totale, moins l'or	...	...	...	...	...	7 824.1	12 104.1	19 931.9	31 297.6	50 042.5
Foreign exchange										
Devises étrangères	...	...	...	...	...	7 098.5	11 439.9	19 235.7	30 887.5	49 635.8
Ireland Irlande										
Total reserves minus gold										
Rés. totale, moins l'or	#5 325.0	5 359.7	5 586.5	5 414.8	4 078.5	2 830.9	778.7	720.0	778.7	871.1
Foreign exchange										
Devises étrangères	4 869.1	4 982.7	5 195.5	4 879.4	3 425.2	2 323.7	514.4	493.8	590.8	609.2
Israel Israël										
Total reserves minus gold										
Rés. totale, moins l'or	22 604.9	23 281.2	23 378.6	24 082.9	26 315.1	27 094.4	28 059.4	29 153.2	28 518.5	42 513.2
Foreign exchange										
Devises étrangères	22 514.8	23 163.0	23 179.1	23 665.0	25 778.4	26 616.0	27 839.0	29 011.0	28 406.0	42 324.0
Italy Italie										
Total reserves minus gold										
Rés. totale, moins l'or	#22 421.8	25 566.5	24 419.4	28 603.1	30 372.2	27 859.0	25 514.7	25 661.7	28 385.0	37 087.6
Foreign exchange										
Devises étrangères	#18 707.7	22 423.2	20 905.3	24 587.8	26 062.0	24 011.1	23 527.9	24 413.2	27 319.2	35 306.0
Jamaica Jamaïque										
Total reserves minus gold										
Rés. totale, moins l'or	554.5	1 053.7	1 900.5	1 645.1	1 194.9	1 846.5	2 169.8	2 318.4	1 878.5	1 767.1
Foreign exchange										
Devises étrangères	553.8	1 053.6	1 899.0	1 644.2	1 194.8	1 846.4	2 169.8	2 318.2	1 878.2	1 767.0

International reserves minus gold *(continued)*
Millions of US dollars, end of period
Réserves internationales, moins l'or *(suite)*
Millions de dollars des E.-U., fin de période

Country or area Pays ou zone	1999	2000	2001	2002	2003	2004	2005	2006	2007	2008
Japan Japon										
Total reserves minus gold										
Rés. totale, moins l'or	286 916.0	354 902.0	395 155.0	461 186.0	663 289.0	833 891.0	834 275.0	879 682.0	952 784.0	1 009 360.0
Foreign exchange										
Devises étrangères	277 708.0	347 212.0	387 727.0	451 458.0	652 790.0	824 264.0	828 813.0	874 936.0	948 356.0	1 003 670.0
Jordan Jordanie										
Total reserves minus gold										
Rés. totale, moins l'or	2 629.1	3 331.3	3 062.2	3 975.9	5 194.3	5 266.6	5 250.3	6 722.0	7 542.0	8 561.6
Foreign exchange										
Devises étrangères	2 628.8	3 330.6	3 061.0	3 975.0	5 193.1	5 264.8	5 249.5	6 720.4	7 539.4	8 558.0
Kazakhstan Kazakhstan										
Total reserves minus gold										
Rés. totale, moins l'or	1 479.2	1 594.1	1 997.2	2 555.3	4 236.2	8 473.1	6 084.2	17 750.8	15 776.8	17 871.5
Foreign exchange										
Devises étrangères	1 253.8	1 594.1	1 997.2	2 554.3	4 235.0	8 471.9	6 083.0	17 749.5	15 775.4	17 870.1
Kenya Kenya										
Total reserves minus gold										
Rés. totale, moins l'or	791.6	897.7	1 064.9	1 068.0	1 481.9	1 519.3	1 798.8	2 415.8	3 355.0	2 878.5
Foreign exchange										
Devises étrangères	772.2	881.2	1 048.1	1 050.0	1 461.0	1 499.0	1 780.6	2 396.0	3 334.6	2 855.7
Korea, Republic of Corée, République de										
Total reserves minus gold										
Rés. totale, moins l'or	73 987.3	96 130.5	102 753.0	121 345.0	155 284.0	198 997.0	210 317.0	238 882.0	262 150.0	201 144.0
Foreign exchange										
Devises étrangères	73 700.3	95 855.1	102 487.0	120 811.0	154 509.0	198 175.0	209 968.0	238 388.0	261 771.0	200 479.0
Kosovo Kosovo										
Total reserves minus gold										
Rés. totale, moins l'or	...	...	...	...	...	...	...	...	646.5	641.0
Foreign exchange										
Devises étrangères	...	...	...	...	...	...	...	...	646.5	641.0
Kuwait Koweït										
Total reserves minus gold										
Rés. totale, moins l'or	4 823.7	7 082.4	9 897.3	9 208.1	7 577.0	8 241.9	8 862.8	12 566.0	16 660.0	17 112.8
Foreign exchange										
Devises étrangères	4 244.5	6 504.4	9 191.1	8 357.0	6 640.5	7 347.4	8 380.4	12 177.6	16 285.6	16 611.0
Kyrgyzstan Kirghizistan										
Total reserves minus gold										
Rés. totale, moins l'or	229.7	239.0	263.5	288.8	364.6	528.2	569.7	764.4	1 107.2	1 152.9
Foreign exchange										
Devises étrangères	224.6	238.3	262.2	288.2	354.3	508.3	564.5	731.1	1 093.4	1 097.6
Lao People's Dem. Rep. Rép. dém. pop. lao										
Total reserves minus gold										
Rés. totale, moins l'or	101.2	139.0	130.9	191.6	208.6	223.2	234.3	328.4	532.6	628.7
Foreign exchange										
Devises étrangères	101.1	138.9	127.5	185.5	189.5	207.9	220.2	313.7	517.1	613.6
Latvia Lettonie										
Total reserves minus gold										
Rés. totale, moins l'or	872.0	850.9	1 148.7	1 241.4	1 432.4	1 912.0	2 232.1	4 353.4	5 553.4	5 027.6
Foreign exchange										
Devises étrangères	868.9	850.8	1 148.6	1 241.3	1 432.2	1 911.7	2 231.9	4 353.1	5 553.1	5 027.2
Lebanon Liban										
Total reserves minus gold										
Rés. totale, moins l'or	7 775.6	5 943.7	5 013.8	7 243.8	12 519.4	11 734.6	11 887.1	13 376.4	12 909.9	20 244.5
Foreign exchange										
Devises étrangères	7 727.3	5 895.4	4 965.8	7 190.9	12 460.8	11 672.4	11 828.7	13 313.3	12 844.1	20 181.8
Lesotho Lesotho										
Total reserves minus gold										
Rés. totale, moins l'or	499.6	417.9	386.5	406.4	460.3	501.5	519.1	658.4	...	...
Foreign exchange										
Devises étrangères	493.5	412.6	381.5	401.0	454.4	495.3	513.5	652.7	...	...

International reserves minus gold *(continued)*
Millions of US dollars, end of period
Réserves internationales, moins l'or *(suite)*
Millions de dollars des E.-U., fin de période

Country or area Pays ou zone	1999	2000	2001	2002	2003	2004	2005	2006	2007	2008
Liberia Libéria										
Total reserves minus gold										
Rés. totale, moins l'or	0.4	0.3	0.5	3.3	7.4	18.7	25.4	72.0	119.4	160.9
Foreign exchange										
Devises étrangères	0.4	0.2	0.4	3.3	7.3	18.7	25.4	71.9	119.3	139.0
Libyan Arab Jamah. Jamah. arabe libyenne										
Total reserves minus gold										
Rés. totale, moins l'or	7 279.7	12 460.8	14 800.5	14 307.4	19 584.0	25 688.8	39 507.8	59 289.2	79 404.7	92 313.3
Foreign exchange										
Devises étrangères	6 225.5	11 407.7	13 749.0	13 159.4	18 309.8	24 336.3	38 235.2	57 907.3	77 897.5	90 803.4
Lithuania Lituanie										
Total reserves minus gold										
Rés. totale, moins l'or	1 195.0	1 311.6	1 617.7	2 349.3	3 372.0	3 512.6	3 720.2	5 654.4	7 565.8	6 279.7
Foreign exchange										
Devises étrangères	1 190.6	1 310.2	1 599.3	2 295.9	3 371.9	3 512.5	3 720.1	5 654.3	7 565.6	6 279.6
Luxembourg Luxembourg										
Total reserves minus gold										
Rés. totale, moins l'or	#77.4	76.6	105.6	151.7	279.9	298.4	241.1	218.1	143.6	334.6
Foreign exchange										
Devises étrangères	0.3	0.1	0.1	0.2	88.9	143.9	166.7	156.0	93.8	258.4
Madagascar Madagascar										
Total reserves minus gold										
Rés. totale, moins l'or	227.2	285.2	398.4	363.3	414.3	503.5	481.3	583.2	846.7	982.3
Foreign exchange										
Devises étrangères	227.0	285.1	398.2	363.2	414.2	503.3	481.2	583.1	846.6	982.0
Malawi Malawi										
Total reserves minus gold										
Rés. totale, moins l'or	246.4	243.0	202.5	161.5	122.0	128.1	158.9	133.8	216.6	...
Foreign exchange										
Devises étrangères	243.0	239.6	198.8	158.3	118.2	123.3	154.6	129.6	212.9	...
Malaysia Malaisie										
Total reserves minus gold										
Rés. totale, moins l'or	30 588.2	28 329.8	29 522.3	33 360.7	43 821.7	65 881.1	69 858.0	82 132.3	101 019.0	91 148.8
Foreign exchange										
Devises étrangères	29 670.0	27 432.2	28 632.9	32 419.1	42 772.4	64 905.9	69 376.9	81 723.6	100 635.0	90 605.1
Maldives Maldives										
Total reserves minus gold										
Rés. totale, moins l'or	127.1	122.8	93.1	133.1	159.5	203.6	186.3	231.4	308.3	240.6
Foreign exchange										
Devises étrangères	124.8	120.5	90.8	130.6	156.7	200.7	183.6	228.5	305.3	237.6
Mali Mali										
Total reserves minus gold										
Rés. totale, moins l'or	349.7	381.3	348.9	594.5	952.5	860.7	854.6	969.5	1 087.1	1 071.1
Foreign exchange										
Devises étrangères	337.1	369.7	337.4	582.4	938.4	846.2	841.2	955.4	1 071.9	1 056.1
Malta Malte										
Total reserves minus gold										
Rés. totale, moins l'or	1 788.0	1 470.2	1 666.2	2 209.3	2 728.7	2 732.0	2 576.4	2 976.8	3 785.4	#368.3
Foreign exchange										
Devises étrangères	1 701.9	1 385.8	1 582.4	2 115.3	2 624.5	2 621.7	2 473.0	2 865.0	3 662.0	#288.3
Mauritania Mauritanie										
Total reserves minus gold										
Rés. totale, moins l'or	35.3	46.2	36.7	70.1	27.0	33.7	64.5	187.2	197.8	...
Foreign exchange										
Devises étrangères	35.3	45.9	36.5	69.9	26.9	33.7	64.3	187.1	197.8	...
Mauritius Maurice										
Total reserves minus gold										
Rés. totale, moins l'or	731.0	897.4	835.6	1 227.4	1 577.3	1 605.9	1 339.9	1 269.6	1 780.3	1 742.7
Foreign exchange										
Devises étrangères	689.1	857.1	796.3	1 184.5	1 519.2	1 544.7	1 289.2	1 226.3	1 739.9	1 693.4

71
International reserves minus gold *(continued)*
Millions of US dollars, end of period
Réserves internationales, moins l'or *(suite)*
Millions de dollars des E.-U., fin de période

Country or area Pays ou zone	1999	2000	2001	2002	2003	2004	2005	2006	2007	2008
Mexico Mexique										
Total reserves minus gold										
Rés. totale, moins l'or	31 782.2	35 508.8	44 740.7	50 594.4	58 955.6	64 140.7	74 054.1	76 270.5	87 109.2	95 126.1
Foreign exchange										
Devises étrangères	30 992.0	35 142.0	44 384.0	49 895.0	57 739.9	62 777.9	73 014.6	75 447.7	86 309.4	93 994.1
Micronesia (Fed. States of) Micronésie (Etats féd. de)										
Total reserves minus gold										
Rés. totale, moins l'or	92.7	113.0	98.3	117.4	89.6	54.8	50.0	46.6	48.5	40.0
Foreign exchange										
Devises étrangères	91.2	111.6	96.9	115.8	87.8	52.9	48.2	44.7	46.4	37.9
Mongolia Mongolie										
Total reserves minus gold										
Rés. totale, moins l'or	136.5	178.8	205.7	349.7	236.1	236.3	430.3	926.0	1 195.6	...
Foreign exchange										
Devises étrangères	136.3	178.7	205.6	349.5	235.9	236.1	430.1	925.8	1 195.4	...
Montenegro Monténégro										
Total reserves minus gold										
Rés. totale, moins l'or	...	...	...	58.2	63.7	81.8	204.0	432.7	732.4	478.4
Foreign exchange										
Devises étrangères	...	...	...	58.2	63.7	81.8	204.0	432.7	721.8	467.8
Montserrat Montserrat										
Total reserves minus gold										
Rés. totale, moins l'or	14.0	10.4	12.5	14.4	15.2	14.1	13.9	14.6	14.5	11.7
Foreign exchange										
Devises étrangères	14.0	10.4	12.5	14.4	15.2	14.1	13.9	14.6	14.5	11.7
Morocco Maroc										
Total reserves minus gold										
Rés. totale, moins l'or	5 689.4	4 823.2	8 473.9	10 132.7	13 851.1	16 336.6	16 187.4	20 340.7	24 123.3	22 103.8
Foreign exchange										
Devises étrangères	5 507.5	4 612.0	8 262.0	9 914.5	13 634.1	16 107.0	16 008.0	20 182.1	23 980.0	21 976.0
Mozambique Mozambique										
Total reserves minus gold										
Rés. totale, moins l'or	654.0	723.2	713.2	802.5	937.5	1 131.0	1 053.8	1 155.7	1 444.7	1 577.7
Foreign exchange										
Devises étrangères	653.9	723.1	713.2	802.4	937.4	1 130.9	1 053.6	1 155.5	1 444.5	1 577.6
Myanmar Myanmar										
Total reserves minus gold										
Rés. totale, moins l'or	265.5	223.0	400.5	470.0	550.2	672.1	770.7	1 235.6	...	...
Foreign exchange										
Devises étrangères	265.3	222.8	399.9	469.9	550.1	672.1	770.5	1 235.4	...	...
Namibia Namibie										
Total reserves minus gold										
Rés. totale, moins l'or	305.5	259.8	234.3	323.1	325.2	345.1	312.1	449.6	896.0	1 293.0
Foreign exchange										
Devises étrangères	305.4	259.8	234.2	323.0	325.1	344.9	312.0	449.4	895.9	1 292.8
Nepal Népal										
Total reserves minus gold										
Rés. totale, moins l'or	845.1	945.4	1 037.7	1 017.6	1 222.5	1 462.2	1 499.0	...	...	...
Foreign exchange										
Devises étrangères	836.9	937.9	1 030.4	1 009.8	1 213.1	1 452.5	1 490.2	...	...	...
Netherlands Pays-Bas										
Total reserves minus gold										
Rés. totale, moins l'or	#9 885.7	9 642.5	9 034.3	9 563.3	11 167.0	10 654.8	8 986.0	10 802.4	10 269.7	11 476.4
Foreign exchange										
Devises étrangères	6 286.8	7 003.9	5 930.3	6 017.4	7 335.5	7 209.6	7 078.2	9 327.0	8 748.7	9 368.9
Netherlands Antilles Antilles néerlandaises										
Total reserves minus gold										
Rés. totale, moins l'or	265.0	260.7	301.1	398.9	372.9	415.4	545.4	495.0	660.9	818.9
Foreign exchange										
Devises étrangères	265.0	260.7	301.1	398.9	372.9	415.4	545.4	495.0	660.9	818.9

Country or area Pays ou zone	1999	2000	2001	2002	2003	2004	2005	2006	2007	2008
New Zealand Nouvelle-Zélande										
Total reserves minus gold Rés. totale, moins l'or	4 455.3	3 952.1	3 564.7	4 962.8	6 085.4	6 947.4	8 892.7	14 068.5	17 247.2	11 153.0
Foreign exchange Devises étrangères	4 025.0	3 618.9	3 161.2	4 481.8	5 413.7	6 438.8	8 693.6	13 916.0	17 124.1	10 955.4
Nicaragua Nicaragua										
Total reserves minus gold Rés. totale, moins l'or	509.7	488.5	379.9	448.1	502.1	668.2	727.8	921.9	1 103.3	1 140.8
Foreign exchange Devises étrangères	509.5	488.4	379.6	448.1	502.0	667.7	727.5	921.5	1 103.2	1 140.7
Niger Niger										
Total reserves minus gold Rés. totale, moins l'or	39.2	80.4	107.0	133.9	260.1	258.0	249.5	370.9	593.0	702.1
Foreign exchange Devises étrangères	26.1	69.2	95.9	121.6	244.7	243.7	236.9	357.8	579.3	687.4
Nigeria Nigéria										
Total reserves minus gold Rés. totale, moins l'or	5 450.3	9 910.9	10 456.6	7 331.3	7 128.4	16 955.6	28 279.6	42 298.7	51 334.2	53 001.8
Foreign exchange Devises étrangères	5 450.0	9 910.4	10 455.8	7 331.0	7 128.0	16 955.0	28 279.0	42 298.1	51 333.1	53 000.4
Norway Norvège										
Total reserves minus gold Rés. totale, moins l'or	23 807.3	27 597.4	23 277.5	31 999.8	37 220.0	44 307.5	46 985.9	56 841.6	60 839.6	50 949.8
Foreign exchange Devises étrangères	22 545.7	26 706.9	22 197.5	30 692.1	35 890.2	43 078.2	46 377.4	56 181.4	60 294.1	50 214.1
Oman Oman										
Total reserves minus gold Rés. totale, moins l'or	2 767.5	2 379.9	2 364.9	3 173.5	3 593.5	3 597.3	4 358.1	5 014.1	9 523.5	11 581.9
Foreign exchange Devises étrangères	2 697.3	2 310.9	2 277.0	3 064.8	3 466.6	3 484.5	4 308.7	4 970.2	9 485.1	11 541.1
Pakistan Pakistan										
Total reserves minus gold Rés. totale, moins l'or	1 511.4	1 513.4	3 640.0	8 078.3	10 941.0	9 799.0	10 032.8	11 543.1	14 044.0	7 194.2
Foreign exchange Devises étrangères	1 511.0	1 499.0	3 636.0	8 076.0	10 693.0	9 554.0	9 817.0	11 327.6	13 829.0	7 011.5
Panama Panama										
Total reserves minus gold Rés. totale, moins l'or	822.9	722.6	1 091.8	1 182.8	1 011.0	630.6	1 210.5	1 335.0	1 935.1	...
Foreign exchange Devises étrangères	805.0	706.8	1 075.5	1 165.7	992.5	611.4	1 192.5	1 315.9	1 915.4	...
Papua New Guinea Papouasie-Nvl-Guinée										
Total reserves minus gold Rés. totale, moins l'or	205.1	286.9	422.6	321.5	494.2	632.6	718.1	1 400.7	2 053.7	1 953.4
Foreign exchange Devises étrangères	204.3	274.5	413.6	315.0	489.9	631.2	717.4	1 400.0	2 052.9	1 952.6
Paraguay Paraguay										
Total reserves minus gold Rés. totale, moins l'or	978.1	762.8	713.5	629.2	968.9	1 168.1	1 297.1	1 702.2	2 461.5	2 844.6
Foreign exchange Devises étrangères	845.9	632.6	584.3	486.8	811.2	1 001.1	1 140.3	1 532.0	2 383.9	2 767.3
Peru Pérou										
Total reserves minus gold Rés. totale, moins l'or	8 730.5	8 374.0	8 671.9	9 339.1	9 776.8	12 176.4	13 599.4	16 733.3	26 856.5	30 271.5
Foreign exchange Devises étrangères	8 730.1	8 372.5	8 670.1	9 338.3	9 776.4	12 176.1	13 598.9	16 732.4	26 852.7	30 262.5
Philippines Philippines										
Total reserves minus gold Rés. totale, moins l'or	13 269.7	13 090.2	13 476.3	13 329.3	13 654.9	13 116.3	15 926.0	20 025.4	30 210.6	33 192.9
Foreign exchange Devises étrangères	13 143.2	12 974.8	13 352.7	13 200.5	13 523.3	12 979.5	15 800.1	19 891.4	30 071.4	33 047.2

71

International reserves minus gold *(continued)*
Millions of US dollars, end of period
Réserves internationales, moins l'or *(suite)*
Millions de dollars des E.-U., fin de période

Country or area Pays ou zone	1999	2000	2001	2002	2003	2004	2005	2006	2007	2008
Poland Pologne										
Total reserves minus gold										
Rés. totale, moins l'or	26 354.7	26 562.0	25 648.4	28 649.7	32 579.1	35 323.9	40 863.7	46 371.1	62 966.8	59 305.6
Foreign exchange										
Devises étrangères	26 107.1	26 319.9	25 161.6	27 959.2	31 724.9	34 552.8	40 486.9	46 107.0	62 720.3	58 931.0
Portugal Portugal										
Total reserves minus gold										
Rés. totale, moins l'or	#8 427.1	8 908.7	9 666.6	11 179.1	5 875.9	5 174.1	3 478.7	2 063.6	1 257.8	1 309.4
Foreign exchange										
Devises étrangères	#8 005.7	8 539.2	9 228.2	10 655.8	5 248.8	4 631.2	3 173.4	1 835.3	1 044.4	1 022.0
Qatar Qatar										
Total reserves minus gold										
Rés. totale, moins l'or	1 304.2	1 158.0	1 312.7	1 566.8	2 944.2	3 395.9	4 542.4	5 382.7	9 416.4	9 649.5
Foreign exchange										
Devises étrangères	1 228.2	1 079.1	1 190.8	1 404.2	2 758.1	3 225.4	4 456.5	5 307.1	9 345.0	9 553.0
Republic of Moldova République de Moldova										
Total reserves minus gold										
Rés. totale, moins l'or	185.7	222.5	228.5	268.9	302.3	470.3	597.4	775.5	1 333.7	1 672.4
Foreign exchange										
Devises étrangères	185.4	222.1	227.8	268.6	302.2	470.2	597.4	775.3	1 333.5	1 672.3
Romania Roumanie										
Total reserves minus gold										
Rés. totale, moins l'or	1 526.3	2 469.7	3 922.5	6 125.3	8 040.0	14 616.4	19 872.1	28 066.2	37 194.1	36 868.4
Foreign exchange										
Devises étrangères	1 516.2	2 468.7	3 915.7	6 123.0	8 039.7	14 615.8	19 871.5	28 065.9	37 193.6	36 746.9
Russian Federation Fédération de Russie										
Total reserves minus gold										
Rés. totale, moins l'or	8 457.2	24 264.3	32 542.4	44 053.6	73 174.9	120 809.0	175 891.0	295 568.0	466 750.0	412 548.0
Foreign exchange										
Devises étrangères	8 455.4	24 262.6	32 538.1	44 050.8	73 172.1	120 805.0	175 690.0	295 277.0	466 376.0	411 494.0
Rwanda Rwanda										
Total reserves minus gold										
Rés. totale, moins l'or	174.2	190.6	212.1	243.7	214.7	314.6	405.8	439.7	552.8	596.3
Foreign exchange										
Devises étrangères	159.7	189.5	199.8	233.6	184.9	284.4	379.8	416.8	528.7	564.9
Saint Kitts and Nevis Saint-Kitts-et-Nevis										
Total reserves minus gold										
Rés. totale, moins l'or	49.6	45.2	56.4	65.8	64.8	78.5	71.6	88.7	95.8	110.4
Foreign exchange										
Devises étrangères	49.5	45.1	56.3	65.6	64.7	78.3	71.5	88.6	95.7	110.3
Saint Lucia Sainte-Lucie										
Total reserves minus gold										
Rés. totale, moins l'or	74.5	78.8	88.9	93.9	106.9	132.5	116.4	134.5	153.7	142.8
Foreign exchange										
Devises étrangères	72.5	77.0	87.1	91.9	104.7	130.2	114.2	132.2	151.2	140.3
Saint Vincent-Grenadines Saint Vincent-Grenadines										
Total reserves minus gold										
Rés. totale, moins l'or	42.6	55.2	61.4	53.2	51.2	75.0	69.5	78.7	87.0	83.7
Foreign exchange										
Devises étrangères	41.8	54.5	60.8	52.5	50.4	74.2	68.8	77.9	86.2	82.9
Samoa Samoa										
Total reserves minus gold										
Rés. totale, moins l'or	68.2	63.7	56.6	62.5	83.9	86.1	81.8	80.7	95.4	87.1
Foreign exchange										
Devises étrangères	64.2	59.8	52.8	58.3	79.3	81.3	77.3	75.9	90.2	81.9
San Marino Saint-Marin										
Total reserves minus gold										
Rés. totale, moins l'or	144.1	135.2	133.5	183.4	252.7	355.6	354.0	479.1	647.8	706.8
Foreign exchange										
Devises étrangères	138.4	129.6	127.9	177.3	245.9	348.3	347.2	471.8	639.8	698.7

International reserves minus gold *(continued)*
Millions of US dollars, end of period
Réserves internationales, moins l'or *(suite)*
Millions de dollars des E.-U., fin de période

Country or area Pays ou zone	1999	2000	2001	2002	2003	2004	2005	2006	2007	2008
Sao Tome and Principe Sao Tomé-et-Principe										
Total reserves minus gold Rés. totale, moins l'or	10.9	11.6	15.5	17.4	25.5	19.5	26.7	34.2	39.3	...
Foreign exchange Devises étrangères	10.9	11.6	15.5	17.3	25.4	19.5	26.7	34.1	39.3	...
Saudi Arabia Arabie saoudite										
Total reserves minus gold Rés. totale, moins l'or	16 996.9	19 585.5	17 595.7	20 610.4	22 620.0	27 290.9	26 530.0	27 522.9	33 760.2	30 342.4
Foreign exchange Devises étrangères	15 490.0	18 036.0	14 796.0	16 715.0	17 662.0	23 273.0	24 074.0	25 971.0	32 308.0	28 223.0
Senegal Sénégal										
Total reserves minus gold Rés. totale, moins l'or	403.0	384.0	447.3	637.4	1 110.9	1 386.4	1 191.0	1 334.3	1 660.0	1 601.4
Foreign exchange Devises étrangères	398.6	381.2	438.0	626.3	1 098.2	1 376.7	1 187.4	1 331.8	1 657.3	1 598.6
Serbia Serbie										
Total reserves minus gold Rés. totale, moins l'or	154.4	391.5	1 004.7	2 166.0	3 410.8	4 095.9	5 627.9	11 647.7	13 892.6	11 122.9
Foreign exchange Devises étrangères	154.4	371.7	996.1	2 165.0	3 410.4	4 095.8	5 597.7	11 638.9	13 891.8	11 120.7
Seychelles Seychelles										
Total reserves minus gold Rés. totale, moins l'or	30.3	43.8	37.1	69.8	67.4	34.6	56.2	112.9	40.8	63.8
Foreign exchange Devises étrangères	30.3	43.7	37.1	69.8	67.4	34.6	56.2	112.9	40.7	63.8
Sierra Leone Sierra Leone										
Total reserves minus gold Rés. totale, moins l'or	39.5	49.2	51.3	84.7	66.6	125.1	170.5	183.9	216.6	...
Foreign exchange Devises étrangères	18.6	43.9	50.9	60.6	32.1	74.1	137.7	154.7	185.8	...
Singapore Singapour										
Total reserves minus gold Rés. totale, moins l'or	77 047.1	80 170.3	75 677.0	82 221.2	96 245.5	112 579.0	116 172.0	136 260.0	162 957.0	174 193.0
Foreign exchange Devises étrangères	76 508.2	79 723.4	75 152.9	81 566.6	95 474.4	111 845.0	115 712.0	135 814.0	162 517.0	173 649.0
Slovakia Slovaquie										
Total reserves minus gold Rés. totale, moins l'or	3 370.7	4 022.3	4 141.0	8 808.7	11 678.1	14 417.5	14 900.7	12 646.6	18 032.1	17 854.2
Foreign exchange Devises étrangères	3 369.9	4 021.8	4 140.3	8 807.5	11 676.8	14 416.1	14 899.4	12 645.2	18 025.8	17 804.9
Slovenia Slovénie										
Total reserves minus gold Rés. totale, moins l'or	3 168.0	3 196.0	4 330.0	6 980.2	8 496.9	8 793.4	8 076.4	7 036.1	#979.8	868.1
Foreign exchange Devises étrangères	3 058.8	3 110.0	4 244.3	6 852.6	8 343.1	8 662.3	8 013.1	6 987.1	#942.0	809.9
Solomon Islands Iles Salomon										
Total reserves minus gold Rés. totale, moins l'or	51.1	32.0	19.3	18.2	37.2	80.6	95.4	104.4	119.1	89.5
Foreign exchange Devises étrangères	50.4	31.3	18.7	17.5	36.4	79.7	94.6	103.6	118.2	88.7
South Africa Afrique du Sud										
Total reserves minus gold Rés. totale, moins l'or	6 353.1	6 082.8	6 045.3	5 904.2	6 495.5	13 141.3	18 579.1	23 056.9	29 588.6	30 583.5
Foreign exchange Devises étrangères	6 065.3	5 792.7	5 765.1	5 600.8	6 163.7	12 794.3	18 259.6	22 720.1	29 234.2	30 237.8
Spain Espagne										
Total reserves minus gold Rés. totale, moins l'or	33 115.0	30 988.9	29 582.3	34 535.7	19 788.4	12 388.8	9 677.6	10 822.2	#11 480.2	12 413.7
Foreign exchange Devises étrangères	31 329.5	29 516.4	27 905.5	32 590.4	17 512.8	10 481.4	8 594.1	10 088.2	10 792.0	11 540.0

71

International reserves minus gold *(continued)*
Millions of US dollars, end of period
Réserves internationales, moins l'or *(suite)*
Millions de dollars des E.-U., fin de période

Country or area Pays ou zone	1999	2000	2001	2002	2003	2004	2005	2006	2007	2008
Sri Lanka Sri Lanka										
Total reserves minus gold										
Rés. totale, moins l'or	1 635.6	1 039.0	1 286.8	1 631.0	2 264.9	2 132.1	2 650.9	2 836.7	3 515.0	2 562.9
Foreign exchange										
Devises étrangères	1 569.1	976.4	1 225.9	1 563.6	2 193.2	2 057.6	2 581.0	2 762.0	3 432.6	2 487.2
Sudan Soudan										
Total reserves minus gold										
Rés. totale, moins l'or	188.7	#137.8	49.7	248.9	529.4	1 338.0	1 868.6	1 659.9	1 377.9	1 399.0
Foreign exchange										
Devises étrangères	188.7	#137.8	49.7	248.8	529.1	1 338.0	1 868.5	1 659.9	1 377.9	1 399.0
Suriname Suriname										
Total reserves minus gold										
Rés. totale, moins l'or	38.5	63.0	119.3	106.2	105.8	129.4	125.8	215.4	400.9	433.3
Foreign exchange										
Devises étrangères	27.3	52.7	109.6	95.9	94.7	118.0	115.5	204.9	390.4	423.3
Swaziland Swaziland										
Total reserves minus gold										
Rés. totale, moins l'or	375.9	351.8	271.8	275.8	277.5	323.6	243.9	372.5	774.2	751.9
Foreign exchange										
Devises étrangères	363.6	340.1	260.5	263.6	264.1	309.5	231.0	358.9	759.9	737.9
Sweden Suède										
Total reserves minus gold										
Rés. totale, moins l'or	15 019.0	14 862.6	13 976.9	17 127.4	19 681.1	22 157.7	22 090.1	24 777.8	27 044.4	25 896.4
Foreign exchange										
Devises étrangères	13 522.0	13 757.0	12 740.0	15 520.0	18 015.0	20 640.0	21 382.0	24 074.0	26 382.0	25 127.0
Switzerland Suisse										
Total reserves minus gold										
Rés. totale, moins l'or	36 321.0	32 272.1	32 005.6	40 154.7	47 652.5	55 496.6	36 297.3	38 093.7	44 474.2	45 060.9
Foreign exchange										
Devises étrangères	34 176.0	30 854.0	30 141.0	38 164.0	45 560.0	53 634.0	35 421.0	37 364.0	43 867.0	44 151.0
Tajikistan Tadjikistan										
Total reserves minus gold										
Rés. totale, moins l'or	55.2	92.9	92.6	89.5	111.9	157.5	168.2	175.1	...	...
Foreign exchange										
Devises étrangères	55.1	85.0	87.7	87.7	111.0	156.2	162.8	171.6	...	...
Thailand Thaïlande										
Total reserves minus gold										
Rés. totale, moins l'or	34 062.8	32 015.9	32 354.8	38 046.4	41 076.9	48 664.0	50 690.7	65 291.4	85 221.3	108 661.0
Foreign exchange										
Devises étrangères	33 804.7	31 933.2	32 349.5	38 042.2	40 965.1	48 497.5	50 502.0	65 147.1	85 110.1	108 317.0
TFYR of Macedonia L'ex-R.Y. Macédoine										
Total reserves minus gold										
Rés. totale, moins l'or	429.9	429.4	745.2	722.0	897.7	905.0	1 228.5	1 750.6	2 082.3	1 920.3
Foreign exchange										
Devises étrangères	428.7	428.7	742.9	715.9	897.4	904.2	1 227.7	1 747.6	2 080.8	1 919.0
Timor-Leste Timor-Leste										
Total reserves minus gold										
Rés. totale, moins l'or	...	...	...	43.5	61.3	182.4	153.3	83.8	230.3	210.4
Foreign exchange										
Devises étrangères	...	...	...	43.5	61.3	182.4	153.3	83.8	230.3	210.4
Togo Togo										
Total reserves minus gold										
Rés. totale, moins l'or	122.1	152.3	126.4	205.1	204.9	359.7	194.6	374.5	438.1	580.0
Foreign exchange										
Devises étrangères	121.5	151.9	125.8	204.4	204.2	359.2	194.1	373.9	437.5	579.4
Tonga Tonga										
Total reserves minus gold										
Rés. totale, moins l'or	24.5	24.6	23.8	25.1	39.8	55.3	46.9	48.0	65.2	69.8
Foreign exchange										
Devises étrangères	22.1	22.3	21.4	22.5	36.9	52.2	44.0	44.9	61.9	66.4

71

International reserves minus gold *(continued)*
Millions of US dollars, end of period
Réserves internationales, moins l'or *(suite)*
Millions de dollars des E.-U., fin de période

Country or area Pays ou zone	1999	2000	2001	2002	2003	2004	2005	2006	2007	2008
Trinidad and Tobago Trinité-et-Tobago										
Total reserves minus gold										
Rés. totale, moins l'or	945.4	1 386.3	1 907.1	2 027.7	2 451.1	3 168.2	4 960.8	6 585.7	6 693.7	9 442.6
Foreign exchange										
Devises étrangères	945.4	1 386.2	1 876.0	1 923.5	2 257.8	2 993.0	4 885.8	6 530.9	6 657.4	9 380.4
Tunisia Tunisie										
Total reserves minus gold										
Rés. totale, moins l'or	2 261.5	1 811.1	1 989.2	2 290.3	2 945.4	3 935.7	4 436.7	6 773.2	7 850.8	8 849.3
Foreign exchange										
Devises étrangères	2 207.3	1 780.9	1 962.2	2 260.2	2 912.9	3 895.0	4 405.6	6 741.4	7 816.8	8 812.9
Turkey Turquie										
Total reserves minus gold										
Rés. totale, moins l'or	23 345.9	22 488.4	18 879.2	27 068.6	33 991.0	35 669.1	50 579.0	60 891.9	73 383.9	70 427.7
Foreign exchange										
Devises étrangères	23 191.0	22 313.0	18 733.0	26 884.0	33 793.0	35 480.0	50 402.0	60 710.0	73 155.8	70 231.0
Uganda Ouganda										
Total reserves minus gold										
Rés. totale, moins l'or	763.1	808.0	983.4	934.0	1 080.3	1 308.1	1 344.2	1 810.9	2 559.8	2 300.6
Foreign exchange										
Devises étrangères	760.8	804.5	981.5	931.1	1 075.5	1 307.4	1 343.1	1 810.8	2 559.5	2 300.4
Ukraine Ukraine										
Total reserves minus gold										
Rés. totale, moins l'or	1 046.4	1 352.7	2 955.3	4 205.3	6 683.2	9 490.7	18 988.0	21 844.6	31 786.0	30 800.6
Foreign exchange										
Devises étrangères	980.7	1 103.6	2 704.3	4 177.0	6 662.0	9 489.5	18 987.0	21 843.2	31 783.2	30 791.9
United Arab Emirates Emirats arabes unis										
Total reserves minus gold										
Rés. totale, moins l'or	10 675.1	13 522.7	14 146.4	15 219.4	15 087.8	18 529.9	21 010.3	27 617.4	77 238.8	31 694.5
Foreign exchange										
Devises étrangères	10 377.1	13 303.9	13 918.2	14 897.2	14 731.5	18 209.0	20 867.7	27 511.9	77 161.9	31 556.6
United Kingdom Royaume-Uni										
Total reserves minus gold										
Rés. totale, moins l'or	#33 297.4	38 773.6	34 188.7	37 549.9	35 348.5	39 942.3	38 467.2	40 697.8	48 958.1	44 348.3
Foreign exchange										
Devises étrangères	#27 504.7	34 163.4	28 843.1	30 979.8	28 645.4	34 081.7	35 853.9	38 888.6	47 497.8	41 550.3
United Rep. of Tanzania Rép.-Unie de Tanzanie										
Total reserves minus gold										
Rés. totale, moins l'or	775.5	974.2	1 156.6	1 528.8	2 038.4	2 295.7	2 048.8	2 259.4	2 886.4	2 862.9
Foreign exchange										
Devises étrangères	761.5	961.1	1 143.6	1 515.2	2 023.1	2 280.1	2 033.8	2 244.2	2 870.4	2 847.5
United States Etats-Unis										
Total reserves minus gold										
Rés. totale, moins l'or	60 499.6	56 600.4	57 633.7	67 962.3	74 894.1	75 890.0	54 083.8	54 853.9	59 524.3	66 607.0
Foreign exchange										
Devises étrangères	32 182.1	31 238.3	28 981.0	33 818.0	39 721.8	42 718.3	37 838.1	40 943.5	45 803.8	49 583.6
Uruguay Uruguay										
Total reserves minus gold										
Rés. totale, moins l'or	2 081.2	2 478.9	3 097.1	769.1	2 083.2	2 508.5	3 074.1	3 085.3	4 114.3	6 352.8
Foreign exchange										
Devises étrangères	2 031.3	2 431.9	3 050.4	763.5	2 079.4	2 507.3	3 067.8	3 084.2	4 114.0	6 348.7
Vanuatu Vanuatu										
Total reserves minus gold										
Rés. totale, moins l'or	41.4	38.9	37.7	36.5	43.8	61.8	67.2	104.7	119.6	115.2
Foreign exchange										
Devises étrangères	37.1	34.8	33.5	32.0	38.8	56.5	62.2	99.3	113.8	109.4
Venezuela (Bolivarian Rep. of) Venezuela (Rép. bolivarienne du)										
Total reserves minus gold										
Rés. totale, moins l'or	12 277.3	13 088.5	9 239.5	8 487.1	16 034.7	18 375.4	23 918.8	29 417.3	24 196.1	33 098.1
Foreign exchange										
Devises étrangères	11 708.0	12 633.0	8 825.0	8 038.0	15 546.0	17 867.0	23 454.0	28 933.0	23 686.0	32 581.0

71

International reserves minus gold *(continued)*
Millions of US dollars, end of period
Réserves internationales, moins l'or *(suite)*
Millions de dollars des E.-U., fin de période

Country or area Pays ou zone	1999	2000	2001	2002	2003	2004	2005	2006	2007	2008
Viet Nam Viet Nam										
Total reserves minus gold										
Rés. totale, moins l'or	3 326.2	3 416.5	3 674.6	4 121.1	6 224.2	7 041.5	9 050.6	13 384.1	23 479.4	23 890.3
Foreign exchange										
Devises étrangères	3 324.7	3 416.2	3 660.0	4 121.0	6 222.0	7 041.0	9 049.7	13 382.5	23 471.8	23 882.0
Yemen Yémen										
Total reserves minus gold										
Rés. totale, moins l'or	1 471.5	2 900.3	3 658.1	4 410.5	4 987.0	5 664.8	6 115.4	7 511.5	7 715.4	8 111.4
Foreign exchange										
Devises étrangères	1 295.1	2 815.6	3 639.6	4 365.6	4 982.0	5 613.5	6 096.6	7 504.4	7 715.4	8 110.9
Zambia Zambie										
Total reserves minus gold										
Rés. totale, moins l'or	45.4	244.8	183.4	535.1	247.7	337.1	559.8	719.7	1 090.0	1 095.6
Foreign exchange										
Devises étrangères	45.3	222.5	116.5	464.8	247.2	312.2	544.0	706.4	1 080.2	1 085.0
Zimbabwe Zimbabwe										
Total reserves minus gold										
Rés. totale, moins l'or	268.0	193.1	64.7	83.4	...	...	...	...	...	...
Foreign exchange										
Devises étrangères	266.5	192.5	64.3	82.9	...	...	...	...	...	...

Source:
International Monetary Fund (IMF), Washington, D.C., the database on International Financial Statistics, last accessed July 2009.

Source:
Fonds monétaire international (FMI), Washington, D.C., la base de données de Statistiques Financières Internationales, dernier accès juillet 2009.

1   For statistical purposes, the data for China do not include those for the Hong Kong Special Administrative Region (Hong Kong SAR) and Macao Special Administrative Region (Macao SAR).

1   Pour la présentation des statistiques, les données pour la Chine ne comprennent pas la Région Administrative Spéciale de Hong Kong (Hong Kong RAS) et la Région Administrative Spéciale de Macao (Macao RAS).

Total external and public/publicly guaranteed long-term debt of developing countries
Millions of US dollars

Total de la dette extérieure et dette publique extérieure à long terme garantie par l'Etat des pays en développement
Millions de dollars des E.-U.

A. Total external debt [&] • Total de la dette extérieure [&]

Developing economies	2002	2003	2004	2005	2006	2007	2008	Economies en développement
Total long-term debt	**1 858 791**	**1 976 479**	**2 079 545**	**2 048 665**	**2 195 467**	**2 602 309**	**2 785 694**	**Total de la dette à long terme**
Public and publicly guaranteed	1 344 595	1 423 845	1 466 660	1 331 287	1 234 553	1 312 490	1 406 863	Dette publique ou garantie par l'Etat
Official creditors	757 547	797 929	812 495	718 107	641 723	670 085	684 164	Créanciers publics
Mulitlateral	352 169	375 305	387 127	375 016	348 460	372 999	391 701	Multilatéraux
IBRD	109 606	107 727	104 755	99 089	95 489	96 858	99 831	BIRD
IDA	100 539	113 982	124 497	121 694	98 665	108 844	111 098	IDA
Bilateral	405 378	422 624	425 368	343 092	293 263	297 086	292 463	Bilatéraux
Private creditors	587 048	625 916	654 165	613 179	592 830	642 405	722 699	Créanciers privées
Bonds	373 902	410 342	435 410	401 679	407 602	447 846	461 701	Obligations
Commercial banks	153 199	158 913	167 339	166 837	145 816	159 777	192 549	Banques commerciales
Other private	59 947	56 660	51 416	44 664	39 412	34 782	68 449	Autres institutions privées
Private non-guaranteed	514 195	552 635	612 885	717 378	960 914	1 289 819	1 378 831	Dette privées non garantie
Undisbursed debt	**217 910**	**237 429**	**232 032**	**224 422**	**215 216**	**221 988**	**...**	**Dette (montants non versés)**
Official creditors	176 419	180 285	186 002	189 034	185 709	192 751	...	Créanciers publics
Private creditors	41 491	57 144	46 031	35 388	29 507	29 237	...	Créanciers privées
Commitments	**116 985**	**144 915**	**139 562**	**161 834**	**134 889**	**162 972**	**143 364**	**Engagements**
Official creditors	52 522	52 488	53 082	65 882	60 222	70 752	...	Créanciers publics
Private creditors	64 462	92 427	86 480	95 953	74 667	92 220	...	Créanciers privées
Disbursements	**228 271**	**277 730**	**354 379**	**425 257**	**503 626**	**684 147**	**572 388**	**Versements**
Public and publicly guaranteed	114 217	130 510	145 025	146 326	137 072	159 580	139 770	Dette publique ou garantie par l'Etat
Official creditors	45 610	49 895	46 916	46 001	54 907	57 228	62 225	Créanciers publics
Multilateral	31 452	37 459	33 217	34 264	39 818	42 080	43 469	Mutilatéraux
IBRD	9 954	11 404	10 333	9 575	12 372	10 618	13 878	BIRD
IDA	6 768	6 563	7 835	7 114	6 715	7 341	6 603	IDA
Bilateral	14 158	12 435	13 699	11 736	15 090	15 148	18 756	Bilatéraux
Private creditors	68 607	80 615	98 109	100 326	82 165	102 352	77 545	Créanciers privées
Bonds	38 937	46 896	59 933	64 097	53 484	68 257	37 479	Obligations
Commercial banks	24 542	27 078	33 843	31 978	23 976	30 197	36 220	Banques commerciales
Other private	5 128	6 641	4 333	4 250	4 704	3 898	3 845	Autres institutions privées
Private non-guaranteed	114 054	147 221	209 355	278 931	366 553	524 567	433 152	Dette privé non garantie
Principal repayments	**236 041**	**264 152**	**292 156**	**320 250**	**381 391**	**382 507**	**385 258**	**Remboursements du principal**
Public and publicly guaranteed	119 346	138 042	131 902	153 189	194 291	123 506	114 023	Dette publique ou garantie par l'Etat
Official creditors	54 107	62 940	57 993	76 935	99 146	51 988	52 673	Créanciers publics
Multilateral	30 348	35 463	30 329	26 845	36 806	26 476	27 513	Multilatéraux
IBRD	15 809	17 126	15 024	12 274	17 445	11 133	11 064	BIRD
IDA	1 241	1 345	1 546	1 634	2 052	1 951	2 293	IDA
Bilateral	23 760	27 477	27 664	50 090	62 340	25 512	25 160	Bilatéraux
Private creditors	65 239	75 102	73 909	76 255	95 145	71 517	61 350	Créanciers privées
Bonds	26 497	34 645	34 696	41 876	59 991	40 182	28 926	Obligations
Commercial banks	27 398	29 611	30 882	25 649	25 666	23 974	19 243	Banques commerciales
Other private	11 343	10 846	8 332	8 729	9 488	7 361	13 181	Autres institutions privées
Private non-guaranteed	116 695	126 110	160 254	167 060	187 100	259 001	271 623	Dette privée non garantie
Net flows	**-7 770**	**13 578**	**62 223**	**105 008**	**122 234**	**301 640**	**187 276**	**Apports nets**
Public and publicly guaranteed	-5 129	-7 533	13 122	-6 863	-57 219	36 074	25 747	Dette publique ou garantie par l'Etat
Official creditors	-8 497	-13 045	-11 077	-30 934	-44 239	5 239	9 552	Créanciers publics
Multilateral	1 105	1 997	2 888	7 420	3 012	15 603	15 956	Multilatéraux
IBRD	-5 855	-5 722	-4 691	-2 699	-5 072	-514	2 814	BIRD
IDA	5 527	5 218	6 289	5 481	4 663	5 391	4 310	IDA
Bilateral	-9 602	-15 042	-13 965	-38 354	-47 251	-10 364	-6 404	Bilatéraux
Private creditors	3 368	5 512	24 199	24 071	-12 980	30 835	16 195	Créanciers privés
Bonds	12 440	12 250	25 237	22 221	-6 507	28 075	8 553	Obligations
Commercial banks	-2 857	-2 533	2 961	6 329	-1 690	6 223	16 977	Banques commerciales
Other private	-6 215	-4 205	-3 999	-4 479	-4 784	-3 463	-9 335	Autres institutions privées
Private non-guaranteed	-2 641	21 111	49 101	111 871	179 453	265 566	161 529	Dette privée non garantie

72

Total external and public/publicly guaranteed long-term debt of developing countries *(continued)*
Millions of US dollars

Total de la dette extérieure et dette publique extérieure à long terme garantie par l'Etat des pays en développement *(suite)*
Millions de dollars des E.-U.

A. Total external debt [&] • Total de la dette extérieure [&]

Developing economies	2002	2003	2004	2005	2006	2007	2008	Economies en développement
Interest payments	**79 886**	**84 781**	**81 497**	**90 151**	**99 901**	**118 840**	**127 257**	**Paiements d'intérêts**
Public and publicly guaranteed	55 500	58 696	56 416	63 317	57 706	60 396	63 237	Dette publique ou garantie par l'Etat
Official creditors	23 714	23 381	21 804	23 949	19 848	19 902	20 299	Créanciers publics
Multilateral	13 361	11 889	10 773	10 616	11 744	12 898	11 944	Multilatéraux
IBRD	6 299	5 042	4 080	4 113	4 911	5 584	4 201	BIRD
IDA	694	702	897	898	838	773	804	IDA
Bilateral	10 353	11 492	11 031	13 333	8 105	7 004	8 355	Bilatéraux
Private creditors	31 786	35 316	34 612	39 368	37 857	40 494	42 938	Créanciers privées
Bonds	21 696	24 887	25 673	30 047	28 271	30 202	30 387	Obligations
Commercial banks	7 703	7 970	6 950	7 700	8 003	8 419	10 507	Banques commerciales
Other private	2 387	2 459	1 990	1 621	1 583	1 873	2 044	Autres institutions privées
Private non-guaranteed	24 385	26 084	25 082	26 834	42 195	58 443	64 020	Dette privée non garantie
Net transfers	**-87 656**	**-71 203**	**-19 274**	**14 857**	**22 333**	**182 800**	**60 019**	**Transferts nets**
Public and publicly guaranteed	-60 629	-66 229	-43 293	-70 180	-114 925	-24 322	-37 490	Dette publique ou garantie par l'Etat
Official creditors	-32 211	-36 426	-32 881	-54 883	-64 087	-14 663	-10 747	Créanciers publics
Multilateral	-12 257	-9 893	-7 885	-3 197	-8 732	2 705	4 012	Multilatéraux
IBRD	-12 154	-10 765	-8 771	-6 812	-9 984	-6 098	-1 388	BIRD
IDA	4 832	4 515	5 392	4 582	3 825	4 617	3 506	IDA
Bilateral	-19 955	-26 533	-24 996	-51 686	-55 355	-17 368	-14 759	Bilatéraux
Private creditors	-28 418	-29 803	-10 413	-15 297	-50 837	-9 659	-26 742	Créanciers privées
Bonds	-9 256	-12 637	-435	-7 826	-34 778	-2 127	-21 834	Obligations
Commercial banks	-10 560	-10 502	-3 988	-1 370	-9 692	-2 196	6 470	Banques commerciales
Other private	-8 602	-6 664	-5 989	-6 100	-6 368	-5 336	-11 379	Autres institutions privées
Private non-guaranteed	-27 026	-4 974	24 019	85 036	137 258	207 122	97 509	Dette privées non garantie
Total debt service	**315 927**	**348 933**	**373 654**	**410 401**	**481 293**	**501 347**	**512 903**	**Total du service de la dette**
Public and publicly guaranteed	174 846	196 739	188 318	216 506	251 997	183 902	177 260	Dette publique ou garantie par l'Etat
Official creditors	77 822	86 321	79 797	100 884	118 995	71 890	72 972	Créanciers publics
Multilateral	43 709	47 352	41 101	37 461	48 550	39 374	39 457	Multilatéraux
IBRD	22 108	22 168	19 105	16 387	22 356	16 716	15 266	BIRD
IDA	1 935	2 048	2 442	2 532	2 890	2 724	3 097	IDA
Bilateral	34 113	38 969	38 695	63 423	70 445	32 516	33 516	Bilatéraux
Private creditors	97 025	110 418	108 522	115 622	133 002	112 012	104 287	Créanciers publics
Bonds	48 193	59 533	60 368	71 923	88 262	70 384	59 313	Obligations
Commercial banks	35 102	37 581	37 832	33 349	33 668	32 393	29 750	Banques commerciales
Other private	13 730	13 305	10 322	10 350	11 072	9 235	15 224	Autres institutions privées
Private non-guaranteed	141 081	152 194	185 335	193 895	229 296	317 445	335 643	Dette privées non garantie

[&] The following abbreviations have been used in the table:
   IBRD: International Bank for Reconstruction and Development
   IDA: International Development Association

[&] Les abréviations ci-après ont été utilisées dans le tableau :
   BIRD : Banque internationale pour la reconstruction et le développement
   IDA : Association internationale de développement

Total external and public/publicly guaranteed long-term debt of developing countries
Millions of US dollars

Total de la dette extérieure et dette publique extérieure à long terme garantie par l'Etat des pays en développement
Millions de dollars des E.-U.

B. Public and publicly guaranteed long-term debt • Dette publique extérieure à long terme garantie par l'Etat

Country or area Pays ou zone	1998	1999	2000	2001	2002	2003	2004	2005	2006	2007
Afghanistan Afghanistan	...	...	...	...	...	...	...	...	1 635.4	1 961.5
Albania Albanie	506.1	583.4	921.3	970.9	994.8	1 231.9	1 402.7	1 372.2	1 575.4	1 787.0
Algeria Algérie	28 484.2	25 897.3	23 440.5	20 852.9	21 288.1	21 850.0	20 394.6	15 480.3	3 872.0	3 755.6
Angola Angola	9 099.6	8 713.0	8 084.8	6 982.7	7 530.9	7 620.0	8 146.6	10 332.2	8 247.2	10 474.1
Argentina Argentine	75 524.5	79 131.4	81 633.4	82 994.5	87 313.1	94 061.8	98 016.0	54 225.1	60 745.9	66 110.3
Armenia Arménie	568.6	651.4	675.1	715.6	818.5	877.2	960.7	922.5	1 037.3	1 272.4
Azerbaijan Azerbaïdjan	314.2	528.4	737.4	784.5	1 046.0	1 288.4	1 372.2	1 278.0	1 446.3	1 748.4
Bangladesh Bangladesh	15 098.7	15 995.2	15 167.7	14 741.0	16 403.5	18 083.0	19 186.4	17 922.6	18 836.4	20 150.5
Belarus Bélarus	796.4	709.1	688.9	664.3	748.6	710.0	744.4	785.6	841.9	2 337.9
Belize Belize	279.8	337.5	553.2	645.4	775.6	945.2	923.2	972.5	992.0	1 036.7
Benin Bénin	1 472.0	1 472.9	1 441.9	1 505.4	1 689.2	1 726.2	1 831.1	1 744.7	768.6	851.9
Bhutan Bhoutan	171.0	181.8	202.2	265.2	376.9	481.5	593.3	636.7	697.3	775.0
Bolivia Bolivie	4 294.1	4 245.3	4 136.5	3 126.2	3 517.2	4 159.8	4 557.1	4 568.2	3 176.7	2 149.6
Bosnia and Herzegovina Bosnie-Herzégovine	...	2 240.1	1 956.5	1 780.3	2 030.8	2 316.5	2 686.3	2 555.8	2 829.6	3 014.0
Botswana Botswana	524.7	484.5	437.8	378.9	472.4	484.7	488.0	437.6	384.1	380.0
Brazil Brésil	98 636.6	92 514.5	96 129.8	96 129.0	99 148.4	99 503.3	96 818.2	93 933.0	84 301.9	79 956.9
Bulgaria Bulgarie	7 972.8	7 777.6	7 671.4	7 386.6	7 479.9	7 676.2	7 413.7	5 075.2	5 065.9	5 242.7
Burkina Faso Burkina Faso	1 287.1	1 359.1	1 225.7	1 312.8	1 406.6	1 596.6	1 863.4	1 878.6	1 003.2	1 268.4
Burundi Burundi	1 082.1	1 053.1	1 036.0	985.6	1 104.3	1 251.9	1 326.8	1 229.6	1 291.3	1 344.1
Cambodia Cambodge	2 261.4	2 292.9	2 328.1	2 392.8	2 587.3	2 868.4	3 079.7	3 154.8	3 317.7	3 537.1
Cameroon Cameroun	9 352.2	8 711.4	8 453.7	8 038.1	8 531.0	9 552.9	8 790.9	6 085.4	2 270.4	2 204.2
Cape Verde Cap-Vert	239.0	306.0	312.6	339.4	378.2	428.0	448.5	458.7	504.3	559.5
Central African Rep. Rép. centrafricaine	840.9	825.9	795.6	756.7	982.2	902.5	921.6	864.2	855.2	835.7

72

Total external and public/publicly guaranteed long-term debt of developing countries *(continued)*
Millions of US dollars
Total de la dette extérieure et dette publique extérieure à long terme garantie par l'Etat des pays en développement *(suite)*
Millions de dollars des E.-U.

B. Public and publicly guaranteed long term debt • Dette publique extérieure à long terme garantie par l'Etat

Country or area Pays ou zone	1998	1999	2000	2001	2002	2003	2004	2005	2006	2007
Chad Tchad	945.5	1 004.4	987.7	977.5	1 138.8	1 405.5	1 527.7	1 494.7	1 627.5	1 712.5
Chile Chili	5 004.8	5 654.6	5 255.2	5 581.2	6 799.5	8 046.3	9 426.0	9 096.5	9 448.7	9 377.9
China Chine	99 399.3	99 196.4	94 841.5	91 759.3	88 595.1	85 308.3	89 751.3	85 043.8	88 033.5	87 653.4
Colombia Colombie	16 751.3	20 222.6	20 806.3	21 773.6	20 669.8	22 784.5	23 772.4	22 555.3	25 002.9	27 688.6
Comoros Comores	219.8	213.9	207.0	222.2	244.6	265.4	273.3	257.3	259.8	279.2
Congo Congo	4 167.3	3 857.1	3 687.5	3 563.8	3 900.0	4 342.8	5 520.6	5 087.6	5 244.8	4 807.1
Costa Rica Costa Rica	3 026.7	3 183.3	3 503.6	3 511.3	3 372.0	3 848.7	3 555.0	3 244.1	3 428.5	3 749.8
Côte d'Ivoire Côte d'Ivoire	10 799.7	9 699.1	9 063.5	8 602.7	9 110.3	9 700.5	11 091.5	9 973.1	10 828.3	11 651.3
Croatia Croatie	4 924.8	5 523.2	6 111.3	6 424.5	7 685.4	10 111.1	11 654.3	10 035.3	11 109.0	14 211.5
Dem. Rep. of the Congo Rép. dém. du Congo	9 214.4	8 262.3	7 880.2	7 586.5	8 845.4	10 161.3	10 125.0	9 412.1	9 848.2	10 853.0
Djibouti Djibouti	263.8	248.4	237.9	235.7	296.1	355.5	382.1	376.6	426.0	439.8
Dominica Dominique	95.3	96.7	145.8	192.5	199.4	205.2	225.1	221.8	218.0	214.7
Dominican Republic Rép. dominicaine	3 482.4	3 584.1	3 311.3	3 790.3	4 029.9	5 424.9	6 152.1	6 078.5	6 439.6	6 545.6
Ecuador Equateur	12 947.3	13 383.9	11 177.7	11 113.4	11 104.4	11 231.4	10 537.2	10 597.9	10 065.1	10 446.9
Egypt Egypte	27 643.3	26 108.6	24 338.2	25 162.7	25 687.4	27 064.3	27 020.0	25 794.0	25 495.5	26 940.2
El Salvador El Salvador	2 336.9	2 542.5	2 710.1	2 975.9	4 414.8	4 814.8	4 858.0	4 775.2	5 587.3	5 443.9
Eritrea Erythrée	146.1	252.6	298.0	394.9	489.2	605.1	704.0	723.0	781.4	855.7
Ethiopia Ethiopie	9 613.6	5 361.8	5 326.8	5 561.3	6 318.7	7 031.3	6 332.0	5 898.0	2 166.8	2 543.8
Fiji Fidji	136.7	118.5	99.5	86.3	96.0	110.6	119.6	112.5	119.3	274.1
Gabon Gabon	3 835.4	3 293.0	3 453.5	3 041.3	3 240.9	3 394.8	3 800.1	3 582.4	3 858.5	5 177.0
Gambia Gambie	433.6	431.1	437.9	435.3	507.3	566.6	620.3	625.0	688.3	704.3
Georgia Géorgie	1 301.0	1 309.1	1 273.9	1 310.6	1 444.9	1 564.0	1 593.1	1 494.4	1 466.1	1 543.2
Ghana Ghana	5 004.0	5 144.2	4 994.4	5 253.5	5 755.7	6 422.5	5 892.6	5 738.6	1 895.6	3 047.4
Grenada Grenade	107.2	112.1	179.8	183.9	294.1	300.1	346.7	391.5	447.7	468.1
Guatemala Guatemala	2 428.6	2 531.9	2 539.7	2 928.4	3 097.7	3 426.6	3 794.5	3 687.5	3 920.8	4 213.6
Guinea Guinée	3 126.4	3 061.0	2 940.4	2 843.9	2 972.5	3 154.0	3 187.7	2 930.5	2 979.9	3 048.0
Guinea-Bissau Guinée-Bissau	874.3	834.2	715.5	627.2	662.3	712.6	738.0	671.3	695.0	730.5
Guyana Guyana	1 197.9	1 129.8	1 123.8	1 094.9	1 144.8	1 216.6	1 141.2	1 041.2	923.3	582.8

Total external and public/publicly guaranteed long-term debt of developing countries *(continued)*
Millions of US dollars

Total de la dette extérieure et dette publique extérieure à long terme garantie par l'Etat des pays en développement *(suite)*
Millions de dollars des E.-U.

B. Public and publicly guaranteed long term debt • Dette publique extérieure à long terme garantie par l'Etat

Country or area Pays ou zone	1998	1999	2000	2001	2002	2003	2004	2005	2006	2007
Haiti Haïti	986.5	1 045.0	1 043.0	1 031.3	1 065.9	1 210.1	1 225.0	1 277.9	1 346.1	1 500.4
Honduras Honduras	3 949.2	4 121.3	4 210.8	3 860.7	4 058.7	4 423.3	4 831.8	4 092.3	2 985.9	1 942.5
India Inde	84 611.3	86 410.3	80 050.9	78 818.4	82 256.5	84 668.3	89 027.7	80 302.7	63 798.8	74 419.0
Indonesia Indonésie	67 528.8	73 917.3	69 646.6	68 493.7	71 271.7	73 913.1	71 822.5	71 728.8	67 117.4	68 707.9
Iran (Islamic Rep. of) Iran (Rép. islamique d')	7 712.0	5 732.0	4 706.6	5 291.5	6 604.0	8 933.4	9 984.9	10 492.5	11 095.9	11 145.9
Jamaica Jamaïque	2 979.8	2 888.3	3 763.9	4 312.7	4 604.7	4 576.2	5 284.5	5 550.5	6 015.8	6 372.2
Jordan Jordanie	6 498.3	6 714.2	6 182.8	6 632.3	7 071.7	7 172.6	7 227.2	6 877.7	7 142.9	7 318.0
Kazakhstan Kazakhstan	3 037.8	3 360.1	3 622.5	3 450.2	3 210.4	3 469.4	3 232.9	2 176.8	2 136.2	1 697.7
Kenya Kenya	5 513.2	5 344.1	5 045.5	4 710.7	5 244.7	5 823.9	6 071.0	5 770.3	5 806.3	6 121.9
Kyrgyzstan Kirghizistan	933.9	1 134.4	1 220.3	1 256.8	1 397.3	1 584.5	1 742.4	1 664.8	1 824.7	1 895.5
Lao People's Dem. Rep. Rép. dém. pop. lao	2 387.5	2 479.3	2 458.6	2 455.4	2 619.7	1 892.0	2 033.6	1 987.5	2 242.5	2 445.9
Latvia Lettonie	404.2	864.8	827.1	978.2	1 123.6	1 238.1	1 580.3	1 318.2	1 553.3	1 808.7
Lebanon Liban	4 047.1	5 328.8	6 574.5	8 952.4	13 829.1	14 781.0	17 456.3	17 902.3	18 981.2	19 789.2
Lesotho Lesotho	660.6	661.0	656.7	578.5	628.5	672.6	721.6	618.9	616.0	644.8
Liberia Libéria	1 092.3	1 062.3	1 040.1	1 011.8	1 064.6	1 126.8	1 176.9	1 114.7	1 115.3	909.6
Madagascar Madagascar	4 096.1	4 358.2	4 205.8	3 786.7	4 130.1	4 615.8	3 486.7	3 178.8	1 235.7	1 424.5
Malawi Malawi	2 304.1	2 586.4	2 544.1	2 468.8	2 670.1	2 934.5	3 295.6	3 061.8	788.9	807.0
Malaysia Malaisie	18 154.5	18 930.1	19 233.7	24 156.3	26 414.7	25 399.6	25 570.3	22 449.3	22 598.8	18 440.9
Maldives Maldives	183.4	194.1	184.7	180.7	223.0	259.5	331.7	325.4	377.8	425.9
Mali Mali	2 833.1	2 813.6	2 671.0	2 642.5	2 517.8	2 910.1	3 135.5	3 101.7	1 624.4	1 988.5
Mauritania Mauritanie	2 048.9	2 147.8	2 028.5	1 936.3	1 938.0	2 076.3	2 081.7	2 079.3	1 395.4	1 437.0
Mauritius Maurice	1 124.4	1 135.2	827.8	761.0	830.6	921.7	853.8	723.5	585.5	572.3
Mexico Mexique	87 044.7	87 910.7	81 488.2	94 230.4	99 517.9	106 659.8	108 507.0	108 481.9	96 094.1	105 379.1
Mongolia Mongolie	650.0	841.1	833.4	823.7	949.0	1 137.5	1 306.6	1 266.7	1 361.0	1 565.7
Montenegro Monténégro	...	...	...	...	...	...	...	...	1 228.1	1 164.0
Morocco Maroc	20 688.6	18 813.5	17 238.9	15 349.9	14 369.2	14 456.9	14 105.2	12 441.4	13 495.8	15 670.3
Mozambique Mozambique	6 030.8	4 872.3	4 734.4	2 571.7	2 886.7	3 164.0	3 711.5	3 719.4	2 354.1	2 532.8
Myanmar Myanmar	5 052.7	5 337.1	5 241.6	5 006.5	5 390.8	5 857.4	5 646.6	5 195.7	5 233.6	5 515.9

Total external and public/publicly guaranteed long-term debt of developing countries *(continued)*
Millions of US dollars

Total de la dette extérieure et dette publique extérieure à long terme garantie par l'Etat des pays en développement *(suite)*
Millions de dollars des E.-U.

B. Public and publicly guaranteed long term debt • Dette publique extérieure à long terme garantie par l'Etat

Country or area Pays ou zone	1998	1999	2000	2001	2002	2003	2004	2005	2006	2007
Nepal Népal	2 615.6	2 960.8	2 827.2	2 672.8	2 947.8	3 139.3	3 299.9	3 130.1	3 285.2	3 484.8
Nicaragua Nicaragua	5 493.3	5 636.5	5 350.0	5 294.9	5 430.9	5 751.2	3 965.3	3 870.0	3 169.1	2 143.7
Niger Niger	1 444.5	1 458.6	1 466.6	1 416.9	1 602.8	1 887.3	1 793.6	1 782.3	755.3	862.7
Nigeria Nigéria	23 445.0	22 357.7	30 019.9	29 218.1	28 057.1	31 350.2	32 637.3	20 342.2	3 908.7	3 814.7
Pakistan Pakistan	26 140.2	28 134.7	27 173.2	26 436.2	28 015.7	30 768.6	30 878.1	29 472.4	32 277.9	35 917.2
Panama Panama	5 417.4	5 676.3	5 703.8	6 326.8	6 404.7	6 481.5	7 215.0	7 492.0	7 774.2	8 266.6
Papua New Guinea Papouasie-Nvl-Guinée	1 430.0	1 466.7	1 454.0	1 370.2	1 438.8	1 504.5	1 445.1	1 266.4	1 225.5	1 156.1
Paraguay Paraguay	1 590.6	2 074.5	2 059.8	1 981.0	2 045.4	2 200.6	2 430.5	2 265.2	2 234.7	2 194.9
Peru Pérou	19 288.4	19 467.3	19 215.3	18 881.7	20 914.9	23 031.5	24 676.9	22 497.7	22 111.2	19 669.4
Philippines Philippines	29 172.9	34 770.6	33 744.5	29 210.2	32 318.6	36 146.7	35 981.2	35 364.1	36 750.8	37 894.8
Poland Pologne	34 160.6	32 180.3	29 775.3	24 040.9	27 543.7	33 251.0	34 737.8	35 093.9	39 247.8	43 597.7
Republic of Moldova République de Moldova	796.5	719.1	852.8	792.0	825.8	848.2	754.3	699.7	736.1	778.5
Romania Roumanie	6 636.7	5 632.6	6 583.0	7 028.7	9 028.7	11 723.6	13 661.9	13 329.9	14 204.5	15 238.0
Russian Federation Fédération de Russie	121 574.3	121 188.3	110 988.5	103 765.3	96 059.2	99 027.7	103 403.7	76 827.1	56 427.3	70 396.4
Rwanda Rwanda	1 120.5	1 162.5	1 147.3	1 163.6	1 305.4	1 416.5	1 543.4	1 419.6	389.3	455.5
Saint Kitts and Nevis Saint-Kitts-et-Nevis	124.4	133.8	152.7	214.7	260.9	314.9	313.3	292.6	289.5	272.9
Saint Lucia Sainte-Lucie	133.6	140.9	167.6	166.0	210.7	235.0	256.6	248.9	256.4	267.4
Saint Vincent-Grenadines Saint Vincent-Grenadines	107.9	161.4	163.3	162.4	172.8	194.0	223.0	246.3	241.0	199.3
Samoa Samoa	154.3	156.6	147.3	143.3	156.8	177.7	185.7	177.3	205.9	226.0
Sao Tome and Principe Sao Tomé-et-Principe	245.3	295.2	284.4	290.6	309.7	332.0	346.6	323.1	336.4	147.3
Senegal Sénégal	3 509.9	3 373.8	3 208.5	3 169.4	3 531.0	3 943.6	3 557.4	3 539.8	1 658.3	2 029.0
Serbia Serbie	6 461.1	6 194.6	6 178.0	6 177.5	7 535.0	8 129.0	8 122.4	7 621.4	7 472.7	8 224.0
Seychelles Seychelles	199.6	211.0	219.7	220.7	283.7	328.8	345.0	397.2	494.8	526.3
Sierra Leone Sierra Leone	1 060.8	1 033.3	972.8	1 033.6	1 176.8	1 337.0	1 434.4	1 350.2	1 256.5	308.2
Solomon Islands Iles Salomon	113.7	125.3	120.7	130.9	150.2	151.3	155.3	144.1	150.8	147.0
Somalia Somalie	1 886.4	1 859.4	1 825.1	1 794.7	1 859.9	1 936.1	1 949.1	1 881.5	1 922.6	1 978.8
South Africa Afrique du Sud	10 667.8	8 173.3	9 087.7	7 941.0	12 427.1	14 120.1	13 793.4	15 661.6	13 939.8	13 868.1
Sri Lanka Sri Lanka	8 063.6	8 412.9	7 944.1	7 499.7	8 400.4	9 158.8	9 847.5	9 651.8	10 317.4	11 878.6

Total external and public/publicly guaranteed long-term debt of developing countries (*continued*)
Millions of US dollars

Total de la dette extérieure et dette publique extérieure à long terme garantie par l'Etat des pays en développement (*suite*)
Millions de dollars des E.-U.

B. Public and publicly guaranteed long term debt • Dette publique extérieure à long terme garantie par l'Etat

Country or area Pays ou zone	1998	1999	2000	2001	2002	2003	2004	2005	2006	2007
Sudan Soudan	9 225.9	8 852.0	10 142.8	10 337.2	10 641.0	11 109.8	11 547.3	11 074.8	11 663.4	12 337.4
Swaziland Swaziland	272.9	280.0	262.9	262.2	311.3	355.4	353.9	351.1	353.8	356.7
Tajikistan Tadjikistan	702.6	741.3	755.1	761.6	901.1	911.8	807.1	828.6	842.4	1 065.4
Thailand Thaïlande	28 087.6	31 305.8	29 462.5	26 218.1	22 533.8	17 711.6	15 310.7	13 627.7	11 703.8	9 841.5
TFYR of Macedonia L'ex-R.Y. Macédoine	1 063.2	1 146.4	1 205.8	1 169.5	1 292.0	1 466.2	1 573.2	1 653.7	1 575.6	1 520.0
Togo Togo	1 325.3	1 286.6	1 227.6	1 191.9	1 323.4	1 484.4	1 605.2	1 446.3	1 553.5	1 654.6
Tonga Tonga	64.1	68.5	64.7	62.3	71.6	84.7	85.2	81.1	84.0	89.6
Tunisia Tunisie	9 675.3	10 246.5	9 684.3	10 227.0	12 381.5	14 853.0	16 230.6	14 794.5	15 425.4	16 579.1
Turkey Turquie	50 010.6	50 205.3	55 867.6	53 764.6	59 697.4	63 123.0	67 337.1	61 908.7	67 132.9	75 170.9
Turkmenistan Turkménistan	1 869.8	2 311.2	2 271.3	1 855.9	1 583.1	1 402.4	1 226.6	877.8	730.5	648.2
Uganda Ouganda	3 401.0	2 994.2	3 051.3	3 304.9	3 564.5	4 158.3	4 425.6	4 216.4	1 107.7	1 575.1
Ukraine Ukraine	8 971.9	9 590.4	8 141.8	8 098.6	8 272.1	8 890.9	10 589.5	10 458.4	9 537.8	10 568.2
United Rep. of Tanzania Rép.-Unie de Tanzanie	6 086.9	6 316.3	5 732.0	5 276.1	5 720.7	5 723.8	6 226.7	6 219.7	2 928.8	3 683.9
Uruguay Uruguay	5 108.2	5 079.6	5 512.6	6 030.6	6 683.8	7 468.2	7 813.3	7 779.2	8 596.9	9 615.7
Uzbekistan Ouzbékistan	2 660.7	3 565.2	3 763.5	3 905.4	4 005.5	4 149.0	4 115.2	3 626.9	3 296.6	3 085.9
Vanuatu Vanuatu	55.2	64.5	73.1	70.2	76.5	82.0	83.6	71.9	72.0	74.0
Venezuela (Bolivarian Rep. of) Venezuela (Rép. bolivarienne du)	28 034.9	27 653.9	27 432.5	24 915.3	23 063.8	24 155.6	26 133.3	30 927.5	27 159.2	27 494.2
Viet Nam Viet Nam	19 873.7	20 479.4	11 586.1	11 436.3	12 178.6	14 363.3	15 630.7	16 433.5	17 517.5	19 371.8
Yemen Yémen	5 231.8	5 372.3	4 059.2	4 276.8	4 497.4	4 744.5	4 799.3	4 717.1	4 997.6	5 343.2
Zambia Zambie	5 326.3	4 505.4	4 443.7	4 826.6	5 264.5	5 582.3	5 852.7	3 954.7	972.7	1 136.5
Zimbabwe Zimbabwe	3 194.6	2 982.3	2 774.1	2 678.8	3 020.7	3 388.1	3 564.2	3 217.0	3 408.8	3 734.7

Source:
World Bank, Washington, D.C., the *Global Development Finance* (GDF) database, last accessed September 2009.

Source:
Banque mondiale, Washington, D.C., la base de données de "Global Development Finance" (GDF), dernier accès septembre 2009.

Technical notes: tables 70-72

Table 70: Foreign exchange rates are shown in units of national currency per US dollar. The exchange rates are classified into three broad categories, reflecting both the role of the authorities in the determination of the exchange and/or the multiplicity of exchange rates in a country. The *market rate* is used to describe exchange rates determined largely by market forces; the *official rate* is an exchange rate determined by the authorities, sometimes in a flexible manner. For countries maintaining multiple exchange arrangements, the rates are labelled *principal rate*, *secondary rate*, and *tertiary rate*. Unless otherwise stated, the table refers to end of period and period averages of market exchange rates or official exchange rates. For further information see *International Financial Statistics* and www.imf.org.

Table 71: Total Reserves Minus Gold is the sum of the items Foreign Exchange, shown in this table, as well as Reserve Position in the Fund, and the U.S. dollar value of SDR holdings by monetary authorities.

Foreign Exchange includes monetary authorities' claims on non-residents in the form of foreign banknotes, bank deposits, treasury bills, short- and long-term government securities, ECUs (for periods before January 1999), and other claims usable in the event of balance of payments need.

Table 72: The data on external debt for developing countries *were* extracted from *Global Development Finance 2008*, published by the World Bank. In this table, developing countries are those in which 2008 GNI per capita was below $ 11,906.

The World Bank Debtor Reporting System (DRS) maintains statistics on the external debt of developing countries on a loan-by-loan basis. The estimated total external indebtedness of developing countries is a combination of DRS data and other information obtained from creditors through the debt data collection systems of other agencies such as the Bank for International Settlements (BIS) and the Organization for Economic Co-operation and Development (OECD), supplemented by market sources and estimates made by country economists of the World Bank and desk officers of the International Monetary Fund (IMF).

Long-term external debt is defined as debt that has an original or extended maturity of more than one year and that is owed to non-residents and is repayable in foreign currency, goods, or services. Long-term debt has three components: a) public debt, which is an external obligation of a public debtor, including the national government, a political subdivision (or an agency of either), and autonomous public bodies; b) publicly guaranteed debt, which is an external obligation of a private debtor that is guaranteed for repayment by a public entity; and c) private non-guaranteed external debt, which is an external obliga-

Notes techniques : tableaux 70 à 72

Tableau 70: Les taux des changes sont exprimés par le nombre d'unités de monnaie nationale pour un dollar des Etats-Unis. Les taux de change sont classés en trois catégories, qui dénotent le rôle des autorités dans l'établissement des taux de change et/ou la multiplicité des taux de change dans un pays. Par *taux du marché*, on entend les taux de change déterminés essentiellement par les forces du marché; le *taux officiel* est un taux de change établi par les autorités, parfois selon des dispositions souples. Pour les pays qui continuent à mettre en œuvre des régimes de taux de change multiples, les taux sont désignés par les appellations suivantes: "taux principal", "taux secondaire" et "taux tertiaire". Sauf indication contraire, le tableau indique des taux de fin de période et les moyennes sur la période, des taux de change du marché ou des taux de change officiels. Pour plus de renseignements, voir *Statistiques financières internationales* et www.imf.org.

Tableau 71 : Le total des réserves, déduction faite de l'or, correspond à la somme de tous les éléments de change figurant dans ce tableau, ainsi qu'à la situation des réserves du fonds, et à la valeur en dollars des États-Unis des droits de tirage spéciaux détenus par les autorités monétaires.

Les éléments de change comprennent les créances détenues par les autorités monétaires sur des non-résidents sous forme de billets de banque étrangers, de dépôts bancaires, de bons du Trésor, d'effets publics à court et à long terme, d'unités monétaires européennes (pour les périodes antérieures à 1999) et d'autres éléments utilisables si la situation de la balance des paiements l'exige.

Tableau 72: Les données concernant la dette extérieure des pays en développement sont tirées de "*Global Development Finance 2008*", publié par la Banque. Les pays en développement sont dans ce tableau ceux où le RNB par habitant était en 2008 inférieur à 11 906 dollars.

Le Système de notification de la dette de la Banque mondiale sert à tenir à jour prêt par prêt les statistiques de la dette extérieure des pays en développement. Le total estimatif de la dette extérieure des pays en développement a été calculé en combinant les données du Système de notification avec d'autres informations obtenues auprès des créanciers par le biais des systèmes de collecte de données d'autres organismes, tels que la Banque des règlements internationaux (BRI) et l'Organisation de coopération et développement économiques, ou de sources du marché, et avec des estimations des économistes chargés des pays à la Banque mondiale et au Fonds monétaire international (FMI).

La dette extérieure à long terme s'entend de celle dont la maturité d'origine (ou la maturité après prorogation) est à plus d'un an, contractée auprès de non-résidents et remboursable en devises, en biens ou en services. La dette à long terme comporte trois éléments : a) la dette publique, dette (ou administration relevant de l'un ou de l'autre), et administrations publiques autonomes; b) la dette garantie par une administration

tion of a private debtor that is not guaranteed for repayment by a public entity. Public and publicly guaranteed long-term debts are aggregated.

All data related to public and publicly guaranteed debt are from debtors except for those on lending by some multilateral agencies, in which case the data are taken from the creditors' records. These creditors include the African Development Bank, the Asian Development Bank, the Central Bank for Economic Integration, the Inter-American Development Bank, the International Bank for Reconstruction and Development (IBRD) and the International Development Association (IDA). (The IBRD and IDA are components of the World Bank.)

The data referring to public and publicly guaranteed debt do not include data for (a) transactions with the International Monetary Fund, (b) debt repayable in local currency, (c) direct investment and (d) short-term debt (that is, debt with an original maturity of less than a year).

The data referring to private non-guaranteed debt also exclude the above items but include contractual obligations on loans to direct investment enterprises by foreign parent companies or their affiliates.

Data are aggregated by type of creditor. The breakdown is as follows:

Official creditors:

(a) Loans from international organizations (multilateral loans), excluding loans from funds administered by an international organization on behalf of a single donor government. The latter are classified as loans from governments;

(b) Loans from governments (bilateral loans) and from autonomous public bodies;

Private creditors:

(a) Suppliers: Credits from manufacturers, exporters, or other suppliers of goods;

(b) Financial markets: Loans from private banks and other private financial institutions as well as publicly issued and privately placed bonds;

(c) Other: External liabilities on account of nationalized properties and unclassified debts to private creditors.

A distinction is made between the following categories of external public debt:

– Debt outstanding (including undisbursed) is the sum of disbursed and undisbursed debt and represents the total outstanding external obligations of the borrower at year-end;

– Debt outstanding (disbursed only) is total outstanding debt drawn by the borrower at year-end;

– Commitments are the total of loans for which contracts are signed in the year specified;

– Disbursements are drawings on outstanding loan commitments during the year specified;

– Service payments are actual repayments of principal amortization and interest payments made in foreign

publique, obligation extérieure d'un débiteur privé dont le remboursement est garanti par une entité publique; c) la dette extérieure privée non garantie, obligation extérieure d'un débiteur privé dont le remboursement n'est pas garanti par une entité publique. La dette extérieure publique et la dette extérieure garantie à long terme sont agrégées.

Toutes les données concernant la dette publique et la dette garantie par une entité publique proviennent des débiteurs, sauf celles concernant les prêts consentis par certains organismes multilatéraux, pour lesquels les données proviennent des dossiers des créanciers : il s'agit notamment de la Banque africaine de développement, de la Banque asiatique de développement, de la Banque centrale d'intégration économique, de la Banque interaméricaine de développement, de la Banque internationale de reconstruction et de développement (BIRD) et de l'Association internationale de développement (IDA) (la BIRD et l'IDA font partie du groupe de la Banque mondiale).

Les statistiques relatives à la dette publique ou à la dette garantie par l'Etat ne comprennent pas les données concernant: (a) les transactions avec le Fonds monétaire international; (b) la dette remboursable en monnaie nationale; (c) les investissements directs; et (d) la dette à court terme (c'est-à-dire la dette dont l'échéance initiale est inférieure à un an).

Les statistiques relatives à la dette privée non garantie ne comprennent pas non plus les éléments précités, mais comprennent les obligations contractuelles au titre des prêts consentis par des sociétés mères étrangères ou leurs filiales à des entreprises créées dans le cadre d'investissements directs.

Les données sont groupées par type de créancier, comme suit:

Créanciers publics:

(a) Les prêts obtenus auprès d'organisations internationales (prêts multilatéraux), à l'exclusion des prêts au titre de fonds administrés par une organisation internationale pour le compte d'un gouvernement donateur précis, qui sont classés comme prêts consentis par des gouvernements;

(b) Les prêts consentis par des gouvernements (prêts bilatéraux) et par des organisations publiques autonomes.

Créanciers privés:

(a) Fournisseurs: Crédits consentis par des fabricants exportateurs et autres fournisseurs de biens;

(b) Marchés financiers: prêts consentis par des banques privées et autres institutions financières privées, et émissions publiques d'obligations placées auprès d'investisseurs privés;

(c) Autres créanciers: engagements vis-à-vis de l'extérieur au titre des biens nationalisés et dettes diverses à l'égard de créanciers privés.

On fait une distinction entre les catégories suivantes de dette publique extérieure:

– L'encours de la dette (y compris les fonds non décaissés) est la somme des fonds décaissés et non décaissés et représente le total des obligations extérieures en cours de l'emprunteur à la fin de l'année;

currencies, goods or services in the year specified;

– Net flows (or net lending) are disbursements minus principal repayments;

– Net transfers are net flows minus interest payments or disbursements minus total debt-service payments.

The countries included in the table are those for which data are sufficiently reliable to provide a meaningful presentation of debt outstanding and future service payments.

– L'encours de la dette (fonds décaissés seulement) est le montant total des tirages effectués par l'emprunteur sur sa dette en cours à la fin de l'année;

– Les engagements représentent le total des prêts dont les contrats ont été signés au cours de l'année considérée;

– Les décaissements sont les sommes tirées sur l'encours des prêts pendant l'année considérée;

– Les paiements au titre du service de la dette sont les remboursements effectifs du principal et les paiements d'intérêts effectués en devises, biens ou services pendant l'année considérée;

– Les flux nets (ou prêts nets) sont les décaissements moins les remboursements de principal;

– Les transferts nets désignent les flux nets moins les paiements d'intérêts, ou les décaissements moins le total des paiements au titre du service de la dette.

Les pays figurant sur ce tableau sont ceux pour lesquels les données sont suffisamment fiables pour permettre une présentation significative de l'encours de la dette et des paiements futurs au titre du service de la dette.

73

Disbursements of bilateral and multilateral official development assistance and official aid to individual recipients

Versements d'aide publique au développement et d'aide publique bilatérale et multilatérale aux bénéficiaires

| Country or area
Pays ou zone | Year
Année | Net disbursements (US $) - Versements nets ($E.-U.) | | | |
		Bilateral Bilatérale (millions)	Multilateral[1] Multilatérale[1] (millions)	Total (millions)	Per capita Par habitant
Total	**2003**	**37 153.0**	**15 611.5**	**52 764.6**	...
Total	**2004**	**38 608.5**	**18 870.8**	**57 479.3**	...
	2005	**65 708.9**	**19 490.9**	**85 199.8**	...
	2006	**58 485.7**	**21 820.2**	**80 305.8**	...
	2007	**51 654.8**	**24 330.1**	**75 984.9**	...
Afghanistan	2003	1 199.7	362.8	1 562.5	68.7
Afghanistan	2004	1 701.1	416.5	2 117.6	89.6
	2005	2 166.5	534.7	2 701.1	110.2
	2006	2 404.6	486.8	2 891.4	113.9
	2007	2 992.7	838.2	3 830.9	145.7
Albania	2003	230.3	109.7	340.0	110.1
Albanie	2004	165.0	121.9	286.9	92.6
	2005	178.1	127.4	305.5	98.2
	2006	176.9	118.3	295.2	94.6
	2007	200.6	94.5	295.2	94.2
Algeria	2003	168.8	68.2	237.0	7.4
Algérie	2004	234.7	80.3	315.0	9.7
	2005	266.2	70.4	336.6	10.2
	2006	204.6	-3.8	200.8	6.0
	2007	289.2	92.2	381.4	11.3
Angola	2003	372.2	122.3	494.5	31.6
Angola	2004	1 015.7	131.0	1 146.7	71.1
	2005	247.7	175.9	423.6	25.5
	2006	-55.2	123.8	68.6	4.0
	2007	85.6	137.3	222.9	12.7
Anguilla	2003	1.8	2.1	3.9	311.7
Anguilla	2004	1.4	1.3	2.7	204.1
	2005	4.3	-0.3	4.0	293.4
	2006	0.3	4.1	4.4	313.5
	2007	2.6	2.7	5.3	363.8
Antigua and Barbuda	2003	3.0	2.0	5.0	61.9
Antigua-et-Barbuda	2004	1.2	1.4	2.6	31.4
	2005	6.9	0.2	7.1	85.4
	2006	1.9	1.1	3.1	36.3
	2007	2.1	2.1	4.1	48.0
Argentina	2003	98.2	2.9	101.1	2.7
Argentine	2004	78.5	13.9	92.4	2.4
	2005	77.8	20.5	98.2	2.5
	2006	81.0	34.1	115.1	2.9
	2007	63.8	19.2	82.9	2.1
Armenia	2003	127.4	120.7	248.1	81.1
Arménie	2004	133.1	119.9	253.1	82.6
	2005	126.4	44.4	170.8	55.7
	2006	135.0	76.4	211.5	68.9
	2007	230.7	118.9	349.6	113.8
Azerbaijan	2003	158.5	131.7	290.2	34.9
Azerbaïdjan	2004	92.3	57.5	149.7	17.9
	2005	95.4	87.0	182.5	21.6
	2006	95.2	73.5	168.7	19.8
	2007	109.8	72.8	182.5	21.1
Bahrain	2003	1.1	-0.1	1.1	1.5
Bahreïn	2004	1.4	-0.8	0.6	0.9

73

Disbursements of bilateral and multilateral official development assistance and official aid to individual recipients *(continued)*

Versements d'aide publique au développement et d'aide publique bilatérale et multilatérale aux bénéficiaires *(suite)*

Country or area Pays ou zone	Year Année	Net disbursements (US $) - Versements nets ($E.-U.)			
		Bilateral Bilatérale (millions)	Multilateral[1] Multilatérale[1] (millions)	Total (millions)	Per capita Par habitant
Bangladesh Bangladesh	2003	695.0	687.2	1 382.2	9.3
	2004	632.7	753.6	1 386.3	9.2
	2005	548.4	739.4	1 287.8	8.4
	2006	456.3	742.2	1 198.5	7.7
	2007	663.9	810.9	1 474.8	9.3
Barbados Barbade	2003	2.4	17.3	19.7	78.3
	2004	2.6	26.3	28.8	114.1
	2005	6.0	-8.2	-2.2	-8.6
	2006	3.1	-3.6	-0.5	-2.0
	2007	7.2	13.7	20.8	81.8
Belarus Bélarus	2005	33.8	12.6	46.3	4.7
	2006	38.2	22.9	61.0	6.2
	2007	48.8	15.9	64.6	6.6
Belize Belize	2003	4.2	7.8	12.0	44.3
	2004	3.8	4.5	8.3	30.2
	2005	7.5	5.4	12.9	45.6
	2006	3.7	4.6	8.3	28.8
	2007	8.1	14.3	22.4	76.2
Benin Bénin	2003	196.1	105.8	301.9	41.0
	2004	210.0	181.2	391.2	51.4
	2005	207.6	140.8	348.4	44.3
	2006	228.4	147.0	375.4	46.2
	2007	238.3	229.3	467.6	55.7
Bhutan Bhoutan	2003	52.1	24.7	76.8	124.7
	2004	53.1	25.5	78.6	124.1
	2005	56.9	32.8	89.7	138.1
	2006	51.0	42.9	93.9	141.5
	2007	43.4	45.4	88.8	131.3
Bolivia Bolivie	2003	552.9	385.2	938.1	106.2
	2004	557.3	229.1	786.3	87.3
	2005	437.3	204.1	641.4	69.8
	2006	569.7	269.8	839.5	89.7
	2007	352.7	113.8	466.6	49.0
Bosnia and Herzegovina Bosnie-Herzégovine	2003	331.2	202.0	533.2	141.0
	2004	298.8	351.4	650.2	171.9
	2005	265.6	236.5	502.1	132.8
	2006	320.2	134.8	455.0	120.3
	2007	288.4	134.0	422.4	111.8
Botswana Botswana	2003	27.4	2.1	29.5	16.4
	2004	31.8	16.4	48.2	26.6
	2005	30.0	19.9	49.9	27.1
	2006	36.3	31.0	67.2	36.1
	2007	63.6	39.6	103.2	54.5
Brazil Brésil	2003	184.3	8.4	192.6	1.1
	2004	147.2	8.1	155.2	0.8
	2005	174.3	19.9	194.2	1.0
	2006	74.7	6.5	81.2	0.4
	2007	269.9	25.8	295.7	1.6
Burkina Faso Burkina Faso	2003	265.7	252.6	518.2	40.3
	2004	331.4	306.1	637.5	48.0
	2005	338.4	349.4	687.8	50.0
	2006	385.8	473.8	859.6	60.4
	2007	411.8	505.5	917.3	62.3
Burundi Burundi	2003	121.2	106.2	227.4	32.7
	2004	185.8	173.3	359.0	50.1
	2005	180.3	183.4	363.7	49.3
	2006	222.5	192.8	415.2	54.6
	2007	199.7	266.1	465.8	59.4

73

Disbursements of bilateral and multilateral official development assistance and official aid to individual recipients *(continued)*

Versements d'aide publique au développement et d'aide publique bilatérale et multilatérale aux bénéficiaires *(suite)*

| Country or area
Pays ou zone | Year
Année | Net disbursements (US $) - Versements nets ($E.-U.) | | | |
		Bilateral Bilatérale (millions)	Multilateral[1] Multilatérale[1] (millions)	Total (millions)	Per capita Par habitant
Cambodia Cambodge	2003	319.2	184.3	503.5	37.5
	2004	297.4	161.3	458.7	33.6
	2005	346.5	176.1	522.5	37.7
	2006	347.5	150.5	498.0	35.3
	2007	417.3	196.7	613.9	42.9
Cameroon Cameroun	2003	751.6	142.9	894.5	52.6
	2004	572.1	207.4	779.5	44.8
	2005	331.4	80.9	412.3	23.1
	2006	1 505.3	178.5	1 683.8	92.3
	2007	1 696.8	199.2	1 896.0	101.6
Cape Verde Cap-Vert	2003	90.2	53.3	143.5	310.3
	2004	90.8	51.5	142.3	302.7
	2005	104.1	55.5	159.6	334.2
	2006	98.7	37.8	136.5	281.6
	2007	114.2	50.4	164.6	334.7
Central African Rep. Rép. centrafricaine	2003	32.4	18.8	51.2	12.9
	2004	54.8	55.0	109.8	27.2
	2005	60.5	29.6	90.1	22.0
	2006	65.3	68.2	133.5	32.0
	2007	117.8	58.5	176.2	41.4
Chad Tchad	2003	95.5	154.9	250.5	26.7
	2004	163.1	164.2	327.4	33.8
	2005	161.7	214.4	376.2	37.5
	2006	152.5	127.8	280.3	27.1
	2007	223.4	128.3	351.7	33.1
Chile Chili	2003	61.4	16.6	78.0	4.9
	2004	25.9	29.7	55.6	3.4
	2005	75.6	75.0	150.6	9.2
	2006	64.3	17.8	82.1	5.0
	2007	98.0	21.4	119.4	7.2
China Chine	2003	1 139.5	174.7	1 314.2	1.0
	2004	1 584.9	62.8	1 647.7	1.3
	2005	1 664.6	40.0	1 704.6	1.3
	2006	1 165.4	12.4	1 177.7	0.9
	2007	1 331.2	35.4	1 366.6	1.0
Colombia Colombie	2003	767.1	32.8	799.8	19.2
	2004	481.7	35.5	517.2	12.2
	2005	571.6	51.8	623.4	14.5
	2006	917.1	69.1	986.2	22.6
	2007	628.9	100.5	729.5	16.4
Comoros Comores	2003	11.1	13.3	24.4	41.4
	2004	13.9	11.6	25.4	42.2
	2005	15.1	7.7	22.8	36.9
	2006	19.9	9.9	29.9	47.4
	2007	19.6	24.9	44.5	68.9
Congo Congo	2003	33.9	35.1	68.9	21.1
	2004	47.8	67.6	115.4	34.5
	2005	1 343.9	85.0	1 428.9	418.2
	2006	169.1	89.1	258.2	74.1
	2007	47.6	65.3	112.9	31.8
Cook Islands Iles Cook	2003	4.6	1.2	5.8	315.3
	2004	5.9	2.9	8.8	467.1
	2005	7.0	0.8	7.8	406.1
	2006	31.0	1.3	32.3	1 668.8
	2007	9.0	0.3	9.3	476.7
Costa Rica Costa Rica	2003	31.0	-3.7	27.3	6.5
	2004	11.4	2.4	13.8	3.2
	2005	25.0	3.7	28.7	6.6

73

Disbursements of bilateral and multilateral official development assistance and official aid to individual recipients *(continued)*

Versements d'aide publique au développement et d'aide publique bilatérale et multilatérale aux bénéficiaires *(suite)*

Country or area Pays ou zone	Year Année	Net disbursements (US $) - Versements nets ($E.-U.)			
		Bilateral Bilatérale (millions)	Multilateral[1] Multilatérale[1] (millions)	Total (millions)	Per capita Par habitant
	2006	20.1	2.5	22.6	5.1
	2007	48.4	2.2	50.5	11.3
Côte d'Ivoire Côte d'Ivoire	2003	281.2	-27.8	253.3	13.7
	2004	196.6	-36.3	160.3	8.5
	2005	129.1	-32.3	96.8	5.0
	2006	198.8	51.4	250.2	12.7
	2007	111.5	54.3	165.8	8.2
Croatia Croatie	2003	80.3	37.9	118.2	26.5
	2004	87.4	32.7	120.1	27.0
	2005	62.6	60.9	123.4	27.8
	2006	68.2	130.6	198.7	44.8
	2007	55.1	107.1	162.1	36.6
Cuba Cuba	2003	59.3	15.2	74.5	6.7
	2004	69.8	26.8	96.6	8.6
	2005	68.0	18.9	86.9	7.8
	2006	56.9	20.7	77.5	6.9
	2007	57.0	30.8	87.7	7.8
Dem. Rep. of the Congo Rép. dém. du Congo	2003	5 009.5	407.2	5 416.7	97.4
	2004	1 165.0	660.5	1 825.5	31.8
	2005	990.1	793.8	1 783.9	30.2
	2006	1 500.4	549.1	2 049.4	33.7
	2007	788.4	427.0	1 215.4	19.4
Djibouti Djibouti	2003	37.0	39.4	76.4	98.3
	2004	39.4	27.2	66.7	84.3
	2005	53.6	23.5	77.1	95.8
	2006	89.5	26.0	115.5	140.9
	2007	75.5	36.9	112.4	134.7
Dominica Dominique	2003	3.4	7.5	10.8	159.9
	2004	10.7	18.3	29.0	428.2
	2005	4.5	10.5	15.0	222.7
	2006	1.8	17.5	19.3	287.1
	2007	3.1	15.9	19.0	283.7
Dominican Republic Rép. dominicaine	2003	60.4	8.2	68.6	7.4
	2004	84.5	-0.1	84.4	9.0
	2005	55.4	20.2	75.5	7.9
	2006	13.0	38.4	51.4	5.3
	2007	25.0	96.4	121.4	12.4
Ecuador Equateur	2003	173.6	1.2	174.9	13.7
	2004	158.5	-0.2	158.3	12.3
	2005	192.7	35.1	227.8	17.4
	2006	170.5	17.6	188.2	14.3
	2007	180.5	31.1	211.5	15.9
Egypt Egypte	2003	775.1	84.1	859.2	11.6
	2004	1 175.6	260.4	1 436.0	19.0
	2005	662.8	241.6	904.3	11.7
	2006	536.8	286.7	823.4	10.5
	2007	787.0	227.0	1 014.1	12.7
El Salvador El Salvador	2003	170.4	21.1	191.4	31.8
	2004	201.7	13.7	215.4	35.7
	2005	162.6	34.2	196.8	32.5
	2006	150.6	5.5	156.2	25.7
	2007	71.5	15.3	86.8	14.2
Equatorial Guinea Guinée équatoriale	2003	17.6	3.3	20.9	36.3
	2004	23.1	6.1	29.2	49.2
	2005	29.7	9.2	38.9	63.9
	2006	18.9	7.5	26.4	42.2
	2007	25.7	5.7	31.4	48.8
Eritrea Erythrée	2003	185.5	130.7	316.1	76.5
	2004	177.5	89.8	267.3	62.1

73

Disbursements of bilateral and multilateral official development assistance and official aid to individual recipients *(continued)*

Versements d'aide publique au développement et d'aide publique bilatérale et multilatérale aux bénéficiaires *(suite)*

Country or area Pays ou zone	Year Année	Net disbursements (US $) - Versements nets ($E.-U.)			
		Bilateral Bilatérale (millions)	Multilateral[1] Multilatérale[1] (millions)	Total (millions)	Per capita Par habitant
	2005	225.8	131.6	357.4	79.9
	2006	63.2	66.8	130.1	28.1
	2007	45.5	106.9	152.3	31.9
Ethiopia Ethiopie	2003	1 033.3	533.7	1 567.0	22.1
	2004	1 024.7	747.2	1 772.0	24.4
	2005	1 184.4	702.2	1 886.6	25.3
	2006	1 024.1	898.6	1 922.7	25.1
	2007	1 242.0	1 146.7	2 388.7	30.4
Fiji Fidji	2003	42.9	7.9	50.8	62.1
	2004	36.4	28.5	64.9	78.9
	2005	38.8	26.8	65.6	79.2
	2006	39.0	18.2	57.2	68.7
	2007	31.6	24.3	56.0	66.7
Gabon Gabon	2003	-41.2	30.1	-11.1	-8.4
	2004	23.5	16.3	39.9	29.7
	2005	29.5	22.9	52.4	38.2
	2006	31.9	-1.2	30.7	22.0
	2007	33.6	16.0	49.6	34.9
Gambia Gambie	2003	19.7	40.0	59.7	41.6
	2004	11.6	43.4	55.0	37.1
	2005	14.7	46.0	60.7	39.8
	2006	25.1	43.5	68.6	43.6
	2007	33.1	36.3	69.4	42.9
Georgia Géorgie	2003	163.9	53.0	216.9	47.4
	2004	209.1	95.4	304.5	67.4
	2005	183.2	102.9	286.1	64.1
	2006	210.4	136.4	346.8	78.6
	2007	244.2	125.4	369.6	84.8
Ghana Ghana	2003	471.4	483.4	954.8	45.6
	2004	913.3	469.7	1 382.9	64.5
	2005	601.6	526.2	1 127.8	51.5
	2006	594.7	580.1	1 174.7	52.5
	2007	708.5	431.5	1 139.9	49.8
Grenada Grenade	2003	8.3	3.4	11.7	114.5
	2004	10.5	5.3	15.8	154.5
	2005	26.0	24.8	50.8	495.5
	2006	3.4	23.6	27.0	262.6
	2007	4.4	19.6	24.0	232.6
Guatemala Guatemala	2003	216.0	29.3	245.4	20.3
	2004	203.7	11.6	215.3	17.4
	2005	219.1	33.0	252.1	19.8
	2006	445.1	36.5	481.6	37.0
	2007	412.4	34.4	446.8	33.5
Guinea Guinée	2003	134.6	107.1	241.6	27.2
	2004	178.3	94.9	273.3	30.2
	2005	126.0	61.0	186.9	20.3
	2006	102.9	54.9	157.8	16.8
	2007	122.2	92.1	214.3	22.3
Guinea-Bissau Guinée-Bissau	2003	97.6	47.7	145.2	103.5
	2004	28.6	47.8	76.3	53.1
	2005	26.8	39.2	66.0	44.8
	2006	39.4	42.7	82.1	54.4
	2007	43.6	79.2	122.8	79.7
Guyana Guyana	2003	28.7	67.1	95.8	126.0
	2004	70.3	77.5	147.8	193.8
	2005	40.0	109.6	149.6	195.9
	2006	46.6	126.3	172.9	226.2
	2007	40.1	83.3	123.3	161.4

Disbursements of bilateral and multilateral official development assistance and official aid to individual recipients *(continued)*

Versements d'aide publique au développement et d'aide publique bilatérale et multilatérale aux bénéficiaires *(suite)*

Country or area Pays ou zone	Year Année	Net disbursements (US $) - Versements nets ($E.-U.)			
		Bilateral Bilatérale (millions)	Multilateral[1] Multilatérale[1] (millions)	Total (millions)	Per capita Par habitant
Haiti Haïti	2003	153.2	59.0	212.2	23.3
	2004	209.1	49.7	258.8	28.0
	2005	283.9	159.5	443.4	47.1
	2006	363.3	216.8	580.1	60.6
	2007	434.3	266.8	701.1	72.1
Honduras Honduras	2003	231.4	155.3	386.7	58.4
	2004	328.4	320.5	648.9	96.1
	2005	456.4	235.3	691.6	100.3
	2006	384.7	203.8	588.4	83.7
	2007	289.6	170.4	460.0	64.1
India Inde	2003	384.3	541.7	926.1	0.8
	2004	14.6	675.6	690.1	0.6
	2005	844.1	875.5	1 719.6	1.5
	2006	653.0	723.9	1 377.0	1.2
	2007	903.2	389.9	1 293.1	1.1
Indonesia Indonésie	2003	1 580.5	164.9	1 745.4	8.2
	2004	-117.4	224.8	107.4	0.5
	2005	2 242.1	216.6	2 458.7	11.2
	2006	602.0	651.6	1 253.6	5.6
	2007	362.1	483.5	845.6	3.8
Iran (Islamic Rep. of) Iran (Rép. islamique d')	2003	102.1	25.8	127.9	1.8
	2004	138.9	32.9	171.8	2.5
	2005	76.9	21.1	98.0	1.4
	2006	70.7	44.3	115.0	1.6
	2007	67.3	21.4	88.7	1.2
Iraq Iraq	2003	2 095.0	70.4	2 165.4	80.6
	2004	4 393.8	139.2	4 533.0	164.5
	2005	21 823.1	49.3	21 872.4	774.6
	2006	8 487.8	226.4	8 714.2	301.8
	2007	8 991.6	82.2	9 073.8	307.7
Jamaica Jamaïque	2003	1.1	2.1	3.1	1.2
	2004	13.3	67.2	80.6	30.4
	2005	11.4	24.8	36.2	13.6
	2006	-0.6	38.1	37.5	14.0
	2007	-17.0	46.2	29.3	10.9
Jordan Jordanie	2003	1 092.2	134.6	1 226.7	233.9
	2004	433.8	147.5	581.2	107.6
	2005	440.2	149.7	589.9	106.0
	2006	361.8	156.9	518.7	90.3
	2007	289.5	182.6	472.1	79.5
Kazakhstan Kazakhstan	2003	228.0	15.3	243.3	16.2
	2004	203.3	21.7	224.9	14.9
	2005	146.2	18.3	164.5	10.8
	2006	96.0	23.3	119.3	7.8
	2007	180.8	-25.9	154.9	10.0
Kenya Kenya	2003	320.3	198.9	519.2	15.3
	2004	470.8	184.5	655.3	18.8
	2005	509.9	244.5	754.4	21.1
	2006	760.1	166.9	927.0	25.2
	2007	824.1	472.8	1 296.9	34.3
Kiribati Kiribati	2003	12.8	5.5	18.4	206.9
	2004	10.1	6.6	16.7	184.6
	2005	21.3	6.5	27.8	302.2
	2006	19.6	5.6	25.1	268.3
	2007	22.4	4.4	26.8	281.4
Korea, Dem. P. R. Corée, R. p. dém. de	2003	77.9	51.7	129.6	5.6
	2004	102.2	47.2	149.4	6.4
	2005	39.4	41.5	80.9	3.4

73

Disbursements of bilateral and multilateral official development assistance and official aid to individual recipients *(continued)*

Versements d'aide publique au développement et d'aide publique bilatérale et multilatérale aux bénéficiaires *(suite)*

| Country or area
Pays ou zone | Year
Année | Net disbursements (US $) - Versements nets ($E.-U.) | | | |
		Bilateral Bilatérale (millions)	Multilatéral[1] Multilatérale[1] (millions)	Total (millions)	Per capita Par habitant
	2006	28.9	23.3	52.2	2.2
	2007	71.7	27.0	98.6	4.2
Kyrgyzstan Kirghizistan	2003	112.6	80.8	193.4	37.8
	2004	109.6	114.3	223.8	43.3
	2005	124.9	83.6	208.6	39.9
	2006	123.6	72.3	195.8	37.1
	2007	118.7	83.3	201.9	37.8
Lao People's Dem. Rep. Rép. dém. pop. lao	2003	189.0	109.9	298.9	52.5
	2004	176.1	89.9	266.0	46.0
	2005	158.8	126.6	285.4	48.5
	2006	187.6	124.1	311.7	52.1
	2007	221.7	132.5	354.2	58.1
Lebanon Liban	2003	118.8	111.1	229.9	58.0
	2004	128.5	138.2	266.7	66.2
	2005	129.5	117.5	246.9	60.5
	2006	388.6	283.4	671.9	162.9
	2007	463.8	167.6	631.4	151.7
Lesotho Lesotho	2003	32.9	47.4	80.3	41.0
	2004	35.1	61.5	96.5	48.8
	2005	39.9	30.2	70.1	35.1
	2006	38.5	34.4	72.8	36.2
	2007	62.3	68.5	130.8	64.4
Liberia Libéria	2003	70.3	36.2	106.5	33.9
	2004	163.0	49.9	212.9	66.0
	2005	143.9	87.5	231.4	69.4
	2006	187.4	80.1	267.5	77.1
	2007	226.5	468.9	695.3	191.7
Libyan Arab Jamah. Jamah. arabe libyenne	2005	16.7	3.4	20.1	3.4
	2006	33.4	2.7	36.2	6.0
	2007	15.2	2.4	17.5	2.8
Madagascar Madagascar	2003	224.9	319.0	543.9	32.7
	2004	684.6	565.8	1 250.4	73.0
	2005	497.6	416.7	914.3	51.9
	2006	261.0	485.0	746.0	41.2
	2007	386.5	500.5	887.0	47.7
Malawi Malawi	2003	308.9	203.8	512.7	39.7
	2004	308.2	193.9	502.1	37.8
	2005	325.3	253.9	579.2	42.4
	2006	397.9	273.9	671.8	47.8
	2007	400.5	323.0	723.5	50.1
Malaysia Malaisie	2003	103.6	4.4	108.0	4.4
	2004	293.8	3.0	296.8	11.8
	2005	17.8	6.9	24.7	1.0
	2006	230.0	9.0	239.0	9.2
	2007	191.7	7.1	198.9	7.5
Maldives Maldives	2003	8.7	9.2	17.9	62.9
	2004	8.8	13.5	22.4	77.6
	2005	39.7	22.5	62.2	212.7
	2006	16.0	19.2	35.2	118.8
	2007	18.0	20.3	38.3	127.4
Mali Mali	2003	271.9	283.7	555.5	49.3
	2004	327.5	254.7	582.2	50.4
	2005	370.7	326.8	697.6	59.0
	2006	398.4	417.8	816.3	67.4
	2007	558.1	455.1	1 013.2	81.7
Marshall Islands Iles Marshall	2003	51.5	5.0	56.5	1 036.3
	2004	49.5	1.6	51.1	919.4
	2005	55.8	0.7	56.5	996.1

73 Disbursements of bilateral and multilateral official development assistance and official aid to individual recipients *(continued)*

Versements d'aide publique au développement et d'aide publique bilatérale et multilatérale aux bénéficiaires *(suite)*

| Country or area
Pays ou zone | Year
Année | Net disbursements (US $) - Versements nets ($E.-U.) | | | |
		Bilateral Bilatérale (millions)	Multilateral[1] Multilatérale[1] (millions)	Total (millions)	Per capita Par habitant
	2006	55.0	^0.0	55.0	949.6
	2007	51.4	0.6	51.9	875.6
Mauritania Mauritanie	2003	136.1	115.8	251.9	89.0
	2004	83.1	104.6	187.7	64.5
	2005	105.2	76.8	182.1	61.0
	2006	93.7	95.9	189.6	61.9
	2007	133.2	208.0	341.2	108.7
Mauritius Maurice	2003	-17.7	2.5	-15.2	-12.3
	2004	14.7	19.9	34.7	27.9
	2005	21.5	10.5	32.0	25.6
	2006	8.5	12.0	20.5	16.3
	2007	43.6	27.3	70.9	55.8
Mayotte Mayotte	2003	166.1	^0.0	166.0	1 010.9
	2004	208.6	-0.2	208.5	1 230.6
	2005	201.9	-0.5	201.3	1 154.1
	2006	337.5	0.1	337.6	1 881.5
	2007	406.9	0.4	407.2	2 208.7
Mexico Mexique	2003	73.6	24.1	97.7	0.9
	2004	78.9	34.8	113.8	1.1
	2005	160.4	27.6	188.0	1.8
	2006	208.9	36.9	245.8	2.3
	2007	79.0	41.2	120.2	1.1
Micronesia (Fed. States of) Micronésie (Etats féd. de)	2003	109.3	3.0	112.4	1 037.4
	2004	85.2	1.1	86.3	792.4
	2005	104.4	1.9	106.4	972.0
	2006	105.9	2.5	108.5	987.8
	2007	110.6	4.2	114.8	1 042.7
Mongolia Mongolie	2003	148.9	86.6	235.5	94.8
	2004	147.4	95.6	243.0	96.5
	2005	126.7	54.0	180.7	70.9
	2006	126.6	45.9	172.5	66.8
	2007	140.3	52.8	193.1	73.9
Montenegro Monténégro	2006	60.3	33.8	94.1	151.4
	2007	44.6	44.3	88.8	143.1
Montserrat Montserrat	2003	36.3	0.2	36.5	7 312.6
	2004	37.4	7.1	44.5	8 308.7
	2005	27.0	0.9	27.8	4 939.6
	2006	24.9	7.4	32.4	5 591.6
	2007	32.5	3.9	36.3	6 183.8
Morocco Maroc	2003	335.7	157.3	492.9	16.5
	2004	393.5	243.7	637.2	21.1
	2005	286.9	315.3	602.1	19.7
	2006	566.7	361.3	928.0	30.1
	2007	627.9	326.3	954.3	30.6
Mozambique Mozambique	2003	697.1	348.9	1 045.9	52.9
	2004	731.3	508.3	1 239.5	61.0
	2005	760.2	528.2	1 288.4	61.8
	2006	938.3	663.2	1 601.5	75.0
	2007	1 073.2	676.8	1 750.0	80.0
Myanmar Myanmar	2003	83.4	34.9	118.3	2.5
	2004	81.5	38.9	120.4	2.5
	2005	77.6	59.2	136.8	2.8
	2006	92.0	41.4	133.3	2.7
	2007	129.3	63.6	192.9	3.9
Namibia Namibie	2003	110.3	33.5	143.8	74.3
	2004	124.0	33.6	157.6	79.9
	2005	88.1	21.8	109.9	54.7
	2006	105.7	38.0	143.7	70.1
	2007	143.5	71.4	214.9	102.9

73

Disbursements of bilateral and multilateral official development assistance and official aid to individual recipients *(continued)*

Versements d'aide publique au développement et d'aide publique bilatérale et multilatérale aux bénéficiaires *(suite)*

| Country or area
Pays ou zone | Year
Année | Net disbursements (US $) - Versements nets ($E.-U.) | | | |
		Bilateral Bilatérale (millions)	Multilateral[1] Multilatérale[1] (millions)	Total (millions)	Per capita Par habitant
Nauru Nauru	2003	16.0	0.1	16.1	1 602.5
	2004	13.6	0.1	13.7	1 355.5
	2005	8.9	0.1	9.0	889.1
	2006	17.3	0.1	17.4	1 717.7
	2007	25.0	0.4	25.4	2 500.0
Nepal Népal	2003	320.4	142.1	462.4	17.7
	2004	318.5	103.6	422.0	15.8
	2005	345.5	75.9	421.3	15.5
	2006	317.5	192.9	510.4	18.4
	2007	377.3	217.1	594.4	21.0
Nicaragua Nicaragua	2003	521.8	309.5	831.2	156.3
	2004	856.3	383.8	1 240.1	230.2
	2005	509.7	252.5	762.2	139.7
	2006	385.5	339.2	724.7	131.2
	2007	493.9	298.6	792.5	141.6
Niger Niger	2003	244.5	216.5	461.0	37.8
	2004	305.7	241.7	547.3	40.0
	2005	254.3	265.7	520.0	39.7
	2006	235.2	278.8	514.0	37.8
	2007	232.7	304.1	536.9	38.0
Nigeria Nigéria	2003	199.8	108.8	308.6	2.3
	2004	314.6	263.2	577.8	4.2
	2005	5 931.5	469.6	6 401.1	45.4
	2006	10 819.6	610.5	11 430.1	79.2
	2007	1 385.2	561.2	1 946.4	13.2
Niue Nioué	2003	8.8	0.1	8.9	5 117.9
	2004	13.8	0.2	14.0	8 307.7
	2005	20.1	1.0	21.1	12 828.5
	2006	8.6	0.4	9.0	5 600.0
	2007	14.0	0.8	14.8	9 486.2
Occupied Palestinian Terr. Terr. palestinien occupé	2003	490.8	455.4	946.2	269.6
	2004	605.3	480.8	1 086.1	298.7
	2005	569.0	526.4	1 095.3	291.2
	2006	754.4	672.9	1 427.3	367.0
	2007	836.4	1 017.4	1 853.8	461.4
Oman Oman	2003	10.5	1.1	11.5	4.6
	2004	2.0	-0.3	1.7	0.7
	2005	3.6	0.7	4.3	1.7
	2006	-14.5	4.4	-10.2	-3.8
	2007	9.6	5.3	14.9	5.5
Pakistan Pakistan	2003	536.3	535.8	1 072.1	6.8
	2004	382.2	1 036.6	1 418.8	8.7
	2005	786.5	697.1	1 483.6	8.9
	2006	1 144.9	931.2	2 076.1	12.3
	2007	976.4	1 201.2	2 177.6	12.6
Palau Palaos	2003	25.3	0.1	25.4	1 274.5
	2004	19.4	0.1	19.5	971.9
	2005	23.4	0.1	23.4	1 164.2
	2006	37.2	0.1	37.3	1 843.8
	2007	21.8	0.4	22.1	1 089.9
Panama Panama	2003	31.3	-3.0	28.3	9.1
	2004	25.3	-1.6	23.7	7.5
	2005	17.3	2.0	19.3	6.0
	2006	19.3	11.3	30.5	9.3
	2007	-139.4	2.5	-136.9	-41.0
Papua New Guinea Papouasie-Nvl-Guinée	2003	218.8	2.1	220.9	38.0
	2004	249.7	19.3	269.1	45.1
	2005	245.3	21.5	266.8	43.6

Disbursements of bilateral and multilateral official development assistance and official aid to individual recipients *(continued)*

Versements d'aide publique au développement et d'aide publique bilatérale et multilatérale aux bénéficiaires *(suite)*

Country or area Pays ou zone	Year Année	Net disbursements (US $) - Versements nets ($E.-U.)			
		Bilateral Bilatérale (millions)	Multilateral[1] Multilatérale[1] (millions)	Total (millions)	Per capita Par habitant
	2006	248.3	27.2	275.4	43.9
	2007	287.4	33.1	320.5	49.9
Paraguay Paraguay	2003	55.4	-5.7	49.8	8.8
	2004	26.4	-6.0	20.5	3.5
	2005	55.0	-6.6	48.3	8.2
	2006	62.1	-8.4	53.8	8.9
	2007	82.7	19.1	101.8	16.6
Peru Pérou	2003	447.7	45.7	493.4	18.2
	2004	439.3	21.6	460.9	16.8
	2005	388.7	62.4	451.0	16.2
	2006	374.9	75.8	450.7	16.0
	2007	171.2	77.8	249.1	8.7
Philippines Philippines	2003	675.4	28.2	703.6	8.5
	2004	413.1	20.8	434.0	5.2
	2005	524.7	27.1	551.8	6.5
	2006	519.4	33.5	553.0	6.3
	2007	547.4	57.3	604.7	6.8
Republic of Moldova République de Moldova	2003	80.4	32.8	113.2	29.1
	2004	76.6	37.0	113.6	29.7
	2005	84.4	77.4	161.8	43.0
	2006	83.5	126.9	210.4	56.7
	2007	93.1	161.0	254.1	69.3
Rwanda Rwanda	2003	213.4	121.4	334.8	38.5
	2004	216.9	272.6	489.5	55.5
	2005	281.3	292.5	573.8	63.8
	2006	321.1	264.2	585.3	63.6
	2007	373.9	336.5	710.4	75.1
Saint Helena Sainte-Hélène	2003	17.6	0.4	18.0	3 697.3
	2004	26.1	0.2	26.2	5 475.2
	2005	22.5	0.1	22.6	4 783.6
	2006	23.1	5.0	28.1	6 057.3
	2007	39.8	3.5	43.3	9 456.1
Saint Kitts and Nevis Saint-Kitts-et-Nevis	2003	-0.3	0.3	^0.0	-0.4
	2004	-0.2	0.9	0.8	16.1
	2005	1.6	1.8	3.4	69.2
	2006	3.6	3.2	6.8	136.6
	2007	3.5	0.9	4.5	88.3
Saint Lucia Sainte-Lucie	2003	4.8	10.0	14.8	91.3
	2004	-23.7	2.3	-21.4	-130.8
	2005	6.5	4.5	11.0	66.3
	2006	2.4	14.2	16.7	99.9
	2007	7.4	9.1	16.6	98.1
Saint Vincent-Grenadines Saint Vincent-Grenadines	2003	3.7	2.6	6.3	58.0
	2004	7.3	3.8	11.1	102.0
	2005	5.7	-0.9	4.8	44.5
	2006	2.3	3.0	5.3	48.5
	2007	47.9	18.5	66.3	608.3
Samoa Samoa	2003	27.0	6.0	33.0	184.5
	2004	24.6	6.0	30.6	171.3
	2005	29.9	13.5	43.4	242.7
	2006	38.3	8.7	47.0	262.5
	2007	29.1	8.1	37.3	208.3
Sao Tome and Principe Sao Tomé-et-Principe	2003	25.5	12.2	37.6	254.9
	2004	21.7	11.7	33.4	222.2
	2005	18.4	14.0	32.4	212.3
	2006	18.3	3.3	21.5	138.7
	2007	31.1	4.9	36.0	228.2
Saudi Arabia Arabie saoudite	2003	9.9	1.7	11.6	0.5
	2004	8.5	1.7	10.2	0.4

73

Disbursements of bilateral and multilateral official development assistance and official aid to individual recipients *(continued)*
Versements d'aide publique au développement et d'aide publique bilatérale et multilatérale aux bénéficiaires *(suite)*

| Country or area
Pays ou zone | Year
Année | Net disbursements (US $) - Versements nets ($E.-U.) ||||
		Bilateral Bilatérale (millions)	Multilateral[1] Multilatérale[1] (millions)	Total (millions)	Per capita Par habitant
	2005	13.0	2.0	15.1	0.6
	2006	11.2	2.8	13.9	0.6
	2007	-144.1	0.5	-143.6	-5.8
Senegal Sénégal	2003	314.4	142.8	457.3	42.7
	2004	755.5	299.1	1 054.6	96.0
	2005	443.8	242.6	686.4	60.8
	2006	509.1	305.3	814.4	70.3
	2007	450.9	374.1	825.0	69.4
Serbia Serbie	2003	853.0	444.2	1 297.2	121.2
	2004	583.7	564.6	1 148.3	104.5
	2005	766.3	280.6	1 046.9	92.8
	2006	1 169.2	407.8	1 577.1	136.2
	2007	476.1	345.9	822.0	69.1
Seychelles Seychelles	2003	4.9	3.2	8.1	98.7
	2004	6.1	2.9	9.0	109.7
	2005	7.9	6.9	14.8	179.1
	2006	7.1	7.5	14.0	176.3
	2007	1.4	1.9	3.4	40.2
Sierra Leone Sierra Leone	2003	208.3	125.3	333.6	70.5
	2004	162.6	212.4	375.1	76.1
	2005	129.2	219.9	349.1	68.3
	2006	179.5	163.7	343.3	65.1
	2007	380.7	154.3	535.1	98.7
Solomon Islands Iles Salomon	2003	56.5	3.7	60.1	133.6
	2004	116.8	4.5	121.3	262.7
	2005	172.3	25.9	198.2	418.3
	2006	178.9	25.5	204.4	420.6
	2007	236.5	12.0	248.6	498.9
Somalia Somalie	2003	113.6	60.1	173.7	21.8
	2004	139.7	58.3	198.0	24.3
	2005	145.0	92.7	237.7	28.4
	2006	263.1	125.8	388.9	45.5
	2007	256.7	123.8	380.5	43.6
South Africa Afrique du Sud	2003	477.3	163.2	640.5	13.7
	2004	459.2	168.3	627.5	13.2
	2005	465.9	213.9	679.8	14.1
	2006	560.6	159.2	719.8	14.8
	2007	597.2	196.2	793.4	16.1
Sri Lanka Sri Lanka	2003	271.0	388.5	659.5	34.4
	2004	337.2	162.0	499.1	25.8
	2005	824.9	282.2	1 107.1	56.7
	2006	485.2	268.7	753.9	38.3
	2007	297.9	263.9	561.8	28.3
Sudan Soudan	2003	332.0	277.8	609.8	16.4
	2004	847.9	118.7	966.6	25.5
	2005	1 454.8	319.7	1 774.4	45.9
	2006	1 518.1	447.0	1 965.2	49.7
	2007	1 666.1	324.1	1 990.2	49.2
Suriname Suriname	2003	4.0	6.8	10.9	22.3
	2004	15.8	8.1	23.9	48.3
	2005	33.5	10.4	43.9	87.8
	2006	55.6	8.2	63.7	126.1
	2007	123.6	27.0	150.6	295.0
Swaziland Swaziland	2003	12.7	20.3	33.0	29.8
	2004	7.3	14.4	21.6	19.4
	2005	20.9	26.3	47.3	42.0
	2006	12.3	23.1	35.3	31.1
	2007	12.1	38.9	51.0	44.3

73

Disbursements of bilateral and multilateral official development assistance and official aid to individual recipients *(continued)*

Versements d'aide publique au développement et d'aide publique bilatérale et multilatérale aux bénéficiaires *(suite)*

Country or area Pays ou zone	Year Année	Net disbursements (US $) - Versements nets ($E.-U.)			
		Bilateral Bilatérale (millions)	Multilateral[1] Multilatérale[1] (millions)	Total (millions)	Per capita Par habitant
Syrian Arab Republic Rép. arabe syrienne	2003	28.8	91.9	120.7	6.7
	2004	15.7	110.9	126.6	6.8
	2005	5.5	73.2	78.7	4.1
	2006	-11.4	63.1	51.7	2.6
	2007	9.1	102.4	111.5	5.4
Tajikistan Tadjikistan	2003	80.3	63.4	143.7	22.5
	2004	91.9	139.0	230.9	35.8
	2005	104.7	134.3	238.9	36.6
	2006	91.8	142.2	234.0	35.3
	2007	106.0	105.6	211.6	31.5
Thailand Thaïlande	2003	-969.3	24.1	-945.2	-14.6
	2004	-3.6	48.7	45.1	0.7
	2005	-214.3	41.0	-173.2	-2.6
	2006	-292.9	77.0	-215.9	-3.2
	2007	-396.2	81.5	-314.7	-4.7
TFYR of Macedonia L'ex-R.Y. Macédoine	2003	179.3	85.1	264.4	130.4
	2004	162.2	83.3	245.5	120.8
	2005	165.4	56.1	221.5	108.8
	2006	131.0	63.1	194.2	95.3
	2007	134.1	56.1	190.1	93.2
Timor-Leste Timor-Leste	2003	147.4	27.3	174.7	192.5
	2004	141.3	19.9	161.1	169.5
	2005	160.1	24.4	184.5	186.1
	2006	173.7	35.0	208.7	202.9
	2007	226.2	50.7	276.9	260.2
Togo Togo	2003	46.3	1.9	48.2	8.5
	2004	52.3	12.0	64.4	11.0
	2005	58.6	23.4	82.1	13.7
	2006	54.8	24.1	78.8	12.8
	2007	64.7	57.5	122.2	19.4
Tokelau Tokélaou	2003	6.2	0.2	6.4	4 801.8
	2004	8.4	0.1	8.4	6 669.3
	2005	15.9	0.1	16.0	13 174.0
	2006	10.7	0.2	10.9	9 215.9
	2007	12.6	0.3	12.9	10 914.5
Tonga Tonga	2003	15.0	10.8	25.8	256.9
	2004	14.9	4.3	19.2	189.5
	2005	24.7	7.0	31.7	311.2
	2006	18.6	2.8	21.4	209.1
	2007	26.5	4.2	30.7	297.8
Trinidad and Tobago Trinité-et-Tobago	2003	5.1	-8.2	-3.1	-2.4
	2004	7.2	-9.3	-2.0	-1.6
	2005	6.1	-8.1	-2.0	-1.5
	2006	4.0	9.3	13.3	10.1
	2007	6.9	13.8	20.7	15.6
Tunisia Tunisie	2003	207.7	94.8	302.5	31.2
	2004	230.8	95.2	326.0	33.3
	2005	268.7	103.3	371.9	37.7
	2006	287.0	154.4	441.4	44.3
	2007	193.9	139.5	333.4	33.1
Turkey Turquie	2003	19.5	145.9	165.4	2.4
	2004	-16.5	308.3	291.8	4.2
	2005	-8.9	410.2	401.3	5.6
	2006	147.1	401.0	548.2	7.6
	2007	237.5	560.4	797.9	10.9
Turkmenistan Turkménistan	2003	16.7	6.7	23.4	5.0
	2004	11.4	7.2	18.5	3.9
	2005	11.9	5.9	17.7	3.7

| Country or area
Pays ou zone | Year
Année | Net disbursements (US $) - Versements nets ($E.-U.) | | | |
		Bilateral Bilatérale (millions)	Multilateral[1] Multilatérale[1] (millions)	Total (millions)	Per capita Par habitant
	2006	5.4	6.1	11.4	2.3
	2007	1.4	8.6	9.9	2.0
Turks and Caicos Islands	2003	1.2	1.0	2.2	83.8
Iles Turques et Caïques	2004	1.2	1.9	3.2	110.1
	2005	3.1	2.1	5.2	170.3
	2006	0.1	-0.5	-0.4	-13.2
	2007	2.6	12.8	15.4	474.8
Tuvalu	2003	5.5	0.4	5.8	603.3
Tuvalu	2004	5.4	2.6	8.0	823.0
	2005	5.9	3.1	8.9	915.8
	2006	12.7	2.6	15.3	1 564.8
	2007	9.0	2.7	11.7	1 192.5
Uganda	2003	587.3	410.6	997.9	37.1
Ouganda	2004	683.9	532.0	1 215.8	43.8
	2005	690.6	502.2	1 192.8	41.6
	2006	938.2	607.9	1 546.1	52.1
	2007	1 002.5	720.5	1 723.0	58.2
Ukraine	2005	232.7	131.7	364.5	7.8
Ukraine	2006	280.6	171.0	451.6	9.7
	2007	244.3	141.0	385.2	8.3
United Rep. of Tanzania	2003	965.6	755.1	1 720.8	46.6
Rép.-Unie de Tanzanie	2004	1 028.7	733.6	1 762.3	46.4
	2005	858.3	618.9	1 477.2	37.9
	2006	991.7	832.2	1 823.9	45.5
	2007	1 830.7	972.6	2 803.2	67.9
Uruguay	2003	7.7	6.2	14.0	4.2
Uruguay	2004	9.9	11.6	21.5	6.5
	2005	2.8	11.3	14.1	4.2
	2006	10.8	9.7	20.5	6.1
	2007	19.9	13.4	33.3	10.0
Uzbekistan	2003	167.5	16.6	184.1	7.2
Ouzbékistan	2004	205.8	25.4	231.2	8.9
	2005	120.8	31.7	152.6	5.8
	2006	92.5	41.4	133.9	5.0
	2007	102.3	45.9	148.3	5.5
Vanuatu	2003	28.2	4.2	32.4	158.2
Vanuatu	2004	34.6	3.1	37.7	179.1
	2005	33.4	6.1	39.4	182.2
	2006	41.4	7.4	48.8	219.6
	2007	52.1	4.5	56.6	248.1
Venezuela (Bolivarian Rep. of)	2003	64.2	16.1	80.2	3.1
Venezuela (Rép. bolivarienne du)	2004	28.4	15.9	44.2	1.7
	2005	20.6	27.2	47.8	1.8
	2006	32.9	23.1	55.9	2.1
	2007	44.6	25.9	70.5	2.5
Viet Nam	2003	967.7	785.5	1 753.2	21.4
Viet Nam	2004	1 184.8	615.1	1 799.9	21.7
	2005	1 252.8	632.5	1 885.3	22.4
	2006	1 306.3	526.5	1 832.8	21.5
	2007	1 488.4	979.2	2 467.5	28.7
Wallis and Futuna Islands	2003	53.6	1.9	55.5	3 749.0
Iles Wallis et Futuna	2004	71.5	1.3	72.8	4 901.7
	2005	71.7	0.4	72.0	4 829.0
	2006	102.0	0.4	102.4	6 825.3
	2007	117.0	0.1	117.1	7 755.6
Yemen	2003	126.6	109.3	235.9	11.9
Yémen	2004	152.7	98.1	250.7	12.3
	2005	132.8	132.6	265.5	12.6

Disbursements of bilateral and multilateral official development assistance and official aid to individual recipients *(continued)*

Versements d'aide publique au développement et d'aide publique bilatérale et multilatérale aux bénéficiaires *(suite)*

Country or area Pays ou zone	Year Année	Net disbursements (US $) - Versements nets ($E.-U.)			
		Bilateral Bilatérale (millions)	Multilateral[1] Multilatérale[1] (millions)	Total (millions)	Per capita Par habitant
	2006	134.8	146.7	281.6	13.0
	2007	167.3	62.9	230.3	10.3
Zambia	2003	591.9	157.0	748.9	66.8
Zambie	2004	745.8	379.2	1 125.0	98.1
	2005	822.5	340.0	1 162.5	99.0
	2006	1 115.2	308.8	1 424.0	118.5
	2007	712.9	275.8	988.7	80.3
Zimbabwe	2003	160.7	25.3	186.0	14.9
Zimbabwe	2004	166.4	20.4	186.8	15.0
	2005	186.8	187.0	373.8	30.0
	2006	199.8	79.4	279.2	22.4
	2007	371.4	101.9	473.3	38.0

Source:
Organization for Economic Co-operation and Development (OECD), Paris, the OECD Development Assistance Committee database, last accessed September 2009. Per capita calculated by the United Nations Statistics Division from the World Population Prospects: The 2008 Revision, mid-year population data.

1 As reported by OECD/DAC, covers agencies of the United Nations family, the European Commission, IDA and the concessional lending facilities of regional development banks. Excluding non-concessional flows (i.e., less than 25% grant elements).

Source:
Organisation de coopération et de développement économiques (OCDE), Paris, la base de données du comité d'aide au développement de l'OCDE, dernier accès septembre 2009. Les données par habitant ont été calculées par la Division de statistiques de l'ONU de "World Population Prospects: The 2008 Revision," d'après les données de la population au milieu de l'année.

1 Communiqué par le Comité d'aide au développement de l'OCDE, comprend les institutions et organismes du système des Nations Unies, la commission européenne, l'Association internationale de développement, et les mécanismes de prêt à des conditions privilégiées des banques régionales de développement. Les apports aux conditions du marché (élément de libéralité inférieur à 25) en sont exclus.

74

Net official development assistance from DAC countries to developing countries and multilateral organizations

Net disbursements: millions of US dollars and as a percentage of gross national income (GNI)

Aide publique au développement nette des pays du CAD aux pays en développement et aux organisations multilatérales

Versements nets: millions de dollars E.-U. et en pourcentage du revenu national brut (RNB)

Country or area Pays ou zone	2003 $ millions	2003 % of GNI % du RNB	2004 $ millions	2004 % of GNI % du RNB	2005 $ millions	2005 % of GNI % du RNB	2006 $ millions	2006 % of GNI % du RNB	2007 $ millions	2007 % of GNI % du RNB	2008 $ millions	2008 % of GNI % du RNB
Total **Total**	**69 065**	**0.25**	**79 431**	**0.26**	**107 078**	**0.33**	**104 369**	**0.31**	**103 487**	**0.28**	**119 760**	**0.30**
Australia Australie	1 219	0.25	1 460	0.25	1 680	0.25	2 123	0.30	2 669	0.32	3 166	0.34
Austria Autriche	505	0.20	678	0.23	1 573	0.52	1 498	0.47	1 808	0.50	1 681	0.42
Belgium Belgique	1 853	0.60	1 463	0.41	1 963	0.53	1 978	0.50	1 953	0.43	2 381	0.47
Canada Canada	2 031	0.24	2 599	0.27	3 756	0.34	3 683	0.29	4 080	0.29	4 725	0.32
Denmark Danemark	1 748	0.84	2 037	0.85	2 109	0.81	2 236	0.80	2 562	0.81	2 800	0.82
Finland Finlande	558	0.35	680	0.37	902	0.46	834	0.40	981	0.39	1 139	0.43
France France	7 253	0.40	8 473	0.41	10 026	0.47	10 601	0.47	9 884	0.38	10 957	0.39
Germany Allemagne	6 784	0.28	7 534	0.28	10 082	0.36	10 435	0.36	12 291	0.37	13 910	0.38
Greece Grèce	362	0.21	321	0.16	384	0.17	424	0.17	501	0.16	693	0.20
Ireland Irlande	504	0.39	607	0.39	719	0.42	1 022	0.54	1 192	0.55	1 325	0.58
Italy Italie	2 433	0.17	2 462	0.15	5 091	0.29	3 641	0.20	3 971	0.19	4 444	0.20
Japan Japon	8 880	0.20	8 922	0.19	13 126	0.28	11 136	0.25	7 679	0.17	9 362	0.18
Luxembourg Luxembourg	194	0.86	236	0.79	256	0.79	291	0.90	376	0.91	409	0.92
Netherlands Pays-Bas	3 972	0.80	4 204	0.73	5 115	0.82	5 452	0.81	6 224	0.81	6 993	0.80
New Zealand Nouvelle-Zélande	165	0.23	212	0.23	274	0.27	259	0.27	320	0.27	346	0.30
Norway Norvège	2 042	0.92	2 199	0.87	2 786	0.94	2 954	0.89	3 728	0.95	3 967	0.88
Portugal Portugal	320	0.22	1 031	0.63	377	0.21	396	0.21	471	0.22	614	0.27
Spain Espagne	1 961	0.23	2 437	0.24	3 018	0.27	3 814	0.32	5 140	0.37	6 686	0.43
Sweden Suède	2 400	0.79	2 722	0.78	3 362	0.94	3 955	1.02	4 339	0.93	4 730	0.98
Switzerland Suisse	1 299	0.37	1 545	0.40	1 772	0.44	1 646	0.39	1 685	0.37	2 016	0.41
United Kingdom Royaume-Uni	6 262	0.34	7 905	0.36	10 772	0.47	12 459	0.51	9 849	0.35	11 409	0.43
United States Etats-Unis	16 320	0.15	19 705	0.17	27 935	0.23	23 532	0.18	21 787	0.16	26 008	0.18

Source:
Organisation for Economic Co-operation and Development (OECD), Paris, the OECD Development Assistance Committee database, last accessed August 2009

Source :
Organisation de coopération et de développement économiques (OCDE), Paris, la base de données du Comité d'aide au développement de l'OCDE, dernier accès août 2009.

Socio-economic development assistance through the United Nations system
Development grants: thousands of US dollars, 2007

Assistance en matière de développement socioéconomique fournie par le système des Nations Unies
Subventions au développement : en milliers de dollars des E.-U., 2007

Region, country or area Région, pays ou zone	UNDP[a] PNUD[a]	UNFPA FNUAP	UNHCR HCR	UNICEF[b]	WFP PAM	IFAD[c] FIDA[c]	Specialized agencies[d] Institutions spécialisées[d]	Other UN funds and programmes[e] Autres fonds et programmes des NU[e]	Total development grants Total subventions au développement
Total **Total**	**4 678 525**	**514 700**	**1 342 014**	**2 516 851**	**2 642 356**	**401 368**	**3 544 393**	**1 583 741**	**17 343 412**
Regional programmes **Totaux régionaux**	**427 077**	**26 200**	**0**	**159 249**	**5 512**	**0**	**1 480 677**	**385 084**	**2 587 917**
Africa [1] Afrique [1]	5 703	14 100	0	27 995	3 283	0	247 019	14 361	327 458
Americas Amériques	3 776	4 600	0	11 185	1 729	0	84 741	1 987	118 713
Asia and the Pacific Asie et le Pacifique	1 988	7 500	0	17 639	500	0	168 080	6 616	220 225
Europe Europe	17 975	0	0	5 420	0	0	106 108	2 219	141 566
Western Asia [1] Asie occidentale [1]	290	0	0	6 035	0	0	82 078	3 769	97 993
Global/Interregional Global/Interrégional	162 176	0	0	90 974	0	0	792 652	356 132	1 446 794
Other countries [2] Autres pays [2]	235 169	0	0	0	0	0	0	0	235 169
Not elsewhere classified [3] **Non-classé ailleurs [3]**	**818 108**	**121 000**	**277 319**	**0**	**143 792**	**0**	**403 998**	**226 555**	**1 990 772**
Total all countries **Total, tous pays**	**3 433 340**	**367 500**	**1 064 695**	**2 357 602**	**2 493 052**	**401 368**	**1 659 718**	**972 101**	**12 764 722**
Afghanistan Afghanistan	199 014	10 700	70 330	78 269	133 713	0	62 787	28 602	583 415
Albania Albanie	7 815	600	875	3 759	0	1 011	2 672	650	17 382
Algeria Algérie	2 913	300	6 697	1 716	13 285	0	3 497	864	29 272
Andorra Andorre	0	0	0	0	0	0	18	0	18
Angola Angola	22 604	2 600	12 073	51 688	4 544	643	17 427	1 111	112 690
Antigua and Barbuda Antigua-et-Barbuda	225	0	0	0	0	0	188	47	460
Argentina Argentine	215 583	600	2 737	3 170	0	3 951	40 455	551	267 584
Armenia Arménie	5 813	600	1 940	3 057	5 388	4 173	2 034	300	23 306
Aruba Aruba	0	0	0	0	0	0	5	0	5
Australia Australie	0	0	1 164	0	0	0	23	0	1 187
Austria Autriche	0	0	1 045	0	0	0	78	0	1 123
Azerbaijan Azerbaïdjan	13 074	900	3 586	2 568	7 836	3 564	1 141	62	32 731
Bahamas Bahamas	14	0	0	0	0	0	366	0	380
Bahrain Bahreïn	1 772	0	0	0	0	0	330	222	2 324
Bangladesh Bangladesh	51 737	7 800	3 998	56 432	77 571	13 023	28 232	3 500	242 293
Barbados Barbade	2 905	0	0	0	64	0	586	1 001	4 556
Belarus Bélarus	16 871	400	1 620	887	0	0	911	122	20 810
Belgium Belgique	0	0	3 380	66	0	0	0	0	3 446

75

Socio-economic development assistance through the United Nations system *(continued)*
Development grants: thousands of US dollars, 2007
Assistance en matière de développement socioéconomique fournie par le système des Nations Unies *(suite)*
Subventions au développement : en milliers de dollars des E.-U., 2007

Region, country or area Région, pays ou zone	UNDP[a] PNUD[a]	UNFPA FNUAP	UNHCR HCR	UNICEF[b]	WFP PAM	IFAD[c] FIDA[c]	Specialized agencies[d] Institutions spécialisées[d]	Other UN funds and programmes[e] Autres fonds et programmes des NU[e]	Total development grants Total subventions au développement
Belize Belize	745	0	0	1 225	145	0	356	90	2 560
Benin Bénin	4 944	2 000	1 774	15 059	2 864	2 844	4 714	309	34 508
Bhutan Bhoutan	3 558	1 100	0	2 835	3 711	1 413	2 243	269	15 129
Bolivia Bolivie	29 748	2 200	0	17 920	7 293	1 918	6 998	2 183	68 261
Bosnia and Herzegovina Bosnie-Herzégovine	19 823	400	7 803	3 222	0	3 340	1 848	196	36 632
Botswana Botswana	7 699	1 400	2 575	3 030	0	0	2 463	962	18 128
Brazil Brésil	192 245	1 500	3 073	15 052	0	4 370	147 129	20 966	385 025
Brunei Darussalam Brunéi Darussalam	0	0	0	0	0	0	43	0	43
Bulgaria Bulgarie	10 743	400	958	1 035	0	0	1 342	187	14 665
Burkina Faso Burkina Faso	10 056	5 100	0	18 434	10 892	6 660	7 830	1 462	60 433
Burundi Burundi	18 583	2 600	25 565	20 036	38 713	3 225	12 658	911	122 350
Cambodia Cambodge	35 912	3 300	1 071	21 215	15 512	4 451	17 504	2 865	114 663
Cameroon Cameroun	6 412	3 100	3 452	9 361	3 356	4 480	7 182	964	38 308
Canada Canada	0	0	1 674	0	0	0	116	0	1 790
Cape Verde Cap-Vert	4 651	1 000	0	856	789	927	2 317	767	11 306
Central African Rep. Rép. centrafricaine	19 805	2 800	4 180	17 717	25 019	0	6 866	987	77 374
Chad Tchad	14 800	2 900	82 378	34 872	72 312	2 752	16 976	6 886	233 876
Chile Chili	13 866	200	0	1 471	0	0	2 035	108	17 810
China Chine	50 657	4 100	4 046	26 826	0	34 640	31 727	4 313	156 310
China, Hong Kong SAR Chine, Hong Kong RAS	0	0	0	0	0	0	20	0	20
China, Macao SAR Chine, Macao RAS	0	0	0	0	0	0	38	0	38
Colombia Colombie	131 674	2 800	13 552	10 465	15 480	1 894	7 410	11 109	194 795
Comoros Comores	3 635	600	0	2 663	0	0	1 641	155	8 694
Congo Congo	7 234	1 800	6 953	8 264	2 648	2 989	7 043	807	37 739
Cook Islands Iles Cook	207	0	0	0	0	0	334	0	541
Costa Rica Costa Rica	3 432	500	1 996	710	0	0	1 532	271	8 440
Côte d'Ivoire Côte d'Ivoire	13 546	6 500	8 747	26 489	23 559	528	11 749	1 496	92 613
Croatia Croatie	8 986	0	3 499	1 126	0	0	1 240	164	15 015
Cuba Cuba	10 627	600	210	1 769	2 301	0	3 790	147	19 444
Cyprus Chypre	16 684	0	787	0	0	0	66	0	17 537
Czech Republic République tchèque	0	0	514	0	0	0	235	6	755
Dem. Rep. of the Congo Rép. dém. du Congo	78 512	13 900	47 849	136 130	76 394	826	60 206	725	414 542

75

Socio-economic development assistance through the United Nations system *(continued)*
Development grants: thousands of US dollars, 2007

Assistance en matière de développement socioéconomique fournie par le système des Nations Unies *(suite)*
Subventions au développement : en milliers de dollars des E.-U., 2007

Region, country or area Région, pays ou zone	UNDP[a] PNUD[a]	UNFPA FNUAP	UNHCR HCR	UNICEF[b]	WFP PAM	IFAD[c] FIDA[c]	Specialized agencies[d] Institutions spécialisées[d]	Other UN funds and programmes[e] Autres fonds et programmes des NU[e]	Total development grants Total subventions au développement
Djibouti Djibouti	1 118	800	3 154	6 869	4 613	478	3 327	6	20 366
Dominica Dominique	280	0	0	0	0	0	259	200	739
Dominican Republic Rép. dominicaine	10 323	1 000	0	2 479	569	1 067	2 827	562	18 833
Ecuador Equateur	16 816	1 100	5 216	4 804	1 034	1 000	4 050	273	34 301
Egypt Egypte	56 328	2 600	11 469	8 025	1 569	10 407	8 571	2 479	101 448
El Salvador El Salvador	17 006	1 400	0	2 087	2 734	5 431	3 835	406	32 900
Equatorial Guinea Guinée équatoriale	3 117	1 600	0	1 244	0	0	1 493	8	7 462
Eritrea Erythrée	14 091	1 900	3 910	17 801	999	4 795	6 009	1 152	50 657
Estonia Estonie	0	0	0	0	0	0	773	0	773
Ethiopia Ethiopie	19 686	11 900	25 351	98 548	166 863	12 838	40 665	3 618	379 468
Fiji Fidji	10 940	0	0	0	0	0	2 474	1 118	14 532
Finland Finlande	0	0	0	0	0	0	74	0	74
France France	0	0	2 747	0	0	0	539	0	3 286
French Guiana Guyane française	0	0	0	0	0	0	32	0	32
French Polynesia Polynésie française	0	0	0	0	0	0	45	0	45
Gabon Gabon	7 275	500	2 443	2 597	0	0	2 911	623	16 348
Gambia Gambie	2 896	700	419	3 202	2 815	1 659	2 267	356	14 315
Georgia Géorgie	8 582	1 500	5 434	3 006	4 381	648	1 322	516	25 389
Germany Allemagne	0	0	2 214	0	0	0	1 111	0	3 324
Ghana Ghana	14 671	2 700	9 188	23 309	4 430	5 052	6 149	1 229	66 726
Greece Grèce	0	0	1 196	0	0	0	706	0	1 902
Grenada Grenade	147	0	0	0	0	410	494	4	1 056
Guam Guam	0	0	0	0	0	0	12	0	12
Guatemala Guatemala	130 007	4 100	0	4 855	6 555	4 821	64 593	777	215 708
Guinea Guinée	6 985	1 500	9 339	13 741	11 928	3 437	7 558	1 168	55 655
Guinea-Bissau Guinée-Bissau	6 429	1 500	0	5 210	5 078	0	2 561	87	20 864
Guyana Guyana	1 597	0	0	1 692	0	1 715	1 818	836	7 658
Haiti Haïti	18 202	4 300	0	14 625	21 742	2 843	6 999	2 498	71 208
Honduras Honduras	60 867	1 900	0	3 077	5 722	7 834	4 266	982	84 649
Hungary Hongrie	0	0	2 258	0	0	0	452	0	2 711
India Inde	49 997	13 500	3 759	107 111	14 879	15 929	65 011	7 206	277 391
Indonesia Indonésie	82 765	5 800	2 105	119 794	42 047	5 978	52 941	6 382	317 813

75

Socio-economic development assistance through the United Nations system *(continued)*
Development grants: thousands of US dollars, 2007

Assistance en matière de développement socioéconomique fournie par le système des Nations Unies *(suite)*
Subventions au développement : en milliers de dollars des E.-U., 2007

Region, country or area Région, pays ou zone	UNDP[a] PNUD[a]	UNFPA FNUAP	UNHCR HCR	UNICEF[b]	WFP PAM	IFAD[c] FIDA[c]	Specialized agencies[d] Institutions spécialisées[d]	Other UN funds and programmes[e] Autres fonds et programmes des NU[e]	Total development grants Total subventions au développement
Iran (Islamic Rep. of) Iran (Rép. islamique d')	6 647	1 300	11 963	5 097	826	0	7 567	2 073	35 473
Iraq Iraq	64 930	2 300	30 779	40 866	12 012	0	55 420	9 317	215 624
Ireland Irlande	0	0	659	0	0	0	0	0	659
Israel Israël	0	0	362	0	0	0	218	0	580
Italy Italie	0	0	3 691	0	0	0	1 328	0	5 019
Jamaica Jamaïque	2 514	0	0	1 834	32	0	1 764	1 368	7 511
Japan Japon	0	0	2 652	0	0	0	2 405	1 072	6 130
Jordan Jordanie	11 822	700	40 541	3 060	516	2 029	3 198	112 173	174 038
Kazakhstan Kazakhstan	8 891	600	2 550	2 506	0	0	1 130	554	16 230
Kenya Kenya	32 197	3 100	53 616	33 068	190 298	6 774	22 771	3 093	344 924
Kiribati Kiribati	0	0	0	0	0	0	895	0	895
Korea, Dem. P. R. Corée, R. p. dém. de	534	1 900	0	18 086	33 699	448	20 671	56	75 394
Korea, Republic of Corée, République de	5 737	0	785	0	0	0	1 649	202	8 456
Kosovo Kosovo	0	1 000	0	3 216	0	0	155	1 242	5 613
Kuwait Koweït	3 993	0	0	0	0	0	184	19	4 196
Kyrgyzstan Kirghizistan	15 532	600	1 424	2 363	0	408	2 074	1 642	24 043
Lao People's Dem. Rep. Rép. dém. pop. lao	12 323	1 500	0	11 033	7 321	4 984	9 931	1 806	49 094
Latvia Lettonie	1 376	0	0	0	0	0	300	0	1 676
Lebanon Liban	23 285	1 800	11 594	15 424	1 709	0	7 647	87 124	148 584
Lesotho Lesotho	4 887	1 300	0	6 837	11 533	3 645	5 522	850	34 574
Liberia Libéria	47 363	4 900	40 626	21 623	34 623	0	10 368	180	159 682
Libyan Arab Jamah. Jamah. arabe libyenne	4 721	0	886	0	503	0	4 047	1 638	11 795
Lithuania Lituanie	1 355	0	0	0	0	0	2 360	2	3 717
Madagascar Madagascar	8 828	3 200	0	26 416	13 891	3 276	9 732	1 403	66 835
Malawi Malawi	19 775	2 800	3 120	33 926	43 212	3 206	7 527	1 382	114 948
Malaysia Malaisie	6 878	600	4 292	2 083	0	0	1 710	658	16 221
Maldives Maldives	8 148	600	0	15 388	0	0	2 164	271	26 571
Mali Mali	18 197	2 900	0	24 010	11 905	5 029	7 288	1 549	70 878
Malta Malte	0	0	50	0	0	0	316	0	365
Marshall Islands Iles Marshall	0	0	0	0	0	0	307	0	307
Mauritania Mauritanie	10 275	2 300	5 337	7 035	19 212	6 938	4 662	378	56 136
Mauritius Maurice	4 922	100	0	-3	0	345	1 613	845	7 822

Socio-economic development assistance through the United Nations system *(continued)*
Development grants: thousands of US dollars, 2007

Assistance en matière de développement socioéconomique fournie par le système des Nations Unies *(suite)*
Subventions au développement : en milliers de dollars des E.-U., 2007

Region, country or area Région, pays ou zone	UNDP[a] PNUD[a]	UNFPA FNUAP	UNHCR HCR	UNICEF[b]	WFP PAM	IFAD[c] FIDA[c]	Specialized agencies[d] Institutions spécialisées[d]	Other UN funds and programmes[e] Autres fonds et programmes des NU[e]	Total development grants Total subventions au développement
Mexico Mexique	16 212	2 100	2 268	4 925	112	1 369	10 704	1 150	38 859
Micronesia (Fed. States of) Micronésie (Etats féd. de)	0	0	0	0	0	0	310	0	310
Mongolia Mongolie	4 909	3 200	222	3 343	0	2 709	5 086	430	19 899
Montenegro Monténégro	3 525	0	2 520	1 097	0	0	784	0	7 925
Montserrat Montserrat	49	0	0	0	0	0	0	0	49
Morocco Maroc	14 375	2 300	1 376	7 518	0	0	8 766	712	35 046
Mozambique Mozambique	16 935	27 000	2 749	44 091	37 553	7 432	13 979	2 609	152 347
Myanmar Myanmar	18 160	3 900	6 442	39 007	11 307	0	17 218	2 790	98 822
Namibia Namibie	6 522	2 000	2 967	3 783	6 369	0	3 051	1 039	25 731
Nauru Nauru	0	0	0	0	0	0	184	0	184
Nepal Népal	24 782	5 000	9 134	22 455	37 318	1 532	14 249	1 256	115 726
Netherlands Antilles Antilles néerlandaises	0	0	0	0	0	0	16	-3	13
New Caledonia Nouvelle-Calédonie	0	0	0	0	0	0	0	82	82
Nicaragua Nicaragua	24 596	4 200	0	7 064	7 597	3 140	5 482	566	52 645
Niger Niger	19 182	4 000	0	38 821	22 666	2 173	15 883	313	103 038
Nigeria Nigéria	48 977	9 800	3 380	94 771	0	7 063	57 549	13 497	235 037
Niue Nioué	471	0	0	0	0	0	80	25	576
Norway Norvège	0	0	0	0	0	0	57	0	57
Occupied Palestinian Terr. Terr. palestinien occupé	0	5 500	0	26 326	69 993	1 188	24 552	463 410	591 000
Oman Oman	0	800	0	615	0	0	1 482	0	2 897
Pakistan Pakistan	48 573	9 000	22 741	101 645	29 727	16 657	58 386	10 748	297 492
Palau Palaos	0	0	0	0	0	0	161	0	161
Panama Panama	233 564	700	1 041	914	34	4 821	14 412	2 030	257 521
Papua New Guinea Papouasie-Nvl-Guinée	3 995	1 900	404	6 471	0	0	5 707	867	19 344
Paraguay Paraguay	32 954	900	0	1 954	0	311	1 150	61	37 329
Peru Pérou	88 135	12 900	0	7 716	6 289	5 955	8 198	4 606	133 800
Philippines Philippines	14 996	5 600	193	16 710	11 588	4 884	11 539	1 533	67 044
Poland Pologne	10 536	0	961	0	0	0	1 042	494	13 034
Portugal Portugal	0	0	59	0	0	0	575	0	634
Puerto Rico Porto Rico	0	0	0	0	0	0	0	46	46
Qatar Qatar	0	0	0	0	0	0	910	535	1 445
Republic of Moldova République de Moldova	11 646	500	652	5 098	0	6 246	1 438	498	26 079

75

Socio-economic development assistance through the United Nations system *(continued)*
Development grants: thousands of US dollars, 2007

Assistance en matière de développement socioéconomique fournie par le système des Nations Unies *(suite)*
Subventions au développement : en milliers de dollars des E.-U., 2007

Region, country or area Région, pays ou zone	UNDP[a] PNUD[a]	UNFPA FNUAP	UNHCR HCR	UNICEF[b]	WFP PAM	IFAD[c] FIDA[c]	Specialized agencies[d] Institutions spécialisées[d]	Other UN funds and programmes[e] Autres fonds et programmes des NU[e]	Total development grants Total subventions au développement
Romania Roumanie	6 000	700	1 069	3 137	0	1 324	4 189	1 386	17 805
Russian Federation Fédération de Russie	12 862	700	14 118	14 162	6 334	0	13 762	5 673	67 612
Rwanda Rwanda	20 970	2 400	6 661	14 492	15 505	9 757	4 960	1 334	76 079
Saint Helena Sainte-Hélène	0	0	0	0	0	0	115	0	115
Saint Kitts and Nevis Saint-Kitts-et-Nevis	16	0	0	0	0	0	329	7	352
Saint Lucia Sainte-Lucie	210	0	0	0	0	0	236	132	578
Saint Vincent-Grenadines Saint Vincent-Grenadines	243	0	0	0	0	0	257	108	608
Samoa Samoa	1 878	0	0	0	0	0	1 484	163	3 525
Sao Tome and Principe Sao Tomé-et-Principe	2 162	400	0	1 082	956	900	1 174	163	6 837
Saudi Arabia Arabie saoudite	10 935	0	2 162	1 378	0	0	16 364	0	30 839
Senegal Sénégal	13 795	2 700	6 574	10 280	6 418	6 972	7 744	3 679	58 163
Serbia Serbie	20 589	200	23 614	2 007	0	0	4 045	6 586	57 040
Seychelles Seychelles	0	0	0	0	0	0	1 049	53	1 102
Sierra Leone Sierra Leone	38 012	2 700	9 803	19 107	12 350	631	5 577	845	89 023
Singapore Singapour	0	0	47	0	0	0	179	23	249
Slovakia Slovaquie	0	0	512	0	0	0	473	60	1 045
Slovenia Slovénie	0	0	193	0	0	0	338	0	531
Solomon Islands Iles Salomon	26	0	0	0	0	0	1 938	6	1 970
Somalia Somalie	56 781	4 200	12 577	62 727	67 678	0	36 104	3 191	243 258
South Africa Afrique du Sud	4 065	1 300	6 812	8 306	893	0	7 435	4 695	33 506
Spain Espagne	0	0	1 276	0	0	0	534	0	1 811
Sri Lanka Sri Lanka	19 609	3 500	20 642	49 827	42 776	4 703	18 374	6 042	165 473
Sudan Soudan	158 278	21 600	75 580	182 534	565 233	6 403	80 726	2 757	1 093 110
Suriname Suriname	0	0	0	0	0	0	458	39	497
Swaziland Swaziland	1 123	900	0	6 954	11 155	1 880	4 729	34	26 776
Sweden Suède	0	0	2 075	0	0	0	877	0	2 952
Switzerland Suisse	0	0	662	2 129	0	0	75	0	2 866
Syrian Arab Republic Rép. arabe syrienne	6 448	2 700	55 390	4 203	6 412	6 008	6 820	42 885	130 865
Tajikistan Tadjikistan	18 374	700	938	4 868	7 780	0	5 280	2 653	40 593
Thailand Thaïlande	11 282	1 200	14 540	15 123	0	0	7 262	3 853	53 260
TFYR of Macedonia L'ex-R.Y. Macédoine	5 118	0	3 250	2 037	0	968	1 112	24	12 509
Timor-Leste Timor-Leste	27 224	2 000	938	8 959	8 576	0	4 514	123	52 333

Socio-economic development assistance through the United Nations system *(continued)*
Development grants: thousands of US dollars, 2007

Assistance en matière de développement socioéconomique fournie par le système des Nations Unies *(suite)*
Subventions au développement : en milliers de dollars des E.-U., 2007

Region, country or area Région, pays ou zone	UNDP[a] PNUD[a]	UNFPA FNUAP	UNHCR HCR	UNICEF[b]	WFP PAM	IFAD[c] FIDA[c]	Specialized agencies[d] Institutions spécialisées[d]	Other UN funds and programmes[e] Autres fonds et programmes des NU[e]	Total development grants Total subventions au développement
Togo Togo	31 296	1 200	200	7 887	1 896	0	4 086	426	46 991
Tokelau Tokélaou	287	0	0	0	0	0	49	0	336
Tonga Tonga	0	0	0	0	0	0	1 017	0	1 017
Trinidad and Tobago Trinité-et-Tobago	4 849	0	0	0	0	0	1 066	877	6 792
Tunisia Tunisie	2 043	300	377	1 042	0	6 026	3 238	371	13 396
Turkey Turquie	21 411	3 300	7 832	6 756	0	3 118	7 681	103	50 201
Turkmenistan Turkménistan	2 614	800	729	2 818	0	0	193	1 222	8 375
Turks and Caicos Islands Iles Turques et Caïques	0	0	0	0	0	0	5	0	5
Tuvalu Tuvalu	0	0	0	0	0	0	203	0	273
Uganda Ouganda	12 960	5 800	32 402	61 714	112 907	12 113	20 527	1 602	260 025
Ukraine Ukraine	25 648	3 000	3 112	9 053	0	0	4 696	944	46 452
United Arab Emirates Emirats arabes unis	3 058	0	590	0	0	0	361	165	4 175
United Kingdom Royaume-Uni	0	0	1 683	0	0	0	41	0	1 724
United Rep. of Tanzania Rép.-Unie de Tanzanie	18 938	3 600	37 033	21 363	39 687	16 738	16 745	1 444	155 547
United States Etats-Unis	0	0	3 781	0	0	0	736	0	4 517
Uruguay Uruguay	13 815	1 300	0	1 145	0	1 891	3 417	147	21 777
Uzbekistan Ouzbékistan	14 546	900	164	9 655	0	0	1 578	855	27 698
Vanuatu Vanuatu	0	0	0	0	0	0	1 946	11	1 956
Venezuela (Boliv. Rep. of) Venezuela (Rép. boliv. du)	28 951	1 800	3 663	2 526	0	8 735	3 129	487	49 291
Viet Nam Viet Nam	12 681	5 200	220	13 616	0	10 326	15 900	2 726	60 761
Yemen Yémen	10 604	1 400	6 560	9 760	6 532	6 771	10 123	192	51 942
Zambia Zambie	6 521	2 300	10 731	15 088	18 859	3 578	8 944	3 461	69 481
Zimbabwe Zimbabwe	4 648	4 900	1 851	30 212	97 913	0	9 834	1 540	150 899

Source:
United Nations, *Comprehensive statistical analysis of the financing of operational activities for development of the United Nations system for 2007, Report of the Secretary-General* (A/64/75).

The following abbreviations have been used in the table:
IFAD: International Fund for Agricultural Development
UNDP: United Nations Development Programme
UNFPA: United Nations Population Fund
UNHCR: United Nations High Commissioner for Refugees
UNICEF: United Nations Children's Fund
WFP: World Food Programme

Source:
Nations Unies, *Analyse statistique globale du financement des activités opérationnelles de développement du système des Nations Unies pour 2007, Rapport du Secrétaire général* (A/64/75).

Les abréviations ci-après ont été utilisées dans le tableau :
FIDA : Fonds international de développement agricole
PNUD : Programme des Nations Unies pour le développement
FNUAP : Fonds des Nations Unies pour la population
HCR : Haut Commissariat des Nations Unies
UNICEF : Fonds des Nations Unies pour l'enfance
PAM : Programme alimentaire mondial

75

Socio-economic development assistance through the United Nations system *(continued)*
Development grants: thousands of US dollars, 2007

Assistance en matière de développement socioéconomique fournie par le système des Nations Unies *(suite)*
Subventions au développement : en milliers de dollars des E.-U., 2007

[a] Total of central resources and UNDP-administered funds.
[b] Includes programme assistance less UNDP-financed expenditures.
[c] Loan disbursements.
[d] Expenditures by FAO, IAEA, ICAO, ILO, IMO, ITU, UNESCO, UNIDO, UPU, WIPO, WHO, WMO and the World Tourism Organization.
[e] Expenditures by ITC, UNAIDS, UNCTAD, UNEP, UN-Habitat, UNODC, UNRWA, the Office for the Coordination of Humanitarian Affairs and the Peacebuilding Support Office.

[a] Y compris ressources centrales et fonds gérés.
[b] Comprend l'aide aux programmes moins les dépenses financées par le PNUD.
[c] Versements au titre de prêts.
[d] Dépenses engagées par la FAO, l'AIEA, l'OACI, l'OIT, l'OMI, l'UIT, l'UNESCO, l'ONUDI, l'UPU, l'OMPI, l'OMS, l'OMM et l'Organisation mondiale du tourisme.
[e] Dépenses engagées par le CCI, ONUSIDA, la CNUCED, le PNUE, ONU/Habitat, UNODC, l'UNRWA, le Bureau de la coordination des affaires humanitaires et le Bureau d'appui à la consolidation de la paix.

1 Due to a different regional classification, some regional expenditures in Northern Africa may be reported under Western Asia.

2 Regional expenditures reported with no further breakdown.
3 Expenditures reported with no further breakdown.

1 En raison de différences de classification régionale, il se peut que certaines dépenses régionales relatives à l'Afrique du Nord soient incorporées au total pour l'Asie occidentale.

2 Dépenses régionales non détaillées dans le rapport.
3 Dépenses communiquées sans autre ventilation.

Technical notes: tables 73-75

Table 73 presents estimates of flows of financial resources to individual recipients either directly (bilaterally) or through multilateral institutions (multilaterally).

The multilateral institutions include the World Bank Group, regional banks, financial institutions of the European Union and a number of United Nations institutions, programmes and trust funds.

The source of data is the Development Assistance Committee of OECD to which member countries reported data on their flow of resources to developing countries and territories, countries and territories in transition, and multilateral institutions.

Additional information on definitions, methods and sources can be found in OECD's *Geographical Distribution of Financial Flows to Aid Recipients* and www.oecd.org.

Table 74 presents the development assistance expenditures of donor countries. This table includes donors' contributions to multilateral agencies; therefore, the overall totals differ from those in table 73, which include disbursements by multilateral agencies.

Table 75 includes data on expenditures on operational activities for development undertaken by the organizations of the United Nations system. Operational activities encompass, in general, those activities of a development cooperation character that seek to mobilize or increase the potential and capacity of countries to promote economic and social development and welfare, including the transfer of resources to developing countries or regions in a tangible or intangible form.

Expenditures on operational activities for development are financed from contributions from governments and other official and non-official sources to a variety of funding channels in the United Nations system. These include United Nations funds and programmes such as contributions to the United Nations Development Programme, contributions to funds administered by the United Nations Development Programme, and regular (assessed) and other extra budgetary contributions to specialized agencies.

Data are taken from the latest report of the Secretary-General to the General Assembly on operational activities for development.

Notes techniques : tableaux 73 à 75

Le *tableau 73* présente les estimations des flux de ressources financières mises à la disposition des pays soit directement (aide bilatérale) soit par l'intermédiaire d'institutions multilatérales (aide multilatérale).

Les institutions multilatérales comprennent le Groupe de la Banque mondiale, les banques régionales, les institutions financières de l'Union européenne et un certain nombre d'institutions, de programmes et de fonds d'affectation spéciale des Nations Unies.

La source de données est le Comité d'aide au développement de l'OCDE, auquel les pays membres ont communiqué des données sur les flux de ressources qu'ils mettent à la disposition des pays et territoires en développement et en transition et des institutions multilatérales.

Pour plus de renseignements sur les définitions, méthodes et sources, se reporter à la publication de l'OCDE, *la Répartition géographique des ressources financières de aux pays bénéficiaires de l'Aide* et www.oecd.org.

Le *tableau 74* présente les dépenses que les pays donateurs consacrent à l'aide publique au développement (APD). Ces chiffres incluent les contributions des donateurs à des agences multilatérales, de sorte que les totaux diffèrent de ceux du tableau 73, qui incluent les dépenses des agences multilatérales.

Le *tableau 75* présente des données sur les dépenses consacrées à des activités opérationnelles pour le développement par les organisations du système des Nations Unies. Par "activités opérationnelles", on entend en général les activités ayant trait à la coopération au développement, qui visent à mobiliser ou à accroître les potentialités et aptitudes que présentent les pays pour promouvoir le développement et le bien-être économiques et sociaux, y compris les transferts de ressources vers les pays ou régions en développement sous forme tangible ou non.

Les dépenses consacrées aux activités opérationnelles pour le développement sont financées au moyen de contributions que les gouvernements et d'autres sources officielles et non officielles apportent à divers organes de financement, tels que fonds et programmes du système des Nations Unies. On peut citer notamment les contributions au Programme des Nations Unies pour le développement, les contributions aux fonds gérés par le Programme des Nations Unies pour le développement, les contributions régulières (budgétaires) et les contributions extrabudgétaires aux institutions spécialisées.

Les données sont extraites du dernier rapport annuel du Secrétaire général à la session de l'Assemblée générale sur les activités opérationnelles pour le développement.

Annex I

Country and area nomenclature, regional and other groupings

A. Changes in country or area names

In the periods covered by the statistics in the *Statistical Yearbook*, the following changes in designation have taken place:

Brunei Darussalam was formerly listed as Brunei;

Burkina Faso was formerly listed as Upper Volta;

Cambodia was formerly listed as Democratic Kampuchea;

Cameroon was formerly listed as United Republic of Cameroon;

Côte d'Ivoire was formerly listed as Ivory Coast;

Czech Republic, Slovakia: Since 1 January 1993, data for the Czech Republic and Slovakia, where available, are shown separately under the appropriate country name. For periods prior to 1 January 1993, where no separate data are available for the Czech Republic and Slovakia, unless otherwise indicated, data for the former Czechoslovakia are shown under the country name "former Czechoslovakia";

Democratic Republic of the Congo was formerly listed as Zaire;

Germany: Through the accession of the German Democratic Republic to the Federal Republic of Germany with effect from 3 October 1990, the two German States have united to form one sovereign State. As from the date of unification, the Federal Republic of Germany acts in the United Nations under the designation "Germany". All data shown which pertain to Germany prior to 3 October 1990 are indicated separately for the Federal Republic of Germany and the former German Democratic Republic based on their respective territories at the time indicated;

Hong Kong Special Administrative Region of China: Pursuant to a Joint Declaration signed on 19 December 1984, the United Kingdom restored Hong Kong to the People's Republic of China with effect from 1 July 1997; the People's Republic of China resumed the exercise of sovereignty over the territory with effect from that date;

Macao Special Administrative Region of China: Pursuant to the joint declaration signed on 13 April 1987, Portugal restored Macao to the People's Republic of China with effect from 20 December 1999; the People's Republic of China resumed the exercise of sovereignty over the territory with effect from that date;

Myanmar was formerly listed as Burma;

Palau was formerly listed as Pacific Islands and includes data for Federated States of Micronesia, Marshall Islands and Northern Mariana Islands;

Saint Kitts and Nevis was formerly listed as Saint Christopher and Nevis;

Serbia, Montenegro: As of 1992, data provided for Yugoslavia refer to the Federal Republic of Yugoslavia which was composed of the two republics of Serbia and Montenegro. On 4 February 2003, the official name of the

Annexe I

Nomenclature des pays ou zones, groupements régionaux et autres groupements

A. Changements dans le nom des pays ou zones

Au cours des périodes sur lesquelles portent les statistiques, dans l'*Annuaire Statistique* les changements de désignation suivants ont eu lieu:

Le *Brunei Darussalam* apparaissait antérieurement sous le nom de Brunei;

Le *Burkina Faso* apparaissait antérieurement sous le nom de la Haute-Volta;

Le *Cambodge* apparaissait antérieurement sous le nom de la Kampuchéa démocratique;

Le *Cameroun* apparaissait antérieurement sous le nom de République-Unie du Cameroun;

République tchèque, Slovaquie: Depuis le 1er janvier 1993, les données relatives à la République tchèque, et à la Slovaquie, lorsqu'elles sont disponibles, sont présentées séparément sous le nom de chacun des pays. En ce qui concerne la période précédant le 1er janvier 1993, pour laquelle on ne possède pas de données séparées pour les deux Républiques, les données relatives à l'ex-Tchécoslovaquie sont, sauf indication contraire, présentées sous le titre "l'ex-Tchécoslovaquie";

La *République démocratique du Congo* apparaissait antérieurement sous le nom de Zaïre;

Allemagne: En vertu de l'adhésion de la République démocratique allemande à la République fédérale d'Allemagne, prenant effet le 3 octobre 1990, les deux Etats allemands se sont unis pour former un seul Etat souverain. A compter de la date de l'unification, la République fédérale d'Allemagne est désigné à l'ONU sous le nom d'"Allemagne". Toutes les données se rapportant à l'Allemagne avant le 3 octobre figurent dans deux rubriques séparées basées sur les territoires respectifs de la République fédérale d'Allemagne et l'ex-République démocratique allemande selon la période indiquée;

Hong Kong, région administrative spéciale de Chine: Conformément à une Déclaration commune signée le 19 décembre 1984, le Royaume-Uni a rétrocédé Hong Kong à la République populaire de Chine, avec effet au 1er juillet 1997; la souveraineté de la République populaire de Chine s'exerce à nouveau sur le territoire à compter de cette date;

Macao, région administrative spéciale de Chine: Conformément à une Déclaration commune signée le 13 avril 1987, le Portugal a rétrocédé Macao à la République populaire de Chine, avec effet au 20 décembre 1999; la souveraineté de la République populaire de Chine s'exerce à nouveau sur le territoire à compter de cette date;

Le *Myanmar* apparaissait antérieurement sous le nom de Birmanie;

Les *Palaos* apparaissait antérieurement sous le nom de Iles du Pacifique y compris les données pour les Etats fédérés de Micronésie, les îles Marshall et îles Mariannes du Nord;

Saint-Kitts-Et-Nevis apparaissait antérieurement sous le nom de Saint-Christophe-et-Nevis;

Serbie, Monténégro : Les données fournies pour la Yougoslavie à partir de 1992 se rapportent à la République fédérale de Yougoslavie, qui était composée des deux républiques de la Serbie et du Monténégro. Le 4 février 2003, la

"Federal Republic of Yugoslavia" was changed to "Serbia and Montenegro". On 3 June 2006, Serbia and Montenegro formally dissolved into two independent countries. When data are available separately for Montenegro and/or Serbia, they are shown under the respective heading.

Timor-Leste: Formerly East Timor;

Former *USSR*: In 1991, the Union of Soviet Socialist Republics formally dissolved into fifteen independent countries (Armenia, Azerbaijan, Belarus, Estonia, Georgia, Kazakhstan, Kyrgyzstan, Latvia, Lithuania, Republic of Moldova, Russian Federation, Tajikistan, Turkmenistan, Ukraine and Uzbekistan). Whenever possible, data are shown for the individual countries. Otherwise, data are shown for the former USSR;

Yemen: On 22 May 1990 Democratic Yemen and Yemen merged to form a single State. Since that date they have been represented as one Member with the name 'Yemen'.

It should be noted that unless otherwise indicated, for statistical purposes, the data for China exclude those for Hong Kong Special Administrative Region of China, Macao Special Administrative Region of China and Taiwan province of China.

B. Regional groupings

The scheme of regional groupings given below presents seven regions based mainly on continents. Five of the seven continental regions are further subdivided into 21 regions that are so drawn as to obtain greater homogeneity in sizes of population, demographic circumstances and accuracy of demographic statistics. This nomenclature is widely used in international statistics and is followed to the greatest extent possible in the present *Yearbook* in order to promote consistency and facilitate comparability and analysis. However, it is by no means universal in international statistical compilation, even at the level of continental regions, and variations in international statistical sources and methods dictate many unavoidable differences in particular fields in the present *Yearbook*. General differences are indicated in the footnotes to the classification presented below. More detailed differences are given in the footnotes and technical notes to individual tables.

Neither is there international standardization in the use of the terms "developed" and "developing" countries, areas or regions. These terms are used in the present publication to refer to regional groupings generally considered as "developed": these are Europe and the former USSR, the United States of America and Canada in Northern America, and Australia, Japan and New Zealand in Asia and Oceania. These designations are intended for statistical convenience and do not necessarily express a judgement about the stage reached by a particular country or area in the development process. Differences from this usage are indicated in the notes to individual tables.

"République fédérale de Yougoslavie", ayant changé de nom officiel, est devenu la "Serbie-et-Monténégro". Le 3 juin 2006, la Serbie-et-Monténégro s'est officiellement dissoute pour former deux États indépendants. Lorsque des données sont disponibles séparément pour la Serbie et le Monténégro, elles sont présentées dans leurs catégories respectives.

Timor-Leste: Ex Timor oriental;

L'ex-*URSS*: En 1991, l'Union des républiques socialistes soviétiques s'est séparé en 15 pays distincts (Arménie, Azerbaïdjan, Belarus, Estonie, Géorgie, Kazakhstan, Kirghizistan, Lettonie, Lituanie, République de Moldova, Fédération de Russie, Tadjikistan, Turkménistan, Ukraine, Ouzbékistan). Les données sont présentées pour ces pays pris séparément quand cela est possible. Autrement, les données sont présentées pour l'ex-URSS;

Yémen: Le Yémen et le Yémen démocratique ont fusionné le 22 mai 1990 pour ne plus former qu'un seul Etat, qui est depuis lors représenté comme tel à l'Organisation, sous le nom 'Yémen'.

Il convient de noter que sauf indication contraire, les données statistiques relatives à la Chine ne comprennent pas celles qui concernent la région administrative spéciale de Hong Kong, la région administrative spéciale de Macao et la province chinoise de Taiwan.

B. Groupements régionaux

Le système de groupements régionaux présenté ci-dessous comporte sept régions basées principalement sur les continents. Cinq des sept régions continentales sont elles-mêmes subdivisées, formant ainsi 21 régions délimitées de manière à obtenir une homogénéité accrue dans les effectifs de population, les situations démographiques et la précision des statistiques démographiques. Cette nomenclature est couramment utilisée aux fins des statistiques internationales et a été appliquée autant qu'il a été possible dans le présent *Annuaire* en vue de renforcer la cohérence et de faciliter la comparaison et l'analyse. Son utilisation pour l'établissement des statistiques internationales n'est cependant rien moins qu'universelle, même au niveau des régions continentales, et les variations que présentent les sources et méthodes statistiques internationales entraînent inévitablement de nombreuses différences dans certains domaines de cet *Annuaire*. Les différences d'ordre général sont indiquées dans les notes figurant au bas de la classification présentée ci-dessous. Les différences plus spécifiques sont mentionnées dans les notes techniques et notes de bas de page accompagnant les divers tableaux.

L'application des expressions "développés" et "en développement" aux pays, zones ou régions n'est pas non plus normalisée à l'échelle internationale. Ces expressions sont utilisées dans la présente publication en référence aux groupements régionaux généralement considérés comme "développés", à savoir l'Europe et l'ex-URSS, les Etats-Unis d'Amérique et le Canada en Amérique septentrionale, et l'Australie, le Japon et la Nouvelle-Zélande dans la région de l'Asie et du Pacifique. Ces appellations sont employées pour des raisons de commodité statistique et n'expriment pas nécessairement un jugement sur le stade de développement atteint par tel ou tel pays ou zone. Les cas différant de cet usage sont signalés dans les notes accompagnant les tableaux concernés.

Africa
Sub-Saharan Africa
Eastern Africa

Burundi
Comoros
Djibouti
Eritrea
Ethiopia
Kenya
Madagascar
Malawi
Mauritius
Mozambique

Réunion
Rwanda
Seychelles
Somalia
Uganda
United Republic of
   Tanzania
Zambia
Zimbabwe

Middle Africa

Angola
Cameroon
Central African Republic
Chad
Congo

Democratic Republic of the
   Congo
Equatorial Guinea
Gabon
Sao Tome and Principe

Southern Africa

Botswana
Lesotho
Namibia

South Africa
Swaziland

Western Africa

Benin
Burkina Faso
Cape Verde
Côte d'Ivoire
Gambia
Ghana
Guinea
Guinea-Bissau
Liberia

Mali
Mauritania
Niger
Nigeria
Saint Helena
Senegal
Sierra Leone
Togo

Northern Africa

Algeria
Egypt
Libyan Arab Jamahiriya
Morocco

Sudan
Tunisia
Western Sahara

Americas
Latin America and the Caribbean
Caribbean

Anguilla
Antigua and Barbuda
Aruba
Bahamas
Barbados
British Virgin Islands
Cayman Islands
Cuba
Dominica

Jamaica
Martinique
Montserrat
Netherlands Antilles
Puerto Rico
Saint Kitts and Nevis
Saint Lucia
Saint Vincent and the
   Grenadines

Afrique
Afrique subsaharienne
Afrique orientale

Burundi
Comores
Djibouti
Erythrée
Ethiopie
Kenya
Madagascar
Malawi
Maurice
Mozambique

Ouganda
République-Unie de
   Tanzanie
Réunion
Rwanda
Seychelles
Somalie
Zambie
Zimbabwe

Afrique centrale

Angola
Cameroun
Congo
Gabon
Guinée équatoriale

République centrafricaine
République démocratique
   du Congo
Sao Tomé-et-Principe
Tchad

Afrique australe

Afrique du Sud
Botswana
Lesotho

Namibie
Swaziland

Afrique occidentale

Bénin
Burkina Faso
Cap-Vert
Côte d'Ivoire
Gambie
Ghana
Guinée
Guinée-Bissau
Libéria

Mali
Mauritanie
Niger
Nigéria
Sainte-Hélène
Sénégal
Sierra Leone
Togo

Afrique septentrionale

Algérie
Egypte
Jamahiriya arabe libyenne
Maroc

Sahara occidental
Soudan
Tunisie

Amériques
Amérique latine et Caraïbes
Caraïbes

Anguilla
Antigua-et-Barbuda
Antilles néerlandaises
Aruba
Bahamas
Barbade
Cuba
Dominique
Grenade

Iles Turques et Caïques
Iles Vierges américaines
Iles Vierges britanniques
Jamaïque
Martinique
Montserrat
Porto Rico
République dominicaine
Sainte-Lucie

Dominican Republic	Trinidad and Tobago	Guadeloupe	Saint-Kitts-Et-Nevis
Grenada	Turks and Caicos Islands	Haïti	Saint-Vincent-et-les Grenadines
Guadeloupe	United States Virgin Islands	Iles Caïmans	Trinité-et-Tobago
Haiti			

Central America / Amérique centrale

Belize	Honduras	Belize	Honduras
Costa Rica	Mexico	Costa Rica	Mexique
El Salvador	Nicaragua	El Salvador	Nicaragua
Guatemala	Panama	Guatemala	Panama

South America / Amérique du Sud

Argentina	French Guiana	Argentine	Guyane française
Bolivia	Guyana	Bolivie	Iles Falkland (Malvinas)
Brazil	Paraguay	Brésil	Paraguay
Chile	Peru	Chili	Pérou
Colombia	Suriname	Colombie	Suriname
Ecuador	Uruguay	Equateur	Uruguay
Falkland Islands (Malvinas)	Venezuela	Guyana	Venezuela

Northern America [a] / Amérique septentrionale [a]

Bermuda	Saint Pierre and Miquelon	Bermudes	Groenland
Canada	United States of America	Canada	Saint-Pierre-et-Miquelon
Greenland		Etats-Unis d'Amérique	

Asia / Asie

Eastern Asia / Asie orientale

China	Democratic People's	Chine	Japon
China, Hong Kong Special	Republic of Korea	Chine, Hong Kong, région	Mongolie
Administrative Region	Japan	administrative spéciale	République de Corée
China, Macao Special	Mongolia	Chine, Macao, région	République populaire
Administrative Region	Republic of Korea	administrative spéciale	démocratique de Corée

South-central Asia / Asie centrale et du Sud

Afghanistan	Maldives	Afghanistan	Maldives
Bangladesh	Nepal	Bangladesh	Népal
Bhutan	Pakistan	Bhoutan	Ouzbékistan
India	Sri Lanka	Inde	Pakistan
Iran (Islamic Republic of)	Tajikistan	Iran (République islamique d')	Sri Lanka
Kazakhstan	Turkmenistan	Kazakhstan	Tadjikistan
Kyrgyzstan	Uzbekistan	Kirghizistan	Turkménistan

South-eastern Asia / Asie du Sud-est

Brunei Darussalam	Myanmar	Brunei Darussalam	République démocratique
Cambodia	Philippines	Cambodge	populaire lao
Indonesia	Singapore	Indonésie	Singapour
Lao People's Democratic	Thailand	Malaisie	Thaïlande
Republic	Timor-Leste	Myanmar	Timor-Leste
Malaysia	Viet Nam	Philippines	Viet Nam

Western Asia / Asie occidentale

Armenia	Occupied Palestinian	Arabie saoudite	Jordanie
Azerbaijan	Territory	Arménie	Koweït
Bahrain	Oman	Azerbaïdjan	Liban
Cyprus	Qatar	Bahreïn	Oman
Georgia	Saudi Arabia	Chypre	Qatar

Iraq	Syrian Arab Republic	Emirats arabes unis	République arabe syrienne
Israel	Turkey	Géorgie	Territoire palestinien occupé
Jordan	United Arab Emirates	Iraq	Turquie
Kuwait	Yemen	Israël	Yémen
Lebanon			

Europe

Eastern Europe

Belarus	Republic of Moldova
Bulgaria	Romania
Czech Republic	Russian Federation
Hungary	Slovakia
Poland	Ukraine

Northern Europe

Channel Islands	Latvia
Denmark	Lithuania
Estonia	Norway
Faeroe Islands	Svalbard and Jan Mayen
Finland	Islands
Iceland	Sweden
Ireland	United Kingdom
Isle of Man	

Southern Europe

Albania	Malta
Andorra	Portugal
Bosnia and Herzegovina	San Marino
Croatia	Serbia and Montenegro
Gibraltar	Slovenia
Greece	Spain
Holy See	The former Yugoslav
Italy	Republic of Macedonia

Western Europe

Austria	Luxembourg
Belgium	Monaco
France	Netherlands
Germany	Switzerland
Liechtenstein	

Oceania

Australia and New Zealand

Australia	Norfolk Island
New Zealand	

Melanesia

Fiji	Solomon Islands
New Caledonia	Vanuatu
Papua New Guinea	

Micronesia-Polynesia
Micronesia

Guam	Nauru
Kiribati	Northern Mariana Islands
Marshall Islands	Palau

Europe

Europe orientale

Bélarus	République de Moldova
Bulgarie	République tchèque
Fédération de Russie	Roumanie
Hongrie	Slovaquie
Pologne	Ukraine

Europe septentrionale

Danemark	Irlande
Estonie	Islande
Finlande	Lettonie
Ile de Man	Lituanie
Iles Anglo-Normandes	Norvège
Iles Féroé	Royaume-Uni
Iles Svalbard et Jan Mayen	Suède

Europe méridionale

Albanie	Grèce
Andorre	Italie
Bosnie-Herzégovine	Malte
Croatie	Portugal
Espagne	Saint-Marin
Ex-République yougoslave de	Saint-Siège
Macédoine	Serbie-et-Monténégro
Gibraltar	Slovénie

Europe occidentale

Allemagne	Luxembourg
Autriche	Monaco
Belgique	Pays-Bas
France	Suisse
Liechtenstein	

Océanie

Australie et Nouvelle-Zélande

Australie	Nouvelle-Zélande
Ile Norfolk	

Mélanésie

Fidji	Papouasie-Nouvelle-Guinée
Iles Salomon	Vanuatu
Nouvelle-Calédonie	

Micronésie-Polynésie
Micronésie

Guam	Kiribati
Iles Mariannes	Micronésie (Etats fédérés de)
septentrionales	Nauru

Micronesia (Federated States of)	Iles Marshall	Palaos

Polynesia		*Polynésie*	
American Samoa	Samoa	Iles Cook	Samoa
Cook Islands	Tokelau	Iles Wallis-Et-Futuna	Samoa américaines
French Polynesia	Tonga	Nioué	Tokélaou
Niue	Tuvalu	Pitcairn	Tonga
Pitcairn	Wallis and Futuna Islands	Polynésie française	Tuvalu

C. Other groupings

Following is a list of other groupings and their compositions presented in the *Yearbook*. These groupings are organized mainly around economic and trade interests in regional associations.

Andean Common Market (ANCOM)
    Bolivia
    Colombia
    Ecuador
    Peru
    Venezuela

Asia-Pacific Economic Cooperation (APEC)
    Australia
    Brunei Darussalam
    Canada
    Chile
    China
    China, Hong Kong Special Administrative Region
    Indonesia
    Japan
    Malaysia
    Mexico
    New Zealand
    Papua New Guinea
    Peru
    Philippines
    Republic of Korea
    Russian Federation
    Singapore
    Taiwan Province of China
    Thailand
    United States of America
    Viet Nam

Caribbean Community and Common Market (CARICOM)
    Antigua and Barbuda
    Bahamas (member of the Community only)
    Barbados
    Belize
    Dominica
    Grenada
    Guyana
    Haiti
    Jamaica
    Montserrat
    Saint Kitts and Nevis
    Saint Lucia

C. Autres groupements

On trouvera ci-après une liste des autres groupements et de leur composition, présentée dans l'*Annuaire*. Ces groupements correspondent essentiellement à des intérêts économiques et commerciaux d'après les associations régionales.

Marché commun andin (ANCOM)
    Bolivie
    Colombie
    Equateur
    Pérou
    Venezuela

Coopération économique Asie-Pacifique (CEAP)
    Australie
    Brunei Darussalam
    Canada
    Chili
    Chine
    Chine, Hong Kong, région administrative spéciale
    Etats-Unis d'Amérique
    Fédération de Russie
    Indonésie
    Japon
    Malaisie
    Mexique
    Nouvelle-Zélande
    Papouasie-Nouvelle-Guinée
    Pérou
    Philippines
    Province chinoise de Taiwan
    République de Corée
    Singapour
    Thaïlande
    Viet Nam

Communauté des Caraïbes et Marché commun des Caraïbes (CARICOM)
    Antigua-et-Barbuda
    Bahamas (membre de la communauté seulement)
    Barbade
    Belize
    Dominique
    Grenade
    Guyana
    Haïti
    Jamaïque
    Montserrat
    Sainte-Lucie

Saint Vincent and the Grenadines
Suriname
Trinidad and Tobago

Saint-Kitts-Et-Nevis
Saint-Vincent-et-les Grenadines
Suriname
Trinité-et-Tobago

Common Market for Eastern and Southern Africa
(COMESA)
    Angola
    Burundi
    Comoros
    Democratic Republic of the Congo
    Djibouti
    Egypt
    Eritrea
    Ethiopia
    Kenya
    Madagascar
    Malawi
    Mauritius
    Namibia
    Rwanda
    Seychelles
    Sudan
    Swaziland
    Uganda
    Zambia
    Zimbabwe

*Marché commun de l'Afrique de l'Est et de l'Afrique
australe* (COMESA)
    Angola
    Burundi
    Comores
    Djibouti
    Egypte
    Erythrée
    Ethiopie
    Kenya
    Madagascar
    Malawi
    Maurice
    Namibie
    Ouganda
    République démocratique du Congo
    Rwanda
    Seychelles
    Soudan
    Swaziland
    Zambie
    Zimbabwe

Commonwealth of Independent States (CIS)
    Armenia
    Azerbaijan
    Belarus
    Georgia
    Kazakhstan
    Kyrgyzstan
    Republic of Moldova
    Russian Federation
    Tajikistan
    Turkmenistan
    Ukraine
    Uzbekistan

Communauté d'Etats indépendants (CEI)
    Arménie
    Azerbaïdjan
    Belarus
    Fédération de Russie
    Géorgie
    Kazakhstan
    Kirghizistan
    Ouzbékistan
    République de Moldova
    Tadjikistan
    Turkménistan
    Ukraine

European Union (EU)
    Austria
    Belgium
    Bulgaria
    Cyprus
    Czech Republic
    Denmark
    Estonia
    Finland
    France
    Germany
    Greece
    Hungary
    Ireland
    Italy
    Latvia
    Lithuania
    Luxembourg

Union européenne (UE)
    Allemagne
    Autriche
    Belgique
    Bulgarie
    Chypre
    Danemark
    Espagne
    Estonie
    Finlande
    France
    Grèce
    Hongrie
    Irlande
    Italie
    Lettonie
    Lituanie
    Luxembourg

Malta	Malte
Netherlands	Pays-Bas
Poland	Pologne
Portugal	Portugal
Romania	République tchèque
Slovakia	Roumanie
Slovenia	Royaume-Uni
Spain	Slovaquie
Sweden	Slovénie
United Kingdom	Suède

Least developed countries (LDCs)	*Pays les moins avancés* (PMA)
Afghanistan	Afghanistan
Angola	Angola
Bangladesh	Bangladesh
Benin	Bénin
Bhutan	Bhoutan
Burkina Faso	Burkina Faso
Burundi	Burundi
Cambodia	Cambodge
Central African Republic	Comores
Chad	Djibouti
Comoros	Erythrée
Democratic Republic of the Congo	Ethiopie
Djibouti	Gambie
Equatorial Guinea	Guinée
Eritrea	Guinée équatoriale
Ethiopia	Guinée-Bissau
Gambia	Haïti
Guinea	Iles Salomon
Guinea-Bissau	Kiribati
Haiti	Lesotho
Kiribati	Libéria
Lao People's Democratic Republic	Madagascar
Lesotho	Malawi
Liberia	Maldives
Madagascar	Mali
Malawi	Mauritanie
Maldives	Mozambique
Mali	Myanmar
Mauritania	Népal
Mozambique	Niger
Myanmar	Ouganda
Nepal	République centrafricaine
Niger	République démocratique du Congo
Rwanda	République démocratique populaire lao
Samoa	République-Unie de Tanzanie
Sao Tome and Principe	Rwanda
Senegal	Samoa
Sierra Leone	Sao Tomé-et-Principe
Solomon Islands	Sénégal
Somalia	Sierra Leone
Sudan	Somalie
Timor-Leste	Soudan
Togo	Tchad
Tuvalu	Timor-Leste
Uganda	Togo
United Republic of Tanzania	Tuvalu
Vanuatu	Vanuatu

Yemen
Zambia

Mercado Común Sudamericano (MERCOSUR)
Argentina
Brazil
Paraguay
Uruguay

North American Free Trade Agreement (NAFTA)
Canada
Mexico
United States of America

Organisation for Economic Cooperation and Development (OECD)
Australia
Austria
Belgium
Canada
Czech Republic
Denmark
Finland
France
Germany
Greece
Hungary
Iceland
Ireland
Italy
Japan
Luxembourg
Mexico
Netherlands
New Zealand
Norway
Poland
Portugal
Republic of Korca
Slovakia
Spain
Sweden
Switzerland
Turkey
United Kingdom
United States of America

Organization of Petroleum Exporting Countries (OPEC)
Algeria
Indonesia
Iran (Islamic Republic of)
Iraq
Kuwait
Libyan Arab Jamahiriya
Nigeria
Qatar
Saudi Arabia
United Arab Emirates
Venezuela

Marché commun sud-américain (Mercosur)
Argentine
Brésil
Paraguay
Uruguay

Accord de libre-échange nord-américain (ALENA)
Canada
Etats-Unis d'Amérique
Mexique

Organisation de coopération et de développement économiques (OCDE)
Allemagne
Australie
Autriche
Belgique
Canada
Danemark
Espagne
Etats-Unis d'Amérique
Finlande
France
Grèce
Hongrie
Irlande
Islande
Italie
Japon
Luxembourg
Mexique
Norvège
Nouvelle-Zélande
Pays-Bas
Pologne
Portugal
République de Corée
République tchèque
Royaume-Uni
Slovaquie
Suède
Suisse
Turquie

Organisation des pays exportateurs de pétrole (OPEP)
Algérie
Arabie saoudite
Emirats arabes unis
Indonésie
Iran (République islamique d')
Iraq
Jamahiriya arabe libyenne
Koweït
Nigéria
Qatar
Venezuela

Southern African Customs Union (SACU)
　　Botswana
　　Lesotho
　　Namibia
　　South Africa
　　Swaziland

---

a　The continent of North America comprises Northern
　America, Caribbean and Central America.

Union douanière d'Afrique australe
　　Afrique du Sud
　　Botswana
　　Lesotho
　　Namibie
　　Swaziland

---

a　Le continent de l'Amérique du Nord comprend l'Amérique
　septentrionale, les Caraïbes et l'Amérique centrale.

Annex II

Conversion coefficients and factors

The metric system of weights and measures is employed in the *Statistical Yearbook*. In this system, the relationship between units of volume and capacity is: 1 litre = 1 cubic decimetre (dm^3) exactly (as decided by the 12th International Conference of Weights and Measures, New Delhi, November 1964).

Section A shows the equivalents of the basic metric, British imperial and United States units of measurements. According to an agreement between the national standards institutions of English-speaking nations, the British and United States units of length, area and volume are now identical, and based on the yard = 0.9144 metre exactly. The weight measures in both systems are based on the pound = 0.45359237 kilogram exactly (Weights and Measures Act 1963 (London), and *Federal Register announcement of 1 July 1959: Refinement of Values for the Yard and Pound* (Washington D.C.)).

Section B shows various derived or conventional conversion coefficients and equivalents.

Section C shows other conversion coefficients or factors which have been utilized in the compilation of certain tables in the *Statistical Yearbook*. Some of these are only of an approximate character and have been employed solely to obtain a reasonable measure of international comparability in the tables.

For a comprehensive survey of international and national systems of weights and measures and of units' weights for a large number of commodities in different countries, see *World Weights and Measures*.

Annexe II

Coefficients et facteurs de conversion

L'*Annuaire statistique* utilise le système métrique pour les poids et mesures. La relation entre unités métriques de volume et de capacité est: 1 litre = 1 décimètre cube (dm^3) exactement (comme fut décidé à la Conférence internationale des poids et mesures, New Delhi, novembre 1964).

La section A fournit les principaux équivalents des systèmes de mesure métrique, britannique et américain. Suivant un accord entre les institutions de normalisation nationales des pays de langue anglaise, les mesures britanniques et américaines de longueur, superficie et volume sont désormais identiques, et sont basées sur le yard = 0.9144 mètre exactement. Les mesures de poids se rapportent, dans les deux systèmes, à la livre (pound) = 0.45359237 kilogramme exactement (*Weights and Measures Act 1963* (Londres), et *Federal Register Announcement of 1 July 1959: Refinement of Values for the Yard and Pound* (Washington, D.C.)).

La section B fournit divers coefficients et facteurs de conversion conventionnels ou dérivés.

La section C fournit d'autres coefficients ou facteurs de conversion utilisés dans l'élaboration de certains tableaux de l'*Annuaire statistique*. Certains coefficients ou facteurs de conversion ne sont que des approximations et ont été utilisés uniquement pour obtenir un degré raisonnable de comparabilité sur le plan international.

Pour une étude d'ensemble des systèmes internationaux et nationaux de poids et mesures, et d'unités de poids pour un grand nombre de produits dans différents pays, voir *World Weights and Measures*.

A. Equivalents of metric, British imperial and United States units of measure
A. Equivalents des unités métriques, britanniques et des États-Unis

Metric units / Unités métriques	British imperial and US equivalents / Equivalents en mesures britanniques et des Etats-Unis		British imperial and US units / Unités britanniques et des Etats-Unis	Metric equivalents / Equivalents en mesures métriques
Length — Longueur				
1 centimetre – centimètre (cm)	0.3937008	inch	1 inch	2.540 cm
1 metre – mètre (m)	3.280840	feet	1 foot	30.480 cm
	1.093613	yard	1 yard	0.9144 m
1 kilometre – kilomètre (km)	0.6213712	mile	1 mile	1609.344 m
	0.5399568	international nautical mile	1 international nautical mile	1852.000 m
Area — Superficie				
1 square centimetre – (cm^2)	0.1550003	square inch	1 square inch	6.45160 cm^2
1 square metre – (m^2)	10.763910	square feet	1 square foot	9.290304 dm^2
	1.195990	square yards	1 square yard	0.83612736 m^2
1 hectare – (ha)	2.471054	acres	1 acre	0.4046856 ha
1 square kilometre – (km^2)	0.3861022	square mile	1 square mile	2.589988 km^2
Volume				
1 cubic centimetre – (cm^3)	0.06102374	cubic inch	1 cubic inch	16.38706 cm^3
1 cubic metre – (m^3)	35.31467	cubic feet	1 cubic foot	28.316847 dm^3
	1.307951	cubic yards	1 cubic yard	0.76455486 m^3
Capacity — Capacité				
1 litre (l)	0.8798766	British imperial quart	1 British imperial quart	1.136523 l
	1.056688	U.S. liquid quart	1 U.S. liquid quart	0.9463529 l
	0.908083	U.S. dry quart	1 U.S. dry quart	1.1012208 l
1 hectolitre (hl)	21.99692	British imperial gallons	1 British imperial gallon	4.546092 l
	26.417200	U.S. gallons	1 U.S. gallon	3.785412 l
	2.749614	British imperial bushels	1 imperial bushel	36.368735 l
	2.837760	U.S. bushels	1 U.S. bushel	35.239067 l

Metric units Unités métriques	British imperial and US equivalents Equivalents en mesures britanniques et des Etats-Unis	British imperial and US units Unités britanniques et des Etats-Unis	Metric equivalents Equivalents en mesures métriques
Weight or mass — Poids			
1 kilogram (kg)	35.27396 av. ounces	1 av. ounce	28.349523 g
	32.15075 troy ounces	1 troy ounce	31.10348 g
	2.204623 av. pounds	1 av. pound	453.59237 g
		1 cental (100 lb.)	45.359237 kg
		1 hundredweight (112 lb.)	50.802345 kg
1 ton – tonne (t)	1.1023113 short tons	1 short ton (2 000 lb.)	0.9071847 t
	0.9842065 long tons	1 long ton (2 240 lb.)	1.0160469 t

B. Various conventional or derived coefficients

Air transport

1 passenger-mile = 1.609344 passenger kilometre
1 short ton-mile = 1.459972 tonne-kilometre
1 long ton-mile = 1.635169 tonne kilometre

Electric energy

1 Kilowatt (kW) = 1.34102 British horsepower (hp)
1.35962 cheval vapeur (cv)

C. Other coefficients or conversion factors employed in *Statistical Yearbook* tables

Roundwood

Equivalent in solid volume without bark.

Sugar

1 metric ton raw sugar = 0.9 metric ton refined sugar

For the United States and its possessions:
1 metric ton refined sugar = 1.07 metric tons raw sugar

B. Divers coefficients conventionnels ou dérivés

Transport aérien

1 voyageur (passager) – kilomètre = 0.621371 passenger-mile
1 tonne-kilomètre = 0.684945 short ton-mile
0.611558 long ton-mile

Energie électrique

1 British horsepower (hp) = 0.7457 kW
1 cheval vapeur (cv) = 0.735499 kW

C. Autres coefficients ou facteurs de conversion utilisés dans les tableaux de l'*Annuaire statistique*

Bois rond

Equivalences en volume solide sans écorce.

Sucre

1 tonne métrique de sucre brut = 0.9 tonne métrique de sucre raffiné

Pour les États-Unis et leurs possessions:
1 tonne métrique de sucre raffiné = 1.07 tonne métrique de sucre brut

Annex III

Tables added and omitted

A. Tables added

The present issue of the *Statistical Yearbook* includes the following tables which were not presented in the previous issue:

Table 38:	Fabrics
Table 39:	Footwear with uppers of leather
Table 43:	Pesticides
Table 44:	Pig iron and crude steel
Table 47:	Passenger cars
Table 48:	Refrigerators for household use
Table 49:	Washing machines for household use
Table 50:	Machine tools
Table 51:	Trucks
Table 55:	CO_2 emission estimates
Table 57:	Threatened species
Table 58:	Water and sanitation
Table 61:	Patents

B. Tables omitted

The following tables which were presented in previous issues are not presented in the present issue. They will be updated in future issues of the *Yearbook* when new data become available:

- Population in urban and rural areas, rates of growth and largest urban agglomeration population
- Food supply
- Daily newspapers
- Implicit price deflators
- Employment by economic activity
- Oil crops
- Livestock
- Fertilizers
- Meat

The following table has been discontinued:

- Sulphuric acid

Annexe III

Tableaux ajoutés et supprimés

A. Tableaux ajoutés

Dans ce numéro de l'*Annuaire statistique*, les tableaux suivants n'ont pas été présentés dans le numéro antérieur, et ont été ajoutés :

Tableau 38:	Tissus
Tableau 39:	Chaussures à dessus en cuir naturel
Tableau 43:	Pesticides
Tableau 44:	Fonte et acier brut
Tableau 47:	Voitures de tourisme
Tableau 48:	Réfrigérateurs à usage domestique
Tableau 49:	Machines à laver et à sécher le linge, de type ménager
Tableau 50:	Machines-outils
Tableau 51:	Camions
Tableau 55:	Estimations des émissions de CO_2
Tableau 57:	Espèces menacées
Tableau 58:	Access à l'eau et l'assainissement
Tableau 61:	Brevets

B. Tableaux supprimés

Les tableaux suivants qui ont été repris dans les éditions antérieures n'ont pas été repris dans la présente édition. Ils seront actualisés dans les futures livraisons de l'*Annuaire* à mesure que des données nouvelles deviendront disponibles:

- Population urbaine, population rurale, taux d'accroissement et population de l'agglomération urbaine la plus peuplée
- Disponibilités alimentaires
- Journaux quotidiens
- Déflateurs implicites des prix de produit intérieur brut
- Emploi par activité économique
- Cultures oléagineuses
- Cheptel
- Engrais
- Viande

Le tableau suivant a été discontinué :

- Acide sulfurique

Statistical sources and references

A. Statistical sources

1. Carbon Dioxide Information Analysis Center, *Global, Regional, and National CO$_2$ Emissions Estimates from Fossil-Fuel Burning, Hydraulic Cement Production, and Gas Flaring* (Oak Ridge, Tennessee, USA); web site http://cdiac.esd.ornl.gov.
2. Food and Agriculture Organization of the United Nations, *FAO Statistical Yearbook* (Rome); web site http://faostat.fao.org.
3. _____, *FAO Yearbook of Fishery Statistics, Aquaculture production* (Rome).
4. _____, *FAO Yearbook of Fishery Statistics, Capture production* (Rome).
5. _____, *Global Forest Resources Assessment 2005* (Rome); web site www.fao.org/forestry/fra2005.
6. International Civil Aviation Organization (Montreal); web site www.icao.int.
7. International Labour Office, *Yearbook of Labour Statistics* (Geneva); web site http://laborsta.ilo.org.
8. International Monetary Fund, *Balance of Payments Statistics Yearbook* (Washington, D.C.); web site www.imf.org.
9. _____, *International Financial Statistics* (Washington, D.C.).
10. International Parliamentary Union (IPU), *Women in National Parliaments* (Geneva)
11. International Sugar Organization, *Sugar Yearbook 2008* (London).
12. International Telecommunication Union, *World Telecommunication/ICT Indicators Database 2009, 13th Edition* (Geneva); web site www.itu.int.
13. Organisation for Economic Co-operation and Development, *Development Co-operation Report* (Paris); web site www.oecd.org.
14. _____, *Geographical Distribution of Financial Flows to Aid Recipients* (Paris).
15. United Nations, *Demographic Yearbook 2007* (United Nations publication, Sales No. B.10.XIII.1).
16. _____, *Energy Statistics Yearbook 2006* (United Nations publication, Sales No. 09.XVII.4).
17. _____, *Industrial Commodity Statistics Yearbook 2006* (United Nations publications, Sales No. 10.XVII.12 H).
18. _____, *International Trade Statistics Yearbook 2007*, PDF (United Nations publication, Sales No. 10.XVII.2 H).
19. _____, *Monthly Bulletin of Statistics*, various issues up to October 2009 (United Nations publication, Series Q).
20. _____, *National Accounts Statistics: Main Aggregates and Detailed Tables, 2007* (United Nations publication, Sales No. E.09.XVII.9)

Sources statistiques et références

A. Sources statistiques

1. "Carbon Dioxide Information Analysis Center, *"Global, Regional, and National CO$_2$ Emissions Estimates from Fossil-Fuel Burning, Hydraulic Cement Production, and Gas Flaring"* (Oak Ridge, Tennessee, USA); site Web http://cdiac.esd.ornl.gov.
2. Organisation des Nations Unies pour l'alimentation et l'agriculture, *Annuaire Statistique de la FAO* (Rome); site Web http://faostat.fao.org.
3. _____, *Annuaire statistique des pêches, production de l'aquaculture* (Rome).
4. _____, *Annuaire statistique des pêches, captures* (Rome).
5. _____, *Evaluation des ressources forestières mondiales 2005* (Rome); site Web www.fao.org/forestry/fra2005.
6. Organisation de l'aviation civile internationale (Montréal); site Web www.icao.int.
7. Bureau international du Travail, *Annuaire des statistiques du Travail* (Genève); site Web http://laborsta.ilo.org.
8. Fonds monétaire international, *"Balance of Payments Statistics Yearbook"*, (Washington, D.C.); site Web www.imf.org.
9. _____, *Statistiques financières internationales*, (Washington, D.C.).
10. Union interparlementaire, *Les femmes dans les parlements* (Genève)
11. Organisation internationale du sucre, *Annuaire du sucre 2008* (Londres).
12. Union Internationale des télécommunications, *"World Telecommunication/ICT Indicators Database 2009, 13th Edition"* (Genève); site Web www.itu.int.
13. Organisation de Coopération et de Développement Economiques, *Coopération pour le développement, Rapport* (Paris); site Web www.oecd.org.
14. _____, *Répartition géographique des ressources financières allouées aux pays bénéficiaires de l'aide,* (Paris).
15. Nations Unies, *Annuaire démographique 2007* (publication des Nations Unies, No de vente B.10.XIII.1).
16. _____, *Annuaire des statistiques de l'énergie 2006* (publication des Nations Unies, No de vente 09.XVII.4).
17. _____, *Annuaire des statistiques industrielles par produit 2006* (publications des Nations Unies, No de vente 10.XVII.12 H).
18. _____, *Annuaire statistique du commerce international 2007*, PDF (publication des Nations Unies, No de vente 10.XVII.2 H).

21. _____, *Operational activities of the United Nations for international development cooperation, Report of the Secretary-General, Addendum, Comprehensive statistical data on operational activities for development for the year 2007 (A/64/75).*

22. _____, *World Population Prospects: The 2008 Revision* (United Nations publication, Sales No. 09.XIII.5).

23. United Nations Educational, Scientific and Cultural Organization Institute for Statistics (Montreal); web site www.uis.unesco.org.

24. World Bank, *Global Development Finance*, vols. I and II, (Washington, D.C.); web site www.worldbank.org.

25. World Conservation Union (IUCN) / Species Survival Commission (SSC), Gland, Switzerland and Cambridge, United Kingdom, "IUCN Red List of Threatened Species", 2004, 2006 and 2008; web site www.iucnredlist.org.

26. World Health Organization (WHO) and United Nations Children's Fund (UNICEF), *the WHO/UNICEF Joint Monitoring Programme for the Water and Sanitation* (Geneva and New York)

27. World Intellectual Property Organization, *World Intellectual Property Indicators 2009* (Geneva); web site http://www.wipo.int.

28. World Tourism Organization, *Yearbook of Tourism Statistics, 2009 edition* (Madrid); web site www.world-tourism.org.

B. References

29. International Labour Office, *International Standard Classification of Occupations, Revised Edition 1968* (Geneva, 1969); revised edition, 1988, *ISCO-88* (Geneva, 1990), revised edition, 2008, *ISCO-08* (Geneva, 2007).

30. International Monetary Fund, *Balance of Payments Manual, Sixth Edition* (Washington, D.C., 2009).

31. United Nations Statistics Division, *Classifications of Expenditure According to Purpose: Classification of the Functions of Government (COFOG), Classification of Individual Consumption According to Purpose (COICOP), Classification of the Purposes of Non-Profit Institutions Serving Households (COPNI), Classification of the Outlays of Producers According to Purpose (COPP),* Series M, No. 84 (United Nations publication, Sales No. E.00.XVII.6).

32. _____, *Energy Statistics: Definitions, Units of Measure and Conversion Factors*, Series F, No. 44 (United Nations publication, Sales No. E.86.XVII.21).

33. _____, *Energy Statistics: Manual for Developing Countries*, Series F, No. 56 (United Nations publication, Sales No. E.91.XVII.10).

19. _____, *Bulletin mensuel de statistique*, différentes éditions, jusqu'à octobre 2009 (publication des Nations Unies, Série Q).

20. _____, *"National Accounts Statistics: Main Aggregates and Detailed Tables, 2007"* (publication des Nations Unies, No de vente E.09.XVII.9).

21. _____, *Activités opérationnelles du système des Nations Unies au service de la coopération internationale pour le développement, Rapport du Secrétaire général, Additif, Données statistiques globales sur les activités opérationnelles au service du développement pour 2007 (A/64/75).*

22. _____, *"World Population Prospects: The 2008 Revision"* (No de vente 09.XIII.5).

23. Institut de statistique de l'Organisation des Nations Unies pour l'éducation, la science et la culture (Montréal); site Web www.uis.unesco.org.

24. Banque mondiale, *"Global Development Finance, Vols. I et II,"* (Washington, D.C.).

25. Union mondiale pour la nature (UICN) / Commission de la sauvegarde des espèces, Gland, Suisse, et Cambridge, Royaume-Uni, "La liste rouge des espèces menacées de l'UICN", 2004, 2006 et 2008 ; site Web www.iucnredlist.org.

26. Organisation mondial de la santé (OMS) et Fonds des Nations Unies pour l'enfance (UNICEF), *la Programme commun OMS/UNICEF de surveillance de l'eau et de l'assainissement* (Genève et New York)

27. Organisation Mondiale de la Propriété Intellectuelle, *Indicateurs mondiaux relatifs à la propriété intellectuelle pour l'année 2009* (Genève); site Web http://www.wipo.int.

28. Organisation mondiale du tourisme, *l'Annuaire des statistiques du tourisme, 2009* (Madrid); site Web www.world-tourism.org.

B. Références

29. Organisation internationale du Travail, *Classification internationale type des professions, édition révisée 1968* (Genève, 1969); édition révisée 1988, *CITP-88* (Genève, 1990). édition révisée 2008, *CITP-08* (Genève, 2007).

30. Fonds monétaire international, *Manuel de la balance des paiements, sixième édition* (Washington, D.C., 2009).

31. Division de statistique de Nations Unies, *"Classifications of Expenditure According to Purpose: Classification of the Functions of Government (COFOG), Classification of Individual Consumption According to Purpose (COICOP), Classification of the Purposes of Non-Profit Institutions Serving Households (COPNI), Classification of the Outlays of Producers According to Purpose (COPP)"*, Série M, No 84

34. _____, *Handbook of Vital Statistics Systems and Methods*, vol. I, *Legal, Organization and Technical Aspects*, Series F, No. 35, vol. I (United Nations publication, Sales No. E.91.XVII.5).

35. _____, *Handbook on Social Indicators*, Studies in Methods, Series F, No. 49 (United Nations publication, Sales No. E.89.XVII.6).

36. _____, *International Recommendations for Industrial Statistics*, Series M, No. 48, Rev. 1 (United Nations publication, Sales No. E.83.XVII.8).

37. _____, *International Standard Industrial Classification of All Economic Activities*, Statistical Papers, Series M, No. 4, Rev. 2 (United Nations publication, Sales No. E.68.XVII.8); Rev. 3 (United Nations publication, Sales No. E.90.XVII.11).

38. _____, *International Trade Statistics: Concepts and Definitions*, Series M, No. 52, Rev. 1 (United Nations publication, Sales No. E.82.XVII.14).

39. _____, *Methods Used in Compiling the United Nations Price Indexes for External Trade*, volume 1, Statistical Papers, Series M, No. 82 (United Nations Publication, Sales No. E.87.XVII.4), volume 2 (United Nations publication, sales No. E.91.XVII.8).

40. _____, *Principles and Recommendations for Population and Housing Censuses*, Statistical Papers, Series M, No. 67 (United Nations publication, Sales No. E.80.XVII.8).

41. _____, *Provisional Guidelines on Statistics of International Tourism*, Statistical Papers, Series M, No. 62 (United Nations publication, Sales No. E.78.XVII.6).

42. _____, *Standard International Trade Classification, Revision 3*, Statistical Papers, Series M, No. 34, Rev. 3 (United Nations publication, Sales No. E.86.XVII.12), *Revision 2*, Series M, No. 34, Rev. 2 (United Nations publication), *Revision*, Series M, No. 34, Revision (United Nations publication, Sales No. E.61.XVII.6).

43. _____, *Supplement to the Statistical Yearbook and the Monthly Bulletin of Statistics, 1977*, Series S and Series Q, Supplement 2 (United Nations publication, Sales No. E.78.XVII.10).

44. _____, *System of National Accounts, Studies in Methods*, Series F, No. 2, Rev. 3 (United Nations publication, Sales No. E.69.XVII.3).

45. _____, *System of National Accounts 1993*, Studies in Methods, Series F, No. 2, Rev. 4 (United Nations publication, Sales No. E.94.XVII.4).

46. _____, *Towards a System of Social and Demographic Statistics, Studies in Methods*, Series F, No. 18 (United Nations publication, Sales No. E.74.XVII.8).

47. _____, *World Weights and Measures* (United Nations publication, Sales No. E.66.XVII.3).

(publication des Nations Unies, No de vente F. 00.XVII.6).

32. _____, *Statistiques de l'énergie: définitions, unités de mesures et facteurs de conversion*, Série F, No 44 (publication des Nations Unies, No de vente F.86.XVII.21).

33. _____, *Statistiques de l'énergie: Manuel pour les pays en développement*, Série F, No 56 (publication des Nations Unies, No de vente F.91.XVII.10).

34. _____, "*Handbook of Vital Statistics System and Methods*, Vol. 1, *Legal, Organization and Technical Aspects*", Série F, No 35, Vol. 1 (publication des Nations Unies, No de vente E.91.XVII.5).

35. _____, *Manuel des indicateurs sociaux*, Série F, No 49 (publication des Nations Unies, No de vente F.89.XVII.6).

36. _____, *Recommandations internationales concernant les statistiques industrielles*, Série M, No 48, Rev. 1 (publication des Nations Unies, No de vente F.83.XVII.8).

37. _____, *Classification internationale type, par industrie, de toutes les branches d'activité économique*, Série M, No 4, Rev. 2 (publication des Nations Unies, No de vente F.68.XVII.8); Rev. 3 (publication des Nations Unies, No de vente F.90.XVII.11).

38. _____, *Statistiques du commerce international: Concepts et définitions*, Série M, No 52, Rev. 1 (publication des Nations Unies, No de vente F.82.XVII.14).

39. _____, *Méthodes utilisées par les Nations Unies pour établir les indices des prix des produits de base entrant dans le commerce international*, Série M, No 82, Vol. 1 (publication des Nations Unies, No de vente F.87.XVII.4), Vol. 2 (publication des Nations Unies, No de vente F.97.XVII.8).

40. _____, *Principes et recommandations concernant les recensements de la population et de l'habitation*, Série M, No 67 (publication des Nations Unies, No de vente F.80.XVII.8).

41. _____, *Directives provisoires pour l'établissement des statistiques du tourisme international*, Série M, No 62 (publication des Nations Unies, No de vente 78.XVII.6).

42. _____, *Classification type pour le commerce international (troisième version révisée)*, Série M, No 34, Rev. 3 (publication des Nations Unies, No de vente F.86.XVII.12), *Révision 2*, Série M, No 34, Rev. 2 (publication des Nations Unies), *Révision*, Série M, No. 34, Révision (publication des Nations Unies, No de vente F.61.XVII.6).

43. _____, *Supplément à l'Annuaire statistique et*

48. World Health Organization, *Manual of the International Statistical Classification of Diseases, Injuries and Causes of Death*, vol. 1 (Geneva, 1977).

49. World Tourism Organization, *Methodological Supplement to World Travel and Tourism Statistics* (Madrid, 1985).

50. _____, *Recommendations on Tourism Statistics*, Statistical Papers, Series M, No. 83 (United Nations publication, Sales No. E.94.XVII.6).

au bulletin mensuel de statistique, 1977, Série S et Série Q, supplément 2 (publication des Nations Unies, No de vente F.78.XVII.10).

44. _____, *Système de comptabilité nationale,* Série F, No 2, Rev. 3 (publication des Nations Unies, No de vente F.69.XVII.3).

45. _____, *Système de comptabilité nationale 1993,* Série F, No 2, Rev. 4 (publication des Nations Unies, No de vente F.94.XVII.4).

46. _____, *Vers un système de statistiques démographiques et sociales, Etudes méthodologiques,* Série F, No 18 (publication des Nations Unies, No. de vente F.74.XVII.8).

47. _____, *"World Weights and Measures"* (publication des Nations Unies, No. de vente E.66.XVII.3).

48. Organisation mondiale de la santé, *Manuel de la classification statistique internationale des maladies, traumatismes et causes de décès,* Vol. 1 (Genève, 1977).

49. Organisation mondiale du tourisme, *Supplément méthodologique aux statistiques des voyages et du tourisme mondiaux* (Madrid, 1985).

50. _____, *"Recommendations on Tourism Statistics,* Statistical Papers", Série M, No. 83 (publication des Nations Unies, No. de vente E.94.XVII.6).

	Population		Gender / Femmes			Education		Communication			National accounts / Comptabilités nationales							
Table	8	9	10	11	12	13	14	15	16	17	18	19	20	21	22	23	24	Tableau
Afghanistan	•	•	•	•	•	•		•	•	•	•	•	•					Afghanistan
Albania	•	•	•	•	•			•	•	•	•	•	•				•	Albanie
Algeria	•	•	•	•	•	•		•	•	•	•	•	•	•			•	Algérie
American Samoa	•			•				•	•									Samoa américaines
Andorra	•		•	•	•			•	•		•		•			•		Andorre
Angola	•	•	•	•	•	•	•	•	•	•	•	•	•	•				Angola
Anguilla	•			•	•						•	•	•					Anguilla
Antigua and Barbuda	•		•	•	•	•		•	•	•	•	•	•					Antigua-et-Barbuda
Argentina	•	•	•	•	•	•	•	•	•	•	•	•	•	•	•		•	Argentine
Armenia	•	•	•	•	•	•	•	•	•	•	•	•	•	•			•	Arménie
Aruba	•			•	•	•		•	•	•	•	•	•					Aruba
Ascension	•																	Ascension
Australia	•	•	•	•	•	•	•	•	•	•	•	•	•	•	•	•	•	Australie
Austria	•	•	•	•	•	•	•	•	•	•	•	•	•	•	•	•	•	Autriche
Azerbaijan	•	•	•	•	•	•	•	•	•	•	•	•	•	•	•		•	Azerbaïdjan
Bahamas	•	•	•	•	•	•	•	•	•	•	•	•	•	•			•	Bahamas
Bahrain	•	•	•	•	•	•	•	•	•	•	•	•	•	•				Bahreïn
Bangladesh	•	•	•	•	•	•	•	•	•	•	•	•	•	•			•	Bangladesh
Barbados	•	•	•	•	•	•	•	•	•	•	•	•	•				•	Barbade
Belarus	•	•	•	•	•	•	•	•	•	•	•	•	•	•			•	Bélarus
Belgium	•	•	•	•	•	•	•	•	•	•	•	•	•	•		•	•	Belgique
Belgium-Lu?embourg																		Belgique-Lu?embourg
Belize	•	•	•	•	•	•	•	•	•	•	•	•	•			•	•	Belize
Benin	•	•	•	•	•	•	•	•	•	•	•	•	•					Bénin
Bermuda	•			•	•	•	•	•	•	•	•	•	•	•				Bermudes
Bhutan	•	•	•	•	•	•		•	•	•	•	•	•	•			•	Bhoutan
Bolivia	•	•	•	•	•	•		•	•	•	•	•	•	•	•		•	Bolivie
Bonaire																		Bonaire
Bosnia and Herzegovina	•	•	•	•	•	•		•	•	•	•	•	•					Bosnie-Herzégovine
Botswana	•	•	•	•	•	•	•	•	•	•	•	•	•				•	Botswana
Brazil	•	•	•	•	•	•	•	•	•	•	•	•	•	•			•	Brésil
British Indian Ocean Terr.																		Terr. brit. de l'océan Indien
British Virgin Islands	•			•	•	•	•				•	•	•					Iles Vierges britanniques
Brunei Darussalam	•	•	•	•	•	•	•	•	•	•	•	•	•				•	Brunéi Darussalam
Bulgaria	•	•	•	•	•	•	•	•	•	•	•	•	•	•		•	•	Bulgarie
Burkina Faso	•	•	•	•	•	•	•	•	•	•	•	•	•	•			•	Burkina Faso
Burundi	•	•	•	•	•	•	•	•	•	•	•	•	•					Burundi
Cambodia	•	•	•	•	•	•	•	•	•	•	•	•	•					Cambodge
Cameroon	•	•	•	•	•	•	•	•	•	•	•	•	•	•			•	Cameroun
Canada	•	•	•	•	•	•	•	•	•	•	•	•	•	•			•	Canada
Cape Verde	•	•	•	•	•	•	•	•	•	•	•	•	•			•		Cap-Vert
Cayman Islands	•			•	•	•		•	•	•	•	•	•					Iles Caïmanes
Central African Rep.	•	•	•	•	•	•	•	•	•	•	•	•	•					Rép. centrafricaine
Chad	•	•	•	•	•	•	•	•	•	•	•	•	•					Tchad
Channel Islands		•																Iles Anglo-Normandes
Chile	•	•	•	•	•	•	•	•	•	•	•	•	•	•			•	Chili
China	•	•	•	•	•	•	•	•	•	•	•	•	•	•				Chine
China, Hong Kong SAR	•	•	•		•	•	•	•	•	•	•	•	•	•	•		•	Chine, Hong Kong RAS
China, Macao SAR	•		•	•	•	•	•	•	•	•	•	•	•	•	•		•	Chine, Macao RAS
Christmas Is.																		Ile Christmas
Cocos (Keeling) Islands																		Iles des Cocos (Keeling)
Colombia	•	•	•	•	•	•	•	•	•	•	•	•	•	•			•	Colombie
Comoros	•	•	•	•	•	•		•	•	•	•	•	•					Comores
Congo	•	•	•	•	•	•	•	•	•	•	•	•	•					Congo
Cook Islands	•			•	•	•		•			•	•	•			•		Iles Cook
Costa Rica	•	•	•	•	•	•	•	•	•	•	•	•	•		•		•	Costa Rica
Côte d'Ivoire	•	•	•	•	•	•	•	•	•	•	•	•	•	•	•	•	•	Côte d'Ivoire
Croatia	•	•	•	•	•	•	•	•	•	•	•	•	•	•	•		•	Croatie
Cuba	•	•	•	•	•	•	•	•	•	•	•	•	•				•	Cuba
Curaçao																		Curaçao
Cyprus	•	•	•	•	•	•	•	•	•	•	•	•	•	•	•		•	Chypre
Czech Republic	•	•	•	•	•	•	•	•	•	•	•	•	•	•	•		•	République tchèque
Dem. Rep. of the Congo	•	•	•	•	•	•	•	•	•	•	•	•	•					Rép. dém. du Congo
Denmark	•	•	•	•	•	•	•	•	•	•	•	•	•	•	•		•	Danemark
Djibouti	•	•	•	•	•	•	•	•	•	•	•	•	•				•	Djibouti
Dominica	•		•	•	•	•		•	•	•	•	•	•					Dominique
Dominican Republic	•	•	•	•	•	•	•	•	•	•	•	•	•	•	•		•	Rép. dominicaine

	Finance		Labour, wages and prices — Main d'œuvre, salaires et prix				Agriculture, forestry and fishing — Agriculture, forêts et pêche				Manufacturing — Industries manufacturières						
Table	25	26	27	28	29	30	31	32	33	34	35	36	37	38	39	40	**Tableau**
Afghanistan		•	•				•	•	•	•	•					•	Afghanistan
Albania	•	•	•	•		•	•	•	•	•	•	•	•			•	Albanie
Algeria	•	•	•			•	•	•	•	•	•	•		•		•	Algérie
American Samoa						•	•										Samoa américaines
Andorra				•		•							•				Andorre
Angola	•						•	•	•	•	•					•	Angola
Anguilla	•	•	•			•				•							Anguilla
Antigua and Barbuda	•	•	•			•				•							Antigua-et-Barbuda
Argentina		•	•	•	•		•	•	•	•	•	•				•	Argentine
Armenia		•	•	•			•	•	•	•	•	•			•	•	Arménie
Aruba	•	•				•				•							Aruba
Ascension																	Ascension
Australia		•	•	•	•	•	•	•	•	•	•	•		•		•	Australie
Austria	•	•	•	•	•	•	•	•	•	•	•	•				•	Autriche
Azerbaijan	•	•	•	•		•	•	•	•	•	•	•	•	•		•	Azerbaïdjan
Bahamas	•	•	•			•	•									•	Bahamas
Bahrain		•	•	•		•	•			•							Bahreïn
Bangladesh	•					•	•	•	•	•						•	Bangladesh
Barbados	•	•				•	•	•		•	•					•	Barbade
Belarus	•		•	•		•	•	•	•	•	•	•	•	•	•	•	Bélarus
Belgium		•	•	•	•		•	•		•						•	Belgique
Belgium-Luxembourg							•	•	•								Belgique-Luxembourg
Belize	•	•	•			•	•									•	Belize
Benin	•	•				•	•									•	Bénin
Bermuda			•			•				•	•						Bermudes
Bhutan			•			•	•	•	•	•						•	Bhoutan
Bolivia	•	•				•	•	•	•	•	•	•			•	•	Bolivie
Bonaire																	Bonaire
Bosnia and Herzegovina			•	•			•	•	•	•						•	Bosnie-Herzégovine
Botswana	•		•	•		•	•	•	•	•					•	•	Botswana
Brazil	•	•	•	•		•	•	•		•	•	•	•		•	•	Brésil
British Indian Ocean Terr.										•							Terr. brit. de l'océan Indien
British Virgin Islands				•						•							Iles Vierges britanniques
Brunei Darussalam			•			•	•	•			•					•	Brunéi Darussalam
Bulgaria	•	•	•	•	•	•	•	•	•	•	•	•	•	•		•	Bulgarie
Burkina Faso	•	•				•	•	•	•	•						•	Burkina Faso
Burundi	•					•	•	•	•	•	•					•	Burundi
Cambodia			•			•	•	•	•	•						•	Cambodge
Cameroon	•					•	•	•	•	•	•					•	Cameroun
Canada	•	•	•	•	•	•	•	•	•	•	•					•	Canada
Cape Verde	•	•				•		•			•						Cap-Vert
Cayman Islands			•			•				•							Iles Caïmanes
Central African Rep.	•					•	•	•	•	•	•					•	Rép. centrafricaine
Chad	•					•	•	•	•	•	•					•	Tchad
Channel Islands										•							Iles Anglo-Normandes
Chile	•	•				•	•	•	•	•	•	•		•	•	•	Chili
China	•		•	•		•	•	•	•	•	•	•	•		•	•	Chine
China, Hong Kong SAR	•	•	•	•	•	•				•	•	•	•	•	•	•	Chine, Hong Kong RAS
China, Macao SAR	•	•	•	•		•				•	•	•	•	•	•	•	Chine, Macao RAS
Christmas Is.																	Ile Christmas
Cocos (Keeling) Islands																	Iles des Cocos (Keeling)
Colombia																•	Colombie
Comoros	•						•	•		•	•						Comores
Congo	•						•	•	•	•	•					•	Congo
Cook Islands			•			•				•							Iles Cook
Costa Rica	•		•	•		•	•	•	•	•	•					•	Costa Rica
Côte d'Ivoire	•					•	•	•	•	•						•	Côte d'Ivoire
Croatia	•					•	•	•	•	•	•	•	•			•	Croatie
Cuba		•	•	•		•	•	•	•	•	•	•	•	•		•	Cuba
Curaçao					•												Curaçao
Cyprus	•	•	•	•		•	•	•		•	•	•	•		•	•	Chypre
Czech Republic	•	•	•	•	•	•	•	•	•	•	•		•	•	•	•	République tchèque
Dem. Rep. of the Congo	•					•	•	•	•	•	•					•	Rép. dém. du Congo
Denmark	•	•	•	•	•	•	•	•	•	•	•		•	•	•	•	Danemark
Djibouti										•	•						Djibouti
Dominica	•	•	•			•				•						•	Dominique
Dominican Republic		•	•	•		•	•	•	•	•	•	•	•			•	Rép. dominicaine

	Manufacturing / Industries manufacturières											Energy / Energie		Environment / Environnement					
Table	41	42	43	44	45	46	47	48	49	50	51	52	53	54	55	56	57	58	Tableau
Afghanistan		•										•	•	•	•	•	•	•	Afghanistan
Albania	•	•		•								•	•	•	•	•	•	•	Albanie
Algeria	•	•		•		•		•		•	•	•	•	•	•	•	•	•	Algérie
American Samoa													•	•	•		•	•	Samoa américaines
Andorra														•	•		•	•	Andorre
Angola		•		•								•	•	•	•	•	•	•	Angola
Anguilla												•	•	•	•	•		•	Anguilla
Antigua and Barbuda												•	•	•	•	•	•	•	Antigua-et-Barbuda
Argentina	•	•		•	•	•	•	•	•		•	•	•	•	•	•	•	•	Argentine
Armenia	•	•								•		•	•	•	•	•	•	•	Arménie
Aruba												•	•	•	•	•	•	•	Aruba
Ascension														•					Ascension
Australia	•		•	•			•	•	•			•	•	•	•	•	•	•	Australie
Austria	•	•	•	•						•		•	•	•	•	•	•	•	Autriche
Azerbaijan	•	•		•		•	•	•				•	•	•	•	•	•	•	Azerbaïdjan
Bahamas																		•	Bahamas
Bahrain	•				•							•	•	•	•	•	•	•	Bahreïn
Bangladesh	•	•		•		•	•					•	•	•	•	•	•	•	Bangladesh
Barbados	•	•											•	•	•	•	•	•	Barbade
Belarus	•	•		•		•	•	•	•	•	•	•	•	•	•	•	•	•	Bélarus
Belgium	•	•	•	•								•	•	•	•	•	•	•	Belgique
Belgium-Luxembourg	•																		Belgique-Luxembourg
Belize												•	•	•	•	•	•	•	Belize
Benin		•										•	•	•	•	•	•	•	Bénin
Bermuda												•	•	•	•	•	•		Bermudes
Bhutan		•										•	•	•	•	•	•	•	Bhoutan
Bolivia	•	•										•	•	•	•	•	•	•	Bolivie
Bonaire																			Bonaire
Bosnia and Herzegovina	•	•		•	•							•	•	•	•	•	•	•	Bosnie-Herzégovine
Botswana														•	•	•	•	•	Botswana
Brazil	•	•		•	•	•	•	•	•	•	•	•	•	•	•	•	•	•	Brésil
British Indian Ocean Terr.														•			•	•	Terr. brit. de l'océan Indien
British Virgin Islands														•	•		•	•	Iles Vierges britanniques
Brunei Darussalam		•										•	•	•	•	•	•	•	Brunéi Darussalam
Bulgaria	•	•		•	•	•						•	•	•	•	•	•	•	Bulgarie
Burkina Faso		•										•	•	•	•	•	•	•	Burkina Faso
Burundi												•	•	•	•	•	•	•	Burundi
Cambodia		•										•	•	•	•	•	•	•	Cambodge
Cameroon		•			•							•	•	•	•	•	•	•	Cameroun
Canada	•	•										•	•	•	•	•	•	•	Canada
Cape Verde												•	•	•	•	•		•	Cap-Vert
Cayman Islands														•			•	•	Iles Caïmanes
Central African Rep.												•	•	•	•	•	•	•	Rép. centrafricaine
Chad												•	•	•	•	•	•	•	Tchad
Channel Islands														•					Iles Anglo-Normandes
Chile	•	•	•					•	•			•	•	•	•	•	•	•	Chili
China	•	•	•	•	•			•	•			•	•	•	•	•	•	•	Chine
China, Hong Kong SAR		•										•	•				•	•	Chine, Hong Kong RAS
China, Macao SAR		•										•	•		•		•		Chine, Macao RAS
Christmas Is.																		•	Ile Christmas
Cocos (Keeling) Islands																		•	Iles des Cocos (Keeling)
Colombia	•	•		•								•	•	•	•	•	•	•	Colombie
Comoros												•	•	•	•	•	•	•	Comores
Congo		•										•	•	•	•	•	•	•	Congo
Cook Islands														•	•	•	•	•	Iles Cook
Costa Rica	•	•										•	•	•	•	•	•	•	Costa Rica
Côte d'Ivoire		•										•	•	•	•	•	•	•	Côte d'Ivoire
Croatia	•	•	•	•	•					•		•	•	•	•	•	•	•	Croatie
Cuba	•	•			•		•		•	•		•	•					•	Cuba
Curaçao																			Curaçao
Cyprus		•										•	•	•	•	•	•	•	Chypre
Czech Republic	•	•	•	•	•							•	•	•	•	•	•	•	République tchèque
Dem. Rep. of the Congo	•	•										•	•	•	•	•	•	•	Rép. dém. du Congo
Denmark	•	•	•	•		•	•	•	•	•	•	•	•	•	•	•	•	•	Danemark
Djibouti												•	•	•	•	•		•	Djibouti
Dominica												•	•	•	•	•	•	•	Dominique
Dominican Republic	•	•		•								•	•	•	•	•	•	•	Rép. dominicaine

	Science and technology / Science et technologie			International merchandise / Commerce international des marchandises			International tourism and transport / Tourisme international et transport				BoP / BdP	International finance / Finances internationales			Development assistance / Aide au développement			
Table	59	60	61	62	63	64	65	66	67	68	69	70	71	72	73	74	75	**Tableau**
Afghanistan				•								•			•		•	Afghanistan
Albania				•			•	•	•	•	•	•	•	•	•		•	Albanie
Algeria	•	•	•	•			•	•	•	•		•	•	•	•		•	Algérie
American Samoa	•			•			•	•										Samoa américaines
Andorra				•				•									•	Andorre
Angola				•													•	Angola
Anguilla			•	•														Anguilla
Antigua and Barbuda			•	•				•	•	•		•	•	•			•	Antigua-et-Barbuda
Argentina	•	•	•	•	•		•	•	•	•	•	•	•	•	•		•	Argentine
Armenia	•	•		•			•	•	•	•	•	•	•	•	•		•	Arménie
Aruba				•			•	•			•	•						Aruba
Ascension																		Ascension
Australia	•	•	•	•	•	•	•	•	•	•	•	•		•		•	•	Australie
Austria	•	•	•	•	•	•	•	•	•	•	•	•				•	•	Autriche
Azerbaijan	•			•			•	•	•	•	•	•	•	•	•		•	Azerbaïdjan
Bahamas				•			•	•	•	•	•	•	•	•			•	Bahamas
Bahrain				•			•	•	•	•	•	•	•	•			•	Bahreïn
Bangladesh				•			•	•	•	•	•	•	•	•	•		•	Bangladesh
Barbados				•			•	•	•	•	•	•	•	•	•		•	Barbade
Belarus	•	•		•			•	•	•	•	•	•	•	•	•		•	Bélarus
Belgium	•	•	•	•	•	•	•	•	•	•	•	•		•	•		•	Belgique
Belgium-Luxembourg											•							Belgique-Luxembourg
Belize				•			•	•	•	•	•	•	•	•			•	Belize
Benin				•			•	•	•	•		•	•	•	•		•	Bénin
Bermuda		•		•			•	•	•	•								Bermudes
Bhutan				•			•	•	•	•		•	•	•	•		•	Bhoutan
Bolivia	•	•		•			•	•	•	•	•	•	•	•	•		•	Bolivie
Bonaire				•			•	•										Bonaire
Bosnia and Herzegovina	•			•			•	•	•	•	•	•	•	•	•		•	Bosnie-Herzégovine
Botswana	•	•		•			•	•	•	•	•	•	•	•	•		•	Botswana
Brazil	•	•	•	•	•		•	•	•	•	•	•	•	•	•		•	Brésil
British Indian Ocean Terr.																		Terr. brit. de l'océan Indien
British Virgin Islands							•	•										Iles Vierges britanniques
Brunei Darussalam	•	•		•			•	•	•	•	•	•					•	Brunéi Darussalam
Bulgaria	•	•	•	•			•	•	•	•	•	•	•	•			•	Bulgarie
Burkina Faso	•	•		•			•	•	•	•		•	•	•	•		•	Burkina Faso
Burundi				•			•	•	•	•		•	•	•	•		•	Burundi
Cambodia	•	•		•			•	•	•	•		•	•	•	•		•	Cambodge
Cameroon	•			•			•	•	•	•		•	•	•	•		•	Cameroun
Canada	•	•	•	•	•	•	•	•	•	•	•	•				•	•	Canada
Cape Verde	•			•			•	•	•	•		•	•	•	•		•	Cap-Vert
Cayman Islands				•			•	•										Iles Caïmanes
Central African Rep.	•			•			•	•	•			•	•	•	•		•	Rép. centrafricaine
Chad				•			•	•				•	•	•	•		•	Tchad
Channel Islands																		Iles Anglo-Normandes
Chile	•	•	•	•			•	•	•	•	•	•	•	•	•		•	Chili
China	•	•		•			•	•	•	•	•	•	•	•			•	Chine
China, Hong Kong SAR	•	•	•	•	•	•	•	•	•	•	•	•	•	•			•	Chine, Hong Kong RAS
China, Macao SAR	•	•	•	•	•	•	•	•	•	•	•	•	•	•			•	Chine, Macao RAS
Christmas Is.																		Ile Christmas
Cocos (Keeling) Islands																		Iles des Cocos (Keeling)
Colombia				•			•	•	•	•	•	•	•	•			•	Colombie
Comoros				•			•	•	•	•		•	•	•	•		•	Comores
Congo				•			•	•	•	•	•	•	•	•	•		•	Congo
Cook Islands				•			•	•						•			•	Iles Cook
Costa Rica	•	•		•			•	•	•	•	•	•	•	•	•		•	Costa Rica
Côte d'Ivoire	•			•			•	•	•	•	•	•	•	•	•		•	Côte d'Ivoire
Croatia	•	•		•			•	•	•	•	•	•	•	•			•	Croatie
Cuba	•	•	•	•			•	•	•	•	•						•	Cuba
Curaçao				•			•	•										Curaçao
Cyprus	•	•	•	•			•	•	•	•	•	•	•	•			•	Chypre
Czech Republic	•	•	•	•			•	•	•	•	•	•	•	•			•	République tchèque
Dem. Rep. of the Congo	•	•		•													•	Rép. dém. du Congo
Denmark	•	•	•	•	•	•	•	•	•	•	•	•				•	•	Danemark
Djibouti				•	•		•	•	•		•	•	•	•	•		•	Djibouti
Dominica				•	•		•	•	•			•	•	•	•		•	Dominique
Dominican Republic				•			•	•	•	•	•	•	•	•	•		•	Rép. dominicaine

Table	8	9	10	11	12	13	14	15	16	17	18	19	20	21	22	23	24	Tableau
Ecuador	•	•	•	•	•	•		•	•	•	•		•	•	•	•	•	Equateur
Egypt	•	•	•	•	•	•	•	•	•	•	•	•	•	•		•	•	Egypte
El Salvador	•	•	•	•	•	•	•	•	•	•	•	•	•	•	•		•	El Salvador
Equatorial Guinea	•	•	•	•	•	•		•	•	•	•	•	•					Guinée équatoriale
Eritrea	•	•	•	•	•	•	•	•	•	•	•	•	•					Erythrée
Estonia	•	•	•	•	•	•	•	•	•	•	•	•	•	•	•	•	•	Estonie
Ethiopia	•	•	•	•	•	•	•	•	•	•	•	•	•					Ethiopie
EU-25		•																UE-25
EU-27																		UE-27
Euro Area																		Zone euro
Faeroe Islands	•			•				•	•		•							Iles Féroé
Falkland Is. (Malvinas)	•																	Iles Falkland (Malvinas)
Fiji	•	•	•	•	•	•	•	•	•	•	•	•	•	•	•	•	•	Fidji
Finland	•	•	•	•	•	•	•	•	•	•	•	•	•	•	•	•	•	Finlande
France	•	•	•	•	•	•	•	•	•	•	•	•	•	•	•	•	•	France
French Guiana	•	•			•						•	•		•				Guyane française
French Polynesia	•	•			•						•	•		•				Polynésie française
Gabon	•	•	•	•	•	•		•	•	•	•	•	•				•	Gabon
Gambia	•	•	•	•	•	•	•	•	•	•	•	•	•	•	•	•	•	Gambie
Georgia	•	•	•	•	•	•	•	•	•	•	•	•	•	•	•		•	Géorgie
Germany	•	•	•	•	•	•	•	•	•	•	•	•	•	•	•	•	•	Allemagne
Ghana	•	•	•	•	•	•	•	•	•	•	•	•	•	•	•		•	Ghana
Gibraltar	•				•													Gibraltar
Greece	•	•	•	•	•	•	•	•	•	•	•	•	•	•	•	•	•	Grèce
Greenland	•							•			•	•						Groenland
Grenada	•	•	•	•	•	•		•	•	•	•	•		•				Grenade
Guadeloupe	•	•		•							•	•						Guadeloupe
Guam	•	•			•			•	•									Guam
Guatemala	•	•	•	•	•	•		•	•	•	•	•	•	•	•		•	Guatemala
Guernsey	•																	Guernesey
Guinea	•	•	•	•	•	•		•	•	•	•	•	•					Guinée
Guinea-Bissau	•	•	•	•	•	•	•	•	•	•	•	•	•	•				Guinée-Bissau
Guyana	•	•	•	•	•	•	•	•	•	•	•	•	•					Guyana
Haiti	•	•	•	•	•	•		•	•	•	•		•				•	Haïti
Holy See	•																	Saint-Siège
Honduras	•	•	•	•	•	•		•	•	•	•	•	•	•	•	•	•	Honduras
Hungary	•	•	•	•	•	•	•	•	•	•	•	•	•	•	•	•	•	Hongrie
Iceland	•	•	•	•	•	•	•	•	•	•	•	•	•	•	•	•	•	Islande
India	•	•	•	•	•	•	•	•	•	•	•	•	•	•	•	•	•	Inde
Indonesia	•	•	•	•	•	•	•	•	•	•	•	•	•	•	•		•	Indonésie
Iran (Islamic Rep. of)	•	•	•	•	•	•	•	•	•	•	•	•	•	•	•		•	Iran (Rép. islamique d')
Iraq	•	•	•	•	•	•		•	•	•	•	•	•					Iraq
Ireland	•	•	•	•	•	•	•	•	•	•	•	•	•	•	•	•	•	Irlande
Isle of Man	•																	Ile de Man
Israel	•	•	•	•	•	•	•	•	•	•	•	•	•	•	•	•	•	Israël
Italy	•	•	•	•	•	•	•	•	•	•	•	•	•	•	•	•	•	Italie
Jamaica	•	•	•	•	•	•		•	•	•	•	•	•	•		•		Jamaïque
Japan	•	•	•	•	•	•	•	•	•	•	•	•	•	•	•	•	•	Japon
Jersey	•							•		•								Jersey
Jordan	•	•	•	•	•	•	•	•	•	•	•	•	•	•	•	•	•	Jordanie
Kazakhstan	•	•	•	•	•	•	•	•	•	•	•	•	•	•	•		•	Kazakhstan
Kenya	•	•	•	•	•	•	•	•	•	•	•	•	•	•	•			Kenya
Kiribati	•	•	•	•	•	•	•	•	•	•	•	•						Kiribati
Korea, Dem. P. R.	•	•	•	•	•			•			•							Corée, R. p. dém. de
Korea, Republic of	•	•	•	•	•	•	•	•	•	•	•	•	•	•	•	•	•	Corée, République de
Kosovo											•		•					Kosovo
Kuwait	•	•	•	•	•	•	•	•	•	•	•	•	•	•				Koweït
Kyrgyzstan	•	•	•	•	•	•	•	•	•	•	•	•	•	•	•			Kirghizistan
Lao People's Dem. Rep.	•	•	•	•	•	•	•	•	•	•	•	•	•					Rép. dém. pop. lao
Latvia	•	•	•	•	•	•	•	•	•	•	•	•	•	•	•	•	•	Lettonie
Lebanon	•	•	•	•	•	•	•	•	•	•	•	•	•	•	•	•		Liban
Lesotho	•	•	•	•	•	•	•	•	•	•	•	•	•	•	•			Lesotho
Liberia	•	•	•	•	•	•		•	•	•	•	•						Libéria
Libyan Arab Jamah.	•	•	•	•	•	•		•	•	•	•	•	•					Jamah. arabe libyenne
Liechtenstein			•	•	•			•	•	•			•					Liechtenstein
Lithuania	•	•	•	•	•	•	•	•	•	•	•	•	•	•	•	•	•	Lituanie

	Finance		Labour, wages and prices — Main d'œuvre, salaires et prix				Agriculture, forestry and fishing — Agriculture, forêts et pêche				Manufacturing — Industries manufacturières						
Table	25	26	27	28	29	30	31	32	33	34	35	36	37	38	39	40	Tableau
Ecuador	•		•	•	•	•	•	•	•	•	•	•	•			•	Équateur
Egypt	•	•	•	•		•	•	•	•	•	•	•	•	•		•	Égypte
El Salvador		•	•		•		•	•	•	•	•	•			•	•	El Salvador
Equatorial Guinea	•					•	•		•	•						•	Guinée équatoriale
Eritrea							•	•	•	•							Érythrée
Estonia		•	•	•		•	•	•	•	•	•	•	•	•	•	•	Estonie
Ethiopia	•	•	•			•	•	•	•	•	•					•	Éthiopie
EU-25																	UE-25
EU-27																	UE-27
Euro Area	•	•															Zone euro
Faeroe Islands			•				•			•							Îles Féroé
Falkland Is. (Malvinas)							•	•		•							Îles Falkland (Malvinas)
Fiji	•		•				•	•	•	•	•	•	•			•	Fidji
Finland		•	•	•	•	•	•	•	•	•	•	•	•	•	•	•	Finlande
France		•	•	•	•	•	•	•	•	•	•	•				•	France
French Guiana			•				•	•	•	•						•	Guyane française
French Polynesia			•	•			•		•	•							Polynésie française
Gabon							•	•	•	•	•	•				•	Gabon
Gambia	•						•	•	•	•	•					•	Gambie
Georgia		•	•	•	•	•	•	•	•	•					•	•	Géorgie
Germany		•	•	•	•	•	•	•	•	•	•	•	•	•	•	•	Allemagne
Ghana	•	•					•	•	•		•	•				•	Ghana
Gibraltar			•	•		•	•									•	Gibraltar
Greece		•	•	•	•	•	•	•	•	•	•	•	•			•	Grèce
Greenland			•				•		•	•							Groenland
Grenada	•	•					•			•							Grenade
Guadeloupe			•				•		•							•	Guadeloupe
Guam				•	•		•			•							Guam
Guatemala		•	•	•			•	•	•	•	•	•	•			•	Guatemala
Guernsey																	Guernesey
Guinea	•						•	•	•	•	•						Guinée
Guinea-Bissau	•	•					•	•	•	•	•					•	Guinée-Bissau
Guyana	•	•	•	•			•	•	•	•	•	•	•			•	Guyana
Haiti							•	•	•	•	•					•	Haïti
Holy See																	Saint-Siège
Honduras			•				•	•	•	•	•					•	Honduras
Hungary	•	•	•	•		•	•	•	•	•	•	•	•	•	•	•	Hongrie
Iceland	•	•	•		•		•	•	•	•	•	•					Islande
India	•	•	•	•	•	•	•	•	•	•	•	•	•			•	Inde
Indonesia	•	•	•		•		•	•	•	•	•	•				•	Indonésie
Iran (Islamic Rep. of)		•	•		•	•	•	•	•	•	•	•	•	•	•	•	Iran (Rép. islamique d')
Iraq	•	•	•		•		•		•	•		•	•	•		•	Iraq
Ireland		•	•	•	•	•	•	•	•	•	•	•			•	•	Irlande
Isle of Man			•	•						•						•	Île de Man
Israel	•	•	•	•	•	•	•	•	•	•	•						Israël
Italy		•	•	•	•	•	•	•	•	•	•	•	•		•	•	Italie
Jamaica		•	•	•	•	•	•	•	•	•	•	•				•	Jamaïque
Japan	•	•	•	•	•	•	•	•	•	•	•	•	•	•	•	•	Japon
Jersey			•	•	•												Jersey
Jordan	•	•	•	•		•	•	•	•	•		•				•	Jordanie
Kazakhstan	•	•	•				•	•	•	•	•	•	•	•	•	•	Kazakhstan
Kenya	•	•	•				•	•	•	•	•	•	•		•	•	Kenya
Kiribati																	Kiribati
Korea, Dem. P. R.							•	•	•	•	•						Corée, R. p. dém. de
Korea, Republic of	•	•	•	•	•	•	•	•	•	•	•	•	•	•		•	Corée, République de
Kosovo			•														Kosovo
Kuwait	•		•				•	•		•	•				•		Koweït
Kyrgyzstan		•	•			•	•	•	•	•	•		•	•	•	•	Kirghizistan
Lao People's Dem. Rep.	•	•	•			•	•	•	•	•	•					•	Rép. dém. pop. lao
Latvia	•	•	•	•	•	•	•	•	•	•	•	•	•	•	•	•	Lettonie
Lebanon	•	•	•				•	•	•	•	•		•			•	Liban
Lesotho	•		•				•	•	•	•	•				•		Lesotho
Liberia							•	•		•	•					•	Libéria
Libyan Arab Jamah.	•		•				•	•	•	•	•						Jamah. arabe libyenne
Liechtenstein			•														Liechtenstein
Lithuania	•	•	•	•	•	•	•	•	•	•	•	•	•	•	•	•	Lituanie

	Manufacturing / Industries manufacturières											Energy / Energie		Environment / Environnement					
Table	41	42	43	44	45	46	47	48	49	50	51	52	53	54	55	56	57	58	Tableau
Ecuador	•	•	•	•				•				•	•	•	•	•	•	•	Equateur
Egypt	•	•	•		•			•	•	•		•	•	•	•	•	•	•	Egypte
El Salvador	•	•		•								•	•	•	•	•	•	•	El Salvador
Equatorial Guinea												•	•	•	•	•	•	•	Guinée équatoriale
Eritrea		•										•	•	•	•	•	•	•	Erythrée
Estonia	•	•	•	•								•	•	•	•	•	•	•	Estonie
Ethiopia	•	•										•	•	•	•	•	•	•	Ethiopie
EU-25																			UE-25
EU-27																			UE-27
Euro Area																			Zone euro
Faeroe Islands												•	•	•	•	•	•		Iles Féroé
Falkland Is. (Malvinas)												•	•	•	•	•	•		Iles Falkland (Malvinas)
Fiji		•										•	•	•	•	•	•	•	Fidji
Finland	•	•	•	•	•	•	•	•	•	•	•	•	•	•	•	•	•	•	Finlande
France	•	•		•	•	•		•	•			•	•	•	•	•	•	•	France
French Guiana		•										•	•	•	•	•	•	•	Guyane française
French Polynesia												•	•	•	•	•	•	•	Polynésie française
Gabon		•										•	•	•	•	•	•	•	Gabon
Gambia												•	•	•	•	•	•	•	Gambie
Georgia		•		•						•	•	•	•	•	•	•	•	•	Géorgie
Germany	•	•	•	•	•	•	•	•	•	•	•	•	•	•	•		•	•	Allemagne
Ghana		•		•	•	•						•	•	•	•	•	•	•	Ghana
Gibraltar												•	•	•	•	•	•	•	Gibraltar
Greece	•	•	•	•				•	•			•	•	•	•	•	•	•	Grèce
Greenland												•	•	•	•		•	•	Groenland
Grenada												•	•	•	•	•	•	•	Grenade
Guadeloupe		•										•	•	•	•		•	•	Guadeloupe
Guam												•	•	•	•		•	•	Guam
Guatemala	•	•		•								•	•	•	•	•	•	•	Guatemala
Guernsey																			Guernesey
Guinea		•										•	•	•	•	•	•	•	Guinée
Guinea-Bissau												•	•	•	•	•	•	•	Guinée-Bissau
Guyana												•	•	•	•	•	•	•	Guyana
Haiti		•										•	•	•	•	•	•	•	Haïti
Holy See																			Saint-Siège
Honduras	•	•										•	•	•	•	•	•	•	Honduras
Hungary	•	•	•	•	•	•	•	•	•	•		•	•	•	•	•	•	•	Hongrie
Iceland		•			•							•	•	•	•	•	•	•	Islande
India	•	•	•	•	•	•	•	•	•	•	•	•	•	•	•	•	•	•	Inde
Indonesia	•	•	•	•	•		•	•	•	•		•	•	•	•	•	•	•	Indonésie
Iran (Islamic Rep. of)	•	•	•	•	•	•	•	•	•	•	•	•	•	•	•	•	•	•	Iran (Rép. islamique d')
Iraq	•	•		•								•	•	•	•	•	•	•	Iraq
Ireland	•	•	•	•		•		•			•	•	•	•	•	•	•	•	Irlande
Isle of Man														•					Ile de Man
Israel	•	•										•	•	•	•	•	•	•	Israël
Italy	•	•	•	•	•							•	•	•	•	•	•	•	Italie
Jamaica		•										•	•	•	•	•	•	•	Jamaïque
Japan	•	•			•	•		•	•	•		•	•	•	•	•	•	•	Japon
Jersey																			Jersey
Jordan	•	•		•														•	Jordanie
Kazakhstan	•	•	•	•	•	•	•	•	•	•	•	•	•	•	•	•	•	•	Kazakhstan
Kenya	•	•	•	•	•							•	•	•	•	•	•	•	Kenya
Kiribati												•	•	•	•	•	•	•	Kiribati
Korea, Dem. P. R.	•	•		•								•	•	•	•	•	•	•	Corée, R. p. dém. de
Korea, Republic of	•	•	•	•	•	•	•	•	•	•	•	•	•	•	•	•	•	•	Corée, République de
Kosovo																			Kosovo
Kuwait	•	•			•			•				•	•	•	•	•	•	•	Koweït
Kyrgyzstan	•	•										•	•	•	•	•	•	•	Kirghizistan
Lao People's Dem. Rep.		•										•	•	•	•	•	•	•	Rép. dém. pop. lao
Latvia	•	•	•				•	•				•	•	•	•	•	•	•	Lettonie
Lebanon	•	•										•	•	•	•	•	•	•	Liban
Lesotho					•									•		•	•	•	Lesotho
Liberia		•										•	•	•	•	•	•	•	Libéria
Libyan Arab Jamah.	•	•										•	•	•	•	•	•	•	Jamah. arabe libyenne
Liechtenstein														•	•		•	•	Liechtenstein
Lithuania	•	•	•					•		•	•	•	•	•	•	•	•	•	Lituanie

Table	Science and technology / Science et technologie			International merchandise trade / Commerce international des marchandises			International tourism and transport / Tourisme international et transport				BoP / BdP	International finance / Finances internationales			Development assistance / Aide au développement			Tableau
	59	60	61	62	63	64	65	66	67	68	69	70	71	72	73	74	75	
Ecuador	•	•		•	•								•	•	•		•	Equateur
Egypt	•	•	•	•			•	•	•	•		•	•	•	•		•	Egypte
El Salvador	•	•		•			•	•	•	•		•	•	•	•		•	El Salvador
Equatorial Guinea				•								•	•		•		•	Guinée équatoriale
Eritrea							•	•				•			•		•	Erythrée
Estonia	•	•	•	•			•	•	•	•		•	•	•			•	Estonie
Ethiopia	•	•		•			•	•	•	•		•	•	•			•	Ethiopie
EU-25				•														UE-25
EU-27				•														UE-27
Euro Area											•	•	•					Zone euro
Faeroe Islands	•			•							•							Iles Féroé
Falkland Is. (Malvinas)																		Iles Falkland (Malvinas)
Fiji				•			•	•	•	•		•	•	•			•	Fidji
Finland	•	•	•	•	•	•	•	•	•	•		•	•			•	•	Finlande
France	•	•	•	•	•	•	•	•	•	•		•	•			•	•	France
French Guiana																	•	Guyane française
French Polynesia				•													•	Polynésie française
Gabon	•						•	•	•	•		•	•	•	•		•	Gabon
Gambia	•						•	•	•	•		•	•	•	•		•	Gambie
Georgia	•	•	•	•			•	•	•	•		•	•		•		•	Géorgie
Germany	•	•	•	•	•	•	•	•	•	•			•			•	•	Allemagne
Ghana				•														Ghana
Gibraltar				•														Gibraltar
Greece	•	•	•	•			•	•	•	•		•	•			•	•	Grèce
Greenland	•			•														Groenland
Grenada				•			•	•	•	•		•	•	•	•		•	Grenade
Guadeloupe							•	•										Guadeloupe
Guam	•						•	•									•	Guam
Guatemala	•						•	•	•	•		•	•	•	•		•	Guatemala
Guernsey																		Guernesey
Guinea							•	•	•			•	•	•			•	Guinée
Guinea-Bissau				•			•	•	•	•		•	•	•			•	Guinée-Bissau
Guyana				•			•	•	•	•		•	•	•			•	Guyana
Haiti				•			•	•	•	•		•	•	•	•		•	Haïti
Holy See																		Saint-Siège
Honduras	•						•	•	•	•		•	•	•			•	Honduras
Hungary	•	•	•	•	•		•	•	•	•		•	•				•	Hongrie
Iceland	•	•	•	•	•	•	•	•	•	•		•	•				•	Islande
India	•	•	•	•	•		•	•	•	•		•	•	•			•	Inde
Indonesia	•	•		•			•	•	•	•		•	•	•			•	Indonésie
Iran (Islamic Rep. of)	•	•					•	•	•	•			•	•			•	Iran (Rép. islamique d')
Iraq							•	•	•			•	•		•		•	Iraq
Ireland	•	•	•	•	•	•	•	•	•	•			•			•	•	Irlande
Isle of Man																		Île de Man
Israel		•	•	•	•		•	•	•	•		•	•				•	Israël
Italy	•	•	•	•	•	•	•	•	•	•			•			•	•	Italie
Jamaica		•	•	•	•		•	•	•	•		•	•	•			•	Jamaïque
Japan	•	•	•	•	•	•	•	•	•	•		•	•			•	•	Japon
Jersey																		Jersey
Jordan	•	•		•	•		•	•	•	•		•	•	•			•	Jordanie
Kazakhstan	•	•		•			•	•	•	•		•	•	•	•		•	Kazakhstan
Kenya	•	•	•	•			•	•	•	•		•	•	•	•		•	Kenya
Kiribati				•			•	•							•		•	Kiribati
Korea, Dem. P. R.				•						•					•		•	Corée, R. p. dém. de
Korea, Republic of	•	•	•	•	•	•	•	•	•	•		•	•				•	Corée, République de
Kosovo													•					Kosovo
Kuwait	•	•					•	•	•	•		•	•				•	Koweït
Kyrgyzstan	•	•	•				•	•	•	•		•	•	•			•	Kirghizistan
Lao People's Dem. Rep.	•	•					•	•	•	•		•	•	•			•	Rép. dém. pop. lao
Latvia	•	•	•	•	•		•	•	•	•		•	•				•	Lettonie
Lebanon				•			•	•	•	•		•	•	•			•	Liban
Lesotho	•	•					•	•	•	•		•	•	•			•	Lesotho
Liberia							•	•	•	•		•					•	Libéria
Libyan Arab Jamah.				•	•		•	•	•	•		•			•		•	Jamah. arabe libyenne
Liechtenstein							•	•										Liechtenstein
Lithuania	•	•	•	•	•		•	•	•	•		•	•				•	Lituanie

Table	8	9	10	11	12	13	14	15	16	17	18	19	20	21	22	23	24	Tableau
Luxembourg	•	•	•	•	•	•	•	•	•		•	•	•	•		•	•	Luxembourg
Madagascar	•	•	•	•	•	•	•	•	•	•	•	•	•	•			•	Madagascar
Malawi	•	•	•	•	•	•		•	•	•	•	•	•	•			•	Malawi
Malaysia	•	•	•	•	•	•	•	•	•	•	•	•	•	•	•	•	•	Malaisie
Maldives	•	•	•	•	•	•	•	•	•	•	•	•		•	•			Maldives
Mali	•	•	•	•	•	•	•	•	•	•	•	•	•	•			•	Mali
Malta	•	•	•	•	•	•	•	•	•	•	•	•	•	•	•	•	•	Malte
Marshall Islands	•		•	•	•	•		•	•	•	•							Iles Marshall
Martinique	•		•		•				•		•		•					Martinique
Mauritania	•	•	•	•	•	•	•	•	•	•	•	•	•					Mauritanie
Mauritius	•	•	•	•	•	•	•	•	•	•	•	•	•	•			•	Maurice
Mayotte	•	•						•	•									Mayotte
Mexico	•	•	•	•	•	•	•	•	•	•	•	•	•	•	•	•	•	Mexique
Micronesia (Fed. States of)	•	•	•		•			•	•		•		•					Micronésie (Etats féd. de)
Monaco	•		•	•	•						•							Monaco
Mongolia	•	•	•	•	•	•	•	•	•	•	•	•	•	•	•	•	•	Mongolie
Montenegro	•	•		•	•	•	•	•	•	•	•	•	•					Monténégro
Montserrat	•					•	•								•			Montserrat
Morocco	•	•	•	•	•	•	•	•	•	•	•	•	•				•	Maroc
Mozambique	•	•	•	•	•	•	•	•	•	•	•	•	•	•				Mozambique
Myanmar	•	•	•	•	•	•	•	•	•	•	•	•	•	•				Myanmar
Namibia	•	•	•	•	•	•	•	•	•	•	•	•	•	•				Namibie
Nauru	•		•		•	•					•							Nauru
Nepal	•	•	•	•	•	•	•	•	•	•	•	•	•	•				Népal
Netherlands	•	•	•	•	•	•	•	•	•	•	•	•	•	•	•	•	•	Pays-Bas
Netherlands Antilles	•	•	•	•	•	•			•		•	•	•	•				Antilles néerlandaises
New Caledonia	•		•	•	•			•	•	•	•	•	•	•				Nouvelle-Calédonie
New Zealand	•	•	•	•	•	•	•	•	•	•	•	•	•	•	•	•	•	Nouvelle-Zélande
Nicaragua	•	•	•	•	•	•	•	•	•	•	•	•	•	•	•	•	•	Nicaragua
Niger	•	•	•	•	•	•	•	•	•	•	•	•	•	•				Niger
Nigeria	•	•	•	•	•	•	•	•	•	•	•	•	•					Nigéria
Niue	•				•	•												Nioué
Norfolk Island	•																	Ile Norfolk
Northern Mariana Islands	•			•					•									Iles Mariannes du Nord
Norway	•	•	•	•	•	•	•	•	•	•	•	•	•	•		•	•	Norvège
Occupied Palestinian Terr.	•	•		•	•		•	•	•	•	•	•	•	•				Terr. palestinien occupé
Oman	•	•	•	•	•	•	•	•	•	•	•	•	•	•			•	Oman
Pakistan	•	•	•	•	•	•	•	•	•	•	•	•	•	•	•		•	Pakistan
Palau	•		•	•	•	•	•	•	•		•	•						Palaos
Panama	•	•	•	•	•	•	•	•	•	•	•	•	•	•	•		•	Panama
Papua New Guinea	•	•	•	•	•	•		•	•	•	•	•	•	•				Papouasie-Nvl-Guinée
Paraguay	•	•	•	•	•	•	•	•	•	•	•	•	•	•			•	Paraguay
Peru	•	•	•	•	•	•	•	•	•	•	•	•	•	•	•	•	•	Pérou
Philippines	•	•	•	•	•	•	•	•	•	•	•	•	•	•			•	Philippines
Pitcairn	•																	Pitcairn
Poland	•	•	•	•	•	•	•	•	•	•	•	•	•	•	•	•	•	Pologne
Polynesia	•																	Polynésie
Portugal	•	•	•	•	•	•	•	•	•	•	•	•	•	•	•	•	•	Portugal
Puerto Rico	•	•						•	•	•	•	•	•	•		•		Porto Rico
Qatar	•	•	•	•	•	•	•	•	•	•	•	•	•	•				Qatar
Republic of Moldova	•	•	•	•	•	•	•	•	•	•	•	•	•	•	•	•	•	République de Moldova
Réunion	•	•						•	•	•	•	•						Réunion
Romania	•	•	•	•	•	•	•	•	•	•	•	•	•	•	•		•	Roumanie
Russian Federation	•	•	•	•	•	•	•	•	•	•	•	•	•	•	•		•	Fédération de Russie
Rwanda	•	•	•	•	•	•	•	•	•	•	•	•	•					Rwanda
Saba																		Saba
Saint Eustatius																		Saint-Eustache
Saint Helena	•			•														Sainte-Hélène
Saint Helena ex. dep.	•																	Sainte-Hélène sans dép.
Saint Kitts and Nevis	•		•		•	•	•	•	•	•	•	•	•					Saint-Kitts-et-Nevis
Saint Lucia	•	•	•	•	•	•	•	•	•	•	•	•	•	•				Sainte-Lucie
Saint Maarten																		Saint-Martin
Saint Pierre and Miquelon	•																	Saint-Pierre-et-Miquelon
Saint Vincent-Grenadines	•	•	•	•	•	•	•	•	•	•	•	•	•		•			Saint Vincent-Grenadines
Samoa	•	•	•	•	•	•	•	•	•	•	•	•	•					Samoa
San Marino	•		•	•	•		•		•	•	•	•	•		•	•		Saint-Marin
Sao Tome and Principe	•	•	•	•	•	•	•	•	•	•	•	•	•					Sao Tomé-et-Principe

	Finance		Labour, wages and prices Main d'œuvre, salaires et prix				Agriculture, forestry and fishing Agriculture, forêts et pêche				Manufacturing Industries manufacturières						
Table	25	26	27	28	29	30	31	32	33	34	35	36	37	38	39	40	**Tableau**
Luxembourg			•	•	•	•	•	•	•			•				•	Luxembourg
Madagascar	•	•	•	•			•	•	•		•	•	•			•	Madagascar
Malawi	•	•				•	•	•	•	•	•	•	•			•	Malawi
Malaysia		•	•	•	•	•	•	•	•							•	Malaisie
Maldives	•	•	•						•	•	•						Maldives
Mali	•	•	•				•	•	•	•	•					•	Mali
Malta	•	•	•	•			•	•	•	•							Malte
Marshall Islands						•	•			•							Iles Marshall
Martinique			•				•			•						•	Martinique
Mauritania	•	•					•	•	•	•	•					•	Mauritanie
Mauritius	•	•					•	•	•	•	•					•	Maurice
Mayotte										•							Mayotte
Mexico		•	•	•	•	•	•	•	•	•	•	•	•		•	•	Mexique
Micronesia (Fed. States of)							•			•							Micronésie (Etats féd. de)
Monaco										•							Monaco
Mongolia	•	•		•	•		•	•	•	•	•					•	Mongolie
Montenegro		•		•	•		•	•	•			•	•	•	•	•	Monténégro
Montserrat	•	•					•			•							Montserrat
Morocco	•	•	•	•		•	•	•	•	•	•					•	Maroc
Mozambique	•	•					•	•	•	•	•	•	•		•	•	Mozambique
Myanmar	•		•	•			•	•	•	•	•		•			•	Myanmar
Namibia							•	•	•	•	•						Namibie
Nauru							•		•								Nauru
Nepal	•	•					•	•	•	•	•	•				•	Népal
Netherlands			•	•	•	•	•	•	•	•		•				•	Pays-Bas
Netherlands Antilles	•	•	•			•				•							Antilles néerlandaises
New Caledonia			•				•	•	•							•	Nouvelle-Calédonie
New Zealand	•	•	•	•	•	•	•	•	•	•	•	•	•	•		•	Nouvelle-Zélande
Nicaragua			•	•		•	•	•	•	•						•	Nicaragua
Niger	•	•	•	•			•	•	•	•				•		•	Niger
Nigeria	•	•				•	•	•	•	•	•	•	•	•	•	•	Nigéria
Niue			•				•			•							Nioué
Norfolk Island						•											Ile Norfolk
Northern Mariana Islands			•			•	•			•							Iles Mariannes du Nord
Norway	•	•	•	•	•	•	•	•	•	•	•	•			•	•	Norvège
Occupied Palestinian Terr.			•	•	•		•	•	•							•	Terr. palestinien occupé
Oman	•	•			•	•	•	•		•							Oman
Pakistan	•	•	•	•			•	•	•	•	•		•	•		•	Pakistan
Palau										•							Palaos
Panama		•	•	•	•	•	•	•	•	•						•	Panama
Papua New Guinea	•	•				•	•	•	•	•	•					•	Papouasie-Nvl-Guinée
Paraguay	•	•	•	•			•	•	•	•						•	Paraguay
Peru	•	•	•		•	•	•	•	•	•	•	•	•	•			Pérou
Philippines	•	•	•	•			•	•	•	•	•					•	Philippines
Pitcairn										•							Pitcairn
Poland	•	•	•	•	•	•	•	•	•	•	•	•	•	•	•	•	Pologne
Polynesia																	Polynésie
Portugal		•		•	•	•	•	•	•	•	•	•	•	•		•	Portugal
Puerto Rico			•	•		•	•		•			•					Porto Rico
Qatar	•	•	•	•			•	•	•	•							Qatar
Republic of Moldova		•	•	•	•	•	•	•	•	•	•	•			•	•	République de Moldova
Réunion			•			•	•	•	•	•							Réunion
Romania		•	•	•	•	•	•	•	•	•	•	•	•			•	Roumanie
Russian Federation	•	•	•	•	•	•	•	•	•	•	•	•	•		•	•	Fédération de Russie
Rwanda	•	•	•				•	•	•	•	•					•	Rwanda
Saba																	Saba
Saint Eustatius																	Saint-Eustache
Saint Helena			•	•						•							Sainte-Hélène
Saint Helena ex. dep.																	Sainte-Hélène sans dép.
Saint Kitts and Nevis	•	•					•			•	•	•					Saint-Kitts-et-Nevis
Saint Lucia	•	•	•	•			•			•							Sainte-Lucie
Saint Maarten																	Saint-Martin
Saint Pierre and Miquelon						•				•							Saint-Pierre-et-Miquelon
Saint Vincent-Grenadines	•	•	•				•	•		•							Saint Vincent-Grenadines
Samoa			•				•	•		•	•					•	Samoa
San Marino			•	•		•											Saint-Marin
Sao Tome and Principe	•		•				•	•		•						•	Sao Tomé-et-Principe

Table	41	42	43	44	45	46	47	48	49	50	51	52	53	54	55	56	57	58	Tableau
				Manufacturing / Industries manufacturières								Energy / Energie		Environment / Environnement					
Luxembourg	•	•		•								•	•	•	•		•	•	Luxembourg
Madagascar	•	•										•	•	•	•	•	•	•	Madagascar
Malawi		•										•	•	•	•	•	•	•	Malawi
Malaysia	•	•		•		•	•	•				•	•	•	•	•	•	•	Malaisie
Maldives												•	•	•	•	•	•	•	Maldives
Mali		•										•	•	•	•	•	•	•	Mali
Malta												•	•	•	•	•	•	•	Malte
Marshall Islands												•	•	•	•	•	•		Iles Marshall
Martinique		•										•	•	•	•		•		Martinique
Mauritania	•	•		•								•	•	•	•	•	•		Mauritanie
Mauritius												•	•	•	•		•		Maurice
Mayotte														•			•		Mayotte
Mexico	•	•	•	•		•	•	•	•		•	•	•	•	•	•	•	•	Mexique
Micronesia (Fed. States of)													•	•	•		•	•	Micronésie (Etats féd. de)
Monaco														•		•	•	•	Monaco
Mongolia		•		•								•	•	•	•	•	•	•	Mongolie
Montenegro		•		•									•	•			•	•	Monténégro
Montserrat												•	•	•	•		•	•	Montserrat
Morocco	•	•		•								•	•	•	•	•	•	•	Maroc
Mozambique	•	•	•		•							•	•	•	•	•	•	•	Mozambique
Myanmar	•	•			•							•	•	•	•	•	•	•	Myanmar
Namibia					•							•	•	•	•	•	•	•	Namibie
Nauru												•	•	•	•	•	•		Nauru
Nepal	•	•										•	•	•	•	•	•		Népal
Netherlands	•	•		•	•							•	•	•	•		•	•	Pays-Bas
Netherlands Antilles												•	•	•	•		•		Antilles néerlandaises
New Caledonia		•										•	•	•	•		•		Nouvelle-Calédonie
New Zealand	•	•										•	•	•	•	•	•	•	Nouvelle-Zélande
Nicaragua		•										•	•	•	•	•	•	•	Nicaragua
Niger		•										•	•	•	•	•	•		Niger
Nigeria	•	•		•			•	•			•	•	•	•	•	•	•	•	Nigéria
Niue		•										•	•	•	•	•	•	•	Nioué
Norfolk Island														•			•		Ile Norfolk
Northern Mariana Islands														•			•		Iles Mariannes du Nord
Norway	•	•		•	•							•	•	•	•	•	•	•	Norvège
Occupied Palestinian Terr.		•										•	•	•	•		•		Terr. palestinien occupé
Oman		•										•	•	•	•	•	•	•	Oman
Pakistan	•	•		•								•	•	•	•	•	•	•	Pakistan
Palau												•	•	•	•	•	•	•	Palaos
Panama		•										•	•	•	•	•	•	•	Panama
Papua New Guinea												•	•	•	•		•	•	Papouasie-Nvl-Guinée
Paraguay	•	•										•	•	•	•	•	•	•	Paraguay
Peru	•	•	•	•			•					•	•	•	•	•	•	•	Pérou
Philippines	•	•		•								•	•	•	•		•		Philippines
Pitcairn														•			•		Pitcairn
Poland	•	•	•	•	•	•	•	•	•	•	•	•	•	•	•	•	•	•	Pologne
Polynesia																			Polynésie
Portugal	•	•		•		•	•	•	•		•	•	•	•	•		•	•	Portugal
Puerto Rico		•										•	•	•	•		•		Porto Rico
Qatar		•		•								•	•	•	•	•	•	•	Qatar
Republic of Moldova		•		•		•	•	•				•	•	•	•	•	•	•	République de Moldova
Réunion		•										•	•	•	•		•		Réunion
Romania	•	•	•	•	•	•	•	•	•		•	•	•	•	•	•	•	•	Roumanie
Russian Federation	•	•	•	•	•	•	•	•				•	•	•	•	•	•	•	Fédération de Russie
Rwanda												•	•	•	•	•	•	•	Rwanda
Saba																			Saba
Saint Eustatius																			Saint-Eustache
Saint Helena												•	•	•	•		•		Sainte-Hélène
Saint Helena ex. dep.																			Sainte-Hélène sans dép.
Saint Kitts and Nevis												•	•	•	•	•	•		Saint-Kitts-et-Nevis
Saint Lucia												•	•	•	•	•	•		Sainte-Lucie
Saint Maarten																			Saint-Martin
Saint Pierre and Miquelon												•	•	•	•		•		Saint-Pierre-et-Miquelon
Saint Vincent-Grenadines												•	•	•	•	•	•		Saint Vincent-Grenadines
Samoa												•	•	•	•	•	•		Samoa
San Marino														•			•		Saint-Marin
Sao Tome and Principe												•	•	•	•	•	•	•	Sao Tomé-et-Principe

| | Science and technology | | | International merchandise trade | | | International tourism and transport | | | | BoP | International finance | | | Development assistance | | | |
| | Science et technologie | | | Commerce international des marchandises | | | Tourisme international et transport | | | | BdP | Finances internationales | | | Aide au développement | | | |
Table	59	60	61	62	63	64	65	66	67	68	69	70	71	72	73	74	75	Tableau
Luxembourg	•	•	•	•			•	•	•	•	•		•				•		Luxembourg
Madagascar	•	•	•				•	•	•	•	•		•	•	•			•	Madagascar
Malawi				•			•	•	•	•		•	•	•	•		•	Malawi
Malaysia	•	•	•	•	•		•	•	•	•		•	•	•	•		•	Malaisie
Maldives				•			•	•	•	•		•	•	•	•		•	Maldives
Mali	•			•			•	•	•	•		•	•	•	•		•	Mali
Malta	•	•	•				•	•	•	•		•	•				•	Malte
Marshall Islands							•	•		•					•		•	Iles Marshall
Martinique							•	•										Martinique
Mauritania										•		•	•	•	•		•	Mauritanie
Mauritius		•		•	•		•	•	•	•		•	•			•		Maurice
Mayotte															•		•	Mayotte
Mexico	•	•	•	•	•		•	•	•	•	•	•	•	•	•		•	Mexique
Micronesia (Fed. States of)							•	•	•						•		•	Micronésie (Etats féd. de)
Monaco	•	•	•				•	•	•		•							Monaco
Mongolia	•	•		•			•	•	•	•	•	•	•	•	•		•	Mongolie
Montenegro	•	•		•			•	•	•	•	•	•	•	•	•		•	Monténégro
Montserrat							•	•	•						•		•	Montserrat
Morocco	•	•	•	•			•	•	•	•	•	•	•	•	•		•	Maroc
Mozambique	•	•		•			•	•	•	•		•	•	•	•		•	Mozambique
Myanmar	•	•		•			•	•	•	•		•	•	•	•		•	Myanmar
Namibia				•			•	•	•	•		•	•	•	•		•	Namibie
Nauru	•						•	•							•		•	Nauru
Nepal	•			•			•	•	•	•		•	•	•	•		•	Népal
Netherlands	•	•	•	•		•	•	•	•	•	•		•			•		Pays-Bas
Netherlands Antilles											•						•	Antilles néerlandaises
New Caledonia				•			•	•	•								•	Nouvelle-Calédonie
New Zealand	•	•	•	•			•	•	•	•	•	•	•	•		•		Nouvelle-Zélande
Nicaragua	•	•		•			•	•	•	•		•	•	•	•		•	Nicaragua
Niger	•			•			•	•	•	•		•	•	•	•		•	Niger
Nigeria	•			•			•	•	•	•	•	•	•	•	•		•	Nigéria
Niue				•			•	•							•		•	Nioué
Norfolk Island																		Ile Norfolk
Northern Mariana Islands							•	•										Iles Mariannes du Nord
Norway	•	•	•	•	•		•	•	•	•	•	•	•	•	•	•	•	Norvège
Occupied Palestinian Terr.	•			•			•	•	•						•		•	Terr. palestinien occupé
Oman				•			•	•	•	•		•	•		•		•	Oman
Pakistan	•	•	•	•			•	•	•	•	•	•	•	•	•		•	Pakistan
Palau							•	•	•						•		•	Palaos
Panama	•	•		•			•	•	•	•	•	•	•	•	•		•	Panama
Papua New Guinea				•			•	•	•	•		•	•	•	•		•	Papouasie-Nvl-Guinée
Paraguay	•			•			•	•	•	•	•	•	•	•	•		•	Paraguay
Peru	•	•	•	•	•		•	•	•	•	•	•	•	•	•		•	Pérou
Philippines	•	•	•	•			•	•	•	•	•	•	•	•	•		•	Philippines
Pitcairn																		Pitcairn
Poland	•	•	•	•			•	•	•	•	•	•	•	•			•	Pologne
Polynesia																		Polynésie
Portugal	•	•	•	•	•		•	•	•	•	•		•		•	•		Portugal
Puerto Rico							•	•	•								•	Porto Rico
Qatar				•			•	•	•	•		•	•				•	Qatar
Republic of Moldova	•	•	•	•	•		•	•	•	•	•	•	•	•	•		•	République de Moldova
Réunion							•	•										Réunion
Romania	•	•	•	•	•		•	•	•	•	•	•	•	•			•	Roumanie
Russian Federation	•	•	•	•	•		•	•	•	•	•	•	•	•			•	Fédération de Russie
Rwanda				•			•	•	•	•	•	•	•	•	•		•	Rwanda
Saba							•											Saba
Saint Eustatius							•	•										Saint-Eustache
Saint Helena																	•	Sainte-Hélène
Saint Helena ex. dep.																		Sainte-Hélène sans dép.
Saint Kitts and Nevis				•			•	•	•	•		•	•		•		•	Saint-Kitts-et-Nevis
Saint Lucia		•	•				•	•	•	•		•	•		•		•	Sainte-Lucie
Saint Maarten							•	•	•									Saint-Martin
Saint Pierre and Miquelon																		Saint-Pierre-et-Miquelon
Saint Vincent-Grenadines	•	•		•			•	•	•	•		•	•		•		•	Saint Vincent-Grenadines
Samoa		•					•	•	•	•	•	•	•	•	•		•	Samoa
San Marino							•	•	•				•				•	Saint-Marin
Sao Tome and Principe				•			•	•	•	•	•	•	•	•	•		•	Sao Tomé-et-Principe

	Population		Gender / Femmes			Education		Communication			National accounts / Comptabilités nationales							
Table	**8**	**9**	**10**	**11**	**12**	**13**	**14**	**15**	**16**	**17**	**18**	**19**	**20**	**21**	**22**	**23**	**24**	**Tableau**
Saudi Arabia	•	•	•	•	•	•	•	•	•	•	•	•	•	•	•		•	Arabie saoudite
Senegal	•	•	•	•	•	•	•	•	•	•	•	•	•	•	•		•	Sénégal
Serbia	•	•	•	•	•			•	•	•	•	•				•	•	Serbie
Serbia and Montenegro			•					•	•	•	•	•						Serbie-et-Monténégro
Seychelles	•													•	•	•		Seychelles
Sierra Leone	•	•	•	•	•	•	•	•	•	•	•	•	•	•	•	•		Sierra Leone
Singapore	•	•	•	•	•	•		•	•	•	•	•	•	•	•	•		Singapour
Slovakia	•	•	•	•	•	•	•	•	•	•	•	•	•	•	•	•	•	Slovaquie
Slovenia	•	•	•	•	•	•	•	•	•	•	•	•	•	•	•	•	•	Slovénie
Solomon Islands	•	•	•	•	•	•		•	•		•	•	•					Iles Salomon
Somalia	•	•	•	•	•			•	•	•	•	•	•					Somalie
South Africa	•	•	•	•	•	•		•	•	•	•	•	•	•	•		•	Afrique du Sud
Spain	•	•	•	•	•	•	•	•	•	•	•	•	•	•	•		•	Espagne
Sri Lanka	•	•	•	•	•	•		•	•	•	•	•	•	•	•		•	Sri Lanka
Sudan	•	•	•	•	•	•		•	•	•	•	•	•	•	•	•		Soudan
Suriname	•	•	•	•	•	•		•	•	•	•	•	•	•				Suriname
Svalbard and Jan Mayen Is.	•																	Svalbard et îles Jan Mayen
Swaziland	•	•	•	•	•			•	•	•	•	•	•				•	Swaziland
Sweden	•	•	•	•	•	•	•	•	•	•	•	•	•	•	•		•	Suède
Switzerland	•	•	•	•	•	•	•	•	•	•	•	•	•	•		•	•	Suisse
Syrian Arab Republic	•	•	•	•	•	•	•	•	•	•	•	•	•	•				Rép. arabe syrienne
Tajikistan	•	•	•	•	•			•	•	•	•	•	•				•	Tadjikistan
TFYR of Macedonia	•	•	•	•	•	•	•	•	•	•	•	•	•	•	•	•	•	L'ex-R.Y. Macédoine
Thailand	•	•	•	•	•	•	•	•	•	•	•	•	•	•	•		•	Thaïlande
Timor-Leste	•	•	•	•	•	•	•	•	•	•	•	•	•				•	Timor-Leste
Togo	•	•	•	•	•	•	•	•	•	•	•	•	•	•				Togo
Tokelau	•																	Tokélaou
Tonga	•	•	•	•	•	•		•	•	•	•	•	•	•				Tonga
Trinidad and Tobago	•	•	•	•	•	•		•	•	•	•	•	•	•	•		•	Trinité-et-Tobago
Tristan da Cunha	•																	Tristan da Cunha
Tunisia	•	•	•	•	•	•	•	•	•	•	•	•	•	•	•		•	Tunisie
Turkey	•	•	•	•	•	•	•	•	•	•	•	•	•	•		•	•	Turquie
Turkmenistan	•	•	•	•	•			•	•	•	•	•	•				•	Turkménistan
Turks and Caicos Islands	•			•	•			•	•		•	•	•					Iles Turques et Caïques
Tuvalu	•	•	•	•	•			•	•	•	•	•						Tuvalu
Uganda	•	•	•	•	•	•		•	•	•	•	•	•				•	Ouganda
Ukraine	•	•	•	•	•	•	•	•	•	•	•	•	•	•	•	•	•	Ukraine
United Arab Emirates	•	•	•	•	•	•	•	•	•	•	•	•	•	•				Emirats arabes unis
United Kingdom	•	•	•	•	•	•	•	•	•	•	•	•	•	•	•	•	•	Royaume Uni
United Rep. of Tanzania	•	•	•	•	•	•	•	•	•	•	•	•	•	•	•		•	Rép.-Unie de Tanzanie
United States	•	•	•	•	•	•	•	•	•	•	•	•	•	•	•	•	•	Etats-Unis
United States Virgin Is.	•	•						•	•	•								Iles Vierges américaines
Uruguay	•	•	•	•	•	•		•	•	•	•	•	•	•	•		•	Uruguay
Uzbekistan	•	•	•	•	•	•		•	•	•	•	•	•				•	Ouzbékistan
Vanuatu	•	•	•	•	•			•	•	•	•	•	•	•	•		•	Vanuatu
Venezuela (Boliv. Rep. of)	•	•	•	•	•	•	•	•	•	•	•	•	•				•	Venezuela (Rép. boliv. du)
Viet Nam	•	•	•	•	•	•		•	•		•	•	•					Viet Nam
Wallis and Futuna Islands	•																	Iles Wallis et Futuna
Western Sahara	•	•																Sahara occidental
Yemen	•	•	•	•	•	•	•	•	•	•	•	•	•	•	•		•	Yémen
Zambia	•	•	•	•	•	•		•	•	•	•	•	•				•	Zambie
Zanzibar											•		•					Zanzibar
Zimbabwe	•		•	•	•	•		•	•	•	•	•	•	•	•		•	Zimbabwe

	Finance		Labour, wages and prices / Main d'œuvre, salaires et prix				Agriculture, forestry and fishing / Agriculture, forêts et pêche				Manufacturing / Industries manufacturières						
Table	25	26	27	28	29	30	31	32	33	34	35	36	37	38	39	40	**Tableau**
Saudi Arabia			•			•	•	•		•	•						Arabie saoudite
Senegal	•	•				•	•	•	•	•	•					•	Sénégal
Serbia	•	•	•	•	•	•		•	•	•		•	•	•	•	•	Serbie
Serbia and Montenegro			•	•			•	•	•	•		•	•			•	Serbie-et-Monténégro
Seychelles	•	•	•			•	•			•		•	•				Seychelles
Sierra Leone		•	•			•	•	•		•						•	Sierra Leone
Singapore		•	•	•		•	•			•	•					•	Singapour
Slovakia	•	•	•	•	•	•	•	•	•	•	•				•	•	Slovaquie
Slovenia	•	•	•	•	•	•	•	•	•	•			•	•	•	•	Slovénie
Solomon Islands		•					•	•	•	•						•	Iles Salomon
Somalia							•	•	•	•						•	Somalie
South Africa	•	•	•	•	•	•	•	•	•	•	•			•		•	Afrique du Sud
Spain		•	•	•	•	•	•	•	•	•	•	•	•	•	•	•	Espagne
Sri Lanka	•	•	•	•		•	•	•	•	•	•		•			•	Sri Lanka
Sudan			•				•	•	•	•	•					•	Soudan
Suriname			•				•	•	•	•						•	Suriname
Svalbard and Jan Mayen Is.																	Svalbard et îles Jan Mayen
Swaziland	•	•					•	•	•	•						•	Swaziland
Sweden	•	•	•	•	•	•	•	•	•	•	•	•	•	•	•	•	Suède
Switzerland	•	•	•	•	•	•	•	•	•	•	•		•			•	Suisse
Syrian Arab Republic	•	•	•		•	•	•	•	•	•						•	Rép. arabe syrienne
Tajikistan	•		•				•	•	•	•	•		•	•	•		Tadjikistan
TFYR of Macedonia	•	•	•	•		•	•	•	•	•		•	•			•	L'ex-R.Y. Macédoine
Thailand	•	•	•	•	•	•	•	•	•	•	•		•			•	Thaïlande
Timor-Leste							•	•									Timor-Leste
Togo	•	•					•	•	•	•	•					•	Togo
Tokelau										•							Tokélaou
Tonga			•				•			•						•	Tonga
Trinidad and Tobago	•	•	•	•	•	•	•	•	•	•						•	Trinité-et-Tobago
Tristan da Cunha																	Tristan da Cunha
Tunisia		•	•		•	•	•	•	•	•		•	•				Tunisie
Turkey	•	•	•	•	•	•	•	•	•	•	•	•	•			•	Turquie
Turkmenistan							•	•		•				•			Turkménistan
Turks and Caicos Islands			•							•							Iles Turques et Caïques
Tuvalu			•				•	•		•							Tuvalu
Uganda	•	•	•				•	•	•	•	•	•	•	•		•	Ouganda
Ukraine	•	•	•	•	•	•	•	•	•	•	•	•	•	•	•	•	Ukraine
United Arab Emirates			•				•	•		•							Emirats arabes unis
United Kingdom		•	•	•		•	•	•	•	•		•	•		•	•	Royaume-Uni
United Rep. of Tanzania	•	•	•			•	•	•	•	•	•	•	•			•	Rép.-Unie de Tanzanie
United States	•	•	•	•	•	•	•	•	•	•	•	•	•	•		•	Etats-Unis
United States Virgin Is.				•			•			•							Iles Vierges américaines
Uruguay	•	•	•	•	•	•	•	•	•	•						•	Uruguay
Uzbekistan			•				•	•		•	•	•	•				Ouzbékistan
Vanuatu	•	•					•	•	•	•						•	Vanuatu
Venezuela (Boliv. Rep. of)	•		•		•		•	•	•	•						•	Venezuela (Rép. boliv. du)
Viet Nam	•	•	•	•		•	•	•	•	•	•	•	•			•	Viet Nam
Wallis and Futuna Islands							•			•							Iles Wallis et Futuna
Western Sahara							•	•									Sahara occidental
Yemen		•					•	•	•	•	•		•				Yémen
Zambia	•	•					•	•	•	•	•					•	Zambie
Zanzibar																	Zanzibar
Zimbabwe	•	•		•			•	•	•	•						•	Zimbabwe

Table	41	42	43	44	45	46	47	48	49	50	51	52	53	54	55	56	57	58	Tableau
Saudi Arabia	•			•								•		•				•	Arabie saoudite
Senegal		•										•	•	•	•	•	•	•	Sénégal
Serbia	•	•	•	•	•		•				•		•	•		•		•	Serbie
Serbia and Montenegro	•	•	•	•	•			•	•	•		•			•			•	Serbie-et-Monténégro
Seychelles												•	•	•	•	•	•	•	Seychelles
Sierra Leone		•										•	•	•	•	•	•	•	Sierra Leone
Singapore	•	•		•								•		•	•	•	•	•	Singapour
Slovakia	•	•	•	•	•		•	•		•		•	•	•	•	•	•	•	Slovaquie
Slovenia	•	•	•	•			•					•	•	•	•	•	•	•	Slovénie
Solomon Islands												•	•	•	•	•	•	•	Iles Salomon
Somalia												•	•	•	•	•	•	•	Somalie
South Africa	•	•	•	•	•	•		•	•		•	•	•	•	•	•	•	•	Afrique du Sud
Spain	•	•	•	•	•	•	•	•	•	•	•	•	•	•	•	•	•	•	Espagne
Sri Lanka	•	•		•								•	•	•	•	•	•	•	Sri Lanka
Sudan	•	•					•	•				•	•	•	•	•	•	•	Soudan
Suriname		•			•							•	•	•	•	•	•	•	Suriname
Svalbard and Jan Mayen Is.																		•	Svalbard et îles Jan Mayen
Swaziland														•	•	•	•	•	Swaziland
Sweden	•	•	•	•	•	•	•	•	•	•	•	•	•	•	•	•	•	•	Suède
Switzerland	•	•	•		•							•	•	•	•	•	•	•	Suisse
Syrian Arab Republic	•	•			•			•	•			•	•	•	•	•	•	•	Rép. arabe syrienne
Tajikistan		•			•		•					•	•	•	•	•	•	•	Tadjikistan
TFYR of Macedonia	•	•	•	•	•		•					•	•	•	•	•	•	•	L'ex-R.Y. Macédoine
Thailand	•	•		•		•	•	•	•	•		•	•	•	•	•	•	•	Thaïlande
Timor-Leste												•	•	•	•		•	•	Timor-Leste
Togo		•										•	•	•	•	•	•	•	Togo
Tokelau														•			•	•	Tokélaou
Tonga												•	•	•	•	•	•	•	Tonga
Trinidad and Tobago					•							•	•	•	•	•	•	•	Trinité-et-Tobago
Tristan da Cunha														•					Tristan da Cunha
Tunisia	•	•				•						•	•	•	•	•	•	•	Tunisie
Turkey	•	•	•		•			•	•		•	•	•	•	•	•	•	•	Turquie
Turkmenistan		•										•	•	•	•	•	•	•	Turkménistan
Turks and Caicos Islands												•	•				•	•	Iles Turques et Caïques
Tuvalu														•			•	•	Tuvalu
Uganda	•			•								•	•	•	•	•	•	•	Ouganda
Ukraine	•	•	•	•	•	•	•	•	•	•	•	•	•	•	•	•	•	•	Ukraine
United Arab Emirates	•	•		•	•							•	•	•	•	•	•	•	Emirats arabes unis
United Kingdom	•	•	•	•	•	•	•	•	•	•	•	•	•	•	•	•	•	•	Royaume-Uni
United Rep. of Tanzania	•	•	•									•	•	•	•	•	•	•	Rép.-Unie de Tanzanie
United States	•	•	•		•	•	•	•	•	•	•	•	•	•	•	•	•	•	Etats-Unis
United States Virgin Is.					•							•		•			•	•	Iles Vierges américaines
Uruguay	•	•	•									•	•	•	•	•	•	•	Uruguay
Uzbekistan	•	•	•		•			•				•	•	•	•	•	•	•	Ouzbékistan
Vanuatu												•	•	•	•	•	•	•	Vanuatu
Venezuela (Boliv. Rep. of)	•	•		•	•							•	•	•	•	•	•	•	Venezuela (Rép. boliv. du)
Viet Nam	•	•	•	•		•	•					•	•	•	•	•	•	•	Viet Nam
Wallis and Futuna Islands												•	•	•	•		•	•	Iles Wallis et Futuna
Western Sahara												•	•	•	•		•		Sahara occidental
Yemen		•										•	•	•	•	•	•	•	Yémen
Zambia	•	•										•	•	•	•	•	•	•	Zambie
Zanzibar																			Zanzibar
Zimbabwe	•	•		•								•	•	•	•	•	•	•	Zimbabwe

	Science and technology / Science et technologie			International merchandise trade / Commerce international des marchandises			International tourism and transport / Tourisme international et transport				BoP / BdP	International finance / Finances internationales			Development assistance / Aide au développement			
Table	59	60	61	62	63	64	65	66	67	68	69	70	71	72	73	74	75	**Tableau**
Saudi Arabia	•		•	•			•	•	•	•	•	•	•		•		•	Arabie saoudite
Senegal	•	•		•			•	•	•	•	•	•	•	•	•		•	Sénégal
Serbia	•	•		•	•		•	•	•	•	•	•	•	•	•		•	Serbie
Serbia and Montenegro				•						•								Serbie-et-Monténégro
Seychelles	•	•		•			•	•	•	•	•	•	•	•	•		•	Seychelles
Sierra Leone				•			•	•	•	•	•	•	•	•	•		•	Sierra Leone
Singapore	•	•		•		•	•	•	•	•	•	•	•				•	Singapour
Slovakia	•	•	•	•	•		•	•	•	•	•	•	•				•	Slovaquie
Slovenia	•	•	•	•	•		•	•	•	•	•	•	•				•	Slovénie
Solomon Islands				•			•	•	•	•	•	•	•		•		•	Iles Salomon
Somalia													•	•			•	Somalie
South Africa	•	•		•	•		•	•	•	•	•	•	•	•	•		•	Afrique du Sud
Spain	•	•	•	•	•		•	•	•	•	•	•	•			•	•	Espagne
Sri Lanka	•	•	•	•	•		•	•	•	•	•	•	•	•	•		•	Sri Lanka
Sudan	•	•		•			•	•	•	•	•	•	•	•	•		•	Soudan
Suriname				•			•	•	•	•	•	•	•		•		•	Suriname
Svalbard and Jan Mayen Is.																		Svalbard et îles Jan Mayen
Swaziland				•			•	•	•	•	•	•	•	•	•		•	Swaziland
Sweden	•	•	•	•	•		•	•	•	•	•	•	•			•	•	Suède
Switzerland	•	•	•	•	•	•	•	•	•	•	•	•	•		•	•	•	Suisse
Syrian Arab Republic							•	•	•	•	•	•			•		•	Rép. arabe syrienne
Tajikistan	•	•		•			•	•	•	•	•	•	•	•	•		•	Tadjikistan
TFYR of Macedonia	•	•		•			•	•	•	•	•	•	•	•	•		•	L'ex-R.Y. Macédoine
Thailand	•	•	•	•	•		•	•	•	•	•	•	•	•	•		•	Thaïlande
Timor-Leste													•		•		•	Timor-Leste
Togo	•			•			•	•	•		•	•	•	•	•		•	Togo
Tokelau															•		•	Tokélaou
Tonga				•			•	•	•	•	•	•	•		•		•	Tonga
Trinidad and Tobago	•	•	•	•			•	•	•	•	•	•	•	•	•		•	Trinité-et-Tobago
Tristan da Cunha																		Tristan da Cunha
Tunisia	•	•	•	•			•	•	•	•	•	•	•	•	•		•	Tunisie
Turkey	•	•	•	•	•	•	•	•	•	•	•	•	•	•	•		•	Turquie
Turkmenistan				•			•	•	•	•	•	•	•		•		•	Turkménistan
Turks and Caicos Islands							•	•							•		•	Iles Turques et Caïques
Tuvalu															•		•	Tuvalu
Uganda	•	•	•	•			•	•	•	•	•	•	•	•	•		•	Ouganda
Ukraine	•	•	•	•			•	•	•	•	•	•	•	•	•		•	Ukraine
United Arab Emirates				•			•	•	•	•		•	•				•	Emirats arabes unis
United Kingdom	•	•	•	•	•	•	•	•	•	•	•	•	•			•	•	Royaume-Uni
United Rep. of Tanzania				•			•	•	•	•	•	•	•	•	•		•	Rép.-Unie de Tanzanie
United States	•	•		•			•	•	•	•	•	•	•		•	•	•	Etats-Unis
United States Virgin Is.	•						•	•										Iles Vierges américaines
Uruguay	•	•		•	•		•	•	•	•	•	•	•	•	•		•	Uruguay
Uzbekistan			•				•	•	•	•	•	•	•	•	•		•	Ouzbékistan
Vanuatu				•			•	•	•	•	•	•	•	•	•		•	Vanuatu
Venezuela (Boliv. Rep. of)	•				•				•		•	•	•		•		•	Venezuela (Rép. boliv. du)
Viet Nam	•	•		•			•	•	•		•	•	•	•	•		•	Viet Nam
Wallis and Futuna Islands															•			Iles Wallis et Futuna
Western Sahara																		Sahara occidental
Yemen			•	•			•	•	•	•	•	•	•	•	•		•	Yémen
Zambia	•			•			•	•	•	•	•	•	•	•	•		•	Zambie
Zanzibar																		Zanzibar
Zimbabwe				•			•	•		•		•	•	•	•		•	Zimbabwe

Index

Note: References to tables are indicated by **boldface** type.

A

access, proportion of population with access to water
supply and sanitation coverage. *See* water supply and
sanitation coverage

aggregates, national accounting, relationships among,
193-204, 253

agricultural production, **13**, **331-335**

    method of calculating series, 24-25, 358

    per capita, **13**

    sources of information, 24-25

agricultural products (non-food)

    defined, 328

    prices, **309-316**

    production, **331-335**

    value added by, **178-192**

agriculture, hunting, forestry, fishing, 3, 253

    production, **331-335**

    value added by, **178-192**

aid. *See* development assistance

airline traffic. *See* civil aviation

aluminium

    defined, 431

    production, **413-415**

amphibians. *See* threatened species

apparel industry. *See* textile, wearing apparel, leather and
footwear

arable land, as percentage of total land area, **487-496**, 539

aviation. *See* civil aviation

B

balance of payments, 3, **675-712**

    by category of payment, **675-712**

    definition of terms, 713-714

Balance of Payments Manual (IMF), 713

Balance of Payments Statistics Yearbook, 672

beer, **371-375**, 430

beverage industry. *See* food, beverages, and tobacco
industries

beverages, 253, 329

    as percentage of household consumption expenditure,
213-218

    production, **14-19**, **219-250**

beverages, alcoholic. *See* beer

birds. *See* threatened species

birth, rate of, **11-12**, 24

birth, life expectancy at. *See* life expectancy

boring machines. *See* machine tools

brown coal. *See* lignite

business enterprises, research and development
expenditures, **553-559**, 565-566

C

call money rates. *See* money market rate

capital account

    defined, 714

    in balance of payments, **675-712**

capital formation. *See* gross fixed capital formation

capital goods, 329

    prices, **309-316**

carbon dioxide (CO_2) emissions, **497-504**, 539-540

cars, passenger, **418-419**, 432

cellular mobile telephones

    defined, 143

    subscribers and per 100 inhabitants, **119-130**

cement, **399-405**, 431, 497-504, 539-540

central banks, discount rates, **255-259**, 270

cereals (grain)

    defined,

    production, **9**, **336-342**, 358

chemical industry production, **14-19**, **219-250**, 486, 601

chlorofluorocarbon (CFC) consumption, **505-512**

    method of calculating series, 540

cigarettes, production, **376-380**

civil aviation

    definition of terms, 672

    passengers and freight carried, **658-670**

Classification of the Functions of Government (COFOG),
205-212

clothing and footwear

    as percentage of household consumption expenditure,
213-218, 253

    See also textile, wearing apparel, leather and footwear;
footwear, with uppers of leather

CO_2. *See* carbon dioxide (CO_2) emissions

coal

    defined, 484-486

    production, **9**, **14-19**, **466-483**, 484-486

coke, 484

commodities, 3, **9-10**, 24-25, 358, 430, 484, 600, 713

    conversion tables for, 786

communication, 2, 5, 80, 106, **107-143**. *See also* transport
and communications

communication industry. *See* transport, storage and
communication industries

Compendium of Tourism Statistics (UNWTO), 671-672

compensation of employees to and from the rest of the
world, as percentage of GDP, **193-204**

construction industry, value added by, **178-192**

consumer price index, **317-327**, 329

consumption. *See* government final consumption;
household final consumption

conversion factors, 484, 786

    currency, 599, 601

conversion tables

    for selected commodities, 786

    for units of measure and weight, 785-786

cotton. *See* fabrics

countries and areas

    boundaries and legal status of, not implied by this
publication, ii

    coverage of, in *Statistical Yearbook*, 2-5

    economic and regional associations, **780-784**

    recent name changes, **775-776**

    regional groupings for statistical purposes, **775-784**

    statistics reported for, 599

    surface area, **11-12**, 24, **29-40**, 49

    See also developed countries, economies or areas;
developing countries, economies or areas

croplands, permanent, as percentage of total land area,
487-496

crops, 24, 358, **487-496**, 539

crude oil. *See* petroleum, crude

crude steel. *See* pig iron and crude steel

currency

    conversion factors, 4, 251, 566, 599, 601

    exchange rates, 251-252, 566, 599, 601, **715-724**, 748

current account

    defined, 713

    in balance of payments, **675-712**

current transfers, **193-204**, 253

    defined, 713-714

    in balance of payments, **675-712**

customs area, 599

D

death, rate of, **11-12**, 24. *See also* mortality

defence, national, as percentage of government final
consumption expenditure, **205-212**, 253

Demographic Yearbook (UN), 12, 37, 49

developed countries, economies or areas, ii, 3, **14**, **22**, 25,
143, **569**, **571**, **593**, **596**, 776

developing countries, economies or areas, ii, 2-3, **15**, 25,
49, 143, **597**, **741-747**, 748, **765**, 774, 776

    defined, ii, 3, 776

    development assistance to, 3, **751-772**, 774

    external debt of, **741-747**, 748

development assistance, **751-772**, 774

    bilateral and multilateral, **751-764**

    to developing countries and multilateral organizations, **765**

    United Nations system, **766-773**, 774

Development Assistance Committee (DAC) countries,
development assistance from, **765**, 774

discount rates, **255-259**

    defined, 270

domestic production, prices, **309-316**, 328

domestic supply, prices, **309-316**, 328

drilling machines. *See* machine tools

E

earnings. *See* wages

economic affairs, as percentage of government final
consumption expenditure, **205-212**, 253

economic associations, country lists, **780-784**

economic relations, international. *See* international economic relations

economic statistics, **147-599**

education

as percentage of government final consumption expenditure, **205-212**, 253

as percentage of household consumption expenditure, **213-218**, 253

definition of terms, 105-106

girls to boys, ratio in primary, secondary and tertiary, **67-79**, 81

levels of, primary, secondary and tertiary, number of students, **83-98**

public expenditures on, **99-104**

education sector, research and development expenditures by, **553-559**, 565-566

electrical products. *See* office and related electrical products

electricity, 25, 80, 253-254, 430

consumption, **434-465**

defined, 484, 486

production, **9**, **14-19**, **20-21**, **219-250**, **434-483**

electricity, gas, water utilities

production, **14-19**

value added by, **178-192**

cmissions. *See* carbon dioxide (CO_2) emissions

energy, iii, 2-3, **20-21**, **434-483**, 484-486

energy commodities (solid, liquid, gas and electrical)

consumption, **434-465**

definition of terms, 484-486

production, **20-21**, **434-483**

stocks, **434-465**

trade, **20-21**, **434-465**

Energy Statistics Yearbook (UN), 482

environment, 2-4, **487-541**

environmental protection, as percentage of government final consumption expenditure, **205-212**, 253

exchange rates. *See* currency

exports

as percentage of GDP, **165-177**

defined, 600-601

in balance of payments, **675-712**, 713

index numbers, **10**, **22-23**, **586-592**

purchasing power of, **586-592**

value of, **10**, **569-585**, 599-601, 713

volume of, **10**, **22-23**, **586-598**, 600-602

See also external trade

external debt

definition of terms, 748

of developing countries or areas, **741-747**

external trade (international trade), **10**, **22-23**, **569-602**

as percentage of GDP, **165-177**

method of calculating series, 599-601

value of, **10**, **569-585**, 599-601

volume of, **10**, **22-23**, **586-598**, 600-602

See also exports; imports

F

fabrics, **381-383**. *See also* textile, wearing apparel, leather and footwear

factor income, 253

FAO Yearbook of Fishery Statistics, Aquaculture Production, 359

FAO Yearbook of Fishery Statistics, Capture Production, 359

FAO Global Forest Resources Assessment. *See Global Forest Resources Assessment* (FAO)

finance, international. *See* international finance

financial account

defined, 714

in balance of payments, **675-712**

financial statistics, **10**, **255-269**

sources of information, 270

fish. *See* threatened species

fishing

production, **9**, **349-357**

definition of terms, 358-359

See also agriculture, hunting, forestry and fishing

fixed capital. *See* gross fixed capital formation

food

defined, 358

prices, **317-327**

production, **13**, **219-250**, **331-335**

production per capita, **13**

food, beverages, tobacco, as percentage of household
consumption expenditure, 213-218

food, beverages, tobacco industries, production, **14-19,
219-250**

footwear, with uppers of leather, **384-386**, 430-431

foreign exchange reserves, **10, 725-740**, 748

forest cover, **487-496**, 539

forestry. *See* agriculture, hunting, forestry and fishing

Frascati Manual, 564

free-on-board (f.o.b.), 713

fuel, 106, 253, **466-483**, 484-486, **497-504**, 539-540. *See
also* housing and utilities

furniture, household equipment, maintenance, as
percentage of household consumption expenditure,
213-218

furniture industry. *See* wood and wood products

G

gas. *See* liquefied petroleum gas; natural gas; natural gas
liquids; refinery gas

gas utilities. *See* electricity, gas, water utilities

gender, **51-81**

*Geographical Distribution of Financial Flows to Aids
Recipients* (OECD), 774

Global Development Finance, 747-748

Global Forest Resources Assessment (FAO), 539

gold
monetary, 713
reserves minus, **10, 725-740**

government
research and development expenditures by, **553-559**,
565-566
See also public services

government final consumption
as percentage of GDP, **165-177**
expenditure by function, **205-212**
government finance, **10**
method of calculating series, 253

grain. *See* cereals

gross domestic product (GDP)
distribution by expenditure, **165-177**
method of calculating series, 252
relation to other national accounting aggregates, **193-204**
total and per capita, **147-164**
world, **9**

gross fixed capital formation, as percentage of GDP,
165-177

gross national disposable income, as percentage of GDP,
193-204

gross savings, as percentage of GDP, **193-204**, 253

H

health expenditures
as percentage of government final consumption,
205-212
as percentage of household final consumption,
213-218

hotel industry. *See* trade (wholesale/retail), restaurants and
hotel industries

household equipment. *See* furniture, household equipment
and maintenance

household final consumption
expenditure as percentage of GDP, **165-177**
expenditure by purpose, **213-218**
method of calculating series, 253

housing and community amenities, as percentage of
government final consumption expenditures, **205-212**

housing and utilities, as percentage of household
consumption expenditure, **213-218**

hunting. *See* agriculture, hunting, forestry and fishing

I

imports
as percentage of GDP, **165-177**
defined, 599-601
in balance of payments, **675-712**, 713
index numbers, **22-23**, **586-592**
prices, **309-316**
value of, **10**, **569-585**, **593-598**, 599-601, 713
volume of, **22-23**, **586-598**, 600-602
See also external trade

income

  gross national. *See* gross national income

  gross national disposable. *See* gross national

    disposable income

  See also property income to/from the rest of the world

Industrial Commodity Statistics Yearbook (UN), 375, 383,

    386, 404, 407, 412, 414, 417, 419, 421, 424, 427, 429-

    430

industrial production

  world, **9**

  by region, **14-19**

  index numbers of, **219-250**

  method of calculating series, 25, 253-254

  prices, **309-316**

interest rates, 2, 4, **260-269**, 270

intermediate goods, prices, **309-316**

international economic relations, **567-774**

international finance, 3, **715-750**

International Financial Statistics (IMF), 251, 259, 269-

    270, 600, 712, 714, 723, 740, 748

International Recommendations for Industrial Statistics

    (UN), 430

international reserves minus gold, **10, 725-740**

International Standard Classification of Education

    (ISCED), 105-106

International Standards Industrial Classification of All

    Economic Activities (ISIC) (UN), 3, **14-19**, 25, 80,

    219-250, 253-254, 306, 328

international trade. *See* external trade

International Trade Statistics Yearbook (UN), 599

internet users

  method of calculating series, 143

  number and per 100 inhabitants, **131-142**

inventories (stocks), changes in, as percentage of GDP,

    165-177

investment income. *See* property income to and from the

    rest of the world

iron. *See* pig iron and crude steel

ISCED. *See International Standard Classification of*

    Education

ISIC. *See International Standards Industrial Classification*

    of All Economic Activities

L

labour force, **271-296**

  sources of information, 297

  wages, **299-308**

land

  area and categories (arable, forest and permanent

    crops), **487-496**

  definition of terms, 539

lathes. *See* machine tools

leather. *See* footwear, with uppers of leather

life expectancy, 2, **41-48**, 49

lignite

  defined,

  production, **9, 466-483**, 484-485

liquefied petroleum gas (LPG), 486

  production, **466-483**

lorries. *See* trucks

M

machines, washing. *See* washing machines, for household use

machine tools, **425-427**, 432

mammals. *See* threatened species

manufactured goods

  defined, 601

  external trade in, **10, 593-598**

manufacturing industries

  production, **9, 14-19, 219-250, 361-429**

  sources of information, 25, 253-254, 430-431

  value added by, **178-192**

  wages, **299-308**, 328

market exchange rates (MERs), 251, 748

meat, **9**

metal ores, production, **14-19**

metal products industries, production, **14-19, 219-250**

metals, basic, **14-19, 219-250**

milling machines. *See* machine tools

mineral products, non-metallic, production, **14-19, 219-250**

mining and quarrying, 80, 253, 430

  production, **9, 14-19, 219-250**

  value added by, **178-192**

molluscs. *See* threatened species

monetary gold. *See* gold, monetary

money market rate, **260-269**, 270

Monthly Bulletin of Statistics (UN), 270, 599-601

multilateral institutions, 749

    debt to, **7141-742**

    defined, 774

    development assistance from, **751-764**

    development contributions to, **765**

N

national accounts, **147-218**

    definition of terms, 251-253

    relationships between principal aggregates of,
        193-204, 253

National Accounts Statistics: Main Aggregates and
    Detailed Tables (UN), 251

national income, as percentage of GDP, **193-204**, 253

natural gas

    defined, 484-486

    production, **9**, **14-19**, **466-483**

natural gas liquids (NGL)

    defined, 484-486

    production, **466-483**

net current transfers to and from the rest of the world, as
    percentage of GDP, **193-204**, 253

net errors and omissions

    defined, 714

    in balance of payments, **675-712**

O

office and related electrical products, **14-19**

online databases, 6

"other" economic activities, value added by, **178-192**, 253

Ozone-depleting chlorofluorocarbons (CFC), consumption.
    See chlorofluorocarbon (CFC) consumption

P

paper, printing, publishing, recorded media industries,
    production, **14-19**, **394-398**, 431

paper and paperboard

    defined, 431

    production, **394-398**

parliament, women in, **51-58**, 80

passenger traffic, **658-670**, 672-673

passenger cars. *See* cars, passenger

patents, **560-563**, 566

peat

    defined, 484-485

    production, **466-483**

pesticides, **406-407**, 431

petroleum, crude

    defined, 485

    production, **9**, **14-19**, **219-250**, **466-483**

petroleum products

    defined, 484-486

    production, **219-250**, **466-483**

pig iron and crude steel, **408-412**, 431

plants. *See* threatened species

population

    by sex, **29-40**

    definition of terms, 24, 49

    density, **11-12**

    numbers, rates of increase, **9**, **11-12**, **29-40**

power. *See* housing and utilities

prices

    consumer, **317-327**

    indexes of, **309-327**

    method of calculating series, 328-329

    producer and wholesale, **309-316**

primary commodities. *See* raw materials

primary income, 253

printing industry. *See* paper, printing, publishing, recorded
    media industries

private consumption. *See* household final consumption

producer prices

    defined, 328-329

    indexes of, **309-316**

property income from and to the rest of the world, as
    percentage of GDP, **193-204**

public order and safety, as percentage of government final
    consumption expenditure, **205-212**, 253

public services, as percentage of government final
    consumption expenditure, **205-212**, 253

publishing industry. *See* paper, printing, publishing, recorded media industries

purchasing power of exports, **586-592**, 601

Q

quarrying. *See* mining and quarrying

R

radio receivers, production, **416-417**, 431

rates

discount, **255-259**, 270

exchange, 4, 251-252, 566, 599, 601, **715-724**, 748

interest, 2, 4, **260-269**, 270

money market, **260-269**, 270

treasury bills, **260-269**, 270, 748

raw materials, **309-316**, 328

Recommendation concerning the International Standardization of Education Statistics, 105

refinery gas, 484

refrigerators, household

defined, 432

production, **420-422**

regional associations, country lists, **780-784**

regions, statistical

country lists, **780-784**

purpose of, 2-3

surface area, **11-12**

rents and utilities. *See* housing and utilities

reptiles. *See* threatened species

research and development

expenditures on, **553-559**

personnel, **543-552**

sources of information, 564-566

researchers

defined, 564

number of, **543-552**

reserve positions in IMF, **10**, 748

reserves and related items

defined, 714

in balance of payments, **675-712**

restaurant industry. *See* trade (wholesale/retail), restaurants and hotel industries

restaurants and hotels, as percentage of household consumption expenditure, **213-218**

rest of the world

compensation of employees, property income, and transfers from and to, **193-204**

services from and to, **675-712**, 713

retail trade. *See* trade (wholesale/retail), restaurants and hotel industries

roundwood

conversion factor, 786

defined, 358

production, **9**, **343-348**

S

savings, as percentage of GDP, **193-204**, 253

sawnwood

defined, 431

production, **9**, **387-393**

science and technology, **543-566**

scientists. *See* researchers

semi-finished products. *See* pig iron and crude steel

services from and to the rest of the world. *See* rest of the world

sex, population by, **29-40**, 49

short term rates, **260-269**, 270

social protection, as percentage of government final consumption expenditure, **205-212**, 253

social statistics, **51-106**

special drawing rights (SDRs), **10**, **593-598**, 601, 713, 748

spiegeleisen. *See* pig iron and crude steel

Standard International Trade Classification (SITC) (UN), 600-601

stocks. *See inventories*

storage industry. *See* transport, storage and communication industries

sugar

consumption, **361-370**

conversion factors, 786

method of calculating series, 430

production, **9**, **361-370**

Sugar Yearbook (ISO), 370, 430

System of National Accounts (SNA), 176, 190, 204, 211, 217, 251, 329, 713

systems of trade, 584, 599

T

technicians

    defined, 564

    number of, **543-552**

telephones

    method of calculating series, 143

    number in use and per 100 inhabitants, **107-118**

    See also cellular mobile telephones

terms of trade, **22-23**, **586-592**, 601

tertiary education, **67-79**, 81, **83-98**, 105-106

textile, wearing apparel, leather and footwear, **14-19**, **219-250**, **384-386**, 430

threatened species, **513-524**, 540

tobacco industry. *See* food, beverages and tobacco industries

tobacco products. *See* cigarettes

ton of oil equivalent (TOE)

    defined, 484

    production, trade and consumption of commercial energy in thousand metric tons of, **20-21**, **434-465**

tourism, international, **603-657**

    definition of terms, 671-672

tourists

    arrivals, **603-645**

    inbound, receipts from, **633-645**

    origin and destination, **603-632**

    outbound, expenditures, **646-657**

trade, international. *See* external trade

trade (wholesale/retail), restaurants and hotel industries, value added by, **178-192**

transfer income, **193-204**

transport, storage and communication industries, 253, 486

    value added by, **178-192**

transport and communications, as percentage of household consumption expenditure, **213-218**

transport

    air. *See* civil aviation

    equipment, **14-19**, **219-250**

treasury bill rate, **260-269**, 270

trucks, **428-429**, 432, 540

U

unemployment, **271-296**, 297

units of measure and weight, conversion tables, 785-786

university education. *See* tertiary education

V

valuation of goods, method of calculating, 599

value added, by industry **178-192**

visitors, international

    arrivals, **603-645**

    defined, 671-672

    origin and destination of, **603-632**

W

wages, 2-4, 80, **299-308**

washing machines, for household use, **423-424**, 432

water supply and sanitation coverage, **525-538**, 540-541

water utilities. *See* electricity, gas and water utilities

welfare services. *See* social protection

wholesale prices, **309-316**, 329

wholesale trade. *See* trade (wholesale/retail), restaurants and hotel industries

women. *See* gender

wood and wood products, **14-19**. *See also* roundwood; sawnwood

woodpulp, production, **9**

wool. *See* fabrics

World Debt Tables. See Global Development Finance

World Population Prospects (UN), 24, 48-49, 764

world statistics

    selected series, **9-10**

    summary, **7-25**

World Weights and Measures, 785

Y

Yearbook of Labour Statistics (ILO), 297, 328

Yearbook of Statistics, Telecommunication Services (ITU), 143

Also of interest

World Statistics Pocketbook

The *World Statistics Pocketbook* 2008 is an authoritative and comprehensive compilation of 55 key statistical indicators in convenient country profile format. This edition presents available data for 216 countries and areas, from over 20 international statistical sources, generally for the years 2000, 2005 and 2007. The topics covered include: balance of payments, communication, education and culture, environment, health, industrial production, international trade, labour force, largest urban agglomeration, national accounts, population, refugees, surface area, United Nations membership, etc. The notes on the sources and definitions of the indicators are provided to help users perform further research on the statistics.

Monthly Bulletin of Statistics (MBS)

The *Monthly Bulletin of Statistics* presents current economic and social statistics for more than 200 countries and territories of the world. It contains over 50 tables of monthly and/or annual and quarterly data on a variety of subjects illustrating important economic trends and developments, including population, prices, employment and earnings, energy, manufacturing, transport, construction, international merchandise trade and finance. The online version is available at http://unstats.un.org/unsd/mbs.

To order any of these products, visit the United Nations Sales Section website at https://unp.un.org.

UNdata

UNdata is an internet-based data service for the global user community. It brings many UN statistical databases within easy reach of users through a single entry point. Users can search across a variety of UN system statistical resources with over 60 million records. UNdata is available at http://data.un.org.

Également de l'intérêt

World Statistics Pocketbook

Le "World Statistics Pocketbook" de l'Organisation des Nations Unies, présente, dans un format commode, pays par pays, un ensemble complet d'indicateurs statistiques de base. Sauf exception, l'édition 2008, comprend les données disponibles sur 55 indicateurs pour 216 pays et zones géographiques pour les années 2000, 2005 et 2007 dans les domaines suivants : population, activité économique, agriculture, industrie, énergie, commerce international, transports, communications, situation des femmes, éducation et environnement. Des explications sur les sources et les définitions des indicateurs sont fournies afin de permettre aux utilisateurs de faire des recherches plus approfondies sur les statistiques.

Bulletin mensuel de statistique

Le *bulletin mensuel de statistique* présente les statistiques économiques et sociales de plus de 200 pays et régions du monde. On y trouve une cinquantaine de tableaux regroupant des données mensuelles, annuelles ou trimestriels sur de nombreux sujets qui illustrent d'importantes tendances économiques à long terme touchant la population, les prix, l'emploi et les salaires, l'énergie, les industries manufacturières, les transports, le bâtiment, le commerce international de marchandises et les finances. La version en ligne est disponible à l'adresse http://unstats.un.org/unsd/mbs.

Pour commander ces ouvrages, consultez le site Web de la Section des ventes de l'ONU, à l'adresse https://unp.un.org.

UNdata

UNdata est un service sur internet destiné à l'ensemble des utilisateurs à travers le monde. Plusieurs bases de données statistiques des Nations Unies seront désormais accessibles aisément sur le site ou les utilisateurs pourront rechercher ou télécharger une variété de ressources statistiques du système. UNdata est disponible à l'adresse http://data.un.org.